TRUST TAXATION

Third Edition

TRUST TAXATION

EMMA CHAMBERLAIN and
CHRIS WHITEHOUSE

SWEET & MAXWELL

THOMSON REUTERS

Published in 2011 by Sweet & Maxwell, 100 Avenue Road,
London NW3 3PF
Part of Thomson Reuters (Professional) UK Limited
(Registered in England & Wales, Company No 1679046.
Registered Office and address for service:
Aldgate House, 33 Aldgate High Street, London EC3N 1DL)
For further information on our products and services, visit
www.sweetandmaxwell.co.uk
Typeset by Servis Filmsetting Ltd, Stockport, Cheshire
Printed in Great Britain by T.J. International, Padstow, Cornwall.

No natural forests were destroyed to make this product; only farmed timber was used
and re-planted.

A CIP catalogue record for this book is available from the British Library

ISBN 978–0–414–04335–0

PREFACE TO THE THIRD EDITION

Three years have passed since the Second Edition and again change is the order of the day and has resulted in a substantial rewrite of the original text and an expansion of the book to 56 chapters. As before, a selection of precedents is included (in Appendix I); miscellaneous non-statutory material is in Appendix II and some sample IHT calculations in Appendix III.[1]

On the horizon is the prospect of a general anti-avoidance rule ("GAAR"). Even if introduced, it seems unlikely that this will result in any reduction of the mass (morass?) of tax legislation since specific anti-avoidance measures are unlikely to be repealed whilst lurking in the background is the increasingly nebulous "*Ramsay* principle". Sadly the UK tax system suffers from a surfeit of detail often lacking any coherent principle. Two examples illustrate the problem: first, the lack of consistency underpinning the tax treatment of trusts for disabled beneficiaries[2] and, second, the (hot-off-the-press) disguised remuneration legislation, a masterpiece of vague aspirations combined with detailed and wide-ranging rules setting out "the relevant steps" by virtue of which the unsuspecting taxpayer can be caught.[3] "*All relevant circumstances are to be taken into account in order to get to the essence of the matter*"[4] but the legislation is wide enough to catch those who are not intentionally avoiding tax and who may not know what the essence of the matter is or what relevant circumstances they need to consider.

How past generations of judges would despair of it all! Take, for instance, the famous statement of Rowlatt J. in the *Cape Brandy Syndicate* case[5]:

> "*It is urged . . . that in a taxing Act clear words are necessary in order to tax the subject. Too wide and fanciful a construction is often sought to be given to that maxim, which does not mean that words are to be unduly restricted against the Crown, or that there is to be any discrimination against the Crown in those Acts. It simply means that in a taxing Act one*

---

[1] Based on computations originally produced by Robert Jamieson updated by the authors: the faded popular music stars of the 50s and 60s have not been updated.

[2] See Ch.36.

[3] Ch.49 Pity the owner of the family company who wants to know whether he can settle his shares into trust for his children and give the daughter who works in the business a larger stake than the son who works elsewhere! The burden seems to be on the donor to prove that this is not a "relevant arrangement."

[4] ITEPA 2003 s.554A(12).

[5] *Cape Brandy Syndicate v IRC* [1921] 1 KB 64 affirmed [1921] 2 KB 403.

has to look merely at what is clearly said. There is no room for any intendment. There is no equity about a tax. There is no presumption as to a tax. nothing is to be read in, nothing is to be implied. One can only look fairly at the language used . . ."

Or, for a robust approach to the construction of statutory material, consider this from Lord Reid:

"On reading it [TA 1988 s.577(10)] my first impression was that it is obscure to the point of unintelligibility and that impression has been confirmed by the able and prolonged arguments which were submitted to us . . . I have suggested what may be a possible meaning, but if I am wrong about that I would not shrink from holding that the subsection is so obscure that no meaning can be given to it. I would rather do that than seek by twisting and contorting the words to give to the subsection an improbable meaning. Draftsmen as well as Homer can nod, and Parliament is so accustomed to obscure drafting in Finance Bills that no one may have noticed the defects in this subsection."[6]

Of course, not all blame for the legislative mess can be laid at the door of successive governments which have been faced with the wholly unprincipled activities of the tax avoidance industry. When Treasury Minister, Dawn Primarolo, was want to talk of the need to fight fire with fire:

"Faced with such figures [of tax avoidance schemes], the Committee will not be surprised to hear that the Government decided to take action. It is not enough to tackle new arrangements and future avoidance. The Government wanted to send a clear message that artificial avoidance of that kind is not acceptable. Those who devise and market such schemes, and the people who take advantage of them, need to understand that and not assume that avoidance is risk-free. Such schemes have grown so rapidly because they are regarded as a one-way bet. The essential point is that nothing really changes. For example, let us consider somebody who wants to ensure that the house they live in is not part of their taxable estate, but they want to remain living there. They see their adviser, sign a series of papers and pay a substantial fee, even though there might be a relatively small amount of work in it. The client goes home, the paperwork is filed and the arrangements are designed to unscramble when the client dies and have no lasting effect. The only real effect is inheritance tax savings that can run into thousands of thousands of pounds or more. Given that perception of risk and rewards, it is not surprising that people and advisers have found such schemes increasingly attractive. The clause [introducing the POA charge] gives notice that that is a false perception."[7]

More recently the Coalition Government published a Consultation Paper on High Risk Tax Avoidance Schemes[8] envisaging the imposition of an addi-

---

[6] *Fleming v Associated Newspapers Ltd* [1982] 2 All ER 574, HL.
[7] *Hansard*, Standing Committee Debates, May 28, 2004 col.238.
[8] In May 2011 discussed in Ch.56. The paper was heavily criticised in its underlying assumptions by most of the professional bodies.

tional financial penalty equal to a percentage of the tax underpaid (as well as the "normal" penalties surcharges and interest!) on those using "*a high risk tax avoidance scheme . . . a scheme that uses contrived arrangements to seek tax advantages in circumstances where they are not intended to be available . . .*" In the meantime we have seen increased penalties of up to £1 million for those who fail to disclose reportable tax avoidance schemes and the extension of DOTAS to inheritance tax.

Trusts and settlements have unfortunately become a pawn in this battle: the concept of a trust has been stretched to breaking point with judges forced to grapple with fundamental issues such as what core principles must underlie any valid trust.[9] Symptomatic of the problems has been the astonishing growth of so-called *Hasting-Bass*/mistake claims[10] resulting from either the settlor or his trustees falling foul of an unanticipated tax charge and seeking a get-out-of-gaol free card. Although the Court of Appeal has attempted to assert "traditional values" we have not heard the last of the matter since it surely cannot be right that a trustee who fails to take professional advice may be in a better position when things go wrong than one who has.

In some respects Lord Palmerston, with his adherence to gunboat diplomacy,[11] is a model for British Governments of the 21st Century with their enthusiasm for foreign adventures. If only they would instead follow his lead in domestic affairs:

> "*there is really nothing to be done. We cannot go on adding to the Statute Book ad infinitum. Perhaps we may have a little law reform; but we cannot go on legislating forever . . .*"[12]

The authors are indebted to Andrew Strivens who is recovering well after reading (and commenting on) a goodly portion of the manuscript and to Elouise Dale, first among legal secretaries, who has taken charge of the whole project and rewritten sections where necessary.

The law is stated at November 1, 2011.

EMC
CJW

---

[9] See Millett L.J. in *Armitage v Nurse* [1998] Ch 241: "*(there is) an irreducible core of obligations owed by the trustees to the beneficiaries and enforceable by them which is fundamental to the concept of a trust. If the beneficiaries have no rights enforceable against the trustees there are no trusts*" and see Ch.2 for a discussion of different foreign entities.

[10] See 1.22.

[11] Notably in the affair of Don Pacifico when Palmerston remarked "*As the Roman, in days of old, held himself free from indignity, when he could say 'Civis Romanus sum' [I am a Roman Citizen], so also a British subject, in whatever land he may be, shall feel confident that the watchful eye and the strong arm of England will protect him from injustice and wrong*" (Hansard 3, 112, June 25, 1850, 444).

[12] Quoted in Southgate "*The Most English Minister*" (1966, Macmillan) at p.528.

CONTENTS

PART I: GENERAL

PART II: INCOME TAX

PART III: CAPITAL GAINS TAX

PART IV: INHERITANCE TAX

22. INHERITANCE TAX, RESERVATION OF BENEFIT AND PRE-OWNED ASSETS INCOME TAX—AN INTRODUCTION

23. THE 2006 IHT RULES—AN OVERVIEW

24. IHT DEFINITIONS AND CLASSIFICATIONS

25. CREATION OF SETTLEMENTS

26. THE TAX TREATMENT OF QUALIFYING AND NON-QUALIFYING INTERESTS IN POSSESSION AND REVERSIONARY INTERESTS INCLUDING VALUATION ISSUES, LEASES, RELIEFS, *MELVILLE* SCHEMES AND SALES

APPENDICES

GLOSSARY

AEA 1925	Administration of Estates Act 1925
CA 1985, 2006	Companies Act 1985, 2006
CGTA 1979	Capital Gains Tax Act 1979
CPA 2004	Civil Partnership Act 2004
CRGA 2010	Constitutional Reform and Governance Act 2010
CTA 2009, 2010	Corporation Tax Act 2009, 2010
FA 0000	Finance Act 0000
FLRA 1969, 1987	Family Law Reform Act 1969, 1987
FSMA 2000	Financial Services and Markets Act 2000
IA 1986	Insolvency Act 1986
ICTA 1988	Income and Corporation Taxes Act 1988
IHTA 1984	Inheritance Tax Act 1984
IPFDA 1975	Inheritance (Provision for Family and Dependants) Act 1975
ITA 2007	Income Tax Act 2007
ITEPA 2003	Income Tax (Earnings and Pensions) Act 2003
ITTOIA 2005	Income Tax (Trading and Other Income) Act 2005
LPA 1925	Law of Property Act 1925
MHA 1983, 2007	Mental Health Act 1983, 2007
PAA 1964, 2009	Perpetuities and Accumulation Act 1964, 2009
RTA 1987	Recognition of Trusts Act 1987
TA 1988	Taxes Act 1988
TA 1925, 2000	Trustee Act 1925, 2000
TCGA 1992	Taxation of Chargeable Gains Act 1992
TIOPA 2010	Taxation (International and Other Provisions) Act 2010
TMA 1970	Taxes Management Act 1970
TOLATA 1996	Trusts of Land and Appointment of Trustees Act 1996
VTA 1958	Variation of Trusts Act 1958
WA 1837	Wills Act 1837

TABLE OF CASES

xxix

TABLE OF STATUTES

1

li

lv

TABLE OF STATUTORY INSTRUMENTS

PART I: GENERAL

This introductory section provides an overview of a number of background matters before looking at the income tax, capital gains tax and inheritance tax treatment of trusts in detail (see Pts II, III and IV respectively). Part V covers specialist areas.

Ch.1 considers the nature of a trust, sham trusts, the *Hastings-Bass* rule, mistake, perpetuities and accumulation issues from the UK perspective. Ch.2 considers the categorisation of foreign entities including foundations, grantor trusts and usufructs and their tax treatment under UK law. Ch.3 deals with the residence and domicile of individuals. Ch.4 deals with the residence of trusts and companies. Ch.5 provides an overview of the taxation of non-residents and non-UK domiciliaries.

CHAPTER 1

THE TRUST

- Anatomy of a trust **(1.01)**
- Trustees' powers **(1.09)**
- The settlor **(1.14)**
- The trustees **(1.15)**
- Sham trusts **(1.18)**
- Taxation issues **(1.20)**
- *Hastings-Bass* and mistake **(1.22)**
- Accumulation and perpetuity issues **(1.39)**

I ANATOMY OF A TRUST

Much ink has been spilt in an attempt to define a trust. Rather like the **1.01** elephant,[1] however, it is easier to describe than define and the following (derived from Professor Keeton's *Law of Trusts*) is suggested as expressing the main ingredients:

> "*an equitable obligation binding the trustee to deal with property over which he has control either for the benefit of the beneficiaries (of whom he may be one) or for a charitable purpose or, exceptionally, for non charitable purposes*".

A number of the elements in this definition are worthy of further comment.

"An equitable obligation"

This points to the origin of the trust which was developed by courts of **1.02** Chancery.[2]

---

[1] Or a farmhouse, see Twiddy, *Taxation* (June 15, 2000) p.277.
[2] Some date the earliest trusts to Crusaders who before departing for the Holy Land would transfer their lands to a third party to hold for their benefit until they returned, otherwise for their heir.

"Property"

1.03   A trust is a legal relationship involving property which can be of any type, real or personal, tangible or intangible and, if the earliest trusts largely involved land, today the majority exist to hold intangibles such as stocks and shares. Note that until the trustee is the owner of some item of property the trust has not been constituted. It is common practice:

   (i)   to establish the trust in "pilot" form (the settlement deed will commonly refer to the trust fund as comprising a nominal sum, typically £10, together with such other property as may later be added)[3];

   (ii)   then to add further property using the appropriate mode of transfer.[4]

Trustee

1.04   This is the person who holds the property (but is best described as the nominal rather than legal owner since the property may be equitable, such as an undivided interest in land) on trust for the benefit of the equitable owners (the beneficiaries). He is a fiduciary and as such subject to the duties of good faith laid down over the years by the courts of Chancery. Some would describe his obligations as "wholly burdensome". Historically, a trustee was not entitled to remuneration unless this was expressly provided for in the trust instrument and generally may not profit from his trust;[5] this strict rule has now been modified, however, for English law trusts. Even where there is no express provision in the trust instrument to allow trustees to charge, unless the trust is a charitable trust, a trust corporation can always charge whilst a professional trustee can also charge provided that he is not the sole trustee and the other trustees agree in writing.[6]

Beneficiaries

1.05   These comprise the equitable owners of the property so that if land is transferred to A to hold on trust for B for life remainder to C absolutely, B and C comprise the beneficiaries who are together absolutely entitled to the land in the eyes of equity. Accordingly, they can if they so wish bring the trust to an end.[7]

   Trusts may be set up for charitable purposes or, exceptionally, for non-

---

[3]   For pilot trusts, see Ch.41. The Chancery lawyer would consider there to be a single settlement made up of the original property and the additions (whether or not these were added by the original settlor or another). Additions can, however, create problems in the tax arena: see, for instance, 24.26 and 31.32.

[4]   Note, however, that the settlor can declare that he holds specified property on trust: in this case he is his own trustee and no transfer of property is required.

[5]   See, for instance, *Boardman v Phipps* [1967] 2 AC 46.

[6]   TA 2000 s.29.

[7]   *Saunders v Vautier* (1814) 4 Beav 115; *Re Smith, Public Trustee v Aspinall* [1928] Ch 915.

charitable purposes. Generally non-charitable purpose trusts are not valid under English law with a few limited exceptions[8] because there is no individual beneficiary who can compel performance of the trusts. The position is different in many foreign jurisdictions[9] where legislation has been passed to provide for an enforcer.[10]

"Dramatis personae"

As can be seen from the above, any trust will involve three characters: the settlor, the trustee and the beneficiaries. Commonly in family trusts the same individual will perform a multiplicity of roles: it is, for instance, common for the settlor to be one of the trustees (in this way he can retain a measure of control over the property) and it may be that he is also one of the beneficiaries. **1.06**

EXAMPLE 1.1

Sid transfers shares into the names of himself and his son to be held on trust for Sid for life with remainder to his son and daughter in equal shares:

  (i) Sid is settlor, trustee and life tenant (interest in possession beneficiary);
  (ii) his son is a trustee and also entitled in remainder.

The Protector[11]

A protector is largely unknown in UK trusts but common in offshore trusts. Sometimes there is a committee which acts as protector. His role is to consent to the "big" decisions affecting the trusts, e.g. who should be given the capital. Usually he will also have power to replace trustees. He should not generally be given more extensive powers, especially if he is a UK resident because this may cause problems if the trust is intended to be non-UK resident.[12] The trust property should not be vested in him and he should not have power to initiate action. **1.07**

---

[8] There is a line of anomalous cases on tombs, monuments and animals: a trust of land to be used as a recreation ground for employees of a company was held to be valid in *Re Denley's Trust Deed* [1969] 1 Ch 373. Wills containing legacies for the erection and maintenance of tombs, for maintenance of the testator's animals and for the promotion of foxhunting have been held valid on the basis that the legacy can be paid to the legatee who can then use it to carry out the trust: these are called "trusts of imperfect obligation". If the legatee does not use the legacy for the purposes specified the residuary beneficiaries can claim it for themselves so the trust is indirectly enforceable by them. It was noted in *Re Endacott* [1960] Ch 232 that these cases were "*troublesome, anomalous and aberrant*" and should not be increased.
[9] For example, Bermuda; Cayman Islands; British Virgin Islands; Isle of Man and Jersey.
[10] This is discussed further in Ch.2.
[11] He occupies a fiduciary role but will not normally be a trustee.
[12] See Ch.2 in relation to foreign law trusts.

1.08   There may be attractions for a settlor in establishing trusts in flexible form.

EXAMPLE 1.2

(i)   A sets up a trust under which his daughter is entitled to a life interest, with remainder to her two children in equal shares. This is commonly called a *fixed* trust: the daughter is entitled to income (but not to capital) and her children to capital on her death; *contrast*

(ii) B sets up a trust under which the trustees are given discretion to pay income to such of C, D, E, F and G as they think fit with power to accumulate the balance and with a power to appoint capital amongst those beneficiaries in their discretion. They also have power to add persons as beneficiaries. The trust is a *flexible discretionary trust*.

It is common to set up a trust that combines features of (i) and (ii).

(iii) C sets up a trust that gives his daughter a life interest but with power to advance her capital; the trustees are also given power to end her life interest and appoint the trust fund on different trusts (whether discretionary or otherwise) for her or other beneficiaries.

Whereas in (i) the interests are fixed so that if the daughter has a need for capital the trustees have no power to give it to her; in (ii) and (iii) the trustees' powers are sufficiently wide to cater for any eventuality although in the case of (iii) unless and until the trustees do exercise their powers the daughter continues to receive the income. It is desirable for the settlor to provide guidance for the trustees of a flexible trust in the form of a non-binding letter of wishes. This can, and should, be revised by the settlor during his lifetime in the light of changed circumstances. Note that even if the trustees have no power to accumulate income (e.g. because the accumulation period has expired) if they retain a discretion over who can receive the income the trust is discretionary.

II TRUSTEES' POWERS

1.09   Commonly these are divided into administrative (concerned with the running of the trust fund, e.g. powers to invest the capital) and dispositive (powers to distribute income and divide capital amongst the beneficiaries). This division is not, however, wholly satisfactory with some powers being of a hybrid nature (the power for trustees to be remunerated; the power to make appropriations, etc).

1.10   It is dispositive powers which are usually of most concern in the sphere of taxation. For instance:

(i) if a beneficiary is entitled to the income as it arises (i.e. has an interest in possession) then for income tax purposes whilst the trustees are accountable for basic rate tax, any higher rate liability is that of the beneficiary. The IHT treatment of trusts historically distinguished between trusts with and without an interest in possession. Whilst FA 2006 has largely eroded that distinction, there is still an IHT category of trust with a "qualifying" interest in possession;

(ii) the statutory power of maintenance in TA 1925 s.31 has both a vesting and a divesting effect. For instance, a trust "for A contingent on attaining 21 absolutely" will result in A becoming entitled to the income at 18 (albeit that capital entitlement depends on his becoming 21). By contrast a trust which gives a minor beneficiary a right to income ("to A for life" when he is aged two) is converted into a contingent interest and until he becomes 18 the trustees have power to apply income for his maintenance and accumulate any balance.

The statutory power of advancement in TA 1925 s.32 is equally important. **1.11** Normally this is extended to permit the advancement of 100 per cent of the presumptive share of a beneficiary. A major use of the power in practice is not, however, to give the beneficiary his capital interest in the settlement before he is entitled to it, but to apply that capital for his "benefit". This word has been given the widest meaning by the courts and enables trustees to postpone the beneficiary's entitlement to capital if that is considered to be for his benefit. Normally this will be by the making of a "settled advance".

EXAMPLE 1.3

> Under the Bloggs Family Trust, Sid is entitled to a substantial slice of the capital at age 30. He is currently aged 28 and, as a result of the operation of TA 1925 s.31 in receipt of income. The trustees have a widened power of advancement which enables them to apply Sid's share of the capital for his benefit. Sid is currently a hopeless case and will fritter away the capital if it is paid out to him at 30. The trustees accordingly exercise their widened s.32 power to give Sid a right to income for life with a reserved power to give him capital at any time in their discretion and, subject to that, declare trusts for Sid's wife and young children.[13]

The exercise of both the power of advancement and of trustee powers of **1.12** appointment is circumscribed by the terms of the power (e.g. it cannot be used to benefit non-objects[14]) and by the rule that for the purposes of income accumulation and perpetuities any trusts which are created are governed by

---

13 The exercise of the power in circumstances such as this has important tax implications. For instance, had Sid taken capital at 30, a CGT charge might have arisen as a result of the deemed disposal provided for in TCGA 1992 s.71: however, if the trust is "modified" by the making of a settled advance (rather than a new settlement created) this charge will have been avoided. See generally Ch.12 and note that there may also be significant IHT implications in extending the life of a settlement.

14 Note, however, that non-objects may incidentally benefit if, in the case of the power of advancement, such an exercise is for the benefit of the object of the power.

the periods prescribed in the settlement. In effect the exercise of the power is "read-back".

1.13   A distinction can be drawn (which is especially important for CGT purposes) between powers "in the wider" and "in the narrower" form. The former enable the trust property to be held on new trusts (in effect wholly removed from the old trusts) whereas the latter is a power to modify the existing trusts. A s.32 power is a wider power[15] whereas the normal power of appointment is a modifying narrower form power. This, however, is merely the broadest generalisation and the precise terms of the particular power should be considered.[16] For example, an express power of advancement may be drafted in such a way that it can only be exercised so as to give the beneficiary capital outright and a settled advance cannot be made.[17] Sometimes the power requires the consent of another such as the settlor or protector.[18] The formalities required by the settlement as to how the power is exercised must be checked in every case. For instance, does it need to be exercised by deed or is a trustee resolution sufficient? Ideally, settlements should contain a power of advancement, a power of appointment and a power of resettlement. Sometimes the power of resettlement (which allows the trustees to transfer property to another trust "freed and released from the trusts of this settlement") stipulates that the beneficiaries of the new trust must be identical to those of the transferring trust.[19]

III THE SETTLOR

1.14   As has already been mentioned, the settlor may be a trustee and may also be a beneficiary of his trust. It is relatively common for him to be one of the trustees: many settlors wish to have a say in the running of their trust and wish to continue to manage the property. It is, however, important to appreciate that once he becomes a trustee the settlor is a fiduciary and that the property is no longer his to do what he wants with. A failure to appreciate this can lead to actions for breach of trust or even for the trust to be treated as a sham! For a settlor to be a beneficiary of his trust has significant tax implications: for instance he will then be taxed on the income of the trust.[20] He may also find that he is caught by either the IHT reservation of benefit rules or by the

---

[15] Many modern settlements give the trustees an express power to transfer property to the trustees of another settlement under which the same persons (or at least some of the same persons) can benefit.

[16] Even if there is a wider form power, it can be exercised narrowly: i.e. to modify an existing settlement rather than to create a new one. See, for instance, *Swires v Renton* [1993] STC 490 and Example 1.3, above.

[17] Avoid powers such as "*the trustees may pay or transfer funds to a beneficiary for his own use and benefit absolutely.*"

[18] For reasons set out in Ch.20 it is usually inadvisable to give beneficiaries power to consent to the exercise of a power of advancement, especially if the beneficiary is the life tenant. This can not only cause capital gains tax problems but where the life tenant consents to the exercise of a power of advancement that ends his life interest, it arguably makes him the settlor of the income for income tax purposes. See *D'Abreu v IRC* [1978] STC 538 and *IRC v Buchanan* [1957] 2 All ER 400.

[19] Of course the power of advancement can also be exercised in a "wider form" to resettle assets but it is sometimes convenient to have a separate power of resettlement.

[20] The income and capital gains tax implications of settlor-interested trusts are considered in Ch.7.

pre-owned assets income tax charge. There is, however, no general rule of transparency and each tax has to be considered separately.

IV THE TRUSTEES

The initial trustees will be chosen by the settlor who will often retain a power **1.15** to appoint new trustees during his lifetime. The standard power in TA 1925 s.36 allows for the appointment of a replacement trustee in certain circumstances (e.g. if a trustee is dead) as well as the appointment of additional trustees. It is not uncommon in practice for problems to arise in identifying the trustees and specifically when persons who have not been validly appointed purport to act as trustees. Often the problem is not identified for many years at which point there is a nightmare of invalid appointments and exercises of discretion.

Did a trustee retire?

The trust deed may contain express provisions dealing with retirement. If **1.16** it does not statutory provisions will apply. It is important to ensure that the appropriate requirements are satisfied. If they are not, the outgoing trustee will not be discharged and any future trustee actions requiring unanimity will be ineffective; there may also be residence issues arising for the trust if supposedly retired trustees continue in office. *Jasmine Trustees Ltd v Wells & Hind (A Firm)*[21] illustrates the mayhem that can ensue from failed retirements.[22]

In 1968 Major-General and Mrs Coaker became the original trustees of a discretionary settlement in favour of their children and remoter issue. Clause 18 of the trust deed incorporated the statutory power of appointing new trustees. The following events then occurred:

(i) In 1982 they appointed the Investment Bank of Ireland (IBI) and T to be trustees and purported to resign. Their intention was to leave IBI and T as the sole trustees. Both were non-resident. Sadly, while this document was effective to appoint IBI and T as new trustees, it was not capable of discharging Major-General and Mrs Coaker because the two new trustees were not both "individuals" within the then requirements of TA 1925 s.37(1)(c). Major-General Coaker and Mrs Coaker therefore remained as trustees.

(ii) In 1983 Major-General Coaker died.

---

[21] [2007] EWHC 38 (Ch). See also [2007] STC 660. *Yudt v Leonard Ross and Craig* ITELR 531.
[22] As originally drafted TA 1925 ss.37 and 39 did not allow a trustee to be discharged or retire without a new appointment unless at least two *individuals* or a trust corporation remained. Since 1889 a company had been a "person" (Interpretation Act 1889 s.19) but was it an individual? Mann J. in the *Jasmine* case held that companies were not individuals for this purpose which was very unfortunate for the settlement in question. (TLATA 1996 replaced "individuals" with "persons" so this particular trap no longer exists.)

9

(iii) In 1985 T purported to retire appointing a non-resident individual (G) to replace him. T was not discharged as two individuals were not left and G's appointment was invalid as Mrs Coaker did not join in.

(iv) From 1987 onwards various retirements and purported appointments of new non-resident trustees took place together with appointments of trust property. Because Mrs Coaker and T did not participate in the various appointments, they were all invalid.

(v) In 1989 T died.

(vi) In 1996 Mrs Coaker died.

There were two problems for the trust:

(i) It remained onshore until the death of Major-General Coaker, came back onshore in 1989 with the death of T and then became offshore again on the death of Mrs Coaker. The Revenue, therefore, raised assessments for capital gains tax and income tax.

(ii) The appointments of capital were invalid having been made by the wrong people.

Trustees and lack of capacity

1.17 Losing capacity is a ground for removal and replacement of a trustee under TA 1925 s.36(1). However, the trustee continues in office until removed so decisions and appointments made will be invalid if made by the other trustees without removing the incapable trustee.

EXAMPLE 1.4

Ann, Ben and Chris are the trustees of the AAA Settlement. Chris loses capacity. Ann and Ben take no steps in relation to Chris but continue to act alone. All their actions are ineffective.

If the trustee has a beneficial interest, approval must be obtained from the Court of Protection for his replacement.[23] This requires payment of a £400 application fee.

V SHAM TRUSTS

1.18 If the settlement is a sham then the trust is ineffective and there has been no disposal for capital gains tax purposes nor transfer of value for IHT.[24] The

---

[23] TA1925 s.36(9).
[24] For a discussion of sham trusts in the context of divorce see Ch.38 and *A v A & St George Trustees* [2007] EWHC 99 (Fam). The leading case on the definition of sham is *Snook v London*

three elements necessary to establish that a trust is a sham under English law[25] are:

(i) the settlor intends the assets to be held on terms different to those set out in the trust deed;

(ii) the trustee also intends the assets to be so held or goes along with the settlor's intention in a reckless manner; and

(iii) both parties intend to give a false impression of the position to third parties or to the court.

Intention should not be confused with motive. If the settlor had the motive of avoiding creditors when setting up the trust this would not make the trust a sham. However, a sham arises if the documents executed by the parties to the transaction were intended to present to third parties the appearance of creating legal rights and obligations different from the actual legal rights and obligations.

In *Hitch v Stone*[26] the Court of Appeal stated that

"it is of the essence . . . that the parties to a transaction intend to create one set of rights and obligations but do acts or enter into documents which they intend should give third parties, in this case the Revenue or the court, the appearance of creating different rights and obligations".[27]

There has been some debate about whether both parties (trustees and settlor) must intend the deception from the outset or whether it is enough if the settlor alone intends something different to that which is contained in the trust deed. In the Jersey case of *Re Esteem Settlement; Abacus (CI) Ltd v Sheikh Fahad Mohammad al Sabah*[28] a claim based on a unilateral sham was rejected. The Court held:

"in our judgment, in order for a trust to be a sham, both the settlor and the trustee must intend that the true arrangement is otherwise than as set out in the trust deed . . . in order to succeed, the plaintiffs will need to establish that, as well as the settlor, the trustee intended that the assets would be held upon terms otherwise than as set out in the trust deed or alternatively went along with the settlor's intention to that effect without knowing or caring what it had signed and that both parties intended to give a false impression of the position to third parties or to the court."

In that case although the trustees had always implemented requests of the settlor they had given genuine consideration to those requests and the trust

& *West Riding Investments* [1967] 2 QB at 801 and see *Lewin on Trusts* 18th edn, para.4.19 and following.

[25] Although the Jersey Courts have followed suit. *Mackinnon v The Regent Trust Company* [2005] JCA 066 sets out how the principles formulated in English law sham cases apply to Jersey law trusts.

[26] [2001] STC 214.

[27] See also *Rahman v Chase Bank* [1991] JLR 103 and *Midland Bank v Wyatt* [1995] 3 FCR 11 where the trust was held to be a sham.

[28] [2003] JRC 093; [2004] WTLR 1.

had been properly managed and administered. There was no evidence that the trustee took the trusteeship on any basis other than set out in the trust deed, i.e. there was no common intention to mislead.

1.19   The approach of the Jersey Courts to sham trusts was later approved in the English High Court in *Shalson v Russo*[29] where Rimer J. stated:

> "*I respectfully regard the approach adopted by the Royal Court in the Abacus case as correct. It is not only squarely in line with the guidance given by the Court of Appeal in Snook and Hitch, it also appears to me to be correct in principle. When a settlor creates a settlement he purports to divest himself of assets in favour of the trustee, and the trustee accepts them on the basis of the trusts of the settlement. The settlor may have an unspoken intention that the assets are in fact to be treated as his own and that the trustee will accede to his every request on demand. But unless that intention is from the outset shared by the trustee (or later become so shared), I fail to see how the settlement can be regarded as a sham. Once the assets are vested in the trustee, they will be held on the declared trusts, and he is entitled to regard them as so held and to ignore any demands from the settlor as to how to deal with them. I cannot understand on what basis a third party could claim, merely by reference to the unilateral intentions of the settlor, that the settlement was sham and that the assets in fact remained the settlor's property . . . if the donee accepted the gift on the footing that it was a genuine gift, the donor's undeclared intentions cannot turn an ostensibly valid disposition of his property into no disposition at all. To set that sort of case up the donee must also be shown to be a party to the alleged sham. In my judgment, in the case of a settlement executed by a settlor and a trustee, it is insufficient in considering whether or not it is a sham to look merely at the intentions of the settlor. It is essential also to look at those of the trustee.*"

VI TAXATION ISSUES

1.20   Generally speaking the trust is a separate taxable entity distinct from both the settlor and the beneficiaries. Hence trustees are responsible for the making of tax returns and payment of tax due. This has resulted in avoidance opportunities in times when the rates of tax applicable to trusts have been less than those which apply to individuals. Recent governments have generally raised tax rates for trusts so that they equate to the highest rates that apply to an individual in order to prevent advantages arising when property is held in trust.

1.21   The ill-starred trust modernisation programme sought to develop common definitions of basic trust concepts in the realm of income tax and CGT (although not IHT!). For the tax lawyer a "settlement", especially in the realm of income tax[30], sometimes has a far wider meaning than the normal usage of that word (wider, for instance, than it would be understood by a chancery lawyer). It can include an outright transfer of assets (as where a father opens a bank account for his minor child) as well as an "arrangement". By contrast,

---

[29] [2003] EWHC 1637.
[30] See ITTOIA 2005 s.620.

12

the IHT definition is narrower[31] and corresponds more to the traditional chancery idea of a settlement. Applying these concepts to foreign entities is not always easy.[32]

VII HASTINGS-BASS AND MISTAKE

The complexity of UK tax law has led to trustees making mistakes. Similarly, **1.22** settlements may be created without appreciating that the settlor will incur a substantial tax liability. In recent years a large body of case law has developed with trustees seeking to escape from decisions that they regretted by invoking the so-called rule in *Hastings-Bass* and the doctrine of mistake being used to set aside the unwanted gift or settlement.

Virtually all the decisions on *Hastings-Bass* and mistake were at First Instance. In the early cases HMRC were not represented. When they subsequently were represented, they argued that the line of cases was wrong in allowing professional advisers to escape from the consequences of their mistakes in an unjustifiable way. The response from the courts to these arguments was that they were too late in the day. The case law at First Instance was too well settled to overturn; only the Court of Appeal could change it. Finally, in two appeals heard together, *Pitt v Holt* and *Futter v Futter*,[33] the Court of Appeal got its chance and declared that the law had taken "*a wrong turn*".

What was thought to be the ratio decidendi of *Hastings-Bass*[34]

The following statement by Buckley L.J.[35] had been regarded as the ratio deci- **1.23** dendi of the *Hastings-Bass* case:

> "*To sum up the preceding observations, in our judgment, where by the terms of a trust (as under section 32) a trustee is given a discretion as to some matter under which he acts in good faith, the court should not interfere with his action notwithstanding that it does not have the full effect which he intended, unless (1) what he has achieved is unauthorised by the power conferred upon him, or (2) it is clear that he would not have acted as he did (a) had he not taken into account considerations which he should not have taken into account, or (b) had he not failed to take into account considerations which he ought to have taken into account.*"

In the subsequent case of *Mettoy Pension Trustees v Evans*[36] Warner J. said at 1624B:

---

[31] See IHTA 1984 s.43 and Ch.24. See also Ch.9 for a further discussion of settled property.
[32] See Ch.2.
[33] [2011] EWCA Civ 197.
[34] [1975] Ch 25.
[35] At 41F–H.
[36] [1990] 1 WLR 1587.

> "*I have come to the conclusion that there is a principle which may be labelled 'the rule in Hastings-Bass'. I do not think that the application of that principle is confined . . . to cases where an exercise by trustees of a discretion vested in them is partially ineffective because of some rule of law or because of some limit on their discretion which they overlooked. If, as I believe, the reason for the application of the principle is the failure by the trustees to take into account considerations that they ought to have taken into account, it cannot matter whether that failure is due to their having overlooked (or to their legal advisers having overlooked) some relevant rule of law or limit on their discretion, or is due to some other cause.*
>
> *It is not enough, however, for the principle to apply, that it should be shown that the trustees did not have a proper understanding of the effect of their act. It must also be clear that, had they had a proper understanding of it, they would not have acted as they did.*"

1.24   The Court of Appeal has now concluded that the true ratio of *Hastings-Bass* is very much more limited. On Warner J.'s decision in *Mettoy* Lloyd L.J. said at [72]:

> "*The principle on the basis of which the judge decided this aspect of the case cannot, in my judgment, be found in the decision in Re Hastings-Bass itself. What the trustees did in relation to the Mettoy pension scheme was within their powers.*"

Mummery L.J. said at [227]:

> "*these appeals provide examples of that comparatively rare instance of the law taking a seriously wrong turn*".

The correct ratio decidendi

1.25   According to Lloyd L.J. the true ratio of the *Hastings-Bass* case was set out at [40H–41C] of Buckley L.J.'s judgment and is as follows:

> "*Trustees considering an advancement by way of sub-settlement must apply their minds to the question whether the sub-settlement as a whole will operate for the benefit of the person to be advanced. If one or more aspects of the provisions intended to be created cannot take effect, it does not follow that those which can take effect should not be regarded as having been brought into being by an exercise of the discretion. That fact, and the misapprehension on the part of the trustees as to the effect that it would have, is not by itself fatal to the effectiveness of the advancement . . . If the provisions that can and would take effect cannot reasonably be regarded as being for the benefit of the person to be advanced, then the exercise fails as not being within the scope of the power of advancement. Otherwise it takes effect to the extent that it can.*"

When can the exercise by trustees of a dispositive power be set aside?

Lloyd L.J. concluded that Lightman J. had been correct when he said in **1.26**
Abacus v Barr[37] that to challenge the exercise of a discretion successfully, there
must have been a breach of duty by the trustees. He identified two types of
case in which the exercise of discretions can be challenged. In one the exercise
is void; in the other voidable.

(i) If what is done is not within the scope of the power, it will be void. For
   instance:

   - A procedural defect, such as the use of the wrong kind of docu-
     ment, the failure to obtain a necessary prior consent or the wrong
     people executing the document.[38]
   - A substantive defect, such as an unauthorised delegation, or an
     appointment to someone who is not within the class of objects
     (cases of a fraud on a power are similar).[39]
   - A defect under the general law, such as the rule against perpetui-
     ties, the impact and significance of which will depend on the extent
     of the invalidity.

(ii) If what is done is within the terms of the power, but the trustees have in
   some way breached their duties in respect of that exercise, then (unless it
   is a case of a fraud on the power) the act is not void but it may be voidable at the instance of a beneficiary who is adversely affected (subject to
   equitable defences and the court's discretion).

If a third party purchaser has acquired trust property as a result, he may have
an indefeasible title if he gave value without notice of the breach of fiduciary
duty but in such a case the beneficiary's interest would attach to the proceeds
of the sale.[40]

What are the duties of a trustee?

Trustees are under a duty of care, obliging them to exercise such skill and care **1.27**
as is reasonable in the circumstances. They have to weigh benefits and take into
account relevant factors when exercising a discretionary power. It is not possible to lay down any absolute rule as to the matters which trustees ought to
take into account when considering the exercise of a power of advancement or
some other dispositive power. For instance, in many cases fiscal consequences
may be relevant considerations which the trustees ought to take into account.
Circumstances will differ from one trust to another, and even within one trust

---

[37] [2003] EWHC 114 (Ch).
[38] For example in the case of *Jasmine Trustees Ltd v Wells & Hind*—see above at fn.21 many
   documents were invalid because they had been executed by people who were not the
   trustees!
[39] See the striking case of *Turner v Turner* [1984] Ch 100, where the trustees executed documents
   prepared on the instructions of the settlor without considering the exercise of their discretion.
[40] See *Foskett v McKeown* [2001] 1 AC 102 at 127F–G (Lord Millett).

they may change from time to time or according to the nature of the particular exercise under consideration.

Professional advice

1.28 Where tax matters are relevant it is likely to be the duty of the trustees to take proper advice. But where trustees have taken advice from appropriate and reputable advisers on how to proceed in a tax efficient manner which they follow, they will not be in breach of duty if that advice turns out to be wrong. Hence, in the absence of any other basis for a challenge, the trustees will not be in breach of their fiduciary duty for a failure to have regard to relevant matters. Accordingly in such a case the trustees' act is not voidable. Lloyd L.J. accepted:

> "that this distinction makes potentially vulnerable an act done by trustees who fail to take any advice, whereas the same act done in the same circumstances by trustees who take advice which proves to be incorrect is not vulnerable. That is said to reduce significantly the protection afforded to beneficiaries by the Hastings-Bass rule. I accept that the point of the principle is to protect beneficiaries rather than trustees. I also accept that a claim by beneficiaries against the trustees themselves may often be precluded by an exoneration clause in the trust deed. It may also be . . . that a claim against the professional advisers of the trustees would face problems even if liability can be established, because different loss may be suffered by different people, not all of whom may have a claim against the advisers. Recognising those points, nevertheless I see no anomaly in the distinction that I have drawn. It arises from the need to find a breach of trust in order to set aside an act of the trustees which is within their powers . . . One practical consequence, if I am right, is that if in future it is desired to challenge an exercise by trustees of a discretionary power on this basis, it will be necessary for one or more beneficiaries to grasp the nettle of alleging and proving a breach of fiduciary duty on the part of the trustees. Only rarely would it be appropriate for the trustees to take the initiative in the proceedings."

Was relief available in the cases being appealed?

1.29 No. Applying the principles set out above as the trustees in both *Futter* and *Pitt v Holt* had acted within their powers and taken and relied on proper advice, the exercise of their discretion was not voidable.[41]

---

[41] Many of the decided First Instance cases would be decided differently as a result of the Court of Appeal decision. For instance, *Green v Cobham* [2002] STC 820; *Abacus Trust Co v NSPCC* [2001] STC 1344 and *Sieff v Fox* [2005] EWHC 1312 (Ch), all of which involved mistakes as to the impact of CGT, and *Burrell v Burrell* [2005] STC 569 involving a mistake as to IHT.

The equitable jurisdiction to set aside a voluntary transaction for mistake

There is a long standing equitable jurisdiction to set aside voluntary disposi- **1.30**
tions which are vitiated by fraud, undue influence, unconscionable bargains
and mistake. However, there are differences in the case law as to the type of
mistake required. In *Pitt v Holt* application had been made to set aside the
transaction on the basis of mistake as well as *Hastings-Bass* so the Court of
Appeal considered the various tests.

An early case was the Court of Appeal and House of Lords decisions in
Ogilvie v Littleboy[42] and *Ogilvie v Allen*[43] dismissing an application to set aside
various voluntary dispositions to charity which a wealthy widow had come to
regret. In the Court of Appeal Lindley L.J. said:

> "*Gifts cannot be revoked, nor can deeds of gift be set aside, simply because
> the donors wish they had not made them and would like to have back the
> property given. Where there is no fraud, no undue influence, no fiduciary
> relation between donor and donee, no mistake induced by those who derive
> any benefit by it, a gift, whether by mere delivery or by deed, is binding on
> the donor.*
>   *. . . In the absence of all circumstances of suspicion a donor can only
> obtain back property which he has given away by showing that he was under
> some mistake of so serious a character as to render it unjust on the part of
> the donee to retain the property given to him.*"

Lord Halsbury L.C. in the House of Lords referred to setting aside transactions where "*misunderstanding on both sides may render it unjust to the giver
that the gift should be retained.*"

Another case decided in 1909 illustrates a different basis for the jurisdic- **1.31**
tion. In *Lady Hood of Avalon v Mackinnon*,[44] Lady Hood had power under
her marriage settlement to appoint capital to her two daughters. In 1888 she
appointed half the fund to her elder daughter. In 1902 and 1904 she appointed
sums to her younger daughter. Having forgotten the appointment to her elder
daughter, Lady Hood made a further appointment to her in an attempt to
achieve equality between the two. When she discovered the duplication of
gifts she applied to have the gift set aside. Eve J. said that forgetting the earlier
disposition was equivalent to a mistake:

> "*It seems to me that when a person has forgotten the existence of a pre-
> existing fact, and assumes that such fact did not pre-exist, he is labouring
> under a mistake, and he acts on the footing that the fact really did not
> pre-exist.*"

On that basis, and satisfied that the last appointment was made under a
mistake with regard to the existing facts, he held that she was entitled to have
the appointment set aside.

[42] (1897) 13 TLR 399.
[43] (1899) 15 TLR 294.
[44] [1909] 1 Ch 476.

1.32   In *Gibbon v Mitchell*[45] the plaintiff had a protected life interest under
a settlement, and a limited power to appoint an annuity to a surviving
spouse, and subject to that the capital was held on trust for his children.
For tax planning reasons he wished his children's interest in the fund to be
accelerated and was advised that he could achieve this by surrendering his
life interest. He did so but because the life interest was protected, a discretionary trust was created.[46] The beneficiaries of this discretionary trust
included all his children, whenever born, and not, as he wished, his present
children.

Millett J. referred to a number of cases where voluntary dispositions were
set aside for mistake. He summarised these cases as follows[47]:

> "In my judgment, these cases show that, wherever there is a volun-
> tary transaction by which one party intends to confer a bounty on
> another, the deed will be set aside if the court is satisfied that the dis-
> ponor did not intend the transaction to have the effect which it did. It
> will be set aside for mistake whether the mistake is a mistake of law or
> of fact, so long as the mistake is as to the effect of the transaction itself
> and not merely as to its consequences or the advantages to be gained by
> entering into it"

He held that the plaintiff was mistaken as to the effect of the deed of surrender in that he believed that the effect of surrendering his life interest would
be that his two children would become entitled to the fund immediately and
absolutely.

1.33   There have been suggestions that *Ogilvie* and *Gibbon* propounded different tests but Lloyd L.J. said there was no incompatibility. He referred
to a later passage in *Gibbon* where what Millett J. said was much closer to
Ogilvie:

> "Mr. Gibbon did not merely execute the deed under a mistake of law as to
> the legal consequences of his doing so. He executed it under a mistake as
> to its legal effect. The deed itself shows that to be the case. Since its effect
> was not that which he intended, he is entitled to have it set aside. Equity
> acts on the conscience. The parties whose interest it would be to oppose
> the setting aside of the deed are the unborn future children of Mr. Gibbon
> and the objects of discretionary trust to arise on forfeiture, that is to say
> his grandchildren, nephews and nieces. They are all volunteers. In my judg-
> ment they could not conscionably insist upon their legal rights under the
> deed once they had become aware of the circumstances in which they had
> acquired them."

The requirement in *Gibbon* that the mistake be as to the effect not
the consequences is significant as it rules out a remedy where a donor
understands the effect of a transaction but is mistaken as to the fiscal
consequences.

---

[45] [1990] 1 WLR 1304.
[46] For protective trusts, see TA 1925 s.33.
[47] At 1309D–F.

The test for mistake

Lloyd L.J. reviewed the sometimes conflicting case law (on-shore and off-shore) over the last 150 years and concluded that the correct test as a matter of authority and of principle was a combination of *Gibbon v Mitchell, Lady Hood* and *Ogilvie v Littleboy*:

- There must be a mistake on the part of the donor either as to the legal effect of the disposition (*Gibbon*) or as to an existing fact which is basic to the transaction (*Lady Hood*).

- The mistake must be of sufficient gravity as to satisfy the *Ogilvie v Littleboy* test, which provides protection to the recipient against too ready an ability of the donor to seek to recall his gift.

- The fact that the transaction gives rise to unforeseen fiscal liabilities is a consequence, not an effect, for this purpose, and is not sufficient to bring the jurisdiction into play.

Lloyd L.J. considered *Re Griffiths (Deceased)*[48] where a substantial gift made by a man who did not know that he had terminal cancer was set aside. The donor had been advised to take out life assurance to cover the possibility of death within seven years but had decided not to bother:

> "*I wonder whether the judge would have come to the same conclusion on the law (quite apart from the facts) if the case had been argued in a fully adversarial manner. It seems to me that there would have been a strong argument for saying that, having declined to follow the recommendation that he should take out term insurance, Mr Griffiths was taking the risk that his health was, or would come to be, such that he did not survive. If that was the correct view, it seems to me that the answer to the Ogilvie v Littleboy test would have been that it was not against conscience for the recipients of the gift to retain it. Ogilvie v Littleboy was cited by the judge, but he did not pose the question derived from that case in terms when he came to state his conclusion. I do not criticise the judge, given the limited argument before him, but I do question his conclusion. I do not see what there was in the case that could have justified a favourable answer to the Ogilvie v Littleboy test.*"

Applying the test to the facts in *Pitt v Holt*

Mr Pitt was left brain damaged after a road accident and received £1.2 million in agreed damages. His wife was appointed his receiver. Acting on the advice of financial advisers Mrs Pitt transferred the lump sum to a discretionary

---

[48] [2008] EWHC 118 (Ch); [2009] Ch162. In this case Lewison J. commented, "*in my judgment, a mistake about an existing or pre-existing fact, if sufficiently serious, is enough to bring the jurisdiction into play. If and to the extent that Millett J intended to restrict the scope of the equitable jurisdiction to a mistake about the effect of the transaction, I respectfully disagree.*"

settlement. The settlement was not a trust for the disabled under IHTA 1984 s.89 and so IHT was payable both on creation and on 10-yearly anniversaries. No one ever considered the impact of inheritance tax. Englehart QC sitting as a Deputy Judge had set aside the settlement on the basis of *Hastings-Bass*, but had said that he would not have done so on the basis of mistake.[49] Lloyd L.J. agreed that it could not be set aside on the basis of mistake. The respondents need to show three things in order to succeed:

(i) that there was a mistake,

(ii) that it was a relevant type of mistake,

(iii) that it was sufficiently serious to satisfy the *Ogilvie v Littleboy* test.

Mrs Pitt did hold a belief as to the tax effects which were mistaken as regards IHT. The mistake was probably serious enough to satisfy the *Ogilvie v Littleboy* test. However, the fact that there was a liability to pay IHT was a consequence, not an effect, of the transaction. Equally, the fact that the trustees came under a secondary liability to pay the tax was a consequence. The legal effect was the creation of the trust on its particular terms. Each aspect of the charges to IHT upon the creation of the settlement, the assignment of the trust property to the trustees, and the course of dealings with the trust property under the settlement has to be regarded as a consequence of the transaction, not part of its legal effect:

> "*Mrs Pitt is entitled to feel that she has been badly let down by the advice that she was given, and the failure of her advisers to address the question of IHT, especially as the liability could have been avoided so easily. However, it seems to me that her remedy for that (and likewise that of the Futter family for the corresponding errors in their case) lies not in the realms of equity but by way of a claim for damages for professional negligence.*"

1.37   The decision in *Pitt v Holt* is at variance with the approach taken in a number of cases in the Jersey courts and other offshore jurisdictions. For example, in *Clarkson v Barclays Private Bank (Isle of Man) Ltd*[50] the plaintiff had emigrated to Spain from the UK and in order to protect his assets from income tax and death duties set up a discretionary trust in the Isle of Man. He transferred sums to it in 1987 in the belief that those payments would not give rise to any charge to IHT. However, he was deemed domiciled at that time in the UK with the result that a liability to IHT arose on the transfers. Deemster Kerruish held that there was no rational basis for restricting setting aside the transaction to circumstances where a mistake had been made as to the operative effect of that transaction. There could be recovery of the gifted property where the mistake was so serious as to render it unjust for the donee to retain the property, *irrespective of the precise nature of the mistake.*

1.38   Similarly in *Re Betsam Trust*,[51] as a result of a misunderstanding of IHTA 1984 s.267 a married couple wrongly believed that a trust they had created had no IHT liability. The Manx Courts set aside the voluntary transaction on

---

[49] See [2010] EWHC 45 (Ch).
[50] [2007] WTLR 1703.
[51] [2009] WTLR 1489.

the ground of mistake, deciding that *there was a broad equitable jurisdiction to set aside a voluntary transaction on the ground of a mistake as to its fiscal consequences*. In *Mr and Mr P Capital Asset Protection Plan Trust*[52] a UK domiciled married couple settled the proceeds of their business (£1 million) into a non-charitable purpose trust in July 2006. They were advised that this would save inheritance tax and that they could still benefit from the trust. There were many flaws in the arrangements including the fact that the trustees had no power to make loans to the settlors so that the settlors did not have ready access to the funds. In effect their life savings were frozen. The transfers of cash into the trust were set aside on the basis of mistake and the annuity contracts were declared void. See also *In the Matter of the R Remuneration Trust*[53] where the settlor added nearly £3 million to a Jersey "remuneration trust" and *In the matter of the A Trust and Article 11(2) of the Trust (Jersey) Law 1984*[54] where in both cases the Royal Court set aside the trusts on the ground of mistake. Whether the Jersey, Manx and Guernsey Courts will alter their approach to take account of the ratio in *Pitt v Holt* (and *Futter* in relation to *Hastings-Bass* applications) remains to be seen.[55]

VIII ACCUMULATION AND PERPETUITY ISSUES

When exercising dispositive powers trustees must keep in mind perpetuity and accumulation issues. The rule against perpetuities prescribes a period within which the interests of beneficiaries are required to vest.[56] The rule against excessive accumulations restricts the period during which income can be added to the trust capital rather than distributed as income. Both rules have recently been overhauled but generally only in respect of new settlements and will trusts (settlements set up on and after April 6, 2010 and wills executed on or after that date). In practice, trusts will be encountered which were originally set up many years ago and accordingly it is necessary to set out briefly the rules which have applied at different times. **1.39**

Trusts created before July 1, 1964

For these trusts the common law rule of perpetuities applies and all interests must vest during the period of the lifetimes of one or more persons living **1.40**

---

[52] [2008] JRC 159.

[53] [2009] JRC 164A.

[54] [2009] JRC 245.

[55] Early indications are that they will not! The Royal Court of Jersey *In the matter of the S Trust* [2011] JRC 117 decided that a gift of shares to a Jersey resident trust was voidable on the grounds of the donor's mistake. The test to be applied, the court decided, was whether the donor was under some mistake of so serious a character as to render it unjust for the donee to retain the property. It had to be shown that the donor would not have entered into the transaction but for the mistake (which could include a mistake as to the fiscal consequences of the gift). The distinction drawn in the English courts between the effects of a transaction and its consequences was rejected.

[56] The rule does not apply to charitable trusts or to trusts that are subject to a power of revocation reserved by the settlor. See *Lewin on Trusts* 18th edn, para.5.92.

when the trust is created plus 21 years. "Royal lives" clauses are commonly found, e.g.:

> *"the period ending 21 years after the death of the last survivor of the issue living on the date of the settlement of his late Majesty King George V"*.

This means that the dispositive powers of the trustees must be exercised during this period and in a manner which complies with the rule against perpetuities. The problems caused by this perpetuity rule can be demonstrated by the following example. The settlor, S, makes a gift of property to his eldest son, A, who is not yet married. The trust provides that the property is to be held on trust for A for his life and then for his widow for her life and on her death in equal shares to the children of A then living absolutely. The gifts for the children will not necessarily vest within the perpetuity period. Although the gift to A the son, giving an immediate interest in possession, is not void, and A's widow must take within 21 years of the death of A, the gift to the children may not vest in the perpetuity period because the widow, who is not a life in being, may die more than 21 years after A. No children of A have yet been born so they are not lives in being. On that basis the interests of the children would fail.

Interests given by an appointment under a special power or by exercise of an advancement-type power must vest within the perpetuity period running from the date when the settlement was created. Hence, if the instrument is exercised after July 1964 the perpetuity period cannot be changed to a fixed period so pre-1964 trusts are stuck with a lives in being period albeit now operating on a "wait and see" basis.

Trusts established from 1964 to 2010

1.41 PAA 1964, which came into force on July 16, 1964, modified the operation of the common law rule in two main ways. First, it allowed settlors to specify a fixed perpetuity period of up to 80 years as an alternative to a lives in being clause. Secondly, it introduced a system of "wait and see" which provided that where an interest in property could vest outside the perpetuity period and so would be void at common law, that provision was not automatically void but a wait and see rule applied. Did the property in fact vest in the perpetuity period? If so the provision was valid, otherwise void. So in the example above the interests of the children would only be void if they were not born within 21 years of S or A's death. This applied to existing pre-1964 trusts.

The position from April 6, 2010

1.42 The Law Commission proposed reforms of the rule against perpetuities and the rule against excessive accumulations of income in its 1998 report (No.251 *The Rule Against Perpetuities and Excessive Accumulations*). The recommendations were accepted by the Government in 2001 but no parliamentary time was available to deal with it and it was not until April 2009 that the Perpetuities and Accumulations Bill was introduced into the House of Lords using a new procedure developed to help clear the backlog of unimplemented Law Commission Reports. It was implemented as PAA 2009, coming into force on April 6, 2010.

The Act provides for a mandatory perpetuity period of 125 years to replace **1.43** the two alternatives of (i) a life or lives in being plus 21 years (at common law) or (ii) a specified number of years, not exceeding 80 years (under the 1964 Act). The new 125-year period takes precedence over whatever the trust instrument may say. The Act applies to trusts taking effect and wills executed on or after April 6, 2010. Trusts already in existence and wills executed before April 6, 2010 are, therefore, not generally affected.

However, PAA 2009 s.12 allows trustees of existing trusts to opt for a fixed period of 100 years where the perpetuity period is defined by reference to a life or lives in being and it is difficult, or not reasonably practicable, to ascertain whether the lives have ended. Trustees must execute a deed stating that they believe there is such a difficulty and that the instrument is to be treated as if it specified a period of 100 years (no other period is possible).

PAA 2009 s.6(2) provides that the perpetuity period for an instrument created in the exercise of a special power of appointment will begin on the date on which the instrument creating the power took effect. The rule is different for trusts created under a general power of appointment which is exercised after April 5, 2010. Here, the perpetuity period will be 125 years beginning on the date on which the power is exercised, not the date on which it was created.

The "wait and see" rule is retained.

Most practitioners will continue to include a trust perpetuity period. For **1.44** instance:

> *"The 'Trust Period' shall mean the period ending on the last day of the period of 125 years from the date of my death which period (and no other) shall be the perpetuity period for this settlement."*

Some jurisdictions adopt a longer period than 125 years. Jersey and **1.45** Guernsey do not have a rule against perpetuities. Both formerly had a 100 year rule providing that the trust had to terminate on the expiration of 100 years from the date of its creation. Under this rule it was not sufficient for the interests to vest within that period; the trust must actually end.[57] By contrast, under English law the beneficiaries' interests must vest during the perpetuity period but the beneficiary does not need to take absolutely at the end of such period.

---

[57] Trusts (Jersey) Law 1984 art.15 now provides *"unless its terms provide otherwise, a trust may continue in existence for an unlimited period. No rule against perpetuities or excessive accumulations shall apply to a trust or to any advancement, appointment, payment or application of assets from a trust. Except where the terms of a trust provide to the contrary any advancement, appointment, payment or application of assets from that trust to another trust shall be valid even if that other trust may continue after the date by which the first trust must terminate."* Hence, the duration of an old Jersey trust with a fixed period ending in (say) 2040 may be extended by transferring assets to a new trust with an unlimited period. Of course, such a transfer may have capital gains tax implications.

EXAMPLE 1.5

The perpetuity period for the Jenkins Discretionary Trust was 80 years from the creation of the trust in 1970. Just before the expiry of that period the trustees irrevocably exercised their powers of appointment to give Sally (aged 21) a life interest in the entire trust fund with remainder to her daughter, Rosamund (aged 2) absolutely. Both the beneficiaries have interests which are vested at the end of the perpetuity period and the trust will therefore continue until Sally's death. The trustees' administrative powers continue but there are no longer any dispositive powers (e.g. the statutory power of advancement under TA 1925 s.32 has ended).

Application of the rules to pensions

1.46 When an individual joins a pension scheme he enters into a new settlement. This will fix the perpetuity date if property is transferred into another settlement. For instance, if a member joins the scheme on April 4, 2010 the old rules apply (in the absence of a term of years being selected, this will be the life of the member plus 21 years[58]) but if the member joins on April 6, 2010 the new rules apply (125 years). If setting up a trust to receive death benefits (sometimes called a "spousal by-pass trust"), it is desirable to tie the perpetuity period into that of the pension trust.

But there is a difficulty: the new trust will have the mandatory 125 year period from date of settlement whereas the assets transferred from the original pension scheme may be subject to the old perpetuity period. The solution is that although the perpetuity period of a new trust is mandatory, it is possible to limit the "Trust Period". (There is also "wait and see".) Accordingly in the new trust:

(i) the perpetuity period *must be* 125 years; however

(ii) the deed should define the *Trust Period* by reference to the permitted period under the pension trust (commonly life of member plus 21 years). This is the period within which interests must vest and so will ensure compliance with the pension perpetuity period. (In any event the "wait and see" principle ensures that the transfer into the by-pass trust will not be void ab initio.)[59]

---

[58] Other persons may be included as "relevant lives", e.g. the member's spouse and children alive at the time when he joined the scheme.
[59] See the precedent at A1.5.

Varying the dispositions of a will under IHTA 1984 s.142[60] to create a settlement

EXAMPLE 1.6

> Aaron died on August 6, 2009 leaving his estate to his wife, Frida, absolutely. On August 6, 2010 she executes a deed of variation by which she settles the estate on a life interest trust (IPDI) for herself, remainder on discretionary trusts for her issue. *Note*:
>
> (i) the variation is read-back for *IHT purposes*, i.e. it is as if Aaron had set up the trust in his will;
> (ii) but for all other purposes Frida creates the trust on August 6, 2010 and the 125 year perpetuity period applies.
>
> Contrast the position if the will had set up a trust which was varied (e.g. by one beneficiary assigning his interest to another): in this case the date of the will determines the relevant perpetuity period (on these facts the old law applies).[61]

Other problems—short trust periods and exercising powers of appointment

Even if the perpetuity period for the settlement has not ended, the trust deed **1.47** may specify that any power of appointment can only be exercised within a Trust Period which may be shorter than the perpetuity period and may have expired! Sometimes the settlor specifies that the trustees must exercise dispositive powers within (say) 40 years of the date of the settlement! It is important that a Trust Period is not confused with the perpetuity period. In the above example, it will usually be possible for the trustees to exercise their powers within the 40 year Trust Period and as part of that appointment give themselves new powers of appointment which are exercisable within the (longer) perpetuity period.

EXAMPLE 1.7

> The X Will Trust has perpetuity period which is specified to be the lives of his children living at X's death plus 21 years. All four children of the testator are still alive when he dies. The will also gives the trustees a power of appointment in favour of the Beneficiaries (being the issue of the testator) to be exercised during the Specified Period (which ends on January 31, 2009) and in default of such appointment the

---

[60] See further Ch.39.
[61] Note also the variation of trusts case of *Wyndham v Egremont* [2009] EWHC 076 (Ch) in which the settlement was given a new perpetuity period but the court concluded that this did not involve the creation of a new settlement for CGT purposes (i.e. there was no deemed disposal): see further 12.21.

children take equally. The trustees do not want the trust to end and the children would prefer the fund to be held for their children born now or in the future. In 2008 the trustees exercise their power of appointment in terms that they have power to pay or apply capital at any time during the perpetuity period at their discretion to Beneficiaries alive now or born during the perpetuity period. Future born issue can then benefit.

Accumulations[62]

1.48   The statutory rules against excessive accumulations (there has never been a common law rule limiting accumulations) was abolished in the case of settlements created after April 5, 2010 and for will trusts when the will is executed after that date. It is now, therefore, possible to accumulate throughout the lifetime of a settlement. Existing trusts, however, remain bound by the old restrictions.

PAA 2009 does not override provisions in trust documents so the unrestricted power to accumulate will be subject to any express limitations in the trust instrument. For new trusts it is, therefore, important to update precedents. Trust instruments have commonly been drafted to give trustees powers to accumulate income limited to "the accumulation period" which is typically 21 years from the instrument taking effect.

Today the period should be defined as *"the accumulation period shall be the Trust Period"*[63]

1.49   Many trusts remain governed by the pre-2010 restrictions on accumulations which were as follows.

Section 164 of LPA 1925 and PAA 1964 provide for six specific periods during which income can be accumulated. Where a direction or power to accumulate exceeds the relevant statutory period (but not the common law perpetuity period) it is void as to the period in excess.[64] The four periods set out in s.164(1) LPA 1925 are:

(i) the life of the grantor/settlor;

(ii) 21 years from the death of grantor/settlor /testator (usually only appropriate for wills, life policies (non-income producing) held in trust);

(iii) the duration of the minority of persons living or *en ventre sa mare* at the

---

[62] The rule against excessive accumulations is a statutory rule that restricts the period during which the income may be accumulated and came about as a direct response to the case of *Thellusson v Woodford* (1805) 11 Ves Jr 112: it was feared that an unrestricted power to accumulate would result in such a concentration of wealth in private hands that it might compromise the economic independence of the nation or even threaten the power of the crown. The rule applies to charitable trusts but does not extend to corporate settlors. It does not apply to the administrative retention of income to smooth out the effect of fluctuations, allowing retention in good years and distribution in bad ones.

[63] Alternatively do not define an accumulation period but instead allow trustees to accumulate income as part of their general dispositive powers, all of which must be exercised during the Trust Period.

[64] See Thomas, *Powers*, 1st edn, para.4.69.

death of grantor/settlor/testator (rarely used—the period is shorter than the period of 21 years from the death of the settlor);

(iv) the duration of the minorities of any person who would, if of full age, be entitled to the accumulated income (this does not permit accumulation after a beneficiary attains 18 and would not apply if the trustees have an overriding power of appointment).

The other two periods set out in s.13 of the 1964 Act are:

(v) 21 years from the date of making the disposition. This is the most common period selected by settlors; and

(vi) The duration of the minority of any person in being at that date.

For existing trusts where the accumulation period has expired, what are the options? **1.50**

(i) The trustees must distribute income if they have no power to accumulate but they may not want to do this.

(ii) They could invest the trust fund so as to minimise income but this may be seen to be unduly restrictive.

(iii) They could move trust assets into a wholly-owned company which declares no dividends but this may have adverse tax implications, for example, such a transfer would be a disposal for capital gains tax purposes.

(iv) They could appoint a contingent interest in the whole of the trust fund to a minor so that income can be accumulated under s.31 TA 1925 until the child reaches 18 and then revoke that interest. This has no inheritance tax or CGT implications.

(v) They could change the governing law of the trust to a jurisdiction such as the Jersey or Guernsey which has no rule against accumulations. However, the trustees need an express power to change the governing law.[65] Article 8 of the Convention on the Law Applicable to Trusts and on their Recognition, as brought into force by RTA 1987, supports the ability to give a valid new accumulation period if the law of the trust has been validly changed. It is not thought that this will result in the creation of a new settlement (and consequent deemed disposal) for CGT purposes.

(vi) The trustees could, if they have sufficient powers, transfer the income they receive in Trust 1 to a new Trust 2 which has a longer accumulation period. The new trust would be one that benefits the existing beneficiaries of Trust 1. The income so transferred becomes capital in the hands of the recipient trustees who can then accumulate future income.

---

[65] *Chellaram v Chellaram No.2* [2002] 3 All ER 17.

CHAPTER 2

CATEGORISATION OF FOREIGN ENTITIES AND TRUSTS

I INTRODUCTION

2.01   The growth in the number of "international rich" has led to the increased use of offshore structures to hold wealth, which is often situated in a number of different countries. Such structures may not be tax driven: in many cases dynastic reasons prompt a wealthy family member to establish a structure to hold assets for his heirs. He wants to protect the assets from dissipation as a result of divorce, spendthrift children, or unwise business ventures and to secure an orderly succession of assets between various branches of the family. He may want to avoid the fragmentation of his wealth or the split up of a particular company. In some cases lifetime gifts can legitimately defeat forced heirship provisions or other legislation that restricts testamentary freedom.[1] Privacy and the desire to avoid probate in a number of different jurisdictions are other factors.

2.02   Although trusts are popular vehicles, many international families (especially from a civil law background) are unfamiliar with such structures and prefer to use something over which they can exercise more control. Members of a family resident in one jurisdiction may require entities different from those needed by another branch. An entity may be considered a settlement for inheritance tax purposes but may not be settled property for capital gains tax.[2] This chapter briefly considers the alternative structures, usually

---

[1] For example in some Sharia law countries it is permitted to make lifetime gifts where the donor is not on his death bed without having to follow Sharia law requirements in the division of the estate

[2] The income tax "settlement" provisions in ITTOIA 2005 ss.619–648 contain a wide definition of settlement designed, in the words of Lord Hoffmann in *Jones v Garnett* [2007] STC 1536 "*to prevent people from reducing their tax liability by settlements, gifts or similar arrangements which*

offshore, that the private client adviser will come across and considers their possible UK tax treatment.

Inheritance tax

IHTA 1984 s.43(2) defines "settlement" in the following terms: 2.03

> "'*Settlement' means any disposition or dispositions of property, whether effected by instrument, by parol or by operation of law, or partly in one way and partly in another, whereby the property is for the time being—*
>
> > (a) *held in trust for persons in succession or for any person subject to a contingency, or*
> >
> > (b) *held by trustees on trust to accumulate the whole or part of any income of the property or with power to make payments out of that income at the discretion of the trustees or some other person, with or without power to accumulate surplus income, or*
> >
> > (c) *charged or burdened (otherwise than for full consideration in money or money's worth paid for his own use or benefit to the person making the disposition) with the payment of any annuity or other periodical payment payable for a life or any other limited or terminable period,*
>
> *or would be so held or charged or burdened if the disposition or dispositions were regulated by the law of any part of the United Kingdom; or whereby, under the law of any other country, the administration of the property is for the time being governed by provisions equivalent in effect to those which would apply if the property were so held, charged or burdened.*"

Note, in particular: 2.04

(i) the application of a fiction if the dispositions were regulated by UK law would they have created a settlement as defined in (2)(a)–(c);

(ii) the requirement to look at the law of another country and see if the administration of the property is governed by provisions equivalent in effect to those which would apply if there was a settlement within the above provisions. The words "*equivalent in effect*" are somewhat imprecise: do they mean that the entity must be administered like a trust (e.g. so that those administering the property occupy a fiduciary position and must act in the interests of the beneficiaries?) or is it sufficient that the position is "broadly similar" to that of a trust?

(iii) section 43(4) makes provision to deal with the situation where Scots law applies: in particular a "settlement" includes "*a deed creating or reserving a proper liferent of any property whether heritable or moveable*".

transfer income or income-producing assets to their minor children or under which they or their spouses retained an interest".

CGT position

2.05   There is nothing similar in the CGT legislation which defines "settled property" as:

> "*property held in trust other than property to which section 60 applies and references, however expressed, to property comprised in a settlement are references to settled property*".[3]

The approach to be adopted

2.06   Questions arise as to whether foreign entities such as foundations establishments and usufructs are settlements companies or merely nominee arrangements. An analysis should first be made of how that foreign entity actually operates and its legal characteristics under its governing law. UK tax law must then be applied to establish how those legal characteristics are to be categorised for UK tax purposes.[4]

2.07   What can make the position particularly problematic is:

(i) in some cases two foreign entities with the same title are set up quite differently under their individual constitutions[5] with the result that (say) one is a settlement but the other is not. Each structure must be examined separately and one cannot assume that entities with the same name will be taxed in the UK in the same way;

(b) it is sometimes unclear how the entity operates in practice. It may be described as a trust and take effect as such under the foreign law in question, but in reality operates as a nominee arrangement;

(c) an entity may be treated as a settlement for the purposes of one tax but not another. There is evidence that HMRC are taking a more sophisticated approach nowadays and arguing that (say) a US grantor trust is a settlement for inheritance tax purposes but not for capital gains tax purposes.

2.08   The UK identification adopted is usually important. For instance, if a particular entity is a trust for inheritance tax purposes and holds a UK house then it is exposed to 10-year charges and if set up by a UK domiciliary entry charges may have been incurred.

---

[3] TCGA 1992 s.68. Section 60 excludes property held by nominees and on bare trusts: see 9.02 and following.
[4] See *Memec v IRC* 71 TC 77; [1998] STC 754, CA considering whether the structure is transparent or opaque.
[5] Similar problems can arise in determining whether a US limited liability company is transparent or opaque.

II FOUNDATIONS[6]

They are creatures of statute and the legislation of each jurisdiction differs. **2.09**
They are most associated with Liechtenstein but are also found in other civil
jurisdictions such as Austria, Switzerland, Panama, St Kitts, Seychelles,
Nevis, Anguilla, Antigua, Malta and the Netherlands Antilles. Jersey has also
introduced legislation allowing the establishment of foundations.[7]

Like a company a foundation is a separate legal entity which owns assets in **2.10**
its own right. The foundation can only be liable for debts up to the value of
those assets. This is in contrast to trusts where trustees do not have separate
legal personality; do not beneficially own the assets and can be made personally liable for trust debts. A foundation is incorporated by entry on a register
and, like a company, has a name and registration number. However, unlike
a company it has no shareholders: it is not "owned" by anyone.[8] It can last
indefinitely.

The "founder" (equivalent to a settlor) provides the assets and sets out in **2.11**
the declaration or articles (similar to a memorandum and articles of association) how the assets should be administered and how they be dealt with while
he is alive and after his death. There may also be bye-laws supplementing the
articles. The founder often reserves certain powers in the articles such as power
to change the bye-laws: revoke or add or exclude beneficiaries or remove the
Foundation Council. In some jurisdictions, such as Liechtenstein, the reservation of too many powers can now prevent the Foundation being properly
constituted.

The property is usually held "for persons in succession" or with the power **2.12**
to accumulate income. In that sense a foundation looks like a trust. It has a
Council or Board which administers the foundation.

It may have named beneficiaries or be established for specified purposes.
For example, some foundations are used like a purpose trust as the holding
vehicle for the shares in a private trust company which in turn acts as trustee
and holds the assets of the family.

It is not always clear what rights beneficiaries have against the Council to **2.13**

---

[6] Foundations are called *stiftungs* in Liechtenstein. They were originally used for religious or
charitable purposes.
[7] The Foundations (Jersey) Law 2008 became effective in 2009. Jersey and Bahamas are the only
common law jurisdictions that have established a foundations law, although the Isle of Man is in
the process of enacting the Foundations Bill 2010 and Guernsey is expected to pass legislation in
2011. The Jersey foundation is a separate legal entity that can hold assets in its own name although
it may not directly acquire immovable Jersey property or engage in commercial trading. It has
features of both companies and trusts. It is incorporated by a qualified person and registered in
the Register of Companies but governed by the Foundations Law, its charter and its regulations.
A foundation need not have an initial endowment (unlike a trust) and its objects in Jersey can be
charitable or non-charitable or to benefit particular persons. The regulations are confidential,
setting out the objects and will make provision for the appointment of council members one
of whom must be a person regulated in Jersey to carry on trust business. The charter is a public
document. A particular feature of the Jersey foundation is the requirement for the regulations to
provide for the appointment of a guardian to ensure that the council carries out its functions. It
has a role similar to that of an enforcer in a Jersey purpose trust. The founder is not necessarily the
settlor – he does not have to be the person endowing the foundation. A beneficiary has no rights in
the assets of the foundation unless specifically granted these in the constitution but can approach
the Jersey court in the event of a grievance. The foundation is not obliged to provide information
to any person unless required by the court or by its internal regulations.
[8] Compare a company limited by guarantee.

enforce the terms of the foundation nor whether the duties and obligations of the Council members are fiduciary or merely contractual. This can vary from jurisdiction to jurisdiction and from foundation to foundation. If contractual, who can enforce the contract apart from the founder while he is alive? It appears that even where the founder has reserved rights to control the Council, the beneficiaries may often have limited rights to hold the Council to account and the foundation is only subject to some form of limited state official supervision.[9] That does not accord with a trust arrangement where there is:

> *"an irreducible core of obligations owed by the trustees to the beneficiaries and enforceable by them which is fundamental to the concept of a trust. If the beneficiaries have no rights enforceable against the trustees there are no trusts."*[10]

2.14   In some cases the founder and members of his family after his death retain rights to demand the property and only if the property is not demanded does it go according to the terms of the foundation.[11] In other cases the foundation is required to apply assets for particular purposes and for particular beneficiaries so looking more like a trust.

2.15   In fact, a foundation could probably meet the requirements of a settlement but may not always do so. The position must depend upon the actual terms in each case and an entity can be a foundation without being a trust. In some cases it may be no more than a nominee arrangement with the property still in effect belonged to the original owner. This might be the position where the founder retains extensive rights.[12] The question is whether the founder has retained so many rights that he has not alienated the assets or whether he has alienated the assets and the arrangement is simply subject to a power of revocation.

2.16   In the joint declaration between HMRC and Liechtenstein signed on August 11, 2009[13] it was agreed that the Liechtenstein Stiftung is, prima facie, to be regarded as a trust and an anstalt as a company. However:

> *"the parties recognise that the ultimate UK taxation consequences for UK taxpayers will depend on the particular facts as is the case where UK or*

---

[9] Exceptionally Malta makes provision to deal with the rights of beneficiaries vis-à-vis the council. The Bahamas provides that a beneficiary has a right to receive accounts and information. In other jurisdictions this right to information can be excluded if the Founder so decides. Panama allows beneficiaries to apply to the court for removal of the Council and the right to contest its decisions.

[10] *Armitage v Nurse* [1998] Ch 241.

[11] In the United States foundations have been held to be revocable trusts even though they have a separate legal existence. (However, the UK would not necessarily accept that all revocable grantor US trusts are settled property: see 2.19.) In other jurisdictions courts have declined to treat trusts and foundations as the same. See for example *Norway v Olsen* (2003) 5 ITELR 77 where the Supreme Court of Norway rejected the notion that Liechtenstein stiftung could be regarded as equivalent to a Norwegian family foundation. Although both trusts and foundations contained a division of ownership rights, trusts could not be regarded as owning property in the same way as foundations.

[12] See International Manual 336940, *"foundations, establishments and associations may be legal entities in their country of formation. They may have some of the characteristics of charities, charitable trusts or family settlements. They will usually be unincorporated bodies governed by a board of trustees but some of them may be incorporated and governed by a board of directors."*

[13] Memorandum of Understanding relating to Taxes.

other common law entities or fiduciary relationships, such as trusts, are involved."

In Liechtenstein the 2008 Foundation Act (called StiG) came into force in April 2009 and, in part, governs pre-existing foundations. Disclosure rights for beneficiaries are now exclusively determined by the 2009 Act for all foundations. A purely circular purpose consisting of no more than the management of assets is not valid. A foundation deed which restricts the foundation's purpose to the management of assets and makes reference to beneficiaries only by giving the foundation council or founder full authority to nominate beneficiaries in the future through bye-laws, is not regarded as validly constituted and the courts may no longer permit the formation of a foundation in two such separate steps. Overall, foundations appear to have moved nearer to the concept of a trust. **2.17**

III ESTABLISHMENTS[14]

An establishment is also a creature of statute. It is a separate legal entity and, as noted above, is generally treated as opaque and a company by the HMRC although it can vary in form considerably. There is usually a board of directors: articles and bye-laws although beneficiaries not shareholders. It operates on the basis that a supreme authority holds the "founder's rights" and these rights include determining the beneficiaries, amending the articles and bye-laws, appointing and removing the directors and ending the establishment. Such founder's rights do not die with the founder but can be assigned and may be held by a separate council. Often they are held by a third party as nominee for the founder. The rights could be regarded as a contractual arrangement with the establishment like a *chose in action*, or they could be regarded as something like a general power of appointment over the establishment or even an interest in possession which might then make the establishment look more like settled property. The very flexibility of establishments makes it difficult to characterise them but in general HMRC regards them as companies. **2.18**

IV US GRANTOR TRUSTS

Valid trust or nominee arrangement?

Grantor trusts are commonly used in the United States for estate planning purposes and are treated as transparent for US tax purposes. They are often set up to avoid probate delays and can cause inheritance tax problems for US citizens who are deemed UK domiciled since if the property is settled for UK inheritance tax purposes the donor has created a relevant property trust with a potential entry charge. **2.19**

The settlor is often the sole trustee; the trust is revocable; income and capital **2.20**

---

[14] In Liechtenstein, an anstalt.

is paid to the settlor on demand and the duties of the trustees are owed exclusively to the settlor. He usually has an unrestricted power of amendment and while he is alive no one else can receive any capital or income. This is akin to a nominee arrangement rather than a settlement.

2.21 Of course, the mere fact that the trust is revocable does not mean it is not a settlement or that it is a sham. However, the fact that it is called a trust under US law does not mean it is a valid trust under UK law. In a UK trust, the trustees must owe fiduciary duties to the beneficiaries: i.e. there must be an element of "trust" and the trustees need to have discretions and powers in relation to the trust fund.[15] The trustees should not be simply holding the assets on behalf of the beneficiaries in a nominee/agency arrangement.

2.22 *Lewin on Trusts*[16] notes:

> "*the reservation by the settlor of large beneficial powers and interests may leave the lifetime trusts declared in favour of others so squeletic as to be considered illusory.*"

But he also accepts that retained powers do not necessarily turn the settlement into a testamentary disposition and goes on to say

> "*it is not thought that the reservation even of very considerable rights and powers would make the trusts illusory during the settlor's lifetime unless the settlor was virtually the equitable owner of the trust property during his life.*"[17]

Shams

2.23 It is important to distinguish between a trust which is a sham because its stated terms are never intended to take effect (but if they had been so intended then it would have been a valid trust) and a document that despite its name does not take effect as a trust as its terms demonstrate that the settlor retains overall control of the assets.[18]

2.24 The starting point is the intention of the settlor—did he intend to create a substantive trust and give up dominion and control of the assets or just enter into an agency or nominee arrangement. Then ascertain what, if any, discretions are vested in the trustees while the settlor is alive. Is there any succession element or does the settlor simply amend the class of beneficiaries from time to time with effect from his death: in which case it looks more like a will (probably invalidly executed under UK law since two witnesses will not usually have been involved).

---

[15] See *Armitage v Nurse* [1988] Ch at 253 CA.

[16] 18th edn, para.1–14.

[17] A settlement can be revocable and still a valid trust for UK tax purposes as *Melville* and IHTA 1984 s.5(2) illustrate. English courts are familiar with revocable lifetime trusts and are not necessarily going to regard them as testamentary in nature or a nomineeship: see *Baird v Baird* [1990] 2 AC 548 but compare *AG v Jones and Bartlett* (1817) 3 Price 368, 391 and *Jeffries v Alexander* (1860) 8 HLC 594. Revocable life interest trusts were commonly used as a method of avoiding probate duty in 19th century England.

[18] Sham trusts are considered at 1.18 and following.

In *BQ v DQ*,[19] the donor had the right to revoke and amend the trust during **2.25** his lifetime and the instrument provided that the entire net income and so much of the principal as the trustee shall determine, shall be paid to the donor. Somewhat surprisingly, it was held that the trusts were void on the basis of the cumulative effect of the trust documents taken with the de facto situation. Crucial to this decision was Art. VIII(H) which said that:

> "*the written approval by the donor of any trust transaction during his lifetime shall be a complete release of the trustee of any liability or responsibility of the trustee to any person with respect to this transaction.*"

If Art. VIII(H) had been coupled with a more obviously independent trustee, the judge may not have come to the same conclusion because the trustee could have been called to account and clearly did have some discretionary powers.

For US tax purposes, there is no practical difference between: **2.26**

(i) a trust with power vested in the settlor to direct that income and capital is paid to him; to amend and revoke the trust but for the trustees to be able to pay income to someone else if he does not so direct; and

(ii) a trust where the trustees have no discretions to distribute any income or capital during the settlor's lifetime (while he remains of full capacity) with a power to amend and revoke vested in the settlor.

However, for UK purposes (ii) may not be a settlement. Consider the following typical clause:

> "*During the Donor's lifetime all of the net income of the trust shall be paid to the Donor or as the Donor directs. In addition payments of principal in such amounts as may be requested at any time or times by the Donor including the entire trust principal shall be paid to the Donor or as he directs. If the Donor becomes incapacitated . . . so much of the net income and principal as the trustees determine may also be paid to or applied for the benefit of persons dependent upon the Donor for support and persons designated by the donor in writing prior to such incapacity. Any such income not so paid or applied may be added to principal or held for like payment, application or addition at such later time or times as the trustees determine. Upon the Donor's death the trust property including any property added to the trust following the Donor's death shall be disposed of as hereinafter provided . . . upon the death of the Donor all trust property not otherwise disposed of shall be paid to the executor administering the estate of the Donor for disposition in accordance with the terms of the will of the Donor submitted to probate.*"

It is not thought that this creates a settlement. It might be argued that unless **2.27** and until the settlor directs the trustees to pay out capital and income then it is

---

[19] [2011] WTLR 373.

held on succession for certain named beneficiaries on his death. Some support for this approach is *Thompson v Browne*[20] where it was commented:

> "*if there be anything in [an earlier decision] to support the notion, that where a person by deed settles property to his own use during his life, and after his decease for the benefit of other persons, a power of revocation reserved in such a deed alters the character of the instrument and renders it testamentary . . . It can only be said that, if this were law, a great number of transactions of which the validity has never been doubted would be liable to be impeached.*"

2.28 However, in the above clause the settlor has the sole right to direct how income and capital should be paid during his lifetime and the trustees have no independent discretion. He can ask for it at any time and the trustees have no ability to withhold such payment. Even if income is accumulated and added to capital during the settlor's lifetime because he chooses not to direct the trustees, that capital still has to be paid out as he directs. The position would alter if the settlor lost capacity when it would seem that a trust will then arise.[21]

V USUFRUCTS

2.29 Usufructs are commonly found in civil law countries, notably in France and Spain. Although usually over land, they can be created over moveable property. So Art.578 of the French Code Civile provides that:

> "*an usufruct is the right to enjoy property belonging to another, as if its owner, at the expense of preserving that property.*"

The owner of the right is the usufructuary and the owner of the property subject to the right is called the encumbered owner or *nu-propriétaire*. The usufructuary is responsible for the upkeep of the property.[22]

Features of a usufruct over land

2.30 The following features are commonly found:

(i) the usufructuary has the right to enjoy the fruits (use) of the property during his lifetime. This right can be renounced; charged voluntarily and seized by third parties although it is generally thought to be inalienable because of its connection with the person of the usufructuary;

(ii) the interests of both the usufructuary and the "bare title owner" are registered in the relevant property register;

(iii) this division of property title can occur on death (with someone being

---

[20] (1825) My 6K. 32.
[21] This may have UK tax consequences if the settlor is at that stage UK domiciled.
[22] In Scotland a "proper liferent" is a form of usufruct.

given a usufruct in the property and other persons given the bare title) or by a voluntary act of the owner of the property or a buyer;

(iv) on the acquisition of a usufruct and bare title tax will be split and shared between the usufruct and the bare title owners according to a formula which takes the age of the usufructuary as the working base;[23]

(v) on the death of the usufructuary this "interest" (which will cease) does not form part of his estate for inheritance tax purposes. Hence no probate is needed in respect of this asset. The bare owners will then "consolidate" their title at the land registry by producing the death certificate and payment of any transfer tax owing.

Approach of HMRC

Generally HMRC have treated a usufruct as equivalent to a life interest for inheritance tax purposes.[24]   **2.31**

As a general impression the usufruct has some similarities with a lease for life and some with a life interest. It is not, of course, either: the relationship is not one of landlord and tenant and there is no trust of the property. The creation of a usufruct does not involve the creation of a settlement as that term is commonly understood. However the definition of "settlement" in s.43(2) is extended to catch the situation whereby: **2.32**

> "*under the law of any other country, the administration of the property is for the time being governed by provisions equivalent in effect to those which would apply if the property were so (i.e. as in the basic definition) held charged or burdened*".

It is far from clear what is meant by the "administration" of the property: there is, of course, nothing equivalent in a usufruct to the powers of trustees or even of a Settled Land Act life tenancy. Further, are the provisions "equivalent in effect" to a life interest trust? Again it is thought that the answer is no. The personal rights of use given to the usufructuary are far removed from an equitable interest in a trust fund (or legal title in the case of SLA settlements) enjoyed by an English life tenant.   **2.33**

Consequences if a usufruct is an IHT settlement

A number of apparently bizarre consequences would ensue: **2.34**

(i) if created before March 22, 2006 then the interest in possession will be qualifying and so on the death of the usufructuary the full value of the property (i.e. both usufruct and bare title) may be taxed;

---

[23] So if at the time of sale the usufructuary was in his early 60s it is thought that 40% of the total value of the property will be attributed to his interest.

[24] An alternative possibility would be to treat it as a lease for life.

(ii) if created after that date there will be a relevant property trust with the possibility of anniversary and exit charges;

(iii) the creation of the usufruct after March 21, 2006 may accordingly involve a chargeable transfer with (once the settlor's nil rate band is exhausted) a 20 per cent tax charge;

(iv) if an owner retains a usufruct in land and gives away the bare title (which has some similarities with an *Ingram* arrangement) then he would appear to be caught by the reservation of benefit rules[25];

(v) the bare title is a reversionary interest. If the arrangement has been set up by a non-UK domiciliary who, for instance, grants a usufruct to his mother whilst retaining the bare title this (given that the property is not UK situs) will be an excluded property settlement.

Is it a lease?

2.35 There is no extension in the natural meaning of a lease for IHT purposes to similar non-UK arrangements and accordingly it is not thought that there is any way of treating the usufructuary as a tenant for life and the bare owner as the landlord, with there being a settlement for IHT purposes under s.43(3).

CGT treatment

2.36 The UK/France Double Tax Treaty provides that for UK capital gains tax purposes a usufruct is an interest in land.[26] The interests of the usufructuary and bare title owner are not the same, i.e. this is not a case of co-ownership and the nearest analogy for these purposes would appear to be with the position of a leasehold and freeholder.

2.37 It would appear to follow that the creation of a usufruct will involve the owner in making, for CGT purposes, a part disposal of the land. If, for instance, the usufruct was retained and bare title given away then the gain of the disponer would be calculated in accordance with the part disposal rules.[27]

2.38 On the death of the usufructuary HMRC comment that:

> "*If the correct analogy is that the particular arrangement has the characteristics of settled property then it is treated as such . . . a usufruct governed by French law would be regarded as a non-trust arrangement as it is broadly similar to a Scottish proper liferent.*"[28]

---

[25] FA 1986 s.102A: for *Ingram* schemes see 22.18 and 43.38. Contrast the position if the usufruct was over a chattel: see Ch.44.

[26] See UK/France Double Tax Convention (June 19, 2008) Art.6(2) which provides that a usufruct of immovable property, "*shall have the meaning which it has under the law of the Contracting State in which the property in question is situated*". In France it is an interest in land.

[27] Account would doubtless be taken of the values put on their respective interests in, e.g. France or Spain, as the case may be.

[28] CGTM 31305.

The CGT legislation provides that:

> "*on the death of (a) liferenter the person (if any) who, on the death of the liferenter, becomes entitled to possession of the property as heir shall be deemed to have acquired all the assets forming part of the property at the date of the deceased's death for a consideration equal to their market value at that date.*"[29]

In other words, there is a tax-free uplift on the death of the usufructuary. Of course, if there is a pre-March 22, 2006 IHT settlement, the death of the usufructuary will result in an IHT charge on the value of the property. But it would appear that usufructs created after that time will involve relevant property settlements (so that at most there may be an exit charge at the rate of something below six per cent on the death of the usufructuary) but the CGT uplift still applies!

What is it?

If one concludes that it is not sufficiently analogous to a settlement then the usufruct arrangement falls to be treated on its own terms (it is sui generis). The respective rights enjoyed by the parties will need to be valued in the usual way. A lifetime surrender of the usufruct may, for instance, be a PET or chargeable transfer: on death it would seem that the usufruct will have a nil value as it comes to an end.   2.39

VI DELAWARE LLCS

The tax problems raised by foreign entities are well illustrated in the case of *George Anson v HMRC*. Anson was a participant in a Delaware limited liability company, HarbourVest Partners LLC. He was a UK resident non-domiciliary and was taxed on the remittance basis. He remitted his income from the LLC (on which he had paid tax in the US on the basis that the profits arose to him directly) and HMRC sought to assess Mr Anson to tax on the basis that the income remitted from the LLC was dividends on which no US tax credit could be given. HMRC contended that in English law, the LLC was opaque: it carried on its business as principal and the members of the LLC were not liable for debts. They denied Mr Anson treaty relief for the US tax he had paid on his LLC profits because for UK tax purposes he had received something different namely dividends.   2.40

The First Tier Tribunal decided that members of an LLC have interests akin to the interests of a Scottish partner and that the interest was transparent for UK tax purposes. They considered that the test for the purposes of treaty relief under the UK/US treaty was whether Anson was subject to tax computed by reference to the same profits or income as that on which he was taxed in the US. They decided that the members of the LLC were entitled   2.41

---

[29] TCGA 1992 s.63(2).

to their profits as they arose and therefore that Anson was taxed on the same income in the UK as in the US, and as such was entitled to relief under the treaty. This was overruled by the Upper Tier Tribunal which decided that he was not taxed on the same profits. The Upper Tribunal pointed particularly to s.18–701 of Delaware LLC Act which stated that members of the LLC have no interest in the specific LLC property. Hence Anson did not have a proprietary interest in any of HarbourVest's assets or profits. Mann J. distinguished LLCs from Scottish partnerships which are recognised as income transparent even though the partnership itself owns its assets.

2.42   In the alternative Anson also claimed that the anti-avoidance provisions now contained in ITA 2007 s.720 applied so that as transferor he was deemed to be entitled to his share of the profits of the LLC anyway for UK tax purposes and thereby obtained treaty relief. At the time of writing the Upper Tier Tribunal has still to consider this point.

CHAPTER 3

RESIDENCE AND DOMICILE STATUS OF INDIVIDUALS

I INTRODUCTION

Relevance of residence and domicile

An individual's "residence" and "domicile" is critical to his UK tax liability.   **3.01**
Domicile rather than residence is important for IHT purposes although a person's residence can be relevant in relation to deemed inheritance tax domicile and the pre-owned assets income tax rules.[1]

Trustees need to know the residence and domicile status of the settlor and   **3.02**
of beneficiaries to whom they wish to make distributions: both can have a material effect on the tax position of the trust and the tax liability on distributions from it. For example:

(i) a UK domiciled or deemed domiciled settlor who sets up a trust will   **3.03**
generally be liable to inheritance tax if the value of the assets settled exceed his nil rate band. The trustees (whether or not UK resident) can be secondarily liable for that inheritance tax and for future inheritance tax due on each 10-year anniversary[2];

(ii) IHTA 1984 s.218 imposes a reporting IHT obligation on professionals[3]

---

[1] See Chs 31 and 34 and 3.107.
[2] Even non-resident trustees must therefore check if the settlor was deemed domiciled in the UK at the date of the trust or funding of the trust. For reporting obligations and penalties where tax is not paid, see Ch.56.
[3] Other than a barrister.

including trustees who *"in the course of a trade or profession [are] concerned with the making of a settlement and know or have reason to believe that the settlor was domiciled in the UK and that the trustees are not or will not be resident in the UK"*;

(iii) a UK resident settlor who has set up a trust, wherever resident, is liable to income tax on the trust income if it is settlor-interested with a right of reimbursement from the trustees. A UK domiciled and resident settlor will have a similar right of reimbursement against offshore trustees for capital gains tax on gains realised by the trustees. The trustees need to allow for this liability[4];

(iv) a beneficiary's residence and domicile has a material effect on how trustees structure distributions and on disclosure to the tax authorities. For example, if a beneficiary of an offshore trust is a US citizen, there are likely to be severe penalties in the US if the beneficiary fails to disclose the existence of the trust even if he has received nothing from it. If a beneficiary is UK resident but foreign domiciled then it may be preferable to make capital distributions to him if these can first be matched with pre-April 2008 trust gains.

Knowing when a taxpayer acquires UK residence is also relevant for the purposes of paying the £30,000 charge.[5]

3.04   This chapter discusses:

(i) the rules governing the residence status of an individual for UK tax purposes. The new statutory residence rules that are expected to come into effect from April 2012 are also considered briefly;

(ii) the meaning of domicile under English law.

Ch.5 examines the UK tax consequences of non-UK residence and foreign domicile.

When is an individual UK resident?

3.05   Whether someone is resident in the UK is the subject of limited statutory provisions[6] and generally the matter is governed by case law and practice. There is no statutory test akin to that found in other countries such as the United States or Ireland which partly accounts for the current mess. During the 2008 Finance Bill debates the Treasury Minister, Jane Kennedy, announced that she would consider further the option of a comprehensive statutory residence test if the professional bodies and HMRC could agree common ground. After much discussion with representative bodies, in June 2011 the Treasury/HMRC finally produced a consultation paper setting out, in some detail, a statutory residence test. The consultation paper

---

[4] See Ch.7 for income tax and Ch.19 for capital gains tax of offshore trusts.
[5] £50,000 in certain cases from April 6, 2012: see Ch.5.
[6] See ITA 2007 ss.829–832.

has been received positively and it is intended to be enacted from April 6, 2012.[7]

For the moment, taxpayers must self-assess (and in some cases guess!) their **3.06** residence status taking into account the various (and often conflicting) case law. HMRC do not give residence rulings. For many the position will be clear-cut, e.g. they have moved abroad with family, given up their home and are working full-time abroad. For others the position will be more marginal: they may leave family here, work abroad part-time, have several homes in different countries and spend perhaps 70 to 90 days in the UK each year, possibly working here as well. It is not easy in such cases to say categorically whether the person is UK resident and the residence status of a person is often investigated many years later when the taxpayer is unlikely to have retained all the evidence required to show non-UK residence.[8] The proposed statutory test should remove many areas of uncertainty but the taxpayer will still need to retain good evidence of his days in the UK: what he did when here, and where and how he spent his time abroad.[9]

II THE CURRENT STATUTORY RULES

There are limited statutory rules governing residence and until recently confu- **3.07** sion arose as to how these should be interpreted.

Rule for leavers

ITA 2007, s.829[10] imposes income tax on those who have left the UK for the **3.08** purposes of only occasional residence abroad. The individual is charged to income tax as if he was still residing in the UK. There is no reported case where this alone has resulted in a liability to tax. Although in *Levene*[11] the taxpayer was found to have left the UK for only occasional residence abroad, he was held to have been resident in the UK under common law all along. In *IRC v Combe*[12] the taxpayer went to serve an apprenticeship in New York for three years and that was not found to be for the purpose of occasional residence abroad.

In *Reed v Clark*[13] the taxpayer was absent for only a little over a year but **3.09** this was held to be a distinct break in the pattern of his life and throughout his absence he had made his permanent home and place of business in California.

---

[7] See further 3.67: draft legislation has not yet been published.
[8] See for example the salutary case of *Hankinson v IRC* [2009] UK FTT 384 and 3.00 below.
[9] See 3.67 below.
[10] Formerly TA1988 s.334. Section 829 does not apply to capital gains tax since ordinary residence alone (without residence, if that is possible) renders a person subject to capital gains tax.
[11] [1928] AC 217.
[12] [1932] 17 TC 405.
[13] [1985] STC 323. Nevertheless in the Supreme Court decision of *Gaines-Cooper* (see 3.51) it was held that there was some distinction (see para.16) and that s.829 could operate as an independent charging provision and the concept of distinct break was particularly relevant to s.829.

It was held that his residence in California was not occasional. The Judge noted:

> "*A person's occasional residence is contrasted with his usual or ordinary residence . . . in my view a year is a long enough period for a person's purpose of living where he does to be capable of having a sufficient degree of continuity for it to be properly described as settled. Hence depending on all the circumstances the foreign country can be the place where for that period he would be ordinarily and not just occasionally resident. I appreciate that this construction may give little scope in practice for the operation of [s829] as an independent charging provision . . . but I do not find this consideration sufficiently compelling to require the language to be given a different meaning."*

3.10   In *Grace*,[14] HMRC having at one point agreed that s.829 did not apply and that Grace had not left the UK for the purpose only of occasional residence abroad, then argued at the rehearing that they were not bound by this concession and that his residence in Cape Town was not occasional but for settled purposes as part of a regular order of his life adopted voluntarily.[15] The argument was dismissed but the fact that they felt able to make it demonstrates the difficulties of s.829. In the Supreme Court decision of *Gaines-Cooper* (see 3.51) it was held that there was a distinction between losing one's settled abode (necessary under general law) and having a settled purpose abroad (necessary to avoid being caught under s.829).

Rule for arrivers

3.11   A second statutory income tax rule is ITA 2007 s.831[16] which operates where an individual is in the UK for some temporary purpose and not with a view to establishing residence. If he spends 183 days or more in the tax year in the UK then regardless of his actual residence status, his relevant foreign income is taxable and he is treated as UK resident in relation to employment income. In determining whether the conditions of ss.831 and 832 are met, living accommodation in the UK is ignored.

3.12   In *Grace* the Court of Appeal finally confirmed that ss.831 and 832 are not substantive rules of residence but confer relief where the temporary visitor is UK resident or impose tax if he exceeds the 183 day threshold as if he were resident even if in fact he is not. The Court of Appeal also confirmed that what has to be temporary is not the individual's presence but his purpose, i.e. are his reasons for being in the UK casual or transitory.[17]

---

[14] The case was first heard by Special Commissioner Nuala Brice who found in favour of the taxpayer: see [2008] STC (SCD) 531 reversed on appeal by HMRC to the High Court: see [2008] EWHC 2708 (Ch). The taxpayer appealed to the Court of Appeal successfully [2009] EWCA Civ 1082 and it was then remitted back to the First Tier Tribunal for a complete rehearing where he lost: see [2011] UKFTT 36.

[15] For a full discussion of *Grace* see 3.29.

[16] Formerly TA 1988 s.336.

[17] See also *Cooper v Cadwallader* [1904] 5 TC 101.

Full-time work

The other statutory income tax rule is in ITA 2007 s.830[18] which applies for income tax purposes if an individual works full-time in a foreign employment or a foreign trade. Any UK living accommodation is ignored in determining whether he is UK resident. All duties other than incidental duties (narrowly defined) must be performed outside the UK. Note that this does not say he is non-UK resident, only that accommodation is ignored in determining the question of residence.

3.13

Midnight test

For the statutory rules, the calculation of 183 days in the UK now[19] includes midnights in the UK unless the individual is a passenger in transit. HMRC have also indicated that they will include midnights in applying residence generally. If a midnight is spent in the UK in transit it is ignored. However, the individual must not engage in activities substantially unrelated to their transit through the UK. Similar changes were introduced for gains and employment income.[20] However, in determining residence under general law it is clear that HMRC do not consider that they are bound to count only midnights and the case law itself demonstrates that in some circumstances where a person is coming regularly in and out of the UK all days of presence can be counted.

3.14

MPs and members of the House of Lords

From 2010–11 they are deemed resident, ordinarily resident and domiciled in the UK for all tax purposes. This applies even if that person is a Member of Parliament for only part of the tax year and regardless of whether or not they are on a leave of absence.[21]

3.15

III PROBLEMS IN DETERMINING RESIDENCE STATUS UNDER CURRENT CASE LAW

The current case law is uncertain and often contradictory. Why is this?

---

[18] Formerly TA 1988 s.335.
[19] FA 2008 s.24 amended ITA 2007 s.831 from April 6, 2008.
[20] TCGA 1992 s.9 and ITA 2007 s.832.
[21] See Pt 4 of CRGA 2010.

The issue is determined as a question of fact rather than principle

3.16 The first problem is that the issue of residence has always been treated as one of fact, and so decided cases mostly consist of judges deciding whether or not the Commissioners were entitled to find as they did. As Viscount Summer said in *Levene v IRC*[22]:

> "*the legislature partially transfers to [the appellate commissioners] the function of imposing taxes on individuals, since it empowers them in terms so general that no one can be certainly advised in advance whether he must pay or can escape payment*".

In the same case, Viscount Cave emphasised that "reside" has no special meaning for tax purposes and it is possible to reside in two places:

> "*Probably the most difficult case is that of a wanderer who, having no home in any country, spends part only of his time in hotels in the UK and the remaining and greater part of his time in hotels abroad. In such cases the question is one of fact rather than one of degree and must be determined in all the circumstances of the case. If, for instance, such a man is a foreigner who has never resided in this country, there may be great difficulty in holding that he is resident here. If he is a British subject, the Commissioners are entitled to take into account all the facts of the case*".

In *Lysaght*,[23] Lord Summer unhelpfully noted:

> "*a man is taxed where he resides. I might almost say he resides wherever he can be taxed*".

Like any fact finding expedition it can result in similar cases being decided differently.

Out of date case law

3.17 Another reason for the unsatisfactory state of the law is that until recently the case law was largely out of date. *Levene* and *Lysaght* are often regarded as the leading cases but date from the 1920s when air travel was almost non-existent and the Channel Tunnel had not been built.[24] Both were British subjects who had sold their homes and left the UK. In *Levene*, he visited the UK in the summer months, taking medical advice and attending to family and personal matters and staying in hotels. He owned no permanent home abroad. In *Lysaght*, he had a home in Ireland but came to the UK for a week every month to attend board meetings. Both were

---

[22] [1928] AC 217.
[23] (1928) 13 TC 511.
[24] It may be asked why there were no major cases apart from *Reed v Clark* from the 1930s until the 1990s. Presumably this was because both tax payer and HMRC were happy to rely on IR20 (or its earlier equivalent).

held to be UK resident. The day count for Mr Levene was rather higher than for Mr Lysaght who was present in the UK for 101 days, 94 and 84 days over three years. The latter was held to be marginal but nevertheless resident here.

Misinterpretation of the "available accommodation" rule

Another problem has been confusion over the relative importance to be given the retention of accommodation in the UK. Until 1993 HMRC practice[25] was to regard a taxpayer as UK resident if he had accommodation available to him in the UK and he set foot in the UK for even a day during the year unless he was working full-time abroad. In the 1993 Budget, the then Conservative Government announced its intention to abolish this "available accommodation" rule. However, instead of simply enacting that accommodation should be disregarded in determining residence for all purposes, it merely amended the predecessor legislation to ITA 2007 ss.831 and 832 so that the relevance of accommodation remained unchanged for the purposes of the general law.
 3.18

It is clear from the case law that there never was an available accommodation rule in the sense stated by HMRC, i.e. someone was not automatically UK resident under general law if he set foot in the UK for a day simply because he had a UK house. Both *Gaines Cooper*[26] and *Grace* confirm that it is merely one factor to be taken into account under general law.
 3.19

Levene suggests that available accommodation does mean a lower day count will result in residence.[27] However, compare *Withers v Wynyard*[28] where the taxpayer was held to be non-UK resident under general law despite spending three and a half months here in that year and owning a lease and using a London flat. It appears that the quality of residence is also important and having a UK home may suggest a greater intention to settle here. Someone who comes in and out of the UK at infrequent unplanned intervals is much less likely to be treated as UK resident than someone who comes to the UK for continuous periods of time staying in the same place each time, even if overall the period spent in the UK is the same.

More recently in *High Tech International v Deripaska*,[29] *Cherney v Deripaska*[30] and *Yugraneft v Abramovich*[31] (all non-tax cases but where the same criteria apply in determining residence) accommodation was not decisive since all of them were held to be non-UK resident for the purposes of serving
 3.20

---

[25] See IR20 (1992 edition): called the "available accommodation" rule.
[26] See later citations.
[27] See also *AG v Coote* (1817) 2 TC 385 where the taxpayer lived in Ireland but used a house in London: held to be UK resident and the difficult case of *Cooper v Cadwalader* (1904) 5 TC 101 where the taxpayer leased a shooting lodge in Scotland and used it for two months every year when on holiday. He lived and worked full-time in New York for the rest of the year; the Court of Session held this meant he was resident in Scotland. If correct this would mean many foreigners are UK resident who only spend two months here in their London flats!
[28] (1938) 21 TC 724.
[29] [2006] EWHC 3276.
[30] [2007] EWHC 965.
[31] [2008] EWHC 2613.

proceedings despite having accommodation here.[32] The individuals concerned had UK houses which they used and they also had houses elsewhere, but it was held that the quality of their use of their houses resembled that of a hotel. It was not a place where they *"habitually and normally resided for a settled purpose"*. Hence, they were held to be non-UK resident.

3.21   It is clear from these cases that the accommodation rule has been misinterpreted by HMRC in determining a person's residence status under general law, otherwise all of these people would have been UK resident. Critically, in *Gaines-Cooper* it was conceded, without further discussion, that the mere existence of available accommodation meant that the taxpayer was UK resident in 1992–93 prior to the rule change. This concession has made a material difference to the taxpayer because he became a leaver rather than an arriver in 1993–94 and therefore had to show a distinct break: see 3.46. Although under general law accommodation should not make one automatically resident, for the purposes of IR20 which Gaines-Cooper was then forced to rely upon it was regarded as making him automatically UK resident, and he then had to leave: see paras 2.7–2.9 of IR20. It should be noted that the Supreme Court accepted there was an available accommodation rule at last for the purposes of interpreting IR20 that made Gaines-Cooper UK resident in 1992–93 (see para.23 of Lord Wilson's judgment and para.74 of Lord Mance's decision) but it was not directly relevant to the point they were asked to consider.

3.22   The conclusion is that available accommodation continues to be relevant in determining whether someone has "left" the UK for the purposes of general law although it is not relevant in determining whether someone has come to the UK for a temporary purpose under the statutory test. It is also specifically ignored if someone leaves the UK for full-time employment abroad.[33] In the proposed statutory test, *"accessible accommodation"* is regarded as one connecting factor in determining residence status, confirming that it is relevant but not conclusive.[34]

3.23   It is clear that if a person has a home elsewhere that foreign home is relevant in determining his residence status in the UK. The importance of this point is often underestimated. A person can be resident in more than one country but the Court of Appeal said in *Grace* that, while not decisive, the existence of a home elsewhere must be taken into account. Again, this is reflected in the proposed statutory residence test. If a person has a home in the UK and nowhere else, it is proposed that from April 6, 2012 they are treated as conclusively resident in the UK.

3.24   Note that to be *"available"* under current case law the accommodation does not have to be owned by the taxpayer if it is available to him: see *Lowenstein*[35] where the house was owned by a foreign company owned by the taxpayer. The same approach is proposed in the statutory test, where the reference is to *"accessible accommodation"*.[36]

---

[32] Abramovich spent an average of 141 whole or part days in the UK in the calendar years 2003 to 2007, and 68 complete days. He had available accommodation and made regular visits in connection with his substantial business interest, Chelsea Football Club. Despite this, Clarke J. held that for the purposes of s.41 of CJA he was non-resident in 2007.

[33] See ITA 2007 s.830.

[34] Which is not intended to change the status of the majority of individuals so one must assume that it aims to reflect at least to some extent the current law.

[35] (1926) 10 TC 424.

[36] See definitions in 3.72.

Day count test

The correct day count test under general law is at present unclear. In the past **3.25** it was generally considered to be an average of 90 days[37] but it is clear that day count is only one (albeit perhaps the most important) factor in determining residence. Moreover what days should be counted as days of residence in the UK? All days of presence, or only midnights? Can someone be UK resident if not present here at all in the tax year: *Rogers v IRC*[38] held that this was possible.

Settled place of abode

It remains unclear whether the test of residency is simply whether the UK is **3.26** the settled or usual place of abode of the taxpayer or whether multiple factors need to be looked at; alternatively are multiple factors merely evidence of whether a taxpayer has a usual or settled place of abode in the UK? See *Dubai Bank Ltd v Abbas*[39] where the Court of Appeal noted:

> "*a person is resident . . . in a particular part of the UK if that part is for him a settled or usual place of abode . . . a settled or usual place of abode connotes some degree of permanence or continuity . . . depending on the circumstances of the particular case time may or may not play an important part in determining residence. For example a person who comes to this country to retire and who buys a house for that purpose and moves into it, selling all his foreign possessions and cutting all foreign ties, would be likely to have been held to become immediately resident here. In other cases it may be necessary to look at how long the person concerned has been here and to balance that factor with his connections abroad*".

In that case the defendant's wife and son lived in a flat in London and he spent some two months per year in England. The Court of Appeal held he was not UK resident. The flat was owned by a company. The taxpayer had been involved in its acquisition and refurbishment but stated he stayed in hotels rather than at the flat and asserted he was effectively separated from his wife.

However, in *Shepherd v IRC*,[40] the Special Commissioner summarised the **3.27** case law as follows:

> "*From these authorities I derive the following principles: (i) that the concept of residence and ordinary residence are not defined in the legislation; the words therefore should be given their natural and ordinary meanings (Levene); (ii) that the word 'residence' and 'to reside' mean 'to*

---

[37] On the basis of HMRC practice but see *IRC v Combe* and *IRC v Zorab* where visits were close to six months per year.
[38] (1879) 1 TC 225—a master mariner who did not set foot in the UK in the tax year was still held to be UK resident: see also *D Farquhar v HMRC* [2010] UK FTT 231.
[39] [1996] EWCA Civ 1342.
[40] 78 TC 389.

dwell permanently or for a considerable time, to have one's settled or usual abode, to live in or at a particular place' (Levene); (iii) that the concept of 'ordinary residence' requires more than mere residence; it connotes residence in a place with some degree of continuity (Levene); 'ordinary' means normal and part of everyday life (Lysaght) or a regular, habitual mode of life in a particular place which has persisted despite temporary absences and which is voluntary and has a degree of settled purpose (Shah); (iv) that the question whether a person is or is not resident in the United Kingdom is a question of fact for the Special Commissioners (Zorab); (v) that no duration is prescribed by statute and it is necessary to take account of all the facts of the case; the duration of an individual's presence in the United Kingdom and the regularity and frequency of visits are facts to be taken into account; also, birth, family and business ties, the nature of visits and the connections with this country, may all be relevant (Zorab; Brown); (vi) that a reduced presence in the United Kingdom of a person whose absences are caused by his employment and so are temporary absences does not necessarily mean that the person is not residing in the United Kingdom (Young); (vii) that the availability of living accommodation in the United Kingdom is a factor to be borne in mind in deciding if a person is resident here (Cooper) (although that is subject to s336); (viii) that the fact that an individual has a home elsewhere is of no consequences; a person may reside in two places but if one of those places is the United Kingdom he is chargeable to tax here (Cooper and Levene); (ix) that there is a difference between where a British subject has established a residence in the United Kingdom and then has absences from it (Levene) and the case where a person has never had a residence in the United Kingdom at all (Zorab; Brown); (x) that if there is evidence that a move abroad is a distinct break that could be a relevant factor in treating an individual as non-resident (Combe); and (xi) that a person could become non-resident even if his intention was to mitigate tax (Reed v Clark)."

A similar multi-factor test was adopted by Levison J. in the High Court in *Grace*.[41]

The concept of distinct break

3.28   *Grace*[42] was a long running case and demonstrates many of the problems with the current law: in particular the difficult question of whether a distinct break is needed for those who leave the UK and whether a higher burden is imposed on them. It is discussed in some detail below because in the Court of Appeal the factors that are important to consider in determining residence were clearly laid out. It now seems clear that the taxpayer who wants to become non-UK resident must keep to a lower day count in the UK than a foreigner coming to or visiting the UK who wishes to remain non-UK resident. A distinction between arrivers and leavers is reflected in the proposed statutory

---

[41] See also *Gaines-Cooper v HMRC* at 3.46.
[42] See fn.14 for citations.

residence test: leavers must have fewer connecting factors in the UK if they want to lose non-UK residence or spend less time here.

The Grace case

Grace appealed against a notice of determination that he was ordinarily resident in the UK for the six years from 1997–98 to 2002–03 inclusive. The Special Commissioner decided in his favour that he was neither resident nor ordinarily resident in the UK. The Revenue successfully appealed this decision and Lewison J. concluded that the Special Commissioner had made errors of law in arriving at her decision and, further, that the only possible conclusion from the primary facts was that Grace was resident in the UK. On appeal the Court of Appeal[43] unanimously concluded that the Special Commissioner had misdirected herself but that there was *not* only one possible conclusion and therefore the decision had to be remitted to the First Tier Tribunal (Tax Chamber) which had by then replaced the Special Commissioners. That re-hearing took place at the end of 2010 with the decision released in 2011. In the event, Grace was held to be UK resident and ordinarily resident under general law.   **3.29**

The facts of that case were as follows. Grace was a British citizen born in South Africa in 1952 and he lived there until 1979. He qualified as an airline pilot and worked for UK airlines from 1987. He lived in the UK from 1986 and owned a house near Gatwick. In August 1997, the first year when he claimed to be non-UK resident, he set up home in South Africa and bought a house there in 1998 but continued to work for British Airways, retaining his house near Gatwick which he shared at one point with a girlfriend. He used his house before and after flights and when sick. He spent at least some of his remaining time when not flying in South Africa. He remained on the UK electoral roll and continued to use his UK bank and credit cards. It was accepted throughout that he had a well-structured social network in South Africa; a doctor and dentist; had purchased land there; joined clubs there; his most important personal effects were in South Africa. However, the UK property was fully furnished with computer and broadband access with vacant possession and he remained on the electoral roll. Post was sent to that address and he kept a car in the UK. He had had no contact with his children or wife for over 30 years and he planned to retire to South Africa when he was 60.   **3.30**

The Court of Appeal noted: **3.31**

(i) The word *"reside"* is a familiar English word which means *"to dwell permanently or for a considerable time, to have a settled or usual abode to live in or at a particular place"*.

(ii) Physical presence in a particular place does not necessarily amount to residence in that place where, for example, a person's physical presence there is no more than a stop-gap measure. In considering a person's presence, one must consider the amount of time he spends in that place: the nature of his presence and his connection with that place.

---

[43] [2009] EWCA Civ 1082.

(iii) Residence in a place connotes some degree of permanence, continuity or expectation of continuity.

(iv) Short but regular periods of physical presence may amount to residence, especially if they stem from the performance of a continuous obligation such as a business obligation, and the sequence of visits excludes the elements of chance and of occasion: see *Lysaght*.

(v) Although a person can have only one domicile at a time, he may reside in more than one place or in more than one country.

(vi) It is wrong to conduct a search for the place where a person has his permanent base or centre adopted for general purposes or to look for his real home.[44]

(vii) Although residence must be voluntarily adopted, a residence dictated by the exigencies of business will count as voluntary residence: see *Lysaght*.

(viii) Where a person has had his sole residence in the UK, he is unlikely to be held to cease to reside in the UK unless there has been a definite break in his pattern of life: see *Re Combe*. See also 3.34 below.

(ix) No duration is prescribed by statute and it is necessary to take into account all the facts of the case: the duration of an individual's presence in the UK and regularity and frequency of the visits. Also birth, family and business ties, the nature of business and the connections with the country may all be relevant: see *Zorab*[45] and *Brown*.[46]

(x) The availability of living accommodation in the UK is a factor to be borne in mind in deciding if a person is resident here: see *Cooper v Cadwalader*.

(xi) The fact that an individual has a home elsewhere is of no consequence. A person may reside in two places. However, the fact that a home elsewhere is of no consequence is not to be understood as meaning that the other home is entirely irrelevant to the necessary enquiry. That would be inconsistent with the obligation to take into account all the facts of the case. But the existence of another home is not decisive because of the possibility of simultaneous residence in several places. In fact, the point that Mr Grace spent relatively little time in South Africa did turn out to be relevant.

(xii) There were only two respects in which a person's state of mind is relevant in determining ordinary residence. First, the residence must be voluntarily adopted; and second there must be a degree of settled purpose: see *Shah*.

3.32 When the case was remitted back for rehearing to the First Tier Tribunal the judge considered whether Grace needed to make a distinct break as a UK resident leaving the UK. This point had already been considered by Moses

---

[44] See *Shah v Barnet London BC* [1983] 2 AC 309.
[45] *IRC v Zorab* (1926) 11 TC 289.
[46] *IRC v Brown* (1926) 11 TC 405.

L.J.[47] where he concluded that, construed as a whole, paras 2.7–2.9 of IR20[48] required the taxpayer to show that he had left the UK permanently or indefinitely and to visit no more than the maximum number of days expressed. Moses L.J. went on to say that in order to show that the taxpayer had left permanently or indefinitely, the taxpayer needed to demonstrate a distinct break and in particular that "*he had severed his ties to the extent that his previous social and family ties in the UK are no longer retained*".

It was acknowledged by the First Tier Tribunal that these comments were relevant in interpreting IR20 not necessarily in deciding residence under general law. The judge commented: **3.33**

> "*My conclusion from this is that in Gaines-Cooper and Levene, the Court of Appeal considered a distinct break with the UK was essential if a person is claiming to have left the UK permanently or indefinitely for the purposes of s334 and therefore IR20. This is not surprising: unless there has been a distinct break with the UK a person will only have left temporarily. However I find that the Court did not, as it did not need to, consider whether a distinct break is essential for someone shedding common law residence. On the contrary, all their comments on distinct break are in the context of it as a test of permanent or indefinite absence abroad.*" (at [35])

However, the Tribunal noted that it was unlikely that residence would be lost unless there was a distinct break: **3.34**

> "*Someone who has had UK residence needs to demonstrate that they have lost it, which is something a non UK resident does not have to do in order to demonstrate that they are not UK resident. The deciding cases on the common law meaning of residence have not held that it is essential that a distinct break is shown. However, although I agree with (Counsel for the taxpayer) that it is not essential to show a distinct break, it must be difficult to show that UK residence has been lost unless a distinct break in the taxpayer's pattern of life has occurred. I can envisage a set of circumstances where a taxpayer gradually runs down his connections with and presence in the UK to the extent that ultimately he becomes non resident without actually ever one year or another making a distinct break. However the point is not relevant in the context of this case where it is not suggested that Mr Grace gradually ran down his connections with the UK. The question is whether the change in circumstances in September 1997 were sufficient to convert his resident status to non resident: so in practice Mr Grace will have to show a sufficient break in his pattern of life.*" (at [38])

However, some of Lord Wilson's comments in the Supreme Court decision in *Gaines-Cooper*[49] suggest it is necessary to have a distinct break to lose UK residence under general law, or at least some break in "the pattern of the taxpayer's life".

---

[47] In the judicial review proceedings of *Davies and James* (1) *Gaines-Cooper* (2) [2010] EWCA Civ 83 at [2] and Supreme Court decision [2011] UKSC 47. See 3.38.

[48] For IR20, see 3.38.

[49] [2011] UKSC 47.

3.35 Despite the original decision in *Grace* by the Special Commissioners, at the rehearing new witness statements and evidence was produced, and HMRC were allowed to introduce log books and diaries for some of the years in dispute. As a result the day count became much more adverse for Grace. HMRC's argument was that the pattern of UK work was predictable with regular short stays.

3.36 The First Tier Tribunal found in HMRCs favour for the following reasons:

(i) Grace in fact spent some leisure time in Horley and although his visits were short, nevertheless they were very frequent. His house was not like a hotel for him: he kept his car parked there; he paid council tax and received mail; he read his post; he caught up on paperwork and he had a girlfriend who lived with him there.

(ii) He had a social life here, at least for 2000–01, but the fact that he spent most of his social life in South Africa did not mean that he could not be resident in the UK. Like *Lysaght*, he was here for the purposes of employment. He spent a third to a half of the year neither in the UK nor in South Africa. Although there was a distinct decrease in the amount of time spent in the UK in September 1997 he was not in the UK merely for the purposes of work because the greater part of his time spent in the UK was in fact enforced rest days at intervals of about four to five days between work flights. He did have a settled abode in the UK because he was predictably staying at his house once a month. His presence in the UK was not a stop gap but indefinite and he had an expectation of continuity.

(iii) He had a real home in Cape Town and he had a different nature of life in South Africa but his social life was not greatly different before and after September 1997 in the UK.

(iv) His occupation of his own house gave a different quality to his time in the UK than if he had stayed in hotels. A very important part of his life, namely his employment, remained in the UK, and he had a home here. He did not demonstrate a sufficient break. He simply went from being a person resident in one country to being a person resident in two.

The Barrett case

3.37 The question of whether the taxpayer had "left" the UK was also considered in the *Barrett* case.[50] He was a director and major shareholder of a successful management services company in the entertainment industry. He claimed to have left the UK on April 5, 1998 and was out of the UK for more than 12 months apart from various visits of short duration. He returned to the UK on April 7, 1999 and sought to rely on *Reed v Clark*[51] to establish non-UK residence. But he was unable to demonstrate to the satisfaction of the Special Commissioner that he did in fact leave the UK on April 5, 1998, one of the reasons being that his switch card was used in the UK on April 6 and 7! The taxpayer's case was of no merit but it is notable that the Special Commissioner

[50] *Barrett v RCC* [2008] STC (SCD) 268.
[51] [1985] STC 323; 58 TC 528.

re-emphasised there the need for a distinct break and investigated the facts carefully.

IV HMRC PRACTICE AND JUDICIAL REVIEW

IR20: "Residents and non-residents: liability to tax in the United Kingdom"

The fact that the case law on residence was a mess did not really matter for much of the latter half of the 20th century, as HMRC formulated practical rules, published in the booklet IR20 "*Residents and non-residents*". These rules operated more or less unchanged from the 1940s and gave rise to the belief that if you did not spend more than 90 days in the UK each year you would not be treated as UK resident. IR20 was withdrawn from April 6, 2009 and replaced by HMRC 6. HMRC 6 has itself been revised and a rather clearer (although still unsatisfactory) version produced in December 2010. **3.38**

IR20 was described as a concession and could not be used for tax avoidance purposes. It was prefaced by the comment that it set out only the main factors to be taken into account and that each case had to be determined on its own facts. But even with those qualifications, IR20 seemed to be a clear statement of practice which could be relied on by taxpayers in cases which clearly fell within its terms.[52] Even before it was withdrawn disputes had surfaced over its interpretation, no doubt reflecting the more mobile workforce; the ease of travel in and out of the UK and the fact that a day count test alone in determining residence was proving inadequate to stop significant tax leakage. **3.39**

Coming to the UK

Under IR20 an individual was stated to be UK tax resident for a tax year if he met one of the following conditions: **3.40**

(i) he was physically present in the UK for 183 days or more: "the 183 day rule".[53] Until April 6, 2008 it was normal practice to ignore days of arrival and departure. From April 6, 2008 midnights were included in the 183 day computation unless the person was "*in transit*"[54];

(ii) he visited the UK regularly on average 91 days or more in each tax year. The average was taken over a period of up to four years from the year of departure (so does not include days in years when he was UK resident): the "91 day rule";

(iii) he came to the UK with the intention of residing here permanently or for at least three years, in which case he was resident (and ordinarily resident) in the UK from the date when he arrived;

[52] Cf. *R v IRC, Ex p MFK Underwriting Agents Ltd* [1989] STC 873 at 892 per Bingham L.J.
[53] See ITA 2007 ss.831 and 832.
[54] See 3.14.

(iv) he came to the UK for a settled purpose (e.g. to take up employment) which meant he remained in the UK for at least two years. In this situation he was also resident in the UK from the date he arrived;

(v) he intended from the start to make regular visits of the type described in (ii), in which case he was treated as resident and ordinarily resident from April 6 of the first tax year;

(vi) he decided, before the fifth year, that he was going to make such visits, in which case he was resident and ordinarily resident from the beginning of the tax year in which he made that decision;

(vii) he was both UK resident and ordinarily resident and had left the UK only for occasional residence abroad.

Leaving the UK

3.41 An individual leaving the UK was therefore regarded as non-resident under IR20 if he satisfied the 183 and 91 day[55] rules and fell into one of the following categories:

(i) he had emigrated permanently;

(ii) he or his spouse had left the UK to work full-time abroad under a contract of employment or on a self-employed basis for a period which included at least one complete tax year;

(iii) he went abroad for some other settled purpose which lasted for at least one complete tax year.

An individual who departed without satisfying any of the above was treated as remaining UK resident. However, if, in fact, he satisfied the 183 and 91 day rules for three complete tax years his status was reviewed.

3.42 IR20 therefore suggested that residence was basically a question of counting days and given that days of arrival and departure did not normally count as days in the UK before April 6, 2008, it was possible in theory for an individual living abroad to work for four days each week in the UK for 45 weeks in the year and still be non-resident.

3.43 In *Tax Bulletin 52*[56] HMRC began to move away from a pure day count when they stated that mobile workers who retained a home and settled domestic life in the UK but worked abroad in the week to such an extent that they were under the 90 day limit (e.g. lorry drivers) nevertheless remained UK resident.

3.44 IR20 broke down further in *Shepherd v HMRC*,[57] where an airline pilot's claim to have been non-resident was examined in detail and rejected by the Special Commissioner. Although he satisfied the conditions of IR20 in terms of a strict day count, HMRC contended that this was not enough to estab-

---

[55] i.e. was not physically present in the UK for 183 days or more and did not spend an average of 91 days or more in each tax year over four years in the UK.

[56] April 2001.

[57] [2005] STC (SCD) 644; [2006] STC 1821.

lish non-residence. Subsequently, the High Court confirmed that the Special Commissioner had not misdirected herself in law but had accurately set out the legal test that she was required to apply. In *Shepherd* the taxpayer spent half the year outside the UK flying. He rented a flat in Cyprus and was in the UK for less than 90 days from 1999 to 2000 (excluding days of arrival and departure). However, he continued to live mostly in the matrimonial home when returning to the UK (despite being separated from his wife) and was not granted an immigration permit in Cyprus until February 2000. He had to be in the UK before and after each flight. The Special Commissioner concluded that he had never left the UK: there was no distinct break in the pattern of his life and even if he was resident in Cyprus during that year this was not sufficient to lose UK residence.

Matters came to a head in *Gaines-Cooper*,[58] the most celebrated case on non-residence. **3.45**

The Gaines-Cooper litigation

The saga began in October 2006. Gaines-Cooper was English by birth and at no time gave up his British passport. He was born in 1937 and owned a home in the UK through an offshore structure. He began a manufacturing business in the Seychelles in 1975; bought a house there and was granted a residency permit. In 1976 to 1980, he let his UK house and, in fact, ended up letting his Seychelles house between 1976 and 1979 for financial reasons. He spent 50 days or less per year in the UK in that period and appears to have been treated as non-resident for exchange control purposes. He spent between 100 and 200 days per year in the Seychelles from 1976 to 1980. He was also carrying on business and living in California from 1979 to at least 1986. However, he had international businesses operating in many different places, in the Seychelles, California and the UK. In 1993, he remarried and his second wife was Seychellois. She had been living in the UK since 1977 and in 1994 she took British nationality. After her marriage, she spent most of her time in the UK home working in the UK operation. Their child, James, was born in 1998 and went to school in the UK until 2005. **3.46**

Gaines-Cooper argued that he was non-resident from 1993 to 1994 onwards on the basis of IR20.[59] However, before proceedings began, he made a significant concession: he accepted that he was UK resident in 1992−93 because of what was then perceived to be the "available accommodation" rule. As noted above, it is not thought that this concession was necessary. If he had not made it, he could have argued that he had never come to the UK and was therefore not a leaver. He would not then have had to show a distinct break. Hence, he would not have had to satisfy the greater criteria that the Court of Appeal has held was required under IR20 for leavers.

A key part of Gaines-Cooper's case was that he had spent less than 91 days a year in the UK ignoring days of arrival in and departure from the UK.[60] **3.47**

---

[58] [2007] STC (SCD) 23; domicile status affirmed [2008] STC 1665; judicial review application in *R. (Davies) v HMRC* [2010] STC 860.

[59] He also claimed to have acquired a domicile of choice in the Seychelles: see 3.87.

[60] Which meant he could fly in on Saturday and out on Sunday to avoid the visit being counted.

The Special Commissioners did not follow the day-counting rules in IR20 but adopted a midnight test. The result was that until at least 2000–01 he was held to have spent more than 120 midnights in the UK for all years after 1992–93. The Special Commissioners expressly did not follow IR20 but applied the case law. They took a multi-factor approach, similar to that set out above,[61] in particular:

(i) he had a settled abode in Henley where he dwelt permanently or indefinitely;

(ii) he spent more time in the UK than he spent in the Seychelles or anywhere else;

(iii) he had both family and business ties in the UK;

(iv) his wife and son lived in the UK and his wife considered herself UK resident;

(v) he purchased and restored expensive UK business property.

The Special Commissioner decided that he was not a visitor who was in the UK for temporary purposes but an ordinarily resident individual who had left the UK merely for occasional residence abroad. He was not here for a casual purpose but rather in pursuance of "the regular habits of life":

> "A decision to visit the UK on a large number of days each year to be with one's wife and child is not a temporary purpose".

3.48   Gaines-Cooper did not challenge the decision of the Special Commissioners on his residence status although he did appeal on the domicile point, losing that case as well in the High Court. However, he pursued judicial review proceedings on the residence issue on the basis that he had followed the terms of IR20, and therefore had a legitimate expectation that HMRC would apply it, *regardless of whether those terms accorded with the actual law.*

3.49   In Brief 1/2007 issued in early 2007, HMRC effectively asserted what they later argued in the judicial review proceedings, namely that even if they were bound by IR20 as a matter of principle, Gaines-Cooper had not satisfied IR20 because he had misinterpreted the 90 day rule which applied only to individuals who had left the UK or to visitors coming here. It did not apply in determining whether an individual had "left" the UK in the first place. In deciding this latter question, Brief 1/2007 stated that HMRC considers all relevant evidence, including the pattern of presence in the UK and elsewhere. Hence, the retention of family and accommodation would suggest the individual had not left. HMRC summarised the position as follows:

> "In considering the issues of residence, ordinary residence and domicile in the Gaines-Cooper case, the Special Commissioners needed to build up a full picture of the taxpayer's life. A very important element of the picture was the pattern of his presence in the UK compared to the pattern of his presence overseas. The Special Commissioners decided that, in looking at these patterns, it would be misleading wholly to disregard days

---

[61] See the discussion of the *Grace* case at 3.29.

of arrival and departure. They used the taxpayer's patterns of presence in the UK as part of the evidence of his lifestyle and habits during the years in question. Based on this, and a wide range of other evidence, the Special Commissioners found that he had been continuously resident in the UK. From HMRC's perspective, therefore, the 91-day test was not relevant to the Gaines-Cooper case since the taxpayer did not leave the UK."

Gaines-Cooper pursued his judicial review proceedings along with two other taxpayers, Messrs Davies and James. He said he had abided by the terms of IR20 and therefore should be treated as non-resident. He had a legitimate expectation that HMRC would follow their own guidance and had relied on it to his detriment. HMRC initially resisted this, because of words in the Preface to IR20 which said: **3.50**

> *"The booklet offers general guidance on how the rules apply, but whether the guidance is appropriate in a particular case will depend on all the facts of that case"*;

and because of words in para.1.1 which said:

> *"This booklet sets out the main factors that are taken into account, but we can only make a decision on your residence status on the facts in your particular case"*;

despite the unequivocal wording of Chs 2 and 3. They also argued that IR20 cannot be allowed to produce a different result in any individual case from the strict law of residence because to have issued such a booklet would have been *"ultra vires"*, outside HMRC's *"care and management"* powers; and further, that once a person's residence status on the strict law has been decided against him by the Tax Tribunal, any *"legitimate expectation"* the person had to be treated as non-resident would have become *"illegitimate"*.

HMRC therefore strongly resisted Gaines-Cooper's application for permission to bring judicial review proceedings.

The judicial review decision

Judges in the Administrative Court refused permission to bring judicial review proceedings, but the Court of Appeal (Ward, Dyson and Moses L.JJ.) disagreed and criticised HMRC for even resisting the granting of permission. At the substantive hearing in November 2009,[62] HMRC accepted that they were bound by IR20 Ch.2 (*"Leaving the UK"*) and Ch.3 (*"Coming to the UK"*), if a person fell clearly within its wording. There was, however, dispute over what the words actually meant. They also argued that since Gaines-Cooper had already had a Special Commissioner's hearing in which he was held to be UK resident for the years in dispute he could not now rely on IR20. **3.51**

The Court of Appeal considered that it was important to the smooth running of the tax system that HMRC should have power to issue booklets

---

[62] See *R (Davies) v IRC* [2010] STC 860; EWCA Civ 83.

like IR20, intended to make the law intelligible to the average citizen, and that people should be entitled to rely on such booklets even if the result might be more favourable to the individual than the strict law. Hence the argument that Gaines-Cooper could not rely on IR20 contrary to the Special Commissioners' decision was wrong.

Once HMRC had accepted that in theory they could be bound by IR20 and any other guidance their main argument was that neither Gaines-Cooper (nor Messrs Davies/James) actually satisfied IR20. Davies and James claimed that they had left the UK and worked full-time abroad and the case therefore required the Court of Appeal to consider both IR20 para.2.2 ("*working abroad*") for Davies and James and paras 2.7 and 2.8 ("*leaving the UK permanently or indefinitely*") for Gaines-Cooper. HMRC argued that both paragraphs required you to "leave" the UK in the strict resident/non-resident sense, and that the day-count rules only apply once you have "left". If that were right, it would make IR20 completely useless, because you still have to apply the strict law to determine whether you have become non-resident in the first place.

3.52   The Court of Appeal decided HMRC was bound by IR20:

> "*The real difficulty lies not in imposing well established public law obligations on the Revenue, but in the interpretation of the assurances that the Revenue has given and their application to the facts relating to the particular taxpayers.*"

All the taxpayers lost but the decision makes three important points in relation to IR20:

   (i)   in the case of IR20 para.2.2, the taxpayer must demonstrate that he has left the UK to work full-time abroad and has done so for the whole of the relevant tax year. However, he does not have to demonstrate a distinct break from the UK;

   (ii) in the case of paras 2.7–2.9, the taxpayer must demonstrate a distinct break from former social and family ties within the UK;

   (iii) the number of visits to the UK does not establish non-resident status but once that status is acquired, the number of visits to the UK may result in it being lost.

3.52A   Davies, James & Gaines-Cooper appealed to the Supreme Court and their case was heard in July 2011. Judgment was handed down on October 19, 2011 and the Court of Appeal decision was affirmed by a majority of four to one with Lord Mance dissenting.[63] Although the taxpayers lost the case, it has confirmed the important principle that HMRC:

> "*accepts that a taxpayer has a legitimate expectation that HMRC will apply the guidance of IR20 to the facts of his particular case and, if satisfied that the facts and evidence fall within one of the circumstances in*

---

[63]   See *R (on the application of Davies v HMRC* and *R (on the application of Gaines-Cooper) v HMRC* [2011] UKSC 47.

Chapter 2 of IR20 indicating a certain residence treatment, will treat him accordingly".

Hence other taxpayers whose residence status is challenged by HMRC in respect of years prior to April 2009 (when IR20 was withdrawn) will be able to rely on IR20 provided of course they satisfy its terms.

In the leading judgment, Lord Wilson found in favour of HMRC: **3.52B**

> *"The reference to visits to the UK therefore underlines the need for a change in the individual's usual residence and therefore by ready inference for a distinct break in the pattern of his life in the UK."*

In his view, although poorly written and confusing, paras 2.7 to 2.9 of IR20 required the taxpayer to leave the UK in a more profound sense, namely permanently or indefinitely or for full-time employment, to take up residence abroad and to relinquish "his usual residence" in the UK. The paragraphs did show that any property retained was required to be used for the purpose only of visits rather than as a place of residence. Even if the requirement for a distinct break was unclear, the wording in these paragraphs was sufficiently confusing that it could not be relied upon!

The taxpayers also argued that even if IR20 itself did not create a legitimate expectation, nevertheless the Revenue's own settled practice was in line with the pure day count test. On this point Lord Wilson held that there was insufficient evidence. He considered that when HMRC scrutinised claims, they did not in fact adopt a settled practice different from that set out in IR20. *"The Appellants' evidence to this effect was far too thin and equivocal."*

Counsel for the taxpayers further failed in his submission that in determining whether employment had lasted for a whole tax year, one could argue that a later tax year of full employment was sufficient to mean someone could be non-UK resident in an earlier tax year. In their case the full-time employment did not cover the whole of the first full tax year in question (which was when the disposal showing a gain took place). In subsequent tax years they had continued to work abroad fulltime and had done so for entire tax years but it was held that this could not relieve them from liability in the first year when they had not worked full time abroad for the entire year.

Hence in the end all three taxpayers had to fall back on paras 2.7 to 2.9.   **3.52C**
They failed to demonstrate that they had gone abroad to live outside the UK for three years or more or at least for a settled purpose within the terms set out in IR20. The only difference is that in the case of *Davies & James* their residence status has not yet been tested as a matter of general law. Hence they may win on this basis.

Many will disagree with the decision.   In a powerful dissenting judgement   **3.52D**
Lord Mance commented thus at para.89:

> *"The references* [in paras 2.7 and 2.8] *to going abroad permanently or to live outside the UK for three years or more and to a 'stated aim' of living abroad permanently or indefinitely are directed most obviously to the taxpayer's intention regarding the overall duration of his or her absence rather than to the quality of absence or the nature of any return visits or continuing British connections. Further, it is clear that the words 'Leaving the UK permanently or indefinitely' cannot and do not precisely or accurately reflect*

all the paragraphs above which they appear. Thus the only requirements under the first part of paragraph 2.9 are (i) going abroad (ii) 'for a settled purpose' which is expressly defined to include 'a fixed object or intention in which you are going to be engaged for an extended period of time.'

...In my opinion, paragraph 2.9 is designed to assist taxpayers who never intended to leave permanently or indefinitely but can show a settled purpose of lesser duration. The second part of paragraph 2.9 deals with situations where there was neither an intention to go abroad permanently or indefinitely nor any settled purpose. It covers two possibilities: one that the taxpayer can subsequently say and show that he has acquired an intention to leave the UK permanently (or, one would presume though this is not expressed, for three years or more); the other that his actual absence covers three years from departure. This second possibility looks on its face at the period for which he is abroad again without focusing on the quality of absence."

He then went on to comment that para.2.1, which deals with people who *"usually live in this country and only go abroad for short periods"* cannot be regarded as matching any of the taxpayers' lifestyles during the relevant periods.

> *"I do not find any express terms of paragraph 2 of IR20 or in particular in the words 'permanently or indefinitely' direct support for any requirement for a distinct break. Looking at the matter more broadly, it would seem to me remarkable that, if any such requirement were intended, it was not clearly expressed. The guidance is intended to be useful as well as reliable. The requirement for a distinct break from family and social ties in the UK would certainly be a 'main factor'...and in its uncertainty would also be matters of obvious concern to many taxpayers. How (for example) does one demonstrate a distinct break from family ties in a world where spouses or partners may live and work in different countries but meet regularly in one or the other?"*

He added in para.95:

> *"The further references in paragraph 2.8 to the exclusion from this 91 day average period of days spent here due to exceptional circumstances such as the illness of yourself or a member of your immediate family do not fit with an expectation of a distinct break of social or family ties to the UK. The reference in all versions of IR20 from November 1993 on to a person being able to have property available for use in the UK during his visits here also militates against the requirement for a distinct break."*

He concluded that:

> *"The natural meaning of Chapter 2 in all its versions since at least 1993 is that rather than apply the case law test of a distinct break they introduced (and for public law purposes substitute) a series of specifically delineated cases, into which, if a taxpayer falls, he or she will be treated without more as not resident or ordinarily resident in the UK. I repeat that the suggestion that the distinct break test is implicit in the language of paragraphs 2.5 to 2.9 (though not in that of paragraph 2.2) appears to me remarkable*

in the light of the obvious importance of such a factor if it were envisaged. Paragraphs 2.5 to 2.9 of IR20 are essentially futile, indeed positively misleading, if they are reading as incorporating or reiterating the difficult case law test of a distinct break, and moreover imposing a further specific restriction (the 91 day average limit) to the taxpayer's disadvantage. I appreciate that in the Appellants' cases the view may be taken that it is desirable and appropriate that HMRC should be able to tax as ordinarily resident persons with the lifestyle and connections in the UK of these Appellants. That is a moral or fiscal judgment which may well reflect the strict law (and evidently does so in the case of Mr Gaines-Cooper) but it does not follow that it is the conclusion to be drawn from the guidance in IR20 which HMRC issued, in the interests of good governance, clarity and transparency for the benefit of individuals, to explain the combination of the law and practice by reference to which such individuals could direct their affairs."

He then roundly rejects Lord Wilson's judgment:

"To treat IR20 as pregnant with the detailed implications listed in para 45 or in some way informing an ordinarily sophisticated taxpayer of a need for a multi factorial evaluation of his or her circumstances and for a distinct break runs contrary not only to the wording and sense of the document itself but also to its genesis and purpose; so also, to treat IR20 as so unclear as to communicate nothing to which the legal effect can be given on the means by which non residence status might be acquired."

Lord Mance did not consider whether the Appellants could show a clear and unequivocal practice prior to 2005.

HMRC 6

This replaced IR20 in April 2009 and was far less prescriptive. It was amended **3.53** in December 2010 but is heavily caveated throughout to avoid any argument that it raises a legitimate expectation. About the only useful part on which a taxpayer can rely relates to those working full-time abroad:[64]

> *"8.5 Leaving the UK to work abroad as an employee*
>
> *If you are leaving the UK to work abroad full-time, you will only become not resident and not ordinarily resident from the day after the day of your departure, as long as:*
>
> > - *you are leaving to work abroad under a contract of employment for at least a whole tax year*
> > - *you have actually physically left the UK to begin your employment abroad and not, for example, to have a holiday until you begin your employment*
> > - *you will be absent from the UK for at least a whole tax year*

---

[64] Interpreted to mean (by HMRC) no more than 10 days working in the UK.

- *your visits to the UK after you have left to begin your overseas employment will*

  - *total less than 183 days in any tax year, and*
  - *average less than 91 days a tax year. This average is taken over the period of absence up to a maximum of four years.*

8.6 Returning to the UK after working abroad

If you were not resident and not ordinarily resident when you were working abroad and you return to the UK when your employment ends, you will be not resident and not ordinarily resident in the UK until the day before you return to the UK. You will become resident and ordinarily resident on the day you return to the UK unless you can show that your return was simply a short visit to the UK between two periods of full-time employment abroad.

However, if you have previously been resident in the UK and are returning to become resident here again after a period of residence abroad, you might need to consider whether your absence from the UK was a period of 'temporary non-residence'. If you were temporarily non-resident in the UK, this may affect your liability to UK tax when you return to become resident in the UK again."

V ORDINARY RESIDENCE

3.54 This has been an area of increasing inquiry by HMRC. A difficulty is that HMRC guidance has probably been wrong for some years and the case law is a mess. The consultation paper on the statutory residence test proposes abolishing it!

Ordinary residence is relevant for tax purposes in two main areas. First, an individual is not liable to income tax under the transfer of assets provisions[65] if UK resident but not ordinarily resident. Second, a person who is resident but not ordinarily resident in the UK is liable to tax on his UK earnings but his foreign earnings are taxable only on the remittance basis.[66] If he is resident and ordinarily resident he is liable to tax on the whole of the earnings from the employment, irrespective of how little of those earnings are earned in the UK.[67]

3.55 HMRC's amended HMRC 6[68] states that if an individual comes to the UK permanently or with the intention of staying for at least three years, then that individual will be treated as ordinarily resident in the UK. The wording of para.7.5 has also changed so that *"if after three complete tax years, a pattern*

---

[65] ITA 2007 ss.720−735.

[66] ITEPA 2003 s.26.

[67] The remittance basis applies to chargeable overseas earnings (ITEPA 2003 s.22). This enables a UK resident and ordinarily resident foreign domiciled person who claims the remittance basis to pay tax only on UK earnings. However, this is more restrictive than s.26 since it requires the employer to be resident outside the UK and for all the duties of the employment to be performed wholly outside the UK. Two separate contracts are therefore required. Under s.26 there is no requirement that all the duties are performed abroad and it can be a single contract with a UK employer.

[68] From December 2010.

has emerged that these visits total more than 91 days on average and your visits continue, then you will become resident and ordinarily resident in the UK from the start of the next tax year." Previous guidance had indicated that if the individual continued to visit the UK he would become ordinarily resident at the start of the fifth year where visits averaged 91 days or more per tax year over a four-year period.

What is the position of those who do not intend to come to the UK for more than three years but are resident on arrival and are coming for a settled purpose such as work?

The leading authority on the meaning of ordinary residence is *Shah v Barnet London Borough Council*,[69] a case relating to student grants. The House of Lords decided that foreign students who were allowed into the UK on education visas for a limited period could be ordinarily resident here. Lord Scarman stated: **3.56**

> "*I unhesitatingly subscribe to the view that 'ordinarily resident' refers to a man's abode in a particular place or country which he has adopted voluntarily and for settled purposes as part of the regular order of his life for the time being, whether of short or of long duration.*"

This suggests that to be "ordinarily resident" an individual must be resident but with some added quality to make it "ordinary". However, some tax legislation, notably TCGA 1992 s.2, proceeds on the assumption that an individual can be ordinarily resident without being resident. A similar view was expressed by the Special Commissioners in *Gaines-Cooper v HMRC*.[70] But this is probably wrong. In both *Levene v IRC*[71] and *Reed v Clark*[72] it was assumed "*the concept of ordinary residence involves actual residence, in the sense referred to with the added quality of continuity.*"

Recent case law has mainly concerned those coming to the UK on short term work assignments who wished to take advantage of ITEPA 2003 s.26. In *Genovese v HMRC*,[73] the taxpayer came to the UK on a short-term banking assignment in July 1998 and took a series of one year leases of a flat commencing in September 1998. In 2002–03, he purchased a house. The Special Commissioner considered that for residence to be ordinarily or habitual it must have a pattern and continue for a sufficient time and suggested a minimum period of three years was necessary to establish that the pattern had become habitual. He concluded that from September 2001 the taxpayer had become ordinarily resident. The taxpayer had by then held short term tenancies for a full three years. Accordingly he was ordinarily resident from April 6, 2001. **3.57**

A contrary approach was taken by the same judge sitting in the First Tier Tribunal in *Tuczka v HMRC*.[74] In this case he came to the conclusion that a period of residence of less than three years can be sufficient to establish ordinary residence for tax purposes; that decision was upheld by the Upper Tribunal. The taxpayer arrived to take up employment in July 1997 and lived **3.58**

[69] [1983] 1 All ER 226.
[70] [2007] STC 1665 at 1702, [190].
[71] [1928] AC 217 at 225.
[72] [1985] STC 323.
[73] [2009] SPC 00741.
[74] [2010] UKFTT 33; affirmed [2011] UKUTT 113.

in rented accommodation until he bought a property in early 1998. In July 1998 he filed Form P86 indicating that the expected duration of his stay was two and a half to three years. The Tribunal decided he became ordinarily resident at some stage during 1998−99 as his purpose, namely the employment, was by then settled. They rejected his argument that because in 1998−99 he had no intention to stay in the UK indefinitely he was not ordinarily resident. He argued that he intended to return to Austria within two and a half years: he risked having his employment terminated without notice and he brought to the UK only minimal personal belongings. However, by 1998 he had found a flat, been joined by his girlfriend and worked here. He had accordingly established a settled pattern of living and that was sufficient to make him ordinarily resident even within three years of arrival. An intention to reside indefinitely is needed to establish domicile but not ordinary residence.

3.59   The Upper Tribunal's decision seems correct in law: the purpose of coming to work in the UK is a settled purpose, and so may result in ordinary residence immediately even if the taxpayer does not acquire accommodation and presumably even if he leaves within three years, although in both cases the taxpayers stayed beyond the initial three year period.

3.60   IR20 had stated that a person arriving in the UK without an intention to stay for at least three years would only be treated as ordinarily resident from the start of the tax year following the third anniversary of his arrival or, if earlier, from the start of the tax year in which they decided to remain in the UK for three or more years. In other words the length of their intended residence rather than the reason for their presence in the UK was seen as the important element in determining ordinary resident. In the light of the case law, IR20 seems wrong or at least misleading.

3.61   HMRC 6 still contains references to the three year period but is more circumspect. It states:

> "*if you are treated as ordinarily resident solely because you have accommodation here and you dispose of the accommodation and leave the UK within three years of your arrival, you may be treated as not ordinarily resident for the duration of your stay if this is to your advantage . . . If you come to the UK for less than three years, you might not be ordinarily resident but there are many factors to consider.*"

The Tribunal's emphasis in *Tuczka* was on the purpose for which the taxpayer came to the UK rather than the intended length of residence. HMRC 6 refers to this "settled purpose" in the context of ordinary residence and assumes that a purpose cannot be settled unless it is likely to continue for a certain period, noting:

> "*if you come to the UK for a settled purpose, for example to live or work in the UK for three years or more you will be ordinarily residenct from when you first arrive.*"

This might be taken to suggest that a settled purpose can only be established if you intend to stay in the UK for more than three years but the Tribunal was clear this was not the case.[75]

---

[75] They may have been influenced in the *Tuczka* case by the fact that he had in fact stayed beyond the three years. However, it cannot be the case that if a taxpayer intended to leave within three

In *Turberville v HMRC*[76] the taxpayer left the UK in July 2001 to work **3.62** in Texas on a contract which was expected to last until retirement. He and his wife owned two homes in England which they kept, and took a flat in Texas. The unexpected collapse of his employer's business led to him being made redundant in October 2002. He left the US and took a lease on a flat in Monaco from December 1, 2002. In 2002–03 he spent 140 whole days in the UK partly in connection with the company's liquidation and 52 part days.

The questions for the Tribunal were whether his decision to take up employment in the US meant that he lost ordinary residence in the UK and whether his return to the UK for three months restored his ordinary resident status. It found that on the facts taken together the period of return after redundancy did not mean that the taxpayer became ordinarily resident in the UK as there was not the necessary degree of settled purpose. There had been a distinct break in the taxpayer's life in July 2001. In this case the two UK properties were, in the Tribunal's view, "*fairly neutral*". They key point was that he was not back in the UK for settled purposes as part of the regular order of his life.

VI PRACTICAL POINTS FOR THOSE WISHING TO BECOME NON-UK RESIDENT

For those who want complete certainty as to their residence status how can **3.63** they best ensure that they are not resident and ordinarily resident in the UK and that their absence from the UK is not for occasional purposes?[77]

The easiest option is to follow HMRC 6 guidelines and work full-time abroad (as employee or self-employed or as a mixture of the two) for at least one complete tax year limiting days in the UK to no more than 90 days per tax year. There is no need to give up accommodation and family ties here. A spouse could remain here. The work must actually begin by the start of the tax year for which he is claiming non-UK residence and span a full tax year. Duties in the UK should be confined to incidental duties although HMRC now accept that up to 10 days non-incidental work in the UK is acceptable.

HMRC will examine claims to work full-time abroad where the sums at stake are large, particularly if the taxpayer is working for a company he controls. In *Hankinson v HMRC*[78] the taxpayer was not able to prove he had worked full-time abroad at any time in the year let alone for a complete tax year. He had to pay over £30 million of tax at stake with penalties and interest.

Another option is to leave the UK for a complete tax year, not set foot in **3.64** the UK for a complete tax year and base oneself firmly in one place abroad, i.e. rely on *Reed v Clark*. A wanderer, i.e. a person who does not settle in any

---

years but he later changed his intentions his status retrospectively would be changed for the earlier years before the change of intention. HMRC proposes to deal with this in the statutory residence test by abolishing ordinary residence and introducing a "work day" relief for the first three years of arrival not based on intention.

[76] [2010] UKFTT 69 (TC).
[77] See s.829 ITA 2007.
[78] [2009] UKFTT (384) TC; [2010] STC 2640 (UT) which emphasises that HMRC examines the records of an employee's movements in great detail.

particular place abroad would not satisfy this test. It is necessary to have a permanent home abroad.

3.65   Other taxpayers who retain accommodation and family ties here, do not work full-time abroad and may even do some limited work in the UK, will be in an uncertain position until the enactment of the statutory residence test.[79] They need to demonstrate a clear break from the UK. In these circumstances what steps should they take to improve their position if they want to claim non-residence status?

3.66   First, demonstrate that the taxpayer has a settled base outside the UK. Do not wander round the globe. Ensure that all the following is sent to that base abroad and not kept in the UK:

(a) Official post and personal correspondence, e.g. pension forms, State pension, tax returns, tax correspondence, life insurance forms, passport, identity card, any renewal forms, health cover renewals, bills, mobile phone registration.

(b) Bank accounts moved abroad; all bank statements sent to new address.

(c) Re-register gun licence and driving licence, car registration issued to place abroad.

In addition consider the following:

(d) Move society, club and sport memberships abroad.

(e) Same with church, arts, restaurant or social membership.

(f) Doctor, optician and dentist to be abroad; register accordingly with local practice.

(g) Office and secretary should not be retained in the UK; avoid a UK office base of any sort; surrender UK directorships.

(h) Registration for local taxes should be evidenced and retained.

(i) Take out no new ISAs or any other investment that requires residence in the UK.

(j) Spend more time in the place abroad than anywhere else—six months minimum. Accept that taxpayer is resident there for tax purposes. Do not argue something different to different tax authorities.

(k) Keep detailed notes of visits to the UK and evidence of when the taxpayer came and what was done in the course of those visits.

(l) Keep all boarding passes and receipts evidencing days of entry and exit.

(m) Keep details of work done abroad, keep detailed daily diary.

(n) Have few possessions in the UK, i.e. keep minimal clothes and all personal items, e.g. books, papers, clothes, etc abroad.

(o) Pets—if possible take abroad.

(p) Visit the UK for irregular (not regular) purposes, e.g. to see friends

---

[79] i.e. like *Grace* and *Gaines-Cooper*.

rather than for any settled purpose. Do not return to the UK in between trips abroad. Return to base.

(q) Minimise days spent in the UK if accommodation retained here, e.g. to under 70.

(r) Monitor website, internet, etc and ensure entries are consistent with what is being said to HMRC about residence status.

VII THE PROPOSED STATUTORY RESIDENCE TEST

In June 2011 the Government published a proposed statutory residence test to come into effect on April 6, 2012. The test will have three parts: **3.67**

- Part A contains conclusive non-residence factors that would be sufficient in themselves to make an individual not resident.
- Part B contains conclusive residence factors that would be sufficient in themselves to make an individual UK resident.
- Part C contains other connection factors and day counting rules which will only need to be considered by those whose residence status is not determined by Part A or Part B.

In the rare situations where an individual satisfies one of the conditions in both Part A and Part B, for example someone whose only home is in the UK but who spends very few days in the country in a particular tax year, Part A will take precedence and the individual will be non-UK resident in that year.

Part A: conclusive non-residence

Part A of the test will conclusively determine that an individual is not resident in the UK for a tax year if they fall under any of the following conditions; namely they: **3.68**

- were not resident in the UK in all of the previous three tax years and they are present in the UK for fewer than 45 days in the current tax year; or
- were resident in the UK in one or more of the previous three tax years and they are present in the UK for fewer than 10 days in the current tax year;
- leave the UK to carry out full-time work abroad, provided that they are present in the UK for fewer than 90 days in the tax year and no more than 20 days are spent working in the UK in the tax year.

An individual who does not fall within Part A would not necessarily be UK resident. They would instead need to consider Part B or Part C. **3.69**

Part B: conclusive residence

3.70 Provided Part A of the test does not apply, an individual will be conclusively resident for the tax year under Part B if they meet any of the following conditions, namely they:

- are present in the UK for 183 days or more in a tax year; or
- have only one home and that home is in the UK (or have two or more homes and all of these are in the UK); or
- carry out full-time work in the UK.

The following example from the Treasury paper illustrates how Part B determines residence status:

Situation	Residence outcome
Mrs C is married and lives in New York with her husband and young children. She works for an international company with offices in London, Paris and Madrid. In 2012–13 she is asked to work on a project in the London office and spends 200 days in the UK. The project lasts for fewer than nine months. She stays in a hotel and is joined by her husband and family during the summer. She retains her home in the US.	Mrs C is resident in the UK under Part B of the test because she spends 183 days or more in the UK. If she spent fewer than 183 days in the UK, she would need to consider Part C of the test. None of the other criteria in Part B apply to her.

Part C: other connection factors and day counting

3.71 Part C applies only to those individuals whose residence status is not determined by Part A or Part B and, therefore, whose circumstances are less straightforward. Part C reflects the principle that the more time someone spends in the UK, the fewer connections they can have with the UK if they want to be non-resident. It also incorporates the principle that residence status should adhere more to those who are already resident than to those who are not currently resident. It is perhaps instructive in highlighting the areas that HMRC consider important at present.

Under Part C an individual simply needs to compare the number of days he spends in the UK against a small number of clearly defined connection factors. Individuals who know how many days they spend in the UK and how many relevant connection factors they have will find it straightforward to assess whether they are UK resident.

3.72 The following connection factors are relevant, but only when linked to the amount of time the person spends in the UK:

- Family—the individual's spouse or civil partner or common law equivalent (provided the individual is not separated from them) or minor children are resident in the UK;

- Accommodation—the individual has accessible accommodation in the UK and makes use of it during the tax year (subject to exclusions for some types of accommodation);
- Substantive work in the UK—the individual does substantive work in the UK (but does not work in the UK full-time);
- UK presence in previous year—the individual spent 90 days or more in the UK in either of the previous two tax years;
- More time in the UK than in other countries—the individual spends more days in the UK in the tax year than in any other single country.

These connection factors are combined with days spent in the UK into a "scale" **3.73** to determine whether the individual is resident or not. It is proposed to have separate "scales" for arrivers and leavers, reflecting the principle that it should be harder for leavers to relinquish residence than for new arrivers to acquire it.

Individuals not resident in all of the previous three tax years (arrivers)

If an individual was not resident in all of the three tax years preceding the **3.74** year under consideration, the following connection factors may be relevant to their residence status, if they occur at any point in the tax year, namely the individual:

- has a UK resident family;
- has substantive UK employment (including self-employment);
- has accessible accommodation in the UK;
- spent 90 days or more in the UK in either of the previous two tax years.

The way these connection factors are combined with days spent in the UK to determine residence status for arrivers is as follows:

Days spent in the UK	Impact of connection factors on residence status
Fewer than 45 days	Always non-resident
45–89 days	Resident if individual has four factors (otherwise not resident)
90–119 days	Resident if individual has three factors or more (otherwise not resident)
120–182 days	Resident if individual has two factors or more (otherwise not resident
183 days or more	Always resident

In effect this means that an arriver who keeps his midnights to under 90 can never become UK resident, even with family and accommodation here.

Individuals resident in one or more of the previous three tax years (leavers)

3.75   If the individual was resident in one or more of the three tax years immediately preceding the tax year under consideration, the following connection factors may be relevant to their residence status, if they occur at any point in the tax year, namely the individual:

- has a UK resident family;
- has substantive UK employment (including self-employment);
- has accessible accommodation in the UK;
- spent 90 days or more in the UK in either of the previous two tax years;
- spends more days in the UK in the tax year than in any other single country (not relevant for arrivers: see 3.74).

The way these connection factors are combined with days spent in the UK to determine residence status for leavers is as follows:

Days spent in the UK	Impact of connection factors on residence status
Fewer than 10 days	Always non-resident
10–44 days	Resident if individual has 4 factors or more (otherwise not resident)
45–89 days	Resident if individual has 3 factors or more (otherwise not resident)
90–119 days	Resident if individual has 2 factors or more (otherwise not resident)
120–182 days	Resident if individual has 1 factor or more (otherwise not resident)
183 days	Always resident

In effect a leaver who is not working full-time abroad and spends up to 89 midnights in the UK in the tax years after departure and retains accommodation here will need to ensure his family are also non-UK resident and that he does not do substantive work here.

Other aspects of the proposed test

3.76   *Split years*: steps will be taken to legislate Extra Statutory Concession (ESC) A11, so that a tax year can be split into periods of residence and non-residence in certain circumstances when an individual comes to, or leaves, the UK part way through a tax year. Split year treatment will apply where an individual:

- comes to the UK to take up permanent residence; or

- leaves the UK to take up permanent residence abroad; or

- loses UK residence when leaving to work full-time outside the UK.

The intention is broadly to recreate the circumstances in which split year treatment currently applies and to put it on a statutory footing.

Anti-avoidance provisions: the test will include an anti-avoidance five year   **3.77**
rule for some forms of investment income along the lines of CGT. In particular, it will apply to dividends paid by closely controlled companies that reflect profits that have built up during a period of residence and which are then taken out during a short period of non-residence.

The new five-year rule will not apply to all types of income that are received when a person is non-resident. For example, it will not apply to earnings from employment or self-employment or to normal types of regular investment income, such as bank interest or dividends from listed companies.

Definitions are set out in Pt 4 as follows.   **3.78**

Full-time work abroad: a person has full-time work abroad if they leave the   **3.79**
UK to perform work abroad and are:

- employed abroad under one or more contracts of employment (including consecutive employments) or hold offices which have combined total hours of 35 hours per week or more; or

- carrying on one or more trades or professions wholly abroad where 35 hours of work per week or more is undertaken on average.

In either of these cases the work must be carried out for at least one full tax year if it is to be classed as full-time work abroad.

When a person is working full-time abroad, no more than 20 working days   **3.80**
can be performed in the UK in any one tax year. This limit will be reduced pro rata if the individual is treated as being not resident for part of a year under the split year rules.

The person must be present in the UK for fewer than 90 days. This limit will be reduced pro rata if the individual is treated as being not resident for part of a year under the split year rules.

Working day: a working day is any day on which three hours or more of   **3.81**
work is carried out. If an individual carries out fewer than three hours of work, the day will not count towards the threshold of 20 working days for the purposes of full-time working abroad. Even if an individual is not present in the UK at the end of the day, they will still be treated as working in the UK on that day if they have worked in the UK for three hours or more. Where individuals work in the UK for less than three hours on a particular day, they will be expected to have sufficient records to demonstrate this fact.

Day of presence in the UK: the definition of a day of presence in the UK   **3.82**
remains unchanged and includes midnights. The extent to which days spent in the UK due to exceptional circumstances can be ignored is still under consideration.

Family: an individual is treated as having family in the UK (and therefore a   **3.83**
connecting factor for Part C purposes) in a tax year if either of the following applies:

- the individual's spouse, civil partner or common law equivalent (i.e. co-habitee) is resident in the UK in that tax year or any part of that tax year. This does not include a spouse, civil partner or common law equivalent if they are separated from the individual under a court order or a separation agreement or where the separation is likely to be permanent; or

- the individual has children under the age of 18 who are resident in the UK and the individual spends time with those children (one to one or with others present), or lives with them, for all or part of 60 days or more during the tax year. It will not matter whether these days were spent with the child in the UK or elsewhere.

3.84   A child will not be treated as being resident in the UK for these purposes if their residence is mainly caused by time spent at a UK educational establishment. This will be when the child spends fewer than 60 days in the UK when not present at the educational establishment and the child's main home is not in the UK.

3.85   *Accommodation*: an individual has UK accommodation if residential property:

- is accessible to be used by them as a place of residence; and

- is used by them or their family in the year as a place of residence.

3.86   *Substantive employment (including self-employment)*: an individual is treated as having substantive employment or self-employment in the UK (and therefore a Part C connecting factor) if they work in the UK for 40 or more days in the tax year. The definition of a working day is any day in which more than three hours of work is undertaken. This includes a day where the person is not in the UK at the end of that day.

VIII DOMICILE

3.87   Domicile is a concept of private international law.[80] Persons who are not UK-domiciled benefit from a more favourable tax regime.[81]

The domicile of a person is, in general, the place or country where he permanently resides or has his home or which is determined to be his permanent home by rules of law. His home is that place or country in which he resides with the intention of remaining permanently or with regard to which he retains that intention though no longer in fact resident. A person cannot be without a domicile or have more than one domicile at a time.

3.88   A domicile may be a *domicile of origin*, a *domicile of choice* or a *domicile of dependence*. These three concepts are discussed briefly below. There is also a concept of *deemed domicile*, but only for for IHT purposes.[82]

---

[80] It affects the ability to make a claim under IPFDA 1975. For a full discussion, see *Dicey, Morris and Collins Conflict of Laws* (14th edn) 2006 at Ch.6. See the *Agulian* case below.
[81] See Ch.5.
[82] Discussed in Ch.31.

Domicile of origin

This is the domicile of an individual at his birth. At common law it is his **3.89** father's domicile, unless he is illegitimate or born posthumously, in which case he takes his mother's domicile.[83] This domicile is retained until the person (not being a minor) acquires another domicile by choice or until, during his minority, the parent acquires another domicile of choice, when the child acquires that as a domicile of dependence.

In *Barlow Clowes International v Henwood*[84] it was held that the taxpayer needed to establish "*a singular and distinctive relationship with the country of his supposed domicile of choice*" in order to demonstrate that he had lost his domicile of origin. It was not enough that he had rejected his country of origin if he had no settled intention to live permanently in another jursidiction. It was noted that once a domicile of choice was acquired, the loss of it should not be easily inferred:

> "*it is likely that many people will be as attached to a domicile of choice they have acquired as to a domicile of origin which they enjoyed origi-nally. The law should reflect that fact . . . it seems to me that as a general proposition the acquisition of any new domicile should in general be treated as a serious allegation because of its serious consequences. None of the authorities cited to us preclude that approach and such an approach ensures logical consistency between two situations where the policy interest is to be protected. However what evidence is required in a particular case will depend on the application of common sense to the particular circum-stances.*" (at [91])

It was expressly noted that as a matter of law a domicile of choice is not lost if a person merely moves from the place of his domicile of choice without having decided whether to move permanently provided that he retained an intention to reside permanently in the place of his domicile of choice.

A domicile of choice

This is acquired when a person voluntarily fixes his sole or chief residence **3.90** in a particular place with an intention of continuing to reside there for an unlimited time.[85] He must intend to abandon his previous domicile. In a sense therefore the acquisition of a domicile of choice involves an actus reus (physi-cal presence in the territory) accompanied by the requisite mental state (mens rea). A domicile of origin will not be lost, even though a person has left that country with no intention of returning, if he has not decided definitely in which other country he will live.

The domicile of a person born in England of parents domiciled here is ipso **3.91** facto English, but if, for example, on attaining his majority he emigrates he

---

[83] Adopted children take the adoptive parent's domicile as their domicile of origin.
[84] [2008] EWCA Civ 577.
[85] *In the Estate of Fuld (No.3)* [1966] 2 WLR 717.

will not lose his domicile of origin and acquire a domicile of choice until he settles in a particular country with an *intention* of living permanently or indefinitely in that place. Residence alone is not enough.[86] If he afterwards decided to leave that State without intending to return, his domicile of origin would revive[87] and if he died before acquiring a new domicile of choice his domicile at death would accordingly be English.[88]

3.92   Residence in a particular state must be freely chosen and not prescribed by necessity, such as the duties of office, the demands of creditors, or relief from illness,[89] and must be general and indefinite in its future contemplation. The tendency of many decisions has been to emphasise the adherence of the domicile of origin, and to attach less significance to residence, however long, as an indication of a change of domicile.[90] The case of *Agulian v Cyganik*[91] bears this out.

In the Estate of Fuld,[92] Scarman J. said concerning the intention necessary to acquire a domicile of choice:

> "*If a man intends to return to the land of his birth upon a clearly foreseen and reasonably anticipated contingency, eg the end of his job, the intention required is lacking; but if he has in mind only a vague possibility, such as making a fortune . . . such a state of mind is consistent with the intention required by law.*"

This passage was approved by the Court of Appeal in *Buswell v IRC*[93] and in *IRC v Bullock*[94] where Buckley L.J. said[95]:

---

[86] A person cannot be domiciled in Canada, Australia or the United States (or indeed the UK!) which are federal states: domicile requires connection to a particular territory subject to a single system of law. Hence, each state is a separate territory for the purposes of domicile and one must be domiciled in a particular state or province. Difficulties can arise where a person moves from one state to another and he has a domicile of choice rather than origin in that state and a domicile of origin in the UK. If he ceases to reside in one state so that he has lost his domicile there then unless he immediately takes up residence in another state his domicile of origin revives.

[87] See *Udny v Udny* (1869) LR 1 Sc & Div 441.

[88] *Re Clore (No.2)* [1984] STC 609.

[89] See *Re Mackenzie (No.2)* [1941] Ch69, concerning a domiciled Australian who for the last 54 years of her life had lived in mental homes in England.

[90] *Winans v Att Gen* [1904] AC 287; *IRC v Bullock* [1976] 1 WLR 1178.

[91] [2006] EWCA Civ 129. The deceased had been born in Cyprus in 1939. He had fled for safety reasons to London in 1957 but retained family in Cyprus. He bought land there and in 1972 returned to his home village intending to live there permanently. In 1974 Turkey invaded and occupied Northern Cyprus and he returned to London with his daughter. His daughter later returned to Cyprus but by his death he had lived in London for 43 years. He retained a Cypriot ID Card and lived the life of a Greek Cypriot in the UK, talking Greek and watching Cypriot TV. He got engaged to Renata Cyganik in 1999 and married her in 2003. He died unexpectedly shortly thereafter and, apart from leaving £50,000 to Renata, the rest of his estate went to family members. She made a claim under IPFDA 1975. For her claim to be successful she needed to demonstrate that the deceased had died UK domiciled. HMRC accepted that he was not domiciled here under general law (albeit deemed domiciled here for inheritance tax purposes). The judge at the High Court held that the deceased had acquired an English domicile of choice but the Court of Appeal overturned this decision. The High Court judge over-emphasised the importance of the marriage and the evidence was not sufficiently convincing to establish the change of domicile. Contrast *Holliday v Musa*.

[92] [1968] P 675; [1966] 2 WLR 717.

[93] [1974] 1 WLR 1631.

[94] [1976] 1 WLR 1178.

[95] At 1185.

> "*I do not think it is necessary to show that the intention to make a home in the new country is irrevocable or that the person whose intention is under consideration believes that for reasons of health or otherwise he will have no opportunity to change his mind. In my judgment the true test is whether he intends to make his home in the new country until the end of his days unless and until something happens to make him change his mind.*"

In the *Bullock* case, the taxpayer's domicile of origin was in Canada. His matrimonial home was in England, but he intended to return to Canada if he survived his wife. The Court decided that this contingent intention prevented him from acquiring an English domicile. In the words of Buckley L.J.:

> "*The question can perhaps be formulated in this way where the contingency is not itself of a doubtful or indefinite character: is there a sufficiently substantial possibility of the contingency happening to justify regarding the intention to return as a real determination to do so upon the contingency occurring rather than a vague hope or aspiration?*"

These principles were applied with a different result in the Estate Duty case of **3.93** *Re Furse, Furse v IRC*[96] where an American citizen with a domicile of origin in Rhode Island had lived in Sussex for the last 39 years of his life, making annual visits to the US. His intention was to return permanently to the US when he became incapable of living an active physical life on his wife's farm in Sussex. It was held that he died domiciled in England, because the contingency of returning was too vague and indefinite and permitted of almost infinite adjustment to meet his wishes.

In *Re Shaffer, Morgan v Cilento*[97] the question was whether the playwright **3.94** Anthony Shaffer, who died in London, had abandoned his English domicile of origin. The judge held that he had established a domicile of choice in Queensland and his English domicile of origin had not revived before his death, i.e. he had not abandoned his domicile of choice. His intention to return to Queensland may have been withering but it had not actually changed by the time of death.

A domicile of choice, unlike a domicile of origin, can be abandoned without **3.95** the acquisition of a new domicile; but it is still necessary to show both a change of residence and a change of intention. It appears, therefore, that where a person loses mental capacity, having acquired a domicile of choice outside the UK, even if he becomes resident in England he will not lose his domicile of choice because he does not have the necessary intention to cease residing in the country of that domicile.[98]

In *Allen v Revenue and Customs Commissioners*[99] the Special Commissioner **3.96** decided that an elderly woman had not lost her domicile of choice in Spain (despite her UK domicile of origin and the fact that she had lived with relatives in the UK in the last few years of life) because she maintained a foreign home ready at all times for her occupation and it was clear that she would have

---

[96] [1980] STC 596.
[97] [2004] WTLR 457.
[98] Once acquired a domicile of choice is not lost according to *Dicey* unless two conditions are satisfied: "*A person abandons a domicile of choice in a country by ceasing to reside there and by ceasing to intend to reside there permanently or indefinitely, and not otherwise.*"
[99] [2005] STC (SCD) 614.

returned to Spain if she could have persuaded relatives to look after her there. She had purchased a house in the UK shortly before death so this decision is somewhat surprising but the Special Commissioner was influenced by the fact that though she had an English domicile of origin she had spent very little of her adult life in the UK.

3.97   It has been held by the House of Lords that a person in the UK illegally may acquire a UK domicile. While the illegality of the residence is a factor in deciding whether such a person has a genuine intention to remain in the UK, nevertheless it will not in itself mean they cannot acquire a UK domicile of choice.[100]

3.98   Most recently in *Holliday v Musa*[101] the Court of Appeal held that a Cypriot had abandoned his domicile of origin and acquired a domicile of choice in England. It confirmed that the correct test to apply is not whether the relevant person intended to return to his country where he had a domicile of origin but rather whether he intended to settle permanently in the particular jurisdiction where domicile is claimed.[102]

Standard of Proof

3.99   It is sometimes said that it is more difficult to prove the replacement of a domicile of origin than that of a domicile of choice because *"its character is more enduring, its hold stronger, and less easily shaken off"*: *Winans v Att Gen.*[103] The standard of proof in the case of abandonment of a domicile of origin goes beyond a mere balance of probabilities.[104] It was said in *Re Lloyd-Evans*[105] that in either case both the intention and the act must be demonstrated to be unequivocal.

3.100   In *Re Flynn*[106] Megarry J. considered that the standard of proof for abandonment of a domicile of choice is the civil standard of a balance of probabilities, and not proof beyond reasonable doubt, subject to the overriding consideration that abandonment is (as Scarman J. had said in *Fuld* in relation to *acquisition* of a domicile of choice) *"not to be lightly inferred from slight indications or casual words"*.

Domicile of dependence

3.101   At common law, the domicile of a married woman was the same as that of her husband[107] and her domicile of origin was not revived by reason only of her becoming a widow.[108] This "dependent domicile" was abolished, with effect

---

[100] See *Mark v Mark* [2005] 3 All ER 912.
[101] [2010] EWCA Civ 335.
[102] The facts were similar to *Agulian* and the result is surprising.
[103] [1904] AC 287 at 290.
[104] *Henderson v Henderson* [1967] P 77 at 80.
[105] [1947] Ch 695, 707.
[106] [1968] 1 WLR 103.
[107] *Lord Advocate v Jaffrey* [1921] 1 AC 146.
[108] *Re Wallach, Weinschenk v Treasury-Solicitor* [1950] 1 All ER 199.

from January 1, 1974, by the DMPA 1973. Under s.1(1), which extends to the whole of the UK, the domicile of a married woman at any time after December 31, 1973, instead of being the same as her husband's by virtue only of marriage, is to be ascertained by reference to the same factors as in the case of any other individual capable of having an independent domicile. This is qualified by s.1(2) under which, where immediately before January 1, 1974 a woman was married and had her husband's domicile by dependence, she is to be treated as retaining that domicile (as a domicile of choice, if it is not also her domicile of origin) unless and until it is changed by acquisition or revival of another domicile either on or after January 1, 1974. Such a change is unlikely to come about except as the result of divorce or separation, since it is not open to a wife (any more than to a husband) to choose a domicile of choice in a different country unless it is supported both by the fact of residence there and by the necessary intention of permanent or indefinite residence there. It is not enough that the wife has a house in another country and lives there for 10 weeks in the year.[109]

As regards minors and pupils, under s.3(1), which extends to England and **3.102** Wales and Northern Ireland (but not to Scotland), the time at which a person first becomes capable of having an independent domicile is when he attains the age of sixteen or validly marries under that age. In Scotland a child can acquire an independent domicile when out of pupillarity (i.e. at the age of 14 for a boy or 12 for a girl).[110]

Section 4, which extends to England and Wales, Scotland and Northern **3.103** Ireland, relates to the dependent domicile of a child as at any time after December 31, 1973, when his father and mother are alive but living apart. Under s.4(2) the child's domicile at that time is to be that of his mother if (a) he then has his home with her and has no home with his father; or (b) he has at any time had her domicile by virtue of para.(a) and has not since had a home with his father.

Obtaining a domicile ruling from HMRC

HMRC would not give a ruling on a person's domicile unless it is relevant to **3.104** the determination of a current tax liability. Their practice until August 2010 for income tax and CGT purposes was set out in *Tax Bulletin 29*. If the individual had not yet submitted a tax return, HMRC would continue to give a written ruling for that tax year if a DOM1 form or P86 was submitted before the return was due. Otherwise the individual had to self-assess by ticking the boxes on the non-residence pages of a return; claiming foreign domiciled status and HMRC might then choose to investigate as part of an enquiry.

An alternative strategy, particularly if the person had been UK resident for **3.105** some years but was not yet deemed domiciled (for IHT purposes) and wanted a ruling quickly, was for him to settle foreign situate property of (say) £350,000 into a trust (i.e more than the nil rate band). The trust was then reported to HMRC requesting confirmation that the person was not UK domiciled. If he was considered not UK domiciled no IHT was due. If, however, he was

[109] *IRC v Duchess of Portland* [1982] 2 WLR 367.
[110] *Arnott v Groom* (1846) 9 D 62.

UK domiciled the transfer was chargeable. The authors' experience was that HMRC scrutinised a person's domicile with some rigour if this route was used. Until recently HMRC had to give a ruling if the tax at stake was over £10,000. However, on August 24, 2010 HMRC issued Brief 34/10 stating that no domicile rulings would be given for IHT purposes at all unless there was a "significant risk of loss" of tax and that the taxpayer should expect a forensic examination of his life. HMRC are now keen to interview taxpayers who claim a foreign domicile.

3.106   Any domicile ruling is relevant and valid only for the year in which it is given but if the person's personal circumstances do not change it is unlikely that HMRC will take a different view in later years. Of course continued residence in the UK beyond what was originally anticipated can in itself be evidence of change of intention and therefore a relevant circumstance which might give rise to a different domicile ruling.

Deemed domicile[111]

3.107   Even if a person is domiciled outside the UK under general law; he may be deemed domiciled in the UK for inheritance tax purposes if one of two conditions is satisfied[112]:

(i)   If he was domiciled in the UK on or after December 10, 1974 and was domiciled in the UK (under general law) within the three years immediately preceding the transfer in question. This catches the taxpayer who was domiciled in the UK under general law and then emigrated. In this case, for three years (but not three tax years) from the acquisition of a new domicile he retains a deemed UK domicile.

(ii)   If he was resident for income tax purposes in the UK on or after December 10, 1974 and was UK resident for income tax purposes in not less than 17 out of the 20 tax years ending with the income tax year in which he made the relevant transfer. This catches the foreign domiciliary who has lived in the UK for a long time even though he retains his foreign domicile under general law. "Residence" is used in the income tax sense and does not require residence for a period of seventeen complete years only residence for a tax year. In determining residency, available accommodation is ignored.

3.108   Until April 6, 2005 the concept of deemed domicile applied only for inheritance tax purposes. From that date someone who is UK deemed domiciled can also suffer an income tax charge under the pre-owned assets income tax regime.[113]

---

[111] See also Ch.31.
[112] IHTA 1984 s.267.
[113] See Ch.34.

CHAPTER 4

RESIDENCE OF TRUSTEES AND COMPANIES

- Trustee residence (**4.01**)
- Exporting UK trusts (**4.13**)
- Importing a trust (**4.40**)
- Corporate residence (**4.43**)

I TRUSTEE RESIDENCE

When is a trust non-resident? Position before April 6, 2007

The rules on trust residence changed from April 6, 2007. Before that date, a **4.01** trust was non-UK resident for CGT purposes when a majority of the trustees were neither resident nor ordinarily resident in the UK *and* the general administration of that trust was ordinarily carried on outside the UK.[1] A trust was non-resident for income tax purposes only if either all the trustees were non-UK resident or, if there were mixed residence trustees, the settlor was neither resident nor domiciled in the UK at the date he created the settlement or added property to it.[2] The general administration test was not relevant for income tax purposes.

Further, there was a let-out for CGT purposes for professional trustees. **4.02** In essence, where a person who was resident in the UK carried on a business consisting of or including the management of trusts and was acting as a trustee in the course of that business he was treated in relation to the trust *for capital gains tax purposes only* as non-resident provided that the whole of the settled property consisted of or derived from property that was provided by someone not at the time of making that provision domiciled, resident or ordinarily resident in the UK. Note, however, that this let-out did not apply for income tax purposes and so was of limited use unless the trust was a non-settlor-interested interest in possession trust, in which case UK income tax would be payable by reference to the source of the income and the tax status of the life tenant, so that the residence of the trust was not relevant.[3]

---

[1] TCGA 1992 s.69(1).
[2] See FA 1989 s.110.
[3] See 6.10.

4.03 The test for residence of trustees became the same for income tax and capital gains tax purposes.[4] Where a trust is created by a settlor who is resident, ordinarily resident *or* domiciled in the UK, all the trustees must be resident outside the UK if the trust is to be non-resident. So if the settlor is not UK domiciled but is UK resident (or vice versa) at the date of setting up or subsequently adding property to the trust, all trustees must be non-resident.

However, if the settlor is non-resident and non-UK domiciled at the time he funds the trust (including any additions or resettlements) it is only necessary that there is one non-resident trustee for the trust to be treated as non-resident for both income tax and capital gains tax purposes. (This is broadly the same as the income tax position before April 6, 2007.) It does not matter if the settlor subsequently becomes UK resident or domiciled provided that he does not add to the trust. Nor does it matter if there are two UK resident trustees if there is one non-UK resident trustee. Note that the place where the administration of the trust is carried out is no longer relevant for capital gains tax purposes and the exemption for professional trustees was abolished on the basis that it constituted "state aid".[5]

4.04 If the trust property is transferred from one trust to another, the residence and domicile of the settlor has to be tested both at the time the original trust was funded and at the time of the transfer.[6] If there are multiple settlors of a trust, all such persons must be non-UK resident and domiciled at the date they settled or added funds to the trust or at the time of any resettlement. Otherwise if there are mixed residence trustees the trust will be UK resident.

4.05 The status of the settlor at the time of death is determinative if the trust was set up by his will or on his intestacy.

EXAMPLE 4.1

> Mr A was not resident or domiciled in the UK when he died leaving assets in trust. The trustees comprise two friends resident in the UK and one non-UK resident friend. The trust was non-resident for income tax purposes but until April 6, 2007 was resident for capital gains tax purposes unless one of the UK friends was acting as a trust professional. From April 6, 2007 it is no longer UK resident for capital gains tax unless the trustee carries on a business in the UK through a permanent establishment, branch or agency in the UK.[7]

---

[4] FA 2006 Sch.12 amended TCGA 1992 s.69. The wording is different, however, because of the rewrite of income tax. See ITA 2007 s.475 replacing TA 1988 s.685E and compare TCGA 1992 s.69(2)−(2E).

[5] It must be doubted whether this is correct. Cyprus now has the "international trust" which allows Cyprus resident trustees to act in Cyprus without the trust being treated as resident there for tax purposes where the settlor and beneficiaries are not resident in Cyprus. This matter is subject to an ongoing debate between the CIOT/STEP and Treasury.

[6] TCGA 1992 ss.68B and 69(2C).

[7] See 4.06.

By contrast:

EXAMPLE 4.2

Mr A was resident but not domiciled in the UK when he died in 2005 leaving assets on a will trust. The trustees comprise one UK resident and two non-UK residents and the general administration of the trust is carried on abroad. The testator-settlor's status is tested at death. Accordingly the trust was initially UK resident for income tax purposes but non-resident for capital gains tax. From April 6, 2007, however, it became UK resident for both taxes.

Branch agency or permanent establishment

FA 2006 introduced an important additional condition for trustees that applies for both income tax and CGT purposes from April 6, 2007. TCGA 1992 s.69(2D) states that: **4.06**

> "*a trustee who is not resident in the UK shall be treated as if he were resident in the UK at any time when he acts as trustee in the course of a business which he carries on in the UK through a branch, agency or permanent establishment there*".[8]

Acting as a trustee "*in the course of a business*" means the business of providing professional trustee services for a fee. The terms "*branch, agency or permanent establishment*" have been the subject of great controversy. In July 2009 HMRC issued guidance on the position[9] and further guidance has been issued by STEP and CIOT that has been agreed with HMRC.[10] Bear in mind that if a trust becomes UK resident even for a day this can have disastrous capital gains tax consequences because on exporting the trust again there is a deemed disposal of all the trust assets at market value with the result that the worldwide gains of the trust become subject to UK tax.[11]

If the settlor was neither UK domiciled nor resident at the time he funded the trust, the problem can be avoided by having one non-resident individual trustee who is unpaid. Then the trust cannot become UK resident even if one of the other professional trustees carries on business in the UK through a branch, agency or permanent establishment. However, for trusts where any settlor was UK resident or domiciled at a time when the trust was funded or any resettlement was made, this strategy will not work and it is not always convenient or possible to have a lay trustee. **4.07**

HMRC accept that for trustees the "branch" and "agency" tests apply to **4.08**

---

[8] The comparable income tax provisions are found in ITA 2007 ss.474–476 although following the rewrite they are now expressed in slightly different terms from the capital gains tax provisions.
[9] See [2009] SWTI 2334.
[10] See [2010] SWTI 2459.
[11] See 4.22.

non-corporate trustees and the "permanent establishment" test to corporate trustees. Corporate non-resident trustees therefore need only be concerned about being treated as UK resident if they have a permanent establishment (as opposed to a branch or agency) in the UK.[12] Essentially it requires a fixed place of business in the UK through which all or part of the business of the company is carried on or an agent acting on behalf of the company who has and habitually exercises in the UK authority to do business on behalf of the company.

4.09   Agents of independent status acting in the ordinary course of business are excluded as are investment managers within the terms of the investment management exemption. Hence, UK professionals such as lawyers and accountants providing services on an arm's length basis to the trustees will not mean the trust has a permanent UK establishment.[13] HMRC accept this applies even if the trustee and the service provider are members of the same group provided that the terms of engagement are commercial. Similarly an investment manager cannot be a permanent establishment of the trustee even if within the same group provided that he acts on commercial terms, carrying out normal investment transactions such as investment in stocks and shares, securities, unit trusts, options, futures etc.[14] Options and futures relating to land are excluded.

4.10   The Commentary to the OECD Tax Model Convention (referred to in the HMRC Guidance Annex) provides further details on the meaning of "permanent establishment". A fixed place of business includes a place of management, a branch, office, factory or building site. So this could include the case where meeting rooms are regularly used by trustees in the UK to meet beneficiaries. (The rooms do not necessarily have to be owned or leased although the HMRC Guidance assumes this.)

4.11   The test is applied on a trust by trust basis. So while a trustee for more than one trust might be acting as a trustee in relation to one trust at a fixed place of business in the UK, it must be considered separately whether he is acting as a trustee through a fixed place of business in the UK in connection with another trust.

4.12   So far HMRC appear to have taken a fairly sensible line in interpreting the term "permanent establishment". However, it does appear to have deterred trustees from using UK advisers, e.g. in relation to investment or legal advice, when the service can be obtained elsewhere.[15] Where a non-resident corporate trustee has a UK resident director or employs a UK relationship manager to liaise with the beneficiaries, care is needed. Generally trustee meetings should always be outside the UK and regular use of UK premises for trustee/beneficiary meetings should be avoided. The core business of the trust (which HMRC regard as including the general administration of the trust: investment strategy and decisions as to distributions) should take place outside the UK. Hence even if the trustees meet the settlor or beneficiaries in the UK, this should be more in the nature of fact-finding and discussion. The ultimate decisions should be taken (and be seen to be taken) outside the UK. There should be a

[12] For the definition of "permanent establishment" see CTA 2010 ss.1141–1153 discussed at 4.36. This definition is incorporated into the CGT and income tax legislation: ITA 2007 s.989 and TCGA 1992 s.288.

[13] See Example 3 of HMRC Guidance.

[14] For the complete list, see Investment Manager (Specified Transactions) Regulations 2009.

[15] STEP, banks and other bodies have suggested this.

formal report before the trustees when they come to make that decision and minutes should demonstrate that the matter was genuinely discussed at that meeting and not merely rubber-stamped.

II EXPORTING UK TRUSTS

Emigration of trusts

A trust will become non-UK resident if the UK trustees retire in favour of non-residents. As noted above, all the new trustees must be non-UK resident unless all persons who have funded the settlement were neither resident nor domiciled in the UK when they did so (or at the date of any resettlement). **4.13**

Can a trust emigrate?

Most modern trusts have an express provision to allow the appointment of non-resident trustees. What is the position where no such express power has been inserted?[16] **4.14**

It is clearly possible for UK trustees to retire in favour of non-resident trustees without either the sanction of the court or express provision in the trust deed. The appointment of foreign trustees is never void but could in certain circumstances be challenged by beneficiaries as improper. Pennycuick V.C. in *Re Whitehead's Will Trusts*[17] noted:

> "*The law has been quite well established for upwards of a century; that there is no absolute bar to the appointment of persons resident abroad as trustees of an English trust. I say 'no absolute bar' in the sense that such an appointment would be prohibited by law and would consequently be invalid. On the other hand, apart from exceptional circumstances, it is not proper to make such an appointment, that is to say, the court would not, apart from exceptional circumstances, make such an appointment; nor would it be right for the donees of such a power to make an appointment out of court. If they did, presumably the court would be likely to interfere at the instance of beneficiaries. There do, however, exist exceptional circumstances in which such an appointment can properly be made. The most obvious are those in which the beneficiaries have settled permanently in some country outside the UK and what is proposed to be done is to appoint new trustees in that country.*"[18]

Judicial attitudes have changed since then so that provided that the export can be shown to be for the beneficiaries' advantage (for instance in saving tax) then **4.15**

---

[16] See *Lewin on Trusts* (18th edn) para 14.45 and following.
[17] [1971] 2 All ER 1334.
[18] In that case he approved the appointment of Jersey Trustees where the beneficiaries had lived there since 1959. Cf. *Re Weston's Settlements* [1969] 1 Ch 223 where the Court of Appeal refused to sanction a similar arrangement in relation to Jersey where the beneficiaries were young and had only lived there three months.

even if the beneficiaries are not living in that country the courts are not likely to interfere. Millett J, noted in *Richard v Hon A B Mackay*[19]:

> "*in the conditions of today, when one can have an international family with international interests, and where they are as likely to make their home in one country as in another . . . I doubt the language of Sir John Pennycuick is really in tune with the times. In my judgment, where the trustees retain their discretion . . . the court should need to be satisfied only that the proposed transaction is not so inappropriate that no reasonable trustee could entertain it.*"

4.16   HMRC cannot object to the appointment since they do not have locus standi but it is sensible to include in any trust instrument an express power providing for appointment of non-resident trustees along with a provision preventing the removal of a trustee on the grounds of absence from the UK for more than 12 months. The trust instrument should also contain a power to change the proper law of the trust (which may be convenient if the trustees move to a different jurisdiction).[20]

4.17   TA 1925 s.37(1)(c) shall be considered when considering the export of a trust unless it has been expressly excluded. It provides as follows:

> "*It shall not be obligatory, save as hereinafter provided, to appoint more than one new trustee where only one trustee was originally appointed, or to fill up the original number of trustees where more than two trustees were originally appointed, but, except where only one trustee was originally appointed, and a sole trustee when appointed will be able to give a valid receipt for all capital money, a trustee shall not be discharged from his trust unless there will be either a trust corporation or at least two persons to act as trustees to perform the trust.*"

A trust corporation does not include a corporate trustee in offshore jurisdictions.[21] Hence, the appointment of new trustees may be valid, but UK resident trustees do not get a good discharge (and the trust is likely to remain UK resident) unless there are at least two non-resident trustees. Until January 1, 1997 the non-resident trustees had to include at least two individuals but this was changed by TLATA 1996 Sch.3 para.3(12). *Jasmine Trustees v Wells & Hind*[22] confirmed that references to "*individuals*" cannot include a corporate trustee and, therefore, prior to 1997 it was necessary for UK trustees to retire in favour of two individuals not two persons unless there was express provision to the contrary in the trust deed.

---

[19] [2008] WTLR 1667 and *Lewin on Trusts* (18th edn) para.14.45 and following.
[20] See A1.4 cl.13.3. For further discussion on the CGT and IHT implications of changing the proper law, see Ch.12.
[21] See TA 1925 s.68.
[22] [2007] STC 660. See Ch.1.

Advantages of exporting a trust

Moving a trust offshore is usually undertaken in order to obtain all or some **4.18** of the following benefits: protection from the possible reintroduction of exchange control[23]; deferment or even avoidance of CGT and income tax; better protection from creditors and defeating matrimonial claims. So long as the UK resident settlor (and any spouse or civil partner) are excluded from any possibility of benefit or power to enjoy, income tax will be avoided in the case of a non-resident discretionary trust unless UK resident and domiciled beneficiaries receive trust income or the trust owns assets such as rental property in the UK or a beneficiary ordinarily resident in the UK receives a benefit and the trust structure produces "relevant income".[24] Note however that a UK resident and domiciled settlor will still be taxed on trust gains under TCGA 1992 s.86 if any of his children and grandchildren are beneficiaries even if he is excluded.[25]

For CGT purposes, non-resident trusts have significant advantages for **4.19** foreign domiciliaries because s.86 does not apply to them irrespective of whether they are remittance basis users.[26] Accordingly, if the trust realises gains on the sale of a UK situated asset there is no capital gains tax charge unless and until the trust provides benefits or capital payments to the settlor or beneficiary in the UK. By contrast, if the foreign domiciled, UK resident settlor owned UK assets directly he would be taxed on an arising basis on any gains realised by the trust. However, offshore trusts can cause problems for remittance basis users in some cases when they receive benefits in the UK.

EXAMPLE 4.3

> George is the resident but foreign domiciled settlor of an offshore trust established some years ago which owns two houses. He lives in the trust's UK house and the other (Italian) house is rented out. The trust sells the Italian house realising a gain of £100,000 in May 2010. No gains were realised prior to 2008 by the trust. It is estimated that the benefit to George of living rent-free in the UK house is £30,000 pa. Although there are no gains on the UK house (because it has not been sold and would in any event qualify for main residence relief) nevertheless he pays tax under TCGA 1992 s.87 on £90,000 (three years of benefits matched to the gains) with £10,000 unmatched gains carried forward. In 2011 when he receives a further benefit of £30,000 the balance of the surplus gains (i.e. £10,000) is matched to that benefit so that he pays tax on £10,000.
>
> By contrast, if he had owned the UK house directly and not through the trust there would be no capital gains tax charge. Although there are ways

---

[23] Surely unlikely now but a genuine fear in the 1980s/90s
[24] ITA 2007 s.731 and following. See Ch.8.
[25] See Ch.19.
[26] By remittance basis users is meant those who claim the remittance basis of taxation and (in the case of those who have been UK resident for more than seven years) pay their £30,000/£50,000, see Ch.5.

of minimising the above tax charge (e.g. by distributing the £100,000 to him abroad in the year when it is realised[27]) foreign domiciled beneficiaries can pay tax by reference to gains on assets which are different from the asset or capital they actually enjoy in the UK.[28]

4.20 If the settlor was UK domiciled but is now dead, offshore trusts allow capital gains tax to be deferred and a gross sum to be reinvested even if all the beneficiaries are UK resident and domiciled. However, the supplemental charge referred to in Ch.19 may make the tax advantages marginal for UK resident and domiciled beneficiaries unless the trust is seen as a long term roll-up investment vehicle or the beneficiaries are likely to become non-resident for more than five years; or some of the beneficiaries are remittance basis users. In the case of non-resident beneficiaries the trust gains can be "washed out" by making payments to those beneficiaries abroad in the tax year prior to the UK resident and domiciled beneficiary receiving capital.[29]

4.21 The deferral of income tax for discretionary trusts may be seen as another advantage, particularly where distributions are not anticipated for some years to come: the fund can be invested outside the UK and returns rolled-up gross. By contrast if the trust is a UK resident discretionary or accumulation trust, then income suffers tax at 50 per cent (42.5 per cent on dividends).[30] If the beneficiary becomes non-UK resident, he can receive income distributions tax-free, e.g. dividends from an underlying company.

The CGT export charge[31]

4.22 When UK resident trustees retire in favour of non-resident trustees, they are deemed to dispose of the assets in that settlement immediately before "the relevant time" and immediately to reacquire those same assets. This deemed disposal is closely modelled on that which applies when a person becomes absolutely entitled to settled property and on the exit charge which is levied when a non-UK incorporated company ceases to be UK resident. Section 80(1) defines the phrase "relevant time" as meaning any occasion when trustees become non-UK resident provided that *the relevant time falls on or after March 19, 1991*.

4.23 Since the deemed disposal takes place "immediately before" the relevant time, the disponors are the retiring UK trustees who, given that the CGT year cannot generally be split,[32] also remain liable for gains realised by the new trustees in the tax year in which they are appointed.[33] Who is liable to pay the export charge? Because the deemed disposal is by the retiring UK trustees they are primarily responsible to pay the tax. It is therefore important that they retain sufficient assets or security to cover this liability.

---

[27] See Ch.19.
[28] In the above example there should not be any income tax charge under ITA 2007 s.720 but if George was merely a beneficiary rather than the settlor there might in certain circumstances be a charge under s.735: see Ch.8.
[29] See Ch.19.
[30] See Ch.6.
[31] TCGA 1992 s.80(2).
[32] ESC D2 does not apply to trustees.
[33] SP 5/92 para.2.

EXAMPLE 4.4

> Trustees of the Leather Trust own valuable land. The settlor is dead. The land shows a substantial gain. They decide that they wish to sell the land. If they sell the land they realise a gain taxed at 28 per cent. They, therefore, decide instead to retire in favour of Jersey resident trustees in February 2011 and in May 2011 the Jersey trustees sell the land.
>
> The effect of TCGA 1992 s.80 is that there is a deemed disposal of the land in February 2011 and therefore that the original trustees realise a gain at that point. They suffer tax at 28 per cent and must pursue the Jersey trustees for the money if they have not made a sufficient retention to cover this tax.[34]

4.24 TCGA 1992 s.82 further provides that if the CGT is not paid by those trustees within six months of the due date, any former trustees of that settlement who held office during the "relevant period" can be made accountable. The latter have a right of recovery against the retiring trustees who retired in favour of the non-resident trustees. The relevant period (broadly) means the 12-month period ending with the emigration (although not backdated before March 19, 1991). Assume, for instance, that A and B (two professional trustees) retire on January 1, 1999 in favour of two family members. Those family trustees subsequently (on July 1, 1999) retire in favour of two non-UK resident trustees, C and D, such retirement being without the prior knowledge of A and B. On these facts, the appointment of C and D constitutes the "relevant time" for s.80 purposes and any tax arising as a result of the deemed disposal will therefore be payable on January 31 in the following tax year (i.e. on January 31, 2001). If not paid within six months of that date HMRC may demand the CGT from all or any of A, B and the family trustees. However, a former trustee can escape liability if he shows that "*when he ceased to be a trustee of the settlement there was no proposal that the trustees might become neither resident nor ordinarily resident in the UK*".[35] It is advisable to include a clause in trustee deeds of retirement stating that all trustees acknowledge that the emigration of the trust was not in mind at the date the trustee stepped down. If there is power for the settlor or protector to remove trustees so that a UK trustee can be removed without consent and a non-resident person appointed, some provision should be made in the trust instrument for that removed trustee to be given security for any tax on the future export of the trust.

4.25 The deemed disposal is of "defined assets" which (predictably) includes all the assets that constitute the settled property at the relevant time. It does not include UK assets used for the purpose of a trade carried on by the trustees through a UK branch or agency because those assets remain within the UK tax net even after the trustees become non-resident: hence there is no need to subject them to the deemed disposal. Nor does the deemed disposal extend to assets if, before the relevant time, gains accruing on them would have been protected by a double tax treaty.[36]

4.26 Section 81 deals with "involuntary" exports and imports. Assume that the

---

[34] See 37.37 for an example where triggering a capital gains tax disposal by exporting the trust may be desirable in order to crystallise gains before the life tenant's death in a reverter to settlor trust.
[35] TCGA 1992 s.82(3) and SP 5/92 para.5.
[36] TCGA 1992 s.80(5).

trustees of a settlement are Adam (UK resident) and Cedric (a Jersey-resident accountant) who does all the paperwork and performs the administrative tasks for the trustees. The settlor was UK resident at the date he set up the trust so that it is UK resident. Adam dies with the result that the conditions laid down in s.69(1) are satisfied and the trust ceases to be UK resident. On these facts, there was no intention to export the trust. Imposing an exit charge in such a case would be unjust and s.81 prevents the charge arising *provided that* within six months of Adam's death UK trustees are again appointed. Not surprisingly, the exit charge remains in force for those defined assets that are disposed of during the period of non-UK residency (i.e. between the death and the resumption of UK residence).

4.27   Finally, the converse situation (a non-resident settlement becoming UK resident because of the death of a trustee) is provided for in s.81(5)–(7). Reverting to non-resident status within six months of the death will not generally trigger the s.80 exit charge subject only to an exception where the period of UK residence has been used to add assets to the settlement claiming hold-over relief on that transfer. In that case, resuming non-resident status will result in a deemed disposal at market value of such assets. *Green v Cobham*[37] illustrated the difficulties that could arise when a trustee who was a professional trustee retired from his business and hence ceased to be a professional, so that the trust inadvertently became UK resident for capital gains tax purposes.[38]

Bed and breakfast schemes

4.28   *Davies v Hicks*[39] concerned the interaction of the bed and breakfast rules for shares with the exit charge on the export of a settlement. The bed and breakfast provisions are designed to prevent the creation of a capital loss by the sale and subsequent repurchase of the same assets. Prior to April 6, 2008 TCGA 1992 s.106A provided that where securities were sold they had to be identified with securities of the same class acquired by the same person in the period of 30 days. This eliminated any loss assuming that the values remained similar. The argument successfully run in *Hicks* was that when UK trustees sold shares and retired in favour of non-UK trustees who reacquired the shares within 30 days, s.106A required the shares disposed of to be identified with the securities reacquired, thereby eliminating any gain which would otherwise have arisen under the export charge (unless in that short period the shares had increased in value). Did s.106A(5)(a) deem the shares to remain in trustee ownership throughout as HMRC maintained[40] or did the trust emigrate with cash? Park J. decided that there was nothing in s.106A that deemed the trustees still to hold shares at the date of export:

> "*I cannot accept in this case that a provision which was intended to identify which shares acquired by a particular taxpayer should be matched with shares sold by the same taxpayer can be deemed to have had effects going far beyond that and requiring it to be imagined, for a quite different statu-*

---

[37] [2002] STC 820 and see Ch.1 for a consideration of the current scope of *Hastings-Bass*.
[38] Given the abolition of the professional trustee exemption after April 5, 2007, the case is largely of historic interest.
[39] [2005] STC 850. The decision has been reversed by legislation: see 4.33.
[40] See *IR Tax Bulletin*, April 2001 and their Example 2 for further details.

tory purpose, that the assets held by the taxpayer at a different time did not consist of the actual assets then held by him, but rather consisted of different assets altogether."[41]

Round the world scheme

This loophole was often combined with what was known as a "round the world" scheme. The trust was exported from the UK without an emigration charge and then a disposal of shares could take place protected by treaty relief as set out below. The round the world scheme was also used for trusts already non-UK resident that held assets pregnant with gains otherwise chargeable on the settlor under TCGA 1992 s.86. It involved trustees resident in (say) Jersey retiring in favour of trustees resident in a foreign jurisdiction with a suitable UK double tax treaty. While in that country (e.g. New Zealand) the new non-resident trustees sold trust property but, before the end of the same tax year, UK resident trustees were appointed. The aim was to avoid TCGA 1992 ss.86 and 87 charges by ensuring that at no time was there a single and continuing body of trustees with dual-resident status: the sections were considered to be inapplicable because trustees were resident in the UK at some time in the year of assessment albeit at a *different* time from that of the disposal. Arguably, s.77[42] would not apply to tax the settlor either because the treaty would protect the gain. **4.29**

Smallwood v HMRC[43]

This was a "round the world" scheme (designed to avoid s.86)[44] and so was concerned with the residence of a trust but is relevant to companies in that the question of "effective management" for the purposes of the double tax treaty was considered by the Court of Appeal. The chronology was as follows: **4.30**

(i) 2000–01: the sole trustee was a Jersey resident corporate trustee holding trust property (shares) pregnant with gains;

(ii) December 2000: the Jersey trustee resigned and the settlor (under a power reserved in the settlement) appointed a Mauritius associate as trustee in its place;

(iii) January 2001: shares held by the trust were sold;

(iv) March 2001: Mauritius trustee resigned in favour of settlor, making the trust UK resident.

[41] There is some analysis of how far deeming provisions should be taken generally in [26] of the judgment. Arguably the same analysis could apply to avoid capital gains tax on export of a trust where there is no actual sale and reacquisition but merely a deemed disposal and reacquisition of securities by virtue of s.106A itself!

[42] TCGA 1992 s.77 then charged the settlor to tax on trust gains of a UK resident settlement. This ceased from April 6, 2008.

[43] [2010] STC 2045.

[44] See Ch.19.

The intention was that s.86 would be avoided because it only applied where the trust was UK resident throughout the tax year. In this case, the trust was UK resident in part of the year which meant that it was deemed to be UK resident throughout the tax year.[45] However, it was hoped to relieve the gain by the use of the UK/Mauritius double tax treaty: art.13(4) of which gave sole taxing rights to the country of residence of the alienator at the time of the disposal. As the gains were realised when the trust had a Mauritius trustee the trust was resident only in Mauritius at the date of disposal.

4.31   The Court of Appeal decided that the tie-breaker provision in the residence article came into operation because the trust was chargeable to tax in both states: the trust was taxable in Mauritius because of its actual residence and taxable in the UK because of its residence from March 2, 2001 and therefore deemed to be resident throughout the tax year. Under the tie-breaker clause, residence was then determined by where the effective management of the trust was. The Court of Appeal decided that the effective management was in the UK on the basis that the scheme was:

> "*devised in the UK by Mr Smallwood on the advice of KPMG Bristol . . . and the events carefully monitored and orchestrated by KPMG. There was a scheme of management of this trust which went above and beyond the day to day management exercised by the trustees for the time being and the control of it was located in the UK*".

4.32   This decision is surprising in the light of the opposite conclusion in *Wood v Holden* that merely relying on advice did not mean the directors of Eulalia had ceded effective control.[46] Indeed the Court of Appeal in *Holden* rejected attempts by HMRC in *Wood v Holden* to suggest that the "real decisions" lay in the UK rather than elsewhere because initiatives and advice emanated from the UK:

> "*there was discussion at the [Special Commissioners] hearing as to what happened 'in real life'; where there were 'real decisions'; what happened in 'a real sense' and whether all that happened was a piece of paper. I decline to use such language so as to avoid the effect of what actually happened; the transaction was conducted by [the corporate director as the director of Eulalia and in the Netherlands]. [The corporate director] might have had every incentive to carry it out but it had the right to refuse if it wished and the power to do so.*"

Anti avoidance measures

In 2003 the Revenue amended the CGT article in the Mauritius and Canada Treaties to discourage trusts from emigrating there to avoid CGT. In 2004 the

---

[45] TCGA 1992 s.2(2).
[46] It is difficult to see that the test of effective management is materially different from central management and control.

New Zealand treaty was likewise amended.[47] Under F(No.2)A 2005 s.33 a new TCGA 1992 s.83A was inserted to stop the round the world scheme generally.

FA 2006 s.74 amended TCGA 1992 s.106A by inserting s.106(5A) to prevent **4.33** a trust holding shares from being exported without an emigration charge by disapplying the bed and breakfasting rules where the person making the disposal of securities reacquired them at a time when he was non-resident or treaty non-resident. This reversed the decision in *Davies v Hicks*.

Split year treatment

Gains on disposals made in the tax year of migration are fully chargeable **4.34** on the UK resident trustees who retire in favour of non-resident trustees because the split year concession in ESC D2 has never applied to trusts. CGT is payable even if the disposal takes place by new trustees who are resident in a territory whose treaty with the UK gives that territory sole taxing rights over capital gains.[48] In any event, as the decision of the Court of Appeal in *Smallwood* illustrates, where the trust is resident in both jurisdictions during the course of a single tax year (albeit at different times during that year), the tiebreaker clause must be applied to determine the residence status of the trustees. If overall the effective management of the trust was still in the UK at the date of the disposal then even though the trustees may be resident abroad when the assets were sold the trust will be treated as resident in the UK for CGT treaty purposes.

European dimension

In *de Lasteyrie du Saillant v Ministere*,[49] a French individual moved from **4.35** France to Belgium and as a result was taxed in France on the unrealised increase in the value of the shares which he held in a French company. The ECJ held that this was likely to restrict freedom of establishment by acting as a disincentive for individuals who wanted to move elsewhere in the EU although taxing individuals on a return after a brief stay abroad may be acceptable. In *N v Inspecteur van de Belastingdienst* (C-470/04) the ECJ confirmed that a

---

[47] The amendments to the treaties typically provided that the tiebreaker provisions allowing Mauritius or the relevant country sole taxing rights on gains where the alienator was resident there did not apply "*in respect of gains from the alienation of any property on a person who is a resident of that State at any time during the fiscal year in which the property is alienated, or has been so resident at any time during the six fiscal years immediately preceding that year.*" Previously the Mauritius treaty read as follows:

> "*(5) The provisions of paragraph (4) of this Article shall not affect the right of a Contracting State to levy according to its law a tax on capital gains from the alienation of any property derived by an individual who is a resident of the other Contracting State and has been a resident of the first-mentioned Contracting State at any time during the five years immediately preceding the alienation of the property.*"

[48] See TCGA 1992 s.83A. With effect from March 17, 2005 TCGA 1992 s.83A provides that gains are chargeable if realised in the year of departure from the UK even if the new trustees are resident in a treaty country which has sole taxing rights over capital gains.

[49] [2005] STC 1722 ECJ.

member state can still assess a departing resident in respect of gains or income accrued at the time of emigration provided that this does not give rise to an immediate charge to tax: i.e. the tax charge is deferred until the asset is sold. It seems then that some limited form of exit charge may be upheld but that the current blanket and immediate exit charges on emigration of trusts may not be lawful under EU law.

Disposals in year of migration/income tax and offshore income gains

4.36 As noted above, gains accruing on disposals after the emigration of a trust but in the same tax year remain fully chargeable. The trustees cannot rely on split year treatment for gains because ESC D2 does not apply to trusts. There is no deeming of income on emigration of a trust. HMRC accept that the foreign trust income of a discretionary trust arising in the same tax year as the emigration but after that date is free of tax. Offshore income gains are triggered when the trust emigrates as there is a deemed disposal of the offshore fund.

Capital payments

4.37 The gains in TCGA 1992 s.87 pool of a non-resident trust are attributed to beneficiaries who receive capital payments in the same year as the gains accrue or who have received capital payments in earlier years when gains are subsequently realised. A capital payment is brought into account for these purposes if it was received when the trust was UK resident but was made in anticipation of a disposal by the trustees when non-resident.

Beneficial interests

4.38 The disposal of a beneficial interest in an offshore settlement is generally chargeable to CGT.[50] Of course, there is then the possibility of a double tax charge—once on the disposal of the beneficial interest and again when the beneficiary receives capital by virtue of s.87. A measure of relief is given under s.85: if the settlement was formerly UK resident and has migrated, any beneficiary whose interest was created or acquired before the date of migration is deemed to acquire the interest at its market value at the relevant time. The relief does not apply if before being resident in the UK the trust had been non-resident and at the relevant time had unallocated trust gains within a s.87 or Sch.4C pool.[51]

[50] TCGA 1992, s.85.
[51] TCGA 1992, s.85(10): see Ch.20.

Trustee borrowing

Any trustee borrowing should be paid off before emigration if it is not within **4.39** the let-outs in Sch.4B. Outstanding trust borrowing under Sch.4B will become relevant once the trust is non-resident (unless the trust was settlor-interested in which case it was already relevant).[52]

III IMPORTING A TRUST

This is easily achieved by appointing UK resident trustees. No gain is triggered **4.40** on entry into the UK because no deemed disposal occurs. Accordingly there is no rebasing of the trust assets to market value and trustees become liable to CGT if they are resident in the UK during any part of the tax year. It may therefore be worth rebasing the assets in the tax year prior to immigration if the trust is not within the settlor s.86 charge.[53] Curiously HMRC apply split year income tax treatment to immigrating trusts.[54] There is no change to the IHT position of the trust on immigration since this depends on the domicile of the settlor when the settlement was made and the situs of the asset at any relevant time.

Advantages of importing a trust

Immigration may be attractive for the following reasons: **4.41**

   (a) The family may prefer to have UK resident trustees who are less expensive, particularly if family members are appointed. Check that there is provision in the trust deed to allow beneficiaries to be appointed as trustees.

   (b) If the settlor and his spouse/civil partner are excluded but the trust is for the benefit of children and grandchildren the settlor may dislike the fact that he is liable under s.86 TCGA 1992 for trust gains if he is UK domiciled and resident. It may be awkward for him to claim reimbursement of the tax. Once the trust immigrates he ceases to be liable although the trustees will suffer CGT at 28 per cent. Of course an alternative option may be to ensure that a pre-1998 settlement is kept offshore but varied so that it is solely for the benefit of the settlor's grandchildren and remoter issue and so is outside the s.86 charge.[55]

   (c) If the trust is interest in possession and the beneficiaries are UK resident and domiciled or the majority of its income is UK source then there may be little income tax advantage in retaining the trust offshore since the income is fully taxable.

---

[52] See Ch.19.
[53] See Ch.19.
[54] See Tax Return Guide 2010.
[55] See Ch.19.

Disadvantages of immigration

4.42   There can be significant disadvantages in immigration:

(a) The trust may continue to be governed by the foreign law which could be inconvenient. It may be better to exercise the power to change the proper law to English if that is permitted.

(b) Worldwide income of a non-settlor-interested discretionary trust becomes subject to UK income tax at 50 per cent (42.5 per cent for dividends).[56]

(c) Income distributions by discretionary trustees fall within ITA 2007 ss.493–498 and hence tax at the trust rate (50 per cent) must be withheld from any distribution. Of course the beneficiary may be able to reclaim some or all of the tax. However, this is more cumbersome than the position of a non-UK resident trust where the trust simply pays the beneficiaries gross, without withholding tax, and the beneficiaries then pay tax at their own rates.[57]

(d) If the trust has received significant UK dividends or other UK source income while non-UK resident it will have paid UK tax. That "tax pool" cannot be carried forward once the trust immigrates and is therefore lost.[58]

(e) Future offshore income gains, even of an interest in possession trust, become chargeable on the trustees at 50 per cent once the trust immigrates.[59]

(f) Capital distributions from a UK resident trust can be chargeable to tax twice: if there is a deemed disposal of an asset by the trustees at a gain (e.g. when a beneficiary becomes absolutely entitled)[60] then the trustees pay CGT at 28 per cent. And if there is an unmatched pool of gains in the trust that was realised when it was non-UK resident, capital distributions made after immigration can be matched to that pool and subject to CGT on the beneficiary.[61] Alternatively if there is outstanding available relevant income within the trust structure at the time it immigrates that income will be matched to capital distributions in priority to any unmatched capital gains.

(g) If an underlying company immigrates along with the trust (which may be hard to avoid if the trustees are the directors) then future profits will be subject to corporation tax. This may not mean that any more tax is payable if gains of the non-resident company are taxed under TCGA 1992 s.13 but the position needs to be considered carefully.[62]

(h) Once imported the trust cannot be exported again without an exit

---

[56] See Ch.6.
[57] See Ch.6.
[58] See Ch.8: ITA 2007 s.497(2).
[59] See Ch.6.
[60] Hold-over relief may be available, e.g. if the trust is a relevant property settlement for IHT purposes: see TCGA 1992 s.260.
[61] See TCGA 1992 s.89.
[62] See Ch.54 for taxation of non-resident companies.

charge. If a beneficiary is likely to become non-UK resident at a future date, immigration may be seen as a poor option.

(i) The treatment of losses needs to be considered carefully. If the trust was within s.86 when offshore and now immigrates, any unused s.86 losses are wiped out. By contrast, if the trust has s.87 losses carried forward then such losses can be used in the future against trust gains realised when the trust becomes UK resident.[63]

IV CORPORATE RESIDENCE

The tax treatment of non-resident companies

A non-resident company (whether owned by an individual or a trust) benefits **4.43** from the following UK tax treatment:

(a) Foreign income is not subject to UK tax.

(b) UK rental income is subject to basic rate income tax. Note that the company is not subject to corporation tax on such income. This is a significant advantage over a non-resident individual or discretionary trust receiving UK rental income since the individual can be subject to higher or additional rate tax on such income[64] and the discretionary trust will pay tax at 50 per cent.[65]

(c) In the case of dividends and interest, the tax is restricted to the tax withheld at source.

(d) If the company is trading in the UK through a permanent establishment ("PE") then it pays corporation tax on the profits of such establishment.[66]

(e) Gains realised by the company are not taxed on the company unless the chargeable gains accrue on UK assets of the PE or the trade carried on through it.

The above rules cover the tax treatment of the company itself. There are of course a separate set of anti-avoidance rules to tax the individual or trust which owns the company in respect of the corporate gains or income.[67] In

---

[63] See Ch.19.

[64] A resident of the Channel Islands, Isle of Man and EEA national will qualify for personal allowances ITA 2007 s.56.

[65] See ITA 2007 ss.971 and 972 and The Taxation of Income from Land (Non-residents) Regulations (SI 1995/2902). A non-resident individual can receive rent gross under the non-resident landlord scheme but must undertake to operate self-assessment in respect of his rental income.

[66] See s.1141 CTA 2010 for definition of PE: a company has a permanent establishment if it has a fixed place of business in the UK or an agent has and habitually exercises authority in the UK to do business on behalf of the company. Agents of independent status acting in the ordinary course of business are not deemed to constitute a permanent establishment. Brokers and independent managers are deemed to be independent agents in certain circumstances. A branch, office, or construction site are all deemed to be a fixed place of business.

[67] These are discussed in Chs 8 and 19. Broadly a non-resident individual shareholder will not

addition, if a non-resident company becomes UK resident and then emigrates there will be an exit charge on emigration.[68]

What is a non-resident company?

4.44   The CTA 2009 rewrite introduced the concept of the UK resident and non-UK resident company.[69] The definition is unhelpful: a UK resident company is a company resident in the UK and a non-UK resident is a company which is not resident in the UK. FA 1988 s.66 introduced the statutory rule deeming a company incorporated in the UK to be regarded for all tax purposes as resident here.[70] Hence, the central management and control test (discussed below) does not apply to UK registered companies. However, if a company is incorporated in the UK but its place of effective management is situated in another state and under the tie-breaker clause in that treaty it is treated as resident in that state, it is deemed for all UK tax purposes to be non-resident.[71] HMRC's view is that this provision can only apply if the relevant double tax country contains a tie-breaker article.[72]

Foreign incorporated companies—central management and control

4.45   The leading case on company residence is *De Beers Consolidated Mines v Howe*,[73] where the House of Lords held:

> "*A company resides for the purposes of income tax where its real business is carried on . . . and the real business is carried on where the central management and control actually abides.*"

HMRC's current Statement of Practice[74] emphasises that company residence is ultimately a question of fact, depending on where central management and control is exercised. Their approach is to ascertain (a) whether the appointed directors do, in fact, exercise central management and control; (b) if they do,

be subject to these anti-avoidance rules. The resident individual taxed on an arising basis will be subject to tax on the company gains and income on a worldwide basis under respectively TCGA 1992 s.13 and ITA 2007 ss.720–730. The UK resident individual who is a remittance basis user will be subject to tax as follows: (a) the arising basis applies and higher rate income tax is payable on UK source income and CGT on corporate gains from the disposal of UK situated property (b) the remittance basis applies to all other corporate income and gains. The tax treatment of trusts owning offshore companies will depend on whether the trust is UK resident and on the domicile and residence status of the beneficiaries: see Ch.19.

[68] For the taxation of non-resident companies see Ch.54.
[69] See s.1319.
[70] See now CTA 2009 s.14. There is a limited exception to the incorporation rule that operates if the UK registered company was carrying on business before March 15, 1988 and had become non-resident before then pursuant to certain Treasury consents: see CTA 2009 Sch.2.
[71] CTA 2009 s.18.
[72] See *Tax Bulletin 14*. For a discussion of the place of effective management, see *Smallwood* at 4.30 above.
[73] [1906] AC 455. See, more recently, *Wood v Holden* discussed at 4.50.
[74] SP 1/90.

where do they exercise it and (c) if they do not, who does exercise management control and where. HMRC have also recently issued guidance relating to subsidiaries of UK groups based in treaty jurisdictions where they appear to accept that directors can be UK resident and participate in board meetings by telephone from the UK without making that company UK resident.[75]

In *De Beers* the mining company was incorporated in South Africa with **4.46** some general meetings held there. The diamonds were mined in South Africa and sold in London. A majority of the directors resided in London and under the company's articles and in fact, the London meetings were intended to exercise overall control. The London board had power, at any time, to overrule the local South African board even though they did not often do so, i.e. there was at least passive oversight and tacit control by the London directors and the South African directors did on occasion take instructions from London. The House of Lords held that the company was UK resident: in applying the central management and control test, the question was how the company in fact managed its affairs.

In considering central management and control, essentially one is looking **4.47** at the decision making process in relation to business policy, e.g. where are major contracts negotiated; where is the appointment of directors exercised; where are the strategic decisions taken? Even if the right to control is not often exercised, is its existence in fact based from the UK?[76] This may be inferred if there is a controlling shareholder. Do the articles give some overriding rights or veto to a UK shareholder or director? Is the shareholder the person with all the expertise who is the dominating influence? This can be particularly problematic where the non-resident company is not merely holding investment assets but carrying on a trade or enterprise that requires input from the UK resident shareholder.

Usurpation

In *Bullock v Unit Construction Company Limited*[77] although the articles **4.48** expressly said that all decisions and management and control had to be in the hands of the local directors of a number of South African subsidiaries, the board in the UK had caused the local directors to stand aside on certain matters of importance with the result that the terms of those articles were no longer relevant. The board in the UK had simply taken over or "usurped" the running of the African subsidiaries who rubberstamped decisions already taken in London. Although the High Court and Court of Appeal had held that the subsidiaries were non-UK resident on the basis that the constitutional management and control lay in South Africa (per the articles) the House of Lords reversed this on the basis that it was actual conduct that determines residence. If the parent company had told the subsidiaries what it wanted them to do but then let them make their

[75] INTM 120150.
[76] See *Mitchell v Nobel* 6 TC 372.
[77] [1960] AC 351. In this case the taxpayer UK company successfully argued for the UK residence of the subsidiaries in order that losses sustained by those companies could be set against the profits of the UK holding company.

own decisions the companies would have been non-resident.[78] However, the parent company had "usurped" the subsidiary company boards.

4.49   In *Untelrab Ltd v McGregor*[79] an offshore subsidiary company was held to be non-resident on the facts and HMRC did not appeal from the Special Commissioners' decision. The offshore subsidiary's board met in Bermuda and its role was to provide loans to other group members. The UK parent company issued guidelines for the operation of the company and made requests that loans should be made to particular subsidiaries. It was decided that, on balance, the finance was ultimately decided in Bermuda and not London, even though the company did not always undertake independent consideration of the loan proposals. The board had generally independently examined the terms of finance and proposals made by the parent company and would have refused improper loans. It may be regarded as a marginal case.

Wood v Holden[80]

4.50   A decision of the Court of Appeal, this concerned a tax avoidance scheme involving a Dutch company (Eulalia Holding BV) set up by PwC. The scheme required Eulalia to be managed in Holland and so a resident of the Netherlands under the UK Double Tax Treaty in order to avoid a charge under TCGA 1992 ss.13 and 86 on the settlor in respect of gains realised by Eulalia on a subsequent sale of a subsidiary company. The company lost before the Special Commissioners but the High Court and the Court of Appeal held that Eulalia was non-UK resident.

4.51   One difficulty for the company in demonstrating that control and management was abroad was that the sole director had relatively little to do. The corporate director resolved to buy and sell shares of the subsidiary but there was no evidence as to how the purchase price had been fixed nor of any advice being requested or given by the directors of Eulalia. The corporate director did not appear to give consideration to the price suggested by PwC who introduced the purchaser to Eulalia. The Special Commissioners decided that the only acts of management and control were the making of the board resolutions and the signing or execution of documents in accordance with those resolutions.

> "*We do not consider that the mere physical acts of signing resolutions or documents suffice for actual management . . . What is needed is an effective decision as to whether or not the resolution should be passed and the documents signed or executed and such decisions require some minimum level of information. The decisions must at least to some extent be informed decisions. Merely going through the motions of passing or making resolutions and signing documents does not suffice. Where the geographical location of the physical acts of signing and executing documents is different from*

---

[78]   In the case of *R v Dimsey* [1999] STC 846 it appears that HMRC successfully obtained a conviction for conspiracy to cheat the public revenue on the basis that the business of the company was really conducted by Mr Chipping in the UK: the board does not seem to have met.

[79]   [1996] STC (SCD) 1.

[80]   [2006] STC 443.

the place where the actual effective decision that the documents be signed and executed is taken, we consider that the latter place is where the central management and control actually abides."

Although no file notes or actual reviews of any legal documentation could be produced, board meetings did take place and one officer of the corporate director gave written evidence that it was the general practice of the corporate director to have documents reviewed by legal counsel. Unlike *Unit Construction*, the local board was not by-passed. In the light of these findings of fact Park J. held that the Special Commissioners' decision was wrong:

> *"The role of the foreign company's board had not been usurped and the mere fact that the decisions made by the directors were part of a preplanned tax avoidance scheme where PriceWaterhouse were the 'overall architects' was not enough. There can be no doubt that AA Trust [the corporate director] took those decisions in Amsterdam and nonetheless so by reason of having been recommended to take decisions by PriceWaterhouse in Manchester."*

He noted obiter that just because the corporate director may not have had sufficient information to properly discharge its duties as director did not invalidate the decision itself. A genuine decision to buy and sell had still been taken.

The Court of Appeal upheld Park J.'s judgment. The Special Commissioners had made two findings of fact which meant that the company must be resident in the Netherlands. The first was that the directors were not by-passed: i.e. their role was not usurped; second that there was nothing surprising in the fact that the directors accepted the agreement prepared by PwC and that the managing directors of the company did decide to sign and execute documents. There was no evidence that PwC had dictated the decision which the company was to make. There was no basis for refusing to treat a decision that was made in connection with that activity as an effective decision on the ground that the directors made no other decisions:

> *"ill-informed or ill-advised decisions taken in the management of a company remain management decisions."*

The case is important for the following reasons:

4.54

(a) The fact that a company is included within a group structure for the purposes of a tax scheme does not alter the residence of that company;

(b) "Influence" is not the same as control; a board may act under the influence of another person but that does not mean the board has ceased to exercise central management and control;

(c) A decision of the board is still effective even if made without complete information or full consideration;

(d) Even if the company's activities are small, e.g. it buys and sells shares on just one occasion, this does not necessarily mean that the particular decision cannot be validly taken by an overseas board. This is relevant for many offshore structures where the offshore company may be doing very little other than acting as a passive investment vehicle for a property occupied by a beneficiary.

Laerstate BV v HMRC[81]

4.55 This was not so much a case of the foreign board's role being usurped rather that the sole foreign director was a business associate of the shareholder and was dictated to by the 100 per cent UK resident shareholder. The board never functioned as a board of management or met properly. There was just one dominant person who made the strategic business decisions. If the board had met regularly in one place abroad and taken decisions on a properly informed basis (even if the requests came from the shareholder) the outcome would have been different.

Practical points on company residence

4.56 The following points should be noted in relation to non-resident companies:

1. Consider the basis on which UK shareholders are involved. Their role must be as shareholder not director. Are there special provisions in the articles conferring powers on certain UK residents, e.g. the settlor of a trust? If so, they should be powers of veto rather than active powers. Do the directors have the requisite skill to take properly informed decisions? Although *Wood v Holden* indicates that a director does not need to be fully informed to make a genuine decision nevertheless it is much safer if the directors can positively demonstrate proper expertise and understanding of their role and the strategic decisions required to run a company.

2. Avoid input into the decision making process of the company being unstructured and unrecorded. If the business expertise of a lay client or shareholder is needed, then this should be formalised with reports submitted to the board. The directors can then consider such advice and this can be recorded in writing. Avoid the appearance of rubber stamping by always retaining emails and telephone attendance notes. If a shareholder makes a request to the Board then this should be formally considered and recorded in the minutes.

3. Is there anything to suggest that the role of the directors has been usurped (per *Unit Construction*) or dictated to (per *Laerstedt*)? Is there a UK resident 100 per cent shareholder or a UK director? If so, particular care is needed. The board must show it gives genuine and informed consideration to its decisions. Clearly this is easier to show if there is a paper trail that can be produced.

---

[81] [2009] UK FTT 209 (TC); and see [2010] PCB 260.

4. Ensure the board of even a passive investment vehicle meets at least twice yearly and preferably in the same jurisdiction. A "wandering" board is unhelpful in establishing non-residence. Even if the company holds one asset, such as a property which produces no income, the board should still review the company's investment and business interests and determine (for instance) whether to retain or sell the investment.

5. Retain board minutes which are detailed and give reasons for decisions. Ensure that all the directors who are present are minuted as present.

6. Where the board is considering a large or complex transaction reports and draft documents should be submitted well in advance so that they can be given proper consideration.

7. Instructions should be given by the board to third parties not through an agent or the UK resident settlor. When conducting negotiations with third parties (e.g. an estate agent), ensure that the directors establish contact first with the third party even if they request the agent to deal with a UK resident on day to day tasks. The final decision (e.g. on sale or purchase) should always be clearly taken by the directors *abroad* and communicated to the third party by the directors not by the UK resident.

8. Written resolutions should not be signed in the UK even if prepared in advance of the board meeting and signed in escrow. So, for example, a UK resident director or officer of the corporate director should not sign resolutions in advance while in the UK.

Burden of proof

If HMRC claims that a foreign incorporated company is resident in the UK   **4.57**
and is therefore subject to tax, the taxpayer will need to prove that it is not
UK resident.[82] Although in *Untelrab Ltd v McGregor*[83] the burden of proof
that a foreign incorporated company was UK resident was cast on HMRC, in
Wood v Holden it was assumed the burden of proof was on the taxpayer. In any
event, once the taxpayer has brought evidence to show that a foreign registered
company is not UK resident, he has satisfied the evidential burden and then
HMRC must bring evidence to show that the company is in fact UK resident.

[82] See TMA 1970 s.50(6).
[83] [1996] STC (SCD) 1.

CHAPTER 5

TAXATION OF NON RESIDENTS AND FOREIGN DOMICILIARIES—BASIC PRINCIPLES

- Tax liability of non-residents (**5.01**)
- Temporary non-residence (**5.09**)
- Tax regime for foreign domiciliaries (including the remittance basis charge; what is a remittance; currency gains; offshore trusts; situs; losses and 2011 consultation document) (**5.21**)

I TAX LIABILITY OF NON-RESIDENTS

General comments

5.01 Before April 6, 2008 many foreign domiciliaries were not greatly concerned about whether they were UK resident. They were often present in the UK for limited periods of time—maybe over 90 days—but could easily live off capital and avoid remitting income from outside of the UK. The main effect of being a UK resident was the effect on their inheritance tax position since at some point they would become deemed UK domiciled.[1] In practice, even this could largely be dealt with by ensuring that the foreign domiciliary transferred foreign assets into a trust before there was any possibility of acquiring deemed domiciled.

5.02 Since April 6, 2008 it has become much more important to establish a foreign domiciliary's residence status each year since this will determine whether they are liable to pay the £30,000 or in some cases (from April 6, 2012) £50,000 annual remittance basis charge and whether they need to claim the remittance basis. In addition the foreign domiciliary is now generally required to make a formal claim for the remittance basis and to submit a tax return each year.

5.03 A non domiciliary who first became UK resident in 1995–96 and has remained here ever since will become *deemed UK domiciled* for inheritance tax purposes in his 17th year of UK residence on April 6, 2011. A resident individual who has a deemed UK domicile in 2011–12 will only lose it if he emigrates on or before April 5, 2012 and is non-resident for all of 2012–13, 2013–14, 2014–15 and 2015–16. He will then lose his deemed domicile with

---

[1] See IHTA 1984 s.267 and Ch.31.

effect from April 6, 2015 (and can therefore set up excluded property trusts in that year), but only if he remains non-resident throughout 2015–16. If he returns in the course of that tax year he will not have lost his deemed domicile.

Income tax

5.04 UK resident and domiciled individuals or foreign domiciliaries who do not claim the remittance basis[2] are liable to tax on their worldwide income, irrespective of whether that income is received in the UK. By contrast, if an individual is UK resident, but not UK domiciled and he claims the remittance basis, tax liability is normally limited to:

(i) UK investment income (but not Irish source income since April 6, 2008);

(ii) offshore investment income, to the extent that this income is remitted to the UK.

Non-UK domiciled individuals will, therefore, be best advised to hold investments offshore to minimise the impact of UK income tax.

5.05 Non-UK residents are liable to tax on investment income arising in the UK but the tax payable is normally limited to the amount deducted at source. The exception to this is UK income from land, which is fully subject to UK tax, subject to a deduction for the usual expenses (e.g. agents' fees and interest on a loan to purchase the property) and with a credit for any tax collected at source from the tenants or property agents. The practical effect is that non-UK residents can avoid UK tax on bank interest and higher rate tax on dividends. Interest can be paid gross if the individual provides a declaration to the bank or building society that he is not ordinarily resident.[3] There is no tax payable on UK dividends.[4]

Capital gains tax

5.06 An individual who is resident or ordinarily resident in the UK during any part of the year of assessment is taxed on his worldwide chargeable gains made during that year.[5] There are two qualifications to this general proposition.

First, an individual who is resident and a remittance basis user in the UK is liable to CGT only on such gains on overseas assets as are remitted to the UK.

Secondly, where the gain is realised from disposals of overseas assets and cannot be remitted to the UK because of local legal restrictions, executive action by the foreign Government or the unavailability of the local currency, CGT will only be charged when those difficulties cease.[6]

---

[2] See 5.21 onwards.
[3] See ITA 2007 s.858. See Ch.8 for the tax position of non-UK resident trusts.
[4] See ITA 2007 s.811.
[5] The meaning of residence for CGT purposes is discussed further in Ch.3.
[6] TCGA 1992 s.279.

5.07   A person who is neither resident nor ordinarily resident in the UK is generally not liable to CGT on gains even from a disposal of assets situated in the UK.[7] His domicile or the situs of the assets is generally irrelevant. Hence non-UK resident trusts do not generally suffer CGT. In order to prevent UK residents avoiding tax by transferring all their assets into off-shore trusts which then realise gains, a series of provisions have been introduced to catch gains realised by offshore trusts where the settlor/beneficiary is UK resident.[8]

5.08   However, there are three exceptions to the basic rule as follows:

(i) A non-UK resident individual (or trust) is subject to CGT if trading in the UK through a branch or agency. In this event the branch or agency assets are subject to tax.[9] The charge cannot be avoided by removing assets from the UK or by ceasing to trade in the UK. In both cases a deemed disposal at market value will occur (compare the deemed disposal which results from the emigration of a UK resident company).

EXAMPLE 5.1

Jon is non-UK resident and owns a portfolio of UK let properties in London and UK farmland which he farms through a manager. He sells all the UK land. No tax is payable on gains in respect of the let properties but he is subject to CGT in respect of gains on the UK farmland although a roll-over claim could be made into another trade.[10] If he had sold the farming business prior to becoming non-UK resident and rolled-over the gain by reinvesting in the assets of a new business situated abroad there is no claw back of relief.[11] Alternatively he could transfer the business to a company as a going concern prior to migration.

(ii) There are special rules to tax temporary non-residents who return within five years. These rules affect gains realised while abroad or (in the case of foreign domiciliaries) foreign gains or income realised while UK resident but remitted when non-UK resident.[12]

(iii) There is a claw back of the held-over gain if an individual emigrates.[13] There are similar claw back provisions if a gain has been deferred using EIS relief and the individual then emigrates.[14]

---

[7] TCGA 1992 s.2.
[8] See Ch.19.
[9] TCGA 1992 s.10.
[10] See TCGA 1992 ss.152–160.
[11] TCGA 1992 s.152 onwards. See Ch.13 for full details on the position for non-residents in relation to rollover relief.
[12] See 5.09 below.
[13] See TCGA 1992 s.168 and Ch.18. See 4.35 for consideration of exit charges under EU law.
[14] See Ch.16.

FA 1998 introduced the concept of temporary non-residence for CGT pur- **5.09**
poses.[16] An individual who is "temporarily non-resident" (as defined below)
is taxed on certain gains realised whilst non resident but only when he returns
to the UK. It is important to realise that whether someone is "resident" and
"ordinarily resident" is interpreted for CGT purposes in the same way as for
income tax purposes.[17] A taxpayer's residence is determined for a complete
tax year so that an individual resident in the UK at any time during that year
is prima facie taxed on gains realised at any time during the year.[18] It is only
by concession that the year can be split into periods of residence and non-
residence: see ESC D2.[19]

An "entry charge" has been introduced so that if the following conditions **5.10**
are satisfied an individual who becomes non-resident is taxed on his return to
the UK on gains realised during the period of non-residence:

(i) the individual was UK resident or ordinarily resident for at least some
part of four of the seven tax years preceding the year of departure;

(ii) the individual becomes non-UK resident for less than five complete
consecutive tax years;

(iii) during his period of absence from the UK he has disposed of assets
which he had owned when he left the UK or he receives capital payments
from an offshore trust[20] or a trust of which he was the settlor realises
a gain in circumstances where he would be taxed on those gains on an
arising basis if he were UK resident and domiciled[21]; or gains from an
offshore company are attributed to him.[22]

In these situations, the individual is taxed as if the gains accrued to him in **5.11**
the year of return to the UK. Because no distinction is made between one
intervening year and another it follows that the CGT annual exempt amount
is only available for the year of return (that being the year in which the gains
are deemed to accrue) and that losses realised in later intervening years of non-
residence may be offset against gains from earlier years deemed to accrue in
the year of return. (This is an exception to the general rule that losses cannot
be carried back.) The rate of tax in a year of return from 2008–09 to 2010–11
is 18 per cent even if the disposal took place prior to then. Any past taper
relief that might have been available under the pre-2008 regime is ignored
although any indexation is preserved. The rate of tax on immigrations after
April 5, 2011 is 28 per cent assuming the individual is a higher rate taxpayer.
Note, however, that the 18 per cent rate of tax continued for immigrations in

[15] TCGA 1992 s.10A(9ZA) and ITA 2007 s.832A.
[16] As amended by F(No.2)A 2005 inserting s.10A. These rules came into effect from March 17,
1998.
[17] See Ch.3 for rules on residence.
[18] TCGA 1992 s.2.
[19] From March 17, 1998 ESC D2 was amended to limit the circumstances when the year may be
split and is considered further below.
[20] TCGA 1992 s.87.
[21] TCGA 1992 s.86.
[22] TCGA 1992 s.13.

2010–11 whether or not return to the UK within five years occurred before or after June 22, 2010.[23] All gains treated as arising in 2010–11 are deemed to accrue before June 23, 2010.

EXAMPLE 5.2

> Emma leaves the UK in 2008–09, emigrating to Germany. In 2010–11 she is forced to return due to the illness of her mother. She arrives back in the UK on August 4, 2010. During 2009–10 she realised gains on assets acquired before she had left the UK of £200,000. These gains are deemed to accrue before June 23, 2010 and are taxed at the 18 per cent rate. If she had delayed her return to 2011–12 the rate of tax increased to 28 per cent.

5.12 Unlike the US or France the Government chose not to impose an "exit charge" on individuals becoming non-UK resident.[24] Instead, they simply extended the length of period it was necessary for the individual to stay abroad before any CGT advantages could be obtained. It is thought this was partly because of EU constraints on the imposition of an exit charge. A number of further points should be noted about these provisions:

(i) the temporary non-residence rule applies to losses as well as gains;

(ii) it does not (with certain exceptions) apply to disposals of assets which the taxpayer acquired at a time when he was non resident[25];

(iii) the normal limitation period for CGT assessments is extended to two years after January 31 next following the year of return in order to catch gains made in the year of departure, otherwise HMRC would on occasion be out of time in collecting tax on disposals;

(iv) gains (and losses) are calculated in the normal way at the time when the asset is disposed of, as if the taxpayer were then UK resident. Tax will, however, be charged at rates current in the year of return so even though the disposal was made in a year of non-residence when the rate might have varied from 40 per cent to 10 per cent, if the taxpayer returns within five years but between April 6, 2008 and April 5, 2011 the rate is 18 per cent (on the gain calculated after indexation if relevant). If the taxpayer returns after April 5, 2011 the rate of tax is 28 per cent for a higher rate payer;

(v) there are special rules to prevent a possible double charge under TCGA 1992 ss.86 and 87;

---

[23] Presumably the government felt that it would have been too difficult for an individual to fix their date of re-entry into the country to a particular part of the tax year given that at present there are disputes about whether the taxpayer is UK resident in a particular tax year at all. See F(No.2)A 2010 Sch.2 para.19.

[24] Except in limited circumstances, e.g. where gains had been held-over or deferred. See Ch.18 for hold-over relief and Ch.16 for EIS relief. See EU position at 4.35.

[25] Section 10A(3): *"the after-acquired assets rule"*.

(vi) if a taxpayer returned within five years of leaving but before April 6, 2008, taper relief was given by reference to the period of ownership of the asset until sale not the period up to the date of return to the UK. If a taxpayer returns after April 6, 2008 but within five years of leaving having made the disposal before April 5, 2008 then gains are computed with the benefit of indexation but not taper relief[26];

(vii) until the Budget in 2005 it was thought that the charge on re-entry to the UK within five years could be neutralised by relief under a double tax treaty (see s.10A(10)). HMRC do not accept this view was ever correct and since March 16, 2005 it is now expressly provided that treaties cannot override the s.10A charge (see s.10A(9C)).[27]

The concept of temporary non-residence has been extended in two ways. First, with effect from April 6, 2008, non-domiciliaries who leave the UK for less than five years, having been here for at least four of the seven years preceding the tax year of departure, and relevant foreign income or foreign chargeable gains that arose before departure are remitted to the UK during the period of absence, are taxed in the year of return.[28] **5.13**

Before April 2008 the foreign domiciliary already paid tax on gains by virtue of s.10A if he had been in the UK for a minimum of four years, left, and returned within five years if: **5.14**

(a) he disposed of UK situate assets while non-resident which were acquired before leaving the UK; or

(b) he disposed of foreign assets while non-resident which were acquired before he left the UK and remitted the proceeds to the UK in or after the year of return.

---

[26] Return in 2011–12 is the last year when this could apply.

[27] Section 10A was stated to be *"without prejudice to any right to claim relief in accordance with any double taxation relief arrangements"* (s.10A(10)). Hence it had been assumed that a capital gains article in a standard double tax treaty (such as that between Belgium and the UK) which gave sole taxing rights on disposals of most assets to the country where the alienator was resident at the time of disposal, would apply to prevent a charge under s.10A in the year of return. However, while HMRC originally accepted the view that a Treaty can override a charge under s.10A this is no longer the case. F(No.2)A 2005, s.32(6) simply deletes s.10A(10). The change has effect in any case in which the year of departure is 2005–06 onwards.

FA 2005 also introduced changes for taxpayers who became dual resident, i.e. those treated under the tie-breaker provisions as resident in the foreign state (so treaty non-resident) but who never ceased to be resident or ordinarily non-resident in the UK. They did not need to rely on a five-year absence provided they maintained residence in both states and under the tie-breaker provisions would be treated as resident in the foreign state. However, whenever a person becomes treaty non-resident in or after 2005–06 they will be treated as non-resident for the purposes of s.10A. Hence, they will need to do their full five years abroad in order to avoid a CGT charge on disposals of assets. As with non-residents generally, assets acquired and disposed of while treaty non-resident will not be subject to the five-year rule.

Although a treaty non-resident taxpayer will now be treated as non-resident for the purposes of s.10A, gains attributed to him under the ss.86 and 87 offshore settlement regime and TCGA 1992, s.13 will not be postponed until the tax year of arrival back in the UK. In effect, gains attributed under such provisions will continue to be taxed as at present, i.e. on the basis that the taxpayer is treated as resident in the UK throughout the time.

[28] See ITA 2007 s.832A and TCGA 1992 s.10A(9ZA).

These rules continue to apply. Note that if he is not a remittance basis user in the year he returns to the UK then if he has realised gains on a foreign situate asset during the period of absence, he will be taxable even if he does not remit them. This is because they are deemed to be realised in the year of his return so in order to avoid tax he needs to claim the remittance basis and not remit the gains.[29] The rate of tax if immigration occurred during the course of 2010–11 in (a) and (b) is 18 per cent. If the remittance of the foreign asset in (b) above occurs after April 5, 2011 then the rate of tax is 28 per cent assuming the foreign domiciliary is a higher rate taxpayer.

5.15   FA 2008 extended this to catch foreign chargeable gains realised when the individual was UK resident but remitted while non-UK resident or relevant foreign income realised prior to departure but remitted in a year of non-residence. The gains or income are treated as remitted in the year of return.[30]

5.16   Second, if an individual returns within five years of leaving, any offshore income gains realised in his absence are treated as arising in the tax year of his return.[31]

5.17   The consultation document on a statutory residence test published in June 2011 proposes extending the temporary non-residence rule to certain types of investment income received when absent. At present if a taxpayer becomes non-UK resident for (say) 18 months,[32] and during that period he receives a large dividend from his private company there is no tax due.

5.18   The position for foreign domiciliaries can be summarised as follows:

(a) foreign chargeable gains and relevant foreign income realised prior to leaving and remitted while non-UK resident: taxed under TCGA 1992 s.10A(9ZA) and ITA 2007 s.832A in the year of return. The rate of tax on gains is 18 per cent if the return is before June 23, 2010.

(b) foreign gains realised prior to leaving and remitted after return: taxed under s.12 at the rate prevailing when remittance occurs. If remittance occurs in 2010–11 then the rate of tax is 18 per cent on gains remitted before June 23, 2010 and thereafter 28 per cent;

(c) foreign gains realised while non-UK resident and remitted when UK resident: taxed on remittance unless asset acquired while non-UK resident;

(d) foreign gains realised and remitted while non-UK resident on assets acquired while UK resident. Taxed under s.10A.

---

[29] A common mistake is for the foreign domiciliary to decide after a short period of absence that he will come back to the UK and settle here permanently. If he returns with this intention then all foreign chargeable gains realised in the period of absence will be taxed on his return whether or not he remits them.

[30] Again the 18% rate would apply for remittances of gains in 2010–11 whether before or after June 23, 2010.

[31] The Offshore Fund (Tax) (Amendment) Regulations 2009 (SI 2009/3139) reg.23 with effect from December 1, 2009. See Ch.53.

[32] Perhaps following the *Reed v Clark* approach: see Ch.3.

EXAMPLE 5.3

Andrew was domiciled in the UK but on March 30, 1999 he left to take up a three-year contract of employment in Belgium. His broker liquidated his portfolio on April 3 and, during his absence, Andrew sold his UK house and a valuable picture given to him by his wife as a leaving present. He returned to the UK in March 2004 after having extended his original contract. The CGT position is as follows:

(1) Andrew remains resident in the UK in the tax year 1998–99 so that the disposal of shares on April 3, 1999 is chargeable.[33]

(2) Because Andrew returned to the UK in March 2004 he had not been absent for five complete tax years so that the disposal of the house is prima facie brought into charge in tax year 2003–04 (his year of return). Likewise the sale of the picture that, because it was acquired from a spouse, is not excluded under the after-acquired assets rule. Andrew may try to claim protection under the double tax treaty with Belgium so that his gain on the picture will be exempt from CGT (the gain on the real property could be protected under the treaty). It was thought by practitioners that although the gain is deemed to accrue to the taxpayer in the year of return (when he became UK resident) HMRC accepted that if the gain was actually realised at a time when he was resident in Belgium, treaty relief could apply. This view has now been rejected by HMRC.

(3) If Andrew acquires an asset such as a picture in the tax year after departure and sells the picture in the tax year before he returns to the UK, any gain is not chargeable. Similarly any loss would not be allowable.

(4) If Andrew had gone abroad on or before March 16, 1998 he would not be chargeable on gains made while not resident or ordinarily resident even though he may return within five years.

EXAMPLE 5.4

Facts as above except that Andrew was not UK domiciled but had become non-UK resident for four years after having spent (say) 10 years in the UK previously. Foreign chargeable gains realised or relevant foreign income arising while he was a UK resident and subject to the remittance basis are not taxable unless and until remitted. If he remitted such gains or relevant foreign income to the UK in the four years of non-residence he is taxed in the year of return. If he remits such gains or relevant foreign income to the UK in the years after returning to the UK such gains or income are taxable under general principles.

---

[33] ESC D2 does not apply: see 5.19.

Split year treatment

5.19   As already discussed, CGT is charged on individuals resident or ordinarily resident at any time during a tax year on gains made during the course of that year. ESC D2, however, enables the year to be split so that gains arising after a person ceases to be resident are untaxed whilst gains arising before he becomes UK resident are similarly outside the tax net. Observe the following restrictions:

(i) the concession does not apply to trustees;

(ii) like any concession it will not apply *"if any attempt is made to use it for tax avoidance"*[34];

(iii) in the case of an individual who becomes UK resident on or after April 6, 1998, split-year treatment will only apply if he has satisfied the five year test. An individual leaving the UK on or after March 17, 1998 will only benefit from split-year treatment if he was not resident in the four out of seven years of assessment preceding that of his departure. Therefore, in Example 5.3 Andrew could not benefit from split-year treatment for gains realised in the year of departure even if he leaves the UK permanently and therefore for more than five years.

Planning points

5.20   CGT losses should be realised prior to departure. Care should be taken to ensure that arrangements with a potential purchaser, made before going non-resident, do not amount to a disposal at that time. HMRC may argue that there was a binding agreement or contract for sale reached on or before the date of emigration or (if split year treatment does not apply) in the year of departure.

Furthermore if shares in a company have been sold in consideration of receiving shares or loan notes issued by the purchasing company, HMRC may argue that s.135 does not apply.[35] Even if a clearance has been obtained under s.138 this will be invalid if the taxpayer had definite plans to go abroad at the time of the sale and he did not disclose this in the clearance.

EXAMPLE 5.5

Philip owns all the shares in a manufacturing company, P Ltd. He receives an offer from a rival company to buy P Ltd for £20 million cash. Philip and the purchaser reach an informal agreement on terms in February 2007. Philip emigrates in March 2007 and the actual agreement is signed on April 6, 2007. HMRC may ask to see the papers surrounding the sale

---

[34] See *R v IRC, Ex p Fulford-Dobson* [1987] STC 344: QB 978.
[35] See Ch.17 and the *Snell* case.

in order to establish whether a binding oral agreement had been reached in February before Philip left the UK.

Alternatively Philip sells the company in March just before emigration in consideration of receiving guaranteed loan notes from the purchaser which he then cashes six months after the sale in October 2007. In the light of *Snell*, HMRC may well successfully argue that there was a chargeable disposal in March 2007 when the loan notes were then cashed and that TCGA 1992 s.137(1) applies so that there is no s.135 relief.

In this example, if Philip returned within five years but after April 5, 2008 even if the gains had been realised on disposals in 2007–08 the rate of tax on return before April 6, 2011 would be 18 per cent. Any past taper relief entitlement would be ignored. Indexation would be preserved. If he returns in his fifth year of non-residence, i.e. 2011–12, then the rate is 28 per cent.

III THE NEW REGIME FOR FOREIGN DOMICILIARIES

FA 2008 Sch.7 introduced important changes to the way in which foreign **5.21** domiciliaries who are UK resident are taxed. A detailed survey of all these changes is outside the scope of this book but the main income tax and capital gains tax changes with effect from April 6, 2008 can be summarised as follows:

(a) The definition of "remittance" has been made comprehensive.[36] Remittances in specie are caught as are gifts between connected persons.[37]

(b) *Loans* It is no longer possible to use relevant foreign income or foreign employment income to pay interest on debts taken out abroad with the exception of limited transitional provisions.[38]

(c) *Remittance basis charge* A £30,000 charge, "the remittance basis charge", is payable if the foreign domiciliary was UK resident in seven of the last nine tax years prior to the year of assessment and over the age of 18.[39] This is the price to be paid if the foreign domiciliary wants to avoid being taxed on his worldwide income and gains. He will still be taxed on any actual remittances. Around 5,400 individuals paid the charge in 2008–09. The June 2011 consultation document on the Taxation of Foreign Domiciliaries announced that it will be retained for those who

---

[36] See ITA 2007 s.809L.
[37] See Ch.44 for the position on remittances of art and chattels and the limited exceptions.
[38] The position on pre-March 2008 loans is subject to grandfathering arrangements in Sch.7 para.90. Before March 12, 2008 money was often lent abroad to an individual, to enable him to acquire an interest in UK residential property. Repayment of the debt or of any guarantee was secured on the property. The relevant foreign income was used outside the UK before April 6, 2008 to pay interest on the debt and this was not treated as a taxable remittance. That position continues under transitional arrangements provided that the terms of the pre-April 2008 loan are not varied and certain other conditions are satisfied. It only covers a loan for the purchase of residential property that is occupied by the foreign domiciliary. The transitional provisions do not cover the position where foreign employment income was used to pay interest and these arrangements continue. The use of foreign employment income to pay interest on such a debt will be treated as a taxable remittance from April 2008.
[39] ITA 2007 s.809H.

have been resident in at least seven of the nine preceding tax years. However, a new £50,000 charge will be introduced with effect from April 6, 2012, for adults with unremitted overseas income and capital gains of £2,000 or more who have been resident in the UK in at least 12 of the 14 preceding tax years and who elect to be taxed on the remittance basis in that year. The Government has estimated that around 3,500 such individuals will choose to pay the higher £50,000 charge in 2012–13, but around 3,500 will move to the arising basis. This means that those who arrived in 2000–01 or earlier years must pay £50,000 from 2012–13 to claim the remittance basis. Those who arrived between 2001–02 and 2005–06 inclusive must pay £30,000.

(d) All those who claim the remittance basis (even if they have only just arrived in the UK and are not liable to pay the remittance basis charge) lose their entitlement to the income tax personal allowance and the annual capital gains tax exemption.

(e) Mixed fund rules prescribe an order determining whether income or gains has come out of an account.[40]

(f) Loss relief for foreign gains is available if an election is made.[41]

(g) Payments for UK services and goods made abroad can in certain circumstances be made out of relevant foreign income or foreign chargeable gains.[42]

(h) Changes to the temporary residence rules.[43]

(i) Offshore trust capital gains tax rules can now apply to foreign domiciliaries.[44]

(j) Changes to the transfer of assets legislation.[45]

(k) Income source-ceasing ended. If the source-ceased income arose many years ago but was not brought into the UK before April 6, 2008 it cannot now be brought in without a tax charge unless that income has been used to purchase an asset before March 12, 2008.[46]

(l) Transitional rules in FA 2008 Sch.7 para.86(2) protect certain property and cash brought in before April 6, 2008.[47]

(m) Transitional rules in FA 2008 Sch.7 para.86(3) protect any property other than money (not only art) brought into the UK after April 5, 2008 where purchased with relevant foreign income before March 12, 2008.[48]

---

[40] ITA 2007 ss.809Q–S.
[41] TCGA 1992 s.16ZA.
[42] ITA 2007 s.809W.
[43] See 5.09.
[44] See Ch.19.
[45] See Ch.8.
[46] See FA 2008 Sch.7 para.86(3).
[47] See Ch.44 for further details.
[48] See Ch.44 for further details.

What is a "remittance basis user"?

From April 6, 2008, to obtain the benefit of the remittance basis for foreign   **5.22**
chargeable gains, foreign employment income or relevant foreign income an
individual must generally claim to be taxed on a remittance basis unless he
comes within limited exceptions.[49] He is then a "remittance basis user". If he
claims the remittance basis he will lose all personal allowances and the annual
capital gains tax exemption (from the first year of UK residence).[50] In addition, if he has been UK resident in at least seven out of the nine tax years
immediately preceding the tax year in question and is over 18 he must pay
£30,000 for the privilege of retaining the remittance basis. If he does not opt
to pay the £30,000 charge he will pay tax on an arising basis.[51] The £30,000
charge is in addition to any tax due on foreign income and gains remitted to
the UK. It is a tax charge on nominated unremitted income and gains rather
than a stand-alone charge. Those who elect to pay the charge must nominate
an amount of overseas income and capital gains of at least £1 which is deemed
to generate an additional tax charge of £30,000.[52] This nomination ensures
that the £30,000 is a tax charge on overseas income and gains rather than a
stand-alone levy. The legislation was structured in this way primarily to ensure
that US citizens could claim a foreign tax credit for the £30,000.[53] The remittance basis charge has been controversial for US citizens who already pay tax
on a worldwide basis and faced the prospect of paying £30,000 to the UK
government with no prospect of a credit for such tax against their US liability.
The IRS ruling confirms that in order to obtain a US credit against the UK
tax, US citizens need to nominate sufficient foreign income or gains to ensure
that UK tax is generated of at least £30,000 if the income or gains were in fact
remitted. The US citizen cannot nominate merely £1 of income.

There are ordering rules to ensure that if nominated income or gains is, in   **5.23**
fact, remitted and other untaxed income and gains remain unremitted, then that
unremitted income and gains is deemed to be remitted before the nominated
income and gains.[54] Any foreign income or gains (including the nominated
income or gains) can be used to pay the £30,000 charge direct to HMRC from
abroad without this being treated as a taxable remittance. However, difficulties
can then arise if the foreign domiciliary changes his mind; for example, he may

---

[49] i.e. he has been here for less than seven years and has no UK income or gains and remits no
foreign income or gains to the UK. If he has been resident here for seven or more years then
the remittance basis does not need to be claimed and the £30,000 levy does not need to be paid
and there is no loss of personal allowances if his overseas unremitted income and gains do not
exceed £2,000 pa.

[50] Sections 809C–G.

[51] If he opts to be taxed on an arising basis this has no bearing on his domicile status under
general law.

[52] ITA 2007 s.809C.

[53] The US IRS issued ruling 2011–19 confirming that the remittance basis charge is creditable for
US income tax purposes.

[54] The "worst" sort of income is then generally deemed to be remitted first. It is therefore common
for an individual to keep the nominated income or gains in a segregated account. The Government
proposes to amend the legislation with effect from April 2012 to allow individuals to remit the
first £10 of nominated income or capital gains free of tax. In many cases where an individual only
nominates £10 of income anyway this will avoid the need to set up a separate nominated account. It
would be helpful if this relief could be backdated to April 2008 to avoid some of the complexity that
has arisen where a foreign domiciliary has inadvertently remitted nominated income in the past.

pay the charge on account and then find that he has insufficient foreign income or gains to make paying the charge worthwhile or he has ended up remitting most of his foreign income or gains to the UK anyway. In these circumstances if he opts for the arising basis of taxation having already paid the £30,000 on account to HMRC out of his foreign income or gains, although it can be repaid to him it will then have been treated as remitted in which case further tax will be due on the £30,000! Do not pay the charge out of foreign income or gains unless the remittance basis user is certain that he will not change his mind. The foreign domiciliary can opt in and out of the charge depending on the level of his overseas gains and income each year.[55] The charge applies only to adults, so becomes payable in the year a person turns 18. Married couples both have to pay the charge if they want to avoid tax on their respective personal foreign income and gains. The first £30,000 was due in January 2010 for 2008–09 and applied to anyone UK resident continuously since 2001–02. If the £30,000 charge is paid from an offshore source direct to HMRC by cheque or electronic transfer, it will not itself be taxed as a remittance. If the sum is repaid (e.g. the individual decides not to claim the remittance basis and amends his tax return) it will be taxed as a remittance at that point.[56]

5.24   Foreign domiciliaries therefore can:

(i) be remittance basis users not liable to the remittance basis charge (because they have not been in the UK for long enough). They will still lose their personal allowances and annual exemption;

(ii) be remittance basis users liable to pay the £30,000 (£50,000 from April 2012) charge;

(iii) be taxed on an arising basis but still foreign domiciled under general law. In that case they will obtain the benefit of the capital gains tax transitional reliefs relevant for offshore trusts[57];

(iv) be any of the above but deemed domiciled in the UK for inheritance tax purposes if they have been resident in the UK for 17 out of the last 20 tax years.[58]

What constitutes a remittance?[59]

5.25   The definition of remittance in s.809L ITA 2007[60] was extended for both foreign income and gains. It aims to set out a comprehensive code to determine what is a remittance on or after April 6, 2008.

---

[55] Watch payments on account if the foreign domiciliary opts in and out of the remittance basis, e.g. where the foreign domiciliary has paid £30,000 on account for 2011–12 and then decides when filing his return for that year in January 2013 to opt for the arising basis if he has paid the £30,000 to HMRC out of past untaxed income or gains that is effectively a remittance of such income or gains to the UK.

[56] Section 809V.

[57] See FA 2008 Sch.7, paras 120–127. See Ch.19.

[58] If deemed domiciled, they may also be subject to pre-owned assets income tax if the relevant conditions are satisfied: see Chs 31 and 34.

[59] See s.809L. Further details are discussed in Ch.7 in relation to settlor-interested trusts.

[60] Introduced by FA 2008.

It catches remittances in specie or gifts to other family members. In the past **5.26** it had been possible for individuals to buy an asset using foreign income and bring the asset to the UK without this being taxed provided the asset was sold here. Similarly an individual could give foreign income or gains to another person, often a family member. Provided the gift was made outside the UK it was a gift effected abroad and the sums received were capital in the hands of the recipient. As long as the sums gifted were not used for the financial benefit of the donor, no taxable remittance occurred when they were brought into the UK.[61]

However, where income or gains arise after April 5, 2008 and are gifted **5.27** to a "relevant person" (widely defined to include spouses, cohabitees, minor children and minor grandchildren, trusts and companies from which any of the above can benefit) the later transfer of such sums by the relevant person to the UK even by way of investment will result in a deemed remittance and tax will be payable by the donor. The residence of the recipient is irrelevant. Nor does the donor need to receive any benefit to be treated as making a taxable remittance.[62]

Section 809L provides that income or gains of an individual is treated as **5.28** remitted to the UK if Conditions A and B are met; or if Condition C is met; or if Condition D is met.

Condition A is that money or other property is brought to, received in or used in the UK by or for the benefit of a relevant person or a service is provided in the UK to or for the benefit of a relevant person.

Condition B is that:

(i) the property, service or consideration for the service is wholly or in part income or chargeable gains; or

(ii) derives wholly or in part and directly or indirectly from the income or chargeable gains and in the case of property or consideration is property or consideration given by a relevant person; or

(iii) the income or gains are used outside the UK directly or indirectly in respect of a relevant debt; or

(iv) anything deriving from the income or chargeable gains is used in respect of the debt.

Condition C covers gifts of qualifying property to non-relevant persons where a relevant person still benefits. The benefit by that person is, however, disregarded:

(i) if the property or service is enjoyed virtually to the entire exclusion of all relevant persons[63]; or

(ii) if full consideration is given for the enjoyment; or

---

[61] *Carter v Sharon* [1936] 1 All ER 720; *Grimm v Newman* [2002] STC 84.

[62] A transitional rule protects foreign income or gains arising before April 6, 2008. If the foreign domiciliary gives such income or gains to a relevant person who then remits no tax charge arises provided he receives no benefit himself.

[63] In this respect the same approach will be followed as for the reservation of benefit rules: de minimis enjoyment will be ignored.

(iii) if enjoyment is on the same terms as members of the general public.

EXAMPLE 5.6

Adult son is given abroad A's relevant foreign income. There is no remittance by A. The son uses it to buy a house in the UK. A visits as a guest occasionally. There is no taxable remittance, but if:

(1) A becomes infirm and moves in this is a taxable remittance when first enjoyed by A (see s.809L(6)); but
(2) A moves in but pays a market rent. No taxable remittance.

Condition D counteracts reciprocal arrangements but is incomprehensible!

5.29   *Relevant person* is defined[64] as the individual; spouse; cohabitee; civil partner; minor child or minor grandchild; company in which any of the above are participators; trusts where any of the above are beneficiaries and anybody connected with such a company or trust. However, in relation to gains and income arising before April 6, 2008 the definition was restricted to the individual foreign domiciliary. The effects of these changes can be seen in the following examples.

EXAMPLE 5.7

(1) A sells foreign land at a gain and gives the proceeds to his wife who invests them in the UK in shares. There is no benefit to A but A is taxed on the gain unless it arose from a disposal made before April 6, 2008 in which case there is only a taxable remittance if A benefits.

(2) B sells foreign shares at a gain in 2009 and gives the proceeds to his adult son (non-UK resident) who settles them into trust which invests in the UK. Arguably B cannot benefit from the trust but his minor grandchild can. There is a taxable remittance. The position would be different if B had sold before April 6, 2008. B may not know that his adult son has set up a trust nor that it had invested in the UK! Equally it may be argued that an absolute tracing rule is not required because there is no time limit to the tracing exercise and no means by which the original donor can easily trace what the donee has done with the money. The donor has no statutory indemnity. Presumably there must be some conscious intention on the part of the donor that the donee will give it to a relevant person.

(3) C gives relevant foreign income to his adult son abroad who invests it in the UK. There is no taxable remittance by either person even if son is UK resident since it is capital in the son's hands and an adult son is

---

[64] In s.809M.

not a relevant person in relation to C. But if the son then sells the UK shares and gives the proceeds to a trust which subscribes in the capital to an underlying company which invests in the UK and the trust is one from which C and his spouse can benefit, then this is a taxable remittance unless the gifted interest arose prior to April 6, 2008.[65]

Currency gains

Foreign domiciliaries often hold bank accounts denominated in a currency other than sterling. They convert the currency into sterling only on remittance. Foreign currency bank accounts are chargeable assets for capital gains tax so that any withdrawal of funds from such an account constitutes a part-disposal of the asset and a capital gain or loss can arise. Calculations of gains and losses have become extremely complicated, not least because there is no annual capital gains tax exemption to cover de minimis gains; there is dispute between HMRC and practitioners over the correct way to calculate foreign currency gains.[66]

5.30

The June 2011 consultation paper produced by the Treasury proposes that all sums within an individual's foreign currency bank account will be removed from the scope of capital gains tax. This is welcome development. It is not yet known whether this will apply to offshore trusts or if the exemption will be applied retrospectively to April 6, 2008 if the individual so elects.

5.31

Use of trusts

Offshore trusts are discussed further in Ch.19 in the context of capital gains tax; in Ch.53 in the context of offshore gains, and in Ch.8 in the context of income tax. A few points are, however, worth making at this stage. If assets are held in an offshore trust then the situs of the assets while in trust is irrelevant in relation to capital gains tax but the source of the income is relevant for income tax. The foreign domiciliary is not subject to capital gains tax under TCGA 1992 s.86, whether or not a remittance basis user, and there is no capital gains tax on disposals of UK situated assets by the non-resident trustees. What triggers the tax charge is if a benefit or capital payment is provided to the beneficiary.

5.32

This should be contrasted with the income tax provisions where the source of the income affects the charge on the foreign domiciliary. A transferor is taxed on an arising basis on trust or company income which he has power to enjoy and which is UK source whether or not he receives it and a

---

[65] The position would be more debateable if they were not actually beneficiaries but there was power to add the settlor/spouse or any other relevant person. The answer partly depends on the meaning of "derived" and partly on whether the power to add a relevant person means the trust itself becomes a relevant person.

[66] See HMRC notice at [2010] SWTI 37.

non-transferor is taxed on an arising basis if a benefit received abroad can be matched to UK relevant income within the structure.[67]

5.33   It is no longer sound advice for a foreign domiciled taxpayer, who is UK resident, to hold all foreign assets which are likely to show a gain in a trust. The use of a trust will avoid CGT on UK situated assets but can complicate the remittance rules.[68] Instead of looking at the gain on the actual asset and whether that gain has been remitted it is necessary to compute all the gains of the trust. Even if the capital payment or benefit received by the foreign domiciliary is not derived from an asset which shows a gain, if the trust as a whole has realised gains then a capital gains tax charge can arise.[69]

Before April 2008 trusts were also used as a means of avoiding capital gains tax: foreign assets pregnant with gain could be gifted into trust and rebased to market value. On later disposal of the asset by the trustees, there was no taxable remittance even if the proceeds were paid back to the donor and he brought them to the UK. The gain "disappeared"! That position has now changed for gifts made after April 5, 2008.[70]

When is an asset situate outside the UK for capital gains tax purposes?

5.34   The situs of the assets is irrelevant for capital gains tax purposes if the asset is held in an offshore trust structure. However, it will be relevant where the individual holds foreign assets direct or the individual owns at least 10 per cent of an offshore company which holds the foreign assets because in these cases the remittance basis can only apply where the asset is foreign situated. Otherwise gains will be taxed on an arising basis irrespective of whether the individual is foreign domiciled or claims the remittance basis.

5.35   TCGA 1992 s.275 provides that the situs of any intangible asset will be in the UK if any right or interest comprised in the asset is governed by, exercisable in or enforceable under or is subject to the law of the UK. The same is true of futures or options over intangibles situated in the UK because the situs of futures or options is governed by the situs of the underlying asset. Furthermore, all shares (including bearer shares) in and debentures of UK incorporated companies, whether registered or not, are treated as situated in the UK. The general rule is that debts are situated where the creditor is resident (wherever secured). However, a judgement debt is situated where the judgement is recorded; a bank account owned by a foreign domiciliary is not situated in the UK unless it is denominated in sterling or is in a branch in the UK. So non-UK foreign currency accounts of non-domiciliaries are situated outside the UK. Goodwill is situated where the business is carried on.[71]

---

[67] See Ch.8.
[68] As noted in Ch.19.
[69] Unless the foreign domiciliary is a remittance basis user and all benefits and capital payments are received and retained outside the UK.
[70] See ITA 2007 s.809T and Example 19.23 for a consideration of the position where assets pregnant with gains are settled after April 5, 2008.
[71] For other rules see TCGA 1992 ss.275A–C.

Losses

Until April 6, 2008 there was no relief for overseas losses realised by a foreign **5.36**
domiciliary. FA 2008 Sch.7, however, has introduced limited loss relief for
overseas losses if a foreign domiciliary, on the remittance basis, so elects.[72]
Unless and until the foreign domiciliary elects into the remittance basis he
obtains relief for foreign losses because he is taxed on an arising basis. Once
he elects for the remittance basis, if he does not elect to use foreign losses in
that first year, any future losses will not be allowable even if in a later year he
chooses to be taxed on an arising rather than remittance basis.

EXAMPLE 5.8

Barry arrives in England and sells his Portuguese property for a gain of
£50,000 and his French shares for a loss of £40,000 after allowing for currency
gains and losses. The Portuguese property was sold for £150,000 so one third
of the proceeds was gain. He remits £20,000 from the Portuguese sale proceeds
in 2007 to the UK thinking that his net gain (ignoring his annual exemption)
is at worst £10,000 after deducting the loss. Under the old rules he is treated as
remitting only a proportion of the gain so one third of the £20,000 is treated
as remitted gain. None of the loss on the French shares is allowable. Of course
if he keeps the proceeds of the French shares separate from the Portuguese
property proceeds and then remits only the French proceeds he does not remit
any gain and no tax is due (but no loss relief is given).

If he remits in 2008–09 from the Portuguese bank account then the gain is
treated as coming out first so a £20,000 remittance would be treated as representing £20,000 gain. However, some loss relief is given if claimed.

Schedule 7 introduced a limited form of loss relief. A number of conditions **5.37**
must be satisfied:

(i) an election must be made in the first year when the remittance basis is
claimed. If no election is made, foreign losses of that tax year and all
future tax years will not be allowable losses even if the individual later
opts to be taxed on an arising rather than remittance basis unless he
accepts he is domiciled in the UK under general law;

(ii) foreign chargeable gains remitted to the UK in a tax year later than that
in which the foreign asset was disposed of cannot be reduced by losses
of any year later than that in which the gains arose.[73]

EXAMPLE 5.9

A, a remittance basis user, realised foreign gains of £50,000 in 2009.
He realised foreign losses in 2010–11 and remitted the £50,000

---

[72] See Sch.7 para.62 and s.16ZA TCGA 1992 as amended.
[73] Section 16ZB.

gains in 2011–12. He cannot use the losses to reduce the taxable remittance.

(iii) If the remittance basis is claimed for the tax year in which the foreign chargeable gains arise, the allowable losses are deducted first from foreign chargeable gains that both arise and are remitted in that tax year, then against foreign chargeable gains arising but not remitted in that year and then from any UK chargeable gains arising in that year.

EXAMPLE 5.10

B, a remittance basis user, realises foreign gains of £50,000 in 2008–09, foreign losses of £60,000 and UK losses of £3,000. He realises gains on UK assets of £15,000 and remits £20,000 of the gains. The losses (including UK losses) are set against the remitted gains first (£20,000) and then against the remaining unremitted foreign gains arising in that year (but not against foreign gains in earlier years) and then against the UK gains, leaving £2,000 of UK gains chargeable.

5.38 The election is irrevocable. Foreign (or UK) personal losses cannot be deducted against gains chargeable under TCGA 1992 s.87 nor against gains which arose in a year prior to the losses (even if they are remitted in a year after the losses arose).[74] It is not possible to separate out the gain from the original capital and remit only the capital. The position is different from a separation of income and capital.

EXAMPLE 5.11

Pauline, a remittance basis user, invested £1 million in shares in a German bio-tech company, BTI Limited. These produce dividends each year which is paid into her overseas income account and kept abroad so she avoids income tax. She eventually sells the BTI shares for £2 million. She remits £1 million to the UK from her capital account. She cannot successfully argue that the £1 million represents the original capital and that the gain has not been remitted even if the sale proceeds have been split up. Before April 6, 2008 HMRC would tax her on half the remittance on the basis that remittances are treated as taxable gain in the proportion that the gains bear to the total amount in the account.[75] However, after April 5, 2008 remittance of the first £1 million is treated as entirely gain.[76]

The dividend income that has been paid into the overseas income account can continue to be segregated and is not taxable unless remitted.

---

[74] See Ch.21.
[75] See old CG Manual 25401.
[76] See ITA 2007 s.809Q which deals with the remittance of income and gains where transfers are made out of mixed funds.

Other exemptions

Specific exemptions have been introduced for foreign domiciliaries in rela- **5.39**
tion to assets purchased with relevant foreign income or foreign chargeable
gains.[77]

New business investment relief

In June 2011 the Government announced in a consultation paper on foreign **5.40**
domiciliaries a radical proposal to encourage investment in the UK. If
enacted, the practical effect of this relief may be that foreign domiciliaries
from April 6, 2012 will only pay tax on their UK source income and UK gains
plus their overseas income and gains remitted for their personal benefit. One
of the damaging aspects of the FA 2008 changes was that overseas income or
capital gains remitted to the UK by foreign domiciliaries or relevant persons[78]
was liable to UK tax regardless of the purpose for which they were used. This
was a significant disincentive for foreign domiciliaries to invest in the UK
because such investment could often result in an immediate tax charge. A
foreign domiciliary would often have insufficient "clean capital" or not have
segregated foreign income or gains in the past adequately.

The Government now proposes to allow tax-free remittances for investment **5.41**
in the following types of business, classed as "qualifying businesses":

(i)   businesses carrying out a trading activity;

(ii) businesses undertaking a development or letting of commercial property;

(iii) businesses carrying out a mixture of the above.

Residential lettings are excluded from relief. Presumably farming is included
although the position on holiday lets remains unclear. Leasing of tangible
moveable property such as yachts, cars, furniture and pictures or the provision
of personal services are excluded activities. The Government is considering
whether investment should be permitted in companies carrying on qualifying
businesses that are listed on a recognised Stock Exchange or on AIM.

The overseas income and gains must be invested through the vehicle of **5.42**
a company if they are to be classed as tax-free remittances. However, the
company could be owned by a holding company, trust, partnership or the
individual direct. So, foreign domiciliaries will be able to invest in UK businesses using funds held in offshore companies and trusts without attracting a
tax charge on the remittance.

The company can be funded through a mixture of share and loan capital. **5.43**
Hence if a foreign domiciliary lends £1 million of relevant foreign income to
a qualifying company there is no taxable remittance at that point. This is very

---

[77] These are discussed in Ch.44 and are particularly relevant to art and personal possessions.
[78] Widely defined to include most trusts set up by the settlor, co-habitee, spouse, minor children,
minor grandchildren.

different from other reliefs such as EIS which require the investment to be in the form of share capital not loans.

5.44 The tax relief will not be restricted to investment in businesses that are resident in the UK or carrying out trades wholly or mainly in the UK. It will be possible for the foreign domiciliary to invest in a non-UK resident company as long as the company has a permanent establishment in the UK. In most cases the foreign domiciliary will want to invest in a non-resident foreign-incorporated company for other tax reasons even if the company has a permanent establishment in the UK.

5.45 There is no requirement to hold a majority ownership stake in the company. Nor is there any upper or lower limit on the amount of overseas income or capital gains that can be remitted for investment purposes. There are no restrictions on the investor's connections to the business in which they invest.[79] Hence, the investor can work for or be a director of the business and draw commercial remuneration. However, he will not be allowed to take money out of the business for personal purposes, e.g. loans from the company or remuneration that is not commercial. The investment can be in a company where members of the family work and draw remuneration.

5.46 There are no restrictions on the length of time for which the investment must be held. If the investment is sold then the overseas income or capital gains remitted must be taken out of the UK within two weeks of the individual receiving the money. The amount of overseas income or capital gains used to fund the qualifying investment will be treated as coming out first on disposal of the investment before any capital gain.

If the original investment remains in the UK for longer than two weeks[80] it will be treated as a taxable remittance. However, the effect of the relief is that a foreign domiciliary will pay tax on the UK source income generated by the investment (e.g. in the form of dividends out of the company) but the seed capital used to finance the investment will be protected from tax even if it is derived from or represents foreign income or chargeable gains that would otherwise be taxable on remittance.

5.47 Foreign domiciliaries will not be allowed to sell an existing business to a new company set up in 2012 and funded by overseas income or gains. Hence, if a foreign domiciliary funded an existing business in 2009 using clean capital (to avoid a taxable remittance of foreign income or gains) he cannot replace that capital by selling it to a foreign company after April 6, 2012. It is not clear what the position would be if he wanted to invest in a new business in 2011 by way of loan. If the loan was repaid after April 6, 2012 would the repayment of the loan at that point be treated as a taxable remittance?

5.48 The Government suggests a minimum compliance burden on an individual who claims the relief on their tax return; he will give details of whether he has remitted income or capital gains to the UK for investment in a qualifying business, how much has been remitted and in what businesses the funds have been invested.

The consultation paper suggests that the relief only needs to apply to those who are taxed on the remittance basis. However, individuals paying tax on an arising basis will often need the relief because they may well want to remit foreign income and gains realised in previous years when they were on

---

[79] Again contrast this with EIS income tax relief. See Ch.16.
[80] Or whatever period is eventually agreed.

the remittance basis. Similarly those who have become temporarily non-UK resident but return within five years would want to be able to claim the relief if they invest in the UK using foreign income or chargeable gains during the period of non-residence.

It is not clear how the mixed fund rules will interact with the new relief. **5.49** If, for example, the taxpayer brings in money from a mixed fund to invest in the UK will this be treated as clearing out the mixed fund account as per the normal ordering rules and what happens if the UK investment is subsequently realised and the money comes back out of the UK? Can it then be put in a new offshore account? If so this would be a means of cleaning up existing mixed accounts. The untaxed income or gains could be used for the UK investment and the clean funds then remitted for personal expenditure.

PART II: INCOME TAX

The next section is mainly concerned with income tax. Ch.6 considers the tax treatment of UK resident trusts which are not settlor-interested whilst Ch.7 looks at settlor-interested UK resident trusts and includes a consideration of the (significantly reduced since 2008) CGT implications. Finally Ch.8 deals with the income tax treatment of non-UK resident trusts, both settler-interested and non-settlor-interested.

CHAPTER 6

INCOME TAX OF NON-SETTLOR-INTERESTED TRUSTS—UK RESIDENT

This chapter considers the income tax position of UK resident trusts which are not settlor-interested. UK resident settlor-interested trusts are considered in Ch.7 and non-resident trusts in Ch.8.

I DEFINITIONS

As discussed in more detail elsewhere,[1] part of the "trust modernisation" **6.01** process involved introducing a series of definitions of settled property, settlor and trustees.

Settled property

TA 1988 s.685A first defined settled property (and this was rewritten in ITA **6.02** 2007 s.466 in almost identical terms):

> "*for the purposes of the Tax Acts unless the general context otherwise requires, settled property means any property held in trust other than property held by a person as nominee for another, property held by a*

---

[1] See Ch.7 for the income tax and capital gains tax definition of settlor, Ch.9 for capital gains tax definitions of settled property and Ch.4 for residence and trustees.

person as trustee for another person who is absolutely entitled as against the trustee and property held by a person as trustee for another person who would be absolutely entitled if he were not an infant or otherwise under a disability."[2]

Settlor

6.03   TA 1988 ss.685B–D introduced a definition of settlor[3] rewritten in ITA 2007 s.467. A person is a settlor in relation to the settlement if the settlement was made, or treated as having been made, by that person. He is treated as having made a settlement if he has entered into it or he has provided property directly or indirectly for the purposes of the settlement or if the settlement arose on his death and any of the settled property is property of which he was competent to dispose immediately before his death.[4] A person ceases to be a settlor in relation to a settlement if no property of which he is the settlor remains in the settlement; he has not undertaken to provide property for the purposes of the settlement in the future, and he has not made reciprocal arrangements with another person for that other person to add cash in the future.

6.04   Where property is transferred between settlements for less than full consideration then the settlor of the transferor trust becomes a settlor of the transferee trust. However, this rule is disapplied in relation to a transfer of property at less than full consideration that occurs in any one of the following circumstances[5]:

(a) by the assignment by a beneficiary of settlement 1 to the trustees of settlement 2 of an interest in settlement 1;

(b) by the exercise of a general power of appointment;

(c) by a variation of a settlement established under a will or intestacy. So if property is first settled by the variation of a will then generally the person who was entitled to the property immediately before the variation is treated as the settlor.[6] However, if a settlement arose on the death of a person (whether created by will or arising on intestacy) and it is varied by the beneficiaries so that the property becomes comprised in another settlement, then the deceased is still treated as the settlor.[7]

---

[2] Note the extended definition of settlement for the purposes of the charge on the settlor: see 7.04.

[3] See Ch.7.

[4] See ITA 2007 s.467 and Ch.7 and compare the capital gains tax provisions which are very similar.

[5] See ITA 2007 ss.470–472.

[6] ITA 2007 s.472.

[7] See ITA 2007 s.473. See also Ch.9 in relation to similar capital gains tax provisions and Ch.39 for variations.

Example 6.1

(a) In 1990 X (aged 90) settled property on a fixed interest life interest trust for his daughter A remainder to his grandchild B (whether or not alive at A's death). A is 60 and still going strong. B is 35 and at the point of death. B's remainder interest is excluded property for inheritance tax purposes[8] and he assigns her interest to a discretionary trust for her own children. B not X is the settlor of the discretionary trust for income tax purposes.

(b) Y is the life tenant of an interest in possession trust set up by his grandfather. Under the terms of the trust he has a testamentary general power of appointment. He exercises it by will to appoint on trust for his grandchildren. X not the grandfather is the settlor of the new trust.[9]

(c) Z died intestate leaving a wife and adult children. Under the intestacy rules, his children took half the residuary estate outright and the balance was left on interest in possession trusts for his widow, remainder to such of his children as are alive on his death.[10] The widow and children enter into a deed of variation so that all the residuary estate is now left on flexible interest in possession trusts for the widow and then to the issue of Z (including children) but with wide overriding powers to end the interest in possession of the widow at any time. It would appear that Z is the settlor as to half the residuary estate (i.e. that half settled on his death) and the children are the settlors of the other half to which they were absolutely entitled on his death and which is now held on interest in possession trusts for the widow. This is inconvenient! Theoretically the widow is entitled to and taxed on half the income (i.e. the half where the children are not treated as the settlors). In respect of the other half she is entitled to receive income as life tenant but the children are liable to pay tax on it under ITTOIA 2005 s.624 with a right of reimbursement.[11] If the widow is only a basic rate taxpayer and the children are higher or additional rate taxpayers this will result in more tax being payable.

Trustees

TA 1988 s.685E(1)[12] provides that the trustees of a settlement are to be treated as a single person, distinct from the persons who may from time to time in fact be trustees. Previously there was no express statutory rule deeming trustees to be a single person for income tax purposes although case law achieved much the same result.[13] The section provides that the trustees of a settlement are a single person even if some are trustees of one fund and

6.05

---

[8] See IHTA 1984 ss.47 and 48(1).

[9] For the advantages in doing this see Ch.38.

[10] Note that the position would be different if D had died leaving a will which gave property on interest in possession trusts for his widow and then to such of his children who survive her. In these circumstances the children only have a contingent interest.

[11] See Ch.7 for the income tax treatment of settlor-interested trusts.

[12] Importing TCGA 1992 s.69(3) into income tax. It is rewritten as ITA 2007 s.474.

[13] See for example *IRC v Berrill* [1981] STC 784.

others trustees of another fund. It should be read subject to the ability to make a sub-fund election which is discussed further at 12.42 and 6.11. There is now a common trustee residence test for income tax and capital gains tax purposes.[14]

II TAXATION OF TRUSTEES OF FIXED INTEREST TRUSTS

Liability of trustees for tax at basic rate

6.06 Trustees of UK resident trusts where the beneficiary is entitled to the income as it arises are, from April 6, 2008, subject to income tax at the basic rate (20 per cent for 2011–12) on all the income produced by the trust fund other than dividends where they are charged at the dividend ordinary rate (see 6.33 and 6.19).[15] They are not allowed to deduct their personal allowances nor those of any beneficiary.[16] Nor are the trustees allowed a deduction for any trustee management expenses.[17] It is important to be clear what is meant in this context by trustee management expenses. HMRC put the matter as follows:

> "*In managing a trust the trustees may incur expenses in the course of exercising their duties and powers. These are 'trust management expenses' (TMEs). TMEs are not like any other expenses for tax purposes.*
> *There is a common misconception that TMEs are on a par with tax deductions for trading. Where a trust carries on a trade, the normal trading income rules apply to the computation of the profit/loss of that trade. In contrast, TMEs are expenses incurred in the capacity of trustee, not in any other capacity such as a trader. They are not related to the expenses or deductions of a trade or rental business. Even if a large trust is run like a business, for TMEs purposes the rules for allowable trading deductions are not in point. A separate set of principles, legislation and case law apply. The more common tax notions of 'capital' and 'income', e.g. construction of a new building versus repairs, do not apply. What is relevant is 'capital' and 'income' in trust law, which is completely separate.*
> *The allowance of TMEs for tax purposes is based to a large extent on trust law.*"[18]

6.07 Some receipts such as share buy-backs, offshore income gains, lease

---

[14] See Ch.4.
[15] See, for instance, ITTOIA 2005 s.8 under which the trustees are the persons liable because they are the persons receiving or entitled to the profits and see TMA 1970 s.71. For the position when the income is taxed on the settlor under the anti-avoidance rules, see Ch.7.
[16] Of course some sources of income provide for a deduction of expenses in arriving at the taxable sum, e.g. trading income. For the tax position of settlor-interested trusts, see Ch.7. For the position where the life tenant is a remittance basis user or non-resident, see 6.10 below.
[17] See TSEM 8310 and *Aikin v Macdonald's Trustees* (1894) 3 TC 306.
[18] See TSEM 8005. Note that although TMEs cannot be deducted by the trustees for basic rate purposes, they may be deducted if the trustees of a fixed interest trust are liable for tax at the trust rate on capital receipts: see 6.57.

premiums and accrued interest are capital as a matter of trust law but taxed as income for tax purposes. These receipts do not become the income of the life tenant and the trustees of a fixed interest trust (as well as of a discretionary or accumulation trust) will be liable to pay tax on them at the special trust rate (now 50 per cent).[19] However, such deemed income can benefit from the standard rate band of £1,000[20] even if the trust is a fixed interest trust.[21]

Special income tax and capital gains tax treatment is given if the trust is **6.08** for a vulnerable beneficiary and an election is made. The income tax liability is then computed as if the beneficiary had received the income directly, i.e. by applying his own rates and allowances.[22]

An assessment to income tax at basic rate may either be made on the trus- **6.09** tees directly (e.g. where they receive income from letting land) or they may receive investment income with tax deducted at source (e.g. bank interest) when the tax deducted will satisfy the trustees' liability. The dividend rates of income tax apply to both UK and many categories of foreign dividends[23] and are 10 per cent basic rate, 32.5 per cent higher rate and 42.5 per cent additional rate.[24] Hence there is no further liability for the trustees on UK or certain foreign dividends[25] since such dividends are deemed to carry a tax credit[26] satisfying the 10 per cent basic rate.[27]

UK trustees of an interest in possession trust are always subject to basic rate **6.10** tax on UK source income (with a credit for any tax deducted at source) but if the life tenant is non-UK resident the trustees are not chargeable in respect of the beneficiary's share of income received from abroad.[28] That income is omitted from the Trust and Estate Tax Return and the trustee has no liability. Similarly HMRC accept that the trustees' liability on the share of income from abroad payable to a beneficiary who is a remittance basis user is limited to the amount remitted to the UK.[29]

Assessments can be made in the name of any one or more of the relevant **6.11** trustees, i.e. the trustees to whom the income arises and any subsequent trustees.[30] Where a sub-fund election has been made for capital gains tax purposes[31] ITA 2007 s.477 applies the sub-fund legislation for income tax purposes. A sub-fund election cannot be made earlier than April 6, 2006 but if made, the trustees of the sub-fund are treated as separate from the trustees of the principal settlement.

---

[19] See ITA 2007 s.481 and 6.58 below.
[20] The standard rate was £500 in 2005–6 and has been £1,000 from 2006–7 onwards: see 6.33.
[21] ITA 2007 s.491 for further details of standard rate band.
[22] See Ch.36.
[23] ITTOIA 2005 ss.397 and 397A.
[24] ITA 2007 ss.8 and 19.
[25] Except where the life tenant is a remittance basis user in which case the dividend income is charged at the basic rate not the dividend ordinary rate because remittance basis users do not obtain the benefit of the lower dividend rates.
[26] This is one-ninth of the net dividend: so if £90 is paid as a dividend the credit is 1/9 x £90 = £10.
[27] The tax position of the beneficiary is discussed further at 6.15.
[28] See TSE 3160 and *Williams v Sanger* 7TC 387.
[29] See TSE 3165.
[30] FA 1989 s.151(2)(a).
[31] Under TCGA 1992 Sch.4ZA. Discussed at 12.42.

EXAMPLE 6.2

The trustees run a business. The profits of that business are calculated in accordance with the normal rules under ITTOIA 2005 and are subject to basic rate income tax in the trustees' hands. A change of trustees does not result in the discontinuance rules applying.[32] If a sub-fund election is made over part of the fund which is producing (say) investment income then the trustees of that sub-fund are not relevant trustees in respect of income tax due on the business income (and vice versa).

Submitting a return

6.12 In exceptional cases, trustees of interest in possession trusts do not have to complete a return. If there are professional trustees acting; there is no untaxed income arising or any such income is mandated directly to a beneficiary, and no capital gains tax arise, the trustees are not required to submit a return but have to undertake to notify HMRC of any change in their circumstances. The beneficiary will be directly assessed on any income and the trustees must notify HMRC of the name and address of the beneficiary.[33] HMRC will also generally allow trustees not to submit a return where the only asset of the trust is a residential property which is occupied rent-free by a beneficiary under the terms of the settlement.

Bare trusts[34]

6.13 In general trustees are not required to make returns/pay tax in respect of bare trusts. Thus if they receive income, such income should be paid to the beneficiary who is responsible for tax on it. However, with the agreement of the beneficiary the bare trustees may voluntarily return income (but not capital gains) and account for tax at the appropriate rate.[35]

III TAXATION OF THE INTEREST IN POSSESSION BENEFICIARY

6.14 A UK resident beneficiary who is entitled to the income of a UK trust as it arises (or is entitled to have it applied for his benefit) is subject to income tax for the year of assessment in which that income arises, even if none of the money is paid to him during that year.[36] In passing it should be noted that although the inheritance tax treatment of such a beneficiary may have

[32] ITTOIA 2005, ss.258, 361.
[33] See TSEM; 3040 TMA 1970 s.76.
[34] See generally, *Tax Bulletin*, February 27, 1997.
[35] Bare trusts are considered in Ch.42.
[36] *Baker v Archer-Shee* [1927] AC 844 HL.

changed on March 22, 2006 there was no change for income tax purposes.[37] Hence, a beneficiary could have a non-qualifying interest in possession for inheritance tax purposes but will be subject to the same income tax regime as a beneficiary with a qualifying interest in possession.

Source of the income

The general rule is that the beneficiary entitled to the income of an English **6.15** law trust is treated as directly entitled to the underlying income and so the trust is not the source of the income (despite the fact that the beneficiary is only taxed on the net amount that he receives after deduction of management expenses). So if the assets are situated in the UK he has UK source income and if they are abroad he has foreign source income.[38] Other jurisdictions where you look to the underlying source of the income (i.e. the trust is treated as transparent) include Jersey, Guernsey, Isle of Man, Bahamas, Cayman Islands and New Zealand (called "Baker jurisdictions"). By contrast, in "Garland jurisdictions"[39] the fixed interest beneficiary is not regarded as having a specific interest in each and every trust asset but only a right against the trustees so that the trust is not transparent. These include New York, India and New Jersey.[40] In *R (on the application of Huitson) v HMRC*[41] the *Baker* principle was considered in some detail, the judge doubting (at [52]) that it should be applied in every context and suggesting, obiter, that the principle may not apply to trust trading profits, i.e. the income paid to the life tenant may not be the same as the trustees' trading profits.

The question of whether a trust is treated as transparent can be relevant in **6.16** the following situations:

(i) where foreign domiciled beneficiaries are life tenants the source of the income may be important in terms of the remittance basis. Similarly where the trust receives income that is exempt in the hands of a non-resident life tenant such as interest on FOTRA (exempt government securities) trustees can arrange to receive interest gross and pay this to the non-UK resident without deducting tax;

(ii) if a life tenant receives UK or foreign dividends and he is to enjoy the 10 per cent, 32.5 per cent and 42.5 per cent rates and notional tax credit then the trust must be transparent;

(iii) before April 6, 2008 the point could be relevant in the context of source ceasing. The underlying assets could be sold and source ceasing achieved: this has no tax advantages after April 5, 2008.

---

[37] For the IHT changes see Ch.23.
[38] See *Baker v Archer-Shee* above.
[39] From the decision in *Archer-Shee v Garland* (1931) 15 TC 693, where a different result was reached on the basis of evidence that the law of New York was different from that of the UK.
[40] HMRC publish a list—see *http://hmrc.gov.uk/cnr/nr_trusts.htm#baker_garland_countries* for their views. A liferent (life interest) under a Scots trust is not transparent but this position has been explicitly reversed in tax legislation for UK resident Scots trusts: ITA 2007 s.464.
[41] [2010] EWHC 97 (Admin).

Dividend income

6.17   The life tenant is entitled to the non-repayable tax credit in respect of UK dividends.[42] The dividend income is grossed up by the tax credit and tax is charged on the beneficiary at the appropriate dividend rate on that grossed-up sum. The effective tax rate on UK dividends on the amount actually received is therefore nil for a basic rate tax payer, 25 per cent for a higher rate tax payer and 36.11 per cent for an additional rate taxpayer.

EXAMPLE 6.3

An interest in possession trust receives UK dividend income of £900. A one-ninth tax credit (£100) applies to the dividend.

Trustees' position

The trustees receive gross income of £1,000 with a £100 credit and no further tax is due from them.

Beneficiary's position	£
Net income (as above)	900
Grossed up	1,000
Tax credit	100

(a) If the beneficiary is a non-taxpayer or basic rate taxpayer there is no further tax liability but the non-taxpayer cannot reclaim the £100 tax credit.

(b) If the beneficiary is a higher rate taxpayer he pays 32.5 per cent tax on £1,000 less £100 credit = £225 tax (i.e. 25 per cent of £900).

(c) If the beneficiary is an additional rate taxpayer he pays 42.5 per cent on £1,000 less £100 credit = £325 tax (i.e. 36.11 per cent of £900).

Note that remittance basis users are not entitled to the benefit of the dividend rate.

Foreign dividends

6.18   Before 2008–09, foreign dividends were taxed at the same rates as UK dividends, using the 10 per cent and 32.5 per cent rates but with no 10 per cent tax credit attached to them.[43] From the tax year 2008-9, however, foreign dividends

---

[42] See ITTOIA 2005 s.398.

[43] The dividend rates did not generally apply to remittance basis users although the position was different in 2005–06 and 2006–07 where due to a flaw in the legislation remittance basis users were able to claim the benefit of the dividend rates. Remittance basis users do not have the

received by a "minority shareholder" can also attract the non-repayable 10 per cent tax credit. The holding of the shareholder had to form less than 10 per cent of the distributing company's entire issued share capital.[44] The company could be resident in any foreign jurisdiction. In applying the 10 per cent threshold, it is necessary to aggregate any shares that the life tenant held personally and shares in other trusts in which he was life tenant. (Shares form part of that life tenant's holding *"to the extent that the person is beneficially entitled to the shares or to a distribution arising in respect of the shares (or both)"*.) These rules remain unchanged except that from April 22, 2009 a minority shareholder is an individual owning less than 10 per cent of a class of share capital, not the entire issued share capital.

Life tenants of "transparent" trusts are therefore treated as receiving the foreign dividend directly for the purposes of the credit rules whether or not the trustees first receive it. **6.19**

From April 22, 2009, the rules were extended to dividends received by an individual owning a 10 per cent or greater share in a non-resident company provided that the company is from a qualifying territory. So if the trustees' holding is 10 per cent or more a tax credit is available if the company is resident in a qualifying territory.[45] A qualifying territory is any territory with which the UK has concluded a double tax treaty containing a standard non-discrimination article.[46] For example all EU countries, United States, Japan, China and Switzerland are qualifying. It does not cover low tax jurisdictions such as Jersey, Guernsey, Isle of Man, Bermuda or Liechtenstein. Further, certain types of companies in some qualifying territories (even in the European Union) do not qualify for the tax credit if they benefit from special tax treatment, e.g. certain companies in Cyprus, Barbados, Jamaica, Luxembourg, Malaysia and Malta, although in practice it is relatively easy to site the company in one of these jurisdictions and obtain the benefit of the tax credit but with minimal additional tax in the country of residence. **6.20**

For instance, where the trustees wholly own a Jersey or other offshore holding company there is no available tax credit on dividends received by the life tenant. Moreover, even if that company itself receives UK or foreign dividends from the shares it owns, no credit is given to the life tenant for tax on those dividends. However, if the dividend is received by the trustees under deduction of foreign withholding tax then the beneficiary is eligible to receive the benefit of both the dividend tax credit if the company is in a qualifying territory, and the foreign tax credit although the foreign tax credit may be restricted under the terms of a double tax treaty with the UK. **6.21**

Trustee expenses[47]

The income to which the beneficiary is entitled is that which is left in the trustees' hands after they have paid deductible trust expenses (called trust management expenses or TMEs) and discharged their income tax liability. **6.22**

---

benefit of the dividend rates now (and also lose their personal allowances and annual capital gains tax exemption: see Ch.5).
[44] ITTOIA 2005 ss.397AA(2) and 397C.
[45] ITTOIA 2005 s.397AA(4).
[46] ITTOIA 2005 s.397BA.
[47] HMRC has published revised guidance on trustee management expenses at TSEM 8000–8790.

6.23   What are allowable trustee management expenses in the context of fixed interest trusts?[48] ITA 2007 s.500 provides explicit rules about the way in which expenses incurred by trustees in connection with fixed interest trusts reduce the amount of the beneficiary's income for tax purposes:

> "*the expenses are incurred by the trustees in the current tax year or in an earlier tax year and . . . are chargeable to income by the trustees under a term of the settlement or in accordance with any law . . . and the beneficiary's entitlement . . . is reduced by reference to the expenses.*"[49]

6.24   In the case of interest in possession trusts, "allowable" TMEs do not constitute a tax deduction as such because they represent part of the income that the beneficiary is not entitled to. The provisions of the trust deed or any relevant court order affecting the trust as well as case law are relevant factors in deciding if the expense was correctly deducted from the income.[50] So if a trust deed authorises the trustees to discharge capital expenses to improve land out of income this will reduce the amount of the life tenant's income for higher and additional rate purposes.[51]

EXAMPLE 6.4

Geoffrey is the life tenant of a trust fund. The trustees exercise their overriding powers before October 6, 2008 and partially end his qualifying interest in possession in favour of his son Edward who takes a transitional serial interest. Under the terms of the appointment, Edward's fund is primarily liable to bear any inheritance tax in the event of Geoffrey dying

---

See also 6.47.

[48] See TSEM 8300.

[49] This is a précis of ITA 2007 s.500.

[50] See also 6.35. Case law includes *Murray v CIR* (1926) 11 TC 133 and *MacFarlane v CIR* (1929) 14 TC 540 and *Lord Wolverton v CIR* HL 1931 (income used to pay insurance policies not part of life tenant's income); see also cases where trustees' payments were treated as income of the life tenant, e.g. *Lord Tollemache v CIR* 1926 11 TC 277—trustees paid rates on a house occupied by the life tenant. The life tenant was treated as receiving income of this amount. Similarly in *Sutton v CIT* 1929 14 TC 662 where the Court of Appeal held that the amounts paid by the trustees for the expenses of keeping up the house were the life tenant's income, i.e. the sums were not trustee expenses at all but rather distributions. So if trustees pay council tax or electricity bills of the occupying life tenant this would be regarded as funding his personal liability and therefore be part of his income. See *Tax Bulletin* August 2005 and *HMRC v Clay Discretionary Trust* [2009] STC 469: see 6.47.

[51] For a general consideration of trustee expenses, see 6.35 and following. Case law includes *Murray v CIR* (1926) 11 TC 133 and *MacFarlane v CIR* (1929) 14 TC 540 and *Lord Wolverton v CIR* HL 1931 (income used to pay insurance policies not part of life tenant's income); see also cases where trustees' payments were treated as income of the life tenant, e.g. *Lord Tollemache v CIR* (1926) 11 TC 277—trustees paid rates on a house occupied by the life tenant. The life tenant was treated as receiving income of this amount. Similarly in *Sutton v CIT* 1929 14 TC 662 where the Court of Appeal held that the amounts paid by the trustees for the expenses of keeping up the house were the life tenant's income, i.e. the sums were not trustee expenses at all but rather distributions. So if trustees pay council tax or electricity bills of the occupying life tenant this would be regarded as funding his personal liability and therefore be part of his income. For a detailed consideration of what expenses are, as a matter of law, properly chargeable to income see the *Peter Clay* case noted above.

within seven years. They take out a decreasing seven year term assurance policy on Geoffrey's life which is part of Edward's fund and pay the annual premiums out of his income (under an express power in the trust deed). Edward is entitled to the net income after such premiums (and other allowable expenses) are paid. Accordingly, whilst the trustees pay basic rate tax on the gross income, Edward pays higher rate tax on the net income he actually receives (with a credit for the basic rate tax paid by the trustees on that income). In the absence of an express power to pay premiums out of income it is a capital expense being for the benefit of the whole trust fund.

The order of set off of allowable TMEs

Section 503 prescribes an order for the reduction of the life tenant's income **6.25** by expenses. UK dividend income is reduced first, then dividends from non-resident companies, then savings income and then other income. This relatively generous treatment of expenses does not apply if the trust has non-UK resident beneficiaries and some of the beneficiary's income is untaxed income.[52] The trustees' expenses otherwise available to reduce the beneficiary's income are reduced in the same proportion as that which such non-taxable income bears to the total trust income.

The beneficiary's tax return

The beneficiary receives a net sum which must be grossed-up in order to **6.26** find the sum which enters his total income computation and is entitled to a credit for some of the income tax paid by the trustees; not, however, for the full amount in cases where management expenses have been deducted.[53] Depending on his other income and allowances, a beneficiary may be entitled to reclaim all or some of the tax paid by the trustees. Alternatively, he may be liable for tax at the higher or additional rates or the dividend rates.

EXAMPLE 6.5

An interest in possession trust receives rental income £1,000 and bank interest £800 (lower rate tax of £200 has been deducted at source) in 2011–12. The trustee pays TMEs properly chargeable to income of £250.

Trustee's position

	Rent (£)	Interest (£)
Gross income	1,000	1,000
Tax due	200	200
Net income	800	800

[52] See s.501.
[53] *Macfarlane v IRC* [1929] SC 453.

The trustee receives credit for the tax deducted at source from the bank interest (£200) but has to pay £200 tax on the rent; TMEs do not affect the trustee's position. If the trustees has incurred agency fees or other rental expenses these reduce the rental income and therefore the tax due on that income.

Beneficiary's position

	Rent (£)	Interest (£)
Net income (as above)	800.00	800.00
Minus TMEs (set primarily against savings income)	Nil	(250.00)
800	550.00	
grossed up (@ 20%)	1,000.00	687.50

In this example the entries on the form R185 (Trust Income) given by the trustees to the beneficiary would be:

	Net amount	tax credit	taxable amount
Rent	800.00	200.00	1,000.00
Interest	550.00	137.50	687.50

6.27 The beneficiary uses the information on form R185 to make his self-assessment, or to claim a repayment. Note the complication of the 10 per cent savings rate: the interest is taxed at 10 per cent in the hands of the beneficiary if the beneficiary's total income from all sources is less than his combined personal allowance plus £2,560 (for 2011–12). In the above example the beneficiary is taxable on £1,687.50 and given credit for £337.50 tax (although the trustees have in fact paid £400 tax and received gross income of £2,000).

Taxing an annuitant

6.28 An annuitant under a trust is not entitled to income of the trust as it arises; instead he is taxed on the income that he receives. The trustees deduct income tax from the annuity[54] and the beneficiary is given credit for the basic rate tax deducted at source in the usual way.

IV TAXATION OF TRUSTEES OF DISCRETIONARY AND ACCUMULATION TRUSTS

6.29 As noted previously, trustees are not liable to income tax at the higher rate because they are not individuals. However, the RAT (rate applicable to trusts)

---

[54] ITA 2007 ss.898 and 899.

as well as the £1,000 standard rate band applies to discretionary or accumulation trusts. Since 2010–11 the trust rate has been 50 per cent. The trusts in question are those where there is income arising to trustees in any year of assessment so far as it:

(i)   is income which is to be accumulated or which is payable at the discretion of the trustees or any other person (whether or not the trustees have power to accumulate it)[55];

(ii) is not income from service charges held in trust by a relevant housing body;

(iii) is not, before being distributed the income of any person other than the trustees[56];

(iv) is not income arising under a trust established for charitable purposes only[57]; and

(iv) exceeds the income applied in defraying the expenses of the trustees in that year which are properly chargeable to income (or would be so chargeable but for any express provisions of the trust).[58]

Broadly, trusts which contain a power for trustees to accumulate income, and trusts which give the trustees discretion over the distribution of the income, are caught. In *IRC v Berrill*[59] the settlor's son was entitled to the income from the trust fund unless the trustees exercised a power to accumulate it. Vinelott J. held that TA 1988 s.686 (the forerunner of ITA 2007 s.484) applied because the income was "*income . . . which is payable at the discretion of the trustees*". "*Discretion*" is wide enough to cover a power to withhold income.   **6.30**

The phrase "*income which is to be accumulated*" in ITA 2007 s.480 presumably refers to income which the trustees are under a duty to accumulate. A mere power to accumulate is not sufficient, although it usually means that the income "*is payable at the discretion of the trustees*" within s.480(2). The section does not apply to income which is treated as that of a person other than the trustees, for instance, where a beneficiary has a vested interest in the income (e.g. a life tenant). The type of settlement considered in *Pearson v IRC*,[60] in which the income of a life tenant could be taken from him after it had arisen by the exercise of a power to accumulate it, is subject to the special rate as the income still belongs to the trustees.   **6.31**

Trustees' liability[61]

Trustees are liable to pay income tax under ITA 2007 s.479 as follows: **6.32**

---

[55] ITA 2007 s.479(1).
[56] ITA 2007 s.480. This will exclude the situation where it belongs to an interest in possession beneficiary or is taxed on the settlor. For the position when the income is taxed on the settlor, see s.620 and Ch.7.
[57] ITA 2007 s.479(1)(b). Income produced by pension funds is likewise outside the charge.
[58] ITA 2007 s.484.
[59] [1981] STC 784.
[60] See *Pearson v IRC* [1981] AC 753; [1980] 2 All ER 479 HL; and Ch.22.
[61] ITA 2007 s.479.

(i) tax at the trust rate (loosely called the additional rate or the rate applicable to trusts "RAT"): which is 50 per cent.[62] Thus, where interest etc has been received subject to tax of 20 per cent then the trustees have a further 30 per cent tax to pay.

(ii) on dividends: at 42.5 per cent. Dividend income from UK companies is received with a non-repayable tax credit of 10 per cent. So a dividend of £90 carries a tax credit of £10 producing gross income of £100. This is subject to tax at the trust dividend rate of 42.5 per cent of which 10 per cent is met by the tax credit leaving a further 36.11 on the net amount actually received to be paid by the trustees.[63]

As noted later, certain capital receipts such as offshore income gains, lease premiums, etc are treated as income for the purposes of s.479 and subject to the 50 per cent tax rate (and, of course, the 50 per cent rate applies whether the trust is fixed interest or discretionary).

Standard rate band

6.33 For 2006–07[64] and subsequent tax years the first £1,000 of income taxable at the RAT for discretionary or accumulation trusts will, depending upon the source of the income, be taxed not at 50 per cent but at either the basic (20 per cent),[65] or dividend ordinary rate (10 per cent).[66] This is called "the standard rate band". It applies to income after deduction of allowable trust management expenses. The total maximum tax saving is £200.

It will be appreciated that less tax is then credited to the tax pool which may be a factor in determining the size of distributions. Of course, if there is a sizeable tax pool or income is being accumulated this will not matter and tax is then saved. In fact, the main advantage of the provision is compliance. For trusts where income is £1,000 or less and tax has already been deducted at source there is no further liability and no need to submit a tax return. Where trust income comprises both interest/rental income as well as dividends dividend income is treated as the highest slice of trust income for the purposes of the standard rate band. Hence, the rental income is deemed to form the lowest part of that total income followed by interest and then dividend income.

6.34 ITA 2007 s.492 inserted an anti-fragmentation rule to stop settlors setting up multiple trusts each with £1,000 bands. Where the settlor has made more than one settlement the £1,000 slice must be divided equally between the trusts in existence in the tax year subject to a minimum band of £200 for each

---

[62] Until 2004–05 the rate was 34% on all income with the exception of dividends. From 2004–05 the rate was increased to 40% to "align" it with the higher rate of tax for individuals. From 2010–11 it increased to 50%.

[63] As with other income, the rate was increased from 2004–05 and then again from 2010–11.

[64] The standard rate band was first introduced from 2005–06 and at that time comprised the first £500 of taxable income.

[65] Before 2008–09 one had basic rate income taxed at 22% and savings income taxed at 20%. The change from 2008 to 20% on all income apart from dividends is a welcome simplification despite the controversy it caused.

[66] Section 686D TA 1988 as inserted by FA 2005 s.14 and amended in FA 2006 to raise the limit from £500 to £1,000. The standard rate band is now in ITA 2007 s.491.

settlement. If a settlement has multiple settlors, s.492 is applied to it on the basis of the settlor who has made most settlements. The section operates no matter how long ago the settlement was made[67] and whether or not the settlements are inter vivos or testamentary, produce income, are settlor-interested or interest in possession. Unlike the capital gains tax rules, non-resident trusts have to be counted. If a sub-fund election is made then the sub-fund is treated as a separate settlement for the purpose of dividing the £1,000.[68]

Trustee expenses

Such expenses are not deductible in the hands of the trustees for income tax purposes whether the trust is discretionary or interest in possession.[69] As we have seen, while such expenses are not taken into account in the taxation of the trustees of an interest in possession trust they are allowed in calculating the income of the beneficiary for tax purposes, i.e. in establishing what is the net income to which the beneficiary is *entitled.*   **6.35**

The position is different for discretionary and accumulation trusts where trustees may offset TMEs "properly chargeable to income" against trust income for the purpose of determining the income which is chargeable at the trust rate (RAT) or the dividend trust rate.[70] The terms of the trust deed cannot alter what is deductible for such trusts: it is a question of what expenses are to be set against income as a matter of law.   **6.36**

EXAMPLE 6.6

An accumulation/discretionary trust has the following income:

Dividends £90 net; bank interest £800 net (£200 tax deducted at source).

The trustees have spent £120 on allowable TMEs.

The income tax position is as follows:

TMEs are set first against dividend income, and any excess against the savings income.

	£		£
Dividends gross	100	Bank interest gross	1,000
Less TMEs grossed			
up at dividend rate			
$90 \times 100/90$	100		

---

[67] Compare the capital gains tax position on annual exemptions: see Ch.11.
[68] Whether all this complexity is seriously worth the paper it is written on is debateable. Few people would set up trusts to take advantage of the £1,000 allowance!
[69] See also 6.47 for HMRC's view on the very limited nature of trust management expenses and *Carver v Duncan* [1983] STC 310.
[70] Income so relieved remains subject to the basic rate or dividend ordinary rate.

Less excess TMEs 30 grossed up at 100/80 =	(37.50)
Net taxable income	962.50

£962.50 is taxable at the RAT (50 per cent). As this income has already suffered tax at the lower rate (20 per cent) the further tax to pay is:

£962.50 @ 30% = £288.75

V TAXATION OF DISCRETIONARY BENEFICIARIES

6.37 A discretionary beneficiary has no right to income but is merely the object of the trustees' discretion. However, any payments that he does receive are charged as his income and he receives a credit for the tax paid by the trustees and attributable to that payment.[71] As the trust is discretionary, that tax is at the rate applicable to trusts (50 per cent from April 6, 2010). When the income is distributed this is a new source of income and the beneficiary cannot look through to the underlying assets of the trust. Accordingly no distinction is made between dividend income, savings income and other income in the hands of the beneficiary. All such distributions are taxable under ITTOIA 2005 s.683 as annual payments in the hands of the beneficiary. The payment carries a tax credit of 50 per cent[72] and the beneficiary may also reclaim all or part of that credit depending on his tax position.

6.38 Once an irrevocable decision has been taken by the trustees to retain income as a part of the capital of the fund, the sum accumulated loses its character as income and is treated in the same way as the original fund: i.e. as capital.[73] It follows that the income tax suffered on that income (at 50 per cent) may be irrecoverable[74] and that no further income tax will be charged on the accumulations when they are eventually paid out to the beneficiaries as capital (although such distributions may have capital gains tax and inheritance tax consequences). In deciding whether it is more advantageous to accumulate income or to pay it out to beneficiaries as income, trustees need to consider, inter alia, the tax position of the individual beneficiaries.[75]

EXAMPLE 6.7

In 2011–12 trustees receive non-dividend income of £10,000. A, B, C and D are four discretionary beneficiaries. A has no other income and has an unused personal allowance; B is a basic rate taxpayer (not entitled to the

---

[71] See below for how this operates in relation to the tax pool.
[72] See 6.72 and following.
[73] See Ch.29 for consideration of whether such income has been accumulated and has become capital or is merely "retained".
[74] It will be credited in the tax pool and hence may be used, e.g. if tax rates rise: see 6.45.
[75] Under TA 1925, s.31(2) as amended by the FLRA 1969, s.1(3), Sch.1 Pt I and by TA 2000, s.40(1), Sch.2, para.25 the trustees may apply accumulations of income for the maintenance of the relevant beneficiary: the tax treatment of these payments is obscure. The better view is that they are capital payments.

savings rate); C is subject to tax at a marginal rate of 40 per cent and D is subject to tax at a marginal rate of 50 per cent. The trustees are deciding whether to pay income to any one or more of the beneficiaries or whether to accumulate it. The position is further complicated because the receipt of even a small amount of trust income (as an income rather than capital distribution) by a beneficiary could result in pushing their total income above £100,000 with the result that their personal allowances then reduce. This can mean that relatively small amounts of trust income can result in high marginal rates of tax for an individual beneficiary.

The following tax consequences ensue ignoring the standard rate band:

(1) trustees are subject to tax at 50 per cent on the trust income (i.e. £5,000 tax).
(2) the trustees decide to pay all the net income of £5,000 to A he is entitled to a repayment of tax as follows:

	£
Income (£5,000 × 100/50)	10,000
Deduct: personal allowance (2011–12)	6,475
Income chargeable to tax	3,535
Income tax:	
£3535 at 20%	707
Deduct: Tax treated as paid	5,000
Tax refund	(4,293)

(3) the trustees pay the income to B (the basic rate taxpayer), he is not entitled to a refund of any tax at the basic rate, but, depending on the amount of his other income, may obtain a refund of the extra 30 per cent tax paid by the trustees;
(4) the trustees pay the income to C (the higher rate taxpayer), C can reclaim 10 per cent;
(5) the trustees pay the income to D (the additional rate taxpayer). No further tax is due;
(6) the trustees accumulate the income, the £5,000 tax paid is irrecoverable (it goes into the "tax pool")[76] and the net income of £5,000 is converted into capital.

6.39 From a tax viewpoint, the trustees should avoid payments to C and D: consider paying all or part of the income to A and B, and accumulate any balance. Note that even if the trust deed provides that accumulated income can be paid out in later years and treated as current year income, HMRC do not accept that this means it is an income distribution on which a tax credit can be claimed.[77] Merely having a provision in the trust deed[78] that past accumulations can be paid out as current year income is not sufficient.

[76] See 6.42 for the tax pool.
[77] See 6.65 for a consideration of when payments are income in the hands of the beneficiary.
[78] Or relying on s.31(2) TA 1925. HMRC do not accept that the concluding words of s.31(2)

Non-resident beneficiary's liability

6.40 A non-resident beneficiary of a UK discretionary trust who receives income treated as net of tax may claim relief in respect of the tax exemption on FOTRA securities or under the terms of a double taxation agreement, where such relief would have been available had the beneficiary received the income directly instead of via trustees. Repayment may also be claimed where the beneficiary is not chargeable to UK tax in those circumstances. Relief is only granted if the payment is out of income which arose to the trustees within the six years before the end of the tax year in which the payment was made to the beneficiary.[79]

Dividends

6.41 The position is more complex when the income distributed is dividends. The rules, which came into effect on April 6, 1999, have resulted in a basic higher or additional rate beneficiary being in a worse position if he receives such income via a discretionary trust than if he had personally owned the shares and hence directly received the dividend.[80]

EXAMPLE 6.8

(i) *Position when individual personally owns shares/is an interest in possession beneficiary in a trust*

B, a higher rate taxpayer, receives a net dividend of £900 from the shares which he owns in Family Co Ltd.

	£
Gross dividend	1,000
Tax at 32.5%	325
Deduct: Tax credit (10%)	(100)

have the effect of de-capitalising the accumulations. Where it is known that such accumulations have been released, e.g. by reference to trusts accounts or trustees' resolution, HMRC would argue that what has been received by the beneficiary is received as capital (*Stevenson v Wishart* [1987] STC 266—a beneficiary will normally receive releases of capital as capital). The phrase "*as if they were income arising in the then current year*" is regarded as simply meaning that the trustees are bound by the proviso to s.31(1), just in the same way as they would be if they were deciding whether or not to release current income to or for the benefit of the minor.

[79] See ESC B18. For the position on payments from non-resident trusts see Ch.8.
[80] The life tenant under a fixed interest trust is in no worse position than the outright owner of the shares, given that the tax treatment is "transparent". As a result of the FA 2006 changes in the IHT treatment of trusts the problem in the case of discretionary trusts may be solved by appointing the beneficiary an interest in possession in the shares before the dividend is declared: see A1.19.

Tax payable	225 (or 25% on the net amount received of £900)

Net cash in hand £900 – £225 = 675.

If B had been a basic rate taxpayer he would have been left with cash in hand of £900 since there would have been no further tax to pay.

(ii) *Position if dividends channelled through a discretionary trust*

But consider the position if the £900 net dividends had been distributed to B out of a discretionary trust:

(1) *B is a higher rate taxpayer*; he receives a net distribution of £450 with a credit of £450 (representing tax at 50 per cent).

	£
Gross income	900
Deduct: Tax credit at 50%	450
Reclaim tax of 10%	90
Net cash in hand	540

In effect he does not get the benefit of the dividend rate.

(2) *If B is a basic rate taxpayer*:

	£
Gross income	900
Tax payable by B at 20%	180
Deduct: Tax credit (50%)	450
Repayment due	270

Net cash in hand £450 + £270 = £720

Again he is worse off (by £180) than if the trust was interest in possession because he does not get the benefit of the dividend rate.

By contrast, the non-taxpayer is no worse off than if he had received the dividend direct: in both cases (using the above figures) he ends up with £900 cash in hand since he reclaims all the 50 per cent tax credit.[81]

---

[81] In the light of this disparity in treatment, trustees should consider converting the trust (in whole or in part) into an interest in possession for the relevant beneficiary. Usually this can be done by a simple deed of appointment which can be revocable. In this way some flexibility as to who gets the income is preserved. Such appointments are "nothings" for IHT purposes: see Ch.26. For a precedent, see A1.19.

6.42   As noted above, payments from discretionary trusts represent a new source of income. This means that without special provisions, no credit would be given to the beneficiary for the tax already borne by the trustees. Instead he would receive an income distribution and pay tax on it despite the fact that the trustees had already paid tax. ITA 2007 s.494 therefore provides a tax credit for the beneficiary: trustees operate deduction at source in relation to income distributions to beneficiaries but offset the tax to be deducted on those distributions against tax already paid on their income as it arose (the "tax pool"), i.e. the tax already paid is credited against the tax that is now to be deducted. These rules only apply to UK resident trusts.[83]

6.43   The trustees must provide the beneficiary with a statement showing the grossed up amount of the payment: the sum deducted under s.494 and the actual amount of the discretionary payment.[84]

If the trust is UK resident but has received foreign income which has suffered foreign tax, the foreign tax does not go into the tax pool but ESC B18 allows the beneficiary credit for the foreign tax insofar as the foreign income arose in the tax year of the payment or in the five previous tax years.

6.44   Section 496 provides that when the trustees calculate the income tax that they must pay when they distribute income, they can reduce the payment by the total amount of tax in the tax pool available for that year. So if they make a payment of £50 to a beneficiary this is treated as a gross payment of £100 on which £50 tax has been deducted. If the tax pool only contains tax of £30 then the trustees must pay another £20. If the trust tax pool contains tax of £60 then no further tax is due and the pool is reduced to £10. If the trust has accumulated income in the past then it may have a substantial tax pool.[85]

6.45   The tax pool is the sum of the tax suffered by the trustees on income that has already been taxed under ITA 2007 ss.479 and 491 (i.e. at the trust rate or the new standard rate). It comprises tax actually paid by the trustees together with tax credits. However, from April 6, 1999 the tax credit at 10 per cent on dividend income cannot enter the tax pool. This is to ensure that the general principle that the credit is irrecoverable will not be breached by the dividend being channelled through a trust. Needless to say, this greatly complicates the position and may increase the tax burden on the beneficiary. Of course, the increase in the rate to 50 per cent means that the tax pool may well be insufficient to cover the tax owing when the trustees make distributions because past income will have been taxed at a lower rate (so that the amount in the tax pool is correspondingly low).

The beneficiary, if taxable at a lower rate, can claim repayment of all or part of the income tax the trustees have deducted.

---

[82]   ITA 2007 ss.494–498.
[83]   Section 493(1)(b).
[84]   See ITA 2007 s.495.
[85]   This tax pool's running total started on April 5, 1973 for a trust which then had income available for distribution.

EXAMPLE 6.9

On April 6, 2011 a discretionary trust had a tax pool brought forward of £498. In 2011–12 the trust receives non-dividend income of £2,000 on which it pays tax at 50% = £1,000. During that year, the trustees exercise their discretion to distribute income of £1,600. This is treated as a gross sum of £1,000 × 100/50 = £2,000 from which income tax at 50% = £1,000 has been deducted. The trustees must account to HMRC for £1,000, but have a credit of £498 plus £1,000 = £1,498 so that no further tax is payable and this leaves £498 tax carried forward in the "tax pool".

Dividend income and the tax pool

When dividend income is received and then distributed by trustees the position is more complex: **6.46**

(i) that income is taxed at the "dividend trust rate" of 42.5 per cent (32.5 per cent until 2010–11);

(ii) only tax actually paid by the trustees is credited to the tax pool: therefore on a cash dividend of £90 the tax pool is credited with £32.49 tax (effectively 36.11 per cent of the net dividend)[86];

(iii) if the net income remaining is then distributed the trustees are accountable for tax at 50 per cent on the grossed up distribution in the normal way.

EXAMPLE 6.10

Dividend income is received by discretionary trustees and dealt with as follows:

	£
Dividend received	900
Tax credit (1/9th)	100
Gross income	1,000
Deduct: Tax @ 42.5%	425
Income after tax	575
Tax due from trustees	425
Deduct: Tax credit	100
Additional tax due	325

---

[86] See ITA 2007 s.493 formerly TA 1988 s.687(3).

149

Amount credited to tax pool	325
Cash in hands of trustees	575

If the trustees accumulate the net income there is no further income tax to pay and £575 becomes capital. But if the trustees distribute that income:

(1) the non-repayable tax credit cannot be added to the tax pool, and so
(2) if the trustees distribute to a beneficiary the whole of the income after tax, the position is:

	£
Net income distribution to beneficiary	575
Addition for tax @ 50%	575
Gross income of beneficiary	1,150
Tax due under s.496	575
Deduct: Tax credited to tax pool	325
Shortfall	250

In this situation, unless there is a balance in the tax pool brought forward in order to "frank" the whole amount of the tax of £575, the shortfall has to be funded from other sources. In such cases the trustees may therefore have to adopt an alternative strategy. For instance, they may take the view that the distribution to the beneficiary and the tax payable under s.496 must be wholly met from the net of tax income received, £575 in the above example. To achieve this, the distribution to the beneficiary must be limited to 50 per cent of the cash dividend received. Continuing the example above, the result would be:

	£
Distribution to beneficiary £900 × 50%	450
Addition for tax @ 50%	450
Gross income of beneficiary	900
Tax due	450
Deduct: Tax credited to tax pool	325
Balance paid by trustees	125

This is met out of the cash balance held by the trustees of £575 less the net payment to the beneficiary of £450 = £125.

TMEs are not deductible in calculating the trustees' liability to tax at the basic   **6.47**
rate but may be deducted in arriving at the amount of income chargeable at
the rate applicable to trusts.[87] The rewritten legislation in ITA 2007 s.484(5)
provides for the deduction of expenses if:

> "*(a) they are expenses of the trustees; and*
> *(b) they are properly chargeable to income, ignoring the express terms*
> *of the settlement.*"

In *Carver v Duncan*[88] trustees paid premiums on policies of life assurance out   **6.48**
of the income of the trust as they were permitted to do under the trust deed.
The House of Lords held that the payments were not deductible[89] which was
limited to expenses properly chargeable to income under the general law. As
the life assurance premiums were for the benefit of capital they should have
been borne by capital. Accordingly the express provision in the instrument did
not bring the sums within the section.

Lord Templeman stated that income "*must bear all ordinary outgoings of*   **6.49**
a recurrent nature, such as rates and taxes, and interest on charges and encum-
brances". However, just because an expense is recurrent it does not mean
that it is of an income nature. For instance, the annual premiums in that case
were "*a recurrent charge but not an ordinary outgoing*". He cited *Re Bennett*[90]
as authority for the proposition that an "*ordinary outgoing*" was a payment
"*made in order to secure the income of the property*". Expenses incurred for
the benefit of both the income and capital beneficiaries must, he concluded,
be charged to capital.

Peter Clay case[91]

In this case, expenses totalled £249,871 for the tax year for a discretionary   **6.50**
trust one of six similar trusts with the same trustees. Non-executive trustees
were paid fees for their limited time in attending meetings. An executive trustee
devoted 30 hours per week to the six trusts. The investments were diversified
on a worldwide basis, leading to work dealing with double tax treaties and
withholding taxes in about 17 countries and monitoring the interest rates
on the currencies. The legislation (now in s.484) refers to expenses properly
chargeable to income but there is no statutory definition of such expenses. The
taxpayer argued that many expenses are incurred for the benefit of the trust
property as a whole but are still properly chargeable to income. The correct
test was whether the expense was an ordinary outgoing of a recurrent nature
that was necessary or designed to maintain income.

---

[87] Note, however, that if the trust is settlor-interested they are not deductible against the settlor's
liability: see 7.19.
[88] [1985] AC 1082. *Carver* has been followed in the *Clay* case which is considered at 6.50. See also
TSEM 8001–8790.
[89] Under TA 1988 s.686(2)(d) (now ITA 2007 s.484).
[90] [1896] 1 Ch 778.
[91] [2008] STC 928.

6.51   HMRC maintained that any expenses which benefited both capital and income beneficiaries could not be apportioned between income and capital but were to be charged entirely to capital and that the only expenses attributable to income are those paid in order to secure that income. This applied particularly to the investment managers' fees which amounted to £176,000. The taxpayer contended that much of this work related to advice on the investment of trust income which had been accumulated.

6.52   The Special Commissioner decided that the trustee had a general obligation to maintain a fair balance between the interests of income and capital beneficiaries so the trustees should allocate proportionately expenses between income and capital unless they were exclusively capital expenses.[92] The High Court[93] rejected this proposition (based on the statement in *Carver v Duncan* that the payment of the fees of the investment advisers which were incurred for the benefit of the fund as a whole would be properly chargeable to capital). There was potential conflict between the first proposition in *Carver* that income must bear all ordinary outgoings of a recurrent nature such as rates and taxes and capital must bear all costs charges and expenses incurred for the benefit of the whole estate since some expenses might fall into both categories, e.g. buildings insurance. However, the judge held that he was bound by the principle that where the expense was incurred for the benefit of the whole estate it must be paid out of capital.

6.53   The Court of Appeal[94] concluded that there were three categories of trust expenses:

(i)   those incurred for the benefit of the estate as a whole (i.e. for the benefit of both income and capital beneficiaries);

(ii) those incurred exclusively for the benefit of the income beneficiaries;

(iii) those incurred exclusively for the benefit of the capital beneficiaries.

Expenses falling into categories (i) and (iii) are wholly charged to capital. Expenses within (ii) wholly to income. However, when there is an expense within (ii) that is not separately recorded, the overall expense can be apportioned on a time basis (if there are no time records the trustees should make a reasonable estimate). As a result the Court permitted the apportionment of the executive trustees' fees and bank charges; custodian fees and professional fees for accountancy and administration.[95]

Specific illustrations

6.54   HMRC gives a number of specific examples of how expenses fall to be treated under the general law.[96] For instance, the following expenses may be deducted against income:

---

[92] [2007] STC (SCD) 362 and see *Re Duke of Norfolk's Settlement Trusts* [1979] 1 Ch 37 at 62 and TA 1925 s.22(4).
[93] [2008] STC 928.
[94] *RCC v Peter Clay Trust* [2009] STC 469.
[95] For the approach of HMRC to apportionment see TSEM 8162–8168.
[96] See TSEM 8700 and following.

(i) *accountancy/preparation of trust accounts*: time spent calculating the trust's income (but not gains) and time spent on the collection of income;

(ii) *preparation of the trust tax return*: more likely to be income than capital because of the obligation to return income each year. Similarly, time spent on repayment claims;

(iii) *tax advice*: only where it exclusively benefits the income beneficiary;

(iv) *bank loan/overdraft*: whether the interest is deductible from income depends on the use of the moneys borrowed. For instance, interest on a loan to purchase an income producing property (but not, apparently, a loan to pay IHT);

(v) *income distributions*: the costs (e.g. in trustee deliberation time) is deductible;

(vi) *insurance premiums for trust assets*: generally not deductible, but exceptionally allowed where:

    (a) building insurance for a property; and
    (b) the lease contains an obligation to insure; and
    (c) the trustees are the lessees; and
    (d) the property is occupied by beneficiaries in accordance with the terms of the trust; and
    (e) neither the beneficiaries nor any tenants are under an obligation to pay the premiums;

(vii) *penalties and tax related interest*: penalties are not deductible: interest may be if it relates to income tax.

Timing issues

It was decided in *Peter Clay* that trustees can use a cash basis or an accruals **6.55** basis provided they are consistent. This has changed since the case; ITA 2007 s.485 makes it clear that trustees' expenses are deductible when incurred rather than when paid.

Resumé

TME's are different in kind from expenses of a trade or letting which are **6.56** deducted in arriving at the taxable profit. They comprise the running costs of the trust and their treatment depends on whether *as a matter of trust* law they are capital or income. To be deductible for discretionary trusts the expenses must be incurred *solely* for the benefit of the income beneficiary (e.g. in the collection/calculation of his income). By contrast expenses incurred for the benefit of the trust fund as a whole are payable out of capital: this will include the majority of trust expenses. TMEs should be grossed up at the appropriate rate.[97] So, if TME's are £1,000, which have been paid out of net income, the gross equivalent is:

---

[97] For the order of set off, see 6.25.

(a) £1,110 if paid out of dividends (grossed up at 10 per cent);

(b) £1,250 if paid out of savings or other income. (Before tax year 2008–09 if paid out of non-savings income they would have been grossed up to £1,282). Now the grossing up is only at the basic rate of 20 per cent.

In the case of trusts in which part of the fund is held on an interest in possession trust and part on discretionary trusts IR 392 requires the trustees to make a just and reasonable apportionment of TME's between the income of the trustees and the income of the beneficiaries who are entitled to it. In reality, it is likely that more expenses will be attributed to the portion of the fund held on discretionary trusts where there is additional tax and accounting work.

VIII CAPITAL RECEIPTS TAXED AS INCOME

6.57   From June 22, 2010 all trustees suffer CGT at a rate of 28 per cent (previously 18 per cent from April 6, 2008 and before that 40 per cent).[98] In certain circumstances capital receipts are *deemed* to be income and taxed at 50 per cent (although they can benefit from the standard rate band if appropriate).

FA 2006 introduced a new s.686A[99] to gather together the various cases where capital receipts of trustees are taxed as income. This section can apply to interest in possession trusts as well as to discretionary trusts. It is the trustees not the life tenant (or discretionary beneficiaries) who are liable for the tax since the receipts form part of the capital not the income of the trust fund (and therefore are not distributed to the life tenant).

6.58   The capital receipts taxed as income include[100]:

(i) *share buy-backs:* when trustees sell shares back to the company (a "share buy-back") the proceeds are generally taxed as income.[101] A potential difficulty arose with shares sold by the trustees of a settlor-interested trust in that the income distribution would be taxed in the settlor's hands but there would be no TCGA 1992 s.37 reduction against the capital gain since this is only given to the person making the disposal, i.e. the trustees. Consequently the trustees would also suffer a capital gain based on the same sale proceeds. However, HMRC confirmed that they would apply TMA 1970 s.32 to eliminate the capital gain in such cases.[102]

The 2006 buy-back provision was defectively drafted in relation to discretionary trusts in that the wording of s.686A meant that on a buy-back of shares the whole of the payment by the company to the trustees was

---

[98] For the CGT position of trustees, see Ch.11
[99] This section is now rewritten in ITA 2007 s.482.
[100] But see ITA 2007 s.482 for full list.
[101] TA 1988 s.686A(2) inserted by FA 2006 s.89 Sch.13 para.3 in respect of payments made from April 6, 2006. See Ch.17 for further details of the capital gains treatment.
[102] This enables HMRC to reduce all or part of a tax charge if they are satisfied the taxpayer has suffered tax more than once for the same transaction.

taxable including the original subscription price, not just the element representing the distribution.[103] The position was corrected in FA 2007 with effect from April 6, 2006[104];

(ii) *accrued income profits*[105];

(iii) *ITA 2007 s.752* and following *(old TA 1988 s.776)*: capital receipts on a sale of land can be taxed as income if the land was acquired or developed with a view to realising a gain[106];

(iv) *Lease premium payments*: the grant of a lease for a period which does not exceed 50 years in consideration for the payment of a premium, results in part of the premium being taxed as income.[107] For instance, if the trustees grant a lease for 35 years for a premium of £100,000, part of that premium is taxed as income.[108] The trustees suffer tax at 50 per cent on such deemed income[109];

(v) *Offshore income gains*[110]: since such gains often arise in non-resident trusts and the tax treatment differs according to whether the trust is settlor-interested or not, they are discussed separately at Ch.52. The complexity of these provisions, involving as they do both the transfer of assets rules and the offshore capital gains tax legislation, is horrendous! The main point to remember is that such gains are taxed at 50 per cent not 18 per cent. There is no annual capital gains tax exemption. From April 6, 2008 there is a big disincentive to realising offshore income gains as opposed to "normal" gains. Further, a beneficiary with a qualifying[111] interest in possession who dies will trigger an income tax charge on such gains: there is no tax-free uplift;

(vi) *Gains from contracts for life insurance*[112];

(vii) *Profits from deep discounted securities*.[113]

Accrued income profits and stock dividends

The accrued income scheme applies to trustees[114] (and, unlike personal representatives, trustees do not benefit from the de minimis £5,000 exemption). **6.59**

---

[103] See Ministerial Statement issued on October 9, 2006 by the Paymaster General.
[104] See ITA 2007 s.482 type 1(b).
[105] See 6.59.
[106] TA 1988 s.686A(2)(j).
[107] ITTOIA 2005 s.277, TA 1988 s.686A(2)(d).
[108] ITTOIA 2005 s.277.
[109] Before April 6, 2006 the income tax charge was limited to basic rate.
[110] See TA 1988 ss.757–764.
[111] For IHT purposes, see Ch.26.
[112] ITTOIA 2005 s.467.
[113] ITA 2007 s.482.
[114] Formerly TA 1988 ss.710–728 rewritten as ITA 2007 s.619.

Example 6.11

UK resident trustees hold £100,000 in nominal value of Government stock paying interest at five per cent pa on June 30 and December 31. They sell that stock *cum div* to a third party X on September 30, 2011 for £99,780:

(1) *Trust tax position*: subject to income tax in 2011–12 on three months' accrued interest (£1,250) for the period from June 30, 2011 (the last payment date) to September 30, 2011 (disposal or settlement date).

(2) *X's tax position*: assuming that he retains the stock until December 31, 2011, he will then be subject to income tax on the interest paid as follows:

Interest payment to December 31, 2011	£2,500
Deduct accrued interest purchased (July 1 to September 30)	£1,250
Reduced amount taxable	£1,250

(3) Had the sale been *ex div* so that the interest payment of £5,000 to December 31, 2011 was retained by the trustees, the trust would be taxed on £1,250 of that figure and the balance of £1,250 (i.e. interest from the date of disposal to the date of sale) would be taxed in X's hands.

6.60 Where the assets of a trust include shares in a company and the trustees receive shares either as a stock dividend or on the demerger of the company, it can be uncertain whether in terms of trust law the shares received are an addition to income or capital. The courts have generally taken the view that the presumed intention of the settlor should be carried out. So if there is an express provision in the trust deed which covers the receipt of stock dividends, this is relevant in deciding whether the shares received belong to the income beneficiary or to the capital of the trust.

The position can be complex but the rules, briefly, are as follows:

(i) a distribution of shares by way of simple bonus issue to trustees will be treated as capital of the trust.[115]

(ii) In the absence of a discretion for the trustees to determine whether demerged shares are to be treated as income or capital, on an indirect demerger the trustees can treat the receipt of shares under the demerger as capital of the trust.[116]

(iii) On a direct demerger the demerged shares are generally received by the trustees as income of the trust, being a dividend out of accumulated profits under company law.[117]

---

[115] *Bouch v Sproule* (1887) 12 App Cas 385.
[116] See *Re Lee (Deceased)* [1993] 3 All ER 926.
[117] See *Hill v Permanent Trustee Company of New South Wales Ltd* [1930] AC 720. The *Tax*

(iv) Stock dividends: The effect of the Court of Appeal decision in *Howell v Trippier*[118] is that stock dividends received by a discretionary trust are taxable at the dividend trust rate with a credit for tax at the dividend ordinary rate.[119]

The Law Commission in its Report[120] was critical of the current law on the basis of its inappropriate and unpredictable results, complexity and its uncertainty in application to novel arrangements. It recommended that trustees should have a power of allocation. This power would allow trustees, taking the trust's receipts over a given period, to allocate all or part of one or more trust receipts as necessary in order to ensure that a balance was kept between classes of beneficiaries entitled to capital and to income. This would be coupled with a statutory requirement to balance investment returns arising under a power of allocation, applying solely in the context of the exercise of the power of allocation. **6.61**

It also recommended that shares distributed in a tax-exempt demerger[121] should be classified as capital for trust law purposes. This would classify as capital shares received as a result both of direct and indirect demergers. We also recommend that when such a distribution is made, trustees should have a power to make a payment of capital to beneficiaries interested in income where otherwise there would be prejudice to those beneficiaries. **6.62**

On March 22, 2010 Bridget Prentice, the then Parliamentary Under-Secretary for Justice, said: **6.63**

> "*The Government have carefully considered the report and are pleased to announce that they accept the Law Commission's recommendations. It is now intended to consult on these reforms and the proposed draft legislation.*"

IX SUPPLEMENTING INCOME WITH CAPITAL

Capital distributions from a UK resident trust to beneficiaries are not generally subject to income tax.[122] Once an accumulation of income is made, a subsequent distribution of that accumulated fund is generally a distribution of capital and tax accordingly in the hands of the beneficiary.[123] **6.64**

If, however, a beneficiary is entitled to a fixed amount of income each year which is to be made up out of capital should the trust fail to produce the **6.65**

Bulletin October 1994, Issue 13 sets out the way in which HMRC tax the receipt of such shares.

[118] [2004] STC 1245.

[119] See (SWTI) 2005 276.

[120] "*Capital and income in trusts: classification and apportionment*" published May 7, 2009.

[121] The Law Commission would have preferred to make a recommendation in relation to all demergers but was unable to do so because the introduction of flexibility in treatment of receipts would have impacted on the tax treatment of interests in possession and might have caused an interest in possession trust to lose its status as such for both income tax and, where relevant, inheritance tax purposes.

[122] The position is different if the distribution is from a trust with "relevant income" because it is or has been non-UK resident and has accumulated income: see further Ch.8.

[123] See *Stanley v IRC* [1944] 1 All ER 230.

requisite amount of income, such topping-up payments are taxed as income in his hands.[124] In other words, to determine whether a sum forms part of a beneficiary's total income, it is necessary to ascertain, not whether the sum arises from capital or income of the trust, but whether it is received by the beneficiary "in the quality of income".

EXAMPLE 6.12

(1) The testator's widow has been left an annuity of £4,000 a year; the trustees are required to pay it out of the capital of the trust fund if the income is insufficient. The widow is liable to income tax on the payments that she receives whether paid out of income or capital because they are annual payments.

(2) The settlor's widow is given an annuity of £4,000 a year and, in addition, the trustees have the power "*to apply capital for the benefit of the widow in such manner as they shall in their absolute discretion think fit*". Any supplements out of capital may escape income tax because the widow has an interest in both income and capital, and payments out of capital are treated as advances of capital rather than as income payments.[125]

6.66   HMRC has in the past considered that payments made out of trust capital can be taxed as income in the hands of a recipient beneficiary even when the payments are not paid in augmentation of an income entitlement: the income nature of the payment in the hands of the recipient can be discovered by looking at its size, recurrence, and purpose. In *Stevenson v Wishart*[126] discretionary trust income was paid out in full each year to a charity and capital sums were then paid to one of the beneficiaries who had suffered a heart attack. The purpose of the payments was to cover medical expenses and the cost of living in a nursing home. HMRC's argument that these sums were paid out for an income purpose and were therefore subject to income tax was rejected both at First Instance and by the Court of Appeal. Fox L.J. stated:

> "... *there is nothing in the present case which indicates that the payments were of an income nature except their recurrence. I do not think that is sufficient. The trustees were disposing of capital in exercise of a power over capital. They did not create a recurring interest in property. If, in exercise of a power over capital, they chose to make at their discretion regular payments of capital to deal with the special problems of [the beneficiary's] last years rather than release a single sum to her of a large amount, that does not seem to me to create an income interest. Their power was to appoint capital. What they appointed remained capital.*"

---

[124] See *Brodie's Will Trustees v IRC* (1933) 17 TC 432; *Cunard's Trustees v IRC* [1946] 1 All ER 159 CA.

[125] The trustees should resolve to make top-up payments in the exercise of their discretion to pay capital: avoid making such payments "automatically".

[126] [1987] 2 All ER 428, [1987] 1 WLR 1204 CA.

The Court of Appeal stressed the exceptional nature of nursing-home payments. Fox L.J., for instance, stated that such expenditure, although involving day-to-day maintenance, was emergency expenditure of very substantial amounts which would usually fall outside normal income resources. The Court of Appeal noted that the mere fact of recurrence was not in itself sufficient to make the payments income.

It is understood that HMRC currently treat advances or appointments **6.67** out of trust capital as capital in the hands of the recipient beneficiary unless:

(i) the payments in question are designed to augment income[127];

(ii) the payments in question really amount to an annuity[128]; or

(iii) the trust instrument contains a provision authorising the use of capital to maintain a beneficiary in the same degree of comfort as had been the case in the past.

Why does it matter if a distribution is income or capital

Whether distributions are income or capital in the hands of the beneficiaries **6.68** is relevant in tax terms for the following reasons:

(a) If payments are income distributions the beneficiary receives a tax credit of 50 per cent but the UK resident trustees may have insufficient in the tax pool to frank that credit and have more tax to pay.[129]

(b) An income receipt may push the beneficiary into higher rates of tax or result in the loss of personal allowances.

(c) An income receipt may enable a basic rate or non-taxpayer to reclaim some or all of the 50 per cent tax paid by the discretionary trustees.

(d) If a distribution is capital exceptionally the beneficiary may be taxed on it as relevant income[130] or be subject to capital gains tax[131] but will receive no tax credit for the income actually paid in the past by the trustees. The trustees will not deduct 50 per cent tax.

(e) If a distribution is capital then the trustees may have to pay inheritance tax on it given that it may be a distribution out of a relevant property settlement, unless the beneficiary suffers income tax on the receipt or the trust is an excluded property settlement.[132]

---

[127] See *Jackson's Trustees v IRC* (1942) 25 TC 13.
[128] See *Cunard's Trustees v IRC* [1946] 1 All ER 159 CA.
[129] See 6.45 above.
[130] See Ch.8—this could apply even if the trust is now UK resident if it has a pool of relevant untaxed income that arose while the trust was non-UK resident or it has received transfers from other non-resident trusts that have a pool of available relevant income.
[131] If the trust has stockpiled gains which have not yet been matched. The trust may have been non-UK resident in the past or have received capital from another trust with stockpiled gains. See Ch.19.
[132] See Ch.29.

(f) If a distribution is capital then any benefit of ESC B 18 is lost (foreign or UK tax credits.)[133]

X TA 1925 S.31[134]

6.69 The effects of s.31 (which may be excluded or modified by the trust instrument) may be stated in the following propositions:

(i) If a minor is absolutely entitled to the capital even though the income is retained by the trustees, it belongs to the minor. Therefore, ITA 2007 s.479 is inapplicable because the income is that of a person other than the trustee; were the minor to die, both capital and income accumulations would belong to his estate and pass on his intestacy. The income is taxed on the minor (or the parent if he is the settlor): see Ch.7.

(ii) If a minor has a vested interest in income only (for example if the trust is to Z for life when Z is seven years old), the trustees may accumulate that income. Were the minor to die the accumulations would not pass to his estate. In this case s.31 has a divesting effect and for income tax purposes the accumulated income is subject to the rate applicable to trusts because it does not belong to any particular beneficiary as it arises. In *Stanley v IRC*[135] it was stated that

> "*s.31 has effected a radical change in the law. [The beneficiary] is, in fact, for all practical purposes in precisely the same position as if his interest in surplus income were contingent*".

(iii) If a beneficiary is contingently entitled to trust capital on attaining an age in excess of 18, s.31 vests the income of that contingent interest in the beneficiary from the age of 18.[136] In this case the section has a "vesting effect." This provision was significant in the context of accumulation and maintenance trusts in which capital entitlement was deferred until age 25 (or later). The beneficiary normally becomes entitled to income at 18 as a result of the operation of s.31 unless specifically excluded. Where the age of capital vesting was over 25, s.31 of TA 1925 could save a trust from falling outside the accumulation and maintenance trust rules before March 22, 2006.[137]

---

[133] See Ch.8.
[134] i.e. TA 1925 s.31 as amended by FLRA 1969 s.1(3), Sch.1, Pt I and by TA 2000 s.40(1), Sch.2, para.25.
[135] *Stanley v IRC* [1944] KB 255, [1944] 1 All ER 230 CA.
[136] TA 1925 s.31(1)(ii) as amended by FLRA 1969 s.1(3), Sch.1 Pt I.
[137] See Ch.30.

CHAPTER 7

INCOME TAX AND CGT ISSUES ARISING IN RELATION TO SETTLOR-INTERESTED UK RESIDENT TRUSTS

Precedent

I GENERAL POINTS

This chapter considers the capital gains tax and income tax position of trusts   **7.01** which are settlor-interested or trusts where anti-avoidance provisions result in the income being taxed on the settlor. The capital gains taxation of non-resident trusts which are settlor-interested[1] is dealt with in Ch.19 so this chapter looks at the capital gains tax position only where the trust is settlor-interested and UK resident.

There is no coherence in the legislation. A trust can be settlor-interested   **7.02** for capital gains tax purposes but not for income tax purposes. It can be settlor-interested if non-UK resident but cease to be so once imported; it can be settlor-interested for certain capital gains tax purposes but not for others[2]; and it can be settlor-interested for capital gains tax and income tax purposes but yet there is no reservation of benefit for inheritance tax purposes.[3] Now

---

[1] The capital gains tax definition of a settlor-interested UK resident trust is different from the definition of a settlor-interested non-UK resident trust. See below and Ch.19.

[2] For example the rules on what is a settlor-interested trust are different for Sch.4A purposes and for s.165 TCGA 1992 (hold-over relief) purposes.

[3] For example, a settlor might be excluded but his wife and children only can benefit. This would

that discretionary/accumulation trusts pay income tax at 50 per cent on all but the first £1,000 of income (unless they receive dividend income in which case the rate is 42.5 per cent on the gross and 36.11 per cent on the net)[4] and all UK trusts pay 28 per cent capital gains tax on gains[5] it is questionable whether some of this anti-avoidance legislation is necessary. The settlor often obtains no great advantage in diverting income to a trust[6] or receiving capital benefits but the anti-avoidance legislation remains on the statute book and greatly complicates compliance. Similarly, now that hold-over relief has been abolished for gifts to settlor-interested trusts some legislation is redundant. The Government took the opportunity to repeal Sch.4B (transfers of value) in relation to UK settlor-interested trusts but is Sch.4A really needed now (deemed disposal where beneficiary sells an interest in a settlor-interested trust)?

II SETTLEMENTS IN WHICH THE SETTLOR RETAINS AN INTEREST FOR INCOME TAX PURPOSES[7]

7.03 This section includes settlements where the income is taxed on the settlor, even if the settlement is not strictly settlor-interested, namely:

(i) a settlement where the settlor retains an interest[8]; and

(ii) a settlement on unmarried minor children of the settlor[9];

(iii) capital payments including loans to the settlor.

WHAT IS A SETTLEMENT?

7.04 A "settlement" for income tax purposes is widely defined as follows:

> "*includes any disposition, trust, covenant, agreement, arrangement or transfer of assets. . .*".[10]

not generally involve a reservation of benefit for inheritance tax purposes unless s.102A FA 1989 was breached: see Ch.33. Similarly the trust could provide that the settlor could only benefit from capital in limited circumstances, e.g. if all the earlier trusts failed. In these circumstances this would be a "carve-out" for inheritance tax purposes (see Ch.22) but generally such a trust would be settlor-interested for capital gains tax and income tax purposes.

4 See Ch.6.
5 In respect of disposals from June 23, 2010 F(No.2)A 2010 Sch.1.
6 Contrast the position in the 1970s when the income of discretionary trusts was taxed at 45% but the income of individuals at rates of up to 83% or for unearned income 98%.
7 The income tax settlement provisions were enacted piecemeal during the 20th century and finally rationalised (to some extent!) in 1995 becoming TA 1988 s.660A–G and s.677–682A. They were re-enacted into plain English(!) by ITTOIA 2005 in Ch.5 of Pt V.
8 ITTOIA 2005 s.624.
9 Although not strictly settlor-interested we discuss the anti-avoidance provisions in this section.
10 ITTOIA 2005 s.620(1) on the scope of this provision, see the *Arctic Systems* case at 7.65 and following.

HMRC do not regard the definition as applicable only to spouses and minor children. It applies to any arrangement for income to be payable to a person other than the settlor provided that the settlor has an interest in the settlement where the arrangements are:

(i) bounteous; or

(ii) not commercial; or

(iii) not at arms length; or

(iv) in the case of an outright gift between spouses, wholly or substantially a right to income.[11]

Note especially that a settlement requires the settlor to give bounty: commercial arrangements are not caught.[12]

There are notable differences between the income tax and CGT definitions of "settlor-interested trusts": **7.05**

(i) the meaning of "settlement" is much wider for income tax purposes and can include more than just a trust;

(ii) a trust which benefits minor children of the settlor is not settlor-interested for income tax purposes although distributions to those children may trigger anti-avoidance provisions. Contrast the capital gains tax definition of settlor-interested;

(iii) capital gains tax and income tax have different "backward tails". In the case of hold-over relief, a claw back charge can arise if the trust becomes settlor-interested within six years after the tax year of the disposal into trust on which the gain was held-over. In the case of income tax, future trust income can be taxed on the settlor if he has received a capital sum from the trust in the previous 10 years whether or not the trust is otherwise settlor-interested.[13]

Who is the settlor?

Settlor is defined as any person by whom the settlement was made.[14] A person who: **7.06**

(i) has made or entered into the settlement directly or indirectly;

(ii) has provided or undertaken to provide funds directly or indirectly for the purposes of the settlement; or

---

[11] See HMRC TSEM 4200.
[12] *IRC v Plummer* [1979] STC 793; *Bulmer v IRC* [1966] 3 All ER 801: by contrast the IHT definition is not so limited: see Ch.24.
[13] ITTOIA 2005 ss.619 and 646. Note that a "settlement" is widely defined for these purposes: see ITTOIA 2005 s.620. On "arrangements" see *Butler v Wildin* [1989] STC 22; 61 TC 666.
[14] ITTOIA 2005 s.620 although see also FA 2006 Sch.13 inserting TA 1988 ss.685B–D (now ITA 2007 s.467) which defines settlor for general purposes without repealing ITTOIA 2005 s.620.

(iii) has made with any other person a reciprocal arrangement for that other person to make or enter into a settlement[15]

is a settlor.[16]

Where a settlement has more than one settlor, each settlor is treated as the only settlor of a deemed separate settlement, with rules as to the property and income which is to be treated as belonging to that separate settlement.[17]

When is a trust settlor-interested for income tax purposes?

7.07 A settlor has an interest in the settlement for income tax purposes[18] if the property or any related property[19] is or will or may become payable to or applicable for his benefit or that of his spouse[20] in any circumstances, including cases where the trust fund reverts to the settlor under a revocable settlement, or the settlor is a discretionary beneficiary (or could be added as such).[21] However, there is an exception for a tax year in which the settlor is not UK domiciled or not resident or ordinarily resident in the UK and if settlement income arising in that tax year is exempt by virtue of his domicile or residence. For example, non-UK source income of an offshore trust arising to a UK resident foreign domiciliary.[22] Where income is excluded under this rule it may be treated as arising in a subsequent year in which it is remitted to the UK and is then taxable on the settlor at that time on the assumption that if the settlor was entitled to the income he would be chargeable to UK tax on it by reason of his residence in the UK.[23]

7.08 The settlor is *not* deemed to have an interest in settled property if and so long as none of that property, and no related property, could become payable to or applicable for the benefit of the settlor or the spouse or civil partner of the settlor, except in the event of:

(i) the bankruptcy of a beneficiary[24];

(ii) an assignment of or charge of his equitable interest by a beneficiary[25];

(iii) in the case of a marriage settlement, the death of both parties to the marriage and of all or any of the children of the marriage[26]; or

---

[15] Compare the definition of settlor for capital gains tax purposes at 9.24 and for inheritance tax purposes at 24.19.

[16] See *Crosland v Hawkins* (1961) 39 TC 493 CA and *Mills v IRC* [1974] STC 130 HL.

[17] Compare inheritance tax provisions on multiple settlors: see Ch.24.

[18] See ITOIA 2005 ss.624–648.

[19] In this context related has the same meaning as "derived" which is discussed at 7.09. Property can be related and derived even if not in the subject settlement: see *West v Trennery* discussed at 7.57.

[20] Spouse includes, since December 5, 2005, a registered civil partner.

[21] ITTOIA 2005, s.624.

[22] ITTOIA 2005 s.648(2)(3).

[23] The effects of this rule are discussed further in Ch.8.

[24] ITTOIA 2005, s.625(2)(a).

[25] ITTOIA 2005, s.625(2)(b).

[26] ITTOIA 2005, s.625(2)(d).

(iv) the death of a child of the settlor who had become beneficially entitled to the property or any related property at an age not exceeding 25.[27]

In addition, by s.625(3) a settlor is not regarded as having an interest if:

> "*there are no circumstances in which the property can become payable [for the settlor] during the life of a person other than on the bankruptcy of that person or the assignment of that person's interest and the person is alive and under 25 years old*"

There is some odd drafting in these provisions, especially in (iv) and in the s.625(3) exclusion. It would seem likely that (iv) is intended to permit property to revert to the settlor on the death of a child under the age of 25 (i.e. the wording should have read "*would have become beneficially entitled*"). If this is correct then it applies in the typical accumulation and maintenance settlement where the attainment of 25 was the condition of entitlement. It will be noted that s.625(3) is not limited to a child of the settlor. **7.09**

EXAMPLE 7.1

(1) A settles property on his two adult daughters C and D aged 39 and 40, as concurrent life tenants. Because he has not disposed of the remainder interest, it is held on a resulting trust for him. A has retained an interest in the trust fund with the result that the income is taxed as his.

(2) If the trust was for "C and D at 25, capital if they reach 30 in equal shares" there is a resulting trust in favour of A if C and D both die before 30. However while C and D are under 25 A has not retained an interest because "during the life" of C and D and while they are alive and under 25 A cannot benefit.[28] However, once C and D reach 25 the trust becomes settlor-interested. Note that C and D do not need to be his issue. The let-out is intended to protect the typical old-style A-M trust where the settlor wanted to benefit a young person but ensure that the property reverted to him if the child died under 25. So "to A at 25 remainder to the settlor if A dies before 25" would not be settlor-interested because while A is alive and under 25 the settlor cannot benefit.

If there is a power to revoke the trusts (whoever possesses that power) and as a result the trust fund may revert to the settlor or his spouse or civil partner, the income of the fund is treated as belonging to the settlor because the property "*will or may*" become payable to or applicable for the benefit of the settlor etc.[29] If, under the terms of a discretionary settlement, any person has, or may **7.10**

---

[27] ITTOIA 2005, s.625(2)(e). See ITTOIA 2005, s.625(3) preventing any charge if a person is alive and under 25 years and during whose life the property cannot become applicable for the benefit of the settlor (or his spouse) save in the event of bankruptcy, assignment or charge. A typical accumulation and maintenance trust with a long-stop provision for the settlor or his spouse was thus covered while the children were under 25.

[28] See ITTOIA 2005 s.625(3).

[29] ITTOIA 2005, s.625(1).

have, the power to pay income or property to the settlor or his spouse/civil partner, then the income arising under the settlement is treated as belonging to the settlor.[30]

7.11   The nature of the interest which the settlor must retain has given rise to some discussion. A power to participate in the management of the trust is not sufficient; likewise, the possibility that a beneficiary might make a gift to the settlor is ignored; and HMRC accept that if the trustees agree to pay the inheritance tax that arises on the creation of the settlement, this does not amount to the retention of an interest.[31] The possibility of inheriting an interest by will or on the intestacy of a beneficiary does not give the settlor any interest in the settled property unless and until the possibility has become a reality. So for example "to my child absolutely at 35 but if he dies before then the interest shall pass to those beneficiaries entitled under his will or intestacy" would make the trust settlor-interested.

LOANS BY THE SETTLOR

7.12   Where a settlor has lent interest-free to the trustees or provides a guarantee for trust borrowing, it has been held that the settlor has an interest in the settlement.[32] Does the settlor have an interest if the trustees enter into a commercial transaction with him? For example, the settlor may sell or buy property at market value from the trust. This is not regarded as giving the settlor an interest. It also appears that a loan on commercial terms to or from the settlor is not regarded as giving him an interest in the settlement[33] since it is not an application for his benefit, although it may cause problems under the capital receipts rule.[34]

SPOUSES/CIVIL PARTNERS

7.13   If a settlement is made on the spouse (or civil partner) of the settlor, income is taxed as the settlor's unless the spouse or civil partner is given an "outright gift" and meets the following conditions[35]:

   (i) Condition A is that the gift carries a right to the whole of the income;

   (ii) Condition B is that the property is not wholly or substantially a right to income.

So, for example, a gift of non-voting preference shares to a spouse is treated as a gift of income. Furthermore, a gift is not an outright gift if it is subject to conditions or there are any circumstances in which the property (or any related

---

[30] ITTOIA 2005, s.625(1).
[31] See SP 1/82.
[32] See *Jenkins v IRC* (1944) 26 TC 265 and *IRC v Wachtel* (1970) 46 TC 543.
[33] See *Vestey's Executors v IRC* (1949) 31 TC 1 at 83(HL).
[34] See 7.45.
[35] See ITTOIA 2005 s.626.

property) is payable to the donor or is applicable for the benefit of the donor or will or may become so payable or applicable.[36]

The settlor's spouse or civil partner does not include: **7.14**

(i) a spouse/civil partner from whom the settlor is separated under a court order or a separation agreement;

(ii) a spouse from whom the settlor is separated where the separation is likely to be permanent (normally HMRC accept that a separation of 12 months is likely to be permanent);

(iii) the widow or widower of the settlor; or

(iv) a person to whom the settlor is not married or in a civil partnership but whom the settlor may later marry or enter into a civil partnership with.[37]

EXAMPLE 7.2

Mr A transfers ordinary shares to Mrs A absolutely. The income on those shares is taxed as Mrs A's income. If Mr A settles shares on trust for Mrs A for life, remainder to their son then the income is taxed as Mr A's.[38]

However, if Mr A settles shares on trust for Mrs A by way of provision on   **7.15**
their divorce, he is not taxed on the income provided that this is payable to her even if he retains some interest in the capital.[39] Section 627 is wider than the let out in s.625(4) because it does not simply exclude separated spouses from the definition of spouse but allows the settlor to remain a beneficiary of the capital. However, the trust has to be made on divorce or separation as part of the financial provision for the other party.

EXAMPLE 7.3

A is life tenant and settlor of a settlement. As part of the provision that he is required to make on divorce he agrees under court order that the trustees can revoke his life interest and appoint a similar life interest to his wife.[40] He can continue to receive capital at the trustees' discretion. Does this fall within the protection of s.627? The income must arise *"under a settlement made by one party to a marriage by way of provision for the other"* under a court order or after dissolution. The income

---

[36] See the *Arctic Systems* case discussed at 7.65.

[37] Disapplying the decision in *IRC v Tennant* (1942) 24 TC 215. Compare the capital gains tax and transfer of assets legislation where the mere possibility of future spouses or civil partners benefiting will make the trust settlor/transferor interested.

[38] See also ITTOIA 2005, s.626: *Young v Pearce; Young v Scrutton* [1996] S.T.C. 743. For the application of the settlement rules in the context of shares in family companies owned by spouses, see the *Arctic Systems* case and other case law outlined at 7.65 and following.

[39] See s.627(1).

[40] This may have inheritance tax implications after October 5, 2008.

arises under a settlement which was not originally made for this purpose. Accordingly on a narrow construction it is not within the protection of s.627 and A will be taxed on all the income.[41]

If A assigned his life interest to a new settlement for his wife made on divorce the position would be clearer.[42]

CHARITY LET-OUT

7.16   The charge on the settlor does not apply to income which arises under a trust, the trustees of which are resident in the UK, if it is given by the trustees to a charity in the year of assessment in which it arises, or if it is income to which a charity is entitled under the trust.[43]

Tax consequences of a settlor-interested trust

7.17   The 1991 Revenue Consultative Document "*Trusts*" stated

> "*where a settlor can benefit from a settlement it is right to treat the settlement income as still belonging to him or her; the settlor may be in much the same position as if the assets in the settlement had been retained in direct ownership.*"

This remains the aim in ITTOIA 2005 s.624 which deems the income arising under the settlement to be that of the settlor if it arises from property in which he has an interest.

7.18   More specifically, the trust income is treated for all tax purposes as that of the settlor and is treated as the highest part of his income.[44] If the settlor exercises his right of recovery this liability is borne by the trustees or beneficiaries.[45] In calculating the ultimate liability to income tax the settlor is allowed the same deductions and reliefs as if the income had actually been received by him. So, for example, the settlor takes the benefit of the dividend rates on both UK and foreign income.[46]

7.19   HMRC accept that the normal property income rules apply in calculating the income assessable on the settlor or transferor under the settlements legislation.[47] ITTOIA 2005 s.272 states that profits of a property business are calculated in the same way as the profits of a trade. Hence in calculating the income tax of a settlor-interested trust a deduction is permitted for interest

---

[41] An alternative view is that the appointment and consent constitute a separate settlement for income tax purposes under which the income does arise and this settlement *is* made on the dissolution of the marriage.

[42] See Ch.49.

[43] ITTOIA 2005, s.628.

[44] See ITTOIA 2005 s.619A.

[45] See 7.26 and following for who actually pays the tax and how it can be recovered.

[46] See ITTOIA 2005 ss.397/397A and Ch.6.

[47] See Property Income Manual 1045 (and also RDRM Ch.1 in relation to foreign rental income). They apply the same rule to the transfer of assets legislation.

paid on loans (even loans from connected parties) where the money borrowed is wholly and exclusively incurred for the purposes of the property rental business. HMRC will generally challenge a loan to the value of more than 80 per cent of the property.[48]

Non-residence of settlor

Foreign issues are discussed in Ch.8 but the position in relation to foreign resident settlors and UK resident trusts is dealt with here. Broadly if the settlor is non-resident foreign income is not deemed to be his although the UK source income (subject to withholding tax) is deemed to be his whether the trust is UK resident or not. This is on the basis that (per s.648(2)): **7.20**

> "*references to income arising under a settlement [and taxed on a non-resident settlor] do not include income arising under the settlement in that tax year in respect of which the settlor, if actually entitled to it, would not be chargeable to income tax by deduction or otherwise because of not being UK resident.*"

EXAMPLE 7.4

(1) A UK resident trust is life interest for a beneficiary X (a UK resident domiciliary) and receives UK dividends and interest and foreign source interest. It is settlor-interested and the settlor is not UK resident. The foreign source income is not deemed to be the settlor's and such income is taxed on X.[49] But the UK source income (both dividends or interest) is taxed on the settlor (not on X) because it is chargeable on the settlor. The settlor has no further income tax liability if tax has been deducted at source or has a tax credit.[50]

(2) Facts as in (1) above except that the trust receives gross UK interest. ITA 2007 s.811 limits the tax on UK source income to the tax withheld, deducted at source or given as a credit when payable to a non-resident. If the non-resident settlor had received such income personally there would be no tax because of s.811. Although s.812 normally imposes UK tax on such income where the trust has any UK resident beneficiary, does it apply where the UK source income is deemed to be that of the settlor or does s.811 take priority? It is thought, given the wording of s.648(2), if the income is not chargeable to income tax at all, then it is not treated as the settlor's so s.812 applies not s.811. The result is that X suffers tax on the UK interest received gross. However, if the trust income was UK dividend income then the income is deemed to be the non-resident settlor's under

---

[48] Trust management expenses do not reduce the income taxable on the settlor: see s.624(1A). This can complicate the collection of tax—see 7.30.

[49] Because s.648(2) excludes it.

[50] The settlor is, in effect, taxed on the same basis as if he had received the income personally and it is disregarded income: no additional or higher rate tax is therefore due.

s.624 since he is chargeable to tax on it (albeit with no further tax due) and ITA s.811 applies so there is no further tax for X to pay. Tax is treated as having been paid at source on the dividend.[51] If the trust income was rental income then the settlor (but not X) would be liable to tax on it.

7.21   It can be seen that in these circumstances where the settlor is non-UK resident and the life tenant is UK resident it is sometimes better to keep the trust settlor-interested in order to minimise the tax on UK source income subject to withholding tax or a tax credit (e.g. dividends).

EXAMPLE 7.5

> The adult children of a non-resident settlor are the life tenants of a non-settlor-interested trust (resident or non-UK resident). The settlor is excluded from all benefit. They assign their life interests to the settlor before October 6, 2008.[52] The income then is taxed as the settlor's (both as a matter of trust law and under the deeming provisions in s.624). The trust receives UK dividends. The settlor pays no further tax on such income.[53]

7.22   If, in the above example, the trust had been settlor-interested because (say) the settlor had a remainder interest, this does not involve a reservation of benefit for inheritance tax purposes (the retained interest is a carve-out); there is no POAT charge (because the settlor is non-UK resident); but the tax charge on UK source income subject to withholding tax is reduced. The children do not pay income tax on the income they receive as life tenants and instead since the trust is settlor-interested the income is treated as the settlor's. In the case of dividends, for example, no further tax is payable.

Pre-owned assets income tax (POAT)

7.23   An additional effect if the trust is settlor-interested because the settlor (as opposed to his spouse or civil partner) can benefit, then is that there may be a pre-owned assets income tax charge if the trust owns intangibles. This is wholly separate from the "normal" income tax charge being related to the value of the settled property not to the income it produces.[54] The question of who actually pays the income tax due is a complicated issue that is discussed at 7.00.

---

[51]   See ITTOIA 2005 s.399.
[52]   A capital gains tax charge under s.85 or s.76 would arise if the trust had been or was non-UK resident or had received property from a non-resident trust. An inheritance tax charge would arise if the assignment was made after October 5, 2008 because the settlor would then not take a qualifying interest in possession: see Ch.27.
[53]   For inheritance tax purposes the settled property is back in his estate.
[54]   FA 2004 Sch.15 para.8: see Ch.34.

Income of a company

A tax charge does not arise on the settlor under s.624 if the only income in the trust structure arises in a company owned by the trust. This is not "settlement" income[55] unless the settlor had given property directly to the company when owned by the trust since this is within the income tax definition of "settlement".[56]

7.24

EXAMPLE 7.6

(1) A settles shares on trust under which he can only benefit if all the beneficiaries die so that there is a resulting trust to A. The settlor has an interest in the settlement. The trust produces £1,000 income in 2011–12 on which A is taxed at 50 per cent (tax is £500) with a right of reimbursement. The POA charge under para.8 also applies given that the settled property is intangibles and A does not reserve a benefit (because the retention of the reversionary interest is a carve-out). If the settled property is worth £1 million, A pays an additional tax of four per cent (for 2011–12) × £1 million = £40,000 less tax paid under s.625 (£500) = £39,500 under POAT![57]

(2) A UK resident trust gives a life interest for X but is revocable by the settlor (UK resident and domiciled). The settlor has retained an interest for income tax purposes. The income is payable to X but taxed on the settlor under s.624. There is no tax liability on X and trustees pay basic rate tax, the settlor higher or additional rate (see 7.35). If the income is UK dividend income and the settlor is a higher rate taxpayer he effectively pays 25 per cent tax on the amount received. If an additional rate taxpayer he will pay further tax at an effective rate of 36.11 per cent.

Separate funds

In calculating the income tax charge do not include income which arises from property in which the settlor has no interest or which he did not settle.[58]

7.25

EXAMPLE 7.7

(1) In 2005 the settlor set up a trust which was divided into two funds A and B. Fund A sets up a life interest for his child X but he remains a

---

[55] Following the repeal of certain provisions in 1989: see TA 1988 s.681(3).
[56] See *Chamberlain v IRC* (1943) 25 TC 317. Of course income of an offshore company may well fall within ITA 2007 s.720 (discussed in Ch.8).
[57] This is discussed further in Ch.34.
[58] See TSEM 4200.

discretionary beneficiary. Fund B is life interest for his grandchildren and neither he nor his spouse/civil partner retain any interest. He is only taxable on the income of Fund A. He will pay income tax at his highest marginal rate with the benefit of the same deductions and reliefs as if the income were his.

(2) As above except that an uncle of the settlor adds property to Fund A which produces £100,000 income. X is taxable on that income not the settlor. The settlor continues to be taxed on the income of Fund A that derives from property he settled.

Additional income tax complications arise where the UK resident trust is settlor-interested but the settlor is non-domiciled. These are discussed in Ch.8.

DISCRETIONARY/ACCUMULATION TRUSTS—WHO PAYS THE TAX?

7.26 The income of such a settlor-interested trust is treated for all income tax purposes as the income of the settlor alone.[59] It is treated as the highest part of his income and is taxed under whichever part of the UK tax code would have applied if it had actually been his income.[60] Logically therefore the settlor should account for all the tax on the income and then recover it from the trustees under ITTOIA 2005 s.646. This is particularly the case given that income taxed on the settlor is deemed to retain its original character.

7.27 In fact, FA 2006 s.89 changed the way in which trustees of settlor-interested discretionary/accumulation trusts were taxed so that they were no longer exempt from liability at the special trust rates. The result is extraordinary complexity with unnecessary reclaims, particularly as discretionary trustees pay at a rate of 50 per cent and many settlors pay tax at rates of 40 per cent or less.[61]

7.28 The starting point is ITTOIA 2005 s.646(8) which states that nothing in ss.624–632 is to be read as excluding a charge to tax on the trustees as persons by whom any income is received. HMRC's interpretation of this[62] is that the trustees of a discretionary/accumulation settlor-interested trust are obliged to pay tax (at 50 per cent from 2010–11 under ITA 2007 s.479 or at the 42.5 per cent dividend rate) and make returns. This is despite the fact that income is expressly excluded from ITA 2007 s.479 if, before being distributed, it is the income of any person other than the trustees.[63]

7.29 The settlor then receives a credit for the tax paid by the trustees: i.e. they are treated as having paid it on behalf of the settlor and it is available to be used

---

[59] ITTOIA 2005 ss.624(1) and 629(1).
[60] ITTOIA 2005 s.619.
[61] Before April 6, 2010 usually trustees of settlor-interested accumulation/discretionary settlements paid tax at the same rate (40%) as the settlor since the settlor was a higher rate taxpayer.
[62] See *Tax Bulletin* 84, August 2006.
[63] See s.480(3)(a). However, HMRC do not consider that the settlement code deems the income to be that of the settlor not the trustees for the purposes of avoiding a charge to 50% on the trustees under s.479.

against the settlor's own tax liability. Tax paid by the trustees on behalf of the settlor does not enter the "tax pool".

The settlor must return the trust income on his tax return. If he is not a 50 per cent taxpayer he then reclaims any overpaid tax from HMRC! Section 646(5) as amended from 2010–11[64] now requires the settlor to repay any tax reclaimed to the trustees (since they have actually paid it on his behalf) and the settlor can require HMRC to issue a certificate showing the amount of the repayment due which he has to hand to the trustees. (HMRC cannot give such details to the trustees without the consent of the settlor.) So if he is a 40 per cent taxpayer he can reclaim 10 per cent but must then pay it to the trustees who paid the tax. It might have been simpler to make the settlor pay the right amount of tax from the start and then leave him to recover that tax from the trustees without involving HMRC in repayment claims!

The difficulties are compounded in that even if the settlor is a 50 per cent taxpayer the tax paid on behalf of the settlor by the trustees is unlikely to be correct. The settlor's actual liability will usually be greater than the tax deducted by the trustees. For example, the settlor receives no relief for trust management expenses but is taxed on the gross income of the trust. In calculating the tax on the trustees they are liable for income tax at the basic rate band on the first £1,000 and at 50 per cent on the remaining income.[65] Accordingly, the amount charged on the settlor will therefore be greater than the amount paid by the trustees if he is a 50 per cent taxpayer. ITTOIA 2005 s.646(1) enables the settlor to recover additional tax paid by him from the trustees. If the settlor fails to claim reimbursement then HMRC consider that this could be a transfer of value for IHT purposes. They accept when the settlor repays an overpayment of tax to the trustees he does not make a chargeable transfer for IHT purposes. **7.30**

Distributions to beneficiaries

If the trustees distribute the income to the settlor as a beneficiary of the trust he is not taxable on that distribution since he has already been taxed on the income.[66] **7.31**

If the trustees distribute the income to UK beneficiaries other than the settlor it is not taxed again as it has already been taxed as the settlor's. Before FA 2006, the trustees did not show discretionary payments at all and the beneficiary never showed the payment in his return although strictly one could argue this was a new source of income in his hands. From April 6, 2006 the recipient is treated as having paid income tax at the top rate on the actual amount of the payment made which is not grossed up.[67] He has no further tax liability in respect of the payment but no part of the tax can be repaid or set against liability arising from any other income of the beneficiary. Hence, the beneficiary cannot set such income against any trading losses nor reclaim it if a basic rate taxpayer. The trustees do not need to gross up such payments **7.32**

---

[64] See F(No.3)A 2010 s.7 amending ITTOIA 2005 s.646(5) and (6) with effect from 2010–11.
[65] ITA 2007 ss.479 and 491 and see Ch.6.
[66] Before April 5, 2006 due to TA 1988 s.687(1). From April 6, 2006 such discretionary payments to the settlor are taken out of charge by ITTOIA 2005 s.685A(5).
[67] ITTOIA 2005 s.685A(3).

and they have no effect on the tax pool. They should show them only in the additional information box of the trust return.

7.33   One difficulty after April 5, 2006 was that since such distributions were included in the beneficiary's total income/gains they might push other income/gains into a higher rate of tax since under the statutory ordering rules, income distributions from a trust were charged on a beneficiary before savings and/or dividend income. However, FA 2008 amended this with retrospective effect so that income distributions from settlor-interested discretionary/accumulation trusts are treated as the highest part of the recipient's income for all income tax purposes except for the purposes of top slicing relief for life insurance bonds.[68] This ensures that other income is not pushed into higher rates. However, the income distributed from the settlor-interested trust remains part of the beneficiary's total income and may therefore affect tax reliefs and benefits which are means tested, e.g. age allowance, student loan repayments.[69]

Fixed interest trusts

7.34   If the trust is fixed interest (e.g. a life interest trust) the trustees are subject to basic rate tax on all the income irrespective of whether it is settlor-interested.

Settlor is the life tenant

7.35   If the interest in possession beneficiary is the settlor then s.624 does not apply to the income that he actually receives. This is because it is his income anyway so the deeming provision is not necessary. The settlor, however, may pay higher and additional rate tax in the same way as any life interest beneficiary. In addition, sums treated as income for tax purposes (such as accrued income, payments of a lease premium, profits from land etc, share buy-backs)[70] but which as a matter of trust law constitute trust capital are taxed on the settlor under s.624. Further the settlor will pay tax under s.624 on any income that was used to pay income expenses. He can reclaim tax suffered under s.624 from the trustees.

Settlor not the life tenant

7.36   If the life tenant is someone other than the settlor but the trust is settlor-interested as noted above, the trustees still pay basic rate tax. The income is not taxed as that of the life tenant beneficiary (because the settlement code takes such income away from him) but is taxed on the settlor with a credit for the basic rate tax paid by the trustees. The settlor must pay higher and additional

---

[68] Section 685A(5A). As amended by s.67 FA 2008 with effect from 2006–07. See December 2007 and April 2008 *IHT & Trusts Newsletters* for further details.

[69] Note that different rules apply to settlor-interested trusts if the settlor is non-UK domiciled and the trust income is unremitted by the settlor or the trustees. See Ch.8.

[70] See ITA 2007 s.481.

rate tax if applicable. He can then reclaim such higher or additional rate tax that he has paid from the trustees.

HMRC outline a few unusual examples affecting the taxation of settlor-interested trusts in TSEM at 4513 set out below.

7.37

> "*(i) Trust is partially settlor interested*
>
> *The income tax paid by trustees for a tax year may be paid partly on income attributable to a settlor and partly on income from property from which a settlor is excluded from benefit. The tax paid on income attributable to the settlor does not enter the tax pool—see TSEM4512. Tax paid on other income enters the tax pool in the normal way—see TSEM3756 onwards,*
>
> *Example*
>
> *A settles property into the A discretionary settlement. The settlement consists of two funds.*
>
> *Fund A contains a house which is let and a block of shares in A plc.*
>
> *Fund B contains a block of shares in B plc.*
>
> *Under the terms of the settlement the settlor and any spouse or civil partner of the settlor are excluded from benefiting from Fund B.*
>
> *In 2009–2010 the income of the trustees (and tax paid on that income) is as follows:*
>
> **Fund A**
>
> | | | *Tax due from trustees* | |
> |---|---|---|---|
> | *Rental Income* | *£10,000* | *£1,000 @ 20%* | *£200* |
> | | | *£9,000 @ 40%* | *£3,600* |
> | *Dividend Income* | *£5,000* | *£5,000 @ 32.5% (of which* | *£1,625* |
> | | | *10% satisfied by tax credit)* | |
> | *Tax paid* | | | *£5,425* |
>
> *The settlor is given credit for the tax paid on the income attributable to the settlor – £5,425. Where the tax paid by the trustees exceeds the settlor's own income tax liability the tax (excluding the £500 non payable tax credit attached to the dividends) may be repaid to the settlor.*
>
> **Fund B**
>
> | | | | |
> |---|---|---|---|
> | *Dividend Income* | *£15,000* | *£15,000 @ 32.5% (of which* | *£4,875* |
> | | | *10% satisfied by tax credit)* | |
> | *Tax paid* | | | *£4,875* |

As the settlor is excluded from benefiting from Fund B, this tax is not available to the settlor. The normal rules apply and £3,375 of the tax paid (£4,875 less £1,500 non payable tax credit attached to the dividends) enters the tax pool.

(ii) Trust ceases to be, or becomes, settlor interested

A trust may cease to be settlor interested part way through a tax year, for example when the settlor dies. Similarly, a trust may become settlor interested part way through a tax year, for example the settlor may marry or enter into a civil partnership with an existing beneficiary of the trust.

Where this happens the tax paid by the trustees should be apportioned on a time basis so the part is available to cover the settlor's liability and the other part dealt with in the normal way.

Example

In 2009–2010 the income of the trustees (and tax paid on that income) is as follows:

		Tax due from trustees	
Savings Income	£10,000	£1,000 @ 20%	£200
		£9,000 @ 40%	£3,600
Tax paid			£3,800

The settlor of the trust dies on 5 January 2010. The trust ceases to be settlor interested on that date because Section 624 ITTOIA applies only to income arising under a settlement during the life on the settlor.

The settlor is taxed on £7,500 and is given credit for £2,850 (75% of £3,800).

The balance of the tax, £950 goes into the tax pool."

III PAYMENTS TO MINOR UNMARRIED CHILDREN OF THE SETTLOR[71]

7.38   Income produced by a settlement which is paid during the settlor's lifetime to or for the benefit of the settlor's minor unmarried child is normally taxed as the income of the settlor in the tax year when it is distributed. (Of course if the income arises under a settlement in which the settlor retains an interest it is taxable on the settlor under ITTOIA 2005 s.624 anyway so this provision does not apply.)

---

[71] ITTOIA 2005 s.629.

Where the total income paid to the child under such a settlement does not exceed £100 in any year (the £100 limit is per parent settlor) it will not be taxed on the settlor. If income is accumulated under an irrevocable settlement of capital for a child, the income is not taxed as that of the settlor. However, if payments are later made out of the trust fund to the child at a time when the child is still under 18 and unmarried these are treated as the settlor's income up to the amount of the accumulations.[72] In such cases the payment is not taxable on the child. The trustees will have already accounted for tax at the relevant rate in the year the income arose. The tax rate ultimately chargeable on the settlor depends on when it is paid to the child. It is chargeable at the settlor's marginal rates and carries a credit for the tax paid by the trustees.

EXAMPLE 7.8

D settles shares on discretionary trusts for the benefit of his three infant unmarried children A, B and C in equal shares contingent on attaining the age of 21 years. If the income of the fund is £20,000 per year gross, the income tax position (for the tax year 2008–9) is as follows:

(1) The trustees are liable for tax on the first £1,000 of income (depending on the source of income) at either the basic, lower or dividend ordinary rate.[73]

(2) If the balance of the income (after the payment of tax at 40 per cent or the 32.5 per cent dividend rate) is accumulated (and note that the payment of expenses properly charged to income[74] is excluded from the calculation of retained income for the purposes of calculating the charge on the settlor on later distributions to children), it is not treated as the income of the settlor.

(3) If, later in 2011–12, the income is paid to a minor child of the settlor, it is treated as income of the settlor in that tax year. So if £1,200 is paid to, or for the benefit of, A, the result is that D's income is increased by £1,200 which must be grossed up.[75] In 2011–12 this involves grossing up at the 50 per cent rate producing a gross payment of £2,400. The settlor (D) is given credit for the £1,200 tax paid by the trustees. He can reclaim some of that tax if he is not a top rate taxpayer but must reimburse tax to the trustees.[76] Hence where the settlor is not a 50 per cent taxpayer consider making income distributions to his minor children in order to recover some of the tax suffered by the trust.

(4) The legislation prevents the children's personal allowances and lower rate bands being used to reclaim tax paid by the trustees.[77]

[72] ITTOIA 2005 s.629.
[73] ITA 2007 s.491 assuming the settlor established only one trust: see Ch.6.
[74] For tax purposes see Ch.6.
[75] ITA 2007 s.494(1) treats the payment *"as if it were made after the deduction of a sum representing income tax at the trust rate on the grossed up amount of the discretionary payment."* Note that s.493 expressly extends this treatment to a payment which is treated for income tax purposes as the income of a settlor under ITTOIA 2005 s.629.
[76] See s.646(5) as amended by F(No.3)A 2010.
[77] See Ch.6 for further details of how this would work if the distributions were made to minor

But if income is paid to an adult child or other beneficiary this reduces the available retained income which can be taxed on the settlor if distributions are made to his minor children.

(5) If all the net income which has been accumulated is distributed amongst the three minor beneficiaries (and, therefore, treated as the settlor's income), any further distributions to the beneficiaries will be capital.[78]

(6) If a UK resident settlor is deemed to receive the income of an overseas trust he can, by concession, claim relief for tax paid by the trustees.[79]

(7) If the trust had been an interest in possession trust for A, B and C so that the income was paid to them the trustees will only have paid basic rate tax. The settlor may then be liable for up to a further tax with a credit for the income tax already paid. He can recover this additional tax from the trustees.

7.40 Section 619 makes it clear that the trust income (whether the trust is fixed interest or discretionary) is charged on the settlor at whatever rate the income would have been charged if it had actually been his income. So, for example, if the trust income comprised dividend income and the trust was a fixed interest trust, the settlor would in respect of distributions before April 6, 2010 be liable to pay a further 25 per cent on the net amount paid to the minor children (32.5 per cent of the gross).[80] After that date he is taxed at 36.11 per cent on the net amount (42.5 per cent on gross dividend). He can then reclaim this from the trustees.

7.41 Five other general matters should be noted:

(i) "*child*" is widely defined to include a stepchild,[81] an illegitimate child, and an adopted child,[82] but does not include a foster child;

(ii) the definition of "*settlement*" for these purposes includes a transfer of assets and an arrangement[83];

(iii) if the settlor is not the parent of the child beneficiary, the above provisions do not apply; hence settlements funded by grandparents can be advantageous from an income tax point of view[84];

(iv) discretionary income payments made on or after April 6, 2006 to unmarried minor children of a settlor, where that child is a vulnerable person for the purposes of FA 2005 and the trustees have made a claim under FA 2005 s.25 for special income tax treatment, do not give rise to a charge to tax on the settlor[85];

---

grandchildren of the settlor or other non-taxpayers who were not minor children of the settlor.
[78] Which may, of course, lead to a CGT charge under TCGA 1992 s.71: see Ch.11.
[79] See ESC A93 for the full text of the concession and Ch.8.
[80] See Ch.6.
[81] ITTOIA 2005 s.629(7)(a).
[82] TA 1988 s.832(5).
[83] *Thomas v Marshall* [1953] AC 543; [1953] 1 All ER 1102 HL. Parents may therefore create a settlement if they waive their entitlement to dividends in the family company as a result of which their minor children benefit.
[84] See Ch.6.
[85] See Ch.36.

(v) the settlor can recover any tax he has to pay although since the trust top rate is now 50 per cent it is unlikely he will pay any further tax unless (a) the trust is an interest in possession trust for his minor children in which case the trustees will only have paid basic rate tax (b) the income now being distributed to the children arose in an earlier year when the trustees paid tax at a lower rate or (c) there are significant trust management expenses. If the settlor is a 40 per cent (or less) taxpayer, distributions out of a discretionary trust to his minor children will result in a tax reclaim.

Revocable settlements

There must be no power to terminate the trust in circumstances where the fund could revert to the settlor since otherwise he will be taxed on the income under s.624 (as a settlement in which he has retained an interest). It does not matter whether the power to terminate is given to the settlor or to a stranger. The settlement must be irrevocable. Furthermore, the income or assets from the fund must not be payable, according to the terms of the settlement, to or for the benefit of the settlor or his spouse except for payments made after the death of the child beneficiary or on the bankruptcy of the child, or on a purported charge or assignment of assets by the child. Therefore, a settlement is irrevocable if the child is given a protected life interest under the standard trusts,[86] and if the settlement is to revert to the settlor on the death of the child beneficiary. Finally, a settlement is not irrevocable if it can be determined by act or default of any person. For example, a settlement that will terminate if the settlor ceases to be employed in a specified employment is not irrevocable. Bare trusts are caught by these provisions and all income (over £100) is taxed on the settlor as his income.[87]

7.42

IV RECEIPT OF CAPITAL BENEFITS[88]

These provisions are aimed at preventing the settlor or his spouse (or civil partner) obtaining any benefit (including a loan) from a settlement in which the income may be taxed at a lower rate than that which would have applied had the settlor retained it. They generally apply only where the trust is not settlor-interested (because otherwise the settlor would normally be taxable on all the trust income anyway). Hence, they usually catch loans to the settlor/spouse/civil partner from the trust rather than capital payments since the trustees would not have power to pay capital to a settlor if he was excluded as a beneficiary. More bizarrely they catch the situation where the settlor or spouse/civil partner has lent money to the trust (on any terms) and the trust repays the loan. The repayment of the loan by the trustees is treated as the

7.43

---

[86] See TA 1925 s.33 as amended by FLRA 1987 s.33(1), Sch.2 para.2.
[87] See Ch.42 for the position before 1999.
[88] ITTOIA 2005 ss.633–643.

payment of a capital sum to the settlor.[89] Unlike the provisions taxing the settlor on trust income under s.624 or under s.629, the settlor has no right to recover this tax from the trustees. The provisions do not apply if the capital payment is otherwise than by way of a loan or repayment of a loan and is for full consideration in money or money's worth. So a purchase by the trustees from the settlor or spouse of an asset at full value will not be caught but a loan from the settlor or spouse that is subsequently repaid by the trustees will be! A payment to the settlor's widow or widower is not caught.

When are these provisions relevant?

7.44   With the increase in the trust rate to 40 per cent from tax year 2004–05 and 50 per cent from 2010–11 one would have thought that HMRC would accept that these provisions are largely redundant for UK resident discretionary trusts because when capital payments are matched to trust income arising from 2004–05 onwards, the notional tax credit is usually equal to the potential liability of the settlor and no further tax will be due. However, they are a great complication. They are relevant where the trust is not settlor-interested and:

(a) capital benefits to the settlor are matched to trust income that has been taxed at a lower rate. For example, if a capital benefit provided now is matched to income arising prior to 2004–05 in these years the notional tax credit was lower;

(b) trust income arising after April 2004 comprises dividend income because the notional tax credit will not be 40/50 per cent and further tax is then due from the settlor;

(c) the trust is non-UK resident when no tax will have been paid on non-UK source income.

In calculating the available income up to the end of a tax year when a capital payment is made, matching is made against income of an earlier tax year before that of a later tax year.[90] This means that where a settlor receives a capital benefit from a trust with undistributed income arising before 2004–05 (or even before 2010–11) he could suffer additional tax if he is a higher rate or additional rate taxpayer even though there may be significant trust income in later years that has been taxed at higher rates. When these provisions apply the settlor has no right to recover any additional tax that he pays from the trustees.[91]

---

[89] See *De Vigier v IRC* [1964] 2 All ER 907, where the settlor's wife lent money to the trustees to enable them to take up a rights issue. The settlor was taxable on the money applied in later repayment of that loan.
[90] See ITTOIA 2005 s.640(4).
[91] Contrast the position under ss.624 and 629.

How s.633 operates

Capital sums such as loans to the settlor (or to his spouse or to a company **7.45** connected with him[92] from the trust are matched with undistributed "available" income of the trust and taxed as the settlor's income.

A "capital sum" covers any sum paid by way of loan (whether or not on commercial terms) or a repayment of a loan and any sum paid otherwise than as income and which is not paid for full consideration in money or money's worth.[93] Hence an outright distribution of capital to the settlor or spouse is a capital sum and if the settlor is then excluded he will be taxable on all future available income arising in the next 10 years. A capital sum is treated as paid to the settlor if it is paid to a third party at his direction or as a result of his assignment,[94] but is only caught to the extent that it is less than, or equals, the income available in the settlement. *Available income* means the total amount of undistributed income in the trust but deducting:

(a) any income already taxed on the settlor under s.624 (settlor-interested trust) or s.629 (capital payments to his minor children); and

(b) income used to pay expenses properly chargeable to income; and

(c) an amount equal to tax at the trust rate on undistributed income of the current and previous years.[95]

An excess capital payment is not charged in the year of receipt, but may be charged later if income arises in the settlement in any of the next 10 years following the year in which it is paid[96] until the whole of the capital sum has been treated as income of the settlor. Any part of the capital sum which has not been matched with available income at the end of 10 years following the year in which it is paid cannot be treated as income of the settlor.[97]

The capital sum is treated as income of the settlor grossed up at the trust **7.46** rate applicable in the year of the capital receipt. This is irrespective of the personal tax position of the settlor or the source of income; the settlor is entitled to credit for tax actually paid by the trustees in earlier tax years when the income arose, but not to any repayment of that tax if he is a lower rate tax payer. If when he has included the grossed up income he is a 50 per cent tax payer then he pays 50 per cent on that income with a credit for the tax actually paid by the trustees. In that respect, the legislation is very different from that applying to settlor-interested trusts under ss.624 and 629 where the settlor can recover any tax paid and is taxed by reference to the source of the income and so, for instance, obtains the benefit of the dividend rate.

As income arising to the UK discretionary trustees in 2004–05 and later **7.47**

---

[92] The settlor may inadvertently fall foul of these provisions because the trustees have lent to a company controlled by him.

[93] ITTOIA 2005 s.634(1).

[94] ITTOIA 2005 s.634(5) e.g. the settlor assigns a loan owed to him to a trust.

[95] There are special rules if income was used to pay interest by the trustees.

[96] ITTOIA 2005 s.633(4).

[97] ITTOIA 2005 s.633(3)–(5).

years is taxed at 40 per cent (from 2010–11 50 per cent),[98] the notional tax credit will often fully cover the charge on the settlor. However, further tax will be due if the trust had received dividend income in that time or the payment has to be matched to "available income" of earlier tax years. If the trust is non-UK resident there is no such notional tax relief and the settlor could be taxed at 50 per cent by reference to the available trust income (which is grossed up at 0 per cent if the income arises abroad to a non-UK resident trust) with the right of recovery. If the trust has always been a fixed interest trust then there is generally no available income anyway against which the capital payment is matched.

EXAMPLE 7.9

(1) In 2010–11 the settlor makes a loan of £100,000 to his settlement which the trust then repays in full. If the trust is a life interest trust for the settlor's adult children then the settlor suffers no income tax charge since there is no available income. By contrast, if the trust is discretionary and income is accumulated no liability arises on the settlor when he makes the loan, but on repayment he is treated as receiving a capital sum and the income of the settlement will be treated as the income of the settlor to the extent of available income. The £100,000 is grossed up at the trust rate prevailing in the year of the capital receipt = £200,000. Tax due from the settlor (assuming he is an additional rate taxpayer) is £100,000 (50% × £200,000). However, if the trust has accumulated net interest of £100,000 all arising from 2004–05 and there is no available undistributed income arising in prior years the notional tax on this is £66,666 and this is credited against any further tax due from the settlor. If there is insufficient accumulated "available" income for the year in which the loan was repaid, the income of subsequent years is treated as that of the settlor in those later years up to the amount of the repayment but while the trust is UK resident and receives sufficient undistributed income which is taxed at 50 per cent no tax should be due.[99]

(2) The trust lends money to the settlor's spouse on fully commercial terms. He has received no benefit from the loan and does not retain an interest in the trust. Nevertheless, he is taxed on any accumulated trust income grossed up at 50 per cent up to the amount of the loan with a credit for the tax actually paid by the trustees in the past on that income. Again note that if some of the accumulated income to which the capital payment is matched arose in years prior to 2004–05 then the notional tax credit will not be 50% and additional tax will be due from the settlor if he is an additional rate or higher rate taxpayer. He cannot recover that tax from the trust.

(3) The following example is adapted from TSEM Manual. Emma puts

---

[98] Apart from the first £1,000, unless it is dividend income.
[99] Whilst the trust suffers tax at 50% there should be no additional tax to pay.

£200,000 into a discretionary trust in favour of her minor children on May 1, 2007. The money is invested and income arises as follows:

2007–08 Income £15,000 charged £1,000 @ 20%
£14,000 @ 40% Tax = £5,800

2008–09 Income £20,000 charged £1,000 @ 20%
£19,000 @ 40% Tax = £7,800

2009–10 Income £15,000 charged £1,000 @ 20%
£14,000 @ 40% Tax = £5,800

2010–11 Income £12,000 charged £1,000 @ 20%
£11,000 @ 50% Tax = £5,700

No payments are made to the children so no income is treated as the income of Emma under ITTOIA 2005 s.629. On May 1, 2010 Emma (an additional rate taxpayer) borrows £30,000 from the trustees. She is treated as receiving income grossed up at 50 per cent = £60,000.

The undistributed income of the trustees is £36,900 (£62,000 less the tax of £25,100 paid on that income). The grossed up amount is chargeable to income tax at her marginal rate of tax but a notional credit is given for tax at the trust rate in force for the years in which the income arose to the trustees. The loan is matched with income of earlier years first.

		£
Loan to settlor		30,000
Grossed up @ trust rate		60,000
Tax due from Emma	(60.000 @ 50%)	30,000
Less notional tax:		
Years to 2009–10:	50,000 @ 40%	20,000
2010–11	10,000 @ 50%	5,000
Total notional tax		25,000
Further tax due from settlor		5,000

(4) Henry's wife is a discretionary beneficiary of a UK resident trust set up by Henry. The income has been taxable on Henry as a settlor-interested trust. In 2010–11 the trustees make a capital payment to the wife of £100,000 and then exclude her irrevocably. They are still married and living together. The trust ceases to be settlor-interested. However, since a capital sum has been paid to the settlor or spouse the available income of the trust continues to be taxable on Henry (albeit only if undistributed). Contrast the position under ITA s.727 discussed in Ch.8 (at Example 8.5(2)) where in theory all future income can be taxable on the transferor once he has received a capital sum even if paid to someone else.

183

7.48   In summary where a loan or capital payment to the settlor or his wife made between 2004–05 and 2009–10 is matched wholly with income arising to trustees in those years there will generally be no further tax liability on the settlor if the trust is UK resident as the notional tax relief will fully cover the charge unless the trust income comprises dividends or is non-UK resident. This also applies where a loan or capital payment made in 2010–11 or later is matched wholly with income arising to trustees in 2010–11 or later years. However, where the trust is UK resident and the loan or capital payment is matched with undistributed income for a tax year where the rate of the notional tax credit is less than the marginal rate of the settlor then a liability will arise on the settlor.[100] The scope of s.633 is therefore wider than often appreciated since a settlor can still be taxable on the settlement income even after total exclusion. One way round this may be to advance the settlor assets in specie rather than cash since ITA 2007 s.727 and ITTOIA 2005 s.633 are thought only to apply where a sum of money is paid to the transferor or settlor. Some doubt as to this is raised by *Irving v HMRC* [2008] STC 597 where it was held that a transfer of shares to an employee that could immediately be converted into cash was equivalent to a sum of money. However, this was in the particular statutory context and it is notable that the provisions in ITEPA 2003 Pt 7A and in particular s.554C differentiate between payments of a sum of money and transfers of assets confirming the two are seen as different. Identical language defining capital sum is used in ITTOIA 2005 s.634 and ITA 2007 s.628 (see Ch.8). It is notable that in ITTOIA 2005 s.643(3), which covers capital sums and associated payments paid to settlors by corporate bodies and is discussed in the following paragraph, transfers of assets are specifically included in the definition of associated payments. It is difficult to see why transfers of assets would have been included as an associated payment if transfers of assets in specie were already encompassed in the definition of "payment of capital sums". It should be noted that if the settlor (or transferor under ITA 2007 s.727 in relation to offshore trusts) incurs any liability he has no right of reimbursement against the trustees under either section. It may therefore be sensible (at least to avoid a charge under the settlement provisions in s.633) for the trustees to convert the trust to an interest in possession trust to avoid any income being accumulated. The problem arises equally in the case of offshore trusts where a UK resident settlor has received a capital sum. However if the settlor and spouse are excluded and the settlor is a remittance basis user neither ITTOIA 2005 s.633 nor ITA 2007 s.727 can impose future liability on the settlor if the trust has no UK source income. If the offshore trust is still a relevant person in relation to the settlor however it will be necessary for the trust to avoid remittances of income to the UK. At least in relation to s.633, liability lasts only for 10 years after the tax year of payment and only to the extent that income is not distributed as it arises. Liability under s.727 is not so time limited and can arise even if the income is paid to someone else.

---

[100] For the position in respect of loans to foreign domiciliaries: see Ch.8.

Capital sums paid by a company connected with the settlement

The charge also applies to a capital sum received by the settlor from a body **7.49**
corporate connected with the settlement where the trustees have made an associated payment to the company. The payment by the company is deemed to
have been made by the trustees. An associated payment in relation to a capital
sum paid to a settlor means any capital sum paid to a company by the trustees
and any other sum so paid or asset transferred, for less than full consideration,
provided that it is made within five years before or five years after the date on
which the sum is paid to the settlor. Generally, a company is connected with
a settlement if it is a close company and the participators include the trustees
of the settlement.[101]

V CAPITAL GAINS TAX

The importance of a UK trust being settlor-interested

From April 6, 2008, gains arising within the trust are no longer taxed on **7.50**
the settlor. Nevertheless, whether or not a trust is settlor-interested remains
relevant since no hold-over relief is available for transfers into such a settlement.[102] Further, trusts which are or have been settlor-interested can be
caught by Sch.4A if the settlor or another beneficiary disposes of his beneficial
interest for consideration. The result is a deemed disposal of the underlying
trust assets.[103]

The following were consequences of a trust being settlor-interested before **7.51**
April 6, 2008:

(i) Gains arising within the trust were treated as accruing to the settlor
and regarded as forming the highest part of the amount on which he
was chargeable to capital gains tax (the "s.77 charge.") He had a right
of reimbursement against the trustees.[104] The gains deemed to accrue
to the settlor were reduced by allowable losses of the trust. The settlor
could then use any personal losses (to the extent these had not already
been used against personal gains) to reduce the trust gains. Surplus
trust losses could not be used against the settlor's personal gains. Taper
relief was then given in the normal way but the trust annual exemption
was not available.[105] Disposals by settlor-interested trusts from April 6,
2008 are no longer taxed on the settlor and so gains and losses accrue

---

[101] ITTOIA 2005 ss.637(8) and 641.
[102] See Ch.18. Of course there is generally no hold-over relief on a gift into a non-resident trust
whether or not settlor-interested. Although see 4.35 for EU issues and TCGA 1992 s.239
(transfers to EBT).
[103] See Ch.20 for disposals of beneficial interests. Sch.4A only applies to settlor-interested trusts
or trusts which were settlor-interested in the previous two years.
[104] TCGA 1992, s.78: note the conditions that needed to be satisfied to claim reimbursement. The
capital gains tax had to be paid by the settlor who then received a certificate from the Inspector
before he could claim reimbursement.
[105] For computational aspects and further details on loss relief, see Ch.21.

only to the trustees and are taxed at 28 per cent. The annual exemption is available to the trust and if there are other trusts will now have to be pro-rated between more trusts.[106] Surplus personal losses can no longer be set against trust gains.

(ii) Trust losses were relieved differently for settlor-interested trusts.[107]

(iii) Schedule 4B (transfers of value), which no longer applies to UK resident settlor-interested trusts was relevant to transfers of value made before April 6, 2008.

What is a settlor-interested trust for CGT purposes?

7.52   A settlor of a UK resident trust is treated as having an interest in his settlement in any tax year, if one of two conditions is met[108]:

(i) Any property which may at any time be comprised in the settlement, or any derived property is, or will, or may become, payable to or applicable for the benefit of the settlor, his spouse, civil partner[109] or dependent children[110] in any circumstances whatsoever[111]; or

(ii) Any of the settlor; spouse; civil partner or dependent children enjoys a benefit deriving indirectly or directly from the property which is comprised in the settlement or from any derived property.

A dependent child is an unmarried child under the age of 18 years who does not have a civil partner. Child includes a stepchild.

Condition (i) looks at the terms of the settlement and is focused on whether the trustees could benefit any of the above. Condition (ii) focuses on actual rather than potential benefits received (e.g. a loan or rent-free occupation of a trust house). Note that a settlor who has any interest, however small in a settlement (even if he is excluded from some part of an appropriated fund) has retained an interest in the settlement.[112]

---

[106] See 11.09.

[107] See Ch.21. In particular a loss realised and carried forward in a settlor-interested trust from April 6, 2008 cannot reduce future trust gains.

[108] TCGA 1992 s.169F.

[109] With effect from December 5, 2005. Civil partners capable of receiving benefits or actually receiving benefits were brought into s.77 by the Tax and Civil Partnerships Regulations SI 2005/3229. The possibility of a future civil partner was ignored in determining whether UK resident settlements were settlor-interested for s.77 purposes. The position is different in respect of UK trusts where hold-over relief is needed or in respect of non-UK resident trusts. Future civil partners should be expressly excluded from non-UK resident settlements, since the possibility of future civil partners benefiting can mean that the trust is settlor-interested. HMRC have indicated in correspondence that they would not consider pre-December 2005 offshore trusts to be settlor-interested merely because of the possibility that the settlor might contract a civil partnership if the general context showed no intention to benefit a civil partner. The question of whether spouses/civil partners/cohabitees can benefit can also be relevant in determining whether the trust is a relevant person for the purposes of the remittance rules: see Chs 3 and 8.

[110] With effect from April 6, 2006: see s.77(2A).

[111] Section 169F(2) and (3A).

[112] See *West v Trennery* [2005] STC 214 and especially the comments of Lord Millett. This definition does not apply to non-resident trusts. An offshore trust is "qualifying" and gains are taxed

EXAMPLE 7.10

In 1996 Henry sets up a trust in which he is the life tenant. In 2005 the trust is divided into two funds A and B. He retains an interest in possession in Fund A but Fund B is held on trust for his grandchildren and he and all defined persons in (ii) above are excluded from any benefit. Although for income tax purposes he will not be taxed on the income in Fund B nor for inheritance tax purposes treated as reserving a benefit in Fund B, for capital gains tax purposes he was until April 6, 2008 taxed on gains realised within both Funds A and B. A sub-fund election might have avoided the problem.[113] Even though he is excluded from Fund B, if he adds assets to that Fund he cannot claim hold-over relief unless a sub-fund election is made.[114]

7.53 Even if the trust is settlor-interested within the above definition, there is no restriction on hold-over relief on gifts to UK resident trusts nor is there a claw-back of relief if any of the following conditions are met:

(i) The only defined person who can benefit is the settlor's spouse or civil partner and the settlor and spouse/civil partner are separated in circumstances where the separation is likely to be permanent.[115] The legislation does not attempt to catch cohabitees.[116]

(ii) The settlor dies during the tax year before the material time.[117]

(iii) The terms of the trust are such that although a dependent child could, in principle, benefit, the settlor does not have living dependent children, i.e. no account is taken of future dependent children.[118] Nor is account taken of children who are minors and can benefit but can only benefit at 18.[119] However, unlike s.77(3) and (3B) which excluded future spouses or civil partners as well as future born dependent children,[120] it appears that s.169F treats a trust which could benefit future civil partners or spouses as one which is settlor-interested from the start, even though the settlor is unmarried. Hence, in these circumstances there is no hold-over relief.[121]

(iv) a widow or widower or a surviving civil partner is not a defined person.

on the settlor under TCGA 1992 s.86 if (broadly) the settlor, spouse/civil partner/children (whether or not minors), grandchildren or their spouses can benefit: see Ch.19.

[113] On whether a sub-fund election was possible: see Ch.12.

[114] See Ch.12.

[115] See s.169F(4)(a); this mirrors s.77(3)(c) now repealed.

[116] cf. the remittance rules and ITA 2007 s.809M (definition of relevant person in relation to trusts).

[117] So if the trustees conferred a benefit on the spouse after the settlor had died this would not result in a claw-back of hold-over relief. This mirrors s.77(6)(a).

[118] See s.169F(4B) which mirrors s.77(3B).

[119] Cf. ITA 2007 s.809M and see Ch.18.

[120] So gains realised by a trust which could benefit future spouses and future born dependent children were not taxed on the settlor under s.77 if he was excluded reversing the effect of *Unmarried Settlor v IRC* [2003] STC (SCD) 274.

[121] See TCGA 1992 s.169F(4B) which specifically provides that no account is taken of a term of a settlement relating to dependent children at any time when the individual has no dependent children but does not mention spouses/civil partners.

EXAMPLE 7.11

Harry set up a UK resident trust for his children, grandchildren and any surviving spouse. All his children are adult. The possibility of having children in the future is ignored until such time as he does have children. Similarly, the fact that his wife can benefit after his death does not make the trust settlor-interested. If, however, the trust could benefit a *future* spouse of Harry's while he is alive then in theory it is settlor-interested even if he is not married or he is married to a spouse who is excluded.[122] Hold-over relief is denied.

7.54 Even if the settlor and spouse can potentially benefit, the settlor is not treated as having an interest in the trust if no actual benefit is enjoyed by him, or his spouse/civil partner and one of the following conditions are met:

(a) none of the property or derived property comprised in the settlement can become payable or applicable for the benefit of settlor or spouse/civil partner except, in the case of a marriage settlement, on the death of both parties to, and of all the children of, the marriage[123]; or

(b) none of the property or derived property comprised in the settlement can become payable or applicable for the benefit of settlor or his spouse/civil partner except on the death of a child of the settlor who had become beneficially entitled to the property while aged 25 or under.[124] Derived property includes income from the property.

---

[122] HMRC do not comment except to note at CGTM 35150 that the list of exceptions is shorter than for income tax purposes. Unless there is express provision to the contrary, the case law is clear that the settlor still has an interest in the settlement if it allows benefit to be conferred on a future spouse however hypothetical. This is the effect of the decisions in *IRC v Tennant* (1942) 24 TC 215 and *Unmarried Settlor v IRC* [2003] STC (SCD) 274. In the first of these cases the settlor had an overriding power of appointment and in the second the trustees had an unrestricted power to add beneficiaries. In both cases, the settlor was unmarried, but had he married in the future the power could, as a matter of construction, have been exercised in favour of the future spouse. This, it was held, was sufficient to render the settlement settlor-interested within the meaning of the then income tax and capital gains tax provisions. The income tax provisions in ITTOIA 2005 s.620 and the pre-repeal version of TCGA 1992 s.77 removed this as respects UK resident settlements. They specifically excluded from the term "spouse" any person to whom the settlor is not currently married but may later marry. Unfortunately, equivalent exclusions are not found in the hold-over relief provisions or indeed in relation to non-resident trusts: see TCGA 1992 Sch.5.

[123] So if the trust fund reverted to the settlor's estate on the death of all parties this would not be settlor-interested. This mirrors the old s.77(4)(c).

[124] This mirrors the old s.77(4)(d) but note ss.77(4)(a) and (b) are omitted. The wording is far from straightforward. Note that the settlor's entitlement can only arise if the following conditions are met:

(a) the child becomes entitled to both income and capital (at the latest) by age 25; and

(b) he then dies.

It is very odd for trusts to be drafted in this way: a common trust would give the income or capital to the child contingently on attaining 25, failing which it is to revert to the settlor. But that does not fall within the wording. Such a trust would be settlor-interested for capital gains tax purposes but not for income tax purposes: see 7.09.

Example 7.12

(1) Harry set up a UK resident trust for his grandchildren who take at 25. He can benefit from capital if all his grandchildren die before attaining 25 leaving no issue. The trust is settlor-interested for capital gains tax hold-over relief purposes since none of the above exceptions apply. (Harry would not be regarded as reserving a benefit for inheritance tax purposes given that his retained interest involves a carve-out but he would be regarded as having an interest for pre-owned assets income tax purposes and, indeed, for income tax purposes generally.)[125]

(2) If, however, the trust had been for the benefit of his adult children and provided that they became beneficially entitled to trust property or derived property on or before 25 (so for example they took entitlement to capital not merely income at age 25) and subject to that the trust property reverted to Harry on their deaths the trust is not settlor-interested for hold-over relief purposes! It is assumed that this provision would allow the children to take an absolute defeasible interest and Harry could only benefit if they then die.

7.55 Additional exceptions (previously available under s.77 and which still apply for income tax purposes) do not apply (and have never applied) in relation to deciding whether a trust is settlor-interested for hold-over relief purposes. For instance, s.77(4)[126] provided that a trust was not settlor-interested if:

(a) no property could become payable to the settlor except in the event of the bankruptcy of some person who was or might become beneficially entitled to the property or an assignment of the property being made by such person, nor

(b) while some person was alive and under 25, the property could not become payable during that person's life to the settlor or spouse except in the event of that person becoming bankrupt or assigning or charging his interest.[127]

Derived property

7.56 "Derived property" is defined in s.169F(2)[128] and its meaning was considered in *West v Trennery*[129] where the House of Lords held that property can be related or derived property even if it is no longer in the settlement.

Derived property was originally defined in s.77(8) as:

---

[125] See 7.08 and following and Ch.33.
[126] And the equivalent income tax provisions: see 7.08.
[127] See further 7.09 and Example 7.1(2).
[128] The term was also found in s.77(2) and is in the income tax provisions at ITTOIA 2005 s.625 (where the concept of "related property" is given the same meaning).
[129] [2005] STC 214.

> "*income from that property or any other property directly or indirectly representing proceeds of, or of income from, that property or income there from.*"

Given the confusions that this definition caused (discussed in *Trennery*), it was amended in FA 2006[130] and s.77(8)[131] read:

> "*derived property in relation to any property means—*
>
> (a) *income from that property;*
> (b) *property directly or indirectly representing*
>
> (i) *proceeds of that property; or*
> (ii) *proceeds of income from that property; or*
>
> (c) *income from property which is derived property by virtue of paragraph (b) above.*"

West v Trennery

7.57 In *West v Trennery* the taxpayer had submitted that the pre-2006 definition was limited to income from that property, or from any other property. He was successful before the Special Commissioners[132]; lost in the High Court[133]; won at the Court of Appeal[134] and lost in the House of Lords.[135] The case involved two UK resident trusts with almost identical terms. They were used to affect a flip-flop scheme[136] designed to reduce the rate of capital gains tax on a trustee disposal from 40 to 25 per cent.[137] Each settlement created in April 1995, gave the settlor an initial interest in possession and so was settlor-interested. On April 4, 1995, the settlor transferred shares to Trust 1 and held-over the gain (restrictions on hold-over relief were only introduced in 2003). On the same day those trustees borrowed 75 per cent of the value of the shares (giving a mortgage over the shares) and transferred this sum to Trust 2. On April 5, 1995 the trustees of the first settlement excluded the settlor and all other defined persons as beneficiaries. It remained interest in possession (with the intention that gains should only be taxed at 25 not 40 per cent). In the following tax year the trustees of Trust 1 sold the shares and realised the gains, 75 per cent of the sale proceeds were used to repay the borrowings. The 25 per cent left over was used to pay the capital gains tax due. Nothing was left in Trust 1. All the value represented by the shares was in Trust 2.

---

[130] See Sch.12 para.13.
[131] Now repealed but the same wording is found in TCGA 1992 s.169F(6).
[132] [2002] STC (SCD) 370.
[133] [2003] EWHC 676 (Ch).
[134] [2004] STC 170.
[135] [2005] STC 214.
[136] Discussed in Chs 12 and 19.
[137] From April 6, 2004 all UK trusts paid capital gains tax at 40% so that the scheme ceased to have any relevance after that date. In any event since *Trennery* was ultimately lost by the taxpayer it was hard to see any justification for Sch.4B continuing to apply to UK resident trusts which have never been non-resident or received property from a non-UK resident trust. It was finally repealed for such trusts from April 6, 2008.

If the first trust was settlor-interested in the second tax year, the gains **7.58** would have been taxable at 40 per cent on the settlor and the scheme would have failed. HMRC therefore needed to show that in the tax year of sale, the settled property of Trust 1 or any derived property was payable or applicable for the benefit of the settlor in any circumstances whatsoever. They initially presented three arguments:

(i) the cash transferred to the second settlement remained derived property in relation to the first settlement and hence the first settlement remained settlor-interested;

(ii) the settlor retained a benefit because he had made the borrowing as one of the trustees; was personally liable for the borrowing and had a right of indemnity out of Trust 1;

(iii) on the construction of the documents the settlor had not been excluded from the first settlement because he could still benefit from Trust 1 through an advance to another settlement in which he was a potential beneficiary.

The High Court decided in favour of HMRC on (i) but held that (ii) and (iii) failed. The High Court decision in favour of HMRC on (i) was reversed by the Court of Appeal,[138] the two secondary arguments ((ii) and (iii)) decided in favour of the taxpayer in the High Court were not appealed by HMRC.

So far as (ii) and (iii) were concerned, Peter Smith J. in the High Court held **7.59** that the fact that as trustee the settlor had an implied right of indemnity did not mean he had a derived benefit. This was just:

> "*a normal right, which is an incident of trusteeship. The settlor has no personal benefit from that right of indemnity as it only vests in him in his capacity as trustee.*"[139]

He also held that the settlor does not have an interest in a settlement just because he could theoretically benefit if there was a transfer of the funds from Trust 1 to a transferee trust where he could be added as a beneficiary. He distinguished *IRC v Botnar*[140]: if the settlor could only benefit by the independent act of a third party, s.77 did not apply. His decision was presumably reached on the basis that the trustees and the settlor did not intend that the power to transfer funds to another settlement would be used to enable the money to be passed to the settlor. Ideally when excluding the settlor from the first trust the draftsman should have provided that the trustees could not exercise any of their dispositive powers (including any power to transfer to another settlement) in such a way as to benefit the settlor or his spouse. The decision is helpful in cases where this has not been done.

As already noted, the High Court decided that (i), namely that the property **7.60** in Trust 2 was derived property from Trust 1, succeeded. Derived property included property outside the settlement and moneys raised by loan must be

---

[138] [2004] STC 170. The Court of Appeal decision was in turn reversed by the House of Lords.
[139] This may be relevant in the inheritance tax context, for example in the application of FA 1986 s.103 where a donor may incur liabilities as a trustee: see Ch.33.
[140] [1999] STC 711.

derived from the mortgage of the shares. However, the Court of Appeal held that property could only be derived property if it was settled property in the chargeable (first) settlement. As it was not comprised in that settlement it was not derived property.

7.61   Like the Court of Appeal, the House of Lords rejected the taxpayer's first contention that s.77(8) applied only to income from the originally settled property and not capital.[141] However, they also rejected the taxpayer's other argument, that once the borrowed funds reached Trust 2 they were no longer derived property. They decided that the definition of derived property was not so limited. The mortgage of the shares meant that the money borrowed represented the proceeds of the shares. Section 77(8) referred to "*the proceeds of the property*" not the proceeds of sale of that property and therefore could include proceeds of a mortgage secured on the shares. Lord Millett attempted to put some limits on this and suggested that the cash appointed to the second trust ceased to be derived property once the first settlement sold the shares, for then the property which the borrowed money represented had gone. Lord Walker, however, did not impose any such limits and summarised the position as follows:

> "*In my opinion the £770,000 [the borrowings] started off as derived property (and was also, for a matter of hours or minutes, property comprised in the first settlement). It continued to be derived property after it was appointed out of the first settlement. The effect of the taxpayer's argument would be to cut off the operation of the derived property provision at the very moment when it started to have some work to do. The economic effect of the arrangements was to transfer about three quarters of the value of the shares to the second settlement, but without any disposal of the shares for CGT purposes . . . the Section 77 requirement that the chargeable settlement should, in the year of assessment in question, contain some property to which the derived property can be linked provides some restriction on its scope but I would accept that it does not meet every possible hard case.*"

7.62   The case illustrates that great care is required if the intention is to avoid a trust becoming settlor-interested or to ensure it is no longer settlor-interested. For example, if the settlor made a gift into a non-settlor-interested trust and claimed hold-over relief, and the trustees borrowed and appointed the borrowings to new trusts which were (even if incidentally) capable of benefiting the settlor then on the basis of *West* there may be a claw back of hold-over relief. Presumably the same meaning of derived property applies for income tax purposes in relation to related property.[142]

---

[141] The amendment to s.77(8) made by FA 2006 which is reflected in s.169F was designed to put this beyond doubt.

[142] See ITTOIA 2005 ss.625 and 626. Flip-flop schemes were also carried out by offshore trusts on a similar basis to avoid a charge under s.86. "Derived property" is not used in the offshore trust legislation albeit TCGA 1992 Sch.5 does refer to relevant property which can include property provided by the settlor "or property representing that property". The proceeds of a mortgage could still represent that property: see Ch.19.

Definition of settlor[143]

The general meaning of settlor for capital gains tax purposes is discussed in Ch.9. However, s.169E contains its own definition as follows: **7.63**

> *"a person is a settlor in relation to a settlement if:-*
>
> *(a)   he is an individual, and*
> *(b)   the settled property consists of, or includes, property originating from him."*

This is the same definition as was used for the purposes of s.77 except that it was not limited to individuals. It is different from the definition in s.68A which refers to persons (not individuals) who have provided or undertaken to provide property directly or indirectly for the purposes of the settlement. The difference arises out of the fact that hold-over relief under TCGA 1992 ss.165 and 260 is only available in the first place if an individual makes the disposal.

Section 169E states that property is treated as *"originating from a person"* if he has provided it directly or indirectly for the purposes of the settlement or if another person has provided it pursuant to reciprocal arrangements. It also includes property which wholly or partly represents property originating from the settlement.[144]

For s.77 purposes a person was only a settlor in relation to that part of the trust property originating from him or property which represented such property, including accumulated income of the property. If no such property was left in the settlement he ceased to be the settlor in relation to it.[145] However, if the trust becomes settlor-interested as to *any part of the property* comprised in it, a claw-back of any held-over gain can be triggered[146] even if the held-over gain relates to a disposal by a different settlor. The result is that additions by (say) a beneficiary can trigger a tax charge on the original settlor.[147] This may have been an accident of drafting but HMRC appear to take the point.[148] **7.64**

VI THE SCOPE OF THE SETTLEMENTS LEGISLATION— RECENT CASE LAW

The Arctic Systems Case[149]

The case concerned an IT specialist who had worked as an employee for several years. However, in 1992, he was made redundant and, following discus- **7.65**

---

[143] See 9.23.
[144] The definition is broadly similar to that in s.68A and the old s.79 and is found in Sch.5 for the purposes of s.86 although s.86 does not refer to *"for the purposes of the settlement"*.
[145] See also TGCA 1992 s.68A(6).
[146] See Example 18.23.
[147] See s.169C(2).
[148] See CGTM 66923.
[149] *Jones v Garnett* [2007] STC 1536 HL

sions with his wife, he decided to set up his own consultancy business. At an early stage, it became clear to Mr Jones that he would have to form a limited company because the IT agencies and their clients would only deal with companies. As a result, on the advice of his accountants, Mr Jones and his wife acquired two shares in an off-the-shelf company called Arctic Systems Ltd, for which they each paid £1. Mr Jones was the sole director. As is customary with many small companies, he did not have a written service contract. Mrs Jones was the company secretary and she also undertook all the administrative work such as book-keeping, invoicing and liaising with clients—she spent, on average, five hours per week on company business. The company paid them both a modest salary which was intended to meet their "basic needs", with the balance of the profits (after deduction of tax) being distributed as dividends. In his capacity as director, it was Mr Jones' decision as to when and in what sum dividends should be declared.

7.66   HMRC considered that the settlement provisions applied to the dividends received by Mrs Jones so that they were taxed as the income of her husband. The case was heard in 2004 by two Special Commissioners who, very unusually, could not agree on the outcome.[150] Accordingly, the presiding Special Commissioner (Dr Brice) exercised her casting vote for the dismissal of Mr Jones' appeal against the tax assessment. Mr Jones appealed to the High Court.

7.67   In the High Court,[151] Park J. found in favour of HMRC. A unanimous Court of Appeal then found in favour of the taxpayer.[152] There were two substantive issues on which the Court of Appeal had to make a determination:

(i) whether there was a settlement within the statutory definition[153]; and

(ii) if so, whether it could be taken out of the charge to income tax by the let-out for outright gifts to a spouse.[154]

7.68   In the words of Sir Andrew Morritt:

> "*The answer to the first question depends on the proper construction and application of the long-standing provisions to be found in ss.660A–660G ICTA 1988 in the light of the guidance afforded by a number of reported cases decided since 1939 (this is a reference to Copeman v Coleman (1939)). The answer to the second question depends on the true construction and application of s.660A(6) ICTA 1988.*"

He said that the formation of Arctic Systems did not constitute a settlement because it involved no "bounty" and the manner in which Mr and Mrs Jones subsequently ran the company in terms of salaries and dividends did not form part of an arrangement that constituted a settlement. Carnwath L.J. noted:

> "*for the first time [the Revenue] seek to apply the concept [of settlement] to what has been found to be a normal commercial transaction between*

---

[150] [2005] STC (SCD) 9.
[151] [2005] STC 1667.
[152] [2006] STC 283.
[153] TA 1988 s.660G(1). See now ITTOIA 2005 s.620(1).
[154] TA 1988 s.660A(6). See now ITTOIA 2005 s.626.

two adults, to which each is making a substantial commercial contribution albeit not of the same economic value."

Sir Andrew Morritt noted:

"*the Court [is not required] to ignore the increasing tendency for married couples to be involved in the business of each other on a commercial non-bounteous basis. Such involvement may take the form of a partnership or a company in which each own shares. Though one spouse may generate the income of the firm or company, the services of the other may be just as commercially important in providing the essential administrative, accounting, support and back-up services.*"

He added:

"*In this case, there can be no doubt but that the arrangement was or included the acquisition by Mrs Jones of her share in the company. Equally, there can be no doubt that the acquisition on its own was for full value in the context of a joint business venture to which both parties made substantial and valuable contributions. If the arrangement is confined to such acquisition, then I would agree with counsel for Mr Jones that it cannot constitute a settlement for the purposes of S660G(1) ICTA 1988 . . .*

The 'bounty' on which HMRC necessarily rely is that provided subsequently and in fact by the combination of the demand and charge-out rate for the services of Mr Jones, the salary in fact paid to Mr Jones, the other commitments of the company and the dividend subsequently declared and paid by the company to Mrs Jones. All these additional elements depended on the will of Mr Jones or on wholly extraneous factors. He did not commit himself to working for the company at any particular rate of salary or at all. His charge-out rate necessarily depended on the demand for his services and the going market rate. Whether any and, if so, what profits were made depended not only on the difference between Mr Jones' charge-out rate and salary but the level of the company's overheads and other commitments. If the company made profits, whether to declare any and, if so, what dividend was a matter for Mr Jones as the sole director and controlling shareholder.

For my part, I do not think that these elements can be included in the 'arrangement'. They did not form any part of a structure of things or combination of objects; their uncertainty and fluidity is the converse of an arrangement. It is not that they were not legally enforceable, they were not settled at all. No doubt Mr and Mrs Jones hoped for the best, but it cannot be said that they had arranged it. Without these elements, there was no element of bounty and no settlement within the statutory definition."

He therefore concluded that there was no settlement:

"*In the absence of any service agreement between the company and Mr Jones,[155] I am unable to accept that the payment of modest salaries to Mr*

---

[155] Unlike many of the earlier settlement disputes (which typically involved parents settling income from the benefit of their children), there was *no* contract or mechanism in place at the outset either:

Jones was any part of the arrangement. Similarly, the declaration of the dividends was not arranged in advance; it was dependent on the trading fortunes of the company. Further, as counsel for Mr Jones submitted and as I accept, the fact that the structure being set up might lend itself in the future to some tax mitigation is irrelevant to the existence of an element of bounty."

7.69 On the question of the possible application of TA 1988 s.660A(6), Sir Andrew Morritt said that, if there had been a settlement, it would not have helped the taxpayer because:

 (i) there was no outright gift of a share from Mr Jones to his wife, but that if there had been;

 (ii) an ordinary share is *not* substantially a right to income.

7.70 HMRC appealed to the House of Lords who decided in favour of the tax-payer but for different reasons! In Lord Hoffmann's opinion Sir Andrew's analysis was divorced from reality because this was not a normal commercial arrangement between two adults. Mr Jones would never have entered into the arrangement with someone with whom he was dealing at arm's length. The arrangements contained the "necessary element of bounty" to constitute a settlement:

> *"Authority for taking a broad and realist view of the matter may be found in several cases of which the most relevant is Crossland v Hawkins . . . Mrs Jones could not have been issued with a share without the agreement of her husband and when he agreed to that arrangement it was expected that he would take a low salary and that substantial dividends would be distributed. That was the advice which they had received from the accountant. And that was what happened . . . the decisions were tax driven and not commercially driven. And it was necessary, in order to gain the tax benefit, that Mr Jones should in a broad sense, transfer some of his earnings to his wife."*

7.71 However, he found that the transfer of the share to his wife *had* been an outright gift between spouses within s.626 so that the charging provision in s.624 did not apply. Once one accepted that there had been bounty the fact that she bought it for £1 did not mean there was no gift. Mr Jones' consent to the transfer of a share with expectations of dividend to Mrs Jones for £1 gave the transfer the element of bounty and made the transfer a gift. But the share was not wholly or substantially a right to income even if its value arose from the expectation that it would generate income. It was an ordinary share conferring a right to vote and to participate in the distribution of assets on a winding up etc. HMRC also argued that the transfer of the share was not the whole of the arrangement which included the provision of services by Mr Jones and the dividend policy. This was rejected and it was held that the transfer of the share

 – to agree the future income of the business; or

 – to decide on what might be done with any such income (e.g. the payment of salaries or dividends at a later date). Compare for example, *Crosland v Hawkins* [1961] Ch 537.

was the essence of the arrangement. The expectation of other future events gave that transfer the necessary element of bounty but *the events themselves did not form part of the arrangement*. The arrangement must be identified by the constituent parts of the legal structure at the start and not by what is done later in using the structure for its intended purpose. Baroness Hale tentatively suggested that the Revenue's argument might have been easier to understand by adopting a year on year approach—looking at the level of salary drawn each year. If each spouse made a financial contribution and received equal contributions there would be no settlement in that year but there could be in other years. However, as she noted *"there are many variations and permutations"* and she did not pursue this line.

Following the case the Treasury issued the following statement in July 2007:   **7.72**

> *"The Government is committed to maintaining fairness in the tax system. The case has brought to light the need for the Government to ensure that there is greater clarity in the law regarding its position on the tax treatment of 'income splitting'. ...it is the Government's view that individuals involved in these arrangements should pay tax on what is, in substance, their own income and that the legislation should clearly provide for this. The Government will therefore bring forward proposals for changes to legislation."*

Draft legislation was published on December 6, 2007 to discourage "income-   **7.73** shifting". These proposals, set out in new ITA 2007 ss.681A–681F were the subject of widespread criticism. They not only reallocated dividends in the case of husband and wife companies but also extended to partnerships and could in some cases affect trust arrangements. The Chancellor announced that a further period of consultation was necessary and deferred the start of the new regime. More recently there has been a further consultation on the taxation of small businesses carried out by the Office for Tax Simplification[156] mainly focused on IR35 although there may be further developments in this area.

Of course, the case arose because different tax burdens are imposed on   **7.74** similar types of income, namely dividends and salary. It might also be questioned why the Government as a matter of policy is happy to let property or savings assets be divided between spouses to allow the lower-earning spouse to use his or her personal allowances and basic rate bands but earned income cannot be so diverted. It is not easy to identify what is in substance another person's income where individuals work together in a family business including partnerships where all members are exposed to commercial risk.

HMRC have continued to pursue cases involving husband and wife com-   **7.75** panies or companies where income is diverted to minor children with mixed success.

For example, in *Patmore v HMRC*,[157] HMRC were unsuccessful. The   **7.76** facts of that case were unusual principally because the wife made a genuine contribution of capital for her shares. Mr Patmore started to work for an engineering company soon after it was established, and subsequently became a director. As at 2000, Mr Patmore owned 15 of the 100 issued shares, with

---

[156] See *Small Business Review*, March 2011.
[157] [2010] SFTD 1124.

the remainder owned by the company's founder and his family. At around that time, the company's founder announced that he wished to retire and wanted to sell the business. This led to the founder and his family selling their 85 shares to Mr Patmore and his wife. The total purchase price was £320,000, payable in three instalments over about 20 months. The initial instalment of £100,000 was raised by way of mortgage on the Patmore's jointly-owned family home, the remaining two instalments were to be funded by dividends paid out of the company's post-sale profits. Of the 85 shares acquired, Mr Patmore was allocated 83 (bringing his total to 98) and Mrs Patmore took two shares. However, a couple of months later, the company renamed the shares as A shares and created a new class of shares, B shares, of which 10 were issued, all to Mrs Patmore. Over the next few years, dividends were paid on both classes of shares, bringing Mrs Patmore's dividend income to about 40 per cent of the total paid by the company.

HMRC challenged the arrangement, arguing that Mrs Patmore's dividend income ought to be assessed on Mr Patmore under the settlements code. They failed because they were unable to prove that Mr P had conferred any bounty. Mrs Patmore was getting a disproportionate dividend in relation to her actual shareholding but that differed from her contribution. As the judge held:

> "Mrs Patmore was jointly liable with Mr Patmore on the mortgage and the [share purchase instalment] debt. She contributed equally to him in the purchase of 85 shares. In return, she was given a mere two shares and was later allocated 10 B shares with no rights to a dividend . . . I struggle to see any element of bounty by Mr Patmore."

The judge instead interpreted the facts as one involving a constructive trust— in this case, although Mr Patmore owned a greater proportion of the shares, some of his shareholding was to be treated as beneficially held for his wife. Ultimately, the judge considered that Mrs Patmore was beneficially entitled to 42.5 per cent of the company (being one half of the shares acquired by the couple in 2000). For this reason, the overall arrangement generally fell outside of the scope of the settlements code. The settlements legislation could, however, apply to the extent that Mrs Patmore's income exceeded this 42.5 per cent share.

7.77   In *Buck v HMRC*[158] the 99 per cent majority shareholder (the husband) waived his entitlement to the company dividends, thereby channelling the company's profits to his then wife. The Special Commissioner decided that the only gift element was the right to the dividend income itself, meaning that the statutory let-out for gifts between spouses could not apply. The total dividends payable were effectively a fixed monetary amount so that any shareholder waiving his entitlement was thereby increasing that of another shareholder, thus conferring bounty. If the dividends had been calculated on a fixed amount per share (with each share of the same class receiving the same dividend) then any individual shareholder waiving his entitlement would not have increased that of another shareholder thereby generating no element of bounty. In this case the dividend value of £35,000 per share could not have been met from the company's reserves if all share-holders had taken up their right to the dividend thereby proving the exist-

---

[158] [2009] STC (SCD) 6.

ence of arrangements to confer bounty as the dividend of £35,000 could only legally have been declared in the first place with prior knowledge of the waiver.

7.78 The *Bird* case[159] concerned arrangements benefiting minor children (the children took a 60 per cent shareholding and thereby received dividends). Again, it was held to be within the scope of the settlements code; the statutory let-out in s.626 did not apply, as its scope is limited to arrangements between spouses and civil partners.

THE SCOPE OF "SETTLEMENTS LEGISLATION"—SUMMARY

7.79 It should be remembered that the following have all been held to be settlements for income tax purposes:

(a) the release or assignment by a life tenant or other beneficiary of his interest under a settlement[160];

(b) the creation of a company by which a taxpayer is engaged to provide services for a modest salary with the company then providing the taxpayer's services for a much greater amount[161];

(c) the provision of funds and work for a company owned by minor children with minimal share capital where the parents lent money to the company, guaranteed bank borrowings and caused the company to enter into a development project[162];

(d) the creation of preference shares issued to children or spouses with the company then paying exceptional dividends on those shares[163];

(e) the gift or sale at an undervalue of shares in a company whereby husband works at a modest salary and dividends are paid on both shares.[164] As noted above this was held to be an arrangement but protected as an outright gift;

7.80 As the House of Lords made clear in *Jones* the question of whether there is an arrangement or settlement must be identified at the time it is made; subsequent events may be evidence of the intention of the parties at the time of the arrangement but are not part of the arrangement itself. So in that case the establishment by the taxpayers of the corporate structure, together with their common intention to take shares in it and to avoid tax was the arrangement. It is not clear whether the holder of a life interest who consents to termination of his life interest becomes a settlor.[165] *IRC v Mills* and *Butler v Wildin* might suggest that the provision of services is a settlement. However, the House of Lords noted that it is the provision of funds not the provision of services

---

[159] [2009] STC(SCD) 81.
[160] See *IRC v Buchanan* (1957) 37 TC 365.
[161] See *IRC v Mills* [1974] STC 130.
[162] See *Butler v Wildin* [1989] STC 22.
[163] See *Copeman v Coleman* (1939) 22 TC 594 and *Young v Pearce* [1996] STC 743.
[164] See *Jones v Garnett* [2007] UKHL 35.
[165] See *D'Abreu v IRC* (1978) STC 538.

that makes the person a settlor. Hence, if services are provided to a trust or a company on arms' length terms, there is no settlement.

VII MAKING A TRUST NON-SETTLOR-INTERESTED—POINTS TO WATCH

7.81   In many cases it becomes necessary to exclude the settlor from a trust. For example, where there is a continuing reservation of benefit a UK domiciled settlor should be excluded: this will involve a deemed PET under FA 1986 s.102(4). The settlor may not need access to the trust income any longer and with to avoid paying tax under the settlement provisions.

7.82   If the settlor/spouse/civil partner is excluded, in the following tax year the settlor will not be subject to tax on the settlement income.[166] However, this is not the case if the trust has lent or distributed capital funds to the settlor, which are then repaid and there is future undistributed trust income that is matched to that capital receipt.[167]

7.83   Moreover as discussed in Ch.8 the position is different under the transfer of assets regime and if the settlor has at any time received a capital distribution then he can in theory continue to be taxed on the income of a non-UK resident company held by the trust whether or not he receives it and even after he has been wholly excluded.[168]

Drafting issues

7.84   To ensure the trust is not settlor-interested for income tax purposes, it is not necessary to exclude the settlor's widow or cohabitee, only the settlor or his spouse/civil partner. It may also be necessary for the settlor to assign any interest he has in remainder (e.g. under a resulting trust) to ensure that the trust is no longer settlor-interested. Check the default trusts in the deed and that the settlor's estate could not take in default if the contingent interests failed.

7.85   For example, a trust "for A for life and then to B at 25 and in default to the grandchildren of the settlor who are living at the end of the Trust Period" would be settlor-interested because there is a resulting trust in favour of the settlor, however remote. The settlor needs to assign his reversionary interest. The trust should instead have been drafted "for A for life, B at 25 and in default to the issue of the settlor living at the date of this deed in equal shares". This creates exhaustive trusts with no possibility of reverter to the settlor or his estate.

7.86   If a trust is made non-settlor-interested this may have POAT implications.[169]

7.87   Finally if a decision is taken to exclude the settlor, ensure that the settlor/spouse/civil partners are fully excluded and not just from the particular trust but also from benefiting under any future exercise of the trustees' discretion to create a resettlement.

---

[166] Under ITTOIA 2005 s.624.
[167] See 7.45 above.
[168] See ITA 2007 ss.728 and 729 and Example 8.5(2).
[169] See Ch.34.

CHAPTER 8

INCOME TAX OF NON-RESIDENT TRUSTS—THE FOREIGN DIMENSION

- Settlor-interested trusts (**8.01**)
- Non-settlor-interested offshore structures (**8.38**)
- Summary of how the provisions operate for foreign domiciled settlors and beneficiaries (**8.62**)

This chapter considers the income tax treatment of non-resident trusts, looking first at settlor-interested trusts before considering the taxation of non-settlor-interested trusts. In general, a non-resident trust can still be useful as a way of sheltering income if the trust is discretionary: all trust income is foreign source and the settlor/spouse/civil partner are wholly excluded from any benefit.[1] In these circumstances income can be rolled up free of UK tax until it is distributed to a UK resident and domiciled beneficiary. However, as explained at 8.38, a UK resident beneficiary will find it difficult to avoid tax when he receives distributions from the trust (whether of income or capital).

I SETTLOR-INTERESTED TRUSTS[2]

The settlements legislation

The basic rules for determining whether a trust is settlor-interested for the **8.01** purposes of the settlements legislation have been considered at some length in Ch.7 in relation to UK resident trusts. The rules for determining whether a trust is settlor-interested for income tax purposes operate in the same way for non-resident settlements. Hence, the income of an offshore trust is prima facie assessable as the settlor's under ITTOIA 2005 Pt 5 Ch.5 if he is UK resident. If the settlor is not UK resident then foreign source trust income that arose while he was non-resident cannot be taxed on him if he later becomes UK

---

[1] Or the settlor is dead or non-resident.

[2] For when trustees are non-UK resident, see Ch.4. For settlor-interested UK trusts, see Ch.7. For taxation of foreign domiciliaries, see Ch.5. For offshore trusts and capital gains tax provisions, see Ch.19. For offshore income gains and non-resident trusts, see Ch.53. For taxation of offshore companies, see Ch.54.

resident even if the trust income is then remitted by the trust or the settlor.[3] As a result, trust income arising prior to the settlor becoming UK resident should be segregated from income arising subsequently whether it is retained in the trust or distributed to the settlor.

Non domiciled settlors

8.02 The settlements legislation can apply to settlors taxed on the remittance basis as well as to UK domiciliaries but foreign source income of the trust is excluded from charge on the settlor unless and until that income is remitted to the UK by any relevant person, including the settlor.[4] Income received by a settlor-interested trust can also be assessed on the settlor or "transferor" under the transfer of assets (TOA) legislation[5] but in cases of overlap the settlement code takes priority.[6] The remittance basis user who is the settlor remains fully assessable to UK source income of the trust. However, the non-resident discretionary trustees in receipt of UK source income are account-able for tax at 50 per cent and the settlor must then claim any overpaid tax back.[7]

8.03 The relevant provisions that provide for the remittance basis are in ITTOIA 2005 s.648. Subsection (3) provides that:

> "and if for a tax year section 809B, 809D or 809E of ITA 2007 (remit-tance basis) applies to the settlor, references in this Chapter to income arising under a settlement include in relation to any relevant foreign income arising under the settlement in that tax year only such of it as is remitted to the UK (in that tax year or any subsequent tax year) in circumstances such that if the settlor remitted it, the settlor would be chargeable to income tax."

Section 648(5) states that:

> "where subsection (3) applies, the remitted income is treated for the pur-poses of this Chapter as arising under the settlement in the tax year in which it is remitted."[8]

The question of whether a trust's income has been remitted by the settlor is determined by the general rules in ITA 2007 so, for example, if the trust (a relevant person) invests foreign source trust income in the UK this is treated as a remittance by the settlor.

---

[3] See ITTOIA 2005 s.648(2). Similarly there is no charge under the TOA legislation if the trans-feror is non-resident when the income arises.

[4] See ITA 2007 s.809L and Ch.5 for further details of remittance basis and meaning of "relevant person" which includes the trust and any company owned by the trust.

[5] ITA 2007 ss.720–730.

[6] Section 624 deems the trust income to be the income of the settlor alone for income tax pur-poses so it is not then treated as the income of the person abroad, the trustees.

[7] See Ch.7 for the mechanics.

[8] This wording was amended by FA 2009 with effect from April 22, 2009.

Transitional rules for pre-April 6, 2008 relevant foreign income

FA 2008 s.86(4) provides that for remittance purposes, in relation to pre-April **8.04**
6, 2008 relevant foreign income of the individual, references to a relevant
person are solely to the individual. So if a remittance basis user gives pre-
April 6, 2008 relevant foreign income[9] to his spouse abroad in 2010 and she
remits it but does not benefit the donor, there is no taxable remittance by
the donor. The domicile of the spouse is irrelevant: it is capital in her hands.
For this reason many remittance basis users have kept pre-April 6, 2008
relevant foreign income separate from post-April 5, 2008 relevant foreign
income so it can be used by relevant persons other than the individual in the
UK.

What is the position in relation to pre-April 2008 relevant foreign income **8.05**
arising within the trust? Although not free from doubt, it is thought that if
income arose to a settlor-interested discretionary trust (or to a trust where the
settlor is the life tenant) before April 6, 2008 but is remitted after that date,
s.648(5) (which states that income is treated as arising under the trust in the
year in which it is remitted) does not mean that it is taxable as post-April 5,
2008 income if a relevant person other than the settlor (e.g the trustees) remits
it. So, in effect, there is an exemption to ensure that pre-April 2008 income of
the settlement is not taxed on a remittance by someone other than the settlor.[10]

EXAMPLE 8.1

(1) A settlor-interested non-resident trust received foreign source income in
2005. This was paid to the settlor in 2005–06 and he remits it in 2009. He
pays tax on that income (and would have done so under the pre-April 6,
2008 rules). But if he gives it to his wife abroad and she remits it there is no
taxable remittance provided that he does not benefit from the remittance.

(2) If the trust received foreign source income in 2005, has not distributed
it to the settlor and invests it in the UK in 2009 there is no taxable
remittance. The trust is not a "relevant person" in relation to pre-April
2008 income. Of course, it is necessary for the trustees to have kept such
income separate from post-April 5, 2008 income.

Remittances and relevant persons

Foreign source income whenever arising which is given away by the settlor **8.06**
to a non-relevant person is not taxed when remitted by that person provided
neither settlor nor any other relevant person receives any benefit from it.[11]

---

[9] i.e. investment income such as dividends, interest, trust income.
[10] FA 2009 inserted para.86(4A) in Sch.7 of FA 2008 with effect from April 6, 2008 to make it clear
that the definition of relevant person in relation to settlement income that arose prior to April 6,
2008 is still restricted to the settlor even if not remitted until after 2007–08.
[11] See ITA 2007 s.809N.

If a settlor gives away post-April 2008 personal relevant foreign income to a trust which is a relevant person[12] and the trust remits it to the UK that is a taxable remittance by the settlor. Similarly, if relevant foreign income arises to the trustees after April 5, 2008 and it is brought to the UK by the trust (which is a relevant person), that is a taxable remittance by the settlor.

Assume in all the examples in Example 8.2 below that the trust is non-UK resident and that the settlor is a remittance basis user.

EXAMPLE 8.2

(1) A settlor-interested discretionary trust receives relevant foreign income from trust investments in 2009 which is distributed at the trustee's discretion to the settlor's niece abroad as income. The niece remits the income. There is no taxable remittance by the settlor since a niece is not a relevant person. There may be a tax charge on niece if she is UK resident since even if she is a remittance basis user, on the above facts she has remitted the income distributed to her. Even if the trust accumulates the income and then confers a benefit on the niece in the UK there is a tax charge on the niece under the transfer of assets provisions.[13] Of course, the settlor continues to be liable to UK tax on any UK source income whether or not paid to the niece.

(2) If the trust is a life interest trust for the niece then UK source income is still taxed as the settlor's if the trust is settlor-interested but the relevant foreign income is taxed on the niece if she is UK resident and domiciled. If she is not UK resident there is no tax charge either on the niece or settlor on foreign source income whether or not it is remitted. If she is a remittance basis user she but not the settlor is taxed if the income distributed to her is remitted to the UK. If the foreign source income is paid to her and retained by her abroad there is no tax charge on her or the settlor. Hence, foreign source income of a settlor-interested fixed interest trust (with the life tenant being someone other than the settlor) is not taxed on the settlor even if the life tenant remits the income provided the life tenant is not a "relevant person" in relation to the settlor.

(3) In 2010 the settlor settles his post-April 5, 2008 personal relevant foreign income into a trust from which neither he or any relevant person can benefit. The trust is not itself a relevant person. If the trust then remits that income (e.g. by investing it in the UK) there is no taxable remittance by the settlor.

(4) The trust can benefit the settlor's spouse and is therefore settlor-interested. It can also benefit the settlor's minor children. If foreign income arises and is invested in the UK that is taxable on the

---

[12] i.e. it can benefit any of the settlor/spouse/civil partner/cohabitee/minor children/minor grandchildren.
[13] See 8.10 and following.

settlor as a remittance by a relevant person.[14] If the trust makes distributions of foreign income to the spouse (a remittance basis user) which she remits that is also taxable on the settlor as the spouse is a relevant person in relation to the settlor.

(5) The settlor has pre-April 6, 2008 source ceased income which he cannot remit to the UK tax-free. He gives that income to a trust which buys a UK house for his occupation. That is a taxable remittance because he benefits from the remittance (because of the transitional rules the trust is not a relevant person).

UK resident trusts with foreign source income

If UK resident discretionary trustees of a settlor-interested trust receive income and the settlor is a remittance basis user, the tax treatment is as follows:

8.07

(i) the settlor is taxable on an arising basis on UK source income (the same is true of a non-resident trust which receives UK income). Note the trustees pay the tax at 50 per cent and then the settlor reclaims if he is not an additional rate taxpayer[15];

(ii) the trustees pay UK tax on foreign source income. The income is not within s.648(3) nor taxed on the settlor under s.619 unless and until remitted. Hence, it is trust income which is received by the UK trust and taxed under normal principles.

If the trust contains a life interest for another beneficiary who is not a relevant person in relation to the settlor and the trust receives relevant foreign income which is not remitted by the trust but paid to the beneficiary then the trust is liable to basic rate tax and the beneficiary to higher or additional rate tax if he is UK domiciled and resident.

8.08

If the UK resident trust is settlor-interested and received foreign source income which is remitted by the settlor or any other relevant person (including the trust or any life tenant) then the settlor is liable for the tax not the life tenant. If the life tenant is a relevant person in relation to the settlor but is himself taxed on the arising basis but does not remit the income to the UK, the life tenant not the settlor will be liable to UK tax.

Trust management expenses do not reduce the income taxable as the settlor's where the settlement is settlor-interested.[16]

8.09

---

[14] Although note the proposed new rules on investment by foreign domiciliaries intended to come into effect from April 6, 2012: see Ch.5.
[15] See 7.26 for the convoluted mechanics.
[16] See 6.47.

The transfer of assets (TOA) legislation[17]

8.10 An individual who is resident and domiciled in the UK might seek to avoid UK income tax by transferring income-producing assets to a non-UK resident entity not subject to UK income tax. In the case of trusts, this is prevented by s.624 since any income arising at the trust level will be taxed on the settlor if he retains an interest in it. However, as noted in Ch.7, income arising in a company is not generally caught by the settlement legislation and therefore separate anti-avoidance rules are required where assets are transferred to offshore companies. These used to be found in s.739 TA 1988 but were rewritten and are now in ITA 2007 s.720 and following. Below is a brief summary of the provisions and the points that practitioners need to consider.

8.11 The relevant wording in ITA 2007 s.720(1) is as follows:

> *"The charge under this section applies for the purpose of preventing the avoidance of liability to income tax by individuals who are ordinarily UK resident by means of relevant transfers."*

So the code does not apply to those who are UK resident but not ordinarily resident (although in most cases such persons will not be UK domiciled either and therefore will be subject to the remittance basis). The transfer of assets code only applies to individuals not (for example) to charities or companies.

EXAMPLE 8.3

> George, UK resident, ordinarily resident and domiciled, owns investment property in France that produces substantial letting income. He transfers it to a non-UK resident company in return for shares or loan stock. This was done for UK tax reasons.
>
> Section 720 operates to treat the income of the company as George's. He is taxed on all income of the company on an arising basis. A foreign incorporated company which was UK resident would still be within s.720. So if the above company was UK resident (because of UK management and control) but foreign incorporated, George will still be taxed on all the income of the company even though the company also pays corporation tax! In practice a credit is given for any tax paid by the company. This is particularly relevant when an offshore company receives UK source rental income. This income is subject to basic rate tax in the hands of the company[18] and the transferor will be given a credit for that tax. The motive defence, discussed at 8.26 below, does not apply.

---

[17] ITA 2007 ss.720–730.
[18] See Ch.54.

Conditions for s.720 apply

Condition 1: a "relevant transfer" must occur .[19] This is a transfer of assets and   **8.12**
as a result of that transfer or associated operations, income becomes payable
to a person abroad;

Condition 2: the individual[20] has power to enjoy that income (whether now
or later) or receives or is entitled to receive a capital sum.

If these conditions are met, the income of the non-resident person is then
taxed as that of the transferor.[21] Parliamentary debates when the sections were
first enacted make it clear that they were only intended to catch transferors.
The House of Lords decided otherwise in *Congreve v IRC*,[22] but that decision
was itself overruled in *Vestey v IRC*.[23] Unlike the settlement provisions there
is no right to recover any tax paid.

Sections 726 and 730 introduce the remittance basis for foreign source   **8.13**
income where the transferor is a remittance basis user.

The person to whom the income is payable can be a trust, a company, or an   **8.14**
individual. The transfer of assets code is not, therefore, confined to offshore
trusts and companies owned by such trusts. The person to whom the income
arises need not be the transferee: it can be any other person to whom the
transferee has transferred the assets or assets representing them by way of an
associated operation.[24]

The question of when a transfer of assets occurs has been considered in a   **8.15**
number of cases including *IRC v Brackett*[25] where the taxpayer provided services to a Jersey company for no consideration and it was held that there was
a transfer of assets (being services performed under the contract of employment) and that the profit generated by the taxpayer's activities was income
payable to the company as a result of that transfer.[26] The section can apply if
the assets transferred were already abroad when the transfer is made.

---

[19] Defined in ITA 2007 s.716.
[20] Defined in s.714(4) to include the transferor's spouse or civil partner.
[21] Note that *Vestey v IRC* [1980] AC 1148 which involved a transfer of properties to non resident
   trustees restricted the scope of s.720 to the original transferor of the assets or his spouse. This
   resulted in separate legislation (ITA 2007 s.731 onwards) to bring into charge those individuals
   other than the transferor who received benefits as a result of the arrangements.
[22] (1948) 30 TC 163.
[23] [1980] STC 10.
[24] An associated operation is defined in ITA 2007 s.719 to mean an operation of any kind effected
   by any person in relation to any of the assets transferred, or representing the same, or the
   income arising from such assets or any accumulations of income and whether effected before
   or after or at the same time as the transfer. A will can be an associated operation although it
   is not clear whether a will or death is a transfer.
[25] [1986] STC 521.
[26] See also *IRC v Willoughby* [1997] STC 995 (transfer of assets by the taxpayer to a life office
   in consideration of the issue of personal portfolio bond); *IRC v McGuckian* [1997] STC 908
   (transfer of shares in a private company) and *Carvill v IRC* [2000] STC (SCD) 143 (transfer of
   shares in a UK holding company to an offshore holding company in consideration of a share
   issued by that company. Dividends paid by the UK company).

EXAMPLE 8.4

Anna, domiciled and resident in the UK, transfers the shares of her foreign company to an offshore trust. She is excluded but her spouse (from whom she is separated) can benefit. Dividends declared by the company are trust income but are not taxable on Anna because the trust is not settlor-interested. She cannot benefit and she is separated from her spouse. However, the trust income is within s.720 and taxable on Anna. (There is no similar let out where the spouse is separated.) The income of the company is also taxable on Anna under s.720. If the company is UK resident and incorporated and never declares dividends then even if the trust is non-resident there is no tax charge on Anna. No income has arisen to any person abroad. However, if the company is UK resident and owned by a foreign holding company which in turn is owned by a trust, and declares a dividend to the holding company then that income (viz the dividend) is taxable on Anna.

Overlap with the settlement legislation

8.16 If the trust was settlor-interested (e.g. because Anna in the above Example could benefit) then she is taxable on the trust income under s.624. It is not then taxed again under s.720.[27] Because Anna would be liable for tax under s.624 she has a right of recovery to the extent the tax liability on the settlement income has been paid by the trustees. She separately pays income tax on any foreign resident company income under s.720 (with no right of recovery albeit a credit for any UK source tax paid by the company, e.g. on UK rental income). If the company dividends the income as it arises to the trust she will pay tax on that income under s.624 not s.720. HMRC do not tax her under both s.720 on the company income and then again on the trust income. Accordingly non-resident companies should therefore generally distribute the income to the trust as it arises where the trust is settlor-interested and the settlor is UK resident.[28]

When is there power to enjoy the income?

8.17 Predictably, the situations when an individual has power to enjoy income are widely drawn.[29] So, for example, if an individual transferred assets to a trust where he and his spouse/civil partner were not beneficiaries but could be added he would be treated as having power to enjoy. If he and his spouse/civil partner are excluded from the trust but there is power for the trust to transfer assets to a trust from which they can benefit then he may be treated as having power to

---

[27] ITTOIA 2005 s.624 takes priority over ITA 2007 s.720.
[28] See Ch.54.
[29] See ITA 2007 s.723.

enjoy.[30] If benefits in kind (such as rent-free accommodation) are conferred on the transferor even if he is not a beneficiary of the trust then s.720 is in point and he is taxed on the relevant income. Even if the transferor does not receive the income of the trust or company he can be taxed if he has power to do so or he can control the application of income. So a taxpayer who owned all the voting shares in a foreign company was held to have power to enjoy because he had power to control the income. A mere power to appoint trustees should not in itself mean the appointor had power to enjoy within s.720 but a transferor who retained a power of appointment over income or capital which he could exercise in favour of himself or his spouse/civil partner has power to enjoy. A transferor who could be added as a beneficiary has power to enjoy.

Charge where capital sums received (ss.727–729)

Even if the transferor has no power to enjoy the income, he can be caught **8.18** under the capital receipts provisions.

This condition is met if the individual receives or is entitled to receive any **8.19** capital sum, whether before or after the relevant transfer or in any earlier tax year he has received any capital sum whether before or after the relevant transfer and the payment of that sum or the entitlement is connected with any relevant transaction. Note that entitlement to capital means more than just being able to benefit at the discretion of the trustees. So if, for example, a transferor can benefit from capital only at the trustees' discretion but he never actually receives any capital sum and he is then excluded from all benefit (and note his spouse/civil partner must also be excluded) he is no longer taxed on the income arising within the overseas structure. If, however, he has received a capital sum in the past and is then wholly excluded, this does not stop all the income being taxed on him in the future until he dies. So once the transferor has received a capital sum,[31] liability under s.727 can in theory remain forever. The capital sum is not treated as income: it is the trigger for deeming future income (or past income) within the structure to be the transferor's. In the Explanatory notes to the ITA rewrite, however, it was stated "*in practice, where entitlement to a capital sum has ceased, HMRC do not pursue further liability under s739(3)*". It is not known if in fact HMRC would pursue liability where the transferor had received a capital sum and was then excluded. The explanatory notes are ambiguous but do not confirm in terms that someone who has actually received a capital sum ceases to be exposed to future liability.

The uncertainty has created problems since April 6, 2008. Before that date **8.20** many foreign domiciliaries would not have worried on the basis that such TOA income was foreign source and not remitted. However, to avoid a charge under the TOA provisions now, the foreign domiciliary would need to continue to opt for the remittance basis. If he decides to be taxed on the arising basis, exclusion from his offshore structure may not be sufficient to avoid a tax charge on all foreign source income if he has received a capital sum in the past,

---

[30] See *IRC v Botnar* [1999] STC 711 (although query the position if, unlike *Botnar*, the power of resettlement did not expressly exclude power to transfer assets to a trust where the settlor could benefit but there was no intention to benefit the transferor).
[31] Apart from a loan which has been repaid: see 8.21.

see Example 8.5(3). In summary, if the transferor is merely a discretionary object, has received no capital sums (apart from loans from the trust which he has repaid) and is later excluded then his liability under s.720 ceases in the tax year after exclusion. However, if he has received a capital sum, however small in the past, then theoretically he could continue to be taxable on all future income whether or not he is excluded. This can be particularly harsh given that there is no right of reimbursement.

What is a capital sum?

8.21   Capital sum[32] includes:

(i) any sum paid or payable by way of loan to the transferor (although if the loan has been repaid by the transferor and the transferor is excluded then liability under s.727 ceases for future years); or

(ii) a sum paid to him by way of repayment of a loan. So a settlor who lends money to an offshore company which then repays the loan is taxed on the offshore company's income until he dies even though he may have given the company shares away, e.g. into a trust. This is the case even if he is excluded from all benefit. Compare (a).Note that if the settlor assigns a debt to Trust 2 and Trust 1 repays Trust 2, the settlor is still treated as receiving a capital sum. See s.278(5).

(iii) any other sum not being income which is paid or payable otherwise than for full consideration in money or money's worth: e.g. a capital advance. At 7.45 we discuss at some length the definition of capital sum and whether it includes a payment of assets in specie.

EXAMPLE 8.5

(1) X transfers assets to an offshore trust from which he and his wife are excluded but a loan is made to him or his wife even on fully commercial terms. He falls within the transfer of assets provisions until the loan is repaid.

(2) X settles shares in an offshore company on trusts from which he is a potential beneficiary. The trust makes a capital payment to him and then excludes him and his wife. It is thought that he continues to be taxable on all the income.[33]

(3) X is a foreign domiciliary who has lived in the UK for 10 years. His personal income is mostly UK source and he decides to opt for the arising basis in the future. He is the settlor of a trust which owns an offshore

---

[32] Section 728.

[33] In *Vestey* it was suggested in the High Court that the charge was limited to the amount of the capital sum received but this was rejected by the House of Lords. See, however, 8.19 for the comments of the Rewrite Team.

company that receives substantial foreign investment income. He was repaid a loan by the company some years ago and has been excluded (from benefit under the trust) since 2009. Nevertheless he could be subject to tax on all future company income.[34]

(4) X is the transferor of a trust with an underlying company. He is the life tenant of the trust but dies in the course of the year. Offshore income gains are triggered by his death.[35] Actual income also arises in the company after he has died but in the same tax year. It is thought that he is not taxed on the actual income (although Condition A refers to power to enjoy in the tax year, Condition B in s.721 could be read as restricting this to income arising prior to his death).[36] It is arguable that he is also not taxed on the offshore income gain triggered by his death on the basis that such offshore income gains are treated as arising immediately after his death.[37]

Liability

Where a transferor is caught by s.728 he is assessed to income tax on all the non resident's income but only to the extent that it arose by virtue or in consequence of the relevant transfer of assets and any associated operations. As a result, the purchase of an existing offshore company with an existing income stream is not within the section.[38]   **8.22**

The transferor is entitled to such deductions and reliefs as he would have been allowed had he and not the company (or other non resident entity) actually received the income. If the income within the company or trust has already suffered basic rate tax, this will not be collected again from the UK resident. However there is no right of recovery of the tax from the overseas entity. It appears that the transferor is assessable only on the income from assets he transferred and not from any other income generated within the overseas entity. The income on which he can be assessed includes accrued income profits[39] and offshore income gains.   **8.23**

Take the common structure of an offshore trust which holds assets through a holding company. Suppose the company receives income and then declares a dividend? In practice HMRC do not charge income tax twice in these circumstances.[40] However, double tax charges arise where there is a UK domiciled transferor of a trust where its holding company receives income which is taxed on the transferor and then the company is liquidated or sold. Even if the trus-   **8.24**

---

[34] HMRC have stated informally on one case seen by the authors that where the capital sum was paid some years ago the settlor can now be excluded and continuing liability under ss.720–730 will cease.

[35] See Ch.53.

[36] Although the wording in the rewrite is not clear. The position was clearer under s.739 of TA 1988.

[37] If he is liable to pay income tax on such gains then there is no inheritance tax deduction because they are not personal offshore income gains: see Ch.53.

[38] See Ch.54 fn.7 (taxation of non-resident companies).

[39] See Ch.6.

[40] See Ch.54 for further details.

tees make no capital payment if the company shares show a gain on disposal that gain is taxed on the transferor under TCGA 1992 s.86.[41]

8.25   If the transferor has suffered tax under ss.720 or 727 but the income is only subsequently distributed to him then it is not deemed to form part of his income again for income tax purposes.[42] Accordingly, where the transferor has already paid income tax, the trustees should not liquidate the company but ensure that it pays a dividend which is then paid to the transferor. Of course it may be difficult to identify the company income charged under ss.720 and 727 with the payments later made from the trust. For UK domiciled and resident settlors it will therefore often be preferable to ensure that all income in the overseas structure is paid out to them as it arises to avoid future problems.

Motive test[43]

8.26   There is complete exemption from the TOA charge if the individual satisfies HMRC that one of two conditions is met. This is called the *motive or purpose defence*.[44] For post-December 4, 2005 transactions[45] an individual will avoid liability if either of the following condition is satisfied:

   (i) *Condition A*: it would not be reasonable to conclude from all the circumstances of the case that tax avoidance was the purpose, or one of the purposes, for which the relevant transactions or any of them were effected, or

   (ii) *Condition B*: all the relevant transactions were genuine commercial transactions and it would not be reasonable to conclude that any of the relevant transactions was more than incidentally designed for the purpose of avoidance.[46] In practice this condition is more commonly satisfied. A commercial transaction can be effected only in the course of a trade or business.

Condition A is failed if any purpose however small involves tax avoidance. An incidental tax avoidance purpose is permitted in Condition B. Taxation is defined to include any form of UK tax including inheritance tax and national insurance contributions but not foreign taxes.

8.27   For pre-December 5, 2005 transactions[47] a slightly different motive test operated. An individual avoided liability if either:

   (i) *Condition A*: avoiding liability to taxation was not the purpose or one of the purposes for which the relevant transactions or any of them were effected; or

   (ii) *Condition B*: the transfer and any associated operations were genuine com-

---

[41] See Ch.54.
[42] ITA 2007 s.743(4).
[43] Sections 736–742.
[44] ITA 2007 ss.736–742.
[45] ITA 2007 s.737.
[46] ITA 2007 s.737(3).
[47] ITA 2007 s.739.

mercial transactions and not designed for the purpose of avoiding liability to taxation. (Commercial transactions are not defined, cf. s.737 above.)

In relation to pre-December 5 transactions taxation is not defined but is thought to cover all UK taxes but not foreign taxes although possibly not national insurance contributions.

There is no clearance procedure and the onus is on the taxpayer to show that **8.28** the motive defence applies. He must show that the conditions are fulfilled and a motive defence should be disclosed clearly on any self assessment returns.[48] If the motive test is satisfied, all UK tax is not necessarily avoided since income arising directly to the trustees can still be taxed under s.624 if the trust is settlor-interested and capital distributions can be taxable under s.87 (or gains taxed under s.86 if the settlor is UK resident and domiciled).

The key phrase, of course, under both the pre- or post-December 2005 **8.29** tests is "tax avoidance", and the House of Lords in *IRC v Willoughby*[49] distinguished between tax avoidance and tax mitigation. That case concerned an investment in offshore personal portfolio bonds which the House of Lords held involved tax mitigation since those bonds were subject to a tax regime specifically provided for by Parliament. Lord Nolan noted:

> "*It would be absurd in the context of s741 (now ITA 2007 s737) to describe as tax avoidance the acceptance of an offer of freedom from tax which Parliament has deliberately made. Tax avoidance within the meaning of s741 is a course of action designed to conflict with or defeat the evident intention of Parliament.*"

Even if tax has been avoided, the taxpayer may still be able to rely on the fact that this was not the purpose of the transaction. Section 737 tells us how the purpose of a transaction is to be ascertained: examine all the circumstances of the case and then ask what conclusions as to purpose it would be reasonable to draw. The intentions and purposes of advisers and of those who design or affect any of the transactions are taken into account.

There has been a long debate about whether the tax avoidance motive **8.30** involves a subjective or objective test. HMRC stated in RI 201:

> "*if a transaction actually involves tax avoidance that is considered by the Revenue to be one of its purposes, even if the transferor did not form the subjective intention of avoiding tax.*"

But can it be right to say that the transfer has a tax avoidance purpose just because it saved tax even if the transferor had no tax avoidance in mind? If that is the case then there is no point in having a test because HMRC will argue that it saved tax the transaction had a tax avoidance purpose!

In *Beneficiary v IRC*[50] the Special Commissioners rejected an objective **8.31** test as they did in *Carvill v IRC*.[51] In *Beneficiary*, the settlor created a Jersey discretionary settlement in favour of his granddaughter in order to give

---

[48] See *Tax Bulletin*, April 14, 1999.
[49] [1997] STC 995.
[50] [1999] STC (SCD) 134.
[51] [2000] STC (SCD) 143.

her independence but transferred cash from a UK account to Jersey. It was decided that UK tax was a matter of indifference to the settlor, although a secondary point was whether taking advantage of an express inheritance tax relief was avoidance or mitigation. More recently in *Burns v HMRC*[52] two sisters who transferred UK land into a wholly Jersey company unsuccessfully sought to rely on the motive defence. The Special Commissioner decided that since the purpose of the transfers included avoidance of higher rate income on the rental income and inheritance tax the matter involved avoidance not mitigation of tax.[53]

8.32   Is there any real difference between the pre- and post-December tests? HMRC obviously consider that the post-December test imports a more objective flavour and certainly the requirement to look at the purposes of the individual's advisers is new in being set out expressly. But the emphasis is still on the purpose of those who carried out the transactions. Another difference is that under the old test an associated operation undertaken for tax avoidance could only jeopardise the defence if it resulted in income becoming payable to a person abroad.[54] Under the new test, a tax motivated associated operation can result in a structure losing its s.737 protection even if the associated operation does not in itself generate any income. All income within the structure (including pre-December 5, 2005 income) becomes taxable if Condition A is failed because of an associated operation.

EXAMPLE 8.6

X a non-resident, foreign domiciled settlor held all his assets through a wholly owned company. He lived all his life in Hong Kong. In his will he leaves the shares in his company on discretionary HK resident trusts for his far-flung but warring family, who are variously resident in the USA, Hong Kong and the UK. He never takes any UK tax advice. The motive test is satisfied. Over the next few years the trustees take UK tax advice and are advised that the UK resident beneficiaries are better off receiving benefits in the form of capital distributions from the trust. Accordingly the trustees ensure that no dividends are paid by the company. Instead only interest-free loans are made by the company to the trust and this continues beyond December 2005.[55] The trustees then use these funds to make capital payments to the beneficiaries. It is arguable that the motive test is failed given the associated operation of the loan to the trust followed by the capital payment, even though the loan does not generate any income.

---

[52] [2009] (STC) SCD) 165.
[53] He noted: "*indirectly retaining a UK real property and simply achieving a technical change in status by putting the property into a non-UK resident company in a case where one of the purposes is to achieve the potential inheritance tax advantage implicit by effecting those steps, does seem to me to cross the border between mitigation and tax avoidance.*" Cf. *Swift v HMRC* [2010] SFTD 553 where a Delaware LLC was considered to satisfy the motive defence (this matter was not considered on appeal: see *RCC v Anson* [2011] UKUT 318) and see 2.50.. The motive test is also relevant to non-transferors discussed below since if it can be satisfied a non-transferor who receives a benefit will not be taxable under ITA 2007 s.735.
[54] See *IRC v Herdman* [1969] 1 All ER 495 HL and *Tax Bulletin 40*, April 1999.
[55] This may cause Sch.4B problems: see Ch.19.

Foreign domiciled transferors

8.33
Sections 726 and 730 provide a remittance basis for non-UK domiciled transferors who are taxed on the remittance basis. Under the pre-April 6, 2008 legislation, ITA 2007 ss.726 and 730 precluded a tax charge on the transferor if:

(i) the transferor was non-UK domiciled in the tax year when the income arose;

(ii) had the income in fact been his, he would not have been chargeable on it by reason of his domicile.

UK source income (e.g. rental income payable to a foreign company) was therefore taxable on the arising basis (even if the company was owned by a trust). However, foreign income of the trust or company had the benefit of the remittance basis. It was generally accepted that before April 6, 2008 a remittance of that foreign income was not taxed unless made in the year in which the income arose. Section 720(3) focused "*on the amount of income treated as arising in the tax year.*" Sections s.726 and 730 stated that the transferor was not chargeable to income tax under s.720 in respect of such income if he was not domiciled in the UK and:

> "*if the income had in fact been the individual's income because of being so domiciled the individual would not have been chargeable to income tax in respect of it.*"[56]

So, although it was clear that remittances in the year when the income arose were caught, there was no provision charging subsequent year remittances. Hence although trust income was caught under the settlement code by virtue of s.648 if subsequently remitted, income of companies was not caught if later remitted by the transferor. For example, loans could be made out of the accumulated income by the company to the transferor. Alternatively the company could be liquidated and the trust receive the income from the company as a capital rather than income distribution.

8.34
It was also unclear whether tax was only charged if the remittance was by the transferor (i.e. following distribution to him) or whether a remittance by the person abroad (e.g. the trust) counted. So, for example, if trust income was accumulated and used to subscribe for shares in a holding company which then used the cash to buy a commercial property in the UK, it was unclear whether this resulted in a tax charge on the transferor. However, it was clear that remittance by a third party (e.g. if the trust distributed to a daughter who then remitted) did not result in the transferor being chargeable.[57]

8.35
Sections 726 and 730 were redrafted in FA 2008 to treat the income arising under s.721 to the individual as "deemed income" if the transferor is a remittance basis user. If it is UK source then he is taxed on an arising basis as before. If the income is foreign then s.726(3) "*treat(s) the foreign deemed income as relevant foreign income of the individual*" and 726(4) "*treat(s) so much of the income within s721(2) as would be relevant foreign income if it*

---

[56] See also the earlier legislation in TA 1988 s.743(3).
[57] Although this might result in a separate charge on the daughter under ITA 2007 s.735.

were the individual's as deriving from the foreign deemed income". This is a lot of deeming! Hence, if the income accruing to the person abroad is remitted by the transferor or any other relevant person (including the trust) then a tax charge arises on the transferor. This is the case even if the income is remitted in a subsequent year and includes a remittance by the person abroad (assuming that person is a relevant person). So a company owned by a trust which invests its foreign income in the UK would involve a taxable remittance by the transferor.[58]

8.36   What about pre-April 6, 2008 income which has arisen to the foreign entity? FA 2008 Sch.7 para.170 provides that *"the amendments made [to s726 and 730] have effect for the tax year 2008/9 and subsequent tax years."* However, pre-April 6, 2008 income accruing to the person abroad but remitted after April 5, 2008 is not caught by these rules as the condition in s.726(1)(a) is not met and therefore the income does not become deemed income caught under the new rules: i.e. s. 809B, D or E (remittance basis user claim) could not have applied in those years. Hence, pre-April 2008 income remitted to the UK by the company or any relevant person apart from the transferor is not taxable on the transferor unless he benefits. As with trust income, such income must be kept separate from post-April 2008 income.

8.37   Foreign domiciliaries who are transferors need to be careful about the transfer of assets code for the following reasons:

(i)   in order to avoid a charge on all the income in the structure on an arising basis they will need to be remittance basis users, not merely foreign domiciled, i.e. to make a claim for the remittance basis and (if they have been resident here for seven out of the last nine years) pay the annual charge[59];

(ii)   future income within the structure will be taxed if remitted in a subsequent year by the transferor (who is the remittance basis user) and by any other relevant person including the trust or company;

(iii)   pre-April 6, 2008 income should be kept segregated (a) because it may not be taxable anyway if remitted in a subsequent year and (b) because it will not be taxable if it had been used to purchase an asset prior to March 12, 2008 even if the asset is subsequently remitted or even sold in the UK.[60]

II NON-SETTLOR-INTERESTED OFFSHORE STRUCTURES

Liability of offshore trustees

8.38   Non-UK resident trustees are liable to income tax only on UK source income, e.g.

---

[58] Although note the proposals announced in the June 2011 Consultation document and discussed in Ch.5.

[59] Compare the capital gains tax regime where a foreign domiciled settlor who is not a remittance basis user is not taxable under s.86 on trust gains: see Ch.19.

[60] See the transitional provisions in FA 2008 Sch.7 para.86(3) and Ch.5.

(i) profit from the business of renting UK land;

(ii) dividends from UK companies (with a 10 per cent non repayable tax credit);

(iii) interest (e.g. on a UK bank account which may have suffered a 20 per cent withholding tax at source);

(iv) trading income.[61]

If the trust is accumulation or discretionary non-resident trustees are subject to the normal 50 per cent trust rate subject to the starting rate on the first £1,000.[62]

8.39 To reduce the 50 per cent tax charge, the trustees often hold UK sited income producing assets through offshore companies where the trust is not settlor-interested or the settlor is non-UK resident. In that case the tax on the rent payable to the company is reduced to 20 per cent.[63] Of course, there may also be inheritance tax advantages in holding UK land through offshore companies if the settlor was not UK domiciled or deemed domiciled. There may be some capital gains tax disadvantages in holding assets through trusts (i.e. doubling up on capital gains) and there may be SDLT charges if the land is transferred by the trustees into a company.[64]

No UK beneficiaries

8.40 If the non-resident trust has no UK resident beneficiaries or there are potential UK resident beneficiaries but the trust is fixed interest for a beneficiary who is not UK resident, then income tax is limited[65] to tax on rental or trading income. Bank and building society interest can be paid gross if the life tenant beneficiary makes a declaration to the bank or building society that he is not ordinarily resident in the UK or if the trust is discretionary; no beneficiaries who could receive income are ordinarily resident and the trustees make the appropriate declaration.[66] There is no further tax on dividend income.

UK beneficiaries

8.41 If the non-resident trust is a fixed interest trust for a beneficiary who is UK resident or the trust is discretionary and some or all of the beneficiaries are ordinarily resident then ITA 2007 s.812 applies. For fixed interest trusts all the

---

[61] See the rules in ITA 2007 ss.811 and 812 outlined at 8.39.

[62] *IRC v Regent Trust Company* [1980] STC 140. Note the potential collection problems for HMRC and see ESC B18 discussed at 8.43. For discussion of the taxation of such trusts generally see Ch.6.

[63] See Ch.54 for the taxation of offshore companies.

[64] Note that if land is held by a trust where the UK resident transferor does have power to enjoy then there is no advantage in transferring it to a company. The transferor is taxable on the UK rental income (with a credit for any tax deducted) irrespective of his domicile.

[65] Under ITA 2007 s.811.

[66] See ITA 2007 s.858.

UK source income is charged at 20 per cent (with no further tax on dividends). For discretionary trusts all the UK source income of the trust is then charged to UK tax at the dividend trust rate or the trust rate in the same way as if the trust were UK resident (but with the benefit of the starting rate on the first £1,000 of income).

EXAMPLE 8.7

(1) The Strivens life interest trust is a Jersey resident trust for Andrew for life remainder to his children. Andrew is not the settlor[67] and is non-UK resident although his children Charlotte and Luke are UK resident. The trust receives non-UK source income (not taxable) and UK dividends and gross interest. There is no further tax liability on the UK dividends given that Andrew is not UK resident and can obtain the benefit of ITA 2007 s.811. There is no tax liability on the interest if Andrew has made the appropriate declaration.

(2) If the trust was discretionary for Andrew and his children then the trustees are liable to tax at the trust or dividend upper rate given that the children are UK resident.

Distributions to UK resident and domiciled beneficiaries

8.42 If non-resident trusts make income distributions to UK resident beneficiaries then even though the trust income may have suffered UK income tax, there is no credit under ITA 2007 ss.493–498 for the trustees' tax when distributions are made.[68] Section 494 only applies to UK resident trusts. Further, the trustees can set off only a proportion of their trust management expenses against the trust's UK income,[69] viz the same proportion of the expenses as the UK income bear to the total income. Without any relief the income distributed to the beneficiary suffers further tax on the net sum distributed.[70]

8.43 ESC B18 gives limited relief.[71] It allows the beneficiary to claim the same credit for the trust's UK tax as he would have obtained if the trust had been UK resident. However, the benefit of the concession is difficult to obtain and the following conditions must be satisfied:

(i) the trustees must be fully up to date with trust tax returns and all tax due on UK income paid;

(ii) the UK tax credited can be that for the tax year of the distribution and the previous five tax years although it is not clear how six years' tax credit can be used and yet the condition below be satisfied; crucially the

---

[67] For the position of settlor-interested trusts see Ch.7.
[68] See Ch.6.
[69] ITTOIA 2005 s.487.
[70] There is no tax charge on the trustees simply because they make the distribution since ITA 2007 s.496 only applies if the trustees are UK resident.
[71] See A2.40.

payment to the beneficiary must be an income distribution (even if not paid out of the actual UK income) and the trust income is set against such distributions on a last in first out basis and foreign and UK source income treated as distributed rateably. Hence the most recent trust income is paid out first (so it may be foreign).

EXAMPLE 8.8

A discretionary trust receives in the same tax year UK source income of £100 gross (£50 net) on which £50 tax is paid (ignoring the starting rate) and foreign source income of £260 (net £200) on which foreign tax of £60 has been paid. The trust makes an income distribution of £100 in that tax year. The beneficiary can claim a tax credit for UK tax on only one third of that distribution and there is no credit for the foreign tax. If the foreign income arose in 2008–09 and the UK source income in 2007–08 and the distribution was made in 2008–09 then given that the income in the year of distribution is more than the income distributed, all the distribution is treated as being made out of the foreign income and no tax credit is available. If however the distribution was £300 then one could look back to the previous year and obtain a UK tax credit on one-third of the distribution.

If the UK income is dividend income the trust tax credited to the beneficiary does not include the 10 per cent notional tax credit but only the extra tax (36.11 per cent in 2011–12) paid by the trustees on the net amount received. If the beneficiary is a basic rate tax payer and all the distribution can obtain the benefit of the credit then there is no further tax liability.

If in the above example all the trust income comprised UK rental income on which 50 per cent tax is paid by the trustees then the UK beneficiary can claim a full 50 per cent credit for the distribution.

Immigration of the trust

If a trust immigrates into the UK then any credit for UK tax suffered while **8.44** the trust was non-UK resident is lost. The past uncredited UK tax does not pass into a new tax pool. A trust should therefore not be imported if income distributions to be made to UK resident beneficiaries and the credit for UK tax suffered by the trustees on UK income claimed.[72]

Transfer of assets provisions (TOA): ITA 2007 ss.731–735A

It would be easy for non-resident trustees to minimise income tax charges for **8.45** UK resident and domiciled beneficiaries by accumulating foreign income and

---

[72] See ITA 2007 s.497(2) and explanatory notes to ITA 2007 change 89.

then distributing it as capital. While a beneficiary might be subject to capital gains tax on such distributions if the trust had realised gains or did so in the future[73] the tax rate on such distributions would only be 28 per cent from 2011–12 (or a maximum 44.8 per cent with full supplemental charge) and the beneficiary would have the benefit of his annual capital gains tax exemption.

8.46   To stop this, the TOA legislation imposes an income tax charge on capital distributions to UK resident beneficiaries (who are not the settlor or transferor).[74] The beneficiary can be subject to income tax on a capital distribution by reference to a notional pool of *"relevant income"* which pool includes income both at the trust level and in any underlying companies which has not been used in expenses, distributed as income or been allocated to prior distributions taxable under the provision. (So capital distributions to non-residents or to non-individuals such as charities do not reduce the pool of relevant income unless the income has been kept physically segregated and is used to make the distribution.)

8.47   Non-UK resident trustees therefore need to keep a record of all available relevant income from the start of the trust or, if later, from March 10, 1981 (when the rules taxing non transferors were first introduced). These provisions apply only to income arising to the overseas entity. So where a company or trust has always been UK resident the provisions do not apply (since all such income will have been subject to UK tax anyway). But if a trust has been non-UK resident and then immigrates the provisions can apply to capitalised income that arose while the trust was non-UK resident. In addition if a company is foreign incorporated but UK resident the provisions can apply.[75] However, if an overseas trust owns a UK resident and foreign incorporated company no relevant income arises unless and until dividends are declared.

When do the TOA provisions apply?

8.48   Sections 731–735A have effect where a relevant transfer occurs and the individual ordinarily resident[76] in the UK receives a benefit provided out of assets available for the purpose as a result of a transfer or any associated operation. However, unlike s.720,[77] an individual is only assessed to income tax to the extent of any benefit he receives. The benefit includes a cash advance, a loan, free use of property or the transfer of an asset. The benefit is taxed as the income of the UK resident in the year of receipt to the extent that it does not exceed the relevant income of the non resident trust or company in the tax years up to and including the year when the benefit is paid. If the benefit received exceeds the relevant income of those years, any excess is carried

---

[73] See Ch.19.

[74] Transferors are taxed separately on trust income under ITTOIA 2005 s.624 and under the TOA rules in ITA 2007 s.620 on foreign income in any other overseas entity (e.g. a company wholly owned by the trust).

[75] See ITA 2007.

[76] The TOA provisions do not apply to the transferor unless he is ordinarily resident in the year in which the income arises and do not apply to a non transferor unless he is ordinarily resident in the year in which the benefit is conferred (ITA 2007 s.732(1)(b)). However, a benefit received when UK resident can be taxed by reference to available relevant income which arose when the non transferor was not UK resident.

[77] See 8.14.

forward and set against the first available relevant income of future years until it is used up. The same income cannot be charged to tax twice[78] so where several beneficiaries receive benefits the relevant income is allocated amongst them in such proportions as may be just and reasonable.

EXAMPLE 8.9

(1) Paul is a beneficiary of a non-resident trust set up by his father in 1999. His father has been dead for many years and the trust has accumulated income (both at the trust level and in holding companies) and has realised some capital gains. In 2008 the trustees make a capital payment of £10,000 to Paul (resident and domiciled) in the UK. The payment is first matched to relevant income and to the extent there is insufficient relevant income it is then charged to capital gains tax if there are unmatched trust gains. In this case, the payment is £10,000 and the relevant income is £100,000. That payment is matched to relevant income and subject to income tax (so will not have the benefit of any CGT exemptions) and the relevant income is reduced to £90,000. Only when all that relevant income has been reduced by other capital payments to UK residents will any capital distribution be subject to capital gains tax.

(2) This assumes of course, that the motive defence is not in point.[79] If Paul successfully argues that this is available then he is not subject to income tax (because the payments are capital and s.731 does not apply) but he will be subject to capital gains tax on the payments if there are trust gains. [80]

The available relevant income may have suffered UK or foreign tax as it arose **8.49** but a beneficiary is charged to tax on the amount received with no tax relief. So, in Example 8.9, Paul (a higher rate taxpayer) will pay tax of £4,000 on the £10,000 irrespective of whether the trust or any holding company has received UK income which has suffered tax.

Prior to the FA 2008 changes, it was preferable for a UK resident and domiciled beneficiary to pay income tax at 40 per cent rather than capital gains tax at 64 per cent. Between April 6, 2008 and June 22, 2010 the maximum capital gains tax rate was 28.8 per cent. Even now it is only 44.8 per cent while the maximum income tax rate is 50 per cent for a top rate taxpayer. Hence Paul may want to try and match capital payments to gains rather than income.

Trustees wishing to utilise the annual capital gains tax exemptions of ben- **8.50** eficiaries need to ensure either:

(i) that there is no available relevant income which could be subject to income tax under s.731 nor any offshore income gains[81]; or

(ii) that the motive test applies.

[78] Section 743.
[79] See 8.23.
[80] See Ch.19.
[81] Discussed in Ch.53.

How to reduce relevant income

8.51 Income does not become relevant income if it is distributed as income as it arises even if the distribution is to a non-resident. Just because the trust is a fixed interest trust does not mean there is no relevant income. There may be deemed income such as accrued income profits in the trust[82] as well as offshore income gains. The trust may also have a holding company in which income has been accumulated. All of that company income counts as relevant income.

EXAMPLE 8.10

> The X trust (with a deceased settlor) owns an investment company, X Limited. The X trust is a life interest trust for A (UK resident and domiciled) but X Limited has received dividends from UK and foreign companies, some of which have had tax deducted at source and that income (£100,000 net) has not all been paid up to the trust.
>
> The pool of relevant income is £100,000. The trustees also have capital cash of £10,000 at the trust level which they lend to beneficiary A interest-free. A is taxed on the benefit of the loan ($4\%^{83} \times £10,000 = £400$ benefit). This £400 reduces the relevant income but A receives no credit for the UK or foreign taxes paid by X Limited.

8.52 A difficult question is when relevant income ceases to be "available". A benefit paid to a non-resident does not have available relevant income allocated to it. Hence distributions to non-residents do not generally reduce the pool of relevant income although relevant income ceases to be available if, on the facts, the distribution is identifiable with the income (e.g. the distributed funds had been kept segregated in banking (not merely accounting) terms). So if in Example 8.10 the shares of X Limited were transferred to a non-UK resident or sold to a third party then the available income in the trust would then be nil (since all trust income has been paid out to the life tenant and X Limited with its undistributed income has now gone).

8.53 It is often difficult to keep track of relevant income. For example, offshore trusts frequently own offshore companies and dividends are paid from the company to the trust. Does the retained income at the level of the company cease to be available relevant income as and when it is paid up to the trust? If not there will be double counting in that income arises in the company and the same income is in fact paid up to the trust level. It is believed that once the company's retained income has been distributed, it is no longer capable of being counted although it becomes relevant income at the trust level.[84]

---

[82] ITA 2007 Pt 12 Ch.2.
[83] The Official Rate of interest in 2011–12.
[84] See 8.55.

Foreign domiciled beneficiaries: the position before April 6, 2008

More complicated problems arise in relation to foreign domiciliaries who are **8.54** ordinarily UK resident. Section 735 originally provided a remittance basis but it was not a standard remittance basis in that *first*, the individual could not be domiciled in the UK, *secondly*, the benefit conferred by the trustees could not be received in the UK and *thirdly*, there could be no relevant UK income within the structure. So for the relief to be available, s.735 required all benefits to be received abroad and all relevant income in the trust/company structure to be foreign. This was a significant disincentive for investment in the UK.

EXAMPLE 8.11

> Debbie is the UK resident foreign domiciled beneficiary of an offshore trust. The settlor is dead. In 2007 she receives a benefit of £20,000 in the form of a large interest-free loan made to her abroad. She does not remit the money to the UK. A company owned by the trust has received UK rental income of £10,000. There is also significant foreign income of £100,000. HMRC considered that Debbie was taxed on up to £10,000 by reference to the UK income. She receives no credit for the tax paid by the company.

ITA 2007 ss.731–735 contains no rules to determine: **8.55**

  (i) which year's income was allocated to a benefit;

 (ii) within each year, which entity's income was so allocated so that where a trust owned a number of different companies which income was matched first; and

(iii) within an entity's income of a given year how the allocation was made as between UK and non-UK income. The legislation did not require UK income to be allocated first. If a trust had only UK domiciled beneficiaries it was irrelevant because they would all be taxed. If the trust had a mixture of beneficiaries it was highly relevant to know which source of income has been matched to which benefit. The taxpayer would argue that all the UK income was allocated to the distributions to the UK domiciliary leaving the foreign income to be allocated to the distributions to the foreign domiciliary who did not remit. Of course, if the legislation had prescribed an order, e.g. UK income out first, then this could have facilitated avoidance; trustees could make distributions of income to UK domiciliaries in the tax year prior to distributions abroad to the foreign domiciliaries and hence wash out the "tainted UK income".

All that was said was that income could not be taken into account more than **8.56** once in taxing the transferor under ss.720–730 or a non transferor under ss.731–735. If there was a choice as to who to allocate income to, it is made by

HMRC on a just and reasonable basis.[85] In the above example it is assumed that all the UK income is allocated to the benefit. At least before April 6, 2008, a case could have been made for saying the opposite and that none of the UK income was allocated to that beneficiary (or that income was prorated).

8.57   Further difficulties arose (and still arise after April 2008) where distributions are made in the same tax year to different beneficiaries. How is UK income matched between them? How is the beneficiary to self-assess because he will not necessarily know what relevant income has been allocated to other beneficiaries?

8.58   What happens if the UK income is paid by way of dividend to the trust level? As income moves up the structure, it arguably cannot be relevant income more than once. So once a company distributes profits or retained profits comprising relevant income, that ceases to be available in the company. It becomes income at the next stage up the chain and so available there. If right, this, inter alia, means UK income at company level is converted to non-UK income at the next level (assuming the company is non resident). On that basis if in the above example the company paid a dividend to the trust and then a distribution was made to Debbie in the next tax year she would not suffer tax if the benefit was received abroad.

It was believed by some that if the benefit or the relevant income was received/remitted to the UK in a subsequent year, there could be no tax charge. This followed from the framework of ITA 2007 ss.730–732 and the absence of a provision charging subsequent year receipts/remittances. If right, it meant that s.735 was more an exemption than a remittance basis.[86]

The position from April 6, 2008

8.59   Section 735 was rewritten as ss.735 and 735A by FA 2008. If the foreign domiciled beneficiary is a "remittance basis user"[87] and the income treated as arising to him under s.732 is foreign income of the transferee (i.e. of the trust or company), then it is classified as foreign deemed income which is "*treated as relevant foreign income*".[88] Section 735(4) then implies that the deemed income is taxable if either the relevant income which relates to any part of that foreign deemed income or a benefit which relates to any part of that foreign deemed income is remitted. So the remittance basis applies and there is a tax charge if the beneficiary remits the benefit related to the deemed foreign income or the beneficiary or any relevant person (including the trust or company) remits the actual foreign income related to the deemed income. This is a lot of deeming!

8.60   Section 735A imposes matching and identification rules which appear to match income of earlier years before later years and within the same year to match UK relevant income before foreign income. It is not clear whether one goes back to the latter of 1981 or the trust's inception when matching or whether

---

[85] ITA 2007 s.743.

[86] See, for example, Clarke *Offshore Tax Planning* (14th edn), para.57.10 and cf. Kessler *Taxation of Foreign Domiciliaries* (6th edn), para.17.35 and Michael Flesch QC in *GITC Review*, Vol.1 issue 2, p.16 where he argues that all that matters is the place of receipt at the time the benefit is conferred and a subsequent remittance is irrelevant.

[87] See Ch.5.

[88] Section 735(3).

the matching only applies to income arising from April 6, 2008 onwards (with a pool of unmatched income brought forward under the old rules).

Unlike the CGT provisions, the source of the income is still relevant in determining whether there is a taxable remittance. If the beneficiary enjoys the benefit outside the UK he can still be taxed if UK income has arisen and remains in the structure. In practice it may be possible to deal with the UK income problem by dividending it up through the structure so it ceases to be available UK relevant income and becomes foreign source income.   **8.61**

III SUMMARY OF HOW PROVISIONS OPERATE FOR FOREIGN DOMICILED SETTLORS AND BENEFICIARIES

Non-transferor trusts (i.e. not settlor-interested nor within ITA 2007 ss.720–730)

In taxing capital distributions on beneficiaries, consider matters in the follow-   **8.62** ing order:

  (i) whether there is any available relevant income,

  (ii) whether there are unmatched offshore income gains (OIGs),[89]

  (iii) whether there is any Sch.4C pool of gains,[90]

  (iv) whether there are any normal s.2(2) trust gains.[91]

The concept of "available" relevant income is technical and complex and   **8.63** working out the available pool can take much analysis. It depends on a number of factors including:

  (i) whether the companies/trustees have kept income segregated (and excluded the transferor from benefiting from this income);

  (ii) whether income has been paid away as it arises so is no longer available;

  (iii) whether the income has arisen in one structure but there has been more than one transfer, i.e. if different income producing assets were transferred into a trust at different times the position is more complicated;

  (iv) whether the particular beneficiary on whom a benefit is being conferred can benefit from the pool of relevant income. Some trusts set up structures under which income is paid away to another trust or ring-fenced in a pool that excludes certain beneficiaries of the first trust, so that there is no relevant income pool from which they can benefit.

  (v) whether there are fixed interest securities with accrued income or deep discount securities. The accrued income or deep discount is all added to the pool of relevant income;

[89] See Ch.53.
[90] See Ch.19.
[91] See Ch.19.

(vi) whether there have been capital distributions to UK resident beneficiaries to which past relevant income has been allocated so that the pool has been reduced. The question of how relevant income should be allocated between different beneficiaries, particularly where distributions have been made in different tax years is controversial. It is arguable that once a pool of relevant income has been allocated to one beneficiary then that particular amount cannot be reallocated to another beneficiary even if it was not taxable in the first beneficiary's hands or the first beneficiary received a capital distribution of less than the amount then in the pool.

(vii) whether a trust has received value or property from another trust or company, e.g. have loans been written off, appointments of capital made or assignments of interests been made between trusts? In that event the relevant pool from the first trust may arguably be taxed on beneficiaries receiving capital distributions from the second;

(viii) if income has been paid from the companies up to the trusts as income, do not double count that income in calculating the pool: there is only one set of income;

(ix) whether the relevant income has already been taxed on the transferor under ITA 2007 ss.720–730.

8.64 In most cases trustees will tend to treat the trust and company as together having a single combined pool of relevant income. This pool comprises all income of past and current years within the companies and trusts (ignoring entities from which a beneficiary is excluded) which has (a) not been distributed to any UK resident beneficiary and (b) not been used in paying income expenses. Assuming there is available sufficient relevant income, the capital distribution is then treated as the income of the recipient beneficiary.

EXAMPLE 8.12

X, a remittance basis user who is a beneficiary (but not settlor) of a trust receives a capital payment or benefit worth £1 million.

The pool of unallocated relevant income over all years including current year = £600,000.

X pays income tax on £600,000 subject to the remittance basis. If he does not remit then there is no tax on X and arguably the relevant pool has still reduced.

£400,000 unmatched capital payment.

Offshore income gains (OIGs)

8.65 In Example 8.12 above the capital distribution exceeded the available pool of income by £400,000. It is then necessary to go to the next stage and look at gains. If there are any unallocated offshore income gains (i.e. gains realised on the disposal of non-reporting offshore funds)[92] in that year such gains are then matched to the balance of the capital distribution. These are taxed at income tax rates but subject again to the remittance basis.[93]

EXAMPLE 8.12 CONTINUED

X receives	£1,000,000
Matched to relevant income	£600,000
Unmatched balance	£400,000
OIGs	£300,000

£200,000 of the £300,000 OIGs were realised pre-April 2008. £50,000 of the £100,000 OIGs were realised after April 2008 but accrued prior to April 6, 2008.

The effect of the rebasing election means that X is chargeable only on the balance of £50,000 OIGs accruing post-April 6, 2008 (and only if remitted).[94]

Unmatched balance of capital payment c/f = £100,000. So £300,000 OIG are matched but only £50,000 taxed.

CGT on "ordinary trust gains"

Once all the relevant income and OIGs have been matched then assuming **8.66** there are no Sch.4C gains[95] the capital distribution is matched to ordinary trust gains (i.e. currency gains, equity gains and gains arising within the investment companies on disposals of equities and non roll up funds and disposals of the investment company shares [i.e. any other trust gains except OIGs]). If such trust gains or "s2.(2) amounts" are matched with a capital payment to X in the year a gain accrued, capital gains tax would in principle be charged on the remittance basis at 28 per cent under TCGA 1992 s.4.[96] The charge can, however, rise to a maximum of 44.8 per cent if there is a delay in making the capital payment after the gain is realised.[97]

However, no charge arises to capital gains tax if and to the extent that the **8.67** rebasing election provides relief, i.e. gains arising after April 6, 2008 on any assets throughout the structure but accruing before then are not chargeable. Nor are gains on disposals made prior to April 6, 2008 taxable on the beneficiary. Gains

---

[92] See Ch.53.
[93] As explained in Ch.53, there are, briefly, two mechanisms of charge on OIGs: ITA 2007 ss.731–735 (*"the transfer of assets code"*) and TCGA 1992 s.87 (*"the s.87 code"*). Regulation 20 of The Offshore Funds (Tax) Regulations 2009: SI 2009/3001 applies the charging provisions under the s.87 code (*the primary rule*) and reg.21 applies the transfer of assets charging provisions (*the secondary rule*).
[94] See Ch.53.
[95] Discussed in Ch.19 and at 8.68 below.
[96] See TCGA 1992 s.87B.
[97] TCGA 1992 s.91. See Ch.19.

are however matched on a last in first out basis (LIFO) so that gains realised after April 2008 are always chargeable first although the benefit of the rebasing election (if made) is that only gains accruing after April 6, 2008 are taxed.

EXAMPLE 8.12 CONTINUED

> X has £100,000 unmatched capital payment. In the year of distribution the trust or underlying company has realised £200,000 capital gains. Those gains accrued after April 2008. None of the transitional reliefs apply and X will pay tax at 28 per cent subject to the remittance basis. If however the gains realised in fact accrued say 75 per cent before April 6, 2008 and 25 per cent post-April 2008 then 75 per cent of the £100,000 capital payment escapes tax even on remittance.[98]

8.68 An added complication is if the trust incurred significant trust borrowing. Unless the borrowing is applied for "normal trust purposes" (e.g. payment of trust expenses) then an additional pool of gains can arise under TCGA 1992 Sch.4B because the trustees are treated as making a deemed disposal of a proportionate part of all the settled property. The same capital gains tax transitional provisions apply (rebasing, etc) but the computational exercise becomes worse since gains then have to be calculated on a deemed disposal of the entire trust fund or a proportionate part if the conditions in Sch.4B paras 11(2) or (3) are satisfied rather than on actual disposals.

8.69 In summary, there are various provisions that can apply to tax a capital payment made to a non-transferor beneficiary who is a remittance basis user if he remits such sums to the UK. The priority between these tax provisions is:

(i) transfer of assets (ITA 2007 ss.731–735): subject to income tax;

(ii) OIGs (primary and secondary codes. Regulations 20 and 21 of The Offshore Funds (Tax) Regulations 2009): subject to income tax;

(iii) Schedule 4C gains—generally subject to capital gains tax;

(iv) future s.2(2) amounts—subject to capital gains tax (see 8.57).

8.70 If a capital payment is not fully matched in the year of payment to all the above it remains available to be matched against future relevant income, OIGs, Sch.4C gains or s.2(2) amounts (and therefore potentially taxable if remitted) in that same order of priority. One exhausts the pool of available relevant income, OIGs etc through all tax years before moving onto the next category. This is explained further in Ch.19.

---

[98] See Ch.19 for transitional reliefs and rebasing election.

Even more complicated provisions apply to tax a capital payment made to a **8.71** remittance basis taxpayer who is the settlor of a trust if he remits such sums to the UK. The priority between these tax provisions is:

(i) Settlement provisions (ITTOIA 2005 s.624) in relation to trust income;

(ii) Transfer of assets (ITA 2007 s.720);

(iii) OIGs (ICTA 1988 s.762);

(iv) Transaction in securities code (ITA 2007 s.684) in respect of extraction of value from underlying companies only;

(v) Schedule 4B gains;

(vi) Section 2(2) amounts (i.e. gains taxed under s.87B).

Hence, if a capital payment can be matched to income it is income tax, not **8.72** capital gains tax, which will bite since these provisions take priority. Note though that the actual income must be remitted to the UK for a tax charge to arise. If foreign income is kept abroad and segregated by the transferor or trust then benefits can be conferred on the transferor without a tax charge arising.

However, as the trust is a relevant person in relation to the settlor, if it remits **873** any foreign trust or company income (including OIGs) to the UK, the transferor will suffer a tax charge on such remittance[99] whether or not the same is paid out to him.[100]

Where the transferor of a settlor-interested trust or a company owned by **8.74** such a trust can benefit from the offshore structure and that structure receives UK source income, that income is taxable on the transferor on an arising basis even though he is a remittance basis user. The tax charge is not reduced if a UK resident remittance basis user moves the income-producing asset into an offshore structure from which he can benefit.

[99] Under ITA 2007 s.809L.
[100] This is subject to certain limited transitional reliefs discussed in Ch.5 and at 8.06 above.

PART III: CAPITAL GAINS TAX

The CGT treatment of settlements has been subject to significant amendments since 1998. The FA 1998 substantially altered the taxation of offshore trusts, froze indexation relief and introduced taper relief. The FA 2004 restricted hold-over relief in the case of UK resident settlor-interested trusts and the FA 2006 enacted "modernisation" proposals for the taxation of trusts and further extended the definition of a settlor-interested trust. FA 2008 reduced the rate of capital gains tax for trusts to 18 per cent, abolished taper relief and indexation for disposals on or after April 6, 2008 and repealed TCGA 1992 s.77 which had imposed a CGT charge on the UK resident settlor of a UK resident settlor-interested trust.[1] For most disposals made by UK resident trusts after June 22, 2010 the rate of CGT increased to 28 per cent.[2]

In this part, Ch.9 sets out the key CGT definitions in relation to the taxation of trusts. Ch.10 considers CGT issues on the creation of a settlement. Ch.11 looks at actual disposals by trustees of UK resident settlements and the rates of tax payable. Ch.12 considers deemed disposals. Chs 13 to 17 look at the various business reliefs available to trustees (including entrepreneurs' relief, roll-over relief and share exchanges) and Ch.18 is concerned with the hold-over relief provisions on disposals into and out of trusts. Ch.19 considers the regime for non-resident trusts and the changes for foreign domiciliaries. Ch.20 deals with the capital gains tax position on the disposal of beneficial interests by beneficiaries and Ch.21 looks at the loss relief provisions for trusts and trustees. For the capital gains tax treatment of personal representatives, see Ch.40 and for the position of settlor-interested UK resident trusts see Ch.7.

---

[1] The concept of a settlor-interested trust has not been abolished. For example, it is still relevant to hold-over relief and in relation to Sch.4B and 4C TCGA 1992. See Ch.7 for settlor-interested trusts, Ch.18 for hold-over relief and Ch.19 for Schs 4B and 4C.

[2] Unusually the changes in rates were not made effective until the day after the Budget announcement.

CHAPTER 9

CGT DEFINITIONS

- "Settled property" **(9.02)**
- Meaning of absolute entitlement **(9.09)**
- The definition of settlor including multiple settlors, corporate settlors, resettlements and post-death variations **(9.23)**
- Single or multiple settlements **(9.39)**
- Definition of trustees **(9.46)**
- Disposals **(9.49)**

The legislation taxes gains on settled property and not (generally) the value **9.01** of the interests of the individual beneficiaries. Actual disposals by the trustees and certain deemed disposals may therefore trigger a charge: in other words, the legislation is primarily concerned with the gain or loss arising on the disposal of an asset which is comprised in the trust fund. Hence, disposals of beneficial interests are normally exempt.[3] The creation and termination of a settlement may trigger actual or deemed disposals of "the assets" or "settled property" and therefore lead to a capital gains tax charge.

I "SETTLED PROPERTY"

"Settlement" is not defined, but "settled property"[4] is *"any property held in* **9.02** *trust"*[5] with the exception of certain trusts detailed in TCGA 1992 s.60.

---

[3] See generally Ch.20.
[4] As amended by FA 2006 Sch.12 although the amendment merely adds the words *"and references however expressed to property comprised in a settlement are references to settled property"*.
[5] TCGA 1992 s.68. For the purpose of the capital payment rules and the tax charge under s.87 (relevant for trusts which are or have been non-UK resident) the extended income tax definition of a settlement is adopted: see TCGA 1992 s.97(7) as amended by FA 1998 s.129(2) and by FA 2000 Sch.26 Pt II para.4. Hence, for this purpose settlement includes any disposition, trust, covenant, agreement, arrangement or transfer of assets (see ITTOIA 2005 s.620(1) and Ch.7) but some element of bounty must be present: see *IRC v Plummer* [1979] STC 793. HMRC also accept that for the purpose of the settlor charge under s.86, a settlor is a person who has provided bounty to his settlement. Note, however, that generally the definition of settled property is capable of applying to commercial settlements lacking any element of bounty.

When is property not settled for capital gains tax purposes?

9.03 In the following situations, although there is a trust, the property is not settled property but is treated as belonging to the beneficiary. In addition, settled property does not include property which is held by personal representatives in the course of the administration of an estate.[6]

(i) Assets held by person as nominee or as bare trustee

9.04 Property is not settled where assets are held by a person as nominee for another person or as trustee for another person absolutely entitled as against the trustee. The provision covers both nomineeships and bare or simple trusts.[7]

EXAMPLE 9.1

> A parent settles a house on bare trust for his adult son giving the trustees administrative powers over the property.[8] The property is not settled property for capital gains tax purposes. Instead, the house is treated as belonging to the son so that the son's unused annual capital gains tax exemption will be available in respect of any gains made on a disposal by the bare trustee. The son is absolutely entitled as against the trustees in that he has the exclusive right (subject only to satisfying any outstanding charge, lien or other right of the bare trustees to resort to the asset for payment of duty, taxes or other outgoings), to direct how the house shall be dealt with. The fact that the trustees may be given administrative powers to deal with the property does not make it settled property. The acts of the trustees are treated as the acts of the beneficiary.[9] Hence, disposals of the property between nominee or bare trustee and the beneficiary are disregarded for capital gains tax purposes.[10]

(ii) Property held on trust for a minor or person under a disability

9.05 Property is not settled where it is held on trust for any person who would be absolutely entitled to that property but for being a minor or other person under a disability.[11]

---

[6] Of course a trust (and therefore settled property) may be established by will and the PRs will commonly become trustees at the conclusion of the administration.

[7] Bare trusts likewise do not fall within the definition of "settlement" for IHT purposes: see IHTA 1984 s.43 and Ch.42.

[8] For bare trusts, see Ch.42 and see A1.2 for a precedent.

[9] See s.60(1).

[10] For example, if a person only becomes absolutely entitled to settled property on attaining the relevant age, e.g. 21, the trustee is then deemed to have disposed of the assets for market value at that time and to have reacquired them as bare trustee at that value (see TCGA 1992 s.71). However, when the trustee is a bare trustee and transfers the asset to the beneficiary that provision does not apply since there is no settled property.

[11] TCGA 1992 s.60(1).

Example 9.2

(1) A and B hold property for C aged 11 years absolutely. Because of his age C cannot demand the property from the trustees. There is a settlement for income tax although not for inheritance tax purposes.[12] For CGT purposes C is a person who would be absolutely entitled but for his minority and therefore, he is treated as owning the property which does not comprise settled property. Hence, in addition to his annual exemption being available on any disposal of the property, when C reaches 18 there is no deemed disposal and no capital gains tax charge at that time.

(2) A and B hold property on trust for D, aged 12 years, contingent upon his attaining the age of 18 years. As with (1) above the beneficiary would be absolutely entitled were it not for his minority. D, however, is not entitled to claim the property from the trustees *because of the provisions of the settlement* which require him to satisfy an age contingency. Unlike (1) above, D's entitlement is contingent upon living to a certain age, so that, were he to ask the trustees to give him the property, they would refuse because he has not satisfied the contingency.[13] This, therefore, is settled property for the purposes of CGT.

(iii) Trust for two or more persons jointly absolutely entitled

Property is not settled where it is held on trust for two or more persons **9.06** who are or would be jointly absolutely entitled. The word "jointly" is not limited to the interests of joint tenants, but applies to concurrent owners and so covers more than one beneficiary concurrently entitled "in the same interest".[14] Joint ownership covers a number of different situations as follows.

---

[12] See 24.05.

[13] See *Tomlinson v Glyn's Executor and Trustee Co* [1970] Ch 112; [1970] 1 All ER 381 CA. In this case, a settlor conveyed investments to trustees to hold in trust for such of the beneficiaries as shall attain the age of 21 or marry under that age. It was held that the beneficiaries were not absolutely entitled as against the trustees but for being infants because infancy was not the only impediment preventing the absolute entitlement. Their interests were defeasible and contingent. Hence, the property was settled for capital gains tax purposes.

[14] See *Kidson (Inspector of Taxes) v Macdonald* [1974] Ch 339; [1974] 1 All ER 849; [1974] STC 54. It was argued that property was not nominee property if the co-owners were tenants in common since s.60(1) refers to persons who are *jointly* entitled. This argument was rejected: it was held that jointly meant concurrently or in common. In *Stephenson v Barclays' Bank* [1975] 1 WLR 882; (1978) 1 All ER 625 and in *Booth v Ellard* [1980] 3 All E.R. 569; [1980] 1 WLR 1443 CA, the question was whether the holders of successive interests (e.g. life interest and vested remainder interest) could be regarded as absolutely entitled if they were sui juris and together entitled to terminate the trust under the rule in *Saunders v Vautier* 41 ER 482. Such beneficiaries are jointly absolutely entitled but it was held that their interests have to be concurrent rather than consecutive for the purposes of s.60.

EXAMPLE 9.3—STATUTORY TRUSTS OF LAND

A and B purchase Blackacre as tenants in common. The land is held on a trust of land as a result of LPA 1925 ss.34 and 36,[15] but for the purposes of CGT the property is not settled and is instead treated as belonging to A and B equally.[16]

EXAMPLE 9.4—POOLING ARRANGEMENTS

T and his family own 72 per cent of the issued share capital in T Ltd (their family company). In 1989 they entered into a written agreement as a result of which the shares were transferred to trustees and detailed restrictions, akin to pre-emption provisions in private company articles, were imposed. The beneficial interests of T and his family were not, however, affected in the sense that each shareholder had a beneficial interest corresponding to the shares transferred. It was just that the disposal of the beneficial interests was restricted. Subsequently, the shares were transferred back to the various members of the family in the same proportions. In such a "pooling arrangement" the shares are treated as nominee property with the result that there is no disposal for capital gains tax purposes either on the creation of the trust or on its termination.[17]

9.07 Similar arrangements are often entered into when parcels of land are transferred to trustees to secure better management of the whole but the individual share of each transferor in the whole corresponds to the land he contributed. This is not uncommon where the ownership of parcels of land are split between different owners and they receive offers for the whole from a developer: they will often fare better in negotiations where they pool the land and operate together.

9.08 At one time HMRC considered that on a partition of real property each co-owner disposed of his undivided interest in the whole in consideration of the separate parcel he received on partition and, by concession, gave a form of roll-over relief.[18] In the light of *Jenkins v Brown*[19] it would appear that a partition which mirrors the underlying beneficial interests is not a disposal anyway so that no concession is needed.

---

[15] LPA 1925, ss.34 and 36 as amended by TOLATA 1996, ss.5 and 25(2), Sch.2 paras 3, 4 and Sch.4.

[16] *Kidson (Inspector of Taxes) v Macdonald* [1974] Ch 339; [1974] 1 All ER 849; [1974] STC 54.

[17] Cf. *Booth v Ellard* above; and see *Jenkins v Brown* [1989] 1 WLR 1163; *Warrington v Sterland* [1989] STC 577 in which a similar result was arrived at in the case of a pooling of family farms. See Ch.52 for a discussion of pooling in the context of partnerships.

[18] ESC D26: now classified as "obsolete".

[19] [1989] 1 WLR 1163.

II MEANING OF ABSOLUTE ENTITLEMENT

It is the concept of absolute entitlement that lies at the root of the situations in TCGA 1992 s.60 where trust property is not settled. TCGA 1992 s.60(2) provides as follows:

> "*It is hereby declared that references in this Act to any asset held by a person as trustee for another person absolutely entitled as against the trustee are references to a case where that other person has the exclusive right, subject only to satisfying any outstanding charge, lien or other right of the trustees to resort to the asset for payment of duty, taxes, costs or other outgoings, to direct how that asset shall be dealt with.*"

EXAMPLE 9.5

(1) J is entitled to an annuity of £1,000 a year payable out of settled property held in trust for X absolutely. The property is settled for capital gains tax purposes.[20]

(2) *Contrast*: L surrenders his qualifying interest in possession in July 2006 whereupon the settled property is held for M absolutely. M is "absolutely entitled" for CGT purposes although the trustees may insist on retaining assets to cover the risk of an IHT charge were L to die within seven years.[21] Note the fact that the trustees retain the property and can use it to satisfy their lien does not mean it is settled property.[22]

TCGA 1992 s.60(2) does not offer any guidance on the question of when a beneficiary has the exclusive right to direct how the asset in the settlement shall be dealt with. Under trust law, beneficiaries are not able to issue such directions unless they have the right to end the trust by demanding their share of the property.[23] Difficulties may arise in a number of circumstances. For example, suppose a beneficiary is one of a class and he satisfies the age contingency but the class has not yet closed.

9.09

9.10

---

[20] *Stephenson v Barclays Bank Trust Co Ltd* [1975] 1 All ER 625; [1975] STC 151. The annuity is not a charge or outgoing and so causes the property subject to the annuity to be settled property.

[21] The surrender is a potentially exempt transfer for IHT purposes. If L did not have a qualifying interest in possession, e.g. he had an interest in possession that had arisen after March 21, 2006 which was not an immediate post-death interest, transitional serial interest or disabled person's interest then his surrender would not be a PET because the property in the trust is not included in his estate for inheritance tax purposes. There would, however, be an inheritance tax exit charge given that a relevant property settlement has ended and CGT hold-over relief would be available.

[22] See *X v A* [2000] 1 All ER 490 where the trustees were entitled to retain the assets against prospective and contingent environmental liabilities and to receive remuneration in the meantime. The amount of the retention should be calculated on the basis of what is, on reasonable but not fanciful assumptions in favour of the trustees, the worst case. The trustee may invest and manage the retained fund in accordance with the powers conferred by the trust instrument or by law, taking account of his own interests by virtue of his right of indemnity but acting impartially as between himself and the beneficiaries. In *Re Lewis* [1939] Ch 232 a fund was finally distributed after 47 years in court!

[23] See, e.g. *Re Brockbank, Ward v Bates* [1948] Ch 206; [1948] 1 All ER 287.

EXAMPLE 9.6

Property is held on trust for such of the settlor's children as attain 21 years. The settlor has four children and has become incapable of having further children.[24] The property remains settled property even after the children attain 21 until the settlor dies unless the trustees apply to Court which can then give authority to distribute the trust fund.[25]

Crowe v Appleby and appropriations

9.11 What happens when one of a number of beneficiaries has become entitled to a portion of the fund but other beneficiaries have not yet satisfied the relevant contingency?

EXAMPLE 9.7

A trust fund is held for the settlor's three daughters (A, B and C) contingent upon attaining 21 and, if more than one, in equal shares. A, the eldest, is 21 years old and is, therefore, entitled to one-third of the assets.

Whether she is absolutely entitled as against the trustees to that share for *capital gains tax purposes* will depend upon the type of property held by the trustees. The general principle is that she is entitled to claim her one-third share, but not, in exceptional cases, when the effect of distributing that portion of the fund would be to damage the interests of the other beneficiaries. When the settled assets comprise land in England and Wales, this will be the result because the asset would often have to be sold to raise the necessary money.[26]

Hence, if the fund comprises land, A is not absolutely entitled for capital gains tax purposes when she reaches 21; therefore, the settlement continues in respect of all the land until it is sold by the trustees (in which event A takes one-third of the cash); or alternatively all three daughters satisfy

---

[24] As in *Figg v Clarke* [1997] STC 247.

[25] It is assumed that the trust does not provide for the class to close when the first child attains 21.

[26] See *Crowe v Appleby* [1976] 2 All ER 914 CA and in particular the decision of Goff J. at High Court level (51 TC 457) which decided that if the settled property was land in England or Wales there was no occasion of absolute entitlement on the satisfaction of any contingency other than the final one. The land as a whole remained settled property and so any disposal of it is a disposal by the trustees. The position is different in relation to Scottish law trusts (even if the land is situated in England) and to land in Northern Ireland or the Irish Republic where the beneficiary can call upon the trustees to convey to him an undivided share in the property (see *Stenhouse's Trustees v Lord Advocate* [1984] STC 195 SC). See further HMRC's Capital Gains Manual CG37540 and following. and *Snell's* Equity, 32nd edn at para.29.02 where it is concluded that the rule is limited to a trust comprising land; a single valuable chattel but does not extend to a substantial holding of private company shares. HMRC comment at CGTM 37540 that land owned by an English law trust in England, Wales or Scotland (but not Northern Ireland) is within the scope of *Crowe v Appleby*.

the contingency, or die before 21 years. Only then will the fund cease to be settled because one or more persons will, at that point, become jointly absolutely entitled to the property.[27]

By contrast if A is entitled to demand her share (as would generally be the case if it were an investment portfolio), her one-third share of the fund ceases to be settled (even though A may leave her share in the hands of the trustees who will then hold those assets as bare trustee for her).

Even in relation to assets such as an investment portfolio which are readily divisible into shares, HMRC do not regard the beneficiary as having become absolutely entitled if the trustees have an express power of appropriation and do not exercise it.[28] In such cases they will treat A as absolutely entitled only when the trustees exercise that power (and only in respect of the assets so appropriated). **9.12**

Hence, if no appropriation is made HMRC consider that the settlement continues until all beneficiaries are together absolutely entitled (or the asset in question is sold, if earlier).[29] It is questionable whether this view is correct since it means that under almost any trust no beneficiary will become entitled to capital on reaching a specified age unless the trustees exercised their express or implied power of appropriation.[30]

Further, this practice can produce apparently bizarre results. For instance, assume that A becomes entitled at age 25 to half the trust fund: his brother B will become entitled to the other half in two years time. The fund comprises some assets pregnant with gain and others showing neither gain nor loss. The trustees might appropriate the latter to A so that no CGT will be payable. In this connection: **9.13**

(i) It might be said that in so doing they were acting unfairly vis-à-vis B since his share will be diminished by the CGT payable on the CGT deemed disposal when he becomes entitled.[31]

(ii) HMRC's practice on appropriations is at odds with the following statement of Walton J. in *Stephenson v Barclay's Bank*:

> "*When the situation is that a single person who is sui juris has an absolute vested beneficial interest in a share of the trust fund, his rights are not, I think, quite as extensive as those of the beneficial interest holders as a body. In general, he is entitled to have transferred to him (subject, of course, always to the . . . rights of the trustees . . .) an aliquot share of each and every asset of the trust fund which*

---

[27] For problems that can arise on a division of a controlling shareholding: see *Lloyds Bank Plc v Duker* [1987] 3 All ER 193; [1987] 1 WLR 1324 and 9.12 below. A is, of course, entitled to one-third of the income. For IHT purposes he is treated as the owner of one-third of the trust property.

[28] See CGTM37521. It is thought that a similar approach should be taken in cases where there is only an *implied* power to appropriate. However, HMRC do not appear to recognise that trustees have such implied powers of appropriation under general law. See generally on implied powers *Lewin on Trusts*, 18th edn, paras 36–62.

[29] At CGTM 37531: "*until this power [of appropriation] is exercised the beneficiary cannot claim any specific asset and therefore it cannot be said that he or she is absolutely entitled to a fractional share of everything*".

[30] For the SDLT effects of an appropriation between funds: see Ch.51.

[31] See TCGA 1992 s.71.

*presents no difficulty so far as division is concerned. This will apply
to such items as cash, money at the bank or an unsecured loan, stock
exchange securities and the like. However, as regards land, certainly,
in all cases, as regards shares in a private company in very special
circumstances (see Re Weiner's Will Trusts) and possibly (although
the logic of the addition in fact escapes me) mortgage debts (see Re
Marshall per Cozens-Hardy MR) the situation is not so simple, and
even a person with a vested interest in possession in an aliquot share
of the trust fund may have to wait until the land is sold, and so forth,
before being able to call on the trustees as of right to account to him
for his share of the assets."*[32]

Private company shares

9.14 The case law on private company shareholdings is unsatisfactory. Walton J.
in the above case commented that in this case there is usually no difficulty
in saying that a beneficiary who has become entitled to a percentage of the
shareholding capital *has* become absolutely entitled since he can call for the
number of shares equivalent to his percentage entitlement to be transferred to
him. However, there are exceptions.

9.15 In *Lloyds Bank Plc v Duker*[33] the testator divided his 99 per cent shareholding in a private company between his wife and other beneficiaries. The testator's wife became entitled to forty six-eightieths of the residue including the
shares and on her death the beneficiary of her estate called upon the trustees to
transfer to her estate 574 shares in the company, being the equivalent number
of shares equal to forty six-eightieths of the total. It was held that, since the
block of 574 shares was worth more per share than minority holding, the
transfer of shares to the wife's estate would carry markedly more than forty
six-eightieths in total value and that accordingly, to ensure equality per share
among the beneficiaries, the trustees were under a duty to sell the shares so
that the wife's estate took forty six-eightieths of the residuary estate by value.
The company owned a luxury hotel and accordingly the court may have been
influenced by the fact that the asset of the company was land. Also the majority owner of the shares had a power to remove and appoint directors whereas
a minority holding could not unlock the assets. Hence, it was held that on the
particular facts of the case the wife's estate did not become absolutely entitled
for capital gains tax purposes unless and until there was a sale of shares.

9.16 By contrast, in *Re Weiner Deceased*[34] the estate held 75 per cent of the
shares in a private company and 45 per cent was ordered to be distributed
outright on the basis that this could not be worth more per share than the
shares in the block that stayed with the trustees, i.e. no one was advantaged or
disadvantaged by the distribution of a specific number of shares in satisfaction of a beneficiary's interest in the shareholding.

The position taken by the courts therefore seems to be that except in relation
to land in England and Wales only in unusual circumstances is a beneficiary

---

[32] See Ch.12.
[33] [1987] 1 WLR 1324; [1987] 3 All ER 193.
[34] [1956] 1 WLR 579.

not treated as absolutely entitled for CGT purposes when attaining the specified age for absolute entitlement.[35] For instance in *Re Marshall* it was said:

> "*Speaking generally, the right of a person who is indefeasibly entitled to an aliquot share of property to have that share transferred to him is one which is plainly established by law.*"

The position in relation to land

It appears that *Crowe v Appleby* does not apply where the trustees merely own an equitable interest in land.　**9.17**

EXAMPLE 9.8

W dies in 2007 leaving her beneficial half share in the family home on discretionary trusts for her four children. Her husband owns the other half share and is after her death the sole legal owner. The trustees advance one-quarter of their half share to the eldest child. He becomes absolutely entitled to that share for CGT purposes.

Crowe v Appleby applies where trustees have been left land by the settlor from the outset but what happens if trustees subsequently acquire land? Should the rule also apply then? Apparently it does with the result that the trustees could by judicious land purchases defer a beneficiary's absolute entitlement.　**9.18**

EXAMPLE 9.9

The testatrix, W, leaves her residuary estate on trust for her three children (A, B and C) contingent on attaining the age of 25. On her death the estate is made up of cash and quoted shares. The children are all minors. Just before the eldest child is 25 the trustees invest in real property so that by the time the eldest child, A, is 25 the entire trust fund comprises residential properties. The trustees do not exercise their powers of appropriation (for example, by allocating one house to A's share and another house of equal value to B and C's share). Instead the entire trust fund continues to be held in undivided shares. A does not become absolutely entitled to a share of the settled property at 25. If the trustees later sell a house, one-third of that value belongs to A absolutely but the rest remains in trust.[36] If the trustees use all the sale proceeds to buy another property then one third of that property still belongs to A absolutely.

---

[35] See *Re Sanderman's Will Trust* [1937] 1 All ER 368 at 372 and in *Re Marshall* [1914] 1 Ch 192.
[36] Note that if A dies there was a base cost uplift for capital gains tax purposes but only as to his one-third share in the entire trust fund: see Ch.12. But note the impact of the FA 2006 changes for IHT purposes: see A2.323 and Example 9.10.

9.19 Suppose there are more complex trusts over the land, e.g. in 2010 a brother and sister are each given life interests in half the trust fund following the death of their parent. These are qualifying interests in possession for IHT purposes being immediate post-death interests. Because the sister has no children the brother's children will take absolutely on the termination of the life interests.

If the brother dies in 2011, his children become entitled to one-half of the trust fund (the moiety in which the brother had enjoyed a life interest) for IHT purposes. However, the children will not be absolutely entitled for capital gains tax purposes until the death of the sister or the earlier sale of the land. Assume the land is not sold and the sister dies in 2012. At that point the brother's children become entitled to the whole trust fund and there is a deemed disposal of the land.[37] For capital gains tax purposes there is a base cost uplift to market value as to one-half on the sister's death in 2012 and as to the other half share on the death of the brother in 2011. However, any increase in value on the brother's half share between 2011 and 2012 is subject to CGT at 28 per cent such CGT being payable by the trustees.[38]

How do the IHT and CGT rules interact in relation to settled property where the trust ends only on the death of the last life tenant? Consider the following.

EXAMPLE 9.10

Thomas died in 1977 leaving a portfolio of properties on interest in possession trusts for his four children A, B, C and D remainder to their children per stirpes. By 2011 all his children apart from D have died but the trustees never made any specific appropriation or sold the land and therefore the grandchildren are not absolutely entitled for CGT purposes. Each fund also holds other assets in the form of cash and shares. On the deaths of each of A, B and C there was a CGT uplift to market value and the IHT due on each settled share was discharged out of that fund.[39]

In 2011 D, the final surviving child dies and the trust now ends. There is a CGT uplift on his share on his death; all the grandchildren now become absolutely entitled for CGT purposes (even if minors). The trustees have, in effect, disposed of the entire land portfolio at market value and any CGT

---

[37] Under TCGA 1992 s.71: see Ch.12.

[38] See also Ch.12 for problems arising out of *Crowe v Appleby*. In particular, there is no hold-over relief in 2011 under TCGA 1992 s.260 on the brother's share because in 2011 there is no chargeable transfer for inheritance tax purposes (since it had become comprised in his children's estates in 2011). How is the brother's share valued on his death in 2011? Where he owns half outright a discount of 10% or 20% would be relevant for inheritance tax purposes (depending on the type of property involved: see Ch.26) and therefore assuming inheritance tax was chargeable on his death and the value of the land has been ascertained this would be the trustees' base cost for capital gains tax purposes: see TCGA 1992 s.274. However, if the brother died with a qualifying interest in possession in the trust fund, despite the fact that the trustees own all the land, given there are separate qualifying IIPs it is thought that a discount would be applicable. See IHTA 1984 s.50, Ch.26 and A2.323 for HMRC's views on the inheritance tax/capital gains tax interaction in *Crowe v Appleby* situations and the further discussion in Ch.12.

[39] The trustees could have claimed instalment relief on the land on each of A, B and C's deaths and would have presumably paid the IHT from the liquid assets of each fund.

payable on A, B and C's shares (being taxed at 28 per cent on the gain realised by the trustees) is the liability of the trustees and is payable out of each share. It is the trustees who make the deemed disposal and they retain a lien over each share until the tax due on the deemed disposal is discharged.[40] The gain on each share is likely to be different since the market value of each one quarter share of the land at the death of A, B and C will be different. So for example in the case of A's share, the gain will be the difference between market value on the death of D and the value at A's death. It is likely that less IHT was paid on A, B and C's death but more CGT is due now in respect of those shares.

If the beneficiaries later agree to sell the land portfolio then they may realise a further gain depending on whether the land has increased in value since D's death. This is a gain realised by the beneficiaries themselves not by the trustees (even if the trustees still hold legal title) and therefore they can use their annual exemptions and personal losses against any gains realised.

Where A, B, C and D between them have had a large number of children it is possible that the trustees may be asked to appropriate or partition the land so that on the death of D properties are transferred to each branch of the family in satisfaction of their respective shares. This is often much more convenient. For example, A's family may be quite content to retain long term the properties if they are owned solely by them but less keen to retain a portfolio of properties in which their cousins also have an interest. Assuming the values are equal so that each of A, B, C and D's families now receive separate portfolios of properties, what is the CGT position?

It is thought that this partition is a non-event for CGT purposes and does **9.20** not trigger any further disposal since trustees may distribute assets to the beneficiaries under a scheme of division rather than proportionately. HMRC note at CGTM 37104:

> "*in this situation there are good grounds for saying that there is a chargeable disposal by each beneficiary by way of an exchange of assets. Similarly, specific assets may be appropriated by trustees to a beneficiary who has become absolutely entitled to a proportion of the settled property. In this case, the exchange is between the trustees and the beneficiary. It is, however, possible that the principles of Warrington v Brown* [41]*may be applicable in these two situations so that there is no second disposal following shortly after the section 71(1) occasion. If the trustees and beneficiaries seek to apply those principles, no objection should be made, although any attempt to treat a subsequent disposal of an asset on an inconsistent basis should be resisted*".

HMRC's hesitancy in accepting there is no further disposal made by the trustees when an appropriation or partition is made between families who are absolutely entitled is puzzling. The trustees now satisfy each beneficiary's undivided absolute interest in the whole estate by appropriating assets to them. Although they are not appropriating specific assets to an individual

---

[40] Of course HMRC will not care out of which share the trustees actually pay the CGT provided it is paid. The beneficiaries will be concerned that each share bears the correct amount of tax.

[41] *Warrington (Jenkins) v Brown* [1989] STC 577, confirms that there is no disposal of assets when a beneficiary withdraws the same piece of land that he put into the common pool: see Example 9.4.

beneficiary but specific assets to the beneficiaries of one family this should not in itself make any difference to the principle that no CGT disposal has arisen. It is also not clear why the word "shortly" is used in the above statement after absolute entitlement. The trustees can distribute the assets to the beneficiaries in satisfaction of their absolute entitlement as soon as feasible given that the liabilities needed to be ascertained and settled before the trustees can release the property. It may be some time before the trustees are in a position to make a partition but they can then satisfy each beneficiary's entitlement as they think appropriate usually with the beneficiary's agreement.[42]

9.21 Although HMRC may seek to argue that *Crowe v Appleby* can also apply to land held by personal representatives where part is then vested in a legatee absolutely (e.g. a charity) in the authors' opinion this is not correct. The position is discussed further in Ch.40.

9.22 A person can become "absolutely entitled" to assets without being "beneficially" entitled.[43]

III THE DEFINITION OF SETTLOR INCLUDING MULTIPLE SETTLORS, CORPORATE SETTLORS, RESETTLEMENTS AND POST-DEATH VARIATIONS

9.23 As part of the so-called trust modernisation process a new definition of settlor was inserted into the legislation.[44] Section 68A now defines the meaning of settlor; s.68B considers the identity of the settlor in the case of transfers between settlements, and s.68C identifies the settlor when there is a variation of a will or intestacy.

9.24 Settlor means:

> *"the person or any persons who has made or is treated . . . as having made, the settlement" (and a person is treated as having made a settlement if)* *"(a) he has made or entered into a settlement directly or indirectly or (b) the settled property or property from which the settlement is derived, is*

---

[42] What is the SDLT position where trustees satisfy each beneficiary's undivided absolute interest in land by appropriating specific areas of land to them equal to the value they hold in the pool trust? The trustees may choose to appropriate specific assets to each individual beneficiary or alternative specific assets to the beneficiaries of each fund A to D who then hold those appropriated assets jointly. FA 2003 Sch.4 para.6 states:

> *"in the case of a land transaction giving effect to a partition or division of a chargeable interest to which persons are jointly entitled, the share of the interest held by the purchaser immediately before the partition or division does not count as chargeable consideration".*

The SDLT Office has confirmed to the authors that this can apply not only where each individual beneficiary becomes entitled to a specific asset but also where a group of beneficiaries (for example those beneficiaries of family A) become so entitled to the land between them. To the extent equality money has to be paid by one family to another family because one family receives properties of greater value than the other SDLT will be due on that cash.

[43] Hence, property can pass out of one settlement into another settlement if the trustees of the latter have become absolutely entitled as against the trustees of the former: see 7.55; *Hoare Trustees v Gardner* [1978] STC 89 and *Roome v Edwards* [1981] STC 96.

[44] See TCGA 1992 s.68A inserted by FA 2006. The equivalent provision in the income tax legislation is ITTOIA 2005 s.620: see Ch.7.

or includes property of which he was competent to dispose immediately before his death and the settlement arose on his death, whether by will, on his intestacy, or otherwise"[45]

and

"*A person is, in particular, treated . . . as having made a settlement if—*

(a) *he has provided property directly or indirectly for the purposes of the settlement, or*
(b) *he has undertaken to provide property directly or indirectly for the purposes of the settlement."*[46]

A person can become a settlor by exercising a general power of appointment to settle property.

Where A enters into a settlement in accordance with reciprocal arrange-   **9.25**
ments with B, B not A is treated as having made A's settlement and vice versa.

EXAMPLE 9.11

A and B agree to make settlements for each other's children. The settlements are reciprocal and hence, for income tax, CGT and IHT purposes, A is the settlor of B's trust and vice versa. If the children are minor then the settlements will be settlor-interested for CGT purposes and income may be taxed on the settlor. (But note that A has not disposed of the assets that B put into settlement and nor has B disposed of A's assets.)

For inheritance tax and capital gains tax purposes the definition of "set-   **9.26**
tlement" and "settled property" does not require there to be an element of bounty and so commercial settlements such as employee benefit trusts fall within the definition.[47] So far as the definition of "settlor" is concerned, however, the basic requirement is that he should "provide" property which the courts in *CIR v Leiner*[48] (an income tax case) decided introduced a requirement of bounty. A settlor is someone who gifts property into trust, not a person who sells property on arms length terms to the trustees. HMRC have accepted, in the context of the settlor charge for offshore trusts that a similar interpretation of bounty applies for CGT purposes.[49]

---

[45] TCGA 1992 s.68A(2)(a) and see similar provisions for income tax purposes in ITA 2007 s.467(1).
[46] This is similar to the definition of settlor in ITA 2007 s.467 and see also ITTOIA 2005 s.620 and IHTA 1984 s.44 which refer to a person making a settlement. For UK resident settlements whether a trust is settlor-interested will now only be relevant (at least for capital gains tax purposes), on a transfer of assets into the trust. If the trust is settlor-interested then hold-over relief is denied. See Ch.7 for further comments on definition of settlor.
[47] See CGTM 33240. Note there the definition of settlement for s.87 purposes does, however, require bounty: see Ch.19.
[48] 41 TC 589.
[49] *Tax Bulletin* 16.

Where someone becomes a settlor by adding property to a trust but that property is subsequently distributed to a beneficiary he ceases to be a settlor for income tax and CGT purposes.[50] It may be difficult to identify property which has been provided by different settlors.[51]

EXAMPLE 9.12

Mr P transfers a house into a trust which had been set up by his father and already holds £1 million cash. Subsequently the house is sold for £500,000 and the proceeds distributed to the beneficiaries. Mr P ceases to be settlor of the trust. The father remains the sole settlor of the remaining assets.[52]

9.27 This definition of settlor also raises the question of whether when a person who is not the original settlor adds property to an existing settlement he has created a new separate settlement or becomes a settlor of the existing settlement.[53] As a matter of trust law it is common for additions to be merged with the existing trust property and treated as one fund for all purposes and there is nothing in the CGT legislation to displace this treatment.

9.28 Was a new definition of settlor needed? There is a specific definition in the case of non-UK resident settlor-interested trusts in Sch.5 para.7. That definition of settlor is related to the settled property comprised in the settlement rather than to the making of the settlement:

> "*A person is a settlor . . . [for the purposes of s.86] in relation to a settlement if the settled property consists of or includes property originating from him*".

Paragraph 8 then sets out the meaning of "originating" to include property provided by any person and reciprocal arrangements. The definition in s.68A did not amend these provisions and the result is potentially confusing where more than one person has added to the trust since the above definition does not seem to envisage that a person can be a settlor only in relation to that part of the settled property that he has added.[54]

---

[50] TCGA 1992 s.68A(6)(a) and ITA 2007 s.469.

[51] For a discussion of when property provided by different settlors is comprised in a single settlement: see 9.28.

[52] See also Ch.7 for multiple settlors and ITTOIA 2005 ss.644 and 645 and below at 9.00 For income tax and CGT purposes in relation to any given settlor the property and income comprised in the settlement are now restricted to that originating from him. This reverses with the decision in *Lord Herbert v IRC* (1943) 25 TC 93 where it was held that where there was more than one person who was the settlor of the trust, none of them could be assessed to income tax because there was no machinery for apportionment between them.

[53] See the discussion at 9.28 regarding single or multiple settlements. Compare IHTA 1984 s.44(2): in the case of multiple settlors when "*the circumstances so require*" the property is treated as comprised in separate settlements.

[54] Note also that the widened income tax definition applies for the purpose of the capital payments regime in s.87.

Corporate settlors

It should be noted that Sch.5 para.8(4) expressly provides in the context of   **9.29**
non-UK resident trusts that where a close company gives property to a trust
participators of that company are treated as the settlors for CGT purposes.
There is nothing comparable in the IHT legislation.[55] Hence, it is not possible for an individual to give funds to a company which then funds a trust
and argue that the individual is not the settlor of the offshore trust. However,
a transaction between a company and a trust will not normally make the
participators of the company settlors of the trust if it is carried out on arms
length terms because nothing has been "provided".

HMRC also take the view that provision of property to a company wholly   **9.30**
owned by a trust is provision of property for the purposes of the trust and
therefore makes the provider a settlor.[56] However, a contrary view was taken
in the *Coombes* case where a non UK resident gave £1,000 to trustees who
acquired an offshore Newco. A UK domiciliary then gave £700,000 to Newco
which purchased UK land later sold at a substantial gain. It was held he was
not the settlor for s.86 purposes because the trust participation in the company
was not property which originated from the settlor despite the fact that he gave
money to the company. HMRC argued that the increase in the value of the
shares resulting from the gift meant that the settled property originated from
the UK taxpayer but this was rejected by the High Court. The individual may
have provided property for the purposes of the settlement but the question for
s.86 purposes was whether he had provided *settled* property for the purposes
of the trust.

Resettlements

The term "resettlement" is not a term of art. Broadly, a resettlement is said   **9.31**
to occur when the trustees of one trust transfer (in the exercise of a power in
that trust deed) trust property to the trustees of another trust. In such cases,
there will be a deemed disposal of the property under TCGA 1992 s.71(1)
given that the trustees of the recipient trust have become absolutely entitled
to it (it does not matter that they are the same persons as the transferor
trustees since they become entitled to the property in a different capacity).[57]
The term is, however, also used in the context of trust reorganisations: for
instance, where the beneficiaries (all of whom have legal capacity and are
in agreement) and the trustees agreed to vary the terms of the trust. The
best illustration of such rearrangements is the resettlement associated with
the strict settlement of land when (usually) life tenant and remainderman
would "resettle" the property. In such cases it is a question of fact whether a
person has become absolutely entitled to the trust property so that a deemed
disposal occurs.[58]

---

[55] Schedule 5 para.8 is defective as illustrated in the case of *Coombes v IRC* [2008] STC 2984 discussed at 9.30.
[56] See SP 5/92 in the context of s.86 and offshore trusts.
[57] See generally *Hoare Trustees v Gardner* [1978] 1 All ER 791, s.71(1) and 12.31.
[58] See 12.31.

9.32   In cases where the amounts involved are sufficient to justify the costs involved, it is possible to apply under VTA 1958 for a new perpetuity period. In *Wyndham v Egremont*,[59] substantial funds were held on trust. The perpetuity period was 20 years from the death of the last survivor of the issue, whether children or more remote, of His Late Majesty King George V living on May 20, 1940. Given the ages of the remaining Royal Lives in being, the youngest of whom (HRH Princess Alexandra) is 72, the period would expire in the not too distant future and as the current life tenant was only 26, in his lifetime. This would deprive the life tenant's eldest son of an interest in the fund and would trigger a substantial CGT charge on the deemed disposal. Blackburne J. approved a variation which inserted a new perpetuity period (the last survivor of the legitimate issue, whether children or more remote, living on July 24, 2009 of His Late Majesty King George V and the Fifth Baron Leconfield) which significantly postponed the deemed disposal. Section 1(1) of the 1958 Act authorises the court to approve an arrangement varying (or revoking) all or any of the trusts of a will, settlement or other disposition. It does not authorise the court to approve a resettlement. There is no bright-line test for determining what is or is not a resettlement. In *Re Ball's Settlement Trusts*[60] Megarry J. stated that:

> "*If an arrangement, while leaving the substratum effectuates the purpose of the original trusts by other means, it may still be possible to regard that arrangement as merely varying the original trusts, even though the means employed are wholly different and even though the form is completely changed.*"[61]

9.33   When a resettlement or trust reorganisation occurs the following issues can arise:

(i) Who is the settlor of the resettled property?

(ii) What is the effect of such a resettlement in capital gains tax terms: is there a new settlement and hence a deemed disposal of the settled property or does the property remain comprised in the original settlement in which case there is no disposal? The latter question is discussed in 10.55.

Who is the settlor of the resettled property?

9.34   TCGA 1992 s.68B contains specific identification provisions.[62] The settlor of the property disposed of by the trustees of settlement 1 is treated from the time of the transfer as having made settlement 2 and is a settlor of settlement 2 in respect of the transferred property. If there is more than one settlor of the original settlement, how is the transferred property apportioned between them?

---

[59] [2009] EWHC 2076 (Ch). For further discussion see 12.31.
[60] [1968] 2 All ER 438.
[61] For further consideration of resettlements and deemed disposals: see 12.31.
[62] See Examples 9.11 and 9.12.

EXAMPLE 9.13

A and B jointly establish a settlement. A settles a house and B settles shares. The shares are transferred to settlement 2 one year later when they are worth 25 per cent of the whole of settlement 1. Is B the sole settlor of settlement 2 (and does B cease to be a settlor of settlement 1) or are both A and B the settlors of settlement 2 as to 75/25 per cent? Section 68B(3)(b) states that *"except where the context otherwise requires"* both are settlors of a proportionate part of the transferred property. Presumably in this case *"the context"* would require B to be the sole settlor.[63]

When trustees exercise a power in the wider form to create a new settlement **9.35** it is the person who provided the settled property, not the trustees who is the settlor, and such person has always as a matter of trust law been treated as the settlor, so were these new provisions required?[64] Previously there was no mechanism to apportion income or gains where there was more than one settlor of the trust and these provisions correct that.

Instruments of variation[65]

The basic rule is that where the variation creates a settlement that would not **9.36** otherwise have existed; the deceased is not treated as the settlor for income tax and capital gains tax purposes.[66]

EXAMPLE 9.14

Frederick, a non-UK domiciliary, dies leaving his foreign property absolutely to his son. His son is UK domiciled and therefore executes a deed of variation under which the property is settled on trust for himself and his children. Reading-back for inheritance tax purposes, results in Frederick being treated as the settlor of an excluded property settlement. For capital gains tax purposes, however, the son is the settlor.[67]

---

[63] The income tax wording for transferred property in ITA 2007 s.471 is much more explicit providing that B would be the sole settlor of settlement 2.

[64] See *West v Trennery* [2005] 1 All ER 827 which did not cast doubt on the settlor rather than the trustees being the settlor of the transferee trust. The question in that case was whether the trust was settlor-interested and the point that the settlor might not be the person who originally settled the funds was not even raised. The case is discussed in detail in Ch.7. Another question is whether the two settlements should be treated as one settlement either as a matter of trust law or under tax law. Normally the answer would be no but note the extended definition of settlement for capital gains tax purposes in ss.86 and 87 and for income tax purposes: see *Chinn v Collins* [1981] 1 All ER 189.

[65] See Ch.39

[66] See TCGA 1992 s.68C and ITA 2007 s.472.

[67] See *Marshall v Kerr* [1994] 3 All ER 106 HL.

9.37   Contrast the position where a variation ends a trust set up under the will and establishes a new trust. In these circumstances the deceased is treated as the settlor.[68]

EXAMPLE 9.15

> William dies leaving his property on life interest trusts for his spouse and then to his adult children outright. Spouse and children execute a deed of variation setting up new trusts for the grandchildren. The settlor is the deceased (and therefore if the trust is non-UK resident s.86 does not apply (because he is dead) and it is subject to TCGA 1992 s.87). Similarly, for income tax purposes the settlor is William. Hence the income is not taxed on children or spouse even if they can continue to benefit from the trusts.

9.38   More complicated scenarios can arise when there is an intestacy and the whole estate is varied.

EXAMPLE 9.16

> Andrei dies intestate domiciled in the UK. Half his estate passes on life interest trusts for his spouse and then to his children outright. The other half passes directly to his adult children. The spouse and children get together and between them vary the entire estate so an amount equal to his unused IHT nil rate band is left to his children and the remainder on life interest trusts for the spouse and then to the children (so that the IHT spouse exemption is available). In these circumstances, as to half the estate Andrei is the settlor for capital gains tax and income tax purposes; for the other half the widow and children are the settlors. How does this work in practice? For capital gains tax s.77 (which formerly taxed the settlor on gains realised by trustees of a settlor-interested trust) has been repealed and all gains are taxed on the trustees anyway irrespective of who is the settlor. However the income tax position is more complex. The widow is the life tenant and entitled to all the income. The children remain beneficiaries of the residuary trust fund. Are they taxed as settlors on a proportion of the income to which they would otherwise have been entitled even though all of it passes to widow, with a right of reimbursement to the children? These and other problems relating to variations are discussed in Ch.39.

IV SINGLE OR MULTIPLE SETTLEMENTS

9.39   The question of when a separate settlement arises as the result of the trustees exercising a dispositive power of appointment or advancement is discussed at 12.00.

---

[68] See further Ch.39.

However, the problem of whether there are two trusts or one can arise in other contexts, for instance:

(i) The testator may in his will leave different property on separate trusts for different beneficiaries. Is there one trust or two?

(ii) A settlor may add property to a trust. Is this to be treated as a new settlement for capital gains tax purposes or merely an addition?

(iii) A different person may add property to an existing trust. Is this a separate trust?

There is no general definition of the term "settlement" in the capital gains **9.40** legislation.[69] As statute is silent, the court approaches the meaning of the terms "settlement" and "settled property" in the manner explained by Lord Wilberforce in *Roome v Edwards*.[70]

> "*There are a number of obvious indicia which may help to show whether a settlement, or a settlement separate from another settlement, exists. One might expect to find separate and defined property; separate trusts; and separate trustees. One might also expect to find a separate disposition bringing the separate settlement into existence. These indicia may be helpful, but they are not decisive. For example, a single disposition, e.g. a will with a single set of trustees, may create what are clearly separate settlements, relating to different properties, in favour of different beneficiaries, and conversely separate trusts may arise in what is clearly a single settlement, e.g. when the settled property is divided into shares. There are so many possible combinations of fact that even where these indicia or some of them are present, the answer may be doubtful, and may depend upon an appreciation of them as a whole.*
>
> *Since 'settlement' and 'trusts' are legal terms, which are also used by businessmen or laymen in a business or practical sense, I think that the question whether a particular set of facts amount to a settlement should be approached by asking what a person, with knowledge of the legal context of the word under established doctrine and applying the knowledge in a practical and common-sense manner to the facts under examination, would conclude.*"

Offshore trusts

The definition of "settlement" and "settlor" in ITTOIA 2005 s.620 applies in **9.41** relation to the TCGA 1992 s.87 charge on offshore trusts but so as to include a settlement arising under a will or intestacy.[71] That section defines a "settlement" as including, "*any disposition, trust, covenant, agreement, arrangement or transfer of assets. . .*".

---

[69] Save for the special definition that applies in relation to TCGA 1992 ss.87–97 where the trustees of the settlement are neither resident nor ordinarily resident in the UK.

[70] [1982] AC 279 at 292 and 293.

[71] See TCGA 1992 s.97(7).

This is not an exhaustive definition. Its object is to extend the term "settlement" beyond its ordinary meaning.[72] The inheritance tax legislation provides generally for separate settlements when there are different settlors.[73]

Why does it matter whether there is one trust or two?

9.42 This can be important for a number of reasons: for example:

(i) Each trust has its own annual exemption. Trusts made by the same settlor will have to share this equally. If there are multiple settlors of one trust then one annual exemption is given for the whole trust. Where the settlors have set up a number of other settlements, the exemption given is calculated by reference to the settlor who set up the greater number of settlements! So if a trust holds property settled by A who had set up 10 other trusts, the annual capital gains tax exemption is the minimum.[74] It cannot be increased by B (who has not made any other trusts) adding £100 to the trust.

(ii) A loss realised by the trustees can be set against gains of the same settlement. If assets are comprised in different trusts then the loss in one cannot be set against the gain in the other.

(iii) If the trusts are offshore or have been offshore it will be important to know whether one is dealing with one trust or two for the purpose of determining s.87 gains and capital payments.

(iv) Trustees of a single settlement are liable for the capital gains tax resulting from the disposal of any asset comprised in the settlement, even if the assets are vested in different trustees of a sub-fund who may be resident abroad.[75]

(v) If a settlor is non-resident and not UK domiciled at the date the trust was set up then the trust will not be UK resident if there is one non-UK resident trustee. However, if a person who is UK resident or domiciled later adds funds to the trust (rather than sets up a new trust) then the trust becomes UK resident as to the entirety of the assets.[76] Similarly if trustees resettle property at a time when the settlor is UK resident or UK domiciled and there is one UK and one non-UK resident trustee then, the trust becomes UK resident.

Single Instrument—Multiple Trusts?

9.43 HMRC considers[77] that one instrument can create separate settlements if:

---

[72] There is no extended meaning of settlement for the purpose of the s.86 charge on the settlor but the same definition of settlor is adopted thereby incorporating the requirement of bounty.
[73] IHTA 1984 s.44(2).
[74] See Ch.11.
[75] See for example *Roome v Edwards* [1981] 1 All ER 736 HL.
[76] See Ch.4.
[77] See CGTM 33296–CGTM33305.

(i) there are from the outset two or more segregated funds, each held on separate trusts;

(ii) the funds continue to be held on separate trusts in all circumstances. However, if there is a default provision under which one fund will accrue to another if the trusts of that fund fail this is suggestive of a single settlement;

(iii) there are no assets held in common.

However, the above criteria are no more than indications of whether there is a single settlement although (i) is the most important. The question may be difficult to determine in the case of a will which commonly appoints the same trustees and uses trusts in a similar form but different beneficiaries and different assets. It is not uncommon for trustees to hold assets in separate funds within the same settlement and how the fund has been administered *after* the trusts have been constituted cannot determine whether or not there is a single settlement. For example, if a will sets up two trusts the fact that the trustees administer them as one does not change the legal position. In the end it is a matter of construction of the instrument.

In *Bond v Pickford*[78] the Court of Appeal had to decide whether an exercise by trustees of a special power of appointment had created a new settlement. Slade L.J. pointed out that in such a case one relevant test, following the exercise of the power, was to ask:

> "*Do the trustees of the original settlement still have duties to perform in regard to the relevant assets in their capacity as trustees of that [original] settlement?*"

This test may be relevant in deciding whether or not there is a separate settlement in relation to trusts derived from dispositions of a will. If, once the executors of the will have transferred assets to A and B as trustees of one disposition in that will and neither the executors nor C and D as the trustees of a second separate disposition in the will have any duties to perform in regard to those assets, then it is difficult to see how A and B, as trustees of the first disposition in the will, can be trustees of the same settlement as C and D (the trustees of the second disposition in the will).

Indeed it is clear from the judgment of Lord Wilberforce quoted above that, in principle, a will may create two separate settlements. Where there is "separate and defined property; separate trusts; and separate trustees" the fact that there is an initial identity of the dispositive provisions applicable to the two funds does not prevent there being two separate settlements. Even if the trustees are the same this is not conclusive of there being a single settlement.

Additions to trusts

Under general law when property is transferred to the trustees of an existing settlement by the original settlor and accepted by them as an addition to

9.44

9.45

---

[78] [1983] STC 517.

the funds subject to the trusts of that settlement, that further property is not regarded as being subject to a separate settlement.[79] Where property is transferred to an existing settlement by someone other than the original settlor it is more likely that a new trust has been created.[80] One should look at whether there are separate trusts governing beneficial entitlement, separate trustees and separate administration, although none of these factors is conclusive. And often he will wish the addition to be administered as one fund along with the original settled property.

V DEFINITION OF TRUSTEES

9.46   The trust modernisation exercise resulted in a common definition of residence for income tax and capital gains tax purposes.[81] Trustees of settled property are and continue to be treated as a distinct, single and continuing body for capital gains tax purposes. Hence, the trustees make disposals for capital gains tax purposes in their capacity as trustees and the taxation affairs of the trust are entirely separate from the taxation affairs of the individuals who act from time to time as trustees. There is generally no capital gains tax "event" on a change of trustee[82] because they are treated as a single and continuing body.[83]

9.47   Section 69(3) provides that trustees are a single continuing body of persons even if some of the property comprised in a settlement is vested in one set of trustees and some in another. This would arise where property is appropriated to separate trustees of a sub fund without the appointment creating a new settlement.[84]

9.48   HMRC need only assess one trustee to recover capital gains tax.[85] For the liability of retired trustees when a trust subsequently becomes non-resident, see Ch.4. Non-UK resident trustees are not generally liable for capital gains tax[86] although tax on gains attributed to the settlor under s.86 may be recoverable from them.

VI DISPOSALS

9.49   A disposal must occur before a capital gain or loss can arise. In the context of settled property, capital gains tax disposals can be actual or deemed

[79] See *Playfair Palmer v Playfair* [1951] Ch 4 where a father had created a settlement on the marriage of his child and subsequently left a legacy by will to the trustees to be held by them on the trusts of that settlement. It was held that the will did not create a separate settlement.
[80] See CGTM 33320.
[81] See Ch.4: note that the harmonised residence test took effect from April 6, 2007 (not from April 6, 2006 when the other modernisation changes were introduced).
[82] Unless the trust becomes non-resident: see Ch.4. Note the importance of ensuring that trustees properly retire and are validly appointed: see further Chs 1 and 4.
[83] FA 2006 Sch.12 amended TCGA 1992 s.69 to state that trustees are to be treated as a single person rather than as "*a single body of persons*". It is not clear what (if any) the practical effect of this change was.
[84] See *Roome v Edwards*: unless a sub-fund election was made: see 12.42.
[85] TCGA 1992 s.65(1). Hence, a trustee can be accountable for gains accruing in respect of any of the assets of the settlement even if he has never controlled them himself, e.g because they are held in a separate sub-fund by other trustees.
[86] See Ch.19.

but the term "disposal" is not itself defined in the legislation and does not generally include a transaction where an asset is not acquired but is merely extinguished (although if a capital sum is derived from assets the assets are in that event deemed to be disposed of).[87] An actual disposal is generally taken to mean the transfer of ownership of an asset by one person to another.[88] A deemed disposal does not necessarily require this. The meaning of disposal was considered in *Jerome v Kelly*[89] where the House of Lords concluded that a contract to sell land is not itself the relevant disposal. TCGA 1992 s.28(1) fixes the time of disposal as the date of exchange of contracts but this does not in itself deem the contract to be the disposal. The meaning of disposal was further discussed in *Underwood v CRC*.[90] The position is complex where contracts are exchanged but not completed or are subject to further sub-sales.

Disposals of assets comprised in a trust fund will arise in any of the circumstances set out below. Some of these are "deemed disposals" and some are actual disposals. Generally a deemed disposal by trustees is treated as taking place at market value with a deemed reacquisition of the property by the trustees at that value: **9.50**

(i) When assets are transferred into a trust by the settlor, either on creation of the settlement or by subsequent additions.[91]

(ii) On the death of a beneficiary entitled to a qualifying interest in possession in the settled property.[92]

(iii) If a beneficiary becomes absolutely entitled to the settled assets as against the trustees.[93]

(iv) On actual disposals of assets by the trustees during the course of administering the trust.

(v) On the occasion when the trustees of a trust become non-resident or are treated as such under a double tax treaty.[94]

(vii) On transfer of assets from one trust to a different settlement.

(viii) On certain occasions where trustees make a transfer of value linked with trustee borrowing.[95]

(ix) When a sub-fund election is made.[96]

In addition, beneficiaries disposing of their beneficial interests under the settlement are, in limited circumstances, taxed on the value of those interests.[97]

---

[87] TCGA 1992 s.22.
[88] See *Welbeck Securities Ltd v Powlson* [1987] STC 468 and *Kirby Thorn EMI* [1987] STC 621. In *MacNiven v Westmoreland Investments Ltd* [2001] UKHL; [2001] STC 237 it was held the term disposal is a commercial concept and not a term of art.
[89] [2004] STC 887.
[90] [2008] STC 1138.
[91] TCGA 1992 s.22.
[92] See Ch.12.
[93] TCGA 1992 s.71: see Ch.12.
[94] TCGA 1992 s.80 and see Ch.4.
[95] TCGA 1992 Sch.4B and 4C and see Ch.19.
[96] FA 2006 Sch.12 and see Ch.12.
[97] See Ch.20.

CHAPTER 10

CGT ON CREATION OF A SETTLEMENT

- Disposals to trustees **(10.01)**
- Hold-over relief **(10.03)**
- Instalment option and double charges **(10.06)**
- Rates of tax on transfers into trust on or after April 6, 2008 and the effect of the 2010 changes **(10.09)**

I DISPOSALS TO TRUSTEES

10.01 When an asset becomes settled property there is a disposal of the asset settled for CGT purposes.[1] That disposal by the settlor is treated as taking place at market value[2] whether the settlement is revocable or irrevocable, and whether or not the settlor or his spouse is a beneficiary.[3] If chargeable

---

[1] See TCGA 1992 s.70 and *Berry v Warnett* [1982] STC 396. In that case the taxpayer first transferred shares to a nominee and then directed that nominee to hold the shares upon trust for him for life and subject thereto upon trust for a reversioner who paid the taxpayer full value for his reversionary interest. The taxpayer argued that there was only a part disposal because of the life interest retained and that because consideration had been paid for the reversion he had not made a gift in settlement. The former legislation in CGTA 1979 s.53 referred to gifts into settlement but TCGA 1992 s.70 refers to transfers into settlement. The House of Lords held that the transfer to the nominee was not a disposal which requires the transfer of beneficial title rather than the legal transfer of title but that a disposal arose when the taxpayer gave the direction to the nominee, i.e at the point the shares became settled property. The fact that the settlor retains a life interest or is a trustee does not mean that the disposal is not a complete disposal for capital gains tax purposes. (Contrast the position under the reservation of benefit rules where if the settlor retains a life interest he is treated as making a gift of the remainder interest not of the entire settled property.)

[2] *Turner v Follett* (1973) 48 TC 614. Note that gifts into a settlement can be treated as taking place at no gain no loss if the settlement is an employee benefit trust: see TCGA 1992 s.239. See Ch.49 for further details.

[3] See TCGA 1992 s.70. This contrasts with jurisdictions such as the United States where disposals to grantor trusts can be treated as non-events for capital gains tax purposes and the trust is fiscally transparent and taxed as if the assets were still owned by the settlor. The consultation on the modernisation of trusts considered whether to make settlor-interested trusts fiscally transparent for capital gains tax purposes (being more in line with the inheritance tax treatment prior to March 2006 of trusts where the settlor took an interest in possession) In the event the inheritance tax changes in the FA 2006 moved away from the idea of fiscal transparency in these circumstances. In 2006, the capital gains tax legislation extended the definition of what is settlor-interested to include trusts benefitting minor children as well as spouse, civil partner and settlor without making such a trust fiscally transparent. Hence, a settlor could be taxed on

256

assets are settled, a chargeable gain or allowable loss may result, calculated according to the usual capital gains tax rules. The rules on hold-over relief are discussed in detail in Ch.18. The capital gains tax regime since April 2008 is considered in the next chapter and the income tax and capital gains tax regime for UK resident settlor-interested trusts is considered in Ch.7. The two most important changes for trustees to be aware of are as follows:

(a) from April 6, 2008 all gains were initially taxed at the flat rate of 18 per cent irrespective of how long the asset had been owned or the type of trust. Gains were no longer indexed. However, the CGT rate for trustees increased to 28 per cent for disposals on or after June 23, 2010.[4] Unlike individuals who are basic rate or non-taxpayers, trustees pay CGT at the highest rate of 28 per cent with a limited annual CGT exemption.

The only limited exception to this is when trustees qualify for entrepreneurs' relief in which case their effective rate of tax on disposals of certain business assets on or after June 23, 2010 in respect of gains of up to £5 million was reduced to 10 per cent and from April 6, 2011 the £5 million ceiling on relief was doubled to £10 million. However, as Ch.14 explains, the conditions that trustees must satisfy to obtain entrepreneurs' relief are onerous and the availability of the relief also depends on the relevant beneficiary agreeing to such a claim;

(b) the gains of UK resident settlor-interested trusts are no longer taxed on the settlor.[5]

As the settlor and his trustees are connected persons,[6] any loss resulting from the disposal by the settlor to the trustees is only deductible from a gain on a subsequent disposal to *those trustees*. There is, however, no restriction on the use of losses where the settlement is created for charitable, cultural or recreational purposes and the persons benefiting from the trust are not connected with the settlor.[7]

10.02

gains arising in a settlor-interested trust yet the disposal of assets by him into such a trust was treated as taking place at market value and no hold-over relief was available. FA 2008 CGT changes repealed ss.77–79; hence a settlor is no longer taxed personally on gains realised by a settlor-interested trust but hold-over relief on gifts to such trusts is still not available. The FA 2008 changes have therefore accentuated the move towards taxing all trusts as separate entities for both inheritance tax and capital gains tax purposes rather than treating the trust as part of the settlor's estate.

[4] The abolition of indexation was justified on the basis that the CGT rate was low at 18% and that this would provide welcome simplification. However, though there has been a subsequent increase in the rate of CGT to 28% for almost all trusts and many individuals there has been no reintroduction of indexation or taper relief. No doubt if the rate of CGT increases further there will be increased calls to index gains so that only real gains are actually taxed. The wheel will then have come full circle!

[5] In this respect we have returned to the regime operating until April 5, 1988 when gains were taxed at the flat rate of 30%. In 1988 the rule was altered so that gains were taxed (in the case of individuals) at their marginal rate of income tax. From 1998 this rule still operated except that taper relief could reduce the effective rate of tax.

[6] TCGA 1992 s.18(3) and 286(3). For a consideration of the connected person rule, see *Tax Bulletin*, Issue 6, February 1993, p.56.

[7] See TCGA 1992 s.18(4).

Example 10.1

Ambitious wishes to sell his investment portfolio which is standing at a substantial capital gain. He also owns farmland which has fallen in value (and which he wishes to retain). Consider the following:

(i) Ambitious settles both the shares and the farmland into a trust under which he retains an interest in possession (the trustees also have a power to pay or transfer capital to him).

(ii) The disposal to the trustees triggers the gain (on the shares) and loss (on the land). The loss can be used to reduce the chargeable gain realised by Ambitious. The trust acquires the shares and land at market value at the date when they are transferred to the trustees.

(iii) The trustees may then sell the shares and subsequently transfer the cash and farmland back to Ambitious.

Note that if Ambitious had transferred the shares to one trust and the land to another although both trusts are connected with him he cannot set the loss on the land against the gain on the shares—the disposals must be to the same connected party.

Beware of (a) any suggestion that the arrangement is a sham[8] and (b) the IHT position on the creation of new settlements after March 21, 2006. Before that date such a transfer would have been neutral for inheritance tax purposes because the settlor was treated as continuing to own the property beneficially. Hence, no transfer of value arose. After March 21, 2006, however, such transfers are prima facie chargeable transfers for inheritance tax purposes irrespective of any interest retained by the settlor.[9]

II HOLD-OVER RELIEF

10.03 A gain arising on the disposal of assets into trust may be held-over[10]:

(i) under TCGA 1992 s.165 if the assets in question are "business assets";

(ii) under TCGA 1992 s.260(2)(a) *"if the disposal is made otherwise than under a bargain at arm's length and is a chargeable transfer within the meaning of IHTA 1984 . . . and is not a potentially exempt transfer"*. As a result of the 2006 changes in the IHT treatment of settlements, in most cases the creation of a settlement will now involve a chargeable transfer.[11]

---

[8] Sham trusts are considered at 1.18.
[9] There is a limited let out for self-settlements where the settlor has reason to believe that he will become disabled and for interest in possession trusts for a disabled person: see Ch.36.
[10] See Ch.18.
[11] These changes are considered in detail in Ch.22 onwards.

It is important to bear in mind that for disposals made on or after December 5, 2003 no hold-over relief is available under either s.165 or s.260 if the trust is "settlor-interested".[12] (FA 2008 did not change this although gains later realised by the settlor-interested trust after the asset has been settled into trust are no longer taxed on the settlor.) For disposals made into trust prior to April 6, 2006, only if the settlor, his spouse or civil partner could benefit was the trust treated as settlor-interested. For disposals into trust from April 6, 2006,[13] however, a trust is settlor-interested if the settlor, spouse, civil partner and any unmarried minor child or stepchild of the settlor can benefit.[14]

EXAMPLE 10.2

> In July 2010 X sets up a life interest trust for his wife. Although a chargeable transfer for IHT purposes, no hold-over relief is available because the trust is settlor-interested. In 2012 the trustees—exercising a power to pay or apply capital—advance the trust fund to Mrs X. On the termination of the trust there is an IHT "exit" charge and CGT hold-over relief is available. The restriction on hold-over relief for settlor-interested trusts only applies on disposals *into* the trust not out of it.[15]

If the trust becomes settlor-interested within a prescribed period (six years after the end of the tax year in which the disposal takes place) there is a clawback of any hold-over relief that has been claimed.[16] **10.04**

EXAMPLE 10.3

> (1) On April 6, 2006 A sets up a UK resident trust for the benefit of his children. One of his children is under 18. Unless that child is excluded from benefit until he or she reaches 18 there is no hold-over relief on creation of the trust. If hold-over relief is desired, consider the exclusion of children while minors,[17] or provide that no income or capital can be distributed to children of the settlor while they are minors. If they are the only beneficiaries the trustees could be required to accumulate income during their minority so that no distributions can be made.

---

[12] There is a minor exception for a transfer of business assets into a disabled trust which is settlor-interested: see Chs 7 and 36.
[13] TCGA 1992 s.77(2A) as amended.
[14] The definition of a settlor-interested trust is considered in greater detail in Ch.7. If the settlor has no minor children alive—albeit that if they were alive they could benefit—this does not make the trust settlor-interested. Spouse for this purpose includes a registered civil partner but not a separated spouse or cohabitee. (Contrast the provisions in FA 2008 Sch.7 where the definition of relevant person for the purposes of the remittance rules includes cohabitees: see Ch.3.)
[15] For the deemed disposal on the ending of the trust: see Ch.12.
[16] Instalment relief may be available in respect of the tax owing: see TCGA 1992 s.281 and 10.06. Clawback is discussed further in Ch.18.
[17] See A1.22.

(2) B sets up a UK resident trust for his children (all of whom are adult but the class is open) in June 2006. He and his wife are excluded from benefit. Hold-over relief is available even though unborn minor children could benefit. In 2009 A divorces and remarries and his new wife has a child aged 8 who becomes his stepchild. Unless that stepchild is at that point excluded from benefit, at least until he reaches 18, the trust becomes settlor-interested within the claw-back period and there is a clawback of the held-over gain.[18]

10.05 What if property is transferred to a bare trust for the settlor's minor unmarried child? In this situation the property is not settled for CGT or IHT purposes.[19] The result is that the disposal is to the child and hence hold-over relief will be available if the property is business property qualifying within TCGA 1992 s.165. Moreover, on a later disposal by the bare trustee the annual capital gains tax exemption of the beneficiary is available to set against the chargeable gain even though he is the minor unmarried child of the settlor.[20]

III INSTALMENT OPTION AND DOUBLE CHARGES

Instalment option

10.06 If hold-over relief is not available (or is clawed back), any tax due may be paid (by election in writing by the settlor) by 10 equal yearly instalments if the settled assets consist of any of the following:

(i) an interest in land;

(ii) shares or securities of a company which immediately before the disposal gave the settlor control;

(iii) any other unlisted shares or securities whether or not giving control.[21]

The first instalment is due on January 31 following the end of the tax year of disposal and the unpaid tax will attract interest which will be payable with each instalment. The outstanding balance and accrued interest may be paid at any time by the settlor. Any unpaid tax becomes immediately payable if the trust subsequently disposes of the asset for valuable consideration. If the settlor does not pay the tax then HMRC can recover the tax from the trustees if an assessment is made not later than two years from the date when the tax became payable. The trustees are then entitled to recover that tax from the donor.[22]

---

[18] It is assumed that the trust defines children to include step children.
[19] See Ch.42.
[20] Contrast the income tax position: see Ch.42.
[21] TCGA 1992 s.281.
[22] TCGA 1992 s.282.

Double tax charges

Where a settlor transfers assets into a settlor-interested trust is there a potential double inheritance tax/capital gains tax charge? He cannot claim hold-over relief and he could be liable for inheritance tax if the gifted assets exceed his unused IHT nil rate band. HMRC have commented as follows:

> "[we] agree that in theory there can be a double charge to IHT and CGT on a transfer into a settlor-interested trust—assuming IHT business property or agricultural relief does not apply and the transfer is over the £285,000 [in 2011/12 £325,000] limit. However where the transfer is a chargeable transfer for IHT the IHT is allowed as a deduction in computing the chargeable gain on the [subsequent] disposal by the transferee (s.260(7) TCGA). Also under s.165 IHTA if the donee pays the CGT on the transfer the tax reduces the value of the transfer for IHT. So in practice there is no double charge."

A settlor who has to pay both capital gains tax and inheritance tax on transferring assets to the trust may not agree with this analysis! It ignores the possibility that if the settlor pays the capital gains tax and inheritance tax on the original transfer into trust one tax cannot be deducted by the settlor against the other. If the settlor does not pay the capital gains tax on the gift then it is true that any such tax borne by the donee (and not recovered from the settlor) as a result of an assessment by HMRC under TCGA 1992 s.282 can reduce the value transferred by the settlor for inheritance tax purposes.[23] Alternatively, if there is a hold-over relief claim on a disposal by an individual to a trust and the trustees subsequently dispose of the asset, the gain includes both the held-over and any subsequent gain. In computing the gain the trustees can deduct any inheritance tax charged on the original disposal into trust. If this inheritance tax only becomes chargeable or is increased because the donor fails to survive seven years the CGT deduction is accordingly adjusted.

EXAMPLE 10.4

> In July 2008 father settles assets worth £312,000 into trust for his adult children claiming hold-over relief under s.260. The held-over gain is £40,000. He has made some large PETs two years previously but no chargeable transfers so there is no immediate inheritance tax payable. However, he dies three months later with the result that the whole of his nil rate band is allocated to the PETs and the assets passing into the discretionary trust are fully chargeable to inheritance tax at 40 per cent. The inheritance tax is deductible against the chargeable gain accruing to the trustees on a later disposal of the asset but only up to the held-over gain of £40,000. Hence, even though inheritance tax of £124,800 (40% × £312,000) is payable the deduction is limited to £40,000.

[23] IHTA 1984 s.165.

IV RATES OF TAX ON TRANSFERS INTO TRUST ON OR AFTER APRIL 6, 2008 AND THE EFFECT OF THE 2010 CHANGES

(i) Disposals between April 6, 2008 and June 22, 2010 inclusive

10.09 If a settlor disposed of assets into trust between April 6, 2008 and June 22, 2010 inclusive, he paid CGT at 18 per cent on any gains realised whether he was a higher rate or basic rate income tax payer and however long he had owned the assets.[24] Before April 6, 2008 the settlor could have suffered tax at 40 per cent on a disposal if he was a higher rate taxpayer and no taper relief was available. However, at that time the rates of tax could, in practice, be considerably lower than 40 per cent if full taper relief was available[25] or he was not a higher rate taxpayer. Further, an indexation allowance was also available if the asset had been acquired prior to April 6, 1998. Taper relief and indexation were abolished from April 6, 2008 and a March 1982 value (or cost at date of acquisition if later) has been substituted in all cases.

(ii) Disposals on or after June 23, 2010

From June 23, 2010 the position is more complicated for settlors. The CGT rate for disposals by individuals remains at 18 per cent where his total taxable gains and income are less than the upper limit of the income tax basic rate band (which is £37,400 for 2011–12). However, a 28 per cent rate applies to gains or parts of gains above that limit.

EXAMPLE 10.5

Baffled has:

1. taxable income of £27,400 (after all deductions and personal allowances);
2. he made the following CGT disposals into his children's trust:

   a. in May 2010 on which a gain of £17,000 was realised;
   b. in November 2010 with a gain of £25,100.

The CGT annual exemption in 2010–11 was £10,100 and Baffled is not entitled to entrepreneurs' relief. The basic rate limit was £37,400.

Baffled's CGT liability is as follows

1. Deduct the annual exemption against the later gain since this may be taxed at higher rates (viz £25,100 – £10,100) leaving £15,000.

---

[24] This ignores the possible availability of entrepreneurs' relief which is discussed in Ch.14.
[25] See Ch.11.

2. Tax the May gain at the (pre-June 23) rate of 18%.
3. Tax the remaining November gain:

    a. as to £10,000 at 18%;
    b. as to £5,000 at 28%.

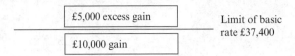

Disposals in 2011–12 taking into account personal allowances and annual exemptions

EXAMPLE 10.6

George, who is under 65, has taxable income of £37,000 for the year ended April 5, 2012. He has no other income for 2011–12 but he makes a chargeable gain on a transfer of assets into trust (before deduction of the annual exemption) of £40,000. The gain does not qualify for entrepreneurs' relief. His capital gains tax liability on the disposal into trust for 2011–12 is computed as follows.

Taxable income £37,000

Deduct Personal allowance (£6,475)

Income taken into account for the purposes of calculating the CGT rate is £30,525

Unused part of the basic rate band (£37,400 – £30,525) = £6,875

Chargeable gain is £40,000

Deduct Annual exemption (£10,100)

Taxable gain £29,900

£6,875 of the gain is taxed at 18% = £1,237 tax

£23,025 of the gain is taxed at 28% = £6,447 tax

Total tax due on gift into trust is £7,684

The above examples illustrate that while the capital gains tax regime after April 5, 2008 was relatively straight forward, from June 22, 2010 the position has been complicated once more by the change in rates and the linkage of the rates to the income of the taxpayer. There will obviously be winners and losers. For those settlors who would have paid capital gains tax at 40 per cent on a gift of a non-business asset to a trust prior to April 6, 2008 (assuming no hold-over relief available) the rate of 18 per cent initially looked attractive. However, for disposals on or after June 23, 2010 the settlor will now often pay CGT at 28 per cent. If the settlor would have qualified for the maximum non-business assets taper relief under the old

10.10

rules,[26] he would have paid tax at only 24 per cent even if he had been a higher rate taxpayer.

10.11   In some cases consideration should be given to revoking a hold-over relief claim made on disposals into trust before June 23, 2010 in order to take advantage of the lower rates of CGT prevailing before June 23, 2010.

EXAMPLE 10.7

On May 4, 2010 Gregory transferred land qualifying for agricultural property relief and showing a gain of £100,000 into a trust for his adult children. He had no personal losses and had used up his annual exemption. He did not wish to pay CGT of £18,000 on that disposal or claim instalment relief under s.281 TCGA 1992 and therefore decided to hold-over the gain.[27]

The trustees sold the land in April 2011 realising a total gain of £120,000. They will pay tax at 28 per cent on the entire gain of £120,000 in January 2013 = £33,600 CGT ignoring any annual exemption. If the hold-over relief claim is now revoked[28] then the settlor will pay £18,000 CGT due in January 2012 and the trustees will pay CGT at 28 per cent on the remaining £20,000 gain = £5,600. This tax is due in January 2013. Hence, the total tax payable is £23,600, a tax saving of £10,000.[29]

Rates of tax payable by trustees

10.12   The current rate payable by trustees for disposals on or after June 23, 2010 is 28 per cent.[30] For a consideration of when it will be worthwhile for trustees to advance the asset with hold-over relief to the beneficiary and let the beneficiary realise the gain rather than the trustees, see Example 11.1.

---

[26] Having held the asset for at least 10 years.

[27] See Ch.18. It is possible to hold-over the entire gain if the property is agricultural even if some of the value is attributable to hope value.

[28] This will be possible since the disposal of land took place in 2010–11. The tax return is therefore due by January 2012 and the claim can be revoked before January 31, 2013. See Ch.18.

[29] This ignores any annual CGT exemption or the fact that tax is payable earlier if the hold-over claim is revoked.

[30] For a summary of rates of tax payable by trustees in years prior to 2011–12, see Ch.11.

CHAPTER 11

ACTUAL DISPOSALS

- Overview (**11.01**)
- Rates and payment of CGT—the old and new regimes; settlor-interested trusts (**11.03**)
- Exemptions and reliefs including losses (**11.08**)
- The CGT regime from April 6, 2008 (**11.14**)
- Avoidance issues (**11.33**)

I OVERVIEW

A charge to capital gains tax may arise as a result of either actual or deemed disposals of property by trustees.[1] Notice, however, that, on a change of trustees, when trust property is transferred from the old to the new trustees, there is no charge to capital gains tax[2] because they are treated as a single person.[3] From April 6, 2008 to June 22, 2010 all trust gains, whether or not the trust was settlor-interested and whether the trust was interest in possession or discretionary, were taxed at a rate of 18 per cent.[4] The rate of CGT on disposals by all UK resident trustees from June 23, 2010 is 28 per cent.[5] Trustees are generally only entitled to one half of the full capital gains tax annual exemption although this is restricted where the settlor has established more than one trust.[6] Trustees can set losses and the annual exemption against gains realised in 2010–11 in the most beneficial way (thereby relieving the post-June 22 gains before pre-June 23, 2010 gains since the latter are taxed at a lower rate).   **11.01**

When chargeable assets are sold by trustees normal CGT principles apply in calculating the trustees' gain (or loss). If the disposal generates a loss it may be set off against trustees' gains of the same tax year or of future years. However, if the loss is still unrelieved when the trust ends it cannot be transferred to   **11.02**

---

[1] Deemed disposals are considered in Ch.12.
[2] Unless the trustees cease to be UK resident: see Ch.4.
[3] TCGA 1992 s.69(1) as amended by FA 2006.
[4] Contrast the position prior to April 6, 2008 when the trustees were taxed at 40% before taper relief unless the trust was settlor-interested in which case the settlor was taxed on trust gains at 10%, 20% or 40% (as the case may be). See further Ch.7. Non-resident trusts are subject to a different charging regime which is considered in Ch.19.
[5] The only exception is when entrepreneurs' relief is available: this is discussed in Ch.14.
[6] This is discussed at 11.09.

a beneficiary who has become absolutely entitled to all or part of the trust fund (although the loss can be set against gains realised by the trustees on the deemed disposal which occurs at that time).[7] Only when a beneficiary becomes absolutely entitled to trust assets so that the trustees make a deemed disposal *and that deemed disposal* produces a loss can that loss be passed on to the beneficiary and be used against his future gains. Even then the loss is "ring-fenced" in his hands so that it can only be offset against a gain on a future disposal of *those* trust assets.[8]

II RATES AND PAYMENT OF CGT—THE OLD AND NEW REGIMES; SETTLOR-INTERESTED TRUSTS

11.03   CGT attributable to both actual and deemed disposals of settled property on or after June 23, 2010 is payable by the trustees at the 28 per cent rate. If the tax is not paid within six months of the due date for payment, it may be recovered from a beneficiary who has become absolutely entitled to the asset (or proceeds of sale from it) in respect of which the tax is chargeable. The beneficiary may be assessed in the trustees' names for a period of two years after the date when the tax became payable.[9]

When trustees advance assets to a beneficiary and hold-over relief is claimed[10] the trustees are at risk of the postponed tax becoming payable if the beneficiary subsequently emigrates within six years[11] after the end of the tax year during which he became entitled to the asset. Retaining assets, or taking a secured indemnity from the relevant beneficiary, is therefore sensible in such cases.[12]

The old CGT regime

11.04   In brief the position is as follows:

1. In 1996–97, interest in possession trusts paid tax at 24 per cent; discretionary trusts were taxed at 34 per cent.

2. In 1997–98 interest in possession trusts paid tax at 23 per cent and discretionary trusts at 34 per cent.

3. From 1998–99 to 2003–04 inclusive, all trusts paid capital gains tax at 34 per cent.

4. From 2004–05 this uniform rate was increased to 40 per cent.

---

[7] See 21.21.
[8] See 21.21.
[9] TCGA 1992 s.69(4).
[10] See Ch.18.
[11] See TCGA 1992 s.168.
[12] See Ch.18 on hold-over relief.

The rates from 1998–99 until April 6, 2008 were charged on trust gains after deducting any available taper relief.

In cases where a beneficiary would be taxed at a lower rate (or had unused losses or an unused annual exemption) it was sometimes advantageous for the trustees to transfer the assets to the beneficiary before their disposal and claim hold-over relief so that the disposal was made and the gain realised by the beneficiary.[13]

THE NEW CGT REGIME—POST-APRIL 5, 2008

From April 6, 2008 to June 22, 2010 the regime was simple and for this reason a number of standard tax planning techniques became redundant. For example, the option of allowing a beneficiary rather than the trustees to realise a gain initially became less worthwhile after April 5, 2008 since all gains realised by trustees and individuals were taxed at the same flat rate (namely 18 per cent). Therefore, unless the beneficiary had losses or an unused annual capital gains tax exemption the same amount of tax was payable whoever realised the gain. However, with the introduction of differential CGT rates between beneficiaries and trustees for disposals made on or after June 23, 2010 the trustees now pay CGT at 28 per cent whereas a lower rate of CGT (18 per cent) will be payable by the beneficiary if he is a lower rate income taxpayer or non-taxpayer and if he realises the gain. **11.05**

EXAMPLE 11.1

The trustees of a discretionary trust are planning to sell land and transfer the net proceeds of sale to the beneficiary Robin. Assume that neither trust nor Robin has an available annual exemption or capital losses but Robin has no taxable income. If in January 2011 the trustees sell land worth £200,000 at a gain of £100,000, then CGT at £28,000 is payable. Net proceeds of sale are £172,000. These are distributed to Robin.[14]

Alternatively the trustees could transfer the land worth £200,000[15] to Robin holding over the gain under TCGA 1992 s.260. The transfer of value for the purposes of calculating the IHT exit charge is £200,000 with no deduction for the gain held-over. If Robin then sells the land, £43,875 of the gain is taxed at 18 per cent and the balance at 28 per cent. The total CGT is £23,612.50 and the CGT saving is £4,387.50 (£28,000 − £23, 612). On the other hand, the trustees are potentially liable to a higher exit charge because IHT is payable on a transfer of value of

---

[13] Accrued taper relief of the trustees was lost if a hold-over claim was made. For the circumstances when hold-over relief is available, see Ch.18.

[14] IHT may be payable on these net proceeds given that there is an exit charge on capital distributions from relevant property trusts, see Ch.29.

[15] Note that the trustees would need to transfer the whole of the land to Robin—transferring a part would not make him absolutely entitled for CGT purposes if the settled property comprised English land, see Ch.9 and *Crowe v Appleby*.

£200,000 not £172,000. In practice the trustees may be reluctant to do this for a relatively small saving in tax. If a hold-over claim is made the trustees should ensure that they are protected from a later CGT charge if the beneficiary fails to pay.[16] One option is to appoint the land to the beneficiary absolutely but retain legal title. The trustees then sell the land on behalf of the beneficiary and can ensure that tax is paid out of the proceeds.

CGT ON SETTLOR-INTERESTED TRUSTS FROM APRIL 6, 2008[17]

11.06 From April 6, 2008 the trustees are liable to pay capital gains tax on trust gains realised by UK resident settlor-interested trusts in the same way as with any other trust. Capital gains tax due on such trust gains is no longer assessed on the settlor. There are several points arising from this. First, whether or not a trust is settlor-interested is still relevant in determining whether hold-over relief is available on transfers of assets into trusts and between trusts. Second, a trust may not be settlor-interested for income tax purposes[18] but may be settlor-interested for capital gains tax purposes if the beneficiaries include dependent children. Third, the income tax provisions on settlor-interested trusts are unchanged. Fourth, the settlor of a trust that was settlor-interested for capital gains tax purposes before April 6, 2008 may be worse off under the new regime if he has or will realise significant personal losses. Before April 6, 2008 he could have set off his losses against trust gains if he had insufficient personal gains to absorb those losses; now he is no longer able to do so.[19]

When is a trust settlor-interested?

11.07 A settlor has an interest in a settlement if one of two conditions is met:

(i) If any property which is or may at any time be comprised in the settlement (or any derived property) is or will or may become payable to or applicable for the benefit of the settlor, his spouse, his civil partner,[20] or (from April 6, 2006) a dependent child in any circumstances whatsoever; or

(ii) Such persons enjoy a benefit deriving directly or indirectly from property which is comprised in the settlement or any derived property.[21]

These conditions are discussed further in Ch.7 but note:

---

[16] See Ch.18.
[17] See Ch.7 for further details.
[18] See Ch.7.
[19] Note also that the change affects trusts for vulnerable beneficiaries discussed in Ch.36.
[20] With effect from December 5, 2005.
[21] TCGA 1992 s.77(2)(b) and (2A) as amended in FA 2006. For the meaning of "derived property" see *West v Trennery* [2005] UKHL 5; [2005] STC 214 HL and Ch.7.

(a) if a minor child of the settlor can potentially benefit from the trust but if there is no such person at present alive, then the trust is not settlor-interested until such child is born;

(b) the 2006 extension to include minor children applied to disposals made by trustees of existing as well as new trusts from April 6, 2006.

EXAMPLE 11.2

Eric set up a discretionary trust for his minor children in 2004. He and his wife are excluded from all benefit. He claimed hold-over relief under TCGA 1992 s.260 on the transfer of land into the trust.[22]

In July 2007 the trustees sold the land and realised a significant gain. His children were still minors at that point. The gains were taxed on Eric but he had unused personal losses with the result that no tax was payable. If, however, the disposal took place in July 2011 then the trustees (not Eric) pay tax and no loss relief is available for Eric.

III EXEMPTIONS AND RELIEFS INCLUDING LOSSES

A number of exemptions and reliefs are available for trustees who dispose of **11.08** trust assets, namely:

1. **Main residence exemption:** this may be available for a residence occupied by a beneficiary and which is settled on either discretionary or interest in possession trusts.[23]

2. **Annual exemption:** see 11.09 below.

3. **Death exemption:** the tax-free uplift on death is available for trusts on the death of a beneficiary with a qualifying interest in possession, but not on the death of a beneficiary with a non-qualifying interest in possession. This is discussed further at 12.12 and following.[24]

4. **Roll-over relief:** postponement relief on the replacement of business assets is available if the trustees are carrying on an unincorporated business or are in partnership,[25] see Ch.13.

5. **Roll-over relief on the incorporation of a business**[26]**:** this relief is again a postponement of, rather than an exemption from, CGT. It applies when

---

[22] Which he was able to do because the transfer into trust took place before April 6, 2006, and note that the 2006 change in the definition of a settlor-interested trust did not involve any claw-back of hold-over relief in respect of an earlier transfer into trust.

[23] TCGA 1992 s.225 as amended by the FA 2004 s.117, Sch.22; and see *Sansom v Peay* [1976] 3 All ER 375; [1976] 1 WLR 1073. In general it does not matter that the beneficiary pays a rent for use of the property: see Ch.43.

[24] Note that there is no tax-free uplift if the gains are offshore income gains. See Chs 19 and 53.

[25] See TCGA 1992 ss.152–159 as amended.

[26] See TCGA 1992 s.162.

there is a disposal of an unincorporated business as a going concern to a company and that disposal is wholly or partly in return for an issue of shares in that company, see Ch.15.

6. **EIS deferral relief:** relief for re-investment under the enterprise investment scheme is available in respect of all UK resident trusts provided that (broadly) all the beneficiaries are either individuals or charities,[27] see Ch.16.

7. **Trusts for vulnerable beneficiaries:** these qualify for special income and CGT treatment.[28]

8. **Entrepreneurs' relief:** see Ch.14.

9. **Hold-over relief:** discussed in Ch.18.

Annual exemption and the use of losses

11.09 Trustees are generally entitled to one half of the annual exemption available to an individual.[29] However, if the settlement is one of two or more made by the same settlor after June 6, 1978 then the half annual exemption has to be divided by the number of settlements made by the settlor after that date and each then has an exempt amount equal to the greater of the figure resulting from that division and one-tenth of the individual exempt amount.[30] In carrying out the division, include settlor-interested trusts[31] and trusts established by the will of the settlor on his death but charitable trusts, non-resident trusts and retirement benefits and compensation funds are ignored.[32] Until 1997–98 brought forward losses could be carried forward if the annual exempt amount would otherwise be wasted. From April 6, 1998 this has not been possible for current year losses: any allowable losses for the year are deducted even if this reduces the net gains below the annual exempt amount. Brought forward losses, however, are only deducted to the extent required to reduce the net gains to the annual exempt amount. An unused annual exemption cannot be carried forward.

EXAMPLE 11.3

Trustees of a settlement make the following gains and incur the following losses (assume that their annual exemption is £4,800 throughout):

---

[27] See TCGA 1992 s.150C and Sch.5B as inserted by FA 1995 and as amended.
[28] See Ch.36.
[29] TCGA 1992 Sch.1 para.2. For 2011–12 this is £5,300.
[30] TCGA 1992 Sch.1 para.2(4).
[31] Note that from April 6, 2008 a trust annual exemption can reduce gains realised by a settlor-interested trust since the settlor's annual exemption is no longer available unlike the position prior to April 2008 where a settlor-interested trust resulted in the gains being chargeable on the settlor and it was only his annual exemption that could be used. Both before and after April 6, 2008 the presence of a UK resident settlor-interested trust restricts the annual CGT exemption available for other trusts. This can be relevant where a trust is imported: see Ch.19.
[32] Sch.1 para.2(7).

Tax Year	Gain (£)	Loss (£)
Year 1	5,000	10,000
Year 2	8,500	4,500
Year 3	10,000	–

In *Year 1* no CGT is payable and the trustees will carry forward a loss of £5,000: their annual exemption for the year is wasted. In *Year 2* the loss for the year reduces the gain to £4,000 which is covered by the trustee's annual exemption. The carried forward loss of £5,000 is therefore taken to Year 3. In *Year 3* that loss reduces the gain to £5,000 so that after deducting their annual exemption the trustees are taxed on £200 at 28 per cent = £56.

HMRC Manual at CG 18092 considers when a settlement is "made" for the purposes of determining whether it was pre- or post-June 1978: **11.10**

> "*You should construe the word 'made' as referring to the various means by which a separate settlement may come into existence. This includes straightforward new deeds of settlement, assignments, appointments and transfers to new settlements but NOT additions to the settled property of an existing settlement.*"[33]

EXAMPLE 11.4

(1) Emma set up three trusts. Trust 1 was made in 1975 but she added most of the funds to it in 1977. Trust 2 was set up in 1981 and is non-UK resident and Trust 3 is UK resident and was made and funded in 1999. In these circumstances Trust 3 has a full trust annual exemption for 2011–12 of £5,300. However, if Trust 2 becomes UK resident then the trust annual exemption is divided between them from that tax year and they each receive £2,650. Note that if Trust 2 then realises £2,500 of gains and Trust 3 realises no gains in 2011–12, the unused annual exemption of Trust 3 cannot be set against Trust 2 gains. Trust 1 will not have a restricted annual exemption and is not taken into account in determining the exemption available to the other two trusts.

(2) Doris set up 10 UK resident trusts in 2008. The 2011–12 exemption for each trust is one tenth of the individual annual exemption, i.e. £1,060).[34] For 2010–11 the annual exemption can be relieved against trust gains in the most favourable way and so will generally be set against gains realised after June 22, 2010 first since these gains are taxed at the higher rate of 28 per cent (unless entrepreneurs' relief is available).

---

[33] Contrast this with their views on additions and new settlements in the inheritance tax context: see Ch.24.

[34] Note the slightly different position where the trust arises as a result of a sub-fund election: see 12.42.

Taper relief

11.11   Taper relief was abolished for disposals on or after April 6, 2008. Prior to that date trustees qualified for taper relief in the same way as individuals. (Note that gains realised by a non-resident trust before April 6, 2008 and which are now stockpiled and so taxable under s.87 retain the benefit of taper relief despite the fact that the effective rate of tax on capital payments has been reduced.)[35]

After full business taper relief, in 2007–8 trustees were taxed at an effective rate of only 10 per cent on disposals of business assets (40 (the full CGT rate) × 25 per cent). After 10 years' ownership, trustees were taxed at an effective rate of 24 per cent on non-business assets (40 × 60 per cent). Particularly relevant was the point that accrued taper relief was lost if a hold-over election was made (typically, on the creation or ending of a trust). In considering whether an asset owned by a trust qualified for business or non-business taper relief one had regard not only to the trustees' position but also to that of the beneficiary in the case of interest in possession trusts.

11.12   Under the taper relief regime, trusts were useful as an "umbrella", in that a change of beneficial entitlement in a continuing trust did not affect the length of the trustees' ownership period because there was no disposal of the settled property. Hence, taper relief could continue to accrue, which was especially important for non-business assets.

EXAMPLE 11.5

> In 1998 Henry settled shares into trust for himself for life in order to crystallise his retirement relief.[36] The shares were later sold with the benefit of taper relief and the trustees reinvested the net proceeds in equities in 2000. In 2005, Henry was excluded from any benefit and the children were given interests in possession. There was no disposal by the trustees and therefore no interruption to the non-business assets taper relief period. However, from April 6, 2008 all accrued taper relief was lost and the length of ownership of the trust property makes no difference to the tax rate. Any gain is taxed at a flat rate (now 28 per cent).
>
> One of the anomalies of the taper relief regime was that from April 6, 2004 commercially let assets could qualify for business assets taper relief if used in a trade carried on by an unlisted trading company, most partnerships or a sole trader irrespective of whether the owner of the land or any beneficiary of the relevant trust was carrying on that trade or had any connection with it.

---

[35] See Ch.12.
[36] Before March 22, 2006 this was a non-event for IHT purposes. Retirement relief was progressively reduced from 1998 being finally abolished in 2003.

EXAMPLE 11.6

Trustees own farmland which is let (a) to a neighbouring farmer or (b) to an unquoted farming company. The farmland became a business asset in the trustees' hands from April 6, 2004. In the second case because the company was a qualifying company[37] business assets taper was available to the trustees from April 6, 2000.[38] Sometimes trustees owned a portfolio of commercial properties. If any were let to unlisted companies, partnerships or sole traders then the trustees were entitled to business assets taper relief albeit any gain would be apportioned between the pre- and post-April 2004 periods of ownership with only the post-April 5, 2004 period qualifying for business assets taper relief.

While the taper relief legislation did not make radical distinctions between individuals and trustees, it is noteworthy that the conditions necessary for trustees now to qualify for entrepreneurs' relief are much more onerous than for individuals and the relief is not available on a disposal of land let to third parties.[39] **11.13**

IV THE CGT REGIME FROM APRIL 6, 2008

On October 9, 2007 the then Chancellor, Alistair Darling, announced a major simplification of the taxation of capital gains which would apply to disposals on or after April 6, 2008. These changes in can be summarised as follows[40]: **11.14**

 (i) A single rate of charge to CGT at 18 per cent for individuals, trustees and personal representatives, irrespective of the type of asset or how long it had been held or whether the disponer was a higher rate or basic rate taxpayer and irrespective of the type of trust.[41]

 (ii) Taper relief and the indexation allowance were abolished. Therefore disposals of assets first acquired before April 1998 no longer benefitted from an indexation allowance.

 (iii) The "kink test" for assets held at March 31, 1982 was abolished.[42] Rebasing to March 31, 1982 became compulsory.

 (iv) Halving relief was abolished.[43]

 (v) The share identification rules were simplified.[44]

---

[37] See TCGA 1992 Sch.A1 para.6(1)(b).
[38] See TCGA 1992 Sch.A1 para.5(2)(b).
[39] It is possible that if the land is let to a qualifying beneficiary for use in his business it could qualify for entrepreneurs' relief as a disposal of trust business assets but the conditions are onerous: see Ch.14. Compare the conditions re associated disposals by individuals where payment of rent does cause problems.
[40] The changes were contained in FA 2008 Sch.2.
[41] Subsequently increased (in some cases) for disposals after June 22, 2010 by F(No.2)A 2010.
[42] FA 2008 Sch.2 para.57 and following.
[43] FA 2008 Sch.2 para.72 and following.
[44] FA 2008 Sch.2 para.84.

(vi) TCGA 1992 ss.77–79 were repealed and gains realised by trustees of settlor-interested trusts no longer taxed on the settlor. Nor do Schs 4B and 4C (transfers of value linked to trustee borrowing) apply to a UK resident settlor-interested trust with no s.87 stockpiled gains.[45] Related to this were certain changes to the taxation of the income and gains of trusts for vulnerable persons (which are often settlor-interested) to ensure (broadly) that the tax paid in respect of such income and gains was no higher than would be the case if the income and gains arose directly to the vulnerable person.

(vii) The definition of trading company and trading group, previously found in Sch.A1 (taper relief), was inserted as a new s.165A because it remained relevant to hold-over relief claims.

(viii) Subsequently the Government bowed to business pressure and announced an entrepreneurs' relief on the disposal of business assets whereby gains up to £1 million were effectively taxed at 10 per cent.[46]

Taxpayers were not given an option to elect for a deemed disposal and reacquisition of their assets at market value on April 5, 2008 which would have allowed them to lock in any accrued taper relief or indexation allowance albeit at the price of paying capital gains tax earlier. Finally, bear in mind that the changes had effect only for the purposes of CGT and did not apply to corporation tax. Therefore trustees owning companies will still need to be aware of the indexation allowance (taper relief never applied to companies) in relation to gains realised by an underlying company.

Winners and losers under the new capital gains tax regime

11.15 The new regime brought winners and losers. In the context of trusts the main losers were trusts able to benefit from full business assets taper relief; trusts where indexation was significant and trusts with deferred or rolled-over gains which would have qualified for full business assets taper relief under the old regime (these are discussed further below). Those individuals who paid basic rate tax on gains (20 per cent) were almost invariably worse off under the new regime given the loss of taper relief and indexation. This affected beneficiaries who had received assets from trusts with the benefit of a hold-over relief and were expecting to pay capital gains tax at lower rates when the asset was eventually sold.[47] However, overall the new regime tended to benefit trusts (since these paid tax on gains at 40 per cent), higher rate taxpayers and those trusts or individuals owning assets with little taper relief. In particular, trusts with non-business assets, including portfolios of investments such as let residential properties and equities. These assets qualified for non-business assets taper relief so that the minimum CGT rate for a trust was 24 per cent but

---

[45] i.e. this assumes that the trust did not realise gains while non-UK resident which are stockpiled: see Ch.19.

[46] See Ch.14. The ceiling was increased to £2 million (disposals from April 6, 2010); to £5 million (disposals from June 23, 2010) and to £10 million (disposals from April 6, 2011).

[47] A basic rate taxpayer paid at an effective rate of 12% after maximum non-business assets taper relief.

only if the asset had been owned by the trustees at March 17, 1998 (i.e. for 10 complete years). Such trusts, after April 5, 2008, initially paid tax at only 18 per cent, however short the period of ownership: a 25 per cent reduction in the tax bill. Even in respect of disposals from June 23, 2010 the rate of tax is still only 28 per cent.

Beneficiaries who receive capital payments under the offshore trust regime **11.16** which are taxed under TCGA 1992 s.87. At a CGT rate of 18 per cent plus the maximum supplementary charge, the overall rate in respect of capital payments received before June 23, 2010 and matched to gains realised on or before April 5, 2011 was 28.8 per cent (maximum) rather than 64 per cent in 2007–08 and earlier years. Even where capital payments are now matched to gains and taxed at the higher 28 per cent rate, the supplemental charge means that the maximum rate is still 44.8 per cent.[48] Moreover, where the asset was disposed of prior to April 6, 2008 the stockpiled gain going into the s.87 pool will have been calculated with the benefit of taper relief. When a capital payment is made between April 6, 2008 and June 22, 2010 inclusive and matched to such tapered gains the effective tax rate is then at a maximum of 18 per cent with the supplemental charge. Many trustees therefore made capital payments to beneficiaries prior to June 22, 2010 in order to get rid of the stockpiled gains at acceptable rates.

The disparity in an income tax top rate of 50 per cent as compared with 18 **11.17** per cent CGT rate led inevitably to an increase in the latter. With effect from June 23, 2010 all trusts now pay CGT at 28 per cent. With the loss of taper relief and indexation this will adversely affect trusts holding assets on a long-term basis.

TRUSTS WHICH HAD BENEFITTED FROM FULL BUSINESS ASSETS TAPER RELIEF

This included trusts of some commercially let property (see Example **11.18** 11.6 above) and trustees who owned shares in a family trading company. Entrepreneurs' relief is generally less generous for trusts than taper relief.

EXAMPLE 11.7

The trustees of the Palmer Discretionary Trust have owned farmland since 1981. Its value in 1982 was merely agricultural, (say) £100,000. Indexation to 1998 brought the base cost to £204,700. The land has been let for many years to a local farmer who farms it. It now has some hope value, being on the edge of a town but in a green belt area so that its value is anything between £700,000 and £1million. The trustees have received an offer to buy the land for £800,000.

(i) If the sale had occurred in 2007–08   £

Sale proceeds   800,000

---

[48] See Ch.19 for a detailed analysis of these provisions in F(No.2)A 2010.

Less indexed base cost	(204,700)
Untapered chargeable gain	595,300
Gain after taper relief entitlement [49]	287,727.85
Tax at 40 per cent	115,091.15

(ii) If the sale had occurred in 2008–9

Chargeable gain is £700,000 (£800,000—the 1982 value) taxed at a flat rate of 18 per cent. *Tax is £126,000.*

(iii) If the sale occurs in 2011–12

The chargeable gain is £700,000 taxed at a flat rate of 28 per cent. Tax is £196,000.

Some trustees, in anticipation of an increase in rates, elected to make a sub-fund election over those assets pregnant with gain before June 23, 2010 in order to trigger a deemed disposal and "capture" the lower rate.[50]

TRUSTS HOLDING ASSETS WITH SIGNIFICANT INDEXATION

11.19   Farmland owned at March 31, 1982 usually attracted significant indexation relief (as in Example 11.7). Note however, that if a hold-over claim had been made on a disposal that took place before April 6, 2008, then although the transferor's accrued taper relief was lost, the gain on which the transferee paid tax in the future was the gain *after* indexation. Hence, (where a gift and a hold-over relief or roll-over claim were made before April 6, 2008) the indexation was effectively "banked". Accordingly, although indexation has been abolished it may still be relevant if (a) no gain/no loss transfers took place between spouses before April 6, 2008 or (b) gains have been deferred, rolled over or held-over on disposals of assets before April 6, 2008. Trustees will still need to calculate the base cost of such assets with the benefit of indexation.

TRUSTS WHO HAD ROLLED-OVER A GAIN ON A BUSINESS ASSET

11.20   The chargeable gain on the asset currently held is taxable at 28 per cent whereas if the trustees had not made the roll-over claim the gain, under the taper relief regime might have been taxed at 10 per cent.

---

[49] The business asset taper relief period ran from April 6, 2004 to April 6, 2007 (three years) and the non-business period from April 6, 1998 to April 6, 2004 (six years). The total period of ownership was nine years. Hence, one third of the gains (£198,433) received BATR so that 25 per cent of one third of the gain was taxed (£49,608.25) and two thirds of the gain (£396,866) received maximum non-BATR (with the bonus year) so 60% of two thirds of the gain was taxed (£238,119.60). The end result was that £287,727.85 gains were chargeable after taper.

[50] See 12.42.

EXAMPLE 11.8

In January 2007 the trustees sold farmland which they farmed and rolled-over all the gain into new farmland. They made a roll-over claim to avoid paying 10 per cent tax on the indexed gain on the original farmland. However, on a disposal of the replacement farmland after June 22, 2010 the gain rolled-over as well as any subsequent gain is taxed at 28 per cent (although note that the gain rolled over is the indexed gain before taper relief).[51]

TRUSTS WITH DEFERRED GAINS

Trustees may hold a business asset gifted by the settlor which was subject to a **11.21** hold-over election when the trust was set up. It might have qualified for full business assets taper relief but the held-over gain will now be taxed at 28 per cent on a future disposal. Similarly, trustees may have advanced a business asset to a beneficiary, holding-over the gain in the expectation that the beneficiary would also eventually sell with the benefit of a 10 per cent rate. In these circumstances the settlor and trustees need to consider whether the hold-over relief claim should be revoked.[52] In general, revocation of a hold-over claim can be made within the normal time limits for amending a tax return. (For example, if a hold-over relief claim is made on a disposal in 2007–08 it could be revoked by the person making the claim at any time before January 31, 2010.) In some cases, the decision not to revoke a hold-over claim may have been made on the assumption that the eventual gain would be taxed at 18 per cent not 28 per cent. Of course that assumption is now wrong and often it will be too late to revoke the claim.

EXAMPLE 11.9

Dan settled shares in his unlisted trading company on trust for his grandchildren in 2006–07. The shares qualified for business assets taper relief and a hold-over claim was made when Dan's tax return was submitted in January 2008.[53] Although Dan's taper relief was forfeited it was anticipated that on a later sale after two years the trustees would have the benefit of taper relief and so pay tax at 10 per cent. Dan considered revoking the claim before January 2009. The trustees would then have acquired the shares at full market value and only future gains would then be taxed In fact Dan did not want to pay immediate tax at 10 per cent and decided not to revoke the claim on the basis that 18 per cent payable by the trust was an acceptable rate. Now when the trustees come to sell the shares the rate of tax is 28 per cent. It is too late to revoke the hold-over relief claim.

---

[51] Entrepreneurs' relief may relieve the gain but the conditions are onerous for trustees: see Ch.14 and 13.19 for options in this situation.

[52] A claim to hold-over a gain on creation of the trust is made by the settlor alone. He is therefore the only person who could revoke that claim and would then suffer a CGT charge.

[53] Under TCGA 1992 s.260 rather than s.165.

11.22 Similar consequences may have arisen when beneficiaries became absolutely entitled to settled property.

EXAMPLE 11.10

> The beneficiaries of the C Discretionary Trust set up in May 1997 became absolutely entitled in March 2007 to residential garages which had always been let by the trustees. The trustees therefore made a deemed disposal. The garages qualified for full non-business assets taper relief and had a significant indexed base cost. If a hold-over claim was made when the trustees' tax return was submitted in January 2008 the beneficiaries acquired the garages at their indexed base cost but without any taper relief. If a hold-over relief claim was not made, then the trustees would have paid tax at a rate of 24 per cent on the indexed base cost when the trust ended in 2007.

Qualifying corporate bonds (QCBs)

11.23 Trustees may have sold shares in a company in exchange for a QCB so that the gain was deferred until disposal of that QCB. Before April 2008 taper relief would have been available when the QCB was eventually encashed. On the subsequent disposal of a QCB acquired before April 6, 2008, the original gain will be taxed without the benefit of taper relief (although entrepreneurs' relief is given if the disponer would have qualified at the date of disposal of the original shares and indexation has been banked). However, trustees are unlikely to qualify for entrepreneur's relief. If the trustees acquire QCBs after April 5, 2008 they can now choose whether to claim entrepreneurs' relief (if they otherwise qualify) on the deferred gain rolled into the QCB.[54]

Kink test and halving relief

11.24 Trustees may have owned assets which benefited from the kink test or halving relief. They may now find that their assets have a lower base cost[55].

Share identification and pooling

11.25 There are rules for the identification of shares and securities and other "fungible" assets which cannot be distinguished from one another.[56] Before 2008 it was necessary to have a complex order of identification, based upon the dates when the

---

[54] See Ch.17.
[55] The kink test and halving relief are considered below at 11.30 and following.
[56] TCGA 1992 ss.104–106A and 109.

shares were acquired, because taper relief depending on how long an asset was owned. Shares disposed of on any given day were identified with shares acquired on that day (the "same day rules") and within the next 30 days (the "bed and breakfasting rules"), then with shares acquired from April 1998 (on a LIFO— "last in first out"—basis), and then with shares in up to three separate pools.

The abolition of the kink test, taper relief and indexation meant that a simpler system now applies: the LIFO rules were replaced and all shares of the same class in the same company are treated as forming a single "section 104" holding regardless of when they were originally acquired. However, the same day and bed and breakfasting rules remain unchanged, and shares are identified under those rules before they are identified with shares in the share pool.

The allowable expenditure in respect of the new pool is the market value at **11.26** March 31, 1982 of all securities that were owned at that date and the cost (or acquisition value) of all securities acquired from April 1982. Disposals are treated as a part disposal of that asset.

EXAMPLE 11.11

The X Trust acquired the following shares:

> (a) in 1986, 600 shares for £10,000 (these shares benefitted from an indexation allowance which brought the base cost up to £16,890);
> (b) in April 1999, 300 shares for £7,000;
> (c) in April 2007, 200 shares for £6,500.

Consider the position if a disposal occurred at the following times:

(i) Pre-April 6, 2008 disposal

The trust sold 400 shares in November 2007 for £18,000 (£45 per share). It was treated as disposing of the April 2007 shareholding first and then 200 shares out of the 1999 shareholding. It had no taper relief on the April 2007 shareholding but 30 per cent non-business assets taper relief on the shares acquired in 1999. Accordingly its tax liability was as follows:

> (i) 200 shares cost £6,500; sale proceeds £9,000 (£45 per share); gain is £2,500.
> (ii) 200 shares cost £4,666 (£23.33 per share); sale proceeds £9,000; gain after 30 per cent taper is £3,033.

The £5,533 gain after taper was taxed at 40 per cent = £2,213.

(ii) Disposal between April 6, 2008 and June 22, 2010

If the sale of 400 shares took place in June 2008 for the same price then it is treated as a part disposal out of a pool of 1,100 shares with a total unindexed base cost of £23,500 (£21.36 per share). The base cost of those 400 shares will be £8,544 and the capital gains tax will be £18,000 − £8,544 = £9,456 × 18 per cent = £1,702.

For disposals after June 22, 2010 the tax increased to £2,648, more than in either of the above scenarios.

(iii)   Sale of entire holding before April 2008

If the Trust sold the entire shareholding in June 2007 receiving sale consideration of £49,500 (1,100 × £45) then the CGT calculation would be:

- On the 200 shares: gain of £2,500 (as above).
- Gain on the next 300 shares after taper relief is £13,500 – £7,000 = £6,500 × 70 per cent = £4,550
- Gain on the remaining 600 shares is £27,000 – £16,890 = £10,110. After full non-business assets taper relief the gain is £6,066.

Hence the total gain = £2,500 + £4,550 + 6,066 = £13,116 taxed × 40 per cent = £5,246.

(iv)   Sale of entire holding in June 2008

If the Trust sold the entire shareholding in June 2008 for £49,500 then one simply deducted the £23,500 unindexed base cost from the sale consideration. The gain was £26,000 and tax at 18 per cent was £4,680.

(v)   Sale of entire holding in June 2011

If the Trust sold in June 2011, then the tax at 28 per cent is £7,280.

The taxpayer is slightly better off on either a part or whole disposal under the new rules until June 23, 2010. Thereafter he is worse off than under either the pre- or post-April 2008 regimes but the calculations are easier.

Rebasing issues

11.27   The compulsory rebasing to March 31, 1982 meant that the kink test and halving relief were abolished for disposals after April 5, 2008.

11.28   The "kink test"[57] only affected assets that were owned on March 31, 1982. It provided that the gain (or loss) on the disposal of that asset was the lower of two amounts: the gain (or loss) calculated by reference to the original acquisition cost of the asset (and any other allowable expenditure on it), and the gain (or loss) based on treating the value of the asset on March 31, 1982 as the total allowable expenditure up to that date. It was possible prior to April 6, 2008 to elect for the actual March 31, 1982 market value to be used without considering the kink test. Its abolition results in all assets owned on March 31, 1982 having a cost equal to their market value on that date. In most cases this will make little difference and of course it saves keeping past records and greatly simplifies the tax calculation.

11.29   However, rebasing to 1982 was disadvantageous in the following cases:

(a) where several taxpayers purchased all the share capital of a company before 1982. Each acquired only a minority holding and if the overall value of the company showed little increase prior to 1982, an election was not appropriate. The acquisition cost was based on an assets value (viz a fraction of the total cost of acquiring the company), whereas

---

[57] TCGA 1992 s.35.

the 1982 value of each taxpayer's holding was arrived at on a minority basis;

(b) if assets were acquired before 1965 time apportionment (which exempted gains accruing prior to 1965) might have been more attractive than a 1982 value particularly where the asset had not grown in value. This was often be relevant to trusts which owned landed estates for many years with no intervening uplift in value on a deemed disposal (for example on the death of a life tenant);

(c) where assets had fallen in value between date of acquisition and 1982 (relevant in the case of some works of art);

(d) where halving relief was available.

The kink test

Before April 6, 2008 assets the taxpayer owned on March 31, 1982 were deemed to have been sold by that person and immediately reacquired by him at market value on that date but this rebasing did not apply automatically in certain cases unless an election[58] was made. In particular, automatic rebasing did not operate where the effect of taking market value at March 31, 1982 (compared to not doing so) would be to: **11.30**

(a) turn a gain into a loss;

(b) turn a loss into a gain.

In the above cases there was deemed to be neither a gain nor a loss on the transaction.

(c) increase the gain (the smaller gain was taken); or

(d) increase the loss (the smaller loss was taken).

EXAMPLE 11.12

A trust sells a Lowry picture ("Men on way to football match") for £150,000. It had been acquired for £11,000 in 1975 and was worth £50,000 in 1982. In this case rebasing was beneficial. However, if the picture was sold for £40,000 then the trust realised a loss (based on the 1982 value) and a gain (based on the 1975 figure). Under the kink test the transaction was treated as taking place on a no gain no loss basis unless an irrevocable election was made by the trustees for rebasing to apply to all disposals of assets in the trust on March 31, 1982. This election could be made at any time before April 6, 1990 and (if no relevant disposal was made by that time) could still be made by January 31 two years after the end of the tax year of the first relevant disposal (being a

[58] See 11.28.

disposal by the taxpayer of 1982 assets).[59] From April 6, 2008, irrespective of whether the trust has made the election, all assets are rebased to March 1982 values.

Halving relief

11.31 When assets were rebased in 1982 an anomaly arose in the interaction of rebasing with hold-over relief and roll-over relief. In the case of hold-over relief the anomaly arose if (i) the disponer owned the asset on March 31, 1982, (ii) the hold-over disposal occurred between then and April 6, 1988 and (iii) the recipient disposed of the asset after April 6, 1988.

In the case of roll-over relief the anomaly arose where (i) the old asset was acquired before March 31, 1982, (ii) the roll-over disposal occurred between then and April 5, 1988 and (iii) the new asset was disposed of after April 6, 1988.

11.32 In both cases part of the gain on the post-April 5, 1988 disposal accrued before March 31, 1982; however, rebasing did not apply because the taxpayer making that disposal did not then own the assets. In this case, the legislation did not adopt the logical course of deeming the gifted or the new asset to have been owned by the disponor on March 31, 1982. Instead, an arbitrary relief was given[60]: the amount otherwise deducted from the acquisition cost of the donee or (in the case of roll-over relief from the acquisition cost of the new asset) was reduced by half. Halving relief had to be claimed within two years of the tax year when the post-1988 disposal was made.

Its abolition[61] in respect of disposals by individuals and trustees from April 6, 2008 could have an adverse effect for trustees where a gifted asset has not yet been disposed of.

EXAMPLE 11.12

The X trust was given land by Claude in 1985 worth £300,000 which he had acquired in 1970 for £120,000. He made a hold-over relief election and the trust was treated as acquiring the land at a cost of £120,000. It was worth £200,000 in 1982. If the trust had sold the land in 2007/8 for £500,000 the gain would have been £500,000 less the cost of £120,000 and indexation on £120,000 since 1985 (say £95,000). Hence the chargeable gain was £285,000.

If a claim for halving relief was made then acquisition cost would have been increased by half the held-over gain of £180,000 to £305,000 (£120,000 + £95,000 + £90,000). So the chargeable gain would have been reduced by £90,000 to £195,000 and taxed at an effective rate of 24 per cent (if a non-business asset) resulting in tax of £46,800.

---

[59] See SP 4/92 for HMRC's view on certain types of disposal which were disregarded for this purpose.
[60] TCGA 1992 Sch.4.
[61] Sch.4 now applies only for the purposes of corporation tax: see FA 2008 Sch.2 para.76.

(i) Later disposals

By contrast, if the disposal was made in 2008–9 then the trust was treated as having acquired the asset for £120,000. The resultant chargeable gain of £380,000 taxed at 18 per cent = £68,400. If the disposal was delayed until 2011–12 the tax increases to £106,400.

(ii) Advancing the asset to a beneficiary before 2008

If, however, the trustees had advanced the land to a beneficiary in (say) 2006, making a claim for halving relief and holding over the gain, the beneficiary would have acquired it at the higher indexed cost with the benefit of halving relief, i.e. £305,000. Any tax charge on that deferred gain continues to take into account halving relief and indexation. Accordingly the beneficiary sold for £500,000 in 2008–9 the chargeable gain was £195,000 and tax (at 18 per cent) £35,100. This increased to £54,600 for disposals after June 22, 2010 if the beneficiary is a 28 per cent taxpayer.

V AVOIDANCE ISSUES

The 2008 regime represented a substantial simplification on what went before **11.33** but the fact that gains are now taxed at a lower rate than income may not always be advantageous. For example, setting trading losses against capital gains is now less useful because such losses will now only be relieved at 28 per cent not at 40 per cent (or even 50 per cent) However, as a result of the differential rates, there is now an incentive to convert income into capital. To combat this, there are a range of weapons available to HMRC including:

(i) treating the transaction as trading so that the profit is subject to income tax;

(ii) invoking the legislation concerning transactions in securities[62];

(iii) invoking the legislation dealing with transactions in land[63];

(iv) invoking the legislation dealing with the sale of a right to income[64];

(v) applying existing case law on what is an income receipt.

Trading or investment

Is the transaction one of trading rather than investment? If so, the profit **11.34** is subject to income tax rather than capital gains tax.[65] This is particularly

---

[62] ITA 2007 ss.682–688 replacing ss.682–694 from March 22, 2010.

[63] ITA 2007 s.752.

[64] ITA 2007 s.773. The legislation was designed to prevent tax avoidance by an individual who receives a capital sum for a right to his future earnings from an occupation. This provision was originally introduced to counter the sale of personal services by (especially) actors and other entertainers for a capital sum in order to avoid income tax. HMRC have confirmed to the CIOT that this legislation should not apply to trusts, eg on the sale of a life interest.

[65] TCGA 1992 s.37 gives primacy to income tax over capital gains tax.

relevant to land transactions: an asset may have been acquired as an investment and subsequently become appropriated to trading stock, or vice versa. Some developers may have held land as an investment but now want to develop it and accordingly appropriate it to trading stock. This triggers a deemed disposal[66] which would have qualified for taper relief in 2007–8 provided that no election had been made for it to be treated as a no gain no loss disposal. Generally the lower rate of tax on gains favours crystallising the profit on the asset at the time it is appropriated to trading stock, i.e. before commencement of trading.

11.35   A number of the factors have a bearing on whether a trade exists or not: the so-called "badges of trade".[67] The relevant factors include (especially in the case of land)[68]:

(a) Has the taxpayer carried out a similar transaction before? If so he is more likely to be a trader: see *Page v Pogson*.[69]

(b) Has the taxpayer been involved in other similar types of operation? Where a person is closely associated with land transactions as a builder or developer, there is a presumption that the transactions are subject to income tax.

(c) What did the taxpayer intend when he purchased the property? If to hold land as an investment or for his use and enjoyment, this would indicate that the land was not trading stock. (*Taylor v Good*[70]).

(d) Has the taxpayer personally used and enjoyed the asset? If he occupies a house as his residence then again this would indicate the land is not trading stock.

(e) The nature of the asset. If the asset can be used to generate an investment return it is more likely to be regarded as an investment asset. For example is the land income-producing? If the rents from the land exceed the outgoings it is more likely to be an investment than if the opposite were true.

(f) How was the asset acquired? If it was acquired by inheritance or gift it is less likely to be considered a trading asset.

(g) How long has the asset been held? A short timescale between purchase and sale is suggestive of trading.

(h) Is there too much land for the taxpayer's personal use? Surplus land may indicate a trading intention.

---

[66] Under TCGA 1992 s.162.
[67] *Marson v Morton* [1986] STC 463.
[68] Where an individual buys and sells quoted shares it is unlikely that HMRC will accept this is a trading activity and that gains are trading profits even if the shares are bought and sold on a frequent basis; otherwise the individual would be entitled to income tax loss relief when shares are sold at a loss! Normally HMRC resist this on the basis that the individual is not properly regulated to act as a trader. See *Salt v Chamberlain* [1979] STC 750 where an individual made losses though the buying and selling of quoted securities with the intention of making a profit. It was held that "*where the question is whether an individual engaged in speculative dealings is carrying on a trade, the prima facie presumption would be that he is not.*"
[69] (1954) 35 TC 545.
[70] [1974] STC 148.

(i) Has the taxpayer carried out work on the asset to make it more saleable? Has he applied for planning permission?

(j) How was the purchase of the asset financed? Short-term borrowing is indicative of a trading activity.

Transactions in securities

A "transaction in securities" includes the purchase; sale or exchange of securities; the issue of new securities and the altering of rights attached to securities. The aim is to prevent the conversion of an income profit into a capital gain, e.g. drawing profits out of a company by way of liquidation rather than as a dividend. **11.36**

The original provisions applied until March 23, 2010 where the effect of the transaction was that income tax or corporation tax was reduced or avoided, i.e. a tax advantage was obtained in any of the five circumstances listed in A–E in ITA 2007 s.686–690. The legislation did not apply where the transaction was carried out either for bona fide commercial reasons or in the ordinary course of making or managing investments and did not have as its main objective or one of its main objectives obtaining a tax advantage.

In July 2009 a consultation paper was published with the aim of simplifying the legislation and making it more focused, so that instead of catching all transactions in securities and then filtering out certain "acceptable" transactions, only transactions undertaken with a main purpose of securing a tax advantage were caught. New legislation was then introduced from March 24, 2010.[71] In particular although the definition of a transaction in securities is not narrower, one of two prescribed conditions (Condition A or B) must now be met, both of which require the receipt of consideration. ITA 2007 s.685 merges the two provisions formerly contained in ss.689 and 690 (circumstances D and E) and now applies only to close companies[72] rather than relevant companies. **11.37**

Condition A covers the situation where a person receives relevant consideration as a result of one or more transactions in securities: **11.38**

(a) in connection with the distribution transfer or realisation of assets of a close company; or

(b) the application of assets of a company to discharge liabilities; or

(c) the direct or indirect transfer of assets of one close company to another close company where income tax is not borne on that consideration.

Condition B requires that the person: **11.39**

(a) receives relevant consideration in connection with one or more transactions in securities;

(b) two or more close companies are concerned in the transaction; and

---

[71] See FA 2010 Sch.12.
[72] Or non-resident companies that would otherwise be close.

(c) the person does not pay or bear income tax on the consideration.

This would cover the sale of shares in a close company which has assets available for distribution to another company in return for shares or securities. So, in effect, the distributable assets of company A are received in the form of shares in company B.

A detailed consideration of this legislation is outside the scope of this book but case law that is still relevant to taxpayers who are considering transactions includes *CIR v Cleary*[73] where the shareholders sold their shares in one company to another company at market value and they owned both companies. The transaction was held to be a transaction in securities. In *CIR v Joiner*[74] the company sold its business to a new company which was controlled by the shareholder of the old company. The old company, J Limited, was placed into liquidation. Again, the transaction was not undertaken for bona fide commercial reasons and the income tax legislation applied. However, "ordinary" liquidations should not generally be caught. By contrast, if the shareholder sets up a company which trades for a short period, then is liquidated and then a new company is set up shortly thereafter the position might be different.

11.40   Unlike the previous legislation, the new legislation applies only to close companies and will not apply if more than 75 per cent of the shares in a close company are transferred to an unconnected party.[75] This means that clearance is no longer necessary in relation to transactions that are disposals or takeovers, a major improvement.

Transactions in land[76]

11.41   This legislation is designed to tax property dealing profits and development profits as income where they would not otherwise be taxable as trading profits. It mainly affects trusts that realise a gain of a capital nature from a disposal of land. That gain is subject to income tax at 50 per cent whether the trust is discretionary or interest in possession and irrespective of the fact that the gain is trust capital and is not payable to the life tenant.[77] It applies equally to non-residents and UK residents holding UK land, whether directly or through a company. Typical situations include the landowner who obtains planning permission and sells the land obtaining a slice of future development profits.[78]

---

[73] [1967] 2 All ER 48.
[74] [1975] 1 All ER 755.
[75] ITA 2007 s.686.
[76] Formerly TA 1988 s.776, now ITA 2007 s.752.
[77] See ITA 2007 s.482 and see Ch.6. Note that other amounts are also treated as income and taxed at 50% under s.482 irrespective of the nature of the trust, including accrued income profits, the proceeds of share buy-backs (effectively taxed at 36.11 per cent on the amount received after the tax credit: see 17.39), offshore income gains (see Ch.53), deep discount profits and gains from contracts for life assurance. In all cases these are trust capital in the hands of the trustees and so are not payable to the life tenant.
[78] See *Page v Lowther* [1983] STC 799. The Court of Appeal held that a tax avoidance motive was not a pre-requisite. The legislation may be invoked where non-residents sell development land and HMRC can direct the purchaser to withhold tax if the land is under contract. Settlors who have diverted gains to trusts can also be assessed: see s.759(6) and *Yuill v Wilson* [1980] STC

Trustees who own land that has development potential and is sold for development should consider this legislation carefully.

Other ways of taxing capital as income

The courts will apply a *Ramsay* type approach to artificial transactions seeking to convert income into capital. Relevant case law includes *Ramsay v CIR*,[79] *Furniss v Dawson*,[80] *Craven v White*,[81] *MacNiven v Westmoreland Investments Ltd*.[82] At the time of writing the possible introduction of a general anti-avoidance provision is being considered by an independent committee chaired by Graham Aaronson QC which is due to report in November 2011.

11.42

---

460. They can be treated as providing the opportunity to realise a gain to another person. Of course, the section does not apply where the land is held through a trading company as trading stock and the profit on the disposal of the land will in due course be subject to corporation tax.

[79] [1981] STC 174.
[80] [1984] AC 474.
[81] [1989] AC 398.
[82] [2001] STC 237. See generally Ch.5.

CHAPTER 12

DEEMED DISPOSALS OF TRUSTEES

- General principles (**12.01**)
- Beneficiary becoming absolutely entitled (**12.05**)
- Death of a qualifying interest in possession beneficiary (**12.12**)
- Resettlements (**12.21**)
- Variation of settlements and change of governing law (**12.26**)
- "Anti flip-flop" legislation (**12.40**)
- Sub-fund elections (**12.42**)

I GENERAL PRINCIPLES

12.01   When a deemed disposal occurs, trustees are deemed to have disposed of the trust assets at their then market value and immediately to buy them back again at the same value. This can lead to a CGT charge on the trustees. However, in some cases the resultant gain can be held-over (usually as the result of a joint election of trustees and the beneficiary) whilst in others (notably on the death of a qualifying interest in possession beneficiary) the trust may benefit from a tax-free uplift in the value of the trust fund.

12.02   When a beneficiary became absolutely entitled to settled property before June 16, 1999 any allowable loss which had accrued to the trustees in respect of property which was, or was represented by, the property to which he had become entitled, was (assuming that the loss was not used by the trustees) treated as accruing to him.[1] This included losses resulting from the deemed disposal to the beneficiary as well as losses carried forward by the trustees from preceding tax years. From that date, however, losses only pass to a beneficiary in limited circumstances and will often be of no use to him.[2]

12.03   If the trustees do not pay the tax due on the deemed disposal within six months from the date when it became payable, and the asset in respect of which the chargeable gain accrued is transferred to a person absolutely entitled to it as against the trustees,[3] that person may be assessed and charged in the name of the trustees within two years from the time when the tax became

---

[1] Section 71(2) as originally enacted.
[2] Ch.21 considers the loss regime for trustees generally and, also see s.79A, which prevents non-beneficiaries from using trust losses by purchasing interests in trusts.
[3] For the meaning of "absolutely entitled" as against the trustees: see 12.05.

payable.[4] The beneficiary cannot be assessed to tax on more than the chargeable gain and where only part of the asset is transferred he cannot be assessed for more than a proportional part of that amount.

EXAMPLE 12.1

> In 2011–12 A became absolutely entitled as against the trustees to a piece of land. The trustees do not pay all the tax on the resultant deemed disposal. A can be assessed for the tax. If A and B had become jointly absolutely entitled in equal shares each would be responsible for half the tax.

Deemed disposals can arise in the following situations: **12.04**

(i) When a beneficiary or the trustees of another trust become absolutely entitled to assets comprised in the trust fund.[5]

(ii) On the death of a person with a qualifying interest in possession in the settled property.[6]

(iii) On the trustees becoming neither resident nor ordinarily resident in the UK.[7]

(iv) On the disposal of an interest in a settlor-interested trust for consideration.[8]

(v) Where trustees of certain trusts make a transfer of value linked with trustee borrowing.[9]

(vi) On a sub-fund election being made.[10]

II BENEFICIARY BECOMING ABSOLUTELY ENTITLED[11]

At the time when a beneficiary becomes absolutely entitled as against the **12.05** trustees to all or any part of the settled property, the trustees are deemed to dispose of the assets which comprise that settled property at their market value at that time and to re-acquire them at that value. The various reliefs and exemptions available to trustees on an actual disposal are available on the deemed disposal, e.g. principal private residence relief. Any tax is the trustees' liability since they are deemed to make a disposal. After the deemed disposal the trustees hold the assets as bare trustees for the beneficiary: it does not matter whether or not the assets are actually transferred to him. The property

---

[4] TCGA 1992 s.69(4).
[5] TCGA 1992 Sch.71(1).
[6] TCGA 1992 ss.72 and 73.
[7] Discussed in Ch.4.
[8] TCGA 1992 Sch.4A: discussed in Ch.20.
[9] TCGA 1992 Sch.4B and C: see also Ch.19.
[10] TCGA 1992 Sch.4ZA.
[11] TCGA 1992 s.71(1).

ceases to be settled property and so future disposals of the property are by the beneficiary.

EXAMPLE 12.2

> Shares in D Ltd are held by trustees for S absolutely, contingent upon attaining the age of 25 years. S has just reached 25 and the shares are worth £100,000. The trustees' base cost is £25,000. Because S is now absolutely entitled to the settled property the trustees are deemed to sell the shares (for £100,000) and to reacquire them (for £100,000). On the sale they have realised a chargeable gain of £75,000 (£100,000 – £25,000). The shares are now deemed to be S's property so that if he directs their sale and, say, £107,000 is raised, he has a chargeable gain of £7,000 (£107,000 – £100,000). His annual exemption is available against that gain.

12.06 As already discussed,[12] absolute entitlement means that the beneficiary has the right to direct how the asset is to be dealt with. A person who is a minor or of mentally incapacity is still treated as being absolutely entitled if this is the only reason for his not being able to give an effective direction to the trustees.[13] A person can be absolutely entitled although the property is subject to a charge or lien in favour of the trustees for taxes, costs or other outgoings.[14]

Absolute entitlement may occur under the terms of the settlement or it may result from the exercise of the trustees' dispositive powers. Normally absolute entitlement means absolute beneficial entitlement. However, trustees of another trust can become absolutely entitled to settled property for these purposes.[15]

EXAMPLE 12.3

> The terms of the Hibiscus Trust (which holds cash and quoted shares) provide for beneficiaries to become entitled to income in equal shares at 18 and for them to take capital at 25. The beneficiaries, A B and C, are over the age of 18. A reaches 25 in 2006 and receives her one-third share of the trust fund.[16] The other two beneficiaries B and C are 22 and 20 at

---

[12] See Ch.9.
[13] TCGA 1992 s.60(1).
[14] TCGA 1992 s.60(2) and see the discussion in Ch.9 of *Crowe v Appleby*. TCGA 1992 s.60(2). See also *X v A* [2000] 1 All ER 490: although the beneficiary who has attained an absolute and vested interest in the trust property is entitled to have it transferred to him this right is subject to the trustees' lien and if there are reasonably foreseeable liabilities (albeit remote or contingent) which may affect the trust fund they can retain part or all of the property. However, this does not mean that the beneficiary is not absolutely entitled to the property for CGT purposes (and for IHT purposes the settlement is at an end).
[15] See 12.21, below on resettlements.
[16] The transfers to A and B are non-events for IHT purposes since they already have qualifying interests in possession: see IHTA 1984 s.53(2) and Ch.26. The transfer to a separate trust for C may give rise to an immediately chargeable transfer by C with the second trust falling within

present. The trustees decide to reorganise the trust. They advance B her share of the capital absolutely (a deemed disposal). They then transfer C's share to another trust for her benefit. The trustees of the second trust are absolutely (albeit not beneficially) entitled to the property so that there is a further deemed disposal.[17]

When do beneficiaries become absolutely entitled?

HMRC have been known to argue that where trustees resolve to advance an asset (such as land) to a beneficiary and the resolution is not recorded in a deed, the beneficiary does not become absolutely entitled until title to the property is transferred to him, on the basis that the trustees are not bound by the resolution and the beneficiary cannot enforce it without consideration unless it is under deed. This can make a difference if the tax legislation changes between the date of the resolution and the date of the transfer (e.g. if rates of tax rise) or if the property increases in value. **12.07**

In the eighteenth edition of *Lewin on Trusts*, the editors note:

> *"It is a matter of construction of a resolution of the trustees, having regard to the objective meaning of the language used in the context in which the resolution was made and the surrounding circumstances, whether they have advanced assets to a beneficiary absolutely or merely facilitated a future advance to the beneficiary by entitling him to apply for a transfer of the assets to him in exercise of the trustees' powers of advancement."*[18]

In *Cameron v M. & W. Mack (E.S.O.P.) Trustees Ltd*,[19] which concerned an employee benefit trust, the trustees resolved in the following terms:

> *"IT WAS RESOLVED to earmark the following numbers of shares for the under mentioned individuals with a view to such shares being advanced to such individuals for their own absolute use and benefit freed from the Trusts of the Settlement as and when requested by each of them."*

The claimant was one of the *"under mentioned individuals"*. Upon being dismissed from his employment, he applied for the transfer of his "earmarked" shares. The trustees refused. The court held that the term was used to describe the process of identifying the particular shares for which a beneficiary was entitled to apply and that the resolution did not amount to the exercise of the power to transfer part of the trust fund to or for the benefit of the claimant. It was not until the trustees acceded to a request and

---

the relevant property regime. If, however, C only attained 18 after March 22, 2006 the trust of C's share would, from that time, fall within the 18–25 regime thereby resulting in an exit charge when the property was re-settled: see generally Ch.35.

[17] In each case (i.e. when A and B and the trustees) become absolutely entitled to settled property the trustees make a deemed disposal under TCGA 1992 s.71.

[18] At 39–31.

[19] [2002] WTLR 647.

transferred the shares to the employee that the power to transfer the trust property was exercised.

12.08   However, it is not thought that *Cameron's* case necessarily supports the HMRC view. It (implicitly) confirms that a power to pay or apply may be exercised by resolution. Whereas in that case, the context indicated that "earmarking" was a stage preparatory to, and independent of, the exercise of the power to transfer, in most cases where the trustees resolve to advance capital to a beneficiary there is nothing to suggest this two-stage process.

Lewin further notes[20] *"in general no formality is required for the exercise of a power but statute imposes formalities in certain cases and the settlor may . . . impose formalities."* Hence the settlement may provide that a particular power has to be exercised by deed and the exercise of a power by will, must comply with the formal requirements of WA 1837 as to signing and attestation. The exercise may require the consent of someone or require that the instrument exercising the power should specifically refer to that power. There is no general jurisdiction to dispense with such requirements although in certain cases equity may make good a defective execution (for example if it can be shown that the trustees intended to exercise the power and the defects are only ones of form).

In some cases statute imposes formal requirements: for example the creation of an interest in land can be effected only in writing signed by the person creating it.

Several beneficiaries becoming absolutely entitled

12.09   Difficulties can arise when several beneficiaries become absolutely entitled to a share of the trust fund. Does each beneficiary become absolutely entitled to a proportionate share of each and every asset or can the trustees decide who gets what, e.g. where one beneficiary is non-UK resident the trustees may decide to appropriate the assets that show the least gain to him and the ones showing the most gain to the UK resident beneficiary where a hold-over election is possible. Dicta in *Stephenson v Barclays Bank*[21] suggests that each beneficiary becomes entitled to an aliquot share but if there is a subsequent appropriation, HMRC in practice accept that a beneficiary has become absolutely entitled to the actual assets appropriated to him.[22]

Crowe v Appleby problems

12.10   Problems may arise where a beneficiary becomes entitled to a share in land but the remaining shares are still subject to the trusts of the settlement.[23] If a beneficiary is not treated as absolutely entitled for capital gains tax purposes,

[20] See para.37–166 and following.
[21] [1975] 1 All ER 625; [1975] STC 151.
[22] CG Manual para.37105. Normally trustees are given express powers of appropriation by the settlement: in other cases a power may be implied (see *Lewin*, at para.36.62). Note that the statutory power in AEA 1925 s.41 is limited to personal representatives.
[23] For a detailed discussion on absolute entitlement, see 9.09.

there will be no deemed disposal and this may in turn affect the hold-over relief position.

EXAMPLE 12.4

In 1996 Andrew set up a trust of a commercial property for his children Charlotte and Luke. They each become entitled to one half of the income and capital on reaching 25. (This was an "accumulation and maintenance trust" for IHT purposes.) Charlotte became 25 in 2007 and Luke 25 in 2009. They did not take interests in possession until reaching 25.

When Charlotte reached 25 in 2007, for CGT purposes she did *not* become absolutely entitled to one-half of the land. Until the land is sold, Luke reaches 25 or dies under that age (when Charlotte will inherit his share), whichever is the earlier, the trust continues and no deemed disposal is made by the trustees. Hence only in 2009 on Luke's 25th birthday do the trustees make a deemed disposal of the settled property when all the beneficiaries are together absolutely entitled.

For inheritance tax the position is quite different. The trusts over Charlotte's share ended on her 25th birthday when there was no IHT exit charge.[24] She is treated from 2007 as entitled to the half share in the property and, if she died after that date, it would form part of her estate for inheritance tax purposes and be taxable. This means that when Charlotte becomes absolutely entitled to her share for CGT purposes in 2009, CGT hold-over relief is not available under TCGA 1992 s.260 (in particular relief available on the ending of an accumulation and maintenance trust given by s.260(2)(d) does not apply since that trust ended—in respect of Charlotte's share—when she became 25).[25]

As a result of the 2006 changes in the IHT treatment of settlements, the taxation of Luke's share when it vests in 2009 is not what was envisaged when the trust was set up.[26] From April 6, 2008 the s.71D regime applied to the share so that when Luke became 25 an IHT exit charge occurred.[27] As a result CGT hold-over relief will be available under s.260 in respect of any gain accruing on that share.

---

[24] IHTA 1984 s.71(4)(a) and see Ch.30.
[25] If Charlotte died before 2009, she was—for IHT purposes—the owner of 50% of the property (and is, of course, entitled to the income from that moiety). Does the CGT death uplift apply? TCGA 1992 s.72(1) deals with the death of a beneficiary entitled to an interest in possession in all or any part of the settled property but since Charlotte took her interest in possession after March 21, 2006 it is not a qualifying iip within TCGA 1992 s.72(1)(b). Therefore (say HMRC) there is no deemed disposal for CGT purposes and no uplift: see A2.326 (Question 35).
[26] The IHT changes in respect of accumulation and maintenance trusts are described in detail in Ch.30.
[27] From April 6, 2008 the trust of Luke's share fell within IHTA 1984 s.71D (inserted by FA 2006).

Extending the settlement

12.11   In the above example, the trustees could have made a settled advance[28] before Luke became 25 in 2009 so that he did not take his share outright (and hence Charlotte would not become absolutely entitled to her share for capital gains tax purposes). The settled advance could provide for Luke to be given an interest in possession with continuing trusts for his spouse and children. In these circumstances an IHT exit charge (at the date of the settled advance) will arise under the s.71D regime and the trust will henceforth fall within the relevant property regime (with 10-year charges and exit charges) but a deemed disposal for capital gains tax purposes will be avoided. The CGT result of making the settled advance was as follows:

(i) The trust continued for CGT purposes (i.e. *Crowe v Appleby* was, in effect, extended).

(ii) There was no deemed disposal in 2009 when Luke became 25; the property remained settled for capital gains tax purposes.

(iii) On Luke's share, however, IHT charges may arise under the relevant property regime and, were he to die, because his interest in possession is non-qualifying for IHT purposes, there will be no CGT uplift. Accordingly, if the trust then ends there will be a deemed disposal for capital gains tax purposes.[29]

(iv) There is no inheritance tax payable on Charlotte's share (because she is already treated as owning it) but no hold-over relief is available on the ending of the trust in respect of that share.

III DEATH OF A QUALIFYING INTEREST IN POSSESSION BENEFICIARY

12.12   If property ceases to be settled property on the death of a person with a *qualifying interest in possession*[30] a deemed disposal at market value by the trustees takes place under s.71(1) but no chargeable gain accrues unless the gains are offshore income gains: i.e. gains on non-qualifying funds.[31] On all other types of property there is an uplift in the value of the settled property but without any charge. There is no loss relief if the deemed disposal results in a loss. This exemption from charge does not apply to any part of the gain which represents a gain held-over at the time when the trust was created or if on the death of the life tenant the settled property reverts to the settlor absolutely.[32]

---

[28] Assuming they have a widened power of advancement. Care would need to be taken to ensure that the exercise of the power did not create a new settlement for CGT purposes: see A1.21.

[29] A hold-over relief election may be made to postpone any gain.

[30] For the meaning of this term, see Chs 24 and 26.

[31] See TCGA 1992 s.73(1)(a) and Ch.53.

[32] See Ch.37. If the death of the beneficiary causes the property to revert to the settlor absolutely, the "reverter to disponer" exception applies. The death of the beneficiary in these circumstances does not lead to a charge to inheritance tax and so the normal uplift but no charge provisions of capital gains tax are modified to ensure that there is no double benefit. Therefore,

This corresponds to the normal capital gains tax principle that on death there is an uplift but no charge.[33]

EXAMPLE 12.5

T was the life tenant of a pre-March 2006 interest in possession trust containing property settled by his mother in 1986 with the benefit of hold-over relief. The gain held-over was £20,000. On T's death, the held-over gain of £20,000 becomes chargeable but any additional gain is wiped out.[34] It will be possible to make a further hold-over claim to avoid paying tax on the £20,000 gain if T's death is a chargeable transfer for IHT purposes.[35] From March 22, 2006 unless T's spouse or civil partner takes absolutely or on interest in possession trusts,[36] on the death of T it is inevitable that there will be a chargeable transfer and therefore the clawed back gain on entry into the trust can generally be held-over again. So if, for example, on T's death the trust fund passes on interest in possession trusts or outright to his children IHT will be payable and therefore the gain can be held-over.

EXAMPLE 12.6

Property consisting of shares in Z Ltd (a UK company) and offshore non-distributor funds (e.g. hedge funds) is held on UK resident trusts set up in 1996 by Mr X for C for life, or until remarriage and thereafter to D absolutely. The trust is not settlor-interested.

(1) If C dies there is a deemed disposal and reacquisition of the Z Ltd shares at their then value by the trustees (s.71), but capital gains tax is not charged (s.73). The settled property then belongs to D.
(2) By contrast if C had remarried, his interest in possession ceases and the trust ends. C makes a PET in favour of D but CGT may then be chargeable on Z Ltd shares and income tax on the offshore funds. There is no CGT uplift on the lifetime termination of C's

---

the death causes a deemed disposal and reacquisition, but for such a sum as ensures that neither gain nor loss accrues to the trustees (a no gain/no loss disposal): TCGA 1992 s.73(1)(b). Note, however, that the reverter to disponer IHT exemption also applies if the property reverts to the settlor's widow/widower/surviving civil partner within two years of his death and in this case the normal death uplift is not disapplied. On reverter to settlor trusts, see Ch.37. For the triggering of the earlier held-over gain, see Ch.18.

[33] TCGA 1992 s.73 as amended by FA 1996 Sch.39 para.6. Commonly the uplift in CGT value will be the same as the value taken for IHT purposes. Note, however, that there will be cases where the IHT value is not "ascertained" (i.e. agreed with HMRC) and in this situation reliance cannot be placed on the figure submitted for IHT purposes when it becomes necessary to determine the uplifted CGT value: see TCGA 1992 s.274.

[34] See TCGA 1992 s.74.

[35] Hold-over relief is then available under TCGA 1992 s.260. Contrast the position if mother had given T the asset outright in 1986 and hold-over relief had been claimed. In these circumstances there is no clawback of the held-over gain on T's death.

[36] In which case the IHT spouse exemption is available: T's spouse can take a TSI: see Ch.27.

interest. No hold-over relief is available on the Z Ltd shares unless the shares qualify as business property.[37]

(3) On C's death or remarriage, there is a disposal of the hedge funds because the trust ends and, in any event, death occasions a disposal of the trust assets at market value for CGT purposes.[38] In both cases the offshore income gain is subject to income tax at the rate applicable to trusts (currently 50 per cent)[39] on the trustees.[40]

12.13 If the life interest had subsisted in part only of the fund, the death of the beneficiary results in an uplift of the appropriate portion of each asset in the fund.[41]

Termination of an interest in possession on death when the settlement continues[42]

12.14 The death of a beneficiary entitled to a qualifying interest in possession, in cases where the settlement continues, results in a deemed disposal and reacquisition of the settled property by the trustees at its then market value. CGT is not imposed, and the purpose of this provision is the familiar one of ensuring a tax-free uplift.[43] The termination of an interest in a part of the fund, where the settlement continues, results in a proportionate uplift in the value of all the assets.[44]

EXAMPLE 12.7

Property is held in a trust set up in 2003 for A for life and then for his daughter D contingently on attaining 25. A dies in 2007 when D is aged 20 and the income is accumulated until she becomes 25.[45] The CGT consequences are:

---

[37] IHTA 1984 s.165.
[38] TIOPA 2010 ss.354–363 and The Offshore Fund (Tax) Regulations 2009 (SI 2009/3001) for the taxation of offshore funds. Where C dies but the trust does not end the position on offshore funds is discussed at Ch.53.
[39] ITA 2007 s.482 imposing 50% rate in 2010–11 and 2011–12.
[40] For the position for UK resident and non-resident trusts generally that hold non-qualifying funds: see Ch.53.
[41] TCGA 1992 s.73(2) as amended.
[42] See TCGA 1992 s.72 as amended by FA 1996 Sch.39 para.5.
[43] TCGA 1992 s.72(1)(a).
[44] See TCGA 1992 s.72(1) as amended by FA 1996 Sch.39 para.5(2); note that similar rules apply if a beneficiary entitled to an interest in possession dies, albeit that the interest continues (e.g. an estate *pur autre vie*) and to certain annuity interests: TCGA 1992 s.72(3) and (4) as amended. Until 1996, ss.72 and 73 were expressed in terms of life interests before being extended to include other interests in possession, e.g. an interest in possession terminable on a beneficiary attaining a certain age.
[45] If on the death of A the daughter was entitled to the income of the settlement (i.e. had an interest in possession) then for IHT purposes this would be a transitional serial interest given that A had died before April 6, 2008 so that D is treated as entitled to the capital of the trust fund (under IHTA 1984 s.49(1)) with the consequence that on attaining 25 no IHT charge arises and CGT hold-over relief is not available (unless the assets qualify as business assets under TCGA 1992 s.165).

(1) *Death of A*. There is a deemed disposal of the property and a tax-free uplift (although not on any offshore income gains in the trust fund which are taxed on the trustees if the trust is UK resident and not settlor-interested).[46] The settlement continues because D has not attained 25 and is, for IHT purposes, taxed as a relevant property settlement.

(2) *D becomes 25*. There is a further deemed disposal and capital gains tax at 28 per cent may be charged on any increase in value of the assets (apart from the offshore funds) since A's death. However because there is an IHT exit charge, CGT hold-over relief is available[47] on the settled property (apart from the offshore funds).

(3) *Offshore funds*. These are not assets eligible for hold-over relief and any profits realised on the deemed disposal when D becomes 25 will be taxed at 50 per cent on the trustees. The trustees should reserve for this tax before distributing the net amount to the beneficiary.

Again, the full tax-free uplift on death does not apply to a gain held-over on the creation of a settlement which becomes chargeable.[48] There is, however, a deemed disposal and base cost uplift where a beneficiary entitled to an interest in possession dies without that interest in possession coming to an end, e.g. if his interest is an interest *pur autre vie* so that it passes under his will.[49]   **12.15**

EXAMPLE 12.8

(1) Settled property is held on trust to pay the income to A for his life, subject thereto to B for life and subject thereto for C absolutely. B's death during the lifetime of A will not have any CGT consequences (no base cost uplift and no deemed disposal) and nor will it have any IHT consequences.

(2) In 2004 Bert assigned his interest in possession in the family settlement to his daughter Babs. Babs enjoyed a qualifying interest in possession and, on her death before Bert, there is a tax-free uplift in the settled property. The interest (an estate *pur autre vie*) will pass under Babs' will but note that the settlement will now fall into the IHT relevant property regime unless Babs' spouse takes the interest.

Assignments of life interests

Assume that property is held on trust to pay the income to A for life and remainder to such of B, C and D as survive him and if more than one in equal shares. If A surrenders his life interest, it cannot be known which of B, C and   **12.16**

---

[46] For a contrary view: see Ch.53.
[47] Under TCGA 1992 s.260(2)(a).
[48] Unless another hold-over election is possible under TCGA 1992 s.260: see Ch.18 and above. Since March 22, 2006 unless the assets pass to a surviving spouse there will generally be a chargeable transfer and therefore the clawed back gain is usually eligible for hold-over relief.
[49] TCGA 1992 s.72(2).

D will become absolutely entitled to the settled property until A's death and their interests are not accelerated. The income arising until A's death will be distributable among such of them as are for the time being living. The property remains settled property and falls into the relevant property regime for inheritance tax purposes. When A dies B, C and D (if all living) take absolutely and there will be a deemed disposal under TCGA 1992, s.71(1). This does not result from the termination of an interest in possession on the *death* of the person entitled to it and so a chargeable gain could accrue (although, given the IHT exit charge, this may be held-over).

12.17   Different problems arise if the life tenant assigns rather than surrenders his interest in possession: consider the following:

EXAMPLE 12.9

X and Y were beneficiaries under the will of their father who died some years ago. X was given a life interest in half the residue of the estate with remainder to his children. Y took the other half absolutely. In 2005 X and Y assigned their respective life and absolute interests to a trust for their mother for life, reverter to them. What is the IHT and CGT analysis in these circumstances?

Y's position is straightforward. There is no base cost capital gains tax uplift on the mother's death (because the property reverts to the disponer) but no inheritance tax charge because of reverter to settlor relief. (The creation of the settlement in 2005 will have been a PET for IHT purposes and may have triggered a CGT gain.)

X's position is more complicated. On mother's death before X there could be both an IHT charge and a CGT charge. There are in effect two items of settled property involved here: the property settled in the head settlement that will pass to X's children on X' death and the life interest settled in the subsidiary settlement (mother's trust). X was deemed to make a transfer of value of the underlying capital for IHT purposes when he assigns his life interest and on the termination of mother's interest *pur autre vie* (which is a pre-2006 qualifying interest in possession) she is treated as having disposed of the underlying settled property for inheritance tax purposes.[50] If the termination of mother's interest occurs before October 5, 2008 X then becomes entitled to the interest in possession again. Can one argue that reverter to settlor relief is due because the capital is deemed to revert to him?

12.18   HMRC consider that in these circumstances X takes a transitional serial interest (if mother dies before October 2008) but that there is a charge on the mother's death before October 6, 2008 since no reverter to settlor relief is due.[51] If mother dies after October 5, 2008, X again takes an interest in pos-

---

[50] See IHTA 1984 s.51.

[51] See *Thomas v IRC* [1981] STC 382 and Ch.37 for reverter to settlor relief. It is accepted that where a beneficiary assigns a qualifying interest in possession to another person prior to October 5, 2008 the assignee's interest *can* qualify as a transitional serial interest because the

session but this will be relevant property since he acquires a new interest in possession after October 2008.

Nor will there be capital gains tax uplift on mother's death or on earlier surrender of her interest *pur autre vie*. Section 72(2) TCGA 1992 does not apply because there can be no disposal or deemed disposal of the underlying settled property on mother's death; for capital gains tax purposes the only settled property comprised in mother's trust is a life interest. The assets in the original will trust remain at the original base cost on the death of mother (albeit there is no actual or deemed disposal of those underlying assets at her death). Matters would be different if X had assigned his life interest to mother outright rather than on life interest trusts. In these circumstances capital gains tax uplift would be available.[52]

The meaning of a qualifying interest in possession[53]

Any interest in possession to which an individual became entitled before March 22, 2008 is a qualifying interest in possession. With effect from that date TCGA 1992 ss.72 and 73 were amended[54] so that if the interest in possession arises on or after that date there is no deemed disposal or base cost uplift to market value on the death of the beneficiary (whether or not the property remains settled) unless: **12.19**

   (i) the interest is an immediate post-death interest (an IPDI); or

   (ii) a transitional serial interest (a TSI); or

   (iii) a disabled person's interest within IHTA 1984 s.89B(1)(c) or (d); or

   (iv) a 18–25 trust where the person dies under 18; or

   (v) a bereaved minor trust.

The effects of these changes can be summarised as follows:

EXAMPLE 12.10

Husband dies in 2007 leaving his assets on interest in possession trusts as to half for his wife and as to the other half for his child with remainders over. (TA 1925 s.31 is excluded and so if the child is a minor he will have an immediate entitlement to income.) In both cases there is an IPDI.[55] Accordingly on the death of wife or of the child IHT will be chargeable and a CGT base cost uplift is available.

---

assignee's interest will be within the original settlement (and in this case mother and X have interests within one compound settlement). For TSIs see 27.16 and following.

[52] For a full discussion of the IHT treatment of assignments of interests in possession see 27.19 onwards.

[53] See further Ch.26.

[54] As a result of the IHT changes in the taxation of settlements and especially of the limitations on *qualifying* interests in possession: see 26.02.

[55] IHTA 1984 s.49D: for the meaning of an IPDI, see Ch.28.

If the wife or child's interest is terminated inter vivos and the remainder beneficiaries take absolutely this is a PET for IHT purposes by the beneficiary and a deemed disposal for capital gains tax purposes at market value.[56] No hold-over relief is available unless the settled property qualifies as business assets within TCGA 1992 s.165.

EXAMPLE 12.11

Husband has an interest in possession on a pre-March 22, 2006 trust. He dies in 2009 and his wife then becomes entitled to a successive interest in possession. The wife's interest is a transitional serial interest (a TSI)[57] and the spouse exemption will prevent any IHT charge on the husband's death. Both interests are "qualifying" and so on both husband and wife's deaths there is a base cost uplift for CGT purposes.

EXAMPLE 12.12

Father dies leaving his estate on a bereaved minor trust for his two children, Amy and John. They are each given entitlement to income at 16 and Amy dies aged 17. There is no inheritance tax charge[58] but a base cost uplift for CGT purposes.[59]

EXAMPLE 12.13

Mother dies leaving her estate on trust for her only child Mary at 25. Mary becomes entitled to the income from the age of 16.[60] She dies aged 17, and base cost uplift for capital gains tax purposes is available even if the property remains settled.[61] There is no inheritance tax charge.[62] If Mary died *after* reaching 18 *but before* 25 there would be no base cost uplift for capital gains tax purposes but an inheritance tax exit charge on the ending of the s.71D trust.[63] CGT hold-over relief will be available if the trust ends at that time.[64]

---

[56] Under TCGA 1992 s.71.

[57] For the meaning of a TSI see 27.16 and following.

[58] IHTA 1984 s.71B(2)(b). This is a better inheritance tax position than would have been the case under the old accumulation and maintenance regime where, if an infant child had become entitled to an interest in possession, the property would have been subject to tax on the child's death.

[59] TCGA 1992 s.72(1B).

[60] This is an 18–25 (s.71D) trust for IHT purposes unless Mary becomes entitled to income within two years of her mother's death in which case s.144 operates reading-back the iip as an IPDI: see Chs 35 and 39.

[61] Under TCGA 1992 s.72(1A)(b). IHTA 1984 s.71E(2)(b).

[62] IHTA 1984 s.71E(2)(b).

[63] IHTA 1984 s.71F(2). A special charging regime is provided for in IHTA 1984 s.71F.

[64] Under TCGA 1992 s.260: see Ch.18.

If the 18–25 trust is extended by the making of a settled advance so that Mary does not take outright at 25 but instead is given a life interest, there is then an inheritance tax charge[65] When she dies there is no inheritance tax charge unless the trust then ends (in which case there is an exit charge) and there is no capital gains tax uplift since the property is within the relevant property regime. Hold-over relief will, however, be available.

EXAMPLE 12.14

Mother left her estate on trust for her daughter Mary at 30 with Mary being entitled to income at 18 and default trusts over. She was aged 12 at the time of her mother's death. At 18 her interest in possession will not be qualifying (it is not an IPDI) and nor is the trust an 18–25 (s.71D) trust. It falls within the IHT relevant property regime. On Mary's death before or after 18 there is no inheritance tax payable unless the trust then ends (in which case there is an IHT exit charge) and no base cost uplift for capital gains tax purposes. If the trust ends on Mary's death there is a deemed disposal[66] and hold-over relief under TCGA 1992 s.260 will be available.

EXAMPLE 12.15

H sets up a trust during his lifetime giving his adult child an immediate interest in possession. Before March 22, 2006 the child would have a qualifying interest in possession so that if he died there would be a CGT base cost uplift on the settled property. Unless the child is disabled this is no longer the case for trusts set up after March 21, 2006. Instead the settlement falls under the IHT relevant property regime and the child's interest in possession is not qualifying. Hence, on his death there is no base cost uplift for CGT purposes. Nor is there an IHT charge unless the trust then ends in which case there is an exit charge under the relevant property rules and a deemed disposal for CGT purposes[67] with hold-over relief being available under s.260.

Impact of deemed disposals

When it is not possible to postpone payment of the tax by a hold-over election, **12.20** the ending of a settlement may prove prohibitively expensive. In the case of a qualifying life interest settlement it may be preferable to wait for the tax-free uplift on death: by contrast, in the case of discretionary trusts, because there is a chargeable transfer for inheritance tax purposes, hold-over relief under s.260 will

---

[65] For the calculation of the rate of charge under s.71F: see Ch.35.
[66] Under TCGA 1992 s.71(1).
[67] Under TCGA 1992 s.71(1).

be available. Consider whether in a particular case it will be possible (and if so desirable) to postpone absolute vesting and therefore the s.71 deemed disposal.

EXAMPLE 12.16 (POSTPONING THE DEEMED DISPOSAL)

> Before March 22, 2006 Fred set up an interest in possession trust for his son then aged 21. His son is entitled to capital at 30 and is now aged 28. The trustees do not think it is wise for the son to take capital in two years' time nor do they wish to suffer a CGT charge on the ending of the trust. Therefore, they exercise their widened power of advancement to make a settled advance which has the effect of continuing the interest in possession trust for the son and then provides for an interest in possession trust for his wife remainder to his children absolutely. The trustees also retain a power to advance capital to the son.

> *If the trustees made the settled advance before October 6, 2008*

> The result was that the interest taken by the son was either a transitional serial interest[68] or a nothing because the existing interest continued.[69] If it was a transitional serial interest any subsequent interest in possession for the son's spouse cannot be a transitional serial interest and will not qualify for spouse exemption but the son will make an immediately chargeable transfer.

> *Exercise of the power after October 5, 2008*

> Any interest in possession taken by the son will not (on HMRC's view) be qualifying and therefore the trust will become subject to the relevant property regime. There will be a transfer of value by the son and an IHT charge with the property becoming held on a relevant property trust).[70] There is then no CGT base cost uplift on his subsequent death because his life interest was not qualifying.

As can be seen from the above example care needs to be exercised before extending the life of a settlement: taking steps to avoid absolute entitlement in order to ensure no gains are triggered may have unsatisfactory IHT consequences.[71]

IV RESETTLEMENTS

12.21 When property passes into a new settlement (e.g. as a result of the exercise of a power in the trust instrument) a CGT charge may arise[72] since there is a

---

[68] On TSIs: see 27.16 and A2.243 (Questions 5 and 6).
[69] See the discussion in 27.22 onwards on whether the exercise of a power of advancement in such cases creates a new interest in possession.
[70] Consider also whether the property will be taxed on his death for inheritance tax purposes because he has reserved a benefit: see FA 1986 s.102ZA.
[71] For consideration of when an advancement or appointment creates a new interest in possession: see 27.22 onwards.
[72] Under TCGA 1992 s.71(1).

deemed disposal *"on the occasion when a person becomes absolutely entitled to any settled property as against the trustee"* which wording is capable of applying when new trustees (even the same trustees in a different capacity) become so entitled to the property.[73] Exactly when a resettlement occurs remains a matter of some uncertainty.[74] However, the question is of some importance for the following reasons quite apart from the s.71 deemed disposal:

1. The annual exemption is given to the trustees of a settlement. If there are several settlements then each has its own annual exemption which varies according to the number of post-June 1978 settlements.

2. Losses of one trust cannot be set against gains of another.

3. The capital gains tax assessment is made on the trustees of the settlement, not on the trustees of separate funds within a settlement. Hence, if there is no resettlement but merely separate funds, the trustees of one fund can be liable for tax on the gains of the other.

4. If assets are moved from one fund to another within a settlement there is no capital gains tax disposal and generally no SDLT liability. However if assets are transferred from one trust to another then that is a disposal of assets and there may also be SDLT implications if assets are exchanged between settlements (see 51.12).

5. For IHT purposes, the appointment of assets from one interest in possession trust onto a new interest in possession trust after March 21, 2006 did not give rise to a transitional serial interest. By contrast, the creation of a new interest in possession within the existing trust was a transitional serial interest prior to October 5, 2008.

6. The assets of each trust are generally valued separately for capital gains tax purposes. So for example if a trust holds 51 per cent shareholding this will be worth more than two trusts holding 25 and 26 per cent each.[75]

In *Roome v Edwards*,[76] Lord Wilberforce stressed that the question whether **12.22** a new settlement had been created should be approached *"in a practical and common sense manner"* and suggested that relevant indicia included separate and defined property, separate trusts and separate trustees, although he emphasised that such factors were helpful but not decisive and that the matter ultimately depended upon the particular facts of each case. He contrasted special powers of appointment which, when exercised, did not usually result in a resettlement of property, with wider powers (e.g. of advancement) which permit property to be wholly removed from the original settlement. A

---

[73] See *Hoare Trustees v Gardner* [1979] Ch 10; [1978] 1 All ER 791 and note especially that s.71(1) does not require a person to be "beneficially" absolutely entitled.

[74] The concept of resettlement is discussed at 9.31 in some detail. See especially *Roome v Edwards* [1982] AC 279; [1981] 1 All ER 736 HL; *Bond v Pickford* [1983] STC 517 CA; and *Swires v Renton* [1991] STC 490. HMRC concede at CGTM37803 that if the form of the transaction does not give a clear cut answer you have to ask "what is the overall impression of the results of the transaction?"

[75] For the valuation of IHT joint interests and consideration of IHTA 1984 ss.50–52: see Ch.26.

[76] [1982] AC 279.

Statement of Practice[77] gives some guidance on when the exercise of a power of advancement or appointment is not treated as creating a new settlement.

EXAMPLE 12.17

A family trust was created in discretionary form in 1965, since when 90 per cent of the assets have been irrevocably appointed on various interest in possession trusts, with the remaining 10 per cent being held on accumulation and maintenance trusts for beneficiaries who are all minors.[78] The various funds are administered by the original trustees of the 1965 discretionary trust. On these facts the property has remained comprised in the original settlement for CGT purposes. Accordingly:

(1) Even if separate trustees are appointed for, e.g. those assets held on interest in possession trusts, the trustees of the original 1965 trust remain liable for any capital gains tax attributable to that portion of the assets.

(2) Only one trust annual exemption is available for gains realised in any part of the settled fund.

(3) Losses realised in one fund may reduce the chargeable gains realised in another.

(4) Whether the trust deed should make any provision for "compensating" that part of the fund which produced the capital loss is a matter which should be considered by the trust draftsman.[79]

12.23 The indicia detailed by Lord Wilberforce were applied by the Court of Appeal in *Bond v Pickford*.[80] There the power which the trustees exercised was to apply capital for the benefit of a beneficiary by allocating assets to him either absolutely or contingently. It was submitted by HMRC that the result of the exercise of the power of allocation was to create a new settlement, rendering the trustees of the new settlement absolutely entitled against themselves in their capacity as trustees of the original settlement and thereby giving rise to a deemed disposal of the allocated property. The Court of Appeal, however, held that a new settlement had not been created. It emphasised the importance of considering each case on its own facts and drew a distinction between powers "*in the wider form*" which authorise the trustees to remove assets altogether from the original settlement and powers "*in the narrower form*" which when exercised merely alter an existing trust. The exercise of a power in a narrower form could not create a new settlement. It was necessary to consider objectively both the nature of the trustees' powers and their intention in exercising them.

---

[77] See SP 7/84 and 12.25.
[78] All these appointments occurred before the FA 2006 changes in the IHT taxation of settlements. Old style accumulation and maintenance trusts lost their privileged IHT treatment on April 6, 2008.
[79] For the availability of a sub-fund election: see 12.42 and following.
[80] [1983] STC 517.

The Court of Appeal's approach in *Bond v Pickford* was followed by Hoffmann   **12.24**
J. in *Swires v Renton*[81] where the intention of the trustees in exercising their
power, objectively assessed from the terms of the relevant deed, rebutted the
inference that a new settlement had been created even though the power in
question was a power in a wider form which could have been used to transfer
property to a new settlement.

SP 7/84 emphasises the following matters: **12.25**

1. each case must be considered on its own facts and by applying established legal doctrine in a practical and common-sense manner;

2. a deemed disposal cannot arise unless the power exercised by the trustees or the instrument conferring the power gives the trustees authority
   to remove assets from the original settlement by subjecting them to the
   trusts of a different settlement, i.e. it is a power *"in the wider form"*;

3. even if such powers in the wider form exist, a deemed disposal will still not
   occur if the exercise is revocable, or the trusts declared of the advanced
   or appointed funds are not exhaustive, so that there exists a possibility at
   the time when the advancement or appointment is made that the funds
   covered by it will, on the occasion of some future event, cease to be held
   upon such trusts, and once again become held on the original trusts of the
   settlement. HMRC also consider it unlikely that a deemed disposal will
   arise if duties in relation to the appointed assets still fall on the trustees
   of the original settlement in their capacity as trustees of that settlement.
   Although it may be appropriate to consider whether a separate settlement
   is established when there are separate trustees this factor in itself is by
   no means conclusive. It is not uncommon to have different trustees of
   different sub-funds which are all part of one settlement[82];

4. a power to pay or apply capital (e.g. a s.32 power) is a power in the wider
   form and can be exercised to effect a resettlement. So long as power has
   been exercised for the benefit of the advanced beneficiary he need not be
   the sole beneficiary of the new trust[83];

5. in the case of a power of appointment, the question is whether it is a
   power in the wider or narrower form, i.e. do the trustees have power to
   take assets out of the settlement or do they only have power to declare
   new trusts which are "read-back" into the existing settlement. Generally
   when exercising an appointment type power, the trustee is merely (as
   it were) filling in a gap which the settlor left when establishing the
   settlement.[84]

---

[81] [1991] STC 490.
[82] TA 1925 s.37(1)(b) provides for the possibility of separate trustees being appointed over part
of the trust property; TCGA 1992 s.69(3) provides that where part of the property comprised
in the settlement is vested in one set of trustees and part in another they should be treated as
together constituting a single body of trustees.
[83] See *Pilkington v IRC* [1964] AC 612; *Re Halstead's Will Trusts* [1937] 2 All ER 570; *Re
Hampden Settlement Trusts* [1977] TR 177.
[84] See *Muir v Muir* [1943] AC 468. Of course this may be a matter of terminology since some

Whether a change in governing law results in a resettlement is considered at 12.32 below.

V VARIATION OF SETTLEMENTS AND CHANGE OF GOVERNING LAW

Variation by the beneficiaries

12.26   Trusts may be varied by the agreement of all the beneficiaries who are sui juris and together entitled to the entirety of the beneficial interests. Trusts may also be varied where some beneficiaries are not sui juris (e.g. minors or unborns) by recourse to the VTA 1958 which empowers the court to consent to the variation on behalf of such beneficiaries (including any unborns) provided that it is for their benefit. The CGT position is a matter of some uncertainty but the following matters are relevant:

(1) any variation requires the consent of all the beneficiaries who must therefore be of full age and mentally competent[85];

(2) in *Re Brockbank*[86] all the beneficiaries asked the trustees to retire in favour of replacements and the court decided that the trustees were entitled to refuse to do so. The beneficiaries acting together could, if they wished, have achieved their objectives by ending the trust and then resettling the property with their preferred trustees.[87] It is therefore sometimes said that the beneficiaries can only achieve their goals by creating a new settlement;

(3) the issue for CGT purposes is, however, different. Any charge to tax must be based on a deemed disposal under TCGA 1992 s.71, i.e. on a person or persons becoming absolutely entitled to the settled property as against the trustees. The question of whether there is a "new" settlement or a "resettlement" has to be approached against this background.

EXAMPLE 12.18

A settlement was set up by a now deceased settlor with A as life tenant and B, his son, as absolute remainderman. In 2005, A and B agreed to change the trust so that they will become joint tenants for life (both with

---

practitioners would argue that if the power—albeit to appoint property—permits the transfer of assets into a separate trust, then it is not a power of appointment stricto sensu but rather an advancement type power to transfer or apply assets.

[85] See generally *Saunders v Vautier* (1841) 4 Beav 115 (fixed trusts) and *Re Smith, Public Trustee v Aspinall* [1928] Ch 915 (discretionary trusts). Under the 1958 Act the role of the court is to supply the missing consents for those who do not have capacity.

[86] [1948] Ch 206.

[87] There will commonly be compelling tax reasons making this unattractive. TLATA 1996 Pt II to some extent reversed this decision.

qualifying interests in possession) and subject to that B's children will be absolutely entitled if they reach 18. The trustees agree that they will hold the trust property on these revised terms and with the same administrative powers. The agreement is contained in a "deed of modification of the X settlement".

On facts such as these it is difficult to see that a person has at any time become absolutely entitled to the trust property. Neither A nor B have done so and nor have they required the trustees to transfer the property to a new settlement of their own creation. The authors are therefore of the view that such a modification (even if called a resettlement!) does not give rise to a CGT charge.[88] **12.27**

It would appear, however, on the basis of Example 12.19 below which is taken from the HMRC CG Manual at 37903 that in Example 12.18, HMRC disagree and not only *would* they treat A as the settlor of the life interest taken by B (because A has surrendered part of his income and is therefore the settlor for income tax purposes) but B would be treated as the settlor of the remainder interest now passing to his children. **12.28**

HMRC note at 37900:

> "*Where there is a variation of a trust . . . it is necessary to identify the settlor. If the conclusion taken is that there are no new settlements then for CGT purposes the identity of the settlor is unaffected. However if, in effect, interests in income have passed from one person to another, the former may well be the settlor of an arrangement for Income Tax purposes.*"

These comments (and the example which follows) are concerned with identifying the settlor and the property settled. For instance, the commentary refers to a settlement of income for income tax purposes whilst in the example it is assumed that two new settlements have been created with P as the settlor of one and B and Q as the settlors of the other. What is being settled is, in each case, an interest under the original settlement. Does this mean that there is a deemed disposal of the assets in the original settlement? The Manual says that the variation in the example below "*is considered to terminate the settlement*" but it is difficult to see how the requirement for absolute entitlement in s.71 has been met. If there is no new settlement then as they note above HMRC consider that the identity of the settlor is unaffected for CGT purposes. However, they consider that the settlor does change in the example below because there has been a new settlement.

EXAMPLE 12.19 (FROM HMRC MANUAL)

Under a settlement made by X, A and B are each entitled to half the income. On A's death his son P will get half absolutely. On B's death her daughter Q will get half absolutely. The values of their respective interests are, say:

A's life interest £60,000

---

[88] A is the settlor for income tax purposes with regard to the income interest he has given up and so will be taxed on the income arising to B on the joint life interest.

P's remainder £40,000

B's life interest £75,000

Q's remainder £25,000

Under the variation, executed when all the beneficiaries are adults, which is considered to terminate the old settlement:

A takes 30 per cent of the property,

20 per cent goes to a new accumulation and maintenance settlement for P's children,

B takes 25 per cent of the property,

the rest is held for Q for life with a remainder to Q's son R.

P should be regarded as the settlor, for the purpose of the annual exempt amount, of the accumulation and maintenance settlement, because this is how his share has been dealt with. B and Q should be regarded as the settlors of the other settlement.

Note in the above example HMRC have assumed that P and Q's share is now held on new trusts.

Court variations

12.29   If the variation requires the consent of the court under VTA 1958, what is the position? The House of Lords decision in *IRC v Holmden*[89] provides strong support for the proposition[90] that so long as an arrangement under VTA 1958 is carefully drafted so as to make it clear that the intention is that the old settlement is to continue in existence, albeit in a varied form, the Order of the Court does not bring the existing settlement to an end but merely varies it.

12.30   HMRC are believed to accept that the question of whether there has been a revocation determining a trust or a variation of a trust which continues to exist is one of construction.[91] Where a perpetuity period is extended (not uncommon in variations of old settlements and often a major reason for seeking a variation) it is sometimes suggested that they may be more inclined to argue that a new settlement has been created but it is not invariably the case that a new perpetuity period means that there is a new settlement. Indeed HMRC note that it would be "exceptional" for a new trust to arise out of a variation. These matters have now been considered by the court in the case discussed in the next paragraph.

12.31   In *Wyndham v Egremont*[92] the court approved a variation of the trust on behalf of unborn beneficiaries. One of the benefits was the substitution of a new "Vesting Day" (in effect a new perpetuity period). The existing period

[89] [1968] 1 All ER 148.
[90] The case was concerned with estate duty rather than capital gains tax.
[91] See CGTM 37884 which indicates that the same principles apply to both variations by agreement and variations under the 1958 Act.
[92] [2009] EWHC 2076 (Ch) and see also 9.32 for the facts of the case.

308

was likely to end during the lifetime of the current interest in possession beneficiary and when that happened a substantial capital gains tax charge would result. Giving judgment Blackburne J. noted:

(i) that the 1958 Act should be viewed as a statutory extension of the rule in *Saunders v Vautier*[93] (viz that all beneficiaries can join in modifying the terms of their trust). Accordingly what varies the trust is the agreement of the beneficiaries not the court order;

(ii) the court could agree a new perpetuity period: see for instance *Re Holt's Settlement*[94] in which advantage was taken of PAA 1964 to obtain a new 80-year period with a 21-year accumulation period;

(iii) not every variation will involve a resettlement. He cited the remarks of Lord Wilberforce in *Roome v Edwards*[95] and concluded that the arrangement which he approved involved a variation of the existing trusts but not a resettlement. Specifically he commented that:

> "*the trustees remain the same, the subsisting trusts remain largely unaltered and the administrative provisions affecting them are wholly unchanged*"

(iv) he concluded that the variation did not result in a capital gains tax deemed disposal under s.71(1). On this matter he noted:

> "*This view cannot of course bind HM Revenue and Customs who, I should note, were approached with a view to commenting on a joint opinion of counsel to the effect that the variations of the pre-arrangement trusts effected by the arrangement would not give rise to adverse tax consequences but who declined - as I understand it in accordance with a change of practice in such matters - to be joined to the proceedings or to comment one way or the other on counsel's opinion or otherwise to make any representations.*"

Change in governing law

Concerns have been expressed that a change in the governing law of a settlement necessarily results in a new settlement and therefore a deemed disposal of the settled property for CGT purposes. In the current global era the governing law of both UK resident and non-resident trusts is often changed: if the trusteeship moves from Jersey to Bermuda, it may be inconvenient to keep the trust subject to Jersey law since the Bermudan trustees then need to seek Jersey legal advice every time they wish to exercise their powers. Usually there is an express power to change the governing law of a trust and trustees frequently exercise such a power[96] but more conservative trustees may refuse to change the governing law for fear of adverse UK tax consequences arising if there is

12.32

---

[93] (1841) 4 Beav 115; [1835–42] AER Rep 58.
[94] [1969] 1 Ch 100.
[95] See 12.22.
[96] Where there is no express power the question of whether there is a resettlement may be more

a resettlement. How well-founded are these concerns? The problem is a very real one since trustees frequently do want to change the proper law. Certainly an express power to change the proper law should always be inserted in the trust deed.

HMRC views

12.33   It is not thought HMRC argue that a change in proper law is necessarily a resettlement although it may be preferable to ensure that under the new law it is specified that no interests can vest beyond the original perpetuity period applicable under the settlement as first drafted (whether or not this is actually necessary as a matter of trust law and even if it may be seen as unduly restrictive), i.e. one should try to look at "what is the overall impression of the results of the transaction".

There is no relevant CGT authority on the specific point of whether a change in the governing law in itself constitutes a resettlement although there are a number of estate duty cases cited below which suggest that it is now. The question for capital gains tax purposes remains whether the new trustees become absolutely entitled to the property as against the old trustees at any time during the process (see s.71 TCGA 1992) and it is difficult to say that any new set of trustees becomes so entitled even if the governing law is changed and/or the perpetuity period is extended.

Trust law position

12.34   *Underhill and Hayton*[97] notes (without further analysis) that the Supreme Court of Delaware in *Wilmington Trust Company v Wilmington Trust*

uncertain. In *Duke of Marlborough v Attorney-General (No.1)* [1945] Ch 78, the Court of Appeal noted (at 85) that:

> "*It may well be the case that the proper law of a settlement can be changed by subsequent events, but we do not see how this can happen without the concurrence of beneficiaries agreeing to a change in the proper law and thereby, in effect, making a new settlement.*"

This view was adopted in *Parker and Mellows: the Modern Law of Trusts* (9th edn) where in para.23–063 it states:

> "*there will nevertheless be a deemed disposal for the purposes of capital gains tax where the change of applicable law is made pursuant to the agreement of the beneficiaries; this is because for at least a moment of time the beneficiaries will be absolutely entitled to the trust property as against the trustees. However, it is not thought that a deemed disposal would be a consequence of a change of applicable law pursuant to an express provision in the trust instrument.*"

This also seems to be the view of Dicey & Morris in *Conflict of Laws* (13th edn) at para.29–020. The authors are not convinced that the absence of an express power to change the proper law means that implementing such a change will be a resettlement.

[97] *Law Relating to Trusts and Trustees*, 17th edn (London, 2006) at para.102.164.

Company[98] considered that a new settlement resulted from a change in proper law. Underhill notes that it could also be said:

> ". . . *such a power* [to change the governing law] *is like a power of appointment that permits the creation of a sub-trust within the umbrella of the original or head trust, so that a change from English to Suntopian law is only permitted because the English 'birth' law so decrees and the English trust should be treated as a continuing subsisting head trust when the applicable law is changed to Suntopian law, so that any provisions of Suntopian law (eg as to perpetuities and accumulations or to trusts always being revocable or irrevocable in limited circumstances) which go beyond provisions of English law are inoperative.*" This is sometimes expressed as the "umbrella principle".

Although *Wilmington* is the trust case cited (as above) in support of the argu-   **12.35**
ment that a change in governing law involves a resettlement, in the authors' view it is not relevant: it is not a case where the proper law as such was changed or where the courts decided that there was a resettlement. A New York domiciled donor executed a deed of trust under which shares were transferred to his wife upon certain trusts for her benefit and for the benefit of their children. By a provision of the deed, a majority of the adult beneficiaries, subject to the approval of the donor during his lifetime, could change from time to time the trustee to any trustee in any state possessing certain qualifications and, in such event, it was directed that such successor trustee "shall hold the said trust estate subject to all the conditions herein *to the same effect as though now named herein*". Subsequently, the original trustee was authorised to transfer and deliver the trust property to the Wilmington Trust Company in Delaware. The question was whether as a result of the italicised words, on a change of trustee Delaware law applied to the trusts in which case a subsequent deed of appointment would be valid. There was no express change as such in the proper law.

Nevertheless, the Supreme Court of Delaware held that the italicised words "*must be accepted as authorizing a removal of the 'seat' of the trust from its original location, and its re-establishment under the law of another jurisdiction.*" The decision of the Court does not, in terms, state that a change in the governing law must ipso facto amount to a re-settlement. Rather, it focuses on whether or not there is a change in the "seat" of the trust. It is not made clear whether "seat" refers merely to the physical location of the trustees or to a more fundamental concept such as the jurisdiction that governs the trust. Throughout the judgment, the concepts of "seat" and "governing law" do not appear to be clearly distinguished. In any event once the Court had concluded that the appointment of a new trustee amounted to a removal of the seat from one jurisdiction to another, it went on to say (without any explanation or analysis) that such removal led to "its *re-establishment* under the law of another jurisdiction".

Matthews summarises[99] the arguments for and against the proposition that   **12.36**
a change in proper law entails a new trust. These begin (at para. 16.2) from

---

[98] (1942) 24 A 2d 309.
[99] In *Trusts: Migration and Change of Proper Law* (Oxford, 1997).

the starting point of the conceptual difficultly inherent in a change of governing law:

> "*How can a particular trust, which exists only as a viewpoint of certain facts by a given legal system, pass out of that legal system and into another, whilst remaining the same trust? As the original legal system ceases to have anything to do with the matter, surely the original trust ceases to exist, to be replaced (perhaps) by a similar trust under the new proper law, which law, viewing the same set of acts, regards a trust as in existence? This is heady stuff indeed.*"

In posing the question of whether a change in proper law entails a new trust, Professor Matthews states (at para. 16.3) that "*[t]here is certainly professional opinion to the effect that it does in English law, although this view is not universally shared*". He then returns to the umbrella principle noted above, commenting that the original system of law can be "big" enough to encompass other systems, i.e. to accept within its own rules the possibility of a change to another system:

> "*Thus a change from, say, English law to New York law does not mean the trust leaves the English system at all. It continues as the creature of that system, although now having subtly different effects and consequences. The exercise of a power to change the proper law is thus equivalent to the exercise of a complex power of appointment.*"

This means that the original system "can never be completely thrown over, but is always there in the background". This argument is, in effect, the "umbrella" argument referred to in *Underhill and Hayton* above. It is supported by several estate duty cases.[100]

12.37   Of other authors, Thomas and Hudson[101] note that powers to change the governing law raise "difficult questions" and suggest that such a power (if it be valid at all) at most permits—and should be restricted to—a change to a law that does not involve infringement of mandatory provisions of the initial governing law (including perpetuities). They go on to note that "*[e]ven then the old law will not have been eradicated, since the new law will operate under its umbrella*". This approach appears to be borne out by art.10 of the Hague Trusts Convention which indicates that, as far as the Convention is concerned, the trust after the change of law is the same one as existed before the change.[102]

---

[100] See for example *Re Levick's Will Trusts* [1963] 1 WLR 311. See also *Philipson-Stow v IRC* [1961] AC 727 where a testator who died domiciled in England bequeathed his residuary estate on trust for the deceased for life. The will expressed the intention that it should be construed in accordance with the law of England but the House of Lords held that the proper law regulating the passing of the share of the foreign land was that of the lex situs, i.e. South African law. There was no suggestion that the land was subject to a separate settlement from the remaining trust property and in fact it was accepted that when the foreign immovable property was sold the lex situs might change in which case there might be a change in proper law. "The proper law may change with a change in the subject-matter." It was not suggested that a single trust could not contain more than one asset subject to different law or that a change in the proper law results in a resettlement. In other words the question of proper law under which the assets were held was not seen as sufficiently fundamental to result in a new settlement.

[101] *Law of Trusts*, 2nd edn (Oxford), para.41.47.

[102] In his book on *The Hague Trusts Convention* (Oxford, 2002) Professor Jonathan Harris com-

The point has become relevant for IHT as well as CGT following the legislative changes introduced from March 22, 2006. If there is a qualifying pre-March 22, 2006 interest in possession and a change in governing law results in a resettlement, the interest in possession of the beneficiary is no longer qualifying.[103] In *Dymond's Death Duties,* 15th edn (1973), the authors analyse the old case law (prior to the days when most settlements had an express power to change the proper law) in the context of estate duty in depth and conclude presciently that there is not necessarily a new settlement for estate duty purposes on a change in proper law even without an express power. They note:

> "*The Philipson-Stow decision appears to have sounded the death-knell to the doctrine (suggested by some of the remarks in Marlborough) that the proper law of an instrument is immutable* [and hence any change in the law meant a new settlement]; *and although the Levick decision has a freezing effect on the proper law of wills there seems no sound reason for freezing the proper law of inter vivos settlements if this is contrary to the intentions either of the original settlor or of beneficiaries who have in effect constituted themselves new settlors. That being so, it is suggested that,* **even during the continuance of a settlement,** *a change of proper law ought logically to be possible in exceptional circumstances (and otherwise than by a change from movables to immovables or vice versa . . . it is difficult to see any reason why the law should forbid him to bring about the necessary change of proper law."*[104]

Conclusion

All the above suggests that a change in the governing law of a trust does not   **12.39**
invariably or, even usually, give rise to a re-settlement for either IHT or CGT
purposes, particularly if exercised pursuant to the operation of law (as in the
estate duty cases) or under an express power in the trust deed.

VI "ANTI FLIP-FLOP" LEGISLATION

These measures were introduced by FA 2000[105] and were aimed at "flip-   **12.40**
flop" arrangements commonly used in offshore trusts to avoid triggering a
s.86 charge.[106] The legislation was, however, widely drafted and capable of
catching UK resident settlor-interested trusts. Schedule 4B was repealed
with effect from April 6, 2008 in relation to UK resident settlor-interested
trusts. Accordingly this legislation is now only relevant where the trust is non-
resident or has been non-UK resident and has s.87 gains.[107]

---

ments at p.305: "*It may be said to be implicit in Article 10 that the 'one trust' approach is adopted for Convention purposes . . .*"
[103] See transitional serial interests and Ch.27.
[104] See p.1306 [bold added].
[105] See TCGA 1992 s.76B, Sch.4B as inserted by the FA 2000 s.92(1), (2), Sch.25: See Ch.7.
[106] For the s.86 charge: see Ch.19.
[107] See Ch.19.

12.41   In brief the scheme that Sch.4B was intended to counteract ("the flip-flop scheme") involved the following steps:

(i) in tax year 1 the trustees of Trust 1 borrowed money against the security of the trust assets and advanced the cash to a new settlement under which the settlor could benefit; and

(ii) in the same tax year but after the transfer of cash, the trustees of Trust 1 excluded the settlor and his spouse so it was no longer a settlor-interested trust (or in the case of an offshore settlement excluded the wider class necessary to make it non-settlor-interested)[108]; and

(iii) in tax year 2, the trustees of Trust 1 realised gains by disposing of their assets. These were thought not to be chargeable on the settlor (who had been excluded from the trust) and (prior to 2004) were taxed at only 25 per cent; and

(iv) distributions to the settlor were made from Trust 2 using the cash borrowed. The cash realised from the sale in Trust 1 was used to repay the borrowing.

In relation to UK resident trusts the flip-flop scheme was eventually held not to have worked because of the definition of "derived property".[109] For the position on offshore trusts see Ch.19.

VII SUB-FUND ELECTIONS[110]

12.42   From April 6, 2006 trustees of a settlement can elect for a fund or other specified portion of settled property to be treated as a separate settlement for capital gains tax purposes. This election is also effective for income tax purposes.[111] The election can apply to both UK resident and non-resident trusts although the capital gains tax effects will be very different in each case. It is useful in cases where trustees lack an express power to transfer assets to a new settlement or do not want to do so because of the IHT implications but are prepared to countenance a disposal for CGT purposes. It is thought possible to have a sub-fund subject to a different governing law.

12.43   The election cannot be revoked once made. It cannot be made before April 6, 2006 or after the second January 31 following the tax year to be affected by the election. In other words, if the election is to be deemed to have been made for 2010–11 it must be made by the time the enquiry period has ended on January 31, 2013.[112] The election is treated as taking effect from a specified date which must be shown on the election form SFE1. It must be signed by all trustees of both principal and sub-fund settlements and the form requires confirmation

---

[108] See Ch.19.

[109] See *West v Trennery* [2005] STC 214 HL and 7.57 for further discussion.

[110] TCGA 1992 Sch.4Z inserted by FA 2006 Sch.12 para.6.

[111] For income tax, see ITA 2007 s.477.

[112] The election procedure is in TCGA 1992 Sch.4ZA, paras 10–13. These paras provide that the election must be made by each trustee of the principal settlement (it would appear therefore that the trustees of the sub-fund do not have to consent). The election must specify the date from which it is to take effect which must not be later than the date on which it is made: see para.2(1).

that the four conditions are satisfied at the date when the election is treated as taking effect and details of the trusts, property, settlors and beneficiaries.

Conditions necessary to make a sub-fund election

The four conditions are the same for income tax and CGT purposes: **12.44**

(i) the principal settlement must not itself be a sub-fund settlement;

(ii) there must be some property left in the principal settlement which is not in the sub-fund;

(iii) there cannot be jointly-held assets between the principal settlement and the sub-fund;

(iv) there is no person who is a beneficiary under both the principal settlement and the sub-fund (except in certain limited circumstances).

Note that a principal settlement may have more than one sub-fund but sub-funds cannot themselves split into further sub-fund settlements. When the trustees already administer two separate funds within one trust they can decide which is to be the sub-fund and which the principal settlement but in fact the election does not need to follow the same split as the funds. For example, a sub-fund election could be made over all but £10 of the settled property and there will be a deemed disposal of the whole trust fund bar £10, irrespective of whether such settled sub-fund property is itself divided into more than one fund.

Since the principal settlement is for income tax and capital gains tax purposes **12.45** a continuation of the settlement as it was before the election in the past it was thought better to make the sub-fund election over those funds which contain assets which show the least gain. With the confidently anticipated increase in CGT rates from 18 to 28 per cent in 2010 a number of trusts opted to use the sub-fund election to trigger an early disposal thereby capturing the lower CGT rate.

One advantage of this procedure was that it gave trustees time to determine **12.46** whether or not to make the election and trigger a (backdated) deemed disposal. Hence provided the trust satisfied the sub-fund conditions as at June 22, 2010, trustees can make the election at any time on or before January 31, 2013 with effect from that date.[113] This would then trigger a deemed disposal capturing the lower capital gains tax rate. This was especially useful if the trustees were not sure if a particular asset would go up or down or whether they were likely to sell it in the near future and thereby trigger actual gains.

EXAMPLE 12.20

On June 21, 2010 trustees held two funds: fund A comprising private company shares pregnant with gain and likely to be sold in early 2012

---

[113] June 22, 2010 was the date when the CGT rate changed: see Ch.11.

on trust for X, Y and Z and Fund B (houses) on flexible trusts for (inter alia) X, Y and Z. All of X, Y and Z have qualifying pre-March 2006 interests in possession in Fund A and discretionary interests in Fund B.

The trustees want X, Y and Z to continue to be able to benefit from both funds but also capture the 18 per cent rate on the shares. They do not want to trigger a gain on the houses. On the other hand the company may not in the end be sold and the trustees are reluctant to trigger the gain on the shares and pay tax early if the company sale falls through. They could resettle Fund A but then X, Y and Z will lose their qualifying IIPs. They therefore reorganise Fund B so that on June 21 2010 it is now the principal fund held for W for his life (a non-qualifying IIP) and then for X Y and Z. The latter can only benefit on W's death. A sub-fund election is made over Fund A with effect from June 21 after the company shares have been sold in January 2013.

The result is a deemed disposal of Fund A shares as at June 21, 2010. There is no change to the IHT position. Note that if the election is to be effective then the conditions need to be in place at a specified earlier date. They cannot be put in place later.

12.47 Condition 4[114] that *"no person will be a beneficiary under both the sub-fund settlement and the principal settlement"* is the most onerous. However, a person is not to be regarded as a beneficiary under a settlement if property becomes payable to him by reason only of his marrying or entering into a civil partnership with a beneficiary under the settlement; the death of a beneficiary under the settlement; or the exercise by the trustees of the settlement of a power of advancement (but only a power of advancement in the statutory form or similar and not a power of advancement over the entire fund). Further, a person is not regarded as a beneficiary, if he can benefit only from the failure or determination of protective trusts.[115] The policy reason for this condition remains unclear and it is less restrictive than at first sight appears.[116]

EXAMPLE 12.21

The Frank Trust was set up in 2000 and gives an interest in possession to Frank (the settlor). He divorced in 2007 and the trustees were ordered to transfer half the fund into a separate interest in possession settlement for Frank's wife (as part of the financial arrangements). However that new settlement would be regarded as a relevant property settlement for IHT purposes.[117] Instead they varied the existing trust and appointed

[114] See 12.44 above.
[115] TCGA 1992 Sch.4ZA para.9(2).
[116] See 12.48 below and Example 12.20 when XYZ have continuing trusts in both funds.
[117] And hence subject to anniversary and exit charges: see Ch.23. This assumes that a new interest in possession arising in a separate settlement cannot be a transitional serial interest: See Ch.27 and A2.259.

an interest in possession to the wife over half the existing trust property which took effect as a TSI (provided that it was done before October 6, 2008).[118] The trustees also wished to have separate capital gains tax settlements so that losses on one fund are not set against gains on the other fund and so that CGT and income tax are assessed on separate sets of trustees who are issued with separate returns and can produce separate accounts.[119]

If a sub-fund election is made, although there will be a deemed disposal of the property in the wife's fund from the date the election is treated as taking effect, from that point onwards they can operate as two separate trusts for CGT purposes. It is likely that their children (assume they are adult) will benefit under both funds on the death of either parent. However, if the children can only benefit on the death of a parent and not by the exercise of overriding powers of appointment then condition 4 is not broken and a sub-fund election can be made. Similarly, if the children can only benefit by exercise of the statutory power of advancement then the condition is not breached.

12.48 The election conditions require the sub-fund not to be the whole of the property comprised in the settlement and it cannot comprise an interest in an asset held jointly with the principal settlement. However, there is nothing to stop the trustees electing that all but, say, £10 is subject to a sub-fund election. The £10 fund will then be the principal fund. As noted above the sub-fund does not need to mirror any actual funds of the trust. Condition 4 restricts a beneficiary from being a beneficiary under both the sub-fund settlement and the principal settlement. However the same person can be a beneficiary of all the sub-fund settlements if more than one sub-fund is created, provided they are not also a beneficiary of the principal settlement. Moreover the condition that a person is not regarded as a beneficiary under a settlement if property comprised in the settlement or any derived property *"will or may become payable to him or applicable for his benefit by reason only of the death of a beneficiary under the settlement or the exercise of a [statutory] power of advancement"* may be less onerous than first thought.[120]

So in Example 12.20 if W is 80 and dies shortly after the sub-fund election has been made, X Y and Z then become beneficiaries of both funds again.

---

[118] Prior to April 6, 2008 one unfortunate consequence was that for as long as the settlor could benefit from any of the settled property (even if wholly excluded from the wife's part) he would continue to be taxed on all trust gains under TCGA 1992 s.77. This is no longer the case.

[119] From 1996–97 onwards CGT may be assessed on any one or more of the relevant trustees unless a sub-fund election is made. The relevant trustees are those in office at any time in the tax year when the chargeable gains accrue. From 2006–07 onwards ITTOIA 2005 s.685E provides for the same result for income tax purposes. If the trustees of one fund also wish to protect their fund from claims by creditors in respect of speculative ventures carried out by trustees of the other fund a resettlement of the assets, not just a sub-fund election, is needed.

[120] Nor is he regarded as a beneficiary if property becomes payable to him by reason only of his marrying or entering into a civil partnership with a beneficiary under the settlement.

Effects of making an election

12.49   The effects are as follows:

1. The CGT annual exempt amount[121] will be split between the funds.

2. The sub-fund election triggers a deemed disposal of the settled property in the sub-fund so that capital gains tax may be payable by the UK resident trustees at the rate prevailing at the time of the deemed disposal. A hold-over claim can be made under the normal rules.[122] If the settled property comprises non-qualifying funds (e.g. hedge funds or offshore funds which have not got distributor status) then there is an income tax charge on the UK resident trustees.[123]

3. In the case of non-resident trusts, there is a deemed disposal, no hold-over relief but the trustees will not be liable for tax. The settlor may suffer a tax charge under s.86 or if that section does not apply, the deemed gains may be added to the pool of s.87 gains. Presumably the sub-fund then takes a proportionate part of the total s.87 gains as at the end of that tax year by virtue of s.90 and the s.87 pool in the principal fund is reduced accordingly.[124] In the case of offshore income gains, there will either be an income tax charge on the transferor under ITA 2007 s.720 if an election is made or the OIGs may become relevant income for the purposes of s.731 or s.87 gains.

4. The allowable losses on the deemed disposal of any assets which the trustees of the sub-fund settlement are treated as acquiring can be used against gains on certain disposals of the assets to which they have become absolutely entitled, but not otherwise.

5. The two funds self-assess and submit income tax returns separately. Where the settlor can benefit from one fund and not the other, a sub-fund election means that he is only taxed on the income of the fund from which he can benefit. If an election is not made he is taxed on the entire income of the trust even though he may be able to benefit from one part.

12.50   If desired it may be possible to avoid a CGT charge on the deemed disposal where the trust is UK resident by ensuring that the conditions for hold-over relief are satisfied.

---

[121] The annual exemption is not split fractionally between all existing trusts made by that settlor in the way provided for in Sch.1; instead the existing exemption that would have been given to the principal settlement but for the election is divided equally between the principal settlement and the sub-fund trust: TCGA 1992 Sch.A1 inserted by FA 2006 Sch.12 para.44.
[122] See 12.50.
[123] At 50% (2011–12).
[124] See s.90 and Ch.18.

EXAMPLE 12.22

The Strivens Will trust was set up on the death of the wife and involved flexible life interest trust (an IPDI) for the surviving spouse (H). The trustees revoke part of H's life interest and declare discretionary trusts of discrete property for his children. H makes a chargeable transfer for inheritance tax purposes. If the other conditions for a sub-fund are met, an election can be made under which the specified date is the date of the exercise of the power and hold-over relief under s.260(2)(a) applies on the deemed disposal.[125]

---

[125] HMRC Manual at CG 33331 suggests that hold-over relief would not be available if the children were under 18 on the basis presumably that the trust was settlor-interested. But it is difficult to see how this is right given that W is the settlor and is dead and H is not consenting to the exercise of the power.

CHAPTER 13

ROLL-OVER RELIEF

- Basic conditions (**13.01**)
- Computation of the gain (**13.11**)
- Claiming the relief (**13.12**)
- The effect of the changes in April 2008 (**13.16**)
- Relevance of roll-over relief to trustees (**13.19**)

A number of exemptions and reliefs are available to trustees who dispose of business assets. These reliefs are also available to individuals but there are certain points of particular relevance to trusts. These reliefs are considered in Chs 13 to 17 and a table summarising the different conditions for all the reliefs and their order of priority can be found at the end of Ch.17.

I BASIC CONDITIONS[1]

13.01 Roll-over relief applies where a person carrying on a trade disposes of assets used in that trade and within certain time limits replaces them with new "qualifying" assets which are used on their acquisition in his trade. Note that unlike incorporation relief it is not available if the person is carrying on a business rather than a trade (e.g. commercial property lettings).[2] Holiday lettings can be treated as a trade for roll-over relief purposes and farming, market gardening and commercial woodlands are all trades. The relief must be claimed (unlike incorporation relief which is automatic) and involves a CGT postponement rather than an exemption. Any gain accruing on the old asset is carried forward to the new asset since the gain is rolled-over and deducted from the acquisition cost of the new asset. Tax is therefore postponed until that asset is sold and not in turn replaced.

13.02 It is not necessary to trace the money used to pay for the new assets to the money received from the old so the sale proceeds do not need to be kept in a separate bank account before reinvestment and indeed the legislation envisages that the new asset can be purchased prior to the disposal of the old.

---

[1] TCGA 1992 ss.152–159. Roll-over relief takes precedence over entrepreneurs' relief see CG Manual 64136. Only the chargeable gain not qualifying for roll-over relief is eligible for entrepreneurs' relief, e.g. if not all of the sale proceeds are reinvested. See further Ch.17 and 15.11.

[2] See *Griffiths v Jackson and Pearman* 56 TC 58.

However, the old assets or the proceeds of the old assets *"must be part of the resources available to the taxpayer when the new assets are acquired."*[3] HMRC consider that s.152 merely requires an equivalent amount to the proceeds of disposal (or deemed proceeds on a deemed disposal) to be invested in the new asset but do not accept that roll-over relief is available on the deemed reacquisition and disposal of the same asset, e.g. when a sub-fund election is made.[4]

Roll-over relief may be available on: **13.03**

(a) the disposal of an asset by way of gift based on the amount of considera-tion deemed to have been received;

(b) where actual consideration passes on a transaction between connected persons and an increased or reduced consideration has to be substituted;

(c) on an exchange of assets if the remaining requirements of s.152 are satisfied;

(d) on a deemed acquisition of a qualifying asset, for example under TCGA 1992 s.62 when a person acquires an asset as a legatee.[5]

The new and old assets do not need to be the same type of qualifying asset or **13.04** used in the same trade but the trade must be carried on by the same person.[6] Hence, in the context of trusts it does not matter if the beneficiaries of the trust change between disposal and reinvestment but the trustees must make the reinvestment if they have realised the gain.

For full relief, the old assets must have been used only for the purposes of **13.05** the trade throughout the trader's period of ownership but there are appor-tionment provisions where the asset was used partly for trading and partly for non-trading purposes or was only used for part of the period of ownership in the trade. It does not matter if the old asset ceases to be used for the purposes of a continuing trade before being sold[7] but roll-over relief is lost where the new asset is purchased and not *"on the acquisition taken into use"* for the trade. The courts have considered the meaning of these words and how quickly after acquisition the asset must be used.[8] It is possible to accept reasonable delay

---

[3] See the difficult decision of *Watton v Tippett* [1997] STC 893 where the taxpayer purchased freehold land and buildings for a single price and within 12 months of that purchase sold part and claimed roll over relief on the land and buildings retained by him. The court rejected his claim on the basis that it was necessary to identify the asset acquired and disposed of and the retained land had not been acquired as such. A part disposal of a single asset did not count. The position would have been different if two separate properties had been purchased even if for one single unapportioned consideration. See also correspondence between HMRC and CIOT (CIOT/TIR/11/91) and CG Manual 60790. A trader may apply funds eligible for roll-over relief in improvement expenditure on an existing asset or on acquiring an additional interest in an asset already used for trading purposes: see ESC D 25.

[4] TIR 11/91; 1991 (STI) 1097.

[5] CGTM 60790.

[6] Section 152(8) deems two or more trades carried on by the same person to be a single trade.

[7] See *Richart v J Lyons & Co Ltd* (1989) 62 TC 261: the relief is restricted on the basis that the asset has not been used throughout the ownership period but it is not lost.

[8] See *Campbell Connelly & Co Ltd v Barnett* [1992] STC 316. *"On acquisition"* was held to mean the date of completion, not the date of exchange. However, where two or more interests in the same asset are acquired it is the date on which the first of these interests was acquired that the "immediately" test is applied. So in *Campbell Connelly* a freehold reversionary interest was acquired in January. The property was subject to a lease and an underlease. The company only

between the "*acquisition*" and the subsequent "*taking into use*" but not mere dilatoriness.[9] HMRC note at 60830:

> "*If the asset is ready for use when possession is obtained, it must be taken into qualifying use without delay. The asset may, however, need minor alterations or adaptations or the claimant may need, for example, to obtain stock or to engage staff before the asset can be taken into use. Relief should not be denied solely on the grounds that the asset has not been brought into use as soon as it is acquired, provided that it is brought into use as soon as is practicable after the acquisition and without unnecessary delay. The question is to be decided on the facts and circumstances of the case taking account of the nature of the trade and the asset concerned. In most cases, it is expected the interval will be short. For example, taking over a public house but not opening until after the next licensing may be acceptable but taking over a hotel as a going concern in May but not opening until October would be unacceptable (unless the hotel is, for example, in a ski resort and the main season is in the winter). The interval may be longer but still acceptable if the trade is a seasonal one. If the asset is acquired after the end of the season but is not taken into use until the beginning of the new season, the delay may be acceptable. Examples might include an aircraft used for crop spraying or an ice cream kiosk in a seaside resort.*"

Qualifying assets

13.06   "*Qualifying assets*" are listed in s.155 and are:

(a) land and buildings;

(b) fixed plant and machinery;

(c) ships, aircraft, hovercraft;

(d) satellites, space stations and spacecraft;

(e) goodwill;

acquired the underlease in September of the same year and went into occupation then. The Court of Appeal concluded that failure to use the property by reference to the first acquisition in January precluded any claim for roll-over relief. Mere intention to use the land once possession could be obtained was not sufficient.

[9] See *Milton v Chivers* [1996] STC (SCD) 36. ESC D24 states that qualifying assets may be treated as if they were taken into use on the acquisition where capital expenditure is incurred on enhancing the value of the asset; and the improvement works begin as soon as practicable after acquisition and are completed within a reasonable period; and the asset is taken into use (and in the case of land or buildings, occupied) only for the purposes of the trade as soon as is practically possible after completion of the work; and the asset is neither let nor used for any non-trading purpose in the period between acquisition and taking into use for trade purposes. This interpretation of the statutory wording "*which on the acquisition are taken into use*" in TCGA 1992 s.152(1) was given judicial approval by Sir Richard Scott in *Steibelt v Paling* [1999] STC 594 when he commented "*I regard D24 as being a very sensible attempt by the Revenue to indicate how it believes the language of the 1992 Act in this regard should be applied.*" HMRC therefore regard D24 as a legitimate interpretation of the legislation rather than a concession. See also CGTM 60850.

(f) milk and potato quotas;

(g) ewe and suckler premium quotas;

(h) fish quota;

(i) payment entitlement under the single payment scheme;

(j) rights of a member of Lloyd's syndicate.

If the new asset is a depreciating asset (one which is a wasting asset or which will become one within 10 years)[10] s.154 makes special provision to prevent the gain being rolled-over and written off over the life of the new asset. Instead, the rolled-over gain is held in suspense until the earliest of disposal of the new asset: it ceasing to be used in the trade or the expiration of 10 years.

Neither the old nor the new assets need to be situated in the UK for roll-over relief to apply and relief can be claimed where an individual (but not a trustee)[11] becomes non-resident between the disposal of the old asset and the acquisition of the new one. (However, if the individual or trustee is already non-resident and the old asset is used in a UK trade the new asset must also be so used.)[12] Shares are not qualifying assets and roll-over relief is not available on disposals of shares.[13]   **13.07**

Expenditure on new buildings or additions to existing buildings occupied and used for the trade qualifies for relief.[14] By concession,[15] relief may also be given for gains on disposals of old assets against: **13.08**

(a) capital expenditure on improvements to qualifying assets which are either already in use (and for land and buildings, occupied) for the purposes of the trade or which are taken into trade use (and occupation) on completion of the enhancement work; and

(b) the cost of acquisition of a further interest in qualifying assets which are already in use (and occupation) only for trade purposes.

In both cases, expenditure on improvements or on the acquisition of the further interest is to be treated as the acquisition of new assets which are taken into trade use on the acquisition.[16]

Roll-over relief is not available where the trade is a trade of dealing in or developing land and the reinvestment is in land that would form part of the trading profits: i.e. the trader cannot roll-over the gain into land that is going to be developed (trading stock) although he could roll-over the gain into land that is being used in his business, e.g. into a new office headquarters.   **13.09**

---

[10] A lease for a 60-year term is a depreciating asset. A wasting asset is defined as one with a predictable life not exceeding 50 years.

[11] TCGA 1992 s.80(6). Note the limited exception in s.80(7).

[12] Section 159.

[13] Gains on disposals of shares could, however, be sheltered through EIS relief: see Ch.16.

[14] Section 155 Class 1A(1).

[15] ESC D22 and D25.

[16] See CGTM 60431.

13.10 The new asset must be bought within one year before or three years after the disposal of the old.[17] Hence the new asset can be purchased before the disposal of the old asset. HMRC have discretion to extend the four-year period where the taxpayer intends to acquire the new assets but does not do so for reasons outside his control and acquires the asset as soon as possible thereafter. The exercise of HMRC's discretion to extend the time limits can only be challenged by judicial review.[18] Although once acquired the new asset must as soon as possible be taken into use for the purposes of the taxpayer's trade, if the asset is brought into use and then the trade ceases but the asset is retained or the asset ceases to be used in the trade, there is no claw back of relief until the asset is disposed of.

II COMPUTATION OF THE GAIN

13.11 Unlike EIS relief,[19] s.152 requires that all the consideration from the old assets is invested in the new assets. If the amount not reinvested is greater than the gain then no relief is due.[20] Or to put it another way, if the purchase price of the new asset does not exceed the acquisition cost of the old, all the gain is chargeable. If the amount not reinvested is less than the gain, relief is restricted to the extent of the difference between the two. So capital gains tax is payable on the amount not reinvested. If trustees know that the acquisition price of the new asset will be too low to enable any roll-over relief to be claimed they should consider transferring part of the old asset to a beneficiary prior to sale, claiming hold-over relief.[21]

Relief should not be claimed where the taxpayer makes an allowable loss on the sale of the old asset since the loss cannot be added to the base value of the new asset. Nor should it be claimed if the gain does not exceed the taxpayer's annual exemption and the taxpayer cannot roll over only a part of the gain after deducting the annual exemption.

EXAMPLE 13.1

(1) A trust purchased land in 1999 for £100,000. It farmed the land until April 2009 when it was sold for £500,000 thereby realising a gain of £400,000. No indexation or taper relief was due. The trust bought more land for £600,000. Tax on all the gain of £400,000 can be deferred and

---

[17] See s.152(3).
[18] See *R (on the application of Barnett) v IRC* [2004] STC 763. An extension may be granted even if an asset was acquired within the time limit which could have qualified for roll-over relief but the taxpayer chose not to make a claim on this asset in preference to another asset: see (1991) STI 1097. It is sufficient if an unconditional contract for acquisition of the new asset is entered into within the specified period even if completion occurs after the three years.
[19] See Ch.16.
[20] See s.153.
[21] See Example 13.1(5).

the base cost of the replacement land reduced to £200,000. If, however, the trust reinvests only half the proceeds of sale, e.g. it buys new land for £250,000 then relief is restricted. The amount not reinvested is £250,000 which is less than the gain of £400,000 so some relief is due. The difference is £150,000 which is the gain rolled over. The base cost of the new asset is accordingly £250,000 less £150,000 = £100,000. Capital gains tax remains payable on £250,000, i.e. on over half the gain even though half the proceeds were reinvested. If the trust wanted full roll-over relief there is nothing to stop them reinvesting a further £250,000 in another asset used in the same or different trade within the required time limits.

(2) If the farmland had been used for the trade for only 8 out of the 10 years that it was in the trust (having been let during the first two years), the maximum gain capable of being rolled-over is 80 per cent of £400,000 = £320,000. If the trust reinvests only £320,000 then there is no further restriction of roll-over relief because the proceeds attributable to the business use are equal to the amount reinvested. If the trust reinvests say £250,000 then relief is further restricted.

(3) If in (1) above the trust had purchased new land costing only £100,000 no relief would have been due. The trust would pay tax on £400,000.

(4) If in (1) above the farmer was not a trust but an individual (A) then he could transfer half the farmland before sale to his wife. His gain would then be £200,000 (on a base cost of £50,000) and his share of the proceeds £250,000. If he reinvested in farmland costing £100,000, he is eligible for relief of £50,000. His base cost for the new asset is £50,000. H and W are between them taxed on a gain of £350,000 rather than £400,000. This device could be used so that H transfers say 80 per cent of the land to W leaving him with sale proceeds of 20 per cent = £100,000 which are then fully reinvested. H and W are then taxed on £320,000 gain between them.

(5) Similarly if trustees carry on the farming trade and know that not all the sale proceeds are to be reinvested, they could transfer (say) 80 per cent of the land to a beneficiary claiming hold-over relief[22] leaving them with 20 per cent of the land on which they receive sale proceeds of £100,000. They reinvest all the proceeds they receive and claim full roll-over relief. The beneficiary pays tax on £320,000 (£400,000 sale price on 80 per cent less base cost of £80,000). Prior to April 2008 it was undesirable to do this because of the loss of taper relief: the beneficiary would pay at a higher rate of tax than the trustees. Now that all chargeable gains are taxed at a flat rate of 28 per cent irrespective of how long the asset is held[23] this option could be considered.

III CLAIMING THE RELIEF

A claim for relief must be made in writing and must specify: **13.12**

- the identity of the claimant;
- the old assets which have been disposed of;

---

[22] Under s.165: see Ch.18.
[23] Unless qualifying for entrepreneurs' relief, for which see Ch.14.

- the amount received for each of those assets;

- the date of disposal of each of those assets;

- the new assets which have been acquired;

- the date of acquisition of each of those assets or the dates on which unconditional contracts for the acquisition of each of those assets were entered into;

- the cost of each of those assets; and

- the amount of the proceeds from each of the old assets which has been used to acquire each new asset.

HMRC Helpsheet HS 290 contains a claim form. The completed form can be attached to the Capital Gains supplementary pages of the self-assessment tax return.

Time limits for claims

13.13   As no time limit is specified, the general time limits apply.[24] A claim made on or after April 1, 2010 must generally be made within four years of the end of the tax year or accounting period to which it relates. A capital gains tax claim made before April 1, 2010 had to be made within five years after January 31 following the tax year to which it related. In effect, these changes mean that the time limit for roll-over relief claims for years from 2005–06 was shortened to four years. So the time limit for making a claim in respect of the tax year 2011–12 is April 5, 2016. In the case of a "discovery" assessment which is *not* for making good loss of tax brought about carelessly or deliberately (or, for assessments made before April 1, 2010, loss of tax attributable to fraudulent or negligent conduct), the time limits are extended. So:

(a)   any "relevant" claim, election, application or notice which could have been made or given within the normal time limits of the Taxes Acts may be made or given within a year of the end of the chargeable period in which the assessment is made; and

(b)   any "relevant" claim, etc previously made or given, except an irrevocable one, can, with the consent of the person(s) by whom it was made or given (or their personal representatives), be revoked or varied in the manner in which it was made or given.

Provisional claims

13.14   On the introduction of Self Assessment a change was made to allow the taxpayer to obtain relief before the acquisition of the new assets on making

---

[24] TMA 1970 s.43 and FA 1998 Sch.18 para.55 apply as modified in FA 2008 s.118, Sch.39 paras 12 and 45; SI 2009/403.

a declaration of an intention to reinvest in their Self Assessment Return. Provisional relief can be obtained for disposals in 1996–97 and for subsequent years and the tax otherwise due is postponed even if the reinvestment has not yet been made.[25] If the reinvestment is not in fact made then the relief is withdrawn.

Withdrawal of claims

The taxpayer can amend a claim made in the return up to 12 months after the filing date of the return. This includes a withdrawal of the claim altogether. In some cases taxpayers withdrew roll-over relief claims where the old taper relief regime proved better than the post-April 2008 regime.   **13.15**

IV THE EFFECT OF THE CHANGES IN APRIL 2008

An asset may have been disposed of before April 6, 1988 and a roll-over relief claim made on the acquisition of a new asset. If the old asset had been acquired before April 1, 1982 no account was taken of rebasing so TCGA 1992 Sch.4 (halving relief) gave an arbitrary relief in relation to an eventual disposal of the new asset.[26] Where trustees or individuals sell the new asset on or after April 6, 2008 the rolled-over gain comes back into charge without the benefit of halving relief although with indexation.[27]   **13.16**

Another point to bear in mind is that when trustees sold an asset before April 5, 2008 and reinvested the proceeds, it was the gain before taper that needed to be reinvested. If the trustees then sell the new business asset on or after April 6, 2008 no business assets taper relief is available. So in many cases trustees (and individuals) will ultimately pay at a higher CGT rate on the disposal of the new asset than if they had not claimed roll-over relief on the disposal of the old asset (10 per cent if full business assets taper relief had been available on the disposal of the old asset).   **13.17**

EXAMPLE 13.2

(1) Trustees rolled-over gains by reinvestment in a new asset before April 6, 1988 (say in 1987) after selling an asset which they had acquired in January 1982. They sold the new asset in June 2008. In computing the chargeable gain, indexation but not halving relief is available on the rolled-over gain.

(2) In June 2007, trustees reinvested sale proceeds from the disposal of farm-land (which occurred in June 2006) into new land which was sold in June 2009 for £1 million. There is no taper relief on any of the sale proceeds

---

[25] See TCGA 1992 s.153A and CGTM 60702 for further details.
[26] See Ch.11.
[27] See TCGA 1992 ss.35A and 56.

even though when the old farmland was sold in 2006 full business assets taper relief was available. Under the old rules, taper relief would have been available on the disposal of the new asset but only if the new asset was a business asset owned for at least two years. Under the 2008 rules, no taper relief is available even if the gain on the disposal of the old asset would have qualified. The calculation of the gain rolled over in 2007 on the disposal of the old asset does not change. This rolled-over gain was the gain after indexation relief up to 1998 but calculated before taper relief. So if in 2007 after deduction of the indexed base cost of the old asset the gain was (say) £320,000 then in June 2009 that is the amount that must be deducted from the final proceeds of £1 million in computing the chargeable gain. Do not recompute the rolled-over gain without indexation!

(3) If the trustees decided to sell the asset in March 2008 then no taper relief would have been available on the new asset because it had not been owned for two years.

(4) In (2) and (3) above, the trustees could have decided not to make a roll over relief claim (or to make a provisional claim under s.153A which is then withdrawn) in respect of the 2006 disposal; then full business assets taper relief would have been available on the disposal of the old asset (but with tax payable in January 2008). The gain on the disposal of the new asset does not receive taper relief but the base cost of the new asset is higher.

13.18   Where provisional or final roll-over relief claims have been made on disposals of old assets before April 6, 2008 the taxpayer may reinvest the proceeds in a new asset but now consider withdrawing the provisional or final claim in order to maximise business assets taper relief on the old asset. Of course, this crystallises the capital gains tax liability earlier but potentially at lower rates. The taxpayer will then hold the new asset with a higher base cost. For claims made where the proceeds were reinvested after the disposal but before April 6, 2009 the time limits will generally have expired and a claim cannot be withdrawn.[28]

V RELEVANCE OF ROLL-OVER RELIEF TO TRUSTEES

13.19   Relief on replacement of business assets is available if the trustees are carrying on an unincorporated business or are in partnership.[29] Relief cannot be claimed when trustees merely own an asset which is used by a beneficiary in his trade or provided for use by a company which they own. In this respect the conditions for roll-over relief are the opposite of those required for entrepreneurs' relief where a qualifying beneficiary not the trustees needs to be carrying on the trade! It is most likely to be in the business of farming that roll-over relief will be relevant to trustees.

---

[28]   So a taxpayer who sold in March 2008 and acquired a new asset for his trade in say May 2009 would have filed a return in 2009–10 making any provisional claim final. He can withdraw this claim at any time before January 2012.

[29]   See TCGA 1992 ss.152–159 as amended.

For roll-over relief purposes the trustees (whatever the type of trust) must **13.20** carry on the trade and so would need to enter into a partnership (e.g. with the beneficiary) or to trade themselves as trustees. They need to ensure that they have power under the trust deed to carry on a trade and are suitably protected from liability.[30] Where the business is already in existence (e.g. trustees inherit the business of the deceased testator) in the absence of express authorisation they can only carry it on for such reasonable time as is necessary to enable them to sell it as going concern.[31]

An alternative if the trustees are not trading is for the trustees to transfer **13.21** the asset to the beneficiary carrying on the trade before any sale if hold-over relief would then be available.[32] The beneficiary could then bring the asset into use for his trade and six months later dispose of it. There is no restriction in a subsequent roll-over relief claim by the beneficiary if the asset is used by the beneficiary for the entire period of his ownership and the gain is reinvested. By contrast, if the trustees sell the asset and advance the proceeds to the beneficiary no relief will be due.

EXAMPLE 13.3

> Trustees own farmland which has been let to the life tenant for many years. The life tenant wishes to carry on his farming business on more profitable land. The trustees have three options: *first*, they can retain the land and let it to a new tenant, not necessarily a beneficiary. There is no disposal so no capital gains tax arises. *Secondly*, they can sell the land and give the life tenant the proceeds or reinvest the proceeds themselves in new land to be farmed by the life tenant. In that case capital gains tax is charged at 28 per cent. *Thirdly*, they can advance the farmland to the life tenant (claiming hold-over relief).[33] The life tenant can then bring the land into his business for a few months and then sell it along with the rest of his business, claiming roll-over relief on the entire gain including the held-over gain and reinvesting the proceeds in new land.

Non-resident trustees

As noted above, s.80(6) disallows roll-over relief where trustees have become **13.22** non-UK resident between the date of the disposal of the old asset and the acquisition of the new asset. This anti-avoidance provision does not apply

---

[30] See *Lewin on Trusts*, 18th edn, at para.36–80. The STEP standard provisions give trustees power to trade. In the absence of a power in the trust deed, trustees have no power to carry on a continuing trade.

[31] By contrast trustees may retain or acquire shares in trading companies even if there is no express authorisation under the trust instrument: see TA 2000 s.3(1) although *Lewin* notes: "*they owe a duty to supervise the management of the company in such a case . . . [and] we do not consider that trustees lacking a power to carry on a business may circumvent that restriction by arranging for the incorporation of a company and acquiring its shares so that a business may instead be carried on by the company*": see paras 36–80.

[32] See Ch.18 for hold-over relief.

[33] See Ch.18.

where trustees are non-UK resident both before and after the disposal of the old asset or where the trustees become non-UK resident after the disposal of the old assets provided the new assets are UK situated and used in a trade carried on in the UK through a branch or agency.[34]

13.23 Generally roll-over relief is not needed where trustees were non-UK resident before the disposal of the old asset because they are not subject to capital gains tax. Hence, the anti-avoidance provision in s.80(6) is not relevant. However:

(1) if the trust is within s.86[35] and the trade is carried on outside the UK by the trustees, roll-over relief is useful because rolling-over gains can avoid a tax charge on the settlor and the new asset can later be sold by the trustees at a time when the settlor is non-UK resident;

(2) in addition if the trade in which the old asset was used is carried on by non-resident trustees through a branch or agency in the UK then roll-over relief is necessary to avoid a charge under s.10 on a disposal of the UK situate asset. However, in this case (as with non-resident individuals) the new trade must also be carried on in the UK for the relief to be available.[36]

13.24 The main difference between individuals and trustees in the context of non-residence is that UK resident individuals can claim roll-over relief if they become non-UK resident between the date of disposal of the old asset and acquisition of the new, even if their non-resident status takes the rolled-over gain outside the CGT charge (because the reinvestment is from assets used in a UK trade, branch or agency to assets used in a foreign trade) while an emigrating trust cannot do this as a result of s.80(6).[37] However, an individual who is already non-UK resident is subject to the same restrictions as trustees who were non-resident at the date of the disposal of the old asset: if the old asset was used in a trade in the UK then the reinvestment must be in new assets also used in a trade in the UK.

---

[34] Section 80(7).

[35] See Ch.19.

[36] TCGA 1992 s.159.

[37] The old assets are not chargeable assets under s.10A if the individual is UK resident at the date of disposal so s.159(1) does not apply.

CHAPTER 14

ENTREPRENEURS' RELIEF[1]

I BASIC PRINCIPLES

Background

Entrepreneurs' relief was announced in January 2008 by the then Labour Government under some political pressure. The relief replaced taper relief for disposals on or after April 6, 2008. For 2008–09 and 2009–10 the relief (if claimed by the taxpayer) applied to gains of up to £1 million on disposals of "qualifying business assets". The relief resulted in gains of up to this amount effectively being taxed at 10 per cent. Thereafter the 18 per cent flat rate applied. This is a lifetime limit per taxpayer: it can be used in respect of a single disposal or set against a number of disposals.   **14.01**

For disposals on or after April 6, 2010 the £1 million lifetime limit was raised to £2 million. This lasted less than three months since for disposals from June 23, 2010 the lifetime limit was again raised, this time to £5 million. Thereafter gains were taxed at 18 per cent or 28 per cent depending on whether the individual was a higher rate taxpayer.[2] From April 6, 2011 the relief was again increased, this time to £10 million. The mechanics of the relief operate slightly differently before and after June 23, 2010 but the basic entitlement conditions remain the same. Note though that the change in mechanics does adversely affect offshore trusts.   **14.02**

The relief can be claimed on more than one occasion up to a lifetime total of (now) £10 million gains. Disposals before April 6, 2008 do not affect the limit except in the case of deferred gains on which entrepreneurs' relief is claimed under transitional rules.   **14.03**

---

[1] FA 2008 Sch.3 and TCGA 1992 s.169H and following.
[2] For trustees, 28%.

14.04   The relief is a curious mixture of business assets taper relief and the old retirement relief.[3] Originally the relief was relatively unimportant: the maximum tax saving that it could bring was £80,000 (eight per cent of £1 million). It is now worth a maximum of £1.8 million in tax savings.[4] Trustees, in particular, need to be more careful now to secure entrepreneurs' relief when it may be available given (a) the increased relief and consequent tax savings (b) the rate of CGT if entrepreneurs' relief is not available is no longer 18 per cent but 28 per cent for trusts and (c) often when the relief only sheltered gains of up to £1 million it was unlikely that the beneficiary would have any "spare" entrepreneurs' relief to sacrifice to the trust.[5]

Mechanics of entrepreneurs' relief—computation

14.05   For disposals between April 6, 2008 and April 5, 2010 entrepreneurs' relief reduced the relieved element of any capital gain up by four-ninths leaving the residue of five-ninths to be reduced by annual exemption or losses.[6] That unrelieved gain was also eligible for hold-over relief if the disposal was a gift. Subject to these possible deductions, this meant there was an effective rate of 10 per cent on gains of up to £1 million.

For disposals after June 22, 2010 all gains up to the relevant threshold are taxed at 10 per cent. The balance of unrelieved gain is taxed at 18 per cent or 28 per cent, depending on the circumstances of the taxpayer. The four-ninths formula is no longer used: it is simply a flat rate 10 per cent rate that applies to all gains of up to £10 million. This new basis of computation has had an effect on deferred gains and reorganisations even where the disposal took place prior to June 23.[7]

EXAMPLE 14.1

> David sold 50 per cent of the shares in his trading company D Ltd in May 2008 for £2.5 million. Derek sold 12 per cent for £600,000. All conditions for entrepreneurs' relief are satisfied by David and Derek. The gain on David's disposal is £2 million and the gain on Derek's disposal is £500,000.

---

[3] Where the legislation uses terms that also appeared in the retirement relief legislation, they are intended to have the same meaning (except where the entrepreneurs' relief legislation specifically provides a different meaning) (Treasury Explanatory Notes to the 2008 Finance Bill). See also HMRC Capital Gains Manual CG64010.

[4] i.e. 18% x £10 million (18% being the difference between 10% if relief available and 28% if not).

[5] For the mechanics of the relief as it applies to trusts: see 14.23.

[6] TCGA 1992 s.169N. Note that when calculating the gain eligible for entrepreneurs' relief the gains and losses arising on the same business disposal must first be aggregated by the sole trader even if the disposal of the business takes place over several tax years. So, if Roger had sold his consultancy business realising a gain of say £100,000 on the freehold of the main office and a loss of £40,000 on the disposal of a subsidiary office then the loss is deducted to reach a net gain of £60,000 which is added to any gains from the sale of the goodwill of the business to reach the £1 million limit. Do not deduct the loss on the second office from gains realised on disposals of other assets not part of the business.

[7] See Ch.17 for details.

David's CGT liability

	£
Proceeds	2,500,000
Gain	2,000,000
Less entrepreneurs' relief (4/9 × £1 million)	(444,444)
Taxable gain (£555,556 + £1 million unrelieved)	1,555,556[8]
Tax at 18%	280,000

Effective rate of tax on total gain is 14%

Derek's CGT liability

	£
Proceeds	600,000
Gain	500,000
Less entrepreneurs' relief (4/9 × £500,000)	(222,222)
Taxable gain	277,778
Tax @ 18%	50,000

Effective rate of tax on total gain is 10%

As the examples below illustrate, if gains realised on a disposal of the business **14.06** were substantially above £5 million the taxpayer was worse off for disposals between June 23, 2010 and April 5, 2011 because of the increased CGT rate. If gains of up to £5 million were realised then the taxpayer was generally better off if the disposal is made after June 22.[9] For disposals after April 6, 2011 the taxpayer is better off on gains of up to £10 million.

EXAMPLE 14.2—DISPOSAL IN MAY 2010

(1) In May 2010, Roger sells his business, Consultancy Inc, which he has owned since 1990, realising a net gain of £2 million.

Entrepreneurs' relief 4/9 × £2 million = £888,888

Chargeable gain = £1,111,112

Tax at 18% = £200,000. This is an effective rate of 10%.

(2) The facts are as above, except that Roger sells his business in May 2010 realising a gain of £5 million. After entrepreneurs' relief (as in (1)) gain chargeable to CGT at 18% = £4,111,112 giving tax of £740,000 and an effective rate of 14.8%.

(3) Facts as above except that Roger sells his business in May 2010 for £10

---

[8] This is eligible for hold-over relief if the disposal is a gift. See priority of reliefs at the end of Ch.17.
[9] However, watch deferred consideration: see Ch.17.

million. After entrepreneurs' relief gain chargeable to CGT at 18% = £9,111,112 × 18% giving tax of £1,640,000 and an effective rate of 16.4%.

EXAMPLE 14.3—DISPOSAL IN JULY 2010 (WHEN CGT RATES INCREASED TO 28 PER CENT)

(1) Roger sells his business in July 2010 for £2 million.

Roger's capital gains tax liability for 2010–11 is calculated as follows.

Chargeable gain qualifying for entrepreneurs' relief £2 million

Capital gains tax payable (£2 million × 10%) = £200,000

(2) Roger sells his business in July 2010 for £5 million. CGT payable = £500,000 (10% × £5 million).

(3) Roger sells his business in July 2010 for £10 million. CGT payable is:

First £5 million taxed at 10% = 500,000

Balance £5 million taxed at 28% = £1,400,000

Total tax = £1,900,000

Effective rate of tax = 19%

If Roger sold the business for £10 million in July 2011 the entire gain would benefit from entrepreneurs' relief giving a tax rate of 10%.

Aggregation of gains and losses

14.07 When a business is sold some disposals of the business assets may crystallise gains and other disposals may create losses. Before calculating entrepreneurs' relief the gains and losses arising on the same business disposal must be set off.[10] This condition applies even if the disposal of the business is spread over two or more tax years.

The aggregation rule in TCGA 1992 s.169N also applies where a shareholder disposes of shares or securities in his personal company. Some may be sold at a profit and others may generate a loss, depending on the base cost for each type of security. In this situation the gains and losses still need to be aggregated before entrepreneurs relief can apply to the net gain. It is not clear how this will work in practice if the disposals are spread over more than one tax year.

Once the losses arising on the disposal of assets in the business have been aggregated with gains from disposals of assets of that same business any other losses brought forward or arising in the same tax year are set off against any residue of the gain after entrepreneurs' relief has been applied.

---

[10] TCGA 1992 s.169N(1).

The basic rules for individuals

Entrepreneurs' relief applies to: **14.08**

(a) Gains made on the disposal of all or part of a trading business carried on by the individual either alone or in partnership for at least 12 months. This covers sole traders and partners and includes professions and vocations, but does not include a property letting business other than furnished holiday lettings.[11] The business must be owned by the individual throughout the period of one year ending with the date of disposal (so a property to be sold might attract relief if it was let as furnished holiday accommodation for this period). It does not need to be sold to only one purchaser or as a going concern.[12] It may be difficult to distinguish between a sale of part of the business and a disposal of the assets used in that business. If there is a disposal of assets, not an interest in the business which is continuing, no relief is due on that disposal.[13]

(b) Gains made on disposals of assets following the cessation of a business where the assets were formerly used in the business and disposed of up to three years after the cessation of the business. The business must have been owned by the individual throughout the period of one year immediately prior to the cessation. This also covers gains on disposals of shares where the business had ceased trading by the time the shares were disposed of, if the disposal date falls up to three years after the date the company ceased to be a trading company or to be a member of a trading group.

(c) Gains made by an individual on the disposal of shares in a trading company[14] where that individual was an officer or employee of the company or of another company in the same group of companies ("the employment condition") and held at least five per cent of its ordinary shares with voting rights ("the ownership requirement"). The company

[11] Note in relation to letting of furnished holiday accommodation, HMRC announced on April 22, 2009 that the provisions were also to apply to property in the European Economic Area (EEA) (HMRC Technical Note April 23, 2009). A number of further changes to the furnished holiday accommodation rules were provided for in FA 2011. With effect from April 6, 2012, the minimum period over which a qualifying property must be available for letting to the public in the relevant period is increased from 140 days to 210 days in a year and the minimum period over which a qualifying property is actually let to the public in the relevant period increased from 70 days to 105 days in a year. A period of grace will allow businesses that do not continue to meet the "actually let" requirement for one or two years to elect to continue to qualify throughout that period. (HMRC Tax Information and Impact Note "Furnished Holiday Lettings", December 9, 2010).

[12] Section 169I(3).

[13] See further 14.14.

[14] The definitions of trading company, trading group and holding company are imported directly from the taper relief legislation. Accordingly, even if a trading company holds non-trading assets or has non-trading activities this has no effect on entrepreneurs' relief provided the non-trading activities are not substantial, i.e. more than 20 per cent of the company's business. This is especially relevant in the 12 months prior to disposal. In cases where the 20 per cent limit is breached, consider a restricting to separate trading from investment assets. A disposal for entrepreneurs' relief purposes includes a sale, gift, deemed disposal on a beneficiary becoming absolutely entitled, the liquidation of a company, or a share buy-back receiving capital gains tax treatment. See *Tax Bulletin* Nos 53 and 62.

must be his personal company for one year and the individual must be an officer or employee throughout the period of one year ending with the date of the disposal[15] or those conditions must be satisfied through-out the period of one year ending with the date on which the company ceases to be a trading company and that date is within the period of three years ending with the date of the disposal.[16] If a business is incor-porated and the company shares are then sold within a year it appears that there is no entrepreneurs' relief even if the business had been owned for many years. In that case, it may be better to elect to disapply incor-poration relief.[17]

14.09 All the above are termed "material disposals" under s.169I:

(d) *Associated disposals.*[18] Where an individual qualifies for entrepreneurs' relief on a disposal of shares or securities or is a member of a part-nership who is entitled to relief on the disposal of his interest in the partnership, relief will also be available in respect of any "associated disposal" of an asset which was used in the business. For example, if a company director owns the premises from which the company carries on its business and sells the premises at the same time as he sells his shares in the company, the sale of the premises may count as an "asso-ciated disposal" and any gain attract entrepreneurs' relief. The relief due on an associated disposal is restricted where the asset in question was not wholly in business use throughout the period it was owned or if rent has been charged. However, associated disposals are not relevant to trustees.

The basic rules for trustees[19]

14.10 Entrepreneurs' relief applies only if all the following conditions are satisfied:

(a) at the date of disposal a beneficiary of the trust has an interest in pos-session which is not for a fixed term; and

(b) the beneficiary in question is either carrying on the business personally or as a partner, or is an officer or employee of the company and owns five per cent of the voting shares personally; and

---

[15] Section 169I(6).
[16] This does not help shareholders who are officers or employees, get sacked because of an inter-nal board dispute and then sell their shares. No entrepreneurs' relief is due. The company or the other shareholders may not have the resources to buy back the shares. It has been suggested by the CIOT that the individual is given a three-year period of grace after resigning in which to sell the shares. It is difficult to know why the Government thought it necessary to have a 5% threshold *and* an employee condition. One or the other had been sufficient for business assets taper relief.
[17] See Ch.15 for further details. Contrast the inheritance tax position where (because of the replacement property provided) business property relief could still be claimed on the company shares.
[18] Sections 169K and 169P.
[19] Sections 169J and 169O.

(c) the beneficiary elects jointly with the trustees to "transfer" his unused entrepreneurs' allowance in part or whole to be set against gains realised by the trustees; and

(d) throughout a period of one year ending not earlier than three years before the disposal (1) the company was the qualifying beneficiary's personal company and he was an officer or employee or (2) the business assets were used by the qualifying beneficiary in his own business or in a partnership of which he was a member and that beneficiary ceased to carry on the business (or be a partner) on the date of disposal or within three years before that date.

II THE RULES IN DETAIL

Disposals of shareholdings

The shareholding must meet the five per cent threshold without including **14.11** shares held by associates or shares held in another capacity, for instance as a trustee of a settlement. Where shares are held in the joint names of a married couple or civil partners, each spouse is deemed to have a 50 per cent beneficial interest in the whole shareholding. However, there is no aggregation of the shares held by spouses: each spouse must separately satisfy the five per cent ownership requirement and the officer/employee condition.

So in Example 14.1, if David's wife was an officer or employee of the company and owned at least five per cent of the shares for more than a year then she would have her own lifetime allowance of £10 million (from April 6, 2011). David could transfer some of his shares to her in the year prior to the sale and appoint her an officer of the company. She does not need to own all the shares for a year prior to disposal, only five per cent or more. Then more of the total gain would be protected by relief. However, if the transferor spouse was left with less than five per cent shares at the date of disposal, no relief would be available.

The shares disposed of by the individual do not have to be ordinary shares. **14.12** As long as ordinary voting shares in the company are held at the minimum threshold level of five per cent, any other disposals of shares or securities in the company can qualify for relief. The shareholder may make several disposals of shares in the same company at different times and claim entrepreneurs' relief on all gains made as long as the employment and ownership requirements are met for the required one-year period in respect of each disposal.

The shareholder must be either an officer or employee of the company in which he disposed of shares.[20] However, if the company was a member of a trading group, the employment condition is satisfied if the shareholder was employed by another company of that group. The employment does not need to be full-time or paid.

It is not necessary for the individual to cease working in the company nor **14.13** for the company to cease operating. Nor does the legislation require any minimum disposal of shares. So as noted above sales of shares can be made on

[20] TCGA 1992 s.169I(6)(b).

different occasions and all may qualify for entrepreneurs' relief provided the conditions are satisfied in the one-year period prior to each disposal. However, if the company has ceased trading in the previous three years, entrepreneurs' relief is also available on a disposal of shares (typically on liquidation) provided that the individual satisfied the ownership and employment requirements in the one-year period prior to cessation. As already noted there is no relief if an employee is dismissed or retires while still owning shares. Unless he sells before he ceases to work in the company (or crystallises the gain e.g. by transfer into a trust) relief is lost

EXAMPLE 14.4

Andrew is the managing director of an IT company in which he has a five per cent stake.[21] He decides he wants a change of lifestyle and gives six months notice. Under the articles he can keep the shares for up to one year after leaving at which point they must be sold to the company. The company does not at present have the resources to buy the shares. He should transfer them to a private trust for his own or his family's benefit (business property relief should be available) while he is still a director in order to crystallise his entrepreneurs' relief.[22]

Disposals of a business by a sole trader

14.14 The minimum ownership test of one year must be satisfied. However, the conditions are harder for unincorporated businesses because there must be a *disposal of all or part of the business* (even if not sold as a going concern) and not merely a disposal of business assets.[23] The retirement relief cases offer some guidance on what is a disposal of a part of a business rather than merely of assets. *McGregor v Adcock*[24] established the "interference test", i.e. where the impact of the sale on the business was considered to see what had changed. If the sale made a significant difference to the way the business operated then there had been a sale of part of the business; if not then the sale was one of assets only which would not qualify for relief. In the days of retirement relief HMRC treated disposals of 50 per cent or more of the farmland occupied by the farmer as a disposal of part of the business.[25]

---

[21] Ignore the employment related securities rules and Pt 7 ITEPA 2003 and assume that his shares will qualify for capital gains tax not income tax treatment.

[22] This assumes the articles permit him to make transfers of the shares in this way. The buyback of shares should qualify for capital treatment: see Ch.17. An alternative is to do a buy back of shares now but with a deferred completion date.

[23] Where the assets are sold after the business has ceased then relief may be due as a post-cessation disposal. Where assets are sold and the trade continues no relief is due.

[24] [1977] STC 206. The case involved a disposal of less than five acres of farmland out of 35 acres owned by the taxpayer.

[25] See also *Atkinson v Dancer* [1988] 61 TC 598; [1988] STC 758. which involved a sale of nine acres out of 89 acres where the taxpayer failed to obtain relief; *Mannion v Johnston* [1988] 61 TC 598; [1988] STC 758 and *Pepper v Daffurn* 66 TC 68 [1993] 466 where the taxpayer failed to show that there was a disposal of part of the business and compare *Jarmin v Rawlings* 67 TC

Example 14.5

Sandy, an eminent cellist who performs round the world, gives up performing as he nears retirement and now only teaches. He decides to sell his Amati cello and receives an offer of £1 million. He has not sold part or all of his business merely an asset used in the business. He has not as such ceased trading assuming his teaching is in a self-employed rather than employed capacity and so he cannot rely on the post-cessation disposal rules. No entrepreneurs' relief is available. Even if the business ceased (e.g. his only teaching work was as an employee) if he had stopped using his cello some years previously there would be no relief. The asset must be in use at the date the business ceased.[26]

Disposals by partners[27]

14.15 There are three special rules to ensure that disposals made by an individual partner attract relief as if he had been a sole trader:

(a) where an individual transfers assets to a partnership, on the occasion of him joining that partnership and the partnership takes over his business[28];

(b) where a partner disposes of the whole or part of his interest in the partnership[29];

(c) where any partner disposes of a business asset he is treated as if he had owned the whole of the partnership business.[30]

Where a sole trader merges his business with an established partnership the relief in (a) and (b) will ensure that any gains arising on the transfer of assets between those partners, either the new partner transferring his assets, or the existing partners transferring an interest in the partnership assts (such as goodwill), may be covered by entrepreneurs' relief.

Post-cessation disposals

14.16 When a sole trader ceases trading he may retain some of the business assets for disposal at a later date. Entrepreneurs' relief can still apply to these later disposals if the individual owned the business throughout the period of one

---

130; [1994] STC 1005 where the taxpayer succeeded in arguing that he had made a disposal of the dairy farming business. See also *Wase v Bourke* 68 TC 109; [1996] STC 18 and *Barrett v Powell* 70 TC 432; [1998] STC 283.

[26] See 14.16 below.
[27] TCGA 1992 s.169I(8).
[28] TCGA 1992 s.169I(8)(a).
[29] TCGA 1992 s.169I(8)(b).
[30] TCGA 1992 s.169I(8)(c).

year ending with the date on which the business ceased to be carried on and the disposal is within three years after the date the business ceased.[31] The business owner does not have to make any disposal of his business for the post-cessation relief to operate. The only requirement is that the business has ceased to operate (whether before or after April 6, 2008). Such a disposal is still a "material disposal of business assets" within s.169I and the relief is more generous than for associated disposals (which are only relevant to partnerships and companies).

The date the business ceased is a question of fact.[32] The condition may cause difficulties where, for example, farmland is sold but the individual carries on farming for that season.

14.17   The asset in question must have been a "relevant business asset" and in use for the purposes of the business at the time when it ceased.[33] Curiously the asset does not need to be in use for the business (or owned) for any minimum length of time. Relevant business assets are defined in s.169L and can include any assets (including goodwill) used for the purposes of the business carried on by the sole-trader or partnership, but not including "excluded assets", namely shares and securities or other investment assets. However, there is no restriction on how the asset is used between the date the business ceased and the disposal of the asset. The owner can let the asset at a commercial rent in the three-year period or use the asset in a different business. (Contrast the position for associated disposals.)

Assets that have a mixed business and non-business use can qualify as relevant business assets. There is no restriction that requires the asset to be used wholly for the purposes of the business at the date of cessation provided it is part of the business.

Associated disposals[34]

14.18   An associated disposal of business assets can only occur in connection with:

(a) the disposal of shares or securities in a company; or

(b) the disposal of a partnership interest.[35]

14.19   In order to obtain relief, three conditions must be satisfied. First there must be a material disposal of business assets. So, if a shareholder disposes of shares but is not an employee or officer or if the company is not his personal company there is no entrepreneurs' relief on the associated disposal.[36]

Assuming that the shareholder or partner makes a material disposal, so that Condition A is satisfied, Condition B requires that the individual makes the disposal as part of his withdrawal from participation in the business carried

---

[31] TCGA 1992 s.169I(4).
[32] See CGTM 64105.
[33] Section 169I(2)(b).
[34] FA 2008 Sch.3, s.169K.
[35] Sole traders have the more flexible post-cessation relief set out at 14.16 above.
[36] Condition A in s.169K.

on by the partnership or company.[37] (This may require some reduction in work but not necessarily the partner retiring completely.)

Condition C requires that the asset was used for the purpose of the business for at least one year prior to the disposal of the shares or partnership interest or the cessation of the company's or partnership's business if earlier.[38] **14.20**

There is no specified time limit during which the associated disposal must be made, but the HMRC guidance,[39] stipulates that both the disposal of the shares or partnership interest and the associated disposal of the asset must be caused by the same event and that there should be no significant time interval between the material and associated disposals. They have laid down guidelines as to when a later disposal of an asset can be accepted as an associated disposal, namely if the disposal occurs: **14.21**

- within one year of the cessation of business; or

- within three years of the cessation of business and the asset has not been leased or used for any other purpose at any time after business ceased (cf. post-cessation disposals by a sole trader); or

- within three years of the material disposal provided the asset has not been used for any purpose other than that of the business.

Section 169P(4) imposes four additional restrictions on associated disposals. If any of the following apply the amount of the gain arising on the associated disposal of the asset, which would be subject to entrepreneurs' relief, is reduced on a "just and reasonable" basis: **14.22**

(a) the asset has only been used by the business for part of the period of ownership by the individual, e.g. land was let to a third party before being let to the qualifying company of the individual;

(b) only part of the asset has been used for the purposes of the business, e.g. the top floor of an office is let for residential purposes and the bottom floor is used as offices by the partnership;

(c) the individual concerned has only been involved in carrying on the business whether personally, as a partner of the partnership or employee/officer of the company for part of the time during which the asset was used by the business, e.g. where an individual was a salaried partner before becoming a full partner;

(d) any payment of rent was made for the use of the asset by the personal company or partnership for a period after April 5, 2008.

Where the rent paid is less than a full market rent for the use of the asset the gain is restricted proportionately.[40]

[37] TCGA 1992 s.169K(3) and (5).
[38] TCGA 1992 s.169K(4).
[39] CGTM 63995.
[40] See Example 14.7(2) below for a way round the rent restriction if the asset is owned by a trust and let to the partnership.

14.23 We have gone into some detail in relation to entrepreneurs' relief for individuals because unless the basic conditions are understood mistakes will be made in applying the relief to trustees. However, where action is taken in advance, trustees and the qualifying beneficiary may be able to secure greater entrepreneurs' relief than would otherwise be the case. It is therefore important to review trust structures which hold assets used in the family business or company shares. A key point is that entrepreneurs' relief is not available at all for discretionary trusts. Relief is only available if:

   (i) there is a "qualifying beneficiary" at the time of the trust asset disposal. An individual is a qualifying beneficiary if he or she has, under the terms of the settlement, an interest in possession (otherwise than for a fixed term)[42] in:

      (a) the whole of the settled property; or
      (b) a part of the settled property which consists or includes the trust business assets which have been disposed of[43]; and

   (ii) the trustees make a disposal of shares[44] or assets which are used (or previously used) in the business carried on by the qualifying beneficiary (either alone or in partnership)[45]; and

   (iii) the relevant condition is met; namely either:

      (a) throughout a period of one year ending not earlier than three years before the date of the disposal the trading company is the qualifying beneficiary's personal company and he is an officer or employee; *or*
      (b) throughout the period of one year ending not earlier than three years before the date of disposal the trust assets were used for the purposes of the business carried on by the qualifying beneficiary (whether as sole trader or partner) and the qualifying beneficiary ceased to carry on the business on the date of disposal or within the period of three years before that date.

14.24 As can be seen from the above, whether or not the trustees carry on a business or own five per cent of the shares is irrelevant. It is the qualifying beneficiary who needs to satisfy the conditions, i.e. carry on the business or own the five

---

[41] TCGA 1992 s.169T; 1690.

[42] So an interest in possession which can be terminated by exercise of the trustees' overriding powers is acceptable but an interest in possession for six months is not. This was confirmed by Jane Kennedy, Financial Secretary to the Treasury, during the Committee Stage on the Finance Bill on May 13, 2008.

[43] Section 169J(3). See 14.31 for the position where there are several interest in possession beneficiaries not all of whom may be qualifying.

[44] It does not matter that the trustees own less than 5% of the shares provided that the qualifying beneficiary owns at least 5% of the trading company.

[45] Note that the assets cannot be investment assets nor shares in an investment company. Nor can the trustees qualify for associated disposals, e.g. if the assets are owned by the trustees but used in a company owned as to 5% by a qualifying beneficiary no relief is due. Settlement business assets are either shares or assets used in the business carried on by the beneficiary.

per cent shareholding. However, if the trustees are conducting a business in partnership with a qualifying beneficiary the gain arising on the disposal of a trust asset used in the partnership will attract relief if the qualifying beneficiary ceases to be a partner at the time the trust asset is sold or in the previous three years.[46] In relation to companies, if the qualifying beneficiary does not own at least five per cent of the shares personally (as well as being an officer of the company) then no relief is available to the trustees. Although s.169J(4)(a) refers to "*the qualifying beneficiary's personal company*" this is not decided by reference to the trust holding shares but by reference to the individual's personal holding.[47]

Note, however, that no disposal of the beneficiary's personal company shareholding or business is required. The personal shareholding can be retained and the company can continue with the beneficiary working there even after the trustees' disposal. By contrast, in the case of an unincorporated business, the beneficiary must cease to carry on the business on or *prior to the trust disposal* whether or not the beneficiary actually disposes of the business, e.g. he might retire as partner but the partnership continues.

Curiously it does not seem necessary for the interest in possession to have existed for a minimum period of time prior to the disposal of trust business assets or in the period when the company was the beneficiary's personal company. The legislation requires the interest in possession to exist at the date of the disposal and the conditions in s.169J(4) seem merely to require the relevant interest in possession beneficiary at that date to have owned five per cent of the shares personally and be an officer of the company for a year or be carrying on the business for a year but not for him to have been a qualifying beneficiary for a year. HMRC guidance, however, indicates that they consider that there needs to be a qualifying beneficiary for at least one year prior to the disposal. **14.25**

No relief is due to trustees unless the qualifying beneficiary has not exhausted his £10 million lifetime allowance at the date of the trustees' disposal and he is willing to allow the trustees to use it. However, it is not possible to restrict the claim to a specified amount on any particular disposal: it is an all or nothing claim. The beneficiary must agree to the trustees using a sum which is the lesser of his unused lifetime allowance and the amount of gain realised by the trustees so the legislation requires that any claim by the trustees to take advantage of the beneficiaries' unused relief must be signed by the beneficiary in question as well as by the trustees. For example, assume that both beneficiary and trustees own shares and they sell on the same day. If the individual makes gains personally of £10 million he cannot use (say) half his lifetime allowance on those personal gains and agree that the trustees can take the balance. Only if he has insufficient personal gains to use up the lifetime allowance or makes no claim on his own disposal can the lifetime allowance be used by the trust. So if he claims relief against any personal gains, entrepreneurs' relief must be used fully first against those gains. If, however, the trustees sold shares the day before the beneficiary, entrepreneurs' relief could be claimed on all the trustees' gain, with the balance then being available on the gains realised by the beneficiary personally the following day. Similarly, he cannot assign a percentage of his lifetime allowance to the trustees in the hope **14.26**

---

[46] See s.169J(5).
[47] See s.169S(3).

of using the balance at a later date. If the trustees realised gains of up to £10 million and the beneficiary agreed to "transfer" his lifetime allowance, then all of that allowance has to be used on the trust gains. Only if the gain arising to the trustees is less than the unused lifetime allowance will the beneficiary be able to carry forward an unused part.

14.27 In the case of shares it is possible to make separate qualifying disposals on which entrepreneurs' relief can be claimed. For example, the sale of the shares could be structured to take place on separate dates so beneficiary and trustees realise gains on each disposal. Then the beneficiary could claim entrepreneurs' relief on his disposal and agree to the use of his lifetime allowance on a disposal made by the trustees.

14.28 A beneficiary may not want to use entrepreneurs' relief to shelter personal gains that he has made on the disposal of a business if, for example, he has substantial personal losses which can be used to shelter those gains. Alternatively it is possible that the beneficiary does not intend to dispose of his own company shares and therefore it is sensible to use the relief on the trustees' disposal. Another reason why the beneficiary may not need his own lifetime allowance is that he may have ceased to carry on the business but all the valuable assets are held by the trust so all the gains are made within the trust.[48]

14.29 Trusts can also be useful where an asset is used by a partnership and rent is charged. No relief is due on an associated disposal if the asset is owned by an individual and rent charged. But if the same asset is owned by the trust and rent charged to the partnership then entrepreneurs' relief can still be claimed: not under the associated disposal provisions but under the basic relief for trustee disposals.

EXAMPLE 14.7

(1) Chris owns 10 per cent of the shares in a trading company of which he is a director. The other 90 per cent is owned by a trust in which he is the interest in possession beneficiary. Both Chris and the trust satisfy the conditions for entrepreneurs' relief. When the company is sold, if Chris claims the relief on the disposal of his personal shares then entrepreneurs' relief is allocated first to that disposal and then in respect of the trust gains (if he agrees). Chris must make a separate claim in respect of his own personal gains within the time limits as well as sign the trustees' claim within those time limits. However, Chris does not have to make a claim on his personal gains and could if he wishes elect that the whole of his £10 million relief is allocated to the trustees. But if he makes gains of (say) £500,000 personally he cannot claim £400,000 entrepreneurs' relief and agree that the trustees take the balance. He must use the relief against all the £500,000 gains if he wants to use it at all and then transfer the balance of the lifetime allowance to the trustees. Further, he cannot agree that only a proportion of the unused balance is allocated to the trustees. So if the trustees realise gains of £2 million then they can take £2 million

---

[48] Section169M(2). Since the beneficiary cannot sign the trustees tax return HMRC say that this means the joint claim should accompany the trustees' tax return or else be sent to the trustees' tax office separately.

of his remaining lifetime allowance if he agrees leaving him with £7.5 million lifetime allowance to carry forward. However, he cannot agree that the trustees take only £1.5 million of his lifetime allowance.[49]

(2) Chris is also a partner in a firm of solicitors working one day a week. The trustees own the premises on which the law business is carried on and charge rent. Chris retires as partner in 2009 and in 2010 the trustees sell the premises. Entrepreneurs' relief is potentially available on the trustees' disposal if Chris agrees since the building is being used in a business carried on by the beneficiary. It does not matter that the property is let. By contrast if Chris had owned the property personally and let it to the partnership no relief would be available on the associated disposal. (Note that Chris could not transfer let land owned personally by him and used by the partnership to a trust claiming hold-relief if he was a beneficiary because the trust would be settlor-interested).

The £10 million limit is by reference to each qualifying beneficiary. So, one has to consider previous claims by the qualifying beneficiary in respect of his personal gains and previous claims in respect of other trust gains (associated with the same qualifying beneficiary) which are all taken into account. Hence, there is no advantage in holding shares in a company via different settlements with the same qualifying beneficiary because the £10 million limit remains the same. However, where trustees of the same settlement have different qualifying beneficiaries in relation to settled property there is no reason why the trustees cannot claim more than one unused lifetime allowance if each beneficiary agrees. **14.30**

Where two beneficiaries have interests in possession in settled property (whether shares or other business assets) but only one of them works in the business, entrepreneurs' relief cannot be claimed on the non-working beneficiary's proportion.[50] Of course, the inheritance tax changes in 2006 have facilitated tax planning in that it is possible to ensure that the trust is reorganised 12 months before a disposal so as to maximise the relief. **14.31**

Where there is more than one qualifying beneficiary (i.e. both work in the business and have five per cent each), s.169O operates to treat the trustees' gain as a number of separate smaller gains to which the £10 million cap in s.169N(4A) is then separately applied. **14.32**

For example, where a settlement has two qualifying beneficiaries, each entitled to half of all the income from the trust assets, and there was a qualifying disposal realising a gain of £8 million on July 2011 and all the conditions are met with respect to both beneficiaries (neither of whom has made a claim and both of whom are willing to let the trustees benefit from their unused allowance), the entire gain would be covered such that the trustees would pay tax at the rate of 10 per cent on the entire £8 million with each beneficiary having £6 million of unused allowance to carry forward.

[49] Note that if the trustees also own the building from which the company trades there is no entrepreneurs' relief on this building. The trustees do not qualify for relief on an associated disposal.

[50] See s.169(O). The level of relief that can be assigned to the trustees is restricted to the relevant proportion, i.e. the qualifying beneficiary's entitlement to share in the income during the material time. See s.169O(6), i.e. the latest period of one year ending in the three years before the date of the disposal of the trust asset in question.

EXAMPLE 14.8

(1) The White Trust has three equal interest in possession beneficiaries (A, B and C) each of whom works in the family trading company and owns five per cent if the shares in the company personally.[51] The Trust also owns a significant part of the shares in the company which is to be sold. Each beneficiary can assign his unused lifetime allowance on a disposal of the shares to the Trust so that the Trust may end up with £30 million (£10 million per beneficiary) of gains being sheltered.

(2) Facts as above but C is not a qualifying beneficiary. One third of the gain will not be eligible for relief. However, the trustees may have power to revoke his interest and appoint further interests in possession to A and B. After the shares are sold the "extra" interests in possession of A and B could be revoked and C resumes his interest again. This has no inheritance tax consequences. Make sure that all the interests in possession are revocable to maintain flexibility![52]

(3) Facts as above except that the trust is discretionary although all three of its principal beneficiaries work in the business and own five per cent of the shares personally. The trustees could appoint them revocable interests in possession a week prior to the disposal so as to enable the relief to be claimed.[53] This appointment has no inheritance tax consequences.

(4) Facts as above except that the trust is a discretionary trust and none of the working beneficiaries own five per cent personally although the trust's shareholding is 60 per cent. The trustees should advance five per cent of the shares to each beneficiary, appoint each of them a revocable interest in possession in the balance and ensure that each beneficiary is an officer or employee of the company. After 12 months relief will be available.

(5) The trust is discretionary and has three main beneficiaries but only one of them works in the company and owns five per cent of the shares. The Trust could appoint a revocable interest in possession in all the shares to that one beneficiary.

(6) The trust is interest in possession but the settled property comprises a house and shares (of similar value) to which two beneficiaries are jointly entitled. Only one of them is a qualifying beneficiary for entrepreneurs' relief purposes. The trustees might appropriate the trust assets so that the working beneficiary has an interest in possession in the shares and the non-working beneficiary an interest in possession in the house. If the interests in possession are qualifying pre-March 2006 interests for inheritance tax purposes some care is needed to ensure that the fund in which

---

[51] It does not matter whether the interests are "qualifying" for IHT purposes or not: i.e. they may all have come into existence after March 21, 2006.

[52] Of course if the beneficiary has a qualifying interest in possession (i.e. generally one that arose before March 22, 2006) then termination of that interest in possession will have inheritance tax consequences.

[53] HMRC consider that the interest in possession must subsist for at least one year prior to disposal but this view seems wrong on the wording of the legislation.

each beneficiary has an interest in possession remains of the same value. However, if the interests in possession are non-qualifying for inheritance tax purposes and are revocable the trustees could appoint the beneficiary an interest in possession in all the shares without having to worry about the inheritance tax position or whether each beneficiary has an interest in possession of equal value. Of course the type and amount of income taken by each beneficiary will change. There should be no SDLT charges if land and shares are swapped between sub-funds. See 51.12.

(7) The trust is interest in possession with 10 equal family beneficiaries and owns a farm which is let to the family farming partnership in which all beneficiaries are partners. The trustees sell all the land to a developer realising a gain of £50 million and the partnership ends. The beneficiaries all allow the trustees to use their relief. The entire gain suffers a 10 per cent tax rate.

Death of non-qualifying interest in possession beneficiary

Where a beneficiary with a non-qualifying interest in possession dies and **14.33** the trust ends there is then a deemed disposal for capital gains tax purposes. There is no uplift to market value in the trust property because he has a non-qualifying interest in possession.[54] In these circumstances HMRC accept that if the beneficiary met the qualifying conditions up to the date of death then an entrepreneurs' relief claim can be made provided that both the trustees and the personal representatives of the beneficiary join in making the claim.

Claiming the relief

As already noted, entrepreneurs' relief must be claimed by both the trustees **14.34** and the qualifying beneficiary.[55] The jointly signed paper claim will normally be submitted with the tax return for the tax year in which the gain arose, although where no tax return is issued, or the return has already been submitted, the claim may be made by letter to HMRC. It must be made by the first anniversary of January 31 following the tax year in which the gain arose. The claim may be withdrawn within the same period. A joint claim by trustees and beneficiary must also be made by both of them within the time limits.

EXAMPLE 14.9

Trustees sell shares in January 2009 (2008–9) and can qualify for entrepreneurs' relief. The trustees and the qualifying beneficiary must jointly elect to claim the relief on or before January 31, 2011.

---

[54] See TCGA 1992 s.73(2A). See Ch.12 for details of the deemed disposal and Ch.24 for the definition of non-qualifying interest, i.e. a post-March 21, 2006 interest.
[55] TCGA 1992 s.169M.

14.35 The authors do not consider that there is an addition to the settled property if the beneficiary elects with the trustees to claim the relief.[56] The trustees end up paying less tax but this is no different from a joint election for principal private residence relief which also has to be signed by trustees and beneficiary. Moreover the beneficiary is not "transferring" the relief under the terms of the legislation but merely making a joint election. Neither "property" nor value has been added by him.

Deferred consideration loan notes and share for share exchanges

14.36 The complicated interaction of deferred consideration transactions with entrepreneurs' relief is discussed further in Ch.17. Trustees are particularly disadvantaged in relation to QCBs.

IV OFFSHORE ISSUES

14.37 The HMRC Guidance on entrepreneurs' relief does not cover issues relating to remittance basis users or offshore trusts. It is understood that HMRC accepts that the relief can be claimed by remittance basis users and that the delay between the time when the gains arise and when the remittance is made is no bar on the claiming of relief provided a valid claim is made. It appears that the relief limit that applies with respect to remittance basis gains is that which is in force when the gains arise not when the gain is remitted.

Since June 23, 2010 when the four-ninths discount provisions were removed, it is not clear how the mixed fund rules operate for remittance basis users where foreign chargeable gains qualifying for relief are realised in excess of the entrepreneurs' relief limits then in force. For example, if a foreign chargeable gain of say £15 million is realised in 2011–12 does entrepreneurs' relief apply to the first £10 million remitted so that the 10 per cent rate applies to all of it with future remittances of gains over this limit taxed at 28 per cent or is a blended rate used? If the latter it may be better for the remittance basis user to opt for the arising basis of taxation in the year of disposal.

Another point is that by the time the gain is remitted the individual may be out of time for making an entrepreneurs' relief claim: TCGA 1992 s.169M requires an election for relief to be made before the first anniversary of January 31 following the tax year in which the disposal takes place. The remittance basis user should therefore make a protective claim in the event that he thinks it is possible that he may want to remit the gain later.

EXAMPLE 14.10

In August 2008 gains of £5 million are realised by X, a remittance basis user, on the disposal of a foreign situated business. The proceeds are kept

---

[56] So that the beneficiary does not become a settlor of the trust.

in an offshore bank account and remitted to the UK in August 2010. The £1 million lifetime limit in force in 2008–9 applies. Presumably 4/9 deduction applies to the gain rather than the special 10 per cent tax rate. If that is right, this would mean that the taxable portion of the gain will be taxed at 28 per cent (giving an effective 15.6 per cent tax rate on the £1 million gain benefiting from relief) with the £4 million excess being taxed at 28 per cent. The claim must be made by January 31 following the tax year in which the gain was realised.

It is believed that HMRC accept that relief could apply to TCGA 1992 s.86 gains **14.38** charged on the settlor of an offshore trust under the June 2010 rules it is unclear how s.86(4)(b) operates in relation to disposals after June 22, 2010 where the gain itself is no longer reduced by four-ninths and then taxed. This states:

> "*those gains should be treated as forming the highest part of the amount on which the settlor is chargeable to capital gains tax for the year*".

In these circumstances is the 10 per cent rate available or does s.86(4) take priority? Following the changes from June 23, 2010 the chargeable gain itself is no longer reduced. It is the tax rate that is reduced to 10 per cent. Similarly in relation to s.87 gains: the relief does not exempt the gains after June 22, 2010 it merely reduces the rate of tax. In these circumstances can the 10 per cent rate ever be available given that the pool of gains attributed to beneficiaries does not distinguish between gains on different types of assets and the gain is taxed on the beneficiary at his rates.[57]

Non-residence

Another issue relates to individuals who are temporarily non-resident but **14.38A** subject to UK CGT under TCGA 1992 s.10A, and who wish to make a claim for entrepreneurs' relief. For example, if a sale of shares eligible for entrepreneurs' relief takes place when the individual is non-UK resident but he returns within five years the gain is treated as accruing to the taxpayer in the year of return. However, the date of disposal for entrepreneurs' relief is at the time of the sale of the shares. TCGA 1992 s.169M requires an election for relief to be made before the first anniversary of January 31 following the tax year in which the disposal takes place and so the individual may find himself out of time in making the claim. He may need to make a protective claim.

V ENTREPRENEURS' RELIEF AND PERSONAL REPRESENTATIVES (PRS)

PRs are not entitled to entrepreneurs' relief. Normally it is not necessary because **14.39** there is an uplift to market value on death on all the deceased's property;

---

[57] The authors are grateful to Kevin Slevin for pointing out these anomalies in respect of ss.86 and 87.

including shares or business property owned by the deceased. However, if the administration of the estate is protracted and the business assets are retained by the PRs a gain may arise. In these circumstances they may wish to avoid selling the business assets or shares during the course of administration and instead vest them in a qualifying beneficiary.

EXAMPLE 14.11

> Ronald dies in 2010. The PRs wind up the estate by 2012 and at that point transfer a 100 per cent shareholding to the residuary beneficiary Mary, daughter of Ronald. Mary has never had any personal shareholding but worked in the business for many years and the shares show a substantial gain since 2010. She sells the shares three months later. Is she entitled to entrepreneurs' relief? Clearly she would be if she had owned five per cent of the shares herself for over one year. However in this case she has only owned shares for three months.
>
> The authors consider that she is entitled to relief since she is treated as owning the shares since the date of death for capital gains tax purposes.[58] Apparently HMRC do not accept this view and argue that she must already own five per cent personally if she is to obtain relief on the shares now being transferred to her or else own those transferred shares for a further 12 months.[59]

VI COMPARISON OF BUSINESS ASSETS TAPER RELIEF AND ENTREPRENEURS' RELIEF

14.40 Entrepreneurs' relief is more restrictive than the old business assets taper relief ("BATR"), particularly for trustees. HMRC apparently did not want the relief to be available to trustees, presumably on the basis that they are not entrepreneurs. These simple comparisons with business assets taper relief illustrate the key differences and remind trustees of what to watch for:

    (i) maximum taper relief resulted in an effective tax rate of 10 per cent on all gains for a higher rate taxpayer, five per cent for a basic rate taxpayer. Maximum entrepreneurs' relief results in an effective 10 per cent rate on the first £10 million of gains whether a higher or lower rate taxpayer;

    (ii) maximum non-business assets taper relief resulted in gains being taxed at 24 per cent for a higher rate taxpayer or trust. All gains other than those qualifying for entrepreneurs' relief are now taxed at 28 per cent for trusts whatever the period of ownership;

---

[58] See s.62(4) TCGA 1992.
[59] Schedule A1 para.4(5), in the context of business assets taper relief made provision for the legatees but this was for legatees who did not qualify for relief in their own right but where PRs could. This is not the position for entrepreneurs' relief where PRs can never qualify for relief.

(iii) taper relief required a two-year holding period for full BATR and a 10-year holding period for maximum non-business assets taper relief. Full entrepreneurs' relief is available after one year;

(iv) BATR was available without limit. Entrepreneurs' relief is subject to a £10 million lifetime maximum (albeit this is per qualifying beneficiary not per trust);

(v) the "trading company" and "holding company of a trading group" tests in entrepreneurs' relief are taken from the business taper relief legislation[60];

(vi) entrepreneurs' relief requires an individual to own at least five per cent of the ordinary share capital and at least five per cent of the voting rights must be exercisable by that individual by virtue of that holding, i.e the company has to be his personal company. This was only a requirement for BATR where the company was listed and the vendor was *not* an officer or shareholder. There was no minimum shareholding requirement for shareholders of unlisted companies after 2000 or for shareholders of listed companies where the shareholder was an employee;

(vii) entrepreneurs' relief generally requires a disposal of a business or part thereof where the business is unincorporated (or if no disposal then a cessation of the business). In this respect it is closer to retirement relief. BATR was available on a disposal of assets, whether or not part of the business was being disposed of;

(viii) entrepreneurs' relief requires the shareholder to be a director or employee of that company (and in the case of trusts is only available where the interest in possession beneficiary is a director or employee and owns five per cent in his own right). BATR did not require the beneficiary or shareholder to be a director or employee unless the company was listed and the shareholder owned less than five per cent;

(ix) neither entrepreneurs' relief nor BATR have any minimum age requirement or requirement to retire although associated disposals do require some withdrawal from participation in the business;

(x) discretionary trusts could claim BATR. Entrepreneurs' relief is not available to discretionary trusts whether or not the trustees themselves carry on the trade or own five per cent of the shares[61];

(xi) a trust was entitled in its own right to taper relief irrespective of any personal entitlement of the beneficiary. Trustees do not have their own £10 million entrepreneurs' relief allowance. Each interest in possession beneficiary has to agree to assign to the trustees all or part of his unused lifetime entrepreneurs' relief allowance by entering into a joint election;

(xii) entrepreneurs' relief must be claimed. Taper relief was given automatically;

---

[60] TCGA 1992 Sch.A1.
[61] The trustees should therefore consider appointing an interest in possession to an appropriate beneficiary: see Example 14.8(3).

(xiii) entrepreneurs' relief is available only on shares in trading companies or disposals of trading businesses. An individual shareholder or trustee of a *non-trading* company could qualify for BATR where the individual or eligible beneficiary was an officer or employee of the company and the individual or trust did not have a material interest in the company[62];

(xiv) it was possible to obtain BATR on disposals of let land used in a third party's business. It is not possible to claim entrepreneurs' relief on let land owned by an individual even if used by a partnership or company of which the individual is a member. However, there is apparently nothing to stop trusts letting land to a qualifying beneficiary for use in his business or partnership. This is still a disposal of a trust business asset rather than an associated disposal. By contrast, a trust cannot claim entrepreneurs' relief on the disposal of land used in the qualifying beneficiary's personal company whether or not rent is charged. This is not a trust business asset and the rules for associated disposals do not apply to trusts. The rules on deferred consideration are more complex.[63]

---

[62] "Material interest" was defined as more than 10% of voting rights, the right to receive dividends, issued shares of any class or the right to receive assets in a winding up: see FA 2001 s.78 retrospectively applied to periods after April 5, 2000.
[63] See Ch.17.

CHAPTER 15

INCORPORATION RELIEF

- Basic principles **(15.01)**
- Tax planning opportunities **(15.05)**
- Election to disapply relief **(15.08)**
- Interaction with other reliefs **(15.11)**

I BASIC PRINCIPLES[1]

As with roll-over relief,[2] this relief is a postponement of, rather than an exemption from, capital gains tax. It applies when there is a disposal of an unincorporated business *as a going concern* by an individual sole trader, partnership or trust to a company and that disposal is wholly or partly in return for an issue of shares in that company. There is no requirement for the business to continue as a going concern for a particular period after the transfer.[3]   **15.01**

Gains made on the disposal of chargeable business assets will be deducted from the value of the shares received (the gain is rolled into the shares) and the relevant business assets are acquired by the company at market value. Note that "business" has a wider meaning than "trade" and may include the trade of managing a landed estate[4], the commercial letting of furnished holiday accommodation or managing a portfolio of investment properties. There appears to be no restriction on incorporating a UK business into a foreign incorporated company; this may be relevant for remittance basis users who   **15.02**

---

[1] See TCGA 1992 s.162.
[2] Discussed in Ch.13.
[3] See *IRC v Gordon* below.
[4] See CG 65712. But note that the transfer of a single let property to a company would probably be insufficient. See *American Leaf Blending Co v Director-General of Inland Revenue* [1978] STC 561 where Lord Diplock noted:

> "*in the case of a private individual it may well be that the mere receipt of rents from property that he owns raises no presumption that he is carrying on a business. In contrast . . . in the case of a company incorporated for the purpose of making profits for its shareholders any gainful use to which it puts any of its assets prima facie amounts to the carrying on of a business.*"

The word "business" may be interpreted differently as between individuals and companies.

wish to recite the asset for tax planning reasons, e.g. they want to settle foreign situated assets into trust with a view to IHT saving.[5]

Conditions for the relief to apply

15.03 First, the business must be transferred as a going concern; a mere transfer of assets does not qualify.[6] Second, a transfer of all the assets of the business excluding only cash[7] but including goodwill[8] must occur.[9] Relief will not be available if the owner wishes to keep any business assets such as land and buildings out the company for SDLT or commercial reasons.[10] If only part of the total consideration given by the company is in shares and the rest is in cash or loan notes relief is restricted. However, the assumption of liabilities of the business by the company is not treated as additional consideration for this purpose.[11] Third, the transfer must be made wholly or partly in exchange for shares. Fourth, the shares must be issued by the company to the transferor. So relief will be lost or restricted where shares are also issued to the transferor's spouse or children.[12]

EXAMPLE 15.1

> Chris transferred his business to a company in 2010. The gain arising on the assets was £50,000 and the consideration comprised £80,000 in shares and £20,000 in cash. Chris sold the shares in 2012 for £120,000. 80 per cent of the gain can be held over as calculated below.

[5] Note, the effect of TCGA 1992 ss.13 and 14A that charges CGT on disposals of UK assets owned by foreign incorporated companies. In order to avoid s.14A applying the shares would then have to be settled into trust by a foreign domiciled person: see Ch.19. There is no CGT charge on the trustees or the foreign domiciled settlor if the foreign incorporated company then sells the UK assets. The CGT charge is based on whether a beneficiary has received capital payments from the trust.

[6] HMRC refer in CGT Manual at 65715 and following to an Australian case *Reference under the Electricity Commission (Balmain Electric Light Co Purchase) Act 1950*. In *Gordon* it was described as meaning that "*its doors are open for business*".

[7] Usually the capital account of the business owner or partner is withdrawn before incorporation to ensure no tax on withdrawal rather than it being locked up in the company where subsequent withdrawals by way of dividend will be taxable on a higher rate or additional rate taxpayer.

[8] Valuation of goodwill may in itself create problems beyond the scope of this book. See *Balloon Promotions Ltd v HMRC* [2006] STC (SCD) 167.

[9] If land is transferred to the company in consideration of the issue of shares watch SDLT: see 51.17. The SDLT charge is based on the market value of the land. This may be a reason to keep the land out of the company.

[10] If the land is to be kept out of the company and simply used by the company then only 50 per cent BPR will be available. However, there are often commercial reasons to keep the business premises out of the company. If rent is charged no entrepreneurs' relief is available. One way of preserving incorporation relief would be to first create a lease out of the freehold property (e.g. transfer freehold property into joint ownership with the spouse and then the couple grant a lease to the business owner). On incorporation the lease rather than the freehold is assigned to the company and the freehold reversion retained by the individuals.

[11] See ESC D 32. This is presumably regarded as an interpretation rather than a concession since it has not been replaced by legislation.

[12] For hold-over relief on gifts to companies: see Ch.18.

Gain held over in 2010 is £50,000 × £80,000/(80,000 + 20,000) = £40,000

Gain in 2012: Proceeds £120,000. Cost £80,000 less gain held over (£40,000) = £40,000

Gain ignoring any entrepreneurs' relief = £80,000[13]

15.04 The rules for trustees apply in the same way as for individuals, i.e. where there is a disposal of an unincorporated business as a going concern by trustees and that disposal is wholly or partly in return for shares in that company, the gain may be rolled-over into the shares. The gain arising on the transfer of assets is deducted from the value of the shares received in the company. The relief will be less commonly used by trustees who rarely trade as an unincorporated business (and as already noted, the relief is not available on a mere transfer of assets). However, it can be used successfully by individuals in conjunction with trusts in order to maximise inheritance tax planning opportunities particularly where the donor may not survive seven years.[14]

II TAX PLANNING OPPORTUNITIES

15.05 The relief is useful where a business is to be sold by an individual or trust to a purchaser, the assets stand at a large gain and the purchaser refuses to buy shares. If the trustees first incorporate the business as a going concern the company can then sell the trade and assets at market value and no capital gains tax charge arises until the shares are sold.[15] This arrangement does not work if the trustees had ceased to run the business as a going concern before incorporation and were simply selling off assets.

15.06 Another advantage of this arrangement is that the business can be incorporated by an individual as a trading company, the company shares then given into trust with the benefit of BPR[16] and then the company can sell the trading assets and reinvest the proceeds in an investment business without any claw back of relief.

EXAMPLE 15.2

Henry is elderly and farms land with substantial development value. He wishes to give this away before he stops farming. He incorporates the farming business as a going concern[17] becoming a director of the

---

[13] For the interaction with entrepreneurs' relief, see 15.11.

[14] See Example 15.2 below.

[15] See *Gordon v IRC* [1991] STC 174. The Special Commissioner decided that the business had not been sold as a going concern because its end (namely the sale of assets) was "*too clearly and too closely in sight*" but the taxpayer's appeal against this decision was allowed on the basis that (a) the only point of time at which to test whether a business is being transferred as a going concern is the time of transfer (b) the business had continued uninterruptedly beyond that point and (c) the existence of a planned sale of assets was not inconsistent with the continuation of the trade.

[16] Note the replacement rules in IHTA 1984 s.107(3).

[17] He would not claim entrepreneurs' relief: incorporation relief takes priority and is

company and then after one year he gives the shares to a trust for his children with business property relief (for IHT purposes)[18] and entrepreneurs' relief (for CGT purposes) on the shares under TCGA 1992 s.169M.[19] After farming it for six months the company sells the land and invests the cash in let property. The land had been rebased to market value on incorporation so any gain is likely to be small. If Henry died within seven years, there would be no claw back of relief provided that the original shares are retained by the trustees.[20]

15.07 Incorporation is sometimes used as a way of sheltering gains accruing on the disposal of an unincorporated UK business prior to migration. The business is transferred to a company claiming s.162 relief and since the shares are not a business these can be sold after migration without a branch or agency charge under TCGA 1992 s.10. As noted above, it is also possible for a foreign domiciliary to resite the business by transferring it to a foreign incorporated (whether UK resident or non-resident) company with incorporation relief. He could also (if not yet UK deemed domiciled) then settle the foreign situated shares into trust to obtain IHT and CGT savings.

III ELECTION TO DISAPPLY RELIEF

15.08 Section 162A allows the taxpayer to elect that s.162 (which is otherwise automatic if the conditions are satisfied) is disapplied. This section was intended to benefit those taxpayers whose shares acquired on incorporation were not held long enough to attract the maximum level of business assets taper relief. As incorporation relief was applied before taper relief, it was sometimes beneficial not to claim incorporation relief if the company was to be sold shortly after incorporation.

15.09 Section 162A has not been repealed despite the abolition of taper relief; a taxpayer will wish to disapply incorporation relief in the following circumstances:

(a) the incorporation occurred before April 6, 2008 and the sale of shares took place soon after— there is no business assets taper relief on the sale of the shares; entrepreneurs' relief is not available if the shares have not been owned a year and was of limited value before June 23, 2010;

(b) the taxpayer did not carry on a trade and the incorporation of the investment business took place between April 6, 2008 and June 23, 2010 with a sale of shares occurring soon after that date. It will generally be better

---

preferable because it rebases the assets without using up his lifetime allowance. See Ch.14 for entrepreneurs' relief. If all the gain is rolled-over into the shares no chargeable gain arises against which entrepreneurs' relief would be given.

[18] IHTA 1984 s.107 allows IHT relief even though the company shares have not been owned for two years provided that the business had been carried on for the required period.

[19] For entrepreneurs' relief the shares would need to be owned for one year before a claim can be made. Otherwise he would need to claim hold-over relief under s.260 TCGA 1992. Since Henry is elderly he is unlikely to use his lifetime allowance (currently £10 million) on other disposals. However he may not want to wait a year before making the gift.

[20] See IHTA 1984 s.113A(3)(b).

to make a s.162A election because no entrepreneurs' relief is available on a disposal of the shares but the gain on incorporation would only be taxed at 18 per cent or on the subsequent sale of the shares after June 22, 2010 at 28 per cent. If an election is made to disapply incorporation relief the gain is no longer rolled into the shares which have a higher base cost;

(c) the taxpayer carries on a trade that he incorporates but the shares are subsequently sold within a year. In that case no entrepreneurs' relief is available on the shares which have not been owned for a year. It is better to claim it on the incorporation so that the shares have a high base cost but this will only be possible if an election is made to disapply incorporation relief: see Example 15.3.

The time limits for making the necessary s.162A election are as follows: **15.10**

(1) the second anniversary of January 31 next following the tax year in which the incorporation took place. So if the business is incorporated in 2010–11, the election must be made by January 2014; but

(2) if the shares acquired at the time of the incorporation have all been disposed of by the end of the tax year following that in which the transfer of the business took place, the election must be made no later than the first anniversary of the January 31 next following the tax year in which that transfer took place. So if incorporation took place in 2010–11 and the shares were sold or given away in 2011–12, the election must be made by January 31, 2013 (i.e. within the normal time limits for amending a self-assessment return).

EXAMPLE 15.3

(1) Emma runs a shop which she purchased for £500,000 in 2003. In March 2007, she incorporates her business (value then was £1.5 million) in consideration of the issue of shares in S Ltd. S Ltd is then sold in March 2009 for £2 million. If she does not elect to disapply incorporation relief, in March 2009 she will obtain entrepreneurs' relief on £1 million gain and pay 18 per cent on the balance of £500,000 gain. Total tax bill = £190,000.

If she makes a s.162A election then she obtains full business assets taper relief in 2007 on £1 million gain (£100,000 tax) and can claim entrepreneurs' relief on the £500,000 gain in March 2009 (£50,000 tax). Total tax is therefore £150,000. She will need to make the s.162A election by January 31, 2010.

She must claim entrepreneurs' relief by January 31, 2011 (on or before the first anniversary of January 31 following the tax year in which the disposal for which relief is sought is made.).

(2) John owns a significant portfolio of investment properties. In 2009 he incorporates the business despite the SDLT cost. His CGT rate (without incorporation relief) would have been 18 per cent. In 2011 he sells

the company shares unexpectedly in order to raise funds for another business venture. His rate of tax on the shares is then 28 per cent. No entrepreneurs' relief is available on the disposal of the shares given it is an investment company. Although John might have kept the shares and the company sold the properties without a tax charge (since the properties were acquired by the company at market value in 2009) he would then have had to extract cash from the company and at that point either income tax or CGT charges would have arisen, depending on the method chosen. It is therefore better that he elects to disapply incorporation relief. The acquisition cost of his shares will then not be reduced by the rolled over gain.

(3) Chris incorporates his trading business but sells the shares shortly afterwards. No entrepreneurs' relief is due. It is better that he claims the relief on incorporation so that the base cost of the shares is uplifted.

IV INTERACTION WITH OTHER RELIEFS

15.11 HMRC guidance states that incorporation relief is automatic if the conditions apply and an election to disapply the relief has not been made.[21] There is, however, some uncertainty in respect to the order of priority between entrepreneurs' relief and incorporation relief before June 23, 2010. HMRC's view (not explicit in CGTM64135-147) is that incorporation relief takes precedence over entrepreneurs' relief on the disposal of a business: i.e. that entrepreneurs' relief is only available on any part of a gain that remains after any roll-over has been made.

15.12 So if in Example 15.3(1) Emma incorporated the business in March 2009, she cannot on HMRC's view claim entrepreneurs' relief first and then incorporation relief on the balance of the chargeable gain. If she does not elect to disapply incorporation relief there is no entrepreneurs' relief.[22] If she claims entrepreneurs' relief and disapplies incorporation relief the value of the shares is uplifted but there may be no benefit if the company sells the assets at a substantial gain and everything is extracted by way of dividend rather than liquidation. She will have used up her lifetime allowance for nothing. However, some practitioners considered that before June 23, 2010 entrepreneurs' relief could be claimed even if an election to disapply incorporation relief had not been made: the chargeable gain was first reduced by four ninths (entrepreneurs relief) and then the reduced gain was subject to incorporation relief.[23]

15.13 Certainly, from June 23, 2010 entrepreneurs' relief no longer reduces the assessable gain but instead provides for the chargeable gain to be taxed at the reduced rate of 10 per cent, i.e. entrepreneurs' relief is not applied to reduce the chargeable gain arising. If an incorporation occurs and some gain is left assessable (e.g. because not all the consideration is in the form of shares with some being given in cash or loan notes) the taxpayer can claim entrepreneurs' relief only on that part of the gain and therefore apply the 10 per cent rate

---

[21] The priority of reliefs generally is discussed in Ch.17.
[22] See s.169N(1) and (4).
[23] See McKie in PCB (2009) at p.20 for a statement of the contrary view.

to the extent it falls within his lifetime allowance. Entrepreneurs' relief is not given first with incorporation relief claimed on the balance.

In considering whether to use incorporation relief to defer the gain or disapply incorporation relief and claim entrepreneurs' relief to reduce tax on the gain one should consider:
15.14

- Whether the company shares are likely to be sold in the future and if so whether they will then qualify for entrepreneurs' relief. For example a trust may not be able to claim entrepreneurs' relief if there is no qualifying beneficiary at that time. Equally company shares owned by an individual may be held until his death in which case there will be the usual death uplift to market value.

- Is the tax payable now using entrepreneurs' relief likely to be less than the tax payable in the future on the deferred gain? For instance, CGT rates may increase whilst the conditions for entrepreneurs' relief may in the future become more onerous.

- Are there any sales of other businesses likely in the future where the individual may need to use his lifetime allowance given by entrepreneurs' relief?

CHAPTER 16

ENTERPRISE INVESTMENT SCHEME (EIS) DEFERRAL RELIEF[1]

- The scope of the relief (**16.01**)
- Qualifying conditions (**16.10**)
- EIS relief and trusts (**16.14**)
- Transitional provisions—interaction with entrepreneurs' relief (**16.18**)

I THE SCOPE OF THE RELIEF

16.01   The enterprise investment scheme (EIS) replaced the business expansion scheme (BES) on January 1, 1994. It is part of a long history of successive governments trying to encourage investment in small companies by offering a range of income and capital gains tax reliefs, to individual investors who subscribe for shares.[2] They are always introduced with great fanfare. Take, for instance, in 1983 Geoffrey Howe announcing the introduction of BES:

> *"These proposals will transform the position of unquoted trading companies seeking outside equity. It is a further move towards removing the bias in the tax system against the personal shareholder and a further measure to encourage wider share ownership. By concentrating help on those companies which do not have ready access to outside capital the scheme will assist many more small or medium companies to realise their undoubted potential for growth."*

16.02   The Coalition Government has published a consultation document which looks at the EIS and venture capital trust schemes and sets out a number of reform options aimed at improving their effectiveness as well as offering a new scheme aimed at seed investment: the Business Angel Seed Investment Scheme (BASIS). Over the years, all the schemes have been dogged by a prolifera-

---

[1] TCGA 1992 Sch.5B and see paras 17 and 18 for trustees.
[2] In 1981 the Conservative Government launched the business Start-Up Scheme that then became the new Business Expansion Scheme. BES was withdrawn in 1993 and replaced by the Enterprise Investment Scheme. At the time of writing in July 2011 the Coalition Government has published a consultation paper with the aim of considering a new relief to run along-side Venture Capital Trusts and Enterprise Investment Schemes–the Business Angel Seed Investment Scheme (BASIS). EIS is designed to address the equity gap that has been found to exist between £250,000 and £2 million where SMEs find it hard to access capital.

tion of complex rules, rigidly applied by HMRC to disallow investor's relief. Without a change in attitude by HMRC in applying the rules purposively where genuine investment in qualifying businesses is being made, it is difficult to see that these further initiatives will achieve much.

Tax relief on EIS schemes takes three forms: **16.03**

(i) relief from income tax if the shares are held for three years from the date they were issued or from when the qualifying trade started (if later). Until April 6, 2011 the income tax relief was 20 per cent (now 30 per cent) of the cost of the shares to be set against the individual's income tax liability for the tax year in which the investment was made. The relief can be claimed up to a maximum investment of £500,000, giving maximum tax relief in any one year of £100,000 (to April 5, 2011) now increased to £150,000. However, the relief cannot be set-off against dividend income. From April 6, 2012 the maximum investment will be increased to £1 million. The EU Commission has confirmed that this does not breach state aid rules and therefore the maximum income tax relief will increase to £300,000;

(ii) exemption from CGT on future gains realised on a disposal of the shares in the EIS company if the individual has received income tax relief on the cost of the shares. The shares must be held for three years from the date of issue or the date the trade began (if later). The exemption does not extend to exempt any gains deferred on the original investment; and

(iii) deferment of a charge to CGT on the disposal of any asset where the proceeds are invested in shares of an EIS company.

Only the last relief, deferral relief, is relevant to trustees. They are not eligible **16.04** for income tax relief or CGT exemption and can only claim EIS deferral relief on subscriptions made after April 5, 1998.[3] EIS CGT deferral relief allows UK resident trustees and individuals to shelter gains from the disposal of *any asset* by reinvestment of the *gain* (not the whole sale proceeds) in a qualifying EIS company. There is no minimum period for which the shares must be held: the deferred gain is brought back into charge whenever the shares are disposed of or deemed to be disposed of under the EIS legislation.

This deferral relief is without limit except that from July 19, 2007 the total **16.05** amount that can be raised by a company using EIS relief is £2 million in any 12 month period and the company must not breach the gross assets test (set out in 16.11 below) nor (before April 2012) have more than 50 full-time employees. (If the limit is exceeded, none of the shares issued qualify for EIS deferral relief.) From April 6, 2012 both the gross assets and employee tests are increased as set out at 16.11(d). In addition the annual investment limit for qualifying companies will be increased from £2 million to £10 million. Unlike income tax relief, it does not matter if the investor is connected with the company.[4]

The trustees must within one year before or three years after the original **16.06** disposal upon which the gain has arisen, make the qualifying investment. It

---

[3] Although, they could claim reinvestment relief which was then replaced by EIS deferral relief.
[4] If income tax relief is being claimed the investor must not possess more than 30% of the capital or voting power of the company or be a director except in limited circumstances.

does not matter that the gain being reinvested was from the disposal of a non-business asset. Any gains can be deferred. If part of the gain is reinvested, deferral relief is given on that proportion of the gain.[5] The balance of any gain not reinvested will be chargeable and therefore before April 6, 2008 would have qualified for taper relief. It can qualify for any available annual CGT exemption. The interaction with entrepreneurs' relief is more complex and is explained at 16.18 and following.

Computation of the relief

16.07 The gain that was relieved on disposals before April 6, 2008 was calculated after indexation and retirement relief (the latter only on disposals before April 6, 2003) but before reduction by taper relief. Unlike roll-over relief that reduces the acquisition cost of the new asset, a deferred gain under EIS relief is simply held in suspense and then brought into charge on the occasion of a subsequent chargeable event e.g. the sale of the EIS shares. Before April 2008 no further taper relief was given for the period of deferral.

EXAMPLE 16.1

> In 2004 Giles realised a gain of £100,000 from the disposal of a picture. It is eligible for taper relief but he wanted to avoid paying any CGT. He therefore reinvested the gain in an EIS company. The shares were then sold in March 2008. The £100,000 deferred gain is brought back into charge and he will be able to claim only the same level of taper relief that he would have obtained in 2004.[6]

16.08 UK resident trustees can qualify for EIS deferral relief provided that (broadly) all the beneficiaries are either individuals or charities both at the time the original gain is realised and at the time the trust subscribes for the shares in the qualifying company.[7] As already noted trustees may only claim deferral relief; they cannot claim income tax relief on the reinvestment or capital gains tax exemption on the ultimate disposal of the shares in respect of gains accruing during the period of the EIS investment.

Claims

16.09 The relief can be claimed only after the shares are issued and after the qualifying company sends the investor a form EIS3. The investor must submit Pt 2 of the EIS 3 form with the deferral claim; he can do this on the tax return or

---

[5] It is not necessary to reinvest the actual proceeds of sale derived from the original asset that was sold at a gain.
[6] For the position where EIS shares are sold after April 5, 2008: see 16.18 and following.
[7] See TCGA 1992 s.150C and Sch.5B as inserted by the FA 1995 and as amended. See 16.10 and following.

separately. Claims to relief can be made up to five years after the first January 31 following the tax year in which the investment was made. The deferral relief shares must be issued in the period beginning 12 months before and ending three years after the accrual of the gain on which relief is claimed although HMRC has powers to extend these time limits.[8]

II QUALIFYING CONDITIONS

The rules for EIS deferral relief are complex and it is easy to lose the relief. **16.10** HMRC operate an informal clearance procedure but only in relation to whether the company is a qualifying company, not in relation to whether the other conditions for the relief are satisfied.[9]

A qualifying investment is made when the following conditions are satisfied: **16.11**

(a) the trustees or individual are UK resident. No claim is allowed if the investor is also treated as resident in another country by virtue of double taxation treaty and would not be liable to CGT if the EIS shares were sold at a gain immediately after they were issued;

(b) the investor must subscribe wholly in cash for fully paid-up ordinary non-preferential shares.[10] This can be difficult if the investor does not have full control over the precise timing of the payment and issue of shares. Sometimes the investment goes in before the actual issue of shares on an informal basis. HMRC have in the past regarded this as a loan and no relief is due unless clearly documented as an advance payment for shares. An undertaking to pay cash at a future date will not result in the shares being fully paid. Until the later of three years after the date the shares were issued or three years after the start of the trade such shares must not carry any present or future preferential rights. After that they may do so but arrangements must not be in place for this to occur;

---

[8] In *R (on the application of Devine) v CIR* [2003] QB; 75 TC 679 the taxpayer applied for judicial review over the Revenue's refusal to extend the three-year time limit for reinvestment in the EIS. Moses J. reviewed the evidence and refused the application.

[9] Applications are made to the Small Company Enterprise Centre, 1st Floor Ferrers House, Castle Meadow Road, Nottingham, NG2 1BB.

[10] In the *Blackburn* case [2008] it was held that money informally put into a company with a general intention that it was for shares could be treated as qualifying subscription for shares. A company was incorporated in 1998 to operate a sports club. It made several issues of shares to its controlling director (B). He claimed EIS deferral relief in respect of these shares. The Revenue rejected the claim on the basis that some of the shares were not issued in order to raise money for the purpose of a qualifying business activity, as required by TCGA 1992 Sch.5B para.1(2), and that the other shares failed to qualify because they were caught by the "value received" provisions of TCGA 1992 Sch.5B para.13. The Special Commissioner allowed the appeals in relation to 450,000 of the shares. The Court of Appeal held that a further 590,000 shares qualified for relief, but that the initial allotment of 149,998 shares failed to qualify, since that share issue failed to meet the requirements of TCGA 1992 Sch.5B para.1(2)(f). *HMRC v Blackburn* (and related appeal) [2009] STC 188; [2008] EWCA Civ 1454. Contrast the decision in *Domain Dynamics (Holdings) Ltd v HMRC* [2008] STC (SCD) 1136. The July 2011 Consultation document proposes a period of grace for payment for shares. In F (No.3)A 2010, changes were made to the definition of eligible shares for the purpose of VCT investment, relaxing the restrictions on preferential rights to income and assets. The Government proposes replicating that definition for EIS from 2012.

(c) the company must be a qualifying company as defined in the EIS income tax relief legislation in relation to these shares. So the company issuing the shares (or subsidiaries) must carry on a qualifying trade or research and development. Property development, farming, market gardening, forestry and timber production as well hotel-keeping and the management of nursing or residential care homes, accountancy or legal services, insurance and money lending are excluded trades and a company whose activities comprises more than 20 per cent of these excluded activities cannot qualify for relief. From April 2012 the list of excluded activities will be extended to exclude feed-in tariffs, i.e. businesses in substantial receipt of subsidies to provide a reliable source of income from the generation of electricity.[11] The giving of financial advice is not an excluded trade. A qualifying company can include an AIM listed company or a company on the PLUS Quoted and PLUS Traded Markets but not a listed company. It must not be under the control of or be a 51 per cent subsidiary of another company.[12]

There is no requirement that the qualifying company must be resident in the UK but for shares issued on or after April 6, 2011 the company must have a permanent establishment in the UK and the trade no longer has to be carried on wholly or mainly in the UK;

(d) the gross assets test must be satisfied. The company's gross assets between April 5, 2006 and April 6, 2012 must be no more than £7 million before issue and £8 million after the issue of shares.[13] It must have fewer than 50 full-time employees at the time the shares are issued. From April 6, 2012 the gross assets test becomes £15 million before investment (as it was before April 6, 2006) and the company can have up to 250 employees. Until April 6, 2012 no more than £2 million may be raised by the company in any 12 month period from the scheme;

(e) the money raised by the issue must be used in a qualifying business activity.[14] Broadly for shares issued before April 22, 2009 at least 80 per cent of the money raised must have been used for the purposes of the qualifying business activity within one year of the issue and the remainder within the following year. For shares issued after that date the money raised must be employed wholly (disregarding insignificant amounts) for that purpose by the end of the two years following the issue. The money raised must be used for activities carried on by the holding company or any qualifying 90 per cent subsidiary (or a 90 per cent subsidiary of a 100 per cent subsidiary or a 100 per cent subsidiary of a 90 per cent subsidiary of the parent company);

---

[11] Community interest companies; co-operative societies and trades generating electricity by hydro power or anaerobic digestion will continue to qualify. Solar and wind generation will be excluded unless carried on by the above "community type" entities.

[12] The conditions for whether a company is qualifying are complex: see ITA 2007 ss.187–191 for details.

[13] The limit was lowered from £15 million before and £16 million after the issue with effect from April 6, 2006.

[14] Only the shares that are issued to investors who claim EIS income tax or deferral relief have to be issued to raise money for the purposes of a qualifying business activity. Other shares in the same share issue need not be issued to raise money for that activity.

(f) anti-avoidance rules must not be breached. In particular, relief will be denied or clawed back if arrangements exist for a pre-arranged exit or the investor or his associate *"receives value"*.[15] This is widely defined and can include simply putting in the cash before the share documentation has been competed! In addition, relief is denied if in the period beginning two years prior to the issue of the shares or (if later) with the formation of the company and three years after the share issue ("the relevant period"), a loan-linked investment to the investor or his associate has been made. Loan-linked investments are widely defined (para.15) to include a loan which would not have been made in the relevant period if the individual had not subscribed for the shares. So an arm's length loan from banks is caught if the security includes the shares or the terms of the loan are influenced by the acquisition.

Chargeable events

On the occurrence of a chargeable event the deferred gain is brought back into charge. A chargeable event will arise if: **16.12**

(a) there is a disposal of the EIS shares by the trustees.[16] If only some of the shares are disposed of then only a proportionate part of the gain becomes chargeable;

(b) there is a deemed disposal of the EIS investment, e.g. when a beneficiary becomes absolutely entitled;

(c) the trustees become non-UK resident before the expiry of three years from the later of the date the trade commenced or the shares were issued;

(d) "value" is received from the EIS investment in the "period of restriction", namely one year prior to the issue of the shares and three years after the shares are issued or if later, when the trade commenced;

(e) the shares cease to be eligible shares. This could occur if, for example, the investor is later granted a put option over the shares or receives value from the company during the relevant period (generally ending three years from issue of shares).

Receiving value

An investor is treated as "receiving value" if certain events occur in the period of restriction.[17] These include: **16.13**

---

[15] See 16.13.
[16] Or by the individual unless the individual is transferring shares to his spouse or civil partner on a no gain no loss basis.
[17] Sch.5B para.13.

(a) if shares are bought back;

(b) the company repays a debt owed to the investor pursuant to arrangements connected with the share issue; see *Inwards v Williamson*[18] where relief was not denied but contrast *Optus v HMRC*[19] where the conversion of loan notes into shares was a return of value within para.13(2)(b). See also *Segesta Ltd v HMRC*[20] where a football club in financial difficulties issued shares to a controlling shareholder; deferral relief was denied on the basis that the subscription for further shares had simply been used to repay earlier loans from the shareholder.

(c) the company lends to the investor unless the loan is repaid in full before the share issue[21];

(d) the company provides a benefit to the investor or disposes of an asset to the investor for less than market value or acquires an asset from the investor for above market value or makes a payment to the investor (unless it is reasonable remuneration for acting as an employee, or a commercial rent or commercial interest on a debt).

III EIS RELIEF AND TRUSTS

16.14   Interest in possession trusts[22] are eligible to claim deferral relief; but note that this does not include an interest in possession for a fixed term.[23] All the beneficiaries must be individuals or charities. If some of the beneficiaries are not individuals or charities then only the relevant proportion of the gain may qualify for relief. If a trust was interest in possession at the date of disposal of the original asset (within the specific meaning of the legislation so excluding fixed term interests) but discretionary at the date of the EIS investment (or vice versa) then no relief is due.

---

[18] [2003] STC (SCD) 355.

[19] [2006] STC (SCD) 687.

[20] [2010] UK FTT 235 (TC).

[21] When an investor pays money into an EIS company there must be full paperwork. In particular, to make it clear that the payment of the money into the company is by way of share subscription and is in relation to an issue of shares and for no other reason, and that no debt is to be created. There will be value received where a company "*repays, in pursuance of any arrangements for or in connection with the acquisition of the shares, any debt owed to the individual other than a debt which was incurred by the company on or after the date of issue of the shares.*" Previously the legislation said "*on or after the date on which he subscribed for the shares*". So there must be some form of contract in place before the issue, since if money is simply paid to a company and there is not the appropriate evidence that it was not intended to be a loan then there is a risk that this will produce a debt and hence a return of value problem when the shares are issued.

[22] Whether qualifying, or non-qualifying interests in possession.

[23] See entrepreneurs' relief where a similar condition applies. The obsession with fixed terms is an odd one. If the beneficiary has an interest in possession for five months, that is a fixed term. If he has an interest in possession which is terminable by exercise of the trustees' overriding powers of appointment and they exercise such powers at the end of the fifth month that is not a fixed term interest in possession. It does not matter whether the interest is an IHT "qualifying" interest or not.

EXAMPLE 16.2

In January 2008 the trustees of the Risky Trust (a non-settlor-interested discretionary trust) realised a gain (before taper) of £100,000 from the sale of investments. This qualified for the maximum non-business assets taper relief so the chargeable gain was £60,000. The trustees did not want to pay capital gains tax so decided to reinvest £60,000 in a recruitment agency company which had been established by the settlor some years earlier and wished to expand. The company issues new ordinary fully paid up shares to the trustees in consideration for the £60,000. The trustees still have to pay tax on £40,000 gain which would have received taper relief. If the trustees wanted to avoid paying any capital gains tax the whole pre-tapered gain of £100,000 had to be reinvested. Note that no relief was available if the trustees had previously invested in the company (or its subsidiaries), claimed EIS relief and then realised part of their earlier investment. Nor is relief available if the loan-linked rules or the rules preventing value being received are breached. (For example, the trustees lend to the company and are repaid in the year prior to the issue of shares.) However, it does not matter if the settlor or a beneficiary receives remuneration from the company provided that it is reasonable for the work done. If not reasonable then all relief is forfeited.

It would not matter if the trustees owned 100 per cent of the share capital or only 1 per cent. There is no minimum or maximum percentage limit. Nor does it matter if the trustees already own (say) 40 per cent of the company and then make a further share subscription provided that neither they nor any beneficiary or associate had received value within the previous year.

16.15 The rules on value received by the trustees and loan-linked investments apply if the trustees, any beneficiary or any associate of the beneficiary receives value or a loan-linked investment.[24] Associates include spouses, parents, children and trusts.

EXAMPLE 16.3

Facts as in Example 16.2 above except that money was lent to the company by the trustees, a beneficiary or the settlor and the company repays it during the period of restriction. EIS relief is refused or clawed back.

16.16 A problematic area is what happens on the death of an interest in possession beneficiary. If an individual investor dies then TCGA 1992 Sch.5B para.3(5) provides that despite the deemed acquisition arising on death the deferred gains are not brought back into charge. Nor is the deferred

---

[24] Schedule 5B para.18. Value is also received if a director's account becomes overdrawn and he is an investor or connected to the investor, e.g. a beneficiary.

gain revived if there is a subsequent sale by the executors so in effect death wipes out the deferred gain. However, para.3(5) does not apply on the death of a beneficiary with a qualifying interest in possession with the result that there is a chargeable event and the gain appears to come back into charge.

16.17   The following examples from HMRC Manual[25] illustrate some practical problems for trustees.

EXAMPLE 16.4

(a) The trust fund is held on bereaved minor trusts for the benefit of A, B and C. Each of them will become absolutely entitled to one third of the settled property on reaching age 18. If any of the beneficiaries dies before age 18, D becomes absolutely entitled to their share of the settled property. As all the beneficiaries are individuals all chargeable gains arising on disposals by the trustees will be eligible for deferral relief even though it is not an interest in possession trust.

(b) A, B and C are each entitled to one third of the property, if alive, on their 25th birthday. If none reaches the age of 25, D gets the property. They are entitled to their share of the income, and therefore have an interest in possession, from their 18th birthday. An asset is sold just before the oldest, A reaches his 18th birthday. Therefore, at that date there was no interest in possession. If the trustees acquire qualifying shares after A's 18th birthday HMRC say that relief is still due, because although there is now an interest in possession it is for a fixed period, up to A's 25th birthday. The status of the trust has not changed for EIS purposes because HMRC seem to regard it as remaining a discretionary trust! If A had taken an interest in possession that continued for the remainder of his life apparently relief is not due because the status of the trust has changed from discretionary to interest in possession between the date of disposal and the date of the EIS investment.

(c) A is entitled to 35 per cent of the income of the settlement. The remainder is held on discretionary trusts for B, C and D. The trustees have power to appoint capital to A, B, C and D. The default trust is in favour of X, the local football club, which is not an individual or charity. The legislation provides that A has an interest in possession and a deemed interest in possession is held by the company Therefore only 35 per cent of the gains are eligible for relief. Effectively the interests of B, C and D are ignored.

---

[25] VCT Manual para.41600.

IV TRANSITIONAL PROVISIONS—INTERACTION WITH ENTREPRENEURS' RELIEF

Gain realised and reinvested in EIS scheme before April 6, 2008; subsequent disposal brings deferred gains back into charge after April 5, 2008[26]

First, no taper relief will be available when the suspended gain comes back **16.18** into charge after April 5, 2008. So any taper relief built up prior to the EIS investment will be lost. (When EIS shares were sold prior to April 6, 2008, taper relief on the deferred gain was calculated by reference to the holding period of the original assets sold. The subsequent holding period of the EIS shares was irrelevant: see Example 16.1.)

Secondly, if deferral relief was claimed in relation to a gain arising before April 6, 2008 and the deferred gain comes into charge on or after that date it may be reduced by entrepreneurs' relief if the gain arising on the original disposal would have been eligible for entrepreneurs' relief had the relief been available at that time.[27]

EXAMPLE 16.5

(1) Risky Trust sells a valuable picture in 2003 which qualified for 30 per cent non-business taper relief. The gain before taper but after indexation is £100,000. It reinvests the full £100,000 into an EIS company, claiming deferral relief. (Remember that in order to avoid all capital gains tax the trust has to invest the gross gain before, not after, calculating taper relief: see Example 16.2.) In 2007, the shares in the EIS company are sold for £150,000. £100,000 of this represents the gain deferred and will still qualify for 30 per cent taper relief. The period of ownership from 2003 to 2007 is ignored. The other £50,000 represents the gain during the EIS period and qualified for full business assets taper relief (but not exemption from capital gains tax).[28]

(2) By contrast, if the EIS shares are sold in 2009 the gains deferred will be taxed at 18 per cent but with the benefit of indexation to 1998.[29] Gains accruing during the period since 2003 will also be taxed at 18 per cent but without the benefit of indexation. Entrepreneurs' relief is available under the transitional provision in FA 2008 Sch.3 para.8 if the trustees *would have* qualified for such relief had a claim been made in 2003 and a claim is now made. In the above example the picture would never have

---

[26] FA 2008 Sch.3 para.8.
[27] On the conditions for entrepreneurs' relief: see Ch.14.
[28] Gains accruing during the EIS period can be exempt if the investor is an individual subject to certain conditions. The exemption for gains accruing during the EIS period is never available to trustees.
[29] For reasons similar to those which apply to QCBs it is the chargeable gain after indexation and before taper that is held in suspense. QBCs are considered in Ch.17.

qualified for entrepreneurs' relief so there is no possibility of claiming it on the deferred gain.

(3) Facts as above but the disposal of the EIS shares takes place after June 22, 2010: entrepreneurs' relief is available if the trustees would have qualified at the date of the disposal in 2003 although in the above example they would not have qualified.[30] If they had qualified in 2003 the tax rate remains 10 per cent on gain up to the lifetime allowance despite the different mechanism used in granting entrepreneurs' relief. Gains over the lifetime limit are taxed at the 28 per cent rate for trusts.

(4) Facts as above but the disposal of some EIS shares takes place before June 23, 2010 and some on or after that date. Where a chargeable event in respect of the EIS investments first occurred before June 23 and a valid claim to entrepreneurs' relief was made, that claim reduces the remaining postponed gain by four-ninths up to the lifetime limit applicable at the time of the first disposal and then the reduced postponed gain is liable to CGT at 28 per cent for trusts. This creates an effective rate of 15.6 per cent, i.e. five-ninths of the gain chargeable at 28 per cent. The 10 per cent rate of CGT does not apply to a deferred gain brought back into charge but which has already been reduced by four-ninths because of a pre-June 23, 2010 chargeable event.[31]

Position if gains realised before April 6, 2008 but reinvested after April 5, 2008

16.19 If the gains were realised before April 6, 2008 and the deferral of tax on such gains by reinvestment in an EIS company was made after April 5, 2008 the transitional provision in para.8 can still apply to a later disposal if the trustees would have qualified for entrepreneurs' relief on the disposal made prior to April 2008. The 10 per cent rate will then be available on gains up to the lifetime limit. However, it is hard to see its relevance in these circumstances given that it is much more likely that a trust would qualify for taper relief than entrepreneurs' relief. Hence a trust which has made a disposal before April 2008 qualifying for full business assets taper relief may be better off if no EIS relief is claimed. Instead the trustees pay capital gains tax on the disposal in 2007–08 at an effective rate of 10 per cent. Even if the trust could qualify for entrepreneurs' relief the qualifying beneficiary may not want to use up his lifetime allowance on a disposal by the trust. If the transitional relief in para.8 is wanted, then a claim must be made to HMRC no later than the second January 31 following the end of the tax year in which the first relevant chargeable event occurs (generally the sale of the EIS shares). So if the EIS shares are sold by the trust in August 2009 (2009–10) a claim for entrepreneurs' relief must be made by trustees and beneficiary no later than January 31, 2012.

[30] See F (No.2)A 2010 Sch.1 para.11.
[31] Note that the assessment of the deferred gain is quite separate from the assessment of any capital gain arising on the EIS shares purchased. This may be exempt if the investor is an individual and the other conditions for income tax relief and CGT exemption are satisfied.

Gains realised and reinvested after April 5, 2008 but before June 23, 2010

Where gains on a business asset are realised *after* April 5, 2008 and the indi-   **16.20**
vidual or trustees decide to shelter such gains by reinvesting some of the
proceeds in an EIS scheme then entrepreneurs' relief can be claimed (if available) on part or all of the gains realised on the first disposal provided that first
disposal qualified for the relief then and any balance can be protected by EIS
relief.[32] So unlike the pre-April 2008 position with regard to taper relief,[33] it
is possible first to claim entrepreneurs' relief and then claim EIS relief since
entrepreneurs' relief takes priority over EIS relief.[34] Hence, if a trust realised
£99,000 gains in 2009 on shares qualifying for entrepreneurs relief, it could
claim entrepreneurs' relief (assuming that the qualifying beneficiary agrees to
transfer his lifetime allowance). That gain of £99,000 is reduced by four-ninths
resulting in a chargeable gain of £55,000. The trust invests (say) £60,000 into
an EIS company. The whole of the chargeable gain of £55,000 is deferred since
the investment in EIS shares exceeds £55,000.

However, when the deferred gains of £55,000 come back into charge on a
later disposal of the EIS shares, no further entrepreneurs' relief is available on
the deferred gain[35] even though the lifetime allowance may have increased.
This is because there is no material disposal of business assets. The suspended
gain comes back into charge at 28 per cent.[36]

If the trustees sell a non-business asset such as a picture in 2009 realising a
gain of £100,000 they would have paid tax at 18 per cent. If they reinvest the
gain in an EIS company then on an eventual disposal of the EIS shares the
deferred gain comes back into charge at 28 per cent (or whatever the CGT
rates for trusts are at that time when the deferred gain is crystallised). The
CGT bill has been deferred but the amount of tax has increased!

Disposals and reinvestments after June 22, 2010

An amendment to TCGA 1992 Sch.5B para.1 inserted as para.5A means that   **16.21**
the investor must now choose whether to claim EIS deferral relief and pay
no tax on the gain deferred or not claim EIS deferral relief and instead claim
entrepreneurs' relief.[37] Paragraph 5A excludes deferral relief from applying to
gains chargeable to CGT at the 10 per cent rate. In the authors' view the taxpayer can still claim entrepreneurs' relief up to his lifetime allowance (now £10

---

[32] Note that a beneficiary cannot transfer only part of his lifetime allowance: it is an all
or nothing claim. So in this example if the beneficiary had £1 million unused lifetime allowance
all or none of this would have to be transferred to the trustees: see Ch.14.
[33] And the position on hold-over relief another deferral relief: see 17.41.
[34] See the specific provision in TCGA 1992 Sch.5B para.1(1) and the amendments in
Sch.1 para.9 F(No.2)A 2010 inserting para.5A, modifying sub-para.1(b) for gains on disposals
after June 22, 2010.
[35] The position may be different on the actual gain arising on the disposal of the shares
that accrued during the ownership of the shares if the company shares qualify.
[36] For entrepreneurs' relief, see Ch.14.
[37] See para.5A of para.1 of Sch.5B TCGA 1992 which excludes deferral relief from
applying to gains chargeable to CGT at the 10% rate.

million) and then EIS deferral relief on any balance over the lifetime limit.[38] However, other commentators differ and argue that the investor must either claim EIS relief on the entire chargeable gain or claim no EIS relief and receive only entrepreneurs' relief up to the lifetime allowance. In practice, given the lifetime limit is £10 million it is unlikely that EIS deferral relief will be needed for individuals although trusts may find that they have only a limited amount of entrepreneurs' relief transferred to them. What does seem clear is that a taxpayer realising (say) £5 million gains on an initial disposal of a business cannot claim entrepreneurs' relief on say £2 million of those gains and EIS relief on the balance: he must either claim entrepreneurs' relief on all the gains up to the lifetime allowance or EIS deferral on all such gains if he wants to preserve his lifetime allowance. It is unlikely that a taxpayer will not claim his full entrepreneurs' relief up to the lifetime limit then available given that the deferred gain cannot qualify for entrepreneurs' relief when it is brought back into charge whether or not the company shares would otherwise qualify at that time for entrepreneurs' relief.

It is also worth remembering that whether or not the original disposal on which gains are now being deferred was a business asset, if the EIS company shares into which the gain was deferred are sold and the deferred gain comes back into charge, the investor will pay at the rates prevailing at the time when the deferred gain is crystallised. It is unlikely that CGT rates will go down in the near future so the EIS deferral claim may mean that the investor ends up paying tax at higher rates!

---

[38] This is confirmed at CG Manual para.64135.

CHAPTER 17

SHARE SALES AND DEFERRED CONSIDERATION; EARN-OUTS; SHARE BUY-BACKS; PRIORITY OF RELIEFS[1]

I INTRODUCTION

On a takeover of his company the vendor may receive cash, shares, loan notes **17.01** or qualifying corporate bonds issued by the acquiring company. The consideration may be fixed and ascertainable at the point of sale (even if payment is deferred) or be unascertainable (usually related to the future profits of the company and some form of earn-out). Each of these has different tax consequences that are considered in this chapter.

Take-overs raise particular issues for trustees who are selling shares. If the **17.02** trust shareholding is substantial they may be asked to provide warranties or indemnities to the purchaser.[2] Trustee shareholders should be cautious before providing warranties or indemnities since they must act in the best interests of the beneficiaries of the trust and not expose the trust assets to risk. They should check whether they are authorised under the trust deed to give warranties; should limit any liability to the amount of the trust fund under their control and would be wise expressly to exclude any personal liability.

This chapter considers the position where trustees sell shares in exchange **17.03** for some form of deferred consideration, e.g. QCBs, shares or loan notes. The position has been complicated by FA 2008 CGT changes. Provisions had to

---

[1] See TCGA 1992 ss.135–137 for share exchanges and TCGA 1992 s.116(10) for QCBs.

[2] Warranties are contractual statements made by a seller that amount to assurances as to the condition of the target company or business and the existence of any liabilities. If a warranty turns out to be untrue a buyer may have a claim for damages against the trustees but the buyer will have to show that he has suffered loss. Indemnities are undertakings made by the vendor shareholders to meet specific liabilities which a buyer may incur as a result of an acquisition: e.g. tax indemnities.

be put in place then to protect vendors who had sold shares in exchange for deferred consideration before April 6, 2008 under the old taper relief regime since without some form of transitional relief they would no longer pay the 10 per cent CGT they were expecting to pay on ultimate disposal but instead pay at 18 per cent (now 28 per cent). Often entrepreneurs' relief would not be available on the disposal of the shares or loan notes acquired on exchange. However, as explained at 17.10 onwards, subsequent changes to the way in which entrepreneurs' relief was computed[3] meant that the way in which those transitional reliefs applied was altered, leading in some cases to a doubling in effective tax rates from 10 per cent to 15.55 per cent.

II SHARE EXCHANGES

17.04 If trustees sell shares in exchange for the issue of shares or securities (non-QCBs)[4] in the acquiring company (commonly called "*a paper for paper exchange*") there is neither a disposal of the original shares nor the acquisition of a new holding for capital gains tax purposes. Instead, the original shares and new shares/securities are treated as a single asset acquired when the original shares were acquired.[5] Capital gains tax on the gain made by the trustees (as the disposing shareholder) is postponed until the shares/debentures are sold.[6] If the trustees receive consideration which is partly cash and partly shares then the cash element is treated as a part disposal of the shareholding and s.135 postponement will apply to the balance.

17.05 In order for the section to apply, the following conditions must be satisfied:

(1) the issue of shares must be by the purchasing company (Company B) not one of its subsidiaries and to the shareholders of the target company (A).

(2) company B must generally obtain more than 25 per cent of the ordinary share capital in Company A.[7]

(3) the transaction must be effected for bona fide commercial reasons and not form part of any scheme or arrangement of which the main purpose or one of the main purposes is to avoid a liability to capital gains tax or corporation tax.[8]

17.06 If a clearance is obtained it only confirms that the transaction satisfies (3) above not whether the other conditions are satisfied. In *Snell v HMRC*,[9] a company was sold for a mixture of shares and loan notes. The main shareholder subsequently became non-resident and disposed of his loan notes, free

---

[3] Introduced in F(No.2) A 2010.
[4] Broadly a QCB (TCGA 1992 s.117) is a debt on a security that represents a normal commercial loan expressed in sterling. A non-QCB is a loan note convertible into shares in the acquiring company, carrying the right to subscribe for further shares or loan notes or which contains the right of repayment in a foreign currency at a spot rate prior to redemption.
[5] TCGA 1992 ss.126–131.
[6] TCGA 1992 s.135.
[7] TCGA 1992 s.135(2) Case 1.
[8] TCGA 1992 s.137. An advance clearance is generally sought under s.138.
[9] [2006] STC (SCD) 296 (upheld in the High Court: see [2007] STC 1279).

of capital gains tax, within six months. The Special Commissioner decided that the paper for paper provisions were not intended to be an exemption mechanism for somebody who used them before becoming non-resident:

> "*We find that he had the purpose of becoming non-resident before redeeming the loan notes and accordingly that one of his main purposes, indeed the only main purpose of effecting the arrangement, was the avoidance of capital gains tax*".

So although the exchange itself was effected for bona fide commercial reasons such exchange formed part of a scheme one of the main purposes of which was the avoidance of capital gains tax. The High Court rejected submissions of the taxpayer that it was not tax avoidance but tax mitigation because it was merely using a relief given by Parliament. Nor was it accepted that the intention to go non-resident was not formed at the date of exchange, albeit that it was not a certainty. It was held that s.137 includes the avoidance of a contingent or future capital gains tax liability. See also *Coll v HMRC*[10] where again s.137 was not satisfied: the taxpayer had taken loan notes with a view to going non-resident and thereby avoiding tax even if it was not a certainty.[11]

17.07 If trustees become non-UK resident after an exchange of shares there is an exit charge under TCGA 1992 s.80.[12] However, if vendor trustees are *already* non-UK resident but the trust is subject to tax under TCGA 1992 s.86 because the settlor is UK domiciled and the offshore trust is settlor-interested it will be necessary to satisfy HMRC that there are no plans for the settlor to become non-UK resident (because once he is non-UK resident then the trustees can dispose of the new shareholding and there would be no tax charge on the settlor provided that he did not return to the UK within five years).[13]

III SALES OF SHARES FOR ASCERTAINABLE CONSIDERATION IN CASH

17.08 If the sale is for a cash sum which is *fixed and ascertainable* at the date of the contract, whether or not it is paid immediately, there is an immediate chargeable gain at the date of sale and any reliefs are based on the legislation in force at the contract date. There is no discount for any delay in receipt of the consideration or the fact that it may not be paid. Even if the cash payment is made conditional upon a specified event, e.g. a beneficiary or another shareholder working in the business for a minimum period, or the expiry of one year, the original CGT liability will only be revised if the taxpayer can satisfy the Inspector that part of the consideration has proved irrecoverable.[14] There is no discount for the fact that any consideration may be contingent if it is ascertainable. If the sale consideration is payable over a period exceeding

---

[10] [2010] STC 1849.
[11] If the purchaser had insisted that only loan notes or shares not cash would be paid the position might have been different.
[12] See Ch.4.
[13] See Ch.5.
[14] TCGA 1992 s.48.

18 months, HMRC may allow the vendor to pay the tax in interest-bearing installments.[15]

17.09   If trustees sold shares before April 6, 2008 for a fixed price payable in cash they were unaffected by the FA 2008 changes. Their capital gains tax liability was unchanged and taper relief available. By contrast, if trustees sell shares for cash *on or after* April 6, 2008 there is no taper relief or indexation and the only relevant relief is entrepreneurs' relief which must be considered at the date of the disposal. If a qualifying beneficiary agrees to transfer his entrepreneurs' relief to the trust, then the trustees will want to maximise the value of that relief by ensuring that as much as possible of the consideration is fixed and ascertainable at the date of disposal.

IV SALE FOR DEFERRED CONSIDERATION IN SHARES OR LOAN NOTES

17.10   In many cases trustees and other shareholders sell shares for a mixture of cash and shares/loan notes in the acquiring company. The purchaser may not be prepared or able to pay the entire purchase price in cash at completion and the vendor may not want the purchase price to comprise a fixed cash sum payable over a period of time because he may then have cash flow problems in paying the tax upfront. Hence, the fixed consideration is often deferred and taken in the form of loan notes or shares. It is not dependent on future profits and is ascertainable but simply eases cash flow for the purchaser. By taking shares or loan notes, the date of disposal and therefore the capital gains tax liability is deferred on that part of the gain that is satisfied in shares or loan notes.

Pre-April 6, 2008 sales for shares or loan notes

17.11   Under the pre-April 6, 2008 regime the vendor's period of ownership for taper relief purposes continued after the sale if the deferred consideration comprised shares or non-qualifying corporate bonds (non-QCBs) and so the post-sale period would qualify for business assets taper relief (BATR) if the purchasing company was an unlisted trading company or (if the company was listed) the trust was interest in possession and the beneficiary was employed by the purchaser after the sale or the trustees owned at least five per cent of that listed company.

17.12   Before 2002, many vendors wanted to take shares or non-QCBs in order to continue accruing BATR until these were sold or redeemed because the period of ownership required to obtain full BATR at that time was longer than two years. For deals made between April 5, 2002 and April 6, 2008, however, many vendors already qualified for full BATR at the date of the share sale and did not need non-QCBs or shares to extend their taper relief period.[16] Indeed,

[15] TCGA 1992 s.280 and Ch.18.
[16] If non-QCBs were backed by a commercial bank guarantee this would potentially have brought them within the scope of the limited economic exposure rule in TCGA 1992 Sch.A1 para.10 restricting taper relief. To continue accruing taper relief, the vendor had to be exposed to fluctuations of more than 20% either upwards or downwards in the value of the asset. A loan

trusts in particular often wanted to avoid non-QCBs or shares because they wanted to avoid any risk that the shares/non-QCBs would not qualify for BATR in the future. If, for example, the acquiring company issued the vendor with shares in a listed company and the interest in possession beneficiary stopped working for the group, then from that time the shares ceased to be business assets and the rate of tax started increasing. So in respect of sales taking place before April 6, 2008 the vendors of trading companies would have tended to take any element of deferred consideration in the form of QCBs rather than shares or non-QCBs.

Sale before April 6, 2008; disposal of deferred consideration shares or non-QCBs takes place after April 5, 2008

Where trustees sold shares in exchange for shares or non-QCBs on a disposal **17.13** in 2007–08 or earlier, as explained above, TCGA 1992 ss.126–135 means that capital gains tax is not payable on the disposal until the replacement shares are sold or loan notes redeemed. If the shares or loan notes are disposed of or redeemed after April 5, 2008, there is no indexation and no taper relief. The chargeable gain brought into tax on disposal is the unindexed gain taxed at 18 per cent before June 23, 2010 and 28 per cent thereafter. The only reduction is if entrepreneurs' relief is available at the date of the disposal.[17]

Entrepreneurs' relief is only available (whether the vendor is a trust or **17.14** individual) if the vendor satisfies the conditions for entrepreneurs' relief at the date of the encashment of the shares or non-QCBs. So, if an individual does not possess the requisite five per cent shareholding, or is not an officer or employee of the acquiring company at the date of disposal no relief is due. Similarly, the vendor trust has to satisfy the conditions for entrepreneurs' relief at the date of disposal and the qualifying beneficiary agree to use his unused lifetime allowance.

Hence the trustees may end up paying tax at a higher rate because they may not satisfy the conditions for entrepreneurs' relief at that date. In particular, they may find that the qualifying beneficiary does not satisfy the ownership or working conditions.[18]

Shares in company sold for QCBs before April 6, 2008; QCBs disposed of after April 5, 2008

If the vendor (whether trustee or individual) sells his shareholding in consid- **17.15** eration of the issue of a QCB then the gain on the original shares crystallises but is held in suspense until the QCB is disposed of.[19] This results in a fundamentally different capital gains tax treatment if the QCB is disposed of after

note is unlikely to increase in value and the guarantee meant that the vendor was not exposed to downside risk. The vendor might not then be able to continue to qualify for taper relief. In practice HMRC did not seem to take this point.

[17] TCGA 1992 s.127.
[18] See Ch.14.
[19] TCGA 1992 s.116.

April 6, 2008 but was acquired on a disposal of the target company prior to this date. When the QCB is encashed after April 5, 2008, the deferred gain is simply held in suspense and therefore the computation of the deferred amount will have taken account (if appropriate) of the kink test, halving relief and the indexation allowance. However, any taper relief is lost.[20]

17.16   If the individual vendor received QCBs on a take-over before April 6, 2008 so that the gain was deferred under TCGA 1992 s.116(10) then (as with trusts) the deferred gain is still calculated with the benefit of indexation (because it is merely held in suspense) but in addition entrepreneurs' relief is given (if claimed) on the encashment of the loan notes *if* the relief would have been available on the original exchange when the QCBs were acquired (on the assumption that the entrepreneurs' relief legislation had been in force).[21] The vendor would therefore have had to own five per cent personally in the company at the date of exchange prior to April 2008 as well as be an officer or employee of the target company (not the acquiring company).[22] This transitional relief is only available to individual vendors not trustee vendors. Hence, there is no possibility of entrepreneurs' relief for trusts where the takeover occurred before April 6, 2008 in consideration of the issue of QCBs.

17.17   There are further complicated transitional rules for entrepreneurs' relief where some or all of the QCBs acquired prior to April 2008 are sold after June 22, 2010 by the individual. If the first encashment took place before June 23, 2010 the deferred gain that comes back into charge is reduced by four-ninths and the balance taxed at 18 per cent giving an effective rate of 10 per cent. On a later encashment of QCBs after June 22, 2010 the deferred gain comes back into charge after a reduction of four-ninths and is taxed at 28 per cent giving an effective rate of 15.55 per cent. The rate of tax has increased significantly and the relief is still limited to four-ninths of £1 million despite the increase to £2 million for disposals after June 22, 2010. It is the first encashment date that determines the level of the lifetime limit on the relief to be applied.

Accordingly, if the *first* encashment is not made until after June 22, 2010 then the four-ninths reduction does not apply and the deferred gain is brought back into charge and taxed at 10 per cent up to the lifetime allowance then in force. This is much better since the relief will be based on the lifetime allowance in force at the date of encashment (which is much higher than £1 million) and tax rates of 10 per cent up to that allowance. None of this is, however, relevant to trustees.

EXAMPLE 17.1—PRE-APRIL 6, 2008 TAKEOVER; LOAN NOTES OR SHARES SOLD AFTER APRIL 5, 2008

> In February 2008 the C Discretionary Trust decides to sell its shares in C Ltd, an unlisted trading company for £4.5 million. The trust originally acquired the shares for £200,000 in May 1993 (indexation to April 1998 at

---

[20] This is better than share-for-share or share for non-QCB exchanges where both indexation and taper relief is lost. See Ch.11 for further details of these reliefs.

[21] See FA 2008 Sch.3 para.7.

[22] Entrepreneurs' relief is only available to the person who made the exchange not, for instance, his spouse. The individual vendor may have given some QCBs to his spouse. She needs to give them back to him if he wants to claim entrepreneurs' relief on these shares.

0.152 = £30,400). Assume that the trust qualified for BATR throughout because it always owned at least 25 per cent of the voting shares. The trust is offered (i) £4.5 million cash *or* (ii) five million shares in the purchasing company (being a one per cent shareholding in the acquiring company).

(i) *If the trust takes cash of £4.5 million in February 2008*

	£
Chargeable gain after indexation is	4,269,600
Chargeable gain after taper relief at 75%	1,067,400
Tax at 40% (effective tax rate is 10%)	426,960
Net proceeds after tax	4,073,040

(ii) *If the trust takes no cash and just shares in the purchasing company (Company B) and disposes of them in May 2010 for £4.5 million*

	£
Chargeable gain (no indexation)	4,300,000
Tax at 18%	774,000
Net proceeds after tax	3,726,000

The trust is worse off by £347,040. No entrepreneurs' relief is due unless the conditions are satisfied in May 2010. The trust would therefore need to be made an interest in possession[23] with the interest in possession beneficiary owning at least five per cent of shares personally in Company B and he would also need to be an officer or employee of Company B.

If in the above example the trustees delayed the sale until after June 22, 2010 then the tax rate increased to 28 per cent and the tax bill to £1,204,000. It would certainly then be worthwhile for them to try and secure entrepreneurs' relief on the final encashment of the shares.

(iii) *If the trust took QCBs of £4.5 million in February 2008 and disposed of them after April 5, 2008 but before June 23, 2010 the position would be as follows*

	£
Chargeable deferred gain after indexation is	4,269,600
Tax at 18%	768,528
Net proceeds after tax	3,731,472

There is no possibility of entrepreneurs' relief for the trustees either in relation to the original exchange or the disposal of the QCBs.[24] The

---

[23] Perhaps one year before the sale, although this point is arguable: see Ch.14.
[24] As noted above, on pre-April 6, 2008 exchanges of shares for QCBs *by individuals*, Sch.3 para.7 provides a transitional relief if a claim is made no later than the second January 31 following the end of the tax year in which the first relevant disposal occurs. A relevant disposal is the first occasion after April 5, 2008 when the QCB is redeemed. However, the transitional relief does not apply to pre-April 6, 2008 exchanges of shares for QCBs by trusts.

trustees are therefore better off taking QCBs as in (iii) than shares as in (ii) above because of the preservation of past indexation. However, if entrepreneurs' relief was available on the eventual disposal of the shares given as consideration on the original exchange, then taking shares as in (ii) above is more attractive.

Sales of companies for deferred consideration in shares or non-QCBs from April 6, 2008

17.18   If trustees or individuals sell shares after April 5, 2008 then they may be offered as consideration shares or loan notes (whether non-QCBs or QCBs) in the acquiring company. There are commercial considerations in point: shares are likely to be more risky than the loan notes which are often guaranteed and have a fixed value. In addition trustees need to consider tax issues and this may influence whether the loan notes are structured as QCBs or non-QCBs. They may want shares rather than loan notes in order to preserve the possibility of IHT business property relief particularly if they are approaching a 10-year anniversary.[25]

17.19   There is no taper relief or indexation for disposals after April 5, 2008 and the main issue is the availability of entrepreneurs' relief. Before April 6, 2010 the relief saved a maximum of only £80,000. Now the increase in capital gains tax to 28 per cent combined with the increase in the lifetime allowance has made entrepreneurs' relief worth up to £1.8 million in tax savings.

17.20   Entrepreneurs' relief is only of relevance for trusts where (a) the trust is interest in possession at the date of disposal; (b) the interest in possession beneficiary agrees to the trust using some or all of his lifetime allowance[26]; and (c) the interest in possession beneficiary is an officer or employee of the acquiring company and owns five per cent personally.[27] These conditions will often not be satisfied.

17.21   If the conditions for entrepreneurs' relief are satisfied at the date of takeover the legislation allows the vendor (whether trust or individual) to elect under TCGA 1992 s.169Q[28] to opt out of the normal share for share exchange treatment. This enables the vendor to make full use of entrepreneurs' relief in the tax year of the takeover. If a trust is the vendor the election has to be made by both the trust and interest in possession beneficiary. The trust is then treated as having made a normal capital gains tax disposal with the value of the shares or loan notes (non-QCBs) received in the acquiring company treated as cash consideration. The new shares will have a base cost equal to their market value at the date of the takeover. This will reduce the gain when the new shares or non-QCB loan notes are eventually sold.

17.22   The s.169Q election is made on an all or nothing basis. Before April 2010 (when entrepreneurs' relief was doubled) it was not often attractive because if the total gain was significantly more than £1 million it would simply bring forward the date of payment of tax at 18 per cent on the unrelieved

---

[25] See Ch.45.
[26] See Ch.14 for full conditions.
[27] See Ch.14.
[28] See FA 2008 Sch.3 inserting s.169Q into TCGA 1992. This election cannot be made if the exchange took place before April 6, 2008.

gains. However, now that the lifetime allowance for entrepreneurs' relief has increased so dramatically, in many cases it will cover the entire gain realised by both the beneficiary personally and the trust. 10 per cent tax payable by January 31 after the tax year of the disposal may be seen as a reasonable price to save 28 per cent tax payable later. The trustees must ensure that they have sufficient cash (whether from the deal itself or from other trust assets) to fund the accelerated capital gains tax liability.

EXAMPLE 17.2

> A trust sells its 25 per cent shareholding worth £4.5 million in 2009 with a base cost of £200,000 in exchange for shares or non-QCBs of £4 million and cash of £500,000. A qualifying interest in possession beneficiary is an employee and owns five per cent of the shares personally and agrees to transfer the balance of his unused entrepreneurs' relief. A s.169Q election is made by trustees and beneficiary.

> Entrepreneurs' relief is given against the £500,000 cash element with any balance being set against the shares and non-QCBs. The reduced gain is then chargeable at 18 per cent. It is unlikely that the trustees would want to make the election given that the tax saved will at best be limited to £80,000 and the individual beneficiary may also have used some part entrepreneurs' relief on his personal shareholding leaving less than £1 million lifetime allowance available for the trustees. If however, the sale took place after June 22, 2010 then the election would result in the entire gain being taxed at 10 per cent.

Sales for deferred consideration in QCBs from April 6, 2008

A similar election is available under s.169R where shares are exchanged for QCBs from April 6, 2008 but for takeovers before June 23, 2010 only for individuals. An individual can make a claim under s.169R and any available entrepreneurs' relief at the date of exchange is deducted in arriving at the gain which is held in suspense. It reduces the frozen gains by four-ninths (up to the lifetime maximum). The reduced frozen gain will then be chargeable when the QCBs are sold or redeemed and will be taxed at 18 or 28 per cent. The rate depends on whether the date of the encashment of the bonds is before or on or after June 23, 2010, and if the disposal is after June 22, 2010, whether the taxpayer pays income tax at the higher rate. **17.23**

Shares exchanged for QCBs on or after June 23, 2010

If the takeover occurs after June 22, 2010 then s.169R is modified by F(No.2)A 2010. If entrepreneurs' relief was available on the disposal of the original shares an election can be made by *either individuals as before or (if eligible) trustees and beneficiaries* that the gain is not deferred. Instead, **17.24** it will be assessed not at the time the QCB is encashed but at the time of the takeover. Note this is different from the position prior to June 23, 2010 because:

(i) both trustees and individuals can elect to disapply the deferral provisions; and

(ii) the gain is not held in suspense and charged at the date the loan notes are redeemed but instead charged at the date of the takeover.

Entrepreneurs' relief will then apply and the resulting gain (up to the qualifying maximum) will be charged at 10 per cent. This election effectively disapplies the share for QCB rule in the same way as the election on a share for share exchange. In both cases the date for payment of tax is accelerated to the date when the exchange takes place rather than the date of encashment of the QCBs or the shares.

V EARN-OUTS

(i) Unascertained cash earn-out

17.25   In some cases the vendor will receive a fixed cash sum on completion of the sale with further *unascertainable* cash sums being paid over the next two or three years, calculated using a formula based on the results of the business over this period (an earn-out). The amount to be paid is not ascertained. The rules on earn-outs operate in the same way for individuals and trustees.

17.26   The earn-out is a separate asset for capital gains tax which has to be valued at the time of the disposal (sometimes called a "*Marren v Ingles right*"). Its value forms part of the consideration to be taken into account in calculating the gain on that disposal. Where the deferred consideration is received later, that receipt is consideration for the separate disposal of the earn-out right[29] and a further chargeable gain or allowable loss may arise.[30] CGT on the receipt of the right cannot be paid by installments because the right exists at the date of contract and does not constitute consideration payable in installments. The right is an asset that comes into being at the time of the share disposal and so before April 6, 2008 a new period of ownership for taper relief started at that point. It is not in itself a business asset even though the original shares may have been. So any gain (based on the earn-out payment received less the deductible value of the right) was never eligible for BATR. Nor was it likely to qualify for non-BATR because the right would not have been held for long enough so the gain would have been taxed at 40 per cent.

17.27   Under the post-April 2008 regime any gain realised on the cash earn-out is not eligible for entrepreneurs' relief because the disposal of the right is not a material disposal of relevant business assets.

[29] TCGA 1992 s.22.
[30] *Marren v Ingles* (1980) 54 TC 76.

EXAMPLE 17.3—CASH EARN-OUTS (UNASCERTAINED)

(1) *Under the pre-April 6, 2008 regime.* Trust B sells shares in June 2005 which qualified for full BATR. It received cash of £1 million plus an earn-out based on the results of the company over the next two years to be paid in cash (unascertainable). That earn-out right was valued at £500,000 in June 2005. The trust is taxed on the sale of shares for a consideration of £1.5 million (being the cash plus the value of the earn-out right) with full BATR. However, if the trust received earn-out consideration two years later of (say) £750,000 it would make a gain of £250,000 which would not qualify for any taper relief because the earn-out right was a non-business asset and it had been held for less than three years.[31]

If the earn-out falls below expectation this can result in a capital loss arising on the disposal of the right.[32]

(2) *Under the regime from April 6, 2008.* As above, except Trust B sells its shares in June 2009. The trust (and qualifying beneficiary) is eligible for entrepreneurs' relief then but this is wholly utilised by the £1 million cash and the earn-out right of £500,000 is taxable at 18% in 2009. A further £250,000 is taxable at 28% when the right is satisfied by the payment of the £750,000 assuming that it is paid after June 22, 2010. There is no possibility of entrepreneurs' relief on that additional £250,000 consideration. If the value of the earn-out right combined with the cash does not exceed the lifetime allowance at the date of share sale then both elements are eligible for entrepreneurs' relief.

(ii) Ascertained cash earn-out

If the vendor receives fixed ascertainable earn-out consideration which is merely contingent, e.g. cash of £1 million at completion plus the sum of £500,000 payable in two years time if profits reach a target level then the vendor is taxed on the whole £1.5 million at the date of completion. If the £500,000 is never paid he can reclaim the tax paid. Under the pre-April 2008 regime BATR could be claimed on the £1.5 million assuming all other conditions were satisfied at the date of disposal. Under the post-April 5, 2008 regime, entrepreneurs' relief can be claimed up to the lifetime allowance in force at that time.

17.28

---

[31] It is important in the case of cash earn-outs to receive a reasonable amount of cash consideration upfront not least because all of the tax will have to be paid out of this sum including tax on the value of the right. It is important to obtain an accurate value for the right. Overvaluing it means paying capital gains tax on consideration that is never received and an undervaluation means a loss of BATR (under the old regime) or entrepreneurs' relief (under the new regime) on the excess value of the right. BATR or entrepreneurs' relief is never available.

[32] For disposals of earn-out rights after April 9, 2003 capital losses can be carried back against the gain on the original sale of the shares: see TCGA 1992 s.279A. The vendor has to make an irrevocable election.

(iii) Unascertained earn-outs payable in shares or QCBs

17.29   The vendor may sell his shares for a mixture of cash, QCBs/shares and an unascertainable earn-out in the form of shares or loan notes based on future profitability of the company. The right to receive the *unascertainable* deferred consideration in the form of shares or loan notes would normally be taxable in the same way as if it were to be satisfied by a cash payment along *Marren v Ingles* lines. However, where the *earn-out* can *only* be satisfied by shares and/or loan notes, the right to receive that *earn-out* is deemed to be a non-QCB security which brings the share exchange rules in to play unless the vendor elects otherwise under s.138A. The result is that no upfront capital gains tax charge arises at the date of disposal on the value of the earn-out right. When the earn-out shares/loan notes are issued there is a conversion of the deemed earn-out security into the appropriate shares/loan notes issued (which will be QCBs or non-QCBs depending on what is issued) and again the exchange rules apply. No capital gain therefore arises until those securities received under the earn-out are disposed of.[33]

Pre-April 6, 2008 earn-outs

17.30   Where a disposal involving an unascertainable earn-out took place before April 6, 2008 and the earn-out was to be satisfied by shares or loan notes which had not been issued the vendor might have made an election to disapply s.138A and be taxed on the value of the earn-out right at the date of the original disposal. BATR might then have been available so the earn-out right might be taxed at 10 per cent. The time limit for making an election was the January 31 after the tax year in which the right is conferred. When the earn-out is eventually satisfied, if there is any gain over the value of the right, that increase will be subject to capital gains tax at the rates then prevailing. This route maximised BATR but was only worth doing if the earn-out was likely to be paid fairly soon and was reasonably certain.

17.31   If an election was not made to disapply s.138A, the cash received when the earn-out securities were eventually disposed of could only qualify for entrepreneurs' relief if the conditions for entrepreneurs' relief were satisfied at the date of the encashment but would not qualify for BATR. Although the vendor would not have used up any entrepreneurs' relief allowance on the take-over prior to April 6, 2008, sales of earn-out securities cannot attract any form of entrepreneurs' relief unless the vendor satisfies the ownership and officer requirement in the acquiring company at the date of disposal of the earn-out securities.

---

[33] TCGA 1992 s.138A. Before 2003 the vendor had to opt into s.138A to avoid a *Marren v Ingles* type disposal. If the vendor has an option to take part of the earn-out in cash, the deferral relief offered by s.138A will not be available but the earn-out agreement can be structured so that an identifiable part is satisfied in shares/debentures and the remainder is satisfied in cash and then s.138A relief is available on the shares/debenture earn-out element but an initial tax charge will arise on the cash element.

Takeovers from April 6, 2008 involving earn outs

Where the take-over of the vendor's company takes place after April 5, 2008 **17.32** then until April 6, 2010 the £1 million lifetime entrepreneurs' allowance would often have been used up on the initial cash consideration with nothing left over to cover the value of the earn-out right. So an election to disapply s.138A would not have been made. This may work to the vendor's advantage in the rare cases where the vendor satisfies the conditions for entrepreneurs' relief at the date when the earn-out securities are sold and cash is received since the lifetime allowance has now increased to £10 million and so may cover all the gain on the earn-out.

However, in many cases the vendor will not qualify for entrepreneurs' relief when the earn-out securities are disposed of and therefore will want to maximise entrepreneurs' relief at the time of the take-over. This will increase the likelihood that the vendor will wish to disapply s.138A. In many cases the entire consideration including the value of the earn-out right will be covered by entrepreneurs' relief. Any consideration eventually received which is in excess of the value of the earn-out rate will be subject to tax at 28 per cent by the trustees.

EXAMPLE 17.4

(1) The J interest in possession trust has owned 40 per cent of the issued share capital of Bees Ltd, a trading company, from its formation in 1992. The interest in possession beneficiary, Jeremy, owned the remaining 60 per cent. In May 2004 Bees Ltd was sold to Wasps Plc in exchange for cash of £50,000 and two payments of shares in Wasps Plc, an unlisted company, payable after two and four years dependent on results. In May 2006 the first tranche of earn-out is paid and J Trust receives 40,000 shares and Jeremy 60,000 shares in Wasps. Both sell them in May 2007. In May 2008 each is due to receive a further 40,000/60,000 earn-out shares if profits reach the desired level. The CGT position is as follows:

   (i) *May 2006 earn-out.* There is no CGT liability on the earn-out until the sale in May 2007 assuming that no election to disapply s.138A was made. The earn-out right is a business asset qualifying for BATR when the disposal was made in May 2007 (albeit the sale is of shares).

   (ii) *May 2008 earn-out.* Any earn-out shares received in May 2008 that are sold after June 22, 2010 will be taxed at 28 per cent unless entrepreneurs' relief is then available.

(2) If the takeover had occurred after April 5, 2011 and entrepreneurs' relief is available then the trustees may wish to elect to disapply s.138A in respect of the earn-out right in order to bring the value of the consideration into charge at the time of the original transaction, thus taking advantage of the £10 million lifetime allowance to cover the value of the earn-out right.

Conclusions

17.33   1. It is possible for both trustees and individuals to disapply s.127 on share for share exchanges or share for non-QCB exchanges by making an election under s.169Q in order to maximise entrepreneurs' relief at the date of exchange but this involves an all or nothing election so the whole gain becomes chargeable. It is much more likely to be worthwhile electing under s.169Q now that the lifetime allowance is £10 million because it is unlikely that the total share/non-QCB consideration is substantially in excess of this limit.

2. Trustees cannot make an election on takeovers to disapply the deferral provisions if they received QCBs on takeovers occurring prior to June 23, 2010. See old s.169R. However, thereafter they can make an election to disapply the deferral relief and receive QCBs.

3. The position for trusts receiving deferred consideration is more neutral since June 23, 2010. Prior to that date they could never obtain entrepreneurs' relief if they received QCBs because they could never elect to disapply the deferral provisions. Since June 23, 2010 they can disapply the deferral provisions whether they receive shares or QCBs. There is only any advantage in doing this if the trustees qualify for entrepreneurs' relief at the time of takeover. However, given that there is likely to be unused entrepreneurs' relief on disposals from April 6, 2011 the trustees will often want to disapply the share for share exchanges or deferral relief on QCBs in order to maximise the available entrepreneurs' relief at the date of takeover.

3. Where trustees/individuals take shares or non-QCBs on a takeover, if no election is made under s.169Q to disapply the share for share exchange provisions then entrepreneurs' relief is available on the eventual disposal of the new shares/non-QCBs only if the vendor satisfies the relevant conditions for entrepreneurs' relief at that date. The five per cent voting and working requirements make this more difficult. Entrepreneurs' relief is never available on the encashment of QCBs.

4. Entrepreneurs' relief has become more important in relation to structuring deferred and earn-out consideration now that the lifetime allowance for entrepreneurs' relief has risen dramatically from £1 million to £10 million since the lifetime allowance will probably no longer be used up on the initial cash consideration received on the takeover. If entrepreneurs' relief has not been fully utilised on receipt of the initial consideration but there is a significant earn-out element then make the earn-out ascertainable (in which case *Marren v Ingles* will not apply and the whole contingent consideration is taxed at the date of disposal with the benefit of any available entrepreneurs' relief). It is possible to make the earn-out ascertainable by applying an artificial cap. Tax at 10 per cent will then be paid in January of the following tax year on the maximum capped sum. If the earn-out is not achieved, TCGA 1992 s.48 allows a tax reclaim to be made. The advantage of this approach is that the whole of any potential earn-out will be taxed as part of the initial consideration. This means that a 10 per cent rate of CGT should apply

if the whole consideration including earn-out is less than £10 million. The disadvantage is the cash flow issues if the earn-out is not achieved and a repayment has to be made.

5. Alternatively if the earn-out consideration is unascertained, payable in shares/loan notes and there is unused entrepreneurs' relief at the date of the original takeover, an election to disapply s.138A could be made. Then the vendor will be taxed on the value of the right of the earn-out but with entrepreneurs' relief being available on that value. As high a value as possible should be negotiated for that right depending on how much entrepreneur's relief is available.

6. If entrepreneurs' relief is fully utilised on the initial consideration (excluding any earn-out) then it is better to make any earn-out unascertainable and for it to be satisfied in loan notes or shares with no election to disapply s.138A; the earn-out will be taxed at 28 per cent[34] when encashed but at least the tax is deferred until the earn-out is eventually paid.

VI SHARE BUY-BACKS[35]

A company may purchase its own shares in accordance with CA 2006 **17.34** ss.709–723. Such a purchase is permissible unless expressly prohibited under the Articles of Association.[36] The company must have sufficient distributable profits to pay for the purchase although private companies may also use the proceeds of a fresh issue of shares. In such a case any premium paid on redemption can only be paid out of such proceeds up to the amount of the lesser of:

(a) the amount of the premium paid on the shares being redeemed when they were originally issued; and

(b) the current amount of the company's share premium account including the amount of any premium to be paid on the new shares being issued to finance the purchase of the existing shares.

Private companies, unless expressly prohibited by their Articles of Association, **17.35** can also purchase shares out of capital. In this case, the procedure is more complicated requiring a statutory declaration from the directors as to the solvency of the company looking one year ahead. The declaration requires a report from the auditors to be annexed to it following an enquiry made into the state of affairs of the company.

Before embarking on the purchase the relevant sections of CA 2006 should **17.36** be carefully considered. A particular point to watch is that the purchase price cannot be paid in instalments: the terms of purchase must provide for payment on redemption. However, it is possible to provide in the terms of purchase for shares to be purchased in tranches on different dates which may achieve much

---

[34] Assuming this is the rate of tax then in force and no entrepreneurs' relief is available on the earn-out securities.
[35] CTA 2010 1033 and following, formerly TA 1988 ss.219–229.
[36] Contrast the position under CA 1985 where express authorisation was needed.

the same effect, i.e. a multiple completion buy-back. See **Tax Bulletin** 21 p.4. It is not permissible for a company to purchase partly paid shares.

17.37   If the owner of the shares being purchased is a director of the company or its holding company (or a person connected with the director) the purchase may amount to a substantial property transaction and require approval by the members of the company or the holding company.

Capital gains treatment

17.38 CTA 2010 1033 provides that if certain conditions are satisfied, a purchase by a company of its own shares will not be treated as an income distribution but any profit will be subject to capital gains tax and be taxed at 28 per cent (subject to any available entrepreneurs' relief). The conditions are:

(i) the company is *unquoted*. AIM shares are unquoted;

(ii) it is a *trading* company or a holding company of a trading group;

(iii) the vendor is an individual; trustee; PR of a deceased shareholder or company. He must be *resident* (and in the case of an individual ordinarily resident) in the UK throughout the tax year of sale;

(iv) *period of ownership*. The vendor must generally have owned the shares for five years ending with the transfer. If a settlor transferred shares to a trust or a trust transferred shares to a beneficiary then each person must separately satisfy the five year period. The periods cannot be aggregated. (The only exceptions are husband/wife and deceased/PRs and legatees where aggregation is permissible. In any event for PRs the period is only three years);

(v) *substantial reduction test*. The vendor must substantially reduce his shareholding which means that his interest in the company must decrease by at least 25 per cent after the share buy-back and, of course, the buy-back itself cancels the shares. The vendor's post-sale interest must not be more than 75 per cent of his pre-sale interest (CTA 2010 s.1037). The seller's post-sale entitlement to profits must be no more than 75 per cent of his pre-sale entitlement to profits. This is a particularly difficult test for trustees because in calculating this reduction, all of the settlor's shares, those of his spouse; and any personal shareholding of any beneficiary who may become entitled to a significant interest in the shareholding have to be counted because they are all "associates" of the trustees. Each of their percentage shareholdings will be increased after the buy-back and the substantial reduction has to take this into account. Although other trusts set up by the settlor are associated with the settlor and spouse's personal shareholdings and would count for the purposes of the substantial reduction test if the settlor or spouse sold their shares, other trusts set up by the settlor are not associated with each other[37];

---

[37] *Who are associated persons?* "Associates" are defined in CTA 2010 s.882. Spouses and civil partners are associated with each other and minor children are associated with parents and vice versa. Trustees other than employee benefit trusts are associates of the settlor or any associate

(vi) *connected person test.* After the purchase the vendor must not be connected with the acquiring company, i.e. hold more than 30 per cent of the company's issue ordinary share capital or share and loan capital or voting power: see CTA 2010 s.1037. Again the rights of associates must be included;

(vii) *trade benefit test.* The buy-back must be done for one of two reasons. Either, it must benefit the trade carried on by the company or its 75 per cent subsidiaries and not be done for the avoidance of tax nor to enable the shareholder to participate in profits without receiving a dividend. Buying out a minority discontented shareholder who is stepping down from management might qualify. Alternatively, the whole or substantially the whole of the sale proceeds must be used in discharging an inheritance tax liability charged on a death which could not otherwise be paid without due hardship. The inheritance tax need not be due in respect of the shares. See Statement of Practice 2/82.

For trustees, the trade benefit might be satisfied if, say, the trustees did not wish the company to pursue certain higher risk opportunities for expansion, particularly if their beneficiaries were not directly involved in the business. A clearance application can be made to HMRC to establish whether the trade benefit test is satisfied. In one recent case HMRC accepted that the trade benefit was satisfied where the trustees wished to pursue a safer option which would maximise dividends for their life tenants who were not employees in the business but the remaining shareholders were directors/employees and wanted to plough back all the profits in expansion. The trustees were pressing for a sale of the entire company. A beneficiary of the trust should not remain an employee or director.

If, however, capital gains tax treatment cannot be obtained for a buy-back **17.39** of the shares then the sale proceeds after deducting the original subscription price (not the base cost) are taxed as an income receipt and the trustees from April 6, 2010 are taxed at the special rate for trustees (an effective rate of 36.12 per cent on the net cash received).[38] Note, however, that income tax treatment often generates a capital loss which can be carried forward and used against any future gains realised by the trust.[39] On any buy-back of company shares 0.5 per cent stamp duty is payable by the company. Even if the buy-back of shares is subject to income tax, as a matter of trust law the proceeds are trust capital and not income of a life tenant.

of the settlor and also associated with any person "*who is or may become beneficially entitled to a significant interest in the shares*". An interest is significant if its value exceeds 5% of the value of all settled property. If the settlor sells his shares, his spouse's (or civil partner's) shareholdings plus those of his minor children and all trusts he set up are therefore associated with him. In calculating the substantial reduction and connected party tests, all these shareholdings must be included. If a beneficiary sells, any trusts in which he is capable of benefiting by more than 5% are associated with him along with those of his spouse or minor children. If any trust sells, then the settlor, the spouse of that settlor plus any beneficiary who might receive more than 5% from the trust are associates of that trust but the other trusts are not associates of that trust nor is the spouse or minor child of the beneficiary associated.

[38] ITA 2007 ss.481–482.

[39] The loss will effectively be the difference between the subscription price and the unindexed base cost (earliest date of acquisition is now March 1982).

EXAMPLE 17.5

The Warriner Trust owns 25 per cent of the shares in T Limited and has done so for many years. The trust was an old-style "A-M" trust which was set up for the benefit of the settlor's grandchildren. Two of the grandchildren have taken interests in possession (which are non-qualifying) since March 2006. The shares are the only asset of the trust. Two of the grandchildren are children of a son who is the managing director of the business, owns 30 per cent of the shares and has ambitious expansion plans. The other two are children of a daughter who has no interest in the business. The son has announced that no dividends can be paid for the next 10 years because all profits have to be ploughed back into the company although he has just increased his own salary substantially. The trustees feel uneasy about his track record and would prefer to sell their shares in order to diversify the trust fund and to invest in assets which produce income for the grandchildren. They are particularly anxious for those grandchildren whose parents have no involvement in the business. After some negotiation it is agreed that the company will buy-back all the trust's shares.

If the buy-back is taxed as an income distribution then the trustees will pay tax at 36.11 per cent (i.e. 42.5 per cent of the gross distribution) on the amount received (less the original subscription price) but this sum is received as trust capital. The trustees would obviously prefer capital treatment to apply. The ownership, residence and trade benefit conditions are met. However, they will need to ensure that the connected party and substantial reduction tests are met. If the settlor or his spouse still have personal shareholdings these have to be taken into account. If the son could benefit from the trust then he is a beneficiary with a significant interest and his personal shareholding would also need to be added back to determine whether the tests are satisfied. For instance, the provisions of the trust may need to be amended before the buy-back to ensure that the son (who has a substantial personal shareholding) can never benefit from the trust and is therefore not associated with it.

VII CONCLUSIONS AND COMMENTS ON PRIORITY OF RELIEFS

17.40 The last five chapters have highlighted the complexity of the CGT business reliefs for trusts and the different conditions that have to be satisfied. Trust modernisation was meant to ensure that holding assets in a trust was largely neutral compared with holding assets personally but the conditions imposed on trusts in connection with business reliefs are often more onerous than for individuals.

17.41 Below is a summary of some of the traps mentioned in these last five chapters:

(i) Roll-over relief requires the trustees to carry on a trade. Entrepreneurs' relief requires the interest in possession beneficiary to carry on a trade.

(ii) None of the reliefs apart from EIS and entrepreneurs' relief distinguish between interest in possession and discretionary trusts. A discretionary trust cannot claim entrepreneurs' relief and EIS can be restricted in the case of discretionary trusts with non-individuals as beneficiaries.

(iii) EIS relief does not permit changes in the terms of the trust between sale and reinvestment and imposes restrictions on the class of beneficiaries.

(iv) The "substantial reduction" and "connected party" tests must be watched particularly carefully where companies buy-back shares from trustees if capital treatment is desired.

(v) The conditions on share for share exchanges are complex but generally following the increases to the lifetime allowance in April 2011 to £10 million, trustees should maximise any available entrepreneurs' relief at the date of takeover by receiving cash or electing to disapply the share for share exchange provisions or QCB deferral provisions. They should either take ascertainable earn-out or make a s.138A election on unascertainable earn-out if they have unused entrepreneurs' relief at the date of takeover. Tax will be paid earlier but at a lower rate.

(vi) In relation to company shares it may be relatively easy to secure entrepreneurs' relief for trusts by ensuring that appropriate reorganisations of the beneficial interests in the shares take place prior to disposal. Trustees should review the position to ensure that shareholdings are structured in the best way.

(vii) Where rent is charged for use of an asset by a company or partnership there is no entrepreneurs' relief if the owner of the asset is an individual. This restriction could be avoided if the asset is held by the trustees and the trustees charge the company or partnership a rent for using it in the business.

A summary of the various reliefs and transitional rules in table form is set out below. **17.42**

Business reliefs for trustees

Roll-over relief (s.152)

Conditions	Claim needed	Time limits	Relief given	Points	Transitional rules
Trustees must trade. Not investment businesses.	Yes. 4 years from end of tax year of disposal. Can make provisional claim.	Reinvest 1 year before or 3 years after disposal.	Deferral.	Bring new assets into use immediately. Must reinvest all proceeds for max relief.	28% on gains rolled-over on sale of business even if pre-April 08 roll-over claim made. Gain is before taper if rolled-over pre-April 2008 but then after indexation.

391

Entrepreneurs' relief (ER) (TCGA 1992 ss.169H–S)

Conditions	Claim needed	Time limits	Relief given	Points	Transitional rules
Beneficiary must have IIP and qualify in his own right for one year prior to disposal. Trading co or business only. Not available for discretionary trust.	Joint election by trustees and beneficiary. Beneficiary cannot select level of relief to be taken by trustee once he agrees to transfer his unused relief.	First anniversary of January 31 following tax year of disposal.	Up to £10 million gains taxed at 10%.	Available for trustees on let land used by beneficiary in his trade. But material disposal of business required (or of company shares).	

Share for share exchange (TCGA 1992 s.135T)

Conditions	Claim needed	Time limits	Relief given	Points	Transitional rules
Available to all trusts if conditions are satisfied.	Automatic unless trustees/ individuals elect to disapply: s.169Q.	N/A	CGT rolled-over into new shares. Deferral.		No indexation on rolled-over gain. No taper. ER for trusts or individuals only if conditions satisfied when new shares sold. Otherwise 28 per cent tax for trusts.

Share buy-backs (CTA 2010 ss.1033–1043)

Conditions	Claim needed	Time limits	Relief given	Points	Transitional rules
Available to all trusts if conditions are satisfied.	Automatic if conditions met.	N/A	Proceeds subject to capital gains tax at 28%.	Watch substantial reduction and connected party tests.	

Shares for QCBs (TCGA 1992 s.116(10))

Conditions	Claim needed	Time limits	Relief given	Points	Transitional rules
Available to all trusts.	Automatic but individuals and trustees can elect to disapply deferral relief on disposals after June 22, 2010 (s.169R).	N/A	Gains on original shares held in suspense.		No taper relief on past gains. Indexation given on suspended gain only if pre-April 6, 2008 takeover. ER for individuals on pre-April 08 disposals only if conditions satisfied at date of exchange. Sch.3 para.7. No entrepreneurs' relief for trustees on pre-June 2010 takeovers involving QCBs.

EIS Relief (TCGA 1992 Sch.5B)

Conditions	Claim needed	Time limits	Relief given	Points
Can defer tax on any gains. Reinvestment in trading co required. All trusts can qualify but certain restrictions on beneficiaries.	Yes.	Invest one year before or three years after original disposal.	Tax on gain is deferred if gain reinvested.	No income tax relief or CGT exemption. Watch loans to and from companies.

Incorporation relief (TCGA 1992 s.162)

Conditions	Claim needed	Time limits	Relief given	Points	Transitional rules
Any business whether or not trading. All trusts. Transfer of trade required not just assets.	Automatic but can disapply relief by s.162A election.	Elect to disapply s.162 by second January following tax year of incorporation. Election should be made if shares are sold within a year and entrepreneurs' relief could have been claimed on incorporation in the absence of incorporation relief.	Gain on assets is rolled into shares and the assets are rebased.	No ER on pre-April 2008 deferred gains where the gain brought into charge after April 2008 on disposal.	Since June 23, 2010 no ER if incorporation relief available on entire gain.

Summary of priority of reliefs

17.43 We have referred to the various priority of the reliefs in earlier chapters. A summary is given below:

1. **Roll-over relief and incorporation relief:** this takes priority over entrepreneurs' relief. Entrepreneurs' relief is calculated by reference to the gain chargeable after it has been reduced by roll-over relief. If the full gain is rolled-over, the part left chargeable can then attract entrepreneurs' relief.[40]

2. **Incorporation relief.** For incorporations after June 22, 2010 incorporation relief takes priority. Entrepreneurs' relief cannot be claimed first followed by incorporation relief on the reduced gain. Only if a capital gain is left assessable after the incorporation (e.g. where some of the consideration is in cash rather than shares) can entrepreneurs' relief be claimed. An election can, however, be made to disapply incorporation relief altogether in which case entrepreneurs' relief can be claimed if available.[41]

3. **Hold-over relief.**[42] This takes priority over entrepreneurs' relief. Only if there is a sale at an under-value or two separate disposals (e.g. gifts of shares on different occasions) can entrepreneurs' relief be claimed on the gain not held-over. It is not possible to claim entrepreneurs' relief and then hold-over the balance of the gain.

4. **EIS relief.**[43] Entrepreneurs' relief took priority over EIS relief for disposals before June 23, 2010. The gain deferred under EIS relief was the gain after being reduced by entrepreneurs' relief. From June 23, 2010 the taxpayer must choose whether to claim EIS deferral relief and pay no tax on the gain deferred or not claim EIS deferral but instead reduce the rate of tax by claiming entrepreneurs' relief.[44] It is not possible to claim EIS deferral on the balance of the gain chargeable after entrepreneurs' relief is given (on up to £10 million gains). In practice, now that the lifetime allowance has increased to £10 million it is unlikely that EIS deferral will be needed anyway on disposals of trading companies because gains are unlikely to exceed that limit. Only if the taxpayer wants to preserve his lifetime entrepreneurs' relief allowance will he be interested in EIS deferral relief. In these circumstances he must choose which one he wants.

5. **Share for share exchanges or share for non-QCB loan notes.** No entrepreneurs' relief is available on the share for share exchange unless an election is made to disapply the share for share exchange relief. Entrepreneurs' relief is available on the eventual encashment of shares if the conditions for entrepreneurs' relief are satisfied at the date of encashment.

---

[40] See CGTM 64136 for HMRC comments.
[41] This may be advisable if it is likely that the company shares will be sold within a year after incorporation since entrepreneurs' relief will not then be available.
[42] See CGTM 64137.
[43] See CGTM 64135.
[44] See Sch.5B para.1(5A) TCGA 1992.

6. **Share for QCB exchange.** No entrepreneurs' relief is available on exchange or eventual encashment of QCBs for trusts. From June 2010 trustees can disapply deferral relief on takeover consideration paid in QCB shares.

7. **Earn-out provisions.** Trustees can receive ascertainable cash earn-out or may elect to disapply the earn-out provisions under s.138A. This maximises entrepreneurs' relief on the take-over.

CHAPTER 18

CGT HOLD-OVER RELIEF

- Background (**18.01**)
- Gifts of business assets (s.165 relief) (**18.20**)
- Gifts subject to an immediate IHT charge (s.260 relief) (**18.48**)
- Disposals to a settlor-interested trust (**18.61**)
- Payment of tax by instalments on gifts and sales at an undervalue (**18.67**)
- Principal private residence relief and s.260 hold-over (**18.71**)
- Double charges: relief for IHT against CGT (**18.76**)
- Tax planning and hold-over relief (**18.78**)

I BACKGROUND

An overview of the law

18.01   Gifts and other non-arms-length disposals are treated as taking place at market value. As a result a gain can accrue to a donor even though he has received nothing for the assets and has not generated any cash to pay the tax. In 1978 a form of hold-over relief was introduced for gifts of business assets.[1] This was extended the following year[2] which made it possible to postpone the payment of CGT on the majority of lifetime gifts, whatever the asset (including gifts into trust).[3] Provided that a joint election was made by donor and donee, the donor was treated as disposing of, and the donee as acquiring, the asset for its market value at the date of the gift minus the chargeable gain which was held-over. This postponement of tax could continue until the asset was sold because if the donee in turn made a gift of the asset, a further hold-over election was available. In the event that the donee died still owning the asset, the entire gain was wiped out by the death uplift in value. (There was an exception for gifts into trusts on which hold-over relief had been claimed.)[4]

18.02   In his 1989 Budget speech, however, the then Chancellor of the Exchequer Nigel Lawson announced the repeal of general hold-over relief for disposals

---

[1] CGTA 1979 s.126.
[2] By FA 1980 s.79.
[3] The relief given by FA 1980 s.79 (now repealed) was extended to include deemed disposals of settled property by FA 1982 s.82(1).
[4] See 18.08.

of property made on or after March 14, 1989, citing as justification the fact that it:

> "*was introduced . . . in 1980, when there was still capital transfer tax on lifetime gifts, in order to avoid a form of double taxation. But the tax on lifetime giving has since been abolished, and the relief is increasingly used as a simple form of tax avoidance.*"[5]

Position after 1989

After March 1989, the main occasions when hold-over relief has been available are: **18.03**

(i)   gifts of business assets;

(ii)   gifts of property qualifying for inheritance tax agricultural property relief;

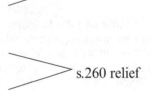

s.165 relief

(iii)   transfers into and out of trusts which are immediately chargeable for IHT purposes;

(iv)   transfers out of accumulation and maintenance; BMTs and s.71D trusts.

s.260 relief

Settlor-interested trusts

The opportunities for taking advantage of hold-over relief were severely **18.04** curtailed from December 10, 2003 when the relief was taken away in respect of gifts to settlor-interested trusts. The aim was to stop hold-over relief being used as part of an inheritance tax avoidance scheme (a "*Melville*"[6] scheme). From April 6, 2006 the definition of settlor-interested trusts was widened to include trusts where the dependent minor children of the settlor could benefit and hold-over relief was also denied on transfers to these trusts. The result was to reduce even further the opportunities to claim hold-over relief irrespective of whether the gift was immediately chargeable to inheritance tax.[7] These changes (and also the restrictions on the availability of principal

---

[5] As a reasoned statement this does not bear close scrutiny because there was (and is) still a potential inheritance tax charge on all lifetime gifts.

[6] As discussed at 31.53, a *Melville* scheme involved a chargeable transfer into a discretionary trust but by limiting the loss to the settlor's estate an immediate charge to IHT was avoided. The loss to the estate was kept low by reserving to the settlor a general power of appointment exercisable after (say) three months. For a further discussion of *Melville* schemes and their uses under the current inheritance tax regime: see Ch.31.

[7] Note that transfers *out* of settlor-interested trusts to individuals are not affected and can qualify for hold-over relief. From April 6, 2008 the settlor no longer pays capital gains tax on gains realised by settlor-interested trusts but hold-over relief is still denied on gifts into settlor-

private residence relief when a hold-over claim is made) are considered at 18.71 and following.

Priority of reliefs

18.05 Relief under s.260 takes priority to hold-over relief for gifts of business assets under s.165 in those cases where a disposal would meet the conditions for both reliefs. This may benefit the transferor if there would be some restriction of hold-over relief under s.165 (e.g. because the assets had not been used as business assets throughout the qualifying holding period).[8] Given that most disposals into trust after March 21, 2006 will be into relevant property settlements, s.260 is likely to be most relevant.[9]

Employee trusts

18.06 In the case of gifts to employee trusts, TCGA 1992 s.239 affords relief from CGT by providing that the disposal is for such consideration as to ensure that there is neither a gain nor a loss. This section applies automatically where the conditions are met, in priority to hold-over relief. A claim is not required.[10]

18.07 When is hold-over relief relevant to trustees?

(i) on the inter vivos creation of the trust which will involve a disposal of assets by the settlor by way of gift;

(ii) on the transfer of chargeable assets to a beneficiary, e.g. in the exercise of a trustee power of advancement;

(iii) on a deemed disposal under TCGA 1992 s.71 when a person becomes absolutely entitled to settled property against the trustees.[11] Not only will there be a deemed disposal on the ending of a trust (e.g. when a beneficiary becomes entitled to the trust fund) but also if there is a resettlement of the property.[12]

EXAMPLE 18.1

The trustees of the Scraggs Discretionary Trust No.2 have wide powers of appointment and advancement:

---

interested trusts. The definition of settlor-interested trust is in TCGA 1992 s.169F. See further 18.61 below.

[8] See 18.20.

[9] See also 18.10 for the interaction of hold-over relief with other reliefs.

[10] For further details see Ch.49.

[11] For a consideration of the tax charge imposed by s.71, see Ch.12.

[12] For a consideration of when a resettlement occurs for CGT purposes, see Ch.11.

(i) They appoint Blackacre on trusts under which Ronnie Scraggs—who is disabled—becomes entitled to an interest in possession:

- *for IHT purposes* Blackacre is now held on a qualifying interest in possession trust[13] and hence there is a charge on the ending of the relevant property regime;
- *for CGT purposes*, however, the settlement is continuing and there is no disposal of Blackacre; hold-over relief is not required.

(ii) They advance Whiteacre (which is farmland) to Reggie Scraggs who intends to farm it in-hand:

- *for IHT purposes*: subject to the availability of agricultural property relief[14], an exit charge will arise when the property leaves the settlement;
- *for CGT purposes*: hold-over relief under s.260 will be available on a claim being made (note that this will take priority over any s.165 relief).

(iii) They transfer two Railway Cuttings to another family discretionary trust (the No.1 Trust):

- *for IHT purposes*: s.81 of IHTA 1984 prevents any charge and the property is treated as remaining comprised in the Scraggs Discretionary Trust No.2;
- *for CGT purposes*: the property has passed into a new settlement (i.e. the No.1 Trust, the trustees of which have become absolutely entitled to it as against the No.2 Trustees) but because there is no chargeable transfer for IHT purposes, s.260 hold-over relief is not available. Of course this may not matter if (a) two Railway Cuttings is the main residence of a beneficiary entitled to occupy it under TCGA 1992 s.225 or (b) if it is a business asset so that hold-over relief is available under s.165.

18.08 If hold-over relief is claimed when the trust is set up, the subsequent death of an interest in possession beneficiary in circumstances where there would normally be a tax-free uplift does not wipe out the held-over gain which becomes chargeable.[15] However the payment of tax may be postponed if the conditions exist for a further hold-over election (as would be the case if IHT was charged on the ending of the interest in possession).

EXAMPLE 18.2

(1) Lady Noyan's mother settled assets into a (qualifying) interest in possession trust for her daughter in 1988, claiming hold-over relief. Lady Noyan died in 2011 and the assets pass to her son David outright. This is a chargeable transfer for IHT purposes and hold-over relief can be claimed in respect of the gain originally held-over by the mother in

---

[13] See 28.02.
[14] See Ch.46.
[15] TCGA 1992 s.74 and see Example 12.05.

1988. Note that any gain accruing on the assets during the lifetime of the Settlement is wiped out on Lady Noyan's death.

(2) As above except David takes a (non-qualifying) interest in possession on his mother's death. Again this is a chargeable IHT transfer and hold-over relief can be claimed on the original gain.

(3) Contrast the position if Lady Noyan's interest in possession is terminated while she is alive: if David takes outright then this is a PET by Lady Noyan. No hold-over relief is available unless the property qualifies as agricultural or business. Even if Lady Noyan dies within seven years, capital gains tax may be payable on the disposal out of the trust. It may be possible for the trustees to claim instalments relief under TCGA 1992 s.281.[16]

(4) If the trustees end Lady Noyan's interest and David takes either on interest in possession or discretionary trusts arises there is no disposal for capital gains tax purposes. Hence hold-over relief is not needed. This is an immediately chargeable transfer for inheritance tax purposes.[17]

18.09 As Example 18.2(3) illustrates, in some cases it may be worthwhile advancing business or agricultural property outright to the person with a qualifying interest in possession just before their death in order to eradicate any held-over gain on the way into the trust. Such an advancement has no inheritance tax consequences[18] and all the gain now subject to a further held-over claim on the way out of the trust will be wiped out on the death of the beneficiary when the asset is rebased to market value.

Claiming hold-over relief/interaction with other reliefs

18.10 Relief under ss.165 and 260 is not given automatically; it depends on the appropriate claim being submitted.[19] The claim must be made by the transferor and the person who acquires the asset ("the transferee") or, where the trustees are the transferee, by the transferor alone.[20] Hence, on creation of a settlement only the settlor makes the election. The time limit for making a claim is four years after the end of the year of assessment in which the disposal occurred.[21] Where the gifted asset is not subject to any restrictions for partial non-business use under Sch.7[22] it is possible to make a hold-over relief claim without a formal determination of the market value of the asset or a computation of the gain.[23] HMRC are not bound by any valuations, however, and if this procedure is used it is not possible to revoke the hold-over claim.

---

[16] See 18.67.
[17] Note that Lady Noyan must be excluded from the ongoing trusts to avoid a reservation of benefit: see FA 1986 s.102ZA and Ch.33.
[18] IHTA 1984 s.53(2).
[19] TMA 1970 s.43. From 1996–97 onwards, the claim must be on form IR295: *Relief for Gifts and Similar Transactions*.
[20] TCGA 1992 s.165(1)(b); s.260(1)(c).
[21] TMA 1970 s.43(1)(a). Previously it was five years after the January 31 next following the year of assessment but this was altered by FA 2008 with effect from April 1, 2010.
[22] See 18.25.
[23] For the conditions to be satisfied, see SP 8/92 and *Tax Bulletin* April 1997.

Otherwise revocation can be made within the normal time limits for amending a tax return. (For example, if a hold-over relief claim is made for a disposal in 2011–12 it can be revoked by the persons making the claim at any time before January 31, 2014.) As the paragraphs below illustrate it may be useful to be able to revoke a claim where tax rates have increased particularly if the held-over gain is clawed back because the trust has become settlor-interested or the transferee emigrates.[24]

Given the potential loss of taper relief (and now entrepreneurs' relief) if there is any risk that the beneficiary may become non-resident within six years after the end of the tax year to which the claim relates (with the result that hold-over relief is then clawed back)[25] it may be better to wait before making the hold-over claim rather than making the claim and then revoking it or making a claim and letting the gain be clawed-back. The tax bill is not the same if a hold-over relief claim is never made or made and revoked compared with if a claim is made and then the gain is later clawed back.[26] It is not just the loss of reliefs. If the gain is clawed-back at a time when tax rates have raised, the tax bill increases. Hence, the position in respect of past held-over claims on disposals before April 6, 2008 has been complicated by the change in rates; the abolition of taper relief and indexation and the introduction of entrepreneurs' relief. **18.11**

Disposal and claw back prior to April 6, 2008

If the disposal in respect of which a held-over claim was made occurred before April 6, 2008 and there was any risk of a claw-back then it was generally better under the old regime to pay the tax and not make a claim until the last possible moment (at which point the tax would be repaid). This was because if any taper relief was available on the disposal it was lost if a held-over claim was made. Even if there was subsequently a claw-back of the held-over gain, taper relief did not become available on that gain: it was lost for good.[27] If no hold-over claim was made then tax was paid on the gain after taper relief. If a hold-over claim was subsequently made, that tax could be repaid. **18.12**

Disposal before April 6, 2008 and clawback on or after April 6, 2008

However, the abolition of taper relief and the reduction in capital gains tax rates has made the decision less clear cut where the disposal took place before April 6, 2008 and the claw-back occurs afterwards. Generally, if the gain only qualified for non-business assets taper relief or if it qualified for any indexation allowance, it was better to make the hold-over claim even if the deferred gain is subsequently clawed back. The computation of the deferred gain that **18.13**

---

[24] See 18.12.
[25] See 18.39.
[26] The gain can be clawed-back if the individual donee becomes non-UK resident or the trust becomes settlor-interested within the claw back period. See 18.39 and 18.63.
[27] This is so whether the event triggering clawback of the held-over gain occurs before or after April 6, 2008: see 18.13.

later comes into charge is the gain after halving relief, the kink test and indexation allowance if appropriate and that gain is then taxed at 18 or 28 per cent, i.e. at lower rates than before April 6, 2008.

EXAMPLE 18.3

Trustees of a discretionary trust advance assets worth £150,000 which have been owned by them for 15 years to a beneficiary in January 2008. The gain before non-business assets taper relief and after indexation (to 1998) is £100,000 and they can hold-over this gain under s.260. The beneficiary acquires the assets at a cost of £50,000. If the trustees do not make the claim, tax has to be paid by January 31, 2009 but full non-business assets taper relief reduces the gain to £60,000 so the capital gains tax is 40% × £60,000 = £24,000. A claim for hold-over relief could be made at any time before January 31, 2014.

If a claim is made in January 2009 it must be revoked before January 31 2010.

If the beneficiary becomes non-UK resident in (say) January 2010 (a claim having been made), then the held-over gain is clawed back and is deemed to accrue immediately before the beneficiary becomes non-resident.[28] The result is that capital gains tax is now paid on the gain after indexation but before taper of £100,000. However, when the gain becomes chargeable the rate of capital gains tax is only 18 per cent so the tax is £18,000. This is less than if no hold-over relief claim had been made. By contrast, if the beneficiary did not become non-UK resident until after June 22, 2010 then the held-over gain that is clawed back becomes chargeable at the rate of 28 per cent, i.e. £28,000 tax and it is too late to revoke a claim!

If, however, full business assets taper relief had been available on the original disposal even if there was no significant indexation allowance, then the capital gains tax position would be worse if a hold-over claim was made and then clawed back even before June 2010 since the held-over gain that becomes chargeable is the gain before taper. So the rate of tax on the deferred gain is 18 per cent not 10 per cent.

Disposal and claw-back after April 6, 2008

18.14　As noted above, capital gains tax is charged on the clawed-back gain at the rates prevailing at the date of claw-back not the date of the original disposal. If rates increase after a disposal on which a claim has been made then trustees are particularly vulnerable if there is a claw-back of the held-over gain because they may not have retained enough to pay the tax.[29]

---

[28] See s.168(1) TCGA 1992.
[29] See 18.42 below.

Example 18.4

Trustees transfer a share portfolio to a beneficiary of a discretionary trust in January 2009, holding over the gain. The beneficiary emigrates in 2011. The gain is clawed back and capital gains tax is charged at 28 instead of 18 per cent (the rate at the time of the deemed disposal). The trustees should revoke the claim before January 31, 2012.

If the beneficiary did not emigrate until 2013 it would be too late to revoke the claim but the trustees may not have reserved enough to pay the tax then due. The only safe way is for trustees to keep a reserve of at least 40 per cent (which assumes CGT rates will not rise above 40 per cent) or take a charge over the beneficiary's property. Although the beneficiary is primarily liable for the tax, if he does not pay it within 12 months from when it is due, then the trustees can be assessed. One problem is that the trustees cannot know what rates of tax are likely to be in force when the gain is clawed-back and therefore the amount to reserve.

The interaction of hold-over relief and entrepreneurs' relief for disposals after April 6, 2008 and before June 23, 2010[30]

This is a further factor that can complicate the decision on whether to make a hold-over claim. Hold-over relief reduces the chargeable gain that would otherwise have accrued on the disposal.[31] Section 169N(4) originally stated that the chargeable gain accruing at the time of the disposal is the amount after entrepreneurs' relief. This is different from the way that taper relief operated since it had tapered the chargeable gain.[32] Hence, it would seem that the held-over gain would be the gain after claiming any available entrepreneurs' relief, i.e. entrepreneurs' relief took priority over hold-over relief. However, HMRC did not agree with this[33] taking the view that if a hold-over claim is made then no chargeable gain will arise and therefore there will be no "relevant gain" for the purposes of s.164N(1). Hence a claim for entrepreneurs' relief could only be made if hold-over relief was not made or was claimed but was restricted because some consideration was paid.

18.15

Interaction of hold-over relief and entrepreneurs' relief for disposals after June 22, 2010

Entrepreneurs' relief for disposals made after June 22, 2010 no longer reduces the assessable gain.[34] Instead all or part of the chargeable gain is simply taxed at the reduced rate of 10 per cent. So if a gain is made after

18.16

---

[30] See also Ch.17.
[31] See TCGA 1992 ss.260(4) and 165(4).
[32] See TCGA 1992 s.2A.
[33] See CGTM 64137.
[34] Section 169N(4) has been modified.

June 22, 2010 and a hold-over claim made, it is clear that entrepreneurs' relief cannot be applied first and then the balance of the gain held-over. If the disposal involves a sale at an under-value in a non-arm's length transaction so that part only of the gain is held over then entrepreneurs' relief can be claimed (if available) in respect of the assessable gain not held-over, i.e. the sale price.

18.17 The taxpayer may consider transferring assets at separate times. So, for example, half the shares could be gifted on Day 1 on which entrepreneurs' relief is claimed but no hold-over relief and the balance of the shares are then gifted on Day 2 and hold-over relief is claimed. What is not now possible is to give all the shares on Day 1 and claim hold-over relief on only part of the gain and entrepreneurs' relief on the balance. Either entrepreneurs' relief must be claimed or hold-over relief but not both.[35]

Disposal and claw back after April 5, 2008 — entrepreneurs' relief

18.18 If a disposal is made after April 5, 2008 (whether before or after June 22, 2010) that would have been eligible for entrepreneurs' relief but a hold-over claim is made, if that held-over gain subsequently comes back into charge due to emigration of the transferee[36] or the trust becoming settlor-interested, entrepreneurs' relief is not available then even if the transferee would otherwise qualify for relief in his own right. This is because there is no qualifying business disposal: it is simply that the chargeable gain is deemed to have accrued to the transferee immediately before emigration (or when a trust becomes settlor-interested to the transferor at the date it becomes settlor-interested). The whole gain comes into charge at the rates prevailing then.

EXAMPLE 18.5

In January 2010 beneficiary A becomes absolutely entitled to shares in a trading company qualifying for hold-over relief under s.165. If A had agreed, the disposal could also qualify for entrepreneurs' relief since A had an interest in possession and satisfied the other conditions. However, no entrepreneurs' relief claim is made and the gain is held-over.

In February 2012 A emigrates. The held-over gain is clawed back and even if all other conditions are satisfied no entrepreneurs' relief on that held-over gain is available. Moreover, the gain is now taxed at 28 per cent not the lower 18 per cent rate that would have been payable in January 2010 even ignoring any entrepreneurs' relief.

---

[35] Their general view was that roll-over, incorporation and hold-over relief took priority over entrepreneurs' relief. See s.169N(5)(a) which states that relevant gains are to be computed in accordance with the provisions of this Act fixing the amount of chargeable gains which apparently HMRC consider gives priority to other reliefs.

[36] For example, because the trust becomes settlor-interested or the donee emigrates: see 18.39 and 18.63.

If, however, A had agreed to a claim by the trustees, entrepreneurs' relief could have reduced the gain in 2010 but HMRC state that no hold-over relief would then have been available on any unrelieved balance.[37] Hold-over relief must be claimed on either all the gain or none of it.

In the past there was no point in a donor who qualified for taper relief giving the asset to the donee and making a hold-over claim if the donee then sold the asset shortly afterwards. All accrued taper relief would be lost. With entrepreneurs' relief the donor may want to "save" his relief and in some cases it may be worth making a hold-over claim on gifts and not claiming entrepreneurs' relief in order to maximise entrepreneurs' relief between various members of the family. **18.19**

EXAMPLE 18.6

Father owns all the shares in a trading company and in January 2010 sold them to a third party for £3 million; any entrepreneurs' relief was at that time limited to gains of up to £1 million. If, however, he had two children who work in the business he could have transferred one third of the shares to each of them in 2009, a year before the sale. He could have held-over the gain on the shares, not making any claim for entrepreneurs' relief. A year later in January 2010 all three individuals sell to the third party. Entrepreneurs' relief can protect the whole £3 million gain. Provided each individual member of the family owns at least five per cent of the shares personally for the year prior to disposal and is an employee or officer and has not already used his lifetime allowance, then he can claim entrepreneurs' relief. Even if the family sell all the shares within a year of the gift, entrepreneurs' relief is still available on the gain made by each individual provided that such individual owned five per cent personally and worked in the company in the year prior to disposal. The gifted shares do not need to have been owned for a year if the individual already owned five per cent personally. Of course, since the lifetime allowance for entrepreneurs' relief has now increased substantially it is less likely that families will need to operate these arrangements.[38]

---

[37] As noted earlier, on HMRC's view, if entrepreneurs' relief is claimed on disposals before or after June 22, 2010, no hold-over relief claim can be made to relieve any balance of unrelieved gain. Most practitioners consider that this is wrong and that before June 2010 hold-over relief could be claimed on that part of the gain not qualifying for entrepreneurs' relief.

[38] For disposals on or after April 6, 2010 the £1 million lifetime limit was raised to £2 million. This lasted less than three months since for disposals from June 23, 2010 the lifetime limit was again raised, this time to £5 million. Thereafter gains were taxed at 18% or 28% depending on whether the individual was a higher rate taxpayer. From April 6, 2011 the limit was again increased this time to £10 million. The mechanics of the relief operate differently before and after June 23, 2010 but the basic entitlement conditions remained the same. See Ch.14.

Availability of relief

18.20   Under TCGA 1992 s.165, hold-over relief is available (subject to the restrictions noted below) on a disposal of business assets.[39] There must be a disposal by an individual or trust and the disposal must be of a chargeable asset "*otherwise than under a bargain at arm's length*". Relief may therefore be available for both gifts and undervalue sales. The donee can be any UK resident "person", a term which includes individuals, trustees and companies.[40] A claim must be made: the relief is not automatic.

Definition of business assets

18.21   An asset is a business asset for the purposes of relief if[41]:

(a) It is, or is an interest in, an asset used for the purposes of a trade, profession or vocation carried on by:

- the transferor; or
- his personal company[42] (whether or not a trading company although it must carry on a trade in which the asset is used); or
- a member of a trading group of which the holding company is his personal company; or

(b) It consists of shares or securities of a trading company,[43] or of the holding company of a trading group, where:

- the shares or securities are not listed on a recognised stock exchange; or

---

[39] Note that gifts to companies of freehold or leasehold land by a connected person are chargeable to SDLT on the basis of the market value of the land: FA 2003 s.53.

[40] However, note the restriction if the gifted property is shares or securities and the donee is a company: see 18.33.

[41] TCGA 1992 s.165(2) as amended by FA 1993 s.87 Sch.7 para.1(1) and by FA 2000 s.90(3) and FA 2008 Sch.2 para.34.

[42] "*Personal company*" is defined in TCGA 1992 s.165(8)(a) (as substituted by FA 1998 s.140(4)) as "*in relation to an individual, a company the voting rights in which are exercisable, as to not less than 5 per cent, by that individual*".

[43] From April 6, 2008 the definition of trading company and trading activities etc is found at s.165A as substituted by FA 2008 but no changes to the meaning of trading company have been made since April 6 2003. From April 6, 2003 a more restrictive definition of trading company and trading group was introduced in the hold-over relief legislation: FA 1998, s.140(4) and see now new s.165A as substituted by FA 2008. For gifts before April 6, 2003, a trading company was a company whose business consisted wholly or mainly of the carrying on of a trade or trades. The wholly or mainly requirement was much less restrictive than the definition used from April 6, 2003 for hold-over relief claims and derived from the old taper relief legislation. A trading company is "*a company carrying on trading activities which activities do not include to a substantial extent activities other than trading activities*": see TCGA 1992 s.165A. "*Substantial*" considered by HMRC to mean an 80% rather than "a more than" 50% test on trading activities. Cf. business property relief discussed in Ch.45.

- the trading company or holding company is the transferor's personal company.[44]

18.22 A mere disposal of assets suffices: it is not necessary for the disposal to be of part of a business.[45] An individual who transfers an asset used in a trade carried on by a partnership of which he is a member can claim relief whether or not he ceases to be a partner.[46]

18.23 Whether an asset is used for the purposes of a trade may sometimes be a moot point: for instance, would the relief be available on a gift of a valuable Munch oil painting ("The Sick Child") which has adorned the offices of a funeral parlour for many years?

18.24 "Trade" has its normal meaning but is extended to include the commercial letting of furnished holiday accommodation and the occupation of woodlands managed on a commercial basis with a view to profit.

Partial hold-over relief

18.25 Where an asset has not been used as a business asset throughout its period of ownership, e.g. land has been used as to 50 per cent during ownership for the purposes of a trade and 50 per cent as let investment property, the held-over gain is reduced by reference to the period of ownership when it was not used as a business asset. The period before March 31, 1982 is included in the computation even after April 6, 2008. Similar restrictions occur where the asset is a building or structure which was only partly used for a qualifying purpose during the period of ownership and in this case the restriction is in accordance with what is *"just and reasonable"*.[47]

18.26 Hold-over relief on a transfer of *shares* is restricted where the company owns chargeable assets that are not business assets *but only* where *either* the transferor was able to exercise at least 25 per cent of the voting rights at any time in the 12 months before the transfer *or* the transferor is an individual and the company was his personal company at any time in the 12 months before the transfer.

18.27 When relief is restricted, the held-over gain is reduced by multiplying it by A/B where A is the market value on the date of the transfer of the company's chargeable business assets and B is the value on the same date of all the company's chargeable assets. This can give rise to anomalies. For example, since the restrictions are by reference to the company's assets on the date of the transfer, if the transferor has control of the company, he could arrange that before making the gift the company disposes of any chargeable non-business assets that would otherwise restrict hold-over relief. The company would be liable to corporation tax on the disposal but this would avoid a restriction on hold-over relief for the donor.

18.28 From April 2003 a transferor has faced the more restrictive *"substantially a trading company"* test for determining whether shares can qualify for

---

[44] Contrast entrepreneurs' relief where it is necessary for even an unlisted company to be the taxpayer's personal company. See Ch.14.
[45] Contrast entrepreneurs' relief and see Ch.14.
[46] Cf. entrepreneurs' relief and see Ch.14.
[47] TCGA 1992 Sch.7 paras 5 and 6. However, note the uncertainty concerning "mixed" assets used by the interest in possession beneficiary in his trade: see 18.26.

hold-over relief in the first place *as well as* the pre-April 2003 provisions for restricting hold-over relief where a company owns non-business chargeable assets.[48]

EXAMPLE 18.7

A has owned a pub chain for eight years and all the pubs have been used in his sole trade for three years. He then lets one pub (Pub A) for five years before bringing it back into business use as part of the chain. Hold-over relief (under s.165) on a gift of that pub into an interest in possession trust set up in 2004 is restricted to three-eighths of the gain. (If a gift of Pub A was made to the trust in 2009 there would be no entrepreneurs' relief (unless exceptionally the trade had ceased) because the gift is of a single asset not part of a disposal of the business).

If in 2009 A disposed of his entire pub business, including Pub A, by a gift to his children the disposal is a material disposal and there is no restriction on entrepreneurs' relief by reference to the previous non-business use of Pub A. It is thought that he can claim hold-over relief on the balance of the gain not protected by entrepreneurs' relief with an appropriate restriction for non-business use.[49] However, if Pub A was owned by A and used by a partnership of which A was a member (having not been used in a business for some years prior to that), A would need to dispose of his partnership interest and substantially reduce his activities as partner before he could obtain entrepreneurs' relief. In addition, there would be a restriction in entrepreneurs' relief on Pub A by reference to the earlier non-business use.[50] Hold-over relief under s.165 would arguably be available on the balance of the gain not protected by entrepreneurs' relief although there would still be a restriction for the non-business use.[51] So neither entrepreneurs' relief nor hold-over relief under s.165 provide protection in respect of the entire gain.

[48] Note that entrepreneurs' relief is not so restricted: sales of company shares can qualify for full relief if the company is "substantially" a trading company even if some of the assets in the company comprise investment assets. Nor is entrepreneurs' relief restricted if (say) there is a disposal of part or all of a business (a material disposal) and some of the assets were not used in the business for the entire period of ownership or were partly used for other purposes provided that the asset was used in the business and therefore a relevant business asset at the date of disposal of the business.

However, entrepreneurs' relief is restricted where there is an associated disposal of assets (e.g. some of the assets are owned by the vendor personally and used by the partnership or his personal company and there is a material disposal of the business) and the assets have not been used exclusively for business purposes throughout the period of ownership or (since April 2008) have been rented to the partnership (TCGA 1992 s.169P).

[49] Although see 18.15 for interaction with entrepreneurs' relief. HMRC disagree with this interpretation. For disposals after June 22, 2010 entrepreneurs' relief cannot be claimed first followed by hold-over relief on the unrelieved gain. Entrepreneurs' relief is available only on that part of the gain that does not qualify for hold-over relief (e.g. because some consideration was paid).

[50] See Ch.14.

[51] Note that HMRC disagree.

If the taxpayer had farmed land and then let it for agricultural use there is **18.29** no restriction of hold-over relief provided that the land qualified for IHT agricultural property relief at the date of disposal.[52]

Business assets hold-over relief for trustees[53]

The requirements for relief are modified when business assets are owned **18.30** by trustees. Broadly, the relevant business asset must *either* be used for the purposes of a trade, profession or vocation carried on by the trustees *or* by a beneficiary with an interest in possession in the settled property.[54] In the case of a disposal of shares in a trading company, either that company must not be listed on the Stock Exchange or, alternatively, at least 25 per cent of the voting rights at the company's general meeting must be exercisable by the trustees.[55]

It is not necessary for the beneficiary to have a qualifying interest for IHT purposes.[56]

EXAMPLE 18.8

A trust set up in May 2006 owns land which is used by Fred in his trade. Fred has an interest in possession in the land. Hold-over relief is available to the trustees on a disposal of the land (e.g. if they advanced the land to Fred). Note that it is only necessary for Fred to have the interest in possession *immediately before* the disposal.[57]

Arguably, the provisions restricting relief where the asset is not wholly used **18.31** for business purposes throughout the period of ownership apply only if the trustees use it for their trade not if the interest in possession beneficiary uses it in his trade.[58] Where trustees own land which is used partly by an interest in

---

[52] See TCGA 1992 Sch.7 paras 3 and 6(2): see Ch.46.

[53] TCGA 1992 Sch.7 paras 2 and 3.

[54] Contrast the rules on entrepreneurs' relief and roll-over relief in Chs 13 and 14 which are less generous. Roll-over relief is only available if the trustees carry on the trade; entrepreneurs' relief is only available if the interest in possession beneficiary is carrying on the trade.

[55] TCGA 1992 Sch.7 para.2 as amended by FA 2000 s.90(3) and by FA 2004 s.116, Sch.21 para.9.

[56] The meaning of a "*qualifying*" interest in possession is considered at 28.02.

[57] This is similar to the rules for entrepreneurs' relief: the beneficiary needs an interest in possession immediately before the disposal of trust business assets but not an interest in possession for 12 months. Note that HMRC do not agree with this view and consider the beneficiary needs to have had an interest in possession for 12 months to qualify for entrepreneurs' relief.

[58] See Sch.7 para.(4)(2)(c) and para.5 which refer to the trustees being the transferor but do not discuss the position where the interest in possession beneficiary is using the land. Para.5 can never be satisfied by the interest in possession beneficiary because he is not the transferor; the restriction is imposed by para.5 on the transferor if the asset was not used for the purposes of the trade by the transferor throughout the period of its ownership and by para.6 if the asset is only partly used for business purposes. By definition the asset is not being used by the trustees as transferor if the asset is being used by the life tenant in his trade. If para.5 needs to be satisfied, para.2(2)(a)(ii) giving relief to an interest in possession beneficiary who uses the asset in his trade would be meaningless. Whether HMRC would argue that the interest in possession beneficiary is treated as the transferor in these circumstances and therefore has to use the asset for trading purposes throughout his period of ownership is not known.

possession beneficiary for his trade and partly by a third party hold-over relief is restricted to what is just and reasonable under para.6. There is no requirement for the beneficiary to have a particular type of interest in possession.[59]

EXAMPLE 18.9

As in Example 18.8 above except that Fred only uses some of the land for his trade. The other land is let out to a third party who uses it in his trade as a car park. Hold-over relief is restricted. In practice these restrictions are unlikely to be a problem since most land that is used by the beneficiary in his trade or is owned by the trustees is farm land on which there will be hold-over relief anyway, whoever carries on the farming business. It does not matter that the farm land is let out by the trustees provided agricultural property relief is available.

18.32 The restrictions on the amount of hold-over relief in the case of a disposal of shares in unlisted companies are less onerous for trustees than individuals.

EXAMPLE 18.10

Trustees hold a 20 per cent share in an unlisted trading company. A beneficiary becomes absolutely entitled to the shares as against the trustees. The trustees claim hold-over relief. Even if the company owns some investments, there is no restriction on the claim (para.7(1)(b) only refers to individuals). Note, however, that if the trustees own 25 per cent or more of the voting rights in the company there is a restriction even if the company is unlisted (see para.7(1)(a)).

Assume that the trustees owned 25 per cent of the shares and that the business assets (goodwill, plant and machinery and a freehold interest in a property used for the company's business) are worth £1,295,000 and the chargeable non-business assets (let property and quoted shares) are worth £1,105,000. Total chargeable assets are therefore worth £2,400,000. The chargeable gain is £150,000.

The held-over gain is reduced from £150,000 to the following:

$1295/2400 \times £150,000 = £80,937.$

The balance remains chargeable subject to any deduction for entrepreneurs' relief.

The restriction on hold-over relief could have been avoided if the trustees had disposed of one per cent of their shares at least 12 months before the deemed disposal when the beneficiary became absolutely entitled.

---

[59] Contrast entrepreneurs' relief where the beneficiary has to have an interest in possession which is not for a fixed term.

Restrictions on gifts to companies

From November 9, 1999 it has not been possible to claim hold-over relief on **18.33** the transfer of shares or securities to a company. The relief was withdrawn because it was being exploited in tax avoidance schemes. However, it is still possible to claim hold-over relief on transfers of *other assets* to a company.[60] HMRC confirmed in *Tax Bulletin* 50, December 2000 that disposals to a trust with a corporate trustee were not subject to the restriction:

> *"under s.69(1) the trustees of a settlement are treated for capital gains tax purposes as being a single and continuing body of persons distinct from the persons who may from time to time be the trustees. The transfer is therefore treated for all purposes of capital gains tax as a transfer to trustees and not a transfer to a company."*

A similar result applies when there is a transfer of shares to a company which **18.34** is acting as trustee of a bare trust. The gift is regarded as a transfer to the beneficiary.

Calculation of the held-over gain

It is the chargeable gain which is held-over. The chargeable gain is calculated **18.35** by reference to market value of the asset at the date of the gift.

For gifts made before April 6, 2008 the held-over gain could be reduced by indexation up to April 1998. If any held-over gains on pre-April 6, 2008 gifts come back into charge after April 6, 2008 that held-over gain continues to be reduced by indexation. However, for gifts made after April 5, 2008 the held-over gain cannot be reduced by any indexation on the gifted asset that accrued up to April 1998.

Where gifts were made prior to April 6, 2008 the gain held-over was always the gain *before* calculation of any taper relief. The transferees' qualifying holding period for taper relief purposes started at the date the gift was made, with the result that the period of ownership of the transferor did not count. Of course the transferee will not be eligible for any taper relief after April 5, 2008, however long he has held the asset and so the entire gain including any held-over gain is the untapered gain.[61]

---

[60] This provision restricting gifts of securities to companies was first introduced in FA 2000 and was inadvertently repealed for disposals on or after April 6, 2003. For a period of some four months between April and October taxpayers were able to give shares to companies and claim hold-over relief. The error was spotted and the provision was then re-enacted. The press release dated October 21, 2003 announced with effect from that date (not from December 5, 2003) that s.165 gifts relief is denied on the transfer of shares or securities to a company. A classic case of the tax system being so complicated that everyone lost the plot!

[61] Taper relief operated as a reduction in the rate of tax charged on a disposal so could not reduce the held-over gain.

EXAMPLE 18.11

Christopher gave shares in a unlisted trading company into an interest in possession trust for his children in July 2005. The shares were acquired by Christopher in January 1989 for £1,000 and in July 2005 were worth £51,500. The hold-over relief claim was made by Christopher alone.[62]

	£
Christopher's gain is	51,500
Less indexed base cost (say)	(1,500)
	50,000

The effect of the hold-over relief claim is that Christopher has no CGT liability on the gift and the trustees' base cost of the shares is reduced to:

	£
Deemed consideration	51,500
Less held-over gain	(50,000)
	1,500

Note that the trustees obtained all of Christopher's indexation allowance but none of his taper relief. If the gift had been made after April 5, 2008 the gain held-over is the unindexed gain. If in the above example the trustees dispose of the shares after April 5, 2008 for (say) £100,000 there is no taper relief but the held-over gain is still £50,000, i.e. reduced by indexation.

Assume that all the children work in the company and have qualifying interests in possession and each owns five per cent of the shares. On a disposal by the trustees, entrepreneurs' relief would be available on the entire gain of £98,500 including the held-over gain. (This assumes that each of the children agree to use their lifetime entrepreneurs' relief allowance.) If, however, there is a clawback of the held-over gain under s.169C because the trust becomes settlor-interested in (say) 2009 there is no entrepreneurs' relief available even if all other conditions are satisfied because there is no qualifying disposal; the chargeable gain is simply treated as accruing at the time the trust becomes settlor-interested.[63]

18.36   HMRC do not require a formal valuation of the asset transferred *unless* (before April 6, 2008) there was a possibility that indexation will create a loss *or* (after April 5, 2008) where there is an interaction between hold-over relief and other reliefs such as entrepreneurs' relief *or* where the transfer is a sale at an under-value.[64] It is not, however, possible to make a partial claim for hold-over relief, e.g. to reduce the gain to the level of the transferor's annual exemption. However, the held-over amount could be restricted by making the transfer for an amount of consideration that produces the required gain or (depending on the type of asset involved) by making gifts in separate tranches.

---

[62] See 18.10 for who needs to make the claim.
[63] See 18.63.
[64] See 18.10 on claims generally.

Sales at under-value

Where the actual consideration for the transfer exceeds the expenditure on the **18.37** asset that is allowable in calculating the gain, the held-over gain is reduced by that excess. Where the consideration does not exceed the allowable expenditure, the whole gain is held-over.

EXAMPLE 18.12

In Example 18.11, if the trustees had paid Christopher £10,000 for the shares in July 2005, hold-over relief would have been reduced by the excess of £10,000 (actual consideration) over £1,000 (the allowable cost before indexation) namely £9,000. The gain held-over would therefore be:

	£
Chargeable gain as calculated above	50,000
Less reduction	(9,000)
	41,000

Christopher would therefore have a chargeable gain of £9,000 and the trustees' base cost of the shares would be £51,500 – £41,000 = £10,500, equivalent to the actual consideration paid plus the indexation allowance of £500 on Christopher's original base cost.

Non-residence of donee

No hold-over relief is available if the transferee is neither resident nor ordinar- **18.38** ily resident in the UK or is regarded as resident elsewhere under a double taxation agreement.[65] Nor is hold-over relief available if the transferee is a dual resident trust[66] or the transferee is a company that is controlled by a person or persons who are neither resident nor ordinarily resident in the UK and connected with the transferor.[67] This can affect UK trustees where a beneficiary who becomes absolutely entitled is non-resident: in such cases, no hold-over relief claim is possible under either ss.165 or 260.

Subsequent emigration and claw-back

A held-over gain becomes chargeable if the transferee is an individual who **18.39** becomes neither UK resident nor ordinarily resident within six years after

[65] TCGA 1992 s.166.
[66] TCGA 1992 s.169.
[67] TCGA 1992 s.162.

the end of the year of assessment in which the disposal on which hold-over relief is claimed took place if the transferee still owns the asset at that time.[68] The rate of tax charged on the clawed-back gain is the rate prevailing at that date of claw-back not the date of the original disposal. Again this can affect trustees who have made a hold-over claim when a UK resident beneficiary becomes absolutely entitled to the settled property and that beneficiary emigrates within six years. The trustees are chargeable on any clawed back gain if the donee fails to pay the tax within 12 months of the tax becoming payable.[69] They may have reserved insufficient tax. No assessment can be made on the trustees under this provision more than six years after the end of the year of assessment when the relevant disposal was made.[70] In practice this means that if a beneficiary becomes non-resident more than four years from the end of the year of assessment in which the trustees make the disposal the trustees are no longer at risk. For example, if a beneficiary becomes absolutely entitled to the settled property in January 2009 (tax year 2008–09) and hold-over relief is claimed, no assessment can be raised on the trustees after April 5, 2015. If the beneficiary emigrates in 2013–14 (i.e. in the fifth year after the disposal) capital gains tax is not due until January 2015. If the beneficiary does not pay it then the trustees cannot be charged for 12 months, i.e. until January 2016 by which time HMRC are out of time to assess the trustees.

18.40   If the transferee is a trust rather than an individual (e.g. there is a transfer between settlements or a gift into trust) and the trust becomes non-resident on or after March 19, 1991 there is no claw back of the held-over gain. This is because an exit charge is imposed on emigration of a trust in respect of all the unrealised gains, not just the held-over gain.[71] There is a deemed disposal under TGCA 1992 s.80 not merely a clawback of the held-over gain. In principle therefore, entrepreneurs' relief would be available if all the other conditions are satisfied.

Calculating the clawed back gain

18.41   Where emigration of the individual transferee occurs, a chargeable gain equal to the held-over gain is deemed to accrue to him *immediately before* he becomes non-resident. If emigration occurred before April 6, 2008 the transferee was not charged tax on the transferor's gain *but was deemed to have a gain equal to the held-over gain and the held-over gain did not qualify for taper relief.* In other words neither the transferor nor the transferee benefited from taper relief.[72] By contrast, trusts which emigrated under s.80 and suffered an exit charge were entitled to taper relief (because there was a disposal not merely a clawback of the gain held-over) but only based on the transferee trustees' period of ownership of the asset.[73]

18.42   As already noted, if the transferee does not pay the tax within 12 months of the due date of payment, the deemed gain can be assessed on the transferor in

---

[68] TCGA 1992 s.168(1).
[69] TCGA 1992 s.168(7).
[70] Section 168(8).
[71] TCGA 1992 s.80: see Ch.4.
[72] See TCGA 1992 s.2(A)(3).
[73] See Ch.4.

the name of the transferee within six years of the end of the year of assessment in which the disposal took place on which hold-over relief was claimed.[74] The transferor can recover any tax paid from a transferee but this might be difficult if the transferee has left the UK. Hence, trustees should ensure that they make provision for the possibility of the beneficiary's emigration. One option would be to postpone making the hold-over relief claim until the last possible moment, namely four years after the end of the year of assessment and only make the claim if the donee is still UK resident.[75] However, then the trustees would have had to pay the CGT on the gain which would only be repaid once the claim was made. An alternative, which is more common, is for the trustees to retain sufficient assets to cover the tax at stake or to obtain security from the beneficiary. One difficulty in calculating the retention is to allow for a tax rate increase: see Examples 18.3 and 18.13.

EXAMPLE 18.13

Sandra, an interest in possession beneficiary of a pre-March 2006 trust, becomes absolutely entitled to let land qualifying for agricultural property relief[76] on attaining 30 in 2009. She is UK resident and the trustees decide to make a hold-over relief claim rather than pay tax at 18 per cent. They do not take a charge over the property. Sandra then emigrates in January 2011 and sells the land free of CGT at a time when she is non-resident. The gain held-over is clawed back and CGT at 28 is assessed on Sandra. If Sandra fails to pay the tax by January 2013,[77] the trustees can be assessed for that tax. It would be attractive for the trustees to revoke the claim in these circumstances so that they can pay capital gains tax at the lower 18 per cent rate that was available in 2009.

There is no claw back on emigration of the transferee if he goes abroad for **18.43** full-time employment, none of the duties of which are performed in the UK *and* the transferee again becomes resident or ordinarily resident in the UK within three years of his emigration and still owns the asset in question.[78]

It is questionable whether the claw-back charge on individuals (or indeed **18.44** an exit charge on trusts) would be upheld by the European Court where the donee emigrates to a country within the European Union. It may be said that such a charge represents a restriction on freedom of establishment of nationals of a Member State in the territory of another Member State (see art.43) *or* a restriction on freedom of movement of capital (whether or not between Member States: see art.56). The UK Government specifically chose not to impose an exit charge on the emigration of individuals in 1998.[79] In *van*

---

[74] See fn.36 above.
[75] On claims for relief, see 18.10.
[76] On APR, see Ch.46.
[77] A year after it is due.
[78] TCGA 1992 s.168(5).
[79] See *de Lasteyrie du Saillant v Ministère* [2004] 6 ITELR 666. The taxpayer moved from France to Belgium with the result that he was taxed on the increase in value of certain securities. Despite the fact that the French tax code contained provisions permitting suspension of payment and would exonerate taxpayers entirely at the end of a five year period if they had still retained the assets, it was held that the exit charge was a disproportionate obstacle to freedom

Hilten—van der Heijden[80] a Netherlands national emigrated to Switzerland. She died in Switzerland and her heirs were assessed to inheritance tax in the Netherlands on the basis that a Netherlands national who died within 10 years of having ceased to reside there should be deemed to have been resident there at the time of his death. The European Court held that national legislation which would discourage a national who wished to transfer his residence to another Member State and thus hinder his freedom of movement could not for that reason alone constitute a restriction on the movement of capital. The taxpayer lost the argument but HMRC are presumably aware that exit charges on the emigration of trusts and the claw-back of held-over gains on the emigration of an individual may be vulnerable if challenged by taxpayers. The hold-over relief provisions have not been extended to other areas of the tax legislation.[81] Of course, the opportunities for avoidance might be too great if a hold-over claim was made; the transferee taxpayer then became non-UK resident and he was able to argue against a claw back of the held-over gain.

18.45 A disposal by the transferee to his spouse or civil partner is ignored for the purposes of determining whether the emigrating transferee has disposed of the asset. Hence, there is still a claw back if the transferee emigrates after a disposal to the spouse.[82] If the transferee does dispose of the asset after the claw back charge has been made, no reduction to his base cost is made in respect of the held-over gain otherwise there would be a double capital gains tax charge.[83]

18.46 The claw back of the held-over gain on emigration is reduced by half if the donor acquired the asset before March 31, 1982; the gift took place between then and April 5, 1988 and the recipient emigrated on or after April 6, 1988.[84]

Agricultural Property

18.47 Land qualifying (or which would qualify on a chargeable transfer being made) for 100 per cent or 50 per cent IHT agricultural property relief is specifically included as a business asset for CGT purposes.[85] Hope value in the land also qualifies for hold-over relief even though the hope value does not itself qualify for agricultural property relief.[86]

---

of establishment. The taxpayer was subject to disadvantageous treatment in comparison with the person who maintains his residence in France. (Contrast the *Hilten* case below where the taxpayer was not disadvantaged by emigrating compared with staying in the Netherlands.) The Courts held in *Lasteyrie* that the transfer of a person's tax residence outside the territory of a Member State does not in itself imply tax avoidance (stopping tax avoidance being regarded as a permitted exception to the article).

[80] [2006] WTLR 919.

[81] This is discussed in relation to sub-fund elections: see Ch.11.

[82] TCGA 1992 s.168(3) but note that if there is a claw-back future disposals by the spouse or civil partner shall be taken into account as if they had been made by the transferor with the base cost being calculated as if hold-over relief had not been given.

[83] See TCGA 1992 s.168(10).

[84] Sch.4 para.4.

[85] TCGA 1992 Sch.7 para.1. Let agricultural land therefore attracts relief. As to when agricultural property relief is available, see Ch.46.

[86] It may attract business property relief for IHT purposes: see Chs 45 and 46.

EXAMPLE 18.14

As in Example 18.13 Sandra becomes absolutely entitled to agricultural land valued at £2 million, with £1.5 million hope value. Hold-over relief can be claimed on the entire gain. Note, however, that if Sandra had not been entitled to a qualifying interest in possession for at least two complete years immediately prior to the disposal, the land would not have been eligible for agricultural property relief and therefore no hold-over relief would have been available.[87]

III GIFTS SUBJECT TO AN IMMEDIATE IHT CHARGE
(s.260 RELIEF)

Availability of relief[88]

Hold-over relief is available on a gift or undervalue sale if the relevant disposal **18.48** *"is a chargeable transfer within the meaning of the Inheritance Tax Act 1984"*, or would be such a transfer but for the availability of the annual exemption.[89]

Hence relief under s.260 is available on a gift to UK resident trustees which **18.49** is not a potentially exempt transfer and on the transfer of property out of a settlement (typically the deemed disposal on its termination) which is not a potentially exempt transfer by a beneficiary. This category embraces the creation or termination of a relevant property settlement (i.e. almost all lifetime gifts to trusts after March 22, 2006 and, before that date, gifts to discretionary trusts).[90] However, a gift to a settlor-interested trust cannot qualify for relief.[91] A transfer out of a non-UK resident trust will qualify provided that it is a chargeable transfer *and* provided that the recipient is UK resident.[92]

---

[87] See Ch.46. If, however, Sandra's interest had been non-qualifying (e.g. came into being after March 21, 2006) then there is no need for it to be in place for two years.

[88] See TCGA 1992 s.260 as amended.

[89] The transfer of a business or of agricultural property qualifying for relief from inheritance tax is eligible for relief under TCGA 1992 s.260 because these reliefs reduce the *value* of the chargeable transfer but do not prevent there being such a transfer. As to business and agricultural property relief, see Chs 45 and 46.

[90] Assume that A becomes absolutely entitled to property held in a discretionary trust. For IHT purposes this is a chargeable occasion since the property ceases to be relevant property (see IHTA 1984 s.65(1)(a): note two exceptions—*first* if the transfer occurs within three months of the creation of the settlement or of an anniversary charge and *second* if it occurs within two years of the death of a testator who has created the trust so that there is "reading-back" under IHTA 1984 s.144). Although this is not a chargeable transfer as such "*references in this Act to chargeable transfers shall be construed as including references occasions on which tax is chargeable under Chapter III Part III of this Act.*" (IHTA 1984, s.2(3)). HMRC accept that CGT hold-over relief is available in such cases on the basis that the requirement for there to be an IHT chargeable transfer is met: see (1989) STI 844.

[91] TCGA 1992 ss.169B–G inserted by FA 2004 s.116, Sch.21 paras 4, 10(4) with effect for disposals after December 9, 2003. The definition of a settlor-interested trust was modified by FA 2006 from April 6, 2006: see Ch.7.

[92] Hence, a transfer between two relevant property trusts will not qualify because it is not chargeable (see IHTA 1984 s.81: the property is treated for IHT purposes as remaining comprised in the original settlement).

18.50   Because s.260 specifies that to come within its terms the disposal must be to and by either an individual or the trustees of a settlement,[93] gifts to and by companies do not qualify[94] even though they may be chargeable transfers for IHT purposes. It is not necessary for IHT to be *paid* for hold-over relief to be available. It is, however, necessary for there to be a chargeable transfer.

EXAMPLE 18.15

> Charlotte settles investment property on trust for her brother Luke in 2011.[95] The trust is not settlor-interested. The investment property is worth £325,000, i.e. is within her nil rate band. No IHT is payable but hold-over relief under s.260 is still available. Note that if Charlotte and her husband Alex own the property equally and settle their respective shares in a single trust, then this is treated as a gift by each of them.[96] If the property is worth (say) £650,000 the transfer each makes falls within their respective nil rate bands and no IHT is payable. Both may claim hold-over relief.

18.51   There is no hold-over relief under s.260 on the disposal of a property to a beneficiary within three months of the settlement being established (nor within three months of an IHT anniversary charge) because there is no IHT exit charge.

18.52   If in the above example Charlotte transferred assets to a trust where the loss to her estate did not exceed her annual inheritance tax exemption, hold-over relief is still available even though there is no chargeable transfer. At first sight this might be thought surprising because s.260 requires a chargeable transfer; a chargeable transfer is a transfer of value which is not an exempt transfer and s.19 says that transfers of value not exceeding the annual exemption are exempt. However, s.260(2)(a) gives relief if a disposal is a chargeable transfer *"but for s19 of IHTA 1984"*. Hence a transfer of value which is within the inheritance tax annual exemption can still qualify for hold-over relief.

18.53   In some cases this is important because the loss to the donor's estate might be small but the chargeable gain on the assets transferred high. For example in *Melville* schemes[97] the loss to the donor's estate for inheritance tax purposes often fell within his annual exemption but the gain on the assets gifted was substantial. However, there must be some loss to the donor's estate. Otherwise it is not a transfer of value and therefore cannot be a chargeable transfer. In rare cases an asset might show a significant gain but its disposal would not result in any loss to the donor's estate for inheritance tax purposes.

---

[93] TCGA 1992 s.260(1) as amended by FA 2000 s.90(2) and by FA 2004 s.116, Sch.21 para.5(1), (2).
[94] Unless, of course, the gift to a company is of a business asset (other than shares and securities) when relief may be available under TCGA 1992 s.165 as amended: see 18.29, above. A gift *by* a company can never qualify for hold-over relief.
[95] This will be a relevant property settlement.
[96] For IHT purposes they will be treated as creating two settlements: see IHTA 1984 s.44(2).
[97] Discussed at 31.53.

EXAMPLE 18.16

(1) A is the remainderman of a trust that was previously non-resident. His interest is excluded property for inheritance tax purposes because he did not purchase it and he is not the settlor.[98] He assigns his interest to a discretionary trust for his issue. This is not a chargeable transfer for inheritance tax purposes albeit a disposal of a chargeable asset for capital gains tax purposes. No hold-over relief is available.

(2) B is the owner of a freehold that is subject to a lease for life. The lease for life was granted by B's father to his daughter C for no consideration and B was then gifted the freehold interest. C is now 90 and frail. For capital gains tax purposes the freehold interest has substantial value because the lease will end on C's death. For inheritance tax purposes, the freehold interest is not excluded property but under s.170 IHTA 1984 the freehold interest is worth nothing (because on the death of C the entire value of the property is then taxed under s.43 as if she had an interest in possession). B wishes to give the freehold interest to a trust for his children because it produces no income for him and is an appreciating asset. However, there is no hold-over relief on the gift because it is not a chargeable transfer since there is no loss to his estate resulting from the gift.

18.54 Hold-over relief is also available in the following situations where the relevant transfer is exempt from any IHT charge[99]:

(i) gifts to political parties[100];

(ii) gifts to maintenance funds for historic buildings and for disposals out of settlement to such funds;

(iii) gifts of designated property; and

(iv) gifts of works of art.

A-M trusts and trusts for children

18.55 Section 260 relief was available for a disposal which, by virtue of IHTA 1984, s.71(4), *"does not constitute an occasion on which IHT is chargeable"*.[101] This dealt with the situation where an accumulation and maintenance trust came to an end as a result of the property vesting in the beneficiary absolutely.[102] For instance, if the settlement had been set up in 1990 and provided for the property to be held on trust for B contingent on attaining the age of 18, then when he became 18 in 2005:

---

[98] See IHTA 1984 s.48.
[99] See TCGA 1992 s.260(2) as amended by FA 1998 s.165, Sch.27 Pt IV.
[100] TCGA 1992 s.60(2)(b)(i).
[101] TCGA 1992 s.260(2)(d).
[102] For the meaning of a s.71 accumulation and maintenance trust, see Ch.30.

- there was no IHT charge as a result of s.71(4) and

- CGT hold-over relief was available.

18.56 In practice, the relief rarely applied since most accumulation and maintenance trusts became interest in possession (usually when the beneficiary attained 18) and so, when capital vested (usually when the beneficiary was 25), CGT hold-over relief under s.260 was not available because at the time when the deemed disposal occurred *it was no longer an accumulation and maintenance trust*. By contrast, when the beneficiary became entitled to income at 18, although the nature of the trust changed for IHT purposes, for CGT the same settlement continued, there was no disposal and so no occasion for s.260 to apply. This CGT problem on the ending of accumulation and maintenance trusts produced what was commonly called a *"time bomb trust"*. Of course, since March 22, 2006 it has not been possible to set up new accumulation and maintenance trusts and existing accumulation and maintenance trusts ceased to qualify as such from April 6, 2008 unless they satisfied the revised terms of s.71 which require capital vesting no later than age 18. Section 260(2)(d) remains relevant to these trusts.

EXAMPLE 18.17

The Hawkes Trust was an accumulation and maintenance trust created in 2005 for four grandchildren all aged between 5 and 10 at March 2006. The trust terms provide for children to take income and capital at 25. Before April 6, 2008 the trustees modified the trust so that the grandchildren must now take capital outright at 18. When each grandchild reaches the age of 18 and takes his share of the capital, hold-over relief can be claimed.

18.57 If a beneficiary of an existing accumulation and maintenance trust becomes entitled to the income (e.g. at 18) it will no longer affect any later claim for hold-over relief when they become absolutely entitled to capital. Because the trust was not modified before April 6, 2008 it ceased to meet the revised A-M requirements and fell into the relevant property regime. The interest in possession is not qualifying and therefore hold-over relief is available under s.260(1) when the beneficiary takes capital at 25.

EXAMPLE 18.18

Facts as in Example 18.17 except that the Hawkes Trust provides for grandchildren to take income at 18 and capital at 30. No changes to the terms of the trust were made before April 6, 2008 and so from that date it fell into the relevant property regime. There is no capital gains tax disposal when the grandchildren reach 18 and no hold-over claim is necessary. When they reach 30 they take the capital outright and hold-over relief is available.

As already indicated, FA 2006 prevented any new accumulation and maintenance trusts being set up. It is, however possible, to set up bereaved minor and s.71D (18–25) trusts but these are far more restrictive in scope since they can only be created by will and in favour of a child of the testator. There were limited transitional provisions to allow existing accumulation and maintenance trusts to be converted into s.71D trusts prior to April 6, 2008.[103] For s.71D and bereaved minor trusts, hold-over relief is only relevant when they come to an end and FA 2006 has amended s.260 to provide for relief to be available.[104]

EXAMPLE 18.19

(1) Facts as in Example 18.18 above except that the Hawkes Trust provides for grandchildren to take income at 18 and capital at 25. On April 6, 2008 it fell into the 18–25 (s.71D regime) for IHT purposes. When the grandchildren reach 25 a hold-over relief claim is available since there will be an inheritance tax charge under s.71D.[105]

(2) Jasper dies on April 23, 2011 and by his will leaves property to his son Conrad on attaining the age of 25.

  (i) Jasper has created a s.71D (18–25) trust for IHT purposes;
  (ii) Conrad will become entitled to income at 18 as a result of TA 1925 s.31;
  (iii) at 25 an IHT exit charge will arise (usually calculated by reference to the seven years from his eighteenth birthday) and CGT hold-over relief, under s.260(2)(a), will be available. Note that if Conrad became absolutely entitled to the assets before his eighteenth birthday hold-over relief would be available under s.260(2)(db), albeit that there is no IHT exit charge. If Conrad becomes absolutely entitled to the assets at any time between 18–25 there is a charge to IHT under s.71F and therefore hold-over relief is available under s.260(2)(a).[106]

Offshore trusts and hold-over relief

Hold-over relief under s.260 may be important where transfers are being made out of an offshore trust.

---

[103] Bereaved minor and s.71D trusts are considered in detail in Ch.35.
[104] See TCGA 1992 s.260(2)(da) (trusts for bereaved minors) and (db) (age 18–25 trusts) inserted by FA 2006 Sch.20 para.32.
[105] See Ch.35.
[106] The fact that the tax charged is nil (e.g. because the trust falls within the IHT nil rate band) does not mean no hold-over relief is available. Contrast the position on a transfer of assets out of the settlement within the first quarter of the commencement of a relevant property settlement or the first quarter after a 10-year anniversary of a relevant property settlement when there is no inheritance tax charge (see IHTA 1984 s.65(4)) and therefore no hold-over relief.

EXAMPLE 18.20

The trustees of an offshore settlement set up by a UK resident and domiciled settlor (which is settlor-interested) own assets which show substantial unrealised gains. The trust is discretionary and the trustees resolve to advance all the assets to UK resident beneficiaries (including the settlor). The beneficiaries become absolutely entitled to the property and hold-over relief is available. There is no charge under s.86 on the settlor. Note, however, that if the trustees had previously realised capital gains (stockpiled gains under s.87 not having been matched to earlier capital payments) these gains will be charged on the beneficiaries since the trustees have made a capital payment.[107]

If the trust was an accumulation and maintenance trust for the children and the trustees advanced them the assets, hold-over relief would be available provided that the conditions of s.71(4) are met (i.e. that the trust still met the A-M requirements).

Restrictions on Relief under s.260

18.60 The same restrictions on UK residents and emigration of the donee[108] and the same computational aspects[109] as outlined above in relation to s.165 apply to relief under s.260. The same exclusion of taper relief in the computation of the held-over gain applied on gifts and other disposals made prior to April 6, 2008.[110] Note also the problems that arise as a result of *Crowe v Appleby* when interests vest on attainment of a specified age but the beneficiary is not "absolutely entitled" for CGT purposes.[111]

IV DISPOSALS TO A SETTLOR-INTERESTED TRUST

18.61 Hold-over relief under ss.165 and 260 is not available if there is a disposal into a trust in which the settlor is interested.[112]

EXAMPLE 18.21

On December 10, 2003 X transferred shares in his family company into a life interest trust for himself with a view to restarting the taper relief clock

---

[107] "Stockpiled gains" and the operation of s.87 is considered at 19.27 and following.
[108] See 18.39.
[109] See 18.35.
[110] See 18.35.
[111] See 9.11 and 12.10 for discussion of *Crowe v Appleby* and see A2.327 (Questions 34 and 35).
[112] See FA 2004 s.116, Sch.21 which provides that relief to settlor-interested trusts under TCGA 1992 ss.165 or 260 as amended is not to be available on certain transfers. This had effect in relation to disposals on or after December 10, 2003: see FA 2004 Sch.21 para.10.

(this was in order to lose a "tainted" taper relief period). Hold-over relief under s.165 was not available so that the disposal may have triggered a chargeable gain. (Note, however, that disposals *out of* settlor interested trusts remain eligible for hold-over relief if the transferee is not a settlor-interested trust.) By contrast, if X had made the disposal into trust on December 9, 2003 hold-over relief would have been available.

The main target of the change was "*Melville*[113] *schemes*", which depended upon s.260 hold-over relief being available for a transfer into a settlor-interested discretionary trust although the change also struck at arrangements to restart the taper relief clock.[114] From April 6, 2006 the extension of the definition of settlor-interested trusts to include trusts for dependent children[115] further restricted the opportunities for claiming relief. Hold-over relief continues to be denied on any transfers to settlor-interested trusts (including trusts for dependent children) made after April 5, 2008 even though gains made by those trusts are no longer taxable on the settlor under TCGA 1992 s.77.

Curiously where gifts of business assets are made to minor children outright **18.62** rather than into trust there is no restriction on hold-over relief.

Claw back of hold-over relief

If a trust becomes settlor-interested within the relevant period (defined as six **18.63** years after the end of the year of assessment in which the disposal is made) there is a claw-back of any held-over gain unless the settlor has died before the material time.[116] When the relief was clawed back prior to April 6, 2008 the same problems regarding the availability of taper relief and the increase in capital gains tax rates arose as discussed at 18.11. The gains and losses were determined on the basis that taper relief never applied. Similarly any relief clawed-back under s.169C if the trust becomes settlor-interested cannot qualify for entrepreneurs' relief as discussed at 18.13 and following.

EXAMPLE 18.22

A transfers two investment properties, both commercially let, into a trust in June 2011. Even if the trust is interest in possession for his daughter, provided that the daughter is adult and that the settlor and his wife (civil partner) and any living minor children are excluded from benefit, hold-over relief is available because A has made a chargeable transfer for IHT purposes. It does not matter if the transfer falls within A's IHT nil rate band.

[113] *Melville v IRC* [2001] EWCA Civ 1247; [2002] 1 WLR 407; [2001] STC 1271, CA. See also 31.53.
[114] In practice, the tainted pre-2000 taper relief period had become less of a problem with the passage of time.
[115] Defined as an unmarried (including a child who has not entered into a civil partnership) minor child or step-child of the settlor.
[116] Defined as the time when the trust becomes settlor-interested.

If, however, A's daughter was a minor dependent child, hold-over relief would not be available. Accordingly, if A wanted her to benefit while still a minor he would have to pay inheritance tax at 20 per cent to the extent the value of the investment property exceeded his available nil rate as well as capital gains tax on the chargeable gain. No deduction is given to A for one tax against the other.[117]

EXAMPLE 18.23

In 2010 A sets up a trust for his children. One of his children is under 18. If that child can benefit there is no hold-over relief. In the light of this, A ensures that his minor children are excluded from all benefit until they cease to be dependent.

However, assume that three years later an adult child pays money into the trust. The trust becomes settlor-interested in relation to *the person* who has added property to the settlement because the child is a beneficiary. In those circumstances, even though the original settlor is not a beneficiary and the trust is not settlor-interested in relation *to him*, nevertheless there is a claw-back of the held-over gain.[118] A is subject to tax on the entire gain held-over. If the trustees have disposed of trust assets already or do so in the future, their gains/losses are computed on the basis that there was no hold-over claim. If the trustees themselves claimed hold-over relief on a payment out, the claim made by the trustees is computed on the basis that there was no gain held-over on the original gift from the settlor.[119] The settlor, A, may therefore wish to obtain an indemnity from the trustees to cover any tax liability for which he may become liable if the trustees inadvertently accept property from a beneficiary.

Exceptions[120]

18.64 The restrictions on hold-over relief into settlor-interested trusts do not apply in the following circumstances:

---

[117] See 18.76.

[118] See s.169C condition 1 which refers to "*A settlor who has an interest in the settlement.*" It is enough for either condition 1 or condition 2 to be satisfied. There is no claw-back if the transferor who claimed hold-over relief has died in the claw-back period: TGCA 1992 s.169C(6).

[119] The Budget 2006 explanatory notes on this part of the legislation were misleading:

"*the second condition prevents the first condition being side-stepped by the use of a chain of transfers which interposes one or more intermediate settlements or individuals between an individual and a settlement of which he is a beneficiary and to which he wishes to transfer an asset and obtain the benefit of gifts relief.*"

Subsequent questions raised by the Opposition in Committee did not suggest that the clause should be read in such a limited way.

[120] See TCGA 1992 s.169D.

(i) In the case of a gift to trustees of a maintenance fund for a historic building if they have elected under ITA 2007 s.508 that income arising under the settlement or part of the settlement involved is not to be treated as income of the settlor for the tax year in which the disposal is made[121];

(ii) In the case of a gift into a trust for a disabled beneficiary (whether or not such person is the settlor)[122] two conditions must be satisfied:

    (a) *immediately* after the making of the disposal the settled property is held on trusts which secure that, during the lifetime of a disabled person, not less than half of the property which is applied, is applied for the benefit of the person concerned (the *capital* condition) and that person is entitled to not less than half of the income arising from the property or no such income may be applied for the benefit of any other person or no interest in possession subsists in the settled property (the *income* condition)[123];

    (b) if immediately after the making of the disposal, one or more settlors is "an interested settlor" or will or may acquire such an interest under subsisting arrangements, each such settlor is a disabled beneficiary.[124]

For these purposes a settlor is an "interested settlor" only if he has an interest in the settlement or there are arrangements under which he will or may acquire such an interest.[125] In other words, the settlor can only benefit if he is disabled but spouses and other minor children can benefit whether or not disabled. In deciding whether the trust falls within the exception it is irrelevant that the settlor's spouse/civil partner or dependent children can benefit (or whether they are disabled).[126] The only requirements are that the trust must satisfy the requirements outlined above that it is for a disabled person and that, if he can benefit, the settlor is a disabled person.   **18.65**

As a result of the IHT changes in the taxation of settlements[127] most new inter vivos trusts set up after March 21, 2006 result in an immediate IHT charge (since the relevant property regime applies) and so s.260 hold-over relief may be available. This treatment does not, however, apply if the trust establishes a "disabled person's interest" for *inheritance tax purposes*[128] because in that case the creation of the trust will be either a potentially exempt transfer by the settlor or, as in Example 18.24(1), spouse exempt.[129]   **18.66**

---

[121] TCGA 1992 s.169D(1).

[122] For the definition of disability, see TCGA 1992 s.169D(7) and Ch.36.

[123] The requirements are different from those laid down in FA 2005 s.34(2) which gives special CGT treatment to qualifying trusts for disabled persons, and are also different from the requirements necessary to obtain the full annual CGT exemption: see Ch.36.

[124] Note that this does not mean that the settlor has to be a beneficiary of the trust, merely that *if he is, he must be disabled*.

[125] See TCGA 1992 s.169D(5). Confusingly this provision is not therefore concerned with a "settlor-interested" trust but rather with whether the settlor can benefit!

[126] TCGA 1992 s.169D(5).

[127] See Ch.23.

[128] This term is defined in IHTA 1984 s.89B: see Ch.36.

[129] For instance, if the trust is set up for a disabled child or grandchild, IHTA 1984 s.49(1A) applies s.49(1) so that the disabled person is treated as owning the trust capital and so the definition of a PET in s.3A(1A)(c)(i) or (ii) is met.

Accordingly, hold-over relief will then not be available under s.260 of TCGA 1992 (although may be available under TCGA 1992 s.165 if the assets settled are business assets).[130]

EXAMPLE 18.24

(1) A sets up a settlement which is for the benefit of his disabled wife excluding himself from all benefit. Provided that the conditions relating to the use of income and capital in s.169D(3) are met this will be a qualifying trust with the result that CGT hold-over relief under s.165 will be available provided that the normal conditions for that relief are met. The fact that his minor children may also benefit does not matter, even though they are not disabled. However, if A can benefit there is no hold-over relief.

(2) A sets up a settlement which is for the benefit of his disabled nephew and which satisfies the conditions in s.169D(3). His wife and children who are not disabled can benefit. He is excluded. Provided that the normal conditions for relief under s.165 are met hold-over is available. If A can benefit there is no relief.

(3) A sets up a trust for himself, his wife and children. He is disabled. The capital and income conditions are satisfied. Hold-over relief may be available.

V PAYMENT OF TAX BY INSTALMENTS ON GIFTS AND SALES AT AN UNDERVALUE

18.67 Where gifted property shows a gain and no hold-over relief is available,[131] the transferor will be liable to pay capital gains tax by January 31, following the tax year of disposal. In these circumstances some relief is provided.[132] For gifts of land, shares of a company controlled by the transferor or unlisted shares, where the transferor may elect to pay the tax by 10 equal yearly

---

[130] Can one obtain hold-over relief under s.260TCGA 1992 if a gift of non-business assets is made into a trust that satisfies s.169D(3)? This is possible only if the trust that is established does not create a disabled person's interest for inheritance tax purposes and it is difficult to see how it could satisfy the conditions in s.169D(3) and not also be a disabled person's interest for inheritance tax purposes. If the disabled person is given an entitlement to income in only half the settled property and the capital condition in s.169D(3) is satisfied, it is possible that this does not satisfy s.89B(c) of IHTA 1984 which requires an interest in possession in the settled property—here the beneficiary has an interest in possession in only half the settled property. It would be odd if such a gift was treated as a PET as to half and hold-over relief is then available on the other half held on discretionary trusts. The legislation on disabled trusts is a mess!

[131] For example, because the gift is of non-business assets and is not to a trust or the gift is to a settlor-interested trust; if hold-over relief is available but not claimed (e.g. because the transferor fears that capital gains tax rates will rise) then no instalment relief can be claimed unless hold-over relief is available but the amount of the chargeable gain exceeds the amount which can be held over, e.g. there is some restriction on relief.

[132] By TCGA 1992 s.281.

interest-bearing instalments. The first instalment is due on the normal due date for payment of capital gains tax, i.e. January following the tax year of disposal.

Relief is lost if the asset is subsequently disposed of for any consideration by the transferee and the transferee is connected to the transferor. Relief is also lost if the transferee's successor sells the asset. For example, A gives land to his son B who one year later gives it to C (an unconnected person in relation to A) who immediately sells it. A is no longer entitled to instalment relief after C sells it. **18.68**

If hold-over relief is clawed back because the trust becomes settlor-interested then the chargeable gain deemed to accrue to a transferor under s.169C(7) is also eligible for instalment relief if the other conditions for the relief are satisfied. Relief will not be available if the asset in question has been sold. The relief also applies to gifts into trust or on the ending of a trust where a person becomes absolutely entitled to the settled property as against the trustees. **18.69**

Consideration paid in instalments[133]

A separate relief is given if consideration for the disposal of an asset is payable to the vendor by instalments over a period exceeding 18 months. HMRC may at its discretion allow the person making the disposal to opt to pay the tax by instalments. There is no requirement for him to satisfy HMRC that he would otherwise suffer undue hardship nor are any assets specified. The size and frequency of the instalments are entirely at the discretion of HMRC, but the period over which they are paid: **18.70**

(a) must not exceed eight years; and

(b) must end not later than the date on which the last instalment of the consideration is payable.

VI PRINCIPAL PRIVATE RESIDENCE RELIEF AND S.260 HOLD-OVER

These provisions targeted a CGT saving scheme involving the second home. **18.71**

EXAMPLE 18.25

X owns a second home which has increased in value since he bought it. In due course he wants to sell but meanwhile his (unemployed) son has agreed to live in the property to obtain principal private residence (PPR) relief. X therefore puts the property into a discretionary trust claiming hold-over relief under s.260. It is envisaged that after the son

[133] TCGA 1992 s.280.

(a beneficiary of the trust) has occupied the property as his PPR it will be sold and the entire gain (including the held-over gain) will be exempt from CGT. This arrangement is not effective:

(1) If X or his spouse (or civil partner) or dependent children (including stepchildren) are beneficiaries. The trust is "settlor-interested" and so hold-over relief is not available. This change affected disposals into trust on or after December 10, 2003 (April 6, 2006 in the case of dependent children).

(2) If none of the above can benefit under the trust, the gain can be held-over but PPR relief will not be available on either the held-over gain *or any gain accruing whilst the house is in the trust*,[134] i.e. it is not possible to combine a hold-over claim with PPR relief on the property.[135] There is a similar restriction if the house is taken out of the trust by a hold-over election.

EXAMPLE 18.26

Amy owns a house which is not her main residence. It shows a chargeable gain of £50,000 and is worth £250,000. In January 2007 she transfers it into a trust for her adult children from which she, her spouse and minor children are excluded. She makes a hold-over election under s.260. One of her children occupies the property as his main residence. The trustees sell the property in December 2007 realising a gain of £75,000. The entire gain is taxable on the trustees including the £25,000 gain arising during the period of ownership of the trustees. If, however, Amy revokes[136] her hold-over relief election then the trustees can claim principal private residence relief on a gain of £25,000 arising during their period of ownership but Amy will be subject to CGT on her £50,000 gain (albeit with the benefit of taper relief).

18.72 Transitional rules[137] dealt with the situation where the house had been put into trust before December 10, 2003 or taken out of the trust with a hold-over claim and principal private residence relief was available on such earlier periods of ownership. Broadly speaking it was important in such cases to trigger a disposal at the earliest available opportunity as the following examples show.

EXAMPLE 18.27

X set up a discretionary trust on March 10, 2003 into which he transferred his second home purchased for £100,000 in 2006. Its value was

---

[134] Contrast s.74 TCGA 1992 imposing a claw-back charge on the death of the life tenant only by reference to the hold-over gain of the gain subsequently accruing after the gift into the trust.

[135] TCGA 1992 s.226A inserted by FA 2005 s.117, Sch.22 paras 6 and 7(3) effective for disposals made after December 9, 2003.

[136] For time limits on revocation, see 18.10.

[137] TCGA 1992 s.226A as inserted by FA 2004 s.117, Sch.22 para.6, with the transitional provisions in FA 2004 Sch.22 para.8.

then £250,000; the gain held-over was £150,000. X is a beneficiary under the trust[138] and the property is occupied by X's son who moved in on June 1, 2003. Assume there was a disposal of the property on March 10, 2004, when it is worth £300,000.

	£	£
Disposal proceeds		300,000
Deduct: Acquisition cost	250,000	
Less: Held-over gain	150,000	
Base cost for the trustees		100,000
Gain		200,000*
Deduct: Main residence relief		
(including last 36 months)[139]		
£200,000 × (275/365)		150,685
Chargeable		
***£200,000 × (90/365)		49,315
Deduct: Annual exemption (say)		3,950
Taxable gain		45,365
Tax payable at 34%**		15,424**

* Less incidental costs of acquisition and disposal

** 40% for disposals by trustees after April 5, 2004

*** Period from December 10 to date of disposal

18.73 Paragraph 8 of Sch.22 to FA 2004 introduced a "*post-commencement period*" defined as the period beginning on December 10, 2003 and ending on the date of disposal. Main residence relief is restricted to that part of the gain referable, on a time basis, to the period of ownership up to December 10, 2003. The exemption given for the last 36 months of ownership is not available if any part of the period of ownership falls on or after December 10, 2003.

EXAMPLE 18.28

The period of ownership is one year. Principal private residence relief is available up to December 10, (because looking back three years from the date of disposal this will cover all the period from March 2003) but not for the period from December 10, even though this period falls within the last three years of ownership. If the trustees had delayed selling the property until (say) March 2006 and the gain was still

---

[138] That did not matter in the case of disposals into trust before December 10, 2003.
[139] TCGA 1992 s.223(2)(a).

£200,000, main residence relief would only be available on 275/1095 of the gain (i.e. on £50,228) and the chargeable gain would be 820/1095 = £149,772.

Distributions to beneficiaries

18.74 Note how the rules apply if the trustees have distributed the property to a beneficiary before or after December 10, 2003 and the beneficiary occupies as his main residence expecting to obtain principal private residence relief in due course.

EXAMPLE 18.29

In December 1992 John settled cash into a discretionary trust for his children. The trustees purchased a house. In November 2001 the trustees advanced the property to Harry, his son, who has been in occupation as his main residence for most of the trustees' period of ownership. A hold-over claim was made because not all the gain realised by the trustees was covered by principal private residence relief. Harry continued to occupy the property as his main residence until he sold the house in January 2009. In these circumstances because Harry's allowable expenditure is reduced as a result of the trustees' hold-over relief claim he is not entitled to main residence relief on the entire gain. The transitional rule applies because the gift out of the trust on which a hold-over relief claim was made occurred before December 2003. Effectively Harry will receive main residence relief from November 2001 up to December 10, 2003 but thereafter no relief. *The longer he owns the property after December 10, 2003, the less relief will be available.*[140]

18.75 In cases where the time limits have not expired the trustees might revoke the hold-over claim so that there is a small gain on the transfer out to Harry and then he can acquire the property at market value and claim main residence relief for the entire gain arising during his period of ownership.

Suppose in Example 18.29 that the trustees had advanced the property to Harry after December 9, 2003. In those circumstances if they claimed hold-over relief it would appear that no transitional relief is available to Harry because the relevant earlier disposal took place after December 9, 2003. Hence Harry loses the benefit of *any* principal private residence relief.

In general, when trustees transfer property to beneficiaries which has either been subject to a hold-over relief claim in the past or is now subject to a claim, the position shall be reviewed if the beneficiary is in occupation of the property as his main residence.

---

[140] Watch inheritance tax after March 21, 2006: previously he could have set up an interest in possession trust for himself with no inheritance tax consequences.

A settlor transferring assets into a settlor-interested trust faces potential **18.76**
double tax charges. He may pay inheritance tax on the gift into the settlement
at 20 per cent (to the extent the value exceeds his unused IHT nil rate band)
as well as capital gains tax at 28 per cent on the chargeable gain. No relief
for the inheritance tax is given when calculating the chargeable gain on the
transferor's gift.[141]

If, however, a hold-over claim is made (the trust is not settlor-interested) **18.77**
relief is given for the lesser of the inheritance tax attributable to the value of
the asset and the amount of the held-over gain in calculating the chargeable
gain subsequently realised when the transferee trustees dispose of the asset.[142]
It does not appear to matter whether the transferor or transferee paid the
inheritance tax on the transfer into trust.[143] The relief is the smaller of the
inheritance tax attributable to the value of the asset and the amount that
would be the transferee's chargeable gain on the disposal ignoring any relief
for the inheritance tax due. Hence the relief cannot create a loss.

EXAMPLE 18.30

(1) In July 2011 X sets up a life interest trust for his wife. Although a chargeable transfer for IHT purposes, no hold-over relief is available because
the trust is settlor-interested. Assume that he pays IHT of £5,000 and
CGT of £40,000. He cannot deduct one tax against the other. He dies
in 2010 and further IHT is due of £5,000. The trustees pay this. If the
trustees sell the asset there is no relief for the IHT against the chargeable
gain.

(2) If however, a hold-over relief claim could have been made on the initial
gift into trust, the trustees can deduct the lesser of the IHT attributable
to the value of the property settled and the chargeable gain held-over
against the gain on the sale.

(3) Assume in (1) that there is no sale. In 2014 the trustees—exercising a
power to pay or apply capital—advance the trust fund outright to Mrs
X holding over the gain. On a subsequent disposal by Mrs X she can
deduct the lesser of the inheritance tax payable on the termination of
the trust (the "exit" charge) and the chargeable gain held-over on a subsequent disposal of the asset by her.

(4) As in (1) except that Mrs X dies in 2012 before the asset is sold
whereupon the trusts end with the property being held for the couple's
daughter absolutely. There is an IHT exit charge because of the ending

---

[141] See 10.08 for further analysis where the donor does not pay the capital gains tax.
[142] See TGCA 1992 s.260(7) and s.165(10) and IHTA 1984 s.165 when the donee pays the
CGT. See also 10.08 and Example 10.4.
[143] The settlor may have paid the initial 20% inheritance tax on a gift to relevant property
settlement which will involve grossing up (see Ch.29). However relief is only given on the value
transferred excluding grossing up.

of the trust but CGT hold-over relief is available on any gain accruing during the trustees' period of ownership. The position is better than in (3) above where both Mr and Mrs X could end up paying inheritance tax at 40 per cent on the property. Care should be taken before breaking up relevant property trusts and placing the assets in the hands of elderly beneficiaries.

(5) On March 22, 2006 Mrs Y is entitled to a qualifying interest in possession which ends with her death in 2011 when the trust also ends. The value of the settled fund is taxed as part of Mrs Y's estate at 40 per cent and there is a CGT uplift to market value. No hold-over claim is available and none is needed.

VIII TAX PLANNING AND HOLD-OVER RELIEF

Opportunities

18.78 Limited tax planning using hold-over elections remains possible as follows:

(a) Exits from relevant property trusts (whether or not settlor-interested) can benefit from capital gains tax hold-over under s.260. Hence *Melville* schemes established before December 10, 2003 could be completed provided that the appointee was an individual (not a new trust) or the terms of the existing trust are merely varied.

(b) Hold-over relief may be used to extract funds from offshore trusts without triggering a capital gains tax charge on the settlor.[144]

(c) If a gain was held over on creation of the trust and the qualifying life tenant is elderly consider ending the trust while the life tenant is still alive.

EXAMPLE 18.31

Chris settles farmland qualifying for hold-over relief into trust for his sister Dot in 2005, Dot taking a qualifying interest in possession. On Dot's death the assets will pass on interest in possession trusts to Dot's child (this will be a relevant property trust). Dot is elderly and in poor health and when she dies the held-over gain on the way into trust will come into charge although a further hold-over claim could be made at that point.

Instead the trustees advance the farmland to Dot outright.[145] This has no inheritance tax consequences since she is treated as owning the

---

[144] Under TCGA 1992 s.86: see Ch.19.
[145] Under an express power in the settlement.

underlying assets.[146] The trustees again hold-over the gain on the farm-land. On Dot's death the held-over gain disappears and the farmland is rebased to market value.

(d) The use of a nil rate band relevant property trust for inheritance tax planning may still be attractive.[147] The key is that the trust must not be "settlor-interested".

EXAMPLE 18.32

X puts shares in his investment company into a discretionary trust for the benefit of his grandchildren. He can:

(1) limit the value transferred to his available nil rate band for inherit-ance tax;
(2) include his adult children; minor children can also be included provided that they cannot benefit until they reach 18;
(3) make an election for capital gains tax hold-over relief under s.260(2)(a) of the 1992 Act.

Traps

A gift made within seven years of the donor's death can result in the worst **18.79** of all worlds. The gift may be immediately chargeable to inheritance tax or become so if the PET fails but there is no tax-free uplift for capital gains tax because the donor did not own the asset at the date of death.[148]

Note also that a claw-back of a held-over gain can result be a disaster because of the loss of entrepreneurs' relief although in some cases, as Example 18.13 illustrates, if the gain is clawed back it may be taxed at lower rates after April 5, 2008.

Before any hold-over relief election is made, consider whether entrepre- **18.80** neurs' relief is available on the disposal and if it is likely that tax rates will increase in the future. It may be preferable to take advantage of entrepreneurs' relief and not claim hold-over relief, particularly now that the lifetime allow-ance is £10 million. For many taxpayers this limit will never be reached. If hold-over relief is claimed on a gift which was eligible for entrepreneurs' relief the eventual tax bill may be higher if the donee does not qualify for entrepre-neurs' relief on a later disposal of the asset.

---

[146] IHTA 1984 s.53(2).
[147] As to nil rate band discretionary trusts, see Chs 29 and 38.
[148] Consider whether there may be a way out if the donor was in ill health at the date of the gift and did not know this: see 1.35 and *Re Griffiths* [2008] STC 776.

CHAPTER 19

OFFSHORE TRUSTS

- Background (**19.01**)
- UK domiciled and resident settlors (**19.13**)
- Foreign domiciled settlors (**19.26**)
- Taxation of UK resident and domiciled beneficiaries (**19.27**)
- Taxation of foreign domiciled UK resident beneficiaries (**19.49**)
- Anti "flip-flop" legislation and Schs 4B and 4C (**19.69**)
- Information requirements for offshore trusts (**19.79**)
- Conclusions (**19.80**)

I BACKGROUND

19.01 The CGT rules on offshore trusts are complex and since 1991 have been subject to almost continuous legislative change. Until FA 2008 the rules did not significantly affect foreign domiciliaries who were not subject to either s.86 (the settlor charge) or s.87 (capital payments regime for beneficiaries). Hence gains could be realised by offshore trusts (and their underlying companies) without any capital gains tax concerns for either the trustees or the foreign domiciliary. The main problem for the foreign domiciliary if he received a capital payment or benefit from a trust, was income tax and in particular the transfer of assets (TOA) provisions.[1]

EXAMPLE 19.1

> Giles is a beneficiary of an offshore trust. He is not UK domiciled but is UK resident and the settlor (now deceased) was not UK domiciled. Some trust income has been distributed as it arises but there is over £2 million income retained in a holding company and at the trust level ("relevant income"). The trust has realised significant gains (both on non-distributor and distributor funds).[2] In 2006 he received a capital payment of £1 million that he remits to the UK.

---

[1] See Ch.8.
[2] These are discussed further in Ch.53. The regime changed from December 1, 2009. Non-

The tax position in 2005 was that Giles did not pay capital gains tax because, before 2008, s.87 did not apply to foreign domiciled beneficiaries. However, unless the motive defence applied or (possibly) the payment received from the trust is derived from a transfer of assets into the trust which has never produced relevant income, in 2006 he will suffer an income tax charge at 40 per cent on the capital by reference to the pool of relevant income, taxable on the remittance basis.[3]

If he receives the capital payment in 2008–09 his tax position is no different. The TOA provisions take priority so the payment remains subject to 40 per cent income tax. However, once the relevant income pool has been exhausted he is then potentially subject to tax on any trust gains subject to the remittance basis if applicable and the rebasing election. These are discussed further below.

19.02 This CGT exemption for foreign domiciliaries who held assets in trust was in stark contrast to the position of UK resident domiciliaries where, since 1998, the offshore trust regime has resulted in penal tax charges and heavy compliance costs. One of the ironies of FA 2008 is that it significantly improved the tax position of UK domiciliaries in the context of offshore trusts—instead of paying tax at rates of up to 64 per cent the maximum charge until June 23, 2010 was 28.8 per cent as a result of the introduction of a flat CGT rate of 18 per cent. Even after the rates changed from June 23, 2010 the maximum charge is 44.8 per cent. Moreover, a change in FA 2008 to the matching rules from first in/first out to last in/first out meant that the "interest" charge is now less on some capital payments.

19.03 However, FA 2008 worsened the position of foreign domiciliaries who are UK resident: for the first time they became subject to capital gains tax (under TCGA 1992 s.87) if they received capital payments from offshore trusts on or after April 6, 2008.[4]

19.04 Of course offshore trusts are not the only offshore vehicles available: offshore companies, mutual funds and offshore investment bonds can also be used to mitigate UK tax. This chapter considers the following:

(i) the tax treatment of non-UK resident trusts in cases where the settlor is UK resident and domiciled;

(ii) the tax treatment of non-UK resident trusts when the settlor is not resident in the UK (wherever domiciled);

(iii) the tax treatment of non-UK resident trusts when the settlor is not UK domiciled but is UK resident;

(iv) the taxation of UK resident and domiciled beneficiaries of a non-UK resident trust;

(v) the taxation of UK resident and non-domiciled beneficiaries;

(vi) flip-flops and other offshore matters.

reporting offshore funds are collective investment schemes which do not have "reporting status". An offshore income gain accrues when a material interest in a non-reporting fund is disposed of. Many offshore funds such as hedge funds are non-reporting funds.
[3] The position on offshore income gains also needs to be considered: see Ch.53.
[4] The new regime for foreign domiciliaries is summarised at 19.11 and is discussed at 19.49.

Overview

19.05   Non-resident trustees do not pay capital gains tax. Hence, anti-avoidance legislation is needed to ensure that when UK residents set up offshore trusts or receive benefits from such trusts, capital gains tax is charged. Successive governments have therefore introduced increasingly complex legislation to try and ensure that the use of offshore trusts does not bring tax advantages. This complexity can work for or against a beneficiary and can be unfair. For example, s.87 provides that when a capital payment is made to a beneficiary it is matched to available trust gains up to the amount of the payment (rather than matched pro rata between trust capital and gains). This can have arbitrary results.

EXAMPLE 19.2

> A and B are beneficiaries of a non-resident trust set up by their deceased father. They are both UK resident and domiciled. The fund is now worth £1.5 million. They become entitled to capital at 40. The trust has realised gains in the past of £200,000 and no capital distributions have been made. A is the first to reach 40 in 2009 and receive his share of £750,000. The entire trust gains are matched to his capital payment. As he is UK resident and domiciled he pays capital gains tax on the £200,000 gains of £57,600 (assuming a rate, including "interest", of 28.8 per cent). Assume the trust realises no further gains and the next payment is to B a year later at which point the trust is ended. B pays no tax because all the trust gains have been washed out. A ends up with less than B. The position would be even worse for A if the trust had realised (say) £750,000 gains. In that case all his capital payment is matched to trust gains and taxed at 28.8% = £216,000. For the position if further gains are realised after A has received his capital payment see 19.32 below.
>
> If however, A is not UK resident then there is no tax when he receives his share of the trust fund but the trust gains have still been "washed out". The result is that B can then receive his share tax-free (assuming the trust realises no further gains before it is ended).[5]

Summary of changes

19.06   **From 1965 to 1981:** FA 1965 s.42 imposed a charging system for non-UK resident trusts that led to major difficulties and was ultimately abandoned in 1981.

19.07   **From 1981 to 1991:** FA 1981 s.80 introduced a charging system based on capital distributions received by UK domiciled and resident beneficiaries provided that the trust had been established by a UK domiciled settlor. This is

---

[5] This is discussed further at 19.40.

now the s.87 charge. One consequence was that offshore trusts could be used to defer indefinitely the payment of CGT and, in addition, there was no exit charge when a UK trust migrated. Hence, even if the trust was one that could benefit the settlor, no capital gains tax charge arose when gains were realised, despite the settlor being UK resident and domiciled. It was only when capital payments were made to him that any tax was suffered. This meant that potentially there was an indefinite deferral of capital gains tax with no penalty paid for that deferral. UK domiciled settlors therefore found that there was no disadvantage in holding assets through offshore trusts. If the trust realised gains no tax was payable until distributions were made to the settlor who by that time might have left the UK. In the meantime the trustees could invest the gross gain. Trusts with foreign domiciled settlors were at an even greater advantage because neither they nor any beneficiaries (whether UK domiciled or not) were subject to capital gains tax on capital payments from the trusts.

From 1991 to 1998: major changes were made by FA 1991: **19.08**

(i) *"Interest" charge*: to "encourage" trustees to distribute capital as soon as the gain arose, an interest charge was imposed on UK resident and domiciled beneficiaries receiving capital payments if the trustees delayed in distributing gains. The intention was to impose a higher rate of tax on offshore trusts where gains were realised but were not immediately taxed. Despite the maximum penalty being an extra 24 per cent tax charge (so that higher rate taxpayers could end up paying at a rate of 64 per cent), this did not encourage the re-importation of trusts or the distribution of capital.

(ii) *Settlor charge*: FA 1991 provided that new non-resident trusts set up after March 18, 1991 by UK resident and domiciled settlors where the settlor, his spouse or children and their spouses could benefit were subject to an immediate CGT charge ("the s.86 charge") on the settlor if gains were made (these were known as "settlor-interested trusts"). Hence the deferral advantages were lost for new trusts set up by UK resident and domiciled settlors unless the beneficiaries were grandchildren or other persons apart from children, settlor or spouses.

However, trusts set up and funded by foreign domiciled settlors (whether before or after 1991) were not affected by any of these changes even if all the beneficiaries were UK domiciled or resident: gains realised by these trusts were not subject to CGT even if capital payments were made to UK resident and domiciled beneficiaries. As noted in Example 19.1 the transfer of assets regime under TA 1988 s.740[6] might cause a problem in such cases.

Offshore trusts set up by UK domiciled and resident settlors before March 18, 1991 continued to operate under the old deferral regime and were therefore able to avoid the capital gains tax s.86 charge on gains provided that there was no "tainting".

---

[6] Now ITA 2007 s.731.

Example 19.3

Andrew, a UK resident domiciliary and higher rate taxpayer, in 1990
settled assets on interest in possession trusts for himself and then to his
children. The gain was held-over and then the trust emigrated. (At that
time there was no claw-back of the held-over gain.) The trust fund comprised only shares in a private trading company. In 1997 the company
was sold. The trustees realised gains of £2 million but these are not
taxable unless and until Andrew or another beneficiary receives capital
payments. As long as Andrew and his children do not receive capital distributions in excess of their unused annual capital gains tax exemption
each year, no tax is paid. The s.87 gains can gradually be "washed out".
Provided the disposal was made before March 1998 (see 19.08 below)
this tax treatment remains broadly unchanged: capital payments can be
limited to the unused annual exemption each year. If capital payments
were made to Andrew in excess of his exemption before April 6, 2008 then
the excess could have been taxed at 64 per cent in his hands as a higher
rate taxpayer. If such capital payments are made to him between April
6, 2008 and June 22, 2010 inclusive then he is taxed at 28.8 per cent.[7] For
capital payments received thereafter he is taxed at 44.8 per cent.

(iii) *Exit charge*: From March 19, 1991 an exit charge was levied on UK
trusts which emigrated.[8] This stopped the sort of arrangements in
Example 19.3 above: on emigration of Andrew's trust after March 18,
1991 the held-over gain would be triggered.[9]

FA 1998 changes

19.09 There were further changes involving:

(1) from April 6, 1998, an extension of the s.86 settlor charge to settlements
created before the 1991 changes. This meant that almost all the pre-
1991 trusts which had been set up by UK domiciled settlors wanting
to defer capital gains tax were now caught. Hence, from March 1998 a
UK domiciled settlor pays tax on an arising basis on all trust gains if
the trust can benefit "defined persons" and the settlor is alive. While the
trust is non-UK resident this remains the case even after April 5, 2008.
Of course, if the trust is imported then the trustees rather than the settlor
pay tax on future gains;

---

[7] See 19.45. F(No.2)A 2010 Sch.1 para.22 introduced a transitional rule in respect of capital
payments received before June 23, 2011 that are matched to gains realised before April 6, 2011.
The tax rate plus supplemental charge if applicable is 18% even if the trust gains are realised
June 23, 2010 and April 5, 2011. See 19.12. Note that if capital payments are received after
June 22, 2010 or capital payments are received before June 23, 2010 but matched to trust gains
realised after April 5, 2011 then the higher 28% rate applies (assuming that the beneficiary is a
higher rate taxpayer).
[8] See TCGA 1992 ss.80–84 and Ch.4.
[9] See Ch.4.

(2) including "grandchildren" in the class of "defined person" for the purpose of the settlor charge if the trust was established or tainted after March 16, 1998;

(3) extending the capital payments charge under s.87 on UK resident and domiciled beneficiaries who received payments from offshore trusts even when the settlor was not domiciled or resident in the UK when setting up the trust or subsequently;

(4) widening the tax charge on disposals of beneficial interests in a settlement[10];

(5) new rules to ensure that a settlor or beneficiary could not avoid the ss.86 and 87 charges by becoming non-resident unless they left the UK for at least five years.[11]

This process was continued by anti-avoidance measures in FA 2000, FA 2003 and F(No.2)A 2005 mainly aimed at stopping the circumvention of the settlor s.86 charge or the beneficiary s.87 charge.

19.10

FA 2008 changes

(1) The s.86 settlor charge remains restricted to UK domiciled settlors. Non-UK domiciled settlors are not subject to tax under s.86 even if they opt to be taxed on an arising basis on worldwide income and personal gains, i.e. they are not remittance basis users.[12]

19.11

(2) The capital payments charge under s.87 applies to all beneficiaries wherever domiciled, including the settlor.

(3) A remittance basis user will be liable to CGT only if a capital payment is remitted to, or a benefit received in the UK.

(4) Capital payments made to non-UK domiciliaries before April 6, 2008 will not be taxed even if matched with post-April 5, 2008 gains and irrespective of whether the beneficiary is a remittance basis user provided that he is still foreign domiciled at the time of matching.

(5) Non-UK domiciliaries are not taxed on capital payments after April 5, 2008 where these are matched with pre-April 6, 2008 gains, whether or not the beneficiary is a remittance basis user.

(6) Trustees have an option to rebase assets within trusts and certain underlying companies at April 6, 2008.

(7) Transitional rules apply to payments made between March 12, 2008 and April 5, 2008.

---

[10] See Ch.20.
[11] See Ch.3.
[12] Foreign domiciliaries who are UK resident but claim the remittance basis are called "remittance basis users". See Ch.5 for further details of remittance basis users. Once they are UK resident for seven years they must pay the annual £30,000 charge and lose their personal allowances from the date of arrival if they claim the remittance basis: see 5.21.

(8) The situs of assets on which the trust gain is realised is irrelevant to the remittance basis. What matters is whether the beneficiary has remitted the capital into the UK under the extended remittance rules in ITA 2007 s.809L[13] or received the benefit in the UK.

(9) The first-in first-out rule will no longer apply to match gains with capital payments.[14] Instead capital payments will be matched first to gains of the current year before being matched to gains of earlier years on a LIFO basis.

(10) Gains which have already been realised prior to April 6, 2008 will still have the benefit of any taper relief albeit they will only be taxed at 18 per cent if matched to capital payments made between April 6, 2008 and June 22, 2010.

Changes in F(No.2)A 2010

19.12   Three changes were introduced that affect the rates of capital gains tax. *First*, Sch.1 para.22 provides that any capital payments received after June 22, 2010 whether matched to trust gains realised before or after this date, are taxed at 28 per cent in the hands of the beneficiary assuming that he is a higher rate taxpayer. (The rate is 18 per cent if and insofar as the beneficiary has not utilised or fully utilised his income tax basic rate band (£37,400).)

Secondly, if a capital payment is received before June 23, 2010 but matched to trust gains realised before April 6, 2011 (whether or not after June 22, 2010) then the rate of tax is still a flat rate 18 per cent. Hence many trustees deliberately realised gains before April 6, 2011 where there were unmatched capital payments in order to secure the lower rate.

Thirdly, for 2010–11 any trust gains that are chargeable on the settlor under s.86 continue to be taxed at the flat rate 18 per cent whether these gains are realised before or after June 22, 2010.[15]

II UK DOMICILED AND RESIDENT SETTLORS

19.13   The present legislation is contained in TCGA 1992 s.86 and Sch.5. It applies at any time in a tax year if three conditions are satisfied:

(i) the settlor is resident and UK domiciled[16];

---

[13] See Ch.5.
[14] See 19.32.
[15] See para.21. They are treated as accruing before June 23, 2010.
[16] If he is non-UK resident then there is no s.86 charge even if UK domiciled unless he returns within five years of leaving or was not UK resident in four out of the seven years immediately preceding his departure: see Ch.5. Note that if the trust realised gains in, say, 2006 when the settlor was non-UK resident and the settlor returns within five years but after April 5, 2008, such gains are deemed to accrue to him in the year of return (unless otherwise attributed to beneficiaries under s.87) and are taxed on him at 18% if he returns before April 6, 2011 (without any taper relief): see TCGA 1992 ss.86A and 10A(2). If he returns after this date within five

(ii) the settlement is a qualifying settlement; and

(iii) the settlement is non-UK resident throughout the tax year. (If it was UK resident for even part of a tax year then it is UK resident for the entire tax year and from April 6, 2008 the trustees are taxed on any gains.)

When these conditions are satisfied, gains realised by the trustees, which would have attracted a UK CGT charge had the trustees been resident, are taxed as gains of the settlor at a flat rate of 18 per cent up to April 6, 2011 and thereafter at 28 per cent if he is a higher rate taxpayer. The gains are treated as the top slice of his overall gains for the year concerned. Such gains can be reduced by the "personal" losses of the settlor and his annual exemption if available.[17] If the settlor is not interested in the settlement (e.g. because all relevant defined persons have been excluded) then the fact that he is resident and domiciled in the UK will not result in any tax charge on him. If the settlor has died then there is no tax charge under s.86 in the year of death.

"Settlement" and "settlor" are defined as for income tax[18] to include an **19.14** arrangement (so bounty is required) and settlor includes a testator or intestate when the settlement arises under a will or intestacy.[19]

EXAMPLE 19.4

(1) Fred set up and funded[20] an offshore trust in 1999. It is one from which he can benefit and he is UK domiciled and resident.[21] The trustees sell a picture realising a gain of £1 million in 2006–07. The trustees do not pay any tax. Fred, however, is liable to pay the capital gains tax although he has a right of reimbursement against the trustees.[22] The trustees have no annual exemption although trust losses can reduce the trust gains taxed on Fred.

If the trustees had realised losses of £500,000 in an earlier year these losses can be carried forward set against the gains and so reduce the tax charge on Fred. If the trustees had owned the picture on March 16, 1998, non-business assets taper relief based on their period of ownership is available to reduce the gain charged on Fred in 2006–07.[23] Hence the net gain after the losses will be £500,000 and after taper relief of 35 per

years of leaving they are taxed at 28% if he is a higher rate taxpayer even if realised in, say, 2007–08 when he might have had some taper relief!

[17] See Ch.21.
[18] See ITOIA 2005 s.620(1) and Ch.7.
[19] TCGA 1992 s.87(6) as amended by FA 2008.
[20] A person is a settlor if the settled property consists of or includes property originating from him—Sch.5 para.6. The provision can be direct or indirect and reciprocal arrangements are countered. However, some bounty must be involved (so commercial arrangements such as offshore employee benefit trusts set up to motivate staff are outside s.86). Moreover if there is one settlor X who settles £1 million and Y adds, say, £100 to the trust, Y can only be taxed on the gains arising from the £100 not from the gains arising on £1 million.
[21] If Fred was non-UK domiciled, s.86 does not apply. If he was non-resident then again it does not apply (although note the rules on temporary non-residence which can result in a charge if he returns to the UK within five years of ceasing to be resident: see Ch.5).
[22] Such right of reimbursement is not treated as a capital payment under s.87 TCGA 1992.
[23] Taper relief was abolished in respect of disposals after April 5, 2008.

cent he will be taxed on a gain of £325,000 at (say) 40 per cent. This is an effective rate of 26 per cent on the net gains.

(2) If the trust was imported to the UK in 2006–07 in the tax year after the losses had been realised those losses could not be set against the gain subsequently realised when the trust was UK resident.[24]

(3) If Fred dies during the course of the 2006–07 tax year, no gains realised by the trustees can be attributed to him in that year under s.86.

(4) If the disposal was in 2008–09 and the trust was imported in that tax year (whether before or after disposal) no gains would be taxed on Fred. Instead the gains would be taxed on the trustees at 18 per cent until June 22, 2010 and thereafter at 28 per cent. (If a trust is UK resident for any part of the year it is UK resident for the whole year.)

(5) If Fred leaves the UK and during the period of his non-residence the trust realises gains, he is not taxed on those gains unless he returns to the UK within five years of departure.[25] If he does return within five years then trust gains are taxed on him at 18 per cent if he returns before April 6, 2011 and thereafter at 28 per cent if he is a higher rate taxpayer.

The settlor is given a statutory right to recover any s.86 tax that he suffers from his trustees, but the extent to which this right may be enforced in a foreign jurisdiction remains uncertain.[26]

When is a settlement "qualifying"?

19.15   Section 86 originally applied to "qualifying settlements" which were defined in Sch.5 para.9 as non-UK resident settlements created "*on or after 19 March 1991*" which could benefit defined persons. Pre-March 1991 settlements were therefore generally outside the scope of the rules (and were known as "golden trusts") but para.9(2) provided that in four situations such settlements could *become* qualifying settlements (see further SP 5/92): this is known as "tainting".

19.16   Tainting could arise if any one of four conditions was satisfied on or after March 19, 1991:

(i) Property or income was added to the trust (by anyone, unless the transaction was at arm's length).

(ii) The settlement was UK resident and became non-UK resident.

(iii) The terms of the settlement were varied so that a defined person became for the first time a person who would *or* might benefit from the trust.

(iv) A defined person (within para.9(7): see definition of defined persons at 19.16 below) who was not capable of benefiting from the trust before March 19, 1991 enjoyed a benefit for the first time.[27]

---

[24] For the loss relief provisions, see Ch.21.
[25] See rules on temporary non-residence in Ch.5.
[26] See CGTM 38321 and 19.22.
[27] See SP 5/92 for examples of tainting.

When does tainting occur?

EXAMPLE 19.5

The Chamberlain Family UK Trust was set up in 1983. In 1997 the trustees become non-UK resident. Not only did that event trigger an exit charge[28] but, in addition, because the settlement was exported after March 18, 1991 it became a "qualifying settlement".

EXAMPLE 19.6

A Jersey settlement was set up in 1989 by a UK resident and domiciled settlor for his grandchildren:

(a) In 1994, a court order was obtained whereby the beneficial class was widened to include the settlor's children. This had the effect of turning the trust into "a qualifying settlement". By contrast, in settlements where the trustees have *always* had the power to add beneficiaries and exercised that power to add a "defined person" after March 1991 it was not thought that the terms of the trust had been varied so that it became a "qualifying settlement". (In SP 5/92 it is stated that *where the terms of the trust include a power to appoint anyone within a specified range to be a beneficiary, exercise of that power after March 19, 1991 will not be regarded as a variation of the settlement*. When the trustees have a general power to add anyone the position is unclear); or

(b) the trustees distributed funds to the settlor's spouse who was not a beneficiary. The effect of this breach of trust was to convert the trust into "a qualifying settlement" since she was now a person who had enjoyed a benefit (and was a "defined person") and she was not a person who might have been expected to have enjoyed such a benefit from the settlement after March 18, 1991; or

(c) on April 1, 1992 the son of the settlor added property to his father's trust. An addition, whether by the settlor or another, had the effect of turning the trust into a "qualifying settlement" and the son is taxable under s.86 in respect of gains realised from property added by him. Also the father will henceforth be taxed on all other gains. This provision had to be watched carefully: it did not apply in cases where there was an accretion to settlement funds (e.g. where the trust received dividends or bonus shares from a company in which it had investments) nor if the settlor added property to discharge the administrative expenses of the *trust* (not an underlying *company*) to the extent that such expenses could not be discharged out of trust income.[29]

---

[28] For the exit charge, see Ch.4.
[29] On the meaning of "administrative expenses" see SP 5/92 and especially para.26.

1998 changes to the meaning of qualifying settlements[30]

19.17 As noted above, the 1991 changes did not persuade taxpayers to repatriate their *existing* trusts. Such trusts could still realise gains tax-free and the beneficiaries might emigrate before receiving capital payments. Although the 1991 changes reduced the number of *new* offshore trusts, the settlor could still set up an offshore trust for his grandchildren and obtain capital gains tax deferral advantages on his existing offshore trusts.

The FA 1998 changes introduced a more onerous regime for the emigration of individuals[31] and extended the settlor s.86 charge to *all* non-resident settlements, even those created before 1991 and irrespective of tainting in cases where the trust was settlor-interested and the settlor was UK domiciled and resident. In addition, the definition of "defined persons" was extended to include "grandchildren" or their spouses if the trust was established or tainted after March 16, 1998.

Who are defined persons?

19.18 Before March 17, 1998, the settlor was only treated as having an interest in the settlement if the trust was set up on or after March 19, 1991 and any of the following "defined persons" could benefit[32]:

    (i) settlor or spouse/civil partner[33];

    (ii) child or stepchild of the settlor or spouse/civil partner of child or step-child (even if adults);

    (iii) any company controlled by any or all of the above and any company associated with such a company.

From March 17, 1998, if any of the above can benefit then the trust becomes settlor-interested (whenever established) and so gains are taxed on the settlor even if the trust was established prior to 1991. However, there were special provisions made for protected trusts discussed at 19.20.

The list of defined persons was formidable and it was particularly worthy of note that children (including step-children) *of whatever age* were included. Note the trap that exists for a settlor in cases where a UK trust has been created in favour of his children which is then exported. Although the settlor

---

[30] FA 1998 s.132.
[31] See Ch.3.
[32] Sch.5 para.9.
[33] Civil partners are defined persons with effect from December 5, 2005. See *Tax Bulletin* 80 December 2005. HMRC have confirmed that civil partners should be expressly excluded from trusts set up after December 2005 if it is intended that defined persons should not benefit. However, what is the position with regard to settlements established prior to December 5, 2005 which would not necessarily have expressly excluded civil partners? The mere possibility of a future civil partner benefiting, e.g. if the trustees have power to add to the class of beneficiaries would be enough to make the trust qualifying. HMRC have said in a letter to STEP that the "*introduction of the Civil Partnership Act 2004 will not alone result in a change of status for non-resident settlements that are not regarded as settlor-interested under existing law.*"

is otherwise excluded from all benefit under the trust, the effect of the export is to create a qualifying settlement with the result that gains will be taxed as the settlor's since defined persons (his children—even if they are geriatric adults) will or may benefit.

The only exclusion of real significance from the list of defined persons **19.19** was grandchildren and this omission was rectified by FA 1998. In respect of offshore trusts created on or after March 17, 1998 the list of defined persons was extended to catch:

(a) any grandchild of the settlor or his spouse;

(b) the spouse or civil partner of any such grandchild; and

(c) companies controlled by such persons and companies associated with such companies.

Note that grandchildren trusts established before March 17, 1998 are not brought within the settlor charge unless the trust is tainted (e.g. by the addition of further property). Therefore, if the settlor wishes to avoid a s.86 charge a trust established before March 17, 1998 must be limited exclusively for the benefit of the grandchildren and their issue.

Protected trusts

The s.86 settlor charge was avoided if during a transitional period (which **19.20** lasted until April 6, 1999) all "defined persons" were excluded from benefit. Alternatively, the charge was avoided if the beneficiaries were before April 6, 1999 limited to infant children of the settler, grandchildren, unborn persons, future spouses etc, albeit that these persons would be within the class of "defined persons". Such a trust was known as a "protected settlement".[34] A settlement cannot become protected after April 6, 1999. If the trust was made protected during that period then gains realised from March 17, 1998 to April 5, 1999 were not taxed on the settlor. Otherwise gains realised during that period were deemed to accrue in the following tax year, i.e. on April 6, 1999.

EXAMPLE 19.7

The Brown Jersey Trust was set up in 1988. The settlor, Neil, is a UK domiciled and resident life tenant. The trust provides for remainder to his infant children. With the introduction of the 1998 changes, the trustees in the exercise of powers under the settlement:

(1) appointed half the fund to Neil absolutely. This was a deemed disposal by the trustees on which Neil was subject to CGT both on the gains realised by the trustees from the disposal and on

[34] See TGCA 1992 Sch.5 para.9(10A).

445

stockpiled gains realised prior to March 1998 since he had received a capital payment[35];

(2) the trustees, before April 6, 1999, excluded Neil from all benefit in the trust with the result that, as the only beneficiaries were his infant children, the settlement became a "protected settlement". So long as it retains this status, future gains will not be taxed on Neil as the settlor;

(3) protected settlement treatment is lost if the settlement is tainted. In addition, privileged treatment ceases in a year where the conditions are not satisfied: notably in the tax year following a beneficiary attaining 18 (the year after the first child of Neil becomes 18). At that point the children could be excluded altogether and the trust fund held only for his grandchildren (if appropriate).

Making the trust non-qualifying

19.21 A settlement which is qualifying because it benefits defined persons can be made non-qualifying and the settlor will then escape the s.86 charge on future trust gains provided that the trust is non-qualifying for the entire tax year when the gain is made. If the trust was set up before March 17, 1998 and has not been tainted then it can be made non-qualifying at any time by ensuring that the only beneficiaries are grandchildren and remoter issue.[36]

EXAMPLE 19.8

Peter set up an offshore trust for himself, his issue and his brothers and sisters and their issue in 1990. He is domiciled and resident in the UK. The trust has realised no gains since 1998. It has not been added to or tainted. In 2008–09 the trustees want to realise a substantial gain from the sale of land. Provided that Peter, his spouse, children and their spouses and any company controlled by them are permanently excluded from any benefit in the tax year *before* the disposal (i.e. in 2007–08), then gains realised by the trustees in the following tax year will not be taxed on Peter. The only beneficiaries will then be his siblings, their issue and his grandchildren and remoter issue. None of these are defined persons in respect of settlements established *before* March 17, 1998. Note that the settlement is *not* a protected settlement and therefore the change in beneficiaries does not need to be done prior to April 1999 but can be done at any point provided the trust has not been tainted after March 16, 1998. Grandchildren of the settlor can be retained within the class of beneficiaries.

If no change to the class of beneficiaries is made in 2007–08, any gains realised in the next tax year by the trustees will be taxed on Peter under s.86 unless he dies in that year or the trust is immigrated. If he dies then

---

[35] See 19.33.
[36] This is different from making the trust protected which could only be done before April 6, 1999.

no capital gains tax is payable. Tax may be due under s.87 when capital payments are made if it realised gains prior to 1998.[37] If the trust is immigrated to the UK then the immigration does not in itself trigger any tax and the trustees pay tax not the settlor. If the terms of the trust are later changed so that only Peter's grandchildren can benefit, it will fall outside the s.86 regime.

Reimbursing the UK settlor for tax on trust gains

As noted earlier, the settlor is given a statutory right to recover any s.86 tax that he suffers from the trustees but the extent to which this right may be enforced in a foreign jurisdiction is uncertain.[38] It is not, however, thought that a right of reimbursement is the same as the enforcement of foreign revenue laws: see Lord Mackay of Clashfern in *Williams & Humbert Ltd v W & H Trade Marks (Jersey) Ltd*[39] where he commented that:

19.22

> "*the existence of (an) unsatisfied claim to the satisfaction of which the proceeds of the action will be applied appears to me to be an essential feature of the principle (that foreign revenue laws will not be enforced)*".

The proper law of the settlement may also be relevant: if it is English law, in practice reimbursement may be easier to enforce.[40]

Other problems for the settlor within the s.86 charge

Divorce can present problems which were exacerbated by the 2006 inheritance tax changes.

19.23

EXAMPLE 19.9

On his divorce in 1989, Paul set up a Jersey trust for the benefit of his children under which he was prohibited from benefiting. He is estranged from his children. In 2000 the children become absolutely entitled to the trust fund leading to a gain of £2 million. Paul is taxed on this gain with no prospect of recovering tax either from the trustees or his children.[41] If the trust has been made UK resident, future gains would not

---

[37] See 19.33.
[38] See CGTM 38321.
[39] [1986] AC 368 HL.
[40] See *Trusts and Estates Law and Tax Journal*, July/August 2004, p.5 and Ch.56.
[41] See, however, the Jersey case of *Re the T Settlement* (2002) 4 ITLR 820 where the settlor was expressly excluded from benefit but the Court nevertheless permitted a variation of the trust in order to allow the trustees to reimburse her the capital gains tax due under s.86. It was held that the variation would be for the benefit of unborn beneficiaries since benefit included the discharge of certain moral obligations on their behalf.

become taxable on Paul since it will no longer be a settlor-interested trust because all his children are adult. For many settlors trust immigration became the only option.[42]

EXAMPLE 19.10

John and Carolyn divorce in 2007. They are both resident and domiciled in the UK. John's main asset is the offshore trust which he set up in 1991 and in which he has an interest in possession. It has £1 million of stock-piled s.87 gains[43] and £500,000 unrealised gains. The trust is worth £4 million. It is agreed that Carolyn should get half of this. However, if a payment of £2 million is made to her or John outright, there will be s.87 gains attributed to the recipient of £1 million since these are treated as coming out first. The payment may also trigger unrealised gains on the deemed disposal which are taxed on John.

Accordingly, the parties decide to split the trust assets but to retain them in the trust structure. Before March 22, 2006, half the trust fund could have been advanced over to a UK resident interest in possession trust for Carolyn with John excluded (assuming that the trustees had appropriate power to do this). Although this may have triggered s.86 gains on the settlor if the transfer itself realised gains (and posed certain s.87 risks for the wife if the transfer could be regarded as a capital payment to her) at least John would not be taxed on the future gains of the new trust.[44] £500,000 of the s.87 stockpiled gains would be transferred to the new trust under s.90. The two trusts could then operate independently.

However, if half the settled property of the 1991 trust is transferred to a separate interest in possession trust for Carolyn this cannot qualify as a qualifying interest in possession after March 22, 2006, but will instead fall within the relevant property regime.[45] If the transfer to the new trust is a chargeable transfer, there is 20 per cent inheritance tax since IHTA 1984 s.10 does not apply to transfers out of trusts.[46] Hence, it may be necessary to keep the funds within the existing trust and have one fund held on interest in possession trusts for Carolyn (which will qualify as a transitional serial interest if set up before October 6, 2008)[47] and one fund retained on interest in possession trusts for John. However, even though John is excluded from Carolyn's share, he still suffers capital gains tax on all future gains unless the trust is brought back to the UK. Moreover losses in one fund (say John's) could end up being set against gains in Carolyn's fund which may be undesirable. The trustees have to submit one tax return and are liable for all the tax on both funds. Moreover,

---

[42] Bear in mind that trust immigration will mean the annual CGT exemption may be split among more trusts, and s.86 losses cannot be carried forward once the trust is UK resident.

[43] See 19.31.

[44] Once they are separated for the purpose of the s.86 charge it does not matter that his former spouse benefits.

[45] This is discussed further in Ch.27.

[46] See 26.26.

[47] On transitional serial interests, see 27.15.

the spouse who received the first capital payment gets charged on all the stockpiled gains. These capital gains tax problems could be avoided if a sub-fund election was made under FA 2006 Sch.12 (see TCGA 1992 Sch.4ZA) and UK trustees are appointed over Carolyn's fund. Watch the conditions necessary for sub-fund elections—in particular condition 3. John will need to be excluded from Carolyn's fund and vice versa and their children should only be able to benefit on the death of either life tenant or by exercise of the statutory power of advancement.[48]

The effect of a sub-fund election is as follows: **19.23A**

1. there is a deemed disposal and John will be charged on any gains realised from that disposal under s.86. It will therefore be sensible to ensure that the sub-fund comprises assets that do not show a gain so that the deemed disposal does not trigger s.86 gains;

2. TCGA 1992 s.90 applies and there is a transfer of s.87 gains to the new settlement (being the assets comprised in the sub-fund). Since half the funds are going into the sub-fund, £500,000 stockpiled gains move across into the sub-fund. The result is that if Carolyn receives a payment of £1 million before John she is not taxed on all the £1 million gains. This is fairer because they can each receive capital payments and pay tax on a due proportion of stockpiled gains, rather than the beneficiary who receives the first capital payment being taxed on all the gains up to the value of that payment;

3. assume the sub-fund comprises assets that are held on interest in possession trusts for Carolyn and that this sub-fund was created before October 2008 so she has a TSI (a qualifying interest in possession for inheritance tax purposes). Any future gains realised by the trustees of that sub-fund will still be taxed on John while the trustees are non-UK resident. Hence it may be preferable to appoint UK resident trustees over that sub-fund in order to avoid a tax charge on John in respect of future gains.

The end result of all this legislation has been that offshore trusts are rarely **19.24**
set up by UK domiciliaries. Further anti-avoidance measures were passed in FA 2000, FA 2003 and F(No.2)A 2005 including the anti-flip-flop legislation discussed at 19.69. The FA 2008 changes encouraged the further break up of trusts because capital could be distributed and taxed at a top rate of 28.8 per cent (if the full supplemental charge applied) instead of 64 per cent.[49]

Losses and ss.86 and 87

See Ch.21 for a consideration of the position on losses. **19.25**

---

[48] For sub-fund elections, see 12.42.
[49] Now that trust gains are charged at 44.8% (with the supplemental charge) the position will no doubt change back again.

19.26 The legislation under which gains realised by offshore trusts are taxed on the settlor under s.86 only applies in years when the settlor is both domiciled *and* either resident or ordinarily resident in the UK. Gains realised in other years are not taxed on the settlor and neither are gains realised in the tax year when the settlor dies. Thus s.86 does not apply to offshore trusts if the settlor is not UK domiciled and resident. This is still the case even after April 6, 2008 and the settlor does not need to be a remittance basis user. However, even for foreign domiciled settlors the position has changed since April 6, 2008 since if they are beneficiaries, any UK resident beneficiary of an offshore settlement can be taxed on benefits received if gains are realised by the trustees. Hence the s.87 rather than the s.86 regime applies. The s.87 regime for foreign domiciliaries is discussed at 19.49.

EXAMPLE 19.11

> John (domicile of origin Italian) is the settlor and life tenant of an offshore trust that realises substantial gains in 2011. He is aged 50 and until now has successfully claimed he is not UK domiciled even though he has lived in the UK for many years. He does not pay tax on any gains realised by the trustees under s.86 even if he is not a remittance basis user. However, if he receives benefits or capital payments in the UK then as a beneficiary he will be subject to tax under s.87B.[50] If in 2010–11 he becomes UK domiciled because he now has no intention of leaving the UK, he will be taxed on an arising basis under s.86 on all gains realised by the trustees from that tax year onwards, whether or not they make capital payments to him.

IV TAXATION OF UK RESIDENT AND DOMICILED BENEFICIARIES

19.27 TCGA 1992 ss.87 and following apply to non-resident trusts in respect of gains made from 1981–82 onwards where the trustees are not resident nor ordinarily resident in the UK during the tax year. Note, however, that if the s.86 (the settlor charge) applies, no s.87 gains can arise. Until April 6, 2008 TCGA 1992 ss.87 and following applied only to tax UK resident *and* domiciled beneficiaries on capital payments or benefits received from an offshore trust or a UK trust which had "stockpiled gains". From that date UK resident but foreign domiciled beneficiaries can also suffer a capital gains tax charge but only if capital payments are remitted to the UK.

---

[50] See 19.49.

Basic rules for UK domiciled and resident beneficiaries

Prior to March 17, 1998, for s.87 to apply (even for UK resident and domiciled beneficiaries), the settlor had to be domiciled *and* either resident or ordinarily resident in the UK at some time during the tax year or when the settlement was made. Hence, if the settlor was UK domiciled and resident at the date of the trust's creation the rules of s.87 *always* applied. If the settlement was originally created by a non-domiciled settlor, who subsequently became a UK resident domiciliary, it was caught but only for those years when the settlor was UK resident and domiciled and it ceased to be caught on his death. Trusts set up by non-resident but UK domiciled settlors were also not caught by s.87 until the settlor became resident here. **19.28**

EXAMPLE 19.12

> In 1995 P set up an offshore trust while domiciled in Hong Kong. Three beneficiaries are UK domiciled and resident but one is non-UK domiciled. Until March 1998 none of the beneficiaries suffered CGT under s.87. There is no s.86 charge. Only post-March 1998 gains are charged on the beneficiaries.

As a result of disquiet caused by the "*Robinson Trust*", capital payments received by UK resident and domiciled beneficiaries on or after March 17, 1998 are potentially subject to capital gains tax under s.87. The residence and domicile of the settlor became irrelevant. Section 87*ff* was therefore extended to all non-resident trusts (or trusts which had realised gains while non-resident which had not been taxed under s.86) irrespective of when they were set up and whether or not the avoidance of UK tax was one of the motives of the settlor. However, in the case of trusts set up by a non-domiciled settlor only those trust gains realised after March 16, 1998 were attributable to beneficiaries.[51] **19.29**

EXAMPLE 19.13

> (1) Giles, domiciled and resident in France, settled his holiday home in Nice in an overseas trust in 1980 for his daughter, Nina, who is domiciled and resident in England. He is also a beneficiary. The trust realised significant gains between 1980 and 1998. From March 17, 1998 capital payments (including the use of the property by Nina) are subject to capital gains tax under s.87 on Nina but only if the trust realises gains from that date, unless Giles becomes UK resident and domiciled. Assuming that no chargeable gains are realised, any tax charge will be postponed until, for instance a beneficiary becomes entitled to the property or it is sold.

---

[51] Equally any losses realised before March 17, 1998 were not allowable: see Ch.21.

(Note (1) that the property may benefit from main residence relief so there may be no chargeable gains in any event and (2) that Nina's beneficial interest is a chargeable asset.)

If Giles becomes UK resident but not domiciled then there is still no charge under s.87 on Nina by reference to the pre-1998 gains and no charge on Giles under s.86. However, Giles could be subject to tax under s.87B TCGA 1992 if he receives benefits in the UK after April 5, 2008.[52] Nina will be taxable under s.87 by reference to all gains realised by the trust after March 17, 1998 if she receives any benefit from the trust irrespective of where the benefit is received.

(2) The trustees of a non-UK settlement set up by Irek, a Russian dancer now deceased, hold the trust property for Irek's four grandchildren; two of whom, A and B, are now resident and domiciled in the UK. The other two C and D are UK resident but not UK domiciled. Any capital payments made by the trustees to A and B prior to March 17, 1998 are not taxable even if gains are realised post-March 16, 1998. Gains and losses accruing to the trustees before March 17, 1998 and capital payments received before March 17, 1998 are wholly ignored. However, if the trustees realise gains after March 16, 1998, any capital payments A and B receive after March 16, 1998 can be taxed on them. No payments to C and D are taxable if made prior to April 6, 2008 whenever the gains are realised unless they become UK domiciled and resident at the date the capital payment is matched to the gain. So if the trustees make unmatched capital payments to C and D in February 2008 and realise gains in February 2009, provided neither C nor D are domiciled in the UK at that time[53] the payment is matched to those gains (and reduces the stockpile) but no tax is payable. If however say C was UK domiciled by February 2009 then he would pay capital gains tax at 18 per cent even though the capital payment had been received at a time when he was not UK domiciled.[54] If payments are made to C and D after April 5, 2008 then they are generally taxable if they can be matched to post-April 5, 2008 gains.

(3) J moved to Hong Kong in 1920 and when domiciled there settled his non-UK property on trust for his UK descendants who become absolutely entitled to the property in 2005 when the trust period ended. On this occasion a tax charge arose and since the beneficiaries received a capital payment on becoming absolutely entitled it was necessary for them to include in their tax returns a calculation showing gains realised by the trust since March 17, 1998, including gains realised on the deemed disposal when they become absolutely entitled.

Only gains not taxed under s.86 become s.87 gains but trust gains can be subject to tax under s.86 if disposals are made by the trustees and the settlor or

---

[52] See 19.49.
[53] Under general law—they do not have to be remittance basis users but must be foreign domiciled at the date of matching.
[54] The same point applies to non-residents. For this reason it is sensible to ensure that if a beneficiary has received substantial capital payments while non-UK resident or foreign domiciled, such payments are matched to trust gains realised at a time when that status continues.

another beneficiary can also pay tax under s.87 on different gains if there are unmatched trust gains that were not previously taxed under s.86 and capital payments are made.

Operation of the s.87 charge[55]

The charging system under s.87 operates as follows: **19.30**

(a) Trust gains ("stockpiled or s.2(2) gains")

The trust gains for each year are calculated on the assumption that the trustees   **19.31** are UK resident (*"the amount on which the trustees would have been chargeable to tax . . . if they had been resident and ordinarily resident in the UK in that year"*, see s.87(4) as inserted by Sch.7 para.108 FA 2008). Non-resident trustees are *not* entitled to the benefit of a CGT annual exemption, but the normal uplift in value in the settled assets will occur on the death of a qualifying interest in possession beneficiary[56]; the principal private residence exemption may apply and taper relief is applied to reduce any gain from *a disposal made prior to April 6, 2008*. For trust disposals on or after April 6, 2008 there is no taper relief but even if capital payments are made after that date, if matched to pre-April 2008 gains then such gains are still calculated taking into account the taper relief available at the date of disposal. In computing this total, gains made by offshore companies owned by trusts may be attributed to the trustees.[57] The position regarding entrepreneurs' relief is problematic: see 14.37.

Matching

If s.2(2) trust gains are not "matched" to benefits received by a beneficiary in   **19.32** that year they are carried forward and matched to future benefits. In addition, if benefits have been received in the past which have not yet been matched to trust gains then the gains realised in a later year are matched to the earlier benefits. To the extent that trust gains realised in a particular year cannot be matched to past or current year benefits they are carried forward and become *"stockpiled"* and matched to future benefits. Hence, the stockpiled gains go up or down depending on the level of benefits received in any year. Gains can be matched to benefits received by non-residents (even though there is no tax charge on such non-residents) and so can be "washed out". As noted previously, FA 2008 now provides a different matching rule. Instead of gains being matched on a first-in first-out basis, they are now matched on a last-in first-out basis.

---

[55] See FA 2008 Sch.7 paras 108 and following. for position from April 6, 2008.
[56] See 12.12.
[57] See TCGA 1992 s.13(10).

EXAMPLE 19.14

Trust has the following history of gains and capital payments

Gains	Capital payments
1997: £100 gain	£200

Gain all matched. Capital payment b/f is 100

1999: £200 gain	£300

£100 gain matched to 1997 capital payment and £100 to the 1999 capital payment

£200 unmatched capital payments c/f

2005: £5,200 gains	£4,000

Gains of £200 matched to 1999 capital payment leaving £4,000 to be matched to the 2005 capital payment

£1,000 gains c/f from 2005.

2009: £2,000 gains	£2,000

The 2009 gains are all matched to the 2009 capital payment leaving the 2005 gains still to be c/f. They will only be matched to future capital payments if no later gains are realised in or before the tax year of a capital payment. This will reduce the supplementary charge—discussed further at 19.48.

(b) Capital payments

19.33 The gains realised by the trustees will be attributed to the UK resident and domiciled beneficiaries and subject to CGT to the extent that they receive "capital payments" unless otherwise taxed as income. A "capital payment" is widely defined[58] to include, inter alia, the situation where a beneficiary becomes absolutely entitled to the trust property as well as to the "*transfer of an asset and the conferring of any other benefit*". This can include, for example, rent-free occupation of houses owned by a trust, use of pictures owned by a trust as well as loans to beneficiaries. A tax charge can arise in relation to a UK domiciliary even if the benefits are received outside the UK.

"*Received*" is given an extended definition under s.97(5) and includes a payment received by a beneficiary directly or indirectly, applied in payment of any debt of his, otherwise paid or applied for his benefit or received by a third party at his direction.

"*Beneficiary*" is also given an extended meaning: if a person who is not a beneficiary receives a capital payment he is deemed to be a beneficiary under s.97(8) unless an actual beneficiary can be treated as receiving the payment. Payments to UK charitable beneficiaries are treated as capital payments so

---

[58] See TCGA 1992 s.97(1) and (2).

s.2(2) trust gains can be allocated to them albeit they are exempt from capital gains tax.[59] Hence trust gains can be washed out by payments to charitable beneficiaries.

Loans and benefits in kind

In *Billingham v Cooper; Edwards v Fisher*[60] it was decided that the provision **19.34** of an interest-free loan which was repayable on demand conferred a benefit on the borrower (a beneficiary of the trust) every day for which the loan was left outstanding. That benefit was a "payment" within s.97(2) and a capital payment by virtue of s.97(1). The value of the benefit could be quantified retrospectively and the legislation would be applied year by year. Two other matters are worthy of note:

(1) It was accepted that a fixed period loan (e.g. for 10 years) conferred a benefit once and for all at the date of the loan and that there was no subsequent conferment of a benefit.

(2) The Court of Appeal rejected the argument that no benefit was received (or its value was nil) on the basis that if interest had been charged it would have gone to the beneficiary (who was life tenant of the settlement). The following extract from the judgment of Lloyd J. at First Instance[61] was expressly approved by the appeal court:

> "*It seems to me that the legislation does not call for or permit a comparison of the position that the recipient might have been in if a different transaction had been undertaken by the trustees. There are too many different possible comparisons for that to be a tenable approach. The proper comparison is with the position of the recipient if the actual loan had not been made rather than if some other transaction had been entered into. The recipient of the actual loan, if it had not been made, would not have had the use of the money lent.*
>
> *It seems to me that this is particularly clear from the fact that the sections are directed to attributing gains not only to beneficiaries but also among beneficiaries in circumstances in which more than one beneficiary has received a capital payment, which of course is not true of either of these cases.*
>
> *I accept it is not sensible to suppose that the person entitled to income has a special status which exempts him from this treatment or requires him to be treated more favourably than other beneficiaries.*"

[59] Under s.256 TCGA 1992.
[60] [2001] STC 1177, CA.
[61] [2000] STC 122.

Settled advances

19.35 More controversially, HMRC have been known to argue that a settled advance by the trustees in favour of a particular beneficiary can be a capital payment within s.97. Suppose the trustees of a discretionary offshore trust with a dead UK domiciled settlor decide that they wish to defer a beneficiary's absolute entitlement to capital at 25. The beneficiary is UK domiciled and resident and would otherwise become entitled to one third of the trust fund and be subject to capital gains tax on the stockpiled gains (if he is the eldest child he may have the disadvantage of being taxed on all the stockpiled gains so far realised and effectively then "wash out" the gains to the benefit of the others: see Example 19.2).

The trustees have no overriding powers of appointment but they do have a wide power of advancement and, therefore, exercise this power so as to make a settled advance for the benefit of the eldest child by way of resettlement of one third of the trust fund (say £2 million) so that he does not become absolutely entitled.[62] Is this a capital payment? Even if he has no right to demand the capital can HMRC successfully argue that he has received a capital payment up to the value of the assets advanced? The beneficiary may only be given a revocable life interest and in these circumstances can he really be taxed on the whole capital value?

19.36 Section 97(2) provides that a payment includes the conferring of any benefit and s.97(5)(b) then states that a payment is received by the beneficiary if it is paid or *"applied for his benefit"*. The power of advancement can only be exercised if it is for the benefit of a beneficiary. It has been suggested that the precise terms of the settlement under which a child takes is irrelevant and the value of that interest is also immaterial because if the application is for his benefit it is squarely within s.97(5)(b). The alternative view is that s.97(5)(b) is concerned with payments made to a third party but where the beneficiary still receives full value and s.90 has a separate mechanism for carrying forward outstanding trust gains to a new settlement. For example, payments made to the school in settlement of fees that are a parent's liability on behalf of a child could be classed as payments applied for the benefit of a parent. In the above example the beneficiary had not in reality received anything like £2 million since the actual value of his settled interest is far less than this. If the first view is correct and the s.87 charge applies to the full value of the capital advanced he would have to pay capital gains tax out of his personal funds yet he has received no capital personally.

19.37 In *Burton v HMRC*,[63] HMRC argued that a settled advance made for the benefit of a settlor by means of a resettlement to another trust in which he was a beneficiary was a capital payment equal to the amount advanced. The Tribunal did not reject the notion that the advance to the new trust was a capital payment but held that it was of nil value. A valuation is required in all cases where a benefit is not an outright transfer. In *Herman v HMRC*[64] a resettlement followed by a distribution out of the transferee trust was treated as a capital payment received indirectly from the original settlement. (In *Burton* no distributions had been made out of the second settlement so this point was not considered.) However, in that case the transfer to a new trust and subsequent distribution were part of a pre-planned scheme executed in a very short timescale.

---

[62] Such "settled advances" are considered in Ch.1.
[63] [2009] UK FTT 203 (TC).
[64] [2007] STC (SCD) 571.

The valuation of capital payments is important in a number of situations. For **19.38** example, if an offshore trust holds English situated land to which three UK resident beneficiaries become entitled at 30. When A reaches 30, he becomes absolutely entitled for inheritance tax purposes but not for capital gains tax purposes.[65] The same is true of B. Only when C reaches 30 (assuming the land is still unsold) do the beneficiaries become absolutely entitled for capital gains tax purposes. When A and B reached 30 they each took indefeasible interests in the capital. That was presumably a benefit under the capital payments rules given their interests were no longer contingent and could be sold or assigned by them. The valuation of that benefit must be done under TCGA 1992 s.97(4) (given it is not an outright transfer of cash). It is likely that the economic benefit or value of what they received then was fairly small: a purchaser of their interests would not have been able to mortgage it or sell or develop the land without the trustees' co-operation. But he would have paid something for the opportunity of getting hold of the development potential.

The value of what A and B received then when they each reached 30 does **19.39** not reduce the value of what they eventually receive on absolute entitlement when C becomes 30 or on sale of the land if earlier. In this respect it is similar to the benefit of a loan. If A receives an interest-free loan, the taxable benefit is the interest-free element; if the loan is written off then the value of the loan is taxable. The benefit on write off of the loan is not reduced by the earlier benefit of no interest payments.

(c) Method of attribution

Trust gains are attributed to *all* beneficiaries who receive capital payments as **19.40** follows. The first beneficiary (taking the tax year as a whole) to receive a payment has[66] attributed to him all the gains then realised by the trustees to the extent of the benefit which he receives. This can produce unfair results: see Example 19.1. The problem may be avoided by a sub-fund election: see Example 19.10.

When more than one capital payment is made in a single tax year, gains are attributed to the payments pro rata.[67] If a capital payment is made at a time when there are no trust gains, subsequent gains may be attributed to that beneficiary (s.87(4)). Finally, if no capital payments are made, trust gains are carried forward indefinitely until such a payment occurs (s.87(2)). (For the position of a non-UK domiciled or resident beneficiary who receives capital payments, see 19.49 below.)

EXAMPLE 19.15

A non-resident discretionary settlement has four beneficiaries, two of whom (A and B) are UK domiciled. Over three years the fund has no

---

[65] See *Crowe v Appleby* [1976] 2 All ER 914, CA. and 9.18 and 12.10.
[66] Unless he is not resident here and the trust is caught by the FA 2003 changes: see 19.69.
[67] TCGA 1992 s.87(5).

income and makes the following net gains and capital payments. No capital payments have been made to any non-UK resident or non-UK domiciled beneficiaries.

	£	A £	B £
Year 1			
Capital payments		10,000	5,000
Net gains £6,000 apportioned		4,000	2,000
Capital payments c/f		6,000	3,000

	£	A £	B £
Year 2			
Capital payments		3,000	6,000
Including payments b/f		9,000	9,000
Trust gains	20,000		
Amount apportioned	18,000	9,000	9,000
Gains c/f	2,000		

	£	A £	B £
Year 3			
Capital payments		15,000	5,000
Trust gains	10,000		
Gains b/f	2,000		
Amount apportioned	12,000	9,000	3,000
Capital payments c/f		6,000	2,000

(d) ITA 2007 s.731 tie-in

19.41 A capital payment made by trustees may be treated as income in the hands of the beneficiary under ITA 2007 s.731.[68] Such payments are charged to income tax up to the relevant income within the trust structure including subsidiary companies for that year; income from previous years is included to the extent that such income has not already been charged to a beneficiary. It is only the excess that is treated as a capital payment for the purpose of the apportionment of trust gains.

[68] See Ch.8.

So in the above example if the trust had accumulated income of £5,000 in year 1, £5,000 of the capital payment would be subject to income tax at up to 50 per cent if made after April 2010 and the other £5,000 would be subject to capital gains tax at 18 per cent (between April 6, 2008 and June 22, 2010).

(e) Payments to the non-UK resident /domiciled beneficiary can help the UK resident and domiciled beneficiary

As discussed already, prior to April 6, 2008 a beneficiary who received a capital payment was only subject to CGT on the attributed gains if UK domiciled and resident.[69] Accordingly, a non-UK resident or domiciled beneficiary could have trust gains attributed to him but *not suffer any tax on those gains*. Such gains were washed out and so distributions to non-residents or foreign domiciliaries could reduce the s.87 charge for a UK resident domiciliary. **19.42**

The UK beneficiary cannot deduct his personal losses from the gain attributed to him under s.87[70] (contrast the position of a settlor beneficiary and s.86 gains and losses) but may deduct his annual exemption and the balance would, before April 6, 2008, then attract tax at 10, 20 or 40 per cent as appropriate with the surcharge where relevant (see 19.45). Gains realised before April 6, 2011 and attributed to a beneficiary in respect of capital payments made on or after April 6, 2008 and before June 23, 2010 attract capital gains tax at 18 per cent (plus the surcharge if applicable bringing the maximum charge to 28.8 per cent). In calculating the beneficiary's liability, s.87 gains will be treated as the *lowest part* of his total gains for the year (thereby enabling him to benefit from his annual exemption and, in appropriate cases, reducing any interest surcharge). **19.43**

A charge under s.87 can be deferred so long as the trustees avoid making capital payments. The charge can be avoided altogether if: **19.44**

(i) payments are made to a non-UK resident; or

(ii) payments are made to a non-UK domiciled beneficiary who (in relation to capital payments made after April 6, 2008—see post) does not remit and is taxed on a remittance basis or can benefit from transitional reliefs; or

(iii) distributions are made to UK resident and domiciled beneficiaries which do not exceed their annual capital gains tax exemptions.

Following the introduction of the "temporary non-residents" charge by FA 1998, difficulties can arise if a settlor—who would otherwise be subject to the s.86 charge—ceases to be UK resident. As a result the capital payment rules in s.87 will apply, but if the settlor returns to the UK within five years of his departure gains during his absence will be attributed to him on his return (see Ch.5). To prevent a double charge such gains will not include capital payments made to UK resident and domiciled beneficiaries (although note that no deduction is made for payments to non-resident beneficiaries: see TCGA 1992 s.86A).

[69] Old TCGA 1992 s.87(7).
[70] Although he can deduct his personal losses from gains attributed to him under Sch.4C. See 19.78 and Ch.21.

(f) The supplementary (interest) charge from April 6, 2008

19.45   A "supplementary" charge may apply to beneficiaries who receive capital payments on or after April 6, 1992. From April 6, 2008 it can therefore apply to capital payments to UK resident foreign domiciliaries. The charge operates as an interest charge on the delayed payment of CGT following a disposal of chargeable assets by non-resident trustees. It is, however, limited to a six-year period and, therefore, the time covered by the charge begins on the *later* of (a) December 1 in the tax year following the year in which the disposal occurred, and (b) December 1 six years before December 1 in the year of assessment following that in which the capital payment was made. The rate of charge is 10 per cent pa of the tax payable on the capital payment (this percentage may be amended by statutory instrument). The minimum period is two years so the minimum charge is 20 per cent. For a higher rate taxpayer, the effective maximum rate on which he could be charged under s.87 was 64 per cent prior to April 6, 2008, reduced to 28.8 per cent for capital payments received after that date and before June 23, 2010 even if matched to gains realised before April 6, 2008 or gains realised between June 23, 2010 and April 5, 2011.

19.46   If on April 6, 2011 there are any unmatched capital payments that were made before June 23, 2010 then as and when further trust gains are realised they are no longer taxed at a flat rate of 18 per cent. When matched to those pre-June 23, 2010 capital payments they are taxed at 28 per cent if the beneficiary is a higher rate taxpayer. Equally if capital payments are made after June 22, 2010 then whether or not they are matched to trust gains realised before or after this date the flat rate of 18 per cent no longer applies. Instead they are taxed at 28 per cent if the beneficiary is a higher rate taxpayer. The supplemental charge if appropriate will also apply (e.g. where a capital payment made after June 22, 2010 is matched to gains realised some years earlier.)

EXAMPLE 19.16

The Allegri Trust realises capital gains in the tax year 1998–99 and a capital payment was made to a UK domiciled and resident beneficiary X on July 1, 2004:

(1) That beneficiary X will be assessed to CGT on the capital payment received (at the then rates of, say, 40 per cent).

(2) The interest charge will apply for the period from December 1, 1999 to November 30, 2005 at four per cent per annum so that the interest charge continues to run after the capital payment has been made. In all, six years were subject to the additional charge (being 24 per cent) thereby giving a capital gains tax rate of 64 per cent (40 + 24) Note that if the beneficiary does not suffer a CGT charge—for instance because he is able to set his annual exemption against the gains attributed to him—there is no interest charge.

460

(3) If he receives the capital payment on or after April 6, 2008 in, say, 2009 and the gains to which such payments are matched qualify for the maximum surcharge he is taxed at 28.8 per cent.

(4) If he receives the capital payment on June 22, 2010 the rate of tax is still 28.8 per cent. If he receives the capital payment on or after June 23, 2010 then the rate of tax is 44.8 per cent. Note though that since April 2008 the capital payment must be matched to the gains realised most recently, thus reducing the likelihood of the supplementary charge applying. See Example 19.14 above.

19.47 The precise mechanics governing the supplementary charge are complex. Prior to April 6, 2008 capital payments were matched first with total trust gains at April 6, 1991 and then on a first-in first-out basis. Trustees were given at least 12 months in which to distribute gains since the interest charge did *not* apply to gains realised in the same or immediately preceding year of assessment. See Example 19.14.

19.48 From April 6, 2008 capital payments to both UK and non-UK domiciled beneficiaries are matched with gains on a last-in first-out basis.[71] This is advantageous because the interest charge is less where trust gains have been realised in recent years.

V TAXATION OF FOREIGN DOMICILED UK RESIDENT BENEFICIARIES[72]

19.49 Capital payments made from April 6, 2008 to non-UK domiciled beneficiaries will generally be chargeable to tax and matched with gains on a last-in first-out basis. The remittance basis will apply if the non-UK domiciled beneficiary is a "remittance basis user"[73] in the year when trust gains are treated as accruing to him. This will be so whether the trust gains accrue in respect of UK or non-UK assets. A capital distribution will be treated as remitted if the distributed property is received in or brought to the UK. Benefits-in-kind will be treated as remitted if enjoyed or used in the UK.

With an exception for capital payments made between March 12, 2008 and April 6, 2008, the 2008 legislation does not change the tax position of non-UK domiciled beneficiaries who received capital payments on or before April 5, 2008 and does not tax non-UK domiciled beneficiaries on future capital payments where these are matched to trust gains realised prior to April 6, 2008. This is so irrespective of whether the non-UK domiciled beneficiary is a remittance basis user and the date of matching. (Note that the beneficiary must be foreign domiciled at that date.).

19.50 Surplus capital payments brought forward from 2007–08 will not be taxed unless the non-UK domiciled beneficiary is both resident and domiciled in the

---

[71] See FA 2008 Sch.7 para.112.
[72] See FA 2008 Sch.7 paras 108 onwards and s.87ff as amended.
[73] i.e. where he has claimed the remittance basis under ITA 2007 s.809B or is entitled to it under s.809C.

UK when trust gains are treated as accruing to him or they can be matched to offshore income gains or relevant income.

Capital payments before March 12, 2008

19.50A Surplus capital payments to non-UK domiciled beneficiaries made before March 12, 2008 can be franked against post-April 5, 2008 trust gains, although only to the extent that there are no capital payments made after April 5, 2008 to which the post-April 5, 2008 gains can be attributed on a LIFO basis. No charge will arise whether or not the beneficiary is a remittance basis user because the payment was received prior to April 6, 2008.[74]

Capital payments between March 12 and April 6, 2008

19.50B Capital payments made to non-UK domiciled beneficiaries between March 12, 2008 and April 5, 2008 which are not matched to pre-April 6, 2008 gains are subject to a special rule. They will be left out of account in 2008–09 and subsequent years for the purposes of s.87 and are not matched to trust gains at all unless the beneficiary becomes UK domiciled in the future in which case such surplus capital payments can be matched to trust gains then realised.[75] This transitional rule will be relevant where a beneficiary received significant capital payments in that period and these would otherwise have been matched to trust gains. The interaction of this rule with the transfer of assets provisions and offshore income gains is discussed in Ch.53.

EXAMPLE 19.17

(1) A receives £1 million payment from the trust on March 13, 2008. This cannot be matched to pre-April 2008 gains. In 2008–09 the trust realises gains of £1 million. These are not matched to that capital payment which is still not taxed. In 2009–10 A becomes domiciled in the UK. The trust realises gains which can then be matched to the March 13, 2008 payment.

(2) If A had received the £1 million payment on March 11, 2008, the payment would have been fully matched to the 2008–09 gains. No tax is payable even if A is not a remittance basis user. The gains are "washed out". There is no tax charge on A in 2009–10 when he becomes domiciled here.

The rule will have no adverse effect on A if he never becomes UK domiciled.

19.51 Surplus trust gains brought forward from 2007–08 and treated under s.87(4) as accruing to non-UK domiciled beneficiaries by virtue of capital payments

---

[74] FA 2008 Sch.7 para.124. Note that the foreign beneficiary must still be non-domiciled at the date of matching.
[75] FA 2008 Sch.7 para.125.

made on or after April 6, 2008 will not be taxed unless the non-UK domiciled beneficiary has become both resident and domiciled in the UK. Although the capital payment is received after April 5, 2008, if it is matched to trust gains realised prior to April 6, 2008 or to the pre-April 6, 2008 element of any gain on a rebasing election, it is not necessary in this case for the non-UK domiciled beneficiary to be a remittance basis user.

EXAMPLE 19.18

(1) B, a foreign domiciliary, receives £1 million payment from the trust in 2008–09 and remits it to the UK. No gains are realised by the trust in 2008–09 but there are surplus gains brought forward from 2007–08 of £2 million. The payment is matched to those gains and no tax is charged on B, whether or not he is a remittance basis user.[76] If gains had been realised in 2008–09 of £500,000 these would have been matched first to the capital payment and the balance of £500,000 matched to the 2007–08 gains so then B would have paid tax at 18 per cent on half the capital remitted (assuming he was a remittance basis user: if B is a foreign domiciliary taxed on an arising basis he will pay tax at 18 per cent on £500,000 gains whether or not remitted). It is unclear what the position is if B only remits half the capital to the UK—can it be treated as comprising that capital matched to pre-April 2008 trust gains and therefore not taxable? It is thought that the gains and capital payments remitted are examined over the entire year and a proportionate part taxed.

(2) B, a remittance basis user, receives £1 million payment in 2008–09 and does not remit it to the UK at any time while UK resident. No tax is payable even if the payment is matched to post-April 2008 gains because it has not been remitted.[77]

Trusts which are non-UK resident on April 6, 2008 have the option to elect for rebasing to market value as at April 6, 2008 in relation to all assets held by the trust both directly and by its underlying companies.[78] The effect is that the pre-April 6, 2008 element of any trust gains treated as accruing to non-UK domiciled beneficiaries after that date will not be taxed. In most cases trustees made the election when there was any possibility of foreign domiciled beneficiaries and the trust had assets showing unrealised gains at that date. Minimal disclosure is required. The trust simply needs to complete a form giving the name of the trust and trustees. The names of the settlor or beneficiaries are not required.[79]

Any supplemental charge under s.91 for remittance basis users will be calculated based on the year in which the capital payment is made by the trustees, not the year in which it is remitted to the UK by the non-UK domiciled beneficiary.

19.52

---

[76] See Sch.7 para.124.
[77] See s.87B—remittance basis. In determining whether capital has been remitted consider the wider rules in s.809L and Ch.5.
[78] FA 2008 Sch.7 para.126.
[79] See 19.55 for rebasing.

EXAMPLE 19.19

B, a higher rate taxpayer, receives £1 million payment for the trust in 2008–09 which is matched to gains realised in that tax year (and assume no rebasing election is made). He remits it to the UK in 2012. The tax rate is 18 per cent. If, however, the trustees had only made the payment to him in 2012 the supplemental charge would have operated if the capital payment was matched to 2008–09 gains.[80] Moreover the rate of tax is now 28 per cent.

19.53 When a capital payment is made on or after April 6, 2008:

- trust gains of the current year will be treated as accruing to the beneficiary before gains of previous years, and trust gains of later previous years before those of earlier previous years; and

- current year capital payments will be matched with trust gains before capital payments of previous years and capital payments of later previous years before those of earlier previous years;

- there is still no charge to tax on capital payments to non-UK resident beneficiaries, although capital payments made on or after April 6, 2008 will be matched to trust gains in the same order as for other beneficiaries (LIFO). A distribution to a non-UK resident beneficiary could be advantageous for a foreign domiciled UK resident beneficiary if there is a large pool of pre-April gains. The payment to the non-resident washes out the most recent gains which would otherwise be taxed on the foreign domiciliary allowing capital payments made the next tax year to the UK resident foreign domiciliary now to be matched to pre-April 2008 gains which gains are not chargeable on foreign domiciliaries. A payment to a non-UK resident beneficiary is less advantageous for the UK domiciled beneficiary because the most recent gains are washed out leaving him subject to tax on earlier gains which carry the supplemental charge.

19.54 Note that one looks at the position over the entire year not on a payment by payment basis. The result is that:

(i) remittance basis users will be taxable on a remittance basis in relation to trust gains accruing to them under s.87 if and to the extent that the trust gains and the capital payments relate to the period after April 5, 2008. If they are not remittance basis users, they will be taxed on an arising basis;

(ii) even if the capital payment relates to trust gains made after April 5, 2008 and the payment is remitted, there is no tax payable if the payment is matched to a trust gain deemed to accrue before April 6, 2008 on a rebasing election: see 19.51.

---

[80] Note that the last-in first-out matching rule now applies so later gains of the trust will be treated as distributed first.

(iii) if payments are made to non-resident and UK resident beneficiaries in the same tax year, the gains are pro-rated between them.

Rebasing[81]

The trustees of any trust which is non-UK resident as at April 6, 2008, what-   **19.55**
ever the domicile of the settlor, have the right to elect that, for one limited purpose, the following assets will be deemed to have been reacquired at market value on April 6, 2008:

(a) assets owned by the trust on April 6, 2008;

(b) assets owned by an underlying company on April 6, 2008, insofar as:

   (i) on the disposal of any such asset the gain (if any) is apportionable to the trust under s.13(10); and
   (ii) it would have been so apportionable if in fact realised on April 6, 2008.

The election cannot be made on an asset by asset basis and, once made, will apply to all assets of the trust and any underlying companies. It is irrevocable and must be made on or before January 31 following the tax year in which the first of the following occurs:

• a capital payment is made to any beneficiary (or person treated as a beneficiary) who is UK resident; or

• a part of the trust fund which is less than the whole is transferred after April 5, 2008 to a new settlement in circumstances where s.90 applies.

The earliest possible election was January 31, 2010. In most cases unless they were certain that there were never likely to be foreign domiciled beneficiaries, trustees have made the election. HMRC allow the election to be made early even if no capital payment to a UK resident beneficiary or resettlement has yet been made. An election is still possible provided there has been no reset-tlement and no capital payment made to a UK resident beneficiary. Note that if capital distributions have been made but taxed as income under the transfer of assets legislation the time limits do not start running.

The election will not in itself trigger a deemed disposal. The one limited   **19.56**
purpose of the election is simply that, when there is a later actual disposal of the asset, the trust gains realised on that disposal will be split between the pre-April 6, 2008 and post-April 5, 2008 elements. Non-UK domiciled beneficiaries will not be taxed insofar as any capital payments are matched to the pre-April 6, 2008 element of gain. There will still be one trust pool but trustees will need to keep a record of pre-April 6, 2008 and post-April 5, 2008 gains for the purposes of being able to tell non-UK domiciled beneficiaries whether they are taxable. Obviously for gains realised in 2008–09 it is likely

---

[81] FA 2008 Sch.7 para.126.

that much of the gain represents a pre-April 2008 element and will therefore not be taxable.

19.57 The availability of any reliefs on the disposal (such as main residence relief) will be given by reference to the rules prevailing at the date of the actual disposal not the position on April 6, 2008. Where the gain on an actual disposal is reduced by a relief, the relief is apportioned pro rata between the pre-April 6, 2008 and post-April 5, 2008 elements of gain. However, in relation to main residence relief, the way in which rebasing operates can result in anomalies. Where a beneficiary occupied the property as his main residence before April 2008 but not after this date, the total main residence relief is not pro rated between the pre- and post-April 2008 elements of gain. Hence, rebasing may not result in any lower tax charge. However, where the beneficiary occupies the property as his main residence after April 5, 2008 but not before, the rebasing election can effectively eradicate any chargeable gain for a foreign domiciliary. All the pre-April 2008 element of gain is not taxed because of rebasing and the post-April 2008 element of gain is not chargeable because of the main residence relief.[82]

19.58 The election has no impact on the calculation of the supplemental interest charge nor does it accelerate any charge under s.86 on a UK domiciled and resident settlor. This is because the election does not alter the fact that the entire gain continues to be treated for all purposes as having arisen only on the date of actual disposal, even if part of the gain is allocated to the pre-April 6, 2008 pool for the purposes of determining whether a non-UK domiciled beneficiary is taxable under s.87.

19.59 Where a capital payment made after April 5, 2008 is less than the trust gains, the LIFO rule means that the gains of later years will be treated as accruing to the beneficiary before the gains of earlier years. Where a rebasing election has been made by the trustees the legislation provides that the post-April 5, 2008 element of the trust gains of a given year will be treated as accruing proportionately with the pre-April 6, 2008 element in respect of capital payments made on or after April 6, 2008. It is not possible to be worse off by making an election. If the chargeable gain is higher on rebasing (e.g. because all main resident relief accrued before April 2008—see 43.154) the lower gain is taken.

EXAMPLE 19.20

A receives £100,000 payment in 2008–09. He is a remittance basis user. The trust realises gains of £1 million in that year of which £100,000 accrued post-April 2008 and £900,000 before April. It makes a rebasing election. The 2008 Budget Note indicated that all the £100,000 payment would be matched to the post-April 2008 element of gain with the result that all of it is taxable if remitted. In fact para.127(4) provides that the realised gain is matched proportionately so one-tenth represents the post-April 5, 2008 element and nine-tenths the pre-April 2008 element. Even if the whole £100,000 is remitted, only one-tenth is taxable.

19.60 If A is foreign domiciled but not a remittance basis user then whether or not he remits the £100,000 payment, one-tenth will still be taxable but the part

---

[82] See 43.154 for further details.

attributable to the pre-April 2008 element will not be taxed. Since any gain resulting from a rebasing election will not be brought into account on April 6, 2008 but only when the asset is disposed of, the notional pool of pre-April 6, 2008 gains will fluctuate in the future because:

(a) when assets owned on April 6, 2008 are disposed of at a gain, the pool of pre-April 6, 2008 gains will increase; and

(b) capital payments will reduce the pre-April 6, 2008 pool to the extent that there are no post-April 5, 2008 gains to which the payment can be allocated in that year.

EXAMPLE 19.21

(a) B who is foreign domiciled but not a remittance basis user received a capital payment in January 2008 of £1,000. The trust had no stock-piled gains at that time. It makes a rebasing election. It realises a gain in 2010 of £3,000—pre-April 2008 element is £1,000 and post- is £2,000. One-third of pre-April 2008 element gain is matched to capital payment. None of it is taxed because the payment was received before April 2008 but the matching rules will affect the taxability of future capital payments.

(b) C (a remittance basis user) receives a £1,000 capital payment in January 2010. The trust gain in that year is £3,000—pre-April element is £1,000 and post- is £2,000. Two-thirds of the capital payment is taxable if remitted since it is matched to the post-April 2008 element. If only part of the £1,000 is remitted presumably only a proportionate part of the post-April 2008 gain is taxed. If C is not a remittance basis user then one-third is still not taxed (because it relates to a pre-April 2008 element) and the balance is taxed on an arising basis.

Should a foreign domiciliary use offshore trusts?

Do the 2008 changes mean that foreign domiciled settlors should no longer set up offshore trusts? Before April 6, 2008 although offshore trusts produced few income tax advantages for the foreign domiciliary they brought huge capital gains tax advantages: gains on foreign assets held personally could effectively be eradicated by giving them to an offshore trust. Gains realised by trustees on assets held within the trust were not taxable even if capital payments were made. The foreign domiciliary did not have to worry about foreign currency gains. The position has become much more complicated!   **19.61**

First, it is no longer possible to wash out unrealised gains by giving a foreign asset to a trust.   **19.62**

EXAMPLE 19.22

Elouise, non-UK domiciled, buys £200,000 worth of shares in the German company Z Limited using capital. In 2005 she settles the shares in an offshore trust from which she can benefit at a time when they are worth £1 million. Under the pre-April 6, 2008 rules there was no deemed remittance and the trust acquired the shares at market value of £1 million. If the trustees sold the shares for £1.5 million two years later realising a gain of £500,000 and then paid capital to the settlor in the UK there was no taxable remittance by Elouise of either the £800,000 pre-settlement gain or the £500,000 post-settlement gain since neither TCGA 1992 ss.86 nor 87 applied and s.12 was not applicable. The gains had been "washed out". Even if the trustees had reinvested the proceeds in UK assets and sold at a gain and paid out the proceeds to her in the UK, there would still have been no tax chargeable on Elouise.

19.63 The new rules have altered this so that gains cannot be "washed out" by use of trusts.[83]

EXAMPLE 19.23

Facts as in Example 19.22 except that Elouise settles the shares into trust in 2010. The trust acquires the shares at market value and there is no deemed remittance at that point. However, if the trust sells the shares and pays (say) £300,000 to Elouise or her spouse, minor child or grandchildren, cohabitee or company owned by her and the £300,000 is brought to the UK, Elouise is treated as having remitted £300,000 of £800,000 pre-settlement gain and is taxed accordingly. If the trust invests any part of the proceeds of sale in the UK, that is also a taxable remittance.

In addition, a beneficiary who receives a capital payment from the trust will also suffer a s.87 charge based on the trust gains of £500,000. The s.87 charge will fall on the person who receives the capital payment (not necessarily on Elouise). If, however, the trustees had paid the £300,000 to her adult son resident here, then Elouise is not taxed on £300,000 pre-settlement gain and the son will be liable to tax under s.87 by reference to the trust gains of £500,000 only.

If Elouise had settled the shares into trust in 2005 but no payment was made to her until (say) 2009, the question arises as to whether the pre-settlement gains of £800,000 can in future be taxed on her under ITA 2007 s.809T or whether she is only taxed under the s.87 settlement code on trust gains of £500,000. The let-out in Sch.7 para.86(4) makes it clear that if the trustees distribute to a spouse or other relevant person, Elouise cannot be taxed on the £800,000 pre-settlement gains because references to a relevant person are restricted to her as the donor. However, the

---

[83] See ITA 2007 s.809T.

position is less clear where payments are made to Elouise herself which are derived from the sale proceeds of the asset. The better view is that gains on pre-April 2008 gifts to trust are not taxed on Elouise even if the payment to her is made after April 6, 2008 although, of course, she could now be taxed under s.87 on trust gains of £500,000.

There are further complications. It is no longer sound advice for a foreign **19.64** domiciled taxpayer who is UK resident to hold all foreign assets which are likely to show a gain in a trust. The use of a trust will avoid or at least defer CGT on UK situated assets but can complicate the remittance rules. Instead of looking at the gain on the actual foreign asset and determining whether that gain has been remitted it will be necessary to compute all the stockpiled gains of the trust.

EXAMPLE 19.24

An offshore trust owns a portfolio of shares and a UK house occupied by B. The trust sells the shares at a gain and reinvests the proceeds. B pays tax on the gain even though nothing has been distributed to him because the trust gains are matched to his capital benefits from the occupation of the house (s.87B).

Compare the position if H (a foreign domiciliary) occupies a UK house which **19.65** qualifies as his main residence. He owns it personally. There is no capital gains tax on sale (due to main residence relief) and no tax charge on the benefit of his occupation. The main tax problem is that he will pay inheritance tax on his death but this could be dealt with by insurance: see Ch.43.

UK houses: washing out gains

Assume that H occupies a UK house but it is owned in an offshore company **19.66** which in turn, is owned by a trust. He has no inheritance tax exposure. He is treated as receiving a taxable benefit equal to rent-free occupation of (say) £50,000 pa but there is no tax charge as long as the trust makes no gains on or after April 6, 2008.

EXAMPLE 19.25

In 2017–18 the company sells the house realising gains of £1 million. Assume most of the gains accrued post-April 5, 2008 and therefore all of these gains are potentially taxable on him. H has received benefits of £500,000 in the UK since April 2008. He now pays capital gains tax because the gains can be matched to the past benefits. If, however, the trustees make a capital distribution of £1 million to him in 2018 in the same tax year as the sale and he keeps this capital abroad then that capital payment is matched to the trust gains first. In 2018 he has therefore received total benefits of £1,050,000 of which £50,000 was received in the UK. He therefore pays tax on the remittance basis but only on £50,000 gains. If the trust realises further gains in future tax years, those gains (if not matched to capital payments made in the same year) can be taxed on him by reference to the earlier benefits. If no capital payment was made in tax year 2017–18 the capital gain is matched to the earlier capital payments and taxed (since such payments were received in the UK).[84]

19.67 In summary, if B can ensure that no gains are realised at a time when he is UK resident or, if they are, that they are matched to capital payments made to him abroad, then he can receive UK benefits without significant tax liabilities. The position becomes more complicated where the trust holds more than one asset. The timing of capital payments can be important.

EXAMPLE 19.26

Assume as above that the trustees hold a UK house through a company. The house is occupied by B who receives taxable UK benefits. The trustees sell the company in 2010–11 for a gain of £1 million having made a rebasing election. All the gain realised on the disposal accrued pre-April 6, 2008; the trustees should not make a cash distribution to B abroad in 2010–11. If they do, they are "wasting" tax-free gains on a capital distribution that would not be taxed on B anyway because he receives it abroad and does not intend to remit it.

If they do not make any distributions to him in that tax year all of those £1 million gains (deemed to accrue pre-April 2008 "*pre-April 2008 election gains*") would then be matched to the earlier capital payments of £500,000 (i.e. the occupation of the house) and no tax is payable on B even though the capital payment was received after April 5, 2008. £500,000 gains are carried forward to be matched against future capital payments. However, since these gains are also pre-April 2008 gains they are not taxed on B in the future even if he is not a remittance basis user.

Hence, it is better to match pre-April 2008 election gains to capital payments received in the UK by the foreign domiciliary because no tax is paid and match post-April 2008 election gains to capital payments received outside the UK.

Conclusions

19.68 Where trustees have made a rebasing election and they have several assets they wish to sell and have unmatched capital payments they should consider the position carefully. If asset 1 shows mainly a pre-April 2008 accrued gain and asset 2 shows mainly a post-April 2008 gain and capital payments have all been

---

[84] A similar example is given in Ch.44 in relation to the use of chattels.

received in the UK by a foreign domiciliary, sell asset 1 in the tax year before the sale of asset 2. If, however, capital payments have been received outside the UK by a remittance basis users and are never likely to be remitted, then sell asset 2 first so chargeable post-April 2008 gains are matched to the payments received abroad. Remember that the use of a company may double up gains and therefore tax charges!

VI ANTI "FLIP-FLOP" LEGISLATION AND SCHS 4B AND 4C

19.69   FA 2000 sought to stop flip-flop schemes by introducing Schs 4B and 4C in TCGA 1992. It applies to all offshore settlor-interested trusts and trusts with stockpiled gains but no longer to UK settlor-interested trusts.

EXAMPLE 19.27

A simple flip-flop scheme before FA 2000 worked as follows:

1. Trustees of the A Trust, a non-UK resident trust, which has no stockpiled gains and only unrealised gains, borrow against the security of the trust assets and advance the cash to the B Trust (which includes the settlor as a beneficiary); they then exclude "defined persons" from the A Trust;
2. A Trust disposes of assets to pay off the loan, whilst the cash is advanced out of B Trust to the settlor.

Under this arrangement no gains were read through to the B Trust (because there were no stockpiled gains which had been realised before Year 2) so that the distribution (in Year 2) from B Trust was tax-free. Further, the only disposal in the A Trust occurred at a time when the settlor charge did not apply. A Trust was non-UK resident so no CGT arose on the trustees.

19.70   The FA 2000 legislation applies if:

1. the trustees make a transfer of value on or after March 21, 2000; and
2. the transfer of value is linked with outstanding trustee borrowing (it does not matter if the borrowing was taken out prior to that date); and
3. the trust is within ss.86 or 87 TCGA 1992, in the tax year.[85]

If Sch.4B applies there is a deemed disposal with the result that the settlor of a non-UK resident trust within s.86 may pay capital gains tax on gains from such a disposal at 18 per cent of gains from April 6, 2008 up to June 22, 2010 and thereafter 28 per cent plus supplemental charge.[86] Any such deemed gain realised by a non-resident trust outside the s.86 charge would also fall to be

---

[85] Note that since April 6, 2008 it no longer applies to UK resident settlor-interested trusts.
[86] See Ch.11. Note that following further changes in April 2003, the Sch.4C pool will comprise

taxed on the beneficiaries in future because such gain goes into a Sch.4C pool and can be taxed on UK resident and domiciled beneficiaries in receipt of capital payments from the settlement. If the pool was created prior to April 6, 2008 then Sch.4C does not apply to foreign domiciliaries or gains in the pool cannot be washed out by payments to non-residents and foreign domiciliaries. Where the transfer of value occurs after April 5, 2008 then the Sch.4C pool can be attributed to foreign domiciled beneficiaries resident in the UK. There is no motive test.

If Sch.4C losses are realised these can be set off against the beneficiary's personal gains.

What is a transfer of value "linked" to trustee borrowing?

19.71 By linked is meant that at the time of the transfer there is outstanding trust borrowing. The transfer does not need to be made using the borrowed money. Note that loans to the trust from underlying companies wholly owned by the trust, from beneficiaries or settlors are caught just as much as commercial loans. However, loans to companies owned by the trust are not trustee-borrowing although will be transfers of value if the loans are made by the trustees. Trust borrowing is outstanding until repaid. Borrowing which is applied for normal trust purposes is disregarded. Normal trust purposes involve:

(i) expenditure such as a payment in respect of ordinary trust assets, e.g. buying shares or securities, houses, tangible properties and payments in connection with a business carried on by the trustees;

(ii) discharging a pre-existing loan which has been applied for normal trust purposes;

(iii) bona fide expenses incurred by the trustees in administering the settlement or any of the settled properties.

19.72 Expenditure on intangibles such as insurance policies is not normal expenditure. In addition a simple debt such as a bank deposit is not covered so in theory trustees who borrow and then deposit the monies in a bank account are not making an application of the borrowings for normal trust purposes.[87] There are other problems, e.g. when must the expenditure on ordinary trust assets occur, i.e. must it be as a direct application of the borrowing? What about repairs to property? This is not allowable expenditure within TCGA 1992 s.38 so in theory does not qualify. HMRC, however, stated that they would regard such expenditure as being for normal trust purposes under Sch.4B on the basis that it is reflected in the state or nature of the asset at the time it is incurred.

19.73 Particular care must be taken when trustees borrow and then lend to underlying companies. Such simple debts are not ordinary trust assets: accordingly the trustees need to subscribe for shares or securities in the company. The

---

not only the gains realised on the deemed disposal under Sch.4B but all unmatched stockpiled gains at the end of the tax year in which the transfer of value occurs: see 19.77.

[87] *Tax Bulletin* 66 however commented that this is not a transfer of value. Hence if trustees borrow £500, deposit £300 and pay £200 to X, they are treated as making a transfer of value of £200 but outstanding trust borrowing is £500. See Example 19.29.

asset must be held by the trustees immediately after the transfer of value. HMRC have indicated that they would regard borrowing incurred to buy real property as continuing to satisfy the normal trust purposes test even if the property is subsequently let provided that it remains part of the trust fund. Bona fide current expenses include income and capital expenses and the payment of capital taxes but do not cover making a reserve in respect of future expenditure or borrowing taken out to pay off old unpaid debts or expenditure in administering any underlying holding company. This is because the expenditure must be incurred in administering the *settlement* or on the *settled property*.

What is a transfer of value?

A transfer of value is not the same as an IHT transfer of value. Trustees are treated as making a transfer of value if:

19.74

   (i) they transfer an asset to any person *either* for no consideration *or* for a consideration which is less than market value; or

   (ii) they lend money or any other asset to a person; or

   (iii) they issue a security.[88]

The effect of the legislation

As noted above if the transfer of value is linked to trustee borrowing, there is a deemed disposal under Sch.4B. The disposal is deemed to occur at the date when the transfer of value is made and is of all the chargeable assets which are retained in the trust immediately after the material time. Even if there is only a small transfer of value linked to trustee borrowing there is still a deemed disposal but only of a proportion of each of the assets in the settlement. See Example 19.29 for part disposals under Sch.4B. The deemed disposal is triggered even if the transfer of value is not actually funded or in any way related to the trustee borrowing; all that is necessary is that at the material time there is trustee borrowing which is outstanding. The base cost of the trust assets will be uplifted on the deemed disposal in the normal way.

19.75

This prevented the use of old-style flip-flop schemes which had effectively worked by borrowing, transferring the cash to a new trust and then excluding the settlor and all defined persons from the first trust. The realisation of gains in the first trust was delayed until the tax year after the settlor had been excluded. The intention was to avoid a s.86 charge on future gains.[89]

However, FA 2000 introduced a loophole that enabled trustees to reduce or eliminate stockpiled gains that could be attributed to beneficiaries on future capital payments under s.87. This loophole was contained in TCGA 1992

19.76

---

[88] See *Tax Bulletin* 66.
[89] They were also used in relation to UK settlor-interested trusts when gains were taxed at higher rates than non-settlor interested trusts: see Ch.7 and *West v Trennery*.

s.90(5)(a) which prevented s.87 gains from being carried across to the transferee settlement (Trust B) to the extent that the transfer was (under Sch.4B) linked with trustee borrowing. The legislation that had aimed to stop s.86 avoidance thus opened up extensive opportunities for s.87 tax avoidance as illustrated in the following example:

EXAMPLE 19.28

> Offshore Trust A has £1 million stockpiled gains and is worth £1 million. It holds mostly cash or assets showing no gain. It borrows £1 million and in 2002 appoints all the borrowed funds of £1 million to Trust B. Since there was a transfer of value linked to trustee borrowing, s.90(5)(a) provided that the stockpiled gains of £1 million did not pass across into Trust B. Trust B took £1 million free of the stockpiled gains. There was a deemed disposal of the assets remaining in Trust A but since these showed no gains (or maybe the settlor was dead or not UK domiciled so that such gains would not be immediately taxable anyway) this did not matter. There was nothing to go into the Sch.4C pool.
>
> See however, *Herman v HMRC*[90] where the scheme was held not to work. In that case Trust B made a payment to a beneficiary as part of an overall plan and it was held that the amount was received "indirectly" from Trust A and would be taxed under s.87. Hence the scheme did not avoid a capital gains tax charge even as the FA 2000 legislation was originally drafted!

19.77   Such "s.90 schemes" were widely used in an attempt to get rid of the stockpiled gains which could not easily be washed out in cases where all the beneficiaries were UK resident. The Government response to the s.90 avoidance scheme was aggressive and "retroactive".[91] These changes are complex but the effects can be summarised as follows:

(i) The changes are relevant wherever trustees of a settlement have made a transfer of value linked to trustee borrowing after March 20, 2000 even if the original settlement (Trust A in the above example) has subsequently ceased to exist. Since, as noted above, a transfer of value linked to trustee borrowing can occur in a number of unexpected instances where there is no avoidance motive, the position must be checked wherever trustees have borrowed.

(ii) The provisions do not affect beneficiaries who have received capital payments from Trust B prior to April 9, 2003. Thus in the above example if Trust B had distributed the entire £1 million to the relevant beneficiaries before April 9, 2003, such beneficiaries are not caught by the FA 2003 legislation and the payments are tax-free provided that the s.90 scheme works (it may fail for other reasons, e.g. if Trust B was a sham or it was part of a scheme: see *Herman* above).

[90] [2007] STC (SCD) 571.
[91] FA 2003 s.163 amended Sch.4C.

(iii) FA 2003 now provides that the Sch.4C pool comprises not only the Sch.4B gains realised on the deemed disposal *but also any outstanding s.87 gains* in the transferor settlement at the end of the tax year in which the transfer was made. Thus in the above example, Trust B no longer takes £1 million cash free of the s.87 gains. All those s.87 gains fall into the Sch.4C pool (along with any deemed Sch.4B gains) and can be allocated to any future payments made to beneficiaries of either Trusts A or B.

(iv) The fact that (as in the above example) no gains may be realised on the deemed disposal under Sch.4B is irrelevant. If there is a transfer of value linked to trustee borrowing then the anti-avoidance legislation is triggered and a Sch.4C pool is formed comprising the Sch.4B trust gains plus the unmatched s.87 stockpiled gains.

(v) For the purposes of calculating any Sch.4C pools arising before April 6, 2008, the outstanding s.87 gains are calculated ignoring payments to non-resident or foreign domiciled beneficiaries in the tax year of the transfer of value (or subsequently) although payments to such beneficiaries that took place prior to April 9, 2003 can reduce the s.87 stockpile.

(vi) The old s.87 stockpile in Trust A is reduced to nil. There is just one Sch.4C pool overhanging both trusts.

EXAMPLE 19.29

In 2003–04, Trust A borrows £2 million and appoints the cash to Trust B in June 2003. There is a deemed disposal of all the settled property held by the trustees of Trust A as at June 2003 (say shares in X Ltd worth £600,000 with a base cost of £100,000) which disposal, therefore, realises a Sch.4B gain of £500,000 (ignoring taper relief). The level of stockpiled s.87 gains in Trust A at the end of 2003–04 is £1 million. The Sch.4C pool is therefore £1.5 million and can be attributed to future capital payments made to beneficiaries out of either Trust.

B then makes distributions of £1.5 million to A and B, both not domiciled in the UK, and the following tax year Trust B distributes the balance of the fund, being £500,000, to C who is UK resident and domiciled. The distributions to A and B do not reduce the Sch.4C pool of gains (which remains at £1.5 million) although A and B do not suffer a CGT charge. C pays tax on the entire £500,000 distributed to her. Similarly, if Trust A makes any distributions to A and B, such distributions will not reduce the Sch.4C pool and future capital payments to UK resident and domiciled beneficiaries such as C will be taxed. Note that because the Sch.4C pool arose prior to April 6, 2008 even if capital payments are made to non-domiciliaries after April 6, 2008 they cannot have any gains in pre-Sch.4C pools attributed to them.

(vii) The risk of triggering a transfer of value prior to April 6, 2008 was not only that one created a deemed disposal of the remaining assets in the original settlement but also that one had lost the opportunity to structure future capital payments tax efficiently—gains could not be "washed out" by making distributions to non-chargeable beneficiaries. However, from April 6, 2008 this has changed. There are no changes to the taxation of pre-April 2008 Sch.4C pools and those Sch.4C pools still cannot be washed out by payments to non-domiciliaries. However, a Sch.4B transfer of value on or after April 5, 2008 will result in the creation of a separate Sch.4C pool. This means that gains in Sch.4C pools coming into existence on or after April 6, 2008 will be able to be matched with capital payments to non-UK domiciled beneficiaries but the remittance basis will apply.

(viii) The deemed disposal of the remaining settled property means that those assets are rebased for all future purposes. Note, however, that under Sch.4B there is only a deemed disposal of the settled property, not of assets held in trust companies.

19.77A   A difficult issue is when a part disposal arises under Sch.4B. Assume the following facts: the trust owns a house worth £800,000 originally purchased with borrowings of £300,000 and ready cash of £100,000. It therefore shows a gain of £400,000. The £300,000 is not outstanding trust borrowing since it was applied for normal trust purposes. The trustees later borrow a further £400,000 on the security of the house; they put £100,000 on deposit and advance £300,000 to a beneficiary. This is a transfer of value of £300,000 and outstanding trust borrowing is £400,000 as defined in para.5. (The cash is not regarded as applied for normal trust purposes even if it is later reinvested in shares.) The transfer of value is less than outstanding trust borrowing and therefore Sch.4B para.11(2) applies. The deemed disposal is VT (value transferred) = £300,000 over EV (effective value of the remaining chargeable assets—defined in para.12(3)). EV is £500,000 since the original borrowing used to acquire the asset must be deducted. Hence the deemed disposal is three fifths of the settled property (60 per cent) realising a Sch.4B gain of £240,000.

If the Trustees reinvested the cash of £100,000 in chargeable assets rather than putting it on deposit, the transfer of value would be equal to the outstanding trust borrowing but less than the net value of the remaining chargeable assets (still £500,000). Paragraph 11(3) applies.   The deemed disposal is of a proportion given by TB (outstanding trust borrowing) / EV. Hence £300,000/£500,000 = 60%. The Sch.4B gain is the same.

EXAMPLE 19.30

Facts as in Example 19.29 except that Trust A actually sold the X Ltd shares 11 months later in May 2004 for £700,000. The gain realised then would be £100,000 (which gain will not fall into the Sch.4C pool unless a further transfer of value is made). The shares were rebased to £600,000 as a result of the deemed disposal.

(ix) In Example 19.29 taper relief was available on the deemed disposal in June 2003 calculated on a period of ownership from the date of acquisition up to June 2003. However, no further taper relief was available on the actual disposal in May 2004 because the shares had not been held for 12 months. The actual gain of £100,000 realised on a later actual disposal of X Ltd shares is a s.87 gain which is not attributed to Trust B does not pass into the Sch.4C pool and can still be washed out on future payments by Trust A to non-resident or non-domiciled beneficiaries. It is only the Sch.4C gains that could not be washed out.

(x) The interest surcharge can also apply to Sch.4C gains and to maximise the adverse effects although note that one year's supplemental tax is levied if the capital payment is only one year after the gain is realised. Again the FIFO rule has been changed to LIFO from April 2008. Gains of post-April 5, 2008 Sch.4C pools are attributed to capital payments before gains of pre-April 2008 Sch.4C pools and Sch.4C gains are attributed before later s.87 gains.

(xi) There are wide anti-avoidance provisions catching further transfers to other trusts. Thus if in this example either Trust A or Trust B makes a further transfer of value creating a further Sch.4C pool then that pool can be visited on any of the beneficiaries who receive capital payments from Trusts A, B or C even if, say, the beneficiaries are excluded from the Trust which made the further transfer of value.

(xii) One new and potentially useful aspect is the ability to wash out Sch.4C gains on post-April 2008 pools by payments to foreign domiciliaries. However, once a Sch.4C pool is created it must be fully exhausted before any s.2(2) trust gains are matched if they are realised later.

EXAMPLE 19.31

A trust borrows in 2009 an amount equal to 90 per cent of the trust fund and transfers the cash to a new settlement. That is a transfer of value which triggers a deemed disposal (possibly only if part of para.11(3) applies) and Sch.4B gains of, say, £1 million. These go into a new Sch.4C pool. The trust has three beneficiaries: A – non-UK resident; B – resident and not domiciled and C – resident and domiciled. The trustees make a capital payment to A: this does not reduce the Sch.4C pool. They make a capital payment to B abroad—this reduces the Sch.4C pool even though he is not chargeable unless and until he remits.

If in later years either trust realises further gains these will not fall into the Sch.4C pool but cannot be matched to payments to B or C until the Sch.4C pool is exhausted. Hence the supplemental charge will be higher because the Sch.4C gains were realised earlier.

Schedule 4C gains and personal losses

In some cases trustees may wish to trigger a deemed disposal under Sch.4B in order to create a pool of Sch.4C gains and move the existing s.87 gains into that pool. If a capital payment is made to a UK resident beneficiary who has **19.78** personal losses, such Sch.4C gains attributed to the beneficiary on the capital payment can be reduced by the personal losses. By contrast trust gains in the s.87 pool cannot be reduced by personal losses. Watch the targeted anti-avoidance rule on losses discussed further in Ch.21.

VII INFORMATION REQUIREMENTS FOR OFFSHORE TRUSTS[92]

19.79   FA 1994 widened the information provisions to catch all non-resident trusts, not just those in which a defined person retains an interest. Accordingly, they apply to additions to an existing trust; to the establishment by a UK resident and domiciled settlor of a foreign settlement and indeed to a foreign settlement created by a non-UK resident and domiciliary who subsequently becomes resident and domiciled and, finally, to the export of a UK trust. In all cases details of the date when the settlement was created; name and address of persons delivering the return and details of the trustees must be provided.[93] The draft legislation on Sch.7 published in January 2008 proposed extending these reporting requirements to all offshore trusts set up by UK resident foreign domiciliaries but in the event the proposals were dropped.

VIII CONCLUSIONS

19.80   The harshness of the offshore regime for UK domiciliaries and in particular the fact that capital gains were effectively taxed at up to 64 per cent led to a proliferation of tax schemes in the early 1990s, followed by the inevitable anti-avoidance legislation. The reduction in the rate of capital gains tax to 18 per cent on April 6, 2008 reduced the number of such schemes and encouraged people to break up offshore trusts with mainly UK beneficiaries particularly where the settlor was UK domiciled and still alive. The matching of capital payments to gains on a last-in, first-out basis further encouraged earlier repatriation of gains.

UK domiciliaries who received capital payments before June 23, 2010 found that their rate of tax reduced from a maximum 64 to 28.8 per cent. This was often regarded as an acceptable price to pay and many pre-1991 trusts set up by UK settlors were then ended. The rate of tax for capital payments made from June 23, 2010 has increased to 44.8 per cent maximum.

19.81   For foreign domiciliaries, the FA 2008 changes greatly complicated their tax position. For the first time offshore trusts with foreign domiciled beneficiaries needed to consider the pattern of trust gains and distributions. Although it is possible with careful planning to avoid or at least mitigate capital gains tax on capital payments, the regime is highly complex. When added to the heady mix of transfer of assets provisions and the legislation on offshore income gains, many foreign domiciliaries may despair. Whether all this will raise much revenue for the Exchequer remains to be seen. Most foreign domiciliaries have by now arranged their affairs so as to avoid remitting any funds from offshore

---

[92]   TCGA 1992 s.98A, Sch.5A.
[93]   The reporting duty is on the transferor or, on the export of a trust, the trustees: see also Ch.56.

trusts to the UK and/or ensured that assets such as UK houses are no longer held in trust structures. Alternatively, where trusts are needed to hold assets from which the foreign domiciliary can benefit in the UK these assets are held in dry trusts. The capital gains tax position can then be managed: as soon as gains are realised they are "washed out" by payments abroad in the same tax year equal to the gain to a remittance basis user or non-resident.

CHAPTER 20

THE DISPOSAL OF A BENEFICIAL INTEREST

- The basic rule **(20.01)**
- Disposal of an interest in a non-UK resident settlement or in a settlement which was at any time non-resident or which has received property from such a settlement **(20.06)**
- Sale of an interest in a settlor-interested trust **(20.19)**
- Tax planning issues **(20.29)**

I THE BASIC RULE

20.01   There is no charge to CGT when a beneficiary disposes of an interest in settled property even though an equitable interest in settled property is an asset for capital gains tax purposes.[1] Section 76(1) provides that:

> "*no chargeable gain shall accrue on the disposal of an interest created by or arising under a settlement . . . by the person for whose benefit the interest was created by the terms of the settlement or by any other person except one who acquired, or derives his title from one who acquired, the interest for a consideration in money or money's worth, other than consideration consisting of another interest under the settlement.*"

The rationale is that the settled property itself is subject to capital gains tax[2] so that to charge tax on the interest of a beneficiary would be a form of double taxation. There is, however, a growing list of exceptions resulting from tax avoidance schemes which have sought to exploit the basic exemption.

20.02   In brief the general exemption will not apply:

(i) once the interest has been purchased for money or money's worth (see 20.03);

(ii) if the interest is in a non-resident settlement (see 20.06);

---

[1] TCGA 1992 ss.21(1)(a) and 76(1) as amended by FA 1998 s.128(1)(a), cf. the disposal of an interest in an unadministered estate (see Ch.39).

[2] See Ch.11.

(iii) if the interest is in a settlement that has at any time been non-resident or received property from a non-resident settlement (see 20.17);

(iv) if the interest is in a settlor-interested trust (see 20.19).

Position of a purchaser

Once a beneficial interest has been purchased for money or money's worth, a **20.03** future disposal of that interest whether by gift or sale (unless by the original beneficiary under the settlement) will be chargeable to CGT. The consideration does not have to be "full" or "adequate", i.e. any consideration however small will turn the interest into a chargeable asset. An exchange of interests by beneficiaries under a settlement is not treated as consideration so that a later disposal of either interest will not be chargeable.[3]

EXAMPLE 20.1

(1) A is the remainderman under a settlement created by his mother. He sells his interest to his friend B for £350,000. No CGT is charged on A. If B resells the remainder interest to C for £410,000, B has made a chargeable gain of £60,000 (£410,000 – £350,000). The gain is taxed at 28 per cent if B is a higher rate taxpayer. Note that the s.76(1) exemption is not available because there has been an acquisition of a beneficial interest for consideration. Further, if B gave the remainder interest to C (or if he becomes absolutely entitled to the settled property)[4] there is a disposal of his equitable interest which can result in a chargeable gain or loss because B was the purchaser of the interest which has as a result become a chargeable asset.

(2) If A (the original remainderman) had paid cash to the settlor as consideration for entering into the settlement and later gifted or sold the interest to B, no chargeable gain (or loss) would accrue on that disposal by A because A was the person for whose benefit the interest was created. However, a subsequent disposal of the interest by B would be chargeable (even if B had been gifted the interest by A) because A had paid for the interest so B acquires title through a person who furnished consideration.[5]

(3) If A, the original remainderman, had not purchased his interest and gave it to B who then sold it to C there would be no charge on either A or B because they are not purchasers. There would, however, be a charge on C as and when there was any further disposal of the beneficial interest.

---

[3] Compare the inheritance tax changes in FA 2006 s.157 amending s.48 of IHTA 1984 under which consideration for sales of interests in excluded property settlements can include exchanges of interests within a settlement: see Ch.31.

[4] See 20.04.

[5] See also TCGA 1992 s.16(2) and *Berry v Warnett* [1982] 1 WLR 698.

20.04 When a life interest is sold, the wasting asset rules may apply on a subsequent disposal of that interest by the purchaser. In general, if the predictable life expectation of the life tenant is 50 years or less then a life interest is wasting. The predictable duration of life interests in settled property and of annuities must be ascertained from actuarial tables approved by HMRC[6] and is not based on the medical condition of the life tenant. If the life interest is a wasting asset this increases the capital gain because the acquisition cost of the asset is written off on a straight line basis. So even if the life interest does have a 1982 value the gain could still be substantial.[7]

EXAMPLE 20.2

(1) Andrew is the life tenant of a UK resident trust. He held the life interest in March 1982 at which time it was valued at £100,000 with a predictable life of 40 years. He sells it in March 2009 to Bill, an unconnected person, for £90,000 (at a time when its actuarial value was estimated at 13 years).

	£	£
Disposal consideration on sale		90,000
Allowable cost	100,000	
Deduct (27/40 × £100,000)	67,500	32,500
Gain		57,500

Andrew pays tax at 18% (the CGT rate in 2008–09) = £10,350

(2) If Andrew dies in March 2011 the life interest is extinguished. B has an allowable loss as follows:

	£	£
Disposal consideration on death of Andrew		Nil
Allowable cost	90,000	
Deduct (2/13 × £90,000)	13,847	76,153
Allowable Loss		(76,153)

Purchaser becoming absolutely entitled to any part of the settled property ("the s.76(2) charge")

20.05 The termination of the settlement may result in the settled property vesting in a purchaser of the remainder interest (of course, he may also become entitled

---

[6] See TCGA 1992 s.44(1)(d).
[7] See CGTM 38020.

to such property in other situations, for example if an advancement is made to or for his benefit). As a result, that purchaser will dispose of his purchased interest in return for receiving the settled property.[8] The resultant charge that he may suffer[9] on the disposal of his equitable interest does not affect the deemed disposal by the trustees (and possible CGT charge on them).[10] Hence, there is a possibility of double capital gains tax charges: one on the trustees and one on a beneficiary.

EXAMPLE 20.3

> Assume in Example 20.1(1) above, that C becomes absolutely entitled to the settled property which is then worth £900,000. He has realised a chargeable gain of £490,000 (£900,000 – £410,000). In addition, the usual deemed disposal rules under TCGA 1992 s.71(1) operate to tax the trustees' gains (if any) on the disposal of the underlying assets.[11]

II DISPOSAL OF AN INTEREST IN A NON-UK RESIDENT SETTLEMENT OR IN A SETTLEMENT WHICH WAS AT ANY TIME NON-RESIDENT OR WHICH HAS RECEIVED PROPERTY FROM SUCH A SETTLEMENT

20.06 TCGA 1992 s.85(1) provides that the disposal of an interest in a non-resident settlement is chargeable: the basic exemption conferred by s.76(1) is excluded although it is provided that no charge arises if the beneficiary becomes absolutely entitled to any part of the trust fund.[12] The s.85 charge is not limited to sales of trust interests. It can apply where the original life tenant of a non-UK resident trust surrenders his interest for no consideration and the trusts continue.

EXAMPLE 20.4

> A is life tenant of a non-UK resident trust.[13] He surrenders his life interest for no consideration and the assets become held on discretionary trusts. He is treated as making a disposal of his life interest and is taxed on any gain: i.e. on the difference between his base cost (likely to be nil given that he is the original beneficiary[14] unless the trust had been

---

[8] TCGA 1992 s.76(2).
[9] It may be that he makes a loss but that is unlikely.
[10] Under TCGA 1992 s.71(1).
[11] Compare the position if the potential charge arises under s.76(1A) because the trust has been non-UK resident: see 20.17.
[12] TCGA 1992 s.85(1).
[13] Or a UK resident trust that has received property from a non-UK resident trust.
[14] An original beneficiary will have no acquisition cost because there is no corresponding disposal when he acquires his interest. TCGA 1992 s.17 prevents market value being substituted on the beneficiary becoming entitled to his interest.

exported after being set up[15] or he had the interest in March 1982) and the actuarial market value of his interest. Any gain is taxed at 28 per cent assuming he is a higher rate taxpayer. His interest is likely to be a wasting asset. Note, however, that there is no disposal by the trustees since the property continues to be settled. If A's life interest was a pre-March 2006 qualifying interest in possession then the termination of that interest is also a chargeable event for inheritance tax purposes.[16] If A's life interest ended because he became absolutely entitled to the settled property there is no tax charge: see s.76(2).

Involuntary termination

20.07 What happens if the interest of a beneficiary in an offshore trust terminates not as a result of any voluntary action on his part (such as a sale or surrender), but by an act of the trustees, e.g. where a life interest is terminated by the trustees under a power reserved to them in the settlement? For capital gains tax purposes the termination will not amount to a disposal by the beneficiary. Whilst it is true that under that legislation certain involuntary disposals (e.g. a sale under a compulsory purchase order) are subject to charge (so that a voluntary act on the part of the disponor is not always required), in these cases there is a transfer of assets as opposed to a mere forfeiture of rights. (Of course, if the interest of the beneficiary was revocable by the trustees at any time it would have little value to that beneficiary so, in any event, there would be no gain on a disposal).

If the trustees, therefore, exercise overriding powers of appointment in the case of a non-UK resident trust and terminate a life interest and make an appointment on continuing trusts for children, there is no CGT charge on the life tenant because he has not disposed of his beneficial interest.

Consents

20.08 What is the position if the trustees can exercise their overriding settlement powers only with the consent of the life tenant? Is there a disposal by the beneficiary who consents in these circumstances?[17] A classic example is when the trustees exercise their power of advancement in favour of remainder beneficiaries and the life tenant's consent is required under s.32 of TA 1925. Does it make a difference if the beneficiary in question releases the requirement for his consent before any advancement by the trustees is in contemplation?

20.09 In the authors' view, the giving of consent or the release of such consent by a beneficiary is not a disposal of a beneficial interest under the settlement although it may make him the settlor for income tax purposes if the result is that entitlement to income passes to someone else. Giving consent is not

[15] See 20.15.
[16] Ch.23.
[17] This issue is considered in the context of variations of trusts: see 9.60 and 12.29. It is not thought that the release of consent rights has any inheritance tax consequences as they are settlement powers: see IHTA 1984 ss.47A and 272.

in itself a disposal of a beneficial interest: it has merely enabled the trustees to exercise an overriding power which has had the effect of terminating that interest. In the past, HMRC have indicated that if no consideration is given for the consent (or any release of it) there is no disposal of his interest by the beneficiary.[18]

20.10 That is not the end of the matter, however, since a further question arises, namely is the *release* of a consent or the actual giving of consent the disposal of a separate asset for capital gains tax purposes namely a *chose in action*?[19] If so, variations of any settlement whether UK resident or not, where the beneficiary has to consent might be problematic! If this asset is not settled property, is there a charge under other provisions of the capital gains tax legislation apart from ss.76 and 85, e.g. under ss.22, 24, 29 or 30? It would appear odd to create a new chargeable asset in connection with settled property given that the beneficiary already has a beneficial interest under the trust (in addition to the ownership of the trust property by the trustees), since that could lead to double or even triple charges. However, in general consent rights are an asset for capital gains tax purposes since the holder can stipulate for payment before exercising them.[20] Any money or money's worth which he derives from the consent rights is taxable as a capital gain under TCGA 1992 s.22. Alternatively if he gives up his consent rights even for nil consideration could this be a depreciatory transaction triggering an adjustment on any disposal of the life interest under the capital gains tax value shifting rules?[21] It is thought not since s.30 will operate only where there is a tax-free benefit, i.e. a benefit which is not required to be brought into account in computing the recipient's income and gains. It might be said instead that the consent to a termination of the life interest triggers a deemed disposal of the life interest under TCGA 1992 s.29(5). Again this can be dismissed: that subsection applies where an asset is subject to a right or restriction, not where it has the benefit of it.

20.11 The other point is that even if the consent requirement is a form of proprietary right or interest, assuming the consent right is not exercised for any consideration, on its own it would have a negligible value: without the life interest which it "protects" it is of no use to anyone other than, possibly, a remainderman in whose favour the power of advancement could be exercised.[22] The position might be different if, for example, the life tenant was not

---

[18] An alternative view taken by some advisers is that if the life tenant releases his right to consent to the termination of (say) a life interest or consents he has subjected his income interest to the exercise of an overriding power by the trustees. In these circumstances there is a resettlement of the beneficial interest for capital gains tax and income tax purposes and he is the settlor. However, see CG Manual paras 37881 and 37882 onwards which note that where the trustees with the consent of the beneficiaries vary the terms of a trust, if the property is held on continuing trusts it is treated as a mere variation of the terms of the existing settlement and not a disposal for capital gains tax purposes. Even if the variation is such that there is a disposal, the assumption is that it is a disposal of the underlying assets not of the settled interest itself.

[19] The right might be an asset within s.21(1)(c) TCGA 1992 being "*any form of property created by the person disposing of it or otherwise coming to be owned without being acquired.*" However, one would need a specific deeming provision to tax such right given that a disposal does not cover a transaction in which an asset (here the right) is not acquired but merely extinguished. See *Welbeck Securities Ltd v Powlson* [1987] STC 468. See the following footnotes for discussion of whether any of the deeming provisions might apply.

[20] See *O'Brien v Benson's Hosiery Ltd* [1979] STC 835.

[21] TCGA 1992 s.30.

[22] The position though remains unsatisfactory. Similar problems arose in the inheritance tax context in relation to a power of revocation where it was held in *Melville v IRC* [2001] STC

merely giving up the right to consent to the exercise of a statutory power of advancement but was surrendering a power of appointment which allowed him to appoint the fund to any person.[23]

Surrenders and the s.86 charge

20.12   The effect of s.85 is that even if the settlor wants to be excluded from a non-resident trust (along with all defined persons) in order to avoid a s.86 capital gains tax charge on the settlor on future disposals of settled property by the trustees,[24] it may not be possible to do this easily without triggering a different capital gains tax charge on the beneficial interest itself if the terms of the trust are such that the settlor will only be excluded if he surrenders his life interest.[25] It is clear that the surrender of an interest *will* be regarded as a disposal of the beneficial interest and so the settlor could be liable to CGT (although the life interest is likely to have a low or nil base cost).[26] The fact that the trust has become resident in the UK would not prevent a charge.[27] However, there is no charge in the case of both UK resident and non-resident trusts where the beneficiary who has become entitled to the interest (other than by purchase) becomes absolutely entitled.

EXAMPLE 20.5

(1) The trustees of a pre-1991 offshore trust hold the property on interest in possession trusts for the settlor and subject thereto on interest in possession trusts for his children. The settlor wishes to carry out inheritance tax planning. The trustees have no power to terminate his life

---

1271 that the power was a separate asset with value. In the inheritance tax context, the position was eventually dealt with by legislation: see IHTA 1984 s.47A.

[23] It is thought desirable (out of abundant caution) for the beneficiary to release his right to consent before any termination of his interest is in contemplation rather than consenting to an advancement which terminates his life interest. The consent right more obviously has a value as a separate piece of property if the giving of the consent directly results in the termination of his life interest (and the other concern that it is a disposal of the beneficial interest under the settlement itself is greater in these circumstances). Sections 24 and 29(5) are the deeming sections which might be problematic if there is a concern that the right to consent or the release of that right is a separate chargeable asset although HMRC would still have to show that the asset has value. Section 24 deems a disposal to arise on the occasion of the entire loss, destruction or extinction of an asset whether or not a capital sum is received. If the right to consent has been released or extinguished it is conceivable that there might be a disposal but the problem (if there is one) could be avoided if the right is released only for a period of time, e.g. the life tenant releases his right to consent for one year. Section 29(5) provides that if an asset is subject to any description of right or restriction, the extinction or abrogation in whole or in part of the right or restriction by the person entitled to enforce it, shall be a disposal by him of the right or restriction. It is thought, in any event, that the right has little value. This is strengthened if the right is surrendered well before any appointment or advancement terminating the interest is effected.

[24] See Ch.19.

[25] For the s.86 charge and taxation of offshore trusts generally, see Ch.19.

[26] Although note that the life interest may have a 1982 base cost (but still be a wasting asset) or have been uplifted to market value if the trust was exported: see s.85(3) and 20.15.

[27] See 27.22.

interest and so he surrenders his interest for no consideration. As a result, the successive interest in possession trusts for the children take effect and (if the surrender was affected before October 6, 2008) these will be transitional serial interests for inheritance tax purposes and the settlor makes a PET.[28] However, since the trust is offshore and the settlor has made a disposal of his beneficial interest this is subject to capital gains tax and he is taxed on any gain. The life interest has a nil-base cost in his hands (assuming he did not hold it in 1982) although if the disposal occurred in 2006–07 he would be entitled to non-business assets taper relief. If he had held his life interest since before March 1998 he would have obtained nine years taper relief so (assuming that he was a higher rate tax payer) he would have been taxed at a rate of 26 per cent. If he surrendered his life interest in 2008–09 then any chargeable gain was taxed at 18 per cent.

(2) If the settlor became absolutely entitled to the property then there is a disposal of the settled property and he is treated as disposing of his beneficial interest in consideration of obtaining that property but no charge arises (s.76(3)).[29]

It is desirable to ensure that offshore trustees have wide overriding powers of appointment, exclusion etc in order to enable them to rearrange the beneficial interests without the consent or any action being required of a beneficiary which might trigger unexpected charges under s.85.

Foreign domiciliaries

Do the same problems arise for UK resident foreign domiciled beneficiaries? **20.13** Suppose a UK resident foreign domiciled beneficiary who is a remittance basis user[30] gifts his beneficial interest in an offshore settlement. There is no immediate tax charge if the gain on such beneficial interest is not remitted to the UK[31] and the beneficial interest is foreign situs. There are accordingly two questions: when are gains remitted and what is the situs of the beneficial interest?

Where underlying assets are held by trustees as bare trustees or nominees **20.14** for the foreign domiciled beneficiary then it is the situs of the actual assets that is relevant.[32] However, where the beneficiary has an equitable interest under a settlement it is not thought that the situs of the underlying assets is relevant. In these circumstances the situs for capital gains tax purposes seems to be determined by the law of the trust or possibly depends on where the trustees are resident.[33] Accordingly, the beneficial interest of a life tenant or remainderman under a foreign law settlement with non-UK resident trustees will not be situated in the UK. Nevertheless, a tax charge could arise if the foreign domiciliary

---

[28] For TSIs, see 27.16 and following.
[29] Note that a purchaser of a beneficial interest will be charged under s.76 if he becomes absolutely entitled to the settled property wherever the residence of the trust.
[30] See Ch.5.
[31] See FA 2008 Sch.7 and ITA 2007 s.809L to determine when income and gains are remitted to the UK and see Ch.5.
[32] See *Re Clore* [1982] STC 625 at 633 and TCGA 1992 s.60.
[33] See *Re Smith, Leach v Leach* [1898] 1 Ch.89.

sold his interest under the trust for consideration and remitted the proceeds to the UK for himself or any relevant person.

EXAMPLE 20.6

Dmitri is the life tenant under a Jersey law settlement set up in 1998. He is not domiciled or deemed domiciled in the UK but has been resident here for 10 years. The trustees are resident in Jersey. He wishes to surrender his life interest in favour of his son who is also not UK domiciled but takes a life interest on termination of Dmitri's interest. The trust is an excluded property trust for inheritance tax purposes since it holds no UK situated assets so that there are no inheritance tax issues. Assume the trustees have no overriding powers. The tax position is as follows:

(1) If Dmitri surrenders his life interest then his son takes a life interest which will not be a qualifying interest in possession unless Dmitri surrenders his interest prior to October 6, 2008 in which case son takes a transitional serial interest. However, s.82 does not apply (because Dmitri is not UK domiciled) and the settlement is an excluded property trust. Even if the trust becomes a relevant property settlement on the termination of Dmitri's interest there are no 10-year charges unless the trust holds UK situated property directly at that time and there is no entry charge on the termination of Dmitri's interest in possession.

(2) If Dmitri surrenders his life interest for no consideration then there is a capital gains tax charge unless he is a remittance basis user.[34] If he is[35] then no capital gains tax is payable unless property derived from the gain is remitted to the UK for the benefit of Dmitri or any other relevant person.[36] (A minor child or grandchild, spouse or cohabite, are all relevant persons.) A foreign chargeable gain is treated as accruing to Dmitri on the disposal of his beneficial interest but he receives no actual consideration. Section 809T applies and the beneficial interest is treated as deriving from the chargeable gains. In this case though the beneficial interest (i.e. Dmitri's life interest) has disappeared so it is hard to see how there can ever be a taxable remittance!

(3) If however, Dmitri assigned his life interest to his wife (so that she took an interest *pur autre vie*) there could be a tax charge on Dmitri[37] if his wife sold that interest and remitted the proceeds to the UK. By contrast, if Dmitri assigned his life interest to his adult son his son could sell that interest and remit the proceeds to the UK without creating a tax charge for Dmitri but if son settled the proceeds into a trust for his own minor children and the trust

[34] See Chs 5 and 19.
[35] See s.809B as inserted by FA 2008 Sch.7.
[36] See ITA 2007 s.809L and Chs 5 and 19.
[37] Under ITA 2007 ss.809L and T.

remitted the proceeds then Dmitri would be caught even if he
could not benefit under that trust.[38]

(4) If Dmitri sold his interest to a third party or a relative and then
either he or any relevant person remitted the proceeds to the UK
there would be a tax charge on Dmitri.

Export of UK resident trust

If the trust was originally UK resident, the appointment of non-resident **20.15**
trustees triggers an exit charge on the assets in the trust.[39] Some protection
against a double charge is given if a beneficial interest is subsequently disposed
of by s.85(3):

> *"For the purpose of calculating any chargeable gain accruing on the
> disposal of the interest, the person disposing of it shall be treated as
> having:*
>
> *(a) disposed of it immediately before the relevant time, and*
> *(b) immediately reacquired it, at its market value at that time."*

The relevant time is the date of emigration. The relief in s.85(3) only applies
to a beneficiary whose interest was created or acquired before the date of
emigration.[40] If the trust resumes UK residence there is no relief on the
subsequent disposal of a beneficial interest since the trustees do not satisfy
the basic condition in s.85(1).

The purpose of s.85(3) is to fix the acquisition cost of the disponor at the
date when the trustees emigrated (i.e. the acquisition cost of his beneficial
interest which might otherwise be nil is rebased to market value at that time).
The relief only applies where s.80 (exit charge on emigration of the trust)
applies so if a trust emigrated before March 1991 (i.e. before s.80 was introduced) there was no rebasing of the beneficial interests.

EXAMPLE 20.7

The X trust was set up in 1988 with J being entitled in remainder on
the death of his sister, K who enjoys an interest in possession. The
trustees became non-UK resident on March 20, 1996 and J disposed of
his remainder interest shortly afterwards (whether for consideration or
otherwise). It was worth £150,000 at the date of disposal.

(1) J has made a chargeable disposal.[41]
(2) In order to compute his chargeable gain, if any, the market value

---

[38] For details of relevant persons, see Ch.5.
[39] See Ch.4.
[40] TCGA 1992 s.85(4).
[41] TCGA 1992 s.85(1).

of his remainder interest when the trust became non-resident on March 20, 1996 must be ascertained.

If the trust later became UK resident again no relief under s.85(3) would be available if J subsequently disposed of his interest and he would realise a chargeable gain.[42]

In- and-out schemes

20.16 Section 85(3) was amended to prevent what was termed "the in-and-out scheme". Assume that a non-resident trust had stockpiled gains which would be taxable on a UK resident and domiciled beneficiary under s.87 if he received capital payments. It was a cash fund. UK trustees were appointed so that the trust became resident and subsequently it was exported (by the appointment of further non-resident trustees). On export, s.85(3) operated to increase the base costs of all the beneficial interests but, given that the trust comprised only cash, there was no exit charge under s.80 on the settled property. As a result, a beneficiary could later sell his beneficial interest, e.g. to a non-UK resident who would not be concerned about the stockpiled gains. This enabled the beneficiary to enjoy the value of the trust without any capital gains tax charge under s.87. From March 21, 2000,[43] however, the disposal of a beneficial interest in a non-resident settlement which had stockpiled gains at "the material time" (i.e. when it ceased to be UK resident) cannot benefit from the uplift in value under s.85(3). There is still an uplift if the trust emigrated at a time when it had no such gains.

EXAMPLE 20.8

(1) Facts as in Example 20.7 above except that the X Trust emigrated in 1989. There will, however, be no uplift in J's remainder interest because emigration occurred before the introduction of s.80 so s.85(3) would not provide relief.[44]

(2) If the X Trust became resident in the UK in 1996 and emigrated again in 2001 then if at the time of emigration in 2001 there were no stockpiled gains because all the gains realised prior to 1996 had been distributed there is an uplift in the value of beneficial interests.

(3) However, if the Trust became UK resident in 2005 and J then disposed of his remainder interest, s.85(3) will not apply and his interest is not rebased. Relief under s.85(3) only operates if s.85(1) applies,[45] i.e. the X Trust is non-UK resident at the time when the interest is sold. If the

---

[42] Because of the charge under TCGA 1992 s.76(1A): see 20.17.
[43] The amendment to TCGA 1992 s.85 applies where the material time, within the meaning of TCGA 1992 s.85(10), falls on or after March 21, 2000: FA 2000 s.95(5).
[44] TCGA 1992 s.85(2)(a).
[45] See s.85(2)(b).

Trust is back in the UK, then s.76(1A) does not give a similar relief and since the charge is under s.76(1A) rather than s.85 there is no rebasing.

Disposals of interests in UK trusts that had been non-UK resident or received property from a non-resident trust ("the s.76(1A) charge")[46]

Disposals of beneficial interests in a UK resident trust which was at any time non-UK resident or non-UK resident under a double tax treaty (or which had received property from a non-UK resident trust) were brought into charge in respect of disposals occurring on or after March 6, 1998.[47] This provision aimed to stop schemes designed to avoid a charge on gains which had accrued in foreign trusts by repatriating the trusts with the beneficiary then disposing of his interest. If, however, the beneficiary in question becomes absolutely entitled to the settled property no s.76(1A) charge arises.[48]

20.17

EXAMPLE 20.9

In 1997, offshore trustees of a pre-1991 settlor-interested trust disposed of assets realising a gain which could not then be charged on the settlor under s.86[49] and was stockpiled. The settlor wanted to receive capital from the trust fund but could not sell his interest without triggering a s.85 CGT charge. The trust was therefore imported in 1998 and then he was able to sell his beneficial interest under the settlement to a bank (by this time the settlement held cash) tax-free. The bank was non-UK resident and therefore did not care about the fact that there were s.87 gains in the settlement.

As amended with effect from March 6, 1998, s.76(1A) now catches the disposal of *any* beneficial interest under a settlement if the trust has at any time been non-resident or if the UK trust has received property from a non-resident settlement. There is no charge if, or to the extent that, the beneficiary becomes absolutely entitled to the trust property (since this will trigger the charge on the stockpiled gain). Note though that there is no relief from s.76(1A) if the trust emigrated with no stockpiled gains, the beneficiary had an uplift in the value of his beneficial interest under s.85(3) and the trust then returns to the UK. In that case the beneficiary does not seem to take an uplifted base cost.

The provision is wide-ranging. Consider the following:

20.18

---

[46] TCGA 1992 s.76(1A), (1B) and (3).
[47] TCGA 1992 s.76(1A), (1B) and (3).
[48] TCGA 1992 s.76(3).
[49] See Ch.19.

EXAMPLE 20.10

A UK trust was set up to benefit children of the settlor in 1996. It has never been non-resident. Children of the settlor are life tenants entitled to capital at 30. One of the beneficiaries wishes to sell his interest to a purchaser in 2008. Just before he affects the sale the trustees receive £1,000 of property from an offshore settlement. The result is that the whole of the UK settlement is tainted and therefore a disposal of *any* of the beneficial interests by a beneficiary will be taxed.

III SALE OF AN INTEREST IN A SETTLOR-INTERESTED TRUST[50]

20.19 The rules relating to the sale of an interest in a settlor-interested trust took effect from March 21, 2000 and when they apply *the trustees*, provided that they are UK resident, are treated as disposing and reacquiring trust assets at market value (i.e. there is a deemed disposal). Until April 6, 2008 capital gains tax was charged at either the settlor-rate (if the settlor was then interested in the trust) or at the normal 40 per cent rate (if the trust was no longer settlor-interested but had been so in the previous two years) and in the latter case could be recovered by the trustees from the beneficiary who sold the interest. Schedule 4A has been retained even though TCGA 1992 ss.77–79 (which taxed settlors on gains in their trusts if they retained an interest) have been repealed. Therefore if a UK resident trust is settlor-interested a Sch.4A charge can still arise but will be charged on the trustees, albeit the trustees retain the right to recover the tax from the person who disposed of the interest.

Basic conditions

20.20 The following conditions need to be satisfied for a charge under Sch.4A to arise:

(i) the trust must be UK resident;[51]

(ii) the trust must be settlor-interested or have been so in the previous two tax years or have received property from a trust which was settlor-interested in the previous two years. Note that a trust which comprises property derived from more than one settlor but where only one of the settlors is UK resident and has an interest is wholly within the provisions of Sch.4A so any disposal by a beneficiary will trigger a charge on the trust assets even if those assets had not been settled by that UK resident settlor[52];

---

[50] TCGA 1992 Sch.4A as inserted by FA 2000 Sch.24.
[51] Sch.4A para.5.
[52] Sch.4A para.7.

(iii) the settlor must in the tax year in which the disposal takes place or in any of the previous five tax years have been resident or ordinarily resident in the UK[53];

(iv) there must be a disposal of any interest created by or arising under a settlement for consideration. A disposal by any beneficiary, not just the settlor, is caught.

If the conditions are satisfied there is a deemed disposal of all the underlying assets of the settlement at market value. The tax is always paid by the trustees after April 5, 2008 but is recoverable from the person who disposed of the interest.[54] Note that there cannot be a charge on both the deemed disposal of the underlying assets and the disposal of the equitable interest in the trust. The disposal that produces the lower gain is disregarded. This will generally mean that the disposal of the equitable interest will be ignored unless the beneficiary has previously purchased it or the trust has been non-UK resident.[55]   **20.21**

When is a settlor interested in his trust?

This is determined in accordance with s.169F(2)–(6), i.e. if the settlor, his spouse (other than a separated one), civil partner or minor child can or could benefit from the trust.[56] A trust is not settlor-interested if the settlor dies in the year of assessment.[57] However, the legislation applies not only if the trust is settlor-interested when the beneficial interest is sold but also if the trust contains property derived from any trust which was settlor-interested at any time in the previous two years. Notice that the disposal can be by *any* beneficiary: the legislation is not limited to disposals by the settlor. The settlor must, however, be either resident or ordinarily resident in the UK[58] or have been so in any of the previous five tax years. Years of UK residence before 1999–2000 are disregarded.   **20.22**

The mischief under attack

The intention was to prevent exploitation of the TCGA 1992 s.76(1) exemption by individuals who gifted assets into trust with the benefit of hold-over relief (instead of selling the assets), retained an interest under the trust and then sold the exempt beneficial interest free of capital gains tax. A simple scheme which the legislation was intended to stop (as set out by HMRC in CG 35101) would have been something like this: **20.23**

---

[53] Sch.4A para.6.
[54] Sch.4A para.11.
[55] Sch.4A para.10.
[56] See Ch.7.
[57] From April 6, 2006 if living dependent children of the settlor are beneficiaries this made a trust settlor-interested.
[58] The definition of a settlor-interested trust is considered in Ch.7.

- A owns a valuable holding of unlisted shares in a trading company which he wishes to sell to B.

- He creates a settlement under which he has the life interest and his son C has the remainder.

- He transfers the shares to the settlement, claiming hold-over relief under TCGA 1992 s.165.

- He sells his life interest to B and C sells his remainder interest to D, B's son. The price would be based on the current market value of the shares, with some discount for potential future capital gains tax.

- B and D are appointed trustees of the settlement.

- B and D now have full control as beneficiaries and as trustees. They could get the shares out of the trust, using a TCGA 1992 s.165 hold-over claim to prevent CGT arising. But this would involve some liability under TCGA 1992 s.76. Alternatively they could simply leave the assets in the settlement.

On the sale by A and C the legislation provides that there is a deemed disposal of the trust assets. However, the scope of the legislation is much wider than the above and can catch different transactions.

EXAMPLE 20.11

(1) In 1999 D settled unlisted shares and made a hold-over election under s.165 to avoid the payment of CGT.[59] He became absolutely entitled to those assets on attaining 35 (which was, say, four months later). Before the four months elapsed he sold this interest to E and F, trustees of a second settlement with realised capital losses. As a result:

    (a) under general principles the sale by D of his interest did not attract a CGT charge[60];
    (b) when E and F become absolutely entitled as trustees a further hold-over election was available, and when they disposed of the assets they could reduce the resultant gain by their unused trust losses.

    In these circumstances TCGA 1992 Sch.4A provides that when D sells his interest the trustees of the first trust make a deemed disposal of the trust property and until April 6, 2008 the tax charge was borne by D as the settlor. The deemed disposal of the underlying assets cannot qualify for hold-over relief under either ss.165 or 260 because it is deemed to be in a bargain at arm's length. However, if D sells his equitable interest in the trust on or after April 6, 2008 there is a deemed disposal by the trustees but the tax charge is now on them at 18 per cent (until June 23, 2010 and

---

[59] Such an election is no longer possible: since December 2003 hold-over relief is not available on transfers into settlor-interested trusts: see Ch.18. See also 21.26 and TCGA 1992 s.79A which restricts the use of trust losses where any person connected with the original transferor purchases an interest in a settlement.

[60] TCGA 1992 s.76(1) as amended by FA 1998 s.128(1)(a).

thereafter at 28 per cent) not on D although the trustees can recover the tax from D under para.11. The mischief which Sch.4A aims to stop is now fairly limited given the restrictions on hold-over relief introduced in 2003.

(2) Valuable land in St Ives was settled in 1990 and X, the current life tenant, is the settlor. His son, Y, is the remainderman but X shows no sign of dying so in 2011 Y decides to sell his interest to raise much-needed cash. X knows nothing about this. TCGA 1992 Sch.4A applies and the trust suffers a CGT charge. Note that the tax charge is not on the value of the beneficial interest of Y but on the underlying assets. There is no motive test. The trustees pay tax at 28 per cent but can recover this from Y. The residence of the beneficiary is irrelevant.

Consideration

Consideration means actual consideration but excludes another interest in the same settlement save one previously disposed of for value. It does not include the incidental costs of a transaction.[61]   **20.24**

The charge

The deemed disposal is of all the trust assets even if the consideration is minimal unless one of two exceptions applies: **20.25**

(i) where the interest being sold is an interest in a specific fund in which case the deemed disposal is restricted to assets in that fund.[62] So if B is the life tenant of Blackacre and C is the life tenant of Whiteacre and the trust has been settlor-interested within the previous two years, the sale by B of his interest results in a disposal of Blackacre but not Whiteacre;

(ii) where the interest is in a specific fraction of the income or capital in which case the deemed disposal is of that fraction of the underlying assets. So if B and C were joint life tenants of the whole of the settled property and only B sold his life interest, there is a disposal of 50 per cent of the settled property.

Since the deemed disposal is made by the trustees, liability for tax prima facie falls on them. Before April 6, 2008 if the settlement was within s.77 the settlor was liable but could recover the tax from the trustees unless he was the disponer of the interest. If the settlement was not settlor-interested in the year of disposal the trustees were directly liable. If the trustees bear the tax under Sch.4A they are entitled to recover it from the person who disposed of the beneficial interest. In Example 20.11(2), X could recover his tax from the trustees who would in turn recover it from Y.[63]   **20.26**

---

[61] See *Tax Bulletin* 66, August 2003.
[62] Para.8(1).
[63] TCGA 1992 Sch.4A para.11.

20.27   Paragraph 13 has complicated provisions to deal with delayed completion. What happens if the contract to sell the beneficial interest and completion of the sale are in different tax years? The beginning of the disposal is when the contract is entered into or, if earlier, when an option is granted. Effective completion is when the buyer becomes unconditionally entitled to the beneficial interest. If they are in different tax years, the disposal takes place in the year of effective completion and the residency test of the settlor and the trustees are applied by reference to both years. In addition, the rules as to whether the settlement is settlor-interested are applied for the year of completion.

20.28   It is curious that Sch.4A remains on the statute book. Since December 2003 hold-over relief has no longer been available on transfers into settlor-interested trusts and therefore the sort of schemes considered in Example 20.11(1) are no longer possible. It is hard to see why HMRC would want to catch Example 20.11(2) anyway. Presumably HMRC wish to retain Sch.4A in order to deal with the possibility of a settlor selling his exempt interest under the trust in the future when the trust assets show a large unrealised gain.

IV TAX PLANNING ISSUES

UK resident trusts

20.29   Where the trust has always been UK resident, is not settlor-interested (and was not settlor-interested in the previous two years) and has not received property from a non-UK resident trust then sales of exempt interests by beneficiaries are still a possibility. There is no capital gains tax for the beneficiary who can walk away with cash. He does not need the consent of the trustees. However, it is often the case that the beneficiary in question does not have a valuable interest worth selling: for instance, if the trustees can defeat such interest by exercise of powers of appointment or advancement then no purchaser will want to buy it and any purchaser will also want to ensure that he is not subject to capital gains tax on a later disposal of that interest. Moreover, even if the beneficiary sells to a non-resident this does not help if the trust then sells assets and realises gains. Similarly if the beneficiary sells to a UK charity the charity pays no tax but the trustees continue to pay tax on any disposals of the underlying assets. Even if the trust is settlor-interested a beneficiary could still sell his interest without a tax charge arising provided the settlor is not UK resident.

Offshore trusts

20.30   Schedule 4A does not apply to non-resident trusts but, of course, there is no exemption for disposals of beneficial interests. However, where settlor-interested offshore trusts contain assets showing large unrealised gains, the disposal of a beneficial interest in the settlement by a beneficiary could still be attractive. This was particularly the case prior to April 6, 2008 because of the taper relief position. Often a beneficial interest had been held for longer than the trust assets and therefore qualified for more taper relief. In addition there was no supplemental charge.

EXAMPLE 20.12

N is the UK resident and domiciled life tenant and settlor of an offshore trust which was set up in 1995. N's son is the remainderman entitled to capital on N's death. Since the trust is non-UK resident the s.76(1) exemption will not apply so that if N sells his life interest this will be a chargeable disposal. The capital gain will be calculated under normal principles (the life interest will be a wasting asset). If the sale of a life interest takes place during 2007–08 tax year, N would have a qualifying holding period of nine years plus an additional year under TCGA 1992 s.2A(8)(b) for taper relief purposes. He would therefore pay at an effective tax rate of 24 per cent on any gain he makes on the disposal of his life interest. Any disposal of the trust assets would probably be taxed at a higher rate on N under s.86 unless they were business assets because the investments are likely to have changed over the years and therefore non-business assets taper relief would be less.

However, from 2008–09 the rate of tax will be the same whether N sells his life interest or the trust sells its investments. The question then comes down to whether the base cost of the life interest (generally a wasting asset and one with a nil acquisition cost in the above example) is less than the base cost of the assets comprised in the trust and also whether the trust contains any stockpiled gains. In this case the gains would necessarily have been realised prior to March 1998 (because after then the gains would have been taxed on N under s.86 anyway) and will therefore be subject to the maximum supplemental charge.[64] If N sells his life interest then he receives the cash and there is no possibility of a s.87 charge because he is simply realising an asset that he owns personally. However, if the trust sells settled property then it is the trust that receives the capital albeit N is taxed under s.86. If the trustees then advance the cash to N there is a further tax charge on N under s.87 at an effective rate of 28.8 per cent if there are stockpiled gains and the capital payment was made before April 2011. If the capital payment to N is made after April 5, 2011 the rate of tax for N is 44.8 per cent.

IHT link-up

The inheritance tax implications of any disposal by an individual of his inter- **20.31**
est in possession (whether the trust is offshore or not) need careful consideration and are discussed in some detail in Ch.26.[65] If N's qualifying interest in
possession is worth £50,000 actuarially but the value of the settled property
in which his interest subsists is £150,000 and he receives £50,000 for the sale

[64] See Ch.19.
[65] IHTA 1984 ss.51(1) and 52(1).

497

of his life interest he will have made an IHT transfer of value of £100,000 (£150,000 – £50,000). He cannot rely on the no gratuitous intention exemption in IHTA 1984 s.10 because that only relieves dispositions that would otherwise have been transfers of value. The disposal of a life interest in a settlement is not itself a transfer of value[66] but a deemed ending of the interest. If the sale of the life interest is to a company, such as a bank, this would be an immediately chargeable transfer. If the transferee is an individual it would be a PET (a TSI until October 6, 2008: thereafter the disposal will result in a chargeable transfer into a relevant property trust).[67]

Summary

20.32 Whether the disposal of a beneficial interest is subject to capital gains tax depends on a number of factors:

1. Does it fall within the standard exemption under s.76, i.e. if the trust has always been UK resident and not received any property from a non-UK resident trust and there has been no past purchase of the beneficial interest then it is not a chargeable asset when disposed of. However, if the trust is UK resident and has been or is settlor-interested watch Sch.4A even if the beneficiary is disposing of an exempt interest. A remainderman who sells his interest may inadvertently trigger a tax charge on the trustees which they will seek to recover from him.

2. If the equitable interest is a chargeable asset has there been a disposal of that interest which is chargeable, e.g. has the beneficiary made a disposal of it at all or have the trustees merely terminated the interest? Has the beneficiary become absolutely entitled to assets of a non-resident trust (in which case the beneficial interest is treated as being disposed of but no charge arises)?

3. If there is such a disposal does the interest being disposed of have any value? For example, where the trustees take away a particular beneficiary's right to capital and they do not need the consent of the person with the interest, that interest is of little market value.

4. If the interest does have value and a disposal would be chargeable, is the disponer of the interest a foreign domiciled beneficiary? If so does the remittance basis apply and could there be a remittance under s.809L?

---

[66] See s.51(1)(a).
[67] See 27.14 for the IHT treatment of a termination of a qualifying interest in possession. See Ch.26 for sales of life interests.

CHAPTER 21

LOSS RELIEF

I BASIC PRINCIPLES

The changes in 2008 to the capital gains tax regime affected the use of capital losses in three ways. **21.01**

First, although capital losses were not themselves tapered, the effect of TCGA 1992 s.2A(1) meant that prior to April 6, 2008 losses had to be deducted from gains before the application of taper relief. This was the case both for current year losses and for those brought forward from earlier years. The abolition of taper relief meant this is no longer relevant. Losses are deducted from gains and the net gains then taxed at a flat rate of 28 per cent.[1]

Secondly, before April 6, 2008 gains and losses realised by UK resident settlor-interested trusts were treated as accruing to the settlor and tax was charged on him. From April 6, 2008 this is no longer the case. This has had an impact on losses realised before April 6, 2008 by such trusts which have been carried forward.

Thirdly, until April 6, 2008 losses realised on assets situated abroad by a foreign domiciliary were disallowed. This changed: an irrevocable election can be made to obtain loss relief on foreign situated assets. Losses realised by non-residents are not allowable unless they return to the UK within five years of leaving.[2]

---

[1] See Ch.11 for rates of tax. Prior to June 23, 2010 gains were taxed at 18% and therefore losses relieved gains at that rate. Losses realised in 2010–11 (where gains can be taxed at either 18 or 28% depending on whether they were realised before or after June 23, 2010) can be set off against gains in the way that gives the most favourable result. Hence losses can be relieved against gains that would otherwise be taxed at 28%.

[2] See Ch.5 for further details and TCGA 1992 s.2(1).

Otherwise the basic principles remain the same.

21.02 Section 2(2) provides for the deduction of current year losses first and then for the deduction of brought forward losses. Current year losses must be deducted from current year gains in full and can therefore result in a wasted annual exemption. However, brought forward losses are only deducted against gains in later years to reduce those gains to the amount covered by the annual exemption and not to zero.

EXAMPLE 21.1

A realises gains of £14,000 and losses of £13,000 in the same tax year. All the losses have to be used leaving only £1,000 gains to be covered by A's annual exemption. If the losses had been brought forward from previous years then they would have reduced the gains to £10,600 (the 2011–12 annual exemption) leaving no tax to pay in 2011–12 and £10,600 losses to carry forward for future use.

21.03 Section 2 applies to individuals, trustees, companies and personal representatives. Section 2(3) prevents the carry-back of losses except that allowable losses made by the deceased in the tax year of death may be deducted from chargeable gains accruing to him in the three tax years preceding the tax year of death (assuming that they cannot be used in the year of death and taking gains accruing in a later year before gains in an earlier year).[3]

21.04 Losses are computed in the same way as gains.[4] Hence assets that cannot realise a chargeable gain (such as a house qualifying for main residence relief or chattels worth less than £6,000 or debts owned by an original creditor) cannot generate allowable losses.

21.05 A loss on a disposal to a connected person is deductible only from chargeable gains arising on other disposals to that same person while he is still connected.[5]

21.06 Trustees carrying on a trade are in certain circumstances entitled to set trading losses against capital gains. The applicable rules are the same as for individuals.[6] The relief requires an election and capital gains may be used only to the extent that the trading loss cannot be used against the taxpayer's other income for the tax year. The trading loss is set against gains after such gains have already been reduced by capital current year and brought forward losses but ignoring the annual exemption. Hence, claiming a trading loss can mean that an annual exemption is wasted. If full relief is not available in the year when the trading loss is incurred, the balance can be carried-back and set against gains in the immediately preceding tax year. Given that losses set against income are relievable at 50 per cent but losses set against gains are relievable only at 28 per cent it is unlikely that many trustees will want to make the election.

---

[3] TCGA 1992 s.62(2). Personal losses can never be deducted against s.87 trust gains attributed to beneficiaries: see *Futter v Futter* [2010] STC 982 and 1.23.

[4] TCGA 1992 s.16(1). On disposals before November 30, 1993 indexation could increase a loss or turn a gain into a loss but from that date this was no longer possible.

[5] See Ch.10 and Example 10.1.

[6] FA 1991 s.72.

EXAMPLE 21.2

Discretionary trustees have taxable income of £10,000, trading losses of £50,000, chargeable gains of £40,000 and allowable capital losses of £10,000. The taxable income is reduced to nil and an election is made for £40,000 of trading losses to set against gains. The chargeable gains are first reduced by the capital losses leaving £30,000 gains to use against the trading losses. The trustees' annual exemption is effectively wasted. There are £20,000 trading losses left to carry back.

Under self-assessment a loss is not allowable unless the taxpayer gives notice to HMRC in relation to the year of assessment in which the loss accrues.[7]

II ANTI-AVOIDANCE

21.07 With effect for disposals from December 6, 2006, FA 2007[8] introduced a new "targeted anti-avoidance rule" (TAAR) to deny loss relief where the loss arises in consequence of arrangements the main purpose of which is to secure a tax advantage.[9] The tax advantage does not have to be secured for the person who realised the loss. The aim (in the words of the Guidance Notes[10]) is:

> "*to restrict the use of capital losses resulting from the arrangements where tax avoidance is the main purpose or one of the main purposes of the arrangements . . . [but] the new legislation [will not] ordinarily prevent a genuine loss on a real disposal of an asset from being set-off against a person's own gains, including the case where, before the real disposal that gives rise to the genuine loss, the person acquires the relevant asset from a spouse at no gain no loss under s58.*"

However, it is hard to see on the wording of the legislation that the TAAR is so restricted!

21.08 HMRC consider that "purpose" is wider than "motive" and imports an objective test: i.e. one has to look at the overall context. However, in looking at the main purpose of the arrangements one has to look at the objectives of the person who undertook the transaction and therefore his state of mind at the time (which is surely a subjective test). A tax advantage is obtained if capital gains tax, corporation tax or income tax are reduced or avoided. Read literally the legislation seems to deny loss relief for any loss unless the ability to deduct the loss was not one of the main purposes of the transaction. The legislation

---

[7] TCGA 1992 s.16(2A).

[8] See TCGA 1992 s.16A.

[9] FA 2006 had already introduced targeted anti-avoidance rules restricting losses of corporate bodies. The TAAR introduced in FA 2007 blocked all capital gains tax loss schemes, whether undertaken by companies, individuals, trustees or personal representatives.

[10] Published in draft in July 2007. The final version of the Guidance is in Appendix II at A2.17.

is not limited to denying relief where there "is no genuine commercial loss" as the guidance notes suggest.[11]

21.09 Several examples in the guidance notes (Examples 11 to 14 and 18) are relevant to trusts, three of which create "acceptable" losses and one of which does not. In some of the Examples the facts are unlikely. For instance, in Example 12 of the Guidance it is improbable that the trustees would have sold the asset to a third party. The trustees could have transferred the asset to beneficiary Z and realised the loss on the deemed disposal anyway if they had already realised gains in that tax year. Similarly in a variation of Example 12, Example 13 envisages that the trustees are administering a discretionary trust for a number of beneficiaries, and Z is one of that class of beneficiaries. The trustees sell a capital asset and realise a chargeable gain. In the same year, they also sell an asset which is standing at a loss. The loss can be set against the gain, and so no CGT is payable in that year. Also in that year, the trustees advance funds to a number of the beneficiaries, including Z, who uses the sum that he receives to buy the asset on which the loss has been realised by the trustees. Again the facts are improbable. But the suggestion in Example 13 that this is acceptable only because the trustees have also advanced cash to a number of beneficiaries is worrying. Suppose they had advanced cash only to the beneficiary who wanted to buy the asset? Why should this make a difference to loss relief?[12]

21.10 Example 14 of the Guidance gives the more likely example of a trust distributing assets that show both gains and losses to a beneficiary in the same year with the intention that the loss incurred on the transfer of the second asset is set against the gain arising on the transfer of the first asset. HMRC comment that:

> "*To decide whether the TAAR will operate to make the claimed losses disallowable it is necessary to determine whether arrangements have been entered into with a main purpose of securing a tax advantage. The main purpose test is operated by looking at the main purpose of the participants in entering into these arrangements. This requires an analysis of the overall economic objective of the arrangements, and whether that objective is being fulfilled in a straightforward way, or whether additional, complex or costly steps have been inserted. In this case, the trustees have arranged to dispose of the two assets in the same tax year, and have done so. The economic consequence of the transactions, namely the realisation of a gain on the transfer of the first asset and a loss on the transfer of the other, matches the tax outcome. There have been no additional, complex or costly steps inserted into the arrangements. These factors suggest that the main purpose of the arrangements was not to secure a tax advantage. The two disposals have been made with a view to taking advantage of the statutory relief in s2(2) in a straightforward way. In such a case the TAAR will not apply and the losses will be available to set against the chargeable gains.*"

This example does not say what would happen if the beneficiary immediately sold one of the assets back to the trust. Presumably HMRC would argue that

---

[11] The CIOT vigorously protested against this guidance (which can be changed at any time and is only subject to judicial review) which conflicts with the legislation.

[12] It may be that in these examples HMRC have in mind the anti-avoidance provisions restricting loss relief when losses are realised on transfers of assets to beneficiaries: see Example 21.7 below.

this was a "complex" step designed to use the losses or that the main purpose of the arrangement was the realisation of the loss.

Example 18—trustees make a deliberate transfer of value

> "*A body of trustees who fall within the terms of Schedule 4B*[13] *have outstanding borrowing which has not been used for trust purposes The trustees intentionally make a transfer of value which triggers a charge under Schedule 4B, and as they expect this transaction results in a capital loss. The trustees have realised chargeable gains in the same year, and claim to set the loss against those gains.*
>
> *... The fact that the trustees have deliberately triggered the operation of the schedule is an indicator that one of their main purposes was to secure the advantage of the capital loss. In such a case, the TAAR will apply and the loss will not be an allowable loss."*

This gives no assistance on when trustees are likely to be regarded as "deliberately" triggering Sch.4B. They may have made an inadvertent transfer of value.

HMRC have said that they will operate a limited post-transaction clearance **21.11** system for trustees in the final year of the settlement but will not give COP 10 advice in respect of transactions which in their view may have been undertaken for the purpose of avoiding tax.[14]

III LOSSES OF UK RESIDENT SETTLOR-INTERESTED TRUSTS

The rules dealing with the tax treatment of a loss in a settlor-interested trust **21.12** have changed with bewildering rapidity as can be seen from the following survey.

Regime from April 1998 to April 2000

With the introduction of taper relief the capital gains tax regime for settlor- **21.13** interested trusts was changed. From April 1998 to April 2002 the gains of settlor-interested trusts were attributed to settlors under TCGA 1992, ss.77 (if UK resident) and 86 (if non-UK resident).[15] The original rule was that, where there were attributed gains, taper relief would already have been taken into account in computing that gain; therefore, settlors could not deduct their personal (untapered) losses from the tapered trust gains attributed to them. And trust losses were not attributed to settlors and so could not be deducted from personal gains.

An individual who had unrelieved personal capital losses and whose only chargeable assets were held in a settlor-interested trust could not, therefore, use those personal losses against attributed trust gains.

---

[13] Schedule 4B is considered in Ch.19.
[14] TAXREP 30/07 issued by the ICAEW, STEP, CIOT and the Law Society.
[15] See Chs 7 and 19 respectively.

21.14   This harsh position was changed by FA 2002 which provided that trust gains attributed to settlors for 2003–04 onwards (whether in respect of UK or non-UK settlor-interested settlements) would be the amount of the trust gains *before* the deduction of taper relief. If the settlor had personal capital losses, he had to set them against his own chargeable gains first, but any surplus losses could then be deducted from the (untapered) trust gains attributed to him. Taper relief by reference to the trustees' period of ownership was *then* applied. The settlor was assessed to tax on these tapered gains after loss relief and was entitled to claim from the trustees of the settlement reimbursement of any tax paid.

21.15   There was no election procedure and the relief was mandatory. The settlor could not choose to set personal losses against attributed trust gains in priority to personal gains even if that gave a better taper relief position. A settlor could elect for these rules to apply for the tax years 2000–01, 2001–02 and 2002–03. Elections could be made for one, two or all three of these years no later than January 31, 2005.[16] If the settlor was chargeable on gains from more than one settlement, the election for years 2000–01 to 2002–03 could be restricted to specified settlements.

Settlors of settlor-interested trusts have never been able to set attributed trust losses[17] against personal gains.

21.16   Accordingly the tax position when trust gains were charged on the settlor in respect of between April 2002 and 2008 was as follows:

(a) calculate trust gains before taper relief but setting off trust losses against gains in the order specified by the taper relief rules so that the gains that would qualify for the highest percentage of taper relief were left in charge;

(b) set off the settlor's personal losses against personal gains;

(c) set off remaining personal losses against untapered trust gains in the order specified by the taper relief rules. Losses brought forward were only set off to the extent necessary to reduce the untapered gains to the level of the settlor's annual exemption;

(d) reduce the remaining gains by the taper relief to which the trustees would have been entitled.

The settlor's annual exemption was first set against settlor-interested trust gains and only the balance set against personal net gains after taper relief.

Example 21.3

The D settlement, a UK resident trust, realised trust gains after taper relief of £6,000 in 2003–04. These were charged on the settlor Richard. Richard also had personal gains of £11,000 before taper relief, personal

---

[16] See s.2(5) TCGA 1992, as amended by FA 2002 Sch.11. Sch.11 also added paras 6–8.
[17] See Example 21.4.

losses in the year of £2,000 and personal losses brought forward of £14,000.

The annual exemption of Richard for 2003–04 of £7,900 was first set against the trust gains of £6,000 leaving £1,900 of the exemption available.

Richard's personal losses *of that year* of £2,000 are then set against personal gains of £11,000 leaving net personal gains of £9,000.

Losses brought forward are then set against net gains of £9,000 to the extent needed to bring them down to the balance of the annual exemption. This requires the use of £7,100 of the losses (£9,000 − £1,900).

The remaining losses brought forward (£14,000 − £7,100 = £6,900) are carried forward.

If the D settlement had realised £100,000 trust gains *before* taper relief and Richard had the same level of personal gains and personal losses, all the remaining brought forward losses of £6,900 would be set against the £100,000 trust gains. Richard would have then been taxed on the net trust gains of £93,100 but after deduction of taper relief. (Note that the personal losses brought forward and current year losses had first to be deducted against the personal gains before being deducted against trust gains.)

21.17 As already noted trust losses could not be set-off against personal gains of the settlor although in the above example if the trust had realised losses of £6,000 in the same tax year these would have reduced the trust gains assessable on Richard to nil.

EXAMPLE 21.4

The D settlement (UK resident) has losses of £100,000 realised at a time when it was settlor-interested. Richard the settlor has personal gains of £50,000. He cannot set the trust losses against the personal gains. Fiscal transparency only worked one way!

21.18 If a UK resident trust realised losses at a time when it was not settlor-interested and then realised gains during a period after it had become settlor-interested (e.g. because a dependent child was born who could benefit) and this all occurred before April 6, 2008 the losses realised in the earlier period could not be set against the gains realised in the later period.[18] Of course from 2008 such losses can now be used even if the trust remains settlor-interested!

---

[18] TCGA 1992 s.77 stated that where *chargeable gains accrue to the trustees of a settlement* from the disposal of the settled property and after making any deduction provided for by s.2(2) TCGA 1992, there remained an amount on which the trustees would be chargeable to tax, the trustees shall not be chargeable to tax in respect of those gains but chargeable gains "*shall be treated as accruing to the settlor in that year.*" Section 2(2) provides that capital gains tax shall be charged on the "*total amount of chargeable gains accruing to the person chargeable in the tax year after deducting losses accruing to that person in an earlier year.*" The difficulty is that the losses accrue to the trustees as the chargeable person when the trust is not settlor-

Regime from April 6, 2008

21.19 Gains of UK resident settlor-interested trusts are no longer taxed on the settlor but on the trustees.[19] The result is that personal losses of the settlor can no longer be used against trust gains (to the extent that they have not been used against current year personal gains). Personal losses can, however, continue to be used against offshore trust gains charged on the settlor under TCGA 1992 s.86.[20]

EXAMPLE 21.5

A UK resident settlor-interested trust realises gains of £100,000 in 2008–9. The settlor has personal losses brought forward of £50,000 and was hoping to use them against the trust gains since he has no personal gains and is unlikely to realise any. The personal losses can no longer be used to reduce the trust gains. Settlors of UK resident trusts with large brought forward personal losses or who were likely to realise losses in the future will no longer be able to use them to shelter trust gains. The trustees pay tax at 18 per cent on their gain in 2008–09 (28 per cent on disposals after June 22, 2010).

Note, however, that there are special rules in relation to gains and losses of settlor-interested vulnerable trusts which are discussed in Ch.36 and see below for the position of offshore trusts where personal losses can still relieve s.86 gains.

The position from June 23, 2010[21]

21.20 Gains realised by UK resident trusts are taxed at 28 per cent for disposals on or after June 23, 2010. TCGA 1992 s.4B provided that losses and the annual exemption could be deducted in the most beneficial way which was beneficial in 2010–11 when the rate increased from 18 per cent.

---

interested while the gains after it becomes settlor-interested are treated as accruing to the settlor. Hence, the trust losses can only be set against gains realised when the trust ceases to be settlor-interested because it is only at that point that the gains become chargeable on the trustees. From April 6, 2006 a trust became settlor-interested if a dependent child could benefit.

[19] TCGA 1992 s.77 was repealed from April 6, 2008.
[20] See 21.34.
[21] As inserted by F(No.2)A 2010 Sch.1 para.2. Note that the transitional provisions which allowed the 18% rate to continue for gains realised in 2010–11 by offshore trusts within the s.86 charge or in relation to gains attributed to beneficiaries under s.87 in 2010–11 did not apply to UK resident trusts. See Ch.19 for further details.

Example 21.6

The trustees of the Gibbon Trust have the following gains and losses for 2010–11:

May 2010 – gains of £20,000

June 1, 2010 – losses of £10,000

July 2010 – gains of £30,000

The losses can be set against the gains realised in July 2010 because these are taxed at a higher rate. The trust annual capital gains tax exemption can also be set against the gains realised in July 2010. In some cases trustees deliberately triggered gains prior to June 23, 2010 in order to capture the lower capital gains tax rate.[22]

IV LOSS RELIEF WHEN A BENEFICIARY BECOMES ABSOLUTELY ENTITLED[23]

21.21 When a beneficiary becomes absolutely entitled to the settled property, there is a deemed disposal of that property by the trustees at market value and the trustees are deemed immediately to reacquire it at the same value.[24] The deemed disposal ends the capital gains regime of the trust and, even if the assets remain under the control of the trustees,[25] future gains or losses on those assets will be realised by the beneficiary. Any gains or losses arising because of the deemed disposal are trust gains or losses.

21.22 Where a person has become absolutely entitled to settled property as against the trustee, there is only a restricted relief allowing trust losses *on the deemed disposal* itself to be transferred to the beneficiary to be set against future gains realised by him. This is because the allowable loss is transferred to the beneficiary only in so far as it has not been used by the trustees against gains accruing to them on that disposal or against earlier disposals in the same tax year.[26] Accordingly, a trust loss:

> *"shall be treated to the extent only that it cannot be deducted from pre-entitlement gains of the trustee, as an allowable loss accruing to the beneficiary (instead of to the trustee)"*

but this only occurs if the following conditions are satisfied:

(i) the loss must accrue on the deemed disposal when the beneficiary became absolutely entitled;

---

[22] This was done by an actual disposal or by making a sub-fund election. See Ch.12 for further details.

[23] Section 71(2).

[24] TCGA 1992 s.71 and see Ch.12.

[25] For example, to satisfy liabilities or the lien of the trustees. Subject to that the trustees hold the assets on a bare trust for the beneficiary.

[26] TCGA 1992 s.71(2) and (2A).

(ii) the trustee must have no "*pre-entitlement gain*" against which to set the loss. A pre-entitlement gain is a gain realised on the deemed disposal or before the deemed disposal but in the same tax year. If there are such gains the trustee must set the deemed disposal loss against them before using any other trust losses (e.g. losses carried forward from earlier years or losses on other disposals).[27] This rule takes priority over the rule that losses realised in 2010–11 can be set against gains in the most favourable way.[28] Later gains of the trustees in the same tax year are ignored and cannot be set against this loss even if the trustees would prefer to do this. So if in Example 21.6 the losses had been realised on a transfer of an asset to a beneficiary that loss would have to be set against the May 2010 gain not the July gain[29];

(iii) the beneficiary must in the future realise a gain on that property which gave rise to the deemed disposal loss or, in the case of an estate or interest in land, on any derivative asset.

When all these conditions are met(!) the gain on the property sold by the beneficiary may be offset by the trustees' deemed disposal loss. The loss is deducted from the gain before any other loss relief of the beneficiary.

21.23   Where there are two settlements and the trustees of one trust become absolutely entitled as against the trustees of the other, the trustees of the second settlement take the benefit of the loss on the deemed disposal.

EXAMPLE 21.7

In March 2004 Kate becomes absolutely entitled to one-half of the assets in her mother's trust. At that time the trustees have unused brought forward capital losses of £50,000 and Asset A to which Kate becomes entitled is worth £40,000 less than when acquired by the trustees. She also receives Asset B which shows a loss of £20,000.

Note:

(1) None of the realised brought forward losses of £50,000 will pass to Kate: they remain available for use by the trustees against future disposals of the remaining trust property.[30]

---

[27] See s.71(2D) for ordering rules.

[28] The ordering rules in s.71 are expressed to apply "*notwithstanding any other rules contained in this Act*".

[29] Although there is no official form that the beneficiary needs to complete it is sensible for the trustees to supply him with a statement of the loss and all relevant details so he has the information available for future use. For instance, the trustees could provide the beneficiary with a letter confirming the tax district and reference of the trust and certify that:

"*in accordance with TCGA 1992 s71 you became entitled on [date] to a loss of £[amount] from the disposal of the following asset, which loss may be used by you to offset your own chargeable gains realised from the disposal of that asset.*"

[30] Before June 15, 1999 if the trustee could not deduct the loss from chargeable gains which accrued to him in the same tax year as that in which the deemed disposal occurred, he could transfer the benefit of that loss to the beneficiary and if the trustee had brought forward losses which he could not use, he could transfer the benefit of them to the beneficiary. So the

(2) The loss that occurs on the s.71 deemed disposal (£40,000 on Asset A and £20,000 on B) passes to Kate but only to be set against future gains on a disposal of *that* property. If, however, the trustees could use all or part of the £60,000 losses either against gains realised earlier in the same tax year or against gains arising on the s.71 deemed disposal (e.g. if other assets showing a gain became vested in Kate) then to that extent the loss would not be passed to Kate.

(3) Kate cannot set the loss on Asset A against a later gain on Asset B, only against a subsequent gain on Asset A, despite the fact that both assets were deemed to be disposed of on the same occasion.

(4) The transfer of losses from the trustees to a beneficiary is mandatory if the trustees have no pre-entitlement gains. The trustees cannot set such losses off against their own gains realised later in the same tax year or in a later tax year. For this reason trustees may want to sell the asset to a third party and let the beneficiary buy it back.[31]

Costs incurred in transferring trust property[32] to the beneficiary can be added to the base cost of the transfer of the asset to the beneficiary (hence reducing his future gain or increasing his loss) even though he did not incur that expenditure himself. It is sensible for the trustees to give him details of these costs so he knows what his base cost is. SP2/04 gives a list of scale charges for corporate trustees which can be used as a guide by other trustees. Trustees have a choice of using actual costs incurred on a deemed disposal or the scale rates. For example, £25 per holding is the authorised allowable expenditure (even though such cost may not be incurred) on a transfer of quoted shares to a beneficiary. **21.24**

Alternatively, HMRC practice[33] is to allow the trustee to deduct such costs on transfer to a beneficiary in the computation of the gain or loss realised by the trustees on the deemed disposal of that asset by the trustees if the beneficiary waives his entitlement. This is despite the fact that the trustee usually incurs such expenditure after the beneficiary has become absolutely entitled and when the trustee is holding as bare trustee so strictly such expenses should not be set against gains which accrued to the trustees before this time. **21.25**

Valuation fees incurred by the trustees (but not the cost of disputing the valuation) are allowable. Similarly actual costs incurred on the deemed disposal (separately from costs of transfer to a beneficiary) are allowable by the trustees.[34]

beneficiary could use all these losses without restriction and he could offset them against gains accruing on the disposal of his own assets which had never been held within the trust. Those were the days!

[31] See 21.08 above for HMRC commentary on whether this is caught by the TAAR provision.

[32] See TCGA 1992 s.64(1)(b). HMRC have agreed with TACT a scale of expenses which will be allowable in respect of the transfer of assets to beneficiaries by corporate trustees which are members of TACT. See SP 2/04 reproduced in A2.15.

[33] See CGTM 33523.

[34] See also *IRC v Chubb's Trustee* (1971) 47 TC 353. Note that s.38(4) prevents *deemed* incidental costs from being deducted on a deemed disposal. However, in *Chubb* where a trust was terminated by arrangement between beneficiaries and trustees, it was held that barrister's and

21.26 TCGA 1992 s.79A[35] restricts loss relief for trustees. Before this change it had been possible for non-beneficiaries to utilise unrelieved trust losses as illustrated in the following example.

EXAMPLE 21.8

> The Chamberlain discretionary trust (UK resident) has unrelieved capital losses of £250,000. John adds assets to the settlement which have an unrealised gain of (say) £250,000 holding-over the gain.[36] The trustees then appoint the property to beneficiary Ben absolutely contingently on his being alive in seven days time. John purchases Ben's interest and therefore at the end of seven days becomes absolutely entitled to the trust property. The analysis was as follows:
>
> (i) John added property but avoided any chargeable gain by making a hold-over election[37];
>
> (ii) On the deemed disposal under TCGA 1992 s.71(1), the gain realised by the trustees on John's added property would be wiped out by the carried forward trustee loss. John would therefore purchase back his property with the benefit of a tax-free base cost uplift.

21.27 Section 79A prevents the trustees' losses from being set against a previously held-over gain. The basic requirements for the section to apply are that:

(i) assets must be added to a settlement and a hold-over relief claim made;

(ii) the transferor or a person connected with him must purchase an interest in the settlement. (Hence, it does not catch additions by an existing beneficiary; although no hold-over relief would be available for such an addition,[38] the beneficiary could add assets that appreciate in value later.)

With the exclusion of hold-over relief for transfers into a settlor-interested trust, it is thought that s.79A is redundant.[39] The following could, however, be considered.

---

solicitor's costs incurred in advising on the arrangements were allowable against the trustees' gains, as was stamp duty.

[35] Introduced by FA 2000 s.93.

[36] He could not hold over the gain if the trust was non-UK resident.

[37] Note the introduction of the settlor-interested restriction on hold-over relief on December 5, 2003.

[38] Since the trust is settlor-interested in relation to that beneficiary.

[39] This is a further addition to the armoury of anti-avoidance provisions on losses. The connected persons rule means that losses on disposals by the settlor to the trust can only be set against gains realised from disposals to the same trust. Section 71(2A) stops trust losses being

EXAMPLE 21.9

Giles set up a non-settlor-interested discretionary trust for the benefit of his adult children and the trust has unrelieved capital losses of £1 million carried forward. He settles land into the trust and holds-over the gain. The land is agricultural property and qualifies for inheritance tax relief so that the IHT entry charge is avoided. The trustees then sell the land and the gain on the land can be reduced by the losses carried forward.

VI OFFSHORE TRUSTS AND LOSSES

Section 87 gains and losses

The tax treatment of trust gains attributed under s.87 to UK residents and domiciled beneficiaries of offshore trusts following the receipt of a capital payment is completely different from that which applies to UK resident trusts.[40] Section 87 gains cannot be set against the beneficiary's personal losses since ss.2(4) and 62(2A) isolate such gains from any losses realised by the beneficiary personally.[41] **21.28**

However, losses realised by the offshore trustees[42] can be deducted against future s.87 gains realised by them and thereby reduce the amount of s.87 gains attributable to a beneficiary who receives a capital payment.[43] This is the case even if the trust later becomes UK resident and realises gains.[44]

EXAMPLE 21.10

The Z Settlement is an offshore settlement primarily for the benefit of Angel and the settlor is dead. In 1998 it realises £100,000 gains. These are not taxed on the trustees or any beneficiary but go into the s.87 pool because no previous capital payments have been made.

---

passed out to beneficiaries except in very limited circumstances; s.79A prevents gains being brought in and used against trust losses.

[40] See Ch.19.

[41] The disallowance of personal losses against s.87 gains was introduced in 1998 because s.87 gains were calculated after taper relief and to allow personal losses to reduce s.87 gains would be to allow loss relief against tapered gains. Despite the abolition of taper relief in 2008 and representations made by the CIOT and other bodies, FA 2008 did not allow losses to be set against s.87 gains. For a disastrous error see *Futter v Futter* [2010] STC 1899.

[42] Assuming that the trust is not within s.86 TCGA 1992.

[43] See ss.87(4) and 97(6) which allows losses (including brought-forward losses) to be set against trust gains despite the fact that the trustees are non-UK resident and s.16(3) normally disallows such losses for non-residents.

[44] Section 97(6) allows losses realised in a year of non-residence to be carried forward and used against gains in a later year and says nothing about the trust needing to be non-UK resident in that later year.

In 1999 the trust realises £40,000 losses. The losses cannot be carried back.

In 2000 the trust realises £30,000 gains. The 1999 losses are set against this gain thereby reducing it to zero. There are unrelieved losses of £10,000.

In 2001 the trust makes a capital payment of £60,000 to Angel.

The trust's s.87 pool at the end of 1999–2000 is £100,000 gains with £10,000 losses brought forward which cannot be set against the £100,000 gains but can reduce future trust gains. The payment to Angel is matched to £60,000 gains. (This is the case even if she is not UK resident.) The trust pool of gains at the end of 2001–02 is therefore £40,000 gains (100 – 60). The unrelieved losses of £10,000 can be used to reduce future trust gains.

Gains attributed to a beneficiary under s.87 cannot be reduced by that beneficiary's personal losses. So even if Angel has £10,000 personal losses these cannot reduce the s.87 trust gains attributed to her.

If the trust became UK resident then the £10,000 unused losses could be set against the future gains of the trustees despite the fact that the trust is by then UK resident. Similarly if the losses are realised by the trust when UK resident they could be set against later gains realised by the trustees when non-UK resident.[45]

21.29 Because s.87 losses realised by offshore trustees are not passed out to the beneficiary the restrictions in s.71(2)–(2D) referred to in 21.22 above do not apply.

EXAMPLE 21.11

Sarah becomes absolutely entitled to securities on reaching 25 and the offshore trust (not settlor-interested) realises a loss on the disposal of £10,000. This loss is carried forward and set against future gains of the trustees. Such losses are realised by non-resident trustees: see s.16(3). Section 87(4) provides that the losses realised by the trustees in the particular tax year can be taken into account in computing the s.2(2) trust gains but they are not allowable for use by the beneficiary: s.97(6) makes it clear that the losses can be carried forward to reduce future s.2(2) gains. The section 2(2) trust gains pool is an arithmetical construct; the beneficiary is not taxed on the actual gain realised by the trustees or the gains on the share of property appointed out to him but by reference to a *pool* of gains.

---

[45] TCGA 1992 s.97(6) gives loss relief only to those losses realised when the trust is non-UK resident but this would not appear to stop such trusts claiming loss relief under s.2(2) where the losses have been realised when the trust was UK resident even if the gains are realised when the trust was non-UK resident (provided it was not then within s.86).

Section 87 losses cannot reduce ss.86 or 77 gains

If losses have been realised in the trust prior to a period when it becomes **21.30** a "qualifying" settlor-interested trust[46] and trust gains are realised after it became qualifying (e.g. in the case of a "pre-1991 trust"), the existing realised s.87 losses cannot be used to reduce future gains which are taxed on the settlor. Such gains may only be reduced by losses that are also realised during the period of the settlor charge.[47]

The existing losses from the period when the trust was non-qualifying are kept "in suspense" and may be used against future trust gains arising *after* the settlor charge has ceased to apply, e.g. after the settlor has died or the trust has become UK resident and ceased to be settlor-interested. So in the above example, if the trust became settlor-interested in 2005[48] the trust losses of £10,000 could not be used to reduce any gains taxed on the settlor under s.86. However, if the trust was imported in 2008–09 future trust gains could be reduced by those "s.87" losses carried forward.

However, if the trust had been imported before April 6, 2008 and remained **21.31** settlor-interested (within s.77) then no s.87 losses realised while the trust was non-UK resident could reduce the gains charged on the settlor under s.77 although those losses (still held in suspense!) could reduce gains realised after April 5, 2008. What a mess!

EXAMPLE 21.12

Chris, a tax adviser, died in 2008–09, suffering a heart attack after reading FA 2008. He had created a non-UK resident settlement in the mid-1980s. He was UK domiciled. Capital payments have not been made by the trustees and the gains (losses) of the settlement are as follows:

Tax year	£ Gain (loss)
1986–87	2.5 million
1987–88	(1 million)
2000–01	(0.4 million)
2006–07	0.5 million
2007–08	(0.2 million)
2008–09	0.5 million

Chris' family now wish to import the trust and there are some assets in the trust showing an unrealised gain and some showing an unrealised

---

[46] i.e. the losses were realised at a time when s.87 rather than s.86 applied. The trust may later fall within s.86, e.g. if the settlor becomes UK domiciled or as a result of the FA 1998 changes.
[47] See TCGA 1992 Sch.5 para.1.
[48] For example, the settlor was not dead but instead was non-resident until that tax year but then returned to the UK.

loss. In 2009–10 the trust is imported by the appointment of UK resident trustees.[49]

(1) Gains will be taxed at 18 per cent from April 6, 2009 to June 22, 2010 and thereafter at 28 per cent. Note that the stockpiled gains realised in the past (£2.5 million) remain on the clock until such time as they are matched against capital payments made to beneficiaries.[50]

(2) The trust had become settlor-interested on March 17, 1998.[51] Chris was subject to capital gains tax on trust gains under s.86 while the trust was non-UK resident.[52] The loss realised in 1987–88 (which is a s.87 loss realised before the trust becoming settlor-interested) could not be used against gains realised by the trust in 2006–07 when settlor-interested. However, the £400,000 s.86 loss realised in 2000–01 reduced the £500,000 gain so Chris was charged on a net £100,000 gain in 2006–07. The loss realised in 2007–08 can only be used against future s.86 gains.

(3) The loss of £1 million in 1987–88 may be offset against future trust gains realised when the trust is not within s.86 including gains realised by UK resident trustees: s.97(6). It can be set against the £500,000 gain in 2008–09. Although this gain was realised when the trust was offshore and still settlor-interested, since Chris died in that year s.86 does not apply. Hence, the gain in 2008–09 is a s.87 gain that can be relieved by the earlier s.87 loss.

(4) Note however that the 2007–08 loss is a s.86 loss and is now what HMRC term "clogged", i.e. unusable since Chris has died.

No loss relief for pre-1998 losses where settlor non-domiciled or non-UK resident.

21.32   FA 2008 Sch.7 para.118 preserves the disallowance of gains and losses accruing to trustees before March 17, 1998 where the settlor was not UK domiciled or not UK resident.

EXAMPLE 21.13

Elouise is the settlor of a trust set up in 1988. She was domiciled in Queensland, Australia at all times but is UK resident. The trust realised gains and losses as follows:

---

[49] Or from April 6, 2007 by appointing just one UK resident trustee. Alternatively if the trust retains non-UK resident trustees it can still be imported for capital gains tax purposes *until April 6, 2007* merely by switching the general administration of the trust to the UK. After that date a UK resident trustee would need to be appointed: see Ch.4.
[50] TCGA 1992 s.87A.
[51] See Ch.19.
[52] And would have been taxed under TCGA 1992 s.77 if the trust had become UK resident.

	£
1989	100,000
1995	(900,000)
2005	800,000
2007	(700,000)
2009	100,000

The trustees made a capital distribution to Elouise's husband, Alex, in 2007 of £300,000. He is UK domiciled and resident. They made a further distribution of £200,000 to Elouise in 2009.

(1) All gains and losses of the settlement realised before March 17, 1998 are ignored. Gains and losses realised after that date (whether before or after 2008) are s.87 gains and even though the trust is settlor-interested s.86 does not apply to foreign domiciled settlors whether or not they are remittance basis users.[53]

(2) The trust has realised losses of £900,000 in 1995 but none of these can reduce the 2005 gains. These losses are lost. Therefore Alex pays tax under s.87 on the full £300,000 payment which is matched to the 2005 gains. £500,000 gains and £700,000 losses are carried forward. The £700,000 losses can be used to reduce the 2009 gains to nil leaving £600,000 carried forward.

(3) The distribution of £200,000 to Elouise in 2009 is matched to current year gains first. There are no current year gains left after deduction of losses. Hence, the capital payment is matched to the £500,000 pre-2008 gains carried forward and it is not taxed even if Elouise is not a remittance basis user (since the payment is matched to pre-2008 gains). There are £300,000 pre-2008 gains to be carried forward to match against future capital payments. Although the trust is settlor-interested it is not within s.86.

(4) If Elouise became UK domiciled then the trust would fall within s.86. Any unused s.87 losses realised before that tax year would be stranded s.87 losses until she became non-UK resident, non-UK domiciled or died (or all defined persons were excluded).[54]

Losses of offshore trusts within Sch.4C

In contrast to s.87, Sch.4C gains can be offset against personal losses. The **21.33** provision restricting loss relief under s.2(4) is confined to TCGA 1992 ss.87 and 89. This might encourage trustees to engineer a deliberate transfer of value linked to trustee borrowings in order to generate trust losses on a non-settlor-interested trust.

---

[53] See Chs 4 and 19. Hence, even if someone has been UK resident for seven or more years but is not a remittance basis user because they do not pay the £30,000 charge, s.86 does not apply if they are not UK domiciled.

[54] i.e Elouise, spouses, civil partners, children, grandchildren, etc: see Ch.19.

VII LOSSES OF OFFSHORE TRUSTS WITHIN S.86[55]

21.34   The rules are complicated but can be summarised as follows:

1. Losses realised when the trust was either UK resident or was non-UK resident but not within s.86 are not allowable against gains arising when the trust is non-UK resident and within s.86 but are allowable against gains realised when the trust is non-UK resident and within s.87.[56]

2. Losses realised when the trust was non-UK resident and within s.86 ("s.86 losses") are not allowable against gains realised when the trust was non-UK resident and not within s.86. Nor are they allowable against gains realised from April 6, 2008 if the trust becomes UK resident whether or not (prior to 2008) it remained settlor-interested.[57]

3. Personal losses can still be set against s.86 gains subject to the same ordering rules that used to operate for s.77: see 21.11 above.

4. A trust set up by a foreign domiciled settlor can never be within s.86 whether or not he is a remittance basis user until he becomes UK domiciled under general law and therefore all such gains and losses realised by the non-UK resident trust are within s.87.

EXAMPLE 21.14

Charlotte is a UK domiciled and resident and since 1999 the life tenant of a non-resident trust which she established and which realises losses of £100,000 in 2000. These are s.86 losses. The trust is then imported but otherwise the terms are not changed. The trust realises gains in 2003–04 of £50,000. The losses cannot be set against the gains even though the gains were (at that time) taxed on Charlotte under s.77 because realised by a settlor-interested trust. If the trust had remained non-resident the position would have been different.[58] Hence, there is a danger in importing a trust which has unused s.86 losses.

21.35   In the above example, if Charlotte had died in 2003–04 the losses realised in 2000 became unusable (wherever the trust is resident). Trust gains realised in the tax year of her death but before her death cannot be relieved against the s.86 losses because the trust is not in the s.86 regime in the tax year of her death. These gains would go into the s.87 trust pool.

---

[55]   See TCGA 1992 Sch.5 para.1.

[56]   See Sch.5 para.1(6).

[57]   The general rule is that losses realised by non-residents are not allowable (s.16) and therefore losses realised by non-resident trustees are only allowable under the specific provisions of the legislation in relation to either ss.87 or 86.

[58]   Section 86 and Sch.5 para.1(2) provide a specific mechanism for deducting losses against gains chargeable on the settlor under s.86 but this did not carry over to allowing such losses to be deducted from gains realised by the trust when it became UK resident and the gains became chargeable on the settlor under s.77 TCGA 1992.

After Charlotte's death there are no unrealised trust gains since her inter- **21.36**
est was a qualifying interest in possession for IHT purposes and hence there
was a base cost uplift to market value which eradicated unrealised trust gains.
Note however, that unrealised gains within underlying trust companies and
realised s.87 gains are not eradicated by Charlotte's death. So if the trust
had realised s.87 gains of £10,000 made in February 1991 (before it became
settlor-interested and which have not been distributed) and the trust ends on
her death, UK resident and domiciled beneficiaries are treated as receiving
capital payments and can be taxed on such s.87 gains.

Personal losses may be set off against gains of non-resident trusts attributed **21.37**
by virtue of s.10(A) to a settlor returning to the UK after a period of non-UK
residence.[59]

VIII LOSSES IN AN UNDERLYING OFFSHORE COMPANY

The loss regime for gains realised by a non-UK resident close company is quite **21.38**
different from the loss relief regime for trusts. The taxation of companies is
discussed further in Ch.54.

---

[59] However, there is an restriction where the amount to be attributed to the returning
settlor in respect of the gains of a non-resident trust has been reduced because such gains have
already been attributed to the beneficiaries of the trust under s.87: see Ch.19.

PART IV: INHERITANCE TAX

The IHT treatment of settlements was radically altered by FA 2006. In this Part, Ch.22 provides a general introduction to IHT, to the reservation of benefit rules and to pre-owned assets income tax whilst Ch.23 gives an overview of the 2006 changes. The following chapters then consider the taxation of settlements in detail: Ch.24 sets out the fundamental IHT definitions including the definition of an interest in possession. Ch.25 deals with the IHT consequences of establishing a settlement and Ch.26 with qualifying interest in possession trusts.

Prior to March 22, 2006 all interest in possession trusts set up by individuals were "qualifying"[1] but from that date very few inter vivos interest in possession trusts will be qualifying. The beneficiary is deemed to own the settled property for inheritance tax purposes only if he has a qualifying interest in possession. The position of pre-March 22 interest in possession trusts and the transitional regime introduced by FA 2006 is considered in Ch.27. Ch.28 considers when qualifying interest in possession trusts can be created today. Ch.29 deals with relevant property settlements: before the 2006 changes these comprised mainly discretionary trusts but the central object of the 2006 changes was to apply this tax treatment to all settlements with relatively few exceptions. Ch.30 looks at the accumulation and maintenance trust from the standpoint of existing trusts given that new qualifying accumulation and maintenance trusts cannot be established. What this will mean in terms of making provision for minors and older children is considered in Ch.35, which provides an in-depth treatment of bereaved minor and s.71D trusts. Ch.31 considers the inheritance tax treatment of excluded property settlements and various IHT issues relevant to foreign domiciliaries. Ch.32 discusses the deductibility of debts and Chs 33 and 34 look at the reservation of benefit and POA rules in detail.

---

[1] A "qualifying" interest in possession means that the relevant beneficiary is treated for inheritance tax purposes as beneficially entitled to the underlying settled property in which his interest subsists.

CHAPTER 22

INHERITANCE TAX, RESERVATION OF BENEFIT AND PRE-OWNED ASSETS INCOME TAX—AN INTRODUCTION

- Potentially exempt transfers (PETs) (**22.02**)
- Gifts from companies (**22.06**)
- The charge on death (**22.08**)
- Reservation of benefit (**22.10**)
- *Ingram* and *Eversden* (**22.17**)
- Application of the reservation of benefit provisions generally (**22.21**)
- Avoiding the reservation of benefit rules (**22.30**)
- Impact of the pre-owned assets charge (**22.38**)

Inheritance tax is charged on an individual who makes a transfer of value (typically a gift) during his lifetime and on his estate at death.[1] Various exemptions and reliefs are available to prevent certain kinds of transactions from giving rise to a charge. For example, gifts between spouses are normally exempt from IHT,[2] as are family maintenance dispositions[3] and gifts of modest amounts.[4]   **22.01**

I POTENTIALLY EXEMPT TRANSFERS (PETS)

The majority of lifetime transfers made by individuals became PETs in 1986. The name is something of a misnomer since such a transfer is treated as exempt unless the transferor dies within seven years of its making. Hence they might more properly have been called "potentially chargeable transfers". Initially the definition of a PET did not include transfers into an interest in possession trust or the deemed transfer of value on the inter vivos termination of an interest in possession but that restriction was removed in 1987. From   **22.02**

---

[1] Death is a "deemed" transfer of value under IHTA 1984 s.4(1). Note that a "person" (including therefore a company) can make a transfer of value but only an individual can make a chargeable transfer of value. A transfer of value made by a close company can be apportioned amongst its participators (see IHTA 1984 s.94(1)).

[2] IHTA 1984 s.18.

[3] IHTA 1984 s.11. See *McKelvey (PRs of McKelvey Deceased) v RCC* [2008] STC (SCD) 944 and 35.56 for further comment on this exemption.

[4] IHTA 1984 s.19 (annual exemption), s.20 (small gifts) and s.21 (normal expenditure out of income). In the latter case the exemption can be used to make substantial IHT savings given that there is no prescribed ceiling on the payments: see *Bennett v IRC* [1995] STC 54.

that date it was generally the case that all lifetime transfers of value were PETs with only limited exceptions, of which the most significant was for transfers into and out of discretionary trusts which remained immediately chargeable.

The changes in the IHT treatment of settlements have, however, had a significant impact on the PET definition. From March 22, 2006 whilst virtually all unsettled lifetime gifts made by individuals remain PETs the majority of settled gifts will not qualify and instead will be immediately chargeable.

EXAMPLE 22.1

(1) S settles property on his son for life, remainder to the son's children. Prior to March 22, 2006 such a transfer would have been a PET by S. From that date, however, it is immediately chargeable.

(2) S settles property on trust for his minor grandchildren at 18. Prior to March 22, 2006 S would have made a PET (into an A-M trust). From that date, however, S's transfer is immediately chargeable.

(3) Under a settlement established in 2000 (i.e. a pre-March 22, 2006 settlement) A is the current life tenant followed by a life interest for his eldest son. Prior to March 22, 2006 the termination of A's life interest during his lifetime (e.g. by a deed of surrender or by the trustees exercising a power in the settlement) would have been a PET with his son being treated as the owner of the settled property in accordance with the provisions of IHTA 1984 s.49(1). From that date, however, this result only followed if the termination had occurred during a transitional period (which ended on October 5, 2008). Thereafter any termination in favour of an interest in possession for the son has resulted in A making an immediately chargeable transfer of value with the settled property then falling into the relevant property charging regime. The son has to take outright on the termination of A's life interest for A to be treated as making a PET.[5]

22.03   It was common for family settlements to provide for a life interest to (say) a child of the settlor with a successive life interest for that child's spouse. Often such trusts had started life as A-M settlements for the children of the settlor which had then been converted into interest in possession trusts for those children on or before they became 25.[6] Giving a successive life interest to the child's spouse was attractive for two reasons: *first* out of a wish to benefit the spouse but *secondly* because the transfer of value on the ending of the son's life interest would then be spouse exempt[7] but the spouse would not become absolutely entitled to the property.[8] The 2006 changes have restricted such planning in the future. It is still possible to provide for a surviving spouse through

[5] See IHTA 1984 s.3A(7).
[6] The requirements for old style A-M trusts are considered in Ch.30 including the requirement that income or capital must vest in a beneficiary no later than age 25.
[7] Note that the spouse or civil partner must be UK domiciled: IHTA 1984 s.18(2).
[8] Commonly the trustees will possess overriding powers to end the spouse's life interest which, if exercised, would result in that spouse making a PET. Note also that the property would benefit

an interest in possession (an IPDI) trust set up in the will of the deceased. However, for existing pre-budget interest in possession trusts, future use of the spouse exemption will be restricted. Suppose that the son of the settlor had an interest in possession on March 22, 2006. Until October 6, 2008 spouse exemption was available if property passed on interest in possession trusts for the spouse of the son whether the son's interest ended inter vivos or on death.[9] After October 5, 2008, however, spouse exemption has only been available on an inter vivos termination of the son's interest in possession if his spouse took outright. However, if the pre-budget interest in possession ends on the son's death after October 5, 2008 and the spouse then takes on interest in possession trusts, spouse exemption is still available under the transitional rules.[10]

In addition, where the spouse has already taken a transitional serial interest, the inter vivos termination of that spouse's life interest is now only a PET if at the time when the interest ends the settlement also ceases. Hence, property cannot be tied up in trust indefinitely without falling into the relevant property regime. It is no longer possible for a person to set up a new inter vivos settlement for the benefit of his spouse and qualify for spouse exemption.[11]

22.04 If it is felt desirable to retain the property in trust beyond the life tenant's death without it becoming relevant property, one option would be for the trustees to give the qualifying interest in possession beneficiary a general power of appointment exercisable on his death. The qualifying interest in possession beneficiary is treated as beneficially entitled to the property for IHT purposes at death so giving him a general power of appointment will not result in additional IHT on death. The beneficiary could then exercise that power by will and appoint on interest in possession trusts for the intended beneficiaries. These trusts will be IPDIs. There are no CGT concerns because the settled property is revalued on the death of the life tenant.[12]

22.05 These changes resulted from amendments to the PET definition which took effect on March 22, 2006. From that day PETs have been limited:

(i) To outright gifts from one individual to another individual or out of a qualifying interest in possession trust to an individual[13];

(ii) To gifts from an individual into a disabled trust or from a qualifying interest in possession into a disabled trust[14]; or

(iii) To a gift into a bereaved minor's trust on the ending of an immediate post-death interest (an IPDI).[15]

---

from the CGT free uplift on the child's death. Consider using a general power of appointment to continue this treatment: see 38.15 and 22.04.

[9] See 27.16.

[10] This assumes that the surviving spouse is UK domiciled or deemed domiciled: see ss.18 and 49D IHTA 1984.

[11] See Ch.25: save in the event that it qualifies as a disabled person's interest within s.89B.

[12] See further Ch.38 and A1.17.

[13] In cases where an individual is entitled to a qualifying interest in possession, he is treated as entitled under IHTA 1984 s.49(1) to the property in the settlement. Accordingly the creation of such trusts before March 22, 2006 fell within the PET definition being treated as a gift to another individual: see s.3A(2).

[14] See ss.3A(1A)(c)(ii) and 89.

[15] See s.3A(1A)(c)(iii). For IPDI's and bereaved minor trusts, see Chs 28 and 35.

Given the fact that no new qualifying inter vivos interest in possession settlements can be created from March 22, 2006[16] an inter vivos gift to an interest in possession trust is no longer treated as a gift to an individual within s.3A(1A)(c)(i) (and so it will not be a PET) unless it is a gift to a disabled trust within s.3A(1A)(c)(ii). Nor can the termination of a qualifying interest in possession in a settlement take effect as a gift to an individual within s.3A(1A)(c)(i) after October 5, 2008 unless:

(a) the interest in possession being terminated is a qualifying interest in possession[17]; and

(b) on inter vivos termination of such an interest in possession the settled property passes to an individual outright.

However, as noted above the termination of a qualifying interest in possession may not constitute a gift to an individual but may still be a PET within s.3A(1A)(c)(ii) or (iii) if the gift is to a disabled person's trust or a bereaved minor trust.

II GIFTS FROM COMPANIES

22.06   A gift from a company to an individual can never be a PET. If the company is not a close company, no chargeable transfer of value arises anyway. If the company is a close company the transfer of value is apportioned to the participators (who are deemed to make the transfer) but cannot be a PET.[18]

Nor can a gift to a close company from an individual take effect as a PET. A PET (as defined in s.3A) requires that either (a) "*the value transferred is attributable to property which by virtue of the transfer, becomes comprised in the estate of that other individual*" (being the individual to whom the gift is being made) or (b) "*so far as that value is not attributable to propety which becomes comprised in the estate of another person, to the extent that, by virtue of the transfer, the estate of that other individual is increased.*"

EXAMPLE 22.2

A gives £100,000 to B Ltd which is wholly owned by B. This is not a PET by A to either B or B Ltd. Section 3A(2)(a) does not apply because although the property becomes comprised in the estate of the company it does not become comprised in the estate of an individual. Section 3A(2)(b) does not apply because it can only operate "*so far as that value is not attributable to property which becomes comprised in the estate of another person*" and in this case the property does become comprised in the estate of another person (the company). It does not matter that B's estate is increased.

[16] Save for a disabled person's trust within s.89B: see generally Ch.36.
[17] For example, an IPDI.
[18] IHTA 1984 s.3A(6).

The disparity in the IHT treatment of settled and unsettled gifts by individuals   **22.07**
is striking. Not only has the "inheritance tax transparency" of new interest in
possession trusts been removed so that most trusts are taxed as separate entities rather than as part of the estate of the life tenant, but gifts into trust are
generally taxed more harshly than gifts to individuals. The 2008 capital gains
tax changes have increased the shift towards trusts being taxed as a separate
entity rather than as part of the estate of the settlor.[19]

III THE CHARGE ON DEATH

IHT is chargeable on a person's death as if immediately before he died he had   **22.08**
made a transfer of value and the value transferred thereby was equal to the
value of his estate at that time.[20] For this purpose a person's estate is the
aggregate of all the property to which he is beneficially entitled, except that
immediately before his death his estate does not include excluded property.[21]
Since for IHT purposes a person entitled to a qualifying interest in possession
in settled property is treated as beneficially entitled to the property in which his
interest subsists, on the death of such a person the settled property will form
part of his estate and be subject to IHT.[22]

Calculating the charge on death

This involves the following: **22.09**

(i) Valuing all property in his estate immediately before his death (for the
definition of "property" see IHTA 1984 s.272).

(ii) The estate may be swollen by settled property in which the deceased had
enjoyed a qualifying interest in possession and by the value of property
in which the deceased had reserved a benefit.

(iii) Excluded property is left out of account.[23]

---

[19] Generally governments have wavered between taxing trusts as part of the estate of an individual beneficiary and taxing them as separate entities. There has rarely been a consistent
approach taken between the different taxes or even within the same tax. For example, in some
cases inheritance tax and capital gains tax reliefs are given by reference to the status or characteristics of the interest in possession beneficiary and in others by reference to the status or
characteristics of the trust.

[20] IHTA 1984 s.4(1). For an example of the difficulties that can arise in valuing property *immediately before* death, see *Arkwright v IRC* [2004] STC (SCD) 392 (reversed [2004] STC 1323).
See also *Price v RCC* [2011] SFTD 52 for a further consideration of the related property rules.
Note that the value of the estate is arrived at after deducting liabilities: see s.5(3). For liabilities
generally, see Ch.32.

[21] IHTA 1984 s.5(1).

[22] IHTA 1984 s.49(1). Again this is subject to the excluded property rules: see Ch.31. Primary
responsibility for payment of the tax is on the trustees of the settlement. For the treatment of
liabilities, see *St Barbe Green v IRC* [2005] STC 288 and Ch.32. A major consequence of the
2006 legislation is to restrict the creation of new qualifying interest in possession trusts.

[23] IHTA 1984 s.5(1) and for the meaning of excluded property see IHTA 1984 ss.5 and 48, Ch.31.

(iv) The value of business and agricultural property may be reduced by either 100 or 50 per cent: this is business property relief (BPR) and agricultural property relief (APR).[24]

(v) Liabilities are deducted from the value of the property in the estate provided that such liabilities were incurred "*for a consideration in money or money's worth*" (IHTA 1984 s.5(5)).[25] IHT is calculated on the net value of the estate with the nil rate band applying up to £325,000[26] and thereafter tax being charged at a flat rate of 40 per cent.[27]

(vi) Property must be valued at "*the price which the property might reasonably be expected to fetch if sold in the open market*"[28] immediately before death. In this connection note the following:

    (a) no discount is allowed for the fact that all the property is put onto the market at the same time;

    (b) in certain cases a change in value of the assets resulting from the death may be taken into account (e.g. a loss of goodwill in an owner-occupied business on the death of the sole proprietor)[29];

    (c) in general the IHT value will become the CGT acquisition cost of a legatee inheriting the assets of the deceased[30];

    (d) if liabilities exceed the deceased's "free estate" they cannot be used to reduce the value of settled property in which he had an interest in possession[31];

---

[24] See Chs 45 and 46.

[25] Special rules apply to artificial debts, see FA 1986 s.103: see 32.31 and 38.56. In general, a liability secured on property will be deducted from the value of that property: see IHTA 1984 s.162(4) and for business property relief see IHTA 1984 s.110. The consideration does not have to have been received by the deceased. Hence, if mother incurs a debt of £1,000 by paying for her daughter's holiday that debt has been incurred for consideration and is deductible.

[26] For 2011–12 and years up to 2014–15.

[27] If the deceased had made chargeable transfers or PETS within seven years of his death these may exhaust his IHT nil rate band since they are cumulated with his estate at death for the purpose of calculating the tax payable. In the event that tax is payable on lifetime transfers as a result of death within seven years primary responsibility for that tax rests with the donee: IHTA 1984 s.199(1)(b) and for the contingent liability of the deceased's personal representatives, see IHTA 1984 ss.199(2), 204(8) and for their right of recovery s.211(3).

[28] IHTA 1984 s.160.

[29] IHTA 1984 s.171.

[30] This will, however, only be the case if the value has been "ascertained" for IHT purposes which will not be the case, e.g. if the assets passed to the deceased spouse; qualified for 100% APR or BPR or if the deceased's estate fell within his IHT nil rate band: see TCGA 1992 s.274 and *Tax Bulletin*, April 1995 p.209. See *Stonor (executors of Dickinson) v IRC* [2001] STC (SCD) 199 where it was held that the executors could not substitute the higher sale price on the sale of assets in the estate for the probate value where the estate was left to charity because no values had been "ascertained" for inheritance tax purposes. A higher sale price can only be substituted where more inheritance tax is then paid. This decision is based on the principle that substitution of the sale proceeds can only be allowed for inheritance tax purposes on a claim made by an "appropriate person" defined as a person who is liable for inheritance tax (IHTA 1984 s.190(1)). Presumably in that case the executors had wanted to increase the probate value in order to avoid or reduce a capital gains tax charge on a subsequent sale by them when the assets had increased in value from probate. Unless the executors could show that the value was actually wrong at the date of death and was in fact higher, the fact that the asset had increased in value since death did not mean they could substitute that higher value for probate purposes.

[31] This is the effect of *St Barbe Green v IRC* [2005] STC 288. It was accepted in this case that the value of trust property is the net value *after* deducting liabilities. For a discussion on whether

(e) there are certain special inheritance tax valuation provisions. See, for example, ss.167 (valuation of life policies), 170 (leases for life), 161 and 176 (related property). Where property valued on death as "related property" is sold within three years after the death, or land is sold within four years of death, or listed securities within one year, for less than the death valuation, the PRs may substitute a lower figure for the death valuation and so obtain a reduction in the IHT paid on death. This lower figure will also form the death value for CGT so that the beneficiary cannot claim CGT loss relief.

IV RESERVATION OF BENEFIT

Capital Transfer Tax had been a comprehensive cradle to grave tax whereby **22.10** transfers both inter vivos and on death were taxable. With the introduction of the potentially exempt transfer in 1986, however, the majority of inter vivos transfers ceased to be immediately taxable and escaped tax altogether provided that the transferor survived the transfer by seven years. This raised the possibility of taxpayers giving away their assets and suffering no IHT charge on that gift but retaining the use of those assets until death. Such arrangements would have driven a coach and horses through the tax and it was to deal with them that the reservation of benefit rules were introduced in 1986.[32] In the event these rules proved inadequate to stop the avoidance of inheritance tax by "*cake and eat it*" arrangements and were bolstered by an income tax charge from April 6, 2005 (the pre-owned assets—or "POA"—charge).[33]

The fundamental provision in the reservation of benefit minicode which **22.11** determines whether an individual has reserved a benefit is s.102(1) FA 1986, the essential part of which is as follows:

> "*this section applies where, on or after 18th March 1986, an individual disposes of any property by way of gift and either—*
>
> *(a) possession and enjoyment of the property is not bona fide assumed by the donee at or before the beginning of the relevant period; or*
>
> *(b) at any time in the relevant period the property is not enjoyed to the entire exclusion, or virtually to the entire exclusion, of the donor and of any benefit to him by contract or otherwise;*
>
> *and in this section 'the relevant period' means a period ending on the date of the donor's death and beginning seven years before that date, or, if it is later, on the date of the gift.*"

liabilities of the free estate will be available to reduce the value of reservation of benefit property which is included in the deceased's estate, see Ch.32.

[32] It might be more accurate to say reintroduced since they had been in force at the time of estate duty and the 1986 legislation was very largely identical to its predecessor. See further Ch.33.

[33] The change only applies if the arrangement is not caught by the reservation of benefit rules: see FA 2004 Sch.15 para.11(3)(5)(a) and generally the authors' "*Pre-Owned Assets and Estate Planning*", 3rd edn, 2009 and Ch.34.

For this purpose, by FA 1986 Sch.20 para.6(1)(c), a benefit which a donor obtained by virtue of associated operations of which the disposal by way of gift is one, is treated as a benefit to him by contract or otherwise.

22.12 Notice two key points. *First*, that what activates the provisions is a "gift" made by an individual. There is no definition of gift which will therefore bear its normal meaning as a transfer of property with donative intent.[34] In any event, the use of "gift" as the triggering event distinguishes the reservation of benefit minicode from the rest of the IHT legislation where the key event is the making of a transfer of value. As a result, in certain circumstances there can be a transfer of value for IHT purposes which is not a gift and this dichotomy has been exploited by taxpayers.[35]

Secondly, that what can trigger the rules once a gift has been made, is that the property is not enjoyed to the entire exclusion of the donor. This can mean de facto enjoyment. Hence, once a gift has been made it is never safe for the donor to enjoy benefits or otherwise use the property (i.e. there is no seven-year period after which the slate is wiped clean). Note also that it is possible for a reservation of benefit to arise if the gifted property is not enjoyed "virtually" to the donor's entire exclusion whether or not the donor receives any benefit. The full consideration let-out in Sch.20 para.6 only applies in relation to the occupation of land or chattels. So even if there is no benefit to the donor a reservation of benefit can arise. For example, if shares are gifted by a partner to another person who then sells the shares and lends the cash back to the partnership charging a commercial rate of interest, there will be a reservation of benefit: see *Chick v Commissioner of Stamp Duties of New South Wales.*[36] The question is one of fact: has the donor been excluded from the property? See also *Commissioner of Stamp Duties of New South Wales v Permanent Trustee Company New South Wales*[37] where a daughter made loans to her father of property which he had gifted to her. In that case the loans were interest-free, but even if they had been interest bearing there would still have been a reservation of benefit.

Let-outs

22.13 The legislation provides that certain disposals by way of gift which would otherwise result in property being subject to the reservation of benefit provisions are taken outside the ambit of those provisions. For example, FA 1986 s.102(5) excludes a disposal of property by way of gift which qualifies for the IHT spouse exemption.[38] Some of these let-outs are also incorporated into

---

[34] See IHTM 14315. Note, however, FA 1986 s.102ZA (inserted by FA 2006) which deems a beneficiary whose interest in possession has terminated to make a gift of "*the no longer possessed property*": see Ch.33.

[35] The main instance involved the termination of an interest in possession in circumstances where although the beneficiary made a transfer of value he did not make a gift so that if he continued to enjoy the use of the settled property the reservation of benefit rules were inapplicable. FA 2006 sought to prevent this by extending the meaning of gift to cover the termination of a life interest: see FA 1986 s.102ZA inserted by FA 2006 and Ch.33. HMRC take the view that there can be a gift without a transfer of value, see IHTM 14315.

[36] [1958] AC 435.

[37] [1956] AC 512.

[38] It was this exemption which was exploited in the *Eversden* case: see 22.19 and 43.43.

the pre-owned assets regime so that a transaction which qualifies for favoured treatment under the reservation of benefit provisions generally also does so for the purposes of the income tax charge.[39]

When the conditions in s.102(1) are satisfied, the property in question is prima facie "property subject to a reservation" and so caught by the reservation of benefit provisions. In certain cases, anti-avoidance legislation has the effect that property may be caught even though these requirements are not satisfied. Conversely, there are various ameliorating provisions that mean that even if s.102(1) requirements are satisfied or the anti-avoidance provisions are prima facie infringed there is not necessarily a reservation of benefit problem.

Full consideration[40]

A key let-out is provided by FA 1986 Sch.20 para.6(1)(a) which provides that **22.14** in the case of land and chattels the:

> "*retention or assumption by the donor of actual occupation of the land or actual enjoyment of an incorporeal right over the land or actual possession of the chattel shall be disregarded if it is for full consideration in money or money's worth*".

EXAMPLE 22.3

(1) Jake gives his house "Marigold" to his daughter Sissie. He continues to occupy the property under an assured shorthold tenancy paying a full market rent. He is outside the reservation of benefit provisions and not subject to the pre-owned asset charge.

(2) As in (1) above but Sissie and her family also occupy the property and Jake merely uses the converted loft space. If he now wishes to escape the reservation of benefit provisions by paying a full rent (which will also prevent a POA charge) it is thought that this will be calculated by reference only to the loft space which he occupies (i.e. that he need not pay a rent for the whole property).

(3) Bill gave a 50 per cent share in his house to his brother Ben some years ago. Ben has now moved to Manila. Bill wishes to pay full consideration to avoid the reservation of benefit rules applying to the gifted half share but what is full consideration for the use of Ben's 50 per cent share in the property? No guidance is given in the legislation but to be "on the safe side" 50 per cent of a rent for the whole would undoubtedly suffice.

---

[39] A good example is "sharing arrangements" considered in detail at 43.94.

[40] For the view of HMRC see IHTM 14341 where it is stated that "*it is unlikely that any such arrangement could be overturned if that taxpayer can demonstrate that it resulted from a bargain negotiated at arm's length by parties who were independently advised and which followed the normal commercial criteria in force at the time it was negotiated*". See also 43.101.

22.15 The following further points may be noted about the full consideration let-out:

(i) That the consideration must be full throughout the occupation of the property by the donor. If at any stage less than full consideration is paid, the donor will reserve a benefit. Hence normal commercial rent reviews should be incorporated into any tenancy agreement and should be observed! Ideally the parties should be able to show that the consideration has been negotiated between independent valuers.[41]

(ii) Whereas the pre-owned asset legislation sets out in some detail the terms of the lease on which the "rental value" of the property is arrived at,[42] FA 1986 gives no guidance on how "full consideration" is to be determined. It must, however, take into account all the terms of any letting so that if the donor takes over responsibility for repairing, insuring the property, etc this may reduce the amount to be paid in rent. This flexibility is not available under the POA legislation.

(iii) The full consideration let-out provides the basis for a widely used chattel scheme involving a gift and leaseback of the chattels. Its attraction is that the actual rent paid in such cases is relatively small.[43]

(iv) Whilst full consideration will commonly involve the payment of rent the requirement may also be satisfied by the payment of a premium: for instance Jake in Example 22.3(1) does not want the uncertainties of a series of assured shorthold tenancies with the risk in the future of substantial rent increases which he might not be able to afford. Accordingly he negotiates a lease for his life with Sissie for which he pays a commercial premium.[44]

(v) The POA charge does not apply where the full consideration exemption for reservation of benefit applies.[45] Note that if the donor ceases to pay full consideration but continues to use or enjoy the gifted property he then falls within the GWR legislation but remains outside the POA charge.

(vi) The full consideration let-out only applies to land and chattels. As explained at 22.09 even if there is no benefit to the donor, if he is not excluded from gifted property (other than land or chattels) then a reservation of benefit can arise.

The donor's spouse (or civil partner)

22.16 One point should be noted in passing concerning the scope of the GWR provisions, namely that there is nothing in s.102(1) which makes property

---

[41] Separate valuers negotiating on the rent that should be paid on a standard short hold tenancy would be unusual but it is certainly advisable to have separate valuers acting for each party where full consideration arrangements relate to chattels or the arrangements over the land are unusual, e.g. if a premium is payable on a lease for life. Any valuations should be in writing and retained by the taxpayer.

[42] FA 2004 Sch.15 paras 4 and 5.

[43] See further Ch.44.

[44] For the taxation of rent and any premium paid on the grant of a lease, see ITTOIA 2005, Pt 3.

[45] Sch.15 para.11(3)(5(d).

which the donor has given away and which the donor's spouse (but not the donor) is capable of enjoying or from which she benefits "property subject to a reservation" in relation to the donor.[46] On the contrary, the legislation confers favourable treatment on gifts to spouses (unless the spouse exemption is restricted because the donor is UK domiciled and the donee spouse is not). This approach is also adopted (albeit with some significant differences) for the purposes of the POA charge.[47]

EXAMPLE 22.4

Silas establishes a discretionary trust of shares under which the beneficial class:

(i) includes Silas. He is therefore caught by the reservation of benefit rules.[48] If Silas is not a named beneficiary but the trustee has power to add any person (including Silas) as a beneficiary it is thought that the position is the same;

(ii) alternatively Silas is wholly excluded from benefit but his wife can benefit under the trust. Silas is not within the reservation of benefit rules because he cannot benefit and nor does the POA charge apply since para.8 is only relevant if the settlor can benefit under the trust.

V INGRAM AND EVERSDEN

Two IHT cases, *Ingram* and *Eversden*, are particularly important and will be reviewed briefly. **22.17**

The *Ingram* case[49]

Lady Ingram owned real property which she wished to give to her children and grandchildren subject to retaining the right to occupy the property during her life. To achieve this she transferred the property to her nominee. The next day, acting on her directions, he granted her a 20-year rent-free lease and on the **22.18**

---

[46] A benefit to the donor's spouse is, however, relevant under FA 1986 Sch.20 para.7 (policies of life insurance). Also, the fact that the donor's spouse has a right or enjoys property may have adverse implications for the donor in respect of gifts of land under FA 1986 s.102A.

[47] See FA 2004 Sch.15 para.10(1)(b)–(c).

[48] See *IRC v Eversden* [2002] STC 1109 before Lightman J. where it was accepted by both parties that this was the case. The effect of settlor-interested trusts falling within the reservation of benefit rules is that the para.8 POA charge on settled intangible property is inapplicable. Note that there is no reservation if (i) the settlor retains a life interest in his settlement or (ii) if he retains a remainder interest in circumstances where the "carve-out" principle applies: see Ch.26.

[49] [1995] STC 564: on appeal [1997] 4 All ER 395; [1997] STC 1234, CA; reversed [1999] STC 37 (HL). For *Ingram* schemes see generally 43.38. For the use of *Ingram* schemes in current planning, see 43.85.

following day transferred the property, encumbered by the lease, to trustees who immediately executed declarations of trust whereby the property became held for the benefit of her children and grandchildren (to the exclusion of Lady Ingram).

Following her death, HMRC issued a determination that, under the reservation of benefit rules, the property was deemed to be comprised in her estate immediately before she died. The House of Lords found unanimously for Lady Ingram's executors. The lease was valid, but even if it was not, the property given away was the encumbered reversion. Their Lordships stressed that it was important to identify precisely what property had been given away by the donor and what (if anything) she had retained. Continued enjoyment of the latter did not amount to a reservation in the former (arrangements of the type adopted in this case are known as "shearing" operations). Not long after the House of Lords' decision, anti-avoidance legislation, intended to nullify the effect of the decision in relation to land, was introduced (now FA 1986 ss.102A–C).[50]

The *Eversden* case[51]

22.19 In 1988 Mrs S settled the family home, which she then owned, upon trust to hold the same for herself as to five per cent absolutely and as to 95 per cent upon the trusts of a settlement under which her husband, Mr S, was the life tenant. After his death the trust fund was to be held upon discretionary trusts for a class of beneficiaries which included Mrs S.

During their joint lives Mr and Mrs S occupied the family home: Mr S under the terms of the settlement, and Mrs S by virtue of her retained interest as a tenant in common. After Mr S's death in 1992 Mrs S continued in occupation. In 1993 the trustees sold the house and, out of the proceeds, including Mrs S's five per cent share, acquired a replacement property and an investment bond. Thereafter Mrs S owned a five per cent share in the replacement property and the bond. She died in 1998 having, in the interim, been in sole occupation of the replacement property, but having received no benefit from the bond. HMRC argued that the entirety of the replacement property (and the bond) should be included in her estate immediately before she died by reason of her enjoyment of it.

The Court of Appeal unanimously rejected HMRC's appeal. The case was argued solely on the application of s.102(5) of FA 1986 which provided that a disposal of property which was a spouse exempt transfer was outside the scope of the reservation of benefit rules. HMRC sought to restrict the size of gift to which the spouse exemption applied by arguing there was a mismatch in the legislation between "gift" and "transfer of value". Although when Mrs S created the settlement she may have made a transfer of value to her husband

---

[50] Because this legislation was closely targeted to catch the *Ingram* scheme (a) it did not prevent similar arrangements involving chattels (although these are now caught by the POA legislation) and (b) it did not catch reversionary lease arrangements provided either that the donor had owned the property for at least seven years before entering into the scheme or had acquired it for full consideration. Such arrangements are, however, caught by the POA legislation.

[51] *Essex (Executors) v IRC* [2002] STC (SCD) 30; affirmed sub nom *IRC v Eversden (Greenstock's Executors)* [2002] STC 1109 affirmed [2003] STC 822, CA. See further Ch.33 and 43.43.

of her 95 per cent interest, for the purpose of the reservation of benefit provisions she also made a series of gifts consisting of the equitable interests given to the various beneficiaries under the settlement and the exemption in s.102(5) was confined to the gift (of the life interest) which she made to her husband.

Carnwath L.J., with whom Brooke L.J. and Nelson J. agreed, rejected HMRC's argument. *Ingram* was concerned solely with the nature of the interest retained by the donor and was decided in a different context. The same applied to the *Perpetual Trustee*[52] case. Neither was concerned with and neither addressed the position of successive interests forming part of a gift into a settlement. Carnwath L.J. held that it was not possible to introduce conceptual subtleties into s.102(5) without distorting the language.

Given s.49(1),[53] Mrs S had made a transfer of value of the whole of the settled property to her husband and to him alone. Section 102(5) applied to that transfer, and so Mrs S did not reserve a benefit. There was nothing in s.102 to modify the effect of s.49(1). If this caused problems then he concluded that they were for Parliament to correct.

Anti-*Eversden* legislation

Unsurprisingly, FA 2003 s.185 introduced ss.102(5A)–(5C) into FA 1986 in **22.20** order to reverse the Court of Appeal's decision. These provisions had effect in relation to disposals made on or after June 20, 2003. *Eversden* schemes set up before that date were thus unaffected by the new provisions whether or not the spousal interest in possession had already been terminated.[54]

Section 102(5A) provides that s.102(5)(a) (the spouse exemption) does not apply if or, as the case may be, to the extent that the four conditions are satisfied:

(1) the property becomes settled by virtue of the gift[55];

(2) by reason of the donor's spouse (who is referred to as "the relevant beneficiary") becoming beneficially entitled to an interest in possession in the settled property, the disposal is or, as the case may be, is to any extent within the spouse exemption because of s.49(1);

(3) sometime after the disposal during the donor's lifetime the relevant beneficiary's interest in possession comes to an end; and

(4) on the occasion when the interest in possession comes to an end, the relevant beneficiary does not become entitled to the settled property or to another interest in possession in the settled property.

---

[52] *Comr for Stamp Duties for New South Wales v Perpetual Trustee Co Ltd* [1943] AC 425 PC.
[53] To the effect that a qualifying interest in possession beneficiary is treated as beneficially entitled to the settled property: note that the scope of s.49(1) was severely limited by FA 2006. See 28.02.
[54] But they can still fall within the POA legislation.
[55] Note therefore that if the property is already settled the anti-avoidance provision does not apply.

For this purpose: (i) the disposal of an interest is treated as the termination of that interest; and (ii) references to any property or to an interest in any property include references to part of any property or interest.[56]

Section 102(5B) then provides that to the extent that s.102 applies by virtue of s.102(5A), s.102 has effect as if the disposal by way of gift had been made immediately after the relevant beneficiary's interest in possession came to an end. These anti-avoidance provisions were thus targeted directly at future *Eversden* schemes.

EXAMPLE 22.5

> H settles the house in which he lives on interest in possession trusts for his wife W in July 2003. The gift is spouse exempt (provided W is UK domiciled). H does not reserve a benefit. In December 2003 the spousal interest is terminated by the trustees. He is still living in the house. H is then treated as reserving a benefit in the house. Note that if W's interest is terminated on or after March 22, 2006 (for example, in favour of the children) and both live in the house, both of them are treated as reserving a benefit in the house, H under s.102(5A) and W under s.102ZA! There is no POA charge in either case.

If, however, the property had been settled into trust for W before June 20, 2003 and W's interest in possession is terminated before or after that date H is not treated as reserving a benefit but would then be subject to a POA charge unless the termination arose on W's death or on termination either H or W became absolutely entitled to the property.

VI APPLICATION OF THE RESERVATION OF BENEFIT PROVISIONS GENERALLY

22.21 When the GWR provisions apply, they have two consequences, namely a claw-back of the gifted property on death under s.102(3) and a deemed PET under s.102(4).

Claw-back on death: s.102(3)

22.22 Section 102(3) provides that if, immediately before the death of the donor, there is any property which in relation to him is property subject to a reservation then, to the extent that the property would not otherwise form part of the donor's estate at that time, that property shall be treated as property to which he is beneficially entitled.[57] This is important in two ways.

---

[56] FA 1986 s.102(5C).

[57] It follows that property subject to a reservation in relation to an individual does not form part of his estate until immediately before his death (assuming that the reservation is then continuing). This view is not affected by s.102(4): see 22.27 below.

Property comprised in the taxpayer's estate

That s.102(3) does not operate with respect to property which already forms **22.23** part of the deceased's estate immediately before he dies is hardly surprising because the reservation of benefit provisions are designed to prevent an individual from enjoying property which has ceased to form part of his estate. If the property is part of his estate, there is no reason to apply the reservation of benefit provisions to it. A benefit can be reserved in excluded property but because it is excluded it will not be taxed as part of the individual's estate on death.[58]

Excluded property

Section 102(3) is not itself a charging provision. It merely provides that the **22.24** deceased is to be treated as beneficially entitled to the property in question immediately before his death. The charge on death is then imposed on the property comprised in a person's estate, not on property to which he is beneficially entitled.[59] However, in many cases the point is not important, because the general rule is that a person's estate is the aggregate of all the property to which he is beneficially entitled.[60] That rule, however, is subject to one important qualification, namely that, immediately before a person's death his estate does not include excluded property. So, where the property which is subject to a reservation is excluded property no charge will be imposed on a person's death in respect of it, notwithstanding that under s.102(3) he was treated as beneficially entitled to it immediately before he died.[61]

The position in respect of non-settled property is straightforward. Assume X, who is not domiciled in the UK for IHT purposes, dies having reserved a benefit in respect of a house in Florida. As non-UK situs property the house treated as owned by X is excluded property and no problems arise. However, if on his death X had become domiciled or deemed domiciled in the UK the property would not have been excluded property.

Change the facts and assume that the house was owned by a settlement **22.25** which X had created when he was domiciled outside the UK. If he dies domiciled abroad the position will be exactly as it was in the first example. But what if X dies domiciled in the UK, e.g. under the IHT deemed domicile rules?[62] In that case the question is which rules apply for determining whether or not the house is excluded property for the purposes of the reservation of benefit rules. If the fact that the house is settled property is ignored, the house will be prevented by X's UK domicile from being excluded property. If, on the other

---

[58] Property will form part of the donor's estate if he owns it at the time of his death or then enjoys a qualifying interest in possession in it. See Ch.31 for how the provisions operate in relation to excluded property.

[59] IHTA 1984 s.4.

[60] IHTA 1984 s.5(1).

[61] Excluded property is defined in IHTA 1984 s.6 and, in the context of settlements and interests in settled property, see IHTA 1984 s.48.

[62] See IHTA 1984 s.267. For a consideration of the IHT domicile rules, see 31.04 and following and 3.107.

hand, account is taken of the fact that the house is settled property and the rules for determining whether or not settled property is excluded property are applied, the house will remain excluded property notwithstanding that X has become domiciled in the UK.[63] HMRC now accept that the property will remain excluded and that any subsequent change of domicile by the settlor is ignored.[64]

Exemptions

22.26   The fact that s.102(3) operates to claw-back property into the deceased's estate does not necessarily mean that such property will be subject to IHT on the deceased's death.[65] Such a result will be avoided if the property qualifies for a relief such as business property relief.[66]

Because property subject to a reservation is in the actual ownership of the donee it will not generally qualify for, e.g. the spouse exemption on the donor's death because it will not then become comprised in that spouse's estate.[67]

Cessation of reservation: the deemed PET under s.102(4)

22.27   Section 102(4) provides that if, at any time before the end of the "relevant period"[68] any property ceases to be property subject to a reservation, the donor is treated as having at that time made a disposition of the property by a disposition which is a PET.[69]

Business relief and agricultural relief

22.28   In certain cases the rules governing the availability of business property relief and agricultural property relief are relaxed so that property which is subject to

---

[63] IHTA 1984 s.48(3) provides that non-UK situs property comprised in a settlement is excluded property provided that the settlor was non-UK domiciled when he made the settlement.

[64] The view of HMRC is at IHTM 14396: see further Ch.31.

[65] It may, for instance, fall within his IHT nil rate band.

[66] See Ch.43 and note the conditions necessary if gifted property in which a benefit is reserved is to qualify for agricultural property relief or business property relief.

[67] For the spouse exemption, see IHTA 1984 s.18. For HMRC's views, see IHTM 14303, "... *the GWR rules are fictitious treatments created only for the purposes of preventing IHT avoidance. They do not affect the actual devolution of the property in real life so the gifted property does not actually pass on death under the will or intestacy.*" However, see Ch.34 and 43.49 in the context of home loan schemes where this analysis may be flawed when an election has been made to opt into reservation of benefit.

[68] The "*relevant period*" means a period ending on the date of the donor's death and beginning seven years before that date or, if it is later, on the date of the gift: FA 1986 s.102(1).

[69] Note that the property is not treated as forming part of the taxpayer's estate. HMRC accept that if the property becomes comprised in the donor's estate (for instance if the gift is unscrambled) this does not give rise to any charge on the deemed PET because there is no loss to the donor's estate.

a reservation may qualify for relief on the basis that a notional transfer by the donee can include the donor's ownership and occupation periods in determining whether relief is due.[70]

A possible misunderstanding

The reservation of benefit rules sometimes give rise to a misunderstanding, **22.29** the view being mistakenly taken that where an individual reserves a benefit he is (for IHT purposes) treated as though he had never given the property away. This is incorrect. The rules operate by clawing the property back into his estate immediately before he died for the purpose only of imposing an IHT charge on it, or by providing for a notional PET if he ceases to reserve a benefit but they do not deem the property never to have left his estate.

It accordingly follows that:

(i) As a matter of general law the property is comprised in the estate of the donee so that IHT will be payable on that person's death.

(ii) There is no CGT uplift on the death of the donor even though the reservation of benefit rules result in an IHT charge on the property.[71]

(iii) It is the donee who is primarily liable to pay any IHT owing on the reservation property resulting from the death of the donor.[72]

(iv) The property is not treated as forming part of the donor's estate for IHT purposes while he is alive. This can sometimes be relevant for POA purposes, for example in relation to home loan schemes which are discussed in Ch.34 and at 43.53 in detail.

VII AVOIDING THE RESERVATION OF BENEFIT RULES

Inevitably taxpayers have sought to reduce their estates for IHT purposes by **22.30** making PETs of property whilst at the same time wishing to retain benefits (e.g. the use of income) from the property gifted. In some cases the taxpayer may be content simply to know that he will be able to obtain benefits from the gifted property if the need arises.

It is a testimony to the success of such arrangements that the Government felt it necessary to introduce the pre-owned assets charge. What therefore were the arrangements entered into by tax payers which have led to this new tax?

---

[70] FA 1986 Sch.20 para.8: See Ch.45.
[71] See TCGA 1992 s.62 for the CGT rules on death.
[72] IHTA 1984 s.200(1)(c), 204(9), 211(3) and see Ch.56.

The Home Loan (Double Trust) Scheme

22.31   This was probably the single most important reason for the introduction of the legislation.[73] The authors consider that, if correctly implemented, the scheme is not caught by reservation of benefit but from April 6, 2005 is likely to be subject to the POA charge.[74]

The use of cash gifts

22.32   An apparent weakness in the reservation of benefit legislation is that whilst there are tracing provisions which may apply if the original property given is switched into a new property, these rules do not apply to an outright gift of cash. Hence if Albert were to give his son Sidney £400,000 which Sidney uses to purchase a house for occupation by Albert it is not considered that there is any reservation of benefit in the house. Not surprisingly, the POA regime includes detailed provisions to catch cash contributions to the purchase of property which is then occupied. They will still escape inheritance tax but instead suffer the POA charge if made after April 5, 1998 and the donor occupies the house or uses the chattel purchased with the cash within seven years of the gift.[75]

Reversionary lease arrangements

22.33   As noted above, they are not caught by the anti-*Ingram* legislation provided that either the property has been owned more than seven years before the arrangement was entered into or that it was purchased for full consideration at any time. They are not caught by reservation of benefit[76] but are within the POA charge.

[73] HMRC intend to attack some of these arrangements on the basis that they fall within the reservation of benefit net because the debt is repayable on demand. This will not, however, prevent the POA charge from applying in respect of the property occupied because that property is still reduced by the excluded liability which is not treated as part of the donor's estate just because he has reserved a benefit in it. More recently they have indicated a willingness to attack *all* home loan schemes: see HMRC guidance notes reproduced at A2.67 and 43.49 for details of home loan schemes.

[74] There are arguments against this view. See Ch.34 and 43.53.

[75] See Ch.34 and 43.97.

[76] However, note the decision of the First Tier Tribunal in *Buzzoni v RCC* [2011] UKFTT 267 (TC) in which the deceased had owned a long lease on a property in Knightsbridge. See also 33.13 and 43.85. In 1997 she obtained the consent of the freeholder to grant an underlease (for a period expiring two days before the headlease) to a settlement for her children. The underlease commenced in 2007, 10 years after it was granted (it was therefore a reversionary lease). The underlease contained some 11 pages of covenants given by the undertenant which reflected the covenants which the deceased had given in the headlease. The Tribunal decided that:

   (i) the gift of the underlease took place in 1997, not in 2007 when it fell into possession;

   (ii) the deceased's gift was qualified by the covenants given by the under tenant (e.g. to pay the service charge; the advance service charge and to keep the property in repair). This

Chattel schemes

These avoided the reservation rules either by a shearing arrangement or by satisfying the full consideration exemption. Whilst the former are within the POA charge, the latter—which rely on the full consideration let out[77]—are not. **22.34**

***Ingram* land schemes**

Arrangements carried out since March 1999 have been caught by the reservation of benefit legislation but pre-1999 arrangements are caught by the POA charge. *Ingram* schemes are still relevant for some lifetime planning: see 38.54 and 43.85. **22.35**

***Eversden* schemes**

New schemes are within the 2003 legislation and caught by the reservation of benefit provisions but "revenge" has been taken on past schemes via the POA charge. **22.36**

Reverter to settlor schemes

Further changes were made to the POA legislation with effect from December 2006 to catch reverter to settlor trusts that were designed to circumvent both reservation of benefit and POA. Such trusts can avoid reservation of benefit but are now caught by POA.[78] **22.37**

involved a reservation of benefit and the only way of avoiding this would have been for the deceased to give away a bare underlease, i.e. an underlease without any covenants in favour of the deceased. The Tribunal stressed that as a matter of law it was possible to have a lease without covenants: the essential feature of a lease is a right of possession for a finite time. This is the property interest which could have been gifted without a reservation;

(iii) the position might have been different if the licence to sublet had required the under tenant to enter into a covenant directly with the freeholder (the head landlord) to pay the service charge directly to him;

(iv) it rejected the argument that the covenants conferred no benefit on the deceased because they merely reimbursed her for her liabilities under the headlease;

(v) the fact that mirror covenants might have been implied by law even in the absence of an express provision does not affect the position; they could equally amount to a reservation and should have been excluded.

It should be noted that no benefits accrued under the underlease to the deceased until that lease took effect in possession in 2007. The deceased died in 2008.

[77] See 44.01 and following for chattel arrangements.
[78] See Ch.37.

22.38 The pre-owned assets charge is one of a number of measures designed to combat tax avoidance. Specifically it was announced that:

> "*action will be taken against avoidance of the Inheritance tax rules for gifts with reservation, where the former owner continues to enjoy the benefits of ownership of an asset*".[79]

It was originally envisaged that the income tax charge would be free-standing and largely independent of the reservation of benefit provisions in FA 1986. Changes resulting from the consultation process, however, resulted in a close linkage of the charge with that legislation, for instance:

(a) the charge does not apply if the asset in question is caught by the reservation of benefit rules and so will form a part of the taxpayer's estate at death[80];

(b) the charge does not apply if the taxpayer "opts into" the reservation of benefit rules by making an election[81];

(c) a number of exemptions from the reservation of benefit legislation also apply to the income tax charge, e.g.:

- gifts to charities and political parties;
- gifts to housing associations and for national purposes;
- maintenance funds for historic buildings;
- employee trusts.[82]

(d) situations where the benefit is excluded from a reservation of benefit charge are also excluded from a POA charge[83] (for example de minimis benefits; a benefit for which full consideration is provided and occupation of land by a donor at a time when he has become unable to maintain himself)[84];

(e) a transaction is excluded from the POA charge if the property was transferred (by sale or gift) to the transferor's spouse or gifted into an interest in possession trust under which the spouse enjoyed an interest in possession.[85] This mirrors the spouse exemption in the inheritance

---

[79] Pre-Budget Report 2003 "*The strength to take the long-term decisions for Britain: Seizing the opportunities of the global recovery*": December 10, 2003. A consultation paper was issued the following day.

[80] FA 2004 Sch.15 para.11(3) and (5).

[81] FA 2004 Sch.15 paras 21–23. For instance a pre-1999 *Ingram* scheme did not fall within the reservation of benefit legislation but the taxpayer is subject to the income tax charge unless he makes this election or (more likely) ceases to occupy the property or pays a market rent. The election must be made on Form IHT 500 and in the case of "existing arrangements" caught by the charge on April 6, 2005, the deadline was January 31, 2007. But the election process is deeply flawed: see generally Ch.34.

[82] FA 1986, s.102(5)(d)–(i) as amended by the FA 1989 s.171(5) and (6).

[83] i.e. situations dealt with in FA 1986 Sch.20 para.6.

[84] FA 2004 Sch.15 para.11(5)(d).

[85] FA 2004 Sch.15 paras 10(1)(b)–(c) and (2)(a)–(b) but note that the income tax charge can apply if the spouse's interest in possession ends otherwise than on death.

tax legislation although note that for POA purposes (unlike inheritance tax) the spouse's domicile is irrelevant.[86] Even the qualification that the income tax rules may apply if the spouse's interest in possession ends otherwise than on death, mirrors the qualification in the inheritance tax legislation which was introduced to reverse the *Eversden* decision.[87] Note, however, that if the spousal interest in possession ends on the death of the spouse, reservation of benefit can still apply to the donor if the disposal into trust was made after June 19, 2003. POA would not apply if the spousal interest in possession ends on the death of the spouse, whether or not the disposal into trust was made before or after June 19, 2003. Hence, where the settlor transferred property into an interest in possession trust for his spouse prior to June 19, 2003 and the spouse then dies there is no reservation of benefit or POA problem for the settlor (although unless the property passes back to the settlor on the spouse's death there may be inheritance tax payable on the spouse's death);

(f) the charge does not apply if the disposal of property involved a redirection of a deceased's estate (for example by a deed of variation falling under IHTA 1984 s.142)[88];

(g) the charge does not apply in cases where an interest in land is given away and both donor and donee occupy the property ("sharing arrangements").[89] Nor does it apply if the donor gives away cash and the donee uses that cash to buy a share in a new property with the donor;

(h) disposals of property before March 18, 1986 are ignored: this is in accordance with the reservation of benefit charge which was only introduced in respect of gifts made on or after that date.[90]

There are, however, significant differences. For example, there is no similar let out in the POA legislation to that in s.102A where an *Ingram* scheme is carried out over seven years (i.e. at least seven years elapses between the creation of the lease and gift of the freehold). Most importantly, POA can potentially apply to any disposal of land or chattels even if the disposal is a sale for full consideration, i.e. even if there is no element of gift. Inheritance tax only applies where there is a transfer of value and the reservation of benefit rules depend on a gift. This can result in a POA charge where no inheritance tax saving was intended or indeed achieved. The obvious example is on a sale of an interest in land between connected parties.[91]

---

[86] See FA 1986 s.102(5)(a) which incorporates the spouse exemption in IHTA 1984 s.18.
[87] See FA 1986 s.102(5A).
[88] FA 2004 Sch.15 para.16.
[89] FA 2004 Sch.15 para.11(5)(c) and see FA 1986 s.102B(4). See 31.57.
[90] FA 2004 Sch.15 paras 3(2)(a), 3(3), 6(2)(a), 6(3), and 8(2). Note that outright cash gifts made before April 6, 1998 are ignored in applying the contribution condition: see para.10(2)(c) and 34.13.
[91] See further 34.11 and 43.126.

The basics of the POA charge

22.39   The legislation provides separately for an income tax charge to apply to:

(a) land[92];

(b) chattels[93]; and

(c) intangible property comprised in a settlement in which the settlor retains an interest.[94]

22.40   As regards land the conditions for operation of the charge are as follows:

(a) an individual must occupy land (this is "the relevant land"); and

(b) either the "disposal condition" or the "contribution condition" must be satisfied in respect of that land.

Hence, let land can never be caught by the POA charge even if the disposal condition is satisfied.

22.41   The "disposal condition" is that at any time after March 17, 1986 the individual owned an interest in the relevant land (or in other property which the relevant land replaced) and disposed of all or part of his interest. Certain disposals are ignored (they are "excluded transactions"): namely arm's length sales of whole or part of the interest in the land to an unconnected party or, if the sale is to a connected party, a sale of the whole interest in a "*transaction such as might be expected to be made at arm's length between persons not connected with each other*". Hence, an arm's length sale to a relative is excluded[95] but note that the exclusion is not applicable to sales of part of the property or where the sale is at an undervalue.

22.42   The "contribution condition" is met where the individual directly or indirectly provides any of the consideration used to purchase an interest in the relevant land. In many ways this is the most significant condition, because the reservation of benefit rules rarely caught cash gifts.[96] For instance, if G gives his daughter £100,000 in 1999 which she later uses to purchase a house which G occupies within seven years of the gift, the reservation of benefit rules are inapplicable but the income tax charge will apply to G in respect of his contribution.[97] The contribution condition not only catches cash gifts but can apply where property is transferred and then later sold by the transferee and used to purchase a house or chattels which is then occupied or used by the original transferor.

---

[92] FA 2004 Sch.15 paras 3–5.

[93] FA 2004 Sch.15 paras 6 and 7.

[94] FA 2004 Sch.15 paras 8 and 9.

[95] FA 2004 Sch.15 para.10(1). Compare IHTA 1984, s.10 and note that an arm's length sale to a relative of the whole interest of the taxpayer in his main residence (other than any right expressly reserved by him) will lead to neither reservation of benefit nor income tax charges (some very limited forms of "equity release" within the family are hence permitted although sales of part at full value are within the POA charge after March 8, 2005).

[96] See 22.32 above.

[97] The failure of the reservation of benefit rules to deal with this situation is because of the limited tracing rules in FA 1986 Sch.20.

The charge, in the case of land, is on the appropriate rental value for **22.43** the land during the tax year. The tax charge suffered by G (on the benefit derived from his occupation) will be based on a market rent for the house. Accordingly, if the house could be let for £2,000 per month the income tax charge on G for that year will be on a benefit of £24,000. (If G is a higher rate taxpayer he will therefore have to pay £9,600 in tax.[98]) There are two situations where part only of the full rent is taxed. *First*, if the taxpayer contributed part only of the purchase price and, *secondly*, if he disposed of part only of the interest in the relevant land.

The basic principles for chattels are the same: the key difference lies in **22.44** valuing the benefit derived from the use of the chattels which is calculated on the basis of the interest that would be payable at a prescribed rate (currently set at four per cent) on an amount equal to the value of the chattels. In practice, the chattel charge catches *Ingram* chattel arrangements (where the taxpayer reserves a lease in the chattel and gives away the freehold interest). Given the exemptions set out in para.11(5)[99] it does not catch the more common arrangements in which the chattel is given away and then rented back for full consideration.

The third area of charge (intangibles held in a settlement) depends upon **22.45** the settlor falling within ITTOIA 2005 s.624 in respect of income produced by the settlement, i.e. he must have reserved an interest in the settlement (ignoring any interest reserved for his spouse or civil partner). In such cases the "para.8" charge is again calculated on the basis of an annual rate of interest (currently four per cent) being applied to the property in the settled fund. The types of settled property which may lead to the charge arising are generally stocks and shares and insurance policies: the para.8 charge will not apply to land (whether or not let or occupied) nor to chattels held in a trust. This charge, catching capital assets that could be applied for the benefit of the settlor, is aimed at *Eversden* schemes under which intangible property, such as an insurance bond, was routed through the spouse (using the inheritance tax exemption) into a discretionary trust under which the settlor could benefit, but which was outside the reservation of benefit rules.[100]

An important limitation to the POA charge when the property is comprised in the taxpayer's estate

Assume that J continued to use property which had been settled under an **22.46** *Eversden* arrangement[101] but which is then unscrambled so that the property is appointed back to J.

In such circumstances it is inappropriate for the income tax charge to apply on the basis of J's use or occupation of the property and it is accordingly excluded.[102] This exclusion from charge, along with that which applies when

---

[98] The detailed provisions for calculating the chargeable amount are in FA 2004 Sch.15 paras 4 and 5. See also the Charge to Income Tax by Reference to Enjoyment of Property Previously Owned Regulations 2005: SI 2005/724 fixing valuation dates.
[99] i.e. the exemptions in FA 2004 Sch.15 para.11(5)(d).
[100] See Ch.33.
[101] As to *Eversden* arrangements, see 22.19 and 43.43.
[102] FA 2004 Sch.15 para.11(1) but note that this exemption from charge is limited when the value

the arrangement is caught by the reservation of benefit rules, is crucial in limiting the width of the charging provisions. It ensures that the tax is closely focused and only operates in situations where the taxpayer has escaped from the inheritance tax net. It also means that innocent transactions will normally escape: for instance, an arrangement under which M gifts her flat to her daughter in order to avoid paying nursing home fees is not subject to POA because M reserves a benefit.[103]

22.47 With the 2006 restrictions on creating qualifying interests in possession, the scope of this limitation has been limited. For instance, a further way of seeking to avoid the future imposition of nursing home fees has been for taxpayers to transfer property into a life interest trust for themselves. Before March 22, 2006 that would have been a nothing for IHT purposes (no reduction in the estate of the taxpayer) and for POA purposes, because the property was in the taxpayer's estate, the POA charge was inapplicable. From March 22, 2006, however, the trust created will be taxed as a relevant property settlement and the interest in possession as non-qualifying so that the property will not be treated as remaining comprised in the taxpayer's estate. The POA charge may still be avoided if the taxpayer has reserved a benefit in the settlement.[104]

of the person's estate is reduced by an excluded liability: see FA 2004 Sch.15 para.11(6) and (7). See also s.80 FA 2006, 37.31 and 34.36.

[103] Note however, that if M had prior to March 22, 2006 settled her flat on qualifying interest in possession trusts for herself and the flat was then sold and a new property was purchased which M occupies as the interest in possession beneficiary, s.80 FA 2006 arguably imposes a POA charge from December 5, 2005, although HMRC state that there is no POA charge if M had an interest in possession throughout in the settled property. See A2.226 and Ch.34. If M settles her house into an interest in possession trust after March 22, 2006 her interest cannot be qualifying and the trust is a relevant property settlement but one in which M reserves a benefit. There is no s.80 POA charge. See further 34.19.

[104] On this question of when a life tenant will reserve a benefit in a relevant property trust after March 2006 see the *Eversden* case and 22.19 and 43.43 and Ch.33 generally.

CHAPTER 23

THE 2006 IHT RULES—AN OVERVIEW

- Background to the changes (**23.02**)
- The IHT treatment of settlements set up on and after March 22, 2006 (**23.08**)
- Exceptional cases: new settlements which are not taxed under the relevant property regime (**23.12**)
- Will drafting options (**23.19**)
- Existing settlements (**23.25**)
- Comments and conclusions (**23.31**)

The Budget on March 22, 2006 included proposals to *"align the inheritance tax treatment for trusts"*.[1] These proposals, heavily amended in certain respects, were given statutory force by FA 2006 s.156 and Sch.20. This chapter provides an overview of what was changed and the following chapters in this part will then consider the position in greater detail.

23.01

I BACKGROUND TO THE CHANGES

The Capital Transfer Tax (and subsequently IHT) treatment of trusts was based upon a fundamental division between interest in possession trusts on the one hand and other settlements ("relevant property trusts") on the other. In the case of the former, the legislation provided for the interest in possession ("IIP") beneficiary to be deemed to be the beneficial owner of the trust property.[2] Accordingly, on his death that property would be aggregated with his free estate and tax imposed on the total value.[3] This method of charging

23.02

---

[1] See 2006 Budget Note (BN) 25.

[2] IHTA 1984 s.49(1).

[3] Such aggregation could affect property values: for instance, if a taxpayer owned 25% of the shares in X Ltd and a further 26% were held in a trust in which he had an interest in possession the value of the combined shareholding would be arrived at on the basis of a controlling interest. It could also affect the availability of BPR: see IHTA 1984 s.105(1)(b) and Ch.45. Note, however, that aggregation has its limitations. For instance, as a result of the wording of IHTA 1984 s.52(1) the termination of an interest in possession during the beneficiary's lifetime results in a transfer value based not on the fall in value of his estate (including the value of the settled property) but on *"the value of the property in which his interest subsisted"*. The tax planning opportunities thereby afforded are considered further at 26.26. The issue of liabilities is similarly instructive in revealing the limits of aggregation. In *St Barbe Green v IRC* [2005]

the IIP beneficiary was of long standing dating back to the introduction of estate duty in 1894. It may be noted that its premise is fictional: in the real world an interest in possession beneficiary has no right to the capital of the settlement—the hallmark of his interest is a right to income (or to the use of trust property).[4]

23.03   Non-interest in possession trusts were subject to a wholly different regime. For convenience such trusts were commonly referred to as "discretionary trusts" but that oversimplified the position since the taxing regime applied to all trusts other than qualifying IIP settlements.[5] Especially in the light of the 2006 changes, it is important to use a different terminology to describe such trusts and in this book the term "relevant property settlement" is used.[6]

23.04   The taxation of such trusts has enjoyed a somewhat chequered history. In the days of estate duty, discretionary trusts were for many years untaxed (no property "passed" on the death of a beneficiary) and the belated attempt to impose a charge in 1969 (by attributing capital to beneficiaries who had received income payments out of the trust) was a failure. A radical new system was therefore unveiled when Capital Transfer Tax was introduced in 1975 and which abandoned all attempts to attribute the trust property to a particular (or to a number of) beneficiaries on the basis of trust distributions received. Instead, the trust itself was taxed as a separate entity. Initially the tax charge was penal (with a top rate of 75 per cent) and during a "transitional period" many discretionary trusts were converted into other—and more favourably taxed—types of settlement. In the main the favoured vehicle was the accumulation and maintenance trust (A-M Trust) which was a settlement without an interest in possession and which received privileged treatment.[7] Broadly speaking, provided that the relevant conditions were met the normal CTT/IHT charges were avoided so that the property could be held in and pass out of that trust without a charge arising. It is little wonder that such trusts became popular and, although intended to provide a vehicle to ensure that settled gifts to minors received parity of treatment with gifts to adults, the generously drafted legislation meant that the privileged treatment could continue until a beneficiary attained 25 and, because it was possible to pick and choose between beneficiaries, the trust could be drafted with a high degree of flexibility. Commonly, therefore the A-M Trust was used as the vehicle to hold the family wealth with the initial non-interest in possession trusts being replaced by IIP trusts by the time the beneficiary became 25 and the trustees then being given overriding powers of appointment in favour of a wide class of beneficiaries.[8]

23.05   The 1975 treatment of relevant property settlements was overhauled in 1982 and the system then introduced continues in force. Such trusts are subject to charges every 10 years (the "anniversary" charge) and, if property ceases to

---

STC 288, Mann J. concluded that the personal liabilities of the deceased could not be deducted from the value of the settled property in which he had enjoyed an interest in possession (see further a detailed analysis of this decision Ch.32).

[4] See, for instance, IHTA 1984 s.51 and TLATA 1996 ss.12 and 13.

[5] IHTA 1984, s.58(1) also provided that certain other settlements did not comprise relevant property. Qualifying IIP is defined in IHTA 1984 s.59.

[6] The charge under IHTA 1984 Ch.3 Pt 3 is on settlements which contain "relevant property".

[7] IHTA 1984 s.71.

[8] The trust considered by the court in *Burrell v Burrell* [2005] STC 569 is typical of the highly flexible trusts that were employed.

be held on such trusts, there is then an "exit" charge. In 1982 the top rate of anniversary charge was cut to 15 per cent; in 1984 that came down to 9 per cent and in 1986 to the present 6 per cent. Bearing in mind that the rate of charge on a qualifying IIP trust is at a top rate of 40 per cent[9] this can hardly be described as penal.

One other background point of great significance is that the lifetime estab- **23.06** lishment of IIP and A-M trusts was generally a potentially exempt transfer (a PET) with the result that provided the settlor survived for seven years no tax was payable. By contrast the creation of a relevant property settlement was immediately chargeable.[10]

Diagrammatically the pre-March 22, 2006 position can be represented as **23.07** follows:

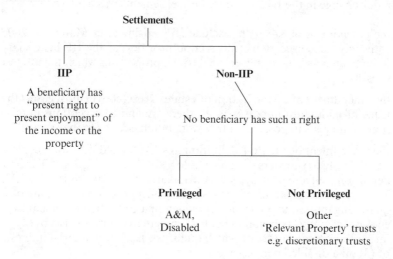

[9] This will be the case if the IIP beneficiary dies having used up his IHT nil rate sum. Of course, the 40% rate was commonly avoided *either* by ensuring that on the death of the IIP beneficiary the trust fund was held for the benefit of his spouse (or civil partner) so that relief under IHTA 1984 s.18 was available if the recipient spouse was UK domiciled or neither spouse was UK domiciled *or* by lifetime tax planning given that the inter vivos termination of the IIP was commonly a potentially exempt transfer.

[10] PETs were introduced in 1986 but only in the following tax year were they extended to include the lifetime ending of an IIP. The change was considered desirable to ensure a level playing field for settled and unsettled lifetime gifts. The justification for the separate treatment of discretionary trusts was that property was passing into a separate taxable structure: i.e. was ceasing to be comprised in the estate of any individual taxpayer. It should also be borne in mind that the way in which the IIP treatment worked meant that if A settled property on himself for life that was a "nothing" (since his estate was not reduced in value) whilst if on his death the settled property passed to his spouse for life that was a spouse exempt transfer. As limited compensation for the IHT charge on the creation of a relevant property settlement CGT hold-over relief was generally available under TCGA 1992 s.260 (although note the exclusion, from December 10, 2003, of settlor-interested trusts from relief (and from s.165 relief) in order to stop "*Melville*" schemes: see 26.16). The definition of a settlor-interested trust for CGT purposes was widened from April 6, 2006: see Ch.7.

23.08 With few exceptions,[11] "new" settlements are taxed as "relevant property" settlements under IHTA 1984 Pt III Ch.III.[12] As a result:

(i) The lifetime creation of a settlement will generally be a chargeable transfer rather than—as had been the case—a PET;

(ii) The trust will be subject to IHT anniversary and exit charges.[13]

23.09 This major change in the IHT treatment of settlements was achieved by:

(ii) the amendment of s.49(1) to exclude IIPs arising after March 21, 2006 with only three exceptions (this section provides for the IIP beneficiary to be treated as beneficially entitled to the property in which the interest subsists);

(iii) the amendment of s.5 (definition of estate) to exclude (in most cases) the value of an interest in possession[14]; there are limited exceptions in relation to interests in possession that were purchased for money's worth[15];

(iv) the amendment of the PET definition in s.3A: the old definition continued to apply to transfers of value made before March 22, 2006. The new definition—effective for transfers on and after that date—is in s.3A(1A). This preserves the status of the transfer which arises on the ending of a qualifying interest in possession provided that either the settlement then ends or the property becomes held (1) on bereaved minor trusts or (2) on interest in possession trusts which qualify as transitional serial interests or (3) on a disabled person's trust.[16]

Note: (1) In all other cases the beneficiary will make an immediately chargeable transfer and the continuing settlement will be taxed under the relevant property regime.

---

[11] See 25.12 below.

[12] In the past it has been convenient to refer to these rules as taxing non-interest in possession (or discretionary) trusts. With the extension of the charge to include some settlements in which there is an interest in possession this practice has become misleading: better to say that the charge under these provisions is on "relevant property" as defined in IHTA 1984 s.58 (which has, of course, been amended).

[13] BN 25 stated that the inter vivos creation of new trusts will automatically attract CGT hold-over relief given that it will involve a chargeable IHT transfer: this, however, is not the case because of the exclusion of hold-over relief for disposals into a settlor-interested trust. This is discussed further in Chs 10 and 18.

[14] The definition of a "reversionary interest" in IHTA 1984 s.47 has not been amended and does not include an interest in possession which is not therefore excluded property under IHTA 1984 s.48. This exclusion of the value of an interest in possession from the relevant beneficiary's estate opened the door to tax planning opportunities and was, as a result, restricted by an amendment in FA 2010: see ss.52 and 53.

[15] See FA 2010 s.53.

[16] See 27.16 for TSIs and Ch.36 for disabled person's trusts: see also s.81A(2) for further limitations to the definition of PET. A transfer of a reversionary interest by a settlor e.g. to his son cannot be a PET following the FA 2010 changes (see IHTA 1984 s.81A) but a transfer of the reversionary interest to a spouse or charity would still qualify for exemption: see 26.46 for further details.

(2) Consider the following situation:

C has a qualifying IIP (given that the assignment of B's remainder interest occurred prior to March 22, 2006). What happens on the inter vivos termination of A's life interest in (say) 2009? At that point the Trust 1 property will fall into Trust 2. C has always had, and continues to have, a qualifying IIP although the value of his interest has now increased. Does A make a PET or a chargeable transfer? In the authors' view A makes a PET since the conditions in s.3A are satisfied.[17] Both A and C have qualifying interests in possession that arose pre-March 2006.

BN25 (issued at the time of the 2006 Budget) indicated that additions **23.10** of property to an existing trust would be treated as a new settlement for these purposes but there was no specific provision to this effect in FA 2006. Presumably therefore HMRC are relying on the wording of IHTA 1984 s.43(2)—the definition of "settlement"—to produce this result.[18]

PETs AND IIPs

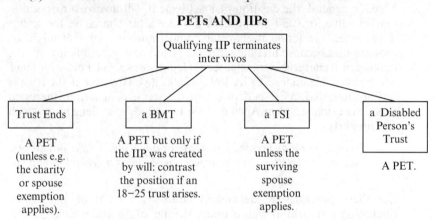

Trust Ends	a BMT	a TSI	a Disabled Person's Trust
A PET (unless e.g. the charity or spouse exemption applies).	A PET but only if the IIP was created by will: contrast the position if an 18–25 trust arises.	A PET unless the surviving spouse exemption applies.	A PET.

Practical Advice

The main impact of the change is in the tax treatment of the creation or **23.11** variation of settlements inter vivos since, unless the trust is one for a disabled person,[19] the settlor will make an immediately chargeable transfer for IHT purposes. The practical consequences are:

(i) that PETS are now generally limited to outright gifts. Settled gifts involve an immediately chargeable transfer[20];

(ii) lifetime trusts are generally limited to:

- gifts up to the amount of the settlor's available IHT nil rate band (£325,000 for 2011–12 and future years until 2014–15). Bear in mind that both spouses (including civil partners) can establish nil

---

[17] Note that this view is not accepted by HMRC. They consider that A makes a chargeable transfer to Trust 2. See further 27.18.
[18] This issue is discussed further at 24.26 and in Ch.31.
[19] See Ch.36.
[20] With the exception of a gift into a disabled person's trust. See Ch.36.

rate band trusts and that gifts inter se (e.g. to enable both to set up such trusts) are spouse exempt[21];

- gifts into trust of property attracting 100 per cent relief (or of excluded property) so that no IHT is payable on the creation of the trust[22];
- a gift into a bare trust which will still take effect as a PET: see Ch.42;
- gifts into trust falling within the normal expenditure out of income exemption.[23]

Needless to say advisers have sought ways of avoiding the IHT "entry" charge which resulted from the 2006 changes. This led to the development of "*Melville Mark III schemes*" discussed at 26.16; to the amendment of the IHT legislation in FA 2010 with a view to prevent their use and, as a result of concerns about the development of future schemes, the limited extension (from April 5, 2011) of DOTAS to IHT[24];

(iii) CGT problems remain—indeed have been exacerbated as a result of FA 2006. In general, the creation of a settlement will involve a disposal at market value for CGT purposes and hence a tax charge on the settlor if the asset transferred is chargeable and showing a gain. It might be thought that because lifetime settlements will now generally involve the making of a chargeable transfer for IHT purposes, CGT hold-over relief will be available under TCGA 1992, s.260(2)(a). However, if the trust is settlor-interested, relief is denied and the scope of a settlor-interested trust was extended from April 6, 2006 to include a settlement in which any property:

"*is or will or may become payable to or applicable for the benefit of a child of the (settlor) at a time when the child is a dependent child of his*".

For these purposes a "dependent child" is a child of the settlor (including a stepchild) who is under the age of 18 and who is unmarried and does not have a civil partner.[25] This will not, of course, deny hold-over relief to grandchildren's settlements and does not apply if at the relevant time the settlor has no dependent children or dependent children are excluded while unmarried and under the age of 18. So a settlement in favour of the children of the settlor at a time when he only has adult children will attract hold-over relief despite the fact that he might in the future have a further child. There is, however, the risk of a claw-back if a child is born in the period beginning with the making of the disposal and ending six years after the end of the year of assessment in which the disposal occurred and the child is not excluded while under 18.[26] To avoid this risk it will be desirable to limit the class of beneficiaries to the settlor's adult children or to provide that minor children can only benefit once the claw-back period has expired[27];

---

[21] IHTA 1984 s.18.

[22] See IHTA 1984 Pt V, Chs I and II.

[23] See IHTA 1984 s.21.

[24] These matters are discussed in detail in Ch.18.

[25] TCGA 1992 s.169F (3A), (4A) and (4B) inserted by FA 2006 Sch.12 para.4. See Ch.7 on settlor-interested trusts and Ch.18 on hold-over relief.

[26] TCGA 1992 s.169C and see 10.11 for further details of how the claw-back charge is calculated.

[27] For a suitable clause, see A1.22.

(iv) if a lifetime settlement is to be set up, the form of the settlement no longer affects its IHT treatment. Whether the trust gives a beneficiary an entitlement to income (which would be an interest in possession but not a qualifying interest in possession for inheritance tax purposes); is fully discretionary, or gives trustees power to maintain and accumulate for infant beneficiaries it will be a relevant property settlement and hence subject to the usual anniversary and exit charges. In practice therefore the decision as to the form of the settlement may be:

(a) a discretionary trust for maximum flexibility; or

(b) one which limits the beneficiaries e.g. to grandchildren with a view to the fund being used to pay school fees and gives the trustees powers to accumulate any surplus income; or

(c) a trust which provides a person with a right to income which may be beneficial for income tax purposes.[28] There will, of course, be no CGT uplift on the death of that beneficiary (since he no longer has a qualifying interest in possession for IHT purposes) but nor will the assets of the trust be aggregated with his free estate on death.[29]

III EXCEPTIONAL CASES: NEW SETTLEMENTS WHICH ARE NOT TAXED UNDER THE RELEVANT PROPERTY REGIME

The exceptional cases are:

23.12

- Disabled trusts[30];
- Bereaved minor trusts[31];
- Section 71D trusts[32];
- IPDI trusts.[33]

(i) Disabled trusts

Disabled trusts which fall under IHTA 1984 s.89 have the same tax treatment as before FA 2006 changes (for instance, the inter vivos creation of the trust

23.13

---

[28] Notably in avoiding the charge under ITA 2007 s.479 (currently at 50%) and the penal levy on the distribution of dividend income: see 6.41.

[29] For the CGT rules on the death of a life tenant see 12.12. Whilst the uplift continues to apply to interests in possession in existence on March 22, 2006 it only applies to interests arising after that date in limited circumstances (i.e. to IPDI; TSI; bereaved minor interests and s.71D trusts if the beneficiary dies under 18 with an interest in possession and to a disabled person's interest trust under s.89B(1)(c) or (d)). See Ch.31 and 25.08 for a consideration of the reservation of benefit position where the settlor is the life tenant of a trust made after March 21, 2006.

[30] Discussed further in Ch.36.

[31] Discussed also in Ch.35.

[32] Discussed also in Ch.35.

[33] See Ch.28.

is a PET). Further, the definition of a disabled person's trust was widened in that Act. A trust is now a disabled person's trust if:

(a) it satisfies the conditions of an old style IHTA 1984 s.89 trust (i.e. discretionary, certain restrictions on capital distributions while disabled person is alive);

(b) under IHTA 1984 s.89A it is a self-settlement without an interest in possession made on or after March 22, 2006 by a person with a condition expected to lead to disability and which satisfies certain conditions as to capital distribution[34];

(c) if the trust is an interest in possession trust for a disabled person set up after March 21, 2006 (no restrictions on capital distributions)[35]; or

(d) if the trust is a self-settlement and is an interest in possession trust set up by a person whose condition makes it likely that he will become disabled and certain conditions are satisfied as to the distribution of capital.[36]

Both (c) and (d) involve actual rather than deemed IIPs. In all cases the disabled person is treated, under s.49(1), as the beneficial owner of the settled property and so the creation of such a settlement may be a PET or in the case of self-settlements, a nothing.[37]

(ii) Bereaved Minor Trusts

23.14   Trusts for a "bereaved minor" (BMT) are defined in IHTA 1984 s.71A. Such trusts can only be set up by will; must benefit a minor child of the testator and must provide for capital to vest at 18.[38] Statutory trusts for minors which arise on intestacy are also included. The tax treatment of these trusts is similar to that which applied to accumulation and maintenance trusts, i.e. no anniversary charge and nor is there a charge on the minor becoming absolutely entitled to the property nor when s.71A ceases to apply as a result of the death (under the age of 18) of the minor.[39] CGT hold-over relief is available on the ending of this trust.[40]

---

[34] As with a s.89 trust, there is a deemed interest in possession so that the creation of the trust is a "*nothing*".

[35] IHTA 1984 s.89B(1)(c).

[36] IHTA 1984 s.89B(1)(d).

[37] IHTA 1984 s.49(1A)(b) and note that the CGT uplift is available on the death of the disabled person (which is not the case with ss.89 and 89A Trusts). See Ch.36 for disabled trusts.

[38] It is tempting to see this as something akin to the accumulation and maintenance trust under IHTA 1984 s.71. However, the differences are striking: a bereaved minor trust can only be set up by will; in favour of a minor child of the testator and must vest capital in him at 18. It does not matter that the minor has an interest in possession in the income before age 18.

[39] The existence of the s.32 power of advancement (including the usual widened power to allow 100% of the presumptive share to be advanced and an equivalent express power) is specifically dealt with in s.71A(4) and s.71B(2)(c). Some flexibility is permitted in giving the trustees powers of selection amongst beneficiaries under the age of 18.

[40] TCGA 1992 s.260(2)(da) and note that the death uplift is available on the death under 18 of the minor with an interest in possession (TCGA 1992 s.72(1A)).

(iii) Section 71D Trusts

23.15 The then Labour Government responded to criticism that vesting capital at age 18 was often inappropriate by introducing a new regime for age 18–25 trusts ("s.71D trusts").[41] Broadly speaking the same conditions have to be met as for a BMT so that:

(a) the provisions only apply to trusts set up in the will of a deceased parent[42];

(b) whereas BMTs require absolute vesting at 18, s.71D trusts require capital and income to vest in the beneficiary (a bereaved child) not later than the attainment of age 25;

(c) as with BMTs, the mere existence of the statutory power of advancement —even widened by the exclusion of the 50 per cent restriction in TA 1925 s.32(1)(a)—or of an express power "to the like effect" will not prevent the trust from satisfying the s.71D requirements.[43] Pending entitlement to capital the beneficiary must either be entitled to the income, or if it is accumulated, it must be accumulated for his benefit and there must be no power to apply income for the benefit of any other person.

The tax treatment of s.71D trusts is as follows:

(A) while the beneficiary is under the age of 18, as for BMTs (i.e. old style A-M treatment with no anniversary or exit charges);

(B) once the beneficiary attains 18 a special charging regime laid down in s.71F applies: in general up to age 18 there is no IHT charge but if the beneficiary dies after 18 but before 25 or the trust ends after the beneficiary reaches 18 or the trust property becomes held on continuing trusts there is a special exit charge. There are no 10-year anniversary charges while the trust satisfies the conditions in s.71D.

For instance, if a parent died when his daughter A was aged six and under the terms of his will capital is to vest in her at 25, then a tax charge will arise calculated as follows:

---

[41] See IHTA 1984 ss.71D–G.

[42] Although note that existing A-M trusts could be converted before April 6, 2008 into s.71D trusts even if the trust had been set up by someone other than the parent or the parent is still alive. The provisions also apply to trusts established under the Criminal Injuries Compensation Scheme and to trusts arising by virtue of a variation (under IHTA 1984 s.142(1)) of the will of the deceased parent dying after March 21, 2006 or by virtue of a "reading-back" event under IHTA 1984 s.144. See also Ch.30.

[43] Overriding powers of appointment which might be exercised to divert the property away from the bereaved child mean that the trust will not fall within s.71D. For the certainty required by s.71A(3)(a) and s.71D(6)(a)—"*will . . . become absolutely entitled*"—compare s.71(1)(a) and see *Inglewood v IRC* [1981] STC 318 at 322. For the meaning of "powers to the like effect" see IHTA 1984 s.88, *Law Society Gazette*, March 3, 1976 and SPE7. Some flexibility is permitted in that the trustees can be given powers of selection whilst a child is under the age of 25.

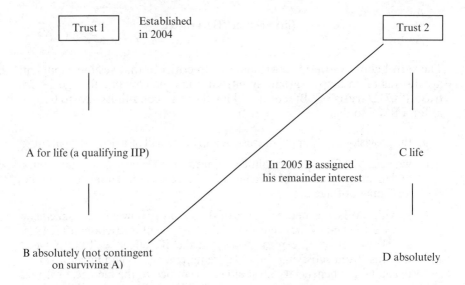

Trust 1 — Established in 2004 — Trust 2

A for life (a qualifying IIP)   C life

In 2005 B assigned his remainder interest

B absolutely (not contingent on surviving A)   D absolutely

(I) to age 18 no IHT;

(II) from 18–25 IHT is calculated in accordance with IHTA 1984, s.71F at a maximum rate of 4.2 per cent on the value of the property when the trusts cease to qualify as 18–25 trusts.[44] If A dies during this period there is an inheritance tax charge irrespective of whether the trust ends. There is no inheritance tax charge if a 10-year anniversary arises during this period.[45]

(iv) IPDI trusts

23.16   An immediate post-death interest in possession (IPDI) trust will be taxed as an old style interest in possession, i.e. the property in the settlement will be treated as beneficially owned by the IIP beneficiary.[46] An IPDI trust can only be established by a will[47] and the Finance (No. 2) Bill 2006 as originally published severely limited the scope for establishing such trusts. These restrictions were swept away as the result of a startling U-turn performed by HM Paymaster General in Committee. Accordingly life interest trusts in a will (including, but not limited to, trusts of residue for a surviving spouse or civil partner) will be IPDIs (provided that the beneficiary becomes entitled to the interest in pos-

---

[44] Section 71F(3) provides that the amount of tax shall be arrived at by multiplying the chargeable amount (the value of the property in the settlement to which the beneficiary becomes entitled: grossing up may apply if the entitlement is to part only of the fund) by the relevant fraction (30% of the number of completed quarters (fortieths) from when the beneficiary became 18 to the vesting of the property) and multiplied by the settlement rate (a maximum of 20%). Hold-over relief under TCGA 1992 s.260 will be available on the ending of the s.71D trust.

[45] Contrast the position if the trust had been taxed under the relevant property regime. If A died after 18 there would be no inheritance tax exit charge unless the trust ended but there could be a 10-year anniversary charge depends on when the anniversary date of the creation of the trust fell.

[46] IHTA 1984 s.49(1A)(iii).

[47] Including a will varied by an instrument falling under IHTA 1984 s.142.

session on the death of the testator) irrespective of any overriding powers of appointment/advancement vested in the trustees.[48]

Old, pre-2006, wills drafted to settle residue on trusts for the spouse for life did not therefore require amendment. However, care needs to be taken in administering such a trust since: **23.17**

(a) any termination of the spouse's interest is—since March 22, 2006— treated as a gift by the spouse for the purposes of the reservation of benefit rules[49];

(b) in general the inter vivos termination of the interest will only be a PET if the settlement ends at that point (e.g. if the trusts are for A for life remainder to B absolutely and A's life interest is ended by an advancement to B, A is treated as making a PET). By contrast, if the settlement continues, the continuing trusts will fall into the relevant property regime and so the spouse will be treated as making an immediately chargeable transfer. This would for instance, be the case if after A's life interest the property was held on trust for her son for life. A surrender by A of her interest would therefore involve an immediately chargeable transfer (tax being charged at the lifetime rate of 0 or 20 per cent with a supplemental charge if A were to die within seven years). The only exception is if, on the termination of the life interest, the property is held on a bereaved minor's trust (in such a case A will make a PET) or if the son is disabled so that the trust is one for a disabled person.[50]

The new structure for taxing settlements may be represented diagrammatically as follows: **23.18**

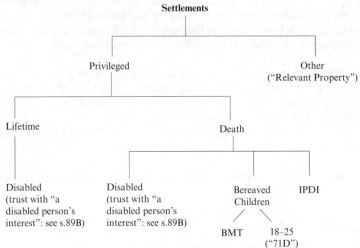

[48] If the beneficiary is the testator's spouse or civil partner the exemption under IHTA 1984 s.18 will therefore be available if the spouse/civil partner is UK domiciled: see further Ch.28.
[49] See FA 1986 s.102ZA (inserted by FA 2006). As a result appointments revoking the interest in possession and establishing a nil rate band trust under which the spouse could still benefit are now caught by the GWR legislation. Note, however, that the change was not retrospective so that terminations before March 22, 2006 were unaffected. See Ch.34.
[50] IHTA 1984 s.3(1A)(c)(iii). For the question of whether an IPDI can be converted into a disabled person's trust, see Ch.36.

23.19 The exceptional cases considered above are—save only in the case of disabled trusts—concerned with will trusts. In IHT terms, the will draftsman therefore has greater variety of trust at his disposal than the trust draftsman. The following matters are worthy of note.

23.20 Standard IHT planning advice in the case of spouses and civil partners had been to ensure that both IHT nil rate bands were utilised. On the death of the first spouse/civil partner, this was commonly achieved by the use of a nil rate band discretionary trust, frequently constituted by a debt or charge.[52] However, the introduction, from October 9, 2007, of transferable unused IHT nil rate bands in the case of a surviving spouse or civil partner who died on or after that date resulted in a radical reconsideration of the position. In some cases, it will be sensible to leave everything to the survivor so that IHT on the first death will be nil and on the death of that survivor, two nil rate bands will be available to set against the tax charge. However, there may still be attractions in the use of a nil rate band discretionary trust. For instance:

(a) to shelter property which is likely to increase in value by an amount greater than rises in the nil rate band or to obtain the benefit of a discounted value[53];

(b) in cases where the surviving spouse has remarried after the death of the first spouse and his estate may benefit from an additional nil rate band (so, in effect, three nil rate bands are potentially available);

(c) to preserve flexibility bearing in mind that a future government might repeal the transferable nil rate band legislation and that any nil rate band discretionary trust that is set up can be broken up with the benefit of "reading-back" under IHTA 1984 s.144 within two years of death.

All these matters are explored in greater detail in Ch.38. In general, as the dust has settled on the 2007 changes, it can be seen that a variety of options and alternative approaches are available to the will draftsmen. No longer is it the case that there is a single standard IHT efficient will.

23.21 So far as gifts to the surviving spouse (or civil partner) are concerned, an IPDI trust will be attractive:

(a) in cases where the testator wants to preserve the capital, e.g. for children of an earlier marriage;

(b) to avoid the risk of future nursing home fees being payable out of the couple's combined estate;

(c) in enabling the trustees to exercise overriding powers of appointment to cause PETS to be made by the survivor but note that from March 22, 2006 the spouse will only be treated as making a PET (rather than an

---

[51] See also Ch.38.
[52] See generally Ch.38.
[53] See generally 38.18. The freezing of the nil rate band for years up to and including 2014–15 is an important factor. Consider also in such cases the use of a number of pilot trusts designed to secure full nil rate bands for each such settlement.

immediately chargeable transfer) if the appointment is (1) to another beneficiary absolutely, (2) to a disabled person trust or (3) into a bereaved minor's trust.[54] The former advantage—that the spouse could continue to benefit from property that had been appointed away from her without falling into the IHT reservation of benefit rules or the pre-owed asset income tax charge—has been removed by FA 2006 in respect of appointments after March 21, 2006.[55]

In cases other than family wills for the first spouse to die (e.g. in the case of wills for the surviving spouse), if minor children are to benefit then the following trust options are now available: **23.22**

(1) a bereaved minor trust for the testator's children which has the attraction of A-M treatment once set up but which involves the vesting of capital at 18 with only limited flexibility permitted[56];

(2) a s.71D trust under which capital must vest no later than age 25. However, there may be an IHT charge after the child attains 18. There is only the same limited flexibility as with the bereaved minor trust.[57] It appears likely that testators will prefer to use the s.71D trust instead of the bereaved minor's trust. It may be that the latter will therefore become something of a dead letter[58];

(3) set up an IPDI trust for the minor children. This will, for some testators, be the most attractive option since the interest in possession can be highly flexible: there can be overriding powers enabling the interest both to be enlarged and to be terminated. And, of course, it offers the prospect of the property remaining settled without IHT charges for longer periods than is permitted under either bereaved minor or s.71D trusts. Two other points to note:

(a) TA 1925 s.31 must be excluded if the minor is to have the interest in possession which is necessary for an IPDI trust[59];

(b) if the minor child were to die IHT would be payable on the termination of the IPDI;

---

[54] But not into a s.71D trust (i.e. a trust for children of the deceased at an age no later than 25): see IHTA 1984 s.3A(1A)(c)(i)–(iii) inserted by FA 2006 Sch.20 para.9.

[55] See FA 1986 s.102 ZA and Sch.20 para.4A both inserted by FA 2006 Sch.20 para.33. See further Ch.33.

[56] The flexibility comes in the form of a widened power of advancement which could be used—if the trustee considered such exercise to be for the "benefit" of the beneficiary—to make a settled advance and thereby postpone the vesting of capital beyond the age of 18: see IHTA 1984 s.71A(4); 71B(2)(c) both inserted by FA 2006 Sch.20 para.1. Once a settled advance has been made, the trusts that it creates will fall within the relevant property regime unless they provide for the vesting of capital at 25 and so come within s.71D. HMRC also accept that trustees can be given power to select amongst children under the age of 18: see generally A2.371 and following.

[57] A settled advance is possible to postpone vesting at 25. There is no 20% entry charge into the relevant property regime but thereafter the trust will be subject to the anniversary and exit charges applicable under the relevant property regime.

[58] Bear in mind that if a s.71D trust is ended by a transfer of assets to the beneficiary no later than the age of 18 there is no IHT liability. IHT will only arise if the trust continues beyond age 18. Hence. in using a s.71D trust there is the ability to enjoy all the benefits of a bereaved minor trust if vesting capital at 18 becomes appropriate. However, there is also the advantage that the trust can be kept in being for a further seven years if this is desirable.

[59] See Ch.38 and A1.10.

(4) set up a relevant property trust for the minor;

(5) leave the property on a bare trust for the minor. The property will form part of the minor's estate and he will be entitled to demand it from the trustees when he becomes 18.[60]

23.23 So far as other beneficiaries are concerned (e.g. adult children/grandchildren) the option of using a bereaved minor or s.71D trust[61] is not available and so the possibilities, if a trust is required, are narrowed to:

- an IPDI,

- a relevant property trust, or

- a bare trust.

23.24 Testators should remember that if an IPDI trust is set up for (say) a son, a subsequent interest in possession for the son's spouse will not qualify for the spouse exemption on the son's death. That successive life interest is not an IPDI: hence on the son's death the settled property does not become comprised in his spouse's estate and so the exemption under IHTA 1984 s.18 is not available. The spouse must take outright if spouse exemption is to be obtained.[62]

V EXISTING SETTLEMENTS

(i) General advice

23.25 As a rule of thumb the 2006 changes meant that it was desirable to review all settlements in existence of March 22, 2006 given that the IHT treatment when set up may have changed. In some cases a review should have been undertaken as a matter of urgency, e.g. in the case of accumulation and maintenance trusts where the transitional period ended on April 6, 2008. This section considers the position of each of the main existing settlements likely to be encountered in practice.

(ii) Discretionary Trusts

23.26 A trust which was discretionary in form on March 22, 2006 was unaffected by the changes save that it is no longer possible for a qualifying interest in possession (falling within IHTA 1984 s.49(1)) to arise in the future.[63] This means that:

---

[60] See Ch.42 for a consideration of what happens if the property in the bare trust is settled by an advance made before the beneficiary reaches 18.

[61] This trust is, of course, available for a child of the testator who has not attained 25.

[62] For a consideration of the use of general powers of appointment to create a successive IPDI for the survivor see 38.49 and following.

[63] Unless the trust is converted into one for a disabled person.

(a) the trustees of such trusts may consider appointing an interest in possession to a beneficiary so as to reduce the 50 per cent income tax charge on income paid out to him. This is a nothing for inheritance tax purposes and does not result in any exit charge. It is not a disposal for CGT purposes. But the corollary is that appointing an interest in possession to a beneficiary will no longer avoid a 10-year charge[64];

(b) such an appointment will not cause a new two-year ownership period to begin in the cases of APR and BPR since the trustees are now treated as continuing to own the relevant business or agricultural property[65];

(c) appointing an interest in possession (which can be revocable) may bring capital gains tax advantages in the context of entrepreneurs' relief.[66] The interest in possession can be revoked later without any inheritance tax consequences[67];

(d) prior to March 22, 2006 the trustees of a discretionary trust might transfer assets to a new interest in possession trust, claiming hold-over relief under TCGA 1992 s.260 and suffering an exit charge. For resettlements after that date there is no exit charge even if the new trust is an interest in possession trust because the settled property remains relevant property.[68] Accordingly, since the appointment is not a chargeable transfer there is no hold-over relief under s.260.[69]

(iii) A-M Trusts[70]

So far as existing A-M trusts are concerned, the old rules of s.71 continued to apply until April 6, 2008 (in effect a two-year transitional period) or until a beneficiary became entitled to income (if earlier) but only apply thereafter if the terms of the trust provide for one or more beneficiaries to become entitled to the settled property (and not just an interest in possession in it) at 18. In the event that the terms of the trust did not so provide on or before April 6, 2008 the trust then fell within the "relevant property" charging regime or, if capital must vest at 25 and the other conditions were met, within the s.71D trust regime. There was no IHT exit charge when the trust ceased to satisfy the amended s.71 requirements.[71]

23.27

---

[64] It used to be common for trustees of nil rate band discretionary trusts to appoint a beneficiary an interest in possession just prior to the 10-year anniversary in order to avoid a 10-year charge. There was no exit charge if the value of the assets when settled was under the nil rate band, irrespective of the value at the date of the appointment.

[65] See *Burrell v IRC* [2005] STC 569 where business property relief was not available because an accumulation and maintenance trust had ended with the beneficiary becoming entitled to an interest in possession and that beneficiary had not enjoyed the interest for the requisite two years when it was terminated by an appointment of the property onto discretionary trusts. See Example 45.3.

[66] See Ch.14.

[67] Section 102ZA (deeming an interest in possession beneficiary to make a "gift" for reservation of benefit purposes) does not apply if the interest is non-qualifying.

[68] See IHTA 1984 s.81.

[69] There might be hold-over relief under s.165 if the new trust is not settlor-interested.

[70] See also Ch.30.

[71] FA 2006 Sch.20 para.3 and for the application of the s.71D regime, see IHTA 1984 s.71D(3)–

(iv) Practical Advice for A-M trusts

23.28 There was no right or wrong answer to the question of how an existing A-M trust should have been modified (if at all) to cope with the changed IHT treatment assuming, indeed, that suitable powers existed to enable the terms of the trust to be changed.[72] The transitional period ended on April 5, 2008 and many A-M trusts were amended to ensure that they fell within the 18–25 regime. Many more were doubtless overlooked, however, and the adviser faced with the difficulty of determining the correct IHT treatment of a pre-March 2006 settlement, originally drafted in A-M form, needs to bear in mind the following matters:

(a) if a beneficiary became entitled to an interest in possession before March 22, 2006, the A-M trust ended and the interest is "qualifying". On or after that date, the interest does not qualify and that portion of the settled property will therefore have become held on a relevant property trust. Of course, from April 6, 2008, the entire trust will fall into this regime unless the terms of the trust were such that it then satisfied the revised A-M requirements (viz capital vesting at 18) or met the conditions for 18–25 trusts;

(b) bear in mind that when a trust ceased to qualify as a s.71 A-M trust there was no exit charge and this included the cases where it ceased to qualify as a result of the changes that came into force on April 6, 2008;

(c) if the trust ceased to qualify for continued A-M treatment in 2008 and did not meet the conditions to be a s.71D trust at that time then, although it falls within the relevant property regime from that date, there is no immediate IHT charge and future charges will only accrue from the time when it becomes a relevant property trust (i.e. from April 6, 2008). For many this represented a price worth paying to keep the property in a highly flexible settlement given that the property was not comprised in any beneficiary's estate for inheritance tax purposes;

(d) the trust will benefit from CGT hold-over relief in all cases: viz if it remains a s.71 trust; if it satisfies the s.71D conditions (provided no distribution is made within three months of the beneficiary becoming 18) or it becomes a relevant property trust;

(e) the change in the rules may have resulted in an unequal treatment of beneficiaries: for instance, if beneficiary A obtained an interest in possession in (say) one-quarter of the fund in 2005 there is no way that the other beneficiaries can be given an interest in possession after March 21, 2006 which will receive the same IHT treatment (unless they are disabled).[73]

(4). See also Ch.30. Note that if during the transitional period a beneficiary became entitled to an interest in possession in the property then whilst there was no IHT exit charge on the ending of the A-M trust the resulting IIP trust came within the relevant property charging regime unless the conditions for a s.71D Trust were met *at the time when the beneficiary took an interest in possession*.

[72] Otherwise an application to court was necessary.

[73] See Ch.36.

(v) Interest in possession trusts

So far as an existing interest in possession trust is concerned the old tax treatment will continue (viz the settlement will not be relevant property) but on the ending of that interest the tax position will depend on whether or not the settlement then ends. If it does then the usual tax treatment applies: i.e. the settled property is comprised in the beneficiary's estate and so he may, for instance, make a PET[74]; a spouse exempt transfer or a chargeable transfer. By contrast, if the trust does not end then the general principle is that he will make a transfer into a relevant property settlement.[75] This was, however, subject to an exception for "transitional serial interests" (TSI) which arose before October 6, 2008.[76] Note, however, that a surviving spouse (or civil partner) may acquire a TSI on the death of the first spouse who enjoyed a qualifying IIP whenever that occurs. **23.29**

(vi) Practical Advice for IIPs

1. Existing IIP trusts should have been reviewed before the end of the transitional period. **23.30**

2. Until October 6, 2008 there was the opportunity to replace the then current interest in possession by one or more replacement interests in possession. Note however that if A's interest was replaced by a similar interest for B and if B's interest were in turn replaced before October 2008 by a similar interest for C then C's interest would not have been a transitional serial interest (consequently on the termination of B's interest the trust would have become subject to the relevant property regime and B would have made a chargeable transfer of value). Contrast the position if A's existing interest in possession was ended before October 2008 and replaced by interests in possession for each of B and C in half the trust fund. B and C both have transitional serial interests.[77]

3. Assume A is the life tenant and it is envisaged that his spouse (or civil partner) will thereafter benefit from the property. The IHT spouse exemption will be available if:

    (i) on the ending of A's interest the trust ends with the property passing to Mrs A absolutely;

---

[74] See IHTA 1984 (1A) read with s.3A(2).

[75] This is because no new IIP can arise after March 21, 2006 within s.49(1) (except for IPDI, disabled trusts, and subject to the transitional relief for a "TSI").

[76] The original deadline of April 6, 2008 was extended to October 6, 2008 by FA 2008 s.141.

[77] See 27.15 and following and see Ch.27 generally for further consideration of the transitional serial interest conditions. There are some who consider that the trust must have been entirely interest in possession prior to March 22, 2006 for transitional serial interests to be created or that the pre-March 2006 interest in possession must be entirely ended for a transitional serial interest to arise. The authors do not consider that either view is correct for the reasons set out there.

(ii) A had died or surrendered his interest before October 6, 2008 (Mrs A then took an interest in possession in the trust fund which was a qualifying transitional serial interest). (Note that if A surrendered his interest and the property passed back on interest in possession trusts to him on the death of Mrs A this will not be a qualifying interest in possession and no spouse exemption is available on Mrs A's death);

(iii) A dies on or after October 6, 2008 and Mrs A becomes entitled to an interest in possession in the trust fund.[78]

Relief is not therefore available today if A surrenders his interest and Mrs A becomes the interest in possession beneficiary. In this situation there will be a relevant property settlement and A will make a chargeable transfer.

4. The changes in the IHT rules had an impact on standard divorce arrangements (see Ch.50). The main problem in the case of existing trusts is illustrated by the following example.

EXAMPLE 23.1

A has been married for 20 years and has a life interest in a settlement set up by his father many years before his marriage. In November 2010 A separates from his wife and since the main family wealth is in the trust it is agreed that the trustees will appoint his spouse a life interest in part of the fund as part of the divorce settlement and at a time when the parties are still married. In these circumstances A is taxed as if he had made a transfer of value but as he has not actually made a transfer of value IHTA 1984 s.10[79] cannot apply and post-October 2008 the interest taken by the spouse will not be a TSI and so the spouse exemption will not apply. It would be possible for the trustees to advance the property to the spouse absolutely so that the spouse exemption applies but this may not be what A wants and may trigger capital gains tax charges.[80] Compare the position if A had owned the property outright. In these circumstances a settlement made by A for his wife is not subject to an immediate IHT charge because it is protected by IHTA 1984 s.10 although the settlement will be taxed in accordance with the provisions of the relevant property regime. Hence, every 10 years the trust will suffer a 10-year charge with an exit charge on final termination or on earlier distributions of capital.

---

[78] IHTA 1984 s.49D.

[79] Section 10 provides (broadly) that a disposition is not a transfer of value if it is shown that it was not intended to confer a gratuitous benefit on any person. Hence a settlement in satisfaction of matrimonial claims might be thought to be within its protection. Unfortunately the restrictive wording prevents this.

[80] See further, for a consideration of the possible application of IHTA 1984 s.11 and Ch.50. See also Example 19.10 for the use of a sub-fund election.

1 The 2006 changes have radically altered the IHT treatment of life- **23.31**
time giving: PETs are now, broadly speaking, limited to outright gifts.
Government's (and doubtless HMRC's) dislike of trusts is apparent and
the "level playing field" treatment for outright gifts and gifts into trust
has been abandoned. Looking to the future will the scope of PETs be
further restricted or will they be abolished?[81]

2. Once property is in a "relevant property" settlement the current IHT
rates are far from penal with a top rate of tax on 10-year anniversaries
of six per cent.[82] However, there is no certainty that this rate will be
retained: an increase to 10 per cent, for instance, would have the effect
of producing an annual trust wealth tax of one per cent.

3. It is unlikely that much use will be made of bereaved minor trusts
given the restrictions on their use and the unacceptably early outright
vesting age. It is more likely that 18–25 trusts will be set up (which can
be "extended" by the making of a settled advance before the beneficiary
becomes 25). For those wishing to make lifetime gifts to minors (whether
children or grandchildren) there may be attractions in using a bare trust
albeit that income and capital will have to be paid out at 18 (subject to
the possible exercise of a power of advancement).[83]

4. Continuing use is being made of lifetime trusts falling within the settlor's
IHT nil rate band or normal expenditure out of income exemptions or
to hold 100 per cent relievable or excluded property.

5. It is likely that many old settlements will continue to cause difficulties
with advisers having to bear in mind the "old" as well as the "new" IHT
rules. For instance, difficulties may arise in the area of interest in possession trusts where some reorganisation occurred after March 21, 2006
and before October 6, 2008. Questions such as did that reorganisation
create one or more transitional serial interests, or did it leave all (or at

---

[81] The Office of Tax Simplification in its final report of March 2011 commented:

> "*2.30 We consider that a more appropriate approach to the inheritance tax reliefs is to con-
> sider the scope and operation of inheritance tax with reference to the original and desired
> policy rationale, and thus to consider individual reliefs in context. In addition, any review of
> inheritance tax needs to include a review of the taxation of trusts, which are often used to
> pass family assets between generations.*
>
> *2.31 The Inheritance Tax Act 1984 was not considered by the Tax Law Rewrite project, and
> a complete review of the tax would enable the policy rationale for various provisions to be
> analysed, reliefs to be reviewed and, where necessary, either repealed, simplified or increased
> in line with inflation, and a simpler system overall to be considered . . .*
>
> *2.33 In the light of all this our conclusion is that there should be a proper review of inherit-
> ance tax, whether by HMRC, HM Treasury or the OTS. This would clearly be a longer
> term project. In short, this is a tax that needs a 'top down' review of the sort alluded to in
> 2.3 above.*"

[82] In 1975 the introduction of CTT resulted in a top rate on trusts of 75% and the 1982
overhaul had a top rate of 15% (reduced to 9% in 1984 and to the present 6% in 1986).

[83] See Ch.42.

least some) of the pre-March 2006 interests intact, are likely to arise in the future. This question will become particularly relevant where, for example, on the death of the interest in possession beneficiary, his or her spouse takes an interest in possession. If the deceased beneficiary has a pre-March 2006 interest in possession then the spouse takes a transitional serial interest and spouse exemption is available on the deceased beneficiary's death. If, however, the deceased beneficiary had been given a new interest in possession by the reorganisation then the surviving spouse cannot take a transitional serial interest and so there is no spouse exemption.[84]

6. For the future it will be important to know whether the exercise of a power of appointment or advancement is a "nothing" for inheritance tax purposes or creates a new interest. For example, a beneficiary may currently be entitled to a qualifying interest in possession but become entitled to capital on reaching 40 in 2012. The trustees wish to defer his entitlement to capital by exercising a power of advancement in 2011. Does this result in the creation of a new interest in possession (which would no longer be qualifying) or is it a "nothing" for inheritance tax purposes? This and related questions are discussed in Ch.27.

7. Future interest in possession settlements will not (save in the cease of disabled trusts), involve the aggregation of settled property with the free estate of the beneficiary.

---

[84] See further Ch.27. Note that it may be possible for the trustees to confer a general testamentary power of appointment on the deceased beneficiary which is then exercised by him so as to create an IPDI in favour of his surviving spouse: see 38.55 and 28.19.

CHAPTER 24

IHT DEFINITIONS AND CLASSIFICATIONS

- Meaning of "settlement" and related terms (**24.01**)
- When is there a disposition creating a settlement? (**24.11**)
- Who is the settlor? (**24.18**)
- Additions by the settlor including loans to trusts and the implications of borrowing by interest in possession trusts (**24.26**)
- Classification of settlements (**24.35**)

This chapter considers the definition of "settlement" for IHT purposes and what is meant by an interest in possession. Two preliminary points are worthy of note:

(i) that the 2006 changes were concerned with the IHT treatment of settlements and have had the result that there is now a striking difference between outright gifts and settled gifts.[1] Hence, understanding the width of "settlement" for IHT purposes is vital;

(ii) that the vast majority of new settlements will now be subject to the "relevant property regime"[2] but the meaning of an "interest in possession" remains significant both in the context of old settlements and because of the limited situations in which new qualifying interest in possession trusts can be set up.

I MEANING OF "SETTLEMENT" AND RELATED TERMS

"Settlement" is defined in s.43(2) as[3]:   **24.01**

"*. . . any disposition or dispositions of property, whether effected by instrument, by parol or by operation of law, or partly in one way and partly in another, whereby the property is for the time being:*

(a) held in trust for persons in succession or for any person subject to a contingency, or

---

[1] See 23.11 and following.
[2] Explained in Ch.27.
[3] Commercial arrangements may be caught because there is no requirement that the settlor must have a donative intent (contrast the position for income tax and for the ss.86 and 87 CGT charge: see *IRC v Plummer* [1980] AC 896; [1979] 3 All ER 775 HL).

(b) *held by trustees on trust to accumulate the whole or part of any income of the property or with power to make payments out of that income at the discretion of the trustees or some other person, with or without power to accumulate surplus income, or*

(c) *charged or burdened (otherwise than for full consideration in money or money's worth paid for his own use or benefit to the person making the disposition) with the payment of any annuity or other periodical payment payable for a life or any other limited or terminable period, . . .*

(3) A lease of property which is for life or lives, or for a period ascertainable only by reference to a death, or which is terminable on, or at a date ascertainable only by reference to, a death, shall be treated as a settlement and the property as settled property, unless the lease was granted for full consideration in money or money's worth; and where a lease not granted as a lease at a rack rent is at any time to become a lease at an increased rent it shall be treated as terminable at that time."

EXAMPLE 24.1

(1) Property is settled on A for life remainder to B and C absolutely in equal shares (this is a "fixed", interest in possession, trust). The property is "held in trust for persons in succession" within IHTA 1984 s.43(2)(a). If A, B and C are adult they can between them bring the trust to an end[4] but until they do so the property continues to be settled.

(2) Property is held on trust for "such of A, B, C, D, E and F as my trustees in their absolute discretion may select" (this is a discretionary trust and falls within IHTA 1984 s.43(2)(b)).

(3) Property is held on trust "for A (currently aged six) contingent on attaining 18 years" with a default gift over. This settlement falls within IHTA 1984 s.43(2)(a).

(4) Property is held on trust by A and B as trustees for Z absolutely (a bare trust). For IHT purposes there is no settlement and the property is treated as belonging to Z.[5]

(5) A and B jointly purchase Blackacre. This gives rise to a statutory trust of land[6] with A and B holding the land on trust (as legal joint tenants) for themselves as either beneficial joint tenants or tenants in common. For IHT purposes there is no settlement and the property belongs to A and B equally.[7] This would appear to be the case even if the purchase is made on the basis that A allows B sole occupation of the property rent-free.

---

[4] See *Saunders v Vautier* (1841) 4 Beav 115.
[5] See 24.05 and for the (similar) capital gains tax position see Ch.9 and, for bare trusts generally Ch.42.
[6] LPA 1925, ss.34 and 36 as amended by TLATA 1996 s.5, Sch.2.
[7] For the (similar) capital gains tax position, see Ch.9.

(6) A grants B a lease of Blackacre for B's life at a peppercorn rent. This is a settlement for inheritance tax purposes and A is the trustee of the property.[8] Under LPA 1925 s.149(6) the lease is treated as being for a term of 90 years which is determinable on the death of B.

(7) A settles property in his will on "trust for my wife for life and then to my children absolutely" but with overriding powers of appointment in the trustees enabling them to vary or end the trusts in the 125-year trust period. On the death of wife the property continues to be settled because the children have a defeasible absolute interest.[9] The words in s.43(2)(a) "subject to a contingency" cover an interest that can be defeated, e.g. by marriage or by exercise of the trustees' powers of appointment.

(8) A gives Blackacre to B "absolutely subject only to a power vested in me to transfer such property to anyone in the world including myself." This is in the authors' view not settled property. B takes an absolute interest which is defeasible by the exercise of the general power of appointment which A has retained. Under s.5(2) A is treated as beneficially entitled to Blackacre and it is not part of the estate of B. The legislative draftsman did not intend to include an absolute interest which is defeasible by the exercise of a general power of appointment to be settled property unless there is some element indicating a settlement (such as another contingency) since he contemplates in s.5(2) that a person A may have a general power of appointment "over property other than settled property".[10]

(9) If A gave Blackacre "to B for life and then to C but subject to my power to revoke the settlement at any time" this would be settled property[11] and A is not treated as owning the property (although he may have reserved a benefit in it for inheritance tax purposes given that he has power to benefit from it).[12]

(10) A gives his ex-wife a house as part of the divorce settlement. The intention is to make an absolute gift to wife in order to avoid any entry charge on creation of a settlement.[13] However, A wants to ensure that his wife cannot pass it to her new husband or any children of the second marriage or sell it and spend the cash. The terms of the divorce settlement state that on sale of the property the proceeds are to be held in a separate account with wife entitled to the income and that wife cannot mortgage the property without consent. Any cash must be invested in specified securities or

---

[8] IHTA 1984 s.45. As to the position where a lease is treated as a settlement, see 24.04 and 24.09. This situation does not produce a settlement for the purposes of other taxes. It is believed that HMRC treat a usufruct as an IHT settlement on the basis of this provision. It is far from certain that this treatment is correct since the rights confirmed on the usufructuary are different from those enjoyed in a UK lease. Note that the foreign law extension is in relation to s.43(2) not 43(3). A usufruct is not generally regarded as a settlement for capital gains tax purposes. For offshore structures, see Ch.2.

[9] Note also that if wife's interest in possession (which is an IPDI) ends during her lifetime then this will not be a PET but a chargeable transfer because the children do not take absolutely but on continuing trusts. Care is needed when varying will trusts. See Ch.38.

[10] See *Kempe (PRs of Lyons deceased) v IRC* [2004] STC (SCD) 467.

[11] See *Perry v Astor* (1935) 19 TC 255.

[12] Note that A *would* be treated as owning the property if he had a general power and it was a superannuation scheme since the settled property regime is excluded and s.5(2) applies: see s.151(4).

[13] See Ch.50.

a replacement property only for occupation by wife and she must leave it to her children in her will. The legal title must be registered in the names of persons whom A can trust. Such conditions are likely to be regarded as creating a settlement for inheritance tax purposes. In practice to achieve A's wishes and ensure the house is ring-fenced from the wife's other assets there is little alternative to creation of a settlement.[14]

24.02 The provisions of the relevant instrument should be considered carefully in deciding whether property is settled.

EXAMPLE 24.2

In 2011 A settles property on trust for his son but subject to the trustees' powers to appoint trusts in favour of his daughter's children. The property is settled while the daughter is alive but she dies without issue then the son becomes absolutely entitled without any possibility of defeasance. The settlement falls into the relevant property regime when A settles the property; the son does not take a qualifying interest in possession while his sister is alive and the property is not part of his estate for inheritance tax purposes, being subject to 10-year charges. On his sister's death the son takes outright and there is then a disposal for capital gains tax purposes (with hold-over relief available under TCGA 1992 s.260)[15]; there is a potential exit charge for inheritance tax purposes and the property then becomes part of the son's estate.

If a beneficiary can unilaterally bring the trust to an end, the property is not settled. So if A settles property on trust to accumulate the income for 21 years and then to transfer the property and accumulations to B (without requiring him to reach a specified age) then B is able to end the settlement at any time and the property is not settled.[16]

Foreign entities

24.03 Section 43(2) contains an express extension to catch foreign law entities: a settlement arises if property is for the time being held in trust or would be so held if the disposition were regulated by the law of any part of the UK or "*whereby under the law of any other country, the administration of the property is for the time being governed by provisions equivalent in effect to those which would apply if the property were so held*". Questions arise as to whether foreign entities such as foundations, establishments or so-called "grantor" US-style trusts are settlements, companies or merely nominee arrangements for inheritance tax purposes: see Ch.2.

---

[14] The options are discussed in Ch.50. See Examples 19.10 and 23.1.
[15] Provided that the settlement does not end in a three-month period following a 10-year anniversary of the settlement: see IHTA 1984 s.65(4).
[16] *Saunders v Vautier* (1841) 4 Beav 115.

When is Property "Held in Trust for Persons in Succession"?

In *IRC v Lloyds Private Banking Ltd*[17] the relevant terms of the deceased's **24.04** will were as follows:

> *"(1) While my Husband Frederick Arthur Evans remains alive and desires to reside in the property and keeps the same in good repair and insured comprehensively to its full value with Insurers approved by my Trustee and pays and indemnifies my Trustee against all rates taxes and other outgoings in respect of the property my Trustee shall not make any objection to such residence and shall not disturb or restrict it in any way and shall not take any steps to enforce the trust for sale on which the property is held or to realise my share therein or obtain any rent or profit from the property.*
> *(2) On the death of my said Husband Frederick Arthur Evans I devise and bequeath the said property known as Hillcroft Muzzy Hill, Astwood Bank, near Redditch to my daughter Kathleen Roberts-Hindle absolutely."*

The court decided that the effect of this clause was that the deceased's husband was given a right to occupy the property which was equivalent to an interest in possession[18] so that the property was settled within s.43(2)(a).[19] In practice, the issue has most commonly arisen when a will set up a "nil rate band discretionary trust" containing the deceased's share in the property and, the property having been occupied by the surviving spouse, the question was whether an interest in possession had come into being.[20]

Section 43(2)(b) and bare trusts for minor beneficiaries

Consider the position when property is held in trust for a minor absolutely.[21] **24.05** Because of his age the beneficiary is not entitled to demand either the income or the capital from the trustees who will (unless it has been excluded) have the standard power to apply income for the maintenance of the beneficiary and to accumulate any surplus under TA 1925 s.31. Does it follow that this arrangement is a "settlement" within s.43(2)(b)? It is thought not, since the minor is, of course, entitled to all the income produced by the property: the fact that all or part is retained by the trustees does not mean that it is being accumulated in the sense envisaged by s.43(2)(b). In essence, the power to retain income is being used administratively by the trustees rather than dispositively. Hence, was the infant beneficiary to die before attaining 18 all the property (including the retained income) held by the trustees for him would

---

[17] [1998] S.T.C. 559.
[18] See further on rights of occupation, 24.45.
[19] See also *Woodhall (personal representatives of Woodhall) v IRC* [2000] STC (S.C.D.) 558; *Faulkner v IRC* [2001] STC (SCD) 112; *IRC v Eversden* [2002] EWHC 1360; [2002] STC 1109 per Lightman J. at [27] (the issue of whether there was an interest in possession in the settled property was not considered on appeal); *Oakley (personal representatives of Jossaume Deceased) v IRC* [2005] STC (SCD) 343.
[20] See also SP 10/79.
[21] In the light of the 2006 changes in the IHT treatment of trusts there may be attractions in setting up such bare trusts: see Ch.42.

form part of his estate.[22] HMRC have confirmed that a bare trust is not an IHT settlement[23].

Leases for Life

24.06   Section 43(3) brings four kinds of lease into the definition of a settlement:

(i) a lease for life or lives;

(ii) a lease which is terminable on death (and note that if a lease is granted without any provision for the payment of a commercial rent but at any time will become a lease at an increased rent it is treated as terminable at that time: hence a provision for the payment of a commercial rent on the death of the tenant will result in the lease being treated as a lease for life);

(iii) a lease for a period ascertainable only by reference to a death; and

(iv) a lease terminable at a date ascertainable only by reference to a death.

The life in question need not be that of the beneficiary.[24]

24.07   Prior to March 22, 2006 the tenant would have been treated as enjoying a qualifying interest in possession in the let property and the landlord as entitled to a reversionary interest (in the freehold or head lease which would not be excluded property given that he is treated as the settlor albeit it would have no value under the special valuation provisions in IHTA 1984 s.170 unless value has been provided by the lessee).[25] From March 22, 2006 the inter vivos grant of such a lease has involved the creation of a relevant property settlement by the landlord.

24.08   An important exception is that a lease for life is not treated as a settlement if it is granted for full consideration in money or money's worth or to the extent that consideration is paid. It is believed that HMRC accept that this exclusion will apply when the owner of property carves out and retains a non-commercial lease for life and gives away the freehold or where property is transferred on the understanding that a lease for life at less than a commercial rent will be granted back to him.[26]

EXAMPLE 24.3

In 1998, X entered into the following arrangement in relation to his main residence. First, he granted a lease to a nominee for the rest of his (X's) life and then he gave away the encumbered freehold to (or on trust for) his daughter. Note the following:

---

[22] See further *Capital Taxes*, 1984, at p.66 (N. Warren).
[23] See A2.320.
[24] A statutory tenancy is not regarded as a lease for life: see IHTM 16.91.
[25] So if A grants B a lease for two thirds of the market value consideration, B is treated as having an interest in possession in one third of the property while A is treated as owning the remaining two thirds. See ss.43(3), 50(6) and 170.
[26] See CTO Advanced Instruction Manual at E15 (now withdrawn) although the same statement does not appear in the revised IHTM.

(1) This arrangement is a form of *Ingram* scheme (sometimes called a shearing operation) designed to circumvent the reservation of benefit rules. In essence, X continues to occupy the property by virtue of his retained lease and retains no benefit from the gifted freehold. Changes in FA 1999 prevented the use of *Ingram* schemes to circumvent the reservation of benefit rules and existing schemes were then caught by the POA legislation from April 6, 2005. However, *Ingram* and other carve-out schemes can still be relevant in some lifetime planning: see 43.42.

(2) In *Ingram*, a 20-year lease had been carved out. It would, however, have been more satisfactory to tailor the lease to the life of the taxpayer thereby avoiding the problems were he to live too long or to die too soon! What put advisers off carrying out the arrangement in this way (and as set out in the example above) was the risk that the retained lease, being for X's life, involved the creation of a settlement. As noted above, HMRC appear to have taken the view that no settlement would result because the lease was granted for full consideration. It is, however, difficult to see the basis for this approach. Even if X had given the property to his daughter on the understanding that she would grant him a lease-back (which the House of Lords accepted in *Ingram* was equally efficacious to circumvent the reservation of benefit rules) it is hard to accept that the lease so granted is in return for consideration furnished by X. In reality, what he is doing is making a conditional gift ("I will give you the freehold if you grant me a lease for the rest of my life") comprising the encumbered freehold interest.

Query whether the position would be different if X sold the encumbered freehold interest to his daughter and retained a lease for life or for a term of years (in the absence of any gift this transaction is infected by neither GWR nor POA problems and may therefore have some attractions). Can it now be said that X has furnished consideration for the lease? Obviously if he had sold the freehold for its full value (say £1 million) and subsequently procured a lease for life for which he had paid a market premium (say £400,000) so that after set off the daughter ended up paying £600,000 for the encumbered freehold full consideration has been paid. If this is correct then even if there is a single transaction essentially involving the sale of an encumbered freehold for £600,000, the same result should follow.[27]

Meaning of Trustee

The ordinary meaning is given to the term "a trustee", although it also includes any person in whom the settled property or its management is for the time being vested.[28] In cases where a lease for life is treated as a settlement the landlord is the trustee (and is the person liable for tax on the death of the lessee).

24.09

---

[27] Commercial sale and lease-back arrangements normally involve the sale of the freehold interest followed by a lease-back for which a full rent is payable. See 43.126.

[28] IHTA 1984 s.45. Presumably this is directed at foreign law entities such as foundations which may not have trustees.

24.10   As is discussed at 26.42 and following:

(1) reversionary interests (future interests) are generally excluded property in the hands of the beneficiary[29];

(2) a non-qualifying interest in possession is not generally an asset in the estate of the beneficiary[30];

(3) a settlement power, defined in IHTA 1984 s.47A as *"any power over, or exercisable (whether directly or indirectly) in relation to, settled property or a settlement"*, is not "property" for IHT purposes,[31] i.e. it is left out of account in arriving at a person's IHT estate under s.5. Further the purchase of a settlement power involves a transfer of value by the purchaser who is treated as getting nothing for his money.[32] The introduction of these provisions from April 17, 2002 was intended to prevent *Melville* schemes which had relied on the retention of a power to revoke the settlement preventing the settlor from making a substantial transfer of value on its creation. In the event, Mark II *Melville* schemes were quickly developed which relied on the retention of a reversionary interest in the settled property.[33]

II WHEN IS THERE A DISPOSITION CREATING A SETTLEMENT?

24.11   Difficulties have arisen in identifying, for CGT purposes, when property has been resettled (i.e. when a new settlement has been created out of an existing settlement).[34] Difficulties may also arise when it is necessary to determine whether the settlor has created one or more settlements.[35] Similar problems may arise for inheritance tax and the definition of "settlement" may not help to resolve these problems.[36] In *Hatton v IRC*[37] it was held in a blatant tax avoidance scheme that where two settlements were made by reference to each other or the first was made with a view to facilitating the making of the second settlement they constituted a single settlement made by a disposition effected by associated operations. Under the *Ramsay* principle, the creation of the two settlements constituted a preordained series of transactions and (in the case) the mother had made a single composite transaction and was the settlor.

---

[29] See 26.31.
[30] See Ch.25.
[31] See IHTA 1984 s.272.
[32] See IHTA 1984 s.55A.
[33] *Melville* schemes are considered at 26.45 and 31.53.
[34] See 12.21.
[35] See 9.39.
[36] See, for example, *Minden Trust (Cayman) Ltd v IRC* [1984] STC 434; affirmed [1985] STC 758, CA; and *Tax Bulletin*, Issue 27, February 1997, p.398. With the 2006 changes in the IHT taxation of settlements, because the majority of new settlements fall within the relevant property regime IHTA 1984 s.81(1) will generally treat the property involved in any resettlement as remaining comprised in the first settlement.
[37] [1992] STC 140.

Contrast *Rysaffe* where it was held that a number of pilot settlements were not made by reference to each other and were not associated.

Difficulties can also arise where one will sets up several trusts. Are they **24.12** separate settlements or merely separate sub-funds within one settlement? i.e. can one disposition set up two trusts?[38] The wording of s.43 suggests not where several dispositions are made in a single instrument but HMRC note that[39] *"where trusts are made at the same time by a single deed or will, they are likely to be separate but related trusts"*. The test applied seems to be the capital gains tax rather than any analysis of the wording in s.43.[40] So if the trusts established in the will exist independently of each other they are separate trusts even if the trustees are the same and there is a possibility of cross-accruers. Since the settlements will be "related settlements"[41] in a will it is unlikely to make much difference for inheritance tax purposes whether they are one trust or several. However for CGT and SDLT reasons it will be highly relevant: see 51.12.

EXAMPLE 24.4

(1) Each year S creates a discretionary trust of £3,000 (thereby utilising his annual IHT exemption) and his wife does likewise. Accordingly, at the end of five years there are 10 mini-discretionary trusts. As a matter of trust law, and assuming that each settlement is correctly documented and constituted, there is no reason why this series should be treated as one settlement. So far as the IHT legislation is concerned the settlements are not related settlements made on the same day[42]; the "associated operations" provisions would seem inapplicable[43]; and the principle in *WT Ramsay Ltd v IRC*[44] although of uncertain ambit, could only be applied with difficulty to a series of gifts. Each settlement should, of course, be fully documented.[45]

(2) On June 1, 2011, A sets up an interest in possession trust for his son for life and the trustees are given wide powers to transfer all or part of the trust fund into another settlement—whenever established—under which the son can benefit. On December 1, 2011 the trustees transfer the assets

---

[38] For a discussion of the position from the capital gains tax perspective, see Ch.9.

[39] See IHTM 42232.

[40] For the CGT position, see Ch.9. For SDLT see 51.12.

[41] For the meaning of "related settlements", see IHTA 1984 s.62.

[42] See IHTA 1984 s.62.

[43] See IHTA 1984 s.268, and see *Rysaffe Trustee Co (CI) Ltd v IRC* [2002] STC 872; affirmed [2003] EWCA Civ 356; [2003] STC 536, in which it was decided that for the purposes of the IHTA 1984 s.43 "disposition" had its ordinary meaning and was not extended to cover a disposition effected by associated operations. In general terms, therefore, provided that a trust lawyer would conclude that separate settlements had been established, albeit with identical property (in *Rysaffe*, private company shares), the IHT legislation must be applied on that basis.

[44] *WT Ramsay Ltd v IRC* [1982] AC 300 HL.

[45] It is common for separate discretionary trusts to be created of substantial life insurance policies. Such trusts will normally be on identical terms, with the same trustees, but established on consecutive days. Each trust will contain a separate item of property (a particular insurance policy). It is understood that HMRC had taken the view that such a series of settlements fell within IHTA 1984 s.268 (associated operations) and so could be treated as a single settlement. In the light of the *Rysaffe* case this argument is not thought to be tenable and the authors believe has been abandoned.

into a protective life interest trust that had been established for A's son in 2007. The IHT position is as follows:

   (i) by creating the settlement on June 1, 2011 A has made a chargeable transfer for IHT purposes. The settlement is subject to the relevant property regime;

  (ii) the transfer of assets on December 1, is ignored for IHT purposes and they are treated as remaining comprised in the original settlement.[46] It will therefore be necessary for the trustees to keep the transferred assets separate from the existing assets in the transferee trust for the purposes of completing the appropriate IHT returns.[47]

It may be important to know whether property is comprised in one settlement or two in order to judge whether it is subject to a qualifying interest in possession.

EXAMPLE 24.5

A is entitled to a pre-March 2006 life interest in a settlement, remainder on discretionary trusts for his sister's children. A wants to make provision for his own children. There are no powers for the trustees or A to do this. Accordingly on September 5, 2008 A assigns his life interest on interest in possession trusts for his two children B and C. They therefore take an interest *pur autre vie*. Is the life interest comprised in a new settlement (in which case it did not qualify as a transitional serial interest)[48] or should this be regarded as one compound settlement comprising settled property with two settlors for different purposes? The life tenant A is deemed by virtue of IHTA 1984 s.49(1) to have settled the capital for inheritance tax purposes by virtue of his assignment. The question is discussed further in Ch.27 and see also HMRC correspondence at A2.259 where it is accepted that where a beneficiary assigns a qualifying interest in possession to another person the assignee's interest can qualify as a transitional serial interest because the assignee's interest will remain within the original settlement.

The impact of IHTA 1984 s.81[49]

24.13   For the purpose of the relevant property charge[50] when property ceases to be comprised in one settlement by becoming comprised in a separate settlement it is to be treated as remaining comprised in the first settlement.[51]

---

[46] IHTA 1984 s.81(1): see 24.13.
[47] For CGT purposes the transfer will be a disposal and may result in charge under TCGA 1992 s.71 and note that hold-over relief will only be available if the assets are business assets within TCGA 1992 s.165: see 18.55.
[48] For the meaning of a transitional serial interest, see Ch.27.
[49] See also 41.11.
[50] i.e. IHTA 1984 Pt III, Ch.III.
[51] The section does not apply if before becoming comprised in the second settlement a person becomes beneficially entitled to the property.

EXAMPLE 24.6

(1) Tom puts property into a life interest trust (Trust 1) for his children in 2011 but the trustees have power to transfer all or any part of the trust fund into a qualifying settlement (defined as any settlement in which the children can benefit). In 2013 the trustees exercise this power to transfer the entire trust fund into a family discretionary trust (Trust 2) which Tom had set up in 2000.

The property is treated—for IHT purposes—as remaining comprised in the 2011 settlement. Hence, the first 10-year charge will be in 2021, etc. Note that there is no such rule for other taxes so that the transfer may give rise to a CGT charge[52] whilst as a matter of trust law the assets will normally merge with whatever property is already in the 2000 settlement.

(2) In 2011 X settles funds on trust for A remainder to B absolutely if B attains 35. B is 35 next year and before becoming absolutely entitled he assigns his contingent remainder interest to a new discretionary trust for his issue. No IHT entry charge arises on the settlement by B of his remainder interest. In 2012 A's interest ends and the settled property moves into Trust 2. It would appear that B is the settlor of Trust 2. For the purposes of calculating future 10-year anniversary charges and exit charges of Trust 2 does this run from 2011 or 2012 and is it based on A or B's cumulative total? There are two possible answers. First, s.81 applies with the result that it is based on A's cumulative total and calculated from 2011. However, for ROB and all other IHT (and tax purposes generally) the settlor of Trust 2 is B not A. The second answer is that s.81 does not apply because of the exclusion which applies when *"any person becomes beneficially entitled to the property (and not merely to an interest in possession in the property)"*. The first settlement ends because B satisfied the contingency of attaining age 35. Of course, the difficulty with this answer is that at the relevant time B no longer enjoyed his interest and at that time no person did become absolutely beneficially entitled to the property. Moreover, if s.81 is not intended to apply it is difficult to make sense of the words in s.81(3) which expressly exclude assignments of reversionary interests made before December 10, 1981.

Section 81 only applies for the limited purposes of the relevant property **24.14** regime. As Example 24.5 illustrates, if there is a qualifying interest in possession in settled property then it will still be necessary to know whether property has been resettled. Moreover it appears that s.81 does not apply in determining whether the settlor is liable to inheritance tax under IHTA 1984 s.201(1)(d). Similarly, in Example 24.6(1) the trustees of Trust 1 do not remain liable for the 10-year charge that arises on the settled property in Trust 2. In Example 24.6(1), if the majority of the trustees of Trust 2 are non-resident then the

---

[52] See Chs 18 and 22. Hold-over relief will only be available if the property is a business asset within TCGA 1992 s.165. Hold-over relief is not available under s.260 because there is no inheritance tax payable—the property is treated as remaining in the first settlement for inheritance tax purposes.

transferred property is comprised in a non-resident trust for inheritance tax purposes. Do not look at the residence of the trustees of Trust 1.

24.15   A side effect of the 2006 changes has been a growing use of pilot trusts: viz the creation of a number of separate discretionary settlements inter vivos on different days to which the settlor will subsequently add substantial property, for instance by will after his death. Whilst it is important to show that a number of separate settlements have been established, it would seem that if all the settled property were subsequently to be merged into a single settlement the effect of s.81 is to preserve the existence of the individual settlements for IHT charging purposes. Obviously if it is likely that assets may be transferred to a new trust it is desirable for a trust deed to contain an express power to resettle.[53]

The impact of IHTA 1984 s.80

24.16   Before March 22, 2006, s.80 provided that:

(i)   if a settlement was established which conferred an immediate interest in possession on either the settlor or his spouse; then

(ii) for the purposes of the relevant property regime[54] it was not to be treated as comprised in a settlement at that time;

(iii) instead when the property was no longer held on trusts under which either of those persons was entitled to an interest in possession, the property was then to be treated as comprised in a separate settlement made by the settlor or spouse (as the case may be) who last ceased to be beneficially entitled to an interest in possession in it;

(iv) reference to spouse included references to the settlor's widow or widower and registered civil partner;

(v)   although the commencement of the relevant property settlement was accordingly deferred, 10-year anniversary charges ran from the date when the settlement was initially created with the settlor/spouse interest in possession.[55]

EXAMPLE 24.7

X, who died on March 20, 2006 provided in his will:

(a) for a nil rate band discretionary trust; and

(b) for the residue to be held on an interest in possession trust for his wife with remainder on a discretionary trust for his issue.[56]

---

[53] See Ch.42 (pilot trusts) and A1.1.
[54] i.e. IHTA 1984 Pt III, Ch.III.
[55] IHTA 1984 s.61(2).
[56] This was a relatively standard family will of the time since it used up X's nil rate band and the residue (held on a qualifying interest in possession trust) was spouse exempt.

For IHT purposes:

(a) by virtue of s.80, for the purposes of the relevant property regime, the trust of residue is treated as arising on the termination of the spouse's life interest. Note, however, that the anniversary charges will be dated by reference to March 20, 2006 when the trust was set up on X's death;

(b) accordingly, the trust of residue is not a "related settlement"[57] to be taken into account in taxing the nil rate band discretionary trust since (1) the settlor is not the same and nor (2) were the settlements created on the same day.

With the 2006 changes in the IHT treatment of settlements, s.80 was amended (from March 22, 2006) so that it will now only apply to new settlements which confer a "postponing interest" on either the settlor or his spouse.[58] A "postponing interest" is defined as either an IPDI[59] or disabled person's interest.[60] In Example 24.7 therefore, the IHT consequences are unchanged since the trust of residue is an IPDI.[61] If the interest in possession ends on the death of the surviving spouse but the trust continues (as in the Example) and she settles her free estate by trusts set up in her will then those trusts will be related to the interest in possession settlement. She could of course, avoid this by leaving her free estate in her will to pilot trusts set up by her during her lifetime.[62] **24.17**

III WHO IS THE SETTLOR?

The question of who is the settlor of a settlement is important for the following reasons: **24.18**

(a) liability for inheritance tax;

(b) reservation of benefit;

(c) whether the settled property is excluded property;

(d) calculating the 10-year and exit charges in the case of a relevant property settlement.

In the majority of cases it is not difficult to identify the settlor because there is usually one settlor who has created a settlement by a "disposition" of property (which may include a series of associated operations).[63]

IHTA 1984 s.44(2) states:

> "*Where more than one person is a settlor in relation to a settlement and the circumstances so require, this Part of this Act (except Section 48(4)*

---

[57] For the definition of a "related settlement" see IHTA 1984 s.62.
[58] IHTA 1984, s.80(4)(a) inserted by FA 2006 Sch.20 para.23.
[59] "Immediate post-death interest": See Ch.28.
[60] IHTA 1984 s.80(4)(b) inserted by FA 2006 Sch.20 para.23. For a disabled person's interest, see IHTA 1984 s.89B and 28.
[61] For the offshore implications of s.80, see Ch.31.
[62] See Ch.41.
[63] IHTA 1984 s.272. See *Hatton v IRC* [1992] STC 140 and fn.20 above.

to (6)) shall have effect in relation to it as if the settled property were comprised in separate settlements".

Thomas v IRC[64] indicates that this provision normally only applies where an identifiable capital fund has been provided by each settlor. The fund is then treated as two separate settlements in the case of relevant property trusts where both the incidence of the periodic charge and the amount of inheritance tax chargeable may be affected. This can be relevant where, for example, husband and wife transfer a jointly owned property into a discretionary trust. For inheritance tax purposes this involves two separate settlements and each trust has the benefit of the relevant settlor's unused nil rate band.

24.19   "Settlor" is defined (in terms similar to the income tax and CGT definition) as follows[65]:

"In this Act 'settlor', in relation to a settlement, includes any person by whom the settlement was made directly or indirectly, and . . . includes any person who has provided funds directly or indirectly for the purpose of or in connection with the settlement or has made with any other person a reciprocal arrangement for that other person to make the settlement."[66]

In *Fitzwilliam v IRC*[67] HMRC argued that where trustees of a will trust exercised their power of appointment to confer a remainder interest on the daughter and the daughter settled that interest in a new trust shortly thereafter, the real settlor of the settlement was the deceased. Although it was accepted that the deceased was the settlor for trusts purposes (because the appointment by the trustees was read-back under his will) the House of Lords held that he was not the settlor for inheritance tax purposes. The deceased had not provided property for the purposes of or in connection with the settlement made by the daughter because:

"the words 'for the purpose of or in connection with' connote that there must at least be a conscious association of the provider of the funds with the settlement in question. It is clearly not sufficient that the settled funds

---

[64]   *Thomas v IRC* [1981] STC 382. See also 12.16 and 12.19.

[65]   IHTA 1984 s.44(1).

[66]   In *Hatton v IRC* [1992] STC 140 Chadwick J. considered the impact of the associated operations provisions of IHTA 1984 s.268 on the question of multiple settlors and settlements. He concluded in that case that the first settlement was made with a view to enabling or facilitating the making of the second (within the meaning of the IHTA 1984 s.268(1)(b)). Accordingly, there was a disposition by associated operations which was treated as a single disposition of property into a composite settlement. Given the nature of the property settled by these two settlors, the judge was then forced to conclude that each settlor had made the entirety of the composite settlement. This approach (treating each settlor as having established one separate settlement of the entirety of the settled property) would, the judge suggested, also apply to reciprocal settlements. In a simple case A would settle property on X for a limited interest in possession remainder to A and as a quid pro quo B would settle property on Y for an initial interest in possession remainder to B. In both cases the reverter to settlor provisions would at first sight apply on the termination of X and Y's respective interests. Once it is accepted, however, that A is also a settlor of B's trust and *vice versa* (see IHTA 1984, s.44(1)) that analysis does not hold good. Instead, because B is a settlor of "A's settlement" on the termination of X's limited interest an inheritance tax charge may arise. The judge viewed the situation as one in which A and B were settlors of two separate settlements rather than accepting the view that B should be seen as "a dominant settlor" of A's trust.

[67]   [1993] STC 502.

should historically have been derived from the provider of them. If it were otherwise, anyone who gave funds unconditionally to another which that other later settled would fall to be treated as the settlor .. of the funds. It is clear that in the present situation there cannot possibly have been any conscious association of Earl Fitzwilliam with Lady Hastings' settlement."

Bear in mind, however, that IHTA 1984 s.81 provides that for the purposes of the relevant property charging regime, when property ceases to be comprised in one settlement and becomes comprised in another (without in the interim any person becoming absolutely entitled to the property) then it is treated as remaining comprised in the original (the transferor) settlement. This means that the settlor of the original settlement remains the settlor (for the purpose of the relevant property charge) of the property albeit that it is comprised in a separate settlement that might have been made by a different settlor. **24.20**

EXAMPLE 24.8

In 2007 Andrew set up a trust for son Luke for life remainder to his daughter Charlotte absolutely. Luke has a non-qualifying IIP. Five years later Charlotte assigns her remainder interest (which is excluded property) into a new settlement ("Trust 2") for her own children with power to add beneficiaries apart from herself. Charlotte does not make a transfer of value since the reversionary interest is excluded property. Andrew is not the settlor of Trust 2. Accordingly, there is no reservation of benefit problem even though Andrew could be added as a beneficiary (provided he is not actually added nor benefits after the interest falls in). However, Charlotte as the settlor of Trust 2 should be excluded from Trust 2 in order to avoid a reservation of benefit when the remainder interest falls in on the death of Luke. Trust 2 is a relevant property trust but there are no charges while it only holds the remainder interest. After Luke's death, 10-year charges can arise but the tax is calculated by reference to Andrew's cumulative total not Charlotte's.[68]

Companies as settlors

What is the position when a close company settles property into trust?[69] A transfer of value by a close company is apportioned to the participators of **24.21**

---

[68] Note that if Luke had a qualifying IIP and his life interest was ended during his lifetime it would be necessary to exclude him from Trust 2 in order to avoid a GWR under FA 1986 s.102ZA.

[69] Unlike the capital gains tax and income tax definitions of settlement, no bounty is required for a settlement to arise for inheritance tax purposes and therefore a commercial settlement set up by a company to incentivise workers is a settlement for inheritance tax purposes even though it is not a settlement for income tax or capital gains tax purposes. This is why TCGA 1992 ss.86 and 87 and the settlement income tax provisions do not generally apply to EBTs: see Ch.49.

that company. Does this mean that the participators are also the settlors for IHT purposes or is the company the settlor?

Charge on creation of settlement

24.22   The IHT legislation makes provision for a charge to arise when any close company wherever it is incorporated gifts property to a trust. The company's transfer of value is apportioned amongst its participators.[70] However, no apportionment is made to participators if s.94(2)(b) applies. This states that in relation to persons not UK domiciled or deemed domiciled for inheritance tax purposes:

> "*if any amount which otherwise be apportioned to an individual who is domiciled outside the UK is attributable to the value of any property outside the UK that amount shall not be apportioned.*"

Hence, if a close company (wherever incorporated) makes a transfer of value of foreign situated property no amount is apportioned to any foreign domiciled participator.

24.23   The above illustrates that if company X is a foreign incorporated company that would be close if UK resident but the participators are UK domiciliaries, the foreign status of the company will not in itself prevent a transfer of value being apportioned and charged on those individuals even though the foreign company settles the funds and may be the settlor for IHT purposes. This is because a transfer of value by a foreign incorporated close company cannot be excluded property within s.3(2) because s.6 provides that for property to be excluded the person beneficially entitled to it must be an individual foreign domiciliary and a body corporate is not an individual. Hence, property to which the company is beneficially entitled cannot be excluded property.[71]

10-year anniversary and exit charges

24.24   When a foreign incorporated close company controlled by UK domiciled participators settles foreign assets into trust, can the trust be an excluded property settlement and thereby not subject to 10-year and exit charges? In order to be excluded property it is necessary that at the date when the property was settled the conditions in IHTA 1984 s.48(3) were satisfied: namely that the settlor was not domiciled in the UK and the property comprised in the settlement at any relevant date (e.g. a 10-year anniversary) is situated outside the UK. While the capital gains tax legislation specifically deems the participator to be the settlor there is no similar provision in the inheritance tax legislation[72]. This is presumably because in that legislation there is a separate code to apportion transfers of value to the individuals. But there is no further provision that the

---

[70] IHTA 1984 s.94.
[71] See Ch.31.
[72] TCGA 1992 Sch.5 para.8(4) which makes express provision to treat shareholders and other participators as settlors providing property where a close company is the settlor.

participators are deemed to be the settlors of the trust when a close company funds a settlement.

Section 44 refers not only to the person who makes the settlement but also **24.25** to those who provide property directly or indirectly. So the person named as the settlor in the trust document is not necessarily the only settlor for tax purposes. However, provided no shareholder or employee was providing services at an under-value to the company or diverted future rights to the company it is not possible to say that the individual shareholders could be treated as settlors for IHT purposes. *IRC v Mills*[73] emphasises that it is not the provision of services as such but of funds which results in someone being a settler, i.e. where someone is not paid properly for their services or agrees that bonuses should be paid to a trust. On that basis it would be possible for a foreign incorporated company to settle foreign assets (e.g. cash) into a trust that is excluded in the future from 10-year and exit charges even if the participators are UK domiciled. An entry charge could still arise on the participators but the settled property is excluded. See the issues raised by corporate settlors in the context of EBTs in Ch.48.

IV ADDITIONS BY THE SETTLOR INCLUDING LOANS TO TRUSTS AND THE IMPLICATIONS OF BORROWING BY INTEREST IN POSSESSION TRUSTS[74]

Where there is one settlor who adds property to his settlement is this one set- **24.26** tlement or two? The question is significant in relation to:

(i) discretionary trusts (especially with regard to timing and rate of the periodic and exit charges);

(ii) where excluded property is comprised in a settlement[75]; and

(iii) when a settlor adds property to a pre-March 22, 2006 settlement in which there existed on that date an interest in possession or which was A-M in form.

As a matter of trust law, there is generally a single settlement where a single fund is held and managed by trustees for one set of beneficiaries, so that such additions do not lead to the creation of separate settlements. In general, if it would be advantageous to have two settlements it is desirable that a separate settlement deed should be drawn up.

Approach of HMRC

The Budget Note BN25 issued by HMRC on March 22, 2006 stated that: **24.27**

---

[73] 49 TC 367 at 408.
[74] An addition by any other person will generally be treated for IHT purposes as creating a separate settlement: see 24.11.
[75] See 31.32 for a discussion of additions in the context of excluded property trusts.

> "*the new rules will apply . . . to new trusts, additions of new assets to existing trusts and to . . . other IHT relevant events in relation to existing trusts.*"

In effect, therefore, HMRC treat the addition as creating a separate settlement which is in line with the views previously expressed in the context of excluded property trusts.[76] The view is thought to be based on the wording of s.43(2) which defines a settlement as "*any disposition or dispositions of property . . .*"[77] Presumably, the HMRC view is that each disposition of property represents a separate settlement. However, the contrary could be argued from s.43, i.e. that several dispositions can create a single settlement.

Whilst it is the case that a settlement only arises when property is transferred to trustees it would be surprising to a property lawyer to be told that every time such a transfer is made a separate settlement is created. On such an analysis establishing a trust in pilot form (e.g. with a small sum of money) and then adding substantial assets subsequently would result in two separate settlements.

It is difficult to point to a specific provision in the IHT legislation which contradicts general trust law and, in particular, s.67 which deals with additions to relevant property settlements proceeds on the assumption that those additions are to be taxed as part of the settlement to which they were added.[78] If they were to be taxed as a separate settlement, there would have been no need for the section! Further, treating additions as comprised in a separate settlement was not a point taken by HMRC in the *Rysaffe* litigation.[79] HMRC point to ss.60 and 67 as suggestive that additions to interest in possession trusts are somehow different from additions to relevant property settlements taxed under Ch.III because the relevant property regime specifically deals with additions and clearly envisages one settled fund, while Ch.II dealing with interest in possession trusts contains no such provisions.[80] However, it is difficult to see any justification for the HMRC view that an addition to an existing settlement where property becomes comprised in the settlement is a new settlement "made" at that time.[81] There is no provision in Ch.II that deems a new settlement to arise. It is thought that FA 2006 should have referred to property "becoming comprised in a settlement" after March 21, 2006 if additions to a pre-March 22, 2006 interest in possession trust were to be taxed on the basis that they created a new settlement.

---

[76] See also A2.332.

[77] Consider also IHTA 1984, s.267(3)(a) which has a different tax regime depending on when settled property "becomes comprised" in the settlement. However these words suggest that in the absence of any express provision property is not taxed differently depending on when it "becomes comprised" in the settlement.

[78] Other provisions in Ch.III, Pt III are to the same effect: for instance IHTA 1984 s.81 is needed only because the assumption is that otherwise the added property would be comprised in the transferee settlement. It would be bizarre if a different meaning was to be attributed to settlement for the purposes of Pt III and, of course, the s.43 definition is said to be for the purpose of "the Act".

[79] And see fn.43 above.

[80] Section 60 provides "*in this Chapter references to the commencement of a settlement are references to the time when property first becomes comprised in it*".

[81] It seems to conflict with s.46A (contracts of life insurance) which suggests that property added (e.g. by way of premium payments) is not a separate trust but that the interest in possession after the addition is a different interest in possession.

Comments and Conclusions

In the authors' view therefore the statement in BN 25 (and RI 166) is either **24.28** wrong or at least inaccurate. Clearly though it is the intention of BN 25 that additions of property to an existing interest in possession trust should be taxed on the basis that they involve the creation of a new relevant property settlement. As discussed above, it is difficult to accept that this result follows on the basis that a separate settlement has been created. An alternative and perhaps better argument for the HMRC view would be to consider the definition of an interest in possession in s.49(1): specifically that section does not apply to an interest in possession "in settled property" to which a person becomes beneficially entitled after March 21, 2006 (with only relatively few exceptions): see s.49(1A). Although the Budget Notice does not so argue, it might be said that the interest in possession only arose in the new property (i.e. in that part of the settled property) when it was added. The taxpayer would appear to have difficulty in arguing successfully that his interest in possession in "settled property" was an interest in possession which arose before March 22, 2006 in respect of property added to the trust after March 21, 2006. Hence, even if he can show an addition does not create a new trust, this would not help him if the interest in possession in the settled property was treated as arising after March 21.

The legislation on transitional serial interests ("TSIs") and existing A-M trusts deals specifically with the added property problem. A TSI can only be created in property then (i.e. immediately before March 22, 2006) comprised in the statement (see s.49C(2)(b)).[82] In the case of A-M trusts the transitional rules apply to the settled property immediately before March 22, 2006 (see s.71(1A)(a)). No advantage could therefore be gained from adding to an A-M trust.

Adding value to an existing settlement

Different considerations arise where value rather than property is added to a **24.29** settlement by the settlor. This can arise where, for example, a settlor forgives a debt owed to him by the trustees improves a house owned by the trustees or gives property to a company owned by the trustees. In this case the authors consider that a new settlement is not created when value is added. Consider especially the following:

(1) adding value does not result in any change in the property comprised in the settlement. For instance, if a settlement owns all the shares in a company, a gift of property to that company will not result in the addition of any property to the settlement;

(2) in the case of IIP and A-M trusts, there will be no change in the property that had been subject to those trusts immediately before March 22,

---

[82] It therefore follows that even if the addition of property to an existing IIP trust did not involve the creation of a new settlement (and so was a PET) it will not be possible for a subsequent IIP in that property to qualify as a TSI.

2006, and so it is not thought that the various transitional provisions considered above will apply. Accordingly adding value to a pre-March 2006 IIP settlement will not involve the creation of a separate settlement. As a result, where the settlor adds value to a qualifying IIP settlement he will make a PET given that the effect of the addition is to increase the estate of a beneficiary[83];

(3) is the position the same if value is added by a person other than the settlor? Whilst that person might conceivably fall within the definition of a settlor in IHTA 1984 s.44[84] as the person indirectly providing funds for the purpose of or in connection with the settlement, it is difficult to see that the addition of value creates a separate settlement since the s.43 definition of settlement requires there to be a disposition of property whereby the property becomes held on trust. In this case the same property is already held on trust. Assume, for instance, that a life tenant pays for improvements to a dwelling house owned by the trust which he occupies. Any attempt to say that he has created a new settlement as a result of the value added (quite apart from the difficulties thrown up by the s.43 definition) also encounters obvious practical difficulties: in particular, what property is comprised in this new settlement? The money that he expended on the improvements has disappeared and will (to some extent) be reflected in the enhanced value of the property comprised in the existing settlement. In a case where the beneficiary discharges administration fees of a settlement, it is not even possible to point to property in the settlement benefiting from an enhanced value.

Approach of HMRC

24.30   In their original response to the STEP/CIOT questions on Sch.20,[85] HMRC:

(1) did not draw any distinction between additions of property and of value nor according to whether the addition was made by the settlor or a third party;

(2) accept that if cash is given to trustees and spent (for instance, on administrative expenses), although a new settlement resulted from the value added, it ceased to exist at the moment when the money was spent (i.e. it had at best an ephemeral life!);

(3) however, if the money was spent on improvements to trust property, HMRC suggested that it was necessary to determine what proportion of the value of that settled property was represented by the improvements and that value would be comprised in a separate settlement.

In July 2008, however, they announced that they were giving further thought to their previously expressed views on additions and that further guidance

---

[83] IHTA 1984 s.3A(1A)(c)(i) and (2)(b). It is thought that subs.(2)(b) is concerned with additions of value given that subs.(2)(a) is concerned with the addition of property.
[84] See 24.18.
[85] See A2.332.

would be produced in due course. This is not surprising! The exercise envisaged in their original answer has a surreal quality but lacks much technical analysis of tax legislation! Over three years later further guidance has not, however, been issued!

Loans to trusts

What is the position where a qualifying pre-March 2006 IIP trust borrows **24.31** funds (e.g. from the settlor), to improve the settled property or on the security of an existing property to acquire properties? Does it matter that such loans are interest-free and repayable on demand? There are two separate issues: has property been added to the settlement and is each property that is purchased with the borrowings derived from or does it represent settled property in which a qualifying interest in possession subsisted prior to March 2006? Alternatively is the new property purchased with the loans held on relevant property trusts?

The making of an interest-free loan repayable on demand is not a transfer **24.32** of value provided that the value of the loan is equal to the amount of the debt. HMRC apparently consider that it involves a gift for reservation of benefit purposes because there is an intention to confer bounty. The argument is that the property disposed of is the interest foregone albeit no benefit is retained by the settlor. That would suggest HMRC may consider that the interest-free element of the loan *is* added property. If that view is correct then the increased value represented by the interest foregone is held on non-qualifying interest in possession trusts. The loan monies themselves are not added property. However, the authors consider it difficult to argue that something that has never existed and never been owed or paid (namely the interest) constitutes a gift *or in itself involves an addition to the settled property*. It may be a benefit to the trustees or life tenant but that is a different matter. The position would, of course, be different if the loan was interest-bearing and then the settlor forgave the interest.[86] In any event HMRC may not need to argue that an interest-free loan involves a gift. FA 1986 Sch.20 para.5(4)(b) specifically deems the settled property derived from the loan to be gifted property for GWR purposes if the lender also gives property to the trust.[87]

Are funds borrowed by qualifying interest in possession trusts held on relevant property trusts?

The second issue is when the trust is a qualifying IIP whether the loan monies **24.33** are themselves held on qualifying IIP trusts. One must first identify the settled

---

[86] For POAT purposes HMRC accept that an interest-free loan does not satisfy the contribution condition because there is no "provision" of consideration. See HMRC guidance on POAT and question 32 at A2.186. On the other hand a loan to a trust is regarded as a settlement for income tax purposes by the lender: see Ch.7.
[87] See Chs 32 and 33. The provision can easily be avoided by ensuring that the lender does not make a gift to the trust. His spouse could instead set up the trust with a nominal sum.

property in which the qualifying interest in possession subsisted at March 22, 2006. So if, after March 22, 2006, X lends the trustees of the IIP trust £1 million there is no change in the value of the settled property at that stage. However, it is not possible to say that the cash that was lent was held on qualifying interest in possession trusts as at March 2006. It did not exist at that time! On that basis there are two separate funds and the property represented by the cash is relevant property (initially worth nil but increasing as the property values increase). If, therefore, the trust holds one property on qualifying IIP trusts and borrows to acquire a second property the latter becomes held on relevant property trusts (subject to a debt), there is no inheritance tax charge on the life tenant's death on that second property but 10-year charges may arise on the net equity.

24.34   The authors, however, feel that these arguments and conclusions are far removed from a common sense approach to the position. Can it really be the case that every time a pre-March 2006 IIP settlement borrows money the result is to create a relevant property trust? A more sensible conclusion would be that if the trustees borrow on the security of the existing property then they are simply exercising investment powers and "turning to account" the existing settled property, particularly if they borrow on commercial terms. So the borrowed funds have grown out of the existing settled funds and represent the same.[88]

V CLASSIFICATION OF SETTLEMENTS

24.35   Settlements for IHT purposes can be divided into three categories[89]:

(i) Category A: a qualifying interest in possession settlement. For example, where the property is held for a tenant for life under a pre-March 2006 trust who, by virtue of his interest, is entitled to the income and therefore has "an interest in possession". That beneficiary is treated as owning the underlying capital for inheritance tax purposes.

(ii) Category B: a relevant property settlement; for example a trust where trustees are given a discretion over the distribution of the income or the settlement (being post-March 21, 2006) contains an interest in possession which is not qualifying. In the case of a discretionary trust, beneficiaries have the right to be considered by the trustees when the latter exercise their discretions; the right to ensure that the fund is properly administered, and the right (even if it is a discretionary trust)[90] to

---

[88] See *West v Trennery* [2005] 1 All ER 827. The case of *Barbe Green* (see Ch.32) might suggest that no new IIP arises. However, FA 1986 Sch.20 para.5 (in the context of reservation of benefit) provides that settled property derived from or represented by a loan is treated as comprised in the original gift by the settlor for reservation of benefit purposes. This is the case whether the loan is on commercial terms or not. This is unhelpful because it suggests that a loan from the settlor is not otherwise comprised in the original gifted property.

[89] Ignoring disabled trusts which are subject to the Category A tax regime and are therefore deemed to be qualifying interest in possession trusts even in cases where a beneficiary is given no entitlement to income.

[90] See *Re Smith* [1928] Ch 915.

join with all the other beneficiaries to bring the settlement to an end.[91] However, they have no entitlement to income or capital. In the case of a non-qualifying interest in possession the beneficiary has a right to receive income but not capital. In Category B the trust is taxed as a separate entity and is subject to 10-year charges, exit charges etc. Whether the relevant beneficiaries die or are excluded is generally irrelevant to the inheritance tax position.[92]

(iii) Category C: these comprise special or privileged trusts. They are not subject to the Category A or B regimes and may be either discretionary or give entitlement to income.[93] Bereaved minor and 18–25 trusts fall into this category.

To place a particular trust into its correct category is important for two reasons. First, because the inheritance tax treatment of each category is totally different both in respect of the occasions on which tax is charged and the tax rates. Secondly, a change from one category to another normally gives rise to an inheritance tax charge. For example, if a qualifying interest in possession ceases, whereupon the trust property becomes held on discretionary trusts, the settlement moves from Category A to Category B, and a chargeable occasion (the ending of a life interest) has occurred.[94] A 20 per cent entry charge may arise. If property moves from Category B to Category A[95] then there is an exit charge of six per cent maximum. Property cannot generally move from Category B to Category C[96] although property could move from Category A to Category C: for instance, an IPDI trust could end and the settled property then be held on a BMT or s.71D trust.

The 2006 changes have reduced the significance of this classification because virtually all new (i.e. post-March 21, 2006) settlements fall into Category B (i.e. they are subject to the relevant property regime). However, it is still possible to create a qualifying interest in possession trust on death (an IPDI) whilst trusts for a disabled person—whether inter vivos or on death—can fall into Category A.[97] The fact that two trusts which give entitlement to income may be taxed completely differently adds to the confusion: in the pre-March 2006 days all trusts which gave entitlement to income were taxed in the same way. Under the new regime a trust that looks as if it is an IPDI might in fact be a bereaved minor trust. Similarly what looks like a s.71D trust may turn out to be an IPDI.[98] And, of course, knowing what is meant by a qualifying interest in possession is also important in the context of existing settlements.

24.36

---

[91] Cf. the position on foreign entities, see Ch.2.

[92] Unless reservation of benefit is in point or the death of a beneficiary causes the settlement to end, thereby resulting in an IHT exit charge: see Ch.33.

[93] Compare the old accumulation and maintenance trust which ceased to qualify if a beneficiary became entitled to income. So it was a discretionary trust, albeit with favourable tax treatment. In the case of s.71D or bereaved minor trusts it does not matter whether the beneficiary has an entitlement to income or not. It is the capital conditions that determine whether such trusts qualify for favoured status.

[94] This event has never been a potentially exempt transfer: see the limitation in IHTA 1984 s.3A(1)(c) as inserted by FA 1986 s.101, Sch.19 para.1.

[95] Only possible now if the Category A trust is a disabled trust.

[96] Although note the "reading-back" effect of IHTA 1984 s.144: see Ch.39.

[97] Note though that a "deemed" qualifying interest in possession could arise even if the trust was discretionary: see ss.89 and 89A.

[98] See 38.17, Example 35.5 and 35.29.

Meaning of an "interest in possession"

24.37 Normally trusts can easily be slotted into their correct category. Trusts falling within Category C are carefully defined so that any trust not specifically falling into one of those special cases must fall into Category B.[99] Problems are principally caused by the borderline between Categories A and B where the division is drawn according to whether the settlement has an interest in possession or not. In the majority of cases no problems will arise: at one extreme stands the life interest settlement; at the other the discretionary trust. What, however, of a settlement which provides for the income to be paid to A, unless the trustees decide to pay it to B, or to accumulate it; or where the trust property is enjoyed in specie by one beneficiary as a result of the exercise of a discretion (for example, a beneficiary living in a dwelling house which is comprised in the assets of a discretionary trust)? To resolve these difficulties, the phrase an "interest in possession" needs definition. The legislation does not assist; instead, its meaning must be gleaned from an HMRC press release[100] and the speeches of the House of Lords in *Pearson v IRC*[101] which largely endorsed the statements in that press release.

The view of HMRC

24.38 According to HMRC[102]:

"... *an interest in settled property exists where the person having the interest has the immediate entitlement (subject to any prior claim by the trustees for expenses or other outgoings properly payable out of income) to any income produced by that property as the income arises; but ... a discretion or power, in whatever form, which can be exercised after income arises so as to withhold it from that person negatives the existence of an interest in possession. For this purpose a power to accumulate income is regarded as a power to withhold it, unless any accumulation must be held solely for the person having the interest or his personal representatives.*

On the other hand the existence of a mere power of revocation or appointment, the exercise of which would determine the interest wholly or in part (but which, so long as it remains unexercised, does not affect the beneficiary's immediate entitlement to income) does not ... prevent the interest from being an interest in possession."

The first paragraph is concerned with the existence of discretions or powers which might affect the destination of the income after it has arisen and which

---

[99] Although note that a will trust "for my children at 25" giving them entitlement to income would be an IPDI Category A trust if the children were or became entitled to income within two years of death: see Ch.39.

[100] i.e. HMRC Press Release of February 12, 1976.

[101] *Pearson v IRC* [1981] AC 753; [1980] 2 All ER 479 HL. The term "interest in possession" is used in TLATA 1996 and in the CGT legislation where it is assumed that it will bear the inheritance tax meaning.

[102] See HMRC CG36321.

prevent the existence of any interest in possession (for example a provision enabling the trustees to accumulate income or to divert it for the benefit of other beneficiaries). The second paragraph concerns overriding powers which, if exercised, would terminate the entire interest of the beneficiary, but which do not prevent the existence of an interest in possession (for example the statutory power of advancement or a power of appointment). Provisions dealing with the payment of administrative expenses may be problematic! It has always been accepted that expenses charged on the income can be ignored in deciding whether there is an interest in possession so long as such payments were for "outgoings properly payable out of income". However, the presence of a clause in the settlement providing for expenses of a *capital* nature to be so charged was originally considered by HMRC to be fatal to the existence of any interest in possession. This was held to be wrong in *Pearson v IRC* where a clause permitting the trustees to apply income in payment of administrative expenses of a capital nature did not preclude a beneficiary from having an interest in possession. HMRC now accept this.[103]

Pearson v IRC[104]

Both capital and income of the trust fund were held for the settlor's three adult **24.39** daughters in equal shares subject to three overriding trustee powers:

(i) to appoint capital and income amongst the daughters, their spouses and issue;

(ii) to accumulate so much of the income as they should think fit; and

(iii) to apply any income towards the payment or discharge of any taxes, costs or other outgoings which would otherwise be payable out of capital.

The trustees had regularly exercised their powers to accumulate the income. What caused the disputed tax assessment was the irrevocable appointment of some £16,000 from the fund to one of the daughters. There was no doubt that, after the appointment, she enjoyed an interest in possession in the appointed sum; but did she already have an interest in possession in the fund? If so, no inheritance tax would be chargeable on the appointment[105]; if not, there would be a charge because the appointed sums had passed from a "no interest in possession" to an "interest in possession" settlement (Category B to Category A).

HMRC argued that the existence of the overriding power to accumulate and the provision enabling all expenses to be charged to income deprived the settlement of any interest in possession. It was common ground that whether such powers had been exercised or not was irrelevant in deciding the case. The overriding power of appointment over capital and income was not seen as endangering the existence of any interest in possession (see the second paragraph of the Press Release).

[103] See ICAEW Guidance Note December 14, 1992: see Ch.6.
[104] *Pearson v IRC* [1981] AC 753; [1980] 2 All ER 479 HL.
[105] As to the IHT treatment of advancements to a life tenant or absolute entitlement on the satisfaction of a contingency, see 26.28.

For a bare majority in the House of Lords the presence of the overriding discretion to accumulate the income was fatal to the existence of an interest in possession. "A present right to present enjoyment" was how an interest in possession was defined and the beneficiaries did not have a present right. Their enjoyment of any income from the trust fund depended on the trustees' decision whether or not to accumulate. No distinction was to be drawn between a trust to pay income to a beneficiary (with an overriding power to accumulate), and a trust to accumulate (with a power to pay). Therefore, in the following examples there is no interest in possession:

- to A for life but the trustees may accumulate the income for the benefit of others; and

- a provision that the income shall be accumulated but the trustees may make payments to A.

Income rights and rights of occupation

24.40 HMRC comment:

> "*The right of residence gives an interest in possession to the beneficiaries in occupation. If the trusts provide that in addition to these occupants, a further beneficiary [who has no right of use and enjoyment] shall have a right to the income of the property, that beneficiary takes no immediate interest in possession the interest in income is displaced by the interests in possession of the occupants [see SP10/79 last paragraph]. Where a house is given to A for life on condition that he permits B to reside there with him, it is considered that A has the sole interest in possession. B has no interest in the house. This view which also applied for estate duty, might seem debateable, but it accords with the Pearson case – Pearson v IRC [1981] AC 753. A can, from the beginning, refuse to let B into the property and thereby lose his own life interest but whether he does that or not there is nothing B can do about it. A can later terminate his occupation, which on these facts also terminates B's occupation (the obligation being personal to A).*"[106]

Flexible interests in possession

24.41 In practice these remain extremely popular[107] and operate as follows:

(i) the interest in possession may be terminated by the trustees exercising an overriding power of appointment. However, until the trustees exercise that power the beneficiary is entitled to the income. Normally the consent of the relevant beneficiary is not required although he will often be one of the trustees;

---

[106] IHTM 16103. The valuation of an interest in possession where the life tenant shares occupation or income with a number of other qualifying life tenants is discussed in Ch.26.
[107] See Ch.25.

(ii) the trustees have power to advance capital to or for the benefit of the interest in possession beneficiary.

A high degree of flexibility is built into this structure: to some extent these trusts were a substitute for "full blown" discretionary trusts. A further attraction was that they provided a vehicle to circumvent the GWR/POA legislation.[108] In simple terms, if the interest in possession beneficiary suffered a termination of his interest he did not make a gift and therefore if he continued to use or benefit from the trust assets the GWR/POA legislation did not apply. FA 2006, by extending the concept of a "gift" to the transfer of value treated as happening on the termination of an interest in possession, has generally stopped this avoidance technique by extending the scope of the GWR legislation.[109] However, flexible interest in possession trusts are likely to remain popular for the following reasons:

(a) An IPDI is a qualifying interest in possession trust. Thus if property is left to the surviving spouse of the deceased, it will be exempt from inheritance tax and the spousal interest in possession can then be revoked and property given to the (say) children as a PET by the surviving spouse.

(b) Although the reservation of benefit rules mean that the spouse cannot generally benefit after the interest in possession is terminated it is possible to circumvent these rules in relation to land.[110]

(c) Flexible interest in possession settlements have capital gains tax advantages in the context of hold-over relief and entrepreneurs' relief.[111]

(d) It is often convenient and tax efficient to give a beneficiary entitlement to income for income tax reasons.[112] However, it will often be desirable to make this entitlement revocable to maintain flexibility.

Problems remaining after *Pearson v IRC*[113]

The test laid down by the majority in the House of Lords provides some **24.42** certainty in a difficult area of law and the borderline between trusts with and without an interest in possession is reasonably easy to draw. Where there is uncertainty about the entitlement of a beneficiary to income, it is likely that the settlement will fall into the "no interest in possession" regime. The following paragraphs consider some of the difficulties remaining after the case.

[108] This is considered in Ch.33.
[109] The legislation is, however, narrowly drafted and appears to leave open the possible use of shearing arrangements: see 43.85.
[110] See 43.85.
[111] See Chs 14 and 18.
[112] See 6.41 and 35.05.
[113] For a recent illustration see *Trustees of the Fairburn or Douglas Trust v RCC* [2008] STC (SCD) 338.

(i) Dispositive and administrative powers—can trustees use the income of the life tenant to pay capital expenses?

24.43 For there to be an interest in possession the beneficiary must be entitled to the income as it arises. Were this test to be applied strictly, however, even a standard life interest trust might fail to satisfy the requirement because trustees can always deduct permitted management expenses from the gross income, so that few beneficiaries are entitled to all the income as it arises.[114] This problem was commented on by Viscount Dilhorne in *Pearson v IRC*[115] as follows:

> ". . . *Parliament distinguished between the administration of a trust and the dispositive powers of trustees . . . A life tenant has an interest in possession but his interest only extends to the net income of the property, that is to say, after deduction from the gross income of expenses etc properly incurred in the management of the trust by the trustees in the exercise of their powers. A dispositive power is a power to dispose of the net income. Sometimes the line between an administrative and a dispositive power may be difficult to draw but that does not mean that there is not a valid distinction.*"

In *Pearson v IRC* the trustees had a discretion to apply income towards the payment of any taxes, costs or other outgoings which would otherwise be payable out of capital. Was this power administrative (in which case its presence did not affect the existence of any interest in possession) or dispositive (fatal to the existence of such an interest)? HMRC took the view that the existence of this power was a further reason for the settlement lacking an interest in possession.[116] Viscount Dilhorne for the majority in the House of Lords decided that the power was administrative. Lord Keith similarly noted:

> "*I consider that a distinction is properly to be drawn between powers directed to the preservation of the trust estate for the benefit of the life tenant and remainderman alike and discretionary powers the exercise of which is intended to have an effect upon the actual benefits which the beneficiaries as such became entitled, by virtue of their several interests, to receive. It is not at all appropriate in my view to [equate] a power to execute repairs with a power to distribute income at discretion from the point of view of a person who is entitled to receive any income not dealt with under the powers.*"

24.44 HMRC now accepts that a power to pay capital expenses out of income (which may be useful given that it may be impractical to sell capital assets if the trust lacks liquidity) if exercised will not prevent there being an interest in possession in the trust. Acceptable though this argument may be for management expenses, is it convincing when applied to other expenses and taxes (e.g. capital gains tax and inheritance tax) which would normally be payable out of the capital of the fund? In *Miller v IRC*[117] the Court of Session held that

---

[114] See Ch.6.
[115] *Pearson v IRC* [1981] AC 753 at 774 and 775; [1980] 2 All ER 479 HL at 486.
[116] See further *Carver v Duncan* [1985] STC 356 and IHTM 16067.
[117] [1987] STC 108 Ct of Sess.

a power to employ income to make good depreciation in the capital value of assets in the fund was administrative. (There was no requirement for the income previously arising and not paid out to be made good when capital was realised.) It should be stressed that the House of Lords did not have to decide whether HMRC's contention was correct or not and that Viscount Dilhorne's observations are obiter dicta.

The point is one of considerable practical importance. It is no longer possible to add property to existing interest in possession trusts without concerns that the added property becomes relevant property. In the context of pre-2010 discretionary trusts the trustees may no longer have a power of accumulation and have to distribute income. How far can they retain such income to pay capital expenses or is such retention an unauthorised accumulation? Moreover what is the income tax position of an interest in possession beneficiary where trustees have used income to pay capital expenses? For example, they have funded payment of IHT out of income. Is he subject to higher rate tax on the net income after payment of such expenses or does he pay higher rate tax on the gross income having received only the net?[118] These points and the trust law issues arising out of trustees using income to pay capital expenses are discussed in more detail in Chs 1 and 6.

(ii) Power to allow beneficiaries to occupy a dwelling house: *Judge (Personal Representatives of Walden Deceased) v HMRC*[119]

Mr Walden died on January 28, 2000 and in his will left his residuary estate **24.45** on discretionary trusts for his wife and relatives. The matrimonial home was separately dealt with by cl.3 of his will which was in the following terms:

> "*I GIVE free of tax and of any monies secured thereon by way of legal charge or otherwise to my Trustees ALL THAT my interest in the property known as and situate at 30 Perrymead Street London SW6 OR the property in which I am at my death ordinarily resident or in which I have then last been ordinarily resident UPON TRUST with the consent in writing of my Wife during her lifetime to sell the same with full power to postpone sale for so long as they shall in their absolute discretion think fit and to hold the net proceeds of sale and other monies applicable as capital and the net rent and profits until upon the trusts and with and subject to the powers and provisions of my Residuary Fund (as hereinafter defined) as an accretion thereto AND I DECLARE my Trustees during the lifetime of my Wife to permit her to have the use and enjoyment of the said property for such period or periods as they shall in their absolute discretion think fit pending postponement of sale she paying the rates taxes and other outgoings and keeping the same in good repair and insured against fire to the full value thereof in some office of repute nominated by my Trustees in the names of my Trustees.*"

---

[118] The trustees pay basic rate tax on the net income without any deduction for expenses: see Ch.6. For trust management expenses, see 6.06, 6.22, 6.35 and 6.47.
[119] [2005] STC (SCD) 863.

Mrs Walden had lived in the property for many years with her husband (although it appears that she had no beneficial interest in it) and on his death his executors and trustees[120] wrote to her in the following terms:

> *"I would confirm that under clause 3 of your late husband's will, 30 Perrymead Street is the sole asset of a Life Interest Trust and you will enjoy the occupancy of the property during your lifetime . . . you will be responsible for the actual payment of the premiums [for buildings insurance cover] as well as all the household bills etc. including council tax . . .*
>
> *Under Clause 4 of the will the residue of the estate is to be held on a discretionary trust for the benefit of yourself, your nephew and niece and also their children. As trustees we have the responsibility of exercising our discretionary powers under the terms of the will and also under trust law when considering making payment of capital and income to the discretionary beneficiaries . . .*
>
> *This discretionary trust is slightly different in as much that you, as the surviving spouse, is not nominated as the 'primary beneficiary'. . ."*

The letter was written on the basis that Mrs Walden had been given an interest in possession in the property (then worth £625,000) and the IHT return was completed accordingly with the result that no IHT was payable on his death.

Mrs Walden continued to live in the property until her own death on October 3, 2003. The appellants took out letters of administration to her estate and in the IHT return her estate was valued at £392,344. However, they were advised that Mrs Walden had not enjoyed an interest in possession in the property under cl.3: instead it was comprised in a discretionary trust and so did not fall to be aggregated[121] for the purpose of calculating the tax due on her free estate. HMRC thereupon issued a notice of determination because they were of the view that cl.3 had created an interest in possession.[122]

24.46 The Special Commissioner decided, in favour of the appellants, that cl.3 did not give Mrs Walden an interest in possession in the property and nor had she at any later time acquired such an interest. The following points may be noted:

(i) for Mrs Walden to have an interest in possession it was necessary for her to have "a present right to the present enjoyment of" (the property)[123]

---

[120] Commercial Union Trustees Ltd (subsequently Norwich Union).

[121] Under IHTA 1984 s.49(1).

[122] The trustees of Mr Walden's will were not represented at the hearing. From the perspective of HMRC either tax on the property would fall due on Mrs Walden's death (as they contended before the Commissioner) or, failing that, the IHT return on Mr Walden's death was incorrect and instead of a spouse exempt gift, cl.3 by creating a discretionary trust would have resulted in a substantial liability to IHT at that time. That charge would fall on the executors and trustees of Mr Walden's estate who would not be protected even if in receipt of a certificate of discharge. Given the time delay interest would also be payable. Further if the house was sold after Mrs Walden's death—as was likely—there would be no CGT uplift on her death and so the question of availability of CGT main residence relief would fall to be considered in the light of SP10/79 (which was not mentioned before the Special Commissioner).

[123] *Pearson v IRC* [1980] STC 318 at 323 (Viscount Dilhorne) and for a right to occupy constituting an interest in possession, see *IRC v Lloyds Private Banking* [1998] STC 559.

and she would not have such a right if the trustees had a discretion as to whether or not she should occupy it;

(ii) clause 3 was defectively drafted and posed serious problems of construction. The clause provided for the property to be held on a trust for sale (with any sale being dependant on Mrs Walden's consent) and pending any sale, rent and profits (if any) were to be held on the discretionary trusts of residue. In the final words of the clause dealing with occupation by Mrs Walden "for such period or periods as they [viz the Trustees] shall in their absolute discretion think fit" the Special Commissioner discerned the clear intention that the trustees retained a discretion to allow Mrs Walden "to reside in (the property) for no period or for any period".

Whilst the decision that no interest in possession existed, given the concluding words of cl.3, is understandable, the result, taking into account other factors, may be thought somewhat surprising. For instance: **24.47**

(i) it meant that IHT was payable on Mr Walden's death and, even allowing for the ability to pay by instalments over 10 years, the result might have been to force a sale of the property. Mrs Walden was substantially younger than her husband and it might therefore have been thought that his intention would have been to defer the payment of tax until her death. It would be surprising if his overriding concern—as was suggested—was to avoid the value of the property being taxed on his wife's death;

(ii) the structure of the will might suggest, given that the residue established a discretionary trust, that the purpose of cl.3 was different and was designed to confer rights—in excess of those enjoyed by a discretionary beneficiary—on Mrs Walden;

(iii) it was not argued on behalf of HMRC that the letter by the trustees to Mrs Walden (set out above) had the effect of giving her an interest in possession in the property: "rather the evidence supported the view that (the trustees) thought that an interest in possession had been created by the will."[124]

---

[124] The trustees, presumably because they were acting under a misapprehension as to the legal effect of cl.3, did not validly exercise their discretion to confer a right of occupation on Mrs Walden. And yet even had they appreciated that the trust conferred a discretion on them, is it conceivable that they would have come to any other conclusion? The property had been Mrs Walden's home for many years and although it was accepted that she had no equitable interest therein she would surely have been entitled to at least the use the property if she had raised a claim under the 1975 Act. Although 15 years younger than her husband she in fact only survived him by three years: had she continued to live in the property for (say) a further 10 years would a court have concluded that she never had any right to occupy so that if the trustees discovered the true position she could have been evicted (or does she at some point obtain protection on the basis of a "legitimate expectation"?). The reference in the will to Mrs Walden being responsible for the payment of taxes, outgoings etc on the property must in the light of the decision be analysed as a fetter on the trustees' discretion: viz the trustees can only allow her to occupy on these terms. It might, however, also be viewed as laying down the terms on which she has the right to occupy with the consent to sale requirement being seen as protection for that right.

The wider significance of the case

24.48 Although widely reported in the national press it is difficult to accept that this case lays to rest the uncertainties that have arisen over when an interest in possession exists when property is held in a discretionary trust.[125] Bear in mind that the case involved a severely deficient will and, of course, a trust which owned the entire house so that the trustees could—if they wished—have permitted a beneficiary to occupy. By contrast, in the "usual" case it is only a beneficial share of the property which passes on the first spouse's death into a discretionary trust. The issues involved are then quite different.[126] The *Walden* decision is of some significance in confirming that mere usage (occupation) does not by itself prove that there is a right to occupy: this must be conferred by the trustees.

Does it matter after March 21, 2006?

24.49 Because new inter vivos qualifying interest in possession trusts cannot be set up after March 21, 2006[127] it might be thought that the problem that arose in both *Lloyds Private Banking* and *Walden* will not arise in the future. Note, however:

(i) that wills can still create qualifying interest in possession trusts (IPDIs) so that the *Lloyds Private Banking* decision remains of importance;

(ii) that if a will establishes a discretionary trust then if an interest in possession is created within two years of death that is read-back as an IPDI. Hence in what circumstances an interest in possession can be considered to arise (as in *Walden*) remains an important issue.[128]

Discretionary Trust owning a house/share in a house

24.50 In recent years it has been suggested that HMRC take the view that if on the death of H his share of the matrimonial home is left by will on discretionary trusts (in practice usually a nil rate band discretionary trust) for a class of beneficiaries which includes Mrs H (who owns the other share in the property and, with the death of H, will usually be the sole legal owner) then if Mrs H continues to occupy the property exclusively after H's death she will be considered to enjoy an interest in possession in the share held under the trusts of

---

[125] It is uncertainties of this type which led to the proliferation of debt/charge schemes in an attempt to ensure that the deceased's IHT nil rate band was utilised. On the question of CGT it is interesting to speculate on the position in *Walden* since it may be argued that Mrs Walden did indeed occupy under the terms of the trust so that the requirements of TCGA 1992 s.225 are met. By contrast, in the case of an equitable share (only) held in a trust the availability of the relief is less clear cut: see 38.25 and 43.26.

[126] See 38.24.

[127] Save only in favour of disabled beneficiaries: see Ch.36.

[128] See IHTA 1984 s.144 (3)–(6) as inserted by FA 2006 Sch.20 para.27.

H's will. No case has been taken to the Commissioners on this point and the *Walden* case offers no support for this view of HMRC. The following matters are especially worthy of note:

(i) what the trustees own is a beneficial share in the property which does not give them any rights to sell/let the freehold interest;

(ii) Mrs H is in occupation by virtue of her own equitable interest and it seems unlikely that the trustees would persuade a court either to order a sale of the property or to force the payment of a rent[129];

(iii) the trustees may take the view that, having been left a share in the property, their best course of action is to ensure that the property is being properly maintained and insured by Mrs H and, subject to that, to retain it as an appreciating asset.[130]

Recently HMRC appear to have agreed with this view at least where a share in the original property has been left on discretionary trusts and the authors' experience is that they have usually dropped arguments that an interest in possession has been conferred by the trustees on the survivor.[131]

A power to allow beneficiaries to occupy a dwelling house may exist both in settlements which otherwise have an interest in possession and in those without. The mere existence of such a power is to be ignored; problems may only arise if and when it is exercised.[132] SP 10/79 indicates that if such a power is exercised to allow, for a definite or indefinite period, someone other than the life tenant to have exclusive or joint right of residence in a dwelling house as a permanent home, there may be an inheritance tax charge on the partial ending of that life interest. In the case of a fund otherwise lacking an interest in possession, the statement suggests that the exercise of the power will result in the creation of an interest in possession and therefore an inheritance tax charge would arise.   **24.51**

Whether this view is correct is arguable; in *Swales v IRC*[133] for instance, the taxpayer's argument that the mandating of trust income to a beneficiary was equivalent to providing a residence for permanent occupation (and accordingly created an interest in possession) was rejected by the court. In practice, however, any challenge could prove costly to the taxpayer, and trustees who possess such powers should think carefully before exercising them.[134]

(iii) Interest-free loans to beneficiaries

It is thought that the view (once held by HMRC) that an interest-free loan to   **24.52**
a beneficiary out of a discretionary trust created an interest in possession for

---

[129] Consider TLATA 1996 ss.12–15.
[130] A difficult question is then whether on sale of the property the trustees are entitled to claim the CGT principal private residence exemption in respect of their share in the property. Is Mrs A entitled to occupy it "under the terms of the trust" so that the requirements of TCGA 1992 s.225 are met? See further 38.25 and 43.26.
[131] See further Ch.43 and A2.363 for the views of HMRC.
[132] See 24.45 above.
[133] *Swales v IRC* [1984] 3 All ER 16.
[134] See also TLATA 1996 ss.12 and 13.

the beneficiary has now been abandoned.[135] It is difficult to see any merit in the argument. As that beneficiary becomes a debtor of the trust (to the extent of the loan), one wonders in what assets his interest could subsist; the money loaned belongs to him absolutely.

(iv) Position of the last surviving member of a discretionary class

24.53   If the class of beneficiaries has closed, the sole survivor must be entitled to the income as it arises so he enjoys an interest in possession. Of course, this will not generally be a qualifying interest in possession after March 22, 2006. When the class has not closed, however, trustees have a reasonable time to decide how income is to be distributed and, if a further beneficiary could come into existence or be added before that period has elapsed, the current beneficiary is not automatically entitled to the income as it arises so that there is no interest in possession.[136] Likewise, the trust remains discretionary if the class has not closed and the trustees have a power to accumulate income.

---

[135] The problem can arise in relation to nil rate band discretionary will trusts where the debt scheme is implemented: see 38.18 and 38.36.

[136] *Re Trafford's Settlement: Moore v IRC* [1985] Ch 32; [1984] 1 All ER 1108. Query whether the likelihood of a further beneficiary being born in the future is a relevant factor.

CHAPTER 25

CREATION OF SETTLEMENTS

- Background **(25.01)**
- Charge to tax in respect of settlements created on or after March 22, 2006 **(25.02)**
- Reservation of benefit on setting up a trust **(25.06)**
- Impact of the pre-owned assets charge **(25.10)**
- The importance of the 2006 changes **(25.11)**

I BACKGROUND[1]

There is no immediate IHT charge on inter vivos gifts into settlement if these can qualify as potentially exempt transfers (PETS). Before March 22, 2006 an inter vivos transfer to a trust was generally a PET if the trust was (a) interest in possession or (b) an accumulation and maintenance trust or (c) a disabled trust.[2]

    Nor did an inheritance tax charge arise in the circumstances set out in the following example.

25.01

EXAMPLE 25.1

(1) In 2005 S settled £500,000 on trust for himself for life with remainder to his children. As S, the life tenant, was deemed to own the property in the trust (and not simply a life interest in it) his estate had not fallen in value (a "nothing"). Nor did he reserve a benefit because the property was still comprised in his estate.

(2) In 2004 S settled £500,000 on trust for his wife for life, remainder to his children. S's wife was treated as owning the property in the trust so that S's transfer was an exempt transfer to a spouse.

---

[1] For the CGT consequences of establishing a trust, see Ch.10. Given that no consideration is being paid by the trustees the creation of the trust involves neither SDLT nor SD charges. For "sham" trusts, see 1.18.

[2] IHTA 1984 s.3A(1)(c) as inserted by FA 1986 s.101, Sch.19 para.1.

An immediate charge at half (lifetime) rates was, however, imposed if a discretionary trust was created inter vivos.[3]

II CHARGE TO TAX IN RESPECT OF SETTLEMENTS CREATED ON OR AFTER MARCH 22, 2006

25.02 All inter vivos settlements set up on or after March 22, 2006 are within the charging regime for relevant property trusts with the exception only of a trust for a disabled beneficiary falling within the definition of "a disabled person's interest" in IHTA 1984 s.89B.[4] Accordingly, as had been the case in respect of discretionary trusts before March 22, 2006:

(i) the creation of the trust will be an immediately chargeable transfer by the settlor and so tax will be payable if the value transferred exceeds the settlor's available IHT nil rate band[5];

(ii) CGT hold-over relief will be available unless the trust is settlor-interested.[6]

EXAMPLE 25.2

Taking the settlements considered in Example 25.1 and assuming that they were set up on or after March 22, 2006 the position is as follows:

(1) S establishes a relevant property trust and it is irrelevant that he has retained a life interest. IHT will therefore be payable (at 20 per cent) on the excess transferred above his available IHT nil rate band. The value of the interest retained is ignored in valuing S's estate so that the fall in value is £500,000 (with, if appropriate, grossing up).[7] No longer is the property still comprised in his estate (because he does not enjoy a qualifying interest in possession within s.49(1)).

Is S taxed on the settled property on his death? The actuarial value of the life interest is not taxed on his death because it is ignored when valuing his estate.[8] Could HMRC successfully argue that the retention of a life interest involves a reservation of benefit? It may be said that the retention of the life interest is a carve-out, i.e.

---

[3] The fact that a gift of shares transferred into a discretionary trust was not a potentially exempt transfer and that IHT was immediately chargeable led to a successful professional negligence claim. The solicitor and counsel advising the settlor failed to point out the adverse IHT consequences of creating a discretionary settlement when an interest in possession trust should have been considered: see *Estill v Cowling Swift and Kirchin* [2000] Lloyd's Rep PN 378.

[4] On trusts for a disabled beneficiary, see Ch.36.

[5] In general the charge is at half the IHT death rates, i.e. 0% up to £325,000 (tax year 2011–12) and at 20% on the excess. If tax is paid by the settlor grossing up will apply: see 25.04, below.

[6] See Ch.18.

[7] See Ch.29.

[8] See IHTA 1984 s.5(1)(a)(ii).

that what he has given away is the remainder interest in which he has reserved no benefit.[9] He has not gifted the right to receive the income because he has retained it. Hence the value of the settled property is not taxed on his death under the reservation of benefit rules in FA 1986 s.102(3).

This carve-out argument would not apply if the trustees had a power to apply capital for his benefit which would be viewed as the retention of a benefit in the gifted remainder interest. What would be the position if the trustees could terminate his life interest by exercising an overriding power but did not do so? Has the trustees' omission to act conferred a benefit on the settlor so that the GWR rules apply? The HMRC analysis of home loans suggests they might consider this a GWR.[10] However, they do not consider that the retention by the settlor of a remainder interest involves a reservation of benefit even if the trustees have power to stop him taking under that interest. For example, estate preservation bond plans involve the bond being settled into trust and maturing at stated intervals. In the event that the trustees do not exercise their overriding powers to appoint to the beneficiaries the bond then reverts to the settlor. The trustees have no power to appoint in the settlor's favour but have a power to stop him taking.[11] The authors are of the view that the benefit of the settlor derives from the retained interest and cannot be attributed to the trustees' failure to take it away and that the approach adopted in estate preservation plans is correct.

Further the carve-out argument does not apply if the gifted property is an interest in land, given the wider provisions of FA 1986 s.102A.[12]

If the arrangement is not caught by reservation of benefit the question of a pre-owned assets income tax charge becomes relevant. For example, if the property which was settled comprised cash and S retains an entitlement to income, he would be subject to POA under FA 2004 Sch.15 para.8 since none of the let-outs apply (para.11(1) ownership exemption does not apply). It might be possible for S to circumvent this POA charge by settling cash if the trustees immediately invested it in let property (then the para.8 charge is inapplicable and because S is not in occupation the land charge under para.3 does not apply). POA is also avoided if S settles let chattels.

(2) The creation of this trust for the spouse will likewise be taxed as a relevant property settlement and no spouse exemption will be available. Assuming that the settlor has not himself reserved any benefit, the reservation of benefit provisions do not apply just because his spouse is a beneficiary.

[9] See further 25.08 below.
[10] See 43.37.
[11] See Ch.47.
[12] For tax planning involving a settlement of an undivided share in let commercial property with the settlor keeping the rent by virtue of his life interest, see Ch.55.

(3) If the settlor retains a remainder interest then this is not in itself a ROB but POAT could apply.

Will Trusts

25.03   The long standing IHT rules continue to apply to the creation of will trusts: generally tax is charged unless, e.g. the spouse exemption applies (as in para. (2) of Example 25.1). Even after the 2006 changes it remains possible to create a qualifying interest in possession trust by will: known as an IPDI ("immediate post-death interest").[13]

EXAMPLE 25.3

> By her will Miranda left a pecuniary legacy of £200,000 to her son James for life remainder on discretionary trusts for his children and the residue of her estate to her husband Tony for life remainder to the UFO society. She died in 2007: both James and Tony have IPDIs. Accordingly while the gift on trust for James is chargeable (but falls within Miranda's nil rate band) the gift of residue is spouse exempt. Therefore tax is payable on the death of each of James and Tony if they still have the interest in possession on the value of the settled property subject to that interest. There are no 10-year charges or exit charges while they each retain their IPDI. Note that if Tony's interest in possession ends during his lifetime and the trust continues (e.g. in favour of his children) then the trust falls into the relevant property regime from that date and Tony makes a chargeable transfer. Assume James' interest in possession also ends (whether or not at a different date or at the same time as Tony's) and that each trust then becomes discretionary. Even though both trusts were established in the same will because one trust gave a spouse an immediate qualifying interest in possession they are not related settlements.[14]

Liability to tax[15]

25.04   If IHT payable on creation of a settlement is paid by the trustees, the settlor does not as a result retain an interest in the settlement for income tax purposes.[16] If the IHT is paid by the settlor then he will suffer a greater fall in the value of his estate and this process is known as grossingup.

---

[13] See Ch.28.
[14] See s.80 and Ch.23.
[15] For the duty to deliver accounts and information see IHTA 1984 s.216 as amended and for the reporting requirements when non-resident trusts are established, see IHTA 1984 s.218. See also Ch.35.
[16] SP 1/82. As to whether an agreement that the trustees should pay inheritance tax amounts to a reservation of benefit, see (1987) 84 *L.S. Gaz. No. 14*, 1041.

EXAMPLE 25.4

In June 2011, S transfers Blackacre worth £625,000 into an interest in possession trust for his son. This is an immediately chargeable transfer by S and, assuming that he has a nil rate band of £325,000 available, the IHT position is as follows:

   (i) If S pays the tax the transfer of value, ignoring S's annual exemption (s), will be grossed up as follows:

	£
total chargeable transfer of value	625,000
deduct nil rate amount	325,000
(a) amount chargeable	300,000

Gross up (a) by multiplying it by 100 divided by $(100 - R)$ where R is the rate of IHT applicable (this is 20 per cent). The calculation is—

$£300,000 \times 100/80 = £375,000.$

Hence, S's total transfer of value is £700,000 and his tax liability £75,000.

   (ii) If the trustees pay the tax, the chargeable transfer is limited to £300,000 and tax payable is £60,000. Note also that in this case the tax can be paid by instalments over 10 years.[17]

25.05 Primary liability for inheritance tax arising during the course of the settlement rests upon the trustees. Their liability is limited to the property which they have received or disposed of or become liable to account for to a beneficiary and such other property which they would have received but for their own neglect or default.

If, however, trustees fail to pay, HMRC can collect IHT from any of the following[18]:

  (i) Any person entitled to an interest in possession in the settled property. The liability of such person is limited to the value of the trust property, out of which he can claim an indemnity for the tax he has paid.[19]

  (ii) Any beneficiary under a discretionary trust up to the value of the property that he receives (after paying income tax on it) and with no right to reimbursement from the trust for the tax he is called upon to pay.

---

[17] IHTA 1984 s.227.

[18] See IHTA 1984 s.201(1) and Ch.56.

[19] IHTA 1984 s.200(1)(c) which catches a person who at any time after death is entitled to an interest in possession in the property. This is, of course, wholly unreasonable given that in no sense does the beneficiary own the capital in the settlement. Indeed since March 21, 2006 the beneficiary is not even deemed to own the underlying capital. See A2.362 for the comments of HMRC when this point was raised by CIOT/STEP.

(iii) The settlor, where the trustees are resident outside the UK, because, if the trustees do not pay, HMRC cannot enforce payment abroad. A settlor who pays tax has a right to recover it from the trust.

III RESERVATION OF BENEFIT ON SETTING UP A TRUST

25.06 The creation of inter vivos settlements can lead to reservation of benefit problems or exceptionally to an income tax charge on the settlor under the pre-owned asset rules. The matters set out in the following paragraphs are especially worthy of note.

(i) Settlor appoints himself a trustee

25.07 If the settlor appoints himself a trustee of his settlement, that appointment does not by itself amount to a reserved benefit. A settlor may therefore retain some control over the settled property. If the terms of the settlement provide for his remuneration as trustee, however, there may be a reservation in the settled property.[20] One way of overcoming this is for the settlor-trustee to be paid by an annuity, as such an arrangement will not constitute a reserved benefit and the ending of that annuity will not lead to any IHT charge.[21]

Particular difficulties are caused if the settlor-trustee is a director of a company whose shares form part of the trust fund. The general rule of equity is that a trustee may not profit from his position and this means that he will generally have to account for any director's fees that he may receive. It is standard practice, however, for the trust deed to provide that a trustee need not in such cases account for those fees[22] and when the settlor-trustee is allowed to retain fees it is arguable that he has reserved a benefit in the trust assets. HMRC have, however, indicated that they will not take this point so long as the director's remuneration "involves the continuance of reasonable commercial arrangements".[23]

(ii) Settlor reserves an interest for himself

25.08 If the settlor reserves an interest for himself under his settlement, whether he does so expressly or whether his interest arises by operation of law, there may be no reservation of benefit since he is making a partial gift (this is a species of "carve-out").

---

[20] *Oakes v Comr of Stamp Duties of New South Wales* [1954] AC 57; [1953] 2 All ER 1563 PC. It is understood that HMRC do not at present take this point: see IHTM 14334 provided "the fee is entirely reasonable."

[21] IHTA 1984 s.90. The retention of an annuity is seen as a "carve-out", i.e. as property not being settled on the trustees.

[22] See, for instance, A1.4 cl.11.2.

[23] See HMRC letters of February 19, 1987, March 5, 1987, and May 18, 1987.

EXAMPLE 25.5

S created a settlement for his minor son, absolutely on attaining 21 years. No provision is made for what should happen if the son were to die before that age, and so there is a resulting trust to the settlor. However, the settlor has not reserved a benefit. Instead, he has made a partial gift, i.e. a gift of the settled property less the retained remainder interest in it.[24]

If the settlor is one of the class of beneficiaries in a discretionary trust, however, he is not entirely excluded from the trust property. In view of the limited nature of a discretionary beneficiary's rights[25] he cannot be treated as making a partial gift. Hence, he will be treated as having reserved a benefit in the entire settled fund despite the fact that he may receive no benefit from it.[26] By contrast, the inclusion of the settlor's spouse as a discretionary beneficiary does not result in a reserved benefit. Were that spouse to receive property from the settlement however, which was then shared with or used for the benefit of the settlor, HMRC may argue that he has reserved a benefit.

(iii) Gift to a spouse

The reservation of benefit rules did not apply to an exempt gift to a spouse. **25.09** Accordingly, prior to June 2003 it was possible to channel a benefit through a spouse.

EXAMPLE 25.6

In 2000, A settled property on a revocable life interest for his wife B and subject to that on discretionary trusts for a class of beneficiaries which included A. B's life interest is terminated after six months. A had not reserved any benefit since the gift was spouse exempt although he was one of the objects of the discretionary trust.[27]

This avoidance of the reservation of benefit rules was prevented for disposals after June 19, 2003 by the anti-*Eversden* legislation: see Ch.43.

[24] *Stamp Duties Comr (New South Wales) v Perpetual Trustee Co Ltd* [1943] AC 425; [1943] 1 All ER 525 PC; see also *Cochrane v IRC* [1974] STC 335 where the settlor expressly reserved surplus income. For a general consideration of so-called "shearing operations" see *Ingram (executors of Lady Ingram) v IRC* [2000] 1 AC 293; [1999] STC 37 HL and 22.14 and 43.34. The interest retained must be identified with some precision: classically it will be a reversionary interest. If this could be accelerated by the exercise of an overriding power of appointment, query whether a reservation of benefit then arises.

[25] See *Gartside v IRC* [1968] AC 553; [1968] 1 All ER 121 HL.

[26] See *IRC v Eversden* [2003] EWCA Civ 668; [2003] STC 822 and *PRs of Lyon Deceased v RCC* (2007) SWTI 1816; SpC 616. It is thought that the position is different if the settlor, although not a discretionary beneficiary, is capable of becoming such a beneficiary (e.g. under a power to add to the class of beneficiaries). Only when he is added does he reserve a benefit.

[27] See *IRC v Eversden* [2003] EWCA Civ 668; [2003] STC 822 at [25].

(iv) Cash gifts

As explained at 43.74 and in Ch.34, outright cash gifts are not subject to the tracing provisions and are therefore a way of circumventing the reservation of benefit provisions.[28] However, cash gifts to a settlement are not within FA 1986 Sch.20 para.2 but have their own tracing provisions in para.5. Hence, if A gives cash to a trust which then purchases property in which he lives, he has reserved a benefit. Paragraph 5 does, however, contain inadequate tracing provisions in respect of property coming out of the trust and these weaknesses are considered at 34.15 (and see Example 34.5).

IV IMPACT OF THE PRE-OWNED ASSETS CHARGE

25.10 The pre-owned assets charge is considered in Ch.34.

V THE IMPORTANCE OF THE 2006 CHANGES

25.11 By providing that the creation of a lifetime settlement cannot be a PET[29] the 2006 legislation:

(i) drew a sharp distinction between the IHT treatment of settled and unsettled gifts;

(ii) has meant that most new settlements that have been created since the changes either:

(a) fell within the settlor's IHT nil rate band;
(b) comprised business or agricultural property attracting 100 per cent relief;
(c) fell within the normal expenditure out of income exemption[30];

(iii) in cases where a settlor wishes to settle a sum in excess of his available nil rate band and the relieving provisions noted above are not available the 20 per cent entry charge that will be imposed is a considerable deterrent. Inevitably schemes were devised to circumvent this charge (typically "*Melville Mark III schemes*") which in turn led to amending legislation and to the extension of DOTAS to this area of IHT.[31]

---

[28] See Sch.20 para.2(b) FA 1986.
[29] The one exception is the creation of a disabled person's trust.
[30] IHTA 1984 s.21.
[31] See further Ch.56 for disclosure and Ch.26 for *Melville* schemes.

CHAPTER 26

THE TAX TREATMENT OF QUALIFYING AND NON-QUALIFYING
INTERESTS IN POSSESSION AND REVERSIONARY INTERESTS
INCLUDING VALUATION ISSUES, LEASES, RELIEFS, MELVILLE
SCHEMES AND SALES

Precedent

I BACKGROUND

Not all interest in possession trusts contains a "qualifying" interest in   **26.01**
possession. As a result of changes effected by FA 2006, inter vivos settlements set up after March 21, 2006 will only be qualifying if the interest is
a disabled person's interest within IHTA 1984 s.89B(1)(c) or (d).[1] A non-
qualifying interest in possession settlement is taxed in accordance with the
relevant property regime.[2] It remains possible to set up a qualifying interest
in possession trust by will (this is an "IPDI")[3] and the definition of a qualifying interest in possession extends to an interest in possession to which an

---

[1] This provision was inserted by FA 2006 Sch.20 para.6 in respect of trusts created on or after
    March 22, 2006. See 26.02 for the full definition, and Ch.36.
[2] i.e. under IHTA 1984 Pt III Ch.III: see s.59(2) as amended by FA 2006 Sch.20 para.20.
[3] "Immediate Post Death Interest": see IHTA 1984 s.49A inserted by FA 2006 Sch.20 para.5.

individual was entitled on March 22, 2006 and (in limited circumstances) to a successive interest in possession in that settlement (a "transitional serial interest").[4]

EXAMPLE 26.1

(1) Under the Willie Wonker trust, which was set up in 1999, Willie is entitled to an interest in possession. On his death his son, Dilly, takes an interest in possession with remainder over to a chocolate charity. Willie has a qualifying interest in possession. If his interest ended before October 6, 2008 Dilly, in turn, became entitled to a qualifying interest in possession (a TSI). If, however, Willie's interest ends on or after that date, Dilly's interest will not be qualifying and the trust will be taxed as a relevant property settlement.[5]

(2) Mindful of the attentions of his creditors, Nasty put his assets into a life interest trust for his wife in 2007. Mrs Nasty does not enjoy a qualifying interest in possession. The trust is taxed as a relevant property settlement.[6]

(3) By his will Theakston leaves his entire estate to his son for life, then to his daughter-in-law for life with remainder to his grandchildren. On Theakston's death—whenever that occurs—the son enjoys a qualifying interest in possession (an IPDI[7] if the death is after March 21, 2006 otherwise a qualifying IIP under the old rules). The daughter-in-law's successive life interest will also be qualifying but only if Theakston dies before March 22, 2006 so that at that date the son has a qualifying interest in possession and her interest vests in possession either before October 6, 2008 or, if later, on the son's death (in these cases it will be a transitional serial interest).

26.02 This chapter is concerned with the IHT treatment of qualifying interests in possession. It is therefore important to bear in mind:

(i) that in considering whether the provisions discussed in this chapter apply the first stage is to consider whether the settlement creates an interest in possession[8]; and

(ii) if it does, whether that interest is qualifying.

---

[4] IHTA 1984 s.49B–E inserted by FA 2006 Sch.20 para.5.
[5] Transitional Serial Interests are considered in detail at 27.16 and following.
[6] Note that the spouse exemption is not available on creation of the trust: see Example 25.2.
[7] IPDIs are considered in detail in Ch.28.
[8] Notice that the tax changes in FA 2006 did not affect the meaning of an interest in possession for IHT purposes: see 24.37 and following. Of course in the case of new inter vivos settlements the question will generally be irrelevant for inheritance tax purposes although whether someone has an interest in possession (even if not qualifying) can affect the availability of certain capital gains tax entrepreneur's relief, and has income tax implications: see Chs.6 and 14. Some settlement deeds provide that the term "interest in possession" when used in the deed is to have its IHT meaning. It follows that such a definition does not present a problem post-FA 2006 although this drafting practice is likely to end with the restriction of qualifying status in the case of new interest in possession settlements.

II IHT TREATMENT OF A BENEFICIARY ENTITLED TO A QUALIFYING IIP

The beneficiary entitled to income of a trust (typically the life tenant) is treated as owning that portion of the capital of the trust fund: **26.03**

> *"a person beneficially entitled to an interest in possession in settled property shall be treated for the purposes of the Act as beneficially entitled to the property in which the interest subsists."*[9]

This rule is a fiction because in no real sense is the interest in possession beneficiary the owner of the capital in the fund. For IHT purposes, however, the capital forms part of his estate, so that on a chargeable occasion inheritance tax is charged on the trust fund at his rates. The settlement itself is not a separate taxable entity (contrast the rules for relevant property trusts),[10] although primary liability for any tax falls upon the trustees.[11]

III THE MEANING OF A REVERSIONARY INTEREST

As the interest in possession beneficiary (typically a life tenant) is treated as owning all the capital in the trust, other beneficiaries with "reversionary interests" own nothing. "Reversionary interest" is defined in the legislation as: **26.04**

> *"a future interest under a settlement, whether it is vested or contingent (including an interest expectant on the termination of an interest in possession which, by virtue of section 50 . . ., is treated as subsisting in part of any property)".*[12]

Generally, reversionary interests are excluded property and can be assigned without charge to IHT.[13] The term does not catch the interests of discretionary beneficiaries because such rights as they possess, notably to compel due administration of the trust, to be considered and jointly to wind up the trust, are present rights. Their interests are neither in possession nor in reversion. Two further points may be noted:

(1) to a trust lawyer the term a "reversionary interest" is limited to an interest that reverts to the settlor. The IHT definition is wider than this and

---

[9] IHTA 1984 s.49(1).
[10] As to the treatment of relevant property trusts, see Ch.29.
[11] IHTA 1984 s.201.
[12] IHTA 1984 s.47.
[13] It follows that the assignment of a reversionary interest can have advantageous IHT consequences in terms of tax planning (for CGT purposes no chargeable gain will normally result on any assignment: see TCGA 1992 s.76(1) as amended by the FA 1998 s.128 and Ch.20). For instance, assume that A is entitled to a qualifying IIP and is aged 80 and on his death the property passes to B, aged 79, absolutely. There is the prospect of two IHT charges on the trust if A and B were to die in that order. Whilst a measure of quick succession relief might be available (see IHTA 1984 s.141) the IHT position would be improved if before A's death B assigned his remainder interest, e.g. to his young grandson.

embraces both reversionary and remainder interests. So for example, in a trust which is A for life, then B for life and then C absolutely, both B and C have reversionary interests for inheritance tax purposes while A is alive and C has a reversionary interest while B is alive;

(2) a non-qualifying IIP is not a reversionary interest (it is a present interest) but receives special treatment with its value being excluded from the estate of the beneficiary by IHTA 1984 s.5(1)(a)(ii) and (1A).[14]

IV THE NATURE OF A NON-QUALIFYING IIP

26.05 The fictional entitlement posited by s.49(1) does not apply. However, a beneficiary who enjoys a non-qualifying interest in possession in a trust fund[15] may still have the benefit of a valuable *chose in action*. For IHT purposes:

(i) the interest is not a reversionary interest (so that it is not thereby made excluded property); but

(ii) IHTA 1984 s.5(1)(a)(ii) and (1A)[16] provide (subject to the 2010 amendment considered below) that the estate of a person does not include a non-qualifying interest in possession.

Interestingly, therefore, a potentially valuable asset has been taken out of the IHT net.

EXAMPLE 26.2

Jason sets up a settlement on June 1, 2006 giving his son, Fleece, then aged 30, an interest in possession. Sadly Fleece dies, wholly unexpectedly, shortly afterwards.

For IHT purposes the interest in possession is non-qualifying and Jason has created a relevant property settlement. On Fleece's death his estate does not include the interest in possession. Of course, if the settlement ends at that time the normal "exit" charge under the relevant property regime may apply.[17]

---

[14] But note the amendment made by FA 2010 to prevent IHT avoidance arrangements where the interest was purchased so that IHTA 1984 s.10 prevented any charge from arising at that time. See further 26.06 and Example 26.3.

[15] i.e. one that arose post-March 21, 2006 and is not a transitional serial interest. See for instance A1.19 for the appointment of such an interest out of a discretionary trust. The appointment can be revocable and may have income tax advantages.

[16] Inserted by FA 2006 Sch.20 paras 7 and 10.

[17] See Ch.29. At 2011–12 rates the exit charge will be at something less than 6%.

After FA 2006 the following schemes were devised to exploit the fact that non-qualifying interests in possession were not chargeable to IHT.[18]   **26.06**

EXAMPLE 26.3

Mr X (an unconnected party) enjoys a fixed life interest in a settlement established in 2007, the assets of which are worth £1 million. For IHT purposes the interest is non-qualifying. The actuarial value of that life interest (taking into account the age of Mr X and income produced by the assets) is £100,000. Cunning purchased the interest for £100,000. The IHT consequences before December 9, 2009 were as follows:

(i)   Cunning's estate for IHT purposes was reduced by £100,000 (given that no value was included for the life interest);
(ii) the arrangement was commercial so that the reduction in value did not give rise to an IHT charge: see IHTA 1984 s.10(1);
(iii) the disposal of the life interest by Mr X would not normally rise to a CGT charge[19];
(iv) if Mr X's interest had been a "qualifying" interest in possession its sale would have had IHT consequences[20] but as it is non-qualifying its disposal does not trigger the charging mechanism under the relevant property regime;
(v)   Cunning could leave his interest per autre vie to his children in his will or give the income interest away during his lifetime.

Tax analysis: IHT—does s.10 IHTA 1984 apply?

In most cases Cunning would buy the income interest from an unconnected   **26.07**
third party but in principle he could also buy it from a family trust where another (preferably young) relation had an income interest that was non-qualifying. Either way it was necessary for the income interest to be fixed and not capable of termination by the trustees otherwise it would have no commercial value.[21] In some cases the trust provided for a fixed term income interest of, say, 90 years. This had the advantage that its value did not depend on the health or life expectancy of any particular individual.

For the scheme to work it was not only necessary to satisfy the condition in   **26.08**
s.10(1)(a) or (b) viz that:

"*(a) the disposition was made in a transaction at arm's length between persons not connected with each other or, (b) such as might be excepted*

---

[18] They were not chargeable because of IHTA 1984 s.5(1)(a)(ii), (1A).
[19] See TCGA 1992 s.76(1) and Ch.20.
[20] See IHTA 1984 s.51 and 26.12.
[21] For ascertaining its commercial value, see 28.00.

to be made in a transaction at arm's length between persons not connected with each other",

but also to satisfy the condition in the opening words of s.10(1), i.e. that the transfer of value was not intended or made in a transaction intended to confer any gratuitous benefit on any person. Although the purchase (i.e. the initial transaction itself) was not intended to confer any gratuitous benefit on the vendor of the income interest (since it took place on a fully commercial basis) the subsequent assignment by gift of that life interest or even leaving it by will could be an associated operation within the extended definition of transaction in s.10(3) and intended to confer a gratuitous benefit. Section 10 protection would not then be available. The reference to gratuitous intent in s.10 is not confined to the parties to the transaction itself.

26.09   It might therefore be argued that in purchasing the interest and thereby reducing his estate (by the £100,000 cash) there *was* an intention by Cunning to confer a gratuitous benefit on his family who will eventually receive the purchased income interest IHT free, whether by way of inter vivos gift or via the will. There were greater concerns about s.10 if Cunning was on his death bed when the interest was purchased because then he was doing so with the aim of conferring an IHT free benefit on someone else.

26.10   The s.10 defence is a more robust one if it can be shown that Cunning wanted an income stream that was coincidentally outside of his estate for IHT purposes. The longer the gap between the initial purchase by Cunning and his death or subsequent assignment by way of gift, the harder it was for HMRC to argue that there was gratuitous intent behind the initial purchase, although the definition of associated operations in s.268 is wide enough to embrace a subsequent assignment.[22] Cunning paid for an interest which will last longer than his life. The interest will accordingly pass under his will usually to other family members or into trust. There is therefore, arguably a latent gift aspect to the transaction which could be construed as a gratuitous intention. Equally it could be regarded as a good investment, i.e. Cunning is paying for an income stream.

26.11   The authors are of the view that if Cunning purchased the interest *without* an immediate intention that he would give it away and the income interest produced a fixed yield then the disposition was not made in a "transaction including a series of transactions and any associated operations intended to confer any gratuitous benefit."[23]

Tax analysis: CGT

26.12   For CGT purposes any inter vivos gift of the income interest by Cunning is a chargeable event for CGT purposes. TCGA 1992 s.76(1) would normally apply to prevent a charge but this is disapplied because Cunning *purchased* the interest.[24] No CGT charge should arise on the onward gift by Cunning as

---

[22] See also *Macpherson v IRC* [1988] STC 362.
[23] See comments of Lord Jauncey in *Macpherson*.
[24] TCGA 1992 s.76. The s.76(1) exemption is also disapplied where trustees are (or have been) resident outside the UK. Quite often in the above scheme the income interest was purchased

the value of the income interest is likely to be worth less actuarially than the amount he paid for it, taking into account purchase costs. A loss (connected) should result.[25] CGT problems may, however, arise if the trustees have power to advance capital to the holder of the life interest for the time being and later do so in favour of Cunning's issue.[26]

Terms of trust

The terms of the settlement must not have given power for the trustees to invest in non-income producing assets but instead, often required the trustees to engineer a minimum level of income for the holder of the income interest which if necessary was to be made up out of capital. Further, the trustees must have had no power to terminate the income interest. Most schemes provide for fixed term of 90 years rather than an interest for life. The whole aim of the scheme was to ensure that the income interest was commercially valuable: hence the trustees must not have had a power to advance capital to another person without the consent of the holder of that income interest.

26.13

Other issues

The scheme raised other issues including the following:

26.14

1. *Borrowing*: consider the position if Cunning had insufficient funds to purchase the income interest. He could borrow commercially but this was expensive. One option was for the purchaser to borrow from a bank which then took security over the trust funds. The difficulty was that all the trust income was then being used to fund the borrowing costs thereby removing any argument that the purchase was being done to provide him with a secure income. In addition the bank liability reduced the value of an asset in his estate not chargeable to IHT anyway.

2. *Who is the settlor?* The trust fund must have been settled in advance of discussions being held with Cunning as to the possible purchase of a trust interest. Even if the trust was set up specifically with a view to the sale of the trust interest, the original settlor must not have had a specific purchaser in mind and the trust fund must actually be settled with cash by the purchaser. Difficulties arose if the settlor merely lent to the trust and then put the money in when he received the cash for the income

from a non-UK resident trust set up by a foreign domiciled settlor after 2006 who did not have to worry about the entry charge for IHT purposes: see TCGA 1992 s.85.

[25] The income interest is not a wasting asset if the unexpired term is for more than 50 years.

[26] The CGT charge arises under s.76(2) if:

- the interest being disposed of by the donee (the issue in the illustration) was purchased by a previous holder (i.e. Cunning); and

- the donee has become absolutely entitled (as against the trustees) to assets in the settlement as the holder of the interest.

interest from the purchaser. At the time of the purchase of the interest the trust would have been valueless!

3. *Excluded property*: as noted above the trust was often set up by a non-UK domiciliary and contained non-UK situs assets. Initially therefore the settlement contained excluded property for IHT purposes.[27] However, when a UK domiciled individual purchased the income interest, the property in the settlement ceased to be excluded property and became relevant property for IHT purposes even if the assets remained non-UK situs.[28]

HMRC response: the FA 2010 changes

26.15 Whatever the strength of HMRC's case with regard to s.10, HMRC decided to legislate against these schemes and FA 2010 s.53 amended IHTA 1984 s.5(a) (a)(ii). This section generally excludes the value of a non-qualifying interest in possession from the estate of the beneficiary. However, a new subs.(1B) was inserted. This has the effect of making the purchased income interest "qualifying" and so the value of the trust fund will form part of the beneficiary's estate (see s.49(1)) if:

(i) he was domiciled in the UK on becoming beneficially entitled to it; and

(ii) he became so entitled because of a disposition which was prevented from being a transfer of value by IHTA 1984 s.10.

Accordingly if Cunning in the above Example purchased X's income interest on or after December 9, 2009, he would be treated as owning (for IHT purposes) the value of the trust fund (£1 million).

26.16 In the common situation where property is settled on trust for A with life remainder to B, during A's lifetime B has a reversionary interest which is excluded property for IHT purposes. When A dies, however, B becomes entitled to the settled property which forms part of his chargeable IHT estate. In exceptional cases reversionary interests are not excluded property and FA 2010 ss.52 and 53 also introduced anti-avoidance legislation to combat their use in *Melville* III planning schemes.[29] Again these changes were effective from December 9, 2009.

VI CONSEQUENCES OF THE S.49(1) FICTION AND HOW TO VALUE JOINT INTERESTS IN POSSESSION

26.17 The value of the settled property is aggregated with the value of the estate of the interest in possession beneficiary. The consequences of this on the death of the beneficiary are illustrated in Example 26.8 below. However such aggrega-

---

[27] IHTA 1984 s.48(3).
[28] IHTA 1984 s.48(3B).
[29] See further 26.45.

tion does not apply for all purposes. For instance, if the beneficiary's free estate is insufficient to discharge his personal liabilities these cannot be deducted, for IHT purposes, against the value of settled property in which he had enjoyed an interest in possession.[30] In *St Barbe Green v IRC*[31] the deceased died with an insolvent estate and was the life tenant in certain assets under three family settlements. Mann J. held that the net liabilities were not available to reduce the estate beyond the value of the free estate's assets that were available to meet them.[32]

The beneficiary entitled to a qualifying interest in possession is treated as being the beneficial owner of the trust property, or an appropriate part of that property. If there is more than one such beneficiary, it is necessary to apportion the settlement property between those beneficiaries.[33] A beneficiary who has the right to all the income of the fund for a period shorter than his lifetime (however short the period) is still treated for IHT purposes as owning the entire settled fund.

26.18

In cases where a beneficiary is not *only* entitled to income but is entitled to use the capital assets in the fund, he is treated as owning those assets.

Joint interests

How are joint interests in possession or interests in possession in only part of the settled property taxed? IHTA 1984 s.50 sets out to cover this point but leaves a number of ambiguities. Section 50(1) states that where a person is entitled to only part of the income of the settled property his interest is taken to subsist in such part of the property as bears to the whole the same proportion as the part of the income to which he is entitled. So if he is entitled to 40 per cent of the income he is treated as having an interest in possession in 40 per cent of the capital. The position where a beneficiary is entitled to a fixed amount of income each year is discussed below since slightly different valuation principles apply.[34]

26.19

Section 50(5) provides that where a person is not entitled to any income of the property but is entitled jointly or in common with others to the use and enjoyment of the property his interest shall be taken to subsist in such part of the property as corresponds to the proportion which the annual value of his interest bears to the aggregate of the annual values of his interest and that of

---

[30] It will be appreciated that as a matter of general law creditors of the deceased in such a case will have no right to claim against settled assets (save in exceptional cases, e.g. where the settlement had been set up by the deceased to put assets out of their reach).

[31] [2005] STC 288 and Ch.32.

[32] He was influenced by the decision in the estate duty case of *Re Barnes* [1938] 2 KB 684 of Lawrence J. who in the context of that legislation had commented that "*I do not see how, in determining the value of an estate, allowance can be made for debts beyond the value of the assets out of which the debts are to be met*". Mann J. concluded that, despite the different wording in IHTA 1984 s.5(3) which requires liabilities to be taken into account in arriving at the estate of the taxpayer, Parliament would not have intended to change the estate duty position and allow a deduction in the situation where the property in question is not accountable for the payment of the debts. A similar result will occur in the case of property treated as part of a deceased's estate under the reservation of benefit rules: see Ch.32.

[33] IHTA 1984 s.50(1).

[34] See 26.20.

the others. Annual value is not defined! The meaning of this section remains obscure.[35] It requires the person in question to be entitled only to the use and enjoyment of the property jointly or in common with other persons and not to any income of the property. What is the position if A and B presently occupy property but could let it and keep the rent?

At IHTM 16103 HMRC comment:

> "*The beneficiary may very well be entitled to a great deal of income from the rest of the settled fund but that does not affect the application of s50(5). If the interest carries the right to let the property and receive a share of the income s50(5) does not apply but s50(1) produces the same result.*"

This view is confirmed in Dymond at para.16.638 "*What purports to be merely a joint right of residence may carry the right to let the property and receive a share of the income. In such a case s50(5) does not apply but s50(1) gives a similar result.*"

26.20   Section 50 was relevant in *Woodhall v IRC*[36] where the deceased's will provided that no sale of the family home was to take place whilst any of his three children "shall desire to live there" and the executors and trustees were to permit the children "or each or any of them to occupy the same". The net proceeds of sale were to be divided among the three children equally. After the deceased died in 1957 one of the children left the family home in 1958 and died in 1971. A second child, E, had apparently already left the family home in 1957 and a third child, A, lived there until he died in 1997. It was not disputed that the property was settled but the Revenue argued that by virtue of his sole occupation of the property A had an interest in possession in the entirety albeit one which was defeasible by reason of the right of E the surviving non-occupying beneficiary to occupy with A if he chose to do so. A's personal representative argued that A had no interest in possession at all or if he did under s.50(5) it subsisted in only half the house. It was decided that A had an interest in possession in the property but since E was also entitled to use and enjoy it s.50(5) applied and therefore A had an interest in possession in only half the property. Section 50(5) applied because the beneficiaries only had a right of occupation.[37]

EXAMPLE 26.4

> A and B are jointly entitled to occupy property which is worth £750,000. They are only entitled to occupy the property not to any income if they were not in occupation and therefore s.50(5) applies. That entitlement arose prior to March 22, 2006 and therefore they have qualifying IIPs.

---

[35] IHTA 1984 s.50(5). It is a moot point whether the decision by trustees of land under TLATA 1996 s.13 to exclude an interest in possession beneficiary from occupying trust property changes the IHT position: See "Trusts of land: the new Act" 94 *LS Gaz* January 22, 1997 at p.30.

[36] [2007] STC (SCD) 558.

[37] Note that the value of A's interest was not discounted: this question was not considered in the case.

The capital value of the property must be apportioned to A and B in proportion to the annual value of their respective interests. If their interests are equal the apportionment will be as to 50 per cent each. If A dies, the value of his half share is aggregated with his free estate and the value of his nil rate band apportioned pro rata.[38]

Can the value of a joint interest be discounted?

When s.50(5) applies (as in *Woodhall*) it provides that: **26.21**

> *"(the beneficiary's) interest shall be taken to subsist in such part of the property as corresponds to the proportion which the annual value of his interest bears to the aggregate of the annual value of his interest and that or those of the other or others."*

HMRC comment that:

> *"the importance of section 50(5) is that it ensure that the beneficiary's interest is valued as a fraction of the whole with no question of a joint property discount."*[39]

Similarly, they take the view that when part of an interest in the whole or part of the settled property ends, s.52(4)(a) has the same effect since it provides that:

> *"the tax chargeable . . . on the coming to an end of part of an interest shall be charged as if the value of the property (or part) in which the interest subsisted were a correspondence part of the value of the whole."*

It might be said that the wording of s.52(4)(a) admits of no uncertainty since it expressly deals with the *value* of the part of the interest which has ended. By contrast, s.50(5) is dealing with the identification of the property in which the interest subsists, not with the value of that property. Accordingly, in *Woodhall* the subsection determined that A's interest was in 50 per cent of the property but it does not then deal with the valuation of that share in the property. Indeed, it is thought that the subsection is performing the same function as s.50(1) which, in the context of a beneficiary being entitled to part only of the income of the property, states:

> *"the interest shall be taken to subsist in such part only of the property as bears to the whole the same proportion as the part of the income to which he is entitled bears to the whole of the income."*

---

[38] In practice, difficulties may arise (especially when construing trusts set up by will) in deciding whether a beneficiary is given a right to occupy a particular property (so that if the property is sold or he ceases to occupy his IIP ends) or whether he has a life interest in that property and in any proceeds of sale if it was to be sold. In the latter case the IIP continues even after sale of the property and after the beneficiary ceases to occupy it. See A2.363 and following for correspondence with HMRC on SP 10/79.

[39] IHTM 16102.

Again, nothing is being said about value, merely about identifying the property in which the interest subsists.

26.22   The authors would draw the following conclusion on valuation:

(i) a beneficiary entitled to an interest in possession in the entirety of the trust fund is treated as the beneficial owner of the property in the settlement.[40] If the settlement owned a 50 per cent share in commercial property, normal valuation principles would be applied in determining the size of any discount for joint ownership[41];

(ii) if a beneficiary has a joint interest in possession in the settled property, s.50(1), (2) and (5) identify the share of the property attributable to that share. The next stage is to value the share: HMRC at IHTM 16101 appear to accept this by commenting that in such cases "*the property to be valued is the share itself with any appropriate discount for joint ownership*";

(iii) if it is necessary to value part of a joint interest (e.g. which is surrendered inter vivos) then s.52(4)(a) provides that what is taxed is a proportionate part of the interest. But, of course, the interest itself may still benefit from a discount in valuation under (ii). Accordingly the purpose of s.52(4)(a) is to prevent any possibility of a second discount (a point noted in the example at IHTM 16101).

EXAMPLE 26.5

(1) Adam died in 2011. He was the interest in possession beneficiary in a trust set up in 2007 by his late father's will and which contains a 50 per cent share in the family home (the other 50 per cent interest is owned by Adam's mother).

In valuing the trust's share the usual discount for joint ownership will apply (so if the house is worth £500,000 the settled share will be £250,000 less a 10% discount = £225,000).

(2) On the facts of *Woodfall*, A died entitled to an interest in possession in 50 per cent of the house held in the settlement. The value of that 50 per cent interest should be discounted in calculating the tax due on this death.

(3) Mavis was joint life tenant with her sister Madge of their main residence, "The Soeurs". The trustees exercise a power of appointment to terminate Mavis' interest as to 50 per cent and appoint the same to her brother Jasper (accordingly the beneficial interests are now Madge 50 per cent; Mavis 25 per cent; Jasper 25 per cent). Under s.52(4)(a) the tax charge is calculated by reference to the value of Mavis' original share. Accordingly, if the house is worth £500,000 the value of Mavis' 50 per

---

[40] IHTA 1984 s.49(1).

[41] Of course if the beneficiary personally owned the other 50% interest, the entirety is comprised in his estate and so no question of a discount arises on his death (contrast the position if his interest ended during his life when the settled share has to be valued in isolation: see s.52(1)).

cent share (discounted) is £225,000 and the partial termination of her interest results in her making a chargeable transfer of £112,500.

VII BENEFICIARY ENTITLED TO A FIXED INCOME (INCLUDING AN ANNUITANT)

Difficulties may arise where one beneficiary is entitled to a fixed amount of income each year (for example an annuity) and the remaining income is paid to another beneficiary. (Assuming that the annuity interest and remaining income interest give the beneficiaries qualifying IIPs under s.49(1).) If the amounts of income paid to the two were compared in the year when a chargeable event occurred, a tax saving could be engineered. Assume, for instance, that the annuity interest terminates so that IHT is charged on its value. The proportion of capital attributable to that interest and, therefore, the IHT, would be reduced if the trustees had invested in assets producing a high income in that year since then a relatively small proportion of the total income would be payable to the annuitant who would be treated as owning an equivalently small portion of the capital. By contrast, when a chargeable event affects the interest in the residue of the income (for example, through termination of the trust) the trustees could switch the assets into low income products, thereby achieving a similar reduction in inheritance tax. **26.23**

IHTA 1984 s.50(3) is designed to counter such schemes by providing that the Treasury may prescribe higher and lower income yields which take effect as limits beyond which any fluctuations in the actual income of the fund are ignored.[42]

EXAMPLE 26.6

The value of the assets settled in 2005 is £500,000; annual income £40,000: i.e. eight per cent. A is entitled to an annuity of £5,000 a year; B to the balance of the income. If there is a chargeable transfer affecting the annuity, then apply s.50(3) because actual income is higher than the specified higher rate.

Assume that the prescribed higher rate is six per cent on the relevant date; the calculation is: Notional income = 6% of £500,000 = £30,000. A's annuity is £5,000; as a proportion of income it is £5,000/£30,000; A's share of the capital is, therefore, 5/30 × £500,000 = £83,333.

This calculation is used whenever the actual income yield exceeds the prescribed higher rate. The calculation cannot lead to a charge in excess of the total value of the fund. If the actual income figures had been used, A's share of capital would be 5/40 × £500,000 = £62,500.

When a chargeable transfer affecting the interest in the balance of the income occurs, if the actual income produced falls below the prescribed

---

[42] See the Capital Transfer Tax (Settled Property Income Yield) Order 1980 SI 1980/1000.

lower rate, the calculation proceeds as if the fund yielded that rate. If both interests in the settlement are chargeable on the same occasion, the prescribed rates do not apply because the entire fund is chargeable.

VIII LEASE TREATED AS A SETTLEMENT

26.24 When a lease is treated as a settlement (a lease for life or lives not granted for full consideration), prior to March 22, 2006 the tenant is treated as owning the whole of the leased property save for any part treated as belonging to the landlord.[43] To calculate the landlord's portion it is necessary to compare what he received when the lease was granted with what would have been a full consideration for the lease at that time.[44]

EXAMPLE 26.7

(1) Land worth £100,000 is let to A for his life in 2005. The landlord receives no consideration so that A is treated as owning the whole of the leased property (i.e. £100,000). The granting of the lease is a transfer of value by the landlord of £100,000.This was a PET in 2005 (assuming A was not the landlord's spouse).

(2) As above, save that full consideration is furnished by A for the grant of the lease. The lease is not treated as a settlement.[45] No inheritance tax will be chargeable on its creation as either the landlord's estate does not fall in value or the transaction falls within IHTA 1984 s.10 (essentially commercial transactions which are not transfers of value).

(3) Partial consideration (equivalent to 50 per cent of a full consideration) is furnished by A so that the value of the landlord's interest is 50% of £100,000 = £50,000. The value of the tenant's interest is £50,000 and the granting of the lease is a transfer of value of £50,000.

(4) Assume the facts are as in (1) above except that the land is let to A for life in 2007. The landlord is treated as making a transfer of value of £100,000 but this is now a chargeable transfer not a PET. A is not treated as owning any part of the leased property and the arrangement has created a relevant property settlement.

(5) Father leases land worth £300,000 to his daughter for life and retains the freehold interest. He is treated as making a transfer of value to his daughter of £300,000 and a part disposal for capital gains tax purposes. The freehold interest is not excluded property but has no value in his estate for inheritance tax purposes: see IHTA 1984 s.170. Five years later, when his daughter is seriously ill, he settles the freehold interest into a trust for his adult son. This still has no value for inheritance tax

---

[43] See 24.06.
[44] IHTA 1984 ss.50(6) and 170.
[45] As to the meaning of "settlement", see 24.01.

purposes so is not a chargeable transfer. However, the settled gift of the freehold interest is a disposal for capital gains tax purposes and is valued according to normal commercial principles so that it may well show a gain. That gain cannot be held-over under TCGA 1992 s.260 because no IHT chargeable transfer has occurred.

IX WHEN IHT IS CHARGED

26.25 IHT may be charged whenever a qualifying interest in possession terminates. This may occur inter vivos or on death.[46] There are two types of termination: actual and deemed. Actual terminations occur where the interest in possession of the beneficiary ceases (e.g. on his death or because the terms of the settlement provide for the interest to end on the occurrence of a specific event such as remarriage) or ends because the trustees exercise overriding powers which terminate the interest in possession.

Deemed terminations occur where the interest in possession continues but the person who was entitled to that interest ceases to own it. For example, a life tenant assigns his interest in possession to another person.[47]

(i) Actual terminations

26.26 The IHT charge is calculated on the basis that the life tenant had made a transfer of value at that time and the value transferred had been equal to the value of the property in which his interest had subsisted.[48] The transfer of value made by the (former) life tenant may either be a PET (and so exempt from IHT provided that he survives by seven years) or immediately chargeable. In general:

(i) if the settlement ends (as in Example 26.7 below) he will make a PET;

(ii) if, however, the settlement continues he will make an immediately chargeable transfer since the continuing trusts will be taxed under the relevant property regime.[49]

In cases where IHT becomes payable in respect of the termination of an interest in possession in part only of the trust fund it is thought that the tax must be borne by that portion of the fund.

---

[46] For the charge on lifetime terminations, see IHTA 1984 s.52 and note that the disposal of an interest (e.g. an assignment for value) is treated as the coming to an end of the interest: IHTA 1984 s.51. The charge on death of the interest in possession beneficiary arises as a result of the combination of IHTA 1984 ss.49(1) and 4(1).

[47] See 27.19 for the various permutations involving assignments of life interests and reversionary interests.

[48] IHTA 1984 s.52(1).

[49] The only exceptions are (1) if his interest was replaced before October 6, 2008 by a TSI when the termination was a PET or (2) on his death by a successive life interest for his spouse/civil partner (when the spouse exemption applies) or (3) (at anytime) by a "disabled person's interest" within s.89B.

EXAMPLE 26.8

> £100,000 is held on a qualifying IIP trust for A for life or until remar-
> riage and thereafter for B absolutely. If A remarries, his life interest
> terminates and he makes a transfer of value of £100,000 which will
> be a PET. (The trustees should be aware of the IHT position and not
> transfer the trust assets to B without suitable protection in case A dies
> within seven years.)
>
> If A never remarried, but consented to an advancement of £50,000 to
> B, his interest ends in that portion of the fund and he makes a transfer
> of value of £50,000 (a PET). Assume that three years later, A surrenders
> his life interest in the fund, now worth £120,000. This is another transfer
> of value (a further PET).

Notice that in all cases of the inter vivos termination of the interest in possession, any tax charge is levied on a value transferred which is "equal to the value
of the property in which his interest subsisted".[50] The principle of calculating
loss to the donor's estate (as is normally the case for IHT purposes) does not
apply in these cases.

EXAMPLE 26.9

> (1) Jackson has a qualifying interest in possession in a family trust which
> owns 20 per cent of the shares in the family investment company. He
> owns a further 35 per cent personally. Jackson surrenders his interest
> in possession and the shares in the trust pass to his daughter Lee. For
> the purpose of valuing Jackson's transfer of value only the property
> in the settlement is taken into account, i.e. the value of a minority 20
> per cent shareholding. Contrast the position if Jackson died when the
> aggregation of the trust shareholding with his personal sharehold-
> ing would result in an IHT charge based on the value of a 55 per cent
> shareholding.[51]
>
> (2) Assume that the settlement has owned a 60 per cent shareholding and
> that Jackson's IIP was in 25 per cent of the trust fund. It is thought that
> for the purposes of valuing the transfer of value on the termination
> of his interest he is treated under s.49(1) as owning 25 of a 60 per cent
> shareholding valued on a majority basis. He is *not* treated as transferring
> a 15 per cent shareholding valued on a minority basis.

Since on an actual termination of the qualifying IIP the beneficiary is
deemed to make a transfer of value under s.52(1) it would appear that the
"no gratuitous intention, commercial transactions" exemption in s.10 is not

[50] IHTA 1984 s.52(1).
[51] HMRC formerly took the view that in the case of lifetime terminations the settled shares were
required to be valued as part of Jackson's whole estate so that the value transferred would be
based on a 20% disposal out of a majority shareholding. The practice was abandoned in March
1990.

available.[52] Even if he received consideration for consenting to that termination arguably this would not reduce the value transferred. Section 52(2) does not apply because the interest is not *being disposed of* by him but is ended by the trustees. For instance, assume that the life tenant agrees to the advancement of half the settled property in which he has a qualifying IIP so that it becomes held on IIP trusts for his former spouse. The consent is given as part of the arrangements on a divorce settlement. Section 10 does not give protection against the transfer of value. The IIP for his spouse is not qualifying after October 6, 2008 (it cannot be a TSI after this date), hence there is a chargeable transfer with (possibly) 20 per cent IHT payable on the ending of the IIP.

(ii) Deemed Terminations

If the beneficiary disposes of his beneficial interest in possession that disposal **26.27** "*is not a transfer of value, but shall be treated . . . as the coming to an end of his interest*".[53] The absence of gratuitous intent does not prevent an IHT charge on the termination of beneficial interests in possession. The value transferred is the value of the settled property in which the interest had subsisted less any consideration received for the disposal. Note that the beneficiary cannot rely on "the no gratuitous intention, commercial transactions" exemption in s.10 IHTA 1984 because s.10 only relieves dispositions that would otherwise have been transfers of value. The disposal of a life interest in the settlement is not itself a transfer of value.

EXAMPLE 26.10

(1) A assigns his life interest to C by way of gift. For IHT purposes it is as if that life interest had terminated and A has made a transfer of value. C becomes a tenant *pur autre vie* and when A dies C's interest in possession terminates so raising the possibility of a further IHT charge.

(2) If, instead of gifting his interest, A sells it to C for £20,000 (actuarial value) at a time when the property in the trust fund was worth £100,000, A's interest is treated as terminating and the transfer of value is equal to the fall in his estate of £80,000 (£100,000 − £20,000).[54]

---

[52] Section 10 requires there to be a disposition by the taxpayer but s.52(1) merely deems him to make a transfer of value. For the possibility of s.11 applying when an IIP is assigned as part of a divorce arrangement see Example 26.14 below.

[53] IHTA 1984 s.51(1).

[54] IHTA 1984 s.52(2): note that if the consideration received by the IIP beneficiary is a reversionary interest in the property or any other interest in the settlement, no deduction is allowed for the value of such an interest (see 26.30). Note also that s.52(2) applies only to an interest which "comes to an end *by being disposed of* by the person beneficially entitled thereto" and not to actual terminations of the qualifying IIP either directly under s.52(1) or on death. In Example 26.10(1) C, the assignee may in appropriate cases have taken a transitional serial interest (a TSI): see 27.16.

(iii) Partitions/Vesting of Capital in IIP Beneficiary

26.28 A partition of the fund between life tenant and remainderman causes the interest in possession to terminate and the life tenant makes a transfer of value equal to the value of that portion of the trust fund passing to the remainderman.

EXAMPLE 26.11

> A (the life tenant) and B (the remainderman) partition a £100,000 fund in the proportions 40:60. A is treated as making transfer of value of £60,000 (£100,000 – £40,000). Any tax payable will come out of the fund to be divided.[55]

26.29 If all or part of the capital of the fund is paid to the interest in possession beneficiary (normally under an express power in the trust deed or as the result of a partition), or if he becomes absolutely entitled to the capital (for example on satisfying a contingency), his interest in possession determines pro tanto, but he does not make a transfer of value because there is no fall in the value of his estate.

EXAMPLE 26.12

> Property is settled on an IPDI trust for D for life, capital at 30. (D is 18 at the date of the testator's death and therefore takes a qualifying IIP since he is entitled to the income of the settlement.)[56] At age 30, that interest terminates, but, as he is now absolutely entitled to the capital, he does not make a transfer of value. There is a deemed disposal of the settled property for CGT purposes.[57]

(iv) Purchase of a Reversionary Interest[58]

26.30 As the interest in possession beneficiary owns the settled property for IHT purposes it follows that his potential tax bill could be reduced were he to purchase a reversionary interest in the settlement. To prevent this result, the reversionary interest is not valued as a part of the life tenant's estate at the time of its purchase (thereby ensuring that his estate has fallen in value); and the commercial bargain exemption[59] does not apply, thereby ensuring that the fall in value may be subject to charge even though there is no donative intent.

---

[55] *Executors of Patch (Deceased) v RCC* [2008] STC (SCD) 453.
[56] TA 1925 s.31 as amended by FLRA 1969 s.1(3) Sch.1 Pt I TA 2000 s.40(1), Sch.2 para.25.
[57] See 12.05.
[58] See IHTA 1984 ss.10 and 55(1) as amended by FA 1987 s.58, Sch.8 para.1 and 26.45 for *Melville* schemes.
[59] As to dispositions not intended to confer a gratuitous benefit on any person see IHTA 1984 s.10 as amended and earlier comments at 26.07.

Assume, for instance, that B has £60,000 in his bank account and is the life tenant of a fund with a capital value of £100,000 (on his death the fund passes to C absolutely). For inheritance tax purposes, B is treated as owning £160,000. If B were to purchase the reversionary interest in the settlement from C, however, for its market value of £60,000, the result would be as follows:

(i) B's estate would not appear to have fallen in value. Originally it included £60,000; after the purchase it includes a reversionary interest worth £60,000 since it ceased to be excluded property once purchased by B.[60]

(ii) B's estate now consists of the settlement fund valued at £100,000 and has been depleted by the £60,000 paid for the reversionary interest so that a possible charge to inheritance tax on £60,000 has been avoided.

However, as the reversionary interest is not valued as part of B's estate, by paying £60,000 for it B has made a transfer of value of £60,000. This will be a chargeable transfer by B. C previously owned a reversionary interest worth £60,000 and now has cash of £60,000. The reversionary interest was part of his estate even though not taxed on his death (because it was excluded property) and therefore the £60,000 he receives has not increased his estate. So far as C is concerned the transaction is a "nothing", albeit that he has replaced excluded property (which would not have been chargeable on his death) with cash (which will be).

(v) Depreciatory Transactions

When the value of the trust fund is diminished by a depreciatory transaction entered into between the trustees and a beneficiary (or persons connected with a beneficiary), tax is charged as if the fall in value of the trust fund were a partial termination of the interest in possession.[61] A commercial transaction lacking gratuitous intent is not caught by this provision. In *IRC v Macpherson*[62] the value of pictures held in a trust fund was diminished by an arrangement with a person connected with a beneficiary that, in return for taking over care, custody and insurance of the pictures, he was entitled to keep the pictures for some 14 years. Although this arrangement was a commercial transaction, lacking gratuitous intent when looked at in isolation, it was associated with a subsequent operation (the appointment of a protected life interest) which did confer a gratuitous benefit so that the exception for commercial transactions did not apply and the reduction in value of the fund was subject to charge.

26.31

---

[60] IHTA 1984 s.48(1)(a).
[61] IHTA 1984 s.52(3): contrast the differently worded provisions in IHTA 1984 Pt III Ch.III (relevant property) and in the bereaved minor trust and 18–25 (s.71D) legislation.
[62] [1989] AC 159; [1988] 2 All ER 753 HL.

EXAMPLE 26.13

Trustees grant a 50-year lease of a property worth £100,000 at a peppercorn rent to the brother of a reversionary beneficiary. The brother is connected to the beneficiary.[63] As a result the property left in the settlement is the freehold reversion worth only £20,000. The granting of the lease is a depreciatory transaction which causes the value of the fund to fall by £80,000 and, as it is made with a person connected with a beneficiary, IHT may be levied as if the interest in possession in £80,000 had ended. (Contrast the position if the lease had been granted to the brother in return for a commercial rent.) Note that this deemed transfer of value cannot be a potentially exempt transfer: see IHTA 1984 s.3A(6).

If, however, the trustees grant a lease to another trust which benefits the brother, and the settlor of both trusts is dead this would not be caught by s.52. The trustees of each trust are not connected with each other or the beneficiaries.

X EXEMPTIONS AND RELIEFS

(i) Reverter to Settlor or Spouse

26.32   This exemption is considered in Ch.37.[64]

(ii) IHT Exemptions

26.33   The spouse exemption may be available on the termination of the qualifying interest in possession if the person, who then becomes entitled to the settled property, is the beneficiary's spouse or civil partner. The surviving spouse must take the settled property outright if the qualifying interest in possession arose after March 21, 2006 (i.e. it was a transitional serial interest or an IPDI). If the qualifying interest in possession arose prior to March 22, 2006 the spouse can take an interest in possession which qualifies as a transitional serial interest on the death of the first spouse. In both cases the full spouse exemption is not available unless:

1. both deceased and transferee spouse are domiciled or deemed UK domiciled; or

2. both deceased and transferee spouse are not domiciled and not deemed UK domiciled; or

---

[63] See IHTA 1984 s.272 and TCGA 1992 s.286.
[64] See IHTA 1984 s.53(3)–(5) for lifetime transfers and s.54(1) and (2) for the exemption on death. For CGT position see TCGA 1992 s.73(1)(b) as amended by FA 1996 s.201, Sch.39 para.6(2), (4) and (5).

3. transferor spouse is not domiciled or deemed UK domiciled but transferee spouse is domiciled or deemed UK domiciled.

Instead only a £55,000 exemption is available if transferor spouse is deemed domiciled or is domiciled in the UK and transferee spouse is not.[65]

In addition, the interest in possession beneficiary's annual exemption and the exemption for gifts in consideration of marriage may be available on the inter vivos termination of the interest if the beneficiary so elects.[66] Although there is no duty to report the making of a potentially exempt transfer, the life tenant should within six months give the appropriate notice to the trustees indicating that he wishes the transfer to be covered by his relevant exemption. If this procedure is carried out, the appropriate exemption will be available if needed.

(iii) Estate Duty—Surviving Spouse Exemption

The continuation of the estate duty relief available when property was left on death to a surviving spouse in such circumstances that the spouse was not competent to dispose of it (for example was given a life interest) is preserved by IHTA 1984.[67] The first spouse must have died before November 13, 1974 and the relief ensures that tax is not charged on the termination of the surviving spouse's interest in the property (whether that occurs inter vivos or on death). **26.34**

(iv) Excluded Property

If the settlement contains excluded property, inheritance tax is not charged on that portion of the fund.[68] **26.35**

(v) Dispositions for Maintenance of Family

If the interest in possession is disposed of for the purpose of maintaining the beneficiary's child or supporting a dependent relative, IHT is not charged.[69] Section 51(2) provides that it shall not be treated as coming to an end. **26.36**

---

[65] See IHTA 1984 s.18.
[66] See IHTA 1984 s.57.
[67] See IHTA 1984 s.273, Sch.6 para.2. Note that if the surviving spouse's interest is terminated during the spouse's lifetime there is no base cost uplift for capital gains tax purposes. In these circumstances it is generally preferable to let the surviving spouse retain the interest in possession until death in order to obtain the capital gains tax uplift.
[68] See Ch.31.
[69] IHTA 1984 ss.5(1) and 53(1).

EXAMPLE 26.14

> H is a life tenant under a settlement set up by his father in 1980. He assigns that life interest to his wife in 2009 as part of the arrangements made on their divorce. Assuming this is within s.11 as being for her maintenance, s.51(2) prevents this from being a transfer of value.[70]

(vi) Charities

26.37 Tax is not charged if on the termination of the interest in possession the property is held on trust for charitable purposes.[71]

(vii) Protective Trusts

26.38 The forfeiture of a protected life interest is not chargeable.[72]

(viii) Variations and Disclaimers

26.39 Dispositions of a deceased (made by will, on intestacy or otherwise) may be redirected after death by means of an instrument of variation or disclaimer without incurring a further IHT charge. Disclaimers are possible in the case both of settlements created by the deceased on his death[73] and for pre-existing settlements in which the death has resulted in a person becoming entitled to an interest in the settled property.[74] Variations, on the other hand, are only permitted in the case of settlements created on death by the deceased, not for settlements in which the deceased had been the beneficiary.

EXAMPLE 26.15

> If A by will leaves a life interest to his wife remainder to their daughter, Mrs A can accelerate the daughter's interest by a disclaimer of her life interest. Alternatively, if Mrs A has already received income from the interest (so that it is too late to disclaim), she may achieve the same result by a variation.

---

[70] See IHTA 1984 s.11 and see *McKelvey (Executor of McKelvey Deceased) v RCC* [2008] STC (SCD) 944 and Ch.50.

[71] IHTA 1984 s.23.

[72] As to protective trusts, see IHTA 1984 ss.73, 88 and 28.09.

[73] See IHTA 1984 s.142 as amended by the FA 1986 s.101(1), (3) and Sch.19, para.24 and by the FA 2002 s.120(1).

[74] IHTA 1984 s.93.

(ix) Quick Succession Relief

This relief mirrors that for unsettled property. The first chargeable transfer **26.40** may be either the creation of the settlement or any subsequent termination of an interest in possession (whether that termination occurs inter vivos or on death).[75] Relief can therefore be engineered by the life tenant surrendering or assigning his interest (contrast unsettled property when it is only available on a death).[76]

(x) Reliefs for Business and Agricultural Property[77]

If a settlement with a qualifying IIP contains business property, that property **26.41** is treated as belonging to the life tenant who as the transferor must fulfil the conditions for relief.

Similar principles operate for agricultural relief, i.e. the life tenant must satisfy the conditions of two years' occupation or seven years' ownership.[78]

XI TAXATION OF REVERSIONARY INTERESTS[79]

(i) Reversionary interests and excluded property

As reversionary interests are generally excluded property their disposition **26.42** will not lead to an IHT charge. This is because IHTA 1984 s.5(1)(b) provides that the estate of a person immediately before his death does not include excluded property (so preventing any charge to that property on death) and s.3(2) provides that for the purposes of identifying a transfer of value "*no account shall be taken of the value of excluded property which ceases to form part of a person's estate as a result of a disposition*" (so preventing any charge on the lifetime gift of excluded property). It will be appreciated that apart from these provisions, excluded property is generally taken into account for IHT purposes: accordingly if a reversionary interests is purchased for full consideration there is no diminution in the purchaser's estate (given that the value of the reversionary interest will be equal to the consideration paid).[80]

---

[75] See IHTA 1984 s.141.
[76] For variations and disclaimers, see Ch.39 and note that the variation of a will involving the redirection of an interest in possession after the death of the beneficiary may not be possible under s.142.
[77] IHTA 1984 ss.103–124C. With the availability of relief at 100% it is crucial to ensure wherever possible that the qualifying conditions are met: see Chs 45 and 46.
[78] As to business property relief, see IHTA 1984 ss.103–114.
[79] IHTA 1984 s.48(1).
[80] Note the special rule if a reversionary interest is purchased by a beneficiary with a prior interest in the settlement: see 26.30 above.

(ii) When reversionary interests are not excluded property

26.43 In the following cases reversionary interests are not excluded property and on any disposition they will need to be valued. The value to be brought into account will be the market value of the interest calculated on an actuarial basis.[81]

(i) A disposition of a reversionary interest which has at any time, and by any person, been acquired for a consideration in money or money's worth[82];

(ii) A disposition of a reversionary interest if it is one to which either the settlor or his spouse is, or has been, beneficially entitled[83];

(iii) The disposition of a reversionary interest where that interest is expectant upon the termination of a lease which is treated as a settlement. However, since the landlord's reversion has a nil value for inheritance tax purposes[84] unless consideration has been received, in practice IHT is not charged on a disposition of it.

The above can be illustrated by the following examples.

EXAMPLE 26.16

(1) In 1996 a trust was set up by father for daughter (D) for life, remainder to son (S) if he is alive on daughter's death. S assigns his contingent remainder interest to a discretionary trust. The interest is excluded property and there is no tax charge even if S dies within seven years of the assignment. However, if S is alive at D's death the remainder interest falls in. If the trust can benefit S then he has reserved a benefit in the trust. The fact that he gave away excluded property does not mean the reservation of benefit rules do not apply. It is just that they have no relevance until D dies. If S is excluded from the trust it is not thought that the gift is caught by s.102. (The concern might be that the donee does not have possession and enjoyment until the property becomes an interest in possession but it is thought this view is wrong.)[85]

(2) Facts as above except S is fed up waiting for his sister to die and sells his interest to his niece. This interest is not excluded property in the hands of the niece (and is also a chargeable asset in the hands of the niece for capital gains tax purposes).

(3) Father sells his daughter a short term interest in possession for six months for full consideration with remainder to himself. He gives away that reversionary interest. In the absence of s.48(1)(b) the reversionary

---

[81] For the definition of a reversionary interest see 26.04 and for the offshore dimension see 31.57.
[82] IHTA 1984 s.48(1)(a).
[83] IHTA 1984 s.48(1)(b).
[84] IHTA 1984 s.48(1)(c) and see special valuation provisions in IHTA 1984 s.170.
[85] See *Dymond's Capital Taxes* 5A.216.

interest would have been excluded property and so no transfer of value by him on the gift of the valuable reversionary interest. Section 48(1) prevents this. Note that the reversionary interest is not excluded property for either the father or the donee.

(v) The deemed disposition when the reversionary interest of a settlor/ purchaser vests in possession

As already noted a reversionary interest is defined as *"a future interest under a settlement"*. In many cases (but not, of course, all) that interest will vest in possession at which point the interest will be a present interest and will cease to be excluded property. Normally this will not give rise to any IHT charge.

26.44

EXAMPLE 26.17

Property is settled on trust for A for life, then B for life with a remainder interest in C. During A's lifetime, B and C have reversionary interests which comprise excluded property. On A's death, B's life interest vests in possession and ceases to be excluded property. Of course, unless his interest is qualifying it is excluded from the value of his estate: see 26.05. On the death of B, C becomes absolutely entitled to the trust fund: his excluded property reversionary interest ends. Note that if B died before A his reversionary interest will not attract a tax charge on his death because it is excluded property.

These rules were exploited in a tax avoidance scheme, commonly known as a *Melville Mark III* Scheme, which operated as follows:

26.45

EXAMPLE 26.18

S settles £500,000 on trusts under which at the end of 30 days he becomes entitled to the income of the trust for a period of 90 years. (For the first 30 days of the settlement the income is accumulated or distributed to others: there are default trusts at the end of the 90-year period.)

The IHT analysis was as follows:

(i) When S created the settlement his 90-year right to income was a future interest and accordingly a reversionary interest.

(ii) Because S was the settlor, that interest was not excluded property and so in calculating the fall in value of his estate when he set up the settlement, it has to be valued. It is likely that the interest will be worth close to £500,000 so that S will have set up this relevant property trust with a small chargeable transfer.

(iii) At the end of 30 days, S becomes entitled to the income and the reversionary interest ends. There is no IHT charge and the interest in possession that S enjoys is non-qualifying and has no value in his estate. At this point, therefore, there is a substantial fall in value of S's estate but no occasion of charge has arisen (specifically S does not make a disposition of property!). The normal entry charge on creation of the settlement has accordingly been avoided.

26.46 To prevent such arrangements, FA 2010[86] inserted a new s.81A ("reversionary interests in relevant property") into IHTA 1984. This provides when a reversionary interest in relevant property owned by a purchaser or by the settlor or his spouse or civil partner (known as a "relevant reversioner") comes to an end *"by reason of the reversioner becoming entitled to an interest in possession in the relevant property"* then the beneficiary is to be treated as making a disposition of the reversionary interest at that time. Accordingly, in the above Example, at the end of 30 days S will make a transfer of value (equal to the value of the reversionary interest) which cannot be a PET.[87]

(v) Settled reversionary interests[88]

26.47 Where an individual settles a reversionary interest (so that the interest itself becomes settled property as opposed to being merely an interest in settled property) the position is more complicated. If the reversionary interest is part of the trust fund of another settlement, e.g. because the reversioner ("R") has settled his reversionary interest under Trust A into a separate Trust B, it is not excluded property just because the settlor of Trust A was non-UK domiciled even if the reversionary interest is situated outside the UK.[89]

Instead, the position is that if (i) the reversionary interest itself is situated outside the UK and (ii) the settlor of the reversionary interest (i.e. R) is not domiciled in the UK at the time he settled it into Trust 2 it is excluded property.[90] However, if R retains his reversionary interest in Trust 1 it is not excluded property if one of the exceptions above applies unless he is domiciled abroad and it is foreign situated.

EXAMPLE 26.19

(1) H leaves foreign property on IPDI trusts for his wife W for life and then to his son S. Assume this is Trust 1 and it is an excluded property trust because H is not UK domiciled at death. S sells his reversionary interest to P. The trust under which the IPDI/reversionary interest subsists is a Jersey law trust with Jersey resident trustees. The reversionary interest

---

[86] By s.52.
[87] IHTA 1984 s.81A(2). This legislation came into effect in respect of reversionary interests to which a relevant reversioner becomes beneficially entitled on or after December 9, 2009.
[88] IHTA 1984 s.48(1), (3)–(3A).
[89] A reversionary interest under a trust is a *chose in action* and situated where it is properly recoverable: i.e. where the trustees reside or possibly where the proper law of the trust is rather than where the trust assets are situated.
[90] See IHTA 1984 s.48(3).

is not excluded property in P's hands even though the Jersey trust is an excluded property settlement unless P is not UK domiciled and the reversionary interest is itself foreign situate (which it will be if the trust is foreign law with foreign trustees).

(2) If P settles the reversionary interest into Trust 2, the settled property of Trust 2 is the reversionary interest. It is thought that despite the wording in s.48(3) the trust fund of Trust 2 comprises excluded property if P is not UK domiciled and the reversionary interest is foreign situate

(3) Assume in the above example that son does not sell his interest to P but simply settles the interest away on Trust 2. Son is UK domiciled. Trust 1 comprises excluded property. Trust 2 comprises the reversionary interest and this is not excluded under s.48(3) wherever it is situate. However, until W dies it is thought that the reversionary interest is excluded property (none of the exceptions to s.48(1) in 26.27 above applies). Therefore there is no transfer of value on the gift by son into trust. There are, therefore, no 10-year charges in Trust 2 until the termination of wife's interest when then the reversionary interest falls in. Note that the settled property in Trust 2 is not excluded after W has died (even though the original settlor H was not domiciled here). The aim of the legislation is to ensure that gifts of reversionary interests by beneficiaries of excluded property trusts are not taxed more or less adversely than gifts of reversionary interests by beneficiaries of non-excluded property trusts where the donor of the reversionary interest is UK domiciled.

CHAPTER 27

WHEN IHT IS CHARGED ON QUALIFYING INTEREST IN POSSESSION TRUSTS (INCLUDING TRANSITIONAL RELIEF)

- Overview (**27.01**)
- How the rules operated before March 22, 2006 (**27.05**)
- The charging regime after March 21, 2006 (**27.14**)
- Transitional serial interests (TSIs) (**27.15**)

I OVERVIEW

27.01 As discussed in Ch.26:

(a) The interest in possession beneficiary is treated as the beneficial owner of the capital in the settlement.[1]

(b) IHT may be payable on the termination of that interest which may occur during the lifetime of the beneficiary or on his death. There are also circumstances where, for IHT purposes, the interest is deemed to terminate.

(i) When tax is not payable on a termination

27.02 IHT will not be payable on the termination of a qualifying interest in possession if on that occasion the transfer is exempt from charge.

EXAMPLE 27.1

Property is held in trust for A for life with remainder to charity. On the termination of A's interest, whether that occurs inter vivos or on death IHT is not chargeable because of the exemption for gifts to charity.[2]

---

[1] IHTA 1984 s.49(1).
[2] IHTA 1984 s.23.

Note, however, that the charity exemption will not be available if on A's death the charity taking is a foreign charity which does not benefit from the charity exemption[3] or the property is held on discretionary trusts before being applied for charitable purposes. There is generally no "two year" grace period although see Ch.39 for possible ways of reorganising even inter vivos settlements after death so as to secure retrospectively spouse or charitable exemption.[4] If the trustees want to retain discretion they could instead ensure that on A's death the property passes to charity but on defeasible trusts so that the trustees retain power to appoint to other (non-charitable) beneficiaries. Preferably restrict the exercise of such powers to a period of less than 12 months from death. If the trustees release such overriding powers within a year of death (or the ability to exercise such powers expires automatically within the year of death), then the charitable gift becomes absolute and s.23(2) gives relief. If the trustees prefer they can instead appoint some or all of the property to non-charitable beneficiaries within the year from death and then charitable exemption will be lost. However, at least they retain some discretion on A's death to benefit non-charities if they wish.

A similar result will occur if on the termination of A's life interest the property is held in trust for his spouse or civil partner absolutely. In this case the spouse exemption will prevent the IHT charge from arising.[5] **27.03**

(ii) When the termination is a potentially exempt transfer (a PET)

FA 2006: **27.04**

(i) severely restricted the scope for creating qualifying interests in possession; and

(ii) limited the PET definition so that (in general terms) a PET only applies to outright rather than settled gifts.

---

[3] For the revised definition of charity, see FA 2010 Sch.6 Pt I: it is envisaged that the IHTA 1984 s.272 definition will be repealed. The effect will be to extend IHT relief to charities in the EEA.

[4] *Bailhache Labesse Trustees Ltd v RCC* [2008] SpC 006. On the death of the life tenant, the property became held on discretionary trusts. Within 12 months of his death, the trustees appointed the property absolutely in favour of two charities. The taxpayer's argument that no tax was payable on the settled property when the life tenant died because of the charity exemption under IHTA 1984 s.23 was rejected. Section 23(1) excepted a transfer of value to the extent that value transferred was attributable to property given to charity. In this case, the transfer of value occurred on the life tenant's death when the trust became discretionary. It was only subsequently (by virtue of the trustees' appointment) that the property was given to charity. Nor can IHTA 1984 s.144 apply to the discretionary trust so that the appointment cannot be read back to the date of the deceased's death. That section deals with property settled by will on discretionary trusts. In this case, the settlement was inter vivos. In order to secure exemption the default beneficiaries would need to have disclaimed their interest in favour of charity (see IHTA 1984 s.93) and the trustees exercised their powers appropriately to get rid of the discretionary interests: see Ch.39.

[5] IHTA 1984 s.18. This assumes that the spouse or civil partner is UK domiciled or that both life tenant and spouse are not UK domiciled: see Ch.26.

It follows that if on the inter vivos termination of a qualifying interest in possession the settlement continues the beneficiary will not make a PET[6] whereas if it ends at that time he will do so.[7] This contrasts strikingly with the rules that had applied before March 22, 2006. Then the termination of an interest in possession was generally treated as a PET—whether or not the settlement ended—unless there were continuing discretionary trusts. To deal with existing interest in possession trusts, FA 2006 provided for a measure of transitional relief which extended the PET definition (and qualifying interests in possession) to what the legislation termed "transitional serial interests" or "TSIs".[8]

II HOW THE RULES OPERATED BEFORE MARCH 22, 2006

(i) The scope of the PET regime

27.05 FA 1986 originally restricted the definition of a PET[9] to exclude the creation of interest in possession settlements and chargeable occasions occurring during their continuance (e.g. the termination of the interest). This limitation, which cut across the principles of neutrality in the taxation of settlements and the fiction that the life tenant owned the settled property, was imposed because of concern that the interest in possession trust would otherwise be used in schemes for IHT avoidance. It was feared that an interest in possession trust would be set up by a PET (thereby avoiding an immediate tax charge); terminated (thereby triggering an IHT charge but calculated according to the IHT rate of the chosen life tenant who would be a "man of straw"); and replaced by a discretionary trust. In this fashion the settlor would, in effect, create a discretionary trust by means of a potentially exempt transfer. In the event F(No.2)A 1987 extended the scope of the PET to interest in possession trusts, but continuing fears of abuse led to the introduction of complex anti-avoidance rules which are considered below.[10]

27.06 Accordingly, an actual or deemed termination of an interest in possession which occurred during the life of the relevant beneficiary was a potentially exempt transfer provided that the property was, after that event:

- held for one or more beneficiaries absolutely (so that the settlement was at an end); or

- for a further interest in possession; or

- on accumulation and maintenance or disabled trusts.

---

[6] Subject only to the rules for disabled person's trusts and for transitional serial interests (discussed at 27.15).

[7] If there is an inter vivos termination of a non-qualifying interest in possession this is generally a non-event for inheritance tax purposes unless the settlement ends, in which case there could be an exit charge: see IHTA 1984 s.52(2A) and 65(1)(a).

[8] See 27.15 and following.

[9] As to potentially exempt transfers see IHTA 1984 s.3A as inserted by FA 1986 s.101, Sch.19 F(No.2)A para.1 and amended by ss.96(1)–(3), 104(4), Sch.9 Pt III. The definition has of course been further amended (restrictively) by FA 2006.

[10] As to the anti-avoidance provisions, see 27.08.

In these cases, IHT was therefore only payable if the interest in possession beneficiary died within seven years of the termination of his interest so that the PET failed. If the above requirements were not satisfied (for example where after the termination the fund was held on discretionary trusts) there was an immediate charge to tax on the termination of the interest in possession and the anti-avoidance rules could be triggered.[11]

EXAMPLE 27.2

(1) In 2003 S settled property on his daughter D for life, remainder to charity. In 2005 D died. The creation of the trust was a potentially exempt transfer and the anti-avoidance rules did not apply because the trust ended on D's death. The charity exemption[12] prevented a charge to tax from arising.

(2) In 2004 S settled property on a stranger, N, for life or until such time as the trustees determined his interest and thereafter the property was to be held on a discretionary trust for S's family and relatives. The creation of the trust was a potentially exempt transfer; a later termination of N's life interest was a chargeable transfer which could trigger the anti-avoidance rules if it occurred within seven years of the making of the settlement (IHTA 1984 s.54(A)).[13]

(3) In 2004 S settled property on D, his daughter, for life remainder to her twins at age 21 years. D surrendered her life interest in 2005 when the twins were (a) 17 years; or (b) 18 years; or (c) 21 years. The creation of the trust was a PET by S. If the life interest was surrendered at (a), the fund was then held on accumulation and maintenance trusts (a PET by D); if surrendered at (b), the transfer was to the twins as interest in possession beneficiaries (again a PET by D)[14]; if surrendered at (c), the twins were absolutely entitled and so the settlement ended (a PET by D). Note that on the surrender of the life interest D made a potentially exempt transfer. The anti-avoidance provisions do not apply to deem S to have made a further transfer of value in 2005, because no relevant property trusts arise.[15]

(ii) Charge on the death of the interest in possession beneficiary before March 22, 2006

As the assets in the settlement were treated as part of the estate of the deceased life tenant at the time of his death, IHT was charged on the settled fund at the estate rate appropriate to his estate. The tax attributable to the settled property was payable by the trustees. Notice that although the trustees

27.07

---

[11] See 27.08.
[12] IHTA 1984 s.23.
[13] See 27.08.
[14] They became entitled to interests in possession at 18 as a result of TA 1925 s.31.
[15] See 27.08.

pay this tax, the inclusion of the value of the fund in the deceased's estate could increase the estate rate, thereby causing a higher percentage charge on his free estate.

EXAMPLE 27.3

(1) A settlement consists of securities worth £500,000 and is held on trust for A for life with remainder to A's son B for life. A dies on December 1, 2005 and the value of his free estate is £300,000; he had made a chargeable lifetime transfer of £75,000 six years before his death. The tax rate on transfers up to £275,000 is 0 per cent, thereafter 40 per cent (tax year 2005–06). Inheritance tax was calculated as follows:

  (i) Chargeable death estate: £300,000 + £500,000 (the settlement) = £800,000.
  (ii) Join the inheritance tax table at £75,000 (point reached by lifetime transfers).
  (iii) Calculate death inheritance tax: £200,000 at 0% and £600,000 at 40% = £240,000.
  (iv) Convert to estate rate:
  $$\frac{240,000}{800,000} \times 100 = 30\%.$$
  (iv) Inheritance tax attributable to settled property is 30% of £500,000 = £150,000.

If shortly before his death A had given away a further £200,000 by a PET that transfer is rendered chargeable because of his death within seven years. That transfer—along with the earlier £75,000 transfer—will exhaust his available IHT nil rate band. On his death the chargeable estate is therefore £600,000 which is taxed at 40 per cent giving a liability of £240,000 which is now payable as to £200,000 by the trustees of the settled property.

(2) Since the nil rate band is allocated against the first transfer of value difficulties may arise if the life tenant's interest in possession was terminated inter vivos. For example, suppose H left his residuary estate worth £300,000 on interest in possession trusts for his second wife W. The trustees terminate W's interest in possession three years after H's death in favour of the children of the first marriage. This is a PET by W of (say) £325,000 (assuming this is the value of the settled property at that time). She made no earlier gifts.

W dies five years from the date of the termination. At her death the nil rate band is (say) £350,000. Her free estate passes to her own children. They find that £325,000 of the nil rate band has been used up on the transfer of value to H's children leaving only £25,000 available to set against the free estate which passes to them.

(iii) The anti-avoidance rules

A non-interest in possession trust (typically a discretionary trust) could not **27.08**
be set up by a potentially exempt transfer, and this prohibition was reinforced
by rules designed to prevent a settlor with a high cumulative total channelling
property into such a trust via an initial short lived interest in possession in
favour of an individual with a nil or lower IHT cumulative total.

(a) When the rules applied

The three prerequisites were that: **27.09**

  (i) an interest in possession trust was set up by means of a PET[16];

  (ii) it terminated either as a result of the life tenant dying or by his interest
ceasing inter vivos; and

  (iii) at that time a non-interest in possession trust (other than an accumulation and maintenance settlement) came into being.

If the termination occurred within seven years of the creation of the original
interest in possession settlement and at a time when the settlor was still alive,
the anti-avoidance rules applied.[17]

(b) Operation of the rules

The IHT charge on the property at the time when the interest in possession **27.10**
ended was the higher of two calculations. *First,* the IHT that would arise under
normal charging principles: i.e. by taxing the fund as if the transfer had been
made by the life tenant at the time of termination of his interest. The rates
of charge were either half rates (where there was an inter vivos termination)
or full death rates when termination occurred because of the death of the life
tenant. *By contrast,* the second, alternative calculation deemed the settled
property to have been transferred at the time of termination by a hypothetical
transferor who in the preceding seven years had made chargeable transfers
equal in value to those made by the settlor in the seven years before he created
the settlement. For the purpose of this second calculation half rates were used.

EXAMPLE 27.4

    In 2003 S settled £190,000 on trust for P for life or until remarriage
and thereafter on discretionary trusts for S's relatives and friends. His

---

[16] So one way of avoiding the provisions was to settle property on interest in possession trusts for
the spouse so that the gift was spouse exempt. The spouse's interest in possession could then
be terminated and discretionary trusts arise.
[17] See IHTA 1984 ss.54A, 54B as inserted by the FA (No.2) 1987 s.96(1), (6), Sch.7 para.1.

cumulative total at that time of chargeable transfers was £140,000 and he had made PETs of £85,000. P remarried one year later at a time when she had made chargeable transfers of £50,000; PETs of £45,000; and when the settled property was worth £210,000.

(1) The anti-avoidance provisions are relevant because the three conditions for their operation are satisfied.

(2) IHT would normally be calculated at P's rates, i.e. on a chargeable transfer from £50,000 to £260,000. Under the anti-avoidance rules, however, the tax may be calculated by taking a hypothetical transferor who has S's cumulative total at the time when he created the trust; therefore on this calculation the £210,000 will be taxed as a chargeable transfer at IHT rates from £140,000 to £350,000. The second calculation will be adopted because a greater charge to IHT results. This tax must be paid by the trustees.

(3) Assume that either S or P died after the termination of P's interest in possession. This may result in a recalculation of the IHT liability (the PETs made by that person in the seven years before death become chargeable). So far as the anti-avoidance rules are concerned, however, the basis on which the IHT calculation was made in the first place is not altered. In this Example, as the greater tax was produced by taking the hypothetical transferor, the subsequent death of P is irrelevant since it cannot be used to switch the basis of computation to P's cumulative total. By contrast, the death of S may involve an additional IHT liability since his potentially exempt transfers of £85,000 may now become chargeable and therefore included in the hypothetical transferor's total when the settlement was created.

(c) Escaping from the anti-avoidance rules

27.11 The following points should be noted:

(a) If the interest in possession continued for seven years the anti-avoidance rules did not apply; nor did they apply if the settlor had died by the time the relevant interest in possession had come to an end;

(b) The anti-avoidance rules did not apply if the settlement had been created without an immediate interest in possession (for example if the settlor started with an accumulation and maintenance trust which subsequently turned into an interest in possession trust), or if the settlement was created by means of an exempt transfer (for example, if a life interest was given to the settlor's spouse and that interest was subsequently terminated in favour of a discretionary trust);

(c) Trustees could prevent the anti-avoidance rules from applying if, within six months of the ending of the interest in possession, they terminated the discretionary trust either by an absolute appointment or by creating a further interest in possession; and

(d) It was always possible to channel property into a discretionary trust by a PET, if an outright gift was made by A to another individual B (a PET) who then settled the gifted property on the appropriate discretionary trusts. (The settlement was a chargeable transfer by B but taxed at B's rates so that, if he had made no previous chargeable gifts a full nil rate band would be available to him.)[18]

(d) Effect of the FA 2006 changes

So far as new trusts are concerned the anti-avoidance rules are in the main a dead letter since inter vivos settlements can no longer create a qualifying interest in possession and be set up by a potentially exempt transfer. Hence the only possible application of the rules in respect of *new* settlements will be on the creation of a disabled person's trust falling within IHTA 1984 s.89B. However, looking at the four situations covered in s.89B, the anti-avoidance rules will not apply to self-settlements (s.89B(1)(b) and (d)); whilst s.89(1)(a) deals with a deemed rather than an actual interest in possession. Accordingly, the only scope for the rules is in respect of a new interest in possession being created for a disabled person within s.89B(1)(c): see generally Example 27.5 below. **27.12**

Settlements already in existence on March 22, 2006 may, of course, still be affected by the charge. The position is as follows: **27.13**

(a) on the termination of the current interest in possession—whether inter vivos or on death—s.54A will apply if there is then a chargeable transfer and there are continuing relevant property trusts. Obviously s.54A will be irrelevant if the trusts end at that point[19];

(b) in one case the current interest in possession may end, inter vivos, in circumstances where although the settlement continues the beneficiary is treated as making a PET. This is if the replacement trusts involve a disabled person's interest. Section 54A is inapplicable at this stage (because there is no chargeable transfer) but may apply in the future on the inter vivos termination of that interest or on the death of the beneficiary if that disabled person's interest ends within seven years of the original PET by the settlor and the settlor is still alive at the date the relevant property trusts arise.

III THE CHARGING REGIME AFTER MARCH 21, 2006

The changes in the IHT treatment of settlements which took effect from March 22, 2006 had the following results: **27.14**

---

[18] HMRC might argue that A is the indirect settlor having directly or indirectly provided the funds. See *Hatton v IRC* [1992] STC 140. However, even if A was treated as the settlor of the discretionary trust this would not mean HMRC could argue that A not B had made the chargeable transfer because A's estate is not diminished by the setting up of the trust—the gift has already been made to B. HMRC would have to show that the gift by A to B was a sham.

[19] Curiously the reference is only to a termination on the *death* of the person entitled to the disabled person's interest or TSI: see s.54A(1A) IHTA 1984. But it is thought that s.54A can apply on inter vivos terminations of a disabled person's interest or TSI if the other conditions are satisfied.

(i) it is generally no longer possible to set up a new lifetime settlement with a qualifying interest in possession;

(ii) the termination of a qualifying interest in possession can (subject to (iv) below) only be a PET if the settlement comes to an end at that time;

(iii) likewise exemptions from the tax (e.g. the spouse exemption) will only apply if on the termination the settlement ends;

(iv) there were, however, transitional rules which generally operated until October 5, 2008 whereby if an interest in possession which existed on March 22, 2006 was replaced during that period by a new interest in possession it was a transitional serial interest and the relevant beneficiary was treated under s.49(1) as beneficially entitled to the settled property.[20] In the case of spouses (including civil partners) there is a further extension of this relief after October 5, 2008 provided that the successive life interest arises on the death of the spouse who had enjoyed an interest in possession on March 22, 2006.

EXAMPLE 27.5 (NEW TRUSTS)

(1) In December 2009 Doris set up a life interest trust for her disabled son, Phil.[21] That transfer is a PET by Doris. Assume that Phil dies in 2012 whereupon the property passes to his siblings outright.

    (i) Phil had enjoyed a qualifying interest in possession;

    (ii) accordingly the value of the settled property is aggregated with his free estate and the IHT charge on his death calculated as in Example 27.3 above;

    (iii) if the trustees had been given overriding powers of appointment[22] which they exercised before Phil's death to terminate his life interest and appoint the property on continuing interest in possession trusts for his siblings the termination of Phil's life interest would be an immediately chargeable transfer since the continuing settlement now becomes a relevant property trust. Similarly if Phil died within seven years of the original settlement and the settled property then became held on relevant property trusts s.54A can apply. For example if the settled property was worth £325,000 at Phil's death and his free estate had a nil value and he had made no life time gifts, the trust fund would fall within his nil rate band and there would be no charge on his death. However, if the settlor had made chargeable transfers of (say) £100,000 in the seven years prior to December 2009 then the alternative calculation is made

---

[20] IHTA 1984 s.49(1A)(c); 49B–E inserted by FA 2006 Sch.20 para.5 with effect from March 22, 2006 and as amended by FA 2008.

[21] Disabled trusts are considered at Ch.36. The settlement in this case created a disabled person's interest falling within s.89B(1)(c).

[22] Note that unlike a disabled person's trust within s.89, there are no restrictions on the application of capital during Phil's lifetime if an interest in possession trust is created for a disabled person: capital can be transferred to anyone on termination of his interest whether inter vivos or on death.

(whether Phil's interest ends inter vivos or on his death) with the result that the trustees pay tax at 20 per cent on £225,000 excess. (Note that chargeable transfers made by the settlor in the period between 2009 and the date of Phil's death or earlier termination of his life interest are ignored for the purposes of this calculation.)

In these circumstances the alternative calculation outlined in Example 27.4 has to be made unless the settlement is ended within six months of the termination of Phil's interest and the beneficiaries take the settled property outright. Given that on the coming to an end of the disabled person's interest any continuing trusts will now always be subject to the relevant property regime, it will be desirable to take appropriate steps to prevent s.54A inadvertently applying.[23] Therefore ensure that if a disabled person's trust is set up within s.89(B)(1)(c) the settlement ends automatically on the termination of the disabled person's interest within seven years of being established unless there are good reasons for it to continue.

(2) By his will Reg (who died on Christmas Day 2010) left his estate on life interest trust to his second wife, Thelma with remainder over on life interest trusts for his three adult children. Twelve months after Reg's death the trustees terminate Thelma's life interest. For IHT purposes:

   (i) on Reg's death the spouse exemption applied (the interest in possession for Thelma was an IPDI)[24];
   (ii) on the termination of Thelma's interest in possession she made an immediately chargeable transfer and the continuing trusts fall within the relevant property regime.[25]

EXAMPLE 27.6 (EXISTING TRUSTS)

(1) Jake became entitled to a life interest in his family settlement on January 1, 2000. He surrenders that life interest after March 22, 2006 as a result of which the trust property passes outright to his son, Jason. Jake makes a PET.

(2) As above but as a result of the surrender the trust fund becomes held on continuing interest in possession trusts for Jason. If the surrender occurs before October 5, 2008 Jake made a PET and Jason was entitled to a transitional serial interest. If it occurred on or after October 6, 2008 Jake made an immediately chargeable transfer with the property becoming held on a relevant property settlement. If the settlor established the trust within seven years of the termination of Jake's interest in possession then s.54A can apply in the latter case.

---

[23] The trustees may not be aware of the problem until more than six months has elapsed from Phil's death. It is not possible then to prevent the s.54A provisions from applying.
[24] The meaning of an IPDI is considered in detail at Ch.28.
[25] Under the pre-March 22, 2006 regime this would have been a PET by Thelma. Note also that if Thelma continues to benefit from the settled property, the reservation of benefit rules will apply: see FA 1986 s.102ZA and Ch.33.

27.15 It is worth stressing at the start of this section that, as the name implies, transitional serial interests were intended to afford a measure of transitional relief when the new rules taxing settlements were introduced in 2006. Accordingly they can only occur in existing (pre-March 22, 2006) settlements in which there was at that time an interest in possession. Further, because the "transitional period" has now ended[27] a TSI can today only occur in two situations:

(i) when on the death of the pre-March 22 interest in possession beneficiary, his spouse or civil partner becomes entitled to an interest in possession in the trust fund[28];

(ii) when an insurance policy held on interest in possession trusts prior to March 22, 2006 remains held on interest in possession trusts after the death of the previous beneficiary(ies).[29]

It is also worth bearing in mind that many settlements were modified during the transitional period and questions will arise in the future as to whether what was done involved the creation of a transitional serial interest or, perhaps, and doubtless unintentionally, had the effect of turning the settlement into a relevant property trust.

Finally, it is apparent that even where the original settlement was set up before March 22, 2006 and subsequent assignments of interests under that settlement also took place before March 22, 2006 the new legislation can still radically affect the tax treatment of such trusts.[30]

Definition of a TSI

27.16 A TSI is a qualifying interest in possession so that the beneficiary is treated as owning the capital in the settlement.[31] It follows from this that when the TSI arises this can be as the result of a PET by the previous interest in possession beneficiary.

Four conditions must be satisfied.

1. *Condition 1*: the settlement commenced before March 22, 2006 and immediately before March 22, 2006 "the property then comprised in the settlement was property in which" a person had an interest in possession ("the prior interest"). Note that it does not matter if the person who had the pre-March 2006 interest in possession was a company or an individual: the successor can still take a transitional serial interest

---

[26] IHTA 1984 ss.49B–E inserted by FA 2006 Sch.20 para.5. FA 2008 s.141 extended the transitional period from April 6 to October 5, 2008 inclusive.

[27] From October 6, 2008.

[28] See 27.32.

[29] See 27.33.

[30] See 27.19 onwards.

[31] IHTA 1984 s.49(1A)(c) inserted by FA 2006 Sch.20 para.4.

although if a company's interest in possession terminated this would not be a PET.

2. *Condition 2*: that the prior interest ended on or after March 22, 2006 but before October 6, 2008.[32] Note that the prior interest could end inter vivos or on death. It did not matter if the prior interest was ended by the beneficiary assigning[33] or surrendering it or if it ended by exercise of the trustees' overriding powers of appointment or advancement.

3. *Condition 3*: on the termination of the prior interest someone immediately becomes entitled to an interest in possession in the settled property.

4. *Condition 4*: the person with the current interest does not have a disabled person's interest and nor does s.71A ("bereaved minor trust") apply.

EXAMPLE 27.7

Under the Baggins trust, set up in 2001, Bilbo was entitled to an interest in possession on March 22, 2006. On January 1, 2007 he surrendered that interest as a result of which his cousin Frida became entitled to a life interest in the trust fund. The IHT position is as follows:

(i) Bilbo had been entitled to an qualifying interest in possession and Frida became entitled to a TSI;
(ii) Frida is therefore treated as owning the capital in the settlement and Bilbo made a PET when his interest terminated.[34]

In general[35] a TSI must arise before October 6, 2008: Condition 2 in IHTA **27.17** 1984 s.49C(3) provides that the prior interest (viz the interest in possession in existence on March 22, 2006) must come to an end "at a time on or after March 22, 2006 but before October 6, 2008" and the current interest (the TSI) must arise at that time. It follows that the prior interest in possession can be superseded only once. A second successive interest in possession even if arose during the transitional period was not a TSI.

EXAMPLE 27.8

(1) Take the example of the Baggins trust (in Example 27.7 above) and assume that after Bilbo has surrendered his interest Frida assigned her interest to her brother before October 6, 2008. This was treated as the termination of Frida's interest[36] and the brother became entitled to an

---

[32] Extended from April 6, 2008 by FA 2008 s.141.
[33] Section 51 provides that where A assigns his interest in possession to B it is treated as coming to an end even though the life interest in fact continues (with B having an interest pur autre vie). Hence, Condition 2 is satisfied.
[34] See the PET definition in IHTA 1984 s.3A(1A): the transfer constitutes a gift to another individual within (1A)(c)(i).
[35] But subject to the special rules for spouses: see 27.32.
[36] See Example 27.7, above.

interest in possession *pur autre vie*. Frida had been entitled to a TSI but the brother is not: accordingly, the termination of Frida's interest was immediately chargeable and the trust is now subject to the relevant property regime.

(2) Suppose that the Baggins Trust had been set up in 2005 for Bilbo by Mr T who is still alive. Bilbo's interest is ended in 2007 and Frida takes a qualifying interest in possession (a transitional serial interest). Now suppose that Frida dies in 2009, i.e. within seven years of the settlement being established. If the trusts do not end on Frida's death (or within six months) then the settled property will be one in which no qualifying interest in possession subsists. In these circumstances s.54A can apply.[37] The calculation at 27.10 has to be made.[38]

27.18 There was considerable confusion about the conditions to be satisfied for a TSI to arise.[39] In particular:

(i) It was suggested that the prior interest (in the above example Bilbo's interest) had to wholly end during the transitional period and moreover terminate at the same point in time as the replacement interest. So, for example, if Bilbo's interest in possession was ended as to half in favour of interest in possession trusts for Frida in 2007 and the remaining half ended in favour of Freddie in January 2008, the prior interest (being the whole of Bilbo's interest in possession) did not end in 2007 and so Frida did not enjoy a transitional serial interest. On this reading, only Freddie took a transitional serial interest when the entire prior interest was terminated. The authors do not consider that this is correct: all that was necessary was for the prior interest to end *at least in part* of the settled property. The wording of s.49C(1) merely refers to B (the holder of the current interest which is the transitional serial interest) being entitled to an interest in possession in settled property in which a prior interest had existed. Condition 2 requires the prior interest to have come to an end but this is simply a timing provision to ensure that the prior interest must come to an end in *that part of the settled property* which is now comprised in the current (TSI) interest before October 6, 2008 ("the current interest"). The "current interest" is merely defined as an interest in possession in settled property and does not require all the settled property subject to the pre-March 22, 2006 life interest to become comprised in the current interest. Hence, if A had a pre-March 22, 2006 life interest this was capable of being ended as to half in favour of D before October 2008 with D taking a TSI. A would make a PET of half the value of the settled property to D.[40]

---

[37] See IHTA 1984 s.54A(2A) inserted by FA 2006 Sch.20 para.16 and 27.08.

[38] IHTA 1984 s.54A(1)(a) and (2). Note that s.54A can apply even if it is the successive interest in possession that ends. Section 54A would also apply on inter vivos termination of Frida's transitional serial interest if relevant property trusts then arose.

[39] See CIOT/STEP letter to HMRC and replies in A2.353 and following.

[40] What if the trustees appropriated assets between funds, e.g. A's prior interest is ended in 50% of the trust fund with his son and daughter each taking interests in possession (TSIs as long as this occurred before October 6, 2008). The trust fund included two houses, both of equal value and amounting in all to 50% of the value of the trust fund. The trustees subsequently decided that son should take one house and the daughter the other house and so appropriated

(ii) A similar misconception is that the prior interest (being the qualifying pre-March 2006 interest in possession) must have subsisted in the entire settled fund. Take the case of an accumulation and maintenance trust in which A had become entitled at the age of 18 in 2005 to an interest in possession in (say) one-quarter of the trust fund. If that interest was replaced by a successive interest in possession before October 6, 2008 would that interest be a TSI?[41] The definition of prior interest as "the property then comprised in the settlement [being] property in which [the person] was beneficially entitled to an interest in possession" has been interpreted as meaning that an interest in possession must subsist in the entire trust fund at March 22, 2006 (even if a number of different persons enjoyed interests in possession in the trust fund). Hence, in the above example it has been argued that Condition 1 was not complied with. It is true that *"the property then comprised in the settlement"* is not a helpful wording in s.49C(2), implying as it does the entirety of the trust fund; it would have been better to have referred back to the fund in which the current interest arises and defined the prior interest so that it read:

> *"immediately before 22 March 2006 the settled property in which B takes a current interest was property in which B or some other person was beneficially entitled to an interest in possession."*

Nevertheless, the authors consider that the conditions in relation to the prior interest must be read in the context of the current interest and refer to the same settled property.[42] Otherwise B's current (transitional) interest could subsist in entirely different property from the prior interest which would lead to greater anomalies. For example, if A had settled £10 on life interest trusts for himself in 2005, then this was a qualifying interest in possession and constitutes the prior interest if he then added £200,000 in 2007; this was a non-qualifying interest in possession. Assume next that his interest in £210,000 was wholly terminated in June 2008 in favour of B who took an interest in possession. A was beneficially entitled to £10 (the prior interest) which ended and B took an interest in possession in settled property of £210,000 (the current interest). If "prior interest" could be taken to mean different property from "current interest" then B takes a transitional serial interest in £210,000 because on that basis the legislation does not require B's interest in possession to be in settled property which was comprised in the trust immediately before March 22, 2006 or for any qualifying interest in possession to have subsisted in that settled property since March 22 until June 2008.

(iii) What if the prior life interest ended and the current interest came into existence under a different settlement? Consider the position if A was

the properties to their respective shares. Was this a further termination of the son/daughter's interest in possession which would therefore take the interests out of the TSI regime? It is not thought so: both were entitled to a TSI in 50% of the settled property and an appropriation of specific assets to satisfy that entitlement does not change the position. This has been agreed by HMRC: see A2.245. For the SDLT implications of the appropriations see Ch.51.

[41] See, for example, PTPR Vol.12 issue 1"What to do with trusts created before 22 March 2006?" (Mullan).

[42] A view which is confirmed in the STEP/CIOT correspondence: see A2.234. HMRC regard themselves as bound by this.

entitled on March 22, 2006 to a life interest and subject to that the settled property passed to B absolutely. In December 2006, B assigned his remainder interest into a trust giving his daughter C a life interest remainder to grandchildren. A died in 2007 and the trust fund therefore passed on interest in possession trusts for C. Was C's interest in possession a TSI? No, even if both settlements commenced before March 22, 2006. The reference in Condition 1 to "the settlement" indicates that the prior and current interest must be comprised in a single settlement.[43] This could create problems where a life tenant was getting divorced and it was desirable to have the settled property which is transferred for the benefit of the other spouse when held in a separate settlement.

(iv) Consider the position when the prior life interest ends and the trust property becomes held on trust for an existing pre-March 2006 interest in possession beneficiary. Suppose, for example, that under Trust 1 A was entitled to Blackacre for life, remainder to his son, and that the son assigned his absolute remainder interest prior to March 22, 2006 into Trust 2 under which B was entitled to a interest in possession? In these circumstances the property comprised in Trust 2 was excluded property and B had a qualifying interest in possession in that settled property. When A died in (say) January 2008, what was previously excluded property in Trust 2 was replaced by Blackacre but B still had the same qualifying interest in possession albeit in different property. It is thought that this is not a transitional serial interest but a pre-March 2006 qualifying interest in possession and that the position would be the same even if A died after October 5, 2008.[44]

The assignment of a qualifying interest in possession

27.19   If the person with the prior life interest (A) assigned his life interest (the prior interest) to C in 2007, C took an interest *pur autre vie* and C's interest was a TSI. The original interest in possession of A ("the prior interest") came to an end by virtue of the assignment[45] and so Condition 2 was met.[46]

EXAMPLE 27.9

Under the terms of a pre-2006 will trust property is held on trust for A for life (being the second wife of the deceased testator) and then to the testator's children from his first marriage. A assigned her life interest to her own daughter C in 2007. This gave the daughter a TSI.

(1) *If A dies before C*
   If A dies within seven years of the assignment inheritance tax will be payable on her failed PET. But if the settled property contin-

---

[43] See especially s.49C: HMRC have confirmed this view: see A2.255.
[44] See A2.258. This view is not accepted by HMRC.
[45] See IHTA 1984 s.51(1)(b).
[46] See A2.259.

ues to remain held in trust on A's death this involves a chargeable transfer by C (whose TSI has ended) and the trustees may be liable for 20 per cent inheritance tax on the excess over C's available nil rate band. Even if the trust ends on A's death, C's interest in possession is still terminated with the result that C is treated as making a PET and inheritance tax could be payable if C dies within seven years. Again the trustees would be liable for this tax[47]. Moreover on A's death there is no capital gains tax uplift in the value of the settled property (because A was not entitled to the interest in possession at death). So on the inter vivos termination of the interest in possession if the trust then ends there may be capital gains tax to pay (and no hold-over relief unless the trust fund comprises business property).

(2) *If C dies before A*

If C dies before A (whether before or after October 6, 2008) then there will then be a capital gains tax uplift with the interest *pur autre vie* passing according to C's will or intestacy. The interest *pur autre vie* loses its favoured qualifying IIP status on C's death. Accordingly no spouse exemption will be available even if C's spouse is left the interest *pur autre vie* so inheritance tax will be payable on the then value of the trust fund. Note that if C had been assigned the IIP prior to March 22, 2006 then C's spouse could take a qualifying TSI in C's interest *pur autre vie* since C enjoyed a qualifying IIP.

On these facts, some reorganisation of the trust before A or C's deaths would be advisable. For example, the settlor's children and C could agree a partition of the trust prior to any death. Note also that when A assigned her life interest she was the settlor of the income for income tax purposes so that if the assignment is to her minor child C, A will continue to be taxed on such income while C is a minor.[48]

Matters become more complicated if A assigned her life interest onto new interest in possession trusts (e.g. to C for life and then to C's children). The life interest itself is the settled property of the settlement created by A.[49] On C's death before A the property passes not under her will but according to the terms of the settlement. It is doubtful if C's interest was a transitional serial interest if the new settlement was set up after March 21, 2006[50] but before October 6, 2008. It also appears that on the death of C before A, even if the new settlement is a qualifying interest in possession (e.g. because A settled her life interest on trust for C prior to March 22, 2006) there is no capital gains tax uplift.[51] This is because there is no disposal of the underlying settled property of the original head settlement on C's death; for CGT purposes the

27.20

---

[47] Further C may not be best pleased at this use of her IHT nil rate band.
[48] ITTOIA 2005 s.620.
[49] Cf. the position where a reversionary interest becomes settled property and see Ch.26.
[50] Although see *Thomas v IRC* [1981] STC 382 where it was held that in the case of an assignment of a life interest on protective trusts there was no separate fund which could be treated as comprised in a separate settlement and hence the property remained subject to the trusts of the first settlement.
[51] TCGA 1992 s.72(2) does not apply.

only settled property comprised in the new settlement is a life interest. The assets in the original trust remain at the original base cost on the death of C (since there is no actual or deemed disposal of those underlying assets at her death). There may, of course, be income tax implications for A if C is her minor child.

EXAMPLE 27.10

A trust was established in 2000 by X under which A is entitled for life with remainder to B absolutely. Consider the following alternative scenarios:

(1) *In June 2008*: A assigns her life interest to C absolutely. This is a TSI in the hands of C and a PET by A. On A's death the TSI ends and C makes a PET since the trust ends (B is absolutely entitled). If C died before A, the interest *pur autre vie* will pass under C's will or intestacy. IHT will be charged on the value of the settled property at the date of C's death. The interest is no longer a qualifying IIP and there is no spouse exemption even if it passes to C's spouse. There is a CGT uplift on the value of the settled property on C's death; or

(2) *In June 2005*: A assigns her life interest to C absolutely. This is a pre-March 2006 qualifying IIP in the hands of C and a PET by A. As in (1), on A's death the interest of C ends and C makes a PET because the trust ends. On C's death before A, the interest passes to C's spouse and will be a TSI and so qualify for the spouse exemption. IHT will otherwise be payable on C's death. There is the usual CGT uplift in the value of the settled property on C's death; or

(3) *In June 2009*: A assigns her life interest to C absolutely. This is a chargeable transfer by A equal to the value of the settled property since C's interest is not a qualifying IIP. There is no IHT on C's death since the trust falls into the relevant property regime with 10 year charges. No CGT uplift on C's death; or

(4) *In June 2005*: A assigns her life interest on an IIP trust for C, remainder to D. C's position during A's lifetime is as in (2) above. On C's death before A there is no CGT uplift. If A resettles her life interest after March 21, 2006 but before October 6, 2008 then C cannot take a TSI (since this is a new settlement); or

(5) *Settlement of B's reversion*: A retains her life interest but in 2005 B settles his remainder interest on trust for C for life, remainder to D. Whether A dies before or after October 5, 2008, on A's death C retains his qualifying IIP, albeit the value of the property in the trust has increased. By contrast, if B had resettled his absolute reminder interest after March 21, 2006 on trust for C for life this would create a qualifying IIP trust. It is not a TSI since A's interest has not ended, and in any event there is a new settlement for all purposes except for the relevant property rules in Ch.III.[52]

---

[52] See IHTA 1984 s.81.

However, B's resettlement is not a PET or a chargeable transfer whenever the assignment is made because it is of excluded property.

A TSI can be a "new" interest with a "new" beneficiary

A TSI can arise even though that interest did not exist on March 22, 2006 and, indeed, the beneficiary might not even have been born at that date.   **27.21**

EXAMPLE 27.11

On March 22, 2006 Jim was entitled to an interest in possession subject to which the trust fund was held on discretionary trusts for his issue. On April 1, 2006 Jim's son Jake was born and on April 1, 2007 the trustees terminated Jim's interest and made an appointment in favour of Jake for life.[53] Jake acquires a TSI and Jim made a PET.

Suppose that Jim was entitled to a qualifying pre-March 22, interest in possession and that the trustees have a power to apply capital for his benefit. On his death the trust fund passes to his children. Jim, however, is ill and the trustees want to ensure that his wife takes an interest in possession in order to secure spouse exemption on Jim's death. Accordingly, they make a settled advance for the benefit of Jim by providing that (subject to his existing interest in possession) on his death his wife becomes entitled to an interest in possession. Provided that the exercise of the power is made subject to Jim's existing life interest and does not alter that interest but merely makes provision for the position on his death, it is thought that the spousal interest in possession will qualify as a transitional serial interest whenever Jim dies.[54]

When does a "new" interest arise?

Sometimes the question will arise as to whether the interest in possession in existence on March 22, 2006 has been replaced by a new interest in possession. The legislation assumes that the beneficiary of the prior interest can be the *same* person as the beneficiary of the current interest (the TSI: see s.49C(2)(b) *"which B or some other person"*). Any such replacement occurring during the transitional period was a TSI but thereafter it will result in a relevant property settlement coming into being (and the beneficiary making a chargeable transfer).   **27.22**

---

[53] It will be important to exclude TA 1925 s.31 otherwise Jake will not take a qualifying interest in possession because the trustees will have power to accumulate income and Jake will only be entitled to those accumulations if he survives till 18.

[54] See s.49D and 27.32 below. In general, care is needed when exercising powers of appointment and advancement to avoid disturbing pre-March 22, 2006 interests in possession unnecessarily: see A1.21.

EXAMPLE 27.12

Property was settled on trust for A contingent on attaining 25 absolutely (with default trusts). He was 18 on June 6, 2005 when he became entitled to the income under TA 1925 s.31:

(i) he therefore enjoyed an interest in possession on March 22, 2006 and will become entitled to capital on June 6, 2012. At that time there will be no IHT charge.[55] There may, however, be a CGT charge[56] and, of course, the trustees may have concerns (e.g. if he is a wastrel) at his becoming entitled to the trust capital;

(ii) assume that the trustees have a power which enables them to apply all the capital of the trust fund for A's benefit (typically a widened s.32 power). They may choose to do this by making a settled advance[57] whereby A retains an entitlement to income for the rest of his life with the trustees having power to advance him capital and, subject thereto, there are trusts for A's children. This:

> (a) will not create a new settlement for CGT purposes provided that the power is exercised *"in the narrower form"*[58];
>
> (b) *IHT analysis*: A enjoyed an interest in possession (to income until age 25) which was extant on March 22, 2006. If the settled advance is made before October 6, 2008 this will either be a nothing (on the basis that his existing interest in possession continues) or a TSI; if it is a TSI, no spouse exemption will be available if A's spouse takes an interest in possession on A's death.[59]

27.23   HMRC considers a new interest for A has arisen (so A uses up the TSI relief).[60] They take the view that *"it seems reasonable"* to treat the exercise of the trustees' power as bringing "the prior interest" (in the wording of s.49C) to an end and replacing it with "the current interest" (the TSI). Support for this view may be found in the wording of s.49C which makes it clear that the same person can enjoy both interests. However:

(i) it may be said that the interest enjoyed by A was a right to income and capital at 25 but as a result of TA 1925 s.31 income vested early (at age 18). The trustees had a power to apply capital for his benefit before the age of 25 which they did by leaving the right to income untouched but postponing any entitlement to capital. Viewed in this way it may be said that A's right arose at 18 and has never been terminated or replaced;

(ii) the position would appear to be different if A was given income till 25 when his entitlement ceased in favour of B but the trustees had power to

---

[55] IHTA 1984 s.53(2).

[56] Hold-over relief will only be available if the property comprised business assets within TCGA 1992 s.165.

[57] See generally *Pilkington v IRC* [1964] AC 612: *Re Hampden's Settlement Trusts* [1977] TR 177; [2001] WTLR 195 and 1.21.

[58] See *Swires v Renton* [1991] STC 490.

[59] For the operation of the spouse exemption see 27.32.

[60] See A2.248.

advance capital and income for his benefit at any time whilst he enjoyed the interest in possession. If they exercised this power to give him a life interest then it may be said that the original interest was of limited duration (bearing in mind that A could receive neither income nor capital at the age of 25 under the terms of the original provision) and has been replaced by a new interest in possession for his life.

Why it matters if a "new" interest arises

It will be necessary to know whether a new interest in possession arises for two reasons. First, will spouse exemption be available on A's death if his spouse then takes an interest in possession? This is only possible if A's interest is neither a new interest nor a transitional serial interest. Second, if the advancement is made in A's favour after October 5, 2008 and A's interest is "new" then it cannot be a qualifying interest in possession and as a result of the power being exercised the trust falls into the relevant property regime (with potentially a 20 per cent entry charge and 10-year charges). If A's interest is not new then a power of advancement can be exercised after October 5, 2008 without adverse tax consequences. **27.24**

HMRC accept that in a number of closely analogous situations a "new" interest in possession does not arise.[61] So, for instance, if A was given a life interest on attaining 25 but, as a result of TA 1925 s.31, became entitled to income at 18 it is accepted that a new interest does not arise at 25: there is a single continuing right to income. It has been suggested that there is a distinction between this and the settled advance in Example 27.10 which lies in the fact that *"A's interest arises under the terms of the settlement and not from the exercise of the trustees' powers"*. It, however, seems a little odd to draw a distinction on this basis since the exercise of trustee powers is, for many purposes (for instance perpetuity and accumulation) "read back" into the settlement and treated as (in effect) filling in the gaps left by the settlor. **27.25**

In the authors' view A need not take a new interest in possession in Example 27.12 when the power of advancement is exercised to postpone his entitlement to capital. Care does, however, need to be exercised by the trustees in wording the instrument which exercises the power. For instance, if that document states that the property is to be held on trusts which wholly replace those in the original settlement then it makes it difficult to argue that A's position in respect of his entitlement to income has not altered.[62] Instead, the trustees should refer to a "modification" of the existing trusts and to a "continuation" of A's income interest during his lifetime: see further the precedent at A1.21. **27.26**

IHT position if the same beneficiary receives a "new" interest

In some cases it may be quite clear that the same beneficiary has received a new interest in possession. For example, the trustees may have revoked A's **27.27**

---

[61] See A2.353 and following.
[62] Consider also whether this could involve the creation of a new settlement for CGT purposes with the risk of a CGT charge: see Ch.12.

interest in possession by the exercise of an overriding power of appointment and given him a new interest in possession. If the replacement occurred during the transitional period a common sense view was that the IHT position must be neutral. Before the change the beneficiary enjoyed a qualifying interest in possession as a result of which the capital of the settlement was taxed as part of his estate: when he became entitled to the new interest which is a TSI it has exactly the same consequences so that there was no diminution in the value of his estate. However, the IHT legislation is not that straightforward!

(i) IHTA 1984 s.52(1) provides that if an interest in possession comes to an end during the lifetime of the relevant beneficiary[63] tax shall be charged as if he had made a transfer of value equal to the then value of the settled property;

(ii) Section 52(1) is, however, subject to s.53(2) which provides:

"Tax shall not be chargeable under s52 above . . . if the person whose interest in the property comes to an end becomes on the same occasion beneficially entitled to the property or to another interest in possession in the property".

27.28   At first sight, therefore, all was well and no charge arose when the "prior interest" of A is replaced by a TSI for A. On the basis of this exemption from charge a number of "settled advances" were made in the immediate aftermath of the FA 2006 changes. However, it was also noticed that the wording of s.53(2) was sufficiently wide to permit the following arrangement.

EXAMPLE 27.13

A enjoys an interest in possession until age 30 when he becomes entitled to capital. The trustees are concerned that a substantial CGT charge will arise at that time and wish to obtain the benefit of CGT hold-over relief. Consider the position if they waited until the end of the transitional period and then, in exercise of their widened power of advancement, gave A a life interest but retained a power to advance him capital which they subsequently exercised in his favour. The IHT analysis was as follows:

(i) HMRC consider that A's life interest is a "new" interest in possession (see 27.23);

(ii) because it arose outside the transitional period it cannot have been a TSI: instead the settlement then fell into the relevant property regime;

(iii) any charge on the ending of A's qualifying interest in possession was, however, prevented by s.53(2) which disapplied the charge provided that A obtained a replacement interest in possession whether or not that interest was qualifying;

(iv) because the settlement was within the relevant property regime, the

---

[63] This includes the situation when the interest is assigned and does not, as a matter of property law, end: see IHTA 1984 s.51.

advancement of capital to A triggered an exit charge (which will be small) and CGT hold-over relief was available.

HMRC were made aware of this "loophole" in the legislation and their (pre-dictable) response was to look for a way of denying that any such loophole existed. Their solution was to invoke s.53(2A) which restricted the scope of s.53(2) and which they considered prevented it applying in the situation illustrated in Example 27.11 above. Section 53(2A) was in the following terms: **27.29**

> "*Where—*
>
> > *(a) a person becomes beneficially entitled on or after 22 March 2006 to an interest in possession in settled property, and*
> > *(b) the interest is not a disabled person's interest.*
>
> *Sub-section (2) above applies in relation to **the coming to an end of the interest** with the omission of the words 'or to another interest in possession in the property'*"

However, this provision (read naturally) dealt with:

(i) the arising of an interest in possession on or after March 22, 2006 in circumstances where it was a TSI. Note that the possibility of it being a disabled person's interest is expressly excluded and, given that we are only concerned with qualifying interests in possession—otherwise the s.52 charge would not in any event be relevant—that leaves only a TSI interest;

(ii) the coming to an end of the interest which, in the context, must surely refer to the TSI interest.

The limitation thus imposed is hardly surprising since any replacement interest in possession cannot be qualifying and hence the continuing trusts fall into the relevant property regime so that there is a diminution in the estate of the beneficiary and an IHT charge would be the natural outcome.

Hence it was thought that s.53(2A) was irrelevant in a case such as that considered in Example 27.11. HMRC did not agree, however, and took the view that the words "*the coming to an end of the interest*" in that subsection were capable of applying to the termination of *any* qualifying interest in possession including a pre-March 22, 2006 interest which was replaced by a TSI in favour of the same beneficiary. This view would have produced a grotesque result given that it could have applied even if A's replacement interest was a TSI (as in Example 27.12). The property would remain comprised in the beneficiary's estate but the trust would still suffer an IHT entry charge at 20 per cent if the value of the settled exceeded the beneficiary's nil rate band (and did not qualify for business property relief or agricultural property relief).[64] **27.30**

---

[64] This HMRC view was also at variance with answers given in the correspondence: there was no hint in that correspondence of a tax charge arising in this situation.

27.31 After a considerable period of uncertainty, the matter was sorted out in the 2008 Budget which repealed and replaced s.53(2A) with the following:

> *"(2A) Subsection (2) above applies by virtue of the person becoming beneficially entitled on or after 12 March 2008 to another interest in possession in the property only if that other interest is-*
>
> > *(a)   a disabled person's interest, or*
> > *(b)   a transitional serial interest;*
>
> *and that is the case irrespective of whether the person's beneficial entitlement to the interest in possession in the property which comes to an end is one which began before, or on or after, 22 March 2006."*[65]

This achieves what had doubtless been the intention all along, namely:

(a) that s.53(2) gives protection if the prior interest is replaced by a TSI for the same beneficiary; but,

(b) the loophole illustrated in Example 27.13 has been closed: it is not possible to use s.53(2) to avoid the entry charge into a relevant property trust.

An incidental result was that because of the uncertainty generated by the protracted correspondence with HMRC on the scope of the old s.53(2A) the transitional period for interest in possession trusts was extended from April 6 to October 5, 2008.

The spouse/civil partner extension ("s.49D interests")

27.32 As mentioned above in connection with s.49C, a TSI must come into existence before October 6, 2008 (i.e. during the transitional period). Section 49D, however, contains a limited extension of the time limit but only if the following conditions are met:

(i) the settlement must have commenced before March 22, 2006 and immediately before that date "F" was beneficially entitled to an interest in possession in the trust property (*"the previous interest"*) (*Condition 1*);

(ii) the previous interest came to an end on or after October 6, 2008[66] on the death of F (*Condition 2*);

(iii) immediately before F died E was the spouse or civil partner of F (*Condition 3*);

(iv) on F's death E became entitled to an interest in possession in the settled property (*"the successor interest"*) (*Condition 4*);

---

[65] FA 2008 s.140: the amendment was treated as having come into force on March 22, 2006 (as if the old s.53(2A) had never been inserted into IHTA 1984).

[66] If it ended before this date s.49C applied to treat it as a TSI.

(v) section 71A (bereaved minor trusts) does not apply to the property in which the successor interest subsists and the successor interest is not a disabled person's interest (*Condition 5*).[67]

If the above conditions are met then E's interest in possession is a transitional serial interest and accordingly the spouse exemption applies on F's death.[68]

Note especially the following:

(i) this TSI can arise at any time: the only limiting factors are that it must be on the death (not inter vivos termination) of the previous interest and the beneficiary must be the surviving spouse or civil partner;

(ii) it is not necessary for the marriage/civil partnership to have been in place on March 22, 2006.

EXAMPLE 27.14

Under the Wilko Family Settlement, Willie (then aged 19) was entitled to an interest in possession in half the trust fund on March 22, 2006. In 2020 he marries Wilhelmina, and under a power in the settlement appoints her a successive life interest in his share. He dies soon afterwards. The IHT position is as follows:

(i) Wilhelmina's interest in possession is a TSI since the conditions in s.49D are met. Accordingly, the spouse exemption will apply on Willie's death, no IHT will be payable and the CGT tax-free death uplift will apply. Note that the same arguments about whether Willie's interest needs to be in the entirety of the settled property are raised by the wording of s.49D given the definition of "previous interest" in s.49D(2): see Condition 1. Again it is thought that the settled property to which Condition 1 refers is the same settled property as the successor interest taken by the spouse/civil partner and that there is no problem.

(ii) contrast the position if Willie surrendered his interest inter vivos thereby accelerating that of his wife. Her interest is now **not** a TSI (the requirements of s.49D are not met since her interest in possession does not arise on Willie's death). Hence the property becomes subject to the relevant property regime and Willie has made an immediately chargeable transfer (which may be a disaster!).

[67] So if the spouse is a disabled person and the other conditions for a disabled person's trust are satisfied (see Ch.36) s.49D does not apply. However, spouse exemption can still be available (assuming the conditions on domicile etc are satisfied under s.18: see Ch.24) on the death of F. Note however that if E ceased to be a disabled person (however unlikely) and had taken an actual rather than deemed interest in possession within s.89B(c) then the interest in possession would arguably cease to be a qualifying interest in possession. If E took a deemed interest in possession under s.89 and then ceased to be disabled the position may be different: see Ch.36.

[68] See IHTA 1984 s.18.

Contracts of life insurance—s.49E interests

27.33 IHTA 1984 s.49E deals with settlements of life insurance policies in place on March 22, 2006.[69] The definition of a TSI is extended in such cases so that:

(i) until October 6, 2008 the normal rules for TSIs apply but thereafter;

(ii) provided that successive interests in possession arise on the deaths of each of the previous interest in possession beneficiaries, each one is a TSI whether or not the new IIP beneficiary is the spouse of the deceased person.

This treatment continues until the settlement ceases to contain rights under the pre-March 22, 2006 life insurance contract whereupon on the death of the then interest in possession beneficiary any subsequent interest in possession will not be a TSI.[70]

Planning with TSIs

27.34 Many existing interest in possession trusts were reorganised before the October 6, 2008 deadline. If no such reorganisations were done, the spouse/civil partner extension still continues to be available on the death of a beneficiary who held an interest in possession on March 22, 2006.

EXAMPLE 27.15

Sharon is the life tenant of a family settlement established in 2005. The trustees have an overriding power of appointment in favour of Sharon, any spouse or civil partner of Sharon and her issue. In 2020 when aged 40 she marries Jude. The trustees should consider exercising their power of appointment to give Jude a successive interest in possession after Sharon's death which will be a TSI (whenever Sharon dies) so that the spouse exemption will be available and the trust will benefit from a CGT uplift. Note:

(i) the appointment must only take effect after the termination of Sharon's interest occurring on her death (and may be made terminable until that occurs);

(ii) Jude could be given a revocable interest in possession in order to preserve future flexibility.

27.35 It is likely that some of the reorganisations (many carried out in a hurry just before the end of the transitional period) will have been defective and will not have created TSIs.

---

[69] See also IHTA 1984 s.46A–B inserted by FA 2006 Sch.20 para.11.
[70] IHTA 1984 s.49E(4) and Ch.46 for interests subsisting in contracts of life insurance.

EXAMPLE 27.16

Jasper, aged 70, and the life tenant of his family's settlement, agrees with the trustees that before October 6, 2008, they will exercise their settlement powers to replace his interest with a life interest for his grandson Julian, then aged two. Unless the trustees ensure that Julian becomes entitled to the income (which will normally involve excluding TA 1925 s.31) then he will not take a TSI with the result that Jasper will make an immediately chargeable transfer rather than a PET and the settlement will be subject to the relevant property regime.

27.36 There may be uncertainty as to whether a TSI has been created in situations where the same beneficiary has received an enlarged interest (for instance, when a settled advance has been made in his favour: see 27.00). If the correct analysis is that no new interest came into being, then on that beneficiary's ("B") death a surviving spouse or civil partner may take a TSI. Even if there is any doubt about whether B took a new interest in possession the trustees may still want to give B's surviving spouse a revocable interest in possession and argue the position out with HMRC. At best the spouse exemption is available on B's death with capital gains tax uplift. On revocation of the surviving spouse's interest the property can then pass outright to the children as a PET by that spouse with no capital gains tax due. Much will depend on the precise terms of the trust and how the advancement is drafted.[71]

27.37 Where TSIs have been created for inheritance tax purposes (e.g. to make provision for the life tenant's children), ensure that the life tenant ("B") whose interest has been terminated has been excluded for reservation of benefit purposes.[72] Otherwise, the inheritance tax planning will be nullified. For example, if the trustees have reserved powers of revocation and appointment over the children's interests in possession and B could benefit under those powers there will be reservation of benefit problems. It may not be too late to correct the position. For example, if they have such powers, the trustees could release their ability to make any future appointment in favour of B (the previous life tenant). The cessation of reservation of benefit would be a deemed PET by B under FA 1986 s.102(4).

Income tax issues

27.38 In some cases the TSI will have been created with the consent of the life tenant rather than by the exercise of overriding trustee powers.

EXAMPLE 27.17

A is the pre-March 2006 life tenant of an interest in possession trust. The trustees have power to advance or appoint capital on trust for his

[71] For a way of securing the spouse exemption by the creation (via a general power) of an IPDI, see Ch.38.
[72] See FA 1986 s.102ZA and Ch.33.

children but only with his consent. He consents to them appointing transitional serial interests to his children. His interest in possession is accordingly terminated. It is arguable that his consent makes him the settlor for income tax purposes.[73] If this is right then not only does A need to be wholly excluded from the continuing trusts for inheritance tax purposes but he will need to be excluded for income tax purposes. Indeed both he *and* his spouse/civil partner will need to be excluded to avoid the income being taxed on him under ITTOIA 2007 s.624. In this example if A's children were minors then any income arising during their minority (which has to be paid out to them in order for their interests to be TSIs) will be taxed on A.

27.39 In some cases A may retain a remainder interest but be excluded as a discretionary object of the trustees' powers. The retention of such an interest would not generally be regarded as a reservation of benefit for inheritance tax purposes (being a carve-out) but if A is treated as the settlor for income tax purposes this might cause income tax problems. Moreover there could be a pre-owned assets income tax problem if the settled property in which he retains a remainder interest comprises intangibles![74]

---

[73] See *D'Abreu v IRC* [1978] STC 538.
[74] FA 2004 Sch.15 para.8. Query whether it could be argued (as HMRC accept in the case of certain insurance-based schemes) that the reversionary interest is held on a separate, bare, trust: see Ch.34.

CHAPTER 28

IMMEDIATE POST-DEATH INTERESTS AND OTHER QUALIFYING INTERESTS IN POSSESSION

- Meaning of qualifying interest in possession after FA 2006 (**28.02**)
- Immediate post-death interests (IPDIs) (**28.10**)
- Other qualifying interests (**28.23**)

The hallmark of a qualifying interest in possession is that the relevant ben-   **28.01**
eficiary is treated as beneficially entitled to the property in which the interest
subsists (IHTA 1984 s.49(1)) and that the relevant property regime does not
apply (IHTA 1984 ss.58(1) and 59). This chapter considers in detail one of the
three qualifying IIPs that can arise after FA 2006, namely immediate post-
death interests.

I MEANING OF QUALIFYING INTEREST IN POSSESSION AFTER FA 2006

Section 49 provides that the following are qualifying interests in possession: **28.02**

(i) an interest to which an individual becomes entitled before March 22, 2006[1];

(ii) an interest to which a company is entitled if (1) the business of the company consists wholly or mainly in the acquisition of interests in settled property and (2) the company acquired the interest for full consideration in money or money's worth from an individual who was beneficially entitled to it.[2] From March 22, 2006 the interest purchased must be qualifying in accordance with the new rules[3];

---

[1] IHTA 1984 s.59(1)(a)(i) inserted by FA 2006, Sch.20 para.20.
[2] IHTA 1984 s.59(2)–(4) and note that there are special rules, (1) where the interest was acquired before March 14, 1975 and (2) where the company is an insurance company licensed to carry out contracts of long-term assurance.
[3] Hence, the company must purchase an interest which immediately before the purchase is an IPDI, a pre-March 2006 interest, a transitional serial interest or a disabled person's interest within s.89B(1)(c) or (d), i.e. an actual not a deemed interest in possession. If a company acquired an interest in possession in property to which ss.71A or 71D applied then it appears that ss.71A and 71D will not apply from the date of the purchase and the settled property will no longer be subject to those special regimes.

661

(iii) if the individual becomes beneficially entitled to the interest on or after March 22, 2006 and it is:

- an immediate post-death interest; or
- a disabled person's interest; or
- a transitional serial interest.

An interest in possession owned by a close company

28.03   When the interest in possession is owned by a close company (whether or not one whose business is mainly dealing in trust interests) the intention is that participators in the company are treated as beneficially entitled to it in accordance with their interests in the company.[4] When the company became entitled to the interest in possession on or after March 22, 2006 these provisions apply if:

(a) the interest is an IPDI or transitional serial interest[5]; or

(b) if the interest in possession was acquired on or after December 9, 2009 when the company is UK domiciled and became entitled to the interest *"by virtue of a disposition which was prevented from being a transfer of value by section 10"* (essentially commercial bargains).[6]

28.04   The relevant property settlement charging provisions do not apply if:

(i) the business of the company consists wholly or mainly of acquiring interests in settled property;

(ii) the acquisition was for full consideration in money or money's worth from an individual who was beneficially entitled to the interest; and

(iii) if the individual became entitled to the interest on or after March 22, 2006 that it was either an IPDI or a TSI.[7]

28.05   Under s.101 the participators are treated as the persons entitled to the interest in possession and the IHT treatment then, presumably depends on the application of s.5 (meaning of estate) and s.49(1) (a qualifying interest in possession beneficiary treated as owning the capital in the settlement). Before the 2009 amendments to the IHT legislation (see 28.06), it is difficult to see how these provisions could produce the intended result given that:

(i) a pre-March 22, 2006 interest in possession was not included in s.101(1A);

---

[4] IHTA 1984 s.101(1). For the operation of these provisions, see *Powell-Cotton v IRC* [1992] STC 625.

[5] IHTA 1984 s.101(1A): note disabled person's interests are not included.

[6] IHTA 1984 s.101(1A) inserted by FA 2010 as part of the legislation to counter *Melville Mark III* schemes.

[7] IHTA 1984 s.59(2): note that the section was not amended by FA 2010.

(ii) even in the case of an interest which was a TSI or IPDI in the hands of the original beneficiary, there is no provision to say that it continues to be a TSI or IPDI (as the case may be) once purchased by the company. In the absence of such a provision, the basic rule is that the purchased interest will cease to be qualifying, i.e. it will not fall within the deeming provision in s.49(1) so that the participators are not deemed to own the settled property (and the interest in possession itself did not form part of a person's estate).[8] However, for the purposes of the relevant property regime the interest was "qualifying" so that there were no anniversary or exit charges imposed on the settlement. A shambles!

The 2009 changes have restored a measure of sanity by providing: **28.06**

(i) that any interest in possession purchased on or after December 9, 2009 is outside the relevant property regime;

(ii) that it is treated as a qualifying interest for the purposes of s.49(1) so that the value of the settled property is deemed to be in the estate of the holder of the interest. This value can therefore be attributed to the participators;

(iii) section 5 is amended to reinstate the interest as part of the beneficiary's estate.

EXAMPLE 28.1

(1) A is the pre-March 22, 2006 interest in possession beneficiary of the X Trust. The actuarial value of his interest is £100,000. The settled property is worth £1 million. Y Limited (whose business consists entirely of buying interests in settled property) buys A's interest in possession in November 2008 (after the end of the transitional period) for £100,000. The s.10 exemption (no gratuitous intent) does not apply to A[9] and he is treated as making a transfer of value of £900,000.[10] The company has a qualifying interest in possession so that the settlement is not relevant property.[11] However, given that the purchase was before December 9, 2009 and the interest was neither a TSI nor an IPDI, the rules apportioning the interest to the participators do not apply. Accordingly whilst the interest in possession is owned by the company, no IHT is levied on the settlement!

(2) Even if A's interest which the company purchased in 2008 was either an IPDI or TSI, because there is nothing to deem it to continue to be such, there is still no attribution of value under s.49(1) to the participators.

(3) By contrast, if the purchase occurs on or after December 9, 2009 then the value of the settled property will be attributed to the participators and the relevant property regime will not apply.

[8] IHTA 1984 s.5(1)(a)(ii).
[9] See Ch.26.
[10] IHTA 1984 s.52(2).
[11] IHTA 1984 s.59(2).

28.07   A few further points. If the company:

(i) is gifted the interest by the original beneficiary then the relevant property regime applies and there is no charge under s.101 on the participators;

(ii) if the company is left an IPDI by the will of a deceased testator then it would appear that there is both an apportionment of value to the participator under s.101 and the relevant property regime also applies to the settlement (a double whammy!);

(iii) if the company purchases the interest on or after December 9, 2009 then there will be an apportionment of value to participators but the relevant property charge will also apply unless the business of the company is wholly or mainly that of acquiring interests in settled property (a further double whammy!).

Interests in residue

28.08   A beneficiary who is entitled to the residue in an unadministered estate is treated as if residue had been administered, i.e. as if he had the interest from the death of the deceased. Although the section refers to an "interest in possession" it is thought to apply equally to an absolute entitlement to residue. In valuing that beneficiary's estate, no reduction in value is allowed for delay or costs of the administration.[12]

Protective Trusts[13]

28.09   These trusts are subject to special rules. Essentially if the initial interest is forfeited (e.g. because of the bankruptcy of the beneficiary) with the result that a discretionary trust arises, for IHT purposes the interest in possession is deemed to continue.[14] From March 22, 2006 these rules only apply to new trusts if the interest in possession is an immediate post-death interest; a disabled person's interest or a transitional serial interest.[15] In line with the policy behind the 2006 changes it is no longer possible to create a qualifying protective trust inter vivos with the exception only of a disabled person. If the initial interest in possession arose before March 22, 2006 and is then forfeited after March 22, 2006 (e.g. because of the bankruptcy of the beneficiary) the ben-

---

[12] IHTA 1984 s.91: see A2.260.
[13] Commonly protective trusts are set up using the statutory model in TA 1925 s.33. Occasionally the terms are expressly set out in the trust instrument. In recent years the flexible life interest trust has been more frequently employed.
[14] IHTA 1984 s.88 (pre-1978 protective trusts fell within the defectively drafted s.73). The section applies to settled property which is *"held on trusts to the like effect as those specified in section 33(1) of the Trust Act 1925"*. HMRC considers that this means trusts *"not materially different in their tax consequences"*. They consider that the extension of the list of potential beneficiaries *"to, for example, brothers and sisters is not regarded as a minor variation"*. See SP E7.
[15] IHTA 1984 s.88(3)–(6) inserted by FA 2006 Sch.20 para.24.

eficiary continues to be treated as beneficially entitled to a qualifying interest in possession.

EXAMPLE 28.2

(1) A is entitled to a protected life interest in a trust set up by his father in 2003. In 2011 he becomes bankrupt and the settled property as a result becomes held on discretionary trusts for A and his family. He is treated for inheritance tax purposes as if his interest continued and the trust therefore faces a tax charge on his death. There will, however, be no capital gains tax uplift.[16]

(2) W becomes entitled to a protective life interest under the will of her late husband who died in 2009. This is an IPDI. W becomes bankrupt in 2011 and the interest in possession is forfeited so that the fund becomes held on discretionary trusts. W is treated for inheritance tax purposes as if her qualifying interest in possession continued.[17] Again there will be no base cost uplift for capital gains tax purposes on the death of W.[18]

II IMMEDIATE POST-DEATH INTERESTS (IPDIS)

IHTA 1984 s.49A states that where a person (L) is beneficially entitled to an interest in possession in settled property it is an IPDI only if four conditions are met: **28.10**

(i) *Condition 1*—the settlement must be "effected by will or under the law relating to intestacy"[19];

(ii) *Condition 2*—the person entitled to the interest in possession ("L" in the legislation) must have become beneficially entitled to it "on the death of the testator or intestate";

---

[16] Because there is no equivalent provision in the CGT legislation deeming A to have a continuing interest in possession after the forfeiting event.

[17] The same analysis would apply if W had a transitional serial interest or a disabled person's interest which was held on protective trusts.

[18] Is the capital gains tax position on the death of W any different in respect of post-March 2006 protective trusts? In the above example, s.88(5) IHTA 1984 states that "*this Act shall apply as if that interest in possession were a continuation of the immediate post death interest*". So the immediate post-death interest continues for inheritance tax purposes until W's death. Section 72(1B) TCGA 1992 states that there is a deemed disposal and reacquisition on the death of W if "*the interest is an immediate post death interest within the meaning given by s.49A of IHTA 1984*". Can one argue that W is *deemed* to have an immediate post-death interest and therefore the capital gains tax uplift applies? It is thought not. A prior condition for s.72(1B) to apply at all is that an interest in possession terminates on the death of a person entitled to it (see s.72(1) and (1A)). An interest in possession is given its normal meaning in this context and where the discretionary trusts were triggered prior to the death of the principal beneficiary; no interest in possession has terminated on the death.

[19] An IPDI may arise on intestacy when the deceased leaves a surviving spouse and issue. The spouse will be entitled to a life interest in one-half of the residue of the estate: see AEA 1925 s.46(1)(i).

(iii) *Condition 3*—s.71A (bereaved minor trust) does not apply to the property and nor is the interest a disabled person's interest[20];

(iv) *Condition 4*—Condition 3 must be satisfied at all times since the interest in possession arose at death.

28.11 BN 25 commented that the IPDI trust must be for:

> "*the benefit of one life tenant in order of time whose interest cannot be replaced (more than one such trust may be created on death so long as the trust capital vests absolutely when the life interest comes to an end).*"

This statement of intent was reflected when the 2006 Finance Bill was published in a provision designed to limit the overriding powers possessed by the trustees to ensure that the trust must end when the interest in possession terminates. Various restrictions were inserted to prevent an interest in possession being ended without L's consent. It would have been difficult to satisfy the conditions as drafted (for instance, a standard form power of advancement would have disqualified the trust from IPDI status!). Not surprisingly there was an outcry from the professional bodies given that the effect of the clause would also have been to deny spouse exemption in the majority of wills which had included a settled gift to the spouse or civil partner. As a consequence the Government performed a somewhat ungracious U-turn with the result that all interest in possession trusts established on death will be IPDIs: the existence of overriding powers which could be exercised to terminate the IPDI (with or without the consent of the beneficiary) and extend the life of the trust are irrelevant.

28.12 The original BN 25 proposal was ill thought out. Government policy required two things:

(i) that flexible interest in possession trusts should not be used as a way of circumventing the reservation of benefit rules. However, this was separately dealt with in FA 2006[21] and did not require the definition of an IPDI to take this problem into account;

(ii) that trusts should not be a vehicle for avoiding the payment of IHT. Given that qualifying interest in possession trusts and the definition of a PET are dealt with elsewhere in FA 2006 again it was unnecessary to seek to define an IPDI restrictively so as to ensure that at its termination the settlement ended. If the settlement does not end on the termination of the IPDI then in most cases it will simply fall into the relevant property regime at that point (with an IHT entry charge).

---

[20] Bereaved minor trusts receive a similar IHT treatment to that which applied to accumulation and maintenance trusts (see Ch.30) whilst disabled person's interests are qualifying interests in possession so that they do not need IPDI status (see Ch.36). Having said that, if a disabled person ceases to be disabled, then his interest in possession ceases to be a disabled person's interest and cannot revert to IPDI status.

[21] See FA 1986 s.102ZA.

EXAMPLE 28.3

In his will Jones leaves his entire estate on a flexible interest in possession trust for his wife Olive. He dies in December 2010 and the trustees then terminate Olive's interest in £300,000 which they appoint on discretionary trusts for a class of beneficiaries including Olive. The rest of the estate will be held on continuing trusts after Olive's death. The IHT position is that:

  (i) Olive's interest in possession is an IPDI.

  (ii) The termination of that interest in £300,000 takes effect as an immediately chargeable transfer by Olive[22] and because she is not excluded from benefiting under the discretionary trust she is treated as reserving a benefit in the appointed property which will therefore be taxed as part of her estate when she dies.[23]

  (iii) On Olive's death the value of the settled property in which her interest in possession subsists will be taxed along with her free estate. The continuing trusts will in future be taxed under the relevant property regime unless they satisfy the conditions of s.71A (bereaved minor trust) or s.71D (18–25 trust) or create a disabled person's interest (see s.89B).

  (iv) If Olive's interest in possession is terminated inter vivos whereupon the property is held on continuing trusts she will make an immediately chargeable transfer unless those trusts fall within s.71A (bereaved minor)[24] or constitute a disabled trust in which case Olive will make a PET.[25]

  (v) Hence, it is not possible to provide for qualifying interest in possession trusts for the *grandchildren* of the testator on termination of Olive's IPDI whether this occurs during her lifetime or on death. Any further interest in possession trusts will be non-qualifying and involve a chargeable transfer by Olive. One could provide for s.71D trusts to arise on Olive's death or during her lifetime if the testator's children were under 25. A BMT could be appointed for the testator's minor children. However, (unlike a BMT) the creation of s.71D trusts on an inter vivos termination of Olive's interest is a chargeable transfer not a PET even though such trusts are taxed according to the special regime in s.71F.[26]

---

[22] Note that the chargeable transfer is not made by Jones: see IHTA 1984 s.80 as amended.

[23] FA 1986 s.102ZA inserted by FA 2006.

[24] See IHTA 1984 s.3A(1A)(c)(iii) and (3B). It should be noted that if the ending of the IPDI results in property being held on trusts within s.71D (18–25 trusts) then the termination will not be a PET. It is difficult to see any justification for this different treatment.

[25] IHTA 1984 s.3A(1A) inserted by FA 2006 Sch.20 para.9. Note that s.3A(1A)(c)(ii) refers to a gift into a disabled trust, namely a trust to which s.89 applies (s.3A(1A)(3A)): in addition if an interest in possession trust for a disabled person is set up after March 21, 2006 because that will result in a qualifying interest in possession (see IHTA 1984 s.59(2)(c)) its establishment on the inter vivos termination of an IPDI will also be a PET since the transfer will fall within IHTA 1984 s.3A(1A)(c)(i) as a gift to another individual.

[26] See Ch.35.

28.13   Diagrammatically the position can be represented as follows:

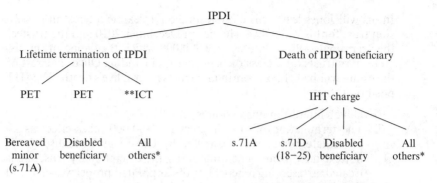

* All these trusts taxed as relevant property settlements unless a s.71D trust.
** Immediately chargeable transfer.

Condition 1

28.14   An IPDI will arise in the following circumstances:

(i) If the property becomes settled by the will into an interest in possession trust. Note that an IPDI can be created in favour of any person: it is not limited to an interest in possession trust for a spouse[27];

(ii) Established on intestacy: for instance, the statutory trust of residue which will occur when the intestate is survived by spouse and children;

(iii) Established as the result of an instrument of variation falling within IHTA 1984 s.142(1)[28];

(iv) Established as a result of IHTA 1984 s.144 (two year trusts). In brief, if the will establishes a trust which is not an interest in possession and within two years of death an event occurs (e.g. a trustee appointment) which causes the property *"to be held on trusts that would, if they had in fact been established by the testator's will, have resulted in (an IPDI) subsisting in the property."*[29]

then the Act shall apply as if the will had set up an IPDI.

[27] IPDIs may be attractive vehicles for minor beneficiaries: see 35.58.
[28] See Ch.39.
[29] IHTA 1984 s.144(3)–(6) inserted by FA 2006 Sch.20 para.27.

EXAMPLE 28.4

(1) Alf's will leaves everything to his daughter when he dies in early 2009. Within two years of his death she enters into a variation within s.142(1) whereby Alf's estate (less his nil rate band) is settled on interest in possession trusts for Rosa, Alf's wife. The variation has established an IPDI.[30] Spouse exemption is therefore available in respect of the residue of Alf's estate.

(2) Thomas' will leaves his property on discretionary trusts. On January 1, 2011, within two years of Thomas' death, the trustees appoint:

   (i) £300,000 on an interest in possession trust for Thomas' son, Gordon;
   (ii) the residue on an interest in possession trust for Thomas' surviving civil partner, Jonny.

By virtue of s.144 the appointments are "read back" into the will resulting in the creation of two IPDIs.

(3) Susie leaves property to her husband Tom for life provided that he survives her for 28 clear days. Tom duly survives and takes an IPDI. The standard survivorship clause does not prevent the interest in possession arising on the death of Susie.[31]

This is ambiguous. Does it mean that the actual vehicle which contains the settled property has to be established by will or is it sufficient that the property which is subject to the interest in possession is settled as a result of the provisions of the will?[32] HMRC have confirmed that the latter is the correct interpretation.[33] So it is not necessary that the will itself establishes the trust; it could add the property to an existing interest in possession trust set up by the deceased.[34]

28.15

EXAMPLE 28.5

Carlo is a US citizen who is deemed UK domiciled. His wife Lottie is also a US citizen who is UK deemed domiciled. In order to avoid US probate duty, Carlo's will leaves his residuary estate into a trust estab-

---

[30] IHTA 1984 s.142(1) provides that for all purposes of the Act the variation shall be treated as having been effected by the deceased. This is sufficient to satisfy Conditions 1 and 2 in s.49A: see 39.14.

[31] See IHTA 1984 s.92 which provides for a form of "reading back" and A2.226.

[32] The wording reads "*the settlement was effected by will or intestacy*" but this could mean "the settlement of the settled property in which L was entitled to an interest in possession was effected by will or intestacy".

[33] See A2.280.

[34] Or the will could add it to an existing interest in possession trust set up by someone other than the deceased. In both cases the property added is still subject to an IPDI. Of course, the property already in the existing trust will generally be relevant property if the trust was set up after March 21, 2006.

lished in 1989 which created an interest in possession for Lottie. Is this an IPDI? The settlement of the property was effected by the will albeit it passes into an existing settlement.

Condition 2

28.16   The requirement that L became beneficially entitled to the interest in possession on the death of the testator/intestate means that an entitlement which arises subsequently, albeit as a result of a trust established in the will, does not suffice.

EXAMPLE 28.6

(1) Jim's will settled his chattels on life interest trusts for his son remainder to his grandchildren. After Jim's death in 2010 the trustees exercise their powers to terminate the son's interest and appoint the chattels on interest in possession trusts for Jim's grandson. Although the grandson enjoys an interest in possession in a trust set up by will it is not an IPDI. Hence on the termination of his interest the son makes an immediately chargeable transfer and the trust falls into the relevant property regime.

(2) On Jessie's death in 2010 her will provided for her assets to be held on discretionary trusts. After some three years the trustees appoint her husband a life interest. This is not an IPDI; the trusts continue to fall into the relevant property regime (for IHT purposes the appointment is a "nothing").[35]

Condition 3

28.17   An interest in possession can subsist in a bereaved minor's trust and the definition of a disabled person's interest includes an interest in possession trust established for that person. It is not intended that the IPDI regime should apply in either case. In the case of bereaved minor trusts this is understandable since they are subject to a wholly different IHT charging regime. By contrast it is a little difficult to see why the disabled person's interest needs to be distinguished. The relevant trust must be one which gives an interest in possession to a disabled person within IHTA 1984 s.89B(1)(c) and this creates a qualifying interest in possession in the same way as an IPDI.

---

[35] It is irrelevant that the appointment is read back into the original settlement for perpetuity and accumulation purposes. If the appointment had occurred within two years of Jessie's death reading-back under s.144 would have resulted in the husband having an IPDI and the spouse exemption applying: see 39.61.

This suggests that a will trust which creates an IPDI initially may subsequently cease to satisfy the requirements. For instance, if a minor child of the testator was given an immediate interest in possession on his parent's death and capital at 30 then his interest is an IPDI. (If later the trustees exercised their overriding powers to defer his absolute entitlement at 30 then arguably the child would take a new interest in possession which would not qualify as an IPDI. See Ch.27 for a consideration of when a new interest in possession arises.)[36]

28.18

If, however, the trustees exercised a power of appointment to vest capital in him contingently on attaining the age of 18 then the trust would now fall within s.71A as a bereaved minor's trust and so be outside the IPDI definition. The consequences of this happening are considered in Ch.35.

A "pecking order"

A bereaved minor trust requires capital to vest at 18 but so far as income is concerned either the minor must be entitled to the income as it arises (i.e. he enjoys an interest in possession) or no such income may be applied for the benefit of any other person (so that unless it is applied for the minor's maintenance it will be accumulated).[37] The potential overlap with the IPDI trust when the minor is given an immediate interest in possession is resolved in favour of the bereaved minor trust which takes precedence.[38] A similar overlap is possible between a s.71D (18–25) trust and an IPDI since the definition of the former requires capital to vest no later than age 25 pending which the beneficiary must either be entitled to income as it arises (i.e. enjoy an interest in possession) or, as with s.71A, "no such income may be applied for the benefit of any other person". In this case the IPDI takes precedence: see IHTA 1984 s.71D(5)(a).

28.19

Hence, in considering what type of trust is set up in a will when the beneficiaries are bereaved minors, the "pecking order" is:

(1) BMT;

(2) IPDI;

(3) 18–25 (s.71D).

---

[36] This suggests that when drafting wills it is unwise to specify any age at which an IPDI beneficiary takes capital. Otherwise if at a later date it is felt desirable to defer capital entitlement in part or whole, e.g. for capital gains tax reasons, it could have unfortunate inheritance tax complications given that the beneficiary may (depending on the particular powers) be regarded as taking a new interest in possession. It is better to give the beneficiary an IPDI for his life with overriding powers of appointment giving flexibility and a power to advance him capital at the trustees' discretion: see Ch.38.

[37] IHTA 1984 s.71A(3)(c).

[38] IHTA 1984 s.49A(4)(a).

The different tax treatment accorded to these trusts and the danger of, for instance, intending to create a s.71D trust but ending up with an IPDI means that the will draftsman needs to pay particular attention to the pecking order: see further 35.13.

General powers of appointment

28.20 A general power of appointment enables the donee of the power to exercise it in his own favour, i.e. if he wishes he can appoint himself the owner of the property. General powers may be exercisable by deed or deeds, will or codicil or as the instrument creating the power provides. Notice, in particular, that it can be made exercisable by will. Unsurprisingly, the donee of such a power is treated for some purposes as if he owned the property. This means that if he exercises the power to establish a settlement then he is the settlor of a new settlement. Accordingly there will be a new 125-year perpetuity period and a different period in the instrument creating the power is ignored. For IHT purposes:

> (i) IHTA 1984 s.5(2) provides that the donee of a general power "*shall be treated as beneficially entitled to the property or money*" (which is subject to the power). For these purposes, a general power is defined as a power enabling the donee "*to appoint or dispose of property as he thinks fit*". However, s.5(2) is crucially limited: it does not apply if the property is settled. And, of course, in the majority of cases, a general power is exercisable over settled property which will not therefore be treated as in the beneficial ownership of the donee of the power;

> (ii) in cases where the property is settled a general power is a "*settlement power*" within the definition of IHTA 1984 s.47 ("*any power over or exercisable (whether directly or indirectly) in relation to settled property or a settlement*"). A settlement power is not "property" for IHT purposes.[39]

EXAMPLE 28.7

> Clara's will settles her estate on trust for her daughter, Daphne, for life, remainder to her grandchildren but gives her husband, Robert, a general power of appointment exercisable by will over the estate. Clara's will creates an IPDI for her daughter. When Robert dies (whether or not he exercises the power) the value of Clara's trust fund is not included in the value of his estate and nor is the power itself included.[40]

General powers and IPDIs

28.21 Assume in Example 28.7 that Robert exercised the general power to provide that the trust fund should be held on trust for his son, Richard, for life, remain-

---

[39] IHTA 1984 s.272.
[40] See further Ch.31 for a consideration of settlement powers and non-UK domiciliaries.

der to Richard's children. Because Robert is exercising the power by will and creating a settlement of property, Richard's interest will be an IPDI. The four Conditions set out above are met: specifically the settlement (a "new" settlement) has been effected by Robert's will and Richard became entitled to his interest in possession on the death of the testator (Robert). It is, of course, a striking feature of this Example that, although Robert is creating a new settlement, the settled property is not comprised in his estate for IHT purposes. HMRC accept that on facts such as these Richard enjoys an IPDI.[41]

For the practical use of general powers in IHT planning to circumvent the restriction on the use of life interests trusts to create a succession of interests, see 38.55. **28.22**

III OTHER QUALIFYING INTERESTS

A "DISABLED PERSON'S INTEREST"

The term is considered in detail in Ch.36. It is defined in IHTA 1984 s.89B and comprises the following: **28.23**

(i) an interest in possession which a disabled person is treated as enjoying under a trust falling within s.89. This covers the "deemed" interest in possession set up under a pre-2006 disabled trust[42];

(ii) an interest in possession which is deemed to arise under a self-settlement made on or after March 22, 2006 by a person with a condition expected to lead to a disability. Again this is a deemed interest in possession[43];

(iii) an interest in possession in a settlement to which a disabled person becomes entitled on or after March 22, 2006. In this case the settlement contains an interest in possession (i.e. this is not a case of deemed interest) and note that the settlement can be established either by will or inter vivos by any person[44];

(iv) a self-settlement (as in (ii) above) which gives an interest in possession to a disabled person. Again this is not a case of a deemed interest in possession.

The amended PET definition[45] includes a transfer of value by an individual after March 22, 2006 which is a gift to a disabled trust (defined as a trust to which s.89 applies).[46] This means that the creation of a disabled trust within (i) can be by a PET. In the case of (ii) and (iv) above, because both are self-settlements with the settlor retaining a qualifying interest in possession, there **28.24**

---

[41] See A2.273. It is not necessary for the instrument which created the general power to have been a will: it could have been a settlement.

[42] See 36.30 and following. Although the settlement does not give the disabled person a right to income he is deemed to have an interest in possession.

[43] See IHTA 1984 s.89A inserted by FA 2006 Sch.20 para.6 and Ch.36.

[44] IHTA 1984 s.89B(1)(c) inserted by FA 2006 Sch.20 para.6.

[45] IHTA 1984 s.3(A)(1A)(c)(ii) inserted by FA 2006 Sch.20 para.9.

[46] IHTA 1984 s.3A(1A)(3A) inserted by FA 2006 Sch.20 para.9.

is no diminution in the settlor's estate (hence the creation of the settlement is a "nothing"). In the case of (iii) above the creation of the settlement will be a PET on the basis that it involves a gift to another individual within s.3A(1A)(c). In the event that an IPDI (or indeed a pre-March 22, 2006 interest in possession trust) ends and the property thereupon becomes held upon trusts which create a disabled person's interest, the relevant beneficiary whose interest has ended makes a PET.

A transitional serial interest

28.25 The meaning of this term is considered at 27.16.

EXAMPLE 29.2

(1) S creates a discretionary trust on January 1, 1999. The first anniversary charge will fall on January 1, 2009; the next on January 1, 2019 and so on. If the trust had been created by will and the testator had died on December 31, 2005, that date marks the creation of the settlement.[10]

(2) On January 1, 2004 S created a flexible accumulation and maintenance trust.[11] On April 6, 2008 the trust ceased to qualify as accumulation and maintenance because of the amended s.71 requirements which came into force on that day.[12] It therefore, became a relevant property settlement. The first anniversary charge will fall on January 1, 2014.[13]

(3) Q set up a £10 trust on June 1, 2000 to which he added property on his death on September 1, 2007. The trust commenced on June 1, 2000 when property (£10) first became comprised in it.[14]

(4) T set up three pilot discretionary trusts on consecutive days in August 2004; by his will £300,000 is added to each trust when he dies on September 1, 2007. For each of the three settlements 10-year charges run from their date of commencement (see (3) above) and if the trusts were subsequently to be consolidated (by the trustees of two of the settlements exercising a power in their settlement to transfer assets to the third) they would still, for IHT purposes, be treated as three separate settlements (see IHTA 1984 s.81(1)).[15]

(5) S settled property on August 1, 2002 on trusts under which his wife is given a (qualifying) life interest with remainder on trusts for his grandchildren. As a result of s.80, for the purposes of the relevant property regime, the property is treated as being comprised in a settlement made by S's wife at the time when her interest ends. However, the 10-year anniversaries run from August 1, 2002 when the original trust was established.[16]

(6) X receives a legacy from his father. He executes a deed of variation whereby he varies it into a discretionary trust for his children and the deed of variation is read back for inheritance tax purposes.[17] The 10-year charge is calculated by reference to father's death since the trust commences at the date of death and is treated as made by the deceased.[18]

---

[10] IHTA 1984 s.83.

[11] For a consideration of A-M trusts and the transitional rules that applied, see Ch.30.

[12] The trust was not amended to provide for vesting of capital and income at 18 or so as to fall within s.71D: see 35.35.

[13] Note, however, that the charge is calculated by reference to the period during which the trust qualified as a relevant property settlement, i.e. from April 6, 2008. See 29.22.

[14] This trust is sometimes referred to as a "pilot settlement". In practice, would-be settlors may well execute a trust instrument but fail to constitute the trust by vesting property in the trustees. In such a case the trust will only commence for IHT purposes when the trustees receive property, for instance on the death of the settlor (and this, of course, may be precisely what the pilot trust was intended to avoid!). For pilot trusts, see Ch.41.

[15] Section 81(1) is discussed at 24.13.

[16] IHTA 1984 s.61(2): see further 24.16.

[17] Under IHTA 1984 s.142.

[18] See Ch.39 for post-death variations.

29.04 Apart from the anniversary charge, IHT is also levied (the "exit charge") on the happening of certain events (the most important of which is the ending of the trust, e.g. by the outright appointment of capital to a beneficiary). In general, the tax then charged is a proportion of the last periodic charge. Special charging provisions operate for chargeable events which occur before the first 10-year anniversary when the first periodic charge is levied.

II CREATION OF THE SETTLEMENT

29.05 The creation of the settlement will, generally, be a chargeable transfer of value by the settlor (it cannot be a potentially exempt transfer). The following matters should be noted:

(i) If the settlement is created inter vivos, grossing-up applies unless the inheritance tax is paid out of the settled property.

EXAMPLE 29.3

Ann, who had made no previous chargeable transfers, settles £335,000 on discretionary trusts in June 2011. She has already used her annual exemption.[19] The first £325,000 falls within her nil rate band and therefore inheritance tax is payable on the balance of £10,000 at 20 per cent. If Ann pays the inheritance tax on the gift, her estate falls in value by £335,000 plus the inheritance tax payable on the £10,000, i.e. Ann is charged on the cost of the gift by treating the £325,000 as a gift net of tax. Therefore the part of the gift on which inheritance tax is payable (£10,000) must be grossed up to reflect the amount of tax payable by using the formula:

100 / 100 – R where R is the rate of inheritance tax applicable to the sum in question.

The calculation is £10,000 × 100/80 = £12,500 gross (IHT is £2,500).

Hence, if Ann pays the tax the total cost of the gift for Ann is £335,000 + £2,500 = £337,500. The trust receives £335,000.

If the trustees pay the tax the total cost of the gift to Ann is £335,000, the IHT liability is £2,000 (20% × £10,000) and the trust ends up with £333,000.

Note that once the transferor's cumulative total exceeds her nil rate band, tax is levied at 25 per cent of the excess if the transferor pays the tax. So if in the above example Ann had already made chargeable trans-

---

[19] Earlier gifts in the same tax year are given the benefit of the annual exemption. If A made an outright gift of £3,000 this would not be a PET but an exempt transfer in its own right. Therefore he cannot make a gift to a discretionary trust later in the tax year and claim the annual exemption.

fers of £325,000 then a further chargeable transfer of £325,000 would attract tax of £81,250 on Ann.

(ii) The cumulative total of chargeable transfers made by the settlor is crucial because it forms part of the cumulative total of the settlement on all future chargeable occasions (i.e. the settlor's transfers do not drop out of the cumulative total after seven years when calculating 10-year anniversary and exit charges). Hence, to calculate the correct IHT charge it is essential that the trustees know the settlor's cumulative total at the date when he created the trust.[20] If the settlor made earlier lifetime gifts which were PETs they are treated as exempt transfers unless and until the transferor dies within the following seven years and are therefore not cumulated in calculating inheritance tax on subsequent chargeable transfers unless the transferor dies within seven years.[21]

(iii) A "related settlement" is another settlement created by the same settlor on the same day as the discretionary trust (other than a charitable trust). Generally such settlements should be avoided.[22]

(iv) Additions of property by the original settlor to his settlement should be avoided unless the settlor has made no previous PETs or chargeable transfers and the additions are all within his unused nil rate band. If property is added by a person other than the original settlor, the addition is treated as a separate settlement for inheritance tax charging purposes.[23]

Particular problems may arise for the trustees if the settlor dies within seven years of creating the trust. If this happens, potentially exempt transfers made before the settlement was created and within seven years of his death become chargeable so that tax on creation of the settlement and the computation of any exit charge[24] made during this period may need to be recalculated. If extra tax becomes payable, this is primarily the responsibility of the settlement trustees and their liability is not limited to settlement property in their hands at that time. Given this danger it is prudent for trustees who are distributing property from the discretionary trust within the first seven years to retain

29.06

---

[20] If, as a result of the settlor's fraud, wilful default or neglect, there is an underpayment of inheritance tax, HMRC may recover that sum from the trustees outside the normal six year time limit. In such cases the time limit is six years from the date when the impropriety comes to the notice of HMRC (IHTA 1984 s.240(3)). Obviously a problem would arise for trustees if at the time when the underpayment came to light they held insufficient assets to discharge the extra inheritance tax because they could be made personally liable for the tax unpaid. HMRC have stated that where the trustees have acted in good faith and hold insufficient settlement assets they will not seek to recover any unpaid tax from them personally.

[21] See Example 29.4.

[22] As to the calculation of IHT on property in a related settlement, see 29.08 below. Note that it is only the value of property comprised in the related settlement immediately after it commenced which is included so if two trusts of £10 were set up on the same day they would be related property settlements but subsequent additions would not be related. Charitable trusts are not related settlements. Settlements established in a will are related unless IHTA 1984 s.80(4) applies (this provides that a trust setting up an IPDI or disabled person's interest for a surviving spouse (or surviving civil partner) is treated as only taking effect on the coming to an end of the "postponing interest": see 24.17).

[23] See IHTA 1984 s.44(2) and 24.18.

[24] As to exit charges, see 29.07 below.

sufficient funds or take suitable indemnities to cover their contingent inheritance tax liability.[25]

EXAMPLE 29.4

Bird makes the following transfers of value:

(1) June 2005; £500,000 to his sister Cyd (a potentially exempt transfer).
(2) May 2009; £325,000 to a family discretionary trust.
(3) In May 2010 the trustees distribute the entire trust fund to the beneficiaries and in May 2011 Bird dies.

As a result of his death, the 2002 potentially exempt transfer is chargeable (the resultant IHT is primarily the responsibility of Cyd) and in addition tax on the creation of the settlement must be recalculated. When it was set up the potentially exempt transfer was ignored so that the transfer fell within Bird's nil rate band. With his death, however, inheritance tax must be calculated, at the rates in force in May 2006, on transfers from £500,000 to £785,000. In addition, no IHT will have been charged on the termination of the trust in May 2010 and therefore a recomputation is again necessary, with the trustees being primarily accountable for the resulting bill.

III EXIT CHARGES BEFORE THE FIRST 10-YEAR ANNIVERSARY

29.07 An exit charge arises whenever property in the settlement ceases to be relevant property.[26] Therefore, if the trustees appoint property to a beneficiary absolutely or if (before March 22, 2006) an interest in possession arose in any part of the fund, there is an inheritance tax charge on the value of the property ceasing to be held on relevant property trusts. A charge is also imposed if the trustees make a disposition as a result of which the value of relevant property comprised in the settlement falls (a "depreciatory transaction": notice that there is no requirement that the transaction be made with a beneficiary or with a person connected with him).[27]

If the resultant IHT is paid out of the property that is left in a continuing trust, grossing-up applies.

The exit charge does not apply to a payment of costs or expenses (so long as fairly attributable to the relevant property), nor does it catch a payment which is income of any person for the purposes of income tax.[28]

---

[25] Note also the "PET trap". When PETs are made within seven years following a chargeable transfer and the settlor survives seven years from the chargeable transfer but dies within seven years of the PET, more inheritance tax can be paid than if no PET had been made. This is because, in assessing the tax due on the failed PET, the settlor's cumulative total at the time of the PET has to be calculated *taking into account* the chargeable transfer. This will affect the tax payable by the donee of the PET.

[26] IHT 1984 s.65(1).

[27] Contrast the position of interest in possession trusts, see 26.31.

[28] IHTA 1984 s.65(5).

Calculation of the settlement rate

29.08 The rate of tax charged is based on half the full inheritance tax rates (sometimes called the lifetime rates) even if the trust was set up under the will of the settlor. The rate of tax actually payable is then 30 per cent of those rates applicable to a hypothetical chargeable transfer which is the sum of the following:

(a) the value of the property in the settlement immediately after it commenced[29];

(b) the value (at the date of the addition) of any added property; and

(c) the value of property in a related settlement (valued immediately after it commenced).[30]

No account is taken of any rise or fall in the value of the settled fund and the value comprised in the settlement, and in any related settlement, can include property subject to a qualifying interest in possession.

29.09 Tax on this hypothetical transfer is calculated by joining the IHT table at the point reached by the cumulative total of previous chargeable transfers made by the settlor in the seven years before he created the settlement. Other chargeable transfers made by the settlor on the same day as the settlement are ignored and, therefore, if the settlement is created on death, other gifts made in the will or on intestacy are ignored.[31]

29.10 The tax is converted to an average rate (the equivalent of an estate rate) and 30 per cent of that rate is then taken. The resultant rate (the "settlement rate") is used as the basis for calculating the exit charge.

EXAMPLE 29.5

Jasper settles £340,000 on discretionary trusts on April 1, 2006. His total chargeable transfers immediately before that date stood at £85,000. Jason pays the inheritance tax due on creation of the settlement. If an exit charge arises before the first 10-year anniversary of the fund (April 1, 2013) the settlement rate would be calculated as follows:

(1) Calculate the hypothetical chargeable transfer. As there is no added property and no related settlement it comprises only the value of the property in the settlement immediately after its creation (i.e. £340,000).

(2) Cumulate the £340,000 with the previous chargeable transfers of Jasper (i.e. £85,000) = £425,000. Taking inheritance tax rates current at the time when the exit charge arises, tax on transfers between £85,000 and £425,000 is £20,000 (using tax year 2011–12 rates with a nil rate band of £325,000).

---

[29] This will be the net value, i.e. if the trustees paid tax on the creation of the trust this will reduce the value of the property in the settlement.
[30] IHTA 1984 s.68(5).
[31] See IHTA 1984 s.68(4)(b) as amended by the FA 1986 s.101(1), (3), Sch.19 para.18. Of course other trusts created by the will may be related settlements.

(3) The tax converted to a percentage rate is 6.15; (20,000 / 340,000) 30 per cent of that rate produces a settlement rate of 1.85 per cent.

Tax charge

29.11 The charge is on the fall in value of the property in the settlement.[32] To establish the rate of charge, a further proportion of the settlement rate must be calculated equal to one-fortieth of the settlement rate for each complete successive quarter that has elapsed from the creation of the settlement to the date of the exit charge. That proportion of the settlement rate is applied to the chargeable transfer (the "effective rate").

EXAMPLE 29.6

Assume in Example 29.5 that on March 25, 2010 there was an exit charge on £20,000 ceasing to be relevant property. The effective rate of inheritance tax is calculated as follows (using 2009–10 rates):

(1) Take completed quarters since the settlement was created, i.e. 15.
(2) Take fifteen-fortieths of the "settlement rate" (1.85%) to discover the effective rate = 0.694%.
(3) The effective rate is applied to the fall in value of the relevant property. The inheritance tax is, therefore, £138.80 if the tax is borne by the beneficiary; or £139.77 if borne by the remaining fund (as a result of "grossing-up").

29.12 There is no charge on events that occur in the first three months of the settlement[33] or, when the trust was set up by the settlor on his death, on events occurring within two years of that death.[34] Note, however, that if the trustees of a relevant property trust appoint a beneficiary an interest in possession on or after March 22, 2006 the property remains relevant property (unless the beneficiary is disabled or the trust was set up by will so that reading-back under s.144 applies to create an IPDI)[35] and no exit charge arises. Similarly, if property is appointed to another settlement (other than a disabled trust) no exit charge will arise even if the new trust is an interest in possession trust. Such events are "nothings".[36]

The rate of tax is charged by reference to the initial value of the settled property which has encouraged the use of nil rate band discretionary trusts. Provided that the settlor had not exhausted his IHT nil rate band so that the

---

[32] Hence, if the trust had a 55% shareholding in a company and the trustees appointed a beneficiary a 15% shareholding the loss of control in the trust would be taken into account.
[33] IHTA 1984 s.65(4).
[34] IHTA 1984 s.144(2).
[35] IHTA 1984 s.89B. For s.144, reading-back and IPDIs, see 39.60.
[36] In practice it is relatively common for discretionary trustees to appoint a revocable interest in possession (e.g. to a beneficiary with only a small income) in order to avoid the 50% income tax rate that applies to such trusts: for a precedent revocable deed of appointment A1.19.

initial transfer of value on creation of the settlement was taxed at 0 per cent, capital distributions before the first tenth anniversary will be free of inheritance tax. Note, however, that if the property originally settled was business or agricultural property qualifying for relief (so that either the value put into the settlement was nil or reduced to come within the settlor's nil rate band) a tax charge can arise if the property ceases to be settled within the first 10 years if at that time it did not qualify for APR or BPR.[37]

EXAMPLE 29.7

(1) On May 1, 2011, Z settles £325,000 on discretionary trusts for his issue. He has made no previous chargeable transfers or PETs so that this is a "nil rate band discretionary trust". The value of the settled property increases dramatically to £2 million which on April 30, 2021 the trustees appoint absolutely to Z's two sons. There is no IHT exit charge payable (since that charge is calculated by reference to the value of the property originally settled in 2011).

(2) Contrast the position if on April 30, 2021 the trustees had merely appointed the sons' interests in possession in the trust fund. This is a "nothing" for IHT purposes; the settlement continues to be taxed under the relevant property regime and the 10-year charge on May 1, 2021 will be based on the then value of the settled property (£2 million).

(3) Likewise, note that if the trustees had determined to appoint out sufficient property to reduce the value of what remains in the settlement so that it falls within the then nil rate band then although there will be no exit charge on April 30, 2021, that value will be included in the settlement's cumulative total for the purpose of calculating the anniversary charge on May 1, 2021.[38]

IV CHARGE ON THE FIRST 10-YEAR ANNIVERSARY

The charge is levied on the value of the relevant property comprised in the set‑ **29.13** tlement immediately before the anniversary[39] and at first sight no distinction appears to be drawn between income and capital in the fund. HMRC accept, however, that income only becomes relevant property, and therefore subject to charge, when it has been accumulated.[40] Pending accumulation, the income is not subject to the anniversary charge and can, therefore, be distributed free from any exit charge. The crucial question is, therefore, at what moment is income accumulated? Obviously, when an irrevocable decision to that effect has been taken by trustees and it may also occur after a reasonable time for distribution has passed.[41] The legislation gives no guidance on what property is

[37] See generally Chs 45 and 46.
[38] See further 29.16.
[39] See IHTA 1984 s.64.
[40] See SP 8/86 and [1989] *Capital Taxes News* Vol.8, May 1989.
[41] But see *Re Locker's Settlement Trusts, Meachem v Sachs* [1978] 1 All ER 216; [1977] 1 WLR

treated as being distributed first, i.e. if an appointment is made by the trustees out of property comprised in the settlement, does it come out of the original capital or out of accumulations of income? As a reduced charge may apply to property which has been added to the trust (such as accumulated income) this is an important omission.[42]

The assets in the trust fund are valued according to general principles and, if they include business or agricultural property, the reliefs appropriate to that property apply, subject to satisfaction of the relevant conditions. Any inheritance tax charged on such property is payable by instalments.[43]

Calculation of the rate of tax

29.14   Half rates are used in calculating the inheritance tax rate and, as with the exit charge[44]; the calculation depends upon a hypothetical chargeable transfer. The calculation is as follows:

Step 1: Calculate the hypothetical chargeable transfer which is made up of the sum of the following:

(i) the value of relevant property comprised in the settlement immediately before the anniversary;

(ii) the value, immediately after it was created, of property comprised in a related settlement; and

(iii) the value, at the date when the settlement was created, of any non-relevant property then in the settlement which has not subsequently become relevant property. So this would include settled property at the date of the settlement which has subsequently been distributed to a beneficiary.[45]

29.15   Normally the hypothetical chargeable transfer will be made up exclusively of property falling within paragraph (i) above. Property within paragraphs (ii) and (iii) above affects the rate of inheritance tax to be charged without itself

---

1323 where income which arose between 1965 and 1968 was still available for distribution in 1977 and it was accepted that it had not been accumulated. In that case a distinction was drawn between a trust where the trustees have a power to distribute and an obligation to accumulate in default of exercise of the power of distribution and a trust where there was an obligation to distribute but a mere power to accumulate. In *Re Locker* there was a direction to distribute income: "the trustees *shall* pay, divide or apply the income of the trust fund to or for the beneficiaries" and the Court held that although in these circumstances it was the duty of the trustees to distribute the trust income within a reasonable time after it came into their hands they could still distribute some years later. The fact that they had failed in their duty earlier did not mean they could not carry it out now: "failure to exercise the permissive power within the proper limits of time left the default trusts standing. In the case of an obligatory power [to distribute] the failure to execute the trust promptly is an unfulfilled duty still in existence . . . the court can permit the existing trustees if willing and competent to do so to repair their own inaction." Cf. *Allen-Meyrick's Will Trusts* [1966] 1 WLR where the power to distribute was discretionary.

[42] As to the reduction in the rate of the anniversary charge for property which has been added to the trust, see 29.21.

[43] See IHTA 1984 ss.103–114, 115–124C, 227 as amended and Chs 45 and 46.

[44] As to exit charges before the first 10-year anniversary, see 22.07.

[45] This will be significant when old A-M trusts have become subject to the relevant property regime after certain of the beneficiaries became absolutely entitled to their shares and IHTA 1984 s.71(4) applied to prevent any tax charge from then arising: see Ch.30.

being taxed. Related settlements are included because transfers made on the same day as the creation of the settlement are normally ignored and, therefore, an inheritance tax advantage could be achieved if the settlor were to set up a series of small trust funds rather than one large fund.[46] Non-relevant property in the settlement is included because the trustees could switch the values between the two portions of the fund.

Step 2: Calculate tax at half rates on the hypothetical chargeable transfer **29.16** by joining the inheritance tax table at the point reached by:

(i) the chargeable transfers including failed PETs of the settlor made in the seven years before he created the settlement; and

(ii) chargeable transfers made by the settlement in the first 10 years (see Example 29.7(3)). Where a settlement was created after March 26, 1974 and before March 9, 1982, distribution payments (as defined by the capital transfer tax charging regime in force between those dates) must also be cumulated.[47]

Discretionary settlements therefore have their own total of chargeable transfers; with transfers over a 10-year period being cumulated (the seven-year period used for individuals is not employed for discretionary trusts). The unique feature of a settlement's accumulation lies in the inclusion (and they never drop out) of chargeable transfers of the settlor in the seven years before the settlement is created.

Step 3: The tax is converted to a percentage and 30 per cent of that rate is **29.17** then taken and charged upon the relevant property in the settlement. For the tax year 2011–12 the highest rate of inheritance tax is 20 per cent (half of 40 per cent). The highest effective rate (anniversary rate) is, therefore, 30 per cent of 20 per cent, i.e. six per cent.

EXAMPLE 29.8

Take the facts of Example 29.5 (i.e. original fund £340,000, exit charge on £20,000; previous transfers of settlor £85,000). In addition, assume that Jasper had created a second settlement of £15,000 on April 1, 2006. The trust fund is worth £345,000 at the first 10-year anniversary.

(1) Relevant property to be taxed is £345,000.
(2) Calculate hypothetical chargeable transfer:

	£
(a) Relevant property, as above	345,000
(b) Property in related settlement	15,000
	360,000
(3) Settlement's cumulative total:	
Settlor's earlier transfers	85,000
Chargeable transfers of trustees in the preceding 10 years	20,000
	105,000

---

[46] This may still be possible if "pilot" trusts are used: see generally Ch.41.
[47] IHTA 1984 s.66(6).

(4) Tax from the table (at half rates) on transfers from £105,000 to £465,000 (£360,000 + £105,000) = £28,000[48] (using 2011–12 rates) so that, as a percentage rate, inheritance tax is 8.12 (28/345)

(5) The effective rate is 30 per cent of 8.12% = 2.43%.
Tax payable is £345,000 × 2.43% – £8,383.50.

V EXIT CHARGES BETWEEN ANNIVERSARIES

29.18 The same events trigger an exit charge after the first 10-year anniversary as before it.[49] The inheritance tax charge is levied on the fall in value of the trust fund with grossing-up, if necessary. The rate of charge is a proportion of the effective rate charged at the first 10-year anniversary. That proportion is one-fortieth for each complete quarter from the date of the first anniversary charge to the date of the exit charge.[50]

EXAMPLE 29.8

Continuing Example 29.8, 15 months later the trustees appoint £25,000 to a beneficiary. The inheritance tax (assuming no grossing-up) will be: £25,000 × 2.75% × 5/40 (five-quarters since the last 10-year anniversary) = £75.94.

If the rates of inheritance tax have been reduced (including the raising of the rate bands) between the anniversary and exit charges, the lower rates apply to the exit charge and, therefore, the rate of charge on the last anniversary has to be recalculated at those rates.[51] So long as the inheritance tax nil rate band remains linked to rises in the retail prices index,[52] recalculation will be the norm.

VI LATER PERIODIC CHARGES

29.19 The principles that applied on the first 10-year anniversary operate on subsequent 10-year anniversaries.[53] So far as the hypothetical chargeable transfer is concerned the same items are included so that the value of property in a related settlement and of non-relevant property in the settlement is always included. The value of the property in the related settlement is always the value immediately after the settlement commenced. Even if the related property trust has been ended, the value at commencement must still be included. Similarly the value of non-relevant property in the settlement

[48] i.e. £360,000 is taxed at 0% on the first £220,000 (£325,000 – £105,000) and 20% on the balance.
[49] As to exit charges before the first 10-year anniversary, see 29.07.
[50] See IHTA 1984 s.69.
[51] IHTA 1984 s.9, Sch.2 para.3 as amended.
[52] See IHTA 1984 s.8 as amended.
[53] As to the charge on the first 10-year anniversary, see 29.13.

at commencement must be included even if it has ceased to be comprised in the settlement. The cumulative total of the fund includes, as before, the chargeable transfers of the settlor made in the seven years before he created the settlement and the transfers out of the settlement in the 10-years immediately preceding the anniversary (earlier transfers by the settlement fall out of the cumulative total). The remaining stages of the calculation are unaltered.

VII TECHNICAL PROBLEMS AND PLANNING

29.20 The basic structure of the charging provisions is relatively straightforward. The charge to inheritance tax is built upon a series of periodic charges with interim charges (where appropriate) which are levied at a fraction of the full periodic charge.

Reduction in the rate of the anniversary charge

29.21 If property has not been in the settlement for the entire preceding 10 years (as will be the case when income is accumulated during that period) there is a proportionate reduction in the charge.[54] The reduction in the rate of tax is calculated by reference to the number of completed quarters which expired before the property became relevant property in the settlement. This proportionate reduction in the effective rate of the periodic charge does not affect the calculation of inheritance tax on events occurring after the anniversary, i.e. any exit charge is at the full effective rate.

There are no provisions which enable specific property to be identified. Therefore, the reduction mentioned above applies to the value of the relevant property in the trust at the 10-year anniversary "attributable" to property which was not relevant property throughout the preceding 10 years. Presumably, therefore, some sort of proportionate calculation is necessary where the value of the fund has shown an increase. Furthermore, if accumulated income is caught by the anniversary charge, a separate calculation has to be made with regard to each separate accumulation, as being property which has not been in the settlement for the whole of the previous decade.[55]

Conundrum

29.22 How are charges on property converted by FA 2006 into relevant property calculated?[56]

---

[54] IHTA 1984 s.66(2).
[55] See SP 8/86 and 29.13 and fn.41 above.
[56] See generally IHTA 1984 s.69(2).

EXAMPLE 29.10

On January 1, 1995 Yves created an accumulation and maintenance (A-M) trust for his three children, each of whom will attain an interest in possession on becoming 25. When Yves made the settlement he had a nil cumulative total and the property he settled was worth £200,000. On January 1, 2005, at the first 10-year anniversary, the trust fund was worth £1 million. Since the trust was still an A-M trust no periodic charge was imposed. All three children were over 18 but had attained 25 by April 6, 2008 when the trust fund became relevant property. It was then worth £3 million.[57]

What happens if there is an exit charge between April 6, 2008 and January 1, 2015 at a time when the trust fund is worth £4 million?

29.23 There are provisions governing this, but they are far from easy to understand. The situation is governed by IHTA 1984 s.69(2) which provides that the rate at which tax is charged is the appropriate fraction of the rate at which it would have been charged at the previous 10-year anniversary if immediately before that anniversary all the property which has since become relevant property had then been relevant property. The effect of s.69(3) appears to be that for this purpose the value to be used is the value of the property at the time when it became relevant property, i.e. £3 million.

If the property in respect of which the exit charge is imposed has not been relevant property throughout the period since the last 10-year anniversary the appropriate fraction is reduced in the usual way, e.g. if the property on which the charge is imposed only became relevant property five years after the last 10-year anniversary the appropriate fraction will be three-twentieths.[58] Previous exit charges do not affect subsequent exit charges.

EXAMPLE 29.10 (CONT'D)

Assume that on January 1, 2010 a part of the settled assets to a value of £750,000 was advanced to Adam just before his 25th birthday. The position is as follows:

(i) an IHT exit charge under IHTA 1984 s.65(1)(a) applies. For CGT purposes, hold-over relief under TCGA 1992 s.260 is available;

(ii) to calculate the IHT exit charge go back to the last 10-year anniversary (January 1, 2005) and calculate what the charge would have been on the basis that relevant property in the settlement immediately before the anniversary was worth £3 million. For these purposes:

  • There was no related settlement.
  • When the settlement was created it contained non-relevant property which has all become relevant property (on April 6, 2008) and so is ignored.[59]

---

[57] See 30.19 for the transitional rules for A-M trusts.
[58] See IHTA 1984 s.69(4).
[59] Contrast the position if capital payments had been made to beneficiaries at a time when the trust was A-M. See further Ch.30.

- So far as the hypothetical chargeable transfer is concerned,[60] the settlor had made no chargeable transfer in the seven years before creating the settlement and nor had there been chargeable transfers out of the settlement in the previous 10 years;[61]

(iii) taking the 2011–12 rates, the nil rate band of £325,000 is deducted leaving £2.675 million to be taxed at 20% = £535,000 so that the rate of tax is 17.8% (545,000 / 3 million) and 30% of this produces a rate of tax of 5.3%;

(iv) normally the charge will be by reference to the number of complete successive quarters in the period from the last anniversary to the day before the occasion of charge.[62] However, the settlement did not contain relevant property at that time and so[63] no quarter which expired before the day on which the property became relevant property is to be counted (unless that day—viz when the trust became relevant property—falls in the same quarter as that in which the exit charge arises when it is taken into account).

In this case there are exactly 20 complete quarters in the period from the last 10-year anniversary (January 1, 2005) to the exit occasion (January 1, 2010) and of these 13 are complete quarters before April 6, 2008 (when the property became relevant property). Hence there are only seven chargeable quarters so the tax rate becomes:

$5.3 \times 7/40 = 0.927\%$

Tax payable on the advance to Adam of £750,000 (ignoring grossing-up) is £6,952.50.

Planning for the anniversary charge

The charge is a snapshot, i.e. it is imposed on property in the settlement at the time of the relevant anniversary. More precisely IHTA 1984 s.64 provides for the charge to apply to relevant property comprised in the settlement "*immediately before a ten year anniversary*". There may in consequence be opportunities for avoiding or mitigating this charge. In the case of a non-domiciled settlor, for instance, ensuring that on the chargeable occasion the property is non-UK situs, will mean that it is excluded property and so not within the definition of relevant property and not within the charge.[64] The fact that the trust property has been UK situated for most of the previous 10-year period does not matter. By contrast, if a trust established by a non-UK domiciled

29.24

---

[60] See 29.14.
[61] Of course there will often be cases when this is not true and the settlor will have followed standard advice and created a discretionary trust to use his nil rate band (a chargeable transfer) before setting up the A-M trust (which he did by a PET). That earlier chargeable transfer will be taken into account if it occurred within seven years of setting up the A-M trust.
[62] IHTA 1984 s.69(4).
[63] IHTA 1984 s.69(4) applying s.68(3).
[64] See IHTA 1984 s.58(1)(f).

settlor holds foreign situated property for 9 out of 10 years but on the 10-year anniversary the trustees own UK situated property then the 10-year charge is reduced to allow for the period during which the settled property was excluded property.[65]

29.25   The value of the relevant property may be reduced by business or agricultural property relief.[66] The normal conditions for that relief must be met: for instance, the trustees must satisfy the two-year ownership requirement for business property relief.[67] The switch into property attracting this relief therefore needs to occur more than two years before the anniversary occasion unless the trust has held business property or agricultural property, sells it before the 10-year anniversary, buys further business property or agricultural property which has been held for less than two years at the 10-year anniversary but the replacement provisions apply.[68] (Broadly these provisions require the trustees to have held the original and replacement business or agricultural property for a combined period of at least two years out of the last five before the anniversary.)[69]

29.26   Distributing property out of the trust just before the anniversary will not affect the rate of anniversary charge given that the rate is calculated by including "amounts on which any charges to tax were imposed under s.65 (the "exit charge") in respect of the settlement in the 10 years before the anniversary concerned". Of course if the settlement were to be wholly broken up before the 10-year anniversary (as may be desirable in the case of a "nil rate band discretionary trust") then the 10-yearly charge will not arise.[70]

Transfers between settlements

29.27   Section 81 prevents a tax advantage from switching property between discretionary settlements by providing that such property remains comprised in the first settlement. Accordingly, property cannot be moved out of a discretionary trust to avoid an anniversary charge; property cannot be switched from a fund with a high cumulative total to one with a lower total; and the transfer of a property from one discretionary fund to another is not chargeable.[71]

Added property

29.28   Special rules operate if, after the settlement commenced (and after March 8, 1982), the settlor makes a chargeable transfer as a result of which the value

---

[65] See IHTA 1984 s.66(2): the property is not relevant property for the full 10-year period so the charge is reduced.
[66] IHTA 1984 ss.103(1) and 115(1) and see Chs 45 and 46.
[67] IHTA 1984 ss.106 and 117.
[68] See IHTA 1984 ss.107 and 118.
[69] Although the conditions are slightly different for tenanted agricultural property.
[70] See further 29.12.
[71] IHTA 1984 s.81 and see (1989) *Capital Taxes News* Vol.8 p.219. See 24.13 and note the use of this provision to "consolidate" pilot trusts.

of the property comprised in the settlement is increased.[72] Note that it is only additions by the settlor that trigger these provisions[73] and that it is the value of the fund which must have increased and not necessarily the amount of property in that fund. A transfer which has the effect of increasing the value of the fund is ignored if it was not primarily intended to have that effect and did not in fact increase the value by more than five per cent.

EXAMPLE 29.11

In 2007 Sid settles stocks and shares in S Ltd and the benefit of a life insurance policy on his life.

(1) Each year Sid adds to the settlement property equal to his annual inheritance tax exemption (£3,000).

(2) Sid continues to pay the premiums on the life policy each year.

(3) Sid transfers further shares in S Ltd to the trust.

The special rules for added property do not apply in either case (1) or (2), because S is not making a chargeable transfer; the first transfer is covered by his annual exemption and the second by the exemption for normal expenditure out of income. The transfer of further shares to the trust, however, is caught by the provisions relating to added property.[74]

If the added property provisions apply, the calculation of the periodic charge which next follows the addition is modified. For the purposes of the hypothetical chargeable transfer, the cumulative total of the settlor's chargeable transfers is the higher of the totals in the seven year period:

(i) immediately before creating the settlement plus transfers made by the trustees of the settlement before the addition; and

(ii) immediately before transferring the added property, deducting from this latter total the transfer made on creation of the settlement and a transfer to any related settlement.

In general, the settlor should avoid additions because they may cause more inheritance tax to be charged at the next anniversary. It will be preferable to create a separate settlement.[75] **29.29**

---

[72] IHTA 1984 s.67(1).

[73] An addition by another person would be treated as creating a separate settlement: see IHTA 1984 s.44(2).

[74] IHTA 1984 s.67 as amended by FA 1986 s.101(1), (3), Sch.19 para.17.

[75] Modern practice is to establish the settlement with a nominal sum (e.g. £10) and then to immediately add substantial assets. Given that the time gap is usually short, it is unlikely that in this period the settlor will make any chargeable transfers and so s.67 will not create problems. Care needs to be exercised, however, if pilot trusts are established inter vivos with the settlor intending to add property to them by his will when he dies. Some years may separate these events and the danger of making chargeable transfers in the interim should be borne in mind.

Example 29.12

In 1987 X made an immediately chargeable transfer of £70,000.

In 1992 on the same day X settled £100,000 on discretionary Trust A and £50,000 on discretionary Trust B.

In 1994 X made another chargeable transfer of £20,000.

In 1999 X added £50,000 to Trust A and £30,000 to Trust B.

In 2002 the first 10-year anniversary charge of Trust A arises. The cumulative total used for working out the hypothetical chargeable transfer[76] is the greater of (i) £70,000 and (ii) £90,000 (£70k + £20k) so £90,000 will apply. If the chargeable transfer in 1994 had instead been made in 1998, i.e. more than 10 years after 1987 the figures would have been (i) £70,000 and (ii) £20,000 so (i) would have been taken.

The sum of £30,000 is ignored because it is a transfer made on the same day as value is added to A. The sum of £50,000 is ignored because it is taken into account in calculating the value used to find the effective rate.

The timing of the exit charge

29.30 Assume that a discretionary trust has been in existence for nearly 10 years and that the trustees now wish to distribute all or part of the trust property to the beneficiaries. Are they better off doing so just before the 10-year anniversary or should they wait until just after that anniversary? Generally it is advantageous to distribute before an anniversary because the inheritance tax payable is calculated at rates then in force but on historic values; i.e. on the value of the fund when it was settled or at the last 10-year anniversary. By contrast, if the trustees delay until after the anniversary, inheritance tax (still at current rates) is then assessed on the present value of the fund.

29.31 Difficulties may arise in the case of a settlement which includes property that qualified for either business relief or agricultural relief when the trust was set up. In this situation, trustees should take care before selling the property and before ending the trust.

For instance, if property is distributed before the first 10-year anniversary, the rate of tax that applies is based upon "*the value, immediately after the settlement commenced, of the property then comprised in it*"[77] which makes no allowance for that property attracting business or agricultural property relief. Of course this will not matter if the property ceasing to be comprised in the settlement qualifies for 100 per cent BPR or APR since then the value transferred will be nil, but if that property has been sold and cash is being distributed a charge will arise.

---

[76] See 29.14 above.
[77] IHTA 1984 ss.68(4) and 69(5)(a).

EXAMPLE 29.13

In 2007 Vince sets up a discretionary trust for his family into which he transfers:

    (i) stocks and shares worth £300,000;
    (ii) 25 per cent of the shares in the family trading company which are worth £1 million but which attract 100 per cent BPR.

In 2011 the trustees:

    (a) advance the stocks and shares (then worth £400,000) to beneficiary A, or
    (b) advance the family company shares (then worth £1.2 million) to A.

The IHT consequences are as follows:

    (i) there is an "exit occasion" in 2011 and the tax rate will be calculated on the basis that the property put into the settlement by Vince was worth £1.3 million (i.e. without any allowance for BPR in the family company shares). If Vince had already used up his IHT nil rate band at the time when he set up the trust (say he had given £500,000 to a close company two years earlier) the rate calculated under IHTA 1984 s.68(4)(5) will be six per cent;
    (ii) if the distribution is of the stocks and shares ((a) above) that rate will be applied to the then value of £400,000 with a reduction based on the number of completed quarters that have elapsed from the creation of the settlement in 2007[78];
    (iii) if however, the distribution is of the relevant business property— still attracting relief at 100 per cent[79]—the tax charge is nil.
    The problem does not arise with exit occasions occurring after an anniversary charge even if the business or agricultural property has been sold immediately after the anniversary (see further Example 45.4).

VIII DISCRETIONARY TRUSTS CREATED BEFORE MARCH 27, 1974

29.32 Discretionary settlements created before March 27, 1974: are subject to special rules for the calculation of inheritance tax which generally result in less tax being charged.

---

[78] IHTA 1984 s.68(2).
[79] Bear in mind that the trustees must satisfy a two-year ownership period to qualify for relief: IHTA 1984 s.106 (BPR) and s.117 (APR).

Chargeable events occurring before first 10-year anniversary

29.33 As the settlement is treated as a separate taxable entity, only transfers made by the settlement are cumulated. Such chargeable transfers were either distribution payments (if made under the regime in force from 1974 to 1982) or are chargeable events.[80] Once the cumulative total is known, the rate of tax is calculated at half rates and the charge is at 30 per cent of that rate.[81]

First anniversary charge

29.34 No anniversary charge applied before April 1, 1983. Therefore, the first discretionary trust to suffer a charge was one created on April 1, 1973 (or 1963, 1953, 1943 and so on).

The amount subject to the charge is calculated in the normal way. In calculating the rate of charge, however, it is only chargeable transfers of the settlement in the preceding 10 years that are cumulated (as the settlement predates capital transfer tax/inheritance tax the settlor has no chargeable transfers to cumulate). Property in a related settlement and non-relevant property in the settlement are ignored. As before, the rate of charge is reduced if property has not been relevant property throughout the decade preceding the first anniversary.[82] The danger of increasing an inheritance tax bill by an addition of property by the settlor[83] is even greater with these old trusts. If such an addition has been made, the settlor's chargeable transfers in the seven-year period before the addition must be cumulated in calculating the rate of tax on the anniversary charge.[84] The effective rate of charge for the anniversary charge is (as for new trusts) 30 per cent of the rate calculated according to half the table rates.

Chargeable events after the first anniversary charge

29.35 The position is the same as for new trusts.[85] The charge is based upon the rate charged at the last anniversary.

IX EXEMPTIONS AND RELIEFS

29.36 Many of the exemptions from inheritance tax do not apply to property in relevant property trusts; for example the annual exemption, the marriage

---

[80] See IHTA 1984 s.65.
[81] See IHTA 1984 s.68(6) as amended by FA 1986 s.101(1), (3), Sch.19 para.18.
[82] As to such reduction in the rate of the anniversary charge, see above.
[83] As to the addition of property by the settlor, see above.
[84] IHTA 1984 s.67(4) as amended by FA 1986 s.101(1), (3), Sch.19 para.17.
[85] As to exit charges after the first anniversary charge and between anniversaries, see 29.18. As to later periodic charges, see 29.19.

exemption, and the exemption for normal expenditure out of income. There is no exemption if the settled fund reverts to either, the settlor or his spouse (and note that if the settlor is a beneficiary the reservation of benefit provisions apply).[86] Business and agricultural property relief may, however, be available, provided that the necessary conditions for the relief are met by the trustees.[87] There is no question of any aggregation of the trust property with property owned by a discretionary beneficiary.

Exit charges are not levied in certain cases when property leaves the settlement, e.g.: **29.37**

(i) Property ceasing to be relevant property within three months of the creation of the trust, or of an anniversary charge, or within two years of creation (if the trust was set up on death)[88] is not subject to an exit charge.

(ii) Property may pass, without attracting an exit charge, to such privileged trusts as employee trusts[89]; maintenance funds for historic buildings[90]; charities (with no time limits)[91]; political parties in accordance with the exemption in IHTA 1984 s.24[92]; national heritage bodies.[93]

If a discretionary fund contains non-relevant property, the periodic and exit charges do not apply to that portion of the fund.

Under IHTA 1984 s.58 property is not relevant property if, although no qualifying interest in possession subsists in the settled property, the property is held on certain special trusts. These are as follows.

(a) Accumulation and maintenance trusts and trusts for bereaved children

For a detailed treatment of accumulation and maintenance trusts and trusts **29.38** for bereaved children see Chs 23 and 27.

(b) Charitable trusts

If trust property is held for charitable purposes only, whether or not for a **29.39** limited time, there is no charge to inheritance tax and the fund is not "relevant property".[94] Transfers to charities are exempt, whether made by individuals or by trustees of relevant property trusts.[95] IHTA 1984 s.70 is concerned with temporary charitable trusts which that section defines as "settled property

---

[86] See Ch.26.
[87] See Chs 45 and 46.
[88] IHTA 1984 s.144 and see *Frankland v IRC* [1996] STC 735 discussed in Ch.31.
[89] IHTA 1984 s.75.
[90] IHTA 1984 s.77, Sch.4.
[91] IHTA 1984 s.76(1)(a).
[92] IHTA 1984 s.76(1)(b).
[93] IHTA 1984 s.76(1)(c), Sch.3.
[94] IHTA 1984 s.58(1)(a).
[95] IHTA 1984 s.76 as amended by FA 1998, ss.143(4)(a), 165, Sch.27 Pt IV.

held for charitable purposes only until the end of a period (whether defined by date or in some other way)"[96] and ensures that when the fund ceases to be held for such purposes an exit charge arises. That charge (which is calculated in the same way as for accumulation and maintenance trusts)[97] will never exceed a 30 per cent rate which is reached after 50 years.

(c) Trusts for the benefit of disabled persons

29.40   See Ch.36.

(d) Pension funds

29.41   See Ch.48.

(e) Employee trusts (EBTs)

29.42   Broadly employee trusts are trusts for the benefit of employees in a particular trade or profession or employment by, or office with, a body carrying on a trade, profession or undertaking and those who are married to or dependent on them.[98]

(f) Compensation funds

29.43   Trusts set up by professional bodies and trade associations for the purpose of indemnifying clients and customers against loss incurred through the default of their members are exempt from the rules for relevant property trusts.[99]

(g) Newspaper trusts

29.44   The provisions relating to employee trusts are extended to cover newspaper trusts.[100]

(h) Maintenance funds for historic buildings

29.45   IHT exemptions are available for maintenance funds where property is settled and the Treasury gives a direction.[101] Once the trust ceases, for any reason, to

[96] IHTA 1984 s.70(1).
[97] As to the calculation of such IHT see 30.18.
[98] See IHTA 1984 s.86(3) and Ch.49.
[99] IHTA 1984 ss.58–63.
[100] IHTA 1984 s.87.
[101] i.e. under IHTA 1984 Sch.4 para.1.

carry out its specialised function, an exit charge occurs, calculated in the same way as for accumulation and maintenance trusts.[102]

(i) Protective trusts

The special treatment accorded to certain protective trusts is considered at 28.04.[103] **29.46**

(j) Excluded property trusts[104]

Key points to consider in the context of the relevant property charging regime are as follows: **29.47**

(a) If trustees of an excluded property trust distribute non-UK situs assets (such as cash in a foreign currency *foreign* bank account) to individual beneficiaries to their accounts abroad, then there is no inheritance tax charge under IHTA 1984 s.68 even if at that time the trust holds other UK situated property. The reason is that excluded property is not relevant property[105] and therefore the charging provision in s.65 is not brought into play when the excluded property ceases to become comprised in the settlement. When a capital distribution of foreign situs property is made to beneficiaries, the property does not *cease* to be relevant property because it is not relevant property in the first place. **29.48**

(b) Any cash payment should be made to an individual beneficiary's off-shore account from the trustees' offshore bank account in order to avoid any argument that the funds only leave the trustees' account when they are already in the UK and UK situated. **29.49**

(c) It may be queried why inheritance tax is not charged when settled property comprising UK situs assets becomes excluded property and thereby ceases to be relevant property. The answer is found in s.65(7) which provides that tax is not charged: **29.50**

"by reason only that the property comprised in the settlement ceases to be situated in the UK and thereby becomes excluded property."

There is, however, one important exception to this: although IHTA 1984 s.48(3A)(a) provides that Authorised Unit Trusts and OEICs are excluded property if the settlement was made when the settlor was not domiciled, trustees should *not* directly reinvest UK situated assets (including cash in a UK bank account) into an Authorised Unit Trust or an OEIC. If they do so, they will trigger an exit charge because the

---

[102] IHTA 1984 s.77, Sch.4 para.8.
[103] See IHTA 1984 s.88.
[104] See Ch.31 and 29.24 above.
[105] IHTA 1984 s.58(1)(f).

exemption in s.65(7) referred to above does not apply where the reinvestment is into an AUT or OEIC. It does not *become* excluded property by ceasing to be situated in the UK but it becomes excluded property because of a specific exemption in s.48(3A). HMRC take this point! Therefore the trustees should move cash from the sale of UK situs assets abroad before reinvesting in AUTs or OEICs (if indeed they decide they want to invest in such assets).

(d) If trustees distribute UK situated property then under s.68(5), although the excluded property itself is not chargeable, the *rate* of exit charge on non-excluded property before the first 10-year anniversary is calculated by reference to a "hypothetical chargeable transfer" which includes the *value* of excluded as well as non-excluded property immediately after the settlement commenced.

29.51 (e) If the UK situated property on which the exit charge is levied has not been relevant property throughout the relevant period because it has been excluded, the rate of exit charge is correspondingly reduced.

29.52 (f) If all the settled property is excluded property at the time of the 10-year anniversary, there is no charge, even if it has been non-excluded property for most of the previous 10 years. The charge is only ever levied on relevant (non-excluded) property at the relevant date. However, if on the 10-year anniversary, some of the property is UK sited, then in calculating the hypothetical transfer in s.66(4)(b), one must include the initial value of the settled property which was then excluded and which has not subsequently become relevant property. Hence even if there is a very small amount of UK property, tax may be payable because of the value of the excluded property at the time when the settlement was made.

29.53 (g) The position between 10-year anniversaries is even more complicated. Even if there is a nil charge on the 10-year anniversary because all the settled property is excluded property, if a distribution of UK situated property is subsequently made, the rate is recomputed because since the first 10-year anniversary some excluded property has become relevant property. Section 69(2)(b) brings in excluded property which has become relevant property, even if it has subsequently returned to excluded property status. Only UK situated property that is distributed is actually taxed but the point still needs to be watched because it can increase the overall rate on that property.[106]

29.54 (h) Sections 80 and 82 also need to be considered.

---

[106] The position in this respect is different from that which applies to business and agricultural property. In the latter case if all the settled property qualifies for 100% business property relief or agricultural property relief at the 10-year anniversary but is then sold, subsequent distributions of non-business property before the next 10-year anniversary are not charged.

EXAMPLE 29.14

The trust was initially a qualifying interest in possession trust for the settlor set up before March 22, 2006. Although the settlor was not UK domiciled when he set up the trust, he died deemed domiciled.

Applying s.80 (since the settlor took an immediate interest in possession in the settled property), the settled property is treated as comprised in a notional trust made at the date of termination of his qualifying interest in possession. Section 82 requires us to look at the domicile of the settlor both at the date when the settlement was made and at the time his qualifying interest in possession came to an end in order to determine whether the trust property is excluded property for the purposes of the relevant property regime. The settlor was foreign domiciled when he established the settlement but deemed domiciled at the date his interest in possession ended.

HMRC accept that the trust assets are not subject to tax under FA 1986 **29.55** s.102(3) on the death of the settlor even if he has reserved a benefit because the reservation of benefit provisions are trumped by IHTA 1984 ss.48(3) and 80–82 only apply for the purposes of Ch.III (relevant property regime). Nor can ss.80–82 impose a charge on termination of his qualifying interest in possession on death of the settlor in the above example. The relevance of these provisions is that the settlor must be domiciled outside the UK at both the start of the settlement and on termination of his qualifying interest in possession in order for the settled property to continue to qualify for excluded property status under s.48(3) after his death for the purposes of the relevant property regime.

However, s.82 only applies for the purposes of s.48(3). It does not catch **29.56** trust assets qualifying for excluded property status under s.48(3A). Hence it is possible to avoid a future exit charge or 10-year anniversary charge after the death of the settlor in the above example by ensuring that at specific dates the trustees hold OEICs or AUTs falling within s.48(3A).

CHAPTER 30

ACCUMULATION AND MAINTENANCE (A-M) TRUSTS

- Background (**30.01**)
- Tax treatment of A-M trusts before March 22, 2006 (**30.05**)
- Tax treatment of s.71 A-M trusts after March 21, 2006 (**30.19**)
- Concluding remarks (**30.33**)

I BACKGROUND

The demise of accumulation and maintenance trusts

30.01 The so-called A-M trust was the creature of the capital transfer tax (later inheritance tax) legislation[1]: the only reason for establishing trusts of the complexity needed to fall within the statutory definition in that legislation was to take advantage of the inheritance tax benefits that were on offer.[2] A-M trusts were often considered under the title "trusts for infant beneficiaries". Of course they were that, but given the somewhat curious conditions that had to be satisfied (notably that it sufficed for income to vest in a beneficiary no later than the age of 25 years)[3] they could also be established for the benefit of children in the age bracket 18–25 years. The trust could also be drafted in the form of a highly flexible (i.e. discretionary) trust, which, because of the special IHT rules, did not give rise to the charges applicable to "pure" discretionary trusts.[4]

---

[1] See IHTA 1984 s.71 as amended by SI 2005/3229 and by FA 2006.

[2] It should be remembered that (by and large) it was only in the area of IHT that tax benefits were conferred. The income of the trust, for instance, was subject to the rate applicable to trusts or the Sch.F trust rate imposed by ICTA 1988 ss.686 and 687 as amended and if trust dividends were distributed to beneficiaries, a further burden resulted given that the tax credit on dividends could not be deducted from the tax payable at the trust rate on distributions to beneficiaries: see Ch.6.

[3] IHTA 1984 s.71(1)(a).

[4] It was a common mistake to assume that once a trust had been established in accumulation and maintenance form, it would continue to satisfy the requirements until it ceased to exist. In fact, the majority of accumulation and maintenance trusts underwent a process of metamorphosis into interest in possession trusts before finally terminating. A failure to appreciate this produced elementary errors, e.g. (a) that there was no inheritance tax charge on the death of a beneficiary of an A-M trust. This was true provided that the trust was still in accumulation and maintenance form, but if the beneficiary had obtained an interest in possession (e.g. at 18 years under TA 1925 s.31 as amended by FLRA 1969 s.1(3),

The flexibility of these trusts combined with their tax advantages explains **30.02**
why the IHT legislation was changed in 2006 leading to the demise of the A-M
vehicle. Speaking in the Standing Committee Debates on June 13, 2006, the
Paymaster-General commented:

> *"It was clear that A and M trusts have been routinely used to shelter
> large amounts of wealth from inheritance tax for long periods of time.
> We are talking about money going into trusts in excess of the IHT
> threshold.*
>
> *Trusts are set up ostensibly to provide for minor children, but that
> often happens in circumstances in which there is no particular need
> for a trust—the sums involved being grossly disproportionate to those
> required to provide for the child and most of the trust assets being
> destined ultimately for other beneficiaries. However, let us park the
> difference between sensible planning that allows children to have a nest
> egg—quite a large one in some cases—and cases in which there are other
> beneficiaries.*
>
> *I have repeatedly said that continued special provisions are justified when
> trusts for bereaved minor children constitute a way to protect children
> should they lose one or both parents, and that is precisely the situation with
> which the provisions of Sch 20 are designed to deal."*[5]

From March 22, 2006 it has not been possible to set up new accumulation and **30.03**
maintenance trusts under IHTA 1984 s.71.[6] Existing trusts, however, continued to receive the old IHT treatment during a transitional period which ended
on April 6, 2008. On that date, however, the wording of s.71(1)(a) changed so
that instead of requiring that:

Sch.1 Pt I, TA 2000 s.40(1), Sch.2 para.25 and CPA 2004 s.261(1), Sch.27 para.5) then his
death resulted in the normal inheritance tax charge associated with the termination of an
interest in possession. (b) CGT hold-over relief was available on the termination of an
accumulation and maintenance trust. This was true only if the trust was in accumulation
and maintenance form at the time when it ceased to exist: 1992 s.260(2)(d). If, however,
the accumulation and maintenance trust had ended as a result of an interest in possession
coming into existence, then on that event there was no liability to capital gains tax (specifically, there was no deemed disposal under TCGA 1992 s.71) and therefore no question of
any hold-over election being either available or needed. If the trust subsequently ended as
a result of the interest in possession beneficiary becoming entitled to the capital, hold-over
relief under TCGA 1992 s.260(2)(d) was not available. (c) That 25 years was the magic age
for all purposes and therefore a settlement on N (aged two years) contingent on his attaining
50 years could not be a qualifying accumulation and maintenance trust. This was wrong; it
would qualify provided that N became entitled to the income of the trust at no later than
the age of 25 years. Correctly identifying the form of the trust remained significant after the
2006 changes given that there were different transitional provisions dealing with accumulation and maintenance and interest in possession trusts in existence on March 22, 2006. Of
course, if a trust was a qualifying accumulation and maintenance trust on that date but a
beneficiary became entitled to an interest in possession during the transitional period which
ran until April 6, 2008 (say on January 1, 2007) then the fund (or that portion of it if the
interest in possession only arose in part), from that date became held on a relevant property
trust (unless it then satisfied the conditions to be an "age 18–25 trust" as set out in IHTA
1984 s.71D inserted by FA 2006).
[5] Rt Hon. Dawn Primarolo MP at col.603.
[6] IHTA 1984 s.71(1A) inserted by FA 2006.

"one or more persons . . . will, on or before attaining a specified age not exceeding twenty five become entitled to it or to an interest in possession in it",

18 replaced the age of 25 and absolute vesting (not just entitlement to an interest in possession) was required. It is likely that the majority of existing settlements then ceased to qualify as accumulation and maintenance because the conditions of the revised s.71(1)(a) were not met.

Establishing new trusts after FA 2006

30.04   The changes that came into effect from March 22, 2006 meant that:

(i) Any lifetime trust will—unless it falls within the definition of a trust which creates a "disabled person's interest"[7]—be immediately chargeable for IHT purposes. It does not matter that the trust is set up for the benefit of the settlor's children, grandchildren or other beneficiaries. There are no longer special rules for inter vivos trusts when beneficiaries take capital or income at a specified age.

(ii) There are special rules for certain *will trusts* but only if these are established by a testator for his own children. First, "bereaved minor trusts", which receive the same IHT treatment as s.71 accumulation and maintenance trusts (no anniversary or exit charges), but which require capital to vest no later than the age of 18. Secondly, "18–25 trusts" which, as the name suggests, enable the capital to vest at any time up until age 25 but which levy an IHT charge once the beneficiary has attained 18 (this may be seen as a "fine" for continuing to use the trust structure).[8]

Nothing will now be served by continuing to draft trusts in A-M form which are designed to satisfy the conditions in IHTA 1984 s.71 when no IHT advantages apply: old style accumulation and maintenance precedents can therefore be consigned to the dustbin of tax history.

30.05   This chapter is concerned with two matters:

(i) The definition of an A-M trust which remains important since— although new A-M trusts falling within the s.71 definition cannot be set up—existing A-M trusts may have been varied so as to preserve their favoured status. Moreover, whether a trust was A-M, interest in possession or a relevant property settlement at March 22, 2006 is important because it affects the tax treatment of the trust going forward. For

---

[7] As defined in IHTA 1984 s.89B inserted by FA 2006 Sch.20 para.6.

[8] The IHT charge does not arise on the beneficiary reaching 18. The exit charge is imposed if the trust ends at any time after the beneficiary reaches 18 with an increasing rate each year up to a maximum of 4.2% if the beneficiary becomes entitled to capital at 25. If the trust does not end when the beneficiary reaches 25 but continues (e.g. because the trustees have made a settled advance: see 10.42 for CGT position) there is an exit charge (maximum rate 4.2%) then as the trust enters the relevant property regime. Thereafter 10-year charges and exit charges arise in the normal way. The main advantage of the s.71D trust is protection from 10-year charges until the beneficiary reaches 25 and in many cases a low or nil rate of charge.

example TSIs cannot be created out of A-M trusts or discretionary trusts. A trust that is described as A-M, may in fact have been a qualifying interest in possession trust at March 22, 2006. Practitioners therefore need to review existing trusts to determine whether that trust satisfied the s.71 conditions on March 22, 2006 or had already become an interest in possession trust.

(ii) How A-M trusts set up prior to March 22, 2006 which have not been ended are taxed following the changes which took effect on March 22, 2006. This chapter discusses the taxation of trusts which have continued to retain accumulation and maintenance status and those trusts which from April 6, 2008 became relevant property settlements.

II TAX TREATMENT OF A-M TRUSTS BEFORE MARCH 22, 2006

Before March 22, 2006, the inter vivos creation of an accumulation and main- **30.06** tenance trust was a potentially exempt transfer[9] and thereafter, so long as the property continued to be held on accumulation and maintenance trusts, the 10 year anniversary charge did not apply[10] and there was no exit charge when the property ceased to be held on qualifying accumulation and maintenance trusts.[11] As a result the IHT treatment of settled gifts to minors was much the same as outright gifts to adults.

The requirements for setting up an A-M trust before March 22, 2006

To qualify for the privileged IHT treatment, an A-M trust had to satisfy the **30.07** three requirements considered below.[12] Failure to do so meant that the normal charging system for relevant property settlements applied. When the requirements ceased to be satisfied (e.g. because a beneficiary became entitled to the trust fund or to an interest in possession in it) IHT was not charged save in exceptional cases.[13]

Requirement 1

The first requirement was that one or more persons (beneficiaries) will, on or **30.08** before attaining a specified age not exceeding 25 years, become beneficially entitled to, or to an interest in possession in, the settled property.[14] The age of 25 years was specified as a maximum age limit and this was a generously late

---

[9] IHTA 1984 s.3A(1)(c) as inserted by FA 1986 s.101, Sch.19 para.1.
[10] See IHTA 1984 ss.58 and 64 as amended by FA 2004 ss.203 and 326, Sch.42 Pt 3.
[11] IHTA 1984 s.71(4). For the unusual occasions when an exit charge arose, see 30.15 below.
[12] IHTA 1984 s.71 as amended by SI 2005/3229.
[13] For the occasions when an exit charge arose, see 30.15.
[14] IHTA 1984 s.71(1)(a).

age when one considers that the primary purpose of these rules was to deal with settlements for minors.

EXAMPLE 30.1

(1) In 2004 property was settled on trust "for A absolutely, contingent on attaining the age of 18 years". A, then aged two, will become entitled to both income and capital at 18 so that Requirement 1 was satisfied.[15]

(2) In 2005 property was settled upon trust "for B absolutely, contingent upon attaining the age of 30 years". B, then aged 3, will not acquire the capital in the fund until after the age of 25 years but Requirement 1 will be met if B acquires an interest in possession no later than age 25. B will do so, because TA 1925, s.31[16] (if not expressly or impliedly excluded) provides that when a beneficiary with a contingent interest attains 18 years, that beneficiary shall then be entitled to the income produced by the fund even though he has not yet satisfied the contingency.[17]

30.09 The requirement that a beneficiary *"will"* become entitled required a degree of certainty. However, the possibility of death before attaining the specified age did not prevent the requirement from being satisfied while the beneficiary was still alive.[18] The word "will" caused particular problems when trustees possessed overriding powers of advancement and appointment (dispositive powers) which, if exercised, could result in entitlement being postponed beyond age 25. So long as the dispositive power could only be exercised amongst the existing beneficiaries and could not be used to postpone entitlement to an interest in possession beyond the age of 25 years, the trust would qualify for A-M status. Accordingly, a power to vary or determine the respective shares of members of the class, even to the extent of excluding some members altogether, was permissible so long as it was limited as indicated.[19]

EXAMPLE 30.2

Under a 2004 settlement, property was held on trust for the three children of A contingent upon their attaining the age of 25 years and if more than one, in equal shares. The trustees were given overriding powers of appointment, exercisable until the first beneficiary attained

---

[15] And note that this trust, by meeting the revised s.71 requirements, continues to receive A-M treatment even after April 5, 2008.

[16] i.e. TA 1925 s.31 as amended by FLRA 1969 s.1(3), Sch.1 Pt I, TA 2000 s.40(1), Sch.2 para.25 and CPA 2004 s.261(1), Sch.27 para.5.

[17] From April 6, 2008 a trust in this form ceased to qualify for A-M treatment and became subject to the relevant property regime: see 30.21 below.

[18] See *Lord Inglewood v IRC* [1981] STC 318; affirmed [1983] 1 WLR 366; [1983] STC 133, CA. A similar requirement is included in the definition of a bereaved minor trust (see IHTA 1984 s.71A(3) inserted by FA 2006) and in the definition of an 18–25 trust (see IHTA 1984 s.71D(6) inserted by FA 2006).

[19] SP/E1 (June 11, 1975) and see the *Law Society's Gazette*, June 11, 1975.

25 years, to appoint the fund absolutely or for an interest in possession to one or more of the beneficiaries as they saw fit.

The property will vest absolutely in one or more of the beneficiaries no later than the age of 25 years. The existence of the overriding power of appointment cannot be exercised other than in favour of the class of beneficiaries and cannot be used to postpone the obtaining of an interest in possession until after a beneficiary has attained 25 years. Requirement 1 was accordingly met.

30.10 The mere existence of a common form power of advancement did not prevent a settlement being A-M. However, such powers can be exercised so as to postpone a beneficiary's entitlement to income beyond the age stated in the trust document and so beyond the age of 25 years[20] and they can, in exceptional cases, result in property being paid to a non-beneficiary.[21] Obviously, if the power was so exercised the trust would cease to meet the s.71 requirements and a charge to IHT could result.[22]

EXAMPLE 30.3[23]

In 2002 property was settled "for the children of E contingent on their attaining 25 years". The trustees were given the following (alternative) overriding powers of appointment:

(1) to appoint income and capital to E's sister F. The mere existence of this power meant that the settlement did not qualify as an A-M trust. There was no certainty that the fund would pass to E's children because the power might be exercised in favour of F.
(2) to appoint income to E's brother G. The same consequence followed because the mere existence of this power meant that the income could be used for the benefit of G.
(3) to appoint capital and income to E's relatives so long as those relatives are no older than 25 years. This power did not cause problems because whoever received the settled fund, whether E's children or his relatives, would be no older than 25 years.

30.11 In *Lord Inglewood v IRC*, at First Instance, Vinelott J. in considering the requirements of s.71(1)(a) distinguished between events provided for in the trust instrument and events wholly outside the settlor's control:

"... *the terms of the settlement must be such that one or more of the beneficiaries, if they or one of them survive to the specified age, will be bound*

[20] See *Pilkington v IRC* [1964] AC 612; [1962] 3 All ER 622 HL.
[21] See *Re Hampden Settlement Trusts* [1977] TR 177; *Re Clore's S.T.* [1966] 1 WLR 955; *X v A* [2006] 1 WLR 741.
[22] See [1975] BTR 437 (which became SP/E2 but in July 1994 was dropped as obsolete) in which HMRC confirmed that the "existence" of a "common form" power would not break the requirement; and see also *Lord Inglewood v IRC* above. The position was confirmed again in Revenue correspondence published in *Taxation Practitioner* (Nov 1995) and see A2.375.
[23] Taken from SP/E1 (June 11, 1975).

to take a vested interest on or before attaining that age . . . Of course, a beneficiary may assign his interest or be deprived of it by an arrangement or by bankruptcy before he attains a vested interest. But he is not then deprived of it under the terms of the settlement, so these possible events, unlike the exercise of a power of revocation or appointment, must be disregarded."[24]

Requirement 2

30.12 No interest in possession must subsist in the settled property and the income from it must be accumulated so far as it is not applied for the maintenance, education or benefit of a beneficiary.[25] Accordingly, once an interest in possession came into being, the settlement ceased to be an A-M trust.[26] If there could be no interest in possession in the income, what was to happen to it? Two possibilities were envisaged by Requirement 2: it could either be used for the benefit of a beneficiary (e.g. under a power of maintenance) or it could be accumulated. The official view was that a pure accumulation trust (without any power to maintain) was within IHTA 1984 s.71, as was an exhaustive trust for maintenance without any power of accumulation.[27]

Requirement 3

30.13 Either:

(i) Not more than 25 years had elapsed since the commencement of the settlement or, if it was later, since the time (or latest time) when Requirements 1 and 2 became satisfied with respect to the property; or

(ii) All the persons who were, or had been, beneficiaries were, or had been, either:

- children of a common grandparent; or
- children, widows or widowers of such grandchildren who were themselves beneficiaries but died before the time when, had

---

[24] *Lord Inglewood v IRC* [1981] STC 318 at 322; and see also [1983] 1 WLR 366 at 372; [1983] STC 133 at 138, CA per Fox L.J. Note the unsatisfactory decision in *Crawford Settlement Trustees v RCC* [2005] STC (SCD) 457, which was compromised on appeal and is thought to be wrong.

[25] IHTA 1984 s.71(1)(b).

[26] This remains the case for existing accumulation and maintenance trusts even though the interest in possession will not be "qualifying" if it arises after March 21, 2006. It can therefore result in the trust ceasing to fall within s.71 and becoming a relevant property settlement: see further 30.20 below.

[27] Care had to be taken in choosing the appropriate accumulation period if the intention was to accumulate income beyond the minorities of the beneficiaries. Various periods are permitted under LPA 1925 s.164 and 165 and under TA 1925 s.31, but some of them (unless further restricted) would have caused the trust to fall outside the definition of an accumulation and maintenance trust. In the case of an inter vivos trust, for instance, a direction to accumulate "during the lifetime of the settlor" would mean that an interest in possession might not arise until after the beneficiaries had attained the age of 25 years; likewise, a provision to accumulate for 21 years when some of the beneficiaries were already over the age of four at the commencement of the settlement would have been fatal.

they survived, they would have become entitled as mentioned in Requirement 1.[28]

Requirement 3 was first introduced in FA 1976 in an attempt to stop the A-M trust from being used to benefit more than one generation. There were two ways in which it could be satisfied. Either the trust must not last for more than 25 years from the date when the fund became settled on A-M trusts; or all the beneficiaries had to have a common grandparent.

EXAMPLE 30.4

(1) In 2004 property was settled on an A-M trust for the children and grandchildren of the settlor. As there was no grandparent common to all the beneficiaries, the trust must not last for longer than 25 years if an exit charge to inheritance tax was to be avoided.

(2) In 2005 property was settled on A-M trust for the children of brothers A and B. As there is a common grandparent the duration of the accumulation and maintenance trust did not need to be limited to 25 years.

There was one case in which two generations could benefit: namely where the original beneficiaries had a common grandparent and one of those beneficiaries had died, substitution per stirpes was permitted. **30.14**

In practice Requirement 3 did not succeed in curbing the use of trusts to benefit more than one generation. In simple terms an A-M trust would be set up for (say) children of the settlor who would be given interests in possession no later than age 25. The trustees, however, would have wide powers of appointment which could then be exercised to terminate the interest in possession and appoint onto fresh A-M trusts for the settlor's grandchildren. The children would make a PET (and doubtless survive seven years!).

Ending of A-M trusts

No IHT was charged when property from an A-M trust became subject to an interest in possession in favour of one or more of the beneficiaries, nor when any part of the fund was appointed absolutely to (or became held on trust for) such a beneficiary. In both cases, the event had to occur on or before the beneficiary became 25. This exemption, together with the exclusion of the anniversary charge, meant that once the property was settled on these trusts **30.15**

---

[28] IHTA 1984 s.71(2) as amended by SI 2005/3229. Once more than 25 years passed from the creation of the accumulation and maintenance settlement and not all the beneficiaries were the grandchildren of a common grandparent, the settlement lost its privileged inheritance tax status. The earliest accumulation and maintenance settlement to lose its status in this way was one created on April 15, 1976, its status being lost on April 15, 2001. The settlement then became a relevant property settlement. Also, when that 25-year period expires, there is an inheritance tax charge at a rate of 21% on the value of the trust assets: see 30.18 below.

there was no further inheritance tax liability (at least until after the beneficiary had obtained an interest in possession).

EXAMPLE 30.5[29]

"... to A absolutely contingent on attaining 25 years". This straightforward trust satisfied the requirements of an A-M trust so long as A was a minor. Consider, however, the following possibilities:

(1) A attained 18 years. A was entitled to the income from the fund and, therefore, Requirement 2 was broken. No IHT was charged on the ending of the A-M trust consequent upon the arising of A's interest in possession.
(2) A attained 25 years. Ordinary principles for interest in possession settlements applied; A's interest in possession came to an end, but no inheritance tax was payable because A as the life tenant was already treated as being entitled to all the property.[30]
(3) A died aged 19 years. Inheritance tax was charged on the termination of A's interest in possession.[31]

30.16 There was nothing to prevent an A-M trust from being created for an open class of beneficiaries, for example, *"for all my grandchildren both born and yet to be born"*. If such a trust was to be created it was desirable to ensure that the class of beneficiaries would close when the eldest obtained a vested interest in either the income or capital. Failure to do so would result in a partial divesting of any beneficiary with a vested interest when a further beneficiary was born, and this could lead to an inheritance tax charge. Class-closing rules could be implied at common law,[32] but it was safer to insert an express provision to that effect. IHTA 1984 s.71(4)(b) provides that tax shall not be charged on the death of a beneficiary before attaining the specified age. It followed that, if the entire class of beneficiaries was wiped out, the accumulation and maintenance trust ceased on the death of the final member, but, whoever then became entitled to that fund, no inheritance tax was payable. When it was necessary to wait and see if a further beneficiary was going to be born, however, this provision did not operate, because it was then not the death of the beneficiary which ended the accumulation and maintenance trust, but the failure of a further beneficiary to be born within the trust period.

Occasions when an exit charge applied

30.17 It was rare for property to leave an A-M trust otherwise than by vesting in a beneficiary and so long as this happened, no inheritance tax was chargeable.

---

[29] In this example it is assumed that A became entitled to the interest in possession before March 22, 2006: a later entitlement has very different consequences: see 30.20 and following below.
[30] IHTA 1984 s.53(2).
[31] IHTA 1984 ss.4, 5 and 49(1).
[32] *Andrews v Partington* (1790) 3 Bro CC 60 at 401.

Provision was, however, made for calculating an exit charge in the following circumstances:

(a) when a depreciatory transaction entered into by the trustees reduced the value of the fund[33];

(b) when the 25-year period provided for in Requirement 3 was exceeded and the beneficiaries did not have a common grandparent[34];

(c) when property was advanced to a non-beneficiary or resettled on trusts which did not comply with the requirements of an A-M trust[35]; and

(d) if the trust ended some time after the final surviving beneficiary had died.

IHT was calculated in these cases on the value of the fund according to how long the property had been held on the accumulation and maintenance trusts.[36] The calculation was made as follows:　**30.18**

(i) 0.25 per cent for each of the first 40 complete successive quarters in the relevant period;

(ii) 0.20 per cent for each of the next 40 complete successive quarters;

(iii) 0.15 per cent for each of the next 40 complete successive quarters;

(iv) 0.10 per cent for each of the next 40 complete successive quarters; and

(v) 0.05 per cent for each of the next 40 complete successive quarters.

Therefore, on expiry of the permitted 25 years, IHT at a rate of 21 per cent was payable. Subsequently, normal relevant property settlement rules applied, so that five years later there would be an anniversary charge. These rules may still be relevant to trusts with young beneficiaries where before April 6, 2008 the trust was altered to require beneficiaries to take capital and income no later than 18. Such trusts remain A-M trusts under the transitional provisions.

III TAX TREATMENT OF S.71 A-M TRUSTS AFTER MARCH 21, 2006

The section is concerned with the IHT treatment of A-M trusts set up before March 22, 2006 (from that date s.71 trusts cannot be set up).[37] Of course, trusts may have been set up as A-M trusts but by March 22 one or more beneficiaries may have acquired interests in possession in all or part of the trust fund. In that event the trust will not be wholly accumulation and maintenance in form on March 22 and this section will only be relevant to that portion of the trust　**30.19**

---

[33] IHTA 1984 s.71(3)(b).
[34] As to the third requirement of an A-M trust, see 30.13 above.
[35] As to requirements of an A-M trust, see 30.07 above.
[36] IHTA 1984 ss.70(6) and 71(5).
[37] IHTA 1984 s.71(1A).

fund which was still held on trusts falling within s.71 on March 22, 2006, i.e. in respect of settled property where no beneficiary had an interest in possession.

The transitional period

30.20 From March 22 to April 6, 2008 the IHT treatment of a s.71 accumulation and maintenance trust did not change. This meant that:

(i) anniversary and exit charges did not apply so that if the trust ended on the occasion when a beneficiary became absolutely entitled to the trust fund (or, indeed, if the trust ended because of the death under the vesting age of the beneficiary) there was no IHT exit charge;

(ii) during this period a beneficiary may have become entitled to an interest in possession and this would have had the following effects:

(a) IHTA 1984 s.71 ceased to apply (Requirement 2 was no longer satisfied) in respect of that part of the fund in which the interest in possession arose[38];

(b) because qualifying interests in possession within s.49(1) cannot generally come into being after March 21, 2006[39] the trust then became a relevant property settlement (i.e. subject to future anniversary and exit charges) unless at the time when the interest in possession arose the conditions for an 18–25 trust were satisfied.[40]

EXAMPLE 30.6

Dod set up an A-M trust for her children on April 1, 1990. Her eldest son, Rufus, became entitled to an interest in possession in one-third of the trust fund on his 18th birthday in 2005. Her second son, Greybeard, took a similar interest on his 18th birthday in 2007. The remaining one-third is held on trust for the third son, Greenmantle, and he will become 18 in 2012. The capital remains settled for Dod's grandchildren. The IHT position of the trust is as follows:

(1) *Rufus' share*: this was held on a qualifying interest in possession trust for him on March 22, 2006. On the ending of his interest after October 5, 2008 (unless his wife or civil partner becomes entitled to a successive interest in possession on his death which is a TSI)[41],

---

[38] There will be no IHT "exit" charge: see IHTA 1984 s.71(4)(a).

[39] IHTA 1984 s.49(1A) inserted by FA 2006.

[40] IHTA 1984 s.71D(3)–(4) inserted by FA 2006. In the case of flexible accumulation and maintenance trusts the requirements in s.71D(3) were not met because although the relevant beneficiary became entitled to an interest in possession he would not become entitled to capital on or before attaining 25 as required by IHTA 1984 s.71D(6). Accordingly it was important to review such trusts before the interest in possession arose since the conditions of s.71D(6) had to be met *at the time* (in such flexible trusts it was likely that the trustees had adequate powers which could have been exercised to ensure that the s.71D(6) conditions were met).

[41] See 27.32.

Rufus will make an immediately chargeable transfer (unless the property is transferred to a beneficiary outright) with the continuing trusts being taxed under the relevant property regime;

(2) *Greybeard's share*: his interest in possession arose after March 21, 2006 and is not "qualifying". There was no IHT exit charge on the ending of the A-M trust[42] but because he did not become entitled to capital at 25, his share of the trust is now taxed under the relevant property regime. There was no entry charge when the trust falls into the relevant property regime[43];

(3) *Greenmantle's share*: this was still held on A-M trusts on April 5, 2008, when it ceased to meet the revised A-M requirements and as capital will not vest in Greenmantle on or before he becomes 25, the relevant property regime has applied from that date. There is no charge when this share of the trust fund ceases to be in the A-M regime.

As will be apparent from the above example, one effect of the 2006 changes is that Dod's children are now taxed differently: probably the last thing that she intended!

What happened on April 6, 2008?

From April 6, 2008 for existing trusts, Requirement 1 in the definition was amended to read, "*one or more persons (beneficiaries) will, on or before attaining a specified age not exceeding 18 years become beneficially entitled to it*" (viz the settled property). As compared to the previous definition note that: **30.21**

(i) The vesting age became 18 rather than 25;

(ii) At that age it is no longer sufficient for an entitlement to income to arise: the beneficiary must become entitled to capital in the settlement (which will therefore end).

Requirements 2 and 3 of s.71 are unamended.

If the trust satisfies these amended requirements it will continue to be taxed under the s.71 provisions. Note especially: **30.22**

(i) that the wording of s.71(1)(a) allows for a degree of flexibility ("*one or more persons*"). It is unnecessary for each beneficiary to take a share in the trust fund: the trustees can retain powers to "pick and choose" between them provided always that the power cannot be exercised so as to postpone vesting of capital beyond the age of 18. The following power will therefore satisfy the requirements of the modified s.71:

---

[42] See IHTA 1984 s.71(4)(a). Note that this provision does not require the interest in possession to be qualifying: hence the IHT exemption on the ending of the A-M trust in this situation has been preserved.

[43] Anniversary charges will be dated from when the A-M trust was originally set up: there is, however, a reduction for the period during which the A-M regime applied and the trust did not comprise relevant property.

"To such of my children as attain the age of 18 years and if more than one in such shares as the trustees shall from time to time by deed or deeds revocable or irrevocable appoint and in default of such appointment in equal shares absolutely at 18 provided that no such appointment shall be made and no such appointment shall be revoked so as to either diminish or to increase the share (or the accumulations of income forming part of the share) or to give a new share (or new accumulations of income) to a child who at the date of such appointment or revocation has reached the age of 18."

Note that the power must not be capable of exercise so as to vary (whether by increase or diminution) the share of a beneficiary who has attained 18[44];

(ii) the inclusion of a widened power of advancement does not prevent the trust meeting the s.71 requirements[45] even though this power may be exercised to prolong the settlement by means of a settled advance: see Example 30.7 below;

(iii) section 71(4) has not been amended so that there is no IHT exit charge on the ending of an A-M trust whether that is because the beneficiary becomes absolutely entitled to the property or takes an interest in possession (even a non-qualifying interest in possession).

EXAMPLE 30.7

In 2004, Dodson set up an A-M trust for his children. He currently has three children but expects to have more. The terms of the trust were amended during the transitional period to meet the revised s.71 requirements and now provide for capital vesting at 18. However, the trustees have a power of appointment along the lines of that set out above and a widened s.32 power of advancement.

Consider the tax position on the happening of the following events:

(1) Dodson's eldest son proves to be "a thoroughly bad lot" and the trustees therefore exercise their power of appointment before he is 18 so that the trust fund becomes held for Dodson's children other than that eldest son. This has neither IHT nor CGT consequences;

(2) Dodson's daughter is appointed a 20 per cent share in the trust fund on her 18th birthday. There is no IHT exit charge and CGT hold-over relief will be available;

(3) Dodson's second daughter is "bad with money" and accordingly on her 18th birthday the trustees exercise their power of advancement for her benefit by giving her an interest in possession in a further 20 per cent share of the fund with trusts over for her spouse and issue. This part of the trust ceases to fall within the A-M

[44] See A2.376.
[45] See 30.09 and A2.375.

712

regime but there will be no IHT exit charge. It is now taxed under the relevant property regime. There are no CGT implications;

(4) the remaining 60 per cent of the trust fund continues to be held on A-M trusts for Dodson's other children (and the class may still be open although it is customary to close the class when the eldest child reaches 18).

It is now too late to convert a pre-March 2006 A-M trust into this new style A-M. The conversion had to be done at the latest by April 5, 2008. The advantages and disadvantages of doing this compared with leaving the trust unaltered or converting it into a s.71D trust are discussed at the end of this chapter.

Falling into s.71D

There will be cases where the A-M trust provided for capital to vest at 25 so **30.23** that the conditions for the operation of IHTA 1984 s.71D were met on April 6, 2008.[46] In this case it is important to be aware of the likely exit charge when capital vests in a beneficiary at 25.

The calculation of the charge under s.71F uses similar principles that **30.24** apply to the calculation of the anniversary charge in the relevant property legislation. It is, however, important to stress the s.71D trusts are not relevant property trusts and, in particular, do not suffer anniversary charges. The only charge is the exit charge which generally will arise when a beneficiary:

- becomes absolutely entitled to the trust property after 18 and before 25; or

- dies having attained 18; or

- when property is applied or paid for his benefit (in this case the trust may end if there is an outright advancement or, alternatively, if a settled advance is made to prolong the trust then there will be a continuing relevant property settlement).

The calculation largely follows the general rules but with one exception as illustrated below.

EXAMPLE 30.8

An accumulation and maintenance trust was set up on January 9, 2000 with £400,000. There were no related settlements and it was the first chargeable transfer of the settlor. The only beneficiary becomes entitled to capital and income at 25 so the trust meets the requirements of s.71D on April 6, 2008. The beneficiary became 18 on May 12, 2006 taking an

---

[46] See A2.371 and following for correspondence dealing with the satisfaction of the s.71D conditions. Note in particular that whilst powers of selection given to the trustees need not create problems, HMRC take the view that the beneficial class must be closed on April 6, 2008.

interest in possession at that time (which is not qualifying given that it arises after March 21, 2006). An interim distribution of £300,000 is paid to the beneficiary on August 19, 2010 when he is 22.

The IHT calculation is arrived at as follows:

(1) Although the distribution is made more than 10-years after the creation of the settlement no 10-year charge arose on January 9, 2010 because the trust was then governed by s.71D.
(2) The exit charge on the distribution is calculated in accordance with IHTA 1984 s.71F. The settlement rate is determined by an assumed chargeable transfer which in this illustration includes only the value of the property when the settlement was made[47] viz
   - Assumed chargeable transfer £400,000 – £325,000[48] = £75,000 so that tax at 20% = £15,000.
   - Effective rate = 15,000/400,000 × 100 = 3.75 × 3/10 = 1.125%
   - £300,000 × 1.125% = £3,375.
(3) There is then a reduction for the number of complete fortieths in the period from the day that the beneficiary attained 18 and ending with the day before the chargeable event (i.e. from May 21, 2006 to August 18, 2010). This gives seventeen-fortieths so that the amount of tax under s.71F(3) is
   £3,375 × 17/40 = £1,434.37
   Note two important points in connection with this special charging regime:
   (i) whereas the relevant property tax charge reduces the sum payable by the number of complete fortieths that the property was not relevant property, in this case the tax is reduced to the number of complete fortieths that the property was subject to s.71D;
   (ii) the tax rate is calculated on the value of the property *when origi-nally settled.* Accordingly in the case of an A-M trust established many years ago this may produce a significantly lower (or no) IHT. For instance, if £325,000 was put into an A-M trust in 1988 with the settlor having made no prior chargeable transfers then, that would now fall within the IHT nil rate band with the result that any exit charge will be zero.

Flexibility

30.25 Many trusts were drafted to retain a degree of flexibility, i.e. to give the trustees power to determine the shares of beneficiaries whilst they are under the age of 25. For the trust to fall within s.71D the relevant power cannot be exercised so as either to increase or diminish the share of a beneficiary once he has attained 25 and HMRC take the view that if the power has been exercised to exclude a beneficiary revocably it is not possible to "bring him back in" by revoking the previous exercise of the power. Accordingly, it will be important when exercising that power to leave the beneficiary with a minimal share which can

---

[47] IHTA 1984 s.71F(9).
[48] The nil rate band for 2011–12.

then be increased (if desired) as the result of the exercise of the power of revocation and reselection.[49] The following clause does not breach the s.71D(6) requirements:

> "*to such of my grandchildren as attain the age of 25 years and if more than one in such shares as the trustees shall from time to time by deed or deeds revocable or irrevocable appoint and in default of such appointment in equal shares absolutely at 25 providing always that no such appointment shall be made and no appointment shall be revoked so as to either diminish or increase the share (or the accumulation of income forming part of the share) of or give a new share (or new accumulations of income) to a grandchild who at the date of such appointment or revocation has reached the age of 25 nor benefit a grandchild who has been excluded from benefit as a result of the exercise of the power.*"

EXAMPLE 30.9

The trustees of an A-M trust are given the power to select (revocably or irrevocably) amongst grandchildren under the age of 25. The definition of beneficiaries in the settlement allows grandchildren born before the eldest attains 25 to benefit but thereafter the class closes. In default of selection the grandchildren take in equal shares absolutely. In considering whether the trust fell within s.71D on April 6, 2008 (when all the beneficiaries are still minor) note the following:

(i) HMRC consider that the class of beneficiaries must be closed on April 6, 2008 if the trust is to meet the s.71D requirements[50];

(ii) Assuming that there are three grandchildren, A B and C then if the trust is to satisfy s.71D, the power of selection must not be capable of benefiting any child once he has attained the age of 25. On or before that age his share must be fixed and the power of selection limited to the shares of B and C (assuming that A, the eldest, has taken his share at 25).

(iii) In the case of A-M trusts it was common to exclude (revocably) a beneficiary just before he became 18 (so as to prevent a right to income under TA 1925 s.31) and then to "bring him back" into the class just before he became 25 so as to vest the intended share in him at 25. HMRC take the view that if it is possible wholly to exclude a beneficiary but then to revoke the exercise of that exclusion the trust does not satisfy s.71D.[51] Accordingly, it will be important to make sure that any beneficiary who is to be reinstated before he becomes 25 is left with a "share" (which can be of a nominal value, for instance 1 per cent of the fund).

---

[49] Similar drafting considerations applied to accumulation and maintenance trusts and so if the settlement contained a power of selection it was likely that it did not infringe the s.71D requirements, subject, however, to the revocation point and the need to close the class.

[50] See A2.377. It is far from clear that HMRC are correct in this interpretation of the legislation since they accept that "B" in the legislation is to be construed in the plural.

[51] Again it is far from clear that this interpretation of the legislation is correct.

Retaining a wide power of advancement

30.26 This is expressly permitted by s.71D(7)(b). It enables the trust to be extended beyond the age of 25 by making a settled advance as in the following Example.

> EXAMPLE 30.10
>
> The Rogers A-M trust provides for Nick to take capital and income at 25. The trustees have a widened s.32 power of advancement:
>
> (i) on April 6, 2008 the trust fell into the s.71D regime; there was no entry charge.
> (ii) Nick will be 25 on January 1, 2012 and the trustees determine to exercise their power of advancement to postpone his entitlement to capital. Accordingly they make a settled advance giving him a life interest, reserving a power to advance capital to him but otherwise declaring trusts in favour of his children.

The IHT consequences are as follows:

(a) When the trustees exercise their power to make the "settled advance", s.71D ceases to apply and there will be an exit charge under s.71F (calculated by reference to the period from April 6, 2008 to the date of the settled advance). The same exit charge arises whether Nick becomes absolutely entitled or the trust continues as a relevant property trust.

(b) The continuing trusts will be subject to the relevant property regime.

CGT tie-in

30.27 While the trusts are within the s.71D regime, CGT hold-over relief will be available[52] if a beneficiary becomes absolutely entitled on or before attaining 18. If capital is advanced to him after that date, there is a chargeable transfer for IHT purposes (by virtue of IHTA 1984 s.2(3)) and hold-over relief is available under s.260(2)(a). Of course once the beneficiary is over 25 (e.g. when the settled advance has extended the settlement) hold-over relief is available under s.260(2)(a) in the normal way because any payment out of capital will be a transfer out of the relevant property regime. If the trustees exercise the power of advancement to postpone his entitlement to capital at 25 then there is no disposal for capital gains tax purposes provided that care is taken with the drafting of the settled advance to ensure that a new settlement is not created.[53]

---

[52] Under TCGA 1992 s.260(2)(db).
[53] See A1.19 for a suitable precedent.

Position if the relevant property regime applies

If the A-M trust fell into the relevant property regime on April 6, 2008 the following consequences ensue.

(i) 10-yearly charges

The trust will be subject to 10-yearly anniversary charges which run from the date when the settlement was first set up.[54] It does not matter that at that time no part of the trust fund comprised relevant property. For instance, if the trust was set up on May 1, 1988, anniversaries run from that date. On May 1, 1998 there was no relevant property in the trust (since it was then within the A-M regime)[55] but on May 1, 2008 there was an anniversary and the trust will at that time comprise relevant property.[56]

30.28

(ii) Reduction for the A-M Period

In calculating the 10-year anniversary charge there is a reduction in the rate of charge:

30.29

> "*Where the whole or part of [the value of the relevant property on the anniversary] is attributable to property which was not relevant property throughout the period of ten years ending immediately before the ten year anniversary concerned*".

And the reduction in the tax rate is by:

> "*One fortieth for each of the successive quarters in that period which expired before the relevant became.. relevant property . . .*" (IHTA 1984 s.66(2)).

In the above illustration the rate of charge which applies on May 1, 2008 anniversary will accordingly be reduced by thirty nine-fortieths.

(iii) Calculating the rate of charge on the 10-year anniversary

The rate of charge depends upon:

30.30

(a) the value of any property put into a "*related settlement*" (viz one set up

---

[54] See 29.06.
[55] IHTA 1984 s.58(1)(b).
[56] Note that if the trust had received property by way of resettlement from another trust then the anniversary charges in respect of that property will run from the date of the first trust. It is therefore important that trustees check whether the settlement they are dealing with has received any property from another trust: see IHTA 1984 s.81 and 24.13.

on the same day: see IHTA 1984 s.62). Note that the value is frozen at the time when the related settlement was made[57];

(b) previous chargeable transfers made by the settlor in the seven years before he created the settlement.[58] It had been standard IHT planning advice before 2006 for taxpayers wishing to set up a discretionary trust (which would involve an immediately chargeable transfer rather than a PET) to make any PETs (whether involving an outright gift or a gift into a qualifying interest in possession or accumulation and maintenance trust) only after first making the chargeable transfer (the value of which would normally be limited to the settlor's IHT nil rate band). Making PETs after immediately chargeable transfers ensured that if the PETs subsequently became chargeable (because of the death of the taxpayer within seven years) it would not affect the calculation of the tax on the discretionary trust set up by the immediately chargeable transfer. Hence, in looking back at what transfers a settlor had made in the seven years before establishing the accumulation and maintenance trust it should not be assumed that there will be none. [59] For some settlors an earlier chargeable transfer will have been made. If the settlor had added property to the A-M trust before March 22, 2006 these additions would have been PETs and have no effect on the cumulative total of the settlor which is taken into account even if those PETs had themselves been preceded by chargeable transfers made since the trust was set up[60];

(c) *"The value immediately after it became comprised in the settlement of any property which was not then relevant property and has not subsequently become relevant property whilst remaining comprised in the settlement".*[61] The meaning of this provision is not immediately obvious but its intention is akin to the related settlement rule: instead of creating two settlements on the same day the settlor might set up a single settlement but divided into a relevant property fund on the one hand and a qualifying interest in possession fund on the other. The value of the latter when the settlement was created will be taken into account in calculating the tax rate to be used when charging the relevant property fund. In the context of A-M trusts which fall into the relevant property regime this provision is significant where property was originally in the settlement but has vested absolutely in a beneficiary before the relevant property regime first applied (as in the following example).

---

[57] See IHTA 1984 s.66(4)(a).
[58] IHTA 1984 s.66(5)(a).
[59] Of course, this is even more likely to have been the case if the A-M trust was set up in (say) 1987 since PETs were only introduced in 1986 and so earlier transfers of value (unless exempt) would have been chargeable.
[60] Note that IHTA 1984 s.67(1) dealing with additions of property to a settlement is only concerned with chargeable transfers. The position would be different if the settlor died within seven years of making the addition.
[61] IHTA 1984 s.66(4)(b).

EXAMPLE 30.11

Dodgey set up an A-M trust on June 1, 1999 by settling £400,000. On April 5, 2008 the eldest beneficiary (Ron) became absolutely entitled to 50 per cent of the value of the trust fund (the entire fund is then worth £1 million); the other half of the fund remains settled on trusts for Dan which ceased to satisfy the revised s.71 requirements on the next day and therefore fell into the relevant property regime. On the 10-year anniversary (which fell on June 1, 2009) there was property originally in the settlement (Ron's fund) which never became relevant property whilst it remained comprised in the settlement.

Accordingly in working out that 10-year charge on June 1, 2009 the value of Ron's fund on June 1, 1999 needs to be taken into account. Presumably this is 50 per cent of the then value of the settlement (i.e. £200,000). The difficulty, however, in applying this part of the legislation is that there is no tracing procedure laid down so unless specific assets were settled into Ron's fund its application depends on what might be termed a "common sense" view of the matter.

(d) *"the amounts on which any charges to tax were imposed under section 65 ['exit charges']... in respect of the settlement in the ten years before the anniversary concerned".*[62]

Taking the facts of Example 30.11 above when Ron became absolutely entitled to his moiety in 2008 no charge arose under IHTA 1984 s.65 since the settlement did not at that time contain relevant property (it was still held on qualifying accumulation and maintenance trusts).

EXAMPLE 30.12

Take the facts of Example 30.11 but assume on January 1, 2009 Dan became absolutely entitled to £250,000, being a half share in the remaining trust fund (then worth £500,000). On that occasion an "exit" charge arose[63] and so when calculating the 10-year anniversary charge on June 1, 2009 the payment of £250,000 will form part of the hypothetical chargeable transfer which is taken into account in fixing the anniversary tax rate.[64]

(iv) Calculating the exit charge

IHTA 1984 s.69 deals with the calculation of the exit charge between 10-year anniversaries. In general, the charges are calculated by reference to the rate **30.31**

---

[62] IHTA 1984 s.66(5)(b).

[63] For the calculation of this charge, see Example 30.13.

[64] Note that there is no reduction for the time when this part of the trust fund was not relevant property. The problem considered in Example 30.11 does not arise since although not originally relevant property Dan's fund has become relevant property at a time when it was comprised in the settlement.

which had applied at the time of the last anniversary.[65] But what if at the time of the last anniversary charge there was no relevant property in the settlement? Optimists might imagine that as the rate of tax at that time must have been nil there will be no exit charges in the following 10 years! Sadly, however, the draftsman had foreseen this eventuality and provided for it in IHTA 1984 s.69(2)(b). In general, the tax is calculated by taking the value of property at the time when it first became relevant property (IHTA 1984 s.69(3)).

EXAMPLE 30.13

The Jackson A-M Trust was set up on September 1, 1990. Assume that Jackson had made no chargeable transfers before 1990. The property settled was then worth £500,000. On April 6, 2008 it became subject to the relevant property regime and it was then worth £1.5 million. On August 30, 2010 the trustees distributed the entire fund (then worth £2 million) to Jim Jackson. The IHT position was as follows:

(i) the last 10-year anniversary occurred on September 1, 2000 when there was no relevant property in the settlement (because at that time the trust was an A-M settlement);

(ii) when Jim received all the trust property there was an IHT exit charge[66] and the rate of tax was arrived at under ss.68 or 69 (see s.65(3)). Section 68 did not apply because there had been a 10-year anniversary; accordingly s.69 was the relevant provision. Under this section it was necessary to calculate what the anniversary tax charge would have been on September 1, 2000:

"if immediately before that anniversary the property had been relevant property comprised in the settlement (s69 (2)) with a value equal to 'the value of the property when it became relevant property' (s69 (3))";

(iii) in the case of the Jackson Settlement, therefore, it was necessary to obtain a valuation of the property in the trust when it first became relevant property on April 6, 2008 since that fixed the rate of tax applying when Jim became absolutely entitled.

Accordingly the tax payable is as follows:

(i) value of property at last anniversary £1.5 million: see s.69(3);

(ii) assumed chargeable transfer £1.5 million – £325,000 = £1,175,000;

(iii) tax at 20% = £235,000 giving an effective rate of $235,000/1,500,000 \times 100 = 15.66\% \times 3/10 = -4.698\%$;

(iv) that rate is then reduced by the appropriate fraction (being the number of complete fortieths in the period from September 1, 2000 to April 6,

---

[65] Allowing for any reduction of IHT rates (including increases in the nil rate band) which have subsequently occurred: see IHTA 1984 Sch.2 para.3.
[66] See IHTA 1984 s.64(1)(a).

2008 (i.e. the time during which the settlement did not comprise relevant property) = 30/40;

(v) the tax charge is accordingly £2 million × 4.698% × 30/40 = £23,498.

(v) CGT upside

Once the settlement falls within the relevant property regime, CGT holdover relief on TCGA 1992 s.260 will normally be available when any property ceases to be comprised in the settlement so that there is a deemed disposal for CGT purposes under TCGA 1992 s.71. In this connection note: **30.32**

(i) a claim for hold-over relief involves a joint election made by trustees and the relevant beneficiaries;

(ii) the fact that the trust is settlor-interested is irrelevant (that only affects the availability of hold-over relief on the creation of a trust).

Practical advice

For some, the paramount objective will have been to keep the settlement in being and, if it was intended that it would continue indefinitely, then at some point it was inevitably going to become subject to the relevant property regime.[67] With this in mind the decision to allow the relevant property regime to apply might have been taken in April 2008 and the following are key points in considering the impact of that regime: **30.33**

(ii) there was no "entry charge" when the trust ceased to qualify under s.71 as A-M on April 6, 2008 (or earlier if a beneficiary had became entitled to an interest in possession in the trust fund between March 22, 2006 and April 5, 2008 inclusive);

(iii) at the next 10-year anniversary the charge will be reduced to allow for the period when the settlement did not contain relevant property[68];

(iv) a full anniversary charge involves a *top rate* of tax of six per cent (being 30 per cent of the top lifetime rate (20 per cent) when the IHT nil rate band has been used up). This may be payable in instalments in the case of certain property.[69]

---

[67] For instance, if the terms are such that it initially falls into s.71D but the trustees subsequently make a settled advance to prolong the settlement after a beneficiary becomes 25. At that point the settlement will suffer a s.71D exit charge and for the future fall into the relevant property regime.

[68] See 29.21.

[69] IHTA 1984 s.227.

(v) exit charges are a fraction of the last anniversary charge (allowing for any reduction in tax rates) and hence will be charged at a rate of something below six per cent;

(vi) once the relevant property regime applies it will generally be possible to end the trust with the benefit of capital gains tax hold-over relief;

(vii) IHT relief may be available on qualifying business and agricultural property.[70]

EXAMPLE 30.14

An accumulation and maintenance trust was set up on January 1, 2000 with £400,000 being settled. There were no related settlements and this was the first transfer of the settlor. The settlement became relevant property on April 6, 2008. In these circumstances:

(a) The first 10-year charge arose on January 1, 2010 when the trust funds were worth £500,000.

(b) The IHT calculation was as follows:

Assumed chargeable transfer = £500,000 – £325,000[71] = £175,000 × tax @ 20% = £35,000

Effective rate £35,000/£500,000 × 100 = 7% × 3/10 = 2.1%

£500,000 × 2.1% = £10,500 reduced by complete fortieths for the time the property was not relevant property, i.e. the period from January 1, 2000 to April 6, 2008 = 33/40 so that tax payable was £10,500 – 33/40 × £10,500 = £1,837.50

30.34 Consider the more complex situation if beneficiaries under the A-M trust take qualifying interests in possession at various dates. As in (1) assume that the A-M was created on January 1, 2000 with £400,000; no related settlements but the settlor had settled £250,000 into a discretionary trust in 1995 (this was an immediately chargeable transfer which will form part of the settlor's cumulative total at the time when he creates the A-M trust). Prior to March 22, 2006 one of the beneficiaries became entitled to an interest in possession in half the funds whilst another took an interest in possession in one quarter of the funds on April 6, 2007. The remaining quarter became relevant property on April 6, 2008. The 10-year charge arose on January 1, 2010 when the settled funds were worth £800,000:

(a) The rate of charge on the anniversary was determined by reference to the assumed chargeable transfer which comprises:

(i) the value of the property to be charged, namely the two quarter shares that are relevant property, therefore, £400,000[72]; and

---

[70] See Chs 45 and 46.
[71] The nil rate band for 2009–10.
[72] IHTA 1984 s.66(4)(a).

    (ii) the value of property immediately after it became comprised in the settlement of property which was not then relevant property and had not become relevant property: viz one half subject to the pre-March 2006 interest in possession so ½ × £400,000 = £200,000;

    (iii) the total assumed chargeable transfer was therefore £600,000.

(b) the assumed chargeable transfer was added to the settlor's cumulative total of transfers at the time when the trust was created so the tax rate was calculated on an assumed aggregate chargeable transfer of:

£850,000 – £325,000[73] = £525,000 × 20% = £105,000

(c) the effective rate then became £105,000/£600,000 × 100 = 17.5% × 3/10 = 5.25%

(d) the tax therefore became £400,000 × 5.25% = £21,000. Of this tax one half was attributable to property that had been relevant property since April 6, 2007,[74] the other half to property that had been relevant property only since April 6, 2008. In both cases the charge was reduced by the number of complete fortieths that the property was not relevant property so:

£10,500 – 29/40 (period from January 1, 2000 –April 6, 2007) = £2,887.50 and

£10,500 – 33/40 (period from January 1, 2000 –April 6, 2008) = £1,837.50

The total tax was therefore £4,725

IV CONCLUDING REMARKS

Practitioners will inevitably be faced with the need to review A-M trusts and their offspring for many years to come, and it will therefore remain important to have in mind not only the "old" A-M rules which will have applied when the trust was first set up (and will explain why a number of the provisions were inserted into the trust instrument) but also to the impact of the FA 2006 changes which may well have resulted in modifications being made to the trust during the transitional period.[75]   **30.35**

It is worth emphasising that advisers were faced with the following main options in the wake of the 2006 changes (and that a choice had to be made between these options before April 6, 2008):   **30.36**

(i) *convert the trust so that it continued in the A-M regime*: of course the A-M trust was always something of an IHT "best buy" and a major attraction of this option was that an open class of beneficiaries could be retained (not possible according to HMRC if the trust was to fall under the s.71D (18–25) regime). This option was therefore likely to be most attractive in a case where substantial A-M trusts had been set up just

[73] The nil rate band for 2009–10.
[74] When a beneficiary took an interest in possession in quarter of the trust fund.
[75] See 30.20.

before the 2006 changes by (say) a youngish father for his children, and it was important that the class remained open since he expected to have (many) more children.

Trustees might not have wished children to take outright at 18 but a power of advancement could be retained. This option "bought time", where the beneficiaries were all very young because it delayed entry into the relevant property regime and therefore avoided 10-year charges that might otherwise have occurred while the children were under 18. However, that time saving came at a price: a child's absolute entitlement to a particular share could only be delayed by exercise of the power of advancement and that power must be exercised for the benefit of that child. The trustees had to give up any overriding powers of appointment to vary the shares of the beneficiaries after 18. Accordingly, if a trust had four beneficiaries, A B C and D, and A is approaching 18, the trustees must let A take outright, or exclude A altogether (so the whole fund is held on trust for B, C and D) or advance A's share so that it is held on continuing trusts for A. If they do the latter, it is unlikely that the terms of a settled advance for the benefit of A can provide powers that allow the trustees to terminate A's interest in favour of B, C and D at any time. Usually the advancement will be for A and any future spouse and children and A's siblings will only benefit if A and his immediate family have all died. Hence it is necessary for the trustees to be reasonably certain of the share each child should take at 18. For landed estates where some flexibility to vary the shares between members of the family later is desirable, this will be awkward[76];

(ii) *do nothing and leave the trust to become subject to the relevant property regime on April 6, 2008*: the desire to keep the settlement in being indefinitely meant that sooner or later it would end up in the relevant property regime. Accordingly, in cases where the beneficiaries were in their early 20s so that the 18–25 regime was of limited attraction, the decision was commonly taken to "bite the bullet", keep all the flexibility offered by the terms of the existing trust and allow the relevant property regime to apply. A key attraction was the absence of any IHT charge on the ending of the A-M trust on April 6, 2008: the real problem with establishing relevant property trusts today is not so much the anniversary charge but the 20 per cent entry charge. Here therefore, was an opportunity to keep a settlement in being (often for many years) which was gratefully accepted in many cases. Such settlements had commonly been drafted flexibly with overriding powers of appointment and wide powers to vary the interests of the various beneficiaries once they had taken an interest in possession. Such powers can continue to be exercised. So long as the relevant property regime charges are not increased above six per cent in the future the tax position may well be acceptable;

(iii) *ensure that on April 6, 2008 the conditions of s.71D (18–25) were met*: in practice a number of widely used A-M precedents provided for capital vesting at 25 and in such cases no action might have been necessary

---

[76] In practice, converting trusts to vest capital at 18 was frequently beset with problems. In a number of the standard precedents there were no appropriate powers available to the trustees.

to ensure compliance with s.71D.[77] One minor downside of the s.71D regime is that if a child dies under 25 the property may be taxed on his death (although not at 40 per cent only at the rates applicable under the s.71D regime). If the settled property is relevant property (or within the new style A-M trust regime) and not within the s.71D regime, no charge arises on the death of a beneficiary. Another problem was the view of HMRC that it was necessary to close the class by the date of conversion so this option was not suitable for trusts where it was likely that future beneficiaries would be born. (It was possible to convert half the trust into a s.71D trust for existing children and hold the remaining settled property on relevant property trusts to cater for future born children but the drafting was tricky and future compliance is likely to prove a nightmare!)

However, the attractions of the s.71D regime generally are:

(a) that anniversary charges are avoided while the beneficiary is under 25;

(b) that the special exit charge provided for in s.71F in many old A-M trusts produced only a small (in some cases microscopic!) charge;

(c) the retention of a wide power of advancement left open the possibility of trustees keeping the settlement in being by in due course making a settled advance. Further, the trust could retain an element of flexibility. However, once the child reaches 25 similar problems concerning flexibility will arise as in (i) above: a child's share (whether nil or 100 per cent) must be fixed by 25 and if the share is retained in trust for the benefit of that child by exercise of the power of advancement, the continuing trusts over that share after 25 are likely to be less flexible. This is because the power must be exercised for the benefit of *that child not the whole class*.[78] Although the power of advancement itself can be exercised so as to confer a power of appointment on the trustees exercisable in the future, care is still required to ensure that overall it can be seen as for the benefit of the particular child.

(3) In a number of trusts, the changes will have produced a compliance nightmare. What was envisaged as a single trust for a family may, as a result of the timing of events, have ended up with (say) one fund with a qualifying interest in possession; a second fund which has fallen into the relevant property regime and a third fund within s.71D. Different occasions of tax and rates of charge will apply to the three funds and a settlor who intended equality between his children will find that his plans have been frustrated.

---

[77] If the trust contained overriding powers of appointment or the beneficiary merely took an interest in possession at 25 some modification was required.
[78] "Benefit" has a wide but not unlimited meaning: see, for instance, *Lewin on Trusts* (18th edn), para.32–02.

CHAPTER 31

EXCLUDED PROPERTY, FOREIGN IHT ISSUES AND NON-DOMICILIARIES

I BASICS

31.01 Inheritance tax is not chargeable on excluded property.[1] In general unsettled property is excluded property if:

(i) the owner is not domiciled in the UK; and

(ii) the property is not situated in the UK.[2]

---

[1] IHTA 1984 s.3(2) and 5(1). Section 3(2) states that no account shall be taken of the value of excluded property which ceases to form part of a person's estate. So a gift of excluded property is not a PET. Section 5 makes it clear, however, that excluded property is part of an individual's estate until the moment *before* his death. So, for example, in assessing the loss to a donor's estate if he makes a gift of non-excluded property, the excluded property in his estate is taken into account.

[2] IHTA 1984 s.6. There are limited exceptions where UK situated assets are excluded property if owned as part of a person's free estate. These exceptions are similar to those discussed for settled property, for example where an individual is non-resident and owns specified government securities. Similarly authorised unit trusts or shares in an open-ended investment company will be excluded if owned by a non-domiciled individual.

Settled property

Property held in a settlement will only be excluded property under UK internal law[3] if both the following conditions are satisfied: **31.02**

(i) the settlor was domiciled outside the UK at the time when he made the settlement: note that the position of the interest in possession beneficiary or the domicile of the settlor at the date of his death is irrelevant[4]; and

(ii) the settled property is not situated in the UK. It will not generally matter if UK situated property is held in an offshore company owned by the trustees[5] because the settled property itself (being the company shares) is not UK situated.

As already noted, the domicile of the beneficiary is normally irrelevant and it   **31.03**
does not matter whether the settlement is an interest in possession or discretionary trust. The residence of the trustees is also irrelevant for inheritance tax purposes although a non-domiciled settlor will normally want the assets to be held in a non-resident trust for capital gains tax purposes.[6] Accordingly, even if a beneficiary is domiciled in the UK, there will be no charge to IHT on the termination of his qualifying interest in possession nor on any payment made by the trustees to him of non-UK situated property from a discretionary trust.

EXAMPLE 31.1

> A, domiciled in Portugal and now deceased, by his will left shares in BVI companies on trust to pay the income to his nephew, B, for life. B is domiciled and resident in the UK. The property is excluded property, being property situated abroad settled by a settlor domiciled at that time outside the UK. There was no charge to inheritance tax on the death of A; further, there is no inheritance tax charge on the ending of B's life interest even though it is a qualifying interest in possession.[7] If A had settled the BVI shares on discretionary trusts for his nephew and issue of B, all of whom were UK domiciled, the property would be, for the same reason, excluded so that the normal relevant property charges would not apply.

---

[3] Ignoring any provisions of the treaties.
[4] But see 31.27 for the effect of ss.80–82 and Ch.33 concerning the reservation of benefit provisions. See also treaty relief for the position where a beneficiary's domicile can make a difference if he has a qualifying IIP and dies treaty domiciled in another state.
[5] Although note the reservation of benefit problems where UK situated property is added to a company: see Ch.31 generally re UK situated property.
[6] See Chs 19 and 4.
[7] If A had died after March 21, 2006 B's interest is an immediate post-death interest (an IPDI): see Ch.28.

If, however, the trustees had exchanged the settled BVI shares for shares in UK companies, the property would no longer be excluded and there would be a charge to inheritance tax on the death of B (if he had a qualifying interest in possession), or the normal relevant property charges would apply if the trust was discretionary.[8]

Deemed domicile

31.04 The general rules on domicile are discussed in Ch.3. Even if a person is domiciled outside the UK under general law he may be deemed domiciled in the UK for inheritance tax purposes if one of two conditions is satisfied[9]:

(a) if he was domiciled in the UK on or after December 10, 1974 (under general law) and within the three years immediately preceding the transfer in question. This catches the taxpayer who was domiciled under general law and has emigrated. For three years (calendar years, not tax years) from the acquisition of a new domicile of choice he will retain a deemed UK domicile;

(b) if he was resident for income tax purposes in the UK on or after December 10, 1974 in not less than 17 out of the 20 income tax years ending with the income tax year in which he made the relevant transfer. This catches the foreign domiciliary who has lived in the UK for many years even though he retains his foreign domicile under general law. "Residence" is used in the income tax sense[10] and does not require residence for a period of 17 complete years only residence for a tax year.

EXAMPLE 31.2

(1) Kim, who is domiciled in New Zealand, came to the UK on April 1, 2000. He therefore first became UK resident in tax year 1999–2000. He will become UK deemed domiciled if he is still in the UK on April 6, 2015 even though he retains his NZ domicile.

(2) Paul had lived in the UK all his life with a UK domicile of origin. In March 2006, however, he moved to Portugal and in August 2010 he decided to remain there permanently. At this time he acquired a domicile of choice in Portugal under general law. Although he has been resident outside the UK for more than three tax years, he remains UK deemed domiciled until August 2013 because he did not lose his domicile under general law until 2010.

Until April 6, 2005 the concept of deemed domicile applied only for inheritance tax purposes. From that date, however, a person who is UK deemed

---

[8] See Ch.19 for the CGT position of the beneficiaries.
[9] Section 267 IHTA 1984.
[10] See Ch.3 and the proposal for a statutory residence test.

domiciled can also suffer an income tax charge under the pre-owned assets income tax regime.[11] Hence, foreign domiciliaries who are deemed domiciled and who are resident in the UK should consider not only their inheritance tax position but also whether they are subject to the pre-owned assets tax.

II TREATY RELIEF

Estate duty treaties

A number of double tax treaties displace the deemed domicile rules on death.[12] **31.05** These treaties are with France, Italy, India and Pakistan. However, they do not displace the deemed domicile rules on inter vivos transfers (so a PET may still become chargeable if the donor dies within seven years).[13] Each treaty has slightly different requirements. In general the treaties provide that inheritance tax[14] is not due on the death of an individual on any property situated outside the UK passing under a disposition regulated by foreign law.[15] So, for example, an Indian who is deemed domiciled in the UK should ensure that his non-UK property passes under a foreign law will or trust. An inheritance tax account is still required on death even if the relevant treaty exempts property from being chargeable in the UK.[16]

EXAMPLE 31.3

In 1997 Cedric, an Indian domiciliary, set up a Jersey law trust under which he retained a qualifying interest in possession at a time when he was deemed UK domiciled. The trust holds only non-UK situated assets.[17] On his death, assuming that he is domiciled in India under Indian law,[18] there is no inheritance tax payable on the settled assets because they are non-UK situate and pass under foreign law. Further,

---

[11] See Ch.34.
[12] See IHTA 1984 ss.158(6) and 267(2).
[13] Section 158(6) provides that the treaties have effect for inheritance tax only in relation to inheritance tax chargeable by virtue of s.4, i.e. the charge on death so failed PETs are not protected.
[14] The treaty (unlike the France, Italy or Pakistan treaties) refers only to estate duty not inheritance tax or taxes "of a substantially similar character" but it extends to capital transfer tax and inheritance tax.
[15] Although in the case of Italy the restriction is limited to UK settlements; a UK law will is still within the treaty exemption if the other conditions are satisfied.
[16] See Ch.40.
[17] There are treaty situs rules but these do not apply to India and Pakistan because Article V (situs rules) only applies if duty would otherwise be imposed on the property under the law of each of the contracting governments. Neither India nor Pakistan imposes any form of death duty so situs is determined under normal rules not under the Treaty.
[18] Not merely domiciled in India under English law. However, recent domicile cases in India have confirmed that Indian domicile is very similar in concept to English domicile. In particular one is not domiciled merely in a particular state India does not have a federal legal system but domiciled in India.

there is no Indian tax payable because India abolished estate duty in 1985. (Note that the treaty does not protect the making of the settlement from being a chargeable transfer if made after March 21, 2006; nor is a relevant property settlement protected from 10-year charges). It would, however, appear to protect Cedric from a charge under the reservation of benefit provisions if, say, he was the settlor of a trust where he did not have a qualifying interest in possession but otherwise reserved a benefit. In calculating any UK tax due on his remaining estate which is UK situate or does not pass under a foreign law disposition, the rates of tax are calculated ignoring the foreign property. Hence if his UK property is within his unused nil rate band no tax is due.

31.06 A foreign domiciled person who is deemed UK domiciled and is within the protection of one of the above treaties should ensure that his assets pass under a foreign law will or trust. Of course, there is a danger that these treaties will be revoked or renegotiated in which case he will become taxable on his world-wide estate. But if the Treaty is not revoked, a foreign domiciliary who makes PETs and dies within seven years will be worse off than if he had retained the foreign assets until death. For an elderly person this presents something of a dilemma but it is thought unlikely that the Treaties will in practice be revoked without prior notice. It is understood that so far very few have claimed the benefit of the Treaties and it is not yet clear how much information HMRC require in considering a claim for Treaty protection. For example, what proof will be necessary to show that someone was domiciled in a particular state in India under Indian law rather than in the UK at death?

EXAMPLE 31.4

Ravi has lived in England for many years but has retained (as a matter of general law) his domicile of origin in the Punjab. He owns a substantial property portfolio in Manchester worth in the region of £5 million. He reserves a benefit in a Jersey law settlement set up some years ago when he was deemed UK domiciled so that it cannot be an excluded property trust. He is terminally ill and, given the UK situs of the portfolio, a substantial IHT liability will arise on his death. Accordingly he borrows £4.7 million, all of which is charged against the portfolio. He transfers the cash to a bank account in Jersey and makes a Jersey law will to dispose of it. On his death:

(i) the value of the portfolio will be reduced by the liabilities charged on it to £300,000 which is covered by his available IHT nil rate band. No account is taken of property situated outside the UK in determining the amount or rate of UK tax.

(ii) the bank account in Jersey is protected by the Indian Treaty and accordingly tax free;

(iii) if Ravi had created a settlement of the cash he would at that time have made a chargeable transfer of value which was outside the Treaty protection[19];

[19] Note that it will be important to ensure the loan is properly charged on the UK property

(iv) The settlement in which he reserves a benefit will also be protected from an IHT charge on his death even though it is not excluded property. If the settlement had been governed by English law then there would have been no protection from a UK tax charge.

Other treaties

In addition to the four estate duty treaties mentioned above which are only relevant to the charge arising on death, there are six other treaties covering IHT: Switzerland, United States, Ireland, the Netherlands, South Africa and Sweden.[20] These generally approach the problem of double taxation not by laying down situs rules but by first resolving problems of dual domicile in favour of a single domicile for the purposes of the treaty and then giving primary taxing rights to the country of treaty domicile and reserving taxing rights to the other country in respect of certain assets such as land and permanent business establishments.[21] Of these six treaties, Switzerland only covers taxes arising on death rather. (As with the estate duty treaties the Swiss treaty applies to IHT charges arising on the death of an qualifying interest in possession beneficiary or where settled property is taxed on the transferor's death under the reservation of benefit provisions.) **31.07**

Generally most countries other than the UK treat a person as domiciled there if they are resident or ordinarily resident in that country. The concept of domicile for UK tax purposes means something quite different.[22] The UK charges IHT on a worldwide basis even if the person has not been resident here for many years if they remain domiciled in the UK. Even if a person is not domiciled in the UK under general law, foreign domiciliaries who have been living in the UK for over 17 years will remain deemed domiciled for three tax years after departure. And unlike other countries the UK will not tax a person on a worldwide basis simply because they are resident in the UK (unless they have been resident in the UK for 17 tax years). In order to counteract this bias in favour of other countries, all but the Irish treaty provide that a person who is a national of the UK but not of the other country and has not been resident in the other country for a minimum period is treaty domiciled in the UK. This preserves the UK taxing rights where a person has not lost their domicile of origin in the UK but happens to die resident in the other country.[23] **31.08**

and there is not also a charge over the cash deposit. See Ch.32 for liabilities and the order of deduction.
[20] South Africa, SI 1979/576; United States, SI 1979/1454; Netherlands, SI 1980/706; Sweden, SI 1981/840; Ireland, SI 1978/1107; Switzerland, SI 1994/3214.
[21] Within this basic idea there are many variations. For example, South Africa reserves taxing rights to the country where the person is not treaty domiciled if he was domiciled there in the 10 previous years. The United States effectively reserves taxing rights to the US where the person is a US citizen. The Swiss treaty allows secondary taxing rights where the person was a national of that country and domiciled there in the five previous years, Of course under UK law the person is not taxed anyway in the UK if he loses his actual domicile and deemed domicile so these provisions would not catch people who had emigrated permanently and been out of the UK for more than three years.
[22] See Ch.3.
[23] Netherlands also requires that the person does not intend to remain indefinitely in the Netherlands and the Swedish agreement requires the person to be domiciled or deemed domiciled in the UK.

31.09   Other cases of dual domicile are resolved in the standard way set out in the OECD Model. So the first tiebreaker test is where a person has a permanent home available to him. Permanent home probably means a residential base not merely a holiday home or an office where the person stays when he visits the UK.[24]

If he has a permanent home in both states or neither, then he is deemed resident where he has his centre of vital interests, i.e. where his personal and economic relations are closer (the former generally being considered more important). If his centre of vital interests cannot be determined then it is where he has a habitual abode, i.e. where does he habitually live? This appears to include someone who lives in a hotel regularly. If he has a habitual abode in both countries, or neither then the final tiebreaker test is nationality.[25] If the person is a dual national or a national of neither country the matter has to be settled by agreement.

31.10   It may be necessary to apply these tests continuously over a 10-year period, since the agreements with South Africa, Sweden and the Netherlands give a secondary taxing right if there was a treaty domicile in the UK within the 10 years preceding the gift or transfer on death, where at the time of the transfer there is a treaty domicile in the other country.

31.11   Treaty relief is particularly relevant for a person domiciled under foreign law who returns to their country of origin (e.g. Switzerland) but dies deemed domiciled in the UK. In these circumstances the treaty will often provide complete relief from the UK death charge except on UK situated property. Many of the treaties such as Sweden and the United States give 50 per cent spousal relief where the foreign national who is deemed UK domiciled transfers property to a foreign domiciled spouse.

---

[24] A permanent home at least suggests it has some sense of being a base for the taxpayer, even if not his main base. The meaning of this has been discussed by the French Conseil d'Etat in Decision No.69.852 of January 26, 1990 (1990) 23–24 Droit Fiscal 800. The taxpayer lived in France and travelled to work in Germany where he had rented an office. He then rented an apartment in Germany where he lived on weekdays returning to his house and family in France at weekends. He was held to have a permanent home in both countries from that time and his vital interests were divided between both states and as his place of habitual abode could not be established so his residence was determined by his French nationality. The Conseil refused to rank one place of residence over another according to subsidiary elements such as whether one place of abode is owned and the other rented or where the taxpayer's family resides. The French Ministry of Foreign Affairs has interpreted permanent home as meaning the place with which the taxpayer has his closest *personal* bonds or relations and that financial and economic links are not important.

The Bundesfinanzhof held that a permanent home meant a special type of domicile used in the sense of a home where a person stays more than occasionally and for more than a short time. See Decision of October 23, 1985 IR 244/82 (1985) BStB.

[25] Centre of vital interests is difficult. Someone can live with their family in one state but work five days a week in another. The Bundesfinazhof case quoted above also considered this where a German worked in Spain for a little over one year. He retained a family home in Germany and was also resident in Spain. He was held to have permanent homes in both countries but the centre of vital interests was Germany because it was certain that he would return there.

Settled property

Treaty relief can be particularly important in connection with settled prop-   **31.12**
erty. The UK generally imposes IHT on settled property on the basis of first
the settlor's IHT domicile (not treaty domicile) at the date the settlement was
made (not the date of death), and second the situs of the settled property.
Nevertheless IHT is restricted in the five treaties where the settlor had a treaty
domicile in the other country at the date of the settlement. So, for example,
even where a person was deemed or actually UK domiciled under UK law but
was treaty domiciled elsewhere, the UK may be able to charge IHT only in
respect of UK land or permanent establishment held by that settlement. The
terms of each treaty must be examined in each case but can assist in enabling
the settlor to avoid an entry charge into a settlement.

On death a treaty can relieve the trust from IHT in the following situations: **31.13**

(a) Treaty relief can apply where the settlor has reserved a benefit in a non-
    excluded property settlement and dies treaty domiciled in the other
    country. The other country will have taxing rights, not the UK, on
    foreign situated property.

(b) Relief can apply where an individual dies with a qualifying interest
    in possession but is treaty domiciled in the other country. The other
    country will have sole taxing rights except on UK situated property.

EXAMPLE 31.5

Henry, a Swedish national, who had lived in the UK for 20 years,
returned to Sweden. Immediately after his return in 2007 he set up a
trust into which he transferred all his property comprising foreign situated shares and cash in Jersey along with UK real estate. He was deemed
domiciled in the UK at the date when he set up the trust.

Under Art.5(4) of the Treaty he is not taxed in the UK on the transfer
into settlement except on the UK real estate since he was not a UK
national. Nor does the trust suffer charges under the relevant property
regime.

The Swiss treaty will not protect the trust from relevant property charges if the   **31.14**
transferor was deemed or actually domiciled in the UK at the date of death
but will assist in protecting the death estate from IHT.

EXAMPLE 31.6

(1) Christophe, a Swiss national, had lived for 20 years in the UK. He
    returned to Switzerland and died there in his third year of residence in
    Switzerland. He retained no home or other assets in the UK and has a
    treaty domicile in Switzerland. On his death he left his estate on an IPDI

trust to his son. There is no UK tax on his death under the treaty (and Swiss tax would generally be limited to around six per cent assuming the gift into trust could be classified as a gift to his son as the primary beneficiary). However, the trust is not an excluded property settlement given that he was deemed UK domiciled when he set it up. Accordingly on the death of the son IHT is prima facie payable (subject to any treaty relief available on the son's death). If the son's qualifying interest in possession terminated during his lifetime then IHT charges could arise both on termination and thereafter under the relevant property regime. The treaty only applies to IHT "insofar as it applies to the estate of a deceased person" not to charges under the relevant property regime.

(2) Christophe was also the life tenant of a trust set up in 1997 by his mother, a UK domiciliary. Christophe has a qualifying interest in possession. On his death after his return to Switzerland there is no UK IHT provided that the trust holds no UK situated assets despite the fact that it is not an excluded property settlement.

Transfer of nil rate band and treaty relief

31.15 On the death of a surviving spouse or civil partner his estate may benefit from the unused nil rate band of the first spouse or civil partner to die. IHTM confirms that where a spouse has died foreign domiciled, having left foreign property (e.g. to his children), then the surviving spouse will have a full transferable nil rate band because there was no chargeable transfer on the death of the first spouse.[26] Similarly if a treaty (such as the Indian treaty) exempts foreign situated property from UK tax then the nil rate band can be transferred to the surviving spouse. If, however, on the first death the property is taxed in the UK but tax is reduced to nil by either double taxation relief or successive charges relief there is no transferable nil rate band available. IHTM 43025 notes:

> "Where, under the terms of a double taxation agreement, an asset is not subject to tax, then if this means that the chargeable estate is below the nil rate band, the amount unused is available for transfer.
>
> However, where there is a liability to tax that is reduced to nil by either double taxation relief or successive charges relief, the nil rate band remains fully used."

III EXEMPTIONS FOR EXCLUDED PROPERTY

31.16 The basic exemptions are:

(a) The estate of a person immediately before his death does not include excluded property.[27]

---

[26] See IHTA 1984 s.8A(2). The transferred nil rate band is considered in Ch.38.
[27] IHTA 1984 s.5(1).

(b) No account is taken of excluded property which leaves a person's estate in determining whether an inter vivos disposition is a transfer of value.[28]

(c) Relevant property (i.e. property in trust which is subject to 10-yearly anniversary and exit charges) does not include excluded property.[29]

(d) Excluded property which is held in a qualifying interest in possession trust is not subject to inheritance tax on the death of the beneficiary or on the inter vivos termination of his interest in possession.

Situs

The "situs" of property is governed by common law rules and depends on the type of property involved, although it is important to remember that the rules can be subject to contrary provisions in double taxation treaties. Briefly, the rules are as follows: **31.17**

(a) Any interest in land is situated where the land is physically located;

(b) Chattels are situated at the place where they are kept. It is therefore important that the foreign domiciliary avoids having chattels in the UK at the date of his death;

(c) Registered shares and securities are situated where they are registered or, if transferable on more than one register, where they would normally be dealt with in the ordinary course of business;

(d) Bearer shares and securities transferable by delivery are situated where the certificate or other document of title is kept[30];

(e) A bank account is situated at the branch which maintains the account although special rules apply to non-residents' foreign currency bank accounts.[31]

UK situate assets

When the settlor is not UK domiciled at the time when he creates a settlement it is important that trustees do not own UK property directly. **31.18**

EXAMPLE 31.7

Eric, a foreign domiciliary, set up a trust in 2003 with foreign currency in an account abroad. The trustees use the cash to invest in a UK property.

---

[28] IHTA 1984 s.3(2).
[29] IHTA 1984 s.58(4)(f).
[30] For the CGT position of bearer shares, see CGT Manual 12452-3 and TCGA 1992 s.275(1)(c) in relation to bearer debt securities to which the above rule does not apply.
[31] See Ch.3.

Eric dies without becoming UK domiciled or deemed domiciled. The IHT position is as follows:

    (i) If the trust had established an interest in possession for Eric, the property is UK situated and taxed on his death as it would be for any UK domiciled beneficiary owning a qualifying interest in possession[32];

    (ii) If the trust is discretionary and Eric is a beneficiary then he has reserved a benefit with the result that there is again a tax charge on his death.[33] In addition because the trust owns UK property on a 10-year anniversary there will be an inheritance tax charge.

31.19   Foreign domiciliaries should take care where a foreign situate gifted asset is transferred into trust and subsequently brought to the UK. This can occur where non-UK situated chattels are put into trust and then brought into the UK or where a UK house is gifted to an offshore company and then transferred from the company to the trust. In these circumstances apart from a charge under the settlement rules, the gift with reservation rules may also result in a charge because the gifted property is not itself excluded property.[34]

31.20   There are three situations when it is particularly important to avoid having UK situated property directly owned by a trust:

    (i) *when settling assets into trust*: if A transfers UK situated assets into a trust for himself and family, this is a chargeable transfer subject to an immediate inheritance tax charge (at 20 per cent to the extent that the value settled exceeds his nil rate band);

    (ii) *on a 10-year anniversary*: when a discretionary trust owns UK property at the time of a 10-year anniversary, the hypothetical transfer used in determining the IHT rate is calculated on the basis of the value of the UK property and also that of any non-UK property which was excluded property when put into the settlement even though that property has remained excluded.[35] Likewise excluded property put into another settlement made by the same settlor and on the same day (a "related settlement") is taken into account. Hence, even if the UK property is within the nil-rate band a charge may arise on a 10-year anniversary[36];

    (iii) *on the death of the settlor*: as noted in Example 31.7 above, if Eric dies and at that time the settlement owns UK situated property, there is a reservation of benefit which cannot be avoided by claiming that the property is excluded property.[37]

---

[32] IHTA 1984 s.49(1).

[33] Section 102(3) FA 1986 is not displaced by s.48(3).

[34] See 31.44.

[35] See Ch.29 for further discussion about the rate of tax charged in relation to excluded property trusts holding UK situated property under the relevant property regime.

[36] IHTA 1984 s.66(4).

[37] See 31.44 below.

When UK situate property can be excluded property if held in trust

Despite the general principle that UK situate property is not excluded property, certain UK assets held in trust are deemed to be excluded property if the
relevant conditions are met. These assets comprise: **31.21**

(i) UK Government securities ("gilts");

(ii) interests in Authorised Unit Trusts (AUTS) and Open Ended Investment
Companies (OEICS);

(iii) non-sterling UK bank accounts.

The rules are different in each case.

Gilts

Gilts[38] which are owned in a settlement where the life tenant has a qualifying interest in possession[39] are excluded property if the person entitled
to the interest in possession is ordinarily resident[40] outside the UK.[41] **31.22**

---

[38] For chargeable events before April 6, 1998 there were two classes of exempt gilts for IHT
purposes, with different conditions attached First Gilts where the conditions required the
individual to be domiciled and ordinarily resident outside the UK. These included (a) 3½%
War Loan 1952 or after, issued under F(No.2)A 1915 s.47. (b) Gilts issued under F(No.2)
A 1931 s.22, where this was the condition set out in the prospectus. Second Gilts, where
the condition required the beneficial owner to be ordinarily resident outside the UK but
domicile was irrelevant. These are essentially all gilts issued on or after April 29 1996. Under
FA 1940 s.60(1), The Treasury has powers to modify the operation of the general exemption from taxation specified in the terms of issue of the security concerned. This power was
exercised so that with effect from April 6, 1998 all gilts were deemed to be FOTRA gilts.
So, for deaths and other chargeable events on or after April 6, 1998, all government securities are excluded property for IHT purposes by reference only to the ordinary residence of
the beneficial owner. The only exception is 3½% War Loan, where the additional domicile
condition continues to apply to deaths or other chargeable events on or after April 6, 1998.
So, in summary:

- FOTRA securities issued before April 29, 1996 will be exempt provided the beneficial
  owner is both domiciled and ordinarily resident outside the UK.

- 3½% War Loan 1952 or after will be only be exempt if the beneficial owner is both domiciled and ordinarily resident outside the UK, even if the chargeable event is after April 6,
  1998.

- All other government securities issued before April 6, 1998 without FOTRA conditions
  will be exempt from that date provided the beneficial owner is ordinarily resident outside
  the UK. Domicile is no longer relevant.

- All other government securities issued after April 29, 1996 will be exempt provided
  the beneficial owner is ordinarily resident outside the UK. Domicile is no longer
  relevant.

[39] i.e. a pre-March 22, 2006 interest in possession, a transitional serial interest or an immediate
post-death interest.
[40] Note that the conditions for establishing domicile and residence for the IIP beneficiary are the
same as for an individual.
[41] See IHTA 1984 s.48(4).

Note that the domicile of the settlor is irrelevant. If the beneficiary is not domiciled in the UK but is UK ordinarily resident the gilts are not excluded property.

EXAMPLE 31.8

A is a UK non-resident interest in possession beneficiary of a will trust established when B died in 2004. He is UK domiciled having decided to leave the UK for a short time. He becomes ill. The trustees decide to protect the inheritance tax position and invest entirely in exempt gilts where only non-UK residence is required. There is no inheritance tax charge on A's death because the gilts are excluded property. It does not matter that A is still UK domiciled nor that B the settlor was UK domiciled.[42]

31.23 If the trust is discretionary and holds UK gilts to benefit from the exemption, none of the beneficiaries must be UK ordinarily resident if the gilts are to be exempt from inheritance tax.[43] The exact wording is, "*all known persons for whose benefit the settled property or income from it has been or might be applied or who are or might become beneficially entitled to an interest in possession in it*" are not ordinarily resident in the UK. If a UK charity is a beneficiary then exemption is not denied.[44] Nor is the exemption denied if there is a possibility that some currently unascertained person, such as an unborn child or future spouse of an existing beneficiary, might become a beneficiary in the future and be UK resident.[45]

However, the reference to the settled property and its income relates to all the property comprised in the particular settlement and not just to the exempt securities. HMRC take the words "*has been or might be applied*" to mean that you will need to consider both past and future or potential application of the property and its income.

Most trusts set up since March 21, 2006 will now be relevant property settlements and will need to satisfy this condition.

EXAMPLE 31.9

A is a discretionary beneficiary of a trust established in 2004. He emigrates. Only if all beneficiaries of the trust are and have always been

---

[42] It is harder to come within this exemption since the FA 2006 changes because a qualifying interest in possession arises only in limited circumstances (although in this case A has an IPDI).

[43] Note that if gilts are transferred from one settlement to another they will only be excluded property if the beneficiaries of both settlements are non-UK ordinarily resident. This prevents gilts from being channelled from a discretionary trust where they were not excluded property to a new settlement. See *Minden Trust (Cayman) Ltd v IRC* [1984] STC 434. When a close company is a beneficiary of a trust any gilts owned by the trust will be excluded property only if all participators in the company are non-UK ordinarily resident, irrespective of the company's residence.

[44] See: IHTM 27249.

[45] See: IHTM 27248.

non-resident will the settled property be excluded. After March 21, 2006 it has not been possible for the trustees to appoint a qualifying interest in possession to A and then purchase exempt gilts to take advantage of the exemption.

There is some debate about whether the gilts have to be registered in the name **31.24** of the trustees or whether they can be held in the name of a nominee. HMRC suggest[46] that excluded property treatment is only available if the gilts are registered in the name of the individual trustees rather than nominees:

> "*If a worthwhile amount of tax is at stake you should investigate the possibility of a last-minute purchase. Except where the available information (e.g. inclusion of sufficient income/interest) reasonably rules out that possibility, you should seek specific confirmation that the gilts concerned were in fact registered in the transferor's, or the trustee's, name(s) at the date of the relevant transfer.*"

It is difficult to discern any rational basis for this view and it is not thought that HMRC maintain this view when challenged. In practice, the gilts exemption is most likely to be useful for the person who is UK domiciled under general law (or is deemed domiciled) but has left the UK and ceased to be ordinarily resident. A person who has emigrated permanently may also find it useful to invest in gilts in order to protect the inheritance tax position until he has lost his deemed domicile. He may be able to borrow on the security of chargeable assets (such as real estate) to invest the proceeds in gilts. The borrowing will then reduce the value of the chargeable assets.[47] The gilts exemption can also be useful for those who wish to settle property while still UK domiciled or to make lifetime gifts.

Example 31.10

(1) Frederick, a Swiss national, returns to Switzerland. He is UK deemed domiciled. He invests in gilts and gives these to his son who is French resident. This is a gift of excluded property and he does not need to survive seven years even if son is UK resident at the date of death. This is because no account is taken of gifts of excluded property.

(2) As above but Frederick decides to settle the property into a trust for his son. The gilts are excluded property and no entry charge arises. However, unless all known beneficiaries are and remain non-UK resident and the trustees retain gilts then the trust is subject to 10-year and exit charges because it is not otherwise an excluded property settlement and is within the relevant property regime. However, even if son is resident in the UK at the date of Frederick's death within seven years of setting up the trust and the trustees have by then sold the gilts it would appear that there is no additional tax payable on the settled gift by Frederick since the trans-

[46] See IHTM 04294.
[47] IHTA 1984 s.162(4).

fer made by Frederick was not chargeable comprising as it did exempt gilts that are for that limited purpose excluded property.

AUTS and OEICS

31.25 The exemption for settled property is different from that applying to gilts. AUTs and OEICS are excluded property unless the settlor was domiciled in the UK at the time when the settlement was made.[48] The residence or domicile of any beneficiary is not relevant. Beware however of the trap outlined at 29.47 in relation to investment in AUTS and OEICS.

Non-sterling UK bank accounts

31.26 A UK bank account is excluded property if it is denominated in foreign currency and the settlor was not UK domiciled when he made the settlement; the trustees are non-resident and the settlement is subject to a qualifying interest in possession in favour of a person neither domiciled nor resident in the UK.[49] This exemption has limited value.

IV IHTA 1984 SS.80–82 TRAPS

31.27 If the settlor or his spouse is the initial qualifying interest in possession beneficiary of the settlement or if they have successive qualifying interests in possession, foreign situs settled property is only excluded property[50] if the settlor was not UK domiciled when the settlement was made and he or his spouse (as the case may be) is non-domiciled when the life interest or the successive life interest ends.[51] This rule applies only for the purposes of the relevant property regime. Prior to FA 2006 it had relatively little impact for foreign domiciliaries who could avoid using relevant property trusts.[52]

EXAMPLE 31.11

(1) In 1997 Jason set up a trust to hold non-UK situs assets when he was not UK domiciled. He took an interest in possession from the outset and there is a successive life interest for his spouse.[53] He died in 2004 UK deemed domiciled and his spouse died in 2007 also UK deemed domiciled. There is no inheritance tax charge on the death of

---

[48] IHTA 1984 s.48(3A) inserted by FA 2003. This rule has applied since October 16, 2002.
[49] IHTA 1984 s.157(4).
[50] See 31.02.
[51] IHTA 1984 ss.80–82.
[52] The provisions are discussed in relation to UK domiciliaries in Ch.29.
[53] Note that if he had taken an interest in possession (say) six months after the funds were settled and in the interim that trust was discretionary, ss.80–82 would not have applied.

either Jason or his spouse because the settlement is an excluded property settlement. Applying s.80, however, on the ending of the interest in possession of his spouse she was UK deemed domiciled and hence the settled property will cease to be excluded and will come within the relevant property regime from that time onwards. Accordingly unless the settlement ends on her death, future 10-year and exit charges will be payable. The one exception to this is if the trust holds AUTS or OEICs at the 10-year anniversary or on payment to a beneficiary.[54]

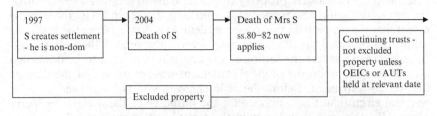

(2) By contrast, if Jason had set up the settlement on or after March 22, 2006 when he was not UK domiciled, then even if Jason had been given an initial interest in possession this would have been irrelevant as s.80 would have no application. The property is excluded property for all IHT purposes.[55]

As a result of the FA 2006 changes foreign domiciliaries should review their trusts in the following circumstances: **31.28**

(a) if the trust was set up prior to March 22, 2006;

(b) if it gave an initial interest in possession to either the settlor or his spouse (or civil partner); and

(c) if the last of the settlor/spouse /civil partner to take a qualifying interest in possession is expected to die deemed or actually UK domiciled.

In these circumstances the trust will either need to end on the last death in order to avoid future 10-year and exit charges or hold AUTS or OEICS at the relevant date. Given that the charge under ss.80–82 is relatively easily avoided by holding AUTs or OEICs (since s.82 does not apply in these circumstances)[56] then the trustees are likely to leave the property in trust rather than for it to become the absolute property of a UK domiciled beneficiary.

Transfers between settlements

When property is transferred between settlements (typically in exercise of an express power in the settlement), for the purposes of the relevant property   **31.29**

---

[54] See 29.47 for further details.
[55] From March 22, 2006 s.80 applies only if the interest in possession is a "postponing interest": see s.80(4). Only IPDIs and disabled interests are postponing.
[56] See s.48(3A).

regime the property is treated as remaining comprised in the first settlement.[57] This section applies whether or not the settlement comprises excluded property. However, IHTA 1984 s.82 also provides that in determining whether the settled property is excluded property, it is necessary to look at the domicile of the settlor of the first settlement at the time it was made and also at the domicile of the settlor of the second settlement at the time when that the second trust was made. Only if both settlors had neither an actual nor deemed UK domicile at the time when each made their trust can the property be excluded property.

31.30   If the trustees transfer property from one trust to another, the settlor of the first settlement is also treated as the settlor of the second settlement to the extent that the property in the second settlement is derived from the first. The settlor has provided the funds indirectly for the purposes of the settlement.[58] In these circumstances the settlor of the first trust will need to be domiciled outside the UK when the original settlement was set up and at the date of the second settlement. Before the 2006 changes, s.82 had not been a major problem given that it only applied for the purposes of the relevant property regime. For instance, if property in the second settlement was held on fixed interest or accumulation and maintenance trusts at a time when a transfer to it was made, then s.82 would not have been relevant. With the restriction on the creation post-March 21, 2006 of new qualifying interest in possession or A-M trusts, however, this is no longer the case since all new settlements generally fall within the relevant property regime. Hence resettlements after the settlor is UK deemed domiciled need to be watched carefully.

EXAMPLE 31.12

(1) Robert settled foreign shares into a discretionary settlement in 2000 when not UK domiciled. He became UK domiciled in 2004. For income tax reasons the trustees decide that they wish to move the income producing assets into a new UK resident trust which is set up in May 2006 and in which Robert is entitled to income. The new trust falls within the relevant property regime and was set up by a UK domiciled settlor. As a result of s.82 the property, transferred from the 2000 settlement ceases to be excluded property for the purposes of the relevant property regime and the usual relevant property charges arise even if the new trust owns non-UK property.[59] Does the exception for AUTs and OEICs apply? Such property can still "be taken to be excluded property" by virtue of s.48(3A) and is not caught by s.82 but s.48(3A) requires the settlor to be domiciled outside the UK when the settlement was made. In the above example, Robert was domiciled in the UK at the date of the second settlement. HMRC argue that the second trust is within the relevant property regime and also subject to the GWR charge at his death since he cannot claim the protection of s.48(3) or (3A) to displace FA 1986 s.102.

---

[57] IHTA 1984 s.81.
[58] See IHTA 1984 s.44.
[59] These charges will be calculated on the basis that the property remains comprised in the original settlement.

(2) By contrast, if the transfer had been made in January 2006 then the new trust would have been a qualifying interest in possession for Robert and s.82 would not have applied. However, it appears that the new trust would still fall outside the protection of the excluded property provisions. Although the property was originally settled when Robert was foreign domiciled, by the date of the resettlement he was UK domiciled and therefore the requirement in s.48(3) and (3A) that the settlor was not domiciled in the UK "at the date the settlement was made" is not satisfied. It is not clear whether the position would be different if the settlor of Trust 2 was say a foreign domiciled settlor as to the initial property settled and the trustees of Trust 1 transferred the property to such a trust. Note also that the residence of Trust 2 is irrelevant to the inheritance tax position.

HMRC have commented on the position where transfers between the two settlements are effected by the trustees, both trusts were set up and funded at a time when the settlor was not UK domiciled but the transfer was made by trustees at a time when one or more of the settlors was UK domiciled. In their view, such a transfer is not caught by s.82 and will remain excluded property generally for all other IHT purposes since both settlements "were made" at a time when each settlor was foreign domiciled.[60] Note that ss.82 and 48(3) and (3A) all refer to when the settlement "was made" not when the property first became comprised in that settlement. **31.31**

EXAMPLE 31.13

> Robert set up two discretionary trusts in 2000 when not UK domiciled. He became deemed domiciled in 2006. In 2007 the trustees transfer non-UK situs property from one trust to another. The property remains excluded for the purposes of ss.82 and 48(3) (and under the GWR regime).

V ADDITIONS OF PROPERTY TO AN EXISTING SETTLEMENT

A controversial issue concerns additions of property to an existing settlement.[61] For instance, what happens when the settlor adds property to his trust after he has become UK domiciled? IHTM 27220 notes: **31.32**

> "*the legislation refers to the settlor's domicile at the time the settlement was made. You must proceed on the basis that, for any given item of property held in a settlement, the settlement was made when that property was put in the settlement. Consult TG or your Team Leader if this view is challenged.*"

---

[60] HMRC note that the position might be different if the settlor had a power of appointment and appointed the assets himself to a new trust although the authors believe this is only right if the settlor exercised a general power of appointment.
[61] This is discussed further in Ch.24.

EXAMPLE 31.14 (TAKEN FROM HMRC MANUAL)

S, when domiciled abroad, creates a settlement of Spanish realty. Later he acquires a UK domicile and then adds some Australian property to the settlement. The Spanish property is excluded property because of S's overseas domicile when he settled that property. However the Australian property is not excluded property as S had a UK domicile when he added that property to the settlement.[62]

31.33 In effect, HMRC consider that every addition to an existing settlement constitutes the making of a new settlement in relation to the added property. The example above makes it clear that adding property to an existing settlement which is excluded does not, in HMRC's view, jeopardise the exemption from inheritance tax for the original property provided that it has been kept segregated. It merely means that the new property does not qualify for protection. In RI 166 HMRC comment, *"if assets added at different times have become mixed, any dealings with the settled fund after the addition may also need to be considered."* Hence, the trustees need to ensure that the original trust property is kept physically segregated from any subsequent additions where such additions are made at a time when the settlor is UK domiciled. Otherwise the existing inheritance tax protection over the assets already settled might be jeopardised:

"The trustees of a settlement should keep adequate records to enable any necessary attribution of the settled property to be made if . . . the settlor has added further assets to the settlement after it was made."

Are HMRC correct that an addition involves the creation of a new settlement?

31.34 This has been discussed in Ch.24 in the context of additions to pre-March 22, 2006 trusts. Section 48(3) refers, in the context of when there is an excluded property settlement, to the relevant time being *"when the settlement was made"* not the time when the property was settled. It is true that property becomes comprised in the settlement at the time when it is added but this is different from saying that a new settlement is "made" when the settlor adds property.

31.35 In general it is not correct to say that there are two separate settlements when property is added to an existing settlement.[63] Accordingly, HMRC have to show that where a person adds property to an existing settlement made by him, two separate settlements are deemed to be made as a result of some provision in the inheritance tax legislation.[64] In fact, HMRC justify their position

---

[62] The same view is repeated in RI 166.

[63] Commonly added property is treated as comprising one fund with the existing settled property.

[64] See *Dymond's Capital Taxes*, para.16.247: *"in general it seems a reasonable inference from the above provisions as a whole that what would as a matter of everyday usage be regarded as a single settlement should only be split into separate settlements where there is a specific statutory direction to that effect or where there is more than one settlor."* Such a direction was found in Sch.5 para.9 FA 1975 for its limited purposes but has not followed through into the inheritance tax legislation.

on the basis of the definitions of settled property and settlement in IHTA 1984 s.43. They consider that each gift to a settlement is a disposition and that each disposition represents a new and separate settlement. However, s.43(2) defines settlement as meaning *"any disposition or dispositions of property"* which suggests that this view is wrong: it envisages that two dispositions can be made to a single settlement.

31.36 HMRC may point out that IHTA 1984 s.60 states that in relation to relevant property settlements and other trusts charged under Ch.III,[65] references to the commencement of a settlement are *"references to when property first becomes comprised in it"*. But this provision does not say that a new settlement commences every time property is added to an existing trust. In any event, there is no need for such a provision in the interest in possession regime because the tax charge does not depend on when property enters a settlement.[66] Indeed s.44 expressly refers to the possibility of two deemed settlements but only where more than one person is a settlor, not in relation to any other circumstances. For the purposes of CGT HMRC accept that a new settlement is not generally made when property is added.[67]

31.37 The case of *Rysaffe v IRC*[68] is unhelpful for HMRC. The Court of Appeal held at [13]:

> *"section 43(2) supplies the definition of settlement to be applied in answering each of these questions [namely what is taken to be a settlement and what is referred to as property comprised in a settlement]. It should be noted that s.43 does not specifically address a numerical question: what is the number of relevant settlements existing in a particular inheritance tax situation. In the absence of specific statutory provisions the answer to the numerical question is to be found in the general law of trusts."*

In that case, an attempt by HMRC to treat five settlements as one (the reverse of what is being argued on additions) was rejected.

Summary of position on additions

31.38 Although it is sensible to follow HMRC guidance and not add to a settlement after a settlor has become UK domiciled, in the light of the *Rysaffe* decision and on the wording of the legislation there is a compelling argument that additions of non-situs assets to an excluded property trust made after the settlor is UK domiciled become excluded property because the property falls within the wording of s.48(3): the settlor was non-domiciled on the commencement date (notwithstanding that further property was added when the settlor was UK domiciled).[69] In any event, there may be a significant chargeable transfer when additions of property are made to a discretionary trust even if the settlor

---

[65] So not qualifying interest in possession trusts.
[66] In the relevant property regime the commencement date of a settlement is important in arriving at 10-yearly anniversaries: see also IHTA 1984 ss.61 and 83.
[67] See Chs 10 and 12.
[68] [2003] STC 536.
[69] One difficulty post-March 21, 2006, however, is that the addition will be a chargeable transfer, at least if made to an existing A-M or discretionary trust and possibly to an interest in

successfully argues that the property falls outside the relevant property regime and the inheritance tax net after that addition.

31.39 If property is added to an existing pre-March 22, 2006 interest in possession trust for the settlor is the addition also held on qualifying interest in possession trusts so that because the settlor is the life tenant there is no transfer of value? This raises slightly different issues which are discussed in Ch.24.

EXAMPLE 31.15

(1) S settles non-situs assets into a discretionary trust in 2005 when not UK domiciled. He becomes deemed domiciled in 2007. He then adds further non-situs property to the trust in 2008. That addition is a chargeable transfer even if the property is comprised in an excluded property settlement thereafter.

(2) S settles assets onto a discretionary trust in 2005 and the trust is converted to a qualifying interest in possession trust for S in January 2006. S could add property to such a trust and contend that there was no transfer of value because there is no loss to his estate.

Gifts to companies

31.40 The difficulties posed by the addition of property to a settlement may be overcome if assets are added to a company wholly owned by the trust so that value (only) is added to the settlement[70]. If the company shares are already held on a pre-March 22, 2006 qualifying interest in possession trust for the settlor who then adds cash or other assets to the company, his qualifying interest in possession continues in the settled property, which is the shares. The value of the trust fund has increased but no property has been added to it.[71]

There are three issues to consider

31.41 *First*, a gift to a company is normally a chargeable transfer and hence the settlor would prima facie be subject to inheritance tax at 20 per cent on the value of the addition (assuming that he has used up his IHT nil rate band). In order to avoid this problem the company shares must be held on a qualifying interest in possession trust for the settlor. It would then be said that the value of his estate immediately after the disposition has not been diminished and

---

possession trust. Conversion of a discretionary trust to a qualifying interest in possession trust for the settlor is not possible under the new regime.

[70] Trustees may establish such a company: it should, of course, be incorporated and managed outside the UK.

[71] For the CGT position when gifts are made to companies, see Ch.18 and *Coombes v IRC* [2008] STC 2984.

so that there is no transfer of value.[72] Commercially one might say that there has been some loss to the settlor's estate because the money is not his to deal with freely because it is now in the company. However, it is not believed that HMRC take this point.

Secondly, it is important to consider how the reservation of benefit rules **31.42** operates. The property is gifted to a company. Assuming that there is a reservation of benefit in that property (because the settlor continues to be able to benefit from it), FA 1986 s.102(3) could apply at his death. It is disapplied on his death, however, if property in which he has reserved a benefit otherwise forms part of his estate on his death. But it is the company shares which form part of his estate on his death not the cash or other assets which he has gifted to the company. Hence, although s.48(3) will protect the shares from an inheritance tax charge, the cash or other assets added to the company will be subject to a reservation of benefit if the settlor were to die domiciled in the UK. It seems preferable then that after the gift the trustees liquidate the company (not declare a dividend)[73] so that the assets become held directly by the trustees. The settlor may reserve a benefit but s.102(3) is then disapplied by s.49 (because of the settlor's qualifying interest in possession) and there is no charge because it is excluded property.

Thirdly by giving cash to the company the settlor has significantly increased **31.43** the value of the company shares. The result is that a substantial gain may be realised when the company is liquidated. That gain will form part of stockpiled s.87 gains which could be disadvantageous for future beneficiaries after his death who are UK resident. Prior to April 6, 2008 this did not matter if all the beneficiaries were foreign domiciled because they were not subject to s.87. However, because such gains will be "post-April 2008 gains", they are now potentially chargeable on a foreign domiciled UK resident beneficiary who receives benefits in the UK.[74]

VI RESERVATION OF BENEFIT ISSUES[75]

It may be argued that if the settlor can benefit from the assets in his trust he **31.44** has reserved a benefit[76]; so that prima facie he is taxed on his death if UK domiciled. On this analysis the settled property rules are overridden by the reservation of benefit rules. However, this appears to be contrary to s.48(3) which states that property is excluded if non-UK situate and held in a settlement made when the settlor was not UK domiciled.

Accordingly, the question is should the deeming provisions in s.102(3), which treat the property as comprised in the settlor's free estate, override s.48(3) which specifically deals with settled property? Should the property be treated as "unsettled" for the purposes only of the reservation of benefit rules? If so, then a settlor who enjoys a qualifying interest in possession in his trust will be in a better tax position than a settlor whose property is held

---

[72] IHTA 1984 s.3(1) and see s.49(1) treating the settlor who is beneficially entitled to an interest in possession as beneficially entitled to the company shares.
[73] Which would be income of the settlor as life tenant.
[74] See Ch.19.
[75] Reservation of benefit is discussed in Chs 33 and 43.
[76] FA 1986 s.102(3).

in a discretionary trust under which he can benefit because if the settlor has a qualifying interest in possession in a trust and dies UK domiciled, s.102(3) is displaced because the property forms part of his estate immediately before his death.[77] It can then obtain the protection of s.48(3) since there is nothing in s.49(1) to displace s.48(3).

31.45 HMRC confirmed in correspondence with the Law Society in 1986[78] that the settled property rules did override the reservation of benefit rules and that there was no tax to pay if the reserved benefit property was excluded property under s.48. This was then confirmed in the CTO Advanced Instruction Manual at D8 but the text was changed in October 2001 indicating that HMRC were reconsidering their position. The IHT Manual then contained contradictory statements. In December 2010, however, HMRC announced that they were revising the Manual: the following statement appears to resolve the difficulties which had risen.

HMRC's revised views

31.46 X creates a settlement of non-UK situs property in which he reserves a benefit at a time when he is not UK domiciled. Subsequently he becomes UK domiciled. HMRC now accept:

(a) that on his death the reservation of benefit charge under FA 1986 s.102(3) does not apply, i.e. the excluded property rules take precedence;

(b) that if he surrenders his interest under the settlement or if the interest ends during his lifetime there is not a deemed PET under FA 1986 s.102(4).

This change corresponds to the widely held view of advisers that in the above situation reservation of benefit should not be an issue. Difficulties may, of course, arise if the settlor adds property to his settlement after he becomes UK domiciled. The revised text of the Manual is as follows:

"IHTM14396—Settled property: Settlement created when the settlor is domiciled outside the UK

Where the settlor was domiciled outside the UK at the time a settlement was made, any foreign property in the settlement is excluded property and is not brought into charge for Inheritance Tax (IHT) purposes (IHTM27220). This rule applies where property is subject to a reservation of benefit even though the settlor may have acquired a domicile of choice in the UK, or be deemed to be domiciled in the UK, at the time the GWR charge arises (IHTM04071).

Reservation ceasing on death

---

[77] IHTA 1984 s.49(1). This section deems the qualifying life tenant to be beneficially entitled to the property but s.48(3) nevertheless tells us it is excluded property if the settlor was foreign domiciled.

[78] *Law Society Gazette* 1986, p.3728.

At the material date FA86/S102(3) deems the donor to be beneficially entitled to property that is, at that time, settled property. As the property in which the reservation subsisted is 'property comprised in a settlement', it is the provisions of IHTA84/S48(3) that are in point. It is the domicile of the settlor at the time the settlement was made that is relevant in deciding whether foreign property in which the reservation subsisted is excluded property.

Example

Henry, who is domiciled in New Zealand, puts foreign property into a discretionary trust under which he is a potential beneficiary (IHTM14393). He dies five years later having acquired a domicile of choice in the UK and without having released the reservation. The property is subject to a reservation on death but it remains excluded property and is outside the IHT charge.

Exceptions to the rule

There are, however, circumstances where this rule does not apply:

- If the trustees had sold the foreign assets so that at the date of death the settled property was invested in UK assets, the exclusion would not apply as the property comprised in the settlement was not situated outside the UK, so IHTA84/S48(3) cannot apply.
- If the donor has acquired a domicile of choice (or is deemed domiciled) in the UK and adds other property to the settlement (irrespective of the situs (IHTM27071) of the property), we regard the donor as creating a separate settlement (IHTM04272). All the trust assets will be property subject to a reservation, but the foreign assets settled when the donor was domiciled outside the UK will be excluded property, whereas the assets settled when the donor was domiciled in the UK will be subject to IHT
- And in the reverse situation, if a donor who is domiciled (or deemed domiciled) in the UK creates a settlement with foreign assets and the settled property remains subject to a reservation at death, the trust assets will be subject to IHT under FA86/S102(3) even if the settlor dies domiciled outside the UK as IHTA84/S48(3) does not apply—as well as being subject to relevant property trust charges (IHTM42000)."

Ending a reservation inter vivos

Unlike s.102(3), FA 1986 s.102(4) does not deem the property to be part of **31.47** the donor's estate or treat it as property to which he is beneficially entitled. Instead it simply deems the donor to have made a PET (i.e. a disposition which is a transfer of value). How does s.3(2) (which states that "*for the purposes of subsection (1) no account shall be taken of the value of excluded property which ceases to form part of a person's estate as a result of a disposition*") interact with s.3(1) which defines the transfer of value?

If it is accepted that the settled property is excluded property, is the value transferred by the deemed PET nil because "no account" is taken of the value of excluded property for the purposes of assessing a transfer of value? Or does the fact that there is a deemed PET mean that there is a transfer of value which overrides s.3(2) and, by definition, cannot be a disposition of excluded property? The difficulty with the latter argument is that it is difficult to see why there should be any difference if the settlor is not UK domiciled. In both cases a deemed PET is made and arguably s.3(2) is overridden. In fact HMRC never considered that a settlor who was not UK domiciled made a PET when a reservation of benefit ceased in non-UK situate property.

31.48   HMRC have recently revised the Manual to deal with this issue as follows:

> *"Where the reservation is released during the donor's lifetime, FA86/ S102(4) treats the donor as making a disposition of the property by a disposition which is a potentially exempt transfer (PET) (IHTM04072). This is different to the basis of the charge arising on death, but as property in which the reservation ceases is 'property comprised in a settlement' the provisions of IHTA84/S48(3) are again in point to decide whether any foreign property is excluded property.*
>
> *As FA86/S102(4) treats the donor as making a disposition, it is the treatment of excluded property when disposition is made that is relevant. IHTA84/ S3(2) states that no account shall be taken of the value of excluded property which ceases to form part of a person's estate as a result of disposition.*
>
> *So as the donor is treated as making a disposition, property is treated as ceasing to form part of their estate. Provided that property is excluded property, IHTA84/S3(2) applies to exclude the assets in which the reservation ceased from charge.*
>
> *The same exceptions to the above will apply as regards*
>
> - *foreign property which is replaced by UK situs property (IHTM27071),*
> - *property added to the settlement when the donor is domiciled in the UK, and*
> - *in the reverse situation outlined above, a charge will arise under FA86/S102(4) if the reservation ceases before the donor's death."*

Section 102ZA and life tenants

31.49   Reservation of benefit questions may also arise when a settlor has settled foreign property into trust at a time when he was not UK domiciled and the trust contains a qualifying interest in possession for the life tenant (who is not necessarily the settlor). What is the position where the qualifying interest in possession is terminated by the trustees but the life tenant continues to enjoy a benefit from the settled property? There is no immediate inheritance tax charge on the termination of his interest in possession if the property is excluded property.[79] The life tenant is deemed to make a gift of the underly-

---

[79] Watch IHTA 1984 s.80 if the settlor is the life tenant and is by then deemed UK domiciled: there is no charge on the termination but thereafter charges under the relevant property regime could apply.

ing property under s.102ZA for reservation of benefit purposes at the time of the termination. If he is domiciled or deemed domiciled here at the date of that gift and continues to reserve a benefit until death the settled property rules under s.48(3) should still override the GWR rules (so that there is no tax charge if the settled property is non-UK situated). HMRC do not comment on this point in their revised statement.

VII POWERS OF APPOINTMENT OVER SETTLED PROPERTY INCLUDING GENERAL POWERS

31.50 It is not uncommon for a foreign domiciled settlor to wish to retain powers of appointment or revocation over the settled property. This may be because he is concerned to retain control over the trust assets or, in some cases, there may be good tax reasons for a settlor to retain such a power. This is particularly true where the settlor or the beneficiaries are US citizens and in US trusts one often sees the power made exercisable subject to the consent of a nominated person. This reflects the general nervousness (from the UK perspective) of giving the settlor (or other beneficiary) an unrestricted power to appoint assets in favour of himself, on the basis that it may make the person a trustee; the trust a sham, or that it may jeopardise the favourable inheritance tax treatment otherwise available on the death of the settlor.

Types of power

31.51 It is not always easy to decide whether the power given is a special power; a general power or a hybrid power. A general power gives the donee[80] power to appoint in favour of anyone in the world including himself. A special power is a power which can be exercised only in favour of certain specified persons or classes, such as issue of the settlor. The donee of the power may himself be an object of the special power. A hybrid power is often described as an intermediate power which gives the donee power to appoint to all persons except a named or specified person or class, e.g. "to any person except the settlor or his estate". A donee with a special power which can be exercised in favour of himself may not in tax terms be treated differently from a donee who has a general power exercisable in favour of anyone including himself.

Does inserting a requirement that the power is only exercisable subject to a consent affect the nature of the power or the tax treatment of the settled property? The case law on the first point is ambiguous. In *Re Dilke*[81] and *Re Phillips*[82] it was decided that the power of appointment was a general power even though it could only be exercised with the consent of the trustees. By contrast in *Re Watts*[83] a power of revocation and reappointment was vested in the settlor and could only be exercised with the consent of the settlor's mother. It was decided that this power was not a general power. It was suggested that there

---

[80] Often the donee of the power is the settlor or the life tenant.
[81] [1921] 1 Ch 34.
[82] [1931] 1 Ch 347.
[83] [1931] 2 Ch 302.

was a distinction between the situation where the consent was in the nature of a veto (as in *Re Dilke* and *Re Phillips*) and the position where the third party was under a duty to consider the beneficial interests which the person exercising the power proposed to appoint and the interests of those who would take in default of appointment (as in *Re Watts*). However, in *Re Churston Settled Estates*[84] Roxburgh J. said that he could find no authority to support such a distinction. He held, following *Re Watts*, that a joint power of appointment exercisable with consent was not a general power. He also decided that a joint power of appointment by itself was not a general power because it could only be exercised with the consent of the other donees of the power.

31.52   *Thomas on Powers* concludes that:

> "... *a power to appoint to an unlimited class of objects, and which is subject to no restriction on the mode or manner of its exercise, may still not be a general power if it is exercisable only with the consent of another person (such a power often being referred to as a consent power)*".[85]

For this proposition, he cites *Re Churston Settled Estates* and also *Re Earl of Coventry's Indentures*.[86] He does, however, note that:

> "*It may be otherwise if consent is required as to the actual exercise of the power and not as to the selection of the appointee*".[87]

In support of this caveat, he cites *Re Dilke*,[88] *Re Phillips*,[89] *Re Watts*,[90] *Re Joicey*,[91] and *Re Triffitt's Settlement*.[92] Later, he states that:

> "*A power which is exercisable only with the consent of trustees is a special and not a general power, unless the consent is required only to the actual exercise of the power and not to the selection or approval of the appointee*".

Whether it is actually possible to separate consent to actual exercise from consent to the choice of appointment must be doubtful.[93] However, it appears

---

[84] [1954] Ch 334.
[85] Sweet and Maxwell (1998) at para.13–10.
[86] [1974] Ch 77.
[87] *Thomas*, para.13–10, fn.26.
[88] *Re Dilke, Verey v Dilke* [1921] 1 Ch 34.
[89] *Re Phillips, Lawrence v Huxtable* [1931] 1 Ch 347.
[90] *Re Watts, Coffey v Watts* [1931] 2 Ch 302.
[91] (1932) 76 Sol Jo 459.
[92] *Re Triffitt's Settlement, Hall v Hyde* [1958] Ch 852.
[93] In *Re Earl of Coventry's Indentures* [1974] Ch 77, Walton J. held that *Re Churston Settlement*, in following *Re Watts*, had overlooked the fact that the latter turned on a question of construction of the terms of the power. He held that, in consequence, the decision in *Re Churston* could not bear the weight placed upon it and he felt compelled to re-examine the question afresh. He considered the question in the context of the rule against perpetuities and observed:

> "*Treating the matter as res integra, I fail for myself to see how a general power which is exercisable only with the consent of a third party can possibly be said to amount to an absolute vested interest in the subject matter of the power in the donee thereof. The plain fact of the matter is that such a person cannot appoint to whomsoever he chooses. He can only appoint in a manner approved by somebody else. The restriction on his ownership arises not from a restriction directly placed upon the possible field of selection by the terms of the power itself, but from the necessity of obtaining the specified consent. But in my judgment if a person can*

that for tax purposes the power may be drafted in such a way as to ensure that the person whose consent is needed acts in a fiduciary capacity so that however wide the class of objects, it will not be a general power or one which will cause a tax problem.[94]

The inheritance tax consequences of a general power over settled property

EXAMPLE 31.16

> A discretionary trust is set up and funded with non-UK situs property at a time when the settlor (S) is not UK domiciled or deemed domiciled. S is given a power of revocation or general power of appointment over the settled property (for US tax reasons). No consent is required. What is the IHT treatment of the power?

The mere inclusion of a power of revocation or general power of appointment in an excluded property settlement should not in itself cause any inheritance tax problems given that it does not matter that S reserves a benefit in the settlement.[95] The result seems counter intuitive: while the donee of a general power is not technically the owner of the property which is the subject matter of the power, for the purposes of the rule against perpetuities the law looks to the substance rather than the form and that property is regarded as beneficially owned by the donee of the power.

However, a power of revocation or general power of appointment which is vested in the settlor will not in itself result in the settled property in respect of which the power is exercisable being treated as property to which the settlor is beneficially entitled for inheritance tax purposes. This is because of the distinction drawn in the inheritance tax legislation between settled and non-settled property: in effect a special regime is applicable to settled property.[96]

> only pluck the fruit with the consent of somebody else it cannot in any meaningful sense be said to be vested in him".

His only reservation was:

> ". . . where in the case of a power exercisable with consent the person or persons whose consent was required upon being applied to said 'yes: exercise the power in any way you please, I (or we) don't care.' It appears to me that so long as such consent had been given and was not withdrawn (and of course unless the power to consent as a whole was capable of and had been duly released it could always be withdrawn) the donee of the power had an unfettered general power, and thus able to claim a fresh start for his appointment from the point of view of the rule against perpetuities."

[94] Except possibly in relation to reservation of benefit where the settlor has the power although this would not generally be an issue in the case of excluded property settlements.
[95] S is probably a named beneficiary anyway so the insertion of a general power of appointment does not cause any additional reservation of benefit problems. If a beneficiary who is not the settlor has the power this would not in itself cause a reservation of benefit to arise in relation to that beneficiary because he has not gifted the settled assets.
[96] The position is slightly different for capital gains tax and income tax but where the settlor is the person with the general power of appointment and he is not UK domiciled, such a power does not usually cause problems.

31.53   IHTA 1984 s.5(2) provides:

> *"A person who has a general power which enables him, or would if he were sui juris enable him, to dispose of any property other than settled property, or to charge money on any property other than settled property, shall be treated as beneficially entitled to the property or money; and for this purpose 'general power' means a power or authority enabling the person by whom it is exercisable to appoint or dispose of property as he thinks fit."*

While the above makes it clear that the existence of the power cannot mean that the holder is beneficially entitled to the settled property, the *Melville*[97] decision disturbed this analysis by treating the power as a separate item of property. For foreign domiciled settlors this was a disaster if they died UK domiciled because the power would be a valuable asset taxed on their death as part of their worldwide estate. In the event, the position was corrected in 2002 (a change deemed always to have had effect) by the combined effect of:

> Section 272: *". . . 'property' includes rights and interests of any description but does not include a settlement power,"* and

> Section 47A: *"In this Act 'settlement power' means any power over, or exercisable (whether directly or indirectly) in relation to, settled property or a settlement."*

31.54   There is, however, one further problem: does the failure to exercise a power of revocation or power to appoint in favour of oneself constitute an omission to exercise a right within s.3(3) IHTA 1984 which provides:

> *"Where the value of a person's estate is diminished and that of another person's estate, or of settled property in which no interest in possession subsists, is increased by the first-mentioned person's omission to exercise a right, he shall be treated for the purposes of this section as having made a disposition at the time (or latest time) when he could have exercised the right, unless it is shown that the omission was not deliberate."*

The better view is that s.3(3) does not apply for two reasons:

(i)   the settlor's estate does not include either the settled property (s.5(2)) or the settlement power (see s.47A). Therefore, the settlor's failure to exercise the power of revocation or of appointment cannot be said to have resulted in the value of his estate having been diminished; and

(ii) the failure to exercise the power does not result in the value of another person's estate, or of settled property in which no interest in possession subsists, being increased. The value of the settled property remains the same.

The authors conclude therefore that the mere inclusion of a power of revocation or of a general power of appointment in a settlement does not prevent

---

[97] *IRC v Melville* [2001] STC 1271, CA.

the property being excluded property nor, in itself, cause an inheritance tax problem for the settlor.

It is not known if HMRC accept this analysis. It has been suggested that **31.55** they might take a s.3(3) point but only if the settled property was not excluded property.[98] Out of abundant caution, however, practitioners may prefer to make the exercise of the power of appointment or revocation subject to consent and provide that the consent is exercisable in a fiduciary capacity.

Exercise of a power of appointment

What are the IHT consequences if the settlor exercises a power of appointment **31.56** or revocation? If he revokes the settlement the assets fall into his free estate and, if he is UK domiciled, will be taxable on his death. But what if the donee of the power (whether or not the settlor) exercises his general power of appointment to appoint the excluded settled property on different trusts or to another person outright? An outright appointment to another beneficiary will not be a PET. If the donee of a general power of appointment is settlor of the original trust and appoints on new trusts this would cause difficulties (a) if there is a resettlement of the assets and (b) if he is domiciled or deemed UK domiciled at that time.

VIII REVERSIONARY INTERESTS[99]

Unlike the term interest in possession, a reversionary interest is specifically **31.57** defined in the IHT legislation. Section 47 provides that it means:

> "*a future interest under a settlement whether it is vested or contingent (including an interest expectant on the termination of an interest in possession which, by virtue of s.50 below, is treated as subsisting in part of any property)* . . ."

The term, therefore, includes an interest dependent on the termination of an interest in possession, whether that interest is vested or contingent. A default interest following a discretionary trust is also a reversionary interest for IHT purposes.

EXAMPLE 31.17

Property is settled on the following trusts:

(1) A for life, remainder to B for life, remainder to C. B and C both have reversionary interests for IHT purposes.

---

[98] The exception for excluded property would be on the basis that s.3(2) directs that for the purposes of s.3(1) no account is taken of excluded property. If all the property concerned is excluded property there cannot be a charge by reference to s.3(3).

[99] For further discussion of reversionary interests see Ch.26.

(2) To A absolutely contingent upon attaining the age of 21. A is currently aged six and has a reversionary interest for IHT purposes.

31.58 The interest of a discretionary beneficiary is not, however a "reversionary interest", being in no sense a future interest. Such a beneficiary has certain rights, particularly the right to be considered by the trustees when they exercise their discretions and the right to compel due administration of the trust but the commercial value of such rights will be nil since the beneficiary has no entitlement to either income or capital.

"Situs" of a reversionary interest

31.59 The courts have not unambiguously decided whether a reversionary interest is an interest in trust assets in specie (in which case it is situated where the trust assets are situated) or a *chose in action* (in which case it is situated where it is properly recoverable) but the better view, certainly in the case of a trust for sale, is that it is a *chose in action*.[100] In other cases the position is unclear; but by analogy with estate duty principles it will be a *chose in action* if the settled assets are personal; but an interest in the settled assets themselves if they comprise land. Since a *chose in action* is normally situated in the country in which it is recoverable,[101] in some cases the reversionary interest will not be situated in the same place as the settled assets. HMRC seem to take the view that a reversionary interest will normally be situated where the trustees reside.

The general exemption

31.60 A reversionary interest is excluded property for IHT[102] wherever situate and regardless of the domicile of the settlor or of the holder of the reversionary interest, subject only to three exceptions designed to counter tax avoidance:

(i) *When it was purchased for money or money's worth*: take a settlement on A for life, remainder to B. B sells his interest to X who gives it to his brother Y. X (a purchaser of the interest) has made a transfer of value (a PET) of a reversionary interest (valued taking into account the value of the settled fund and the life expectancy of A);

(ii) *Where it is an interest to which the settlor or his spouse (or civil partner) is beneficially entitled*;

(iii) *Where a lease for life or lives is granted for no or partial consideration, there is a settlement for IHT*[103] *and the lessor's interest is a reversionary interest*.[104]

---

[100] *Re Smyth, Leach v Leach* [1898] 1 Ch 89.
[101] *New York Life Insurance Co v Public Trustee* [1924] 2 Ch 101.
[102] IHTA 1984 s.48(1).
[103] IHTA 1984 s.43(3).
[104] IHTA 1984 s.48(1)(c).

EXAMPLE 31.18

In 2005, I grants a lease of property worth £30,000 to T for £10,000 for the duration of T's life. I creates a settlement for IHT purposes and T is treated as having an interest in possession and, therefore, as beneficial owner of two-thirds of the property (£30,000–£10,000).[105] I is treated as the owner of one-third of the property (because he received £10,000). His interest in the remaining two-thirds of the property is not excluded property.[106]

FA 2010[107] provides that there will be a deemed disposition of a reversionary **31.61** interest when it is in relevant property (viz in a settlement without a qualifying interest in possession) on the occasion when it ends, if the same beneficiary then becomes entitled to an interest in possession.[108] The disposition that is deemed to be made cannot be a PET. This rule applies if the reversionary interest has been acquired for a consideration in money or money's worth or is owned by the settlor; his spouse or civil partner (viz situations (i) and (ii) above).[109]

The foreign element

As noted above,[110] irrespective of where the settled property in which the **31.62** reversionary interest subsists is situated, the general exemption in s.48(1) along with the three exceptions above applies. Section 48(3), however, states:

"*where property comprised in a settlement is situated outside the UK*

(a) *the property (but not a reversionary interest in the property) is excluded property unless the settlor was domiciled in the UK at the time the settlement was made; and*

(b) *section 6(1) above applies to a reversionary interest in the property, but does not otherwise apply in relation to the property*"

The proviso in (a) appears to exclude the operation of s.48(1) by saying that **31.63** a reversionary interest in settled property situated abroad is only excluded property if the interest is itself situated abroad and owned by a foreign domiciliary.[111] See Example 26.19 for further details.

It is thought that s.48(3) only prevails over s.48(1) in cases of conflict and **31.64** that there is no conflict since the words "but not a reversionary interest" in s.48(3)(a) mean that whether a reversionary interest is excluded property

---

[105] IHTA 1984 ss.50(6) and 170.
[106] See 24.07.
[107] This was done by inserting s.81A into IHTA 1984. The provision is designed to stop *Melville Mark III* schemes: see Chs 26 and 27.
[108] The interest in possession will not (unless the beneficiary is disabled) be qualifying.
[109] See 26.42 onwards for further details.
[110] And see also 26.42 onwards.
[111] See Example 26.19.

depends first on the general rule in s.48(1) and only if s.48(1) does not apply need one look at the rules in s.48(3). Hence, where the settled property in which the reversionary interest subsists is situated outside the UK, the interest can be excluded property under s.48(1) if none of the exceptions in 31.48 above apply and if s.48(1) does not apply relief is still available if the beneficial owner of the reversionary interest is a foreign domiciliary and the reversionary interest itself is situated outside the UK.[112]

31.65   However, where a person settles a reversionary interest (so that the interest itself becomes settled property as opposed to being merely an interest in settled property owned by a beneficiary) the position is more complicated. If the reversionary interest is situated abroad and was settled by a foreign domiciliary then it will be excluded property under s.48(3)(a). If it is situated in the UK or is situated abroad and settled by a UK domiciliary it is thought that the settled reversionary interest can still be excluded property under s.48(1) provided that none of the three exceptions applies.[113]

IX PURCHASED INTERESTS IN EXCLUDED PROPERTY SETTLEMENTS

31.66   Before December 5, 2005, it was possible for a UK domiciliary to take advantage of excluded property trusts to mitigate his inheritance tax by turning chargeable property into excluded property.

EXAMPLE 31.19

> In 2004, A was seriously ill. He intended to leave all his estate worth £9 million to his son. Meanwhile B, an Isle of Man domiciliary, had established an excluded property trust under which he owned a life interest (or a right to income for (say) 90 years) with the remainder interest being owned by his company, B Ltd. A accordingly purchased B's life interest and, via A Ltd, a company which he formed for the purpose, the remainder interest of B Ltd for a total price of £9 million.[114] His chargeable estate was thereby converted into an interest in an excluded property settlement.

31.67   The scheme was vulnerable to attack. For example, if the settlement was established by a foreign domiciliary, B, specifically to sell an interest to A and the settlement was funded out of borrowed monies in anticipation of A buying the interest it is likely that HMRC would successfully contend that A was the

---

[112] Sections 6(1) and 48(3)(b).

[113] Some commentators consider that where a UK domiciliary settles his foreign situate reversionary interest, the settled reversionary interest can never be excluded property because of the s.48(3)(a) proviso.

[114] Note, however, that the value of the reversionary interest is in A Ltd which means that the shares owned by A at his death will have a chargeable value which depends on the likely duration of B's life interest. Were there to be a power to pay capital to the life tenant, that would of course reduce the value.

settlor under IHTA 1984 s.44(1) on the basis that he provided property directly or indirectly for the purpose of the settlement.

FA 2006 s.157[115] put an end to the scheme by inserting s.48(3B) which provides that property in a settlement (including AUTS and OEICS) is not excluded if: **31.68**

> "*(a) a person is or has been beneficially entitled to an interest in possession in the property at any time,*
> *(b) the person is, or was, at that time an individual domiciled in the UK, and*
> *(c) the entitlement arose directly or indirectly as a result of a disposition made on or after 5th December 2005 for a consideration in money or money's worth.*"[116]

Existing schemes were unaffected by the change.

The section is in some ways wide ranging. Unlike TCGA 1992 s.76[117] there is no let-out where the consideration consists of another interest in the settlement. Any type of consideration is enough to bring the section into play. Nor does it appear to matter if someone other than the purchaser took an interest in possession in the settlement or the interest in possession beneficiary subsequently becomes domiciled in the UK but was not at the date of purchase. It is not necessary to acquire a qualifying interest: any interest in possession will be enough to bring the section into play. **31.69**

EXAMPLE 31.20

X, domiciled in India, sets up two settlements—one holding non-UK situated land (Trust 1) and the other holding non-UK shares (Trust 2) for his two children A and B both of whom have life interests and are deemed domiciled in the UK.

Some years later it is agreed that the trusts should be split so that Trust 2 comprising foreign investments is held on trust solely for child A and Trust 1 comprising the land is held on trust solely for child B. A and B consent to the termination of their respective life interests and the trustees of each trust then exercise their powers so that A is excluded from Trust 2 and B is excluded from Trust 1. Both now have an IIP in the whole of their respective trusts.

In these circumstances it appears each child has acquired an interest in possession in settled property for consideration i.e. giving up their interest in the other trust.

Moreover what happens if in the above example A was not UK domiciled at the date he acquired the interest for money's worth but he later becomes domiciled in the UK whilst still entitled to the interest in possession? In these

---

[115] With effect from December 5, 2005.
[116] IHTA 1984 s.48(3B).
[117] See Ch.20.

circumstances he would appear to be caught by s.48(3B) if he is UK domiciled at any time when he owns the interest in possession. Similarly if he is UK domiciled at the date of acquisition but then loses his UK domicile the provision operates. Even if the purchasing life tenant ceases to be entitled to the interest in possession (e.g. he assigns it to someone else) the provision can still operate.[118]

31.70 Having said this, the section is in some ways narrowly drafted. It would appear that it only affects interests in possession not (for example) contingent interests over capital nor a reversionary interest in the settlement. However, if the purchaser of the reversionary interest later obtains an interest in possession, (e.g. because the prior interest in possession is ended immediately after the purchase), then the section applies: as an indirect consequence of the disposition he has become entitled to an interest in possession. Similarly if A, a non-UK domiciliary, buys a reversionary interest in an excluded property settlement and gives it to B (a UK domiciliary) who some time later becomes entitled to an interest in possession then s.48(3B) applies. The consideration does not need to be provided by the UK domiciliary or the person who eventually becomes entitled to an interest in possession.

If the interest in possession is ended or surrendered and then the settled property in which the interest in possession subsisted is sold by the trustees and replaced with cash or other assets it is arguable that on a literal reading the section no longer applies. The beneficiary must be entitled to an interest in possession in "the property" and once those two conditions are no longer satisfied the replacement property can enjoy the protection of s.48(3).

It is not, however, necessary to purchase a *qualifying* interest in possession to be caught by this legislation so care is still required when excluded property trusts with UK domiciled beneficiaries are reorganised because, as the above example illustrates, the consideration does not need to be in money's worth.

Avoiding the rules?

31.71 It is possible to avoid s.48(3B) if there is no interest in possession. So if, for example, a *Pearson* type interest is purchased then it would appear that neither s.48(3B) nor the FA 2010 anti-avoidance provisions in s.5(1B) can apply.[119]

EXAMPLE 31.21

A foreign domiciled settlor transfers £10 million into a non-UK resident trust. The terms of the trust provide that income is to be distributed between the settlor and the reversionary beneficiary (a company wholly owned by the settlor) at the trustees' discretion and in the absence of any such distribution it must be accumulated and such accumulated income will pass to the settlor at the end of five years. The terms of the trust provide that the same process is to be repeated every five years for

---

[118] See s.48(3C)(a) although this seems clear under the wording in s.48(3B) anyway.
[119] See further Ch.26.

the duration of the trust. The settlor's interest is called "the Income Interest" and falls short of a present right to present enjoyment, and is therefore not an IIP.

X, a UK domiciliary, purchases the reversionary interest through a company wholly owned by him. He also buys the Income Interest from the settlor relying on IHTA 1984 s.10.[120] In these circumstances he obtains no entitlement to income and therefore the settled property remains excluded. He is not taxed on the value of his Income Interest at death because it is not an interest in possession. If he gives his Income Interest away during his lifetime then this is valuable property in his estate which is not be excluded; he must survive seven years and ensure the gift is to an individual in order that it takes effect as a PET.

However, the settled property continues to be excluded property for the purposes of the relevant property regime so entry charges as well as 10-year charges are avoided. The Income Interest held by the donee is not itself excluded property (it is not a reversionary interest or an IIP and therefore will be subject to tax on the donee's death).

If the donee acquires an IIP in the settled property later (e.g. the trustees change the terms of the trust to confer an IIP on him) then s.48(3B) would appear to mean that the settled property loses its excluded property protection. What is the position under s.5(1B)? Has the donee become entitled to an IIP "by virtue of a disposition which was prevented from being a transfer of value by section 10". Arguably he has become entitled to the IIP not by reason of the purchase since at that point he had an Income Interest that fell short of an IIP. He has become entitled as a result of the trustees' exercising their discretion to change the terms of the trust. Unlike s.48(3B) which uses the words "the entitlement arose directly or indirectly as a result of a disposition made for consideration" s.5(1B) is more narrowly drafted. On that basis his newly acquired interest in possession continues to fall outside his estate for IHT purposes with the result that there is no IHT charge on his death.

X PRE-OWNED ASSETS INCOME TAX: PROBLEMS FOR FOREIGN DOMICILIARIES

This subject is discussed in Ch.34. 31.72

XI ACCOMMODATION ARRANGEMENTS

These are considered in Ch.43. 31.73

---

[120] For the difficulties in relying on s.10 see Ch.26. However, this may not matter if there is no drop in his estate because he pays no more than the value of the income interest.

CHAPTER 32

LIABILITIES

- The basic rules (**32.01**)
- What liabilities are deductible (including guarantees)? (**32.02**)
- Liabilities and excluded property including situs of debts (**32.07**)
- Liabilities and interest in possession trusts (**32.16**)
- Liabilities and reserved benefit property (**32.21**)
- Foreign domiciliaries and liabilities—maximising the excluded property (**32.24**)
- The artificial debt rule in FA 1986 s.103 (**32.27**)
- Foreign domiciled settlors and FA 1986 s.103 (**32.35**)
- Loans by settlors to trusts and reservation of benefit problems (**32.43**)
- Liabilities in the context of business and agricultural property (**32.46**)

I THE BASIC RULES

32.01   The deduction of liabilities is dealt with in IHTA 1984 s.5 and in Chs I and II of Pt VI: in particular s.162.[1] There is also an anti-avoidance rule that can operate to prevent the deduction of liabilities (even if incurred for full consideration and so deductible under general principles) in FA 1986 s.103. In the context of inheritance tax trustees need to consider four areas[2]:

(i) Trustees often lend to a beneficiary or to the settlor when he is a beneficiary: for example, the trustees of a nil rate band discretionary will trust

---

[1] It is somewhat odd that s.5 includes provisions dealing with liabilities given that it is entitled "meaning of estate". FA 1975 (introducing Capital Transfer Tax) had distinguished between an individual's estate (defined in s.23) and the value of an estate. Property may be included in an estate even though its value is left out of account.

[2] Loans to settlors or beneficiaries may also have capital gains tax or income tax implications. For example, even if a trust excludes the settlor/spouse/civil partner from benefit the settlor may be taxed on all the income of the trust if he receives a loan from the trust whether or not on commercial terms (see ITTOIA 2005 s.633; the capital receipts rule and Ch.7). Or the trust may become settlor-interested for capital gains tax purposes if the trustees confer a benefit on the settlor. A loan to a settlor or a beneficiary who is a relevant person in relation to the settlor may create tax problems for remittance basis user settlors if it is a remittance of the relevant foreign income: see Ch.8. Loans to beneficiaries from offshore trusts may result in income tax charges under ITA 2007 ss.731–735 or capital gains tax charges under TCGA 1992 s.87: see Chs 8 and 19.

762

set up by H may lend to the surviving spouse W. Is the debt deductible on W's death? In the case of a loan to a settlor life tenant is the transaction tax neutral (i.e. the debt is a deduction in the settlor's free estate but an asset of the trust) or is the debt non-deductible under FA 1986 s.103?[3]

(ii) Trustees may incur liabilities to third parties or beneficiaries, e.g. they borrow to purchase a house.[4] Is the debt incurred by the trustees deductible for the purposes of calculating the inheritance tax liability on the trust?[5]

(iii) Trustees of an excluded property settlement may lend to a foreign domiciled settlor. Is the liability deductible by the settlor? Trustees may own both UK property and excluded property and need to know against what property the debt is deductible.[6]

(iv) Trustees may own business or agricultural property. Against what property are trust liabilities deducted?[7]

(v) If Trustees of a pre-March 22, 2006 qualifying interest in possession trust borrow funds and purchase a new property, is this new property held on relevant property trusts or is the new property still part of the qualifying interest in possession settled property?[8]

EXAMPLE 32.1

Jonny is domiciled in China. At the date of his death he owns UK assets worth £1 million and has a Chinese estate worth over £4 million. He owes £1 million to a bank. If the debt is deductible against his UK estate there is no UK inheritance tax payable. His remaining property is excluded property. But if the debt is deductible only against the Chinese property then tax is payable on his UK estate. If the debt is deducted proportionately against the UK and Chinese property then four fifths of the UK estate remains chargeable to tax. IHTA 1984 s.162 lays down rules to determine the deductibility of debts in these circumstances but it is not entirely satisfactory.[9]

II WHAT LIABILITIES ARE DEDUCTIBLE (INCLUDING GUARANTEES)?

Section 5(3) sets out the general rule that in valuing a person's estate at any time his liabilities at that time are to be taken into account. The liability must

32.02

---

[3] See 32.21.
[4] A typical illustration being the double trust/home loan scheme: see Ch.43.
[5] See 32.16.
[6] See 32.32 and 32.35.
[7] See 32.23.
[8] See 24.32.
[9] See 32.07 and following.

be enforceable since no allowance is made for liabilities which are not legally enforceable, except that a debt that is actually paid in the due course of administration of the estate will not be disallowed solely on the ground that it was statute-barred.[10]

32.03 A specialty debt (i.e. a debt under deed), becomes statute-barred on the expiration of 12 years from the date on which the cause of action accrues.[11] The nil rate band debt scheme implemented on the first spouse's death[12] commonly involves a specialty debt. The cause of action accrues when the deed is executed. It is important therefore that the debtor (in this case the surviving spouse) acknowledges the trustees' claim in writing every 12 years. A new 12-year period then runs from the date of acknowledgement.[13] Debts paid under a moral obligation are not enforceable. A debt can be incurred for full consideration provided in favour of another: for instance, if Z agrees to pay £10,000 for an around the world cruise for his aged mother, that debt is incurred for full consideration (the provision of the cruise) and will be deductible on Z's death even though his mother enjoys the benefit (of course the arrangement results in a transfer of value for IHT purposes: a gift by Z to his mother).

32.04 Under s.5(5), liabilities incurred by a transferor (not being imposed by law) are taken into account only to the extent that they were incurred for consideration in money or money's worth.[14] Consideration in money or money's worth does not include marriage. A liability incurred for full consideration will be allowed in full, and one incurred for partial consideration will be allowed in part. Liabilities imposed by law are allowable, whether incurred for consideration or not: for instance taxes, penalties and fines.

EXAMPLE 32.2

A wishes to benefit his son B who is the principal beneficiary of a trust set up by C. The trust owns a property called Castle Mound worth £110,000. A buys the property from the trustees for £200,000 leaving the purchase price outstanding as a debt owed to the trustees. In valuing A's estate the debt of £200,000 is allowable only to the extent of £110,000. There is no transfer of value until he pays the money but when he does so he will make a transfer of value of £90,000. If the money is paid to the trust after March 21, 2006 this is a chargeable transfer by A.[15]

---

[10] *Norton* v *Frecker* (1737) 1 Atk524.

[11] Limitation Act 1980 s.8. IHTM 28384 states: "*a debtor may decide to pay the debt after the expiry of the time limits. Because of this you should allow a debt which is otherwise statute-barred if the personal representatives pay the debt and you receive evidence that the payment has been made.*"

[12] See Ch.38. As consideration is furnished for the debt it can be by a simple agreement: a deed is unnecessary.

[13] Limitation Act 1980 s.29(5).

[14] For the meaning of "*money's worth*", see *Secretan v Hart* [1969] 1 WLR 1599 at 1603.

[15] As a result of FA 2006 changes in the IHT treatment of settlements. Consider also the income tax implications in this example: if A receives a capital payment from a trust (which includes loans whether or not made on a commercial basis) this can result in an income tax charge on him if he is the settlor under the capital receipts rules: see Ch.7. In the above example C not A was the original settlor but A has overpaid for the property by £90,000 so in effect is settling

Under IHTA 1984 s.162(1) a liability in respect of which there is a right to **32.05** reimbursement can be taken into account only to the extent that reimbursement cannot reasonably be expected to be obtained. So a contingent liability under a guarantee will not be deductible if there is little risk of the guarantee being called in. This can be relevant where trustees guarantee a beneficiary's borrowings. Any deduction will be based on the facts existing at the time of the chargeable event and will not necessarily correspond to the net amount, if any, eventually paid out of the trust.

A guarantee debt is normally incurred for consideration in money or money's worth, namely the creditor's granting (or continuing or extending) credit to the principal debtor. Where this is so, there may still be a transfer of value (to the debtor) when the guarantee is given. If the principal debtor is a person of substance, the liability incurred is likely being largely offset by the right of reimbursement, and accordingly any value transferred will be small. On the other hand, guaranteeing the liability of an impecunious principal debtor will constitute an immediate transfer of value when the guarantee is given approximating to the full amount of the liability. If the guarantor is called upon to honour the guarantee, payments made by him to the creditor will not themselves be transfers of value.

EXAMPLE 32.3

(1) A pre-March 22, 2006 interest in possession trust owns £1 million worth of assets. The life tenant, Sid, wishes to purchase a residential property and borrows from the bank. The bank is not prepared to lend unless the trustees guarantee the loan. Any transfer of value made by the trustees when giving the guarantee would be based on the likelihood of it being called in. If Sid's loan is secured on the property purchased this may be seen as unlikely. In any event any transfer of value is passing to Sid the life tenant and so is not chargeable.[16] If Sid dies, the guarantee has to be considered when valuing the trust assets in which he has a qualifying interest in possession.

(2) Assume Sid's interest in possession had arisen after March 21, 2006 so that the relevant property regime applies to the settlement. The trustees enter into the same guarantee arrangement this time in respect of borrowings to fund Sid's business. The bank take no charge on Sid's assets and are relying on the guarantee. Sid has a history of failed businesses. In these circumstances, the trustees are making a depreciatory transfer out of a relevant property settlement at the point of giving the guarantee and there may be an exit charge.[17]

that sum. Moreover if the trust was offshore and A was receiving an interest-free loan consider the effect of the remittance rules. For example, has there been a remittance of relevant foreign income? Is he receiving a benefit that is taxable under either the transfer of assets provisions or the capital payment rules? See Chs 8 and 19.

[16] See IHTA 1984 ss.52(3) and 53(2).

[17] IHTA 1984 s.65(1)(b).

Future liabilities

32.06 IHTA 1984 s.162(2) provides that where a liability falls to be discharged after the time at which it is to be taken into account, it must be valued as at the time at which it is to be taken into account (e.g. on a 10 year anniversary). Accordingly, debts payable at a future date without intermediate interest (or with interest at less than the market rate) will be discounted. This was relevant to the valuation of the debt in the home loan scheme.[18]

III LIABILITIES AND EXCLUDED PROPERTY INCLUDING SITUS OF DEBTS

32.07 Section 162(4) and (5) set out the rules for determining which property is reduced by the liability but do not cover every situation. They are particularly important in the case of excluded property settlements and foreign domiciliaries.

Liabilities charged on property

32.08 The general rule is that liabilities are deducted, as far as possible, from the value of the property on which they are secured.

Section 162(4) provides that a liability which is an incumbrance on any property must as far as possible be taken to reduce the value of that property. Accordingly, the entity to be valued is the property subject to the liability. In *Alexander v IRC*[19] the property could not in fact have been sold burdened by the liability charged on it, but the Court of Appeal applied the principle of *IRC v Crossman*[20] and held that the property must be valued on the basis of what a hypothetical purchaser would pay for it burdened by the liability.

EXAMPLE 32.4

A has a qualifying interest in possession in Fund A of a pre-March 22, 2006 settlement. B has a qualifying interest in possession in Fund B of the same trust. A dies and Fund A comprises a house worth £1m subject to a charge of £300,000. The value of Fund A is reduced to £700,000. If B dies, the charge cannot be deducted against the value of the property in his fund.[21]

---

[18] See Ch.43.
[19] [1991] STC 112.
[20] [1937] AC 26.
[21] See 32.16, below for a consideration of liabilities incurred by trustees.

Charging exempt property

A debt charged on exempt property (e.g. a mortgage on a house left to the deceased's widow) cannot be deducted against chargeable property (e.g. the residuary estate left to children). Similarly a debt charged on instalment-option property cannot be deducted against non-instalment property.

32.09

Foreign liabilities

Section 162(5) provides

32.10

> *"where a liability taken into account is a liability to a person resident outside the UK which neither falls to be discharged in the UK nor is an incumbrance on property in the UK, it shall so far as possible, be taken to reduce the value of property outside the UK."*

HMRC state[22] that if there are debts owing in more than one foreign country, the debts in any one country should be set against the assets in that country and any excess set proportionately against the assets in other foreign countries. There is no statutory basis for this view. HMRC appear to allow an unsecured debt due to a UK creditor (which can be discharged in or out of the UK) to be allowed in full against non-excluded property.[23] However, the position is unclear when the debt is secured on both UK and non-UK property or the liability is to be discharged in the UK but is secured on property outside the UK.[24] In these cases how do s.162(4) and (5) interact?

Section 162(4) prescribes a reduction in the value of the encumbered property; if the debt is not secured on UK property or does not fall to be discharged in the UK, s.162(5) requires the debt to be deducted against the non-UK property. This will generally only matter where there is excluded property or the property in the trust passes to different beneficiaries.

EXAMPLE 32.5

A, non-UK domiciled, dies owning UK land worth £1 million and cash deposited in Jersey worth US $2 million. The UK land passes to his son and the cash is left to his daughter. He owes £500,000 to a Jersey bank. In these circumstances it is thought the £500,000 will be deducted entirely from the US $2 million with the result that inheritance tax is payable in full on £1 million. His daughter receives $2 million less £500,000.

If the debt was owed by A to a UK creditor and is expressed to be dis-

---

[22] IHTM 28394.
[23] IHTM 28395.
[24] The place that is specified in the debt agreement is the place where the debt falls to be discharged. If none is specified the debt will fall to be discharged in the place of residence of the creditor.

charged in the UK then the son pays inheritance tax on only £500,000 and the debt is discharged out of the UK land. However, if the debt is secured on the foreign cash but expressed to be discharged in the UK what is the position?[25]

HMRC take the view that s.162(4) takes priority over s.162(5) so that if the debt is charged on excluded property it is deductible out of this property even if the debt is owed to a UK creditor or expressed to be discharged in the UK.[26] This is thought to be right. The result is that the son pays tax on £1 million and the daughter pays no inheritance tax but receives $2 million less £500,000.

32.11 Trustees of excluded property settlements need to be careful if liabilities may be deductible against settled UK property. Apart from IHT issues, this can cause other problems. First, if the debt is charged against UK property but with the commercial borrowing coming from a foreign bank, HMRC may argue that interest payable on the debt is UK source income. This raises questions about whether income tax should be deducted at source from the interest payments.

Second, if liabilities are incurred by borrowing from another excluded property settlement it is important to ensure that the debt is not a UK situate asset in the hands of the lending trust.

EXAMPLE 32.6

A settles US $1 million on Discretionary Trust 1. He is UK resident but not UK domiciled. Trust 1 lends (whether interest free or on commercial terms) the cash to Trust 2 also set up by A[27] and which buys a UK house. Trust 1 requires security for the loan and takes a charge on the house. The debt is a UK situate asset and Trust 1 faces 10-year and periodic charges. Furthermore, there may be a liability under FA 1986 s.102(3) (reservation of benefit) on A's death if he dies deemed UK domiciled and Trust 1 still owns a UK situate asset.[28] A will generally be a beneficiary of both trusts particularly if the loan from Trust 1 is interest-free. Even if he is not a beneficiary of Trust 1, HMRC may argue that if the loan is repayable on demand the Trustees of Trust 1 have indirectly conferred a collateral benefit on A by not calling in the loan and therefore there is a reservation of benefit in Trust 1 by A. For further discussion on this point see home loans in Ch.43.

---

[25] See also IHTM 28396: "*If the deceased's estate includes both UK and foreign assets you should first deduct any UK debts against the UK assets and the deficiency if any against the foreign assets. Debts are UK debts if one of the following applies: they are owed to creditors resident solely in the UK; they are charged on property in the UK, or they are contracted to be paid in the UK. This practice should be applied notwithstanding the decision in Re Kloebe [1884] 28 Ch. D 175. This was that in the administration of the English estate of a deceased person domiciled abroad, foreign creditors are entitled to be paid along with those resident in the UK in shares proportionate to their respective claims.*"
[26] See IHTM 28395.
[27] Rather than to A personally to avoid FA 1986 s.103: see 32.27.
[28] See Ch.33 for discussion of reservation of benefit and for further discussion of the foreign domiciliary buying a house in the UK see Ch.43.

If the debt is a specialty debt charged on UK land, is the debt situated where the land is located or where the deed is located?[29] The authors believe that the most likely answer is that for inheritance tax purposes the debt is treated as situated where the land is located. The general rule in English Law is that a debt due on a deed (a specialty debt) is situate in the place where the specialty is found at the creditor's death. Where the deed is secured on land and creates an interest in land the position appears to be different although none of the tax cases are directly on the point. The cases do not provide clear support for the proposition that for the purposes of inheritance tax the situs of a specialty secured on land should be the place in which the land is located but it appears that for some purposes the asset will be treated as an interest in land rather than as a specialty debt. This will be relevant to trustees of excluded property trusts who lend to UK resident beneficiaries and want to take security over UK sited land.

32.12

In *Commissioner of Stamps v Hope*[30] the purchase price of land situated in New South Wales was to be paid by 12 promissory notes, falling due at various dates, and the payment of which was secured by a mortgage of the land. At the date of the mortgagee's death, the mortgage deed was kept in Victoria but the debtors were resident in New South Wales. The Privy Council held that the debt was one specialty debt (not two separate contracts one being a simple debt secured in Victoria and another being a specialty debt) situate in Victoria and was not liable to probate duty imposed in NSW. They did not expressly consider the question of whether or not a specialty creating a mortgage of land should be treated differently. In *Walsh v The Queen*[31] the Privy Council considered the situs of debts due to a company by debtors outside Queensland but secured upon real and personal property situated in Queensland. It was held that the:

32.13

> "*personal obligation to pay may not be an asset in Queensland but it does not follow that the debt due, so far as it is charged upon estate within Queensland and gives the creditor a real and preferable interest in that estate, is not an asset [of Queensland] Such an interest is certainly property of the company and property in [Queensland] because it affects the estate which is admittedly situated there.*"

See also *Payne v R*[32] where a debt secured on land in Victoria was held to be liable to duty there even though also evidenced by another document expressed as a specialty debt held in NSW. In *Toronto General Trusts Corporation v R*[33] land in Alberta was mortgaged to a resident of Ontario. The mortgage was represented by two duplicate deeds, one held by the mortgagee in Ontario and the other held in Alberta. It was noted that in these circumstances:

---

[29] See *Dymond's Capital Taxes* at 30.352. cf. *Commissioner of Stamp Duties v Hope* [1891] AC 476 with *Walsh v The Queen* [1894] AC 144 and see *Dicey, Morris and Collins Conflict of Laws* (14th edn) at 22.035. The original commentary on specialty debts at IHTM 27078 has been withdrawn. HMRC now considers that the debt is UK situated on the basis that the debt is located where the land rather than the deed is situated.

[30] [1891] AC 476.

[31] [1894] AC 144.

[32] [1902] AC 552.

[33] [1919] AC 95.

> "*the rule* [that specialty debts are located where the deed is situated] *could not be applied in a sensible manner to the facts of the case: it was equally effective to prove that the debt was situate in Alberta as it was to prove that it was situate in Ontario. The truth appears to be that in such cases the rule gives no guidance on the question of the locality of the debt and regard must be had to the other circumstances of the case..the debts were secured, not only by the personal obligation of the mortgagors but also by mortgages which created interests in lands in Alberta and this fact cannot be put out of account.*"

Of course, in that case the deeds were situated in both jurisdictions so the mortgage deed and security may have been the deciding factor.

32.14   Dicey, Morris and Collins in *The Conflict of Laws* (14th edn), para.22.035 note:

> "*a mortgage of land confers an interest in land and will be held situate where the land is situate, but where it is necessary (e.g for taxation purposes) to distinguish between the situs of the mortgagee's interest in land and that of the mortgagor's personal obligation to repay then the latter if in the form of a specialty will be held situate where the deed is situate from time to time. In the conflict of laws the distinction between the interest in land and the personal obligation is not normally made for the purposes of situs and the asset is regarded as a unity which is situate in the country where the land lies.*"[34]

32.15   Trustees of an excluded property trust are not infrequently asked to lend to UK resident foreign domiciled beneficiaries to fund the purchase of a house or for other expenditure in the UK. The intention is to secure the debt on the house and therefore reduce the value of the house for inheritance tax purposes.[35] If the trustees lend direct and secure the borrowing on the house the debt will be UK situated in the hands of the trustees. Hence it will not be excluded property and may be subject to 10-year charges (or inheritance tax on the death of the life tenant if it is a qualifying interest in possession trust). Lending via a company presents other risks.[36] A further problem is that if the property is secured by a first legal mortgage it appears that this is a regulated activity for the purposes of FSMA 2000.[37] This means that the lender must be authorised under that Act.

IV LIABILITIES AND INTEREST IN POSSESSION TRUSTS

32.16   When a trustee incurs a liability as trustee he has a lien over the trust fund for reimbursement. This can give rise to problems in relation to trusts in which the beneficiary has a qualifying interest in possession. When the trustees have

---

[34] The last statement appears to be based on the decision in *Re Hoyles Bow v Jagg* [1911] 1 Ch 179 which held that a mortgage debt secured by land was an immovable for succession law purposes.
[35] The wider tax implications of this are discussed in Ch.43 and below.
[36] See Ch.43.
[37] See FSMA (Regulated Activities) Order (SI 2001/544) art.61.

borrowed funds and the life tenant dies, inheritance tax is charged on the value of the estate of the individual which includes the property "in which the interest [in possession] subsists."[38] But in what property does his interest subsist—the gross or net value of the settled property? There is nothing in the legislation which specifically reduces the value of the settled property by the liability. Section 5(3) is of no assistance since it provides only that in determining the value of a person's estate his liabilities will be taken into account. In this case the liability is that of the trustees not the life tenant and trustees do not have an estate because they are not beneficially entitled to any property. Similar questions arise on the lifetime termination of an interest in possession where IHTA 1984 s.52 provides that the value transferred is equal to the value of the property in which the interest subsisted. Again one has to determine whether this is a gross or net value.

It would be unjust if the trustees were taxed on the gross value of the settled property without any account being taken of the debt and HMRC have always taken the view that trustees' liabilities are taken into account for inheritance tax purposes.[39] The correct analysis may be that the trustees' lien can be regarded as an incumbrance over the property and therefore s.162(4) can be relied upon to reduce the value of the settled property.   **32.17**

The Barbe Green case

In *St Barbe Green v IRC*[40] the judge adopted a different approach and held   **32.18**
that the value of the property in which the life tenant's interest subsisted was the settled property net of trust liabilities. In that case the deceased, (the 12th Duke of Manchester) died in 2002 with almost nothing in his personal estate but owing around £48,000. He was tenant for life of three settlements worth in excess of £340,000. The trustees sought to deduct from the values of the settlements the amount of the Duke's personal debts. The taxpayers argued that under s.5(1) a person's free estate is aggregated with settled property in which he had an interest in possession so as to form one overall estate. Section 5(3) then states that in determining the value of a person's estate at any time his liabilities at that time shall be taken into account and since a person's estate includes property in which he had an interest in possession the balance of the debt could be deducted against the settled property.

HMRC's argument was that in determining the value of the estate under   **32.19**
s.5(1) one has to take into account the liabilities deducting them from the value of the property which must be used to discharge the liabilities. Since the trust assets were not available to pay the deceased's personal liabilities, those liabilities could not be offset for inheritance tax purposes.

Mann J. commented that there was no inherent reason in the world created   **32.20**
by the inheritance tax legislation under which an interest in possession in settled property was aggregated with free estate why liabilities in the free estate could not also be set off against the aggregated assets of the trust. Read literally, s.5(3) could be taken to mean that personal liabilities reduce the value of

---

[38] IHTA 1984 s.49(1), see Ch.24.
[39] See the (now withdrawn) Advanced Instruction Manual at W56. The deduction of the debt is a significant issue in home loan / double trust schemes: see Ch.43.
[40] [2005] STC 288.

the whole estate—both trust and personal. However, he held that under IHTA 1984 s.49(1) the deceased is beneficially entitled to the property in which the life interest subsists and "property" in this context means the property net of trust liabilities. Therefore, the property of the deceased for the purposes of s.5(1) comprised the personal estate net of liabilities and the settled property net of trust liabilities. Once the free estate is reduced to zero by the personal liabilities, the amount unrelieved has nothing against which it can be offset:

> "*In other words it is at that stage [the stage of determining the value of the property for the purposes of s.5(1)] that the liabilities are dealt with. It is not necessary for s.5(3) to provide for a second time that the debts are to be deducted in arriving at the value for the deceased's property (or estate) and in my view it is not really doing that. It is in part confirmatory but in the main it is intended to provide a qualification . . . to the principle that debts are deductible—the meat of the subsection is in the closing words 'except as otherwise provided by this Act'.*"[41]

V LIABILITIES AND RESERVED BENEFIT PROPERTY

32.21 It is thought that the same reasoning would prevent debts in a taxpayer's free estate being deducted against property which becomes treated as part of his estate under the reservation of benefit rules (see FA 1986 s.102(3)): in no real sense does he "own" the property. The subsection is a "deeming" provision along the lines of s.49(1) considered in the *Barbe* case. However, HMRC accept that, in principle, debts can be deducted in computing a charge under the reservation of benefit provisions where the reserved benefit property itself is subject to a liability and is settled. So it is only the net value of that settled property which falls into the inheritance tax net on the donor's death.

EXAMPLE 32.7[42]

In 1990 the donor settles £1 on discretionary trusts of which he is, and remains until his death in 2000, a beneficiary. Shortly after the creation of the settlement he advances £50,000 to the trustees by way of loan, interest free and repayable on demand. At the time of his death, the settled property comprises £1 cash (representing the original £1 gift into settlement) and the proceeds of an insurance policy (purchased with the borrowed monies) on the donor's life amounting to £250,000. The loan of £50,000 has been repaid at the rate of £2,500 per annum by the trustees and £25,000 is outstanding at the date of death.

The proceeds of £250,000, less the loan of £25,000, are derived from the original loan, and can be treated as part of the death estate. (The balance outstanding under the loan (£25,000) forms part of the free estate.)

---

[41] In the alternative Mann J. held that HMRC's construction of s.5(3) was supported by the estate duty case of *Re Barnes* [1938] 2 KB 684 and that it was correct that liabilities cannot be deducted from assets when the testator's estate is not liable to bear them. A deficit on joint property that passes under the Will (i.e. a tenancy in common) can be set against free assets.
[42] Taken from IHTM 14401.

The above example deals with settled property. Under FA 1986 Sch.20 **32.22**
para.5(4) the settled property from which the loan is derived is treated as
being gifted property for reservation of benefit purposes.[43] Presumably, on
the basis of *Barbe*, the settled property in which the reservation of benefit
subsists is the property net of trust liabilities. There seems no reason to think
that the position is different if the loan is owed by the trustees to someone
other than the donor. For example if, in the case of the home loan scheme,
an election is made into the reservation of benefit provisions to avoid a POA
income tax charge[44] the loan which the property trustees owe to the trustees
of the loan trust (Trust 2) should in principle be deductible against the house
(in which the donor is deemed to reserve a benefit) and the settled property
in which the reservation of benefit subsists is the house net of the liability.
Accordingly the election may in these circumstances not give rise to a significant tax liability.

Incurring debts to reduce the inheritance tax liability of an individual has
been used extensively over the years. The home loan or double trust scheme
is a classic example.[45]

The position is more difficult where the donor reserves a benefit in property **32.23**
that is not settled. For example, A gives his house to B who lets A continue
living there. B then mortgages the property (perhaps borrowing from a trust)
and uses the cash borrowed for other purposes. In these circumstances does
A reserve a benefit in the gross or net value of the house? If the net value it
would be easy to reduce (or extinguish!) the effect of the reservation of benefit
rules by the donee simply charging the reserved benefit property with debt. It is
thought that in the above circumstances A reserves a benefit in the gross value
of the house this being the gifted property.

VI FOREIGN DOMICILIARIES AND LIABILITIES—MAXIMISING
THE EXCLUDED PROPERTY

Many foreign domiciliaries have arranged the ownership of their UK house **32.24**
using a two trust structure. This relies on a foreign sited specialty debt reducing the value of the UK home.[46]

Debts have been used in other contexts by foreign domiciliaries. For **32.25**
example, assume that A is the life tenant of a qualifying interest in possession trust set up by his father before March 2006 who was not UK domiciled.
The trust owns a UK house worth £1 million in which A lives. Because it is
UK sited, the property is not excluded property on A's death. If the trustees
borrow £800,000 charging that debt on the UK property[47] and deposit that
sum overseas (so that it becomes excluded property), the value of the UK situated property is reduced by £800,000.

---

[43] If in the above example the donor's spouse had provided the £1 and the donor himself had
gifted nothing but merely lent money then the reservation of benefit provisions do not apply:
see Ch.33.
[44] See Ch.43.
[45] See Ch.43.
[46] It is discussed further in Ch.43 and 32.15 above. See also 32.27 for the impact of FA 1986 s.103
on foreign domiciliaries.
[47] But see 32.15 above and the difficulties if the trustees take a first legal charge over the property.

If the trust had been set up by a UK domiciled settlor but the life tenant was not UK domiciled, simple borrowing is no use because the cash borrowed will not be held in an excluded property settlement. However, they could advance the borrowings to the life tenant absolutely. The value of the life interest is reduced and if the cash advanced is kept abroad by the non-UK domiciled life tenant, it is not subject to inheritance tax. The capital gains tax implications of this transaction[48] need to be considered carefully if the trust was or had been non-UK resident or contained s.87 stockpiled gains.[49]

32.26 Where trustees of an excluded property settlement own UK situated property directly, borrowing can be used to reduce the inheritance tax charge on the following occasions:

(1) on the 10-year anniversary of a trust that is not a qualifying interest in possession trust. Charge the UK property with trustee borrowing and deposit the cash abroad. After the 10-year anniversary the borrowing can be repaid;

(2) if settled property is being advanced to a beneficiary, advance non-UK settled property rather than UK property otherwise an exit charge will arise if the trust is not a qualifying interest in possession trust. If a UK house is being advanced to a beneficiary subject to debt beware of SDLT[50];

(3) if the settlor has reserved a benefit in the trust ensure that the settled property situated in the UK is reduced by debt to avoid any inheritance tax charge on his death;

(4) on the death of a beneficiary who has a qualifying interest in possession ensure that any UK settled property is reduced by debt.[51]

VII THE ARTIFICIAL DEBT RULE IN FA 1986 S.103

32.27 FA 1986 s.103 restores the estate duty rule disallowing debts for which the consideration was property derived from the deceased or was given by a person who had property derived from the deceased. The section is an important adjunct to the reservation of benefit rules. For instance, if A gives his house to B which he continues to occupy there is a reservation of benefit in the gifted property. But if he were to buy the house back for full consideration which is left outstanding as a debt owing to B then there is no reservation (since the gifted property, the house, is then comprised in his estate). It is in this type of case that s.103 operates to disallow the debt for the purposes of the IHT charge on A's death.[52]

32.28 Sections 103 (1) and (6) makes the deduction of debts or incumbrances incurred or created by the deceased after March 17, 1986, "subject to abatement" to the extent that the consideration consisted of:

[48] See TCGA 1992 Sch.4B.
[49] See Ch.19.
[50] See Ch.51 for possible ways to mitigate or avoid the charge.
[51] For the position under FA 1986 s.103 in relation to settlors and loans from excluded property trusts see 32.32 and following.
[52] Bear in mind that although the debt is disallowed for IHT purposes under this section it remains payable as a matter of law: in effect it is treated as a taxable pecuniary legacy.

(i) property derived from the deceased, ("*Head A*") or

(ii) other consideration given by any person who was at any time entitled to, or amongst whose resources there was at any time included, any property derived from the deceased ("*Head B*").

EXAMPLE 32.8

A gives his son £50,000 in 1997. The son subsequently lends A £45,000. A dies before repaying the loan. The £45,000 cannot be deducted against A's estate for IHT purposes as a result of Head B above. If A repaid the loan before his death, that repayment is deemed to be a PET.[53] The position would be different if the son wrote off the loan since no money or money's worth is being applied by A in reducing the debt as required by s.103(5). It might therefore be preferable for the son to release A from the loan rather than for A to repay it. Then the son makes a PET to Dad.[54]

Section 103(4) limits the meaning of "*property derived from the deceased*" by excluding cases where there is no direct or indirect element of bounty, e.g. where the property was bought from the deceased for full value without any associated operations.

Head B covers situations where the property given by A is not bought **32.29** back by him. For instance, it can apply where A makes a gift to B and B subsequently sells other property he has owned all along to A leaving the price outstanding.

EXAMPLE 32.9

In 2003 H gives a picture to son worth £15,000. The son keeps the picture but lends £16,000 to H. H dies in 2006 and within seven years of the gift. £15,000 of the £16,000 is not deductible from H's estate unless it can be shown that the gift by H was not made with the aim of facilitating the loan by S. In addition the 2003 PET is chargeable because of H's death within seven years. In these circumstances the IHT (Double Charges) Regulations 1987[55] provide some relief.

EXAMPLE 32.10

In 1985 H gives a share in his house (worth £250,000) to his wife, W. The gift is spouse exempt. The purpose of the gift was to ensure that his wife had sufficient property to use up her nil rate band on death. W dies

---

[53] FA 1986 s.103(5).
[54] Note that s.103 only operates to disallow the debt "immediately before" Dad's death: accordingly the release of the debt will increase the value of his estate.
[55] SI 1987/1130 reg.6.

in 1996 leaving her interest in the property on discretionary trusts. The executors assent the share of the property back to H in consideration for him being indebted to the trust for the nil rate sum. In effect, H has bought back the property gifted and the debt is disallowed under Head A (see *Phizackerley* discussed in Ch.43). It does not matter that the gift was made prior to 1986.[56]

32.30 The charge under Head B is relaxed by s.103(2) in two ways. First, the debt can be deducted to the extent that its value exceeds the value of the property given by the deceased.

EXAMPLE 32.11[57]

A gives his son B shares worth £20,000. B lends A out of his separate resources £25,000 at a time when the shares were worth £17,000. A dies and a deduction of £25,000 is claimed. The value in point is the realisable value of the shares at the time the debt was created (not at the time of the gift). So the liability is reduced by £17,000 leaving £8,000 as a valid deduction. (If the shares had been worth £25,000 there is no deduction.)

32.31 Secondly, if, in the last example, it can be shown that the gift by A to B was not made with the aim of facilitating the loan back to A then the debt will not be disallowed on A's death.[58] It is possible to give guidance only in very general terms as to the circumstances in which HMRC will in practice concede that a disposition by the deceased was not made "*with reference to, or with a view to enabling or facilitating*" the giving of the consideration for the liability. The word "shown" in subs.(2)(b), and also in subs.(4), puts the burden of proof on the taxpayer. If it can be shown that when the deceased made the disposition he never contemplated that it might be used to provide consideration for the creation of the debt, it is immaterial that at some later date it had such an effect or was so used; but if the deceased kept his ideas to himself it may be difficult to establish this, though proof that the disposition was made for some *other* specific purpose will be helpful. If the disposition and the creation of the debt were contemporaneous, or nearly so, this difficulty may often prove insuperable, even if there was ostensibly another reason for the gift.

Trusts lending to settlors

32.32 Care is needed when trusts lend to settlors. Suppose that A is the UK domiciled life tenant and settlor of a pre-March 22, 2006 trust. He is in need of funds and the trustees lend him cash.[59] In these circumstances, he is caught by s.103 of the FA 1986. He has incurred a liability personally and the monies

---

[56] When FA 1986 s.103 was introduced: see IHTM 28366.
[57] Set out in IHTM 28369.
[58] See s.103(2)(b).
[59] Loans to settlors have also been a feature of offshore trusts where there are UK domiciled settlors to reduce s.87 charges when they receive capital payments. See generally Ch.19.

lent to him are derived from his earlier gifted property. Accordingly the debt is non-deductible in the settlor's estate but nevertheless is an asset of the trust in which he has an interest in possession and is therefore taxable on his death. So there is double inheritance tax payable on the same asset! It is not clear whether HMRC take this view. It has been suggested that since the qualifying life tenant owns the money borrowed from the trustees and is deemed to own the debt under s.49(1) he cannot borrow from himself and therefore the borrowings are simply ignored for inheritance tax purposes.[60] The authors do not believe that this argument would succeed: it involves using the deemed ownership provisions in s.49(1) more widely than can have been intended. In the real world, the life tenant incurs a legally binding obligation to the trustees.

A similar approach was used in calculating the taxable benefit to a life tenant **32.33** of an interest-free loan in *Cooper v Billingham*.[61] In that case the life tenant argued that an interest-free loan from the trustees conferred no benefit on him for the purposes of the CGT capital payments rule since he was entitled to the income from the trust anyway. This was dismissed in the High Court:

> "*[Counsel for the taxpayer's] other contention is that no benefit is received from the trustees or that the value of the benefit is nil because the benefit, if any, is the non-charging of interest whereas if interest had been charged it would have gone to the borrower in his capacity as the beneficiary entitled to income and thus he was no better off than he would otherwise have been and in that sense got no benefit from the transaction, or in a different sense any benefit he received was from himself. Again, I prefer [Counsel for the Revenue's] submissions. It seems to me that the legislation does not call for or permit a comparison of the position that the recipient might have been in if a different transaction had been undertaken by the trustees. There are too many different possible comparisons for that to be a tenable approach. The proper comparison is with the position of the recipient if the actual loan had not been made rather than if some other transaction had been entered into. The recipient of the actual loan, if it had not been made, would not have had the use of the money lent . . . it is not sensible to suppose that the person entitled to income has a special status which exempts him from this treatment or requires him to be treated more favourably than other beneficiaries. Nor can I accept [Counsel for the taxpayer's] contention that the benefit, and so the payment, was not received from the trustees. Plainly the trustees conferred that benefit since it was they who refrained from calling in the loan. Plainly that omission was of benefit to the borrower . . . I do not accept that the reference which might have to be made in that way to the circumstances of the borrower extends to include his existing interest under the settlement.*"

Similarly the Court of Appeal noted that:

> "*The whole scheme of the legislation requires the court to see what benefit a beneficiary actually receives, in cash or in kind, otherwise than as income or under an arm's length transaction. Any pre-existing beneficial interest*

---

[60] See Kessler "*Taxation of Foreign Domiciliaries*" (9th edn) at 53.7 for a contrary view where it is suggested that a man cannot owe a debt to himself, i.e. there is no deduction for the debt but the debt is not included in the estate—in effect it is ignored.

[61] See [2000] STC 122 and, on appeal, [2001] STC 1177.

> *belonging to the beneficiary is irrelevant. The judge dealt with this point shortly ([2000] STC 122 at 135) but there was no need for him to say more."*

32.34 Section 103 generally does not apply if the debt is not incurred by the donor personally.

EXAMPLE 32.12

> In 2003 Harry entered into a home loan (or double trust) scheme. He sold his residence to the trustees of an interest in possession trust for himself leaving the purchase price outstanding as a debt which he gave away to his son. On Harry's death the debt is not thought to be disallowed under s.103 even though the consideration was given by the trustees who had received property from Harry. This is because the debt was not incurred by Harry but by his trustees. It should be noted, however, that HMRC consider that on these facts the lien which the trustees have against the trust fund involves an incumbrance which arises as a result of Harry's sale to them. Accordingly, for this reason, the debt is disallowed.[62]

VIII FOREIGN DOMICILED SETTLORS AND FA 1986 S.103

32.35 It is not uncommon for foreign domiciled settlors to settle assets and then receive loans back from the trustees.

EXAMPLE 32.13

> A settles foreign cash into a discretionary trust when not UK domiciled. The trust lends him some of the cash some years later under a specialty debt arrangement which is unsecured[63] and he dies owing the trust £1 million at a time when he is deemed UK domiciled. Is the debt deductible against his free estate? Or does s.103 of the FA 1986 apply?

It might be thought that even if s.103 could apply, if A leaves all his free estate to an exempt person such as a charity or spouse[64] there is no problem anyway even if the debt turns out not to be deductible. The difficulty is that not all the property in A's estate will pass to the exempt person—at least part of it has to be repaid to the trust because of the debt. Accordingly, is charitable or spouse exemption denied on the basis that the benefit attributable to the spouse or charity is only the net value? If that were the case, if A died leaving all his

---

[62] See Ch.43.
[63] To avoid the debt being sited in the UK and to avoid it being treated as an incumbrance.
[64] Assuming that the spouse is deemed or actually UK domiciled so that the spouse exemption is available.

free estate to his wife, the debt of £1 million owed to the trustees would fail to qualify for exemption and be taxable. On the other hand it could be argued that if the liability is subject to abatement this is the case for all inheritance tax purposes: the abatement is not just for the purposes of allowing the deduction of the debt. On that basis the deceased's estate is fictionally increased for all purposes and therefore the spouse exemption is available in full. HMRC do not accept this and regard the debt as a chargeable specific gift (although the legislation does not state this).[65]

But does s.103 apply at all to foreign domiciled settlors in these circum- **32.36**
stances? Section 103(4) provides:

> "*If the disposition first mentioned in (3) above [i.e. the original transfer into trust by the foreign domiciliary who is now deceased] was not a transfer of value[66] and it is shown that the disposition was not part of associated operations which included:*
>
> (a) *a disposition by the deceased either alone or in concert or by arrangement with any other person otherwise than for full consideration in money or money's worth paid to the deceased for his own use or benefit or*
> (b) *a disposition by any other person operating to reduce the value of the property of the deceased*
>
> *the first mentioned disposition shall be left out of account for the purposes of subsections (1) and (3) above".*

So if the conditions of this subsection can be satisfied it does not matter whether the transaction comes within Head A or Head B above: the debt will be deductible. In Example 32.13 the disposition first mentioned in (3) is not a transfer of value because the gift into the trust was of excluded property.[67]

However, subs.(4) also requires that the disposition is not part of associated **32.37**
operations which included (a) or (b) above. The loan in isolation is not an operation within (a) or (b)— it is incurred for full consideration because the foreign domiciliary receives the cash in exchange for the debt and it does not reduce the value of his estate. However, the disposition merely has to be part of an associated operation which included (a) or (b). So even if the loan does not satisfy (a) or (b), one could argue that the gift of assets into the trust was not a transfer of value but was a disposition for less than full consideration and therefore that the two are associated operations.

On that basis since the original gift is part of the overall associated opera- **32.38**
tions and is itself within Head A or B of s.103(1), the subs.(4) let out is not satisfied. Section 103(4) is, however, not clear: in determining whether any associated operations include any dispositions such as are referred to in

---

[65] See IHTM 28365.
[66] Note that an inter spouse transfer, although exempted under IHTA 1984 s.18, is a transfer of value. In *Phizackerley v RCC* [2007] STC (SCD) 328, the argument that the transfer involved the maintenance of the donee spouse and so, as a result of IHTA 1984 s.11 ("dispositions for maintenance of family") was not a transfer of value, was unsuccessful. However, it was not doubted that if the taxpayer could show that a disposition was not a transfer of value (and this would include a disposition of excluded property by a foreign domiciled person) s.103(4) excludes s.103 from applying unless associated operations is in point.
[67] IHTA 1984 s.3(2).

s.103(4)(a) or (b) does one disregard the original disposition into trust with which s.103(3) is concerned? If it is right that the transfer of assets to the trust itself falls within s.103(4)(a) the debt is not deductible unless one can show that the loan back to the settlor is not associated with the gift. This is difficult to argue despite *Reynaud v IRC*.[68] The problem with this analysis is that if a foreign domiciliary X (while living abroad and having no connection with the UK) gives property to Y who subsequently lends the sum back to X later, on a later repayment of the debt by X there would be a deemed PET even though X has no connection with the UK. The attitude of HMRC is unknown but it is inconceivable that they would try to argue the point where the borrower was neither domiciled nor resident here! They may take the pragmatic view that if the foreign domiciliary is not deemed domiciled at the date of repayment there is no PET and the loan is deductible. If he is deemed domiciled (or actually domiciled in the UK) at the date of repayment there is a PET and if he is deemed domiciled here at the date of death and the loan is outstanding then the loan is not deductible.[69]

32.39   An alternative reading of s.103(4) would be to limit it to the situation where the initial disposition is non-gratuitous (and is therefore a transfer of value capable of being protected under s.10) but subsequent operations after the initial disposition are for less than full consideration. The draftsman presumably had in mind the situation where the initial disposition was a sale at full market value and subsequent associated operations took place which were non-gratuitous and involved the vendor incurring a debt.

If that is correct and s.103(4)(a) and (b) only catch subsequent gratuitous transfers, then s.103 can never apply to any settlement funded by a foreign domiciliary at a time when he was neither UK domiciled nor deemed domiciled even if the trust lends back to him and he dies UK deemed domiciled with the loan outstanding or repays the debt while deemed domiciled.

Of course if A lent money to B who subsequently (while not UK domiciled) gave foreign property to A but A continued to owe the debt to B, s.103(4) would not give protection even though the gift is not a transfer of value. The gift is clearly a subsequent disposition associated with the loan.

32.40   If a foreign domiciliary who has borrowed from a trust is now UK deemed domiciled what is he to do? If he repays the debt that is (arguably) a deemed PET. However, if he repays it and survives seven years there is no inheritance tax and the loan proceeds are excluded property. His personal estate is reduced. If the loan is written off by the trustees (assuming that they have power to do this) then his (chargeable) free estate has increased in value. Whether or not he has a qualifying interest in possession in the trust if the loan to him personally is written off, then the value of his free estate (that is not excluded property) has been increased and the value of the settled excluded property has been reduced. He can, of course, leave his free estate without difficulty to his spouse or to a charity and obtain the relevant exemption.

32.41   Whether the loan is written off or repaid may therefore depend partly on (a) how likely he is to survive seven years and whether he has the resources to repay the loan and (b) whether he would qualify for the spouse or charity exemption on his death in respect of his free estate. Alternatively the settlor

[68] [1999] STC (SCD) 185 and see the *Rysaffe* case: see Ch.41.
[69] Consider also the deemed PET that can occur under s.102(4) when a reservation of benefit ceases: see Ch.33.

may take the view that (for the reasons set out above) HMRC are misconceived in their view and that there is no difficulty under s.103 if loans are made to the settlor from an excluded property trust even if he is deemed domiciled.

Conclusions

In general, it is preferable for a foreign domiciliary to avoid incurring liabilities personally in respect of trusts which he has funded where he is likely to become UK deemed domiciled.[70] Nor should he give sums to those from whom he has borrowed already.

32.42

If he has incurred a liability to the trust and is now UK deemed domiciled he can either repay the debt and risk a PET but argue that s.103 does not apply if he dies within seven years or let the debt remain outstanding until death and argue that s.103 does not apply on death to disallow the debt. Alternatively the trustees could write off the debt but this will increase the value of his free estate. This is unattractive if he is now UK deemed domiciled.

Generally, it is preferable to avoid loans to the settlor from a trust. Consider lending to the settlor's spouse or to a company owned by the settlor. Section 103 will not then bite although income tax and capital gains tax will still need to be considered.[71]

IX LOANS BY SETTLORS TO TRUSTS AND RESERVATION OF BENEFIT PROBLEMS

Different issues arise when a settlor lends to a trust. The settlor owns an asset in his estate (which may or may not be excluded property depending on his domicile and the situs of the debt).[72] The trustees are entitled to deduct the debt against the value of the settled property. If the trust is an excluded property settlement and some of the assets are situated in the UK and some are not then it is sensible to ensure that the debt is deductible against the UK property. The principles outlined at 32.07 above will be relevant.

32.43

Do the reservation of benefit provisions apply on his death? If a settlor lends property to a trust from which he can benefit, the tracing provisions in FA 1986 Sch.20 para.5(4) apply and property which is comprised in the trust at the date of death and is derived directly or indirectly from a loan made by the settlor to the trustees is subject to tax under the reservation of benefit provisions. Note that this provision does not apply unless the lender has also made a disposal by way of gift to the trust. If a third party or the lender's spouse puts £10 into the trust and the lender then lends sums to it, there is no reservation of benefit. One might object that the lender will pay tax twice: once on the value of the loan which remains in his estate and again on the settled

32.44

---

[70] Alternative options in relation to the family home are discussed in Ch.43.
[71] This may be relevant if the purpose of the loan is to assist with inward investment into the UK taking advantage of the new rules expected to come into effect in 2012: see 5.40.
[72] If it is necessary for the debt to be non-UK situs then consider making it a specialty debt, i.e. under deed and kept abroad although if the debt is owed by non-resident trustees it will not be treated as a UK situated asset.

property. HMRC give a deduction for the loan against the settled property presumably on the basis of *Barbe*, i.e. the settled property is the property net of trust liabilities which are incurred for full consideration.[73]

32.45   Note that if the £10 had been settled by George's wife or a third party then George is not caught by this provision. However, if he makes "a disposal by way of gift and the property comprised in the gift becomes settled property by virtue of the gift", then para.5(4) is triggered. It does not matter whether the loan is interest free or on fully commercial terms. The property derived from that loan falls into his death estate. The aim is to prevent the lender from alienating the growth in value of the property while retaining a right to income. Bear in mind that this assumes that George is a beneficiary of the trust or otherwise benefits from the settled property. If he lends to a trust from which he is excluded from any benefit and he does not actually benefit from the property then no reservation of benefit arises. In general loans to and from settlors of trusts raise a host of tax issues and should be avoided wherever possible.[74]

EXAMPLE 32.14

Henry lends £1 million to a pre-March 22 2006 interest in possession trust for his three brothers jointly and he and his spouse/civil partner are excluded from benefit. He is foreign domiciled and funded the trust with £100. The trust buys UK property occupied rent-free by Henry and his brothers. Henry has reserved a benefit.

The property increases in value to £2.5 million. On Henry's death the entire property is treated as GWR property and is comprised in his estate for IHT purposes but the reservation is presumably in £1.5 million given that there is a deduction for the £1 million owed to Henry. IHT is payable because the settled property is UK situated. On the death of any brother IHT is also payable on his share (subject to the loan).

Henry moves out of the property and is repaid his loan. He has made a deemed PET of the UK situated property under FA 1986 s.102(4). In addition, if there is any income in the settlement this will also be charged on him under the capital receipts rules.[75]

X LIABILITIES IN THE CONTEXT OF AGRICULTURAL AND BUSINESS PROPERTY[76]

32.46   IHTA 1984 Pt VI Ch.1 dealing with liabilities generally provides, inter alia, that "*a liability which is an incumbrance on any property shall, so far as possible, be taken to reduce the value of that property*" (s.162(4)). For the purpose

---

[73] See Example 32.7.
[74] See Ch.55 for checklist for private clients/trustees.
[75] See Ch.7 and ITTOIA 2005 s.633.
[76] See also Chs 45 and 46.

of BPR s.110 contains the following specific provision: "*the value of a business . . . shall be its net value (and) net value . . . is the value of the assets used in the business . . . reduced by the aggregate amount of any liabilities incurred for the purposes of the business*".[77] For APR there is no such qualification.

As a result of s.162(4) liabilities secured on assets which qualify for business **32.47** relief reduce the value of that property for IHT purposes and so effectively reduce or eliminate the availability of the relief even if the liability was not incurred for the purposes of the business.

EXAMPLE 32.15

> Trustees operate a factory which makes widgets. They also own UK equities. They wished to raise funds to pay to a beneficiary and borrowed on the security of the factory. Even though the liability was not incurred for the purposes of the business it reduces the value of that business. By contrast, if the borrowings had been secured on the UK equities, business property relief would have been unaffected.

Encumbrances on investments

Where money has been borrowed on the security of a non-business asset and **32.48** used to purchase an asset which qualifies for business relief, the net effect is that value not qualifying for relief may be converted into value qualifying for relief.

Assume that X borrows money on the security of his home and uses it to set up his internet business. The encumbrance reduces the value of his home, and the business will qualify for business relief. It might be argued that s.110 should apply because the liability has been incurred for the purposes of the business. On that basis it would reduce the value of the internet business rather than the home. However, it is thought that s.162(4) is the governing provision. Contrast the position if the debts were unsecured when s.110 would require the debts to be set against the value of the business assets.[78]

Agricultural property relief

The position is different for agricultural property relief where liabilities are not **32.49** deducted from the value of agricultural property unless they are charged on the property or (exceptionally) the debts charged on non-agricultural property exceed the value of the property on which they are charged.

---

[77] IHTA 1984 s.110.
[78] Is the loan incurred for the purpose of the business? It is thought so, but contrast the position if X had borrowed in order to purchase a business (e.g. from his retiring cousin). See also *Hardcastle (Vernede's Executors) v IRC* [2000] STC (SCD) 532.

EXAMPLE 32.16

A farmer owns a let farm qualifying for 50 per cent agricultural relief and worth £1 million, subject to a mortgage of £500,000 taken out for the purposes of the business. His other main assets are investments worth £500,000. Were he to die, the value of his estate on death would be £1 million made up of the investments plus the farm after deducting the mortgage thereon. Agricultural relief at 50 per cent would then be available on the net value of the farm (i.e. on £500,000) which would reduce that to £250,000 leaving a chargeable death estate of £750,000.

If, however, before his death the farmer arranged with his lender to switch the mortgage from the agricultural land to the investments, the result then would be that on death the value of his estate would, as above, be £1 million made up of the value of the farm (£1 million) since the investments now, after deducting the mortgage, are valueless. Agricultural relief at 50 per cent would then be available on the entire value of the farm leaving a chargeable death estate of only £500,000.

CHAPTER 33

RESERVATION OF BENEFIT AND SETTLED PROPERTY

- Background (**33.01**)
- The meaning of "gift" (**33.03**)
- The carve-out concept in relation to settlements (**33.05**)
- Extension of "gift" to termination of a qualifying interest in possession (**33.18**)
- Settled gifts—tracing provisions (**33.29**)

I BACKGROUND

In Ch.22, the reservation of benefit rules and pre-owned assets income tax **33.01**
(POA) rules were briefly summarised.[1] This chapter looks at these provisions
with particular reference to trusts.[2] In deciding whether an arrangement falls
within either the GWR rules or the POA charge, consideration should first be
given to the GWR position since if these rules are applicable then generally
there is no scope for the POA charge.

Under FA 1986 s.102(1) the rules apply where an individual disposes of any **33.02**
property by way of gift after March 17, 1986 and:

(a) possession and enjoyment of the property is not bona fide assumed by
the donee at or before the beginning of "the relevant period", or

(b) at any time during "the relevant period" the property is not enjoyed to
the entire exclusion, or virtually to the entire exclusion, of the donor and
of any benefit to him by contract or otherwise.

"*The relevant period*" means a period ending at the donor's death and beginning seven years before the death or, if it is later, on the date of the gift. Under
s.102(2) property within subs.(1)(a) or (b) is referred to as "property subject
to a reservation". Whether there is any such property has to be decided
by looking back from the donor's death to the beginning of "the relevant
period".

---

[1] See 22.10 onwards for basic provisions on reservation of benefit; definition of gift; full consideration let-out, spouse exemption, *Ingram* and *Eversden* schemes and the effect of reserving a
benefit.
[2] For a full survey of the reservation of benefit rules see *Dymond's Capital Taxes* at s.5A.

33.03   As noted previously,[3] rather surprisingly, neither s.102 nor Sch.20 contains any definition of the word "gift". IHTA 1984 has a definition in s.42(1), but that is merely for the purposes of Ch.III of Pt II of the Act (allocation of exemptions). In the context of s.102 one might expect "gift" to mean "transfer of value", and the word is used in that sense in subs.(5), which excludes various exempt gifts from the rules. HMRC considers that, in the context of reservation of benefit, "the word must be given its ordinary meaning".[4]

The relationship between a gift and transfer of value was considered in the *Eversden* appeal[5] where, in the context of s.102(5), Carnwath L.J. commented:

> *"Rightly or wrongly (from the purist's point of view), the draftsmen clearly did find it possible to equate a disposal by way of gift with a transfer of value. That is the effect of posing, in the subsection, the question whether the disposal by way of gift 'is an exempt transfer', with specific reference to the provisions of Part II of the 1984 Act, all of which are references to 'transfers of value'."*

These remarks should be read in context: at most they may be considered to imply that any gift will be a transfer of value. The converse (that all transfers of value are of necessity gifts) cannot be deduced from these comments. The fact that a transfer of value into an interest in possession trust was treated as a gift of the entire settled property to the settlor's spouse is not the same as arguing that (for example) the termination of a spousal life interest by the trustees must necessarily be a gift by the spouse because it is a transfer of value.

General exclusion for pre-March 2006 gifts

33.04   It is worth remembering that the reservation of benefit provisions do not apply to any gift made before March 1986. Hence check when a settlement was funded if it was established prior to March 17, 1986.

EXAMPLE 33.1

> Chris settles property on trusts for his daughter Elouise in 1985 but remains a discretionary beneficiary. Although he has reserved a benefit the reservation of benefit rules do not apply. If, however, he added to that trust in 1987, the reservation of benefit provisions would apply to the added property.

---

[3] See 22.10, above.
[4] See IHTM 14315.
[5] For the *Eversden* case, see 22.19 above.

The carve-out concept was summarised in *Ingram v IRC*[16] where Lord   **33.05**
Hoffmann said:

> "*The theme which runs through all the cases is that although the section does not allow a donor to have his cake and eat it, there is nothing to stop him from carefully dividing up the cake, eating part and having the rest. If the benefits which the donor continues to enjoy are by virtue of property which was never comprised in the gift, he has not reserved any benefit out of the property of which he disposed*".

Section 102, he concluded, laid down a rule that if the donor continued to derive any benefit from the property given away, it would be treated as a reservation of benefit unless the benefit could be shown to be referable to a specific proprietary interest which he had retained.

Accordingly, before applying conditions (*a*) and (*b*) at 33.02 above, it is   **33.06**
necessary to identify precisely the property given. For instance, if the donor retains a lease (as in *Ingram*) the freehold reversion is the property of which the donee must assume possession and enjoyment. By contrast, if the donor settles property on discretionary trusts under which he is a possible beneficiary, the property given is the whole of the property transferred to the trustees. If he transfers property for partial consideration the property disposed of by gift is, in effect, the under value.

The *Ingram* principle has been restricted by ss.102A–C, under which a gift   **33.07**
of an interest in land after March 8, 1999 may be a gift with reservation if the donor retains another interest in the same land. However, the first thing to consider is whether there is a gift with reservation under the general rule in s.102. If there is, s.102A does not apply.[6]

The condition in FA 1986 s.102(1)(b), has two limbs. The donor must be   **33.08**
excluded or virtually excluded (1) from the property and (2) from any benefit by contract or otherwise. With the exception of land and chattels, the payment of full consideration for any benefit or enjoyment a donor obtains will not prevent s.102(1)(b) applying. For instance, if A gives his son £100,000 who then lends it to a partnership in which A is a partner, the loan to the partnership will be a reservation even if the partnership pays a commercial rate of interest for the loan.

In the *Chick* case[7] the deceased gave his son a farm, "Mia Mia", in 1934. In   **33.09**
1935 the deceased, the son and another son entered into partnership as graziers and stock dealers on the terms that the deceased should be the manager and that his decision should be final in all matters relating to the conduct of the business, that the business should be conducted on the holdings of the partners (including "Mia Mia") and that the land held by each partner should be his sole property and he should have the sole and free right to deal with it as he might think fit. The partnership continued until the death of the father in 1952, and "Mia Mia" was held dutiable as a gift subject to a reservation. The main points were:

---

[6] See s.102C(7).
[7] [1958] AC 435.

(1) the deceased was not, in fact, excluded from the property, but as a partner enjoyed rights over it;

(2) there was an initial outright gift of the property—not of the property shorn of certain rights. In this respect the case could be distinguished from *Munro v Commissioner of Stamp Duties (New South Wales)*,[8] where the partnership rights existed before the gift was made;

(3) it was immaterial that the partnership was "an independent commercial transaction" and that the deceased gave full consideration for his rights[9];

(4) the question whether the partnership agreement was "related" or "referable" to the gift did not arise. That question is relevant only to the second limb of the section;

(5) it was immaterial that the donee could make no better use of the property. "The sole question is one of fact—was the deceased excluded?" said Lord Simonds in *Chick*. He distinguished *Oakes v Commissioner of Stamp Duties of New South Wales*[10] and *St Aubyn v A-G (No.2)*[11] as cases under the second limb of the section. In the *Oakes* case, residence on the property in a managerial capacity was not regarded as a "reservation", but in the light of *Chick, Oakes* cannot be considered authoritative on the first limb.

Carve-out principle in relation to trusts

33.10 *Ingram* was a case applying the carve-out concept in relation to outright gifts of individuals. How the carve-out principle operates in relation to settled property raises issues of some difficulty. It is clear that where the settlor is a potential discretionary beneficiary then he has reserved a benefit in the settled property whether or not he actually benefits.[12] The position is less clear cut if the settlor is not a member of the discretionary class but the trustees have a power to add beneficiaries which they could exercise to add the settlor. He is, of course, only capable of benefitting if this power is exercised and it may therefore be argued that unless and until that happens he is not capable of benefitting so that there is no reservation of benefit.

Income interest retained by settlor

33.11 What is the position where the settlor retains only the right to income, e.g. a non-qualifying interest in possession and is not otherwise a beneficiary? In *Att-Gen v Heywood*,[13] property was settled on trust to apply the income at the

8 [1934] AC 61.
9 The New South Wales statute had no equivalent of FA 1986 Sch.20 para.6.
10 [1954] AC 57.
11 [1952] AC 15.
12 See *IRC v Eversden* above and *PRs of Lyon (Deceased)* (2007) SpC 616.
13 (1887) 19 QBD 326.

trustees' discretion during the settlor's life for the benefit of him and other persons, or any of them to the exclusion of the others; and it was held that the settlor had reserved an interest within the meaning of the Customs and Inland Revenue Act 1881 s.38(2)(c). This was followed in *Att-Gen v Farrell*,[14] and both cases were approved by the House of Lords in *Gartside v IRC*.[15]

However, in all these cases the settlor had an interest in income as a dis-   **33.12**
cretionary beneficiary rather than a fixed right which he had reserved. In this situation, where the settlor retains an income right and no other rights over the settled property, it is not thought by the authors that this is a reservation of benefit but rather a carve-out. Although in *Eversden* the notion that a settlor could give away a number of different interests in settled property retaining interests in some but not others was rejected, this was specifically stated to be in the context of IHTA 1984 s.49 where a person with a qualifying interest in possession is deemed to own the entire settled property anyway. Leaving s.49 aside, if the settlor retains the right to receive income all he has given away is the remainder interests in capital and if he is wholly excluded from that there is no gift with reservation.[16] A number of commentators disagree on the basis that if it is a reservation of benefit for the settlor to be a discretionary object of the trust it must be a reservation of benefit for him to retain a right to the income.[17]

A recent discussion of the carve-out principle in the context of reversionary   **33.13**
lease arrangements occurred in *Buzzoni v HMRC*[18] where a donor granted an underlease which provided for the donee to pay the service charge and contained various other covenants. It was held that these were not prior independent rights carved out before grant of the underlease to the donee but part of the gifted property and the covenants were of direct benefit to the donor since they could be enforced against the donee. There was a reservation of benefit. The case confirmed, however, that if the donor had granted the same underlease but without covenants in her own favour albeit that under its terms the donee was required to covenant with the superior landlord to pay the service charge direct to that landlord then this would not have involved a reservation of benefit. There would have been the same economic benefit to the donor but a different tax result.[19] This confirms that the legal *form* of the gift and carve-out is important and so it is not surprising that a reserved right to the income does not involve a reservation but being a discretionary object of a trust as to income or capital does!

---

[14] [1931] 1 KB 81.
[15] [1968] AC 553.
[16] Until March 22, 2006 the position was academic because if the settlor retained a right to income he was deemed under s.49(1) to beneficially own the trust fund.
[17] See, for example, Giles Clarke *Offshore Tax Planning* (17th edn), para.55.15 He also suggests (as does McCutcheon in *Inheritance Tax* (5th edn), para.7–41) that the tracing rules in Sch.20 para.5 FA 1986 pose a problem because the property comprised in a settled gift is to be taken as the property from time to time comprised in the settlement and therefore presumably take the view is that it is not possible to have multiple gifts of individual beneficial interests in a settlement, reserving a benefit in only some of them. In response to this it might be argued that the settlor never actually settles the income interest; what he settles is the capital reversion. HMRC's view is not known although their approach to insurance trusts is in line with carve-out principles.
[18] [2011] FTT 267.
[19] See para.65 of the decision.

A retained reversionary interest

33.14   There is no reservation of benefit but a carve-out if the settlor retains a reversionary interest in the settled property as a result of which settled property reverts to him in the event that all the trusts fail.[20] This assumes that the settlor is not a discretionary object under the prior trusts of capital or income. What is the position if the terms of the trust are "to X and Y at the trustees' discretion and in default of any appointment the settled property passes to the settlor absolutely after 10 years." Some insurance trust arrangements are structured in this way.[21] Could it be said that the trustees have conferred a collateral benefit on the settlor by failing to exercise their discretions so as to benefit the beneficiaries, knowing that this will ultimately benefit the settlor? HMRC have raised a similar argument in relation to home loan schemes, where they argue the failure of trustees to call in a demand debt has resulted in a benefit for the settlor by allowing him to continue living in the property.[22] The authors do not consider that such cases give rise to a reservation.

Settlement powers

33.15   If X creates a settlement which he has power to revoke but from which he is otherwise excluded from benefit, the authors' view is that there is a reservation. His power to revoke is a settlement power within IHTA 1984 s.47A and so the power itself is not property comprised in his estate. However, it is not possible to say that the settlement is enjoyed to his entire exclusion because clearly he could benefit from the property simply by revoking the trust.

Settlor acts as trustee

33.16   If the settlor is a paid trustee, HMRC state that they do not consider there is a reservation of benefit if the remuneration is not excessive. A settlor trustee may also be a paid director of a company owned by the trust. As a matter of trust law he must not profit from his trust and any beneficiary can recover the payments for the trust.[23] Hence, most trust deeds provide that a trustee in such a position need not account to the trust in respect of any director's fees even

---

[20] See *Commissioner of Stamp Duties of NSW v Perpetual Trustee Co Ltd* [1943] 1 All ER 525 where the settlor took the trust property back in the event that the son failed to attain the age of 21 years. This was held not to be a reservation. The settlor had given away the contingent interest in the shares from which he had received no subsequent benefit. See also HMRC letter dated May 18, 1987:

> "In the case where a gift is made into trust, the retention by the settlor of a reversionary interest under the trust is not considered to constitute a reservation, whether the retained interest arises under the express terms of the trust or arises by operation of general law e.g. a resulting trust."

[21] See Ch.47.

[22] See Ch.43.

[23] See *Lewin on Trusts* (18th edn) at 20.01 and following.

if they were obtained as a result of his position as trustee. What is the reservation of benefit position? The problem can, of course, arise whether or not the settlor is trustee: for instance if a person gives away shares in a company in which he is a paid director or employee.

In *Oakes v Commissioner of Stamp Duties of NSW*[24] the Privy Council held **33.17** that a reservation of benefit did arise where an individual settled property on trusts where he was entitled to be reasonably remunerated as trustee and he acted as trustee. However, HMRC indicate that they do not regard the reservation of benefit rule as applying where a donor of shares continues to receive remuneration for acting as director provided that this is a continuation of existing reasonable commercial arrangements and the benefits are in no way linked to or affected by the gift.[25] They do not specifically consider the position where the settlor is trustee *and* director. Problems may arise if, in later years when the settlor is elderly, he still wishes to receive a salary from the company without working for it.

IV EXTENSION OF "GIFT" TO TERMINATION OF A QUALIFYING INTEREST IN POSSESSION

HMRC seem to have accepted the general principle that prior to March 22, **33.18** 2006 a termination by the trustees of a life interest was not a gift by the life tenant unless (possibly) the life tenant consented[26] to such termination or (more likely) surrendered the interest himself. In other words, on the inter vivos termination of a life interest in settled property, the question whether the life tenant made a gift (or, in the words of s.102(1), "disposes of property by way of gift") prior to the FA 2006 changes may have depended on the way in which the interest was terminated.

EXAMPLE 33.2

> Under the will of his father who died in 1999, A was life tenant of a house, but the trustees had power (without A's consent) to terminate his interest and transfer the house to his daughter. They did so in 1991, and A continued to live there until his death in 1999. It appears that HMRC accept this was not a gift with reservation.[27] If, however, A had assigned or surrendered his life interest (for instance because the trustees did not have any overriding powers to end his interest), HMRC may consider that A has made a gift "in the real world" and that gift comprises the house.

In the case of an assignment or surrender, the question remains whether A **33.19** has simply enabled a benefit to pass to his daughter or whether he has made a

---

[24] [1954] AC 57.
[25] IHTM 14334–14337.
[26] Although it is difficult to see how the giving of consent could be treated as a disposition of property for the purposes of s.102(1); it is the action by the trustees (e.g. in exercising a power of appointment or advancement) which is the effective disposition.
[27] The position would be different if A's interest had terminated on or after March 22, 2006: see 33.09.

gift of his life interest (which has now ended so that he cannot have reserved a benefit in it) or a gift of the underlying settled property: (i.e the house), in which case his continued occupation involves a reservation of benefit. In the real world A has only given up his life interest. He never owned the house so could not give it away. Of course, IHTA 1984 s.49(1) deems A to be beneficially entitled to the underlying property.[28] Does this fiction along with s.51 (dealing with the disposal of an interest in possession) displace the real world gift and in conjunction with s.52 substitute the gift of the underlying capital as the relevant gift for reservation of benefit purposes? The Court of Appeal comments in *Eversden*, equating gifts with transfers of value, are obviously helpful to the approach of HMRC. However, s.51 says that the disposal of an interest in possession is not a transfer of value but is treated as the coming to an end of the interest and s.52 says that tax is charged:

> "*as if [A] had made a transfer of value and the value transferred had been equal to the value of the property in which his interest subsisted*".

Hence, the legislation goes to considerable trouble to say that no actual transfer of value takes place. Accordingly it is hard to see how the reservation of benefit rules can apply even on a surrender or assignment of a life interest given that no gift has been made of the underlying property in the real world.

33.20   Could HMRC successfully argue that under the tracing provisions in FA 1986 Sch.20 para.2(4)(5) the life tenant continues to have an interest in possession in the settled property even though it has ceased to exist? It is not thought that the deeming provisions extend this far. The authors' experience is that HMRC have dropped claims that the surrender of a life interest is a gift of the underlying settled property for reservation of benefit purposes. It is noteworthy that in the 2006 amending legislation (s.102ZA) the draftsman not only said that the beneficiary was deemed to make a gift but also provided that he was deemed to make a gift of the underlying property. Hence, he pre-empted any argument that even if there is a gift, in the real world it is not a gift of the underlying property.

Changes in FA 2006

33.21   The "loophole" of a life tenant's interest being terminated by the trustees but with the beneficiary continuing to be able to benefit from the settled property was widely used.

EXAMPLE 33.3

Cunning died in 2004 and by his will:

(a) created a nil rate band discretionary trust under which his surviving wife (Electra) was one of the beneficiaries[29];

---

[28] From March 22, 2006 the scope for the operation of this fiction has been much reduced.
[29] It was standard practice to create such trusts to use up the nil rate band of the deceased. The

(b) left his residuary estate on a life interest trust for Electra with the trustees having a power of appointment to allow them to terminate this interest in whole or in part. On Cunning's death the spouse exemption applied to this residuary trust.

In 2005 the trustees exercised their overriding power to terminate Electra's interest in possession in £275,000 (the then nil rate sum) which they appointed on continuing discretionary trusts under which Electra was one of the beneficiaries.

The IHT analysis was that:

   (i) Electra made an immediately chargeable transfer when the interest was terminated but the value transferred fell into her nil rate band and so no tax was payable;

   (ii) although she could benefit under the continuing discretionary trust because she had not made a gift the reservation of benefit rules did not apply.

An obvious attraction of this arrangement was that, as a matter of fact, **33.22** Electra was the main beneficiary of both discretionary trusts so that both income and capital were available should they be needed. However, on her death neither of the trust funds was taxed.[30]

All this changed following the amendments to FA 1986 s.102 inserted by **33.23** FA 2006.[31] The termination of Electra's interest in possession after March 21, 2006 in Example 33.2 is now treated as a gift by Electra under s.102ZA which provides:

> "*For the purposes of section 102 and Schedule 20*[32] *the individual shall be taken . . . to dispose on the coming to an end of the interest in possession of the no-longer-possessed-property by way of gift.*"

The "no longer possessed property" is defined as:

> "*the property in which the interest in possession subsisted immediately before it came to an end . . .*"

Hence, the beneficiary is deemed to make a gift for the purposes of the reser- **33.24** vation of benefit rules. (Note that no attempt was made by the draftsman to change the reservation of benefit rules so that they are triggered by a transfer of value rather than by a gift.) The section is, however, restrictively drafted: in particular in the definition of the no-longer possessed property and by not being extended to s.102A–C (the anti-*Ingram* legislation).

The change affected all pre-March 22, 2006 interest in possession trusts where the beneficiary's interest had not been ended by March 22, 2006 as well

---

position changed from October 9, 2007 with the introduction of the transferable unused IHT nil rate band: see Ch.38.

[30] In some cases matters were taken further with Electra's interest being ended in further amounts of £275,000 which were channelled, via life interest trusts for the children, into further discretionary trusts. Again Electra could benefit and the children's nil rate band was used to create the further discretionary trusts without any IHT charge.

[31] By s.156 and Sch.20 para.33(1), (2) and (4).

[32] But note not, it appears, for the purposes of ss.102A–C (the anti-*Ingram* legislation).

as later qualifying interest in possession settlements. Hence, it is important to remember to exclude the life tenant from future benefits under the settlement when his interest ends in order to avoid reservation of benefit problems.[33]

EXAMPLE 33.4

> H set up an *Eversden* structure putting his house into an interest in possession trust for his wife in May 2003.[34] The trustees terminated her interest after March 21, 2006 whereupon the house became held on continuing trusts for the couple's children. Although H is protected from reservation of benefit by s.102(5) (because the spouse exemption applied to the original gift in settlement and s.102(5A) (the anti-*Ingram* legislation) does not affect transfers into trust before June 20, 2003) the termination of Mrs H's interest in possession causes a pre-owned assets income tax (POA) problem for H if he is in occupation of the house.[35] If Mrs H continues to occupy the house after the termination of her interest she does not suffer POA income tax but she has a reservation of benefit problem because she is deemed to have made a gift for inheritance tax purposes under s.102ZA.

> As a result, both of them must separately pay "rent" to the trustees—H to avoid a POA charge and W to avoid a reservation of benefit charge. HMRC consider that it is the full amount from each.[36]

33.25 The 2006 change has wider implications than might at first be thought.

EXAMPLE 33.5

> Mr B is the life tenant of a trust set up in 1979 by his father.

> (a) *Terminating his interest before March 22, 2006:* before March 22, 2006 the trustees could have terminated his life interest and appointed the settled property on interest in possession trusts for his son (assuming that they had the necessary powers) and Mr B would have made a PET and the son would have a qualifying interest in possession.

> (b) *Terminating the interest during the transitional period:* if they ended the interest after March 21, 2006 but before October 6, 2008 the son took a

---

[33] Note that if the life tenant's interest is ended in favour of the spouse who takes a qualifying interest in possession, e.g. under the transitional serial interest rules, the reservation of benefit rules do not apply to the life tenant because of s.102(5). Section 102(5A) of FA 1986 (the anti-*Eversden* legislation) is not applicable because the property does not become settled by virtue of the gift—it is already settled. Of course, on a later termination of the spousal interest reservation of benefit could apply to the spouse. POA issues may also arise if the settlement holds intangibles and the spouse has an interest in possession but settlor retains an interest since it will not be protected by either FA 2004 Sch.15 para.11 or para.10.

[34] See 22.19 for a discussion of the *Eversden* case.

[35] Since the transaction is no longer an excluded transaction: see FA 2004 Sch.15 para.10(1)(c).

[36] See A2.205.

transitional serial interest (a qualifying interest in possession)[37] and Mr B still makes a PET but he has also made a gift with reservation if he can still benefit from the trusts or continues to occupy the settled property. This is despite the fact that the property was originally settled before 1986 (when the reservation of benefit rules were introduced) and that Mr B was not the settlor.

(c) *Later termination:* if the trustees terminate Mr B's life interest after October 5, 2008 and appoint the property on interest in possession trusts for his son, then Mr B makes a chargeable transfer for inheritance tax purposes because the son does not take a qualifying interest in possession. The property may also be taxed as part of Mr B's estate on his death under the reservation of benefit rules if he has reserved a benefit. In addition, the property is subject to 10-year anniversary charges even while Mr B is alive. There is no base cost uplift for capital gains tax purposes on Mr B's death.

(d) *Spousal terminations:* if Mr B's interest in possession was terminated inter vivos in favour of his spouse before October 6, 2008 this would have been an exempt transfer (because the spouse took a transitional serial interest which was a qualifying interest in possession) and Mr B could continue to benefit from the use of the settled property without a reservation of benefit problem.[38] He is protected from s.102ZA by the spouse exemption in s.102(5). Nor would there have been a POAT problem because Mr B was not the settlor of the trust.[39] This option might have been attractive if it was felt that tax planning could be done later and Mrs B was "a better life" so that in the future her life interest could be terminated and the trust ended in favour, for instance, of the children so that she, not Mr B, would then be treated as making the PET. She but not Mr B would then need to be excluded from benefit on a subsequent termination of her interest.

In some cases a family will wish to retain the settled property in a trust structure for the long term but retain flexibility over inheritance tax planning. In these circumstances a younger person might have been given a transitional serial interest before October 6, 2008 to keep the property out of the relevant property regime even though the original life tenant was not excluded.   **33.26**

---

[37] For "TSIs", see 27.15 and following.

[38] In simple terms s.102(5)(A)–(C) (the anti-*Eversden* legislation) has effect if the following conditions are satisfied: (i) property becomes settled property by virtue of the gift; (ii) because the settlor's spouse has an interest in possession that disposal is spouse exempt; (iii) at a later date during the settlor's life the interest in possession of the spouse ends without that spouse becoming absolutely entitled to the property or to another interest in possession. If the above conditions are met s.102(5B) provides that s.102 is to be applied *"as if the disposal by way of gift had been made immediately after the (spouse's) interest in possession came to an end"*. In this case the property does not become settled property by virtue of a gift by Mr B, it is already settled property, having been settled by his father. Hence the anti-*Eversden* legislation does not apply.

[39] The position would be different if Mr B was the original settlor of a trust set up after 1986. Then POAT could apply if the spouse takes an interest because HMRC argue that this is not an excluded transaction (the property does not become settled on interest in possession trusts by virtue of the gift but is already settled). It is not clear to the authors that HMRC are right in this view: see A2.17.

EXAMPLE 33.6

Mr C, a widower, is the life tenant of a trust settled by his now deceased father which had been set up in 1985. The trust is non-UK resident and has realised substantial gains which are stockpiled.[40] All Mr C's children who will benefit on his death are UK resident and domiciled. If the trust ends on Mr C's death or on earlier termination of his interest, the s.87 gains will be taxed on the children because they take the settled property. If the trust continues after Mr C's death and he dies after October 5, 2008 the children's successive interests in possession are not qualifying and therefore the trust falls into the relevant property regime. One solution would have been to appoint transitional serial interests to the children just before October 6, 2008. Even if Mr C continued to benefit, at least the interests taken by the children were not within the relevant property regime. If he died still reserving a benefit then the property is taxed on his death but this would have been the case if he had retained a life interest. The main downside was that there was no capital gains tax uplift on his death. However, at least the trust has been kept outside the relevant property regime and tax on the stockpiled gains postponed. Further, if Mr C wanted to carry out inheritance tax planning before his death he could cease to reserve a benefit: this results in him making a deemed PET.[41] Diagrammatically the position is as follows:

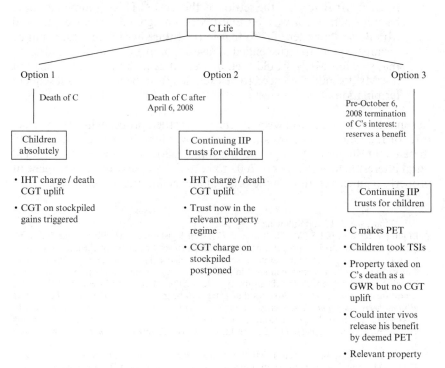

---

[40] See further 19.31.
[41] FA 1986 s.102(4): see Ch.31.

The s.102ZA "loophole"

As already noted the 2006 amending legislation was narrowly drafted. In particular s.102ZA (which deems there to be a gift of the settled property "being the no longer possessed property") does not apply for the purpose of ss.102A–C (the anti-*Ingram* legislation). As a result, a reversionary lease or *Ingram scheme* will still work where the life tenant occupies freehold property owned by the trust, provided that a carve-out is properly made to avoid s.102 FA 1986. It may also be said that if the life tenant retains an interest in possession in the freehold interest after the trustees have granted a reversionary lease to the remainder beneficiary, the life tenant's interest in possession does not come to an end in the freehold interest[42] as is required by s.102ZA(1)(c)). Instead, the value of the freehold property has been devalued by the exercise of the trustees' powers. Section 52(3) IHTA 1984 provides that such a devaluation is treated as a deemed ending of the interest in possession, but this deeming provision does not apply for FA 1986 s.102ZA purposes only for the purposes of "this section" (i.e. s.52). **33.27**

Accordingly it is thought possible to avoid the reservation of benefit rules by ensuring that any benefit retained by the beneficiary is in property remaining subject to the interest in possession trust rather than in the no longer possessed property. Reversionary lease and *Ingram* schemes in the context of settled freehold property are considered further in Ch.43. **33.28**

V SETTLED GIFTS—TRACING PROVISIONS

FA 1986 Sch.20 para.2 deals with the situation where the gifted property is replaced by introducing "tracing" provisions. So if A gives B Whiteacre which is then sold by B who buys Blackacre with the sale proceeds for A to live in, there is a reservation of benefit in Blackacre under the tracing provisions. These provisions do not, however, apply if: **33.29**

(1) there is an outright gift of cash; or

(2) the property given becomes settled property by virtue of the gift.

Instead para.5 provides a self-contained code for tracing where the property becomes settled property by virtue of the gift. In these cases the reservation rules apply as if the property comprised in the gift was the property in the settlement on "*the material date*" (being the date of death or when the reservation of benefit ceased) except in so far as that property neither is, nor represents, nor is derived from, property originally comprised in the gift. **33.30**

Under para.5(5), however, where there is a trust or power to accumulate, accumulations of income arising after the material date are not treated as derived from the gifted property. So, if the reservation ends (with a deemed PET under FA 1986 s.102(4)), accumulations of income arising after that date escape tax. **33.31**

---

[42] FA 1986 s.102ZA(1)(c) requires that "*the interest in possession comes to an end during the individual's life*" and in s.102ZA(3) the "no longer possessed property" means "*the property in which the interest in possession subsisted immediately before it came to an end*".

33.32   Under para.5(2), if the settlement comes to an end at some time before the material date as respects all or any of the property which, if the donor had died immediately before that time, would have been treated as comprised in the gift, then:

> "*(a) the property in question, other than property to which the donor then becomes absolutely and beneficially entitled in possession, and*
> *(b) any consideration (not consisting of rights under the settlement) given by the donor for any of the property to which he so becomes entitled, shall be treated as comprised in the gift (in addition to any other property so comprised".*

However, para.5 does not contain tracing provisions to deal with the position when the beneficiary of the settlement sells the property after he has become absolutely entitled and then uses the proceeds to buy further property from which the donor benefits.

EXAMPLE 33.7

A settles shares on trust for, inter alia, his son. The trustees hold the shares for some years and then sell them and invest in pictures. The pictures are advanced to the son and the trust ended. If A derives some benefit from the pictures (e.g. they hang on his walls) then the tracing rules in para.5(2) apply and he is treated as reserving a benefit. A would therefore need to pay full consideration for his use of the pictures to avoid a reservation of benefit. However, if the son sells the pictures and then buys a house in which A lives (or if he buys more pictures), the reservation of benefit provisions do not apply. Accordingly, one would also need to consider the POA provisions which use the words "property directly or indirectly applied" so that the house which A now occupies would satisfy the condition in para.3 with the result that the POA land charge applies.[43] The POA Regime has better tracing provisions than reservation of benefit so far as settled property is concerned.

33.33   Under para.5(3), where property comprised in a gift is not settled by the gift but is settled by the donee before the material date, paras 5(1) and (2) apply in relation to the settled property as if the settlement had been made by the gift. Property settled by the donee's will or intestacy is treated as settled by him.

Loans made by the donor

33.34   Under para.5(4), where property comprised in a gift becomes settled property either by virtue of the gift or as mentioned in para.5(3), any property which:

---

[43] For the POA charge, see Ch.34.

"(a) on the material date is comprised in the settlement, and
(b) is derived, directly or indirectly, from a loan made by the donor to the
   trustees of the settlement,
shall be treated for the purposes of para.5(1) as derived from property
originally comprised in the gift."

Unlike the rest of para.5, para.5(4) had no counterpart in the estate duty leg- **33.35**
islation in FA 1957 s.38. In the Parliamentary debates during the passage of
the 1986 Finance Bill, the Minister of State explained that para.5(4):

"is concerned with the type of avoidance scheme known as an inherit-
ance trust. The scheme involves setting up a trust with a modest transfer
of assets—the original gift—and then making a substantial interest-free
loan to the trustees. The settlor retains a right to receive benefits from
the trust, but the growth on the interest-free loan is just as much a gift
from the settlor as the original gift itself and, as he has reserved rights to
benefit from the growth, it is right that it should be subject to the gifts-
with-reservation rules."[44]

Consistent with this statement, para.5(4) applies only where the donor gives
property to the settlement and can continue to benefit from it.[45] It does not
catch the case where a donor makes a modest gift to a trustee for one or more
beneficiaries absolutely (a bare trust) and then makes a substantial interest-
free loan to that trustee. Nor does it apply in the situation where someone
other than the lender (e.g. his spouse) establishes the trust to which the lender
then lends money and benefits from the trust. This will protect the future
growth in the trust fund as Example 33.8(1). However, the section can have a
wider impact than is sometimes appreciated: see Example 33.8(2).

EXAMPLE 33.8

(1) S wishes to lend funds to a trust to enable the trustees to buy a house for
    him and his son to live in. His ex-wife funds the trust with £100,000 and
    S lends £1 million to the trust. The trust purchases the house in which
    he and his son live. There is no reservation of benefit. S has made no
    gift to the trust. At S's death the house is worth £2 million and is outside
    S's estate (although the loan is an asset of his free estate and therefore
    chargeable on his death). If S had given £1,000 to the trust the entire
    trust fund would have been subject to a reservation of benefit on his
    death (subject only to a deduction for the loan).

(2) S, is foreign domiciled, in 2005 settled £500,000 into a trust for himself
    and his three brothers. They each take a qualifying interest in possession
    in one quarter of the trust fund. S then borrows from a bank and lends
    the funds to the trust to enable it to purchase a large London house in

---

[44] Official Report, June 10, 1986, cols 423 and 424.
[45] See Ch.32 for further comments on about the effect of para.5(4) in relation to loans made by
the settlor to trust. This is why the settlor is excluded from the standard insurance based loan
trust: see Ch.47.

which they all live. On S's death his share of the trust fund passes to his spouse on qualifying interest in possession trusts (it is a TSI). Although one quarter of the trust fund is therefore spouse exempt the other three quarters is caught by the reservation of benefit rules with no available spouse exemption.

CHAPTER 34

PRE-OWNED ASSETS INCOME TAX REGIME

- The purpose of the charge (**34.01**)
- The charge in outline (**34.06**)
- Land and chattels (**34.09**)
- Exclusions (para.10) (**34.11**)
- Settled intangibles (paras 8–9) (**34.14**)
- Exemptions; the effect of s.80 FA 2006 and excluded liabilities (**34.18**)
- Non-domiciliaries (**34.27**)
- Electing into GWR (**34.40**)

I THE PURPOSE OF THE CHARGE

The pre-owned assets income tax charge was introduced with effect from April 6, 2005 in the teeth of widespread opposition albeit with substantial modifications to the original proposals contained in the Consultation Document of December 11, 2003. The result is that it is necessary to consider not only whether a proposed gift involves a reservation of benefit, but also whether, if it escapes these provisions, it will result in an income tax charge being levied on the transferor.[1] The approach of the draftsman is very different from inheritance tax. The anti-avoidance sections in the inheritance tax legislation generally target specific schemes. Anything else remains excluded. By contrast the POA legislation potentially applies to all disposals of land and chattels (not just gifts) and all intangible property held in a settlor-interested trust. The draftsman then carves out specific exemptions and exclusions. In some cases the exemptions are generous; in other cases the draftsman appears to have overlooked an exemption that might have been thought necessary.   **34.01**

HMRC have published guidance notes on POA (revised at various times since they first appeared in 2005). These are referred to in this chapter and can be found in Appendix II as can an exchange of correspondence (in the form of questions and answers) between STEP/CIOT and HMRC (the "COP 10" letter). At the time of writing the guidance is being substantially revised to   **34.02**

---

[1] The legislation is in FA 2004 s.84 and Sch.15 and all statutory references are to Sch.15 unless otherwise stated. In addition, the primary legislation is supplemented by SI 2005/724 and SI 2005/344. FA 2006 s.80 was introduced to prevent reverter to settlor trusts being used to avoid the POA charge.

appear in the IHT Manual at 44001 and appears in draft in Appendix II.[2] This chapter focuses on the main points that are likely to affect trustees and settlors.

34.03   The main objective of the POA charge was to stop the use of IHT avoidance schemes that circumvented the reservation-of-benefit rules: for instance, an unconditional cash gift by A to his son of £500,000 which is used by the son to buy a flat into which A moves.[3] Apart from discouraging the future use of such arrangements, the legislation also caught past schemes and may be said to have a retrospective (or at least retroactive) effect. There are, however, two significant limitations on the application of the legislation:

> (i) it does not apply to arrangements put in place before March 18, 1986 (this being the date on which potentially exempt transfers and the reservation of benefit rules were introduced: it marked the replacement of CTT by IHT);

> (ii) it does not apply to outright cash gifts made before April 6, 1998 (this is the, probably unintended, effect of Sch.15 para.10(2)(c)).

34.04   Given that the object of the POA charge is to plug holes in the IHT legislation, the charge will not generally apply when the relevant property is comprised in the taxpayer's estate or when, in relation to him, it is property subject to a reservation. It should also follow that in cases where statute provides that the reservation-of-benefit charge does not apply despite the taxpayer having satisfied the basic charging conditions (for instance, where he has given away land and continues to occupy it paying full consideration for his use[4]) then neither should the POA charge apply. Whilst this is generally the case[5] care needs to be exercised, however, since not all the reservation of benefit exclusions have been carried over into the POA legislation. For instance, the grant of a right (e.g. a lease) is not significant if that grant occurred more than seven years before the date of the gift. Hence the reservation-of-benefit rules do not apply if having carved out a lease the taxpayer then waits at least seven years before giving away the encumbered freehold interest.[6] This provision is not, however, carried over into the POA legislation which will therefore apply in such cases.

It should also be noted that the relevant IHT scheme is not affected, i.e. it may still operate to avoid any IHT charge but with the expense of an income tax charge. In a sense, therefore, income tax is the price to be paid for the IHT planning. Reversionary lease schemes,[7] for instance, remain effective for IHT purposes but at a POA cost.

34.05   The POA charge is not subject to a motive test: the fact that the taxpayer may not have intended to avoid inheritance tax is irrelevant. Hence if the taxpayer sells a part of his house to a connected party at full market value then he is subject to POA on that part he has disposed of: the disposal condition is satisfied. No inheritance tax has been saved because the taxpayer is taxed on

---

[2] For a full discussion of the POA regime, see the authors' *Pre-Owned Assets and Estate Planning* (3rd edn 2009) which is also reproduced in *Dymond's Capital Taxes*.
[3] No reservation of benefit because of the deficiencies of the tracing rules in respect of cash gifts.
[4] See FA 1986 Sch.20 para.6(1)(a).
[5] See Sch.15 para.11(5)(b)–(d).
[6] FA 1986 s.102A(5).
[7] See Ch.43 but note *Buzzoni v HMRC* [2011] UK FTT 267 (TC) in which a reversionary lease scheme was caught by the reservation of benefit rules on the basis that covenants were reserved in favour of the donor: see 33.13.

the cash remaining in his estate. (It would be more logical if the POA charge only applied in the event that the taxpayer gave away the cash from the sale but this is not so.) The fact that he has made no gift for inheritance tax purposes is irrelevant. By contrast, if the sale is of the whole house at full market value then there is no POA charge because of the specific exclusion in para.10(1).[8]

II THE CHARGE IN OUTLINE

The first tax year of charge was 2005–06. The taxpayer is assessed on the "benefit" that he is deemed to receive during the course of a tax year. In the case of land and chattels the benefit is arrived at on the basis of the occupation and use enjoyed (hence, the tax charge will cease when the taxpayer ceases to occupy the relevant land or use the chattels). In the case of intangible property (i.e. all property other than land and chattels) held in a settlor-interested trust the charge applies because of the possibility of the taxpayer benefiting under the terms of the trust; hence the charge will cease only if the settlor ceases to be a beneficiary. In accordance with income tax principles the POA benefit must be returned on the taxpayer's tax return and failure to do so may lead to interest and penalties. As part of the self-assessment system, the value of the benefit must be calculated by the taxpayer. In line with general income tax principles, trading losses may reduce the taxable benefit. **34.06**

The taxpayer's election

The taxpayer can elect that income tax shall not apply by opting into the reservation of benefit rules. Two points to note about the election are: **34.07**

  (i) that it must be made on prescribed form IHT 500 and should be submitted to the Capital Taxes division at Nottingham;

  (ii) in the case of existing arrangements (caught in tax year 2005–06) the deadline for making the election was generally January 31, 2007 (the final date for the filing of tax returns for 2005–06). An election made on or before that date has the effect of preventing an income tax charge from applying with effect from April 6, 2005. The election is irrevocable once the January 31 deadline has passed.[9]

The effect of electing into the reservation of benefit rules is to bring s.102(3) (the charge on death) and s.102(4) (the deemed PET on lifetime cessation of benefit) into play. The conditions for the application of these charging provisions (such as the making of a gift after March 17, 1986) are considered to be satisfied by the making of the election. It is important to realise that the election does not result in an unscrambling of the arrangement: it merely affects the IHT position of the donor taxpayer and relieves him from an income tax charge.[10]

The POA charging provisions divide into three parts: **34.08**

---

[8] See 34.12.
[9] See further 34.40 for a consideration of the defective implementation of the election machinery.
[10] See 34.38 below

- Land (paras 3–5);

- Chattels (paras 6–7);

- Intangibles held in a settlor-interested trust (paras 8–9).

This division reflects the fact that the computation of the benefit varies in each case: for instance, whereas the benefit of occupying land is relatively easily calculated on the basis of a market rent for the property, the benefit of using chattels or the possibility of benefiting under a trust of intangibles is less apparent and therefore involves different rules. The charge on land or chattels may apply if either the *disposal* or the *contribution* condition is met. The intangibles charge applies if property was settled by the taxpayer after March 17, 1986 and he retains an interest in the trust under ITTOIA 2005 s.624.[11]

EXAMPLE 34.1

In 2007 Donald put £250,000 into a nil rate band trust under which he was given entitlement to income but was excluded from the capital which was left in trust for his grandchildren. Donald's transfer was a chargeable transfer but no IHT was payable because the value was less than his unused nil rate band. He had an income entitlement but this was not a qualifying interest in possession. Hence, on Donald's death, there is no reservation of benefit.[12] This might be thought the best of all worlds: Donald had kept the income but the capital was not taxed on his death. However, watch POA. Since Donald had an interest in the settlement, while it holds cash or other intangibles he is within the four per cent intangibles charge.[13] If the trust invests in land or chattels there is a charge on Donald if he is in occupation and so the land (or chattels) must be let to avoid a POA charge.[14]

III LAND AND CHATTELS

34.09   The *disposal* condition is met if:

(a) the taxpayer owned an interest in land (or chattels) at any time after March 17, 1986;

(b) at some time after that date he disposed of that interest or of part of it, and

---

[11] Except that if the trust is settlor-interested, only because his spouse has an interest then para.8 does not apply. See also Example 34.7 and 34.27 for limitations of the para.8 charge in the context of foreign domiciliaries.

[12] The arrangements may be seen as a carve-out along the lines recognised by the House of Lords in the *Ingram* case; see though 33.11 for a fuller discussion of whether or not there is a reservation of benefit.

[13] For 2011–12.

[14] See further Ch.43.

(c) that disposal was not an excluded transaction (see below).

It can also apply if the taxpayer owned an interest in other property at any time after March 17, 1986 and disposed of that interest otherwise than by an excluded transaction and the proceeds of the disposal were applied directly or indirectly by another person in acquiring an interest in the land now occupied by the taxpayer. This would catch the situation where A sells or gives land to B; the disposal is not an excluded transaction and A occupies the property. It would also cover A giving a house to B who then sells the house and uses the proceeds to buy another property for A to occupy.

The *contribution* condition is satisfied if:

34.10

(a) another person acquires an interest in land (or chattels) occupied by the taxpayer;

(b) the taxpayer directly or indirectly has provided all or any of the consideration for the acquisition of that land otherwise than by way of an excluded transaction.

This will apply if A gives cash to B who purchases a house for A to occupy. Or A gives cash to B who purchases house 1, sells house 1 and then buys house 2 for A to occupy. It should not apply in the situation where A gives cash to B but B has his own resources to buy a house for A to occupy and uses the gifted funds for another purpose. Some sort of tracing exercise seems to be implied by the legislative words.

The word "provided" which is relevant to the contribution condition is not defined but presumably requires some element of bounty.[15] HMRC seem to accept this in that commercial loans are not regarded as provision. A more difficult question is whether interest-free loans satisfy the contribution condition. Nothing has been provided except the interest foregone. But how can the taxpayer be regarded as providing consideration for the acquisition of land: the "interest" which has not been paid does not exist and has not helped to acquire the land! Moreover, the loan remains part of the taxpayer's estate and is still owed. If a loan is "provision" what happens when it is repaid? Does the contribution condition cease to be satisfied and hence does the POA charge cease? HMRC accept that an interest-free loan does not satisfy the contribution condition at least where the funds have been lent by the occupier of the land.[16] On that basis a settlor who has lent funds to the property trust in a home loan scheme has not "provided" anything and hence if the house is sold and the trustees merely hold intangibles then no POA charge arises.[17]

---

[15] See Ch.7 for meaning of "*provided*" in income tax and capital gains tax contexts.
[16] See A2.188.
[17] Of course an interest-free loan by an individual to a trust would be sufficient to result in him being the settlor for income tax purposes: see Ch.7. Repayment of the loan might trigger further income tax consequences under the capital receipts provisions: see ITTOIA 2005 s.633 and Ch.7.

34.11 There are a number of excluded transactions in the case of the land and chattels charge in para.10 (these exclusions do not apply to relieve a taxpayer from the para.8 intangibles charge). Some of the exclusions may better be described as "safe harbours" rather than exclusions since a transaction can start off as an excluded transaction but later become chargeable. Paragraph 10(1) provides for what is an excluded transaction in relation to the disposal condition; para.10(2) provides for what is an excluded transaction in relation to the contribution condition.

34.12 There are five exclusions in respect of the *disposal* condition:

(i) *Full consideration.* This requires either a disposal of the taxpayer's whole interest in the property (except for any right expressly reserved over the property) either by a transaction made at arm's length with a person not connected with him or by a transaction such as might be expected to be made at arm's length between unconnected persons. A sale of part of the property to an unconnected party (or to a connected party before March 7, 2005) is also excluded as a result of SI 2005/724 reg.5. Commercial arrangements in this area frequently involve "equity-release schemes" and these are therefore outside the POA charge. By contrast, care needs to be exercised if equity release arrangements between members of the family are contemplated. The sale of part of a house to a child, albeit for full consideration, will lead to a POA charge unless exempted under the Regulations (motive is irrelevant).[18] Accordingly the only safe arrangement is as follows:

(a) Dad, who wishes to raise money on his property, carves out a lease for himself for (say) 20 years at a peppercorn rent;
(b) he then sells the freehold—encumbered by the lease—for full consideration.

Dad is protected by para.10 since he is selling his entire interest in the land save only for rights (the lease) which he has retained. There are attractions in this arrangement in terms of tax planning but note (i) that the children who purchase the freehold interest will suffer SDLT on the price paid and (ii) that they will need to have sufficient money to pay full consideration for the freehold. The sale cannot be financed by a gift of cash from Dad otherwise the contribution condition is satisfied and the exclusion does not apply.

(ii) *A transfer or sale to a spouse or (where ordered by the court) a former spouse.*[19] It is not necessary that the spouse is UK domiciled so that this exclusion is wider than the inheritance tax spouse exemption in IHTA 1984 s.18. It does not matter that the spouse subsequently gives the property back to the donor or settles it in trust for him.

---

[18] Of course, it may be that the taxpayer's benefit falls within the de minimis exclusion in cases where only a small interest is sold, see Sch.15 para.13.

[19] Spouse includes a registered civil partner. The transfer may be either a gift or a sale.

(iii) *Gifts (not sales) into trust where the spouse (including civil partner as above) or former spouse takes a beneficial interest in possession.* The exclusion only protects the settlor while the spousal interest in possession continues unless the spouse or former spouse dies.[20] Thus *Eversden* schemes where the spousal interest has already been terminated are subject to the POA charge and consideration should be given to unravelling these arrangements.[21] Although the provision does not state that if the spouse takes an absolute interest in the property (so that her interest in possession is enlarged) the exclusion still applies HMRC take this view. Note also that in HMRC's view the exclusion does not apply where the spouse does not take an interest in possession immediately after the assets are settled but instead the settlor starts off with an interest in possession. It is not necessary for the spouse to take a qualifying interest in possession.

(iv) *A disposal falling within IHTA 1984 s.11* (disposition for maintenance of family).

(v) *A disposal that is an outright gift to an individual and is exempt from IHT by virtue of either IHTA 1984, s.19 (annual exemption) or s.20 (small gifts).*

There are also five exclusions from the *contribution* condition as follows: **34.13**

(i) If the consideration was provided for that person's spouse (or if ordered by the Court, former spouse).

(ii) If on its acquisition property acquired by means of the contribution became settled property in which the spouse (or former spouse) was beneficially entitled to an interest in possession. There is a similar limitation on this exclusion to that discussed above in relation to the disposal condition.

(iii) The provision of the consideration is a disposition within ss.19 or 20 IHTA 1984.

(iv) The provision of the consideration is an outright gift within ss.19 or 20 IHTA 1984.

The above mirrors the exclusions from the disposal condition. The fifth exclusion is, however, only relevant to the contribution condition:

(v) The provision of the consideration was an outright gift of money (sterling or any other currency) and was made at least seven years before the earliest date on which the chargeable person occupied the land or had possession or use of the chattels (as the case may be). HMRC have accepted that cash gifts made before April 6, 1998 are always outside the POA charge.

---

[20] Paragraph 10(3).
[21] See 22.19.

34.14 Paragraph 8 applies to intangible property (excluding chattels, land or an interest in those assets) held in trust. Hence the charge only applies to settled property. Two conditions must be satisfied if the charge is to apply:

> (i) Any income arising under a trust would be treated as income of the settlor under s.624 ITTOIA 2005 if there were such income, although if only the spouse of the settlor (and not the settlor) can benefit then para.8 does not apply.

> (ii) The property in the settlement includes intangible property (including cash) which is or represents property which the individual "settled or added" to the trust after March 17, 1986.

34.15 Whether or not there is a charge therefore depends on:

> (a) the nature of the assets held in the trust: if land or chattels paras 8–9 cannot apply;

> (b) the settlor retaining some sort of interest—note that if the settlor retains an interest the fact that his spouse may have an interest in possession in the settled property will not protect him since para.10 does not apply to intangibles. However, if the spouse alone retains the interest and the settlor cannot benefit then no para.8 charge arises even though the income will be taxed as the settlor's under s.624[22]; and

> (c) the person adding or settling property. So if X lent property to a trust and that loan was repayable on demand, para.8 does not apply.

EXAMPLE 34.2

> In 2005 Dan transfers chattels into a trust in which he retains a remainder interest. Consider these alternatives:

> > (i) He does not use the chattels. HMRC accepts that he has not reserved a benefit (the remainder interest was a retained right); nor will a POA charge under para.6 apply (since he is not in possession/ using the chattels). If the trustees sell the chattels and keep the funds in cash, Dan becomes subject to an income tax charge under para.9. If the trustees then use the cash to purchase land which is let, Dan ceases to be subject to an income tax charge under para.9.

> > (ii) Dan used the chattels but his spouse had an interest in possession in the settlement. There is no POA charge because of the protection of para.10(1)(c) but on selling the chattels and retaining cash the trustees expose Dan to a POA charge even though the spousal interest in possession has not been terminated.

---

[22] See Ch.7 for full discussion of when a trust is settlor-interested.

The chargeable amount under para.9 is arrived at on the basis of interest at the **34.16** prescribed rate (currently four per cent) being charged on to the value of the property comprised in a settlement. In Example 34.2 above, Dan may suffer income tax under para.9 and, as a beneficiary of his trust; income tax under ITTOIA 2005 s.624 tax is still payable as well on the income in the trust. There is no credit for the s.624 income tax, only a deduction against the chargeable amount.

EXAMPLE 34.3

> In Example 34.2 if the trust fund is wholly invested in stocks and shares and worth £1 million and produces income of £40,000 gross, Dan pays income tax under s.624 on that income of (say) £16,000. He also pays para.9 POA tax on the chargeable amount being four per cent (the prescribed rate of interest in 2011–12) of £1 million, £40,000 less £16,000 = £24,000, so further income tax of £12,000 (50 % × 24,000) is due assuming Dan is a top rate taxpayer.

Paragraph 8 is principally aimed at insurance bonds and, in particular, **34.17** *Eversden*–type arrangements. Note, however, that where the settlor merely retains a remainder interest in certain insurance schemes or has affected a loan-and-gift trust, HMRC have accepted that he will not generally be caught by Sch.15.[23] The charge can apply unexpectedly where H starts off with a life interest which then ends and his spouse W takes an interest in possession. He needs to be excluded from any benefit on W's fund going forward. If the fund holds intangibles para.10 does not apply at all and even if the trust holds land or chattels occupied or used by W then para.10 does not apply if the property does not become settled at the time of the gift to the wife. This can be relevant in the context of divorces where a separate fund is carved out for wife from the husband's existing interest in possession. Ensure husband is excluded from any future benefit or consider a sub-fund election.[24]

VI EXEMPTIONS; THE EFFECT OF S.80 FA 2006 AND EXCLUDED LIABILITIES

The exemptions in para.11 apply to land, chattels and intangibles. The most **34.18** important are:

(i) Property in person's estate—para.11(1)the ownership exemption

The charge does not apply to a person at a time when his estate (for IHT purposes) includes the relevant property or property deriving its value from the relevant property (the latter being called here "the derived ownership exemption").

---

[23] See Ch.47.
[24] See Ch.11.

These exemptions mean that the charge will not apply if the property has been returned to the donor (i.e. if the original arrangement has been unscrambled) or if it is held in a trust under which the donor is entitled to a qualifying interest in possession or if he owns outright (or has a qualifying interest in possession in) shares in a company that owns the relevant property (e.g. land which he occupies). The changes in FA 2006 have limited this exemption in two ways.

34.19 *First*, the only qualifying interest in possession capable of being established by lifetime transfer post-March 21, 2006 is a disabled interest or a transitional serial interest. In the case of other interests in possession s.49(1) does not apply and so the property does not form part of the person's estate.

EXAMPLE 34.4

> B sells part of his house to his son for full value. The son then settles it on an interest in possession trust for B. If this settlement is made post-March 21, 2006 B does not take a qualifying interest in possession and therefore the property is not part of his estate for inheritance tax purposes. Hence, he is not protected from a POA charge under para.11(1) nor is he protected under the reservation of benefit provisions because the original disposal was a sale not a gift.

34.20 *Secondly*, s.80 amended para.11(1) Sch.15 with effect from December 5, 2005 so that there is no exemption if the taxpayer did not enjoy a qualifying interest in possession in the property when it was first settled but was appointed one subsequently. The revised legislation can apply if one of two conditions is satisfied:

(i) that the relevant property has ceased to be comprised in the person's estate for inheritance tax purposes (*condition 1*); or

(ii) that the person has directly or indirectly provided any consideration for the acquisition of the relevant property (*condition 2*);

and the following condition is satisfied.

The condition is that if at any subsequent time the relevant property (or derived property) becomes comprised in his estate as a result of IHTA 1984 s.49, then for POA purposes (but no other) the settlor is not treated as having an interest in possession nor as having reserved a benefit in the property. The result is that the settlor is subject to a POA charge because he loses the protection of paras 11(1) or 11(3).

34.21 The difficulty is that s.80 (which was aimed at reverter to settlor trusts)[25] does not distinguish between reverter to settlor trusts and any other trust set up after March 17, 1986 where the settlor has a qualifying interest in possession. It catches not only those transactions in which, for example, land was given away and ceased to be comprised in the settlor's estate but then came back into his estate (condition (i) above). It also catches transactions where the settlor contributed directly or indirectly to the property held in the trust (condition (ii) above).

---

[25] See Ch.37.

It is not generally possible to create new qualifying interest in possession **34.22**
trusts after March 21, 2006 unless the settlor was disabled but the provision
will catch all trusts with qualifying interests in possession established after
March 17, 1986 so B would be caught if he had given property to his son who
then settled it on interest in possession trusts for him before March 22, 2006.

In these circumstances the relevant property is not treated as comprised in
B's estate for the purposes of paras 11(1) and (2) with the result that the POA
charge applies.

The change does not just affect reverter to settlor trusts where, since there **34.23**
is no inheritance tax due on the death of the settlor B, it might be thought
reasonable to impose a POA charge. For example, it could apply where B
ceased to be entitled to a qualifying interest in possession because his wife or
a child took a qualifying interest in possession and he then took a qualifying
interest in possession back in the property at a later date. (It would not apply if
the beneficiary became absolutely entitled to the property rather than merely
taking back a qualifying interest in possession in it.)

Assume, for instance, that in 1987 H set up a trust in which he retains an
interest in possession to which he transferred cash and the trustees purchased
his house "Port Meadow". He may have done this for reasons that have nothing
to do with IHT saving (e.g. he may have been motivated by asset protection considerations or, in the case of US persons, a desire to avoid the need for probate).
The second condition in (ii) above has been satisfied (because the cash has been
spent purchasing the house) even though the property in the trust has always
been comprised in H's estate and H is within the POA charge from December 5,
2005. In fact HMRC do not take this point where the settlor has had a qualifying interest in possession throughout.[26] However, if H's interest in possession
had been ended in favour of son and then H took back an interest in possession
before October 5, 2008 (so it was a qualifying interest in possession: a TSI) then
the POA charge can apply. Paragraph 11(1) does not give protection.

It has a particularly adverse affect on foreign domiciliaries, many of whom
may have initially set up their excluded settlements as discretionary trusts with
cash gifted to the trustees offshore and which then purchased a UK property
(possibly through an offshore company) in which the foreign domiciliary lived.
Just before the house purchase (and before March 22, 2006) the trust was
converted to a qualifying interest in possession trust in order to avoid 10-year
charges on UK property.[27] The result is that property has left the foreign domiciliary's estate and then come back into it. That satisfies the conditions and so
the foreign domiciliary is liable to POA.[28] The foreign domiciliary can elect into
the reservation of benefit provisions and out of POA but results may arise.[29]

Excluded liabilities

In cases where the value of a person's estate is reduced because of an "excluded **34.24**
liability" the relevant property is only treated as comprised in his estate and so

---

[26] See A2.229.
[27] If the excluded property trust was converted into an interest in possession trust while still
holding offshore cash there was no exit charge. Often an excluded property trust started off as
a discretionary trust in order to avoid the IHTA 1984 s.80 charge outlined in Ch.31.
[28] See 34.40 for discussion on the effect of an election in these circumstances.
[29] See 34.26 and following. For the effect of s.80 on foreign domiciliaries generally, see 34.36
onwards.

exempt to the extent that its value exceeds the amount of the excluded liability. Note the following:

(i) a liability is an excluded liability if the creation of the liability and any transaction as a result of which the person's estate included the relevant property were "associated operations"[30];

(ii) in cases where the value attributed in the person's estate is substantially less than the value of the relevant property the exemption does not apply but there is a deduction in the chargeable amount "*by such proportion as is reasonable to take account of the inclusion of the property in his estate*".[31]

The restriction when there is an excluded liability is intended to prevent double-trust/home-loan schemes from falling outside the income tax charge. However, if the taxpayer's estate is not reduced by the excluded liability there is no charge. Consider for example the following:

EXAMPLE 34.5

> Trust 1 was set up by a foreign domiciliary in 1987 and was interest in possession for himself remainder to his wife. It was settled with cash and Trust 1 lent to another interest in possession trust (Trust 2). Trust 2 then purchased a UK house on the open market which is occupied by the foreign domiciliary. The value of the house was reduced by the debt but the debt remains excluded property.

In the above example if loans do not represent provision of consideration for the acquisition of an interest in the property, the contribution condition may not be satisfied anyway. In that event there is no POA charge even if the debt is an excluded liability. (The disposal condition has certainly not been satisfied.)

However, if the contribution has been satisfied, the excluded liability may not be a problem because the debt does not reduce the taxpayer's estate. It reduces his tax liability on his death because the house is reduced in value and the debt is a non-UK situs asset but that is not the same thing. On that basis the debt is an excluded liability but not a relevant excluded liability.[32]

(ii) Property already subject to a reservation of benefit—para.11(3)(5)(a)

34.25 If "*the property or any other property which derives its value from the relevant property would fall to be treated . . . as property subject to a reservation of benefit*" then the taxpayer is not subject to the POA charge. So in Example 34.2 above, if the settlement had been discretionary with Dan as one of the

---

[30] As defined in IHTA 1984 s.268.
[31] See para.11(2).
[32] For a consideration of home loan schemes in the context of foreign domiciliaries, see Ch.43.

beneficiaries, para.8 would not apply since the property would be subject to a reservation of benefit.[33]

(iii) Reservation of benefit let-out

There is an exemption if the gift would have been subject to the reservation-of-benefit provisions except for the s.102B(4) exemption.[34] Even if the original gift was cash and therefore the reservation-of-benefit provisions would not apply nevertheless there is no POA charge.[35] So, where a mother gives cash to her son and they then buy a house jointly, it is thought that there is no reservation of benefit (irrespective of s.102B) and no POA charge.[36]

Similarly, there is an exemption if the gifted property would have been subject to a reservation of benefit except for the let-outs in s.102C(3) and Sch.20 para.6 FA 1986.[37] The full-consideration let-out is the most important one. Despite rather obscure drafting HMRC accepts that "and" in para.11(5)(d) is disjunctive (otherwise the subsection cannot make sense) and therefore full-consideration arrangements involving both land and chattels are protected.[38]

34.26

EXAMPLE 34.6

(1) Father gifts chattels to his sons and pays full market rent for his continued use and enjoyment of them. He is not subject to either reservation of benefit or the POA charge. Similarly if he gives away his house but pays full consideration for his continued occupation, there is no charge.

If the rent is less than market rent, there will be a reservation of benefit and therefore there is still no POA charge because of the let-out in para.11(5)(a). If he gives cash to his son who then buys the chattels and father pays full consideration para.11(8) enables a POA charge to be avoided.[39]

(2) If father gives cash to his son who then buys a house jointly with his father and both occupy the house there is no reservation of benefit and exemption from the POA charge applies. Paragraph 11(8) again deals with this situation and provides that the restriction on tracing through outright gifts of cash is to be ignored, so that the reservation rules are capable of applying and accordingly the exemption for joint ownership and occupation consideration is available.

---

[33] It was accepted in the *Eversden* case that if a settlor could benefit under his discretionary trust he reserved a benefit: see Ch.33.
[34] Paragraph 11(5)(c).
[35] See para.11(3).
[36] See para.11(5)(c) and (8).
[37] Paragraph 11(5)(d).
[38] The consequences for chattel schemes are discussed in Ch.44.
[39] The reservation of benefit rules are treated as capable of applying and therefore the full consideration exemption is available.

34.27 Until December 5, 2005, foreign domiciliaries were, in most cases, protected from tax pre-owned assets charge. Two specific mechanisms afford protection: the let-outs given in para.12 and the para.11 exemptions which are available to taxpayers generally. There is also the basic territorial restriction that the POA charge does not apply to any person for any tax year during which he is not UK resident. This exclusion, in para.12(1), operates irrespective of the domicile of the taxpayer.

Reliefs relevant only to foreign domiciliaries

34.28 These are contained in paras.12(2) and (3) and are as follows:

(i) the basic relief in para.12(2) applies where an individual is not domiciled or deemed domiciled in the UK for IHT purposes and provides that the POA Regime does not apply unless the relevant property is situated in the UK[40];

(ii) in applying the POA Regime to a person who was at any time domiciled outside the UK for IHT purposes, no regard is had to foreign situs property which is excluded property by reason of being comprised in a settlement made by a settlor who was not domiciled in the UK when he made the settlement.[41]

Exemptions relevant to all taxpayers

34.29 The paras.11(1) and (3) exemptions apply regardless of the taxpayer's domicile and regardless of the situs of the property. They have been discussed already[42] but are illustrated in the context of foreign domiciliaries below. Few foreign domiciliaries will be concerned about the intangibles charge since para.8 can only apply if the settled property itself is UK situated intangibles. In most cases UK shares and cash will not be held directly by the trustees but through an offshore company and in that case, para.12(3) protects the offshore company shares and paras 8 and 9 do not apply to the UK shares and cash because they are not held by the trust direct. This contrasts with the charge on land and chattels which can apply whether the property is held directly by the trust or not.

EXAMPLE 34.7(1)

When domiciled in Norway in 1997, Sam set up a Jersey settlement under which she had a qualifying interest in possession. The settlement was

---

[40] See FA 2004 Sch.15 para.12(2).
[41] See FA 2004 Sch.15 para.12(3).
[42] See 34.18.

initially of cash and the trustees then formed a Jersey company which purchased a UK property in which Sam now lives (she has recently become deemed domiciled in the UK). It also holds some UK shares. In considering the effect of the POA charge, the settled property (the Jersey company shares) is, for IHT purposes, excluded property[43] and not subject to POA (being within para.12(3)). The UK house was[44] protected by para.11(1)(b): see Example 34.7(2). The UK shares are not caught by paras 8 and 9 since they are not settled property.

Paragraph 11(1)(b) provides that the POA Regime does not apply to an individual in respect of relevant property if that individual's estate includes property which derives its value from that relevant property ("derived ownership exemption"). **34.30**

EXAMPLE 34.7(2)

Continuing Example 34.7(1), the excluded property (the shares) are treated as comprised in her estate[45] for the purposes of the ownership exemption and those shares derive their value from the UK property occupied by Sam. If this is the case then the POA regime, as a result of the derived ownership exemption, will not[46] apply to the house occupied in the UK. If however, the value of the shares is "*substantially less*" than the value of the house then the POA regime will apply to the difference in value. This could be the case if the trustees lend money to the company to buy the house when HMRC consider that the value of the house is more than the value of the company and the loan does not derive its value from the house.[47]

The POA Regime does not apply to an individual by reference to any property in which he has reserved a benefit ("reserved benefit exemption").[48] The "excluded liabilities" rules do not apply so that even if the reserved benefit property is subject to an excluded liability this will not matter. **34.31**

EXAMPLE 34.8

X dies deemed domiciled in the UK having set up a discretionary trust under which he can benefit which owns non-UK situs property at a time

---

[43] See IHTA 1984 s.48(3).
[44] At least until December 5, 2005: see 34.20.
[45] See IHTA 1984 s.5(1) which provides that a person's estate is the aggregate of all the property to which he is beneficially entitled (as for instance settled property in which that person has a qualifying interest in possession) "except that the estate of a person *immediately before death* does not include excluded property". See also IHTA 1984 s.3(2) providing that the value of excluded property which ceases to form part of a person's estate as the result of a disposition shall not be a transfer of value.
[46] At least until December 5, 2005: see 34.20.
[47] See A2.190. Further, FA 2006 s.80 could now mean that para.11(1) does not apply to give protection because Sam has indirectly contributed to the purchase of a property that she now occupies: see 34.20 and Example 34.11(2).
[48] FA 2004 Sch.15 paras 11(3)(a) and (5)(a).

when he was domiciled outside the UK. On X's death there is no charge on the settled property because, as excluded property, it does not form part of X's estate immediately before he died. But this does not prevent the property from being property subject to a reservation and thereby (in terms of the POA charge) X obtaining the protection of para.11(5)(a).

34.32 The reservation of benefit exemption is extended by para.11(3)(b) to exempt property from the POA charge in which the donor reserves a benefit which derives its value from relevant property ("derivative reserved benefit exemption").

EXAMPLE 34.9

Jude, non-UK domiciled, set up a Jersey discretionary trust which incorporates a Jersey company to acquire a residential property in the UK. Some years later Jude becomes domiciled in the UK. He is a beneficiary of the trust and occupies the property. The IHT/POA analysis is as follows:

  (i) the settlement comprises excluded property (shares in the Jersey company);
  (ii) the property in the trust is not comprised (directly or indirectly) in Jude's estate (i.e. the ownership and derived ownership exemptions are not satisfied);
  (iii) Jude has however reserved a benefit in the property in the discretionary trust[49] (the shares) which derive their value from the UK property. Hence, as a result of the derived reserved benefit exemption the POA charge is excluded.

As with the derived ownership exemption if the trust had lent to the company to enable it to purchase the house then HMRC will not accept that the loan and the shares together derive their value from the house and consider that there may be a POA charge on the different between the value of the house and the value of the company shares. It is odd that HMRC consider that the value of the loan cannot be regarded as derived from the value of the house (rather than from the company's contractual undertakings) given that the loan could not be repaid if the company did not own the house. Foreign domiciliaries should self-assess making full disclosure of any loans if they disagree with the stated HMRC view and/or convert the loan to the company into share capital.

34.33 The legislation does not establish any hierarchy between the para.12 let-outs and the para.11 exemptions. In practice, it is simpler to apply the para.12 reliefs first and, unlike the para.11 exemptions, are not subject to any qualifications. In particular FA 2006 s.80 does not apply to property with para.12 protection.

---

[49] See *IRC v Eversden* [2003] STC 822, CA.

Hence, property contained in a settlement where the settlor has a qualifying **34.34** interest in possession, wherever such property was situate and whether or not owned through a corporate structure, was, as illustrated in the examples above, until December 2005 outside the POA Regime, because of either the para.12 or para.11 exemptions and even if the settlor later became UK domiciled. Similarly, discretionary trusts set up by non-UK domiciliaries were thought to be outside the POA Regime, even where the settled land or chattels were UK situs and owned through offshore companies, and even if the settlor became UK domiciled. This was because the para.12 reliefs were available to the foreign sited property and the para.11(3) exemption relieved the UK property.

There are, however, three ways in which POA can now be a problem for the **34.35** foreign domiciliary who are resident in the UK.

First, as noted above HMRC have now indicated that where a trust or settlor has lent money to a company which owns a house, the company shares are worth less than the house and the loan does not derive its value from the house. This can mean a POA charge on the difference between the value of the company shares and the house even though company shares and loan may be in the settlor's estate.

Secondly, many foreign domiciliaries purchased UK homes using two interest in possession trusts: one owning the debt and the other the house subject to the debt. The idea was that although the debt was an excluded liability within para.11(7), it did not reduce the value of the settlor's estate for POA purposes because he had an interest in possession in the trust which owned it.[50] Nevertheless, the debt reduced the value of the house for inheritance tax purposes. Such structures already in existence may not be affected but after March 21, 2006 it is not possible to create an inter vivos debt trust with a qualifying interest in possession.

Thirdly, and most seriously, FA 2006 s.80 has an adverse effect on foreign domiciliaries where the trust is or has been a qualifying interest in possession trust.

FA 2006 s.80[51]

This has been explained at 34.20 and may be a problem for foreign domicili- **34.36** aries with UK situated assets owned in trusts. Where the assets are non-UK situated and held in trust, the settlor can generally rely on the para.12 reliefs unless the non-UK situated asset is held through a company.[52]

In practice, HMRC accept that where the settlor has retained absolute ownership or a qualifying interest in possession in property or replacement property throughout the period of ownership there is no POA charge. There is also no POA charge if the property is foreign situate and held directly by the trustees because then it has the protection of para.12(3) and 11 is not needed. Nor is there a problem if the UK property is intangibles and held through a company because para.8 does not apply to such property (it only applies to settled intangibles) and no POA protection is needed. It is, of course, unlikely

[50] See para.11(6).
[51] See Ch.34 and FA 2004 Sch.15 paras 11(11) and (12).
[52] See below.

that trustees will hold UK shares directly because of 10-year charges. If the UK property is let land POA does not apply.

34.37   The effect of s.80 on foreign domiciliaries is therefore limited to the following:

>   (a) qualifying interest in possession trusts for someone other than the settlor or discretionary trusts but where the settlor now has a qualifying interest in possession in the property, i.e. the property had left his estate but is now comprised in it again because of IHTA 1984 s.49; and

>   (b) the trust must either own UK land occupied by the settlor or own foreign situate land occupied by the settlor and held in a company and the settlor is now deemed domiciled.[53]

34.38   In these circumstances what are the settlor's options?

>   (a) He can elect into reservation of benefit (although note he may be out of time for making the election unless HMRC accept a late election). The effect of this may not be adverse if by the time the settlor has died the UK property on which he has elected has been replaced by foreign property. In these circumstances the excluded property rules will take priority over the reservation of benefit rules so that any charge under FA 1986 s.102(3) is displaced.[54]

>   (b) The qualifying interest in possession can be ended and discretionary trusts arise. Paragraph 11(12) provides that the property is not "at the subsequent time" to have the protection of paras 11(1) or (3) while the qualifying interest in possession continues. But once the interest in possession has ended para.11(12) ceases to apply. Therefore the settlor obtains the protection of para.11(3) again. This is easy enough to engineer with foreign situated property held in a company even where the property is occupied by the settlor. It is also possible if UK sited property is held in a company but will be more awkward where the UK property is held directly by the trustees.

EXAMPLE 34.10

>   B, a foreign domiciliary, set up a discretionary trust with cash. He remained a beneficiary. The trust then funded a company which bought a UK house.[55] In 2005, the trust was converted into an interest in possession trust for B. If UK real property is occupied by B which is owned by the trustees through the company or directly he is now subject to POA. There is no POA on any UK or foreign shares held in the company structure.

>   If the trust had been interest in possession for B from the outset, HMRC accept that B is not caught by s.80. Nor does it matter if B always had

---

[53] Such property would not have the protection of para.12(3) and therefore would need the protection of para.11(1) or (3).

[54] See also 34.42 for further details of the effect of an election where the taxpayer has a qualifying IIP.

[55] Or possibly holds UK investments.

a qualifying interest in possession and this is now ended so that discretionary trusts arise. In that case the property has now left his estate but it has not come back into it even if he is given an interest in possession later since that interest in possession cannot be qualifying.[56]

Foreign domiciliaries setting up trusts or converting discretionary trusts into interest in possession on or after March 22, 2006 do not need to worry about s.80 because the interest in possession will not be qualifying.   **34.39**

VIII ELECTING INTO GWR

Paragraph 21 provides for a right of election in respect of chattels and land;   **34.40**
para.22 in respect of intangibles. The effect of the election is that the donor is taxed as if he had reserved a benefit in the relevant property which will therefore be taxed as part of his estate for inheritance tax purposes on his death. The POA charge does not apply. The relief is limited; it does not put the individual who has undertaken tax planning in the same position as if the planning had never been undertaken. For example, there is no base cost uplift for capital gains tax purposes on his death so that the donee may face capital gains tax charges on a disposal of the property (particularly in relation to *Ingram* schemes) and the property remains part of the donee's estate under general inheritance tax principles.[57]

In addition in some cases (e.g. *Eversden* schemes) it may be that the property is taxed as part of the original donor's estate but someone else (in this case the spouse) will have made a PET. There is then the possibility of a double inheritance tax charge which is not relieved by the double charges regulations. (By contrast, if the donor has made the PET and reserved a benefit there is relief against a double charge.) Thus some thought must be given as to whether or not an election is the best option.

The donor is not required to notify the donee when making the election   **34.41**
even though the donee will be primarily liable for the inheritance tax due on the donor's death. The legislation provides that the election must be made by January 31 following the end of the initial year (being the first year for which the POA charge applies to the individual in respect of the particular property, etc.) and cannot be revoked after that date although the effect of the election will fall away if the use and enjoyment of the property ceases (the individual will then make a deemed PET under FA 1986 s.102(4)).

The election and interest in possession trusts

If the taxpayer making the election is entitled to an interest in possession in   **34.42**
the relevant property (whether land, chattels or intangibles) then the election

---

[56] Of course if B is deemed UK domiciled there could be adverse inheritance tax implications if his current qualifying interest in possession is ended when IHTA 1984 s.80 may apply so that the property then falls within the relevant property regime of 10-year charges: see Ch.31.
[57] All of which serves to emphasise the penal aspect of the reservation of benefit rules.

disapplies Sch.15 (so there is no POA charge) but paras 21(2) and 22(2) were amended in FA 2006[58] to provide that:

> "(a) the chargeable proportion of the property is to be treated for the purposes of Part 5 of the 1986 Act [reservation of benefit] . . . as property subject to a reservation but only so far as the chargeable person is not beneficially entitled to an interest in possession in the property;

> (b) section 102(3) and (4) of that Act shall apply but only so far as the chargeable person is not beneficially entitled to an interest in possession in the property and

> If the chargeable person is beneficially entitled to an interest in possession in the property sections 53(3) and (4) and 54 of IHTA (reverter to settlor etc) shall not apply in relation to the chargeable proportion of the property."

The end result of all this is as follows:

(1) for those who set up reverter to settlor trusts, there is no longer reverter to settlor relief if the life tenant makes an election.[59] Before March 2006 an individual might give property to his son who then settled it on qualifying interest in possession trusts for his father. On father's death the trust ended in favour of son. Father did not pay POA charge (because he had a qualifying interest in possession and was therefore protected by para.11(1)) and he avoided an inheritance tax charge on death (because father had a qualifying interest in possession which then reverted to the settlor (who was not the original donor). There was no reservation of benefit because s.102(3) disapplies the reservation of benefit provisions as there was a qualifying interest in possession.

EXAMPLE 34.11

A carried out an *Ingram* scheme some years ago in favour of son B. Because of the introduction of the POA charge, in 2005 the scheme was dismantled and B took the property outright. He then settled it on trust for A. The idea was that on A's death the property would revert to B and with the benefit of the reverter to settlor exemption. No reservation of benefit problem arose for A because s.102(3) disapplies the reservation of benefit provisions where the life tenant has a qualifying interest in possession and there was no POA for A because he had a qualifying interest in possession. If, because of the changed POA rules, A makes an election, the effect is that there is no reverter to settlor relief on the property. The son suddenly finds that he faces an inheritance tax charge on the death of his father A!

---

[58] This was related to the s.80 amendment to deal with reverter to settlor trusts, see below.
[59] See 37.28 for further explanation.

(2) As we have seen, s.80 extends much further than reverter to settlor trusts. If a foreign domiciliary elects, then he is treated as having a reservation of benefit on his death but only to the extent that he does not have an interest in possession in the property. So if say the house is held directly by the trust and he has an interest in possession in the whole and elects then there is no POA charge and on his death the position is exactly the same as before—the interest in possession provisions take priority. If by that time the house has been sold and the proceeds invested abroad there is no inheritance tax charge because it is excluded property. If however the house is owned by a company then there would be a charge on A's death because A has an interest in possession in the company shares not the house. Therefore, the house would be fully taxed on his death as a result of the election.

(3) Home loans have always been structured so as to give the settlor an interest in possession. The effect of para.21 seems to be to nullify the adverse inheritance tax effects of an election on home loan schemes. He was beneficially entitled to an interest in possession in the property prior to the election and remains so after the election. On his death there seems no reason why the loan does not continue to be deductible.[60]

Time limits

If the taxpayer is within the de minimis £5,000 exemption (so his taxable benefit did not exceed this limit) then no POA is due and the time limit for making an election does not run.

EXAMPLE 34.12

Miranda sold 20 per cent of her house to her son in April 2006. This is a disposal of land which is within POA since her son is a connected party. However, the taxable benefit is 20 per cent of the market rent in April 2006. That rent is less than £5,000. No POA charge is due. No election need to be (or can be) made. In April 2011 after five years the rental value is reassessed at £8,000 which is over the de minimis limit. Miranda can make an election in January 2013.

Technical difficulties

So far as the form of the election is concerned, HMRC produced Form IHT 500 which they indicated should be completed and sent to Capital Taxes at Nottingham. However, it subsequently transpired that this process suffered from a major procedural defect as follows:

34.43

---

[60] See Ch.43.

(1) the legislation requires the election to be made *"in the prescribed manner"*[61];

(2) *"prescribed"* means *"prescribed by regulations"*;

(3) at the relevant filing date, which was January 31, 2007 for existing schemes, whilst HMRC had issued Form 500 no regulations had been made and hence that form had no legal force and taxpayers who sent in the form make an election in the prescribed manner.

Regulations were subsequently issued[62] which came into effect on November 14, 2007 but nothing was done to deal with the position regarding elections made before that date. Specifically, these regulations do not purport to have (not is it possible to see how they could have) retrospective or retroactive effect.

It is therefore considered that taxpayers must be free to withdraw the form submitted in cases where they elected prior to November 14 (on the basis that such an election would have had no validity anyway) if they wish to retain the IHT benefits of the arrangement which they entered into. They will of course, then be exposed to a POA charge from April 6, 2005. In some cases this may be worthwhile.

EXAMPLE 34.13

Chris, a widower, entered into an Ingram scheme in 1997. He became subject to a POA charge from April 6, 2005.[63] To avoid this he decided to make an election and sent the form in on January 31, 2007. In March 2008 he died unexpectedly. His executors cannot revoke an election if valid but in these circumstances the authors believe that it is an invalid election which they could withdraw. His estate would have to pay POA from April 2005 until March 2008 but the house would not be brought back into charge to inheritance tax on his death.

34.44 It is also far from certain that the election will operate in the way envisaged by HMRC. In particular, all that it does is to treat the property as comprised in the taxpayer's estate at death but normal principles of valuation would then seem to apply so that if the property is burdened by a debt (as is the case in home loan/double trust schemes) then it is only the net value of that property which is subject to IHT. This argument would, of course, be strengthened if the debt were to be charged against the property.[64]

There is a limited power in the legislation for HMRC to accept late elections.[65]

---

[61] See FA 2004 Sch.15 para.23(2).

[62] See SI 2007/3000.

[63] See Ch.43.

[64] See Ch.32 for further discussion about whether debts can reduced the value of property in which a reservation of benefit subsists. Of course debts of the taxpayer's free estate cannot reduce the inheritance tax charged on his death in respect of property that is deemed to be part of his estate on death under the reservation of benefit provisions. But if the property in which the reserved benefit subsists is itself reduced in value by debt then this should be taken into account: see IHTM 14401 and Ch.32.

[65] FA 2007 s.65 see also published HMRC guidance indicating the circumstances in which they will accept a late election:

An election can prove problematic for married couples on the first death **34.45** when the spouse exemption may not be available.[66] However, the FA 2006 changes may have made this less of an issue since the settlor is treated as retaining an interest in possession in the property even after the election has been made and therefore HMRC would presumably accept that spouse exemption is available.

If a person elects, but then pays full consideration for the use of land or chattels on or immediately before making the election, there is no deemed PET and the let out in Sch.20 para.6 applies. The effect is that as long as the person continues to pay full consideration while using the land or chattel, the reservation of benefit rules are disapplied. HMRC accept that in this case no PET arises from making the election and paying full consideration "so long as the taxpayer is paying full consideration at the point of election".[67]

In addition, HMRC consider that if a person elects and then the scheme is dismantled, e.g. the property is appointed back to him so it becomes part of his estate, there is no deemed PET under s.102(4) and the IHT effect of the election falls away.[68]

The Double Charges Regulations 2005 provide some relief from a double **34.46** charge where a home loan scheme has been unscrambled with the debt being written off.[69]

"There may be cases where, given the overall circumstances, we will accept a late election even where the chargeable person cannot show that the reasons for the late election were beyond their control. Essentially, this will be where the chargeable person can show that they were unaware – and could not reasonably have been aware – that they were liable to an income tax charge under this Schedule, and elected within a reasonable time of becoming so aware.

It is likely that such cases will involve a number of relevant features. The chargeable person or their agent should send with their late election a full explanation of the factors that they wish to be taken into account, which may cover (but need not be limited to):

- the nature of the arrangement that led to an income tax charge arising;

- when the arrangement was put in place;

- the advice the chargeable person received at the time the arrangement was put in place and, if later, when this Schedule came into force;

- the circumstances in which they became aware of their liability to an income tax charge under this Schedule;

- any other notable features.

We will only accept a late election where the chargeable person can show that their failure to elect by the relevant filing date is not a result of:

- their taking active steps to avoid both an income tax charge under this Schedule and an inheritance tax charge by virtue of the Gift with Reservation provisions;

- the wish to avoid committing to either an income tax charge or an election pending clarification of the effects of making such a commitment."

[66] See A2.147.
[67] See A2.144.
[68] See A2.144.
[69] SI 2005/3441.

EXAMPLE 34.14

A effected a home loan scheme in 2003. He sold (leaving the price outstanding as a debt) his house to an interest in possession trust for himself and gave away the debt to an interest in possession trust for his children. As a result of the POA charge he wishes to unscramble the scheme and the children and trustees of the debt trust agree to write off the debt. The full value of his house is therefore subject to inheritance tax again. If he dies before 2010, however, he will suffer inheritance tax on the failed PET. Effectively inheritance tax would be charged twice on the same economic value and so there is double charges relief in these circumstances with inheritance tax being paid on the higher of the value of the house or the failed PET but not both. Note that A will pay the POA charge for the period from April 6, 2005 to the date the debt is released unless he makes an election. The children make PETs when the debt is written off if the house is held by A absolutely at the date of the write off. Where the house is still in the trust, the question is whether the addition of value by the children to an existing interest in possession trust for A constitutes a chargeable transfer post-March 21, 2006.[70] It is preferable that the house is removed from the trust before the debt is written off. SDLT charges may be avoided if care is used.

Note however that HMRC accept that where a home loan scheme is dismantled and an election is made, there is no POA due even from April 6, 2005 to the date when the home loan scheme is dismantled. The election is deemed to be effective from April 6, 2005.[71]

[70] See FA 2006 Sch.20.
[71] See correspondence with HMRC on this point at A2.144.

PART V: SPECIALIST TOPICS

This part looks at a number of specialist topics in some detail. Ch.35 considers the taxation of trusts set up for minors and older children. It discusses the options open to parents and other relatives, such as grandparents, who want to make provision for minors and looks in detail at the tax treatment of bereaved minor and 18–25 trusts. Ch.36 considers the tax treatment (income tax, capital gains tax and inheritance tax) of trusts for disabled and other vulnerable beneficiaries. It also considers dispositions for the maintenance of the family. Ch.37 looks at the capital gains, inheritance tax and pre-owned assets income tax treatment of reverter to settlor trusts and the impact of the changes that came into force on December 5, 2005. Ch.38 looks at will drafting and Ch.40 tax issues for personal representatives. Ch.39 examines deeds of variation and two year discretionary trusts whilst Ch.41 considers pilot trusts. Ch.42 deals with bare trusts, their disadvantages and advantages. Chs 43 and 44 cover the inheritance tax and capital gains tax treatment of the family home and chattels. This includes a discussion of main residence relief, the unwinding of house schemes, current options for minimising inheritance tax on the family home, and the position of foreign domiciliaries buying UK property and buying and selling art. Chs 45 and 46 cover business and agricultural property relief. There are then three "commercial" chapters: Ch.47 on life insurance products; Ch.48 pension arrangements and Ch.49 the controversial topic of EBTs. Ch.50 is concerned with trusts in the context of divorce and looks at nuptial settlements, trusts as a financial resource and the impact of the FA 2006 changes. Ch.51 provides an overview of stamp duties. Ch.53 deals with offshore income gains. Ch.52 covers partnerships and Ch.53 offshore income gains. Ch.54 deals with the taxation of non-resident companies, Ch.55 contains a checklist for private clients and trusts with planning ideas, and Ch.56 covers disclosure, compliance and reporting of tax liabilities.

CHAPTER 35

TRUSTS FOR MINORS AND FOR OLDER CHILDREN

- Lifetime options (**35.03**)
- Providing for children and minors by will including priority of trusts (**35.12**)
- Bereaved Minor Trusts (BMTs) including comparison with A-M trusts and pecking order (**35.17**)
- 18–25 (s.71D) Trusts; relationship with IPDIs and other trusts; interaction with s.144 (**35.35**)
- Other death options (**35.56**)

Precedents:

A1.6   Bereaved minor trust
A1.7   18–25 trust (s.71D)
A1.10 IPDI trust for minor children

The IHT changes that came into effect from March 22, 2006 mean that: **35.01**

(i) the setting up of any lifetime trust is—unless it contained a "disabled person's interest"[1]—immediately chargeable for IHT purposes. It does not matter that the trust is set up for the benefit of the settlor's children, grandchildren or other beneficiaries. There are no longer special rules for trusts for beneficiaries under a specified age.

(ii) there are special rules, however, for two will trusts but only if these are established by a testator for his own children. First, "bereaved minor trusts", which receive the same IHT treatment as s.71 accumulation and maintenance trusts (no anniversary or exit charge), but which require capital to vest in the child no later than the age of 18. Secondly, "18–25 trusts" which, as the name suggests, enable the capital to vest at any time up until age 25 but which levy an IHT charge if the beneficiary receives capital after 18 or the trusts continue after the beneficiary has reached 25. The maximum charge is at a rate of 4.2 per cent. (This may be seen as a "fine" for continuing to use the trust structure once adulthood is reached.)

Nothing is served by continuing to draft trusts in a form which was designed   **35.02**
to satisfy the conditions in IHTA 1984 s.71 (i.e. as an old style accumulation

---

[1] See IHTA 1984 s.89B inserted by FA 2006 Sch.20 para.6, and Ch.36.

and maintenance trust) since the IHT advantages have now been withdrawn.[2] Instead, the following options need to be considered by a would-be settlor or testator.

I LIFETIME OPTIONS

Discretionary trusts

35.03 In many cases a discretionary trust will be what the settlor really wants, but before March 22, 2006 he had been put off by the adverse tax consequences. These boil down to the inheritance tax charge at lifetime rates of 0 per cent and 20 per cent (for the tax year 2011–12) when the trust is established inter vivos, and thereafter to anniversary and exit charges.[3] If these charges either do not arise, or can be shown to be manageable, a discretionary trust should be used whenever the settlor wants his trustees to have the flexibility to "pick and choose" between an unlimited class of beneficiaries. Further, if the value of the property to be settled falls within the settlor's IHT nil rate band, or if it comprises property qualifying for 100 per cent business or agricultural property[4] relief, not only will the creation of the trust be free from an inheritance tax charge, but it may well be that subsequent 10-year anniversaries will pass without any charge to tax arising.[5] Even if IHT is payable during the continuance of the trust, the charges currently imposed on discretionary trusts are relatively light: the maximum anniversary charge is levied at only six per cent (tax year 2011–12), whilst exit charges attract tax at only a fraction of that rate.[6]

35.04 Relevant property trusts (including but not limited to discretionary trusts) possess a tax benefit in that CGT hold-over relief may be available both on creation and termination.[7] This is a major advantage of settled as opposed to

---

[2] The position of s.71 accumulation and maintenance trusts already extant on March 22, 2006 is considered in Ch.30.

[3] As to the taxation of discretionary trusts see Ch.29. The truly cautious (some might say wise) would also point out that in recent years governments have been committed to rooting out tax avoidance. Labour Governments, in particular, have shown a deep suspicion of all types of trust, but especially the type of flexible trust epitomised by the full blown discretionary trust. Indeed, the Capital Transfer Tax legislation introduced in 1975 for such "no interest in possession trusts" was widely seen as penal and a form of transitional relief was introduced to enable trustees (at a cut price rate) to switch into a more acceptable form. The current top rate of tax levied at 10-yearly anniversaries is 6% (being 30% of the top lifetime IHT rate which is 20%). This can hardly be described as penal. However, there are fears that the rate will increase in the future: for instance if 50% of the lifetime rate were to be charged this would equate to a 10% charge every 10 years or an annual trust wealth tax of 1%.

[4] See Chs 45 and 46.

[5] This will depend upon: (a) continuance of business and agricultural property reliefs at 100% and the retention of qualifying property; (b) no reduction in the level of the nil-rate band; and (c) increases in the nil-rate band in line with increases in the value of the assets settled.

[6] When it is appreciated that, if the life tenant of a qualifying interest in possession trust dies, tax may be charged at the 40% rate, the relative generosity of the discretionary trust charges becomes apparent. Of course the charge on the ending of an interest in possession was frequently avoided, or at least postponed, by ensuring that the deceased's spouse enjoyed a successive life interest. Judicious use of overriding powers of appointment to terminate the interest in possession (triggering, usually, a potentially exempt transfer by that beneficiary) were also used to avoid the charge.

[7] TCGA 1992 s.260 as amended.

unsettled gifts, because all too often in lifetime estate planning the attractions of the IHT potentially exempt transfer regime are offset by the CGT charge that would arise if a gift were made.[8] An important qualification needs to be made, however, since if the trust is settlor-interested CGT hold-over relief is not available on its creation. Prior to April 6, 2006 a trust was only settlor interested if:

(i) the settlor, or

(ii) the spouse (including, from December 5, 2005, a civil partner) of the settlor,

could benefit under its terms. From April 6, 2006, however, the concept of a settlor-interested trust was extended to include a trust capable of benefiting a dependent child of the settlor.[9]

EXAMPLE 35.1

Richard's first grandchild is born on January 1, 2011 and he determines to establish a trust for the benefit of that child and future grandchildren. He plans to settle (a) a cash sum and (b) investment properties showing a substantial gain.

(1) Before March 22, 2006 his alternatives were:

(a) *an accumulation and maintenance trust*: this was the most likely choice given the age of the one child, and would have been a PET by him for IHT purposes. The main advantages over options (b) and (c) were that it left open the possibility of other children being born later and benefiting and did not give the child an entitlement to income (or capital) at too early an age.

(b) *a bare trust for the child*: this would have been a PET but it was an unlikely option unless Richard was happy for the child to take the trust fund outright at 18.

(c) *an interest in possession trust for the child*: TA 1925 s.31 would need to be excluded. Again this would have been a PET by Richard.

(d) *a discretionary trust*: this would have been a chargeable transfer for inheritance tax purposes but CGT hold-over relief would have been available on the investment properties which was not the case on the other three options.

(2) Since March 22, 2006 Richard has the following options:

(a) if he wants a trust structure then he will make an immediately chargeable transfer for IHT purposes. Accordingly once the value

---

[8] Hold-over relief into a relevant property trust is available even in cases where IHT is not payable because of the availability of the settlor's nil-rate band provided that the trust is not settlor-interested. Hence the attraction of "nil-rate band" discretionary trusts, see Ch.38.

[9] TCGA 1992 ss.169B, 169F as amended by FA 2006. Note that the limitation on hold-over relief does not apply if the settlor does not have dependent children albeit that if he did they could benefit and nor does it prevent hold-over relief being available on payments out of a settlor-interested trust. Settlor-interested trusts are considered in detail in Ch.7 and hold-over relief in Ch.18.

transferred exceeds his available IHT nil rate band (£325,000 for 2011–12) tax at 20 per cent is charged on the excess whatever type of trust is used (apart from a bare trust). If he wishes to settle property worth more than his nil rate band he may still avoid an IHT charge by transferring assets to his wife who makes a similar settlement within her IHT nil rate band.[10] In that way either a single trust worth £650,000[11] or two nil rate band trusts can be set up;

(b) so far as CGT is concerned any cash settled will not create problems and, provided that the trust that he establishes is not settlor-interested (or a bare trust) CGT hold-over relief will be available under TCGA 1992 s.260 in respect of the investment properties;

(c) in terms of the type of trust to be set up, Richard is now freed from the constraints of s.71 (which had to be observed if an accumulation and maintenance trust was to be used) and, given

- that he only has one grandchild, and
- that there is no guarantee that others will be born,

it will be important that he includes other beneficiaries than just grandchildren. It will, for instance, be sensible to include his children as beneficiaries albeit that his wish is to provide for the later generation.[12]

35.05 Richard's options are therefore more limited under the new regime. In one respect though, the tax position is better. Previously if a child was given entitlement to income the settled property would be treated as part of his estate for inheritance tax purposes. Hence, an inter vivos termination of that interest would generally constitute a PET. If Richard now settles assets on interest in possession trusts for his grandchild, this is a chargeable transfer for inheritance tax purposes but the settled property is not treated as part of the child's estate for inheritance tax purposes. The settled property remains within the relevant property regime. This gives the trustees flexibility to change who has entitlement to income without having to worry about any inheritance tax consequences. For example, the eldest grandchild could be given an initial interest in possession in the whole fund (which has attractions in avoiding the 50 per cent income tax rate).[13] If another grandchild is born later, the interest in possession of the first grandchild could be terminated by the trustees in whole or part. That would be a non-event for inheritance tax purposes. Richard can be a trustee and so have a decisive voice in who is to benefit. Income tax compliance is generally easier under an interest in possession trust and the tax treatment of dividend income which is paid out to a beneficiary significantly improved.[14]

Of course, if Richard does not want the grandchildren to be given entitlement to income he may incline to a discretionary trust. Whatever type of trust is used, he can be a trustee and he should supplement the trust with a non-binding letter of wishes which would doubtless be used by the trustees after

[10] Inter-spouse transfers are taxed at no gain no loss: see TCGA 1992 s.58.
[11] Administratively a single trust has attractions: for IHT purposes because there are joint settlors, tax will be charged on the basis that there are two separate trusts. For CGT purposes only a single trust annual exemption will be available, see Ch.11.
[12] This will not give rise to CGT hold-over restrictions provided that *none of his children* is a minor: see Ch.7.
[13] See Ch.6.
[14] See further on flexible interest in possession trusts, 27.05 and 6.41.

his death to determine the direction of the trust. For instance, in the future the class of beneficiaries could be limited to grandchildren and their issue and interests in possession in the trust property for each of the grandchildren could be created or varied as the trustees determine.

As an alternative to using a trust structure, Richard might consider trans- **35.06** ferring the property to a bare trust for the grandchild. Whilst this would have the attraction of being a PET[15] and the grandchild would not, of course, be able to demand either income or capital from the property until he was 18 it is unlikely that these factors will outweigh the disadvantages of:

- no CGT hold-over relief on the creation of the trust for the investment properties;
- Richard would then not create a fund for grandchildren as a class but be making a gift to a single grandchild;
- the child takes capital and income at 18[16] so that there is a lack of flexibility.

Interest in possession trusts

Before March 22, 2006, interest in possession trusts were commonly drafted **35.07** to incorporate a substantial element of flexibility; for example:

(a) the trustees were given power to advance capital to the interest in possession beneficiary[17]; and

(b) the trustees were given overriding powers of appointment which could be used to terminate the interest in possession in whole or in part.

Including provisions such as these explains why such trusts were seen as an alternative to the "pure" discretionary trust. Other factors that encouraged this use were:

(i) the creation of an interest in possession trust inter vivos was a potentially exempt transfer[18];

(ii) the trusts did not suffer IHT anniversary or exit charges[19];

(iii) there was no need to satisfy the onerous conditions for a qualifying accumulation and maintenance trust;

(iv) the termination of the interest in possession by the exercise of overriding powers vested in the trustees commonly resulted in the (former) benefici-

---

[15] For IHT purposes, a bare trust is not a settlement and so the transfer would be treated as an outright gift to the minor beneficiary: see Ch.42.

[16] See Ch.42 for a consideration of the use of the power of advancement to postpone vesting of capital on bare trusts.

[17] In some cases, the interest in possession beneficiary was given the right to call for all or a part of the capital which the trustees might then have been obliged to pay or transfer to him, or which they could only refuse to do by a unanimous resolution.

[18] IHTA 1984 s.3A(2) as inserted by FA 1986 s.101, Sch.19 para.1 and amended by the F(No.2)A 1987 ss.96(1), (2), 104, Sch.9 Pt III.

[19] Although note the charge that arose on the death of the life tenant: see IHTA 1984 s.49(1).

ary making a potentially exempt transfer and the settlement continuing so that no liability to CGT arose; and

(v) a flexible interest in possession trust was used as a vehicle to protect a beneficiary against profligacy and the assets against third party claims.[20]

35.08 However, it always had to be borne in mind that if an interest in possession trust was selected, the death of the beneficiary could result in a substantial IHT charge which was payable by the trustees.[21] It was common therefore for interest in possession trusts to be used for older children (typically over the age of 18) and under that age for the accumulation and maintenance trust to be used. In the (rare) situation where it was desired to give a minor beneficiary an interest in possession, it was important to exclude s.31 of TA 1925 which has the effect of replacing the interest in possession with a power to pay income and to accumulate—during minority—any balance which would only be paid to the minor if he attained 18.[22]

35.09 As Example 35.1 illustrates, however, the position was radically altered by the March 22, 2006 changes. From that date any inter vivos settlement established with an interest in possession has been taxed as a relevant property settlement (unless it involves a disabled person's interest). With this caveat the decision about which type of trust should be used can be taken in the knowledge that the IHT charges on the trust will be the same in all cases.

35.10 For the taxpayer the question is therefore whether he wants to give a right to income to one or more of the beneficiaries. It may be appropriate if the trust is for his children who are in their twenties who may need the income, or if income is going to be paid out to a beneficiary anyway (e.g. to pay school fees), or the trustees want to avoid paying income tax at the 50 per cent trust rate.[23] There are settlors who prefer fixed trusts with the certainty that is provided to the flexibility of the discretionary trust. And, of course, a change in the trust (e.g. on the death of a life tenant or inter vivos termination of his interest in possession) is not a chargeable occasion. IHT charges will only arise every 10 years and when the trust ends.

Bare trusts

35.11 Settlors are sometimes attracted to the idea of creating a trust for the absolute benefit of a minor and the attractions have undoubtedly increased as a result of the 2006 changes in the IHT treatment of settlements. The creation of the trust is a PET because the beneficiary is treated as the owner of the property and so the settlement rules, and anniversary and exit charges, do not apply. The disadvantages of the arrangement are that:

(a) the beneficiary will become entitled to income and capital at age 18 (unless the power of advancement is exercised)[24]; and

---

[20] On protective trusts, see 28.09.
[21] IHTA 1984 s.200(1)(b). In such cases, the life tenant (or trustees) might take out life insurance to cover the tax exposure.
[22] For a suitable exclusion clause, see A1.2 and A1.19.
[23] See Ch.6.
[24] See Ch.42 for a consideration of the implications of this.

(b) on his death inheritance tax will be charged on the value of the settled property which will (whilst he remains a minor) pass on intestacy.[25]

II PROVIDING FOR CHILDREN AND MINORS BY WILL INCLUDING PRIORITY OF TRUSTS

Even after the March 2006 changes, testators have a range of possible trusts that can be used for young children and grandchildren in their wills. These comprise:

    35.12

(i) a qualifying interest in possession trust: (an IPDI)[26] in which the trust property is for IHT purposes treated as belonging to the relevant beneficiary[27];

(ii) a bereaved minor trust: only available for minor children of the testator;

(iii) an 18–25 (s.71D trust): again only available for children of the testator;

(iv) a bare trust;

(v) a discretionary trust (a relevant property settlement).

Priority of trusts

The pecking order of trusts is as follows:

    35.13

(i) BMT takes priority over all others; followed by

(ii) IPDI; and then

(iii) 18–25 trust;

(iv) relevant property trust.

Hence, a will trust for "my children at 25" giving them immediate entitlement to income on death is an IPDI not an 18–25 trust. Similarly, "capital to my children at 18" but giving them income entitlement within two years of death while still minors is a BMT not an IPDI.[28]

---

[25] A bare trust is not a settlement for IHT purposes: see Ch.42. A transfer into a bare trust will therefore be potentially exempt. The income of the trust will be taxed on the settlor if he is the parent of the beneficiary: see ITTOIA 2005 s.629(1)(b). However, the capital is treated as belonging to the minor and so his capital gains tax annual exemption will be available to set against trust gains: see TCGA 1992 s.60.

[26] These have been considered in detail in Ch.28.

[27] Under IHTA 1984 s.49(1).

[28] Beware the effect of s.144. If, say, settled property is held "*on trust for my children living at my death in equal shares at 25*" and one child is 18 at the testator's death or becomes 18 within two years of death, unless TA 1925 s.31 has been modified he takes an IPDI not an 18–25 interest. Section 144 provides for automatic reading-back. The fact that the trustees have not exercised any powers is irrelevant: see Ch.39 and also Example 35.11 below.

35.14   As discussed in Ch.38, before October 9, 2007 the standard family will—made with an eye to IHT saving—normally involved on the death of the first spouse:

(i) use of the IHT nil rate band;

(ii) a spouse exempt gift of residue.

The nil rate band could, of course, have been utilised by making a settled gift to children/grandchildren using one of the trusts listed above but in many cases the preferred option was a nil rate band discretionary trust incorporating debt/charge clauses. The introduction of the transferable unused nil rate for spouses from October 9, 2007 has revolutionised the position since it means that the first spouse can leave all his assets to the survivor without loss of his nil rate band.[29] All in all, it is therefore more likely that trusts for minors and older children will now only feature in the will of the surviving spouse.

35.15   In cases where the will of the first spouse to die leaves residue on an interest in possession trust for the surviving spouse (an IPDI), it will commonly provide for trusts over to take effect on the ending of that spouse's interest. These trusts can qualify as bereaved minor trusts or s.71D (age 18–25) trusts but it is not possible to create successive IPDIs. Accordingly, were the will to provide for residue to be held on trust for the surviving spouse and then for the children of the testator on interest in possession trusts, the trusts for the children would be taxed under the relevant property regime and the surviving spouse would make a chargeable transfer if her interest was terminated or surrendered inter vivos. If the surviving spouse is keen that the children should take IPDIs on her death the trustees would need to advance the capital out to her and then she could set up IPDIs in her will for the children or, alternatively, she could be given a testamentary general power of appointment which she exercises in her will to create these trusts.[30]

35.16   *The options: a diagrammatic resumé*

(a) basic structure:

Spouse 1

Use of nil rate band
(e.g. NRBDT): less
often used today

Residue to spouse 2
may be

Interest in
possession (IPDI)

Outright

In both cases IHTA
1984 s.18 spouse
relief applies

---

[29] See Ch.38 for a consideration of the transferable nil rate and for when nil rate band trusts may still be attractive.

[30] For the use of general powers, see Ch.38 and A1.17.

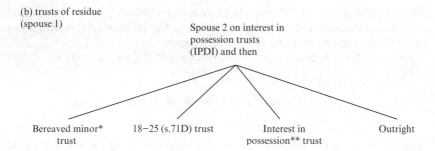

(b) trusts of residue
(spouse 1)

Spouse 2 on interest in
possession trusts
(IPDI) and then

Bereaved minor*   18–25 (s.71D) trust   Interest in   Outright
trust   possession** trust

* If this trust takes effect on the lifetime ending of the spouse's interest in possession then the spouse is treated as making a PET.[31] In all other cases where there are continuing trusts (save for trusts creating a disabled person's interest) the spouse will make an immediately chargeable transfer.

** This will not be a qualifying interest in possession (it will not be an IPDI): hence the relevant property regime will apply.

III BEREAVED MINOR TRUSTS (BMTS) INCLUDING COMPARISON WITH A-M TRUSTS AND PECKING ORDER

The necessary requirements are in IHTA 1984 s.71A and the tax treatment of such trusts laid down in s.71B. The key limiting feature of these trusts is that they can only be set up in favour of a minor child of the testator (hence they cannot be set up for grandchildren) and the trusts must ensure that capital vests at 18. In response to widespread criticism of the latter requirement, the Government during the passage of FA 2006 through Parliament introduced the 18–25 (s.71D) trust which enables the vesting of capital to be postponed until 25, albeit at an IHT cost. Practitioners should consider both options in advising clients on appropriate will trusts for their young children. It is likely that many will wish to use the s.71D trust which provides for some flexibility in the date of capital vesting and the possibility of a postponement even beyond the age of 25. It will therefore be rare for BMTs to be established under the terms of the will[32] unless the testator has a particular wish that his children should take capital and income at 18. An IPDI or s.71D trust for the children is more likely. However, if he leaves residue on IPDI trusts for the surviving spouse and the surviving spouse wishes to terminate her life interest and make PETs for the children, they must either take outright or on BMTs. It is not necessary that the terms of the BMT are set out in the will itself and the trustees may exercise powers of appointment (given to them in the will) to secure that on termination of the spousal IPDI the settled property is held on a BMT.[33] In the case of a BMT if the children are not financially responsible at 18 the trustees can always exercise a power of advancement to defer absolute entitlement at which point the trust will fall into the relevant property regime but

35.17

---

[31] See IHTA 1984 s.3A(1A)(c)(iii) inserted by FA 2006.
[32] Such trusts may arise under the intestacy rules.
[33] See A2.372 and 35.29.

without an IHT charge.[34] Curiously while it is possible to convert the spousal IPDI trust into a s.71D trust on termination of the life interest this would not be a PET by the spouse but a chargeable transfer.

The conditions necessary for the trust to be a BMT are as follows.

(i) Meaning of a "bereaved minor"

35.18   A person who has not attained the age of 18 and at least one of whose parents has died.[35]

(ii) Qualifying trusts

35.19   The trusts for the bereaved minor must either arise under the will of the deceased parent; be established under the Criminal Injuries Compensation Scheme or be held on the statutory trusts for the benefit of a bereaved minor under ss.46 and 47(1) of AEA 1925 (in cases where the parent dies intestate).[36] In cases other than intestacy the trust must satisfy the further conditions in s.71A(3).[37] Only in the cases of intestacy is substitution permitted: this occurs when a child predeceases the intestate leaving issue living at the death of the intestate who stand in his shoes.

EXAMPLE 35.2

(1) By his will A leaves property to his son absolutely on attaining the age of 18, failing which it is to go to A's sister. When A dies his son is aged nine. This is a BMT. Although there is a substitutional provision in favour of the sister, while the son is alive capital and income can only be applied for his benefit and he takes absolutely at 18.

(2) B's will leaves property to his daughter at age 21 with remainders over. Until that age the trustees have power to use income for her maintenance and to accumulate any balance. He dies when she is nine. This is not a

---

[34] The trust could be converted into a s.71D trust at that point if it was felt preferable for the children to take at 25 not 18; then just before 25 their interests could be postponed again at which point the trust would become a relevant property settlement!

[35] IHTA 1984 s.71C inserted by FA 2006 Sch.20 para.1. Given that the trust can only arise under the will of a parent it is a little odd to include the requirement for one of the parents to have died! The definition is modelled on trusts for vulnerable beneficiaries in FA 2005 s.39 which are considered at Ch.36. A person's children are defined for the purposes of s.71 by s.71(8): there is no definition in s.71B. "*Parent*" is defined in s.71H and includes a stepparent.

[36] See IHTA 1984 s.71A(1)(2). The reference to AEA 1925 s.47(1) limits the qualifying trust on intestacy to one for the benefit of the children of the intestate at 18 (i.e. to cases where the deceased left a surviving spouse and issue when the residue is held as to one-half on the statutory trusts for the issue).

[37] i.e. that capital and income can only be applied for the benefit of the bereaved minor who must take at 18.

BMT because capital and income vesting is postponed to 21 but it will qualify as an 18–25 trust.[38]

(3) C dies intestate survived by his three minor children. One, D, marries at 17 has a child but dies in childbirth still aged under 18. This is a BMT. D's one third share vested under the statutory trusts on marriage. Contrast the position if D had died before C leaving a surviving child. The trust still falls within the definition of a BMT and D's child stands in his shoes being contingently entitled to a one-third share.

(4) E's will mirrors the statutory trusts which arise on intestacy. Before E's death a child dies leaving a minor—X. E has two surviving minor children. E's will establishes a BMT in respect of E's surviving children: however the remaining one-third share for E's deceased child does not qualify (now held for X, the minor) and is held on a relevant property trust. The trust does not arise on E's intestacy.

(5) In 2005 (i.e. before the March 22, 2006 changes) Jason died and left his young son, Rufus, then aged eight an immediate interest in possession (TA 1925 s.31 was excluded) with an entitlement to capital at 18. With the passage of FA 2006 the IHT position is as follows:

   (i) this is a BMT[39];

   (ii) if Rufus were to die aged 17 no IHT would therefore be payable despite the fact that he had enjoyed an interest in possession.[40] There is a capital gains tax uplift to market value on his death;

   (iii) if the trustees made a settled advance—along the lines of that considered in Example 35.3(4)—in 2014 then although Rufus' entitlement to capital at 18 is removed no tax is chargeable and this is irrespective of whether his interest in possession terminates.[41] If the trustees defer his entitlement to capital until 25 (whether or not they still allow him to be entitled to the income) then the trust becomes an s.71D trust. Anniversary charges are avoided. There is an exit charge if capital is advanced to Rufus or the trust becomes a relevant property settlement on or before he becomes 25. Curiously, although it was not possible to convert former A-M trusts into s.71D trusts when the beneficiary becomes entitled to income after March 21, 2006, a BMT can be converted into a s.71D trust even though the beneficiary may already have an entitlement to income which he retains. What is odd about this Example is that if Jason had simply left his son an interest in possession in 2005 with no age of capital entitlement the interest would have been a pre-March 22, 2006 qualifying interest in possession. The tax regime is then completely different.

(6) Thomas died in 2005 leaving property on trust for his son Terry (then aged 16) giving him an immediate interest in possession and providing for capital to vest when Terry was 18. The trustees had a wide power of

---

[38] See 33.35.
[39] See s.71A(1) which can apply to property settled before March 22, 2006.
[40] IHTA 1984 s.49(1B).
[41] IHTA 1984 s.53(1A).

advancement which they exercised in 2007 by making a settled advance giving Terry a life interest with remainders over. The analysis is:

(i) the trust was a BMT even though Terry was entitled to a pre-March 22, interest in possession (see Example 35.2(5));
(ii) the settled advance caused the trust to fall outside s.71A (since capital will no longer vest in Terry at 18) but this did not give rise to an IHT exit charge[42];
(iii) as a result of the settled advance the property fell into the relevant property charging regime. Terry's original life interest was not a pre-March 22, 2006 qualifying interest in possession and the interest he took after the settled advance was not a transitional serial interest.[43]

35.20   The requirement that the trust must be established under the will of a deceased parent can be satisfied:

(i) if the trusts arise as the result of an instrument of variation of the deceased's will which is read-back under IHTA 1984 s.142(1)[44];

(ii) if the trusts arise as the result of an event occurring within two years of death leading to a reading-back under IHTA 1984, s.144[45];

(iii) unlike an IPDI,[46] it is not necessary that the property becomes immediately held on these trusts at death: a BMT can, for instance, be preceded by an IPDI, a relevant property trust or an 18–25 trust.[47]

The amendments to s.144—which provide for reading back if the terms of a non-interest in possession trust[48] are modified within two years of death so that the continuing trusts satisfy the requirements of s.71A—are of limited importance. If the conversion occurs within the permitted two year period, reading back ensures that the s.71A trust is effective from death so that there is no question of an exit charge when the existing relevant property settlement ends. But even after that period has passed, conversion into a s.71A trust out

---

[42] See IHTA 1984 s.71B(2)(c).
[43] IHTA 1984 s.49B(5)(a). Contrast the position if the property was held on trust on Thomas' death so that Terry took an immediate entitlement to income but capital vested at 25. Whether or not the testator died before or after March 22, 2006 if Terry had an interest in possession it was not a s.71D trust (see s.71D(5)(c)). If however the testator died before or after March 22, 2006 giving Terry capital and income at 25 but no immediate entitlement to income this would have been a s.71D trust. If after the conversion of a BMT the settled advance gave Terry capital at 25 but retained his income entitlement then this would have been a s.71D trust! See further 35.13 and 35.28 for the "pecking order".
[44] See Ch.39.
[45] Section 144 is considered at in Ch.39. Typically the will establishes a discretionary trust and within two years of death the trustees appoint all or part of the trust property on a bereaved minor trust: see IHTA 1984 s.144(4)(c)(ii), (5) and (6)(b).
[46] See 35.12 and 35.13. An IPDI involves the beneficiary becoming entitled to the interest in possession on the death of the testator.
[47] If the IPDI ends during the lifetime of the interest in possession beneficiary he will make a PET into the BMT: IHTA 1984 s.3A(1A)(iii): contrast the position in the case of 18–25 (s.71D) trusts, see 35.16.
[48] A qualifying interest in possession is, of course, severely limited in its scope after March 22, 2006: see IHTA 1984 s.144(1A) inserted by FA 2006.

of a relevant property trust is possible albeit at the cost of an IHT exit charge. The trust thus created (typically by exercise of a power of appointment) will still be established under the will of the deceased parent and so qualify as a BMT.

Bear in mind the overriding requirement that a BMT must be set up by the will of a deceased parent.

EXAMPLE 35.3

> Elizabeth died in 2009 leaving her property on an IPDI trust for her daughter Emma who is 45. Emma died unexpectedly in 2011 and the property became held on trust for her two minor children in equal shares contingently on reaching 18. Although Emma has died and hence the children are bereaved minors the trust is established under the will of their grandmother not their mother and therefore on the death of Emma the settled property is taxed under the relevant property regime. The power of advancement cannot be exercised to give the grandchildren IPDIs (but contrast the position if Emma had exercised a testamentary general power of appointment to create such trusts).[49]

(iii) Vesting at 18

35.21   The child must, no later than the age of 18, become absolutely entitled to:

- (i) the settled property;

- (ii) any income arising from it; and

- (iii) income which has previously arisen from property held on the trusts and which has been accumulated.

The following matters are worthy of note:

(a) the terms of the trust must "*secure*" that this condition is met. There must therefore be no overriding powers of appointment which could be exercised to divert the property to other persons or to postpone vesting beyond the age of 18. This requirement resembles the provision in s.71 (dealing with accumulation and maintenance trusts) that beneficiaries "*will*" become entitled to property no later than the age of 25.[50] It is not possible for the terms of the trust to secure with absolute certainty that the property will vest at 18 since the beneficiary might die under that age. Rather the trust must provide for vesting at 18 and it must not contain any provisions which could prevent this from happening.

(b) until the age of 18 if any of the settled property is applied for the

---

[49] See Ch.38.
[50] See Ch.30.

benefit of a beneficiary it must be applied for the benefit of the bereaved minor.[51] It is a little difficult to see that this adds greatly to the basic requirement that the trusts must secure vesting at 18;

(c) that until the age of 18 either the bereaved minor is entitled to the income or no income can be applied for the benefit of any other person.[52] Notice therefore, that the minor can enjoy an interest in possession before becoming entitled to capital at 18.[53] Not only must the application of income be for the benefit of the minor but if income is accumulated the accumulations must belong to the minor.[54] In general under TA 1925 s.31 accumulated income passes with the share to a beneficiary who becomes absolutely entitled on attaining 18 (the position is different if the beneficiary then becomes entitled to a life interest).[55]

(iv) Powers of advancement

35.22 The existence of a common form power of advancement (even modified by the deletion of the 50 per cent ceiling) or of an express power "*to the like effect*" to the statutory power or modified statutory power does not prevent the trust from being a BMT.[56] The words "*to like effect*" are found in IHTA 1984 s.88 which refers to trusts to the like effect to those found in TA 1925 s.33 (protective trusts). HMRC in SE7 stated that they would interpret these words as applying to trusts "*which are not materially different in their tax consequences*".
The statement continued:

> "*the Board would not wish to distinguish a trust by reason of a minor variation or additional administration duties or powers. The extension of the list of potential beneficiaries to, for example, brothers and sisters is not regarded as a minor variation.*"[57]

It is thought that the same approach will be applied to s.71A(4). This provision expressly states that if the trustees' powers are subject to a less restrictive limit than one-half this will not mean the condition is breached. However, an express power which excluded the requirement for consent[58] is not thought to satisfy the BMT requirements.

[51] IHTA 1984 s.71A(3)(b).
[52] IHTA 1984 s.71A(3)(c).
[53] Contrast IHTA 1984 s.71(1)(b): the existence of an interest in possession prevented a trust from being an accumulation and maintenance settlement.
[54] See s.71A(3)(iii).
[55] See generally Snell's *Equity* (31st edn), para.12.46 and see *Re Joel's WT* [1967] Ch14.
[56] IHTA 1984 s.71A(4). In practice the existence of a common form power of advancement did not prevent a trust from qualifying as accumulation and maintenance under s.71: see 30.09. See also the similar provision in trusts for vulnerable beneficiaries in FA 2005 s.34(3).
[57] The reference to the trust being not materially different "in their tax consequences" is somewhat odd since this will depend on whether or not they are treated in the same way as a s.33 trust! Protective trusts are considered at 28.09.
[58] This restriction requires the consent of beneficiaries whose prior interest is prejudiced by the proposed exercise of the power: see TA 1925 s.32(1)(c). When the trustees are exercising the power for the benefit of a beneficiary who would otherwise become entitled to capital at 18 and

from qualifying as a BMT, the exercise of such powers may, of course, cause
the trust to cease to be a BMT. In such a case, however, this will not give rise
to an IHT exit charge.[59]

EXAMPLE 35.4

Adam's will leaves the residue of his estate absolutely to his son contingent on attaining 18 absolutely failing which it is to be divided amongst
Adam's siblings. TA 1925 ss.31 and 32 apply and in the latter case there is
power to advance the entire presumptive share of a beneficiary. Adam's
son is aged 10 at his death.

(1) The trust is a BMT. Capital vests at 18; the existence of the modified
statutory power of advancement is ignored and during the son's minority s.31 ensures that income can only be used for his benefit and that he
will become entitled to any accumulations at 18.

(2) On the attainment of 18, the BMT will end with the son becoming absolutely entitled to the trust property. There is no IHT exit charge[60] and
CGT hold-over relief is available.[61]

(3) If the son dies under the age of 18, the BMT ends and again there is
no exit charge[62] and CGT hold-over relief is available. Note that this
is the position whoever takes the property under default trusts that
apply.

(4) The trustees decide before the son attains 18 that it will be for his
benefit that he does not become entitled to the trust property absolutely.
Accordingly they exercise their power of advancement so that he takes
a life interest at 18 with the trustees reserving a power to advance capital
to him in the future subject to which the trust fund is held for the benefit
of his children.[63] His consent is not required. This exercise of the power
has the following results:

(i) it brings the BMT to an end: however there is no IHT exit charge[64];
(ii) provided that the power is exercised "*in the narrower form*" it will
not create a new settlement for CGT purposes so that there will not
be a deemed disposal of the property[65];

may already have an entitlement to income, his consent is not required because his interest is not
being prejudiced. Hence the requirement for consent may not be a practical problem given that
the powers of advancement have to be exercised for the benefit of the particular minor anyway.
If the power of advancement was modified so as to allow the trustees to advance capital of a
share held for a minor for the benefit of *any* beneficiary (including default beneficiaries) rather
than for the benefit of the minor child concerned the condition would not be satisfied.
[59] See IHTA 1984 s.71B(2)(c).
[60] See IHTA 1984 s.71B(2)(a): see 35.20.
[61] TCGA 1992 s.260(2)(da) inserted by FA 2006 Sch.20 para.32.
[62] IHTA 1984 s.71B(2)(b); TCGA 1992 s.260(2)(da).
[63] Such an exercise of the power is commonly termed a "*settled advance*".
[64] IHTA 1984 s.71B(2)(c).
[65] See Ch.12.

(iii) the continuing trusts will be taxed under the relevant property regime for IHT purposes; the son's interest in possession is not "qualifying": specifically it is not an IPDI. There is no base cost uplift to market value on his death[66] and the settled property is not treated as part of his estate for inheritance tax purposes under s.49(1) IHTA 1984.

(5) As in (4) except that the trustees exercise their power to give the son an interest in possession at 18 and also provide for capital to vest in him at 25. The tax consequences are as in (4) above except that the trust now falls within s.71D (18–25 trusts). This means that until the age of 25 the tax position is as set out in 35.29 below. The material differences from (4) are that (a) if the beneficiary dies between 18–25 so that the s.71D trust ends there is an inheritance tax exit charge; (b) the trust is not subject to anniversary charges and (c) when the beneficiary reaches 25, or takes capital earlier, there is an exit charge.

The charge to tax

35.24   This is dealt with in s.71B which provides that IHT shall be payable (1) when settled property ceases to be held on a bereaved minor trust and (2) when trustees make a disposition which has the result of reducing the value of the settled property (a "depreciatory transaction").[67] However the charge on the cessation of the BMT does not apply in three situations[68]:

(i) if the bereaved minor becomes 18 or absolutely entitled under that age (hence there is no exit charge at 18: see Example 35.3(2));

(ii) if the bereaved minor dies under the age of 18 (so that default trusts apply: see Example 35.3(3));

(iii) if the trustees pay or apply the settled property for the advancement or benefit of the bereaved minor (hence a settled advance is not subject to an IHT exit charge: see Example 35.3(4)).

35.25   Apart from depreciatory transactions, it is a little difficult to envisage situations where an IHT charge will arise since the exclusions from charge in s.71B(2) otherwise deal with all the common situations that are likely to arise. Any charge that may arise is calculated in the same way as the exit charge for existing accumulation and maintenance trusts.[69] There are provisions for aggregating the consecutive periods during which the property has previously been held on s.71 (accumulation and maintenance) or s.71D trusts.

---

[66] See TCGA 1992 ss.72 and 73 and Ch.12.
[67] IHTA 1984 s.71B(1).
[68] IHTA 1984 s.71B(2).
[69] IHTA 1984 s.71B(3)(4) and compare IHTA 1984 s.71(5) and see Ch.30. Although rare in practice the situations in which a charge was capable of arising under s.71 were more extensive.

A comparison with accumulation and maintenance trusts

It has been said that bereaved minor trusts are all that is left of the regime **35.26** which applied to accumulation and maintenance trusts before March 22, 2006. That is true in respect of the basic charging regime, i.e. a bereaved minor trust is a privileged settlement and once established does not generally suffer an IHT exit charge.

The differences between the two are, however, striking and include the **35.27** following:

(i) a BMT can only be established by will/intestacy. There is no equivalent to the inter vivos accumulation and maintenance trust;

(ii) a BMT can only be set up for the minor children (including step-children) of the testator. There is no special vehicle available for grandchildren;

(iii) capital must vest at 18 although reserving a wide power of advancement to change this does not take the trust out of the BMT regime unless and until it is exercised. Under the accumulation and maintenance regime it was sufficient for *either* income *or* capital to vest at or before the age of 25;

(iv) there is limited flexibility in the BMT. By contrast, accumulation and maintenance trusts could be drafted in highly flexible form: all that was required was that one or more beneficiaries became entitled to income or capital not later than age 25. This enabled the trustees to exercise powers of selection between their beneficiaries. It also meant that the A-M trust could end with beneficiary A being given an interest in possession in the settled property at 25 but that interest could be (and frequently was!) subject to wide overriding powers of appointment by which the property could, in effect, be resettled for other family members.

(v) CGT hold-over relief is available however a BMT ends: contrast the more restrictive relief that was available for A-M trusts.[70]

(vi) a BMT can give the minor child an interest in possession yet still be a BMT: by contrast, once an interest in possession arose, an A-M trust came to an end (being replaced by an interest in possession trust). There is an advantage in giving a minor an immediate interest in possession in a BMT in that:

(a) it does not affect the IHT treatment BUT
(b) for CGT purposes the death under the age of 18 of the minor will result in the death uplift.[71]

---

[70] See Ch.18.
[71] TCGA 1992 s.72(1B)(b) inserted by FA 2006 Sch.20 para.30 note that the interest (which is not, of course, a qualifying interest in possession) only has to be in existence immediately before the minor's death. There is a similar amendment in TCGA 1992 s.73(2a)(a) dealing with the situation when the settlement ends with the death.

The "pecking order": a BMT or an IPDI?

35.28 What is the position if the parent's will gives the minor an immediate right to income (TA 1925 s.31 is excluded) with capital vesting at 18. Is that a BMT or an IPDI?[72] IHTA 1984 s.49A provides that if the conditions of s.71A are met the interest in possession is not an IPDI (i.e. the BMT rules take precedence).[73]

35.29   The legislation also envisages the possibility of a trust beginning as an IPDI but then becoming a BMT.

EXAMPLE 35.5

> On Dad's death, property is settled on his son on terms which give the son an immediate right to income and vest capital when he becomes 25. At the date of Dad's death the son is aged two.
>
> (i) This is an IPDI since it cannot be a BMT and although capital vests at the requisite age for the purpose of the s.71D trust, IPDIs take precedence.[74]
>
> (ii) Assume however that the trustees exercise their power to advance capital to the child by providing that he will become entitled to capital at 18. Meanwhile he retains the right to income. This will satisfy the conditions in s.71A for a BMT and it would therefore appear that it ceases to be an IPDI trust, instead becoming a BMT. This follows from s.49A(5) which requires that "condition 3" (that s.71A does not apply to the property) *"has been satisfied at all times since L became beneficially entitled to the interest in possession"*.
>
> (iii) The IHT consequence if this was to happen is that the termination of the IPDI will be a PET by the child.[75] The curious result would then be that if the child were to die within seven years before having attained 18, although the ending of the BMT on death under 18 is not chargeable and he has continued to have an interest in possession, the PET fails and so IHT may be payable. Care should therefore be exercised before a trust is converted into a BMT for the life tenant. Moreover, FA 1986 s.102ZA applies: he reserves a benefit and the settled property is chargeable on his death even if he survives seven years (see Ch.34).

Drafting a BMT

35.30 Whereas the drafting of an A-M trust was frequently a matter that required the equivalent of a higher degree in rocket science that is not the case with a

---

[72] For IPDIs, see Ch.28.

[73] Contrast the position of s.71D trusts: see Examples 35.2(5) and (6).

[74] IHTA 1984 ss.49A and 71D(5)(c)(ii).

[75] As a result of the revised PET definitions in IHTA 1984 s.3A(1A)(iii)(3B).

BMT. There is limited room for manoeuvre and the trusts will frequently be straightforward. For instance:

> "*I leave my residue on trust for my daughter Dolly contingently on attaining the age of 18 absolutely and subject thereto [insert default trusts].*"

In the case of more than one child:

> "*I leave my residue on trust for such of my children as [shall survive me and] attain the age of 18 and if more than one in equal shares absolutely and subject thereto [insert default trusts].*"

If a child dies and the property passes to his siblings outright at 18 the share remains subject to the BMT not the relevant property regime.

Substitutionary clauses are, however, problematic: **35.31**

> "*provided that if any child dies before me or before reaching the age of 18 leaving a child or children living at my death or born thereafter who reach the age of 21 then such child or children shall take by substitution and if more than one in equal shares the share of my residue which his her or their parent would have taken had such parent survived me and attained a vested interest*".

Clauses such as this are commonly used in order to preserve equality between the testator's children and their issue. However the definition of a BMT does not generally allow for substitutionary interests.[76] This has the following consequences:

(1) If at the death of the testator all his children are minors and alive this is a bereaved minor trust. If subsequently a child dies in circumstances when the substitution provisions apply then (a) there will be no IHT exit charge but (b) that portion of the fund will become held on a relevant property trust.

(2) If at the testator's death one of his children had predeceased and the substitutionary provisions apply so the child's issue take his share, that share will be held on a relevant property trust. The remaining shares of the minor children qualify as BMTs.

In practice, it is unlikely that a child will die under 18 leaving issue. However   **35.32**
it is not uncommon for grandparents[77] to want to benefit their grandchildren rather than adult children particularly if the adult children predecease.

EXAMPLE 35.6

Andrew has three adult children X, Y and Z. They are all married with children. He leaves his property outright to his children with substi-

---

[76] See Example 35.2(4).
[77] Who cannot create BMTs for their grandchildren.

tutional provisions for grandchildren at 18 if one of the children dies before him. X dies before Andrew leaving three young children who under Andrew's will take X's share in equal shares if they reach 18. Unless they are given immediate interests in possession (which would be IPDIs) their shares will be held on relevant property trusts.

35.33 It will be sensible to include a widened power of advancement in all cases. Some of the potential difficulties posed by substitutionary clauses may then be solved as follows:

> (i) the substitutionary trusts for the deceased's child's issue fall within the relevant property regime (as discussed above) and hence within IHTA 1984, s.144[78];
>
> (ii) if desired, therefore, the trustees could exercise their power of advancement to either terminate the trusts (in which case if the beneficiaries were minor bare trusts would arise) or alternatively could create an IPDI interest for the beneficiaries with capital at (say) 18 or 21.[79] Although absolute parity of treatment would still not be obtained with the surviving children, the disparity that would result if there was a relevant property trust of the substituted share is avoided. Note especially:
>
>> (a) the great advantage of a BMT is the absence of IHT charges during and on the ending of the trust together with CGT hold-over relief;
>>
>> (b) by contrast, an IPDI trust involves an IHT charge on the death of the beneficiary and, although there is no IHT charge when the assets are advanced out to the beneficiary, CGT hold-over relief will only be available if the trust property comprises business assets.[80] However, there is a capital gains tax uplift on the death of a IPDI beneficiary;
>>
>> (c) to leave the substituted share to be held on relevant property trusts means that IHT anniversary and exit charges will arise. Other settlements in the will (e.g. the BMT) will be aggregated (since they are related settlements) in order to work out the rate of charge. And, of course, there will be the administrative inconvenience of part of the trust fund being subject to a different IHT regime with attendant compliance costs.

It remains unsatisfactory that the position under wills is different from that which arises on intestacy: see Example 35.2(3).

To what extent is flexibility permitted?

35.34 The legislation is drafted with reference to a single bereaved minor but it is acknowledged by HMRC that a qualifying trust can be set up for more than one

---

[78] See Ch.39.
[79] For a precedent clause setting up an IPDI interest in possession for a minor, see A1.10. To obtain reading-back under s.144 the interest must arise within two years of the testator's death.
[80] Within TCGA 1992 s.165.

bereaved minor. Hence references to "a bereaved minor" are to be read as including "bereaved minors". It follows that the following flexibility is permitted:

(1) it is not necessary to provide for vesting in equal shares. Provided that a bereaved minor must take at 18 the requirements of the legislation are met;

(2) accordingly, the trustees can be given a power of selection amongst children under the age of 18 which can be used to vary their shares inter se;

(3) however, the limitations on any such power need to be carefully noted. Specifically:

(i) once a child has attained 18 there must be no ability either to increase or decrease his share;

(ii) HMRC consider that it is not possible revocably to use the power to exclude a beneficiary with a view to reinstating him before the age of 18. The basis for the view is that once excluded the child ceases to be a "bereaved minor". Whilst it may be doubted that this view is correct, in practice it is easy enough to overcome the problem. Instead of wholly (revocably) excluding a child from benefit the trustees should leave him with a nominal share which can then be either increased or ended (as may be considered appropriate) when the trustees make a final decision just before his 18th birthday.[81]

IV 18–25 (S.71D) TRUSTS; RELATIONSHIP WITH IPDIS AND OTHER TRUSTS; INTERACTION WITH S.144

These provisions were introduced by the Government in response to criticisms that the BMT was unsatisfactory in requiring capital to vest at 18.[82] Explaining their introduction, the then Paymaster General, the Rt. Hon. Dawn Primarolo, commented as follows: **35.35**

> "*The amendments tabled by the Government make sure that the legislation for trusts for bereaved minors operates in line with our intentions When a trust that is set up for a child in the event of the death of their parent is set to run on until the child is 18 and 25, the amendments provide that charges. . . will apply only after the child's 18th birthday. Amendment No. 384 makes it clear that the term 'parent', in the context of a new trust for bereaved minors, extends to step-parents. Taken together, the amendments mean that the rules will operate fairly, but of course if there is an absolute disagreement on whether the age should be 18 or 25, that cannot be resolved in this Committee; that is where the Government stand on the issue.*"[83]

The basic conditions to be satisfied are the same as for the BMT with the key difference that capital (together with income and accumulations of income)   **35.36**

---

[81] For the view of HMRC, see A2.370 and for a suitable precedent clause, A1.6.

[82] See IHTA 1984 s.71D–G inserted by FA 2006, Sch.20 para.1. As with BMT, trusts created *before* March 22, 2006 can fall within s.71D.

[83] Hansard Standing Committee Debate, June 14, 2006 Col.604.

must vest in the beneficiary no later than the age of 25 (instead of 18). Accordingly:

(i) s.71D trusts can only be set up by will[84];

(ii) the trusts must not be A-M; BMT; IPDI trusts; interest in possession trusts in which the beneficiary became entitled to the interest before March 22, 2006; a TSI; or a disabled trust within IHTA 1984 s.89[85];

(iii) the testator must be the parent (or stepparent) of the beneficiary;

(iv) until the beneficiary becomes entitled to the trust fund (which must not be later than age 25) any capital applied must be applied for his benefit and any income either paid out to him or accumulated for his benefit;

(v) as with BMTs the trusts must "secure" that capital vests not later than the designated age and the existence of the statutory or an express power of advancement is permitted.[86]

EXAMPLE 35.7

In his will Hugh made provision for his children Hattie and Henry (aged 21 and 15 respectively at the time of his death) by dividing his estate between them equally on the following trusts:

(i) *in the case of Hattie's share*: to Hattie absolutely on her surviving to age 25: failing which the share is to be held on wide discretionary trusts;

(ii) *in the case of Henry's share*: to pay the income and capital to Henry at 25 but the trustees have an overriding power of appointment which they can exercise at any time in favour of a wide discretionary class including Hattie and Henry. The trustees can release this power of appointment.

The IHT position is as follows:

(i) *Hattie's share*: because she is aged over 18 she will be entitled to the income from the share.[87] Although capital vests in her at 25 this is an IPDI not an 18.25 (s.71D) trust.[88] Accordingly capital of the share

---

[84] Or under the Criminal Compensation Scheme: see generally IHTA 1984 s.71D(2). The statutory trusts for issue on intestacy will not qualify since they fall under s.71A (a BMT): see IHTA 1984 s.71D(5)(a). As with BMTs, these trusts can also be set up by an instrument of variation and as a result of IHTA 1984 s.144 (in both cases "reading-back" ensures that the trusts are set up on death).

[85] IHTA 1984 s.71D(5). Comprehensive though this list of exclusions would appear to be it is worth bearing in mind that a s.71D trust can arise before March 22, 2006 and that the list does not include a disabled person's interest trust under s.89B (which does not fall within s.89) so that there would appear to be a potential overlap.

[86] See 35.22.

[87] See TA 1925 s.31.

[88] IHTA 1984 s.71D(5)(a)(ii). If Hugh had died before March 22, 2006 then the interest taken by Hattie would be a pre-March 22, 2006 interest in possession and therefore transitional serial interests could have arisen before October 2008. Hence Hattie's capital entitlement could be

will be treated as part of Hattie's estate[89] and when she becomes 25 (so that the trust ends) there will be no IHT charge.[90] If Hattie dies before becoming 25, IHT will be charged on her share.[91] What if Hattie had been 17 when Hugh died? Although she does not have an interest in possession within two years of death and under s.144, when she becomes entitled to income at 18 this will be read-back to Hugh's death and she will be treated as enjoying an IPDI.[92] If Hattie (17 at Hugh's death) were to die there will be no IHT charge if this happens before she becomes 18 but thereafter there will be a charge.[93]

(ii) *Henry's share*: given his age Henry is not entitled to income from his share at the death of Hugh and so does not have an IPDI. Nor do the trusts fall within s.71D given the existence of the overriding power of appointment. Accordingly the share is held on a relevant property settlement. Were the trustees to release their power of appointment within two years of Hugh's death, reading back under s.144 results in the s.71D conditions being met.[94] If they released their power more than two years after Hugh's death the relevant property settlement would be replaced by a s.71D trust and there would be an IHT exit charge.[95]

Taxation of s.71D trusts

There is a price to pay for retaining capital in trust beyond the age of 18. A special charging regime is provided for in IHTA 1984 s.71F–G and the following matters should be borne in mind in approaching these, at first sight, somewhat daunting provisions: **35.37**

(i) the basic charge[96] occurs when settled property ceases to be property to which s.71D applies or where the trustees make a depreciatory disposition[97];

(ii) tax is not, however, charged:

deferred indefinitely and her interest in possession extended if the trustees exercise a widened power of advancement by making a settled advance. The relevant property regime would not have applied. By contrast, on the death of Hugh *after* March 21, 2006 if her capital entitlement is deferred beyond 25, the trust enters the relevant property regime with an entry charge when the power of advancement is exercised. See Example 35.11.

[89] Under IHTA 1984 s.49(1).

[90] IHTA 1984 s.53(2). CGT hold-over relief will not be available unless the assets are business property within TCGA 1992 s.165.

[91] IHTA 1984 ss.49(1) and 4.

[92] This is probably not what the testator and the will draftsmen intended: it means that a different tax treatment will apply to the two children: see further for the "pecking order" 35.13 and 35.28.

[93] Note that if on Hattie's death aged 17 her share became held in trust for Henry at 25, there will be no charge because the property remains held on s.71D trusts.

[94] IHTA 1984 s.144.

[95] A s.71D trust must be established under the will of a deceased parent but does not have to come into effect immediately on death (the position is the same for a bereaved minor trust: see 35.20): contrast IPDIs.

[96] In s.71E(1).

[97] Compare s.71B providing a similar structure for BMT.

- if the bereaved miner becomes entitled to the capital and income of the trust fund on or before attaining 18[98];
- if the beneficiary dies under the age of 18[99];
- if the property becomes held on a BMT for the beneficiary before he is 18[100];
- if the property is paid or applied for the benefit of the beneficiary on or before he attains the age of 18.[101]

(iii) there are also some additional exclusions from charge which have no counterpart in the BMT provisions:

- no tax is charged on a payment of costs or expenses; or
- on a payment or liability to make a payment which will be the income of any person for the purposes of income tax (or would be if he were UK resident)[102];
- in the case of a depreciatory disposition there is no tax charge if the disposition is such that—were the trustees beneficially entitled to the settled property—either IHTA 1984, ss.10 or 16 would prevent there being a transfer of value.[103]

(iv) the tax charge is levied either in accordance with the rules in s.71F or 71G. The former applies in the normal situations, viz:

(a) on the beneficiary becoming absolutely entitled to the settled property on or before the age of 25;

(b) the death of the beneficiary after the age of 18;

(c) when property is paid or applied for the benefit of the beneficiary.

But remember in all cases that there is no charge if these events occur before the beneficiary is 18. The charge is therefore only levied on the period which has expired since the beneficiary's eighteenth birthday (or from when the trust came into being, if later).

35.38   All of which leaves s.71G as the residual charge: it applies when s.71F does not and is therefore concerned with depreciatory transactions.

EXAMPLE 35.8

The Wilton Trust established in the will of their father who died in 2007 provided for the twins Tim and Tom at 25 in equal shares (income is to be

---

[98] IHTA 1984 s.71E(2)(a). Here the trust is taxed in the same way as a BMT up to age 18.

[99] IHTA 1984 s.71E(2)(b). This again mirrors the BMT provisions.

[100] IHTA 1984 s.71E(2)(c). Accordingly if the testator exercises a power of advancement whereby capital is to vest in the beneficiary at 18 it appears that the trust has moved from being a s.71D trust to a s.71A BMT. It is a little difficult to see that this will have major practical implications save that if there is a prior IPDI the termination of that interest is only a PET if a BMT (not a s.71D trust) then arises.

[101] IHTA 1984 s.71E(2)(d) and compare s.71B(2)(c) in the case of BMT.

[102] IHTA 1984 s.71E(3) and see the similar exclusion in the case of relevant property settlements: IHTA 1984 s.65(5).

[103] There is a similar exclusion in the case of relevant property settlements, see IHTA 1984 s.65(6). Section 10 is concerned with dispositions not intended to confer any gratuitous benefit and s.16 with grants of agricultural tenancies. On depreciatory transactions by trustees of interest in possession settlements, see IHTA 1984 s.52(3) and in the case of relevant property settlements, IHTA 1984 s.65(1)(b).

accumulated during the standard 21 year accumulation period). Assume that the value of the fund is £1 million in 2020.

(i) When Tim is 24 in 2020 the trustees make a settled advance of his 50 per cent share giving him an interest in possession with remainder to his wife and children.
(ii) Tom becomes 25 and takes his share absolutely.

The position is as follows:

(a) the Wilton Trust is a s.71D trust when the father dies;
(b) the settled advance brings that trust to an end in respect of Tim's share (because Tim is no longer entitled to capital at 25) and triggers an exit charge under s.71F;
(c) the continuing trusts for Tim fall outside s.71D; he does not have a qualifying interest in possession and sp the relevant property rules apply;
(d) because Tim's trust continues there is no CGT disposal[104];
(e) so far as Tom is concerned his absolute entitlement brings the trust for him to an end; there is an IHT exit charge under s.71F and (because this part of the settlement is ending) a deemed disposal for CGT purposes on which hold-over relief is available.[105]

Calculating the charge under s.71F

The charge closely resembles the relevant property charging regime but because it is intended to tax the period between the beneficiary becoming 18 and the ending of the settlement (a period of, at most, seven years) it is inappropriate to impose an anniversary charge and instead the charge is in the form of a single exit charge. Take the case of Tim (in Example 35.8): his s.71D trust lasted from his 18th birthday until the settled advance was made just before his 24th birthday. Hence, the charge is over a period of just under six years and is calculated as follows:

35.39

(i) calculate the value of the property ceasing to be comprised in the s.71D trust. Tim's share is worth £500,000[106];

(ii) calculate the number of complete quarters in the period beginning with the day on which he became 18 and ending with "the day before the occasion of charge".[107] In this case there are 23 complete quarters and so 23/40 is the number in 40ths.[108] The "relevant fraction" is then 3/10 multiplied by 23/40;

---

[104] The settled advance is drafted to modify the terms of the existing settlement not to create a new settlement.
[105] Under TCGA 1992 s.260(2)(a).
[106] See IHTA 1984 s.71F(4): in this case the IHT will be paid out of Tim's share, not out of the property remaining in the settlement for Tom, and hence grossing-up does not apply.
[107] If the property only became comprised in the s.71D trust after the beneficiary had become 18, take this later time.
[108] IHTA 1984 s.71F(5) and compare IHTA 1984 s.68(2).

(iii) the "chargeable transfer" is arrived at by aggregating (a) the value of the property in the settlement immediately after it commenced *plus* (b) the value, again immediately after it commenced, of property in a related settlement *plus* (c) the value of added property.[109] There is no added property but the value of Tom's share must be included and hence it is necessary to know the value of the whole fund at the time when the twins' father died. Assume that this was £750,000. The chargeable transfer is of this amount treated as made by a hypothetical transferor who had cumulative transfers equal to the chargeable transfers made by the twins' father in the seven years before he died (disregarding any chargeable transfers made by his will). Assume that there were none;

(iv) the tax charge is on the basis of lifetime rates in 2020[110];

(v) the "settlement rate" can now be arrived at, being tax on the chargeable transfer (£750,000) made by a transferor with no cumulative chargeable transfers so that tax will be:

	£
chargeable transfer	750,000
less nil rate	(325,000)[111]
balance	425,000
tax at 20% on balance equals	85,000

this produces a settlement rate of $85,000/750,000 \times 100 = 11.33\%$.

(vi) the amount of tax is given by:

chargeable amount £500,000 × [relevant fraction (23/40) × (3/10) × settlement rate (11.33)]
Working through the bracketed calculations produces 1.95%.
So the tax is £500,000 × 1.95% = £9,750.

35.40 The top rate of charge is 4.2 per cent which would apply if:

(i) the property was held in trust until the beneficiary became 25 and the trust began not later than his eighteenth birthday. Hence the relevant fraction will be 28/40

(ii) the hypothetical transferor has exhausted his IHT nil rate band so that it rate applicable is 20 per cent;

(iii) the calculation is then 28/40 × 30% = 0.21. 0.21 × 20 = 4.2%.

35.41 If the property had simply been treated as falling within the relevant property regime once the beneficiary attained 18 the IHT charge would normally be much the same. However, it might then be collected on the basis of an anniversary charge followed by a final exit charge. For instance, if in Example 35.8 the twins' father had died on October 1, 2008 and Tom had become 18

---

[109] IHTA 1984 s.71F(8).
[110] IHTA 1984 s.71F(8)(c).
[111] Rates in 2020 are unknown. For the purposes of this example, the nil rate in 2011–12 (£325,000) is used.

on October 1, 2017 and 25 in 2024 then there would have been an anniversary charge in 2018 followed by an exit charge in 2024: however, given that the anniversary charge would have made an allowance for the property only becoming relevant property in 2017 (when it ceased to enjoy the "up to 18" protection) the eventual result would have been much the same unless the property had increased in value significantly since death. There is, however, no doubt that the special regime in s.71F is simpler and easier administratively. It has the result that trustees can evaluate the IHT costs of keeping the settlement going with some precision. Taking the worst case scenario (a rate of 4.2% at 25) the position is:

		rate (%)
(i)	distribute capital when Tom is 19	0.6
(ii)	distribute capital when Tom is 20	1.2
(iii)	distribute capital when Tom is 21	1.8
(iv)	distribute capital when Tom is 22	2.4
(v)	distribute capital when Tom is 23	3
(vi)	distribute capital when Tom is 24	3.6.

Calculating the charge under s.71G

As already stated, this charge is limited to depreciatory transactions and is levied on the basis of the charge under s.71B(3)[112] which in turn is modelled on the exit charge for accumulation and maintenance trusts.[113] There are provisions to deal with the situation where, before becoming a s.71D trust, the settlement fell within s.71 when this charge was calculated by reference to the period during which the trust property was subject to both regimes.   **35.42**

EXAMPLE 35.9

The London A-M Trust was set up on April 1, 2000 for Emily and Emilia who were then aged 10 and 8 respectively. Before April 6, 2008 the terms of the trust were varied so as to provide for them to be absolutely entitled to capital at 25. If a charge to tax under s.71G arises in respect of a depreciatory disposition made by the trustees on April 1, 2014 the charge is calculated by reference to a 14-year period. The tax charge is as follows:

(i) first 10 years at 0.25 per cent for each quarter   10 per cent –
(ii) final four years at 0.20 per cent for each quarter 3.2 per cent
                                                        13.2 per cent[114]

---

[112] See Ch.30.
[113] IHTA 1984 s.71(5) incorporating the provisions of ibid. s.70(3)–(8) and (10). In the case of A-M trusts these provisions could provide for a charge at a top rate of 21%.
[114] See IHTA 1984 s.70(6).

Extending the life of a s.71D trust

35.43 As with BMTs the only permitted overriding power is one of advancement.[115] If that power is exercised in the case of a s.71D trust to postpone vesting beyond 25 there will be an exit charge under s.71F and the continuing trusts will fall under the relevant property regime.[116] Diagrammatically the charging regime for a s.71D trust can be represented as follows:

		Vesting at 25	*Settled advance postponing vesting*
0		Age of beneficiary	
		Treated as BMT: no IHT charges	
18			
18		Beneficiary aged 18	
		Special charging regime top rate 4.2% at 25	
25		Beneficiary 25 (IHT charge at a top rate of 4.2%) Trust ends	Settled advance at 25 (IHT) charge at a top rate of 4.2%
			Relevant property settlement (anniversary / exit charges in future)

Converting a s.71D trust into a BMT

35.44 It seems clear that such a conversion can occur: for instance the trustees accelerate the vesting date of capital from 25 to 18 by use of a power of advancement. If this happens the trust ceases to be within the s.71D regime[117] but there is no exit charge.[118] This leads to the question of whether it will ever be desirable to bring the s.71D trust into the BMT regime. In the situation discussed in Example 35.10 below there will be an attraction in so doing.

[115] See Example 35.3(4).
[116] See Example 35.8.
[117] IHTA 1984 s.71D(5)(a).
[118] IHTA 1984 s.71E(1)(c).

EXAMPLE 35.10

(1) Under a will, the residue of the estate is held on trust for the testator's surviving spouse for life (an IPDI)[119] remainder to his son Toby on attaining the age of 25. The trustees have a wide power of advancement. If the spouse is desirous of releasing her interest in possession, the transfer of value that she makes is not a PET but immediately chargeable. If, however, Toby's trust is first modified (by exercise of the power of advancement) to vest capital in him when he gets to 18,[120] and the interest in possession is then surrendered (or terminated) the spouse will make a PET.[121] The trustees could then exercise their powers of advancement again just before he reaches 18 and convert it back into a s.71D trust.

(2) Testator dies leaving his estate on trust for his spouse for life and then on discretionary trusts for his issue. He has four children, all under 25, one of whom (Daisy) is under 18. The trustees exercise their powers so as to provide that subject to the spousal life interest the trust fund is held for Daisy at 18 absolutely. Spouse exemption is preserved on the testator's death. The spouse then surrenders her interest and this is a PET since the trust for Daisy is a BMT. The trustees can then exercise their powers of advancement just before Daisy is 18 so as to convert the BMT into an 18–25 trust for all the children. This triggers no exit charge. Then just before they reach 25 the trustees could exercise their powers again and convert the 18–25 trust into a relevant property trust. There is a small exit charge but the entry charge that would have been payable if a relevant property trust or an 18–25 trust had arisen immediately on termination of the spousal life interest is avoided. A difficulty with this approach is that it is hard to see that it would be for the benefit of Daisy and a valid exercise of the power if the trustees advanced capital on trust for her siblings just before she reached 18. Retaining any wider overriding powers of appointment, e.g. to appoint in favour of persons other than Daisy would breach the BMT requirements.

Converting a BMT into a s.71D trust

If trustees exercise a power of advancement to prevent vesting at 18 but do so in such a way that the conditions of s.71D are met then (a) the trust ceases to be a BMT without an exit charge arising[122] and (b) becomes subject to the s.71D regime: see Example 35.3(5).[123] The trust can then later be converted into a relevant property trust (with a small exit charge). In Example 35.10(3)   **35.45**

---

[119] See Ch.28.
[120] It will, of course, be too late to perform this exercise if Toby is already over 18.
[121] See IHTA 1984 s.3A(1A)(a)(iii) and (3B).
[122] IHTA 1984 s.71B(2)(c).
[123] It is curious that the possibility of a trust moving from ss.71A–71D without an exit charge is not picked up in IHTA 1984 s.71G(3): presumably this is an occasion when Homer—in the guise of the legislative draftsman—has nodded.

the trustees could exercise their powers in favour of Daisy just before she was 18 and hold the property on 18–25 trusts for her; indeed they could further defer her absolute entitlement just before she reached 25. However, the powers must be exercised for Daisy's benefit.

An interest in possession trust?

35.46 Frequently trusts vesting capital at 25 will give the beneficiary a right to income before that age, e.g. as a result of TA 1925 s.31 or because the accumulation period expires before that age. The existence of such an interest:

(i) does not prevent the trust from satisfying the s.71D conditions[124];

(ii) is not a qualifying interest in possession for IHT purposes unless it is in existence when the testator dies (it will then be an IPDI)[125];

(iii) but for CGT purposes will result in an uplifted value (but no charge) in the event that the beneficiary dies before the age of 18.[126] Note, however, that if he dies after that age there is no uplift (although any CGT charge may then be postponed by the making of a hold-over election.[127] This distinction defies rational analysis!

Relationship with IPDIs

35.47 In effect IPDIs take precedence. Accordingly, if the will provides for the child to have an immediate right to income with capital vesting at 25 this is not a s.71D trust but instead gives the child a qualifying interest in possession.[128]

Relationship with s.144

35.48 Given that s.71D trusts must simply be established under the will of the deceased parent, rather than, as in the case of IPDIs also having to take effect from death, it follows that if they result from the conversion of a non-interest in possession trust within two years of death they are read back to the date of death. As a result there is no exit charge on the ending of the relevant property settlement. By contrast, if the "conversion" of the s.144 trust occurs more than two years after the death, a s.71D trust will still come into being but only at that date and therefore with an IHT exit charge arising.[129]

---

[124] See priority of trusts at 35.13 and 35.28.
[125] But note the "reading-back" effect of IHTA 1984 s.144 (see Examples 35.7 and 35.11).
[126] TCGA 1992 s.72(1A)(b) and 73(2A)(b).
[127] Under TCGA 1992 s.260(2)(a).
[128] Contrast the position with a BMT: IHTA 1984 ss.49A and s.71D(5)(c)(ii).
[129] This mirrors the position for s.71A BMT: see 35.20.

Bear in mind that s.144 can also operate to destroy what at first sight would appear to be a s.71D trust.[130]

EXAMPLE 35.11

> Roy dies in 2010. He leaves his entire estate to his three children A, B and C equally at 25. A is 19 when Roy dies, B is 17 and C is 14. At 18 each child will become entitled to income (as a result of TA 1925 s.31)
>
> *Position of A*: he has a right to income when Roy dies which is an IPDI. When he becomes entitled to capital at 25 there will be no IHT charge (IHTA 1984 s.53(2)) and CGT hold-over relief will not be available unless the property is business assets within TCGA 1992 s.165. If he dies before 25 the value of the IPDI fund will be taxed as part of his estate.
>
> *Position of B*: he will become 18 within two years of Roy's death and when this happens s.144 will apply to "read-back" his entitlement to income to the time of Roy's death. He too, therefore, will have an IPDI. Of course, if he died before 18 the trust for him will satisfy the s.71D requirements.[131]
>
> *Position of C*: the trust for C is within s.71D. Accordingly an exit charge may arise in respect of the period from C becoming 18 to 25. At that time CGT hold-over relief will be available.
>
> *Advice*: if Roy had wanted all his children treated the same and had intended the s.71D regime to apply then the will as drafted in this case is a potential disaster. This has resulted from the right to income at 18 given by s.31 which should have been excluded. Instead the will drafts-man should have provided that until 25 the income from each share can be used for the child's maintenance with any balance being accumulated and added to the share.[132]

The choice: BMT or s.71D?

The immediate reaction of many taxpayers is that they would prefer to post- **35.49** pone capital vesting until the child becomes 25 albeit that the trustees will be given a power to advance capital earlier. Further it might be thought that it will be sensible to draft wills with a s.71D trust on the basis that by advancing capital at 18 the trustees can, in effect, obtain BMT treatment. This is broadly

---

[130] See 35.13 for priority of trusts.
[131] And because he died before 18 there will be no exit charge: in effect, it is treated as a BMT.
[132] It is, of course, possible for income to be used to maintain the other children who are under 25 at the time and for any accumulated income to be added to the general capital then held on s.71D trusts. As a result of PAA 2009 allowing unlimited accumulations of income, it will not matter that a child is under four at the time of death since the old 21-year accumulation period no longer applies.

correct but the following factors should be borne in mind before concluding that BMTs are redundant:

(i) IHT will be chargeable once the trust continues after the beneficiary has attained 18 in accordance with the charging regime in IHTA 1984 s.71F; if the beneficiary dies after 18 there is an inheritance tax charge unless the property continues to be held on trust for other children of the deceased who are under the age of 25;

(ii) a PET will arise on the inter vivos ending of an IPDI but only if the continuing trust is a BMT: not if it is a s.71D trust. This will be a chargeable transfer: see Example 35.10[133];

(iii) CGT death uplift is only available if the beneficiary enjoys an interest in possession and dies before the age of 18.[134] In fact the uplift is available whether the trust is a BMT or s.71D trust and the key features of the relief are (a) that the beneficiary must enjoy an interest in possession and (b) must die under the age of 18.

One further factor to bear in mind is that a BMT can always be extended by making a settled advance (assuming the trustees are given a widened power of advancement)[135] and become a s.71D trust[136] which may, in turn, be further extended.[137] The trust can then fall into the relevant property regime after the beneficiary reaches 25 and a wider class can potentially benefit.[138]

Drafting s.71D trusts

35.50 Similar comments to those made in connection with the drafting of BMT are appropriate: specifically, the legislation permits limited flexibility whilst beneficiaries are under 25.

35.51 In many cases it will be attractive to retain what flexibility is allowed, i.e. to give the trustees power to determine the shares of beneficiaries whilst they are under the age of 25. Care needs to be taken to ensure that the relevant power cannot be exercised so as either to increase or diminish the share of a beneficiary once he has attained 25 and HMRC take the view that if the power has been exercised to exclude a beneficiary revocably it is not possible to "bring him back in" by revoking the previous exercise of the power. Accordingly, it will be important to leave the beneficiary with a small share which can then be increased (if desired) as the result of the exercise of the power of revocation and reselection.[139]

---

[133] It is sufficient if the s.71D trust has been converted into a BMT immediately before the interest in possession is terminated.

[134] It will be noted that the top rate of charge is 4.2% at age 25 which some will consider a fair price to pay for continuing the settlement. But, of course, rates may rise in the future.

[135] Specifically it will be desirable for the 50% restriction in TA 1925 s.32(1)(a) to be removed.

[136] See 35.45.

[137] See 35.43.

[138] Note, however, that it may be hard to justify a settled advance as being for the benefit of a beneficiary under 25 if as a result of the advance a wider class can benefit. If the testator wants flexibility between siblings and their issue on distributions of income and capital it is preferable to fall within the relevant property regime from the outset: see Example 35.10(2).

[139] Similar drafting considerations applied to accumulation and maintenance trusts.

The following clause, it is thought, will not breach the s.71D(6) requirements: **35.52**

"to such of my children as attain the age of 25 years and if more than one in such shares as the trustees shall from time to time by deed or deeds revocable or irrevocable appoint and in default of such appointment in equal shares absolutely at 25 providing always that no such appointment shall be made and no appointment shall be revoked so as to either diminish or increase the share (or the accumulation of income forming part of the share) of a child who at the date of such appointment or revocation has reached the age of 25 nor benefit a child who has been excluded from benefit as a result of the exercise of the power."

EXAMPLE 35.12

The trustees are given the power to select (revocably or irrevocably) amongst the testator's children under the age of 25. In default of selection the children take in equal shares absolutely. Note the following:

(a) assuming that there are three children, A, B and C, then if the trust is to satisfy s.71D, the power of selection must not be capable of benefiting any child once he has attained the age of 25. So in the case of the eldest A, on or before he becomes 25 his share must be fixed and the power of selection limited to the shares of B and C;

(b) in the case of A-M trusts, it was common to exclude (revocably) a beneficiary just before he became 18 (so as to prevent him getting a right to income under TA 1925 s.31) and then to "bring him back" into the class of beneficiaries just before he became 25 so as to vest the intended share in him at 25. HMRC take the view that if it is not possible wholly to exclude a beneficiary but then to revoke the exercise of that exclusion the trust does not satisfy s.71D.[140] Accordingly, it will be important to make sure that any beneficiary who is to be reinstated is left with a "share" (which can be of a nominal size, for instance one per cent of the fund).

Retaining a wide power of advancement

This is expressly permitted by s.71D(7)(b). It enables the trust to be extended **35.53** beyond the age of 25 by making a settled advance as in the following example.

EXAMPLE 35.13

The Rogers will trust established on the death of Roy on April 6, 2008 provides for his son Nick (aged 21) to take capital and income at 25 (s.31

[140] It is far from clear that this interpretation of the legislation is correct: see A2.370.

is excluded and so the income may be accumulated until he is 25). The trustees have a widened s.32 power of advancement.

    (a) the trust is in the s.71D regime;

    (b) Nick will be 25 on January 1, 2021 and the trustees determine to exercise their power of advancement to postpone his entitlement to capital. Accordingly they make a settled advance giving him a life interest, reserving a power to advance capital to him but otherwise declaring trusts in favour of his children.

The IHT consequences are:

(1) When the trustees exercise their power to make the "settled advance", s.71D ceases to apply and there will be an exit charge under s.71F (calculated by reference to the period from April 6, 2008 to the date of the settled advance). The same exit charge arises whether Nick becomes absolutely entitled or the trust continues outside the s.71D regime.

(2) The continuing trusts will be subject to the relevant property regime.

Section 71D link with existing accumulation and maintenance trusts

35.54 In general, the object of s.71D is to regulate new will trusts for bereaved children of the testator. However, s.71D(3) and (4) are concerned with something quite different, namely trusts in existence on March 22, 2006 and which on that date satisfied the requirements for an accumulation and maintenance trust.[141] For such trusts there was a transitional period until April 6, 2008 after which the settlement fell within the relevant property regime unless either (i) on that date the trusts provided for vesting of capital at 18 or (ii) as s.71D(3) provides, on that date the settled property was held on trusts for the benefit of a person who had not yet attained 25 and the normal conditions relating to the vesting of the property at 25[142] were met.[143] It is important to realise that in this situation the requirements of s.71D(1) and (2) did not apply. Hence it did not matter that the accumulation and maintenance settlement was not created by will or that the beneficiaries were not the minor children of a testator nor that the settlor was still alive. The majority of accumulation and maintenance settlements were, of course, created inter vivos in favour of the settlor's grandchildren and many have benefited from this legislation.

Section 71D link with pre-March 22, interest in possession trusts

35.55 The position is as follows:

    (i) a s.71D trust can be set up before March 22, 2006;

---

[141] Those requirements are in IHTA 1984 s.71 and are considered in Ch.30.
[142] These are laid down in s.71D(6).
[143] Illustrations of the "conversion" of a s.71 trust into s.71D are given in Example 30.6.

(ii) however, if the beneficiary enjoyed an interest in possession in the property on March 22, 2006, s.49(1) applies to treat him as beneficially entitled to the settled property[144]; and

(iii) s.71D does not apply.[145]

Many A-M trusts in existence at March 22, 2006 did not satisfy the s.71D conditions. If a beneficiary attained an interest in possession after that date but before the trust was varied to qualify as a s.71D trust it was not possible to convert later to obtain s.71D status. In such cases, the beneficiary has a non-qualifying interest in possession and his share falls into the relevant property regime.

EXAMPLE 35.14

X set up an A-M trust in 2005 for his three grandchildren. They each take one third of the income at 25 and the capital of their share at 30. In 2007 the first grandchild reached 25. He became entitled to income and his share ceased to qualify for A-M status. However, his interest in possession is not a qualifying interest in possession and once that grandchild has become entitled to income it is not possible to convert his share into a s.71D trust. The requirement is that the s.71D trust is created out of the A-M trust and that share is no longer held on A-M trusts. Accordingly if the trustees had varied this trust before April 6, 2008 so that all grandchildren become entitled to capital no later than 25, two thirds would then qualify as a s.71D trust but the remaining one third still falls to be taxed under the relevant property regime.

V OTHER DEATH OPTIONS

Bereaved minor and s.71D trusts may well not fulfil the requirements of the testator. For instance: **35.56**

(i) they only enable trusts to be set up for his children and he will often want to benefit grandchildren;

(ii) they require capital and income vesting at either 18 or 25 which he may consider to be unacceptable.[146] Specifically, he may wish to keep the property settled for the indefinite future or wish for flexibility on distributions of income and capital between beneficiaries while they are still young.

The main alternatives available to such testators are: **35.57**

(i) in the case of minor grandchildren, consider the benefits of a bare trust[147]; and

---

[144] Note that IHTA 1984 s.49(1B) only excludes BMT from the operation of s.49(1): see 35.45.
[145] IHTA 1984 s.71D(5)(c)(i).
[146] Of course, the trusts may be extended by settled advances: see 35.23 and following and Example 35.4(4).
[147] See Ch.42.

(ii) where flexibility is felt desirable and where there is a wish to retain a long term settlement structure consider the merits of

    (a) an IPDI, or

    (b) a discretionary trust.

35.58 An IPDI can be set up giving an immediate interest in possession to a minor beneficiary.[148] It will commonly be desirable to give trustees a power to advance capital to that beneficiary rather than to insert a provision giving him capital on attaining a certain age. Flexibility is thereby preserved and in deciding whether to advance capital the trustees can have regard, inter alia, to the CGT position at that time. An alternative whilst giving the beneficiary capital at (say) 30 would be to rely on the trustees to use a power of advancement to postpone that entitlement. It is the difference between[149]:

(i) leaving it up to the trustees to decide if and when the beneficiary gets the capital; and

(ii) giving him the capital at a fixed date but subject to a power for the trustees to stop this happening.

The latter runs the risk of HMRC viewing the continuation of his interest in possession as a "new" interest so that the IPDI has ended. The result would be a relevant property settlement with an entry charge and 10-year charges thereafter as well as a reservation of benefit[150] on the death of the interest in possession beneficiary. A disaster!

35.59 The use of a "full blown" discretionary trust involves an evaluation of the benefits derived from the continuing trust structure as against the costs involved in the periodic IHT charge. Unless the testator wishes the trustees to retain flexibility over who benefits, one option if he is a parent with young children may be to use the s.71D trust so that at least if he dies while the children are young there are no anniversary or other inheritance tax charges. The power of advancement can then be used to extend the trusts later—although it will, of course, have to be exercised for the benefit of that particular child and therefore there is only limited scope for the trusts to benefit a wider class of beneficiaries.

---

[148] See Ch.28 and, for a precedent clause, A1.10.
[149] For HMRC's view on this point, see Ch.27.
[150] See FA 1986 s.102ZA.

CHAPTER 36

TRUSTS FOR VULNERABLE AND DISABLED BENEFICIARIES

- Background matters (**36.01**)
- Income tax rules (**36.06**)
- CGT treatment (**36.22**)
- Inheritance tax: disabled trusts under s.89 (**36.30**)
- IHT: "disabled persons' trusts" after March 21, 2006 (**36.42**)
- Dispositions for the maintenance of family including a dependent relative (**36.56**)

Precedent

A1.03   Disabled person's trust

I BACKGROUND MATTERS

Consider the following scenario. A parent wants to make provision for a disa- **36.01**
bled child who may be mentally incapable or otherwise vulnerable. He does
not want to give the disabled child the money outright since he is worried that
he will lose his means tested benefits. What should he do? This is a particular
worry for parents of a disabled adult child whose wish is to provide properly
for their child and leave him in a secure financial position. In some cases where
there are other children or suitable relatives, the parents may feel able to leave
their estate to that relative and trust him to provide for the disabled child. But
often this option is unsatisfactory. The relative may not want the responsibility
even if he can be trusted and the relative may divorce or die. If the amounts
are large then leaving them outright to the relative is likely to be tax inefficient.

The obvious answer is to settle the funds in a trust. But if the amounts are **36.02**
small then the complexity of a trust may prove costly in terms of professional
fees. And what is the best type of trust? The adviser must consider not only
tax issues but also state benefits. For instance, it is often undesirable if the
whole of the income is paid out for the benefit of a disabled person since this
will result in a loss of means-tested benefits pound for pound. Accordingly, a
discretionary trust is generally better from the benefits perspective because the
mere possibility of receiving capital or income from the trust will not jeopardise the beneficiary's state benefits. The trust can, for instance, buy assets for the
benefit of the disabled person which will improve his quality of life without

jeopardising his benefits. However, the income tax treatment is more complex for discretionary trusts (even if a vulnerable beneficiary election can be made)[1] and no tax-free capital gains tax uplift on death is available. A discretionary disabled person's trust could end up suffering inheritance tax at 40 per cent on the death of the disabled beneficiary as well as not benefiting from the capital gains tax uplift.

36.03   If loss of state benefits is not a concern, tax issues become more important. Here the donor is faced with nonsensical complexity. The definition of a disabled trust is different for each tax; indeed, for capital gains tax purposes different requirements are prescribed depending on whether the objective is to obtain a full annual capital gains tax exemption: hold-over relief or satisfy the conditions for vulnerable beneficiary status! The inheritance tax conditions are difficult to reconcile with the capital gains tax conditions.[2] The inheritance tax legislation at least allows for more than one type of disabled trust; so one can have either an interest in possession or a discretionary trust which will qualify as a disabled person's trust if the other conditions are met.

36.04   With the increase in the income tax rate applicable to trusts,[3] FA 2005 introduced special income tax and capital gains tax treatment for qualifying trusts for vulnerable beneficiaries (disabled persons and bereaved minors), the effect of which was backdated to April 6, 2004.[4] However, the complexity of the legislation and the limited nature of these reliefs make their value questionable. For inheritance tax purposes, disabled trusts are of greater importance as a result of the 2006 changes. This is because all new lifetime trusts, apart from disabled person's trusts, involve the settlor making a chargeable transfer and are subject to the relevant property regime (10-year charges, exit charges etc). However, trusts which create a disabled person's interest can still be set up by a PET and fall outside the relevant property regime.

Who should be treated as disabled or vulnerable for these purposes?

36.05   Calls in the 2006 Finance Bill Standing Committee to adopt the DDA1995 definition of a disabled person for inheritance tax purposes as:

> "*a person who has a physical or mental impairment which has a substantial and long term adverse effect on his ability to carry out normal day to day activities*"

were rejected by the Government.[5] The current definition of mental incapacity, based on MHA 1983 as amended in 2007, is "*incapable by reason of mental*

---

[1] See 36.13.

[2] See IHTA 1984 s.89 and s.89A–B (inserted by FA 2006 Sch.20 para.6) and TCGA 1992 s.3 Sch.1 para.1 amended by FA 1993 s.83 and by SI 1996/2975. See also the different rules on hold-over relief in s.169D discussed in Ch.18. See further 36.55 for the different conditions that apply for capital gains tax and inheritance tax.

[3] At that time to 40%: it is now 50%!

[4] FA 2005 Pt 2, Ch.4 (ss.23–45).

[5] See *Taxation* July 27, 2006 article by Robin Williamson of Low Incomes Tax Reform Group for trenchant criticism of the inheritance tax legislation.

disorder within the meaning of the MHA 1983 of managing his property or administering his affairs." As one Opposition MP said:

> "*Many of those whom we think of as vulnerable are neither disabled nor lacking in mental capacity. It is a class of people that includes the naïve and impressionable as well as the dissolute and insatiable.*"

The 1983 definition does not cater for persons with partial or fluctuating mental capacity or those with a progressive illness (e.g. Alzheimer's) which will in time lead to loss of capacity although the 2007 amendment set out below has improved the position.

II INCOME TAX RULES[6]

To obtain special income tax treatment the trust must be a qualifying trust for vulnerable beneficiaries. Vulnerable beneficiaries fall into two groups: disabled persons and relevant minors. The definition of mental disorder was amended by MHA 2007 with effect from November 3, 2008 by virtue of SI 2008/1900. This affects the definition of disabled beneficiaries generally and is discussed further below.

36.06

Disabled persons

A "disabled person" is a person who is:

36.07

(i) incapable by reason of mental disorder of administering his property or managing his affairs.[7] The definition includes those with learning disabilities that involve significant impairment of intelligence and social functioning, Downs syndrome, depression and bipolar disorder provided in all cases they are incapable of administering their property or managing their affairs. Dependence on alcohol or drugs is explicitly excluded. "Incapable of administering their property etc" is said by HMRC to be a:

> "*subjective test that must be applied in a common sense way and does not call for proof of complete incapacity. Each case must be considered on its own merits. In general the question to be considered is whether, on the balance of possibilities, the person is capable of understanding, absorbing and retaining information including advice relevant to the matters in question sufficiently well so as to enable*

---

[6] FA 2005 ss.23–38. See TSEM 3405 for some long and helpful guidance on this relief.
[7] This definition in MHA 1983 was amended by MHA 2007 with effect from November 3, 2008 to read "*any disorder or disability of the mind.*" Unlike the original sections in the MHA 1983 where those with learning disabilities were excluded the exclusion of those with learning disabilities in the 2007 Act appears only to apply for the various provisions under that Act and has no general read across to tax. Hence, it appears that the definition of mental disorder is now wider and may incorporate those with learning disabilities provided that such a person is unable to manage his affairs (see s.89(4)(a)). This is confirmed in IHTM.

*them to make decisions based upon such information weighing risks
and needs. The focus is on the capacity or ability of the individual
and not the actual outcome."* or

(ii) who is in receipt of an attendance allowance under the Social Security
Contributions and Benefits Act 1992 s.64; or

(iii) in receipt of a disability living allowance under the Social Security
Contributions and Benefits Act 1992 s.71 by virtue of entitlement to the
care component at the highest or middle rate.[8] A person may be treated
as being in receipt of an attendance allowance or disability living allowance provided that they would be entitled to receive the relevant allowances if they were to meet the necessary residence requirements.[9] Note
that people resident in the UK who claim other disability benefits or who
do not claim benefits at all, are excluded.[10]

Relevant minors

36.08   These are persons under the age of 18 who have lost at least one parent.[11]

What are qualifying trusts for income tax purposes?

36.09   Trusts for disabled persons will be qualifying provided that, during the disabled person's lifetime or until the earlier termination of the trusts, any settled

---

[8] Schedule 9 of the Welfare Reform Bill 2011 currently proceeding through Parliament proposes
further amendments to the definitions of disabled and vulnerable beneficiaries of trusts in
IHTA 1984, TCGA 1992 and FA 2005 consequential upon the proposed abolition of disability
living allowance and its replacement by a personal independence payment.
 FA 2005, s.38(1). To qualify for the *middle rate* disability living allowance you must be so
severely disabled physically or mentally that you require: frequent attention from another
person throughout the day in connection with your bodily functions; or continual supervision
throughout the day in order to avoid substantial danger to yourself or others; or prolonged
or repeated attention at night in connection with your bodily functions; or another person to
be awake at night for a prolonged period or at frequent intervals to watch over you in order to
avoid substantial danger to yourself or others (i.e. you must have either daytime or nightime
supervision needs). To qualify for the *highest rate* disability living allowance you must be so
severely disabled physically or mentally that you require: frequent attention throughout the day
in connection with your bodily functions, or continual supervision throughout the day in order
to avoid substantial danger to yourself or others; *and* prolonged or repeated attention at night
in connection with your bodily functions; or in order to avoid substantial danger to yourself or
others you require another person to be awake at night for a prolonged period or at frequent
intervals to watch over you; or you are terminally ill (i.e. you must have both daytime and
nightime supervision needs or be terminally ill). To qualify for *attendance allowance* you must
be aged 65 and either terminally ill or if you were under 65 you would satisfy the conditions
for disability living allowance care component at the highest or middle rate and have done so
throughout a period of six months in the two years before the award begins.
[9] FA 2005 s.38(2).
[10] If, however, the sole reason that the person is no longer in receipt of the relevant allowance is that
he has been admitted into certain types of care or publicly funded accommodation or is receiving
hospital treatment for renal failure then he can continue to qualify as a vulnerable person!
[11] FA 2005 s.39. Note that it does not matter that the minor is married or has entered into a civil
partnership: contrast the definition of a dependent child in the context of settlor-interested
trusts: see Ch.7.

property (i.e. capital) applied for the benefit of a beneficiary must be applied for the benefit of the disabled person[12] and either the disabled person is entitled to all the income (if there is any)[13] or the income may not be applied for the benefit of any other person.[14]

This seems to envisage that if the trusts end while the disabled person is alive, capital can be applied for the benefit of another, non-disabled person. So, for example, if A left property in his will to his children on interest in possession trusts in equal shares with the trusts terminating after five years and it was provided that all capital advancements in respect of each share must be made to the relevant child having the interest in possession during that five-year period then if one child is disabled, the trust is qualifying in respect of that share even though at the end of the five-year period the capital might pass to someone else. This is different from the capital gains tax annual exemption relief and the inheritance tax relief where the restrictions on capital must operate while the disabled person is alive.

36.10 Trusts for relevant minors will qualify only if they are established under the will of a deceased parent of the minor[15] or under the Criminal Injuries Compensation Scheme or as a result of the statutory trusts arising under AEA 1925 for a minor whose relatives have died intestate.[16] Curiously, it appears possible for a trust to qualify where a grandparent has died *intestate* leaving property on trust for that minor whose parent had died. If the grandparent left it to the minor in his *will* it would not do so. Contrast the conditions for s.71A bereaved minor trusts where the trust must be set up by the will or intestacy of the parent.[17]

36.11 Additional conditions are laid down in the case of relevant minors. These are:

(a) that the minor will, on reaching 18, become absolutely entitled to the property, any income arising from it and any income accumulated for his or her benefit before that time; *and*

(b) until that time any of the property that is applied during the minor's lifetime must be applied for his or her benefit; *and*

(c) until that time and while the minor is alive, either the minor must be entitled to all of the income (if any) from the property or no such income may be applied for the benefit of any other person.[18]

36.12 A trust can qualify if the trustees retain the statutory power of advancement. Hence the trustees could defer a minor's entitlement in up to half the trust

---

[12] This does not *require* the distribution of capital but merely imposes restrictions on who can benefit if it is distributed.

[13] Hence, the trust can give the disabled person an interest in possession.

[14] FA 2005 s.34: property is to be distinguished from income and is confined to the capital of the trust fund. Note that the capital condition in the IHT and CGT provisions (described below) only requires that not less than half the settled property which is applied during the disabled person's life must be applied for his benefit. The income tax requirement is that if *any* of the capital is applied for the benefit of a beneficiary it is *all* applied for the benefit of the vulnerable person.

[15] Hence, grandparent trusts set up by will are not covered.

[16] FA 2005 s.35.

[17] For BMTs see Ch.35 and following.

[18] FA 2005 s.35(3)–(4).

fund by making a settled advance before he becomes 18. If they exercise the power the trust ceases to be qualifying.[19] For 2004–05 and 2005–06 the trust only qualified where the statutory advancement power applied. For 2006–07 onwards, an express power to advance up to one half of the capital does not prevent the trusts from being qualifying so long as the provisions are similar to those in TA 1925 s.32.

Special income tax treatment[20]

36.13 The aim is to ensure that the amount of tax charged on income accruing to the trustees is no more than it would have been had the income belonged to the vulnerable person. This apparently simple objective is obscured by some impenetrable drafting.

The amount of the relief is the difference between the total tax paid by the trustees and the vulnerable beneficiary without special treatment and the amount that would be paid if the trust income was deemed to be that of the vulnerable beneficiary. Hence, account will be taken of the beneficiary's other income: personal allowances and the basic rate band.[21] If there are two funds with different beneficiaries and only one beneficiary is vulnerable an election can be made on that fund but trust management expenses have to be apportioned between the two![22]

36.14 Where the trust is settlor-interested, no special income tax treatment is available even though an election can be made.[23] For income tax purposes the income is still taxed on the settlor and the sole effect of the election is that for capital gains tax purposes the gains will be taxed as the beneficiary's gains.

EXAMPLE 36.1

Chris died in 2003 leaving his property in his will to Daisy contingently on her attaining the age of 18 with remainders over. Daisy is currently aged 10. During the tax year 2011–12 the trustees received rental income of £10,000 and dividend income of £25,000 (including the tax credit). They decided to accumulate this for Daisy's benefit. Daisy is a relevant minor and the trust is a qualifying trust. The special income tax treatment is arrived at as follows.

Calculate first the trustees' liability and Daisy's tax liability under the general income tax rules. Compare this with the amount of income tax that would be paid if the trust income of £35,000 was deemed to be that of Daisy. Then reduce trustees' liability to income tax accordingly.

---

[19] In the case of a disabled child they could, of course, exercise the power and the trust could still be qualifying. Cf. the conditions for a trust to qualify as a bereaved minor trust for inheritance tax purposes where an extended power of advancement is permitted.

[20] And capital gains tax: see FA 2005 ss.26–32.

[21] FA 2005 ss.25–29. The reduction is given by reference to the formula TQTI–VQTI, the terms of which are defined in these sections.

[22] See Ch.6 for the tax treatment and meaning of trust management expenses.

[23] FA 2005 s.25(3).

Distributions to Daisy from the trust are ignored in calculating her liability for the purposes of calculating this relief.[24] The trustees end up paying the same amount of tax as Daisy would have paid if the income had arisen directly to her.

However, the trustees cannot simply pay the tax and then distribute the net amount to Daisy. As with all income distributions out of UK resident discretionary and accumulation trusts, the trustees are treated as distributing a net amount from which tax at the rate applicable to trusts (50 per cent) has been deducted. This deduction is treated as a repayable credit in the hands of the beneficiary.[25]

36.15 The trustees must ensure that the tax pool covers the 50 per cent credit if the amount of tax paid by the trustees would normally enter the tax pool[26] is reduced because of a claim to special treatment, the tax that remains payable will enter the tax pool. Given that one of the main problems of discretionary trusts is the calculation of the tax pool and the 50 per cent tax on distributions to beneficiaries, it is difficult to see that this legislation is much more than political window-dressing where income is distributed to beneficiaries. It is not seriously intended to help disabled or vulnerable beneficiaries. The main purpose seems to be to enable the minor or disabled person's personal allowances and basic rate bands to be used without having to distribute the income to the minor or disabled person. This could be useful if the intention is to avoid losing means tested benefits. The easier option of just deeming the income to be the minor's for all tax purposes was not adopted. Instead trustees have to perform two separate calculations and they retain the tax pool.

The election

36.16 In order for the special income tax (and capital gains tax treatment)[27] to apply, the trustees and the vulnerable person (or if a minor, his parent or guardian) must jointly make an election.[28] If there is more than one vulnerable beneficiary each must make the election. Once made, the election is irrevocable. It can be made at any time up to 12 months after the filing date for the trustees' tax return, i.e. 12 months after January 31, following the end of the tax year in question. The earliest tax year to which an election can apply is 2004–05 with the time limit for making an election for that year being January 31, 2007.

36.17 The notice of election must include a statement that the trusts are qualifying trusts; a declaration that all the information included is correct and a declaration by the beneficiary that he authorises the trustees to make the election. Although irrevocable, the election is only effective until either the beneficiary ceases to be a vulnerable person or the trusts cease to be qualifying trusts

---

[24] FA 2005 s.28(5).
[25] ITA 2007 s.493; see Ch.6. So if the trustees distribute all or most of the income, further tax is likely to be payable.
[26] Under ITA 2007 s.498.
[27] See 36.26.
[28] FA 2005 s.37.

or are terminated. The trustees must inform HMRC within 90 days of first becoming aware of any of these events occurring.[29] Once made an election applies for both income tax and capital gains tax purposes.[30] Even though an election is irrevocable, it is possible to make the election and then make an annual claim for one year but not another.[31] This is because in addition to the election, the trustees (not the vulnerable beneficiary) must make an annual claim when submitting the tax return (or within the usual time limits if later, i.e. four years after the end of the relevant tax year).[32]

36.18   An election can be made where a trust has a mixture of vulnerable and non-vulnerable beneficiaries provided that the property held for vulnerable beneficiaries is ring-fenced within a discrete fund. If there is more than one vulnerable beneficiary of the same trust, a separate election is required for each beneficiary for whom the trustees wish to claim the special tax treatment. An election will not be effective in the tax year the vulnerable beneficiary dies but it is possible to have an election in force for only part of a tax year when the special income tax treatment will only apply for the part of the year for which the election applies. For example, an orphan might reach 18 halfway through the year.

EXAMPLE 36.2

> Barbara is the settlor of a trust which she set up for her disabled minor child in June 2006. She and her spouse/civil partner and all other minor children of Barbara's are excluded. Given that all the conditions are met, a vulnerable beneficiary election can be made. If the trust was for several of Barbara's children and only one child was disabled and his funds were held in a discrete fund, an election could be made for that child's fund. The trustees would be assessed to income and capital gains tax on the remaining income and gains in the normal way.

36.19   The special treatment does not apply for income tax purposes if the property in question is property in which the settlor is regarded as having an interest.[33] So, in the above example, if Barbara could also benefit from the trust then the special income tax treatment will not apply. Before April 6, 2008, if the trust was for the benefit of the disabled minor it was settlor-interested for capital gains tax purposes but if this was the only reason why it was settlor-interested then special capital gains tax treatment was not precluded. From April 6, 2008, even if the trust is settlor-interested because Barbara can benefit, this does not preclude special treatment for capital gains tax purposes if the other conditions are satisfied.

---

[29] See s.37(6).
[30] On capital gains tax, see 36.24 and following.
[31] See TSEM 3415.
[32] TMA 1970 s.43(1).
[33] For the purposes of ITTOIA 2005 ss.624 and 625: see Ch.7 and FA 2005 s.25(3).

Non-residence

Trustees who are not resident in the UK can make an election but it is only **36.20** their UK source income which is taken into account in calculating any deduction from the trustees' income tax liability. (They are normally only liable for income tax in respect of UK source income.) If a vulnerable person is non-UK resident then the relief can still be claimed but is computed on the assumption that he is resident and domiciled in the UK!

Personal injury payments

If a trust for a disabled beneficiary is set up as part of a personal injury **36.21** claim, periodical payments are not subject to income tax.[34] This is limited to cases where payments are made to the person entitled to the damages; a person who receives the payments on behalf of that person and a trustee who receives the payments on trust for the benefit of the vulnerable beneficiary. The terms of the trust must provide that the disabled person is, while alive, the only person who may benefit.[35] Where personal injury damages are held on trust for a claimant, such trusts, whether substantive or bare trusts, are disregarded for the purposes of income support and other welfare benefits.[36] All the problems experienced in *Pitt v Holt*[37] could have been avoided if the personal injury award had simply been settled into a bare trust for the husband.[38]

III CGT TREATMENT

There are three separate CGT relieving provisions, two of which cannot be **36.22** combined in a single trust. Only the capital gains tax provisions for vulnerable beneficiaries apply to minors of a deceased parent as well as to disabled beneficiaries.

Annual exemption

Trustees are entitled to the same annual exempt amount as an individual **36.23** (£10,600 for 2011–12 instead of £5,300) if *"for any year of assessment during the whole or part of which settled property is held on trusts which secure that during the lifetime of [the disabled person]"*:

---

[34] ITTOIA 2005 ss.731–734.
[35] While this will satisfy the requirements for income tax vulnerable beneficiary treatment it will not satisfy the requirements of IHTA 1984 s.89: see 36.30 and following.
[36] Income Support (General Regulations) 1987 Sch.10.
[37] [2011] EWCA Civ 197.
[38] For further details in the context of mistake and *Hastings-Bass* see Ch.1. The case is being appealed to the Supreme Court.

(a) not less than one-half of the property which is applied is applied for the benefit of a disabled beneficiary (*the capital condition*);

(b) that disabled beneficiary is entitled to not less than half of the income arising from the property, or no such income may be applied for the benefit of any other person (*the income condition*).[39]

It is not necessary for the beneficiary to be disabled at the time the settlement was made. So a trust could be varied so as to satisfy the conditions if a disabled beneficiary was subsequently born. In considering whether the capital condition is satisfied the statutory power of advancement is disregarded (but not an extended power of advancement in favour of someone who is not the disabled person).If the settlor has made more than one settlement for a disabled person then the full amount is divided between the trusts!

36.24 The definition of disabled person is the same as that adopted for income tax purposes.[40] It is necessary (unlike the vulnerable person's relief) for the income condition to be satisfied throughout the life of the beneficiary. At least half the trust income must either be paid as of right to the beneficiary (so that he has an interest in possession) or at least half the income must be accumulated and not applied for the benefit of another. For 2011–12 the relief is worth a maximum of $28\% \times £5,300 = £1,484$!

Mixed funds

36.25 HMRC note at CGTM 18067:

> "*It is possible that only part of a settlement may fulfil the qualifying conditions. For example, the trust may secure that during the lifetime of the disabled person the income and any capital applied of a specified fund is to be applied as described above. If the fund itself meets the conditions, then the trustees of the settlement are entitled to the main exemption. Paragraph 1 (1) refers to 'settled property' and not to 'all the settled property comprised in the settlement.'*
>
> *By way of contrast if the disabled beneficiary is entitled to an undivided share of the property, as in the example in CG18064, then the tests are to be applied to the whole of the settled property. So if there are three life tenants, each entitled to one-third of the income, and one is disabled, the conditions are not met.*"

See fn.40 in Ch.51 as to the possibility of an appropriation in these circumstances.

Vulnerable beneficiaries

36.26 There is a separate capital gains tax relief for trusts for vulnerable beneficiaries which was introduced in FA 2005 provided that the trust is qualifying and an

---

[39] TCGA 1992 Sch.1 para.1(1).
[40] TCGA 1992 Sch.1 para.1(1)(6).

election is made.[41] An election has to be made for both income tax and capital gains tax purposes although from April 6, 2008 (when the CGT charge on the settlor in respect of settlor-interested trusts ended)[42] it is possible that the trust will obtain special tax treatment for capital gains tax and not for income tax if it is settlor-interested.[43]

36.27 In order to be qualifying the same conditions must be satisfied as in the income tax provisions above (i.e. the trust must be for a relevant minor held on the same conditions as set out in 36.08 or be for a disabled beneficiary held subject to the same conditions as in 36.07). A notable difference from the capital gains tax definition of disabled trust for the purposes of the annual exemption is the legislation requires that if any (not merely up to half) of the capital is applied for the benefit of a beneficiary it must be applied for the benefit of a disabled person and that the disabled person is either entitled to all of the income arising from any of the property or *no* such income may be applied for the benefit of any other person.[44] No relief is given for a tax year if the beneficiary dies in that year.

36.28 The following CGT relief is given:

(1) If the vulnerable person was UK resident, before April 6, 2008 CGT was charged as if he were a settlor in relation to the settlement. It was charged on the vulnerable beneficiary with a right of reimbursement and therefore the beneficiary benefited from his annual exemption and lower rates of tax. Before 2008–09 if the trust was settlor-interested (unless it was settlor-interested solely because the child was a dependent child of the settlor), the election was not effective for capital gains tax purposes.[45] A claim for relief could increase tax liabilities if the individual realised gains of his own and therefore used up his annual capital gains tax exemption because the trust lost its own exemption if a claim was made.

(2) From April 6, 2008, s.31(2) and (3) were repealed and a similar mechanism to income tax introduced. Calculate the trustees' liability to capital gains tax before special treatment and the vulnerable beneficiary's liability to capital gains tax as if the gains arose directly to that person and reduce the trustees' tax liability by the difference. The trustees end up paying the same amount of tax as the vulnerable person would have paid had the gains arisen directly to him. With the increase in the trust rate of CGT to 28 per cent (from June 23, 2010) in many cases the election will be beneficial because the beneficiary will suffer CGT at 18 per cent (and, of course, he may have capital losses as well as a full CGT annual exemption). Note that a trust can be settlor-interested[46] and still obtain special capital gains tax treatment. The income will be taxed on the settlor if settlor-interested[47] but the gains may be taxed by reference to the vulnerable beneficiary. The change in mechanism means that it is no longer possible for a claim for relief to increase the tax liability.

---

[41] The trustees must be resident or ordinarily resident in the UK.

[42] See Ch.7.

[43] See 36.14.

[44] FA 2005 ss.23–37.

[45] See FA 2005 s.30.

[46] For example if another non-disabled dependent child or the settlor can benefit on the death of the disabled child.

[47] For the purposes of ITTOIA 2005 s.624: see Ch.7.

(3) If the vulnerable person is not UK resident the trustees remain liable to CGT but their liability will be reduced by an amount equal to TQTG—VQTG where TQTG is the amount of CGT to which the trustees would, if not for the new rules, be liable in the tax year in respect of the qualifying trust gains, and VQTG is calculated using the formula TLVA-TLVB. Broadly calculate the trustees' actual tax liability without the special treatment; then calculate the tax liability of the vulnerable person including all their personal gains and losses and on the assumption that he is UK resident. Losses brought forward are disregarded and the vulnerable beneficiary is deemed to have given a valid notice in respect of losses realised while non-UK resident (which would not normally be allowable). The trustees' liability is reduced by the difference.

Hold-over relief

36.29 Section 169B disapplies hold-over relief on a gift to a settlor-interested trust.[48] However, if the trust is for a disabled beneficiary and satisfies *either* the conditions to obtain full annual exemption or meets the s.89 inheritance tax conditions then hold-over relief is available even if it is settlor-interested provided that either the settlor is the disabled beneficiary or he is excluded from benefit. In the latter case even if his spouse or civil partner or dependent child can benefit it is not treated as settlor-interested for hold-over relief purposes if the above conditions are satisfied.[49]

IV INHERITANCE TAX: DISABLED TRUSTS UNDER S.89

36.30 IHTA 1984 s.89 provides that a trust which meets the s.89 conditions is not subject to the relevant property 10-year exit and set-up charges as the disabled person is deemed to have a qualifying interest in possession. Hence, a gift to the trust is a PET or if the disabled beneficiary himself set it up it is not a transfer of value.[50] The special treatment of a disabled trust will continue to apply even if the incapacity or disability ceases. The only requirement is that the person met the definition of being a disabled person when the property was transferred into settlement.

36.31 A "disabled person" is defined in s.89(4) as:

> "*a reference to a person who when the property was transferred into settlement was:*
>
> *(a) incapable by reason of mental disorder ...from managing his affairs or administering his property, or*
> *(b) in receipt of an attendance allowance or*

---

[48] See Ch.18.
[49] See TCGA 1992 s.169D and Ch.18.
[50] Until 1981, different provisions regulated disabled trusts: see IHTA 1984 s.74.

(c) in receipt of a disability living allowance at the highest or middle rate."

As discussed earlier at 36.07 the 2007 Act has amended the definition of mental disorder. Favoured treatment is not lost if the person ceases to be disabled[51] after the settlement is made. Note however, that the beneficiary must be disabled at the time when the property is settled, i.e. relief is not available if the beneficiary is not yet born or only becomes disabled after the settlement is made (or at the date of the testator's death in the case of a will trust). If there is a resettlement onto a disabled person's trust where at the date of resettlement the person was disabled but at the date of the original settlement he was not, it is thought that the relevant date is the date of resettlement since that is when property was transferred into a settlement. Contrast the exercise of a power of appointment varying an existing trust which does not have the effect of creating a new settlement.[52]

36.32 The s.89 conditions are that the settled property must be held on trusts which provide that:

(i) during the lifetime of the disabled person, there is no entitlement to income (*the income condition*), and

(ii) not less than half of the settled property which is applied during the lifetime of the disabled beneficiary must be applied for his benefit (*the capital condition*). It does not actually have to be applied for the beneficiary so long as during the lifetime of the beneficiary less than one-half can be applied for the benefit of anyone else. There is no restriction on what happens to the settled property after his death: i.e. the trusts can continue or end. If the trusts continue then the property will be relevant property from the date of the disabled beneficiary's death.

The income condition

36.33 Income can be accumulated during the lifetime of the disabled person and it is therefore possible to provide that the income is either paid to the disabled person (or another) or accumulated. The beneficiary has no entitlement to income and yet income can be paid for his benefit. This ensures that the disabled person does not lose means tested benefits.[53]

36.34 For trusts created (and wills made) before April 6, 2010 (when PAA 2009 came into force) the position with regard to the trustees' power to accumulate income was:

---

[51] IHTM 42823. So if the beneficiary ceases to receive attendance allowance or recovers capacity there is no clawback of relief.

[52] If property is moved from a relevant property trust to a new disabled person's trust then holdover relief should be available under s.260 to avoid a capital gains tax charge on the disposal because there will be an exit charge for inheritance tax purposes.

[53] PAA 2009, effective from April 6, 2010, allows unlimited accumulations of income during the 125-year perpetuity period.

(i) if the disabled person was the settlor it could be accumulated during his lifetime[54];

(ii) it was still possible to satisfy the s.89 conditions after the accumulation period had expired and allow the trust to remain discretionary since the reference to "settled property" is to the capital of the trust fund and so a trust under which some or all the income can be applied for the benefit of a person other than the disabled person would still qualify for favoured treatment.[55]

36.35　Indeed there is no actual requirement that the disabled person should even be a member of the class of income beneficiaries and all or any of the income could be paid to another through out his lifetime. However, such a trust would not qualify for the CGT[56] full annual exemption or as a trust for a vulnerable beneficiary although a disposal of assets into trust could attract hold-over relief. In the case of the vulnerable beneficiary relief (as we have seen) the requirement is that all income must be paid or payable for the disabled person's benefit. It would be possible to qualify for the full annual capital gains tax exemption if income could be accumulated during the beneficiary's lifetime and cannot paid to anyone else during that period.

The capital condition

36.36　The terms of the trust must "*secure*" that not less than half of the settled property which is applied during the life of the disabled person is applied for his benefit. As already noted, this does not require that any capital is applied during the life of the disabled person: it merely lays down restrictions that take effect if any capital is applied. A simple way of meeting this requirement is to provide that during the lifetime of the disabled person he alone is entitled to receive capital advancements (see Precedent A1.23).

36.37　In *Barclays Bank Trust Co Ltd (Trustees of the Poppleston Will Trust) v RCC*[57] the trustees contended that the s.89 conditions were not met because:

(i) they had power during the lifetime of the disabled person to pay capital to "*any person hospital or organisation for the time being having the care of the Beneficiary*" and so could have made payments to (say) the hospital for medical research. This argument was rejected by Vos J. (in the High Court) and the Court of Appeal on the basis that the stated purpose of the trust was to benefit the disabled person and this provision was an additional means of applying property for his benefit.

---

[54] Which is a permitted accumulation period.

[55] Query the position if at the end of the accumulation period (which was, say, 21 years) the disabled person became entitled to the income.

[56] As noted above, to qualify for the full capital gains tax annual exemption, the disabled person must be *entitled* to not less than half the income arising from the trust or no such income may be applied for the benefit of any other person. (The capital requirement is the same as for s.89: the terms of the trust must provide that during the life of the beneficiary not less than half of the settled property which is applied during his lifetime is applied for his benefit.)

[57] [2011] EWCA (Civ) 810.

Accordingly, *"the trust colours the purpose of the power . . . in context the power can only be exercised for the benefit of the (disabled person)"*;

(ii) the statutory power of advancement had been widened and permitted **36.38** capital to be paid to the remainder beneficiaries. The trustees contended that this breached the capital condition because if this power was exercised in full during the lifetime of the disabled person no capital could be applied for his benefit. However, the will also contained a provision that no power in the settlement (including the widened s.32 power) should be capable of being exercised in a manner which would result in the existence of the power preventing there being an interest in possession (which would otherwise be the case). The Court of Appeal confirmed that s.89 gave the disabled beneficiary an interest in possession (albeit that the interest is a deemed not actual interest). Hence, the widened power could not be exercised so as to defeat that interest and therefore the existence of the widened power did not breach the capital condition. It follows that the draftsmen of a s.89 disabled trust should exercise extreme care in relation to widened powers of advancement. The safest course will be to exclude any such power during the lifetime of the disabled person. Instead, insert an express power to pay or apply capital for his benefit[58];

(iii) because the disabled person was free to assign his interest (contrast the **36.39** terms of a standard protective trust) then if he did so no income from the settled property could be applied for his benefit.[59] This argument was also rejected by the Court of Appeal: on the basis that *"the time when the conditions for the application of s89 must be satisfied is 'when the property was transferred into the settlement'"*. And, of course, at that time the terms of the trust secured that the capital condition was met.[60]

Assets in a s.89 trust do not qualify for the CGT uplift on the death of the **36.40** disabled beneficiary because the disabled person only has a deemed interest in possession. Nevertheless the assets are subject to inheritance tax on his death.[61] If trustees advance property to a beneficiary, other than the disabled person during his lifetime this will be treated as a transfer of value by the disabled person.[62] The main advantage of s.89 trusts is that because the disabled person has no right to income there is no loss of means tested benefits.

If the s.89 trust was not acceptable then before the changes of March 22, **36.41** 2006 a straightforward interest in possession trust could have been set up which gave the disabled person a life interest. This was taxed under s.49(1) in the normal way. The following Example illustrates the options available before March 22, 2006.

---

[58] Note that s.89(3) provides that the unextended statutory power of advancement does not give rise to difficulties.
[59] In fact there is no requirement under s.89 that the disabled person must be an income beneficiary. The argument must surely relate to the capital condition.
[60] A similar argument in respect of the conditions for an accumulation and maintenance trust was considered in *Inglewood*: see 30.11.
[61] CGT hold-over relief under TCGA 1992 s.260 would be available if the trust ended.
[62] See IHTA 1984 s.52(1).

EXAMPLE 36.3

(1) A is a disabled beneficiary who has inherited valuable property. With the approval of the Court of Protection his guardian sets up a discretionary trust under which income can be accumulated during his lifetime but if distributed during his lifetime must be paid for his benefit. The terms of the trust also provide that if capital distributions are made, not less than half the trust capital must be applied for his benefit. The trust qualifies under IHTA 1984 s.89 as a disabled trust. No PET is made by A because he is deemed to have an interest in possession so that there is no transfer of value for IHT purposes. On the disabled person's death there will be no CGT base cost uplift but inheritance tax will be payable. The trust will also qualify for the full annual capital gains tax exemption even though income can be accumulated during the life of the disabled person because it is not payable to anyone else during his lifetime. A vulnerable beneficiary election could only be made if the trust provisions were amended so that the capital could only be applied for A's benefit. However he is the settlor so for income tax purposes the income will be taxed on him anyway (under ITTOIA 2005 s.624).[63]

(2) Before March 22, 2006 A settled funds on interest in possession trusts for himself (with remainders over). There was no IHT charge on the creation of the trust because there was no transfer of value since he is deemed to own the underlying property because of his a qualifying interest in possession. On his death there will be a base cost uplift to market value for capital gains tax purposes; and IHT charge and his entitlement to income might result in a loss of means tested benefits.

EXAMPLE 36.4

In 2005 S decided to settle property on trust for his daughter T who was severely disabled. He was concerned about the possibility of T losing means tested benefits. He faced the following choices:

(i) He could settle the funds on interest in possession trusts for T. This would be a PET but T will receive all the income and this may jeopardise means-tested benefits. If the trust provided that any capital distributions made during her lifetime must be to her or applied for her benefit then a vulnerable beneficiary's election could be made and gains and income would effectively be taxed at her rates. If no election was made, the trust would qualify for a full capital gains tax exemption. There is a CGT base cost uplift to market value on the settled property when T dies.

Alternatively:

(ii) He could have settled the funds on discretionary trusts for T and

---

[63] See Ch.7.

provided that any capital distributions must be applied (as to at least half) for T during her lifetime. This would be a PET for inheritance tax purposes because the trust falls under s.89. A vulnerable beneficiary election is not possible. There is no base cost uplift for capital gains tax purposes on the death of T. The full annual capital gains tax exemption is not available but hold-over relief would be available if required.

V IHT: "DISABLED PERSONS' TRUSTS" AFTER MARCH 21, 2006

With the introduction of new rules for the IHT treatment of settlements from March 22, 2006 the preservation and extension of the special rules for disabled trusts is significant in that such trusts are now the only examples of a trust that can be established inter vivos by a PET. Initially FA 2006 made only minor amendments to the regime for disabled trusts. Subsequently more extensive changes were announced.[64] There was a limited change to the definition of "disabled" to bring it into line with the definition used for vulnerable beneficiaries.

36.42

"Disabled person's interest"

This is defined in IHTA 1984 s.89B as follows:

36.43

> "(1) In this Act 'disabled person's interest' means—
>
> (a) an interest in possession to which a person is under section 89(2) above treated as beneficially entitled,
> (b) an interest in possession to which a person is under section 89A(4) above treated as beneficially entitled,
> (c) an interest in possession in settled property (other than an interest within paragraph (a) or (b) above) to which a disabled person becomes beneficially entitled on or after 22nd March 2006, or
> (d) an interest in possession in settled property (other than an interest within paragraph (a) or (b) above) to which a person ("A") is beneficially entitled if—

---

[64] Note that the definition of disabled person was extended to include non-residents who would otherwise qualify but otherwise was not changed. The House of Lords Economic Affairs Committee criticised the lack of consultation between HMRC and the various bodies working in the field and felt that there should be greater alignment of the definitions and that it might be appropriate to include people who do not meet the conditions simply because they do not claim benefits to which they are entitled. For example, the new regime will not necessarily apply to trusts which are ordered to be set up by the courts as part of a personal damages award. In these cases it is not uncommon for the injured party to be in receipt of the lower care component of the disability living allowance and not to be suffering from mental disorder. The 2007 Act has, as noted in 36.07, assisted in allowing a greater range of mental disability to be included. The Welfare Reform Bill 2011 will, when enacted, affect those claiming benefits and introduces changes to the inheritance tax legislation in Sch.9.

(i) *A is the settlor,*

(ii) *A was beneficially entitled to the property immediately before transferring it into settlement,*

(iii) *A satisfies Her Majesty's Commissioners for Revenue and Customs as mentioned in section 89A(1)(b) above,*

(iv) *the settled property was transferred into settlement on or after 22nd March 2006, and*

(v) *the trusts on which the settled property is held secure that, if any of the settled property is applied during A's life for the benefit of a beneficiary, it is applied for the benefit of A."*

36.44 Four different types of trust can qualify within this definition:

Type (i)	s.89 trust	a *"deemed"* interest in possession
Type (ii)	s.89A self-settlement	
Type (iii)	An interest in possession trust	an *"actual"* interest in possession
Type (iv)	An interest in possession trust created by a self-settlement	

36.45   The significance of the concept of a *"disabled person's interest"* is that IHTA 1984 s.49(1A) provides that it is taxed in accordance with the rules in s.49(1), i.e. the beneficiary with the interest (or deemed interest) in possession (the disabled person) is treated as beneficially entitled to the property in which the interest subsists. As a result the inter vivos creation of the trust:

(i) is a PET if made by a person other than the disabled person; *or*

(ii) if made by the disabled person is a "nothing".

36.46 Trusts which give rise to a disabled person's interest are:

(i) *type (i)*: a disabled trust falling within s.89 which have been discussed above[65]: in this case the beneficiary has a "deemed" interest in possession;

(ii) *type (ii)*: a self-settlement within s.89A which also gives rise to a "deemed interest in possession". This is a discretionary trust established by a settlor who has a condition expected to lead to disability;

(iii) *type (iv)*: a self-settlement in which the settlor (with a condition expected to lead to disability) has an interest in possession. An actual not deemed interest in possession;

(iv) *type (iii)*: an interest in possession in settled property to which a disabled person becomes entitled on or after March 22, 2006. Note that the interest can arise in an existing trust or a new settlement can be set up giving the disabled person an interest in possession. This is an actual (as opposed to a deemed) interest in possession.

---

[65] See 36.32 and following.

Self-Settlements (s.89A)[66]

These are settlements set up by persons on or after March 22, 2006 who have a condition expected to lead to a disability within the meaning of s.89(4) (if the settlor is already disabled then the trust will meet the requirements of s.89) (a "*self-settlement*").

The conditions for s.89A to apply are as follows:

36.47

36.48

   (i) the settlor must satisfy HMRC that it was reasonable to expect that at the date of transfer into the trust he had a condition that would lead to him becoming disabled within the s.89 definition.[67] Subsequent improvements in his condition will not affect the tax treatment of the settlement;

  (ii) he is beneficially entitled to the property being settled immediately before it is transferred to the trust.[68] It is not clear whether he has to be entitled absolutely to the property or whether if he has a qualifying interest in possession in the property this is sufficient;

 (iii) during the life of the settlor no interest in possession subsists in the settled property[69]; and

 (iv) the provisions of the trust "*secure*" that if any of the settled property is applied during the settlor's lifetime for the benefit of a beneficiary it is applied for his benefit (*Condition 1*) and also that any power to bring the trust to an end during the settlor's lifetime is such that in the event of the power being exercised either the settlor or another person will then be absolutely entitled to the settled property or a disabled person's interest within either s.89B(1)(a) and (c) will arise (*Condition 2*). If the conditions in s.89A are satisfied the settlor is treated as beneficially entitled to an interest in possession in the settled property (a "deemed" interest). Hence there is no transfer of value on setting up the trust since the settlor's estate is not diminished.

EXAMPLE 36.5

 (1) Jane has just been diagnosed with Alzheimer's. She has not yet lost mental capacity. She settles all her property into trust for herself on discretionary trusts which satisfy the requirements of s.89A. This is not a transfer of value for inheritance tax purposes because she is deemed to have a qualifying life interest. Accordingly it is a "nothing". The property is taxed on her death but with no CGT base cost uplift since she has a deemed not an actual interest in possession.

 (2) Some years later an addition to the settlement is made by Jane's daughter, Ruth. The addition is treated as being comprised in a separate

---

[66] Inserted by FA 2006 s.206(1) and (3).
[67] IHTA 1984 s.89A(1)(b).
[68] IHTA 1984 s.89A(1)(a).
[69] IHTA 1984 s.89A(1)(c).

settlement for IHT purposes[70] which is taxed under the relevant property regime so that Ruth makes a chargeable transfer. If, however, Jane had already lost mental capacity the addition by her daughter would be a PET as the trust would then qualify as a disabled trust under s.89.

36.49 It is far from easy to reconcile Conditions 1 and 2. The reference to settled property in Condition 1 is to "*the capital of*" the settlement. It would appear that whilst Condition 1 is concerned with an advancement-type power (to pay or apply capital), Condition 2 is concerned with a power of appointment and the restriction is intended to ensure that if such a power is exercised during the disabled person's life it must either end the trust (i.e. make an outright appointment) or appoint into trusts creating a disabled person's interest (falling within ss.89B(1)(a) or 89(1)(c)). This requirement makes little sense:

(i) if the trusts are terminated with the disabled person receiving the settled property this is a "nothing" for IHT purposes;

(ii) if another person becomes absolutely entitled the disabled person will make a PET;

(iii) if the property becomes held in the disabled trust he will likewise make a PET.

36.50 In all other cases the disabled person would have made a chargeable transfer when the trusts continued but would that have mattered? It seems to be accepted that property in a s.89A trust can be appointed away from the disabled person so why make it a condition of s.89A status that, in general, the appointment must be absolute. The likely explanation is that it reflects the desire of HMRC to curtail the use of settlements whenever possible.[71]

EXAMPLE 36.6

Sissy, diagnosed with a condition that will lead to disability within the legislation, settles her property on trusts under which:

(i) during her lifetime the trustees have a discretion to pay income to a class of beneficiaries including Sissy and her siblings with power to accumulate any surplus (this satisfies the requirements in s.89A(1)(c)(i): "*during the life of [Sissy] no interest in possession in the settled property subsists*");

(ii) the trust has a power to pay or apply capital for the benefit of any beneficiary but is limited by a proviso that during Sissy's lifetime it can only be exercised in her favour (this satisfies *Condition 1*);

(iii) the trustees also have a wide power of appointment in favour of any of the beneficiaries but again limited so that during Sissy's life the power can only be exercised either to make an outright appointment or to create trusts for a disabled person falling within

---

[70] IHTA 1984 s.44(2).
[71] See Precedent A1.3.

IHA 1984 s.89 or which give the disabled beneficiary an interest in possession.

The IHT consequences are therefore the same once the s.89A trust has been set up as for a s.89 trust. It is very unlikely that Sissy would ever want to use this relief. Why not just set up a trust where she is entitled to the income and which will qualify for relief as a type iv trust?[72] Then she will obtain capital gains tax uplift on death. It is true that her entitlement to income will lose any means-tested benefits but a s.89A trust (type (ii) below) which is discretionary over income will lose the benefit of capital gains tax uplift on death as well as the possibility of creating an IPDI over the property on her death. If she wants a discretionary trust because she is bothered about losing means-tested benefits then her property may not be over the nil rate band anyway. In any event she could still lose any means-tested benefits even with a discretionary trust if she has deliberately deprived herself of such property by way of a self-settlement. In other words s.89A appears to be a relief that will never be used.

36.51

Self-settlement on interest in possession trusts (s.89B(1)(d))

The alternative for a settlor like Sissy in Example 36.6 with a condition likely to lead to disability is to settle property on an interest in possession trust for herself with remainders over. This gives her an actual, as opposed to a deemed, interest in possession. Note also:

36.52

(i) as with the s.89A trusts, the creation of the trust by Sissy will be a "nothing" for IHT purposes;

(ii) because she has an actual interest in possession, a CGT uplift will apply on her death (when, of course, an IHT charge will arise);

(iii) Sissy is entitled to the income which may affect her means tested benefits;

(iv) only *Condition 1* from s.89A is incorporated.

EXAMPLE 36.7

Sissy in Example 36.6 above decided instead of creating a settlement to comply with the s.89A requirements to settle property on an interest in possession trust for herself with remainders on continuing trusts for her children. The trustees are given a power to pay or apply capital which during Sissy's life can only be exercised in her favour. They also have a wide overriding power of appointment which would enable them to terminate Sissy's interest and to appoint the property on continuing trusts or outright for any person in the wide beneficial class. This trust satisfies

---

[72] See 36.52.

the requirements of s.89B(1)(d) and creates a *"disabled person's interest"* for Sissy.

An interest in possession in settled property to which a disabled person becomes entitled (s.89B(1)(d))

36.53   Note that:

> (i) the settlement may have been set up before March 22, 2006 but the disabled interest must arise after March 21;
>
> (ii) there are no restrictions on power to pay or apply capital or to terminate the settlement.

EXAMPLE 36.8

> The Rotham Family Trust was set up in 2000. Jenny had been entitled to an interest in possession but in 2007 this was terminated by the trustees who appointed Rowley, a disabled person, an interest in possession in the settled property. The position is that:
>
> > (i) Rowley's interest is a "disabled person's interest" within s.89B(1)(c) (only if he was disabled in 2000). One way round this restriction is to transfer the property into a new trust for Rowley. Then it is only necessary that he is disabled in 2007;
> >
> > (ii) Rowley's interest cannot be a transitional serial interest and so it does not matter when Jenny's interest was terminated (this could occur after October 6, 2008);
> >
> > (iii) the termination of Jenny's interest involved the making of a PET by her;
> >
> > (iv) it does not matter that the trustees retain overriding powers of advancement/appointment which could be exercised to terminate Rowley's interest.

EXAMPLE 36.9

> (1) A plans to settle property on trust for his disabled child—the trust can be interest in possession or discretionary. If it is interest in possession it is not necessary that capital can only be applied for the benefit of the disabled child. Hence A has more flexibility and can provide that the capital passes to someone else before or after the child's death. An inter vivos transfer by A will be a PET.
>
> (2) Alternatively, if A is a person who can satisfy HMRC that he will become a disabled person, he sets up an interest in possession trust for himself. In this case the terms of the trust must provide that if any

capital is applied during A's lifetime it is applied for the benefit of A. On A's death the trusts can continue (in which case they will fall within the relevant property regime) or end but in either case there will be a 40 per cent tax charge (unless either the spouse or charity exemption applies).

Conundrum: combining type (i) and type (iii) trusts

There is some uncertainly about the correct analysis in the following example:

36.54

EXAMPLE 36.10

In 2005 a settlement was set up for the benefit of the settlor's disabled son, Damian. Damian is entitled to the income of the trust during his lifetime subject to a power for the trustees to accumulate income for a period of 21 years (this is the defined "accumulation period"[73] in the settlement).

The issues arising

(1) At the time when the trust is set up Damian does not enjoy an interest in possession (because of the power to accumulate). However, at the end of 21 years (if he is then alive) he will be entitled to the income (i.e. he will enjoy an interest in possession). Is the income condition[74] satisfied so that the settlement falls under s.89? It is thought that the requirement (that there is no interest in possession in the settlement during the lifetime of the disabled person) must be applied from time to time. Accordingly, at the start of the settlement the condition is met. If it is subsequently broken then the settlement will no longer be a disabled trust within s.89.

(2) That leads to the second issue: namely in 21 years time, if Damian is still alive, what is the IHT effect of the power of accumulation ending? A type (iii) trust is one in which, after March 21, 2006 a disabled person becomes entitled to an interest in possession. That would appear to be the position: s.89B(1)(c) expressly distinguishes the deemed interest in possession under s.89. Accordingly, it is not considered that there is any change in the IHT position: Damian still has a qualifying interest in possession so that he is treated as beneficially entitled to the trust capital. Of course, a change results for CGT purposes since on the subsequent death of Damian (entitled to an interest in possession in the property) there will be a tax-free uplift.[75]

---

[73] Note that as a result of PAA 2009 from April 6, 2010 a settlement for Damian could be drafted giving the trustees the power to accumulate income during his lifetime. This would remove the difficulty since the s.89 income condition would then be met.

[74] See 36.32.

[75] See 12.19 and following.

36.55 The main differences between the various types of trust as listed above can be summarised as follows:

(i) Type (i) and Type (ii) trusts cannot qualify for the capital gains tax uplift on the death of the disabled beneficiary. Type (iii) and (iv) trusts can.[76]

(ii) Type (i) and (ii) trusts must give no entitlement to income: they are drafted as discretionary trusts. Type (iii) and (iv) trusts must give the disabled person or person who may become disabled actual entitlement to income as it arises. In Type (i) and (ii) trusts it is not even necessary that the disabled person receives the income or is an income beneficiary.

(iii) Type (i) trusts require that at least half the capital if applied during the disabled person's lifetime is applied for his benefit. Type (ii) and (iv) trusts require that if any of the capital is applied for a beneficiary during the settlor's life while the trust continues, it is applied for his benefit. Type (iii) trusts do not impose any capital requirements.

(iv) Types (i), (iii) and (iv) trusts do not impose requirements on what is to happen in the event of the trust ending during the disabled person's lifetime. Type (ii) trusts do.

(v) A Type (ii) or (iv) trust must qualify as a disabled person's interest from the outset (by self-settlement). By contrast the other types can arise out of new trusts created from existing settlements (but requiring that the disabled person was disabled at the date the second trust is established and apparently not allowing relief on a mere variation of an existing settlement unless the disabled person was disabled at the date of the original settlement).[77]

EXAMPLE 36.11

Vincent dies in August 2006 leaving his property on IPDI trusts for Chrissy with power to advance her capital and then to her children. Chrissy is aware that she is likely soon to become mentally incapable. She decides that it is preferable she does not have entitlement to income. At her wish the trust is ended by a transfer of the settled property to her. She then sets up a s.89A trust which is discretionary. This is not a transfer of value by her. However, unlike the IPDI there can be no discretion for the trustees to be able to pay all the capital to someone other than Chrissy while she is alive.

The trustees cannot convert the existing IPDI into a s.89A trust because Chrissy is not disabled at the date of Vincent's death. It is questionable whether if they transfer the property to a new (pilot) s.89A trust set up by her that will count as a s.89A trust. (Arguably Chrissy is beneficially entitled to the property before transfer since she has an IPDI in it, and therefore she will be treated as making the transfer into a new self-settlement.)

---

[76] See Ch.12 and s.72(1B) of TCGA 1992.
[77] Section 89A(1), this section applies to *property transferred* by a person A into settlement on or after March 22, 2006 if A was beneficially entitled to the property immediately before transferring it into settlement.

If, however, Chrissy was already disabled at the date of death then the trustees could, assuming that they have appropriate powers and when she is disabled, convert the IPDI into a s.89 (Type (i)) trust and this would be treated as a non-event for inheritance tax purposes because she is already deemed to be beneficially entitled to the property.

EXAMPLE 36.12

Assume the above facts, i.e. that Vincent leaves property on IPDI trusts for his wife Chrissy, who is not disabled. However, some years later Chrissy's adult child Jane who has always been severely disabled is in greater financial need and Chrissy wants to make some provision for her. Can the IPDI trust now be converted into a s.89 disabled trust for Jane (whether discretionary within s.89 or interest in possession within s.89B(c)) such that it remains outside the relevant property regime? If so, is the conversion a PET by Chrissy or a chargeable transfer?

Section 3A(1A)(iii) refers to a *"gift into a bereaved minor's trust"* on the coming to an end of an IPDI but says nothing about a gift into a disabled trust. Section 3A(3B) has detailed provisions for dealing with conversions of IPDIs into BMIs but not for conversions of IPDI into disabled trusts. However, it appears unnecessary to have such provisions since the person with the IPDI is treated as beneficially entitled to the settled property and therefore if their interest is terminated they make a transfer of value. If that transfer of value constitutes a gift to a disabled trust then the gift can take effect as a PET under s.3A(1A)(c)(ii).

If, however, Jane was not disabled at Vincent's death but became disabled during Chrissy's lifetime then the trust could not be converted into a disabled trust. The authors consider that the property could be resettled into a new trust for Jane which is disabled on the basis that at the date the property was transferred into the second settlement Jane was disabled even if she was not disabled at the date the property was originally settled. This would also be a PET by Chrissy.

VI DISPOSITIONS FOR THE MAINTENANCE OF FAMILY INCLUDING A DEPENDENT RELATIVE

In some circumstances IHTA 1984 s.11 may operate to provide relief from an inheritance tax charge. It provides as follows: **36.56**

"*(1) A disposition is not a transfer of value if it is made by one party to a marriage or civil partnership in favour of the other party or of a child of either party and is—*

(a) for the maintenance of the other party, or

(b) for the maintenance, education or training of the child for a period ending not later than the year in which he attains the

age of eighteen or, after attaining that age, ceases to undergo full-time education or training.

(2) A disposition is not a transfer of value if it is made in favour of a child who is not in the care of a parent of his and is for his maintenance, education or training for a period ending not later than the year in which—

(a) he attains the age of eighteen, or

(b) after attaining that age he ceases to undergo full-time education or training;

but paragraph (b) above applies only if before attaining that age the child has for substantial periods been in the care of the person making the disposition.

(3) A disposition is not a transfer of value if it is made in favour of a dependent relative of the person making the disposition and is a reasonable provision for his care or maintenance.

(4) A disposition is not a transfer of value if it is made in favour of an illegitimate child of the person making the disposition and is for the maintenance, education or training of the child for a period ending not later than the year in which he attains the age of eighteen or, after attaining that age, ceases to undergo full-time education or training.

(5) Where a disposition satisfies the conditions of the preceding provisions of this section to a limited extent only, so much of it as satisfies them and so much of it as does not satisfy them shall be treated as separate dispositions.

(6) In this section—

'child' includes a step-child and an adopted child and 'parent' shall be construed accordingly;

'civil partnership', in relation to a disposition made on the occasion of the dissolution or annulment of a civil partnership, and in relation to a disposition varying a disposition so made, includes a former civil partnership;

'dependent relative' means in relation to any person—

(a) a relative of his, or of his spouse or civil partner , who is incapacitated by old age or infirmity from maintaining himself, or

(b) his mother or father or his spouse's or civil partner's mother or father;

'marriage', in relation to a disposition made on the occasion of the dissolution or annulment of a marriage, and in relation to a disposition varying a disposition so made, includes a former marriage;

'year' means period of twelve months ending with 5th April."

888

The section operates by providing that a relevant disposition is not a transfer **36.57**
of value. Accordingly it does not give rise to an IHT liability even if the donor
dies within seven years (or, indeed, immediately) after making the disposition.
The provision is limited to lifetime dispositions (i.e. it does not operate in
respect of transfers made on death).[78]

It will be noted that the section covers a number of situations: for instance, **36.58**
dispositions in favour of children in s.11(1)(b),(2) and (4). Especially relevant
in the context of disabled persons is s.11(3) dealing with dispositions in favour
of a "dependent relative" as defined in s.11(6).

Section 11(3) refers to "care" as well as "maintenance". Neither word is **36.59**
defined but the provision must be reasonable. *Care* is thought to include the
provision of services and *reasonable* presumably means of such amount as is
reasonably necessary having regard to the financial and other circumstances
of the relative and their needs. Note the provision in s.11(5) which enables a
disposition to attract relief even if part of a larger (non-qualifying) disposition. That part which is reasonable falls within the section as illustrated by
the following case.

The McKelvey case[79]

A terminally ill daughter gave two investment properties to her disabled **36.60**
mother (for whom she was caring) intending that they would be sold after
her death and the proceeds used to provide nursing care. The Special
Commissioner decided:

(i) that the greater part of the value transferred (£140,500 out of a total
value of £169,000 for the two properties) was reasonable provision for
the disabled mother. Given that the daughter died soon after making the
gift, the balance was a failed PET;

(ii) whether the provision was reasonable had to be decided in the light of
the circumstances as they were believed to be at the time of the gift. In
this case, the mother did not, in the event, need to sell the properties
to pay for nursing care. The reasonableness test implies an objective
standard, i.e. what would a reasonable man consider to be reasonable
provision at the time of the gift.

It is thought that s.11 may exempt dispositions into trust provided that the **36.61**
relevant conditions are met. For instance, in *McKelvey* the daughter could
have settled the property for the benefit of her mother. Bear in mind, however,
that it is necessary to show that the capital value settled represents reasonable
provision, i.e. it is important that the settlement is drafted to provide for the
capital to be applied for the mother's benefit. Merely giving her an income
entitlement will not suffice.

---

[78] These are not "dispositions" by IHTA 1984 s.4 tax is charged "as if" the deceased had made a
transfer of value.
[79] *McKelvey v RCC* [2008] STC (SCD) 944.

CHAPTER 37

REVERTER TO SETTLOR TRUSTS

- Tax treatment of a revertor to settlor trust before the FA 2006 changes (**37.02**)
- The IHT position from March 22, 2006 (**37.19**)
- The POA position from December 5, 2005 (**37.28**)
- Comments and conclusions (**37.34**)

37.01 Before December 5, 2005, reverter to settlor trusts had been popular for both IHT and CGT planning purposes and as a way of escaping from pre-owned assets income tax charges. However, the pre-Budget statement on December 5, 2005 made it clear that the latter use was to be stopped although the actual legislation was not published until the Finance Bill in April 2006. The new IHT rules taxing settlements, effective from March 22, 2006, apart from largely stopping the creation of new trusts capable of benefiting from reverter to settlor relief, also rendered the IHT position of existing reverter to settlor trusts problematic.

I TAX TREATMENT OF A REVERTER TO SETTLOR TRUST BEFORE THE FA 2006 CHANGES

37.02 A trust which attracted IHT reverter to settlor relief involved the following ingredients:

(i) the trust fund was held on an interest in possession trust since property held in a discretionary trust could not benefit from reverter to settlor relief although before March 22, 2006 it was possible to convert such a trust into a qualifying interest in possession trust[1];

(ii) on the termination of the interest in possession (whether during the lifetime of the beneficiary or on his death) the trust fund had to revert to either:

    (a) the settlor; or

    (b) the settlor's spouse or registered civil partner[2] during his lifetime provided they were UK domiciled; or

---

[1] The trust did not have to start off as interest in possession in order to qualify for reverter to settlor relief.

[2] From December 5, 2005.

(c) the settlor's widow or widower or surviving civil partner provided that this occurred within two years of the settlor's death and that person was UK domiciled;

(iii) the reverter could be absolutely or on interest in possession trusts.

It was not necessary for the settlor to be UK domiciled for relief to be available although in practice it was unlikely that a non-UK domiciled settlor would use such arrangements (except possibly in the case of UK land), because for foreign situated assets he could rely on the excluded property provisions.

Inheritance tax position prior to March 22, 2006[3]

IHTA 1984 ss.53(3) and 54(1) provided that IHT was not chargeable on the termination of an interest in possession (whether on the death of the beneficiary or otherwise) if, when the interest came to an end, the property in which the interest subsisted reverted to the settler, etc (see the above list).[4]   **37.03**

The result, if these conditions were satisfied, was that: **37.04**

(i) IHT was not chargeable if the interest in possession ended during the lifetime of the beneficiary[5]; and

(ii) on the death of the beneficiary the value of the settled property was left out of account in determining the value of his estate immediately before his death.[6]

EXAMPLE 37.1

Angela set up a trust in 2000 for her father Fred for life, reverter to Angela absolutely on the death of Fred or on earlier termination of Fred's interest. The trust owned the house in which Fred lived as his main residence. Fred died in 2005 and the property passed back to Angela:

(i) the creation of the trust was a PET by Angela;

(ii) there was no IHT on the death of Fred as the property then reverted to Angela;

(iii) if, instead, the property had reverted to Angela's spouse while Angela was alive or to her widower within two years of her death, there would still be no IHT payable on the ending of Fred's interest;

(iv) however, if Angela died while Fred was still alive, the property had to revert to Angela's widower within two years of her death in order to secure the relief.[7]

---

[3] For HMRC guidance, see IHTM 04351–3; IHTM 16121–23.

[4] As already noted the reversion in these cases could be absolute or on interest in possession trusts. See IHTA 1984 ss.53(4) and 54(2).

[5] Hence, the ending of the interest in possession was not a potentially exempt transfer: see IHTA 1984 s.53(3) and (4).

[6] This is discussed at 37.07.

[7] This was an important practical point: whilst children may assume that parents die first it does

37.05 The exemption was often used (as in the above Example) when children wanted to provide for their parents or for other elderly relatives. In the above example, CGT principal private residence relief was available to the trustees if the house was sold during Fred's lifetime. This would not have been available if the house had been owned by Angela and she simply allowed Fred to live there. The reverter to settlor relief could also be useful where a settlor wanted to make provision for a minor child but wished to ensure that if the child died before becoming absolutely entitled, the funds would revert to him.[8] Additionally, the trust was sometimes used in a matrimonial context where one spouse was providing for another but wished to retain a long term interest in the assets being transferred. Finally, the exemption was sometimes used in the context of "s.102B sharing arrangements" to deal with the problems that arose if the donee moved out.[9]

37.06 The exemption was only applicable at the point when the settled property reverted to the settlor. Thus, if property was settled on trust for A for life, then to B for life with a reverter to the settlor, C, there was no IHT on the death of B when the property reverted to C but there will have been IHT (subject to the availability of any other reliefs, such as the spouse exemption) on the death of A when it passed in trust for B.

Restrictions

37.07 The IHT relief was *not* available if:

(i) the settlor (or spouse/widow/widower etc as the case may be) had acquired a reversionary interest in the property for a consideration in money or money's worth. This restriction was extended to catch the situation where the settlor acquired the reversion as a result of transactions "*which include a disposition for such consideration (whether to him or another) of that interest or of other property*",[10]

(ii) the relief depended upon a reversionary interest having been transferred into a settlement on or after March 10, 1981.[11]

The first exclusion was designed to prevent tax being avoided in the following way.

---

not always happen. Deaths in the wrong order could result in multiple IHT charges. The reversionary interest was a chargeable asset in Angela's estate: moreover if Angela died within seven years of setting up the trust for her father then the PET would become chargeable irrespective of the position on the death of the father: see Example 37.6.

[8] As discussed below, for relief to be available, the trust for the child had to be interest in possession. It could not, for instance, be in the form of an accumulation and maintenance trust. Of course, such a trust had no income tax advantages because any income would be taxable on the settlor anyway, either because the trust was settlor-interested ITTOIA 2005 s.624 applies) or because it had to be paid out to the minor child (ITTOIA 2005 s.629 applies): see Ch.7.

[9] See 43.94.

[10] IHTA 1984 s.53(6) and 54(3).

[11] IHTA 1984 s.53(5) and see s.54(3).

EXAMPLE 37.2

Assume that Sol settled property on trust for Bill for life some time ago remainder to Bruce. Bill is elderly. The property settled is worth £500,000 and Bruce's reversion is worth £200,000. But for the above qualification the tax that would otherwise have been payable on Bill's death could have been avoided by the settlor Sol purchasing Bruce's reversion for £200,000 with the result that on Bill's death no charge would have arisen (thanks to the reverter to settlor relief) and the £200,000 would have reached Bruce free of tax.

The second qualification was designed to counteract the sort of planning that proved successful in *IRC v Fitzwilliam*.[12]

EXAMPLE 37.3

Many years ago Adam (now deceased) settled property on trust for Bertram for life remainder to Claude. Bertram is now elderly. On the death of Bertram an IHT charge would arise on the ending of his interest in possession. Bertram and Claude might have sought to avoid this charge by:

(i) Claude settling his remainder interest on trusts for Bertram for life with remainder to himself. This would not involve any IHT charge (Claude's remainder interest was excluded property) or any CGT charge[13];

(ii) Bertram then surrendered his life interest under the original settlement: no IHT was payable as he remained entitled to a qualifying interest in possession in the trust fund[14];

(iii) when Bertram subsequently died the property reverted to Claude.

As a result of the second exclusion reverter to settlor relief is not available on Bertram's death since it depends on the transfer of a reversionary trust into a settlement.[15]

HMRC consider that the relief is only available if the property which reverts **37.08** is the underlying property in which the interest in possession subsists. This prevents arrangements which involve a settlement of the interest in possession (not within the statutory restriction considered above which is concerned with reversionary interests).

[12] [1993] STC 502.
[13] See TCGA 1992 s.76(1).
[14] See IHTA 1984 s.53(2). Query whether for CGT purposes there could be a charge on a deemed disposal under TCGA 1992 s.71 on the basis of the property passing into a new settlement.
[15] Of course, this scheme cannot generally be implemented after March 21, 2006 since the new settlement set up by Claude would not give Bertram a qualifying interest in possession unless he was disabled.

EXAMPLE 37.4

Cynthia died in 1994. She left her residuary estate equally between her son Robin (a spendthrift) and her daughter Diana. Robin's interest was left on trust for him for life remainder to his daughter Sarah. Cynthia left the other half of her residuary estate outright to Diana. Unfortunately she made no provision for her husband, John. Therefore in 1995 Robin settled his life interest on trust for his father for life remainder to Robin and Diana settled her absolute interest for her father for his life remainder to her. John is now elderly and the children want to know the inheritance tax and capital gains tax position on his death:

  (i) Robin's settlement involved a termination of his life interest under IHTA 1984 s.51 and a transfer of value under s.52 which was a PET in 1995; Diana's settlement of her absolute interest for her father was also a PET.

 (ii) John is entitled to a qualifying interest in possession in the whole residuary estate. On his death there is no reverter to settlor relief on that share of the property reverting to Robin because it is the life interest which Robin settled (the father taking an interest *pur autre vie*) and not the residuary estate. HMRC consider that there is nothing in IHTA 1984 s.49(1) itself to deem Robin to have settled the underlying capital. He is only the settlor of the life interest. By contrast Diana is settlor of the capital and therefore on John's death reverter to settlor relief is available.

(iii) If John died or the interest otherwise reverted to Robin prior to October 6, 2008 it is understood that HMRC accept that Robin's interest in possession is a transitional serial interest in these circumstances on the basis that the will trust and father's trust can be treated as a compound settlement.[16] If the life interest reverts to Robin because father dies after October 5, 2008 then it can no longer be a qualifying interest in possession and thereafter the trust in which Robin is life tenant is a relevant property trust.

(iv) On John's death there is a capital gains tax uplift in respect of the share reverting to Diana (because what she has settled and is held in trust for him is the underlying capital). However, there is no capital gains tax uplift in respect of the share reverting to Robin. (TCGA 1992 s.72 does not apply.) There is no disposal of the underlying settled property of the original will trust on John's death; for CGT purposes the only settled property comprised in his trust is a life interest. Accordingly the assets in Cynthia's will trust remain at the original base cost. There is no actual or deemed disposal of those underlying assets on John's death or on earlier termination of his interest in possession because those assets are not comprised in father's settlement (at least as far as Robin's interest is concerned).[17]

---

[16] See *Thomas v IRC* [1981] STC 382.
[17] For assignments of life interests and reversionary interests see 27.19 onwards.

Reservation of benefit and reverter to settlor trusts

By retaining a reversionary interest in his settlement, did the settlor reserve a **37.09** benefit? In general the answer was no: the interest retained involved a carve-out, i.e. the settlor retained his interest in reversion and merely gave away the immediate enjoyment of the settled property (the interest in possession).[18] If, however, the trustees had power to appoint the settled funds back to the settlor at any time (i.e. to bring the interest in possession to an end or to appoint an interest in possession in favour of the settlor), then the carve-out argument was less persuasive: see the statements of Lightman J. in the *Eversden* case confirming that a settlor reserved a benefit when he was an object of his discretionary trust.[19]

The remainder interest would have had some value in the settlor's estate because it was not excluded property.[20] However, if the interest could be defeated by the exercise of overriding powers of appointment its value was likely to be nominal.[21] In any event, the planning was done on the basis that the settlor would survive the life tenant. FA 2006 did not change the reservation of benefit rules in so far as they affect the settlor of a reverter to settlor trust.

From the perspective of the life tenant (Y) the position was slightly differ- **37.10** ent. Suppose he had owned the property but given it to X who later settled it on trust for Y with reverter to X. In these circumstances Y reserves a benefit in the property originally given away. However, it was not taxed under the reservation of benefit rules provided the interest in possession continued until his death because the property was comprised in his estate albeit that the value was ignored.[22] As a result reverter to settlor trusts were seen as a way of preserving a "sharing" arrangement when the donee had ceased to occupy the property.

EXAMPLE 37.5

> Clarissa lived in Blueberry Villas with her daughter, Jane. She gave Jane a 50 per cent share in the property relying on FA 1986 s.102B(4) to avoid a reservation of benefit (this is a "sharing arrangement").[23] However, Jane unexpectedly married at the age of 45 and moved out. Clarissa would thereupon be treated as having reserved a benefit in Jane's share. But if (before March 22, 2006) Jane had settled her 50 per cent share on reverter to settlor trusts giving Clarissa a life interest, then because the property was comprised in her estate (as the result of s.49(1)) it

---

[18] This was confirmed in an HMRC letter to the Law Society dated May 18, 1987. See also *Re Cochrane* [1906] 2 IR 200.

[19] The whole concept of a carve-out in reverter to settlor trusts is difficult to reconcile with the decision of the Court of Appeal in *Eversden* (see 22.14) that there is only a single gift to the interest in possession beneficiary.

[20] See IHTA 1984 s.48(1)(b).

[21] If those overriding powers could be exercised in favour of a class of beneficiaries including the settlor then he reserved a benefit.

[22] FA 1986 s.102(3).

[23] See further Ch.33.

was outside the reservation of benefit rules (see FA 1986 s.102(3)) even though, because of the reverter to settlor relief, its value was left out of account when on her death it reverted to Jane.[24]

It might be thought that the distinction between property being comprised in the estate of the deceased life tenant but its value not being taxed is wafer thin but it is a distinction carefully drawn in a number of places in the IHT legislation: for instance, in relation to a business attracting 100 per cent relief (the business assets are in the estate but are untaxed) and in the context of the estate duty exemption for the surviving spouse which is carried over into IHT.[25]

Failed PET

37.11   If the settlor died within seven years of making the settlement, he had made a failed PET. In calculating the transfer of value, the value (if any) of his reversionary interest was taken into consideration.

EXAMPLE 37.6

In February 2000 Alan settled property worth £100,000 on interest in possession trusts for his mother Mischa, remainder to him. His mother had a life expectancy of 10 years. Alan died two years after the settlement was made. At the date of the settlement Alan's reversionary interest was worth £20,000 and therefore the loss to his estate in making the transfer into trust was £80,000. By the time A died, however, his reversionary interest was worth £40,000. On his death he was taxed on the value of the reversionary interest (£40,000) and on the failed PET of £80,000.

A settlor-interested trust

37.12   The settlor retained an interest in the settlement for the purposes of income tax[26] and capital gains tax,[27] and therefore he (rather than the trustees or life tenant) was subject to tax on any settlement income and chargeable gains. Reverter to settlor trusts were therefore commonly used to hold property

---

[24] See FA 1986 s.102(3) which taxes reservation of benefit property on the death of the donor unless the property forms part of her estate immediately before her death. Because of Clarissa's life interest it does form part of her estate but because of the reverter to settlor relief the value is untaxed. The position would be different on an inter vivos termination of the life interest since s.102(4) does not deem the property to be part of the person's estate immediately before termination but simply deems a PET to arise.

[25] By IHTA 1984 Sch.6 para.2.

[26] See ITOIA 2005 s.624.

[27] See TCGA 1992 s.77.

which produced neither income nor chargeable gains, e.g. a family home which was occupied by the life tenant or an insurance bond.[28]

Capital gains tax before March 22, 2006

On the life tenant's death, *if the trust then ended*, the property was deemed to **37.13** be disposed of at no gain no loss and the normal death uplift did not apply. The settlor would therefore receive back the trust assets without a CGT charge but (broadly speaking) at a base cost equal to the market value of the assets when he put them into trust.[29]

For this reason it was normally preferable to ensure that on the death of the life tenant the settlor became entitled to an interest in possession with the trustees having power to advance him capital. This still secured the IHT reverter to settlor relief (because IHTA 1984 s.49(1) deemed the property to be part of his estate) but meant that the death uplift was available for CGT purposes when the life tenant died.[30]

EXAMPLE 37.7

In 1999 Kindly purchased a pleasant riverside flat for his mother which he settled on trusts under which she had an interest in possession and subject thereto on the following (alternative) trusts:

(i) *for Kindly absolutely*: when Mother dies and the property reverts to Kindly, IHT is avoided but there is no uplift in the CGT base cost of the flat so that if it has increased in value and is sold by Kindly after Mother's death the gain will be taxable.[31] Even if Mother occupied the property as her main residence, on her death the trust ends and therefore Kindly cannot claim main residence relief by reference to Mother's occupation because he, not the trustees, now owns the property;

(ii) *for Kindly on interest in possession trusts*: IHT reverter to settlor relief was available. The normal CGT death uplift applies.[32] Some doubt had been expressed as to whether reverter to settlor relief was available where the property reverted to the settlor on interest in possession trusts rather than absolutely but the HMRC Manual confirmed[33] that relief was due (and this was still the case if the reverter took place prior to October 6, 2008 because the settlor

---

[28] Insurance products are considered generally in Ch.47. Many employ a carve-out principle using a settlor interested trust. Note that TCGA 1992 s.77 was abolished from April 6, 2008.

[29] TCGA 1992 s.73(1)(b) which applies if the settlement ends on the death of the interest in possession beneficiary.

[30] TCGA 1992 s.72: there is no logic in the different CGT treatment of a continuing trust which is thought to result from a legislative oversight. It is this aspect that creates a continuing problem for existing reverter to settlor trusts which have continued after October 6, 2008.

[31] See TCGA 1992 s.73(1)(b).

[32] See TCGA 1992 s.72 which does not contain a restriction similar to that in s.73.

[33] At IHTM 16121.

could take a qualifying interest in possession under the transitional serial interest rules);[34]

(iii) *for Kindly's wife either absolutely or on interest in possession trusts*: provided that Kindly was alive when the interest in possession of his mother ends, IHT relief was available under the pre-March 2006 old rules in both cases (and continued to be available in both cases if the mother died before October 6, 2008). For CGT purposes the death uplift was available in both cases (TCGA 1992 s.73(1)(b) only excludes the uplift if the property reverts absolutely to the "disponer" and there is no similar restriction on reverter to spouses of the settlor);

(iv) the same results as in (iii) followed if the property passed to Kindly's widow (either absolutely or on interest in possession trusts) within two years of his death. For CGT purposes the death uplift was (and continues to be) available.

Note that if the property was sold during Mother's life the trustees were entitled to principal private residence relief under TCGA 1992 s.225. It did not matter, for this purpose, what trusts (if any) took effect after the mother's interest in possession.

Putting a house in the trust

37.14 A reverter to settlor trust was therefore often used to obtain principal private residence relief on what was effectively a second home of the settlor.

EXAMPLE 37.8

Eric wanted to purchase a property for the use of his mother. In 2005 he settled cash on interest in possession trusts for his mother, reverter to himself. The trustees had no overriding powers of appointment exercisable in favour of Eric and so he did not reserve a benefit. The trustees purchased the property. On the death of his mother in February 2006 there was no charge to IHT as a result of the reverter to settlor exemption.[35]

If the house had been sold during the mother's lifetime (while she was in occupation or within three years of her ceasing to occupy it) principal private residence relief under TCGA 1992 s.225 would have been available to the trustees, and no chargeable gains would be assessed on the settlor, Eric, under TCGA 1992 s.77.[36] This was advantageous since if Eric had bought the property personally then unless he was also in occupation, no principal private residence relief would have been available on the sale.[37]

---

[34] This is no longer the case as the reverter to Kindly will occur after October 5, 2008: see 37.23.

[35] See IHTA 1984 s.53(3).

[36] Eric would have been assessed to CGT if the sale had taken place before April 6, 2008. After that the trustees are liable for any CGT.

[37] Relief for dependent relatives was abolished in 1988: TCGA 1992 s.226.

POA Regime before December 5, 2005

The POA Regime affected reverter to settlor trusts in two ways. First, HMRC **37.15** considered that the POA charge could apply to the settlor if the trust fund included intangibles.[38] Second, reverter to settlor trusts were sometimes used as a way of avoiding the POA charge.

Dealing with the first point, in the case of Eric and his mother (see Example **37.16** 37.8 above) there was no charge on Eric under the POA Regime. Eric was not in occupation of the property and so the land charge had no application[39] despite the fact that he had either satisfied the disposal condition (if he settled the house) or the contribution condition (if he provided the trust with funds to purchase the house). If Eric moved into the property with his mother, then he would reserve a benefit and so still be outside POA.[40]

Assume, however, that Eric's mother moved into a nursing home in 2007 and the trustees sold the house. At that point the trust holds intangibles (cash) and all the other conditions for the para.8 charge to apply are satisfied.[41] The reservation of benefit exclusion in Sch.15 para.11(3) FA 2004 does not apply because Eric only has a remainder interest in the settlement and this interest was never given away (i.e. it was carved out of the original gift). If Eric wished to keep the trust going to provide income for his mother (although he derives no income tax benefit from this since it is taxed on him) the trustees should invest in assets other than intangibles (for instance, let the house) so that he is not subject to a POA charge.

EXAMPLE 37.9

If the cash from the sale of the house was (say) £1 million, the chargeable amount for POA purposes for the tax year is calculated based on the official rate of interest—in 2011–12 four per cent. Hence, in 2011–12 the chargeable amount for Eric is £40,000 for the year. Assume the cash is held by the trustees for one month before being reinvested in let land. The chargeable amount for the taxable period of one month is £3,333. This falls within the POA de minimis exemption and therefore Eric pays no tax. If, however, the taxable benefit was in excess of the de minimis level: (say) £6,000 for the month, then tax is charged on Eric as follows. Assume also that the cash produces income (e.g. £1,000 in the relevant month), and that Eric is a 50 per cent taxpayer for 2011–12.

Trust income

£500 income tax under ITTOIA 2005 s.624

POA Regime charge

Chargeable amount is

---

[38] FA 2004 Sch.15 para.8.
[39] FA 2004 Sch.15 para.3. See Ch.34 and 34.14.
[40] See FA 2004 Sch.15 para.11(3).
[41] FA 2004 Sch.15 para.8.

£6,000 less £500 = £5,500 × 50% = £2,750 ("deemed income")

Total income tax liability is £3,250 (£2,750 + £500)

In these circumstances there is no benefit to Eric in keeping the trust going since he pays more income tax than if he owned the property outright due to the "deemed income" he is treated as receiving. In these circumstances mother should surrender her life interest so that the trust ends and reverter to settlor relief is available.[42]

37.17   Reverter to settlor trusts were also used to avoid the POA charge.

Example 37.10

> Clara carried out an *Ingram* scheme in 1998 giving the freehold reversion of her house to her daughter Rose.[43] As a result of the introduction of the POA charge on April 6, 2005, Rose settled the freehold reversion in June 2005 on interest in possession trusts for her mother Clara with reverter to Rose. In these circumstances the entire property (freehold and lease) forms part of Clara's estate[44] so that there was no POA charge. Provided that on Clara's death the settled property (the freehold interest) reverted to Rose, relief was available from inheritance tax on Clara's death.[45]

Other uses of reverter to settlor trusts before December 5, 2005

37.18   Apart from their use in providing for aged relatives and to circumvent the POA charge, reverter to settlor trusts were also used in the following situations:

(i) As part of a property purchase arrangement: assume that Dad retained a lease and sold the encumbered freehold of his main residence for

---

[42] If in the above example the trustees had reserved powers to end mother's interest and appoint an interest to Eric there would have been no POA charge on sale of the property because Eric reserved a benefit and so was protected from POA under the ROB exemption in para.11(3). If an interest in possession had been appointed to Eric before October 6, 2008 it would have been a transitional serial interest. The POA charge would not apply: both para.11(1) (ownership exemption) and (3) (GWR exemption) in Sch.15 FA 2004 gave protection. Reverter to settlor relief was available. The property was in Eric's estate for IHT purposes but this was the position anyway under GWR. If an IIP is appointed to Eric after October 5, 2008 then the property is not part of his estate but there is still no POA charge due to the GWR exemption under para.11(3). However, it is unlikely the trustees would do this since by appointing an interest in possession to Eric after October 5, 2008 mother has made a chargeable transfer and there is no reverter to settlor relief.

[43] For *Ingram* schemes, see 22.18 and 43.38.

[44] FA 2004 Sch.15 para.11(1).

[45] The fact that there is no inheritance tax payable on Clara's death does not prevent the property from being part of her estate while she is alive and displacing FA 1986 s.102(3) (gifts with reservation) on her death. Note that the analysis might be different if Clara's interest in possession was ended during her lifetime. In these circumstances was there a deemed PET because her reservation of benefit ceased and s.102(4) FA 1986 was not displaced? If so, Clara's interest in possession had to continue until her death if IHT protection was sought.

full market value. This was outside the POA charge as the result of para.10(1).[46] Funds for its purchase were settled by the children on a reverter to settlor trust for Dad remainder to them. Provided that the trust was appropriately drafted, the CGT death uplift would apply on Dad's death. (Of course, the entire property could have been bought by such a trust if the children had sufficient funds.)

(ii) As part of post-death planning: on Dad's death his half share in the family home was left in his will to his daughter Clara to use up his nil rate band. She settled that interest on reverter to settlor trusts for her Mum (the other beneficial owner, who is in occupation of the property). Main residence relief or death uplift (as appropriate) would then be available on the share held in trust.[47]

(iii) As part of a marketed IHT avoidance scheme: Jim gave his house to his son reserving a shorthold tenancy (on commercial terms) to permit his continued occupation. At the end of that tenancy the son settled the property on a reverter to settlor trust giving Jim an interest in possession. This type of arrangement involved exploiting the distinction between property and value in order to circumvent the POA/GWR rules.

II THE IHT POSITION FROM MARCH 22, 2006[48]

The IHT relieving sections

Sections 53(3) and (4) and 54(1) and (2) were not themselves amended by FA 2006. However, the revised IHT legislation on settlements affects reverter to settlor trusts in two ways. **37.19**

Existing trusts

In order to obtain reverter to settlor relief for existing trusts the property had to revert to the settlor (or his spouse) either absolutely or on qualifying interest in possession trusts so that the settlor etc become "beneficially entitled". Crucially the interest in possession had to be "qualifying" which means in the case of interests arising after March 21, 2006 either is an IPDI; a disabled person's interest; or a TSI.[49] **37.20**

Hence, if the settlor is to obtain reverter to settlor relief for existing trusts it is necessary to satisfy one of two conditions: **37.21**

---

[46] FA 2004 Sch.15 para.10(1) provides that this will be an excluded transaction given that Dad is disposing of his whole interest in the property apart from the rights reserved under the lease.

[47] Although there were potential problems: see Ch.43.

[48] For the changes in the IHT treatment of settlements generally, see 23.02 and following.

[49] IHTA 1984 s.49(1A).

(i) either the settlor (or his spouse/civil partner if the settlor is still alive or had died two years previously) must take *absolutely* on the ending of current the interest in possession; or

(ii) the settlor (or spouse/civil partner if settlor is alive or died two years previously) must take on an interest in possession which is a TSI. This was, however, only possible if the interest in possession for the settlor arose before October 6, 2008.

EXAMPLE 37.11

Eric settled a house on interest in possession trusts for his mother in February 2005. The intention behind the trust was CGT planning.[50] The settlement was drafted so that on mother's death the property would revert to Eric on interest in possession trusts so as to obtain the base cost uplift for CGT purposes.[51]

For reverter to settlor relief to apply, Eric's interest in possession had to vest in possession before October 6, 2008 and therefore mother's interest had to terminate before that date—whether inter vivos or on death. Eric's interest was then a TSI. If mother's interest in possession ended after October 5, 2008 and Eric then takes an IIP there is a chargeable transfer by mother with no reverter to settlor relief and the continuing trust for Eric is subject to the relevant property regime. By contrast, if the trusts provide for Eric or his spouse to take absolutely on the termination of his mother's interest (or if they are so amended) then reverter to settlor relief is available whenever the mother's interest ends. However, the CGT death uplift will then be lost if Eric takes outright (although not if his spouse or civil partner takes outright).

The definition of a TSI can present problems

37.22 In the above example, if mother died and the trust property passed to her widower on interest in possession trusts the spouse exemption is available. The widower takes a transitional serial interest.[52] However, on the death of the widower, *unless* the property reverts to Eric or his spouse absolutely[53] there is an IHT charge. Note even if the widower died before October 6, 2008 and Eric then became entitled to an interest in possession, that interest did not qualify as a transitional serial interest (so no reverter to settlor relief was available) if the widower had become entitled to his successive interest in possession after March 21, 2006 (in effect TSI relief had then been used up!).[54]

---

[50] Either to secure principal private residence relief on a sale of the property during the lifetime of mother or the death uplift.

[51] See 37.13. The trustees would have power to advance the settled property to Eric and thereby the trust could be ended.

[52] Even if mother died after October 5, 2008: see 27.17 and following.

[53] If Eric has died already then it needs to revert to Eric's widow within two years of his death.

[54] For a consideration of transitional serial interests, see 27.17 and following.

Conclusions

All existing reverter to settlor trusts should be reviewed. From October 6, 2008 **37.23** the settlor (or his spouse/civil partner) must take absolutely on the death of the life tenant or on the inter vivos termination of that interest if relief is to be available. In these circumstances, if the settlor takes outright, the capital gains tax uplift will be lost.

There is no change to the reservation of benefit rules. Hence, in Example **37.24** 37.11, even if mother had originally given the property to Eric there is no reservation of benefit problem for her if her life interest ends on her death because the property was comprised in her estate.[55] There would be a deemed PET under FA 1986 s.102(4) if her interest ended during her lifetime and she no longer benefitted from the property.[56]

The position of new trusts

New trusts qualifying for reverter to settlor relief cannot be established on or **37.25** after March 22, 2006 except in very limited circumstances because in few trusts will the life tenant enjoy a qualifying interest in possession.[57]

Accordingly reverter to settlor relief is limited to the following circumstances: **37.26**

(i) If B (the beneficiary who takes the interest in possession) has a disabled person's interest[58];

EXAMPLE 37.12

Justin is severely disabled and unlikely to live more than 10 years. His father settles property on Justin for life remainder to Sylvia (Justin's mother). On Justin's death reverter to settlor relief (and the CGT death uplift) is available. The creation of the trust is a PET by Justin's father.

(ii) If B becomes entitled on or after March 22, 2006 to an immediate post-death interest (an IPDI). In these circumstances the settlor was the testator (who gave B the IPDI by his will) and so reverter relief can only be available if the testator's surviving spouse or civil partner becomes absolutely entitled to the property as a result of B's interest ending within two years of the testator's death (a somewhat unlikely scenario!).

---

[55] See Example 37.10 above.
[56] As a result of FA 1986 s.102ZA (inserted by FA 2006) even if mother had not given the property to Eric for him to settle, if her life interest is terminated on or after March 22, 2006 there is a potential reservation of benefit problem since mother is deemed to have made a gift and so must be excluded from any ongoing benefit.
[57] See IHTA 1984 s.54(2A).
[58] See Ch.36 for disabled trusts.

EXAMPLE 37.13

Andrew died in 2007 leaving his house to his son Paul on an IPDI trust with remainder to Andrew's spouse, Emma, absolutely. Paul dies in 2008 and the trusts end. In these circumstances reverter to settlor relief is available, the house is not taxed on Paul's death and the CGT death uplift applies.

37.27 It is unlikely that Andrew would leave his house to his son Paul rather than Emma but it may occur if, say, Paul had a special need falling short of being disabled.

III THE POA POSITION FROM DECEMBER 5, 2005

37.28 As discussed above,[59] reverter to settlor relief was seen as a way round the POA provisions: see, for instance, Example 37.10.

37.29 Such arrangements should now be reviewed. FA 2006 s.80 amended the POA legislation with effect from December 5, 2005 so that the interest in possession of Clara in Example 37.10 is ignored and the property not treated as part of her estate for the purposes of the POA legislation. Accordingly, from December 5 she is within the POA charge. The change potentially affects all reverter to settlor trusts whenever set up although the income tax charge only applies from December 5, 2005.

37.30 The amending legislation inserted new subparas 11(11) and (12) into para.11 of FA 2004 Sch.15 (dealing with exemptions from charge) as follows:

"(11) Sub-paragraph (12) applies where at any time –

> *(a) the relevant property has ceased to be comprised in a person's estate for the purposes of IHTA 1984, or*
>
> *(b) he has directly or indirectly provided any consideration for the acquisition of the relevant property,*

and at any subsequent time the relevant property or any derived property is comprised in his estate for the purposes of IHTA 1984 as a result of section 49(1) of that Act (treatment of interests in possession).

(12) Where this sub-paragraph applies, the relevant property and any derived property–

> *(a) are not to be treated for the purposes of sub-paragraphs (1) and (2) as comprised in his estate at that subsequent time, and*
>
> *(b) are not to be treated as falling within sub-paragraph (5) in relation to him at that subsequent time.*

---

[59] See 37.17 and following.

(13) For the purposes of sub-paragraphs (11) and (12) references, in relation to the relevant property, to any derived property are to other property–

(a) which derives its value from the relevant property, and
(b) whose value, so far as attributable to the relevant property, is not substantially less than the value of the relevant property."

37.31 This change goes much further than had been indicated in the pre-Budget Press Release of December 2005. It does not just affect reverter to settlor trusts but can apply to any trust set up at any time on or after March 18, 1986 where property was comprised in the taxpayer's estate, left it and then he acquired a qualifying interest in possession in the property again.

EXAMPLE 37.14

In 1987 H set up an interest in possession trust for his wife W into which he put a beneficial interest in his house. He may have done this for tax reasons or for asset protection. This was a spouse exempt transfer for inheritance tax purposes and is protected from any POA charge while W's interest continues.[60] W's interest was terminated on January 1, 2007 and the property reverted to H on an interest in possession trust (which was a TSI and so a qualifying interest for IHT purposes). The property is again comprised in H's estate for inheritance tax purposes as a result of IHTA 1984 s.49(1) but POA is payable by H from January 1, 2007 as a result of the amended legislation.

Notice in this case that the reverter to settlor relief is wholly irrelevant to the taxation of H. The property forms part of his estate as the result of a spouse exempt transfer under a settlement which H created! The key point is that although the property will be taxed as part of his estate his former protection against the POA charge has been removed. Of course, the problem would not arise if H had became absolutely entitled (rather than taking an interest in possession) but this could present CGT problems in cases where, e.g. main residence relief was not available.[61]

By contrast, if W had died rather than her interest being terminated by the trustees, the transaction would remain outside the POA net because of para.10.[62]

37.32 Problems can arise on divorce where one spouse may during the divorce have given assets to the other and receives them back as part of a divorce settlement. In such circumstances it is important that the donor receives them back outright rather than on interest in possession trusts.

---

[60] FA 2004 Sch.15 para.10(1)(c).
[61] There are other problems caused by s.80 which are discussed at 34.36.
[62] Unless the trust then owned intangibles in which case there would be a charge on a benefit equal to 4% (in 2011–12) of the capital value of the intangibles.

37.33 The taxpayer can (subject to the time limits) make an election into reservation of benefit[63]. For instance, in Example 37.10 above, Clara is entitled to a qualifying interest in possession in the freehold interest. On her death, s.102(3) (reservation of benefit) is displaced because she has an interest in possession. The election does not change this.

In addition s.54(1) IHTA 1984 would normally disapply any inheritance tax charge on the death of Clara because the settled property has reverted outright to the settlor Rose. However, if an election into reservation of benefit is made, then Sch.15 paras 21(2)(b)(iii) and 22(2)(b)(iii) provide that reverter to settlor relief is not available where the person is beneficially entitled to an interest in possession in the property. Hence, on the death of Clara the freehold interest will now be taxed as part of her estate for inheritance tax purposes, not because she has reserved a benefit but because she has a qualifying interest in possession and the settled property is deemed to be part of her estate. In these circumstances if the settled property reverts outright to Rose although no reverter to settlor relief is available on Clara's death (and therefore an inheritance tax charge may arise) there is still no capital gains tax uplift because the property reverts to the original disponer, Rose. Hence, if Clara elects, Rose potentially could suffer the worst of all worlds: an inheritance tax charge on Clara's death and a capital gains tax charge when Rose later comes to dispose of the freehold based on the original acquisition cost of the trust. The alternative is that Clara does not make the election under Sch.15 and instead pays income tax (or Rose puts Clara in funds to pay the income tax).

IV COMMENTS AND CONCLUSIONS

37.34 Reverter to settlor relief has been severely curtailed. For instance, the sort of arrangement where Dad leaves his house in his will to his only daughter who then settles it on trust for Mum will no longer attract relief. Such a trust now involves the making of a chargeable transfer for IHT purposes by the daughter and Mum does not have a qualifying interest in possession. Of course, it may be that reverter to settlor relief is not necessary in these circumstances. For instance, if Dad's share in the house is within the IHT nil rate band, then if the daughter settles that share on an inter vivos trust for her mother although this is a chargeable transfer no inheritance tax will be payable (assuming the daughter has made no other chargeable transfers).

On the death of the mother, there is still inheritance tax payable if the trust continues because her entitlement to occupy the property or enjoy its income is ignored for inheritance tax purposes (it is not a "qualifying" interest).[64] However, the trustees may benefit from principal private residence relief so the trust might still be thought worthwhile. (Although there is no uplift on

---

[63] This election is considered in Ch.34.

[64] The relevant property regime applies and tax may be charged if the trust ends at that time (an exit charge) although the value of the settled property means that this is unlikely since it will be covered by the IHT nil rate band.

mother's death this does not generally matter if principal private residence relief is available.) Even if the settlor becomes absolutely entitled so that there is a deemed disposal at market value[65] and any principal private residence relief will reduce the chargeable gain. The daughter acquires the property at market value.

EXAMPLE 37.15

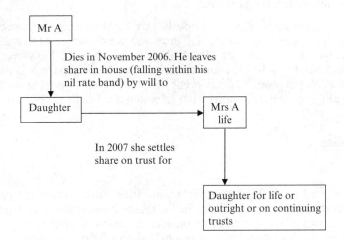

Notes

1. The gift by daughter of her interest in the land is a chargeable transfer not a PET. Since the gift is within her nil rate band this makes little odds.

2. If the house is worth more than the nil rate band at the 10-year anniversary then inheritance tax will be payable but only on the excess above the nil rate band at a rate of six per cent. If Mrs A dies within the first 10 years and the trust is ended, there is no inheritance tax charge even if the house is worth more than the nil rate band at that time.

3. Principal private residence relief for capital gains tax purposes is available if Mrs A is in occupation of the property as her main residence.[66]

4. It does not matter if the daughter or her spouse does not survive Mrs A in terms of the IHT position on Mrs A's death. On Mrs A's death there is no inheritance tax charge because her life interest is ignored for inheritance tax purposes (it is not qualifying).

5. On Mrs A's death there is no base cost uplift for capital gains tax purposes because she does not have a qualifying interest in possession. On disposal of the house by the trustees, however, (whether on a deemed disposal if the trust ends and the daughter takes the house outright or on an actual disposal if the house is sold by the trustees) they are entitled

[65] TCGA 1992 s.71(1).
[66] See TCGA 1992 s.225: see further 43.22.

to principal private residence relief because of Mrs A's occupation of the property as her main residence. Hence capital gains tax will not be a problem.

6. If the daughter dies then she may be treated as having reserved a benefit in the property[67] so that inheritance tax is payable on its value.

7. There is no POA charge unless the daughter occupies the house or the trust fund comprises intangibles and even then only if the daughter does not reserve a benefit. The position is the same as before the 2006 changes. Section 80 is not a problem.

8. Does it matter if Mrs A previously gave the interest in the house to Mr A which is now left to the daughter and which before March 22, 2006 the daughter settled for Mrs A? Is Mrs A subject to POA because of s.80? No, because the transaction between Mr and Mrs A is excluded for POA purposes.[68] In any event Mrs A's interest in possession is not a qualifying interest in possession so would not be caught by s.80.

Other points

37.35   (i) For pre-March 22, 2006 reverter to settlor trusts, review the principal private residence relief. Does the life tenant have a right to occupy under the terms of the settlement? Consider the position particularly carefully where the life tenant also owns a half share of the same property in her own right (as is the case in Example 37.15 above).

(ii) For pre-March 22, 2006 reverter to settlor trusts the POA position should be reviewed for both the settlor and the life tenant. The settlor is not caught if the settled property is a house or chattels and he is not in occupation. But the position is different if the trust owns intangibles. However, s.80 may cause problems for the life tenants of such trusts if they had previously owned the property in question and then given it away to the settlor who settled it.

The best of both inheritance tax and capital gains tax worlds—planning points

37.36   For many taxpayers the original intention behind setting up reverter to settlor trusts was to obtain capital gains tax uplift on death and capital gains tax protection (through principal private residence relief) during the life tenant's lifetime. In Example 37.1 Angela could have retained the house in which Fred lived without any inheritance tax problems on Fred's death. However, her hope was that on Fred's death she could obtain capital gains tax uplift.

As already noted, it is necessary to review pre-March 22, 2006 reverter to settlor trusts where the settlor does not take outright on the death of the life

[67] See Ch.33.
[68] FA 2004 Sch.15 para.10(1)(b).

tenant. To obtain continued inheritance tax protection, change the terms of all existing trusts so that either the settlor takes outright on the termination of the life tenant's interest in possession or (to avoid capital gains tax problems) the settlor's spouse or civil partner takes outright since then the base cost uplift is then available as well as continued inheritance tax protection. If the settlor is worried about divorce then one option would be for the trustees to appoint the spouse an absolute interest but revocable at any time before the life tenant's death. Then if they do divorce the spousal interest can be revoked.

37.37 In some cases the settlor will not be married and therefore using the spouse (or civil partner) will not be an option. Is there any way of obtaining both capital gains tax advantages and inheritance tax protection? Of course the taxpayer may decide that inheritance tax protection is not very useful anyway because the life tenant has few other assets and the house falls within his nil rate band. The figures always need to be calculated before a decision is taken: is it better to pay 40 per cent inheritance tax on the entire value (but starting at a high threshold of £325,000 if the life tenant has no other assets and made no chargeable transfers) or to pay capital gains tax at 28 per cent (for 2011–12) on the gain.

One option might be to trigger the gain while the settlor is alive if the asset held in trust is a house qualifying for principal private residence relief. If the house is sold while the trust continues then principal private residence relief is available. If this is not felt to be desirable another option might be to emigrate the trust. This will trigger a deemed disposal and reacquisition under TCGA 1992 s.80[69] but no chargeable gain on the trustees because of PPR relief. The trustees have then rebased the asset. Only gains arising since emigration will be taxed on the settlor when the life tenant dies. Further, the trust could be immigrated after one complete tax year of non-residence if the family wanted to keep matters straightforward.[70]

37.38 What if the trust property does not qualify for principal private residence relief: e.g. if it is let land or farmland? Or maybe it does qualify for principal private residence relief but the trustees do not want to trigger a gain now. An option might be to engineer a *Crowe v Appleby* situation. Consider the following:

EXAMPLE 37.16

Mother is life tenant of let commercial properties. On her death these pass to her daughter, the settlor. The trustees were hoping for capital gains tax uplift at that point. They revoke mother's life interest in (say) a five per cent share of all the properties (or less if desired) which they appoint on discretionary trusts to the exclusion of mother. (The value of a five per cent share is less than mother's nil rate band.) The result is that the trust fund (the investment properties) now comprises two

---

[69] See Ch.4.
[70] It is not thought that a sub-fund election would work. This election also triggers a deemed disposal for capital gains tax purposes but is not possible unless the trust holds other assets. In addition you cannot have the same life tenant for both funds: for sub-fund elections see Ch.12.

funds, one held on discretionary trusts (five per cent) and one still on qualifying interest in possession trusts for mother (95 per cent). Five per cent of the rent goes into the discretionary fund. Mother has made a chargeable transfer for inheritance tax purposes but the value of the discretionary fund can be kept small. The tax consequences are as follows:

(i) the daughter becomes absolutely entitled to 95 per cent of trust fund for IHT purposes and reverter to settlor relief is available;

(ii) for CGT purposes the daughter is not treated as absolutely entitled to 95 per cent interest because of *Crowe v Appleby*.[71] Accordingly, the settlement continues for CGT purposes with the death uplift applying. Only when the property is sold will the CGT trust end and the daughter become absolutely entitled to 95 per cent of the sale proceeds.

[71] See Ch.9.

Chapter 38

TAX EFFICIENT WILL DRAFTING

- Use of IHT nil rate band before October 9, 2007 (**38.02**)
- The transferable nil rate band (**38.08**)
- Impact on drafting of IHT efficient wills (**38.17**)
- The Nil Rate Band Discretionary Trust (**38.24**)
- BPR/APR and nil rate gifts (**38.46**)
- Dealing with residue with surviving spouse (**38.49**)
- Dealing with residue—no surviving spouse (**38.56**)
- Wills for cohabitees (**38.57**)
- Proposed changes for charitable legacies (**38.59**)

Precedents

This chapter is concerned with drafting IHT efficient wills. Before March 22, **38.01** 2006 the availability of a range of lifetime planning opportunities meant that wills had become of diminished significance. All that has changed since 2006, however, and for many married couples the will is now a principal tool in the battle to save inheritance tax.[1]

The chapter will concentrate on the traditional family will and to simplify the discussion will consider what would be an appropriate will for H who is married to W with two adult children and minor grandchildren. Further, it will be assumed that it is H who will die first and that H and W's combined

---

[1] Unmarried taxpayers will not find the will an especially attractive tax planning vehicle. Same-sex couples may enjoy the advantages of a married couple from December 5, 2005 by registering under CPA 2004.

estate is such that IHT is an issue. Wills for cohabitees are considered, and at the end of this chapter the proposed new relief for charitable legacies.

I USE OF IHT NIL RATE BAND BEFORE OCTOBER 9, 2007

38.02   Prior to October 9, 2007 a married couple would want to ensure that the nil rate band of the first spouse to die was used on his death rather than leaving everything to the surviving spouse. In tax year 2007–08 using two rather than just one nil rate band was worth £120,000 (£300,000 × 40 per cent). However, using the nil rate band of the first spouse to die was not always straightforward.

First, each spouse had to have enough assets in his estate to ensure that if he died first the nil rate band could be used. If he only owned assets of £100,000 at his death his nil rate band could only be used to this extent.[2]

Secondly, unless the couple had a sufficiently large joint estate, they would not want £300,000 to pass direct to their children on H's death because this would leave W financially vulnerable. Further, in many cases the bulk of the family wealth was tied up in the matrimonial home and couples usually disliked the idea of H's share in the home passing outright to the children (especially if the children were from H's first marriage!)[3]

38.03   This usually led to H setting up in his Will a discretionary trust to utilise his IHT nil rate band: the discretionary beneficiaries would include W as well as the children and usually it was envisaged that W would be the principal beneficiary. It was important to ensure that nothing was done which could result in W becoming entitled to a qualifying interest in possession in the trust fund (an IPDI) within two years of H's death since were that to occur the value of the trust fund would then be taxed on her death[4] with the result that H's nil rate band would be wasted.

38.04   A practical problem was to select appropriate assets to go into the trust. A simple solution was to use H's share of the matrimonial home (assuming

---

[2] A deed of variation could not change this by "putting assets into" H's estate. In the situation where assets were unequally split between spouses so that H did not have sufficient assets to cover his nil rate band it was desirable for W to transfer assets to him. This was sometimes referred to as "equalising estates". If the IOU route was to be implemented (see 38.24) then care was needed in connection with the artificial debt rule in FA 1986 s.103 if the estates had been equalised at the time of drafting the wills. See 32.31

[3] See further 38.06. In fact it seems unlikely that, in this situation, the children would succeed in persuading the court to order a sale of the property or to force W to pay them a "rent": note the wide powers of the court under TLATA 1996 ss.14–15. Of course, the children could sell their beneficial share but the price received was likely to be heavily discounted. If a child became bankrupt the normal factors considered by the court on application for an order for sale do not apply. Instead the trustee in bankruptcy can apply to the court having jurisdiction in the bankruptcy where regard will be had to the interests of the bankrupt's creditors as well as to all the circumstances of the case. And 12 months after the bankrupt's assets first vested in the trustee the interests of the creditors are deemed to outweigh all other considerations unless the circumstance of the case are exceptional. At this point it is therefore likely that an order for sale will be made: see IA 1986 s.335A. Another downside was that the children's share would not qualify for CGT principal private residence relief. As a result, in some cases, use was made of a reverter to settlor trust: see 38.07 and Ch.37.

[4] See IHTA 1984 s.144: after the two-year time limit it did not matter since the appointment of an interest in possession after March 21, 2006 is generally a "nothing" for inheritance tax purposes.

that its value[5] equated with his available IHT nil band). However, there were concerns that by virtue of her continuing occupation of the property W would enjoy an interest in possession in the share of the property held in the discretionary trust. Another problem was the CGT position if the property was sold since the availability of principal private residence relief on the share held by the trust will depend on whether W was entitled to occupy the beneficial share of the property under the terms of the settlement.[6]

Constituting the trust by a debt or charge[7]

In many cases the preferred solution was therefore to constitute the discretionary trust by *either* a debt owed to the trustees by W who received all the assets of H's estate *or* by a charge being placed over the assets in H's estate by his executors (typically over his share in the house) which were then assented to W. For many couples the practical results of this arrangement were ideal since W would enjoy the benefit of all the couple's assets whilst H used up his IHT nil rate band on death.

38.05

However, the debt/charge route was not without problems: for instance, what should be the terms of W's debt or of the charge? It would generally be repayable on demand but should it carry interest (rolled-up and so only payable with the principal on W's death) or be index-linked? So far as index linking was concerned—whether by reference to the RPI or to (say) a property index—the tax treatment of the indexed sum in the hands of the trustees was far from clear cut. SDLT could also apply if a debt rather than charge arrangement was used, if W was acquiring an interest in land in consideration of incurring the debt.

Finally, FA 1986 s.103 was capable of operating to disallow the debt on W's death. This would nullify all the tax planning. Section 103 would operate if W had made gifts to H (perhaps as part of an estate equalising exercise) and the debt rather than the charge scheme was used.[8] The case of *Phizackerley*[9] showed that HMRC were not slow to take this point.

---

[5] For the valuation of joint property owned by husband and wife, see *IRC v Arkwright* [2004] EWHC 1720 (Ch) and *Price v RCC* [2010] UKFTT 474 (TC). A half share of a jointly owned house where the house is worth £600,000 will not necessarily be half this (i.e. £300,000). *Arkwright* suggests that a discount should be applied, so that in the above case H's share would not fully satisfy the amount due to the discretionary trustees under the terms of his Will since they are entitled to receive £300,000 but have received a half share worth less than this. This point is also relevant if the IOU scheme is adopted. If the house share is the only asset in H's estate the executors cannot charge it with a debt for more than it is worth. Bear in mind that when the charge is imposed the share may have risen in value: that increased value may be enough to cover a charge for the full nil rate band.

[6] See TCGA 1992 s.225; *Sansom v Peay* [1976] 3 All ER 375 and SP 10/79. It was a difficult balancing exercise to obtain the best of both worlds: i.e. no IHT charge but CGT relief. There are difficult arguments concerning sub-funds under TLATA 1996: see Ch.43 and 43.22.

[7] For a detailed consideration of this topic see 38.36 and following.

[8] It has been suggested that the charge route may also run into s.103 problems if the property is sold by W who then needs the bulk of the proceeds of sale to purchase a replacement property. In this situation the charge will have to be paid off, i.e. the NRBDT trustees will receive part of the proceeds of sale and if W is a donor for the purposes of that section then the trustees should not lend the monies to her. The problem could be overcome by the trustees buying a share in any replacement property along with W.

[9] [2007] STC (SCD) 328: see 38.36.

Outright gifts to children[10]

38.06   If H's estate was sufficiently large this was the easiest way to utilise his nil rate band. In cases where the main value of the estate was represented by the deceased's share in the matrimonial home H might gift his share in the property outright to his children.[11] Say, for instance, that H's beneficial share as a tenant in common was worth £300,000 and that he left it outright to the children.

W's position was that with H's death she would normally become the sole legal owner of the property.[12] She owned beneficially a 50 per cent share in the property and on her death this share would attract IHT. The other share owned by the children would not be taxed: there was no reason to impute the ownership of this share to W. The arrangement was not, however, appropriate in many cases. W may, for instance, be uneasy at the children having rights in the house (especially if the children were from H's first marriage!)[13]

38.07   A major downside was that the children's share would not qualify for CGT principal private residence relief: hence if the house was sold after W's death a chargeable gain could result. Prior to March 22, 2006 this difficulty might have been overcome by the children settling their share on a reverter to settlor trust giving W an interest in possession. Provided that the share reverted to the children on continuing interest in possession trusts this not only secured reverter to settlor relief from inheritance tax on W's death but also the death uplift for capital gains tax purposes. Although this arrangement was stopped by the FA 2006 changes in the IHT treatment of trusts (which largely prevent the creation of new inter vivos qualifying interest in possession trusts) this may not matter. The children could still settle their respective shares in the house on inter vivos interest in possession trusts for W.[14] The share would be within each child's IHT nil rate band so that although they made a chargeable transfer no IHT would be payable. Whether or not the property reverted to them on W's death, her interest in possession was not a qualifying interest in possession and therefore not taxable on her death. Although there was no capital gains tax uplift, if the trustees disposed of the property (whether on termination of the trust or on an actual sale) principal private residence relief available.[15]

---

[10] Or, indeed, to other chargeable persons: for instance, grandchildren or issue of a first marriage.

[11] For problems involved in valuing shares in land in the light of the *Arkwright* decision, see fn.5 above.

[12] See LPA 1925 ss.34 and 35.

[13] It seems unlikely in this situation that the children would succeed in persuading the court to order a sale of the property or to force W to pay them a "rent": note the wide powers of the court under TLATA 1996 ss.14–15. Of course, the children could sell their beneficial share but the price received is likely to be heavily discounted. If a child was to become bankrupt the normal factors considered by the court on application from an order for sale do not apply. Instead the trustee in bankruptcy will apply to the court having jurisdiction in the bankruptcy where regard will be had to the interests of the bankrupt's creditors as well as to all the circumstances of the case. However, 12 months after the bankrupt's assets first vested in the trustee the interest of the creditors outweighs all other considerations unless the circumstances of the case are exceptional. At this point it is therefore likely that an order for sale will be made: see IA 1986 s.335A.

[14] See Example 37.15.

[15] See TCGA 1992 s.225 and 43.22.

In the light of these difficulties, the pre-Budget announcement on October 9, **38.08**
2007 was very welcome. New ss.8A–8C were introduced into IHTA 1984 by
FA 2008 which allow a claim to be made to transfer any unused nil-rate band
(NRB) on the death of an individual to be used against the tax payable on the
death of their surviving spouse or civil partner provided that the survivor dies
on or after October 9, 2007.[16] On the death of the survivor the percentage of
the nil rate band unused on the first spouse's death, expressed as a proportion
of the nil rate band at the time of the survivor's death is added to the survivor's
own nil rate band. Even if the first death took place before October 9, 2007
these provisions apply.[17]

EXAMPLE 38.1

> H died in 1987. On his death none of his then NRB was used because
> his entire estate was left to his wife or to charity. W dies in 2015 having
> made no lifetime gifts when the NRB is £325,000. She can leave up to
> £650,000 tax-free because her nil rate band is increased by 100 per cent
> of £325,000 to £650,000.[18]

---

[16] Note that the changes did not assist cohabitees; for instance, the elderly sisters in *UK v Burden*
[2008] STC 1305. In this case the sisters argued that for IHT to be charged on the death of the
first of them in respect of the property which they jointly owned would be a breach of their
right to the peaceful enjoyment of their possessions as a result of discriminatory tax laws, it
being unfair that they should have to pay tax when a married couple or civil partners would
be exempt. Unrelated cohabitants can choose whether or not to get married and escape IHT,
family members cannot, however committed and stable their relationship. This, they argued,
amounted to discrimination in breach of art.14 of the ECHR taken in conjunction with
art.1 of the First Protocol. This argument was, however, rejected and the court accepted the
UK's argument that the IHT exemption for married and civil partnership couples pursued a
legitimate aim: to promote stable, committed heterosexual and homosexual relationships by
providing the survivor with a measure of financial security after the death of the spouse or
partner. Of course most families will want to sell the house anyway at the point when IHT is
due because the children want to receive cash. However, for carers and cohabitees the current
rules can be harsh. Ireland deals with the situation (at apparently minimal cost) by allowing
capital acquisitions tax to be deferred until such time as both the house is sold **and** the proceeds
are not reinvested in another house. The relief applies where someone lives with the deceased
and the house is their only residence.
[17] HMRC produced tables showing what the nil rate band was:

  (i)   for inheritance tax from March 18, 1986 to the present day;
  (ii) for capital transfer tax from March 13, 1975 to March 17, 1986;
  (iii) for estate duty from August 16, 1914 to March 12, 1975. From 1914–1946 the nil rate band
        was £100 and it should be remembered that not until 1972 did estate duty have a spouse
        exemption (when then introduced this was limited to £15,000). Likewise an exemption for
        gifts to charity (up to £50,000) was only introduced at that time. Inevitably, there will be
        difficulties in producing full documentation establishing an entitlement to an unused nil
        rate band when the death occurred in (say) the 1940s.
[18] The mechanism for claiming H's unused nil rate band is considered below.

Example 38.2

H died in June 2007 having made chargeable gifts of £150,000; 50 per cent of the then NRB of £300,000 is unused. If at the time of W's death the NRB is £325,000, £162,500 can be claimed so increasing W's nil rate band by 50 per cent to £487,500.[19]

Position on the first death (H)

38.09 The size of H's estate is irrelevant: the question is simply what was the then nil rate band and what percentage did he use up either by making a chargeable transfer on death or by chargeable lifetime transfers which cumulated with his estate on death. Note that "M" in the legislation is defined as, *"the maximum that could be transferred by the chargeable transfer made (under s.4) on the person's death"* and must be reduced in a case where the deceased had made chargeable lifetime transfers which were included in his cumulative total. Two further points should be noted:

(i) in the past it had been standard IHT planning to ensure that the estates of spouses were equalised or at least that both had sufficient assets to take advantage of their nil rate bands.[20] From the point of view of the transferability of the nil rate band of the first to die that is irrelevant: it does not matter that H died penniless;

(ii) there is nothing to require the first spouse to die domiciled or deemed domiciled in the UK.

Example 38.3

Ben and Jen had been domiciled for many years in Hong Kong and owned no UK situs assets. However, on Jen's sudden death Ben was left bereft and returned to the UK, resuming his domicile of origin. He died in 2011 owning substantial property. A claim to transfer Jen's unused nil rate band is available to his personal representatives.

38.10 In their *"Frequently Asked Questions"* HMRC comment that on the first death the personal representatives should:

> *"work out what the chargeable amount is and make sure that the surviving spouse is given sufficient documents and information to support the claim that their personal representatives will need to make".*[21]

---

[19] Note that the legislation is more generous than simply allowing for the transfer of any part of the H's unused NRB. It is the unused percentage of the NRB at the time when the survivor dies which is available.

[20] See 38.02.

[21] Obviously this advice is only relevant to deaths from October 9, 2007 when the changes were

It may, in fact, be difficult to do this given that property values will only be agreed with HMRC when tax is at stake: hence if the value of a chargeable transfer clearly falls within the IHT nil rate band of the deceased then its precise value will not be considered by HMRC (it will not be "*ascertained*"). Agreeing the value will therefore have to occur on the second death given that it will affect the size of the unused IHT nil rate band which is capable of transfer. The personal representatives of the first to die should ensure that they obtain written valuations which are retained for the surviving spouse.

Position on the death of the survivor: making the claim

Section 8B indicates that a claim must be made if the unused nil rate band **38.11** of the predeceasing spouse is to be transferred. Normally the claim will be made by the survivor's personal representatives and it must be made in the "permitted period".[22] In the event that they make no claim "*any other person liable to the tax chargeable on the survivor's death within such later period as the Commissioners for HMRC may specify*" can make a claim. The obvious situation where the personal representatives will have no interest in claiming an unused allowance is when any transferred nil rate band will be used to offset the tax on a failed PET for which the donee is primarily liable: see further Example 38.4 below, i.e. the deceased has effectively used up two nil rate bands by PETs which have now become chargeable. The claim can then be made by the donee(s) although it appears they have to wait two years.[23] The claim must be made on the claim form (Form IHT403). The form requires the production of certain documents: these include the death certificate of the first spouse to die; a copy of the will (and any deed of variation effected under IHTA 1984 s.142(1)); the marriage certificate; a copy of the grant of representation; the valuation of assets that passed on that death by a chargeable transfer and a copy of the Form 200/400.[24] Copies of some of the above documents can be obtained even if the originals have been lost. HMRC may have details of the Form 200/400 containing contents of the estate. In general HMRC advise that:

> "*if values are not known, the personal representatives should complete the claim form to the best of their ability and explain the position to HMRC when they make the claim. If there is no evidence that any other assets were chargeable, the personal representatives can make their claim based on the information which they have. . .*".[25]

announced and to estates of persons dying before that date where the administration of the estate is not yet concluded.

[22] The "*permitted period*" is defined as the period of two years from the end of the month in which the survivor dies or, if later, the period of three months beginning with the date on which the personal representatives first act as such. The meaning of the latter words is somewhat imprecise: it might have been expected that the alternative period would have run from the date when the grant of representation was obtained.

[23] Presumably in these circumstances HMRC will accept that a claim can be made earlier.

[24] This form will reveal, inter alia, whether the deceased had made chargeable transfers in the seven years before his death.

[25] HMRC will expect full supporting documentation to be available when the first spouse dies on or after October 9, 2007 but accepts that in respect of earlier deaths "*supporting evidence may not be so readily available*".

38.11   Must the PRs make the claim? Consider the following situation.

EXAMPLE 38.4

> John was first married to Ida who died in 1999 leaving him all her assets. There were two children of the marriage. In 2001 John remarried and when he died his will provided:
>
>   (i) for his second wife, Isla, to be sole executrix;
>   (ii) for a nil rate band gift to his two children from his first marriage;
>   (iii) subject to that, residue to Isla absolutely.

The nil rate band gift to the children is widely drafted (see the wording in Example 38.10(1)) and would appear to involve a gift of John's nil rate band and, provided that it is claimed by the executrix, the unused nil rate band of Ida. Isla refuses to submit the claim and proposes to pay the children only the value of a single nil rate band.

    It is thought that the children can compel her to claim the extra nil rate band and pay them £650,000. It is her fiduciary duty to carry out the terms of John's will under which the children are to receive the maximum sum that can be paid to them without triggering IHT.[26]

Using the transferred nil rate band

38.13   It is important to appreciate that any transferred portion of the nil rate band is used to increase the nil rate band of the survivor *"for the purposes of the charge to tax on the death of the survivor"*. It is therefore not correct to say that a surviving spouse is entitled to two nil rate bands. His estate may be so entitled but he is not. The consequence is that the transferred nil rate band can be used against IHT on the deceased surviving spouse's:

- free estate;

- reservation of benefit property[27];

---

[26] For a contrary view see Kessler and Sartin *"Drafting Trusts and Will Trusts"* (10th edn, 2011) where the authors state at para.18–17:

> *"A claim can only be made by the PRs [John in Example 38.4]. In the absence of any provision in the will John's executors have a discretion whether or not to make the NRB claim . . . so if wife 2 is an executor she has effective power to veto the NRB claim. It is considered that the power of wife 2 to make or refuse a NRB claim should be regarded as a semi-fiduciary power so that other beneficiaries could only challenge a decision not to make a NRB claim where there is bad faith; for wife 2 to consult her own interests in deciding whether or not to allow a NRB claim is to be made is not bad faith."*

The authors go on to suggest that if the executors do not include wife two they should only pay the double NRB to the trust if wife two and her own children are added as beneficiaries.

[27] i.e. property included in his estate at death as a result of FA 1986 s.102(3).

- settled property in which he had enjoyed a qualifying interest in possession[28]; and

- failed PETs and the supplementary charge on immediately chargeable lifetime transfers made within seven years of death.

However, it cannot be used to reduce the tax due in the lifetime of the survivor on gifts which were immediately chargeable: see Example 38.5.

Lifetime gifts of the survivor

It will be appreciated that a lifetime gift may be a potentially exempt transfer **38.14** (such as an outright gift to a child) or immediately chargeable at lifetime (half) rates (such as a gift into a relevant property settlement).[29]

EXAMPLE 38.5

Mrs A died in 1987 having made no lifetime gifts and leaving everything to her husband Mr A. Mr A gave away £650,000 in 2006 to his daughter. He died in March 2011 and since he died within seven years of the gift it is a failed PET. His remaining estate at death is worth £300,000. The lifetime gift is not chargeable—two nil rate bands are allocated against it. The £300,000 left in his estate at death is fully charged at 40 per cent.[30]

If instead of making an outright gift to his daughter Mr A had, in 2007, settled property on her and died within seven years, the IHT position would then be as follows:

(i) The making of the settlement involved an immediately chargeable transfer by Mr A. He has settled £600,000 and had a nil rate band of £300,000 in 2007, leaving a tax charge on £300,000 at 20 per cent (£60,000).

(ii) On his death within seven years additional IHT is payable but because this tax arises on the death of the survivor the unused nil rate band of Mrs A is available and hence no additional tax is charged. There is, of course, no question of any refund of the tax charged when the settlement was created.[31] Hence, in this case the additional nil rate band has only resulted in tax relief at 20 per cent rather than 40 per cent.

---

[28] So that under IHTA 1984 s.49(1) the capital of the settlement is treated as comprised in his estate at death.

[29] Since FA 2006 all new inter vivos settlements will be relevant property and so involve an immediately chargeable transfer except only for a trust in creating a disabled person's interest falling within IHTA 1984 s.89B(1).

[30] In this case it is to be expected that the daughter and not the personal representatives of Mr A will make the claim.

[31] Note that if A had settled £900,000 the immediate tax payable would have been £120,000 (20% × £600,000). On A's death the additional tax at 40% is chargeable on £250,000 (£900,000 − £650,000) only (because of Mrs A's transferred nil rate band) giving tax of £100,000 which is, however, covered by the tax already paid. No extra IHT is therefore payable.

Will trusts of the survivor

38.15   Assume that the surviving spouse W dies in January 2011 and leaves an estate worth £650,000 on discretionary trusts for her grandchildren. If a full transferable nil rate band is available from H's earlier death then tax on the creation of this settlement is nil. However, this relevant property settlement will benefit only from a single nil rate band for the purposes of calculating future tax charges with the result that exit and anniversary charges will arise.[32] This is, of course, consistent with the limited use to which a transferred nil rate band is to be put (viz against tax arising on the death of the survivor). It is possible to avoid this result by the use of pilot trusts, i.e. in her will W leaves £325,000 to each of the pilot trusts that she had set up during her life for her grandchildren. As before there is no tax on death but now both trusts may benefit from a full nil rate band.[33]

The nil rate band maximum

38.16   Section 8A(7) defines the nil rate maximum as the upper portion of the value charged at 0 per cent (for 2011–12 this is £325,000 and this imposes a ceiling on the amount available for transfer under the rules. However, many predeceasing spouses the survivor may have had the maximum value of the unused nil rate bands that can be used against tax on his death is limited to this amount (in effect to one extra nil rate band).

EXAMPLE 38.6

   (i) Tootsie dies in May 2011 pre-deceased by her two husbands Sid and Sad both of whom had left her everything. Her personal representatives can claim an additional nil rate band of £325,000 only;

   (ii) If in (i) above Sid had used up 50 per cent of his nil rate band and Sad 75 per cent of his, then Tootsie's PR's would be entitled to claim 75 per cent (50 per cent for Sid and 25 per cent for Sad) of an additional nil rate band (£325,000 × 75% = £243,750 in 2011–12).

For consideration of the impact of the transferable nil rate band on foreign domiciliaries and the position where the estate of the first spouse qualifies for treaty relief, see Ch.31.

---

[32] IHTA 1984 s.66(3) which assumes a transferor with the chargeable transfers of the settlor in the seven years before he created the trust and then takes the lifetime rates (see IHTA 1984 s.7(2)). The rate before the first 10-year anniversary is similarly calculated: see IHTA 1984 s.68(4).

[33] For the use of pilot trusts, see Ch.41. Arguably W should set up more than two pilot trusts to allow "headroom" (viz room for the assets to grow in value without the risk of future 10-year charges).

III IMPACT ON DRAFTING OF IHT EFFICIENT WILLS

Many couples will welcome the simplicity of leaving everything to the survivor **38.17** absolutely (so that the entire estate is spouse exempt) but still being able to take advantage of two nil rate bands. Bear in mind, however, that this will not always be the best option. For instance:

(i) there may be attractions for a testator protecting capital for children of an earlier marriage and so he will wish to leave only a life interest to the survivor. This will then be an immediate post-death interest (an IPDI) and so spouse exempt. Accordingly a transferable nil rate band will still be available on the death of the survivor;

(ii) a concern that the survivor may eventually go into a nursing home may also encourage the use of a trust in an attempt to shield capital against nursing home fees. Again an IPDI for the survivor would be effective: bear in the mind that the interest in possession can be made revocable by the trustees and so brought to an end if future circumstances make this desirable.[34] Of course, similar protection would be obtained if assets were put into a discretionary trust but only on assets up to a value of the then nil rate band given if a tax charge is to be avoided;

(iii) in the past it had been common when the will of the first spouse to die left everything to the survivor for that person to enter into a deed of variation establishing a nil rate band discretionary trust in order to ensure that the deceased's nil rate band was utilised. This is, of course, no longer necessary.

When will it still be attractive to establish a nil rate band discretionary trust?[35]

More generally the question may be put as to when it will be desirable for **38.18** the first spouse to die to make a chargeable transfer in his will. Consider the following:

1. Mr and Mrs A are wealthy. Given that Mrs A does not need all of Mr A's estate he leaves property to a value of his IHT nil rate band to his children/grandchildren.

2. If the property transferred to the nil rate band trust on the first death is anticipated to outstrip future increases in the NRB, it will still be advantageous to use a NRB trust on the first death. The NRB has, of course, been frozen until the end of the tax year 2014–15: see Example 38.7(2).

3. Two separate nil rate band discretionary trusts may have long-term tax advantages if it is intended to keep the property in trust after the second spouse's death.

---

[34] There may be attractions in terms of future IHT planning for the survivor if a flexible IPDI is used: see 38.54 and 43.85.
[35] For the drafting of nil rate band gifts or trusts, see 38.45.

4. Where H and W have previously been married and their previous partners have died with an unused nil rate band it is desirable to utilise all four nil rate bands: see Example 38.8.

5. Where an estate includes property qualifying for APR or BPR it will generally be preferable not to for the surviving spouse.

Appreciating property

EXAMPLE 38.7

(1) Mrs A died with an unused nil rate band leaving all her property to Mr A. Mr A dies in January 2011 with an estate of £650,000 which is therefore free of inheritance tax. He leaves this on discretionary trusts for his issue and no tax is payable. However, on the 10-year anniversary there will be inheritance tax payable if the value of the settled property exceeds the then value of one nil rate band.[36] By contrast, if Mrs A had set up a nil rate band discretionary trust on her death and Mr A's remaining estate was within his nil rate band on his death and left in trust, then on each trust's 10-year anniversary there would be a nil rate band available to set against the value of the property in that trust.[37]

(2) X dies in March 2010 owning a building plot valued at £325,000. It is, however, anticipated (correctly) that it will be zoned for development in the future and will then be worth 10 times this amount. Consider the following alternatives:

(a) X leaves everything to his wife so that there is a full transferable nil rate band. When she dies in 2014 the land is worth £3 million. Mrs X has an additional nil rate band of £325,000 to set against the land that she inherited; or

(b) X leaves the land on discretionary trusts. This exhausts his nil rate band but the land is not taxed as part of Mrs X's estate on death (even though she may have benefited from the income that it produced as an object of the discretionary trust). The trust can be ended before the first 10-year anniversary without an IHT charge. Of course, in a case like this where the asset is worth the upper limit of the nil rate band when the trust is set up and its value is expected to increase substantially, employing a single discretionary trust will result in 10-year charges given that the value of the property will outstrip increases in the nil rate band. Consider therefore the use of one or more pilot trusts and fragmenting the land ownership between them.[38]

---

[36] See s.66(5) IHTA 1984. Note also that exit charges even before the first 10-year anniversary may also be incurred.

[37] Note also the use of pilot trusts to obtain multiple nil rate bands: see Ch.41.

[38] For pilot trusts, see Ch.41.

(3) Z leaves his beneficial half share in his main residence on discretionary trusts when he dies in March 2010. The then value of the half share was £325,000. When his surviving wife dies in 2014 it has increased in value to £500,000: an increase exceeding the rise in the nil rate band. Some would therefore argue for the continued use of a nil rate band discretionary trust on the death of the first spouse to hold his share of the family home. The IHT and CGT issues that are involved are discussed at 38.25 onwards.

Business and agricultural property[39]

If H's estate includes property which attracts IHT relief at 100 per cent, then leaving that property to W may be considered to be a "waste" in that the spouse exemption will result in the business relief being redundant. The difficulty for the adviser in drafting the will is that it may not be certain that the relevant property attracts relief at 100 per cent; for instance, H may have owned a farming business which diversified.[40] And, of course, the test is not whether the business attracts relief when the will is made but whether it does so at the time of death.[41] Bear in mind also that HMRC will not normally consider the eligibility of property for relief unless tax is at stake. So leaving the property to the children conditional on relief being available otherwise to the spouse will not work since HMRC will not consider whether relief is due. For these reasons making a specific gift of *that business property (without reference to the question of whether or not it qualifies for BPR)* into a discretionary trust is recommended.[42] Bear in mind that if the trust is to continue indefinitely anniversary and exit charges will be avoided so long as the business property is qualifying. If, however, the business were to be sold and the trust received cash then:

38.19

(i) on the next 10-year anniversary a charge will arise given that there is non-relievable property in the settlement;

(ii) if the sale occurs in the first 10 years and the cash is then distributed before the first 10-year anniversary an IHT exit charge may arise despite the fact that no charge arose when the qualifying business assets were settled[43];

---

[39] This is discussed further in Chs 45 and 46.
[40] As, for instance, in *Farmer (Executors of Farmer Deceased) v IRC* [1999] STC (SCD) 321: see Ch.46.
[41] There can be no guarantee that the relief in its present form will continue in the future.
[42] In cases where the availability of the relief is in doubt leaving the property into a relevant property settlement will ensure that HMRC need to consider the availability of relief: in the event of relief being denied the property can be appointed out of the trust to the surviving spouse within two years of death under IHTA 1984 s.144 with the benefit of the spouse exemption being obtained by reading back. In the event of the property attracting relief it may be appropriate to keep the trust but to sell the property to the surviving spouse so that provided he/she owns it for two further years advantage can again be taken of 100% relief (this is sometimes referred to as having "two bites of the cherry"!): see 38.47.
[43] This is because the rate of tax which applies is calculated by reference to the value of the property originally settled with no allowance being given for 100% relief: see further Ch.29.

(iii) if, however, the sale occurs after an anniversary when no tax has been charged because of the property qualifying for 100 per cent relief, no exit charge will arise provided that the cash is distributed before the next 10-year anniversary.

Second marriages

38.20   Where spouses have been widowed and have then remarried it may be desirable for one (or even two) nil rate bands to be utilised in their will.

EXAMPLE 38.8

Jason was predeceased by his wife Laura who left him everything. He has remarried Judith:

(a) on his death his PRs will be entitled to claim Laura's unused IHT nil rate band but if his entire estate is left to Judith this will be wasted. Although her PRs can claim not just any unused nil rate band of Jason but also any further unused nil rate band which Jason's PRs could have claimed, the overall limit of one additional nil rate band means that a nil rate band has been lost;

(b) accordingly, if Jason's will left (at least) a single nil rate band on discretionary trusts that would leave Judith's PRs to claim, in due course, Laura's unused nil rate band. Note especially that it is not necessary for Jason to leave a "double nil rate band" discretionary trust. It suffices that the trust is set up with a single nil rate band;

(c) Judith's will should not leave everything to Jason given that his estate was already entitled to a full nil rate band transfer from Laura. She also should have set up a nil rate band discretionary trust;

(d) in the event that the wills were not correctly drawn the position could be cured by the surviving spouse entering into an appropriate instrument of variation under IHTA 1984 s.142(1);

(e) the position would be further complicated if Judith had been married before and left a widow because her estate is also entitled to an unused nil rate band from her then deceased first husband. There are now four IHT nil rate bands to consider! Ideal IHT planning advice is:

(i) Jason's will should make chargeable transfers equal in value to two nil rate bands (being his own and Laura's). The residue should be left to Judith to take advantage of the spouse exemption;

(ii) Judith's will should be a mirror of Jason's, i.e. she also needs to use up two nil rate bands.

In a case such as this, pilot trusts may offer an attractive way of minimising future IHT charges: see further Ch.41.

Position where a taxpayer has recently died and his Will contains an IHT nil rate band discretionary trust with residue passing to the surviving spouse

If desired the trust can be dismantled by an appointment within two years of death in favour of the spouse which is "read-back" as a result of IHTA 1984 s.144.[44] The effect is that the deceased has not used up any part of his IHT nil rate band which can therefore be used on the survivor's death. Note: **38.21**

(i) if the appointment is to be absolute wait more than three months from the date of death before making it in order to avoid the "*Frankland Trap*"[45] (this is not a problem if the appointment is on an IPDI Trust for the spouse);

(ii) can an appointment be made even before the estate has been administered/property vested in the Trustees? Some wills expressly provide for this to be done but even in the absence of such a clause it is thought that the trustees have all the powers vested in them by the will (in particular that the trust is constituted at death with the trustees being entitled to a *chose in action* to compel due administration of the estate);

(iii) it does not matter that the trust was set up by a Deed of Variation made by the surviving spouse; all that is required is that the appointment is made within two years of the deceased's death (i.e. advantage can be taken of "reading-back" under both IHTA 1984 ss.142 and 144). Nor does it matter if the nil rate band was left into a separate discretionary trust (usually a pilot trust) set up during the first spouse's lifetime.

In the case of earlier deaths (i.e. those occurring more than two years ago) reading-back will not be available and nothing can be done to take advantage of the transferable nil rate band legislation. In these cases it is important to keep the trust in being to ensure that use has been made of the deceased's nil rate band.

Other drafting points

Survivorship clauses: Beware survivorship clauses! In cases where one spouse has insufficient assets to fully use his/her nil rate band, from an IHT perspective, it may be better not to have a survivorship clause.   **38.22**

---

[44] See A1.13. Some commentators have suggested that there may be difficulties in unscrambling a nil rate trust which has been set up with either a debt or charge. Usually the debt is owed by the surviving spouse and the charge is over property that has been assented to her. The effect of appointing the benefit of the debt to her is that it is released. The effect of appointing the benefit of the charge to her is to release the charged property. Given that the trustees will be the original creditors of the debt/charge it is not thought that the appointment gives rise to CGT problems: specifically TCGA 1992 s.251(1) prevents there being a chargeable gain and in the case of a charge it is not thought that a debt on security has been created.

[45] See 39.59.

EXAMPLE 38.9

A and B are civil partners. A has an estate worth £400,000 and B has £200,000. Neither has made any chargeable transfers. Each leaves everything to the other.

A dies first, followed by B two days later.

Without a survivorship clause A's property passes without IHT to B and B has a double nil rate band available.

With a survivorship clause A's property does not pass to B and if it passes to a non-exempt beneficiary, IHT will be payable on the portion in excess of the nil rate band and part of B's nil rate band is wasted. There is no problem if the deaths occur in the opposite order.

38.23 It is important to draft the will so that what a testator wants is achieved. If both his own nil rate and a transferred nil rate band are available then be certain that the clause transfers both if he wants to transfer both or only one if he does not. The point is vital if the residuary estate is left to a charity or the nil rate band is left to one branch of the family and the residuary estate to the other.[46]

IV THE NIL RATE BAND DISCRETIONARY TRUST

38.24 This section considers the nil rate band discretionary trust from two standpoints:

(1) in some cases it will still be attractive for H to set up such a trust rather than leave everything to W[47];

(2) many wills contain such trusts and many such trusts have therefore been set up in recent years.

The discretionary beneficiaries of the trust will normally include W as well as the children and in many cases it is envisaged that W will be the principal beneficiary and will be paid any income that arises. It is important that nothing is done which would result in W becoming entitled to an interest in possession in the trust fund within two years of H's death since were that to occur she would become entitled to an IPDI and the value of the trust fund would be taxed on her death.[48]

A practical problem is to select appropriate assets to go into the trust. At first blush, stocks and shares would seem to be ideal but the income tax treatment of dividends distributed as income to beneficiaries of discretionary trusts produces an unacceptably high income tax rate.[49] However, one benevo-

---

[46] See further 38.45.

[47] Some practitioners may feel that it is safer to continue to draft wills with a NRB trust given that, (i) the trust can easily be unscrambled within two years of death if desired, and (ii) the transferable nil rate band might be abolished in the future.

[48] See IHTA 1984 s.144: after the two-year time limit it will not matter since the appointment of an interest in possession after March 21, 2006 is a "nothing": see Ch.39.

[49] See Ch.6.

lent effect of the FA 2006 changes in the IHT treatment of settlements is that once two years have elapsed from the date of death an interest in possession can be appointed to the surviving spouse which—although of no effect for IHT purposes—will result in the dividend income belonging to the spouse and so the extra income tax charge being avoided.[50]

If a (two-year) discretionary trust over residue is included in a will then do not at the same time create a nil rate band discretionary trust. Instead a cash sum equal to the Deceased's unused nil rate band can be paid out to a child or children by the trustees or kept in trust for them.

The matrimonial home

In many estates the only valuable asset is the matrimonial home. Apart from the house and a few investments and pensions the couple will have no other assets. In this case, the question of what assets should be put into the discretionary trust can be reduced to the choice between putting H's share of the house into the trust (or at least a portion of it up to the value of the IHT nil rate band) or using what is popularly known as the "debt or charge scheme".

38.25

Assume that the decision is taken to put H's 50 per cent share of the matrimonial home into the discretionary trust given that its value[51] equates with his available IHT nil band and there are no other assets in his estate[52] and that W survives for a further six years during which time she continues to occupy the property as her main residence. Given that she is entitled to a 50 per cent share in the equity (as well as being the sole legal owner/trustee) it may be thought that when she dies all that will be taxed is her 50 per cent beneficial share with an appropriate discount. Concerns have been expressed, however, that in a case like this, HMRC may claim successfully that by virtue of her sole occupation of the property W enjoyed an interest in possession in the share of the property held in the discretionary trust.[53]

---

[50] See A1.19.

[51] For the value of joint property owned by husband and wife, see *IRC v Arkwright* [2004] EWHC 1720 (Ch). A half share of a jointly owned house where the house is worth £624,000 will not necessarily be half this, i.e. £312,000. *Arkwright* suggests that a discount should be applied, so that in the above case H's share would not fully satisfy the amount due to the discretionary trustees under the terms of his will. They are entitled to receive £312,000 but have received a half share worth less than this. This point is also relevant if the IOU scheme is adopted. The executors cannot charge a half share of the house with a debt for more than the half share is worth. Additional assets would need to be appropriated to the trustees to make up the difference (or made subject to the charge) unless the trustees decide that any additional amount due to them is appointed to the wife outright within two years of Ted's death (then reading back is obtained under s.144). Bear in mind that when the charge is imposed the share may have risen in value: that increased value may be enough to cover the sum charged. HMRC believe that *Arkwright* was wrongly decided.

[52] It is important that the decision to appropriate the property share into the trust is minuted and desirable for the trustees to protect their interest by having a caution put on the property at the Land Registry. The general principle is that property must be appropriated on the basis of its value at the date of appropriation (and not therefore on the basis of its probate value, if different). It may therefore be that whilst the value of the property share equates with the available IHT nil rate band of the deceased at the time of his death, it has subsequently increased in value so that the personal representatives discover that only a part of the share can be put into the trust (e.g. if the value of the share had increased to £350,000 when the available nil rate band was £312,000, 89.14% (only) can be appropriated to the trust).

[53] The authors are not convinced by such arguments and believe that, if raised, they should be

HMRC's case might be strengthened if the original house was sold and a replacement bought, again for W's sole use within the two years of death. Instead of the argument relying to some extent on trustees' inertia, it might now be said that the trustees have exercised their powers to purchase a property for W's use and have therefore given her a right to immediate possession, the hallmark of an interest in possession.[54]

HMRC's argument analysed

38.26   HMRC's argument appears to centre on the idea that the:

> "*continuation of the deceased's sole occupation of his home . . . arises from a conscious decision of the trustees not to disturb that enjoyment to the exclusion of the others*".

HMRC consider that the trustees must have taken some positive decision to allow the spouse to stay there in sole occupation otherwise they would have been in breach of trust and *Billingham v Cooper*[55] indicates that trustees must be assumed not to have acted in breach of trust. But this assumes that the trustees actually had power to prevent W's rent-free occupation in the first place and that by failing to exercise this power they thereby have conferred occupation rights on her.[56]

A difficulty for HMRC is that whilst s.12 of TLATA 1996 gives the spouse rights of occupation to the property, such rights are derived from her own share not that of the trustees.

38.27   In the authors' view the trustees have no power to prevent the surviving spouse continuing to occupy the property. If the trustees ask her to agree a sale of the property or to pay rent for her occupation the surviving spouse can refuse. If the trustees go to court then the court will look to the provisions of s.12 which emphasise that interest in possession beneficiaries under trusts of land have rights of occupation in the land. In this case, there are no other beneficiaries who have interests in possession (in particular, the trustees have no right to occupy) and who are being excluded and no competing interests which require compensation to be paid. It would therefore be reasonable for the trustees to take the view that a court would be extremely unlikely to order a sale of the property under s.14. The trustees' failure to go to court to obtain an order for sale or seek payment of rent therefore cannot be taken to imply that the trustees have conferred on the spouse exclusive occupation or an interest in possession.[57]

resisted. Since the FA 2006 changes, the task of HMRC has been made even more difficult since they will be forced to argue that any interest in possession arose within two years of the deceased's death in order for it to be qualifying (an IPDI created as a result of IHTA 1984 s.144): otherwise, even if an interest in possession is appointed to the surviving spouse, it is a "nothing".

[54] See Lightman J. in *IRC v Eversden* [2002] STC 1109. Again this must happen within two years of the deceased's death.

[55] [2000] STC 122 affirmed; [2001] 177, CA.

[56] See the *Walden* case discussed in Ch.24 indicating the need for positive action on the part of the discretionary trustees if an interest in possession is to arise.

[57] Normally trustees of a discretionary trust create interests in possession by the exercise (usually by deed) of a power of appointment.

SP10/79[58] makes it clear that for an interest in possession to arise, any power exercisable by the trustees granting the spouse rights over the home has to be expressly drawn and exercised in terms wide enough to confer an exclusive right of residence. For the reasons noted above, there is commonly no reason to think that the trustees have exercised their powers in such a way as regards the original home. In general, the courts are reluctant to imply that decisions or acts have been taken by trustees where there is no evidence that these have been taken (a point emphasised in the *Walden* case).[59]

Section 12 (subject to the limitations set out in that section) confers rights of occupation on an interest in possession beneficiary: it does not say that someone in occupation must have an interest in possession in the entire property. Further there is no need for them to have an interest in possession in the whole property to have rights of occupation.[60]

This analysis is to some extent borne out by the judgment of Lightman **38.28** J. in the *Eversden* case where it appears to be accepted that the trustees only exercised their discretions and conferred rights of occupation in respect of the replacement property because they took the positive decision to use the sale proceeds to buy a property for occupation by the beneficiary. Even then Lightman J. drew back from stating explicitly that the settlor had an interest in possession in the trust assets. In relation to the original property the trustees had not exercised any powers to confer any rights of occupation and the settlor's continued sole occupation did not mean that the trusts ceased to be discretionary trusts.[61]

Advice to trustees

If properly advised, trustees will not simply sit back and do nothing. Any body **38.29** of trustees faced with the situation where the trust fund comprises a beneficial share in a residence occupied by the deceased's spouse's will:

(i) obtain advice as to what their rights are viz à viz the property. It is unlikely that the spouse will be willing to sell and to give the trustees a 50 per cent share of the proceeds and any attempt to persuade the court to order a sale (under TLATA 1996 ss.14–15), as noted above, is unlikely to succeed given the purpose for which the property was bought. Similarly, any attempt to force the spouse to pay a commercial rent (what would that be given that she owns a beneficial 50 per cent share in the property?) will be resisted and there are no competing interests in possession. In many cases the spouse will be unable to afford to pay a rent;

(ii) the trustees should be concerned to ensure that the property is insured and kept in a proper state of repair. Doubtless these are matters that the spouse is attending to but the trustees should take steps to protect their

---

[58] Which was not considered in the *Walden* case.
[59] See 24.44 for a consideration of the *Walden* case.
[60] See *Woodhall v IRC* [2000] STC (SCD) 558: a person can have an interest in possession in land even though he chooses not to exercise any rights of occupation: see Ch.26.
[61] See [2002] STC 1109: see A3.43.

investment. Were there to be a problem this is a matter to bring to the court's attention in an application for sale[62];

(iii) the trustees should register a caution against dealing at the Land Registry to protect their position in the event that the spouse decides to sell the property;

(iv) the trustees may consider selling the beneficial 50 per cent share but there will be difficulties in finding anyone to buy and any purchaser would obtain a substantial discount to reflect the spouse's continued non-rent paying occupation: better still they should be registered as the legal owners of the property with the spouse;

(v) the trustees should consider the range of beneficiaries of their discretionary trust: are any of them in need of either income or capital? In most family arrangements of this type the answer is no but were there to be a problem then it would be a factor to bring to the court's attention in an application to have the property sold.

38.30   In the light of the foregoing, the trustees may feel that they are left with no real alternative but to retain the property: this is likely to be in the best interests of the beneficiaries especially if the property is rising in value. This decision (and the reasons for it) should be evidenced in writing so that the trustees' train of thought is documented. In cases where the original property is sold and a replacement property is to be purchased it may be:

(a) that trust monies will not be needed; or

(b) that the trustees could loan the spouse a sum (repayable on demand) and take security in the form of a legal charge on the new property.[63] Alternatively, once two years have elapsed from death, the trustees may safely convert the trust into an interest in possession settlement and acquire a share in the new property, which will have no adverse IHT implications.

On any sale of the original property it is important that the trustees receive their share of the proceeds and then consider whether they wish to reinvest the cash in a replacement property. The cash should not automatically be put into a new property at the behest of the surviving spouse. The appropriate exercise of the trustees' discretion should be carried out and documented.

CGT downside?

38.31   A further point to bear in mind is the future CGT position if, after W's death, the property is sold. Given that she did not enjoy an interest in possession in the moiety held in trust, there will be no CGT death uplift and the avail-

---

[62] Under s.13(3) the trustees of land may impose reasonable conditions in respect of any beneficiary's occupation of the land.

[63] But always consider whether the surviving spouse is a donor so that FA 1986 s.103 would create difficulties: see 38.36.

ability of CGT principal private residence relief will depend on whether she is in occupation and is entitled to occupy the property under the terms of the settlement.[64] The FA 2006 changes in the IHT treatment of trusts mean that after two years the trustees can appoint the spouse an interest in possession without there being a qualifying IPDI interest. Will that assist in securing principal private residence relief? The conditions for CGT relief are as follows:

(i)   that the beneficiary actually occupies (which she does); and

(ii) that she is entitled to occupy under the terms of the settlement.

Even whilst the trust is discretionary its terms commonly permit any beneficiary to occupy trust property: in *Sansom v Peay*[65] it was considered sufficient that the beneficiary was actually in occupation (by a licence from the trustees) and as a beneficiary of the trust was entitled to occupy by virtue of a power in the trustees. Giving the beneficiary an interest in possession would make the position clearer but the principle should not be different.

However, the question (discussed in Ch.43) is whether even if the trustees have a power under the will to permit beneficiaries to occupy trust property, principal private residence relief can be available under TCGA 1992 s.225 if the trustees do not or cannot exercise such discretions because they have no power to prevent the surviving spouse from occupying the house anyway (as a result of the limited interest that they have been left under the deceased's will). On one reading of s.225, all that is necessary is for the will (expressly or impliedly) to permit beneficiaries to occupy the property. The fact that the spouse occupies in another capacity does not matter. It is desirable though to give the trustees explicit powers in all wills to enable beneficiaries to occupy the property. As a practical matter it seems less likely then that HMRC will query the position.

Loan schemes[66]

In brief, the discretionary trust is constituted either by a debt owed to the trustees by W who has received all the assets of H's estate *or* by a charge being placed over the assets in H's estate (and typically over his share in the house) which are then assented to W. For many couples the practical results of this arrangement were ideal since W enjoyed the benefit of all the assets whilst H had used up his IHT nil rate band on death. However, a number of issues arose, such as:

38.32

(i)   Will the trust be vulnerable to attack as a "sham" or as one in which W enjoys an interest in possession?[67]

---

[64] See TCGA 1992 s.225; *Sansom v Peay* [1976] 3 All ER 375 and SP 10/79.

[65] [1976] STC 494: the case concerned a trust of the entire property.

[66] For documentation, see A1.1.

[67] See *Taxation* April 29, 2004, p.116. In practice it is not thought that this creates a problem provided that the trustees act in a trustee-like manner. They should, for instance, ensure that the debt is secured and hold (once a year?) minuted meetings in which they review the operation of the trust (should they require interest to be charged bearing in mind that the debt will be repayable on demand?) and the needs of their beneficiaries. Of course a qualifying

(ii) What are the terms of W's debt or of the charge? The standard precedents provide for it to be repayable on demand but should it carry interest (rolled-up and so only payable with the principal on her death) or be index-linked? Of course, it is attractive for IHT purposes to ensure that the value of the debt is maintained but the matter was not clear-cut and the following points should be noted:

(a) the trustees will have power to lend money—on whatever terms they consider appropriate—to beneficiaries including W. They could decide not to charge interest/index-link the debt. It is, however, important that the question is considered and the decision of the trustees minuted;

(b) interest which is rolled-up and paid when the principal is paid (usually after W's death) will only attract an income tax charge in the hands of the trustees when it is received[68];

(c) there will be no attraction in providing for either interest or index-linking unless W's estate is reduced by the rolled-up interest/indexed sum on her death. This will be the case provided that the liability has been incurred "*for a consideration in money or money's worth*"[69];

(d) there may be an element of "swings and roundabouts" since the interest while deductible in W's estate (thereby saving IHT at 40 per cent) is subject to income tax in the hands of the trustees when paid at 50 per cent. All or part of this income tax may, however, be reclaimed if the trustees distribute the interest to a non-taxpaying beneficiary or one whose rate of income tax is less than 40 per cent[70];

(e) so far as index-linking is concerned, whether by reference to the RPI or to (say) a property index, the tax treatment of the indexed sum in the hands of the trustees needs consideration. It is not thought that the relevant discounted securities provisions in ITTOIA 2005 Pt 4 Ch.8 apply.[71] Under general principles, capital gains tax will not apply,[72] which means that unless the sum is "interest" (and so subject to income tax) it will be free from tax. "*Interest*" is generally considered to be any payment compensating the lender for the use of his money: however, the uncertainty over whether indexation will produce a return for the lender

interest in possession can only arise if an IPDI comes into existence within two years of death.

[68] For the taxation of interest, see ITTOIA 2005 s.370 and for the meaning of "arising" see *Parkside Leasing v Smith* (1984) 58 TC 282 and *Dunmore v McGowan* (1978) 52 TC 307.

[69] IHTA 1984 s.5(3)–(5) but note FA 1986 s.103 which disallows the deduction of "artificial debts": see 32.31.

[70] Bold spirits have suggested that on the death of W the rolled-up interest should be deducted as a liability in W's IHT return but that the nil rate band trustees may subsequently take the decision to waive payment. It is thought that this will avoid any income tax charge (since those trustees never receive the interest) and that, given the beneficiaries under W's will are likely to be the same persons who benefit under this trust they will be acting properly in so doing. It is common for HMRC to raise a query as to whether the interest has been/is to be paid and, if not, they will disallow it as a deduction in W's estate.

[71] Since it is not a security.

[72] See TCGA 1992 s.251(1).

may indicate that it is in the nature of a gamble and a tax-free windfall.[73]

Charge schemes

These operate as follows. The NRBDT is set up by means of a charge **38.33** created by the PRs over assets in the deceased's estate.[74] Note especially the following:

(a) the charge should be non-recourse, i.e. the trustees can only look to the charged property for payment of the sum owing. Neither the PRs nor any beneficiary to whom the charged property is assented is personally liable to make repayment;

(b) commonly the property charged will be a beneficial share in the matrimonial home. Hence the charge will be over an equitable interest and accordingly not registerable as a legal charge at the Land Registry.[75]

The charge route became the standard method for constituting the NRBDT given that it was thought to avoid the SDLT and s.103 problems that might otherwise arise.[76]

It has been suggested that the charge route may run into problems if the **38.34** property is sold by the survivor who then needs the bulk of the proceeds of sale to purchase a replacement property. In this situation:

(i) the charge will have to be paid off, i.e. the NRBDT trustees will receive their share of the proceeds of sale;

(ii) if s.103 presents problems (i.e. when W is a donor for the purposes of that section) then the trustees should not lend her the monies but there is nothing to stop them acquiring an interest in the replacement house (i.e. becoming co-owners with the survivor). The trustees could then allow the survivor to use their share giving her a life interest once two years have elapsed since death (to avoid IHTA 1984 s.144 applying to "read back" the interest as an IPDI).

SDLT

If H's estate includes an interest in land, will SDLT be in point on the basis **38.35** that W purchases that interest? The current approach of HMRC is set out in

---

[73] Unsurprisingly HMRC did not take this view and considered that an increase in the sum repaid due to indexing is interest, although it is believed they have conceded the position in recent cases.

[74] See A1.8 for clauses in a will permitting the trust to be set up by either a debt or charge and A1.9 for a specimen charge.

[75] This is especially important to avoid the possible imposition of SDLT and disallowance of the liability under FA 1986 s.103.

[76] See 38.35 and following.

the statement *"Stamp Duty Land Tax and Nil Rate Band Discretionary Trusts"* issued on November 12, 2004.[77] From this statement it appears:

(a) that a simple debt arrangement may attract a charge to SDLT on the basis that the surviving spouse is acquiring an interest in land for consideration[78];

(b) that the charge route, whereby the executors charge the deceased's property with payment of the nil rate legacy and then assent the property (burdened by the charge) to the surviving spouse will not give rise to an SDLT liability provided that the spouse does not become personally liable for payment of the legacy and that there is no change in the rights or liabilities of any person in relation to the debt secured by the charge[79];

(c) if the arrangement is the result of an instrument of variation which has established the trust then any debt or charge that may be created is not a land transaction for SDLT purposes.

It has been suggested that HMRC's statement, insofar as it relates to simple debt arrangements, is misconceived but most practitioners will settle for using the charge route on the basis that it is accepted that it will avoid any SDLT charge arising. It is also the preferred route in order to circumvent possible s.103 problems.

The artificial debt provisions

38.36 The inheritance tax attractiveness of the loan trust lies in the debt being fully deducted from the estate of the surviving spouse on death. If, for some reason, the debt is not deductible, H's nil rate band will have been wasted. FA 1986 s.103(1) can apply in two situations:

(i) if on death of the surviving spouse there is an outstanding liability arising from a debt incurred by that spouse; or

(ii) if the outstanding liability arises from an encumbrance created by a disposition made by that spouse.

Note, therefore, that s.103 does not apply if the surviving spouse neither incurred the debt nor made the disposition which created the encumbrance.

---

[77] This is set out in A2.01.

[78] In the case where the only asset in deceased H's estate is his share in the matrimonial home it may be argued that any debt entered into by W must be in consideration for acquiring H's interest (and, of course, to obtain the IHT deduction on W's death the debt must have been incurred for a consideration in money or money's worth). What, however, if H owns personally other assets such as shares which could be appropriated to satisfy the nil rate legacy? In this case there is no obvious reason why SDLT should be payable on the whole value of the land: either an apportionment may be in point or by first appropriating the land to W the trustees could show that the debt was consideration for the acquisition of assets other than land.

[79] In effect any charge must be non-recourse. Note therefore that the executors cannot charge the share in the property for a sum greater than the share is worth. See earlier fn.51 and *Arkwright*.

What then activates s.103 is if all or part of the consideration for the liability has been derived from property originating with the surviving spouse (whether directly or indirectly).

The Phizackerley case[80]

In the case:

38.37

(i) in 1992 Mr P retired and jointly purchased with Mrs P a retirement property;

(ii) Mrs P had never worked during the marriage and hence "*the funds must have been provided by (Mr P)*";

(iii) the joint tenancy was severed in 1996 and Mrs P then made a will (some five days later) establishing a NRBDT and leaving residue to Mr P. She died on April 26, 2000;

(iv) Mrs P's estate was administered with Mr P being assented her share in the property in return for which he "*promised to pay £150,000 (index linked)*" to the trustees ("the debt");

(v) Mr P died in July 2002 leaving an estate of over £500,000. HMRC argued that the debt was non-deductible and the Special Commissioner agreed;

(vi) for the taxpayers it was accepted that Mr P had made a gift to Mrs P in 1992 (as is required if s.103 is to apply) but that it constituted "maintenance" for Mrs P within IHTA 1984 s.11 so that it was not a "transfer of value" and hence the section did not apply (see s.103(4) and note that the spouse exemption does not help because there is still a transfer of value albeit that it is exempt). The Special Commissioner did not accept that the gift of the property share to Mrs P was maintenance.

The result of the decision was that use had not been made of Mrs P's IHT nil-rate band.

More or less all the press coverage was misconceived. There seemed to be an assumption that married couples own property jointly and so how can Mr P have made a gift in 1992? The reality, of course, is that in England there is no "community of matrimonial property". Mrs P would have had a claim on divorce to a share in any property but that raises different issues since the question then is how to provide fairly for both parties. In a similar vein, Mrs P would have had a claim under the 1975 Act had no provision been made for her on her husband's death but that again is dealing with a different situation and has no relevance to the property rights of a married couple during the marriage. It is possible to acquire a proprietary interest in property owned by another but only in limited circumstances, usually by agreement (or some kind of undertaking acted upon) and normally only provided that certain formalities or conditions are met. It is therefore hard to see that the 1992 arrangement can be viewed as anything other than a "gift" by Mr P.

38.38

[80] [2007] STC (SCD) 328.

38.39 Practitioners had been aware of the risk of s.103 applying in this situation for some time so that the decision should not have come as any great surprise to anyone. The case itself was straightforward: Mr P bought back a share in the property which he had given to Mrs P. The couple died in the wrong order: i.e. the donor spouse survived! There would have been no problem had Mr P died first.

38.40 Because the s.103 problem has been long debated, most practitioners, when there was any risk of s.103 applying, established the trust by using the "charge route" or by drafting the will to leave the residue to Mr P on interest in possession trusts (rather than outright). If either of these approaches had been adopted, s.103 would not have applied since it requires the deceased to *either* incur a debt *or* create an incumbrance by way of a disposition made by him. In the case of the charge route, a non-recourse charge is put on the deceased's share of the property by her executors and that charged share is then assented to the survivor who has no personal liability to repay the sum charged. Given therefore that the survivor neither created the incumbrance nor incurred a debt, s.103 will not apply if this approach is adopted. It should also be noted that the charge route has been employed since December 2003 to avoid the risk of an SDLT charge on property acquired by the survivor. Hence the simple debt arrangement is now rarely seen.

An alternative way of avoiding s.103 problems involves settling the residue on a life interest trust for the survivor (an IPDI) so that any debt is incurred by the trustees and not by the survivor and hence s.103 is again circumvented. Of course, the SDLT problem remains and in this case it is also likely that the charge route would be employed.

38.41 One area of uncertainty is in what circumstances HMRC will seek to apply the *Phizackerley* decision. As commented earlier, in this case the position was straightforward, Mr P made a gift to his wife. But what if, like many married couples, they had always jointly owned property with Mrs P making some sort of contribution financially? It seems inconceivable that in such cases HMRC will seek to analyse transfers to find a "gift" element.

Conclusions on constituting the NRBDT

38.42 It has been suggested that since FA 2006 there are fewer risks of any interest in possession arising if the first spouse leaves his or her share of the house on nil rate band discretionary trusts with the surviving spouse in occupation. It has been suggested that if the house is not formally assented to the trust until after two years no risk of an immediate post-death interest can arise but it is thought that this argument is misconceived. The administration of the estate is likely to be completed earlier in which case the beneficial ownership of the land can still vest in the trustees even though the legal ownership must be transferred in writing. In any event the trustees could exercise their discretions over the property even while the administration is continuing. The authors' conclusion is that it is still preferable to satisfy the nil rate band not by a share in the family home but by use of the charge arrangement for the following reasons:

(i) If the surviving spouse takes an interest in possession within two years of death, this is read back under s.144 and will be an IPDI and therefore a qualifying interest in possession. The purpose of the planning to use the deceased's nil rate band has been defeated. The authors do not think that merely allowing the spouse to continue in occupation of the original property could be regarded as conferring an interest in possession whether this occurs before or after March 22, 2006 albeit that difficulties could arise if the original property was sold and a replacement property purchased within two years of the death of the first spouse, not an uncommon situation.

(ii) Capital gains tax main residence relief remains in doubt although the authors consider that it should be available even on the original property.[81]

(iii) Perhaps the biggest argument against putting the share of the house into the discretionary trust is that a substantial increase in property values will mean that on the 10-year anniversary there is an inheritance tax bill to pay.[82] Of course, it may be possible to avoid this by advancing the share in the house outright to a beneficiary such as a child just before the 10-year anniversary[83] but this may not always be practical. One can no longer avoid the 10-year charge by appointing a qualifying interest in possession to the child.

On the other hand the charge route undoubtedly has disadvantages: **38.43**

(i) it can be complicated to set up and explaining it to the couple is not easy;

(ii) s.103 traps have to be watched;

(iii) it has the vulnerability of any inheritance tax scheme which is that the rules could be altered before the relevant death. HMRC do not like inheritance tax planning involving debts and it is not inconceivable that the legislation may be changed in the future. Such changes could be "retroactive" so that such debts are not deductible on the death of the surviving spouse where that spouse has not yet died. Putting a share of the house into a discretionary trust is arguably less vulnerable to legislative change.

Administering NRBDTs set up on a death more than two years ago

Because there is no possibility of unscrambling the arrangement to take **38.44** advantage of the transferable nil rate band by s.144 reading-back, it is important to ensure that the trust is properly administered so that the use of the Deceased's NRB is preserved. Hence:

(i) do not make an outright appointment to the spouse (by contrast appointing on an interest in possession once two years have elapsed from the date

---

[81] See 38.31 and 43.22.
[82] At a maximum rate of 6% on the excess above the then nil rate band.
[83] Since the house was within the nil rate band when it went into the trust there is no exit charge if the trust is ended before the 10-year anniversary.

of death does not create IHT problems: it is a "nothing" and may assist with the income taxation position and generally save compliance costs);

(ii) if established by a debt/charge check that the documentation is in order, e.g. has *Phizackerley*[84] caused problems (bear in mind, however, that if there is a *Phizackerley* problem not a great deal can be done about it!);

(iii) if the charge route over the matrimonial home has been used and the property is now to be sold it will be necessary to pay off the charge. If the surviving spouse then needs all/part of those monies to buy a replacement property the trustees may lend it to her (but not if there is a s.103 problem!) or may buy a share in the property (for his/her occupation);

(iv) if the trust holds a share in the house occupied by the surviving spouse consider the IHT position (is there any reason to think that the spouse has a qualifying interest in possession)? And consider what the CGT consequences will be when the property is sold.

Construing nil rate band clauses

38.45 Wills leaving a nil rate band legacy may be drafted in a variety of different ways. Before October 9, 2007, the general result, in all cases, was to use up the testator's IHT nil rate band. With the introduction of the transferable nil rate band, however, difficulties have arisen. Does the wording used mean that the gift is of only the testator's nil rate band or do the words used mean that a transferable nil rate band from a pre-deceasing spouse is also caught?[85]

EXAMPLE 38.10

Daisy, a widow, makes a will leaving "the nil rate sum" to her collection of distant relations with residue to charity. Her husband had died some years ago leaving her everything. Consider the following alternative ways in which the "nil rate sum" might be defined:

(1) *"the largest sum of cash which could be given without IHT becoming payable in respect of the transfer of value which I am deemed to make on my death"*.

The most that can be given away is Daisy's nil rate band plus that of her deceased husband: hence in 2011–12 the clause operates to give £650,000 to the relatives.

(2) *"The 'Nil Rate Sum' shall mean such sum as is equal to the upper limit of the nil per cent rate band in the table of rates of tax (applicable on my death) in Schedule 1 to the Inheritance Tax Act 1984, less an amount equal to the aggregate of the amount chargeable to inheritance tax of:*

---

[84] [2007] STC (SCD) 328.

[85] For a problem will involving a nil rate band gift see *RSPCA v Sharpe* [2010] STC 975 reversed; [2010] EWCA (Civ) 1474.

(a) *all or any chargeable transfers, including potentially exempt transfers which have become chargeable as a result of my death, made by me during my lifetime in the cumulation period specified in s7(1)(a) of the Inheritance Tax Act 1984;*

(b) *all other gifts, if any, taking effect under my will or any codicil;*

(c) *all or any settled property in which, on my death, I have an interest in possession[86]; and*

(d) *all other property, if any, wherever situate, which is, or which is treated as, property to which I am beneficially entitled immediately before my death (including property subject to a reservation as defined by s.102 of the Finance Act 1986)."*

In this case the reference to the upper limit of the table of rates limits the amount to a single nil rate band (£325,000 in 2011–12).

(3) "such sum as I could leave immediately before my death without IHT becoming payable".

This is also limited to a single nil rate band since any transferred Nil Rate Band is not available immediately before death but only in respect of tax payable on the death.

V BPR/APR AND NIL RATE GIFTS[87]

38.46 A will establishing a nil rate band discretionary trust and leaving residue to the surviving spouse will, in a case where the deceased owned property attracting 100 per cent business or agricultural relief, operate so that part of the benefit of the business or agricultural property relief will accrue to the nil rate trust (i.e. the trustees will receive more than £325,000 (in 2011–12) but not the whole value of the business property) and the remainder of the relief will be attributed to property passing to the spouse and so will be wasted.[88]

EXAMPLE 38.11

The deceased left a nil rate band legacy in the form set out below to his daughter and the residue to his spouse when he died on January 1, 2011. His assets include property eligible for BPR worth £500,000 out of a total estate of £1 million. The deceased made no lifetime transfers.

"I give to my daughter such sum as at my death equals the maximum amount which could be given by this will without inheritance tax becoming payable on my estate."

---

[86] Presumably this should be limited to a "qualifying" interest.
[87] See also 38.19 for a consideration of the drafting issues on BPR.
[88] See IHTA 1984 s.39A.

How much will the daughter take? £325,000? No, the legacy will be reduced by multiplying it by reduced value of estate (after deducting any specific gifts qualifying for relief) (R) divided by the unreduced value of the estate (after deducting any specific gifts qualifying for relief) (U). A legacy with an IHT value of £325,000 will actually be twice that amount.

Accordingly the daughter will take £650,000, the IHT value of which will be reduced to £325,000 thereby being covered by the deceased's nil rate band as follows—

$$£650,000 \times \frac{£500,000 \text{ (R)}}{£1,000,000 \text{ (U)}} = £325,000$$

This may be good news as more assets are passed to the daughter tax-free. If, however, the testator is concerned that the spouse may be left with too little, it is possible to include a cap on the amount to pass under the legacy. Also, part of the BPR has been lost. To obtain the full benefit of the 100 per cent relief ensure that a specific chargeable gift of the BPR property is made.

"Two bites at the cherry" relief

38.47 Assume that H owns a farm qualifying for 100 per cent APR and worth £1 million. It is envisaged that W will take over the business after his death but if he leaves her the farm APR will be wasted. Consider therefore the following:

(i) the farm is left to his daughter. IHT is not payable because of the relief;

(ii) after his death the farm is sold to W with the daughter receiving £1 million in cash;

(iii) once W has owned the farm for two years, APR will be available on her death;

(iv) in addition the daughter can be given a cash legacy of the nil rate sum.

Note in connection with the above:

(i) SDLT will be payable by W on the acquisition of an interest in land;

(ii) there is no clawback of APR or BPR if the property is sold (however soon!) after H's death;

(iii) if it is desired to protect W's position she could be given an option to purchase the farm in the will;

(iv) if W has insufficient money to purchase the farm, leave all or part of the purchase price outstanding as an interest-free loan from the daughter. Watch FA 1986 s.103 if the wife has made any earlier gifts to daughter or makes gifts in the future.

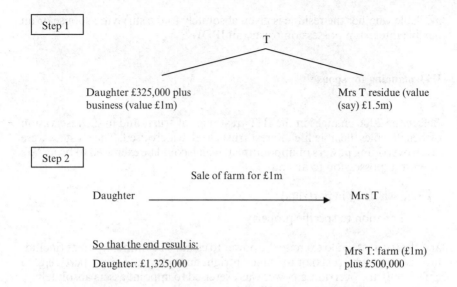

Step 1

T

Daughter £325,000 plus
business (value £1m)

Mrs T residue (value
(say) £1.5m)

Step 2

Sale of farm for £1m

Daughter ⟶ Mrs T

So that the end result is:

Daughter: £1,325,000

Mrs T: farm (£1m)
plus £500,000

Leaving the business into a discretionary trust

38.48 If the business property is put into a discretionary trust the availability of the IHT relief must be considered by HMRC since IHT is at stake.[89] When the position is known (provided that this occurs within two years of the deceased's death) then the trustees:

(i) if it is agreed that the property attracts 100 per cent relief, may leave it on discretionary or other trusts for the children or appoint it outright to them;

(ii) if relief is not available the trustees shall appoint it to the deceased's surviving spouse so that the spouse exemption will prevent IHT from arising.[90]

VI DEALING WITH RESIDUE WITH SURVIVING SPOUSE[91]

38.49 It is common for the first spouse to leave the residue of the estate to the surviving spouse to take advantage of the spouse exemption.[92] This exemption is

---

[89] Assuming that the business is worth more than the available nil rate band.

[90] This is the effect of "reading back" under IHTA 1984 s.144 as to which see Ch.39. This assumes, however, that HMRC give a determination on the availability of relief before the expiry of the two-year period. Disputes on business property relief or agricultural property relief may drag on beyond the two-year period and reading back cannot be obtained if an appointment is made after the two-year period. It is important to submit the probate papers as soon as possible after the death to obtain a view from HMRC.

[91] In this section when we refer to spouse, we also include civil partner in the term.

[92] See IHTA 1984 s.18. Even if W does not need this property it should not be left to the children on H's death given that it will attract a 40% IHT charge. Better to leave it to W and for her to make lifetime gifts (PETs) to the children.

available whether the residue is given absolutely to the surviving spouse or on flexible interest in possession trusts (an IPDI).[93]

IHT planning for spouse

38.50 Before the 2006 changes in the IHT treatment of trusts and in the reservation of benefit rules, flexible life interest trusts were widely used. The trustees were given overriding powers of appointment which could be exercised to bring W's interest in possession to an end:

- in whole or in part; and
- in relation to specific property

and the trustees could exercise the power to establish continuing trusts (including discretionary trusts) or to make outright appointments of property, e.g. to children. If the overriding power was exercised to appoint assets absolutely to the children then W made a PET.

Link up with reservation of benefit and the pre-owned assets regime before March 22, 2006

38.51 Assume that the trustees exercised their power of appointment to create a small (value £275,000) discretionary trust under which the family (including W) could benefit. The tax analysis prior to March 22, 2006 was as follows:

(i) the termination of W's interest in possession was a chargeable transfer but given that she had not used up her nil rate band no IHT was payable (notice that although W is not the settlor, it is her nil rate band which is relevant given that she makes the transfer of value)[94]; and

(ii) whilst the IHT legislation provides that W makes a "deemed" transfer of value,[95] before the changes in FA 2006, it was not considered that she made a "*gift*" as required if the reservation of benefit rules were to apply nor was it thought that she made a disposal of property or settled property for the purposes of the pre-owned asset legislation.[96]

The upshot was that the discretionary trust so established could be used, at the trustees' discretion, as a vehicle to benefit W during her life without the trust being subject to IHT on her death (it was exactly comparable to the nil rate band discretionary trust set up in H's will). W therefore had the comfort of knowing that assets to a value of over half a million pounds were available in the two trusts for her use but would not attract an IHT charge on her death.

---

[93] IPDI's are considered in detail in Ch.28.
[94] See IHTA 1984 s.80(1).
[95] See IHTA 1984 s.52(1).
[96] The position was less clear-cut if she had to consent to the exercise of the power whilst if she surrendered her interest it was thought that she had made a gift. See 20.09 and Ch.33.

DIAGRAMS SHOWING H'S ESTATE HELD ON TWO SEPARATE DISCRETIONARY TRUSTS WITH THE REMAINING RESIDUE ON FLEXIBLE LIFE INTEREST TRUSTS FOR W

STEP 1 (H's Will)

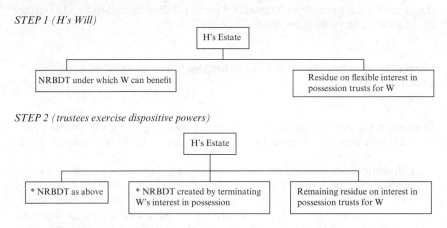

STEP 2 (trustees exercise dispositive powers)

* Not taxed on W's death even though she benefits from both

Impact of FA 2006

This strategy was nullified from March 22, 2006 as a result of an amendment to the reservation of benefit rules. New s.102ZA[97] provides that if:

  (i) an individual became entitled to an interest in possession in settled property before March 22, 2006; or

 (ii) on or after that date becomes entitled to such an interest if it was qualifying (i.e. an IPDI; disabled person's interest or a TSI); and

(iii) that interest comes to an end during the individual's life,

the individual is deemed to dispose of the settled property in which the interest had subsisted[98] by way of gift for the purpose of the reservation of benefit rules. As a result, if the trustees exercised their power of appointment to terminate W's interest in possession on or after March 22, 2006 then she will be treated as making a gift for GWR purposes so that, if she continues to benefit under a discretionary trust created by the appointment, the property will be taxed as part of her estate on her death.[99]

This amendment only applied in respect of the termination of interests in possession on or after March 22, 2006. Accordingly if W's interest had been terminated before that date, the GWR rules did not apply.[100]

The 2006 amendment was, however, drafted restrictively. All that the

38.52

38.53

---

[97] Inserted into FA 1986 by FA 2006 s.156, Sch.20 para.33(1), (2) and (4).
[98] Called the "*no-longer-possessed property*": see FA 1986 s.102ZA(2) and (3).
[99] FA 1986 s.102(3): for a general consideration of the GWR legislation, see Ch.33.
[100] FA 2006 Sch.20 para.33(4).

interest in possession beneficiary is deemed to gift is "*the no-longer-possessed property*". Hence, it is thought possible to effect an *Ingram*-style carve out arrangement whereby the IPDI is terminated in (say) the freehold interest in the matrimonial home with a leasehold interest being carved out and retained in the interest in possession trusts.[101]

Should the surviving spouse be left residue absolutely or on interest in possession trusts?

38.54   In considering whether to leave a surviving spouse residue absolutely or on an interest in possession trust, the following points should be borne in mind:

(i) in some cases the testator will wish to give his spouse a life interest (supplemented by a power in the trustees to pay capital to her) in order to preserve the capital for (say) children of an earlier marriage.[102] However, a surviving spouse who is merely left a life interest with no right to capital is likely to have a claim under IPFDA 1975 and hence it is important that she is made aware of what is proposed and is content with the arrangement.

(ii) A life interest can be useful in ring-fencing assets if the surviving spouse (in the example W) remarries. Any new spouse of W is less likely to be able to claim the capital if it is left on trust for W if W dies or divorces[103];

(iii) if property is given to the spouse outright the spouse can make gifts which will be PETs. If the residue is settled, however, the inter vivos termination of the spouse's interest in possession will only be a PET by the spouse if:

(a) the settlement thereupon ends, or
(b) the property then becomes settled on a bereaved minor's trust,[104] or
(c) it becomes held on trusts under which there is a disabled person's interest;

(iv) if residue is given to the spouse outright the spouse can only make gifts if s/he has mental capacity or an application is made to the Court of Protection. If left on trust the trustees can take the decision as to whether the spousal interest should be terminated in whole or part and PETs made;

(v) if the surviving spouse is left the residuary estate outright, she can establish IPDIs for the children by will. If, however, the first spouse leaves residue on IPDI trust for the surviving spouse, no further IPDIs can be created in H's will to take effect after W's death[105];

---

[101] This is looked at in detail in Ch.43. See 43.85.
[102] Protecting capital against future nursing home fees is also a consideration in many cases.
[103] See further Ch.50.
[104] Note that if the property becomes held on s.71D (age 18–25) trust this is not a PET. The continuing trusts must provide for capital to vest at 18 (i.e. fall within s.71A): see Ch.35.
[105] But consider circumventing this restriction by giving W a general power of appointment: see further 38.55 and following and also 28.19.

(vi) if the testator leaves his residuary estate on IPDI trusts ensure that the trustees have wide overriding powers. If the trust is drafted too restrictively, e.g. there is no power to advance capital to the spouse and the trustees have no power to end the spousal life interest, one is likely to end up in the worst of all worlds. If the testator is worried about giving the trustees too much power consider making the surviving spouse one of the trustees. The trustees must act unanimously so the spouse is assured that the life interest cannot be terminated without her consent. Ensure that there is express power in the will to enable trustees to act even if they are beneficially interested in the exercise of their powers and also insert a power of self-dealing.

EXAMPLE 38.12

H dies leaving the residue of his estate outright to W. They have three children one of whom—Doug—is a spendthrift and a drug addict. At the age of 30 he has spent all the inheritance left to him by his aunt and is now in debt. If W dies she can leave the property on IPDI trusts for her children and so protect the capital so that Doug does not have access to it except at the discretion of the trustees. If, however, H leaves residue on IPDI trusts for W, on her death if the trusts continue for the children for IHT purposes the relevant property regime will apply. However, since in this case there will be IHT on W's death anyway however the property passes, it might be thought preferable to suffer the 10-year charges in exchange for greater control over Doug's share which could be left on continuing trusts. Alternatively, give W a general testamentary power of appointment which she could then exercise by will to give Doug an IPDI.[106]

(vii) There may be capital gains tax advantages in transferring the property into trust for W. Future disposals that might trigger gains can be minimised.

EXAMPLE 38.13

H dies leaving residue outright to W. One of the assets is an investment property. Five years later W decides to settle it on trust for her children. It shows a large gain. She can transfer the property into an inter vivos trust; this is a chargeable transfer for IHT purposes but provided she, any spouse and any dependent children are excluded from benefit the gain can be held-over.[107] If instead H had left the investment property on interest in possession trusts for W, the trustees could terminate her interest at a later date and appoint the property on continuing trust for the children. Although the IHT treatment is

[106] See 38.55.
[107] Under TCGA 1992 s.260.

the same (this is a chargeable transfer by W)[108] for capital gains tax purposes the appointment is merely a variation of the existing settlement and there is no disposal by the trustees. Hence no hold-over relief claim is needed.[109] Therefore, W's minor dependent children can continue to benefit (although W would need to be excluded for reservation of benefit reasons).

(viii) If property is left outright to the spouse, s/he cannot make lifetime gifts on trust for the children which take effect as PETs.[110] They will be chargeable transfers. By contrast if the spouse is given an IPDI in the will which is then terminated so that the property becomes held on bereaved minor trusts during her lifetime this will be a PET. Given the restricted scope of bereaved minor trusts,[111] however, it is not thought that this difference in treatment between settled and unsettled gifts is likely to be significant in encouraging the widespread use of an IPDI trust for the surviving spouse.

(ix) A flexible IPDI may enable shearing arrangements to be effected with a view to IHT saving on the spouse's death: see 43.85.

General powers of appointment[112]

38.55 As explained in detail at 28.19 a general power of appointment over settled property can enable property to remain in a series of IPDI trusts.

A general power of appointment over settled property is not "property" for IHT purposes and the donee of the power is not treated as beneficially entitled to the property merely by virtue of holding that power. Hence, in Example 38.12 above, H could settle the property on IPDI trusts for W and give her a general power of appointment exercisable by her will over the trust fund. If W exercised the general power by will to provide that one third of the trust fund should on her death be held on trust for Doug for life his interest will be an IPDI. The four conditions for IPDI treatment are met: specifically the settlement (a "new" settlement) has been effected by will (W's will) and Doug became entitled to his interest in possession on the death of the testator (W). Note especially:

(i) the settled property is, of course, comprised in W's estate because of the IPDI but this is not considered significant[113];

---

[108] See 24.15 for the effect of IHTA 1984 s.80.
[109] There is therefore no concern about the claw-back charge or "settlor-interested" restriction: see Ch.18.
[110] Save only for trusts which create a disabled person's interest under IHTA 1984 s.89B.
[111] Considered in detail at Ch.35.
[112] For the meaning of a general power see Ch.31.
[113] The general power of appointment could be conferred on someone other than W but of course has to be exercised by will to enable the ongoing trusts to qualify for IPDI status. If say H's best friend has the general power the settled property is not part of his estate for IHT purposes but on the friend's death he has appointed in favour of Doug. Hence the IPDI of W then ends while W is still alive in favour of Doug. This is presumably a PET by W. If the friend dies after W then W's IDPI will already have ended.

(ii) it is essential if an IPDI is to be created for the general power to be exercised by the will of the donee. Accordingly consider limiting the terms of the power so that it is only exercisable by will;

(iii) the person who is given a general power is free to exercise it in favour of any person (that is the nature of general power). In the Example, therefore, if W remarried she could appoint the property to her new husband.

VIII DEALING WITH RESIDUE—NO SURVIVING SPOUSE

In broad terms the options are: **38.56**

(i) outright gifts (e.g. "*to my children equally*");

(ii) IPDI trusts. It is important to bear in mind that although the main use of the IPDI is a trust for a surviving spouse any interest in possession trust set up in a will is an IPDI.[114] This is the only option for a grandparent who wishes to leave assets on trust for his grandchildren but avoid the relevant property regime. Section 31 of TA 1925 must be excluded if the intended beneficiaries are minors.[115]

EXAMPLE 38.14

Donald, a lonely widower, wishes to make provision for his grandchildren Charlotte and Luke but he is anxious they do not receive capital at too early an age. (His children are already well provided for.) He therefore leaves his residuary estate in equal shares to his grandchildren on interest in possession trusts with capital vesting at 30. When he dies they are still minors. Section 31 of TA 1925 has been excluded. The trusts are IPDIs and the grandchildren receive the income equally. The trusts are not taxed under the relevant property regime. However, just before Charlotte reaches 30, the trustees decide to defer her capital entitlement in order to avoid suffering a large capital gains tax charge on her share of the assets. They exercise the widened power of advancement included

---

[114] Combining a nil rate band discretionary trust with an IPDI trust of residue for the surviving spouse will not lead to a problem of "*related settlements*". In general for the purpose of calculating the rate of IHT on a relevant property trust (such as the nil rate band discretionary trust) the value of property in a settlement set up by the same settlor on the same day must be taken into account: see IHTA 1984 s.62 (definition of a related settlement); s.83 (will trusts are treated as commencing on the date of death); s.66(4)(c), s.68(5)(b). However, when the IPDI trust is for the benefit of the surviving spouse the property is—for the purpose of the Ch.III relevant property charge—*not* treated as having become comprised in the settlement at the date of death but only on the termination of that interest in possession (see IHTA 1984 s.80(4) inserted by FA 2006 Sch.20 para.23). Hence the related settlement rules will not apply. This protection is not, however, available in other cases where an IPDI trust is set up and therefore it is important to avoid the combination of a nil rate band discretionary will trust with an IPDI for any person other than the surviving spouse.

[115] For a suitable precedent, see A1.17.

in the settlement. HMRC consider that when they extend her interest in possession they take the trust outside the IPDI regime since her interest in possession is a "new" one which is now within the relevant property regime.[116] The result is that capital gains tax is deferred but her share is henceforth subject to exit charges and anniversary charges and she has made a chargeable transfer with inheritance tax being payable at 20 per cent on the excess over her nil rate band. Moreover, since Charlotte was the life tenant and has not been excluded from the settled property, after the termination of her qualifying interest in possession the reservation of benefit rules apply. The property therefore remains subject to inheritance tax on her death. Even if the settled property passes to her spouse outright on her death there is no spouse exemption. Because her interest in possession is no longer a qualifying interest there is no capital gains tax uplift on her death.[117] All in all, *a tax disaster!*

By contrast, if Donald had not inserted an age for capital to vest in Charlotte the trustees would not have needed to defer her capital entitlement and she would continue to have held a qualifying interest in possession until her death (or earlier termination of that interest). The settled property would be taxed only on her death (with spouse exemption if the settled property then passed to her spouse outright) and with a capital gains tax uplift. The trustees could be given power to apply capital for Charlotte should this be desirable. There will be no IHT if she is given the capital[118] but CGT hold-over relief will then only be available on business assets within TCGA 1992 s.165.

(iii) a relevant property settlement: such a trust will fall within IHTA 1984 s.144 and so provide up to two years flexibility[119];

(iv) a bare trust: this may be attractive, e.g. for minor grandchildren of the testator[120];

(v) a bereaved minor or s.71D (18–25) trust: may be used when the testator wishes to leave assets to his children who are aged under 25. These trusts are considered in detail in Ch.35. There is no reason why the BMT or s.71D trust has to be set up in the will itself. If the estate is left on discretionary trusts the trustees can exercise their powers at any time and alter the terms of the trust to secure that the BMT or s.71D conditions are met.[121] Hence, it is probably better to leave residue on discretionary trusts and then take a view after the death of the testator as to whether it is worthwhile to set up BMTs or s.71D trusts. Much will depend on the ages and circumstances of the children at that time.

---

[116] This may be doubted: see 26.34.

[117] See ss.72 and 73 TCGA 1992 and 7.46.

[118] IHTA 1984 s.53(2).

[119] Section 144 is considered in detail at 39.55 and following.

[120] See further Ch.42.

[121] See Ch.35 for further comment. If the trust is altered more than two years after death, s.71D or BMT treatment can be secured from that date but there is no reading-back to the date of death so until the point of conversion the settled property is within the relevant property regime and may suffer an exit charge.

EXAMPLE 38.15

John, a young widower, leaves his residuary estate on discretionary trusts
for his only son Ben. When the Will was drafted Ben was only four. If
John dies when Ben is aged say seven, it may well be sensible to convert
the trust into a BMT within two years of his death so that anniversary
and exit charges are avoided over the next 11 years. Just before Ben is 18
the trustees could:

(a) let Ben take the capital so that the trusts end and there is no exit
charge and CGT hold-over relief is available; or
(b) make a settled advance deferring his capital entitlement until 25.
The trust is thereby converted into a s.71D trust without any exit
charge and anniversary charges are avoided until he is 25. Just
before Ben is 25 the trustees can consider whether they wish to
defer his capital entitlement again. Whether he takes outright or
the trusts continue there is an exit charge at 25. If the trusts continue the relevant property regime applies from that date; or
(c) make a settled advance so Ben does not take capital at any
specified age. The settled property falls into the relevant property
regime when the advance is made.

If, however, John dies when Ben is 21 the trustees may consider it is
more appropriate to give Ben the property outright or create an IPDI. In
either case they should exercise their powers within two years of death so
that reading back under s.144 is obtained.[122] Unlike a BMT or a s.71D
trust, an IPDI cannot be created out of a discretionary will trust more
than two years after the testator's death.

VIII WILLS FOR COHABITEES

The absence of the spouse exemption is a major problem. It may also be the **38.57**
case that both parties have children from earlier liaisons who they wish to
provide for. A possible strategy is as follows.

EXAMPLE 38.16

Ron and Roz live together but have no intention of marrying. Both have
children from earlier relationships. Their combined estates (roughly
equal in value) are in the region of £1 million. Their basic wish is for the
survivor to have the use of all the property for life and thereafter for it
to pass to the relevant children. The possibilities are:

(i) for Ron (the wills would be identical) to leave Roz a flexible IPDI
with remainders to his children. This will achieve the wishes of

[122] See Ch.35 for a detailed review of BMTs and s.71D trusts.

the couple (the IPDI could be made inflexible if Ron did not want capital to be capable of being applied for Roz's benefit) but at an IHT cost. In rough and ready terms this would be:

On Ron's death:

	£
Taxable estate	500,000
Less NRB	325,000
	175,000
Tax at 40%	70,000

On Roz's death

Value of IPDI trust	430,000
Free estate	500,000
	930,000
Less NRB	325,000
	605,000
Tax at 40%	242,000
Tax on Ron's property	104,000

Left for Ron's children	500,000
Less tax on Ron's death	70,000
Less tax on Roz's death	104,000
	326,000

38.58   The charge on Ron's death is unavoidable but it is something of a disaster for there to be a second charge on Roz's death (and, of course, not only is Ron's property taxed at that time but it takes the benefit of part of Roz' nil rate band). An alternative strategy would therefore be:

EXAMPLE 38.16 CONTINUED

(ii) Ron establishes two lifetime pilot trusts into which he leaves his estate on death (each therefore receives (net) £215,000). Under these trusts Roz can benefit (and can be given a life interest after two years when the danger of a s.144 read-back has gone) and, after her death, the property can be appointed out of the trusts to Ron's children. By this arrangement the trusts will not form part of Roz's estate at death (which will, on the above figures, be £500,000 with a tax liability of £70,000) and both trusts should benefit from a full IHT nil rate band so that when they are ended there will be no IHT charges.[123]

IX PROPOSED CHANGES FOR CHARITABLE LEGACIES

The Coalition Government announced in the 2011 Budget a new incentive for charitable giving: a lower rate of IHT will apply where people leave a charitable legacy of 10 per cent or more of their estate when they die. A consultation document was produced with a view to the change being applicable for deaths on or after April 6, 2012. **38.59**

The intention is that when a will leaves charitable legacies of at least 10 per cent of the net estate, a 36 per cent rate of IHT (compared with the main IHT rate of 40 per cent) will apply to the chargeable estate. Whether or not the 10 per cent threshold has been met (the 10 per cent test) will be determined by comparing: **38.60**

   (i) the total value of charitable legacies for IHT purposes; and

  (ii) the value of the net estate for IHT purposes as reduced by:

      (a) any available nil rate band;

      (b) the value of property passing to a surviving spouse or civil partner (i.e. the spouse exemption); and

      (c) other IHT reliefs and exemptions (e.g. business or agricultural property relief) apart from the charitable legacy itself.

If the 10 per cent test is passed, the chargeable estate will qualify for the reduced rate of IHT.

EXAMPLE 38.17 (TAKEN FROM THE CONSULTATION DOCUMENT)

An estate is valued at £850,000 and the available nil rate band is £325,000. The minimum charitable legacy to pass the 10 per cent test is calculated as follows:

	Now	From April 2012
Estate value	£850,000	£850,000
Less charitable legacy	−£52,500	
Less available nil rate band	−£325,000	−£325,000
Net estate for 10% test purposes	£525,000	
Less minimum charitable legacy		
to pass 10% test	−£52,500	
Taxable estate	£472,500	£472,500

[123] For a consideration of pilot trusts, their uses and advantages, see Ch.41.

IHT due   @ 40%   £189,000   @ 36%   £170,100

The amount left for distribution to non-charitable beneficiaries (i.e. the estate value less any charitable legacy and IHT due) would be:

£608,500   £627,400

With no charitable legacy, the amount available for beneficiaries would be £640,000 (the estate value less IHT due (£210,000) on the estate). The charitable legacy results in a reduction in the amount left to other beneficiaries of:

£31,500   £12,600

As a proportion of charitable legacy   60%   24%

38.61 So under the current rules the effective cost of a charitable legacy of £100 to the remaining beneficiaries is £60. Following the introduction of the charitable legacy incentive, where an estate qualifies for the reduced rate of 36 per cent, the effective cost of a charitable gift will fall. For example, where exactly 10 per cent of the net estate is given to charity, each 100 per cent of that legacy will reduce the IHT due on the estate by £76—so the effective cost of the charitable legacy to the remaining beneficiaries is only £24. Of course, a charitable legacy will still result in an overall cost to the beneficiaries compared to not leaving anything at all to a charity in a will! The measure will reduce that cost but not to such an extent that the reduction in IHT would exceed the amount of the charitable legacy. Because the benefit of the reduced rate will be dependent on whether or not the amount of the charitable legacy is sufficient for the estate to pass the 10 per cent test there will be a "cliff edge" effect. Where the amount of the charitable legacy is close to the critical 10 per cent point, a small difference to the amount of the legacy could have a much larger impact on the estate's IHT liability. Deeds of variation may prove popular!

38.62 The legacy will need to be:

(1) left to a body that is a charity for UK tax purposes, that is, a charity or other organisation in the UK, European Union Member State, Iceland or Norway that would be a charity under the law of England and Wales (if it were located in England or Wales); or

(2) settled in trust to be used for charitable purposes only;

(3) left to a Community Amateur Sports Club.

38.63 In cases where the estate's IHT liability is based only on assets within the free estate, the 10 per cent test will operate as follows:

(1) identify the amount of the estate that is charged to IHT (this will be the net value of the estate after deducting all available exemptions and reliefs and any available nil-rate band);

(2) add back the value of the charitable legacies. The result is the "baseline" for the 10 per cent test;

(3) compare the baseline amount with the value of the charitable legacy.

If the value of the charitable legacy is at least 10 per cent of the baseline, the entire estate will be charged to IHT at the reduced rate.[124]

Nil rate band reduced by lifetime gifts

The value of gifts made in the seven years prior to death may reduce the nil **38.64** rate band available to the estate on death. A reduced nil rate band will increase the baseline for the 10 per cent test as shown in Example 38.18.

EXAMPLE 38.18

An estate is valued at £850,000 at death. Two years before the death, the deceased made a substantial gift of £400,000. The will provides for a charitable legacy sufficient for the estate to qualify for the reduced rate.

The available nil rate band at death was used by the lifetime gift and is therefore zero. The 10 per cent test is:

	£
Net free estate	850,000
Less available nil rate band	0
Net estate for 10% test purposes	850,000
Less minimum charitable legacy to pass 10% test	−85,000
Taxable estate	765,000
IHT due at 36%	275,400

The minimum charitable legacy needed to pass the 10 per cent test is £85,000 and is greater than the amount of £52,500 shown in Example 38.17 even though the value of the estate at death is the same. The lifetime gift within seven years of death has eliminated any nil rate band that may otherwise have been available.

Cases where the IHT estate includes more than the free estate

For the purposes of calculating whether a reduced rate of tax is due, the net **38.65** estate of the deceased may include:

(1) jointly owned property;

(2) reservation of benefit property;

(3) property in which the deceased had a qualifying interest in possession.

[124] See Example 38.17.

38.66   It is not yet clear how the 10 per cent test will apply in these circumstances and what assets should benefit from the reduced rate. The consultation document raises a number of other practical issues including the position on excluded property, grossing up and the position of PRs. Depending on the results of the consultation, draft legislation is likely to appear by December 2011.

38.67   It may be thought that the complexities of the measure outweigh its likely benefits to charity.[125] As a matter of principle is it right that such a complex relief should be introduced when the Government has set up an Office of Tax Simplification to simplify the tax system? HMRC themselves had to issue a revised consultation paper because of errors in the first version! Taxpayers (unless they have a short life expectancy) may question whether the relief will still be in existence at the date of their death and therefore whether it is worth making any specific provision in the will. Nevertheless for those interested in using the relief a draft precedent (prepared before the legislation has been produced) is provided at A1.16.

---

[125] The tax cost of the relief is estimated at £170 million pa.

CHAPTER 39

DEEDS OF VARIATION, DISCLAIMERS AND OTHER POST-DEATH REARRANGEMENTS

- Variations: inheritance tax treatment (**39.04**)
- Variations: CGT treatment (**39.33**)
- Variations: income tax (**39.41**)
- Variations: impact of the POA charge (**39.44**)
- Variations: Stamp duty and SDLT (**39.45**)
- Disclaimers (**39.47**)
- Section 144: discretionary will trusts (**39.55**)

Precedents

A1.11 Deed of Variation (a) severing beneficial joint tenancy and (b) creating a nil rate band discretionary trust with debt/charge provisions
A1.12 Disclaimer of a life interest where life tenant has died within two years of the deceased
A1.13 Revocable appointment of IPDI from a discretionary will trust

This chapter is concerned with post-death rearrangements, namely: **39.01**

  (i) Instruments of variation;

 (ii) Disclaimers;

(iii) Section 144 (two-year discretionary trusts).

Instruments of variation remain a valuable planning tool in the taxpayer's armoury conferring four advantages, namely:

(1) that the relevant beneficiary does not make any transfer of value;

(2) that the reservation of benefit rules will not apply even if he continues to use or enjoy the redirected property;

(3) that they are outside the pre-owned assets charge;

(4) they enable a person who wishes to effect lifetime planning (e.g. for his children) to set up qualifying interest in possession trusts (IPDIs) not falling within the relevant property regime.

39.02 In the "real world":

(i) it is not possible to vary a deceased's will; and

(ii) any variation is accordingly a gift by the person who is redirecting the property.

Section 142, however, creates a fictional world which extends as far as enabling beneficial joint tenancies to be, in effect, severed after the death of one of the joint tenants.[1] The fiction only extends for tax purposes; it does not affect the validity of any gift in the real world.[2] It is sometimes suggested that a foreign law will cannot be varied unless the law governing the will's validity permits this. However, this must be wrong, the gift is not being made by the deceased in the real world; it is being made by the person making the variation. Therefore if that latter person can make the gift validly then the statutory tax fiction can operate if a statement for reading back is made. Of course, if the beneficiary of the will varies a gift that he receives under the will and he opts for reading back under the UK tax legislation this does not have any effect for the purposes of foreign taxes. He is giving away assets and if the assets are foreign sited or the beneficiary is domiciled abroad this may well have foreign tax consequences. For example, US beneficiaries can vary gifts that they receive under wills and opt for reading back but this has no effect for US tax purposes where they may well have made a reportable disposition.

It follows that any gift made by a beneficiary by an instrument of variation is still a voluntary disposition that can be attacked by his creditors if he is insolvent since in the real world it is not deemed to be made by the deceased. This may also have an effect on means-tested benefits or care home fees as well as claims by ex-spouses given that the beneficiary has deliberately deprived himself of property or resources.

39.03 It is not necessary for other beneficiaries under the will to agree to any variation. Nor is it necessary for those who benefit under the variation to be a party to and sign the variation although this is often done. It should also be borne in mind that if the interests of the other beneficiaries under the will being varied are not affected then there is no need for them to be parties to the variation. So, for example, if X leaves his shares in X Limited to his three sons A, B and C who do not speak to each other, A can still vary his shares in favour of his spouse and children even if B and C object unless of course the company articles prohibit such transfers. Bear in mind that the transfer provisions in the articles may allow transfers on death to family relatives but not permit lifetime transfers except to other shareholders. For these purposes, the variation is a lifetime transfer so that the transfer provisions need to be checked with this in mind.

At present a consultation is proceeding on the possible introduction of a

---

[1] The extent of the "deeming" that is required by s.142 was considered in the context of multiple variations of the same property in *Russell v IRC* [1988] STC 195. For a precedent affecting a severance, see A1.11.

[2] See 39.14 below for a consideration of whether variations can be made into trusts not established at the date of death.

reduced rate of IHT for non-charitable residuary beneficiaries (36 per cent instead of 40 per cent) in cases where charitable legacies exceed 10 per cent of the net estate. If this is enacted as anticipated from April 6, 2012, then deeds of variation may be executed to take advantage of this relief. For example, where the net charitable gift is just under 10 per cent, a slight increase in favour of the charity may secure an overall saving for the non-charitable residuary beneficiaries of the estate.[3]

I VARIATIONS: INHERITANCE TAX TREATMENT

If a beneficiary varies the dispositions of property comprised in a deceased's **39.04** estate in accordance with the conditions laid down in IHTA 1984 s.142(1), then, "*this Act shall apply as if the variation had been effected by the deceased.*"

It is commonly said that the terms of the variation are "read back" into the deceased's will.[4]

Requirements under IHTA 1984 s.142

(i) Statement for reading back: From August 1, 2002, no formal election for **39.05** reading-back is required but the variation will be read-back to death and treated as effected by the deceased if the instrument of variation itself contains a statement that this is intended.[5] Only if more IHT becomes payable as a result of the variation does it have to be sent to HMRC within six months[6] and the personal representatives must then be parties to the instrument as well as the person effecting the variation.[7]

The requirement to include the reading back statement in the deed of variation itself has removed some flexibility. Under the old pre-2002 regime it was possible to wait for up to six months before making an election. Now a decision has to be taken when the instrument is made.[8]

(ii) The property must be comprised in the deceased's estate: s.42 only applies **39.06** to property comprised in a person's estate immediately before his death. Excluded property is within this definition[9] but not settled property in which

---

[3] See "*A new incentive for Charitable Legacies*" (Consultation document, June 10, 2011) and Ch.38.
[4] Of course, it should be remembered that variations are not confined to the situation where the deceased left a will but also apply to dispositions of property taking effect under the intestacy rules and to property passing by survivorship under a beneficial joint tenancy.
[5] Typical wording is "*the provisions of IHTA 1984, s.142(1) and of TCGA 1992, s.62(6) shall apply to the variation effected by this instrument.*" Of course it may be desirable to opt for reading back for one tax (e.g. IHT) but not the other (CGT). See *Wills v Gibbs* [2008] STC 808 where the omission of the reading back statement was rectified by the court.
[6] IHTA 1984 s.218A inserted by FA 2002 s.120(2) and (4).
[7] IHTA 1984 s.142(2A) substituted by FA 2002 s.120(1)(7). Note that personal representatives can only decline to make a reading back statement "*if no, or no sufficient, assets are held by them in that capacity for discharging the additional tax*".
[8] A statement of intent is not required for a disclaimer. However if one is not included it precludes the instrument from being treated as a variation in the event that the conditions for a disclaimer are not met: IHTM 35058.
[9] For the meaning of excluded property, see Ch.31.

the deceased had a qualifying life interest so that it taxes no part of his estate at death.[10] It will also include jointly owned property[11] but not gift with reservation property.[12] Although HMRC have confirmed that a deceased's joint tenant's interest passing by survivorship can be redirected by deed of variation, it is not thought that as a matter of law a surviving joint tenant can make an effective disclaimer.[13] Variations are possible even if the beneficiary has only been given a life interest by the will but the beneficiary in question can, of course, only vary what he has—in this case the life interest.

39.07 *(iii) Requirement for writing*: whether it effects a variation or a disclaimer, the instrument must be in writing. This does not necessarily mean that a deed is required, but it is thought that a variation can only receive the favourable tax treatment if effective in property terms, which means that the variation has to be binding and enforceable.[14] To obtain the tax advantages there must generally be no extraneous consideration[15] and therefore a deed is invariably used.

39.08 *(iv) Parties*: the variation or disclaimer must be made by the persons who benefit as a result of the deceased's dispositions, i.e. all parties who are prejudiced by the deed of variation must agree it. Anyone can benefit from that deed—not necessarily members of the family—including limited companies.[16]

39.09 *(v) Parties who vary must be sui juris*: a minor cannot be a party to a deed of variation without the court's consent on his behalf, although obviously he can benefit under someone else's deed of variation. Provided that the minor's interest under the will or intestacy is not adversely affected, a variation can go ahead without his consent. For example, if the will creates a trust in which the remainder interest is left to a minor, there is no objection to any prior interest being the subject of a deed of variation. However, a deed of variation cannot be used to take away an interest of the minor beneficiary and replace it with

---

[10] See IHTA 1984 s.142(5). However HMRC accept that settled property in which the deceased had an interest in possession but also had a general power of appointment which he exercised by will is capable of variation under s.142: see IHTM 35072.

[11] Whether the jointly held property is realty or personalty such as bank accounts. See the words "*or otherwise*" in s.142(1). Note that if the property is beneficially owned by three joint tenants, one dies and only one of the surviving joint tenants wishes to vary the jointly held property he can do so by "severing" the joint tenancy: for s.142 purposes it is only his share which is treated as passing to whoever he designates. The other surviving joint tenant's interest is unaffected.

[12] Although note that a disclaimer of settled property can be made under IHTA 1984 s.93: see 39.52. On the disclaimer of a life interest, see 39.51.

[13] For a precedent variation incorporating a severance, see A1.11.

[14] But see IHTM 35022: "*you can accept a letter or note from the beneficiary redirecting their inheritance as a valid variation so long as the document conforms to the guidelines and otherwise meets the conditions in s.142*".

[15] On consideration, see 39.11.

[16] It is not necessary to include the personal representatives as parties (only if extra tax is payable: see fn.5 above) but as a matter of practice this is commonly done and is obviously important if the estate has not been fully administered. It is also common practice to include the person benefiting from the variation as a party: again this is not strictly necessary but it does mean that he has signified his acceptance of the gift. If the variation establishes trusts the designated trustees will normally be joined to indicate their consent to act. Assume that by will S leaves property to his wife for life and on her death to her daughter if she is then living or, if dead, to her children and the daughter is aged over 55 with one adult child. HMRC accept that a variation can be made by the wife, daughter and adult child and that as a result of *Re Pettifor's Will Trusts, Roberts v Roberts* [1966] Ch 257 the daughter is presumed to be past the age of child bearing so that there is no question of adversely affecting the interests of unborn children: see IHTM 35048.

a different interest even if the minor will benefit overall. Such a variation can only go ahead with the approval of the court.

The Inheritance Tax Manual states that:

> "*an IoV which adversely affects the interests of minor or unborn benefici-aries can achieve total validity only by obtaining the approval of the Court (on an application under the Variation of Trusts Act or under the Court's inherent jurisdiction). A parent's signature on behalf of a minor is not sufficient.*"[17]

Personal representatives can stand in the shoes of a deceased beneficiary, if **39.10** the beneficiary died after the testator, for the purposes of effecting a deed of variation or making a disclaimer ("double death variation").

EXAMPLE 39.1

> Brother died in December 2010 leaving everything to his sister who died six months later in June 2011. The sister left all the property to her children. A double charge (subject to quick succession relief) has arisen in respect of the brother's property. Even if the beneficiaries benefiting under the variation are those who would have taken under the sister's will in any event, so that there is no movement overall in the beneficial inter-ests, it does not appear that HMRC will object to the sister's executors varying the brother's will in favour of the sister's children.[18] Note that if the brother had left everything to his sister who had lost capacity before her death her attorneys (even if acting under an enduring or lasting power of attorney) cannot vary her interest under brother's will while she is alive. They have to obtain the consent of the Court of Protection. If she dies within the two-year period, however, her personal representatives may carry out a variation even though she did not have capacity.

(vi) No consideration payable[19]: s.142(1) does not apply to a variation or dis- **39.11** claimer which is made for any consideration in money or money's worth other than consideration consisting of the making of a variation or disclaimer in respect of another of the dispositions made under the will.[20] So, for example,

---

[17] IHTM 35045.
[18] HMRC consider that it must be shown that the personal representatives were acting with the consent of the persons who would take under the deceased's will. Commonly this consent is stated in a recital to the variation, see *Tax Bulletin* February 1995, p.194.
[19] See IHTM 35100.
[20] However, IHTM 35094 states that where the deceased is domiciled abroad, then if the facts are as in the Example below "*you should refer [such] cases immediately to the TA Team Leader without making any preliminary enquiries.*"
   EXAMPLE T dies domiciled in Switzerland. He has a London house worth £1 million (non-excluded property) which he leaves to his son and excluded property (such as gilts and foreign property) worth the same amount left to his spouse or charities. A variation is made so that the son now gets the excluded property and the spouse or charities get the London flat. If T was domiciled here such rearrangement would appear to be uncontroversial because although there is consideration it is a rearrangement within the terms of the will. However HMRC appear to object to the above.

if X leaves Blackacre to A and Whiteacre to B they can each swap their properties by a deed of variation, even if they are not of equal value. The variation is a non-event for IHT and CGT purposes.[21] However, any external consideration is not permitted so that if B gives A Whiteacre in consideration of A giving B another property he already owns the redirection of Whiteacre does not fall within IHTA 1984 s.142.[22] The donor who makes the deed of variation should pay the legal costs, not the personal representatives or donee, and there must be no understanding that the donee beneficiary will give the property back to the donor at any later date.

Where there is a deed of variation or disclaimer in favour of the deceased's surviving spouse, so that less IHT becomes payable as a result of the spouse exemption, HMRC are likely to raise questions designed to elicit whether lifetime gifts are contemplated by the surviving spouse in favour of the varying beneficiaries, i.e. whether there is some consideration in that the spouse intends to give property to the children who varied the will in her favour or whether the variation is a sham.

39.12 *(vii) Two-year time limit*: the variation or disclaimer must be made "within two years after a person's death". Hence if the deceased died on January 1, 2010 the last day for making the variation is generally assumed to be December 31, 2011.[23]

Link-up with Reservation of Benefit

39.13 HMRC accept that *"this Act"* in s.142(1) includes all the IHT legislation which includes the reservation of benefit legislation in FA 1986. Hence a redirection of property will not be caught by these rules even if the beneficiary continues to derive a benefit from it.

EXAMPLE 39.2

On her husband's death in June 2011, Joyce is left his entire estate including the couple's seaside cottage ("Fishnets") worth £300,000. By deed of variation falling within s.142(1), she transfers this property to her son Barney. Joyce continues to use the property on a regular basis.

---

[21] For the SDLT position see 39.46 below.

[22] Assuming that the exchange is a commercial bargain, the arrangement will not have IHT implications. There may, however, be CGT charges and an SDLT charge.

[23] It might be argued that the two-year period commenced from the day *"after a person's death"* and hence the last day might be January 1, 2012. The question is whether the day of death is included or excluded in calculating the two-year period or whether the two-year period runs from the instant of death in which case it would expire on January 1, 2012 at 10.00 if the deceased had died on January 1, 2010 at 10.00! The statutory rule of interpretation is that fractions of a day will normally be disregarded when the occurrence of a particular event starts or stops the period running and hence the period begins not at the instant the relevant event (here the death) occurs but either at the commencement or the termination of the day during which the death occurs. There is no known case on the point but HMRC are believed to consider that the day of death is included in calculating the two-year period.

Tax analysis

(a) The variation is read back into her husband's will and falls within his hitherto unused IHT nil rate band.

(b) Joyce should also consider whether to make a statement reading back for CGT purposes: this will be desirable if the property has increased in value since her husband's death by more than Joyce's annual exemption.[24] Otherwise she will be treated as making a disposal of the house at market value and she will be taxed on any gain.

(c) Although Joyce continues to derive a benefit from the use of the property she is not within the reservation of benefit rules given that, because of reading-back, she has never made a gift of the property. Likewise she is not caught by the pre-owned assets income tax charge.[25]

Variations and trusts

The property passing under a will or intestacy can be varied into a trust. For **39.14** instance, if Joyce in the above example varied the property into a discretionary trust from which she could benefit, this is not treated as a gift by her for IHT purposes and hence, the reservation of benefit rules do not apply. The new trust would, of course, be a relevant property settlement. What if she varied her interest into a trust (set out in the deed of variation) under which she took an immediate interest in possession and opted for reading back for IHT purposes? Her interest in possession will be an IPDI[26] treated as set up by her husband and is spouse exempt. She will be taxed on her death as if she owned the property beneficially since she has a qualifying interest in possession under IHTA 1984 s.49A. A common misconception is that a variation cannot vary property into a trust that was not in existence at the deceased's death. This confuses the issue. The deceased is not making a gift "in the real world"; the person making the gift is the person making the variation. Hence, it does not matter that he varies in favour of persons or trusts not in existence at the date of the deceased's death. Accordingly the person making the variation can either set up a trust in the variation itself or establish a trust with £10 prior to the variation and then vary into that trust. Both ways effect a gift that is perfectly valid in the real world. If a statement for reading back is made then that is just a tax fiction. It does not mean that the deceased has made the gift in the real world; it is simply a statutory fiction that deems such gifts to be made by the deceased for inheritance tax and capital gains tax purposes. In the "real world" the gift has still been made by the person making the variation.[27]

---

[24] The CGT provisions are in TCGA 1992 s.62(6)–(10). The "reading back" is more limited in its effect under the CGT legislation: see 39.31.

[25] See 39.44.

[26] For the meaning of an IPDI, see 28.10.

[27] HMRC state at CG31600 "*Strictly speaking, the instrument of variation does not actually vary the will itself, but only the effects of the will.*" See *Glowacki v HMRC* [2008] STC (SCD) 188 where the variation was phrased in a curious way.

If the trust is set up by the beneficiary and he then varies property he receives outright into that trust, then any perpetuity or accumulation period will run from the date the trust is set up not from the date of death of the deceased. The position is different if the variation varies a trust set up by the deceased in the will itself.

The deceased may have set up pilot trusts during his lifetime and property can be added to them by a deed of variation.[28]

IHT position after FA 2006 when the variation establishes a settlement

39.15 When considering the IHT regime for variations made on or after March 22, 2006 there are six possibilities to consider:

(i) Testator dies after March 21, 2006 and variation is made with reading back for IHT purposes.

(ii) Testator dies after March 21, 2006 and a variation is made with no reading back for inheritance tax purposes.

(iii) Testator dies before March 22, 2006 and a variation is made with reading back before March 22, 2006.

(iv) Testator dies before March 22, 2006 and a variation is made before March 22, 2006 but with no reading back.

(v) Testator dies before March 22, 2006 and a variation is made after March 21, 2006 but with reading back.

(vi) Testator dies before March 22, 2006 and a variation is made after March 21, 2006 with no reading back.

Each of these possibilities will be considered in turn.

39.16 *Testator dies after March 21, 2006 and variation is effected with reading back for inheritance tax purposes*

EXAMPLE 39.3

Maurice left the matrimonial home (wholly owned by him at his death) on trust for his widow for life then to his children for life with remainders over. He died in 2007. She surrendered her life interest so that her children took immediate interests in possession and made a reading back statement. The children's interests qualified as IPDIs. IHT may be payable on Maurice's death but the widow can continue to live in the home without a reservation of benefit problem.[29]

---

[28] For pilot trusts, see Ch.41.

[29] Note that unless she retains some interest in the home as a beneficiary of the trust or the children live in it no principal private residence relief will be available on the eventual sale of the property: see Ch.43 and TCGA 1992 s.225. Contrast the position if the trustees had terminated

Instruments of variation can still be used to take advantage of a deceased's foreign domicile.

EXAMPLE 39.4

> Joyce inherits non-UK situs property from her uncle who died in 2007 domiciled in Monaco. She enters into a deed of variation (with reading back) so that the property becomes held on interest in possession trusts for herself with the trustees having power to advance her capital. The trustees are UK resident but the trust owns only non-UK situs assets. The trust is treated as having been set up by the uncle in his will giving Joyce an IPDI and is an excluded property settlement. It does not matter that the trust is UK resident nor that the interest in possession beneficiary is UK domiciled. The important determinant of the IHT treatment is where the assets are situated at the date of Joyce's death[30] and the domicile of the settlor when he died (the uncle for IHT purposes). Even if the trustees hold UK situated assets directly during Joyce's lifetime the trust is not within the relevant property regime because it is an IPDI. (Of course, in such a case there would be a risk of Joyce dying while the trustees held UK assets and IHT then being payable.) The trust is an excluded property settlement only while (or to the extent that) it holds non-UK situated assets.[31]

For CGT purposes, Joyce is treated as the settlor.[32] She has a qualifying interest in possession and so for capital gains tax purposes there will be a base cost uplift to market value on her death.[33] Even if there were ongoing trusts after Joyce's death, provided that the trustees do not own UK situated assets, the trust property remains excluded for IHT purposes. Of course, if the trustees do own UK situated assets directly then they will need to consider the relevant property regime charges because after Joyce's death the trust will fall into that regime even if her children become entitled to interests in possession. **39.17**

Testator dies after March 21, 2006 and a variation is effected with no reading back for IHT purposes

If in Example 39.3 the widow of Maurice did not make a reading back statement, then spouse exemption continues to be available on Maurice's death but she is treated as making a chargeable transfer because the interests of her children cannot be IPDIs; the settlement falls within the relevant property regime. On the death of the children their interests do not form part of their estates **39.18**

---

her interest in possession (or if the widow did not opt to read back) when the reservation of benefit rules would be in point: see Chs 33 and 43.

[30] Since it is an IPDI if the trust holds UK situated assets at the date of Joyce's death inheritance tax would be payable.

[31] Excluded property settlements are considered in detail in Ch.31.

[32] See Ch.9.

[33] See TCGA 1992 s.72 and Ch.12.

for inheritance tax purposes. The widow cannot continue to benefit from the trust, e.g. by living in the house rent-free otherwise she will reserve a benefit.[34]

Testator dies before March 22, 2006 and a variation is completed (with reading back) before March 22, 2006

EXAMPLE 39.5

> Maurice left the matrimonial home (wholly owned by him) on trust for his widow for life remainder to his children for life. He died in 2005. The widow surrendered her life interest in February 2006 and opted for reading back. There was a chargeable transfer from Maurice to the children on his death (which might fall within his IHT nil rate band) and the children took qualifying interests in possession under the pre-FA 2006 regime. The wife could continue to benefit from the settled property (e.g. by living in the house) without any reservation of benefit since she opted for reading back under s.142 and so the gift was made by Maurice for all IHT purposes.[35]

39.19   *Testator dies before March 22, 2006 and a variation is effected before March 22, 2006 with no reading back*

EXAMPLE 39.6

> Facts as in Example 39.5 except that the widow did not opt for reading back. The children took life interests which were qualifying interests in possession (since they arose under the pre-March 2006 regime). The surrender of her life interest in February 2006 was a PET by the widow. At that time, s.102ZA was not in force. However, because her life interest was surrendered rather than terminated by the trustees, then there is a concern that if she benefits from any ongoing trusts she is caught by the reservation of benefit rules because she made a gift.[36]
>
> As the widow's interest had been terminated by the trustees before March 22, 2006, the reservation of benefit rules do not apply.[37] The spouse exemption was available on her husband's death and she needed to survive her PET by seven years to avoid an IHT charge. If she retained (say) a five per cent interest in possession, the trustees may claim principal private residence relief on the eventual sale of the property.

39.20   *Testator dies before March 22, 2006 and a variation is made with reading back on or after March 22, 2006*

---

[34] See FA 1986 s.102ZA inserted by FA 2006, and consider carve-out schemes in Ch.43 which avoid s.102ZA.

[35] See 39.14, above.

[36] See 33.19 and following. It is far from clear that these concerns are well founded. Any gift she makes is of her life interest which has disappeared! See 33.20 for further discussion.

[37] She has not made any gift. The position was changed for terminations after March 21, 2006 by FA 2006, Sch.20 Pt 5 inserting new s.102ZA into FA 2006.

EXAMPLE 39.7

Maurice left the matrimonial home (wholly owned by him) on trust for his widow for life remainder to his children for life. He died in 2005 and the widow carried out a variation after March 21, 2006 so that her children took immediate interests in possession. She opted for reading back. There was a chargeable transfer from Maurice to the children on his death (which might fall within his IHT nil rate band) and the children took qualifying interests in possession even though the variation was completed after March 21, 2006. The IHT legislation applies "as if the variation had been effected by the deceased" and at the date of the deceased's death it was still possible to set up qualifying interests in possession. The wife can continue to benefit from the property (e.g. by living in the house) since the gift was made by Maurice for IHT purposes.[38]

EXAMPLE 39.8

Maurice died in 2005 leaving all his property to his wife. In June 2007 she varied his will leaving his unused nil rate band on A-M trusts for his children who take income at 25 and capital at 30. This was treated as an A-M trust falling within IHTA 1984 s.71. From April 6, 2008, however, the trust fell into the relevant property regime unless its terms were altered (before April 6) to either vest capital at 18 or to make it an 18–25 trust.[39]

Testator dies before March 22, 2006 and a variation is effected (with no reading back) on or after March 22, 2006

In these circumstances any ongoing trusts set up by the variation will be within the relevant property regime.   **39.21**

Multiple variations

It is not possible for more than one variation to fall within s.142(1) in respect   **39.22**
of the same property[40] (so if father varies in favour of son and reads back any further variation by the son of the same property will not be within s.142). However, there can be a number of variations made at different times within

---

[38] Note that since the children have pre-March 22, 2006 interests in possession in both Example 39.5 and Example 39.7 it was possible for replacement interests in possession to be set up before October 6, 2008 and for those interests in possession to be transitional serial interests. For what is meant by a TSI, see 27.16. Even after October 5, 2008 a beneficiary's spouse or civil partner can take a TSI provided that this comes into existence on the death of the beneficiary.

[39] See further Ch.35.

[40] *Russell v IRC* [1988] STC 195.

the two-year period in relation to the same estate, provided that each variation deals with separate property. Note also that:

(i) a variation (read back under s.142(1)) can be combined with the ending of a two-year discretionary trust which gave rise to a separate reading back under s.144[41];

(ii) there can be multiple disclaimers and a disclaimer can be combined with a variation.[42]

Rectification

39.23 If a deed of variation is made and contains an error (for example, a gift is stated to be free of tax instead of subject to tax),[43] rectification may be possible but a court application is required for it to be accepted by HMRC even if the parties are in agreement that an error has been made.[44]

Appointments and advancements followed by variations

39.24 If an appointment is made out of a discretionary will trust within two years of death, and read back under IHTA 1984 s.144,[45] a deed of variation may subsequently (but still within two years of the death) be made by the beneficiary who has been appointed the property. IHTA 1984 s.142 will apply if a statement for reading back is made. Similarly HMRC accept that the following rearrangement of the trust interests prior to the variation being made is effective:

EXAMPLE 39.9

A will leaves property to Beth contingent on her attaining the age of 25. There is a wide power of advancement. At the date of death, Beth is over 18 and so entitled to the income under TA 1925 s.31. The trustees exercise their power of advancement so that she becomes absolutely entitled to the property. Beth then redirects that property to her son and opts for reading back under s.142(1). Assuming that the two-year time limit is met, HMRC accept that this is an effective variation and the gift

[41] See 39.24.
[42] See 39.49 onwards.
[43] As was the case in *Ashcroft v Barnsdale* [2010] STC 2544.
[44] Be careful that you restrict any nil rate band trust set up in a deed of variation to the value of the NRB *in force at the date of death*: see *Martin v Nicholson* [2005] WTLR 175. In this case the variation created a legacy of £200,000. This was the figure for the NRB at the time when the variation was executed but the NRB at the date of death was only £154,000 so prima facie £46,000 was chargeable to IHT. Fortunately the court rectified the instrument. For a failure to include the reading back statement, see *Wills v Gibbs* [2008] STC 808.
[45] See 39.55.

to the son is treated as made by the deceased not Beth even though Beth had not been absolutely entitled to the property at the date of death. In other words the trustees can put the beneficiary in a position after death so that he is capable of making a variation even if the beneficiary was not absolutely entitled to the property at the date of death.

Typical uses of variations

(i) Variations were often employed to use the otherwise wasted nil rate **39.25** band of the deceased person. For example, where the will left everything outright to the surviving spouse, he could execute a deed of variation varying up to the deceased's unused nil rate band in favour of their children or on discretionary trusts. With the introduction of transferable unused nil rate bands between spouses and civil partners,[46] it is likely that few such variations will now be made.[47]

(ii) Variations may be made to take advantage of the introduction of the transferable nil rate band for spouses. For instance, if Bob left his nil rate band to his daughter, within two years of his death, she could vary his will to pass the benefit to her mother. This will result in the spouse exemption applying on Bob's death and his unused nil rate band being available on the survivor's death.

(iii) Variations can be used to maximise reliefs such as BPR and APR.[48]

(iv) The estate of a beneficiary alive at the date of the deceased's death can be increased by a variation made after that beneficiary's death. For instance, if H dies leaving his entire estate to his daughter and W (H's wife) dies shortly afterwards without sufficient assets to use up her IHT nil rate band, the daughter can vary H's will in favour of W.[49]

(v) A variation may be used to redirect a posthumous increase in the value of an estate without any IHT charge. Assume that the death estate was worth £300,000 but increased in value after death so that it became worth £500,000. The will had left everything to the widow. She could by instrument of variation provide for a legacy of £300,000 to herself with residue passing to her children. Under IHTA 1984 ss.36–42 the value of the death estate (£300,000) will be wholly attributed to the spouse exempt legacy.

Variations and short lived trusts[50]

Section 142(4) imposes a special rule where a *"variation . . . results in property* **39.26** *being held on trust for a person for a period which ends not more than two years*

---

[46] From October 9, 2007.
[47] See 38.24 for when NRBDT remain attractive.
[48] On will drafting for APR and BPR property, see Ch.38.
[49] See *Tax Bulletin*, February 1995, p.94.
[50] See IHTM 35133.

after the death." The disposition taking effect at the end of this period will be treated as if it had taken effect on death.

EXAMPLE 39.10

> Daughter is left property by her father on his death in 2010. By a read back deed of variation she sets up an interest in possession trust (an IPDI) in favour of her stepmother (to whom her father was married at his death) which will end automatically one year after the father's death whereupon the property will revert to the daughter. The object of the exercise—to obtain the benefit of the spouse exemption on the father's death—is frustrated by s.142(4). As a result of this provision the father's estate will be treated as if it had been left direct to the daughter.
>
> If the variation gave the stepmother a life interest and she died within two years of the father's death, it is the death not the variation that results in the trust ending within two years of death and HMRC accept that s.142(4) does not apply. (They will collect IHT on the death of the stepmother!)
>
> What happens if the variation creates a terminable life interest and the trustees terminate the interest within two years of the deceased's death? Is it the variation which results in the termination of the trust (on the basis that it creates the terms allowing the termination) or is it the act of the trustees? The position is unclear. To avoid arguments ensure that a terminable life interest created by variation for a surviving spouse lasts for at least two years from the date of the deceased's death.[51]

39.27 *Varying life interests where the life tenant has died*

EXAMPLE 39.11

> A dies leaving in his will a life interest to B, remainder to charity and B dies within two years of A's death. In these circumstances there would have been IHT payable on the death of A. However, if the property can be treated as passing direct from A to the charity there is no IHT payable. Can A's will be varied so that the life interest in favour of B is deleted? This could have been done while B was alive by a surrender or disclaimer of his life interest. Can it be done by his personal representatives after B's death?

In the December 2001 issue of the *IHT Newsletter*, HMRC stated:

> "*It is a pre-requisite if the provisions [of s.142(1)] are to have any impact that a real life disposition or transfer took place so that the transferor can*

---

[51] The terminable life interest does not need to last two years from the date of the variation.

decide whether or not to make an election in order to trigger the deeming provisions."[52]

HMRC's view is that the deceased cannot be deemed to bring about effects which the beneficiaries cannot or do not bring about in the real world. Since the life interest of B in the above example has already ended, his personal representatives cannot effect a variation of it.

In *Soutter's Executry v IRC*[53] the deceased, Miss Soutter, left a *"free life-rent and useful occupation of the house at Drevaburn as long as Miss Greenlees wishes to reside there."* **39.28**

Miss Soutter died in November 1999 and her estate was under the inheritance tax threshold. Miss Greenlees lived in the house until she became ill. She died in November 2000 and her estate was substantially over the inheritance tax threshold. The executors and beneficiaries of both estates executed a deed of variation purporting to remove the liferent provision in Miss Soutter's will.

The Special Commissioner decided that in order for a right to be assigned or renounced it must belong to the assignor at the date of the assignment. There can be no assignment of something that does not exist. The executors of Miss Greenlees never held the liferent (which ended with her death) and so had nothing to assign. Although a deed of variation is deemed to be made by the deceased that is only a deeming for tax purposes. It cannot affect the law of property nor the question of whether those making the deed of variation had any right to do so.

The decision has been heavily criticised, rightly so the authors believe. An alternative view is that the sense of s.142 is to deem the deed of variation to take effect at Miss Soutter's death and therefore the fact that the liferent did not exist at Miss Greenlees' death is irrelevant. What is varied is the disposition of property made by Miss Soutter and this could be done by removing the liferent. **39.29**

The executors pointed out that the position was no more unusual than a beneficiary spending a cash legacy (so that he no longer had the property) and then varying the disposition of the will conferring the legacy. HMRC accept that in these circumstances a variation is effective. Similarly, where property such as a house has been sold after death, HMRC accept that the beneficiary can execute a deed of variation in respect of the house.

It may be said that *Soutter* does not apply in England, particularly where the life interest is in income producing property and income arises between the two deaths which belongs to the (deceased) life tenant. And, of course, it is possible for the life tenant of a will trust to vary his life interest while alive within two years of the death of the testator or to disclaim it. Thus if Miss Greenlees had executed a variation the day before her death this would have been effective.

EXAMPLE 39.12

Bramwell leaves his estate, worth £325,000 on his death in 2011, to his sister Charlotte for life remainder to his younger sister Emily. Tragically

---

[52] And see IHTM 35042.
[53] [2002] STC (SCD) 385.

Charlotte dies a year after Bramwell, leaving her estate (also worth £325,000) to Emily. Income of £450 was paid in respect of Charlotte's life interest.

(1) No IHT was payable on Bramwell's death but on that of Charlotte tax of £130,000 (40% × £325,000) was payable (quick succession relief being of no value).

(2) Ideally Emily wishes that Charlotte had never benefitted from the life interest but as she received income during her life the interest cannot be disclaimed by her personal representatives.

(3) Consider, however, Charlotte's personal representatives executing a variation in which the life interest property (together with interest accruing on it since Bramwell's death) is redirected in favour of Emily.

39.30 In summary, HMRC accept that:

(i) a life tenant can vary or disclaim before death;

(ii) a life tenant's PRs can disclaim the benefit of a life interest if it had not been accepted by the deceased life tenant.[54]

Varying settled property

39.31 Section 142 does not apply to property in which the deceased had a qualifying interest in possession at the time of his death.[55]

EXAMPLE 39.13

Alan died in 2011 leaving his free estate to his child Ben outright. Alan was the life tenant of a pre-March 2006 trust set up by his mother and which on his death passed to Ben for life remainder to Ben's children living at Alan's death. Ben can vary the free estate (e.g. by passing it to Alan's spouse so as to obtain the spouse exemption) but cannot vary the destination of the settled property. However, Ben could disclaim his life interest under IHTA 1984 s.93[56] so that the settled property is treated as passing directly from Alan to Ben's children. Note:

(1) on Alan's death the settled property became held on relevant property trusts. Accordingly it did not become comprised in Ben's estate (contrast the position if Alan had died before October 6, 2008 when Ben would have taken a TSI)[57];

(2) the effect of Ben's disclaimer is that on Alan's death the settled property vests absolutely in Ben's children and so no relevant

---

[54] On disclaimers, see 39.47.
[55] IHTA 1984 s.142(5).
[56] IHTA 1984 s.93 is considered at 39.52.
[57] For TSI's see Ch.27.

property charges will arise. There will be the usual CGT uplift on Alan's death.

A common problem is where a pre-March 22, 2006 life tenant dies and the **39.32** settled property does not pass on TSI trusts or outright to the spouse. IHT is then payable.[58] In these circumstances there may be scope for obtaining spouse exemption on death by the use of s.93 combined with the judicious use of trustees' powers of appointment to give the deceased life tenant's spouse a short-term interest in possession.[59]

II VARIATIONS: CGT TREATMENT

Subject to conditions, which are the same as for IHT, any variation of the **39.33** deceased's will or of the intestacy rules, or any disclaimer, made within two years of the deceased's death may be treated:

(1) as if it were not a disposal: TCGA 1992 s.62(6)(a); and

(2) "*this section shall apply*" as if it had been effected by the deceased or, in the case of a disclaimer, as if the disclaimed benefit had never been conferred.[60]

As with IHT, the instrument must be in writing made within two years of **39.34** the death and the variation (or disclaimer) must not be made for a considera-tion in money or money's worth other than consideration consisting of the making of a variation or disclaimer in respect of another of the dispositions: see Example 39.14 below. The variation can be made regardless of whether the administration of the estate is complete or whether the property has already been distributed in accordance with the original disposition. The same prop-erty cannot be subject to more than one variation.

TCGA 1992 s.62(10) defines the assets of which a deceased person was **39.35** competent to dispose and which are capable of being varied. This property is slightly different from the property capable of variation for inheritance tax purposes. It includes jointly owned property but excludes settled prop-erty over which the deceased had a general power of appointment. Such property is capable of variation for inheritance tax purposes but cannot be varied with reading back for capital gains tax purposes. HMRC also deny reading back for capital gains tax purposes in relation to an interest in partnership assets which passes automatically to the surviving partners although a variation of such property is capable of reading back for inherit-ance tax purposes.[61]

---

[58] Sometimes the life tenant has a power to appoint an income interest to his spouse but fails to exercise this power.

[59] This is discussed further at 39.53.

[60] TCGA 1992 s.62(6)(b): the difference in wording to s.142(1), "*this section*" as opposed to "*this Act*", is significant: see 39.13.

[61] See CG 30362 and compare IHTM 35073 although a partnership interest cannot be varied with reading back for inheritance tax purposes where value is given.

EXAMPLE 39.14

A dies leaving a house, Blackacre, to B and a second house, Whiteacre, to C. B would rather have Whiteacre and C would rather have Blackacre. They enter into a deed of variation so that A is deemed to have left Whiteacre to B and Blackacre to C. Although each enters into the variation in consideration of the other also varying his interest, this does not prevent reading back for both CGT and IHT purposes. Accordingly B will take Whiteacre and C Blackacre at probate value.

EXAMPLE 39.15

Andrew is entitled under his mother's will to a picture worth £100,000. Within two years of his mother's death Andrew varies the will so that the picture (now worth £150,000) passes to his brother Robert. Provided that the appropriate statement for reading back is made, this will be treated as if his mother's will had provided for the picture to pass to Robert who will acquire it at its market value at death (£100,000) as legatee.[62]

"Reading back" (TCGA 1992 s.62(7) as amended)

39.36 Before August 1, 2002, reading back did not apply to a variation unless the person or persons making the instrument so elected within six months of the instrument (or such longer period as the Board might allow). From that date, as with IHT, the requirement for a separate election was abolished: if "reading back" is desired the instrument of variation itself must now so provide.[63]

In many cases, it will be desirable that the variation is read back for both CGT and IHT purposes. This is not necessary, however, since the decisions can be taken independently of each other with the result that a taxpayer may decide to read back for IHT purposes without doing so for CGT and vice versa. Careful thought should be given to this matter. Consider the following.

EXAMPLE 39.16

(1) A's will leaves quoted shares worth £100,000 to his daughter. By instrument of variation, she transfers the shares within two years of A's death to her mother (the testator's surviving spouse). The shares are then worth £110,000.

---

[62] If the picture had increased in value since the mother's death by no more than Andrew's CGT annual exemption then Andrew should not opt to read back since the gain is then exempt and Robert will acquire the assets at its market value at the date of the variation: see Example 39.16.
[63] See 39.04.

For IHT reading back will be desirable as the result will be to reduce the testator's chargeable estate at death by £100,000 since the shares are now an exempt transfer to a surviving spouse.

For CGT if the daughter makes a chargeable disposal, her gain will be £110,000 – £100,000 = £10,000 which will be covered by her annual CGT exemption. Her mother will then acquire the shares at the higher base cost of £110,000. Hence, she should not make the reading back statement for CGT purposes.

(2) A will leaves quoted shares worth £100,000 to the testator's surviving widow. After they have risen in value to £140,000 she decides (within the permitted time limit) to vary the will in favour of her daughter.

For IHT it is debatable whether the disposition should be read back. If it is, £100,000 will constitute a chargeable death transfer so that, if the deceased's nil rate band has already been exhausted, tax will be charged at 40 per cent. If it is not, the widow will make a lifetime gift (a PET) of £140,000 that, if she survives by seven years, will be free of tax. On the other hand, if it is likely that she will only survive her husband by a few weeks, then it will be necessary to consider whether it is better for £100,000 to be taxed as part of her dead husband's estate or for £140,000 to be taxed on her death.

For CGT the disposal should be read back into the will since otherwise there will be a chargeable gain of £140,000 – £100,000 = £40,000.

Generally, reading back is desirable for capital gains tax purposes when the administration of the estate is not completed in order to avoid any "*chose in action*" problems.[64]

Who is the settlor?

Marshall v Kerr[65] considered the question of who was the settlor for CGT **39.37** purposes when a deed of variation with election for reading back was made. The testator had died in 1977 domiciled in Jersey and Mrs Kerr (UK resident and domiciled) became entitled to one-half of the residuary estate. By a variation executed in January 1978 and made before the administration of the estate had been completed, her half share was to be retained by the PRs (a Jersey resident company) as trustees for, inter alia, Mrs Kerr. In due course gains were realised by those trustees and capital advanced to Mrs Kerr. If Mrs Kerr was the settlor capital payments made to her would attract a CGT charge.[66] Given that she had transferred property to trustees, on general principles she would be treated as the settlor of that trust: but was this conclusion displaced by the deeming provisions in s.62(6) whereby if a variation is made within two years of death—provided that the appropriate statement is included—it takes effect "*as if the variation had been effected by the deceased*"?

---

[64] See CGTM 31900 and following for a somewhat puzzling interpretation of the position.
[65] [1994] STC 638 HL. The case did not affect the IHT treatment of instruments of variation and disclaimer: see RI 101 (February 1995).
[66] See TCGA 1992 s.87 which is discussed in Ch.19.

39.38   HMRC succeeded in the House of Lords by taking a point not argued in the lower courts. While accepting that s.87 took effect subject to the various deeming provisions contained in s.62, the argument was that nothing in the latter section prevented Mrs Kerr from being treated as a settlor. Lord Browne-Wilkinson analysed matters as follows:

(1)   Two assumptions were made in the lower courts, neither of which was correct: first, that the variation constituted a settlement of assets comprised in the testator's estate and, secondly, that those were assets of which the testator was competent to dispose and so were acquired by the PRs under TCGA 1992 s.62(1).

(2)   When the variation was made the estate was unadministered and hence Mrs Kerr did not dispose of specific assets but of a *chose in action*: namely her right to have the estate properly administered. Although an asset for CGT purposes, this was not an asset owned by the deceased, and so was not an asset of which the deceased had been competent to dispose.

(3)   The disposal of the *chose* was not itself subject to charge because of TCGA 1992 s.62(6)(a).

(4)   Under s.62(6)(b) the interest of the "new" beneficiary is deemed to arise under the will of the deceased with the result that:

"an asset of which the deceased was competent to dispose at the death which is not sold in the course of the administration but is vested in the varied beneficiary is deemed to have been acquired by the varied beneficiary as legatee under the Will."

The "new" beneficiary is therefore only deemed to acquire qua legatee if two conditions are satisfied. First, the asset must be one of which the deceased was competent to dispose and, secondly, that asset must be vested in the varied beneficiary as legatee. The process of administering the estate cannot be ignored: assets acquired by the PRs during administration are treated as if that acquisition were by the legatee who is not treated as acquiring those assets at death.

(5)   Given that Mrs Kerr settled a *chose in action*, it followed that the trustees could not trace their ownership of the settled property to the PRs and thence back to the date of death. There was therefore nothing to displace the general proposition that Mrs Kerr was the settlor of the property. It would appear from the judgment of Lord Browne-Wilkinson that a similar conclusion would be arrived at even if the estate had been fully administered.[67]

Statutory provisions

39.39   The position was put on a statutory footing by FA 2006 Sch.12 which introduced provisions identifying the settlor for CGT purposes where there is a

---

[67] And see CGTM 37888 but note the criticism of the case in *Taxation*, May 3, 2002, p.105.

variation of a will or intestacy which sets up new trusts.[68] These provide that if property becomes settled property as a result of the variation, the person making the variation is the settlor. However, if property was already settled under the will or intestacy and then becomes comprised in another trust as a result of the variation, the deceased person, and not the person making the variation, is treated as the settlor for CGT purposes. This is presumably because if several persons act to vary their entitlements under a will trust and re-settle the assets in a new trust, it would be difficult to establish who is the settlor.

39.40

The position is unclear where a variation merely amends or varies a will trust rather than transferring the property to a new settlement or where the person making the variation (e.g. the life tenant) simply varies their own interest under the settlement. Does the settled property then become comprised in a new trust? Is the life tenant the settlor of the new trust? It is thought not. Suppose the life tenant assigns her interest to a discretionary trust under which income is rolled up. If the trustees then make gains, it was thought that before April 6, 2008 she was not taxed on those gains even though she was a beneficiary under the trust.[69]

EXAMPLE 39.17

(1) Frederick died leaving his foreign property absolutely to his son. Frederick was not UK domiciled. His son was. His son therefore executed a deed of variation under which the property he inherited was settled on trust for himself and his children. For inheritance tax purposes with reading back, Frederick is treated as a settlor of an excluded property settlement. For CGT purposes, however, the son is treated as the settlor.

(2) Sydney died leaving his property on life interest trusts for his spouse and then to his children outright. Spouse and children execute a deed of variation setting up a new trust for grandchildren. The settlor is Sydney.

(3) Barry, domiciled in Portugal, leaves his Portuguese villa and moneys in his Swiss bank account to his son Chris who is UK resident and domiciled. By a variation of the terms of his will made within two years of Barry's death, the property is settled on discretionary trusts with Jersey resident trustees for the benefit of Chris, his spouse and his issue, who include two minor children.

For IHT purposes, reading back ensures that the settlement is of excluded property. Hence the trust is not subject to IHT and there is no 10-year anniversary or exit charge provided that no UK situs assets are part of the trust property on these occasions.

For CGT purposes, the settlement has been created by Chris, a UK resident domiciliary, so that the charging provisions in TCGA 1992 s.86 ff will apply given that he can benefit from the trust.

---

[68] TCGA 1992 s.68C inserted by FA 2006: see Ch.9.
[69] The charge on the settlor under TCGA 1992 s.77 was abolished from April 6, 2008.

For income tax purposes, the trust is settlor-interested and whether it is onshore or offshore, Chris pays tax under ITTOIA 2005 s.624 on all trust income.[70]

III VARIATIONS: INCOME TAX

39.41 The income tax legislation contains no provisions similar to those in IHT and CGT. Accordingly the original beneficiary under the will or intestacy used to be taxed in respect of any relevant income arising between the date of death and the date of execution of any deed of variation affecting the property. However, from April 6, 1995 residuary beneficiaries are taxed on a receipts basis and so if, before the deed of variation, income has not been distributed to the original beneficiary, that income will be assessed on the new beneficiary when it is paid to him.

39.42 Provisions in TA 1988 s.685D (now ITA 2007 s.467) identify the settlor for income tax purposes when a deed of variation is made and which are the same for CGT.[71] Thus, when the variation creates a settlement that would not otherwise have existed, the person making the variation (not the deceased) is treated as the settlor. Where a variation alters an existing will trust set up under the will by setting up a new one, the deceased is treated as the settlor.

39.43 Since there are no provisions for reading back in the income tax legislation, if a beneficiary varies his share of the estate on trusts in favour of his minor unmarried children he will be regarded as the settlor. He is not taxed on the income if he and spouse are excluded from benefit but if income is paid out to the children while minor then it is taxed as his income.[72]

IV VARIATIONS: IMPACT OF THE POA CHARGE

39.44 A disposition is disregarded for the purposes of the POA charge if, by virtue of IHTA 1984 s.17, it is not treated as a transfer of value by the chargeable person.[73] That section provides that a variation to which s.142 applies is not a transfer of value, and hence the person making the deed of variation will not be caught by the pre-owned asset charge. So in Example 39.2 Joyce can continue to benefit from the assets without a pre-owned assets income tax problem.[74]

In cases where the residue of a deceased's estate is left to the surviving spouse absolutely, she might effect a variation to create flexible life interest trusts for herself.[75] In that event, whilst the variation would fall within s.142(1)—since it

---

[70] See Ch.7 and 39.42 below.
[71] See 39.40.
[72] ITTOIA 2005 s.629. See Ch.7 for further discussion of the capital gains tax and income tax implications where an intestacy is varied by all the beneficiaries.
[73] In FA 2004 Sch.15 para.16 ("*change in distribution of deceased's estate*").
[74] IHTA 1984 s.17 performs something of a "*belt and braces*" function in that it says that Joyce does not make a transfer whilst s.142 deems the disposition to have been made by the deceased. Had s.142 stood alone, it might have been argued that Joyce had still made a transfer of value.
[75] The advantages of such trusts are considered at 38.54 and 43.85.

involves a redirection of property—it would not involve any transfer of value by the surviving spouse (whose estate would not be diminished). Hence, s.17 would be irrelevant. It has, however, been confirmed by HMRC (despite the somewhat unfortunate wording in para.16) that such a variation is not caught by the POA charge.[76]

V VARIATIONS: STAMP DUTY AND SDLT

Before the introduction of SDLT on December 1, 2003 an instrument of variation attracted £5 fixed duty unless certified under the Stamp Duty (Exempt Instruments) Regulations 1987. Most post-death variations were certified under category L as being a disposition for which no consideration was given. However, certification under category M was required where there was consideration: for instance Beneficiary A gave the London flat left to him in the will to B in consideration of Beneficiary B giving the house in the country left to him in the will to A.   **39.45**

The current position is as follows: **39.46**

1. There is no SDLT on the variation of a disposition of land[77];

2. Stamp duty is limited to instruments affecting the transfer of shares or securities. HMRC accept that instruments of variation are not subject to Stamp Duty and do not need to include any certification.[78]

VI DISCLAIMERS

A beneficiary's right to disclaim property given to him derives from the general law. HMRC adopt the following principles: **39.47**

(1) the beneficiary must not have accepted any benefit from the property he purports to disclaim;

(2) the disclaimer must not be conditional;

(3) the only disclaimer that can be made by joint tenants is a disclaimer made by them all[79];

(4) the disclaimer must be of the whole of the benefit from the gift, e.g. a legatee cannot disclaim part of a legacy. However, authority to the contrary may be found in *Guthrie v Walrond*,[80] where Fry J. took the view that it depended on the testator's intention, and *Dewar v IRC*,[81] where Maugham L.J. said:

---

[76] See A2.76.
[77] FA 2003 Sch.3 para.4.
[78] See *IHT Newsletter*, April 2004.
[79] Re *Schär, Midland Bank Executor & Trustee Co Ltd v Damer* [1951] Ch 280.
[80] (1883) 22 Ch D 573.
[81] [1935] 2 KB 351.

> *"I conceive that there is no doubt that in the case of pecuniary legacies the legatee is entitled to disclaim part of the legacy if he likes".*

HMRC therefore accept that a partial disclaimer of residue is possible under Scots law[82] or where specifically permitted in the will.[83] They also accept that if a beneficiary is given two separate gifts by will, for instance, a pecuniary legacy and a share of residue, he may accept one and disclaim the other. Generally a disclaimer should be made by deed since it is not being made for consideration.

39.48 Unlike a variation, a reading back statement is not necessary in the case of a disclaimer: if property is disclaimed it will pass automatically to the person next entitled under the will or on intestacy. For instance, if a specific legatee disclaims the property will form part of the residue and pass to the beneficiary who is entitled to that residue. If the residuary beneficiary disclaims then (depending on the terms of the will) the property may pass on intestacy.

39.49 Whereas multiple variations of the same property falling within s.142(1) are not possible,[84] the same restriction does not apply to disclaimers (so A may disclaim a pecuniary legacy which falls into residue and B may disclaim that residue). It is also considered that a disclaimer can be combined with a variation: in the above illustration A having disclaimed the pecuniary legacy, B may then redirect that out of the residue (for instance to C) by an instrument of variation.

39.50 A disclaimer may be a way round HMRC's view that deeds of variation are not possible in the case of a life interest once the life tenant has died.

EXAMPLE 39.18

> Mr Smith dies in 2007 leaving his wife a life interest (an IPDI) with remainder to children alive on his death. His wife dies six months after him. Can a disclaimer of her life interest be effected? If she has not accepted the interest (e.g. received income or any other benefit from it) the answer is thought to be yes. Is there a problem if the IPDI trust owned a share in a house in which wife lived when she owned the other share? Would HMRC consider that wife had accepted the life interest because she had continued to live in the house? It is not thought that such an argument would necessarily succeed. Arguably she was living in the house by virtue of her half share and neither the trustees nor she did anything which constituted an acceptance of the deceased's half share.[85]

HMRC accept that disclaimers of a life interest after death are, in principle, possible:

---

[82] SP E18. Partial disclaimers are also permitted by many states in the USA (e.g. California and New York).

[83] Partial disclaimer was the subject of correspondence in *Capital Taxes News & Reports*, July 1989, pp.246–248.

[84] See 39.22.

[85] The position would be different if she had agreed with the trustees the terms for her continued occupation of the property.

"if the situation had been that it was possible for the life tenant's executors to disclaim his life interest as a matter of general law, then that should fall within the protection of section 142."[86]

HMRC consider that in order to disclaim the life interest of a deceased life **39.51** tenant under general law there must be some property to give up: i.e. some undistributed income. However, is this correct? Whilst a variation is a disposition or gift of property made by the beneficiary, a disclaimer is a refusal to accept something, which is altogether different. It is arguable that executors can refuse to accept something on behalf of the deceased life tenant (accrued or undistributed income or the right to receive the same or even an interest of no value which would however increase the IHT burden on the deceased's free estate) even if they cannot give away something that has ceased to exist.

In the IHT Manual it is stated disclaimers of a life interest are allowed where owing to ill health, ignorance or lack of time the deceased was never in a position to accept or disclaim.

Disclaiming under IHTA 1984 s.93

Section 93 deals with the situation where a person becomes entitled to an inter- **39.52** est in settled property but disclaims that interest. It provides that *"the Act shall apply as if he had not become entitled to the interest"*. Note:

(i) the disclaimer must not be for a consideration in money or money's worth (and there is no saving for another interest under the settlement);

(ii) although no time limit is specified, the requirement that the interest must not have been accepted and no benefit been obtained from it imposes its own time restriction.

Because s.142 does not apply to settled property in which the deceased had **39.53** enjoyed a life interest, s.93 may sometimes assist in enabling the beneficiary who then becomes entitled to disclaim that entitlement.[87] Note, however, that HMRC do not accept a disclaimer of settled property can be made under s.93 where the deceased life tenant also had a general power of appointment which he exercised.[88] They consider that it is then part of the death estate and s.142 must be used not s.93.[89]

So if, for example, X is the life tenant of a settlement set up by his father and he exercises a testamentary general power of appointment to appoint on

---

[86] See IHTM 35042: note, however, *Re Smith* [2001] 3 All ER 552.
[87] See Example 39.19 and IHTM 35164.
[88] See IHTM 35165 and IHTM 35072.
[89] See IHTM 35072:

> *"Settled property (IHTM16000) in which the deceased had an interest in possession (IIP) (IHTM16061) is excluded from the death estate for the purposes of Section 142(1) IHTA 1984 by Section 142(5) IHTA 1984. However we do not apply that exclusion to settled property*
> * *in which the deceased had a beneficial IIP, if*
> * *the deceased had and exercised by Will a general power of appointment over it.*

trust for his daughter J, HMRC state that when such a power is exercised the property is treated as settled by him under his will and becomes part of his death free estate. In practice this will only matter if more than two years have elapsed since the deceased life tenant's death.[90] The position is different in relation to special powers of appointment.

EXAMPLE 39.19

The terms of a settlement set up in 2001 provided:

(1) that the property was held on trust for X for life (a qualifying interest in possession). X also had a power, exercisable by will, to appoint his wife a successive life interest;
(2) subject to the above, for X's children contingent on them attaining the age of 25 but subject to an overriding power of appointment for a class of discretionary beneficiaries including X's children, his siblings and their issue and with a power for the trustees to add (e.g. X's surviving spouse) to the class of beneficiaries.

X died in 2011 without exercising his power to appoint his widow a successive life interest. His two children are in their 30s.

Tax treatment

(i) The trust fund is taxed as part of X's estate on death with no spouse exemption.

(ii) The continuing trusts for the children fall into the relevant property regime.

Proposed reorganisation

It is desired to take advantage of the spouse exemption on X's death.

> *Where both these conditions are satisfied, you should treat the settled property as part of the death estate for the purposes of Section 142(1) IHTA 1984.*
> *The taxpayers may seek to extend this treatment, to cases where the deceased*
>
> - *had exercised the general power of appointment by deed*
> - *had a general power but had not exercised it, or*
> - *had a general power but not a beneficial IIP in the trust property.*
>
> *Where this occurs, you should ask them to demonstrate the grounds on which they consider the particular situation falls within the scope of the legislation. Then, if they press, or if they appear to have a persuasive argument, you should refer the case to TG."*

[90] See IHTM 35165 *"if the deceased had an interest in possession and they had and had exercised by will a general power of appointment over the property we regard that property as part of the deceased's estate at death and any disclaimer must meet the conditions of s142 rather than s93."*

(i) It is not possible to use s.142(1) to vary the provisions of the settlement (a simple rearrangement whereby the children vary their entitlement in favour of their mother is not read back).

(ii) Accordingly consider the following:

    (a) the trustees add Mrs X to the class of beneficiaries and make an appointment in her favour (either absolutely or, more likely, on a life interest trust);

    (b) the children disclaim their interests in the settlement (and any income produced since X's death) under IHTA 1984 s.93. As a result it is as if they had not become entitled to the interest.

The result is that on X's death the default trusts in favour of his wife takes effect with the benefit of the spouse exemption.

39.54 What if at the time of X's death the children were minor so that the court needs to approve a disclaimer on their behalf? It may be said to be for the ultimate benefit of the children that IHT is saved (by obtaining the spouse exemption) especially if the appointment in favour of the spouse is only for a limited period (e.g. it gives her the income for (say) six months) therefore approval should be forthcoming. The arrangement put to the court for approval should expressly provide for acceleration of income on the termination of the children's interests so that events subsequent to that date of death (the spousal appointment) can be taken into account for the purposes of identifying the person who takes the undisposed income on disclaimer.[91]

VII SECTION 144: DISCRETIONARY WILL TRUSTS

39.55 Section 144(1) deals with:

- property comprised in a person's estate immediately before his death which is settled by his will (this includes the case where property is given by will to a lifetime discretionary trust that had been set up by the deceased)[92]; and

- within two years of the testator's death, and

- before any interest in possession has subsisted in the property[93]; and

- an event occurs which would normally lead to an IHT charge (e.g. property is appointed onto new trusts outside the relevant property regime or to a beneficiary outright).[94]

---

[91] *Lewin on Trusts* (18th edn), para.8–37. The doctrine of acceleration does not generally apply to interests under appointments unless an intention to do so is present: *Lewin* para.8–32 and *Craven v Brady* (1867) LR 4 Eq 209. To this end the disclaimers should include a suitable declaration of intention to accelerate the income.

[92] A s.144 trust can, however, be established by an instrument of variation.

[93] The meaning of "interest in possession" has changed for these purposes as a result of the FA 2006 alterations to the IHT treatment of settlements: see IHTA 1984 s.144(1A).

[94] This condition had to be modified to deal (especially) with IPDIs. It resulted in the "*Frankland Trap*": see 39.59.

In these circumstances, provided that the further conditions set out below are met, there is no charge on the ending of the discretionary trust and for IHT purposes it is as if the will had provided that the property was to be held as it is, in fact, held after the event.

39.56   Assuming that the above conditions are met, if the trustees distribute property within the prescribed period to the testator's surviving spouse, that property benefits from the spouse exemption, being treated as having been left by the testator to his spouse. The relevant property trust is, in effect, ignored. Similarly, if the trustees distribute the property to a charity within two years of death, the charitable exemption applies.

The 2006 changes

39.57   The section was amended three times in the course of the 2006 Finance Bill's progress through Parliament in order to accommodate the new regime for the IHT treatment of settlements. The result is a drafting mess and a trap for the unwary. As amended s.144 now reads as follows:

> "*144 Distribution etc from property settled by will*
>
> *(1) Subsection (2) below applies where property comprised in a person's estate immediately before his death is settled by his will and, within the period of two years after his death and before any interest in possession has subsisted in the property, there occurs:*
>
> > *(a)   an event on which tax would (apart from subsection (2) below) be chargeable under any provision, other than section 64 or 79, of Chapter III of Part III of this Act, or*
> > *(b)   an event on which tax would be so chargeable[95] but for section 75 or 76 above or paragraph 16(1) of Schedule 4 to this Act.*
>
> *(1A) Where the testator dies on or after 22nd March 2006, subsection (1) above shall have effect as if the reference to any interest in possession were a reference to any interest in possession that is*
>
> > *(a)   an immediate post-death interest, or*
> > *(b)   a disabled person's interest.*
>
> *(2) Where this subsection applies by virtue of an event within paragraph (a) of subsection (1) above, tax shall not be charged under the provision in question on that event; and in every case in which this subsection applies in relation to an event, this Act shall have effect as if the will had provided that on the testator's death the property should be held as it is held after the event.*
>
> *(3) Subsection (4) below applies where—*
>
> > *(a)   a person dies on or after 22nd March 2006,*

---

[95] See the *Frankland* case considered at 39.59.

(b) property comprised in the person's estate immediately before his death is settled by his will, and

(c) within the period of two years after his death, but before an immediate post-death interest or a disabled person's interest has subsisted in the property, there occurs an event that involves causing the property to be held on trusts that would, if they had in fact been established by the testator's will, have resulted in—

(i) an immediate post-death interest subsisting in the property, or

(ii) section 71A or 71D above applying to the property.

(4) Where this subsection applies by virtue of an event—

(a) this Act shall have effect as if the will had provided that on the testator's death the property should be held as it is held after the event, but

(b) tax shall not be charged on that event under any provision of Chapter 3 of Part 3 of this Act.

(5) Subsection (4) above also applies where—

(a) a person dies before 22nd March 2006,

(b) property comprised in the person's estate immediately before his death is settled by his will,
an event occurs—

(i) on or after 22nd March 2006, and

(ii) within the period of two years after the testator's death, that involves causing the property to be held on trusts within subsection (6) below,

(d) no immediate post-death interest, and no disabled person's interest, subsisted in the property at any time in the period beginning with the testator's death and ending immediately before the event, and

(e) no other interest in possession subsisted in the property at any time in the period beginning with the testator's death and ending immediately before 22nd March 2006.

(6) Trusts are within this subsection if they would, had they in fact been established by the testator's will and had the testator died at the time of the event mentioned in subsection (5)(c) above, have resulted in—

(a) an immediate post-death interest subsisting in the property, or

(b) section 71A or 71D above applying to the property."

The provisions deal with three different scenarios:

Settlement ending

39.58   Section 144(1) and (2) deals with the straightforward case of testator leaving assets on discretionary trusts and outright appointments being made to spouse or other beneficiaries (or the settlement automatically ending, for instance after 23 months).

EXAMPLE 39.20

> Ron dies in 2007 and leaves all his property on discretionary trusts for his spouse, children and remoter issue. The Executors pay inheritance tax on the entire estate. A year after his death, the trustees appoint the house to his widow outright. That is read-back to Ron's death, i.e. it is treated as a gift by Ron to his spouse which is spouse exempt. There is no charge on the ending of the trust and a tax repayment of IHT can be claimed.

39.59   Beware the trap in *Frankland v IRC*[96] and avoid making any appointments within three months of death if reading-back is desired. In that case the trustees of a discretionary will trust appointed an interest in possession to the deceased's spouse within three months of the death. They expected to obtain relief under s.144(1)(a) and s.18; but because of s.65(4) there was no exit charge on the termination of a trust within three months of its creation and so no event which would bring s.144 into play (this is because "reading back" is only available if there occurs an event "*on which taxed would be chargeable*" and there was no such event).[97] Disastrously, the spouse exemption was not available! An appointment onto disabled trusts where reading-back is desired must similarly be delayed for three months after the death.

Appointments on continuing IPDI or s.71A or s.71D trusts

39.60   Section 144(3) and (4) deals with the position where the testator dies on or after March 22, 2006 and the trustees appoint the property on continuing interest in possession trusts for the deceased's spouse or other beneficiaries (an IPDI trust) or on bereaved minor or s.71D trusts. It was necessary to amend s.144 by adding the new sections because giving a beneficiary an interest in possession is (since the 2006 changes) not "*an event on which tax would (apart from s.144) be chargeable*"[98] so there would have been no reading back and so the relevant property regime would continue and there would be no IPDI.[99]

---

[96] [1997] STC 1450, CA. Note that the actual decision was reversed by the 2006 changes since an interest in possession created within three months of death is read back as an IPDI. What must now be avoided is an absolute appointment or appointment on to disabled trusts within three months.

[97] See IHTA 1984 s.68(2).

[98] Because it is ignored for IHT purposes.

[99] This is because an IPDI must take effect on the death (see IHTA 1984 s.49A(3)) so that reading

It might have been easier to take out the words "*an event on which tax would*   **39.61**
be chargeable" in s.144(1)(b) but, initially, to get out of this Catch 22 situation
the Government amended s.144 to allow reading back on appointments out
of discretionary trusts to an IPDI s.71A or s.71D trust but only if the death
occurred after March 21, 2006.

EXAMPLE 39.21

> Donald dies in 2007 leaving his estate on discretionary trusts. The
> trustees appoint his wife Elizabeth a life interest within two years of
> Donald's death. This is an IPDI and reading back operates so that
> spouse exemption is obtained even if the appointment is made within
> three months of death.[100]

Deaths pre-March 22, 2006

The above change did not cover the taxpayer who died before March 22, 2006   **39.62**
leaving property on two-year discretionary trusts when the trustees had not
exercised their powers of appointment on March 22, 2006. In such a case they
could not bring themselves within s.144 unless the appointment was outright
or on disabled trusts. Appointing on continuing trusts had no effect for IHT
purposes and the relevant property regime would continue.

This omission was corrected by insertion of s.144(5) and (6). The result is   **39.63**
that if in Example 39.22 Donald had died in January 2006 (i.e. before March
22, 2006) and the trustees only exercised their powers of appointment to
appoint on continuing trusts on July 1, 2006, there is reading back if those
trusts are IPDI or s.71A or s.71D.

Drafting and using s.144

Section 144 enables the executors to maximise the reliefs (including business   **39.64**
property relief and agricultural property relief) available on the testator's
death taking into account the position at that time. It is desirable for the
testator to leave a non-binding letter of wishes to act as guidance for the trustees in these circumstances. There is no need to draft the will so that the trust
ends automatically within two years of death unless the testator particularly
wants to ensure that certain default trusts come into effect. The discretionary
trust can continue for the full perpetuity period if thought desirable although
s.144 will not apply to appointments made after the two-year period has

---

back is imperative. The position of s.71A and s.71D trusts is different since they merely have
to be "established under the will": hence all that reading back does is to avoid the exit charge
when the relevant property settlement ends.
[100] Contrast outright appointments within three months or appointments on disabled trusts: see
39.59.

elapsed. Any 10-year charge and any exit charge arising more than two years after death will be calculated from the date of death in the usual way.

When can powers of appointment be exercised?

39.65 At one time HMRC took the view that the trustees of a discretionary trust created by a will could not exercise their powers until assets had been vested in them by the executors. This meant either at completion of the administration of the estate or by an express assent of the property. This might lead to unnecessary cash flow problems where there was a surviving spouse since probate had to be obtained and IHT paid before any appointment could be made in favour of a spouse.

It is now accepted by HMRC[101] that there is no requirement that residue must be ascertained and assented to will trustees before the powers granted by a will can be exercised. In each case the time at which a valid exercise of those powers may be made is a question of construction of the particular will concerned. If the will defines "my trustees" as the executors and trustees of the will for the time being and the Trust Period begins from the date of death with "my trustees" having the power of appointment, HMRC accept that the trust is validly constituted at the date of the testator's death and that the executors in their capacity of trustees can exercise their powers during the administration.

Appointing to existing trusts

39.66 Can s.144 be used to appoint to existing trusts? Consider the following.

EXAMPLE 39.22

(1) A dies in 2011 leaving his estate on discretionary trusts. In 2005 he had set up the inter vivos Binns Life Interest Trust for his wife with £10. The trustees of the will trust appoint the estate within two years of death onto the Binns Life Interest Trust. Is this an IPDI? The settlement of the property is effected by the will and, although the trust itself was not set up by will, an IPDI trust has been established.[102]

(2) B had created six pilot discretionary settlements all on different days before his death. The will adds assets to those trusts. In this situation:

---

[101] See *Capital Taxes News*, July 1998 p.98. It is common to give the trustees power to make an appointment even though the administration of the estate is not complete and assets have not been assented to them. See also *Fitzwilliam v IRC* [1993] 3 All ER 184.

[102] HMRC agree: see A2.279. In this case the Binns Life Interest trust is a "pilot" settlement. It might, however, have been set up with substantial assets and then added to by the will trustees. This would raise the question of whether additions of property to a pre-March 22, 2006 interest in possession trust are to be taxed as new settlements. For IPDIs generally see Ch.28.

(a) each trust may benefit from a full nil rate band[103];

(b) but the trustees of the recipient trusts have two years flexibility under s.144 to make amendments to their trusts which, in respect of the property added, are read back into A's will. Note that if an absolute appointment out of the pilot trusts is made within three months of the 10-year anniversary of the commencement date of the pilot trust there is no reading back because of the *Frankland* trap.

(3) Dmitri established four pilot trusts during his lifetime. In his will he made a nil rate band gift (which caught both his nil rate band and the unused nil rate band of his pre-deceasing wife Ludmilla)[104] to trustees to hold on discretionary trusts with a power given to the trustees to transfer the trust fund to any other settlement that Dmitri had established. The residue of the estate was left to charity. After his death the trustees divided the trust fund into four (£650,000/4 = £162,500) paying one such quarter share to the trustees of each of the four lifetime settlements. The IHT position is as follows:

(a) on Dmitri's death no IHT is payable because of the availability of two nil rate bands and the charity exemption;

(b) by dividing the trust fund into four and paying it into the pilot trusts it was expected that each of those settlements would benefit from a full nil rate band and that the sum settled (being half the nil rate band) would allow for growth in the value of the trust fund without any prospect of a tax charge in the future (the property in each trust would need to double in value before the IHT threshold was reached). However IHTA 1984 s.81[105] provides that for the purpose of the IHT relevant property charging regime all the property remains comprised in the transferor (i.e. in the will) trust.[106] And this trust will benefit from only a single nil rate band.[107] Accordingly no use has been made of the lifetime pilot trusts. In a case such as this, Dmitri's will should have left the property directly to the lifetime trusts: there should have been no will trust acting as a distributor.

CGT problems

There is a potential capital gains tax danger in s.144 trusts. If an absolute appointment is made out of the trust within two years from the date of death, it is automatically read back under s.144 for IHT purposes and so there is no capital gains tax hold-over relief available under TCGA 1992 s.260 (because the appointment does not generate a chargeable transfer). There is no CGT **39.67**

---

[103] See the *Rysaffe* case and Ch.41.
[104] For the drafting of nil rate band gifts, see Ch.38.
[105] For s.81 see 24.12.
[106] Note that s.144 is irrelevant: it only applies if within two years of death property ceases to be comprised in a discretionary trust (e.g. by outright appointment or appointment onto life interest trusts). In this case the property remains in a discretionary trust (the pilot settlements).
[107] The transferred nil rate band only reduced tax on the death of the surviving spouse: it cannot reduce future settlement charges.

equivalent to s.144. In practice, however, if the estate is not fully administered at the date of the appointment, HMRC accept that the beneficiaries take qua legatees at probate value. Indeed, this is the case whether or not the trustees hold on discretionary trusts.[108] So, for example, where the deceased left property on IPDI trusts for his spouse and the trustees then end her interest and appoint the property outright to the children, provided that the executors have not assented the property to the trustees and the administration of the estate is still continuing, the children take as legatees and there is no chargeable gain even if the assets have increased in value since death. Whether or not more than two years has elapsed since death is irrelevant for this purpose.

Using s.144 to deal with trusts for children

39.68 If a will creates a trust for grandchildren who take income at 25 and capital at 30 and the trustees wish to prevent it being treated as a relevant property trust, they can appoint (provided that they have suitable powers) in such a way that the trust is now IPDI for each grandchild or a s.71A or s.71D trust. Reading back is obtained provided the normal two-year requirement is met.

The unexpected operation of s.144

39.69 An event can happen, within two years of death, which triggers the operation of s.144 and which may have been unforeseen.

EXAMPLE 39.23

> In his will, Unlucky left his residuary estate to his son, Soo, contingent on his attaining the age of 25. The will draftsman had intended to create an 18–25 trust[109] for Soo but because he was 17 at the time of Unlucky's death, TA 1925 s.31 applied when Soo became 18 to vest income in him.[110] An interest in possession therefore came into existence within two years of Unlucky's death and is read back as an IPDI for Soo. The IHT and CGT consequences are therefore quite different from what had been intended when the will was made.[111]

---

[108] *Cochrane's Executors v IRC* [1974] STC 335; *IRC v Matthew's Executors* [1984] STC 386; CGTM para.31432.

[109] See generally Ch.35.

[110] For the vesting effect of s.31, see Ch.1.

[111] These are explored in detail in Ch.35 but note in particular that at 25 CGT hold-over relief will not be available on the ending of the trust (unless it comprises business assets) while if Soo were to die before 25 the value of the settled property will be taxed as part of his death.

The two-year trap and nil rate band discretionary will trusts

It has been suggested that a deceased spouse's share in the matrimonial home **39.70** should be settled on nil rate band discretionary trusts and that the surviving spouse could be appointed an interest in possession which will not make the house part of her estate because it is not qualifying IPDI. However because of s.144 such an appointment will take effect as an IPDI for the spouse (even if made within three months of death) and the whole property will therefore be taxed on her death. Accordingly, wait for two years before making that appointment.

Impact of the introduction of the transferable nil rate band[112]

Some families will wish to take advantage of the introduction of a transferable **39.71** nil rate band in cases where on the death of the first spouse a nil rate band discretionary trust (frequently holding a debt or charge)[113] has been provided for in the will.[114] In general, provided that two years have not elapsed from the date of death, it will be possible to end the trust by an appointment in favour of the surviving spouse (either absolutely or an IPDI trust) with reading-back under s.144. This will ensure that the spouse exemption applies and the deceased's nil rate band is therefore unused and hence can be claimed by the survivor's PRs after her death.

In unscrambling the now unwanted discretionary trust, it is important to **39.72** observe the appropriate formalities: for instance:

(i) ensure that the decision is taken by all the trustees. It is not unusual to find that some of the persons chosen in the will to be "executors and trustees" of the estate fail to take out a grant of probate, particularly where all the partners of a firm are appointed. The fact that they do not become executors does not affect their position as a trustee. Persons wishing to decline both offices should make a formal disclaimer to that effect;

(ii) end the trust by either a deed or written resolution which can be produced to HMRC when, on the death of the surviving spouse, a transferred nil rate band is being claimed by his personal representatives. Bear in mind that the will shows that the nil rate band was used: accordingly evidence to the contrary (showing a s.144 appointment/advancement with reading back) is essential. In practice, the trust will most commonly be ended by an outright appointment to the surviving spouse which will normally require the trustees to execute a deed. Exceptionally an advancement-type power may be used which does not prescribe any formalities. Nevertheless, for the reasons given above, there should at the very least be a written resolution exercising the power.

---

[112] See Ch.38.
[113] See Ch.38.
[114] Probably executed before the introduction of the transferable nil rate band.

39.73   Note also the following:

(1) it is not considered necessary to vest property in the trustees before the appointment: trustees have rights from the death of the deceased which means that the trust is fully constituted at that time and that the trustees can exercise their powers of appointment (see 39.00);

(2) if the trust has been established with the benefit of a debt (usually owed to the trustees by the surviving spouse) the effect of an appointment in her favour will be to extinguish that liability. In the case of a charge (usually over property which has passed to the spouse) the effect will be to cause a release of the property charged[115];

(3) it is possible to combine s.142 (variations) and s.144;

EXAMPLE 39.24

In June 2007 Dad left everything to Mum. Fearful of wasting his IHT nil rate band, in September 2007 she varied his will to create a nil rate band discretionary trust. In December 2008 (after the introduction of the transferable nil rate band) the trustees appoint the trust fund to Mum absolutely.

Note that all the events take place within two years of Dad's death. Mum's variation is read back under s.142(1) and uses up his nil rate band. However, the subsequent appointment to Mum is in turn read back under s.144 thereby resulting in a restoration of the spouse exemption and the availability of Dad's now unused nil rate band on the death of Mum.

(4) Once two years have elapsed from the death it is not possible to unscramble the arrangement. Any appointment after that time to the surviving spouse will take effect outside s.144 so that there is no reading back and even though the trust property becomes comprised in the survivor's estate the tax treatment of the deceased is unchanged and there is no restoration of his nil rate band.

How far does reading back in s.144 go?

39.74   Discretionary will trusts are frequently used in order to maximise business property relief and agricultural property relief.[116] In effect, the relevant assets are left on discretionary trust in order to force HMRC to give a view on the availability of relief. If relief is not given, then the assets can be appointed to the surviving spouse or civil partner with the benefit of spouse exemption.

---

[115] It is not thought that CGT problems will arise: see TCGA 1992 s.251(1). It is not thought that the typical charge arrangement involves a "debt on security": HMRC consider that "security" means loan stock or similar security, e.g. of any government or company.
[116] See Chs 44 and 45.

Concerns have sometimes been expressed that if the trustees have sold the **39.75** assets by the time they come to make an appointment to (say) the children no relief is available. This is not correct. Business property relief is given by reference to the status of the property at the time of the deceased's death and subsequent sales have no effect on that. Accordingly, relief cannot be secured retrospectively. If, for example, the deceased's interest in a company or partnership is left on discretionary trusts and contains significant excepted assets, there is no scope for the trustees to take out the excepted assets and appoint these to the spouse with the remaining business assets passing to the children with 100 per cent relief. What the deceased has left in his will is an interest in shares or an interest in the partnership not an interest in the underlying assets.[117] It is the shares or the partnership interest that have to be valued and the relief given accordingly. Accordingly, if X dies owning a partnership interest which comprises 10 per cent in value of the excepted assets and the partnership is dissolved after death with the trustees appointing 10 per cent of the net proceeds to the spouse and 90 per cent to the children, the relief is pro rated between spouse and children irrespective of whether all the excepted assets or cash from those excepted assets is appointed to the spouse.

---

[117] A partnership interest is not transparent for inheritance tax purposes even if the deceased's capital account is said to be satisfied by particular assets owned by the partnership.

CHAPTER 40

CAPITAL TAX ISSUES FOR PERSONAL REPRESENTATIVES

- General (**40.01**)
- Valuation of assets at death (**40.07**)
- CGT losses of the deceased (**40.12**)
- Sales by PRs (**40.13**)
- Losses of the PRs (**40.19**)
- Transfers to legatees (**40.20**)

Precedent

A1.23   Appropriation by PRs in favour of charity creating a bare trust

I GENERAL

Free estate

40.01   The assets of the deceased of which he was competent to dispose are deemed to be acquired by the personal representatives (PRs) at their market value at death. This results in an uplift in the value of the assets but no charge to CGT.[1] Hence, death generally wipes out capital gains. The deceased is not treated as being competent to dispose of assets over which he had a power of appointment[2] but is regarded as being competent to dispose of his share of jointly owned property (even if on his death the share passes by jus accrescendi).

EXAMPLE 40.1

Included in the deceased's estate on his death in November 2010 is a Stanley Spencer painting, "the Arisen", that the deceased had acquired in 1940 for £10,000. It is worth £250,000 at death. The gain of £240,000

[1] TCGA 1992 s.62(1). It involves an acquisition of assets without a corresponding disposal.
[2] TCGA 1992 s.62(1).

is not chargeable. Instead his PRs acquire the asset at a new base cost of £250,000.

PRs are deemed to have the residence, ordinary residence and domicile of the deceased at the date of his death, but the remittance basis—which may be available to a UK resident but non-domiciled individual in respect of a disposal of non-UK situs assets—does not apply to PRs.[3] PRs are also charged on the gains of non-resident companies apportioned under TCGA 1992 s.13.[4]   **40.02**

Like trustees, PRs are treated as a single and continuing body of persons, and liability can be imposed on any PR. HMRC will, therefore, assess UK PRs on the estate's worldwide gains even though those PRs may have no control over foreign assets which are vested in foreign PRs. Any one of them is assessable and chargeable on behalf of the body as a whole. Because PRs are deemed to take the deceased's residence status, UK resident PRs of a non-resident deceased are outside the charge to capital gains tax. However, this exemption only applies while they are acting in their capacity as PRs; once they become trustees, they are taxed as UK residents. The vesting of property by the PRs in non-resident trustees pursuant to the provisions of the will is not a capital gains tax disposal.[5]   **40.03**

Death of an interest in possession beneficiary

Held-over gains on entry into a trust are not wiped out on the death of the interest in possession beneficiary although gains on assets accruing over the trust's period of ownership, when the beneficiary has a "qualifying" interest in possession are generally wiped out on his death provided that the property does not revert to the settlor.[6]   **40.04**

EXAMPLE 40.2

T was the life tenant of a pre-March 22, 2006 interest in possession trust and a picture had been settled with the benefit of hold-over relief. The gain held-over was £20,000 and the base cost £10,000. On T's death, the picture is worth £100,000. The held-over gain of £20,000 is chargeable and only the balance of the gain (£70,000) is wiped out on T's death.[7] It is, however, possible to make a further hold-over claim to avoid paying tax on the £20,000 if T's death is a chargeable transfer for IHT purposes.[8]

---

[3] See TCGA 1992 ss.62(3) and 65(2).
[4] See Ch.54.
[5] See TCGA 1992 s.62(4).
[6] See TCGA 1992 ss.72 and 73.
[7] See TCGA 1992 s.74.
[8] See Example 12.5 for further details of this. It is accordingly desirable for the picture to form part of T's chargeable estate, i.e. not to pass under the terms of the trust to a surviving spouse

40.05 FA 2006 amended TCGA 1992 ss.72 and 73 so that if the interest in possession arises on or after March 22, 2006 there is no deemed disposal or base cost uplift to market value on the death of the interest in possession beneficiary unless:

(a) the interest was an immediate post-death interest (IPDI); or

(b) a transitional serial interest (TSI); or

(c) a disabled person's interest within IHTA 1984 s.89B(1)(c) or (d); or

(d) an 18–25 trust where the beneficiary had an interest in possession and died under 18; or

(e) a bereaved minor trust and the minor had an interest in possession.

EXAMPLE 40.3

(1) Jacob died in 2007 leaving the residue of his estate on interest in possession trusts for his wife June and child Jade jointly and thereafter for the survivor. Both take an IPDI. On the death of either, inheritance tax will be chargeable on the ending of the IPDI (on a 50 per cent share of the trust fund) and there is a capital gains tax base cost uplift on that part.

(2) Husband had an interest in possession in a pre-March 2006 trust. He died in 2009 and his wife took a successive interest in possession. This was a transitional serial interest[9] and, on both deaths, there is a base cost uplift for capital gains tax purposes (on the husband's death the spouse exemption applies for IHT: on the wife's death the trust fund is taxable).

(3) Father dies leaving his estate on a bereaved minor trust for Amy who is given an immediate entitlement to income. She dies at 17.[10] There is no inheritance tax charge[11] but a base cost uplift for capital gains tax purposes.[12]

(4) Suki dies leaving her estate on trust for her only child Mary at 25 and, subject thereto, to her nephew. Under the terms of the trust Mary becomes entitled to the income from the age of 16.[13] If Mary dies under 18, having already become entitled to income, there is a base cost

---

in a situation where the spouse exemption would apply. Contrast the position if hold-over relief is claimed on an outright gift when the death of the donee wipes out the held-over gain.

[9] Under IHTA 1984 s.49D: see 27.32.

[10] This is not an IPDI because a bereaved minor interest takes priority.

[11] IHTA 1984 s.71B(2)(b).

[12] TCGA 1992 s.72(1B).

[13] Note that, if she is entitled to the income immediately on the death of mother or becomes so entitled within two years of mother's death, this will be an IPDI and there will be inheritance tax payable on Mary's death. This is because the IPDI trust take priority over the s.71D trust. Further, if she becomes 18 within two years of Suki's death IHTA 1984 s.144 operates to read-back the interest as an IPDI. Therefore, if mother dies when Mary is 14 the interest taken by Mary is an IPDI: see further 35.13.

uplift for capital gains tax purposes under TCGA 1992 s.72(1A)(b) but there is no inheritance tax charge.[14]

If Mary dies after reaching 18 but before 25 there is no base cost uplift for capital gains tax purposes but there is an inheritance tax exit charge.[15]

(5) Alternatively if Suki left her estate on trust for Mary at 30, with Mary taking an entitlement to income at 18 then unless Mary becomes 18 within two years of mother's death (in which case the interest becomes an IPDI as a result of the operation of IHTA 1984 s.144), that interest is not "qualifying" for inheritance tax purposes and the trust falls into the relevant property regime. On Mary's death, if the trust continues there is no inheritance tax payable and no base cost uplift for capital gains tax purposes. If the trust ends on Mary's death there is an IHT exit charge and CGT hold-over relief is available under TCGA 1992 s.260.

If an individual gives business assets to a donee and they claim hold-over relief **40.06** under TCGA 1992 s.165 there is a claw back of relief if the donee becomes non-UK resident.[16] If the donee does not discharge the CGT liability the donor will be liable[17] with a right of reimbursement against the donee. However, it is believed that HMRC accept that no liability can attach to the PRs in respect of that liability if no assessment has been raised during the lifetime of the deceased donor.

II VALUATION OF ASSETS AT DEATH

The assets of the deceased are valued at their open market value at the **40.07** date of death.[18] There is no reduction in the CGT value when business or agricultural property relief reduces the value transferred for IHT purposes. Unlike inheritance tax where the deceased is deemed to make a transfer of value immediately before death,[19] for capital gains tax purposes the notional acquisition occurs at the moment after death. In *Larter v Skone James*[20] the taxpayer argued the contrary in order to sustain an argument that a Revenue assessment for capital gains tax due on death was out of time (at that time capital gains tax was payable on death) but was unsuccessful.

If the value of the asset which forms part of the deceased's estate has been **40.08** "ascertained" for the purposes of inheritance tax that value will constitute the CGT acquisition cost of the deceased's PRs.[21] When the IHT related property rules apply the resultant figure may be artificially high.[22] In cases where the deceased's estate does not attract IHT (e.g. because it is wholly left to a

---

[14] IHTA 1984 s.71E(2)(b).
[15] IHTA 1984 s.71F(2).
[16] TCGA 1992 s.168.
[17] TCGA 1992 s.168(7).
[18] TCGA 1992 s.62(1)(a).
[19] IHTA 1984 s.4.
[20] [1976] STC 220.
[21] TCGA 1992 s.274.
[22] See Ch.38 fn.5.

surviving spouse or a charity; or where the property qualifies for 100 per cent agricultural or business relief; or falls within his nil rate band) the value will not be ascertained and so the figure returned on the IHT account will not fix the CGT value.[23] If the value of the assets is not ascertained for inheritance tax purposes then the normal capital gains tax valuation rules apply.[24] Market value is defined as the price which any asset might reasonably be expected to fetch on a sale in the open market. There is no reduction because all the assets are placed on the market at the same time.

40.09   In the case of unquoted securities the level of information available to a prospective purchaser in the hypothetical market is deemed to be:

> *"all the information which a prudent prospective purchaser of an asset might reasonably require if he were proposing to purchase it from a willing vendor by private treaty and at arm's length".*[25]

40.10   Where property valued on death as "related property" is sold within three years after the death, or land is sold within four years of death, or listed securities within one year, for less than the death valuation, the PRs may substitute a lower figure for the death valuation and so obtain a reduction in the IHT paid on death.[26] Not surprisingly, this lower figure will also form the death value for CGT so that the PRs cannot claim CGT loss relief. As an alternative to reducing the estate valuation, the PRs may prefer to claim a CGT loss on the disposal. This would be advantageous where they have made chargeable gains on disposals of other assets in the estate and where no repayment of IHT would result from amending the value of the death estate. Note, though, *Stonor (executors of Dickinson) v IRC*[27] where it was held that the executors could not substitute a higher sale price for probate value where the estate was left to charity because no values had been "ascertained" for inheritance tax purposes. A higher sale price can only be substituted where more inheritance tax is then paid. This decision is based on the principle that substitution of the sale proceeds can only be allowed for inheritance tax purposes on a claim made by an "appropriate person" defined as a person who is liable for inheritance tax.[28] In that case the executors had wanted to increase the probate value in order to avoid a capital gains tax charge on a subsequent sale by them since the assets had increased in value after death. Unless the executors could show that the value was wrong at the date of death and was in fact a higher value, the fact that the asset had increased in value since death did not mean they could substitute the higher value for probate purposes.

40.11   Ideally, for CGT purposes, the PRs want a high value for the assets because of the tax-free uplift, whereas in the case of estates where IHT is payable they want as low a value as possible. Generally, since IHT will be levied on the entire value on the asset not just on the gain and charged at 40 per cent

---

[23]   See *Tax Bulletin*, April 1995, p.209.
[24]   TCGA 1992 s.272.
[25]   TCGA 1992 s.273(3). See *Clark (executor of Clark Deceased) v Green* [1995] STC (SCD) 99 and *Administrators of the Estate of Caton (Deceased) v Couch* [1995] STC (SCD) 34 regarding the level of information this involves.
[26]   See IHTA 1984 s.190 in relation to land and s.178 in relation to securities.
[27]   [2001] STC (SCD) 199.
[28]   IHTA 1984 s.190(1).

rather than the CGT rate of 28 per cent, a low valuation is preferable unless the assets in question qualify for business property relief or agricultural property relief or are otherwise exempt from IHT (e.g. because of the spouse exemption).

III CGT LOSSES OF THE DECEASED

40.12 Losses of the deceased in the tax year of his death must be set against gains of that year. Any surplus loss at the end of the year of death can be carried back and set against chargeable gains of the deceased in the three tax years preceding the year of death, taking the most recent year first.[29] Any tax reclaimed will, of course, fall into the deceased's estate for IHT purposes! Losses carried back are not set against the gains of any year if and to the extent that they would cause the annual capital gains tax exemption to be wasted.

IV SALES BY PRS

40.13 A sale of the deceased's chargeable assets by his PRs is a disposal for CGT purposes and will be subject to CGT on the difference between the sale consideration and the market value at death. PRs pay tax at the following rates:

  (i) 34 per cent until April 6, 2004;

 (ii) for disposals on or after that date until April 6, 2008 at 40 per cent;

(iii) for disposals from April 6, 2008 to June 23, 2010 at 18 per cent;

(iv) from June 23, 2010 at 28 per cent.

These rules apply even if the beneficiaries under the will would not themselves be subject to CGT (typically because they are UK charities or non-residents). In appropriate cases, therefore, assets should be vested in the beneficiary before sale.[30]

Tax rates

40.14 The "simplified" capital gains tax regime introduced from April 6, 2008 was generally beneficial for estates. Taper relief (which was abolished) had not generally been relevant to PRs because they had to hold the non-business asset for a minimum of three years to obtain even five per cent taper and tapered gains were still taxed at a flat rate of 40 per cent. By contrast, from April 6, 2008 PRs paid capital gains tax at only 18 per cent however long the asset has been owned. That changed from June 23, 2010, however, with the rate of CGT for

[29] TCGA 1992 s.62(2).
[30] See further 40.20 and following and A1.23.

personal representatives being increased to 28 per cent (the top CGT rate). As a result there will be cases where PRs will be advised not to sell an appreciating asset themselves (suffering tax at 28 per cent) but to vest it in a beneficiary for him to sell at the lower 18 per cent rate.[31]

Allowable deductions

40.15 The normal deductions for the incidental expenses of sale are available and PRs can also deduct an appropriate proportion of the cost of the administration of the estate that is necessary to put themselves in the position of being able to sell: e.g. solicitors costs of obtaining probate and of obtaining valuations.[32] Although HMRC publish a scale of allowable expenses for the cost of establishing title (see SP 8/94), PRs may claim to deduct more than the "scale" figure when higher expenses have been incurred. A deduction for the costs of obtaining the grant is only available where the PRs themselves sell the assets in the course of administration not where the beneficiaries under the will dispose of the asset. Nor is the cost of obtaining probate allowable where the asset is transferred to a beneficiary under the will.[33]

Where an asset is transferred to a legatee the PRs may either deduct the cost of the transfer from the gains accruing to them on the sale of other assets or the beneficiary can add the cost of the transfer to the market value at which he is deemed to acquire the asset and thereby reduce his future chargeable gain. There is no deduction for the expenses of negotiating with HMRC or of any related proceedings concerning valuation.[34]

Entrepreneurs' relief

40.16 On the *sale* of an asset by the PRs all gains arising since death are taxed 28 per cent, PRs are not entitled to entrepreneurs' relief. However, for entrepreneurs' relief purposes, the period of ownership by the PRs can be incorporated within the legatee's period so as to increase the amount of relief available but only if the legatee has separately, since before the death, owned at least five per cent voting shares in the trading group in their own right and is an officer or employee. It is understood that if the PRs assented (say) a five per cent shareholding to a beneficiary after death and that beneficiary satisfied all other conditions but did not own five per cent of the shares until the assent, the legatee would need to hold the shares for a further 12 months from the date of assent before relief would be available. It is questionable whether this is correct. The issue for entrepreneurs' relief is whether the legatee is deemed to have all the voting rights of the PRs since date of death by virtue of s.62(4)

---

[31] The rate of CGT applicable to individuals depends on their income tax position. To the extent that they have any unused income tax basic rate band (extending for 2011–12 to £37,400) gains are taxed at 18%. Once that band is exhausted the top 28% rate applies.

[32] *IRC v Richards' Executors* [1971] 1 All ER 785; 46 TC 626 HL and see *Administrators of the Estate of Caton v Couch* [1997] STC 970; 70 TC 10, CA.

[33] See SP 2/04: A2.447.

[34] *Caton v Crouch* [1997] STC 970.

(b) which states, "*the legatee shall be treated as if the PRs' acquisition of the asset had been his acquisition of it*".[35]

EXAMPLE 40.4

In 2009 Marx left 10 per cent of the shares in CP Ltd to the managing director, Engels. The shares are vested in Engels two years after Marx's death and he promptly sells them. Although Engels' ownership period is related back to Marx's death, for Engels to qualify for entrepreneurs' relief HMRC consider that the company must already have been his personal company, i.e. Engels must own personally at least five per cent voting rights in the company for one year prior to the sale of any shares. Either he has to hold these shares for a further 12 months before sale or have owned at least five per cent other voting shares in his own right for at least 12 months.

The CGT annual exemption

40.17 PRs enjoy an annual exemption from CGT of £10,600 in the tax year of death (for 2011–12) and in each of the two following tax years they receive the full CGT annual exemption. Thereafter they have no exemption, so that if it is then intended to sell property in the estate and that sale will result in a chargeable gain, it may be advantageous to vest the asset in the appropriate beneficiary for him to sell if he has an unused annual capital gains tax exemption.

EXAMPLE 40.5

(1) Mack died in May 2009. In June 2011 a valuable Greek vase then worth £100,000 (probate value in 2009 £40,000) is to be sold. Administration of the estate has not been completed. The proceeds of sale will be split equally between Mack's four children. The following possibilities should be considered:

  (a) the PRs could first appropriate the vase to the four children who could then sell it taking advantage of four CGT annual exemptions (£42,400 in all being £10,600 each in 2011–12). The resultant gain (say £17,600) is attributed equally between the children and may be taxed at 18 per cent (£3,168) or 28 per cent (£4,928) or a mixture of the two. *Accordingly, the maximum total tax bill will be £4,928*; or

  (b) the PRs could themselves sell the vase and realise gains of £60,000. No annual exemption will be available (since more than three years

---

[35] Contrast the (now repealed) taper relief provisions: see, in particular, TCGA 1992 Sch.A1 paras 4(5)) and 5(5). See 14.39 for further details.

have elapsed since death) and the rate of CGT will be 28 per cent. *Accordingly, the maximum tax bill will be £16,800.*

(2) Different issues arise when an asset is to be sold and the residuary beneficiary who will be entitled to all or the bulk of the proceeds of sale is not subject to CGT (e.g. because they are a UK charity or non-UK resident).[36]

Principal private residence relief

40.18 When PRs dispose of a dwelling house which, both before and after the death, was occupied by a person who was entitled on death to the whole, or substantially the whole, of the proceeds of sale from the house, either absolutely or for life, PRs were by concession given the benefit of the private residence exemption from CGT (ESC D5). The concession addressed the sort of situation where a house-owner died and his widow and perhaps some children occupied the house. "Substantially the whole" meant 75 per cent of the proceeds. The concession did not cover disposals of part of the house or an interest in the house or grounds. Nor did it help a child who moved into the house after the death of the father. FA 2004 gave statutory force to the ESC and ensured that the position for PRs is on the same statutory footing as the capital gains tax exemption available to trustees.[37] The inserted s.225A provides that relief is available if the person or persons who occupied the house as their main residence immediately before and after the death are together entitled to at least 75 per cent of the net proceeds of disposal (or an interest in possession in the same). Disposals of part of an interest in a house are covered. A specific claim for relief is required by the PRs. "Net proceeds of disposal" are the disposal proceeds realised by the PRs less any allowable incidental costs, but on the assumption that none of the proceeds is needed to meet the liabilities of the estate, including any inheritance tax liability.[38] A claim for main residence treatment is required and must be a joint notice by the PRs and the individuals entitled to occupy. If principal private residence relief is not available to the PRs because a relevant beneficiary of the estate was not in occupation before the death but moved in after death the PRs should assent the house to the beneficiary and let him make the sale.

EXAMPLE 40.6

(1) Sid and his brother Sad live in Sid's house. On his death, Sid leaves the house to Sad who goes on living in it. The property has to be sold by the PRs to pay for Sid's funeral. Any gain will be exempt under s.225A. If Sad was not in occupation at the date of death but is now in occupation,

---

[36] See 40.20. Note also that beneficiary may have carried forward CGT losses which will be available to reduce the gain on sale by that beneficiary.
[37] See TCGA 1992 s.225 but note that the exemption for PRs is still highly restrictive.
[38] TCGA 1992 s.225A(4).

the PRs could assent the house to Sad for him to sell. Even if he has not been in occupation for the entire period since death, the fact that the last 36 months of ownership will be exempt in any event[39] means that Sad obtains principal private residence relief if he has occupied the property for at least some of that period. However, the PRs may have insufficient property left in the estate to pay all the costs and tax. The difficulty is that the PRs cannot easily assent part of the house to Ben and retain part to pay costs: HMRC (wrongly, in the authors' view) do not accept that this is a valid appropriation.[40]

(2) Patrick dies leaving his Dorset estate including a farmhouse to his two children Eric and Ernie. Eric lives in the house but Ernie has a main residence in London. The sons want to retain the house for the foreseeable future. If the house is assented to them jointly, Eric will obtain principal private residence relief on a future sale of his share but there is no principal private residence relief on Ernie's share. If, instead, Eric and Ernie enter into a deed of variation putting the house into a trust where each takes an IPDI (conferring entitlement to income with power to advance capital), the inheritance tax position is no different, but TCGA 1992 s.225 means that principal private residence relief will be available in future on the entire gain when the trustees sell the house as long as Eric occupies as his main residence, even if Ernie is not in occupation and owns a London house as his main residence.[41]

V LOSSES OF THE PRS

Losses made by the PRs on disposals of chargeable assets during administration can be set off against chargeable gains on other sales made by them. Any surplus losses at the end of the administration period cannot be transferred to beneficiaries.[42] Accordingly, when PRs anticipate that a loss will not be relieved, they may prefer to transfer the loss-making asset to the relevant beneficiary so that he can sell it and benefit from the loss relief. If PRs realise losses then they should ensure that they sell an asset realising a gain before the administration of the estate is complete in order to utilise the loss relief. Even if the asset to be sold has not been formally assented to a beneficiary, if the administration of the estate is complete because the residue is ascertained, HMRC may consider that the loss is not allowable against the gain realised on the sale on the basis that the disposal is being made by the PRs who have become bare trustees for the beneficiaries.[43]

40.19

---

[39] TCGA 1992 s.223(1).

[40] Similar issues arise in relation to appropriations of part to charities: see 40.20.

[41] The example illustrates the relative generosity of the relief for trustees under TCGA 1992 s.225.

[42] Contrast losses made by trustees on a deemed disposal under TCGA 1992 s.71 which can in limited circumstances be passed to a beneficiary when the trust ends: see Ch.21.

[43] See HMRC CGTM 30730. Note that artificially created losses on disposals after December 5, 2006 may be restricted under FA 2007 which inserts TCGA 1992 s.16A, and see guidance notes issued by HMRC on July 19, 2007.

40.20 On the transfer of an asset to a legatee, the PRs make neither a gain nor loss for CGT purposes and the legatee acquires the asset at the PRs' base cost together with the expenses of transferring the asset to him. The base cost will in appropriate cases be a fraction of the probate value: for instance, if a 60 per cent shareholding (valued at death as a majority holding) is split between the deceased's four sons each will receive a 15 per cent holding with a base cost equal to one-quarter of the probate valuation of the 60 per cent holding.

EXAMPLE 40.7

The PRs transfer the picture (see Example 40.1) to the legatee (L) under the will in March 2011 when it is worth £300,000. The cost of valuing the picture as a part of the whole estate in November 2010 was £1,000 and the PRs incurred incidental expenses involved in its transfer in March 2011 of £150. L subsequently sells the picture in July 2013 for £330,000. On the transfer by the PRs to L, no chargeable gain accrues to the PRs and L's base cost is:

	£
Market value at death	250,000
Valuation cost	1,000
Expenses of transfer	150
Base cost of L	251,150

When L sells the picture in July 2013 for £330,000 he is charged to CGT on his gain that is £78,850 (£330,000 – £251,150) as reduced by any allowable expenditure that he has incurred and an annual CGT exemption. The rate of tax on the net gain is 28 per cent.[45]

40.21 A "legatee" is defined in TCGA 1992 s.64(2) as any person taking under a testamentary disposition or on intestacy or partial intestacy, whether beneficially or as a trustee. This definition covers only property passing under the will or intestacy to a beneficiary and to the extent that a beneficiary contracts with the PRs to purchase a particular asset or to obtain a greater share in an asset he is not taking that asset qua legatee. In *CG Manual* 30772 HMRC cite *Passant v Jackson*[46] as authority for the view that, where a residuary legatee pays a balancing sum to the executors in order to acquire a property in the deceased's estate, he does not acquire the asset qua legatee. However, in that case, the residuary legatee wished to retain a property worth more than the net

---

[44] TCGA 1992 s.62(4).
[45] Subject to any part being taxable at 18%.
[46] [1986] STC 164, CA.

value of the estate. He paid the executors a balancing payment to cover the shortfall and they executed an assent in his favour. On a subsequent disposal, the legatee sought to include both the probate value of the property and the sum he paid to the executors in his acquisition cost but this claim was rejected. The court said nothing to suggest that on the original acquisition by him from the executors he did not acquire qua legatee and although he was not allowed to include the cash sum he paid the executors to reduce the overall gain on the later sale, which is a very different point.

A *donatio mortis causa* is treated for these purposes as a testamentary disposition and not as a gift, so that the donee acquires the asset at its market value on the donor's death and the donor is not treated as having made a chargeable gain.

Difficult questions may arise when a person receives assets under a trust **40.22** created by will or under the intestacy rules. Does he receive them as a legatee (in which case there is no charge to CGT) or as a beneficiary absolutely entitled as against the trustee, in which case there is a deemed disposal which may be chargeable if the property has increased in value?[47] The answer depends upon the status of the PRs (have they turned into trustees at the relevant time?) and the terms of the will.[48]

During the course of administration PRs are the sole owners of the deceased's assets, albeit in a fiduciary capacity[49] so that there is no trust of particular assets at that time (although the beneficiaries will own a *chose in action* comprising a right to compel due administration of the estate). *Livingston* confirms that a beneficiary has no direct or proprietary interest in the residuary estate of the deceased while it is still being administered. The right of a beneficiary is limited to a right against the executors or administrators to have the estate properly administered and the residue ascertained and disposed of according to the Will or law.[50]

Accordingly, if, before the completion of administration or the vesting of assets in themselves as trustees (whichever first occurs), the property ceases to be settled for CGT purposes, when it is transferred to the relevant beneficiary he will take qua legatee (see Example 40.8(2) below).

EXAMPLE 40.8

(1) T dies leaving his house on trust for his three children all of whom are over 18, in equal shares absolutely. Whether the children receive the assets before the administration is completed or after the executors have assented to themselves as bare trustees for the children does not matter since they take as legatees. For CGT purposes joint ownership does not result in the property being settled.[51]

---

[47] See TCGA 1992 s.71: see Ch.12.
[48] See *Cochrane's Executors v IRC* [1974] STC 335 and *IRC v Matthew's Executors* [1984] STC 386.
[49] *Stamp Duties Comr (Queensland) v Livingston* [1965] AC 694.
[50] In *Raymond Saul & Co v PR of Bernard Hemming (Deceased) and Trustee in Bankruptcy of Hemming* [2008] EWHC 2731 (Ch) it was confirmed that the residuary legatee has no present property interest in any of the individual assets forming the estate while it is being administered or any immediate interest of a proprietary nature in residue.
[51] TCGA 1992 s.60: see further Ch.12.

(2) T dies in 2011 leaving his property on trust for his widow for life and then for his three children absolutely, all of whom are over 18. If the widow dies *before the executors become trustees*, any distributions to the children will be received by them as legatees since, for CGT purposes, the trust ended on the widow's death. If, however, the widow dies *after* the executors have become trustees, the property is then settled, so that the children receive assets as persons absolutely entitled as against the trustees with a consequent deemed disposal under TCGA 1992 s.71 (there will be no charge in this case even if the assets have increased in value since T's death because the event leading to their entitlement is the death of the life tenant who took an IPDI so there is a death uplift: contrast the position if the interest had terminated inter vivos).

(3) Z leaves his residuary estate by will on discretionary trusts. Within two years of his death the assets are distributed amongst his children so that:

(a) for IHT purposes, IHTA 1984 s.144 ensures that the distributions are "read back" into Z's will[52];
(b) although hold-over relief under TCGA 1992 s.260 is not available,[53] provided that the children become entitled during the administration period and the assets are not vested in the trustees first, HMRC accept that the children take qua legatees. Normally the trustees would make an appointment directing the executors (usually themselves) to hold the asset absolutely for the children. Then when the administration is complete the executors transfer the asset to the children pursuant to that appointment and they then take qua legatees. Furthermore HMRC's view is that such appointment does not involve the disposal of a *chose in action* by the trustees (which would be disastrous since the *chose* would have a nil base cost since it has been acquired in circumstances where there is no corresponding disposal).[54]

40.23 When the former matrimonial home of the deceased passes to his surviving spouse there is an uplift in the base cost of the property on death in the usual way. On a subsequent disposal by that spouse, any gain since death will be exempt from CGT if the house has been occupied as that spouse's main residence. Even if it has not, by virtue of TCGA 1992 s.222(7), the deceased's period of ownership is deemed to be that of the surviving spouse in deciding what proportion of the gain (if any) is chargeable.

EXAMPLE 40.9

T bought a house in 2001 for £50,000. It was his main residence until his death in 2005 when it was worth £250,000. His wife (W) whom he married just before his death never lived there with him, but became entitled to the house on his intestacy. T's administrators transferred the

---

[52] See Ch.39.
[53] See Ch.39.
[54] See *Taxation Practitioner,* September 1995, p.23.

house to W in 2006. She occupied it as her main residence after T's death until 2007 and then went abroad until 2011 when she returned and sold the house for £350,000.

For the purpose of the main residence exemption, W can claim that she has occupied the house as her main residence for nine out of the 10 years that it has been in the ownership of herself or T, i.e.:

W is, therefore, charged on a proportion of the gain:

2001–05 (4 years)	Occupied by T as his main residence
2005–07 (2 years)	Occupied by W
2007–11 (4 years)	Abroad from 2003 but last three years of ownership disregarded[55]

(1) Sale consideration (£350,000) – base cost (£250,000) = £100,000 (assuming no other allowable expenses).

(2) Fraction chargeable: £100,000 × 1/10 = £10,000.

Were it not for s.222(7), she would be charged on a larger proportion of the gain, i.e.:

£100,000 × 1/6 = £16,667

Of course, if the husband had not occupied it during his period of ownership, s.222(7) could prove disadvantageous to the wife because then her period of ownership would be 10 years of which only half would qualify for principal private residence relief.

Vesting assets in a charity

Assume that the estate includes land which is showing a substantial gain over probate value and which is to be sold. The residuary beneficiary is a UK charity. If the PRs sell the land in the course of the administration, tax at a rate of 28 per cent will be payable: by contrast, if the land is assented to the charity which sells it no CGT will be payable.[56] In cases where the estate is to be divided amongst several charities the PRs may appropriate the land in partial or entire satisfaction of the charities' entitlement and hold it as bare trustees for those charities.[57] The charities may then direct the trustees to sell and the sale will then be taxed on the basis that it was done by the charities so that the s.256 exemption will apply.[58] In *Prest v Bettinson*,[59] the deceased left his residuary estate to be divided between four charities and one non-charitable body. On sale, the PRs were assessable on the entire gain. The PRs should

40.24

[55] TCGA 1992 s.223(1).
[56] See TCGA 1992 s.256.
[57] For a specimen appropriation, see A1.23.
[58] For the CGT treatment of bare trusts, see Ch.42.
[59] [1980] STC 607.

have appropriated the entirety of the assets showing gains to the charities and non-charity to obtain exemption.[60]

40.25   What if the PRs need part of the sale proceeds (e.g. to pay administration costs), and the estate comprises land which has increased in value since death? One suggestion is to appropriate part of the land before sale to the charity. Unfortunately, HMRC dispute that an appropriation of a share in the land is effective for capital gains tax purposes. They argue that *Crowe v Appleby*[61] applies so that the charity does not become absolutely entitled to the land qua legatee. The High Court decision in that case is authority for the proposition that in order for a person to become absolutely entitled as against the trustees, in the case of land it is not enough for the beneficiary to become entitled to a share if another share remains settled. HMRC consider that unless the charities can direct how their share in the property is to be dealt with, they are not absolutely entitled as against the PRs so that the gain does not accrue to the charities but to the executors in their capacity as trustees of the estate.

40.26   In the authors' view while the charities do not have a beneficial interest in the assets in the executors' hands during the course of administration, once they have been appropriated an interest in land (e.g. a 50 per cent share) it is not clear that their position is comparable to a beneficiary under a trust: specifically s.60(2) is dealing with settled property not property where the beneficiaries of the residuary estate are absolutely entitled. It is not the case that any person owning an undivided share in land is subject to the *Crowe v Appleby* principle. For example, it does not apply in relation to equitable interests in land held by trustees (so if two joint owners own land equally and one settles his 50 per cent share on continuing trusts, the other 50 per cent owner is not suddenly no longer absolutely entitled). Even if the charities are not absolutely entitled it is arguable that they still acquire the assets as legatees within TCGA 1992 s.62(4) and hence the charity is treated as if the executors' acquisition of the asset had been its acquisition.[62]

EXAMPLE 40.10

> A dies owning a house worth £1.3 million at his death and his will leaves his residuary estate (which mainly comprises the house) to charity after cash gifts totalling £800,000 which are chargeable. The executors need to sell the house to raise cash to pay the inheritance tax and the cash gifts. Two years after A's death, the house has increased in value by £300,000. If the charity sells the house and the exemption for disposals by charities[63] applies, there is no capital gains tax payable. As a matter of general law, there is, of course, no difficulty in any executor appropriating "any part of the real or personal estate" in or towards satisfaction of any legacy or any other interest or share in his property. Accordingly, it is thought that the executors could appropriate a specified share in the house to charity.

---

[60] Similar considerations apply if the legatee is non-UK resident and so outside the CGT net.
[61] [1976] 1 WLR 885, CA and see 51 TC 457 (High Court decision of Goff J.).
[62] See s.64(3).
[63] See TCGA 1992 s.256.

Alternatively, the PRs can assent the whole of the interest in the house to the **40.27** relevant charity, subject to a lien for the PRs' debts and liabilities, including payment of the legacies to the non-charitable beneficiaries.[64] *Crowe v Appleby* does not apply because there are no continuing trusts. The charity may then direct the PRs (as bare trustees) to sell the house, and any gain on the sale will then accrue to the charities and not to the PRs. The amount required to pay the legacies etc is retained by the PRs.

A difficulty with this approach is that although the gain accrues on a disposal by the charity, the second condition for exemption in TCGA 1992 s.256 may not be satisfied because the proceeds of sale are not entirely "*applicable and applied for charitable purposes*". Some of the proceeds are used for non-charitable purposes in the payment of expenses and discharge of non-charitable legacies. It is not that the charity is in breach of any charity law by satisfying the charge (because it takes the land subject to such charge in the first place), but it is hard to say that the proceeds are all being applied for charitable purposes. (The position is different from the common situation where a charge is granted by the charity to secure borrowings taken out by the charity and those borrowings are used by the charity for other charitable purposes.)

In the right circumstances a further alternative is to divide the land up physi- **40.28** cally into separate plots. Then the charity could be made absolutely entitled to the entirety of one plot rather than to an undivided share of the entirety, and the PRs could retain other plots and sell them (paying capital gains tax on those parts alone).

Perhaps the easiest option is for personal representatives to sell the land **40.29** at its base cost to the charities. No chargeable gain will arise on the sale by the PRs.[65] They can then use the purchase price to pay the legacies and the debts, and distribute any balance left to the charity. The charity will then sell the land, without having to pay anything back to the PRs. Thus, the entire gain accrues to the charity and is applied for charitable purposes. This raises a number of practical issues, e.g. does the charity have to pay the cash upfront to the executors before it has received cash from the sale? In addition, it seems that there is an SDLT charge on the sale to the charity because the charity does not hold the land for qualifying charitable purposes or as an investment from which the profits are applied to the charitable purposes of the purchaser.[66]

In any event, if the assets are vested in the charity, HMRC may require evi- **40.30** dence that the charity has approved the sale and complied with the provisions of the Charities Act 1993.

---

[64] See AEA 1925 s.36(10).
[65] TCGA 1992 s.257.
[66] FA 2003 Sch.8 para.1(1).

CHAPTER 41

PILOT TRUSTS

- What is a pilot trust? (**41.02**)
- Related settlements (**41.04**)
- The attraction of pilot trusts (**41.06**)
- Adding property (**41.07**)
- Merging the trusts (**41.16**)
- Typical uses of pilot trusts (**41.17**)
- Miscellaneous technical points and traps (**41.25**)

Precedents

A1.1   Pilot discretionary trust
A1.18   Clause leaving property to pilot (lifetime) trusts

41.01   Relevant property settlements are subject to anniversary charges every 10 years and to exit charges. Exit charges are normally calculated by reference to the rate of tax calculated on the previous anniversary (though there are special rules for exits in the first 10 years).[1] In calculating the tax a settlement may benefit from the IHT nil rate band provided that the settlor had not made chargeable transfers in the seven years before he created the settlement. The great attraction of pilot trusts is therefore to allow a settlor to create a number of settlements each of which can benefit from a full IHT nil rate band when calculating exit charges and 10-year charges. One effect of the changes in FA 2006 is that such trusts have become more widespread, being used in conjunction with IHT efficient wills and in lifetime planning.

I WHAT IS A PILOT TRUST?

41.02   A pilot trust is established with a nominal sum (typically £10) with the intention that substantial assets will subsequently be added.[2] There is no magic

---

[1] See generally Ch.29.
[2] Remember, however, that a trust is not constituted until the trustees have received property to be held according to its terms: hence it is necessary to ensure that the stated nominal sum (typically £10) is handed over or held by the solicitor who has established the trust on behalf of the trustees. Some insurance companies set up their pilot trusts with an unused first class postage stamp. 10-year anniversaries run from the date of commencement of the pilot trust, not from

about a pilot trust: it is a standard form discretionary trust with the "initial trust fund" defined as the sum of £10 and (usually) with a statement indicating that it is intended that further property shall be added to it.[3] The settlor will normally create a number of pilot trusts and even if they are identical (e.g. with the same trustees; beneficiaries; and trust powers) they will be separate settlements[4] (accordingly, in order to distinguish them, each should be given a separate name—for instance "the Tomkins No.1 Discretionary Trust"; "the Tomkins No.2 Discretionary Trust" and so on).

Do the trusts need to be different? They were not in *Rysaffe* and while the **41.03** High Court seems solid enough it is not clear what Mummery L.J. in the Court of Appeal meant by the following:

> *"[26] In my judgment, approval of the judge's reasoning is sufficient to dispose of this appeal. In those circumstances I am reluctant to express any view on the opinions expressed by the judge on other questions, which it is not necessary to decide, namely whether the five settlements were created by 'associated operations' and, if so, whether the result would be that there was only one settlement, rather than five settlements, for the purposes of the 1984 Act."*

The claim by HMRC that there was one settlement by associated operations was rejected by the Court of Appeal and the latter did not see it necessary to consider whether they should be treated as a single settlement for any other purposes of the IHT legislation. It may do no harm for each settlement to be different in some way in their terms, e.g. class of beneficiaries, ultimate default beneficiary etc.

II RELATED SETTLEMENTS

The definition of *"related settlements"* requires the settlor to be the same and the **41.04** settlements to commence on the same day.[5] It is not necessary for both trusts to be relevant property settlements for them to be related. So, for example, a discretionary trust can be related to a qualifying interest in possession trust.[6] When a will establishes two or more settlements they will therefore normally be related.[7]

---

the date of any addition. It is also necessary for the trustees to retain the initial (nominal) property settled until further property is added: otherwise the trust will end!

[3] It is, in fact, modern practice to set up virtually all settlements in pilot form and then (immediately) add property to them: for instance by completing stock transfer forms in favour of the trustees. Sometimes the settlement instrument includes an assignment of the settled property (e.g. a life insurance policy) and on other occasions the settlement deed may recite that certain property has already been transferred into the name of the trustees to be held on the trusts which are then set out.

[4] Note the cases of *Rysaffe Trustee Co (CI) Ltd v IRC* [2003] STC 536 and *Reynaud v IRC* [1999] STC (SCD) 18 in which HMRC sought unsuccessfully to tax a number of identical settlements as a single composite settlement.

[5] IHTA 1984 s.62.

[6] Unless the interest in possession trust (whether inter vivos or not) is for the settlor or spouse: see IHTA 1984 s.80 and see fn.7.

[7] Note, however, the exception if one of the settlements creates an IPDI in favour of the testator's surviving spouse (or civil partner) when IHTA 1984 s.80 provides that the settlement only commences on the termination of that spouse's interest in possession. In this situation because

Related settlements should normally be avoided since the value of property in a related settlement immediately after it commenced may affect the IHT rate charged on the "other" settlement.[8] Note, however, that if two trusts are set up on the same day, both with £10, they are related settlements but it is only the value immediately after the related trust commenced which is taken into account in calculating the rate of tax for the other trust. Subsequent additions to the related settlement are ignored. Hence, in the area of pilot trusts the related settlement rules do not generally create difficulties. For instance, 40 trusts can be executed on the same day so long as the substantial property is added later. It is often administratively convenient to set up the trusts on the same day! If the related property rules do pose a problem, that can be avoided by ensuring that settlements commence on different days so that the rules will not apply.

EXAMPLE 41.1

> As part of an IHT planning exercise (see Example 41.8) Jack the Lad sets up 40 identical pilot trusts on July 1, 2011. In each case the initial settled property is £10. For IHT charging purposes the settlements are "related" and accordingly, in working out the tax rate that applies to either settlement £390 (being the value of the settled property initially comprised in the 39 related settlements) is included. This is de minimis and will often not outweigh the convenience of creating all the settlements at once rather than consecutively over a period of 40 days.

41.05   If it is desired to set up more than one trust in a will, all the settlements will commence on the death of the testator and will therefore be related. Pilot trusts cannot be established by varying property into trusts set up by the deed of variation itself (because such pilot trusts are deemed to be established by the deceased and commence at the date of death as a result of reading-back under IHTA 1984 s.142). These difficulties can, however, be avoided by establishing one or more pilot trusts during the lifetime of the testator to which he then adds property by his will.

EXAMPLE 41.2

> Silus' will establishes:
>
>   (i)   a trust for his grandchildren;
>   (ii) life interest trusts for each of his three children;
>   (iii) a life interest trust of residue for his surviving civil partner George.

a surviving spouse is treated as creating the settlement when her interest terminates (typically on death) this may be related to any other settlement that the spouse sets up in her Will but is not related to any other settlement created by the original deceased testator. Hence, it will be desirable for the survivor to use pilot trusts to receive property to be settled on death: see 41.04. Curiously although related settlements, the 10-year anniversary for the trust created in the testator's will runs from the date of the testator's death not the date of the spouse's death: see 41.28 below for further details

[8]   See, for instance, in relation to the 10-year charge IHTA 1984 s.66(4)(c).

Trust (i) creates a relevant property settlement; (ii) and (iii) establish IPDIs.

Trusts (i) and (ii) are related settlements and so the value of the property in the trusts in (ii) will be included in calculating the rate of tax applicable to the relevant property settlement (i). The trust in (iii) falls within IHTA 1984 s.80 and so is treated as arising on George's death (or on the earlier termination of his interest). The tax treatment of the grandchildren's trust would have been improved if Silus had established the trust in pilot form during his lifetime and then added property to it by his will.

EXAMPLE 41.3

Tom, a widower, wishes to leave £900,000 on trusts for his grandchildren at the age of 25 (all are currently young minors). If a single trust is set up in Tom's will that trust will suffer 10-yearly and exit charges because the value of the relevant property exceeds the IHT nil rate band. A similar result will occur if three separate trusts—one for each grandchild—are employed in the will (as a result of the related settlement rules). However, contrast the position if:

(i) Tom, who has made no chargeable transfers, sets up three pilot trusts during his lifetime for grandchildren; and
(ii) In his will he puts £300,000 into each of those trusts.[9]

The IHT position is as follows:

(1) Tom makes a chargeable transfer on his death of £900,000 (note that the tax due on his death is not reduced by the use of pilot trusts);
(2) each settlement will benefit from a full IHT nil rate band (in effect therefore T has set up three nil rate band discretionary trusts).

Diagrammatically the position is as follows:

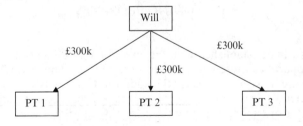

It is important that the pilot trusts are in existence when the will is made, i.e. the gift in the will must be to an existing settlement.[10] A gift by will to an existing trust may be drafted as follows:

---

[9] Of course he is not limited in the number of pilot trusts that he sets up and should allow some leeway in case the value of the trust fund increases by more than rises in the IHT nil rate band. In the above example, consider therefore the use of (say) six pilot trusts each with a £150,000 trust fund.
[10] See generally *Re Edwards' Will Trust* [1948] Ch 440 and contrast *Re Jones* [1942] Ch

"Specific Legacy[11]
> *I give my shares in [insert name] Limited*[12] *to the trustees of the [insert name] Discretionary Settlement 201[insert year] to be held by those trustees on the trusts set out in a deed of settlement dated [insert date] and made by me as settlor and the Original Trustees (as therein defined)."*[13]

III THE ATTRACTION OF PILOT TRUSTS

41.06   Provided that the testator has not used up any part of his IHT nil rate band at the time when he creates the trust then that trust will benefit from the full IHT nil rate band (£325,000 for 2011–12). Note carefully:

(i)   it is therefore necessary to consider what chargeable transfers the settlor has made in the previous seven years. These will mainly comprise settlements that he has created (all of which involve, since March 22, 2006, immediately chargeable transfers)[14];

(ii)   if the settlor has made PETs in the last seven years then these may, of course, become chargeable and so reduce or extinguish the nil rate band available to any trust that he sets up. Accordingly, to be sure of that settlement benefitting from a full nil rate band wait until the seven-year period has expired. Of course, some settlors may be willing to "take a risk", being wholly confident that the PET will not fail and not wishing to delay setting up the pilot trusts;

(iii)   as already noted it is essential that the initial sum settled be transferred to the trustees so that the settlement commences on the date when the document is executed. It is also important that this sum is not spent before further property is added to the trust. Were it to be so, then as the trust would have no property it would cease to exist and would only recommence when further property was transferred to the trustees.

IV ADDING PROPERTY

41.07   Pilot trusts will be established with the intention that the settlor will add substantial property to those trusts either during his lifetime or on death by his will. There are no special rules for the addition of property to a pilot trust so that the general rule is that the settlor will make a chargeable transfer for IHT purposes. It is often forgotten that the attraction of pilot trusts lies in reduced

---

328. It is important that the terms of the lifetime trust are not altered e.g. by an appointment, after the Will is executed: see 41.30.

[11] See also A1.14.

[12] Or as the case may be.

[13] It is important that the settlement is in existence at the time when the will is made: it needs to be identified with precision (e.g. by name and date). The terms of the settlement should not be changed before the death of the settlor unless the will is re-executed after the change.

[14] Save only if the trust is disabled when its creation will be a PET.

IHT charges on the settlements once created. But the settlor still has to get the property into those settlements![15]

It is important to realise that, assuming that the settlor has set up more **41.08** than one pilot trust, he <u>must add property to all the trusts on the same day</u>. Specifically he must not put assets into PT1 on day one, then into PT2 on day two and so on. The reason lies in the IHT relevant property charging rules which provide that <u>in calculating tax on a settlement instead of taking into</u> <u>consideration the chargeable transfer of the settlor in the seven years before he</u> created <u>the settlement, his total chargeable transfer in the seven years before</u> the addition <u>will be substituted if these are greater.</u>[16] But, and this is obviously fundamental, <u>transfers on the same day as the addition are ignored</u>.

EXAMPLE 41.4

Jane established two pilot trusts (PT1 and PT2) on October 1, 2010. On December 1, 2011 she adds £150,000 to each. In 2010 she had made no chargeable transfers and that remained the case at the time of the addition in 2011. The fact that she made a chargeable transfer (£150,000 to the "other" trust) on the day of the addition is irrelevant.

Contrast the position if she had added £150,000 to PT 1 on December 1 and £150,000 to PT2 on December 2, 2011. PT1 would still benefit from a full IHT nil rate band but the tax charge on PT2 would take account of the £150,000 transfer to PT1 (in effect therefore the nil rate band for that trust would be reduced, for 2011–12, from £325,000 to £175,000).

Apart from making sure that property is added to all the trusts on the same **41.09** day, it is also <u>important to check that the settlor has not made any other</u> <u>chargeable transfers in the seven-year period before the addition</u>. Often pilot trusts are funded by lifetime additions of property which are made soon after the trusts are set up so that this is unlikely to have happened. In the case of additions by will, however, which may happen some years after the trusts are created, there may be a problem.

EXAMPLE 41.5

Jim, with an unused IHT nil rate band, set up two pilot trusts on December 1, 2003. On his death on November 5, 2011 he leaves £325,000 to each of the trusts (as well as establishing a nil rate band discretionary trust in his will) with the residue passing to his civil partner:

(i) It is important to check what chargeable transfers Jim had made in the seven years before his death (i.e. from November 5, 2004). If, for instance, he had made a deathbed gift of £500,000 to his

---

[15] For situations where pilot trusts are commonly used, see 41.17 and following.
[16] IHTA 1984 s.67(3).

grandson then that figure will be included in taxing the pilot trusts: so they will have no IHT nil rate band.

(ii) Note that if this was not the case—so that the pilot trusts each benefit from a full nil rate band—then the will discretionary trust will also benefit from a full nil rate band. This is because Jim set up no related settlements in his will and other chargeable transfers on the same day (to the two pilot trusts) are ignored.

41.10 This example illustrates that there may be cases where adding property to a lifetime trust by will turns out to be undesirable. In such cases consider redirecting the property by using IHTA 1984 s.144 reading-back.[17]

The perils of IHTA 1984 s.81

41.11 The simplest way of adding property to a pilot trust by will is to make a specific gift to that trust.[18] In some cases, however, wills have been drafted leaving the property on a discretionary trust set up in the will itself with the will trustees being given power to transfer property out of that trust into the various pilot trusts that the testator established during his lifetime. This is a disaster! IHTA 1984 s.81(1) provides that:

> "*where property, which ceases to be comprised in one settlement becomes comprised in another then, unless in the meantime any person becomes beneficially entitled to the property (and not merely to an interest in possession in the property) it shall for the purposes of this Chapter[19] be treated as remaining comprised in the first settlement.*"

As a result, for IHT charging purposes, the property will never reach the lifetime trusts but will remain in the will discretionary trust. Only one nil rate band will be available and the pilot trusts wasted.[20]

Spousal by-pass trusts and s.81

41.12 It is increasingly common for a pilot trust to be set up to receive death benefits that may be payable under the settlor's pension arrangements.[21] If the sums involved are substantial it is sometimes suggested that more than one spousal by-pass trust should be established in order to benefit from a multiplicity of nil rate bands. Given, however, that the pension arrangement itself involves a trust, s.81 will be relevant and so even if the death benefit is paid into a number

---

[17] See 41.15.

[18] See, for instance, A1.14.

[19] i.e. IHTA 1984 Pt III Ch.III (the relevant property provisions).

[20] It is a misunderstanding to believe that IHTA 1984 s.144 could cure this problem: this section only provides for "reading-back" if an event happens within two years of death whereby property ceases to be held on relevant property trusts. A way of correcting this using a deed of variation is discussed at 41.13. See also, on s.81, 24.12.

[21] See further Ch.48.

of trusts it will, for IHT charging purposes, remain comprised in the trust set up when the settlor took out the pension. This means that only one nil rate band may be available, although this will depend on whether the settlor had made chargeable transfers in the seven years before taking out the pension. Of course, if he has a number of separate pension policies then each of these pension trusts may benefit from a full nil rate band (in effect the death benefit is already held on separate trusts which may enjoy the same advantage as pilot trusts). Accordingly whilst the taxpayer should arrange for the death benefit to be paid into a pilot spousal by-pass trust, there is no point in establishing more than one such trust.[22] In fact if the death benefits from a number of different pensions are paid into one trust, that trust can claim the benefit of more than one nil rate band on any 10-year anniversary (assuming the settlor made no chargeable transfers before joining each pension plan).

Deeds of variation

It has already been noted that property cannot be varied into pilot trusts **41.13** created by the deed of variation with any IHT benefits.[23] However, one could vary property passing under a will into existing pilot trusts set up by the deceased while he was alive. It would also be possible (at least from the inheritance tax perspective) to appoint property out of a discretionary trust set up in the will to a beneficiary outright within two years of death. That transfer is subject to reading back under s.144. The beneficiary can then vary the property appointed to him into pilot trusts *set up by the deceased* and s.142 gives the same beneficial effects as if the deceased had left the property himself to the pilot trusts. The key issue is to set up the pilot trusts during the deceased's lifetime.

A variation into pilot trusts set up by the person making the variation (e.g. **41.14** he may set up five trusts with £10 each) will not mean that the pilot trust treatment can be obtained in respect of the deceased's property. Section 44 has the result that the settlor of each pilot trust will be the beneficiary as to £10 but the deceased as to the varied property. The "separate settlements" rule applies so they are treated as separate trusts for IHT purposes commencing in each case on the date that each settlor added property. Accordingly, unless the variation can be made into trusts already set up by the deceased during his lifetime, the property is being varied into several new trusts made by the deceased but all treated as commencing on the date of his death. Hence they are all related settlements.[24]

The operation of IHTA 1984 s.144

If property is added to a pilot trust by the settlor's will then, assuming that **41.15** the trust does not contain an interest in possession,[25] the conditions for the

---

[22] *Air Jamaica Ltd v Charlton* [1999] 1 WLR 1399 at 1409: see 48.48.
[23] See 41.05.
[24] Because they are separate settlements, the 10-year anniversary on the £10 will be different from the 10-year anniversary on the added deceased's property.
[25] See IHTA 1984 s.144(1A).

operation of s.144 are met given that *"property is settled by (his) will"*. It is therefore possible to "undo" the pilot trust by an appointment onto IPDI trusts within two years of death if desired.[26]

EXAMPLE 41.6

1. Ron, by his will, added £200,000 to a pilot trust which he had set up before his death. The trustees appoint that sum to Ron's surviving civil partner, Ted, within two years of Ron's death. Under s.144 that appointment is read back so that the gift to Ted is exempt under IHTA 1984 s.18.

2. Penny's will adds £300,000 to a discretionary trust which he had set up with £300,000 more than seven years ago. The result of the addition is that the trust will suffer 10-year charges given that its value will exceed the IHT nil rate band. Accordingly within two years of Penny's death the trustees appoint the added £300,000 on an IPDI trust for Penny's daughter. This will be read-back under s.144 and be taxed as a separate settlement with a qualifying interest in possession.[27]

V MERGING THE TRUSTS

41.16 It will often be desirable for a number of pilot trusts to be run as one. Apart from saving expenses there can then be a diversified portfolio of the total sum settled. This can be achieved without forfeiting the IHT advantages as a result of IHTA 1984 s.81(1). As noted above,[28] this provides, for the purposes of the relevant property regime, that when property ceases to be comprised in one settlement by being transferred to another settlement, it is treated as remaining comprised in the first settlement.

Example 41.7

Zed created three pilot trusts (PT1, PT2 and PT3) into each of which he left £300,000 on his death. The trustees of PT1 and PT2 transfer their trust funds to PT3 (in exercise of a power in the settlement deeds). On the 10-year anniversary the value of the assets in PT3 is £1.5 million and the nil rate band is £550,000. For IHT purposes, one-third of the property is treated as remaining in each of PT1 and PT2 as a result of s.81. Each trust therefore has assets worth £500,000 and a nil rate band

[26] Section 144 will not, of course, apply to the £10 originally settled.
[27] An appointment on separate discretionary trusts would not be effective because of IHTA 1984 s.81: see 41.11.
[28] See 41.11.

of £550,000 so that no tax is due.[29] For CGT and SDLT the fact that the assets are now held in a single trust may be advantageous: see 51.12.

VI TYPICAL USES OF PILOT TRUSTS

The addition of property to a pilot trust will normally involve the settlor in making an immediately chargeable transfer for IHT purposes with the result that an IHT charge is incurred. Pilot trusts are accordingly particularly attractive if they can be set up in situations where this charge is avoided. The following are cases where the use of pilot trusts ought to be considered. In general, whenever the taxpayer wishes to establish a long term settlement (i.e. one which will involve 10-year anniversary occasions) he should consider whether fragmenting his gift into a number of settlements will be advantageous.[30]   **41.17**

First case: using up two IHT nil rate bands on death

Jason is a widower with (on his death) the benefit of the unused IHT nil rate band of his deceased first wife. On his death he wishes to leave his estate worth £650,000 to his second wife, Judith, who is a widow and whose estate will also benefit (on her death) from two IHT nil rate bands. Ideal IHT planning advice is for Jason (and Judith) to make wills which use up their two available IHT nil rate bands. In Jason's case, therefore, he may do this by setting up a discretionary trust under which Judith and the children from his first marriage will be beneficiaries. If he were to set the trust up by his will then no IHT will be payable on its creation (because of the availability of the two nil rate bands) but on a 10-year anniversary the IHT charge will only take into account the availability of the settlor (Jason's) nil rate band. Hence at current rates and values a tax charge of three per cent would arise. He ought instead: **41.18**

(a) to establish two lifetime pilot discretionary trusts;

(b) then make a will leaving the benefit of a single nil rate band to each of the two trusts.

As a result, the IHT position on Jason's death will be unaltered but the availability of a nil rate band for both trusts may ensure that there are no 10-year anniversary charges.[31] Should Jason prefer he could establish a single lifetime

---

[29] For all purposes except the calculation of the IHT relevant property charge, PT1 and PT2 have ceased to exist. In the event of any future IHT being payable it is the trustees of PT3 (who hold all the assets) who are liable.

[30] Note the CGT consequences of creating a multiplicity of settlements: in general, the annual exemption will be divided amongst them: see TCGA 1992 Sch.1: see 41.25. This may, however, be considered "small beer". However, note SDLT and CGT disadvantages if there are later transfers of assets between different settlements rather than between funds of the same settlement: see 51.12.

[31] See A1.18 for clauses adding property to a pilot trust by will. Consider whether Jason would

pilot trust (to which he adds property by his will) and set up the other trust in the will itself.

Second case: the substantial relevant property settlement

41.19 Jack is a widower and wishes to leave his £2 million estate on trusts for his collection of grandchildren and great-grandchildren. He accepts that a substantial IHT liability will arise on his death. He envisages that trust being kept in being for many years to provide a long term fund to be used by the family as the need arises.[32] To avoid substantial 10-year charges on the trust fund, Jack should establish (say) eight pilot trusts between which he can then divide his estate at death. Given that the usual conditions are met, each will benefit from a full IHT nil rate band and, for administrative convenience (and CGT and SDLT advantages: see 51.12), they can subsequently be merged into a single settlement.[33]

Third case: using 100 per cent relievable property

41.20 The availability of relief prevents any IHT entry charge if the property is settled. Putting the property into pilot trusts may be particularly attractive if it is envisaged it will be sold and the cash invested in non-relievable property.[34]

EXAMPLE 41.8

Jack the Lad owns all 200 issued shares in Jetsam Ltd which deals in fine art and rare books. He has recently received an offer to sell the business for £10 million which he is minded to accept and envisages settling the proceeds on trust for his relatives. He will not need any of the monies (he owns a number of betting syndicates).

As soon as a binding contract for sale of the business is concluded, Jack will cease to benefit from business property relief.[35] The settlement of the cash will accordingly be a chargeable transfer by Jack giving rise to a substantial IHT entry charge. The resultant settlement will also suffer 10-year charges.

The following is a more tax efficient alternative:

Settling the shares into pilot trusts: Jack creates (say) 40 pilot trusts to which he then transfers his shares (five per trust). That transfer will

---

be best advised to have more than two (perhaps four) pilot trusts to allow for future growth in value of the trust assets.

[32] A settlor like Jack will benefit from PAA 2009 which enables settlements to be set up with an extended 125-year perpetuity period and for income to be accumulated (if so desired) throughout this period.

[33] See 41.16.

[34] For the availability of business and agricultural property relief, see Chs 45 and 46.

[35] IHTA 1984 s.113 but note the replacement property provisions in IHTA 1984 107.

benefit from business property relief. The sale then goes ahead (the trustees entering into the sale contract) and cash is received by the settlements. The IHT entry charge has been avoided and, provided that the usual conditions are met, each settlement will benefit from a full IHT nil rate band.

A number of points of detail should be noted about the above Example: **41.21**

(a) An IHT clawback charge will arise in the event that Jack dies within seven years of transferring the shares into trust assuming that the trustees have by then sold the shares and not purchased qualifying replacement property.[36] Were this to happen the transfers become chargeable (so that the advantage of avoiding an IHT entry charge is lost). However, the benefit of the pilot trusts (each having a full IHT nil rate band) remains and, because of a lacuna in the clawback rules, it does not matter whether or not the shares were put into the pilot trusts on the same day[37].

(b) Consideration needs to be given to the CGT position. The transfer of the shares involves a chargeable disposal by Jack but he may elect for any gain to be held-over.[38] However, the position regarding entrepreneurs' relief needs to be taken into account and Jack may wish to hold-over on only some of the transfers thereby incurring a charge on the others that will benefit from entrepreneurs' relief. Bear in mind that the trusts will not benefit from that relief unless they retain the shares for 12 months on interest in possession trusts[39] and the other conditions are satisfied.

(c) It is easier to fragment ownership of a business which is operated through a limited company by transferring shares. Difficulties arise if the business is run by a sole trader or through a partnership.

Fourth case: taking advantage of the normal expenditure out of income exemption

This exemption is available for gifts out of the income of the taxpayer provided that such gifts are "normal" (i.e. are part of a pattern of payments) and do not have the effect of reducing his standard of living.[40] **41.22**

---

[36] For the clawback rules, see IHTA 1984 s.113A. Note that there is no clawback if the business rather than the shares are sold and the trust still retains the company shares even if the company then holds cash or investment assets: see Ch.45 and Example 15.2.

[37] This is because, although the rules impose a charge on the transfer of the shares into the trust, they do not operate to increase the cumulative total of chargeable transfers made by the settlor, i.e. they do not go onto his "clock": see s.113A(2).

[38] Under TCGA 1992 s.260, given that the trust is not "settlor-interested": see Ch.7.

[39] For entrepreneurs' relief, see TCGA 1992 ss.169H–169R and Ch.14. It is arguable that an interest in possession is not needed for 12 months to obtain entrepreneurs' relief. What is required is that the interest in possession beneficiary owns shares personally for 12 months and is a director or employee of the company.

[40] See IHTA 1984 s.21 and the leading cases of *Bennett v IRC* [1995] STC 54 and *McDowall v IRC* [2004] STC (SCD) 22.

EXAMPLE 41.9

Zed has surplus income of £600,000 each year. To take advantage of the s.21 exemption he settles £200,000 into each of three pilot trusts which he establishes. Note:

(1) the entry charge is avoided because of the availability of the exemption;
(2) given that the conditions are met, each trust will benefit from a full IHT nil rate band;
(3) as the payments are exempt from IHT, it does not matter if the sums are paid into the trusts on different days, i.e. this is not the classic pilot trust arrangement where the additions must be made to all the trusts on the same day. In fact, it is unnecessary to use pilot trusts: the sums could be settled directly into the three trusts although to avoid the related settlement rules the trusts should be set up on different days.[41]

Fifth case: wills for cohabitees

41.23 The major difficulty in these cases is the absence of the spouse/civil partner exemption which means that any property left to the surviving cohabitee may be taxed twice.

EXAMPLE 41.10

Jean, a divorcee, has an estate worth £600,000. She lives with Len, a confirmed bachelor, who has an estate of a similar size. Jean would like to leave half her estate on trust for the children of her marriage and half on life interest trust for Len. If both trusts are established by her will:

(1) Len's trust will be an IPDI and its value will therefore aggregate with his estate on death;
(2) the children's trust will be a relevant property settlement and Len's trust will be a related settlement.

Instead Jean should establish two pilot discretionary trusts into which she divides her estate. Once two years have elapsed from her death Len can be given an interest in possession in "his" trust without it being aggregated with his estate on death. There is no "reading-back" under s.144 and he takes a non-qualifying interest in possession.

---

[41] For the reporting obligations when the normal expenditure out of income exemption is being used, see Ch.56.

Sixth case: maximising BPR on death

Pilot trusts can also be useful in a similar situation to the third case above **41.24** when the business is likely to be sold after death but the taxpayer wishes to keep the proceeds in trust. Having a number of pilot trusts can reduce future 10-year charges on the settled property.

EXAMPLE 41.11

> X dies leaving all his property qualifying for BPR into a number of discretionary pilot trusts and the residue to his wife outright. No IHT is payable on his estate. The wife subsequently agrees to buy the business property from the trustees using the cash she has been left, cash from her own resources or agreeing that the purchase price shall remain outstanding as a debt.[42] After the sale, the trustees will no longer hold property qualifying for BPR. The pilot trusts reduce future 10-year anniversary charges. On wife's death (assuming she survives the sale by two years)[43] there is no IHT payable on the business property. In effect the same business property has been used twice to obtain relief. (This is sometimes referred to as "two bites of the cherry relief".)[44]

VII MISCELLANEOUS TECHNICAL POINTS AND TRAPS

The downside of multiple settlements

Setting up a series of pilot trusts will restrict the annual capital gains tax **41.25** exemption and standard rate band[45] of the trusts. Hence if husband and wife have another active trust holding shares and other property on which gains are regularly realised and which currently benefits from the £1,000 standard rate band they should be warned that setting up pilot trusts will mean the annual capital gains tax exemption and standard rate band of that active trust will be reduced.[46] In addition, later transfers of assets between separate settlements

---

[42] Watch FA 1986 s.103 if she gave property to the deceased: see *Phizackerley.* The debt may not be deductible.

[43] Since a minimum two-year period of ownership is required. She would not qualify for the succession provisions since she acquires by purchase not inheritance.

[44] See 38.47.

[45] See 6.33 and 11.09.

[46] Trustees are generally entitled to half the annual capital gains tax exemption appropriate to an individual. However, if the settlement is one of two or more made by the same settlor after June 6, 1978 then the half annual exemption has to be divided by the number of settlements made by the settlor after June 6, 1978 and each then has an exempt amount equal to the greater of the figure resulting from that division and one-tenth of the individual exempt amount. In carrying out the division, the number of settlements includes settlor-interested trusts and trusts

will be <u>CGT disposals</u> and may have <u>SDLT disadvantages</u> (contrast transfers between sub-funds of a single settlement: see 51.12).

Joint settlors

41.26 Can a pilot trust be set up by husband and wife jointly each settling £10 and then each adding to it in his or her will? <u>This has risks</u>. It is clear for reasons set out at 41.12 that <u>property added in the will must be added to a trust set up by the same settlor, i.e. husband cannot add to a trust set up by wife</u>. IHTA 1984 s.44(2) will simply treat the property added by husband in his will to the wife's inter vivos trust as <u>comprised in a separate settlement set up</u> on the <u>husband's death</u>.

41.27 In theory, you could have joint husband and wife settlements with each of them constituting a settlement with £10. Section 44 would then treat them as settlor of separate £10 settlements. When husband dies, it may be said that property left to the trust by his will is treated as added to the settlement set up by him. However, it is preferable to avoid joint trusts and have separate settlements. This avoids any argument about who initially settled the property into trust or any suggestion that one spouse settled all the funds.

The s.80 trap

41.28 The taxpayer, having set up lifetime pilot trusts, may wish to provide first in his will for a surviving spouse or civil partner and then, after that person's death, put the property into the pilot trusts. In effect, what is envisaged is a spouse exempt IPDI followed by a gift over into the trusts. <u>Unfortunately, as a result of the operation of IHTA 1984 s.80, this arrangement will not work to achieve what the taxpayer wants</u>.

41.29 The section applies in the situation where a settlor creates a settlement with a "postponing interest",[47] being a qualifying interest in possession for either the settlor or his spouse (or civil partner). The section provides that "*for the purposes of this Chapter*" (viz Pt III Ch.III dealing with the taxation of relevant property settlements) the <u>property is treated as becoming comprised in the relevant property settlement on the termination of the postponing interest with that settlement being treated as made by the beneficiary whose interest in possession has ended.</u>

established by the will of the settlor on his death but charitable trusts, non-resident trusts and retirement benefits and compensation funds are ignored. See 11.09.

[47] A "*postponing interest*" is defined in IHTA 1984 s.80(4)(b) as an immediate post-death interest (an IPDI) or a disabled person's interest. This reflects the FA 2006 changes in the IHT taxation of settlements which limited the occasions when a "*qualifying*" interest in possession can arise. The postponing interests are qualifying interests in possession. See 24.157

EXAMPLE 41.12

Jamie established four lifetime pilot trusts and, in his will, left his estate on an IPDI trust for his wife, Jools, with the remainder gift into the two trusts. On Jamie's death:

(1) the IPDI trust for Jools takes effect and the estate is spouse exempt;
(2) on Jools' death, the property passes to the four relevant property settlements created by Jamie. However, for IHT purposes s.80 applies and Jools is treated as making four relevant property settlements. The normal consequences of a settlor adding to his pilot trust therefore do not apply: instead it is Jools (a separate settlor) who is treated as making new settlements. The four settlements will be related to each other and if Jools creates any further settlements in her will, those settlements will be related to the four settlements.
(3) Jools could either disclaim her interest or effect a deed of variation within two years of Jamie's death which would, as a result of reading-back, result in Jamie adding property to his pilot trusts.
(4) Note that the 10-year anniversary is from Jamie's death not Jools's. See s.61(2).

Subsequent changes to pilot trusts

Care is needed if a pilot trust is set up; a will is then executed leaving property to that trust but the trust is subsequently changed before the testator's death. In these circumstances it is necessary to re-execute the will after the alteration to the trust. Otherwise the gifted property in the will passes on the terms of the trust as it existed when the will was made.[48] The gift by will to a trust altered or set up after the will is executed breaches WA 1837 s.9 unless, exceptionally, the trust is altered or set up by the testator signing in the presence of two witnesses. Deeds of appointment varying trusts are not normally executed in this way.   **41.30**

As noted above the beneficial use of pilot trusts in wills depends upon the settlor having an unused nil rate band when he sets them up **and** ensuring that he does not make transfers of value between setting up the trusts and his death or inter vivos additions of property.[49]   **41.31**

---

[48] See *Re Edwards* [1948] Ch 440 and *Re Schintz* [1951] Ch 870.
[49] IHTA 1984 s.67.

CHAPTER 42

BARE TRUSTS

- General points (**42.01**)
- Uses (**42.04**)
- Taxation of a bare trust (**42.06**)
- Deferring absolute entitlement (**42.16**)

Precedent

A1.2   Bare trust

I GENERAL POINTS

42.01   A bare trust is commonly one in which a single beneficiary has an immediate and absolute title to both income and capital.[1] The beneficiary is entitled to the entire equitable interest in the trust fund and his entitlement is not subject to any contingency. It is sometimes said that the trustee has no discretion in respect of the trust property other than the stewardship of that property on behalf of the beneficiary. However, the bare trustee is a fiduciary so that, for example, the rule against self-dealing and against making secret profits applies.[2] Further, a trust for a minor or an incapacitated person who is absolutely entitled to the property gives the trustees active duties to perform: for instance, in respect of the management and investment of the trust fund.

42.02   It remains uncertain how far, in the absence of express provision, a trustee is required to give effect to directions given by an absolute beneficiary of full age and capacity other than a direction to transfer the trust property to him or as he directs. A beneficiary of full capacity can direct the retirement of trustees[3] and give directions in relation to the insurance of trust property.[4] If

---

[1] This will not always be the case: there will be a bare trust if at the conclusion of the administration of an estate, property is held for A and B who are jointly absolutely entitled. Insurance companies produce a bare trust (for instance, as part of a discounted gift plan) which can be for any number of beneficiaries (who are given a fixed share of the totality).

[2] See Thomas & Hudson, *Law of Trusts*, OUP 2010 (2nd edn), para.1.27 and PCB, 2005, 226 and 336. See also *Lewin on Trusts* (18th edn), para.1–21.

[3] See TLATA 1996 ss.19 and 20.

[4] TA 1925 s.19(2).

the bare trustee holds shares in a company it is unclear whether he must vote in accordance with the directions of the beneficial owner who is of full capacity.[5]

A bare trust falls within the definition of a trust of land in s.1(2)(a) of **42.03** TLATA 1996. The trustees are entitled to deal with the property held under the trust as though its absolute owner.[6] It is also clear that at least parts of TA 1925 and TA 2000 apply to bare trustees.[7] Hence the trustees are under the statutory duty of care in s.1 of TA 2000. It has been suggested[8] that even where the beneficiary is of full capacity the trustees are also intended to have the general investment power under s.3 TA 2000 and possibly also the power to acquire land under s.8; the power to delegate to agents under s.11 and powers concerning remuneration under ss.28 and 29. The statutory powers of maintenance and advancement in ss.31 and 32 TA 1925 do not apply to an adult beneficiary but do apply to bare trusts for minors.[9] An absolute trust for a minor may be varied under VTA 1958.[10] To avoid any doubt on the question of what powers a bare trustee has it is sensible to set out the express powers and duties conferred on the trustee in the trust instrument.[11]

Take care where property is added to an existing bare trust and different beneficiaries are intended to benefit. For example if a disponer declares in 2007 that he holds 10 shares in X Limited for "all my children now living" and he has another child in 2008, he needs to execute a new declaration of trust if he wants to transfer more shares and include the new born child as a beneficiary. If he transfers the shares to "all my children living in 10 years' time" this creates a settlement and involves an IHT chargeable transfer.

II USES

Sometimes a bare trust is used where a donor wishes to transfer the property **42.04** immediately but there are formalities or restrictions which will delay (or event prevent) the passing of legal title, such as obtaining a consent or giving notice to a third party. This may happen in the case of shares in a private company which commonly cannot be transferred without obtaining the consent of other shareholders or until other shareholders have decided an option to purchase them. An effective transfer of the beneficial ownership can, however, still take place under a declaration of trust (if the articles do not prohibit this). A bare trust can therefore be used to transfer the beneficial interest immediately with legal title to follow later. If the property is registered land the beneficiary's interest may be protected on the land register by entry of the trustee restriction. Bare trusts have increasingly been used in connection with

---

[5] See *Re Kirkpatrick* [2005] NZHC 469 where it was held that there is no such obligation and compare *Re Castiglione's Will Trusts* [1958] Ch 549 at 558.

[6] TLATA 1996 s.6(1).

[7] See *X v A* [2000] 1 All ER 490.

[8] See *Lewin on Trusts* (18th edn), para.1–25.

[9] See *D v O* [2004] EWHC 1036.

[10] See *CD (A Child) v O* [2004] EWHC 1036 (Ch) and s.1(1)(a) of the 1958 Act which applies where capital is held for a beneficiary absolutely but the beneficiary cannot call for it only because he is a minor. In *CD v O* the judge authorised an application for the extension of the statutory power of advancement in a case where insurance policy proceeds were held on bare trust for the minor, deciding that he had sufficient jurisdiction to do this under VTA 1958.

[11] See A1.2.

discounted gift schemes and to hold the proceeds of life policies for persons others than the life assured.[12]

42.05 *"Blind trusts"* are usually bare trusts. They are used where an individual puts assets into a trust for himself on terms which allow the trustees to buy and sell trust assets as they see fit but without informing him. Such a trust is often used by a politician who will then not declare an interest in any of the assets in the trust given that s/he does not know at any time what assets are owned by the trust. A transfer into the bare trust is not a disposal for capital gains tax purposes if the disponer is the absolutely entitled beneficiary so does not trigger chargeable gains (it is a nothing). Nor is it a transfer of value for inheritance tax purposes.

III TAXATION OF A BARE TRUST

42.06 In general, the beneficiary of a bare trust should return the trust's income and gains on his personal tax return and the trustees are not required to make a return. Although the trustees may pay the tax due to HMRC on behalf of a beneficiary, it is the beneficiary who is chargeable to tax.[13]

Income tax

42.07 Prior to the FA 1999 changes (which came into force on March 9, 1999), bare trusts enabled a parent to avoid paying income tax on a minor child's income which was derived from property which he had settled on that child. During minority income was neither paid to or for the child's benefit nor accumulated in the formal trust sense[14] but was retained by the trustees until the child reached 18.[15] The child's personal allowance and lower rate bands could be set against the income. The income was not paid out to the child until 18 because he could not give a receipt, although it could be applied for his benefit. However, provided the income was not so used while the child was under 18, the provisions in TA 1988 s.660B (now ITTOIA 2005 s.629) which tax a settlor on his minor child's income from the settlement were not triggered.

42.08 Bare trusts created on or after March 9, 1999[16] no longer have these income tax advantages. From that date, if a parent settles property on a bare trust for a minor unmarried child then the income in excess of £100 per annum is taxed on the settlor (parent) as it arises.[17] Bare trusts already in existence at

---

[12] See Ch.47. Note also "sharing arrangements" which will normally involve a declaration of trust where the beneficial interest in property is held on trust for two or more owners in equal or unequal shares: see Ch.43.

[13] Subject to the parental settlement provisions: see ITTOIA 2005 s.629; Ch.7 and 42.07. See also TSEM 1030.

[14] Even if TA 1925 s.31 is not excluded, for income tax purposes if the beneficiary has an indefeasibly vested interest in the trust income and capital and the trustees have discretion over the use of income for the benefit of the minor and must accumulate the balance, it will still be a bare trust rather than a settled property. For an alternative, see A1.2.

[15] Or earlier marriage (or entering into a civil partnership) TA 1925 s.31(2)(i).

[16] As a result of FA 1999 s.64.

[17] See ITTOIA 2005 s.629, previously TA 1988 s.660B(1)(b) which refers to income which during

that date were unaffected although no property should be added since if it is added an apportionment of income is made on a just and reasonable basis. The income assessed on the settlor is taxed at his highest marginal rate but he is entitled to recover from the trustee the amount of tax so paid (although it has to be paid by him to HMRC first before he has a statutory right to reimbursement). "*Child*" is widely defined to include a step-child, an illegitimate child and an adopted child.

Capital gains tax

Despite the loss of income tax advantages on parental bare trusts, these trusts are still used by parents or grandparents in order to utilise the capital gains tax annual allowance of minors. This is particularly useful when a parent has a number of children. Because the property is held on trust "*for any person who would be [absolutely] entitled but for being an infant or other person under a disability*" it is not settled for CGT purposes.[18] Capital gains are therefore taxed as the child's gains with the benefit of a full capital gains tax exemption (£10,600 for 2011–12). The capital gains tax assessments must be made on the beneficiary in his tax district (not on the trustees) and he is responsible for self-assessment.   **42.09**

A disposal of assets into a bare trust is treated as a disposal to the beneficiary (unless the beneficiary of the bare trust is also the disponer, as in the case of blind trusts). Accordingly, if the trust assets are being held on trust for a beneficiary under a disability (e.g. a minor), there is no disposal when he reaches 18 and he can claim the assets because he is treated as having owned them throughout.   **42.10**

Hold-over relief is available on a gift of a business asset into a bare trust. The restrictions[19] on hold-over relief for trusts for dependent children ("settlor-interested" trusts) are only relevant if the property is settled and therefore do not apply to the bare trust.   **42.11**

It follows that if a parent sets up a bare trust for his minor child the trustee should not invest in high income-producing assets (since the income is taxed on the parent). But it is desirable to generate sufficient gains each year to use up the child's capital gains tax annual exemption.   **42.12**

EXAMPLE 42.1

> Trustees hold property on trust for Charlotte absolutely (she is aged eight). Because of her age, Charlotte cannot demand the property from the trustees until she is 18 but for CGT purposes she is treated as owning the assets in the trust fund. Compare the position if the trust deed provided for the property to be held on trust for Charlotte contingent upon

the life of the settlor is paid to or for the benefit of an unmarried child of the settlor or "would otherwise be treated ...as income of an unmarried minor child of the settlor": see Ch.7.

[18] See TCGA 1992 s.60 and 9.0.
[19] See Ch.18.

her attaining the age of 18. In these circumstances, Charlotte is not absolutely entitled to the property which is therefore settled property for capital gains tax purposes.[20] It does not matter that the trustees have a statutory (or express) power of advancement and can in fact take away her absolute entitlement if they exercise these powers before she is 18. Unless and until the trustees make a settled advance, the property is not settled property for CGT or IHT purposes.[21]

Inheritance tax

42.13   Is a bare trust for an infant beneficiary a settlement for inheritance tax purposes? If it is then after March 21, 2006 its creation will be a chargeable transfer.

EXAMPLE 42.2

> S declares that he holds a house on trust for his infant daughter D. Nothing is said about TA 1925 s.31 which therefore applies and enables trustees to use income for the benefit of the child and accumulate any surplus. If this creates a settlement for inheritance tax purposes, S has made a chargeable transfer and the trust is within the relevant property regime with 10-year and exit charges. By contrast, if the gift is treated as a gift to D absolutely (despite the trustees' discretion to withhold income under s.31) then S's transfer is a PET, namely an unsettled gift to the child.

Under IHTA 1984 s.43(2)(a), "settlement" is defined to include property held on trust to accumulate the whole or any part of the income or with power to make payments out of that income in their discretion.[22] If TA 1925 s.31 has not been excluded might this be sufficient to make the property settled on the basis that the trustees can withhold income or distribute it at their discretion? It is thought not since the accumulations belong to the infant's estate, i.e. the retention of income under TA 1925 s.31 is not an accumulation for s.43 purposes because the retention of income is more in the nature of an administrative power. Hence, even if TA 1925 s.31 is not excluded, a gift of property to "my infant son absolutely" will be a PET as an outright gift. After some hesitation, HMRC confirmed that a bare trust is not a settlement for IHT purposes.[23]

42.14   On the death of the beneficiary, the trust property (including any accumulations of income) is treated as the beneficiary's so that if the child dies (whether before or after 18) the funds form part of his estate for inheritance tax purposes.

42.15   If the child dies before the age of 18 the property will pass under the intes-

---

[20] See 9.09 and 12.05.
[21] See 42.16 and following.
[22] IHTA 1984 s.43(2)(b).
[23] See A2.321.

tacy rules, normally to the child's parents. After the age of 18 the fund will pass according to the will of the child (or his intestacy if there is no will). At 18[24] the child can call for the trust property to be transferred to him. If the child is handicapped, the effect of any bare trust on means-tested state benefits should be considered.

IV DEFERRING ABSOLUTE ENTITLEMENT

Bare trusts have increased in popularity following the FA 2006 changes in the inheritance tax treatment of settlements.[25] Donors need to bear in mind that the beneficiary is absolutely entitled and on reaching 18 can call for the trust property unless the trustees have previously exercised a power of advancement to defer vesting by making a settled advance. **42.16**

There would appear to be no reason why the trustees of a bare trust cannot exercise a power of advancement before a child reaches 18 to make a settled advance for his benefit which postpones the vesting of the capital although the trustees will need to justify using their powers in this way.[26] It will, therefore, be desirable for the bare trust to contain an express power of advancement, otherwise the trustees will be relying on the statutory power in TA 1925 s.32 which is limited to one half of the beneficiary's entitlement.[27] **42.17**

If the power of advancement is exercised in this way it will involve a disposal by the beneficiary for capital gains tax purposes since the property now becomes settled. Capital gains tax charges may arise if the asset shows a gain and it is not thought that hold-over relief is available since the trust is settlor-interested.[28] **42.18**

Does it constitute a chargeable transfer by the beneficiary for inheritance tax purposes? To be chargeable a transfer must be a transfer of value which IHTA 1984 s.3(1) defines as: **42.19**

> "*a disposition made by a person (the transferor) as a result of which the value of his estate immediately after the disposition is less than it would be but for the disposition.*"

There is no statutory definition of disposition. It is said to be an ordinary English word of wide meaning and can embrace any act by which ownership

---

[24] 16 in Scotland.

[25] See the precedent in A1.2. Most insurance companies have produced a discounted gift plan using a bare trust

[26] It is thought that the statutory power in TA 1925 s.32 will be implied and that an express power—permitting the advancement of 100 per cent of the child's interest—may be included in the trust document: see A1.2 cl.7. *Lewin on Trusts* (18th edn) at 1.34 confirms this but notes that once the child becomes 18 the power is destroyed so cannot be exercised after this date. See 1–25 and *Pilkington v IRC* [1964] A.C. 612 at 641.

[27] Note the Law Commission Consultation Paper published in May 2011 on ss.31 and 32 of TA 1925. The proposal there is to extend the power to pay or apply capital to or for the benefit of a trust beneficiary to the whole, rather than one-half, of the beneficiary's share of the trust fund. See also Ch.1.

[28] See Ch.18.

of property is lost.[29] In this case the beneficiary has not intentionally divested himself of his beneficial ownership of the property and it is not in his control; the relevant act has been done by the trustees. On that basis it might be argued that although there is a disposition it has not been made by the person whose estate is diminished and therefore there is no chargeable transfer by the minor. IHTA 1984 s.3(3) deems there to be a disposition:

> "*where the value of a person's estate is diminished and the value of . . . any settled property is increased by the first-mentioned person's omission to exercise a right.*"

However, it is difficult to see that the beneficiary has omitted to exercise a right. If the exercise of the power of advancement is not a chargeable transfer then there is no 20 per cent entry charge although any continuing trust will be taxed under the relevant property regime.[30] Unlike IHTA 1984 s.52 which imposes a tax charge if a qualifying IIP ends, whether or not voluntarily, there is nothing in the IHT legislation to impose a charge where the disposition is not effected by the owner. For the same reason it is not clear that the beneficiary is a settlor for IHT purposes. Although s.44 (the definition of settlor) includes any person who has provided funds, albeit directly, to the trust, the "provision" has not been made by the minor.

42.20   Do the reservation of benefit provisions apply? The beneficiary has not made a gift so FA 1986 s.102 is not in point. Nor is it clear that s.102ZA is in point: this only applies where (a) there is a termination of an individual's interest in possession in settled property and (b) (in relation to post-March 21, 2006 interests) the interest in possession is a transitional serial interest, IPDI or disabled person's interest. The interest that is ended by the trustees exercising the power of advancement is not an interest in *settled property* for inheritance tax purposes at all. If this analysis is right, the bare trust can be terminated just before the minor is 18 by exercise of a widened s.32 power of advancement. The property will then be held on relevant property trusts but there is no 20 per cent entry charge and no reservation of benefit by the minor. It is likely that HMRC will strongly resist these conclusions on the basis that the trustees are making a disposition on behalf of the minor and that is sufficient to trigger an entry charge!

42.21   For capital gains tax and income tax purposes HMRC consider that the minor beneficiary is the settlor. The CGT legislation provides that "*a person shall be chargeable to capital gains tax in respect of chargeable gains accruing to him*" without requiring the person to make the disposal himself. (They take a similar view where the court consents to a variation of trust on behalf of a minor beneficiary.)[31] For capital gains tax this no longer matters once the trust has been established because even if the relevant property settlement is settlor-interested there is no tax charge on the beneficiary in respect of trust gains. It does matter, however, if the assets being settled by exercise of the trustees'

---

[29] IHTA 1984 s.272 states that "disposition" includes a disposition effected by associated operations but says nothing further. See *Ward v IRC* [1956] A.C. 391 and see IHTM 4023. HMRC do not refer to the need for the transferor to have made the disposition.

[30] Unless it creates a disabled person's interest within IHTA 1984 s.89B.

[31] See CG 37902 and also *Mills v IRC* 49 TC 367 where a minor actress aged 14 had her earnings paid into trust.

powers of advancement show a gain and hold-over relief is therefore desirable: a hold-over claim is not possible on disposals to settlor-interested trusts.

For income tax purposes the beneficiary will often be entitled under the terms of the settled advance to receive all the income and therefore he is taxed on it as life tenant. The main difference if the beneficiary is treated as the settlor for income tax purposes is that no deduction is possible for trust management expenses so that the beneficiary is taxed on the gross income whether or not he receives all of it. He will also be taxable on any deemed income such as the proceeds of share buy-backs.[32]

---

[32] See Ch.7 for full discussion of income tax in ITTOIA 2005 s.624, and 17.34 for share buy-backs.

CHAPTER 43

TRUSTS AND HOUSES: CAPITAL GAINS TAX AND INHERITANCE TAX CONSIDERATIONS

I CAPITAL GAINS TAX—PRINCIPAL PRIVATE RESIDENCE RELIEF

Principal private residence relief

43.01 The capital gains tax exemption provided for in TCGA 1992 ss.222–226B is available on a gain arising on the disposal, by gift or sale of:

(i) a dwelling house which is the taxpayer's only or main residence, or

(ii) land held for occupation and enjoyment with that residence as its garden and grounds up to the permitted area. The permitted area is half a hectare or such larger area as is required for the reasonable enjoyment of the dwelling-house.[1]

This excludes from capital gains tax what for the majority of people is their most substantial asset.[2] The exemption is extended in certain circum-

---

[1] TCGA 1992 ss.222–224.

[2] In its interim report, recommending that the relief be retained, the Office of Tax Simplification commented that:

> "*4.4 The relief ensures that an individual can replace their home with another without the proceeds of sale from the first home being diminished by a charge to capital gains tax. When the relief was introduced in Finance Bill 1965 it was seen as an important concession for*

stances to include dwellings which are settled property lived in by one or more beneficiaries.[3]

Meaning of dwelling house and residence

The term dwelling-house is not defined in the legislation but its dictionary definition, *"a house occupied as a place of residence"*, has been approved by the Court of Appeal.[4] The term includes flats as well as houses and can include caravans with the necessary degree of permanence.[5] A distinction has been drawn between a residence and temporary accommodation. It appears that there must be some continuity of occupation intended if the house is to qualify for relief: the question is one of fact and degree.[6] The burden of proof is on **43.02**

> *owner-occupiers, not only to encourage home ownership as an attractive investment but also to assist both social and labour mobility.*
>
> *4.5 The rationale for the relief remains as valid today as in 1965, if not more so, as not only is the measure a simplification for many taxpayers but we would expect that without this relief the residential property market could stagnate.*
>
> *4.6 The repeal of this relief would potentially bring everyone who sells their main home within the charge, which could lead to an additional 800,000 individuals completing a self-assessment tax return (although some of these may already file a return)."*

[3] TCGA 1992 s.225: see 43.19.

[4] *Lewis v Lady Rook* [1992] STC 171 at 177.

[5] *Makins v Elson* [1977] STC 46 where the taxpayer bought land intending to build a house on it. In the meantime he lived on the land in a caravan. He never built the house and later sold both land and caravan at a profit. The caravan was held to be a dwelling house: it was connected to mains services, etc. Compare *Moore v Thomson* [1986] STC 170 where the court held that since there was no supply of water or electricity the caravan in question was not a dwelling house.

[6] See *Goodwin v Curtis* [1998] STC 475, CA where the taxpayer contracted to buy a farmhouse in 1983 but in March 1985 instructed agents to sell it. On April 1, 1985 he left his wife, completed the purchase and moved in. On April 3, 1985 the taxpayer completed the purchase of another property and on May 3, 1985 he sold the farmhouse and moved into the other property. The General Commissioners held that one month's residence did not mean he was entitled to the exemption. The nature, quality, length and circumstances of the taxpayer's residence did not establish the expectation of continuity. The Court of Appeal held that this finding was open to them on the facts. His occupation was a stop-gap measure. The taxpayer made a gain of over £100,000! More recently in *P Favell v HMRC*, FTT [2010] UKFTT 360 (TC), TC00642. a market trader (F) purchased a flat in 1999. He transferred it to his son in June 2003. In his tax return, he did not declare any gain on the disposal. HMRC issued an assessment charging CGT, and F appealed, contending that he was entitled to principal private residence relief under TCGA 1992 s.223(3) as he had occupied the flat during 2001 after temporarily splitting up with his partner, but had resumed living with her later in the year (and had subsequently married her). The First-Tier Tribunal reviewed the evidence and dismissed the appeal, observing that F had produced *"no documentary evidence (bills, bank statements, correspondence etc) to show that he had occupied the property"*. F had failed to discharge the burden of proof that the property had been his only or main residence.
A similar decision was reached in a subsequent case where the First-Tier Tribunal found that the appellant had never occupied an apartment as his main residence. See *A Metcalfe v HMRC, FTT* [2010] UKFTT 495 (TC), TC00753. Similarly see *Miss A Bradley v HMRC, FTT* [2011] UKFTT 49 (TC), TC00927. See also *JT Moore v HMRC, FTT* [2010] UKFTT 445 (TC), TC00710 where the taxpayer lived in a property for two months while renovating it. The First-Tier Tribunal reviewed the evidence and dismissed the appeal, finding that his fiancée had refused to live in the property and that M had never occupied it as his main residence. See also *M Springthorpe v HMRC, FTT* [2010] UKFTT 582 (TC), TC00832.

the taxpayer to show that he has occupied it as his residence, as the cases cited below show. Minimal occupation without any expectation of continuity (e.g. where the taxpayer is living in the property while renovating it with a view to onward sale), would not usually qualify.

Two or more units

43.03   A single dwelling-house may comprise several units. For example, country houses may have separate staff quarters, garages or stables. There is a substantial body of conflicting case law on when the relief is available and the question may be particularly relevant to trustees since large properties are often held in a trust.

The entity test

43.04   In *Batey v Wakefield*[7] a separate bungalow within the grounds of the taxpayer's house and used by a caretaker to enable him to perform the duties of his employment with the taxpayer was considered by the Court of Appeal to be exempt from capital gains tax on its sale. The fact that the bungalow was physically separate from the main dwelling house was considered to be irrelevant.

> "*A dwelling-house or a residence, can comprise several dwellings which are not physically joined at all.*"

This decision was followed in *Williams v Merrylees*[8] where it was noted by Vinelott J. that:

> "*what one is looking for is an entity which can be sensibly described as being a dwelling house though split into different buildings performing different functions.*" (the entity test)

The curtilage test

43.05   However, in *Markey v Sanders*[9] Walton J. ignored the entity test and suggested two alternative tests: *either* the buildings must be closely adjacent and occupation of the secondary building had to increase the taxpayer's enjoyment of the main house *or*, looking at the group of buildings as a whole, it must be possible to regard them as a single dwelling-house. In this case a staff bungalow 130 metres away from the main residence and standing in its

[7] [1982] 1 All ER 61.
[8] [1987] STC 445.
[9] [1987] STC 256.

own grounds was not closely adjacent and so could not be treated as part of a single residence.

The Court of Appeal reviewed these decisions in *Lewis v Rook*[10] where a cottage which had been occupied by the taxpayer's gardener some 200 yards from the main house was sold. The cottage was visible from the house so that the taxpayer could signal to the cottage if she wanted assistance. The Court reversed the High Court decision and concluded that no building could form part of a dwelling house that included the main house unless the building was *"appurtenant to and within the curtilage of the main house"* ("the curtilage test"). Hence, main residence relief was not available on the cottage. The entity test was rejected (even though it had previously been adopted by the Court of Appeal in *Batey*).

43.06

In *Honour v Norris*[11] the judge rejected as *"an affront to common sense"* the taxpayer's claim that a number of separate flats in a square could constitute a single dwelling house.

HMRC set out their approach in RI 75 (August 1994) and, unsurprisingly, they apply the curtilage test from *Lewis v Rook*. Their statement emphasises the smallness of acceptable curtilage that will qualify for relief. A wall, fence or road separating two buildings normally prevent them from being in the same curtilage.

However, the view that curtilage must necessarily mean a small area may not be correct. *Secretary of State for the Environment Transport and the Regions v Skerritts of Nottingham Ltd*[12] was an appeal against a listed building enforcement notice where the statute defined a listed building as including *"an object or structure within the curtilage of the building which forms part of the land."* The issue was whether a stable block was part of the curtilage of the main house. Robert Walker L.J. noted:

43.07

> *"in my respectful view this court went further than it was necessary to go [in a right to buy case Dyer v Dorset Country Council]*[13] *in expressing the view that the curtilage of a building must always be small or that the notion of smallness is inherent in the expression. No piece of land can ever be within the curtilage of more than one building, and if houses are built to a density of twenty or more to an acre the curtilage of each will obviously be extremely restricted. But Nourse LJ [in Dorset] recognised that in the case of what the now moribund Settled Land Act 1925 refers to as a principal mansion house . . . the stables and other outbuildings are likely to be included within its curtilage. I also respectfully doubt whether the expression curtilage can usefully be called a term of art. It is . . . a question of fact and degree."*

It can be dangerous to use a judicial interpretation of one statute in support of another, but nevertheless, these comments are suggestive that smallness is not a necessary characteristic in determining curtilage and that everything depends on the nature of the properties in question.

---

[10] [1992] STC 171.
[11] [1992] STC 304.
[12] [2001] QB 59; [2000] 3 WLR 511.
[13] [1988] 3 WLR 21.

More than one residence

43.08 When the taxpayer has two residences, only the property which is his main residence qualifies for relief. He can, however, elect by notice to his tax district for one to be treated as his main residence[14] but note that an election is a choice between residences: it cannot be made on a property that is not being used by him as a residence (e.g. a let property). The election must be made within two years of the acquisition of a second or subsequent residence[15] although it can be backdated by two years. Once made, a notice can be varied at anytime. In the absence of an election the question of which property is the main residence is a question of fact.

In the absence of an election, determining which property is factually the main residence can sometimes be difficult, particularly as the taxpayer now has to self-assess their position. No hard and fast rules can be laid down. In some cases the taxpayer may spend more nights in one house than the other (e.g. a flat in London occupied while the taxpayer is at work) but still regard his country house as his main home. CG Manual 64552 lists various criteria which it suggests are useful in deciding which is the main residence. Some of these are open to question. For example, it is suggested that the place to which the tax return or other third party correspondence is sent might be the main residence but often such correspondence will go to an office address and not a home address so sending it to one of two homes cannot be regarded as particularly significant! HMRC suggest the location of the individual's place of work is relevant but a second home may be bought precisely to ease a long commute.

Other factors listed in the Manual are in the authors' view more important, such as where the taxpayer keeps valuable items; where the family of a married person is based; where the taxpayer is registered to vote. One should look at where the taxpayer intends to return to on a regular basis or which property

---

[14] TCGA 1992 s.222(5).

[15] *Griffin v Craig-Harvey* [1994] STC 54. Each time there is a change in the individual's combination of residences a new period begins and there is a new opportunity to make a nomination. Where a dwelling house is acquired, the date on which there is a new combination of residences will not necessarily be the date of acquisition, it will be the date on which the dwelling house was first used as a residence. Similarly, where an individual ceases to use a dwelling house as a residence, the date on which there is a new combination of residences will be the date on which the dwelling house is no longer used as a residence, it will not necessarily be the date on which that dwelling house is disposed of. If two dwelling houses have been owned for more than two years but one of them has been let, the taxpayer can still make an election within two years of the second house ceasing to be let. This gives taxpayers the opportunity to make an election where more than two years has elapsed: let the second property out for a period, then cease to let it and occupy it again as a residence.
Example taken from HMRC manual
An individual has a single residence until April 1, 2008. On that date she acquired a dwelling house and immediately began to use it as a second residence. She has until March 31, 2010 to nominate which of these residences is to be treated as her main residence.
On November 23, 2008 she acquired another dwelling house and began to use it as a third residence on June 1, 2009. A new period for nominating begins on June 1, 2009 giving her until May 31, 2011 to nominate which of her three residences is to be treated as her main residence.
On September 30, 2009 she ceased to use one of her dwelling houses as a residence and subsequently disposed of it on November 30, 2009. A new period for nominating therefore begins on September 30, 2009; she has until August 31, 2011 to nominate which of her two remaining residences is to be treated as the main residence.

he would base himself in were it not for the demands of work or other commitments. The amount of time spent in each is not necessarily conclusive.

If a taxpayer owns one property and occupies the other under a tenancy **43.09** (rather than a licence) an election that the owned property is the main residence should be made to avoid potential problems although note the concession in the next paragraph. Similarly, if trustees own property which is occupied by a beneficiary who also owns or rents other property, an election should be made.

If a person owns a residence and rents another one under a tenancy not **43.10** merely a licence then it is a residence within s.222. However, the individual may not realise this and as such may be unaware that they must nominate which residence is to be treated as the main residence before the time limit for making a notice expires.

ESC D21 provides that where for any period an individual has, or is treated by the Taxes Acts as having more than one residence, but his interest in each of them, or in each of them except one, is such as to have no more than a negligible capital value on the open market (e.g. a weekly rented flat, or accommodation provided by an employer) the two-year time limit laid down by s.222(5)(a) TCGA 1992 for nominating one of those residences as the individual's main residence for capital gains tax purposes will be extended where the individual was unaware that such a nomination could be made. In such cases the nomination may be made within a reasonable time of the individual first becoming aware of the possibility of making a nomination, and it will be regarded as effective from the date on which the individual first had more than one residence.

Therefore, in cases where the interest in the second property has no more than a negligible capital value ESC D21 extends the time limit until a reasonable time after the person is first made aware that a nomination is needed.

EXAMPLE 43.1

(1) Trustees own a large mansion house occupied by the beneficiary and his family under the terms of the settlement. The beneficiary also owns a *pied à terre* in London. Factually the mansion house is the main residence but the beneficiary is likely to sell the London flat first. If an election is made by trustees and beneficiary on the mansion house it can be switched later to the flat. Even if the election on the flat is only for a period of one month, the last three years of ownership on the flat will be exempt.[16] So the mansion house loses one month of exemption but overall there is likely to be a tax saving for the beneficiary. Of course,

[16] CGTM 64510:

"*Two or more residences: Variation of a notice [May 2010]*"

A notice given under TCGA 1992 s.222(5) can be varied by a further notice at any time. The further notice can be backdated to be effective from up to two years from the date that it was given.

A variation will often be made when a disposal of a residence is in prospect or the disposal has already been made and the individual making the disposal wishes to secure the final period exemption. See CG64985+.

the beneficiary may decide that since the mansion house is never likely to be sold it is better to elect on the *pied à terre* for the entire period of ownership.

(2) Terry, a Swiss national, rents a flat in London where his family live and where he works but he also owns his family home in the Swiss Alps where the family spend all the holidays. It is not clear which is his main residence as a question of fact. D21 would allow him to make an election on the Swiss chalet even if the two-year period has expired. Note that if Terry also owned a house in the UK or France as well as renting the London flat, then D21 cannot be used to extend the two-year time limit.

Calculating the gain

43.11 No part of the gain accruing on the disposal of a dwelling house is chargeable if it has been the taxpayer's only or main residence throughout his period of ownership. If it has been his only or main residence during part of that time only a fraction of the gain is exempt. In calculating the gain, an individual's period of ownership cannot start before March 31, 1982. When he has acquired different interests in his residence at different times, his period of ownership is treated as starting with the first acquisition which would be taken into account in computing his allowable expenditure even if that interest did not in itself entitle him to live in the property.

"Permitted" periods of residence

43.12 Certain periods of non-residence are disregarded:

    (i) an individual who intends in due course to occupy a dwelling as his only or main residence may be treated as occupying it as a residence for such time as he is living in job-related accommodation[17];

    (ii) if the dwelling house was the individual's only or main residence at some time (but not necessarily immediately) before and after the period of absence and during the period of absence he had no other house eligible for relief, then the following periods of absence can be treated as periods when the residence was the only or main residence of the taxpayer even if it is let:

        (a) any period of three years. In practice, HMRC allow relief for three years even if there is a longer period of absence;

For example, where an individual with two residences validly nominates house A, they may vary that nomination to house B at any time. The variation can then be varied back to house A within a short space of time. This will enable the individual to obtain the benefit of the final period exemption on house B with a loss of only a small proportion of relief on house A."

[17] TCGA 1992 s.222(8).

(b) any period, however long, during which the individual works in an employment or office entirely outside the UK; or

(c) any period, not exceeding in total four years during which by virtue of a reasonable condition imposed by his employer he cannot live in his own house.

Business use and entrepreneurs' relief

If part of a dwelling-house is used exclusively for the purposes of a trade or business the gain must be apportioned and no principal private residence relief is due on that part of the gain.[18] Entrepreneurs' relief may be due if the taxpayer conducts his business from home and he has disposed of his entire business.[19] He must dispose of the house not more than three years following the disposal of the business.

43.13

EXAMPLE 43.2

Zac works as a lawyer from his home which is owned by his family trust. One quarter of the rooms are used exclusively for the purposes of the business. On sale in 2011 the trustees make a gain of £100,000. The CGT computation is as follows:

	£
Gain	100,000
Exempt as main residence[20]	75,000
Chargeable gain	25,000

The last three years

The last three years of ownership is exempt in any event (even if the individual is living elsewhere) if the property has been his main residence at any time during the period of ownership and in this case even if the actual residence occurred only before March 31, 1982, disposals will still qualify for the last 36 months exemption.[21]

43.14

---

[18] In the case of disposals before April 6, 2008, that gain did not qualify for full business assets taper relief and therefore the rate of tax was not 10 per cent as might have been expected. This was because TCGA 1992 Sch.A1 para.9 provided that where the asset was used for both business and non-business purposes the chargeable gain had to be apportioned on a pro rata basis into a business and non-business gain prior to the application of taper relief.

[19] See Ch.14.

[20] See 43.21 for trustees' main residence relief.

[21] The restriction of the period of ownership to the period since March 31, 1982 applies only to s.223, the section determining the amount of the relief, and not to s.222, the section which governs whether relief is available.

Letting exemption

43.15   Where the dwelling house has been let as residential accommodation a further relief may be available under s.223(4) TCGA 1992. This relief applies to a disposal after April 5, 1980 which attracts main residence relief. Relief is due under s.223(4) TCGA 1992 where:

(i)   a gain to which s.222 TCGA 1992 applies accrues to an individual; and

(ii)   part or all of the dwelling house has at some time in the owner's period of ownership been let as residential accommodation; and

(iii)   a chargeable gain arises by reason of the letting.

The amount of the relief is the lowest of:

(a)   the amount of private residence relief given by s.223(1)–(3) TCGA 1992; or

(b)   for disposals:

- April 6, 1980 to April 5, 1983 £10,000
- April 6, 1983 to March 18, 1991 £20,000
- from March 19, 1991 £40,000; or

(c)   the amount of the chargeable gain arising by reason of the letting.

If the property is held in the joint names of husband and wife, then in effect each of them can qualify for up to £40,000 letting exemption. There is no need to reoccupy the property after the period of letting.

EXAMPLE 43.3

Donald purchased a house in the Lake District in May 2000 for £100,000. He used this as his second home for five years. He elected for it to be his main residence for one year in May 2004. In May 2005 he let it for two years before transferring it into the joint names of himself and his wife and selling it in May 2010 for £500,000.

The total gain is £400,000 spread evenly over a period of ownership of 10 years, i.e. £40,000 pa.[22]

It was his main residence for one year by election. Therefore the last three years' ownership are exempt in any event. The two let years are also exempt since up to £80,000 of gain can be protected. The result is that six out of the 10 years are effectively exempt from capital gains tax leaving £160,000 gain chargeable at 18 per cent. If he had not made an election in May 2005 it would be worth Donald making an election within two

---

[22] Do not time apportion by reference to the actual increases over each period: the apportionment of gain is done evenly over the 10 years.

years after it ceased to be let. This enables him to access the last three years of ownership exemption and the letting exemption.

Garden and grounds

Land of up to half a hectare is exempt if it is used for the taxpayer's own occupation and for the enjoyment of his residence. Larger grounds can obtain relief if "*required for the reasonable enjoyment of the house, having regard to its size or character*".[23] Otherwise an apportionment of the gain must take place in relation to the excess land.   **43.16**

There is no definition of grounds but HMRC consider that land surrounding the residence and in the same ownership is grounds of the residence unless it is used for some other purpose such as agriculture or business. Land which has previously been used for business purposes can obtain relief if it constitutes garden or grounds at the time of disposal provided that it is for enjoyment with the house. Hence there is no relief on the sale of a part of a garden after the disposal of the house.[24]   **43.17**

EXAMPLE 43.4

> Trustees own a house with one acre of garden. The house is occupied by an elderly life tenant. The bottom half of the garden has been fenced off for development for some years and is overgrown. It will not qualify for relief even though within the permitted area. If, however, the trustees take down the fence and bring the land back into the garden (say) a year before the sale then on a disposal (whether of that land or of the house and garden) relief is available on all the gain.[25]

In the *Tax Bulletin* for February 1992 HMRC noted that, in general, land is treated as garden or grounds qualifying for relief if it is "*enclosed land . . . for ornamental recreation, surrounding or attached to a dwelling house or other building*".   **43.18**

A number of factual questions should be asked when considering the availability of relief on land of over half a hectare: is the excess acreage let? Is it being sold off and the house retained? How big is the house? What is the period, style and locality of house? Are there comparables? What is the historical association of the land with the house: has it been recently acquired? Has there ever been a time when the grounds were not part of the house? How

---

[23] TCGA 1992 s.222(2). The issue is one of fact: what is required for the reasonable enjoyment of the house as a residence. It is an objective test requiring one to look at the size and character of the dwelling house. The leading case is *Longson v Baker* [2001] STC 6 where the judge rejected a claim that paddocks could qualify on the grounds that the keeping of horses are not necessary in order to enjoy a house as a residence. In *Green v IRC* [1982] STC 485 HMRC accepted that grounds of 15 acres were required for the reasonable enjoyment of a mansion of 23,374 square feet.

[24] *Varty v Lynes* [1976] STC 508 and *Tax Bulletin* August 1994, Issue 12.

[25] See further the *Henke* case discussed at 43.20.

much would appear to be garden to the ordinary observer? Contemporaneous evidence is important and the owner should take photographs prior to the sale. It can be difficult to convince HMRC that all the extensive grounds are part of the house if an enquiry is made into the tax return over two years after the disposal and no evidence of the position is available. Access to the house may be denied by the new owners or the house may have been radically altered.

43.19   The word "grounds" is presumably intended to extend the concept beyond land which is specially cultivated or regularly tended to include paddocks and meadowland but this can be difficult if the land is in agricultural use. Are there obvious physical boundaries on the property or the beginnings of a wild area, e.g. by ditches or an abrupt change in ground level? Views of the garden from the house are important: do principal rooms face the gardens? What would a reasonable man require for his reasonable enjoyment?

43.20   The question of what land is comprised in the permitted area is seen as an objective test.[26] In *Newhill* the judge said:

> "*required does not mean merely that the occupiers of the house would like to have it or that they would miss it if they lost it . . . required means that without it there will be such a substantial deprivation of amenities or convenience that a real injury would be done to the property owner.*"

In *Henke v RCC*[27] a couple had jointly purchased a freehold plot of land comprising 2.66 acres. They built a house on the land which became their main residence in June 1993. In July 1995 they obtained planning permission for two houses to be built in front of the house and sold these plots in 1999 with the benefit of planning permission. At the time of sale the plots were part of the garden or grounds of the main residence. The houses were built after sale. It was held that the costs of building the original house could not be deducted in computing the gain on the sale of the plots unless reflected in the value of those plots. The permitted area test was to be applied by reference to what was required in the circumstances prevailing at the time of the disposal and was an objective test. The permitted area was not frozen for all time at the moment of purchase. There were two distinct tests for a house and a garden. In relation to a house, the test for principal private residence relief was "at any time". For land the test was whether it was a garden or ground *at the time of disposal*. The Special Commissioner agreed with the DV that in this case the permitted area was 2.03 acres and the apportionment of the sale proceeds of the plots should be on the basis of the respective size of the non-exempt and the exempt areas. A further apportionment was required because the house was built on the land after the land had been acquired and therefore the property had not been occupied as the principal private residence throughout the period of ownership. Again the test was objective. It is not what the taxpayer feels is necessary for his reasonable enjoyment but rather what area of land would a reasonable person require for reasonable enjoyment of the property. The fact that the DV had made a thorough review of comparable properties

---

[26]   *Re Newhill Compulsory Purchase Order* [1938] All ER 163. Note that any apportioned gain may be relatively small being attributed to the least proximate land area: see *Taxation*, February 8, 2001 p.429.

[27]   [2006] STC (SCD) 561.

and made an allowance for the fact that the Henke's main residence was larger than most held sway with the Special Commissioner.[28]

Trustees

Section 225 extends the CGT exemption to a residence which is settled property provided that the trustees satisfy the conditions as to ownership. The relief requires a claim by the trustees and is available if and to the extent that the conditions as to residence are satisfied by one or more beneficiaries who are entitled to occupy the house under the terms of the settlement. Any election between two or more residences has to be signed jointly by the trustees and the beneficiary.

43.21

EXAMPLE 43.5

An interest in possession trust owns a property occupied by Ruth, one of three life tenants. Her two brothers also have interests in possession but live in other properties. Principal private residence relief is available on the whole gain realised by the trust even though Ruth only has an interest in possession in one third of the settled property.[29]

Meaning of entitled to occupy under the terms of the settlement

It is not necessary that the beneficiary has an interest in possession in the settled property for the trustees to claim relief on the gain. In *Sansom v Peay*,[30] the trustees had a discretionary power to permit any beneficiary to occupy upon such terms as the trustees in their discretion thought fit. HMRC argued that the beneficiaries were occupying by licence of the trustees not under the terms of the settlement. However, it was held that:

43.22

> "*the beneficiaries were in occupation pursuant to the exercise by the trustees of a power expressly conferred by the settlement to permit those beneficiaries to go into occupation and remain in occupation. The trustees exercised that power, and the beneficiaries thereupon became entitled to go into occupation and to continue in occupation until the permission was withdrawn. The trustees never did withdraw permission until they required vacant possession in order to complete the exchange. Therefore looking at the matter at the date of the disposal, the beneficiaries were persons who, in the events which have happened were entitled to occupy the house and did occupy it under the terms of the settlement.*"

[28] The taxpayer appeared in person and did not appoint an expert to produce evidence on what could objectively be regarded as to permitted area.
[29] For an illustration of the generosity of the s.225 exemption, see Example 43.6.
[30] [1976] STC 494.

In other words, it suffices that the trustees exercise their discretion to allow occupation and the beneficiary's entitlement to occupy arose from the exercise of that discretion.

43.23   It is also accepted that a beneficiary can pay rent to the trustees to occupy a dwelling house and that this will not in itself prevent relief. For instance, trustees may charge rent to one beneficiary who occupies the house in order to compensate others who do not occupy.[31] However, the position might be different if say a beneficiary paid rent under a formal tenancy agreement.[32]

EXAMPLE 43.6

(1) Three brothers jointly own three cottages and each brother lives in one property as his main residence. The cottages are of unequal value. Each brother could settle his share of each property for the benefit of all three and obtain s.225 relief.[33]

(2) The Cunning family trustees own a cottage in Mortlake High Street which they intend to let commercially. The trusts are discretionary and include powers allowing the trustees to add to the class of beneficiaries. A tenant (Gullible) is found and enters into an assured short hold tenancy. The trustees add him to the class of beneficiaries and after the end of the tenancy sell the property claiming CGT main residence relief. It seems highly unlikely that this claim will succeed. Gullible's occupation derives solely from his tenancy: including him as a beneficiary of the trust is merely an attempt to secure the relief. It is not envisaged that he will in fact take benefits under the trust (indeed he will be excluded from the beneficial class once the tenancy ends).

(3) Miranda was the life tenant of a trust set up by her father and occupies a house which is her main residence. In 2007 the trustees terminated her life interest in favour of her son, giving him a transitional serial interest. In order to avoid a reservation of benefit problem[34] the trustees granted an assured shorthold tenancy to Miranda under which she pays a market rent for her occupation with the income going to her son. The rent is reviewed each year. In these circumstances it seems difficult to see how the trustees can continue to obtain main residence relief once her life interest has been terminated.[35]

43.24   There is no restriction of relief under s.225 where the trust is settlor-interested.[36]

---

[31] See CGTM 65448.

[32] See Example 43.6(3) below.

[33] Note there is no hold-over relief because the trust is settlor-interested. The creation of the settlement will be a chargeable transfer for IHT purposes.

[34] See FA 1986 s.102ZA and Ch.33.

[35] For restrictions on principal private residence relief for trustees and individuals where there has been a previous hold-over relief claim, see 18.71.

[36] Hence, one reason why reverter to settlor trusts became popular: the settlor could settle a house on trust for the occupying beneficiary and principal private residence relief would be available on a later sale: see 37.13 and Example 37.8. The CGT charge on the settlor in the case of a settlor-interested trust was abolished from April 6, 2008.

Capital gains tax problems may arise if a deceased leaves a share of the house **43.25** on discretionary trusts and his surviving spouse owns the other share benefi- cially and continues in occupation.[37] HMRC may raise a number of points:

(i) If there is no power in the will for trustees to allow a beneficiary to occupy the house, the conditions of s.225 are not satisfied because he is not occupying *"under the terms of the settlement"*. It might be argued, however, that where discretionary trustees acquire a half share in prop- erty by way of gift not purchase they have an implied power as a matter of general law to retain such property for occupation by a beneficiary if they so choose and so that the beneficiary is entitled to occupy under the terms of the settlement even if there is no express power in the will.[38]

(ii) The provisions of the TLATA1996 should be considered. In these cases the legal owner will usually be the surviving spouse and the discretionary trustees merely trustees of an equitable interest in the land (a sub-trust). Section 12 of this Act does not give them rights of occupation nor does it give the discretionary beneficiaries of the sub-trust such rights.[39] HMRC may therefore argue that the trustees of a sub-fund over land have no power to allow any beneficiary to occupy the trust property.

(iii) The surviving spouse occupies by virtue of his personal share and not as a result of his or her position as a beneficiary under the settlement.[40]

One response to these arguments is that if the trustees have an express power **43.26** under the will to allow a beneficiary to occupy the property then the fact that the relevant beneficiary also occupies for some other reason (e.g. personal ownership), makes no difference: relief is still due. The words in s.225 are *"has been the . . . main residence of a person entitled to occupy it under the terms of the settlement"*. A restrictive reading would suggest that the person has to be entitled as a matter of fact to occupy the house *by virtue of being a beneficiary* so that a nil rate band discretionary trust owning only a share in land would not qualify for relief. However, it is considered that these words should be read more widely so that provided the terms of the settle- ment permit a beneficiary to occupy the property, the fact that beneficiary occupies by virtue of some other interest does not matter. Similarly the fact that the trustees have no power to allow a beneficiary into occupation of the property is irrelevant.

---

[37] See 38.25 for the IHT issues concerning nil rate band trusts.
[38] Cf. *Re Power's Will Trusts* [1951] Ch 1074.
[39] Rights of occupation are only given to a beneficiary with an interest in possession under TLATA 1996 s.12.
[40] Where the trustees have sold the half share and a replacement property has been purchased, albeit that a half share is also owned by the surviving spouse, it is easier to argue that the trus- tees have positively exercised their discretions to confer benefits on the spouse and allow that spouse to occupy qua beneficiary; of course, HMRC might then argue the spouse has been given a qualifying interest in possession although this risk disappears if the new property is purchased more than two years after the death: see IHTA 1984 s.144 and 39.55.

Principal private residence relief and the rebasing election under Sch.7 para.126 FA 2008 for foreign domiciliaries

This is discussed further at 43.154.

Principal private residence relief for personal representatives

43.27   Where personal representatives dispose of a dwelling-house which, both before and after the testator's death, was occupied by a person who is entitled on death to the whole or substantially the whole, of the proceeds of sale from the house, either absolutely or for life, principal private residence relief was originally given by concession (see ESC D5). FA 2004 Sch.22[41] gave statutory force to the concession and provides that relief is available if the person or persons who occupied the house immediately before and after the death are together entitled to at least 75 per cent of the net proceeds of disposal. The relief is discussed further at 40.18.

EXAMPLE 43.7

> Charlotte and her brother Luke live in Charlotte's house. On her death Charlotte leaves the house to Luke who goes on living in it. The property has to be sold by the personal representatives to pay Charlotte's credit card bills. Any gain will be exempt under s.225A.

43.28   In some cases, where a sale of the property is in contemplation but the exemption is not available, it will be important that it is not the PRs who make the sale.

EXAMPLE 43.8

> (1) Bill dies leaving his house on IPDI trusts for his children Charlotte and Luke in equal shares.[42] Charlotte moves into the house immediately on his death but the house will have to be sold. If the executors sell the house, no principal private residence relief is due. Charlotte did not occupy the house before death and even if she had, she is not entitled to substantially the whole sale proceeds. However, if the house is assented to the trustees and they sell the house, principal private residence relief will be available on the entire gain even though Charlotte alone is in occupation.[43]

---

[41] Inserting s.225A into TCGA 1992.
[42] An IPDI trust confers an interest in possession: see 28.10.
[43] See Example 43.5.

(2) If Bill had left the house to his children outright and the personal representatives had vested the property in Charlotte and Luke they, as legatees, are deemed to acquire it at the time of death and at the probate value.[44] Then Charlotte who occupies (but not Luke) will obtain principal private residence relief on any later sale in respect of her share.

Capital gains tax on main residences in the context of divorce

See Ch.50.

II INHERITANCE TAX PLANNING: SOME GENERAL CONSIDERATIONS

In retrospect, the tax planning opportunities available for family homes before December 10, 2003 resemble a golden age: by contrast the current climate makes planning with the family home much more difficult. The first major change was the announcement in the Chancellor's Autumn Statement, delivered (rather late) on December 10, 2003, of the introduction of a pre-owned assets income tax charge.[45] This not only affected future schemes but also past schemes going back to 1986 when the reservation of benefit rules were introduced. The climate that now exists is hostile to "unacceptable inheritance tax planning" on the family home.

43.29

For many taxpayers, the family home is their major asset and one on which they particularly resent paying inheritance tax. Hence the keen demand for schemes that enable a taxpayer to continue to live in the home but to avoid inheritance tax on it when s/he dies.

43.30

Any professional adviser needs to exercise extreme caution before advising his client to carry out any tax planning with the family home. As far as possible IHT planning should take advantage of the statutory exemptions and reliefs since these are less likely to be attacked or changed. More aggressive planning may well (when discovered) provoke the wrath of an easily enraged Exchequer.[46] It is relatively easy for any Government to change the POA legislation so that income tax can be imposed on an "unacceptable" tax scheme.

Safe inheritance tax planning

Check that the basic IHT exemptions and reliefs (annual exemption; small gifts, and PETs) have been used. Making larger gifts is still possible provided

43.31

---

[44] TCGA 1992 s.62(4).
[45] See Ch.34 for the POA charge. See below for HMRC's change of heart on home loan schemes.
[46] The change of heart and attack on home loan schemes illustrates the difficulties that may arise: see 43.37.

that the donor retains no benefit or interest in the gifted property and that the gift is (generally) outright rather than into trust. More interesting is the normal expenditure out of income exemption which, the courts have decided, has a wider application than had originally been thought to be the case. For a taxpayer in his 50s with substantial surplus earnings it is to be recommended as a way of controlling the growth in value of his estate.[47]

Business property and farming can attract IHT relief at 100 per cent irrespective of the value of the enterprise. This is a crucial valuation relief and should be safeguarded at all costs.[48] For instance, it is important not to depress the value of business property by raising mortgages against it,[49] or to rush into inter vivos tax planning when full relief will be available on death.[50] A well-drafted will may provide a reasonable solution for the married couple.[51] The authors feel that the following arrangements—some of which are considered in detail below—can be considered "safe" in the context of the family home:

(i) sharing arrangements for the family home[52];

(ii) cash gifts taking advantage of the seven-year "window"[53];

(iii) tax planning via deeds of variation[54];

(iv) commercial sales (equity releases)[55];

(v) flexible will planning; and[56]

(vi) carve outs involving qualifying interest in possession trusts.[57]

The family debt scheme

43.32 Typical of more aggressive planning is the following arrangement, a variant of the home loan scheme, between spouses.

---

[47] See IHTA 1984 s.21 and see *Bennett v IRC* [1995] STC 54 and *McDowell v IRC* [2004] STC (SCD) 362. However, gifts made under the normal expenditure out of income exemption are potentially within the POA Regime. Such gifts can avoid an entry charge if settled on trust and if substantial sums are involved consider the use of pilot trusts: see Chs 41 and 55.

[48] Note the development of schemes to utilise the relief based on investing in a portfolio of AIM shares: see generally Ch.45.

[49] See IHTA 1984 s.162(4).

[50] A good example is a gift by a farmer of his farmland and retention of the farmhouse. On his death, because the house is no longer to be a farmhouse, relief will not be available: see *Rosser v IRC* [2003] STC (SCD) 311.

[51] See Ch.38.

[52] See 43.94.

[53] See Ch.34 and 43.116.

[54] Ch.39.

[55] See 43.126.

[56] 43.85 and 38.54.

[57] See 43.85 and see in particular Examples 43.14 and 43.15.

EXAMPLE 43.9

Tobias owns a private investment company, the shares of which show a large unrealised capital gain. Ultimately he intends to give the shares to his children and grandchildren but for the present wishes to continue to run the business; retain the company dividends while getting the value of the shares out of his estate.

He sells the shares at market value to his wife Ruth. The purchase price is left outstanding as a debt owed by Ruth, which is repayable on the last of them to die. Tobias gives the benefit of the debt to his children/grandchildren.

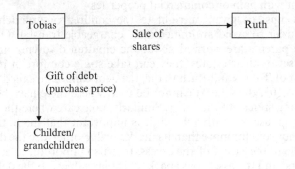

The tax consequences are:

(i) stamp duty is payable by Ruth on the price payable for the purchase of the shares[58];

(ii) there is no capital gains tax payable by Tobias on the disposal of the shares because under TCGA 1992 s.58 the sale to his spouse is treated as taking place at no gain no loss;

(iii) generally the POA Regime does not apply because the transfer is to a spouse (the fact it is a sale not a gift does not matter). A further reason for the Regime not applying is because the charge on intangible property (such as shares) only applies if the property is settled;

(iv) for inheritance tax purposes, the sale to Ruth is a non-event. Even if it is at undervalue, the gift element is spouse exempt (assuming that she is UK domiciled) and so outside reservation of benefit (FA 1986 s.102(5)). The properties are part of Ruth's estate but subject to a debt in favour of the children/grandchildren.[59] On Ruth's death the properties can pass to Tobias if he is still alive subject to the debt. On the last of Tobias and Ruth to die, the debt is repayable. Tobias has made a PET of the debt;

---

[58] The family debt scheme can be used for any type of property (including the family home) but bear in mind that SDLT is now payable at a top rate of 5%. Stamp duty for the shares is at a rate of only 0.5%.

[59] It is of course critical that the debt is deductible on Ruth's death and hence FA 1986 s.103 needs to be born in mind: see 33.27.

provided that he survives seven years there is no inheritance tax on the gift. In any event, there may be a discount on the value of the PET of the debt given that it is not repayable until the death of Tobias and Ruth;

(v) there may be capital gains tax or income tax repercussions on the eventual repayment of the debt, depending on how it is structured[60];

(vi) any dividends arising from the shares is paid to Ruth but may be taxed as Tobias' under the settlement provisions.[61]

43.33 A variant of this scheme would involve a sale of the family home by Tobias to Ruth. Although the property continues to be occupied by Tobias, the transfer to Ruth is an excluded transaction for POA purposes[62] and outside reservation of benefit.[63] The scheme can also be adapted for other assets such as equities pregnant with gain or commercial properties.

43.34 The debt must be given outright to the children or grandchildren (not settled) in order to avoid an immediately chargeable transfer. On the other hand if the parents are worried about the children divorcing and the loan being an asset of their estates, they can take some comfort in the fact that until the last of Tobias and Ruth to die, the debt cannot be called in. Because of FA 1986 s.103, the scheme cannot be used where there have been gifts by the purchasing spouse to the other. Similarly, take care where the asset being sold to one spouse is jointly owned: it is important that the house or other property is not sold for more than its market value otherwise the debt will not be deductible to the extent of the excess. It is also important to ensure that if Ruth dies first and the assets pass back to Tobias subject to the debt that does not involve Tobias taking on any personal liability since otherwise s.103 will apply and a deduction will not be available on his death.

43.35 In practice a major issue is to decide the terms of the debt owed by Ruth. Given HMRC's views on the scope of reservation of benefit it should not be repayable on demand but (say) only after the death of Ruth and Tobias. But should it carry interest and/or be index-linked? For simplicity neither[64] which will mean:

(i) that the value of the PET of the debt is substantially discounted;

(ii) that the base cost of the debt in the hands of the children/grandchildren will be correspondingly low so giving rise to the risk of a substantial CGT charge if it is a chargeable asset[65];

(iii) that the gift is of the current value of the shares. If it is desired to deal with future increases in value then consider combining a share freezer[66] scheme with the family debt arrangement.

---

[60] See further 43.35.
[61] See Ch.7.
[62] FA 2004 Sch.15 para.10(1)(b).
[63] FA 1986 s.102(5).
[64] This avoids income tax on the interest when paid (and HMRC may claim that any increase due to indexation is interest) and also problems later if the scheme has to be dismantled, e.g. on the divorce of the spouses.
[65] For ways of dealing with the CGT problem, see 43.00.
[66] Typically this will first involve issuing bonus growth shares and freezing the value of the existing shares.

A spoiler warning

The family debt scheme involves aggressive (some would say artificial) IHT **43.36**
planning and is precisely the sort of arrangement that successive governments
have sought to prevent. It is closely related to the home loan scheme on which
the Revenue's views have significantly changed. The "new approach" is that
none of these schemes work and they have advanced a number of arguments
as to why this is so.[67] Some of these have no application to the family debt
scheme (since they are concerned with the trusts used in the home loan scheme
which are not replicated in the family debt scheme) but it is to be expected that,
in the current climate, the family debt scheme will be challenged when HMRC
have a suitable case. This is therefore planning for the brave (some would say
for the reckless or foolhardy!).

III THE FATE OF PAST SCHEMES

The main schemes involving the family home were: *Ingram*[68]; *Eversden*[69]; **43.37**
home loan (double trust) and reversionary leases. Although each could take
a number of different forms, most are now caught by POA and so are likely
to be used only in limited circumstances now even if they still work for IHT
purposes. However, note that both *Ingram* and reversionary lease schemes
still have an important role to play in the context of an IPDI trust, e.g. where
husband dies leaving his house on interest in possession trusts for his spouse.
This is discussed further at 43.82 onwards, see also 33.27.

Ingram schemes[70]

Land was divided into different interests and the taxpayer retained a lease **43.38**
which gave him a continued right to occupy the property and give away the
encumbered freehold interest in the land (a "shearing operation").

Divisions of land can be horizontal (as in *Ingram* schemes when a single **43.39**
property is being carved into different slices) or vertical. In *Ingram*, Lord
Hoffmann referred to the history of the reservation of benefit legislation and
noted that the decided cases showed that although its provisions prevent a
donor from *"having his cake and eating it"*, there is nothing to stop him from
"carefully dividing up the cake, eating part and having the rest". He decided the
appeal on the assumption that the lease granted by the nominee (to whom

---

[67] See 43.53.
[68] *Ingram v IRC* [1995] 4 All ER 334; on appeal [1997] 4 All ER 395, CA, reversed [1999] STC 37
HL. See 22.18, 43.42 and 43.85.
[69] *IRC v Eversden* [2003] STC 822.
[70] See Ch.22. For the continued use of such arrangements when a property is settled by will on a
flexible IPDI trust, see 38.54 and in more detail the arrangements described at 43.85 onwards.
Ingram schemes are still be used in the context of an elderly life tenant occupying a house held
in an interest in possession trust. POA problems do not then arise for the reasons set out at
43.85 onwards.

Lady Ingram had transferred the property) came into existence only at the time when the freehold was acquired by the trustees.[71] The trustees never acquired the land free of Lady Ingram's leasehold interest.[72]

43.40   Amending legislation came in the form of new ss.102A–102C inserted into FA 1986.[73] For these provisions to apply:

(i) there must be a gift of an interest in land. Hence, gifts of chattels are not caught nor are sales of a freehold interest subject to a retained lease;

(ii) the donor must retain *"a significant right or interest to the land"* or be party to a significant arrangement in relation to the land.[74]

43.41   Schemes that were carried out before March 9, 1999 are accepted as effective for inheritance tax purposes but when the donor dies the following problems may arise:

(i) *What value is to be attributed to the retained lease?* A lease for more than 21 years gives the donor rights of enfranchisement or possession on expiry of the term which will increase its value. Even if there is no right to enfranchise, the fact that the lease may be non-assignable does not mean it has no value. What has to be valued is what the hypothetical purchaser would pay to have rent-free occupation for the remaining term subject to the same covenants against alienation and the same covenants as to repair.[75] HMRC usually raise two arguments: that there is a special purchaser and that the lease has some marriage value. The donee of the freehold has an interest in purchasing the property and to that extent can be counted as a special purchaser. However, he may have no resources

---

[71] The consequences of such a "contemporaneous carve-out" involved a consideration of the estate duty case of *Nichols v IRC* [1975] STC 278, CA which had concerned a gift by Sir Philip Nichols of his country house and estate to his son, Francis, subject to Francis granting him an immediate leaseback. Goff J., giving the judgment of the Court of Appeal, concluded that such an arrangement involved a reservation of benefit by Sir Philip:

> ". . . we think that a grant of the fee simple, subject to and with the benefit of a lease-back, where such a grant is made by a person who owns the whole of the freehold free from any lease, is a grant of the whole fee simple with something reserved out of it, and not a gift of a partial interest leaving something in the hands of the grantor which he has not given. It is not like a reservation or remainder expectant on a prior interest. It gives an immediate right to the rent, together with a right to distrain for it, and, if there be a proviso for re-entry, a right to forfeit the lease."

In the event the *Nichols* case fell to be decided on the basis of the covenants given by the son in the lease in which he assumed the burden of repairs and the payment of tithe redemption duty, and which amounted to a reservation. The wider statement of Goff J. quoted above to the effect that a leaseback must *by itself* involve a reservation constituted the main authority relied upon by HMRC in *Ingram* (and the comment that the *Munro* case involved a "prior independent transaction" which had subsequently been widely debated). See further the *Buzzoni* case considered at 43.87.

[72] He also noted that a nominee lease was valid as a matter of English law for reasons given by Millet L.J. in the Court of Appeal.

[73] By FA 1999 and taking effect from March 9, 1999.

[74] See further the analysis of a reversionary lease scheme, 43.85.

[75] IHTA 1984 s.160 provides that the market value is the price which the property might reasonably be expected to fetch in a hypothetical sale if sold on the open market at that time.

to fund that purchase. HMRC have also argued that a proportion of the vacant possession premium or marriage value should be allocated to the lease;

(ii) *CGT charge on a sale of the property:* the CGT death uplift will only apply to the leasehold interest. The encumbered freehold is likely to have a low base cost and will not benefit from CGT main residence relief given that the donee does not occupy the property. *Ingram* schemes were, of course, ideal in cases where there was no intention that the family home would ever be sold;

(iv) From April 6, 2005, the pre-owned assets income tax charge will apply given that:

    (a) the donor is in occupation of land; and

    (b) the disposal condition is met in respect of that land.

EXAMPLE 43.10

In 1998, Alexis retained a 20-year, rent-free lease in Blackacre and gave the encumbered freehold to her daughter. Assume that on the POA "valuation date" the value of the interest disposed of (the freehold) is £750,000 and the value of the "relevant land" (the freehold with vacant possession) is £1.5 million. Assume further that the rental value[76] is £15,000 pa. Applying the formula:

R = £15,000

DV = £750,000

V = £1,500,000

Alexis' benefit for POA purposes is therefore £7,500 so that if she is a higher rate taxpayer she will suffer income tax of £3,000.

The benefit is taxed each year whilst Alexis continues to occupy the land. The first "valuation date" was April 6, 2005 with a revaluation required on April 6, 2010.

Practical advice on Ingram schemes in the light of FA 2004 Sch.15

There are limited options open to the taxpayer who has effected an *Ingram* scheme:

    43.42

Option 1: pay the income tax charge: this will either be 40 or 50 per cent (for most individuals) of a full rent for the property but with a discount which aims to reflect the value of the retained lease. In fact, the DV/V valuation method may not truly reflect the value of the lease in the taxpayer's estate (see Example 43.10 above). Given that more than seven years have elapsed since the scheme

---

[76] Calculated in accordance with the provisions of FA 2004 Sch.15 para.5.

was carried out[77] so that the PET of the freehold is outside the IHT net and the taxpayer (or his family) can afford to pay the income tax this may be the best option especially if the taxpayer is in poor health. Bear in mind the following:

(a) The rental value is arrived at on the assumption that the letting is with vacant possession. However, the house may be in need of modernisation and not easy to let. In these circumstances the rental value will be reduced. In arriving at the rent the valuer shall assume that the donor pays all those expenses normally paid by the occupier and the donee bears the costs of repairs and buildings insurance. (The fact that this may not actually be the case does not matter: it is a hypothetical valuation.)

(b) The valuation of the freehold reversion will not take into account marriage value. It should consider the terms of the lease and especially that the lessee is able to live in the property rent-free. A typical *Ingram* scheme was for 15 years, and so if the lease was granted in 1999 it will expire in 2014. The donor will have no right to occupy beyond that date. In these circumstances it may be that the freehold reversion will only be discounted from the vacant possession value on the 2010 revaluation by a relatively small percentage (but, of course, each case will depend on its own facts). The owner of the freehold reversion is not generally required under the terms of the lease to carry out improvements which will increase the value of the property and therefore the DV element.

Option 2: cease to occupy the property: if it is desired to retain the IHT advantage but not pay income tax this is one way out. Of course, alternative accommodation will need to be found! Before surrendering the lease consider carefully the tax implications. For instance, if the lease is assigned to the freeholder (or surrendered) has there has been a disposition of the freehold interest by associated operations at the point of surrender? If so this might be disastrous in IHT terms.[78]

A slightly less radical alternative would be for the donor to occupy part only of the property (e.g. a cottage on the estate). In these circumstances HMRC accept that the income tax charge is limited to the property occupied.

Option 3: donor pays rent or equivalent: there are two options. The first is for the donor (say Alexis) to assign or surrender her lease. She would then no longer have any rights of occupation so that to avoid a reservation of benefit she would need to pay full consideration for that occupation.[79] Such arrangements might not involve paying the same rent as would be due under a commercial assured shorthold tenancy. Instead, the donor could take on responsibility for repairs etc under a tenants repairing lease and reduce the rent payable. Independent valuations should be obtained by both parties. This arrangement is also outside the POA Regime.[80] There is no need for the donor to self-assess nor to obtain valuations of the DV/V figure. Any payments made

---

[77] It is assumed that no new *Ingram* schemes of unsettled property have been carried out since 1999.
[78] This is discussed further in the context of chattel schemes: see Ch.44.
[79] See FA 1986 Sch.20 para.6(1)(a).
[80] FA 2004 Sch.15 para.11(5)(d).

will, of course, be taxable as income in the donees' hands (with a deduction for the usual landlord's expenses).

The alternative option to avoid the POA charge is for Alexis to make payments to the donees *"in pursuance of a legal obligation . . . in respect of the occupation of the land"*.[81] The section does not refer to the payments being rent. Under the terms of the lease the donor is under no legal obligation to pay for her continued occupation; she has a right to occupy rent-free. However, she could put herself under a legal obligation by covenanting with the donee that for as long as she occupies the property she will make payments to him by deed of covenant. Such payments will reduce her POA charge. So if the appropriate rental value is £15,000 and she paid £10,000 under the deed of covenant, she would only be chargeable to POA income tax on £5,000.

Entering into a deed of covenant involves a gift for IHT purposes by the donor because she has no need to do this, having a right to occupy under the lease. However, such payments may fall within the normal expenditure out of income exemption or will be PETs (assuming that the freehold was not gifted into a trust). The payments that she makes under the deed of covenant are not taxable income in the hands of the donee since they are annual payments and so outside the income tax net.[82] Nor are the payments "rent" because no letting business is being run. The donees should self-assess on this basis. Of course, this option depends on the donor being prepared to pay much larger sums to the donees. Instead of paying 40 (or 50 per cent) of the rental value to HMRC she is paying the rental value itself to (say) the children. A difficulty with this arrangement is that if the freehold is held in a trust, payments under the deed of covenant to the trustees might be regarded as additions to a settlement and, after March 21, 2006, may be chargeable transfers unless they come within the normal expenditure out of income exemption.[83]

Option 4: use the election to opt into the reservation of benefit rules: for the individual wishing to remain in occupation of the property and unable/unwilling to pay the income tax charge, making the election was an option. The person who will eventually end up suffering the IHT is the donee. All the IHT savings are lost! For existing schemes the election had to be made by January 31, 2007.[84]

Option 5: take advantage of reverter to settlor relief: before December 5, 2005 the donee could settle their freehold reversion to an interest in possession trust for Alexis and retain the remainder interest. SDLT was not payable although capital gains tax on the disposal of freehold interest was likely. The carve-out ceased and the donor (Alexis) was treated as owning the freehold reversion by virtue of her interest in possession. As a result she reserved a benefit in the property (the reversion) which she had gifted, but the wording of FA 1986 s.102(3) resulted in the reservation of benefit rules being disapplied because of the interest in possession which she enjoyed even though that interest was not taxed on Alexis' death because of reverter to settlor relief. This also, if carried out before December 5, 2005, was exempt from the POA charge.[85]

---

[81] See FA 2004 Sch.15 para.4(1).
[82] ITTOIA 2005 s.727.
[83] See comparable options for leases involving chattels in Ch.44.
[84] But the machinery was defective: see Ch.34.
[85] FA 2004 Sch.15 para.11(1).

This option is no longer available with the closing of the POA loophole[86] and because after the FA 2006 changes it is no longer possible to set up a qualifying interest in possession reverter to settlor trust. This option is accordingly now a non-starter.

Option 6: buying-back the freehold: if Alexis has sufficient resources she could buy back the freehold reversion at market value. Then the entire relevant property (the land) becomes part of her estate and there is no POA charge. The inheritance tax savings are preserved except that the donees now own cash rather than the freehold interest. She would have to pay SDLT on the purchase of the reversion. There may also be capital gains tax for the donees to pay on the sale of the freehold interest (assuming it shows a gain) and, of course, it will not be possible to effect the transaction by leaving the purchase price outstanding as a debt.[87]

Eversden arrangements[88]

43.43   A typical scheme was as follows:

EXAMPLE 43.11

> In May 2003, John settled his house then worth £800,000 on flexible interest in possession trusts for his wife Emma. After six months, Emma's interest in possession was terminated as to 95 per cent of the property with her children then taking revocable interests in possession which conferred rights of occupation (albeit they might choose not to exercise such rights). John and Emma continue to occupy the property.

Diagrammatically the position was then as follows:

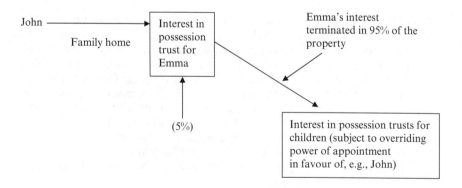

---

[86] From December 5, 2005: see Ch.34.
[87] Because the debt would be disallowed under FA 1986 s.103.
[88] See Ch.22 for a full description of the case.

Tax effects

On a sale of the house during the parents' lifetimes, any gain would qualify for principal private residence relief under TCGA 1992 s.225 because the occupation of the property was by a beneficiary of the trust.[89] In respect of John, the reservation of benefit rules did not apply because of FA 1986 s.102(5) (exempt gifts to spouses).[90] Once Emma's interest in possession was terminated she made an IHT transfer of value[91] which was a PET. She therefore needed to survive seven years for the full IHT savings to be secured. It was not, however, considered that she made a gift (so that the reservations of benefit provisions were not in point even though she continued to benefit from the settled property).[92] New *Eversden* schemes were for all practical purposes stopped from June 20, 2003 by amendments to the reservation of benefit rules and any arrangements completed before that date are caught by the POA Regime.

43.44

Options to avoid the POA income tax charge on Eversden schemes

Option 1: leave the structure in place: if Emma's interest has not yet been terminated it may be sensible to leave the structure in place and do nothing to end it. If the settlor (John) dies, then the spousal interest can be terminated (in part) by the trustees. The POA regime will not apply to the spouse because she has not made a disposal of land[93] and it cannot apply to the settlor because he is dead.

43.45

What happens if Emma dies before John with her interest in possession unrevoked? The POA regime can then never apply to John because the exclusion protects him permanently once Emma has died. The spouse might want her share to pass back to the settlor on revocable interest in possession trusts to avoid an IHT charge on her death.[94] Can the trustees carry out IHT planning at that point, terminating the settlor's interest in possession in part after the death of Emma without a reservation of benefit if he continues in occupation?

---

[89] See 43.26.

[90] See Ch.33.

[91] Under IHTA 1984 s.52.

[92] This is thought to be the case even if she had to consent to the termination of her interest in possession. FA 1986 s.102ZA changed the position in respect of terminations after March 21, 2006. See 22.09 and Ch.33.

[93] Curiously HMRC do not explicitly confirm in the examples in Appendix 1 of the POA Guidance Notes (see A2.62) that it is John rather than Emma who suffers the income tax charge. However, it is not thought that the spouse herself makes a disposal of land for POAT purposes. She may, as the interest in possession beneficiary, have an interest in land (following TLATA 1996 s.12) but if the trustees have terminated her interest in possession she has not made a disposal in the same way that she has not made a gift. Otherwise both settlor and spouse will have made disposals of land and could be caught by the POA Regime and curiously the spouse whose interest has been terminated would not be protected even if the interest in possession trust had been set up after June 20, 2003 because she has made no gift and the reservation of benefit rules do not apply to her. The authors, though, have seen practitioners (wrongly) concerned that the spouse is the person subject to the POA Regime if her interest has been terminated. This is not so; it is the settlor who is caught by the Regime. The spouse has made no disposal for POA purposes.

[94] This interest will be a TSI so that the spouse exemption applies provided that the interest arises on Emma's death.

Prior to March 22, 2006, if the original gift into trust had been made prior to June 20, 2003, the trustees could do this. The fact that the settlor's interest terminated after June 20 (but before March 22, 2006) would not appear to have lost the settlor the inheritance tax protection of FA 1986 s.102(5)(a) in respect of his original gift into trust. However, s.102ZA treats the termination of his life interest as a gift of "the no longer possessed property" and therefore that termination is a new gift by John *as life tenant*. That gift will not be protected by the spouse exemption available on the original transfer into trust. In order to avoid a reservation of benefit by John, if he continues in occupation it is necessary for only part of his interest in possession to be ended. In addition, the children in whose favour the gift occurs would need to occupy the property with John. He can then claim the protection of s.102B(4). Alternatively consider the possibility of an *Ingram* style carve-out as outlined in 43.82 onwards below.

43.46   *Option 2: appoint the house back to John*: if Emma's interest in possession has not yet ended and is now terminated, the trustees could appoint the house back to the settlor, John, to avoid the POA charge. Of course, this means that there is a potential double IHT charge on the value of the house if Emma dies within seven years (the house is in John's estate and Emma has made a failed PET). Emma should not be caught by s.102ZA[95] because her deemed gift on the termination of her life interest is protected by s.102(5)(a)—spouse exemption.

If Emma's interest in possession has been ended and the children now have revocable pre-March 2006 qualifying interests in possession in 95 per cent of the property and the trustees revoke their interests and appoint back the 95 per cent to John and advance the whole property out (95 per cent to John outright and the five per cent retained by Emma to her outright) then the reverter to settlor exemption is available so that the children are not treated as making PETs.[96] The trust has ended but main residence relief is available under TCGA 1992 s.225. The children are treated as making gifts under s.102ZA and must therefore not benefit from the gifted property. In practice this is unlikely to prove a problem.

43.47   *Option 3: pay the income tax charge*: if John (the settlor) is ill it may be worth preserving the IHT advantages and, if necessary, paying the income tax charge. If the value of the house is £800,000 and its rental value is £25,000, John would be taxed on:

$$£25,000 \times \frac{DV}{V\ (£800,000)}$$

The unknown figure is DV: what is the value of the interest disposed of by John? In the above example John owned and disposed of the entire house. Where the spouses owned it jointly and John disposed of only his half interest a significant discount would be available to reduce the DV figure. Following the decisions in *Arkwright* and *Price*,[97] it appears IHTA 1984 s.161(4) has no application and that the value of a half share in a house owned by spouses is

---

[95] See Ch.33.
[96] See IHTA 1984 s.53(3) and (4). The appointment to John must be absolute: for reverter to settlor trusts, see Ch.37.
[97] *Arkwright (PRs of Williams, Deceased)* [2004] EWHC 1720 (Ch); [2004] STC 1323; *Price v RCC* [2010] UKFTT 474 (TC).

not necessarily a mathematical one half of the vacant possession value of the property.[98] In any event, there is nothing comparable to s.161 in Sch.15 and so the general principles of valuing a share (which may result in a discount) will apply. So if John had owned and given away a 50 per cent share of the house, the value of his interest (DV) might be discounted to £340,000, the chargeable amount would then be £10,625, giving rise to a tax liability (for a 40 per cent tax payer) of £4,250 pa. This might be thought an acceptable price to pay to preserve the IHT advantage. Where John gave away the entire house (as in the above example) no discount on the DV figure will be available.

Option 4: *making the election*: should John have made the election into **43.48** GWR?[99] Generally no, because there were three disadvantages:

(i) the 95 per cent share remains part of the children's estate for IHT purposes. An election does not alter the property law consequences of what has happened;

(ii) there would be an IHT charge on the property on the death of John before Emma. No spouse exemption is available;

(iii) if John elects there are potential double charges if Emma died within seven years of the termination of her interest in possession: once on her failed PET and again on the death of the settlor.

Home loan schemes

The home loan (sometimes called the "double trust") scheme was widely **43.49** employed until December 2003. Unlike *Ingram* and *Eversden* schemes, no specific inheritance tax legislation has been passed to stop it although HMRC have indicated that in their view the scheme fails to obtain the anticipated IHT benefits.[100] There was no "single" home loan scheme: rather there were a number of variants. The demand for the scheme was generated by the significant rise in house prices in the 1990s which was not accompanied by a corresponding increase in the IHT nil rate band. The result was that many individuals found that by virtue of owning their home, IHT would be payable on their death and so their wish (to pass the property to their children) would be thwarted.

The structure of a typical home loan scheme

Step 1: S set up a life interest trust (Trust 1: "*the Property Trust*") under the **43.50** terms of which he is a life tenant with the right to enjoy the income of the trust and to enjoy the use of trust property. The trustees were given the usual

---

[98] But note that HMRC do not consider that they are bound by this decision: see R&C Brief 71/07. See also Ch.26 for valuation of interests in jointly owned property.
[99] FA 2005 Sch.15 para.21.
[100] See 43.53.

modern flexible powers: e.g. to advance capital to S or to terminate his life interest. The remainder beneficiaries were S's family.

Step 2: S set up a second (generally) interest in possession trust (Trust 2: "*the Debt Trust*") for the benefit of his children. S was wholly excluded from benefit under this trust.

Step 3: S sold his house to the trustees of the Property Trust (for say £450,000) leaving the purchase price outstanding as a loan.

Step 4: the benefit of the debt owed to S was gifted by him into the Debt Trust (a PET by S).

Diagrammatically the position is as follows:

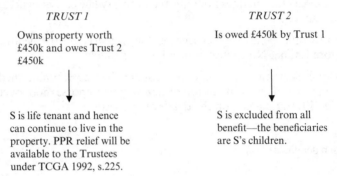

TRUST 1	*TRUST 2*
Owns property worth £450k and owes Trust 2 £450k	Is owed £450k by Trust 1
S is life tenant and hence can continue to live in the property. PPR relief will be available to the Trustees under TCGA 1992, s.225.	S is excluded from all benefit—the beneficiaries are S's children.

43.51 The sale to the Trustees of Property Trust will now attract SDLT: prior to December 1, 2003 (i.e. in the (good old) days of Stamp Duty) duty could be postponed by "resting in contract".

43.52 On S's death it was thought that the position was as follows:

(i) he enjoyed a life interest in the Property Trust and so was subject to IHT on the house.[101] On these facts and assuming no movement in the value of the property, because the debt would reduce the value of the house to nil the net value of the property subject to IHT was nil;

(ii) provided that S survived by seven years, the PET of the debt became an exempt transfer; and even if he did not, there was often a substantial discount if the debt was not repayable until the death of S.

It was in the precise terms of the loan that the schemes varied significantly:

(i) in some cases it was an interest-free demand loan;

(ii) in others it was interest-free but repayable after the death of S;

(iii) sometimes interest was payable and rolled-up with the principal; in other cases the debt was indexed (e.g. by reference to RPI or to a property index);

---

[101] See IHTA 1984 s.49(1). See also the *Barbe Green* case discussed in Ch.32.

(iv) in some cases the loan was structured as a relevant discounted security but repayable on demand and in other cases as a relevant discounted security repayable only on the death of S; and

(v) one arrangement involved the use of a tripartite loan agreement between S and the two sets of trustees, thereby avoiding the necessity for a separate assignment of the debt by S. This was thought to avoid capital gains tax problems on repayment of the debt to Debt Trust (given that the trustees of Debt Trust would not otherwise be the original creditor of the trust).[102]

In some cases the trustees of Property Trust incurred no personal liability for the debt. It could only be satisfied out of the assets of the Trust Fund and the trustees were not permitted to make distributions until the debt had been discharged. In other cases the trustees incurred personal liability (albeit that they probably did not realise this).

HMRC's approach to Home Loan Schemes

43.53 HMRC have now had sight of a significant number of home loan schemes. Their initial approach was published in the POA Guidance Notes in 2005 which stated[103]:

(i) in cases where the loan was repayable on demand because the trustees had not called in the loan they had conferred a significant benefit on the taxpayer in enabling him to continue to reside in the property *"and therefore the debt was not enjoyed to the entire exclusion of any benefit to the vendor(s) by contract or otherwise"*.

(ii) in cases where the debt was only repayable at a time after the death of the life tenant *"since . . . the loan cannot be called in by the loan trustees it is generally thought that these schemes will not be caught as gifts with reservation"*.

43.54 In October 2010, however, the Guidance was revised by the inclusion of the following sentence:

"HMRC is now of the view that these schemes (i.e. those in (ii) above) are also caught as gifts with reservation. Further guidance, including the consequences for the POA charge, will be issued shortly".

In October 2011 the Guidance was further updated. The full text of the revised guidance is at A2.67 but briefly HMRC comment that even where the loan is not repayable on demand home loan schemes do not avoid inheritance tax:

"it is now HMRC's view that as the steps taken under the schemes are a pre-ordained series of transactions a realistic view should be taken of what

---

[102] See TCGA 1992 s.251(1).
[103] See A2.67.

the transactions achieve, as a composite whole, when considering how the law applies. This follows the line of authority founded on W T Ramsay v IRC [1981] 1 AER 865. The composite transaction has the effect that the vendor has made a 'gift' of the property concerned for the purposes of s.102 FA86 and has continued to live there. The property is therefore subject to a reservation of benefit.

It is considered that this approach will apply to all variants of the home loan or double trust scheme and, where it produces a higher amount of tax, will be applied in preference to the position outlined above (reservation of benefit in the debt) *where the loan is repayable on demand."*

It accordingly appears that there are four grounds for attacking the schemes:

(i) if the debt is repayable on demand that involves a reservation of benefit in the debt;

(ii) FA 1986 s.103 applies with the result that the loan was not a valid deduction against the trust fund of the Property Trust;

(iii) the so-called *Ramsay principle* applies so that the gift is to be recharacterised as being of the relevant property and the continued occupation by the taxpayer involves a reservation of benefit;

(iv) alternatively, the scheme involves a series of associated operations so that there is a reservation of benefit in the loan.

It will be noted that these four grounds for arguing that home loan schemes do not succeed in mitigating IHT each have differing consequences: in two cases there is a reservation of benefit in the gift of the loan; in one a reservation of benefit in the property and in the final case a disallowance of the debt in the hands of the trustees. Each of these grounds is considered in greater detail below.

43.55 In response to objections that the POA Guidance, in the light of the new approach adopted by HMRC, was wholly misleading and will have resulted in taxpayers, acting in reliance on that Guidance, paying the POA charge in order to "safeguard" the IHT benefits of the scheme, HMRC commented

"You suggest our guidance is 'categorical'. With respect, whilst I would agree that the guidance as it relates to schemes where the loan is repayable on demand may be so described, I do not think that 'generally thought' can be considered a categorical statement.

As regards the question of fairness between taxpayers, where our view alters, we are bound to apply that revised view to all working cases where the issue has not been settled, as well as to those that arise following the change in view. That is exactly what is happening following legal advice received at the start of this year."

43.56 In fact HMRC's position may now be summarised as being that no home loan schemes are effective in achieving IHT benefits: a far cry from the statement that they are generally thought to be effective to avoid the reservation of benefit rules. In response to suggestions that taxpayers will have relied on the (old) guidance to their detriment HMRC have the following slightly Alice in Wonderland argument:

"You suggest that if we had contended that a reservation of benefit existed in the house, the pre-owned assets charge would not have been paid. Surely this would only have been the case if it was generally accepted that HMRC's view was correct? As this was not the case, would your advice to clients really have been not to pay the POA charge AND deliver an account for IHT purposes on the basis that a reservation of benefit did not exist? Such an inconsistent position would be a risky strategy. If it was the taxpayer's belief (on advice) that a reservation of benefit did not exist, it would follow that the exemption from the POA charge was not available and in self-assessing their liability to income tax it is entirely proper that they should pay the POA charge. I do not see how our guidance would have had a material impact on that decision. And most certainly it could not have influenced whether or not the deceased established the structure in the first place"

Such fantasy speculations do not disguise the fact that the original Guidance was wrong and no longer represents HMRC's views.   **43.57**

Moreover HMRC have failed to take account of the fact that as a result of the original Guidance many taxpayers have paid the POA charge (possibly wrongly if HMRC are correct) and chose not to dismantle their home loan scheme, believing that such scheme was accepted by HMRC. Indeed in many cases after 2003 HMRC *did* accept such schemes, generally allowing a deduction for the debt on the death of the settlor.

By relying on that Guidance, taxpayers have effectively acted to their detriment. HMRC argue that there is no detriment to the taxpayer: if the taxpayer had dismantled the scheme he would still have to pay inheritance tax on death and so he is only worse off to the extent that POAT was paid.[104] This misses the point: in many cases taxpayers *would* have dismantled the home loan scheme if they had thought HMRC might attack the arrangements. Some would also have taken further steps to mitigate inheritance tax, e.g. by a co-ownership scheme or by sale and lease back.[105] The authors are aware of two home loan schemes in the process of litigation.

Analysis of HMRC's arguments on home loan schemes

First Ground: debts repayable on demand

The argument is that by failing to call in the loan, the trustees of the Debt   **43.58** Trust have conferred a benefit on the settlor because he has thereby been able to continue living in his house (which otherwise would have to be sold to

---

[104] Although POAT could be a substantial cost and therefore a substantial detriment. In many cases taxpayers will be out of time to reclaim the POAT paid since the four years has expired. It is not clear whether HMRC will exercise their care and management powers and extend the time limit for reclaiming POAT.

[105] See judgment of *Gaines-Cooper* in Supreme Court discussed in Ch.3 for further comment on whether the initial guidance now estopps HMRC from challenging home loan schemes where the taxpayer can show that he acted to his detriment. Any taxpayer would have to challenge HMRC's change of heart by judicial review proceedings.

pay off the debt). Many such on demand loans were structured so that if the trustees of the debt trust required repayment of the debt before the final repayment date (usually specified to be on a date equal to the likely life expectancy of the settlor) they would only have been entitled to receive the face value of the loan and would have forfeited any rolled-up interest. In other words the trustees of the Debt Trust did much better for their beneficiaries if they waited until the settlor's death. Are the trustees of the Debt Trust required to act to their positive detriment in order to avoid a reservation of benefit problem for the donor?

In any event, the donor derives no benefit from the loan itself. If he derives a benefit at all, it is from occupation of the house, which, on the basis of cases such as *St Aubyn v AG (No.2)*[106] may be regarded as property separate from the gift. A similar point crops up in relation to carve-outs and trusts and also in relation to insurance arrangements. For example, if a life tenant settlor has an income interest but the trustees have the power to terminate his interest and do not do so, is it a collateral benefit conferred on the life tenant?[107] Trusts provide all sorts of indirect benefits for donors which are not regarded as involving a reservation of benefit to the donor. For example, one might argue that a trust set up for the settlor's children and which pays their school fees, leads to a benefit being conferred on the parent-donor which results in a reservation of benefit but HMRC do not take this point. Not all benefits remotely linked to the gift can be said to fall within the reservation of benefit rules.

Second Ground: disallowance of the debt under FA 1986 s.103[108]

43.59   HMRC present the argument as follows:

> "*s.103 is plainly designed to disallow the deduction of artificial liabilities. If a liability is to be taken into account in establishing the value of an estate, then it is capable of being a 'debt' or an 'incumbrance' within s.103. That much seems clear from the opening words of the section. Whilst the loan may not have been secured on the property, will it not have given rise to an equitable lien in favour of the trustees against the property in respect of their indebtedness to the deceased? Will not that lien then be an 'incumbrance' and was it not bought into being ('created') by the disposition? You may argue that as the lien arises by operation of law it was not created by the disposition. But something that arises by operation of law still has to have a trigger, something still has to cause it to come into existence and the only possible trigger here is the disposition made by the deceased. So a liability that is to be taken into account is an incumbrance that was created by a disposition made by the deceased. S.103 therefore operates to abate the loan.*
>
> *Is there another issue here in that if the property is not encumbered by the debt created by the sale of the property to the trust and it is a personal*

---

[106] [1952] AC 15.
[107] This point is discussed in Ch.33.
[108] For a consideration of s.103, see Ch.29.

liability of the trustees, what are the grounds for taking the debt into account in valuing the deceased's estate at death if the trustees cannot have recourse to the trust assets to fund a call to repay the loan?"

The HMRC argument is derived from comments in *McCutcheon on Inheritance Tax*.[109] It should be noted that in that publication the argument having been raised, the editors then reject it on the basis that:

  (i)   the incumbrance was not created by the sale of the property to the trustees: rather it follows from the rights of reimbursement which trustees have against the trust fund[110];

  (ii) the property sold to the trustees was not consideration for any incumbrance: it was consideration for the debt;

  (iii) the trustees have recourse to the trust assets to repay the debt as a matter of trust law.

So far as the final point made by HMRC above is concerned, the majority of debts and liabilities incurred by trustees will be personal liabilities (albeit with a right of reimbursement against the fund) but deductible for IHT valuation purposes.[111] On this basis no debt incurred by a qualifying interest in possession trust set up by a settlor in which he retains a life interest could ever qualify for an inheritance tax deduction. *Barbe* did not suggest this.

Third Ground: operation of the Ramsay Principle

HMRC consider that *Ramsay* applies as follows: **43.60**

"... *the rule is one of statutory construction—we are required to take a realistic view of what the transactions achieve, as a composite whole, when considering how the law applies.*

Lord Hoffmann analysed the nature of the principle in the following terms in BMBF v Mawson 76 TC 446 at para [32]:

'*The essence of the new approach was to give the statutory provision a purposive construction in order to determine the nature of the transaction to which it was intended to apply and then to decide whether the actual transaction (which might involve considering the overall effect of a number of elements intended to operate together) answered to the statutory description. Of course this does not mean that the courts have to put their reasoning into the straitjacket of first construing the statute in the abstract and then looking at the facts. It might be more convenient to analyse the facts and then ask whether they satisfy the requirements of the statute. But however one*

---

[109] (5th edn, 2009), 25–97.
[110] See generally for the right of reimbursement TA 2000 s.31(1) and *Lewin on Trusts* (18th edn, 2008), 29.33. Also *West v Trennery* discussed at 7.56.
[111] See *St Barbe Green v IRC* [2006] STC 288.

approaches the matter, the question is always whether the relevant provision of statute, upon its true construction, applies to the facts as found. As Lord Nicholls of Birkenhead said in MacNiven (Inspector of Taxes) v Westmoreland Investments Ltd [2001] UKHL 6 at [8], [2001] 1 All ER at [8,] [2003] 1 AC 311: "The paramount question always is one of interpretation of the particular statutory provision and its application to the facts of the case."

The statutory provision is s.102 FA'86. Following Lord Hoffmann's approach, we should first analyse the facts. The transactions were part of a widely marketed tax avoidance scheme specifically aimed at circumventing the reservation of benefit provisions. They did so by creating the appearance of a sale, but without any intention that the donor would retain any value on disposal of the property. I do not consider it unreasonable to take the view that a 'sale', where it was always intended that the 'consideration' would be passed on by way of gift can be treated, for all intents and purposes, as a gift of the original property. And it was always the primary purposes of the scheme that the deceased's occupation of (the property) should continue undisturbed.

We must then consider whether the facts, viewed realistically, satisfy the requirements of the statute on a purposive construction. The purpose behind s.102 is well known—where a person makes a disposal by way of gift but they retain a benefit in the gifted property, the property is treated as remaining part of their estate.

Realistically, the transactions, as a composite whole, put the deceased in the same position as if . . . she made a gift of the property and continued to live there—where s.102 would apply without question. Against that backdrop, a purposive interpretation of the word 'gift' in s.102 would reasonably encompass all the steps undertaken as part of a home loan scheme."

The assertion that a sale in the situation where the proceeds are to be given away can be categorised as a gift of the property sold is striking. Does it follow that a taxpayer who sells qualifying business property and settles the proceeds is to be treated as settling the business property? It should also be noted that arguments based on *Ramsay* were given short shrift in the *Ingram* litigation.

Fourth Ground: a series of associated operations

43.61   HMRC put their argument based on associated operations as follows making it clear they regarded this argument as relevant to debts that were repayable only on death:

> "*A further alternative is that the transactions undertaken are associated operations within the meaning of s.268. This is relevant in view of the terms of para 6(1)(c) Sch 20 FA'86. Under that provision, any benefit that the donor obtained by virtue of any associated operations of which the disposal by way of gift was one, shall be treated as a benefit to the donor 'by contract or otherwise'. This is important in view of the second limb of s.102(1)(b)*

FA'86. If it is the case that the arrangements conferred a benefit on the deceased that is referable to the gift, that benefit is to be treated as a benefit by contract or otherwise which falls within s.102(1)(b).

Prior to the transactions taking place the deceased owned [the property] absolutely. After the disposal to the trust took place, s/he was no longer the owner, although as beneficiary under the Property trust, the trustees had the power to allow [her/him] to continue to occupy the property. The sale of the property in exchange for a loan note could, depending on the terms of that note, give the noteholder a significant influence over what was to become of [the property] and the extent to which the deceased could continue to live there undisturbed—which is, of course, an essential part of the scheme.

Whilst the loan note remained in the deceased's hands, its precise terms made little or no difference to her/his circumstances—s/he was unlikely to take any action that would upset her/his enjoyment of her own home. But given that the intention of the scheme was to give the loan note to the trustees of the Second trust, the terms for its repayment take on some significance. Had the loan allowed the noteholder to request repayment on demand, the deceased's ability to continue to live at [the property] undisturbed was at risk. If the noteholder chose to call in the debt, the trustees would almost certainly have to sell the property which would see the deceased lose her/his home.

But by making the loan repayable only after her/his death, the deceased ensured that her/his continued occupation would not be disturbed. That is plainly a benefit to her/him and one that arose directly from the terms of the loan that was given away. The benefit arises within the terms of para 6(1)(c), so the loan note should properly be regarded as subject to a reservation of benefit under s.102(1)(b)".

Even if the gift and prior sale are associated operations within IHTA 1984 s.268 it remains difficult to see how the taxpayer has benefited from them. Specifically there is nothing in the legislation to require an extended meaning to be given to what has been given away and the *Ingram* case provides House of Lords authority for the principle that before seeking to apply the reservation of benefit rules it is necessary to identify precisely what has been given away. In that case, for instance, the fact that the arrangement involved carving out a lease (retained by the taxpayer) and giving away the freehold, did not result in a benefit being reserved in the gifted freehold interest irrespective of the fact that the nature of the gift meant that the freeholder had to allow the donor to continue living in the property.

Audley argument

More recently HMRC have cited the case of *Audley v HMRC*[112] as further evidence the scheme will fail. However, this case related to whether an allowable loss for income tax purposes was realised on the assignment of the relevant discounted security and came down to an analysis of "the price paid" for the loan note. The tribunal held that in effect the loan note (a relevant discounted

43.62

112 [2011] UKFTT 219 (TC).

security) was worth far less than the face value when issued by the trustees of the property trust to the donor in consideration of the transfer of the house to them. However, this point does not have any bearing on whether the loan note is deductible for inheritance tax purposes on the settlor's death. The debt was clearly incurred by the trustees for more than full consideration on the basis of *Audley*. It was not held the loan was a sham and should be ignored. Nor is the case relevant to any of the ROB arguments raised by HMRC.

POA tie-in with HMRC's arguments

43.63 Even if HMRC are right and there is a reservation of benefit in the debt, this does not necessarily mean that there is no POA charge. The relevant property for the purposes of this tax is the house and the donor has satisfied the disposal condition by the transfer into the interest in possession trust. Whilst the para.11(1) exemption applies to the equity in the house, the reservation of benefit property (the loan) does not form part of the donor's estate for inheritance tax purposes while he is alive so that the debt remains an excluded liability and so reduces the value of his estate.[113] HMRC comment in the revised guidance that income tax will be refunded if the litigation results in there being a reservation of benefit in the house. But if there is a reservation of benefit in the debt, HMRC insist that both POAT and IHT is due!

43.64 In any event many home loan schemes have been wound up because of the POA charge that came into operation from April 6, 2005. There were various arguments why the POA Regime might not apply to these schemes[114] but it is thought that the scheme involves an "excluded liability" (the debt) falling within Sch.15 para.11(7) FA 2004.

Excluded liability and the POA charge

43.65 Although the property is part of the settlor's estate for inheritance tax purposes[115] it is subject to an excluded liability in the form of the debt.[116] This provision is intended to operate in the following way: assume that the value of the house is now £500,000 and the debt remains £450,000:

> (i) to the extent that the value of the property exceeds the amount of the excluded liability (£500,000–£450,000) the exemption from POA[117] operates. This is consistent with the general scheme of the legislation since £50,000 is included in the settlor's estate for IHT purposes; and

---

[113] See FA 1986 s.102(3). The position is the same if the debt is disallowed under FA 1986 s.103.
[114] See the authors' *Pre-owned Assets and Estate Planning* (3rd edn, 2009), Ch.17.
[115] As a result of IHTA 1984 s.49(1).
[116] See FA 2004 Sch.15 para.11(7), "*a liability is an excluded liability if (a) the creation of the liability, and (b) any transaction by virtue of which the person's estate came to include the relevant property or property which derives its value from the relevant property or by virtue of which the value of property in his estate came to be derived from the relevant property were associated operations, as defined by s.268 of IHTA 1984*".
[117] In Sch.15 para.11(1).

(ii) but as to the amount of the excluded liability (£450,000), the POA Regime applies (in percentage terms to 90 per cent of the value of the house).

The value of the excluded liability is the face value of the debt plus rolled-up interest as at the valuation date.[118]

Options to avoid the POA charge on home loan schemes

Much will depend on the particular scheme adopted by the taxpayer but the following general points may be noted. **43.66**

Option 1: Pay the income tax and/or consider repaying (part of) the loan

The taxpayer should calculate the POA income tax charge that will be payable. This means obtaining a market value for the house as at the valuation date[119]; identifying the face value of the liability outstanding then plus interest if any and obtaining a rental value of the house at the same date.

EXAMPLE 43.12

A, a higher rate taxpayer, effected a home loan scheme in 2003. On April 6, 2005 the house was worth £1 million with a rental value of £40,000. The loan's face value was £800,000 but its commercial value, given that it was not repayable until A's death, was £400,000. No interest was payable on the debt.

A's income tax charge for the year 2005–06 (and thereafter until the tax year 2010–11) was on a benefit of £40,000 reduced by the amount of property still in his estate. The amount of excluded liability (on HMRC's view) is £800,000 which meant that 80 per cent of the market rent was the deemed benefit, i.e. £32,000 = income tax of £12,800.

A point to bear in mind was that if the annual rental value of the property is less than £5,000 (£10,000 for a married couple) the de minimis exemption excluded the POA charge. A revaluation exercise has to be carried out every five years (e.g. in April 2010, 2015, etc.).

Alternatively, negotiate repayment of the loan if the house is sold and the taxpayer moves to a smaller cheaper house. The two sets of trustees could agree an early repayment of the loan. An actuarial valuation of the loan should be obtained and arm's length negotiations carried out between the two sets of trustees. So, for example, a debt with a face value of £1 million carrying no interest and repayable only on the death of the taxpayers might be discounted **43.67**

---

[118] See A2.128. It is by no means clear that HMRC are correct in this view: it is arguable it should be the commercial value of the debt.
[119] i.e. April 6, 2005 and then April 6, 2010.

by as much as 50 per cent if they were a married couple in their 50s. Once any new house is free of debt the POA charge ceases to apply.[120]

Option 2: Unscrambling the scheme

43.68 There are a variety of ways in which the scheme could be unscrambled. Much will depend on how the debt was structured.

(a) Unscrambling scheme if the debt not a relevant discounted security

43.69 The benefit of the debt could be assigned to the settlor (or settlors if a married couple effected the scheme) and Double Charges Relief will then be available in the event that one of them dies within seven years of the original gift of the debt. There is no further POA charge once the loan is assigned to the settlors whether or not the house remains in trust, because the excluded liability no longer reduces the value of their estates.

Stage 1: If the benefit of the debt is advanced or appointed by the Loan Trustees to the children who assign it to the settlor(s) each child will make a PET. To avoid this, the trustees advance the benefit of the debt contingent on the children being alive in (say) 21 days. During that period the children assign their benefit under the advancement to the settlor(s). (Note that the children retain their existing interests in possession which will terminate only when the contingency is met after 21 days.) So far as the children are concerned this assignment will not have adverse tax consequences since:

(i) for IHT purposes it is of a reversionary interest (viz a future interest under the settlement) which is excluded property[121];

(ii) for CGT purposes the disposal is of an interest under a settlement on which no chargeable gain accrues.[122]

The making of the advancement by the trustees will not have any tax consequences.[123]

Stage 2: at the end of 21 days the settlor(s) becomes absolutely entitled to the debt. The Loan Trust has ended. The debt is not at this point written off. If the settlor were to die within seven years of having entered into the scheme the position (after Stage 1 and Stage 2 have been effected) is as follows:

(i) the taxpayer is taxed on the value of the house in the Property Trust less the value of the debt. Hence any tax charge will be limited to the growth in value of the property above the amount of the debt;

---

[120] If a small debt is left it may be that the "benefit" will fall within the de minimis exemption.
[121] For the definition of excluded property, see IHTA 1984 s.48(1) and Ch.31.
[122] TCGA 1992 s.76(1).
[123] Given that the children wish to assist their parents it is thought that any advancement is for their benefit even if the trustees are aware that the ultimate intention is to assign the debt to the parents.

(ii) the benefit of the debt is in his free estate and accordingly taxed. However, reg.4 of the 1987 Double Charges Regulations prevents there being a charge on both the failed PET of the debt and on the debt itself.[124]

The end result is the unscrambling of the scheme and whilst the settlor has obtained no IHT advantage he will not suffer any IHT double charge.

The tax consequences of Stage 2 are as follows:

(i) the children's interests in possession in the Loan Trust have ended with the absolute vesting of the trust property in the settlor. This does not involve a PET because of the availability of reverter to settlor relief[125];

(ii) on the ending of the debt trust no CGT charge arises provided that the debt falls within TCGA 1992 s.251(1) (which provides that no chargeable gain arises on its disposal).[126]

Diagrammatically the unscrambling arrangement is as follows:

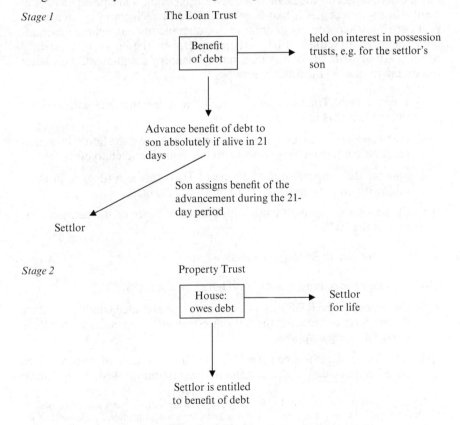

Stage 1   The Loan Trust

Benefit of debt → held on interest in possession trusts, e.g. for the settlor's son

Advance benefit of debt to son absolutely if alive in 21 days

Son assigns benefit of the advancement during the 21-day period

Settlor

Stage 2   Property Trust

House: owes debt → Settlor for life

Settlor is entitled to benefit of debt

---

[124] The taxpayer will need to make a chargeable transfer equal to the value of the failed PET for the relief to be of benefit to him, i.e. he should not leave his estate to his surviving spouse.
[125] See Ch.37: unaffected by FA 2006 Sch.20 as the settlor takes outright.
[126] This is where the various schemes differ: if the debt had been assigned to the trustees of Loan Trust so that they are not the original creditors then any gain may be chargeable. By contrast, if the debt is a relevant discounted security its transfer may trigger an income tax charge.

43.70   So far as the POA charge is concerned once the debt is back in the settlor's estate the excluded liability (viz the debt which affects the house) does not reduce the value of the settlor's estate so that the POA charge does not apply whether or not the debt is then written off.[127] If the debt were to be written off it is not thought that this will involve an addition of property to the settlement so as to lead to a chargeable transfer by the settlor but if this was felt to be a concern then the property could be charged with the debt on a non-recourse basis, then transferred to the settlor (in order to avoid any SDLT charge) and only then released. Double charges relief will be available if the property is back in the settlor's estate.[128]

(b) Unscrambling scheme if debt is an relevant discounted security (RDS)

43.71   If the debt was an RDS then the above method of unscrambling could involve income tax charges for the Debt Trustees if the RDS showed a profit on assignment. (In some schemes it had been structured in such a way as to avoid a profit arising.) Accordingly in order to avoid an income tax charge unscrambling was likely to require either early repayment by the Property Trustees[129] or a release or write off of the loan rather than any assignment. This latter option might involve the following steps:

(i) vary the Debt Trust so that only adults were beneficiaries with no contingent interests in favour of minors;

(ii) the two sets of trustees agree to secure the debt over the house by a non-recourse equitable charge document (agreement and charge)[130];

(iii) appoint the property out of Property Trust to the settlors with them taking on no personal liability to repay the charge;

(iv) the trustees of the debt trust, with the concurrence of the beneficiaries, release the RDS.

43.72   The tax analysis of these steps is as follows:

(i) the release avoids an income tax charge on the RDS;

(ii) the release of the RDS means that there is no excluded liability affecting the property or reducing the settlor's estate with the result that the POA charge no longer applies;

(iii) the POA charge between April 6, 2005 and the date of release might have been avoided if the de minimis exemption applied.[131] Of course

---

[127] Sch.15 para.11(6). It is thought that for these purposes the settlor's estate must be looked at "in the round": viz as the aggregate of the settled property and his free estate (contrast the approach adopted in *St Barbe Green v IRC* [2005] STC 288).

[128] See SI 1987/1130.

[129] In many cases the RDS was structured so that if the Debt Trustees called in the debt before death they received much less than if they waited until death.

[130] The trustees cannot grant a legal charge because they do not have legal title to the property—the legal title generally remained with the vendor under the resting in contracts route.

[131] Sch.15 para.13.

the settlor might have elected into reservation of benefit rules. If the house is back in his estate (free of debt) the effect of the election is nullified[132];

(iv) the property will be fully eligible for the spouse exemption on the death of the settlor and for any other "normal" inheritance tax saving measures;

(v) writing off the debt while the house is still in the Property Trust might be taxed as a chargeable transfer rather than a PET.[133] Hence, the house should be extracted from the trust first (subject to a non-recourse charge) before the debt is written off;

(vi) Can SDLT can be avoided if the transfer of the house subject to the debt back to the parents is structured with a non-recourse charge on the property? The position is debateable.[134] It is clear that if the settlors take on any liability for the debt then SDLT will arise as that is consideration under FA 2003 Sch.4 para.8. In addition, para.8(1A) provides that where:

"(a) debt is secured on the subject-matter of a land transaction immediately before and immediately after the transaction, and

(b) the rights or liabilities in relation to that debt of any party to the transaction are changed as a result of or in connection with the transaction,

then . . . there is an assumption of that debt by the purchaser . . ."

The non-recourse agreement between the two trustees will provide that an **43.73** equitable charge over the house be created in favour of the Debt Trustees, and that the Property Trustees will be *"under no further or personal liability to ensure that the sums due are paid to the Creditors who accept that their only recourse in respect of such sums due is now against the Property by enforcement of their equitable charge."* Hence, the Property Trustees will have no personal responsibility or liability to repay the debt. The only difference is that there is now an equitable charge over the property and the consent of the Debt Trustees is not required to the distribution of the property. Hence, there is a change to the rights of the Debt Trustees but they are not parties to the land transaction.

It might be argued that such an Agreement and Charge *does* change the liabili- **43.74** ties of the Property Trustees in relation to the debt since prior to the Charge they may not have been able to appoint the property out to the parents without the consent of the Debt Trustees and/or under this route they are no longer personally liable for the debt; therefore if it is made in contemplation of the subsequent transfer to the parents there is an SDLT charge on transfer to the parents.

---

[132] See HMRC correspondence, A2.126.

[133] See 31.33 and Ch.24 for a consideration of trust additions.

[134] Note that most home loan schemes were carried out before December 2003 with the sale left resting on contracts so as to avoid stamp duty. On subsequent completion of the sale in favour of the trustees then generally stamp duty rather than SDLT is payable. More usually no completion of the sale takes place and instead when the property is sold to a third party the legal owner conveys it directly at the direction of the trustees to that third party. SDLT is then payable by the third party but not the trustees.

(vii) double charges relief is available if the entire debt is written off and the settlor parents die within seven years.[135]

43.75 The trustees need to give careful thought to their position in effecting any such rearrangement. By giving up trust property in favour of the parents who are excluded from the Debt Trust they are exceeding their powers and this prima facie may be considered void or as a minimum a breach of trust. It is suggested above that as a first step the beneficial class be limited to adults who then consent to the release (children may accept that it is for their benefit that their parents do not suffer an onerous income tax charge). There remains the possibility that excluded minor beneficiaries might challenge the Debt Trustees' decision in the future but this may be considered unlikely. The adult children should be independently advised if they are being asked to provide indemnities to the Debt Trustees.

A better option may be not to write off the debt but for the Debt Trustees to consider asking for early repayment of the loan from the Property Trustees. If the Property Trustees can afford to repay the debt (e.g. they borrow from a bank or have sold the house and have equity) this avoids an income tax charge. The Debt Trustees can perhaps more easily justify an early repayment of the debt rather than a complete write off. Much will depend on the terms of the loan.

Option 3: election into reservation of benefit

43.76 A key matter to bear in mind is the time limit: for a scheme in existence on April 6, 2005 which is within the POA charge, the deadline was January 31, 2007. After that date HMRC consider that it will not be possible to elect although as explained in Ch.34 the authors consider that a later election is not only possible but necessary to be valid. The effects of making the election are considered below but the intention behind the legislation is clear: by electing the taxpayer shall bring himself within the IHT reservation of benefit rules so that on his death the property occupied will be taxed as part of his estate.

43.77 The legislation[136] provides as follows:

(a) if an election is made the POA Regime shall not apply;

(b) s.102(3) and (4) of FA 1986 shall apply;

(c) s.102(3) deals with the situation where on the death of the taxpayer there is property in which he has reserved a benefit and provides that, for the purposes of the IHT charge, the taxpayer is to be treated as beneficially entitled to that property immediately before his death; and

(d) however, s.102(3) only applies to the extent that the property "*would not, apart from this section, form part of the donor's estate immediately before his death.*"[137]

---

[135] See SI 2005/341.
[136] Sch.15 para.21(2)(b).
[137] Curiously this limitation on the operation of s.102(3) is not included in s.102(4) which imposes a deemed PET when a reservation ceases inter vivos.

When the election is made and s.102(3) applies does the restriction continue **43.78**
to apply, i.e. where the taxpayer makes the election can his executors successfully argue that because he had a qualifying interest in possession the property
already formed part of his estate at death so that a charge to IHT will not
arise under the reservation of benefit rules? The wording in s.102(3) does not
impose any restriction for excluded liabilities.

In any event, the amendments made in s.80 FA 2006 (to stop reverter to **43.79**
settlor schemes) expressly state that the chargeable proportion of the property
is to be treated as property subject to a reservation of benefit and s.102(3)
shall apply *but only so far as the chargeable person is not beneficially entitled
to an interest in possession*. On that basis, the additional words in italics seem
to reinforce the argument above that making an election has no adverse effect
for inheritance tax purposes because the reservation of benefit provisions are
disapplied by s.102(3) and the taxpayer is simply treated as holding an interest
in possession in the property with a deduction for the debt.

The IHT 500 form hardly helps because it refers to an election in respect of **43.80**
the land—there is no suggestion that the election is in respect of the debt itself
which would make more sense in the context of home loan schemes.

Option 4: pay rent under a legal obligation by deed of covenant

The taxpayer makes payments under a legal obligation equal to the appro- **43.81**
priate rental value in respect of his occupation.[138] The legislation does not
require the payment of rent as such so that the taxpayer could enter into a
deed of covenant under which he pays to the Property Trustees a sum equal
to the market rent of the property for so long as he remains in occupation. As
annual payments, the sums paid do not suffer income tax in the hands of the
recipient trustees. Otherwise the structure remains unchanged. In connection
with this arrangement note:

(i) payments under the deed are not rent: they are voluntary payments
outside the income tax net[139];

(ii) prior to March 22, 2006, because the payments were to the Property
Trust in which the payer has a life interest there was no transfer of value
for IHT purposes. Now they may be chargeable transfers as additions
to a settlement[140];

(iii) CGT principal private residence relief will not be affected.

Option 4: reverter to Settlor Trust

This involved reorganising the Property Trust to preserve the envisaged inher- **43.82**
itance tax savings whilst avoiding the income tax charge by transferring the
house into a reverter to settler trust. This is now a non-starter given FA 2006

---

[138] See the let out in Sch.15 para.4(1).
[139] See ITTOIA 2005 s.727.
[140] However, the payments may fall within the normal expenditure exemption or within the taxpayer's IHT nil rate band.

s.80 which stops any POA advantages and FA 2006 Sch.20 which imposes an inheritance tax charge on the creation of the trust.[141]

Home loan schemes today

43.83   Old-style home loan schemes in respect of the taxpayer's dwelling house will not be entered into today: *first*, because of the pre-owned assets charge, *secondly*, because of the SDLT charge (rates up to five per cent); *thirdly*, because of Sch.20 and the inheritance tax charges on inter vivos gifts into trusts and *fourthly*, because of the HMRC attack on the inheritance tax efficacy of such schemes. Home loan schemes involving let property using the double trust scheme are no longer attractive given that setting up such trusts will involve immediately chargeable transfers for inheritance tax purposes. Hence, even for those taxpayers who are prepared to argue that the HMRC attack on home loan schemes is misconceived, future schemes are likely to be limited to transfers between spouses.[142] Even then the SDLT charge may make the scheme unattractive in relation to the family home.

SDLT, stamp duty and past home loan schemes

43.84   As noted previously, stamp duty was usually avoided on past home loan schemes by the sale being left "resting in contracts". Legal title remained with the vendor. The stamp duty and SDLT position when the property eventually comes to be sold by the Property Trustees needs some consideration and is discussed further in Ch.51.

We now consider the current inheritance tax planning options that may be available in relation to the family home.

IV CURRENT PLANNING OPTIONS—CARVE-OUT SCHEMES INCLUDING REVERSIONARY LEASE SCHEMES

43.85   The development of reversionary lease arrangements was closely linked to *Ingram* schemes. In particular:

(i) like *Ingram* schemes, reversionary leases involve a shearing operation;

---

[141] See Ch.27 and Ch.34. The restructuring essentially involved the following: (1) The settlor surrendered his life interest in the Property Trust to his children so they became entitled to interests in possession. He was excluded as a beneficiary of the Property Trust; he paid a market rent for his continued occupation. (2) The Children's Trustees then appointed the benefit of the debt (owed to it by the Property Trust) to the Property Trust which now had the same beneficiaries. Alternatively the Children's Trustees wrote off the debt. (3) Subsequently, the Property Trust appointed the house to the children absolutely. (4) The children then resettled the property on a new trust, being a reverter to settlor trust for the settlor (Third Trust). In this case an election under Sch.15 of FA 2004 (para.21), will have adverse consequences because reverter to settlor relief will not be available. See Sch.15 para.21(2)(b)(iii).

[142] See 43.33; "the Family Debt Scheme".

(ii) similar CGT problems could arise in the event of a sale of the property. Hence, they were ideal in cases where it was envisaged that the property would never be sold but would be retained within the family.

Whereas in *Ingram* arrangements, it was necessary first to carve-out a lease and then to gift an encumbered freehold reversion, reversionary leases were a single stage transaction involving only the grant of a lease.

EXAMPLE 43.13

Adam owns Manor Farm which he wishes to pass on to his eldest son, Ben. He wishes to occupy the Manor for the rest of his life. It is inconceivable that the property will be sold outside the family. The scheme operates as follows:

(i) Adam grants Ben a long lease over the property (say 125 years) to take effect in 20 years time.[143] Because the lease does not give Ben occupation rights immediately it is called a deferred or reversionary lease. The terms of the lease do not involve the payment of any rent nor do they impose covenants on Ben[144];

(ii) Adam can continue to occupy the property for the next 20 years because he remains the freeholder;

(iii) The gift of the lease is a PET by Adam and so free from IHT provided that he survives by seven years;

(iv) The freehold interest (of diminishing value) remains in Adam's estate and will be taxed accordingly on his death;[145]

(v) If Adam is still alive at the end of 20 years and wishes to continue to occupy the property he will need to pay Ben a market rent: otherwise he will have reserved a benefit in the lease gifted to Ben.

Reservation of benefit analysis

A continues to occupy by virtue of his retained freehold property: he does not retain a benefit in the gifted property which is the reversionary lease. Like *Ingram* the arrangement is a horizontal carve-out. This analysis was accepted by HMRC in respect of reversionary lease arrangements set up before March **43.86**

---

[143] Could the period of deferral exceed 21 years? This might be desirable if A were (say) in his mid 60s so that he could easily live for another 25 years. This involves a consideration of LPA 1925 s.149(3) which provides *"a term [i.e. lease] at a rent or granted in consideration of a fine, limited to take effect more than 21 years from the date of the instrument purporting to create it, shall be void."* It is thought that a lease which does not involve the payment of any rent (or fine) is outside these provisions.

[144] See *Buzzoni v RCC* [2011] UKFTT 267 (TC) where creating an under lease to the head lease involved the retention of covenants and hence a reservation of benefit: see 33.13.

[145] Could the lease be made to vest in possession on the earlier of 21 years from the date of grant and the death of A (the freeholder)? If so, this would have an obvious attraction in reducing the value of the freehold interest in A's estate. Some concern has been felt that this could convert the reversionary lease into a lease for life under IHTA 1984 s.43(3).

9, 1999. What effect did the 1999 (anti-*Ingram*) legislation have? On its face, the 1999 legislation is targeted specifically at *Ingram* schemes (there was no mention in the accompanying Press Release of other similar arrangements being caught). The argument that reversionary leases are not caught is as follows:

(i) the basic conditions that have to be satisfied for there to be a reservation of benefit are, *first*, that the taxpayer disposes of an interest in land by way of gift (this A undoubtedly does when he grants B the deferred lease). *Secondly*, he must retain *"a significant right or interest or (be) party to a significant arrangement in relation to the land."* Of course A retains his freehold interest—does that satisfy the second requirement?

(ii) the short answer is that it all depends on the facts since *"a right or interest is not significant if it was granted or acquired before the period of seven years ending with the date of the gift."*[146] In the majority of cases, persons wishing to enter into reversionary lease arrangements will do so in respect to property which they have owned for at least seven years. In such cases it is considered that the above let-out applies and so the gifted lease is not property subject to a reservation;

(iii) an alternative argument relies on s.102A(3) which excludes a right, interest or arrangement which enables the donor to occupy the land *"for full consideration in money or money's worth."* If A had originally purchased his freehold interest (whether or not within seven years of the date of the gift) for full consideration then this let out should apply so that again the arrangement remains outside reservation of benefit. Of course, a reversionary lease granted within seven years of A inheriting the property would involve a reservation of benefit because neither of the let-outs is available.

43.87 Initially HMRC took the view that the 1999 legislation caught reversionary leases because:

> *"the occupation [of the donor] is considered to be a significant right in respect of the relevant land and it is thought therefore that a reservation of benefit for inheritance tax will arise. As such, the property will not be subject to the income tax charge."*

Subsequently, however, they recanted and, as the POA Guidance Notes make clear, now accept that such arrangements may not be caught because of the seven-year defence.[147]

Impact of the POA Regime

43.88 Taxpayers such as Adam in Example 43.13 who have entered into reversionary lease arrangements are subject to an income tax charge under the POA Regime from April 6, 2005. The analysis is much the same as for *Ingram*

---

[146] FA 1986 s.102A(5).
[147] See A2.64.

schemes.[148] The practical advice and options available will therefore be much the same. An apportionment of the appropriate rental value will be necessary under Sch.15 para.4. The property gifted (the leasehold interest: DV in the formula) is likely to show a year-on-year increase in much the same way as the freehold reversion in *Ingram* schemes. Once again the fact that a revaluation is only required every five years is generally advantageous for the taxpayer.

Despite this, reversionary lease schemes along with *Ingram* schemes do have a place in future tax planning in two contexts: first where there is an existing pre-March 2006 interest in possession trust where the life tenant is elderly and occupies a house. Secondly, in relation to IPDI trusts set up in a will, often in favour of a surviving spouse. The suggested planning is identical for both.

EXAMPLE 43.14

A is the elderly life tenant of a trust set up by his father in 1985. The trustees wish to carry out inheritance tax planning. The trust owns a large country mansion worth £3 million and the trustees have an overriding power of appointment which can be exercised to terminate (in whole or in part) A's interest.

In 2008 the trustees grant a reversionary lease to a nominee to take effect in, say, 17 years time and the reversionary lease is then appointed to A's son. A is deemed to have made a gift of the no longer possessed property.[149] This involves a PET by A. The freehold interest is still held on interest in possession trusts for A. A has enjoyed a life interest for at least seven years so will be within the protection of s.102A(3). He is not a party to any arrangement given that it was the trustees who took away his interest. Hence, the reservation of benefit rules, do not apply. Section102ZA does not treat the life tenant as making a gift for the purposes of ss.102A–102C but only for the purposes of s.102. Therefore, it is possible for the trustees to carry out a reversionary lease scheme even where the life tenant has not held the interest in possession for seven years. As long as an adequate carve out has been made for s.102 purposes the fact that an arrangement might otherwise be caught by s.102A does not matter.

Could an *Ingram* arrangement be done successfully instead of a reversionary lease scheme in the above example? In theory, yes. However, reversionary lease schemes have two advantages. First, in the above example the life tenant A can rely on the protection of s.102A(3). HMRC have accepted that s.102A would not then apply to treat A as reserving a benefit. Although it is not thought that s.102A applies to the life tenant anyway, this gives an additional layer of protection. However, what is the position if the life tenant has not held the interest in possession for seven years? Is there any advantage in a reversionary lease scheme over an *Ingram* arrangement in these circumstances?

43.89

---

[148] See 43.40.
[149] FA 1986 s.102ZA.

EXAMPLE 43.15

Lord Olly has died, leaving his residuary estate on revocable interest in possession trusts for his wife Lady Olly. The trustees have cash which they use to purchase a substantial freehold property for Lady Olly, where she plans to end her days. They acquire the freehold interest on interest in possession trusts and shortly thereafter appoint a reversionary interest outright to her children. She continues to occupy by virtue of her interest in possession in the freehold interest. In these circumstances the let outs in s.102A(3) and (5) are not applicable. On the basis that ss.102A–102C does not apply to s.102ZA terminations, one might argue that either an *Ingram* or reversionary lease carve out could be effected successfully.

Additional argument in favour of reversionary lease schemes

43.90 There is one further argument in favour of a reversionary lease carve out rather than an Ingram carve out even where the life tenant has not had a qualifying interest in possession in the freehold for seven years. Section 102ZA arguably does not apply to catch the termination of Lady Olly's life interest anyway under the ROB provisions because her interest in possession in the freehold property does not come to an end (as required by s.102ZA(1)(c)). Instead, all that is happening under the reversionary lease scheme is that the value of the freehold property in which she has an interest in possession is being devalued by the exercise by the trustees of their overriding powers of appointment. Section 52(3) IHTA 1984 provides that this will be a deemed ending of the interest in possession, but this deeming provision does not apply for s.102ZA FA 1986 only for the purposes of "this section", i.e. s.52.

43.91 The freehold interest should, following Lady Olly's death, be held on discretionary trusts. This is because, if the freehold passes outright to the children on death (who hold the reversionary lease), there is a risk that HMRC could argue that by virtue of associated operations principle, there was a single gift of the whole of the property to the children at the date of death.

POAT and carve-out schemes

43.91 A major advantage of carrying out a reversionary lease or *Ingram* arrangement within a trust structure is that any POA charge should be minimal. Even if A has made a disposal of an interest in land (which may be doubted) the value of what he has given away as life tenant has a small value namely the right to receive rent or occupy the property after 17 years for the rest of his life.

Capital gains tax and carve out schemes

The reversionary lease has to be appointed outright to the son in Example 43.14 to avoid an entry charge that would otherwise arise if it was settled. However, this is disadvantageous for capital gains tax purposes when the house is sold in the future. The reversionary lease is acquired at a low value and increases in value in the hands of the son without the benefit of main residence relief. In practice the capital gains tax disadvantages can be avoided as follows. Instead of appointing the whole of the reversionary lease outright to the son the trustees instead appoint only a 90 per cent interest outright to him. The remaining 10 per cent interest[150] is held on continuing discretionary trusts for the life tenant's issue to the exclusion of the life tenant. By virtue of *Crowe v Appleby*, the son will not become absolutely entitled as against the trustees to the reversionary lease for capital gains tax purposes and so there has been no disposal by the trustees.[151] Thus, the trustees remain owners of the whole property for capital gains tax but not inheritance tax purposes. There is no capital gains tax uplift to market value on the reversionary lease on the death of the life tenant. However, to the extent that any principal private residence relief is available on the property by virtue of the life tenant A occupying it as the main residence, this will continue to be available and protect both the freehold and reversionary interests: the entire land remains settled for capital gains tax purposes and a beneficiary is in occupation. See s.225 TCGA 1992. The fact that the son is not in occupation does not matter. The same arrangement can be carried out in Example 43.15 above. Lady Olly's children will hold say 90 per cent of the reversionary interest with the balance held on discretionary trusts as a sub-fund of the will trust and Lady Olly will occupy the house as her main residence. On her death the trustees will sell the house and be able to claim main residence relief on the entire gain—both in respect of the freehold and reversionary interests.

43.92

Conclusions on carve-out schemes

While the carve out scheme still has an important place in relation to both pre-March 2006 interest in possession trusts and where the surviving spouse has an immediate post-death interest under a will trust, it will clearly be of limited application elsewhere given the POAT problems. One other restriction is that the scheme does not work well if there is a risk that the life tenant may want to move. In these circumstances the only cash that will pass into the life tenant's fund on the sale of the old property is the cash attributable to the value of the freehold interest and those who hold the long reversionary lease will receive the balance of the sale proceeds. The cash received in the life tenant's fund may not be sufficient to fund a new purchase and there could be difficulties if the children then lend the cash from their share of the sale proceeds back to the life tenant or otherwise help finance a purchase.

43.93

---

[150] Or whatever percentage is thought appropriate in order to keep the discretionary trust within the life tenant's nil rate band and avoid immediate inheritance tax arising.

[151] This assumes the property in question is situated in England or Wales. See 9.18 and 12.10.

V CO-OWNERSHIP/SHARING ARRANGEMENTS (INCLUDING LET PROPERTY)

Position before March 9, 1999

43.94 The IHT treatment of co-ownership arrangements is not entirely straightforward. Before March 9, 1999, the following Ministerial statement (the Hansard Statement) governed the position:

> *"It may be that my Hon Friend's intention concerns the common case where someone gives away an individual share in land, typically a house, which is then occupied by all the joint owners including the donor. For example, elderly parents may make unconditional gifts of undivided shares in their house to their children and the parents and the children occupy the property as their family home, each owner bearing his or her share of the running costs. In those circumstances, the parents' occupation or enjoyment of the part of the house that they have given away is in return for similar enjoyment of the children of the other part of the property. Thus the donors' occupation is for full consideration.*
>
> *Accordingly, I assure my Hon Friend that the gift with reservation rules will not be applied to an unconditional gift of an undivided share in land merely because the property is occupied by all the joint owners or tenants in common, including the donor."*[152]

43.95 This is a puzzling statement. The parents' occupation is surely by virtue of their owning a share in the property: the children are not "allowing" them to live there. The statement also assumes that the house is divided into discrete parts so that the parents' use of the children's part is in return for the parents letting the children use their part. In reality, the parents have the right to occupy the entire property as the owners of an undivided share. Presumably the "full consideration" referred to is intended to be that "I will let you use my 50 per cent of the house in consideration for you allowing me to use your 50 per cent". This is the basis of the supposed 50 per cent ceiling in the size of the gifted share.

However, it is thought that the arrangement is in the nature of a carve-out since the parents' right to occupy the entire property is derived from the interest that they have retained and does not amount to a reservation in the gifted share. This carve-out arrangement was considered in the *Eversden* case where the Special Commissioner and Lightman J. appeared to accept it in relation to the original property, although the latter did not agree there was a carve-out in relation to the replacement property.[153]

If the carve-out argument is right, then the full consideration and therefore the size of the interest retained is irrelevant since even a five per cent retained share confers the right to occupy the property in its entirety. In correspondence between the Law Society and HMRC in 1987,[154] the latter accepted that

---

[152] Statement of Mr Peter Brooke, Minister of State, Treasury Standing Committee G; Hansard, June 10, 1986, col.425.
[153] For the facts of the case, see Ch.22 and 43.44.
[154] Letter dated May 18, 1987.

there could be a gift of an unequal share in the home. However, that statement made it clear that the owners had to remain in joint occupation and that the donee should not pay the donor's share of running costs. It was also seen as important that the donee occupied the property as his family home. The position was substantially altered by the "anti-*Ingram*" legislation in 1999.

Position after March 8, 1999

Gifts of undivided shares in land are now regulated by FA 1986 s.102B. In general, the gift involves a reservation of benefit in cases where the donor continues in occupation.[155] Section 102B(4), however, provides that there is no reserved benefit in the following circumstances: **43.96**

(1) the donor disposes by way of gift, on or after March 9, 1999, of an undivided share of an interest in land;

(2) the donor and the donee occupy the land; and

(3) the donor does not receive any benefit, other than a negligible one, which is provided by or at the expense of the donee for some reason connected with the gift.

Note that there is no longer any requirement for occupation by the donor and donee as the family home. Further, there is no reference to full consideration as the basis for the exemption, so it is thought that the donor is able to give away more than a 50 per cent share in the property. **43.97**

EXAMPLE 43.16

(1) Judith, now widowed, lives in the family home at Sandbanks. Her married daughter lives in south London and comes to stay with Judith with her two young children most weekends and in school holidays. Judith gives the daughter a 50 per cent share in the house. She continues to pay all the outgoings on the property.

   (i) Section 102B(4) will apply given that both occupy the property. The daughter comes and goes as she pleases; leaves possessions in the property; has her own bedrooms etc. From her point of view it is like a second home.

   (ii) The gift is a PET by Judith and note that in calculating the fall in value of her estate her retained 50 per cent share will have a discounted value to reflect the fact of joint ownership. On Judith's death it is this discounted 50 per cent share that will be taxed.

   (iii) Consider the daughter's CGT position assuming that she owns a house in south London. Which is to qualify as her principal private

[155] See s.102B(2).

residence? Consider the use of the election under TCGA 1992 s.222(5).

(2) Some years ago Ben gave a one-third share in his home to his daughter Sheila who lives with him at home and looks after him. He now gifts a further one-third share to his son, an airline pilot who spends most of his time in New York but who stays with Ben ("treats the place like home") when he is in the UK (on average six weeks a year). It is thought that both gifts are protected by s.102B(4).

Occupation

43.98 HMRC give a wide (and in the authors' view) misconceived meaning to "occupation" for the purpose of the para.3 charge in the POA Guidance Notes.[156] It is not clear that the examples cited by HMRC constitute occupation at all for POAT purposes. In any event it is unlikely that the Courts would construe the meaning of occupation in the same way for s.102B purposes since each statute has different objectives. In the authors' view occupation requires some element of control. Mere storage of articles in a house or visits at the invitation of the owner to a home however frequent these visits are, do not constitute occupation.[157]

Expenses

43.99 HMRC are known to dislike arrangements where the donor gives away (say) 90 per cent of the property, and are likely to investigate carefully the third condition set out above: i.e. has the donor received any connected benefits from the donee? That in turn will involve scrutinising how expenses have been split between them.

Under both *Hansard* and s.102B there has been some misunderstanding of precisely how the running costs should be split. A cursory reading of the *Hansard* statement might suggest that running expenses should be split in proportion to the beneficial interests that each has in the property. However, "his share of the running costs", as HMRC subsequently confirmed refers to the donor and donee's actual expenses incurred. Thus, if there is a 90:10 beneficial split in the property, the donee arguably should not pay 90 per cent of the expenses but instead pay no more than the expenses he has actually incurred; when donor and donee live together full-time, this will generally mean a 50:50 split.

In simple terms, just because a person owns 90 per cent of the property, it does not mean that he uses 90 per cent of the gas; electricity and water, and if the donee agrees to pay 90 per cent of those expenses he is therefore conferring

---

[156] See A2.72.

[157] For a detailed consideration of the meaning of "occupation" in the context of both POAT and s.102B see the authors' Dymonds Capital Taxes 33.102 onwards. It is clear that frequent visits to a house by the donor could constitute a reservation of benefit since s.102 is looking at the receipt of *benefits* rather than occupation per se. Visits to a house may be a benefit for reservation of benefit purposes but cannot be regarded as occupation for POAT or s.102B purposes.

a benefit on the donor. The focus is on what collateral benefits, if any, are being provided by the donee in connection with the gift. HMRC do not appear to distinguish between property and living expenses although it may be argued that repair bills should be split in proportion to ownership of the property.

EXAMPLE 43.17

Bob has always occupied his house with his unmarried son, Bill, and has paid all the property expenses. He now gives Bill a share in the property (say 60 per cent) and Bill takes over 60 per cent of the property bills. Nothing else changes in their relationship, Bob continues living in the property (as before) but is now relieved of the worry of paying 60 per cent of the property bills.

   (i) Bob must not receive a benefit (however small?) from Bill which is in some way connected with the gift;

  (ii) there is nothing in the IHT legislation or in common sense to suggest that if Bill does not pay a share of expenses the gift of the 60 per cent is in any sense a "sham"; accordingly;

 (iii) it will be sensible to err on the side of caution. Better for Bob to overpay (or even pay all expenses!) than for there to be a risk that he is in receipt of a benefit. Quite often Bob will be content to do this: it was, after all the arrangement prior to the gift, and children are increasingly happy to be financially dependent on their parents! It may also represent sensible IHT planning for Bob to deplete his estate in this way.

Position under the POA Regime

Prima facie, the POA Regime applies to co-ownership arrangements because there has been a disposal of an interest in land and the donor continues to occupy the property. However, if property *"would fall to be treated as property which is subject to a reservation of benefit"* but for s.102B(4), the land charge does not apply.[158] Since s.102B(4) can only apply to, and therefore protect, post-March 8, 1999 arrangements, the legislation also provides that a disposal made before that time is not subject to the POA Regime if one assumes that had it been made on or after that date it would have qualified for s.102B(4) protection. What is slightly odd about this is that if this particular gift had been made in 1997 it might not have had *Hansard* protection, for instance if the donee was not occupying the property as his family home. The POA Regime does not distinguish between the different conditions required under *Hansard* as compared to s.102B(4) and it may be that HMRC does not, in practice, require occupation as a family home in relation to pre-March 1999 arrangements, even in the inheritance tax context. **43.100**

[158] FA 2004 Sch.15 para.11(5)(c).

Sales of part

43.101 It is somewhat odd that gifts of part falling within s.102B(4) are protected from the POA charge but that sales of part even at full value are not so protected (albeit that such transactions are not gifts and so not subject to the reservation of benefit rules).[159] It is assumed[160] that sales of part at an undervalue are gifts as to the undervalue and may still qualify for protection under s.102B(4) and so exemption from charge under the POA Regime, at least as to the undervalue.

Cash gifts

43.102 What happens if in Example 43.17 Bob does not give an undivided interest in the land to his son but instead gives him cash? For example, Bob gives cash of £100,000 to Bill and together they buy a house worth £200,000, owning it in equal shares and both living there. Section 102B(4) is not in point because Bob has not satisfied the first condition—he has not made a gift of an undivided share in land. But he has not made a gift which is caught by the reservation of benefit rules unless the cash gift was conditional on Bill using it to purchase the property (and then it may be analysed as a gift of a share in the property rather than cash so that s.102B(4) can apply).[161] Does Bob then have a problem under the POA Regime? He has satisfied the contribution and the occupation conditions and therefore prima facie is caught by the land charge. He is not directly protected under the para.11(5)(c) exemption as he does not have s.102B(4) protection. However, para.11(8) provides that in determining whether any property falls within para.11(5)(c) in a case where the contribution condition is met, Sch.20 para.2(2)(b) of FA 1986 (exclusion of gifts of money from the tracing rules) is to be disregarded. The consequences of this deeming appear to be as follows:

  (i) the restriction of tracing through cash gifts for the purposes of reservation of benefit is disapplied;

  (ii) accordingly a gift of cash falls within the general "tracing" rule: viz if the donee ceases to have possession and enjoyment of the gifted property (the cash) then any property which that donee received in substitution for the cash (the share in the purchased property) shall be treated as having been comprised in the original gift;

  (iii) as if the original gift is deemed to be of an undivided share in land then s.102B(4) protection will be available.

43.103 In this situation if the donee ceases to occupy the property so that the s.102B(4) condition is not met the POA protection of para.11(5)(c) is lost and

---

[159] See 43.104.
[160] A2.57.
[161] For the restricted tracing rules in the reservation of benefit legislation, see 33.29.

the gift, although not caught by the reservation of benefit rules, is subject to a POA charge.

Donee dies or ceases to occupy[162]

If either of the requirements of s.102B(4) is broken the gifted share will be **43.104** subject to a reservation of benefit (one way of looking at the position is to say that although the donor has reserved a benefit in the gifted share, the reservation of benefit rules will not apply to him whilst the donee occupies the property and the donor receives no collateral benefit from the donee).

EXAMPLE 43.18

> Sally gives a 50 per cent share in her Reading house to her daughter Shula who is aged 18 and studying at university. After obtaining her degree in media studies, Shula moves out to take up a well paid job in London.
>
> The IHT/POA consequences are as follows:
>
> (i)   Sally no longer has the protection of s.102B(4) because para.(a) is no longer satisfied;
> (ii) accordingly the gifted share is now property subject to a reservation and the charging provisions in FA 1986 s.102(3) and (4) apply;
> (iii) because Sally is caught by the reservation of benefit rules the POA charge does not apply.

As the above example shows, it is important that a gift is only made when it is likely that the joint occupation of the property is going to be long term. Otherwise the position can end up in a mess. It is not, for instance, true to say that Sally is back where she started as a result of falling foul of the reservation of benefit rules: all that these do is to bring the gift back into her estate for IHT purposes either to be taxed at death or to form the subject matter of a lifetime PET. Accordingly should she wish to sell the property in a few years then not only would Shula be entitled to 50 per cent of the proceeds but full CGT main residence relief will not be available on Shula's share, if she no longer occupies the property as her residence.

Reorganising the arrangement

In cases where the donee intends to cease to occupy so that the spectre of a **43.105** reservation of benefit is looming consider the following restructuring options.

---

[162] Although s.102B(4) refers to the need for both donor and donee to occupy the property it is not thought that IHT problems will arise if it is the donor who ceases to occupy (e.g. he may move into a nursing home). In this situation because the donor is not in occupation of the gifted property there is no reservation of benefit: see FA 1986 s.102B(3)(a).

Donor pays a "full consideration" for his occupation of the whole property

43.106 In these circumstances he will not be subject to the reservation of benefit rules[163]; nor will he be subject to the POA Regime which gives protection under para.11(5)(d). There are, of course, difficulties in determining what would be full consideration in this case given that the donor is already entitled to occupy the property as a co-owner. Does he pay the rent that a lodger would pay to share with him or does he have to pay 50 per cent of the full market rent payable as if the property were let with vacant possession? The former is likely to be much lower than the latter! Under the POA Regime the rental value is the full market rent if the property were let with vacant possession; the only unknown factor to determine is the DV—the value of what has been given away. By contrast, in the reservation of benefit legislation, full consideration is not defined. In practice, it is understood that HMRC consider that full consideration in this situation is the appropriate percentage (based on the size of the share given away) of the rent for the whole property.

Donee settles gifted share on a reverter to settlor trust

43.107 An alternative strategy before March 22, 2006 was for the donee to settle the gifted share in the property on a reverter to settlor trust for the donor for life.[164] This is no longer attractive for inheritance tax purposes unless the original donor is disabled. Accordingly if Shula in Example 43.18 settles her share on interest in possession trusts for Sally who is now disabled this will create a qualifying interest in possession and be a PET by Shula. On Sally's death reverter to settler relief is available and s.102(3) FA 1986 is disapplied. However, Sally as the original donor of the share is subject to a POA charge from December 5, 2005.[165]

Practical issues

43.108 A number of practical issues need to be considered before entering into a sharing arrangement. For example, what happens if the donee marries someone whom the donor does not like? That spouse may then occupy the property with the donee. Or suppose that the donor wishes to sell and move somewhere smaller, does he have sufficient funds from his retained share to rehouse himself? Bear in mind that if the donee dies first not only is there inheritance tax payable on his share but the donor will then have to pay full consideration for continued occupation to avoid a reservation of benefit (since the donee, being dead, cannot continue to occupy the property).

---

[163] Because he is protected by FA 1986 Sch.20 para.6.
[164] See Ch.37.
[165] See generally Ch.34.

EXAMPLE 43.19

Sebastian's one substantial asset is Flyte Hall, an Edwardian property worth £1 million. His son, recently divorced, lives with him and, as the arrangement is likely to be permanent. Sebastian gives him a 90 per cent share in the property. Unfortunately the son dies in a motor accident shortly afterwards leaving Sebastian devastated. The son dies intestate and his share in the property passes to his young children who live in London with their mother. Sebastian dies shortly afterwards:

(i) *death of the son*: IHT will be charged on 90 per cent of Flyte Hall. It is always important in entering into a sharing arrangement to consider not just the IHT position of donor but also of donee. Insurance on the life of the son would have been relatively cheap to effect;

(ii) *death of Sebastian*: because he has continued to live in the Hall after the son's death the reservation of benefit rules will result in the entire property being taxed on his death. Double charges relief may be available if he died within seven years of his original gift.

A further concern is whether the gift of a share to an occupying child will disadvantage another child. Assume that Barry has given a half share in his house outright to his youngest son David, and that share was worth £325,000. If Barry dies within seven years of the gift, although David suffers no extra inheritance tax as donee, John, Barry's other son, who has been left the rest of Barry's estate will find that he ends up footing the entire IHT bill—the benefit of the nil rate band has been allocated entirely against David's gift. **43.109**

Other problems can arise if the house increases in value faster than the rest of the estate or the remaining estate has to be used to pay nursing home fees. Suppose Barry gives David a 90 per cent share in the house. The 90 per cent share is worth £325,000 and the 10 per cent retained share £32,000. Barry's other investments such as cash and equities are worth around £300,000 at the time of the gift. He leaves all these to John by will. Unfortunately within three years of the gift Barry becomes ill and has to move into a nursing home. (Although s.102B(4) will thereupon cease to be satisfied, Barry will not fall within the reservation of benefit rules given that he no longer occupies the property.) David remains in the property but all Barry's liquid assets are used to pay the nursing home fees.

Who is the donee?

An outright gift of an undivided share is the most common situation but assume, for instance, that Barry would prefer to settle an interest in the property for the benefit of David (perhaps because David is a disabled child in receipt of state benefit or because it is hoped that the trustees can later equalise any disparities between the children). A gift into a flexible life interest trust for David was before March 22, 2006 considered to fall within the protection of s.102B(4) on the basis that, as life tenant, David is treated **43.110** as owning the property in the settlement[166] and hence was the donee. This remains the position even after FA 2006 but only because David, as a disabled person, can take a qualifying interest in possession so that Barry has made a PET.[167]

If David is not disabled the position is quite different. He would not take a qualifying interest in possession and is therefore not treated as owning the property. The trustees own the property and they do not occupy it and so the protection of s.102B(4) is not available to Barry.

Second homes

43.111 In cases where it is desired to gift a share in a second home not attracting principal private residence relief, the gifted share may be put into a trust[168] and subsequently appointed out to the intended donee (again with the benefit of hold-over relief). The difficulty with this arrangement is reconciling it with the wording of s.102B(4) since the occupying person will not be the original donee of the gift. That will be the trustees and hence it is thought that s.102B(4) will not afford protection so that the share settled by the donor will be caught by the reservation of benefit rules. The problem cannot be corrected later: the original donee has to be the person in occupation. Can this be made to work to the taxpayer's advantage?

EXAMPLE 43.20

A gives a large share in his house to his son B and occupies it with B. B subsequently gives part of that share to his adult children who are not in occupation. In these circumstances is A still protected from reservation of benefit under s.102B(4)? Both donor and original donee still occupy the land so the basic conditions in s.102B(4) are satisfied. B has reserved a benefit since his children are not in occupation but this may not matter in the short-term if B has a reasonable life expectancy and plans to sell up on A's death.

43.112 A simple strategy where the second home shows a chargeable gain would be for a share of the second home to be given away which produces a gain falling within the donor's annual CGT exemption (for 2011–12 this is £10,600). When the property is jointly owned a double exemption (£21,200) is available. This may not result in a substantial slice being given in any one year but the process can be repeated in successive years until the desired percentage has been given away. The main difficulty is obtaining accurate values to make sure that the gain realised stays within the annual exemption.

[166] By virtue of IHTA 1984 s.49(1).
[167] See Ch.36.
[168] In order to obtain the benefit of CGT hold-over relief under TCGA 1992 s.260(2)(a).

Conclusions on the use of sharing arrangements for the main residence

Co-ownership arrangements are one of the safer life time IHT planning **43.113** options provided that the donee continues to occupy the property and the various family and practical issues mentioned above are resolved. The donor can avoid both the reservation of benefit rules and the POA Regime. Bear in mind that the relief is for shared occupation and shared ownership: it is crucial that the donor retains an interest in the property. Give away a 90 per cent share and GWR/POA problems may be avoided: give away a 100 per cent share and the reservation of benefit rules will catch the donor. Similarly a gift of cash used to purchase a 100 per cent interest in the home occupied by the donor results in a POA charge. By contrast if the donor also purchases a share and there is joint occupation, then there is no POA charge!

Co-ownership arrangements for let property

This planning is designed for the situation where clients wish to give away **43.114** the capital value of the let properties but retain the rent. A major obstacle to overcome if an arrangement like this is to succeed in avoiding IHT is reservation of benefit. FA 1986 s.102B(3) does, however, provide an exception to the rules if, (a) the donor gives away *a share* (note *not* his whole interest) in a property; (b) does not occupy the property; but (c) continues to benefit, e.g. by receiving rent from it.

EXAMPLE 43.21

> Assume that Mr and Mrs W have a property worth £100,000 owned 50:50. They give (say) their son a 90 per cent interest (retaining five per cent each) but agree with him that they can keep all the rent. They have made a PET for IHT purposes; no reservation of benefit arises because they do not occupy the gifted property and s.102B(3) provides protection in these circumstances. Of course they make a disposal for CGT purposes so any gain on the property (above their annual exemption) will be taxed.

An alternative to an outright gift would be to settle the gifted share into a **43.115** trust under which the donors retain a life interest. In the above example, Mr and Mrs W would settle the 90 per cent interest on trusts for themselves for life then to (say) the son. Now they are *entitled* to all the income from the property rather than "relying" on the son to allow them to keep it all. The argument is that s.102B(3) protects the donor from any reservation of benefit while the trust holds let property. What happens if the property is then sold and the trustees hold cash or other investments, paying the income to the life tenant? Is the retention of a life interest by the donors a reservation of benefit under general principles? This is discussed further in Ch.33 and although there are varying views the authors' conclude that a reservation of benefit can be avoided with careful drafting. However, while the trust holds intangibles a POAT charge would arise.

There is one significant change in the tax analysis from March 22, 2006 if the settlement route is chosen, namely that the gift into trust is a chargeable transfer rather than a PET. This means that the total value settled by each of Mr and Mrs W should not exceed their available IHT nil rate band. However, it does offer certainty which may be attractive, e.g. if a donee divorces/becomes bankrupt.

VI CASH GIFTS

43.116 Cash gifts have been a fruitful area for IHT planning because of the curiously limited tracing rules.[169]

EXAMPLE 43.22

Jason has lived abroad for many years. In 2010 he gives his daughter, Ruth, £250,000 which she uses to purchase a Suffolk property ("the Crow's Nest"). On his return to England in 2012, Jason occupies the property with Ruth. Jason acquires no interest in the property.

43.117 Jason has made a gift to his daughter and now occupies the property purchased: is he caught by the reservation of benefit rules in FA 1986? The relevant provisions are as follows:

(i) FA 1986 s.102(1) provides that there is a gift with reservation if an individual disposes of any property (here the cash) by way of gift and either, (a) possession and enjoyment of the property is not bona fide assumed by the donee; or (b) at any time in the seven years prior to the donor's death the property is not enjoyed to the entire exclusion or virtually the entire exclusion of the donor and of any benefit to him by contract or otherwise.

(ii) FA 1986 Sch.10 para.6(1)(c) is also relevant. This provides that in determining whether any property which is disposed of by way of gift is enjoyed to the entire exclusion of the donor and of any benefit to him by contract or otherwise, a benefit which the donor obtained by virtue of any associated operations of which the disposal by way of gift is one shall be treated as a benefit to him by contract or otherwise.

(iii) Associated operations are defined by IHTA 1984 s.268 to mean any two or more operations of any kind being, (a) operations which affect the same property or one of which affects some property and the other or others of which affect property representing that property; or (b) any two operations of which one is effected with reference to the other or

---

[169] In FA 1986 Sch.20: see 33.29.

with a view to enabling the other to be effected or facilitating its being effected.

(iv) Finally, Sch.20 para.2 ("substitutions and accretions") deals with substitutions but the paragraph does not apply if the property gifted is cash.[170]

Has Jason reserved a benefit in the cash gifted?

Prima facie it does not appear that there is any reservation of benefit in the **43.118** cash itself because the cash has gone and Sch.20 contains no tracing provisions for outright gifts of cash. There is no direct link between the benefit received (donor living in the property) and the gift of cash. The benefit to Jason of occupying the house does not arise from the gift of cash unless that gift was in some way made conditional on being used to purchase a property.

The property gifted (i.e. the cash) has been enjoyed to the entire exclusion of Jason provided that the gift had not been made conditional on being used to purchase the property: otherwise there is a risk that the gift is in fact of an interest in land or alternatively (and more likely) that Jason is treated as receiving a benefit in the cash gifted because it was made on the basis and on the understanding that he should be allowed to continue in occupation of the purchased property. (The benefit does not need to come from the gifted asset as such if it arises out of the gift.) So, HMRC might consider that Ruth is estopped from denying Jason's occupation once the gift has been made, because he had made the gift under an agreement that she would use the funds to purchase the property

In this case, however, it is difficult to argue that the gift of cash was in reality a gift of the Crow's Nest. On the basis of estate duty cases such as *Sneddon v Lord Advocate*[171] (gift of cash used to purchase shares three days later) and *Potter v Inland Revenue*[172] (gift from donor of cash expressed to be to enable the donee to purchase shares), the subject matter of the gift was nevertheless the cash not the property purchased. The fact that the money was given for a particular purpose does not mean that the gift was subject to a legally enforceable condition.

Effect of the associated operations rule

It is not thought that the associated operations rule affect this conclusion: **43.119** either the arrangement involves a reservation in the gifted property or the reservation of benefit provisions are inapplicable. It might be argued that the

---

[170] Para.2(2)(b). Note also that different rules apply if the original property disposed of by the gift is not cash or is cash which "becomes settled property by virtue of the gift": Sch.20 para.2(2)(a). The rules for settled gifts are in para.5 which treats the gift as being of property comprised in the trust fund from time to time. There is therefore no exemption from the tracing rules for settled cash gifts, although the rules are deficient when property comes out of a settlement.
[171] [1954] AC 257.
[172] [1958] SLT 198.

gift of cash and the purchase of the freehold are associated transactions in that the gift of cash was made with reference to the subsequent purchase and questions of estoppel and conditional gifts are not relevant. But is Sch.20 para.6(1)(c) wide enough to deem the benefit from the associated operation (the purchase) to be a benefit to the donor in the property disposed of (the gift of cash)? If, as is thought, the benefit enjoyed from the associated operation must entrench in some way upon the possession of the actual gifted property in order for there to be a reservation of benefit, then associated operations do not cause an additional reservation of benefit problem. The benefit enjoyed (i.e. the occupation of the house) does not in itself entrench on the gift of the cash. Put another way, the point is that HMRC may be able to establish that Jason has received a benefit from the associated operation made by his daughter (namely the purchase of the property) but they also have to show that the gifted property (i.e. the cash) is not enjoyed to the entire exclusion of any benefit to Jason. Unless the cash gift was conditional or Ruth was estopped from using the cash in any other way, Jason does not enjoy a benefit from the cash as such. The purchase of a property by Ruth combined with her allowing him to live there, benefits him but this is still not a benefit from the cash itself which has been spent.

Approach of HMRC

43.120   In the Manual[173] HMRC accept that the tracing rules do not apply to an absolute gift of a sum of money. This is qualified in two ways:

(i)   if the absolute cash gift is itself subject to a reservation then the sum of money will be taxable; and

(ii) *"a gift which initially seems to be of cash may in reality be a GWR, by associated operations, of other property"*. The example given involves A giving £100,000 cash to B which B uses to buy A's residence (worth £100,000) in which A continues to reside. HMRC comment that *"this is a GWR, by associated operations, of the residence."*

As already noted, it is, however, difficult to see how the associated operations rules can be used to re-characterise a gift as being of property rather than of cash. Of course, the specific example involves a circular arrangement in which the actual cash may never have changed hands. The weakness of the argument appears underlined by the subsequent comments (under the heading "What to do"):

> *"You will not normally raise any enquiries to see if a gift which appears to be of cash may be a gift, by associated operations, of other property. Only ask questions if there is a positive reason for doing so, e.g. where:*
> *the gift is of an odd amount, such as £49,563.15, which suggests it may be related to a purchase by the donee, or*

---

[173] See IHTM14372.

> *there is specific information that the gift was related to the acquisition by the donee of property, especially if the acquisition is from the donor."*

Despite the example cited in the Manual, HMRC appear to take a more circumspect position in the POA Guidance Notes:

> *"where an absolute gift of cash may later be used by the recipient to purchase property occupied or enjoyed by the donor, for example, the application of the reservation of benefit rules to this property is precluded unless the transaction can be shown to be a gift with reservation of benefit by associated operations, of the purchased property."*

Accordingly, it does not follow that all benefits referable to a gift will come within **43.121** s.102. It is not sufficient to take the situation as a whole and find that the donor has continued to enjoy substantial advantages which have some relation to the gifted property. Each advantage must be considered separately to determine whether it is a benefit within the statute.[174] In the authors' view outright cash gifts to an individual will rarely be caught by the reservation of benefit rules.

Impact of the pre-owned asset regime

Given that Jason's gift is not caught by the reservation of benefit rules, it will **43.122** fall within the POA Regime so that he will suffer an income tax charge from April 6, 2005. The following points may be noted:

  (i) Paragraph 3 applies given that Jason is in occupation of the property and that the contribution condition is met.

 (ii) If Ruth had provided some of the purchase price for the "Crow's Nest", para.4(2) requires an apportionment of DV to determine such part of the value of the relevant land as may be attributed to the consideration provided by Jason.

(iii) Although Jason is not in sole occupation, no allowance is made for this in fixing the rental value of "Crow's Nest".

(iv) Note that if Jason acquired a five per cent interest in the new property he would be protected from POA while they are both in joint occupation.[175]

The seven-year defence and cash gifts before April 6, 1998

If the facts are varied so that Jason made the gift to his daughter in March **43.123** 2000 and only returned to England in April 2007 when he occupies the property for the first time, then,[176] the pre-owned asset charge will not apply

---

[174] *Oakes v Stamp Duties Commissioner of New South Wales* [1954] AC 57 at 72 and see *St Aubyn v AG* [1952] AC 15.
[175] See 43.97(ii): cash gifts and co-ownership.
[176] As a result of FA 2004 Sch.15 para.10(2)(c): the arrangement is an excluded transaction.

because the gift was made more than seven years before Jason first occupied the property. Further, only outright cash gifts after April 5, 1998 are caught by the POA Regime even if occupation of the property purchased with the gifted money took place soon after. Accordingly if Jason had made the cash gift in March 1998 and in 2002 took up occupation no POA charge arises even though he occupied the property within seven years of the cash gift.[177]

43.124   Curiously para.10(2)(c) refers to outright cash gifts *"to the other person"* and hence, could include gifts of cash into settlement.[178] As noted above, such gifts are generally caught by the reservation of benefit provisions anyway because the tracing provisions apply but there may be circumstances in which a cash gift into settlement is exempt from the reservation of benefit provisions and also from the POA charge.

EXAMPLE 43.23

> In 2002 Perseus settles cash on interest in possession trusts for his spouse under which he can benefit. Such a transaction cannot be excluded from the POA regime because para.8 arrangements (settlor-interested settlements of intangibles) can never be excluded transactions within para.10. In 2003, the trustees purchase a house with the cash and terminate the spousal interest in possession. The property is rented out until 2010 when Perseus occupies the property. The POA analysis is that provided that Perseus does not occupy the property within seven years of the cash gift he is protected from a charge.[179]

Options for taxpayers

43.125   What are the options for Jason in Example 43.22 if he is caught by the POA charge, e.g. because the cash gift was made on or after April 6, 1998 and he occupied the purchased property within seven years?

> (i) *Election*: Jason could elect for the reservation of benefit rules to apply[180] in order to avoid the income tax charge.
>
> (ii) *Shared occupation*: Suppose Jason gives Ruth cash to purchase a house. Ruth and Jason eventually pool resources and jointly buy a house for their joint occupation. In these circumstances there is no POA charge (see para.11(8) and 43.42, above). If people are going to live together it is desirable for each party to have an undivided share in the land. In

---

[177] See A2.17.
[178] Contrast the wording in para.10(2)(e) which refers expressly to a gift to an individual. The IHT Manual comments that *"a gift is not an outright gift if it is subject to conditions or if it could revert to the donor in any circumstances whatsoever"*.
[179] From March 22, 2006 Perseus will make an immediately chargeable transfer when he sets up the trust.
[180] See Ch.34.

these circumstances there will be no charge under the POA Regime and no reservation of benefit.

(iii) *Improvement*: if Jason gave cash away which was used only to improve, rather than acquire an interest in, a house in which he lives then there is no POA charge or reservation of benefit.

VII SELLING THE FAMILY HOME

One of the (many!) curious features about the POA Regime is the approach taken to sales of land and chattels. Unlike the reservation of benefit legislation, the POA Regime can apply even when no gift has been made. Any disposal of land which the disponer continues to occupy can, in principle, be caught unless it comes within a specific exemption. **43.126**

EXAMPLE 43.24

Rose and Emily, two sisters, have lived together for some years. Rose alone owns the house worth £800,000. She decides to sell, for full consideration, a half share in the property to Emily. (She may want the cash to supplement her lifestyle or may wish to give it away, to other relatives.) Emily pays £400,000 for a 50 per cent share in the property.

(i) Despite the fact that Rose has not made Emily a gift nor made a transfer of value for inheritance tax purposes, she is prima facie caught by the POA Regime. A disposal of the property has been made and Rose continues in occupation. By contrast, if Rose had given the half share to Emily, she would not have a POA charge[181];

(ii) The fact that Emily has paid full consideration for her share does not help Rose: the sale is not protected under para.10(1)(a) because it is not a sale of her whole interest in the land;

(iii) the pre-owned assets charge cannot be reduced under the non-exempt sale provisions because these require a transfer of the whole interest in land.

Regulations extended the POA regime where there are sales of part at full value, namely[182]: **43.127**

(a) an exemption for commercial sales of part (see reg.5(1)(a)); and

(b) certain other sales but only if these occurred before March 7, 2005.

---

[181] As a result of the protection of para.11(5)(c) (incorporating the "sharing arrangements" in FA 1986 s.102B(4)).
[182] SI 2005/724.

Example 43.25

Mary needs to raise cash on her home. After taking financial advice she enters into an equity release scheme with Rest Assurance Inc to whom she sells a 40 per cent share of the property. Under the general terms and conditions Mary is entitled to go on living in the property for the rest of her life. Mary is exempted from any POA charge by reg.5.

43.128 There is also an exemption for connected person disposals provided that, (a) it was such as might be expected to have been made at arm's length between persons not connected with each other; and either (b) the disposal was for a consideration not in money; or (c) in the form of readily convertible assets or the disposal was made before March 7, 2005.

43.129 The upshot is that unless the sale to a connected person occurred before March 7, 2005 Rose in Example 43.24 is caught by the POA charge. Accordingly, she will pay a POA charge on the appropriate rental value of the property. In calculating the POA charge on Rose, allowance will be made for the 50 per cent interest in the land which she retains. The cash of £400,000 is also part of Rose's estate for IHT purposes and similarly a half share in the property is part of Emily's estate.

Sales of whole for full consideration

43.130 What are arguably more controversial arrangements do not appear to be caught by the POA Regime. The starting point for any planning depends on using the exclusion given in para.10(1)(a). This provides a complete protection from the POA charge if the disposal is:

> "*of his whole interest in the property except for any right expressly reserved by him over the property either by a transaction made at arm's length with a person not connected with him or by a transaction such as might be expected to be made at arm's length between persons not connected with each other.*"

The disposal need not be for cash: it can be an arm's length exchange of property.

43.131 One option that has been used in the past (and is still available) is for the whole house to be sold by the individual to a member of his family for full market value. The purchaser can then allow the vendor to live there free of charge. There is no gift so the reservation of benefit provisions do not apply. The cash is part of the vendor's estate for inheritance tax purposes and he can, if he wishes, give it away in due course. This apparently simple transaction does, however, pose a number of problems. There are, for instance, difficulties if the purchaser does not have sufficient cash to pay the purchase price. If he borrows commercially and the vendor then gives him cash to pay off the mortgage then the POA contribution condition is satisfied and a charge arises. In those circumstances, the purchaser might want the vendor to agree to leave the purchase price outstanding as a long-term loan (in which case any subsequent gift of the debt by the vendor would be more problematic for IHT purposes if HMRC's recent attack on debts in the context of home loan schemes succeeds. In this case, the terms of the loan must be the same as those offered by any bank or building society, i.e. it should be on normal commercial terms, interest bearing with interest being paid not rolled up, secured and with the usual deposit paid. It has to be shown that the whole arrangement is a transaction *"such as might be expected to be made at arm's length between persons not connected with each other"*.

43.132 SDLT will be payable by the purchaser who may end up suffering capital gains tax on eventual sale of the property because the vendor who occupies it does not own it. In the past the IHT problem could be solved by the purchaser settling the house on reverter to settlor trusts but this is no longer feasible.[183]

Sale of freehold reversion subject to a lease

43.133 Given the difficulties involved in finding sufficient cash to pay for the purchase of the whole property, an alternative arrangement involves the taxpayer first carving out a lease for himself for a fixed term at a nil or nominal rent, and then selling the freehold interest (subject to that lease) for full market value. There is no gift by the vendor, and therefore the disposal is not caught by the reservation of benefit rules. The freehold has been devalued by carving out the lease. Accordingly, the purchaser has to pay less for the freehold reversion: in the case of a 15-year rent-free lease one might expect the freehold value to be reduced by as much as one half.

Such an arrangement is acceptable for IHT purposes, although it is important to ensure that the proper price is paid so that there is no element of bounty. The valuations are difficult, not least because the transaction is not a common one. There is almost certainly a loss of marriage value; the value of the freehold subject to the lease and the value of the lease are together unlikely to be equal to the current vacant possession value. Should the purchaser pay for the marriage value as well as for the freehold reversion? If so, that will cause a problem under the POA Regime since it is not the sort of transaction that would be made between parties at arm's length.[184]

If, instead, the vendor sells the reversion for a price equal to the value it has in the hands of the purchaser who pays nothing for loss of marriage value, the value of the vendor's estate has been diminished for IHT purposes. Such a transaction will not be a transfer of value if there was no intention to confer a gratuitous benefit on the purchaser.[185] Even if the vendor has made a transfer of value, he has not made a gift for reservation of benefit purposes. The question that remains is whether such a transaction can qualify for para.10(1)(a)(ii) protection from the POA charge. In a commercial transaction between unconnected parties (such as an equity release scheme) the vendor will receive no payment for the loss of marriage value.

43.134 It is important to ensure that when fixing the price for the sale of the encumbered freehold interest, account is taken of the terms of the lease to be retained (i.e. the lease should already be in existence and its terms considered

---

[183] As a result of the 2006 changes in the IHT treatment of settlements: see Ch.37.
[184] See para.10(1)(a)(ii).
[185] IHTA 1984 s.10.

by the valuers). Whilst there is some debate as to whether a lease for life or a lease for a term of years should be granted, the better view is that a lease for life should be avoided because of IHTA 1984 s.43(3): it is hard to argue that such a lease has been acquired for full consideration.

The capital gains tax problems mentioned above are still an issue. If the property is sold, the vendor will obtain principal private residence relief in respect of the lease but the purchaser will find that the freehold reversion is an appreciating asset in his estate which will not qualify for relief.

Funding the purchase price

43.135 Despite the reduced purchase price, difficulties can remain: suppose a purchasing child has insufficient cash to fund the purchase? Perhaps he cannot borrow from his bank and security on the property itself is of limited value because the child only owns the reversion and receives no rent. Can the vendor safely give cash to his child to enable the child to fund the purchase? The reservation of benefit substituted property rules do not apply to non-settled cash.[186] This would, however, cause POA problems. The contribution condition has been satisfied because consideration, namely cash, has been paid by the purchaser for the acquisition of an interest in the land that the vendor occupies and that consideration has been directly or indirectly provided by the vendor.[187]

Conclusions

43.136 IHT planning involving sales of the house (or chattels) to members of the family is still possible even under the POA Regime but considerable care is needed to ensure that the stringent conditions in Sch.15 para.10(1)(a) are satisfied. It is unlikely that HMRC will accept that sales of freehold reversions subject to a retained lease are within the protection of this paragraph without clear evidence of commerciality, and great care must be taken if the purchase money is subsequently given away. SDLT will increase the costs and CGT issues remain a problem if the vendor wishes to move.

VIII FOREIGN DOMICILIARIES AND THE FAMILY HOME— INHERITANCE TAX AND CAPITAL GAINS TAX CONSIDERATIONS

Inheritance tax considerations

43.137 For many years a foreign domiciliary who wished to own, e.g. a house in London, was advised to establish a trust which owned all the shares in an

---

[186] Sch.20 para.2(2)(b).
[187] Of course, the normal limitations on the scope of the contribution conditions apply: for instance, if there had been an outright gift of cash before April 6, 1998 the POA charge will not apply.

offshore company which in turn owned the house. The rationale was that the relevant asset for IHT purposes was the shares in the company which would be held in an excluded property settlement. There then arose a protracted controversy concerning the possible exposure of the foreign domiciliary to a charge to income tax under what was then Sch.E[188] by reason of the benefit of the occupation conferred upon him if he was an actual or a shadow director of the company. The *Dimsey*,[189] *Allen*[190] and *Deverell*[191] cases exacerbated this problem and accordingly new structures were developed.

Offshore "home loan" arrangements

The foreign domiciliary created two trusts. He funded the first trust (Trust 1), which was often discretionary, which in turn funded a company wholly owned by that trust. The company lent the funds to the second trust, under which the foreign domiciliary had an interest in possession and which used the funds to purchase the house. The loan, which was secured on the house, was left outstanding interest-free and repayable on demand.

43.138

Diagrammatically the position was as follows:

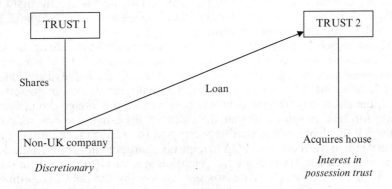

It will be noted that the house is no longer owned by a company so that the shadow director problem no longer applies. An alternative structure was for the discretionary trust to lend the cash by way of a specialty debt to the interest in possession trust with no charge taken over the house. This was thought to make the loan non-UK situated (and in any event both debtor and creditor are non-UK resident) but in order to ensure the IHT deductibility of the debt by the interest in possession trustees, the interest in possession trust held no other property.[192]

43.139

Assume that the company (or discretionary trust) lent to the interest in possession trust £1.5 million all of which the trust used to purchase the house and that 10 years later, when the foreign domiciliary died, the house was worth £2 million. For IHT purposes the value of the property would be reduced by the debt owed to the company and so worth only £500,000. The debt was a

---

[188] Now ITEPA 2003 ss.97–113.
[189] *R v Dimsey* [2001] STC 1520.
[190] *R v Allen* [2001] STC 1537.
[191] *Secretary of State for Trade & Industry v Deverell* [2001] Ch 340.
[192] See IHTA 1984 s.162 and Ch.32.

non-UK situs asset so excluded property in the hands of the discretionary trustees even when a company was not used. The net result was to take the amount of the debt outside the scope of IHT. In many cases the foreign domiciliary and his spouse had successive life interests in the property, so that if the foreign domiciliary's spouse survived him any charge on the excess value of the property was deferred until the death of his spouse. Alternatively any exposure to UK tax was covered by insurance arrangements.

Impact of the POA charge and 2006 IHT charges

43.140   The POA Regime adversely affected the tax effectiveness of some of these arrangements. Although both the para.12(2) basic relief and the settled property para.12(3) relief will operate in respect of the shares in the company (or the debt if it was held directly by the trustees and was non-UK situs), neither of these reliefs is available in respect of the house, because it is situated in the UK and is not excluded property. If the foreign domiciliary has a qualifying interest in possession in the house, the para.11(1) ownership exemption will prima facie be available but only to the extent that the value of the house exceeds the "excluded liability" of £1.5 million. The effect is that the first £1.5 million of the house will be within the POA Regime and their portion of the rent will be subject to annual income tax charges.

43.141   However, Sch.15 para.11(6) provides that there is a POA charge on the debt only "*where the value of someone's estate for the purposes of IHT is reduced by an excluded liability affecting any property*". Accordingly, if the discretionary trust holding the debt was converted into a qualifying interest in possession trust, the effect was that the debt was now part of the foreign domiciliary's estate for IHT purposes so that the value of his estate was not reduced. Although the debt was excluded property and so outside the inheritance tax net at death, nevertheless the POA income tax charge did not apply to the debt as an excluded liability because the condition in para.11(6) was not satisfied: the foreign domiciliary's estate was not reduced by the debt. Accordingly, foreign domiciliaries amended their double trust structure by converting the discretionary trust into an interest in possession trust.[193]

43.142   Since March 22, 2006 it has no longer been possible to convert the discretionary trust into a qualifying interest in possession trust[194] and therefore the trust holding the debt will not be treated as part of the donor's estate and para.11(6) is satisfied—the foreign domiciliary's estate is reduced by the debt even though he reserves a benefit in the debt of the discretionary trust. Reserved benefit property is not treated as part of a person's estate: it is merely taxable on death. Hence, a debt in which the foreign domiciliary reserves a benefit is one that reduces his estate and the POA charge can apply. Moreover those foreign domiciliaries who converted their debt trust into a qualifying

---

[193] Note that the value of the property trust is still reduced by the debt and so that property in the taxpayer's estate is reduced in value. However, the reduction is then comprised in his estate by virtue of the interest in possession in the debt trust. Overall therefore there is no reduction in value of his total estate because of the debt. It is not considered appropriate in this case to consider the two trusts in isolation (contrast the approach of Mann J. in *St Barbe Green v IRC* [2005] STC 288).
[194] See generally Ch.27.

interest in possession trust prior to March 22, 2006 found themselves potentially within the anti-reverter to settlor trust legislation, i.e. back with a POA charge![195]

It could be argued that an election would have no adverse inheritance tax effect if the house is sold by the time the foreign domiciliary dies. Alternatively it might be argued that there is no POA charge anyway because the loan did not satisfy the contribution condition.[196]

Current inheritance tax options for the foreign domiciliary

(a) *Direct ownership*. The risk of IHT may be mitigated by taking out term **43.143** assurance which is written in trust or taken out offshore. If the taxpayer is married then the inheritance tax liability is likely to arise only on the second death and term assurance may be cheap. Perhaps the taxpayer will rely on having sufficient warning of his death to transfer the house into an offshore company moments before death (albeit with an SDLT charge)[197] so that at death he owns only non-situs property. This also avoids the capital gains tax problems associated with holding a house in trust from April 6, 2008.[198] If the trust is a dry structure and holds no other assets then in practice holding the house in trust may not cause future capital gains tax problems under s.87. But if the house is sold (with the benefit of main residence relief so no capital gains tax arises at that point) and the proceeds are reinvested and future gains are made, then these gains can be taxed on the taxpayer under s.87 by reference to his past occupation of the UK house since April 6, 2008.

(b) *Ownership through a company*. In some cases it is still worthwhile for a **43.144** foreign domiciliary to purchase a house in the UK through a company which is owned by a trust, particularly if he is non-UK resident or is likely to remain in the UK for only a few years. (If the company is owned by the foreign domiciliary directly there would be a capital gains tax charge on an arising basis on the foreign domiciliary if the company sells the house while he is UK resident after April 6, 2008. If the company is owned by the trust then s.87 applies but the location of the asset on which any gain is made is irrelevant.) A company provides complete inheritance tax protection. Ensure that the company is funded by way of share capital rather than loan from the trustees to avoid any POA problem.[199] The main immediate risk is income tax due to the shadow director charge but this can be minimised with careful management.[200]

---

[195] See Ch.34 for a further discussion of this mess.
[196] See Ch.34 for a further discussion of this.
[197] See Ch.51.
[198] See Ch.19 and below.
[199] See Ch.34 and A2.00 although it is not thought this view is correct. POA protection should be available under paras 12(3) and 11(3).
[200] Unfortunately the legislation (ITEPA 2003 s.1009) which exempted foreign houses held in a company from any risk of inheritance tax did not apply to UK houses. The risk is that the occupation may be taxable as a benefit in kind under ITEPA 2003 ss.97–113. This normally results in tax on notional earnings each year equal to 4% (the official rate of interest) of the cost to the company of providing the house over £75,000. (Section 106 and see also s.105 ITEPA

One way round the s.106 shadow director income tax charge is for the company to incur no cost in the acquisition of the property. This would mean the foreign domiciliary buys the house and then gives it to a wholly owned company. However, there is SDLT[201] payable and there is a concern that the gifted land remains in his estate for IHT because of the reservation of benefit provisions. Furthermore since April 6, 2008 there are problems given that if the company shares are then gifted to a trust a substantial gain would be realised on the settlement of the shares and eventually taxed on the foreign domiciliary.[202]

A better way of avoiding the shadow director charge is to ensure that trustees and directors are always different and that the beneficiary communicates only with the trustees not the directors. No communications pass between beneficiary and directors that could be considered advice or instruction. In many cases the company grants a short lease up to the trustees who then permit the beneficiary to occupy by licence. The argument then is that the beneficiary is receiving benefits not from the company but from the trustees. It is not thought that ITEPA 2003 Pt 7A applies to shadow directors.

The other problem of corporate ownership since April 6, 2008 where the company is held in trust, is capital gains tax under s.87 on the benefit of the occupation. The house will not qualify for main residence relief given it is held by a company. The result is that on a later disposal of the house or company shares, the foreign domiciliary could be charged under s.87 by reference to the benefit of his past occupation if he is still UK resident at the date gains are realised.[203] As noted below, however, in many cases the capital gains tax problems can be managed by judicious use of capital payments.

43.145   (c)   *Double trust schemes.* Should these be used after March 22, 2006? Obviously no qualifying interest in possession trust can be created so if the relevant property trust holds the UK house it must either do so directly and minimise 10-year inheritance tax charges by the use of debt or hold the house through a company (which increases the capital gains tax risks under s.87). POA issues must also be considered. A variant of a double trust scheme is set out in Example 43.26 below.

43.146   What is the reservation of benefit position on the death of the foreign domiciliary who has funded the purchase of the house? Does the foreign domiciliary reserve a benefit in the UK house and if so can the debt be deducted against the value of the house?

EXAMPLE 43.26

Lilian—a foreign domiciliary—wishes to purchase a house in the UK. In 2007 she settles US$1 million into a debt trust (excluded property and

---

2003.) Hence a house costing £1 million could mean an assessable benefit of £37,000 annually on the foreign domiciliary and income tax at 50% of £18,500. This may well be more than the market rent for the property and even if the foreign domiciliary pays a market rent this will not wholly eradicate the charge although it will reduce the taxable benefit.

[201] FA 2003 s.53.
[202] See s.809T as inserted by FA 2008 Sch.7 and discussed in Ch.5.
[203] See Ch.19 and below for discussion of the new capital gains tax regime from April 6, 2008.

no entry charge). The debt trust will be a relevant property settlement whether or not Lilian takes an interest in possession.

Lilian's father settles $10 on a House Trust. The Debt Trust then lends the cash to House Trust. House Trust (which is also a relevant property settlement) uses the borrowings to buy the house. The house will be subject to 10-year charges but the debt will be deductible in calculating the inheritance tax charge on those occasions. On Lilian's death is there a reservation of benefit from her occupation of the house? She is not the settlor of the House Trust (since she has not given the $10) and the loan is not in itself a gift by her. It is thought that the reservation of benefit provisions should not apply for the reasons set out below. Main residence relief is obtained so there is no s.87 problem until the House Trust makes chargeable gains.

Since there is no initial gift by Lilian para.5(4) cannot apply to cause any reservation of benefit problem in respect of the house.[204] In any event the Debt Trust rather than Lilian is making the loan so para.5(4) should not apply anyway even if she funded the house trust with $10. Accordingly there is no reservation of benefit issue. The only inheritance tax charges are the 10-year anniversary charges which can be predicted and minimised by further borrowing. **43.147**

Although this arrangement works for inheritance tax purposes it has a POA risk in that if one views the loan from the Debt Trust to the House Trust as a contribution, Lilian is within the POA charge in respect of the house which does not have the protection of the reservation of benefit let-out.[205] Nor does it have the protection of para.11(1) since her interest is not a qualifying interest in possession. However, it may be argued that a loan to purchase a house does not satisfy the contribution condition even if it is interest-free.[206] Therefore POA is not a problem. **43.148**

The second option is for Lilian deliberately to bring herself into the reservation of benefit rules to obtain POA protection under para.11(3) but then argue for the inheritance tax deduction of the debt on her death (as well as on any 10-year anniversary of the trust). This could be done by Lilian settling say $10 cash into the House Trust; then lending the house trust the balance of the purchase price and assigning the benefit of the loan to a separate Debt Trust. A concern then is that the reservation of benefit is only in the net equity of the property and so only that element is protected by para.11(3). On the other hand one could presumably argue that the loan element itself was reserved benefit property given Lilan is a beneficiary of the Debt Trust and this loan derives its value from the relevant property (the house). The issue would then arise as to whether the loan is deductible for reservation of benefit purposes against the value of the house on the death of Lilian. Given the problems with home loan schemes this approach seems risky. **43.149**

Moreover there are CGT issues with such structures following the April 6, 2008 changes. Schedule 4B (transfer of value linked to trustee borrowing) can now apply to foreign domiciliaries[207] but this ought not to be in point **43.150**

---

[204] See Chs 33 and 34.
[205] In para.11(3).
[206] See Ch.34 and A2.188.
[207] See Ch.19.

provided the borrowing is applied directly in house purchase for the house is an ordinary trust asset. But in general any trust structure now involves a consideration of capital gains tax issues for the foreign domiciliary whereas if he owned the property directly, capital gains tax would not normally arise because of main residence relief. Accordingly, if the property is owned in a trust structure, the inheritance tax savings must be worthwhile to justify the capital gains tax and POA risks and it is not clear here that they are.

43.151 In conclusion it is thought by the authors that the double trust scheme is now rarely worthwhile for foreign domiciliaries given the POA and reservation of benefit uncertainties and the capital gains tax problems. Moreover even if the POA and reservation of benefit problems can be overcome, there are still potential inheritance tax charges on the house every 10 years and the debt may not be sufficient to eradicate these. Direct personal ownership with appropriate insurance is now the preferred option, or ownership through a company.

Capital gains tax considerations

43.152 Foreign domiciliaries who own the house direct will be in no worse or better position than any UK domiciliary. They will potentially be able to claim main residence relief. Since they are more likely to own more than one house they may well want to make an election for main residence relief as set out at 43.09.

43.153 Where a house is held in a trust, whether or not through a company, and a chargeable gain is realised by the trustees, the latter will need to consider how a beneficiary can avoid a tax charge under s.87B by reference to his occupation since April 2008. The issues here are similar to those that arise in relation to the use of chattels.[208]

EXAMPLE 43.27

> Paul is a remittance basis user in occupation of a house owned by a qualifying interest in possession trust. The trustees also own art and some shares. The benefit of his rent free occupation is estimated at £100,000 pa. By April 6, 2010 he has therefore received £200,000 benefits from the trust since April 6, 2008. The trustees have realised no gains since then.
>
> On April 6, 2010 they realise a gain of £300,000 from the sale of securities and art. In order to avoid a tax charge on Paul by reference to his rent-free occupation of the house, the trustees pay a cash sum of £300,000[209] to Paul or another remittance basis user (or a non-resident) abroad. If paid to Paul he does not remit the cash to the UK. Provided the gain is "washed out" in the year it arises, there is no tax charge on Paul by reference to his occupation in the years before April 6, 2010. There is a small tax charge by reference to his rent-free occupation in 2010–11 but the bulk of the gain has been washed out.

---

[208] See 44.17.

[209] It does not necessarily need to be the cash realised from the sale that is paid out, just an amount equivalent to the gain.

Anomalies can arise where a rebasing election under Sch.7 para.126 FA **43.154** 2008 has been made and the foreign domiciliary has occupied the property as his main residence before but not after April 2008. Paragraph 126 sets out a mechanism intended to limit the tax charge on chargeable gains attributable to foreign domiciled beneficiaries of non-UK resident trusts that accrued before April 6, 2008. However, the effect of the election is that the trustees are treated as acquiring the property immediately before April 6, 2008. If the beneficiary does not occupy after that date then no main residence relief can be claimed to reduce the gain arising under the election mechanism.

EXAMPLE 43.28

A occupies a house owned by an interest in possession trust as his main residence until 2007. He moves out and the trustees sell the house three years later in 2010.

Ignoring the election the trustees will realise no chargeable gain on the house since the entire gain including the last three years' ownership is protected. The effect of the election is to treat the house as being acquired by the trustees on April 2008. Any gain accruing after that date will not be protected from main residence relief. Paragraph 126(8) effectively allows the trustees to take the most favourable option which in this case will be to ignore the effect of the rebasing election.

CHAPTER 44

CHATTEL SCHEMES

- Chattel arrangements (**44.01**)
- Foreign domiciliaries and chattels schemes (**44.17**)

I CHATTEL ARRANGEMENTS

44.01 For some taxpayers, chattel collections (or even the ownership of individual items) raise the spectre of a substantial IHT liability on death. Hence, there has been a demand for an arrangement under which the chattels can be given away (whether outright or into trust for children and issue) whilst at the same time leaving the taxpayer able to continue to use and enjoy them. In recent years two main "schemes" have been employed.

Ingram schemes

44.02 In simple terms the carve-out arrangement blessed by the House of Lords in the *Ingram* case is applied to the chattels[1]: viz the taxpayer retains a lease which enables him to continue to possess the chattels and gifts the "freehold" interest. Doubt was originally expressed as to whether a land shearing operation was capable of applying to chattels but HMRC have accepted that such arrangements are possible.[2] Of course the "*Ingram* scheme" itself was reversed by legislation in FA 1999 but that legislation was expressly limited to land and interests in land.[3]

---

[1] For *Ingram* schemes, see 22.18 and 43.42.

[2] See *Taxation*, October 16, 2003 (Nicholas Brown). In the particular case the chattels in question were individually valued at under £6,000 but collectively had a value of £750,000. A lease for 17 years was retained and on the death of the taxpayers there was seven years left to run on the lease: the PET of the assets (subject to that lease) occurred more than seven years before the death and so was an exempt transfer. The value of the remainder of the lease was then worth £13,000 and the collection of chattels £1,380,000. HMRC initially argued that, unlike land, it was not possible to create different interests in chattels with the result that there had been a gift of the entire interest in the chattels with a contractual arrangement (not involving the payment of full consideration) permitting their use and which amounted to a reserved benefit. See now IHTM 14314.

[3] In the Press Release of March 1999 announcing the blocking of *Ingram* arrangements, it was

1108

Gifts and commercial leaseback: full consideration arrangements

This arrangement has been widely used. The designated chattels are gifted to **44.03** the donee and then leased back to the donor who pays full consideration for his continued use: hence the reservation of benefit rules are inapplicable.[4] In the case of land (to which a similar exemption applies), the commercial rent will frequently be beyond the means of the taxpayer. In the case of chattels, however, there is no ready market in rentals and no standard type of agreement. In practice, experts are engaged by both donor and donee to negotiate a full value for the enjoyment of the chattels. Arrangements are entered into under which there is payment of a relatively small rent (perhaps 0.75–1 per cent of the value of the chattels each year) and the donor/lessee is made responsible for insuring and maintaining the item in question (which will often include the provision of a suitable security system). Similar negotiations are necessary to agree the terms of any rent reviews.[5] The agreement is often made non-assignable by the donor. Some agreements contain price adjuster clauses.[6]

Attitude of HMRC

HMRC attach importance to the parties having the benefit of independent **44.04** advice: see comments in their letter to the Law Society dated May 18, 1987 in relation to land:

> *"whether an arrangement is for full consideration will of course depend on the precise facts. But among the attributes of an acceptable arrangement would be the existence of a bargain negotiated at arm's length by parties who were independently advised and which followed the normal commercial criteria in force at the time it was negotiated."*

HMRC commented in the same letter in relation to chattels:

> *"it would be difficult to overturn an arm's length commercial arrangement entered into by parties who were independently advised."*

However, a number of gift and leaseback schemes have been under considera- **44.05** tion by the Capital Taxes Division which is concerned to ascertain whether full

---

stated that *"if no action were taken, the [Ingram] decision would jeopardise a large part of the tax base. As the decision affects only gifts involving land, the changes to the gifts with reservation rules are limited to such gifts. However, the operation of these rules will be closely monitored and the Government will not hesitate to act to prevent any tax avoidance through other gifts."*

[4] See FA 1986 Sch.20 para.6(1)(a): actual enjoyment of a chattel *"if it is for full consideration in money or money's worth"* is disregarded in applying the reservation of benefit rules.

[5] See generally *Christie's Bulletin for Professional Advisers*, Autumn 1995 (Manisty) and Autumn 1998 (McCall).

[6] An alternative approach suggested by McCall in the above article in *Christie's Bulletin* noted above was for the donor to warrant for himself and his estate that the fee he pays is full consideration for the purposes of Sch.20, para.6 and to covenant that at the end of the term if so required he will make good any shortfall which the donee is able to establish by reference to the warranty. The covenant is made under deed.

value has been paid in "rent". Bear in mind that if it can be shown that there is any element of undervalue, the protection of FA 1986 Sch.20, para.6(1)(c) is lost and the taxpayer will have reserved a benefit. HMRC have queried some gift and lease back arrangements on the basis that if there was no real market in letting country house chattels they do not have to accept a rate agreed by expert valuers. Instead in the absence of a "real world market" they suggested that a Canadian Court of Appeal case[7] provided useful guidance on what constituted full consideration and argued that full consideration was, in reality, the return that the donee would obtain if he invested an amount equivalent to the cash value of the chattels on deposit or in government securities. This would obviously equate much more to the fixed rate return of four per cent chargeable under the POA legislation.

44.06   However, the case was concerned not with full consideration but with benefits to the taxpayer. The shareholder was living in a house built by his company and was paying full market rent for his occupation which was below the rate of return the company could have obtained from investing the cash. The judge decided that in determining the value of the benefit to the taxpayer one should take the cost of providing that benefit to the company into account. Hence the open market rent was not, in all the circumstances, the sole indicator of real value. By contrast, in the case of chattel arrangements one is concerned not with benefits as such to the donor but with whether he has paid full consideration which is a quite different test. Furthermore, in this case the company had used its own cash to build a unique residential property for the taxpayer while in chattel arrangements the donee is simply being given an existing asset which he is likely to want to retain within the family. It is thought that HMRC have not pursued these arguments.

44.07   However, HMRC have argued in some cases that 0.75 per cent–1 per cent is not a fair market value even if it has been "agreed" between two independent "experts". Rigour needs to be applied to the valuation process and some proper analysis of what someone would pay in the real world. Much obviously depends on the nature of the item: a Ferrari sports car leased back to the donor is likely to have a high rental value. Some modern art appears on the walls of banks and lawyers in London and the rent paid there is generally higher than one per cent.

The CGT dimension

44.08   In both carve-out and full consideration arrangements it was important to bear in mind the CGT consequences of disposing of the chattel (or an interest in it). There is a general exemption for chattels which are individually worth £6,000 or less,[8] whilst if the item is a wasting asset then gains are exempt without limit. A wasting asset is one with a predictable useful life of 50 years or less and includes yachts, caravans, animals and all plant and machinery,

---

[7] *Youngman v The Queen* [1991] 90 DTC 6322.
[8] TCGA 1992 s.262(1). Note that there are special rules for sets, TCGA 1992 s.262(4). In the case of more valuable chattels the gift could be into a discretionary trust taking advantage of holdover relief under TCGA 1992, s.260(2)(a) provided that the value was limited to the donor's available IHT nil rate band (so as to avoid an immediate IHT charge) and the trust was not settlor-interested. See Ch.18.

the latter term to include, in HMRC's view, such assets as antique clocks and watches, certain vintage cars and (generally) shotguns.[9]

Impact of the POA Regime

The December 2003 consultation paper made it clear that a main target of **44.09** the new POA charge was chattel schemes: it referred to tax being charged at a specified percentage of capital value in cases where there was no market evidence of an appropriate rent as in the case of "art or antiques". As introduced, the charge under para.6[10] applies to *Ingram* arrangements (in essence the analysis is much the same as in the case of *Ingram* arrangements affecting the land: see 43.42). Hence, the options open to the taxpayer are much the same.

EXAMPLE 44.1

In 2003 Andrew effected an *Ingram* scheme over chattels under which the "freehold" interest in chattels was gifted to an interest in possession trust for his daughter Charlotte. He is now caught by the POA Regime.

If he surrenders his leasehold interest, this may be an associated operation with the result that a transfer of value, equal to the full market value of the chattels (less the earlier transfer), is now made. What happens if instead Andrew assigns his leasehold interest to another member of the family? An assignment should raise no associated operation problems. Could he then pay full consideration for his continued use of the chattels in order to avoid a reservation of benefit? As noted above, full consideration can often be relatively cheap. Does this then protect Andrew from a POA charge by virtue of para.11(5)(d)?

A concern is that "the relevant property" for the purposes of para.11(3) is **44.10** the property disposed of, i.e. both the leasehold and freehold interests. He does not reserve a benefit in respect of the freehold interest merely because he has assigned his lease. To be sure of the full consideration protection he would need to surrender the lease and pay rent direct to the freeholder and as noted above this may cause IHT problems. Could Andrew instead make a payment in pursuance of a legal obligation to the owner of the chattel for his use and possession of the chattel? If he does not assign or surrender the lease the only way he can put himself under a legal obligation is to enter into a deed of covenant.

The amounts of income tax involved may be substantial.

---

[9] *Tax Bulletin*, October 1994 and February 2000: TCGA 1992 s.44. See *Executors of Lord Howard of Henderskelfe (Deceased) v RCC* [2011] UKFTT 493.

[10] Note that FA 2004 Sch.15 para.6(2)(b) refers to a disposal of all or part of his interest in the chattel and para.6(4) treats the creation of a new interest out of an existing interest as the disposal of part of the existing interest. The authors are not aware of reversionary leases being used for chattels.

EXAMPLE 44.2

The encumbered freehold value of the chattels is now £1 million. The market value without the lease is £1.5 million. The appropriate amount is 4%[11] × £1.5 million = £60,000. £60,000 × 1/1.5 = £40,000. Tax on £40,000 (at 50%) = £20,000 pa.

Alternatively Andrew enters into a deed of covenant with the trustees of Charlotte's trust under which he agrees to pay £40,000 being "the appropriate amount". Arguably such amount is not taxable in the hands of the recipient trustees.[12] However, by adding property to a trust he has made a chargeable transfer (unless it is protected as normal expenditure out of income).

44.11 A further option is to enter into a full consideration arrangement and then immediately elect into reservation of benefit. In these circumstances HMRC accept that there is no deemed PET.[13] He would first need to surrender his lease of the chattels. This raises the IHT problems mentioned in Example 44.1—he may be making a significant transfer of value under the associated operations provisions.

44.12 The POA Regime does not apply to full consideration arrangements.[14]

POA alternatives

44.13 The sale of chattels is an excluded transaction if it is a sale of the taxpayer's whole interest in the chattel at market value except for any right expressly reserved by him over it.[15]

EXAMPLE 44.3

Edward owns a valuable picture which shows little gain. He carves out a lease for himself and then sells (rather than gives) the chattel subject to this lease to his son at full market value. The transaction is not a gift and so will not be caught by the reservation of benefit rules and will be excluded from the POA charge. Note that if there is any undervalue element one moves into the problems posed by non-exempt sales. There is no stamp duty payable.

Edward does not need to worry about what constitutes full consideration since he pays no rent. However, he must not have given the cash to his son in order to enable the son to purchase the chattel from him; otherwise he falls foul of the contribution condition.

[11] The official rate of interest for 2011–12.
[12] See 43.42 for a consideration of the use of deeds of covenant in relation to houses.
[13] See A2.144.
[14] FA 2004 Sch.15 para.11(5).
[15] FA 2004 Sch.15 para.10(a).

An alternative option is to use para.10(2)(c), i.e. rely on the gift being made more than six years previously or before April, 1998.   **44.14**

EXAMPLE 44.4

> Edward gives £1 million cash to his son in 2007 who uses it to buy a picture by Magritte. Seven years later the son lends the picture to Edward. He pays no rent. Edward is not caught by reservation of benefit nor does he suffer the POA charge because the gift was more than seven years before benefitting from the Magritte purchased with it.

Consider the shared use and possession of the chattels.   **44.15**

EXAMPLE 44.5

> Luke and Charlotte jointly use a holiday home which contains chattels owned by Luke. He gives a half share in those chattels to Charlotte. For IHT purposes there is no similar relief from the reservation provisions to that contained in s.102B(4) for land. Accordingly Luke's use of the chattels might be seen as in consideration for allowing Charlotte the same level of use.[16] In these circumstances it would probably be unwise for Luke to give Charlotte more than 50 per cent. The preferable analysis is that the gift of a part share in chattels is in the nature of a carve-out and that the donor has a continuing right to use them as a result of his retained share. A POA charge could apply in this case.

A difficulty is that a part owner of a chattel does not have the same rights as a part owner of land or a shareholder of a company. The only relevant legislation is LPA 1925 s.188(1) which states: **44.16**

> "*Where any chattels belong to persons in undivided shares, the persons interested in a moiety or upwards may apply to the court for an order for the division of the chattels or any of them, according to a valuation or otherwise, and the court may make such an order and give any consequential direction as it thinks fit.*"

No cases have been decided on the meaning of s.188 but it is thought that this justifies a discount in the valuation of a half share.[17] As there is no reason to think that the co-owner of chattels has the same rights of use and possession as a co-owner of land,[18] that discount may be substantial.

---

[16] See the *Hansard* statement at 43.94.
[17] See *Christies' Bulletin*, Summer Issue 2005.
[18] Contrast TLATA 1996 ss.12 and 13.

44.17 Foreign domiciliaries often like to enjoy fine art in their UK homes. This raises the following issues:

(a) does bringing the art to the UK or buying art in the UK cause remittance problems if foreign source income or gains have been used to purchase it?

(b) what is the tax position in respect of sales or other disposals of art in the UK?

(c) can the art be protected from IHT if the foreign domiciliary dies and the art is UK situated?

(d) art is often held through trusts: how can CGT and income tax charges on the benefits received by foreign domiciled beneficiaries in the UK be minimised?

44.18 In many ways the issues are similar to those concerning UK houses although in practice, the problems tend to be easier to manage for two reasons: *first*, the chattels can be moved out of the UK if the foreign domiciliary has some warning of his approaching death or wishes to sell them. *Second*, chattels can be resited relatively easily because they can be moved to offshore companies without an SDLT or stamp duty charge. Beware VAT issues if the chattels are transferred for consideration and reservation of benefit issues if they are gifted to a company.

Bringing art and chattels to the UK—remittance problems

44.19 As explained in Ch.3, if a foreign domiciliary buys art or chattels abroad using foreign chargeable gains; foreign employment income, or relevant foreign income and the art is then brought to the UK, prima facie there is a taxable remittance.[19] Property has been brought to the UK by a relevant person and is derived from the income or gains.[20] Similar problems arise if the trustees of a settlor-interested trust (where the settlor is UK resident but foreign domiciled) or a company within that trust uses relevant foreign income[21] to buy art and it is brought to the UK by the trustees, the settlor or any "relevant person".[22]

44.20 However, there are five specific exemptions set out below. Originally these exemptions, apart from the public access provision, only applied if the asset in question derived from relevant foreign income but this restriction was lifted with retrospective effect to April 6, 2008 and they now apply to assets purchased with foreign employment income; relevant foreign income, or foreign chargeable gains.

---

[19] Under ITA 2007 s.809L.
[20] Both Conditions A and B in s.809L are satisfied: see Ch.5.
[21] But they can use trust gains, see Ch.19.
[22] "Relevant person" is explained further in Ch.5 but includes the individual; his spouse or cohabitee; minor children and minor grandchildren; a company he controls; and any trust he has set up which can benefit him or any other relevant person.

The five exemptions are:

(1) public access;

(2) personal use;

(3) repairs;

(4) temporary importation;

(5) de minimis exemption.

Public access[23]

There is no taxable remittance for works of art, antique and collectors' pieces[24] **44.21**
if these are brought to the UK by the individual or any relevant person
(including a trust or company) and the asset satisfies the public access rule, i.e.
the piece is displayed or held at an approved establishment[25] and it is in the UK
for a single period of not more than two years. The definition of works of art
is taken from the indirect tax rules and will not necessarily cover all items that
are publicly displayed. For example, twentieth century furniture, jewellery and
video art will not be covered. The relief can interact with the repair provision
and other exemptions in a somewhat complicated way.[26] The following is taken
from the Remittances Manual at 34150:

EXAMPLE 44.6

(1) Faizal is a UK resident remittance basis user. He is asked by a London
museum, which is an approved establishment, if he will contribute a vase
that he owns to an exhibition that the museum intends to stage. The vase
is derived from Faizal's relevant foreign income. Faizal arranges for the
vase to be shipped to the UK from his holiday home in Switzerland. In
May the vase is received by the museum and is put into secure storage
for one month after which the museum will begin to set up the special
exhibition. The exhibition lasts until the following year in October, at
the end of which the vase is returned to Switzerland. The vase has been
in the UK for 18 months in total. The vase is exempt property so Faizal
has not made a chargeable remittance.

(2) The circumstances are the same as above but this time, at the end of the
exhibition, the vase is not returned to Switzerland. Instead, Faizal asks for
the vase to be sent to a well known restorer in Newcastle to be cleaned. The
restorer keeps the vase in his business premises for a further eight months

---

[23] ITA 2007 s.809Z.
[24] Within the meaning of Council Directive 2006/112. See A2.16 and the Remittances
Manual 37030.
[25] Approved by the National Import Reliefs Unit or other person, premises or institution
designated by HMRC. See also RDRM 34130 and 34510.
[26] Contrast the inheritance tax exemption for works of art.

and then in the following June Faizal arranges for it to be sent back to his home in Switzerland. The vase has been in the UK for 26 months. The vase, purchased using Faizal's relevant foreign income is exempt property under the public access rule for the 18 months from its arrival in the UK in May to the October in the following year. Between October and the following June it is within the temporary importation rule (as it is with the repairer) and so remains exempt property.[27]

Personal use[28]

44.22 This exempts clothing, footwear, jewellery and watches if they are property of a relevant person and are for the personal use of a relevant individual. For example, A uses relevant foreign income to buy a watch for his minor son. No taxable remittance arises provided the asset is not sold here.[29] This exemption does not apply to art.

Repairs[30]

44.23 There is no taxable remittance if an asset is imported to the UK (by the individual or a relevant person) for the purposes of repair (whether or not it satisfies the public access rule) and the repair or restoration is carried out in the UK. So, for example, the importation of boats or pictures purchased with relevant foreign income; gains; or employment income for the purposes of a repair carried out in the UK would be protected under this exemption. However, if relevant foreign income is used to pay for the repair itself this is not protected.

Temporary importation[31]

44.24 If relevant foreign income; foreign chargeable gains, or foreign employment income is used to purchase an asset and the asset is in the UK for 275 days or less there is no taxable remittance. The 275 days is a lifetime, total for each asset not a total per year. However, care is needed if the asset is displayed first to the public and then remains in the UK. The days when it is on public display counts towards the 275 days. If the asset is imported here first for 275 days and then displayed to the public there is no problem![32]

---

[27] Presumably they do not mean the temporary importation rule applies but rather the repair rule applies. See 44.24 below where the 275 days is used up on public display first.

[28] ITA 2007 s.809Z2.

[29] See ITA 2007 s.809Y(3).

[30] ITA 2007 s.809Z3.

[31] ITA 2007 s.809Z4.

[32] See Conditions B and C of ITA 2007 s.809ZA.

De minimis exemption[33]

If the notional remitted amount is less than £1,000 and the property was pur-   **44.25**
chased with foreign income or gains then it is exempt. Each item of property
qualifies for the £1,000 limit.

Transitional rules[34]

Before April 6, 2008 it was common for foreign domiciliaries to use foreign   **44.26**
income to purchase assets and bring these to the UK. A remittance in specie
was not treated as a taxable remittance.[35] The new rules in FA 2008 stopped
remittances in specie but allowed some transitional relief where the asset had
already been purchased. Two transitional reliefs are particularly relevant to
art and chattels.

FA 2008 Sch.7 para.86(2) provides that: **44.27**

> "*if before 6 April 2008, property (including money) consisting of or deriv-
> ing from an individual's relevant foreign income was brought to or received
> or used in the UK by or for the benefit of a relevant person,*[36] *treat the
> relevant foreign income as not remitted to the UK on or after that date (if
> it otherwise would be regarded as so remitted)*".

EXAMPLE 44.7

George, a foreign domiciliary did the following:

(a) gave relevant foreign income to his wife who brought a picture to
the UK on April 3, 2008;

(b) used relevant foreign income to buy UK shares by paying the
broker abroad;

(c) decided that it was likely he would want to sell some pictures by
auction in London and therefore moved all his art work from
Geneva to London on April 3, 2008. All of the art work had been
purchased using relevant foreign income;

(d) gave relevant foreign income to his wife abroad in 2003.[37] She

---

[33] ITA 2007 s.809Z5.

[34] FA 2008 Sch.7 paras 86(2) and (3).

[35] HMRC did, however, always consider that non-monetary assets brought to the
UK were a remittance if purchased out of foreign earnings. See old EIM 40302 from that
time.

[36] Although the remittance is of income arising before April 2008 the definition of relevant
person is the wider definition including an individual's spouse, cohabitee, trust, minor child,
minor grandchild etc. The opening words of para.86(4) which limit the definition of relevant
income to the individual in relation to 2007–08 and prior years make it clear that this does not
apply to paras 86(2) and (3).

[37] Before April 2008 this was not a taxable remittance. A gift abroad (sometimes called
"alienation abroad") of foreign income or gains converted the income or gains into capital
in the hands of the donee and it could then be remitted free of tax. The donee could not

brought the cash to the UK in 2007. This was not a taxable remittance by George under the old rules. She invests the cash in shares which are later sold and she buys a house and art for their joint enjoyment.

In all cases he has the protection of para.86(2) and there is no taxable remittance. Note that this relief only applies if relevant foreign income is used for the purchase of the property brought to the UK not if foreign chargeable gains or foreign employment income are used. So, for example, art purchased with foreign dividend income or foreign interest but not art purchased with foreign chargeable gains. In many cases foreign domiciliaries will not have kept gains segregated from income.

This relief also requires the asset to have been brought to the UK before April 6, 2008 and some proof will be needed of this.

44.28 The second transitional provision is in para.86(3):

> "*if before 12 March 2008 property other than money consisting of or deriving from an individual's relevant foreign income was acquired by a relevant person, treat the relevant foreign income as not remitted to the UK on or after 6 April 2008 (if it otherwise would be regarded as so remitted).*"

EXAMPLE 44.8

(1) A has relevant foreign income which he used to purchase pictures abroad in 2004. The pictures are sold in the UK in 2009. No income tax charge arises. There could be a capital gains tax charge if the pictures show a gain.

(2) B is the settlor and beneficiary of an offshore trust which received foreign income of £1 million in the years prior to 2007–08. By March 12, 2008 all such income had been reinvested in shares and other assets. There is no income tax charge on B if the assets are sold and the income remitted (although there may be other charges on B in respect of trust capital payments: see Ch.19).

give the money or financial equivalence back to the donor but *Grimm v Newman* [2002] EWCA Civ 1621 established that the donee could be the non-domiciliary's spouse and use the gifted money to buy a half share in a UK house owned jointly by the couple. Importance was given in that case to the fact that the donor had no beneficial interest in the monies after the gift. Contrast *Harmel v Wright* [1974] STC 88 where the taxpayer had used his foreign employment income to subscribe for shares in one foreign company which lent the money to a second foreign company which in turn lent the money to the taxpayer who brought it to the UK. The taxpayer was held to have received the income in the UK, Templeman J. observing that emoluments had come in at one end of a conduit pipe going through other pipes and coming out at the other end. The position where gifts were made to a foreign trust set up by the donor is probably similar to that of *Harmel v Wright*, i.e. there is no effective alienation although there are arguments to the contrary. By extending the definition of relevant person to include spouses and cohabitees as well as trusts HMRC stopped alienation along the lines of *Grimm v Newman* after April 5, 2008.

(3) C received foreign dividend income in 2003 which he used to purchase foreign shares in 2004. The proceeds of the shares are not taxable when remitted to the United Kingdom except to the extent that they show a gain.

The tax position of sales or other disposals of art in the United Kingdom

It is easy for foreign domiciliaries to forget that a disposal of art in the United Kingdom may result in a chargeable gain.[38] Capital gains tax can be avoided by taking the art abroad, selling it there and keeping the proceeds abroad. Foreign domiciliaries are liable to capital gains tax on gains realised on UK assets at either 18 or 28 per cent.[39] If they are remittance basis users they have no annual capital gains tax exemption. **44.29**

Before April 2008 foreign domiciliaries would often deal with the capital gains tax problem by making a gift of the asset to an offshore trust (ensuring that at the date of the gift the asset was situated abroad). The gain effectively "disappeared" on the transfer into trust the asset being rebased to market value. There was no cash to remit by the donor. On a subsequent sale by the trustees, even if the asset had increased in value since it had been settled; there was no capital gains tax to pay. **44.30**

This scheme has been partially blocked since April 2008 by ITA 2007 s.809T which provides that:

> *"if foreign chargeable gains accrue to an individual on the disposal of an asset and the individual does not receive consideration for the disposal of an amount at least equal to the market value of the asset, for the purposes of this chapter treat the asset as deriving from the chargeable gains."*

Hence, if the donee is a relevant person (e.g. a trust set up by the settlor from which he can benefit) and brings the asset to the United Kingdom there is a remittance by the donor of the gain realised on disposal into trust. However, if the asset is sold by the donee and the proceeds of the gifted asset are remitted to the United Kingdom by the trust it is not clear that the derivation extends to the sale proceeds. There is no further provision deeming the proceeds of the asset to be derived from the chargeable gains.

Even if the art does not show a gain, foreign domiciliaries also face the problem that bringing art and other chattels into the United Kingdom after April 5, 2008 may in itself be a taxable remittance if the asset was purchased out of overseas income or capital gains and the limited exemptions and transitional provisions above do not apply. Hence if sold the individual is liable to UK income tax or capital gains tax on the initial cost of the asset in question as well as capital gains tax on any gain! **44.31**

In June 2011 the Coalition Government produced a consultation document **44.32**

---

[38] See 44.06 above for further details.
[39] For a remittance basis user paying the £30,000 charge this will always be at 28% because he is deemed to have the requisite level of income or gains to be treated as a higher rate taxpayer. For a remittance basis user who is not paying the remittance basis charge he may not be liable to CGT at 28% if he has insufficient UK source or remitted foreign income or gains. See Ch.5 for further details.

on the taxation of foreign domiciliaries. This acknowledges that if a foreign domiciliary faces a tax charge on remittance of the art for sale even if the proceeds are then taken immediately out of the UK, this makes the UK less attractive as an art market. Accordingly, it has proposed introducing an exemption from April 6, 2012 that would remove the tax charge on remittance of an asset to the UK where it is subsequently sold in the UK. This exemption would cover situations where an exempt asset (likely to be defined as art and antiques) is brought to the UK temporarily and sold. All of the proceeds from any sale have to be taken out of the UK within two weeks of the money being received by the individual. (It is likely that this time limit will be extended and it is intended to apply to the receipt of monies. The time limit is not geared to the date of sale. Sales of fine art are often arranged so that the purchase price is paid in staggered amounts so this will be important.) Of course the UK resident foreign domiciliary will still face a capital gains tax charge if the asset shows a gain. In many cases the art will be held by non-resident trusts in which case it can be sold here without any chargeable gain for the trustees. It is not yet clear whether the proposed exemption will extend to sales in the UK by foreign trusts where the settlor is UK resident.[40]

Inheritance tax protection

44.33 Inheritance tax charges[41] can arise on the following occasions if at that particular time the trustees hold UK situated art directly even if the settlor was foreign domiciled when he established the trust:

(a) on setting up the trust: the art must be non-UK situated when settled;

(b) if the trust is a relevant property trust and UK art is distributed out of the trust or there is a 10-year anniversary and the trustees hold any UK art directly;[42]

(c) on the death of the settlor if at that time the trust holds UK art and he has reserved a benefit in the trust which had been funded after March 17, 1986. Even if the settlor leaves all his property to his spouse, the spouse exemption will not prevent the charge unless the settlor had a qualifying interest in possession[43];

(d) if the beneficiary (whether or not the settlor) has a qualifying interest in possession and dies at a time when the trustees hold UK art.

---

[40] The realisation of a gain by a trust may have other implications if a UK resident beneficiary has received capital payments in the UK but the situs of the asset on which the gain is made does not in itself matter. See Ch.19. If an individual foreign domiciliary sells art in the UK he is subject to CGT on an arising basis on any gain. If a foreign trust sells the art there is no CGT unless and until a beneficiary receives a benefit (and in the case of a remittance basis user receives the benefit in the UK).

[41] See Ch.31.

[42] See Ch.29 for the excluded property rules in the context of relevant property settlements.

[43] In that case FA 1986 s.102(3) will disapply the reservation of benefit provisions.

The last two occasions obviously cannot be predicted and may encourage **44.34**
the trustees to hold UK art through a foreign corporate structure so that the
settled property comprises company shares rather than the art. There is no
stamp duty or SDLT charge on transfer of art to a company. Watch capital
gains tax: although the trustees are not liable to capital gains tax, if the art
being transferred to a company shows a gain then this will have implications
for beneficiaries who have received or will receive capital payments from the
trust.[44]

If the settlor is dead or has not reserved a benefit and the trust is a relevant **44.35**
property settlement then the charge is predictable. The trustees may want
to avoid the complications of a corporate structure and simply resite the
property before every 10-year anniversary. For example, they could move the
chattel out of the UK just before the anniversary and then back again after
the 10-year anniversary has passed.[45]

Until April 6, 2009 Concession F7 operated for foreign owned works of
art that became liable to inheritance tax on a 10-year anniversary or on the
death of an individual.[46] The inheritance tax charge was waived where the
work of art was retained in the UK solely for public exhibition, cleaning or
restoration. This has now been enacted into the IHT legislation[47] in relation
to deaths and 10-year anniversaries occurring on or after April 6, 2009. This
is notably simpler than the exemption for works of art under the remittance
rules described above![48]

Corporate structures

Chattels situate in the UK may be held through companies for inheritance **44.36**
tax protection but a benefit in kind charge can arise if the foreign domiciliary is a shadow director.[49] The taxable benefit is, in effect, 20 per cent of the
market value of the chattel when first provided for use by the employee. So if
a company buys a second-hand aeroplane for £1 million on the open market
and immediately makes it available for the sole use of the director, the taxable

---

[44] See below and Ch.19.
[45] See *Kwok Chi Leung Karl v Commissioner of Estate Duty* [1988] STC 728 and IHTM 4274.
[46] It is not clear that the concession applied to charges arising under the reservation of
benefit rules. The new statutory relief appears to apply to charges arising under the reservation
of benefit rules.
[47] By the Enactment of Extra-Statutory Concessions Order (SI 2009/730) art.13.
[48] Section 5 IHTA 1984 now provides that the estate of a person immediately before his death
does not include excluded property "*or a foreign owned work of art which is situated in the UK
for one or more of the purposes of public display, cleaning and restoration (and for no other
purpose).*" Similarly s.64 provides that a foreign owned work of art that would otherwise be
excluded property which is situated in the UK for the purposes of display cleaning and restoration and for no other purpose is not to be regarded as relevant property.
[49] Under ITEPA 2003 s.203(1). The risk of a shadow director charge is often over-estimated. In
order to be treated as a shadow director ITEPA 2003 s.67 provides that a director includes any
person in accordance with whose directions or instructions the directors of the company are
accustomed to act. See *SS Trade and Industry v Deverell* [2001] Ch 340 for a wide meaning but
see *Ultraframe v Fielding* [2005] EWHC 1638 confirming it does not apply simply because there
is communication between directors and beneficiaries. In practice it is preferable that trustees
and directors are different and that beneficiaries communicate only with trustees. Note that
IPTEA 2003 Pt 7A does not apply to shadow directors.

benefit is 20 per cent of £1 million plus running costs less any sums made good by the director.

However, if the foreign domiciliary pays full consideration for the use of the chattels (which, as noted above, is often not a large sum) there is no benefit and therefore (in contrast to the living accommodation charge) no tax charge. Paying full consideration for the use of the item may, however, not be attractive if that consideration is treated as UK source income taxed on an arising basis and may on occasion raise VAT issues.[50] However, paying rent will not only avoid a shadow director charge but also avoid any capital gains tax issues if the chattels are held in an offshore trust because no taxable benefit is being received in the UK and therefore no s.87 charge can arise.

44.37 Alternatively, hold the art in a dry trust and ensure that when gains are realised they are stripped out in the year they arise.[51]

POAT issues

44.38 Generally foreign domiciliaries have the protection of FA 2004 Sch.15 para.12(3) and 11(3) on the enjoyment of chattels.[52] In one case though, POAT charges can arise. This is where the trust was originally discretionary but a pre-March 22, 2006 qualifying interest in possession was appointed to the foreign domiciled settlor and the trust now holds UK situated chattels either directly or through a company. In these situations a POAT charge can arise as a result of FA 2006 s.80. The chattels will either need to be moved abroad (and held directly by the trustees) or the settlor could make an election into reservation of benefit and immediately pay rent along the lines set out in 44.10 above. Alternatively, his interest in possession could be ended.[53]

How can CGT and income tax charges on the benefits received by foreign domiciled beneficiaries be minimised?

44.39 Problems arise if trustees hold art in a trust which realises gains (whether from the art itself or from other assets). Before April 6, 2008 the foreign domiciled beneficiary was not liable to tax on trust gains. That position was changed by

---

[50] It is argued that where the chattels are being hired out for a full market rent this may constitute an economic activity for VAT purposes, particularly where the owner is a corporate entity. If the VAT threshold is exceeded then VAT will be chargeable. A hire of goods where the effective use and enjoyment takes place in the UK is a supply in the course of furtherance of a business. Business is widely construed: see, for example, the guidance on shooting and VAT published by the British Association for Shooting and Conservation. This is different from the situation where a trustee licenses artwork to a beneficiary on condition that the beneficiary bears the cost of security, insurance and preservation etc. The intention in this case is to secure a trust use rather than carry on a business activity.

[51] See 44.39.

[52] See Ch.34.

[53] This would not have implications under IHTA 1984 s.80 even if by that time he is deemed domiciled here. Section 80 only applies if the property is immediately subject to an interest in possession after it is settled and FA 2006 s.80 generally only applies if it is not! The complications of s.80 for foreign domiciliaries are discussed further at 34.36.

FA 2008 and a foreign domiciled beneficiary can now be liable to capital gains tax on any gains realised by the trust if he has received benefits from that trust since April 6, 2008. Even if he is a remittance basis user if he has been enjoying art in the United Kingdom and the trust realises gains he will prima facie be liable to capital gains tax.[54] The rebasing election[55] may help if the asset has not increased in value since April 2008 but there is likely to be some post-April 2008 element of gain on an ultimate sale.

Even if the trust has no pool of post-April 2008 gains, if it has a pool of **44.40** relevant income available then the beneficiary can also be taxed on the value of benefits received by reference to that available relevant income.[56] For both these reasons it is often suggested that trusts holding art and houses in the United Kingdom should be kept "dry". It is then easier to manage future tax charges.

EXAMPLE 44.9

The trust was set up by B (a non-UK domiciliary) before March 22, 2006. It holds UK situated art used by B for no consideration.[57] The taxable benefit has been valued at £10,000 pa. No tax arises on B unless and until the trust has realised gains.

Years 1–10: Beneficiary B who is UK resident receives taxable benefits from the use of the art of £10,000 pa giving a total of £100,000. The trust is dry, has no other assets and has realised no gains.

Year 11: Trust realises gains of £100,000 when art is sold.

Year 11: Trustees make a capital payment to C of £100,000, a remittance basis user abroad.

Total capital payments made in Year 11 are £110,000.

This payment to C will effectively eliminate any tax charge on B assuming he is currently paying tax on the arising basis. The gain has mostly been washed out in the same tax year it arises by the payment to C abroad of £100,000 and the benefits received in earlier years by B do not come back into charge.[58] B is only taxable on the small amount of benefit received in the United Kingdom for Year 11 and not on the benefits received in earlier years.

Total capital payments made in Year 11 are £110,000. Total gain is £100,000. 9.11 per cent (£9,100) of the gain is attributed to B and 90.9

---

[54] See Ch.19 for further discussion.
[55] See Ch.19 and FA 2008 Sch.7 para.126.
[56] See Ch.8.
[57] This is within B's estate for inheritance tax purposes since even if it is an excluded property trust the trustees are holding UK situated assets directly and on the death of B these will be chargeable either because he has a qualifying interest in possession or because he has reserved a benefit. The trustees may prefer to hold the art through a company. In that event extracting the cash from the company without triggering further gains on the company shares may be problematic. A share buy-back would need to be done and then an amount equal to the gain on the art and the share buy-back would need to be paid to C.
[58] See Ch.19.

per cent (£90,900) of the gain is attributed to C. The gain falls within B's annual CGT exemption. C pays no tax provided that he does not remit the capital.

If B was a remittance basis user he would have no available CGT exemption so would pay tax on the £9,100 gain attributed to him in the United Kingdom. If the sale of the art was delayed until B was non-UK resident, then no remittance basis charge would arise on B provided he did not return to the United Kingdom within five years.[59]

44.41 Note that in the above example even if the beneficiary who was enjoying the art was UK domiciled under general law, there would be no CGT charge on his enjoyment of the chattels while the trust was dry. The same technique of washing out gains by payment to a non-resident remittance basis user abroad could be used.

---

[59] See Ch.3 for residence and foreign domiciliary rules. See Ch.19 for rules on matching on payments from offshore trusts.

BUSINESSES: BPR

Precedents

A1.15 Clause for NRB legacy including business property

I OVERVIEW

This is an area of considerable importance and some difficulty. The importance   **45.01**
derives from the value frequently attributed to the business and, in many cases,
to the availability of 100 per cent relief from IHT.[1] The difficulty arises from the
relatively complex structures that are often employed: a business may operate as
a sole trade; partnership, limited liability partnership or as an incorporated entity
and may be held in a family trust. Many businesses are family run and frequently
adjustments are made to the ownership and running of the business, classically
with parents handing over control and ownership to their children. When the
business is held in a trust it may be managed by the life tenant or by the trustees.

Relationship between APR/BPR

The two reliefs are similar (in that both are concerned with businesses[2]) and   **45.02**
overlap but the following distinctions are worthy of note:

---

[1] See IHTA 1984 Pt V Ch.1 (business property) and Ch.2 (agricultural property). Agricultural
property relief takes precedence over business relief: see IHTA 1984 s.114(1): see 45.02.
[2] In the case of APR see *Dixon v IRC* [2002] STC (SCD) 53 where the relief was not available

(a) APR is given in priority to BPR[3];

(b) differences exist in the treatment of woodlands, crops, livestock, dead-stock, plant and machinery, and farmhouses etc. When APR does not apply, consider whether BPR is available (it can apply to any part of the value transferred not relieved under APR: for instance the hope value of agricultural land);

(c) at one time APR was only available on property situated in the UK, Channel Islands and Isle of Man whereas BPR was not so restricted. After an ECJ decision, FA 2009 changed this, allowing APR and Woodlands relief for property in the EEA. This change is significant in respect of:

   (i) let farmland in the EEA;
   (ii) a farmhouse situated in the EEA.

In both situations BPR (which has always applied to a business any-where in the world) would not have applied to make good the absence of APR.

45.03 Where agricultural property is replaced by business property and vice versa, relief may still be available despite the change. In the *Tax Bulletin* 1994, p.182, the Inland Revenue commented that:

> "*Where agricultural property which is a farming business is replaced by non-agricultural business property, the period of ownership of the original property will be relevant for applying the minimum ownership condition to the replacement property. Business property relief will be available on the replacement if all the conditions for that relief were satisfied. Where non-agricultural business property is replaced by a farming business and the latter is not eligible for agricultural property relief, s.114(1) does not exclude business property relief if the conditions for that relief are satisfied.*
>
>   *Where the donee of the PET of a farming business sells the business and replaces it with a non-agricultural business the effect of s.124A(1) is to deny agricultural property relief on the value transferred by the PET. Consequently, s.114(1) does not exclude business property relief if the conditions for that relief are satisfied: and, in the reverse situation, the farming business acquired by the donee can be 'relevant business property' for the purposes of s.113B(3)(c).*"

If agricultural property was let for seven years, sold and the proceeds rein-vested in business property, the two year period would need to start from the acquisition of the business property because no qualifying trading business was being carried on previously.

---

because there was no history of agricultural production (certainly no commercial activity was undertaken) and the evidence was that the property was merely occupied for the purposes of a private residence. Even for APR it is therefore thought that there needs to be a business (viz the intention to make a profit). See also *Golding v IRC* [2011] UKFTT.

[3] IHTA 1984 s.114(1).

EXAMPLE 45.1

Sixtus has for many years farmed at Praeter Farm. In all, some 300 acres is under cultivation and Sixtus lives in the Grade II listed farmhouse, Praeter Hall. The farm machinery is stored in a magnificent barn and three farm cottages are occupied by farm workers (one has recently retired). Other cottages have been renovated and are now run as furnished holiday lettings. A small area of the land, adjacent to the proposed Suffolk motorway, has development potential. In considering the reliefs available to Sixtus:

(1) first look at APR which will be available on the agricultural value of the land. It may also be given on the farm cottages (including the one occupied by the retired farm worker) and the farmhouse, provided that it is of a "character appropriate" to the property;

(2) business property relief may then be available on the farm machinery and on the "hope" value of the land adjacent to the expressway. It may also be given on the let cottages provided that Sixtus' business is not "mainly" that of holding investments.

In the case of both reliefs, a minimum ownership period has to be satisfied before relief is available: in the case of BPR, a two-year period is required.[4] So far as APR is concerned, s.117 imposes a minimum period of ownership or occupation which is two years when the agricultural property is occupied by the transferor and seven years when occupied by the owner or another (e.g. when the land is let).[5] **45.04**

A clearance procedure

A clearance procedure was introduced from May 1, 2008 for a trial period of six months to cover transfers of business where there was material uncertainty over the availability of business property relief. See HMRC *Brief 25/08*, issued on May 1, 2008. **45.05**

As at December 2008, few clearances had been received *and accepted* by HMRC. The application needed to demonstrate a commercially-significant issue or transaction of the business itself. For example, if the business was considering a restructuring which might jeopardise BPR then clearance could be sought. This might arise where it was expanding in a new area, possibly considering a joint venture type arrangement that might cause BPR problems.[6] **45.06**

---

[4] In recent years the investment in AIM portfolios has become popular for taxpayers who are likely to survive two but not seven years.

[5] In BPR there are rules dealing with replacement property (in s.107 which deals, inter alia, with the incorporation of a business and the formation of a partnership) which were considered in the *Brander* case (see 45.21) and with successions (in s.108). In the case of APR, equivalent provisions are in s.118 (replacements) and s.120 (successions).

[6] Jointly-held companies will only be qualifying trading companies if the holding company holds more than 50 per cent in the joint venture subsidiary so joint ventures need to be structured with care. Otherwise BPR for the whole group could be jeopardised. Similar problems

HMRC did not accept that clearance needed to be given to any shareholder who wanted to know if business property relief was available in respect of his shareholding when no commercially significant issue was at stake: e.g. on a gift of shares.

45.07 However, on January 26, 2009, HMRC announced an extension to the scope of the clearance procedure. HMRC will now give its view of the tax consequences of any transfer of value that involves a change of ownership of a business where this transfer, leaving aside the application of business property relief, would result in an immediate inheritance tax charge and provided that the other conditions are met. Clearances in these changes of ownership cases will remain valid for a limited period of six months. Applications should be sent to IHT Technical Team Nottingham office marked for the attention of "IHT-BPR Technical Team (Clearances)".

This extension means that a donor who wishes to settle shares into trust and can demonstrate that a transaction is genuinely being considered by him may request clearance as to whether the proposed transfer of value will qualify for business property relief. An outright gift to an individual will not qualify for the clearance procedure because it is not immediately chargeable. If the transfer into trust takes place within six months, HMRC remains bound by any positive clearance given, assuming of course, that full disclosure was given. The taxpayer is expected to "put his cards on the table".[7]

II RELEVANT BUSINESS PROPERTY

45.08 The relief applies *"when the whole or part of the value transferred by a transfer of value is attributable to the value of any relevant business property"*.[8] It is expressly provided[9] that references to a transfer of value *"include references to an occasion on which tax is chargeable under Chapter III of Part III"*. The relief may therefore be available in the case of relevant property trusts to prevent or reduce a charge that would otherwise arise on a 10-year anniversary or when a capital distribution is made to a beneficiary (an "exit charge").[10]

45.09 For these purposes, "business"[11]:

(i) includes a business carried on in the exercise of a profession or vocation;

(ii) is not limited to trading activities but will include a property investment business[12]: generally any commercially run operation (it does not include a business carried on otherwise than for gain).[13]

---

might arise where the nature of the business changes (e.g. under new proposed contractual arrangements part of the trading arm is to be sold off or subcontracted) or a holding company is undertaking new activities, not merely holding shares in trading subsidiaries.
[7] See *R v IRC Ex p. MFK Underwriting Agencies Ltd* [1989] STC 873.
[8] IHTA 1984 s.104(1).
[9] In IHTA 1984 s.103(1).
[10] For the anomalies where business property relief is held on a 10-year anniversary or sold just before it see Ch.29 and 45.56.
[11] IHTA 1984 s.103.
[12] But note the significant exclusions from relief in IHTA 1984 s.105(3): see 45.13.
[13] See *Grimwood-Taylor v IRC* [2000] STC (SCD) 39.

"Relevant property business" is exhaustively defined in s.105 as follows: **45.10**

> "*(1) ... in this Chapter 'relevant business property' means, in relation to any transfer of value,—*
>
> *(a) property consisting of a business or interest in a business;*
> *(b) ... securities of a company which are unquoted and which (either by themselves or together with other such securities owned by the transferor and any unquoted shares so owned) gave the transferor control of the company immediately before the transfer;*
> *(bb) any unquoted shares in a company;*
> *(c) ....*
> *(cc) shares in or securities of a company which are quoted and which (either by themselves or together with other such shares or securities owned by the transferor) gave the transferor control of the company immediately before the transfer;*
> *(d) any land or building, machinery or plant which, immediately before the transfer, was used wholly or mainly for the purposes of a business carried on by a company of which the transferor then had control or by a partnership of which he then was a partner; and*
> *(e) any land or building, machinery or plant which, immediately before the transfer, was used wholly or mainly for the purposes of a business carried on by the transferor and was settled property in which he was then beneficially entitled to an interest in possession."*

It should be noted that to obtain relief the transfer of value has to be "attributable to the value of any relevant business property": it does not, however, have to be of relevant business property. Accordingly, relief may be due on a transfer of an asset out of the business: it is not necessary to transfer either the business or an interest in a business to obtain the relief.[14]

The following points should be noted in respect of the definition of relevant **45.11** business property. Relief in each case is at 100 per cent unless otherwise stated:

(i) "*a business*" covers the sole trader or sole practitioner: in practice, it may be difficult to identify which assets are comprised within the business and this is where proper accounts are desirable. In the *Fetherstonehough* case, the life tenant carried on a business using settled land[15];

(ii) "*an interest in business*" catches the share of a partner in either a trading or professional partnership. It is not unusual for trustees to be in a partnership with the principal beneficiary: in such cases a limited partnership may be used with the beneficiary being the general partner;

(iii) *a controlling interest in a company*[16]: there are two separate heads of relief: (b) deals with unquoted companies (including companies dealt

---

[14] See *RCC v Trustees of the Nelson Dance Family Settlement* [2009] STC 802 and 45.25.
[15] See 45.52.
[16] "Control" is defined in IHTA 1984 s.369(1): see Example 45.2 and 45.57.

in on the AIM Market) whilst (cc) deals with quoted companies. In both cases the relief extends to securities (e.g. loan stock) provided that together with any shares owned they gave the taxpayer control of the company. It is accordingly necessary for the securities to carry votes at company meetings for relief to be available. Control of the company does not have to be transferred: it suffices that the transferor had control at the time of the transfer. Relief is limited to 50 per cent in the case of listed companies;

(iv) *unquoted shares*: these can be of any type (ordinary, preferences, deferred, etc.) and there is no minimum holding required[17];

(v) *land, buildings, machinery and plant*: relief is given at 50 per cent if the asset is owned by the taxpayer and used by either a company which he controls or a partnership in which he is a partner.

EXAMPLE 45.2

(1) Ron owns 40 per cent of the shares in Strob Galleries Limited and his wife owns a further five per cent. The remaining 55 per cent of the shares are in a family discretionary trust set up by Ron's father under which Ron and his wife can benefit. Ron personally owns the premises used by the company. On Ron's death the IHT position is as follows:

  (a) 100 per cent relief will be available on the value of Ron's shareholding (assuming that the other conditions for relief, e.g. two-year ownership, are met).

  (b) To obtain 50 per cent relief on the value of the land Ron would need to control the company. His wife's shares are taken into account (they are related property: see IHTA 1984 s.269(2)) but that still leaves him short of the necessary control (more than 50 per cent) to get relief on the property. If, however, the trustees were to appoint Ron an interest in possession in six per cent of the shares then that would suffice to give him control. Note:

    (i)   it does not matter that Ron's interest in possession is not "qualifying" for IHT purposes: s.269(3) attributes the votes of shares comprised in a settlement "*to the person beneficially entitled to the shares*";

    (ii) there is no requirement that Ron must have controlled the company throughout the two years before his death. He must have owned the land etc for this period but the appointment of the "missing" shares can occur just before his death;

    (iii) the appointment of the interest in possession for Ron is a "nothing" in IHT terms: the six per cent shareholding will not be taxed on Ron's death.

(2) Ethan in partnership with Maggie owns the shop from which the business is conducted. In recent years, Maggie has undertaken the bulk of

---

[17] Note that loan capital (even if carrying votes) is not included.

the work and, reflecting this, is now entitled to 80 per cent of the profits, leaving Ethan with 20 per cent. On Ethan's death:

(a) the value of her partnership share will attract 100 per cent relief;
(b) the value of the property will benefit from 50 per cent relief (the size of Ethan's partnership share is irrelevant: all that is necessary is that she is a partner);
(c) Ethan could increase the relief to 100 per cent by transferring the premises to the partnership so that it becomes a partnership asset. If (as is often the case) Ethan wishes to retain the value of the premises then consider transferring it in a "partnership property capital account" which forms part of her estate (i.e. she remains solely entitled to the capital and income attributable to that property). This will also ensure that the transfer to the partnership will not trigger a gain for CGT purposes. An SDLT charge can be avoided if care is used on the split of profits.

(vi) *settled land etc*: this attracts relief at 50 per cent. See further the discussion on the *Fetherstonehough* case at 45.23, 45.40 and 45.51.

III RESTRICTIONS ON BPR

Although "business" is a word of wide import (e.g. it covers a landlord letting **45.12** property with a view to profit), the relief is not available:

> "*if the business . . . consists wholly or mainly of one or more of the following, that is to say, dealing in securities, stocks or shares, land or buildings, or making or holding investments*".[18]

The IHT legislation does not define an investment business but some guidance may be obtained from *Cook v Medway Housing Society Ltd*[19] in which Lightman J. defined "investment" as "the laying out of moneys in anticipation of profitable capital or income return" and further commented:

> "*In determining what is the business of a company . . . it is necessary to have regard to the quality, purpose and nature of the company and its activities, and this includes the full circumstances in which the relevant assets are acquired and retained, including the objects clause in the memorandum of association of the taxpayer and the objects of a society . . . as revealed in its rules. It is relevant to have regard to the actual activities carried on by the taxpayer at the relevant date, but if these are viewed without regard to the taxpayer's past history or future plans they may give only a partial or incomplete picture. The critical question is whether the holding of assets to produce a profitable return is merely incidental to the carrying on of some other business or is the very business carried on by the taxpayer.*"

---

[18] IHTA 1984 s.105(3). Note the "mixed business" cases especially: *Farmer v IRC* [1999] STC (SCD) 321; *IRC v George (Executors of Stedman)* [2003] STC 468, CA; and *Brander (Representatives of Fourth Earl of Balfour) v RCC* [2010] STC 2666.
[19] [1997] STC 90.

45.13 "*Wholly or mainly*" is not defined in the legislation but a sole trader, partnership or company may conduct within a single business[20] two activities. The question is whether looked at in the round, that business is "mainly" (more than 50 per cent) one of holdings investments. If so, no business property relief is due even on that part of the business which is trading. By contrast, if this is not the case (i.e. the investment side is subsidiary) the relief is given on the entirety of the business (including the investments).

45.14 A voluminous body of case law has built up on the application of this test. From this the following general principles can be adduced:

(i) a business involving property letting and management does not attract relief even if the taxpayer is personally involved in the business[21];

(ii) because of the services provided, hotels and bed & breakfast businesses attract relief but the position of furnished holiday lettings[22] is uncertain with, it is thought, everything turning on the extent to which services are provided over and above those of a landlord. HMRC's current approach appears to be to deny relief in all cases;

(iii) caravan parks and mobile homes have provided a particular battleground with some cases giving relief and others not. The Court of Appeal decision in the *Stedman* case is the most authoritative but *Brander* is perhaps the most helpful in relation to landed estates.[23]

The Farmer[24]/Stedman test

45.15 Although emphasising that the matter has to be considered "in the round", a number of factors have been identified in determining whether the business is mainly one of holding investments:

(i) *the overall context of the business* (in *Farmer* the business involved a landed estate with the bulk of the land being used for farming);

(ii) *the capital employed*: was this mainly in the trading activity or the investment part of the business[25];

(iii) the time spent by the employees on the different activities;

(iv) the turnover; and

---

[20] For whether a single business is being carried on or whether there are two separate businesses, see the *Brander* case considered at 45.21.

[21] *Burkinyoung v IRC* [1995] STC (SCD) 29; *Moore (Executors of Martin) v IRC* [1995] STC (SCD) 5; and for the scope of the normal activities of a landlord see the Northern Irish Court of Appeal decision in *McCall and Keenan (PRs of McClean Deceased) v RCC* [2009] STC 990.

[22] Unlike the position for income tax and CGT, there are no special rules in the IHT legislation dealing with furnished holiday lettings.

[23] *IRC v George (Executors of Stedman Deceased)* [2004] STC 147, CA and see *Hall (Executor of Hall Deceased) v IRC* [1997] STC (SCD) 126; *Powell (PRs of Pearce Deceased) v IRC* [1997] STC (SCD) 181; *Furness v IRC* [1999] STC (SCD) 232.

[24] *Farmer v IRC* [1999] STC (SCD) 321.

[25] Note that in *Brander* (see 45.21) the Upper Tier Tribunal accepted that this was to be ignored given that there was no intention to sell the estate.

(v) the profit.

Having identified these factors, the Special Commissioner in *Farmer* commented:

> "*When these factors have been considered it will then be necessary to stand back and consider in the round whether the business consisted mainly of making or holding investments.*"[26]

Dr Brice's approach noted: **45.16**

(1) The business of Home Farm was that of a landed estate, most of the land being used for farming. In the business, the letting of properties was subsidiary to the use of the estate as a farm, the farming being done in a business-like way. The terms of the leases and licences were short, which is unusual for investment properties.

(2) Dr Brice took the capital employed in the business at its probate value of £3.5 million and apportioned £1.25 million to the let property, and the remaining £2.25 million to the farm (this value qualifying for agricultural relief).

(3) The employees and consultants spent far more time on the farm than on the let property.

(4) The farm turnover exceeded the letting turnover in six years out of eight.

(5) In only two years out of the eight did the farm gross profit exceed the lettings gross profit. In every year the net profit of the lettings exceeded the net profit of the farm.

The Special Commissioner decided that the first four factors all supported the **45.17** conclusion that the business consisted mainly of farming; only the fifth supported the opposite view. Accordingly, taking the whole business in the round and without giving predominance to any one factor, the business consisted mainly of farming and not of making or holding investments.

The Court of Appeal in *IRC v George* [2004] STC 147 commented that **45.18** the decision and approach of Dr Brice was "*particularly helpful, not least in its emphasis on the need to look at the business 'in the round'*." It is therefore worth paying close attention to this approach when arguing a case at the First Tier Tribunal. Indeed both *George* and *Brander* highlight the importance of preparing properly for the fact finding tribunal stage given the unwillingness of the higher courts to interfere with that decision if it is a reasonable conclusion on the particular facts.

The Court of Appeal noted in *George*: **45.19**

> "*The section does not require the opening of an investment 'bag', into which are placed all the activities linked to the caravan park, including even the supply of water, electricity, and gas, simply on the basis that they are 'ancillary' to that investment business. Nor is it necessary to determine whether or not investment is 'the very business' of the Company.*

---

[26] [1999] STC (SCD) 321 at [53].

> *The statutory language does not require such a definitive categorisation. In the present context, it gives insufficient weight to the hybrid nature of a caravan site business, as I have explained. The holding of property as investment was only one component of the business, and on the findings of the Commissioner it was not the main component. In my view, the Commissioner's overall approach was correct in law, and he reached a view which was open to him on the facts."*

45.20 This looser approach of looking at things "in the round" was developed further in *Brander*. However, the case is notable for a number of surprising conclusions, in particular the view taken by the Upper Tribunal on appeal that the fact that the capital value of the investment properties comprised in the estate was nearly double that of the non-investment assets was not a factor which needed to be given much weight given it was not envisaged that the property would be sold. Again looked at in the round, they emphasised that it is the overall nature of the business that must be considered. They confirmed that it is necessary to have regard to the period leading up to the date of the transfer not just the position at date of death. The length of the period depends on what is appropriate for the particular business. For example, the year before the death was taken in *Hall* [1997] STC (SCD) 126, a period of three years was used in *Martin* [1995] STC (SCD) 5, and the parties agreed a period of eight years in *Farmer*. In *Brander* Lord Balfour, no doubt taking advice as he became older, took back farms that had originally been let and farmed them in hand after 1999 (four years prior to his death).

The Brander decision

45.21 The case involved a Scottish landed estate comprising, at the date of Lord Balfour's death on June 27, 2003, a total estate of 771.85 hectares (1,907.25 acres) made up of:

(a) Whittinghame Tower Farmhouse;

(b) Whittinghame Mains Farm and Eastfield Farm which were both operated in hand;

(c) Luggate Papple and Overfield Farms which had been let since the 1950s;

(d) parks, woodlands and sporting rights;

(e) 26 let houses and cottages;

(f) two sets of business premises.

In 1968, Lord Balfour inherited a liferent interest in the estate under his father's Will. At the time when the will was made the estate was some 10,000 acres including Whittinghame House, agricultural and forestry land and various houses and cottages. Substantial parts had to be sold off to pay death duties including the House. In November 2002 the estate was released from the life rent, becoming Lord Balfour's absolute property which he then farmed in partnership with his nephew and heir. Note therefore that for the purpose of the two-year ownership test it was necessary to have regard to the position whilst the estate was subject to the life rent as well as the position at death because Lord Balfour himself had owned it personally for less than two years. (It was not disputed that the land was a partnership asset and that he had brought into the partnership as a capital asset otherwise only 50 per cent relief could have been claimed.)

The Upper Tribunal upheld the decision of the First Tier Tribunal in favour of **45.22** the taxpayer and the following matters of significance emerge from the decision.

1. The two-year ownership condition

The Tribunal decided that whilst the estate was held in trust the business was carried on by Lord Balfour and not by the trustees. The Revenue had argued that Lord Balfour merely had a right to the net income and a right of personal occupation and possession, i.e. the life rent was of the net revenue not a right to let the life rented estate. Had this argument succeeded the succession provisions in s.107 would not have applied since Lord Balfour would not have owned relevant business property before November 2002. Hence he would not have satisfied the basic two-year ownership condition in s.106. The Tribunal noted that in the Will the trustees could confer powers on the life renters to work the land, repair property and grant leases. Lord Balfour had something equivalent to a full life rent particularly as the life renter had to bear the losses and profits of management of the farming part.

In succeeding on this point it was necessary for the taxpayer to rely heavily **45.23** on *Finch v IR*[27] where the Court of Appeal (by a majority) decided that settled land used by a life tenant for the purposes of his business qualified for relief under FA 1976 Sch.10, para.3(1)(a)—the equivalent of s.105(1)(a)—on a death before March 10, 1981. They held that the phrase "assets used in the business" in FA 1975 Sch.4 para.14(2), as applied by FA 1976 Sch.10 para.6 (from which s.110 of IHTA 1984 is derived) should be construed literally and would include assets which were not part of the life tenant's own business, provided that they were part of the transfer of value and used in the business.[28]

2. The estate comprised a single business

The in-hand farming business kept separate accounts from those of the trust (as envisaged in the will) and had a separate VAT registration. It was nevertheless decided that the estate was run by Lord Balfour as a single entity making

[27] [1985] Ch 1 also reported as *Fetherstonehaugh v IRC* [1984] STC 261 and discussed at 45.38, 45.40 and 45.51.
[28] *Finch* or *Fetherstonehough* represented a change since before March 10, 1981 settled property could qualify for the reduction if used for the purposes of a business carried on by a company which the life tenant controlled or by a partnership of which he was a member, but the Revenue did not consider that relief was due if the business was carried on solely by the life tenant. Following the FA 2006, it is clear that this case would only be relevant where the assets are held within a settlement where the life tenant is using them in his own business and also has a qualifying interest in possession. In the case of Lord Brander of course, he had taken his qualifying interest in possession many years ago.

no distinction in the daily business activities between the in-hand farming and the rest of the estate. It was held to be a false distinction to hold that Lord Balfour was managing the farming operation himself and the lettings on behalf of the trustees.

Accordingly it was held that the case involved a single composite business. It followed from the *Finch* case that for the purpose of valuing the transfer of value regard was to be had to the value of the trust assets used in the business and not the value of his life rent in those assets.

45.24   While it is helpful to note that merely keeping separate accounts and separate VAT registrations between the trading and investment parts will not invariably mean that BPR is lost, it is clearly sensible to back up "the one estate" argument by running the businesses together and not separately. This is what Lord Balfour did in his day to day practice. HMRC argued that the trustees ran a business separate from that of Lord Balfour's and that it was carried on otherwise than for gain. They lost this argument in the face of the fact that Lord Balfour carried on the management of the entire estate including the lettings both on a day to day basis and in terms of strategic decisions making. The trustees played a passive administrative role. The trustees were not authorised signatories on any bank account and Lord Balfour dealt with the lettings through the solicitors for the trustees. He instigated all forestry work and property disposals and his wishes were always followed. Few meetings of the trustees took place.

3. The composite business was not mainly an investment activity

Although it was accepted that the First-tier Tribunal had been wrong in treating agricultural tenancies as a farming rather than investment activity the error was held to be immaterial. The Upper Tier Tribunal followed the approach of the *Stedman* and *Farmer* cases in determining that this issue must be considered "in the round" and "primarily as a matter of overall impression". The Tribunal rejected HMRC's argument that if the business was a composite business it was mainly trading and accepted the argument run by the taxpayer's counsel that although there were a number of potentially relevant indicia, such as acreage, turnover, profit, time spent, employees and capital values, no one factor was conclusive and the weight attached to a particular factor would vary according to the circumstances of the particular case. There will be circumstances in which a factor which is relevant to one business is not relevant to another. The overall context must always be considered.

45.25   Note the following:

(a) the in-hand farms and woodlands were throughout a non-investment activity and whilst the sporting generated little income it was combined with vermin control throughout the estate and so was a factor on the non-investment side;

(b) both turnover net profit and time spent on the business pointed to the management of the estate being a trading activity;

(c) so far as capital values were concerned the let properties at £4,357,500 way exceeded the trading properties at £2,313,065 but this was only one factor and, given that the long term policy of the estate was to retain land, "*market values were generally immaterial to Lord Balfour's business decisions*". This is possibly the most controversial part of the decision.

This is an important and helpful case for landowners. It confirms the impor-   **45.26**
tance of looking at the estate in the round. Where settled property is held by
the trustees and some of it is let out by the trustees and some farmed by the life
tenant there is now a strong case to ensure that the life tenant runs the whole
estate rather than the trustees carrying on the lettings separately. The trustees
will generally be able to delegate management of the land including lettings to
the life tenant. However, in some cases the lettings activities may significantly
exceed the trading activities and it may then be preferable to demonstrate that
two entirely separate businesses are being carried out on the land—one by the
trustees and one by the life tenant personally in order to avoid losing BPR on
the farming part!

The McCall case[29]

The deceased let 33 acres of farmland which she had inherited from her   **45.27**
husband in 1983 under grazing agreements to local farmers.[30] The land was
zoned for development and when the deceased died, although the agricultural
value was only £165,000, its market value was £5.8 million. Two preliminary
matters should be noted:

1. there is no doubt that APR was available in respect of the agricultural
   value of the land. The issue concerned the availability of business
   property relief on the enhanced value (i.e. on the difference between the
   market value and the agricultural value);

2. the letting arrangements were arranged on behalf of the deceased
   (whose mind rapidly deteriorated after the death of her husband) by
   her son-in-law. The Special Commissioner accepted that it remained her
   business.

So far as the availability of business property relief was concerned, he decided   **45.28**
(and the NI Court of Appeal agreed) that:

1. the activity of tending the land undertaken by the son-in-law coupled
   with the annual letting of the land was just enough to constitute a business. Around 100 hours per annum was spent in weed control; fence
   maintenance; litter and damage control and drainage and water works;

2. but the business consisted wholly or mainly of the holding of investments so that (as a result of IHTA 1984 s.105(3)) business property relief
   was not available. He concluded:

---

[29] [2009] STC 900.
[30] Although there was much discussion of local letting arrangements in Northern Ireland (especially "conacre" or "agistment" arrangements) the agreements in this case were essentially the
same as those employed in England and Wales: accordingly, the lettings were for the period
during which grass was growing, April 1 to November 1. Hence, it is thought that the case is
of general significance.

"The activities of the business do not involve the cutting of the grass and the feeding of it to the cattle but simply making the asset available so that the cattle may live and eat there: the income arises substantially from the making available of the asset not from the other activity associated with it or from selling separately the fruits of the asset: that is the business of holding an investment, and it was the main activity of this business. It was not like a 'pick your own' fruit farm where after months of weeding, fertilising, spraying and pruning, customers are licensed to enter to take the produce and pay by the pound for what they take away: in the business of letting the fields there was less in preparatory work, the fields were let for the accommodation of the cattle as well as for the grazing and the rent was paid by the acre rather than by the ton of grass eaten: it was not a business consisting of the provision of the grass but of the provision of the (non-exclusive) use of the land."

The courts did not accept the taxpayer's argument that the correct analysis of a grazing licence was that it involved the business of selling a grass crop.

45.29   The decision is significant in relation to arrangements in England and Wales. These take a variety of forms: for instance, the grazing licence which may if it grants exclusive possession amount to a short term business tenancy. An alternative, for which the CLA provide a precedent, is a *profit à prendre* under which the grazier is allowed to put cattle on the land to take the grass. What precisely was the arrangement in this case? Girvan L.J. explained the nature of the agistment arrangement as follows:

"The use by Northern Ireland landowners of conacre and agistment arrangements with other farmers is common even though such arrangements have been criticised as unsatisfactory arrangements which do not assist in good land management practices. The fact that such arrangements are common is in part due to their traditional use in Northern Ireland, in part due to a fear on the part of both landowners and graziers and conacre tenants of creating agricultural tenancies with potential adverse legal consequences and in part due to the desire of landowners to retain a degree of control over the land during the period of the contract. What appears clear from the old Irish authorities is that an agistment contract confers on the grazier only a right to graze and not possession of the land in law. They do not create a tenancy. Such an arrangement partakes of the quality of the profit à prendre but one which by way of exception to the normal rules does not require to be created by deed. Such an arrangement bears a close comparison to a contractual licence."[31]

He further commented that the absence of a full and exclusive right of occupation of the land for the grazier and the existence of a right by the owner to enter the land during the period of the agistment did not prevent the business being regarded as the holding of an investment.

45.30   The fact that the deceased did not qualify for business property relief is important when, as in this case, the land has hope value. It will also be significant, however, in deciding whether any house can be a farmhouse: if the correct analysis is that the grazing agreement involves the holding of an invest-

[31] At [16].

ment, then it is difficult to see how the property occupied by the landowner can be a farmhouse.[32]

If only a part of the farmland is subject to a grazing agreement and the bulk **45.31** of the farm is farmed in hand, then on the basis of the "wholly or mainly" test in s.105(3) it is thought that business property relief will be available on all the land.

The Piercy case[33]

The company had been established for property development and had large **45.32** holdings of land for which it received substantial amounts of rent. Although, for corporation tax purposes, it was generally classified as trading, HMRC considered this to be irrelevant, contending that the receipt of substantial rents meant that business property relief was not available since the activities of the company fell foul of s.105(3) in involving mainly the holding of investments.

The Special Commissioner concluded, however, that the business of the **45.33** company involved marshalling sites for development with a view to selling the finished developments. Accordingly, land was held as trading stock and even though it produced a rental income, there was no evidence that it had been appropriated as an investment. Note:

(1) the reference in s.105(3) to a land dealing company (the shares in which do not qualify for business property relief) does not affect building companies:

> "*the only type of land dealing company whose shares fail to qualify for the relief is of some sort of dealing or speculative trader that does not actually develop or actually build on land*";

(2) a company can only conduct the business of holding investments if it has got some investments! In *Piercy*, whilst the company had retained some land, it had not appropriated it as an investment. For instance, the company had acquired land in Islington for residential development but could not proceed because of planning delays. As an interim measure, it had built poor quality limited life industrial workshops on this land (let on short term leases) but with the continuing intention of knocking down these units once residential development became possible. The Special Commissioner concluded that this land had never become appropriated as an investment (incidentally, had it been so appropriated the corporation tax returns of the company over a number of years should have been quite different and, contrary to the arguments of HMRC, the Special Commissioner decided that this was a case where the two taxes "go hand in hand").

The Phillips case[34]

The taxpayer owned shares in eight related family companies, including P Ltd. **45.34** P Ltd made loans to the related companies which were used for the purchase

---

[32] For a consideration of the meaning of farmhouse, see the *McKenna* case at 46.20.
[33] *Executors of Piercy Deceased v RCC* [2008] STC (SCD) 858.
[34] *Phillips (Executors of Phillips Deceased) v IRC* [2006] STC (SCD) 639.

of investment properties. The criteria for making each loan was whether the borrowing company could afford to make the interest payments and whether the value of the purchased property was commensurate with the amount of the loan. All the loans were repayable on demand with no security. P Ltd did not acquire any interest in the shares of the borrowing companies, or in the acquired properties, or any rights in the increased value of the purchased properties. All it was entitled to was the interest payable on the loans. The conclusions of the Special Commissioner were as follows[35]:

> "*At one end of the spectrum of lending could be investment in bonds or debentures but at the other end of the spectrum could be the making of informal unsecured loans which activity amounts to no more than money-lending.*
>   *. . . Thus, in determining what was the business of the company it is necessary to have regard to all the facts in the round. If one starts with the definition (making or holding investments), and asks whether on its ordinary meaning the business of the company fell within it, I think the answer is no. P did not make or hold investments; it made informal loans to its related companies and money lending is not normally regarded as investment . . . the fact that a loan is made to an investment company does not make the making of the loan an investment.*"

The decision suggests that if an investment business is funded by a money-box company, shares in the latter may attract BPR. By contrast a direct investment in the investment business would not!

IV WHAT MUST BE TRANSFERRED?

45.35   It had been generally thought that BPR was only available in the case of unincorporated businesses on a transfer of either the whole business or a part of the business. Whilst this would not present difficulties on the death of the owner, it could present problems in the case of lifetime gifts. In 2002, Nelson Dance[36] settled property forming part of his farming business on to discretionary trusts. This transfer did not involve either the transfer of his entire business nor any part of that business (i.e. it amounted to a transfer of mere assets). He died within seven years of the transfer. The Special Commissioner had to decide whether the original transfer into the discretionary trust qualified for business property relief.[37] He decided, contrary to the unanimous views of the text book writers on the subject, that it did and his decision was upheld in the High Court. The relevant arguments are as follows:

(1)   business property relief is given when the whole or part of the value transferred by a transfer of value is attributable to the value of any relevant business property[38];

---

[35] [2006] STC (SCD) 639 at [32], [33] and [37].
[36] *RCC v The Trustees of the Nelson Dance Family Settlement* [2008] STC (SCD) 792 affirmed [2009] STC 802.
[37] The transfer attracted agricultural property relief but only on the agricultural value of the relevant land which had substantial development potential.
[38] IHTA 1984 s.104(1).

(2) in the IHT legislation value transferred means the fall in value of the transferor's estate;

(3) in the context of business property relief, IHTA 1984 s.110 requires liabilities incurred for the purposes of the business to be deducted in arriving at the net value of that business;

(4) but there is nothing to say that the value transferred must be attributable to the transfer of the whole business or indeed a part of the business;

(5) that is only relevant to the definitions in s.105 which lists property capable of being "relevant business property" (for instance, s.105(1)(a) is dealing with the situation where a taxpayer is a sole trader or, typically, a partner in a partnership).

The decision is significant in allowing individual assets to be stripped out of a **45.36** business: for instance, in the case of a mixed business where there is concern that the investment aspect may become predominant, it will be possible to remove sufficient of the investment assets to ensure that the "wholly or mainly" test in s.105(3) continues to be met. Suppose that a business is predominantly one of house building but has, over the years, acquired a number of tenanted properties. These properties may be transferred out while the business is still "mainly" a trading business. The transfer will attract relief and the remaining business be in less danger of losing relief in the future. Likewise if a business has accumulated a substantial cash reserve which it has been keeping for business purposes so that it is not an excepted asset[39] (as in the *Brown* case)[40] then this, it appears, may be distributed with the benefit of relief.

V THE VALUE OF THE BUSINESS

IHTA 1984 s.110 is as follows: **45.37**

> "*For the purposes of this Chapter—*
>
> (a) the value of a business or of an interest in a business shall be taken to be its net value;
> (b) the net value of a business is the value of the assets used in the business (including goodwill) reduced by the aggregate amount of any liabilities incurred for the purposes of the business;
> (c) in ascertaining the net value of an interest in a business, no regard shall be had to assets or liabilities other than those by reference to which the net value of the entire business would fall to be ascertained."

The section presents a number of problems which the decided cases have done little to resolve. For instance:

---

[39] On excepted assets, see 45.44.
[40] *Brown's Executors v IRC* [1996] STC (SCD) 277.

(i) What are the assets used in the business?

45.38   In the *Fetherstonehough* case the Court of Appeal gave the words a common sense meaning: in that case the tenant for life ran a farming business which used land comprised in the settlement of which he was the life tenant. It accordingly qualified for business relief.[41]

45.39   Oliver L.J. explained the operation of FA 1975 Sch.4 para.14(1) (the forerunner of s.110) as follows:

> "... *in the case of a partnership, there is not generally very much difficulty in ascertaining what the partnership assets are, for this will be apparent from the accounts, but in the case of a sole trader who may have been carrying on business from his private residence and employing in it property which is not segregated from his other property, there may be very considerable difficulty in ascertaining what is and what is not part of 'the business'. The difficulty is a familiar one in the field of construction of wills where a testator bequeaths his business separately from the remainder of his estate ... That, as it seems to me, accounts for the form taken by [s.110(b)], where we are told how the net value to which the tax attributable is to be ascertained. The (provision) is directed, in my judgment, to the case of the decedent who is a sole trader and where what has to be ascertained is not the net value of some interest less than the whole but the value of 'the business'.*
>
> *In such a case there is strictly no such thing as an asset 'of' the business. All the assets of the estate, to the value of which the tax is attributable, are assets 'of' the decedent, and in order to identify which of the decedent's assets can be taken into account in assessing the value of the business, the legislature adopts the only practicable test - were they assets which were 'used in the business'? - it being, as the judge pointed out, necessarily postulated that the assets are assets, the value of which forms part of the value transferred, and therefore which belong to the decedent. Thus the 'assets' and 'liabilities' referred to in the sub-paragraph are not at this stage identified as assets or liabilities 'of' the business. They are simply assets, the value of which is included in the transfer of value, and are to be identified as business assets for the purposes of the ascertainment of the net value by reference to whether they were used by the deceased in his business, just as those of the deceased's liabilities which are to be allowed as a deduction are to be ascertained by asking whether they were incurred by him for the purposes of his business.*
>
> *That test, however, cannot be left unqualified when one comes to the valuation of the alternative with which the paragraph is concerned, for a partner may have no interest at all in some of the assets which are used in the business. They may, for instance, belong to one of the other partners who makes them available gratuitously for partnership purposes. In such circumstances, no conventional valuation of a deceased's partner's share would take into account the value of an asset which, though used in the business, was not owned by the partnership. Take, for instance, the not uncommon case where a medical practitioner allows the partnership of*

---

[41] See further 45.21. Note that as a result of IHTA 1984 s.49(1), land was comprised in his estate. Contrast *IRC v Mallender (Executors of Drury-Lowe Deceased)* [2001] STC 514 when a guarantee over land was used in the business of a Lloyd's Name but not the land supporting that guarantee.

which he is a member to have the use of a surgery attached to or forming part of his private house. In such circumstances, no conventional valuation of any partners' share in the partnership, including that of the landowner himself, would include the surgery as a partnership asset. This, I think, illustrates the purpose of [s.110(c)]. If [s.110(b)] had been left without qualification to govern the valuation not only of 'a business', but also of 'an interest in a business', it would have been arguable that the valuation would have to take the hypothetical surgery referred to above into account.

Thus the paragraph goes on to make it clear that, in valuing a partnership share, property used in the business but not owned by the partnership is not to be taken into account, the valuation embracing only those assets which would have to be taken into account if one were valuing the partnership business as a whole."

In the *Fetherstonehough* case the deceased had carried on a business on settled land in which he was the life tenant. Applying a natural meaning to s.110(b) Oliver L.J. concluded: **45.40**

> *"It seems to me, therefore, that the life interest must, for the purposes of [s.110(b)] be one of the assets which are used in the business (and indeed one of the assets 'of' the business on the judge's narrower construction) whose value must be taken into account. But the value of that asset is part of the value included in the chargeable transfer which is deemed to have taken place, and for this purpose has statutorily to be treated as if it were the interest of an absolute owner [by virtue of s.49(1)].*
>
> *Is there then any ground in logic or as a matter of construction why the same asset should be excluded altogether from the computation of the net value of the business, or should be included at a value less than that statutorily attributed to it in the overall valuation of the transfer of value? . . . It is the inevitable corollary of imagining, as one is directed to do, that the deceased was the freeholder, that the freehold, and not merely his factual life interest, forms part of the farming and forestry business which he carried on."*

The *Hardcastle* case[42] suggests that stock in trade is not an asset used in the business (and accordingly does not benefit from BPR!) This is something of an affront to common sense and it is not thought HMRC follow this decision. **45.41**

(ii) What liabilities are incurred for the purposes of the business?

If the taxpayer borrows to purchase a going-concern business, it is not thought that the liability is incurred for the purposes of the business: it is incurred to buy the business but not for its purposes. By contrast, the typical business overdraft would be a liability incurred as part and parcel of running the business. What of trading losses? In *Hardcastle* the losses of a Lloyd's Name were **45.42**

---

[42] *Hardcastle (Executors of Vermede Deceased) v IRC* [2000] STC (SCD) 532.

not considered to have been incurred for the purposes of the business: rather they were (like profits) the very business itself.[43]

45.43   A further issue arises if a loan incurred for the purposes of the business is secured over non-business property (e.g. over the taxpayer's main residence). Does that liability reduce the value of the business or does IHTA 1984 s.162(4) prevail? That section provides that:

> "*a liability which is an incumbrance on any property shall, so far as possible, be taken to reduce the value of that property*"

In this case it may be said that whilst the liability is to be taken to reduce the value of the property charged, at the same time business property relief is limited to the net value of the business. Section 110 is designed to identify the value of the business for the purpose of giving a valuation relief so that the fact that the liability is separately charged is irrelevant.

(iii) Assets used in the business and excepted assets

45.44   It would appear that the first step is to identify what assets are as a matter of fact used in the business. Having done that, it is then necessary to consider whether any of those assets is an "excepted asset" with the result that its value does not attract relief unless it is land. IHTA 1984 s.112(1) and (2) is in the following terms:

> "*(1)   In determining for the purposes of this Chapter what part of the value transferred by a transfer of value is attributable to the value of any relevant business property so much of the last-mentioned value as is attributable to any excepted assets within the meaning of subsection (2) below shall be left out of account.*
>
> *(2)   An asset is an excepted asset in relation to any relevant business property if it was neither—*
>
> > *(a)   used wholly or mainly for the purposes of the business concerned throughout the whole or the last two years of the relevant period defined in subsection (5) below, nor*
> >
> > *(b)   required at the time of the transfer for future use for those purposes;*[44]
>
> *but where the business concerned is carried on by a company which is a member of a group, the use of an asset for the purposes of a business carried on by another company which at the time of the use and immediately before the transfer was also a member of that group shall be treated as use for the purposes of the business concerned, unless that other company's membership of the group falls to be disregarded under section 111 above.*"

---

[43] The actual result was beneficial to the taxpayer since the losses were deducted against the rest of the taxpayer's estate, i.e. against property which did not attract relief.

[44] See *Barclay's Bank Trust Co Ltd v IRC* [1998] STC (SCD) 125.

Section 112(4) provides that *"where part but not the whole of any land or build-* **45.45** *ing is used exclusively for the purposes of any business and the land or building would but for this subsection be an excepted asset . . . the part so used shall . . . be taken to be such proportion of the value of the whole as may be just."*

Hence, the value of the part used exclusively in the business qualifies for relief and its value will be such proportion of the value of the whole "as may be just". So where a ground floor is used as a shop and the two upper floors are let, although the premises are not used "wholly or mainly in the business" and so are excepted assets, some relief is due. The business part might be valued at more than an arithmetical one-third of the total value of the premises. HMRC state that the DV should report "the higher of (i) the value of the exclusively used part as a separate asset and (ii) the apportioned value of the exclusively used part (apportioning between that and the remainder according to the value which each part contributes to the value of the whole)."

HMRC do not take the point that the domestic use out of hours of say a dentist's waiting room within his house prevents it from being exclusively used for business. See Valuation Office Agency IHTM s.11.32. However, it appears that there must be one room that is used exclusively for business purposes. It is therefore worthwhile ensuring that even on landed estates where agricultural property relief may not be available on the house (or where the agricultural value is significantly below market value), some business property relief is secured on the house by clearly designating part of it for exclusive office use.

In the *Hertford*[45] case, the business in question was that of opening an **45.46** historic house to the public. Ragley Hall was a Grade I listed house and some parts (78 per cent by volume) were open to the public: some parts (22 per cent by volume) were not being occupied by the family. HMRC sought to split the building: arguing that 78 per cent was used in the business (and hence attracted relief) whilst the remainder was not so used. The Special Commissioner (with some hesitation) decided that there was no ground for splitting the asset in this way: common sense suggested that the asset was the whole house which was used in the business.[46] It was accepted by the parties that if this was correct then s.112 would not apply to disallow any of the value from qualifying for relief since *"the asset was used wholly or mainly for the business"* within s.112(2)(a).[47] There was no provision then for apportionment under s.110.

How far can this decision be applied? What, for instance, of a farmhouse **45.47** which fails the "character appropriate" test and so does not benefit from APR?[48] It might be thought that even if it is used in the farming business it will not be "wholly" used and so fall foul of s.112(2)(a) and be an excluded asset with only limited relief under s.112(4) if part is used exclusively. However, if one could argue that the farmland surrounding the house together with the house itself is a single asset for business property relief purposes that, taken as a whole, is used mainly in the business it appears that the house could then qualify for business property relief: "the single estate" argument. The fact

---

[45] *Seymour, Ninth Marquis of Hertford v IRC* [2005] STC (SCD) 177.
[46] A factor was the secondary argument for the taxpayer that the whole building had a business function: *"the entirety of the structure (not merely the first two storeys) is on view to the public"*.
[47] Note that the apportionment provision in IHTA 1984 s.112(3) only comes into play if the asset would otherwise be an excepted asset under the test in s.112(4) and some part is used exclusively for business use.
[48] See 46.20.

that a small part of the estate (i.e. the house) may not be used as much in the business as other parts of the estate would not matter under s.110 so long as the single unit taken as a whole is used mainly in the business. Note that this is a very different approach from agricultural property relief which clearly differentiates between the land and the farmhouse when allocating relief.

VI HOW THE RELIEFS WORK FOR SETTLED PROPERTY

45.48 Both BPR and APR are valuation reliefs: i.e. they operate by reducing the value transferred by a transfer of value. Thus IHTA 1984 s.104(1) provides:

> "*When the whole or part of the value transferred by a transfer of value is attributable to the value of any relevant business property, the whole or part of the value transferred shall be treated as reduced. . .*".[49]

45.49 In the case of settlements with a qualifying interest in possession, any transfer of value will be made by the relevant beneficiary.[50] Hence, in general, he will need to satisfy the conditions for the relief.

45.50 In the case of relevant property settlements, however, the position is different. IHTA 1984 s.103(1) provides that:

> "*references to a transfer of value include references to an occasion on which tax is chargeable under Chapter III of Part III of this Act*".[51]
> (anniversary + exit charges)

Two further provisions are needed to ensure that the reliefs apply to property which is settled:

(i) references to the value transferred by a chargeable transfer include references to the amount on which tax is then chargeable; and

(ii) references to a "transfer" include reference to the trustees of the settlement "concerned".[52]

45.51 The level of relief for trustees is the same as for individuals, i.e.:

(i) 100 per cent relief for all unquoted shares and for businesses belonging to the trust (and for a partnership share in a business owned by the trust)[53];

(ii) 50 per cent relief for controlling shareholdings in listed companies owned by the trust[54];

---

[49] And see the similar wording in s.116(1) in the case of agricultural property. The reduction, in both cases, is either 100 per cent or 50 per cent.

[50] See IHTA 1984 ss.49(1), 52(1) and 4(1).

[51] i.e. anniversary and exit charge.

[52] IHTA 1984 s.103(1)(a)(b) and, for APR, see s.115.

[53] IHTA 1984 s.105(1)(e).

[54] IHTA 1984 s.105(1)(a) and (b). "Listed" means listed on a recognised stock exchange or dealt in on the Unlisted Securities Market. In general securities on AIM are not listed and hence can attract BPR under, (i) unquoted shares. But beware of dual listing on overseas recognised

(iii) 50 per cent relief for land or buildings, plant or machinery owned by the trust but which are used in a business carried on by the interest in possession beneficiary.[55]

(iv) 100 per cent relief on the agricultural value of agricultural property falling within IHTA 1984 s.116(2)(a) and (b) and 50 per cent relief on let agricultural land not attracting 100 per cent relief.

The *Fetherstonehaugh* case[56]

This concerned the availability of relief when land held under a strict settlement **45.52** was used by the life tenant as part of his farming business (he was a sole trader absolutely entitled to the other business assets). The Court of Appeal decided relief was available under s.105(1)(a) on the land in the settlement with the result that the subsequent introduction of 50 per cent (at that time 30 per cent) relief (see (iii)) is apparently redundant in such cases. HMRC accepts that in cases similar to *Fetherstonehaugh* the maximum 100 per cent relief will be available since the land will be treated as an "asset used in the business"[57] and, as its value is included in the transfer of value, the land will be taxed on the basis that the deceased was the absolute owner of it. (Of course, if the interest in possession was not qualifying: (e.g. if it arose after March 21, 2006) this reasoning would not hold good. Relief under (iii) above would, however, still be available.)

For some time after the *Fetherstonehough* decision it remained uncertain **45.53** whether in the case of a transfer after March 9, 1981 the relief would be 50 per cent under s.105(1)(a) or 30 per cent under s.105(1)(e) of the IHTA 1984. Eventually the Financial Secretary to the Treasury wrote a letter[58] confirming that the 50 per cent relief was available "when the circumstances accord with those in the *Fetherstonehough* case". This meant, presumably, that the land and the business must be included in the same transfer of value, as would normally happen on the death of a life tenant.

It appears that the lower rate of relief under s.105(1)(e) can apply only where the transfer of value does not include the transferor's business. The most common case is where the transferor's interest under the settlement comes to an end in his lifetime and he dies within seven years, so that a charge to tax on the land (but not the business) arises under IHTA 1984 s.52(1).[59]

BPR depends upon ownership for a two-year period[60] which has given rise **45.54** to problems when the terms of a trust have changed so that instead of the trust either being accumulation and maintenance or discretionary a beneficiary has become entitled to a qualifying interest in possession.

---

stock exchanges and check whether AIM companies have excessive cash reserves; undertake non-qualifying activities, risks of takeover, acquisition, flotation, insolvency, etc.

[55] IHTA 1984 s.105(1)(cc) and the *Fetherstonehaugh* decision considered at 45.23, 45.38 and 45.52. It may be noted that this part of the legislation has not been amended to reflect the FA 2006 changes in the definition of a qualifying interest in possession. The reference in s.105 is to any interest in possession whether or not qualifying.

[56] [1984] STC 261, CA. Also reported as *Finch v IRC*.

[57] See 45.38.

[58] Published in *CTT News & Reports*, October 1985, p.287.

[59] Query whether the *Nelson Dance* case affects this analysis.

[60] IHTA 1984 s.106: note, however, that there are special rules for replacement property (IHTA 1984 s.107) and for successions (IHTA 1984 s.108).

EXAMPLE 45.3

The Jenkins' accumulation and maintenance trust was set up in 1997 and owns the family wine importing business. In 2004 Jason Jenkins became entitled to an interest in possession on becoming 21. In 2005 the trustees determined that interest by exercising an overriding power of appointment and appointed the property on discretionary trusts for the family. The IHT position is as follows:

(i) In 2004 the accumulation and maintenance trust ended, being replaced by a qualifying interest in possession trust. There was no IHT charge at that time.[61]

(ii) From 1997–2004 the trustees were the owners of the business but in 2004 Jason is treated as the owner for the purposes of IHT business property relief.[62] Accordingly, to qualify for relief he must own the property for a period of two years.

(iii) The termination of his interest in 2004, however, resulted in his making a chargeable transfer[63] which does not attract BPR. To benefit from the relief the trustees should have waited until his interest in possession had been in existence for two years.[64]

45.55 The changes in FA 2006 to the IHT treatment of settlements mean that after March 21, 2006 new qualifying interests in possession will rarely arise. For instance, if Jason's interest had only arisen after that date (so that the trust had continued in accumulation and maintenance form until then) it would not have been a qualifying interest. The trust would have become a relevant property settlement[65] and so the trustees would have continued to be the owners of the business for IHT purposes. And, of course, they would have been entitled to the relief since they satisfied the two-year ownership requirement.

The relevant property charge

45.56 In general the relief will apply in the normal way but note two wrinkles:

(i) in the case of exit charges arising <u>before</u> the first 10-year anniversary, the rate of charge is calculated by reference to:

"*the value, immediately after the settlement commenced, <u>of the property then comprised in it</u>*"[66]

---

[61] IHTA 1984 s.71(4).

[62] See IHTA 1984 s.49(1): Jason is treated as beneficially entitled to the property (i.e. the business) in the settlement.

[63] IHTA 1984 s.52.

[64] See *Burrell v Burrell* [2005] STC 569.

[65] It might have satisfied the requirement for an 18–25 trust but the result would be the same in terms of the trustees continuing to own the property for the purposes of BPR.

[66] IHTA 1984 s.68(5)(a) and for a consideration of the implications of this provision see Ch.29.

which does not permit any reduction to the value of the property settled for either BPR or APR.

EXAMPLE 45.4

(1) A settles property qualifying for 100 per cent business property relief in 2000. In 2006 the business is sold and the cash distributed amongst the beneficiaries. It might be thought that the IHT exit charge in 2006 will be nil on the basis that the value of the property originally settled was, after 100 per cent relief, nil. However, IHTA 1984 s.86 (which deals with the rate of tax before the first 10-year anniversary) provides that the rate is calculated by reference to "*the value, immediately after the settlement commenced, of the property then comprised in it*".[67] Accordingly, it is the value ignoring business or agricultural relief which must be taken and hence the distribution of cash may attract an exit charge.[68]

(2) If, however, the business property remained in the settlement beyond the first 10-year anniversary is then sold and the proceeds paid out to beneficiaries, the IHT position is as follows:

    (a) there will be no 10-year charge (since BPR at 100 per cent is then available);

    (b) the rate of tax charged on the distribution of the cash after sale of the business will be calculated by reference to the appropriate fraction of the rate at which it was last charged rather than by reference to the value of the property in the settlement at the last 10-year anniversary.[69] Assuming, therefore, that the only property in the settlement qualified for relief at 100 per cent so that the rate of tax previously was 0 per cent, the rate of the exit charge will be nil.

(ii) if business property is comprised in a settlement on the occasion of a 10-year charge, relief is available, in the usual way, and if that property is then sold there is no adjustment in the calculation of the rate of the exit charge during the next 10-year period.

EXAMPLE 45.5

The Benji Discretionary Trust was set up on August 1, 2000. On August 1, 2010 it contained shares in Benji Blow-Out Ltd, the family trading company, valued at £1 million and which qualified for relief[70] at 100 per cent. They were subsequently sold for £1.2 million and on July 31, 2020

---

[67] IHTA 1984 s.68(5)(a).
[68] If the trustees had distributed the business property when it attracted relief at 100%, no problem would then arise given that, although tax would be chargeable on the basis of the value of the property originally settled, the charge will be on a nil value.
[69] IHTA 1984 s.69(1).
[70] Under IHTA 1984 s.105(1)(bb).

the trustees appointed the moneys out to the Benji Brothers thereby ending the trust. The tax position is as follows:

 (i) at the time of the 10-year charge in 2010 the value of the property in the settlement was £1 million but this will benefit from 100 per cent relief so that the amount on which tax is charged will be reduced to nil.

 (ii) the sale of the shares will give rise to a CGT charge with no entrepreneurs' relief (see Ch.14).

 (iii) the calculation of the exit charge in July 2020 will depend on the rate charged at the time of the last anniversary, i.e. nil.[71]

"Control"

45.57 This is relevant, for instance, in the case of relief for listed securities and for assets held outside a company.[72] This test is applied at the time when the transfer occurs: it is not necessary for the transferor to have had control of the company during the preceding two years. In applying the control test, IHTA 1984 s.269(3) provides that when shares or securities are held in a settlement the voting powers given to the trustees:

> "*shall be deemed to be given to the person beneficially entitled in possession to the shares*".

Notice that there is no requirement that the interest in possession must be "qualifying".[73]

Succession and replacement provisions

45.58 What happens if an individual or trustees sell property qualifying for business property relief and replace it with other business property that is then subject to a transfer of value within two years? For example, trustees may be approaching a 10-year anniversary and wish to dispose of business property before then, reinvesting in other business property.

 Section 107 offers two ways of obtaining replacement relief when business property is sold and new business property is acquired but the transfer of value occurs at a time when the new business property has not yet been held for the minimum ownership period required under s.106 (two years).

45.59 The first way is to claim replacement relief under s.107(1). Property is treated as satisfying the two-year ownership condition if it replaced other property, and it and the other property and any property directly or indirectly

---

[71] IHTA 1984 s.69(1) and see 3.08.

[72] See IHTA 1984 s.105(1)(b), (cc), (a).

[73] See further Example 45.2 and *Walding v IRC* [1996] STC 13 (incapacity of a shareholder ignored, i.e. his shares still "count" in deciding if a person has control) and *Walker's Executors v IRC* [2001] STC (SCD) 86 (deceased's executors could include his chairman's casting vote in deciding if he had control).

replaced by the other property were owned by the transferor for periods amounting to at least two years in the last five years before the transfer. Any other property concerned must be such that it would (apart from the question of length of ownership) have been relevant business property if the transfer had been made immediately before the property was replaced. The second possibility is to claim replacement relief under s.107(4) (exchanges of shares and company reorganisations) which applies solely to unquoted shares.

EXAMPLE 45.6

> X farmed 1,000 acres of land for many years as a sole trader. In 2009 he settled 40 acres of the land with hope value on trust for his grandchildren, holding over the gain but continued to farm alone. BPR and APR is available on the transfer into trust following *Nelson Dance*. The land is worth £1 million at the date of the gift. In 2011 X spends £1 million on acquiring further land that is then brought into the business. He dies in 2012.
>
> Section 107 does not apply to the gift into trust because the original disposal was not of a business or an interest in a business. The operation of the claw back provisions in relation to the land held by the trustees remains uncertain following the decision in *Dance* although it was not a point HMRC took. However, BPR will be available on the full value of the unincorporated business owned by X including the additional land acquired in 2011. X has owned the relevant business property (the farm) for more than two years. He can inject cash at any time prior to his death in the business and acquire business assets and receive relief. It does not matter that the assets themselves are owned for less than two years.
>
> However, if X gave away his entire farming business to the trust (worth say £5 million) in 2009 and subsequently invested £5 million (from cash resources) in the purchase of a trading company in 2010, does the position change? It would appear that BPR is available at that time on the trading company shares on the basis that the company has replaced the farm. Moreover there is no claw back of relief on the gift into trust assuming that the trustees have continued the business.
>
> No sale proceeds from the farmland have been used to buy the company shares because the farmland was gifted. However, a replacement of one business for another has occurred and the section does not as such require an application of the proceeds of sale.[74]

The replacement rules in s.113A and B apply if business property is given away **45.60** and the donor dies within seven years of his gift and after the gift but before death, business property has been sold by the donee. The additional conditions imposed by s.113A of IHTA 1984 apply to determine whether business relief is available when calculating:

---

[74] For further commentary on s.107 see *Dymond's Capital Taxes* at 24.742 onwards.

(a) the value transferred by a potentially exempt transfer (PET) of relevant business property which proves to be a chargeable transfer (IHTA 1984 s.113A(1)), or

(b) the additional tax chargeable by reason of the transferor's death within seven years on a chargeable transfer, other than a PET, of relevant business property (s.113A(2)). Section 113A(2) does not affect the value of the chargeable transfer for accumulation purposes; this remains as calculated for the tax payable at the time of the transfer.

The intention of s.113A of IHTA 1984 is that relief is available only where relevant business property disposed of by the transferor in his lifetime becomes such, and is retained as such, in the hands of the transferee. Strict adherence to this intention would have harsh consequences in a case where the original property had been replaced by the donee by other qualifying property, and it is relaxed in two instances set out in 45.61 below.

45.61   Section 113A provides:

(a) that the original property must be owned by the transferee throughout the period beginning with the date of the chargeable transfer and ending with the death of the transferor[75]; and

(b) that, subject to subs.(3A), in relation to a notional transfer of value made by the transferee immediately before the death, the original property would (apart from the rule in s.106 (two-year period of ownership) be relevant business property.

EXAMPLE 45.7

Olive gives Phoebe a minority holding of unquoted shares which qualify for business relief at the date of the gift. Olive dies within seven years and tax becomes chargeable on the PET. If Phoebe has sold the shares before Olive's death and banked the proceeds, the relief will not be available subject only to the possibility of replacement relief under s.113B discussed below. Section 113A(3)(a). Similarly the relief will be denied where, though Phoebe has retained the shares, they have acquired a full Stock Exchange listing before Olive dies: s.113A(3)(b). However, if Phoebe has retained the shares but the company remains unlisted albeit has changed in nature, e.g. become an investment company there is no claw back of relief.

EXAMPLE 45.8

Roger has a minority holding of unquoted trading company shares. In 2010, he gives them to his daughter. At the date of the gift, they are s.105(1)

---

[75] This condition that the transferee must retain the property could be breached inadvertently in the past, e.g. where the donee trust was a qualifying pre-March 2006 interest in possession and the trust was converted to a relevant property trust within seven years of the gift (or vice versa).

(bb) property. He dies in July 2016 when the shares are still owned by her and unquoted but the company is no longer trading and instead has sold its business and is renting out properties. There is no claw-back of relief even though the company is now an investment company because s.113(3A)(b) applies and the condition in s.113A(3)(a) is satisfied. The company does not also need to be trading merely unquoted and retained by the donee.

EXAMPLE 45.9

Angus owns 10 per cent of the shares in WER Ltd, an unquoted company. In 1994, he gives all the shares to his daughter. The gift is a potentially exempt transfer (PET). At the time of the gift the shares qualify for business relief at 50 per cent as s.105(1)(c) property.

Angus dies in June 1996. The PET is now chargeable. The additional conditions for relief in s.113A are satisfied. The gift qualifies for a reduction of 100 per cent as s.105(1)(bb) property. It is considered that the 100 per cent reduction will apply for the purposes of cumulation as well as the tax charge on the PET.

45.62 Section 113A is relaxed in the following cases. First, s.113A(6) of IHTA 1984 provides a simple relaxation in cases where shares owned by the transferee immediately before the death in question were issued to him in consideration of the transfer of a business, or an interest in a business, consisting of some or all of the original property, or the shares would, under any of the provisions of TCGA 1992 ss.126–136, be identified with some or all of that property. In such a case the shares are treated as if they were the original property, or the relevant part of it.

Secondly, s.113B, to which s.113A of IHTA 1984 is subject, provides a more complicated relaxation, dealing with cases where the original property is sold and other qualifying property is purchased. Its application is subject to four conditions:

(a) the transferee has disposed of all or part of the original property before the death of the transferor; and

(b) the whole of the consideration received by him for the disposal has been used by him in acquiring other property ("the replacement property").

Condition (b) is very severe. Apparently the relief is lost if anything less than the whole of the consideration is used.

(c) The replacement property is acquired, or a binding contract for its acquisition is entered into, within three years (or such longer period as the Board may allow) after the disposal of the original property (or the part of it concerned); and

(d) the disposal and acquisition are both made in transactions at arm's length or on terms such as might be expected to be included in a transaction at arm's length.

Where the four conditions are satisfied, subs.(3) provides that those in s.113A(3) of IHTA 1984 shall be treated as satisfied if:

(a) the replacement property is owned by the transferee immediately before the death of the transferor; and

(b) throughout the period beginning with the chargeable transfer and ending with the death (disregarding any period between the disposal and acquisition) either the original property or the replacement property was owned by the transferee; and

(c) in relation to a notional transfer of value by the transferee immediately before the death the replacement property would (apart from the rule in s.106) be relevant business property.

45.63   Section 113B(5) of IHTA 1984 deals with the case where the original property has been disposed of, or is subject to a binding contract for sale, on or before the transferor's death within seven years of the gift and no replacement property has been acquired by the transferee before that time. Provided that the replacement property is acquired, or a binding contract for its acquisition is entered into after the death of the transferor but within three years (or such longer period as the Board may allow) after the disposal of the original property or part, s.113B (3) has effect in such a case with the omission of para. (a) and as if any reference to a time immediately before the transferor's death or to the death were a reference to the time when the replacement property is acquired.

This gives the donee a limited three-year period after the sale to decide whether to replace the relevant business property. If the donor dies within seven years of the gift and the donee is still holding cash and the sale took place less than three years before the donee can replace the business asset in order to avoid a clawback of relief. Note that only one replacement of business property can be made and all the net sale proceeds after costs and CGT must be used. It appears that once the donee has made the replacement within the requisite three-year period from sale he is under no obligation to retain the replacement business after the donor's death.

EXAMPLE 45.10

2010—Donald settles his unquoted trading company shares in trust. 100 per cent BPR is available.

July 2011—the trust sells the shares and receives net of tax and costs the sum of £5 million.

2013—Donald dies. Assuming the trustees have not distributed the cash (which would be fatal to a claim) they can now reinvest the cash in a new business. Assume that they do so by June 2014. Can the trustees then immediately thereafter sell the new business on the basis that they have satisfied the replacement provisions and there is no claw back of relief? The authors consider that they can.

EXAMPLE 45.11

A has owned relevant business property (shares) for 30 years. He settles the shares on five trusts for his grandchildren.[76] The shares are sold one year later. Three and a half years after the gift A dies. The trustees of each trust have until three years from the sale (another six months from A's death) to decide whether to reinvest the proceeds from the share sale into relevant business property. Each trust may take a different decision without jeopardising relief for the others.

Contrast the position if A had settled the funds into one trust which had then subsequently resettled the proceeds of sale into a number of different trusts. No replacement relief would be available for the donees under s.113 since they no longer own the gifted property or its sale proceeds. **45.64**

Note that if A settled the shares in trust and the trustees did not sell the shares but instead the company sold its business assets and became an investment company there is no claw-back of business property relief.[77] **45.65**

VII APPLICATION OF THE RESERVATION OF BENEFIT RULES

These are as capable of applying to gifts of business and agricultural assets as to gifts of any other assets. However, the following may be noted. **45.66**

Full consideration let-out

Take the case where father farms land and decides to take the son into partnership, giving him (say) a 50 per cent interest in the land and an accompanying 50 per cent share of all profits. In such a case, it is sometimes argued that there may be no element of gift (it may be a commercial bargain) or the full consideration let out[78] may apply so that there is no reservation of benefit in that gift. **45.67**

Such an argument involves looking at the matter in the round and saying that the benefits in the form of profits should be consistent with the contributions that father and son make in the form of capital and labour. With this in mind the sharing arrangements should stack up commercially.[79] In the above example it is highly unlikely that it could be argued that a transfer of half the land and profits to the son can be justified commercially on the basis that son is working harder in the business than the father. *Boden* involved transfers of goodwill not transfers of capital assets. It may be possible to argue that s.102B(4) (co-ownership and occupation) applies in the above example if the father transfers a share in the land to son and both then farm in partnership.

---

[76] He may have been encouraged to set up five trusts initially in order to take advantage of the pilot trust regime: see Ch.41.

[77] See s.113A(3)(a) IHTA 1984.

[78] In FA 1986 Sch.20 para.6.

[79] See also *Dymond's Capital Taxes* at 9.300 and *AG v Boden* [1912] 1 KB 539.

Both are occupying the land and the father's gift involved a gift of a share in land.

Illustrations

45.68　IHTM provide a number of useful examples of the operation of the reservation of benefit (GWR) rules in the area of businesses and companies including the following:

EXAMPLE 45.12[80]

> Father and son have been in partnership together since 1980 sharing profits equally. The land is owned by the father and occupied by the partnership rent-free without any formal tenancy agreement. In 1989 the father gives the land to the son but the partnership continues to occupy it on the same basis. At the same time the profit sharing ratio is adjusted in favour of the son.
>
> Provided the increase in the son's share of profits represented full consideration in money or money's worth for occupation of the land, FA 1986 Sch.20 para.6(1)(a) will apply and this will not be a GWR.
>
> The father is in effect occupying the land through the partnership and this prima facie constitutes a reservation. However, HMRC accept that the let-out in para.6(1)(a) may be satisfied by an appropriate upward adjustment (in lieu of rent) reflected in the donee's share of the partnership profits. The circumstances of the case must determine what is "appropriate" having regard to what might be agreed under an arm's length deal between unconnected persons. Contrast the position in Example 45.13 below. If the profits were not adjusted in favour of son there would be a reservation of benefit.

EXAMPLE 45.13[81]

> A, who is a partner, withdraws capital from his partnership capital account and gives it to B. B then lends the partnership an equivalent cash sum.
>
> This is a reservation. Though the partnership may pay B a commercial rate of interest for the loan, this payment will not prevent the loan being a reservation. (This is a rare example of a benefit being reserved in a cash gift.)

---

[80] See IHTM 14341.
[81] See IHTM 14336.

EXAMPLE 45.14[82]

A, a farmer, retires and gives his farmhouse, lands and farming assets to his son, but A continued to live in the farmhouse rent-free until his death.

The donor's continued residence in the farmhouse constitutes a reservation so far as that particular property is concerned, but the reservation does not extend to the remainder of the gifted lands and farming assets.

EXAMPLE 45.15[83]

A gives all the shares in his family company to B, it being part of the agreement that B would appoint A to the Board of Directors, a salaried position entitling him to a company car and other fringe benefits.

This would be regarded as the reservation of a benefit to the donor "by contract or otherwise".

EXAMPLE 45.16[84]

A husband and wife each own 50 per cent of the issued capital of a limited company. The company owns the freehold property in which they live. The spouses transfer their shares into an accumulation and maintenance settlement for their grandchildren. They continue to live in the house rent-free until the husband's death.

This is not a GWR. The continued occupation of the property is not referable to the gift (consider, however, POAT issues).

EXAMPLE 45.17[85]

A farmer, on taking his son into partnership, makes a gift to him of a share of all the partnership assets including the land. They then share the profits and losses in the same proportion as they own the partnership assets at commencement. The farmer dies 10-years later.

This is not a GWR. The son has taken possession and enjoyment of the partnership share gifted to him in the form of his share of profits. The father's share of profits is referable to his own partnership share, not the share gifted. (Note that the analysis is not that full consideration is being paid to prevent the GWR provisions from applying but that there was

---

[82] See IHTM 14334.
[83] See IHTM 14334.
[84] See IHTM 14334.
[85] See IHTM 14332.

no reservation in the first place. This may have implications for the POA charge although if the gift is analysed as of a partnership share (a chose in action) rather than of each and every asset (including land) it should not give rise to problems in practice.)

Shared occupation

45.69 Broadly speaking if Dad gives Son a share in his land which they both occupy and Dad receives no benefit, other than a negligible one, from Son, which is for some reason connected with the gift, then there is no reservation in the gifted property.[86]

Application of relief if there is a reservation

45.70 Business (and agricultural) property which is caught by the reservation of benefit rules is treated as comprised in the donor's estate for IHT purposes at his death if the reservation is continuing. Alternatively, if the reservation ceases inter vivos he makes a PET.[87] In both cases, relief may be available to reduce the value of the property subject to charge.[88] The requirements are complex but two sets of conditions need to be satisfied:

(i) at the time of the gift the property has to qualify for relief either as relevant business property or as agricultural property[89]; and

(ii) at the time of the tax charge the property has to satisfy a number of conditions, the basis of which is the concept of a notional transfer by the donee.[90]

In deciding whether the business property relief ownership condition is met,[91] ownership by the donor prior to the gift is treated as ownership by the donee[92] and if the donee dies before the donor (or before the reservation of benefit ceases), his personal representatives or his beneficiaries under his will or intestacy are treated as if they were the donee.[93]

45.71 In general, if the conditions are met the rate of relief is then decided by reference to the notional transfer by the donee. This is, however, subject to the qualification that whether certain stocks and shares are relevant business property is to be decided on the basis that they remained owned by the donor.[94] (This has the effect of preventing aggregation with other property of the donee: however, the restriction is of reduced importance given the

---

[86] See FA 1986 s.102B(4). See Ch.43 for a detailed consideration of this exemption.
[87] This is the effect of FA 1986 s.102(3) and (4).
[88] See FA 1986 Sch.20 para.8 and see IHTM 25381 and following.
[89] See FA 1986 Sch.20 para.8(1).
[90] See FA 1986 Sch.20 para.8(1A)(b).
[91] See IHTA 1984 s.106.
[92] See FA 1986 Sch.20 para.8(2)(a).
[93] See FA 1986 Sch.20 para.8(5).
[94] See FA 1986 Sch.20 para.8(1A)(a).

availability of 100 per cent for minority shareholdings.) Similar rules apply in the case of agricultural property relief: for instance, ownership and occupation by the donor before the gift is treated as that of the donee and in the case of the occupation condition, occupation by the donor after the gift is also treated as that of the donee.[95]

Take the example of Dan who gives his farm (which he has owned and farmed for many years) to his son Phil. Dan continues in occupation until his death 18 months later. The analysis is as follows:

(i) Dan has made a gift which is caught by the reservation of benefit rules and which will be subject to IHT on his death.

(ii) At the time of the gift the property qualified for agricultural property relief.

(iii) At the time of Dan's death, Phil is treated as making a notional transfer of value and has satisfied the ownership/occupation requirement for agricultural property relief to be available.

Reasonable remuneration

A question that frequently arises in the context of a gift of shares in the **45.72** family business is whether the donor can safely continue to be remunerated for working in the business or whether such payment gives rise to a reservation of benefit. The views of HMRC were published in letters dated February 19, 1987 and May 18, 1987. They make the key point that:

> *"the continuation of reasonable commercial arrangements in the form of remuneration and other benefits for the donor's services to the business entered into prior to the gift would not, by itself, amount to a reservation provided that the benefits were in no way linked to or affected by the gift."[96]*

IHTM 14395 gives the following illustration:

EXAMPLE 45.18

The donor transfers shares in an unquoted company into a settlement of which she is trustee (but not a beneficiary). She is entitled to retain remuneration for her services as director of that company.

The continuation of reasonable commercial arrangements governing the remuneration of any other benefits for the donor's services in the

---

[95] See FA 1986 Sch.20 para.8(2).
[96] The problems posed by this statement are many: what for instance is "reasonable" in the context of remuneration? Why must the arrangements pre-date the gift if the rationale for the statement lies in the commerciality of the services? Note that FA 1986 Sch.20 para.6(1)(a) is limited to land and chattels but does the donor receive a benefit within FA 1986 s.102(1)(b) if the consideration represents no more than a fair commercial payment for his services?

company entered into before the gift would not, by itself, amount to a reservation, provided the benefits were in no way linked to or affected by the gift.

On the other hand, if, as part of the overall transaction, including the gift, new remuneration arrangements are made, consider whether the new package amounts to a reservation "by contract or otherwise".

VIII IMPACT OF THE PRE-OWNED ASSETS CHARGE

45.73 There are no provisions in FA 2004 Sch.15 that deal specifically with businesses and farms. Accordingly, the application of the POA regime depends on general principles. It is important to identify the property gifted. For instance:

(i) a gift of shares will only be a problem if the para.8 charge is in point (i.e. because the shares become held in a settlor-interested trust); and

(ii) a gift of a partnership share, as for instance when father gives part of his capital account to his son, in a case where land is a partnership asset is a gift of the share (*chose in action*) and not of an interest in land. Again, therefore, there will only be a problem if the para.8 charge could apply.[97]

In cases where the full consideration let out prevents the reservation of benefit rules from applying to land and chattels, the pre-owned assets charge is equally inapplicable.[98]

Default election

45.74 If the regime would otherwise apply, the election is available to the taxpayer to opt into reservation of benefit.[99] As a result:

(a) no income tax will be payable, and

(b) the asset may attract business or agricultural property relief on the death of the taxpayer or earlier cessation of the reservation.

---

[97] Para.8 will not apply if the gifted property is not held in trust.
[98] See Sch.15 para.11(5)(d). See further Ch.34.
[99] See Ch.34 for a consideration of the election and its defective introduction.

CHAPTER 46

FARMS: AGRICULTURAL PROPERTY RELIEF

- Basics of the relief (**46.01**)
- "Agricultural value" and liabilities (**46.06**)
- The "character appropriate" test (**46.13**)
- What is a farmhouse? (**46.20**)
- When is agricultural property "occupied for the purposes of agriculture"? (**46.22**)
- Getting 100 per cent relief on let property (**46.24**)
- Planning points (**46.25**)

I BASICS OF THE RELIEF

Agricultural property relief (APR) is given on the agricultural value of "agricultural property". Agricultural property is defined in IHTA 1984 s.115(2) which, for convenience, may be divided into three limbs: **46.01**

(i) "agricultural land or pasture" ("*Limb 1*");

(ii) "and includes woodland and any building used in connection with the intensive reading of livestock or fish if the woodland or building is occupied with agricultural land or pasture and the occupation is ancillary to that of agricultural land or pasture" ("*Limb 2*");

(iii) "and also includes such cottages, farm buildings and farmhouses, together with the land occupied with them, as are of a character appropriate to the property." ("*Limb 3*").

It is important to appreciate that it is the agricultural land which is the dominant property: the property in Limbs 2 and 3 is essentially ancillary to the land. **46.02**

The critical issues that arise in connection with APR are: **46.03**

(i) the limitation of the relief to the "*agricultural value*" of the agricultural property;

(ii) in *Limb 3*, the "*character appropriate*" test;

(iii) the meaning of "*a farmhouse*" in *Limb 3*;

(iv) the meaning of *"occupied for agricultural purposes"*;

(v) getting relief at 100 per cent instead of 50 per cent.

46.04   There are two rates of APR: 100 and 50 per cent. The higher 100 per cent relief is available:

(i) if the interest of the taxpayer immediately before the transfer carries the right to vacant possession or to obtain it within 12 months.[1] ESC F17 extends this period to 24 months[2]; or

(ii) property is let on a tenancy beginning on or after September 1 1995. This will include a succession tenancy arising under the AHA 1986.[3]

In other cases relief is generally at 50 per cent.[4]

46.05   As with BPR there is a minimum period of use or ownership before relief is available. There are two alternatives:

(i) occupation by the transferor for agricultural purposes throughout the period of two years before the transfer; or

(ii) ownership for seven years during which it was occupied (by him or another) for agricultural purposes.[5]

II "AGRICULTURAL VALUE" AND LIABILITIES

46.06   APR is given only on the "agricultural value" of agricultural property. "Agricultural value" is defined in s.115(3) as follows:

> *"For the purposes of this Chapter the agricultural value of any agricultural property shall be taken to be the value which would be the value of the property if the property were subject to a perpetual covenant prohibiting its use otherwise than as agricultural property."*[6]

In the *Antrobus* case[7] before the Lands Tribunal, it was agreed that the market value of Cookhill Priory[8] was £608,475 but the Tribunal decided that the agricultural value was only £425,932.50 (i.e. a discount of some 30

---

[1] IHTA 1984 s.116(2)(a). Land let on standard grazing licences (which are for 10 months) meet this requirement.

[2] Note carefully IHTM 24144 which requires a notice to quit to be served before the transfer. The concession can also apply if the property, though let, is valued on an amount broadly equivalent to vacant possession value: see *Exors of Lady Fox v IRC* [1960] AC 1.

[3] See further 46.24 for a consideration of when old tenancies can be replaced in order to take advantage of 100% relief.

[4] Note that CGT hold-over relief under TCGA 1992 s.165 is available if the property attracts APR at either rate: see Ch.18.

[5] IHTA 1984 s.117.

[6] In the case of agricultural within the EEA but outside the UK, the agricultural value, *"is the value as if it were subject to provisions equivalent to that covenant"* (IHTM 24150).

[7] See in the matter of a notice of reference between *Lloyds TSB Private Banking Plc (as PRs of Antrobus Deceased)* and *Peter Twiddy* (IR Capital Taxes) October 10, 2005.

[8] It was accepted by HMRC that this property was a farmhouse: see further 46.20.

per cent on the market value). The taxpayers argued that the property would remain a farmhouse if purchased by someone who carried on a farming business on the land even though he might spend little time in the business.[9] Thus, they would have been unaffected by the s.115(3) covenant since they would have complied with it and as they will be the highest bidders in the market the agricultural value would therefore be equal to the amount which the highest bidder would pay.[10] This was rejected by the Tribunal in the following terms:

> "*A farmhouse is the chief dwelling-house attached to a farm, the house in which the farmer of the land lives. There is, we think, no dispute about the definition when it is expressed in this way. The question is: who is the farmer of the land for the purpose of the definition in section 115(2)? In our view it is the person who lives in the farmhouse in order to farm the land comprised in the farm and who farms the land on a day to day basis. It is likely, although it may not necessarily always be the case, that his principal occupation will consist of farming the land comprised in the farm. We do not think that a house occupied with a farm is a farmhouse simply because the person living there is in overall control of the agricultural business conducted on the land; and in particular we think that the lifestyle farmer, the person whose bid for the land is treated by the appellant as establishing the agricultural value of the land, is not the farmer for the purposes of the provisions.*"[11]

It was considered that the following factors supported this conclusion: **46.07**

(i) the "character appropriate" test which supports the idea of the farmhouse being "the dwelling of a working farmer who requires a suitable house to support his working life";

(ii) the deletion of "mansion house" from the definition of agricultural property in 1975;

(iii) the other elements of the definition, "cottages and farm buildings", support the idea of a working farm;

(iv) HMRC were "not wrong" in treating the s.115(3) covenant in relation

---

[9] The so-called "lifestyle farmer". Giving expert evidence for the taxpayers Mr Clive Beer commented that:

> "*There were at least three ways in which a lifestyle buyer could carry on a farming business without prior experience and without spending much time at the farm. Firstly, the land could be farmed with the assistance of one or more employees, for example a farm manager, or through a contract farming arrangement. Secondly, the land could be farmed in partnership with an active local farmer. Thirdly, the new owner could come to a share-farming arrangement, whereby the landowner would grow grass or other crops for sale to a local livestock farmer, whose cattle or sheep would eat down the crop which he had bought in situ. Whichever of these methods was adopted by the lifestyle farmer, the farmhouse would continued to be occupied by him and used as agricultural property.*"

[10] Mr Beer accepted that the open market value would fall to be discounted for any actual or potential non-agricultural uses of the property to which additional value might be attributable (e.g. any value attributable to sporting rights; development potential or mineral rights). It appears that there were no such factors present in this case.

[11] See further the *McKenna* case: 46.20.

to farmhouses as equivalent to the standard planning AOC for the purposes of establishing values[12];

(v) the conclusion that a farmhouse for s.115(2) purposes was limited to a property occupied by a full-time working farmer meant that the agricultural value under s.115(3) had to be decided on the basis that the covenant would not be satisfied by a "lifestyle" farmer. Accordingly the Tribunal accepted that the 30 per cent deduction in value proposed by HMRC was appropriate[13];

(vi) At the end of its decision the Tribunal considered the value which the property would have:

"on the assumption that our interpretation of the legal position is incorrect and that the demand from the lifestyle farmer may be taken into account in calculating its agricultural value".

On this basis it concluded that the relevant discount would be only 15 per cent thereby giving an agricultural value for the property of £517,203.75.[14]

46.08 This is a significant case being the only reported decision on "agricultural value" and it is, in practice, relied on by HMRC to argue generally for a discount of 30 per cent in the market value of farmhouses. The IHT Manual comments:

"The assessment of agricultural value is a matter for the District Valuer to advise upon. The blanket application of a rule of thumb percentage deduction from market value is not considered to be appropriate, and each case is judged upon its merits following full consideration of all the relevant facts . . . the DV's report should state both the open market and the agricultural value. If you receive a report where the open market and agricultural values of a farmland are said to be the same, you should refer the report with the file to TG (Litigation) to liaise with the DV and provide any further guidance necessary."[15]

46.09 The comments from the Lands Tribunal on who is a farmer for the purposes of s.115(2) (the person who farms the land on a day to day basis and whose principal occupation is likely to consist of farming the land) are debatable and considered further at 46.15.

---

[12] The "agricultural occupancy condition" (AOC) in a planning permission provides that "the occupation of the dwelling shall be limited to a person solely or mainly working, or last working, in the locality in agriculture or in forestry, or a widow or widower of such a person and to any resident dependants" (see *DoE Circular No.11/95*, para.45). The Tribunal considered that in some respects the terms of the AOC were less restrictive than those of the s.115(3) covenant.

[13] There was a dearth of comparable evidence. Three AOC properties were of no assistance and the only comparable used comprised a farm in which there had been an agreement as to agricultural value (a 33.4% discount). It involved a seven bed house with 217.9 acres of land.

[14] The Tribunal considered that there would still be a discount over the open market value of the property since (i) the lifestyle farmer would be buying the property together with all the land whereas (ii) a higher price would be obtained by someone who bought the house and part only of the land and who was not subject to the s.115(3) covenant.

[15] At para.24150.

Enhancement value attributable to development potential is not subject to **46.10** the relief. BPR may apply to this excess value in the case of farmland although probably not in the case of the farmhouse unless one can show that part of it was used exclusively for business purposes in which case limited relief may be due under the excepted assets provisions.[16] The Special Commissioner in the *Higginson*[17] case commented:

> "*A property may command a high price in the open market value because of potential for development; and subsection (3) clearly caters for that situation. But it seems to me that the notional restrictive covenant would have much less of a deprecatory effect in a case where the property has a value greater than ordinary not because of development potential but rather because of what I might call 'vanity value' on account of its site, style or the like. In the light of my decision the point is academic*".

Liabilities

Difficult issues arise in identifying the property against which liabilities are to **46.11** be set.[18] HMRC adopt the following rules:

  (i) debts charged on any property are to be deducted against the value of the property[19];

  (ii) debts not charged on any property should be deducted primarily against property not qualifying for APR;

  (iii) an apportionment is required when a liability is charged on property which is partly agricultural and partly non-agricultural or when property has both agricultural and non-agricultural value. The following illustration is taken from the IHT Manual.

EXAMPLE 46.1[20]

T's estate includes land and buildings with a total value of £1m. Of that £1 million, £800,000 is the value of agricultural property which has an agricultural value of only £100,000 (the remaining £700,000 is development value). A mortgage of £600,000 is charged on the whole of the £1 million land and buildings.

[16] Consider, however, the possible application of the *Hertford* case: see 45.47. It may be possible to argue that the land and farmhouse are one unit—a single estate for business property relief purposes and that since overall that estate is used mainly for business purposes, the entire house qualifies for business property relief. Unlike the provisions in agricultural property relief which clearly differentiate between land and buildings, s.110 does not operate such a distinction or make any apportionment for private use so long as the property as a whole is used mainly in the business.

[17] *Higginson's Executors v IRC* [2002] STC (SCD) 483.

[18] Note that a different rule applies for BPR where the relief is given on the net value of the business: see IHTA 1984 s.110 and 45.37.

[19] See IHTA 1984 s.162(4).

[20] Taken from IHTM 24152.

For the agricultural relief calculation, you should deduct from the agricultural value the proportion of the mortgage attributable to that value. The apportionment is:

£100,000 (agricultural value) × $\frac{600,000}{1,000,000}$ = £60,000

So the value on which the relief is calculated is:

	£
Agricultural value	100,000
Less proportion of mortgage	60,000
Net value for relief	40,000

There is no statutory basis for this method of apportionment and it may be noted that the next section in the Manual is withheld under the Freedom of Information Act!

46.12 It is important that, whenever possible, qualifying agricultural property is not used as security for a loan: charge other property such as a residence not attracting relief or a share portfolio.

EXAMPLE 46.2

Giles farms Wibley Wood, an agricultural estate with an agricultural value of £2 million. He owns a substantial house in the Scottish Borders worth in the region of £750,000. Borrowings in the amount of £500,000 are secured on Wibley Wood. On Giles' death:

(i) relief on Wibley Wood is limited to its value net of the charged liability (viz to £1.5 million);
(ii) the Borders property is fully taxed at (say) 40 per cent giving a tax bill of £300,000.

If before his death Giles had agreed with the lender to switch the charge onto the Borders property then:

(a) full APR would be available on Wibley Wood;
(b) the value of the Borders property would reduce to £250,000 with a consequence tax saving of £200,000.

III THE "CHARACTER APPROPRIATE" TEST

46.13 In the *Antrobus* case[21] the Special Commissioner identified the following factors as being relevant:

---

[21] *Lloyds TSB (PRs of Antrobus Deceased) v IRC* [2002] STC (SCD) 468.

"the principles which have been established for deciding whether a farm-house is of a character appropriate to the property may be summarised as: first, one should consider whether the house is appropriate by reference to its size, content and layout, with the farm buildings and the particular area of farmland being framed (see IRC v Korner[22]); secondly, one should consider whether the house is proportionate in size and nature to the requirements of the farming activities conducted on the agricultural land or pasture in question (see Starke v IRC[23]; thirdly, that although one cannot describe a farmhouse which satisfies the "character appropriate" test one knows one when one sees it (see Dixon v IRC[24]); fourthly, one should ask whether the educated rural layman would regard the property as a house with land or a farm (see Dixon); and, finally, one should consider the historical dimension and ask how long the house in question has been associated with the agricultural property and whether there was a history of agricultural production (see Dixon)."

In *McKenna*[25] the Special Commissioner added a further factor: the rela- **46.14** tionship between the value of the land and the profitability of the land.[26] In that case she concluded that the return from agriculture (a profit of £6,820 in 1998 falling to a loss of £7,975 in 1994) *"would not provide a living income for a person who paid over £3m for the whole estate and so would not attract demand from a commercial farmer"*.[27]

This further factor appears to have heavily influenced the thinking of **46.15** District Valuers to the extent that it has become, in their eyes, the all important factor. The IHT Manual (updated in April 2009) contains the following:

> *"Considering the relationship between the value of the house and the profitability of the land, would the house attract demand from a commercial farmer who has to earn a living from the land, or is its value significantly out of proportion to the profitability of the land? If business accounts have been supplied, copies should be forwarded to the VOA. Business accounts can give a useful indication of the extent of the agricultural activity being carried on although a loss making enterprise is not on its own considered to be a determinative factor."*[28]

The significance of this matter in relation to the character appropriate test may be doubted: in *Antrobus* itself, for instance, the farming operation did not return a profit and it appears that the taxpayer lived off her investment income. The *Golding* case[29] offers a suitable corrective.

---

[22] [1969] SC (HL) 13.
[23] [1994] STC 295 [1994] 1 WLR 888.
[24] [2002] STC (SCD) 53.
[25] See 46.20.
[26] From the evidence of comparables it was clear that Rosteague was at the "top end" of the size of a Cornish farmhouse and that a house of that size would generally have more land. It only came into use as a farmhouse in 1984 (so the historical association was weak) whilst lack of repair went, she considered, to value rather than character.
[27] At [113].
[28] IHTM 24051.
[29] [2011] UKFTT 351 (TC): see 46.16.

46.16   The deceased in the *Golding* case started farming in 1940 on a farm of some 16 acres. After the death of his wife in 1985 he lived alone in an increasingly dilapidated three bedroom farmhouse and, having inherited money, ceased to keep animals and instead sold only a limited production of eggs from 70 free range hens to 15 to 20 regular customers who came to the farm. The taxable farm profit (optimistically put at £1,000 pa) was 25 per cent of his total income (the rest being derived from some relatively small inheritances). HMRC accepted:

(i) that the house was a farmhouse[30]: it was his house; his office and *"an integral part of the land he farmed"*;

(ii) that the farm buildings and land were agricultural property.

Accordingly the sole issue for the Tribunal was whether the farmhouse was "of a character appropriate". In decided that the property met the character appropriate test the following matters are worthy of note:

(i) the decision was based on the approach adopted in the *Antrobus* case[31] and the various factors that the Special Commissioner (Dr Brice) there identified;

(ii) HMRC argued that a functional test was to be applied: it is necessary to consider *"the level of farming activity and the functional requirement or otherwise it generates for a dwelling house"*. This was not accepted: it was noted that in *Antrobus* most years produced farming losses;

(iii) the Tribunal concluded that the question to be asked is:

> *"was the deceased farming? At 80 years of age, it would be unreasonable to expect that to be an extensive activity. In fact if one did, there would be very few farms which would qualify as 'character appropriate'. We do not accept that the lack of a substantial profit is detrimental to a decision that the farmhouse is 'character appropriate'*

(iv) the Tribunal was told that there are over 100,000 farms of a similar or smaller acreage to that of the deceased. The argument presented for HMRC was that the three bedroom property occupied with the small acreage with a limited range of old buildings *"was not suited to modern farming practices . . . (it was) not appropriate to require a dwelling house to be present in order to farm the land"*. The logic of this argument would appear to be to deny relief to (uneconomic) small farms. Much of the argument advanced was concerned not with the facts as they were but with the facts in an ideal farming operation against which the deceased's activities were found wanting.

---

[30] HMRC sought to amend the proceedings to raise the further issue of whether the property was a farmhouse. This was refused but the Tribunal also commented that if they had been asked to consider the point they would have concluded that it was a farmhouse (see para.27).

[31] *Lloyds TSB (PRs of Antrobus) v IRC* [2002] STC (SCD) 468. The factors comprise the appropriateness of the house to the farm land; whether proportionate in size to farming activities; the "elephant test"; the "reasonable man in the Volvo estate" test; the historical dimension.

The decision is a significant victory for the taxpayer and a reverse for the approach adopted by HMRC in recent years that financial considerations are paramount.

Other cases

Starke v IRC[32] concerned the transfer of a 2.5 acre site containing within it a substantial six-bedroomed farmhouse and an assortment of outbuildings together with several small areas of enclosed land which was used as part of a medium-sized farm carrying on mixed farming. The court concluded that the relevant property did not constitute "agricultural land" within the above definition of "agricultural property". The decision is hardly surprising but it does point to the dangers of a farmer giving away the bulk of his farm retaining only the farmhouse and a relatively small area of land. Such retained property will rarely qualify for relief as was emphasised in Rosser v IRC,[33] where the deceased having given away 39 acres of land was left owning only a house, barn and two acres of land when she died. Two acres and (significantly) the barn attracted relief but not the house. **46.17**

Other cases (all decided by the Special Commissioners) may be summarised as follows: **46.18**

- In Dixon v IRC[34] the property comprised a cottage, garden and orchard totalling 0.6 acres. Although surplus fruit was sold it was decided that the property was not agricultural land or pasture: rather there was a residential cottage with land.

- In Lloyds TSB (PRs of Antrobus Deceased) v IRC[35] it was agreed that Cookhill Priory (a listed six-bed country house) was a farmhouse[36] and that the surrounding 125 acres (pus 6.54 acres of tenanted land and buildings including a chapel) were agricultural property. The Special Commissioner decided that the character appropriate test was also satisfied.[37]

- In Higginson's Executors v IRC Ballywood Lodge, formerly a nineteenth-century hunting lodge of six beds with 63 acres of agricultural land; three acres of formal gardens and 68 acres of woodland and wetland around Ballywood Lake, was considered not to be a farmhouse ("not the style of house in which a typical farmer would live").

The character appropriate test must be satisfied in relation to "the property". The Rosser case considered what was meant by "the property" and concluded that: **46.19**

---

[32] [1994] STC 295.
[33] [2003] STC (SCD) 311.
[34] [2002] STC (SCD) 53.
[35] [2002] STC (SCD) 468: "Antrobus I".
[36] It may be noted that this was agreed by HMRC on the basis that Miss Antrobus was a full time working farmer.
[37] See further 46.08 for a consideration of Antrobus II.

"the nexus between the farm buildings and the property in s115(2) is that the farm buildings and the property must be in the estate of the person at the time of making the deemed disposition under s4(1) of the 1984 Act. The alternative view that the farm buildings are in the estate but the property to which they refer is not is untenable. This view would seriously undermine the structure for inheritance tax and create considerable uncertainty about when tax is chargeable and the amount of the value transferred. I would add, however, that estate is defined in the 1984 Act as the aggregate of all property to which the person is beneficially entitled. Property is widely defined in the 1984 Act to include rights and interests of any description. It will therefore cover not only tangible property but also equitable rights, debts and other choses in action, and indeed any rights capable of being reduced to money value."[38]

IV WHAT IS A FARMHOUSE?

46.20   In the leading case[39] Mr McKenna died on January 29, 2003 and his wife, Lady Cecilia, on June 16, 2003. From 1997 they had been the joint owners of the Rosteague Estate. This comprised a substantial Grade II* house (Rosteague House); some 187 acres (of which around 52 were foreshore and 110 agricultural land); various farm outbuildings and a cottage, stable flat and lodge. The estate had originally been purchased by Mr McKenna in 1945 as a second home and only occupied as the main home on his retirement in 1984. Initially the land was tenanted but in 1984 the tenancy was surrendered and thereafter it was contract farmed under a succession of agreements with different contractors. A land agent, acting for the McKennas, was responsible for the management of the land, the farming activities and dealing with the contractors. He purchased a property on the estate and hence was on the spot to supervise and manage the farming operation. At the date of death, Mr. McKenna was aged 91 and had suffered from ill health since 1997. After his death Lady Cecilia, who was aged 92 and who had suffered from ill health since a heart seizure in 1998, entered a nursing home. The Special Commissioner decided that Rosteague House was not a farmhouse.[40]

46.21   The Special Commissioner made the following general comments on the meaning of "farmhouse" in IHTA 1984 s.115(2):

> (a) the wording of the legislation makes it clear that the agricultural land is paramount: other things must be either ancillary or of a character appropriate to the land;

---

[38] [2003] STC (SCD) 311 at [55].

[39] *Arnander (Executors of McKenna Deceased) v RCC* [2006] STC (SCD) 800.

[40] The sale particulars (the estate was sold for in excess of £3 million after the McKennas' deaths) described the house as follows: "*long hall, dining room, library, study, drawing room, flower room, main foyer and stairs, cloakroom, rear hall, kitchen, staff sitting room, back kitchen, seven bedrooms, three bathrooms, sewing room, laundry room, staff flat, detached lodge, cottage, music room, garage, gardens, range of outbuildings*". There was no mention of it being a farmhouse!

(b) there is nothing to suggest that every farm must have a farmhouse: the reference in s.115(2) is to farmhouses generally;

(c) she adopted the definition given in the *Rosser* case[41] as "a dwelling for the farmer from which the farm is managed" and accepted that the Land Tribunal conclusion in *Antrobus II* that "the farmer of the land is the person who farms it on a day to day basis rather than the person who is in overall control of the agricultural busine ss conducted on the land" was a "helpful principle";

(d) the status of the occupier of the property is not the test: rather it is the purpose of the occupation which is relevant;

(e) whether a building is a farmhouse is a matter of fact to be decided on the circumstances of each case and according to ordinary ideas of what is appropriate in terms of size, content and layout in the context of the particular farm buildings and the area of land farmed.

It was the land agent who was responsible for the management of the farming operation (albeit as agent for the McKennas). Hence:

> "*the purpose of Mr. McKenna's occupation of Rosteague House was not to undertake the day to day farming activities. In any event, . . . Rosteague House was larger, grander, more elaborate and more expensive than was required for the reduced farming purposes for which it was in fact used. Its size, content and layout, taken in conjunction with the farm buildings and the particular area of farm being farmed points to the conclusion that it was primarily a rich man's residence rather than a farmhouse*".[42]

V WHEN IS AGRICULTURAL PROPERTY "OCCUPIED FOR THE PURPOSE OF AGRICULTURE"?[43]

The legislation requires the property to be so occupied throughout the period of two (seven) years ending with the death of the owner[44]. In the *McKenna* case, the Special Commissioner commented that: **46.22**

> "*it is clear that neither Mr McKenna nor Lady Cecilia were able to engage in farming matters throughout the period of two years ending with the relevant dates of death*".

This raises the spectre of the aged farmer ending his days in a nursing home with his farmhouse unoccupied. In the *Atkinson* case,[45] the deceased owned farmland including his bungalow which was let to a farming partnership (a new agreement was drawn up in 1996). He lived in the bungalow[46] until

---

[41] [2002] STC (SCD) 311 at [53].
[42] At [92].
[43] See IHTA 1984 s.117.
[44] See s.117(a) and (b).
[45] *Atkinson v Another (Executors of Atkinson Deceased) v RCC* [2010] TC 420; SWTI 2123.
[46] This was not the farmhouse but was considered to be a farm cottage within *Limb 3*.

he became ill some four years before his death. Thereafter he was in hospital and a nursing home. No one lived in the bungalow which remained furnished and contained Mr Atkinson's belongings. During this time the other partners visited the bungalow two or three times a week to collect post etc. Mr Atkinson remained a partner until his death and took part in discussions relating to the farm at least once a week: he occasionally visited the bungalow. It was exempt from council tax because he was residing elsewhere. It appears that Mr Atkinson's partnership share was a small one (e.g. his share of profits was £2,305 out of £77,957 and his partnership interests was worth £42,771 out of £491,138). The First Tier Tribunal decided that APR was available on the bungalow since it was occupied for agricultural purposes:

> "16. 'Occupied' is qualified by the requirement that it be 'for the purposes of agriculture'. But "for the purposes of agriculture' is not further qualified. This no doubt reflects the wide range of activities that can constitute agriculture. It also recognises that the class of properties defined as agricultural property by section 115(2) includes those that are directly used in the functioning of the agricultural activity, such as land and farm buildings, as well as those that are less directly employed but nonetheless provide the structure within which the agricultural activities are conducted. Farm cottages are an example of the latter. Their function is to accommodate people engaged in the relevant agricultural activities. The farm cottages (such as the bungalow in the present case) must perform that function throughout the seven year period; but there is nothing in the Act that prescribes that the accommodation of such people is to be continuous. Nor does the Act provide in what right the person in question (i.e. the person engaged in the agricultural activities) is accommodated in the cottage; it could be the farm owner occupying as such, it could be an employee accommodated under a licence or it could be a partner in the farming business accommodated by agreement between the partners. The reference in subsection (b) of section 117 to the property in question being occupied 'by him or another' indicates as much.

> 17. In the present circumstances the occupation referred to in section 117(b) is the occupation of the three partners in the William M Atkinson & Son partnership as tenant under the agricultural tenancy of the Farm holding. Throughout the period of the partnership the entire holding, the bungalow included, was occupied for the purposes of the partnership's farming activities. The residential buildings, i.e. Abbotson's Farmhouse and the bungalow were used by the partnership to accommodate the partners. For twenty-two years from the time the bungalow was built it housed Mr Atkinson. For the last four years of Mr Atkinson's life the impact of his illness reduced the likelihood of Mr Atkinson being able to return and live in the bungalow until it appears to have become necessary for him to stay permanently in the care home. But he continued to participate in partnership matters and his possessions remained in the bungalow; and from time to time he visited the bungalow. The partners chose to notify the local council that the bungalow was not lived in. Otherwise they did nothing with the bungalow to alter the state of affairs that had subsisted throughout the partnership.

18. Occupation by the partnership continued until Mr Atkinson's death; it was occupation for the purposes of agriculture in the relevant sense because the bungalow was still used to accommodate the diminishing needs of the senior partner."

The decision may not be of any assistance in the case of a farmhouse as opposed to a farm cottage; in the case of the farmhouse, the claim for relief is likely to fail at the earlier stage on the basis that if the owner is in a nursing home and the property is empty so that the house is not the dwelling from which the farm is managed. **46.23**

VI GETTING 100 PER CENT RELIEF ON LET PROPERTY

Relief at 100 per cent is available for land let on farm business tenancies and succession 1986 Act tenancies granted on or after September 1, 1995. Land let on Agricultural Holding Act tenancies granted before September 1, 1995, however, attracts APR at only 50 per cent for the landowner. As a result of the TRIG Reforms[47] of 2006 it may be possible to "convert" a pre-1995 tenancy into a new tenancy thereby securing relief at 100 per cent for the landowner. The mechanics are outside the scope of this book but given the substantial benefits that may accrue to the landlord this is something which should be considered. **46.24**

VII PLANNING POINTS

In relation to agricultural property held in a settlement see the matters noted in relation to BPR at 45.48 and following. **46.25**

So far as the overlap with BPR is concerned, note in particular: **46.26**

(i) on the lifetime disposal of agricultural land with substantial development value, the *Nelson Dance* decision[48];

(ii) when the farming business includes investment properties note the potential for claiming BPR on the entire business: see especially the *Farmer* and *Brander* cases[49];

(iii) if the farmhouse fails the "character appropriate" test, consider the possible impact of the *Hertford* case.[50]

If agricultural property is to be sold and the proceeds settled, consider the use of pilot trusts.[51] Of course, such fragmentation is easier to achieve when the **46.27**

---

[47] See Regulatory Reform (Agricultural Tenancies) (England and Wales) Order 2006 (SI 2006/2805).
[48] See 45.35.
[49] Discussed at 45.15 and 45.21.
[50] See 45.47.
[51] See Ch.41.

business is incorporated. So far as agricultural companies are concerned, APR may be available under s.122 which applies to:

(i) shares or securities of a company when;

(ii) agricultural property forms part of the company's assets and part of the value of the shares or securities can be attributed to the agricultural value of the agricultural property; and

(iii) the shares or securities gave the transferor control of the company.

In cases where the taxpayer does not have control consider the availability of BPR.

Will drafting and business / agricultural property relief

46.28 This important topic is considered at 38.46 and following.

CHAPTER 47

LIFE POLICIES AND OTHER INSURANCE PRODUCTS HELD IN TRUST

- Background (**47.01**)
- Existing trusts (**47.03**)
- Family protection policies (**47.13**)
- Loan trusts (**47.21**)
- Discounted gift plans (DGPs) (**47.23**)
- Flexible reversionary trusts (**47.34**)
- The chargeable event legislation (**47.39**)

I BACKGROUND

There are a wide variety of arrangements involving insurance policies held in a trust of which the following are the most common: **47.01**

(i) *Family protection policies*: typically term assurance policies and second death whole of life policies aimed at providing for the payment of inheritance tax or the provision of a tax-free lump sum in case the main earner dies; these will generally be written on trust so that the proceeds pass to the persons whom the life assured wants to benefit after his death.

(ii) *Trusts of single premium bonds*: a non-income producing investment with a five per cent tax deferred withdrawal facility.

(iii) *Loan trusts*: based on a loan being made to trustees.

(iv) *Discounted gift trusts*: based upon the settlor retaining certain rights in the investment.

(v) *Flexible reversionary trusts*: of increasing use with the attraction of greater flexibility than discounted gift trusts.

Before FA 2006 inheritance tax changes, many of the above were based on flexible interest in possession trusts.[1] Given that (save for a disabled **47.02**

---

[1] Note the differences between Scotland and England/Wales and Northern Ireland: see IHTM 20154 and 20155.

person's interest)[2] it is no longer possible to create new qualifying interest in possession inter vivos trusts it follows that thought needs to be given as to how best to accommodate such arrangements. Consideration also needs to be given to the treatment of existing trusts. HMRC have taken a greater interest in life policies recently. In particular, the account form IHT 400 now incorporates form 410 in respect of life policies which asks for considerably more information than had previously been the case.

II EXISTING TRUSTS

47.03   If a life policy is held in a trust created before March 22, 2006, the transitional rules that apply are as follows:

(i) if the trust was accumulation and maintenance: there were no special provisions and accordingly the normal transitional period until April 6, 2008 ensured that A-M treatment continued until that date but that thereafter the relevant property regime would normally apply[3];

(ii) if the trust was interest in possession: in principle, the tax treatment of the trust will not be affected so long as the policy remains in trust. This result is achieved as follows.

The TSI regime

47.04   Flexible interest in possession trusts envisage a succession of such interests with the settlement continuing to hold the policy until such time as it is encashed. The usual transitional period until October 6, 2008, which allowed the existing interest in possession to be replaced by a transitional serial interest, applied[4] and was extended for existing life insurance trusts.[5]

Premium payments to pre-March 2006 interest in possession and accumulation and maintenance trusts

47.05   HMRC took the view that the addition of property to an existing settlement involved the creation of a new settlement.[6] Concern was expressed that if premiums were paid in respect of existing policies held in trust this could result in the creation of a new relevant property settlement. To provide reassurance

---

[2] IHTA 1984 s.89B.
[3] For a consideration of the treatment of A–M trusts, see Ch.30.
[4] On TSIs, see 27.16 and on life policies see 27.33.
[5] IHTA 1984 s.49E.
[6] For a criticism of this approach, see 24.25 and 31.39. It is thought that the payment of any premium merely maintained rather than increased the policy benefits so that it was in any event debatable whether it involved an addition of property.

the 2006 Finance Bill was amended in Standing Committee by the introduction of:

(i) section 46A to deal with policies held in interest in possession trusts on March 22, 2006;

(ii) section 46B to deal with policies held in accumulation and maintenance trusts on March 22, 2006.

In both cases if a *"premium payable under the contract is paid, or an allowed variation is made to the contract, at a particular time on or after (March 22, 2006)"* then any rights under the contract which, as a result of the payment of the premium or the variation, are comprised in the settlement shall be deemed to have become so comprised (and so that the relevant interest shall be treated as subsisting in them) before March 22, 2006.[7] Note that an "allowed variation" requires that the variation must:

> *"take place by operation of, or as a result of rights conferred by, provisions forming part of the contract immediately before March 22, 2006".*

So, for example, cashing in the existing policy and taking out a new one would not be protected by these provisions although of course premium payments on any new life policy may well be exempt under the normal expenditure out of income rules.[8]

47.06 The intention of these provisions was to ensure that policies that were held on accumulation and maintenance or interest in possession trusts continued to be held on such trusts irrespective of any premium payments made after March 21, 2006 but only so long as the trusts of each settlement were interest in possession or accumulation and maintenance. Most accumulation and maintenance trusts now fall within the relevant property regime.[9] What happens to the premium payments made to such trusts after April 6, 2008?[10] These are no longer protected by s.46B unless the trust then fell within the s.71D regime or became an "18 trust" when the payments continue to be protected.

47.07 It is also provided that if the payment of a premium in such cases involved a transfer of value that transfer is a potentially exempt transfer.[11] It appears that the premium must actually be paid. So if the settlor pays the life company direct then that would be within the scope of ss.46A or 46B. If the settlor added funds to the trust to enable the trustees to pay the premium, strictly that would not be within the scope of these sections, although it is not thought that HMRC would take the point. In any event, most premium payments will not be chargeable transfers of value but exempt as normal expenditure out of income so this is not an important relief.

---

[7] IHTA 1984 s.46(B)(2) providing that such rights shall be treated as falling within a qualifying A–M settlement and that the transfer of value is a PET.

[8] See 47.14.

[9] See Ch.30.

[10] Or earlier if the settlement fell into the relevant property regime before April 6, 2008 because a beneficiary became entitled to income before then.

[11] IHTA 1984 ss.46A(4) and 46B(5).

Extension of transitional serial interest regime

47.08 Also and somewhat surprisingly the Government introduced an extended transitional period in respect of the pre-March 2006 policy held in trust.[12] These provisions are in IHTA 1984 s.49E and were explained by the Paymaster General as follows[13]:

> *"The first condition is that the policy was already held in the settlement on Budget Day[14] and was subject to an interest in possession at that date. The second condition is that the current interest in possession either arose on the death of the person who held the interest on Budget Day, arose on the death of someone holding a transitional serial interest in succession to them, or on the death of someone holding a transitional serial interest by virtue of a previous application of section 49(E). That means that where a person has the interest in possession in a pre-Budget trust holding a life insurance policy, but dies before the person whose life is insured, they can be replaced as the person without an impact and the transitional treatment will continue.[15]*
>
> *The third condition is that the life policy has been held in trust in question throughout the period from Budget Day to the start of the current interest in possession.*
>
> *The fourth condition will mean that transitional serial interest treatment is only due where the interest in question would not also qualify as a trust for a bereaved minor or as a disabled person's interest. That is because it is clear that such trusts are eligible for the same IHT treatment as a transitional serial interest."*

47.09 It is far from clear what justification there was for the extension of transitional serial interest treatment when the trust fund comprises a pre-March 22, 2006

---

[12] See 27.33 for further discussion.

[13] The Standing Committee Debates, January 15, 2006 at Vol.682.

[14] March 22, 2006.

[15] Note that after October 5, 2008 the replacement must occur on death. Compare the extended treatment under s.49D on death of spouse or civil partner: see 27.32 and following. The legislation sets out Condition 2 as follows:

> *"(a) the earlier interest [in possession] came to an end at a time on or after 6 October 2008 (the earlier-interest end-time") on the death of the person beneficially entitled to it and C became beneficially entitled to the present interest (i) at the earlier-interest end time, or (ii) on the coming to an end on the death of the person beneficially entitled to it, of an interest in possession to which that person became beneficially entitled at the earlier-interest end time or on the coming to an end of the second or last in an unbroken sequence of two or more consecutive interests in possession to the first of which a person became beneficially entitled at the earlier--interest end-time and each of which ended on the death of the person beneficially entitled to it or*
>
> *(b) C became beneficially entitled to the present interest—*
>
> > *(i) On the coming to an end on the death of the person entitled to it of an interest in possession that is a transitional serial interest under s49C above or*
> >
> > *(i) On the coming to an end of the second or last in an unbroken sequence of two or more consecutive interests in possession the first of which was a TSI under s49C above and each of which ended on the death of the person beneficially entitled to it."*

life insurance policy. Of course, if that life policy is encashed or lapses or the life assured dies and a new policy is taken out or the trust then invests the cash in different assets neither the new policy nor the other assets will fall within these extended transitional serial interest provisions.

EXAMPLE 47.1

On March 22, 2006 a life insurance policy taken out on the life of X was held on flexible interest in possession trusts for A.

(1) On April 1, 2007 the trustees determined A's interest in possession and appointed an interest in possession for his son, B. B was entitled to a transitional serial interest and A made a PET[16];

(2) On April 1, 2009, B died and the policy became held on interest in possession trusts for his sister, C. She obtains a transitional serial interest.[17] There is a chargeable transfer on B's death. Note that if B died and discretionary trusts arose, a qualifying interest in possession could not then be appointed to C, because the interest in possession must arise immediately on the termination of B's interest. If C died before the life assured and D took an interest in possession then D's interest would also be a transitional serial interest;

(3) On August 1, 2012 the trustees received cash on the death of the life insured X. C died soon afterwards and the cash fund became held in trust for her two children on interest in possession trusts. There was a chargeable transfer on the death of C and her children do not enjoy transitional serial interests (because the life assured has now died) so that the property is now held on relevant property trusts.

Technical aspects

Section 49E only extends TSI treatment, (1) whilst the pre-March 22, 2006 **47.10** policy is held on trust; and (2) the interest arises on death. Hence, if B had surrendered his interest (rather than dying) in 2009, C would not have obtained a TSI. Instead the continuing trust would have fallen within the relevant property regime. As before, B would have made an immediately chargeable transfer.

It is not entirely clear how the special rules for life insurance settlements **47.11** link-in with the s.49D provision under which a spouse can obtain a transitional serial interest after October 5, 2008.[18] Presumably condition 2(a) of s.49E is met in such cases. In the above example, if on B's death his wife had become entitled to an interest in possession and on her death C had taken an interest in possession it is thought - given that the policy is still held in trust— that C obtains a TSI.

[16] Section 49C and not s.49E applies.
[17] Under IHTA 1984 s.49E.
[18] See 27.32.

47.12   There is a gap in the legislation if a beneficiary becomes entitled to an interest in possession before October 6, 2008 which was not a transitional serial interest. For example, if Z had a pre-March 2006 interest in possession in a life policy and then died or surrendered his interest in April 2007, Y could take a transitional serial interest under s.49C. However, if Y then died or surrendered the interest in possession before October 6, 2008, X would not take a qualifying interest in possession. X's interest cannot fall within s.49E (because it arose before October 6) and it cannot be a transitional serial interest under s.49C (which only allows for one transitional serial interest). However, if X were to die after October 5, 2008 and another person W were to become beneficially interested in an interest in possession in the contract, the legislation seems to provide that D's interest in possession would qualify as a transitional serial interest under s.49E. Condition 2(a) requires that D must become entitled "on the death of the person beneficially entitled" to the interest in possession but this does not require C to have had a qualifying interest in possession.

III FAMILY PROTECTION POLICIES

47.13   After March 21, 2006 any trust set up to hold the policy will be a relevant property settlement for inheritance tax purposes. No reporting is usually required because it will generally be within the de minimis limits. In fact in many cases before that date discretionary trusts (viz relevant property settlements) had been used. In general, therefore, the position is unchanged and the following matters may be noted:

(i) the annual premiums will usually be exempt from IHT as a result of the normal expenditure out of income exemption[19];

(ii) the settlement will be subject to anniversary and exit charges. The value of the policy at the relevant time will determine whether tax is payable. Whole of life and term policies whilst providing for a substantial sum assured will have a low surrender value until the death of the life insured or that person becoming seriously ill[20];

(iii) of course, when the life insured dies and the trustees receive cash, on the occasion of a 10-year anniversary the charge will be calculated on the cash value. When substantial insurance is being taken out it is normal to take out a number of policies to cover the desired amount and to employ a number of trusts (ensuring that they are not related settlements). In any event the trustees should review the position shortly before each 10-year anniversary to ensure that the life assured is in good health. If he is not then they could appoint the policy out of the trust before that anniversary. There would be no exit charge (because the value of the property when settled would have been within the nil rate band).[21]

---

[19] IHTA 1984 s.21.
[20] See IHTA 1984 s.167 which in certain circumstances substitutes for market value a premiums paid basis of valuation: it does not apply to the classic IHT term assurance.
[21] See also Ch.41 (pilot trusts).

EXAMPLE 47.2

S wishes to take out life insurance to a value of £2.5 million. To guard against the risk of a substantial IHT charge if the policy is held in a single relevant property settlement:

(1) S creates 10 separate settlements ("pilot trusts")[22] on consecutive days (in each case settling a nominal sum on the trusts);

(2) 10 life policies are taken out and on the same day are assigned to the 10 settlements (one to each).

Given that the settlements are not "related settlements" (since they were not created on the same day)[23] each will benefit from a full IHT nil rate band when calculating charges during the life of each settlement.[24] An entry charge could apply but, in practice, the value of the life policies at the date of settlement is unlikely to exceed the settlor's nil rate band. Provided that the addition is made on the same day to all the settlements, in calculating the charge on any one settlement the additions to the others are ignored.[25] Even if further policies are taken out on different occasions it is still sensible to hold them in separate trusts if the death benefits are worth significantly more than a single IHT nil rate band.[26] It is unlikely that the earlier policies will have used much (if any) of the settlor's nil rate band. Therefore each trust will have its own nil rate band to reduce future 10-year and exit charges. The issue does not arise while the settlor is alive because 10-year and exit charges will be minimal. However, after his death if it is intended to keep the policy proceeds in trust then the advantage of having separate trusts is that each trust will have its own nil rate band to reduce 10-year charges. At a later date the trustees can merge the proceeds into one trust.[27]

The continued payments of premiums by the settlor will not give rise to problems since:

    47.14

(i) if paid directly to the insurance company they will not fall within the s.67 provision dealing with additions to the settlement[28];

(ii) they will not normally involve a chargeable transfer by the settlor since they will either qualify for the normal expenditure out of income or the annual exemption.

---

[22] See Ch.41.

[23] IHTA 1984 s.62.

[24] Assuming that the settlor has not already used this up. The nominal sum settled into trusts 1–9 are of course transfers of value made by the settlor in the seven years before the creation of trust 10 but the amounts will fall within his IHT annual exemption or within the normal expenditure out of income exemption.

[25] IHTA 1984 s.67(3)(b)(i) (added property) and see *Rysaffe Trustees v IRC* [2003] STC 536 which is considered in Ch.24 and at 41.03.

[26] See Ch.41.

[27] IHTA 1984 s.81 provides that for the purposes of the relevant property regime they are still treated as being comprised in the original settlement and therefore each separate fund will retain its own 10-year anniversary and nil rate band, etc.

[28] Even if value has been added (and it may be said that the premium merely maintains the value of the policy) s.67(2) would seem to exclude the payment.

Drafting points

47.15   Some of the standard forms produced by the life companies give the life assured power to appoint trustees followed by a similar power for his spouse. It is not a good idea to give a named spouse power to appoint; even giving the spouse of the life assured for the time being a power to appoint future trustees may not be appropriate if he remarries and the policy is for the benefit of the first family. If the spouse and life assured divorce then s/he will still retain this power. It may not even be sensible to appoint the surviving spouse as trustee. It is easy to overlook these trusts when taxpayers divorce, only to find that on the death of the life assured a long estranged spouse is trustee or has power to appoint trustees.

47.16   Each trust should contain a power to resettle since it may be useful to merge the proceeds of several different life policies held in trust later. As noted above, this has no inheritance tax effect but is administratively attractive.[29]

47.17   The policy is usually written in trust in one of three ways:

    (i) the contract provides that the policy is held on trust for the proposed beneficiary/ies from the inception of the policy;

    (ii) the life assured owns the policy but then executes a trust deed and assigns the policy into trust;

    (iii) the life assured owns the policy and then executes a declaration of trust under which he declares that he holds the policy on trust and appoints an additional trustee/(s) to act with him.

In the latter two cases notice should be given to the insurance company that the policy is now held on trust.

Seven-year reducing policies

47.18   These are taken out to cover the risk of inheritance tax if a PET becomes chargeable. They should not be retained by the donor or life assured since the proceeds of the policy will then be subject to tax on his death. Instead the policy should be given to the donee of the PET (or taken out by the donee on the life of the donor since the donee will have an insurable interest).

47.19   In some cases trustees need to take out a decreasing term policy, e.g. where A's qualifying interest in possession has ended and the settled property has passed to B outright or a transitional serial interest has been created for B. In these circumstances the trustees should ensure that the life policy is not held on interest in possession trusts for A (which sometimes inadvertently occurs if A's interest has only partly ended). The trustees should hold the life policy on separate trusts for the donee. An issue may arise over the funding of the premiums on that policy. Although the payment of an insurance premium is not deductible against the trust income, if it is paid out of income of the life

[29] See Ch.41.

tenant it will reduce the income to which he is entitled and therefore any higher or additional rate tax liability.[30]

If the life assured is the trustee of the policy there should be another trustee to accept receipt of the policy proceeds on the life assured's death. The purpose of the policy is to provide a liquid fund to pay inheritance tax on that death and if he is the sole trustee and the family have to wait until the executors are appointed and probate obtained before a new trustee can be appointed then a main advantage of the policy has been lost. **47.20**

IV LOAN TRUSTS

These trusts are normally structured as in the following example. **47.21**

EXAMPLE 47.3

S establishes a trust for his family from which he and his spouse (including civil partner) are wholly excluded.[31] The form of the trust (whether it is flexible life interest, discretionary, or accumulation and maintenance) is now irrelevant for IHT purposes since it will be taxed as a relevant property settlement. The initial trust fund comprises a nominal sum but S then lends the trustee £1 million on terms that are interest free and repayable on demand. The trustees invest in a single premium bond and use the five per cent withdrawal facility to make partial repayments of the loan to the settlor each year.

The tax position is as follows:

(1) because the loan is repayable on demand S does not make an immediate transfer of value although he may make a gift;
(2) the five per cent withdrawal payments to the settlor are free from tax;
(3) any growth in value of the bond takes effect outside the settlor's estate (the arrangement is sometimes referred to as "*asset freezing*");
(4) the trust may benefit from a nil rate band, and 10-year charges will be on the amount by which the value of the bond exceeds the then outstanding debt.

This trust can be established to invest in any asset: the attraction of a bond lies in the five per cent withdrawal facility. In some cases taxpayers set up both loan trusts and discounted gift arrangements. It is generally recommended that the loan trust be implemented before the discounted gift in case of death **47.22**

---

[30] There will normally be an express power for trustees to pay premiums out of income. In the absence of such a power the premiums are a capital expense.

[31] If the settlor is not wholly excluded then FA 1986 Sch.20 para.5(4)(b) provides that any property directly or indirectly derived from a loan made by the settlor (but not his spouse) to the trust is treated as property in which he has reserved a benefit. See Chs 33 and 34 and 43.147 for further discussion of this provision.

within seven years. The loan trust involves no transfer of value and will not therefore affect the cumulative total of the settlor for the purpose of taxing the discounted gift trust.

V DISCOUNTED GIFT PLANS (DGPS)[32]

47.23 The loan trust affords no immediate IHT advantage to the settlor: the benefit comes with the future growth (if any!) in the value of the bond. By contrast, the DGP can confer immediate benefits. The essence of the plan is that the settlor makes a gift into settlement but retaining certain rights in the insurance bond. Typically the rights retained may be in a series of single premium policies maturing on successive anniversaries of the creation of the settlement or to future capital payments if the settlor is alive at the prospective payment date.

Diagrammatically the position is as follows:

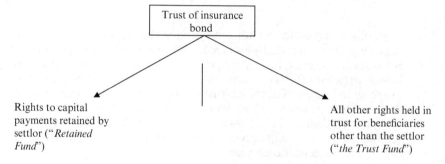

Trust of insurance bond

Rights to capital payments retained by settlor ("*Retained Fund*")

All other rights held in trust for beneficiaries other than the settlor ("*the Trust Fund*")

IHT analysis

47.24 The arrangement is viewed as a "carve-out" or "shearing arrangement" so that provided that the rights retained by the settlor are sufficiently clearly defined and that he is excluded from all benefit in the Trust Fund there is no reservation of benefit.[33]

47.25 One of the attractions of the DGP lies in the "discount". The transfer of value made by the settlor when establishing his trust is the fall in value of his estate and in calculating this it is necessary to arrive at a value for the rights that he keeps in the retained fund. This value will depend on such factors as age, health and sex and on the size of the capital payments that he will receive. For instance, if A, a healthy 70 year old, put £500,000 into a DGP reserving a

---

[32] See IHTM 20423 for a list of the companies offering discounted gift schemes.

[33] The arrangement involves a *chose in action* (viz rights under an insurance bond) which are not capable of separate transfer: i.e. unlike land where a settlor can retain a leasehold interest and transfer only the encumbered freehold, in this case the entire bond must be held in trust but with the rights under it split into a retained fund (for the settlor) and a settled fund (from which he is excluded). On the need for precision in defining the gifted property, see the speech of Lord Hoffmann in the *Ingram* case which is discussed at 43.42 and 43.85.

right to five per cent annual withdrawals of capital over the next 20 years[34] (if he is then alive) a substantial discount will be in order. If it is of (say) 40 per cent then the transfer of value made by A is reduced to £300,000.

The Bower Case[35]

Mrs Bower, aged 90, purchased a discounted gift bond for £73,000. The bond   **47.26** was held in trust under which Mrs Bower retained a five per cent life annuity (equivalent to withdrawals totalling £304.16 per month). She died approximately five months after taking out the policy. It was accepted that she had made a failed PET equal to the premium paid of £73,000 less the value at the time when the policy was taken out, of the Retained Fund (the five per cent withdrawals). The sole issue was what value should be attributed to her retained rights. Note especially:

(i) medical reports indicated that when Mrs Bower took out the policy, her age should be loaded and treated for life expectancy purposes as being 103. Accordingly, on the basis of actuarial tables, her life expectancy was between two and three years;

(ii) HMRC accepted that she had not reserved a benefit and did not enjoy an interest in possession in the whole of the trust fund;

(iii) in their Technical Note[36] HMRC took the view that if a policy was taken out on the life of a person with an age (or adjusted age) in excess of 90, the reserved rights would have a nil or nominal value because genuine life insurance would not be available in such cases. Further, as any buyer of the reserved rights would wish to lay off the mortality risk by taking out such cover, its absence rendered the rights effectively valueless;

(iv) in arriving at the price to be paid by a buyer for Mrs Bower's retained rights, a reduction would be made for the expenses of purchase (for instance, legal expenses and possibly the cost of a further medical examination);

(v) HMRC argued that a purely nominal value of £250 should be attributed to the rights, largely because of the inability to lay off the mortality risk by taking out genuine life cover. This argument was not accepted by the Special Commissioner who concluded:

> "*it seems realistic in this case to say that the buyer need not necessarily be of the risk-averse category who would lay off the mortality risk and then run fairly conventional discounting calculations, but might more appropriately be a speculator*".

This approach was rejected by Lewison J.:   **47.27**

---

[34] To avoid an income tax charge on the excess: see *Sugden v Kent* [2001] STC 158 and 47.39 and following. for the chargeable event legislation.
[35] [2008] STC (SCD) 582 reversed [2009] STC 510.
[36] Dated May 1, 2007: see (2007) SWTI p.1390.

"In asking whether the sale in the open market contemplates that a sale must take place in 'some sort of conventional market manner', it is not at all clear to me that the Special Commissioner appreciated that the hypothetical sale takes place in the real world. He was of course not wrong in saying that he was entitled to consider other possible purchasers, and I do not consider that the possibility of other possible purchasers is necessarily precluded. There must, of course, be an assumed buyer in order to give effect to the statutory hypothesis that the sale takes place.

But although the Special Commissioner was, in my judgment, entitled to consider possible purchasers, he was not entitled to invent them. The assumption of a buyer in order to give effect to the statutory hypothesis in addition tells you nothing about the price which the buyer is assumed to have paid. If in the real world an asset is worthless, the statutory hypothesis does not make it valuable. It is not, in my judgment, lip service to the hypothesis . . . in those circumstances to ascribe a nominal value to an asset. On the contrary, it is the necessary consequence of a finding of fact that an asset is not commercially, as opposed to legally, saleable coupled with the assumption that a sale must be assumed to have taken place."

47.28 The Special Commissioner valued the retained rights at £4,200 as being the price that he considered a speculator would pay. He arrived at this figure as follows:

(i) he started from a "ceiling" calculation of £7,800 which had been arrived at by the insurance company on the basis of the life expectancy of a 103 year old; taking the number of monthly payments she might be expected to draw (2.5 years worth) and then discounting that sum to an equivalent present value by applying a 4.5 per cent interest rate, but allowing no deduction for the expenses of the buyer;

(ii) he then reduced that figure by one-third to allow for mortality risk; the inaccuracy of the life expectancy tables; the lack of competing purchasers; doubts about the medical opinions; and discounting for time;

(iii) finally he deducted £1,000 for estimated legal expenses in acquiring the retained rights;

47.29 He accepted that this method was very much based on the particular facts of the particular case and that his approach "*of simply reducing the price by a 1/3 deduction from a ceiling figure might be much less tempting with a longer life expectancy*". This was scathingly rejected on appeal:

"In paragraph 37 he described his figure as being 'little more than uninformed, but hopefully realistic, guesswork'. Thus, the Special Commissioner himself acknowledged that there had been no evidence before him about how a price payable by a speculator might be calculated. Nevertheless, he went on to produce what he described as 'my calculation and valuation'. The Special Commissioner's method of calculation and valuation is not one that had been put forward by anyone and not put by him to any of the witnesses or parties for comment. This in itself was a breach of the rules of natural justice. But more important for present purposes is that it was *not based on the evidence before the Special Commissioner. It flowed from the Special Commissioner's erroneous conclusion that he was required or entitled to populate the real market in which the hypothetical sale took place with hypothetical speculators who did not share the characteristics of real buyers.*"

Taxing the retained fund

When the taxpayer dies the right to payments under the terms of the retained fund ceases. Does this mean that there is no IHT charge (in effect that the discounted amount is wholly free from charge)? HMRC's practice is to treat the retained fund as valueless but it is far from clear that this is correct. The issue is whether the valuation exercise is to be performed immediately before death taking into account only factors known at that time or with the benefit of hindsight (i.e. with knowledge of the deceased's imminent demise). If the former method were to be adopted (which seems to the authors to be the correct approach) then a reduction in value as a result of the death under IHTA 1984 s.171 would not seem appropriate given that what is coming to an end on death is "*any interest*".[37]

47.30

The POA dimension

The introduction of the POA income tax charge in FA 2004 (with effect from April 6, 2005) led to concerns that discounted gift trusts were settlor-interested trusts which, because they contained intangible property, fell within the para.8 charge.[38] Surprisingly, however, the position was not viewed in this light by HMRC who developed further the analysis adopted for reservation of benefit by concluding that the retained fund had not only been carved out and retained by the settlor but that the rights in it were held on bare trust for the settlor. Hence, the para.8 charge did not apply to this fund[39] and nor did it apply to the trust fund given that the settlor could not benefit under it.[40] It is thought that this argument is flawed since there is no separate property in the retained fund: rather a single asset is held in trust and the settlor is entitled to certain benefits from that asset. Needless to say, many discounted gift arrangements have been established in reliance on this HMRC statement.

47.31

---

[37] The correct valuation procedure was considered in *Arkwright (PR of Williams Deceased) v IRC* [2004] STC (SCD) 89. Oliver L.J. in *Fetherstonehaugh v IRC* [1984] STC 261 at 268 commented (in an obiter dicta) that:

"*The occasion of the deemed transfer of value is, it is true, related to the moment before the death of the deceased but there is nothing in the statute to suggest that the valuation is to be conducted on the basis that the impending demise of the deceased is a known factor which the hypothetical valuer is to take into account*".

[38] For the para.8 charge, see Ch.34.
[39] Because it was not *a settlement* for IHT purposes.
[40] The analysis may be found in the POA Guidance Notes, see A2.68 and following.

47.32 The future of these plans was thrown into doubt as a result of the 2006 changes in the IHT treatment of settlements. The preferred trusts of the trust fund had been flexible interest in possession so that the creation of the trust was a PET. From March 22, 2006 it has no longer been possible to create qualifying interests in possession[41] so that any trust created will involve an immediately chargeable transfer by the settlor. Accordingly, if the (discounted) value transferred exceeds the settlor's available IHT nil rate band tax at 20 per cent is payable on the excess. Further, the settlement so created will be subject to anniversary and exit charges and concern was raised that for this purpose the value to be taxed would include the rights in the retained fund. Such fears appear to be ill founded, however, since correspondence with the HMRC indicates:

(i) that the same approach to that adopted for POA will be followed, i.e. the retained fund will be treated as a bare trust and so as a separate settlement and not therefore aggregated with the trust fund;

(ii) for the purpose of imposing the 10-year charge it will be necessary to value the insurance bond on the basis of what would a purchaser pay for it given that certain rights have been reserved to the settlor (in the form of the retained fund). Hence, the normal discount will apply.

47.33 The main impact of the 2006 legislation has been in limiting the value of the discounted gift to £325,000 (or the settlor's available nil rate band) which is necessary if an immediate IHT charge is to be avoided. For the majority of taxpayers who purchase discounted gift plans, that ceiling will not be a problem. For those wishing to invest more there is the alternative of the trust fund being held on a bare trust for one or more individuals. This would mean that the transfer of value would then be a PET and so the nil rate band restriction is overcome.[42] In effect, there would then be two bare trusts, one of the Retained Fund and the other of the Trust Fund.

VI FLEXIBLE REVERSIONARY TRUSTS

47.34 Not as well-known as DGP, these arrangements are being increasingly marketed by the insurance industry. In brief, the taxpayer invests in a series of single premium policies[43] with specified maturity dates. All of the policies can, however:

(i) be surrendered before the maturity date; or

(ii) be extended beyond the maturity date.

---

[41] There are only restricted exceptions which are not relevant in this context.
[42] See Ch.42 for bare trusts.
[43] Alternatively the arrangement may be set up with the taxpayer making regular payments into the plan.

As with DGP, the policies are settled on trusts under which benefits are retained by the settlor. These retained benefits (carved-out of the settled gift) are in the form of a reversionary interest, i.e. the settlor is entitled to the proceeds arising from any policy when it matures. The flexibility of the arrangement derives from the fact that the trustees have powers which they could exercise to prevent the settlor becoming entitled to the proceeds on maturity. For instance, they could:

(a) exercise an option to extend the term of the policy;

(b) cash-in the policy before the maturity date;

(c) exercise a power of appointment in the trust deed which would have the effect of taking away the settlor's reversionary interest. The settlor is not one of the beneficiaries capable of benefitting under that power.

The tax analysis of the arrangement is as follows: **47.35**

(i) the settlement which holds the policies will be taxed under the relevant property regime if it is either discretionary or interest in possession. This imposes a limit on the amount that can be invested (above £325,000 and an IHT charge at 20 per cent will apply). An alternative is to settle the policies on bare trusts for one or more beneficiaries. The settlor would then make a PET rather than an immediately chargeable transfer;

(ii) the POA analysis follows that for DGPs, i.e. the retained rights of the settlor are held in a separate (bare) trust for his benefit. Because he is excluded from all other benefits which are held on separate trusts the intangibles charge[44] does not apply;

(iii) in terms of the IHT reservation of benefit provisions, it is argued that the arrangement is a carve-out, i.e. the reversionary rights were never given away. So far as the other (gifted) rights are concerned, no benefit has been retained by the settlor. However, in the context of home loan schemes,[45] HMRC consider that there is a reservation of benefit where the trustees have not called in a loan that is repayable on demand because they have thereby conferred a benefit on the settlor. It is, of course, questionable whether any real benefit enures for the settlor by the trustees failing to call in the loan. However, in this case, the fact that the trustees have not exercised their powers so as to prevent the settlor taking the fund absolutely results in a very real benefit to the settlor. This would mean that wherever the settlor has retained an absolute remainder interest in a trust there is a reservation of benefit. However, HMRC do not seem to consider there is a reservation of benefit where the trustees rather than the settlor have powers to terminate or extend the policy. They note at IHTM 14453:

"Example 5

An endowment policy is effected in trust for a named beneficiary if living on the death of the donor/life assured before the termination date of the

---

[44] Under FA 2004 Sch.15 para.8.
[45] Discussed in Ch.43.

policy; otherwise for the donor/life assured. The 'termination date' could include the maturity, the early maturity on guaranteed terms, the surrender of the policy etc.

It is likely that in such a case, the donor can decide when 'termination' should occur. If that is so the donor is not entirely excluded from the gifted property (because he can terminate the policy and claim the proceeds) and the GWR provisions apply."

47.36   It should also be noted:

(i) that the relevant trust (falling within the relevant property regime) may attract IHT anniversary and exit charges;

(ii) that the reversionary interest is a chargeable asset in the hands of the settlor but given the overriding powers of the trustees, it is thought to have only nominal value.

47.37   As compared to the DGP under which the settlor receives an "income" of five per cent each year, the flexible reversionary trust, as its name implies, offers a measure of flexibility: at the maturity date of each policy the settlor can receive the proceeds if he so wishes. If not, the policy can be extended by the trustees or the benefit appointed away from the settlor.

47.38   Both DGP and the flexible reversionary trusts have been developed to hold insurance based products: however, in principle it should be possible to apply the inheritance tax analysis to trusts of other assets: for instance, to units in a unit trust.

VII THE CHARGEABLE EVENT LEGISLATION

47.39   Non-qualifying life policies (that include the sort of investment products with an insurance element outlined above)[46] are subject to a special income tax code.[47] This code now covers both onshore and offshore policies.

47.40   A chargeable event gain arises when a chargeable event occurs. Chargeable events include death; maturity or the partial or entire surrender of the policy and assignment for money's worth.[48] Essentially if more than five per cent of accumulated premiums is withdrawn each year (albeit any unused five per cent can be carried forward to allow a greater surrender in the following year) then the amount in excess of five per cent (or the actual gain if a full surrender occurs) will be chargeable to income tax[49] on the arising basis (whether or not the policy is offshore and held by a remittance basis user and whether or not the proceeds are remitted).[50] There is no charge if the value of any partial surrender in a year is less than five per cent of the premium

---

[46] Mortgage endowment policies are qualifying. Estate preservation bonds, income bonds, etc. are all non-qualifying.

[47] ITTOIA 2005 Pt 4, Ch.9.

[48] See ITTOIA 2005 s.484(1).

[49] Subject to top slicing relief in respect of tax in excess of the basic rate.

[50] In addition if the premium was paid using a remittance basis user's foreign income or gains that were untaxed when they arose any of the 5% withdrawal will be a taxable on a remittance basis user but only if he remits the funds withdrawn to the UK. The amount attributable to

paid. Chargeable event gains are not levied on encashments by non-residents. The temporary non-residence rule requiring five years' non-residence does not apply.[51]

UK resident trusts

47.41 If the settlor of the trust is alive and UK resident then he is taxed on the chargeable event gain whether or not he can benefit from the trust. He has a right of reimbursement.[52] If the settlor is dead[53] or non-UK resident, the trustees pay the tax and the rate on any chargeable event gain is the trust rate of 50 per cent. This charge does not arise if the policy was settled before March 17, 1998: the settlor had died before that date and the policy has not since been varied.[54] If, however, the trustees appoint the life policy absolutely to beneficiaries no chargeable event gain arises on the appointment and the beneficiaries can then encash the policy thus avoiding a charge on the settlor or the trustees and potentially taking advantage of lower rates. No chargeable event arises on the assignment of the policy to the beneficiaries because there is no consideration. The beneficiaries may be non-UK resident in which case tax can be avoided altogether.

Parental settlements

47.42 It is not uncommon for bonds to be held on bare trusts for the minor child of a settlor. In these circumstances do the parental settlement provisions apply on encashment of the bond such that the chargeable event gain is taxed on the parent? R& C Brief 51/2008 confirmed that where a non-qualifying policy is held on bare trusts for the minor, the gains are not assessed to income tax on the settlor but on the minor beneficiary. This is because the minors are the absolute beneficial owners, and therefore ITTOIA 2005 s.465 does not apply.[55] However, the Brief argues that where either or both of the minor child's parents are the settlors of the bare trust, they will remain potentially liable for income tax on chargeable events under the settlement legislation on the basis that the amount is deemed to be their income for tax purposes.[56] This view is doubtful since ITTOIA 2005 s.629 catches *"income arising"* under a settlement. However, while imposing an income tax charge, the chargeable events legislation does not deem the relevant gains to be income. Hence, there is no *"income arising"*.

---

the 5% withdrawal indirectly derives from the original premium paid so Conditions A and B of ITA 2007 s.809L apply: see RDR Manual 33540.

[51] See Ch.5.

[52] See ITTOIA 2005 ss.467(7) and 538.

[53] Unless any gain on the maturity of a policy actually arises on the death of the individual in which case the gain is taxed as his. This would be unusual: most investment policies with an insurance wrapper are written on the lives of more than one person.

[54] See FA 1998 Sch.14 para.7.

[55] Section 465 Condition A applies, i.e. the individual beneficially owns the rights under the policy.

[56] ITTOIA 2005 s.629.

Non-resident trusts[57]

47.43   The transfer of assets legislation applies to chargeable event gains realised by non-resident trusts. Hence, if the trust is one where the transferor or his spouse/civil partner has power to enjoy then he is taxable under ITA 2007 s.720 on chargeable event gains. By contrast, the settlements legislation never applies to chargeable event gains since these are not income arising under a settlement.[58] Otherwise tax is deferred but ITA 2007 ss.731–735 apply to tax benefits received by non-transferors. The remittance basis does not apply since chargeable event gains are not deemed to be relevant foreign income.

---

[57] ITTOIA 2005 s.468.
[58] ITTOIA 2005 ss.620–625 and see Ch.8.

CHAPTER 48

PENSION ARRANGEMENTS

- Background (**48.01**)
- Pension trusts and IHT (**48.15**)
- Lifetime IHT issues (**48.26**)
- ABI Guidance (**48.48**)

Precedent

A1.5   Spousal by-pass trust for pension death benefits

I BACKGROUND

Successive governments have pursued a policy of encouraging individuals   **48.01**
to provide for their own retirement and not to rely on the state pension.
Accordingly pension schemes that are "approved" by HMRC benefit from a
package of tax reliefs, for instance:

  (i) contributions to the scheme are tax deductible[1];

  (ii) the scheme investment income and capital gains are tax-free (so that the
       pension fund is a tax-free roll-up fund)[2];

  (iii) part of the benefits can be paid as a tax-free lump sum.[3]

The tax rules were significantly changed on April 6, 2006 (this was the   **48.02**
Appointed Day or "A Day").[4] A new single set of rules now applies to regulate
the tax treatment of all UK registered pension schemes.

---

[1] Tax relief was available to the individual on contributions based on relevant earnings although
tax relief was available on contributions of up to £3,600, even if relevant earnings were lower
than that. Employer contributions were deductible.

[2] FA 2004 s.186; TCGA 1992 s.271.

[3] Broadly, the lower of 25% of the value of the pension rights and 25% of the member's lifetime
allowance.

[4] Implementing the changes made by FA 2004. The impetus for change can be traced to the
Goode Report of September 1993 and culminated in the HMRC/Treasury report "*Simplifying
the Taxation of Pensions*" in December 2003.

48.03   Before April 6, 2006 four main categories of pension schemes can be identified:

(i) occupational/company schemes;

(ii) personal pension schemes[5];

(iii) retirement annuity contracts;

(iv) unapproved schemes. If the employer provided benefits under such a scheme he did so through a FURBS (funded unapproved retirement scheme) or UURBS (unfunded unapproved retirement benefit scheme). Their tax-free lump sum element plus indexation is protected on values up to A day (April 6, 2006) if payments have qualified for relief, either by virtue of the taxation of employer contributions on the member as earnings or the taxation of all income and gains under the fund. The inheritance tax exemptions continue to apply but only to pre-A day assets that are under a discretionary trust. If contributions are made after A day the tax-free lump sum must be adjusted. Investment gains will be taxable at the rate applicable to trusts and income charged at 50 per cent.

The pre-A Day provisions will remain important for years to come in view of the transitional protections built into the 2004 legislation.

48.04   From April 6, 2006 a single set of rules regulates all UK Registered Pension Schemes[6] which includes occupational pensions; personal pensions and stakeholder pensions. Unapproved schemes (FURBS and UURBS) continue as Unregistered Schemes.[7]

48.05   Transfers can be made between UK registered schemes and also from UK registered schemes to overseas schemes which are regulated as pension funds in their country of establishment. Further, migrants who come to the UK obtain tax relief on contributions to such overseas schemes. The decision in *Equity Trust (Singapore) Ltd v HMRC*[8] is a salutary example of the dangers. A Singapore pension scheme "ROSIIP" had obtained QROPS status and a number of transfers were made to it by UK registered pension schemes. That status was retrospectively withdrawn by HMRC on the basis that on closer examination it did not satisfy the Overseas Pension Schemes Regulations[9] and in particular reg.2. The taxpayer challenged this but the court found in favour of HMRC.[10] The decision is being appealed but unless the taxpayer is successful, HMRC will be able to impose scheme

---

[5] Replacing retirement annuity contracts from January 4, 1988. A SIPP (*Self Invested Pension Plan*) is a variety of personal pension.

[6] A "UK Registered Pension Scheme" has replaced a UK Tax Approved Pension scheme. All pre-April 2006 approved schemes are automatically treated as registered schemes unless before April 6, 2006 they gave notice to opt out of deemed registration.

[7] They are known as Employer Financed Retirement Benefit Schemes (EFRBS).

[8] [2011] EWHC 1463 (Ch).

[9] SI 2006/206.

[10] The appeal was on the question of whether s.5 of the Singapore Income Tax Act 1948 provided a system for the approval or recognition by or registration with the Inland Revenue Authority of Singapore of pension schemes in Singapore for the purposes of Condition B of reg.2(3) and whether it was open to residents of Singapore. HMRC contended that the scheme had not been properly registered with the Singapore authorities and had been treated by them as a foreign trust rather than a pension scheme.

sanction charges on the transferor pension schemes as well as unauthorised payment charges and surcharges on the contributors. No doubt QROPS in other countries such as Hong Kong and Guernsey are also now being examined. Whether HMRC can retrospectively withdraw qualifying status from foreign pension schemes that have previously been given approval, raises separate issues of public law.

A QROPS (a Qualifying Recognised Overseas Pension Scheme) involves the scheme being EEC registered or one that generally corresponds to a UK registered scheme.[11]

48.06

An error in the FA 2004 legislation meant that if a UK pension fund was transferred to a QROPS it would arguably become liable to an IHT charge. Hence, the QNUPS Regulations were introduced which apply to overseas schemes generally (all QROPS will be QNUPS but a QNUPS need not be a QROPS!)[12] So far as QNUPS are concerned there are no reporting requirements to HMRC (so a QNUPS can be established outside the European Community in a country with which there is no double tax treaty). A QNUPS need have no specific investment restrictions (e.g. it can invest in residential property).

48.07

Pension choices from April 6, 2006 to April 6, 2011

The member could take income from a Registered Scheme:

48.08

(i) in the traditional form of a purchased annuity;

(ii) up to age 75 in the form of an unsecured[13] pension (formerly known as "income drawdown");

(iii) from age 75 in the case of money purchase schemes (or Defined Contributions Schemes) the member can (subject to maximum and minimum levels) continue to drawdown the amount of their choice (called an "alternatively secured pension" or "ASP"). This is a restricted version of income drawdown.

"*Protected rights*" are benefits derived from contracting out of the Second State Pension Scheme (SERPS). The consequence is a restriction on benefits if the member is married or in civil partnership when the annuity must be purchased on unisex terms; must include a reduced income for the partner and a minimum payment term in the event of the member's early death.

48.09

---

[11] The transfer to a QROPS is a benefit crystallisation event for the purposes of the member's lifetime allowance. If that allowance is exceeded the chargeable rate is 25%. Note, that there is no further testing against the lifetime allowance so that investment growth in the QROPS can occur unrestricted by that allowance.

[12] The Inheritance Tax (Qualifying Non UK Pension Schemes) Regulations 2010 (SI 2010/0051): "the QNUPS Regulation" effective from January 15, 2010.

[13] Contrast an annuity which is "secure".

The new regime from April 6, 2011

48.10   The Coalition Government introduced in FA 2011 a number of important changes to the pensions regime as follows:

48.11   *Annual allowance*: this effectively sets the maximum tax-relieved contributions during a tax year and from April 6, 2011 it is £50,000 pa. Higher and additional rate taxpayers may be better off under the new rules as they will now be allowed to claim tax relief at their highest marginal rate on contributions of up to £50,000 per annum. Prior to this, from April 6, 2009 many higher earners had their income tax relief restricted to the basic rate on contributions in excess of £20,000. Moreover, the advent of complex carry forward rules means that unused annual allowances can be carried forward, with each year being given a notional annual allowance of £50,000. So if an individual has been a member of registered pension plan since at least 2008–09 and has not used their allowances for the last three years, they may now take advantage of the higher rates of tax relief available. This gives a potential total annual allowance of £200,000 with tax relief at 50 per cent.

48.12   *Lifetime allowance*: from April 6, 2012 the standard lifetime allowance which effectively sets the maximum tax-efficient total pension benefit value is cut from £1.8 million to £1.5 million. If an individual has already been granted enhanced or primary protection from April 6, 2006, then the protection will continue. However, those whose pension funds already exceed or are likely to exceed £1.5 million in the future have an option to elect into fixed protection before April 6, 2012 and protect their pension fund lifetime allowance by fixing it at £1.8 million. However, they cannot then make contributions on or after April 6, 2012.

Taking pension benefits

48.13   Before April 2011 pension benefits generally had to be taken by 75[14] which involved purchasing an annuity or receiving income drawdown. From April 6, 2011 unsecured pension income (USP) and alternatively secured pension (ASP) have been replaced with a single set of rules known as capped drawdown. Capped drawdown applies to all funds in drawdown regardless of the age of the individual with the minimum income limit being set at 0 per cent and the maximum limit being set at 100 per cent of the Government Actuary's Department tables. The maximum income withdrawal that can be made from most drawdown funds on reaching the minimum pension age of 55 will be capped at 100 per cent of the equivalent annuity that could have been purchased with the fund value. The maximum capped amount is to be determined at least every three years until the end of the year in which members reach age 75 following which such reviews are to be carried out annually.

48.14   It is no longer necessary to draw an income from a pension fund by 75 or buy an annuity. Instead the fund can remain invested and uncrystallised until

---

[14] The minimum pension age rose from 50 to 55 on April 6, 2010. Other than on ill-health grounds, a pension cannot (with limited exceptions) be paid before the minimum age is reached.

death. If the individual dies before 75, with the fund uncrystallised (i.e. before the individual draws any pension benefits) then the lump sum death benefits can be paid as a tax-free cash sum even if the individual is in ill-health and defers taking benefits for this reason. Once the fund has crystallised or the member has attained 75, any lump sum death benefit is subject to a fixed income tax charge of 55 per cent. The various inheritance tax charges detailed in ss.151A–151F and explained below, have been repealed. Hence, inheritance tax does not apply with effect from April 6, 2011 to drawdown pension funds remaining under a registered pension scheme including when the member dies after reaching 75. All the anti-avoidance inheritance tax charges applicable to pension schemes where the member omits to take their retirement entitlements are abolished from April 6, 2011 in the case of both registered and unregistered pension schemes.

II PENSION TRUSTS AND IHT

Most pension or annuity arrangements are settlements for IHT purposes within IHTA 1984 s.43(2).[15] The IHT legislation does not provide a blanket exemption for pension scheme benefits: instead there are specific reliefs (e.g. under IHTA 1984 s.151). **48.15**

Relevant property charges

The definition of "relevant property" is settled property in which there is no qualifying interest in possession with the exception (inter alia) of: **48.16**

> "*property which is held for the purposes of a registered pension scheme, a qualifying non-UK pension scheme or a section 615(3) scheme*".[16]

Accordingly FURBS/EFURBS (insofar as contributions are paid after April 6, 2006) are relevant property settlements and taxed in the same way as any other relevant property trust.

Of course, pension (and annuity) rights, would be interests in possession so that an IHT charge might arise on the ending of the pension or annuity and accordingly s.151(2) provides that there is no charge on the fund of a registered pension scheme on the death of the person entitled to the pension or annuity whilst s.151(3) provides for an equivalent exemption when the pension ends otherwise than on death. **48.17**

---

[15] With the exception of contract-based arrangements such as retirement annuity contracts.
[16] IHTA 1984 s.58(1)(d). From April 6, 2006 the old category of "sponsored superannuation schemes" no longer attracts relief (for the meaning of "sponsored superannuation scheme" see IHTM 17122). A s.615(3) scheme is one established in the UK under an irrevocable trust for non-resident employees by employers whose business is wholly or partly outside the UK. The purpose of the trust, is to provide superannuation benefits: in practice the key advantage is that the pension can be received as a tax-free lump sum at whatever age the employee selects. The schemes are treated as registered schemes for the purpose of reliefs from IHT.

The two-year discretionary period

48.18 On the death of a member, ss.58(1)(d) and 151 strictly cease to apply so that a distribution of death benefits in the trustees' discretion would attract the usual exit charge. HMRC, however, apply concessionary treatment allowing the trustees up to two years to make distributions free of tax. Accordingly, "*the death benefits therefore may properly be regarded as remaining held for section 151 purposes pending the exercise of the discretion*".[17]

48.19 The following results follow from this treatment:

(i) if the payment is made in the discretion of the pension trustees to a trust then any further distribution by the trustees of that trust will be taxable in the usual way;

(ii) but if the pension trustees have no discretion, i.e. if they have to make the payment into the trust, then, "*the two year period concession transfers to the trustees of the recipient discretionary trust*".[18]

Death of an ASP member prior to April 6, 2011[19]

48.20 Until April 6, 2001 an IHT charge could arise under s.151A with the value of the ASP funds being treated as the highest part of the member's estate at death. Note:

(i) the charge is on the "relevant amount" defined as the total value of the fund less sums paid out in a relevant dependant's benefits within six months of the end of the month of the member's death[20];

(ii) for these purposes benefits for a relevant dependant include:

(a) a scheme pension;
(b) an annuity;
(c) an unsecured pension;
(d) an ASP; or
(e) paying funds to charity as a lump sum benefit[21];

(iii) if a charge is incurred (e.g. because the funds are applied more than six months after death or applied for the benefit of a non-relevant dependant) the scheme administrator must deliver an account on Form 100 (and event Form 100g). No reliefs or exemptions (such as APR or BPR)

---

[17] IHTM 17123.

[18] IHTM 17124: "*we take the view that the funds concerned remain comprised in a scheme to which section 151 IHTA 1984 applies and so do not constitute 'relevant payments' by virtue of section 58(1)(d)*".

[19] Note ss.151A–151E are repealed in relation to deaths occurring on or after April 6, 2011 by FA 2011 s.65 subject to transitional provisions in FA 2011 Sch.16.

[20] IHTA 1984 s.151A(3)(a) and (b). A "relevant dependant" means a surviving spouse or civil partner and a person who is financially dependent on the member at the time of his death: see s.151A(5).

[21] IHTA 1984 s.151A(4).

are available and nor is the instalment option. The scheme administrator is responsible for the payment of tax due;

(iv) when no charge arises on the member's death the scheme administrator must deliver Form 105 giving details of who inherits the fund. A recapture charge may arise in the future when a relevant dependant (who has received a benefit) dies. However, no recapture charge arises if the dependant's benefits completely exhaust the fund (e.g. the fund is used to purchase an annuity or is paid to charity);

(v) if the deceased's estate includes an interest in an ASP it cannot be an excepted estate.

EXAMPLE 48.1

Maximilian dies aged 82 with an unused IHT nil rate band; a free estate of £300,000 and an ASP fund worth £500,000 which is paid out to a non-financial dependant (his sister, Lucy). The IHT calculation is as follows:

	£
Total estate	800,000
Less NRB	(325,000)
	475,000
Tax at 40%	190,000
Tax attributable to ASP fund	
as the top slice of the estate	190,000

Death of relevant dependant in receipt of benefits before April 6, 2011

The relevant charge is under IHTA 1984 s.151B which applies where: **48.21**

(i) a person was a relevant dependant of a scheme member who had died over the age of 75 and immediately before his death had funds in an ASP;

(ii) the relevant dependant either dies or ceases to be a relevant dependant (e.g. a child becoming 23) and at that time has funds in either a dependant's unsecured pension or a dependant's ASP;

(iii) the designation of funds had occurred within the six-month period from the death of the member.

When these conditions are met, the value of the ASP funds are added to the   **48.22**
scheme member's estate and taxed as the highest part of the value of that estate. The amount of the ASP funds can be reduced if a payment is made to charity within the specified six-month period.

EXAMPLE 48.2

Franz Joseph (FJ) died aged 80 with a free estate of £300,000, which he
left to his children, and an ASP fund worth £500,000. This was used to
pay a dependant's unsecured pension to his surviving spouse Catherine.
On her death the fund is worth £450,000. When FJ died the IHT nil rate
band was £285,000: at the time of Catherine's death it had increased to
£325,000.

Position on FJ's death

	£
Free estate	300,000
Less NRB	(285,000)
	15,000
Tax at 40%	6,000

Recapture charge on Catherine's death

	£
FJ's free estate	300,000
Add value of ASP fund	450,000
	750,000
Less NRB	(325,000)
	425,000
Tax at 40%	170,000

Note:

(1) if there has been a reduction in IHT rates (including an increase in the
nil rate band) the reduced rates are deemed to have been in force at the
time of the member's (FJ's) death;

(2) if FJ had left his entire estate to Catherine his chargeable free estate would
have been nil so that the recapture charge is on £450,000 – £325,000 =
£125,000 (giving tax of £50,000).

The charge under IHTA 1984 s.151C

48.23 This section provides for a charge in cases where the dependant of a member
dies before April 6, 2011 having a dependant's ASP fund in respect of that
member's scheme immediately before his death. The section can only apply if
s.151B does not (i.e. it imposes a fall back charge on the ASP fund).

48.24 In this case, the ASP fund is treated as part of the dependant's chargeable
estate on death (with, as usual, a deduction for payments to charity made
within the specified time).

EXAMPLE 48.3

Jasper died aged 72[22] and his pension fund passed to his surviving civil partner, Simon, who took a dependant's unsecured pension until he became 75 and then a dependant's ASP. At Simon's death the value of his free estate is £500,000; the value of the ASP fund is £250,000 (after the deduction of a £50,000 payment made to charity within six months of the end of the month of Simon's death) and Simon has an unused IHT nil rate band of £325,000. The IHT calculation on Simon's death is as follows:

	£
Free estate	500,000
Value of ASP fund as top slice	250,000
	750,000

Attribute nil rate band (£325,000) to free estate so that tax on the ASP fund is £250,000 × 40% = £100,000.

The income tax charge on ASPs before April 6, 2011

FA 2007 introduced various income tax charges when an individ- **48.25** ual dies whilst in an ASP. For instance, a charge (at 40 per cent) could arise if the minimum income is not paid out in an ASP year. So far as IHT charges under ss.151A–151C are concerned, more significant was the unauthorised payment (UP) charge at a minimum of 55 per cent. This was incurred, for instance, if the remaining fund is redistributed to other members of the scheme or paid out in lump sum form. How this UP charge impacted on the IHT charge depended on which was paid first. Accordingly:

(i) if at the time when the IHT charge fell due (six months after the end of the month of the member's death) no ASP funds had been distributed then IHT was charged on the full value of the ASP funds without any deduction for the payment of income tax. A subsequent UP income tax charge was levied on the funds left after the payment of IHT;

(ii) if, however, an UP income tax charge arose before the IHT fell due, the latter charge was on the value of the funds after the deduction of income tax due on the UP.

The aggregate of the two tax charges was the same but still more than the current fixed 55 per cent.[23]

---

[22] So that s.151B is inapplicable.
[23] For the impact of the UP charge see generally IHTM 17402.

48.26   During the lifetime of the taxpayer he may:

    (i) arrange for his pension death benefits to be held in trust so that they will not be taxed as part of his estate on death;

    (ii) reach pensionable age and decide not to take a pension; or

    (iii) instead of purchasing an annuity, take an unsecured pension (i.e. income drawdown).

There is a concern that pension arrangements may be used as a vehicle in IHT planning: the motivation in (iii) is undoubtedly a wish to avoid taxation on death and in other cases a taxpayer who is terminally ill may decide to forego a pension so that a substantial death benefit will be payable outside his estate.

Income drawdown/failing to take a pension

48.27   As already noted, income drawdown arises when the member has reached pensionable age and instead of purchasing an annuity to provide the pension decides to "draw" income from the pension pot and purchase an annuity later. Before the 2006 changes the deferral had to end at age 75 when the annuity had to be purchased. That is no longer the case, however, although the regime which then applied until April 6, 2011 (Alternatively Secured Pension) was more restrictive than income drawdown (or "Unsecured Pension" as it is now known). Because the member was taking less than his pension entitlement by opting for drawdown, a claim to IHT could arise. All this has changed since April 6, 2011 as noted above. There is no inheritance tax charge now on the crystallised funds.

Omission to exercise a right[24]

48.28   This subsection provides that where the value of a person's estate is diminished and the value of another person's estate or of settled property[25] is increased by the taxpayer's omission to exercise a right then (unless the omission was not deliberate) the taxpayer is treated as making an IHT disposition at the latest time when he could have exercised the right. In the context of pensions HMRC argued prior to April 6, 2011 that a decision not to take benefits in the case of a pensioner who had reached retirement age could come within the section as might a decision to take income drawdown instead of purchasing an annuity.[26] However, note that from April 6, 2006 to April 6, 2011 s.3(3) was subject to the

---

[24] IHTA 1984 s.3(3).

[25] Other than settled property, with a qualifying interest in possession.

[26] The ABI considered that income drawdown was a direct alternative to annuity purchase and so should be treated the same for IHT purposes. HMRC do not accept this argument: see the June 1999 ABI Guidance Note reproduced in IHTM 17102.

provisions in s.12 IHTA 1984 discussed later in relation to registered or qualifying pension schemes or a section 615(3) scheme.[27] In addition, as explained
below, there are arguments against the HMRC argument on s.3(3) even if s.12
was not satisfied. Unfortunately none of these were put forward in *Arnold*. For
deaths after April 2011 the point is likely to be academic.

The Arnold case[28]

The deceased had settled the death benefits payable under her pension on **48.29**
discretionary trusts. Normal retirement age under the scheme was 60 (in fact
a pension could be taken at any age between 50 and 75) but at this time she
had been diagnosed with advanced ovarian cancer (from which she died the
following year) and she did not take a pension. HMRC contended that her
failure to take retirement benefits gave rise to an IHT charge under s.3(3) and
Judge Clark agreed.

The following points arise from his decision: **48.30**

(i) the omission to take retirement benefits was continuing during the
deceased's lifetime: accordingly the disposition was treated as made at
the time of her death (under s.3(3) the disposition is made at the "latest
time" when the right could have been exercised);

(ii) the burden of showing that the omission was not deliberate was on her
executors and there was no evidence to suggest this;

(iii) because of the omission, "*the value of her right to opt for those benefits
(viz the retirement benefits) was lost to her estate and also resulted in the
death benefits becoming payable to the trust*". Judge Clark commented
that, "*the fact that this increase occurred after her death does not prevent
the condition in s3(3) from being fulfilled as there is no reference in the subsection to the time at which the value of the settled property is increased*"[29];

(iv) IHTA 1984 s.10(1) did not apply to treat the disposition as not being a
transfer of value because the settling of the death benefits showed an
intention to confer a gratuitous benefit and:

"*Although I understand that Mrs Arnold's circumstances were likely to
have been such as not to require additional pension income, which would
possibly have increased her income tax liability, I do not consider that this
negates an intention in her mind to confer a gratuitous benefit.*"

(v) the concessionary treatment for surviving spouse and dependants (see
48.26) was not available;

(vi) the diminution in the deceased's estate involved calculating the value of
the "right" to take the pension benefit and the judge concluded that the

---

[27] See s.12(2A)–(2E) inserted with effect from April 6, 2006 and then repealed from April 6, 2011
and substituted by s.12(2ZA) discussed below.
[28] *Fryer (PRs of Arnold (deceased)) v RCC* [2010] S.F.T.D. 632.
[29] Section 3(3) requires the value of settled property to be increased by the omission. For criticism
of this aspect of the decision, see Bramwell in *Taxation*.

benefit would be the lump sum and an annuity guaranteed for a 10-year period. The resultant figure (£89,850) was discounted by 25 per cent to reflect the fact that the annuity was payable over a 10-year period.

Limits on the application of s.3(3)—HMRC view on deaths prior to April 2006

48.31 When the member opted for income drawdown or failed to take any benefit from the scheme immediately on reaching retirement age, HMRC accepted that it would generally be for, *"commercial and retirement planning reasons (. . .a genuine pension arrangement)"*.[30] But if at the time the member deferred (or continues to defer) he was in ill health,[31] then prior to April 6, 2006 HMRC argued that a claim under s.3(3) could arise on the basis that he was unlikely to take his full retirement benefits which would therefore be paid outside his estate. Survival by more than two years after first deferring the pension raised a presumption of good health. In any event, no charge arose if payments under the pension were made to the spouse, civil partner or a financial dependant of the member.[32] That position under s.3(3) was modified from April 2006 and then again from April 2011 and is discussed below.

Arguments against the HMRC view were not put forward in *Arnold*. For example, it could be argued that the last omission occurs just before death when the deceased is terminally ill and at that point is certainly not deliberate. Moreover although the value of the person's estate is diminished by the omission the value of the settled property or another person's estate is not necessarily increased by the omission.

General power to dispose of death benefits

48.32 If the member had a general power of appointment over the pension benefits (specifically a power to appoint them to their estate on death) then they form part of the member's estate on death.[33] HMRC confirm that:

> *"a potential IHT liability is unlikely where the member had a power of nomination in relation to a lump sum death benefit, revocable in life but binding on death, to select from a limited class of survivors. There would be a claim of course if the effect of a revocation is that a lump sum is paid to the legal personal representative as of right."*[34]

48.33 A survivor may be subject to a charge under s.5(2), for instance, if a member died in income drawdown, a surviving spouse (or civil partner or other financial dependant) can:

---

[30] IHTM 17103.
[31] Meaning terminally ill, or in such poor health that their life is uninsurable: see the *Arnold* case at 48.29.
[32] These "concessions" were contained in HMRC's *Tax Bulletin* for February 1992 and the ABI Guidance of 1999: see fn.19. For statutory implementation, see 48.28.
[33] IHTA 1984 s.5(2) as modified by IHTA 1984 s.151(4).
[34] ABI Guidance (June 1999) at para.4.1.

(i) continue in income drawdown;

(ii) purchase an annuity; or

(iii) take a lump sum within two years of the member's death.

If the survivor dies within two years of the member's death as a result of s.5(2) the lump sum is taxed as part of their estate.[35]

The 2006 legislation

With effect from A Day the IHT practice in relation to the application of s.3(3) to members who failed to take a pension or entered into income drawdown was modified by s.12(2A)–(E) that applied from April 6, 2006 to April 5, 2011.[36] The provisions were as follows:

48.34

(i) IHTA 1984 s.12(A)–(G) applied to members of Registered Pension Schemes under the age of 75. Hence, these sections did not apply to FURBS or EFURBS, i.e. unapproved pension schemes;

(ii) for the purposes of s.12(2A) a person was treated as first omitting to take the pension benefits at the earliest date when he could have taken them. If this was before he knew he was ill and he had no gratuitous intention at that point, then by virtue of s.12A onwards, s.3(3) had no further application irrespective of the fact that he could have taken his pension benefits at any time before death so there were further omissions then that may have had a gratuitous intention;

(iii) section 12(2B) then provided that there was no disposition under s.3(3) even if the person did omit to take pension rights at the last time when he could have done so unless s.12(2C) applies;

(iv) section 12(2C) applied if the taxpayer had made an actual pensions disposition within the two years ending with his death knowing he might die during that period. Only at that point would s.3(3) need to be considered.

An "actual pension disposition"[37] included:

(a) taking out a new policy and assigning the death benefits on trust;

(b) assigning on trust the death benefits of an existing policy;

(c) paying further or enhanced contributions to a policy when the death benefits have already been assigned;

(d) deferring taking retirement benefits (e.g. the pension retirement age is 65 and the member who is in ill health defers taking benefits till he is 70, which age he is unlikely to reach);

---

[35] The lump sum is subject to a 35% income tax charge: any IHT charge is accordingly on the net figure.

[36] See IHTA 1984 s.12(2A)–(G) inserted by FA 2004 ss.203(2), 326, Sch.42 Pt 3, with effect from April 6, 2006 until April 6, 2011.

[37] See s.12(2F)(b).

(iv) subsections (2D)(a) and (b) provide that a disposition under s.3(3) is not a transfer of value if the pension scheme death benefits are paid to a relevant dependant[38] or charity.

48.35 These sections provided a more generous treatment than was the position prior to April 6, 2006, since one was generally only required to consider when the deceased first omitted to take the pension and at that point ascertain whether he had any gratuitous intention. The effect of s.12(2A)–(C) was that if a person deferred his pension at a time when he was in good health and had no gratuitous intention at that point and then fell ill, continuing to defer the pension was not an omission taxable under s.3(3) even if he had a gratuitous intention later, provided no further contributions were made. In the case of *PRs of Arnold Deceased v RCC*,[39] as noted above, it was decided that by failing to take a pension at the retirement age of 60 the deceased had "omitted to exercise a right" for the purpose of s.3(3) of IHTA 1984 with the result that the value of that right was to be taxed on her death. If the first omission had occurred after April 2006, then s.12(2A) onwards would have been the relevant provision to consider, although given that she was at that time terminally ill, it is thought that the result would have been the same.

48.36 Hence, in most cases for registered or approved schemes, s.3(3) of the 1984 Act was not an issue even before April 6, 2011, since many people deferred taking their pension with no gratuitous transfer in mind, but in order to maximise their income later. They were in good health when they made the first omission. Provided the deceased avoided making a further scheme contribution at a time when he fell into ill health, no s.3(3) charge could arise even if he could at that point still take his pension (and therefore was making an omission).

48.37 Section 12(2A)–(2G) only applied in relation to registered pension schemes. Hence, any unapproved pension scheme such as an EFURB remained potentially within the scope of s.3(3) if the deceased omitted to draw down his pension at a time when he is in ill-health. (The trustees are not under any obligation to buy an annuity in the case of unapproved schemes but simply to provide the deceased with income from retirement age if he so chooses.) HMRC considered that an omission occurred if the deceased omitted to draw down his maximum income entitlement from the date he could have started taking it even if this was not the normal retirement age. However, whether such an omission was within s.3(3) depended on whether the deceased's omission was deliberate and had any grauitous intent (and presumably also whether the value of the settled property was increased by the omission).

Position from April 6, 2011

48.38 In the case of dispositions from April 6, 2011, FA 2011 s.65 repealed s.12(2A)–(2E) and inserted s.12(2ZA). Section 12(ZA) simply provides that where a person who is a member of a registered pension scheme, a qualifying

---

[38] A relevant dependant meaning the member surviving spouse or civil partner or "someone who is financially dependent on the person at the time": see s.12(2G).

[39] [2010] S.F.T.D. 632.

pension or a s.615(3) scheme omits to exercise pension rights under the pension scheme, s.3(3) does not apply in relation to the omission. This change would appear to embrace unapproved as well as approved pension schemes.

The requirement to secure a pension income by age 75 is removed and there **48.39** is no longer any requirement imposed on registered pension savers to buy an annuity by that age. IHT will not apply to drawdown pension funds even where the individual dies after reaching the age of 75 although IHT will continue to apply to all other lump sums, i.e. those in a non-registered pension scheme. So where previously registered pension funds in drawdown would have been liable to a 35 per cent income tax charge and no IHT if the policy holder was under age 75 and an income tax charge of 55 per cent with IHT at 40 per cent where the policy holder was over 75, now there will be a flat rate recovery charge of 55 per cent for all and no IHT liability if:

(i) the pension scheme member dies having crystallised his benefits (e.g. in income drawdown or where he has set up a lifetime annuity with capital protection); or

(ii) the pension scheme member dies after attaining the age of 75.

It is suggested now that phased or nil drawdown until 75 is the sensible option in most cases because there is no recovery tax charge on uncrystallised funds where the member dies before age 75. Otherwise the 55 per cent charge will apply in respect of any lump sum benefit paid on death if the fund is in drawdown.

Note that contributions made to registered pension schemes when a person **48.40** knows he is in serious ill-health and does not survive the transfer by two years could still be caught by s.3(1).

Death benefits

If the death benefit is payable to the member's estate then IHT will be payable **48.41** on the value of that benefit on the death of the member. Note, however, s.152 which provides that if, on the member's death an annuity is payable under a Registered Scheme to the member's surviving spouse or civil partner or dependant and if at the member's option a sum of money might have become payable to his personal representatives, the member is not (under s.5(2)) to be treated as beneficially entitled to that sum of money.

When death benefits are payable at the discretion of the scheme trustees, **48.42** the death benefits do not form part of the member's estate even if the trustees exercise their discretion to make payments to the estate. In such a case, there is no right to the benefit which could result in it being treated as part of the death estate of the member. Note also SP 10/86 providing that in an approved scheme where the death benefit is held on discretionary trusts no IHT will be charged as a result of the reservation of benefit rules even though the deceased or his personal representatives are potential beneficiaries.[40]

---

[40] HMRC consider that the gift with reservations can apply in the case of unapproved schemes including sponsored superannuation schemes: see IHTM 17073.

Assigning death benefits on to trust

48.43 In general, this will not give rise to IHT charges since the death benefits will have a nominal value. This is on the basis that the member is in good health at the time and so, with a normal life expectancy, is expected to survive to take his retirement benefits whereupon the death benefits will cease to be payable. In practice, HMRC apply the factors set out at 48.34 in this situation, accordingly, if the transfer was made more than two years before the death then, unless there is evidence to the contrary, it is assumed that the member was in good health when he made the transfer.[41]

The use of spousal by-pass trusts (see Precedent A1.5)

48.44 In many cases the death benefits are held by the pension trustees on discretionary trusts for a class of beneficiaries including the surviving spouse or civil partner. In such cases, the deceased may indicate by a letter of wishes (which is not binding on the trustees) how he would like them to exercise their discretions. If the death benefit is paid to (say) the surviving spouse then it will form part of her estate and so may attract a tax charge on his or her death.

48.45 It is for this reason that "spousal by-pass trusts" have become popular. The term is something of a misnomer since the surviving spouse will be a beneficiary (usually the main beneficiary) of the trust (which will be discretionary in form) but (and this is the key advantage) the settled property will not form part of the spouse's estate on death.

48.46 The arrangement is therefore that the pension member will establish a lifetime discretionary trust in pilot form and will then request the pension trustees to pay death benefits to those trustees (it is, of course, necessary to check that under the pension rules they have power to pay to trustees not just named individuals).

48.47 By-pass trusts have given rise to two problems:

(i) ensuring that the perpetuity/accumulation periods for the pilot by-pass trust correspond to that applicable to the pension trust[42];

(ii) whether any advantage would be obtained from establishing a number of pilot settlements so that the death benefits can be divided amongst them. In general no advantage will ensue because of the operation of IHTA 1984 s.81 which will have the effect of treating the property as still comprised in the transferor pension trust. Note, however, that if a number of pension policies have been taken out there will be a number of transferor trusts, each of which may benefit from a nil rate band. This matter is fully explored in the following ABI Guidance Note.

---

[41] IHTM 17071.
[42] This matter is discussed at 1.46.

"ABI Technical Q&A on Pensions and IHT Points: Consolidated version **48.48**

In 2010, the ABI Investment Products Tax Working Group began the process of clarifying key issues relating to pensions and inheritance tax with HMRC. This has been a continuing process with the first guidance published on 11 May 2010. This paper consolidates that guidance with some recently answered questions.

The Q&As from number 3 onwards do not deal with post-1988 pensions which are created by deed poll/board resolution. In the scenarios from number 3 onwards, the contract-based pensions are retirement annuity contracts.

1 Meaning of 'estate' and treatment of LSDB paid as a result of discretion

Where pension scheme administrators have discretion over payment of the LSDB from a trust-based pension, IHTM17123 sets out the position involving a 2 year period for the scheme administrators to consider how to exercise their discretion. It is possible that the scheme administrators choose to exercise their discretion and pay the LSDB to the deceased's executors (in the knowledge that this will be distributed either according to the rules of intestacy or to certain beneficiaries under the deceased's Will). Since payment of the LSDB results from the exercise of the scheme administrator's discretion, we consider that the LSDB does not form part of the deceased's estate on death in terms of s 5 IHTA 1984 and as such no IHT arises either on the transfer from the scheme administrators to the deceased's executors (if within 2 years of date of death) nor on the onward distribution of the LSDB by the deceased's executors.

Question 1a: Can HMRC confirm that they agree with this interpretation?

Answer: Confirmed.

Question 1b: Can HMRC confirm that the IHT position is the same, where the LSDB is paid from a contract-based pension scheme and the scheme administrators similarly make a payment of the LSDB to the deceased's executors in exercise of their discretion?

Answer: Confirmed.

2 Number of settlements, nil rate bands and ten year anniversaries

IHTM17126 deals with the reference date for ten year anniversaries in two different scenarios. One scenario involves a trust-based pension scheme with discretionary powers which makes a discretionary payment to a recipient settlement. IHTM17126 states that ten year charges for the recipient settlement will be taken with reference to the date the member first joined the original pension scheme.

Example: X has three employments during his lifetime, each with individual pension schemes (these are all trust-based pension schemes with discretionary powers). For ease of reference, assume X joined each scheme on

1 January 1980, 1 June 1990 and 1 December 2000. To keep his arrange-ments as tidy as possible for his family in the event of his death, X sets up one family trust (i.e. recipient settlement) with £100 on 1 September 2009. He signs a non-binding letter of wishes for each of his three pension schemes to indicate his preference that the LSDB should be paid to his family trust in the event of his death. X then dies on 10 January 2010 and the pension scheme administrators for all three schemes exercise their powers to pay the LSDB to the X Family Trust within 2 years of death.

Question 2a: Applying the analysis in IHTM17126, there are 4 poten-tial reference dates for ten year anniversaries here: 1 January 2020, 1 June 2010, 1 September 2019 (in relation to the initial £100 gift) and 1 December 2010. Can HMRC confirm its analysis of the scenario here in relation to the number of ten year anniversary dates here?

Answer: Confirmed s81 IHTA applies to give 4 ten year anniversary (tya) dates.

Question 2b: As a follow-on point, what is HMRC's analysis in relation to the available nil rate bands in this scenario? Whilst there is one recipi-ent trust, there are three "feeder" pension scheme settlements, which prompts a query over whether the analysis here is of four settlements, each of which has its own nil rate band as the deceased joined each scheme more than seven years after his last pension scheme joining date, and created the X family trust more than seven years after taking up his last employment.

Answer: Confirmed 4 settlements each with its own nil rate band.

3 Contract-based pension scheme

Taking the facts in 2a above, but with three "feeder" contract-based pension schemes rather than trust-based pension schemes, does HMRC agree with the analysis that there is only one settlement with one nil rate band for IHT purposes (subject to the settlor's cumulative total when he created that settlement), with a commencement date which relates to the recipient settlement only?

Answer: Confirmed. S81IHTA cannot apply in this scenario as there is no initial settlement for IHT purposes and so no movement of property from one settlement to another.

4 SIPP consolidation scenario with trust-based "feeder" pensions

A trust-based pension 1
1988

B trust-based pension 2   D consolidated into   E discretionary trust set
1996   trust-based SIPP in   up with £100 in March
                               February 2008   2008

C trust-based pension 3
2004

The scenario here is that X starts with 3 different pension policies, all of which are trust-based in this example. In February 2008, he consolidates them into a SIPP. In March 2008, he creates a discretionary trust with £100 and a letter of wishes (non-binding) is given to the trustees of the SIPP indicating X's preference that any LSDB should be paid to the discretionary trust. X then dies in March 2010 and the LSDB is paid to the discretionary trust. The question arises as to the number of settlements and nil rate bands in this scenario.

Assume two additional points:

4i there are no new pension contributions paid into pension D – the SIPP is a pure consolidation exercise;

4ii alternatively, there are new pension contributions paid into pension D.

Question 4a: Does HMRC agree with the analysis that in 4i, there are 4 settlements, namely the trusts in A, B, C and E? In this analysis, the SIPP at D is ignored since there were no new pension contributions at that stage. The funds ultimately held in trust E therefore represent 4 settlements, each with a different ten year anniversary date. Settlements A, B and C have a ten year anniversary date with reference to the date the deceased took out the original pensions of A, B and C. The settlement at E has a TYA relating to the date the discretionary trust was created with the £100 cash gift. Can HMRC confirm if it agrees with this analysis?

Answer: Confirmed.

Question 4b: Does HMRC agree with the analysis that in 4ii, there are

5 settlements, namely the trusts in A, B, C, D and E? The contrast with the scenario in question 4a is that in 4b the SIPP does count as a settlement since new pension contributions were made. Can HMRC confirm if it agrees with this analysis?

Answer: Confirmed.

Question 4c: Where there are multiple settlements, as found in both questions 4a and 4b, the administrative task facing the trustees of E could involve multiple IHT100 forms at ten year anniversaries. Does HMRC consider that multiple IHT100 forms are required where IHT is due? Would HMRC agree to a concessionary position where no IHT100 forms were required where no IHT was due, to remove administration for both the taxpayer and HMRC in this situation?

Answer: Where Inheritance Tax is due multiple IHT100s would prima facie be necessary. If difficulties arise tracing the consolidated fund back to trusts A B C D and E then I'm sure we would take a pragmatic approach probably based on some form of pro rata apportionment.

Where it is clear on values that no Inheritance Tax is due we would take a pragmatic approach and where possible not insist on a formal accounting on Forms IHT100.

5 SIPP consolidation scenario with mixture of contract and trust-based 'feeder' pensions

A Retirement annuity contract 1980

B Retirement annuity contract 1986

D consolidated into trust-based SIPP in February 2008

E discretionary trust set up with £100 in March 2008

C Trust-based personal pension 1994

The scenario here is that X starts with 3 different pension policies, one of which is trust-based and two of which are contract-based. In February 2008, he consolidates them into a SIPP. In March 2008, he creates a discretionary trust with £100 and a letter of wishes (non-binding) is given to the trustees of the SIPP indicating X's preference that the LSDB should be paid to the discretionary trust. X then dies in March 2010 and the LSDB is paid to the discretionary trust. The question arises as to the number of settlements and nil rate bands in this scenario.

Question 5a: Does HMRC agree with the analysis that there are 3 settlements and 3 nil rate bands here? The first is pension C, with a TYA date which refers back to the 1994 date. The second is the SIPP at D, with a TYA date which refers to the date the SIPP commenced. The third is the discretionary trust at E. The pensions at A and B are not taken into account for settlement purposes as they are contract-based pensions and therefore there is no property moving between settlements at the point they are transferred to the SIPP, and there is therefore no 'tracing back'. Does HMRC agree with this analysis?

Answer: Confirmed. This is our current analysis for contract based schemes. Our view is that these are not settlements within s43IHTA and in that event s81 IHTA does not apply. The funds transferred from pensions A and B become settled property on their transfer into the SIPP at D.

Question 5b: New pension contributions may or may not be made into the SIPP at stage D. Does HMRC agree that, regardless of whether or not there are new pension contributions, or whether D is simply a pure consolidation exercise, this does not affect the overall number of settlements, which remains the same as in 5a, namely 3 settlements?

Answer: Confirmed.

6 Sequential transfers of trust-based pension arrangements

A trust-based pension 1988

B trust-based pension 1996

C trust-based SIPP 2008

D discretionary trust set up with £100 in March 2008

X's first pension dates back to 1988. In 1996, he established pension B using a transfer value from pension A. Then in 2008, X takes out a SIPP using the transfer value from pension B. In March 2008, he creates a discretionary trust with £100 and a letter of wishes (non-binding) is given to the trustees of the SIPP indicating X's preference that any LSDB should be paid to the discretionary trust. X then dies in March 2010 and the LSDB is paid to the discretionary trust. The question arises as to the number of settlements and nil rate bands in this scenario.

Question 6a: Assume that X made no new pension contributions after pension A, so that the move to pension B and then pension C was effectively just a change of investment wrapper. The analysis here seems to be of two settlements. One is the discretionary trust D, with its TYA relating to its initial £100 gift. There is also a second settlement. This seems to be either the SIPP, or pension A. In either case, the value would be the same, and the only difference would relate to the TYA date, as being either the date of pension A or the date of commencement of the SIPP. Does HMRC agree with the analysis that there are two settlements here, and that pension B is ignored, and if so, what is the appropriate date for the TYA as discussed above?

Answer: Agreed. Section 81 would take us back to Settlement A as setting the appropriate date for the TYA.

Question 6b: Assume now that there are new pension contributions made into pension B, whereas the move from pension B to the SIPP is simply a change of investment wrapper. Does HMRC agree that the analysis here involves 3 settlements, with TYA dates which refer to the dates of commencements of each of A, B and D?

Answer: Confirmed.

Question 6c: Assuming that new pension contributions were made at stages A, B and C, does HMRC agree that the analysis involves 4 settlements, namely A, B, C and D, each with its own TYA reference date?

Answer: Confirmed."

CHAPTER 49

EMPLOYEE BENEFIT TRUSTS

- Background—general tax treatment before December 9, 2010 (**49.01**)
- Definition of an EBT (**49.16**)
- Exit charges when property ceases to be comprised in an EBT (**49.33**)
- Entry charges—general (**49.36**)
- Relief for dispositions by a close company (**49.44**)
- Relief for dispositions by individuals (**49.53**)
- Business and agricultural property relief (**49.56**)
- Disguised remuneration—position from December 9, 2010 (**49.59**)

Precedent

A1.4   Employee benefit trust

I BACKGROUND—GENERAL TAX TREATMENT BEFORE DECEMBER 9, 2010

49.01   Employee benefit trusts (EBTs) were until December 9, 2010 a popular way of rewarding employees. They are trusts (generally discretionary) established with funds provided by employers for the benefit of their employees, past, present or future or for the benefit of dependents or relations of such employees. They can be UK resident or situated offshore. In recent years, offshore EBTs have become more common because of the additional tax advantages:

(i) trust gains are free of capital gains tax in the hands of the trustees;

49.02   (ii) income tax payable by the trustees is limited to UK source income.[1] However, note that this assumes that the transfer of assets provisions, ss.720–730 ITA 2007 do not apply. Normally, these rules only apply to transferors who are individuals. However, a shareholder of a close company can count as a transferor if they procure or have been associ-

---

[1] The rates are the trust rates, i.e. 42.5% dividends and 50% other income. See *Tax Bulletin* April 2004 as to what items of expenditure may properly be claimed as trust management expenses by trustees of discretionary trusts.

ated with the transfer. HMRC may argue that ss.720–730 can apply in respect of EBTs set up by close companies.[2]

In Brief 18/11 HMRC note:

> "*if the employer company is controlled by its shareholder/directors and the offshore employee benefit trust was formed solely for their benefit, the director/shareholders may have procured the transfer into the offshore employee benefit trust and could be considered transferors for the purposes of the income charge.*"

If ss.720–730 apply all income in the employee benefit trust is taxed on the shareholders. HMRC also note that if interest is paid on loans to UK resident beneficiaries (to avoid a benefit in kind charge) the beneficiary must deduct tax at source from payments of interest to the trustees.

By ITA 2007 ss.496A and 496B (formerly ESC A68) to avoid an effective double tax charge, trustees may reclaim tax paid by them when payments made to employees are treated as earnings;

(iii) generally distributions are not subject to capital gains tax under TCGA 1992 s.87 or Sch.4C because if the EBT is a genuine commercial arrangement to attract, retain and motivate staff, there is no element of bounty involved in its setting up. Hence, there is no settlement for s.87 purposes[3]; **49.03**

(iv) tax on earnings can be deferred by making contributions to an employee benefit trust. This is the case even after December 8, 2010 provided there is no earmarking of the fund for the employee. For foreign domiciled employees it was generally better to use offshore trusts: the ability to use the remittance basis, particularly after the employee had left the company, was much greater.[4]

Why establish EBTs?

EBTs are often associated with tax avoidance but they may also have a number of non-tax objectives: **49.04**

---

[2] If so, it may be difficult to argue the motive defence given that the employee benefit trust is offshore to minimise UK tax in the first place. It would be possible to exclude the controlling shareholders so they do not have power to enjoy as transferors, but this is often contrary to the whole purpose behind EBTs.

[3] For the definition of settlement for CGT purposes, see Ch.9. Again this assumes that no gratuitous benefit or bounty is intended on the settlement of the funds by the company. HMRC deny this in relation to inheritance tax (see Brief 18/11 April 2011) and have been known to claim that in some cases ss.86 and 87 do apply because there is bounty. TCGA 1992 Sch.5 deems participators in close companies to be corporate settlors so the s.86 charge apply if there is bounty. If there is bounty, and HMRC can argue that an individual settlor indirectly made the settlement they can also impose income tax under the settlement provisions in ITTOIA 2005 s.620. Their more aggressive approach recently in relation to close companies is in contrast to their statement in *Tax Bulletin* 16 (April 1995) where they noted: "*it is accepted that a trust devoid of bounty is not within either the settlor [s86] or beneficiary [s87] charge legislation. An example would be a genuine commercial arrangement by a company to attract, retain and motivate good quality staff.*"

[4] See 49.08.

(i) They can provide useful cash sums for employees or their dependents in personal financial difficulties. The company can transfer such sums into trust for future use by the trustees at their discretion as they see fit in the event of death or injury of an employee beneficiary.

(ii) They are often used as an incentive: the employee knows that if he increases profitability of the company he may be eligible to receive additional cash payments funded by a trust.

(iii) An employee benefit trust may be set up as a means of creating an internal market for the sale and purchase of non-quoted company shares, e.g. on retirement or resignation of an employee.

(iv) An employee benefit trust may be a way of building up or retaining a large shareholding in friendly hands. The founder knows that his shares can be retained by the trust for the long-term benefit of the company and its employees.

Tax position on contributions to an EBT

49.05 Contributions to an EBT which are held on discretionary trusts are not generally taxable earnings of a particular employee. Hence, even if an employee is taxed later when receiving benefits out of the EBT, a deferral of income tax has been obtained. This is the case even after December 9, 2010 provided that care is exercised in how the funds are held by the trustees and no sub-funds or other type of earmarking takes place.[5]

49.06 Contributions to an employee benefit trust are not necessarily deductible for corporation tax purposes. Although under general principles they are deductible provided that the contribution is revenue in nature and made wholly and exclusively for the purposes of the employer's trade, legislation was enacted to prevent a deduction unless and until the payment was taxed as earnings on the employee.[6] This was to ensure symmetry in the tax system: no deduction until the payments were taxed. Hence, CTA 2009 s.1290 prevents a deduction where it would otherwise be allowed under general principles unless within nine months of the end of the accounting period the money is used by the trustees to meet qualifying expenses or provide qualifying benefits. Qualifying benefits are defined in s.1292 as a payment of money or a transfer of assets which give rise to both an employment income tax charge and a NIC charge or would do so if the duties of the employment were performed in the UK. Loans are expressly excluded. If money is paid out of the employee benefit trust as

---

[5] See *Macdonald v Dextra Accessories Ltd* [2003] STC 749 and *Sempra Metal v HMRC* [2008] STC (SCD) 1062, where HMRC unsuccessfully argued that a contribution became an employee's earnings when allocated to him (even notionally in a sub-fund). It was held that earnings only arise when the fund is unreservedly at the disposal of the employee. This has now been superceded by the new legislation discussed at 49.56. Contributions can be treated as earnings of the employee if earmarked for him.

[6] See FA 1989 s.343 and the House of Lords decision in *Dextra* [2005] STC 1111. The House of Lords eventually held that FA 1989 s.43 did restrict a deduction because the company's contributions were "potential emoluments". In the meantime s.1290 (formerly FA 2003 Sch.24) had been enacted to put the position beyond doubt for contributions made after November 27, 2002. See Revenue Brief 61/09.

qualifying benefits and therefore taxed at a later date then the corporation tax deduction is then available.[7]

If the trust satisfies the conditions of IHTA 1984 s.86 then the settled **49.07** property will not be subject to the normal relevant property 10-year and exit charges and an interest in possession is disregarded provided that it subsists in less than five per cent of the settled property.[8] However, the favoured inheritance tax treatment given to a trust within IHTA 1984 s.86 does not mean that contributions into the EBT are free of inheritance tax. The participators of the close company or an individual making contributions to the EBT will be subject to an IHT entry charge unless certain other conditions apply.[9]

Payments out of the employee benefit trust

Distributions out of the EBT to an employee or former employee[10] are gener- **49.08** ally treated as earnings on which PAYE and NI must be operated.[11] Even if the distribution out of the EBT is made at a time when the employee or former employee is non-resident, the distribution can still be treated as taxable earnings although it may be possible to avoid this if the employee emigrates before his employment ends or receives the distribution when resident in a country with a suitable double tax treaty.

Various ways were sought prior to December 9, 2009 to extract funds or **49.09** value for the employee from the EBTs and avoid the PAYE and NI charge.

Loans

The attraction of the interest-free loan before December 9, 2009 was that even **49.10** while the beneficiary was still employed it was the benefit of the loan rather than its face value that was taxed on the employee as earnings. So, on an interest-free loan of £1 million the tax charge for a top rate taxpayer was not £500,000 as it would have been if he had received the sum of £1 million with the employer having to pay NI at 13.8 per cent. Instead the taxable benefit was four per cent (the official rate of interest for 2010–11) = £40,000 × 50%. PAYE is payable of £20,000. The company would be liable for employer's NI on the taxable benefit (at 13.8 per cent from April 2010) but receive corporation tax

---

[7] In *Sempra Metals* it was held that a corporation tax deduction did not apply even if the beneficial class was not employees but only dependents: s.1290 still applied to prevent a deduction. See also UITF 13 and UITF 32 which capitalises employee benefit trust contributions by showing them as an asset on the company's balance sheet until and to the extent that the assets transferred to the trust vest unconditionally in identified beneficiaries. The effect is to delay the timing of the deduction.

[8] This is less significant after the 2006 changes in the IHT treatment of settlements when new interests in possession will not generally be "qualifying".

[9] See 49.36 and following.

[10] *Bray v Best* [1989] S.T.C. 159 was reversed such that the payments are deemed to be earnings of the last year of the employment: ITEPA 2003 s.30(3).

[11] See *Brumby v Milner* [1976] STC 534 and ITEPA 2003 s.687(4). The employer is liable for the PAYE insofar as the trustees do not pay the tax.

relief. So, on the above figures the net NI cost for the company after corporation tax relief[12] would be £4,416.

49.11   Moreover, once the employment had ceased, the benefit of an interest-free loan made to a UK resident by a non-resident trust could be subject to income tax under the transfer of assets provisions but only to the extent that there was relevant income in the trust from which the employee could benefit.[13] However, the charge under ITEPA 2003 ceased and there was no NI charge. A remittance basis user could receive interest-free loans in the tax years after he had left the employment and pay no tax at all if the loan proceeds were not remitted to the UK. Even if the loan proceeds were remitted to the UK, there was no earnings charge on the former employee and no tax charge under the transfer of assets legislation for non-transferors[14] if there was no relevant income in the trust structure from which he could benefit.

Benefits to family members

49.12   Before December 9, 2010, benefits were often taken out of an EBT by making outright distributions to a family member other than the employee in tax years after his employment had ceased.[15] Care was needed to ensure that cash payments were not made to or for the benefit of the employee's family (e.g. spouse and children) in a way that was of direct monetary value to the employee (for example, to relieve from payment of a liability such as school fees or a settlement of the employee's liabilities to his wife on divorce) or was convertible into cash for the employee. Otherwise this would be fully taxable as the former employee's earnings.[16]

Dividends

49.13   In *Revenue and Customs Commissioners v PA Holdings Ltd*,[17] an employee benefit trust avoided the earnings charge by incorporating a UK resident company, subscribing trust funds into the company and causing the company to declare dividends on preference shares which it had issued to the employees. The Upper Tribunal upheld the finding of the First-Tier Tribunal that, (i) they were both distributions and emoluments; (ii) for income tax purposes, they were taxable as dividends, since Sch.F took precedence over Sch.E; for

---

[12]   Assuming NI of 13.8% and corporation tax at 20%.

[13]   ITA 2007 ss.731–735. Various techniques could be used to minimise or avoid the income tax charge in such circumstances. For example, it might be possible to segregate the income and ensure that the relevant ex-employee and his family are unable to benefit from such relevant income. However, if the trust invested in offshore income funds or accrued income arose, segregation could in practice be difficult to achieve.

[14]   ITA 2007 s.731 and following.

[15]   It was important in these circumstances that the payment to the family member did not satisfy a financial obligation of the employee (e.g. to dependants) otherwise the payment to the family member could be treated as earnings of the former employee. Payments to family members were not effective to avoid the earnings charge while the beneficiary was still employed.

[16]   With no remittance basis available.

[17]   [2010] All ER (D) 207.

NICs purposes, on the other hand, they were taxable as earnings, there being no equivalent to the income tax rule.[18]

Creation of sub-funds

In many cases the employee wanted to know that "his" part of the trust fund **49.14** could not be taken away and accordingly the trustees would notionally allocate or earmark a proportion of cash for his and his family's benefit. This could have inheritance tax implications.[19]

It is not considered that the creation of sub-funds before December 2010 did not in itself generate an income tax liability on the employee. HMRC tried in several cases to argue that the creation of sub-funds[20] or the notional or actual allocation of funds for the benefit of an employee and/or the employee's family or the making of loans was *itself* an occasion of income tax charge. They were unsuccessful in *Dextra* and *Sempra* but another case involving a Scottish football team is being litigated. If correct it would mean that the value of the sub-funds (or the loan) would be fully taxable as earnings.[21]

The disguised remuneration legislation

In any event, to combat the widespread use of such arrangements, the **49.15** Coalition Government introduced the "disguised remuneration" legislation

---

[18] ITEPA 2003 s.716A.
[19] See 49.34.
[20] *Macdonald v Dextra Securities Accessories Ltd* [2003] STC 749 and *Sempra Metals Ltd v IRC* [2008] STC (SCD) 1062.
[21] See "Spotlight 5" issued in 2009 where HMRC showed they have not given up this argument even for periods before December 9, 2010 stating, *"our view is that at the time the funds are allocated to the employee or his/her beneficiaries, those funds become earnings on which PAYE and NICs are due and should be accounted for."* They issued a further statement in March 2011 noting that they were offering employers who have used employee benefit trusts the opportunity to resolve outstanding enquiries:

> *"The Finance (No 3) Bill 2011 introduced new legislation to put beyond doubt that such arrangements or schemes do not work"* (!)

and reiterated their view that even under the existing legislation the schemes did not work. Dave Hartnett suggested:

> *"HMRC's pro-active approach to customers gives them the opportunity to discuss their cases with us and work in partnership to establish how the facts of their case fit within the proposals. For this reason I would encourage customers to come and talk to us."*

In fact there seems little incentive for the employer to co-operate since HMRC simply state that all outstanding PAYE and Class 1 contributions that they allege to be due on contributions to the trust must be settled. Unless the facts of the cases are materially different from those in *Dextra* and *Sempra* it seems hard to see on what basis HMRC can argue that contributions or allocation of sub-funds before December 9, 2010 can be caught and taxed as earnings, even if the sub-funds are irrevocable.

in FA 2011 with effect from December 9, 2010 which is considered at 49.59 and following while HMRC have signalled their intention to scrutinise existing arrangements:

> "*Those intent on avoiding income tax and NICs by using trust arrangements should also be aware that there could be adverse inheritance tax and trust tax consequences regardless of whether they themselves set up the trust. These include IHT charges when contributions are made to the trust, when funds are transferred from a trust to a sub-trust or removed from the sub trust when uncommercial loans are made by the trustees and at the ten year anniversary of the trust.*"[22]

II DEFINITION OF AN EBT

49.16   The conditions for the special IHT treatment of Employee Benefit Trusts (EBTs) are set out in IHTA 1984 s.86 which is in the following terms:

> "*86   Trusts for benefit of employees.*
>
> *(1)   Where settled property is held on trusts which, either indefinitely or until the end of a period (whether defined by a date or in some other way) do not permit any of the settled property to be applied otherwise than for the benefit of—*
>
> > *(a)   persons of a class defined by reference to employment in a particular trade or profession, or employment by, or office with, a body carrying on a trade, profession or undertaking, or*
> > *(b)   persons of a class defined by reference to marriage to or civil partnership with, or relationship to, or dependence on, persons of a class defined as mentioned in paragraph (a) above,*
>
> *then, subject to subsection (3) below, this section applies to that settled property or, as the case may be, applies to it during that period.*
>
> *(2)   Where settled property is held on trusts permitting the property to be applied for the benefit of persons within paragraph (a) or (b) of subsection (1) above, those trusts shall not be regarded as outside the description specified in that subsection by reason only that they also permit the settled property to be applied for charitable purposes.*
>
> *(3)   Where any class mentioned in subsection (1) above is defined by reference to employment by or office with a particular body, this section applies to the settled property only if—*
>
> > *(a)   the class comprises all or most of the persons employed by or holding office with the body concerned, or*
> > *(b)   the trusts on which the settled property is held are those of a profit sharing scheme approved in accordance with Schedule 9 to the Taxes Act 1988. ; or*

---

[22] Spotlight 12 (August 23, 2011).

(c)   the trusts on which the settled property is held are those of a
        share incentive plan approved under Schedule 2 to the Income
        Tax (Earnings and Pensions) Act 2003.

(4)   Where this section applies to any settled property—

(a)   the property shall be treated as comprised in one settlement,
        whether or not it would fall to be so treated apart from this
        section, and
(b)   an interest in possession in any part of the settled property
        shall be disregarded for the purposes of this Act (except
        section 55) if that part is less than 5 per cent of the whole.

(5)   Where any property to which this section applies ceases to be com-
      prised in a settlement and, either immediately or not more than
      one month later, the whole of it becomes comprised in another
      settlement, then, if this section again applies to it when it becomes
      comprised in the second settlement, it shall be treated for all the
      purposes of this Act as if it had remained comprised in the first
      settlement."

49.17 A trust set up by a company that satisfies IHTA 1984 s.86 will be outside the
relevant property regime and notably the 10-year anniversary charge irrespective of the domicile of the company or the situs of the property. The trustees
should not have a power or an obligation under the terms of the trust deed to
pay National Insurance Contributions that otherwise fall to be borne by the
employer. This is because the terms of the trust will then permit, "*any of the
settled property to be applied otherwise than for the benefit of [employees]*",
etc.[23] Note that if the contributing company is foreign incorporated and the
trust holds non-UK situs assets it may be possible to avoid 10-year charges
and exit charges,[24] even if the participators are UK domiciled on the basis the
settlement is of excluded property.[25]

Qualifying beneficiaries

49.18 The section requires the settled property to be held on trusts that do not permit
any of the settled property to be applied otherwise than for the benefit of:

(i)   persons of a class defined by reference to employment in a particular
      trade (see s.86(1)(a));

---

[23] See IHTA 1984 s.86(1). It may be possible to make arrangements, so that the trust only takes
the contribution from the employer company in the first place, subject to the obligation to pay
the NI contributions. This is not in the trust deed but a contractual liability imposed as part
of the terms of the contribution.
[24] In this respect watch loans to UK resident employees or former employees. They need to be
structured as a specialty debt in order to avoid being UK situated property (although HMRC
considers that loans to Scottish debtors are UK situated, even if the loan is by deed and kept
abroad).
[25] See 24.20 for definition of settlor and corporate settlors.

(ii) persons of a class defined by reference to employment by or office with a body carrying on a trade, profession or undertaking (see s.86(3));

(iii) persons of a class defined by reference to marriage to or civil partnership with or relationship to or dependence on the above persons (see s.86(1)(c)).

49.19   Hence, employees (and officeholders, such as company directors) of the same trade who have different employers as well as employees of the same company who undertake different trades can both be included. Under s.86(2), trusts which permit property to be applied for the benefit of the above persons do not lose the relief by reason only that they also permit the property to be applied for charitable purposes (typically this will be when the charity is the default beneficiary or ultimate remainderman).[26] The employer should be expressly excluded from any possibility of benefit. Participators in the company can benefit.[27]

    A number of difficulties result from the definition of qualifying beneficiaries.

49.20   The restriction is that property cannot be applied otherwise than for the benefit of the prescribed class of qualifying beneficiaries. However, the condition is met not only if the prohibition is indefinite but also if it applies for a limited period ("*whether defined by a date or in some other way*"). It would therefore appear, that a trust can be set up in EBT form for (say) 20 years but thereafter may benefit non-qualifying persons.[28] EBT status is accordingly tested from time to time: it will, of course, cease once non-qualifying persons can benefit.[29]

49.21   The use of the disjunctive "or" in s.86(1) indicates that beneficiaries can be restricted to any one class (they may, for instance, be employees, etc of a particular trade within s.86(1)(a) and exclude relatives and dependents within s.86(1)(b)). However, HMRC accept that "or" does not prevent both classes benefitting.[30]

49.22   In s.86(1)(b) "relationship to" an employee appears wide enough to catch all relatives including adopted and illegitimate children. The words "dependence on" are more problematic. HMRC consider that they are restricted to, "*those who are financially dependent*" on the employee, etc. They consider that a child will always be financial dependent until he is 18 or (if later) ceases to be in full time education or vocational training.[31] This restriction in the case of a child may be redundant in that even after that age he will qualify as a relative. More generally, it is accepted that a dependent need not be related to the employee (so a cohabitee may qualify) but it is difficult to see on what basis other forms of dependency are excluded (e.g. emotional dependency should suffice).

---

[26] See IHTM 42914. Note the inheritance tax guidance on EBTs is currently being rewritten so references in this chapter are to the old manual.

[27] IHTA 1984 s.58(1)(b).

[28] See IHTM 42911 and see 42912 (power to alter) which states:

> "*It is immaterial that the trustees, or some other person, may have power to alter the trusts, so that persons outside the specified classes in Section 86(1) IHTA 1984 could benefit. It is similarly immaterial that the existing trusts provide that other persons may benefit in the future. The relief would of course cease to apply if the trusts were altered in that way or if such reversionary trusts came into operation.*"

[29] An exit charge may then arise: see IHTA 1984 s.72.

[30] IHTM 42913.

[31] IHTM 42913.

The beneficiaries may be linked by virtue of employment, etc, by, "*a body* **49.23** *carrying on a trade profession or undertaking*". The use of the wording "undertaking" would encompass any commercial undertaking and is not restricted to trading: it would accordingly include a property investment business. "Body", however, is considered by HMRC not to include a sole trader or partnership (except in Scotland where partnerships are separate legal entities).[32]

The wording of s.86(1)(a) is wide enough to include former employees **49.24** ("*persons of a class defined by reference to employment*") and HMRC accept that although s.86(3) is drafted by reference to present employees, provided that the class of beneficiaries includes all or most of those persons, there is no objection to former employees benefitting.[33] It does not matter that there are more former employees than present employees, provided that all or most of the latter can benefit.

Although most EBTs are discretionary, if a person takes an interest in possession in not more than five per cent of the settled property, this interest in possession is disregarded (so it is not treated as a qualifying interest in possession even if it arose before March 22, 2006). Hence, there is no tax charge on the person's death and the settled property subject to the interest in possession remains outside the relevant property regime.

The trustees can retain power to take the settled property outside the scope **49.26** of s.86 (e.g. by appointing the settled property on narrow trusts for the benefit of one or two employees). The presence of that power will not in itself breach s.86. It is only as and when such power is exercised that the settled property will cease to satisfy s.86 and an exit charge will arise.[34]

The "all or most" test[35]

The rationale for this requirement (which applies if the class of beneficiaries **49.27** is defined by reference to employment by or office with a particular body) is explained in IHTM 42915 as to prevent a qualifying trust being established for the benefit, "*of a small group of employees only . . . such as directors or those with long service or some other elitist group*".

It is important to appreciate that the test takes account only of the employ- **49.28** ees, etc of the body, a majority of which (more than 50 per cent) must be capable of benefitting from the trust. The fact that former employees, relatives and dependants are also capable of benefitting (and may, indeed, amount to a majority of the beneficiaries) is for the purposes of this test irrelevant.

In practice, HMRC operate the following rules: **49.29**

(i) all employees/directors of the relevant "body" are considered and if there is a corporate group structure this brings into account employees etc of all group companies. HMRC comment that:

> "*the exemption would not be available for a contribution to a fund for the sole benefit of the employees of a small subsidiary. This is*

---

[32] IHTM 42925 and for a further consideration of the meaning of "body", see 49.26.
[33] IHTM 42923.
[34] See 49.33. Contrast the restrictions under IHTA 1984 s.13 (see 49.46).
[35] See IHTA 1984 s.86(3)(a).

> *because it would otherwise have been easy to create such a situation artificially in order to benefit a favoured group of a company's office holders or employees."*[36]

It is far from certain that the HMRC interpretation of "body" is correct: normally it would connote a legal entity and, of course, in a group structure each company is a separate legal entity;

(ii) in the case of an international company, employees outside the UK must be included in applying the test;

(iii) employees on probation or who have only served a short period with the employer are included as are part timers and casual labour. HMRC comment as follows[37]:

> *"Where the eligibility for employees to benefit extends only to full-time employees, there may in some cases be a problem. Some industries place heavy reliance on part-timers and casual labour. Some brewers for example who own large numbers of public houses increasingly staffed by managers rather than tenant landlords whose employees are employees of the brewery.*
>
> *Such temporary or irregular employment does not usually qualify the employee for membership of the company's Employee Benefit Trust. Strictly, therefore, such employee trusts can only satisfy Section 86 IHTA 1984 as long as the eligible employees comprise a majority of all (including part-time and casual) employees and this might require in a marginal case a counting of heads every time a distribution is made."*

49.30 It may be noted that HMRC refer in the above extract to the possible need to count heads, *"every time a distribution is made"*. This confirms that whether a trust meets the requirement for an EBT falls to be decided at any relevant time. e.g. when a distribution is made or on the anniversary of setting up the trust.

49.31 In general it is a majority of employees who must be capable of benefitting: self employed workers engaged by the company are not included.[38] HMRC accept that generally consultants are not employees of the business so that their inclusion would cause the trust to fall outside s.86.

EXAMPLE 49.1

Widgit Ltd is a manufacturing company employing a large workforce in Bolton. It also has a retail subsidiary which operates outlets in the North-West.

(1) For the purposes of applying the "all or most" test, HMRC consider that the workforce in both companies has to be considered. Accordingly, if Widgit Ltd has 5,000 employees and its subsidiary has 2,000, then the total of 7,000 employees must be considered.

---

[36] See IHTM 42929.
[37] IHTM 42931.
[38] Difficulties can, of course, arise in a particular case in determining whether a particular individual is employed or self-employed.

(2) If the trust beneficiaries are limited to the employees of Widgit alone this will qualify as an EBT since "most" (i.e. more than 50 per cent) of the 7,000 employees (namely the 5,000 employed by Widgit) are capable of benefitting. Contrast the position if the trust was set up purely for the benefit of the employees of the subsidiary where the trust would not qualify (only 2,000 out of the total 7,000 workforce).

(3) What if the trust is limited to the employees of Widgit who have completed five years' service with the company? Assume that of the 5,000 workforce, 25 per cent have been employed for less than that period. Accordingly those capable of benefitting total 3,750 out of a total workforce of 5,000: still more than 50 per cent so that the requirements for an EBT are still met (53.57 per cent of the 7,000 total) can benefit. But if the company is pursuing a policy of getting its older employees off the payroll and replacing them with (cheaper) new recruits, the position may change. If in the next 12 months, 10 per cent of the older workforce are replaced in this way, then the calculation is:

Total workforce	<u>7,000</u>
Widgit employees	5,000
Ineligible (25%)	1,250
Plus (10% × 3,750)	375
Total ineligible	<u>1,625</u>
Total eligible	<u>3,375</u>
As a % age	48.2%

The trust will therefore cease to be an EBT.

Other practical aspects of the definition

When drafting an EBT consider the following: **49.32**

(i) the trustees' discretion must not be fettered by, e.g. a requirement that the company must consent to distributions. A purely advisory committee is not considered to be a problem. A company can appoint trustees[39];

(ii) do not include as a potential beneficiary the personal representative of a deceased employee. This is because under the terms of the will he may be required to make payments to non-qualifying beneficiaries[40];

(iii) beware trustee remuneration clauses: HMRC consider that if the trustee is a corporation or otherwise not an employee, "*this may well constitute an application of the settled property which would infringe s86(1)*".[41]

---

[39] IHTM 42921.
[40] IHTM 42922.
[41] IHTM 42926.

However, provided that the charges are reasonable (the "going rate") it appears that HMRC will not take this point;

(iv) avoid clauses providing that the powers of the trustees are to be exercised "in the best interests of the company";

(v) trustees may be directed to waive an entitlement to future dividends without infringing s.86 since for this purpose the "settled property" is the capital and not any income produced by it[42];

(vi) the trustees may retain power to alter the trusts on which the property is held to allow persons who are not employees or their dependents to benefit without jeopardising s.86 treatment. If the power is exercised, then at that point an exit charge may arise if the trust falls outside the s.86 regime. The trustees should not have power to pay to another trust whose beneficiaries are not restricted to employees and their dependents.[43]

III EXIT CHARGES WHEN PROPERTY CEASES TO BE COMPRISED IN AN EBT

49.33   If the EBT ceases to qualify under s.86: for example, if irrevocable trusts for the benefit of a particular employee and his family are appointed, an exit charge can arise.[44] The charge is 0.25 per cent per quarter for the first 10 years during which the EBT satisfied the s.86 conditions, 0.20 per cent per quarter for the next 10 years, etc, then 0.15 per cent; 0.10 per cent and 0.05 per cent.[45]

An exit charge is also levied if the trustees make a distribution to, (a) a person who has provided more than £1000 of any of the settled property; *or* (b) has acquired an interest in the settled property for consideration in money's worth; *or* (c) to any participator who holds five per cent or more of the shares if the provider of the settled property is a close company; *or* (d) the trustees make a disposition other than by way of distribution as a result of which the settled property is diminished.

This exit charge does not apply if the distribution is taxed as the income of a beneficiary for the purposes of UK tax or would be if the recipient were UK resident.[46]

49.34   Does the appointment of property on revocable sub-funds in favour of particular employees take the property outside s.86?[47] It can be argued

---

[42] IHTM 42938 and see A1.4.

[43] See IHTM 42922 although it is not clear why a mere power to transfer assets to such a settlement would in itself breach s.86, but a power to alter the beneficial class so as to include non-employees, former employees or their dependents would not do so.

[44] Under IHTA 1984 s.72.

[45] For how the charges operate, see Ch.29.

[46] An appointment on irrevocable trusts, e.g. for the benefit of a former employee and his family may not be treated as earnings and will therefore be subject to an exit charge: see IHTA 1984 s.70(2).

[47] HMRC may argue that an appointment of property on such sub-funds is in itself earnings of the employee although it is thought that this view is misconceived. See 49.14 for the income tax position and also *Postlethwaite's Executors v IRC* considered at 49.51.

that unless and until the sub-funds are revoked, the trusts upon which that settled property is presently held are not for the benefit of a class of persons comprising the majority of employees. Therefore, s.86 is not satisfied and an exit charge arises on the creation of such sub-funds, whether revocable or irrevocable. In Brief 18/11 HMRC appear to consider that sub-trusts are "in general" not s.86 employee benefit trusts and are therefore within the relevant property regime.

However, the contrary argument is that s.86 continues to be satisfied if the appointment is revocable. While the class of beneficiaries under each sub-fund does not include the majority of employees, nevertheless in considering the class of beneficiaries of the trusts as a whole, the trustees must still consider whether they should revoke the deed and benefit other employees. The objects of the trustees' discretion are not limited to the particular employee and his family but continue to include the wider class under the main trust deed because the trustees are required from time to time in exercise of their fiduciary duties to consider whether or not to revoke the deed. On that basis the class of beneficiaries includes not only the family members but the wider employees (albeit the latter might more naturally be regarded as secondary beneficiaries). **49.35**

IV ENTRY CHARGES—GENERAL

A non-close company is not subject to an inheritance tax charge on making contributions to an EBT even if the EBT does not qualify under IHTA 1984 s.86. **49.36**

By contrast, if the company making the contributions to the EBT is a close company then an entry charge could arise on the participators under IHTA 1984 s.94(1) if the close company has made a transfer of value, since that transfer of value is apportioned among the participators according to their respective rights and interests in the company. However, no inheritance tax arises if any of IHTA 1984 ss.10, 12 or 13 apply. HMRC Brief 18/2011 (issued April 4, 2011) sets out HMRC's view on IHT treatment of contributions to employee benefit trusts.[48] If the transfer of value that is apportioned between the individual participators according to their respective interests in the company is below their unused IHT nil rate bands, no charge will arise. Otherwise the charge is 20 per cent on the value transferred in excess of the participator's unused nil rate band. The liability for any inheritance tax charge is the company's under s.94 or, so far as the tax remains unpaid, the participator's under s.202.[49] **49.37**

Before considering ss.10, 12 and 13 it is worth remembering that three other provisions may apply to exempt contributions to the EBT. First, the relevant property regime will not apply (and no entry charges arise) if the participators of the contributing close company are foreign domiciled and the settled property is excluded property.[50] **49.38**

---

[48] This replaced the much criticised Brief 61/2009 (October 14, 2009) which was withdrawn.

[49] Tax is due six months after the end of the month in which the contribution is made, or at the end of April in the year following a contribution made between April 6 and September 30, inclusive.

[50] For the distinction under the relevant property regime between a foreign domiciled close

49.39   Secondly, the contributions may still be exempt from inheritance tax if business property relief is available.[51]

49.40   Third, contributions to the trust *made before April 6, 2006* may have qualified for exemption on the basis that it was a sponsored superannuation scheme and is now an unregistered scheme protected under the transitional A day provisions as an EFRBS (i.e. it is a scheme relating to service in employment and having as one of its objects the provision of retirement or death benefits). That trust will continue to be outside the relevant property regime even if is not within s.86 if no further contributions have been made since April 5, 2006.[52] Payment of trust expenses by the employer after April 5, 2006, will generally not be considered to taint the favoured inheritance tax status of the trust.

Close company apportionments

49.41   A company can make a transfer of value but not a chargeable transfer: see IHTA 1984 s.3(1) which defines a transfer of value as, "*a disposition made by a person*" and s.2(1) defining a chargeable transfer as, "*a transfer of value which is made by an individual*". In the case of close companies, IHTA 1984 Pt IV introduce two deeming provisions into the legislation whereby, *first*, transfers of value made by such a company are attributed to the company's participators and, *secondly*, alterations in the company's share or loan capital (or the rights attaching thereto) which result in value passing out of one person's estate into that of another are deemed to involve a disposition made at the time by the participators.

49.42   So far as the apportionment rules are concerned, *first* there is a set off. A participator to whom a sum is apportioned is entitled to set off against that amount any increase in value in his estate resulting from the company's transfer. While this may seem straightforward, in calculating to what extent the participator's estate has increased in value "*his estate shall be treated as not including any rights or interests in the company*". For instance, if Sid wholly owns Carry-On Ltd which transfers property to him then were it not for this provision, the fall in value of his shares would offset the increase in value occasioned by the transfer, leaving Sid to be taxed on the value of property which becomes comprised in his estate.

49.43   *Secondly*, no apportionment is made if a payment or transfer of assets is brought into account in computing the participator's profit gains or losses for the purposes of income or corporation tax. Loans pose a particular problem: it is thought that a loan repayable on demand will normally not involve the company in making a transfer of value. By contrast a term loan not carrying a commercial rate of interest would involve a transfer of value and, even if the borrower suffers income tax on it, it is difficult to see how it amounts to either a "payment" or "transfer of assets" so that there would appear to be no relief against an apportionment.

company making contributions (which will not in itself avoid the entry charge) and the participators of the company being foreign domiciled see 24.20.

[51] See 49.56.
[52] See para.56(2)(b) Sch.36 FA 2004 which provides transitional relief such that s.151 continues to apply to the EFRBS, so that the funds are not relevant property if no post-April 2006 contributions have been made. See also s.58(1)(d) IHTA 1984.

Section 12

A disposition by a close company to an EBT is not a transfer of value if it is allowable in computing the employer's profits or gains for the purposes of income tax or corporation tax or would be so allowable if those profits or gains were sufficient and fell to be so computed. Although the contribution is revenue in nature and made wholly and exclusively for the purposes of the employer's trade and would therefore be deductible under general principles, as noted earlier, CTA 2009 s.1290 will prevent a corporation tax deduction unless the contribution is taxed as the employee's earnings, i.e. within nine months of the end of year accounting period the money is used by the trustees to meet qualifying expenses or provide qualifying benefits.[53] **49.44**

In HMRC's view there is no "wait and see" provision, so s.12 does not confer inheritance tax exemption unless a deduction is taken in the tax year in which the contribution to the EBT is made.[54] Read literally, this is probably the correct interpretation of s.12, although when the section was drafted it would not have been envisaged that the corporation tax deduction is likely to only become available in a later year. **49.45**

Section 13

If the contribution is not exempted under s.12, it may be possible to obtain relief under s.13 which provides that the contribution is not treated as a transfer of value if the disposition is made by a close company to a trust that satisfies IHTA 1984 s.86, and the persons for whose benefit the trusts permit the property to be applied include all or most of: **49.46**

(i) the persons employed by or holding office with the company; *or*

(ii) the persons employed by or holding office with the company or any one or more subsidiaries of the company.

In Statement of Practice E11 HMRC interpret (ii) as allowing the trust to benefit only employees of a subsidiary company provided that the employees of the holding company comprise a minority of the total employees in subsidiary and holding companies. Hence, a contribution to a fund for the sole benefit of a subsidiary, which does not benefit the majority of the total employees and officers will not qualify:

---

[53] See FA 2003 Sch.24 and *McDonald v Dextra Accessories Ltd* 77 TC 146. The amounts are allowed as "*a deduction for a subsequent period of account so far as – (a) qualifying benefits are provided. . .*" (CTA 2009 s.1290(2)(3)(a)).

[54] See HMRC Brief 18/2011 in which they comment (at para.1.3.2) that "*the relieving effect cannot be given provisionally while waiting to see whether the contribution will become allowable for corporation tax purposes; it is only available to the extent that a deduction is allowable to the company for the tax year in which the contribution is made*".

"where the trust is to benefit employees of a subsidiary of the company making the provision those eligible to benefit must include all or most of the employees and officers of the subsidiary and the employees and officers of the holding company taken as a single class. So it would be possible to exclude all of the officers and employees of the holding company without losing the exemption if they comprised only a minority of the combined class. But the exemption would not be available for a contribution to a fund for the sole benefit of the employees of a small subsidiary. This is because it would otherwise have been easy to create such a situation artificially in order to benefit a favoured group of a company's office holders or employees."

49.47 In addition, the trusts must not permit any of the property to be applied at any time for the benefit of any person who is a participator of five per cent or more in the company (or applied for the benefit of persons connected with the participator).[55] This means that the trust instrument must exclude any possibility of any such benefit being conferred. However, such participators *can* receive a benefit in a form which amounts to a *payment* which is the income of that person for the purposes of income tax or would be the income of such a person if resident in the UK.[56] It is thought that this restriction prevents interest-free loans being made to a participator.[57]

49.48 In Brief 61/2009 HMRC stated:

"Where the trust deed specifically purports to exclude the participators from benefit but nevertheless the participators do benefit in fact, for example:

- *by payment to them of loans or*
- *by assigning funds from the Employee Benefit Trust on sub-trusts for their benefit and that of their family*

then HMRC take the view that s13(2) disapplies s13(1) and the Inheritance Tax charge under s94 arises because the funds have been applied for the benefit of the participators."

It is doubtful this is correct. If the trustees benefit employees who are excluded as beneficiaries this is a breach of trust. In the latest 18/11 Brief, this point has been dropped.

49.49 Where a close company disposes of an asset such as shares to trustees in circumstances such that the disposal is a disposition exempted under IHTA 1984 s.13, then s.239 TCGA 1992 can apply. The effect is that if the disposal is by way of gift or is for a consideration not exceeding the cost of the asset, the disposal and acquisition by the trustees is treated as being made on a no gain, no loss basis. The relief is usually more relevant in relation to gifts of shares to trusts by individual shareholders.[58]

---

[55] In addition s.13(2) excludes any person who has been a participator of 5% or more at any time after, or during the 10 years before, the disposition made by the company into trust.

[56] IHTA 1984 s.13(4)(a). SP E12 comments, *"so even where most of the employees are also major participators or their relatives, an exempt transfer could be made if the trust provided only for income benefit and for the eventual disposal of the capital away from the participators and their families"*.

[57] IHTM 42974.

[58] See 49.53.

This capital gains tax relief is also extended to companies that are not close. As such companies cannot make chargeable transfers, there is no corresponding inheritance tax provision.

Section 10

A distribution to an EBT is not a transfer of value for inheritance tax purposes if it is shown that it was not intended, and was not made in a transaction intended, to confer any gratuitous benefit on any person and it is a transaction which might have been expected to occur if the parties were dealing with each other at arm's length.   **49.50**

If the contributions to an EBT are in lieu of bonuses and are no greater than the bonus would have been, then a s.10 argument may succeed. In *Postlethwaite's Executors v IRC*[59] the Special Commissioner decided that s.10 applied to a £700,000 payment by a company to an offshore unapproved retirement benefit scheme for the benefit of the sole beneficial shareholder. It was decided that the payment did not need to be made under a legal obligation but could be in consideration of past services. It may be argued that the employee benefit trust is merely a means of motivating and retaining good quality service, although this may be harder where all the main employees are also shareholders.   **49.51**

HMRC remain sceptical. They consider that s.10 rarely protects the transfer of funds to an EBT because there is the possibility of a gratuitous benefit (however small!) to, e.g. spouses or children of employees. In Brief 18/2011 they comment that: **49.52**

> "*An EBT is a discretionary trust and to satisfy the conditions of s86 the trustees' discretion must remain unfettered. Given that the potential beneficiaries under an EBT normally include the participators themselves; the employees or former employees; and/or the wives, husbands, civil partners, widows, widowers, surviving civil partners and children and step children under the age of 18 of such employees and former employees; it will normally be difficult to show that the conditions of s10 are met*".

However, in *Postlethwaite* the Special Commissioner rejected HMRC's argument that given the shareholder had died and the sum had become payable to his spouse, this was sufficient to show an intention to confer a gratuitous benefit when the disposition was made.

VI RELIEF FOR DISPOSITIONS BY INDIVIDUALS

Inheritance tax treatment on gifts of shares to employee benefit trust

Under IHTA 1984 s.28(1) a transfer of shares in a close company by an individual is an exempt transfer to the extent that the value transferred is   **49.53**

---

[59] [2007] STC (SCD) 83.

attributable to shares in, or securities of the company which become comprised in a settlement that:

    (i) qualifies under s.86;

    (ii) excludes participators along the lines of s.13(4)[60];

    (iii) in which the trustees:

        (a) hold more than half the ordinary shares in the company; and
        (b) have powers of voting on all questions affecting the company as a whole, which if exercised would yield a majority of the votes capable of being exercised; *and*

    (iv) there are no provisions in any agreement or instrument affecting the company's constitution or management or its shares or securities whereby the condition in para.(iii) above can cease to be satisfied without the trustees' consent.[61]

49.54   This relief is of limited use because of the requirement that the trustees must hold a majority stake but is sometimes used by individuals who wish to ensure that the company will continue to operate after their death when they have no relatives who would be interested in securing its future.

> *Capital gains tax treatment on gifts by individuals to employee benefit trusts*

49.55   The inheritance tax exemption for transfers of shares into settlement by individuals is extended to capital gains tax.[62] The capital gains tax relief applies to any disposal which is, by virtue of IHTA 1984 s.13 deemed not to be a transfer of value or by virtue of IHTA 1984 s.28 deemed to be an exempt transfer. The effect is that the transferor's gain is based on the actual consideration received over cost. So effectively, where shares are gifted or sold for a price not exceeding cost, the consideration received for the disposal is deemed for CGT purposes to be such as gives rise to no gain/no loss. The market value rule is disapplied.

VII BUSINESS AND AGRICULTURAL PROPERTY RELIEF

49.56   What is the position if the close company qualifies for either BPR or APR? These reliefs operate to reduce the value transferred by a transfer of value. The consequences are:

    (i) the shares owned by a participator in the company will benefit from the relief;

    (ii) in the case of a s.94 apportionment there are two transfers of value: the first by the company which is then apportioned to the participators. It

---

[60] See 49.46.
[61] See IHTA 1984 s.75 giving a similar relief from the relevant property exit charge.
[62] TCGA 1992 s.239.

would appear logical to apply business property relief to the first such transfer: viz that made by the company. After all it is only if there is a transfer of value *at that stage* that there is anything to apportion to the participators.[63] What is the relevant property? Presumably the business owned by the company[64] and the transfer of value must be attributable to the value of that relevant business property. As *Nelson Dance*[65] confirms it is not necessary to transfer either the whole business or an interest in it: relief is due if the transfer is merely of assets out of the business. For instance, a cash payment to the EBT where provided that the monies in question are not "excepted assets"[66] the transfer of value may be reduced to nil by the availability of 100 per cent relief.

How do claw back rules in s.113A then operate? If the transferor is the close **49.57** company it is difficult to see that they can be given that a company cannot die as required by s.113A(2)(b) (liquidation is a wholly different matter!) Accordingly to give any meaning to these provisions it would seem that we must look to the deemed transfer of the participator so that it is his death that is relevant.

HMRC have recently accepted that business property relief may be available **49.58** to the close company ("*the company's estate is capable of being relevant business property if it is 'property consisting of a business' (s105(1)(a)*").[67] They stress, however, that:

(i) the business in question must be qualifying within IHTA 1984 s.105(3): accordingly relief is not due if it is wholly or mainly an investment business;

(ii) the property settled into the EBT must not comprise "excepted assets".[68]

VIII DISGUISED REMUNERATION—POSITION FROM DECEMBER 9, 2010[69]

Although commonly referred to as the "disguised remuneration" legislation or **49.59** "Part 7A", it deals—in the words of the statute—with "employment income provided through third parties". As noted previously, it only covers actual office holders and employees, not shadow directors. A typical example is provision through an EBT. The legislation is targeted at arrangements which seek to avoid or defer the payment of income tax. HMRC's draft guidance comments:

---

[63] For a contrary view, see Maston in (2010) P.C.B. at 00.
[64] See IHTA 1984 s.105(1)(a).
[65] *Nelson Dance Family Settlement v RCC* [2008] S.T.C. (SCD) 792 affirmed [2009] S.T.C. 802: see 35.
[66] See IHTA 1984 s.112(2) and *Barclays Bank Trust Co Ltd v IRC* [1998] S.T.C. (SCD) 125.
[67] Brief 18/2011 at para.1.4.
[68] See IHTA 1984 s.112(2).
[69] ITEPA 2003 Pt 7A (inserted by FA 2011 Sch.2). The legislation applies for tax year 2011–12 and following. There are transitional rules and anti-forestalling rules for the period from December 9, 2010 to April 5, 2011.

"Broadly speaking, if third party arrangements are used to provide for what is in substance a reward or recognition, or a loan, in connection with the employee's current, former, or future employment, then an income tax charge arises."[70]

49.60   If the legislation applies then it deems an amount to be employment income ("Part 7A income") and the amount is specifically brought within the ambit of PAYE (so that the tax liability falls on the employer). Although effective from December 9, 2010 certain transitional provisions including some of the provisions dealing with the transfer of assets in specie, do not come into effect until April 6, 2012. Loans made to beneficiaries before December 9, 2010 are not caught by the new regime even if later varied. Loans made between December 9, 2010 and April 5, 2011 inclusive are within the anti-forestalling rules but are excluded to the extent that they are repaid before April 6, 2012. An asset earmarked for an employee before December 9, 2010 does not give rise to a charge but if it is reallocated to another employee after April 6, 2011 this is a relevant step that can give rise to a charge.

49.61   The new rules create a tax charge:

    (i)   on most loans made by third parties including trusts to the employee or former employee;

    (ii) where there is earmarking of money or assets for the employee by a third party; or

    (iii) where there are outright payments of money or transfers of assets to the employee by a third party.

Pre-conditions

49.62   Part 7A income will not arise unless the arrangement *"comes through the s554A gateway"*. In essence:

    (i)   *Condition 1* requires a person (A) to be an employee or a former or prospective employee of another person (B);

    (ii) *Conditions 2 and 3* require there to be an arrangement which it is reasonable to suppose is wholly or partly designed to provide rewards, recognition or loans in connection with A's employment with B (and bear in mind that A might be a former or prospective as well as a current employee). Even if the arrangement meets Condition 1 and either Condition 2 or 3, it will not be through the gateway until a step has been taken which meets Conditions 4 and 5;

    (iii) *Condition 4* requires a relevant third person (e.g. the trustee of an EBT) to take a relevant step. Part 7A will not apply where the employer is providing something directly to the employee and there is no third party involved unless the employer is acting as trustee or the employer undertakes to pay contributions to a relevant third party that are not

---

[70] TEMS 1: Draft Guidance (August 18, 2011).

subject to the annual and lifetime restrictions on pensions tax relief; and

(iv) *Condition 5* it is reasonable to suppose that that step is taken to carry out the relevant arrangement to reward A. The "essence" of the arrangements must always be considered.

EXAMPLE 49.2

In August 2012 Fabio Ltd sets up an EBT for its employees. (This viewed in isolation meets Conditions 1 and 3.) In September the following year, the trustees lend £100,000 to Roger, one of the company's employees. A payment of money by way of loan is a relevant step so that Conditions 4 and 5 are met with the result that Pt 7A income arises. This is employment income of Roger in tax year 2013–14 and tax (collected via PAYE) is payable by Fabio Ltd.

A "relevant step"

A relevant step means one of the three types of step set out in ss.554B–554D: **49.63**

(i) Earmarking (s.554B). This occurs where the third party (including the **49.64** trustees), however informally, identifies a sum of money or asset they hold as being for the benefit of a particular employee. Normally this will lead to a later relevant step (being the payment to A (the employee or person linked to the employee)). There does not need to be any decision as to who is going to benefit from the property subject to the step: simply that there is a step which may lead to A at some later time obtaining some benefit from the property.

(ii) Payment or transfer of an asset—s.554C. This involves a payment of a **49.65** sum of money, including the making of a loan; the transfer of an asset or the granting of a lease which is likely to be for more than 21 years and it must be in favour of a "relevant person" including A or a person "linked" with A; providing security for a loan.[71] The following let-outs should be noted in relation to loans:

(a) As noted previously, loans made before December 9, 2010 are not caught even if the terms are altered, possibly extended. The August draft guidance looks at each alteration on a case by case basis to ascertain whether the alterations are a relevant step.[72]

(b) Writing off an employee benefit trust loan made before December 9, 2010 is not a relevant step under Pt 7A and therefore the tax

---

[71] For person "linked with A" see ITEPA 2003 s.554ZI. It covers persons connected (and formerly connected) with A (for the meaning of "connected" see ITA 2007 s.993); a close company with which A has an association and the 51% subsidiary of such a company.
[72] See TEMP21.

treatment is governed by the rules already in place in ITEPA 2003 ss.62 and 188.

(c) Loans made between December 9, 2010 and April 5, 2011, are subject to Pt7A but only if the loan is still outstanding at April 6, 2012.

49.66   (iii) Making an asset available (s.554D). Where an asset is made available on terms equivalent to transferring the benefit of ownership and enjoyment, tax is charged on the value of the asset transferred. This aims to catch arrangements where A becomes the de facto owner of the asset in all but name. For former employees, s.554D imposes a charge on the entire value of an asset even if it is not owned in all but name if it is made available after the second anniversary of the termination of employment. Although certain employee benefit packages are excluded under s.554G, HMRC insist that such packages must be available to employees generally (interpreted to mean at least 50 per cent of employees of comparable status).

Calculating the Pt 7A income

49.67   It is the value of the relevant step which counts as employment income. Note specifically:

(i) if the relevant step involves a sum of money, its value is that amount. Accordingly if an EBT makes a loan to an employee of £100,000 then the Pt 7A income is £100,000 (in general the repayment of the loan is irrelevant and will not result in repayment of income tax). Tax paid on earmarking steps may become repayable if the arrangements are changed so that the employee ceases to be capable of benefiting from the earmarked property;

(ii) in cases other than a sum of money, the value is the higher of the market value of the asset and the cost of the relevant step;

(iii) these rules take priority over the benefits code:

"if the relevant step is the making of an employment-related loan, the loan give rise to Part 7A income and is not treated as a taxable cheap loan"[73];

(iv) in general the income is A's employment income for the year when the relevant step is taken—although if this is before A's employment starts it counts as A's income in the tax year when it starts;

(v) if A is non-resident in that year the value is reduced to the extent that it is not in respect of duties performed in the UK. But if A had emigrated just before the relevant step then it may be that the step can be attributed to years when A was UK resident so that a full tax charge is imposed[74];

[73] Draft Guidance, TEMP 91.
[74] Draft Guidance, TEMP 94.

(vi) overlap relief may be due if a later relevant step overlaps with an earlier step;

(vii) the employer is obliged to pay PAYE on the value of the relevant step. If the employee does not make good the PAYE to the employer within 90 days then the PAYE itself will become a taxable benefit.

EXAMPLE 49.3

On July 1, 2011 Employer B contributes a freehold property into an offshore EBT.

The property has a market value of £1.2 million. It is immediately allocated into a sub-fund to be applied for the benefit of employee A's spouse and children.

The allocation of the value of £1.2 million into the sub-fund is an earmarking relevant step within s.554B and the arrangement comes through the s.554A gateway. The earmarked amount of £1.2 million counts as employment income of A on July 1, 2011 and is taxable accordingly.

On March 1, 2012 the trustee sells the freehold property and receives net proceeds of £1.1 million.

On March 15, 2012 the trustees uses the proceeds to fund a loan of £1 million to A.

This is a relevant step within s.554C. As the advance of the loan is a step that involves a sum of money, the starting point for working out the value that counts as employment income is the full amount of the sum involved, namely £1 million.

However, this sum is directly referable to the earmarked £1.2 million that has already counted as employment income of A within Pt 7A.

Using the three steps set out above, you calculate the overlap as follows:

Step 1: the value of the earlier relevant step was £1.2 million.

Step 2: the value of the current relevant step is £1 million.

Step 3: you reduce the value calculated at Step 2 by the value calculated at Step 1 (but not beyond nil). So the value of the current relevant step is reduced to nil.

(viii) if a relevant step (other than earmarking) is taken after the death of A the amount which counts as A's employment income instead is the income of the relevant person (for instance, if after the employee's death the EBT trustees make a payment to his widow then she is treated as receiving Pt 7A income).

(ix) There is no exemption under Pt 7A for any employer-financed retirement benefits scheme in respect of contributions on or after April 6, 2011 but the existing tax treatment of payments made out of funds put into an

EFRBS before April 6, 2011 is retained. No step taken under a registered pension scheme can give rise to a charge to income tax under Pt 7A.

EXAMPLE 49.4

In 2016 a retired employee Andrew has a £1 million fund in an EFRBS available to be paid out as a lump sum rather than a pension. The value of the fund as at April 5, 2011 was £700,000. There have been no new employer contributions since April 6, 2011.

The growth in the fund has arisen solely as a result of investment income and capital growth. The growth does not give rise to a charge to income tax under Pt 7A because of the exclusions in ss.554Q and 554R. If the whole amount is paid to Andrew as a lump sum there is no income tax charge under Pt 7A because all the rights accrued before April 6, 2011 including investment income and capital growth. The lump sum is instead potentially liable to income tax as a relevant benefit received under an EFRBS and is therefore employment income under ITEPA 2003 s.394. If Andrew is by then non-UK resident the charge may be mitigated or avoided by a suitable double tax treaty. If the contributions to Andrew's fund were made in part or whole during a period of service overseas then ESC A10[75] may apply to mitigate the s.394 charge.

The future—common problems unresolved

49.68 The scope of Pt 7A has yet to be fully worked out. The following fairly funda- mental areas seem uncertain or at the least very unsatisfactory.

Succession planning

49.69 What is the position in the cases of family companies where the main share- holder wishes to pass on all or part of his shareholding to his children and grandchildren and may choose to do so by outright gift or by gifts into trust? One option (discussed elsewhere in this book) is for him to settle shares in his trading company (qualifying for full business property relief) into a dis- cretionary trust for his issue and their spouses. The settlor is excluded as a beneficiary of the trust. Some of the children of the settlor may be working in the company, some may not. It may well be that (say) the son working in the company ends up receiving more shares from the trust or more benefits from the trust than the daughter who may receive other assets.

49.70 Is there a risk that such an arrangement could be caught by Pt 7A? Clearly there is no desire to reward "A" for the purposes of Pt 7A here (the settlor) since he is excluded from the trust and anyway they are his own shares in the

---

[75] This covers lump sum retirement benefits paid under overseas pension schemes in respect of foreign service.

first place. However, in the common situation where A's children also work in the business, the only let-out appears to be that it is not a relevant arrangement within ITEPA 2003 s.554A(1)(c) because it is not "reasonable" to suppose the arrangement is wholly or partly a means of providing rewards in connection with the children's employment: it is just part of succession planning, i.e. it does not pass what the Revenue called the "s554 A gateway". If this is wrong and there is a relevant arrangement, there will almost inevitably be a relevant step sometime in the future (for example, the payment of a sum of money from the trust to the children) and there is no applicable exclusion at that point.

In most cases it would be hard to see prima facie how the arrangement was: **49.71**

> "*(wholly or partly) a means of providing, or is otherwise concerned (wholly or partly) with the provision of, rewards or recognition or loans in connection with [the children's or the settlor's (as a person linked with the children)] employment. . .with [the company]*",

when no value leaves the company itself as a result of the arrangement. However, a situation where the settlor decides to give more to one child than another (whether shares in the company or other assets) as a specific acknowledgement of his valuable services will be caught. The difficulty is that in family companies there are many scenarios in between these two extremes. It would be ridiculous to tax as earnings contributions of his own shares to trusts simply because some beneficiaries work in the business, even if those who do work in the business end up receiving more.

It may be that the taxpayer can derive assistance from the words "*in essence*" **49.72** in ss.554A(1)(c) and (e). Even where it is arguable that value has been conferred (through a discretionary trust) on a beneficiary partly as son of the settlor and partly as employee of the family company, it may be said that in essence the benefit has been received as son. Section 554A(12) provides that "*all relevant circumstances are to be taken into account in order to get to the essence of the matter*" and in the case where the discretionary beneficiaries include both children who are employees of the company and children who are not, that circumstance would tend to suggest that the essence of the matter was not reward for employment. Even where the working son was the only living beneficiary the authors consider it unlikely that Pt 7A applies in these circumstances since it is not uncommon for a settlor to want to have separate trusts for each branch of the family.[76]

Earmarking before purchase of asset for full consideration

It is not uncommon for employee beneficiaries to sell assets at market value **49.73** to trustees of EBTs. Where the trustees purchase an asset at full market value from an employee beneficiary in exchange for a sum of money, there is a relevant step within s.554C but s.554ZA reduces the value of the relevant step to nil. That provision was specifically inserted in order to provide an exemption

---

[76] Once a relevant third person has decided to reward A in connection with the employment, the choice between doing so with shares in the employer company or, say, cash makes no difference—both can be taxed as earnings.

for sales at market value and was designed to exempt full consideration transactions between trustees and beneficiaries. The example given in the guidance, is of an employee benefit trust buying shares in an employer company from retiring employees and confirming that in these cases, despite there being a payment of a sum of money to the employees, no income tax charge arises.

49.74   However, some practitioners consider there is still a problem under s.554B since a sum of money is being earmarked by the trustees with a view to taking a relevant step under s.554C. Section 554ZA does not say that no relevant step has occurred but merely reduces the value of that relevant step to nil for s.554C purposes.

49.75   HMRC do not seem to regard this as anomalous, stating expressly in their draft guidance that a charge may arise on an earmarking not withstanding that the earmarked assets are subsequently used for an exempt relevant step (other than where the exemption specifically exempts earmarking).[77]

49.76   The employee taxpayer would therefore have to show that there was no earmarking in the first place under s.554B. This section tells us that earmarking is something done with a view to a *"later relevant step"* being carried out. This implies a certain conceptual distinction between the earmarking and the later step, which may not be present where the identification of the money to be used for the purchase, and the purchase itself seem rather to be part of the same transaction.

Appointment from EBT to charity at employee's request

49.77   Where there is a general EBT fund of a substantial value and one or more beneficiaries ask the trustees to exercise their discretions to pay in favour of a UK charity (assume the UK employee is under no financial obligation or duty to pay anything to the charity) and the trustees accede to that request and exercise their discretionary powers to make an outright appointment to the charity, has a relevant step has been taken under s.554C(2) on the basis that the charity has been drawn to the trustees' attention by the employee and the step taken by P at A's request? If so, an appointment made from a IHTA 1984 s.86 employee benefit trust to a UK charity at the request of the employee or former employee, will trigger PAYE and NI on the value of the payment on the basis of this being a relevant step.

---

[77] See draft TEMP20.

CHAPTER 50

TRUSTS AND DIVORCE

- Claiming trust assets on a divorce (**50.03**)
- Nuptial settlements (**50.04**)
- Trusts as a financial resource (**50.19**)
- Pre- and post-nuptial agreements (**50.24**)
- Inherited and pre-marital wealth (**50.34**)
- Anti-alimony and no contest clauses (**50.38**)
- Tax position on divorce (**50.41**)
- Trusts and remittance issues for foreign domiciliaries (**50.54**)

Introduction

Given that approximately two in five marriages end in divorce it is understand-   **50.01**
able that those who have accumulated or inherited wealth wish to keep that
wealth within the family and ensure that the "family property" is not lost on
a divorce. There are three areas where trusts are relevant in a matrimonial
context.

First, parents set up trusts in favour, for instance, of their children to ensure
some continuing control over assets while starting the clock running for inheritance tax purposes. How effective or useful are trusts in protecting assets in
the event of their child's divorce? A couple may settle assets into trusts (particularly offshore trusts) in an attempt to put those assets beyond the reach of
his estranged spouse.

Secondly, trusts are also sometimes set up as part of a divorce settlement.
A spouse may be more inclined to give assets to the other spouse if s/he
knows that they are held in trust for that ex-spouse's benefit rather than
given outright. Hence, trusts can facilitate the reaching of a matrimonial
settlement.

Finally, existing trusts may need to be broken up on divorce so that both
spouses' needs can be satisfied.

The changes to the inheritance tax regime in FA 2006 made the position   **50.02**
more difficult for divorcing couples who might otherwise have used or varied
trusts to settle matrimonial claims. The new remittance rules in FA 2008 have
also presented challenges.

50.03   If a beneficiary under a trust is getting divorced, will the assets of the trust be counted as part of his property? There are a number of possibilities: the Family Courts may regard the trust as a financial resource of the beneficiary or the trust as a nuptial settlement capable of variation by the courts. In cases where the beneficiary has a fixed interest under the trust with no power for the trustees to revoke it, the courts may order the beneficiary to assign such interest to the divorcing spouse.

EXAMPLE 50.1

A is a beneficiary of a trust set up by his father when he was a baby. A has a life interest, is aged 40 and is getting divorced. The settlement will not be regarded as a nuptial settlement[1] but it is possible (although unlikely) that A could be ordered to assign his life interest to his wife so she takes an interest *pur autre vie*.[2] Of course, the right to receive the income is a financial resource.[3] If the trust represents largely inherited or pre-nuptial wealth that is kept segregated from the matrimonial property it appears to be better protected.[4]

II NUPTIAL SETTLEMENTS

The scope of s.24

50.04   The Court has jurisdiction under s.24 of the Matrimonial Causes Act 1973 to make:

"an Order varying for the benefit of the parties of the marriage and of the children of the family or either of them any ante-nuptial or post-nuptial settlement . . . made on the parties to the marriage."

This is much wider than merely taking a trust into consideration as a financial resource because the interests of other beneficiaries, who are not even parties or children of the marriage, can be adversely affected.[5] The courts may

---

[1] See 50.24.

[2] Since A's wife would lose all right to receive the income on A's death such a result might be regarded as unsatisfactory for her. The tax position of interests *pur autre vie* is not straightforward and for assignments after October 5, 2008 has adverse inheritance tax consequences. If A's interest could be ended at any time by the trustees, without the need for his consent, it is obviously not satisfactory for A to assign his interest to his wife since she has something that is for all practical purposes valueless.

[3] How much that resource would be taken into account by a court is discussed further at 50.19.

[4] See 50.34.

[5] In *Brooks v Brooks* [1996] 3 All ER 257 HL, Lord Nicholls expressly stated that the court's power is not confined to varying the interests of the parties to the marriage under the settlement.

also vary a "relevant settlement", i.e. a settlement made during its subsistence or in anticipation of the formation of a civil partnership.[6]

The scope of this power is interpreted widely. The court may make an order **50.05** varying the settlement. Section 24(1)(d) also empowers the court to extinguish or reduce the interest of either party under a marriage settlement other than one in the form of a pension arrangement. Powers of appointment by a party over his own fund can be extinguished although the court will not usually remove the power of appointing new trustees if the relevant party still has an interest in the fund.

In *E v E*[7] the court ordered complete resettlement of part of the trust fund even though it was a Swiss trust with no UK assets and removed both the protector and trustees in relation to that part. The court asserted jurisdiction over non-UK assets, trustees and protectors and were unperturbed by the fact it was a foreign law trust.[8]

The trustees are entitled to be heard in opposition to any proposed variation of their settlement and they can be joined as a third party. The court has to consider whether any proposed variation might adversely affect a minor child of the marriage in which case the child should have the protection of separate representation.[9] A settlement can be varied even if the spouse's interest in it has ended provided it is in existence at decree absolute.[10]

What is a nuptial settlement?

An ante-nuptial or post-nuptial settlement is not defined in legislation but may **50.06** include one made by will or codicil.[11] The terminology, "nuptial settlement", originates from the Matrimonial Causes Act 1859 and is generally considered to involve as a settlement that provides some benefit for either one or both spouses by reference to their married state, i.e. it is in contemplation of marriage although not necessarily in contemplation of a specific marriage. The classic definition of a post-nuptial settlement is found in *Prinsep v Prinsep*[12] where it was stated:

> "*it is upon the husband in the character of husband or upon the wife in the character of wife, or upon both in the character of husband and wife. It should provide for the financial benefit of one or other or both of the spouses as spouses and with reference to their married state.*"

---

[6] CPA 2004 Sch.5 para.7.
[7] [1990] 2 FLR 233.
[8] Article 8 of the Hague Trusts Convention provides for the applicable law of the trust to govern the variation or termination of the trust implying the English Court is precluded from applying s.24 to a settlement governed by an overseas law. However, see *Charalambous* at 50.10 where the English courts invoked art.15.
[9] See *E v E* below and *White v White and King* (1972) 116 Sol Jo 219, CA.
[10] See *Blood v Blood* [1902] LRP 78.
[11] Although it is presumably less likely that a settlement in a will by a deceased person for his child could be regarded as a nuptial settlement since it might be said he has to leave his assets to someone in that situation: he is not making a voluntary gift specifically to provide for the child.
[12] [1929] P 225.

This is not always helpful. A better test may be to ask if the trust has a "nuptial element". For example was it made during the marriage or when the parties were proposing to get married or in contemplation of marriage? Does it hold the matrimonial home?

50.07 There is an important difference between Jersey and the UK in determining what is a nuptial settlement: the Jersey Courts consider this to be limited to a settlement entered into between the parties to the marriage, whereas UK legislation confers jurisdiction over settlements made by anyone provided that it is on the parties to the marriage.[13]

50.08 In *Brooks v Brooks*[14] the term nuptial settlement was to be given a wide meaning and the court stated that s.24 is concerned:

> "with a settlement made on the parties to the marriage. So, broadly stated, the disposition must be one which makes some form of continuing provision for both or either of the parties to a marriage with or without provision for their children."

A settlement can be in respect of a particular marriage and therefore be a nuptial settlement in relation to that marriage even though the spouse of a subsequent marriage might be the person who eventually benefits. (However, curiously, the settlement will only be nuptial in relation to the first marriage because the second marriage will not usually be in contemplation at the time of the first!) The court is entitled to take into account the substance of the transaction but the motive in entering into a settlement is irrelevant.[15] It has no power to vary a settlement made by either spouse which was not made after or in contemplation with the marriage but merely gave the settlor power to appoint an interest to any future spouse.[16] A declaration that the settlement is not a marriage settlement does not prevent it from being a marriage settlement and a settlement with a foreign governing law may be a marriage settlement.

50.09 It is not clear whether the question of whether a settlement is a marriage settlement is determined only at the time the settlement is made or whether subsequent variations or appointments over the settlement can turn a nuptial settlement into a non-nuptial settlement and vice versa. In Example 50.1 the settlement for A is clearly not a nuptial settlement since it was not made on A in the character of husband with reference to his married state. However, if after A's marriage, the trustees varied the trust so as to include the spouse does it become a marriage settlement or does it cease to be such if the spouse and issue are excluded?

50.10 In *Charalambous v Charalambous*[17] the husband argued that the removal of himself and his wife from the class of beneficiaries[18] rendered it no longer a settlement capable of variation under s.24. The High Court rejected this

---

[13] See for example *J v M* [2002] JLR 330 where the trust was not varied in the Jersey Courts and contrast *E v E (financial provision)* [1989] FCR 591 where a discretionary settlement set up by the husband's father, of which H and W were beneficiaries, was varied.

[14] [1996] 3 All ER 257.

[15] *Prescott v Fellowes* [1958] 3 All ER 55, CA where the deed described itself as a settlement on marriage but was nevertheless held not to be a marriage settlement.

[16] *Hargreaves v Hargreaves* [1926] P 42.

[17] [2004] EWCA Civ 1030.

[18] They were removed in January 2001 and the marriage broke down in 2002. The husband had benefited subsequently by substantial loans from the trust to his businesses.

stating that the removal of any "nuptial elements" could not deprive the court of jurisdiction but in any event there were a number of factors which continued to make the trust nuptial. Although husband and wife were removed as beneficiaries they remained joint protectors over the settlement which gave them extensive powers of control; their children remained as beneficiaries and the husband financially benefited from the settlement after he ceased to be a beneficiary. The Court of Appeal upheld the decision but accepted that the removal of the nuptial elements could in some cases deprive the court of jurisdiction, albeit that this had not occurred in the present case. Presumably the reverse could also occur: a non-nuptial settlement could become nuptial if subsequently varied although this point has never been decided. It is assumed that a settlement for the children of the marriage from which the parents are permanently excluded is not a marriage settlement.

The foreign law dimension

50.11 The husband also argued in *Charalambous* that since the settlement was governed by Jersey law, only the Jersey courts had jurisdiction to entertain the wife's claim for an order for variation of the settlement. In the alternative, the husband argued that if the English courts did have jurisdiction only the law of Jersey should be applied (which would have prevented a variation because the trust was on the parties to the marriage but not made by the parties to the marriage). Both the High Court and the Court of Appeal rejected this argument holding that although art.6 of the Hague Convention required that a trust be governed by the law chosen by the settlor, this did not prevent the English court from having jurisdiction in a divorce by virtue of art.15 of the Convention which provided an exception for the "*the personal and proprietary effects of marriage. . .*".[19]

50.12 A separate issue is whether, and if so to what extent, the overseas jurisdiction will recognise and give effect to an English court's order. Questions to consider are:

(a) do local enforcement rules extend to enforcing the English order?

(b) is enforcement prevented by legislation in the relevant country protecting the trust from foreign law orders?

(c) if such legislation exists, is the relevant court nevertheless minded or able to make an order giving effect to the English order?

50.13 The foreign courts have generally rejected interference. In *Minwalla v Minwalla*[20] the Jersey courts criticised an English court's finding that a Jersey law trust was a sham but "as a matter of comity" an order of the English court requiring the trustees of a Jersey trust to transfer significant assets to the wife in satisfaction of an ancillary relief order was upheld. The position might have been different if the trustees had not submitted to the jurisdiction of the English courts. The English Court of Appeal has since stated that the

---

[19] This case preceded the introduction of art.9 of the Trusts (Jersey) Law: see 50.15.
[20] [2005] 1 FLR 771.

assumption of jurisdiction to declare a Jersey trust to be a sham would generally be exorbitant.[21]

50.14 In *Re B Trust*[22] the Jersey Royal Court gave substantive effect to an English judgment but then added:

> "*it would in our view avoid sterile argument and expense to the parties, if the English courts were, in cases involving a Jersey trust, having calculated their award on the basis of the totality of the assets available to the parties, to exercise judicial restraint and to restrain from invoking their jurisdiction under the Matrimonial Causes Act to vary the trust.*"

50.15 Jersey and Guernsey have both introduced legislation to confirm the supremacy of local over foreign law when determining matters affecting local law trusts, their validity and the capacity of those creating them. The new legislation also confirms foreign judgments affecting local law trusts are enforceable only to the extent they are consistent with local law.[23] Any question concerning the validity of a Jersey or Guernsey trust or the existence or extent of powers or the validity of any exercise of such power must be determined under the relevant law and not foreign law. The judgment of a foreign court will not be enforced by a Jersey or Guernsey court if it is inconsistent with these provisions.

50.16 *In the Matter of the IMK Family Trust, Mubarak v Mubarak*[24] the Deputy Bailiff delivered an important judgment on when the Jersey court will enforce an order of the English court purporting to vary the terms of a Jersey trust in the light of art.9. He held that by reason of art.9(4) the Jersey court could not enforce a judgment of the English court under the Matrimonial Causes Act 1973 even where the trustees had submitted to the jurisdiction of the Family Division. If the trustees themselves have no power to make the alteration then the Jersey court will not give effect to such an alteration. Further, the Jersey court has no overriding power to change the terms of a trust; their powers are limited to where it is seen to be in the interests of minor or unborn children to do so. The husband had exercised his powers under the trust to exclude the wife as a beneficiary. The English court's order directed that she should be reinstated as a beneficiary. The Deputy Bailiff held that the court had no power to do this in the light of art.9 of Jersey (Trusts) 1984. However, since in this case all the adult beneficiaries had consented to the English judgment being given effect to in Jersey, although he refused to implement the order of the English court directly, he approved on behalf of the minor and unborn beneficiaries a payment to the wife.[25]

50.17 The position can be summarised as follows:

(a) where the trustees have submitted to the jurisdiction of the English Family Division and taken part in proceedings they may be in some difficulty in arguing subsequently against the enforcement of an order

---

[21] *Charman v Charman* [2007] EWCA Civ 503 and see further 50.19.

[22] [2006] JLR 562.

[23] See Trusts (Jersey) Law 1984 art.9 and the Trusts (Guernsey) Law 2007 s.14 which include provisions similar to those in force in Bermuda and Cayman.

[24] Unreported August 15, 2008.

[25] JRC 136 Royal Court, [2008]; appealed in Jersey: see [2009] 1 FLR 664.

of the Family Division. It was suggested in *Mubarak v Mubarak*[26] that even after the enactment of art.9, where the trustee has submitted to the English jurisdiction, such a judgment is capable of being enforced in Jersey.

(b) even where trustees do not submit to such jurisdiction, the Jersey Court will *not* simply ignore a decision of the Family Division and may well, in the interests of comity, make an order which achieves the overall result contemplated by the Family Division. This was achieved in the *Re B Trust*,[27] not by recognising the variation undertaken by the English court but by directions under art.51 of Trusts (Jersey) Law 1984.[28] It was held that art.9 did not prevent this.

Avoiding a nuptial settlement

It is desirable for settlors to avoid making nuptial settlements. They should **50.18** make provision for their children well before any marriage is in contemplation and not include spouses of the children as potential beneficiaries. In *Hargreaves v Hargreaves*[29] it was held that the settlement was not made in anticipation of marriage even though it was made less than a month before the marriage was agreed. However, it is wise to make provision well before this! Where children are already married, rather than making separate settlements for each married child and his family, the settlor is better advised to create one trust for his children and issue and exclude spouses or widows/widowers. If desired the settlor can insert a power to add beneficiaries. Alternatively, have several trusts but with each trust being expressed as for the benefit of all the issue of the settlor rather than for a particular child.[30]

III TRUSTS AS A FINANCIAL RESOURCE

It is not enough to ensure that a trust is not a nuptial settlement. An interest **50.19** under a trust (even a discretionary interest or a flexible life interest) can be a "financial resource" which the court is entitled to take into account when determining financial provision on divorce. The courts look at the "reality of the situation".[31] They may ignore fine points of trust law. The fact that the beneficiary can be excluded or his interest determined does not mean the courts will disregard the trust if the beneficiary may reasonably expect to receive benefits from it. If there has been a history of capital or income distributions then the trust can be regarded as a financial resource and the beneficiary may face a greater lump sum order or higher maintenance pay-

---

[26] [2009] 1 FLR 664 at [68].
[27] [2006] JLR 562.
[28] See also *Mubarak* at [64]–[72].
[29] [1926] P 42.
[30] It may be worthwhile having separate trusts because of the inheritance tax advantages of pilot trusts: see Ch.41.
[31] *Thomas v Thomas* [1996] 2 FCR 544.

ments against him personally than would have been the case if the trust had not existed. If the beneficiary is excluded from capital but is entitled to income the financial resource may be limited to taking the income into account. Even if the trustees refuse to discharge the beneficiary's liabilities arising from the divorce order the ultimate sanction is that the court can commit the spouse to prison for non-payment.[32]

However, where a spouse receives income from assets over which he has no control the court should not take such income into account other than on the basis of actual receipt. The court should not put improper pressure on the trustees to exercise their discretions for the benefit of the spouse whilst at the same time the court should not be misled by appearances.[33] The position is different where the spouse has effective control over the trust, e.g. is a protector with power to appoint and remove trustees or to consent to distributions of capital.[34] Trustees should not pay funds to a divorcing spouse unless they genuinely believe that doing this is in the best interests of the beneficiary in question.

50.20   As noted above, the courts have taken a robust approach when looking at trusts in divorce cases. In the case of *Charman v Charman*[35] a discretionary offshore trust set up by the husband in 1987 was worth £67 million. The beneficiaries included the settlor/ husband and his issue. The trustees made distributions out of income to Charman until 1997 but not out of capital nor out of capital gains. Charman failed in his argument that the trust assets should be left entirely out of account because they were part of a long term plan to found a "dynastic trust" for the benefit of unborn members of the family. The judge rejected the settlor's contention that this was his true intention:

> *"the failure to indicate any such dynastic plan on the face of any of the letters of wishes . . . is quite frankly incredible"*

Even if that had been Charman's true intention the judge doubted that it would have made much difference. The assets in the trust had been generated during the course of a long marriage and even if the wife had agreed to the husband's plan this would not have assisted Charman's position.

> *"At the end of a marriage of this length for a spouse to be excluded from benefit by such an informal arrangement even if consensual and created at a time when the marriage was sound would be grotesquely unfair."*[36]

---

[32] See the extreme case of *Browne v Browne* [1989] 1 FLR 291, CA. Assets were held in a foreign discretionary trust set up by the wife and all previous requests by the wife for sums to be advanced to her had been granted.

[33] See *Thomas v Thomas*, cited above:

> *"if on the balance of probability the evidence shows that if trustees exercised their discretion to release more capital or income to a husband, the interests of the trust or of other beneficiaries would not be appreciably damaged, the court can assume that a genuine request for the exercise of such discretion would probably be met by a favourable response. In that situation if the court decides that it would be reasonable for a husband to seek to persuade trustees to release more capital or income to him to enable him to make proper financial provision for his children and his former wife, the court would not in so deciding be putting improper pressure on the trustees."*

[34] See *Howard v Howard* [1945] 1 All ER 91, CA and compare *Browne v Browne* (above) and *B v B* [1982] 3 FLR 298, CA and *Minwalla v Minwalla* [2004] EWML 2823; [2005] 1 FLR 771.

[35] [2006] EWHC 1879 (Fam) and the Court of Appeal judgment at [2007] EWHC Civ 503, CA.

[36] It is noteworthy that the Bermudan Trustee (Codan) chose not to participate in the proceedings

The judge went on to make an order for £48 million in favour of the wife, after looking through the trust assets and treating them as if all available to the husband. On appeal, the Court of Appeal approved the decision despite the fact that the husband had received no capital distributions. The trust was not varied but all the assets of the trust were taken into account as a resource of the husband on the basis that the trustees were likely to pay capital if asked. The judgment is not easily enforceable given that the trust assets are overseas and the trustees do not recognise the jurisdiction.

Shams

The Family Division judiciary have generally viewed foreign trusts with scepticism.   **50.21**

> "*These sophisticated offshore structures are very familiar nowadays to the judiciary who have to try them. They neither impress, intimidate nor fool anyone. The Courts have lived with them for years.*"

In some cases trusts have been attacked in divorce proceedings on the basis that they are shams.

In *Minwalla v Minwalla*[37] a husband set up a Jersey trust to hold his shares and properties and the English Family Court held that the trust was void as a sham on the basis that the:

> "*husband never had the slightest intention of respecting even the formalities of the trust deed. . .his intention was that the resources were his and would continue to be his..and the trustees went along with his intentions.*"

In that case the trustees did not see the companies' bank accounts or know where they were operative and were ignorant of the transactions carried out by the companies. When the wife came to enforce the order in Jersey, the Royal Court in "*the Fountain trust case*"[38] did state "*an assumption of jurisdiction by a foreign court to declare a Jersey trust sham to be exorbitant*" although in that case the English order transferring the assets to W *was* enforced.

Lewin on Trusts[39] notes: **50.22**

> "*It is our view that the putative governing law of the trust in each case ought, by analogy with the position in contract, to decide the question of whether or not the apparent arrangements are sham, rather than the lex situs of the trust property concerned. It may also constitute an exorbitant assumption of jurisdiction of an English court to declare a foreign trust a sham, at least in matrimonial proceedings.*"

and refused to produce any information on communications between Codan and Charman on the basis that they did not "consider it in the interests of the trust to participate in a discovery procedure in the English Courts." The UK courts may draw its own adverse conclusions about arrangements even if an order for discovery against a third party may not be enforceable in the overseas court.

[37] [2005] 1 FLR 771 FD.
[38] *In the matter of the Fountain Trust, CI Law Trustees Ltd v Minwalla* [2005] JLR 359.
[39] 18th edn (Sweet & Maxwell 2007), para.4.28.

However, *In the matter of A v A*[40] was a case involving Jersey trustees where the trust was governed by English law and had been set up some years ago by H's parents. Munby J. found that there was no evidence of sham and emphasised the importance of applying the same legal principles as if the question were being determined in the Chancery Division. However, he also stressed that where a spouse sought to obfuscate, hide or mask the reality behind shams, the Family Division should deal with the case robustly, treating:

> "*as one and the same a husband and some corporate or trust structure which it is apparent is simply the alter ego or creation of the husband.*"[41]

Conclusions

50.23   Where the trust was not set up by the divorcing spouse and the assets were settled some time prior to any marriage and for a range of beneficiaries, properly constituted trusts offer some protection on a divorce not least because they provide a clear way of separating pre- and post-marital wealth.[42] The court will often depart from the yardstick of equality where the claimant's financial needs can be met out of other property if there are pre-acquired or inherited assets. Trusts make the existence of the "pre-marital" assets held by each party before the marriage clearer because they are necessarily segregated from personal assets.[43]

---

[40] [2007] EWHC 99 (Fam).

[41] At [18].

[42] See 50.34.

[43] For the general approach of the Courts on divorce see *Miller* and *McFarlane* [2006] UKHL 24. The court looks first at needs with a cross test to the yardstick of equality. The overriding requirement is to produce a fair outcome and essentially "*to give each party an equal start on the road to independent living.*" That does not necessarily mean an equal split of assets. In assessing fairness, one has to look at need, compensation and sharing. *Compensation* is to re-address actual or prospective significant economic disparity between the parties arising from the way they conducted their marriage. For example, where one party has sacrificed their own career or income/capital earning for the benefit of the other spouse. What Baroness Hale described as compensation for "*relationship generated disadvantage*". The third strand is *sharing*. This is based on "*the concept of equality permeating marriage as understood today*" and Lord Nicholls described a husband and wife being now for all practical purposes equal partners in marriage. They commit themselves to sharing their lives, to living and working together and so when the partnership ends each is entitled to an equal share of the assets of the partnership unless there is good reason to the contrary. "*The yardstick of equality is to be applied as an aid not a rule*". Baroness Hale referred to it as sharing the fruits of the matrimonial partnership. In *Miller* several categories of property were distinguished. Lord Nicholls broke these down as follows:

(a) acquired during the marriage otherwise than by inheritance or gift. This is termed the financial product of the parties' common endeavour. Such matrimonial property includes property acquired during periods of pre-marital cohabitation and engagement. Lord Nicholls did not distinguish between matrimonial "family" assets and matrimonial "business and investment" assets. The entitlement of each party to a share of these matrimonial assets was the same however long or short the marriage may have been. In other words the matrimonial property of a short marriage is to be shared—this was the rationale in *Miller*.

(b) the family home is normally regarded as matrimonial property even if brought into the

IV PRE- AND POST-NUPTIAL AGREEMENTS

The position before Radmacher

Where one of the parties is the beneficiary of numerous trusts or has other **50.24**
substantial wealth then it will be desirable to have a pre-nuptial agreement
(PNA) prior to the marriage. The English courts do not ignore a PNA. Until
recently the position has been that they are not obliged to follow its terms and
maintained strongly that their jurisdiction under the Matrimonial Causes Act
1973 cannot be excluded. They can merely take the terms of the PNA into
account as one relevant factor when deciding how to exercise their discretions.
However, it was generally regarded only as one factor and in the case of a long
marriage or where there were children the extent to which it was taken into
account was doubtful.

As a minimum, the key was always to demonstrate that each party had **50.25**
signed the document willingly and in full knowledge. So it was thought that for
a PNA to be considered at all complete disclosure would have to be made of
all wealth before the agreement was signed, including trusts of which a party
was a potential or actual beneficiary along with details of benefits received.

One advantage of a PNA was that it could reduce the need for lengthy dis- **50.26**
closure and valuations in court proceedings. In *Crossley v Crossley*[44] the Court
of Appeal ruled that it is possible to short circuit normal Court procedures
when there is a pre-nuptial agreement, it dismissed Mrs Crossley's appeal
against the High Court decision which ruled that the case could be heard in a
one day hearing. Stuart Crossley successfully requested that the Court "short-
circuit" the normal procedures, given it was a short, childless marriage, both
parties had independent wealth, and a pre-nuptial agreement was in place.

The current position

The ground rules on nuptial agreements generally changed following the **50.27**
Supreme Court decision in *Radmacher v Granatino*.[45] By a majority of eight

marriage by only one of them. In addition, family assets such as bank accounts will generally be regarded as matrimonial property.

(c) for non-matrimonial property, the length of the marriage is of relevance. In the case of
a short marriage, fairness may require that the claimant is not entitled to a share of the
non-matrimonial property and in these circumstances there may be a good reason for
departing from equality. Hence inheritances and gifts and other property that each party
brings to the marriage (apart from the matrimonial home) are less likely to be subject to
a claim or division on a short marriage. Baroness Hale seemed to endorse this part of the
approach in that she noted that if the assets are not family assets or not generated by the
joint efforts of the parties then the duration of the marriage, (i.e. its shortness) may justify
a departure from the yardstick of equality (see [153]).

In Miller the wife obtained an order for £5 million against personal assets of approximately
£20 million after a three-year marriage so the percentage was about 25%.
[44] [2005] EWCA Civ 1581; [2007] EWCA Civ 1491.
[45] [2008] EWCA Civ 1304; (Rev 1) [2009] EWCA Civ 649; (Rev 4) [2010] UKSC 42.

to one the Supreme Court held a husband bound by a German-style marriage contract which he had signed before his marriage at the insistence of his wife's wealthy family. That agreement essentially barred him from making any financial claims on divorce, and would have been binding on the parties in Germany (where the wife was from) and in France (where the husband was from).

50.28   The parties were married for eight years and had two children. Mr Granatino brought financial claims during the divorce process, seeking an order against his wife for housing and an income fund for his ongoing support. He had been an investment banker during the marriage, but at the time of the divorce was studying for a post-graduate degree. The wife owned shares in a family company and her total assets (which she had received from her family) amounted to around £100 million. The High Court awarded the husband £5.5 million. On appeal by the wife, the Court of Appeal found that the husband was a "man of the world" and that despite the fact there had been no financial disclosure or independent legal advice (or indeed a translation of the documents from German), he knew the effect of what he was signing. Accordingly they awarded him £2.2 million by way of a housing fund on loan until the youngest child reached the age of 22 together with a capitalised fund for child maintenance to enable him to support the children when they were with him. On appeal, the Supreme Court dismissed Mr Granatino's appeal, effectively holding him to the terms of the agreement he had signed, subject to some financial provision being made to enable him to satisfy his responsibilities as a father.

50.29   The majority judgment in the Supreme Court declared that the divorce court should:

> *"give effect to a nuptial agreement that is freely entered into by each party with a full appreciation of its implications, unless in the circumstances prevailing it would not be fair to hold the parties to their agreement."*

The criteria for "fairness" would be assessed on a case-by-case basis. The Supreme Court removed the distinction between pre-nuptial and post-nuptial agreements apparently established in *Macleod* discussed below and held that neither type of agreement was contrary to public policy.

Post-nuptial agreements

50.30   In *MacLeod v MacLeod*[46] the Privy Council recognised and upheld a post-nuptial agreement. The couple were American and were married in Florida in 1994 when the husband was 49 and the wife 27. The husband had amassed significant wealth prior to the marriage and, although he retired the following year at age 50 his assets doubled in value during the marriage. The parties moved to the Isle of Man in 1995 and they had five children during their 10-year marriage, aged between 7 and 13 years at the time of the divorce hearing. The couple entered into a pre-nuptial agreement on the day of the wedding (which would have been binding in Florida) which was subsequently varied by two post-nuptial agreements. The second and final deed was entered

---

[46] [2008] UKPC (Isle of Man) 64.

after 14 months of negotiations (with the benefit of legal advice), when the marriage was already in difficulties. That last agreement set out the financial provision that would be made for the wife, in the event of divorce, including capital totalling £1.8 million.

On divorce, the wife argued that all three documents should be disregarded and sought 30 per cent of the husband's pre-marital wealth and 50 per cent of the increase in his assets during the marriage: a claim totalling in the region of £5.6 million. The husband argued that the provision for the wife, as set out in the agreement, should be upheld, although he conceded that an additional sum was needed to provide housing for the children (and the wife as mother) during their minority. However, this should be by way of trust and not as an outright payment to her.

At the first hearing in the Isle of Man, the court held that provision for the wife should be in accordance with the post-nuptial agreement. As to the children they ordered the husband to provide a lump sum of £1.125 million to be paid to the wife, so that she could purchase accommodation sufficient to house her and the five children. The lump sum was to be paid outright and without any restrictions as to how the funds should be invested. Both parties appealed the decision unsuccessfully. The husband then proceeded with his case to the Privy Council wanting the award for housing to be held in trust.

The Privy Council distinguished between pre- and post-nuptial agreements **50.31** and found that there was nothing to stop a couple entering into binding contractual financial arrangements after their marriage governing their life together or the terms of any future separation. Unlike pre-nuptial agreements such contracts would have full legal efficacy if entered into by deed following legal advice and in the absence of undue influence. The "old rule" providing that post-nuptial agreements were contrary to public policy was contrary to modern legal thinking. They acknowledged that although the arrangements lacked generosity of provision for the wife, being much less than she could have expected had there been no agreement, there was no basis for interfering with them.

However, the Privy Council did vary the terms of the parties' agreement in relation to financial provision for the children, finding that it did not provide proper financial arrangements for them. It reversed the earlier decision of the Isle of Man Court that the additional capital provision for housing should go to the wife outright and instead provided that the housing fund be by way of trust, as the husband had wanted.

Taking into account both cases, the current position is therefore that nuptial **50.32** agreements (whether made before or after marriage) are not contractually binding on the English divorce court, and the court will retain its overarching discretion to determine the financial provision to be made on divorce. However, they are not against public policy and the burden is no longer on the financially stronger party to justify that the terms of a nuptial agreement should be upheld. Rather the onus is on the person seeking to get out of the agreement to demonstrate why they should not be held to its terms. The court will look at the effect of the agreement at the breakdown of the marriage, and will not uphold an agreement which results in one partner being left in a position of real need nor where circumstances have radically changed. It is apparently not necessary to have detailed disclosure with independent advice for the agreement to be valid provided the parties understand what they are signing and are not under undue influence.

50.33 On January 11, 2011 the Law Commission published a consultation paper on "Marital Property Agreements" which invited comments on their proposals for reform. These include making qualifying nuptial agreements which have been fairly entered into contractually enforceable providing that the pre-requisites of both parties having had independent legal advice and made full and frank financial disclosure are in place. However, they further suggest that such an agreement would not be enforceable in certain circumstances, for example if it does not meet the needs of the children or leaves a spouse reliant on state benefits.

V INHERITED AND PRE-MARITAL WEALTH

50.34 It remains unclear as to how inherited wealth (including wealth held in trust) should be dealt with on divorce. In the words of Munby J. in *P v P*[47]:

> "*There is inherited property and inherited property. Sometimes. . .the fact that certain property was inherited will count for little. . .on other occasions the fact may be of the greatest significance.*"

Two recent cases, *Robson v Robson*[48] and *Jones v Jones*[49] have been heard by the Court of Appeal with different results. In *Robson* almost the entirety of the husband's wealth (£22 million) was accumulated before the marriage and was inherited from his father. The husband inherited an estate in Oxfordshire on which the family home was situated; a tenancy in respect of the farm estate; an estate in the Scottish Highlands; two London properties and two parcels of development land. The husband appealed against an award in the wife's favour of £8 million, and it was reduced by the Court of Appeal to £7 million. Although the assets were inherited from the husband's family, the parties had jointly elected to live off them.

50.35 The Court of Appeal set down the following principles to be applied in cases involving inherited assets:

(i) the court's overriding objective in the exercise of its discretion must always be to achieve a fair result;

(ii) reference to the principles of need, compensation and sharing (established in the case of *Miller and Macfarlane*[50]) will usually guide the search for fairness;

(iii) the fact that wealth is inherited and not earned does not justify its being treated differently from wealth accrued during the marriage. The nature of the inheritance is relevant, as is the duration of the marriage, together

---

[47] [2005] 1 FLR 576.
[48] [2011] EWCA Civ 1771.
[49] [2011] EWCA Civ 41.
[50] [2006] UKHL 24.

with for how long and in what ways the inheritance has been enjoyed by the parties. The more the wealth has been enjoyed (in substance and in duration) by the married couple the less fair it is to leave it out of account. However:

"where property is acquired before the marriage, or when inherited property is acquired during the marriage, thus coming from a source external to the marriage, then it may be said that the spouse to whom it is given should in fairness be allowed to keep it. On the other hand, the more and the longer that wealth has been enjoyed, the less fair it is that it should be ring-fenced and excluded from distribution so as to render it unavailable to meet the claimant's financial needs generated by the relationship."

(iv) in the exercise of its discretion, the court will strive to meet the needs of both parties even if that results in the division of property and sale of inherited assets.

50.36 In *Jones* the wealth was not inherited but had been partially acquired before the marriage. The parties had been married (a second marriage) for 10 years with no children. The husband's business had been in existence approximately 10 years before the marriage. It was sold for £25 million. The High Court made an award in favour of the husband to reflect the value of the business at the date of the marriage. Although he had no evidence before him on the point, Charles J. found that 60 per cent of the value of the business had been built up before the marriage (£15 million). The wife therefore received £5 million, which was 50 per cent of the difference between that value and the value of the assets as at the date of the trial. This amounted to approximately 20 per cent of the total assets. On appeal by the wife, the Court of Appeal increased her award to £8 million. The reason for this increase was that the court found the value of the business at the date of the marriage to be £9 million rather than £15 million. Fifty per cent of the difference between the revised value of £9 million and the total assets of £25 million was £8 million. The debate was therefore over the value to be attributed to the non-matrimonial assets, i.e. the value of the business as at the date of the marriage.

50.37 If the inherited or pre-marital wealth has been ring-fenced and the couple have not lived off the wealth to any significant extent it is far more likely to be protected in divorce proceedings. In *K v L*[51] court upheld the First Instance decision awarding a lump sum of £5 million to the husband of a 20-year marriage. The wife owned a share in a family business worth £57.4 million and this represented the bulk of the total asset base of £59 million. Crucially the couple had a very modest lifestyle: the family home was worth £300,000 and they spent £80,000 a year. The Court of Appeal held that the wife's shareholding had been ring-fenced as non-matrimonial property and was not intermingled with matrimonial assets. Departure from equal division may even be the usual result in relation to non-matrimonial assets provided the other spouse's needs can be met out of the matrimonial assets.

[51] [2011] EWCA Civ 550.

VI ANTI-ALIMONY AND NO CONTEST CLAUSES

50.38   In some trusts it is provided that trustees cannot exercise powers in favour of a beneficiary if they are doing so to enable him to satisfy claims of a divorcing spouse. The difficulty is that in practice the court may ignore the effect of such a clause. It may be desirable therefore to provide that any beneficiary about to marry must enter into a nuptial agreement before they can be considered eligible to receive future distributions. This gives the beneficiary a good reason to enter into negotiations with the prospective spouse without offence!

50.39   No contest clauses are another device commonly used in offshore trusts. Typically the beneficiary forfeits his interest if he contests the validity of a trust or the trustees' actions. The aim is to discourage litigation by discouraging a divorced spouse or widow from challenging the trustees' actions particularly where these might involve that spouse's issue.[52] For example, the trustees may choose to exclude the spouse of the divorced beneficiary from any future benefit and may also exclude the spouse's issue or limit their benefits. In some cases a no-contest clause will not only purport to exclude the challenging spouse but also his issue.

50.40   A no-contest clause must be certain and reasonable. It appears that a clause preventing the beneficiary from contesting the validity of the trust or a conveyance to the trust is valid but a clause preventing the beneficiary from challenging any exercise of the decision of the trustees may be invalid since this would prevent the beneficiaries being able to enforce the "irreducible core of obligations" that trustees always owe to them.

VII TAX POSITION ON DIVORCE

Capital gains tax

50.41   The main problem for divorcing couples before March 22, 2006 was capital gains tax rather than inheritance tax. Whilst spouses are living together any transfer of assets between them takes place on a no gain no loss basis.[53] This treatment continues for inter-spousal transfers made in the tax year of separation. However, if assets are transferred after the tax year of separation, s.58 no longer applies and such disposals are treated as taking place at market value.[54]

EXAMPLE 50.2

H and W separate in May 2006. Provided that any transfers take place between them before April 6, 2007 they are treated as taking place on

---

[52] *AN v Barclays Private Banking and Trust (Cayman) Ltd* 9 ITELR 630.
[53] TCGA 1992 s.58.
[54] Husband and wife remain connected persons until decree absolute: see TCGA 1992 s.286.

a no gain no loss basis. After April 5, 2007 the transfers are treated as taking place at market value.

Inheritance tax

By contrast, assets can be transferred between husband and wife without attracting an inheritance tax charge up to decree absolute, whether or not they are separated.[55] Only after decree absolute the exemption in s.18 does not apply although two statutory exemptions may still provide relief. First, IHTA 1984 s.10 which provides that a transfer of assets not intended to confer any gratuitous benefit will not be a transfer of value. This exemption will cover transfers of property pursuant to court orders. It can include transfers into trust but not variations of existing interests under trust.[56]

50.42

The second exemption is IHTA 1984 s.11 which provides that a disposition will not be a transfer of value if it is made by one party to the marriage (or civil partnership) in favour of the other party or to a child of either party to the marriage or former marriage and is:

50.43

(i) for the maintenance of the other party; or

(ii) for the maintenance, education or training of the child for a period ending not later than the year ending April 5, in which the child attains 18, or if later, finishes full time education.

In view of the definition of marriage and civil partnership in s.11(6), the relief can apply to dispositions for the maintenance of a divorced spouse or civil partner made on the occasion of the dissolution or annulment of a marriage/civil partnership and the variation of a disposition so made, e.g. on the remarriage of the other party.

In most cases dispositions made on divorce or on termination of a civil partnership are made following arms length negotiations or under the terms of a court order and so are not treated as transfers of value either because they come within s.10 or are not dispositions anyway because the liability is imposed by law under a court order.

50.44

Section 11 is therefore of more use in the context of provision for children.[57] However, it could be useful after a divorce if the parties wish to change maintenance orders between themselves without necessarily obtaining a court order. The authors have seen it claimed successfully where an ongoing maintenance order was capitalised into a lump sum and the husband who provided the sum died within seven years.

---

[55] IHTA 1984 s.18. The Law Society has in the past made representations that the capital gains tax treatment should be similarly extended beyond the tax year of separation.

[56] See Ch.26 and 50.45.

[57] For further consideration of s.11 see Example 26.14.

50.45 In many "big money" cases, it will be desirable that some of the property transferred to the spouse (usually the wife) is retained in trust for her, rather than given to her outright. The other spouse (usually the husband) then feels that there is some guarantee that the assets will eventually pass to the children of the marriage rather than to a future partner of his ex-spouse.

Before FA 2006, a husband could have settled the assets on interest in possession trusts for the spouse and spouse exemption would have been available if the transfer took place before decree absolute. The trust would have been outside the relevant property regime. The spouse could then enjoy the income and use of the assets with control by the trustees and the assets would then pass on to the children on her death.

Since March 22, 2006 all inter vivos transfers into trusts, whether or not interest in possession for the spouse, are chargeable transfers unless the spouse is disabled.[58] The trust property will accordingly fall within the relevant property regime. So a transfer of £500,000 into an interest in possession trust for the spouse may attract a 20 per cent inheritance tax charge on the excess above the £325,000 threshold and the trust will be subject to 10-year anniversary charges and exit charges. However, transfers into trust for a spouse which are made as part of arm's length negotiations or pursuant to a court order are likely to be protected by the s.10 exemption (no gratuitous intention) or alternatively it may be argued that they do not involve a disposition and so cannot involve a transfer of value. The transfer of property is merely in satisfaction of an existing liability imposed by law. Hence, in the above example there should be no immediate inheritance tax to pay on setting up the trust. However, the settled property will be subject to 10-year and exit charges. On the other hand there is no inheritance tax payable on the death of the spouse who has the interest in possession since it is not a qualifying interest in possession.[59] This assumes that the spouse has not "purchased" the interest in possession and is therefore not caught by FA 2010, s.53: see 26.15.

---

[58] See Ch.36.

[59] HMRC generally accept that s.10 applies where each party to the divorce is independently advised so that there is strong evidence of negotiation between the parties. Formerly they considered that this also meant that any transfer by one spouse to the other of assets as part of a divorce settlement was for money or money's worth because the assets were transferred in return for the surrender by the transferee of rights over other property which he would otherwise have been able to exercise. Hence no CGT hold-over relief was available even if the transfer was made pursuant to a court order under Matrimonial Causes Act 1973 on the grounds that the recipient spouse gave actual consideration in the form of surrendered rights which he could otherwise have exercised to obtain alternative financial provision. However, since July 31, 2002 as a result of *G v G* [2002] EWML 1339; [2002] 2 FLR 1143, hold-over relief should be available on transfers of business assets made under Court Order. In *G v G* the court held that neither party was giving up assets or rights as a quid pro quo: the court was exercising the statutory powers vested in it by law. Hence neither party was giving money or money's worth for capital gains tax purposes. HMRC will still not give hold-over relief where there is no recourse to the courts. Does *G v G* undermine the case for s.10 inheritance tax exemption: if hold-over relief is available on transfers pursuant to a court order does the transaction fall within s.10? Presumably there would still be no inheritance tax problem because there is no disposition made by the parties in circumstances where the transfer is made pursuant to court order and therefore no transfer of value.

Example 50.3

In June 2011, as directed by court order in matrimonial proceedings, Mr A settles £10 million on life interest trusts for his wife. This creates a relevant property settlement but there should be no inheritance tax charge since the transfer is protected under s.10. However, every 10 years the trust will suffer a 10-year charge and there will be an exit charge on final termination. The quantum of this tax is unknown in June 2011. It will depend on the value of the settled property and the rate of tax at those relevant 10-year anniversaries.

There is a tension between the practical advantages a trust can bring and the inheritance tax 10-year and exit charges. If a trust is set up there will need to be some provision made as to how future charges will be paid. The IHT rate may increase in future. Is the settlor prepared to pay the charges or set up a cash fund to pay the future charges? **50.46**

The question is whether the advantages of holding assets in trust (and avoiding a 40 per cent inheritance tax charge on the spouse's death) are worth the cost of 10-year charges. Obviously if the spouse dies unexpectedly young it will be better to have held the asset in trust because there is no inheritance tax on that death. Further a trust will result in much greater control over the assets ensuring that they can ultimately pass to the children of the marriage.

If an express trust is not wanted care must be taken to ensure that one is not set up inadvertently. For example, if the court order requires the wife to be able to use of an asset only for her life and to keep the assets separate or for her interest to be terminable in the event of certain conditions such as remarriage, a trust has been set up. Where some form of continuing control over the asset is required it may be worth considering lending cash to the spouse (e.g. to fund a house purchase) but making the loan interest-free and repayable only on the spouse's death. The loan can be secured on the house purchased with the cash by the spouse. Even this route can pose difficulties. For instance, what happens if the spouse decides to move abroad and uses the proceeds to reinvest in a foreign house? How will the loan be secured? Similarly if the spouse remarries and buys a house jointly with her new husband, how will the loan be secured? **50.47**

Matrimonial home

For many divorcing couples the matrimonial home is their most significant asset. As part of the divorce settlement, it is usual for the matrimonial home to be sold and the proceeds split or for one spouse to transfer his interest in it to the other. The sale of the home might occur immediately after the divorce or it might be deferred typically under what is known as a *Mesher* order.[60] HMRC took the view that a *Mesher* order created a settlement[61] and the transfer of **50.48**

---

[60] Called after *Mesher v Mesher and Hall* [1980] 1 All ER 126 in which the court ordered that a house which was jointly owned should be held in trust for both spouses in equal shares and should not be sold until the youngest child reached 17. The wife was at liberty to live in the house rent-free subject to paying all outgoings.

[61] See CGTM 65367.

the house from either or both spouses to themselves as trustees to hold on trust was a disposal for capital gains tax purposes, deemed to be at market value. In practice, principal private residence relief is likely to prevent any capital gains tax charge assuming the transfer into trust takes place within three years of either spouse having vacated the property.[62] When the *Mesher* order terminates (on the children reaching the specified age) the trust ends and there is a deemed disposal back to the spouses (alternatively the order may provide that the house is then to be sold by the trustees within a stated time after a child reaches 18). However, the trustees are entitled to principal private residence relief on the entire gain because one spouse, as a beneficiary, has occupied the house throughout the period of the settlement.[63]

EXAMPLE 50.4

> H and W separate and the house is the main asset. It is agreed that when the children are 18 it will be sold and the proceeds divided between H and W equally. If H and W remain joint owners then on sale (more than three years after H ceases to occupy the property),[64] H will suffer a capital gains tax charge. Before March 22, 2006 the house could instead have been put into an interest in possession trust for wife so that s.225 relief applied to relieve the whole gain, even though part of the proceeds was eventually distributed to H.[65] This is no longer possible without considering the inheritance tax implications. The transfer by both of them is a chargeable transfer and the trust is within the relevant property regime.

Dividing trust assets

50.49 Divorce settlements may not simply involve one spouse transferring assets outright to the other or settling assets owned on trust for the other. The principal financial resource of the family may be the assets already contained in a settlement where one spouse has a life interest and it is desired that the trust should be varied to allow the other spouse to receive benefits. The trustees may not have power to advance capital to either spouse and in any event may be

---

[62] In other cases TCGA 1992 s.225B (enacting ESC D6) may apply and prevent a charge.

[63] TCGA 1992 s.225. The other common arrangement—a deferred charge—has become less popular although remains unaffected by Sch.20. With a deferred charge, one spouse has 100 per cent of the matrimonial home vested in them whilst the other spouse takes a charge, either for a fixed or variable amount. The order will specify when the charge can be realised, for example, when the other spouse dies or remarries or when the children attain a specified age or finish full time education. The tax treatment of a deferred charge is less favourable than a *Mesher* order since when the charge is realised HMRC's view is that the charge is an asset when it is over a percentage of the sale proceeds rather than a fixed amount and the capital gain is calculated on the difference between the amount received and the value of the charge when it was created. If the charge is for a fixed amount the spouse has probably disposed of his entire interest in the house in return for the charge and this charge represents a debt falling within s.251(1) of TCGA 1992.

[64] Because the final 36 months of ownership counts as a period of residence: see TCGA 1992 s.223(1).

[65] Reverter to settlor relief would have applied: see Ch.37.

reluctant to do so if the settlor was, say a spouse's father, who wanted capital to pass to grandchildren. The trust assets may not be readily realisable or the trust may have been offshore and contain significant stockpiled gains which will make an outright distribution of capital expensive. In these circumstances, how can the trust assets best be rearranged?

EXAMPLE 50.5

(1) A has been married for 20 years and has a life interest in a settlement set up by his father some years before the marriage. In June 2011, A separates from his wife and since the main family wealth is in the trust it is agreed that A will assign part of his life interest to his wife so that she takes an interest *pur autre vie*. In these circumstances s.10 provides no protection even if the disposition takes place as part of arms' length negotiations because that section only relieves dispositions that would otherwise have been transfers of value. The disposal of a life interest under IHTA 1984 s.51 is taxed as if A had made a transfer of value but he has not actually made a transfer of value[66]: his interest is merely treated as coming to an end. A will therefore make an immediately chargeable transfer of value.

(2) Contrast the position if A did not assign his life interest but the trustees instead terminated that interest in part and appointed an interest in possession to A's spouse in exercise of their overriding powers. Now A's interest has actually come to an end so s.52 applies. Under s.52(1), tax is charged as if A had made a transfer of value. Can A rely on the s.10 exemption? It is thought not. Although A is deemed to have made a transfer of value the disposition has been made by the trustees. No disposition is made by A of his interest. Further it is difficult to argue that a disposition by the trustees is not intended to confer a benefit on anyone.[67]

In the above example if the couple are still married it would be possible to obtain spouse exemption if the trustees terminated A's interest in part and advance the property to the spouse absolutely. Otherwise for divorces after October 5, 2008[68] the couple will need to consider the potential inheritance tax charges arising both on varying an existing trust to give an interest in possession for A's spouse and in terms of 10-year anniversary charges.   **50.50**

Hence, variations of existing settlements have become more problematic for inheritance tax purposes where the settlor is UK domiciled. It may be possible to argue that a variation of a settlement which gives the spouse a life interest is exempt under IHTA 1984 s.11. HMRC comment in IHTM 4173:   **50.51**

"*if a settlement is made on divorce or termination of a civil partnership or is a variation of an existing settlement, in so far as it is made in satisfaction*

---

[66] IHTA 1984 s.51(1)(a).
[67] See Ch.26.
[68] When it was no longer possible to create a transitional serial interest (a TSI) in favour of the spouse.

of a claim for maintenance of a former spouse or civil partner it is within s11(1)(a) IHTA."

If A was the settlor and not UK domiciled or deemed domiciled then there is no inheritance tax problem about varying existing trusts unless these hold UK situated assets directly.

50.52 In one respect the tax position has improved. Consider a UK resident trust where A is entitled to an interest in possession and he is the settlor. It is agreed in divorce proceedings that a life interest should be given to his wife in part of the trust assets. Although A may be excluded from the fund for his wife, before April 6, 2008 he was still taxed on all the gains arising (although not the income of her fund) even after divorce if he could continue to benefit from any part of the trust (whether or not excluded from her fund). It was not possible to resettle the assets in a separate UK resident trust and obtain favourable inheritance tax treatment because transitional serial interest relief was not available. In these circumstances it was sometimes appropriate to make a sub-fund election under FA 2006 Sch.12.[69]

From April 6, 2008 it does not matter if A continues to have an interest in the UK resident trust for capital gains tax purposes. He is still not taxed on any trust gains which are now taxed only on the trustees. Of course capital gains tax issues are still a problem in the case of offshore settlements since any gains are taxed on A as settlor if he, his spouse, children or grandchildren can benefit from any part of the trust fund.[70]

50.53 Although a transfer on interest in possession trusts from A to A's spouse before October 6, 2008 would have been spouse exempt[71] and A's interest has terminated, the reservation of benefit rules should not apply to A,[72] so that he can continue to be a potential beneficiary in the event of his wife's death. However, the POA regime could apply to A if the wife's part of the trust holds intangibles and A is the settlor. Hence it is desirable that A is excluded from the wife's fund if he is the settlor although if the trust is offshore he will want to retain a right to reimbursement for any capital gains tax payable by him on gains realised from his wife's fund.

VIII TRUSTS AND REMITTANCE ISSUES FOR FOREIGN DOMICILIARIES

50.54 In Chs 5 and 8 we considered the income tax regime of non-resident trusts and the taxation of foreign domiciliaries. This section considers how foreign domiciliaries can best discharge their financial obligations on divorce. Problems arise if the foreign domiciliary's wealth is mainly situated abroad and comprises untaxed income or foreign chargeable gains. Significant sums are also often tied up in trusts set up by foreign domiciliaries for tax and succession reasons.[73] The paying spouse (assume H for the purposes of this discussion)

---

[69] See Ch.12 and Example 19.10.
[70] See Ch.19 and Example 19.10.
[71] TCGA 1992 s.72(1) (being a TSI).
[72] See FA 1986 s.102(5) and Ch.33.
[73] See Ch.29 for excluded property settlements with inheritance tax advantages and Ch.19 for the capital gains tax advantages.

may not want to use "clean" capital funds to pay W or may have insufficient funds. What is the tax treatment of payments by H to W if he gives cash to her abroad in satisfaction of his financial claims and such cash is derived from trust distributions to H which may be relevant foreign income or trust gains? Is this a taxable remittance by H or W?

H's position

There are a number of views as to whether payments made by H to W in respect of a divorce settlement will be a taxable remittance by H if he pays her out of offshore income and/or gains from trust distributions and these are later brought to the UK by W (after decree absolute when W is no longer a relevant person in relation to H). For a taxable remittance by H to arise, both Conditions A and B in ITA 2007 s.809L must be satisfied. It is assumed that Condition B is satisfied because the funds paid to H are derived from foreign income or gains attributed to H. Condition A is satisfied if the money H pays to W is used or received or brought to the UK by or for the benefit of H (or any relevant person in relation to H, i.e. trust, minor child or grandchildren etc) or a service is provided in the UK to or for the benefit of H or any relevant person. W is not a relevant person after decree absolute. At the point H receives any benefit (being the discharge of his liability to W) the money is offshore. The subsequent remittance of the funds by W provides him with no benefit. His obligations have already been settled.   **50.55**

On that basis it is arguable that no tax liability arises on H in respect of payments to W whether or not he pays her pursuant to a court order or a non-binding voluntary agreement provided she does not use the funds to benefit him or a minor child of H's. The settlement of a matrimonial obligation by H out of relevant foreign income or foreign chargeable gains of this kind does not constitute "use" in the UK for the benefit of H. Hence, H could receive an income or capital distribution out of the trust and simply pay W abroad. W should avoid remitting the funds not only until after decree absolute and the court order but she should also wait until both parties' claims are dismissed so that there can be no argument that the funds are in the UK when H receives the benefit of having his claims set aside. H should pay to W's sole account abroad.   **50.56**

W's position

So far as W is concerned she must be certain that the payments to her are coming from H personally not from any trust if she wants to avoid any liability to tax by reference to the pool of trust income or gains. Any order or arrangement will therefore need to specify that the payments come from an offshore account of H in his sole legal name. If W is excluded from the paying trust, it is difficult to see that HMRC could succeed in arguing that in reality the payments from the trustees to H are made for the benefit of W and taxable on her simply because the trustees know H will hand on the monies to her. W cannot be charged to capital gains tax under s.87 as a non-beneficiary if payments   **50.57** are actually made to H the beneficiary. The position may be more problematic under the transfer of assets regime.[74]

50.58   The safest course when trustees want to assist a beneficiary on divorce seems to be as follows:

(i)   W is excluded from the trusts before any trust distribution is made to H;

(ii) H must receive a distribution from a trust before anything is agreed between H and W or before he is directed to pay by court order. The funds are paid and retained by him abroad;

(iii) H pays W to her sole account abroad;

(iv) W does not bring the monies to the UK until after decree absolute and dismissal of all claims by the court. She does not use the funds to benefit minor children or grandchildren of H.

---

[74] Where the legislation is more widely drawn.

CHAPTER 51

STAMP DUTY LAND TAX AND STAMP DUTY

- Stamp Duty Land Tax—an overview (**51.01**)
- Typical transactions encountered by trustees (**51.09**)
- Stamp Duty (**51.24**)

This chapter provides a brief overview of the stamp taxes legislation with particular reference to trusts.

I STAMP DUTY LAND TAX—AN OVERVIEW

From December 1, 2003 stamp duty has no longer applied to any contract, conveyance, transfer, grant, lease, surrender, assignment, release or variation of any interest in land.[1] Instead the purchaser of an interest in or right over land (which broadly means the person deriving the benefit of the transaction such as a tenant or a buyer) may be liable for stamp duty land tax (SDLT) on the chargeable consideration paid.[2] Unlike Stamp Duty, there is no need for any documentation for the tax to be imposed. It is a transaction based tax.

The person acquiring the interest in land is the person liable for SDLT provided that he is a party to the transaction or has given consideration for it. Where the purchaser comprises two or more persons who are jointly entitled to the interest acquired, the liability to pay the tax is joint and several although any of them may in fact discharge it.[3]

The stamp duty legislation did not impose an obligation to stamp an instrument; it merely imposed certain sanctions if the instrument was not stamped. It was therefore viewed as a voluntary tax. SDLT, however, is not voluntary. There is a mandatory requirement on the purchaser in every notifiable SDLT

51.01

51.02

---

[1] As to the meaning of consideration, see 51.08. A chargeable interest in land (see FA 2003 s.43) is defined in s.48 as an estate, interest right or power in or over land in the UK or the benefit of an obligation, restriction or condition affecting the value of any such estate, interest, right or power other than an exempt interest. An exempt interest includes a licence to use or occupy land.

[2] FA 2003 Sch.3A paras 1–4 provides for a number of specific exemptions including transactions where there is no chargeable consideration; transactions in connection with divorce and dissolutions of civil partnerships; assents and appropriations by personal representatives; variation of testamentary dispositions. For trusts and powers in relation to SDLT, see further FA 2003 Sch.16. Disposals to charities are exempt from SDLT.

[3] For the position of trustees, see 51.02 and 51.04.

transaction to pay the tax due and to account to HMRC for that tax on a self-assessment basis. Payment of SDLT is made by sending to HMRC a land transaction return[4] within 30 days of the effective date of the transaction, together with the tax due (calculated by the purchaser).

51.03　A gift is not a notifiable transaction but a return must be completed in cases where tax is chargeable at the zero per cent rate. Notifiable transactions[5] include the grant or assignment of a lease for more than seven years for chargeable consideration or for less than seven years where the chargeable consideration consists or includes a premium in respect of which tax is chargeable at a rate of one per cent or higher or the chargeable consideration consists of or includes rent in respect of which tax is chargeable at a rate of one per cent or higher.

51.04　On delivery of the return and payment of the SDLT, HMRC will issue the taxpayer with a certificate[6] confirming that the return has been delivered. Certain transactions where no SDLT is payable, are not notifiable to HMRC. Instead, the purchaser must complete a self-certificate that no land transaction return is required in respect of the transaction.[7] Without a certificate the Land Registry cannot accept the taxpayer's application for registration of his title.[8]

51.05　Trustees are personally liable for any SDLT (or interest on SDLT) though not penalties. SDLT due can be recovered by HMRC from any one of the "responsible trustees" defined as the persons who are trustees at the effective date of the transaction and any subsequent trustee.[9] The trustee has rights of recovery from the trust fund or from the other trustees as a matter of trust law. The deadline for HMRC enquiries is nine months after the filing deadline.[10] A purchaser who is required to deliver a land transaction return must preserve the requisite records for six years after the transaction or after an enquiry has been completed (if later).[11]

Rates of SDLT

51.06　These are determined by whether the land is residential or non-residential. For 2011–12 the rates are as follows:

	Rate (%)
1. Residential land or property:[12]	
• £125,000 or less[13]	Nil
• £125,001–£250,000[14]	1

---

[4] The prescribed form is HMRC Land Transaction Return Form SDLT1. No longer are the documents produced to HMRC to have stamps impressed on them recording the duty which has been paid; nor is there any need for a particulars delivered ("PD") form.

[5] Defined in FA 2003 s.77.

[6] HMRC Land Transaction Return Certificate, Form SDLT4.

[7] As to self-certification, see FA 2003 s.79(3)(b), Sch.11.

[8] FA 2003 s.79(1).

[9] FA 2003 Sch.16 para.5(3).

[10] FA 2003 Sch.10 para.12(2).

[11] See FA 2003 Sch.10 para.9.

[12] Until September 30, 2012, no SDLT is payable on the first purchase of a zero carbon home with a purchase price not exceeding £500,000. If the purchase price exceeds £500,000, the SDLT liability is reduced by £15,000.

[13] The threshold for properties in disadvantaged areas is £150,000.

[14] First time buyers can claim relief from SDLT on residential transactions up to £250,000 until March 24, 2012.

- £250,001–£500,000 | 3
- £500,001–£1,000,000 | 4
- Over £1,000,000 | 5

2 Non-residential or mixed used land or property[15]:

- £150,000 or less | Nil
- £150,001–£250,000 | 1
- £250,001–£500,000 | 3
- Over £500,000 | 4

Lease rentals (on grant): the Net Present Value (NPV) is charged at 1% on the excess over £125,000 for residential, and 1% on the excess over £150,000 for non-residential or mixed use land.

51.07 SDLT is not a graduated tax but the percentage charge applies to the whole consideration once the threshold is exceeded. There are anti-avoidance provisions for linked transactions. The rate of tax is determined by aggregating the consideration received. For example, if trustees sell half the land to a beneficiary for £125,000 in one month and then the remaining half to him in the next month for the same amount, the consideration is £250,000 and the rate of tax is one per cent. In some cases a transaction will comprise both an acquisition of land and chattels. SDLT is not payable on chattels.[16]

Meaning of consideration

51.08 Many land transactions involving trustees and beneficiaries are outside the SDLT net because of the absence of consideration. Note however, that the following may amount to consideration:

(i) The assumption of debt by a beneficiary on a transfer of land to him out of the trust is treated as a purchase.[17] Even if within the £120,000 threshold for residential property (unless less than £1,000) or £150,000 for non-residential property, an SDLT 1 form must be submitted. The problems this can cause are discussed further below;

(ii) an exchange of interests in land which is treated as two separate transactions[18];

(iii) a partition of land when equality money is paid: the SDLT charge being limited to that equality money[19]; and

(iv) the giving of an indemnity by the purchaser to the vendor. Note, however, FA 2003 Sch.4 para.16A (inserted by Regulation) that an

---

[15] Special rules apply to tax on premiums where the annual rent exceeds £1,000.

[16] FA 2003 Sch.4 para.4 provides for a just and reasonable apportionment of the consideration. See SDLTM 040110 for HMRC's views on what is a chattel or moveable item.

[17] This can arise when a home loan is unscrambled: see 43.53 and 51.23. FA 2003 s.50, Sch.4 para.8 as amended by FA 2004 s.301. In relation to assents and appropriations under wills see FA 2003 s.49, Sch.3 para.3A(2)–(4) as inserted by the FA 2004 s.300(1). This largely replicates the position that had obtained under the previous stamp duty legislation. However, note the wider meaning of assumption of debt: see 51.20.

[18] FA 2003 s.47 as amended by the FA 2004 s.326, Sch.42 Pt 4(2) and by SI 2004/1069.

[19] FA 2003 s.50, Sch.4 para.6.

indemnity for CGT or IHT given to the trustees is not treated as chargeable consideration.[20]

II TYPICAL TRANSACTIONS ENCOUNTERED BY TRUSTEES

51.09 In relation to transactions where land passes into or out of a settlement, the position is as follows:

(i) If the settlor transfers land into a settlement, SDLT will not be payable because a land transaction is exempt from charge if there is no chargeable consideration for the transaction.[21] The trustees must self-certify that a land transaction return is not required in respect of the transaction.[22]

(ii) Trustees who buy and sell land are in the same position, so far as SDLT is concerned, as any other vendor or purchaser.[23]

(iii) If land is appointed out to a beneficiary or, at the end of the trust, becomes vested in a beneficiary and is transferred to him, this will normally be an exempt transaction because of the absence of any consideration. The beneficiary must self-certify that a land transaction return is not required in respect of the transaction.[24]

(iv) If a power of appointment is exercised over a chargeable interest in land and the person in whose favour it is exercised provides chargeable consideration, SDLT will be charged in the usual way.[25] Such situations are rare.

(v) If there is an exchange of interests in land between two family trusts or the acquisition of land for cash by one trust from another, this will attract SDLT in the normal way. If land is switched between the funds of a single settlement (for example land in Fund A is moved to Fund B with securities or land of equivalent value moving in the opposite direction) then in most cases, it is not considered that there is a land transaction, so that SDLT is not relevant.[26]

(vi) If a beneficiary gives up his interest in a trust which holds land (for example a life tenant surrenders his interest) there is no SDLT liability.

---

[20] SI 2006/875.

[21] As to what constitutes chargeable consideration see FA 2003 s.49, Sch.3 para.1, Sch.4 para.1(1).

[22] FA 2003 s.79, Sch.11. As to completion of a self-certificate by trustees, see 51.04 above.

[23] FA 2003 Sch.16, para.4. Reference in the FA 2003 Pt 4 to "purchaser" and "vendor" in relation to a land transaction are to the persons acquiring and the person disposing of the subject matter of the transaction: FA 2003 s.43(4). The trustees are treated as purchasers of the whole of the interest acquired, including the beneficial interest. Hence although the interest in possession beneficiary becomes entitled to an interest in the land he is not a purchaser for SDLT purposes.

[24] FA 2003 Sch.11. An area of doubt used to surround the position if the beneficiary agreed to indemnify the trustees, eg, against future inheritance tax charges. See SI 2006/875 providing that IHT and CGT indemnity given to trustees do not count as consideration.

[25] FA 2003 Sch.16 para.7.

[26] See 51.12.

(vii) In the case of a trust of land, if the life tenant and remaindermen agree to partition the land, for example on an actuarial basis where the life tenant receives 30 per cent and the remaindermen 70 per cent, no SDLT is payable.[27] Where there is a partition involving the payment of consideration only the equality money or other value counts as chargeable consideration.[28]

(viii) The acquisition of a chargeable interest in land by a bare trustee is treated as an acquisition by the beneficial owner of the land.[29] The grant of a lease to a bare trustee is, however, treated as a grant to the trustee, not to the beneficiary.[30]

(ix) Trustees are a single and continuing body so that a change of trustees of a trust fund which includes land, where the new trustees take on existing trust borrowings or agree to indemnify the retiring trustees in respect of claims against them, does not lead to any liability to tax.[31]

(x) If a settlor settles land on an interest in possession trust for his wife under which that interest ends after seven days, subject to which the property is held for the settlor absolutely, then, if during the seven day period the settlor sells his remainder interest to a purchaser, SDLT will be payable. This SDLT avoidance device does not work because the purchaser acquires (in the form of a remainder interest) a significant interest in land on which SDLT is payable.

(xi) In relation to the administration of nil rate band discretionary will trusts[32] a stamp duty land tax liability may arise: for example, on the transfer of the matrimonial home to the surviving spouse if that person is deemed to have given chargeable consideration. As where trustees accept a promise to pay the nil rate sum by the surviving spouse and in consideration of that promise land is transferred to the surviving spouse (or where land is transferred to the surviving spouse and the spouse charges the property with payment of the amount of the nil rate sum pecuniary legacy). In the latter case the charge represents money's worth and so is chargeable consideration for SDLT purposes. However, if the personal representatives charge land with the payment of the nil rate

---

[27] See FA 2003 s.50, Sch.4 para.6 (partition or division of a chargeable interest to which persons are jointly entitled). It is understood that HMRC interpret "jointly entitled" as covering the case where persons are entitled in succession as well as concurrently: cf. the capital gains tax position, for which see *Kidson (Inspector of Taxes) v Macdonald* [1974] Ch 339, [1974] 1 All ER 849; [1974] STC 54.

[28] Sch.4 para.6.

[29] FA 2003 Sch.16 para.3(1) as substituted by the F(No.2)A 2005 s.49, Sch.10 paras 1 and 11 in relation to leases granted after May 19, 2005.

[30] FA 2003 Sch.16 para.3(3).

[31] See in relation to CGT TCGA 1992 s.69(1) and see *Stamp Duty Land Tax Manual SDLTM31750: Application: Trusts and powers* (changes in trustees of a pension fund) and revised SDLT manual at 31745. This is despite the fact that the new trustees are taking on liabilities and therefore might be regarded as giving consideration and so fall outside the Sch.3 para.1 exemption. See Sch.4 para.8(1A) and (1B):

"*A change in the composition of trustees is not a land transaction –this means in particular that there is no charge on such an occasion where trust property is secured by a mortgage or other borrowing.*"

[32] See Ch.38, and 38.36 and A1.9.

sum legacy on a non-recourse basis so that the trustees have no right to enforce payment against the owner of the land, there is no chargeable consideration provided that the assent does not result in change in the rights or liabilities of any person in relation to the debt secured by the charge.

(xii) Trustees of an excluded property settlement may wish to resite UK land by transferring it into a wholly owned company just before the 10-year anniversary.[33]

Pension funds

51.10 When one pension scheme merges with another or there are other transfers of assets between such schemes, to the extent that the assets comprise interests in land and the consideration for the transfer of the transferring pension scheme's assets comprises only the assumption by the receiving scheme of the obligation to pay pension benefits (and any other approved benefits permitted by HMRC) to the members of the transferring scheme, no SDLT charge will arises.[34]

Variations

51.11 For the SDLT position on deeds of variations, see 39.45.

Exchanges within and between trusts

51.12 On the assumption that the SDLT definition of settlement carries the capital gains tax meaning,[35] an exchange of interests in land between funds does not constitute a land transaction because there is no acquisition of an interest in land. At one time HMRC were convinced that SDLT would arise on such a transaction. For instance, if Fund A holds land on accumulation and maintenance trusts and Fund B holds assets on interest in possession trusts and those assets are re-appropriated between the funds then has the life tenant of Fund B acquired an interest in land by (in effect) giving up his life interest over the other assets? Is the life tenant a purchaser? Alternatively, if land were to be exchanged between Fund A and Fund B then could the life tenant be taken to have furnished consideration calculated under the normal rules for exchanges: viz on the basis of the value of his life interest in the land acquired?

---

[33] See 51.17 for transactions with connected companies.
[34] See further *Pension Schemes—Stamp Duty, SDRT and SDLT* (June 6, 2005) available from HMRC.
[35] There is no clear set of SDLT principles as to whether sub-funds of the same CGT settlement are also sub-funds of the same settlement for SDLT purposes. If the SDLT definition of settlement carries the capital gains tax meaning an appropriation between funds is not a land transaction because it does not involve the acquisition of a chargeable interest in land.

Formerly, HMRC maintained that a land transaction could occur on the **51.13** basis that each sub-fund was a separate SDLT settlement but then the question was "who is the purchaser" and what consideration had been paid? HMRC accepted that the possibility of a charge in these cases only arose when there was a transfer of land involving interest in possession funds: in other trusts it was impossible to say that any beneficiary had acquired an interest in land. It was widely felt that this attempt to impose SDLT was misconceived. It was difficult to see how a beneficiary could be said to acquire an interest in land when he was not a party to the exchange and, indeed, might have been unaware of it. Even in the case of an interest in possession trust the life tenant does not acquire any right to the capital, only to the income. Often his life interest would be valueless if the trustees had power to terminate it without his consent. In an effort to clarify matters, it was announced[36] that FA 2006 would contain a provision to ensure that "transfers of assets between sub-funds of a settlement" would not give rise to an SDLT charge on or after July 19, 2006. There was no express commentary as to whether this was because there was no land transaction because a settlement had the same meaning for SDLT purposes as for capital gains tax purposes or because HMRC accepted no chargeable consideration was involved.

The legislation enacted did not, unfortunately, expressly address the point **51.14** at issue.[37] The section provides that the giving of consent by a beneficiary does not mean that there is chargeable consideration for a "re-allocation" of trust property by the trustees but does not in itself say that exchanges can never give rise to SDLT.

However, the wording suggests that HMRC accept that save in the case of **51.15** beneficiary consents there *never was* an SDLT problem on transfers between sub-funds anyway. The professional bodies' subsequent discussions with HMRC regarding appropriation of assets between sub-funds confirmed this, i.e. it was accepted that an allocation of property between sub-funds did not give rise to an SDLT issue and never had.

This only applies to an exchange within two funds of a single trust. An **51.16** exchange of land between two family trusts (with or without payment of any equality money) or the acquisition of land for cash by one trust from another will attract SDLT in the ordinary way. It is therefore important to be clear whether one is dealing with two trusts or one.[38]

EXAMPLE 51.1

Fergus left his residuary estate on trust so that the farmland passed on discretionary trusts for his widow and issue and the family house and quoted shares on an IPDI life interest trust for the widow. Some years later the trustees decide they want to minimise the inheritance tax on the widow's death by "a two bites of the cherry" scheme.[39] They transfer the farmland to the widow's fund and quoted shares of equal value to

---

[36] In the 2006 Budget Day Notes.
[37] FA 2006 s.165.
[38] The same point is true for capital gains tax purposes. See 12.21
[39] See 38.47.

the discretionary fund.[40] The intention is that the farmland will be held by the widow's fund for two years prior to her death so that agricultural property relief will be available.[41]

If the two funds are comprised in one settlement then there is no capital gains tax disposal and no SDLT charge. If the shares and land are held in two separate settlements then each trust makes a disposal of its assets to the other and SDLT will be payable on the acquisition of the farmland by the widow's fund. It may not always be easy to determine whether the will creates two separate trusts or one trust with two separate funds. For inheritance tax purposes IHTA 1984 s.80 means that the IPDI for the widow is treated as held in a separate settlement treated as commencing on the termination of her life interest.[42]

Companies

51.17 Trustees can become involved in transactions involving companies in the following circumstances:

(a) Trustees of a settlement set up by a non-UK domiciled settlor own UK land with a 10-year anniversary approaching. They want to ensure that at the 10-year anniversary the trust holds no UK situated property. Hence they may transfer the land to a wholly owned offshore company.[43]

(b) A foreign domiciled settlor may want to settle UK land. If he gives it to the trust direct there is a 20 per cent entry charge. If he first transfers the land to a wholly owned offshore company and then settles the company

---

[40] This assumes they have sufficient powers to carry out an appropriation. The situation often arises when trustees hold land and investments on qualifying interest in possession trusts for two life tenants in equal shares and it is felt desirable for one beneficiary to own the entirety of the land and the other beneficiary the entirety of the shares. It was held in *Re Freeston's Charity* [1978] 1 WLR 741 that in the absence of an express provision trustees have no power in those circumstances to limit the interest of an income beneficiary to an appropriated part of the fund even where the two assets are of equal value because by doing so they would be altering the nature of the beneficiary's interest, i.e. owning the whole of one asset is not the same as owning half of two assets. The Court of Appeal in *Southgate v Sutton* [2011] EWCA Civ637 appears to have held, notwithstanding *Freeston* that a power of appropriation is an administrative power even if it does incidentally alter a beneficiary's interest and that the trustees can exercise their powers in this way. This is a helpful decision and in accord with similar dicta in *Jenkins v Brown* where it is accepted that if land is pooled there is no disposal. If *Southgate* is wrong the position cannot always be solved simply by effecting an appropriation by use of the power of advancement. The concern then is that if a power of advancement is exercised so as to change the nature of the beneficiary's life interest this could be regarded as a "new" interest in possession and therefore no longer qualifying for IHT purposes. For further discussion see Ch.27. In *Re Z Trust v Rothschild Trust Cayman Islands* [2011] WTLR 735 the court held that a power of appropriation could be exercised so as to effect an exchange between two funds.
[41] Seven years ownership is necessary if the land was not farmed in hand: see Ch.46.
[42] The position would be different if the testator had left an IPDI for someone other than his widow. In these circumstances whether the property was comprised in two separate settlements or not it would be related property and the property left on IPDI trusts would need to be taken into account (at the value on death) when calculating the rate of tax charged on the relevant property: see Ch.29.
[43] See Ch.31 for offshore settlements and excluded property.

shares into trust there is no inheritance tax charge because the shares are excluded property.

(c) Trustees of an excluded property discretionary settlement may want to transfer UK property outright to a beneficiary. If they transfer the land direct to the beneficiary there is an exit charge. If they first transfer it to a company and then transfer the company shares to the beneficiary there is no exit charge wherever the beneficiary is domiciled. The company can then be liquidated and the beneficiary can own the land direct.

The SDLT repercussions of these transactions need careful consideration. FA 2003 s.53[44] imposes an SDLT charge on gifts or other transfers to connected companies irrespective of the consideration paid based on the market value of the property.[45] For example if the value of the property is £510,000 then whatever the consideration actually paid, the property is deemed to pass for a price equal to market value and the cost of transferring the land into the company would be four per cent. A connected person is defined by reference to TA 1988 s.839.   **51.18**

There may be an opportunity to avoid the charge in the example set out in (c) above. If the trust transfers land to a company wholly owned by the beneficiary then the company would not generally be connected with the trust if the settlor was deceased. If it were for the benefit of the beneficiary that the company received the land (which it would be if this avoided an exit charge or the beneficiary was foreign domiciled and therefore did not want to own UK land directly) this would be a way round the charge.

The capital gains tax consequences of a gift of land to a company also need to be considered. The value of the shares is uplifted but with no commensurate increase in their base cost. This may not matter if the shares are subsequently settled into or out of trust because they are then rebased to market value but the point should be considered. Generally it is better to transfer land to a company in consideration of the issue of shares so as to avoid these problems.   **51.19**

EXAMPLE 51.2

A, a foreign domiciliary, gives his UK house to a wholly owned non-resident company. SDLT is payable. There is no inheritance tax event because there is no loss to his estate. The value of the shares has increased but A gives them to a trust. The trust acquires them at market value. There is no inheritance tax on the gift of shares. However, if the trustees later liquidate or dispose of the shares the gain on the original transfer of shares into trust could be taxed on A if the trust invests in the UK or there is otherwise a remittance of the gain by a relevant person.[46]

---

[44] Originally this charge was introduced by FA 2000 s.119 with effect from March 28, 2000.

[45] Section s.53(1) imposes a charge if the purchaser is a connected company or some of the consideration consists of the issue or transfer of shares in a connected company. Sch.3 para.1 (exemption where there is no chargeable consideration) does not apply.

[46] See Chs 5 and 19 and, for the taxation of offshore companies, Ch.54.

The assumption of a liability

51.20 As noted at 51.08, FA 2003 Sch.4 para.8(1) provides:

> "*Where the chargeable consideration for a land transaction consists in whole or in part of:*
>
> *(a) of the satisfaction or release of the debt due to the purchaser or owed by the vendor, or*
>
> *(b) the assumption of existing debt by the purchaser,*
>
> *the amount of debt satisfied, released or assumed shall be taken to be the whole or, as the case may be, part of the chargeable consideration for the transaction.*"

The head (a) covers situations where the property is transferred to a creditor in partial or full satisfaction of a debt. So, for example, if a beneficiary has lent funds to the trustees who then transfer land to him in satisfaction of that debt, this is treated as a sale for SDLT purposes.

51.21 Head (b) is perhaps more common. If land subject to a mortgage is advanced to a beneficiary who assumes liability for the mortgage then that amount of the mortgage is chargeable consideration on which SDLT is payable. This section can be avoided by, for example, the land being advanced to the beneficiary subject to a non-recourse charge so the beneficiary accepts no personal liability to repay the debt.

51.22 However, in order to avoid an SDLT charge it is also necessary to avoid para.8(1A) which provides:

> "*Where:*
>
> *(a) debt is secured on the subject matter of a land transaction immediately before and immediately after a transaction, and*
>
> *(b) the rights or liabilities in relation to that debt of any party to the transaction are changed as a result of or in connection with the transaction,*
>
> *then for the purposes of this paragraph there is an assumption of that debt by the purchaser and that assumption of debt constitutes chargeable consideration for the transaction.*"

For example, if the trustees owe a debt to a bank secured by mortgage and the property is transferred to the beneficiary then it is important to ensure the beneficiary does not take on liability for the debt to avoid a charge under para.8. To avoid a charge under para.8(1A) if the bank agrees to the transfer of the property to the beneficiary subject to the charge the trustees must not be released from liability.

Paragraph 8(1A) can cause particular problems in relation to home loan **51.23** schemes.[47] Trustees of the Property Trust owe a debt to the trustees of the Debt Trust and the debt is generally not secured. The Property Trustees wish to wind up the scheme. The Debt Trustees have advanced the debt to the adult children who now wish to write it off. The parents can then be advanced the home unencumbered by debt. However, the children cannot easily write off the debt while the house is still held in the Property Trust because this would arguably be a chargeable transfer for inheritance tax purposes being an addition of value.[48] The Property Trustees therefore wish to advance the house to the parents subject to the debt and the children can then write off the debt in favour of the parents, thereby making a PET.

The Property Trustees cannot advance the property to the parents free of the debt. The terms of the loan agreement with the Debt Trust prevent the Property Trustees from distributing the assets to beneficiaries without the consent of the Debt Trustees. They therefore first impose a non-recourse charge on the property. The Debt Trustees agree that their consent is not now required to any distribution of the property.

In many cases the debt was originally structured such that the Property Trustees were not made personally liable to repay it and the only recourse of the Debt Trustees was against the assets, for the time being of the Property Trust. The question is whether, as a result of the imposition of the non-recourse charge, there has been a change in the rights or liabilities of the parties to a land transaction. (The creation of the charge is not itself a land transaction.) The rights of the Debt Trustees have been changed (because their recourse is longer to the assets from time to time of the Property Trust Fund but to the property itself.) However, they are not parties to the land transaction between the Property Trustees and the beneficiary. The liabilities of the beneficiary and the Property Trustees have not changed. On that basis there is no SDLT charge.

III STAMP DUTY

The stamp duty regime, with its exemptions, continues to apply to stock and **51.24** marketable securities.[49] Trustees purchasing shares will accordingly suffer stamp duty at 0.5 per cent unless the consideration does not exceed £1,000.[50] FA 2003 limits stamp duty to "instruments relating to stock and marketable securities". "Relating to" is somewhat vague but the position is thought to be as follows:

(i) the usual 0.5 per cent duty will be payable on all purchases of stock and marketable securities subject to the £1,000 de minimis limit;

---

[47] For dismantling options in the case of home loan schemes, see Ch.43 and 43.49 and following.
[48] For the position on additions to trusts after March 2006 see 24.25 and 31.39.
[49] FA 2003 s.125 as amended by the FA 2003 s.296, Sch.39.
[50] See FA 2008 s.98 which introduced a de minimis threshold below which duty is not payable on transfers of stock or marketable securities for instruments executed on or after March 13, 2008 where stamped after March 18, 2008.

(ii) when stock is transferred for no consideration (as, for instance, when it is settled and transferred into the names of the trustees) duty is not payable and prior to FA 2008 the usual certificate (viz that the transfer falls under Category L in the Schedule to the Stamp Duty (Exempt Instruments) Regulations 1987) was included in the stock transfer form. For instruments executed on or after March 13, 2008 the certification procedure is no longer necessary;[51]

(iii) declarations of trust—which formerly attracted a £5 fixed duty stamp—were not stampable after 2003 unless they "relate to stock and marketable securities". However FA 2008 s.99 abolished fixed stamp duty with effect for instruments executed on or after March 13, 2008 and not stamped before March 19, 2008.[52]

51.25 The result is that from March 13, 2008 inter vivos gifts and declarations of trust of stock and securities do not need to be certified and nor do they attract a fixed stamp duty charge.

---

[51] See FA 2008 s.100.
[52] See FA 2008 Sch.32.

CHAPTER 52

PARTNERSHIP STRUCTURES

- Introduction (**52.01**)
- Tax treatment of partnerships including remittance issues for foreign domicillaries (**52.17**)

I INTRODUCTION

With the FA 2006 changes to the IHT treatment of settlements there has been much discussion about using partnerships instead of trusts as a way of avoiding the 20 per cent entry inheritance tax charge[1] and 10-year charges while still keeping some control over the gifted assets. In particular, "family limited partnerships" or FLPs,[2] a vehicle commonly used in the United States, have been promoted as a suitable alternative. **52.01**

A partnership established under the laws of England and Wales is fiscally transparent for capital gains tax and income tax purposes, although for inheritance tax the partners are taxed on the value of their respective interest in the partnership (a *chose in action*) rather than on the underlying assets of the partnership.[3] **52.02**

---

[1] Which applies to the creation of trusts once the settlor has exhausted his nil rate band.
[2] Using the Limited Partnership Act 1907; contrast LLPs registered under the Limited Liability Partnership Act 2000.
[3] In Scotland a partnership is a separate legal entity. See IHTA 1984 s.267 and s.267A for LLPs. IHTM 25094 notes though:

> "*the effect of s267A is that we look through LLPs so that they will be treated in the same way as traditional partnerships. The result of this is that:*
>
> - *Where a traditional partnership incorporates itself as a LLP, a partner's period of ownership for the purposes of qualifying for business (or agricultural) relief will not be regarded as being interrupted.*
>
> - *The normal reliefs and exemptions available to partners in a traditional partnership will also be available to members of a LLP. In particular, Section 10 IHTA 1984 (which provides an exemption for dispositions not intended to confer gratuitous benefit) will apply.*
>
> *A further change is that an interest in a LLP is deemed to be an interest in each and every asset*

Who can enter into partnership?

52.03   Partnerships may have partners who are individuals, trustees or corporate bodies.

Can minors enter into partnerships?

52.04   Minors can enter into partnerships.[4] However, whilst minors can be in partnership, this does not prevent them from repudiating the partnership contract once they become 18, although repudiation would normally have to occur within a reasonable time of the minor turning 18. It is this risk of repudiation that makes it unattractive for minors to enter into partnership.[5]

52.05   An alternative is for the partnership interest to be held by an adult as bare trustee for the benefit of the minor with the adult then entering into the partnership agreement as principal rather than as agent. He will normally prefer to be a limited partner in a FLP rather than a general partner. The bare trustee enters into this FLP as he does any other investment on behalf of the minor. Then the FLP is binding and cannot be repudiated by the child while still a minor and once he is 18 although he could disclaim the gift he would then have to give up all benefit and could not take a share in the assets. By contrast if a minor is a partner he can repudiate the partnership so it is dissolved but claim a share in the partnership assets even where the partnership agreement restricts capital withdrawals.

52.06   If the FLP is structured so that no monies or partnership share can be withdrawn for a fixed period of years the child cannot gain de facto control over the assets. In particular he cannot require the bare trustees to transfer to him his share in the partnership. For this reason, the partnership agreement often specifies that no partnership share can be transferred during the term of the agreement without the consent of all other partners. The bare trustee then continues to hold the share for the absolute use and benefit of the child. However, it is thought that on attaining majority a child could, in practice, get control of his partnership share (irrespective of the terms of the partnership agreement) by application to court. Hence, using the bare trustee route for minors may present the same practical problems as simply making the minor a partner.

> of the partnership, while an interest in a traditional partnership is a 'chose in action', valued by reference to the net underlying assets of the business. This may require you to consider issues of situs of property. In cases of doubt refer to Technical Group (TG) for advice."

The authors consider there is no basis for the view that s.267A results in transparency for inheritance tax purposes for LLPs. LLPs and general partnerships are treated in the same way for inheritance tax purposes. The Manual goes on to say:

> "However, in considering if an LLP is an investment business (IHTM25261), you should look at the nature of the business underpinned by those assets, rather than the nature of the assets themselves, to see whether Section 105(3) IHTA 1984 is in point."

[4] *Alexander Bulloch and Co v CIR* 51 STC 563.
[5] See HMRC's Business Income Manual (BIM) 72065.

What is a partnership?

The majority of trusts own investment property, few directly trade. By contrast the definition of a partnership involves the partners *carrying on a trade, profession or business with a view to profit*. It is a contractual not fiduciary relationship governed by the terms of the relevant partnership legislation and the particular provisions of the partnership agreement. If the "partnership" merely holds an investment asset which does not involve carrying on a business, then it is not in law a partnership but merely co-ownership. However, provided there is active management of the assets and a commercial element to that management (i.e. they are managed with a view to profit) a partnership will, in law, exist.

52.07

HMRC have commented unofficially in the past:

52.08

> "*whether the activities carried on by a particular LLP amount to the carrying on of a business is a question of fact but I think it would only be in exceptional circumstances that letting a building on a commercial basis would not amount to a business*"

Similarly it was noted:

> "*whilst I cannot confirm that holding and managing a portfolio of investments in anticipation of gains and income will always amount to a business, I think it would only be in exceptional circumstances that it would not.*" [6]

Types of partnership

There are three forms of partnership:

52.09

(i) a general partnership formed under the Partnership Act 1890[7];

(ii) a limited partnership formed under the Limited Partnership Act 1907[8]; and

(iii) a limited liability partnership formed under the Limited Liability Partnerships Act 2000.[9]

---

[6] See also the BVCA Memorandum of May 26, 1987 which discusses partnerships in the context of raising funds for investment.

[7] There is no longer a 20-partner limit on general and limited partnerships: this was removed by two Statutory Instruments in 2002. Note that UK LLPs must publish their accounts.

[8] A limited partnership created under the Limited Partnership Act 1907 is one in which at least one of the partners restricts their liability for the debts and obligations of the firm to a predetermined sum instead of bearing unlimited liability. It must be registered with the Registrar of Limited Partnerships in London or Edinburgh as appropriate. A limited partnership consists of at least one general partner (who manages the business and bears unlimited liability to creditors) and at least one limited partner. A limited partner contributes a specified amount of capital on joining the partnership but does not bear any liability to creditors or other partners in excess of its contribution and undrawn profits.

[9] The Limited Liability Partnerships Act 2000 came into force on April 6, 2001. Its main purpose

52.10 Most discussion has focused on FLPs. However, consider the following:

  (i) why is limited liability desired? In practice partnerships as an alternative to trusts tend to be considered when a family owns investment property such as rental houses or a portfolio of shares and securities. Accordingly limited liability is not usually a significant factor;

  (ii) the limited partnership (cp general partnership) is a collective investment scheme and subject to financial services regulation[10];

  (iii) in a limited partnership only the general partner is involved in running the business (if other partners become involved they lose the benefit of their limited liability).

Regulation of FLPs

52.11 Limited partnerships are collective investment schemes within the Financial Services and Markets Act 2000 s.235 since some partners necessarily do not take part in the day to day management and control of the FLP. Hence, the management of the limited partnership must be delegated to an FSA authorised operator. This adds an ongoing layer of cost. It may be possible to get round this by siting the FLP in a non-UK jurisdiction (for example, Jersey).[11] If the FLP holds stock market investments, the authorised person is usually the investment manager.

52.12 Where a general partnership is used and, under the partnership agreement all the partners have day to day control, then the partnership is not a collective investment scheme. A limited liability partnership is not a collective investment scheme under the schedule to the Financial Services and Markets Act 2000 (Collective Investment Schemes) Order 2001.

The typical scenario

52.13 Typically a father wishes to make provision for his minor or adult children or grandchildren but not give them property outright. He enters into an FLP with family members or trustees, providing all the initial cash funding. The

---

and effect was to introduce a new form of legal entity known as a limited liability partnership (LLP) intended to protect legal and accountancy and other professional practices, but the use of LLPs is not restricted to them. Such practices can have partners world-wide who may be concerned about the fact that they have been subject to joint personal liability on matters over which they had little control.

[10] See 52.11.

[11] Note that a Jersey Limited Liability partnership under the LLP (Jersey) 2007 Law is treated as a corporate non-transparent entity by HMRC for tax purposes. A Jersey limited partnership under the 1994 Limited Partnerships (Jersey) Law is not. The use of foreign entities must be considered carefully: see Ch.2. In Anson v HMRC [2011] UK UTB 21 discussed at 2.40 it was held that a US LLC was opaque for tax purposes even though taxed as transparent in the US. See also *Memec v IRC* [1996] STC 1336. HMRC have published a summary of their view on the tax transparency of international partnership vehicles in HMRC International Tax Manual 180020/180030.

trustees will generally be bare trustees holding for the benefit of any minor children and he will gift cash and the bare trustees (and adult partners if any) will then enter into the partnership. As noted above, the child will be treated as the beneficial owner of any partnership share but the bare trustees will be the partners. The father will usually retain a partnership share himself. The father or a company owned by him may be the general partner of a FLP with all the management responsibility; the partnership agreement may provide that the general partner can admit any persons to the partnership without the consent of the other partners, e.g. on the birth of another child that child can be admitted as partner using the bare trustee route.[12] The other partners, including the bare trustees, are limited partners and (as noted previously) may not be entitled to assign their partnership interest or to withdraw capital. They have an economic interest but no management powers. The partnership deed usually directs that distribution of profits is decided by the general partner and the partnership is expressed to last for a fixed period, e.g. 10, 15 or 20 years but on a rolling basis. (It is very difficult for a partnership to be fixed from the outset to endure for as long as a trust.) The children can, in due course, be brought in as directors of the corporate general partner so that they can gradually participate in the management of the business.

52.14 It is possible to draft partnership agreements to include pre-emption provisions for (say) divorcing family members or bankrupt partners to be "bought out" so as to enable the assets to be retained within the family. However, unlike trusts, it is not possible to give the general partner discretion such that the partners' capital entitlements can be varied each year. The partnership agreement could provide that capital cannot be extracted from the partnership during the fixed term without the consent of all the partners and for the senior or general partner to have voting control and discretion as to distribution of income profits (although the IHT reservation of benefit rules should be watched carefully).

52.15 Unlike the position in a discretionary trust, the general partner cannot distribute all the income profits to one partner and none to the others. Any profit shares must be divided in accordance with the partners' respective entitlements under the partnership agreement, i.e. according to the agreed profit sharing ratios even if they are not actually distributed to the partners but reinvested in the partnership. However, the general partner cannot exercise his discretions to withhold distributions of profit share except for the general benefit of the partnership. (Contrast the position of trustees who are under an obligation to consider the interests of all beneficiaries but may exercise their discretion in favour of one or more beneficiaries to the exclusion of others.) Moreover since entitlement to income profits is fixed by the partnership agreement and partners are subject to income tax on their share whether or not the profit is actually distributed, partners are likely to object if they are taxed on profits that are never received because the general partner withholds distribution of the profit shares.

52.16 However, the general partner could be given power to limit the profits actually distributed to an amount equal to each partners' income tax liability and reinvest the balance of profits by crediting these proportionally to each partner's capital share if this is for the general benefit of the partnership. The

---

[12] See 52.03.

general partner may also be given power to agree loans to partners (although watch loans to the donor partner since this could result in IHT reservation of benefit problems).

II TAX TREATMENT OF PARTNERSHIPS

52.17 The often cited tax advantage of a partnership is that it leaves control with the donor but avoids the inheritance tax charges that are often present when settling funds into trust. However, it is worth remembering that the settlement of funds into trust will not incur an inheritance tax entry charge in the following circumstances:

(i) where the value being settled is within the transferor's nil rate band. Consider the use of pilot trusts as a way of minimising future 10-year and exit charges if the settled property increases in value[13];

(ii) where what is being settled comprises surplus income the settlor can make regular gifts out of income into trust: "normal expenditure out of income settlements"[14];

(iii) where what is being settled comprises business or agricultural property qualifying for 100 per cent relief.

In these circumstances trusts are likely to be much easier to operate than any partnership structure and should continue to be used. They provide better protection than partnerships when it comes to protection of assets on divorce or bankruptcy of the family members.[15]

Inheritance tax

52.18 Although the gift of property to other partners by an original donor will be a PET (and avoid any 20 per cent entry charge because it does not involve the creation of a settlement), reservation of benefit must be watched carefully. The donor must enjoy no benefit from the gifted partnership shares and possession and enjoyment must be assumed by the donees. If the donor retains benefits from the income profits, or receives remuneration for managing the partnership, then this can create problems. Later adjustments in partnership shares may also constitute PETs. (By contrast changes in the contingent capital interests taken by beneficiaries or changes in income entitlement will not generally be inheritance tax events in a trust.)

---

[13] See Ch.41.
[14] IHTA 1984 s.21.
[15] Although both trust and partnership interests must be taken into account as financial resources, it may be easier for a court to dissolve or transfer a partnership interest since the limited partner will necessarily have a substantive economic interest in the assets of the partnership. By contrast a beneficiary may only have a contingent or discretionary interest in the capital. Even if the partnership agreement prevents capital withdrawals or assignments of partnership interests within a certain time that capital interest still has economic value. A trustee in bankruptcy can apply to wind up a partnership if just and equitable to do so.

There is no charge every 10 years (unlike trusts). However, the partnership **52.19** share is comprised in the estate of each of the partners and will be taxed on his death (contrast a trust interest which is not generally taxed on the death of a beneficiary). There may be valuation discounts if the partnership share is restricted in some way.[16] HMRC note, however, at IHTM 25120:

> "*A restriction on a partner's right to freely dispose of his partnership share is called a 'Fetter'. In most cases the open market value of the partnership interest is required. Occasionally however the taxable value may be something other than the open market value. Articles of Partnership sometimes provide that a deceased partner's interest in the partnership should pass to the surviving partners:*
>
> - *at a book figure (i.e. the figure at which the capital account stood in the last published balance sheet prior to death); or*
> - *for no payment at all or for a fixed sum.*
>
> *Alternatively:*
>
> - *the surviving partners might have the option to purchase the deceased's share in the business for a fixed price or a balance sheet figure.*
>
> *These provisions in the Articles restrict the deceased's ability to dispose of his partnership interest as he wishes. Once the Articles have been entered into, the partner cannot make a provision in their will to direct how their share in the business will pass (the surviving partners take automatically, or have an option to acquire the deceased's share, though they usually have to pay something to the estate).*
>
> 1. *The rule is that a fetter is to be taken into account for IHT valuation purposes only to the extent that consideration in money or money's worth has been given for it, Section 163(1)(a) IHTA 1984. If the fetter was not granted for full consideration then the open market value of the deceased's interest will be taxable.*
>
>   - *If the fetter was granted before 27 March 1974 other than for full consideration, there is no problem. Simply value the deceased's interest on an open market basis.*
>   - *If the fetter was created after 26 March 1974, the deceased may have made a chargeable transfer by restricting his freedom to dispose of the partnership interest when entering into the Articles of Partnership. You should ascertain an open market value on the*

---

[16] Care should be taken to specify in any partnership agreement how a partnership share is to be valued in the event of a partner retiring or dying. For example, if the partnership agreement specifies that on the death of a partner his share accrues to the other partners the agreement should state whether the surviving partners are expected to pay for this share and whether the share is deemed to accrue at market value or book value. See *Drake v Harvey* [2010] WTLR 1731 where nothing was said in a farming partnership regarding the value to be paid for accruing shares. In the event it was held, following *Cruikshank v Sutherland* [1922] 92 LJ Ch 136 (HL), that where a partnership deed is silent as to the basis of valuation for the purposes of an account, the appropriate value is one that is fair. In *Drake v Harvey* it was held that market value applied.

death and allow against it a deduction for any lifetime transfer agreed to have been made by the deceased at the time he entered into the Articles, Section 163(1)(b) IHTA 1984. For example the deceased took his daughter into partnership in 1995 and by the Deed of Partnership, the share of a deceased partner was to pass to the survivor without payment. The value of the transfer on the creation of the fetter is agreed at £10,000. When the deceased dies in 2000, the open market value of his partnership interest (we ignore the fetter) is agreed at £30,000.

The taxable value on death is £30,000 less £10,000 = £20,000. However, the lifetime cumulative total of £10,000 means that the aggregate total of cumulative chargeable transfers is the same.

2. *If the fetter was granted for full consideration, then only the fetter price will be taxable on the death and you do not need to ascertain an open market value.*
3. *Sometimes, the Articles of Partnership provide that the deceased's share in the partnership is to pass to the surviving partners in return for the payment of an annuity to the deceased's widow or surviving civil partner. Basically, if such an arrangement was made for full consideration, the deceased's partnership interest will be exempt (spouse or civil partner exemption Section 18 IHTA 1984). If the arrangement was not made for full consideration, the open market value will be taxable on death but a deduction will be given against that figure for the capital value of the annuity to the spouse or civil partner which is spouse or civil partner exempt.*
Categories (2) and (3) are relatively uncommon. In the vast majority of cases an open market value at the date of death will be required."

If the partnership agreement provides for automatic accruer on the death of a partner or cross options, this is not treated as a binding contract for sale and does not jeopardise business property relief or agricultural property relief.

IHTM 25292 notes:

"Partners and shareholder directors of companies may enter into agreements between themselves to the effect that

- *when one of them dies before retirement*
- *the surviving partners or directors may purchase the partnership interest or shares of the one who has died.*

The funds for the purchase may be provided by appropriate life assurance policies.

Only most exceptionally does such an agreement constitute a binding contract for sale within Section 113 IHTA 1984. For the agreement to come within Section 113 IHTA 1984 it has to provide

- *for the interest or shares of the deceased partner or shareholder to pass to his or her personal representatives*
- *that the personal representatives are required to sell the interest or shares to the surviving partners or shareholders*
- *who are in terms obliged to buy it or them.*

These requirements are rarely satisfied. When they are, the agreement is called a 'buy and sell' agreement and it prevents the interest or shares concerned qualifying for business relief.

Much more common are agreements under which

a. *the deceased's interest passes to the surviving partners, who are required to pay the personal representatives a particular price, or*
b. *the deceased's interest falls into the estate, but with an option for the surviving partners to purchase it.*

Agreements of these types do not constitute contracts for sale. So they do not prevent the interest from qualifying for business relief by reason of Section 113 IHTA 1984."[17]

Capital gains tax—general points

The capital gains tax treatment of partnerships is generally governed by Statement of Practice D12. Partnerships are treated as transparent for income tax and capital gains tax purposes (they are not treated as a separate legal entity) which means that the members are assessed to tax on the partnership income and gains realised on disposals of partnership assets.[18] So any gains or losses accruing on disposals of partnership assets are taxed on the partners rather than on the partnership. Partners are treated for this purpose as owning fractional interests in each of the partnership assets. Unlike corporate structures partnerships do not suffer a double layer of taxation, first on the corporate profits, then on the shareholders on distributions from the company or on the sale of their shares. **52.20**

Capital gains tax putting assets into partnership

On the *creation* of a partnership there will be CGT issues if the assets transferred show a gain.[19] Before January 2008 HMRC had tended (although **52.21**

---

[17] See Chs 45 and 46 for business property relief and agricultural property relief.
[18] TCGA 1992 s.59. In England, Wales and Northern Ireland a partnership is not a legal person or legal entity distinct from the partners. However, a partnership is a "person" for all purposes of the Taxes Acts unless the contrary intention appears: see Interpretation Act 1978 Sch.1. TCGA 1992 s.59(1) indicates such a contrary intention as it treats partners as persons chargeable to tax on gains arising on disposals of interests in partnership assets.
[19] See HMRC Brief 03/2008.

not consistently) towards the view that an asset introduced would involve a disposal to the extent the introducing partner gave an interest in the asset to the other partners but that this would be treated as done for a consideration giving rise to no gain or loss, i.e. SP D12 was applied not only to the transfers of shares between partners but transfers of assets into partnership. Thus no capital gains tax resulted.

52.22   The Brief (intended to set out a consistent position) instead stated:

> *"We consider that, where an asset is transferred to a partnership by means of a capital contribution, the correct application of the capital gains legislation is that the partner in question has made a part disposal of the asset equal to the fractional share that passes to the other partners.*
>
> *The market value rule would apply, if the transfer is between connected persons or the transaction is other than by way of a bargain made at arm's length."*

It also confirmed the introduction into partnership of an asset which is showing an unrealised gain will generally trigger tax on that gain.

> *"We take the view that a sum credited to the partner's capital account represents consideration for the disposal of the asset to the partnership."*

The "new" approach applied not only to transactions after January 21, 2008 but also to those undertaken before that date if specific advance guidance had not been obtained from HMRC.

52.23   A transfer to a partnership is therefore a disposal (or part disposal if the donor is a partner) and gains realised on such a disposal will, prima facie, be subject to capital gains tax in the hands of the donor. Unlike trusts it is not possible to transfer investment assets to a partnership and hold-over the gain under TCGA 1992 s.260.[20] Are there ways of avoiding this capital gains tax charge?

(i) transferring cash/non-chargeable or assets not standing at a gain is not a problem;

(ii) it is possible to ring-fence the asset transferred into partnership. For instance, if a father transfers investment assets (such as rented property) into partnership his capital share can be expressed to comprise 100 per cent of the (current) value of that property. Future increases *in value* of the asset can belong to the other partners' capital accounts. In these circumstances there is no disposal (but equally no immediate inheritance tax benefits since nothing has been given away). Future capital growth can then be divided between the partners as the partnership provides;

(iii) pooling arrangements: if the partner's interest in the pool of partnership assets reflects exactly the value of his interest in the assets he contributed it may be said that there is no capital gains tax charge.[21] For instance, father and son each transfer a 50 per cent interest in land into

---

[20] Compare gifts to non-settlor interested trusts: see Ch.18 for when hold-over relief can be claimed.
[21] See *Jenkins v Brown* [1989] STC 577.

partnership in which they share 50 per cent of the capital and income profits in order to carry out a development. However, HMRC contend, contrary to the pooling cases such as *Jenkins v Brown*, that when each partner transfers an interest in an asset into partnership they have each made a disposal of their own share in the asset. The answer may depend on the partnership terms: if each is entitled to take his own asset out of the partnership at any time there may be no disposal. *Jenkins v Brown* was a co-ownership case. Contrast *Booth v Ellard*;

(iv) in particular cases the inter spouse "no gain, no loss" rule may apply[22];

(v) if assets put into the partnership are business or agricultural assets, they may qualify for CGT hold-over relief under TCGA 1992 s.165 (and note that the settlor-interested restriction only applies to disposals into trusts), so no CGT charge arises but such assets will generally qualify for business property relief so that a trust could be used without any inheritance tax entry charge.[23]

Disposals by the partnership

Any gains on disposals of assets by the partnership accrue to the partners in their capital sharing ratios.[24] Gains are taxed on each partner at their personal rates and with the benefit of their annual capital gains tax exemptions and any personal losses. Gains will be charged on minor children who are partners not on the parent bare trustee.   **52.24**

Transfers between partners

If there is a change in partnership shares then capital gains tax will arise, e.g. where a partnership holds rental properties and the donor partner reduces his 50 per cent share by, say, 10 per cent, thereby increasing the capital shares of his children there will be a disposal for capital gains tax purposes in the normal way as well as a PET for inheritance tax purposes. Unlike trusts, it is not possible to reorganise members' capital shares without triggering capital gains tax charges.[25] SP D12 para.7 provides for a no gain no loss computation if no consideration changes hands on changes in asset sharing ratios and   **52.25**

---

[22] Under TCGA 1992 s.58.

[23] Partnerships have one advantage over trusts in that gifts of business assets to a minor child of the donor outright are not subject to restriction while gifts of business assets to a trust for a minor child are not eligible for hold-over relief. See Ch.18.

[24] Unless expressly agreed otherwise, the treatment of capital gains and losses follows a profit sharing arrangement. In some cases, it may be difficult to know whether an asset is partnership property or owned by one of the partners and merely used by the partnership. To avoid confusion ensure the partnership accounts accurately state the partnership property and have a declaration of trust confirming whether or not the land is partnership property. This will be particularly relevant where the land qualifies for business property relief: if partnership property it will qualify for relief at 100%, otherwise only at 50%.

[25] Compare the position of trusts where beneficial interests of beneficiaries can be changed and assets exchanged between beneficiaries e.g. new interests in possession appointed or beneficiar-

the transfer is by way of bargain at arm's length. But in the case of a family partnership there is unlikely to be a commercial justification for the change in capital shares.[26] Bear in mind that a transaction between connected persons (i.e. connected otherwise than as partners) is not treated as taking place at arms' length.[27]

Income tax

52.26   The partnership is transparent for income tax purposes.[28] It will constitute a settlement for the purposes of ITTOIA 2005 Pt 5 Ch.5.[29] Hence, if the minor unmarried children of the donor are partners there is no income tax advantage to such a partnership. Generally HMRC accept that the settlement provisions are difficult to apply in other circumstances, e.g. to husband and wife partnerships. For example, if the donor is a member of a partnership with his spouse and adult children and minor grandchildren, he is not regarded as having an interest in all the partnership income only the income of his share. Contrast the position if the donor or his spouse was a beneficiary of a settlement for his children/grandchildren.

SDLT

52.27   SDLT is not payable on the transfer of land into a partnership (whether or not a FLP) so long as the partners are "connected" for the purposes of the legislation (e.g. family members).[30] Note, however, that if a corporate entity is partner then even if the corporate entity is wholly owned by one of the partners, an SDLT charge can arise unless the company takes a minimal share of income profits.

52.28   Anti-avoidance provisions can apply if land is transferred and arrangements are in place for others to join the partnership or for capital to be withdrawn.

52.29   No SDLT should arise on subsequent transfers of partnership interests where the partnership comprises connected parties e.g. family members.[31]

ies excluded without any inheritance tax or capital gains tax consequences. There is no disposal if the reorganisation takes place within the trust: see Ch.11 and 51.42.
[26] It is sometimes claimed that a commercial rationale for increasing the capital share of a child is that the child is undertaking more work in the business. Hence there is no gratuitous intention. It is then argued that there is no PET for inheritance tax purposes and the disposal is protected for capital gains tax purposes by SP D12 para.7. *AG v Boden* [1912] 1 KB 539 is sometimes cited as authority for transfers of partnership interests being commercial where the children were required to work more than the father in the business with the goodwill accruing to the sons on the father's death without payment. However, this only covered transfers of goodwill not transfers of the father's capital interest in the partnership assets.
[27] See TCGA 1992 s.286 for the definition of "connected persons".
[28] ITTOIA 2005 s.848
[29] See Ch.7 and ITTOIA 2005 ss.620–629.
[30] See FA 2003 Sch.15.
[31] See FA 2003 Sch.15

Remittance issues

Although partnerships are treated as transparent for income tax and capital **52.30** gains tax purposes,[32] HMRC do not consider that remittance of foreign income or gains by the partnership is treated as a remittance by the partners in proportion to their respective shares in the partnership. They argue that remittance by a non-UK partnership is not a remittance by the partners because a partnership is not a relevant person; hence if the foreign partnership invests in UK assets, an individual partner who is a remittance basis user does not make a taxable remittance unless what is remitted is used to benefit him.[33] It is not entirely clear what a non-UK partnership is, and HMRC have not opined on the issue. Foreign partnerships have been seen as a useful way of remitting funds for investment in the UK, although with the advent of the new rules for investment in the UK announced in June 2011,[34] it may be that this route will no longer be used.

The Remittances Manual also concludes that where a remittance basis **52.31** user uses his foreign income or gains to make a capital contribution to a UK partnership, he acquires a UK asset, i.e. a share in a UK partnership in exchange for his financial contribution to the partnership, even if the foreign income or gains that he uses to contribute to the partnership are not actually brought to the UK by the partnership at all but placed in the partnership's overseas account and invested only overseas. Presumably a UK partnership means one which is managed and controlled in the UK, although this point remains unclear.

Conclusions

Partnerships have an IHT advantage over trusts in that there is no immediate **52.32** 20 per cent IHT charge on transfer of property into the partnership, and no anniversary charges. Because they are transparent for income tax and capital gains tax purposes, the 50 per cent additional income tax rate and 28 per cent capital gains tax rate can be avoided if the other partners are not top rate taxpayers.

However, the donor still needs to survive for seven years after the date of **52.33**

---

[32] ITA 2007 s.848 and TCGA 1992 s.59.
[33] IDRM para.33530:

> "When a partner makes a capital contribution to a partnership they acquire an asset under partnership law, namely an interest or share in the partnership, which gives them rights to share in future profits and distributions of their capital and any surplus on dissolution of the partnership. A partnership is not a relevant person. Individuals who are partners together in a partnership are not relevant persons by virtue of their role as a partner. . .Offshore partnerships whether trading or investment, may bring partnership funds into the UK to meet trading or investment expenses in the usual course of partnership business. As the funds are brought in by the partnership they are not brought in by a relevant person. In most cases there will be no benefit to a relevant person from the money or other property brought into the UK by the partnership, nor will a service usually be provided in the UK to or for the benefit of relevant person, so Condition A of ITA section 809L is not met. Thus there will be no taxable remittance."

[34] See Ch.5.

the relevant transfer. Unlike gifts to trusts, transfers of investment assets into partnership at a gain are not eligible for hold-over relief and will generally result in capital gains tax. In cases where business property relief or agricultural property relief is available at 100 per cent, a trust is still likely to be the favoured vehicle and will provide better asset protection. Partnerships (like trusts) enable a limited measure of control to be retained by the donor but do not have the same flexibility as a trust in terms of rearranging beneficial interests to take account of changing family circumstances and the needs of beneficiaries. If a FLP is used there are regulatory and compliance costs.

CHAPTER 53

OFFSHORE INCOME GAINS

I INTRODUCTION

A complete explanation of offshore funds would require a separate book **53.01** and one chapter can do no more than outline the basic points. The position has been complicated by the FA 2008 changes to the tax regime for foreign domiciliaries. New legislation was introduced with effect from December 1, 2009. Many offshore trusts hold what used to be called non-distributor funds and are now referred to as non-reporting funds.[1] The original purpose of the rules was to stop people converting income into capital gains by allowing the income to roll-up in the fund. However, in some cases even offshore funds that distribute income regularly will be treated as non-reporting funds so that gains are taxed as income simply because they do not satisfy the necessary reporting requirements. For example, many US mutual funds are non-reporting. The fund managers will have no interest in satisfying UK requirements since most of their investors will be US residents.

Capital gains on what we call "ordinary assets" (i.e. gains on assets that **53.02** are not non-reporting offshore funds) are taxed on individuals at 18 or 28 per cent (with an annual capital gains tax exemption of £10,600 for 2011–12)

---

[1] The main legislation is found in TIOPA 2010 ss.354–363 and The Offshore Fund (Tax) Regulations 2009 (SI 2009/3001) (the 2009 Regulations). These Regulations have been in force since December 1, 2009. However, an understanding of the transfer of assets provisions in ITA 2007 ss.720–735, TCGA 1992 s.87 (capital gains of non-resident trusts) s.13 (gains of non-resident companies) and Sch.4C is also required. The 2009 Regulations were further amended by The Offshore Funds (Tax) (Amendment) Regulations (SI 2009/3139) and by The Offshore Funds (Tax) (Amendment) Regulations 2011. These 2011 Regulations introduced changes to the taxation and classification of reporting funds and how reportable income is to be computed as well as introducing new rules on time limits and clarifying the reporting requirements. They did not change the taxation of investors who hold offshore non-reporting funds.

and on UK resident trusts at 28 per cent with an exemption of £5,300.[2] By contrast gains on non-reporting funds are taxed at the income tax rates of 20, 40 or 50 per cent[3] (with no annual capital gains tax exemption) for individuals and at 50 per cent for UK resident trusts. Hence, the tax position between the two differs markedly. Furthermore foreign domiciliaries obtain no rebasing[4] or pre-April 2008 exemption for offshore income gains accruing or realised before April 6, 2008 if they are taxed under the transfer of assets provisions rather than under TCGA 1992 s.87.

53.03 In order for an offshore income gain to arise, two conditions must be satisfied:

(a) the investor must redeem or otherwise dispose of his interest (e.g. share/units in an offshore fund. Death, takeover and reconstructions are all treated as disposals.[5] Alternatively the investor must receive a distribution from the fund; and

(b) the fund must be a non-reporting fund or if it is a reporting fund at the time of the disposal it was previously a non-reporting fund and an election under reg.48 was not made.[6]

II WHAT IS AN OFFSHORE FUND?

53.04 An offshore fund is defined in TIOPA 2010 s.355(1) as:

"(1) (a) a mutual fund constituted by a body corporate resident outside the United Kingdom,

(b) a mutual fund under which property is held on trust for the participants where the trustees of the property are not resident in the United Kingdom, or

(c) a mutual fund constituted by other arrangements that create rights in the nature of co-ownership where the arrangements take effect by virtue of the law of a territory outside the United Kingdom.

(2) Subsection (1)(c) does not include a mutual fund constituted by two or more persons carrying on a trade or business in partnership.

(3) In this section—

'body corporate' does not include a limited liability partnership, and

'co-ownership' is not restricted to the meaning of that term in the law of any part of the United Kingdom.

(4) See also section 151W(b) of TCGA 1992, section 564U(b) of ITA 2007 and section 519(4)(b) of CTA 2009 (which have the effect that investment

---

[2] See 11.05–09 for rates and exemptions.
[3] Depending on whether the individual is a higher rate taxpayer or not.
[4] See 19.49 and 53.20.
[5] Unless the acquiring entity is itself a non-reporting entity. See regs 35 and 36.
[6] See reg.17 and for further details of the effect of the election see 53.07.

bond arrangements are not an offshore fund for the purposes of section 354)."

A mutual fund

The key term is "mutual fund". This is defined as arrangements which satisfy   **53.05**
Conditions A to C as set out in s.356[7]:

> "*(3)   Condition A is that the purpose or effect of the arrangements is to enable the participants—*
>
> > *(a)   to participate in the acquisition, holding, management or disposal of the property, or*
> > *(b)   to receive profits or income arising from the acquisition, holding, management or disposal of the property or sums paid out of such profits or income.*
>
> *(4)   Condition B is that the participants do not have day-to-day control of the management of the property.*
> *(5)   For the purposes of condition B a participant does not have day-to-day control of the management of property by virtue of having a right to be consulted or to give directions.*
> *(6)   Condition C is that, under the terms of the arrangements, a reasonable investor participating in the arrangements would expect to be able to realise all or part of an investment in the arrangements on a basis calculated entirely, or almost entirely, by reference to—*
>
> > *(a)   the net asset value of the property that is the subject of the arrangements, or*
> > *(b)   an index of any description.[8]*"

What is a Reporting Fund?

The tax treatment on the disposal of an offshore fund depends on whether   **53.06**
or not it has reporting status. To be a reporting fund, it must satisfy a
number of conditions set out in the 2009 Regulations.[9] In particular the fund
must:

---

[7] Previously the reference was to a "collective investment scheme". TA 1988 s.756A(3) referred to FSMA 2000 s.235.
[8] Condition C focuses on exit value but is not met if net value can be realised only on the winding up of the fund. However it is wider than the old definition that provided an investor only realised an offshore income gain if he had the expectation of realising net asset value within seven years (because only then did he have a material interest). See HMRC Offshore Funds Manual for further details of the classification of reporting and non-reporting funds.
[9] See Pt 3.

(i) produce accounts in accordance with international accounting standards or generally accepted accounting practice;

(ii) compute reportable income for each period of account;

(ii) inform participants and HMRC of the amounts distributed per unit and amounts not distributed; and

(iv) apply and be accepted by HMRC as a reporting fund. An existing fund cannot apply retrospectively for reporting status for more than three months before the application.

Undistributed income of a reporting fund is treated as notionally distributed and taxed accordingly as dividend income. Note that even if a fund distributes all its income (so that no income is rolled-up—the mischief that the legislation originally aimed to prevent) this is not in itself sufficient. The offshore fund must also comply with the above requirements and apply to HMRC to be accepted as a reporting fund. HMRC regularly update the list of reporting funds on their website. The fund's prospectus will usually say whether the fund is reporting or not.

53.07   A fund can cease to be reporting by notice to HMRC or if it is in serious breach of the reporting fund requirements. If a fund changes status from non-reporting to reporting then the investor can elect for a deemed disposal of his interest in the fund at market value, when the fund's status changes.[10] The investor will pay income tax at the date of that deemed disposal but capital gains tax on any subsequent increase when eventually disposing of his interest in the fund. If at the time of the change of status the investor's investment is showing a loss the fund is treated on any subsequent disposal as having been a reporting fund throughout. Accordingly, on a later disposal capital gains tax treatment will apply. If no such election is made and the fund shows a gain on change of status then on disposal of a reporting fund that was previously non-reporting, income tax not capital gains tax treatment applies.

III TAXATION OF OFFSHORE NON-REPORTING FUNDS (OIGS)

53.08   No offshore income gain (OIG) accrues until there is a disposal or redemption of an interest in a non-reporting fund[11] or there is a distribution.

53.09   A distribution from a corporate fund is taxed as a dividend in the hands of an individual without the notional one ninth credit (so 10 per cent basic/32.5 per cent higher rate/42.5 per cent top rate and trust rate). If the distribution is from a non-corporate fund it is taxed as income at 20/40/50 per cent as appropriate.

---

[10] Regulation 48.

[11] Or a reporting fund that was previously non-reporting where no election has been made: see 53.07.

What is a disposal?

Disposal generally has the same meaning as for capital gains tax purposes.[12]   **53.10**
This has particular relevance for trusts in the following areas:

(i) a deemed disposal by the trustees on termination of the trust or if a beneficiary becomes absolutely entitled to part of the trust assets triggers a disposal of the trust's interest in the offshore fund so that an OIG may arise. However, no hold-over relief is available to defer the charge even if an inheritance tax charge arises[13];

(ii) a gift of an interest in an offshore fund into trust is a disposal and an OIG could arise which will be taxed on the settlor. Again there is no hold-over relief;

(iii) a sub-fund election may trigger a deemed disposal of units in an offshore fund;

(iv) the death of a beneficiary with a qualifying interest in possession triggers a deemed disposal and reacquisition of the settled property by the trustees.[14] However, there is no uplift to market value similar to that for ordinary capital gains and an offshore income gain is deemed to accrue.[15] If a charge arises it is not deductible against the inheritance tax liability arising on that death[16];

(v) special rules operate in relation to share exchanges: i.e. where an interest in one fund is exchanged for an interest in another fund.[17] Roll-over treatment can apply if the conditions in those sections are satisfied *and* at the time of the disposal both funds are non-reporting provided that at the time of the disposal the new fund is also non-reporting. However, the sections are disapplied if the original fund had been a non-reporting (or non-distributing) fund at any time from January 1, 1984 and the acquiring entity was reporting in the accounting period of exchange. A disposal then occurs. The sections apply to prevent a disposal if the exchange takes place between two funds that are both reporting or between a fund that was formerly distributing in exchange for one that is reporting[18];

(vi) a deemed disposal under TCGA 1992 Sch.4B (transfer of value linked with trustee borrowing) can trigger an OIG[19];

---

[12] Regulation 33. But note that death of the investor and the take-over, or reconstruction of the company are disposals for these purposes.

[13] See Ch.18. Only "ordinary gains", not offshore income gains, are eligible for hold-over relief under TCGA 1992 s.260.

[14] TCGA 1992 s.72. Generally no chargeable gain arises on the deemed disposal on death and instead there is a tax-free uplift but that uplift does not apply to OIGs.

[15] If the individual died owning an offshore fund personally reg.34 deems there to be a disposal with no corresponding uplift. (TCGA 1992 s.62 specifically deems there not to be a disposal but just an acquisition at market value but reg.34 undoes this and provides for a deemed disposal.)

[16] Contrast the position if an individual dies owning offshore funds. In this case the income tax charge arising on the offshore fund is deductible for inheritance tax purposes (see IHTA 1984 s.174).

[17] See TCGA 1992 ss.135 and 136 considered in Ch.17.

[18] See Sch.1 para.3C of the 2009 Regulations.

[19] For what happens to that OIG, see 53.40.

(vii) the emigration of a trust triggers a deemed disposal so that an OIG can arise;

(viii) if non-resident trustees transfer property to a new settlement, TCGA 1992 s.90 applies and a proportionate part of the total pool of OIGs realised in the past and in the tax year of disposal as well as ordinary trust gains are transferred across to the new settlement.[20]

Computation of OIGs

53.11 OIGs are computed in accordance with capital gains tax rules.[21] Before April 6, 2008 the gain was the unindexed gain without taper relief. This remains the case from April 6, 2008 but given the abolition of indexation and taper relief for ordinary chargeable gains the amount of an OIG accruing on a disposal will usually be the same as the amount of chargeable gain if the asset had not been an offshore fund. As explained in 53.18 below, unlike chargeable gains on "ordinary" assets, OIGs are capable of being taxed under two different regimes: the s.87 regime and the transfer of assets regime.

53.12 Losses on an offshore fund cannot be set against other OIGs and are not allowable for income tax purposes although they are allowable for capital gains tax purposes and are allowable against other gains on the same basis as capital losses on ordinary assets.[22] There is no credit for foreign tax paid by the offshore fund (of course tax suffered by the fund reduces its value and so reduces the gain). If the taxpayer owned the offshore fund on January 1, 1984 when the rules were first introduced it is treated as acquired at market value at that time unless the gain is less.

Other points

53.13 The OIG is deemed to be relevant foreign income of the individual.[23] The remittance basis applies to disposals of offshore funds by a remittance basis user.[24] A charitable company or trust is exempt from tax on OIGs.[25] A non-resident is not chargeable on OIGs although a tax charge will arise where a person emigrates (sells the OIG) and returns within five years.[26]

---

[20] See reg.20(3).

[21] See 2009 Regulations reg.39.

[22] See ITA 2007 s.152 and 2009 Regulations reg.42.

[23] Regulation 19(3).

[24] See Chs 5 and 19 for further discussion of remittance basis user and see Ch.54 for when OIGs are realised by companies. See reg.19: offshore gains are deemed to be relevant foreign income so the remittance basis can apply.

[25] See reg.31.

[26] See reg.23 with effect for disposals on or after December 1, 2009.

UK resident trust: not settlor-interested

A UK resident trust is subject to income tax on its OIGs at the trust rate of 50 **53.14** per cent whether the trust is a fixed income trust or discretionary.[27] Of course, the OIG is not actual but deemed income so is not paid to a beneficiary entitled to the income. It is capital for trust law purposes.

UK resident settlor-interested trust

Since an OIG accruing to UK trustees is not "actual income", in the absence **53.15** of express provision it would not fall within ITTOIA 2005 s.624 (settlor taxed on the income of this settlement if it is settlor-interested). Accordingly, Reg 18 provides that the OIG is "treated for all the purposes of the Taxes Acts as income" so is assumed to fall within s.624 and may be taxed on the settlor at his personal rates of income tax. If the OIG arises to a minor under a bare trust arrangement then the gain may be taxed on the settlor/parent under ITTOIA 2005 s.632.[28]

If the settlor is a remittance basis user and the OIG is not remitted by the settlor or any relevant person then it is not charged on the settlor but is taxed on the UK trustees at 50 per cent (and is not taxed if remitted later).

Before December 1, 2009 if the OIG was made by a non-resident company, **53.16** wholly owned by a UK trust, then the settlor did not pay tax under s.624 since it was not trust income.[29] (Of course, the non-resident company did not pay UK tax since it was non-resident.) Instead the OIG was apportioned to a UK participator (the trustees). It was not then taxed on the settlor but on the trustees at 40 per cent (the then trust rate of income tax). Since 2009 OIGs accruing to a wholly owned non-resident company owned by a UK resident trust are taxed on the settlor.[30]

V NON-RESIDENT TRUSTS

Where an OIG accrues to a non-UK resident trust, the trustees are not subject **53.17** to tax on that gain being non-UK resident and the OIG is not deemed to be

---

[27] ITA 2007 s.482.

[28] The legislation assumes this is the case for UK resident trusts. Regulation 20 specifically disapplies the settlement legislation in relation to non-resident settlor-interested trusts.

[29] See Chs 8 and 54 for discussion of company income in the case where the company is owned by a trust.

[30] Regulation 24 treats the OIG as having arisen to the trustees as UK resident participators by virtue of s.13. That is taxed as income and so charged on the settlor. The transfer of assets provisions do not apply because s.13 TCGA 1992 takes priority over the transfer of assets charge. Regulation 21(3) disapplies the transfer of assets provisions in ss.720–729 where the OIG is deemed to arise to a UK resident participator under reg.24.

income arising under the settlement provisions.[31] Therefore, ITTOIA 2005 s.624 does not apply even though the trust may be settlor-interested and the settlor UK resident and domiciled. However, that is not the end of the matter. Instead one has to look at the transfer of assets provisions and the capital payments regime under TCGA 1992 s.87.[32] If the OIGs were realised in an underlying company one must also look at the s.13 charge as applied by reg.24 which treats the offshore income gains as having arisen to the participators.

The interaction of transfer of assets provisions with the capital gains tax provisions

53.18   There are, therefore, two mechanisms to charge OIGs realised by non-resident trusts: ITA 2007 ss.731–735 ("the transfer of assets code") and TCGA 1992 s.87 ("the s.87 code"). Regulation 20 of The Offshore Funds (Tax) Regulations 2009 applies the charging provisions under the s.87 code (*the primary rule*) and reg.21 applies the transfer of assets charging provisions (*the secondary rule*). In both cases the remittance basis is capable of applying. It is important to ascertain which mechanism of charge applies because the transitional provisions in FA 2008[33] only apply if the gain is charged under the primary rule while the motive defence is only available if the gain is charged under the secondary rule. There is a "tie-break" determining whether the primary or secondary rule applies in reg.21(5).

53.19   In most cases for non-transferor trusts,[34] the generally more favourable primary rule under the capital gains tax code will apply. In relation to transferor trusts (wherever the transferor is domiciled) the secondary rule applies unless the OIGs are matched under TCGA 1992 s.87 in the year in which they arise with current year or brought forward capital payments (whether to the settlor or any other beneficiary) and the beneficiary who receives such capital payments is resident (whether or not domiciled) in the UK.

Transitional reliefs

53.20   There are three transitional reliefs in FA 2008 Sch.7 that affect OIGs taxed under the primary rule.

53.21   First, FA 2008 Sch.7 para.126 applies where trustees make a so-called "rebasing election". In that case, in relation to foreign domiciliaries, a chargeable gain accruing in respect of an asset owned by the trustees, or by a company owned by the trustees, is apportioned.[35] Only the part of the gain accruing

---

[31] See reg.22 which limits the application of the code to residents and reg.20(1) which disapplies the settlement code in relation to OIGs of non-resident trusts.

[32] The capital payments regime is applied by reg.20(2) and (3) and the transfer of assets regime by reg.21. These two regulations largely duplicate TA 1988 ss.762 and 762ZA.

[33] See 53.20.

[34] i.e. where the transferor and his spouse/civil partner does not have power to enjoy or where the transferor is not UK resident. See Ch.8.

[35] Paragraph 126(7)–(9).

post-April 5, 2008 is chargeable on a foreign domiciliary. Gains treated as accruing before April 6, 2008 are not taxed.[36]

The effect of a rebasing election is that provided the primary not the secondary rule applies, OIGs treated as accruing prior to April 6, 2008 anywhere within the structure are not chargeable on foreign domiciled beneficiaries albeit they can be allocated to capital payments.

Secondly, under FA 2008 Sch.7 para.124, any chargeable gains or OIGs   **53.22**
arising before April 6, 2008 are not taxable so far as matched with capital payments made before or after that date.[37]

Thirdly, any capital payments made before April 6, 2008 are not   **53.23**
chargeable even if matched to gains or OIGs arising after that date provided at the date of matching that the beneficiary is foreign domiciled. Capital payments made between March 12 and April 5, 2008 cannot be matched to ordinary trust gains arising after April 6, 2008 and therefore remain unallocated but they can be matched to OIGs arising after this date and will not be taxed.

UK domiciled settlors of non-resident trusts

If a non-resident trust (or any underlying offshore company) realises an OIG   **53.24**
then TCGA 1992 s.86 does not apply. Contrast ordinary trust gains which are taxed on a UK domiciled settler.[38]

The UK resident settlor of an offshore trust where he or spouse/civil partner   **53.25**
can benefit may be chargeable to income tax on an OIG under the transfer of assets provisions (under the secondary rule) whether or not he has actually received a benefit or capital sum provided that he has power to enjoy such income (whether of the trust or any underlying company).[39] However, no charge arises if the motive defence applies[40] or the settlor is not UK resident. Moreover no tax charge under the secondary rule will apply if in the year the OIG is realised it is fully matched to a capital payment (whether or not made to the UK domiciled settlor or to another beneficiary) and the recipient of that payment is UK resident.[41]

If a non-UK resident trust from which the UK domiciled settlor and spouse   **53.26**
are excluded benefits his children and realises OIGs, such gains are not taxed on the settlor under s.86 nor under ITTOIA 2005 s.624 nor under the transfer of assets provisions (assuming he has not received a capital sum in the past: see 7.45 and 8.18). Any tax is deferred until such time as a beneficiary receives benefits. That beneficiary will then be taxed under the primary rule if UK resident. The rate of tax will not differ whether taxed under the primary or secondary rules and the transitional reliefs referred to above are only relevant if the beneficiary is foreign domiciled.

Therefore, where a UK resident and domiciled settlor is still alive (provided   **53.27**
he and his wife or civil partner cannot benefit from the trust but his children

---

[36] A similar rebasing relief applies to OIGs in Sch.7 para.101.
[37] See FA 2008 Sch.7 para.100(1)(b).
[38] TCGA 1992 s.86 does not apply to foreign domiciled settlors whether or not remittance basis users. See Chs 5 and 19.
[39] See ITA 2007 s.720–730.
[40] See Ch.8.
[41] See 2009 Regulations reg.21(5).

can) non-reporting funds may be a useful investment vehicle for offshore trusts because tax continues to be deferred. Even if distributions are made, the UK resident minor children have the benefit of income tax personal allowances and the settlor is not taxed on the OIG under the settlement provisions because these do not apply to OIGs realised by non-resident trusts.

On the other hand a UK resident beneficiary will pay income tax to the extent he ever receives benefits which are matched to those OIGs[42] and given that the OIG is deemed income, the rate of tax may be higher than if the OIG was subject to capital gains tax with no annual exemption available.[43] OIGs are always treated as distributed before ordinary trust gains: see Example 53.1 below.

53.28   Even if the settlor can benefit from the trust, as noted above, a charge on the settlor under the transfer of assets provisions can be avoided if the OIG is matched to a capital payment made to a UK resident beneficiary in the year it accrues. Such capital payment could be made to a beneficiary who pays income tax at a lower rate. Distributions of OIGs realised by non-resident non-transferor trusts to the settlor's minor children will not be taxed as the settlor's income under the transfer of assets provisions since these provisions are disapplied and the settlement provisions in ITTOIA 2005 Pt 5 Ch.5 are specifically disapplied to non-resident trusts.

53.29   As noted above, an OIG is not reduced by OIG losses. These are relieved as capital losses against ordinary capital gains and go to reduce the pool of "ordinary s.2(2) trust gains".[44]

EXAMPLE 53.1

A non-resident trust is settlor-interested and the settlor has power to enjoy the income and capital. The settlor is UK resident and domiciled. No charge arises on the settlor under s.86. In 2009 the trustees distribute £100,000 capital equally to his five minor children and in 2010 they distribute a further £20,000.

In 2009—OIGs are £30,000; distributions £20,000 to each of settlor's five minor children.

In 2010—OIGs £30,000; s.2(2) ordinary trust gains are £50,000.

Assume the total pool of OIGs therefore stands at £60,000 and the pool of ordinary trust gains stands at £50,000.

---

[42] Either under the transfer of assets provisions or, if the motive test disapplies those provisions, under TGCA 1992 s.87.

[43] The position was different prior to April 6, 2008 where gains and income were generally taxed at the same rate. OIGs were not taxed on the settlor under TGCA 1992 s.86 and the rate of tax before April 6, 2010 was a maximum 40%. Ordinary trust gains were either taxed on the settlor under s.86 immediately or, if rolled up, could eventually be taxed on higher rate beneficiaries at a rate of up to 64%. Ordinary trust gains are now taxed at 44.8% with full supplemental charge. OIGs can be taxed at up to 50% but at lower income tax rates where the beneficiary is not a top rate taxpayer. Note that the supplemental charge does not apply to OIGs: see reg.20(3). And, as discussed, offshore income gains of a non-resident trust are not taxed on the parent if distributed to the minor children of the settlor.

[44] See Ch.21 and reg.42.

The tax position is as follows:

(1) The LIFO basis does not apply to match the 2010 ordinary trust gains before the OIGs whenever realised. Instead the unmatched OIGs are matched first (on a LIFO basis) through all years and only when all OIGs are exhausted are capital payments matched to ordinary trust gains (assuming there are no unmatched TCGA 1992 Sch.4C gains).[45] If the trust has available relevant income then the benefit must be matched first to this and taxed under the transfer of assets code by reference to that income. The OIGs then remain unmatched until the available relevant income is exhausted.

(2) The five children therefore each pay income tax at their highest marginal rate: in 2009 on £6,000 each (being the 2009 £30,000 OIG) under s.87. They pay on a further £6,000 OIGs in 2010 and at their CGT rate on £10,000 trust gains each in 2010.[46] The OIGs pool for the purposes of the capital payments regime is therefore nil. The capital payments are fully matched. The settlor is not taxed under the transfer of assets provisions (i.e. the provisions in ITA 2007 ss.720–735) even though UK resident and domiciled because the primary rule takes priority. The settlor is not taxed on the income of the minor children.[47]

(3) If, however, the OIGs were not matched to capital payments or the capital payment to which the OIG was matched was one made to a non-resident beneficiary then an amount equal to the OIGs would be taxable on a UK domiciled and resident transferor with power to enjoy under the transfer of assets provisions (see reg.21(4)). In our example since the transferor is UK resident and domiciled, income tax would be charged on him in each year when the OIG arose on an arising basis.

(4) If in the above example the transferor was a remittance basis user[48] then the income tax charge is on a remittance basis but no rebasing is available for the transferor once the transfer of assets provisions apply so pre-April 2008 accrued OIGs can then become taxable. The only exception would be if the motive test applied to prevent a charge under the transfer of assets code. In that event the OIG would not be taxed under the capital payments code in TCGA 1992 s.87.

(5) If the OIG arises to a non-resident company owned by a non-resident trust then the OIG is attributed to the trustees.[49] That

[45] Such Sch.4C gains would only be matched on payments to a foreign domiciled beneficiary if they arose in a post-April 2008 pool: see19.69.

[46] Each child may have an unused capital gains tax exemption in which case no capital gains tax charge arises on the ordinary trust gains. Note that all this is subject to the remittance basis if the beneficiary is a remittance basis user: see Ch.5. If the OIGs all accrued prior to April 6, 2008 and a rebasing election has been made then no tax charge arises on the foreign domiciled UK resident beneficiary even if he is not a remittance basis user. The same transitional reliefs as described in Ch.19 apply. If a proportion of the OIG realised in 2010–11 accrued pre-April 2008 that gain is not taxed under the legislation provided the OIG has not gone into the transfer of assets pool.

[47] See reg.21 which provides that once an OIG is matched with a capital payment under the capital gains tax legislation it cannot become income under the transfer of assets provisions.

[48] i.e. non-UK domiciled and claiming the remittance basis.

[49] Regulation 24.

OIG can then go into the total pool of OIGs taxable under the primary or secondary rules on the same basis as above.

Foreign domiciled settlors of non-resident trusts with power to enjoy—transferor charge

53.30   If an OIG accrues to an offshore trust that is a transferor trust and it is not matched by a capital payment made in that or a previous year to the transferor or to some other UK resident beneficiary (whether or not a remittance basis user) then the transfer of assets provisions (secondary rule) will apply to that OIG so far as the transferor is concerned. Hence, if the transferor is domiciled and UK resident (or foreign domiciled but not a remittance basis user) he will pay income tax on an arising basis under ITA 2007 s.720. Once taxed under the transfer of assets provisions the OIG is then removed from any future charge under the capital payments code as far as any other beneficiary is concerned. If the transferor is a remittance basis user, he pays tax on a remittance basis but henceforth the charge is under ITA 2007 s.720 not under TCGA 1992 ss.87A–87C. This means that no rebasing will be available and there is no exclusion of pre-April 6, 2008 OIGs for the foreign domiciled transferor or beneficiary. If he is a foreign domiciliary claiming the remittance basis he will only pay tax if the OIG is remitted by him or any other relevant person. If he is foreign domiciled and not claiming the remittance basis then the loss of the transitional reliefs may be particularly problematic: he does not need to claim the remittance basis to obtain the benefit of the transitional reliefs but if the secondary rule applies he loses those reliefs and is then taxed on OIGs realised within the trust structure on an arising basis.

53.31   It is therefore important to ensure that in relation to trusts where foreign domiciled UK resident transferors have power to enjoy, OIGs are matched in the year they are realised and the primary rule applies wherever the OIGs has accrued pre-April 2008 gains and a rebasing election has been made. Otherwise the benefit of the capital gains tax transitional reliefs will be lost.

53.32   However, if the motive defence is available it will be better to ensure the secondary rule applies: there is then no charge under the transfer of assets provisions and the transferor will not be taxable on the OIG under the capital payments code either once the secondary rule applies. This can be achieved by not making any payments to UK residents in the year the OIG arises to ensure that the primary rule is disapplied.

In summary the OIGs then cease to be taxable altogether on the transferor provided:

(i) they are not matched to capital payments in the year they arise so are not taxed under the capital payments code; and

(ii) the motive test applies.

53.33   Note also that the March 12 to April 5, 2008 rule[50] does not apply to OIGs. Therefore, if a capital payment has been made to a foreign domiciliary in

---

[50] See 19.46.

that period it can be matched to OIGs arising after that date but will not be taxable under s.87 because the capital payment was received prior to April 6, 2008. This also prevents the OIGs being treated as income in the future for the purposes of the transfer of asset provisions because it has been matched in the year when it arose.

Non-transferor trusts

If the OIG accrues to an offshore trust which is not one where the transferor has power to enjoy[51] and is matched to capital distributions made to a UK resident non-transferor beneficiary (whether in the same or a later year) then prima facie the primary rule (capital payments code) applies and it is not relevant income for the purposes of ITA 2007 ss.731–735 (transfer of assets provisions). Hence, rebasing is available and if the beneficiary is foreign domiciled he will obtain the benefit of the transitional provisions outlined at 19.49.[52]   **53.34**

If the primary rule applies reg.20(5) provides that the beneficiary is treated as making the disposal and hence the offshore income gains are treated as income arising to him. Hence, a higher rate (as opposed to top rate) taxpayer beneficiary will only pay tax on OIGs at 40 per cent while he might pay capital gains tax on ordinary trust gains at 44.8 per cent if the maximum supplemental charge applies.   **53.35**

If, however, the OIG is matched to a capital payment to a non-UK resident beneficiary then although this reduces the OIG pool for s.87 purposes and the non-resident is not taxed[53] the OIG is not treated as arising to a UK resident person. Henceforth, although the OIG cannot be allocated to future payments for the purposes of the capital payments code, the OIGs are relevant income for the purposes of ss.731–735 (and s.720–730) in relation to a subsequent benefit conferred on UK resident beneficiaries.   **53.36**

Before April 6, 2008 this was important for foreign domiciliaries because they were not chargeable to tax at all under s.87 but were chargeable under ss.731–735 (and ss.720–730). From April 6, 2008 the point remains important where OIGs arose or accrued before April 6 or substantial capital payments were made before that date, which have not yet been matched. If the OIGs go into the relevant income pool, the foreign domiciliary will not obtain the benefit of any transitional provisions or rebasing and therefore all the OIGs can be taxed on him albeit under the remittance basis. In other words, an OIG which becomes transfer of assets income cannot subsequently be matched under the capital payments code in TCGA 1992 s.87 et al.   **53.37**

Hence, a foreign domiciliary will generally wish OIGs which arose or accrued prior to April 6, 2008 to be charged under TCGA 1992 s.87 rather than under the transfer of assets provisions in order to take advantage of rebasing and the other transitional reliefs.[54] It is therefore important to ensure that such OIGs are not matched to payments to a non-UK resident unless   **53.38**

---

[51] Or if he does have power to enjoy he is not ordinarily resident in the UK.
[52] Referred to at 53.20 above so that he is not taxed on pre-April 2008 OIGs. As noted in 53.33 unlike ordinary s.2(2) trust gains, a capital payment received between March 12 and April 5, 2008 can be matched to post-April 5, 2008 OIGs and will not be taxed: see 19.50.
[53] Subject to the five-year rule. Regulations 22 and 23.
[54] See Ch.19 for further details.

the motive test is satisfied. If the motive test is available, then the trustees may want to ensure that all OIGs are matched to capital payments to a non-resident so that the secondary rule applies. Then the OIG pool is reduced for the purposes of the capital payments regime and that amount (which would otherwise be taxed under the transfer of assets code) is now exempt from income tax under the transfer of assets legislation.

53.39   Where OIGs have all arisen or accrued post-April 6, 2008 it will matter less to the foreign domiciliary whether he is taxed under the secondary rule (transfer of assets provisions) or the primary rule (capital payments regime) unless the motive test is in point in which case he will want the secondary rule to apply and the trustees should first try and ensure the OIGs are matched to payments to non-residents. Whichever rule applies OIGs are matched to benefits received after any other relevant trust income but before ordinary trust gains or Sch.4C gains and the remittance basis can apply.

TCGA 1992 Sch.4B and 4C 1992

53.40   Before April 6, 2008 although a Sch.4B disposal resulted in the realization of OIGs on the deemed disposal, it was unclear whether that disposal resulted in past or current year unmatched OIGs going into the Sch.4C pool and whether OIGs triggered on the Sch.4B disposal itself entered the Sch.4C pool or remained in the ordinary s.87 OIG pool.[55]

53.41   From April 6, 2008 OIGs triggered on the deemed Sch.4B disposal itself pass into the Sch.4C pool[56] as well as any unmatched OIGs. OIGs are matched to capital payments before any other gains in the Sch.4C pool and before any other OIGs.

EXAMPLE 53.2

(1) An offshore trust realises OIGs of £100,000 in 2008–09 and £50,000 ordinary trust gains. There are unmatched pre-April 2008 capital payments of £100,000 made to a UK resident foreign domiciled beneficiary A. The OIGs are matched first and no tax arises even if the beneficiary is not a remittance basis user and even if the capital payment has been remitted. If, however, the trustees distribute £100,000 to a non-UK resident in 2008–09 or no capital payments are made in that year but earlier unmatched capital payments were made to a non-resident then the OIGs are matched to that capital payment first. There is no tax due then but an amount equal to the OIGs then goes into the transfer of assets pool and can be taxed on A when he receives future benefits on a remittance basis without regard to whether they accrued prior to April 6, 2008.

(2) An offshore trust realises OIGs of £100,000 in 2008–09 all of which accrued prior to April 6, 2008 and a rebasing election is made. No capital payments are made and there are no unmatched capital payments. The

---

[55] Under what was then TA 1988 s.762.
[56] See reg.20(3).

trust is one in which the settlor/transferor X can benefit and is therefore within ITA 2007 ss.720–730. If X is either UK domiciled and resident or UK resident and non-UK domiciled but not a remittance basis user he pays tax on an arising basis even though all the gains accrued before April 6, 2008.

(3) If X the settlor/transferor is non-UK domiciled but UK resident and is a remittance basis user then he pays tax on a remittance basis. However, if those OIGs are later distributed to him they are taxed under ss.720–730 (albeit on the remittance basis) and do not benefit from rebasing.

CHAPTER 54

TAXATION OF NON-RESIDENT COMPANIES

- Introduction (**54.01**)
- Taxation of an individual owning an interest in an offshore company (**54.04**)
- Trustees owning non-resident companies (**54.24**)
- Summary of tax advantages and disadvantages of incorporation (**54.34**)

I INTRODUCTION[1]

54.01   This chapter considers the taxation of non-resident companies owned by UK resident individuals (whether or not UK domiciled) and trusts. It is assumed that the company is situated in an offshore jurisdiction and wholly owned by the individual or trust.

54.02   The non-resident company is not subject to UK tax on its foreign source income. It is liable to corporation tax only if it is trading in the UK through a permanent establishment[2] when tax is charged on such of its profits as are attributable to that permanent establishment.[3] It is not otherwise subject to corporation tax on UK source income and is, at most, subject to basic rate income tax on that income. In the case of UK dividends and payments of interest, the tax is restricted to the tax withheld and so no further tax is due from the company.[4] Accordingly the only type of UK investment income on which a non-resident company is likely to pay tax is rental income from UK real estate and in such a case the company will pay basic rate income tax on that income.[5]

54.03   A non-resident company does not pay tax on capital gains except in respect of gains on assets used in the trade carried on through a permanent establishment in the UK.[6]

---

[1] For the residence of companies, see 4.43.

[2] CTA 2010 s.5(2).

[3] See CTA 2010 s.114(1) regarding the meaning of the term *"permanent establishment"*: essentially a fixed place of business in the UK or where an agent exercises UK authority to do business on behalf of the company: see 4.43.

[4] See ITTOIA 2005 s.399(2) and ITA 2007 s.815.

[5] ITA 2007 s.11.

[6] TCGA 1992 s.10B and see 15.07, 13.07 and 13.22.

II TAXATION OF AN INDIVIDUAL OWNING AN INTEREST IN AN OFFSHORE COMPANY

The transfer of assets legislation

A UK resident and domiciled individual who has put funds into an offshore company and who owns an interest in it will generally be taxed on the income of the company on an arising basis under the transfer of assets provisions, subject only to the motive defence.[7]

54.04

However, in February 2011, the European Commission requested the UK Government to amend the transfer of assets provisions on the basis that they are incompatible with EU law when the company is incorporated and managed in another Member State. The Commission determined that both the transfer of assets provisions and TCGA 1992 s.13[8] are discriminatory and in breach of the EU's Single Market; namely freedom of establishment and the free movement of capital and so contrary to arts 49 and 63 of the Treaty on the Functioning of the European Union and arts 31 and 40 of the EEA Agreement. The result is that investments outside the UK are taxed more heavily than domestic investments and both s.13 and the transfer of assets restrictions are considered to be disproportionate, in the sense that they go beyond what is reasonably necessary in order to prevent abuse or tax avoidance or any other requirements of public interest. Consideration is currently being given by the UK Government as to how to respond. In the absence of a satisfactory response, the Commission may refer the UK to the European Court of Justice.[9]

54.05

EXAMPLE 54.1

(1) A, a UK resident and domiciled individual, forms a non-resident company into which he transfers £1 million in consideration for the issue of fully paid shares. The company buys UK rental property and receives rent. H pays basic rate income tax on the profit from the letting. A is subject to tax on that rental income, albeit with a credit for the tax paid by the company under the transfer of assets legislation. Note that even if the company was owned by a trust, if A had power to enjoy the income of that trust he would be subject to income tax on the rental income.

(2) Facts as above except A is non-UK domiciled and a remittance basis user. He is still subject to UK tax on the rental income (whether or not the company is owned in a trust) because it is UK source.

---

[7] ITA 2007 ss.720–730. The position may be different if the individual purchased shares in a company that already owned its investments, i.e. when the individual bought the company as a going concern. In *Vestey v IRC* [1980] AC 1148 it was held in the High Court that where trustees purchased an insurance company the income of the company was not assessable under these provisions on the basis that it did not arise by virtue of the transfer or any operation associated with the transfer. See also 8.23.

[8] See 54.09.

[9] See CIOT letter dated April 18, 2011 on the Chartered Institute of Taxation website (*http://www.tax.org.uk/* [Accessed September 1, 2011]) for details of the complaint made.

(3) Facts as above except that A is not UK resident. He is not subject to UK income tax on the rent.

Dividends

54.06 Dividends received by a UK resident individual from a wholly owned offshore company are taxed at basic rate (10 per cent), higher rate (32.5 per cent) and additional rate (42.5 per cent) subject only to the remittance basis if applicable. If the individual investor's shareholding (including shares of connected parties) is 10 per cent or more, the 1/9 credit is not generally available.[10] However, if the company is resident in a territory with which the UK has concluded a double tax treaty (for example, Cyprus), it may be possible to secure such a credit.[11]

54.07 Dividends received by a remittance basis user from the offshore company are relevant foreign income and taxed on the remittance basis. Income generated *within* the company (e.g. on its underlying investments) that is treated as arising to the transferor is relevant foreign income if the transferor under the transfer of assets code is also a remittance basis user in the tax year in which the income arises and the income of the company would be relevant foreign income if it were in fact the transferor's.

EXAMPLE 54.2

B, a remittance basis user, is the owner of an offshore company holding rental property in Italy and non-UK shares and securities. B is not taxed on any of the income arising within the company or any dividends unless and until it is remitted whether by B or the company as a relevant person.[12]

Double taxation

54.08 It can be seen from the above that there is scope for double taxation: A in Example 54.1(1) pays higher rate tax on the rental income and potentially further tax as and when the company declares dividends. To deal with this, ITA 2007 s.743(4) provides that where A has been charged to tax on the company's income and it is subsequently received by him it is deemed not to form part of his income again for income tax purposes. This is the case even if the receipt is a new source of income such as a dividend. The position is more problematic when the company distribute to a discretionary trust. Can it then

---

[10] Under ITTOIA 2005 s.397A: see 6.18. If he owns less than 10% the credit is available: see s.397C. Confusingly to obtain the tax credit the shareholder needs to own *less* than 10%. However, to be liable to capital gains tax under s.13 on gains made by the company he needs to own *more* than 10%: see TCGA 1992 s.13(4).

[11] See s.397B(a) and 6.18.

[12] See Ch.5.

be taxed on the settlor again if the trust is settlor-interested under the settlement provisions? Generally HMRC will not assess the dividend again if it is paid to the trust and out to the settlor immediately as income so it is advisable to avoid delay in these circumstances.[13]

But if the company is instead sold or liquidated or a capital distribution is made, the UK resident and domiciled recipient will pay capital gains tax on any gain so realised with no credit for the earlier income tax paid.

Capital gains

Any gains realised by a non-resident company that would be a close company **54.09** if UK resident are apportioned among those participators broadly owning more than 10 per cent of the company under TCGA 1992 s.13.[14] Connected party interests are included in calculating the 10 per cent threshold.[15] No apportionment occurs on gains accruing on the disposal of assets used in a trade carried on by the company abroad and all foreign currency bank accounts and debts are outside the scope of s.13.[16] The chargeable gains that accrue to a non-resident close company are indexed and computed in the same way as those of a UK resident company. Transfers of assets within a non-resident group of companies will generally be "no gain, no loss" disposals for the purposes of s.13 and will therefore not trigger gains on the participators.[17]

Reimbursement

The shareholders or participators have no statutory right to require the **54.10** company to reimburse any tax assessed on them, under either the transfer of assets provisions or the capital gains tax legislation. However, s.13(11) provides that if any tax payable by the participator is, in fact, paid by the company on the participator's behalf, then the amount so paid shall not for the purposes of income tax, capital gains tax or corporation tax be regarded as a payment to the person by whom the tax was originally payable.[18]

Section 13 is targeted at investment gains and, unlike the transfer of assets **54.11** provisions, is not subject to a motive test. The gain is attributed to a participator's interest in the company to the extent of that interest and there is an attribution process that involves looking through multiple layers of intermediate holdings with final attribution being on a just and reasonable basis.[19] When

---

[13] See *Tax Bulletin 40*, April 1999.
[14] The threshold was raised from 5% to 10% by FA 2001 s.80. See s.13(4) which states, *"s.13(2) shall not apply in the case of any participator in the company to which the gain accrues where the aggregate amount falling under that subsection to be apportioned to him and to persons connected with him does not exceed one tenth of the gain."* Participator is defined in CTA 2010 s.454 and can include shareholders and loan creditors.
[15] See TCGA 1992 s.286 for connected persons.
[16] See HMRC Notice of December 10, 2009 reproduced in (2010) SWTI p.45.
[17] See TCGA 1992 s.14(2).
[18] However, it will prejudice the availability of any credit relief under ss.13(5A) or 13(7): see 54.17 and CGTM 57390.
[19] TCGA 1992 s.13(3).

chargeable gains realised by the company are apportioned to UK resident participators, the term "participator" includes any person having a share or interest in the capital or income of a non-resident company, including loan creditors (other than banks).

54.12   A sale or liquidation of the company by the individual participator attracts further capital gains tax at 18 or 28 per cent, depending on whether he is a basic rate or higher rate taxpayer.[20]

54.13   Bear in mind that on the death of the participator there is no tax-free uplifted base cost on the underlying assets of the company only on the company shares themselves.

Double tax treaty relief

54.14   If the company is resident in a country with which the UK has concluded a double tax treaty, giving the other country sole taxing rights over gains accruing to its residents, a s.13 charge may be precluded, provided the company is owned by an individual. Under EU law s.13 may be in breach of freedom of establishment and free movement of capital.[21]

Losses

54.15   Losses realised by offshore companies can be set-off against gains made by the same company in the same year of assessment and against gains made by other non-resident companies which have been apportioned to the same taxpayer in the same year of assessment. They cannot be set against the participator's general personal gains, nor carried forward or back. However, the participator can offset his personal losses against his s.13 gains insofar as the latter are not offset by s.13 losses. It follows that the use of a company may generate unrelieved capital losses.[22]

54.16   If a loss is realised by a company owned by a foreign domiciled participator, such a loss, even on a foreign situs asset, can be set-off against an apportioned gain on a UK asset owned by s.13 company if the gain arises in the same year, whether or not the proceeds of the foreign disposal realising a loss are remitted. However, a foreign s.13 gain cannot be reduced by s.13 losses unless the gain is remitted in the tax year when it is realised.[23]

Relief from double taxation on s.13 gains

54.17   The same economic gain may be taxed twice: once when the company realises the gain on disposal of the underlying asset; and subsequently if the profit

---

[20] For the avoidance of a double charge in such cases, see 54.17.
[21] See 54.05 above.
[22] See Ch.21 for further information on loss relief provisions. See s.13(8) for details of the limited relief on losses and CG 57295.
[23] TCGA 1992 s.14A(4).

represented by the gain is distributed by the company to the participator, whether by way of dividend, sale or liquidation of the company. To deal with this two reliefs are provided.

The first, s.13(5A) relief, is that the person who paid the s.13 tax may deduct the tax paid in respect of the chargeable gain from any CGT or income tax chargeable in respect of a subsequent distribution from the company whether by dividend, distribution of capital or on dissolution of the company. This relief is subject to the following conditions: **54.18**

(i) the distribution of the gain must take place within a specified period of the gain being realised by the company. The specified period begins on the date when the gain is realised by the company and ends on the fourth anniversary of that date or, if earlier, three years after the end of the accounting period in which that date falls[24];

(ii) the company must not have reimbursed the participator who has paid the s.13 tax;

(iii) the gain on which s.13 tax is paid must be distributed as income or capital. There is no relief if the company is sold;

(iv) the second tax charge on distribution must be incurred by the same person as is liable for the s.13 charge. This raises particular problems in relation to trusts.[25]

The second relief, s.13(7) relief, applies without time limit but operates by way of deduction rather than credit. It allows any CGT paid by the participator on the gain apportioned to him under s.13 to be deducted in computing any gain when he disposes of the interest that caused him to be a participator in the first place. This relief is not available if the company reimburses the s.13 tax. It only applies if the participator disposes of his interest in the share capital, not if he receives an income dividend, which will therefore be unrelieved unless he receives it within the time limits specified in s.13(5A) and therefore can claim s.13(5A) relief. It does not apply to non-resident trusts as it only applies if the person realising the gain is the same person who paid the s.13 tax. **54.19**

The effect of these two reliefs is illustrated in the following example. **54.20**

EXAMPLE 54.3

(1) Rodney, a UK resident and domiciled top rate shareholder, owns half the issued share capital in a non-resident close company. He had purchased the shares for £10,000 in 1997. The company sells an asset realising a gain (after indexation) in January 2010 of £100,000. Rodney is charged to capital gains tax on 50 per cent of that apportioned gain at 18 per cent. (£50,000 less his annual exemption of £10,100 = tax of £7,182.) In July 2011 the company is dissolved and Rodney receives a capital distribution of £110,000 thereby realising a gain on

---

[24] TCGA 1992 s.13(5B).
[25] See 54.28 and CGTM at 57366 for examples.

his shares of £100,000. For this year assume he is chargeable to CGT at 28 per cent and has used up his annual exemption. Further tax due on the liquidation of the company is £28,000 less £7,182 (s.13 tax) = £20,818.

(2) If, instead, Rodney sold his shares in the company for £110,000 to a third party after the company had sold its assets then he would be eligible only for s.13(7) relief. On the above figures the s.13 tax would reduce his gain of £100,000 to £92,818 resulting in a further tax liability of £25,989.

Foreign domiciliaries who claim the remittance basis

54.21 Until April 6, 2008, s.13 did not apply if the UK resident participator was not UK domiciled. For disposals by non-resident companies on or after April 6, 2008, s.13 applies to participators who are remittance basis users.[26] The overall effect is that if the company realises gains on foreign situated assets that gain is apportioned to the foreign domiciliary as a foreign chargeable gain and he is taxed on the remittance basis (assuming he is a remittance basis user).[27] Since the company is a relevant person in relation to the remittance basis user, remittance by the company of all or part of the proceeds of disposal results in a tax charge on the foreign domiciled participator.

54.22 If the foreign company realises a gain on the disposal of a UK asset, then the foreign domiciliary is taxed on an arising basis. For instance, if the company owns a UK house which it sells at a gain, that gain is taxed on the UK participator whether or not he is a remittance basis user.

54.23 There is no automatic rebasing to April 6, 2008 in respect of gains within companies owned by foreign individuals so gains accruing prior to that date can still be taxed even if the disposal takes place many years later.

EXAMPLE 54.4

C, a resident non-UK domiciliary who is a remittance basis user, owns all the shares of Guernsey Co, which holds a UK property. The house was acquired in 2005 and by April 2008 was showing gains of £500,000. It is sold in 2015 at a gain of £1 million. All the gains are taxable on C on an arising basis. There is no main residence relief even if he is living in the property. By contrast, if the company had sold the house prior to April 6, 2008, s.13 did not then apply to foreign domiciliaries and so there would have been no tax on C. If C had transferred the company shares into trust immediately prior to the sale in 2015 there is no immediate tax charge on C when the company sells the property although he is taxed under s.87 if he subsequently receives benefits or capital payments from the trust. This planning option is discussed further below.

[26] See TCGA 1992 s.14A.
[27] Section 14A(2).

UK resident trusts

If a UK resident trust owns an offshore investment company which realises **54.24** gains on the disposal of its assets, such gains are attributed to and taxed on the UK resident trustees at 28 per cent by virtue of s.13. If the trust is non-UK resident such gains are attributed to the trust and although not taxed on the trustees, are included in the computation of ss.86 or 87 gains.[28]

In one significant aspect, non-UK resident trusts holding property for UK **54.25** individuals are taxed more favorably than UK resident individuals who hold directly interests in non-resident companies: if the company owns UK land (or other UK situated assets) and realises gains, these are not taxed on an arising basis either on the trustees or the foreign domiciled settlor. The settlor does not need to claim the remittance basis to avoid capital gains tax on gains realised by the trust or company provided he is foreign domiciled by law.

By contrast, a remittance basis user who owns a non-resident company directly is taxed on UK situated gains realised by the company on an arising basis. Moreover, if the trust remits the gain so realised this in itself is not a taxable remittance by the foreign domiciliary even though the trust is a relevant person. A charge under s.87 only arises on the foreign domiciliary if he receives a capital payment or benefit from the trust which he remits. The situs of the asset on which the trust gain is realised is irrelevant. By contrast if the foreign domiciliary owns the company directly and either he or his non-resident company remits the foreign chargeable gain it has realised then there is a taxable remittance.

However, in other ways, trusts owning offshore companies are more **54.26** adversely taxed than individuals. In particular, there is no treaty relief for trustees to preclude a s.13 charge that is apportioned to the settlor or beneficiaries who receive capital payments, since TCGA 1992 s.79B expressly precludes trustee shareholders from enjoying exemption under any treaty.

If the remittance basis user owns personally a non-resident close company **54.27** which is about to realise a gain on a UK situated asset (as in Example 54.4), it is sensible for him to transfer his interest to a non-resident trust before the gain is realised. (A gain will be realised on a gift of the shares to the trust but is not taxable unless remitted: see s.809T.) Then the gain realised on ultimate sale is not apportionable to him but simply increases the trust's pool of gains. It does not matter whether the gain realised by the company is on UK situated or foreign assets.

Non-resident trusts

Gains realised by a non-resident close company owned by a non-resident trust **54.28** are apportioned to the trustees under s.13(10). The trustees are not charged

---

[28] See s.13(10). Trust gains are not as such apportioned to beneficiaries unless they receive capital payments or benefits. See s.13(14).

to tax as they are non-UK resident, but if the trust is within s.86, any apportioned gains are assessed on the settlor. If the trust is not within s.86 (because it is not settlor-interested or the settlor is foreign domiciled whether or not a remittance basis user) the apportioned gains of the trustees go to increase the trust's pool of trust gains.[29]

54.29   As noted, neither the non-resident trustees nor the settlor can claim relief from tax on the gain under s.13(7), as the relief only applies if the person disposing of the participation is identical to the person who pays the tax. The non-resident trustees are disposing of their interest in the company but tax is paid by the settlor in the case of s.86 gains or by a beneficiary in the case of s.87 gains.

Relief for settlor under s.86

54.30   It is accepted that relief is available under s.13(5A) to the settlor if he is assessed under s.86 on the company's gain and this can be an effective way of distributing trust capital.

EXAMPLE 54.5

> X is the UK domiciled and resident settlor and life tenant of an offshore trust. He is a top rate taxpayer. The trust wholly owns Jerseyco which in 2011 realises a gain of £100,000 on the disposal of land wherever situate. The trust also has pre-1998 stockpiled gains of £1 million. No further stockpiled gains have arisen since all trust gains have since 1998 been taxed on X on an arising basis.
>
> X is subject to tax of £28,000 under s.86 in respect of the company's gain.[30] If the company subsequently declares a dividend, X will receive this as life tenant and be able to claim s.13(5A) relief in respect of the s.13 tax paid. Accordingly if the company distributes £100,000, X is subject to tax at 42.5 per cent as an additional rate taxpayer. He will get a tax credit at 28 per cent leaving tax at 14.5 per cent due (£14,500). This does not appear to prevent X from reclaiming the capital gains tax he has suffered under s.86[31] from the trustees. Reimbursement by the company jeopardises the s.13(5A) tax credit but reimbursement by the trustees does not. Hence, X would end up paying £14,500 tax and the trustees would pay £28,000. X would therefore end up with a net receipt of £85,500.

54.31   If in the above example the settlor had a discretionary interest in the settlement (albeit this would be unusual for IHT reasons if he is UK deemed domiciled) then provided the company does not pay the settlor's 13 tax, s.13(5A)

---

[29] See Ch.19 for further details.
[30] When a gain is apportioned to trustees under s.13(10), the settlor will be chargeable under s.86(4) by virtue of Sch.5 para.1(2).
[31] See Sch.5 para.6.

relief should still be available. Again, this does not prevent the settlor claiming reimbursement from the trustees in respect of tax he has suffered under s.86. Nor does it matter that there are stockpiled gains on the clock since the reimbursement is not treated as a capital payment. Note, however, that if the gain realised by the company was paid to the trustees by way of *capital* rather than income distribution from the company and was then paid out to the settlor as a capital distribution he would be treated as receiving a capital payment of £100,000. This payment would be matched to the pre-1998 stockpiled gains and be subject to the maximum supplemental charge. He would pay further tax under s.87 of £44,800 thereby reducing his net receipt to £40,700. It is therefore better for him to receive an income rather than capital distribution.

Relief under s.87

In relation to tax under s.87, the position under s.13(5A) is problematic. If company gains are apportioned under s.13(10) and increase the trustees' pool of gains it is not clear that gains realised on a disposal of the company itself can be relieved from double taxation. HMRC's position remains unknown.   **54.32**

It should also be remembered that UK or foreign tax borne by a company cannot be credited against UK tax charged on beneficiaries who receive distributions from the trust (wherever resident). It is generally accepted, however, that where income has arisen in the company which is paid to the trust as a dividend, there is no doubling up of relevant income for the purpose of the transfer of assets code: see Ch.8.   **54.33**

IV SUMMARY OF TAX ADVANTAGES AND DISADVANTAGES OF INCORPORATION

Advantages of company—for a non-settlor interested non-resident trust

Incorporation provides flexibility as to payment of income to a beneficiary (including a life tenant) because the declaration of a dividend is at the discretion of the directors. This may be attractive if the trustees want to control the flow of income. It may also be useful as a way of keeping a beneficiary below the top rate of tax.   **54.34**

Non-resident trustees of a discretionary trust can continue investing in UK shares through a company without having to pay 42.5 per cent income tax on UK dividend income. If UK dividends are received by non-resident trustees some of this tax can be reclaimed if distributions are made to beneficiaries who pay tax at lower rates. However, the resultant compliance issues can be considerable.[32]   **54.35**

Interest in possession higher rate beneficiaries who are not remittance basis users will generally pay income tax on dividends declared by offshore companies at lower rates if the funds held by the company are invested in assets   **54.36**

[32] See ESC B 18 and Ch.6.

producing non-dividend investment income, e.g. interest. If such interest arose directly to them at the trust level, then rates would be higher. Interest received directly by life tenants is taxed at 20/40/50 per cent. If such interest is received by the company and then paid out to them as dividend income the rates reduce to 10/32.5/42.5 per cent for the individual taxed on the arising basis.

54.37 Gains realised by the company can be distributed by way of dividend to the trust and thence to beneficiaries. Income tax rates are lower for higher rate beneficiaries (40 per cent maximum, 32.5 per cent if life tenant) than capital gains tax rates if capital payments are subject to the full supplemental charge (44.8 per cent). However, in most cases the LIFO rule results in capital payments not being subject to the full supplemental charge and a beneficiary may be able to shelter gains attributed to him under s.87 by the use of his annual exemption.

54.38 FA 2008 and FA 2009[33] give an additional notional tax credit in respect of distributions received by UK resident interest in possession beneficiaries from non-resident holding companies. The credit is only available if the company is incorporated in a suitable double tax treaty country but this can reduce effective rates of tax to those applicable for UK dividend income, i.e. with the benefit of the notional one-ninth tax credit resulting in 0/25 /36.11 per cent tax being paid by the beneficiary on the dividend received.[34]

54.39 Gains realised by the company that are apportioned to the trust are computed with the benefit of indexation.

54.40 Foreign currency gains realised by the company are ignored.

54.41 There is inheritance tax protection if trust has excluded property status.

For settlor-interested trusts

54.42 Companies can provide a way of effectively distributing capital without suffering the full supplemental charge. Value is paid out by way of dividend: see Example 54.5 and 54.28 above.

Disadvantages

54.43 There is a potential doubling up of future gains: on disposals of company shares and on the underlying assets of the company. The capital gains tax rules[35] work very unsatisfactorily for beneficiaries of a non-settlor interested trust.

54.44 On the death of a qualifying interest in possession beneficiary there is a tax-free uplift only on the company shares not on the underlying assets of the company.

54.45 There is no main residence relief in respect of a house owned by a company.

---

[33] By insertion of s.397A into ITTOIA 2005.
[34] See 6.18.
[35] TCGA 1992 s.13.

Risk of shadow director benefit in kind charges.[36]   **54.46**

On a settlor-interested trust a UK resident and domiciled settlor pays tax   **54.47** on an arising basis on all trust and company income under the transfer of assets legislation and further capital gains tax on sale or liquidation of the company. There is no tax relief.[37]

There is restrictive loss relief whether the company is owned directly or by   **54.48** the trust. Section 13 losses cannot be carried forward.

Loss of UK and foreign tax credits where the offshore holding company   **54.49** holds an investment portfolio and receives dividends, e.g. from listed companies. This can be particularly relevant if the portfolio is invested in UK shares. If the UK dividends were received directly by beneficiaries as life tenants the effective rates would be lower: 0/25/36.11 per cent. Under this route they lose any credit for the UK withholding tax on the UK dividends and instead pay at higher rates on dividends from the holding company. This is the reverse of the position in 54.36 where gross interest is received by the company and paid out as dividend. In that case the rates of tax are reduced by use of a holding company. In this case taxed dividends are received by the company and then paid up to the trust as dividend from the holding company. There is no credit for the tax already suffered on the dividends received by the company and the rates of tax on dividends received from an offshore holding company will generally be higher—10/32.5/42.5 per cent.

Corporate residence may be an issue. If the offshore company is managed   **54.50** and controlled from the UK it will be subject to corporation tax.[38]

Potential doubling up of income occurs where it is reinvested by the   **54.51** company rather than paid to the trust when it arises.

Compliance issues arise for a UK resident settlor where the company   **54.52** receives UK rental or other UK source income which the settlor has power to enjoy wherever domiciled. He is taxed on an arising basis on such income with a limited credit for tax paid by the company.

Part 7A issues should be considered althrough bear in mind that shadow   **54.53** directors are outside the scope of this legislation.[39]

---

[36] See Chs 43 and 44 for discussion of benefits arising from the occupation of houses and use of chattels.
[37] See 54.07.
[38] See Ch.4 for rules on residence for trusts and companies: in practice it may be harder to avoid a company becoming UK resident particularly if directly owned by the individual.
[39] See 49.59.

CHAPTER 55

CHECKLIST FOR PRIVATE CLIENTS AND TRUSTS: PLANNING IDEAS

- Points to consider when first receiving instructions in relation to an existing trust (**55.02**)
- Points to consider when advising foreign domiciliaries (including rental properties) (**55.22**)
- Capital gains tax regime for beneficiaries receiving capital payments from offshore trusts (**55.33**)
- CGT and offshore trusts generally (**55.40**)
- Importing an offshore trust (**55.45**)
- Residence—emigration and immigration (**55.50**)
- Advantages and disadvantages of holding assets through an offshore holding company (**55.64**)
- Tax issues to consider on setting up a settlement (**55.65**)
- Making capital distributions to beneficiaries/hold-over relief/absolute entitlement at specified age such as 25 (**55.70**)
- Resettlements vs variations (**55.82**)
- Business reliefs and use of trusts (**55.90**)
- Private residence relief—CGT (**55.108**)
- Disposals of beneficial interests in trusts (**55.113**)
- Losses (**55.118**)
- Lifetime inheritance tax planning—avoiding reservation of benefit (**55.119**)
- Death bed planning (**55.123**)
- Minimising charges under the relevant property regime (**55.130**)
- Will drafting (**55.131**)
- Excluding the settlor from settlor-interested trusts—traps to watch (**55.136**)

55.01 This chapter considers a number of tax planning ideas using trusts and provides a reminder of matters dealt with elsewhere. It also provides a summary of the main tax points that need to be watched in relation to common transactions and situations for private clients and trusts.

We cross refer to the relevant chapter that provides the detailed analysis.

I POINTS TO CONSIDER WHEN FIRST RECEIVING INSTRUCTIONS IN RELATION TO AN EXISTING TRUST

55.02 Check you have a complete set of deeds including the chain of trustees. Have all trustees been validly appointed and retired? See 1.16 and possible traps under TA 1925 ss.37 and 39, before their amendment by Trusts of Land and Appointment of Trustees Act 1996.

Is the person who is defined as "the settlor" a nominal settlor or the person **55.03** who actually funded the trust? Are there others who also added funds? What is the settlor's domicile and residence status at the date of initial funding and when additions were made?

Has there been a resettlement in the past? If so, what was the domicile and **55.04** residence status of the settlor at the date of the resettlement? See Example 55.7 and 4.01. If the transferee trust holds fund derived from another trust, what was the domicile status of the settlor of the other trust? For effect of resettlements on the residence of trust, see 4.03 onwards. For resettlements, generally see 12.21 and 55.82. Has the transferee trust received property from an offshore trust? Watch capital gains tax if there have been disposals of beneficial interests: see 20.06. Check if the transferee trust has stockpiled gains or relevant income that could be taxable on beneficiaries who receive benefits or capital: see 8.00 and 19.49 and 53.17.

What powers does the settlor have? For example, appointment and removal **55.05** of trustees? Consent powers? A testamentary power of appointment?

What is the residence of the trustees? If one trustee is UK resident can one **55.06** rely on the let out in TCGA 1992 s.69(2) and (2)(e): see 4.03.

Is there a Protector with power to consent and, if so, have all necessary **55.07** consents been obtained for earlier appointments?

What dispositive powers do the trustees have? Powers of advancement, **55.08** appointment, resettlement? Are these exercisable within certain time periods? See 1.47. Are certain formalities required for their valid execution, e.g. by deed? Can beneficiaries act as trustees?

Has the accumulation period expired and is the trust discretionary or inter- **55.09** est in possession? If the latter, did the interest in possession arise pre- or post-March 2006 and is it a transitional serial interest: see 27.16.

What is the proper law of the trust? Is there power to change the proper law **55.10** or jurisdiction of the trust? See 12.26

If the entity is a foundation, is it taxed in the UK as a trust or a corporate **55.11** entity? See 2.09.

If the trust is a US trust, it is a grantor trust under US law but is it a nominee **55.12** or substantive trust arrangement under UK law? See 2.19.

Who are the main beneficiaries and where are they resident and domiciled? **55.13** See Ch.5.

Are the beneficiaries or settlor remittance basis users or foreign domiciled **55.14** but taxed on an arising basis? Are any deemed domiciled? If so when did this occur? See 3.87 and Ch.5. Does the trust own an underlying company and if so what is the residence of that company? If non-resident, is management and control situated abroad? See 4.43 and Ch.54.

Is the trust settlor-interested? Can it benefit spouse/civil partner? If so, is **55.15** the settlor UK resident? See Ch.7 for income tax implications. Are the main beneficiaries minor children of the settlor?

Was hold-over relief claimed on a disposal into trust after December **55.16** 2003? If so, watch the CGT claw-back provisions for private residences: see 18.71.

Is the trust fixed interest or discretionary? If fixed interest, are there any **55.17** items of capital that are deemed to be income and taxed at higher rates, e.g. accrued income, etc: see 6.57. Should the trust be made interest in possession in order to reduce 50 per cent rate and maximise tax credits: see 6.4 and A1.19.

55.18 Has a rebasing election been made under FA 2008 Sch.7 para.126? See 19.55.

55.19 Check whether there are any related property settlements: see Ch.29. This may affect the inheritance tax charge under the relevant property regime. Is a 10-year anniversary charge approaching? Remember that the 10-year anniversary charge is from the date of the original settlement not that of any transferee trust. What is the settlor's cumulative total? Are there any related property trusts to consider? Note the position for pre-1974 trusts explained at 29.32.

55.20 Does the trust have a full trust annual capital gains tax exemption or are there other trusts set up by the settlor with which the exemption is shared: see 11.09.

55.21 Diarise dates when beneficiaries reach 25 and s.71D regime ends and any other age when a beneficiary becomes absolutely entitled.

II POINTS TO CONSIDER WHEN ADVISING FOREIGN DOMICILIARIES (INCLUDING RENTAL PROPERTIES)

55.22 *Domicile issues*: where is the relevant person domiciled? How secure is his foreign domicile? Does he have a UK domicile of origin: see Ch.3. Is he likely to lose his foreign domicile and if so do the transitional capital gains tax reliefs for offshore trusts need to be secured now before any change: see 19.55, 53.17 and Example 55.1.

Is he deemed domiciled in the UK for inheritance tax purposes? See 3.107 and Ch.31. If so avoid resettlements. Is the individual claiming the remittance basis or is he merely a foreign domiciliary? See 5.22.

Remember that the tax status of the beneficiary is tested not at the date of capital payment or when the gain is made but at the date of matching: see 19.49 and 55.3 below.

Rental income in offshore structures/transfer pricing issues

55.23 Does the remittance basis user receive or have power to enjoy any UK source income arising in any offshore structure set up by him? If so, such UK income (e.g. rental income) is prima facie taxable on him on an arising basis even if received by a non-resident company or trust: see Ch.8.

Can the tax on such UK source rental income be minimised, e.g. by borrowing abroad to offset the interest against the rental income? A typical structure will involve the non-resident trust buying one or more investment properties, letting them out and receiving rental income. The properties are generally purchased through an offshore company to avoid inheritance tax issues. Accordingly, the trustees lend funds to the company in order to enable it to purchase the properties and the company pays the trust interest on the borrowings out of the rental income. Is the interest tax deductible against the rental income? The interest is normally foreign source and not taxable on a remittance basis user if retained abroad while rent is UK source and taxable on the company at 20 per cent and on the UK resident transferor at higher rate or top rates. It is therefore desirable to minimise the rent and maximise the interest.

ITTOIA 2005 s.272 provides that profits of a property business are calcu- **55.24** lated in the same way as the profits of a trade are computed. A deduction is permitted for interest paid on loans even from connected parties where the money borrowed is wholly and exclusively incurred for the purposes of the property rental business. The settlor is taxed on the net income under ITA 2007 s.727 since this is the amount of income treated as arising to him. See s.746 which gives him the same deductions and reliefs *"as would have been allowed if the income had actually been received by him"*. Hence, the gross receipts are not as such the income deemed to be attributed to the transferor under ITA 2007.[1] Rather it is the profits of the business computed on the basis of normal accounting principles and in accordance with ITTOIA s.272 et al that are treated as the income attributable to the transferor under ss.720–730 ITA 2007.

Avoid having separate companies for each rental property held within a **55.25** trust structure. Otherwise the profits must be calculated separately for each company running its own rental business. This has an impact on how the expenses are apportioned. One cannot deduct expenses of company X against income of company Y on the basis that receipts of both company X and Y are taxed on the transferor. It is the profits of each company after deduction of appropriate expenses that are taxable on the transferor as his available income. Hence, one cannot deduct the interest on global borrowings in the most advantageous way; the interest has to be allowed on normal account- ing principles looking at each company separately and applying the transfer pricing provisions to that proportion of the interest.[2]

Transfer pricing Non-resident landlords are generally required to self-assess **55.26** their profits in accordance with the arm's length principle, i.e. that which would have been found between independent enterprises acting entirely at arm's length.[3] Interest on connected party borrowings can be deductible but the company must demonstrate that the borrowings, when viewed separately for each company, could have been obtained if taken out on an independent arm's length basis. HMRC suggest that acceptable advances will be limited to a range of 65–80 per cent of value albeit acknowledging that one needs to look at the quality of the tenant and the duration of the leases, 85 per cent loan to value is generous. HMRC note in *Tax Bulletin 46,* April 2000 that where a property has subsequently risen or fallen in value and the original loan remains outstanding, no more or less interest can be claimed on that original loan than was due on the original transaction viewed on an arm's length basis.

HMRC acknowledge in *Tax Bulletin 46* that where the value of the property has increased the borrowing capacity of the company, then any refinancing must be examined assuming an arm's length basis at that time of refinancing and in addition the purpose of any additional borrowing needs to be exam- ined. If the refinancing reflects what would have happened between parties at

---

[1] See *Chetwoode v IRC* [1997] STC 64.
[2] See Ch.8.
[3] See ICTA 1988 Sch.28AA para.1A and from 2010–11 in TIOPA 2010 Pt 4 s.146 onwards.

arm's length and the replacement financing is on terms that would have been agreed by such parties, no limitation under TIOPA 2010 Pt 4 will be necessary.

When setting up these arrangements ensure proper loan agreements exist between trust and company. Watch situs of loan (avoid taking security on a UK property else the trust will have a UK situated asset). Source of interest.

55.27   Is the trust a relevant person in relation to the settlor? See 5.21. If so, avoid remittances by the trust or any underlying company: see 8.06.

55.28   Do the transitional provisions in FA 2008 Sch.7 para.86 provide any relief? Can the foreign domiciliary take advantage of the special reliefs for art or chattels: see Ch.44. Have assets that represent pre-March 12, 2008 relevant foreign income been kept segregated? Has pre-April 6, 2008 relevant foreign income been kept segregated? See 5.21.

55.29   Has the foreign dom made an election to use foreign losses? See 5.37.

55.30   Has the trust made a rebasing election? See 19.57 and 53.17.

55.31   Does the trust structure hold offshore income gains and have these been matched to capital payments? Ensure that OIGs are matched in the year they arise for transferor trusts where the transferor is a foreign domiciliary. On tax regime of OIGs for foreign domiciliaries generally: see 53.00.

55.32   For the pros and cons of using offshore trusts for foreign domiciliaries, see 19.61 and Example 19.22. Consider setting up more than one trust for the foreign domiciliary with assets enjoyed in the UK being held in a dry trust and assets enjoyed outside the UK kept in a trust which produces the capital gains and foreign income.

III CAPITAL GAINS TAX REGIME FOR BENEFICIARIES RECEIVING CAPITAL PAYMENTS FROM OFFSHORE TRUSTS

55.33   One way of avoiding a s.87 charge is to have a dry trust where the asset from which the beneficiary benefits is never likely to be sold while he is UK resident or alive. This arrangement works for both foreign and UK domiciliaries. If a UK house is held directly by the trust, main residence relief may be available so that no chargeable gains arise. Watch IHT if the trust is relevant property or the settlor reserves a benefit.

55.34   Where:

(a) trustees own several assets showing gains;

(b) there are unmatched earlier capital payments received in the UK after April 5, 2008 that will therefore be taxable on foreign domiciliaries when matched to post-April 2008 gains; and

(c) one asset shows mainly a pre-April 2008 accrued gain and the other shows mainly a post-April 2008 accrued gain and a rebasing election has been made;

then

(d) sell the asset with the pre-April 2008 gain in tax year 1. The pre-April 2008 gain can be matched to the benefit received in the UK;

(e) if capital payments are made outside the UK, sell the asset showing the post-April 2008 accrued gain first.

If benefits have been received after April 5, 2008 in the UK then avoid match- **55.35**
ing these benefits to post-April 2008 gains by washing out the post-April 2008
gains. This can be done if a capital payment equal to the post-April 2008 gain
is made abroad in the year it is realised.

Timing of capital payments is crucial for foreign domiciliaries: see 19.25–26. **55.36**

EXAMPLE 55.1

> 2007–08 – trust realises gains of £100,000.
>
> 2008–09 – A (a foreign domiciliary) receives £100,000 capital payment
> in the UK; trust realises gains of £80,000. £60,000 of the 2008–09 gains
> accrued pre-April 2008 and £20,000 after April 2008.
>
> Rebasing election made.
>
> Matching operates as follows for A: all the current year gains are
> matched to the capital payment. The 2008–09 gains of £60,000 are not
> chargeable. 2007–08 gains of £20,000 also not chargeable. If A remits the
> £100,000 capital payment to the UK he pays tax on the £20,000 element
> of post-April 2008 accrued gains.
>
> As A is a foreign domiciliary then even if he is not a remittance basis
> user, a rebasing election made by the trustees may further reduce the
> capital gains tax charge if some of the gain realised in 2011–12 is attrib-
> utable to pre-April 2008 periods.[4]

EXAMPLE 55.2

> In March 2005 B settles shares in a company owning a UK house into
> trust. The trust holds no other assets. Rental profit each year is £100,000
> but no tax is due on B until trust gains are realised. Rebasing election
> made.
>
> Trustees sell the company on April 5, 2012 (benefits received in the UK
> by then total £400,000 up to and including 2011–12) realising a gain of
> £1 million.
>
> B can avoid tax if in the year of disposal he is non-UK resident.
>
> If B is UK resident but he is a remittance basis user, then the trustees
> could make a capital payment of £1 million to B which he keeps abroad.
> The s.87 charge is then limited to the capital payment of £100,000
> received in the UK in that year and earlier years' benefits cannot be
> brought into charge because the gain has been fully matched to capital
> payments.
>
> If B is a UK resident domiciliary or he is UK and foreign domiciled but
> not a remittance basis user, the trustees should make the capital payment

[4] See 57.19.

of £1 million to a non-UK resident person or to a remittance basis user abroad.

55.37   Note that the interest surcharge applies by reference to the year of capital payment not by reference to the year of remittance. Hence, if payments are made to X abroad (a remittance basis user) in the same year that the gains are realised and he only remits them 10 years later, there is still no surcharge.[5] However, if trust gains are realised many years previously (even before the beneficiary is UK resident) and the beneficiary receives a benefit when UK resident, if that benefit is matched to the gain on a LIFO basis, the surcharge will apply in full.

55.38   If the beneficiary has received an unmatched capital payment while non-UK resident and the trust gain to which it is matched is only realised after he has become UK resident then he is chargeable (subject to the remittance basis). Hence, ensure all capital payments are matched to trust gains prior to the beneficiary becoming UK resident.

Ensure that the beneficiary and particularly a settlor, takes advantage of all capital gains tax transitional reliefs before there is any risk of losing foreign domicile.

EXAMPLE 55.3

Offshore trust—settlor foreign domiciled but UK resident from 2000–01 to 2009–10.

2010–11 settlor becomes UK domiciled.

Trustees made rebasing election.

2010–11 settlor taxed on all trust gains as well as trust and company income. He loses the benefit of any transitional reliefs in FA 2008.

2011–12 settlor receives a capital payment in 2011 of £1 million. In the same year the trustees realise gains on disposals of assets of £100,000.

Trust gains s.87 pool = £1 million. Of these gains, £500,000 arose before April 2008. The balance arose after this date but of this £300,000 accrued pre-April 2008 and £200,000 accrued post-April 2008.

Settlor pays tax at 28 per cent on £100,000 actual current year gains (s.86).

In addition he is fully taxable on the £1 million capital payment (s.87).

If the settlor had received the £1 million before April 6, 2010, i.e. before he became UK domiciled, he would have paid CGT on only £200,000.

Capture the transitional capital gains tax reliefs early if there is any risk of the settlor or any other beneficiary losing his foreign domicile!

55.39   Isolate the gain from the benefit by a resettlement.

[5] See 19.48.

Example 55.4

Trust 1 holds cash and other investments. Pre-April 2008 gains have been realised by the trustees. The settlor/life tenant receives all income of Trust 1 and is UK resident but not domiciled.

Settlor wishes to receive future benefits in the UK by using art.

2009–10 Trust 1 has realised some post-April 2008 gains (both currency gains and on investments). It makes a capital payment equal to the post-April 2008 gains to the settlor abroad. See s.87A(2). He does not remit it. The payment is matched to the gain even though it is not chargeable.

2010–11 Trust 1 appoints cash to Trust 2 which buys some art for use by the settlor. (Watch inheritance tax on resettlement).

Trust 2 has only pre-April 2008 gains apportioned to it. All the post-April 2008 gains of Trust 1 have been eradicated by the capital payment.

IV CGT AND OFFSHORE TRUSTS GENERALLY[6]

Where offshore trusts are within the s.86 regime consider whether they could be converted into grandchildren's trusts. This is possible where the trust was wholly funded before March 1998 and has not been tainted. A deferral of capital gains tax and income tax can then be obtained: see Ch.19 and in particular 19.19.   **55.40**

Consider payments to a non-UK resident or a non-UK domiciled beneficiary to help the UK resident beneficiary, e.g. by washing out stock-piled gains.   **55.41**

If a UK beneficiary is liable to tax on s.87 gains and has personal losses, consider whether there are any Sch.4C gains that can be realised by the trustees which could then be used against the beneficiary's personal losses: see 19.69 and Ch.21.   **55.42**

Consider importing the trust to avoid a s.86 charge on the settlor.   **55.43**

Consider hold-over relief claims to avoid s.86 charges.   **55.44**

Example 55.5

The "B" Trust is a trust for the settlor's children and grandchildren. It is offshore and therefore within the s.86 regime since the settlor is UK resident and domiciled. Shares held by the trusts are pregnant with gain. Trustees transfer the shares to a beneficiary holding over the gain. No gains are realised by the trustees that can be charged on the settlor. There is a small exit charge for IHT purposes. However, if there is relevant income in the trust this will be matched to any capital payment first; the transfer

---

[6] See Ch.19 generally for the offshore trust CGT regime.

would not then be subject to IHT and therefore apparently not eligible for hold-over relief. See 8.62 for the order in which benefits are taxed.

V IMPORTING AN OFFSHORE TRUST

55.45 Are there unused tax credits which could be used under ESC B18? These will be lost if the trust is imported: see Ch.8.

55.46 Remember that split year treatment does not apply to trusts. Therefore, do not import a trust on April 5 if the intention is that the trust should be non-UK resident that tax year. See 4.40.

55.47 Is the trust presently within the s.86 regime so that gains are taxed on the settler? See Ch.19. If so, does the settlor have any personal losses that can be set against the trust gains? See Ch.21 loss relief provisions. Importing the trust will mean the personal losses can no longer be used. The trust is no longer settlor-interested for capital gains tax purposes.

55.48 Importing the trust has no inheritance tax effect.

55.49 Note that disposals of beneficial interests in the future will be chargeable if a trust has been non-UK resident in the past or received property from a non-UK trust. See 20.26. Stockpiled gains and relevant income will continue to be taxable on beneficiaries who receive capital payments.

VI RESIDENCE—EMIGRATION AND IMMIGRATION

55.50 Watch temporary non-residence rules on pre-emigration RFI and foreign chargeable gains for foreign domiciliaries if absent from the UK for less than five years: see 5.09. Watch capital gains tax position if individual returns within five tax years of leaving: see 5.09.

55.51 If a beneficiary has been non-UK resident for more than five years and is returning to the UK or coming here for the first time check whether capital payments from a trust have been fully matched to trust gains. If not, consider matching in the tax year prior to taking up UK residence: see 5.06.

55.52 If an individual is leaving the UK consider whether any held-over gains will be crystallised: see 5.08 and Ch.18. See also Ch.15 (EIS schemes).

55.53 If an individual is emigrating realise CGT losses prior to departure: see 5.20. If individual is immigrating realise losses after arrival here.

55.54 If an individual is non-UK resident and domiciled or deemed domiciled here, consider use of gilts as a means of avoiding inheritance tax on death or on lifetime gifts. See Ch.31 and 55.123.

55.55 Keep careful records of days spent in the UK: see checklist in 3.63.

55.56 ESC D2: if split year treatment available then capital gains tax is charged only in respect of gains realised on disposals made by individuals (not trusts) after their arrival provided that the individual has not been resident or ordinarily resident in the UK at any time during the five years of assessment immediately preceding the tax year in which he arrived in the UK. The full annual capital gains tax allowance and income personal allowances are available in the year of arrival.

Consider the effect of emigration and immigration on inheritance tax position and domicile status. If the individual returns in his fourth year of non-UK residence he is unlikely to have lost his deemed domicile: see Ch.31. **55.57**

Accelerate disposals on assets showing a gain so these gains are realised in tax year of non-residence. HMRC took the view that the normal matching rules applied to non-residents so that crystallising a gain by a bed and breakfast deal was not possible: see *Tax Bulletin*, April 2001 p.839. However, since March 22, 2006 s.106A(5A) provides that the matching rules do not apply to shares acquired when the person concerned is not resident or ordinarily resident in the UK or is treated as not being so for the provisions of a double taxation agreement. **55.58**

Enter into an unconditional contract with delayed completion if aim is to crystallise gain on an asset while still non-UK resident. Alternatively, transfer assets to a trust or wholly owned company. Note, however, that if the taxpayer is UK domiciled then there will be a chargeable transfer for inheritance tax purposes on a gift into a trust. It may be necessary to sell the asset to the trust in return for an IOU. Consider stamp duty and SDLT if assets are UK situated. **55.59**

Transferring assets to a wholly owned non-resident company should not trigger inheritance tax liabilities because there is no transfer of value but it may be very inconvenient to have assets held in a company. Consider SDLT if UK land is being transferred. **55.60**

Foreign domiciliaries should sort out their bank accounts in the tax year before UK residence commences. Future foreign income arising after acquiring UK residence should be paid into a separate income account that is retained abroad. All pre-emigration income and gains can be placed in a separate "capital" account and can be remitted to the UK. Keep a sterling capital account abroad for easy tax-free remittances to the UK. **55.61**

Once the beneficiary of a trust becomes UK resident consider a rebasing election if one has not already been made. Time limits may start running under FA 2008 Sch.7 para.126. See 19.55. **55.62**

Preserve main residence relief under TCGA 1992 ss.222–224 by reoccupying property. If the individual was UK resident and then left, e.g. for full time employment, and is now returning to the UK, periods of absence from the house can be ignored. Hence, up to three tax years absence or any period of absence throughout which the individual or his spouse worked in full-time employment abroad will still be counted as qualifying periods for the purposes of calculating whether the dwelling house was the individual's only or main residence. However, both before and after the period of absence the individual must occupy the house as his only or main residence. See 43.05 **55.63**

VII ADVANTAGES AND DISADVANTAGES OF HOLDING ASSETS THROUGH AN OFFSHORE HOLDING COMPANY

See 54.34 for the pros and cons. **55.64**

55.65   What is the inheritance tax position of the settlor? If the settlor is domiciled or deemed domiciled in the UK then any lifetime settlement other than for a disabled beneficiary will be an immediately chargeable event. Does he have an unused nil rate band? If the settlor is non-UK resident, consider settlement of gilts. See Ch.31 and Example 55.12. See also death bed planning at 55.127 and Example 55.11.

55.66   Can the settlement be made jointly by a married couple? Consider use of pilot trusts to minimise future charges under the relevant property regime: see Ch.41.

If the property qualifies for BPR check the two-year ownership condition or replacement provisions are satisfied: see Ch.45.

55.67   Could surplus income be transferred into trust without an inheritance tax charge even if in excess of the settlor's nil rate band? See IHTA 1984 s.21. The expenditure must be:

(i) part of the normal expenditure of the donor;

(ii) made out of income (taking one year with another);

(iii) leave the donor with sufficient income to maintain his usual standard of living.

There are two key cases:

Bennett v IRC [1995] STC 54;

McDowall v IRC [2004] STC (SCD) 22.

EXAMPLE 55.6

> Mr A calculates that he will have surplus income of £50,000 pa from his directorship with Quango Inc. He therefore determines to settle this sum each year into a trust for his children and grandchildren. Note:
>
> 1. HMRC say the payments each year must be reported;
> 2. the sum will be taxed as income of Mr A;
> 3. the GWR rules are capable of applying so Mr A must not benefit from the settled property (although he can be a trustee);
> 4. pilot trusts can minimise 10-year charges.[7]

55.68   If the settlor is UK resident and domiciled, is he settling cash or other assets that show a gain? If the latter, can a hold-over claim be made, i.e. will all dependant children plus settlor and spouse be excluded: see Ch.7 and Ch.19. If a remittance basis user, can the settlor settle foreign chargeable assets? The consequences of s.809T are considered at Example 19.23.

55.69   Does the asset settled show a loss? If so, it will be a connected party loss for capital gains tax purposes which cannot be used except against gains realised on other transfers by the settlor to the trustees: see 10.02.

---

[7] See Ch.41.

If the trustees hold an asset pregnant with gain consider whether they can **55.70**
advance it to the relevant beneficiary and claim hold-over relief to defer
capital gains tax. See Example 11.1 and 10.12. For hold-over relief generally:
see Ch.18. If a qualifying interest in possession beneficiary becomes absolutely
entitled to capital a hold-over claim is available only if the property is agricultural or business property.

If a hold-over relief claim is made, consider whether the beneficiary will **55.71**
pay capital gains tax at a lower rate than the trustees (28 per cent) if he sells
the asset? Does he have an annual exemption or personal losses that can be
used to reduce the gain? Note that hold-over relief continues to be available
on transfers out of settlor-interested trusts. However, no hold-over relief will
be available if the capital distribution is taxed on a beneficiary as relevant
income because it will not be a chargeable event for inheritance tax purposes.
See Ch.18. This may have an effect on the settlor if the trust is within s.86. See
Ch.19 and Example 55.3.

If the trustees make distributions to beneficiaries, can any losses be carried **55.72**
forward on the asset being advanced? Ch.21.

If a house is being advanced to the beneficiary which is likely to become his **55.73**
main residence avoid a hold-over relief claim: see 18.71.

Check if the beneficiary is likely to become non-UK resident after becom- **55.74**
ing absolutely entitled. If so there could be a clawback of the held-over gain,
triggering tax at higher rates. See 10.11 and Ch.18.

Check whether there will be an exit charge for inheritance tax purposes on **55.75**
distribution to the beneficiary: see Ch.29. If so, should the beneficiary rather
than the trustees pay the inheritance tax to reduce the amount?

The trustees may want to advance some trading company shares to an indi- **55.76**
vidual beneficiary in order to maximise entrepreneurs' relief if the beneficiary
works in the business but owns less than five per cent personally. See Ch.14
(entrepreneurs' relief).

The trustees must consider whether the beneficiary does become absolutely **55.77**
entitled to the asset being advanced for capital gains tax purposes. Consider
the difficulties if an undivided share in land or private company shares are
advanced to a beneficiary. He becomes absolutely entitled for inheritance
tax purposes but may not do so for capital gains tax purposes. See *Crowe v
Appleby* at 9.18 and 12.10 and following. This may provide opportunities if
the intention is to defer the capital gains tax charge until sale of the property.

Should trustees appropriate specific shares and assets to beneficiaries and **55.78**
how should any powers of advancement be exercised: see 12.10.

If the trust is within the 18–25 regime, remember an IHT exit charge will **55.79**
arise on a beneficiary attaining 25. Hold-over relief available if trust ends: see
Ch.18 for capital gains tax points and Ch.35 for IHT.

Should the trustees consider deferring absolute entitlement by using a **55.80**
settled power of advancement? What are the tax consequences of this if a
s.71D trust? Section 71D exit charge at a max 4.2 per cent but the settled
property will thereafter be within the relevant property regime. No disposal
arises for capital gains tax purposes.

55.81   Where there is an elderly life tenant with a qualifying interest in possession and property was transferred into trust with a hold-over claim and is still held by the trustees, consider transferring that property out to the life tenant while he is still alive with a further hold-over claim (if business property) so that the held-over gain is eradicated on death: see 18.31.

X RESETTLEMENTS VS VARIATIONS

55.82   Do the trustees have power to resettle or only a narrow power of appointment? Can they exercise the power of advancement to resettle assets? See Ch.1. For trust points on resettlements generally, see 12.22.

55.83   For capital gains tax consequences of a resettlement as opposed to a variation, see 12.21 onwards. Bear in mind that if there is a resettlement between two relevant property settlements e.g. non-qualifying interest in possession to a discretionary trust or from discretionary Trust 1 to discretionary Trust 2 there is no hold-over relief unless the property is agricultural or business property because there is no chargeable event for inheritance tax purposes.

55.84   Can the governing law of the transferee trust be different: see 12.30 onwards.

55.85   If there is no power to resettle consider whether it is possible or desirable for the trustees to make a sub-fund election over part of the fund and the best way of doing so? See 12.42.

55.86   When property is transferred between settlements (for instance in exercise of a trustee power to pay or apply property for the benefit of a beneficiary), the property is treated as remaining comprised in the first settlement for the purposes of the inheritance tax relevant property regime.[8] This applies whether or not the settlement comprises excluded property.

55.87   However, IHTA 1984 s.82 also provides that in determining whether the settled property is excluded property, it is necessary to look both at the domicile of the settlor of the first settlement at the time it was made and at the domicile of the settlor of the second settlement at the time that the second trust was made. Only if both settlors had neither an actual nor deemed UK domicile at the time when each made their trust can the property be excluded property: see Ch.31.

55.88   If the trustees transfer property from one trust to another, the settlor of the first settlement is also treated as the settlor of the second settlement to the extent that the property in the second settlement is derived from the first. In these circumstances the settlor of the first trust will need to be domiciled outside the UK when the original settlement was set up and at the date of the second settlement: see Ch.31 for further details.

EXAMPLE 55.7

1. Robert settled foreign shares into a discretionary settlement in 2000 when not UK domiciled. He then became UK domiciled in 2004. For income tax reasons the trustees decide that they wish to move the income

---

[8]   IHTA 1984 s.81: see 24.12 and 41.11.

producing assets into a new UK resident trust which is set up in May 2006 and where Robert is entitled to income. The new trust falls within the relevant property regime and was set up by a UK domiciled settlor. As a result of s.82 the property, transferred from the 2000 settlement ceases to be excluded. 10-year charges arise even if the new trust holds non-UK property.[9]

2. By contrast, if the transfer had been made in January 2006 then the new trust would have been a qualifying interest in possession for Robert and s.82 would not have applied.

3. The residence of Trust 2 is irrelevant to the inheritance tax position.

55.89 What happens if both Trusts 1 and 2 were set up at a time when the settlor was not UK domiciled but the actual transfer between settlements takes place at a time when the settlor is UK domiciled? In these circumstances s.82 should not apply: see Ch.31.

EXAMPLE 55.8

> Robert set up two discretionary trusts in 2000 when not UK domiciled. He became deemed domiciled in 2006. In 2007 the trustees transfer non-situs property from one trust to another. The property remains excluded.

XI BUSINESS RELIEFS AND USE OF TRUSTS

55.90 An individual who has sold his UK trading business and is about to emigrate can reinvest the sale proceeds in a foreign unincorporated business and then emigrate. In these circumstances he can claim rollover relief on the reinvestment and there is no capital gains tax on the subsequent disposal after emigration provided he is non-UK resident for at least five years. see 13.11.

55.91 If the individual has not yet sold the UK business consider transferring it to a company claiming s.162 incorporation relief. He could then emigrate and sell the shares after migration without a branch or agency charge under s.10: see 15.04.

55.92 A foreign domiciliary can re-site his business (even if not trading) by transferring it to a foreign incorporated company claiming incorporation relief. Foreign situated shares can then be settled into trust with no IHT if the foreign domiciliary is not UK deemed domiciled: see Example 15.2.

55.93 Where roll-over claims have been made on disposals of old assets before April 6, 2008 and the proceeds later reinvested in a new asset, consider withdrawal of claim in order to maximise business asset taper relief on the old assets. Roll-over claims in 2009–10 can be withdrawn at any time before January 31, 2012: see 13.15 and 13.18.

55.94 Care is needed to ensure that if trustees defer gains, e.g. by incorporation, by

---

[9] These charges will be calculated on the basis that the property remains comprised in the original settlement.

hold-over or roll-over relief claims or EIS, they do not end up paying more tax at higher rates later. See, for example, 18.4 and following, and consider revoking claims where there is the risk of a claw-back at higher rate: see Example 15.4.

55.95   Similarly consider withdrawal of rollover relief claims or disapplication of incorporation relief where sale occurs within a year of the reinvestment and so no entrepreneurs' relief is available or the rates of capital gains tax are increased: see 13.15 and 15.04.

55.96   Where trustees are trading, consider whether trustees should bring a beneficiary into the business, e.g. as a partner, in order to maximise entrepreneurs' relief: see Ch.14.

55.97   Where trustees are not trading but holding an asset used by the beneficiary in his trade, consider transferring the asset to the beneficiary carrying on the trade before a sale, claiming hold-over relief. The beneficiary could then bring the asset into use for his trade and six months later dispose of it. There is no restriction on a subsequent roll-over relief claim by the beneficiary if the asset is used by the beneficiary and the gain is reinvested. See Example 13.3. Entrepreneurs' relief may also be maximised.

55.98   Trustees should seek to maximise entrepreneurs' relief. Ensure that if shares in a private trading company are owned by the trustees, at least five per cent is vested in the interest in possession beneficiary working in the business personally and that the trust is an interest in possession trust. See 14.23 and following. Ensure sales occur in the correct order to maximise relief: see 14.26 to 14.28. Trusts should be reorganised to maximise relief where one non-qualifying interest in possession beneficiary works in a business and another does not: see Example 14.8.

55.99   If a beneficiary is in partnership or works in a company consider charging rent on trust property used by the partnership or company: see Example 14.7.

55.100   If an individual wishes to make a gift of business property into trust which is to be sold shortly and he is likely to die within seven years with a resulting claw back of BPR, consider the following. Incorporate the trading business first if not already incorporated, taking advantage of incorporation relief. Company shares can then be given into trust with the benefit of business property relief; the company can sell the trading assets and reinvest the proceeds in an investment business without claw back of inheritance tax relief provided the company shares are retained by the trustees: see Example 15.2.

55.101   Where trustees have realised gains on disposals of non-business assets consider use of deferral relief under EIS watching the qualifying conditions and the particular requirements for trusts as set out in 16.14 and following.

55.102   Trustees selling shares in family companies need to consider carefully whether they should receive cash, shares, loan notes or QCBs issued by the acquiring company. The issues are considered in Ch.17: see 17.10 onwards and a consideration of the pre- and post-April 2008 and June 2010 transitional rules.

55.103   Where earn-outs are in point, make the earn-out ascertainable where entrepreneurs' relief has not been fully utilised on receipt of the initial upfront consideration by applying an artificial cap: see 17.33. Similarly, consider disapplying share for share exchanges or share for non-QCB exchanges by making an election under s.169Q to maximise entrepreneurs' relief: see 17.33.

55.104   Consider investment in assets qualifying for business property relief more than two years before any 10-year anniversary. See also *Phillips (Executors* *of Phillips, Deceased) v Revenue & Customs Commissioners.*[10] Trustees may establish a money lending business by incorporating a company which then lends to others.

If a sale of a trading company is imminent and the vendor may die soon   **55.105**
after, then consider selling the company in consideration of the issue of guaranteed preference shares by the acquiring non-listed company. The preference shares can qualify for BPR.

Note that if the property qualifies for 100 per cent BPR on the 10-year   **55.106**
anniversary there is no inheritance tax if the business is subsequently sold and cash is appointed out to beneficiaries in the next 10 years. Contrast the position during the first 10 years if the business is sold and cash distributed. Do not sell an asset qualifying for BPR just before the 10-year anniversary.

Bear in mind, that one result of the 2006 changes to the IHT treatment of   **55.107**
settlements is that once the property has been in the settlement for the qualifying period (two years under s.106)[11] business relief will be available and changes in the form of the settlement (for instance if the trustees appoint an interest in possession) will not affect the position: specifically it will not cause a new two year qualifying period to commence.[12]

XII PRIVATE RESIDENCE RELIEF—CGT

Ensure trustees maximise private residence relief under s.225, i.e. that there   **55.108**
is one beneficiary in occupation and the trustees have power to allow that beneficiary into occupation.

Where trustees have let property, consider terminating the tenancy and then   **55.109**
letting a beneficiary occupy the property until sale. Main residence relief claim can be claimed (plus letting exemption): see Ch.43.

If a hold-over relief claim has been made in the past over a property   **55.110**
which a beneficiary now occupies, consider revoking the hold-over claim or transferring the property out to the beneficiary as soon as possible without a hold-over relief claim in order to maximise main residence relief and the 2003 transitional rules: see Ch.18.

Consider the effect of the rebasing election in the event that main residence   **55.111**
relief is restricted because occupation by a beneficiary did not take place after April 2008: see 43.28 and 19.55.

For IHT and the family home, see 43.85.   **55.112**

---

[10] [2006] STC (SCD) 639.
[11] A similar period applies for agricultural property relief under s.117 if the land is occupied by the trustees for the purposes of agriculture (for the purpose of this provision if the trustees allow a beneficiary—such as the life tenant—to farm the land that this requirement is met). Alternatively agricultural property relief may be due once the land has been owned by the trustees for seven years provided that it was occupied (for instance by a tenant) for agricultural purposes throughout that period.
[12] The only situation where this problem can still arise is if the trustees of a relevant property settlement were to appoint a disabled person an interest in possession within IHTA 1984 s.89B(1) (c). Because that person is treated as beneficially entitled to the property (see IHTA 1984 s.49(1) and (1A)(b)) he will need to satisfy a fresh qualifying period before relief is available; see generally, *Burrell v Burrell* [2005] STC 569.

XIII DISPOSALS OF BENEFICIAL INTERESTS IN TRUSTS

55.113 These raise capital gains tax issues considered in Ch.20 and see in particular 20.32.

55.114 For inheritance tax considerations on assignments including sales of qualifying and non-qualifying life interests see Example 24.5 and 26.06 for sales. For IHT changes in FA 2010, see 26.15. See also 27.09 and 12.16.

55.115 For inheritance tax position on assignments of reversionary interests see Example 24.8, 26.38 and consider the impact of s.81 in 24.6. The anti-avoidance legislation on assignments of remainder interests found in IHTA 1984 s.81A is considered at 26.42.

55.116–7 The inheritance tax position on settlement of reversionary interests when the settlor is foreign domiciled is considered in 26.43.

XIV LOSSES

55.118 See Ch.21. Watch the following with regard to use of losses:

(i) Beneficiaries cannot use personal losses to set against s.87 gains, only against Sch.4C gains.

(ii) A loss on a disposal to connected persons, e.g. a trust, is deductible only from chargeable gains arising on other disposals to that same person while still connected.

(iii) Losses on exempt assets such as houses qualifying for private residence relief cannot generate chargeable losses.

(iv) Watch anti-avoidance TAAR provision in TCGA 1992 s.16(2A) on loss schemes: see 21.07.

(v) Utilise losses of settlor taxable under s.86 against gains in offshore trust before trust returns to the UK and before death of settlor: see Example 21.14 and Example 55.4.

(vi) Check trust losses arising when trust in s.87 regime and outside s.86, e.g. pre-March 1998 position. These can be used even after import of trust: see 21.28. Check whether pre-March 1998 losses carried forward can be utilised again on the death of the settlor: see Example 21.13.

(vii) Watch loss relief when losses realised in an underlying offshore company. There is no ability to carry forward and only limited ability to set such losses against other gains: see Ch.54.

XV LIFETIME INHERITANCE TAX PLANNING—AVOIDING RESERVATION OF BENEFIT

55.119 Section 102B(3)(a) provides that there is no reservation of benefit in cases where there is a gift of an undivided share in land and the donor *"does not* *occupy the land*". Accordingly even if the donor otherwise benefits from the gift, there is no reservation of benefit. At 43.94 and following the authors consider possible options in relation to let properties.

55.120 Consider use of discounted gift schemes in relation to "cake and eat it" arrangements: see Ch.47.

55.121 Planning options in relation to the family home generally including the co-ownership option, home loans, family debt schemes and reversionary leases are discussed further in 43.94 and following.

55.122 Consider the limitations of FA 1986 s.102ZA and the discussion on trust carve-outs at 43.85 and Ch.33. The family home is discussed in the following context.

EXAMPLE 55.9

Trustees carve out a lease and then appoint the encumbered freehold away from an elderly qualifying interest in possession beneficiary.

(i) current position

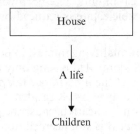

(ii) shearing operation

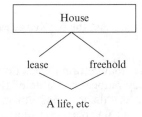

(iii) appointment of freehold interest

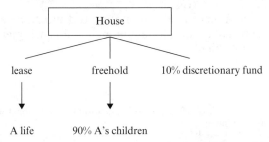

For full inheritance tax and capital gains tax analysis, see 43.85.

Use of gilts

55.123   Gilts held beneficially by a non-UK resident who is domiciled here or in an interest in possession settlement where the life tenant has a qualifying interest in possession[13] will be excluded property.[14] Note that the domicile of the settlor or residence of trust is irrelevant. If the beneficiary is not domiciled in the UK but is UK resident then government securities are not excluded property.

EXAMPLE 55.10

1. A receives a diagnosis of terminal cancer while living in Spain having moved there a year ago. He borrows on the security of all his assets and invests the cash in gilts. The borrowing is secured on the non-gilt assets. His chargeable estate is reduced by the borrowing and the gilts are exempt.

2. B is a non-resident qualifying interest in possession beneficiary of a will trust. B is still UK domiciled having only recently emigrated. The trustees decide to protect the inheritance tax position and invest entirely in exempt gilts where only non-UK residence is required. There is no inheritance tax charge on B's death because the gilts are excluded property. It does not matter that B is still deemed domiciled or that the settlor was UK domiciled.

Gifts for family maintenance and the McKelvey case

55.124–5   IHTA 1984 s.11 provides that certain dispositions are not transfers of value, i.e. that even though they reduce the estate of the disponer they are ignored (see also s.10 dealing with "dispositions not intended to confer gratuitous benefit"). The scope of s.11 has been considered in two cases, *Phizackerley v IRC*[15] (in the context of the non-deductibility of debts under FA 1986 s.103) and *McKelvey v RCC*.[16]

55.126   This exemption can be used in death bed situations, e.g. a parent can provide quite substantial sums for a minor child for their maintenance and education can be quite high!

---

[13] i.e. a pre-March 22, 2006 interest in possession, a transitional serial interest or an immediate post-death interest.
[14] See IHTA 1984 s.48(4).
[15] [2007] STC (SCD) 328.
[16] [2008] STC (SCD) 944. See 36.56

Last minute business property relief injections

Consider the position where trading company shares are wholly owned by the transferor who is very ill. He also owns land personally used by the company. It will qualify for 50 per cent BPR provided he controls the company. If the land is transferred into the company there is SDLT due (see Ch.00) but the land will then qualify for 100 per cent relief. (Section 105(1)(d) IHTA.) **55.127**

Check that the transferor controls the company: this test is applied at the time when the transfer of value occurs: it is not necessary for the transferor to have had control of the company during the preceding two years before death or the relevant date. In applying the control test, IHTA 1984 s.269(3) provides that when shares or securities are held in a settlement the voting powers given to the trustees *"shall be deemed to be given to the person beneficially entitled in possession to the shares"*. Notice that there is no requirement that the interest in possession is *"qualifying"*. **55.128**

EXAMPLE 55.11

Jasper Rougley owns 25 per cent of the ordinary shares in Rougley Make-Up, a successful fashion company. A further 30 per cent shares are held in a discretionary trust established by his father. Jasper owns land as a warehouse used by the company which is currently worth £1 million and he is minded to give it to his daughter:

1. BPR will only be available if the conditions of s.105(1)(d) are met, i.e. Jasper at the time of transfer has control of the company;
2. if the trustees were to appoint him an interest in possession in the 30 per cent shareholding and he was then to transfer the land, relief at 50 per cent would be available. The trustees could then, if they wished, revoke Jasper's interest. This has no inheritance tax implications post-March 21, 2006.

Estate duty treaties

A number of double tax treaties displace the deemed domicile rules in certain cases. These treaties are with France, Italy, India and Pakistan. While the treaties do not displace the deemed domicile rules on inter vivos transfers (so a PET would still become chargeable if the donor died within seven years) they are relevant on death. Ensure for example, that an Indian domiciliary's foreign estate passes under a foreign law will. **55.129**

55.130 The relevant property regime is based on a 10-year anniversary charge calculated using the lifetime rates of IHT. The top rate of charge is six per cent (being 30 per cent of the top lifetime rate which is 20 per cent).[18] Note especially:

(i) that the charge is a snapshot, i.e. it is imposed on property in the settlement immediately before the relevant 10-year anniversary;

(ii) there may in consequence be opportunities for avoiding or mitigating this charge. In the case of a non-domiciled settlor, for instance, ensuring that on the chargeable occasion the property is non-UK situs, will mean that it is excluded property and so not within the definition of relevant property and not within the charge (see IHTA 1984 s.58(1)(f)). The fact that the trust property has been UK situated for most of the 10-year period does not matter. By contrast, if a trust established by a non-UK domiciled settlor holds foreign situated property for 9 out of the 10-years but on the 10-year anniversary the trustees own UK situated property then the 10-year charge is reduced to allow for the period during which the settled property was excluded[19];

(iii) the value of the relevant property may be reduced by business or agricultural property relief.[20] The normal conditions for that relief must be met: for instance, the trustees must satisfy the two-year ownership requirement for business property relief.[21] The switch into property attracting this relief therefore needs to occur more than two years before the anniversary occasion;

(iv) all settlements will have 10-year anniversaries but a charge only arises if at that time the trust includes relevant property and the charge only applies to that relevant property. For instance, an accumulation and maintenance trust set up on April 1, 1994 will have had a 10-year anniversary on April 1, 2004 but, assuming that it was still an accumulation and maintenance trust at that time (or an interest in possession trust), no charge would have arisen under the relevant property regime. The next 10-year anniversary will fall on April 1, 2014;

(v) ensure that property qualifying for BPR is not sold just before a 10-year anniversary.

XVIII WILL DRAFTING

55.131 Both BPR and APR are given at a maximum rate of 100 per cent. HMRC will only consider whether relief is due after the death of the testator if IHT is at

---

[17] See also Ch.29.
[18] IHTA 1984 ss.64 and 66.
[19] See s.66(2): the property is not relevant property for the full 10-year period so the charge is reduced.
[20] IHTA 1984 ss.103(1) and 115(1).
[21] IHTA 1984 s.106.

stake. So a gift to the business to my daughter "if it qualifies for 100% BPR, otherwise to my wife" will not be reviewed by HMRC given that whichever answer they come up with no tax will be payable. If the will has been so drafted it may leave the executors in some uncertainty when it comes to administering the estate!

To qualify for relief in full it is important that there is a specific gift of the property to a chargeable person.[22]   **55.132**

The appropriation by the executors of business/agricultural property to satisfy that legacy will not lead to full relief being due under s.39A(2) since the property was not the subject matter of a specific gift.   **55.133**

38.46 considers alternatives. The solution is: **55.134**

(i) establishing the usual discretionary trust (commonly called an NRBDT);

(ii) putting into that trust the relevant business or agricultural property *without* a qualification along the lines of *"provided that it shall qualify for IHT relief"*. This will constitute a specific gift of the property within s.39A(2) and, because tax will be at stake HMRC must then rule on the availability of the relief; and

(iii) by adding a cash gift of the nil rate band (taking care not to define this as such sum as would not attract an IHT charge but ignoring for this purpose the gift of the business/agricultural property). This is desirable:

    (a) to maximise property going into trust; and
    (b) to ensure that even if the business/agricultural property is worth no more than £325,000 the issue of relief will be determined by HMRC.

By employing a discretionary trust (falling within IHTA 1984 s.144: see Ch.39) it will be possible, once the position of APR/BPR has been agreed with HMRC, to take a view on the future of the trust. For instance, if full relief is given then either the trust may continue or property could be appointed to chargeable persons outright (e.g. to children/grandchildren). By contrast, if relief is not available then an appointment to the surviving spouse may be made to obtain the benefit of spouse relief. Provided that the matter is resolved within two years of death, reading-back will be available; for instance, in respect of the spouse exemption. For further planning ideas, see 38.00 and for maximising the relief for married couples by "two bites of the cherry", see 38.00.   **55.135**

XIX EXCLUDING THE SETTLOR FROM SETTLOR-INTERESTED TRUSTS—TRAPS TO WATCH

EXAMPLE 55.12

X, the settlor, settles foreign assets into an offshore trust in 2007 when foreign domiciled. He was not deemed domiciled here. He remains a

---

[22] See IHTA 1984 s.39A.

beneficiary and the trust invests in a variety of investments. He receives a capital payment in year one but no other capital distributions.

The trust holds most of its assets in an offshore company. He is taxable under the TOA provisions on all such income having power to enjoy it but claims the remittance basis so there is no tax payable: see Ch.8.

Year 15: he no longer wishes to pay the remittance basis charge and has received no capital payments or other benefits from the trust since year one. He is now deemed domiciled here. He is happy that the trust should be appointed entirely for his children. The trustees exclude him and his spouse/civil partner from any possible benefit.

His children remain beneficiaries. X maintains his foreign domicile as a matter of general law although will now be taxed on an arising basis.

What is the tax treatment of X after his exclusion?

55.136 *Inheritance tax*: if the trust is a non-excluded property trust (i.e. settlor was UK domiciled or deemed domiciled when it was set up) there is a deemed PET on his exclusion. However, thereafter the ROB ceases. The seven-year risk may be worth taking. If (as in the example above) the settlor was not domiciled here when the trust was funded but later *becomes* deemed domiciled here and is excluded during his lifetime, then HMRC accept that no inheritance tax charge arises even if he dies within seven years provided the settled property does not comprise UK situated property at the date of his exclusion.[23]

Ensure therefore all trust property is non-UK situated at the date of exclusion of X to avoid a deemed PET risk: see Ch.31.

55.137 *Capital gains tax:* Excluding the settlor and spouse/civil partner is not sufficient to avoid capital gains tax on the settlor if the settlor is actually domiciled here. A s.86 TCGA 1992 charge will still arise on the settlor in respect of all trust gains if the non-resident trust can benefit any defined person (including children and grandchildren and their spouses). However, if the trust was set up and funded entirely before March 17, 1998 and has not been tainted then grandchildren and their spouses can still benefit without breaching s.86. In the above example, X is not yet domiciled in the UK under general law so s.86 does not apply. The exclusion has no capital gains tax consequences for him or the beneficiaries.

55.138 *Income tax:* The capital receipt conditions[24] are met if the individual receives or is entitled to receive any capital sum in a tax year or in any earlier tax year the individual has received any capital sum. Note that the capital receipt condition does not apply if the trust lent to the settlor and has been wholly repaid but loans the other way are caught. Sections 727–730 can apply not merely in the tax year in which the capital sum is received but in subsequent years even if the settlor and his spouse/civil

---

[23] See *IHTM 14396* as amended.
[24] See ITA 2007 ss.728 and 729; 8.18 and 7.45.

partner are by then wholly excluded and do not receive any benefit. X can potentially continue to be taxed on all income under TOA even if excluded: see Ch.8 and 7.45 for possible ways round this.

Drafting issues: ensure that the settlor/spouse/civil partners are excluded **55.139** properly not just from the trust but from any possible exercise of the trustees' discretion, e.g. from resettlements. If they are described as "excluded persons" what does this mean? Is this term defined in the trust?

CHAPTER 56

DISCLOSURE, COMPLIANCE, REPORTING AND ENFORCEMENT
OF TAX LIABILITIES

- HMRC's approach to tax schemes (**56.01**)
- How DOTAS works in relation to direct taxes other than IHT (**56.10**)
- DOTAS and IHT (**56.32**)
- Reporting transfers into and out of trusts (**56.43**)
- Excepted estates (**56.61**)
- Inheritance tax and the penalties regime—liability and reporting (**56.65**)
- Jurisdiction and enforcement issues against non-resident trustees (**56.82**)

I HMRC'S APPROACH TO TAX SCHEMES

56.01   The Disclosure of Tax Avoidance Schemes (DOTAS) regime was introduced in FA 2004 Pt 7. It formed part of the then Chancellor (Gordon Brown)'s plans for curbing tax avoidance. Anti-tax avoidance measures have been continued by the Coalition Government as highlighted in a Consultation Paper published in May 2011 entitled *High Risk Tax Avoidance Schemes.* That paper sets out a three-pronged approach: prevention, detection and counteraction.

Prevention

56.02   In order to deter taxpayers from entering avoidance schemes, HMRC issue *Spotlights.* These publish details of avoidance schemes on the internet and explain why they will be challenged by HMRC or why taxpayers conceded that the schemes do not work. The aim is to discourage taxpayers from entering the schemes in the first place by ensuring that advisers cannot tell clients that the schemes will be free from challenge.

56.03   In addition, a committee has been set up under Graham Aaronson QC to consider the introduction of a general anti-avoidance rule (GAAR). It is due to publish its recommendations before Christmas 2011.[1]

---

[1] The last review considering the possible introduction of a GAAR was by HMRC in 1998; at that time the proposal to introduce a GAAR was heavily criticised by professional bodies and dropped.

Detection

The DOTAS legislation falls under the detection head. It requires those creating and using certain "relevant schemes" to disclose them to HMRC. The regime has two main objectives:

(i) To provide HMRC with early information about the detail of tax avoidance schemes, allowing those schemes to be risk-assessed and, where appropriate, to inform anti-avoidance legislation.

(ii) To identify users of those tax schemes. The regime requires certain persons, normally the promoter of a scheme, to provide HMRC (within strict time limits) with information about how the scheme is intended to work. Users of schemes must also notify HMRC.

Counteraction

The disclosure rules do not give HMRC additional powers of challenge apart from legislation and litigation. This is in contrast to the May 2011 Consultation Paper mentioned above which is focused on the counteraction head. The paper suggests that HMRC should be able to influence the behaviour of potential avoiders who enter "contrived and aggressive tax avoidance schemes" despite warnings in *Spotlights*:

> "*The starting point for such users is that they will retain the use of the money, that would have been payable to the Exchequer absent the avoidance scheme, until such time as enquiries are completed. Provided they can obtain a better return on that money than the rate of interest they will have to pay if the tax eventually becomes payable, they perceive a clear financial incentive to use a tax avoidance scheme, even one whose chances of working (i.e. of delivering the tax advantage it claims to provide) are negligible. For tax avoidance scheme users who see cash flow as a significant incentive to using the scheme, there is also an incentive not to settle matters with HMRC and to extend the dispute for as long as possible. HMRC has incurred significant costs in working up schemes to the point of litigation, only for the users to accept HMRC's arguments at the last moment.*"

The paper proposes removing this cash flow advantage[2] by listing certain high-risk avoidance schemes in regulations which have to be reported to HMRC separately and the users are then subject to an additional charge on any tax found to be underpaid (in addition to penalties). These proposals have been heavily criticised by a number of professional bodies including STEP and the CIOT.

The DOTAS regime for direct taxes came into effect on August 1, 2004 and applied initially to income tax, corporation tax and capital gains tax

---

[2] However, it is doubtful whether there is any significant cash flow advantage given professional fees, interest, penalties and the low rates of interest on money retained by the taxpayer.

but was limited to schemes that concerned employment and certain financial products. It has subsequently been revised several times and extended; in particular, to all avoidance schemes involving income tax, corporation tax and capital gains tax and also to Stamp Duty Land Tax in 2005 and National Insurance Contributions in 2007 and to IHT (to a limited extent) from April 6, 2011.[3]

56.08   The current disclosure rules for direct taxes are set out in FA 2004 ss.306–319 and in a substantial number of supporting Regulations. In August 2011, HMRC published guidance on DOTAS (including inheritance tax) which superseded all earlier guidance. The main changes were:

(i)   confirmation that the bank levy was within the scope of the rules;

(ii) guidance following new rules introduced in FA 2010 which came into force on January 1, 2011. These included:

    (a)   change to the trigger point for disclosure of marketed schemes to ensure early disclosure;

    (b)   an information power to allow HMRC to require intermediaries involved in the marketing of schemes to provide information leading to the identification of the promoter;

    (c)   enhanced penalties for failure to comply with a disclosure obligation;

    (d)   a requirement for promoters to provide periodic lists of clients who have implemented schemes;

(iii) revised guidance following changes to the confidentiality and premium fee hallmarks discussed below and to pensions;

(iv) mew requirements on promoters to provide client lists;

(v)   updated guidance on disclosure of inheritance tax schemes.

56.09   HMRC considers that the disclosure obligation applies to draft legislation that has yet to be enacted.[4]

II HOW DOTAS WORKS IN RELATION TO DIRECT TAXES OTHER THAN IHT

What it applies to

56.10   The DOTAS legislation applies to "notifiable arrangements" and "notifiable proposals".

56.11   *Notifiable arrangements* are arrangements that satisfy the following conditions:

---

[3] See in particular the Inheritance Tax Schemes (Prescribed Descriptions of Arrangements) Regulations 2011 (SI 2011/170) and the form AAG4 (IHT). Separate disclosure regimes apply for VAT and NIC.

[4] For example, schemes that aimed to circumvent the disguised remuneration rules published in draft in December 2010 and enacted in FA 2011.

(i) the arrangements give rise, or might be expected to a tax advantage; and

(ii) the arrangements have the obtaining of that tax advantage as one of their main expected benefits; and

(iii) the arrangements fall within a hallmarked scheme, i.e. any of the types of arrangement specified in Treasury regulations. There are eight types of arrangements known as "hallmarks" (one of these had effect only until December 31, 2010).[5]

A *notifiable proposal* is a proposal for arrangements which, if implemented, would be notifiable arrangements. **56.12**

The concept of *"tax advantage"* is broadly defined and includes not only tax savings but also the deferral of tax payments. **56.13**

Main expected benefit

Whether one of the main benefits that might be expected to arise from the arrangements is a tax advantage, is an objective test that is not affected by the taxpayer's subjective purpose in entering into those arrangements. Tax-driven transactions, where obtaining a tax advantage is the main or only benefit that could be expected from the transaction, are clearly at risk of falling within the disclosure rules. **56.14**

In most cases of transactional tax planning (e.g. joint ventures, acquisitions) obtaining a tax advantage is unlikely to be one of the main benefits of the transaction as a whole; the main benefits are likely to be commercial. **56.15**

SDLT

The disclosure regime includes tax arrangements relating to SDLT where the subject matter of the arrangements is non-residential property with a market value of at least £5 million; residential property with a market value of at least £1 million or mixed property with a total market value of at least £5 million or which includes residential property with a market value of at least £1 million. **56.16**

The main differences that apply in the case of SDLT compared to the disclosure regime for income tax, corporation tax and capital gains tax are: **56.17**

(i) the hallmarks are not applied to limit what is required to be disclosed; however there is a white list of arrangements that are not required to be disclosed;

(ii) disclosure is not required if the arrangements are the same or substantially

---

[5] For details of the hallmarks, see 56.18 and following.

the same as arrangements first made available for implementation before April 1, 2010; and

(iii) some minor differences in respect of the time limits for making disclosure.

Hallmarks[6]

56.18 In brief, the eight hallmarks (that do not apply to SDLT or inheritance tax) are:

(i) *Hallmark 1: Confidentiality from other promoters (reg.6)*: It might reasonably be expected that the promoter would wish to keep the tax saving element of the arrangements confidential from other promoters. HMRC comment in their August 2011 Guidance:

> *"the test would be answered in the affirmative if an element of the scheme were sufficiently new and innovative that a promoter would want the details to remain secret in order to maintain their competitive advantage and ability to earn fees. . . the use of an explicit confidentiality agreement before revealing full details of the scheme to a client by advisers who do not normally use such agreements may indicate that the test is met. However, . . .HMRC would accept the test is not met if the scheme is reasonably well known in the tax community. This can be evidenced from . . .articles in the tax press, textbooks or case law."*

(ii) *Hallmark 2: Confidentiality from HMRC (regs 6 and 7)*: The promoter or the user (where there is no UK promoter) wishes to keep the tax saving element confidential from HMRC and one reason for this is to facilitate continued or repeated use of the tax saving.

(iii) *Hallmark 3: Premium fee (reg.8)*: It might reasonably be expected that a promoter (or a person connected with a promoter) of the same or substantially similar arrangements would, but for the requirement to disclose, be able to obtain a premium fee from a person experienced in receiving services of the type being provided. A premium fee is defined as a fee chargeable by virtue of any element of the arrangements (including the way in which they are structured) from which the anticipated tax advantage arises and which are to a significant extent attributable to that tax advantage or to any extent contingent upon the obtaining of that tax advantage.

(iv) *Hallmark 4: Off-market terms (reg.9)*: This hallmark applied from August 1, 2006 but was abolished with effect from January 1, 2011 as HMRC considered that it was no longer necessary.

(v) *Hallmark 5: Standardised tax products (reg.10)*: The arrangements

---

[6] For detail, see the Tax Avoidance Schemes (Prescribed Descriptions of Arrangements) Regulations 2006 (SI 20006/1543) and, for Hallmark 8, the Tax Avoidance (Prescribed Descriptions of Arrangement) (Amendment). Regulations 2009 (SI 2009/2033).

use standardised documentation and implement transactions that the promoter makes available to more than one person and where it would be reasonable for an informed observer to conclude that the main purpose of the arrangements is to enable the client to obtain a tax advantage.

According to the HMRC Guidance published in August 2011, this hallmark is intended to capture *"mass-marketed schemes"* which are *"tax-driven"*,[7] meaning that without the tax advantage, the arrangements are highly unlikely to be bought by any client. According to HMRC, the fundamental characteristic of standardised tax products is their *"ease of replication"* not, for example, the volume of take-up of the product.[8] Bespoke arrangements will not fall within this hallmark. It only applies where there is a promoter. This does not include a lawyer excluded by legal professional privilege.[9] Arrangements first made available for implementation before August 1, 2006 are excepted from hallmark 5, as are certain arrangements including EIS, VCTs, the corporate venturing scheme, ISAs, approved share options/share incentive plans, EMIs, certain pension schemes are exempted.

(vi) *Hallmark 6: Loss schemes for individuals (reg.12)*: The promoter expects more than one individual to implement the same or substantially the same arrangements and the arrangements are such that an informed observer could reasonably conclude that each of the following apply:

(a) the main expected benefit of those arrangements is the provision of losses to some or all of the individuals participating. Those individuals would be expected to use those losses to reduce their capital gains or income tax liability;

(b) as with the standardised tax products hallmark (with which there is potentially overlap), this hallmark is aimed at tax-driven structures. As with hallmark 5, this hallmark only applies where there is a promoter which does not include a lawyer excluded by LPP.[10]

(vii) *Hallmark 7: leasing arrangements (regs 13 and 14)*: Plant or machinery leases of more than two years duration where the aggregate value of all assets leased is at least £25 million or one of the leased assets is valued at least £10 million and one of the "additional" conditions is met. These are:

(a) a non-corporation tax paying party;
(b) defeasance arrangements;
(c) sale or lease and finance leasebacks.

(viii) *Hallmark 8: Certain pension arrangements*: The arrangements concerned the special annual allowance charge for pension relief purposes.[11] Hallmark 8 applied only from September 1, 2009 and ceased to have effect from April 6, 2011.

---

[7] Paragraph 7.7.2.
[8] Paragraph 7.7.2.
[9] Regulation 5(3).
[10] Regulation 5(3).
[11] See FA 2009 Sch.35. For further details of this hallmark see February 2010 version of HMRC Disclosure of Tax Avoidance Schemes available on their website.

Who must notify?

56.19 The promoter has the primary obligation to disclose notifiable arrangements or proposals. However, liability to make disclosure may also fall on a user who has become party to notifiable arrangements where there is a non-resident UK promoter who does not disclose or where a promoter is prevented from providing all the required information because of legal professional privilege.

Who is a promoter?

56.20 A promoter is any person who, in the course of a "*relevant business*", does either of the following:

 (i) is responsible, to any extent, for the design, organisation or management of the proposed or actual arrangements (a "design promoter"). This includes making a firm approach with a view to making a scheme available for implementation by that person or others;

 (ii) makes a notifiable proposal available for implementation by another person.

56.21 The term "*relevant business*" refers to any trade, profession or business that is carried on by a bank or a securities house or a business that involves providing taxation-related services to others. The definition of promoter can include lawyers, financial advisers, accountants and tax advisers. The obligations apply to both UK and non-UK based promoters.

Exclusions from definition of promoter

56.22 There are exclusions for:

 (i) a lawyer who is prevented from providing all the required information because of the effect of legal professional privilege.[12] This exclusion means that solicitors and barristers are unlikely to be promoters unless the client has waived privilege;

 (ii) where there is no promoter, for example, companies that provide in-house schemes for use within the company or corporate group;

 (iii) employees of promoters and participants in notifiable arrangements;

 (iv) certain other exclusions, the aim of which, according to an HMRC press release of June 22, 2004, is to require only those "*at the heart of*" a scheme to make disclosures.

---

[12] See 56.26.

The exclusion in (iv) means that a person who is only involved in the design **56.23** of a scheme and does not make the scheme available for implementation by others or organise or mange it is not a promoter provided any one of three tests is passed, namely:

(i) *Non-adviser*: persons responsible (to any extent) for the design of the arrangements, but who do not provide tax advice as part of their duties relating to the arrangements (e.g. a lawyer who advises a promoter on the company law aspects or an accountant who advises on accounting aspects);

(ii) *Benign*: persons who, while giving tax advice on the arrangements, are not responsible to any extent for the design of any element of the arrangements that gives rise to the tax advantage (for example, a law firm advising on the correct interpretation of a statutory provision such as whether two parties are connected for the purposes of the Taxes Acts). The advice given must not seek to highlight opportunities to exploit the relevant provisions;

(iii) *Ignorance*: persons who are responsible for the design of some (but not all) of the tax-saving elements of an arrangement and who could not reasonably be expected to have sufficient information to enable them to know whether a notification is required or to provide all the information required in a notification.

When to notify

Generally, promoters must notify a notifiable proposal to HMRC within five **56.24** business days of the *"relevant date"*. The relevant date is the earlier of the date when the promoter:

(i) makes a firm approach to another person with a view to making the scheme available for implementation by that person or others (this trigger was inserted by FA 2010 and had effect from January 1, 2011)[13]; or

(ii) makes a notifiable proposal available for implementation by another person: the scheme must be fully designed and capable of implementation in practice[14] and the promoter must communicate information about the scheme to potential clients suggesting they consider it; or

(iii) becomes aware of any transaction implementing the proposal.

---

[13] HMRC note in 3.6 of the August 2011 Guidance:

> *"This change ensures that a disclosure is triggered as soon as a person takes steps to market the scheme, whether or not it is or could be made available for implementation at the same time or later. The legislation and associated guidance should be read in accordance with that policy intent."*

[14] So if it involves a loan the actual loan provider must be in place and funds available.

56.25   A promoter must also notify within five business days of first becoming aware of any transaction forming part of notifiable arrangements, unless the transaction implements a proposal already notified.[15]

Legal professional privilege

56.26   FA 2004 s.314 expressly preserves legal professional privilege:

> "*Nothing in this Part requires any person to disclose to the Board any privileged information*".

Where a lawyer is involved, it is therefore likely that, unless privilege has been lost or waived, part of the information which must be disclosed will be privileged legal advice. In this situation, the lawyer is excluded from the definition of promoter. In *R (on the application of Prudential Plc) v Special Commissioner of Income Tax*,[16] the High Court ruled that legal advice privilege applied only to legal advice given by lawyers and not to advice given by a non-lawyer, for example, accountants. It concluded that Prudential's case was compelling, accepting that accountants have the expertise to advise on tax law and to do what lawyers do in cases that establish legal advice privilege. However, it determined that precedent prevented the court from developing the law in the way sought by Prudential. This decision was upheld by the Court of Appeal.[17]

Client disclosure, i.e. disclosure by the user of the scheme

56.27   Because of the problem of privilege, the Regulations move the obligation from the promoter to the client or "scheme user" where there is no other promoter. Alternatively, the client has the option of waiving privilege and allowing the promoter to make a disclosure on their behalf. In summary, the scheme user will therefore need to make disclosure where the promoter is based outside the UK and chooses not to disclose; the promoter is a lawyer and legal professional privilege is in issue; or there is no promoter because the scheme user designs and implements his own scheme.

---

[15] In some cases there may be more than one promoter, e.g. the scheme designer and those who provide the scheme under a licensing agreement with the designer. A person who acts solely as an intermediary between a scheme provider and a potential scheme user (that is they seek clients for the provider not themselves) is not a promoter.

[16] [2009] EWHC 2494 (Admin).

[17] See [2010] EWCA Civ 1094.

Promoters must use form AAG[18] to make a disclosure.[19] The notification **56.28** must contain:

> "*sufficient information as might reasonably be expected to enable HMRC to comprehend the manner in which the proposal is intended to operate*".

The promoter must generally make disclosure within five days of the earlier of one of three trigger events.[20] It includes:

(i) the promoter's name and address or otherwise the client's name where the client is disclosing;

(ii) details of the provision by virtue of which the proposal is notifiable;

(iii) a summary of the proposal and any name by which it is known;

(iv) information explaining each element of the proposed arrangements (including the way in which they are structured) from which the expected tax advantage arises;

(v) the statutory provisions on which the tax advantage is based.

HMRC has 30 days from notification by the promoter in which to provide the promoter with a reference number for the scheme. The promoter must then notify the scheme reference number to the client (who may be the scheme user or another adviser who then recommends the scheme to his lay clients who actually enter into the scheme) within 30 days of receiving such notification or if later, within 30 days of when the promoter first becomes aware of the scheme having been implemented.

The scheme user who has been given the reference number must disclose this on his tax return or in certain circumstances on form AAG4.[21]

Companies and individuals using notifiable arrangements which have been notified to HMRC by the promoter must include in their tax return the reference number of the arrangements provided to them by the promoter. The promoter may provide HMRC with details of any other promoter of the same or substantially the same scheme. In the event that the co-promoter is exempt from making his own disclosure of the scheme, he will be sent the scheme number by HMRC and must notify his clients (and if they are advisers who are in turn recommending the scheme to a scheme user must notify the scheme number to the user).

---

[18] Available from HMRC's website.

[19] The form is sent to the Anti-Avoidance Group (Intelligence) at HMRC 1st Floor, 22 Kingsway, London, WC2B 6NR or email at aag@hmrc.gov.uk. There are four different forms available: AAG1 – notification of scheme by promoter; AAG2 notification by scheme user where off-shore promoter does not notify; AAG3 – notification by scheme user where no promoter or promoted by lawyer unable to make full notification; AAG5 – continuation sheet.

[20] For the trigger event, see 56.24.

[21] See para.15.4.1 of the August 2011 Guidance for further details.

Penalties, investigation and enforcement

56.29   Breach of the requirements of the disclosure regime is not a criminal offence. However, failure to make a proper disclosure and failure by a promoter to pass on a reference number to his client may lead to a maximum initial £5,000 civil penalty. Continuing default after the First Tier Tribunal has imposed the initial penalty may lead to a daily default fine of a maximum of £600 for each day for which the failure continues. Failure by a user to include the reference number of a notifiable arrangement in the relevant tax return may result in a £100 penalty for each arrangement, increasing to £1,000 for repeated failures. FA 2007 introduced measures to enable HMRC to investigate cases where it has reasonable grounds to believe that a promoter has failed to comply with the disclosure regime.

56.30   From January 1, 2011 promoters are required to provide quarterly lists to HMRC of clients to whom they have become obliged to issue a scheme reference number during that calendar quarter and failure to do so may result in a penalty.[22]

Introducer provisions

56.31   FA 2010 also included a new category of person for information purposes (an introducer) to describe those who advertise notifiable schemes on behalf of a promoter but whose role does not extend to that of a promoter. An introducer is defined as a person who "makes a marketing contact" in relation to a notifiable scheme but is not involved in the design of the scheme.[23] This might include a solicitor recommending a notifiable scheme to a client.

III DOTAS AND IHT

56.32   DOTAS was extended to IHT on April 6, 2011.[24]

What inheritance tax schemes does DOTAS apply to?

56.33   IHT planning arrangements must be disclosed to HMRC if both the following conditions are met:

   (i) property becomes relevant property as defined in IHTA 1984 s.58(1) as a result of any element of the arrangements; and

---

[22] See FA 2004 s.313ZA and SI 2010/2928 and the August 2011 Guidance at para.14.2.
[23] See FA 2004 s.307(1A).
[24] When the Inheritance Tax Avoidance Schemes (Prescribed Descriptions of Arrangements) Regulations 2011 (SI 2011/170) (the Regulations) came into force. HMRC guidance on the rules is in ss.10 and 11 of the August 2011 Guidance.

(ii) the main benefit of the arrangements is the reduction, deferral or avoidance of the IHT entry charge.[25]

However, even if the above conditions are satisfied, disclosure is only required **56.34** for schemes that are new or innovative. Schemes which are the same or substantially the same as arrangements made available before April 6, 2011 are exempted from disclosure.[26]

The guidance states that "*arrangements*" includes any scheme, transaction or series of transactions. An "*advantage*" is defined very widely as the avoidance, reduction or deferral of a tax charge or obtaining a relief or an increased relief.[27] A "*relevant property entry charge*" is defined as the charge to IHT that arises on a transfer of value made by an individual during his lifetime as a result of which property becomes relevant property.[28] The description does not include the exit and 10-year anniversary charges arising during the lifetime of the settlement nor any other chargeable transfers, e.g. a close company that settles property or a gift by a close company to individuals or a gift by an individual to a close company. Transfers to pilot trusts are not within the Regulations because these arrangements are designed to avoid anniversary charges not entry charges.[29]

A scheme requires disclosure if property becomes relevant property at any point in the arrangements. It does not matter whether property becomes relevant property straightaway or whether it remains relevant property.

How to report an IHT scheme reference number

HMRC has issued the following specific forms for IHT schemes: **56.35**

(i) Form AAG 6 (IHT), which is used for:

(a) promoters to provide scheme reference numbers to clients; and
(b) clients who may be scheme users or intermediaries to provide the scheme reference number to parties to the scheme.[30]

Form AAG 4 (IHT), which is used for scheme users to notify the scheme to HMRC unless it is notified on form IHT100.

A scheme user should notify on form IHT100[31] if: **56.36**

(i) the user is liable to submit an IHT account on form IHT100 in respect of a transaction forming part of the notifiable arrangements, (often there will be no liability to submit an IHT100);

---

[25] See reg.2.
[26] As already noted, the hallmarks are not relevant to IHT. For "grandfathered" schemes, see 56.37.
[27] FA 2004 s.318.
[28] Regulation 2(3).
[29] See Ch.41.
[30] The form is available by clicking the relevant links on the Anti-Avoidance Group website at *www.hmrc.gov.uk/aiu/index.htm*.
[31] For details of Form 100, see 56.43.

(ii) the statutory time limit for submitting the IHT account (12 months after the end of the month of transfer) is no later than the date by which the user must notify the scheme reference number; and

(iii) the user submits the IHT account within that time limit.

Grandfathered arrangements and white list

56.37 Grandfathering provisions exempt arrangements from disclosure if they are of the same or substantially the same description as arrangements that meet any one of the following criteria:

(i) they were first made available before April 6, 2011;

(ii) the date of any transaction forming part of the arrangements falls before April 6, 2011;

(iii) a promoter first made a firm approach to another person in relation to the arrangements before April 6, 2011.[32]

56.38 Paragraph 11.7 of the Guidance contains a white list of grandfathered arrangements. The guidance gives the following examples of evidence needed to show that arrangements are grandfathered:

(i) a clear description of the existence and substance of the arrangement in tax manuals or publications;

(ii) production of an affidavit, where the evidence that the grandfathering rule applies is subject to legal professional privilege;

(iii) a practitioner's own record of when he made an arrangement available or learnt that competitors were making it available.

HMRC white list

56.39 The list in the HMRC Gudance includes schemes that do not fall within the Regulations at all to make the list as extensive as possible. The list is very heavily caveated and HMRC emphasises that:

(i) the list is purely illustrative and should not be regarded as being exhaustive;

(ii) a disclosure should be made if there is any doubt as to whether this is required;

(iii) exemption from disclosure does not indicate that HMRC considers arrangements to be either acceptable or effective, but only that HMRC is already aware of them or that they do not fall within the Description Regulations.

[32] See reg.3.

The guidance preceding the list states that the arrangements on the list may **56.40** need to be disclosed if they:

(i) are part of wider arrangements that fall within the Description Regulations and are not themselves grandfathered;

(ii) are not the same or substantially the same as arrangements already in existence;

(iii) must be disclosed under another part of the DOTAS regime.

The following summary of the HMRC white list uses the same lettering as is **56.41** used in para.11.7 of the August 2011 Guidance:

A. *Arrangements where property does not become relevant property*: these are outside the scope of the Description Regulations.

B. *Arrangements that qualify for reliefs or exemptions*: arrangements that result in property becoming relevant property but qualify for reliefs or exemptions need not be disclosed where there is a single step that qualifies for a relief or exemption (and no other steps are taken in order to gain an advantage). It may be necessary to disclose arrangements that lead to the following, unless it can be shown that they fall within the grandfathering provisions:

    (i) Multiple reliefs or exemptions.
    (ii) More than one application of the same relief or exemption.
    (iii) A single relief or exemption where there are further steps in order to gain an advantage.

It has been suggested by some commentators that where husband and wife jointly settle property into trust using their nil rate bands and annual exemptions as well as the normal expenditure out of income exemption this is disclosable. It is hard to see how this can be the case. HMRC have long been aware of the use of the normal expenditure exemption for gifts of surplus income to relevant property trusts and although not explicitly mentioned, it is clear that they are within the grandfathering rule since HMRC note that more than one application of the same relief does not need to be disclosed if the arrangements can be shown to be covered by the grandfathering rule.

C. *Purchase of business assets for later transfer to a trust*: it is not necessary to disclose the purchase of business assets (whether or not insurance backed) with a view to transferring them to a relevant trust after the two-year qualifying period for BPR, unless there are further steps in the arrangements.

D. *Purchase of agricultural assets for later transfer to a trust*: it is not necessary to disclose the purchase of agricultural assets (whether or not insurance backed) with a view to transferring them to a relevant property trust after the appropriate period to qualify for APR, unless there are further steps in the arrangements.

E. *Pilot trusts*: similarly it is not necessary to disclose pilot trusts established with a nominal sum (regardless of the number of trusts and whether they are created on successive days) where there is no advantage in relation to the entry charge. The tax advantage of pilot trusts is in respect of the 10-year anniversary and exit charges and these are not disclosable under the Regulations.

F. *Discounted gift trusts or schemes*: disclosure is not required where the residual trust is a bare trust, because no property becomes relevant property. Where property does become relevant property, disclosure is not required where the grandfathering provisions apply. By the "residual trust", HMRC presumably means the trust created by the holder of an insurance bond who settles the bond while retaining the right to make capital withdrawals.

G. *Excluded property trusts; disabled trusts; employee benefit trusts; qualifying interest in possession trusts*: these trusts are not relevant property trusts and so need not be disclosed, unless a further element of the arrangements falls within the Regulations and is not itself subject to the grandfathering provisions. So presumably settlement of gilts by a non-resident UK domiciliary into trust where all the beneficiaries are non-UK resident would not be disclosable since the property does not become relevant property. In any event, this is covered by the grandfathering rules since HMRC are well aware of the statutory relief for gilts.[33]

H. *Transfers into relevant property trusts on death*: transfers into relevant property trusts on death, whether under a will or otherwise, need not be disclosed. This is because transfers on death are not relevant property transfers and so fall outside the scope of the Description Regulations.

I. *Changes in the distribution of a deceased's estate*: it is not necessary to disclose the following as there is no transfer of value:

   (i) an after death variation or disclaimer to which IHTA 1984 s.142(1) applies;

   (ii) transfers by a legatee in accordance with the testator's wishes to which IHTA 1984 s.143 applies;

   (iii) an election by a surviving spouse or civil partner under AEA 1925 s.47A to capitalise a life interest arising under the intestacy rules; or

   (iv) the renunciation by a surviving spouse or civil partner of rights under Scottish law within the period mentioned in IHTA 1984 s.147(6); or

   (v) distributions from will trusts that are read-back into the will for IHT purposes under IHTA 1984 s.144.[34]

J. *Transfers of the nil rate band every seven years*: it is not necessary to disclose transfers using the nil rate band every seven years, provided that there is no other step enabling an advantage to be obtained in respect of the entry charge.

K. *Loan to a relevant property trust*: it is not necessary to disclose a loan to a relevant property trust, provided that there is no other step in the transaction except for establishing the trust.

---

[33] See Ch.31.
[34] See Ch.39.

L. *Insurance policy trusts*[35]: neither of the following need be disclosed:

   (i) the transfer to a relevant property trust of rights to benefits payable on death, even where other benefits (such as critical illness benefits) are payable to the settlor;

   (ii) the payment (whether by the settlor or another person) of premiums on a policy held in a relevant property trust.

M. *Chargeable transfer followed by potentially exempt transfer*: it is not necessary to disclose a chargeable transfer made before a potentially exempt transfer so as to ensure that the transferor's nil rate band used for the chargeable transfer, unless there are further arrangements that allow an advantage to be obtained in respect of the entry charge.

N. *Deferred shares*: the transfer of deferred shares to a relevant property trust need not be disclosed, unless the transfer is part of arrangements that enable an advantage to be obtained in respect of the entry charge and the grandfathering provisions do not apply.

O. *Items of national importance*: property does not become relevant property where the following exemptions and reliefs apply:

   (i) exemption for maintenance funds for historic buildings, etc (IHTA 1984 s.27);

   (ii) conditional exemption for heritage property (IHTA 1984 s.30);

   (iii) relief where property enters a maintenance fund (IHTA 1984 s.57A).

P. *Pension death benefits*: it is not necessary to disclose the transfer of pension death benefits to a relevant property trust where the scheme member retains the retirement benefits, unless the transfer is part of arrangements enabling an advantage to be obtained in respect of the entry charge and the grandfathering provisions do not apply.

Q. *Reversionary interests*[36]: it is not necessary to disclose a transfer to a relevant property trust where the settlor retains a reversionary interest if it can be shown that the grandfathering provisions apply.

R. *Transfers that are not transfers of value*: it is not necessary to disclose a transaction if it is not a transfer of value and does not form part of wider arrangements of which one of the main purposes is to avoid an entry charge.

However, it is necessary to disclose arrangements where there is no transfer of value, but the arrangements result in property becoming relevant property and there would have been a transfer of value in the absence of intervening steps in the arrangements, unless the grandfathering provisions apply.

Dispositions that are not transfers of value include:

   (i) Dispositions not intended to confer gratuitous benefit (IHTA 1984 s.10).

---

[35] See Ch.47.
[36] This largely deals with "*Melville* schemes" that often depend on the settlor retaining a reversionary interest: see 26.16.

(ii) Dispositions for the maintenance of family (IHTA 1984 s.11).

(iii) Dispositions allowable for income tax or conferring benefits under a pension scheme (IHTA 1984 s.12).

(iv) Dispositions by close companies for the benefit of employees (IHTA 1984 s.13).[37]

(v) The waiver of remuneration (IHTA 1984 s.14).

(vi) The waiver of dividends (IHTA 1984 s.15).

(vii) The grant of tenancies of agricultural property (IHTA 1984 s.16).

S. *Gifts to companies*: gifts to companies do not result in property becoming relevant property.

Conclusion

56.42 Only in the most straightforward cases, such as a single-step transaction that qualifies for an exemption or relief, can practitioners be sure that they do not need to disclose the arrangements. Where there are any additional steps (including multiple applications of an exemption) practitioners will have to decide whether or not grandfathering applies. It seems likely that the inheritance tax disclosure regime will be extended in the future to cover a wider range of transactions. The penalties for getting it wrong are severe: up to £1m!

IV REPORTING TRANSFERS INTO AND OUT OF TRUSTS

Use of Form IHT100

56.43 Form IHT100 is used to report lifetime transfers of value and chargeable events in relation to trusts (other than the deemed transfer on the death of the interest in possession beneficiary, which is reported in an IHT400 or 205).

56.44 Chargeable events reported in an IHT100 include:

(i) lifetime chargeable transfers of value by individuals (including transfers to relevant property trusts);

(ii) potentially exempt transfers (PETs) that become chargeable because the transferor dies within seven years (but not PETs that do not become chargeable);

(iii) deemed transfers of value by a life tenant on the ending of his qualifying interest in possession;

(iv) in relevant property trusts:

---

[37] Dispositions by close companies are not caught because these are deemed transfers of value by the participators not actual transfers of value and the property does not become settled property.

(a) 10-year anniversaries; and

(b) trust assets ceasing to be relevant property (for example, on distribution to beneficiaries);

(v) in s.71D trusts (bereaved young people):

(a) distributions of assets to a beneficiary who is 18 or over; and

(b) if the trust loses 18–25 status;

(vi) temporary charitable trusts ceasing to have charitable status;

(vii) the ending of an entitlement to conditional exemption from IHT in relation to heritage property;

(viii) the sale of timber where woodlands relief has been claimed on an owner's death.[38]

FA 2006 changed the taxation of trusts in a way that made it necessary to submit IHT accounts more often than in the past since far most property settled into trust became relevant property. HMRC therefore widened the definitions of excepted transfers, terminations and excepted settlements to reduce the number of accounts that need to be submitted where no tax is actually due and the risk of non-compliance is low.[39]   **56.45**

Cases where Form 100 is not required

It is not necessary to submit an IHT100 if the event in question is: **56.46**

(i) an exempt transfer, in some cases;

(ii) an excepted transfer into trust;

(iii) an excepted termination;

(iv) a chargeable event in an excepted settlement.

Exempt transfers

For individuals the dutyto submit an IHT account applies only in respect of *chargeable* transfers[40] not in respect of potentially exempt or exempt transfers.   **56.47**

---

[38] These events are listed in HMRC *IHT Manual*, para.10651 – When to use IHT100.

[39] The rules apply to chargeable events on or after April 6, 2007, although the regulations containing the new rules were not made until March 2008: see Inheritance Tax (Delivery of Accounts) (Excepted Transfers and Excepted Terminations) Regulations 2008 (SI 2008/605). Previously the rules were in the Inheritance Tax (Delivery of Accounts) (Excepted Transfers and Excepted Terminations) Regulations 2002 (SI 2002/1731).

[40] IHTA 1984 s.216(1)(a).

Charlotte gives £3 million to a charitable trust in January 2011. The gift is wholly exempt so that she does not need to submit an IHT100. It does not matter that the gift exceeds the IHT nil rate band (£325,000).

56.48 HMRC state that an IHT100 should be delivered if the normal expenditure out of income exemption is claimed and, without it, there would be an IHT liability because it is a transfer of surplus income into trust in excess of any unused nil rate band.[41] The legal basis behind this view is extremely doubtful.

56.49 For trustees the duty to submit an IHT account applies to any chargeable event in a trust, whether or not an exemption applies.[42] However, in practice, HMRC does not:

(i) require accounts for terminations that are treated as PETs unless the life tenant dies within seven years[43];

(ii) always enforce the requirement for an account of a termination that is wholly exempt.[44]

EXAMPLE 56.2: TERMINATION TREATED AS A PET

Hugh died three years ago leaving his wife a qualifying interest in possession (an IPDI) in an estate comprising land and shares. The remainder interest is left to his adult children. The trustees now terminate the IPDI and divide the capital between the children. The wife is treated as making a PET to the children.[45] There is no need to submit an IHT100 unless the wife dies within seven years. Similarly where a pre-March 22, 2006 qualifying interest in possession was replaced before October 6, 2008 by a TSI in favour of (say) children, this was a PET and no reporting was necessary.

---

[41] IHTM 10652:

"*Where it is claimed that normal expenditure out of income exemption applies and denial of the exemption—either in respect of a single gift (whether it is the first of a planned series of gifts or a gift within a series) or cumulatively taking into account earlier transfers—would mean that there is a liability to IHT, an account should be delivered so that the availability of the exemption can be agreed.*"

[42] IHTA 1984 s.216(1)(b) and (c).
[43] IHTM 10651 and IHT110 guidance, p.5.
[44] IHTM 10831. See also Excepted Settlement Regulations below in relation to settlements without a qualifying interest in possession.
[45] The trustees would normally keep back funds to buy insurance cover against the possibility of the wife dying within seven years of the PET.

Barbara has a qualifying interest in possession. The trustees end her interest in possession in assets worth £1,350,000, which they appoint, (a) as to £1 million to her daughter on qualifying interest in possession trusts (a TSI) in January 2008; and (b) as to £350,000 to charity.

No account is required unless and until Barbara dies within seven years.

Excepted transfers[46]

There is no need to submit an IHT100 on a transfer of property into a relevant **56.50** property trust if the transfer is an *"excepted transfer"*.[47]

Regulation 4 defines an excepted transfer as a chargeable transfer made on or after April 6, 2007 which is an actual (not deemed) chargeable transfer made by an individual, where one of two circumstances apply:

(i) The value transferred is attributable to either cash or quoted shares or securities and that value, together with the transferor's chargeable transfers in the previous seven years, does not exceed the threshold for payment of inheritance tax for the year in which the transfer was made.

EXAMPLE 56.4: TRANSFER OF CASH

Dave gives £100,000 cash to a relevant property trust in January 2011. His full nil rate band of £325,000 is available. This is an excepted transfer, so he does not need to submit an IHT100.

or:

(ii) If the funds settled are not cash or quoted shares, the value of the chargeable transfer together with the transferor's chargeable transfers in the previous seven years, does not exceed 80 per cent of the inheritance tax threshold, and the value of the transfer of value does not in any event exceed the available NRB. For this purpose BPR and APR are not taken into account when calculating the transfer of value.

EXAMPLE 56.5: TRANSFER OF PRIVATE COMPANY SHARES

Chris gives shares in his private family company worth £324,000 to a relevant property trust in January 2011. His full nil rate band of £325,000 is

---

[46] See also 56.33 above.

[47] See Inheritance Tax (Delivery of Accounts) (Excepted Transfers and Excepted Terminations) Regulations 2008 (SI 2008/605). These regulations apply to transfers and terminations made on or after April 6, 2007.

available. This is not an excepted transfer, so he must submit an IHT100 (note that it does not matter that the shares attract 100 per cent business property relief nor that the transfer is within the nil rate band of £325,000).

56.51 The trust can be non-UK resident or UK resident.[48] The excepted transfers regulations can apply in either case to exempt the transferor from an obligation to report. However, in the case of non-resident trusts there is a separate obligation on a professional adviser to report the trust under IHTA 1984 s.218 since the transferor will usually be deemed or actually UK domiciled.[49]

Excepted terminations[50]

56.52 The rules on excepted terminations apply only to "*specified trusts*" being one of the following:

(i) a trust where the beneficiary became entitled to an interest in possession before March 22, 2006;

(ii) an IPDI;

(iii) a TSI;

(iv) a trust for bereaved minors; and

(v) a trust for a disabled person under IHTA 1984 ss.89, 89A or 89B.[51]

56.53 Regulation 5 defines an "excepted termination" as the termination of an interest in possession in a specified trust in one of three circumstances:

(i) The life tenant has given notice (within six months) to the trustees under IHTA 1984 s.57(3) that either his annual exemption or the gifts on marriage or civil partnership exemption applies. Where the value deemed to

---

[48] Contrast the provisions for excepted settlements: if the trust is non-UK resident then reporting of 10-year anniversary charges and exit charges is always required even if no tax is actually payable.

[49] IHTA 1984 s.218 imposes a reporting IHT obligation on professionals, i.e. any person "*in the course of a trade or profession who is concerned with the making of a settlement*". That person (which arguably includes professional trustees) must, within three months, make a return to HMRC but only where the settlor is UK domiciled or deemed domiciled and the trustees are non-resident. Section 218 is not breached if the settlor himself separately returns the details of the settlement to HMRC but if the transfer is not otherwise reported or is an excepted transfer or within the annual exemption of the settlor, this in itself does not relieve the professional from an obligation to report. There is no obligation to report on professionals acting for settlors who are foreign domiciled for inheritance tax purposes: see Ch.31. If the transferor is foreign domiciled and settles non-UK property then there is no relevant property settlement, so reporting is not required under either ss.216 or 218 and the excepted transfer provisions are not relevant. If the transferor is foreign domiciled and settles UK situated land of say 80% of his nil rate band into a non-UK resident trust there is no obligation to report under s.218 but there is a prima facie obligation to report under s.216. However, he does not need to report the settlement, if the excepted transfer conditions are satisfied.

[50] See Inheritance Tax (Delivery of Accounts) Excepted Transfers and Excepted Terminations) Regulations 2008 (SI 2008/605).

[51] Regulations 2(1) and 5(1).

be transferred is covered by the exemptions available, the termination is an excepted termination.

(ii) Where the value in which the interest subsisted is attributable to either cash or quoted shares or securities, and that value together with the value of the beneficiary's chargeable transfers in the previous seven years does not exceed the inheritance tax threshold.

(iii) If the settled property is not cash or quoted shares, where the value of the deemed transfer made on termination, together with the beneficiary's chargeable transfers in the previous seven years, does not exceed 80 per cent of the inheritance tax threshold, and the value of the transfer of value does not exceed the transferor's actual available nil rate band. For this purpose BPR and APR are not taken into account when calculating the transfer of value.

However, it is necessary to submit an IHT100 if a transferor dies within seven years of termination.

EXAMPLE 56.6: ENDING OF IIP WHERE LIFE TENANT'S EXEMPTIONS AVAILABLE

Andrew has a qualifying pre-March 2006 interest in possession. The trustees wish to appoint a sum of cash on trust for Andrew's son Luke. In the previous seven years, Andrew has made chargeable transfers exceeding the nil rate band. This means that the distribution cannot be an excepted termination under the rules applying to transfers of cash or shares.

However, Andrew has not used his £3,000 annual exemption for the current and previous tax year. Accordingly, if the trustees appoint no more than £6,000 to Luke, the distribution is an excepted termination provided that Andrew notifies the trustees that the exemptions are available within six months of the appointment (complying with IHTA 1984 s.57). But if the trustees decide to appoint more than that on trust for Luke they must submit an IHT100. However, if the trustees appointed the cash outright to Luke no reporting is required since this is a PET and not a chargeable transfer.[52]

EXAMPLE 56.7: ENDING OF IIP IN ASSETS OTHER THAN CASH OR SHARES

Fiona has a qualifying pre-March 2006 interest in possession. The trust assets include a small flat in London that she occupies occasionally, but she has decided that she no longer needs to use the flat. The trustees make an appointment replacing her interest in possession in the flat with a new interest in possession for her daughter, Jenny. Jenny's interest in possession is not a qualifying IIP, so the flat becomes relevant property and Fiona makes an immediate chargeable transfer.

[52] See IHTM 10651.

At the time of the appointment (February 2011) the nil rate band was £325,000. In the previous seven years Fiona has made one chargeable transfer of £10,000. The value of the flat is £200,000. Accordingly the total value of the flat and Fiona's previous chargeable transfer is £210,000, which is less than 80 per cent of the nil rate band (£325,000 × 80% = £260,000). The value of the flat is within Fiona's available nil rate band, which is £315,000. This is an excepted termination, so the trustees do not need to submit an IHT100. Note that if the new interest in possession had been appointed during the transitional period before October 6, 2008 no reporting would have been required even if the transfer of value had been well in excess of Fiona's nil rate band because the transfer onto interest in possession trusts for Jenny would have been a potentially exempt transfer and not immediately chargeable.

Death within seven years of a transfer

56.54 Even though the transfer was an excepted transfer or termination, an IHT100 must be submitted if the transferor dies within seven years of a transfer.

EXAMPLE 56.8: LIFE TENANT DIES WITHIN SEVEN YEARS OF TERMINATION OF IIP

Taking the facts in Example 56.7, if Fiona dies five years after her interest in the flat ended, IHT may become payable, but even if it does not the trustees must submit an IHT100 on Fiona's death. It does not matter that the ending of the interest in possession had been an excepted termination.[53]

Excepted settlements

56.55 The Inheritance Tax (Delivery of Accounts) (Excepted Settlements) Regulations 2008 (SI 2008/606) apply to chargeable events on or after April 6, 2007. Different rules applied to events before that date. There is no need to submit an IHT100 if the following apply:

(i) There is no qualifying interest in possession in the trust at the time of the chargeable event.

For this purpose, a chargeable event means an event on which tax is chargeable under one of the following sections of IHTA 1984:

(a) s.64 (the 10-year anniversary charge in relevant property trusts);
(b) s.65 (the exit charge in relevant property trusts); or
(c) s.71D (the exit charge in 18–25 trusts).

[53] Excepted Transfers Regulations 2008 reg.3(2).

(ii) The trustees must always have been <u>UK resident.</u>

For this purpose trustees are UK resident[54] if both: **56.56**

    (a) the general administration of the trust is ordinarily carried on in the UK, and

    (b) all or a majority of the trustees (and where there is more than one class of trustees, a majority of each class) are resident in the UK.[55]

(iii) In addition the trust meets the conditions set out in either para.4(2) or (3).

Para 4(2)

This exception is designed to relieve trustees of pilot trusts of the duty to submit accounts until they receive more substantial assets. The conditions are that:

(a) cash has always been the only trust asset[56];

(b) the settlor did not add any assets to the trust after creating it;

(c) the gross value of the trust assets has never exceeded £1,000;

(d) there are no related settlements.

EXAMPLE 56.9: SMALL CASH TRUST

Hugh creates a discretionary trust with £100 in cash as a pilot trust to receive any death benefits from his company pension scheme. 10 years later:

    (1) he has added no further assets;
    (2) the trustees still hold only the original cash and a small amount of accumulated interest;
    (3) the trustees have always been UK resident.

The trustees do not need to submit an IHT100 on the 10-year anniversary of the trust.

    Paragraph 4(3): **56.57**

(a) the settlor was UK domiciled from the time he created the trust to the time of the chargeable event or his death, whichever is earlier;

(b) there are no related settlements;

---

[54] See Ch.4 for residence of trustees.
[55] Excepted Settlements Regulations 2008 reg.9(b).
[56] So settling a postage stamp will fall outside the exemption. See Ch.41!

(c) the value of the notional chargeable transfer that is used to calculate the rate of IHT does not exceed 80 per cent of the nil rate band. Liabilities and reliefs in IHTA 1984 are not taken into account when calculating the value of the notional transfer for this purpose.

EXAMPLE 56.10: NOTIONAL TRANSFER EXCEEDING 80 PER CENT OF NIL RATE BAND BEFORE RELIEFS

The 10-year anniversary of the X Trust falls in February 2011, when the nil rate band is £325,000. At this time the settlor (who is still alive) has always been UK domiciled and the trustees have always been UK resident. There are no related settlements. The trust holds only agricultural land worth £350,000 and £10,000 in cash. The land qualifies for 100 per cent agricultural property relief, so no IHT arises.

However, reliefs are not taken into account when calculating the value of the notional chargeable transfer. Ignoring APR, the value of the notional chargeable transfer is £360,000. This exceeds 80 per cent of the nil rate band (£260,000). So this is not an excepted settlement and the trustees must submit an IHT100 even though no IHT is payable.

56.58 If trustees do not submit an IHT return because they believe that the trust is an excepted settlement, but later discover that it is not, they must submit a return within six months of the discovery.[57]

Practical points

56.59 If no IHT100 is required, you should still keep records of the chargeable event. The details may be needed in future, for example, because:

(i) an excepted transfer or termination is included in a cumulative total on a later transfer or termination;

(ii) an individual dies within seven years of an excepted transfer or termination;

(iii) the settlor of a relevant property trust dies within seven years of a PET that he made before creating the trust (this affects the calculation of IHT charges in the trust);

(iv) the IHT calculations on a 10-year anniversary of, or distribution from, a relevant property trust affect the calculations on any subsequent distribution before the next 10-year anniversary.

---

[57] Excepted Settlements Regulations 2008 reg.3(3).

Other tax returns

A taxpayer may need to submit other tax returns, depending on the type of **56.60** chargeable event. For example, if an individual makes a chargeable transfer to a new trust, there is a non-statutory obligation to report the creation of the trust on Form 41G(Trust). If the trust is non-UK resident there are also reporting requirements under the capital gains tax legislation.[58]

V EXCEPTED ESTATES

The Inheritance Tax (Delivery of Accounts) (Excepted Estates) (Amendment) **56.61** (No.2) Regulations 2011 came into force on March 1, 2011.[59] The previous regulations specified three categories of excepted estate:

(i) Low value estates which have no liability to IHT because the gross value of the estate plus the chargeable value of certain specified transfers does not exceed the applicable nil rate threshold in the tax year in which the deceased died. The deceased must have made no lifetime chargeable transfers other than specified transfers (cash, tangible movable property, quoted shares, land) of a limited amount.

(ii) Exempt estates which have no liability to IHT because the estate after deducting liabilities and spouse and charity exemptions does not exceed the applicable nil rate threshold in the tax year in which the deceased died. The gross value of the estate plus the value of lifetime transfers must not exceed £1 million and there were the same limitations on the types of chargeable transfer permitted, as with the previous category.

(iii) Non-domiciled estates where the deceased was never domiciled in the UK and the gross value of the estate in the UK was not greater than £150,000 being wholly attributable to cash or quoted shares.

In the case of deaths occurring on or after April 6, 2010 the nil rate threshold **56.62** was increased to take account of a nil rate band transferred from a predeceased spouse or civil partner. The increase was limited to the simple situation where the whole of a nil rate band is transferred. In the April 2011 *IHT and Trusts Newsletter*, HMRC indicated that it expects 75 per cent of estates which do not have to pay tax as a result of TNRB to qualify as excepted estates.

Two other changes took effect in respect of deaths occurring on or after **56.63** March 1, 2011:

(i) To qualify as an excepted estate various conditions have to be satisfied; one is that the deceased died without having made any chargeable transfers during the seven years ending with his death other than

---

[58] See 56.65 below and Ch.19.
[59] Note that they were amended after coming into force to correct a technical omission.

specified transfers not exceeding £150,000. Business and agricultural property relief has never applied when determining the value of these transfers. The new Regulations provide that where transfers exceeding £3,000 in any tax year have been made which are exempt under the normal expenditure out of income exemption, they shall be treated as chargeable transfers for this purpose.

(ii) The Regulations also close an unintended loophole in the original Regulations, reg.4(3)(f) provides that an estate is exempt where the gross value of the estate and lifetime transfers does not exceed £1 million and after deducting the value of property passing to a spouse, civil partner or charity and liabilities, the net value does not exceed the nil rate threshold. For deaths occurring on or after March 1, 2011 at least part of the estate must actually pass to a spouse, civil partner or charity.

56.64 Where an estate qualifies as an excepted estate and benefits from TNRB, the value of the estate and the wording of the oath should follow that used for an "exempt excepted estate". So exact values should be given for the gross and net estate and the oath should contain words confirming that no account is required.[60]

VI INHERITANCE TAX AND THE PENALTY REGIME— LIABILITY AND REPORTING

Delivery of return

56.65 After March 21, 2006, most lifetime gifts made to trusts are immediately chargeable transfers so unless the Excepted Transfers Regulations apply[61] they must be reported. With respect to chargeable lifetime transfers outside the excepted transfers regulations, IHTA 1984 s.216 imposes an obligation on the settlor *and* on the trustees of the settlement to deliver accounts in respect of lifetime chargeable transfers.[62] In *Re Clore (No.3)*[63] the trustees of a settlement, who were all resident outside the UK, contended that though they were liable to pay tax they were not liable to deliver accounts, because of the presumption that legislation does not have an extra-territorial effect. Their argument was rejected by Walton J., who said that the principle of extra-territoriality had been misunderstood. Once it was admitted that the foreign trustees were liable to pay the tax, it followed that they must comply with the relevant administrative machinery.

56.66 If trustees or the settlor fail to deliver an account to HMRC under s.216[64]

---

[60] See *IHT and Trusts Newsletter*, April 2011.
[61] The relevant Excepted Transfers Regulations in force at the date of the transfer should be checked.
[62] IHTA 1984 s.218 imposes an inheritance tax obligation to report non-resident trusts set up by domiciled settlors. TCGA 1992 Sch.5A para.3 imposes a capital gains tax obligation to report non-resident trusts set up by a UK domiciled and resident settlor.
[63] [1985] STC 394.
[64] Fixed penalties also apply to a failure for a professional to deliver an account in respect of setting up any non-resident trust by a UK domiciliary as required under s.218: see s.245A.

and do not have a reasonable excuse[65] then the relevant person is liable to fixed penalties of £100 plus £60 for every day after the day on which the failure has been declared by a Tribunal, until the account has been delivered.[66] This fixed penalty can rise to a maximum of £3,000 but it cannot exceed the tax actually due. Similarly, if an account fails to be delivered by the trustees under s.216(1)(c) before the expiry of 12 months from the end of the month in which the 10-year charge arose[67] there are the same fixed maximum penalties. Note the above are not tax geared penalties: unlike income tax, there are no tax geared provisions for failure to make an IHT return. Schedules 55 and 56 FA 2009 (applied by ss.106 and 107 FA 2009) do provide for tax geared penalties for failure to make an IHTA 1984 s.216 return and failure to pay tax but are not yet in force.

Liability to pay tax

The settlor as the transferor is primarily liable for any inheritance tax arising as a result of lifetime chargeable transfers in trust.[68] The trustees of the settlement are also directly liable to HMRC for inheritance tax on a transfer of value.[69] In a curious and often overlooked provision, a spouse or civil partner of a transferor can also be liable for tax due from the transferor on the chargeable transfer if, at the time of the chargeable transfer, she/he was the spouse or civil partner of the transferor and the transferor made a transfer of value to the spouse or civil partner (whether before or after the gift into settlement).[70]   **56.67**

The primary liability for any 10-year or exit charge falls on the trustees of the settlement under s.201(1)(a) with secondary liability falling on any person for whose benefit any of the settled property or income from it is applied at or after the time the charge arose and/or the settlor (if the trust is non-UK resident).[71] Section 204(6)(b) makes it clear that the settlor is not primarily liable even when there are non-resident trustees.   **56.68**

Time limits

Until April 2011 there was no effective time limit for the collection of inheritance tax.[72] The six year period only ran from when an account had been delivered and tax paid and accepted by HMRC. As from April 1, 2011, s.240 was amended to substitute new subss.(3)–(8) and s.240A inserted. These, for the first time, set out time limits on the collection of inheritance tax: ultimately 20 years where the loss of tax has been brought about deliberately. If   **56.69**

---

[65] See IHTM 36061—HMRC consider very little constitutes reasonable excuse and the burden is on the taxpayer.
[66] See s.245.
[67] IHTA 1984 s.216(6)(c).
[68] See IHTA 1984 s.199(1)(a).
[69] See IHTA 1984 s.199(1)(c).
[70] See IHTA 1984 s.203.
[71] See IHTA 1984 s.201(1)(d).
[72] See IHTA 1984 s.240.

the error was careless then the time limit is six years from the date on which the tax or last instalment of tax became due.[73] Otherwise the time limit is four years.

Penalties

56.70   There *are* tax geared penalties in place for submitting an incorrect (as opposed to no) return whether on lifetime chargeable transfers or on death, so any return that is submitted whether on death or in the case of lifetime transfers should be submitted with care, with reasonable valuations backed up by proper documentation. FA 2007 Sch.24 introduced this new regime for Income Tax, CGT and some other major taxes. FA 2008 Sch.40 extended it to other taxes including IHT and the new penalty regime applies to IHT for all chargeable events that occur on or after April 1, 2009.[74]

The provisions of IHTA 1984 s.247(1) and (2) continue to apply to events before that date under which there is a liability where a person "*fraudulently*" or "*negligently*" furnishes an incorrect account.

56.71   The new regime applies both to persons submitting documents and to third parties providing information to those submitting documents.[75] There are four categories of error[76]:

(i)   inaccurate despite taking reasonable care; no penalties are due;

(ii) "careless" if the inaccuracy is due to failure by the person submitting the document (P) to take reasonable care;

(iii) "deliberate but not concealed" if the inaccuracy is deliberate on P's part but P does not make arrangements to conceal it; and

(iv) "deliberate and concealed" if the inaccuracy is deliberate on P's part and P makes arrangements to conceal it (for example, by submitting false evidence in support of an inaccurate figure).

Penalties are graded depending on the category into which they fall and on whether disclosure was prompted or unprompted. So, for example, in the case of careless errors they range from 0 to 30 per cent of the tax underpaid and in the case of deliberate and concealed errors from 30 to 100 per cent.[77] The new regime applies not only to inheritance tax but also to trustees' tax returns. Further details can be found in the Compliance Manual.

56.72   Where, after any inheritance tax account, information or document has been delivered by any person without negligence, it comes to his notice that it

---

[73] SI 2010/867.
[74] See SI 2009/571 art.2.
[75] FA 2007 Sch.24 para.1A. In the inheritance tax context the new regime applies to submitting an accurate account of appropriate property and the value of that property under ss.216 or 217 IHTA 1984; information or documents due under regulations under s.256 IHTA 1984 (excepted estates); statement or declaration in connection with a deduction, exemption or relief.
[76] See FA 2007 Sch.24 para.3.
[77] See Sch.24 Pt 2.

was incorrect in any material respect or he has underpaid tax, the account is to be treated as having been negligently delivered unless the error is remedied without unreasonable delay.[78]

HMRC discusses penalties at length at IHTM 36102 onwards.[79] They say that they expect a prudent person to: **56.73**

(i) read a form and accompanying notes;

(ii) make the fullest enquiries reasonably practicable before completing a form;

(iii) wait a reasonable time for replies to enquiries;

(iv) provide a copy of any professional valuations of assets he or she may have obtained or estimate the value of the assets only after due consideration; and

(v) check the completed form before signing it.

Hence, under-valuations of property can result in penalties. HMRC say that personal representatives must make it clear where estimated values have been used. In cases where the correct value turns out to be substantially higher, the personal representatives will be asked how their valuation was obtained and to forward copies of any professional valuations. For any penalty to be due there has to be negligence or fault on the part of the taxpayer. HMRC instructions concede that the burden of proving negligence or fraud (now carelessness), should it be disputed and come before the tribunal, is on HMRC. *Robertson v IRC*[80] and *Cairns v HMRC*[81] are the leading inheritance tax cases on penalties. In both cases HMRC failed in their attempt to impose penalties on the solicitors acting as the personal representatives. Both concerned property valuations. In the latter case the Tribunal emphasised that, for these purposes, negligent conduct[82] amounts to more than just being wrong or taking a different view from HMRC. Each case must be considered having regard to its own particular circumstances, taking into account what is reasonably practicable in those circumstances. **56.74**

HMRC comment in the Inheritance Tax Manual in the context of the old legislation that they are particularly looking for cases where: **56.75**

(i) unquoted shares are valued at nominal or par value;

(ii) property values are estimated without any comparisons being made with similar property;

(iii) sales which have already taken place before submission of the account are not reflected in the values given; or

---

[78] IHTA 1984 s.248. The references to fraud or negligence are retained here

[79] Although all the references are to the out of date legislation in s.247 and it has not been updated since April 2009. For more up to date discussion on how HMRC deal with the new categories of careless or deliberate inaccuracy as set out in Sch.24 FA 2007 and now applicable to inheritance tax in relation to an incorrect return see Compliance Manual 81120 onwards and below for examples.

[80] [2002] STC (SCD) 182.

[81] [2009] UKFTT 67 (TC).

[82] The cases were both in relation to chargeable events arising before April 1, 2009 and therefore the old regime under s.247 IHTA 1984 applied which refer to fraud or negligence.

(iv) property is put up for sale at a substantially higher figure than is returned to the Revenue either before or shortly after a Grant Representation is obtained.

56.76 In addition s.247(3) provides (from July 22, 2004) that a person not liable for the tax but who fraudulently or negligently[83] produces any incorrect information or document to HMRC is liable to a fixed penalty of £3,000. Similarly a person who knowingly assists in the submission of incorrect accounts (e.g. they hide a PET that has become chargeable on death) can be liable to a fixed penalty. HMRC give the following examples in the Compliance Manual at 81131 onwards of the four types of inaccuracy under the new legislation which regime is now also applicable to inheritance tax.

56.77 *Inaccurate but took reasonable care:* the following examples from HMRC Compliance Manual are not regarded as careless:

(i) Graeme makes a transposition inaccuracy when filling in his Self Assessment return by writing down his car benefit as £5,190 instead of £5,910.

(ii) Heidi rang our Contact Centre and gave all the relevant details, but despite this she was given inaccurate advice.

(iii) XYZ Insurance Ltd specialises in home insurance. It relies on several agents to sell the insurance policies and to collect the premiums due. The agents are required to send XYZ a periodic report showing details of the policies sold, the amounts of premium, the commission due to the agents and Insurance Premium Tax (IPT). XYZ uses this information to compile its IPT return. Despite having extensive systems in place to capture and process the information, the agents are occasionally late in sending their reports to XYZ. As a consequence, XYZ does not always have all the information it requires in time to compile its IPT returns.

56.78 *Careless inaccuracy:* described as a failure to take reasonable care and regarded by HMRC as similar to negligence. They comment:

> "*People do make mistakes. We do not expect perfection. We are simply seeking to establish whether the person has taken the care and attention that could be expected from a reasonable person taking reasonable care in similar circumstances.*"

HMRC examples include:

(i) Absence of structured record-keeping system to ensure records are accurate.

(ii) Claiming reliefs without checking legislation.

(iii) Not following (presumably correct!) advice from HMRC.

(iv) Repeated errors on VAT returns due to inadequate systems.

---

[83] Note that the references to fraud or negligence are retained here and in IHTA 1984, s.248.

(v) *"Susan is the personal representative of her late mother's estate. Her mother held a number of bank accounts but did not keep any recent bank statements. When she is completing the IHT account Susan does not check the balances on the accounts at the date of death with her mother's bank. Instead she estimates the amounts. This shows a lack of reasonable care."*

Deliberate but not concealed inaccuracy occurs when a person knowingly and intentionally gives HMRC an inaccurate document. Examples given include: **56.79**

  (i) systematically paying wages without accounting for operating PAYE or Class 1 NICs;

 (ii) deliberately describing transactions inaccurately or in a way likely to mislead;

(iii) giving a VAT return to HMRC that includes a figure of net VAT due that is too low because the person does not have the cash at that time to pay the full amount, and later telling HMRC the true figure when they have the funds to pay;

(iv) claiming a deduction for personal expenses of such a size or frequency that the inaccuracy *must* have been known;

 (v) deliberately omitting a known asset from an IHT account (rather than making enquiries about its value) on the basis that the asset can be included in a corrective account later.

Deliberate but concealed inaccuracy: the person has taken active steps to   **56.80** cover their tracks by making arrangements to conceal the inaccuracy, e.g. creating false invoices to support inaccurate figures in the return; backdating or postdating contracts or invoices; creating false minutes of meetings or minutes of fictitious meetings; destroying books and records so that they are not available.

    The following example is given in the context of inheritance tax:

> *"Peter is the personal representative of his late father's estate. Six years before his death, Peter's father gave him a house. Because his father died within seven years of the gift, Peter should declare it in the IHT account as it affects the amount of IHT payable. Peter does not include the gift and, during an enquiry into the account, he produces a Deed of Gift which he has altered to suggest that it was made more than seven years before his father died.*
>
> *Peter has taken active steps to conceal the deliberate inaccuracy by falsifying a document to support the omission of an asset from an IHT account."*

In summary, fixed penalties will arise if an account is delivered late or there is   **56.81** a failure altogether to deliver an account or to pay tax plus interest under s.233 on unpaid tax (in 2011 at three per cent). Tax geared penalties can arise where an account is delivered that is incorrect and taxpayer has not taken reasonable care in the preparation of that account or return. If the actual tax liability is less than the penalty chargeable then the maximum penalty is limited to the amount of tax that is due.[84] It is assumed in all cases that there is no reasonable excuse for the delay.

VII JURISDICTION AND ENFORCEMENT ISSUES AGAINST NON-RESIDENT TRUSTEES

56.82 Where the trust is non-UK resident and charges under the relevant property regime are due, it is likely that HMRC will opt to proceed against any UK resident settlor where possible under s.201(1)(d), or an appropriate s.201(1)(c) beneficiary. The settlor/beneficiary may then be able to claim against the trustees to recover the amount of tax (and penalties) paid. However, there is no statutory obligation for the trustees to reimburse the settlor.[85] Whether the settlor/beneficiary can so claim would depend on whether, for example, the trustees were under an obligation pursuant to the terms of the trust deed or otherwise owed a duty to the settlor/beneficiary to properly account for and discharge the relevant tax liability. Generally trustees located in a foreign jurisdiction have power under a modern trust deed to pay foreign taxes including UK taxes although not necessarily an obligation to do so. In many cases, the trustees will pay the UK tax even where not obliged to do so under the trust deed and even where they have no UK situated property. This is because it is often in the UK resident beneficiaries' best interests. If the trustees pay tax in a timely way, interest and penalties are avoided and therefore the depletion of the trust fund is ultimately less. If HMRC collect the tax from the settlor the trustees may consider exercising their discretions so as to reimburse him assuming he is not excluded from benefit.

56.83 In some cases the settlor may be dead or non-UK resident. The beneficiaries may not be UK based or there may be no UK situated property. Can HMRC then proceed against non-UK resident trustees in the English courts? HMRC must first satisfy the court that an English forum is appropriate for the claim; they then need to be able to enforce the judgment against the trustees' assets in the jurisdiction where they are located.[86]

56.84 The first condition above is relatively straightforward. An English court will have jurisdiction to entertain a claim in personam if the defendant is validly served with process in England or abroad. In the event that the non-resident trustees does not submit to the jurisdiction by nominating an agent resident in England to accept service of proceedings on their behalf, HMRC will have to find a way to validly serve the claim form on the trustees abroad. The relevant provisions are found in CPR Pt 6 and PD6. Generally HMRC would then have to apply to the court for permission to serve the claim form on the trustees under CPR r.6.36. They can obtain permission if they can show that they believe the claim has a reasonable prospect of success and that England and Wales is the proper place in which to bring the claim.

56.85 In *Prestwich v Royal Bank of Canada Trust Co (Jersey) Ltd*[87] (Unreported), the English High Court allowed service out of the jurisdiction on foreign trus-

---

[84] See s.245(5).

[85] Contrast the position under capital gains tax: see TCGA 1992 s.86 and Ch.19.

[86] The trust assets often comprise only a shareholding in a foreign incorporated holding company. It is the holding company which owns the trust assets.

[87] (1998/99) 1 ITELR 565.

tees (in Jersey) of a claim for statutory reimbursement.[88] However, this does not answer the question of whether the Jersey court would have enforced any resulting judgment.

The second condition—enforcing an English judgment—is much more dif- **56.86** ficult. Generally, in the absence of express provisions between the two relevant countries under their double tax arrangements (which often have limited effect),[89] HMRC can only enforce under common law. But foreign courts are unlikely to entertain such an action, either directly or indirectly, on the basis that they will not collect the revenue of a foreign state.[90]

However, there is a distinction between, (1) a claim that seeks to directly or **56.87** indirectly enforce the revenue law of a foreign country; and (2) a claim brought by a private party to recover a sum of money paid by that party by way of tax and/or associated penalty under foreign revenue law. The latter claim may be brought under contract (e.g. to enforce an indemnity) or in restitution, and there is judicial support for saying that this type of claim is not rendered unenforceable by reason of the "foreign revenue law" principle. Thus, trustees who had been personally compelled to pay tax in another jurisdiction could s eek the aid of the English court to be indemnified out of an estate in England.[91] In *Williams and Humbert Ltd v W H Trade Marks (Jersey) Ltd* (a case involving an alleged foreign penal law),[92] the majority of the House of Lords defined the limits of indirect enforcement thus:

> "*No countenance was given in Government of India v Taylor, in Rossano's case. . .nor in Brokaw v Seatrain UK Ltd to the suggestion that an action in this country could ever be properly described as the indirect enforcement of a penal or revenue law in another country when no claim under that law remained unsatisfied. The existence of such unsatisfied claim to the satisfaction of which the proceeds of the action will be applied appears to me to be an essential feature of the principle enunciated in the Buchanan case. . .for refusing to allow the action to succeed.*"[93]

See also *Balkin v Peck*[94] where English trustees of an English trust who had **56.88** distributed the trust fund to the beneficiaries without retaining assets to pay the capital transfer tax on the life tenant's death were able to recover appropriate shares for the CTT liability from the beneficiaries' resident in Australia.

Hence, although a direct claim by HMRC against non-resident trustees for **56.89** unpaid tax and penalties will often fail as any judgment of the English court against the trustees is very unlikely to be enforced by the foreign court as it involves collection of foreign tax, if HMRC proceed against the settlor or beneficiaries who then claim against the trustees for recovery of the tax and

---

[88] Under TCGA 1992 Sch.5 para.6.
[89] See, for example, The Judgments (Reciprocal Enforcement) (Guernsey) Law 1957 which allows registration for enforcement in Guernsey of judgments of the High Court, the Court of Appeal and the Supreme Court of England and Wales, but expressly precludes the registration for enforcement of a judgment where under a sum of money is "*payable in respect of taxes or other charges of a like nature or in respect of a fine or other penalty*" (s.3(2)(b)).
[90] See *Gresh v RBC Trust Company Ltd* [2009/10] GLR 239; *Dicey and Morris* (14th edn), para.5R–019 and the cases there cited.
[91] *Re Lord Cable* [1977] 1 WLR 7; *Re Reid* (1970) 17 DLR (3d) 199.
[92] [1986] AC 368.
[93] [1986] AC 368 at 440–441, per Lord Mackay.
[94] [1988] 43 MSWLR 706.

penalties payable, this right of recovery may well be enforceable through the foreign courts. Of course, it is then necessary for the settlor or beneficiary to have some statutory or other right of reimbursement or indemnity against the trustees which may not always be the case.[95]

---

[95] This may be particularly relevant for capital gains tax falling on the settlor under TCGA 1992 s.86 or income tax due under the settlement provisions where the settlor does have a statutory right of reimbursement. He does not have a statutory right of indemnity in respect of inheritance tax for which he becomes liable. Increasingly, because of the difficulties at common law, the UK is negotiating the right to enforce UK taxes directly through the foreign courts in double tax treaties.

APPENDIX I

PRECEDENTS

PART I: SETTLEMENTS

A1.1   PILOT DISCRETIONARY TRUST

THIS SETTLEMENT is made the ......day of .... 20 [...........] between [...............] ("the Settlor") and [..............] and [...............] ("the Original Trustees")

WHEREAS

(A) The Settlor has paid to the Original Trustees the sum of ten pounds[1] and envisages adding further property to the settlement in the future.

(B) This settlement is irrevocable and shall be known as [*select name, eg Bloggs No 1 Trust*].

(C) The Original Trustees have agreed to act as the first trustees of the settlement.

NOW THIS DEED WITNESSES:

1. DEFINITIONS

   a. In this trust document:

   "Beneficiary"[2] means:
      i. any widow or widower or surviving Civil Partner of the Settlor whether or not remarried or in a civil partnership;
      ii. any child or grandchild of the Settlor whenever born;
      iii. anyone (other than the Settlor) descended from the father or mother of the Settlor;
      iv. anyone who is or has been married to or who is the Civil Partner or former Civil Partner of anyone falling within (ii) or (iii) above;
      v. after the death of the Settlor anyone who may be entitled to inherit all or any part of the Settlor's estate if the Settlor died intestate or under the Settlor's will;
      vi. any person (other than the Settlor) notified in writing by the Settlor during his lifetime to the Trustees[3];
      vii. any body of persons or trust established for charitable purposes only in accordance with the law of England and Wales, notified in writing by the Settlor during his lifetime to the Trustees; and

---

[1] For the requirement that property, albeit of a nominal value, must be put into the pilot trust: see Ch.42.

[2] A wide class of beneficiaries will normally be chosen.

[3] If the class of beneficiaries or trust terms are altered after the execution of a will which is intended to pass property to the trust, then the will should be re-executed confirming that property should be left into the trust as amended.

"Civil Partner" means civil partner as defined in the Civil Partnership Act 2004.

"Trustees" means the Original Trustees and any other trustees for the time being of this trust.

"Trust Fund" means the sum of £10 and all property transferred to the Trustees by any person or persons, at any time held by the Trustees whether by way of accumulation of income, capital appreciation, further settlement or otherwise and all monies, investments, income and other property for the time being representing or arising from the whole or any part of the same.[4]

"Trust Period" shall mean the period of 125 years running from the date of this deed.[5]

b. Words describing relationships include adopted and step children and those tracing their descent through them.

c. Words importing the singular shall include plural and vice versa. Words importing a gender include every gender.

2. THE TRUST PROVISIONS

a. During the Trust Period the Trustees may by deed or deeds appoint that they shall hold the Trust Fund for the benefit of any of the Beneficiaries on such terms as the Trustees think fit.

b. An appointment may create any provisions including discretionary trusts and dispositive and administrative powers exercisable by the Trustees or any other person. An appointment may be revocable during the Trust Period or irrevocable.

c. The Trustees may pay, transfer or apply any part or all of the Trust Fund to or for the advancement or benefit of any Beneficiary or to any fund or settlement in which one or more Beneficiaries is capable of benefitting.[6]

d. Subject to the exercise of the powers in clauses 2(a) to 2(c), the Trustees may accumulate the whole or part of the income of the Trust Fund which income shall be added to the Trust Fund.[7]

3. ULTIMATE TRUSTS

[insert a default beneficiary / beneficiaries][8]

4. TRUSTEES' POWERS[9]

In addition to any other powers conferred on the Trustees by this deed, the Trustees shall have the widest possible powers of administration and management of the Trust Fund as

---

[4] Note that the definition envisages that further property may be transferred to the trustees in the future: see A1.14.

[5] This is the mandatory perpetuity period laid down by the Perpetuities and Accumulations Act 2009. Note, however, that if desired, a shorter Trust Period can be selected (in this case the draftsman must take care to distinguish it from the perpetuity period).

[6] This is a power "in the wider form" and enables the trust fund to be resettled. Note the width of the power: some settlors would limit the recipient trust to one in which *all* the Beneficiaries can benefit or one which the trustees themselves could have set up in exercise of their powers of appointment.

[7] As a result of PAA 2009 all the statutory restrictions on accumulations of income have been removed and it is possible to accumulate throughout the perpetuity period.

[8] This "long-stop" provision is designed to prevent a resulting trust to the settlor. Select one or more living beneficiaries and do not make their entitlement subject to a contingency.

[9] Draftsmen frequently use the STEP Standard Administration provisions in place of this list of powers. For a more comprehensive selection of administrative powers: see A1.5 (Schedule).

if they were absolute owners of the Trust Fund and beneficially entitled to it. In particular:

a. The Trustees may make any kind of investment they could make if they were absolute beneficial owners (and in particular (i) may invest in and retain non-income producing assets situated anywhere in the world and (ii) need not have regard to any rule of law requiring them to consider diversifying the investments).

b. The Trustees may make any disposition of property that they could make if they were absolute beneficial owners.

c. The Trustees may lend all or any part of the Trust Fund to any Beneficiary on such terms (whether or not including provision for the payment of interest and with or without security) as the Trustees in their absolute discretion think fit.

d. The Trustees may borrow on the security of all or any part of the Trust Fund or without giving any security and on such terms as to interest as the Trustees in their absolute discretion think fit.

e. The Trustees may pay or transfer capital or income to the parent or guardian of any minor Beneficiary and the receipt of such parent or guardian shall be a full discharge to the Trustees.

f. The receipt of the treasurer or other proper office in respect of capital or income paid to a charity shall be a full discharge to the Trustees.

g. The Trustees may apply all or part of the Trust Fund in purchasing or maintaining any policy of assurance on the life of any person and shall have all the powers of an absolute beneficial owner in relation to any such policy.

h. The receipt of the Trustees for any money payable under or deriving from any dealing with any policy of life assurance shall be a full and sufficient discharge to the company issuing such policy, which company shall not be concerned in the application of any such monies.

i. In so far as the governing law of this trust permits, the Trustees may delegate in any way the exercise of any of the powers of investment and management of the Trust Fund and may employ agents, discretionary investment managers, nominees and custodians on such terms as the Trustees in their absolute discretion think fit.

j. The Trustees may appropriate all or any part of the Trust Fund as they think fit in or towards satisfaction of the interest of any Beneficiary and may for that purpose place such value on any property as they think fit.[10]

k. Any Trustee (other than the Settlor or any spouse or Civil Partner for the time being of the Settlor) who is a solicitor or other person engaged in a profession or business or any corporate trustee, may charge all usual reasonable professional charges in relation to work carried out in connection with this trust and shall have the power to resign from office as a Trustee.[11]

l. No Trustee shall be precluded from joining in the exercise of any of the powers conferred upon them notwithstanding that he will or may benefit from such exercise or by reason of the fact that he is or may become a Beneficiary provided that at least one other Trustee who takes no benefit is also a party to the exercise.[12]

---

[10] The statutory power of appropriation in AEA 1925 s.41 does not apply to trustees. It is therefore important that they are given an express power.

[11] The settlor should be made aware of this clause and agree its terms.

[12] For difficulties that may be caused by the "self dealing" rule, see *Kane v Radley Kane* [1999] Ch 274 and *Breakspear v Ackland* [2008] EWHC 220 (Ch).

m. The Trustees may by deed (and so as to bind their successors) release or restrict the future exercise of all or any of the powers conferred on them by this trust document or by law.

n. Any legal rule requiring apportionments to be made for the purpose of this trust is excluded and shall not apply.[13]

5. TRUSTEES LIABILITY

No Trustee shall be liable for any loss to the Trust Fund or part of the Trust Fund at any time unless that loss is caused by his own knowing breach of trust.[14]

6. EXCLUDED PERSONS

a. During the lifetime of the Settlor, no part of the capital or income of the Trust Fund shall be capable of being paid or lent or applied to or for the direct or indirect benefit of the Settlor or any spouse or Civil Partner for the time being of the Settlor in any circumstances whatsoever.

b. The prohibition of this clause 6 shall apply notwithstanding anything else contained in or implied by the provisions of this trust document.

7. THE SETTLOR'S POWER TO APPOINT AND REMOVE TRUSTEES[15]

a. During his lifetime and whilst he has capacity, the Settlor shall have power to appoint new and additional trustees and to remove any trustee as long as there shall be at least one corporate trustee or two individual trustees acting after such appointment and/or removal.

b. After the Settlor's death or after he loses capacity, the Settlor's powers in clause 7(a) shall vest in the Trustees.[16]

IN WITNESS etc

---

[13] The complex rules requiring apportionment of income and expenses should be excluded in favour of a receipts/payments basis.

[14] Ensure that the settlor is made aware of and agrees this clause. If professional trustees are used then amend this clause so they are liable for any loss caused by negligence. They will have indemnity insurance to cover this.

[15] It is common for the settlor to have power to appoint trustees: less common for him to have a power of removal.

[16] The pilot trust may have little value in the settlor's lifetime. The settlor may want to appoint a close friend as Protector who has power to appoint trustees after his death. This will be particularly relevant if the trust is non-resident. If the settlor and later his friend are UK resident they cannot be trustees themselves. However, a power of appointment of trustees can be conferred on a UK resident protector.

BARE TRUST[17]

THIS DECLARATION OF TRUST is made the [ ] day of [ ] 20[ ] by [*name*] of [*address*] ('the Donor')

WHEREAS:

(A) The Donor is the legal and beneficial owner of the property described in the Second Schedule ("*the Property*").

(B) The Donor wishes to make provision by way of gift for [*details of beneficiary*] who is under 18 years of age ("*the Beneficiary*") by declaring himself trustee of the Property.

NOW THIS DEED IRREVOCABLY WITNESSES as follows:

1. DEFINITIONS

In this Deed where the context so admits:

1.1 "*the Trust Fund*" shall mean the Property and any additions to the Trust Fund by way of further declaration or otherwise and the assets from time to time representing the said property and additions or any part or parts thereof.

1.2 "*the Trustees*" shall mean the Donor or other the trustees or trustee for the time being of this Declaration.

2. DECLARATION OF TRUST

The Donor declares that from the date of this Declaration the Trustees shall hold the Trust Fund and any income thereof upon the following trusts and subject to the following provisions.

3. BENEFICIAL INTEREST

The Trustees shall hold the Trust Fund and the income thereof upon trust for the Beneficiary absolutely.[18]

---

[17] See Ch.42. A bare trust is not "*settled property*" for CGT purposes nor a "*settlement*" for IHT.
[18] A bare trust can be set up for more than one beneficiary, e.g. "*for my two children Jack and Jill in equal shares*".

4. Power Of Appointment Of Trustees

The power of appointing a new or additional trustee or trustees of this Declaration shall be vested in the Donor during his lifetime and thereafter the statutory power of appointment of trustees shall apply.

5. Administrative powers

Until the Beneficiary attains the age of 18 years the powers and provisions contained in the First Schedule shall apply to the Trust Fund and the income of it.

6. Power Of Maintenance[19]

S. 31 of the Trustee Act 1925 shall not apply to this Declaration to the intent that the Beneficiary shall have the immediate right to the income of the Trust Fund notwithstanding his minority.

7. Extended Power Of Advancement[20]

S. 32 of the Trustee Act 1925 shall apply as if the words "one half of" were omitted from proviso (a) of subsection (1).

THE FIRST SCHEDULE

[*administrative provisions*]

THE SECOND SCHEDULE

[*details of property settled*]

IN WITNESS etc.

---

[19] Failure to exclude s.31 means that the income from the trust may be used by the trustees for the maintenance of a beneficiary under 18 with any balance retained until he becomes 18.

[20] For the use of this power to extend the trust beyond the beneficiary's 18th birthday: see Ch.42.

A1.3   DISABLED PERSON'S TRUST[21]

THIS SETTLEMENT is made the . . . . . . day of . . . .

BETWEEN:

(1) *(settlor)* of *(address)* ('the Settlor') and

(2) *(original trustees)* of *(addresses)* ('the Original Trustees')

WHEREAS

The Settlor wishes to make the settlement set out below and has paid or transferred into the joint names of or placed under the joint control of the Original Trustees the assets described in the Schedule to be held upon and with and subject to the following trusts powers and provisions

NOW THIS DEED WITNESSES as follows:

1 DEFINITIONS AND INTERPRETATION

In this settlement the following expressions have where the context permits the following meanings:

1.1 'the Trustees' means the Original Trustees or other the trustees or trustee for the time being of this settlement and 'Trustee' means each and any of the Trustees

1.2 'the Trust Fund' means the assets described in the Schedule all assets at any time added to it by way of further settlement (whether by the Settlor or any other person) accumulation of income capital accretion or otherwise and all property from time to time representing the same

1.3 'the Principal Beneficiary' means *(disabled person)*

1.4 'the Discretionary Beneficiaries' means:

    1.4.1 any [husband][wife] (whether present or future) or [widower][widow] whether or not remarried of the Principal Beneficiary

    1.4.2 the children and remoter issue of the Principal Beneficiary

---

[21] See Ch.36. The Principal Beneficiary is disabled within the meaning of IHTA 1984 s.89(4). This trust satisfies the inheritance tax conditions for a disabled person's trust and meets the conditions for income tax and CGT vulnerable beneficiary relief.

1.4.3 the spouses (whether present or future) widows or widowers (whether or not remarried) of the persons specified in clause 1.4.2 above[22]

1.5 'spouse' shall include a civil partner registered under the Civil Partnership Act 2004 and 'widow' and 'widower' (and 'remarried') shall be construed accordingly

1.6 'the Trust Period' means the period of 125 years from the date of this deed

2 BENEFICIAL TRUSTS DURING THE LIFETIME OF THE PRINCIPAL BENEFICIARY[23]

2.1 During the lifetime of the Principal Beneficiary the Trustees may from time to time pay or apply the income of the Trust Fund to or for the benefit of the Principal Beneficiary PROVIDED that:

2.1.1 such payment or application shall from time to time be made in such manner and upon such terms and conditions (if any) as the Trustees in their discretion shall from time to time think proper[24]

2.1.2 the Trustees shall accumulate the whole or any part of the income of the Trust Fund that is not paid out under clause 2.1.1 by investing the same and the resulting income of it in any investments by this settlement authorised and adding the accumulations to the capital of the Trust Fund

2.2 The Trustees shall have power in their absolute discretion to pay transfer or apply in any manner to or for the benefit of the Principal Beneficiary the whole or any part or parts of the capital of the Trust Fund

---

[22] It should be considered whether the trustees should be given power to add further beneficiaries so that charities can be included.

[23] This clause is designed to meet the requirements of IHTA 1984 s.89(1) which are that during the life of the disabled person there is no interest in possession in the property and "not less than half of the settled property which is applied during his life is applied for his benefit". Under this precedent, during the lifetime of the disabled person he is the only person to whom capital or income can be applied. This is much more restrictive than the IHT rules require. However, to qualify for the income and capital gains tax relief under the vulnerable beneficiary legislation in FA 2005 ss.23−45 either the disabled beneficiary must be entitled to the income or it may not be applied for the benefit of any other person during his lifetime. Further it is necessary that "if any of the property is applied for the benefit of a beneficiary it is applied for the benefit of the disabled person". The clause meets these two requirements. So far as the enhanced CGT annual exemption is concerned TCGA 1992 Sch.1 para.1(1)) the income requirement is less onerous than that for vulnerable beneficiaries (and so is met) whilst the capital requirement is as for IHT (and so is met). Accordingly it is considered that this form benefits from all three reliefs: viz disabled trusts for IHT; vulnerable beneficiaries for income and capital gains tax and the enhanced CGT annual allowance. Note however, that although the trustees could pay capital to the disabled beneficiary's carers or to a residential home if it is for his benefit to do so, they cannot pay capital for the benefit of anyone else during his lifetime and this may be seen as unduly restrictive. Nor can income be paid to anyone else under this precedent. It may be convenient to pay income to others, e.g. to fund the holiday of the parents of a disabled beneficiary without having to worry about whether this is for the benefit of the disabled beneficiary. The income tax and CGT reliefs available under the vulnerable beneficiary's legislation may not be regarded as worth the loss of flexibility. Note that this precedent will not confer CGT uplift on the disabled beneficiary's death, despite the fact that the trust fund will be treated as part of the beneficiary's estate for IHT purposes. To achieve CGT uplift on death the beneficiary would need to be given actual entitlement to income during the beneficiary's lifetime.

[24] Note that if the disabled beneficiary does not have any entitlement to income his means tested benefits should not be restricted. In fact, the IHT rules would permit all the income to be paid to someone else.

3 BENEFICIAL TRUSTS AFTER THE DEATH OF THE PRINCIPAL BENEFICIARY

3.1 After the death of the Principal Beneficiary the Trust Fund and the income of it shall be held in trust for all or any one or more exclusively of the other or others of the Discretionary Beneficiaries at such ages or times and if more than one in such shares and with such provisions for their maintenance advancement and benefit generally (including discretionary trust powers or provisions) as the Trustees (being at least 2 in number or a trust corporation) shall (due regard being paid to the law concerning remoteness) by deed or deeds revocable or irrevocable made before the end of the Trust Period appoint and in default of and subject to any and every such appointment upon trust for such of the children of the Principal Beneficiary as attain the age of 21 years if more than one in equal shares absolutely

3.2 Subject thereto the Trustees may during the Trust Period pay or apply the income of the Trust Fund to or for the benefit of all or any one or more exclusively of the other or others of the Discretionary Beneficiaries for the time being in existence

3.3 Notwithstanding and in derogation of the above trusts powers and provisions set out in clauses 3.1 and 3.2 (but without prejudice to any prior application of the Trust Fund or the income of it) the Trustees (being at least 2 in number or a trust corporation) shall at any time or times after the death of the Principal Beneficiary have power during the Trust Period in their absolute discretion to pay transfer or apply in any manner to or for the benefit of any one or more of the Discretionary Beneficiaries the whole or any part or parts of the capital of the Trust Fund

3.4 Subject to all the trusts powers and provisions of this settlement and if so far as (for any reason whatever) not wholly disposed of by it the Trust Fund and the income of it shall be held upon trust for *(beneficiary)*

4 ADMINISTRATIVE POWERS

The Trustees shall (in addition to all other powers vested in them by this settlement or by law) have the following additional powers:

4.1 power at their absolute discretion to retain the Trust Fund or any part of it (including any uninvested money) in its actual state and condition for any period and to vary or transpose the mode of investment of the Trust Fund within the range authorised below

4.2 power to invest trust money in the acquisition by purchase or otherwise or upon the security of such property of whatever nature and wherever situated as the Trustees shall in their absolute discretion think fit and so that:

    4.2.1 the acquisition with trust money of property with a view to its enjoyment in kind by the Principal Beneficiary and after his death by any of the Discretionary Beneficiaries shall for the purposes of this settlement be deemed to be an investment of it

    4.2.2 any immovable property which may be acquired for any of the purposes of this settlement (including its enjoyment in kind) may either be vested in the Trustees upon trust for sale with power to postpone sale or held by such persons or person and in such manner as the Trustees may think fit

4.3 power to invest or hold or allow to remain in the name or under the control of some or one only of the Trustees or of any person or persons corporations or corporation as nominee or nominees of the Trustees the whole or such part of the Trust Fund as the Trustees shall in their absolute discretion think fit and the Trustees shall not be liable for any loss to the Trust Fund or income of the Trust Fund occasioned by the exercise of this power

4.4 Power to lend money with or without security to the Principal Beneficiary during his lifetime and thereafter to any Discretionary Beneficiary with or without the payment of interest and upon such terms as to repayment or otherwise as the Trustees in their absolute discretion think fit.

4.5 power (exercisable either expressly or by implication) to allot appropriate partition or apportion any property whatever which (or the future proceeds of sale of which) are for the time being subject to the trusts of this settlement in or towards satisfaction of any share or interest in the Trust Fund or the income of it in such manner as the Trustees shall in their absolute discretion (without the necessity of obtaining any consent) consider just according to the respective rights of the persons interested

4.6 power for any of the Trustees (other than the Settlor or any spouse of the Settlor) to be employed and remunerated as a director or other officer or employee or as agent or adviser of any company body or firm in any way connected with the Trust Fund and to keep as his property (and without being liable to account for such) any remuneration fees or profits received by him in any such capacity notwithstanding that his situation or office may have been obtained or may be held or retained in right or by means or by reason of his position as one of the Trustees or of any shares stock property rights or powers whatever belonging to or connected with the Trust Fund

[5 TRUSTEE INDEMNITY[25]

In the professed execution of the trusts and powers of this settlement no Trustee shall be liable for any loss to the Trust Fund arising by reason of any improper investment made in good faith or for the negligence or fraud of any agent employed by him or it or by any other Trustee although the employment of such agent was not strictly necessary or expedient or by reason of any mistake or omission made in good faith by the Trustee or by reason of any other matter or thing except wilful fraud or dishonesty on the part of the Trustee who is sought to be made so liable]

6 APPOINTMENT OF NEW TRUSTEES

6.1 The statutory power of appointing new or additional trustees as modified below shall apply to this settlement and shall be exercisable by the Settlor during the life of the Settlor and thereafter by the Trustees

6.2 Except where the Trustees include or comprise a trust corporation there shall never be less than 2 Trustees but so that any sole Trustee may act while being such sole Trustee for the purpose of appointing a new Trustee or Trustees but (unless a trust corporation) for no other purpose

6.3 The statutory power of appointing new or additional trustees shall be modified as follows:

6.3.1 any person or persons may be appointed as Trustee or Trustees notwithstanding that such person or persons may be resident domiciled carrying on business or (if a body corporate) incorporated outside the United

---

[25] Only insert this clause if it has been drawn to the Settlor's notice and he has agreed it. Amend if professional trustees are used. They should be liable if they are negligent.

Kingdom and the receipt of such person or persons for the whole or such part or parts of the Trust Fund as may be paid or transferred to such person or persons pursuant to such appointment shall be a complete discharge to any other Trustee or Trustees accordingly

6.3.2 the statutory power of appointing new trustees shall not be exercisable by reason only that a Trustee remains out of the United Kingdom for more than 12 months

6.3.3 the statutory power of appointing additional trustees shall be exercisable notwithstanding that one of the Trustees for the time being is a trust corporation

6.4 Any corporate body may at any time be appointed either as a general trustee or as custodian trustee of this settlement on such terms and conditions as to remuneration (payable out of income or capital) and otherwise in all respects as the person or persons making the appointment shall prescribe or approve and may act by its proper officers in the discharge of its duties as such trustee and in the exercise of the powers and discretions conferred by this settlement or by law

7 TRUSTEES CHARGING PROVISION[26]

The Trustees may employ any of their number (other than the Settlor or any spouse of the Settlor) who may be engaged in any profession or business and any of the Trustees so engaged may charge and be paid all professional or other reasonable costs and proper charges for any business done or services rendered or time spent by him or his firm in connection with the trusts powers or provisions of the settlement whether or not within the usual scope of his profession or business and although not of a nature requiring the employment of a professional or business person

8 EXCLUSION OF THE SETTLOR AND SPOUSE FROM BENEFIT

Notwithstanding anything above contained or implied none of the powers authorities or discretions by this settlement or by law conferred on the Trustees or on any other persons shall at any time or in any circumstances whatsoever be exercisable in any manner which may benefit the Settlor or any spouse of the Settlor and no part of the capital or income of the Trust Fund shall at any time or in any circumstances whatsoever be lent to paid to or transferred to or applied for the benefit of the Settlor or any spouse of the Settlor

[9 CLAUSE HEADINGS[27]

The headings to the clauses of this settlement are for the purposes of information only and are not part of and shall not be used in the construction of this settlement or any part of it]

IN WITNESS etc

---

[26] Ensure that the settlor knows of and approves this clause.

[27] This provision is optional given that even in the event of a conflict between the headings and the clause, it is not thought that the heading would override the express terms of the clause. In other cases (e.g. when the clause contains some ambiguity), the court might consider that using the heading for the purpose of resolving such ambiguity is sensible.

SCHEDULE

Assets

(describe assets referred to in the recital)

(signatures of the parties)

(signatures of witnesses)

EMPLOYEE BENEFIT TRUST[28]

DATE:

PARTIES:

(1) [*COMPANY*] whose registered office is at [*address*] ("the Company" which expression shall, where the context admits, include any company resulting from the amalgamation or reconstruction of the Company); and

(2) [*TRUSTEES*] of [*address*] ("the Trustees").

RECITALS

(A) The Company considers that the loyalty and dedication of its employees (and those of its Subsidiaries) has contributed to the group's prosperity and attainment of a leading position in the field of [*field*]. It also considers that the attraction and retention of a loyal, dedicated and highly motivated workforce is essential to its continuing prosperity and growth (and that of its Subsidiaries). Accordingly the Company wishes to create a settlement for the principal benefit of existing and future employees of the Company and its Subsidiaries, which will give those employees an immediate and direct interest in the continuing prosperity and growth of the group.

(B) The Company has, by resolution of its Board of Directors passed on [ ], approved the establishment of this Settlement and has transferred or delivered to the Trustees or otherwise placed under their control the property specified in the First Schedule. Further money, investments or other property may be paid or transferred to the Trustees by way of addition.

PART 1 - OPERATIVE PROVISIONS

1. **DEFINITIONS AND CONSTRUCTION**

In this Deed, where the context admits, the following definitions and rules of construction shall apply:

1.1. "the Trust Fund" shall mean:

    (a) the property specified in the First Schedule;

    (b) all money, investments or other property paid or transferred by any person to or so as to be under the control of and, in either case, accepted by the Trustees as additions;

---

[28] See Ch.49.

(c) all accumulations (if any) of income added to the Trust Fund; and

(d) the money, investments and property from time to time representing the above;

1.2. "the Trust Period" shall mean the period ending on the earlier of:

(a) the last day of the period of 125 years from the date of this Deed, which period, and no other, shall be the applicable perpetuity period; and

(b) such date as the Trustees shall at any time specify by Deed, not being a date earlier than the date of execution of such Deed or later than date previously specified;

1.3. "Subsidiary" shall mean a company which is a subsidiary of the Company within the meaning of s1159 and Schedule 6 to the Companies Act 2006;

1.4. "the Beneficiaries"[29] shall mean:

(a) the present and future officers and employees and all former officers and employees of the Company and any Subsidiary; and

(b) the spouses, widows, widowers and children or step-children under the age of 18, of the persons who are beneficiaries by virtue of sub-clause 1.4(a).[30]

Neither the Company, any Subsidiary nor any person who shall previously have added property to the Trust Fund, nor the spouse for the time being of any such person, shall be one of the Beneficiaries;

1.5. "Charity" shall mean any trust, foundation, company or other organisation whatever established only for purposes regarded as charitable under the law of England and Wales[31];

1.6. "Excluded Person" any person referred to in s13(2) of the Inheritance Tax Act 1984 and not also referred to in s13(3) of that Act provided that persons within s13(2) shall not be excluded from benefiting in a way permitted under s13(4)[32];

1.7. the expression "the Trustees" shall mean the trustee or trustees for the time being of this Settlement whether original additional or substituted;

1.8. references to the Inheritance Tax Act 1984, the Companies Act 2006 and the Financial Services Act 1986 and to any section of any of those Acts shall include any statutory modification or re-enactment of the Act or section concerned;

1.9. words denoting the singular shall include the plural and *vice versa*;

1.10. words denoting any gender shall include both genders;

1.11. the clause headings are included for reference only and shall not affect the interpretation of this Deed.

2. RETENTION OR SALE OF TRUST FUND

The Trustees shall hold the Trust Fund upon trust in their discretion either to allow the same to remain in the state in which it is received or held for so long as they shall think

---

[29] For the requirements to be satisfied if the trust is to qualify as an EBT: see Ch.49 and A2.379.

[30] IHTA 1984 s.86(1)(b) allows persons to benefit by reference to marriage to; relationship with or dependence on an employee: see generally Ch.49.

[31] See IHTA 1984 s.86(2) and Ch.49.

[32] This allows participators to benefit only if they do not have 5% or more of the share capital/ assets of the company. Note that participators can also benefit without breaching s.13(2) even if they are over this limit if they can only do so in a way that means the payment is taxed as their income or would be so taxed if they were UK resident. See s.13(4). See also cl.14 below.

fit or to sell or convert the same into money. The Trustees may, in their discretion, invest such money in their names or under their control in any of the investments authorised by this Deed or by law, with power from time to time to vary or transpose any such investments for or into others so authorised.

3. Power to receive additional property

The Trustees may, at any time during the Trust Period, accept additional money, investments or other property, of whatever nature and wherever situate, paid or transferred to them by the Company or any other person. Such additional money, investments or other property shall be held upon the trusts and with and subject to the powers and provisions of this Deed.

4. Discretionary trust of capital and income

4.1. The Trustees shall hold the capital and income of the Trust Fund upon trust for or for the benefit of such of the Beneficiaries, at such ages or times, in such shares, upon such trusts (which may include discretionary or protective powers or trusts) and in such manner generally as the Trustees shall in their discretion appoint. Any such appointment may include such powers and provisions for the maintenance, education or other benefit of the Beneficiaries or for the accumulation of income and such administrative powers and provisions as the Trustees think fit.

4.2. No exercise of the power conferred by sub-clause 4.1 shall invalidate any prior payment or application of all or any part of the capital or income of the Trust Fund made under the trusts of this Deed or under any other power conferred by this Deed or by law.

4.3. Any trusts and powers created by an appointment under sub-clause 4.1 may be delegated to any extent to any person, whether or not including the Trustees or any of them.

4.4. The exercise of the power of appointment conferred by sub-clause 4.1 shall:

   (a) be subject to the application, if any, of the rule against perpetuities; and

   (b) be by Deed, revocable during the Trust Period or irrevocable, executed during the Trust Period.

5. Income trusts in default of appointment

The provisions of this clause shall apply during the Trust Period until, subject to and in default of any appointment under sub-clause 4.1.

5.1. The Trustees shall pay or apply the income of the Trust Fund to or for the benefit of such of the Beneficiaries as shall for the time being be in existence, in such shares and in such manner generally as the Trustees shall in their discretion from time to time think fit.

5.2. Notwithstanding the provisions of sub-clause 5.1, the Trustees may at any time in their discretion accumulate the income by investing it in any investments authorised by this Deed or by law and, subject to sub-clause 5.3, shall hold such accumulations as an accretion to capital.

5.3. The Trustees may apply the whole or any part of the income accumulated under sub-clause 5.2 as if it were income arising in the then current year.

6. Power to apply capital for Beneficiaries

The provisions of this clause shall apply during the Trust Period notwithstanding the provisions of clause 5 but subject to any appointment made under sub-clause 4.1.

6.1. The Trustees may pay or apply the whole or any part of the capital of the Trust Fund to or for the benefit of all or such of the Beneficiaries, in such shares and in such manner generally as the Trustees shall in their discretion think fit.

6.2. The Trustees may, subject to the application (if any) of the rule against perpetuities, pay or transfer any income or capital of the Trust Fund to the trustees of any other trust, wherever established or existing, under which any Beneficiary is interested (being a trust under which every person who may benefit is, or would if living be, a Beneficiary of this Settlement), to hold on the terms of that trust, freed and released from the terms of this Settlement, if the Trustees in their discretion consider such payment or transfer to be for the benefit of such Beneficiary.

7. Ultimate default trusts

7.1. Subject as above and if and so far as not wholly disposed of for any reason whatever by the above provisions, the capital and income of the Trust Fund shall be held upon trusts for such of the Beneficiaries as are living at the end of the Trust Period and in equal shares if more than one absolutely.

7.2. Subject to that, if any of the Trust Fund is not effectively disposed of, it shall be held by the Trustees on trust for such Charities as the Trustees shall determine.

8. Beneficiaries' rights during the Trust Period

8.1. No Beneficiary shall have:

(a) any claim, right or entitlement whatever to any part of the capital and income of the Trust Fund, except as provided in this Deed or as the same may arise by virtue of the exercise of any power contained in this Deed; or

(b) any claim, right or entitlement during the Trust Period to call for accounts (whether audited or otherwise) from the Trustees in relation to the capital and income of the Trust Fund, or to obtain any information of any nature from the Trustees in relation to the capital and income of the Trust Fund or in relation to the trusts and powers contained in this Deed.

8.2. The benefits which may from time to time be provided under this Deed shall not form part of any contract of employment between the Company or any Subsidiary and any of their respective officers or employees, and such benefits shall not confer on any such officer or employee any legal or equitable rights against his employer, either directly or indirectly, nor give rise to any cause of action in law against his employer.

8.3. Money paid to, or any other benefit conferred on, any of the Beneficiaries out of the capital or income of the Trust Fund shall not, save as may be required by law in respect of taxation, form part of his wages or remuneration, or count as wages or remuneration for pension or other purposes.

8.4. No officer or employee of the Company, or of any Subsidiary, whose office or employment terminates shall be entitled to any compensation for or by reference to any loss of any right or benefit or prospective right or benefit under this Deed which he might otherwise have enjoyed, whether such compensation is claimed by way of damages for wrongful dismissal or other breach of contract, or by way of compensation for loss of office or otherwise.

9. Administrative powers

The Trustees shall, in addition and without prejudice to all statutory powers, have the powers and immunities set out in Part 2 of this Deed. No power conferred on the Trustees shall be exercised so as to conflict with the beneficial provisions of this Deed.

10. Extended power of maintenance

The statutory provisions for maintenance and education shall apply but so that the power of maintenance shall be exercisable in the discretion of the Trustees and free from the obligation to apply part only of the income for maintenance where other income is available.

11. Extended power of advancement

The statutory provisions for advancement shall apply but so that the power of advancement shall extend to the whole, rather than one half, of the share or interest of the person for whose benefit the advancement is made.

12. Appointment of new trustees

12.1. The power of appointing new trustees shall be vested in the Company.

12.2. A person may be appointed to be a trustee notwithstanding that such person is not resident in the United Kingdom. Remaining out of the United Kingdom for more than 12 months shall not be a ground for the removal of a trustee.

12.3. Any Trustee may retire at any time by giving not less than thirty days' notice in writing to the Company and with effect from the expiry of such notice.

12.4. The Company may by deed remove a Trustee provided that the Trustee being removed is effectually indemnified against liabilities properly incurred as a Trustee. The removal shall take effect upon the receipt by such Trustee of written notice of removal from office.

12.5. On the retirement or removal of a Trustee:

12.5.1. the retired or removed Trustee shall be discharged from his trust; and

12.5.2. a new Trustee shall be appointed if there would otherwise be only one continuing Trustee and that continuing Trustee is an individual.

13. Proper law, forum and place of administration

13.1. The proper law of this Settlement shall be that of England and Wales. All rights under this Deed and its construction and effect shall be subject to the jurisdiction of, and construed according to, the laws of England and Wales.

13.2. The courts of England and Wales shall be the forum for the administration of these trusts.

13.3. Notwithstanding the provisions of sub-clauses 13.1 and 13.2:

(a) the Trustees shall have power to carry on the general administration of these trusts in any jurisdiction in the world. This power shall be exercisable whether or not the law of such jurisdiction is for the time being the proper law of this Settlement or the courts of such jurisdiction are for the time being the forum for the administration of these trusts, and whether or not the Trustees or any of them are for the time being resident or domiciled in, or otherwise connected with, such jurisdiction;

(b) the Trustees may at any time declare in writing that, from the date of such declaration, the proper law of this Settlement shall be that of any specified jurisdiction. No exercise of this power shall be effective unless the law of the jurisdiction specified is one under which this Settlement remains irrevocable and all, or substantially all, of the trusts, powers and provisions contained in this Deed remain enforceable and capable of being exercised and so taking effect;

(c) following any exercise of the power contained in sub-clause 13.3(b), the Trustees shall, by deed, make such consequential alterations or additions to this Deed as they consider necessary or desirable to ensure that, so far as may be possible, the trusts, powers and provisions of this Deed shall be as valid and effective as they were immediately prior to such change;

(d) the Trustees may, at any time, declare in writing that, from the date of such declaration, the forum for the administration of these trusts shall be the courts of any specified jurisdiction.

14. GENERAL RESTRICTIONS ON POWERS

14.1. No discretion or power conferred on the Trustees or any other person by this Deed or by law shall be exercised, and no provision of this Deed shall operate directly or indirectly:

(a) so as to cause or permit any part of the capital or income of the Trust Fund to become in any way payable to or or the benefit of the Company, any Subsidiary or any person who shall previously have added property to the Trust Fund or the spouse for the time being of any such person;

(b) so as to prevent the application of s86 of the Inheritance Tax Act 1984 to these trusts;

(c) so as to cause or permit any part of the capital or income of the Trust Fund to become in any way payable to or applicable for the benefit of any Excluded Person, save by way of a payment which is the income of such person for any of the purposes of income tax (or would be the income for any of those purposes of that person where not resident in the United Kingdom if he were so resident)[33]; or

(d) so as to cause this Settlement to be a collective investment scheme within the meaning of s75(1) of the Financial Services Act 1986.

14.2. The Trustees shall keep such records and accounts as may be necessary to demonstrate the segregation of fund required by sub-clauses 14.1above.

14.3. The prohibitions in sub-clause 14.1 shall apply notwithstanding anything else contained or implied in this Deed.

15. CONSULTATION

In deciding what benefit to confer on any officer to employee or any person who is a Beneficiary by their relationship to an officer or employee the Trustees shall primarily have regard to the contribution made or likely to be made by such officer or employee to the prosperity of the Company or of any Subsidiary, as the case may be. In doing so, the Trustees shall be entitled to consult with, and to rely upon representations made by, the Board of Directors of the Company or of such Subsidiary as to any officer's or employee's contribution.

---

[33] This allows payments to be made to participators of 5% or more but only if they are subject to income tax or would be if they were UK resident. This would appear to allow interest bearing loans to such participators but not interest free loans at least before December 9, 2010 since they would not have been subject to income tax. See IHTA 1984 s.13(4).

16. SHARES

16.1. Subject to clause 16.2, the Trustees shall waive their entitlement to all dividends on shares of the Company comprised in the Trust Fund from time to time.

16.2. The Board of Directors of the Company may, at the request of the Trustees, release the Trustees from the provisions of clause 16.1 for such periods as the Board of Directors shall specify. The release shall be given in writing and may be revocable or irrevocable.

17. ALTERATIONS BY THE COMPANY

The Company may, with the prior written consent of the Trustees, by deed alter or add to any of the provisions of this Settlement provided that no such alteration or addition may impair or adversely affect the rights of any Beneficiary who has become indefeasibly entitled to any interest in the capital or income of the Trust Fund or otherwise alter the restrictions contained in Clause 14 above.

18. IRREVOCABLE SETTLEMENT

This Settlement shall be irrevocable and known as the "[ ] Employee Settlement".

PART 2

Administrative provisions

IN WITNESS etc

SPOUSAL BY-PASS TRUST FOR PENSION DEATH BENEFIT[34]   A1.5

THIS DECLARATION OF TRUST is made the [ ] day of [ ] 20[ ] by [*Name*] of [*address*] and [*Name*] of [*address*] ("the Original Trustees")

WHEREAS

(1) The Original Trustees hold the sum of £10 cash on and with and subject to the following trusts powers and provisions and it is envisaged that further property will in the future be added to this Settlement.

(2) This Settlement shall be irrevocable and shall be known as the [*Name*] Discretionary Settlement.

NOW THIS DEED WITNESSES as follows:

1. DEFINITIONS AND INTERPRETATION

In this Settlement the following expressions have where the context permits the following meanings:

1.1. "**the Trustees**" means the Original Trustees or other the trustees or trustee for the time being of this Settlement and 'Trustee' means each and any of the Trustees;

1.2. "**the Trust Fund**" means the sum of £10 cash all assets at any time added to it by way of further settlement accumulation of income capital accretion or otherwise and all property from time to time representing the same;

1.3. "**the Beneficiaries**" means (subject to the provisions of clause 7)[35] the following persons:

    a. [*Name*];
    b. [*Name*];
    c. [*Name*];
    d. the issue whether children or more remote of the persons described in (b) and (c) above;

---

[34] See Ch.48. The purpose of the trust is to ensure that the pension death benefits are held on discretionary trusts and do not form part of the estate of the surviving spouse (who can, however, benefit as one of the beneficiaries). Hence, these trusts are commonly referred to as "spousal by-pass" trusts.

[35] Normally this will comprise the settlor's surviving spouse/civil partner and issue. Note the power to add/remove beneficiaries in cl.7 which provides attractive flexibility.

e. anyone who is or has been the spouse of the persons described in (b), (c) and (d) above;

and "**Beneficiary**" has a corresponding meaning;

1.4. "**the Trust Period**" means [ ][36];

1.5. "**the Accumulation Period**"[37];

1.6. "**Charitable**" means charitable (and exclusively charitable) according to the law for the time being of England and Wales;

1.7. "**Charity**" means a trust or corporation association society or other institution established only for Charitable purposes and 'Charities' has a corresponding meaning;

1.8. "**Spouse**" shall include a civil partner registered under the Civil Partnership Act 2004 and "**husband**" "**wife**" "**widow**" and "**widower**" shall be construed accordingly;

1.9. "**this Settlement**" shall mean this Declaration of Trust.

2. PRINCIPAL TRUSTS

2.1. The Trustees shall stand possessed of the Trust Fund and the income from it on such trusts and with and subject to such charges powers and provisions whatever in favour or for the benefit of all or any one or more exclusively of the others or other of the Beneficiaries as the Trustees (being at least 2 in number or a trust corporation) in their absolute discretion shall at any time or times during the Trust Period by any deed or deeds revocable or irrevocable appoint (regard being had to the law relating to remoteness).

2.2. Subject as stated above and subject also as is provided in clause 2.3 below any trust appointed under the power contained in clause 2.1 above may be mandatory or discretionary and may create any interest or interests whatever whether absolute or limited and whether vested or contingent and whether in possession or reversion and may divide the property subject to it or the income from it into any shares and may provide for the accumulation of the whole or any part of the income subject to it and any discretionary trust or power may by such appointment be conferred on any person or persons (not necessarily being or including the Trustees) and any such trusts or powers so conferred may authorise the delegation to an unlimited extent of any discretion.

2.3. PROVIDED always that:

a. no exercise of the power of appointment conferred by clause 2.1 above shall affect any capital or income of the Trust Fund (or any share or part of it) previously paid transferred or applied (except merely by accumulation) to or for the benefit of any person under the other provisions of this settlement or any income (except accumulated income) of the Trust Fund (or any share or part of it) accruing prior to such appointment;

---

[36] For the perpetuity difficulties that may arise when the pilot trust is intended to receive benefits from a pre-April 6, 2010 pension scheme see Ch.48. Bear in mind that the perpetuity period of the by-pass trust must be 125 years but the Trust Period can be selected to fit in with the pension trust perpetuity period.

[37] Similar difficulties to those concerning perpetuities arise with restrictions on the accumulation of income: see Ch.1.

b. the Trustees (being at least 2 in number or a trust corporation) may at any time or times before the expiration of the Trust Period by deed or deeds extinguish (or restrict the future exercise of) the power conferred by clause 2.1 above.

3. TRUSTS OF INCOME

3.1. In default of and until and subject to any and every appointment made under the power or powers conferred by clause 2.1 above the income of the Trust Fund shall during the Trust Period be held by the Trustees upon trust to pay or apply or (in the case of a minor) allocate the same to or for the maintenance support or otherwise for the benefit in any manner of all or any one or more exclusively of the others or other of the Beneficiaries for the time being in existence and if more than one in such shares and in such manner in all respects as the Trustees shall in their absolute discretion think fit.

3.2. PROVIDED always that [during the Accumulation Period][38] the Trustees shall not be bound to apply or allocate the whole or any part of the income accruing to the Trust Fund but may pay apply or allocate only so much of the income as the Trustees shall in their absolute discretion think fit and shall accumulate the surplus (if any) of such income in any of the investments authorised by this settlement and shall hold such accumulations as an accretion to (and as one fund with) the capital of the Trust Fund.

4. POWER TO RAISE CAPITAL

4.1. Notwithstanding the trusts powers and provisions of this settlement (but subject to the proviso contained in clause 4.2 below) the Trustees (being not less than 2 in number or a trust corporation) shall have power exercisable in their absolute discretion at any time or times during the Trust Period:

a. to apply the whole or any part or parts of the capital of the Trust Fund for any purpose whatever which the Trustees may think to be for the benefit of any one or more of the Beneficiaries for the time being in existence or to transfer or pay the whole or any part or parts of the capital of the Trust Fund to any one or more of the Beneficiaries for the time being in existence (being of full age) for his her or their absolute use and benefit freed and discharged from the trusts of this settlement;

b. to transfer the Trust Fund or any part of it to the trustees of any other trust or settlement wherever established or existing under which any one or more of the Beneficiaries is or are beneficially interested (whether or not such one or more of the Beneficiaries is or are the only person or persons interested or capable of benefitting under such trust or settlement).

4.2. PROVIDED always that the Trustees (not being less than 2 in number or a trust corporation) may at any time or times during the Trust Period by deed or deeds extinguish (or restrict the future exercise of) the power (but not any of the restrictions applicable thereto) conferred by clause 4.1 above.

5. TRUST ON EXPIRY OF THE TRUST PERIOD

In default of and subject to any and every appointment made under the power or powers conferred by clause 2.1 above and to the exercise of the power to raise capital in clause 4 above the Trust Fund and the future income from it shall from and after the end of the Trust Period be held upon trust absolutely for such of the Beneficiaries as are living at the end of the Trust Period and if more than one in equal shares.

[38] See fn.36.

6. ULTIMATE TRUST

Subject to all the trusts powers and provisions of this settlement and if and so far as (for any reason whatever) not wholly disposed of by it the Trust Fund and the income from it shall be held upon trust for [*Name*] and [*Name*] in equal shares absolutely.

7. ALTERATION OF CLASS OF BENEFICIARIES

7.1. Subject to clause 7.2 below:

    a. the Trustees (being at least 2 in number or a trust corporation) shall have power by any deed or deeds revocable or irrevocable executed during the Trust Period to declare that any individual or individuals whether or not then born or ascertained or any Charity or Charities (other than any individual then a Trustee and other than any individual or Charity previously excluded under the power set out in clause 7.1(b) below) shall from such time and (subject to any future exercise of the power contained in clause 7.1(b) below) either permanently or for such period or periods as shall be specified in any such deed or deeds be included in the class of the Beneficiaries defined in clause 1.3 above;

    b. the Trustees (being not less than 2 in number or a trust corporation) shall also have power by any deed or deeds revocable or irrevocable executed during the Trust Period to declare that any individual or individuals whether or not born or ascertained or any Charity or Charities who or which is or are a member or members (or eligible to be added as a member or members) of the class of the Beneficiaries immediately prior to the execution of such deed or deeds shall from such time and either permanently or for such period or periods as shall be specified in any such deed or deeds cease to be a member or members (or eligible to become a member or members) of such class.

7.2. PROVIDED always that:

    a. no such deed made in exercise of the power conferred by clause 7.1 above shall affect the validity or effect of:

        i. any distribution previously made to or for the benefit of any beneficiary under or pursuant to any power or discretion;

        ii. any transmissible interest (whether vested or contingent) previously conferred on any beneficiary either by clauses 5 and 6 above or under or pursuant to any irrevocable exercise of the power of appointment conferred by clause 2 above or application of capital by clause 4 above; or

        iii. any future distribution to any beneficiary consequent on the absolute vesting in possession of any such interest as is mentioned in clause 7.2(a)(i) above;

    b. the Trustees (being not less than 2 in number or a trust corporation) may at any time or times during the Trust Period by deed or deeds extinguish (or restrict the future exercise of) the power (but not any of the restrictions applicable to the same) conferred by clause 7.1 above.

8. EXCLUSION OF APPORTIONMENT

Where under the trusts for the time being affecting the same there is a change in the person or persons beneficially or prospectively beneficially entitled to the income of any part of the Trust Fund (whether due to the birth or death of any person or for any other reason whatever) the provisions of the Apportionment Act 1870 shall not apply and no apportionment shall be made of income accruing or accrued or of outgoings being expended on the occasion of such change in beneficial entitlement but rather the same shall be treated as having accrued due or become a proper liability on the day of actual receipt or expenditure (as the case may be).

9. ADMINISTRATIVE PROVISIONS

9.1. Subject to clauses 9.2 and 9.3 below the Trustees shall during the Trust Period and during such further period (if any) as the law may allow have the additional powers set out in the Schedule.

9.2. PROVIDED always that the Trustees (being not less than 2 in number or a trust corporation) may at any time or times during the Trust Period by deed or deeds extinguish (or restrict the future exercise of) all or any of the powers (but not any of the restrictions applicable to them) conferred by clause 9.1 above

9.3. If in the administration of the Trust Fund any transaction is in the opinion of the Trustees expedient but the same cannot be effected by reason of the absence of any sufficient power for that purpose conferred by this deed or by law (or by any earlier exercise of the present power) then the Trustees may by deed confer upon themselves either generally or for the purpose of any particular transaction or transactions the necessary power and from the execution of such a deed the Trustees shall have such power as if it had been conferred by this deed.

10. TRUSTEES' CHARGES AND REMUNERATION

10.1. Any of the Trustees who shall be an individual engaged in any profession or business either alone or in partnership shall be entitled to charge and be paid and to retain all professional or other proper charges for any business done or time spent or services rendered by him or his firm in connection with the trusts powers and provisions of this settlement and shall also be entitled to retain any share of brokerage or commission paid to him or his firm by any broker agent or insurance office in connection with any acquisition of or dealing with any investments or property or the effecting or payment of any premium on any policy of insurance subject or intended to become subject to the trusts of this settlement or any such assurance.

10.2. None of the Trustees holding any directorship or other office or employment or retainer in relation to any company all or any of whose shares stock or securities shall at any time be subject to any trusts of this settlement shall be accountable for any remuneration received in connection with such directorship office employment or retainer.

11. CORPORATE TRUSTEES

11.1. A corporation (whether or not a trust corporation) may at any time be appointed to be one of the Trustees on such reasonable terms as to remuneration and charging and otherwise however as shall be agreed at the time when the appointment is made between the person or persons making the appointment on the one hand and the corporation on the other.

11.2. The provisions of the Trustee Act 1925 Section 37 in their application to this settlement shall be varied so that for each reference to "a trust corporation" there shall be substituted a reference to "a corporation (whether or not a trust corporation)".

12. Exclusion of the Self-Dealing Rule

Any of the Trustees may exercise or concur in exercising any powers and discretions given by this settlement or by law notwithstanding that he has a direct or other personal interest in the mode or result of any such exercise but any such Trustee may abstain from acting except as a merely formal party in any matter in which he may be so personally interested and may allow his co-trustees or co-trustee to act alone in relation thereto.

13. Appointment of New Trustees

13.1. The power of appointing a new Trustee or new Trustees shall (subject to clause 13.3 below) be vested in [*Name*] during his life.

13.2. Any individual or corporation may be appointed as a Trustee notwithstanding that such individual or corporation is resident domiciled or incorporated outside the United Kingdom and notwithstanding that as a result of such appointment (or any retirement occurring in connection with it) all or a majority of the Trustees are persons resident domiciled or incorporated outside the United Kingdom.

13.3. It is declared (for the avoidance of any doubt) that the said [*Name*] may at any time or times by deed release (or restrict the future exercise of) the power conferred on him by clause 13.1 above and it is further declared that the provisions of the Trustee Act 1925 Section 36 in their application to this settlement shall be varied so that it shall not be a ground for the appointment of a new Trustee that an existing Trustee has remained out of the United Kingdom for more than 12 months.

14. [Protection of Trustees

14.1. In the professed execution of the trusts and powers of this settlement none of the Trustees (being an individual) shall be liable for any loss arising by reason of any improper investment made in good faith or the retention of any improper investment or any failure to see to the insurance of or preservation of any chattels or the making or revising of any inventory of them or for the negligence or fraud of any agent employed by him or by any other of the Trustees (although the employment of such agent was not strictly necessary or expedient) or by reason of any other matter or thing whatever except wilful and individual fraud or wrongdoing on the part of that one of the Trustees who is sought to be made liable.

14.2. The Trustees shall not be bound or required to interfere in the management or conduct of the affairs or business of any company in respect of which the Trustees shall hold or control the whole or a majority or any part of the shares carrying the control of the company or other the voting rights of the company and so long as there shall be no notice of any act of dishonesty or misappropriation of money on the part of the directors having the management of such company the Trustees shall be at liberty to leave the conduct of its business (including the payment or non-payment of dividends) wholly to such directors.][39]

15. Clause Headings

The headings to the clauses and paragraphs of this settlement are for the purposes of information only and are not part of and shall not be used in the construction of this settlement or any part of it

IN WITNESS etc

---

[39] The Settlor must approve this clause, i.e. it should be drawn to his attention. The same is true of the remuneration provisions in cll.10 and 11.

SCHEDULE

Administrative Powers

1. APPLICATION OF MONEY REQUIRING INVESTMENT

Power as regards any money for the time being subject to the provisions of this settlement and requiring investment to invest or lay out the same in the purchase or otherwise in the acquisition of or at interest upon the security of any shares stocks funds securities policies of insurance or other investments or property (movable or immovable) of whatever nature and wherever situated and whether or not productive of income and whether involving liability or not or upon such personal credit with or without security in all respects as the Trustees shall in their discretion think fit to the intent that the Trustees shall have the same full and unrestricted powers of investing and transposing investments and dealing with trust money and buying or selling property in all respects as if they were absolutely entitled beneficially and so that:

1.1. the acquisition with trust money of property with a view to its enjoyment in kind by a Beneficiary or Beneficiaries in accordance with the provisions of paragraph 22 below shall for the purpose of this settlement be deemed to be an investment of trust money;

1.2. nothing contained in this paragraph shall exclude limit or restrict the power to invest in a legal estate in any land in the United Kingdom conferred by the Trusts of Land and Appointment of Trustees Act 1996 Section 6(3) and the Trustee Act 2000 Section 8(1);

1.3. without prejudice to the generality of paragraph 1 the Trustees shall not be under any obligation to diversify the investments of the Trust Fund;

1.4. any immovable property situated anywhere in the world which may be acquired for any of the purposes of this settlement (including its enjoyment in kind) shall be conveyed to the Trustees either with or without any trust for sale as the Trustees think fit but nevertheless with power to sell the same.

2. RETENTION OF ASSETS

Power to accept or acquire and retain any assets subject or to be subject to the trusts declared by this settlement (including any uninvested money) in their actual state and condition for any period even although the whole or a substantial part of the assets so subject may be producing no or little income or may consist of shares or securities of a single company.

3. TRANSPOSITION OF INVESTMENTS

Power at any time or times to sell or convert or call in any investments or other property for the time being comprised in the Trust Fund or to transpose or convert the same into any other investments or property the acquisition of which with money subject to this settlement is by this settlement authorised.

4. IMPROVEMENTS TO LAND

Power at any time or times to apply any money subject to the trusts of this settlement in making improvements to or otherwise developing or using any land or buildings or in erecting enlarging repairing decorating making alterations to or improvements in or pulling down and rebuilding any buildings which shall be subject to the same trusts.

5. Leases and Mortgaging

Power to lease let license mortgage and charge and to grant tenancies and licences and to accept surrenders of leases tenancies and licences and to enter into and carry into effect any grants agreements or arrangements whatever of or relating to and generally to manage and deal with any land or buildings which shall for the time being be subject to any trusts of this settlement in all respects as if the Trustees were an absolute beneficial owner of such land or buildings and so that no mortgagee or chargee or intending mortgagee or chargee dealing with the Trustees in regard to any such land or buildings shall be concerned to see for what purpose any money is raised or as to the application of such money PROVIDED that nothing in this paragraph shall affect or restrict any power conferred on the Trustees in respect of land situated in England and Wales conferred by the Trusts of Land and Appointment of Trustees Act 1996 Section 6(1) and by the Trustee Act 2000 Section 8(3).

6. Hiring of Chattels

Power to hire out or lend or bail any movable chattels for any period or periods and for any consideration whatever.

7. Mortgaging of Chattels etc

In relation to any property other than land and buildings the like powers of mortgaging charging and entering into and carrying into effect any agreements or arrangements whatever as are given by paragraph 5 above in regard to land and buildings.

8. Borrowing

Power to borrow or raise money for the purposes of mere investment or for acquiring any property either without security or on the security of the whole or part of the Trust Fund and any property so acquired.

9. Guarantees

Without prejudice to the generality of paragraphs 5 and 7 of this schedule power to effect any mortgage or charge under those paragraphs as collateral security for or to guarantee money payable in respect of any loan to a Beneficiary or Beneficiaries upon such terms in all respects as the Trustees shall in their absolute discretion think fit PROVIDED that this power shall not be exercised except in conformity with the beneficial trusts for the time being governing the Trust Fund (or the part of it affected by such mortgage charge or guarantee) and the income from it.

10. Arbitration

Power to refer to arbitration or to the determination of any expert:

10.1 the amount of money to be received or paid on any sale or purchase or exchange;

10.2 the amount of rent or other payment to be reserved by any lease tenancy agreement or licence in respect of the whole or any part of the term or currency of such lease tenancy agreement or licence and the covenants and provisions to be contained in any such lease tenancy agreement or licence;

10.3 the terms for the surrender or other termination of any lease tenancy agreement or licence; and

10.4 all disputes between any tenant or licensee and the reversioner or licensor.

11. Appropriation

Power from time to time to set such a value upon any investments or other property forming part of the Trust Fund as the Trustees shall think fit and to appropriate if they shall think fit any such investments or property at such value in or towards satisfaction of any share or interest under the trusts affecting the same.

12. Valuation

Power at any time or times to have any assets valued for any purpose in such manner as the Trustees shall in their discretion think fit.

13. Promotion of companies

Power to promote or form or join in promoting or forming any company or corporation for the purpose of acquiring or taking on lease or hire for any estate or interest all or any of the assets which are held on the trusts of this settlement or for any other purpose whatever connected with any assets which (or the net proceeds of sale of which) are subject or are to become subject to any of those trusts.

14. Subscription for shares etc

Power to subscribe for all or any of the shares debentures or other securities of any such company or corporation as is mentioned in paragraph 13 above.

15. Sales etc for paper consideration

Power to sell transfer let or hire out for any estate or interest any assets which are subject to any of the trusts of this settlement in consideration of the issue or transfer to the Trustees or their nominees of any stock shares debentures or other securities.

16. Rights attached to investments

Power to exercise or refrain from exercising (either themselves or by proxy) the rights attached to any investments subject to any of the trusts of this settlement in any manner whatever and in particular (without prejudice to the generality of the above) to wind up or dissolve or join in winding up or dissolving any company or corporation and to alter or join in altering any of those rights or any rights attached to any other investments or property.

17. Power to carry on a business

Power from time to time to carry on whether by themselves or in partnership with any other individual or corporation (whether or not such individual shall be beneficially entitled under the trusts of this settlement) any trade or business which they consider to be for the benefit of the beneficiaries under this settlement and in connection with any such trade or business the Trustees may:

17.1 employ all or any part of the capital of the Trust Fund;

17.2 be indemnified out of the Trust Fund against any liability which they may incur in connection with the setting up carrying on or dissolution of such trade or business;

17.3 use for the purposes of the trade or business any land or buildings which are subject to the trusts of this settlement;

17.4 exercise in relation to any such trade or business and the assets thereof any of the administrative powers conferred on the Trustees by this deed or by law including (but without prejudice to the generality of the foregoing) powers of borrowing and charging and of delegation;

17.5 employ or join in employing on such terms as to remuneration and otherwise as they shall think fit any manager and other employees.

18. NOMINEES

18.1 Power to put or leave any shares stocks securities insurance policies or other property whatever (including money) in the name or names of any nominee or nominees for the Trustees and to put or leave any movable chattels for safe keeping in the possession or custody of any person or persons without being responsible for any loss or damage and on such terms and subject to such conditions including remuneration of any such nominee or custodian as the Trustees shall think fit and so that any such nominees or custodians may be or include any one or more of the Trustees.

18.2 The Trustee Act 2000 Sections 16 and 17 shall not apply to this deed.

18.3 The provisions of the Trustee Act 2000 Section 22 shall not apply to any nominee or custodian appointed by the Trustees pursuant to this power.

19. INSURANCE

19.1 Power to effect maintain and deal with any insurance or insurances upon the life of any person or of all or any assets subject to any trusts of this settlement against any risk or risks which the Trustees may consider proper to cover PROVIDED:

    a. that the Trustees shall be under no obligation to insure any such assets to their full value or at all;

    b. that the Trustees may pay all premiums and other costs relating to insurance out of the income or the capital of any property held upon the same trusts under this settlement as such assets.

19.2 All the powers of an absolute owner in respect of any policy or policies forming part of the Trust Fund including the power to surrender convert or otherwise deal with any such policy or policies or any bonuses attaching to them or part of them in such manner as the Trustees shall consider most beneficial to the persons beneficially interested under these trusts.

19.3 Power to apply any money subject to the trusts of this settlement in or towards payment of the premiums or other amounts (if any) necessary for keeping on foot or restoring any policy or policies forming part of the Trust Fund.

20. MAINTENANCE ETC OF CHATTELS

Power to maintain repair improve and alter any movable chattels and to take such steps as they may consider proper for the preservation of any movable chattels or other assets subject to any trusts of this settlement

21. DELEGATION

21.1 Power to delegate all or any of the powers of the Trustees contained in this schedule (including this power) and any administrative power conferred by law (and all or any of the duties and discretions of the Trustees relating to the exercise of such powers) to any person or persons subject to such conditions (if any) and upon such terms (including remuneration and so that in the case of a delegation to two or more persons such delegates may be authorised to act jointly and severally) as the Trustees shall think fit (without being liable for the acts or defaults of any such delegate) and to revoke or modify any such delegation or conditions.

21.2 The Trustee Act 2000 Section 11 shall not apply to this deed.

21.3 The provisions of the Trustee Act 2000 Section 22 shall not apply to any delegate or agent appointed by the Trustees pursuant to the foregoing power.

22. USE OF PROPERTY IN KIND

Power (subject as provided below) to permit a Beneficiary or Beneficiaries (either alone or concurrently or successively) to occupy use or enjoy personally any movable or immovable property which may for the time being be comprised in the Trust Fund upon any terms or conditions whatever which the Trustees may think fit PROVIDED that this power shall not be exercised except in conformity with the beneficial trusts powers and provisions for the time being governing the Trust Fund (or the part of it in which such movable or immovable property is so comprised) and the income from it.

23. LOANS TO BENEFICIARIES

Power (subject as provided below) to lend any money with or without security to a Beneficiary or Beneficiaries with or without payment of interest and upon such terms as to repayment and otherwise in such manner in all respects as the Trustees shall in their absolute discretion think fit PROVIDED that this power shall not be exercised except in conformity with the beneficial trusts powers and provisions for the time being governing the Trust Fund (or the part of it from which such loan is to be made) and the income from it.

24. TRANSACTIONS WITH OTHER TRUSTEES

Power from time to time in their absolute discretion to enter into any agreement or transaction with the trustee or trustees of any other settlement or will (being an agreement or transaction which apart from this present provision the Trustees could properly have entered into if one or more of them had not also been a trustee of such other settlement or will) notwithstanding that the Trustees or one or more of them may also be trustees or a trustee or the sole trustee of such other settlement or will and in like manner in all respects as if none of the Trustees were a trustee of such other settlement or will.

25. POWER TO SIGN CHEQUES

Power to permit any one or more of the Trustees to sign cheques on any bank account in the names of the Trustees and generally to sign orders and authorities to any bank on behalf of the Trustees.

26. ADDITIONS

Power (if the Trustees think fit) to accept any assets which may be transferred or otherwise given to the Trustees as an addition to the capital of the Trust Fund on terms that any inheritance tax that is payable in consequence of such transfer or gift shall be payable out of and borne by the Trust Fund and not by the transferor or donor personally and also power (if the Trustees think fit) to pay any inheritance tax that may from time to time be levied on the Trust Fund or any part of it notwithstanding that some other person or persons may also be liable to pay such tax.

27. RECEIPTS

27.1 Where the Trustees are authorised or required to pay or apply any capital money or income to or for the benefit of any person who does not have the capacity to give a valid receipt for it the Trustees may pay the same to any parent or guardian of such person for the benefit of such person without seeing to the application of it or themselves apply the same for the benefit of such person as may be directed in writing by such parent or guardian and the receipt of such parent or guardian shall be a sufficient discharge to the Trustees.

27.2 The receipt of the person professing to be the treasurer or other proper officer of any charity to which any capital or income may be payable or transferable under this settlement shall be a sufficient discharge to the Trustees.

PART II: WILL TRUSTS AND VARIATIONS

BEREAVED MINOR TRUST

A1.6

(i)   *a single child:*

"I leave the sum of [*e.g. IHT nil rate band*] to my daughter Daisy absolutely contingently on her attaining the age of 18 and subject thereto to my sister Phoebe absolutely".[40]

(ii)   *more than one child:*

"I leave the sum of [*amount*] to such of my children as survive[41] me and attain the age of 18 and if more than one in equal shares absolutely

(iii)   *Flexibility – incorporate a power of selection:*

"I leave the sum of [*amount*] to such of my children as survive me and attain the age of 18 in such shares as my trustees shall appoint and in default equally provided always that the Trustees' power of appointment shall not be exercised to increase or diminish the share of a child who has attained 18 [nor to benefit a child who has been excluded from all benefit as a result of the exercise of the power of appointment]".[42]

(iv)   *Consider adding a widened power of advancement:*

"Section 32 of the Trustee Act 1925 shall apply but with the deletion of the words "one half of" in Section 32(1)(a)."[43]

---

[40] If desired Daisy could be given an immediate right to income (TA 1925 s.31 would need to be excluded): see A1.2 cl.6. The clause would still create a BMT (not an IPDI) and the CGT death uplift would be available in the event of Daisy dying before the age of 18. See Ch.35 for priority issues.

[41] This excludes the substitution provided for in Wills Act 1837 s.33: see *Re Horton* (1979) 88 DLR (3d)264 (Brit. Columbia). Consider, however, whether substitution is desirable.

[42] HMRC accept that limited flexibility is possible in these trusts. Although the wording in the legislation refers to a single bereaved minor beneficiary this must be construed to cover the plural hence a power for trustees to pick and choose between beneficiaries will presumably be acceptable provided that it cannot be exercised in favour of a beneficiary who has already attained 18 or to take away a share from a beneficiary who has attained 18. It is not thought that the words in square brackets are necessary (although HMRC do not agree: see A2.370) and that such a child can be included again provided that he is under the age of 18.

[43] The inclusion of a widened power of advancement does not prevent the trusts from satisfying s.71A. It may be useful if the trustees wish to make a settled advance to prevent vesting at 18: see A2.370.

(i)   *Basic form*

"I leave the residue of my estate to such of my children as shall survive me and attain the age of 25 and if more than one in equal shares absolutely".[44]

(ii)   *Avoiding the risk of an IPDI arising by excluding or modifying the Trustee Act 1925 s.31.*[45]

"The Trustee Act 1925 s.31 (as amended) shall apply to the presumptive shares for the time being in my (residuary estate or as the case may be) under the trusts declared above and the income of the same subject to the following modifications:

(a)   with the substitution in subsection (1)(i) of the words 'the trustees in their absolute discretion think fit' for the words 'may in all the circumstances be reasonable' and the omission of the proviso to subsection (1)

(b)   so that in its application to the presumptive shares in my (residuary estate) of any of my children under the trusts declared in clause xx above in relation to whom the Specified Age (as defined below) exceeds the age of eighteen years s.31 (as modified by clause (a) above) shall have effect as if the age of majority were the Specified Age (the expressions 'infant' 'infancy' and 'minority' therein being construed accordingly) and as if there were substituted the Specified Age for the words 'eighteen years' wherever the same occur in s.31 (as modified)

(c)   the expression 'the Specified Age' in relation to any of my children shall mean whichever is the less of:

(i)   the age which he or she will attain (if he or she so long lives) on his or her last birthday occurring not later than the expiration of the accumulation period or

(ii) the age of twenty-five years.

---

[44] If the trustees subsequently exercise a widened power of advancement to give a minor child an immediate right to income this will not prevent s.71D from continuing to apply although care should be taken not to give a child an interest in possession within two years of death because of "reading back" under s.144 which will create an IPDI. If a minor child dies under the age of 18 there is no IHT charge and, if he had enjoyed an interest in possession, a CGT uplift. Assume that a child dies under the age of 25 and that his share accrues to his siblings; the IHT position is that if the siblings are under the age of 25 so that their shares are held on 18–25 trusts there is no IHT charge. In other cases if the deceased child is over 18 the normal s.71D exit charge will apply to his share

[45] For the "pecking order" see 35.13 and 35.28.

"1.1 The Trustees shall stand possessed of the Trust Fund and the income from it upon trust for such of my children as shall attain the age of 25 years and if more than one in such shares as the Trustees (being at least two in number or a trust corporation) shall by any deed or deeds revocable or irrevocable executed so as to comply with clause 1.3 below appoint and until and subject to and in default of any such appointment in equal shares

1.2 Subject to clause 1.3 below any appointment made in exercise of the power conferred by clause 1.1 above

    1.2.1 may provide for any share or shares in the Trust Fund to be ascertained either by reference to a fraction or fractions of the Trust Fund or by reference to any sum or sums of money or by reference to (or to the value of) any specific assets then forming part of the Trust Fund; and

    1.2.2 may (if the Trustees think fit) expressly provide that the whole or any part or parts of the accumulations of income then forming part of the general capital of the Trust Fund or any part of it or then only forming part of the presumptive share of any such child in the Trust Fund shall therefore go and accrue to and form part of only the presumptive share or shares of any of my children in the Trust Fund or form part of the general capital of the Trust Fund or any part of it but in default of any such express provision all such accumulations of income shall continue to belong to and form part of the general capital to which they belong or (as the case may be) to the presumptive share to which they solely belonged immediately prior to such appointment

1.3 No appointment in exercise of the power conferred by clause 1.1 above shall be made and no such appointment shall be revoked so as either to diminish or to increase the share (or the accumulations of income forming part of the share) of or give a new share (or new accumulations of income) to a child who at the date of such appointment or revocation has attained the age of 25 [nor to benefit a child who has been excluded from benefit as a result of the exercise of the power].

1.4 The Trustees (being at least 2 in number or a trust corporation) may at any time or times by deed or deeds extinguish (or restrict the future exercise of) the power of appointment conferred by clause 1.1 above."

Notes:

1. It is recommended that a widened power of advancement be included which could be used (a) to accelerate vesting so that a child could become absolutely entitled at 18 and thereby avoid an IHT charge[46] or (b) to postpone vesting beyond 25 (a "settled advance").[47]

2. If the will gives the children immediate interests in possession the trust will be an IPDI and not fall within the s.71D regime.[48]

3. If the trustees subsequently exercise a widened power of advancement to give a minor child an immediate right to income this will not prevent s.71D from continuing to apply.[49]

---

[46] See IHTA 1984 s.71E(2)(a).
[47] See 35.36.
[48] See IHTA 1984 s.49A.
[49] So long as the power is not exercised within two years of death otherwise an IPDI will be read back under IHTA 1984 s.144(3)–(5).

4. If a minor child dies under the age of 18 there is no IHT charge and, if he had enjoyed an interest in possession at the date of death, a CGT uplift.[50]

5. Assume that a child dies under the age of 25 and that his share accrues to his siblings; the IHT position is that if the siblings are under the age of 25 so that their shares are held on 18–25 trusts there is no IHT charge. When the siblings are over 25, if the deceased child is over 18 the normal s.71D exit charge will apply to his share.[51]

---

[50] See Ch.35.
[51] See IHTA 1984 s.71F(2)(b).

WILL CLAUSES CREATING A NRBDT AND AN IPDI TRUST OF RESIDUE[52] A1.8

Definitions

6.(1) In clause 7 of this Will where the context so permits the following expressions shall have the following meanings:

(i) "*the Discretionary Beneficiaries*" shall mean subject to the provisions of clause 6(2) below:

      (a) my said [husband/wife]
      (b) my children and remoter issue
      (c) the spouses widows and widowers of the persons mentioned in (b)

and "discretionary beneficiary" shall have a corresponding meaning.

(ii) "*the Trust Period*" shall mean the period commencing with the date of my death and ending one hundred and twenty five years thereafter and such period of one hundred and twenty five years shall be the perpetuity period applicable to the dispositions made by my Will PROVIDED THAT my Legacy Fund Trustees may declare by irrevocable deed that the Trust Period (but not the said perpetuity period) shall terminate on such date as they may specify therein (such date of termination to be earlier than the end of the said period of one hundred and twenty five years but the same as or later than the date of such deed)

(iii) "*the Legacy Fund Trustees*" shall mean [*insert details of trustees*] or other the trustee or trustees for the time being of the Legacy Fund.[53]

(2)(i) SUBJECT to sub-clause (b) below:

      (a) My Legacy Fund Trustees (being not less than two in number or a trust corporation) shall have power by any deed or deeds revocable (during the Trust Period) or irrevocable executed during the Trust Period to declare that any individual or individuals whether or not then born or ascertained or any Charity or Charities (other than any individual then a trustee of the Legacy Fund and other than any individual or Charity previously excluded under the power set out in (b) below) shall from such time and

---

[52] This Precedent creates a nil rate band discretionary trust combined with a spouse exempt IPDI trust of residue. The clause numbers (6–10) are wholly arbitrary!

[53] In drafting the Will it is helpful to designate. "Legacy Fund Trustees" even if they are the same persons as the trustees of the Will.

(subject to any future exercise of the power set out in clause 62(i)(b) below) either permanently or for such period or periods as shall be specified in any such deed or deeds be included in the class of Discretionary Beneficiaries defined in Clause 6(1)(i) above and

(b) The Legacy Fund Trustees (being not less than two in number or a trust corporation) shall also have power by any deed or deeds revocable (during the Trust Period) or irrevocable executed during the Trust Period to declare that any individual or individuals whether or not born or ascertained or any Charity or Charities who or which is or are a member or members (or eligible to be added as a member or members) of the class of Discretionary Beneficiaries immediately prior to the execution of such deed or deeds shall from such time and either permanently or for such period or periods as shall be specified in any such deed or deeds cease to be a member or members (or eligible to become a member or members) of such class.

(ii) PROVIDED always that no such deed made in exercise of either of the powers conferred by sub-clause (i) shall affect the validity or effect of:

(a) any distribution previously made to or for the benefit of any beneficiary under or pursuant to any power or discretion

(b) any transmissible interest (whether vested or contingent) previously conferred on any beneficiary

(c) any future distribution to any beneficiary consequent on the absolute vesting in possession of any such interest as is mentioned in sub-clause (ii)(b) and

(d) the Legacy Fund Trustees (being not less than two in number or a trust corporation) may at any time or times during the Trust Period by deed or deeds extinguish (or restrict the future exercise of) both or either of the powers (but not any of the restrictions applicable to them) conferred by sub-clause (i) above.

Legacy Fund—Nil rate band discretionary trust (with loan/charge provisions)

7. (1) THIS clause shall not take effect unless the gift made to my [*husband/wife*] by Clause [*number*] of my Will takes effect (or but for this Clause would do so).

(2) IN this Clause "*the Nil-Rate Sum*" means the largest sum of cash which could be given on the trusts of this Clause without any inheritance tax becoming due in respect of the transfer of the value of my estate which I am deemed to make immediately before my death.[54]

(3) I GIVE the Nil-Rate Sum to my Legacy Fund Trustees on trust to invest it in exercise of the powers of investment given them by my Will and by law and to hold it and the property which currently represents it ("*the Legacy Fund*") on the trusts and with and subject to the powers and provisions set out in this clause.

(4) DURING the Trust Period my Legacy Fund Trustees (being at least two in number or a trust corporation) may at any time or times:

(i) by deed or deeds revocable (during the Trust Period) or irrevocable appoint that all or any part or parts of the income or capital of the

---

[54] In the event that an additional nil rate band is available (because the testator had been married before and his spouse had predeceased without making use of the IHT nil rate band), the wording of "the nil rate sum" will catch both the deceased's and the transferred nil rate band. Amend if this is not desired.

Legacy Fund shall be held on such trusts (including discretionary and protective ones) in favour or for the benefit of all or any one or more of the Discretionary Beneficiaries and with and subject to such powers (including dispositive and administrative ones exercisable by my Legacy Fund Trustees or any other person) and other provisions as my Legacy Fund Trustees think fit;

(ii) transfer all or any part or parts of the income or capital of the Legacy Fund to the trustees of any Settlement wherever established (whose receipt shall be good discharge to them) to be held free from the trusts of my Will and on the trusts and with and subject to the powers and provisions of that Settlement but only if those trusts powers and provisions are such that (at the time of the transfer) they could themselves have created them under (i) above; and

(iii) pay transfer or apply any part of the Legacy Fund to or for the advancement or benefit of any Discretionary Beneficiary.

(5) IN default of and subject to any exercise of the powers given them by the preceding provisions:

(i) during the Trust Period my Legacy Fund Trustees shall pay or apply the income of the Legacy Fund to or for the maintenance education support or otherwise for the benefit of such one or more of the Discretionary Beneficiaries as my Legacy Fund Trustees may in their absolute discretion think fit but with power to accumulate such income or any part or parts of it (with power to apply the accumulations of past years as if they were income of the current year) and with power (during the Trust Period) to resolve to hold the whole or any part or parts of such income as income on trust for any of the Beneficiaries absolutely and

(ii) on the expiry of the Trust Period my Legacy Fund Trustees shall hold the Legacy Fund as to both capital and income on trust absolutely for such of my issue as are then living and if more than one in equal shares through all degrees according to their stocks and so that no issue shall take whose parent is alive and so capable of taking.

(6) MY Legacy Fund Trustees (being at least two in number) may by deed or deeds (and so as to bind their successors) wholly or partially release or restrict the powers given them by this clause.

(7) ANY other non-residuary gifts made by my Will or any Codicil to it shall have priority to this one.

(8) INSTEAD of satisfying the legacy wholly by the payment of cash (or by the appropriation of property) to the Legacy Fund Trustees my Trustees may:

(i) require the Legacy Fund Trustees to accept in place of all or any part of the Nil-Rate Sum a binding promise of payment made by my Trustees as trustees of any residuary property given by this Will or any Codicil hereto on trusts under which my [*husband/wife*] has an interest in possession for the purposes of Inheritance Tax which debt shall be repayable on demand[55]

(ii) charge all or any part of the Nil Rate Sum on any property which is (or but for this clause would be) given by this Will or any Codicil to it on trusts under which my [*husband/wife*] has an interest in possession for the purposes of Inheritance Tax.[56]

---

[55] This enables a simple debt trust to be created: see 38.24.
[56] This envisages the creation of a charge over the deceased's property: see further A1.9.

(9) THE Legacy Fund Trustees may lend money currently held by them to my spouse.

(10) IN amplification of the foregoing provisions

(i) if my Trustees exercise their powers under (8)(i) above they shall be under no further liability to see that the Legacy Fund Trustees receive the sum promised and if they exercise their powers under (8)(ii) they shall be under no further liability to see that the Legacy Fund Trustees receive the sum secured

(ii) if my Trustees exercise their powers under (8)(ii) above they may give an assent of the property subject to the charge and no one in whose favour the assent is made shall become personally liable for the sum secured

(iii) the Legacy Fund Trustees may require security to be given for any debt to be created by a promise within (8)(i) above or by a loan within (9) and in relation both to such debts (whether or not secured) and to any debt to be secured by a charge within (8)(ii) (all of which shall be debts payable on demand) they

(1) may (subject to the foregoing provisions) impose such terms (if any) as they think fit including terms as to interest and the personal liability of the borrower and terms linking the debt to the Index of Retail Prices or otherwise providing for its amount to vary with the passage of time according to a formula and

(2) may subsequently leave the debt outstanding for as long as they think fit and refrain from exercising their rights in relation to it and waive the payment of all or any part of it or of any interest due in respect of it

and they shall not be liable if my Trustees are or become unable to pay the debt or a security is or becomes inadequate or for any other loss which may occur through their exercising or choosing not to exercise any power given by this sub-clause

(iv) the powers given by this clause are without prejudice to any other powers given by this Will or any Codicil to it or by the general law and are exercisable even though my Trustees and the Legacy Fund Trustees may be the same persons and my spouse may be among them (but they are not exercisable while my spouse is the sole Legacy Fund Trustee) and any of the Legacy Fund Trustees may exercise or concur in existing all powers and discretions given to him by this clause or by law notwithstanding that he has a direct or other personal interest in the mode or result of any such exercise.

IPDI Trust of Residue

8. I GIVE DEVISE AND BEQUEATH all my property both movable and immovable of whatever nature and wheresoever situated except property otherwise disposed of by this Will or by any Codicil hereto unto my Trustees UPON TRUST to sell call in and convert the same into money (so far as not already consisting of money) with power to postpone the sale calling in and conversion thereof (even as regards property of a terminable hazardous or wasting nature) in the absolute and uncontrolled discretion of my Trustees without being liable for loss and to hold the net proceeds and my ready money upon the following trusts:

(1) UPON TRUST to pay thereout (in exoneration of any property which would otherwise be liable for payment of the same) all my funeral and

testamentary expenses and debts and any general legacies given by this Will or any Codicil hereto and any tax or duty arising in respect of my death (even if not a testamentary expense) on all gifts in this Will and any Codicil hereto given free of such tax or duty

(2) UPON TRUST if necessary to invest the remainder after such payment in or upon any investments hereinafter authorised for the investment of trust funds with power to vary and transpose the same

(3) UPON TRUST to stand possessed of such investments and such of my estate as remains for the time being unsold and my ready money and all property from time to time respectively representing the same (hereinafter together called "my Residuary Trust Fund") and the income thereof upon the following trusts.

[Alternative A]

9. *Trusts for the surviving spouse and children*[57]

9.1 THE income of my Residuary Trust Fund shall be paid to my [*Husband/ Wife*] during [*his/her*] lifetime.

9.2 THE Trustees may, at any time during the Trust Period, pay or apply the whole or any part of the Trust Fund in which my [*Husband/Wife*] is then entitled to an interest in possession to [*him/her*] or for [*his/her*] advancement or otherwise for [*his/her*] benefit in such manner as the Trustees shall in their discretion think fit. In exercising the powers conferred by this sub-clause, the Trustees shall be entitled to have regard solely to the interests of my [*Husband/Wife*] and to disregard all other interests or potential interests under my Will.[58]

9.3 Subject thereto the Trustees shall hold the capital and income of my Residuary Trust Fund for such of my children as shall survive me and attain the age of 18 years before the end of the Trust Period, or shall be living and under that age at the end of the Trust Period, and, if more than one, in equal shares absolutely.

[9.4 Consider inserting general power of appointment - see A1.17.]

[Or Alternative B - giving overriding powers to end spouse's interest in possession while spouse is alive]

9. *Trusts for surviving spouse*[59]*and children*

The provisions of this clause shall apply in default of until and subject to any exercise of the powers conferred by clause 10.

9.1 THE income of my Residuary Trust Fund shall be paid to my [*Husband/ Wife*] during [*his/her*] lifetime.

9.2 THE Trustees may, at any time during the Trust Period, pay or apply the whole or any part of the Trust Fund in which my [*Husband/Wife*] is then entitled to an interest in possession to [*him/her*] or for [*his/her*] advancement or otherwise for [*his/her*] benefit in such manner as the Trustees shall in their discretion think fit. In exercising the powers conferred by this sub-

[57] This creates an IPDI trust for the spouse. Amend if residue is given outright to the spouse. Note also, that the wording of cl.7(8) will require amendment if any debt created under cl.7(8)(ii) will be owed by the spouse: see A1.9.

[58] This clause provides an element of flexibility: consider, however, the additional advantages that might arise from giving the trustees a wide over-riding power of appointment: see Alternative B.

[59] The remainder trusts apply (a) on the death of the surviving spouse and (b) in the event that she predeceases the testator. Note that in the latter eventuality the nil rate band trust does not take effect (see cl.7(1)).

clause, the Trustees shall be entitled to have regard solely to the interests of my [*Husband/Wife*] and to disregard all other interests or potential interests under my Will.

9.3 Subject thereto the Trustees shall hold the capital and income of my Residuary Trust Fund for such of my children as shall survive me and attain the age of 18 years before the end of the Trust Period, or shall be living and under that age at the end of the Trust Period, and, if more than one, in equal shares absolutely.

[9.4 Consider inserting general power of appointment - see A1.17.]

Overriding powers

10. MY Trustees shall have the following powers exercisable during the Trust Period [and while my spouse is alive][60]:

10.1 My Trustees shall hold the capital and income of my Residuary Trust Fund in or for the benefit of all or such one or more of the Discretionary Beneficiaries (as defined in clause [6]) at such ages or times exclusive of the other or others of them in such shares or proportions if more than one and with and subject to such powers trusts and provisions for their respective maintenance education or other benefit or for the accumulation of income (including administrative powers and provisions and discretionary or protective trusts and powers to be executed or exercised by any person or persons whether or not being or including my Trustees or any of them and including powers or trusts to accumulate the whole or any part of the income of my Residuary Trust Fund during the Trust Period) and in such manner generally as my Trustees (subject to the application (if any) of the rule against perpetuities) by any deed or deeds revocable during the Trust Period or irrevocable and executed during the Trust Period shall appoint **PROVIDED ALWAYS** that such power may only be exercised by the Trustees during the lifetime of my spouse and provided further that no exercise of this power shall deprive the spouse of any income to which s/he was entitled at the time when it arose or otherwise invalidate any prior payment or application of all or any part or parts of the capital or income of the Residuary Trust Fund made under any other power or powers conferred by my Will or by law.

10.2 For the purpose of giving effect to any such appointment the Trustees shall have power to revoke all or any of the trusts powers and provisions contained in clause 9 including any interest in possession under clause 9 with respect to my Residuary Trust Fund or part or parts thereof to which such appointment relates.

10.3 I declare that provided they are at least two in number or a corporate trustee my Trustees may exercise any or all of the powers contained in this clause whether or not some or all of my Trustees are beneficially interested (either presently or prospectively) in my Residuary Trust Fund and notwithstanding that at the date of such exercise there shall have been no grant of probate or administration in respect of the property over which the said powers shall be executed or that the administration of my estate shall not have been completed.

10.4 The Trustees' powers conferred upon them by the preceding paragraphs of this clause shall include power to transfer pay or apply any part of the capital and income of the Residuary Estate to the trustees for the time being of any settle-

---

[60] Delete words in square brackets if it is intended that the children should not take outright on the spouse's death. The children would then take only defeasible absolute interests at 18 that can be ended by exercise of the cl.10 powers.

ment wherever established (whose receipt shall be a good discharge to them) to be held free from the trusts of the Will and on the trusts and with and subject to the powers and provisions of that settlement but only if those trusts powers and provisions are such that at the time of the transfer they could themselves have created them under clause 10.1 above.

1. Draft Letter from the Executors to the Trustees of the Legacy Fund
(when a charge being imposed by the Executors)

This letter records the agreement that has been reached between us as to the way in which the Legacy Fund is to be constituted.

Under the Will of [*details*] Deceased he provided that the Legacy Fund should have a value equal to the unused amount of his nil rate band and gave the executors power to require the trustees of that fund to accept in place of cash or other property either a binding promise of payment by the surviving spouse or a charge over any property passing to that surviving spouse. At the same time the Trustees may, *inter alia*, impose terms as to the payment of interest or linking the sum outstanding to an appropriate index.

It has now been agreed that you as Trustees will be entitled to the nil rate sum (£[*amount*]) which will be charged over property which will pass to his surviving spouse.[61] In line with the provisions in the Will we as executors will have no further liability to ensure that you receive this amount and when the assets comprised in the residue are transferred to the surviving spouse [*he/she*] will likewise will have no personal responsibility to ensure that you receive the relevant property. Your only recourse therefore is against the charged property.

It is also confirmed that the sum outstanding is repayable on a written demand being made by yourselves either to the executors or, once the assets have been transferred to the surviving spouse to that spouse. *[You have further agreed that the debt shall not carry interest nor be linked to an index.]*

2. Equitable Charge

THIS CHARGE is made the [ ] day of [ ] 20[ ] by [*name*] of [*address*] ("the Executors") of the one part and [*name*] of [*address*] ("the Trustees") of the other part.

SUPPLEMENTAL to the Will ("the Will") of [*details*] Deceased ("the Testator") dated [*date*]

WHEREAS

(1) The Testator died on [*date*] and the Will was proved by the Executors in the [*details*].

---

[61] This assumes that the residue (unlike the clauses in A1.8) passes to the surviving spouse absolutely.

(2) The Legacy Fund and the 'Nil Rate Sum' has the same meaning as in the Will and the Nil Rate Sum amounts to [*amount*].

(3) The Trustees were appointed trustees of the Legacy Fund by clause [*number*] of the Will.

(4) The Executors hold the property described in the Schedule ("the Property").

(5) In exercise of the powers given to them by clause [*number*] of the Will the Executors have required the trustees to accept in place of the Nil Rate Sum a debt to be secured by a charge over the property [and the Trustees have required this sum to be indexed linked by reference to the RPI at the date of the Testator's death].

NOW THIS DEED WITNESSES AS FOLLOWS:

1. In this Deed "the Sum Owing" shall mean the Nil Rate Sum.

2. The Executors hereby charge the Property[62] with the payment to the Trustees of the Sum Owing and the Executors are under no further liability to ensure that the same is paid to the Trustees who accept that their only recourse in respect of the Sum Owing is against the charged property.

3. It is confirmed that in the event that the Executors vest the property in the residuary beneficiary ("the Beneficiary") of the Testator's estate

    (a) they will serve notice in writing on the Trustees and
    (b) the Beneficiary shall not be under any personal liability to ensure that the sum owing is paid to the Trustees.[63]

SCHEDULE

(the Property)

Signed etc

---

[62] The charge will be over property in the Deceased's estate. In many cases the main asset will be a beneficial interest in the main residence. The charge will accordingly be over this asset and will, of necessity, be equitable. Of course, in cases where the Deceased had been sole legal and beneficial owner of the house a legal charge may be employed.

[63] The non-recourse nature of the charge is designed to avoid an SDLT charge arising and to ensure that problems do not arise under FA 1986.

A1.10   IPDI TRUST OF RESIDUE FOR (MINOR) CHILDREN OF THE TESTATOR WITH SUBSTITUTION IN THE CASE OF A PRE-DECEASING CHILD LEAVING ISSUE

I GIVE all my property not otherwise disposed of by this Will or any Codicil to my Trustees:

(1) with power at their discretion to sell all or any of such property when they think fit and to invest the proceeds in any investments hereby authorised and with power from time to time to vary investments for others of an authorised nature.

(2) to pay all debts funeral and executorship expenses legacies and tax.

(3) to hold the remainder and the income thereof ("my Residuary Estate") for such of my children as survive me ("my Children") and if more than one in equal shares but if any of them dies before me leaving a child or children [*who attain the age of [twenty one]*][64] such child or children shall take the share of my Residuary Estate which my deceased child would otherwise have taken and if more than one in equal shares absolutely and PROVIDED ALWAYS that the share in my Residuary Estate of any child of mine ("My Child") shall not vest in him absolutely but shall be retained and invested by my Trustees and held upon the following trusts.

(4) the provisions of sub-clauses (5) to (7) shall apply to the share of the Trust Fund held upon trust for my Child under sub-clause (3). In these provisions, such share is called "The Share" and that one of my Children who is primarily interest in the Share is called the "Life Tenant".

(5) the income of the Share shall be paid to the Life Tenant during his lifetime. If and so long as the Life Tenant is under the age of 18, the Trustees may pay or apply any income of the Share to him or for his maintenance or education or otherwise for his benefit as they shall in their discretion think fit. Any balance of the income shall be retained by the Trustees upon trust for the Life Tenant absolutely. Any such retained income may, at any time, be paid or applied as if it was income arising in the then current year. Section 31 of the Trustee Act 1925 shall not apply to the Share so long as the Life Tenant is under the age of 18.[65]

(6) the Trustees may, at any time or times, during the Trust Period, pay or apply the whole or any part of the Share in which the Life Tenant is then entitled to an interest in possession to him or for his advancement or otherwise for his benefit in such manner as the Trustees shall in their discretion think fit. In exercising the

[64] Complete as appropriate.
[65] It is essential to exclude TA 1925 s.31 if a minor beneficiary is to enjoy an IPDI.

powers conferred by this sub-clause the Trustees shall be entitled to have regard solely to the interests of the Life Tenant and to disregard all other interests or potential interests under this Deed.

(7) the Life Tenant shall have power to appoint his spouse a life or lesser interest (including an interest terminable by the Trustees at any time) in the income of all or any part of the Share. The Life Tenant may make the commencement of such interest dependent upon conditions as to survivorship or otherwise as he shall in his absolute discretion determine [and he may confer on the Trustees the same power for the benefit of his spouse as they have under sub-clause (6) for his benefit]. No such appointment shall be valid unless, at the date if takes effect, the Life Tenant is entitled to an interest in possession in the Trust Fund or the part of the Trust Fund to which the appointment relates.[66]

(8) subject as above, the capital and income of the Share shall be held upon trust for such of the children of the Life Tenant as attain the age of 25 before the end of the Trust Period or are living and are under that age at the end of the Trust Period; and if more than one, in equal shares absolutely.[67]

(9) subject as above, the Share, together with any accrual to it, shall accrue to the other Shares the trusts of which shall not previously have failed or determined (otherwise than by absolute vesting) and, if more than one, equally between them. Each such accrual shall be held upon, with and subject to the same trusts, powers and provisions as the Share to which it accrues.

[66] If desired flexible trusts may be adopted: e.g. the trustees may be given a power of appointment in favour of the Discretionary Beneficiaries (as defined) which could be exercised to terminate the interest in possession of the surviving spouse. A continuing trust for a surviving spouse will not be an IPDI: it will fall into the relevant property regime. Consider as an alternative giving the child a general power of appointment: see 38.55, 28.19 and A1.17.

[67] The continuing trust will, for IHT purposes, be taxed under the relevant property regime.

A1.11   **DEED OF VARIATION (A) SEVERING BENEFICIAL JOINT TENANCY AND (B) CREATING A NIL RATE BAND DISCRETIONARY TRUST WITH DEBT/CHARGE PROVISIONS[68]**

THIS DEED OF VARIATION is made the [ ] day of [ ] 20[ ] by [*name*] of [*address*] ("the Widower")

SUPPLEMENTAL TO the will of [*name*] ("the Deceased") dated [*date*] ("the Will")

WHEREAS

1. The Deceased died on [*date*] and probate of the Will was granted to the Widower out of the District Registry at [*city*] on [*date*];

2. At the date of her death the Deceased and the Widower owned as beneficial joint tenants (1) two accounts with the [*Bank*] Bank numbers [*accounts*] ("the Accounts") and (2) [*Property*][69] ("the Property") all of which assets passed to the Widower by survivorship.

3. In the events which have happened the Widower is the sole residuary beneficiary of the Deceased's estate and is now desirous of varying the dispositions of assets comprised in the Deceased's estate in accordance with the provisions set out in this Deed.

NOW THIS DEED WITNESSES

1. That it shall be deemed that the Widower had immediately prior to the death of the Deceased severed their beneficial joint tenancy in the Accounts and in the Property so that at the date of her death her beneficial half share in the said Accounts and Property formed part of her free estate.

2. That the Will shall be varied as if there were inserted immediately before clause [*number*] the following pecuniary legacy.[70]

[*clause number*] (A) Definitions[71]

---

[68] For a consideration of the debt/charge scheme, see Ch.38. With the introduction, from October 9, 2007, of a transferred nil rate band between spouses it is likely that variations of this type will become relatively uncommon. In the past they were needed to ensure that the deceased spouse's nil rate band was not wasted. However, there are still circumstances where it is attractive for the first spouse to create a discretionary trust in his will: see Ch.38.

[69] For the use of instruments of variation, see Ch.39.

[70] This will normally be the matrimonial home.

[71] Some draftsmen may prefer to set out the trust in a Schedule to the Deed.

In this clause:

(i) "*the Nil-Rate Sum*" means the largest sum of cash which could be given on the trusts of this clause without any inheritance tax becoming due in respect of the transfer of the value of my estate which I am deemed to make immediately before my death[72]

(ii) "*the Trust Period*" means the period starting with my death and ending 125 years afterwards (and that period is the perpetuity period applicable to this clause)

(iii) "*the Beneficiaries*" means my Husband and[73]

    (1) any issue of mine who are alive at the start of or born during the Trust Period and

    (2) anyone who is at any time during the Trust Period the spouse or (whether or not remarried) the widow or widower of any such issue or of any issue of mine who are already dead or die before me

and "*Beneficiary*" shall have a corresponding meaning

(iv) "*my Legacy Fund Trustees*" shall mean [*details*] or such other trustees or trustee for time being of this Legacy Fund.[74]

(B) Declaration of Trust

I GIVE the Nil-Rate Sum to my Legacy Fund Trustees ON TRUST to invest it in exercise of the powers of investment given them by this Will or by law and to hold it and the property which currently represents it ("the Legacy Fund") on the trusts and with and subject to the powers and provisions set out in this clause.

(C) Powers of Appointment and Advancement

DURING the Trust Period my Legacy Fund Trustees (being at least two in number or a trust corporation) may at any time or times

---

[72] Care needs to be taken in defining the "*nil rate sum*". In the event that the wife has been entitled to a transferred nil rate band as a result of a pre-deceasing first husband the definition used in this precedent will catch both her nil rate band and the transferred nil rate band. If this is not desired limit the clause to a single nil rate band e.g.:

> "*The 'Nil Rate Sum' shall mean such sum as is equal to the upper limited of the nil per cent band in the table of rates of tax (applicable on my death) in Schedule 1 to the Inheritance Tax Act 1984, less an amount equal to the aggregate of the amount chargeable to inheritance tax of:*
>
>   *(a) all or any chargeable transfers, including potentially exempt transfers which have become chargeable as a result of my death, made by me during my lifetime in the cumulation period specified by s7(1)(a) of the Inheritance Tax Act 1984;*
>
>   *(b) all other gifts, if any, taking effect under my will or any codicil;*
>
>   *(c) all or any settled property in which, on my death, I have a qualifying interest in possession; and*
>
>   *(d) all other property, if any, wherever situate, which is, or which is treated as, property to which I am beneficially entitled immediately before my death (including property subject to a reservation as defined by s102 of the Finance Act 1986 as amended).*"

[73] If desired further flexibility could be given by permitting the Legacy Fund trustees to add further persons as beneficiaries.

[74] There are attractions in selecting persons other than the Executors to be trustees of the Legacy Fund although in practice it is common for the same persons to act in both capacities. See also (H)(iii).

(i) by deed or deeds revocable or irrevocable appoint that all or any part or parts of the income or capital of the Legacy Fund shall be held on such trusts (including discretionary and protective ones) in favour or for the benefit of all or any one or more of the Beneficiaries and with and subject to such powers (including dispositive and administrative powers exercisable by my Legacy Fund Trustees or any other person) and other provisions as my Legacy Fund Trustees think fit;

(ii) transfer all or any part or parts of the income or capital of the Legacy Fund to the trustees of any Settlement wherever established (whose receipt shall be a good discharge to them) to be held free from the trusts of this Will and on the trusts and with and subject to the powers and provisions of that Settlement but only if those trusts powers and provisions are such that (at the time of the transfer) they could themselves have created them under (i) above; and

(iii) pay, transfer or apply any part of the Legacy Fund to or for the advancement or benefit of any Beneficiary.

(D) Default Trusts

IN DEFAULT of and subject to any exercise of the clause (C) power of appointment

(i) during the Trust Period my Legacy Fund Trustees shall pay or apply the income of the Legacy Fund to or for the maintenance education support or otherwise for the benefit of such one or more of the Beneficiaries as my Legacy Fund Trustees may in their absolute discretion think fit BUT with power to accumulate and add to capital such income or any part or parts of it (and to apply the accumulations of past years as income of the current year) AND with power (during the Trust Period) to resolve to hold the whole or any part or parts of such income as income on trust for any of the Beneficiaries absolutely and

(ii) on the expiry of the Trust Period my Legacy Fund Trustees shall hold the Legacy Fund as to both capital and income ON TRUST for such of my issue as are then living and if more than one in equal shares although through all degrees according to their stocks and so that no issue shall take whose parent is alive and so capable of taking.

(E) Constitution of Trust by Debt or Charge

INSTEAD of satisfying that legacy wholly by the payment of cash (or by the appropriation of property) to the Legacy Fund Trustees my Executors may:

(i) require the Legacy Fund Trustees to accept in place of all or any part of the Nil-Rate Sum a binding promise of payment made by my husband[75]

(ii) charge all or any part of the Nil Rate Sum on any property which is (or but for this clause would be) given by this will or any codicil to it to my husband absolutely[76]

---

[75] These clauses should be incorporated in a will which leaves the residue to the surviving spouse absolutely. See A1.8 for drafting when there is an IPDI for the survivor. This is the "*simple*" debt arrangement. Note also clauses (G)(i); (H).

[76] This is the "*charge route*" which may be employed to avoid FA 1986 s.103 and SDLT problems. The clause enables the executors to impose the charge not just over property passing to the surviving spouse under the residue clause but also over property which would but for this clause pass to that spouse. Take the following example: the value of the Testator's estate is £350,000 of which £325,000 is left on the nil rate band trust leaving only £25,000 in residue. If the trust is to be established by a charge then it is important that the full value of the estate is subject to the charge and not just the £25,000 which passes under the residue clause.

(F) Loans to Beneficiaries

THE Legacy Fund Trustees may lend any money to a Beneficiary or Beneficiaries

(G) Position of my Executors

(i) if my Executors exercise their powers under (E)(i) above they shall be under no further liability to see that the Legacy Fund Trustees receive the sum promised and if they exercise their power under (E)(ii) they shall (to the extent of the value at my death of the property charged) by under no further liability to see that the Legacy Fund Trustees receive the sum secured

(ii) if my Executors exercise their power under (E)(ii) above they may give an assent of the charged property subject to the charge and no one in whose favour the assent is made shall become personally liable for the sum secured.[77]

(H) Powers and Protection of the Legacy Fund Trustees

THE Legacy Fund Trustees may require security to be given for any debt to be created by a promise within (E)(i) above[78] or by a loan within (F) and in relation both to such debts (whether or not secured) and to any debt to be secured by a charge within (E)(ii) (all of which shall be debts payable on demand) they

(i) may (subject to the foregoing provisions) impose such terms (if any) as they think fit including terms as to interest and the personal liability of the borrower and terms linking the debt to the Index of Retail Prices or otherwise providing for its amount to vary with the passage of time according to a formula and[79]

(ii) may subsequently leave the debt outstanding for as long as they think fit and refrain from exercising their rights in relation to it and waive the payment of all or any part of it or of any interest due in respect of it and they shall not be liable if my [husband/wife] is or becomes unable to pay the debt or a security is or becomes inadequate or for any other loss which my occur through their exercising or choosing not to exercise any power given by this clause

(iii) the powers given by this clause are without prejudice to any other powers given by this Will or any Codicil to it or by the general law and are exercisable even though my Executors and the Legacy Fund Trustees may be the same persons and my husband may be among them (but they are not exercisable while my husband is the sole Legacy Fund Trustee) and any of the Legacy Fund Trustees may exercise or concur in existing all powers and discretions given to him by this clause or by law notwithstanding that he has a direct or other personal interest in the mode or result of any such exercise.[80]

---

[77] It is important that no liability is imposed on the recipient of the charged property since (a) this could lead to the disallowance of the debt under FA 1986 s.103 and (b) if liability to discharge the debt is assumed Stamp Duty Land Tax will be payable (if land is involved).

[78] The Legacy Fund Trustees should in the case of the simple debt arrangement give serious consideration to requesting security from the surviving spouse who will (in the majority of cases) have become absolutely entitled to the family home (so that the giving of such security should not pose problems).

[79] It is unlikely that the surviving spouse will wish (or often be in a position) to pay interest on the outstanding debt. Given the power to lend money to a beneficiary, the trustees will often be content to leave the debt interest-free but doubtless repayable on demand.

[80] Frequently the surviving spouse is both executor and legacy fund trustee but it remains important that he/she is not the sole executor or legacy fund trustee and there may be cases where he/she should not act as executor.

3. The provisions of the Inheritance Tax Act 1984, s.142(1) and of the Taxation of Chargeable Gains Act 1992 s62(6) shall apply to the dispositions of property effected by this deed.[81]

IN WITNESS etc

---

[81] For this reading-back election, see Ch.39.

DISCLAIMER OF A LIFE INTEREST WHERE LIFE TENANT HAS DIED WITHIN TWO YEARS OF THE DECEASED[82]

THIS DEED OF DISCLAIMER is made the [ ] day of [ ] 20[ ] by [*name*] of [*address*] ("*the Executors*") acting in their capacity as personal representatives of [*details of the life tenant*][83] ("*the Life Tenant*") who died on [*date*].

WHEREAS:

(A) [*Name*] ("*the Testatrix*") died on [*date*]

(B) Under clause [*number*] of the Will of the Testatrix dated [*date*] ("*the Will*") her residuary estate as therein defined (which property is set out in the Schedule hereto and is called in this deed "*the Trust Assets*") was left upon trust to pay the income therefrom to the Life Tenant during his lifetime or until his remarriage and thereafter to hold the Trust Fund for her children [*details*] in equal shares absolutely.

(C) The Life Tenant died on [*date*] within two years of the death of the Testatrix and the said children of the Testatrix survived her and are therefore entitled to take the Trust Assets in equal shares absolutely.

(D) The Life Tenant had not done any act or thing which could constitute an acceptance of any part of the income of the Trust Assets and the Executors wish to disclaim on his behalf his interest in the Trust Assets.

NOW THIS DEED WITNESSES as follows:

1. THE Executors hereby irrevocably disclaim and renounce all the rights, interest and entitlement of the Life Tenant in the Trust Assets and all other rights, interest and entitlement (if any) that he may have arising under the Will and disclaim and renounce all and any benefit therefrom.

2. THE Executors confirm that the Life Tenant did not accept his interest in the Trust Assets and received no benefit from the same.[84]

IN WITNESS etc

---

[82] For the difficulties in amending the terms of a will after the death of a beneficiary entitled to income, see Ch.39.

[83] See Ch.39.

[84] A disclaimer is only possible if the beneficiary has not received a benefit (i.e. accepted) the interest. In the case of a disclaimer no reading-back statement is required: see Ch.39.

THE SCHEDULE

[details of Residuary Estate disclaimed]

THIS DEED OF APPOINTMENT is made the [ ] day of [ ] 20[ ] by [*name*] of
[*address*] and [*name*] of [*address*] (together "*the Appointors*")

SUPPLEMENTAL TO:

(A) A will dated [*date*] ("*the Will*") made by [*name*] ("*the Deceased*") and

(B) An assent dated [*date*] ("*the Assent*") under which certain freehold land
described in the Schedule to this deed ("*the Property*") was assented to the
Appointors as trustees to hold on the discretionary trusts set out in clause
[*number*] of the Will.

WHEREAS:

1. The Deceased died on [*date*] and the Will was proven on [*date*] at [*City*] District
   Probate Registry.[86]

2. The Appointors are the present trustees of the residuary estate of the Deceased.

3. Under clause [*number*] of the Will the residuary estate of the Deceased (therein
   called "the *Trust Fund*") was held on such trusts in favour or for the benefit of all
   or any one or more of the Discretionary Beneficiaries and in such shares or proportions and with and subject to such powers and provisions for their respective
   maintenance education or other benefit as the Appointors (being at least two in
   number) by any deed or deeds revocable during the Discretionary Period (which
   period is defined in the Will as the period of 125 years from the date of the
   Deceased's death)[87] or irrevocable and executed during the Discretionary Period
   shall appoint.

4. The Discretionary Beneficiaries include the adult children of the Deceased
   namely A and B and their respective spouses widows widowers children and
   remoter issue.

5. The Appointors have not yet exercised their aforesaid powers of appointment
   but are now desirous of revocably exercising their powers under the Will and as
   hereinafter set out.

---

[85] For a consideration of IHTA 1984, s.144 and "reading-back", see Ch.39.
[86] To come within s.144 it is essential the Deceased died within the previous two years.
[87] In some precedents, the discretionary period ends automatically on expiry of two years from
death but it is not necessary to provide for this since it is unduly restrictive.

NOW THIS DEED WITNESSES as follows:

1. EXPRESSIONS used in this deed shall where the context admits have the same meanings as set out in the Will and in this deed "*the Appointed Fund*" means the Property (as described in the Schedule) the net sale proceeds thereof and the assets from time to time representing the same.

2. IN exercise of their powers contained in clause [*number*] of the Will and of every other power them enabling the Appointors hereby revocably appoint and declare that the Appointed Fund and the income thereof shall from the date of this Deed be held upon trust to divide the same into two equal parts of which the first such equal part and the assets from time to time representing the same ("A's Fund") shall be held upon the trusts declared and contained in clause 3 below and of which the second such equal part and the assets from time to time representing the same ("B's Fund") shall be held upon the trusts declared and contained in clause 5 below.

3. THE Trustees shall hold A's Fund and the income thereof upon the following trusts and subject to the following powers and provisions:

    (a) The Trustees shall pay the income of A's Fund to A during the life of A.
    (b) The Trustees may, at any time or times pay, transfer or apply to or for the advancement or benefit (whether absolutely or in trust) of A the whole or any part of A's Fund to which A is then entitled to an interest in possession. In exercising the powers conferred by this sub-clause, the Trustees shall be entitled to have regard solely to the interests of A and to disregard all other interests or potential interests in A's Fund.
    (c) Subject thereto A's Fund and the income thereof shall be held on trust for such of A's children as attain the age of 21 or are living and under that age at the end of the Discretionary Period and if more than one in equal shares absolutely.[88]

4. IF the trusts of A's Fund shall fail the Trustees shall hold A's Fund as an accretion to B's Fund and upon the trusts appertaining thereto (including absolute beneficial interests therein) the trusts of which have not failed and as one fund therewith.

5. THE Trustees shall hold B's Fund and the income thereof upon the trusts contained in clauses 3 and 4 above with the substitution wherever the same appears:

    (a) For A's Fund of B's Fund
    (b) For A of B
    (c) For B's Fund of A' Fund
    (d) For B of A
    (e) For A's children of B's children.

6. THE administrative and other provisions contained in the Will shall continue to apply to the Appointed Fund in so far as those powers and provisions are consistent with the provisions declared by this Deed.

7. THE Trustees shall have power at any time or times before the end of the Discretionary Period by deed or deeds wholly or partly to revoke or vary all or any of the trusts powers and provisions which apply to the Appointed Fund by virtue of this deed and if thought fit by the same or similar deed or deeds to make such fresh appointment in exercise of their said powers of appointment conferred by the Will as they may in their absolute discretion think fit provided that no exercise of their powers of revocation shall invalidate any prior payment or

---

[88] The continuing trusts after A's death will fall under the relevant property regime.

application of all or any part or parts of the capital or income or deprive a beneficiary of income or capital to which he has already become entitled.

8. THE Trustees may by deed or deeds executed during the Discretionary Period release or restrict the future exercise of their power of revocation either wholly or to the extent specified in the relevant deed.

SCHEDULE

[*details of the Property*]

IN WITNESS etc.

A1.14   CLAUSE LEAVING PROPERTY TO PILOT (LIFETIME) TRUST[89]

I give my shares in [*name*] Limited[90] to the trustees of the [*name*] Discretionary Settlement 201[*year*] to be held by those trustees on the trusts set out in a deed of settlement dated [*date*] and made by me as settlor and the Original Trustees (as therein defined).[91]

---

[89] For the use of pilot trusts, see A1.1 and Ch.42.
[90] Or as the case may be.
[91] It is important that the settlement be in existence at the time when the will is made: it needs to be identified with precision (e.g. by name and date).

X Nil rate-band legacy

X.1 In this Clause:

X.1.1 "the Discretionary Beneficiaries" means such of the following as are alive at my death or born during the Trust Period: my [wife/husband/civil partner] children and remoter issue and the spouses widows and widowers and civil partners (whether or not remarried) of such children and remoter issue

X.1.2 "the Trust Period" means the period expiring 125 years from my death which period shall be the perpetuity period applicable to the trusts set out in this Clause

X.1.3 "the Legacy Fund" means:

X.1.3.1 the Specified Sum and my Business Property (as hereinafter defined)

X.1.3.2 all accumulations (if any) of income directed to be held as an accretion to capital and

X.1.3.3 the money investments and other property from time to time representing the above

X.1.4 "the Legacy Fund Trustees" means [*name*] and [*name*] or other trustee or trustees for the time being of the Legacy Fund whether original additional or substituted

X.1.5 "my Business Property"[93] means all my interest in the business known as (*name of business*) ("the Business") including:

X.1.5.1 all goodwill stock vehicles machinery plant and other equipment;

X.1.5.2 all book debts money standing to the credit of the Business at any bank or elsewhere and the benefit of all contracts;

X.1.5.3 any freehold or leasehold premises used by the Business;

X.1.5.4 any property of mine used wholly and exclusively in the Business.

If at the date of my death the name of the Business has changed or if as a result of any amalgamation restructuring rearrangement or sale of the Business my interest is repre-

---

[92] See Chs 45 and 46 for a consideration of business and agricultural property and for the advantages of settling such property into a discretionary trust (along with the nil rate sum).

[93] This definition will require amendment in the event that the testator owns shares in the family business rather than an interest in an unincorporated business.

sented by substituted capital holdings or interests in a new business whether as a sole trader or partner or in a company not being a public limited company then this gift shall not lapse but shall take effect as a gift of such newly named business holdings or interests.

X.1.6 "the Specified Sum" means a pecuniary legacy of the maximum amount which can be given under this Clause without inheritance tax being payable in respect of my death but subject to the following:

X.1.6.1 the Specified Sum shall not exceed the upper limit of the nil per cent rate band (applicable on my death) in the table of rates of tax in Schedule 1 to the Inheritance Tax Act 1984 (or any statutory re-enactment thereof)[94]

X.1.6.2 any other legacy given by my Will or any codicil shall be paid in priority to the Specified Sum and

X.1.6.3 no account shall be taken of the value transferred by the gifts of my Business Property in calculating the Specified Sum.

X.2 If my [wife/husband/civil partner] survives me by 30 days I give to the Legacy Fund Trustees my Business Property and the Specified Sum subject to the payment of inheritance tax.

---

[94] Hence the amount will be limited to one unused NRB not two in the event of the deceased's estate being able to benefit from a transferred unused nil rate band.

DRAFT CLAUSE LEAVING CHARITABLE LEGACY TO MAXIMISE INHERITANCE TAX RELIEF[95]
A1.16

I give to [*name of charity*] such assets[96] to be selected by my executors which are not the subject of a specific gift and which shall have a net value for the purposes of inheritance tax equal to 10% [*or insert larger figure*] of my net estate as defined in Inheritance Tax Act 1984 s[ ] and my executors may appropriate assets to satisfy (or partly satisfy) this legacy without the consent of any beneficiary under my will or codicil.

[The legacy given by this clause shall in no event:

(i) be less than £[ ] whether or not relief under Inheritance Tax Act 1984 s[ ] shall be available; and

(ii) exceed £[ ] even if in consequence of this restriction in the value of the legacy relief shall not be available under Inheritance Tax Act 1984 s[ ].]

---

[95] For the proposal to introduce a reduced (36%) rate of IHT when 10% of the estate is left to charity see 38.59. At the time of writing it is envisaged that this change will be introduced from April 6, 2012 with the necessary legislation being included in FA 2012.

[96] Alternatively leave a sum of a value equal to 10% of the net estate (as defined).

A1.17 CLAUSE CONFERRING GENERAL POWER OF APPOINTMENT FOR LIFE TENANT OVER IPDI TRUST[97]

If at the date of [his/her] death [my spouse] has a qualifying interest in possession in the whole or any part of my Residuary Estate s/he shall have power to appoint by will codicil or other testamentary instrument that such part of my Residuary Estate in which s/he has such qualifying interest in possession at the date of his/her death shall on his/her death be held upon such trusts and provisions (whether absolutely or on continuing trusts) and for such person or persons or charity or charities (including spouse or his/her estate) as s/he shall think fit, freed and discharged from all the trusts of this my Will. [My spouse] may at any time before his/her death release or restrict the future exercise of such general power of appointment.

---

[97] This enables the life tenant to create new IPDI trusts on his or her death thereby keeping the property in trust but outside the relevant property regime (and, in appropriate cases, with the benefit of the spouse exemption). The general power is conferred on the life tenant who has the qualifying interest in possession. This is often the spouse of the deceased testator. However, the power could be conferred on any life tenant.

PART III: SUBSIDIARY DOCUMENTS

DEED OF APPOINTMENT MADE WITHIN TWO YEARS OF THE   A1.18
DEATH OF THE TESTATOR APPOINTING PROPERTY
ABSOLUTELY TO THE SURVIVING SPOUSE

THIS DEED OF APPOINTMENT is made the [ ] day of [ ] 20[ ] by [*name*] of [*address*] and [*name*] of [*address*] ("the Appointors")

SUPPLEMENTAL to the will dated [*date*] ("the Will") of [*Name*] ("the Deceased") who died on [*date*][98]

WHEREAS

1. By clause [*number*] the Will established a nil rate band discretionary trust ("the Trust").

2. [*Deceased's surviving spouse*] ("the Beneficiary")[99] is a member of the class of Beneficiaries as defined in the Will.

3. The Appointors are the present trustees of the Will Trust[100] and are desirous of appointing the assets comprised in the Will Trust (listed in the Schedule to this Deed) to the Beneficiary absolutely.

NOW THIS DEED WITNESSES:

1. In exercise of their power under clause [*number*] and all other relevant powers, the Appointors hereby irrevocably appoint that the property set out in the Schedule shall from the date of this Deed be held upon trust as to both capital and income for the Beneficiary absolutely.

2. All income received by or on behalf of the Trustees from and after the date of this Deed shall be treated as if it had arisen wholly after such date and the Apportionment Act 1870 shall not be applicable to it.

---

[98] "Reading back" under IHTA 1984 s.144 only applies if the appointment takes effect within two years of death.

[99] The Beneficiary is the surviving spouse (or civil partner) of the Deceased and as a result of s.144 (reading back) the trust fund will be spouse exempt (see IHTA 1984 s.18) with the result that (assuming that no other chargeable transfers had been made by the Deceased) his IHT nil rate band will be unused and so may be claimed on the death of the surviving spouse.

[100] Ensure that all trustees execute the deed. If an executor who is also appointed a trustee wishes to renounce as executor, he also needs to resign or disclaim his trusteeship.

SCHEDULE

(Identify property held in the Will Trust)

IN WITNESS etc

APPOINTING A NON QUALIFYING LIFE INTEREST IN POSSESSION IN A DISCRETIONARY TRUST[101]

A1.19

THIS REVOCABLE DEED OF APPOINTMENT is made the [ ] day of [ ] 20[ ] by [*name*] of [*address*] and [*name*] of [*address*] ("*the Appointors*")

SUPPLEMENTAL to a settlement dated [*details of the settlement*] and made between [*names*]

WHEREAS:

1. The Beneficiaries as defined in the Settlement include the children of the settlors and the spouses of such children

2. (X) is a child of the settlors and (Y) is his wife both therefore being members of the class of Beneficiaries.

[3. The Trustees are by clause [*number*] of the Settlement given power to pay, transfer, apply or deal with the whole or any part of the capital or income of the Settlement for the benefit of any one or more of the Beneficiaries and in exercise of that power the Trustees may by deed or deeds appoint capital on such trusts as they in their absolute discretion think fit][102]

4. The Appointors are the present Trustees of the Settlement and are desirous of exercising the said power for the benefit of X and Y as set out in this Instrument.

NOW THIS DEED WITNESSES as follows:

1. In this Instrument "*the Trust Fund*" "*the Trustees*" and "*the Specified Period*"[103] shall have the meanings given to those terms in the Settlement.

2. In exercise of the power conferred on them by clause [*number*] of the Settlement and of any other relevant power the Appointors hereby appoint and direct that from and after the date of this Deed the Trustees shall stand possessed of the Trust Fund upon trust to pay the income thereof to X and Y in equal shares during their joint lives and thereafter to the survivor provided always that the Trustees may at any time or times during the Specified Period by deed or deeds wholly or partly revoke[104] the appointment contained in this clause.

---

[101] See 6.17 and 14.23 for the circumstances when this may be attractive.
[102] Recite details of the power to be exercised as in this illustration.
[103] This will normally be the appropriate perpetuity period within which interests must vest.
[104] The appointment of the interest in possession is a "nothing" for IHT purposes: similarly a future revocation of the interest will have no IHT consequence.

3. All income from the Trust Fund received by or on behalf of the Trustees from and after the date of this Deed shall be treated as if it had arisen wholly after such date and the Apportionment Act 1870 shall not apply to it.[105]

4. Subject to the trust powers and provisions contained in this Deed the Trust Fund and the income thereof shall continue to be held upon and with and subject to the trust powers and provisions declared and contained in the Settlement.[106]

IN WITNESS etc.

---

[105] This clause is desirable to avoid apportionment calculations.
[106] The appointment effects only a modification of the existing trust. Accordingly it does not result in the creation of a new settlement so that there is no CGT deemed disposal.

RESETTLEMENT OF FUNDS FROM DISCRETIONARY TRUST ON NEW TRUSTS[107]

THIS DEED OF RE-SETTLEMENT is made the [ ] day of [ ] 20[ ] by

(1) [*name*] of [*address*] (hereinafter called "the Transferring Trustees")

(2) [*name*] of [*address*] (hereinafter called "the Transferee Trustees")

WHEREAS:

(A) This Deed is supplemental to (i) a settlement dated [*date*] ("the X Settlement")[108] made between [*name*] as settlor of the one part and the Transferring Trustees as the original trustees of the other part whereby certain property was settled upon discretionary trusts and (ii) a settlement dated [*date*] ("the Y Settlement") made between [*name*] as settlor of the one part and the Transferee Trustees as the original trustees of the other part whereby certain property was settled upon [discretionary/interest in possession trusts] for [*give brief details of trusts*].

(B) The Transferring Trustees are the present trustees of the X Settlement.

(C) Pursuant to clause [*number*] of the X Settlement, the Transferring Trustees (*being at least two in number or a trust corporation*)[109] may at any time or times transfer all or any part or parts of the income or capital of the Trust Fund (as therein defined) to the trustees of any settlement wherever established to be held free from the trusts of the X Settlement and on the trusts and with and subject to the powers and provisions of such new settlement [but only if those trusts powers and provisions are such that (at the time of the transfer) the trustees of the X Settlement could themselves have created them under sub-clause [*number*] of the X Settlement][110].

(D) The property listed in the Schedule hereto ("the Property") is for the time being comprised in the Trust Fund of the X Settlement.

---

[107] There is no inheritance tax event on a transfer between two relevant property settlements but there is a disposal for capital gains tax purposes (see IHTA 1984 s.81; TCGA 1992 s71): see Ch.11. Any capital gain cannot be held over under TCGA 1992 s.260 since there is no chargeable transfer but hold-over relief may be available under TCGA 1992 s.165 if the assets comprise business or agricultural property. If the transfer is from a discretionary trust to an interest in possession trust (whether set up before or after March 2006) the property will remain subject to the relevant property regime (because an addition to an interest in possession trust will no longer be treated as held on qualifying interest in possession trusts). So there is no exit charge for inheritance tax purposes.

[108] Insert name and details of transferring settlement

[109] Delete if not applicable

[110] This proviso may not be in the settlement deed: check any restrictions on resettlement and that the trustees have sufficient power to resettle funds!

(E) The Beneficiaries of the X Settlement include A, B and C and their children and remoter issue.

(F) The Transferring Trustees have considered the terms of the Y Settlement and have resolved to exercise their aforementioned power to transfer the Property to the Transferee Trustees to hold on the terms of the Y Settlement, and nothing in the Y Settlement infringes any restrictions on the exercise of such powers or any rule against perpetuities or absolute vesting[111].

(G) The Transferee Trustees have joined in this Deed to accept such property as an addition to the Trust Fund of the Y Settlement.

NOW THIS DEED WITNESSES as follows:

1. **IN EXERCISE** of the power conferred upon them by clause [*number*] of the X Settlement and of all other (if any) powers them enabling, the Transferring Trustees irrevocably resolve determine and direct that the Property shall immediately be transferred to Transferee Trustees to the intent that upon such transfer being made (which has taken place contemporaneously with the execution of this Deed)[112] the Property shall from that time be held on the trusts and with and subject to the powers and provisions of the Y Settlement freed and discharged from all the trusts of the X Settlement and so that all accrued or accruing income of the Property received on or after the date hereof shall be dealt with as if it had accrued after such date (and so that the provisions of the Apportionment Act 1870 shall not apply).

2. **THE** Transferee Trustees hereby acknowledge receipt and acceptance of the Property and will hold the same upon the trusts and with and subject to the powers and provisions contained in the Y Settlement as an addition to and as one fund for all purposes with the trust fund of that settlement and freed and discharged from all the trusts of the X Settlement.

3. **THE** Transferee Trustees hereby jointly and severally covenant with the Transferring Trustees to keep the Transferring Trustees and all other trustee or trustees for the time being of the X Settlement indemnified against all actions, proceedings, claims, demands and costs including fiscal liabilities that might arise in respect of or in connection with the Property or this deed provided that this indemnity shall be limited:

    3.1 to those liabilities which may be notified to the Transferee Trustees or their successors in title within a period of seven calendar years from the date of this transfer; and

    3.2 to the value of the Property at the time it was transferred.

5. **THIS** Deed may be executed in any number of counterparts, all of which taken together shall constitute one and the same deed and any party may enter into this Deed by executing a counterpart.

IN WITNESS etc

THE SCHEDULE

(The Property)

---

[111] Check that the perpetuity and accumulation periods of the transferee settlement are not longer than those of the transferor settlement. For an illustration where the perpetuity rule was infringed in the case of a "settled advance", see *Pilkington v IRC* [1964] AC 612.

[112] In the case of shares (for instance) the transfer will be by stock transfer form.

THIS DEED OF APPLICATION is made the [ ] day of [ ] 20[ ] by [*name*] of [*address*] ("the Trustees")

SUPPLEMENTAL TO a Settlement dated [*date*] and made between [*name*] as Settlor and [*name*] as the Original Trustees ("the Settlement") and to the other instruments listed in the First Schedule to this Deed

WHEREAS

1. By a deed dated [*date*] and made by the Original Trustees ("the [*year*] Deed") J's Fund (as therein defined) became held upon trusts, *inter alia*, under which J is entitled to income and under which he will become absolutely entitled to the assets contained in that Fund on attaining the age of twenty-five years.

2. By clause [*number*] of the Settlement the trustees for the time being of J's Fund are entitled at any time or times before J becomes 25 to apply the whole or any part or parts of the capital of J's Fund for his advancement maintenance education or benefit

3. The Trustees are the present trustees of J's Fund and are desirous of exercising the said power in modification of the existing trusts affecting J's Fund for his benefit in the manner set out in this Deed

NOW THIS DEED WITNESSES:

Definitions

1. In this Deed the following expressions shall where the context permits have the following meanings:

    (i) **"J"** shall mean [*name*] who was born on [*date*]

    (ii) "the Trustees" shall mean the Trustees and the survivor of them or other the trustees or trustee for the time being of J's' Fund

    (iii) "J's Fund" shall have the meaning given to that expression in the [[*year*]

---

[113] Watch any formalities required for the exercise of such a power: eg does the settlement specify that consents must be obtained? If so, does this raise tax issues? See Ch.30.

[114] It is a moot point whether, as HMRC contend, a settled advance operates to create a new interest in possession for the beneficiary: see further Ch.27. If it does then after October 5, 2008, the continuing trusts will fall into the relevant property regime.

Deed] the property now comprised therein being specified in the Second Schedule to this Deed

(iv) "the Perpetuity Period" shall mean the perpetuity period specified in the [ ] Deed.

Application of capital and income of J's Fund

2. The Trustees as trustees for the time being of J's Fund in exercise of their above-recited power and of any and every other power them enabling (but without any intention of hereby creating a separate settlement of J's Fund or the income thereof or any part or parts of the same) **HEREBY RESOLVE DETERMINE AND DIRECT** that J's Fund and the income thereof shall now be and hereby is applied for the benefit of J by henceforth being held by the Trustees (in partial variation[115] of the trusts affecting J's Fund) upon the trusts and with and subject to the powers and provisions hereinafter declared and contained in respect of the same

3. As from the date hereof the Trustees shall stand possessed of J's Fund and the income thereof on the following trusts and with and subject to the following powers and provisions namely:

   (1) The Trustees shall pay the income of J's Fund to J during his life
   (2) J shall have power by deed or deeds revocable during the Perpetuity Period or irrevocable to appoint to [*name*] or to any spouse who shall survive him a life or lesser interest in the income of all or any part of J's Fund

   (3) Subject as aforesaid the Trustees shall hold J's Fund upon trust for all or such one or more exclusively of the others or other of the children of J at such ages or times and if more than one in such shares and with such provisions for their respective maintenance education and benefit generally at the discretion of the Trustees or of any other person or persons as J shall by any deed or deeds revocable during the Perpetuity Period or irrevocable or by will or codicil taking effect by reason of J's death before the end of the Perpetuity Period appoint and in default of and until and subject to any and every such appointment upon trust for all or any of the children of J who shall attain the age of twenty-one years on or before the end of the Perpetuity Period or shall be living and under that age on the expiry of the Perpetuity Period and if more than one in equal shares absolutely and so that such interests shall carry the intermediate income

   (4) Subject thereto J's Fund and the income thereof shall be held on trust for [*details*] absolutely

   (5) Notwithstanding the foregoing the Trustees shall have power at any time or times during the Perpetuity Period to pay or apply the whole or any part of J's Fund to J or for his advancement or otherwise for his benefit in such manner as the Trustees in their discretion shall think fit and after the death of J shall have a like power exercisable in favour of any person appointed an interest in possession in J's Fund under clause 3(2) above

   (6) Section 32 of the Trustee Act 1925 shall apply to the trusts hereinbefore contained with the omission of the words "one-half" from proviso (a) of subsection (1) and the omission of subsection (2)

---

[115] There is no intention to create a new settlement for CGT purposes: the instrument modifies the existing trusts.

Continuance of Settlement terms

4. It is hereby confirmed that the administrative powers and provisions of the Settlement contained in clauses [*numbers*] inclusive shall continue to apply to J's Fund and the income thereof

IN WITNESS etc

FIRST SCHEDULE (details of settlement instruments)

SECOND SCHEDULE (details of property in J's Fund)

A1.22   CLAUSE EXCLUDING DEPENDANT CHILDREN FROM THE DEFINITION OF "BENEFICIARIES"[116]

Definition

The "Beneficiaries" shall mean the existing children of the settlor, namely:

    a. [*details with dates of birth*]

and every other child of the settlor born before the end of the Trust Period[117] but excluding any such child whilst he or she is under the age of 18 and unmarried.

---

[116] This clause should be inserted if the settlor has minor children (or may in the future have such children) and wishes to ensure that the trust is not settlor-interested so that hold-over relief is available on its creation: see further Ch.18. Of course the settlor and spouse must also be excluded.

[117] This defined term is not the perpetuity period (unless it expressly says so) and can usually be shortened if the trustees see fit.

APPROPRIATION BY PRS IN FAVOUR OF CHARITY ON BARE TRUSTS[118]

A1.23

In the estate of [ ] deceased

WHEREAS

1. [ ] ("the Testatrix") late of [ ], died on [ ].
2. The Will dated [ ] was proved by [ ] at the [ ] Probate Registry on [ ].
3. Under the terms of the Will, the XYZ Charity of [ ] is entitled to a one-half share of the residuary estate.

APPROPRIATION

We, [ ], as Personal Representatives of [ ] hereby appropriate 130 ordinary shares of £1 each in ABC plc in part satisfaction of the said Charity's one-half share of the residuary estate of the Testatrix.

As from the date hereof, we declare that we hold the said shares as bare Trustees for XYZ Charity.[119]

Dated this [ ] day of [ ] 20[ ]

Signed

---

[118] For PR's powers of appropriation, see AEA 1925 s.41. No formalities are prescribed for the exercise of this power.
[119] This wording is important in establishing that from the date of the PRs resolution the charity becomes the beneficial owner of the shares. PRs may therefore sell the shares at the direction of the charity with the benefit of the CGT charity exemption.

APPENDIX II

MISCELLANEOUS MATERIAL

1. SDLT and NRBDT: HMRC Statement 12 November 2004[120]

STAMP DUTY LAND TAX AND 'NIL-RATE BAND DISCRETIONARY TRUSTS'

A2.01   We have received a number of enquiries about the interaction between Stamp Duty Land Tax and 'nil-rate band discretionary trusts' ('NRB Trusts'). This note should enable taxpayers and their advisers to decide on the Stamp Duty Land Tax consequences of transactions with NRB Trusts. This note does not cover any taxes other than Stamp Duty Land Tax. Neither does it cover the powers or fiduciary responsibilities of trustees of NRB Trusts, or of personal representatives, under general law. Trustees and personal representatives may wish to take independent legal advice on those aspects.

A2.02   An NRB Trust is commonly established under the Will of a deceased person. The typical form is a pecuniary legacy, not exceeding the nil-rate band for inheritance tax, to be held by the trustees of the NRB Trust ('the NRB trustees') on discretionary trusts for a specified class of beneficiaries. The residue of the estate, often including the matrimonial home, commonly passes to the surviving spouse, although it may pass to residuary trustees.

A2.03   Where the personal representatives discharge the pecuniary legacy by payment of the specified sum to the trustees no Stamp Duty Land Tax issue arises. However in many cases the personal representatives satisfy the legacy otherwise than by payment of the specified sum. It is in these cases that a Stamp Duty Land Tax liability may arise on the transfer of the matrimonial home or other land to the surviving spouse or residuary trustees.

A2.04   The transfer of an interest in land, whether to a residuary beneficiary or to any other person, and whether in satisfaction of an entitlement under a Will or not, is a land transaction for Stamp Duty Land Tax purposes. The question is whether the transferee gives any chargeable consideration for the transfer. Very often a beneficiary gives no chargeable consideration for the transfer of land under a Will. However transactions in connection with NRB Trusts may result in the beneficiary giving chargeable consideration.

A2.05   The commonest examples of such transactions, and their Stamp Duty Land Tax consequences, are as follows:

- The NRB trustees accept the surviving spouse's promise to pay in satisfaction of the pecuniary legacy and in consideration of that promise land is transferred to the surviving spouse. The promise to pay is chargeable consideration for Stamp Duty Land Tax purposes.

- The NRB trustees accept the personal representatives' promise to pay in satisfaction of the pecuniary legacy and land is transferred to the surviving spouse in consideration of the spouse accepting liability for the promise. The acceptance of liability for the promise is chargeable consideration for Stamp Duty Land Tax

---

[120] See generally Ch.38.

1452

purposes. The amount of chargeable consideration is the amount promised (not exceeding the market value of the land transferred).

- Land is transferred to the surviving spouse and the spouse charges the property with payment of the amount of the pecuniary legacy. The NRB trustees accept this charge in satisfaction of the pecuniary legacy. The charge is money's worth and so is chargeable consideration for Stamp Duty Land Tax purposes.

- The personal representatives charge land with the payment of the pecuniary legacy. The personal representatives and NRB trustees also agree that the trustees have no right to enforce payment of the amount of the legacy personally against the owner of the land for the time being . The NRB trustees accept this charge in satisfaction of the legacy. The property is transferred to the surviving spouse subject to the charge. There is no chargeable consideration for Stamp Duty Land Tax purpose provided that there is no change in the rights or liabilities of any person in relation to the debt secured by the charge.

We have also been asked about the consequences for Stamp Duty Land Tax purposes **A2.06** of a Deed of Variation made by beneficiaries after the death of the deceased person. A Deed of Variation may effect a land transaction if it alters the beneficial interests in land, for example by settling land in trust. However, placing a charge on land is not in itself a land transaction. In addition paragraph 4 of Schedule 3 FA 2003 provides that under certain conditions a land transaction effected by a Deed of Variation is exempt from charge.

2. POAT: HMRC GUIDANCE NOTES (4 October 2011 version with 2011 revision to Home Loan/Double Trust Schemes)

HMRC plan to insert a section in their internal Manuals dealing with POAT and will then withdraw this Guidance. This version shows the updates in October 2011.

INCOME TAX AND PRE-OWNED ASSETS GUIDANCE: SECTION 1

CONTENTS

INCOME TAX AND PRE-OWNED ASSETS GUIDANCE SECTION 1

Contents

1. Outline of the charge to income tax

1.1 The circumstances in which the charge applies

A2.07 Section 84 of the Finance Act 2004 gave effect to the provisions of Schedule 15 of that Act. The schedule provides for a charge to income tax on benefits received by a former owner of property. Broadly it applies to individuals (the chargeable person) who continue to receive benefits from certain types of property they once owned after 17 March 1986 but have since disposed of. The schedule has effect for the tax year 2005-06 and subsequent years.

The property within the scope of the charge can be grouped into three headings:

- Land
- Chattels
- Intangible property

If the chargeable person has either disposed of any property within these headings by way of gift or, in some circumstances, sale, or contributed towards the purchase of the property in question and they continue to receive some benefit from the property they are potentially liable to the charge. The benefit may be occupation of the land, use of the chattel or the ability to receive income or capital from a settlement holding intangible property.

The preceding paragraph may suggest that every instance where an individual may **A2.08** have disposed of, or made a contribution to the purchase of, the relevant property will come within the scope of the charge. However, there are several types of transactions relating to land and chattels that are excluded from the scope of the charge. There are also provisions exempting the relevant property from the charge where the property is subject to a charge to inheritance tax or where specific protection from inheritance tax is given by legislation.

If the income tax charge applies the Schedule contains provisions enabling the taxable benefit to be calculated. In the case of the occupation or use of land and chattels the calculation of the taxable benefit will be determined to a large extent by the proportion which the value of the chargeable person's original interest in, or contribution to the purchase, bears to the current value of the property.

The following sections provide more detail on the conditions required for the charge to arise, where the transaction may be excluded or where the property is exempted, and how the benefit is calculated. All references to 'this Schedule' refer to Schedule 15 unless otherwise specified. References to 'the charge' refer to the charge to income tax arising under Schedule 15.

1.2 What property is affected?

The conditions required for the charge to apply are virtually identical where the prop- **A2.09** erty in question is land or chattels but they differ slightly in respect of intangible property.

1.2.1 Land and chattels

The charge applies where the chargeable person occupies any land or uses or possesses **A2.10** any chattels, either alone or with other persons, and either the 'disposal condition' or the 'contribution condition' is met. Paragraphs 3 and 6 of this Schedule define the conditions.

The disposal condition

The disposal condition will apply if the chargeable person, at any time after 17 March **A2.11** 1986, owned relevant land or chattels, or other property whose disposal proceeds were directly or indirectly applied by another person towards the acquisition of the relevant land or chattels, and then disposed of all or part of their interest in the relevant land or chattels (or other property). If the disposal was an excluded transaction (see 1.3.1) the disposal condition will not apply.

Note that the disposal condition will apply to the chargeable person's occupation or use of property even if that property was never actually owned by them. If they gave away other property (apart from cash) to another person who sold such property and used these proceeds to purchase the relevant land or chattel the disposal condition is satisfied, unless it qualifies as an excluded transaction.

A disposition that creates a new interest in land or in a chattel out of an existing interest is taken to be a disposal of part of the existing interest.

The contribution condition

A2.12   The contribution condition will apply if the chargeable person, at any time after 17 March 1986, provided any of the consideration given by another person for the acquisition of an interest in the relevant land or chattel, or for the acquisition of any other property the proceeds of the disposal of which were directly or indirectly applied by another person towards an acquisition of an interest in the relevant land or chattel. As with the disposal condition, if the provision of the consideration qualifies as an excluded transaction, this condition will not apply.

It can be seen that the contribution condition can apply not only where the contribution provided by the chargeable person is directly used to purchase the relevant land or chattel but where the contribution is indirect too. If they provided all or part of the consideration (eg. a cash gift) for the purchase of property by another person, who then sold the property and used the proceeds to purchase the land occupied, or the chattel used, by the chargeable person, the contribution condition is satisfied, unless it qualifies as an excluded transaction (see 1.3.1).

HMRC do not regard the contribution condition set out in Schedule 15, para 3(3) as being met where a lender resides in property purchased by another with money loaned to him by the lender. Our view is that since the outstanding debt will form part of his estate for IHT purposes, it would not be reasonable to consider that the loan falls within the contribution condition [and therefore not reasonably attributable to the consideration (Sch 15, para 4(2)(c)], even where the loan was interest free. It follows that the 'lender', in such an arrangement, would not be caught by a charge under Schedule 15.

1.2.2 Intangible property

A2.13   In contrast to the provisions relating to land and chattels there is only one condition to be met for the charge to apply. Paragraph 8 of this Schedule defines the condition. The charge extends to intangibles that are or represent property settled or added by the chargeable person to a settlement after 17 March 1986 on terms that any income arising from the settled property would be treated under section 624 ITTOIA 2005 (income arising under a settlement where the settlor retains an interest) as income of the chargeable person as settlor and any such income would be so treated even if subsection (2) of that section did not include any reference to the spouse of the settlor. In other words, a charge under paragraph 8 is not triggered where section 624 applies only because the settlor's spouse rather than the settlor has retained an interest. The settlor in this case is, of course, the chargeable person. For example if A sets up a trust for his wife on marriage and he is excluded from all benefit there is no possibility of paragraph 8 applying. However, if he sets up a trust where his wife receives the income but he can benefit if she dies then para 8 could potentially apply subject to any relevant exemptions. In this context 'settlement' has the same meaning as it does for inheritance tax purposes. The definition of 'settlement' can be found in section 43(2) Inheritance Tax Act 1984. The fact that there is no element of bounty does not matter.
Intangible property means assets such as stocks and securities, insurance policies and bank and building society accounts. The provisions of this paragraph do not apply to land and chattels included in a settlement.

1.3 When the charge does not apply

A2.14   There are a number of situations where a charge to tax under Schedule 15 will not arise. Certain transactions are excluded from the charge and there are also exemptions from the charge where certain conditions are met.

1.3.1 Excluded transactions (Sch 15 para 10)

The concept of excluded transactions has no application to intangible property. They only serve to exclude from the income tax charge certain transactions relating to land and chattels.   **A2.15**

For the purposes of the disposal conditions relating to land and chattels, the disposal of any property is an excluded transaction in relation to the chargeable person if

- It was a disposal of their whole interest in the property, except for any right expressly reserved by them over the property, either

    i. by a transaction made at arm's length with a person not connected with them, or
    ii. by a transaction such as might be expected to be made at arm's length between persons not connected with each other.

The exclusion clearly only applies to sales of the entire interest in the property at full market value although the words "except for any right expressly reserved" would envisage the sale of a freehold reversion subject to a lease but only if it was on arms length terms.

Concern was expressed that sales of a part share of property to commercial provid-   **A2.16**
ers of equity release schemes would not qualify as an excluded transaction and an individual would be subject to the charge if he remained in occupation of the land. This concern was recognised in the Regulations to the charge which specifically exempted from the charge disposals of part of an interest in any property by a transaction made at arm's length with a person not connected with the chargeable person. Furthermore, the exemption is extended to disposals of a part share to anyone provided that they were made on arm's length terms and either took place before 7 March 2005, or took place on or after that date for a consideration not in the form of money or assets readily convertible into money.

- The property was transferred to their spouse or civil partner, or former spouse or civil partner where the transfer has been ordered by a court.

- The disposal was by way of gift (or in accordance with a court order for the benefit of a former spouse or civil partner) by virtue of which the property became settled property in which his spouse or civil partner or former spouse or civil partner is beneficially entitled to an interest in possession. The spouse or civil partner must take an interest in possession from the outset. It is not an excluded transaction, however, if the interest in possession of the spouse or civil partner or former spouse or civil partner has come to an end other than on their death. In cases where the spouse or civil partner or former spouse or civil partner has become absolutely entitled to the property, we would accept that the benefit of the exclusion is not lost.

- The disposal was a disposition falling within section 11 Inheritance Tax Act 1984 (disposition for maintenance of family).

- The disposal is an outright gift to an individual and is for the purposes of the Inheritance Tax Act 1984 a transfer of value that is wholly exempt by virtue of section 19 (annual exemption) or section 20 (small gifts).

For the purposes of the contribution conditions relating to land and chattels, the pro-   **A2.17**
vision by the chargeable person of consideration for another's acquisition of any property is an excluded transaction in relation to the chargeable person if

- The other person was their spouse or civil partner, or former spouse or civil partner where the transfer has been ordered by a court.

- On its acquisition the property became settled property in which their spouse or civil partner or former spouse or civil partner is beneficially entitled to an interest in possession. The spouse or civil partner must take an interest in possession from the outset. It is not an excluded transaction, however, if the interest in possession of the spouse or civil partner or former spouse or civil partner has come to an end otherwise than on their death unless the spouse or civil partner or former spouse or civil partner has become absolutely entitled to the property.

- The provision of the consideration constituted an outright gift of cash by the chargeable person to the other person (in this context the "other person" means the person referred to in paragraphs 3(3) and 6(3)) and was made at least 7 years before the earliest date on which the chargeable person occupied the land or had possession or use of the chattel As the earliest date the conditions can be met is 6 April 2005, any provision of consideration by way of an outright gift of cash made before 6 April 1998 will be an excluded transaction.

- The provision of the consideration is a disposition falling within section 11 of the Inheritance Tax Act 1984.

- The provision of the consideration is an outright gift to an individual and is for the purposes of the Inheritance Tax Act 1984 a transfer of value that is wholly exempt by virtue of section 19 or section 20.

1.3.2 Exemptions from the charge (Sch 15 para 11)

A2.18 Property in the estate (para 11(1)) exemption

The charging provisions in schedule 15 relating to land, chattels and intangible property do not apply to a person at a time when their estate for the purposes of the Inheritance Tax Act 1984 includes the relevant property, or other property which

- derives its value from the relevant property, and

- whose value so far as attributable to the relevant property, is not substantially less than the value of the relevant property.

Where their estate includes property which derives its value from the relevant property and whose value, so far as attributable to the relevant property, is substantially less than the value of the relevant property

- the appropriate rental value of the relevant land, or

- the appropriate amount in respect of the chattel, or

- the chargeable amount in relation to the relevant intangible property must be reduced by such proportion as is reasonable to take account of the inclusion of the property in their estate.

For example if Mr B transfers his house to a company wholly owned by him, then provided there are no loans to the company one can say that the value attributable to the company is not less than the value of the house. But if Mr B gave the house to a company which was owned 25% by his wife then the value of the 75% shares he holds would be substantially less than the value of the house. If he has lent money to the company and the company holds the house we take the view that the company's value is less than the house unless (possibly) the loan is charged on the house.

Gifts with reservation Para 11(3) exemption.

The charging provisions also do not apply to a person at a time when, for IHT pur- **A2.19**
poses, the relevant property or property deriving its value from relevant property falls
within the Gifts with Reservation provisions set out in Finance Act 1986.
  The provisions of Schedule 15 are also disapplied if the property

- would fall to be treated as subject to a reservation but for any of sections 102(5)
  (d) to (i) of the Finance Act 1986 (certain cases where disposal by way of gift is
  an exempt transfer for purposes of inheritance tax). But where s.102(5)(h) is in
  point, Schedule 15 is disapplied only when the property remains subject to trusts
  complying with the requirements of Schedule 4, para 3(1) Inheritance Tax Act
  1984 (maintenance funds),

- would fall to be treated as subject to a reservation but for subsection (4) of
  section 102B of the Finance Act 1986 (gifts with reservation: share of interest in
  land), or would have fallen to be so treated if the disposal by way of gift of an
  undivided share of an interest in land had been made on or after 9 March 1999.
  This refers to situations where the chargeable person transfers a share (usually
  50%) of their property to the donee and both the donee and the chargeable
  person continue to occupy the property, paying their share of household
  expenses, or

- would fall to be treated as subject to a reservation but for section 102C(3) of, and
  paragraph 6 of Schedule 20 to, the Finance Act 1986 (exclusion of benefit). This
  refers to situations where the chargeable person continues to use or occupy the
  property but pays full consideration in money or money's worth, or where they
  leave the property but have to move back at a later date due to an unforeseen
  change in their circumstances and are unable to look after themselves because
  of age or infirmity.

Where the contribution condition relating to land or chattels applies, paragraph 2(2)
(b) of Schedule 20 (which excludes gifts of money from the provisions that apply where
property is substituted for the original gift) should be disregarded. For example, if A
gives cash to his son and they buy a home jointly and live together then while they live
together, the POAT charge will not apply.
  Schedule 15 also contains provisions for the chargeable person to elect that the relevant property that would otherwise be subject to the charge be treated as property
subject to a reservation for the purposes of the Inheritance Tax Act 1984. If the election
is made no charge under the Schedule will apply. Full details of these provisions are
given in part 3 of these notes.

Excluded liability

Where at any time the value of a person's estate for the purposes of the Inheritance Tax **A2.20**
Act 1984 is reduced by an 'excluded liability' affecting any property, only the excess of
the value of the property over the amount of the excluded liability can be treated as
comprised in their estate for the purposes of this schedule.
  A liability is an excluded liability if

- the creation of the liability, and

- any transaction by virtue of which the person's estate came to include the relevant property or property which derives its value from the relevant property or
  by virtue of which the value of the property in their estate came to be derived
  from the relevant property, were associated operations, as defined by section 268
  of the Inheritance Tax Act 1984.

The "amount" of the excluded liability will be the face value of the debt, including any rolled up interest or accrued indexation where this has been allowed for under the terms of the agreement. For the purposes of computing the charge under this schedule, it will be sufficient for the debt to be revalued taking into account outstanding interest, or accrued indexation, at the 5 yearly valuation dates. Any reduction of the debt resulting from a repayment can be taken into account as it occurred, and may be reflected in a revised computation of the tax in the relevant year and subsequently.

1.3.3 Residence or domicile outside the United Kingdom (Sch 15 para 12)

A2.21 No charge to tax under this Schedule can arise in relation to any person for any year of assessment during which they are not resident in the United Kingdom.

If a person is resident in but domiciled outside the United Kingdom in any year of assessment, the provisions of this Schedule will only apply to land, chattels or intangible property situated in the United Kingdom.

In applying this Schedule to a person who was at any time domiciled outside the United Kingdom, no regard should be had to any property which is for the purposes of the Inheritance Tax Act 1984 excluded property in relation to them by virtue of section 48(3)(a) of that Act.

A person is to be treated as domiciled in the United Kingdom at any time if they would be so treated for the purposes of the Inheritance Tax Act 1984. Hence the deemed domicile rules will apply for the purposes of this income tax charge.

1.3.4 De minimis exemption (Sch 15 para 13)

A2.22 An exemption from charge under this Schedule applies where in relation to any person in a year of assessment (example 1), the aggregate of the amounts specified below in respect of that year do not exceed £5,000 (example 2). Those amounts are

- in relation to any land to which paragraph 3 applies, the appropriate rental value as determined under paragraph 4(2) – see 2.1 below,

- in relation to any chattel to which paragraph 6 applies, the appropriate amount as determined under paragraph 7(2) – see 2.2 below, and

- in relation to any intangible property to which paragraph 8 applies, the chargeable amount determined under paragraph 9 – see 2.3 below.

Example 1:

The £5,000 is based on the chargeable amount for the year. So if a person is chargeable throughout the whole tax year and the annual benefit is calculated at £5,000 or less they do not have to declare the benefit on their income tax return. If a person is chargeable for only part of the year, say they only become chargeable for the last six months of the year where the full annual benefit would be £8,000, their exposure for the last six months is half that and the benefit of £4,000 would be covered by the de minimis. Where two people are equally chargeable for the whole year in respect of the same property, for example a property with an annual rental value of £8,000, their benefit would be £4,000 each and would be covered by the de minimis. (On the death of one, you should consider former ownership of the property, and the terms of occupation, in deciding whether the whole or a half of the rental value is chargeable on the survivor).

Example 2:

A person is chargeable under Para 3 for a benefit from land with an annual value of £4,000 and under Para 6 for a benefit from a chattel with an annual value of

£3,000. The aggregate benefit is £7,000 and therefore not de minimis. If, in this example, an annual rental of £4,000 is paid to obtain the aggregate benefit, although the net benefit is £3,000 it is not de minimis because the annual open market rental value exceeds £5,000 and therefore the amount of the benefit (£3,000) would need to be declared. A person cannot avoid the tax charge by paying an annual rent to bring himself below £5000.

The de minimis is set against the annual benefit for intangible property after deduction of any tax paid under the headings of Para 9(1) of Schedule 15.

Example:

A person benefits from a settlor interested trust where the benefit is calculated to £7,000 (N). The fund generates income on which tax of £3,000 (T) is payable. The net amount of the benefit (N-T) is £4,000 and is de minimis.The amount of £5,000 does not represent a nil-rate band, therefore where the aggregate charge-able value exceeds £5,000 it is subject to the charge in full. When a taxpayer is chargeable for only part of a year, the £5,000 exemption is not pro-rated.

Where the de minimis exemption under paragraph 13 is not exceeded the transferor cannot make an election because he is not chargeable to income tax under Schedule 15.

1.3.5 Changes in the distribution of a deceased's estate (Sch 15 para 16)

Any disposition made by the chargeable person in relation to an interest in the estate of a deceased person is disregarded for the purposes of this Schedule if under section 17 Inheritance Tax Act 1984 the disposition is not a transfer of value by the chargeable person for IHT purposes. All dispositions covered by section 17, including disclaimers and variations where the provisions of section 142(1) Inheritance Tax Act 1984 apply, will be exempted from the charge by paragraph 16 of this schedule. [see Appendix 1 example]   **A2.23**
   For the purposes of this paragraph 'estate' has the same meaning as it has for the purposes of the Inheritance Tax Act 1984.

1.3.6 Guarantees (Sch 15 para 17)

Where a person ("A") acts as a guarantor in respect of a loan made to another person ("B") by a third party in connection with B's acquisition of any property, the mere giving of the guarantee is not regarded as the provision by A of consideration for B's acquisition of the property.   **A2.24**

INCOME TAX AND PRE-OWNED ASSETS GUIDANCE: SECTION 2

Contents

2. How to calculate the benefit subject to the charge
   2.1   Land
   2.2   Chattels
   2.3   Intangible property
   2.4   Avoidance of double charge to income tax

2 How to calculate the benefit subject to the charge

Where the provisions of paragraphs 3 (land), 6 (chattels) and/or 8 (intangible property) apply to a person in respect of the whole or part of a year of assessment, an amount   **A2.25** equal to the chargeable amount specified by the Schedule is treated as income of theirs chargeable to income tax.

Unless stated otherwise, the approach to valuing property for the purposes of Schedule 15 follows the rule for Inheritance Tax set out in section 160 IHTA 1984. In other words, it is the price that the property might reasonably be expected to fetch if sold in the open market at that time, without any scope for a reduction on the ground that the whole property is to be placed on the market at one and the same time (see paragraph 15 of this Schedule).

The valuation date for property subject to the charge is 6 April in the relevant year of assessment or, if later, the first day of the taxable period.

When valuing relevant land or a chattel it is not necessary to make an annual revaluation of the property. The property should rather be valued on a 5-year cycle. Before the first 5-year anniversary the valuation of the property will be that set at the first valuation date. Thereafter the valuation at the latest 5-year anniversary will apply.

The "relevant land" for the purposes of paragraph 4(5) is the land currently occupied by the chargeable person. Therefore, where a valuation has been carried out in respect of a charge arising under Schedule 15, and within the 5-year cycle the subject property is sold and a smaller less valuable property is purchased for occupation by the chargeable person, then a new valuation will need to be carried out which will be used for the remainder of that 5-year cycle.

The 5-year anniversary is the fifth anniversary of 6 April in the first year of assessment in which the provisions of this Schedule relating to land or chattels apply to the chargeable person. The first valuation date is the date on which the provisions of this Schedule relating to land or chattels first applied to the chargeable person. If there is an interruption in the person's use or occupation of the property and the year of a 5-year anniversary is not a taxable period, the year in which the provisions of this Schedule are applied again will be treated as the next 5-year anniversary.

Example

A is first chargeable to Schedule 15 on 6th April 2005. A valuation is obtained then. He becomes non-UK resident for three years from 6th April 2006 to 6th April 2009. The charge does not apply during this period. He returns to the UK on 7th April 2009. A new valuation is made then and this is the start of the next five year anniversary.

2.1 Land (Sch 15 paras 4 & 5)

A2.26   The chargeable amount in relation to the relevant land is the appropriate rental value, less the amount of any payments which the chargeable person is legally obliged to make during the period to the owner of the relevant land in respect of their occupation.

The appropriate rental value is

$$R \times \frac{DV}{V}$$

R is the rental value of the relevant land for the taxable period.
DV is

- Where the chargeable person owned an interest in the relevant land, the value as at the valuation date of the interest in the relevant land that was disposed of by the chargeable person or, where the disposal was a non-exempt sale, the "appropriate portion" (see final paragraphs of this section below) of that value,

- Where the chargeable person owned an interest in other property, the proceeds of which were used to acquire an interest in relevant land, such part of the value of the relevant land at the valuation date as can reasonably be attributed to the property originally disposed of by the chargeable person or, where the original disposal was a non-exempt sale, to the appropriate portion of that property,

- If the contribution condition applies, such part of the value of the relevant land at the valuation date as can reasonably be attributed to the consideration provided by the chargeable person.

V is the value of the relevant land at the valuation date.

The 'rental value' of the land for the taxable period is the rent which would have been payable for the period if the property had been let to the chargeable person at an annual rent equal to the annual value. The annual value is the rent that might reasonably be expected to be obtained on a letting from year to year if

- The tenant undertook to pay all taxes, rates and charges usually paid by a tenant, and

- The landlord undertook to bear the costs of the repairs and insurance and the other expenses, if any, necessary for maintaining the property in a state to command that rent.

The rent is calculated on the basis that the only amounts that may be deducted in respect of the services provided by the landlord are amounts in respect of the cost to the landlord of providing any relevant services. Relevant service means a service other than the repair, insurance or maintenance of the premises. In other words, if the landlord provides other relevant services, for example the maintenance of the common parts in a block of flats, that are reflected in the rent then the cost of providing those services may be deducted from the rent.

The regulations do not specify the sources from which the required valuations should be obtained. However we would expect the chargeable person to take all reasonable steps to ascertain the valuations, as they would do if, for example, they were looking to let a property on the open market.

Paragraph 4(4) introduces the concept of a 'non-exempt sale' for a disposal which **A2.27** is a sale of the chargeable person's whole interest in the property for cash, but which is not an excluded transaction as defined in paragraph 10. The 'appropriate proportion", which is relevant for ascertaining the "appropriate rental value in paragraph 4(2), can be determined using the formula

$$\frac{MV - P}{MV}$$

Where MV is the value of the interest in land at the time of the sale and P is the amount paid.

Example

A sells his house to his daughter for £100,000. It is worth £300,000. He lives in the house. In these circumstances we would say that only two thirds of the value of the house is potentially within the charge to POAT. However, since he made a gift of that two thirds we would accept that he is protected under para 11(5)(1) reservation of benefit from a charge on that two thirds. Note that if he sold part of his house to his daughter at an undervalue then the non-exempt sale provisions would not apply. So in the above example if he sold half his house to his daughter for £100,000 and that half share was in fact worth £300,000, although he would have reserved a benefit in two thirds of that half share, the £100,000 cash would be subject to POAT.

2.2 Chattels (Sch 15 para 7)

A2.28   The chargeable amount in relation to any chattel is the appropriate amount, less the amount of any payments that the chargeable person is legally obliged to make during the period to the owner of the chattel for the possession or use of the chattel by the chargeable person.

The appropriate amount is

$$N \times \frac{DV}{V}$$

N is the amount of the interest that would be payable for the taxable period if interest were payable at the prescribed rate on an amount equal to the value of the chattel at the valuation date. The prescribed rate is the official rate of interest at the valuation date. The official rate has the meaning given in section 181 of the Income Tax (Earnings and Pensions) Act 2003.

Example

> In 2005/6 A was caught by schedule 15 in respect of an earlier disposal of chattels. The chattels were worth £1,000,000 at the relevant valuation date on 6th April 2005. He will be treated as receiving a taxable benefit of 5% (the prescribed rate in 2005/06) × £1m = £50,000'
>
> Note that the charge is computed differently from land and while any rental payments made to the owner will reduce the amount on which he is chargeable, the fact that he pays a market rent for their use does not prevent an income tax charge arising. Hence if he pays £10,000 rent he will still be taxable on a £40,000 benefit. Tax is due on 31 January 2007 unless A elects.
>
> The provisions for ascertaining DV, V and defining a "non-exempt sale" and the "appropriate proportion" in relation to chattels that are similar to the provisions relating to land (see 2.1 above).

2.3 Intangible property (Sch 15 para 9)

A2.29   The chargeable amount in relation to the relevant property is N minus T.

N is the amount of the interest that would be payable for the taxable period if interest were payable at the prescribed rate on an amount equal to the value of the relevant property at the valuation date. The prescribed rate is the official rate of interest at the valuation date. The official rate has the meaning given in section 181 of the Income Tax (Earnings and Pensions) Act 2003.

T is the amount of any income tax or capital gains tax payable by the chargeable person in respect of the taxable period by virtue of any of the following provisions

- Sections 547, 660A (now s.624 of the Income Tax (Trading and Other Income) Act 2005) or 739 of the Income and Corporation Taxes Act 1988,[121]
- Sections [77 or][122] 86 of the Taxation of Chargeable Gains Act 1992

so far as the tax is attributable to the relevant property.

---

[121] Now the ITA 2007 s.721.
[122] Repealed from April 6, 2008.

Example

Mr A is the UK resident and domiciled settlor of a non-resident settlor inter-ested settlement. (You should assume that Mr A has not reserved a benefit in the settled property nor has an interest in possession in the trust and is therefore subject to the POAT charge).

The settlement comprises 'intangible' property of cash and shares with a value of £1,500,000 at the valuation date. In the tax year 2005/06 the trustees receive income of £60,000 which is chargeable to income tax on Mr A under s.624. A further £150,000 Capital Gains are realised which are deemed to be Mr A's gains by virtue of s.86 TCGA '92. In these circumstances £24,000 Income Tax is payable on the £60,000 and £60,000 in CGT on the £150,000. The tax allowance (T) against the potential Schedule 15 charge is therefore £84,000. The chargeable amount (N) is 5% (the prescribed rate in 2005/06) x £1,500,000 = £75,000. Since the tax allowance is greater than the chargeable amount, a charge under Schedule 15 will not arise.

2.4 Avoidance of double charge to Income Tax

The Schedule contains two provisions to avoid a double charge to income tax arising   A2.30
if the provisions of this Schedule apply.

- If the chargeable person is subject to the charge under more than one provision of this Schedule, i.e. if they were chargeable under paragraph 3 in respect of land they occupied and also under paragraph 8 (intangible property) if the land was owned by a company whose shares had been owned by them and had been settled on trusts of which they were a potential beneficiary, the charge will only apply to the provision that produces the higher amount of tax. If this amount does not exceed the de minimis limit no tax will be payable – the lower amount is disregarded completely.

- If the chargeable person occupies land or possesses or uses a chattel and is chargeable to income tax under the provisions of this Schedule **and** under the benefits code of Part 3 of the Income Tax (Earnings and Pensions) Act 2003, the provisions of Part 3 have priority. Tax will only be chargeable under this Schedule on any amount that exceeds the amount treated as earnings under Part 3.

INCOME TAX AND PRE-OWNED ASSETS GUIDANCE: SECTION 3

Contents

3 The election into Inheritance Tax

3.1 The effect of the election

A2.31 Paragraphs 21 and 22 give the chargeable person the option of electing that any relevant property that would otherwise be subject to the charge be treated as subject to a reservation for the purposes of Part 5 of the Finance Act 1986. If an election is made the property will not be subject to the charge under this Schedule but will instead be subject to a charge to inheritance tax on their death. The charge to inheritance tax will be incurred unless the occupation or use (of property otherwise within this Schedule) ceases permanently (and is not recommenced) at least 7 years before their death or (in the case of land or chattels) the chargeable person pays full consideration for use of the relevant property. If the person is already paying full consideration for use of the land or chattels before making an election and then elects we accept that there is no deemed PET at that point. However, if the person ceases to pay full consideration in the 7 years prior to death and is still in occupation of the property the effect of the election is that they will be subject to an inheritance tax charge on their death.

In the case of a couple who are married or in a civil partnership who jointly owned a property and who are both caught by the provisions of this Schedule, if they both wish to have it treated as property subject to a reservation, they must both make an election. An election by one cannot affect the other. Hence one of them may instead choose to pay the income tax charge in respect of their share, whilst the other may elect for a GWR under paragraph 21.

3.1.1 Land and chattels (Sch 15 para 21)

A2.32 This paragraph applies where the chargeable person is potentially chargeable for any year of assessment by reference to their enjoyment of any land or chattels for the first time. Enjoyment refers to occupation of the land and possession or use of the chattel in question.

The chargeable person may elect that the relevant property, or property substituted for it, shall not be subject to the charge but so long as they continue to enjoy it, the chargeable proportion of the property will be treated as property subject to a reservation and sections 102(3) and (4) Finance Act 1986 will apply.

The 'chargeable proportion' means

$$\frac{DV}{V}$$

where DV and V are the values detailed in section 2.1 of these guidance notes. The valuation dates to be used in these circumstances are

- in the case of property falling section 102(3) Finance Act 1986, the date of death of the chargeable person, and

- in the case of property falling within section 102(4) Finance Act 1986, the date on which the property ceases to be treated as property subject to a reservation.

When calculating DV the transactions to be taken into account should include transactions after the time when the election takes effect as well as before that time.

3.1.2 Intangible property (Sch 15 para 22)

A2.33 This paragraph applies where the chargeable person is potentially chargeable for any year of assessment by reference to any relevant intangible property for the first time.

The chargeable person may elect that the relevant property, or property which it represents or is derived from, shall not be subject to the charge but, provided certain conditions are met, it will be treated as property subject to a reservation and sections 102(3) and (4) Finance Act 1986 will apply. The conditions are

- that the relevant property, or property which it represents or is derived from, remains comprised in the settlement, and

- that any income arising under the settlement would be treated by virtue of section 624 ITTOIA (formerly 660A of the Taxes Act 1988) as income of the chargeable person.

3.1.3 Withdrawal of election

Whether it relates to land, chattels or intangible property the election may be withdrawn or amended during the life of the chargeable person at any time on or before the relevant filing date (see 3.3). If the election is withdrawn the property will be subject to the charge from the tax year 2005-06 or the year on which they would have first become chargeable under this Schedule. **A2.34**

3.2 How to elect

The election must be made on form IHT 500. Guidance on how to complete the form, together with the form itself, can be found elsewhere on this website. **A2.35**

3.3 When to elect

The election must be made on or before 'the relevant filing date', or "such later date as an officer of Revenue and Customs may, in a particular case, allow." **A2.36**

If the chargeable person was subject to income tax from the initial year of the charge, the relevant filing date is 31 January 2007. If they become subject to the charge in a later year of assessment, the relevant filing date is 31 January in the year of assessment immediately following, e.g. if they first became subject to the charge during the year 2007-08, the relevant filing date will be 31 January 2009.

The election takes effect for inheritance tax purposes from the date on which the chargeable person would have first become chargeable under this Schedule but for the election. The earliest year it can take effect is the year beginning 6 April 2005.

3.4 Circumstances in which a late election will be accepted

An event beyond the chargeable person's control

In general, we will accept a late election if the chargeable person can show that an event beyond their control prevented them from sending us the election by the relevant filing date. If the chargeable person was able to manage the rest of their private or business affairs during the period in question, we are unlikely to accept that they were genuinely prevented from delivering the election on time. **A2.37**

Examples of situations that we may consider as an event beyond the chargeable person's control include those where:

- an election was posted in good time but an unforeseen event disrupted the normal postal service and led to the loss or delay of the election.

- the chargeable person's financial records or other relevant papers were lost through fire, flood or theft and the information necessary for the completion of the election could not be replaced in time for it to be completed by the relevant filing date;

- the chargeable person was so seriously ill that they were prevented from dealing with the election before the relevant filing date and from that date to the time the completed election is sent in.

If an illness involves a lengthy stay in hospital or convalescence the chargeable person is expected to have made arrangements for completing and sending in the election on time. But there may be circumstances where this is not possible and we may accept these as a valid reason.

The serious illness of a close relative or partner will be regarded as a valid reason for a delay in electing only if

- the situation took up a great deal of the chargeable person's time and attention during the period from the relevant filing date to the date the completed election was sent in, and
- steps had already been taken to have the election ready on time;

- close relative or partner died shortly before the relevant filing date and the necessary steps had already been taken to have the election ready on time.

Other circumstances

A2.38   There may be cases where, given the overall circumstances, we will accept a late election even where the chargeable person cannot show that the reasons for the late election were beyond their control. Essentially, this will be where the chargeable person can show that they were unaware - and could not reasonably have been aware - that they were liable to an income tax charge under this Schedule, and elected within a reasonable time of becoming so aware.

It is likely that such cases will involve a number of relevant features. The chargeable person or their agent should send with their late election a full explanation of the factors that they wish to be taken into account, which may cover (but need not be limited to):

- the nature of the transaction that led to an income tax charge arising;
- when the transaction was put in place;
- the advice the chargeable person received at the time the transactions were put in place and, if later, when this Schedule came into force;
- the circumstances in which they became aware of their liability to an income tax charge under this Schedule;
- any other notable features.

We will only accept a late election where the chargeable person can show that their failure to elect by the relevant filing date is not a result of:

- their taking active steps to avoid both an income tax charge under this Schedule and an inheritance tax charge by virtue of the Gift with Reservation provisions;
- the wish to avoid committing to either an income tax charge or an election before the 31 January deadline in order to have longer to see which will be the most beneficial course of action.

Changes to HMRC guidance

A2.39   Where HMRC makes changes to its guidance - for example, because we consider that a charge to income tax under Schedule 15 arises from particular transactions that we did not previously regard as giving rise to a charge - we will accept late elections in those cases where the taxpayer can show that they elected as soon as practicable after becoming aware of our revised view.

Changes to the law

Where a change in the law results in a charge arising from particular transactions that did not previously give rise to a charge, we will accept late elections in those cases where the taxpayer can show that they elected as soon as practicable after becoming aware of the change.

A2.40

3.5 Liaison with other parts of HMRC

When we receive a late election, we will consider if sufficient information has been provided to explain why the chargeable person did not elect on time. If it has not, we will write to the chargeable person or their agent for more details.

A2.41

In all cases, we will also contact the chargeable person's income tax office and let them know we have received a late election. Whether we are then able to make a decision on the election may depend on whether or not they have opened an enquiry into the chargeable person's Self Assessment affairs, or whether they intend to do so as a result of the late election (or a combination of the election and other factors).

If there is an ongoing enquiry, or it is intended to open one, then we may not make a decision on a late election until the enquiry is concluded, in case information comes to light during the enquiry that is material to that decision. We may, though, make a decision at an earlier time if the chargeable person's income tax office is satisfied that no further information will be forthcoming that could affect it.

3.6 If we refuse to accept a late election

There is no right of appeal against the refusal to accept a late election, although a taxpayer may seek to challenge such a refusal by way of judicial review. If we do refuse to accept a late election, we will explain our reasons for doing so.

A2.42

If the chargeable person is unhappy about how we have dealt with their case, they may write to the Customer Service & Complaints Manager at:

HMRC Inheritance Tax
Ferrers House
PO Box 38
Castle Meadow Road
Nottingham
NG2 1BB.

If, having taken that step, the chargeable person remains unhappy, they can contact the Adjudicator's Office with any complaints at:

The Adjudicator's Office
Haymarket House
28 Haymarket
London
SW1Y 4SP.

The chargeable person can at any time ask their MP to refer their complaint to the Parliamentary Ombudsman. The Ombudsman will normally expect the complaint to have already been considered by HMRC and by the Adjudicator.

Contents

4 HMRC's approach to certain issues

A2.43   This section of the guidance looks at the HMRC's approach to certain practical issues regarding the pre-owned assets charge under this Schedule.

Examples of how we view particular situations can be found in Appendix 1 to the guidance material.

4.1 Domicile/residence issues

A2.44   Schedule 15 does not apply to a person who is not resident for Income Tax in the United Kingdom in the year of assessment. To be regarded as resident in the UK you must normally be physically present in the country at some time in the tax year. You will always be resident if you are here for 183 days or more in the tax year. If you are here for less than 183 days, you may still be regarded as resident for the year under other tests. If you consider that residency is an issue for you, and one that has not been previously agreed with HMRC, you may wish to consult leaflet IR20 which discusses the position in more detail. The person's domicile in this case is immaterial.

A person's domicile becomes material if that person is resident for Income Tax purposes in the United Kingdom for any year of assessment. If the person is resident in, but domiciled outside, the United Kingdom, only relevant property situated in the United Kingdom will be subject to the charge. As the treatment of domicile for the charge is the same as that for Inheritance Tax, a person's domicile under section 267 Inheritance Tax Act 1984 as well as that under general law is relevant.

A person is deemed domiciled in the United Kingdom under this section if

- they were domiciled on or after 10 December 1974 in the United Kingdom and within the three years immediately preceding the relevant time, or

- they were resident for income tax purposes in the United Kingdom in not less than seventeen of the twenty years of assessment ending with the year of assessment in which the relevant time falls.

The relevant time for the purposes of the charge will be the first day of the year of assessment in question.

Paragraph 12(3) of the schedule provides that if any property situated outside the United Kingdom became comprised in a settlement when the person settling the property was domiciled outside the United Kingdom it will not be subject to the charge.

Even if that person becomes domiciled in the United Kingdom at a later date this property will remain excluded from the charge.

Paragraph 12(3) provides that a charge under this Schedule shall not arise in relation to property regarded as excluded by virtue of section 48(3) IHTA'84. We do not regard this provision as having an impact on paragraph 11 in determining whether there is derived property in the taxpayer's estate, or GWR property in relation to him (see foreign domiciliary example in appendix).

If the person adds property, wherever situated, to the settlement after they became domiciled in the United Kingdom the additional property would be subject to the charge if it falls within the provisions of paragraphs 3, 6 or 8 of the schedule. If applicable the general exclusions and exemptions would still be available, as they would be for any United Kingdom situated property where the person is domiciled outside the United Kingdom.

4.2 Tracing and contributions

An absolute gift of cash is not subject to the inheritance tax reservation of benefit **A2.45** provisions unless the donor retains a benefit in the cash itself. For example, A, who is a partner in a business, withdraws capital from his capital account and gifts this to B, who then lends the partnership an equivalent cash sum. That sum is still on loan to the partnership when A dies. The cash sum is treated as a gift with reservation under section 102(3) Finance Act 1986. But the provisions in paragraph 2 Schedule 20 FA 1986 that enable the reservation of benefit provisions to apply to property that is substituted for the original gift do not apply where the original gift is of cash (para 2(2)(b)).

Thus, where an absolute gift of cash may later be used by the recipient to purchase property occupied or enjoyed by the donor for example, the application of the reservation of benefit rules to this property is precluded, unless the transaction can be shown to be a gift with reservation of benefit, by associated operations, of the purchased property.

These 'tracing' rules do not apply to the application of the income tax charge under this schedule. The arrangement referred to above would satisfy the contribution condition of paragraph 3(3) of this schedule if the contribution was made on or after 18 March 1986. The income tax charge would then apply unless the provision of consideration was an excluded transaction (paragraph 10(3)(2)) or it fell within one of the exemptions from the charge in paragraph 11. For the purposes of the latter paragraph and more particularly sub-paragraphs 11(5)(b), (c) and (d) the restriction on the tracing of cash gifts normally imposed for inheritance tax purposes does not apply when considering whether there is an exemption from the income tax charge (paragraph 11(8) Sch 15).

4.2.1 House sharing

Where people enter into an arrangement whereby they contribute to a shared property **A2.46** (land & buildings) owning venture and whereby they intend to and do in fact share the occupation of and the expenses arising from the occupation of the property **broadly equally**, it is not the intention of Sch 15 FA 2004 to levy an income tax charge on any part of that arrangement. Such circumstances are generally covered by section 102 B (4) FA 1986, which is made applicable to Sch15 by para.11(5)(c). However, if the situation is that the contribution made by each person is not commensurate with their respective enjoyment of the property and / or the expenses were shared unequally, the circumstances may fall to be scrutinised in the context of Sch 15 FA 2004. In such circumstances, a charge to income tax may well result.

4.3 Reasonable attribution

Paragraphs 3(2)(a)(ii) and 3(3) relating to land and 6(2)(a)(ii) and 6(3) relating to chat- **A2.47** tels apply where the chargeable person has either disposed of property and the proceeds of this disposal were used to acquire the relevant property, or where the chargeable person has contributed any of the consideration (directly or indirectly) to acquire the relevant property. Where these provisions apply it is necessary to calculate the proportion of the value of the relevant property that can be reasonably attributed to the property originally disposed of or to the consideration provided. How should this proportion be calculated?

Each case will turn on its own facts and the value of the land disposed of and its ultimate sale price, the consideration provided and the independent financial resources of the recipient will all have to be taken into account when making a reasoned judgement as to the value reasonably attributable.

For example, the disposal condition in paragraph 3(2)(a)(ii) would be met if the chargeable person transferred land to another ("X"), who later sold the land and used the proceeds to purchase a second property which the chargeable person occupies. If the land was valued at £100,000 at the date of transfer, sold for £300,000 and the new property purchased for £150,000, we would consider it reasonable to treat the whole value of the new property to be attributable to the property originally disposed of. If the value of the new property exceeds the proceeds received from the sale of the original property the proportion of the value reasonably attributable to the original property will be reduced. The value reasonably attributable to the new property cannot exceed the final value of the property originally disposed of.

If in the above example X used the sale proceeds to buy another property (Blackacre) which the chargeable person did not occupy but also used his own resources to buy a house (Whiteacre) which the chargeable person did occupy then we will not treat the value of Whiteacre as attributable to the property originally disposed of unless X had borrowed on the security of Blackacre.

If X purchases Whiteacre for £200,000 and half the purchase price (say £100,000) comes from the sale proceeds of the original land given to him and half comes from his own resources we would argue that half the value of Whiteacre was attributable to the property originally disposed of. Note that the reasonable attribution is not limited to the £100,000 originally put into Whiteacre but is half the value of Whiteacre at the relevant valuation date.

4.4 Full or part consideration

A2.48   If the chargeable person's occupation of the relevant land, or enjoyment of the relevant chattel, is for full consideration in money or money's worth, i.e. a full market rent is paid by them for their continued occupation/enjoyment, their occupation/enjoyment is not a reservation of benefit for inheritance tax purposes (para 6(1)(a) Sch 20 Finance Act 1986). This treatment is extended to the income tax charge under this schedule by virtue of paragraph 11(5)(d). Any arrangement or transaction entered into on or after 18 March 1986 where the chargeable person pays full consideration for their enjoyment or occupation of the relevant asset will not be subject to the income tax charge.

If the consideration paid by the chargeable person is less than full consideration, or if they initially pay a full consideration but, over time, this falls below market rates, the asset in question will be treated as subject to a reservation of benefit from the date the chargeable person ceased to pay full consideration. There will be no income tax charge under this schedule provided that the provisions of paragraph 11(5)(a) apply.

4.5 Sales at undervalue

A2.49   The application of paragraph 4(4) in respect of land to which the disposal conditions of paragraph 3(2) applies by virtue of a 'non-exempt sale' is restricted to sales of the whole interest in the property. If there is a sale of part only of the chargeable person's interest in the relevant land, no account can be taken of the consideration actually paid by the purchaser. (for an example see 2.1 above)

As the consideration must be paid in sterling or another currency this sub-paragraph will not apply if the consideration took another form, i.e. if one item of land was exchanged for another. Example: X exchanges his house valued at £800,000, for Y's property valued at £200,000 (Y's property in this example could be taken to mean land, a business, a right, in fact any property other than cash). X continues to live in his former property. Under the provisions of paragraph 4(4) the value of Y's property is not regarded as consideration to be taken into account, and X will be subject to a POA charge on £200,000. On X's death there will be a GWR in respect of a ¾ share of his former property, and his estate for IHT purposes will include the £200,000 from Y.

4.6 Occupation/Possession

Land

Paragraph 3 of the schedule applies where the chargeable person occupies any land that they had either both previously owned and disposed of, or contributed to its acquisition. In this context 'occupation' is construed quite widely. For example, the chargeable person would be regarded as in occupation not only if they were resident in the relevant property but also if they used it for storage or had sole possession of the means of access and used the property from time to time (see Appendix 1). The chargeable person would not be regarded as occupying a property from which they receive rental payments from the person(s) actually in occupation.   **A2.50**

If the person's occupation or use of the property is only very limited in its nature or duration it may not come within the provisions of paragraph 3. Each case will ultimately be decided on the facts and circumstances relating to it. However, in line with the HMRC's Interpretation of inheritance tax and gifts with reservation – RI 55 (November 1993) – some examples can be given of limited occupation that will not bring the chargeable person within paragraph 3. These include

- a house which is the owner's residence but where the chargeable person subsequently stays with the other person for less than one month each year or, in their absence, stays for not more than two weeks each year,
- social visits, excluding overnight stays by the chargeable person as a guest of the owner. The extent of the social visits should be no greater than the visits that may be otherwise be expected if the chargeable person had never previously owned the property, or made a contribution to its acquisition,
- a temporary stay for some short term purpose, for example, while the chargeable person convalesces after medical treatment, or they look after the owner while they are convalescing, or while the chargeable person's own home is being redecorated,
- visits to a house for domestic reasons, for example baby-sitting by the chargeable person for the owner's children,
- a house together with a library of books which the chargeable person visits less than five times in any year to consult or borrow a book,
- land which the chargeable person uses to walk their dogs or for horse riding provided this does not restrict the owner's use of the land.

More significant use of the property may bring the chargeable person within the scope of paragraph 3. Examples are

- a house in which the chargeable person stays most weekends or for more than a month each year,

- a second home or holiday home which the chargeable person and the owner both then use on an occasional basis,

- a house with a library in which the chargeable person continues to keep their own books, or which they use on a regular basis, for example because it is necessary for their work.

Chattels

A2.51   Similar considerations apply to the possession or use of previously owned chattels when the application of paragraph 6 is contemplated. Very limited or occasional use of the chattel in question will not incur an income tax charge under this schedule.

For example, a car used to give occasional lifts (i.e. less than three times a month) to the chargeable person will not be liable to the charge. But if the chargeable person is taken to work every day in the car it is likely an income tax charge will be incurred.

4.7 "Substantially less"

A2.52   Where any relevant property is included in the chargeable person's estate for inheritance tax purposes, or is subject to the inheritance tax reservation of benefit provisions, the value of that property is exempt from the charge (see 1.3.2). If other property that derives its value from the relevant property is included in the estate or is subject to a reservation of benefit the charge will not apply either. However, if the value of that derived property that can be reasonably attributed to the relevant property is "substantially less" than the value of the relevant property, only that proportion of the value of the relevant property that can be reasonably said to be included in the estate is exempted from the charge.

The term "substantially less" is not defined by the legislation but by analogy with the Capital Gains Tax taper relief rules we would regard a reduction of value of less than 20% as not substantially less for the purposes of this Schedule. If the circumstances of a particular case suggest that the "substantially less" provision should be triggered by a reduction of more or less than 20%, it will be judged on its individual merits.

Where the value of the property in the estate is substantially less than the value of the relevant property the appropriate rental value of any land, and the appropriate chargeable amounts relating to chattels or intangible property, for the purposes of this Schedule will be reduced by a reasonable proportion to take into account the property in the estate.

4.8 Double charges

A2.53   The regulations relating to the income tax charge (SI 2005 No. 724) include provisions to avoid a double charge to inheritance tax where the chargeable person elects that the gift with reservation provisions apply to the relevant property. A double charge may arise where the chargeable person makes a gift of property that is a potentially exempt transfer for inheritance tax. If that property is then liable to the income tax charge they may decide to make an election that the property is subject to the inheritance tax reservation of benefit provisions. If they then die within 7 years of the original gift a double charge to inheritance tax will arise – firstly on the original transfer that must now be aggregated with the death estate and secondly on the property subject to the reservation.

The provisions to avoid double charges effectively retain the charge on the transfer that produces the higher overall amount of inheritance tax and reduce the other transfer to nil. The application of these provisions may best be illustrated using an example.

Mr G entered into a lifetime loan scheme (or double trust scheme as it may be known) in June 2003. He sold his house to a trust fund of which he is the life tenant for £500,000. The trustees do not pay the purchase price but give Mr G an IOU instead. Mr G then makes a gift of the IOU (the outstanding purchase price) to a second trust for the benefit of his children. He remains in occupation of the property and, as the outstanding debt reduces the value of the house for inheritance tax purposes to nil (see 1.5.2 and 'excluded liability'), he is liable to the income tax charge from 6 April 2005. To avoid paying the charge he makes an election under paragraph 21 of Schedule 15 that the house is subject to the gift with reservation provisions. Mr G dies in July 2007 and the house is valued at £750,000 at that date.

As the death occurred less than 7 years after the original gift of the IOU it must be aggregated with Mr G's estate when calculating the inheritance tax liability. But the house is also chargeable on the death as a gift with reservation following the election. A double charge to inheritance tax would arise but for the double charges provisions which apply in this instance, as the gifted property (the IOU) represents the proceeds of the disposal of the relevant property (the house). The two potential charges should be considered in isolation. In these examples Mr G's estate is valued at £500,000 and the inheritance tax threshold at the time of writing of £285,000 is used.

Charge to tax using original gift

Gift now taxable		£500,000
Estate		£500,000
Aggregate chargeable transfer		£1,000,000
Taxable gift	£500,000	
Less nil-rate band	−£285,000	
Excess	£215,000	
Tax @ 40%	£86,000	
Taper relief due @ 40%	(£34,400)	
Tax payable	£51,600	
Taxable estate		£500,000
Nil-rate band used against gift		£0
Tax @ 40%		£200,000
Total inheritance tax payable		£251,600

Charge to tax using gift with reservation

Estate	£500,000
Gift with reservation	£750,000
Aggregate chargeable transfer	£1,250,000
Less nil-rate band	−£285,000
Excess	£965,000
Total inheritance tax payable @ 40%	£386,000
(apportioned between estate and gift with reservation)	

In this scenario the charge to tax using the gift with reservation will be used and the charge using the original gift will be reduced to nil by the double charges provisions and disregarded.

Further regulations were made SI 2005 No.3441 to deal with the double charges that may arise where the taxpayer decides to dismantle a "double trust scheme" and return to the position they were in prior to that arrangement.

Example:

Mrs X sells her house to a trust in which she has an interest in possession in exchange for an IOU from the trustees, which she then gifts to a second trust for the benefit of her children. The gift of the IOU is a potentially exempt transfer for IHT purposes and its value will be chargeable if the taxpayer dies within seven years of making it. The "double trust" arrangement is then dismantled e.g. by the cancellation of the IOU, so that the full value of the house will return to her estate and also be subject to IHT on her death. There is therefore the potential for a double charge.

Statutory Instrument 2005, No. 3441, therefore extended the previous regulations by introducing The Inheritance Tax (Double Charges) Regulations 2005, to provide relief from the double charge that would otherwise arise in the above example. As in the previous example, tax is calculated on the basis of the failed PET, and again with the house as an asset of the death estate. Inheritance Tax is then charged on whichever transfer produces the greater tax, and the other transfer is reduced to nil.

It should be noted that the double charges provisions will not always apply when a perceived double charge arises. In particular, if an election is made in respect of property subject to an 'Eversden' type arrangement with the result that the life tenant has made a potentially exempt transfer and the settlor's estate includes property subject to a reservation, both charges to tax are unaffected by the double charges provisions. The provisions only apply where there is a double charge in respect of the same individual.

4.9 Insurance policies

A2.54 There may be certain instances where schemes involving insurance policies fall within the scope of paragraph 8 of the schedule. However, the majority of the more common schemes should not be affected. Examples of those that might be caught can be found in Appendix 1.

Where a charge to tax under this Schedule arises, paragraph 15 of this Schedule requires that the open market value of the policy at the relevant time should be used in establishing the chargeable amount determined under paragraph 9 (see 4.10 below).

4.10 Valuation

A2.55 Paragraph 15 of this Schedule is taken from the wording of section 160 Inheritance Tax Act 1984. This provides that "Except as otherwise provided by this Schedule, the value of any property shall for the purposes of this Schedule be the price which the property might reasonably be expected to fetch if sold in the open market at that time; but that price shall not be assumed to be reduced on the ground that the whole property is to be placed on the market at one and the same time".

INCOME TAX AND PRE-OWNED ASSETS GUIDANCE: SECTION 5

How the charge applies in certain cases

Contents

- Land – straightforward gift or sale of whole
- Land – straightforward gift or sale of part
- Land – equitable interests
- Partnership interests

- Land – lease carve out (Ingram scheme)
- Chattels – lease carve out
- Land – settlement on interest in possession trust (Eversden scheme)
- Intangible property – Eversden scheme
- Land – reversionary lease scheme
- Land – death scheme involving a loan
- Land – lifetime scheme involving a loan (double trust scheme)
- Reservation of benefit in the loan: HMRC's view
- Home Loan or Double Trust Schemes
- Insurance policies
- Land - Occupation
- Post-death variations of an estate
- Foreign domiciliaries – excluded property
- Reverter-to-settlor trusts

Land – straightforward gift or sale of whole

As previously mentioned at 1.3.1 of this guidance, a disposal of property is an excluded   **A2.56**
transaction "if it was a disposal of his whole interest in property", coming within the
provisions of paragraph 10. As this wording makes clear, "his whole interest" is precisely that, and can for example be a half share, or a quarter share of the whole land
if that share is all that he owns.

In 2000 Mr A conveyed his house to his daughter Miss B. He continues to live there.

- While Mr A remains in occupation the property is subject to a gift with reservation for inheritance tax, whether or not Miss B also lives there. The income tax
  charge will not apply by virtue of paragraph 11(5)(a) of this schedule.

- If Mr A pays a full market rent to Miss B for his occupation the property will
  not be subject to a reservation by virtue of paragraph 6(1)(a) Schedule 20
  Finance Act 1986 and the income tax charge will not apply by virtue of paragraph 11(5)(d) of this schedule.

- If the conveyance to Miss B was not a gift but a sale at full market value there will
  be no transfer of value for inheritance tax. The transaction is a disposal for the
  purposes of paragraph 3(2) of this schedule but it is an excluded transaction by
  virtue of paragraph 10(1)(a). An income tax charge will not arise under this schedule.

- If Mr A had carved out a lease of his property for himself, and sold the freehold
  reversion to Miss B, that disposal will be an excluded transaction by virtue of
  paragraph 10(1)(a), provided that the sale was a transaction such as might be
  expected to be made at arms length between persons not connected with each
  other. If this provision has been met an income tax charge under this Schedule
  will not arise. The reversion is regarded as a distinct item of property, and the
  sale was of the entire interest in it. Mr A continued to occupy the house by virtue
  of his leasehold interest, which is a separate item of property. There is of course
  a "marriage" value for the two interests and a truly arms length transaction must
  take account of this along with any other factors.

Land – straightforward gift or sale of part share

In 2001 Mr A conveyed his house into the joint names of himself and his daughter   **A2.57**
Miss B. He continues to live there.

- If Miss B does not occupy the property the half-share gifted by Mr A is subject
  to a gift with reservation for inheritance tax. The income tax charge will not
  apply by virtue of paragraph 11(5)(a) of this schedule.

- If Miss B does not occupy the property but Mr A pays Miss B a full market rent for his occupation of her half-share, the half-share will not be subject to a reservation by virtue of paragraph 6(1)(a) Schedule 20 Finance Act 1986 and the income tax charge will not apply by virtue of paragraph 11(5)(d) of this schedule.

- If Miss B does occupy the property with Mr A and they share the running costs of the property in the same proportion, the half-share will not be subject to a reservation by virtue of section 102B(4) Finance Act 1986 and the income tax charge will not apply by virtue of paragraph 11(5)(c) of this schedule.

- If the conveyance to Miss B was not a gift but a sale at full market value there will be no transfer of value for inheritance tax. The transaction is, though, a disposal for the purposes of paragraph 3(2) of this schedule. Furthermore, the transaction is not an excluded transaction under paragraph 10(1). However, the Regulations provide that, as the sale took place before 7 March 2005, the income tax charge under this schedule will not apply. If the sale had taken place on or after 7 March 2005 Mr A's occupation of the half-share would be subject to an income tax charge if the appropriate rental value exceeds the de minimis limit in paragraph 13. There is a further exception that may apply if the sale was for a consideration not in the form of money or an asset readily convertible into money (see following examples).

- If the sale of a part share had been to a commercial provider of equity release schemes the income tax charge will not apply. This is so whether or not such a sale takes place on or after 7 March 2005.

Land – equitable interests

A2.58 If Miss B acquired her interest in the property by way of an equitable arrangement rather than for cash – for example, she had given up work to care for Mr A on the understanding that she would receive a share of the property in return – the income tax charge will not apply. Regulation 5

In considering whether the conditions were satisfied, we would need information about how the essential elements of the transaction had been arrived at. We do recognise that there is a substantial body of case law dealing with the circumstances in which an interest in a house is acquired in consequence of a person acting to his detriment. The Ministerial Statement had these sorts of situations in mind and we would interpret Regulation 5 accordingly. In particular, we accept that the requirement that "the disposal was by a transaction such as might be expected to be made at arm's length between persons not connected with each other" would be interpreted with such cases in mind. Where the parties had sought separate advice and acted upon it or had obtained a court order confirming the property entitlement, that would reinforce the claim that the conditions were satisfied. But we would not expect parties to such an arrangement to have done this. We recognise that detriment that the acquirer can demonstrate he has suffered can provide consideration for the acquisition of the interest and prevent the transaction from being gratuitous.

Partnership interests

A2.59 The treatment of a share of a partnership interest for Schedule 15 purposes follows that applied for IHT purposes. In other words, we do not regard the partnership interest as transparent, and the disposal of a share is unlikely to give rise to a Schedule 15 charge in any circumstances.

Land – lease carve out (Ingram scheme)

Mr R transfers title to his property to a nominee who then grants Mr R a 20-year lease **A2.60** of the property at a peppercorn rent. The encumbered freehold reversion is then gifted to his son. Mr R continues to occupy the property.

If the transfer was effected on or after 9 March 1999 the property will be subject to a reservation of benefit for inheritance tax by virtue of section 102A Finance Act 1986. No charge to income tax will then arise under this schedule.

If the transfer was effected before 9 March 1999 the arrangement is not caught by section 102A Finance Act 1986 and will be subject to the income tax charge under paragraph 3(2) of this schedule. The value subject to the charge will be the value attributable to the property actually disposed of, calculated in accordance with the formula in paragraph 4(2).

Chattels – lease carve out

The provisions of section 102A Finance Act 1986 only apply to interests in land. If **A2.61** the subject matter of the scheme referred to above is chattels rather than land, therefore, the provisions of this section do not bite. The property will not be subject to a reservation for inheritance tax regardless of when the scheme was actually effected.

It does, however, represent a disposal by the chargeable person who will be subject to an income tax charge under paragraph 6(2) of this schedule. The value subject to the charge will be the value attributable to the property actually disposed of, calculated in accordance with the formula in paragraph 7(2).

Land – settlement on interest in possession trust (Eversden scheme)

Mrs T transfers 95% of her property to a settlement for the benefit of her husband for **A2.62** his life. On his death the property passes to a discretionary trust, of which she is one of the potential beneficiaries. She remains in occupation of the property.

If the transfer was effected on or after 20 June 2003 the property will be subject to a reservation of benefit by Mrs T for inheritance tax by virtue of section 102(5A) Finance Act 1986 and the income tax charge will not apply.

If the transfer was effected before 20 June 2003 the property will not be subject to a reservation of benefit. If the interest in possession of Mrs T's husband continued until his death the property will not be subject to the income tax charge because, although the disposal condition in paragraph 3(2) is met, the transaction is an excluded transaction by virtue of paragraph 10(1)(c).

However if her husband's interest in possession ended during his lifetime the transaction will not be excluded because of paragraph 10(3) and the property disposed of will be subject to the income tax charge. The value of the property will be determined by the formula in paragraph 4(2).

Intangible property – Eversden scheme

Intangible property may also be settled on Eversden-type scheme, i.e. the chargeable **A2.63** person settles cash on interest in possession trusts for their spouse or civil partner, which the trustees then invest in a bond. If the terms of the settlement fall within the definition in paragraph 8 of this schedule similar results to the scheme involving land referred to above apply.

For example, if the spouse or civil partner's interest in possession ends during their lifetime and the property is now held on discretionary trusts of which the settlor is one of the potential beneficiaries, the income tax charge will apply under paragraph 8 if the settlement was effected before 20 June 2003. The charge will be calculated with reference to paragraph 9 of this schedule.

It should be noted that the excluded transaction provisions have no application with regard to intangible property so paragraph 10(1)(c), which may have a bearing in respect of certain Eversden-type schemes involving land, has no relevance here.

If the settlement was effected on or after 20 June 2003 the property is subject to a reservation of benefit for inheritance tax by virtue of section 102(5A) Finance Act 1986 and the income tax charge will not apply.

Land – reversionary lease scheme

A2.64 A reversionary lease scheme, typically, is an arrangement where a donor grants a long lease of his property for say 999 years to the proposed donee, and the lease does not take effect until some future date. An example of this would be where Mr V, who has owned his house since 1990, grants a 999-year lease to his daughter in 1998 but not to take effect until 2018. Mr V continues to occupy the property.

Such schemes entered into before 9 March 1999 are not gifts with reservation of benefit so long as the lease contains no terms that are beneficial to the donor (see example below), and the income tax charge will apply.

For reversionary lease schemes entered into on or after 9 March 1999 HMRC had previously held the view that section 102A Finance Act 1986 would apply to them because the donor's occupation would be a "significant right in relation to the land". If that analysis were correct, the reservation of benefit rules would apply and there would be no income tax charge. However, HMRC now consider that where the freehold interest was acquired more than 7 years before the gift, the continued occupation by the donor would not be a significant right, and therefore, contrary to its previously held view, section 102A cannot apply to the gift because of section 102A(5). If the donor grants a reversionary lease within 7 years of acquiring the freehold interest, section 102A may apply to the gift depending on how the remaining provisions of that section apply in relation to the circumstances of the case.

Bear in mind, however, that, whenever the freehold interest was acquired, a gift may be a gift with reservation of benefit under section 102 Finance Act 1986 if the lease contains terms beneficial to the donor. An example of this may be where the lessee covenants to pay the costs of maintaining the property.

Where the GWR provisions do not apply it will nevertheless be regarded as a disposal of an interest in the relevant land under paragraph 3(2) of Schedule 15, and the charge to income tax will apply, calculated in accordance with the formula in paragraph 4(2), unless the donor elects into the reservation of benefit provisions.

Land – death scheme involving a loan

A2.65 Mr and Mrs S own a house in equal shares as tenants in common. Under the Will of Mr S, assets not exceeding the 'nil-rate band' for inheritance tax pass into a discretionary trust, of which Mrs S is one of the potential beneficiaries. The remainder of his estate passes to Mrs S. Following the death of Mr S in June 2005 his executors transferred his half share of the property to Mrs S and, in return, she executed a loan agreement equivalent to the value of the half-share. No inheritance tax is payable.

The income tax charge under this schedule will not apply here. As Mrs S did not own her husband's share at the relevant time and did not dispose of it the disposal conditions in paragraph 3(2) do not apply. If she did not provide Mr S with any of the consideration given by him for the purchase of his half share the contribution condition in paragraph 3(3) will not apply either. Even if she had provided him with some or all of the consideration the condition will still not apply as it would have been an excluded transaction under paragraph 10(2)(a). In the final scenario, however, the debt would not be allowable for inheritance tax on the death of Mrs S by virtue of section 103 Finance Act 1986.

Land – lifetime scheme involving a loan (double trust or home loan scheme)

There are a number of variants of this scheme – one of the more straightforward types is referred to in the Double Charges section of this guidance (see 4.8) – and if there is no reservation of benefit in the property concerned, the Income Tax charge under this Schedule will apply. (Guidance on whether the loan may be chargeable under the Inheritance Tax reservation of benefit provisions is given at the end of this section).

A2.66

As the chargeable person is usually still occupying the house as the life tenant of an interest in possession trust the exemption in paragraph 11(1) of this Schedule would appear to prevent the charge from applying. However, the value of the property in the estate will be reduced by the debt now owned by the trustees of the second trust in the scheme. For example if the house is valued at £500,000 and the debt is valued at £400,000, only the net value of £100,000 is chargeable to Inheritance Tax. In this scenario the concept of excluded liabilities will apply – paragraphs 11(6) and 11(7) of this Schedule (see 1.3.2). The exemption in paragraph 11(1) is restricted to the value of the relevant property that exceeds the amount of the excluded liability – in this example £100,000. The remaining part of the house will be subject to the charge – in this example four-fifths of the appropriate rental value.

If, in the above example, the debt is expressed as a percentage of the value of the house, the Income Tax charge would be payable on the same percentage of the rental value.

Reservation of benefit in the loan – HMRC's view (revised 2011)

The essence of many of these schemes involves the chargeable person(s) (the vendors) selling their home for full value to a newly formed trust (trust 1) with the sale proceeds left outstanding on loan. An IOU for the loan is gifted to a second trust (trust 2) for the benefit of the vendor's family. The vendor(s) continue to occupy the property under the terms of trust 1, and the loan is repayable to trust 2. Where the loan is repayable on demand, HMRC's view is that the loan will be property subject to a reservation until such time as the trustees call in the loan. The reason for this is that if trust 2 had called in the loan, trust 1 would have been forced either to sell the home to repay the debt, or to seek finance from elsewhere. If the house were sold, then the vendor(s) would have been unable to occupy it under the terms of trust 1. In order to avoid the need for a sale, trust 1 would have had to find a third party willing to lend 100 per cent of the value of the property on the basis of a covenant by the trustees, and security over the house. Even if such borrowing could be obtained, which must be extremely doubtful, it would be prohibitively expensive. Trust 1 could only justify taking on such borrowing if they were financed by the vendor(s) (the life tenants) who would be benefiting from the property by residing in it. On the foregoing basis it is considered that the trustees of trust 2, in not calling in the loan, have enabled the vendor(s) to retain a significant benefit in it, and therefore that the debt was not enjoyed to the entire exclusion of any benefit to the vendor(s) by contract or otherwise.

A2.67

A variant of the scheme described above is where the terms of the loan provide that the debt is only repayable at a time after the death of the life tenant. Since, unlike the position with loans repayable on demand, the loan can not be called in by the loan trustees, it was previously thought that, in general, these schemes would not be caught as gifts with reservation. However, it is now HMRC's view that as the steps taken under the schemes are a pre-ordained series of transactions a realistic view should be taken of what the transactions achieve, as a composite whole, when considering how the law applies. This follows the line of authority founded on W T Ramsay v IRC [1981] 1 AER 865. The composite transaction has the effect that the vendor has made a 'gift' of the property concerned for the purposes of s.102 FA86 and has continued to live there. The property is therefore subject to a reservation of benefit.

It is considered that this approach will apply to all variants of the home loan or double trust scheme and, where it produces a higher amount of tax, will be applied in preference to the position outlined above where the loan is repayable on demand.

The correct approach to double trust or home loan schemes is subject to litigation. If it is held that a reservation of benefit does subsist in the property, the Income Tax charge will not arise. The implications for the Income Tax charge whilst waiting the outcome of the litigation is explained in Income Tax and pre owned assets guidance section 6.

If the loan and not the house is subject to a reservation of benefit this does not mean the vendor can avoid paying Income Tax. The reservation of benefit is in the loan not the house and he has still made a relevant disposal of the house which is subject to an excluded liability and which therefore reduces his estate. Reserved benefit property does not form part of someone's estate while he is alive. (see ss102(3) and (4) FA 1986). In these circumstances if A does not wish to pay the Income Tax charge the debt should either be appointed back to him or written off (in which case the excluded liability ceases to reduce the value of his estate and there is no Income Tax charge from the date the debt is written off or appointed back to him) or he should elect (in which case there is no Income Tax charge at all).

Insurance policies

A2.68   The settlor effects a discounted gift scheme comprising a gift into settlement with certain "rights" being retained by them. The retained rights may, for instance, be a series of single premium policies maturing (usually) on successive anniversaries of the initial investment or on survival, reverting to the settlor, if they are alive on the maturity date, or the settlor carves out the right to receive future capital payments if they are alive at each prospective payment date. The gift with reservation provisions do not apply.

In the straightforward case where the settlor has retained a right to an annual income or to a reversion under arrangements, that right is not property within paragraph 8 as the trustees hold it on bare trust for the settlor. A bare trust is not a settlement for inheritance tax purposes. The settlor is excluded from other benefits under the policy and so this schedule does not apply.

There may be more complex cases where the settlor's retained rights or interests are themselves held on trust. But that would normally be construed as being a separate trust of those benefits in which the settlor had an interest in possession, and no charge to tax will arise under this schedule by virtue of paragraph 11(1).

Even if, in less common cases, the paragraph 11 provisions did not apply so as to exempt the case from charge completely, any charge under this schedule would apply by reference to the value of the rights held on trust for the settlor, not by reference to the value of the underlying life policy.

- The settlor effects a policy and settles it on trust for the benefit of others. He then makes a substantial interest free loan to the trustees, repayable on demand. The trustees use the loan to purchase more policies, and make partial surrenders each year to pay off part of the loan.

This arrangement is not a gift with reservation for inheritance tax. The settlor is not a beneficiary of the trust itself and the making of the loan does not constitute a settlement for the purposes of inheritance tax. No charge to tax will arise under this schedule.

Pension Policies

A2.69   Pension policies may typically provide pension and lifetime benefits for the scheme member, and other benefits that are payable on death at the discretion of the scheme trustees. It is considered that the pension and other lifetime benefits would either represent unsettled property or a trust separate from that on which the death benefits are held. In the arrangement described, both parts can be treated as mutually exclusive and therefore provided the scheme member could not benefit from the trusts governing the death benefits, a charge under this schedule will not arise.

A charge under Schedule 15 will not arise in relation to approved pension arrangements or, from 6 April 2006, pension arrangements under registered schemes. Neither are such arrangements caught as GWR's, as HMRC's statement of practice 10/86 makes clear. Non-registered schemes do not fall within the statement of practice, and so may well come within Finance Act 1986, in which event, the same dispositions would not come within Schedule 15.

Business trusts (or partnership policies)

In some cases, policies are taken out on each partner's life solely for the purposes of providing funds to enable their fellow partners to purchase his/her share from the partner's beneficiaries on their death. The partner is not a potential beneficiary of his/her "own" policy. In such circumstances, a charge to tax under paragraph 8 of this schedule will not arise. **A2.70**

However, in many cases, the partner retains a benefit for themselves, for example they can cash in the policy during their lifetime for their own benefit. In such cases, even if the arrangement is on commercial terms so that it is not a gift with reservation for inheritance tax, the trust is a settlement for inheritance tax purposes and a charge to tax under paragraph 8 will arise.

The valuation of a partner's, or settlor's, interest in a policy for the purposes of paragraph 8 of Schedule 15 should be his share of its open market value as at 6 April each year. That valuation will be relevant for determining the amount of charge for that year of assessment.

Where the policies are term assurances, in the vast majority of cases the policyholder will be in normal health, and therefore it is likely that the chargeable amount, as calculated under paragraph 9 of Schedule 15, will have little marketable value and will fall below the de minimis exemption in paragraph 13. Therefore, a policyholder in normal health at the valuation date may assume that he will survive beyond the term of the assurance, and complete his tax return accordingly. However, in circumstances where the policyholder has been advised that their state of health is such that it casts doubt on their survival to the end of the term of assurance (i.e. there becomes a realistic prospect of the policy paying out and therefore having a material market value), then consideration should be given to obtaining actuarial advice about the value of the policy.

Pre 18 March 1986 Policies settled on trusts

A charge under Schedule 15 does not arise where, before 18th March 1986, a life policy has been contracted and settled on trusts from which the settlor can benefit, even where premiums are paid after this date. **A2.71**

Land – Occupation

Example 1: Mr A gives his house to his daughter in 1987. The disposal condition of paragraph 3(2) has been met. He occupies the property along with his daughter, and later when she moves out, on his own. This was 'relevant land' at all times since 1987, for the purposes of paragraph 3(1), of Schedule 15. It is protected from POAT throughout because it is subject to a reservation of benefit. **A2.72**

Example 2: Mr A sells his house and makes a cash gift to his daughter, who uses the money towards the purchase of a house of her own also using some of her own money. The contribution condition of paragraph 3(3) is met. Within 7 years of this gift he moves in with his daughter and occupies a self-contained part of the house, and has the means of access to the remainder of the property, and actually uses it from time to time. E.g. storing furniture there. In these circumstances, the whole property is considered to be "relevant land" for the purposes of paragraph 3(1). However, while he occupies with his daughter there is no POAT charge due to para 11(8). Had Mr A moved into occupation more than 7 years after the cash gift, the provision of that consideration will be an excluded transaction, coming within paragraph 10(2)(c) of Schedule 15.

Example 3: The scenario is that of example 2, however Mr A does not have means of access to the rest of the house, and his access to the self-contained part is via an external door. He visits the rest of the house only when invited e.g. for Sunday lunch. He stores no furniture there. In this example, only the self-contained part is "relevant land" for the purposes of paragraph 3(1).

Post-death variations of an estate

A2.73 Mrs W is bequeathed a house, which she occupies, under her husband's Will. She completes a deed of variation within two years of her husband's death altering the terms of the Will so that the house passes to her son instead. The deed of variation is effective for inheritance tax purposes as the provisions of section 142(1) Inheritance Tax Act 1984 apply. Although she continues to occupy the house the income tax charge will not apply by virtue of paragraph 16 of this Schedule.

The provisions of paragraph 16 will also apply if the deed of variation referred to above had merely changed Mrs W's absolute interest in the property to a life interest in possession, with her son as remainderman. If her life interest is terminated during her lifetime (but more than two years after her husband's death) and she continues to occupy the property the income tax charge will not apply provided that the deed of variation satisfied the provisions of section 142(1) Inheritance Tax Act 1984. In any event, if her life interest was terminated after 21 March 2006 and she continues to occupy the property the reservation of benefit provisions will apply. (S102ZA FA 1986 as amended by Finance Bill 2006).

Foreign Domiciliaries – excluded property

A2.74 An arrangement that is not uncommon is where a foreign domiciliary settles a trust which owns a UK house through a foreign registered company. The shares in this company (and any loan made to it) are excluded property, coming within the provisions of section 48(3) IHTA '84. Paragraph 12(3) provides that Schedule 15 will have no application to such assets. However in considering the application of paragraph 11 in respect of the house he occupies, the operation of paragraph 12(3) does not mean that the shares (or any loan made to the company) are automatically disregarded in determining whether, for the purposes of paragraph 11, there is derived property which is in the taxpayer's estate or GWR property in relation to him. In these circumstances we would accept that the exemptions in paragraph 11 can apply to the foreign domiciliary.

Reverter-to-settlor trusts

A2.75 Legislation introduced in the 2006 Finance Bill will, from the 5th December 2005, prevent property gifted by the donor but still enjoyed by him as a beneficiary of a reverter-to-settlor trust from escaping an income tax charge under Schedule 15.

Previously the donor could gift property that would then be settled back on him on trusts which allowed him to continue to enjoy the property, but which on his death would revert back to the settlor (the original donee). The property was (for trusts established pre Budget 2006) treated as part of the donor's estate for IHT purposes, but on his death was excluded from a charge to IHT under sections 53 and 54 IHTA'84, as it reverted back to the settlor (the original donee). A charge under Schedule 15 would also not arise because the property was still regarded as part of the donor's estate for IHT purposes.

The new legislation will allow a Schedule 15 charge to apply in situations where the former owner of an asset (or a person who contributed to its acquisition) enjoys the asset under the terms of a trust, and the trust property reverts to the settlor – or to the spouse or civil partner, widow, widower or surviving civil partner of the settlor.

INCOME TAX AND PRE-OWNED ASSETS GUIDANCE: SECTION 6

Home loan or double trust schemes (revised 2011)

As explained in Income Tax and pre owned assets guidance section 5, HMRC is now **A2.75A** of the view that none of the variants of the home loan or double trust scheme succeed in circumventing the reservation of benefit rules. This will affect taxpayers who have put such a scheme into place and are now paying Income Tax in respect of a pre-owned asset. If it is held that a reservation of benefit does exist in the property that was sold to the trust in which the taxpayer retained a life interest, the pre-owned assets (POA) charge will not apply by virtue of paragraph 11(5)(a) Schedule 15 FA'04.

Whilst a decision on the correct treatment of home loan or double trust schemes is awaited, HMRC's approach is that those paying the POA charge as a result of setting up such scheme should continue to do so, in the knowledge that should HMRC's view prevail, all the Income Tax that has been paid under the POA charge will, subject to a claim being made, be repaid (with interest) irrespective of any time limits for repayment that might otherwise apply.

The benefits of taking this option are that it:

- Continues to collect the tax that the taxpayer considers is due.

- Involves no extra costs in making repayments of now, only to have to recover the tax plus interest later should HMRC's view not prevail.

- Involves little or no extra work to regularise the position should HMRC's view not prevail; as the income tax has been paid correctly.

- Avoids any complications should the taxpayer die before the position is settled. If the income tax was repaid, it would only be on the basis that exemption from the POA charge applies. This would mean that the property is subject to a reservation of benefit and the Inheritance Tax due on the estate should be paid accordingly.

Where the taxpayer who put the scheme into place has died and has paid the POA charge either whilst they were alive or through their personal representatives after death, HRMC's approach is that this position too should be left undisturbed until a decision is handed down, as this minimises the future costs and inconvenience should HMRC's view not prevail.

As far as Inheritance Tax is concerned, personal representatives should pay the tax that they consider is due. If this is less than the full amount that would be payable should HMRC's view prevail, they may choose to make a payment on account of the additional Inheritance Tax that would be due so as to reduce future interest charges. Any subsequent repayment of income tax will form an additional asset of the estate.

Where an estate has been settled on the basis of HMRC's previous view of the law, neither the Inheritance Tax nor the POA charge will be re-opened.

3. POAT: CIOT/STEP EXCHANGE OF CORRESPONDENCE WITH HMRC (2005)

Question 1: Deeds of Variation

A2.76   You will recall that the problem relates to the drafting of paragraph 16. This states *"any disposition made by a person ("the chargeable person") in relation to an interest in the estate of a deceased person is to be disregarded for the purposes of this Schedule if by virtue of section 17 IHTA 1984 the disposition is not treated for the purposes of inheritance tax as a transfer of value by the chargeable person"* . Section 17 provides that a variation or disclaimer to which section 142(1) applies is not a transfer of value.

A2.77   The difficulty is that this wording and the Revenue statement in the guidance notes leaves the position ambiguous in certain cases where a spouse of the Deceased has effected a deed of variation. Suppose Mr X dies leaving his estate to his widow who within two years of Mr X's death enters into a deed of variation under which instead of taking her husband's estate absolutely, she decides to settle it on trusts under which she retains a continuing interest in possession with remainders over to her children. This would be a valid deed of variation for inheritance tax purposes, but will it qualify for favoured treatment under the POA Regime? Under section 49(1) of IHTA the widow will, by virtue of her interest in possession under the new settlement, still be treated as owning her husband's estate with the result that she will not make a transfer of value.

A2.78   On a narrow reading it is arguable that the deed is not a transfer of value by virtue of the protection under section 49(1) not by virtue of the protection under section 17 of the 1984 Act and therefore para.16 does not apply to protect the gift. This would matter if the widow's interest later ends but she continues to occupy the property in question.

A2.79   We would argue that section 17 simply states that a variation or disclaimer to which section 142 applies is not a transfer of value anyway and the fact that the variation may not be a transfer of value for some other reason does not matter. Hence the variation is within section 142(1) (assuming all other conditions are met) and the widow is protected from a POA charge under paragraph 16 irrespective of whether her interest in possession later terminates.

A2.80   Is this though the Revenue view? You will understand that deeds of variation setting up a defeasible life interest trust for the spouse are extremely common and will have been done on a very extensive basis since 1986. We recall that in Consultation it was agreed that all deeds of variation falling within section 142(1) would be protected by paragraph 16.

Answer

A2.81   You are concerned here about the situation where an instrument of variation, which takes effect for IHT under section 142(1) IHTA, does not give rise to a transfer of value in any event. For example, Mrs X, who is entitled to her husband's estate under his will, within 2 years of Mr X's death, settles her absolute entitlement on trusts in which she retains a beneficial interest in possession. This is not a transfer of value for IHT purposes, even without the intervention of section 17 IHTA.

We would agree that section 17 applies to all disclaimers or variations that come within section 142(1), even if the variation may not be a transfer of value in any event. As a result, I can confirm that all instruments of variation to which section 142(1) IHTA applies will come within the protection afforded by paragraph 16 of Schedule 15. We will supplement the guidance at 1.3.5 to make this clear. **A2.82**

Question 2: Cash gifts

The position with cash gifts was discussed on several occasions. Suppose a cash gift is made by Jason to his son in January 1997. His son later buys a house and Jason then goes into occupation in March 1998. He satisfies the contribution condition and will be caught under the POA regime unless it is an excluded transaction. The cash gift is an excluded transaction under para.10(2)(c) if "*the consideration constituted an outright gift of money by the chargeable person* (here Jason) *to the other person and was made at least seven years before the earliest date on which the chargeable person met the condition in paragraph 3(1)(a)* " [our underlining]. **A2.83**

The chargeable person is Jason but the earliest date on which he could meet the condition in paragraph 3(1)(a) is when the legislation comes into effect on 6th April 2005. Since the cash gift was made more than seven years before he satisfies the condition it would appear that he is protected from a POA charge despite the fact that he went into occupation shortly after the cash gift. In effect this would mean that such cash gifts made prior to 6th April 1998 will be protected from a POA charge under para.10(2)(c). **A2.84**

We are aware that Martin Haigh suggested this view was correct and that as a matter of policy the Revenue would not object if in effect only cash gifts post-April 1998 are within POA. However the guidance notes imply otherwise although the position is not explicitly stated. What view does the Revenue take on this point? **A2.85**

Answer

Having considered the matter further, we are content to accept that a person could not meet the condition in paragraph 3(1)(a) or paragraph 6(1)(a) of Schedule 15 before the legislation came into effect on 6 April 2005. On this basis, we agree that paragraph 10(2)(c) has the effect of excluding from a charge under Schedule 15 outright gifts of cash made before 6 April 1998. Again we will clarify the guidance on this point.

Question 3: Occupation

At the meetings last year, the meaning of occupation was discussed at some length and there is some helpful commentary on this in the guidance notes. However, it has not dealt with the position where someone gave away the whole land but now occupies only part of the gifted property. **A2.86**

The classic case is where mother has (say) carried out an Ingram scheme on a large estate comprising main house and lodge but then as she becomes elderly has moved out of the main house into the lodge. Her son moves into the main house and mother moves her furniture and possessions down to the lodge and genuinely does not occupy the main house. A less extreme example would be where someone gives away the whole of their house but then ends up living in the self-contained basement flat (a not uncommon scenario in London). **A2.87**

In these circumstances the disposal condition has been satisfied because the person owned an interest in "the relevant land" and has disposed of that interest and occupies "the relevant land". The charge appears to be in relation to the relevant land i.e. the whole amount gifted and there is no provision for pro rating just because someone is now occupying a small part of what they gave away. **A2.88**

A2.89   At the meeting the Revenue said that if someone gave away the whole of an estate but in the end only reserved a benefit by occupying a small self-contained part they would only be subject to reservation of benefit on that part and suggested that the same approach would be adopted for pre-owned assets. Is this in fact the approach that you are going to take? Again many people need to know this in order to calculate their income tax liabilities.

Answer

A2.90   As you say, our guidance notes, principally at paragraph 4.6, set out our views on what constitutes occupation for the purpose of considering whether and to what extent a charge under Schedule 15 arises. This general approach should be applied when considering what constitutes the "relevant land" where an owner has disposed of the whole property but may now be occupying only part of it.

A2.91   Inevitably the facts of individual cases will be relevant in determining the extent of the land that is being occupied by a former owner. As we say at paragraph 4.6, we would construe "occupation" quite widely and believe it goes beyond residence or physical occupation. Thus, in a case where a former owner of property was residing in part of it and had possession of the means of access to the rest of it and used it from time to time, I think we would regard him as occupying the whole property for the purposes of paragraph 3(1) of Schedule 15. On the other hand, where a former owner of property occupies a self-contained part of it and has no access to the remainder which is occupied by others, it would seem reasonable to regard the "relevant land" for paragraph 3(1) purposes as being confined to the self-contained part.

A2.92   I am sure there is scope to expand the guidance on this topic, perhaps by including some examples in the Appendix. We will give this some thought.

Question 4: Funding the POA Charge

A2.93   Some people, particularly those who have carried out *Ingram* schemes, do not want to dismantle the scheme and lose the inheritance tax savings. The donee or other members of the family are prepared to put the donor in funds to pay the income tax each year in order to enable the donor to continue living in the house and to preserve the inheritance tax position. The question then is whether the reimbursement by the donee of the donor's income tax bill could be regarded as a reservation of benefit in respect of the original gifted property. We are talking here only about existing schemes which were carried out before the donor was aware of the possibility of a pre-owned assets charge. Hence the original gift was not in anyway conditional on the donee paying the donor's income tax liability.

It is thought that there is no reservation of benefit and the position is similar to the analysis on cash gifts. In order to avoid a reservation of benefit, in effect, three conditions must be satisfied:

> 1. Possession and enjoyment of the gifted property must be bona fide assumed by the donee. That limb is not in dispute - the donee enjoys the gifted property (the freehold reversion in the case of *Ingram* schemes) irrespective of whether or not the donee pays some cash to the donor to reimburse him for income tax. The original gift was not conditional on the donee paying the tax.

> 2. Section 102(1)(b) states that there is also a reservation of benefit if the actual property itself is not enjoyed to the entire exclusion or virtually to the entire exclusion of the donor. Again the donor (assuming the particular scheme in question has been properly implemented) is excluded from the actual property gifted - say the freehold reversion or the loan or IOU of a double trust scheme.

3. The question then is whether the second limb of section 102(1)(b) is breached i.e. the property has not been enjoyed to the entire exclusion of any benefit to the donor by contract or otherwise. Is the payment by the donee of the donor's income tax liability a collateral benefit conferred on the donor?

It is certainly of benefit to the donor that the donee pays the income tax liability. However, one surely needs to do more than simply identify the benefit which the donor has received from the donee. What one has to show is that the benefit actually entrenches in some way upon the donee's possession and enjoyment of the gifted property or is linked to the property. Otherwise any benefit that the donee gave to the donor in the future however unrelated to the gift would breach the rules.

So if a gift was made of the house now in such a way as to avoid the reservation of benefit provisions but the donee was under some obligation to pay the income tax charge, that might entrench upon the donee's possession and enjoyment of the gifted property and be a reservation of benefit but an undertaking made now by the donee to reimburse the donor for income tax in respect of a gift made some years ago would surely not be a problem.

4. Finally do the associated operations provisions incorporated by para 6(1)(c) alter this analysis: is this a benefit which the donor has obtained by virtue of associated operations of which the disposal by way of gift is one?

The benefit is not enjoyed as part of the arrangements under which the original gifted property was made. The gift of property was made before pre-owned assets regime was envisaged.

The view that there is no reservation of benefit seems to be borne out by the case law. In Oakes *v* Commissioner of Stamp Duties for New South Wales [1954] AC 57 the judicial committee said that it is necessary not merely to find that the settlor continued to enjoy substantial advantages which had some relation to the gifted property but one must consider the nature and source of each such advantage separately. It was specifically held there that the use of the income from the children's shares of the property for their maintenance and education during their minority may have been an advantage to the donor but did not impair or diminish the value of the gift of land to the children or their enjoyment of it.

In the light of this are you able to confirm that if the donee pays the POA income tax liability of the donor in relation to schemes effected prior to the announcement of the pre-owned assets income tax regime in December 2003 there would be no reservation of benefit for the donor?

Answer

I agree with all of your analysis save for a question mark on your paragraph 4. What you say is correct in the context of section 268(1)(b) Inheritance Tax Act 1984, which will be relevant in the great majority of cases. If, however, the source of the income tax monies was derived from the pre-owned assets it may be that section 268(1)(a) could be relevant and a GWR claim be possible.

A2.94

4. POAT: CIOT/STEP COP 10 LETTER – QUESTIONS AND ANSWERS (2006)

SUMMARY OF TOPICS COVERED

Valuation issues

1. Moving properties
2. Calculation of POAT on home loan schemes
3. Reduction of debt on home loan scheme
4. Calculation of POAT charge where mix of intangibles/house on home loan schemes
5. Discounts on DV
6. Commercial group life policies
7. Partnership life policies
8. Pension life policies
9. Pre-1986 life policies
10. Scope of Reg.6: election and home loan schemes/double charges

Home Loan Schemes

11. Assigning debt back to settlor
12. Valuing the excluded liability
13. Commercial borrowing by trust
14. Reservation of benefit on loan. Does POA apply?
15. Which home loan schemes work?

Election

16. Election by one spouse only
17. Effect of election on home loan schemes and s.102(4)
18. Spouse exemption and home loan schemes
19. New elections on change of property
20. Life interest settlor-interested trusts and para.8
21. Elections on home loan schemes—whole house or only on debt part
22. Elections where only part of gifted property caught
23. Late elections
24. Wrong payment of income tax

Equity release

25. Regulation 5 and part disposals. Promissory estoppel

1. VALUATION ISSUES

1.1 Regulation 4 provides that in relation to land and chattels the valuation is by **A2.95** reference to the first valuation date and this valuation is used for a period of 5 tax years. This is favourable to taxpayers where the gifted land increases in value. For instance, in relation to existing Ingram and reversionary lease schemes, one takes the value of the gifted propery as at 6th April 2005 even though the gifted interest (the DV) is likely to increase in value over the next 5 years.

However, the position is unclear where the property is sold and the taxpayer moves to a smaller house.

Example 1

> A Gave £300,000 to his son in April 2000. Son later uses all the cash to purchase a house and contributes none of his own funds. A goes into occupation of house in April 2002. He falls within the contribution condition and is subject to the POA charge from 6th April 2005. The house is worth £1 million on 6th April 2005. He pays income tax in 2005/6 by reference to the rental value of the house.
>
> In 2007 Son sells house and buys a new one for £500,000 into which A moves. In these circumstances there seems to be no mechanism for assessing A to income tax on the rental value of the new house.

Does A continue to pay income tax on a hypothetical rental value of the original £1 million house until 2010?

Similar problems can arise if A moves into a discrete part of the house and only occupies that part, letting the remainder. If he has not done this by 6 April 2005 it would appear that his charge is not reduced for the next 5 years.

Question 1

A2.96   Do HMRC interpret the legislation in this restrictive way or do they take the view that the relevant land for the purposes of para 4(5) is the land that the taxpayer actually occupies and therefore a new valuation is done when the taxpayer first occupies the smaller property or the smaller part? This is on the basis that a new taxable period then starts in which that property or part is the relevant property. The Regulations would then apply on the basis that the first day of such occupation is the first day of the taxable period.

HMRC answer to question 1

A2.97   The "relevant land" for the purposes of paragraph 4(5) is the land currently occupied by the chargeable person. A new valuation should be done when the occupation of that property starts, and we would intend that the new valuation should then be used for the remainder of that 5-year cycle.

1.2 Particular valuation problems arise in relation to the double trust or home loan schemes.

Example 2

B sells his house to a trust in which he retains an interest in possession ("the property trust") and the purchase price of £900,000 is left outstanding as a debt. B gives away the debt. Assume that B is caught by POA and that the debt is an excluded liability. The house is worth £1 million on 6th April 2005 and the debt is £900,000. Based on HMRC's example in the Appendix of the Guidance Notes, B pays income tax on 9/10 of the rental value attributable to the house.

Question 2

A2.98   Can HMRC confirm that this is the view taken? i.e. that where the debt is only a percentage of the value of the house the taxpayer pays income tax on the same percentage of the rental value?

There seems no express provision in para 11 to allow for a percentage reduction in the charge in the event that the property is subject to a debt but has some excess value. We assume from the example in the Appendix that HMRC interpret the interaction of paras 11(6) and (1) and in particular the words "to the extent that" to mean that if the value of the property exceeds the excluded liability by 10% there is a 10% reduction in the charge under para 4.

HMRC answer to question 2

A2.99   We confirm that, where, as in Example 2, the debt is only a percentage of the value of the chargeable property, income tax is payable on the same percentage of the rental value. As you suggest, this follows from the interaction of paras. 11(6) and (1). As far as subsequent valuation cycles are concerned, we would adjust the proportion of the rental value charged to reflect any adjustment to the value of the chargeable property.

1.3 If the debt was reduced to £500,000 (by partial repayment or by writing off) then it would appear that B would pay income tax from that date on half the rental value of the property and that Regulation 4 does not prevent a reduction in the income tax charge on repayment of the debt even if this is done half way through the five year period. Half the value of the property is now deemed to be comprised in the person's estate under para 11(1) and there is no charge on this part.

Question 3

Can HMRC confirm that if the debt "affecting" the property is reduced for any reason the income tax charge reduces by the same proportion even if this reduction occurs during the five year period? **A2.100**

Suppose in the above example the home loan scheme had been effected by a married couple H and W but only H later added the £500,000 to the property trust to enable the property trustees to repay part of the loan. Are we correct to assume that the loan is pro rated so that the excluded liability is reduced for H and W by £250,000 each rather than the repayment just reducing H's share of the excluded liability?

HMRC answer to question 3

We confirm that the income tax charge would be reduced by the same proportion by which the debt affecting the property was reduced. In view of the reference in paragraph 11(6) to "at any time", we confirm that the charge would be reduced even if the reduction of the debt occurred during the 5-year period. **A2.101**

Where the scheme had been effected by a married couple, H & W, we assume that the answer would depend on the precise terms of the property trust. But, assuming that the property is held by H & W equally, the addition by H of £500,000 to the trust would diminish his estate by £250,000 (an exempt transfer to W). On that basis, we would agree that the excluded liability for H & W would be reduced by £250,000 each.

1.4 Suppose that the house is sold by the property trust and the trustees then purchase a smaller property for say £600,000. The debt of £900,000 is not repaid but left outstanding and the spare cash of £400,000 is invested in intangibles to produce an income for B. On a literal reading of Regulation 4 it would appear that B still pays income tax on the market rental of the original property as at the April 2005 valuation (reduced by one tenth). **A2.102**

Question 4

We assume that HMRC consider that once a smaller property is purchased during the five year period, what is valued for the purposes of the POA charge under para 4 is indeed that smaller property. Please confirm. **A2.103**

HMRC answer to question 4

Assuming that the intangibles are held on the original trusts and that the debt of £900,000 is left outstanding, we agree that the smaller property would be within the charge under paragraph 4 and that the intangibles would come within paragraph 8. **A2.104**

In line with the answer to Q1, we would suggest that the paragraph 4 computation should be based on the value of the newer, smaller property with the intangible property being charged under paragraph 8. The parts chargeable under paragraphs 3 (as quantified in accordance with paragraph 4) and 8 should then be arrived at by apportioning the loan rateably between the two components. However if the loan was originally secured specifically on the land, one would calculate the paragraph 3 charge simply by reference to the value of the new, smaller property with the balance of the loan being charged under paragraph 8.

1.5 Suppose husband has given away his 50% share in the home originally owned jointly with his wife. The gift was into an Eversden settlement and is now caught by **A2.105**

POA. In these circumstances, professional surveyors consider that the 50% share should be discounted and hence "the DV" figure be reduced.

Questions of valuation are not specifically addressed in the Guidance Notes but we assume that HMRC accept that, if professionally so advised, a discount for joint ownership would be appropriate for the DV figure.

Question 5

A2.106 Can a standard percentage discount be agreed with HMRC in relation to jointly held interests?

HMRC answer to question 5

A2.107 We agree that the 50% share of the house chargeable under POA should be valued on normal open market principles for the purposes of ascertaining DV. This would imply a discount, but not sure that we can agree a standard discount in advance, any more than we would do for "normal" IHT purposes.

A2.108 1.6 There are difficulties in valuing settled insurance policies caught by para 8. For example, in their Guidance Notes HMRC take the view that life policies settled on a commercial basis by partners or shareholders for each other will be caught under POA if the settlor retains an interest. The settlor will often retain such an interest since there is usually a provision that the life policy will revert to the business owner if he leaves the business before death.

Question 6

A2.109   (a) In these circumstances how does one value the intangible property?

   (b) Would it be based on the surrender value of the life policy?

HMRC answer to question 6

A2.110 Our current view is that a group policy taken out for the partners or shareholders is within the scope of the paragraph 8 charge, because each partner, as settlor, is not excluded from benefit. This appears to be the case whether or not each partner can benefit on leaving the partnership and whether or not the only benefits that can accrue to a partner are those arising on the death of a partner. As far as valuation is concerned, we would expect the value of the policy to be its open market value at the relevant time, not its surrender value.

A2.111 1.7 The comments on life policies taken out by partnerships and other businesses contained at the end of the revised Guidance Notes seem to go directly against Government policy which is to encourage such arrangements (as illustrated by the relieving legislation introduced in FA 2003 s539A for income tax purposes).

Question 7

A2.112 Are HMRC considering an extra statutory concession to relieve such arrangements from the POA charge?

This would appear to be appropriate given that such arrangements are commercial with no donative intent and therefore outside the reservation of benefit provisions.

If the only interest of the settlor in the trust is that the life policy reverts to the settlor if he leaves the business before his death, do HMRC agree that the settlor's interest under such arrangement can be regarded as similar to his interest under discounted gift schemes and therefore outside the POA charge—see 8.1?

HMRC answer to question 7

An Extra Statutory Concession is not in view, as far as we are aware, and we do not **A2.113** think it is for us to comment on whether one would be appropriate. As far as the settlor's interest in the policy is concerned, We are doubtful that there is an exact analogy with Discounted Gift Schemes as you suggest. While this would depend on the terms of the policy concerned, it is not clear to us that the value of the settlor's contingent interest and the value of the interests of the surviving partners can be sufficiently distinguished in the way that we have agreed they can be for Discounted Gifts.

1.8 We should be grateful for some clarification of HMRC policy in respect of **A2.114** pension policies (whether retirement annuity or personal pension policies and whether approved or unapproved). Typically such policies provide that retirement benefits and other lifetime benefits such as a payment on demutualization are held for the absolute benefit of the individual member with death benefits being held on discretionary trusts.

Question 8

HMRC take the view that the analysis on such policies is similar to discounted gift **A2.115** schemes and that the retirement benefits represent separate unsettled property? See 8.1. Can HMRC confirm that the POA Regime does not apply to such pension arrangements? Does their view change if the individual member can benefit from the discretionary trust over the death benefits?

HMRC answer to question 8

(a) As a general rule, the pension and other lifetime benefits for the scheme member **A2.116** and the benefits paid on death are mutually exclusive. On this basis, we would agree that an analogy can be drawn with discounted gift schemes so that the pension benefits would either represent unsettled property or a trust separate from that on which the death benefits are held.

(b) On the basis of the above, we would agree that the POA regime would generally not apply to pension arrangements, where the individual scheme member was not able to benefit from the discretionary trust governing the death benefits.

Valuation problems arise where a settlor takes out a life policy and writes it on trust **A2.117** pre-18 March 1986. The reservation of benefit rules did not apply then and so he is often a potential beneficiary. Suppose that for the last 20 years he has been paying the premiums on such policy. Section 102(6) FA 1986 provides an exemption from reservation of benefit in respect of premiums paid post 17 March 1986 where the policy was taken out before 18 March and the premiums increase at a pre-arranged rate. However, there has been concern that premiums paid post 17 March 1986 would appear to be within the POA Regime.

Question 9

(a) Do HMRC consider that such policies are caught? We would suggest that premi- **A2.118** ums paid since 17 March 1986 are not themselves additions to the settled property if paid direct to the insurance company but merely maintain the value of the settled property and therefore are not strictly within the wording of para 8.

(b) We understand from correspondence in Taxation that HMRC believe POA does apply and apportion the premiums between pre 18 and post 17 March 1986.

(c) In the light of the comment in (a) above will HMRC reconsider their views in respect of payments on such policies?

HMRC answer to question 9

A2.119 In our view, it is correct to regard premiums paid after 17 March 1986 in respect of settled policies as additions to the settled property and so within paragraph 8 if the settlor is a potential beneficiary. As you suggest, the proportion of the settled property chargeable under paragraph 8 is arrived at by apportioning the premiums between those paid pre -18 and post -17 March 1986.

2. HOME LOAN OR DOUBLE TRUST SCHEMES

A2.120 We have a number of specific queries on home loan schemes and would welcome clarification with regard to the following points.

A2.121 2.1 We welcome the provision for the avoidance of a double charge in the event of the GWR election being made. However, as discussed below, the election still has a number of uncertainties. Furthermore Regulation 6 is defective in a number of respects.

Firstly, it should not be limited to gifts into settlements (see Regulation 6(a)(ii)) since in some cases the gift of the debt was outright to a child rather than into trust.

A2.122 2.2 Secondly, Regulation 6 should not be limited to a gift of property representing "the proceeds of the disposal of relevant property".

Many schemes proceeded on the basis of taxpayers lending money to the trustees by a loan agreement and the trustees then using that money to buy the house. The loan does not represent the proceeds of the house. There should be relief in these circumstances.

Question 10

A2.123 Will HMRC in practice apply Regulation 6 to relieve all home loan schemes from a potential double charge where the donor has died having made an election or is Regulation 6 being amended to cover the above points?

HMRC answer to question 10

A2.124 We note your view that Regulation 6 of SI 2005/724 is not wide enough to cover all cases where a double charge may arise after the taxpayer has elected. At this stage, we cannot give an assurance that we will apply the regulation more widely than its terms indicate, but we will pass on your views on this point.

A2.125 2.3 One of the ways that taxpayers are unravelling home loan schemes is to appoint the debt to the children who then assign it back to the settlor thus losing all inheritance tax benefits but at least ensuring (provided that the children took interests in possession under the original trust) that if the settlor dies within 7 years of the original PET, there is relief under the Double Charges Regulations. (This course is often preferable unless double charges relief is to be given for the release of a debt.)

Although there is still an excluded liability in existence, the excluded liability does not appear to be relevant any longer in that it does not reduce the value of the parents' estates under paragraph 11(6) albeit it affects the value of the house. The wording in para 11(6) refers "to the value of the person's estate" and we assume that this means the value of someone's total estate for inheritance tax purposes.

Therefore the fact that the loan continues to reduce the value of the house does not mean that the loan is caught under para 11(6).

Question 11

A2.126 Is the analysis in 2.4 correct (a) in stating that there is relief under the Double Charges Regulations if the children assign the debt back to the settlor and the settlor dies within

7 years of the original gift of the debt and (b) that para 11(6) is no longer in point once the assignment has been effected back to them because the debt no longer reduces the value of their estates?

HMRC answer to question 11

We agree with your analysis in paragraph 2.4(a): the circumstances you have in mind **A2.127** seem to be covered by Regulation 4 of SI 1987/1130. As far as paragraph 2.4(b) is concerned, we agree that paragraph 11(6) would no longer be in point.

2.4 Para 11(6) refers to "the amount of the excluded liability". We seek clarification **A2.128** as to whether this is the face value of the debt (including any rolled up interest or accrued indexation) or the commercial value of the debt.

Example 3

C entered into a home loan scheme. The house is worth £2 million and the debt is repayable on C's death, is linked to the RPI and has a face value of £1.9 million. Its commercial value is discounted due to the fact that it is not repayable until C's death. Allowing for the fact that the debt is linked to the RPI, its market value would be, say, £1.2 million but increasing.

In these circumstances the question is, whether the excess value which is treated as part of C's estate and therefore protected from the POA charge under para 11(1) is:

   (i) £100,000
   (ii) £800,000 or
   (iii) some other figure such as £100,000 less accrued indexation?

Question 12

What is HMRC's view regarding the amount of the excluded liability in the above **A2.129** scenario?

It would appear that the correct view is to take the commercial value of the debt as reducing the person's estate because in reality the property is "affected" by this amount of debt. Obviously the POA charge would become higher as the commercial value of the debt increased towards the end of the donor's lifetime and hence less property exceeded the value of the debt.

HMRC answer to question 12

In our view, the fact that paragraph 11(6) refers to the "amount" of the excluded liabil- **A2.130** ity indicates that it is the face value of the debt, including any rolled-up interest or accrued indexation, that is relevant. In practice, we would only seek to adjust the value of the debt to take account of interest and indexation at the 5-yearly valuation dates, though we would be prepared to allow any reduction of the debt resulting from any repayment be taken account as it occurred and to be reflected in a revised computation of tax in the relevant year and subsequently.

2.5 A common scenario (both for foreign and UK domiciliaries) is where cash is **A2.131** settled into an interest in possession trust for the donor life tenant. The trustees then buy a house for the donor to live in using the gifted cash plus third party borrowings. Although not a home loan scheme, the legislation appears to affect such arrangements.

Example 4

E settles cash of £200,000 into an interest in possession trust for himself in 2003. The trustees purchase a property worth £500,000, borrowing £300,000 from a bank. There are other assets in the trust which can fund the interest but the borrowing is secured on the house which E then occupies.

In these circumstances, one would not expect a POA charge. There is no inheritance tax scheme since the property is part of E's estate and the borrowing is not internal. One would argue that E's estate still includes the house and therefore protection is available under para 11(1). The difficulty is that on one view the loan is an excluded liability within para 11(7) reducing E's estate, albeit it is a loan on commercial terms with a bank.

We would argue that the relevant property for the purposes of para 11 is simply the value of the property net of the commercial borrowing. As this is part of E's estate there is no POA charge.

Question 13

A2.132 Is the above analysis correct?

HMRC answer to question 13

A2.133 We agree with your analysis in paragraph 2.6.
A2.134   2.6 In those home loan schemes where HMRC consider that there is a reservation of benefit in the debt, it would appear that the taxpayer can still face a POA charge—because he has made a disposal of land which is subject to an excluded liability. The fact that he has reserved a benefit in the debt does not make the debt part of his estate such that the excluded liability can be ignored.

Question 14

A2.135 Where there is a reservation of benefit in respect of the loan can HMRC confirm that they would not expect the taxpayer to pay both POA and IHT and that the inheritance tax charge would take priority?

HMRC answer to question 14

A2.136 We agree with the analysis at 2.6. (Even if there is a reservation of benefit in the loan for IHT purposes, it is the land, not the loan, which is the relevant property for POA purposes and para.11, Sch.15 in particular. And although the loan may be property subject to a reservation for IHT purposes, it remains an excluded liability within paras.11(6) and (7), Sch.15 for the purposes of the POA charge.) As matters currently stand, there is no provision to disapply the charge that may arise under Sch.15.

Question 15

A2.137 Will any statement be issued by HMRC as to which home loan schemes of the various types seen they consider do not work for inheritance tax purposes?
    Otherwise taxpayers may self-assess and pay the income tax charge, thinking to preserve the inheritance tax savings but be unaware of HMRC's view.

HMRC answer to question 15

A2.138 We will shortly be issuing updated technical guidance that will include material to identify the circumstances in which we consider a reservation of benefit in the loan exists. Hopefully, this will give some indication to providers of schemes affected whether or not we consider their scheme to be one where a reservation of benefit in the loan exists. This in turn may make it easier for providers to help any clients (or ex-clients) who seek their assistance over completion of their tax return.

3. THE EFFECT OF THE ELECTION

3.1 In the case of a married couple who have sold their jointly owned house to the property trust and given the debt to a second trust, it is assumed that one of them can elect to come within the gift with reservation rules and one can choose not to elect: i.e. it is not necessary for both to make the election.

A2.139

Question 16

Will HMRC please confirm this point?

A2.140

HMRC answer to question 16

As far as we can see, it is possible for one spouse and not the other to elect under paragraph 21.

A2.141

3.2 There is some uncertainty about the effect of the election because para 21 does not as such deem there to be a gift for inheritance tax purposes but simply states that the property is treated as property subject to a reservation.

A2.142

Furthermore in para 21(2)(b)(ii) it is stated that only sections 102(3) and (4) are to apply and not specifically section 102(8) which brings in Schedule 20.

We assume that the wording in para 21(2)(b)(i) referring to the property being treated as property subject to a reservation of benefit for the purposes of the 1986 Act does not limit the scope of the reservation of benefit provisions so that only sections 102(3) and (4) apply.

Example 5

> D effected a home loan scheme. He elects into reservation of benefit and then in April 2010 starts to pay full consideration for the use of his house. Has he made a deemed PET at that point (under s102(4)) and is he protected from a reservation of benefit charge provided he continues to pay a market rent? We assume that HMRC take the view that para 21(2)(b)(ii) does not narrow the effect of 21(2)(b)(i) and the let-outs in para 6 Schedule 20 apply.

Question 17

> (i) Please confirm that on making an election there is a reservation of benefit in the house and not the debt in respect of the home loan scheme and that, once an election is made, all the provisions relating to reservation of benefit in FA 1986 and in particular Schedule 20 apply?

A2.143

> Please also confirm the position on deemed PETs in the example above where the person who elects is already paying full consideration.

> (ii) Suppose A elects into GWR in respect of his home. The house is then appointed back to him absolutely (i.e. the arrangement eg. a home loan scheme, is unscrambled). In these circumstances the reservation of benefit has ceased but the house is back in their estates anyway. Is there a deemed PET under s.102(4)? FA 1986.

HMRC answer to question 17

> (i) We confirm that on making an election under paragraph 21, there would be a reservation of benefit in the house, not the debt in respect of the home loan scheme. In our view, the reference to section 102(4) Finance Act 1986 in paragraph 21(2)(b)(ii) envisages circumstances in which the property ceases to be subject to a reservation and there is nothing to suggest that these would not

A2.144

include circumstances in which the provisions of paragraph 6, Schedule 20 Finance Act 1986 would be in point.

(ii) By analogy with the view we have taken for "actual" gifts with reservation, we believe that the tax treatment for the purposes of Sch.15 would depend on whether or not the taxpayer starts to pay full consideration for the continued use of the house or chattel immediately on making an election or after a period of time. We think it would only be in the latter case that there would be a deemed PET under section 102(4) FA 1986.

(iii) In our view, the provisions of s.102(4) do, in terms, apply, by virtue of para.21(2)(b)(ii), when the taxable property is appointed back to the chargeable person. But the value of A's estate would not be decreased by this deemed PET. On that basis we do not regard the deemed PET by A has having any practical consequences for A, because it would have no value.

A2.145 3.3 We seek clarification of the position on home loan schemes when both spouses elect and one then dies.

Example 6

H and W have effected a home loan scheme. They both elect. On H's death his share in the house is worth £400,000 but is perhaps entirely subject to debt. His share passes to W but the value of her estate is not increased because H's share is subject to the debt. Hence the concern is that the effect of the election is to make H's share taxable immediately on his death by virtue of s102(3) as to £400,000.

In our view it would appear that the spouse exemption is available on the first death since the deceased's share in the house passes to the surviving spouse under the terms of the property trust or otherwise becomes comprised in the survivor's estate as IHTA 1984 requires. This is so even if the value of the debt equals or exceeds that of the house.

Question 18

A2.146 (a) Do HMRC agree with this interpretation? (See also Statement of Practice E13.)

(b) Is HMRC's view that:

1. full spouse exemption is available even if the debt equals the value of the house; or
2. full spouse exemption is available provided the spouse's estate is increased by even a small amount; or
3. spouse exemption is only available to the extent the value of the house exceeds the debt?

HMRC answer to question 18

A2.147 In the circumstances outlined in Example 6, the starting point is the disposals of property that H & W have each made in order to effect a home loan scheme. If then they elect under paragraph 21 and H then dies, we think the effect would indeed be to bring £400,000 into H's estate immediately before his death for IHT purposes by virtue of section 102(3) Finance Act 1986. As far as we can see, there is no scope for spouse exemption as regards this chargeable item as the property disposed of by H in setting up the home loan scheme did not become comprised in the estate of W. Nor, having regard to paragraph 21(3) can we see any scope for reducing the amount charged under section 102(3) FA 1986 by the amount of the debt. Of course, H's estate for IHT purposes will also include his interest in possession in the property trust. We imagine this would consist of his share in the house, subject to the debt. Undoubtedly spouse exemption would be available, but only to the extent that the value of H's share in the house exceeded the debt.

3.4 As noted in 1.5 above there are technical difficulties if the property is sold **A2.148** after an election. Assume that a smaller replacement property is acquired by the trustees but the debt is not repaid. Accepting that the replacement property will be within the para 3 land charge, what of the surplus cash which has been invested in intangibles?

Example 7

Suppose the taxpayer moves out of the home and has made an election. He purchases a smaller replacement house a week later. The balance of the proceeds are invested and he enjoys the income as life tenant.

Question 19

(a) Does a new election need to be made at that point under para 22 in relation to **A2.149** the intangibles part and/or under para 21 in relation to the smaller home?

(b) What happens if the time limits for making the election on the original property have passed?

HMRC answer to question 19

Para 21(2)(a) states that when an election has been made the income tax charge won't **A2.150** apply to the taxpayer's enjoyment of the relevant property "or of any property which has been substituted for the relevant property". From the "any property" we take that to include not only property in the form of land and chattels but also intangible property even though that is subject to a separate paragraph for the election. The equivalent measure in Para 22(2)(a) uses the phrase "or any property which represents or is derived from the relevant property". We think this difference is necessary as it may not be possible to "substitute" intangible property for other intangible property.

But we assume you can convert intangible property into something different and we think an election under Para 22 would similarly cover cases where intangible property is converted into land or chattels and would otherwise be subject to an election under Para 21. So as the paragraphs cover substitutions/derivations, we do not think we require a fresh election when the underlying property changes. In any event, if the taxpayer apparently has an interest in possession in the intangible property, would not paragraph 11(1) be in point assuming a home loan scheme was not involved? As we would not be looking for a fresh election, we assume part (b) of the question is not relevant.

3.5 It may be said that the deeming provision in section 660A(1) TA 1988 (now s624 **A2.151** ITTOIA 2005) is irrelevant to interest in possession trusts where the settlor is life tenant given that there is no question of the income being taxed as that of any other person as envisaged in that provision.

Question 20

Does the para 8 charge apply to cash held in such a trust on the basis that this is a **A2.152** settlor interested trust to which section 660A TA 1988 (now s.624 ITTOIA 2005) is therefore applicable or does the fact that the settlor is the life tenant of this trust preclude the application of section 660A? This would obviously affect the election mechanism. This is relevant to home loan trusts now holding intangibles.

HMRC answer to question 20

A2.153   We are not sure that we can see how the application of section 624 ITTOIA 2005, and therefore paragraph 8 is explicitly precluded per se.

Question 21

A2.154   3.6 When an election is made on a double trust scheme, is this election in respect of the entire land or just the part subject to the debt? Can HMRC confirm the former is correct given that in para 21(3) the DV/V formulation would mean that the entire value of the land equals DV?

HMRC answer to question 21

A2.155   It seems to us that the relevant property in terms of Schedule 15 generally and specifically for the purposes of the election would be the land in its entirety.

A2.156   3.7 The election mechanism does not satisfactorily deal with the position where part of the original gifted property is not within the Regime and part is.

Example 8

Andrew gives his house on interest in possession trusts for spouse Emma in 2000. Her interest in possession is terminated in all but 20% of the fund. Hence the gift ceases to be an excluded disposal in relation to 80%.

Andrew decides to make an election rather than to pay the income tax charge. In these circumstances is the chargeable proportion 100% (being the DV/V figure) or 80%?

It is assumed the latter on the basis that Andrew is chargeable only by reference to his enjoyment of the 80% not by reference to his enjoyment of 100% (see wording in para 21(1)(a)). Hence "the relevant property" on which he can elect is only 80%.

Question 22

A2.157   Do HMRC agree with this analysis?

HMRC answer to question 22

A2.158   We would agree that, in the circumstances set out in Example 8, the "relevant property" would be 80% of it. The use of the formula DV/V, as ordained in paragraph 21(3), would simply mean that all of the 80% would be treated as the chargeable proportion.

A2.159   3.8 Where a taxpayer is doubtful as to whether he is caught by the Regime in the first place he can put full details of his arguments on the additional information pages of the return and presumably would then be treated as having made full disclosure and be protected from a discovery assessment. Of course, even if a taxpayer does obtain finality in one tax year, this will not prevent HMRC raising an enquiry in later years if the taxpayer continued to self assess on the basis that the Regime does not apply to him.

Suppose HMRC do not enquire into the taxpayer's return for 2005/6. In 2006/7 he continues to self assess on the basis that he is outside the Regime; HMRC make an enquiry and it is established that the taxpayer was wrong to self assess on the basis that no income tax was due under the Regime. Possibly a court case clarifies the position or there is a change in legislation which is deemed to have always had effect.

In these circumstances the taxpayer will have missed the deadline for making the election (he first became chargeable under the Regime in 2005 and therefore needed to elect by January 31, 2007) and will have to pay income tax going forward or else try to unravel the arrangement.

Question 23

Will the taxpayer be able to make a late election in these circumstances?   **A2.160**

HMRC answer to question 23

Whether the taxpayer is protected from a discovery assessment in the circumstances   **A2.161**
described will depend on whether the argument he presents is tenable and if not whether he could then be considered negligent in submitting an insufficient self assessment. Tenability would need to be judged against the practice generally prevailing at the time the return was made. We would consider that the taxpayer was bound by the time limit for that year of assessment for making an election regardless of whether HMRC made an enquiry relating to that year or a later year. It would be for the taxpayer to demonstrate that he had a reasonable excuse for failing to make an election in time.

In a situation where a court decision overturns the previous practice or legislation makes changes which is deemed to have always had effect, then the taxpayer would be protected for earlier years and he would be chargeable only from the time the change in practice or legislation was made. It would not be unreasonable to assume he would then have until the deadline for that year of assessment to make an election.

3.9 Another difficulty arises if the taxpayer wrongly pays income tax on the basis   **A2.162**
that he was within the Regime when in fact he was not. This is particularly pertinent in relation to home loan schemes where HMRC appear to accept that some work and some do not.

Question 24

What position will be taken by HMRC in these circumstances? Will the taxpayer (or   **A2.163**
his personal representatives) be able to make a claim for repayment of the tax paid under a mistake of law for 6 years from the date of overpayment?

HMRC answer to question 24

Providers of certain home loan or double trust schemes are already aware that HMRC   **A2.164**
takes the view that the gifts with reservation of benefit legislation applies to them. We will include in our guidance information about the circumstances in which we consider the GWR legislation applies.

If the taxpayer has made an excessive self assessment by virtue of error or mistake in his return then he can claim relief under section 33 of the Taxes Management Act 1970. The time limit for doing so is 5 years from the 31 January following the year of assessment to which the erroneous return relates.

4. REGULATION 5 AND PARA.10(1)(A)—EQUITY RELEASE SCHEMES

4.1 The relief given in Regulation 5 seems unnecessarily restrictive as a matter of prin-   **A2.165**
ciple and we do not fully understand the Ministerial Statement or the Guidance Notes on this. It is suggested that where a child moves into the house to care for an aged parent and acquires an equitable interest in the shared home in consideration for providing caring services, the parent is protected from a POA charge under Regulation 5(b). However, such a disposal does not seem to be by way of a transaction at arm's length between persons not connected with each other. These are not normal com-

mercial arrangements. It is difficult to put a value in advance or even retrospectively on what the services to be provided will actually be worth in terms of a share in the house.

Question 25

A2.166   What evidence is required to satisfy Regulation 5(b)? It will be difficult to establish what would be regarded as an arms length transaction without a court hearing which would generally only occur in the event of a dispute.

HMRC answer to question 25

A2.167   In considering whether regulation 5(b) was satisfied, we would need information about how the essential elements of the transaction had been arrived at. We do recognise that there is a substantial body of case law dealing with the circumstances in which an interest in a house is acquired in consequence of a person acting to his detriment. The Ministerial Statement had these sorts of situations in mind and we would interpret Regulation 5 accordingly. In particular, we accept that the requirement that "the disposal was by a transaction such as might be expected to be made at arm's length between persons not connected with each other" would be interpreted with such cases in mind. We would not therefore expect the parties to have sought separate advice and acted upon it or to have obtained a court order confirming the property entitlement. We recognise that detriment that the acquirer can demonstrate he has suffered can provide consideration for the acquisition of the interest and prevent the transaction from being gratuitous.

A2.168   4.2 Suppose that something that had not been a readily convertible asset and was therefore protected under para 5(1)(b) subsequently became a RCA under ITEPA. We are concerned that a transaction that was previously protected could now lose such protection.

Question 26

A2.169   What happens if the definition of readily convertible asset in ITEPA 2003 changes?

HMRC answer to question 26

A2.170   If the definition of "readily convertible asset" in ITEPA 2003 were to change, I think we would need to review the appropriateness of Regulation 5(2). We are not aware that any such alteration is in prospect, however.

A2.171   4.3 There are difficulties where land is held under one title but is physically discrete—for example, two fields. Suppose father sells one of the two fields to his son for full value and continues to farm in partnership over that field. Does father have a pre-owned assets problem.

Question 27

A2.172   Is the father protected under para 10(1)(a)? Can it be treated as a sale of whole if son becomes beneficially and legally entitled to the entire field even though father is selling only one of the fields?

HMRC answer to question 27

A2.173   The first issue is what constitutes "the property" for the purposes of paragraph 10(1)(a). We think it would be possible to regard each of the two discrete fields as "the property", so the disposal of one of them would be a disposal of the whole interest in that asset. As far as your example is concerned, a sale by father to son would be within paragraph 10(1)(a)(ii) on the basis that father receives a full open market price for his land.

4.4 It is not uncommon for taxpayers to enter into transactions whereby they carve out a lease for themselves and sell the freehold reversion at full market value. Indeed some commercial equity release schemes are structured along these lines. In earlier informal discussions HMRC appeared to agree that the wording in para 10(1)(a) did cover such arrangements but the Guidance Notes suggest there has to be a disposal of the taxpayer's entire interest without any reservation of a lease. The provisions on non-exempt sales of course use a different wording.

A2.174

Question 28

Can HMRC confirm that a disposal of a taxpayer's whole interest in the property "except for any right expressly reserved by him over the property" as set out in para 10(1)(a) is intended to cover a transaction where F has carved out a lease for himself and sold the encumbered freehold reversion for full market value to his son? If so, will the Guidance Notes be amended to confirm this?

A2.175

HMRC answer to question 28

In our view, paragraph 10(1)(a) does cover the scenario you envisage in 4.4. We will amend the Guidance Notes.

A2.176

5. REVERSIONARY LEASE ARRANGEMENTS

5.1 In the case of reversionary lease arrangements, the taxpayer retains the freehold interest giving away a long lease which vests in possession in (say) 20 years time. Assuming that he is within para 3 i.e. that the arrangement does not involve a reservation of benefit, the taxpayer may wish to pay a full rent for his use of the land so as to avoid a POA charge: see Schedule 15 para 4(1). The difficulty is that the owner of the relevant land in this case appears to be himself and he cannot pay rent to himself.

A2.177

Question 29

Does this mean that in the context of reversionary leases this part of the legislation is meaningless? To obtain relief under para 4, will the taxpayer have to transfer his freehold to an interest in possession trust for himself and pay rent to the trustees?

A2.178

HMRC answer to question 29

We agree that it would be difficult for the taxpayer to pay rent to himself in order to avoid a charge under Schedule 15. But, as you suggest, it would be possible to overcome the difficulty.

A2.179

5.2 The Guidance Notes state that reversionary lease arrangements effected post 8 March 1999 are not caught because they are subject to a reservation of benefit. You will be aware that many advisers do not agree with this view. On the basis of HMRC's current advice there is no requirement for a taxpayer to self assess and pay the pre-owned asset income tax charge. If, however, it turns out that HMRC are wrong in their view that post 8 March 1999 reversionary lease schemes are caught by the reservation of benefit rules, pre-owned assets income tax would have been due.

A2.180

Question 30

(a) If HMRC's views are successfully challenged in the courts will the taxpayer be subject to back tax, interest and penalties?

A2.181

(b) We would hope that HMRC would not in these circumstances seek to collect income tax (and interest) in respect of past years but only in respect of future years.

(c) Will it be a requirement for all taxpayers who have done a reversionary lease scheme post March 1999 to put this on their tax return in the white space and explain why they are not paying income tax?

HMRC answer to question 30

A2.182 Our view on the IHT treatment of reversionary leases and, in particular, the application of section 102A Finance Act 1986 to them is under review at the moment. We will be issuing guidance as soon as we can.

6. MISCELLANEOUS PROBLEMS

A2.183 6.1 There are difficulties in determining whether both contribution and disposal conditions have been met in a single transaction and this can be relevant when applying the exclusions in para 10 and the exemptions in para 11.

Para 3(2) provides that the disposal condition is met if the chargeable person owned an interest in the relevant land or "in other property the proceeds of the disposal of which were directly or indirectly applied by another person towards the acquisition of an interest in the relevant land."

Para 3(3) refers to the contribution condition being met where the chargeable person "has directly or indirectly provided, otherwise than by an excluded transaction, any of the consideration given by another person for the acquisition of an interest in the relevant land or an interest in any other property the proceeds of the disposal of which were directly or indirectly applied by another person towards the acquisition of an interest in the relevant land."

Question 31

A2.184 Is the correct analysis of the interaction between the disposal condition and the contribution condition as follows?

1. If the transferred property is itself the relevant land (i.e. is occupied by the donor) only the disposal condition is met.

2. If the transferred property is cash and that cash is used by the donee to buy the relevant land occupied by the donor, only the contribution condition is met. If HMRC agree with this can the Guidance Notes be amended at 1.2.1 which suggest (we think wrongly) that the disposal not the contribution condition is breached if cash is given to the donee who then purchases a property for occupation by the donor.

3. If the transferred property is an asset other than cash, and the donee then sells that asset and uses the proceeds to buy the relevant land, both the disposal and the contribution conditions are met.

4. In such a case Sch 15 para 11(9)(a)(ii) means the relevant land is the relevant property for the purposes of para 11, so that the para 11 exemptions can apply if the other conditions in para 11 are met.

HMRC answer to question 31

A2.185 Taking your four questions in turn:

- If the property disposed of by the chargeable person is the relevant land, we agree that only the disposal condition in paragraph 3(2) is in point.

- If the chargeable person transfers cash, which is then used by the donee to acquire relevant land, we agree that it is the contribution condition in paragraph 3(3) that is in point, not the disposal condition. As you suggest, our guidance at paragraph 1.2.1 needs revising on this point.

- We agree that the contribution condition contemplates circumstances in which a chargeable person has indirectly provided consideration by way of a disposal of assets other than cash. Such a disposal might also meet the disposal condition, as you suggest.

- Paragraph 3 makes it clear that, for the purposes of either the disposal or the contribution conditions, the "relevant land" is the land occupied by the chargeable person. In a case where the contribution condition (paragraphs 3(3) or 6(3), as appropriate) is in point, the "relevant property" for the purposes of the exemptions in paragraph 11 is the "property representing the consideration directly or indirectly provided": We think this must mean provided by the chargeable person. Whether this is the "relevant land must, we think, depend on whether paragraph 3(3)(a) or 3(3)(b) apply.

6.2 The meaning of the "provision" of "consideration" in the context of the contribution condition needs to be clarified. On the basis of the case law the word provided suggests some element of bounty.   **A2.186**

On this basis our view is that if there is a transfer of Whiteacre by A (or another asset) to his son at full market value which is then sold by son and the sale proceeds used to purchase Blackacre for A to occupy this is a breach of the disposal but not the contribution condition because it lacks the necessary element of bounty.

Similarly the provision of a loan on commercial terms by A to his son to enable son to purchase a house which A then occupies in our view does not fall within the contribution condition.

Question 32

Do HMRC agree with this analysis?   **A2.187**

HMRC answer to question 32

Now confirmed that loans are not caught by the contribution condition.   **A2.188**

6.3 Clarification is requested on the position where a house is owned by a company   **A2.189**
but the company is funded by way of loan. The concern is over paras 11(1)(b) and 11(3) (b).

Example 9

B owns 100 £1 shares in X Limited and otherwise funds it by shareholder loan. (Or the house is owned by a company held within an interest in possession trust for B and again the funding for the purchase comes by way of loan from trustees to company.) X Limited buys the house in which B lives. B prima facie falls within the para 3 charge. It would appear that para 11(1) protects him. The shares are not themselves property which derive much value from the house because they are worth substantially less than the house (see para 11(1)(b)(ii)) but the shares and the loan together are comprised in B's estate and between them indirectly derive their value from the house. On that basis para 11(1) does offer full protection.

Question 33

A2.190   Do HMRC agree with this analysis or do they consider that the loan derives its value from the contractual undertakings that oblige the borrowing company to repay?

It would be odd if there is a POA problem when the company is funded by way of loan but not if it is funded by way of share capital.

HMRC answer to question 33

A2.191   In our view, the loan, albeit an asset of B's estate, is not property that derives its value from the relevant property. However, our response to Q32 above would no doubt be applicable here in appropriate circumstances.

A2.192   6.4 How is the charge computed under para 9 when the settled property comprises say a deposit account but also an overdrawn current account at 6th April in the relevant year? Is the POA tax charge based simply on the value of the deposit account without deducting the overdraft?

The definition of relevant property is property which is or represents property which the chargeable person settled. If A settles cash into trust retaining a remainder interest and then the trust invests that cash unwisely e.g. in a hedge fund incurring losses which require the trustees to borrow to settle, is it the net or gross value of the trust fund that is taken in computing the POA charge?

Question 34

A2.193   Can HMRC clarify the above?

HMRC answer to question 34

A2.194   In our view, it is the net value of the trust fund as at 6 April in the relevant year that should form the basis of the computation under paragraph 9.

A2.195   6.5 The excluded transaction provision in para 10(2)(c) refers to an outright gift "to the other person" whereas the wording in para 10(2)(e) refers expressly to an outright gift to an individual. The word person must include trusts and companies. In our view para 10(2)(c) applies to settled gifts and gifts to individuals although of course cash gifts into trust will be caught by the tracing rules in schedule 20 and are therefore generally gifts with reservation if the donor can benefit from the trust and protected anyway under para 11(3).

Question 35

A2.196   Do HMRC agree with this analysis?

HMRC answer to question 35

A2.197   We think the "other person" referred to in paragraph 10(2)(c) must be the person referred to in paragraphs 3(3) and 6(3) as acquiring an interest in the relevant land etc. We agree that such a person need not necessarily be an individual. But we are more doubtful that an "outright" gift of money could include a gift to be held on trusts.

6 PARTNERSHIP ISSUES

A2.198   The Guidance Notes suggest that a partnership is transparent for inheritance tax purposes. While this is true for capital gains tax purposes, as a matter of law a gift of a partnership interest is not a gift of the underlying assets within the partnership.

We therefore do not understand the example given in Appendix 1 which refers to C who gives his son D an interest in the partnership in return for D taking on the day to day running. In these circumstances why is there a disposal of land or chattels at all? There is a fundamental distinction between a firm's capital on the one hand and its individual assets on the other. C's proportionate interest in the capital may be equal to the value of the land or chattels but it is not an interest in the land or chattels itself and therefore he cannot dispose of that land (or the chattels) when he makes the gift of the partnership interest. See Lindley on Partnerships 17th Edn.

Question 36

Are HMRC treating partnerships as transparent for POA income tax purposes? **A2.199**

HMRC answer to question 36

We do not intend to treat partnerships as transparent for the purposes of Schedule 15. **A2.200**
We will amend the example in Appendix 1 of the Guidance that you refer to.
6.7 Certain questions arise in relation to the annual exemption. **A2.201**

Example 10

> X carried out a home loan scheme. In June 2005 he dismantles the scheme. The benefit enjoyed for POA purposes from April to June is £4,000.

Question 37

Will HMRC confirm that : **A2.202**

(a) where the de minimis exemption under para 13 is not exceeded it is not possible for the transferor to make an election because he is not "chargeable to income tax"?

(b) the £5,000 exemption is not pro-rated when a taxpayer is chargeable for only part of the year?

HMRC answer to question 37

We confirm both (a) and (b) are correct. **A2.203**
6.8 In a number of circumstances it is possible for (say) the husband to be caught by **A2.204**
POA charge because he has made a disposal but not a gift and the wife to be caught potentially by gift with reservation.
In these circumstances do they each have to pay full consideration to escape their respective charges?

Example 11

> In 1998 H transfers some properties into a company he wholly owns in consideration of the issue of shares. He has breached the disposal condition. He gives the shares to his wife. In 2003 W gives the company shares to her sons and later both of them occupy one of the properties owned by the company. H and W are not directors of the company.
>
> In these circumstances H might wish to pay rent under paragraph 4 and W might want to pay full consideration under para 6 Schedule 20 in order respectively to avoid a pre-owned assets tax charge and a reservation of benefit situation.

Question 38

A2.205   (a) Is it sufficient that they pay such rent under an assured shorthold tenancy from their joint account and are jointly and severally liable for the rent?

         (b) Or does each person have to pay the full consideration separately?

HMRC answer to question 38

A2.206   It seems to us that Example 11 is dealing with concurrent charges under two separate regimes: Schedule 15, and section 102 Finance Act 1986. In our view, it is arguable that H and W each has to pay full consideration separately in order to meet the separate requirements of paragraph 4(1) Schedule 15 and paragraph 6 Schedule 20 Finance Act 1986.

A2.207   6.9 In 1.3.1 of the Guidance Notes under the bullet points relating to the spouse having to take an interest in possession from the outset it is not clear whether, if the interest in possession of the spouse or former spouse has come to an end other than on their death, the transaction is not an excluded transaction from the outset or whether it becomes so from the time the interest in possession terminates. It must surely cease to be an excluded transaction only from the time the interest in possession terminates.

Question 39

A2.208   Will HMRC please clarify this point and confirm that the transaction only ceases to be an excluded transaction from the date the spousal interest terminates and therefore it is only from that point onwards there is a POA charge. Furthermore para 10(3) states that a disposal is not an excluded transaction if the interest in possession of the spouse comes to an end otherwise than on death of the spouse. Suppose a spouse becomes beneficially entitled to the property absolutely e.g. if the trustees advance the property outright to her so she becomes absolutely entitled. In these circumstances does the excluded transaction protection end? Her interest in possession has ended but only because she has become absolutely entitled to the property.

HMRC answer to question 39

A2.209   In view of the way in which paragraph 10(3) is drafted, it is clear that the transaction ceases to be an excluded transaction only from the time that the interest in possession comes to an end otherwise than on the death of the (former) spouse.

    As far as para.10(3) is concerned, we can see how it might be said that, where a spouse becomes absolutely entitled, the protection afforded by paras.10(1)(c) or 10(2)(b) is no longer available, particularly as the property in question would no longer be settled property. That would be a less than satisfactory result in our view, particularly bearing in mind the related provisions in paras.10(1)(b) and (2)(a). A more satisfactory approach might be to regard the interest in possession, which is not limited in terms of settled property as far as the reference in para.10(3) is concerned, as not coming to an end in these circumstances.

A2.210   6.10 4.6 of the Guidance Notes give some examples of what HMRC consider constitutes occupation and the helpful letter from Mr McNicol dated 22 April 2005 gives further explanation. However, we do not fully understand HMRC's comments in this area. Please could the following common scenarios be clarified so that the taxpayer can self-assess appropriately. This is particularly relevant in relation to holiday homes.

Question 40

A2.211   (a) If there is a right to use a property throughout the year but it is not in fact used by the chargeable person, is it correct that there is no POA charge?

(b) If there is a right to use a property throughout the year and the chargeable person uses the property but it falls within the de minimis limits set out in the guidance notes, is it correct that there is no POA charge?

(c) If there is a right to use a property throughout the year and the chargeable person uses the property for say 3 months of the year there is a POA charge based on the whole year, even though others may have the right to use the property during that period (we are thinking particularly here of holiday homes)?

(d) If there is a right to or actual storage of items in the relevant property but the chargeable person never lives there and the property is occupied by someone else, is it correct that there is no occupation of land within schedule 15?

(e) Would the position of HMRC differ in (d) above if the property remained empty?

HMRC answer to question 40

Before dealing with your individual questions, we think it is worth reminding you of our view that occupation and use should be construed widely and are not confined to physical occupation. **A2.212**

(a) If there is a right to use, but no occupation or use (in the wider sense) by the chargeable person in the year, it is unlikely that there would be a Schedule 15 charge.

(b) We are not sure we can confirm that no Schedule 15 charge would arise in these circumstances. The examples of de minimis use given in paragraph 4.6 of the Guidance Notes do not contemplate (or, at least, do not assume) a right to use in the hands of the chargeable person for the rest of the year. If there is a right to use the property with even a small amount of use, the issue of how in fact the property was used for the rest of the year would need to be considered and whether this use also constituted use by the chargeable person.

(c) We would agree that a Schedule 15 charge based on the whole year would arise.

(d) We think it is difficult to give an assurance that there is no occupation of land under Schedule 15 by the chargeable person, if he is actually storing assets in the property. Particularly if he might have a right of access to these items, the circumstances might suggest that both the chargeable person and the person living in the property were using it.

(e) By saying that the property remains empty, we assume you are envisaging that no-one is living in it. On that basis, if the chargeable person is storing items there, it seems clear that he is using the property for the purposes of Schedule 15.

6.11 The position on non-exempt sales is unclear. It is our view that there is no POA charge because the cash element paid is excluded under the computation in para 4 and the undervalue element is a reservation of benefit anyway and therefore exempted from POA under para 11(3). · **A2.213**

If there is a part exchange at an undervalue with a cash adjustment, i.e. Y transfers Whiteacre worth £800,000 to X in exchange for Greenacre worth £200,000 and X also pays Y cash of £500,000, if at 6/4/05 Whiteacre is worth £800,000 (i.e. total consideration is paid by X of £700,000) we assume that POA is payable only on £200,000. The cash element is excluded under para 4 and the undervalue element is excluded under the reservation of benefit provisions.

Question 41

Is the above analysis correct? **A2.214**

A2.215 We broadly agree with this analysis. (We have assumed that, in order for this question to arise at all, Y continues to occupy Whiteacre after the transfer.)

In more detail, we would regard Y's disposition as one partly by way of gift (as to £100,000) and partly by way of sale (as to the remaining £700,000). In the circumstances envisaged, the proportion of the value of Whiteacre disposed of by way of gift would be treated as property subject to a reservation, thus remaining in Y's estate for IHT purposes and so, by virtue of paragraph 11(3), disapplying paragraph 3 to that extent. And, again in the circumstances envisaged, the disposition by way of sale would not be an excluded transaction and thus would be a non-exempt sale for the purposes of paragraphs 4(2) and (4).

We then need to apply this analysis to the provisions of paragraph 4 that determine how the chargeable amount is to be calculated and, in particular the R x DV/V formula in paragraph 4(2). First, we assume that, in this example, the relevant land would consist of 7/8ths of Whiteacre and, for any taxable period, V, in paragraph 4(2), would be the value of 7/8ths of Whiteacre at the appropriate valuation date. Looking at DV, we agree that, in applying the formula at paragraph 4(4) to arrive at the "appropriate proportion", P would be limited to the cash element of the consideration. Thus, in your example, (MV—P)/MV would be (£700,000–£500,000) / £700,000, or 2/7.

In order to calculate the chargeable amount for a taxable period, let us assume that at the valuation date 7/8 of Whiteacre is worth £875,000 (the whole being worth £1,000,000) and the rental value (R) is £38,500. The appropriate rental value, as prescribed in para.4(4) would therefore be £38,500 × (2/7 × £875,000) / £875,000: in other words, £11,000.

(More simply, the calculation is £38,500 x 2/7.)

7. FOREIGN DOMICILIARIES

A2.216 7.1 Paragraph 12(3) states that no regard is to be had to excluded property. In a case where a trust settled by a foreign domiciliary) owns a UK house through a foreign registered company the shares in the company (and any loan to the company) are excluded property. Concern has been expressed that since para 12(3) says that no regard is to be had to these assets, this in turn means that the shares and loan have to be ignored in applying para 11 and in particular cannot be taken into account in determining whether there is derived property which is in the taxpayer's estate or GWR property in relation to him (which the shares and loans otherwise are). We think that this argument is misconceived but it has been advanced.

Question 42

A2.217 Can HMRC confirm that they agree para 12(3) does not operate in this way and that para 11 can still work to protect the UK house or underlying assets owned by the off-shore company in these circumstances?

HMRC answer to question 42

A2.218 We agree with what you say in paragraph 7.1 about the interaction between paragraphs 12(3) and 11.

8. SCOPE OF THE PARA. 8 CHARGE

A2.219 8.1 In addition to the points raised on valuation, we note that on insurance schemes involving for example quantitative carve outs (for example where the settlor taxpayer is the remainderman in the settlement as in a reverter to settlor trust) the settlor is treated as being outside the POA charge. This is on the basis that his interest in the trust property is either held on bare trust or on a separate trust.

Question 43

Will HMRC confirm that reverter to settlor trusts holding other assets are also outside the para 8 charge?   **A2.220**

HMRC answer to question 43

If you are suggesting that reverter to settlor trusts are outside the scope of sections 624 and 625 ITTOIA 2005, we would be interested to see the reasoning put forward in support of this proposition. In the insurance schemes you mention, which we have agreed do not fall within the said sections 624 and 625 and therefore are outside the scope of paragraph 8, the interests held on trust for the settlor are, as you suggest, carved out of the gift and retained by him. In our view, such schemes are not analogous with reverter to settlor trusts.   **A2.221**

Question 44

There is a potential problem about the wording in para 22(3): if income is treated as income of the chargeable person by virtue of section 660A then due to paragraph 22(3)(b) it shall be treated as property subject to a reservation. Income could be taxed under s660A (now s624 ITTOIA) if only a spouse could benefit and that would not normally bring para 8 into play in the first place although this exclusion is not carried forward once an election is made.   **A2.222**

So if someone elects on intangibles and then he but not his wife is excluded from benefiting under the settlement does this mean that the conditions in para 22(3) are satisfied and hence that he is still treated as having a reservation of benefit? Or does paragraph 22(2)(b)(ii) (which says sections 102(3) and (4) shall apply) mean that if he ceases to reserve a benefit in the property himself the effect of the election falls away so that there is a deemed PET then, even if the conditions in para 22(3) are prima facie satisfied because his wife can still benefit?

HMRC answer to question 44

We lean towards your first interpretation of the effect of para.22(3)(b). If someone is in a position to make an election under para.22(2), he or she must be someone who is (or would be) chargeable under para.8 for that year of assessment. Clearly, the condition in para.22(3)(b) would also be met at that time. It does seem that this condition would continue to be met until such time that both the chargeable person and his or her spouse (or civil partner) were excluded from benefit. At that point, a PET would be deemed to have arisen by virtue of para.22(2)(b)(ii).   **A2.223**

5. POAT: CORRESPONDENCE WITH HMRC ON ELECTIONS (OCTOBER 2006)

A2.224   There is some uncertainty about the actual effect of the election because para 21 does not as such deem there to be a gift for Inheritance Tax purposes but simply states that the property is treated as property subject to a reservation. Schedule 15 provides for what happens if the person ceases to benefit from the elected property but does not provide for what happens if the property actually comes back into a person's estate.

In the COP 10 letter we asked (at question 17) what happens if A makes the election in respect of his home on a home loan scheme (or indeed any other type of Inheritance Tax Scheme). The house is then appointed back to him absolutely i.e. the arrangements are unscrambled. The reservation of benefit has ceased because the house is back in his estate and you confirmed that even if there was a deemed PET under Section 102 (4) FA 1986, appointing the property back to A would have no immediate practical inheritance tax consequences because it is back in his estate anyway. This accords with how the reservation of benefit rules on actual gifts work. (See answer to question 17.)

As you will be aware, many people are unravelling schemes but also wish to make the election in order to avoid an income tax charge from 6th April 2005. If once the property is back in their estates the effect of the election ceases to apply for all inheritance tax purposes (in the same way that a reservation of benefit on gifted property would cease if it was transferred back to the donor) then spouse (and charities) exemption is available. If the election is made and the scheme is not unravelled, spouse exemption is not available.

I am therefore requesting confirmation that HMRC apply the Schedule 15 of FA 2004 legislation on elections in the same way as the reservation of benefit legislation on an actual gift. So even though HMRC would produce the election on any death, on being shown evidence that the property had been appointed back and the scheme entirely unravelled, the election would then be ignored for inheritance tax purposes. Spouse exemption is then available. If that approach is indeed the one HMRC adopt, does it matter if the election is made before or after the scheme is unravelled?

RESPONSE FROM HMRC CAPITAL TAXES NOTTINGHAM: PRE-OWNED ASSETS AND ELECTIONS

A2.225   I can confirm that we do believe that the Schedule 15 FA 2004 legislation on elections should be applied in the same way as the reservation of benefit legislation on an actual gift. As I suggested when you originally raised this question with me on the phone, section 102(3) Finance Act 1986 only has practical force in relation to property that is subject to a reservation immediately before death and only to the extent that it would not form part of the estate in any event.

On that basis, if evidence is produced that property, in respect of which an election under the Schedule 15 legislation had been made, has been appointed back to the estate, we would ignore the existence of the election for the purpose of determining the IHT estate on death.

On your supplementary question, we do not consider the timing of the election to be material. Even if it were made after the unscrambling, the chargeable person would still have been chargeable for the period up to the unscrambling, thus enabling the requirements of paragraphs 21(1) or 22(1), as appropriate, to be met.

6. POAT: CIOT CORRESPONDENCE WITH HMRC ON SECTION 80 FA 2006 (CIOT NOTE JANUARY 2007)

FINANCE ACT 2006 S 80 : NEED FOR POAT ELECTION

A2.226 FA 2006 s 80 amended the income tax charge imposed by the 2004 Finance Act on preowned assets. Unfortunately a drafting error means it has a wider impact than was intended.

The section 80 amendment took effect when it was announced on 5th December 2005. PBRO5 on that date is headed "pre-owned assets and reverter-to-settlor trusts". The text of PBRO5 makes it clear that reverter to settlor trusts are those where the trust property reverts to the settlor or his spouse after termination of another beneficiary's interest in possession. Sections 53 and 54 of the Inheritance Tax Act 1984 are specifically referred to, those being the sections which exempt the trust from the Inheritance Tax otherwise payable on the termination of the beneficiary's interest in possession. For ease of reference it is convenient to refer to that beneficiary as the life tenant and his interest as the life interest.

The drafting error is that the amendment made by s 80 applies not only to trusts where the life tenant is another beneficiary but <u>also to those where the life tenant is the settlor himself.</u>

Where section 80 applies it removes the exemption from the preowned asset charge otherwise applicable where the taxpayer is treated as beneficially entitled to the relevant property for the purposes of Inheritance Tax. Loss of the exemption is thus in point in any case where the life interest vested in the settlor arose before 22nd March 2006 or where the settlor takes an interest in possession after 21 March 2006 and is disabled within the meaning of s89 IHTA 1984. The effect, on the widest view, is that any such life interest exposes the settlor to pre-owned assets tax. Strictly this is only avoided where the asset was settled land or chattels which have at all times subsequently been retained in the trust.

As will be apparent this is an absurd result. The whole point of preowned assets tax is to tax assets which a settlor or donor enjoys despite them not being in his estate for Inheritance Tax purposes. By definition it is not a tax on property to which a settlor or donor is treated as beneficially entitled as such property is fully subject to Inheritance Tax in his hands.

A2.227 As will be seen from the attached correspondence HMRC contend that s 80 does not apply if the life-interest of the settlor has subsisted **at all times** since the inception of the trust. Please note though that there is an exception to this point mentioned below. They have said that this view will be included in revised POAT guidance. On this basis, the difficulties identified above only arise where the initial trusts were discretionary or conferred interests in possession on other beneficiaries. But such scenarios are by no means uncommon, particularly in relation to non domiciliaries who are resident in the UK. A typical case where a non domiciliary would be caught would be where before 22 March 2006 he became entitled to an interest in possession in a UK house owned by a discretionary trust which he had created. Such interest could have arisen either by express appointment prior to the purchase of the house or as a result of SP 10/79.

HMRC have confirmed that the effect of s 80 can be removed by making an election, and that the cost of making the election is merely to disapply the reverter to settlor reliefs in ss 53 and 54 of the Inheritance Tax Act 1984. It is true that s 80 has conferred the right to make an election and it is also the case that in most cases the sole effect of the election is indeed to disapply ss 53 and 54. For this reason an election should be considered urgently in all cases where the settlor did not have an interest in possession when the trust was created but has been appointed one subsequently.

The purpose of this note is to draw attention to the fact that if an election is to be made, then subject to the de minimis exemption mentioned below, it must be made on or before 31 January 2007, i.e. the end of this month. STEP and CIOT are pressing HMRC to introduce amendments to reverse the unintended effect of s 80 as described above. But there is no certainty such amendments will be introduced and an election should therefore be seriously considered.

As the amendments made by s 80 took effect only on 5 December 2005, the amount potentially chargeable to POAT for 2005-06 may be modest. Should the taxable benefit fall within the de minimis exemption, which is £5,000 per taxpayer, no tax is due for 2005-06 and an election will only be needed for 2006-07. It is not possible to make an election on 31 January 2007 if the taxable benefit is under £5000. However, this gives the taxpayer another year to consider his options. An election would then need to be made by 31 January 2008 (assuming the de minimis charge does not also apply for the full year 2006-07).

An election may not be appropriate where the settlor is non domiciled and the asset giving rise to the pre-owned asset charge is land or chattels owned through an offshore company. In such cases an election could expose the land and chattels, and assets representing them to IHT. Specialist advice should therefore be sought. Such cases are comparatively rare because, as indicated above, on HMRC's view s 80 is only in issue if the settlor did not have an interest in possession when the trust was created but only acquired one subsequently. But if the settlor has by now acquired a deemed UK domicile, s 80 potentially impacts on such cases where the land or chattels owned by the company are foreign situs as well as where they are UK situs. (Where the foreign situated land or chattels are owned direct by the trustees then they should be protected from POAT under para 12(3) even if the trust was initially discretionary.)

As a final point, it should be born in mind that on one scenario s 80 can impact on a trust in which the settlor has had a life interest since inception. This is where the trust has been funded by an advance from another trust of which he was settlor but has not at all times had an interest in possession. In those cases too, election should be considered.

Correspondence between CIOT/STEP and HMRC on this point is attached to this note.

Questions from STEP/CIOT

Section 80 amends FA 2004 Sch 15 para 11. The amendments apply where the relevant property is comprised in a person's estate for the purposes of IHTA 1984 s 49 and previously one of two conditions has been met. These conditions are set out in new para 11(11) as follows: **A2.228**

(a) The relevant property has ceased to be comprised in the person's estate for inheritance tax purposes **or**

(b) The person has directly or indirectly provided any consideration for the acquisition of the relevant property.

If at any subsequent time the relevant property or derived property is in his estate for the purposes of s49 IHTA then the effect of s80 is to provide that for POAT purposes (but for no other) the settlor is not treated as having an interest in possession or having reserved a benefit in the property.

The potential difficulty with paras 11(11) and 11(12) is that they do not distinguish between reverter to settler trusts and <u>any</u> trust set up between March 1986 and 22 March 2006 where the settlor has a qualifying interest in possession and would in that event be subject to inheritance tax on his death.

These difficulties arise because paras 11(11) and 11(12) catch not only those transactions where land has been given away and ceased to be comprised in the settlor's estate and then comes back into his estate (condition a above). They also catch transactions where a settlor contributed funds or property to a trust and the trust (or an underlying company) has then used those funds or property representing them to buy the relevant property i.e. the land which is now occupied (condition b above). There is nothing in the words about "any subsequent time" which suggests that under (b) the property had first to cease to be comprised in his estate before being caught by this provision. Indeed if that was the case the words in (a) would be redundant.

A2.229   Are the following cases caught by POAT from 5th December 2005 (the date the change came into effect):

1. In 1987, A sets up an interest in possession trust for himself into which he gifts his house. If the house is still held by the trustees now there is no POAT charge because nothing has left his estate. However assume that the house has since been sold but he retains an interest in possession. The trust holds a mixture of investments and another house that A occupies. Is para 11(11) (b) satisfied on the basis that A has provided consideration for the acquisition of the land which land has subsequently become comprised in his estate.

   A would then have to pay POAT on all the investments from 5th December 2005 for the foreseeable future even though they are prima facie chargeable to IHT in the event of his death. POAT may be due on the new house as well.

2. B is a foreign domiciliary (not deemed domiciled) who before 22 March 2006 set up a discretionary trust into which he transferred cash. He remains a beneficiary of the trust. The trust then funds a company which buys a house (and B will pay income tax under s739 in respect of any UK income). The trust was before 22 March 2006 converted into an interest in possession trust. If there is UK land or there are UK chattels occupied or used by B which are held by the trustees through the company within the interest in possession structure he is now subject to POAT on such property or chattels. (If B is deemed domiciled here then the charge would also apply to non-UK property or chattels occupied or used by him). Even if one reads "subsequent time" to mean some time must elapse between the date when the gift is made and the date the property comes back into B's estate this would still not protect B in this example because the trust was originally discretionary.

3. In June 2006, C, a disabled person, sets up a trust for himself that qualifies as a disabled person's interest within s89B. C puts in cash and the trustees invest in equities or a house that C occupies. C will pay POAT.

A simple amendment that would deal with the problem is to state that section 80 should not apply where the person with the qualifying interest in possession is the settlor. Is this in contemplation?

HMRC response

A2.230   As I understand your concern, it is that the new paragraph 11(11)(b) in Schedule 15 FA04 will catch someone who has settled, say, cash on interest in possession trusts for themselves (either before 22 March 2006, or afterwards if it is a "disabled person's interest") and subsequently occupies property bought by the trustees; or where the property they settled initially has been sold and replaced by other property, while the settlor has retained their interest in possession.

The new paragraph refers to the chargeable person "directly or indirectly [providing] any consideration for the acquisition of the relevant property", and goes on to require that, "at any subsequent time", the relevant property is comprised in the settlor's IHT estate by virtue of their having an interest in possession in it.

In our view, the words "at any subsequent time" should be read as meaning that a POA charge will arise where the consideration leaves the donor's estate, <u>as a result of which that estate is reduced</u>, and later property acquired with such consideration becomes comprised in it again because of their interest in possession. This is consistent with the reasons for Schedule 15.

We do not, therefore, consider that there will be a charge in the scenarios numbered 1 and 3 in your letters, because the assets transferred into trust and any derived assets have always been in the settlor's estate for IHT purposes. We believe that also applies if, in your second scenario, B set up an interest in possession trust from the outset before Budget Day. The taxpayer should self-assess on the basis that no POAT is due and there is therefore no need to put anything about POAT on the tax return or for him to make the election where the settlor has retained an interest in possession throughout and settled the cash or property directly into trust himself (rather than through any other funding vehicle such as another trust). This is because no POAT charge arises under s80 FA 2006.

In summary we do not consider that s.80 has any implications for:

- a settlement of cash on interest in possession trusts for oneself made before 22 March 2006, or made by a disabled person on or after that date, after which the trustees purchase a property in which the settlor resides; or

- the settlement of a house in the same way, which is subsequently sold by the trustees and replaced by other investments or another property.

That remains our view, on the basis that the words "at any subsequent time" mean that new paragraph 11(11)(b) Schedule 15 FA2004 will only be relevant where:

- the consideration in question leaves the donor's estate, as a result of which that estate is reduced; and

- later, property acquired with such consideration becomes comprised in the estate once more by virtue of an interest in possession.

We do not agree that this interpretation makes paragraph 11(11)(a) redundant, since that relates to cases where the disposal condition is met and paragraph 11(11)(b) to cases where the contribution condition is met.

We accept that a POA charge may arise where someone set up a discretionary trust that has subsequently been converted into an interest in possession trust for the benefit of the settlor. (scenario 2 in your example). However, it remains possible in those circumstances to elect out of the charge. So, take the following example:

- H settles a property on discretionary trusts before 22 March 2006;

- also before that date, the trust is converted into an interest in possession trust for H's benefit, with remainder to his wife, W;

- a POA charge therefore arises because of s.80 but H elects.

As we see it, the effects of the election are:

- the chargeable proportion of the property will be treated as subject to a reservation, but only so far as H is not beneficially entitled to an interest in possession in the property *(paragraph 21(2)(b)(i), Schedule 15 FA04)* – i.e. not at all;

- section 102(3) and (4) FA86 will apply, but only so far as H is not beneficially entitled to an interest in possession in the property *(paragraph 21(2)(b)(ii))* – i.e. not at all; and

- the reverter-to-settlor exemptions in s.53(3) and (4) and s.54 IHTA will not apply to the actual interest in possession *(paragraph 21(2)(b)(iii))*.

We do not, therefore, consider that the election affects the availability of spouse exemption on H's interest in possession on his death – or on its termination during his lifetime. That is because, as we have just noted, the election will not cause s.102(3) and (4) FA 86 to apply because of H's interest in possession, so there will be no deemed PET.

CIOT/STEP comment:

A2.231 In the light of the above it will be necessary for practitioners to review urgently all those trusts where the following conditions are satisfied:

1. they were funded between March 1986 and March 2006

2. at the date of funding, the settlor settled funds or property on discretionary trusts or on interest in possession trusts for someone else but before 22 March 2006 he acquired an interest in possession in the settled property.

In these circumstances the UK resident and UK domiciled person (domiciled in the UK under general law) will need to elect by 31 January 2007 but on HMRC's analysis there is no additional inheritance tax payable and the same reliefs and exemptions will be available as would have been due prior to the election.

If the conditions at 1 and 2 above are satisfied, the foreign domiciliary (whether or not deemed domiciled here now) who is resident in the UK and established his trust before he became domiciled here will need to elect by 31 January 2007 if the trust holds directly any UK situated intangibles or the trust directly or through a company holds UK real property that he occupies or UK chattels that he uses and he does not want to pay POAT. (An excluded property trust that holds intangibles through an offshore company structure will not be caught by s80 in any event because para 8 does not apply to the underlying assets of a company and para 12(3) protects the offshore company shares). The settlor who is deemed domiciled here but was not domiciled here when he set up the trust will also need to consider an election on foreign situated land or chattels occupied or used by him where this is held in an offshore company owned by a trust assuming he does not want to pay POAT. However, there are a number of complexities.

Specialist advice should be sought as to the inheritance tax effects of such an election. In general terms an election will increase a foreign domiciliary's inheritance tax bill on his death where the UK situated property is owned by a company and he has an interest in possession in the shares. Otherwise the effect of making an election on UK situated property is likely to be broadly neutral.

7. IHT SCHEDULE 20: CIOT/STEP QUESTIONS AND ANSWERS (UPDATED 2008)

Index of questions and answers

A. Transitional serial interests (TSI)　　　　　　　　　　　　　　A2.232

1. Condition 1 contains the requirement that "immediately before 22 March 2006, the property then comprised in the settlement was property in which B, or some other person, was beneficially entitled to an interest in possession ("the prior interest")".

2. Can it be confirmed that this requirement will be satisfied where B, or some other person, has a beneficial interest in possession in some of the property then comprised in the settlement but not all the property so comprised.

Example 1

Under a trust there are two funds. In Fund A, Mr Smith has an interest in possession. In Fund B, Mr Jones has an interest in possession.

Question 1

Will Condition 1 be satisfied separately in relation to Fund A and/or Fund B?　　A2.233

HMRC Answer

We can confirm that condition 1 can be satisfied separately in relation to both funds.　　A2.234
　　The new s.49C starts from the point of the view of the "current interest" – a beneficial interest in settled property. Given the wide definition of that term in s.43 IHTA, it seems that the beneficial IIP referred to in s.49C(1) can quite easily be in a fund or in property that was previously part of a larger disposition or settlement – and there is nothing to suggest that there must have been a single beneficiary.

Moreover, there is no requirement that the settlement must have been wholly IIP in nature (question 2 below) or that it must have come to an end in its entirety (question 3).

If one can then accept that the property referred to in s.49C(1) is also the property referred to in s.49C(2), and in which the "prior interest" (s.49C(2) & (3)) existed, the concerns raised in questions 1 to 4 fall away.

Question 2

A2.235 Can it be confirmed that Condition 1 will be satisfied in relation to Fund A where Fund B is held not on trusts giving Mr Jones an interest in possession but on discretionary trusts? There is nothing in the wording of s49C to suggest that the pre-Budget interest in possession must subsist in the entire fund.

HMRC Answer

A2.236 We agree.

A2.237 3. Section 49C(3) provides that Condition 2 requires the prior interest to come to an end at a time on or after 22 March 2006 but before 6 April 2008.

Question 3

A2.238 Will Condition 2 be satisfied where the prior interest comes to an end in that period in part only of the settled property in which that interest subsists?

HMRC Answer

A2.239 Yes – see the response to question 1 above.

Example 2

In the example given above, if Mr Smith's interest in possession in Fund A comes to an end in 60% of Fund A and is replaced by an interest in possession in favour of Mr Smith's daughter, but Mr Smith's interest in possession continues in relation to the remaining 40% of Fund A, can it be confirmed that the interest in possession in favour of the daughter will be a transitional serial interest?

HMRC Answer

A2.240 We can confirm this – for the reasons given immediately below.
A2.241 While it has been suggested that Condition 2 requires that the prior interest comes to an end in all the property in which the interest subsists, Condition 2 does not state this and given the definition of current interest it appears that Condition 2 must be construed as referring to the prior interest coming to an end in the settled property concerned in which B takes a current interest but not necessarily in all the settled property of a particular settlement. The "current interest" is merely defined as an interest in possession in settled property and does not in any way require all the settled property comprised in the settlement to be a current interest.

Question 4

A2.242 Please also confirm that the remaining 40% of Fund A continues to satisfy Condition 1 so that a transitional serial interest could be created in that 40% prior to 6th April 2008.

HMRC Answer

We can confirm this.   A2.243

Question 5(1)

Please also confirm that in the above example if 40% of Mr Smith's pre-Budget inter-   A2.244
est in possession is ended as to half for his daughter and half for his son, both son and
daughter take transitional serial interests in their respective shares.

HMRC Answer

We can confirm this.   A2.245

Question 5(2)

If later the trustees wished to appropriate assets between the two funds for son and   A2.246
daughter and the assets were of the same value as the assets previously contained in
each fund, do HMRC accept that such appropriation does not represent the termination of any qualifying interest in possession and therefore does not result in an inheritance tax charge?

HMRC Answer

We agree.

    4. We would be grateful for your views on the circumstances in which the prior   A2.247
interest would be considered to have come to an end and have been replaced by
a current interest. This is relevant because if a prior interest is considered to have
come to an end and have been replaced by a current interest (in favour of the
same beneficiary) there will be no possibility of the interest being replaced by a
transitional serial interest later and the point is particularly important in relation
to spousal relief because spouse exemption will not be available if a spouse of a
life tenant who already has a transitional serial interest takes an interest in possession on the death of that life tenant.

Example 3

Under a pre-Budget 2006 trust a beneficiary A is entitled to the capital contingently on
attaining the age of 30 years. A was 21 on 22 March 2006 and had been entitled to an
interest in possession under section 31 of the Trustee Act 1925 from the age of 18. The
interest is therefore an interest in possession which subsisted on 22 March 2006. Before
2008 the trustees exercise their [enlarged] powers of advancement under section 32 of
the Trustee Act 1925 to defer the vesting of the capital from the age of 30 to the age of
45 and A's interest in possession in the fund will therefore continue until age 45. Clearly
A reaches 30 after 2008 in the above example.

Question 6

 There are two possible interpretations of the above and we should be grateful if   A2.248
HMRC could confirm which view they take.
    Option 1. The exercise of the trustees' powers in this way creates a new interest in
possession for A immediately on exercise of the power of advancement which therefore
takes effect as the "current interest" or "transitional serial interest". Any successive
interest in possession after A's interest in possession has ended cannot then be a transitional serial interest. The property will be taxed as part of A's estate on his death if

he dies with the transitional serial interest. He continues to have a transitional serial interest until termination at 45 or earlier death.

Option 2: A's new interest only arises when A attains the age of 30. Until then he has a pre-Budget qualifying interest in possession.

The new interest cannot take effect as a transitional serial interest at all since on the above facts it will arise after April 2008. Until 30 A will have a pre-Budget interest in possession on the basis that nothing has changed until he reaches 30. Only from 30 will he take a new non-qualifying interest so the settled property will then become relevant property. There will not be an entry charge for A at 30 of 20% due to s53(2) IHTA.

If A dies before reaching 30, then on this analysis his pre-Budget interest will not previously have ended and therefore if his spouse takes an interest in possession this is a transitional serial interest or if his children take interests in possession before 2008 these will be transitional serial interests.

Does the answer to whether option 1 or option 2 applies depend on whether the advancement is drafted in such a way that it extends the interest in possession from 30 without restating A's existing interest in possession until then? Or would any variation of A's interest in possession be regarded as a transitional serial interest from the date of the variation even if the variation only took effect in the future.

HMRC Answer

A2.249 We consider that A's original IIP (until 30) will have "come to an end" when the trustees exercised their power of advancement and been replaced by a new IIP (until 45), which will therefore qualify as a TSI. A's interest is expressed as an entitlement to capital contingent on his attaining 30. It seems reasonable to regard the exercise of the s.32 Trustee Act power as immediately bringing this interest to an end and replacing it with a new one.

NB: As regards HMRC's view on whether a charge arises on the creation of the TSI (or other interest in possession) in these circumstances see also section 141 of Finance Act 2008 which has now removed any suggestion that there could be a charge where A is given a new IIP before October 2008. Note also that there is a third view i.e. that no IIP arises at all if A's entitlement to capital is deferred because his entitlement to income is not as such affected. Much may depend on how the power is exercised and whether it is an advancement or an appointment.

5. An interest in possession might also subsist as follows:

Example 4

A2.250 Under a trust A has a life interest with remainder to his children. The trustees have a power of advancement and exercise such a power to provide that subject to A's existing life interest A's spouse takes a life interest on A's death with remainder to the children at the age of 25. A's interest in possession is not in any way altered.

Question 7

A2.251 Can HMRC please confirm that the exercise of a power of advancement to create an interest in possession for the spouse, which is expressly made subject to A's existing life interest and does not in any way alter that interest but merely comes into effect on his death, will be a transitional serial interest. Similarly, if spouse predeceases A and the advancement on interest in possession trusts for A's children is made subject to A's interest and takes effect before 2008 (e.g. A surrenders his interest) presumably these trusts could also be transitional serial interests.

Assuming that A's present IIP existed before 22 March 2006, we can confirm that the **A2.252** spouse's IIP –whether or not it arises before or after 6 October 2008 - will qualify as a TSI provided that it arises on the <u>death</u> of A and that A is at the date of his death still entitled to a pre-budget interest in possession. Any IIP taken by A's children on the death or earlier termination of A's IIP will also be a transitional serial interest provided that this occurs before 6 October 2008. If A's pre-Budget interest in possession terminates inter vivos in favour of the spouse then the spouse will only take a TSI if this termination occurs before 6th October 2008.

If, however, A's interest was in any way amended (e.g. the trustees exercised powers of revocation and reappointment restating A's interest in possession albeit in the same terms and then declaring interests in possession for A's spouse or for children if she has predeceased), presumably the interests for spouse and children could never be transitional serial interests because A's interest is a transitional serial interest?

HMRC Answer

We agree. **A2.253**

6. Can it be confirmed that an interest in possession can be a transitional serial **A2.254** interest where the interest arises under a different settlement to that in which the original interest subsisted?

Example 5

Under Trust A Mr Smith has an interest in possession and subject to that, the capital **A2.255** passes to Mr Jones absolutely. Mr Jones on 30 December 2006 assigns his reversionary interest into Trust B set up in December 2006 under which his children have interests in possession. Mr Smith's interest in possession then comes to an end on 30 November 2007 at which time the settled property in trust A passes to trust B.

Question 8

Will the interest in possession of Mr Jones' children qualify as a transitional serial **A2.256** interest bearing in mind that the interests arise in relation to the same settled property even though not under the trusts of the original settlement? A similar situation could arise where there is technically a different settlement under which the successive life interest arises due to the exercise of the trustees' powers of appointment in the wider form (as referred to in *Bond v Pickford [1983 (STC 517)]*).

HMRC Answer

Taken with question 9 below. **A2.257**

Question 9

If the difficulty is that Condition 1 is not satisfied because the second settlement is **A2.258** "made" post Budget does it make any difference if the second settlement was made pre-Budget and the interests in the first settlement fall into the second settlement before 2008 to be held on interest in possession trusts. This is a very common situation where there are "trusts over" and there appears nothing in the conditions to prevent this.

HMRC Answer

A2.259   We do not consider that the IIPs of Mr Jones's children will qualify as TSIs whether the second settlement was made before or after Budget 2006.

As we said earlier, s.49C begins from the point of view of the "current interest". Condition 1 requires that "the settlement" in which that interest subsists "commenced" before 22 March 2006.

It goes on to require that, immediately before that date, the property "then comprised" in the settlement – i.e. the same settlement – was subject to the "prior interest".

The IIPs of Mr Jones's children arise under a different settlement (albeit one which happens to hold, following Mr Smith's death, the property that comprised the earlier one) and will not, therefore, qualify as TSIs – and it will make no difference when the settlement was made.

For the same reasons, the exercise of powers of appointment in such a way that assets are removed from one settlement and subjected to the trusts of another will not give rise to TSIs.

Note: where the second settlement was set up prior to 22 March 2006 and the reversionary interest of Mr Jones was assigned into an IIP trust prior to that date STEP/CIOT do not accept that on the death of the life tenant Mr Smith the property then comprised in the second trust (formerly the reversionary interest and now the settled property originally in trust 1) is not subject to a qualifying pre March 2006 IIP. It is however accepted that a TSI cannot arise if property is appointed by the trustees from one IIP trust to another whenever they were set up.

7. Question 10

A2.260   What is the position if the beneficiary holding the pre-Budget interest in possession assigns that interest in possession to another person? Does the assignee's interest qualify as a transitional serial interest? The concern here is that the original interest in possession is not "terminated" by virtue of the assignment, and so the precise terms of the legislation do not appear to have been met.

HMRC Answer

A2.261   We consider that the assignee's interest can be a TSI in this case because the assignor's IIP will have "come to an end" for the purposes of s.49C(3). (The interest will be in the original settlement, so the problem outlined in our response to question 9 will not be an issue).

B Administration of estates

8. Question 11

A2.262   Can it be confirmed that where a will provides that a beneficiary has an interest in possession in residue, that interest in possession will be treated as commencing on the date of death of the deceased and not only when the administration of the estate is completed. This appears to be the case by virtue of Section 91 IHTA 1984.

HMRC Answer

A2.263   We can confirm this.

9. Question 12

A2.264   Can it be confirmed that the position will be the same as in Question 11 above where the interest in possession is in a settled legacy of specific assets not forming part of residue. It seems that this should be the case: *IRC v Hawley* [1929] 1 KB 578.

HMRC Answer

We agree. **A2.265**
This is important for two reasons:

- in order for an interest in possession to satisfy Condition 2 in section 49A for an Immediate Post-Death Interest (IPDI), L must have become beneficially entitled to the interest on the death of the testator or intestate;

- in determining whether an interest in possession is one which subsisted prior to 22 March 2006 where the deceased died before 22 March 2006 but the completion of the administration of the estate was on or after 22 March 2006 there would be difficulties if the pre-Budget interest in possession was not regarded as commencing on the death of the deceased.

10. Question 13

Many wills include a provision which provides that a beneficiary will only take if he **A2.266** survives the testator by a period of time. Please confirm that such a provision would not by itself prevent an IPDI arising.

HMRC Answer

We can confirm this. We consider that s.92 IHTA removes any doubt here. **A2.267**

C IPDIs generally

11. Question 14

Can it be confirmed that if on the death of X a discretionary trust set up in his Will **A2.268** (e.g. a nil rate band legacy trust) is funded by a share in property, and the trustees allow the surviving spouse L to occupy it on an exclusive basis albeit at their discretion along the lines that occurred in *Judge & anor (Representatives of Walden deceased) Sp C 506*, this will not automatically be an IPDI but it will depend on the terms on which she occupies.

HMRC Answer

We agree. **A2.269**

There is a 3 month requirement for reading back under s144 in respect of appointments of absolute interests but this does not apply to appointments of IPDIs. Therefore if the trustees immediately on the death of X or subsequently, conferred exclusive rights of occupation on L this could indeed be an IPDI.

HMRC Answer

We agree. **A2.270**

It appears to us unlikely that mere exclusivity of occupation could in itself be a problem because as Judge confirms a person can occupy exclusively but not have rights which constitute an interest in possession. Indeed if the surviving spouse merely continued in occupation on the same terms as before X's death without the trustees' doing anything positive either way to affect her occupation it would appear they have not exercised their powers so as to give her any IPDI anyway.

A2.271   We agree.

(Indeed it is doubtful that they have any ability under the Trusts of Land and Appointment of Trustees Act 1996 to disturb her occupation if she already owns a half share in the property personally and therefore the trustees have not exercised any power to confer her a present right to present enjoyment which could constitute an immediate post death interest.)

It would be helpful (given how common this situation is) if HMRC could give some guidance on the various scenarios in which they would or would not regard the surviving spouse as taking an IPDI in a property left on nil rate band discretionary trusts in the will if she is already in occupation.

HMRC Answer

A2.272   This will depend on the precise terms of the testator's will or any deed of appointment exercised by the trustees after the testator's death, and we will continue to examine each case on its particular facts.

12. Question 15

A2.273   Can it be confirmed that where a settlement (including a settlement created by will) includes a general power of appointment and that power is exercised by will giving an immediate interest in possession, the interest created over the trust property will qualify as an IPDI?

HMRC Answer

A2.274   We can confirm this.

13. Question 16

A2.275   Can it be confirmed that HMRC takes the view that if an individual (I) leaves by will a gift to a person's estate, when the assets in the estate are held on trusts which qualify as trusts for bereaved minors or age 18-to-25 trusts, the property added pursuant to I's will would also be treated as being held on trusts which qualify as trusts for bereaved minors or 18-to-25 trusts.

HMRC Answer

A2.276   We have assumed that the scenario envisaged here is: I dies leaving a legacy in their will to P; P dies after I but before the legacy has been paid; P's estate is held on trusts that meet s.71A or s.71D. We agree that, in those circumstances, the legacy from I's estate would qualify under those provisions, also.

Example 6

I leaves his estate to his widow for life with remainder to his son S if alive at I's death. S survives I but predeceases the widow leaving a Will under which his estate passes to his children on trusts which qualify as trusts for bereaved minors. The widow dies when the children are aged 10 and 12, so that I's estate falls to be held on the trusts of S's Will. Will the property in I's estate benefit from trusts for bereaved minors status? I is the grandparent but the property is passing according to S's Will.

HMRC Answer

We consider that the property added pursuant to I's will in this example would also fall within s.71A.

A2.277

14. Question 17

If a property is left outright to someone by a will and they disclaim within two years of the deceased's death such that an interest in possession trust takes effect, can HMRC confirm that the trust will qualify as an IPDI?

A2.278

HMRC Answer

We can confirm this.

A2.279

15. Question 18

Can it be confirmed whether, when a will leaves property to an existing settlement (whether funded or unfunded) and under that settlement a beneficiary takes an immediate interest in possession, that interest will qualify as an IPDI. Such arrangements are common for US and other foreign domiciliaries in order to avoid complex probate issues. It might be argued that the interest in possession in the existing settlement does not arise under the will of the deceased. However, there are two arguments against this.

First, HMRC's own analysis is that additions by individuals to existing settlements should be treated as new settlements. Hence the addition by will to an existing settlement is a new settlement set up by virtue of the will.

Secondly, the wording in section 49A Condition 1 refers to "the settlement was effected by will or under the law of intestacy". The question though is what "the settlement" refers to. It would seem that it refers not as such to "the settlement" in the sense of a document but rather to the settlement into trust of the settled property which certainly is effected by will. The same wording is used on deeds of variation under section 142 IHTA and HMRC have always accepted that where property is added by will to a pre-existing settlement there is no reason why the beneficiary of that settlement cannot vary his entitlement.

A2.280

HMRC Answer

We can confirm that the IIP in this scenario would qualify as an IPDI. We agree that "settlement" in this context relates to the contribution of property into the settlement rather than the document under which it will become held.

A2.281

D Trusts for bereaved minors, 18-25 trusts and modified section 71 trusts: Section 71A and section 71D

16. Question 19

Can it be confirmed that trusts otherwise satisfying the requirements of section 71A or section 71D will be regarded as satisfying those conditions where the trusts were appointed under powers contained in the will and were not provided in the will itself at the outset.

A2.282

HMRC Answer

We can confirm this – where the trusts are set up as a result of the exercise of a special power of appointment. We consider the position is different with general powers, on

A2.283

the basis, broadly speaking, that having a general power of appointment is tantamount to owning the property.

Example 7

A2.284   H dies in 2007. His Will leaves an IPDI for his surviving spouse and subject thereto on discretionary trusts for issue of H. The trustees exercise their overriding powers of appointment to create s71A trusts for the children of H. It would appear that the s71A provisions do not need to be incorporated within the Will Trust from the start to qualify for relief but it would be helpful to have this confirmed. Presumably the presence of overriding powers of appointment over capital in favour of surviving spouse would not be treated as breaching the s71A conditions while the s71A interest was a remainder interest.

HMRC Answer

A2.285   We agree (subject to our comments at question 19).

17. Question 20

A2.286   Can it be further confirmed that the analysis in 16 above will apply both where the prior interest in possession is an IPDI and also where there is an interest in possession arising under the will of a person who died prior to 22 March 2006 where the interests will, by definition, not be an IPDI although in all other respects identical to an IPDI.

HMRC Answer

A2.287   We can confirm this.

18. Question 21

A2.288   Can it be confirmed that, where a will contains a gift "to such of my children as reach 18 and if more than one in equal shares" or "to such of my children as reach 25 and if more than one in equal shares" all the interests will qualify as trusts for bereaved minors (or as age 18-to-25 trusts) even though one or more of the children might die after the testator but before the capital vests (so that their shares are divided between their siblings).

HMRC Answer

A2.289   We can confirm this. We consider that each child while alive and under 18/25 has a presumptive share that is held for his or her benefit, and one can apply s.71A or s.71D child by child and presumptive share by presumptive share.

Question 21 A

A2.290   On conversion of an existing pre-Budget a&m trust to s71D status does the class need to close *ab initio* from the date the trust was converted or is it sufficient to say that until someone else is born, the trusts for "B" do qualify as section 71D trusts but not actually close the class?

HMRC answer

A2.291   We consider that a trust in the position where anyone (whether unborn or not) who is not currently benefiting can nevertheless become entitled would not meet the requirements of s.71D(6), since it could not be said for certain that 'B' will become absolutely entitled to the settled property etc. in due course or that no income will be applied for any other person in the meantime. So we take the view that it will be necessary to close the class of beneficiaries for s.71D to apply.

19. Question 22

Can it be confirmed that the answer to Question 21 is not affected by a gift over provision that substitutes the children (if any) of a deceased child who attain a certain age, so that the increase of the siblings' shares is dependent upon whether the child dies childless.   A2.292

HMRC Answer

We can confirm this: the siblings' presumptive shares simply increase (or not) when one of their number dies, depending on whether or not the deceased child had any children of their own.   A2.293

20. Question 23

Can it be confirmed that agricultural property relief (apr) and business property relief (bpr) will apply to charges arising under section 71E. It would appear that these reliefs should be applicable as the charges under section 71D (by reference to section 71E) are charges under Chapter III or Part III IHTA and the reliefs are expressly extended to events of charge under this Chapter (section 103(1) IHTA in relation to bpr and section 115(1) in relation to apr). Further, the formula for calculating the charge under section 71F is similar, in principle, to the charges as calculated under section 65 and section 68 IHTA in relation to exit charges for relevant property generally. Can HMRC confirm this analysis is agreed?   A2.294

HMRC Answer

We agree – for the reasons given.   A2.295

21. Question 24

Section 71E(4) provides that there will be no event of charge where a transaction is entered into by trustees as a result of which the assets held subject to the 18-to-25 trusts are diminished in value, where the disposition by the trustees would not have been a transfer of value under section 10 or section 16 IHTA if they had been beneficially entitled to the trust assets. There is a further exemption in section 71E(3). There are no similar provisions in relation to actions by trustees concerning assets which are held on trusts qualifying under section 71A. Can it be confirmed that in practice HMRC would apply similar principles in relation to events of charge under section 71B for section 71A trusts?   A2.296

HMRC Answer

The provisions in s.71E that the question refers to are not reproduced in s.71B because the charge there arises under s.70 – and s.70 already includes identical provisions at subsections (3) and (4). S.71B(3) says: *"Subsections (3) to (8) and (10) of section 70 apply for the purposes of this section as they apply for the purposes of that section. . ."*   A2.297

22. Question 25

Can HMRC confirm that trusts which are held for beneficiaries as a class (e.g. on trust for such of my children as attain the age of 25 and if more than one in equal shares) will qualify as age 18-to-25 trusts under section 71D(3) and (4) notwithstanding that   A2.298

the class could be diminished by reason of the death of members of the class under the age of 25. While it might be said that the class gift does not fall within the strict wording of section 71D(6)(a) it might be said that nonetheless the assets are held on trust, for the time being, for each child being under the age of 25. HMRC are requested to confirm their view in relation to the continued application of 71D to class gifts where a beneficiary (B) dies before reaching 25 and the assets pass to the other beneficiaries under 25 on s71D trusts. (This is a separate point from the situation where in relation to existing inter vivos a&m trusts the class increases as a result of future beneficiaries being born before the eldest reaches 25.)

HMRC Answer

A2.299   We can confirm this. *CIOT/STEP note: further queries were raised with HMRC on the class closing rules and the application of s71D generally.*[123]

23. Question 26

A2.300   HMRC is asked to confirm that section 71A and section 71D will apply to trusts for a class of children whether or not the assets have been appropriated to each child's share.

HMRC Answer

A2.301   We can confirm this.

24. Question 27

A2.302   There will be a number of circumstances where different sets of beneficiaries under one accumulation and maintenance settlement may require to be treated differently (for example, a settlement for grandchildren where they differ widely in age). Can HMRC please confirm that trusts will qualify as 18-25 trusts or modified section 71 trusts (capital vesting at age 18) if those trusts exist in only part of the settled property. Thus, a settlement might be divided into two sub-funds, one for A's children who are approaching adulthood and for whom an 18-25 trust is appropriate and another for B's children who are very young and where the trustees value retaining flexibility so that that sub-fund will be allowed to fall within the relevant property regime with effect from 6 April 2008 (or be converted into an 18 trust).

HMRC Answer

A2.303   We can confirm this.

25. Question 28

A2.304   There has been some confusion about the interaction of s71D(3) and (4) with s71D(1) and (2). Please confirm that existing A&M trusts set up before the Budget where the settlor may still be alive (and the beneficiary's parent has not died) can qualify for 18-25 status if converted before April 2008 if this occurs immediately after the funds cease to qualify under s71.

HMRC Answer

A2.305   We can confirm that s.71D can apply to existing A&M trusts if the conversion occurs <u>before</u> the funds cease to qualify under s.71 – for the reasons set out in example 8 below.

---

[123] See A2.370 et seq.

Further that there is no inheritance tax charge on conversion of an existing accumulation and maintenance trust to a s71D trust. i.e. that para 3(3) schedule 20 protects all pre-Budget accumulation and maintenance trusts so that there is no inheritance tax entry charge either under s71 or otherwise, at the point the trust starts to qualify for s71D status (or indeed enters the relevant property regime).

A2.306

HMRC Answer

We can confirm this.

A2.307

Example 8

U sets up an accumulation and maintenance trust for his two nieces S and T in 1999. On 22 March 2006 neither has an interest in possession. Currently the nieces take capital at 30 and income at 21. S becomes 21 in January 2007. T becomes 21 in January 2011.

The trustees exercise their powers to ensure that the trusts qualify for 18-25 status in February 2007 i.e. after S has attained entitlement to income (albeit this is not a qualifying interest in possession post Budget). They provide that each child takes capital outright at 25 in a fixed half share. In these circumstances it would appear that S's share cannot qualify for 18-25 status because immediately after the property ceased to be subject to s71 it did not then fall within s71D. T's interest could however qualify under s71D. There is no inheritance tax charge in February 2007 on S's part although there would be a ten year charge in 2009 on her share because this share is now within the relevant property regime and there would be an exit charge when she reaches 25. There are no ten year or entry or exit charges on T's interest until she reaches 25 at which point her share is subject to tax at 4.2%. (This assumes that she does not die before reaching 25).

It would be helpful if this could be spelt out in the guidance notes because trustees need to be aware of the requirement to act swiftly if beneficiaries are about to take entitlement to income. It would also be helpful if examples could be given as to how 18-25 trusts work in practice and their main advantages i.e. to avoid the ten year anniversary charge.

HMRC Answer

We agree with the consequences set out in the example and will incorporate them in guidance.

A2.308

26. Question 29

It would appear that on the death of a child before 18 on a bereaved minor trust or on an 18-25 trust there is no inheritance tax charge even if they are entitled to income (albeit there is a base cost capital gains tax uplift if they are entitled to income).

A2.309

HMRC Answer

We agree – by virtue of s.71B(2)(b) or s.71E(2)(b) and new s.5(1)(a)(i).

It would appear that after a child reaches 18 there is an exit charge on an 18-25 trust if the property ceases to be held on 18-25 trusts but no base cost uplift for capital gains tax purposes whether or not the child has a right to income. Please confirm.

A2.310

HMRC Answer

We can confirm this.

A2.311

Question 30

A2.312 It would appear that, if a child reaches 18 and on his death his share of the trust fund remains on 18-25 trusts for his siblings under cross-accruer provisions, there will be no exit charge at that time. Please confirm.

HMRC Answer

A2.313 We can confirm this.

27. **Question 31**

A2.314 In the HMRC Customer Guide to Inheritance Tax recently published HMRC state under the heading of "What is an age 18 to 25 trust?"
"If the terms of the trust are not rewritten before 6 April 2008 and the trust has not come to an end then existing accumulation and maintenance trusts will automatically become relevant property trusts on the 18th birthday of the beneficiary."
What is the statutory justification for this view. First it is surely the case that an existing A&M trust can become subject to the relevant property regime before 6th April 2008 if a beneficiary takes a post –Budget interest in possession.

HMRC Answer

A2.315 We agree and will amend the Customer Guide.
Second our understanding is that such trusts will become relevant property trusts on the 6th April 2008 or the beneficiary becoming entitled to an interest in possession before that date unless the trust meets the requirements of a s71D trust. If nothing has been done by April 2008 and a beneficiary is not entitled to an interest in possession then the trust falls within the relevant property regime from that date whether or not the beneficiary is a minor. This point needs to be clarified urgently and the information amended.

HMRC Answer

A2.316 We agree. S.71D(5)(b) provides that s.71D does not apply to property to which s.71 applies. A&M treatment will therefore continue up to an including 5 April 2008 if the trusts of the settlement meet s.71, and will fall away on 6 April 2008. If the trusts provide for absolute entitlement at 18 or 25, the settlement will then fall within s.71A or s.71D as appropriate; if they do not, the settlement will be "relevant property" from that date.

28. **Question 32**

A2.317 Please also confirm whether or not hold over relief will be available if assets are distributed within 3 months of a beneficiary's 18th birthday under an 18-25 trust. There will be no inheritance tax charge as there will be no complete quarters since the 18th birthday. In these circumstances is hold over relief denied?

HMRC Answer

A2.318 No. The distribution is still an occasion on which IHT is chargeable – it is just that the charge will be nil. There is no provision in s.71F along the lines of s.65(4).

E Absolute interests

A2.319 29. Where assets are held by a person on bare trusts for minor children section 31 of the Trustee Act is implied in most cases without express reference and will apply unless expressly excluded.

30. It might be said that the application of the section will cause the property **A2.320**
concerned to be settled property within section 43(2)(b) in view of the
provisions for the accumulation of income under section 31(2) of the Trustee
Act. However, the contrary argument is that the accumulations of income are
held for the absolute benefit for the minor concerned and would pass to his
estate if he died under 18 (the minor not being able to give a good receipt) and
the assets are therefore not held in any real sense subject to any contingency
or provision for the diversion of income from the minor. This latter view
seems to be in line with the analysis in the IHT Manual which contemplates
that section 43(2)(b) deals with the position where there is relevant property
held on discretionary trusts (paragraph 4602). The statement in the Inland
Revenue letter of 12 February 1976 where, in the last sentence of the second
paragraph, it is stated that a provision to accumulate income will not prevent
there being an interest in possession if the accumulations are held for the
absolute benefit of the beneficiary, supports the view that section 31 of the
Trustee Act will not in these circumstances cause the relevant property regime
to apply.

31. **Question 33**

Can HMRC confirm that the application of section 31 of the Trustee Act 1925 to assets **A2.321**
held on a bare trust for a minor will not result in the assets being settled property within
the meaning of section 43 IHTA?

HMRC Answer

We confirm that our view is that where assets are held on an absolute trust (ie a bare **A2.322**
trust) for a minor the assets so held will not be settled property within the meaning of
section 43 IHTA 1984 and that this will be the case whether or not the provisions of
section 31 Trustee Act 1925 have been excluded.

There appear to be new and unforeseen capital gains tax problems now where *Crowe* **A2.323**
v Appleby [1975] (STC 502) applies on settled property. The position is complex albeit
common and can best be illustrated by example.

Example 9

In February 2006 Andrew set up a trust for his children Charlotte and Luke.
They each become entitled to one half of the income and capital on reaching
25. Charlotte becomes 25 in 2007 and Luke becomes 25 in 2009. They do not
take interests in possession until reaching 25. The trust only holds one piece of
land.

When Charlotte reaches 25 in 2007 she becomes absolutely entitled for inheritance
tax purposes since Crowe v Appleby has no application for IHT purposes. The
trusts over her share end for inheritance tax purposes before April 6 2008 so there
is no exit charge since she is within the transitional regime. She is treated from 2007
as entitled to the half share in the property and if she died after that date it would
form part of her estate for inheritance tax purposes and hence be potentially
taxable.

There is a further problem. For capital gains tax purposes Charlotte does not
become absolutely entitled to one half of the land. Until the land is sold or Luke
reaches 25 and becomes absolutely entitled (whichever is the earlier) there is no
disposal made by the trustees.

There is no inheritance tax change on 6 April 2008 but from that date Luke's
share is no longer within A&M trust protection but is taxed as an 18-25 trust.

There is no ten year anniversary charge before Luke reaches 25 but if he dies before then there is an inheritance tax charge (likely to be less than 4.2%). As noted above, there is no base cost uplift for capital gains tax purposes.

On Luke reaching 25 in 2009 there is an exit charge on Luke's share of 4.2%.

HMRC Answer

A2.324 (Note: we do not consider this is quite right. We assume that the 4.2% is referred to on the basis of 7/10ths x 6%. However, the charge will not be based on the 7 years from Luke's 18th birthday. S.71F(5)(a) provides that the starting date for calculating the relevant fraction is his 18th birthday "or, if later, the day on which the property became property to which section 71D above applies" – in this case, 6 April 2008).

If the land has not yet been sold there will at that point be a disposal of all the land by the trustees for capital gains tax purposes because both beneficiaries become absolutely entitled. Hold over relief is available on Luke's part under s260 TCGA 1992 but not on Charlotte's part since there is no exit charge. In summary, the trustees will have to pay capital gains tax on any gain on Charlotte's share in 2009 and cannot hold over the gain on that share.

Question 34

A2.325 Prior to the Finance Act 2006, Charlotte would have been treated as having a qualifying interest in possession in her share of the trust assets. If she died before Luke reached 25, there would have been a charge to inheritance tax on her death but because she had a qualifying interest in possession, for capital gains tax purposes, there would be an uplift in base cost on her share of the land under s72(1) TCGA 1992. Post the Finance Act 2006, if Charlotte dies before Luke reaches 25 there will be a charge to inheritance tax but s72(1) TCGA 1992 does not seem to be applicable because Charlotte does not appear to have a qualifying interest in possession which qualifies her for the uplift. Hence she is subject to inheritance tax on her death with no uplift for capital gains tax.

Will HMRC regard her as having a qualifying interest in possession within section 72 for these purposes?

HMRC Answer

A2.326 No – with the result, as stated, that there would be no CGT uplift under s.72(1) TCGA.

Question 35

A2.327 If Charlotte attained 25 in say June 2015 and Luke only reached 25 in 2017 there would be an exit charge on both Luke and Charlotte's shares when each becomes 25 (rate = 4.2%) but hold over relief is only available on Luke's share when the disposal of the land takes place for capital gains tax purposes.

Prior to the Finance Act 2006 there would have been no exit charge when Charlotte reached 25. However, the effect of the new rules is that on reaching 25 Charlotte will now suffer an exit charge but without any entitlement to hold-over the gain which arises when the land is distributed to her when Luke reaches 25. Will HMRC in these circumstances allow hold over relief on both shares?

HMRC Answer

A2.328 No – hold-over relief will be due on Luke's share only.

F Disabled trusts

33. Section 89A(2) appears to conflict with s89A(3). Condition 1 states that if any of the settled property is applied for A it is applied for the benefit of A but Condition 2 envisages that capital <u>could</u> be paid to A or another person on the termination of A's interest during his life provided that the other person became absolutely entitled.   **A2.329**

Question 36

Is HMRC's view that capital can be appointed to someone else on the termination of the trust only if it can be demonstrated that it is for the benefit of A?   **A2.330**

HMRC Answer

No – we do not consider that that condition is in point.   **A2.331**
   Otherwise why does s89A(3) Condition 2 refer to other persons at all?

HMRC Answer

We do not agree with the proposition that there is a conflict between s.89A(2) and (3). Condition 1 refers to the application of "settled property" – i.e. to property that is held on the trusts referred to in s.89A(1)(c). Condition 2, however, is applying conditions that are effective in the event of such trusts being brought to an end.   **A2.332**

G General points

34. **Question 37(1)**

New sections 46A(4) and 46B(5) provide that additions (by way of payment of further premiums) to a pre-Budget interest in possession or A&M trust which holds an insurance policy would not result either in a chargeable transfer or in any part of the trust falling within the relevant property regime.   **A2.333**
   It is understood that HMRC believe that additions of cash or other property to existing pre-Budget interest in possession settlements are subject to the new rules in Schedule 20.
   There are other payments which are often made by settlors or beneficiaries on behalf of a trust. For example, buildings insurance premiums and general maintenance costs, payments to cover trust, administration and taxation expenses.
   It is noted that for the purposes of TCGA 1992 Sch 5 para 9(3) the payment of expenses relating to administration and taxation of a trust are not be treated as the addition of property to the trust. In SP 5/92 the costs of acquiring, enhancing and disposing of a trust asset are not regarded as expenses relating to administration but other property expenses appear to fall within the definition and therefore are not treated as the addition of property to the trust. Would HMRC maintain that the addition of cash or other property to a settlement which may be used either to enhance trust property (eg payment of costs relating to the building of an extension to property) or to purchase other property will be treated as additions but accept that the payment of other trustee expenses (eg trustee fees, buildings insurance premiums and general maintenance costs) will not be treated as chargeable additions?

HMRC Answer

Schedule 5 TCGA is a statutory provision relating to certain, specific circumstances. There is no legal basis on which payments of "other trustee expenses" should not be treated as chargeable additions for IHT purposes.   **A2.334**

Question 37(2)

A2.335 If any of the additions do bring the trust within the new rules, what property within the trust will be caught and how will it be valued? For example, if an addition of cash was made which was then spent by the trustees and HMRC regard this addition as within the relevant property regime (eg an addition to pay expenses or improve properties), how would the proportion of the settled property subject to the new rules be calculated? Would a valuation be needed of the property before and after the improvement? In HMRC's view, do all subsequent post Budget additions need to be kept physically segregated?

HMRC Answer

A2.336 [If a payment of cash was made and then spent immediately on, say, a tax liability or another administration expense, then that short period will be the extent of its time as "relevant property" and there will be no question of having to consider what proportion of the existing settled property represents it going forward.

If a payment was made towards the improvement of a property, then this would appear to require "with" and "without" valuations when there is a chargeable event. [Note added 6 August 2008: HMRC have indicated that they are actively reconsidering this response with a view to producing further guidance shortly.]

It is clearly up to trustees to decide whether to keep post-Budget additions separate from the rest of the trust fund. We think that it may be sensible to do so – or, at least, to keep good records of additions. (The trustees of discretionary trusts already need to do this, of course, in order for the 10-year anniversary value of each addition to be identified correctly in light of the relief in s.66(2) IHTA for property that has not been "relevant property" for a full 10-year period).

35. **Question 38**

A2.337 It is understood that additions to a trust which fall within the normal expenditure out of income exemption will not need to be reported as and when they are made as, following the normal rules, it is not necessary to report exempt transactions? Please confirm.

HMRC Answer

A2.338 We can confirm this.

36. **Question 39**

A2.339 It is not unknown for wills to include a gift of an annuity. Some wills give the executors sufficient powers to enable them to choose how best to satisfy the annuity. In such a case there are typically four methods which executors may use to deal with an annuity.

- Pay the annuity out of residue. In such a case the executors delay the completion of the administration of the estate until the annuitant dies.
- Create an appropriated annuity fund. In such a case the executors appropriate a capital fund of sufficient size to pay the annuity.
- Purchase an annuity. The executors purchase an annuity from an insurance office or life company.
- Commute the annuity. The executors pay the annuitant a cash sum sufficient to allow him to purchase the annuity personally.

The first two options create settled property. Will HMRC confirm that a provision in a will conferring the payment of an annuity upon a person (eg to make a gift of an annuity of £x for life) which the executors satisfy by one of the first two options outlined above will be treated as the creation of an IPDI in favour of the annuitant?

HMRC Answer

We can confirm this.   **A2.340**
   Under s50(2), where a person is entitled to a specified amount (such as an annuity) for any period his interest is taken to subsist in that part of the property that produces that amount in that period. The property in which his interest subsists may therefore vary over time.

Example 10

> Say A is entitled to an annuity of £1,000 and the executors set aside a fund of £40,000 to pay this annuity. In year 1 the income from the £40,000 is £2,000 and half is paid to the annuitant. In year 2 the income from the £40,000 is £1,000 and all the income is paid to A. In year 3 (the year in which the annuitant dies) the income from the £40,000 is £4,000 and a quarter is paid to A. Please could HMRC confirm what property would fall within A's estate on his death (assuming he is treated as having an IPDI) and the basis upon which this has been calculated?

HMRC Answer

We would follow the existing principles set out in s.50(2) to s.50(5) IHTA at the date of   **A2.341**
A's death. (As Dymond, at 16.611, points out, s.50(2) does not give any guidance as to the period over which the income of the settled property should be computed. But the learned authors suggest that looking at the income in the year immediately before the chargeable occasion would normally be a reasonable approach and we would agree.)

H Deeds of variation

Questions have arisen as to the effect of deeds of variation post-Budget.   **A2.342**

37. Example 11

> Testator dies pre-Budget leaving everything outright to X. His will is varied by   **A2.343**
> X and an election made under s 142 to treat the variation as made by the will.

Question 40

Any trust established by the variation will be treated as having been established pre-   **A2.344**
Budget whether or not the variation is actually made pre- or post-Budget. If an interest in possession trust is established under such a variation by X, we assume it will be a qualifying interest in possession given it is deemed to be set up prior to the Budget by the deceased and not by X for inheritance tax purposes and further that it will be possible to create a transitional serial interest in relation to this trust before April 2008. Please confirm.

HMRC Answer

We can confirm this.   **A2.345**

38. Example 12

A2.346   Testator dies post-Budget leaving everything outright to Y. His will is varied to establish ongoing trusts and an election made under s 142 to read the variation back into the will.

Question 41

A2.347   Assuming that the terms of the trusts are appropriate, it is possible to establish IPDIs, 18-25 trusts and BMTs by way of such a variation made by Y. Please confirm. As in question 40 it is assumed that for inheritance tax purposes the settlor is the deceased rather than Y.

HMRC Answer

A2.348   We can confirm this.

39. Example 13

The testator is not domiciled in the UK at his death leaving everything outright to Z. His will dealing with property outside the UK is varied to establish trusts and an election made under s 142 to read the variation back into the will.

Question 42

A2.349   Any trusts established by the variation holding non-UK property will be excluded property trusts whatever the domicile status of Z (the beneficiary making the variation) and whatever the terms of the new trusts. This will be the case whether or not the testator died pre- or post-Budget. Please confirm.

HMRC Answer

A2.350   We can confirm this.
A2.351   **40.** Section 54A IHTA contains certain anti-avoidance provisions that arise where a settlor settles assets into a qualifying interest in possession trust by PET and then the life interest is terminated so that discretionary trusts arise within 7 years. In effect the settlor rather than the life tenant can be treated as having made the chargeable transfer if this yields more tax. S54A(1A) states that where a person becomes beneficially entitled on or after 22 March 2006 to a disabled person's interest or a TSI, s54(1)(b) applies. So if the disabled person or the holder of the TSI dies and relevant property trusts arise, the anti-avoidance provision potentially applies. Nothing is said though in respect of inter vivos terminations of the TSI or disabled person's interest when relevant property trusts arise and the termination occurs within 7 years of the original PET made by the settlor.

Question 43

A2.352   Is it intended that s54A should only apply to interests in possession arising on or after 22 March 2006 if the disabled person's interest or TSI terminates on death rather than inter vivos?

HMRC Answer

A2.353   Section 54A applies both to lifetime terminations of a TSI or disabled person's interest where the other conditions of s54A are satisfied as well as a termination on the death of the life tenant. The fact that s54A(1)(A) refers expressly to death and not to lifetime terminations does not mean that s54A did not cover both scenarios because s54A(1) covered lifetime terminations. We believe s54A can apply to both inter vivos and terminations on death because s.54A (1)(a) refers back to s.52, where s.52 (2A) already provides that, where the person becomes beneficially entitled to the interest in possession on or after 22 March 2006, there will only be a charge under s.52 (1) – and so s.54A will only potentially apply – if the interest is:

- an immediate post-death interest,

- a disabled person's interest, or

- a transitional serial interest.

Submitted to HMRC by The Chartered Institute of Taxation and The Society of Trust and Estate Practitioners on 7 September 2006

Response by HMRC on 3 November 2006 (as amended on 12 December 2006, January 2007 and April 2007)

Note: answer to question 33 added on 4 April 2007 based on letter from HMRC dated 23 March 2007.

Note the change to question 37(2) on 16 July 2008 as a result of discussions with HMRC. Some additional comments have also been added in the notes below the replies to questions 9 and 25.

Changes made throughout to reflect FA 2008 and to add a note after HMRC's response to question 6 on 3 October 2008.

8. IHT SCHEDULE 20: CIOT/STEP CORRESPONDENCE ON TRANSITIONAL SERIAL INTERESTS (MAY 2007)

Finance Act 2006 Schedule 20: pre-existing interests in possession and related matters

A2.354 We are writing about a number of situations (set out in the questions below) where a person (A) was beneficially entitled to an interest in possession in settled property before 22 March 2006. Doubt has been expressed as to whether section 49(1) of the Inheritance Tax Act 1984 will continue to apply in the future, notwithstanding that A will throughout be entitled to the income of the settled property. We consider that, in all those situations, section 49(1) will continue to apply, notwithstanding section 49(1A) which (with exceptions) disapplies that sub-section where the interest in possession is one to which a person becomes beneficially entitled on or after 22 March 2006.

It has been suggested that A will, after that date, become entitled to a different proprietary interest in the settled property. As the Revenue argued in *Pearson v IRC* [1981] AC 753, and all the members of the House of Lords appear to have accepted, for inheritance tax purposes the expression "interest in possession" must be construed as a single phrase. Pearson decided that it means a present right to present enjoyment of the settled property, ie the right to the income from that property as it arises. And in each of the relevant situations, A became entitled to that right before 22 March 2006. Section 49(1A) does not, therefore, in our view, apply.

If we are right about this, then it means that the IHT treatment of the relevant situations will not depend on the accident of the particular drafting technique adopted, with settlements being treated differently notwithstanding that A's rights are the same and without any possible policy justification that we have been able to identify.

We would emphasise that, in each of the examples below, the trustees have not exercised any dispositive powers post-March 2006: the interest taken by A remains throughout merely an entitlement to income and, moreover, an entitlement which is defined under the terms of the settlement prior to March 2006.

We hope that you will be able to confirm that section 49(1) will continue to apply and, therefore, that the same pre-Budget interest in possession will continue to subsist in each of the following examples.

Example 1

(1) Settled property is held on trust to pay the income to A for life contingently on A attaining the age of 25. The trust carries the intermediate income.

(2) A attained the age of 18 on 1 January 2006 and thereupon became entitled to an interest in possession by virtue of section 31 of the Trustee Act 1925. Section 49(1) applies.

In our view, it will continue to apply after age 25, when the express trust to pay income to him comes into effect. On any footing, A has only one interest, being the present right to present enjoyment, brought into possession earlier than would otherwise be the case by section 31.

Question 1 - do HMRC agree?   A2.354

HMRC Answer to Question 1 – We agree.

Example 2

(1) Under a pre-Budget 2006 trust, A is entitled to capital contingently on attaining the age of 25 years. The clause goes on to provide that the trusts carry the intermediate income and section 31 of the Trustee Act is to apply.

(2) The same clause provides that the capital should not vest absolutely on A attaining the age of 25 but should be retained on trust:

    a. to pay the income to A for life, and then
    b. for A's children after A's death,

(3) A attained the age of 18 on 1 January 2006. Section 49(1) applies.

(4) In our view, it will continue to apply after A attains the age of 25 on 1 January 2013, when the "engrafted" trust to pay income to A comes into effect.

Question 2 – do HMRC agree?   A2.356

HMRC Answer to Question 2 – We agree.

Example 3

The facts are the same as example 3, except that the engrafted trusts are contained in a separate clause. In our view, the position is the same, and section 49(1) will continue to apply after A attains the age of 25.

Question 3 – do HMRC agree?   A2.357

HMRC Answer to Question 3 – We agree.

Example 4

(1) A became entitled to income at 25 in January 2006 and section 49(1) applies.

(2) A is contingently entitled to capital at the age of 35, but the trustees retain overriding powers of appointment exercisable during his lifetime. He therefore attains only a defeasible interest in capital in 2016, and the capital remains settled property until his death.

(3) In our view, section 49(1) will continue to apply after A attains the age of 35, notwithstanding that his contingent interest in capital is replaced by a vested but defeasible interest in capital.

A2.358   Question 4 – do HMRC agree?

HMRC Answer to question 4 – We agree.

Example 5

> Presumably, where a transitional serial interest (TSI) arose after 21 March 2006
> but before 6 April 2008 (e.g. a pre-22 March 06 Budget life tenant's interest was
> ended in 2007 and A the new life tenant takes an immediate interest in possession
> and capital at 35 but that capital entitlement is defeasible being subject to any
> exercise of the overriding powers), HMRC would agree that section 49C contin-
> ues to apply to A after he attains the age of 35 for the same reasons, ie that his
> transitional serial interest entitlement continues following his 35th birthday.

A2.359   Question 5 – do HMRC agree?

HMRC Answer to Question 5 – We agree.

In all the above examples, A's interest arises under the terms of the Settlement, and not
from the exercise of the trustees' powers. We think these examples can be distinguished
from the case where a beneficiary is absolutely entitled to capital on reaching a specified
age and the trustees positively exercise their powers to defer that absolute entitlement
and maintain the interest in possession, where we understand that different issues may
arise as set out in the previous reply to queries on Schedule 20 – see questions revised
in © 2007 and in particular Question 6

HMRC Answer - agreed

Interest in possession which continues after death of life tenant

A2.360   In some circumstances, an interest in possession may continue after the death of the
person entitled to the interest up until their death. HMRC have confirmed that a lifetime
assignment of an interest in possession will qualify as a TSI (assuming the other requirements are satisfied - Question 10 of Schedule 20 letter) on the basis that the interest in
possession will have "come to an end" within the meaning of section 49C(3), presumably on the basis of IHTA section 51(1). There is no equivalent provision to IHTA
section 51(1) in relation to transfers on death of an autre vie, but the entitlement of the
prior beneficiary who is holding an interest pur autre vie will have come to an end, even
though the interest itself will not have done so. This may arise, for example, where the
will of the deceased life tenant leaves their residuary estate, which would include their
remaining entitlement to the interest pur autre vie, to their surviving spouse.

Question 6

Do HMRC consider that, when a pre-Budget interest in possession beneficiary who
holds the pur autre vie dies, any interest in possession in such property then taken by
his spouse (or any other person if that occurs before 6 © 2008) will qualify as a transitional serial interest?

   HMRC Answer to Question 6 - Yes. In the circumstances outlined, it would seem that
the death of the beneficiary holding a pur autre vie interest must bring "the prior interest" within the terms of s49C IHTA to an end.

IHTA 1984 section 46B

A2.361   We should be grateful if you would confirm your view in relation to pre-Budget 2006
settled life policies, where a policy is held on section 71 accumulation and maintenance

trusts and the trusts are then converted into trusts within section 71D IHTA. Insurance premiums continue to be paid on the policy.

It is clear that the continued payment of the insurance premiums will be potentially exempt transfers under section 46B(5).

Question 7

Are the added rights arising from the payment of the premiums settled property within section 71D, or are they separate settled property which is within the relevant property regime?

A2.362

There is no equivalent provision in relation to section 71D trusts to section 46B(2), which applies for section 71 trusts where premiums continue to be paid on or after 22 March 2006. Section 46B(2) provides that the rights arising by reference to the payment of the further premiums shall also be within section 71 if they would be but for section71(1A).

The rights arising from the payment of premiums on policies held on trusts where the payments are made after such trust has been converted to section 71D status do not appear to be strictly within section 71D(3), which is necessary for those rights to be held on trusts within section 71D. Section 46B(1) in relation to section 71 trusts refers to sections 46B(2) and (5), but section 46B(3) in relation to section 71D trusts only refers to section 46B(5).

Do HMRC accept that the policy held on section 71D trusts is, in reality, the same asset as that previously held on section 71 trusts and that, in effect, no new rights become comprised in the settlement so that all the policy and its proceeds would be within section 71D?

We would be grateful for HMRC's views on this.

HMRC Answer to question 7 – we do accept that any added rights from the payment of additional premiums would constitute settled property within s71D. If a premium paid once the policy has become property to which s71D applies gives rise to an addition to the settled property the addition will, in our view, automatically become property to which s71D applies.

Section 200

Finally, we note that, under section 200(1)(a), a person with a non-qualifying interest in possession can become personally liable for the tax charged on death, with his liability limited only by reference to the value of the settled property (not the value of his actuarial interest). This seems a somewhat draconian provision, given that the beneficiary is no longer treated as beneficially entitled to the capital. Surely the liability should be limited to the property or income he actually receives? Similarly, in section 201(1) (b), the liability seems anomalous, given that most interests in possession will now be non-qualifying. Why should a beneficiary with a non-qualifying interest in possession have a greater personal liability than a discretionary beneficiary? Can we press for these sections to be reviewed?

A2.363

HMRC Answer – we do not accept that there is an anomaly here. Although an IIP holder whose interest arose before 22.3.06 has been regarded as owning the underlying property for inheritance tax purposes, in reality he has only ever owned a limited interest. The FA 2006 changes do not alter the IIP owner's real position.

9. IHT SCHEDULE 20: CIOT/STEP CORRESPONDENCE ON SP10/79
(September 2007)

Schedule 20 – SP 10/79 and Transitional Serial Interests

A2.364   I am writing on behalf of STEP and the CIOT. We spoke in February about SP10/79. There have been a number of queries raised by members of the representative bodies about the longer term implications of this statement in the light of Schedule 20. Both STEP and the CIOT feel that it is important for these matters to be clarified, so that trustees can be made aware of the IHT implications of decisions they may make relating to property owned by the trust.

SP 10/79 says that (assuming the trustees have sufficient powers) if such a power "is exercised with the intention of providing a particular beneficiary with a permanent home the Revenue will normally regard the exercise of the power as creating an interest in possession." You confirmed that it was not necessary for the trustees to have exercised their powers *in writing* before they could confer an interest in possession. The question of whether they have exercised their powers so as to give a beneficiary a present right to occupy is, in effect, a question of fact which has to be deduced from all the surrounding circumstances and the intentions of the trustees at the relevant time.

Question 1 – when does an interest in possession not arise?

A2.365   One issue that was always unclear is the use of the word "normally" in that SP.

In what circumstances would HMRC *not* regard the exercise of the power by trustees which gives a beneficiary an exclusive right of occupation as *not* creating an interest in possession? *Judge and Judge (Walden's Personal Representative) v HMRC (2005) STC(SCD)863* was a case where the trustees never positively exercised their powers because they did not know that she had, or they thought that she already had, an interest in possession.

HMRC Answer to question 1 - We imagine the instances where we would not regard the exercise of the power by trustees to give an exclusive right of occupation as creating an interest in possession would be rare. But such instances might be where there was no evidence of an intention by the trustees to provide a particular beneficiary with a permanent home or where significant doubt about the intentions of the trustees existed.

Question 2 – when does an SP 10/79 interest arise?

A2.366   It seems that the question of whether an interest in possession has been conferred comes down to whether the trustees have indeed exercised their powers in this way intending to confer exclusive occupation. While HMRC cannot give a definitive answer on a particular case without knowing the facts of that case, if there is evidence that the trustees have indeed *knowingly* exercised their powers so as to give a beneficiary exclusive occupation then we assume that, as a matter of principle, HMRC would consider an interest in possession has been created and, on the same basis, that the trustees could reasonably form a view themselves on this point if the relevant facts justified this conclusion.

Do you agree?

HMRC Answer to question 2 - We agree.

Question 3 - when does an SP 10/79 interest end – replacement properties?

Where it is clear that a beneficiary has acquired an interest in possession pursuant to SP10/79, the question of the nature of that interest in possession then needs to be considered in the light of the transitional serial interest regime.

A2.367

A beneficiary who acquires an interest in possession in line with SP 10/79 merely acquires a present right of occupation. Whether such a beneficiary acquires a right to occupy that *particular* property, or a right to occupy any house for the time being held by the trustees, would seem to depend on the facts and the trustees' intention at the relevant time.

It could be argued that the interest in possession conferred by the trustees will not also include a right to income (assuming that the trustees have merely exercised their powers to allow a beneficiary to occupy property). Hence it is possible that when the land is sold the interest in possession may cease.

Scenario 1

Trustees commonly wish to provide a home for a beneficiary in the long term, with a view to replacing the initial property with another if the beneficiary's family circumstances make this appropriate. They intend from the outset that the beneficiary should have the right to occupy any property owned by the trust, not just the property owned at the time occupation first commences.

A2.368

If the original property occupied by the beneficiary is sold, in practice the sale proceeds will be held with the specific intention of providing another home for the beneficiary by purchase of a replacement property.

In our view, and we understand that this is the view that HMRC have taken in practice in the past, the beneficiary acquires an interest in possession in the property when it is first occupied, and that interest continues even though the property is sold and a replacement property is then purchased and occupied by that same beneficiary. In such cases, there can be no question of the interest in possession coming to an end when the property is sold, and a new interest in possession commencing when the replacement property has been purchased and the beneficiary enters into occupation. If, therefore, the beneficiary began occupation on or before 21 March 2006 and the property is later replaced by another property using the proceeds of sale, the pre-March 2006 interest in possession continues unchanged.

Do you agree?

HMRC Answer to Question 2 - We agree that it is important to review the facts and the evidence of the trustees' intentions to identify the extent of the beneficiary's right of occupation. As far as Scenario 1 is concerned, we would agree with your proposition, on the basis that there is clear evidence that the trustees intended the beneficiary to have the right to occupy any property owned by the trustees for the purpose of providing a home for him.

Question 4 – when does an SP 10/79 interest end – specific property?

Scenario 2

In other cases, the trustees may merely have intended to provide a specific home for the beneficiary by granting him the right to occupy a named property owned by the trust. In such circumstances, the beneficiary's interest in possession could be said to be

A2.369

restricted to that particular property so that, if that property is sold, even though it may be replaced in the future, the beneficiary's interest in possession would end when the first property is sold.

Do you agree?

HMRC Answer to Question 4 - We agree.

Question 5 – transitional serial interests

A2.370 In scenario 2, the trustees may decide to exercise their dispositive powers before the property is sold, but whilst the beneficiary remains in occupation. They may decide to appoint to the beneficiary an interest in possession in the settled property for the time being, irrespective of whether it comprises a house. In a case where, on analysis, the beneficiary had, as at 21 March 2006, a right to occupy a named property only, if the trustees exercise their powers in this way before 6 April 2008, a new interest will be created which, it would seem, qualifies as a transitional serial interest.

The conditions in section 49C would appear to be satisfied in that, before 22 March, the property *then* comprised in the settlement (the particular house) is property in which B was beneficially entitled to an interest in possession (Condition 1). B then becomes beneficially entitled to the current interest at any time before 6 April 2008 (such interest now being different in nature). We appreciate that HMRC may take the view that section 53(2A) applies to impose an entry charge (a point on which I have written separately).

Do you agree?

HMRC Answer to Question 5 - We agree with your analysis that the replacement interest in possession envisaged in Scenario 2 would qualify as a transitional serial interest.

10. SCHEDULE 20: HMRC GUIDANCE ON SECTION 71A TO 71D AND ACCUMULATION AND MAINTENANCE TRUSTS (CIOT/STEP CORREPSONDENCE IN JUNE 2007)

This guidance has been agreed with HMRC. It outlines the way in which HMRC interpret s71 (as amended by FA 2006), s71A and ss 71D-H IHTA 1984. **It should not be regarded as a comprehensive explanation covering all aspects of these sections.** **A2.371**

There are three particular areas of concern, namely:

1. the meaning of "B" in the legislation;

2. the class closing rules;

3. the scope of settled powers of advancement.

1. The meaning of "B" or "bereaved minor" in the legislation

Both s71A and s71D are drafted by reference to a single beneficiary (in s71D called "B" and in s71A called the bereaved minor). However, HMRC consider that it is possible to pluralise B or the bereaved minor to include all beneficiaries within the relevant class provided they are <u>alive</u> at the date the s71A or s71D trust takes effect and are under the specified age. **A2.372**

Accordingly a will trust in the following terms can qualify as a s71A trust:

> "*to such of my children alive at my death as attain the age of 18 years and if more than one in such shares as the trustees shall from time to time by deed or deeds revocable or irrevocable appoint and in default of such appointment in equal shares absolutely at 18 provided that no such appointment shall be made and no such appointment shall be revoked so as to either diminish or to increase the share (or the accumulations of income forming part of the share) of or give a new share (or new accumulations of income) to a child who at the date of such appointment or revocation has reached the age of 18 nor to benefit a child who has been excluded from benefit as a result of the exercise of the power.*"

Note the following:

It is not necessary to fix the shares in which each child takes income and capital while they are all under 18. Hence it is possible to pay out income and capital to the minor children in unequal shares. **A2.373**

The power of selection must not be capable of being exercised so as to vary the share of a child who has <u>already</u> reached 18. Assume three beneficiaries B1, B2 and B3. It is possible to specify at any time before the eldest (B1) reaches 18 the share he is to take but once he reaches 18 any further power of selection can only be exercised between B2 and B3. B1 ceases to be within the definition of "B" in these circumstances.

A2.374   If the power of selection is exercised revocably then it is not possible by revoking that exercise to benefit someone who has been wholly excluded from benefit albeit revocably. If, for example, the whole relevant share is appointed revocably to B3 (but on terms that the appointment could be revoked to confer benefits on B1 or B2) then even though B1 and B2 are under 18 the trust ceases to qualify for s71A status. HMRC consider that it is not possible under the s71A regime for someone who is not currently benefiting to become entitled in the future. Practitioners will therefore need to be careful before exercising any power of appointment revocably.

HMRC do not consider that section 71A is breached merely because a power of appointment might be exercised in this way. Nor is it a problem if, in the above example, the power of appointment is exercised revocably so as to give B1 5%, B2 5% and B3 90%. Since B1 and B2 are not wholly excluded HMRC take the view that they can still benefit under a future exercise of the power since they remain within "B".

A2.375   Nor is there a problem if a beneficiary dies under 18 leaving children in whose favour there will be incorporated substitutional provisions. Hence if B1 dies before 18 leaving children and his presumptive or fixed share passes to those children under the terms of the Will, it is only from that point that the presumptive share of B1 will cease to qualify under s71A and fall within the relevant property regime. The mere possibility that B1 could die before 18 with children taking his share does not breach the s71A conditions. Any power of selection though must not be capable of varying the presumptive share of the deceased B1 once he has died – because B1's children are not within the definition of B and their share must not be increased or deceased after B1 has died.

A2.376   No overriding powers of appointment can be included so that "B's" absolute entitlement could be defeated at 18 although the legislation provides that the existence of an extended power of advancement (ie an express or statutory power of advancement that could be used to defer the beneficiary's capital entitlement by, for instance, providing that his share was to be held on life interest trusts beyond the age of 18) will not in itself cause the trust to fail to satisfy the s71A conditions from the outset. However, if the settled power of advancement is exercised so as to defer vesting of capital at 18 (e.g. by the making of a settled advance) then although there is no charge under s71A on the ending of the bereaved minor trust the relevant share from that point falls within the relevant property regime.

A2.377   All the points above apply to section 71D trusts set up by Will and to accumulation and maintenance ('A&M') trusts which are converted to fall within s71D before 6 April 2008 (or before a beneficiary has attained an interest in possession if earlier). Hence it will be necessary to ensure that any powers of appointment that are retained do not permit a beneficiary's absolute share to be altered after he has reached 25 or defeated on reaching that age and if a power of appointment is exercised revocably it must not be capable of benefiting anyone who has been wholly excluded from benefit (even if under 25 and even if the exclusion was revocable).

2. The class closing rules

A2.378   2.1   Difficult questions arise where an existing A&M trust is converted into a s71D trust. Existing A&M trusts can become s71D trusts provided this happens on the earlier of the beneficiary taking an entitlement to income or by 6 April 2008.[124]

---

[124] It will not be possible to convert an A&M trust into a s.71D trust after the beneficiary has become entitled to income on or after March 22, 2006 because once a beneficiary takes entitlement to income it no longer qualifies as an A&M trust under s71. Section 71D(3)(b) requires conversion of the trusts immediately before the property ceases to be property to which s.71 applies. Hence, it will need to be s.71D-compliant by the time the beneficiary attains an interest in possession. Of course if one beneficiary becomes entitled to income from part of the trust fund the remaining part will remain within the A&M regime and so may be converted subsequently (but before April 6, 2008).

2.2 In the case of existing A&M trusts it is possible that the class of potential beneficiaries will not yet have closed. (This is different from s71A and s71D trusts set up by Will where by definition the deceased parent cannot have any further children, apart from the case of a child en ventre sa mère whose father has died). In the same way that HMRC do not consider "B" can include a beneficiary who has been excluded from benefit (albeit revocably) HMRC do not consider that B can include any unborn beneficiary, again, apart from a child en ventre sa mère.

2.3 So if, for example, an existing A&M trust in favour of the settlor's grandchildren provides that the class closes only when the eldest becomes 25 and the trust currently benefits only B1 and B2 (say grandchildren of a settlor) being the sole living beneficiaries aged 8 and 9, in order to be s71D compliant, the terms of the trust must be amended to exclude any future born beneficiaries. If B1 and B2's parent has a further child in 2009 that child must not be capable of benefiting from the trust fund (except in the event of the death of either B1 or B2 in which case the relevant portion of the trust will from that point fall within the relevant property regime).

2.4 Hence the power to appoint shares must only be exercisable between all or some of the beneficiaries under 25 who are alive at the date of conversion to s71D status. HMRC consider this follows from the drafting in s71D(1)(a),(3)(b)(i) and (6)(a) when taken together.

2.5 This is not the case if an existing A&M trust continues to satisfy the conditions in s71 beyond April 08 because it falls within para 3 schedule 20 FA 2006. A trust which provides for all grandchildren to take outright at 18 will continue to have A&M status under s71, as amended by para 3, Sch 20, beyond April 2008. It will be possible to pay income and capital between them in such shares as the trustees think fit and for future born children to benefit if the trust deed permits this flexibility provided that no child's share can be varied after reaching 18. The class should therefore generally be closed once the eldest child reaches 18.

3. The scope of extended powers of advancement

HMRC accept that the mere possibility of a power of advancement being used to defer entitlement to capital at 18 or 25 does not cause the trust to fail to satisfy the requirements of s71A or s71D given the terms of s71A (4) or s71D(7) respectively. If the power of advancement is exercised in favour of that person so as to create continuing trusts under which the beneficiary's capital entitlement will be deferred beyond the age of 18 or 25 as appropriate, those trusts will fall within the relevant property regime (with either no exit charge in the case of BMTs or with the usual exit charge under s71E, computed according to the provisions in s71F, assuming the proper exercise of the power causes property to be "paid or applied for the advancement or benefit of B"; otherwise, the computation would be under s.71G).

A2.379

HMRC accept that in the case of A&M trusts (including trusts which are modified so that they satisfy the amended s71 definition after 6 April 2008) the mere inclusion of a wide power of advancement is unobjectionable. The exercise of such a power will not trigger an inheritance tax charge if the beneficiary takes absolutely or an interest in possession (albeit not qualifying) on or before 18 (see s71(4) IHTA 1984) and his capital entitlement is deferred beyond 18, although in the latter event, the trust for the beneficiary will thenceforth be a relevant property trust unless it can come within s71D.

11. HMRC BRIEF 18/2011: EMPLOYEE BENEFIT TRUSTS: INHERITANCE TAX AND INCOME TAX ISSUES

Introduction

A2.380   Employment Benefit Trusts are discretionary trusts which seek to reward employees by making payments that favour employees or their families.

This brief sets out HM Revenue & Customs' (HMRC's) current view on Inheritance Tax issues associated with Employee Benefit Trusts. It supersedes and amplifies Revenue & Customs Brief 61/09.

It also includes material on various matters not previously addressed including ongoing Inheritance Tax liabilities of the trust and any sub-trusts it created and the taxation of income arising in offshore Employee Benefit Trusts.

This brief is aimed at agents advising on the Inheritance Tax and trust taxation liabilities of Employee Benefit Trusts.

Existing cases will be taken forward by HMRC on the basis of the views set out in this brief.

All statutory references are to Inheritance Tax Act 1984 unless otherwise stated.

Contents

1. Entry charges payable by a Close Company when it makes a contribution to a s86 Employee Benefit Trust

2. Flat rate exit charge (s72) when property leaves a s86 Employee Benefit Trust

3. Ten year and exit charges in respect of any sub-trusts

4. Payment of ongoing Inheritance Tax liabilities

5. Income Tax assessable under the transfer of asset legislation on income arising in offshore Employee Benefit Trusts

6. Income Tax in relation to UK source income of offshore Employee Benefit Trusts

7. Payment of ongoing trust Income Tax liabilities

8. Contact details and legal references

Part 1 - Entry charges payable by a Close Company when it makes a contribution to a s86 Employee Benefit Trust

1.1 Employee Benefit Trust

A2.381   This part of the brief assumes that the Employee Benefit Trust qualifies as a s86 Employee Benefit Trust in that it is a trust where the funds are held at the trustees' discretion to be applied for the benefit of 'all or most of the persons employed or holding office with the body concerned' (s86(3)(a)).

1.2 Charge on participators (s94)

Where a Close Company (s102(1)) makes a transfer of value (s3) to an Employee Benefit Trust an Inheritance Tax charge arises under s94 unless, broadly, the disposition:

A2.382

- is not a transfer of value under sections 10, 12 or 13
- is eligible for relief

1.3 Transfers of value

Where there is a transfer of value it is apportioned between the individual participators according to their respective rights and interest in the company immediately before the contribution to the Employee Benefit Trust is made. There is an immediate charge of 20 per cent on the value transferred (the contribution) in excess of the participator's unused nil rate band.

A2.383

The liability for the charge to Inheritance Tax that arises under s94 is the company's or, so far as the tax remains unpaid, the participator's (s202).

Inheritance Tax arising under s94 is due six months after the end of the month in which the contribution is made or at the end of April in the year following a contribution made between 6 April and 30 September inclusive. Interest is charged on any unpaid tax from the due date.

1.3.1 Dispositions not intended to confer gratuitous benefit (s10)

A disposition is not a transfer of value when the terms of s10 are met. There is both a subjective test and an objective test; and both tests must be met to satisfy section 10.

A2.384

1.3.1.1 Subjective test - no intention to confer gratuitous intent

The test is not met if there is the slightest possibility of gratuitous intent at the date the contribution is made.

A2.385

1.3.1.2 Objective test - arm's length transaction

To meet the terms of s10 the transaction must either:

A2.386

- have been made at arm's length between persons not connected with each other (as defined in s270)
- was such as might be expected to be made in a transaction at arm's length between persons not connected with each other

An Employee Benefit Trust is a discretionary trust and to satisfy the conditions of s86 the trustees' discretion must remain unfettered. Given that the potential beneficiaries under an Employee Benefit Trust normally include the participators themselves; the employees or former employees; and/or the wives, husbands, civil partners, widows, widowers, surviving civil partners and children and step children under the age of 18 of such employees and former employees; it will normally be difficult to show that the conditions of s10 are met.

1.3.2 Dispositions allowable in computing profits for Corporation Tax (s12)

1.3.2.1 Overview

A2.387 A disposition by a person is not a transfer of value when the terms of s12 are met: broadly, that the disposition is allowable for the purposes of calculating that person's Corporation Tax.

The relieving effect cannot be given provisionally while waiting to see whether the contribution will become allowable for Corporation Tax purposes; and is only available to the extent that a deduction is allowable to the company for the tax year in which the contribution is made.

A deduction in the Corporation Tax accounts can be permanently disallowed by the following:

- capital expenditure disallowed by s74(1)(f) ICTA 1988/s53 CTA 2009

- expenditure not wholly and exclusively incurred under s74(1)(a) ICTA 1988/s54 CTA 2009

Also the timing of a deduction can be deferred to a later period by the following:

- generally accepted accounting practice (UITF32) which capitalises Employee Benefit Trust contributions by showing them as an asset on the company's balance sheet until and to the extent that the assets transferred to the intermediary vest unconditionally in identified beneficiaries

- expenditure subject to s43 FA 1989 (the Dextra decision) - see below

- post 27 November 2002 expenditure subject to Sch24 FA 2003/s1290(2)(3) CTA 2009 - see below

If expenditure is not allowable for any of these reasons then s12 does not apply.

1.3.2.2 Impact of MacDonald (HMIT) v Dextra (2005) UKHL 47 ('Dextra')

A2.388 The Dextra decision applies to contributions made before 27 November 2002.

In that case, the trust deed gave the trustee wide discretion to pay money and other benefits to beneficiaries and power to lend them money. The potential beneficiaries of the trust included past, present and future employees and officers of the participating companies in the Dextra group and their close relatives and dependants. The trustee did not make payments of emoluments out of the funds in the Employee Benefit Trust during the periods concerned. Instead the trustee made loans to various individuals who were beneficiaries under the terms of the Employee Benefit Trust.

The point at issue was whether the company's contributions to the Employee Benefit Trust were 'potential emoluments' within the meaning of s43(11)(a) FA 1989, being amounts 'held by an intermediary with a view to their becoming relevant emoluments'.

The House of Lords held that the contributions by the company to the Employee Benefit Trust were potential emoluments as there was a 'realistic possibility' that the trustee would use the trust funds to pay emoluments. This meant that the company's deductions were restricted. The company could only have a deduction for the amount of emoluments paid by the trustee within nine months of the end of the period of account for which the deduction would otherwise be due. Relief for the amount disallowed would be given in the period of accounting in which emoluments were paid.

1.3.2.3 Restriction of deductions for employee benefit contributions (Sch24 FA 2003)

A2.389 Section 143 and Schedule 24 to the Finance Act 2003 applies to contributions made after 27 November 2002 and prevents a deduction for Corporation Tax purposes until the contribution made for employee benefits is spent by a payment that has been subjected to both PAYE and National Insurance contributions. The position already established in Dextra is therefore effectively formalised by legislation for events on or after 27 November 2002.

1.3.3 Dispositions by Close Companies for benefit of employees (s13)

A disposition is not a transfer of value when the terms of s13 are met. **A2.390**
However, this exclusion does not apply where (amongst other things):

- the contributions by the Close Company are made to an Employee Benefit Trust that does not satisfy s86

- the participators (s102(1)) in the company and any person connected with them are not excluded from benefit under the terms of the Employee Benefit Trust and so s13(2) applies

1.4 Relief from Inheritance Tax - business property relief (s104)

Usually, sections 10, 12 or 13 will not be met and the contribution by the Close **A2.391**
Company will be a transfer of value as a result of a reduction in the value of its estate - the aggregate of the property beneficially owned by the company.
Relief from Inheritance Tax may, however, be available where the value transferred is attributable to relevant business property (s105).
The company's estate is capable of being relevant business property if it is 'property consisting of a business' (s105(1)(a)). However, the availability of business property relief is conditional on whether the transfer meets all the other requirements in Part V, Chapter 1. This means, in particular that:

- the business is not an excluded one, for example a company the business of which consists wholly or mainly of making or holding investments (s105(3))

- the value of the relevant business property transferred is not attributable to any excepted assets (s112)

Business property relief will, therefore, not apply on a transfer of value made by a Close Company that is an investment company.

Part 2 - Flat rate exit charge (s72) when property leaves a s86 Employee Benefit Trust

This part describes charges to Inheritance Tax that can arise in any s86 Employee **A2.392**
Benefit Trust; **even where the original disposition into the trust was not made by a Close Company or individual.**
The charge arises where a payment is made from the Employee Benefit Trust into a sub-trust that is not itself a qualifying s86 Employee Benefit Trust (as outlined at 1.1 above). The charge is a flat rate charge and is dependant on the length of time the property was held subject to the terms of the s86 Employee Benefit Trust. Business property relief will not apply to the flat rate exit charge in these circumstances.
In addition, where there is a non-commercial loan to a participator then an exit charge may arise under s72(2)(b).

Part 3 - Ten year and exit charges in respect of any sub-trusts

In general, sub-trusts are not s86 Employee Benefit Trusts and are, therefore, relevant property trusts for Inheritance Tax purposes (s58). (Full details of 'relevant property trusts' can be found in the Inheritance Tax Manual at page IHTM 42001+.) **A2.393**
Relevant property trusts pay Inheritance Tax on two key occasions:

- on the ten year anniversary of the commencement of the trust (s64) (and every subsequent ten year anniversary)

- when property leaves the relevant property trust or when it ceases to be relevant property (s65)

For both of these occasions a calculation is required in order to establish the Inheritance Tax liability but this charge will not exceed 6 per cent of the value of the trust assets concerned.

For the purposes of the ten year anniversary charge, the anniversary is calculated from the date on which the property became settled (s81), that is, the date the s86 Employee Benefit Trust commenced. However, property can only be treated as relevant property when it leaves the qualifying Employee Benefit Trust.

Where the trustees of a sub-trust decide to bring the trust to an end an exit charge will arise under s65.

The basis of valuation for a charge arising under either s64 or s65 will be an open market value (s160) and will include the value of loans and any accrued interest.

Part 4 - Payment of ongoing Inheritance Tax liabilities

A2.394   Section 201(1) (Settled Property) outlines the persons liable for Inheritance Tax on chargeable transfers arising in respect of trusts, including proportionate charges (s65) and ten year anniversary charges (s64) as well as the flat rate charge (s72) (property leaving employee trusts). Where the transfer is made during the life of the settlor and the trustees are not resident in the UK then the settlor is liable for the ongoing trust Inheritance Tax liabilities (s201(1)(d)).

The settlor of an Employee Benefit Trust will usually be the company, whether or not it is a Close Company.

In addition, where a participator has benefited then s201(1)(c) means that they are liable for the ongoing trust Inheritance Tax liabilities.

Part 5 - Income Tax assessable under the transfer of asset (ToA) legislation on income arising in offshore Employee Benefit Trusts

5.1 Overview

A2.395   It is common for the trust vehicle used as the Employee Benefit Trust to be situated in an offshore jurisdiction and this will potentially give rise to additional liabilities where income arises within the trust.

The ToA legislation was amended by FA 2006 and the legislation applicable following this amendment can be found at s714 ITA 2007, onwards. It came into effect from 6 April 2007. The pre-FA 2006 legislation is contained in s739 ICTA 1988, onwards. There are two potential charges that arise under the ToA legislation - the so-called 'income charge' (s739 ICTA 1988/s720 ITA 2007) and the 'benefits charge' (s740 ICTA 1988/s732 ITA 2007). Each of these are considered in turn.

5.1.1 Income charge

A2.396   The income charge provisions apply to prevent the avoidance of a liability to Income Tax by individuals who are ordinarily resident in the UK where the following conditions apply:

- there is a transfer of assets by virtue or in consequence of which, either alone or in conjunction with associated operations, income becomes payable to a person abroad

- the transferor has the power to enjoy the income

For the income charge provisions to apply the individual on whom the charge arises must be the person who transfers the assets or procures the transfer. If the offshore Employee Benefit Trust is a normal commercial arrangement by a company to reward its employees, the transferor is the employer company; and in such circumstances the income charge is unlikely to be applicable as the transferor and beneficiaries are different people. However, it may be that the employee has transferred a right to receive a bonus into the offshore Employee Benefit Trust and is therefore the transferor. If this is the case the ToA legislation may apply and the employee will be liable to tax on any income arising in the trust.

If the employer company is controlled by its shareholder/directors and the offshore Employee Benefit Trust was formed solely for their benefit, the director/shareholders may have procured the transfer into the offshore Employee Benefit Trust and could be considered transferors for the purposes of the income charge. Whether or not the ToA income charge is then applied will depend on the facts of each case.

5.1.2 Benefit charge

Where the company, not the employee is the transferor the benefit charge may apply. **A2.397**
The benefit charge matches any income arising within the Employee Benefit Trust with any benefits received by the employee. The test is effectively the same as s739 ICTA 1988/s720 ITA 2007 in that where by virtue or in consequence of a transfer income becomes payable to a person abroad, s740(1)(b) ICTA 1988/s732(1)(d) ITA 2007 applies the charge to individuals not liable to tax under the income charge. If a person receives a benefit provided out of assets available for the purpose as a consequence of the transfer, and the trustees are in receipt of income, any benefit provided to a beneficiary is potentially chargeable. The amount of the benefit charged to tax is up to the maximum of either the income or benefit. The benefit charge could, therefore, catch any income arising in the offshore Employee Benefit Trust if it is not caught by the income charge and there are actual distributions by the trustees which are not otherwise chargeable to Income Tax.

Part 6 - Income Tax in relation to UK source income of offshore Employment Benefit Trusts

If an offshore Employment Benefit Trust receives UK source income then, subject to **A2.398**
s811 ITA 2007, the income will be chargeable to tax in the UK and the trustees should make a return of this income to HMRC. Section 811 ITA 2007 limits the scope of the liability to Income Tax of a non-UK resident trust provided that none of the trust's beneficiaries are resident in the UK. As Employee Benefit Trusts are discretionary trusts the trustees will be chargeable to tax at the trust rate under s479 ITA 2007. If the trustees make a discretionary payment out of the trust income to a beneficiary this is treated as untaxed income of the UK resident beneficiary. It does not matter that the trustees have suffered tax on the trust income. The beneficiary returns the income received and can claim relief under Extra Statutory Concession B18.

The trustees of the offshore Employee Benefit Trust or sub-trusts may have advanced interest bearing loans to beneficiaries. If the beneficiaries are resident in the UK then depending on the particular circumstances of each beneficiary the interest will be UK source income in the hands of the trustees and should be reported as such. It is also likely that in such circumstances tax should be deducted at source by the beneficiary paying the interest under s874 ITA 2007.

Where it is contended that the interest is not UK source income, the circumstances surrounding the payment of interest will be closely examined by HMRC.

If the beneficiary does not pay the interest, but the interest is rolled up by the trustees, no immediate tax charge will arise; however, if the interest is subsequently paid or capitalised it is likely that an Income Tax charge will accrue on payment or capitalisation.

Part 7 - Payment of ongoing trust Income Tax liabilities

A2.399 To the extent that income continues to arise within an offshore Employee Benefit Trust and is caught by the transfer of assets legislation the income charge and benefits charge will continue to apply. Likewise if the trustees continue to receive UK source income they will have an ongoing liability to Income Tax and should continue to complete Trust Returns.

Part 8 - Contact details and legal references

8.1 Contact details

A2.400 If you wish to notify the Trusts and Estates business within HMRC of the existence of an Employee Benefit Trust; or, if you wish to discuss settlement of any Inheritance Tax and non-resident trust liabilities that have arisen in respect of an Employee Benefit Trust, then please contact HMRC Trusts & Estates via this link ebtiht.settlementmail-box@hmrc.gsi.gov.uk.

Further information can be obtained by contacting the Helpline on Tel 0845 30 20 900.

8.2 Legal references

Corporation Tax

For accounting periods ending on or after 1 April 2009:

- references to Schedule 24 Finance Act 2003 should be taken to be references to Sections 1290 to 1297 Corporation Tax Act 2009
- references to s74(1)(a) ICTA 1988 should be taken to be references to s54 Corporation Tax Act 2009
- references to s74(1)(f) ICTA 1988 should be taken to be references to s53 Corporation Tax Act 2009

Income Tax

For tax years 2005-06 onwards:

- references to Schedule 24 Finance Act 2003 should be taken to be references to Section 38 to 44 Income Tax (Trading and Other Income) Act 2005
- references to s74(1)(a) ICTA 1988 should be taken to be references to s34 Income Tax (Trading and Other Income) Act 2005
- references to s74(1)(f) ICTA 1988 should be taken to be references to s33 Income Tax (Trading and Other Income) Act 2005
- reference to s739 ICTA 1988 should be taken to be references to s720 ITA 2007
- reference to s740 ICTA 1988 should be taken to be references to s731 ITA 20

Issued 4 April 2011

12. RCC BRIEF 76/09: CHANGES TO THE INCOME TAX CREDIT FOR FOREIGN DIVIDENDS

Introduction

This brief publicises changes that have been made to the scope of the Income Tax credit **A2.401**
for individuals in receipt of dividends from foreign companies. The changes take effect
from 22 April 2009 for the current tax year and affect shareholders in:

- foreign companies with a holding that is 10 per cent or more of the issued share
  capital of the company

- foreign companies with a holding that is 10 per cent or more of a specific class
  of share in the company

- offshore funds

Full details of the changes and how they affect individual taxpayers will be given in the
Notes to the Foreign Pages of the Self Assessment Return.

Background

Dividends received by individuals are currently taxed at headline rates of: **A2.402**

- 10 per cent in respect of basic rate taxpayers
- 32.5 per cent in respect of higher rate taxpayers

However, individuals in receipt of dividends from UK resident companies are entitled
under current law to a non-payable dividend tax credit. Since 6 April 2008, individuals
with shareholdings of less than 10 per cent in foreign companies have also been entitled
to a non-payable tax credit provided that the foreign company is not an offshore fund.
   The dividend tax credit is equal to one ninth of the amount of the dividend. Because
tax is charged on the gross dividend received, including the tax credit, the effective rate
of tax on these dividends is reduced to 0 per cent and 25 per cent.

Changes to be made

Shareholders in offshore funds

There are two changes being made to the tax treatment of distributions from offshore **A2.403**
funds that are companies where an offshore fund is:

- Substantially invested (holds more than 60 per cent of its assets) in interest
  bearing assets, individuals receiving distributions will be treated for tax purposes

as having received interest and not a dividend or other type of distribution. This means that no tax credit will be available and the tax rates applying will be those applying to interest.

- Equity-based, individuals receiving distributions will be entitled to the dividend tax credit irrespective of the size of their holdings or the territory of origin of the fund.

Shareholders in foreign companies with a holding that is 10 per cent or more of the issued share capital of the company

A2.404 The dividend tax credit is being extended to shareholders in foreign companies with a holding that is 10 per cent or more of the issued share capital of the company, subject to conditions:

- the territory of the dividend-paying company must be a 'qualifying territory' (see below)
- the tax credit is not available where the distribution is one of a series of distributions made as part of a tax avoidance scheme, and any dividend-paying company is not resident in a 'qualifying territory
- the company must not be an 'excluded company'(see below)

'Qualifying territory'

A2.405 A 'qualifying territory' is defined as the UK and any territory with which the UK has a double taxation treaty with a non-discrimination article.
The Treasury has the power to make regulations adding to the list of territories that qualify even if the double taxation treaty in question does not contain an appropriate non-discrimination article, or to exclude territories even if the treaty in question does contain such an article.
The following are 'qualifying territories':

Argentina	Australia	Austria	Azerbaijan
Bangladesh	Bangladesh	Barbados	Belarus
Belgium	Morocco	Bolivia	Bosnia-Herzegovina
Botswana	Bulgaria	Canada	Chile
China	Croatia	Cyprus	Czech Republic
Denmark	Egypt	Estonia Reunion	Falkland Islands
Fiji	Finland	France	Gambia
Georgia	Germany	Ghana	Greece
Guyana	Hungary	Iceland	India
Indonesia	Ireland	Israel	Italy
Ivory Coast	Jamaica	Japan	Jordan
Kazakhstan	Kenya	Korea	Kuwait
Latvia	Lesotho	Lithuania	Luxembourg
Macedonia	Malaysia	Malta	Mauritius
Mexico	Mongolia	Montenegro	Myanmar
Namibia	Netherlands	New Zealand	Nigeria
Norway	Oman	Pakistan	Papua New Guinea
Philippines	Poland	Portugal	Romania
Russian Federation	Serbia	Singapore	Slovak Republic
Slovenia	South Africa	Spain	Sri Lanka
Sudan	Swaziland	Switzerland	Taiwan
Thailand	Trinidad & Tobago	Tunisia	Turkey

Turkmenistan	Uganda	Ukraine	USA
Uzbekistan	Venezuela	Vietnam	Zambia
Zimbabwe			

The government has made regulations to exclude from this list companies which are **A2.406** excluded from the benefits of the double taxation agreement with the UK ('excluded companies'). A dividend from an 'excluded company' will be treated as a dividend from a 'non-qualifying' territory and will not get the tax credit. The 'excluded companies' are:

Barbados – companies established under the International Business Companies Act(s)

Cyprus – companies entitled to any special tax benefits under various Cyprus enactments

Jamaica – companies established under enactments relating to International Business Companies and International Finance Companies

Luxembourg – holding companies established under the Luxembourg 1929 and 1937 Acts

Malaysia – companies carrying on offshore business activity under the Labuan Offshore Business Activity Act 1990

Malta – companies entitled to special tax benefits under various enactments.

Shareholders in foreign companies with a holding that is 10 per cent or more of a specific class of share in the company

Since 6 April 2008, an individual with a shareholding of less than 10 per cent of the **A2.407** issued share capital of a foreign company (a 'minority shareholder') has been entitled to the tax credit provided that the foreign company is not an offshore fund. Eligibility to the tax credit is not dependent on the source country of the dividend.

From 22 April 2009, there is an important change in the way the 10 per cent test is applied because the definition of 'minority shareholder' has been altered. A 'minority shareholder' is now defined as a shareholder with less than 10 per cent of a particular class of share in a company. This will have no impact on the vast majority of individuals with foreign shares, but it is possible that some shareholders with, for example, preference shares will no longer qualify as 'minority shareholders'.

A shareholder who no longer qualifies as a 'minority shareholder' will still receive the tax credit if he can meet the 'qualifying territory' test explained above.

Foreign tax credit relief

There is no change to foreign tax credit relief in respect of foreign withholding tax. An **A2.408** individual who is eligible to receive both foreign tax credit relief and the dividend tax credit will get the benefit of both, subject to a ceiling equal to liability to UK income tax in respect of the dividend. 'Excess credits' are lost; they are not repayable and cannot be offset against liability to income tax elsewhere.

Please note that where foreign tax credit relief is restricted under the terms of the Double Taxation agreement with the UK, the amount allowable is calculated on the amount of the foreign dividend, not the amount of the dividend inclusive of the dividend tax credit.

Worked examples:

A basic rate taxpayer receives a net foreign dividend of 76.5 after 13.5 withholding tax is deducted at source.

The UK dividend tax credit of one ninth of the dividend is calculated on the gross dividend $(1/9 \times (76.5 + 13.5) = 10)$.

The amount subject to income tax is the gross dividend plus the dividend tax credit $(90 + 10 = 100)$.

Basic rate taxpayers are subject to the dividend ordinary rate 10% on their grossed up dividend income (100 × 10% = 10).

This taxpayer is entitled to foreign tax credit relief and the UK dividend tax credit (13.5 + 10 = 23.5). The UK tax liability is eliminated but the excess credit cannot be used.

A higher rate taxpayer receives a foreign dividend on the same basis.

The UK dividend tax credit of one ninth of the dividend is calculated on the gross dividend (1/9 × (76.5 + 13.5) = 10).

The amount subject to income tax is the gross dividend plus the dividend tax credit (90 + 10 = 100).

Higher rate taxpayers are subject to the dividend upper rate 32.5% on their grossed up dividend income (100 × 32.5% = 32.5)

Again, the taxpayer is entitled to foreign tax credit relief and the UK dividend tax credit (13.5 + 10 = 23.5). The UK tax liability is reduced to 9 (32.5 − 23.5).

13. ESC B18: PAYMENTS OUT OF DISCRETIONARY TRUSTS

UK resident trusts

A beneficiary may receive from trustees a payment to which TA 1988 s 687(2) applies. **A2.409** Where that payment is made out of the income of the trustees in respect of which, had it been received directly, the beneficiary would—

– have been entitled to exemption in respect of FOTRA securities issued in accordance with FA 1996 s 154; or

– have been entitled to relief under the terms of a double taxation agreement; or

– not have been chargeable to UK tax because of their not resident and/or not ordinarily resident status

the beneficiary may claim that exemption or relief or, where the beneficiary would not have been chargeable, repayment of the tax treated as deducted from the payment (or an appropriate proportion of it). For this purpose, the payment will be treated as having been made rateably out of all sources of income arising to the trustees on a last in first out basis.

Relief or exemption, as appropriate, will be granted to the extent that the payment is out of income which arose to the trustees not earlier than six years before the end of the year of assessment in which the payment was made, provided the trustees—

– have made trust returns giving details of all sources of trust income and payments made to beneficiaries for each and every year for which they are required, and

– have paid all tax due, and any interest, surcharges and penalties arising; and

– keep available for inspection any relevant tax certificates.

Relief or exemption, as appropriate, will be granted to the beneficiary on a claim made within five years and ten months of the end of the year of assessment in which the beneficiary received the payment from the trustees.

Non-resident trusts

A similar concession will operate where a beneficiary receives a payment from discre- **A2.410** tionary trustees which is not within TA 1988 s 687(2) (ie where non-resident trustees exercise their discretion outside the UK).

Where a non-resident beneficiary receives such a payment out of income of the trustees in respect of which, had it been received directly, it would have been chargeable to UK tax, then the beneficiary—

- may claim relief under TA 1988 s 278 (personal reliefs for certain non-residents); and

- may be treated as receiving that payment from a UK resident trust but claim credit only for UK tax actually paid by the trustees on income out of which the payment is made.

The beneficiary may also claim exemption from tax in respect of FOTRA securities issued in accordance with FA 1996 s 154 to the extent that the payment is regarded as including interest from such securities.

A UK beneficiary of a non-resident trust may claim appropriate credit for tax actually paid by the trustees on the income out of which the payment is made as if the payments out of UK income were from a UK resident trust and within TA 1988 s 687(1).

This treatment will only be available where the trustees—

- have made trust returns giving details of all sources of trust income and payments made to beneficiaries for each and every year for which they are required; and

- have paid all tax due and any interest, surcharges and penalties arising; and

- keep available for inspection any relevant tax certificates.

Relief or exemption, as appropriate, will be granted to the beneficiary on a claim made within five years and ten months of the end of the year of assessment in which the beneficiary received the payment from the trustees.

No credit will be given for UK tax treated as paid on income received by the trustees which would not be available for set off under s 687(2) if that section applied, and that tax is not repayable (for example on dividends). However, such tax is not taken into account in calculating the gross income treated as taxable on the beneficiary under this concession.

14. TRUSTEE RESIDENCE: GUIDANCE NOTE AGREED BY HM REVENUE & CUSTOMS ISSUED IN AUGUST 2010 BY ICAEW: CIOT AND STEP

CONTENTS

Section 1: Case Studies

- Trustee carrying out duties for the administration of any trust (Examples 1-12)
- Dependent agent (Examples 13-20)
- Individual non-resident trustee (Examples 21-23)

Section 2: Specific Examples (Examples 24-29)

SECTION 1: CASE STUDIES

In the text below the HMRC Trustee Residence Guidance (Version 1) released on 1 July 2009 is referred to as "the Guidance".

TRUSTEE CARRYING OUT DUTIES FOR THE ADMINISTRATION OF ANY TRUST

There is a suggestion at section 2 of the Guidance that when "*considering whether the corporate trustee is carrying on the administration of a particular trust in the course of their business through the permanent establishment, the frequency of the meetings will be looked at as well as their significance and quality*". The following examples are intended to clarify this aspect of the Guidance. In each case the trustee is the non-UK resident subsidiary of a financial services group.

A2.411

Example 1

The Alpha Trust is subject to English law. The trustee of the settlement is a Trust Company resident in Switzerland, which is a subsidiary of an international bank that has offices and outlets in the UK. Doubts have arisen over the precise scope of some of the provisions in the trust deed, with the result that leading Counsel in London has been instructed to advise. Based on the advice given, the trustee further instructs Counsel to submit an application to vary the terms of the trust deed. In view of the importance attached to the advice received from Counsel, and the application to vary the terms of the trust deed, the trustee has sent a representative to the UK for a month to liaise with Counsel and the trustee"s London solicitors. He stays in the same London hotel throughout this period, and has regular meetings at the London offices of the trustee's solicitors.

A2.412

Analysis

The trustee's representative is present in the UK for a month, holding many meetings with Counsel, the trustee's solicitors and attending Court. Key decisions are still taken by the trustees in Switzerland. The presence of the trustee's representative is in respect of an exceptional event in the trust's life time. It cannot be taken into account in establishing whether or not the Trust Company is acting as a trustee in the course of its business through a permanent establishment in the UK. Although the trustee's representative stays at the same hotel throughout, and attends meetings with the trustee's legal advisers, his occupation/attendance in relation to the Court application and related matters will not constitute a permanent establishment. This is because the occupation/attendance at these places will lack the required degree of permanence required of a fixed place of business. As soon as the Court proceedings are over, the attendance/occupation at these places for this purpose will cease. Even if a permanent establishment could be said to exist, the trustee could not be said to be resident in the UK. As no decisions are taken by the trustee's representative, and he simply acts as directed, none of his activities in connection with the legal proceedings can be considered to be those of the trustee undertaken through a permanent establishment in the UK.

HMRC answer

As set out in the guidance there are 3 examples in considering whether a trust is resident. Before considering whether trust business is conducted through a permanent establishment (PE) it is first necessary to establish whether the trustee company carries on a business through a PE (in some cases they may already have to do this to decide whether there are any profits that need to be returned in UK). Only if the trustee company is carrying on a business through a PE is it necessary then to look at the individual trust and whether the trustee is carrying out the business in relation to a particular trust through that PE. In a number of examples it seemed unlikely that the corporate trustee was carrying on a business through a fixed place of business PE in the UK. It was, therefore, unnecessary to look any further at the activities carried out in relation to a particular trust.

The trust is not resident in the UK because there is no PE in the UK, or to explain, although there was business conducted in the UK the business was not undertaken via a PE.

Example 2

A2.413   As in Example 1, save that the occasion for the trustee's representative being present in the UK is the sale of shares in a UK private company held by the trustee. As before the trustee's representative attends meetings with advisers and reports back to the Trust Company which is resident outside the UK.

Analysis

In Example 1, there is no permanent establishment within the UK, so the trustees could not be said to be UK resident. Even if there were not to be the case the trustee had little choice but to use the UK Courts to vary the terms of the settlement as this was a trust with an English governing law. Similarly, in this example, the trustee has little choice but to send its representative to the UK to liaise with advisers. The key decisions are still taken by the trust company abroad. The analysis is thought to be directly comparable, with the result that none of the activities of the trustee representative in London in connection with the sale can be considered to be those of the trustee undertaken through a permanent establishment in the UK.

HMRC answer

See HMRC answer to Example 1.

Example 3

> The Beta Trust is non UK resident. Its trustee is a Trust Company resident in **A2.414**
> the Isle of Man, which is a subsidiary of an international bank. It has a number
> of beneficiaries, all of whom are currently UK resident. Trust officers from the
> trustee company make regular visits to the UK. They do this to discuss perform-
> ance of the trust's investments with their independent investment advisers who
> are based in the UK and are unconnected with the trust company. They also
> visit the beneficiaries. No other meetings are held with any other advisers except
> for meetings with the trustee's Isle of Man legal advisers as circumstances
> dictate.

Analysis

The fact that no regular meetings are held outside the UK with beneficiaries or advisers has no bearing on whether the trustee is carrying on a business of being a trustee
through a UK permanent establishment constituted by the trust officer when he visits
the UK. There is no permanent establishment on the facts as given, and therefore the
Trust is non-UK resident.

HMRC answer

It is unlikely that the corporate trustee is carrying on a business through a fixed place
of business PE in the UK.

Where a trustee representative is carrying on trust business in the UK they may be
a dependent agent of the trustee, but it still needs to be "habitually" acting in this way
so a one-off event is unlikely to create a dependent agent PE.

Example 4

> Facts are as in Example 3 with the addition that the trustees arrange in 2009/10 **A2.415**
> a meeting with all the beneficiaries to explain the significance of changes to the
> trust deed. The UK is the most convenient location for this meeting which is held
> at a London hotel.

Analysis

The hotel does not constitute a permanent establishment and accordingly the trustees
cannot be UK resident. Even if premises were used that were capable of constituting
a permanent establishment the trustees would not be UK resident. This is because the
purpose of the meeting is auxiliary to the core activities of the trustee, as these would
be the process of deciding on the amendments to the trust deed which was not carried
on in the UK. In addition, a meeting on a single occasion at an hotel would not mean
the trustees are carrying on their core business through a permanent establishment in
the UK. On these facts the trustees are not UK resident in 2009/10.

HMRC answer

See HMRC answer to Example 3.

Example 5

A2.416

The Gamma Trust is non UK resident. Its trustee is a Trust Company resident in Guernsey, which is a subsidiary of an international bank. It has a number of beneficiaries, all of whom are currently UK resident.

The trust property consists of an extensive investment portfolio managed by a UK resident investment management company owned by the parent company.

The contract between the Gamma Trust and the investment manager is on entirely arm's length terms. Before appointing the investment manager the trustee set down the parameters within which the investment manager was to work and targets which it expected to be met in terms of investment performance. The investment mandate is discretionary. The performance of the investment manager is reviewed against the targets set by the trustees on a quarterly basis. The investment instructions and performance targets are also reviewed quarterly and modified where appropriate.

A trust officer from the trustees visits the UK to meet with the beneficiaries on a quarterly basis. These meetings either take place over dinner, at the hotel where the trust officer is staying or in the homes of the beneficiaries. During the quarterly trips to the UK of the trust officer, representatives from the investment management company will also meet with the trust officer to report on the investment performance for the last quarter. The meetings take place either at the offices in the UK of a third party adviser (the accountant) or at the hotel where the trust officer is staying.

No meetings in the UK are held at the offices of the investment fund manager. No other meetings are held with any other advisers except as circumstances dictate for meetings with the trustee's Guernsey legal advisers.

Analysis

The fact that the investment manager is UK resident and in the same group as the non resident trust company does not mean that the trustee is carrying on a business of being a trustee through a UK permanent establishment. The terms on which work is carried out for the trustee are on an arm's length basis and trust officers do not hold meetings with respect to the business of being a trustee of the Gamma Trust at the UK offices of a group company.

Whilst the investment manager has a discretionary investment mandate the terms are the same as offered to other third party clients and no use is made of the investment manager's UK offices. The fact that the trust has no other assets apart from the investment portfolio does not alter this analysis as the trustee has set down instructions on how the fund manager should operate and targets which should be met and the performance of the investment manager is reviewed regularly.

Meetings with beneficiaries are either at restaurants, in the hotel where the trust officer is staying or in the homes of the beneficiaries. As such the trustee cannot be said to be conducting business though a fixed permanent establishment in the UK.

As in Example 3 the fact that no regular meetings are held outside the UK with beneficiaries or advisers is irrelevant.

On these facts the Trust is non-UK resident.

HMRC answer

It is unlikely that the corporate trustee is carrying on a business through a fixed place of business PE in the UK. As the investment manager is on entirely arm's length terms, there is unlikely to be a dependent agent PE. If the trust company is not carrying on a business in the UK through a PE, it is unnecessary to look any further at the activities carried out in relation to the trust.

Where a trust representative is carrying on trust business in UK they may be a dependent agent of trustee, but it still needs to be "habitually" acting in this way.

Example 6

The Delta Trust is non UK resident. Its trustee is a Trust Company resident in Gibraltar. It has a number of beneficiaries, all of whom are currently UK resident. **A2.417**

The trust property consists of an extensive investment portfolio managed by a UK resident investment management company owned by the parent company and a number of UK properties (a UK resident third party letting agent being employed). The trust accounts are also prepared by a UK resident accounting group company.

The contract between the Delta Trust and the investment manager is on entirely arm's length terms. Before appointing the investment manager the trustee set down the parameters within which the investment manager was to work and targets which it expected to be met in terms of investment performance. The investment mandate is discretionary. The performance of the investment manager is reviewed against the targets set by the trustees on a quarterly basis. The investment instructions and performance targets are also reviewed quarterly and modified where appropriate.

The engagement letter between the trustees and the UK resident accounting group company is on arm's length terms.

A trust officer from the trustees visits the UK to meet with the beneficiaries on a quarterly basis. These meetings either take place over dinner, at the hotel where the trust officer is staying or in the homes of the beneficiaries. During the quarterly trips to the UK of the trust officer, representatives from the investment management company will also meet with the trust officer to report on the investment performance for the last quarter. The meetings take place at the hotel where the trust officer is staying.

There are no meetings with the UK resident accounting group company as all communication is by telephone, e-mail or letter/fax.

No meetings in the UK are held at the offices of the investment fund manager or the accounting group company. No other meetings are held with any other advisers except as circumstances dictate for meetings with the trustee's legal advisers in Gibraltar.

All trust decisions are taken outside of the UK after due deliberation.

Analysis

The fact that the UK resident investment manager and the UK resident accountant are in the same group as the non resident trust company does not mean that the trustee is carrying on a business of being a trustee through a UK permanent establishment. The terms on which work is carried out for the trustee are on an arm's length basis and trust officers do not hold meetings to deal with the business of this trust at the UK offices of a group company.

The analysis with respect to the discretionary investment mandate is the same as for Example 5. The analysis with respect to the meetings with beneficiaries is also the same as in Example 5.

As in Example 3 the fact that no regular meetings are held outside the UK with beneficiaries or advisers has no bearing on whether the trustee is carrying on a business of being a trustee through a UK permanent establishment constituted by the trust officer when he visits the UK.

On these facts the Trust is non-UK resident.

HMRC answer

Where services are provided on an arm's length basis then there is unlikely to be a dependent agent PE.

Where a trust representative is carrying on trust business in UK they may be a dependent agent of trustee, but it still needs to be "habitually" acting in this way.

Example 7

A2.418   The Epsilon Trust is non UK resident. Its trustee is a Trust Company resident in Gibraltar. It has a number of beneficiaries, all of whom are currently UK resident.

The trust property consists of an extensive investment portfolio managed by a UK resident investment management company owned by the parent company and a number of UK properties (a UK resident third party letting agent being employed). The trust accounts are also prepared by a UK resident accounting group company.

The contract between The Epsilon Trust and the investment manager is on entirely arm's length terms. Before appointing the investment manager the trustee set down the parameters within which the investment manager was to work and targets which it expected to be met in terms of investment performance. The investment mandate is discretionary. The performance of the investment manager is reviewed against the targets set by the trustees on a quarterly basis. The investment instructions and performance targets are also reviewed quarterly and modified where appropriate.

The engagement letter between the trustees and the UK resident accounting group company is on arm's length terms. A trust officer from the trustees visits the UK to meet with the beneficiaries on a quarterly basis. These meetings either take place over dinner, at the hotel where the trust officer is staying or in the homes of the beneficiaries. During the quarterly trips to the UK of the trust officer, representatives from the investment management company will also meet with the trust officer to report on the investment performance for the last quarter. The meetings take place at the offices of the UK resident accounting group company at the same time as the trust officer drops off the last quarter's accounting records and collects the previous quarter's records. Thus the meetings take place at the UK offices of a Group company.

The quarterly trips to the UK by the trust officer are for the purposes of collecting information. The trust officer makes no decisions whilst in the UK (indeed he or she does not have sufficient authority to make decisions whether in the UK or offshore) and reports back to his or her superiors who make the decisions offshore after due deliberation.

All trust decisions are taken outside of the UK after due deliberation.

Analysis

The analysis with respect to the discretionary investment mandate is the same as for Example 5. The analysis with respect to the meetings with beneficiaries is also the same as in Example 5.

The fact that the UK resident investment manager and the UK resident accounting group company are in the same group as the non resident trust company does not mean that the trustee is carrying on a business of being a trustee through a UK permanent establishment. The terms on which work is carried out for the trustee are on an arm's length basis and trust officers do not hold meetings to deal with the business of this trust at the UK offices of a group company as the meetings are incidental rather than with respect to the business of being a trustee which is all carried out outside the UK.

On these facts the Trust is non-UK resident.

HMRC answer

Where services are provided on an arm's length basis then there is unlikely to be a dependent agent PE.

Example 8

> The Zeta Trust is non UK resident. Its trustee is a Trust Company resident in **A2.419**
> Gibraltar. It has a number of beneficiaries, all of whom are currently UK resident.
>
> The investment performance of the trust was very poor and the trustee decided that it was necessary to replace the investment managers. The shortlist of possible new investment managers was drawn up and all four were UK resident. As such it was decided that the decision would be made after a beauty parade of the four short-listed investment managers. This beauty parade was held in the UK in the conference facilities of the hotel where the trustee representatives were staying. As well as making decisions on the investment manager during the visit to the UK the trustee representatives met with beneficiaries (over lunches and dinners held at various London restaurants) and make decisions as to trust distributions.

Analysis

The business of the trustees with respect to The Zeta trust was clearly carried out in the UK but not at a permanent establishment as the trust company was not acting out of a fixed UK place of business.

On these facts the Trust is non-UK resident.

HMRC answer

Where a trustee representative is carrying on trust business in the UK they may be a dependent agent of the trustee, but it still needs to be "habitually" acting in this way so a one-off event is unlikely to create a dependent agent PE.

Example 9

> The Eta Trust is non UK resident. Its trustee is a Trust Company resident in the **A2.420**
> Isle of Man. It has a number of beneficiaries, all of whom are currently UK resident.
>
> The trust property consists of an extensive investment portfolio managed by a third party UK resident investment management company.
>
> Trustee representatives met with beneficiaries on a quarterly basis (over lunches and dinners held at various London restaurants) and make decisions as to trust distributions.

There are also quarterly meetings between the trustees and the investment managers at which key decisions are taken with respect to the management of the trust property and instructions are given to the fund manager with respect to the trust distribution policy for the upcoming quarter. These meetings take place either at the conference facilities of the hotel where the trustee representatives are staying or at the offices of the investment manager.

Analysis

The business of the trustees with respect to The Eta trust was clearly carried out in the UK but not at a permanent establishment as the trust company was not acting out of a fixed UK place of business.

On these facts the Trust is non-UK resident.

HMRC answer

Where a trustee representatives are carrying on trust business in the UK they may be a dependent agent of the trustee, but it still needs to be "habitually" acting in this way so a one-off event is unlikely to create a dependent agent PE.

Example 10

A2.421

The Theta Trust is non UK resident. Its trustee is a Trust Company resident in the Isle of Man. It has a number of beneficiaries, all of whom are currently UK resident.

The trust property consists of an extensive investment portfolio managed by a UK resident investment management company owned by the parent company.

The contract between the Theta Trust and the investment manager is on entirely arm's length terms. Before appointing the investment manager the trustee set down the parameters within which the investment manager was to work and targets which it expected to be met in terms of investment performance. The investment mandate is discretionary. The performance of the investment manager is reviewed against the targets set by the trustees on a quarterly basis. The investment instructions and performance targets are also reviewed quarterly and modified where appropriate.

A trustee officer meets with beneficiaries on a quarterly basis using the offices of the UK resident investment company. As part of the same visit to the UK there are also meetings with the investment managers to receive their report on investment performance over the last quarter. At the end of each day the trust officer (who does not have the power to make any decisions) reports back the findings from his or her information collection meetings to his or her superiors.

Sometimes after hearing the reports from the trust officer a video conferencing call will be arranged with the trustee representatives and beneficiaries and/or the investment managers to clarify some points. Key decisions are made during the conversations.

Analysis

The fact that the UK resident investment manager is in the same group as the non resident trust company does not mean that the trustee is carrying on a business of being a trustee through a UK permanent establishment. The terms on which work is carried out for the trustee are on an arm's length basis. The analysis with respect to the discretionary investment mandate is the same as for Example 5. The analysis with respect to the meetings with beneficiaries is also the same as in Example 5.

The trust officer used the offices of the UK resident group manager but the business of the trustees is not carried out through these offices as all decisions occur outside of the UK. The fact that there is a video conference call in which key decisions were made does not negate this as the trust representatives who had the power to make the decisions were all offshore when the decisions were made.

On these facts the Trust is non-UK resident.

HMRC answer

Although the offices of the related entity are visited on a regular basis, no decisions are made in the UK, i.e. all decisions are made outside the UK.

Example 11

The Iota Trust is non UK resident. Its trustee is a Trust Company resident in Guernsey. It has a number of beneficiaries, all of whom are currently UK resident. **A2.422**

The trust property consists of an extensive investment portfolio managed by a UK resident investment management company owned by the parent company.

The contract between the Iota Trust and the investment manager is on entirely arm's length terms. Before appointing the investment manager the trustee set down the parameters within which the investment manager was to work and targets which it expected to be met in terms of investment performance. The investment mandate is discretionary. The performance of the investment manager is reviewed against the targets set by the trustees on a quarterly basis. The investment instructions and performance targets are also reviewed quarterly and modified where appropriate.

There are quarterly meetings between the trustees and the investment managers at which key decisions are taken with respect to the management of the trust property and instructions are given to the fund manager with respect to the trust distribution policy for the upcoming quarter. These meeting take place using video conferencing technology such that the trustees are in Guernsey and the investment managers in the UK. As such all trust decisions are taken outside the UK.

Analysis

The fact that the UK resident investment manager is in the same group as the non resident trust company does not mean that the trustee is carrying on a business of being a trustee through a UK permanent establishment. The terms on which work is carried out for the trustee are on an arm's length basis. Whilst the fund managers are in the UK when the quarterly meetings take place the trustee representatives are outside the UK and all decisions are taken outside the UK.

The analysis with respect to the discretionary investment mandate is the same as for Example 5. The analysis with respect to the meetings with beneficiaries is also the same as in Example 5.

On these facts the Trust is non-UK resident.

HMRC answer

It is unlikely that the corporate trustee was carrying on a business through a fixed place of business PE in the UK.

Where services are provided on an arm's length basis (in this case by the investment management company) then there is unlikely to be a dependent agent PE.

Example 12

A2.423
The Kappa Trust was established by a settlor who has never been UK resident. The trustee is a non UK resident corporate trustee, which is a subsidiary of a major international bank.

The trustee has extensive investment interests around the world, including the UK. There are a number of beneficiaries, one of whom lives in the UK. It is the trustee's practice to hold a meeting with their European advisers when they fly through Heathrow, en route to see their advisers in North America. Meetings are held in one of many hotels near the airport. The trustee makes decisions at these meetings on minor administrative aspects and receives legal and tax advice on various European issues. The trustee does not hold meetings at the premises of any subsidiary of their parent company which is based in the UK. UK visits amount to an average of approximately four a year out of a total number of meetings in excess of 20 with other advisers around the world. Major decisions are always taken outside the UK after long periods of discussion.

Analysis

Whilst the meetings in the UK do in part relate to trustee activity and the decisions made will represent core activities there is no degree of permanence as regards the premises used for the business activity. This lack of permanence as regards the premises used means that the decisions made by the trustees have no bearing on whether they are resident in the UK. Even if the premises possessed the requisite degree of permanence the overall activity undertaken by the trustee at the meetings in the UK is relatively minor and insufficient on its own to make the trustee UK resident.

HMRC answer

It is unlikely that the corporate trustee was carrying on a business through a fixed place of business PE in the UK. It is, therefore, unnecessary to look any further at the activities carried out in relation to the particular trust.

DEPENDENT AGENT

A2.424
The Guidance of 1 July 2009 sets out at section 3 HMRC's position where activities are carried on for the trust other than by the non-UK resident trust company. The Guidance states at 3.3 that where, "*say, a UK subsidiary of a non-UK resident trust company is providing services to a trust, then unless the powers granted to it by the non-UK resident trust company are such that it becomes a 'dependent agent with authority to do business on behalf of the non-resident trustee'. . . we will not contend that the UK subsidiary's actions cause the non-UK resident trustee company to have a permanent establishment*". The following examples are intended to clarify HMRC's position. In all of the examples the offshore trustee is a non-resident trust company which is the subsidiary of an international financial services group.

Example 13

A2.425
Mr L is UK resident and is the principal beneficiary of The Lambda Trust which is non-UK resident with a Jersey governing law. The trust owns a number of UK residential properties, and the Trust Company has asked Mr L to advertise for new tenants on their behalf. He passes any details he receives to the trustee, who takes up references and enter into any tenancy agreement direct with the new occupiers.

Very occasionally Mr L may receive a request by the trustee to engage a plumber or an electrician to undertake emergency work in relation to the let properties held by the trust.

Mr L receives no remuneration for any aspect of his involvement, albeit his expenses are refunded.

Analysis.5

Mr L does not have any authority to enter into tenancy agreements on behalf of the trustees. He only engages plumbers or electricians on behalf of the trustee very infrequently. Mr L's involvement lacks the element of frequency or permanence required to make him a dependent agent and thereby deem the trust to have a UK permanent establishment.

HMRC answer

Someone who does not have authority to act on behalf of the trust but does the occasional small task for which they are not remunerated is unlikely to create a dependent agent PE.

Example 14

Mr M is UK resident and is the principal beneficiary of The Mu trust which is non-UK resident with a Guernsey governing law. The trust owns a number of UK residential properties. The trustee employs a UK letting agent but Mr M keeps an eye on the properties to ensure that they are managed properly, as regards the cleaning, gardening, emergency repairs that tradesmen engaged by the letting agents undertake. He reports back to the trustees, so they can authorise that payment can be made.

A2.426

Analysis

Mr M does not have an authority to enter into any tenancy agreement, or engage work to be undertaken for the trustees. He is not a dependent agent and therefore there is no deemed UK permanent establishment.

HMRC answer

Someone who does not have authority to act on behalf of the trust, but does the occasional small task for which they are not remunerated is unlikely to create a dependent agent PE. But if other than occasional then the trust should think about remunerating on arm's length basis to put matter beyond doubt.

Example 15

Mr N is UK resident and is the principal beneficiary of the Nu Trust. Periodically he provides the trustee with a letter of wishes, identifying certain categories of asset or specifically identified investments he would like them to make. The letters are non-binding.

A2.427

Analysis

Mr N is not engaged as an investment adviser by the trustee, and they are free to accept or decline his requests as they feel fit after they have taken appropriate professional advice. Mr N is not a dependent agent.

HMRC answer

If a beneficiary writes to the trustees with a letter of wishes which the trustees are not bound by then that will not create a dependent agent PE. The trust is non-UK resident.

Example 16

A2.428   The trustee of the Xi Incentivisation trust is a corporate trustee resident in Guernsey. The trust itself is an employment benefit trust for the UK employees of Xi International which is a UK resident and quoted company. Representatives from the trust company visit the UK periodically, and attend the offices of Xi International for an update on company performance and strategy. No decisions are taken in the UK. The remuneration committees of Xi international will send a non-binding letter of recommendation to the trustees concerning awards to be made to employees as part of the incentivisation plan. The trustees take considered decisions and make discretionary appointments, but only outside the UK.

Analysis

The trustees are simply collecting information when they visit the UK, and catching up with Xi International on recent developments. The meetings at Xi International's premises will not constitute a permanent establishment. Trustee decisions are only made outside the UK. The trust is resident outside the UK.

HRMC answer

As the activities were simply auxiliary, not "core", they are ignored for the purpose of considering trustee residence status.

  If the trustees had engaged in "core" activities during the visits to the UK, the settlor's premises could be a PE if the meetings were monthly. However, if the meetings were less frequent, this may lack the requisite degree of permanence required of a PE.

Example 17

A2.429   The trustee of the Omicron Incentivisation trust is a corporate trustee resident in Jersey. The trust itself is an employment benefit trust for the UK employees of Omicron International which is a UK resident and quoted company. Representatives from the trust company visit the UK periodically, and meet representatives of Omicron International for an update on company performance and strategy at the London office of a UK sister subsidiary of the corporate trustee. Final decisions as regards future awards are regularly taken at those London meetings.

Analysis

Trustee decisions are taken at the London Offices of sister subsidiary of the Trust company. Hence the Corporate trustee is acting in the UK as a trustee in relation to the Omicron Incentivisation Trust at premises in the UK which constitute a permanent establishment in relation to its own activities. The trust is UK resident.

HRMC answer

Having offices at the disposal of the professional trustee in the UK is likely to create a fixed place of business PE, but only if the activity that is carried out at that PE in relation to a particular trust is a core activity will the trustee be regarded as having a PE for the purposes of that trust.

Example 18

The Pi Settlement has a protector, with powers to appoint and remove trustees **A2.430**
and to prevent certain decisions of the trustee being implemented. The sole
corporate trustee is resident outside the UK. The protector may be UK resident,
or non-UK resident, but if non resident, will visit the UK to see the settlor and/
or the current principal adult beneficiaries from time to time. They may or may
not receive a fee for acting as a protector.

Analysis

In most normal circumstances the protector will not be a trustee, and is not an agent
of the trustees. As a result he or she cannot be a dependent agent. The trust remains
non-UK resident.

HMRC answer

If a protector is appointed then if they are not the trustee and are not a dependent
agent of the trustee then they will not create a PE for the trust.

Example 19

The Rho Trust is governed by Jersey law and has two non-resident trustees. One **A2.431**
trustee is a corporate trustee Sigma Limited which is a professional trustee carrying on trustee business in Jersey and the other trustee is Mr S who is a Jersey
resident lawyer who also carries on a trustee business. The settlor is (and was at
the date of settlement) UK resident.

Sigma Limited and Mr S appoint investment managers in the UK to whom they
delegate investment discretion. The investment manager is unconnected with
both Sigma Limited and Mr S and provides normal investment management
services at an arm's length fee. It has authority to conduct business on behalf of
the trustees. On that analysis the Guidance would accept that in relation to
Sigma Limited the investment manager is an independent agent and would
therefore not constitute a permanent establishment. The position should logically be the same for Mr S. It is true that the Guidance at paragraph 7 suggests
that the independent agent exemption applies only to corporate trustees. There
is scope for suggesting this is the case, in that although section 10(6) TCGA
provides that a branch or agency does not include any person within the exemption in section 82 TMA 1970 (which excluded independent agents from the
definition of branch or agency), section 82 was repealed by Finance Act 1995.
However the reference in section 10(6) to section 82 was not also repealed and it
is possible that section 17(2)(a) of the Interpretation Act 1978 preserves section
82 in the context of section 10(6).

This analysis would mean that the position for individual trustees in relation to
income tax would be worse than that in relation to capital gains tax.

We should welcome HMRC confirmation that in the context of section 10(6)
TCGA the independent agent exemption would in the light of the above analysis
apply to individual trustees for capital gains tax and that, consistently with this,
a similar view would be taken in relation to income tax.

HMRC answer

The independent agent exemption is relevant only to corporate trustees. However, an
independent agent can create a charge to income tax. A key aspect of agency is that the

agent must have authority to do business on behalf of the non-resident, so it won't always make a lot of difference in practice.

HMRC agreed that the position in respect of the reference to s82 TMA 70 in s10(6) TCGA 1992 is not immediately clear and they will clarify it.

Example 20

A2.432   The Tau Trust of which Upsilon Limited, a Jersey corporate trustee, is the trustee appoints Upsilon Investment Management Limited in the UK to manage the investments of the Tau Trust. Upsilon Limited is the holding company of Upsilon Investment Management Limited. Upsilon Investment Management Limited provides investment management services primarily for entities within the Upsilon Group. It operates on arn's length terms on the same basis as that offered to third party unconnected clients but these form a small minority of the clients. Over 70% of the services provided by Upsilon Investment Management Limited are provided to Upsilon Limited and other connected persons.

Example 3a in the HMRC Guidance is similar in dealing with the delegation of investment discretion to a UK investment manager. The example considers that the investment manager should qualify as an independent agent. Reference is made to this being in line with the investment manager exemption.

We assume this is a reference to paragraph 3 Schedule 26 Finance Act 2003. Schedule 26 would seem to be relevant only by analogy because it deals with trading being carried on by the investment manager in the UK on behalf of the non-resident principal (SP1/01(07) (ie as revised July 2007) paragraph 14). It is therefore not relevant where investment transactions are carried out and whether or not the other provisions of Schedule 26 are complied with.

We should welcome HMRC confirmation that where trading is not being carried out by the investment manager on behalf of the non-resident trustee, but merely investment management, then the independent agent exemption will apply without reference to Schedule 26 if the investment manager or other agent is acting on arm's length terms, and that the fact there is a corporate relationship (such as the two entities being in the same corporate group) will not prevent the independent agent status applying.

HMRC answer

It doesn't matter that there is a corporate relationship between the investment manager and the trustee (such as the two entities being in the same corporate group) and this will not prevent the independent agent status applying. This follows the principle in the OECD Commentary on Article 5 that a subsidiary is not automatically assumed to be a dependent agent of its parent.

HMRC confirm that where trading is not being undertaken by the investment manager, but merely investment management, then there should be no difficulty provided the remuneration and terms are arm's length, and it is not necessary in this context that the other requirements of Schedule 26 and SP1/01/07 are satisfied. **17**

INDIVIDUAL NON-RESIDENT TRUSTEE

Example 21

A2.433   The Phi Trust is subject to English law. The trustee of the settlement is a professional lawyer resident in Switzerland. Doubts have arisen over the precise scope of some of the provisions in the trust deed, with the result that leading Counsel in London has been instructed to advise. Based on the advice given, the trustee further instructs Counsel to submit an application to vary the terms of the trust deed. In view of the importance attached to the advice received from Counsel, and the application to vary the terms of the trust deed, the professional trustee comes to the UK for a month to liaise with Counsel and the trust's London solicitors. He stays in the same London hotel throughout this period, and has regular meetings at the London offices of the trust's solicitors.

Analysis

The professional trustee is present in the UK for a month, holding many meetings with Counsel, the trust's solicitors and attending Court. Although the trustee stays at the same hotel throughout, and attends meetings with the trust's legal advisers, his occupation/attendance in relation to the Court application and related matters will not constitute his acting as a trustee in the course of business carried out in the UK through a branch or agency. This is because the occupation/ attendance at these places will lack the required degree of permanence required. The trustee cannot be a branch or agency of himself. As soon as the Court proceedings are over, the attendance/occupation at these places for this purpose will cease.

On these facts the Trust is non-UK resident.

HMRC answer

HMRC accept that the trustee cannot be an agent of himself. There seemed to be an inference that this would not necessarily be so as regards the existence of a branch. HMRC said that overall they would seek to apply the same broad treatment to branch and agencies as for a PE. There seemed to be an inference that the position would be more favourable where there was a governing treaty, and less so where there wasn't.

Example 22

As in Example 21, save that the occasion for the trustee being present in the UK **A2.434** is the sale of shares in a UK private company held by the trustee. As before the trustee attends meetings with advisers.

Analysis

In Example 21, the trustee had little choice but to use the UK Courts to vary the terms of the settlement as this was a trust with an English governing law. Similarly, in this example, the trustee has little choice but to come to the UK to liaise with advisers. The analysis is thought to be directly comparable, with the result that none of the activities of the trustee in London in connection with the sale can be considered to be those of the trustee acting through a branch or agency in the UK.

On these facts the Trust is non-UK resident.

HMRC answer

The short length of time spent in the UK suggested that the trustee was not UK resident. As the trustee could not be an agent of him or herself, it was necessary to establish whether their activities could amount to be being a branch. If the trustee simply took out an office for a month, it was unlikely that they could be said to have established a branch. If they had use of rooms at their independent lawyers, it would not be possible to say that this amounted to a branch. If they had use of a room there and conducted other business from it, it is possible that this might amount to a branch but it was unlikely that this would be the case unless they made use of the accommodation provided in this way for some considerable time.

Example 23

A2.435   The Chi Trust is non UK resident. Its trustee is a professional adviser who is resident in the Isle of Man. The trust's accountant is UK resident and entirely unconnected with the trustee. It has a number of beneficiaries, all of whom are currently UK resident. The trustee makes quarterly visits to the UK (remaining here for two to three days at most). He does this to visit the beneficiaries. Meetings are either held at the homes/places of work of the beneficiaries, at restaurants (over lunch/dinner) or occasionally at the offices of the trust's accountant. At these meetings decisions may be taken with respect to distribution policy. At one meeting held at the accountant's offices legal documentation was signed with respect to a loan to a beneficiary.

On these facts the Trust is non-UK resident.

Analysis

The fact that no regular meetings are held outside the UK with beneficiaries has no bearing on whether the trustee is carrying on a business of being a trustee through a UK branch or agency. There is no fixed place of business in the UK and the trustee cannot be a branch or agency of himself.

HMRC answer

It was agreed that the trustee could not be an agent of themselves.

SECTION 2: SPECIFIC QUESTIONS

OFFSHORE INDEPENDENT TRUST COMPANY; NO GROUP COMPANIES IN UK; NO PREMISES IN UK; ARRANGEMENTS WITH UK PROFESSIONALS

Example 24

A2.436   Tamar Trustees is an independent Jersey trust company. Its shareholders are its four directors, all of whom are Jersey resident. It has no group company or any other affiliated company in the UK. It has no premises in the UK.

CT Legal LLP is a UK law firm which has a good relationship with Tamar Trustees. They have worked together well over the years; the principals known each other well; and they have a number of mutual clients which have been referred in both directions. There are no formal referral arrangements, however, and no exclusivity – both CT Legal and Tamar also refer clients to other firms. There are no financial tie-ups between the firms.

Where the settlor or beneficiaries of one of Tamar's trusts are also clients of CT Legal, the meetings have typically happened at CT's offices in Winchester.

We should welcome confirmation of whether the Winchester premises count as a PE of Tamar in the following cases:

(a) Meetings only take place for mutual clients with both Tamar and CT staff present

HMRC answer

As the meeting rooms are only made available by invitation, there is no right to use them or an automatic expectation of such a right, there is no PE.

(b) CT may occasionally offer the free use of a meeting room to Tamar, to meet their mutual clients even though CT staff do not attend the meeting. **A2.437**

HMRC answer

As the meeting rooms are only made available by invitation, there is no right to use them or an automatic expectation of such a right, there is no PE.

(c) CT may occasionally offer the free use of a meeting room to Tamar to meet new **A2.438** clients. The new clients are not existing clients of CT but CT hope to impress them with the use of their meeting rooms and hopefully sign them up as clients.

HMRC answer

The activity is preparatory so whether or not there is a PE doesn't matter.

(d) CT may occasionally offer the free use of a meeting room to Tamar to meet **A2.439** Tamar's clients. There is no prospect of those clients becoming CT's clients. CT merely offer this facility due to their relationship with Tamar. They do not charge Tamar because the meeting rooms are otherwise empty and so there is virtually no marginal cost to CT in doing so. CT merely benefit from an ongoing good relationship with Tamar.

HMRC answer

The availability of the accommodation is at CT's discretion, so there is no PE.

(e) (f) (g) as in (b) (c) and (d) respectively above, save that Tamar become so used to **A2.440** this arrangement that they no longer call the client partner at CT, but simply contact the CT receptionist and ask if they can have a room in which to meet clients. The CT receptionist occasionally refuses where there are no spare meeting rooms.

HMRC answer

Examples (e) + (f) + (g) – it is doubtful that the meeting room is at the disposal of Tamar, so no PE.

(h) (i) (j) as in (e) (f) (g) save that, while the CT receptionist could theoretically refuse, **A2.441** this has never happened in practice such that Tamar always get a meeting room when they ask.

HMRC answer

Examples (h) + (i) + (j) – there could be a PE if the meetings were frequent enough.

Even if it is found that the trust does have a fixed place of business PE then the trustee will be resident in respect of a particular trust where that trustee's core activities are carried out at that PE.

(k) (l) (m) as in (e) (f) (g) save that CT make a nominal £25 charge for each occasion **A2.442** to cover tea/biscuits etc.

and

(n) (o) (p) as in (h) (i) (j) save that CT make a nominal £25 charge as above.

and

(q) as in (d) save that CT make a £90 per hour charge to Tamar for the use of the meeting room.

HMRC answer

(k) to (q) Payment strengthens the argument that a PE exists, up to (q) where there is a right to occupy.

This was challenged by reference to the analogy of using a room in a hotel. HMRC **A2.443** said that meeting in a hotel room could be a problem if it became known that the trustees were conducting business in a hotel on certain days. However, if different hotels were used it would lack the degree of permanence required. HMRC felt that using a room in a hotel every month for (say) 3 years, could be caught. Meetings which involved an element of discretion were unlikely to be caught. This would apply to meetings at a beneficiary's home or at the settlor's suite of rooms at a hotel – even if these were occupied for long periods would not count as being a place of business for the trust company. There was a discussion as to whether restaurants could ever be a PE; the conclusion was that this was very unlikely. Meetings at adviser's premises unlikely to be an issue. HMRC said they were not trying to catch foreign beneficiary or settlor who visits UK to see his adviser but trustees or advisers who use the same hotel room for a while may be at risk.

Before the trustees could have a PE in the UK, there had to be a requisite degree of permanence. If this was missing, the venue could not be a PE, so it did not matter what was discussed or decided at such meetings. For example, the trustees could come to the UK and meet in a hotel - which they did not regularly use- and make decisions about distribution of trust corpus (a core activity) and this would not make the trust UK resident.

This Example revolves around various circumstances in which premises might be made available. The issue is whether the Jersey trustees have premises at their disposal as they clearly operated from a fixed base when in the UK. This is a example of frequency and degree. Thus, even if Tamar trustees do not have any legal right to occupy the room in the premises of CT, because that room is put at their disposal any repeated use of it where they have some discretion over the use would potentially create a PE. Paying a charge is more likely to suggest room at disposal. Even if it is found that the trust does have a fixed place of business PE then the trustee will be resident in respect of a particular trust where that trustee's core activities are carried out at that PE.

RESERVED POWERS TRUSTS

Example 25

A2.444   Paragraph 10 of HMRC's Guidance refers to the "core" activities of a trust as including:

– the general administration of the trusts;

– monitoring performance of those investments; and

– decisions concerning trust income and whether distributions should be made.

While this may be the case for a conventional "discretionary" trust, however, many (perhaps most) modern trusts will carve out these roles and may give them to different people. Sometimes this is at the request of the settlor who may not come from a culture familiar with trusts and may not want to put all his eggs in one basket. More commonly, however, professional trustees prefer that the investment function is carved out in the trust deed so that they do not assume any personal liability for poor investment performance.

Where this is the case the trust is usually referred to as a "reserved powers" trust or as a "directed" trust.

This needs to be clearly distinguished from the situation where the trust deed gives the powers to the trustees but allows them to delegate. That is NOT the case with a reserved powers trust. Instead the trust deed will simply not give those powers to the trustees in the first place. Some other person will retain or be given those powers.

The most common reserved power is over investments. Typical wording in the trust deed might say "*X shall be the Investment Director of the Trust and shall have power to direct the investment and reinvestment of the Trust Fund. . ... the Trustees shall comply with directions given by the Investment Director. . ...the Trustees shall have no function with regard to the investment and reinvestment of the Trust Fund which shall vest exclusively in the Investment Director. . ...the Trustees shall have no liability whatsoever with regard to the investment and reinvestment of the Trust Fund*".

Typically this power might be reserved by the settlor. Occasionally the trust deed may give this power to a designated investment professional.

Other powers which may be reserved include powers over income and capital. Typical wording in the trust deed might say "*The Trustees shall pay the income of the Trust Fund to such one or more of the Beneficiaries. . ...as X shall from time to time direct.*" Or "*The Trustees shall hold the capital of the Trust Fund upon trust for such one or more of the Beneficiaries. . ...as X shall revocably or irrevocably appoint*".

This power would again typically be reserved by the settlor. Occasionally it might be given to another family member (e.g. the eldest child).

It is common for one or other of these powers to be reserved. It is less common, but there are a number of examples, where both powers will be reserved. In such cases the trustee may have little or no discretion except in emergency situations (typically on the disability or death of the person with reserved powers). It is sometimes queried in such circumstances whether the trust is a "sham". But this is not the case. A "sham" exists where the parties intend a relationship other than that which is evidenced by the documents. Here the relationship is very clearly evidenced. Indeed what is more likely to be a sham is something which purports to be a discretionary trust but where the trustees never truly exercise that discretion! All leading trust counsel agree that provided the terms are clearly set out in the document, there is still a trust in such a situation.

In the light of this the following examples arise:

(a) If the settlor has reserved the investment function to himself do HMRC consider the settlor to be an agency PE of the trustees if he habitually exercises the investment function while present in the UK? Our view is that this is NOT the case. The settlor cannot be a PE of the trustees' business because the investment function is not part of the trustees' business. The trustees' primary and overriding responsibility is to comply with the terms of the trust deed and the trust deed does not give the trustees the investment function in the first place.

(b) As in (a), but the example is whether HMRC consider the settlor himself to be "acting as trustee in the course of a business which he carries on in the UK through a branch, agency or PE". Presumably not on the basis that (1) the settlor may be UK resident anyway (2) as confirmed in the *Armenian Patriarch v Sonsino* case, a person with investment powers is not "acting as trustee" (3) the settlor will not in any event be acting "in the course of a business" carried on "by him" and (4) the PE concept does not (we are told) apply to individuals and an individual cannot be a branch or agency of himself!

(c) (d) as in (a) and (b) but the settlor has reserved rights over income and capital instead of the investment function.

(e) (f) as in (a) and (b) but the settlor has reserved both the investment function AND rights over income and capital.

HMRC answers

If settlor has investment function under trust deed then it cannot be acting as agent of trustee.

To date HMRC weren't aware that they had seen any deeds of a reserved power trust. If they saw such as case then they said that they would obviously want to have a look at the documentation and may want to take further advice, so they were not willing to comment generally on whether a settlor may be treated as the trustee.

INDIVIDUAL NON-RESIDENT TRUSTEE

Example 26

A2.445   Bill Ray moved to Guernsey 10 years ago. He used to practice as an accountant in the UK, but moved to Guernsey on his retirement. He acts as trustee of 25 trusts on an ongoing basis for which he charges a proper fee in order to supplement his retirement income. He accepts that he is "in business" of being a trustee, albeit that it is not a full-time occupation.

Bill Ray has no property in the UK (he sold his UK house when he retired). He visits beneficiaries / settlors of his trusts in the UK, sometimes in their own homes, but often at the Park Lane Hilton, London where he will meet them for lunch. Lunch is held in the restaurant rather than in a booked room.

(a) Does the Park Lane Hilton constitute a branch or agency of Bill Ray's trust-business?

(b) As above, but assume that Bill meets clients solely in their own homes or in restaurants (a different restaurant each time)?

(c) As above, but Bill meets solely in clients' own homes?

(d) In any event can Bill's own presence in the UK constitute a branch or agency? We take the view that while Bill could constitute an agency PE if his business were incorporated, he cannot be a branch or agency of himself. Do HMRC agree?

HMRC answers

(a) No, there is no fixed place of business and no one is acting as Bill Ray's agent.

(b) As above.

(c) The premises are not really at Bill Ray's disposal so, again, there is no branch. (If however Bill Ray maintained an office or other fixed place of business in the UK the availability of that accommodation would be likely to constitute a UK branch.)

(d) Bill Ray cannot be an agent of himself.

NON-RESIDENT SETTLOR

Example 27

A2.446   Sheikh Abdullah is Saudi resident and domiciled. He has no home in the UK, but occasionally comes to the UK (for perhaps 15-20 days a year) for a variety of business reasons. The 15-20 days (midnights) are usually single visits (i.e. fly in one day, fly out the next), but occasionally he may stay in the UK for 2 nights. He stays in one of three main London hotels.

Sheikh Abdullah set up a (sharia-compliant) trust 8 years ago. The trustees are Big Bank Trustees SA who are based in Switzerland. Big Bank Trustees SA is a subsidiary company of Big Bank Inc which has offices throughout the world including an office in Berkeley Square.

The trust is a conventional discretionary (i.e. not reserved powers) trust.

The directors of Big Bank Trustees SA normally meet Sheikh Abdullah twice a year in Riyadh and once a year in Zurich. However, on one occasion, Sheikh Abdullah is so concerned at the investment performance of the trust that he demands an urgent meeting. As it happens he is on a business trip to the UK and one of the directors of Big Bank Trustees SA is also in the UK at the same time. So they arrange to meet at the Berkeley Square office. While there they formulate a new investment strategy for the trust.

Is the Berkeley Square office an PE of Big Bank Trustees SA?

HMRC answer

The same criteria as set out in Example 24 above apply to determine whether Big Bank Inc's office at Berkeley Square is a PE of the Swiss company trustees Big Bank Trustees SA.

A one off meeting, if that was the only meeting involving Big Bank Trustees SA at the Berkeley Square office, would lack the frequency necessary to establish the continuity needed for a PE.

If the Berkeley Square office were a PE, then because formulating a new investment strategy for the trust is core trust business, the trust will be UK resident. If, however, the director of Big Bank Trustees SA met the Sheikh at the Berkeley Square office of Big Bank Inc and listened to his views but did not take any decision or formulate the investment strategy at the offices but did so only when he returned to Switzerland, then no core trust business is being carried on through a PE in the UK and the trust is not UK resident.

See Examples 16 and 17 (on EBTs) for comparable situations.

INDIVIDUAL TRUSTEES

Example 28

Andrew is a qualified and practising solicitor in the Isle of Man. He is appointed as a named individual trustee of a discretionary trust created by a UK domiciled settlor. He is fully remunerated for his service of acting as a trustee (i.e. not merely reimbursed costs). The other trustee is a non-UK resident trust corporation. Andrew and the non-UK resident trust corporation are together the Trustees. The Trustees engage a UK based investment adviser on arm's length terms to advise them on the choice of investments and to manage those investments. The terms of engagement fulfil the agent of independent status exemption in relation to agency PE.

A2.447

Can HMRC please confirm:

(a) Whether, in these circumstances, the agent of independent status exemption only applies to the trust corporation because the PE concept is only relevant to corporate trustees; or

(b) Whether, in these circumstances, the exemption is available because one of the Trustees is a corporate?

(c) Whether they accept that the concept of branch or agency also recognises an exemption for an agent of independent status –see s10(6) TCGA (definition of branch or agency) with its reference to s82 TMA 1970 (now repealed but replaced with essentially similar legislation);

(d) Whether HMRC intend to amend s10 (6) TCGA 1992 with a valid reference to the provisions that replaced s82 TMA 1970. "

HMRC answers

The independent agent exemption is relevant only to corporate trustee.

HMRC agreed that position in respect of reference to s82 TMA 70 in s10(6) TCGA 1992 is not immediately clear and they will clarify it.

15. SP 2/04 (20 AUGUST 2004) ALLOWABLE EXPENDITURE— EXPENSES INCURRED BY PERSONAL REPRESENTATIVES AND CORPORATE TRUSTEES

Expenses incurred by personal representatives

1 Following consultation with representative bodies, the scale of expenses allowable under TCGA 1992 s 38(1)(b), for the costs of establishing title in computing the gains or losses of personal representatives on the sale of assets comprised in a deceased person's estate, has been revised. The Commissioners for HMRC will accept computations based either on this scale or on the actual allowable expenditure incurred. **A2.448**

2 The revised scale is as follows:

3 The revised scale takes effect where the death in question occurred on or after 6 April 2004.

Gross value of estate	Allowable expenditure
A. Not exceeding £50,000	1.8% of the probate value of the assets sold by the personal representatives.
B. Over £50,000 but not exceeding £90,000	A fixed amount of £900, to be divided between all the assets of the estate in proportion to the probate values and allowed in those proportions on assets sold by the personal representatives.
C. Over £90,000 but not exceeding £400,000	1% of the probate value of the assets sold.
D. Over £400,000 but not exceeding £500,000	A fixed amount of £4,000, to be divided as at B above.
E. Over £500,000 but not exceeding £1,000,000	0.8% of the probate value of the assets sold.
F. Over £1,000,000 but not exceeding £5,000,000	A fixed amount of £8,000, to be divided as at B above.
G. Over £5,000,000	0.16 per cent of the probate value of the assets sold, subject to a maximum of £10,000.

Expenses incurred by corporate trustees

4 Following consultation with representative bodies, HMRC have agreed the following scale of allowable expenditure under TCGA 1992 ss 38 and 64(1) for expenses incurred by corporate trustees in the administration of estates and **A2.449**

trusts. The Commissioners for HMRC will accept computations based either on this scale or on the **actual** allowable expenditure incurred.

5 The scale is as follows—

Transfers of assets to beneficiaries etc

A2.450   (i) Publicly marketed shares and securities—

   (A) One beneficiary—£25 per holding transferred
   (B) Two or more beneficiaries between whom a holding must be divided—As (A), to be divided in equal shares between the beneficiaries

   (ii) Other shares and securities—as (i) above, with the addition of any exceptional expenditure

   (iii) Other assets—as (i) above, with the addition of any exceptional expenditure

For the purpose of this statement of practice, shares and securities are regarded as marketed to the general public if buying and selling prices for them are regularly published in the financial pages of a national or regional newspaper, magazine, or other journal.

Actual disposals and acquisitions

A2.451   (i) Publicly marketed shares and securities—the investment fee as charged by the trustees

   (ii) Other shares and securities—as (i) above, plus actual valuation costs

   (iii) Other assets—the investment fee as charged by the trustees, subject to a maximum of £75, plus actual valuation costs

Where a comprehensive annual management fee is charged, covering both the cost of administering the trust and the expenses of actual disposals and acquisitions, the investment fee for the purposes of (i), (ii) and (iii) above will be taken to be £0.25 per £100 on the sale or purchase moneys.

Deemed disposals by trustees

A2.452   (i) Publicly marketed shares and securities—£8 per holding disposed of

   (ii) Other shares and securities—actual valuation costs

   (iii) Other assets—actual valuation costs

6 This scale takes effect for transfers of assets to beneficiaries, actual disposals and acquisitions, and deemed disposals by corporate trustees on or after 6 April 2004.

16. EC COUNCIL DIRECTIVE 2006

Works of Art, Collectors' items and Antiques, as referred to in points (2), (3) and (4) of article 311(1)

PART A   **A2.452**

Works of art

1. Pictures, collages and similar decorative plaques, paintings and drawings, executed entirely by hand by the artist, other than plans and drawings for architectural, engineering, industrial, commercial, topographical or similar purposes, hand-decorated manufactured articles, theatrical scenery, studio back cloths or the like of painted canvas (CN code 9701);

2. Original engravings, prints and lithographs, being impressions produced in limited numbers directly in black and white or in colour of one or of several plates executed entirely by hand by the artist, irrespective of the process or of the material employed, but not including any mechanical or photomechanical process (CN code 9702 00 00);

3. Original sculptures and statuary, in any material, provided that they are executed entirely by the artist; sculpture casts the production of which is limited to eight copies and supervised by the artist or his successors in title (CN code 9703 00 00); on an exceptional basis, in cases determined by the Member States, the limit of eight copies may be exceeded for statuary casts produced before 1 January 1989;

4. Tapestries (CN code 5805 00 00) and wall textiles (CN code 6304 00 00) made by hand from original designs provided by artists, provided that there are not more than eight copies of each;

5. Individual pieces of ceramics executed entirely by the artist and signed by him;

6. Enamels on copper, executed entirely by hand, limited to eight numbered copies bearing the signature of the artist or the studio, excluding articles of jewellery and goldsmiths' and silversmiths' wares;

7. Photographs taken by the artist, printed by him or under his supervision, signed and numbered and limited to 30 copies, all sizes and mounts included.

A2.453   *PART B*

Collectors' items

1. Postage or revenue stamps, postmarks, first-day covers, pre-stamped stationery and the like, used, or if unused not current and not intended to be current (CN code 9704 00 00);

2. Collections and collectors' pieces of zoological, botanical, mineralogical, anatomical, historical, archaeological, Pala ontological, ethnographic or numismatic interest (CN code 9705 00 00).

A2.454   *PART C*

Antiques

Goods, other than works of art or collectors' items which are more than 100 years old (CN code 9706 00 00).

17. HMRC GUIDANCE - CAPITAL GAINS TAX: AVOIDANCE THROUGH THE CREATION AND USE OF CAPITAL LOSSES (FEBRUARY 2010)

Introduction

ANNEX

Introduction   **A2.456**

This guidance explains HM Revenue and Customs' interpretation of section 16A of the Taxation of Chargeable Gains Act 1992 and how the legislation applies. The guidance does not affect a taxpayer's right to argue for a different interpretation, if necessary in an appeal to the First-tier Tribunal.

This guidance is intended to be read in conjunction with the statement on capital losses first published on 6 December 2006 and included as an annex to this guidance. This guidance was first published in draft form on 6 December 2006 and revised and extended before being issued again for comments on 21 March 2007.

The guidance published on 27 July 2006 relating to the anti-avoidance rule for companies remains valid (with the proviso that references to section 8 in that guidance should be read in future as references to section 16A).

Statutory references in this note are to the Taxation of Chargeable Gains Act 1992, unless otherwise indicated.

1. Draft anti-avoidance legislation was published at Pre-Budget Report 2006 targeting arrangements intended to avoid UK tax through the creation and use of contrived capital losses. Final legislation is at section 27 of Finance Act 2007.

2. The legislation applies to capital losses which arise on disposals on or after 6 December 2006 and give rise to a tax advantage. Where the legislation applies to a capital loss, the loss is not to be an "allowable loss" and may not, therefore, be set off against chargeable gains, nor against income, to reduce liability to capital gains tax, income tax or corporation tax. It will replace the legislation which applies currently to capital losses of companies subject to corporation tax, but does not alter its effect. The guidance published on 27 July 2006 relating to the anti-avoidance rule for companies will remain valid (with the proviso that references to section 8 in that guidance should be read in future as references to section 16A). This paper provides guidance on how the legislation will apply in relation to capital gains tax and income tax.

3. Besides continuing to apply to companies liable to corporation tax in respect of chargeable gains, the legislation now applies also to any person liable to tax on capital gains, including individuals, trustees, and the personal representatives of deceased persons. But, because it is targeted at arrangements that are intended to avoid UK tax, most persons will not be affected, nor will it apply to the majority of transactions undertaken. In particular it is unlikely that individuals with a normal portfolio of investments who make disposals in the ordinary course of managing their portfolio would be affected by these new rules because there is currently little evidence to suggest that such individuals undertake the type of arrangements that are targeted by this legislation.

4. The rule does not apply to a simple sale at arm's length of an investment standing at a loss and the setting of that loss against gains, utilising the statutory relief for losses. Such a transaction does not constitute arrangements whose main purpose is to secure a tax advantage, as the main purpose is the disposal of the unprofitable investment.

5. The legislation is intended to have effect where a person enters deliberately and knowingly into arrangements to gain a tax advantage.

6. The effect of the legislation will be to restrict the use of capital losses resulting from the arrangements where the gaining of a tax advantage is the main purpose or one of the main purposes of the arrangements.

"Arrangements" and "tax advantage"

7. This section provides information about the terms "arrangements" and "tax advantage" used in the legislation.

A2.457 *"Arrangements"*

8. The term "arrangements" is widely drawn to include any agreement, understanding, scheme, transaction or series of transactions, whether or not legally enforceable.

9. Whether a transaction forms part of a series of transactions, or a scheme, or an arrangement is in general a question of fact, but this conclusion will follow in

any case where one transaction would not have taken place without another transaction, or would have taken place on different terms without that other transaction. However, it is not necessary that transactions must depend on each other in this way in order that they form part of a scheme or arrangements.

"Tax advantage"   **A2.458**

10. It is a condition for the legislation to apply that the main purpose, or one of the main purposes, of any arrangement(s) is to gain a "tax advantage". This expression is defined in the legislation, and has four legs covering relief from tax, repayment of tax, reduction or avoidance of a charge to tax, and avoidance of an assessment to tax.

11. If a tax advantage arises out of a transaction that is part of the arrangements, the legislation asks whether the main purpose or one of the main purposes of the arrangements (referred to as "a main purpose" in this guidance) is to achieve a tax advantage. The purpose of the arrangements is determined by the purpose of the participants in entering into the arrangements. If any participant who has entered into the arrangements has done so with a main purpose of achieving a tax advantage, that will constitute a main purpose of the arrangements.

12. There is no one factor that determines whether the obtaining of a tax advantage is a main purpose of an arrangement. All the circumstances in which the arrangements were entered into need to be taken into consideration. The circumstances might include:

   • the overall economic objective: this should be considered not only from the perspective of individual participants in the arrangements, but also from any wider perspective, such as that of the settlor or beneficiaries of a settlement whose trustees were participants: for these purposes an economic objective does not include tax motivated reasons;

   • whether this objective is one which the parties involved might ordinarily be expected to have, and which is genuinely being sought;

   • whether the objective is being fulfilled in a straightforward way or whether the introduction of any additional, complex or costly steps would have taken place were it not for the tax advantage that could be obtained.

13. The straightforward use of a statutory relief does not of itself bring arrangements within the TAAR. Equally, the existence of a tax advantage, such as obtaining a deduction for tax purposes, is not enough in itself to show that the arrangements have a main purpose of obtaining a tax advantage.

14. For instance, where there is evidence that a person considered two ways to achieve an economic objective and chose on economic grounds to pursue one of them, the fact that there was a beneficial difference in tax treatment for the chosen route would not meet the main purpose test. Where the potential tax treatment was a factor in choosing between alternative arrangements, then it would still be necessary that securing a tax advantage was a main purpose to the arrangements. There may be situations where the tax advantage secured through undertaking one arrangement rather than another is so significant that this indicates that achieving a tax advantage was a main purpose. This is unlikely to be the case where the arrangements chosen do not involve additional, complex or costly steps included solely to secure or enhance a tax advantage.

15. Where a person has entered into a marketed tax avoidance scheme, this will be taken as an indicator that securing a tax advantage was a main purpose of the arrangements.

16. Hence it will be relevant to draw a comparison in order to consider whether, in the absence of the tax considerations:

- the transaction giving rise to the advantage would have taken place at all;
- if so, whether the tax advantage would have been of the same amount; and
- whether the transaction would have been made under the same terms and conditions.

17. Nothing in the new legislation prevents relief for losses under section 24 where a genuine loss has been incurred on an asset which has been lost or extinguished, etc., or where an asset has genuinely become of negligible value. Nor will the new legislation ordinarily prevent a genuine loss on a real disposal of an asset from being set off against a person's own gains, including the case where, before the real disposal that gives rise to the genuine loss, the person acquires the relevant asset from a spouse or civil partner at no gain/no loss under section 58.

A2.459   Restriction on allowable losses

18. There is evidence to show that a variety of schemes to generate capital losses which the existing legislation was never intended to produce are being marketed and implemented. Typically the schemes involve the generation of a capital loss for tax purposes where there is no genuine economic loss and/or no genuine economic disposal, often through schemes with no economic rationale.

19. The intent of this targeted anti-avoidance rule ("TAAR") is to apply the principle set out in the HMRC statement of 6 December 2006, that relief for capital losses should be available only where a person has suffered a genuine economic loss and made a real economic disposal.

20. This legislation will not apply where there is a genuine economic transaction that gives rise to a real economic loss as a result of a real disposal. In these circumstances there will be no arrangements with a main purpose of securing a tax advantage. Conversely, where there is either no real disposal, or no real economic loss, or any combination of the foregoing, then there are likely to be arrangements in place with a main purpose of securing a tax advantage so the legislation will apply.

21. Nor will the legislation apply where the Act provides that an event is treated as a disposal, such as in the case of a negligible value claim, or where a capital sum is derived from an asset - provided that such an occasion of charge does not form part of arrangements which have been entered into with a main purpose of securing a tax advantage.

22. The effect of the new legislation is that any capital loss arising on a disposal on or after 6 December 2006 does not qualify as an allowable loss when it arises in connection with arrangements having a main purpose of obtaining a tax advantage.

23. In order to prevent abuse where losses are created either for immediate use or for use in future years, the legislation applies even if, at the time the loss arises, there are no chargeable gains from which the loss could otherwise have been deducted.

24. It also prevents abuse where the tax advantage would ultimately have arisen to a person other than the person to whom the loss arises, for example where the trustees of a settlement enter into arrangements to create a loss that would ultimately confer a tax advantage on the settlor because the trustees' gains are, in effect, charged on the settlor.

25. Whilst we will not give advice under Code of Practice 10 in respect of transactions which, in our view, may have been undertaken with the purpose of avoiding

tax, HMRC will provide advice about the interpretation of the wording of the legislation where there is genuine uncertainty, in accordance with the principles set out in Code of Practice 10.

Examples

26. Examples of how the legislation will apply in particular circumstances are set out below. These examples are intended to show how different factors will be taken into consideration in deciding whether or not the TAAR applies in a given set of circumstances. They are not designed as templates for deciding whether a loss is or is not caught by the TAAR in any particular case. That can be determined only in the light of all the actual facts and circumstances.

Example 1 - loss on second-hand life insurance policy

27. An individual, C, acquires a life insurance policy "second-hand" for £1 million. The policy had been issued a few days earlier to a third party for a single premium of (say) £990,000. The policy falls within the income tax regime for 'chargeable event gains'.

28. C surrenders 95% of the policy back to the insurance company, receiving (say) £955,000 for the surrender. A few days later C surrenders the remaining 5% of the policy, receiving (say) £55,000 in final settlement.

29. C's intention is to generate a capital loss broadly equal to the cost to him of acquiring the policy, even though he has made no economic loss. There are two legs to the disposal: it is claimed that the interaction of the income tax rules for chargeable event gains in Chapter 9 of Part 4 of the Income Tax (Trading and Other Income) Act 2005 and the capital gains part-disposal rules mean that the first part-disposal results in neither a chargeable gain nor an allowable loss, while the second results in a loss equivalent to virtually the whole of the £1 million paid by C for the policy, with only a very small chargeable event gain on which C is chargeable to income tax.

30. But any such loss will be generated as a result of arrangements. To decide whether a main purpose of those arrangements is to obtain a tax advantage, it is necessary to look at all the circumstances in which the arrangements were entered into, including the participants' overall economic objective, and whether that objective is being fulfilled in a straightforward way, or whether additional, complex or costly steps have been inserted. In this case, it seems clear that the overall objective of C has nothing to do with investing in the life insurance policy, as the main outcome of the transactions is in fact the tax loss that has been obtained. Furthermore, C has entered into an intricate series of steps the only purpose of which appears to be to deliver this tax loss. This suggests that obtaining the tax advantage was a main purpose of the arrangements, in which case the TAAR will apply and the losses will not be allowable.

Example 2 - capital loss set against income

31. An individual, F subscribes £20 for 20 ordinary shares in a company, G Ltd., which meet the requirements for any loss on disposal of the shares to be relievable against F's income (section 574 ICTA 1988, or, from 6 April 2007, section 131 Income Tax Act 2007).

32. F arranges to sell the shares for their current value to a third party, P. F also grants P an option to sell the shares back for their market value at the time the option is exercised.

33. P injects (say) £1 million into G Ltd. by subscribing for another share at a premium of £999,999. P then exercises the option (within 30 days of F's original sale) and sells the 20 shares back to F for their current value of (say) £1 million.

34. The CGT 'bed and breakfasting' identification rules in section 106A(5) match the shares disposed of (by F) with the later reacquisition, and a loss of £999,980 arises to F. F claims to set this loss off against income. In order to decide whether or not the TAAR applies, it is necessary to determine whether there have been arrangements, and, if so, whether those arrangements were entered into with a main purpose of securing a tax advantage. In the present case, there appears to have been a series of transactions, which would be within the statutory definition of arrangements. To determine whether or not the arrangements were entered into with a main purpose of securing a tax advantage, it is necessary to take account of all the circumstances, including the overall economic objective of the participants in the arrangements, and whether that objective is being fulfilled in a straightforward way, or whether additional, complex or costly steps have been inserted. Here, the intricate series of transactions have the effect of procuring a tax loss unrelated to the economic reality, which suggests that F entered into the arrangements with a main purpose of gaining a tax advantage. In such a case, the new rule will apply and the capital loss will not be an allowable loss, and therefore cannot be set off against F's income (or against F's capital gains).

Example 3 - artificial loss from matched options, etc.

35. A body of trustees, W, takes out two options or futures, designed so that one will yield a loss and the other a corresponding (or similar) gain, depending on how the value of the underlying assets has changed. The contracts are completed so that a loss and a matching (or similar) gain arise.

36. A tax advantage could be obtained by setting the loss on one of the contracts against chargeable gains on some other disposal (in the same year that the loss arises or another year) while the gain on the other contract is perhaps:

- not taxed at all, or

- taxed at a lower rate than the 'saving' achieved by setting the loss against the other chargeable gains, or

- not taxed until a later year.

37. In order to determine whether or not the TAAR applies to these transactions, it is necessary to consider whether or not arrangements have been entered into with a main purpose of securing a tax advantage. The matching contracts are clearly arrangements, so the question is whether the trustees have entered into them with the aim of gaining a tax advantage. This can only be decided by looking at all the circumstances surrounding the arrangements, including the trustees' overall economic objective, and whether that objective has been realised in a straightforward way, or whether additional, complex or costly steps have been inserted. In the present case, the trustees have obtained a loss and a gain, designed to ensure that the loss can be set against real gains, while the gain is either not taxable, or taxable at a lower rate, or perhaps in a later year. So additional and complex steps which have been inserted, and the tax outcome of the transactions does not reflect the economic reality of the situation. These factors suggest that a main purpose of the arrangements was the obtaining of a tax advantage, and so the loss will fall within the terms of the TAAR and will not be allowable.

Example 4 - sale of shares to realise capital loss

38. Mr H, sells shares in a company, S plc, in order to crystallise a loss which can be set against his chargeable gains arising in the year. Unbeknown to Mr H, his wife Mrs H buys shares of the same class in S plc a few days later, at the same price as Mr H sold the original holding.

39. In order to determine whether or not the rule applies to these transactions, it is necessary to consider whether or not arrangements have been entered into with a main purpose of securing a tax advantage. As the statutory definition of arrangements includes a "transaction", both the sale of the shares and their subsequent purchase by Mrs H are arrangements for the purposes of the rule. It is then necessary to consider whether securing a tax advantage was a main purpose of those arrangements, and to do so it is necessary to take account of all the circumstances in which the arrangements were entered into, including the participants' overall economic objective, and whether that objective is being fulfilled in a straightforward way, or whether additional, complex or costly steps have been inserted. Mrs H's decision to acquire shares in S plc was unconnected with Mr H's disposal of similar shares, and Mr H has simply taken advantage of the statutory relief for capital losses in section 2(2) in a straightforward way. Moreover, Mr H has incurred a real economic loss on a genuine disposal to a third party. Mrs H has made a genuine purchase on arm's-length terms. These factors suggest there was no main purpose of obtaining a tax advantage, so these transactions do not fall foul of the TAAR.

Example 5 - sale of shares to realise capital loss

40. Mr H has shares in S plc which are standing at a loss. Mrs H has shares in a separate company, T plc, standing at a gain. Mr H transfers his shares to Mrs H under the no-gain, no-loss rule in section 58 TCGA, and she then sells both holdings of shares. The loss on the shares in S plc covers the gain arising from the shares in T plc, and so no CGT is payable by Mrs H.

41. Taking the spouses together, Mr and Mrs H each have shares which they want to sell. What happens in fact is that they do sell their shares, and the economic consequence is that they realise a gain on one set of shares and a loss on the other set. To decide whether or not the TAAR applies, it is necessary to consider whether there have been arrangements, and whether a main purpose of those arrangements was the securing of a tax advantage. In this case, it seems clear that there have been arrangements, namely the transfer of the shares from Mr H to Mrs H. It is then necessary to look at what the main purpose of Mr and Mrs H in entering into these arrangements was. This can be determined only by looking at all the circumstances surrounding the arrangements. In the present example, Mr and Mrs H wanted to dispose of their shareholdings, and they did this in a straightforward way. They made use of the provisions of section 58 TCGA, which provides the opportunity for spouses (or civil partners) to bring together gains and losses, but again the straightforward use of a statutory relief in this way does not (of itself) bring arrangements within the TAAR. Moreover, the tax outcome of the transactions reflects the economic reality of Mr and Mrs H's situation. In all the circumstances, this suggests that there was no main purpose of achieving a tax advantage, and where there is no such main purpose the rule does not apply.

Example 6 - sale of shares to realise capital loss

42. As in example 4, Mr H sells shares in a company, in order to crystallise a loss which can hen be set against his chargeable gains arising in the year. Mr H makes

arrangements for his wife Mrs H to purchase the same number and class of shares. Mrs H then transfers the shares back to Mr H on the following day. By virtue of section 58 TCGA this is a no-gain, no-loss transaction.

43. To decide whether or not the TAAR applies, it is necessary to consider whether there have been arrangements, and whether a main purpose of those arrangements was the securing of a tax advantage. In this case it is clear that there have been arrangements, as Mr H has arranged for his wife to purchase the same number and class of shares. It is then necessary to look at what the main purpose of Mr and Mrs H in entering into these arrangements was, and to do so it is necessary to consider the overall economic objective of the arrangements, and whether that objective is being fulfilled in a straightforward way, or whether additional, complex or costly steps have been inserted. Clearly the real economic ownership of the shares has remained with Mr H, which suggests that the disposal of the shares was incidental to some other main purpose of the arrangements. The only substantive change here is that a tax loss has been obtained. Since Mr & Mrs H have the same effective holding of shares and no less cash at the end of the arrangements as at the beginning, they have not suffered any corresponding economic loss, which suggests that a main purpose of the arrangements was the securing of that tax advantage. The TAAR will therefore apply and the capital losses claimed by Mr H will not be allowable losses.

44. On a subsequent sale by Mr H any chargeable gain would be greater (or any allowable loss would be smaller) than would have been the case if the arrangements had not been entered into. This does not affect the operation of the TAAR in relation to the losses generated under the arrangements.

Example 7 - sale of shares to realise capital loss

45. The situation may arise where variants on the arrangements in example 6 occur. For example, instead of making arrangements for Mrs H to buy back the same number of shares as had been sold by Mr H, the couple might arrange for a slightly different number of shares to be bought. Or she might purchase the shares and retain them as part of her own portfolio, not transferring them back to Mr H at all.

46. To decide whether or not the TAAR applies in such cases, it is still necessary to consider whether there have been arrangements, and whether a main purpose of those arrangements was the securing of a tax advantage. In each case it is clear that there have been arrangements, and so it is necessary to look at what the main purposes of these arrangements were. All the circumstances surrounding the arrangements have to be taken into account, and to do so it is necessary to consider the overall economic objective of the arrangements, whether that objective is one that the participants might ordinarily be expected to have, whether that objective is genuinely being sought, and whether it is being fulfilled in a straightforward way, or additional, complex or costly steps have been inserted.

47. In a case where a slightly different number of shares has been bought back by Mrs H, but those shares are immediately transferred back to Mr H, it is likely that the securing of a tax advantage would still be one of the main purposes, in which case the TAAR would still apply. But if only a very small proportion of the shares sold by Mr H were then purchased by Mrs H and transferred back to Mr H, or if Mrs H bought the shares and retained them as part of her own share portfolio, it is less likely that the securing of a tax advantage was one of the main purposes of the arrangements, in which case the TAAR would not apply.

Example 8 - sale of shares to realise capital loss

48. A further variant on the situation in example 6 is that Mrs H could buy back the same number and class of shares that had been sold by Mr H, but that she does not do so until, say, 31 days after Mr H has sold the shares.

49. Again, it seems clear that there have been arrangements, and so it is necessary to look at what the main purpose of Mr and Mrs H in entering into these arrangements was. So to determine whether or not the TAAR applies all the circumstances surrounding the arrangements have to be taken into account, considering:

· the overall economic objective of the arrangements,

· whether that objective is one that the participants might be expected to have, and which is genuinely being sought, and

· whether that objective is being fulfilled in a straightforward way, or additional, complex or costly steps have been inserted.

If Mrs H bought back the same number and class of shares which had been sold by Mr H, but did not do so until some weeks after his disposal, it is less likely that the securing of a tax advantage will have been a main purpose of the arrangements, because there will have been a degree of exposure to market fluctuations and therefore a genuine economic risk. As a general rule of thumb HMRC considers that the TAAR will not apply in any case where a sale of shares is followed by their re-purchase after a period exceeding 30 days, provided that the exposure to market fluctuations in that period is real and there are, for example, no additional contracts or arrangements in place that significantly limit any economic risk. This 30 day rule of thumb is derived from the time limit in section 106A(5) TCGA 1992, the rule which operates to counteract so-called "bed and breakfasting" transactions.

Example 9 - sale of shares to realise a capital loss

50. An individual, R, who has realised a chargeable gain in a particular tax year, sells shares in a company, X plc., which are standing at a loss, to an unconnected third party. R wishes to offset the resulting capital loss against the other chargeable gain. 31 days later R buys back the same number of shares in X plc., again from an unconnected third party.

51. To decide whether or not the TAAR applies, it is necessary to consider whether there have been arrangements, and as for example 8, this seems to be the case here. The next question, therefore, is whether the arrangements have a main purpose of securing a tax advantage. As for previous examples, this entails examining all the circumstances surrounding the arrangements, considering their overall economic objective, whether that objective is one that the participants might be expected to have, and which is genuinely being sought, and whether that objective is being fulfilled in a straightforward way, or additional, complex or costly steps have been inserted. In this case, the shares were bought back after the 30 day time limit in section 106A(5) TCGA, so the transaction is not within those "bed and breakfasting" rules. In disposing of the shares in X plc. R has incurred a real economic loss on a genuine disposal to a third party. Provided that R has not entered into some form of contract or agreement to ensure that he is not exposed to a genuine economic risk in respect of the shares during the period they were not in his ownership, this suggests that he has not entered into arrangements with a main purpose of securing a tax advantage. The transactions therefore fall outside the scope of the TAAR.

Example 10 - sale of shares to realise a capital loss

52. R (from example 9) sells the same shares in X plc. to an unconnected third party, again in order to realise a capital loss which can be set against a chargeable gain. However, the contract specifies that R has the right to require the same third party to sell the shares back for their market value within 35 days, provided that the market value has not risen or fallen by more than 5%. R duly buys the shares back after 31 days.

53. Again, it seems clear that arrangements have been entered into, and so the question is whether or not those arrangements have been entered into with a main purpose of securing a tax advantage. To determine whether or not this is the case all the circumstances surrounding the arrangements have to be taken into account, so it is necessary to consider their overall economic objective, whether that objective is one that the participants might be expected to have, and which is genuinely being sought, and whether that objective is being fulfilled in a straightforward way, or additional, complex or costly steps have been inserted. In this example, an additional step has been inserted when compared with the previous example, and the effect of that additional step is that R will suffer no, or very little, real economic risk on the disposal of the shares. Following these transactions R still has the same shareholding in X plc., but he has used the capital losses to secure a tax advantage by reducing the CGT he has to pay, and other than the realisation of the loss there has been no real economic change. As there have been arrangements entered into with a main purpose of securing a tax advantage, the transactions fall within the scope of the TAAR and R's losses will not be allowable losses.

Example 11 - sale of asset by trustees

54. A body of trustees sell a capital asset and realise a chargeable gain. In the same year, they also sell an asset which is standing at a loss in order to crystallise that loss. The loss can be set against the gain, and so no CGT is payable in that year.

55. To decide whether or not the TAAR applies, it is necessary to consider whether there have been arrangements, and whether a main purpose of those arrangements was the securing of a tax advantage. The two disposals will constitute arrangements within the meaning of the new section 16A TCGA, so the issue is whether or not the arrangements have been entered into with a main purpose of securing a tax advantage. To decide this, it is necessary to take account of all the circumstances in which the arrangements were entered into, including the participants' overall economic objective, and whether that objective is being fulfilled in a straightforward way, or whether additional, complex or costly steps have been inserted. In the present case, the trustees have made two genuine disposals, the relief they receive for their loss is explicitly provided for by section 2(2) TCGA, and the tax consequences of the transactions match the real change in the economic ownership of both assets. This suggests that, as indicated in paragraph 4 above, the trustees have not entered into arrangements which have a main purpose of securing a tax advantage and as a result the TAAR does not apply.

Example 12 - sale of asset by trustees

56. A body of trustees sell a capital asset and realise a chargeable gain on disposal to third parties. In the same year, they also sell to a third party an asset which is standing at a loss in order to crystallize that loss. The loss can be set against the gain, and so no CGT is payable in that year. The trustees have also entered into

an agreement with the sole beneficiary of the settlement, Z, that they will appoint funds to him sufficient to allow him to buy the asset on which the loss has been realised from the third party to whom the asset was sold, and Z then does so.

57. Where trustees sell an asset and realise a capital loss in the normal course of administering the trust it is highly unlikely that the rule will apply. This is so even if a beneficiary of the trust later buys the asset from a third party in a genuine arm's length transaction unconnected with the disposal by the trustees, whether from funds advanced to him or her by the trustees, or from his or her own resources. However, the rule is likely to apply if arrangements have been made to manipulate the value of the asset so that the loss claimed by the trustees does not reflect the true economic loss they have sustained

58. As in previous examples, it is clear that arrangements have been entered into, so the question is whether or not there was a main purpose of securing a tax advantage. To decide this, it is necessary to take account of all the circumstances in which the arrangements were entered into, including the participants' overall economic objective, and whether that objective is being fulfilled in a straightforward way, or whether additional, complex or costly steps have been inserted. In the present case, the fact that the trustees are required to administer the trust for the benefit of the sole beneficiary, Z, means that there is a degree of common interest in the outcome of the transactions. However, trust law allows trustees to choose either to sell assets and pass the proceeds to a beneficiary or simply to transfer those assets to him or her, and such a choice is for the trustees to make. Unless there is an additional factor to indicate a degree of manipulation, such as evidence that the loss claimed by the trustees does not reflect their true economic loss on the asset, the rule will not apply.

Example 13 - sale of asset by trustees

59. In a variation of example 12, the trustees are administering a discretionary trust for a number of beneficiaries, and Z is one of that class of beneficiaries. The trustees sell a capital asset and realise a chargeable gain. In the same year, they also sell an asset which is standing at a loss. The loss can be set against the gain, and so no CGT is payable in that year. Also in that year, the trustees advance funds to a number of the beneficiaries, including Z, who uses the sum he receives to buy the asset on which the loss has been realised by the trustees.

60. As in previous examples, it is clear that arrangements have been entered into, so the question is whether or not there was a main purpose of securing a tax advantage. To decide this, it is necessary to take account of all the circumstances in which the arrangements were entered into, including the participants' overall economic objective, and whether that objective is being fulfilled in a straightforward way, or whether additional, complex or costly steps have been inserted. In this example, there are several beneficiaries for whose benefit the trustees are required to administer the trust, which means that the trustees are under an obligation to balance the different beneficiaries' interests in the trust assets. The fact that the trustees have advanced funds to a number of the beneficiaries suggests that the disposals made by the trustees were genuine disposals, effected as part of the normal course of administering the trust. Although one beneficiary has used the funds advanced to him to purchase an asset previously owned by the trustees, this does not of itself mean that the economic objective of the trustees was other than the effective disposal of both the assets, nor that the economic objective of the beneficiary was other than the purchase of the asset on

which the loss was previously realised by the trustees. The fact that the tax outcome for the persons associated with the arrangements matches the economic outcome suggests that obtaining a tax advantage was not a main purpose of the arrangements, and in such a case the TAAR will not apply to disallow the losses.

Example 14 - trustees distributing assets to beneficiaries

61. The trustees of a settlement wish to distribute an asset to a beneficiary of the settlement. They are aware that this will give rise to a chargeable gain. They are also aware that they own a second capital asset which is standing at a capital loss. They therefore transfer that second asset to the beneficiary in the same year. The loss the trustees incur on the transfer of the second asset is set against the gain arising on the transfer of the first asset.

62. Again, to decide whether the TAAR will operate to make the claimed losses disallowable it is necessary to determine whether arrangements have been entered into with a main purpose of securing a tax advantage. The main purpose test is operated by looking at the main purpose of the participants in entering into these arrangements. This requires an analysis of the overall economic objective of the arrangements, and whether that objective is being fulfilled in a straightforward way, or whether additional, complex or costly steps have been inserted. In this case, the trustees have arranged to dispose of the two assets in the same tax year, and have done so. The economic consequence of the transactions, namely the realisation of a gain on the transfer of the first asset and a loss on the transfer of the other, matches the tax outcome. There have been no additional, complex or costly steps inserted into the arrangements. These factors suggest that the main purpose of the arrangements was not to secure a tax advantage. The two disposals have been made with a view to taking advantage of the statutory relief in section 2(2) in a straightforward way. In such a case the TAAR will not apply and the losses will be available to set against the chargeable gains.

Example 15 - investment in EIS shares

63. An individual, J, invests in shares under the Enterprise Investment Scheme (EIS), with a view to securing income tax relief. In order to fund the purchase of the shares J sells a capital asset which is standing at a loss to a third party.

64. To decide whether or not the TAAR applies, it is necessary to consider whether there have been arrangements, and whether a main purpose of those arrangements was the securing of a tax advantage. In this case it is clear that there have been arrangements within the meaning of the legislation, as J has disposed of the capital asset and used the proceeds to fund the purchase of the EIS shares. To decide what J's main purpose was in entering into these arrangements, it is necessary to consider the overall economic objective of the arrangements, and whether that objective is being fulfilled in a straightforward way, or whether additional, complex or costly steps have been inserted. J has made a real disposal of a capital asset in a straightforward way, and has incurred a genuine economic loss. There have been no additional, costly or complex steps inserted into the transactions. The fact that the disposal has been made with a view to using the proceeds to invest in shares which fall within the EIS tax regime does not mean that the arrangements have been entered into with a main purpose of securing a tax advantage, because the straightforward use of a statutory relief does not of itself bring arrangements within the TAAR. Hence the TAAR does not apply.

Example 16 - deferred gain covered by capital loss on EIS shares

65. Y has disposed of a capital asset and realised a chargeable gain, but the gain is deferred because he invests a sufficient amount in shares issued under the Enterprise Investment Scheme (EIS). Unfortunately the EIS company in which Y has invested does not succeed, and the shares later become worthless. Y makes a negligible value claim under section 24(2) and the resulting loss on the shares is set against the original gain that is brought back into charge under the EIS rules, or possibly against Y's income under section 574 ICTA.

66. To determine whether or not the TAAR applies so that the losses Y has realised on the shares in the EIS company are not allowable, it is necessary to decide whether or not arrangements have been entered into with a main purpose of realising a tax advantage. It is clear that there have been arrangements, and to decide whether securing a tax advantage was a main purpose of those arrangements it is necessary to take account of all the circumstances in which the arrangements were entered into, including the participants' overall economic objective, and whether that objective is being fulfilled in a straightforward way, or whether additional, complex or costly steps have been inserted. In this case, Y has made a real investment in an EIS company, and there is nothing to suggest that the EIS company was other than a genuine investment opportunity from Y's perspective. The negligible value claim only creates a disposal for capital gains purposes. No additional, costly or complex steps have been inserted as part of the arrangements; Y is taking advantage of the tax reliefs offered in respect of EIS investments in a straightforward manner. The loss Y suffers on the shares in the company is a real economic loss. Taken together, these factors suggest that there was no main purpose of securing a tax advantage and so Y's loss is allowable. It makes no difference that a gain on the EIS shares may have been exempt. The new legislation does not have any effect on the normal operation of the relief.

Example 17 - capital loss following disposal of company assets

67. M and K are married and between them own all the shares in a property investment company, B Ltd. The shares are standing at a loss but B Ltd owns a valuable property. M and K jointly buy the property from B Ltd. for cash at its open market value and the company distributes its remaining assets, the cash, during its winding up. M and K realise losses on their shares.

68. To decide whether or not the TAAR applies, it is necessary to consider whether there have been arrangements, and whether a main purpose of those arrangements was the securing of a tax advantage. In this case, it seems clear that there have been arrangements, so it is necessary to look at what M and K's main purpose in entering into these arrangements was. This can be determined only by looking at all the circumstances surrounding the arrangements. In the present example, M and K wanted to wind up B Ltd, but also to retain ownership of the valuable property they controlled via the company. The property was purchased by them from the company at market value, and paid for with real consideration, so there was no artificial reduction in the value of the company. The winding-up of the company allowed the shareholders to realise the economic value of their investment in it in a straightforward way. B Ltd. has simply converted value represented by property into the same value represented by cash, and M and K now own the property directly. This, coupled with the fact that the tax effect of the transactions reflects the economic outcome suggests that there was no main purpose of realising a tax advantage, and so the TAAR will not apply.

Example 18 - trustees make a deliberate transfer of value

69. A body of trustees who fall within the terms of Schedule 4B have outstanding borrowing which has not been used for trust purposes (Schedule 4B is a measure introduced to discourage trustees avoiding capital gains tax by incurring debt and advancing funds from the settlement). The trustees intentionally make a transfer of value which triggers off a charge under Schedule 4B, and as they expect this transaction results in a capital loss. The trustees have realised chargeable gains in the same year, and claim to set the loss against those gains.

70. It is necessary to look at the arrangements which have been entered into by the trustees to determine whether these have been entered into with a main purpose of securing a tax advantage. There are arrangements in this case, so the question is whether or not those arrangements were entered into with a main purpose of securing a tax advantage, and to decide this it is necessary to take account of all the circumstances surrounding the transactions. It will be relevant to consider what the trustees' overall economic objective was, and whether that objective is being fulfilled in a straightforward way, or whether additional, complex or costly steps have been inserted. It is significant that Schedule 4B is itself anti-avoidance legislation, intended to counter avoidance of tax on gains by contrived arrangements between settlements. The fact that the trustees have deliberately triggered the operation of the schedule is an indicator that one of their main purposes was to secure the advantage of the capital loss. In such a case, the TAAR will apply and the loss will not be an allowable loss.

ANNEX

HMRC Statement (6 December 2006)

Tax avoidance through the creation and use of capital losses

A2.461   **Purpose of the statement**

1. This statement sets out the principle underlying the new Targeted Anti-Avoidance Rule (TAAR) for capital losses. The rule is aimed at preventing the 'artificial' creation and use of capital losses where there are arrangements and the main purpose or one of the main purposes of those arrangements is to secure a tax advantage.

2. The new TAAR supersedes the TAAR applying to contrived capital losses of companies introduced with effect from 5 December 2005 and found in section 8(2A) to (2C) of the Taxation of Chargeable Gains Act 1992 (TCGA). The principle underlying both TAARs is the same and this statement incorporates the principle for the earlier TAAR.

3. How the legislation is intended to operate, and the types of arrangements to which it will apply, are set out below. We will be consulting with interested parties, and welcome comments from anyone with an interest in this area on whether the draft legislation and draft guidance properly capture and explain the purpose and principle set out in this statement, but not on the principle itself.

Who is likely to be affected?

4. The TAAR will apply to the capital losses of all persons within the scope of tax on chargeable gains. References below to "people" therefore include companies as well as individuals, trustees and personal representatives chargeable to capital gains tax (CGT) on their gains.

5. Most people do not use schemes or arrangements to create capital losses "artificially", nor do they generally use such capital losses in ways unintended by the legislation in order to avoid tax. The schemes and arrangements that this legislation is designed to address can be complex and will have tax avoidance as a main purpose; therefore it will not apply to the majority of people, whose disposals are made in the normal course of managing their investments.

Why the provision is necessary

6. The legislation addresses the contrived creation of capital losses, and prevents such contrived losses being set either against chargeable gains or, in some cases, against taxable income.

7. The provision is necessary because there is evidence from disclosures and other sources that tax avoidance using capital losses is becoming more widespread, and that the intended effect of existing legislation is being circumvented by new avoidance schemes. The evidence includes schemes to create artificial capital losses which may be set off against individuals' taxable income. There are therefore significant new risks of loss of both CGT and income tax, in addition to the risk to corporation tax addressed by the earlier TAAR (see paragraph 2 above). The Government is therefore acting now to prevent the further creation and utilisation of capital losses in circumstances unintended by the legislation.

8. The Government will monitor the impact of the new TAAR, and its effect on people's behaviour, and if necessary will consider whether further action is required.

Principle underlying the TAAR

9. The existing capital gains legislation generally reflects the principle that relief for capital losses should be available only where a person has suffered a genuine commercial loss on a real disposal.

10. However, people are using schemes and arrangements in such a way as to contravene this principle. Therefore the TAAR is necessary to ensure that the capital gains legislation more closely reflects this principle.

General description of the measure

11. The measure applies to "contrived" capital losses arising on disposals made on or after 6 December 2006.

12. Any capital loss arising on a disposal made on or after that day will not qualify as an allowable capital loss when it arises in connection with arrangements that have the obtaining of a tax advantage as one of the main purposes.

13. A further explanation of tax advantage and the main purpose test is set out in the guidance, along with examples of the type of schemes caught.

14. Transactions where a tax advantage is not one of the main purposes will not be caught by the TAAR. Ordinary transactions made in the normal course of managing investments that give rise to a real loss as a result of a real disposal will not be affected by the TAAR.

APPENDIX III

EXAMPLES OF THE IHT CHARGING PROVISIONS FOR RELEVANT PROPERTY TRUSTS[125]

Set out below are eight illustrations of the various IHT charges which can affect relevant property trusts.

---

[125] Supplied by Robert Jamieson MA FCA CTA (Fellow), tax partner in Mercer & Hole and former President of the Chartered Institute of Taxation.

ILLUSTRATION 1—INHERITANCE TAX ON SETTING UP A DISCRETIONARY TRUST; NO GROSSING UP AND DEATH WITHIN SEVEN YEARS

A3.01

On August 31, 2003, Nelson set up a discretionary trust for the benefit of his brother and his brother's family. The trust assets comprised cash and quoted shares totalling £320,000.

Nelson had a cumulative total for IHT purposes of £81,000 as a result of a chargeable transfer made some five years earlier. He had made no other gifts.

The IHT payable in connection with the creation of Nelson's discretionary trust (assumed to be payable by the trustees) was:

		Gross	IHT
	£	£	£
b/f		81,000	–
31.8.03			
Discretionary trust	320,000		
Less: Annual exemptions	6,000		
		314,000	28,000
		395,000	28,000

This calculation, using 2003/04 lifetime rates, is as follows:

	£
On 255,000 − 81,000 = 174,000 @ 0%	–
On 395,000 − 255,000 = 140,000 @ 20%	28,000
	28,000

If Nelson had paid the tax, grossing up would be involved.[126]

Unfortunately, on December 31, 2006, Nelson was killed in an accident. As a result, death rate tax is due in respect of the chargeable transfer on August 31, 2003. This is calculated (using 2006/07 rates) as follows:

---

[126] See Ch.29 for discussion on how grossing up works.

	£
On 285,000 − 81,000 = 204,000 @ 0%	−
On 395,000 − 285,000 = 110,000 @ 40%	44,000
	44,000
Less: Taper relief (20%)[127]	£8,800
	35,200
Less: Tax on lifetime transfer	28,000
ADDITIONAL IHT PAYABLE BY TRUSTEES	7,200

Illustration 1 demonstrated how IHT is computed when a discretionary trust is set up. **A3.02** Now consider the exit charge calculation. On the assumption that we are looking at an exit charge *before* the discretionary trust has suffered its first 10-year charge, there are several factors which have to be taken into account:

(a) the settlor's cumulative total of chargeable transfers at the time when the settlement commenced (Inheritance Tax Act 1984 (s.68(4)(b) IHTA 1984);

(b) the "initial value" of the discretionary trust—this is the actual value of the property which started off within the discretionary trust regime (s.68(5)(a) IHTA 1984);

(c) the length of time for which the property has been in the discretionary trust (s.68(2) IHTA 1984);

(d) the value of the property for IHT purposes which is leaving the discretionary trust (s.65(2) IHTA 1984); and

(e) any property in a related settlement valued at the date of creation of that settlement.

---

[127] Note that the taper relief is applied on the tax due at 40% before deduction of the 20% lifetime tax already paid.

ILLUSTRATION 2—INHERITANCE TAX ON PAYMENT OUT OF DISCRETIONARY TRUST IN FIRST 10 YEARS: APR AND NO GROSSING UP

A3.03 Darin created a discretionary trust on December 20, 1998. His cumulative total of chargeable transfers immediately prior to this settlement was £242,000. Hence, in 1998–99 he had no available nil rate band.

The property which he transferred to the trust was some let farmland which he had owned for many years and which was worth £450,000. Agricultural property relief (APR) of 50 per cent was available (assume that the market value and the agricultural value of the farmland were the same).

Darin had not used his 1998–99 annual exemption. The IHT due was paid by the trustees under the instalment option out of the rental income derived from the let farmland. Thus:

	£	Gross £	IHT £
b/f		242,000	3,800
20.12.98			
Discretionary trust	450,000		
Less: APR (50%)	225,000		
	225,000		
Less: Annual exemption	3,000		
		222,000	44,400
		464,000	48,200

On May 14, 2006, the trustees appointed the farmland (now valued at £800,000) to one of the discretionary beneficiaries absolutely. It still qualified for relief at 50 per cent.[128] The exit charge is calculated as follows (this assumes that the beneficiary paid the relevant IHT):

---

[128] Because the trustees have owned it for more than seven years. The farmland is subject to a pre-1995 tenancy and so only qualifies for APR as 50%. If the trustees were able to persuade the tenant farmer to surrender his Interest and take a post-1995 tenancy then 100% relief would be available.

	£	£
b/f	242,000	–
Initial value (450,000 − 44,400)	405,600	72,520[129]
	647,600	72,520

Note: The initial value is not, for these purposes, reduced by the 50% relief.

IHT at 2006−07 lifetime rates on the initial value is £72,520. This gives an initial rate of:

$$72,520/405,600 \times 100 = 17.8797\%$$

The rate of tax actually payable is:

$$17.8797\% \times 30\% \times 29/40 = 3.8888\%$$

Note: The initial rate is multiplied by 30 per cent and then by the number of complete successive quarters which have elapsed since the start of the trust divided by 40 (see s.68(2) IHTA 1984).

The taxable value of the exit charge is:

	£
Let farmland	800,000
Less: APR (50%)	400,000
	400,000

The IHT paid by the beneficiary amounts to 3.8888% x £400,000 = £15,555.

Note: in working out the rate of tax, take the value of the property at the date it is settled not the date of the exit charge. Ignore APR in calculating the rate of tax. Then tax the property valued at date of exit but after APR.

The calculation of a 10-year anniversary charge is somewhat different. This is shown in Illustration 3 below, along with the rules for computing IHT on an exit *after* a 10-year anniversary. **A3.04**

---

[129] Calculated on the basis of a nil rate band in 2006−07 of £285,000 of which £43,000 was unused (£242,000 – £285,000). Therefore, £362,600 (£405,600 less £43,000) taxed at 20% = £72,520.

ILLUSTRATION 3—10-YEAR ANNIVERSARY CHARGE; SUBSEQUENT PAYMENTS TO BENEFICIARIES

A3.05   Holly set up a discretionary trust on February 3, 1997 at a time when her cumulative total of chargeable transfers was £123,400.

In the 10 years since then, the trustees have made capital appointments of trust property amounting to £130,600.

The first 10-year anniversary charge for Holly's discretionary settlement falls on February 3, 2007 and the quoted shares, cash and other assets still in the settlement on that date are worth a total of £411,000. The IHT due in respect of this 10-year anniversary is computed as follows:

	£
Holly's chargeable transfers prior to trust	123,400
Add: Exit charges	130,600
	254,000
Add: Value of discretionary trust property	411,000
	665,000

IHT at 2006/07 lifetime rates on the value of this discretionary trust property is:

	£
On 254,000 − 285,000 = 31,000 @ 0%	–
On 285,000 − 665,000 = 380,000 @ 20%	76,000
	76,000

Thus:
   76,000/411,000 × 100 = 18.4915%

The rate actually charged is:
   18.4915% × 30% = 5.5475%

Therefore, the trustees must settle an IHT liability of 5.5475% × £411,000 = £22,800.

The relevant legislation for computing a 10-year anniversary charge is in s.66 IHTA 1984. Typically, this will involve an aggregation of:
   (a) the settlor's cumulative total of chargeable transfers made in the seven years prior to the commencement of the settlement (s.66(5)(a) IHTA 1984);

(b) the total of all exit charges imposed in the 10 (*not* seven) years prior to the anniversary in question (s.66(5)(b) IHTA 1984); and

(c) the value of the discretionary trust property still in the settlement on the anniversary date (s.66(4)(a) IHTA 1984).

Tax is charged at current lifetime rates on the value of the discretionary trust property (see (c) above), taking into account what IHTA 1984 calls a "postulated" prior chargeable transfer equal to the sum of (a) and (b) above (s.66(3) IHTA 1984). The purpose of including (b) above is to render ineffective any transfer out of the trust of property just before the 10-year anniversary in order to reduce the value of the trust property subject to the charge.

If, in this illustration, the trustees subsequently made a capital appointment of **A3.06** quoted shares worth £80,000 to Holly's cousin, Valens, who was one of the discretionary beneficiaries, on May 13, 2008, the IHT calculation would proceed as follows by virtue of s.69 IHTA 1984:

(a) the 10-year anniversary charge is recomputed using 2008−09 lifetime rates;

(b) the resulting tax figure is expressed as a percentage of the value of the discretionary trust property on February 3, 2007;

(c) this percentage is multiplied by 30 per cent and then by the number of complete successive quarters which have elapsed since the 10-year anniversary charge divided by 40; and finally

(d) the scaled down percentage is applied to the value of the capital appointment on May 13, 2008 (grossed up, if the trustees, rather than Valens, are to bear the tax).

Thus:

	£
Holly's chargeable transfers prior to trust	123,400
Add: Exit charges	130,600
	254,000
Add: Value of discretionary trust property	411,000
	665,000

IHT at 2008/09 lifetime rates on the value of the discretionary trust property is:

	£
On 254,000 − 312,000 = 58,000 @ 0%	−
On 312,000 − 665,000 = 353,000 @ 20%	70,600
	70,600

This produces:
70,600/411,000 x 100% = 17.1776%

The rate of IHT ascribed to this transaction is:
17.1776% × 30%× 5/40 = 0.6442%

Thus the tax on the appointment which is to be paid by the trustees so that grossing-up applies is:

Note: The gross amount of the exit charge is £80,519 and 0.6442% × £80,519 = £519.

A3.07   The next illustration shows the effect of an exit charge after a 10-year anniversary charge where:

(a) the trust property was wholly eligible for 100 per cent business property relief (BPR) at the 10-year anniversary date; and

(b) the property has since been sold so that it is cash which is appointed out.

ILLUSTRATION 4—INHERITANCE TAX AFTER 10-YEAR ANNIVERSARY WHERE PROPERTY SOLD BUT QUALIFIED FOR BPR AT 10-YEAR ANNIVERSARY

The Pitney Discretionary settlement was established by Mr Pitney on April 5, **A3.08** 1997 with a 40 per cent holding of shares in Tulsa Enterprises Ltd (an unquoted trading company). The beneficiaries comprised Mr Pitney's children and grand-children.

On April 5, 2007, the only assets in the trust were:

(a) shares in Tulsa Enterprises Ltd worth £800,000; and

(b) undistributed cash of £13,600.

Mr Pitney's cumulative total of chargeable transfers prior to April 5, 1997 was nil and there have been no distributions of capital from the trust since it was set up.

The IHT due in respect of the trust's 10-year anniversary on April 5, 2007 is computed as follows:

	£	£
Mr Pitney's chargeable transfer prior to trust		–
Add: Exit charges in 10 years to April 5, 2007		–
		–
Add: Value of discretionary trust property on April 5, 2007:		
Shares in Tulsa Enterprises Ltd	800,000	
Less: BPR (100%)	800,000	
	–	
Cash	13,600	
	13,600	
	13,600	

IHT at 2006–07 lifetime rates on the value of the discretionary trust property is nil.

On February 17, 2009, Tulsa Enterprises Ltd was taken over by a large plc and the trustees received a cash payment of £1,000,000 for their shares. After set-tling their CGT liability of (say) £80,000 on January 31, 2010, the trustees made a capital distribution of £920,000 to the beneficiaries on February 14,

2010 and the trust came to an end. Any undistributed income had already been paid out.

Because the rate of tax on the previous 10-year anniversary, using 2009/10 life-time rates, was 0 per cent, the exit charge on February 14, 2010 is IHT-free. This can be a useful advantage whenever trust property which attracts relief at 100 per cent is sold and cash is then appointed out.

A3.09   Another problem which comes up from time to time is where a settlor has added further property to an existing discretionary trust. Illustration 5 examines the complications where there is an exit charge from such a settlement.

ILLUSTRATION 5—EXIT CHARGE WHEN THERE HAVE BEEN ADDITIONS TO A SETTLEMENT

Presley set up a discretionary trust on August 16, 1997 with cash of £750,000. **A3.10** He had a cumulative total for IHT purposes of £125,000 as a result of a chargeable transfer made in 1993.

On the assumption that no annual exemption was available, the IHT payable in connection with the creation of Presley's discretionary trust (assumed to be payable by the trustees) was:

		Gross	IHT
		£	£
	b/f	125,000	–
16.8.97			
Discretionary trust		750,000	132,000
		875,000	132,000

This calculation, using 1997/98 lifetime rates, runs as follows:

	£
On 215,000 − 125,000 = 90,000 @ 0%	–
On 875,000 − 215,000 = 660,000 @ 20%	132,000
	132,000

The remaining cash was then invested in a portfolio of quoted stocks and shares.

On January 8, 2005, when the settled property included 12,000 ordinary shares in Aaron plc, Presley added a further 120,000 ordinary shares in Aaron plc to the trust and paid the IHT himself. The IHT value for these quoted shares was then 300p per share.

The IHT payable in connection with this addition was (again no annual exemption was available):

	Gross	IHT	Net
	£	£	£
b/f	–	–	–
8.1.05			
Discretionary trust (120,000 × 300p)			360,000
Grossed up	384,250	24,250	
	384,250	24,250	360,000

Note: Presley's earlier chargeable transfers have dropped out under the seven-year rule. His cumulative net transfer of £360,000 exceeds the 2004–05 nil rate band of £263,000 by £97,000, the gross equivalent of which is £97,000 × 100/80 = £121,250. The tax payable is therefore £121,250 – £97,000 = £24,250 and the gross chargeable transfer is £360,000 – £24,250 = £384,250.

On February 1, 2007, the trustees appointed 66,000 ordinary shares in Aaron Plc (now valued at 360p per share) to Priscilla absolutely. She was one of the discretionary beneficiaries and she agreed to pay any tax due.

The initial value of the property originally settled is £750,000 - £132,000 = £618,000. The initial value of the addition (which must also be taken into account when calculating the exit charge—see s.68(5)(c) of IHTA 1984) is £360,000. The exit charge tax is computed as follows:

			IHT
	£	£	£
b/f		125,000	–
Initial value of settlement 618,000			
Initial value of addition 360,000			
		978,000	163,600
		1,103,000	163,600

The IHT at 2006–07 lifetime rates on the combined initial values is £163,600. This gives an initial rate of:

163,600/978,000 × 100 = 16.728%

To the extent that the exit charge comes out of the property originally settled, the initial rate is multiplied by 30% and then by the number of complete successive quarters which have elapsed since the start of the trust—this comes to 37—divided by 40.

However, to the extent that the exit charge comes out of the addition, the number of quarters taken is 37 less the number of complete successive quarters prior to the addition—this comes to 29—and so the fraction becomes 8/40ths.

The IHT payable on the distribution of 66,000 ordinary shares in Aaron Plc (valued at 66,000 3 360p 5 £237,600) to Priscilla is:

Out of property originally settled

16.728% × 30% × 37/40 × 237,600 × 12,000/132,000	1,003
Out of addition	
16.728% × 30% × 8/40 × 237,600 × 120,000/132,000	2,168
	£3,171

Note: The capital appointment to Pricilla is deemed to come pro rata from the property originally settled on August 16, 1997 and from the addition on January 8, 2005.[130]

Note: if both the initial transfer and all subsequent additions fell within Presley's unused nil rate band at the date of each transfer and addition there would be no tax payable on the entry into the settlement and no exit charge on transfer out within the first ten years. (The rate of tax would be 0%.)

The creation of most interest in possession trusts made on or after March 22, **A3.11** 2006 will bring the relevant property regime into play. Illustration 6 below compares the incidence of IHT under the new regime with what a similar trust would have suffered had the pre-March 22, 2006 rules still been around.

---

[130] The special rule in IHTA 1984 s.67 dealing with additions of property is not relevant for an exit charge on February 1, 2007.

ILLUSTRATION 6—INTEREST IN POSSESSION TRUSTS: COMPARISON OF POSITIONS IF PROPERTY SETTLED BEFORE AND AFTER MARCH 22, 2006

A3.12   Cochran set up a life interest trust for his wife, Sharon, on June 1, 2006. Cochran's chargeable transfers prior to the creation of this trust totalled £200,000 and the value of the assets going into the trust was £506,000.

Following Cochran's death in a car accident on April 17, 2017, Sharon remarried on October 3, 2020 and, under the terms of the trust, her life interest terminated. The trust capital went to their three children absolutely.

On the assumptions that the trust property had the following values:

(a) £760,000 on June 1, 2016; and

(b) £890,000 on October 3, 2020

and that 2009/10 tax rates apply to all transactions after the initial setting up of the trust, the IHT payable in respect of this trust is as follows:
Creation of trust on June 1, 2006

	£	Gross £	IHT £
b/f		200,000	–
1.6.06			
Sharon's trust	506,000		–
Less: Annual exemptions	6,000		
		500,000	83,000
		700,000	83,000[131]

Thus £83,000 was payable by the trustees out of the assets settled. Under the pre-March 22, 2006 rules, this would have been an exempt transfer.

10-year anniversary charge on June 1, 2016

---

[131] i.e. £500,000 less unused nil rate band of £85,000 x 20%.

	£
Cochran's chargeable transfers prior to trust	200,000
Add: Value of trust property	760,000
	960,000

IHT at 2009/10 lifetime rates on the value of this trust property is:

	£
On 200,000 − 325,000 = 125,000 @ 0%	–
On 325,000 − 960,000 = 635,000 @ 20%	127,000
	127,000

Thus:

$$127,000/760,000 \times 100\% = \underline{16.7105\%}$$

The rate of IHT actually charged is:

$$16.7105\% \times 30\% = \underline{5.0132\%}$$

Therefore, the trustees must settle an IHT liability of $5.0132\% \times £760,000 = £38,100$. Under the pre-March 22, 2006 rules, there would have been no 10-year anniversary charge.

Termination of trust on October 3, 2020

The value of the property leaving the interest in possession trust on October 3, 2020 following Sharon's remarriage is £890,000. This will be taxed as an exit charge under s.69 IHTA 1984.

The rate of IHT ascribable to this transaction is:
$$5.0132\% \times 17/40 = 2.1306\%$$

If the tax on this appointment is paid by the three children, the liability will be:
$$2.1306\% \times 890,000 = £18,962$$

Under the pre-March 22, 2006 rules, this appointment would have been treated as a potentially exempt transfer made by Sharon and so IHT would only have been due if she had died within seven years of October 3, 2020.

IHT summary

	New rules	Old rules
	£	£
June 1, 2006	83,000	–
June 1, 2016	38,100	–
October 3, 2020	18,962	–
	140,062	Nil

Of course if Sharon had died during this period (e.g. just before the ten year anniversary) then the inheritance tax liability would be more under old rules – $40\% \times £760,000 = £304,000$.

A3.13   The next illustration looks at the position of an accumulation and maintenance trust when the terms of the trust were not modified prior to April 6, 2008, with the result that the trust assets became relevant property on April 6, 2008. The particular point of this example is the calculation of the 10-year anniversary charge.

ILLUSTRATION 7—ACCUMULATION AND MAINTENANCE TRUST: CHARGES FROM APRIL 6, 2008

n December 1, 1998, Faith, whose chargeable transfers totalled £180,000, set up an accumulation and maintenance trust for the benefit of his young nephews and nieces, each of whom was to come into a share of income at the age of 18 and capital at the age of 30.   **A3.14**

Despite learning of the Chancellor's plans for accumulation and maintenance trusts in the Finance Act 2006 (FA 2006), the trustees decided against lowering the vesting age on the ground that, as they put it, "18 is too young for someone to be given a substantial amount of capital".

Accordingly, on April 6, 2008, Faith's trust effectively became a discretionary settlement and the first 10-year anniversary charge arose on December 1, 2008, at which date the trust property was worth £772,000. However, because the assets in the trust had not been relevant property throughout the 10-year period, s.66(2) IHTA 1984 allows the rate at which the tax is charged to be scaled down by 1/40th for each complete successive quarter which had elapsed before the trust assets became relevant property. In this case, 37 quarters expired between December 1, 1998 and April 6, 2008, leaving a fraction of 3/40ths to be applied to the IHT rate. The computation proceeds as follows:

	£
Faith's chargeable transfers prior to trust	180,000
Add: value of trust property	772,000
	952,000

IHT at 2008/09 lifetime rates on the value of this trust property is:

	£
On 180,000 − 312,000 = 132,000 @ 0%	–
On 312,000 − 952,000 = 640,000 @ 20%	128,000
	128,000

Thus:

$$128,000/772,000 \times 100\% = 16.5803\%$$

The rate actually charged is:

$$16.5803\% \times 30\% \times 3/40 = 0.3731\%$$

Therefore, the trustees must settle an IHT liability of $0.3731\% \times £772,000 = £2,880$.[132]

A3.15   The final illustration demonstrates the calculation of the tax charge under s.71D IHTA 1984 where capital vests on an appointment to an age 18–25 trust beneficiary.

---

[132] For the position if the trust had been set up more than 10 years before April 6, 2008, so that a 10-year anniversary had passed, and there was an exit charge before the next 10-year anniversary: see Ch.29.

ILLUSTRATION 8—CHARGE UNDER S.71D REGIME WHEN CAPITAL VESTS IN BENEFICIARY

Holliday died on October 29, 2003 and, in his will, he left part of his estate on trust for his only son, Michael, who had been born on November 26, 1994. The terms of the trust were that income was to be accumulated to the extent that it was not paid out for Michael's maintenance, education or benefit. The trust capital (and any accumulated income) vested absolutely in Michael on his 25th birthday.

This trust was originally an accumulation and maintenance settlement, but, because Michael's vesting age was not amended prior to April 6, 2008, it then became an age 18 to 25 trust. In other words, following Michael's 18th birthday (November 26, 2012), the trust assets were subject to the special charging regime in ss.71E−71G. Accordingly, seven years later, when the trust assets vested on November 26, 2019, there is an exit charge under s.71E IHTA 1984.

On the assumptions:

(a) that the trust assets were worth £520,000 on November 26, 2019;

(b) that the initial value of the trust on Holliday's death (i.e. October 29, 2003) was £268,000;

(c) that Holliday's cumulative total for IHT purposes immediately prior to his death was £149,000; and

(d) that 2009−10 tax rates apply,

the calculation of the IHT on Michael's 25th birthday proceeds as follows by virtue of s.71F IHTA 1984:

	£	IHT £
b/f	149,000	–
Initial value[133]	268,000	18,400

---

[133] Note that the "initial value" may be significantly less than the value of the property in the trust when it ends. The trust may, for instance, have been set up over 20 years ago. Discovering the value of the property at that time may present problems (its original creation may well have been a PET so no IHT value will have been agreed) and it will also be necessary to discover the chargeable transfers of the settlor in the previous seven years. Bear in mind that standard advice was that if a taxpayer wished to make a chargeable transfer (e.g. create a discretionary trust) he should do so before making a PET.

The IHT at 2009/10 lifetime rates on the initial value is £18,400. This gives an initial rate of:

18,400/268,000 × 100 = 6.8657%

The rate of tax actually payable is:

6.8657% × 30% × 28/40 = 1.4418%

Note: 28 quarters have elapsed since Michael's 18th birthday.

The IHT paid by Michael on the vesting of the trust property is 1.4418% ×£520,000 = £7,497.

INDEX

1628

1630

1647

'new' interest with 'new' beneficiary, as, 27.21–27.31
overview, 26.01
planning, 27.33–27.36
s.49D interests, 27.32
s.49E interests, 27.33
spouse extension, 27.32
value of joint IIP
  discounting, 26.21–26.22
  generally, 26.17–26.18
  joint interests, 26.19–26.20
variations, 26.39
vesting of capital, 26.28–26.29

Judicial review
residence, 3.38
when to use, 38.17, 38.54, 43.85

"Kink test"
disposals, and
  generally, 11.30
  introduction, 11.24

Lack of capacity
See **Capacity**

Leases
disguised remuneration, and, 49.65
interest in possession trusts, and, 26.24
meaning of 'settlement', and, 24.06–24.08
usufruct, and, 2.35

"Let-outs"
reservation of benefit, and, 22.13

Liabilities
agricultural property relief, and
  generally, 46.11–46.12
  introduction, 32.49
anti-avoidance rule, 32.01
artificial debt provisions
  foreign domiciled settlors, 32.35–32.42
  generally, 32.27–32.31 [FA 1986, s.103]
  loans to settlors from trust, 32.32–32.34
basic rules, 32.01
business property, 32.46–32.48
charged on property, 32.08
debts under deed, 38.03
deductible liabilities, 32.02–32.06
excluded property
  foreign domiciliaries, 32.24–32.26
  generally, 32.07–32.11
exempt property, on, 32.09
foreign debts, 32.10–32.11
future debts, 32.06
guarantee debts, 32.05
interest in possession trusts, 32.16–32.20
loans by settlors, 32.43–32.45
reservation of benefit
  generally, 32.21–32.23
  loans by settlors, 32.43–32.45
situs of debts, 32.12–32.15
specialty debts, 32.03
statutory basis, 32.01
trustees, and, 32.01

Liability to tax
generally, 56.67–56.68

non-settlor interested offshore trusts, and, 8.38–8.39
non-settlor interested trusts, and
  discretionary trusts tax, 6.32
  fixed interest trusts, 6.06–6.11
settlements, and, 25.04–25.05

Life insurance
accumulation and maintenance trusts
  generally, 47.03
  premium payments, 47.05–47.07
background, 47.01–47.02
chargeable events, 47.39–47.43
discounted gift plans
  Bower decision, 47.26–47.29
  effect of FA 2006, 47.32–47.33
  generally, 47.23
  inheritance tax analysis, 47.24–47.25
  introduction, 47.01
  pre-owned assets charge, 47.31
  taxing retained fund, 47.30
family protection policies
  drafting points, 47.15–47.17
  generally, 47.13–47.14
  introduction, 47.01
  seven-year reducing policies, 47.18–47.20
flexible reversionary trusts
  generally, 47.34–47.38
  introduction, 47.01
interest in possession trusts
  generally, 47.03
  premium payments, 47.05–47.07
loan trusts
  generally, 47.21–47.22
  introduction, 47.01
non-qualifying policies
  generally, 47.39–47.40
  non-resident trusts, 47.43
  parental settlements, 47.42
  UK resident trusts, 47.41
pre-March 22, 2006 trusts
  generally, 47.03
  premium payments, 47.05–47.07
  transitional serial interests, 47.04
single-premium bonds, 47.01
transitional serial interests
  extension of regime, 47.08–47.09
  generally, 47.04
  introduction, 27.33
  technical aspects, 47.10–47.12

Life tenants
settlor-interested UK resident trusts, and, 7.35–7.37

Lifetime allowance
pension schemes, and, 48.12

"Lifetime limit"
entrepreneurs' relief, and, 14.01–14.03

Limited liability partnerships
generally, 52.09
regulation, 52.12

Limited partnerships
generally, 52.10

Milk quotas
roll-over relief, and, 13.06
Minors
18–25 trusts
accumulation and maintenance trusts,
and, 35.54
calculation of charge under s.71F,
35.39–35.41
calculation of charge under s.71G, 35.42
conditions, 35.36
conversion into BMT, 35.44–35.49
drafting, 35.50–35.52
extension of life, 35.43
generally, 35.12
IIP trusts pre-March 22, 2006, and, 35.55
immediate post-death interest, and, 35.47
interests in possession, and, 35.46
introduction, 35.35–35.36
overview, 35.01
powers of advancement, 35.53
priority, 35.13
purpose, 35.35
rate of charge, 35.40
s.144 trusts, and, 35.48
taxation, 35.37–35.38
bare trusts
generally, 35.57
introduction, 35.11
priority, 35.13
bereaved minors trusts
accumulation and maintenance trusts,
and, 35.26–35.27
'bereaved minor', 35.18
charge to tax, 35.24–35.25
conditions, 35.17–35.23
conversion into s.71D trust, 35.45
drafting, 35.30–35.33
generally, 35.12
immediate post-death interest, and,
35.28–35.29
introduction, 35.17
more than one bereaved minor, 35.34
overview, 35.01
powers of advancement, 35.22–35.23
priority, 35.13, 35.28
qualifying trusts, 35.19–35.20
requirements, 35.17
substitutionary clauses, 35.31
vesting at 18, 35.21
capital gains tax, and, 9.05
death options
18–25 trusts, 35.35–35.55
bare trust, 35.57
bereaved minors trusts, 35.17–35.34
diagrammatic resumé, 35.16
discretionary trust, 35.57
generally, 35.12
immediate post-death interest,
35.57–35.58
other, 35.56–35.59
priority, 35.13–35.15
deeds of variation, and, 39.09

disabled persons' trusts, 35.01
discretionary trusts
generally, 35.12
introduction, 35.03–35.06
priority, 35.13
use, 35.59
immediate post-death interest
generally, 35.57–35.58
introduction, 35.12
priority, 35.13
interest in possession trusts, 35.07–35.10
introduction, 35.01–35.02
lifetime options
bare trusts, 35.11
discretionary trusts, 35.03–35.06
interest in possession trusts, 35.07–35.10
partnerships, and, 52.04–52.06
priority of trusts, 35.13–35.15
relevant property trusts
generally, 35.12
priority, 35.13
s.71D trusts
generally, 35.12
introduction, 35.01
priority, 35.13
settlor-interested UK resident trusts, and,
7.38–7.42
Mistake
application to *Pitt v Holt*, 1.36–1.38
available relief, 1.29
duties of trustees, 1.27
equitable jurisdiction, 1.30–1.3
generally, 1.22
professional advice, 1.28
ratio decidendi, 1.23–1.25
setting aside exercise of trustees' dispositive
powers, 1.26
test, 1.34–1.35
Money
family home, and
associated operations rule, and, 43.119
generally, 43.116–43.117
HMRC approach, 43.120–43.121
options for taxpayers, 43.125
pre-April 6, 1998 position, 43.123
pre-owned assets, and, 43.122
reservation of benefit, and,
43.118–43.121
seven-year defence, 43.123–43.124
reservation of benefit, and, 22.32
Motive defence
settlor-interested trusts, 8.26
"Multiple settlements"
capital gains tax, and
additions, 9.45
generally, 9.39–9.40
importance, 9.42
offshore trusts, 9.41
single instrument, 9.43–9.44
Mutual funds
generally, 19.04
offshore funds, and, 53.05

1658

1678